Online Research Aids

Whether students want to investigate the ideas behind a thought-provoking topic or conduct in-depth research for a paper, our online research aids can help them refine their research skills, find what they need in the library or on the Web, and then use and document their sources effectively.

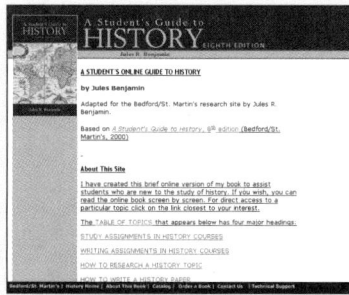

A Student's Online Guide to History, Eighth Edition
www.bedfordstmartins.com/benjamin

Jules R. Benjamin, *Ithaca College*

The online edition of Jules Benjamin's brief yet comprehensive introduction to the study of history contains abbreviated content from the print version and is accessible to students wherever they have a connection to the Internet.

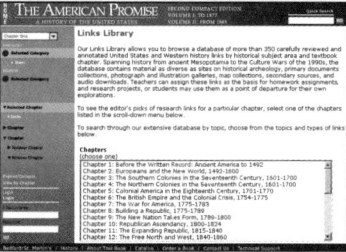

Links Library
www.bedfordstmartins.com/historylinks

Links Library is a database of more than 350 carefully reviewed and annotated American and Western history Web links searchable by topic or by textbook chapter. Spanning history from ancient Mesopotamia to the present, the database contains diverse links to resources such as historical archaeology sites, primary documents collections, photograph and illustration galleries, map collections, secondary sources, and audio.

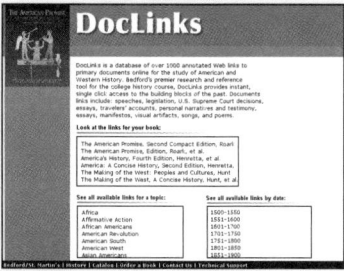

DocLinks
www.bedfordstmartins.com/doclinks

DocLinks is a database of over 1000 annotated Web links to primary documents online for the study of American and Western history. Documents in this database include speeches, legislation, U.S. Supreme Court decisions, essays, travelers' accounts, personal narratives and testimony, essays, e-books, manifestos, visual artifacts, songs, and poems. Documents are searchable by topic and date and are also indexed to the chapters of our major survey textbooks.

Research and Documentation Online
www.bedfordstmartins.com/resdoc

Diana Hacker, *Prince George's Community College*

This online version of Diana Hacker's popular booklet provides clear advice across the disciplines on how to find, evaluate, and integrate outside material into a paper, how to cite sources correctly, and how to format in MLA, APA, CBE, and *Chicago* styles.

www.bedfordstmartins.com/history

THE
AMERICAN
PROMISE

A HISTORY OF THE UNITED STATES

Second Compact Edition

SACRAMENTO RAILROAD STATION *by William Hahn. Fine Arts Museum of San Francisco, Museum Purchase, Gift of M. H. de Young Endowment Fund, 54936.*

THE AMERICAN PROMISE

A HISTORY OF THE UNITED STATES

Second Compact Edition

JAMES L. ROARK
Emory University

MICHAEL P. JOHNSON
Johns Hopkins University

PATRICIA CLINE COHEN
University of California at Santa Barbara

SARAH STAGE
Arizona State University West

ALAN LAWSON
Boston College

SUSAN M. HARTMANN
The Ohio State University

BEDFORD / ST. MARTIN'S
Boston ◆ New York

FOR BEDFORD/ST. MARTIN'S

Publisher of History: Patricia A. Rossi
Director of Development for History: Jane Knetzger
Developmental Editors: Heidi Hood, Gretchen Boger, Louise Townsend
Project Manager: Tina Samaha
Senior Production Supervisor: Joe Ford
Marketing Manager: Jenna Bookin Barry
Associate Editor for New Media: William J. Lombardo
Editorial Assistants: Brianna R. Germain, Rachel L. Siegel, Elisabeth Stark
Production Assistant: Kerri Cardone
Copyeditor: Lisa Wehrle
Text Design: Wanda Kossak
Photo Research: Pembroke Herbert/Sandi Rygiel, Picture Research Consultants & Archives, Inc.
Cartography: Mapping Specialists Limited
Indexer: Maro Riofrancos
Cover Design: Donna Dennison
Composition: TechBooks
Printing and Binding: RR Donnelley & Sons Company

President: Joan E. Feinberg
Editorial Director: Denise B. Wydra
Director of Marketing: Karen Melton
Director of Editing, Design, and Production: Marcia Cohen
Managing Editor: Elizabeth M. Schaaf

Library of Congress Control Number: 2002108121

Manufactured in the United States of America.

7   6   5   4   3
f   e   d   c   b

For information, write: Bedford/St. Martin's, 75 Arlington Street, Boston, MA 02116
(617-399-4000)

ISBN: 0-312-40358-5 (combined edition)
        0-312-40359-3 (Vol. I)
        0-312-40360-7 (Vol. II)

Cover Art: James Leonard, *Wind Machine with Gabriel, Eleanor Roosevelt, and Louis Armstrong.* Smithsonian American Art Museum, D.C./Art Resource, N.Y.

BRIEF CONTENTS

CONTENTS

CHAPTER 1

Before the Written Record: Ancient America to 1492   3

CHAPTER 10
Republican Ascendancy, 1800–1824 211

CHAPTER 11
The Expanding Republic, 1815–1840 235

CHAPTER 26

Cold War Politics in the Truman Years, 1945–1953   671

CHAPTER 27

The Politics and Culture of Abundance, 1952–1960   697

CHAPTER 30

Retreat from Liberalism, 1968–2000   773

CHAPTER 31

The End of the Cold War and the Challenges of Globalization, 1975–2003   809

APPENDICES

Chapter Bibliographies and additional Online Appendix materials are available at www.bedfordstmartins.com/roarkcompact.

MAPS, FIGURES, AND TABLES

SPECIAL FEATURES

PREFACE

THE COMPACT EDITION OF *The American Promise: A History of the United States* grew from the authors' desire to provide a fresh alternative for fellow instructors searching for the most teachable and readable text available: a unique midsized book that pairs all the color, pedagogy, and features of a full-length text with a briefer narrative at a lower price. The unique size of the Compact Edition allows us to meet the needs of students and instructors who want the flexibility of a briefer text without sacrificing coverage or readability. In writing the Second Compact Edition, we continued to draw from our experiences as longtime teachers of the survey course to help us identify the essentials of American history as well as the stories and voices that make this history memorable for students. Our collective experience teaching introductory American history in a wide range of institutions, from community colleges and state universities to private colleges and research institutions, taught us that the survey course is the most difficult to teach and the most difficult to take. It is this knowledge that has informed every decision we have made in creating this text.

Our teaching experience was invaluable in making the choices necessary to create the Second Compact Edition from its parent text, *The American Promise,* Second Edition. To preserve the narrative strengths of *The American Promise,* all of the authors revised their own chapters. To maintain the strong story line and balanced narrative in a midsized format, we reorganized material and combined thematically related sections throughout the text. In short, we did not create the Second Compact Edition simply by cutting; we also reimagined, reorganized, and rewrote.

Our experience as teachers also informed the framework of our text. Most survey texts emphasize either a social or political approach to history; by focusing on one, they inevitably slight the other. In our classrooms, students need **both** the structure a political narrative provides and the insights gained from examining social and cultural experiences. To write a comprehensive, balanced account of American history, we focused on the public arena—the place where politics intersects social and cultural developments—to show how Americans confronted the major issues of their day and created far-reaching historical change.

We also thought hard about the concerns most frequently voiced by instructors: that students often find history boring, unfocused, and difficult and their textbooks similarly lifeless and overwhelming. How could our text address these concerns and help introductory students understand and remember American history's main events and developments? We decided to explore fully the political, social, economic, and cultural changes that students need to understand by connecting them to individuals who experienced history as it happened. To make each chapter more memorable and to portray the diversity of the American experience, we stitched into the narrative the voices of hundreds of contemporaries—from presidents to pipefitters—whose ideas and actions shaped their times and whose efforts still affect our lives. By incorporating a rich selection of authentic American voices, we sought to create a vivid and compelling narrative that captures students' interest and sparks their historical imagination.

Our title, *The American Promise,* reflects our emphasis on the power of human agency and our conviction that American history is an unfinished story. For millions, the nation held out the promise of a better life, unfettered worship, representative government, democratic politics, and other freedoms seldom found elsewhere around the world. But none of these promises came with guarantees. And promises fulfilled for some meant promises denied to others. As we see it, much of American history is a continuing struggle over the definition and realization of the nation's promise. That hope, kept alive by countless sacrifices, has been marred by compromises, disappointments, and denials, but it lives today. Abraham Lincoln, in the midst of what he termed the "fiery trial" of the Civil War, pronounced the nation "the last best hope of

Earth." Ideally, *The American Promise,* Second Compact Edition, will help students become aware of the legacy of hope bequeathed to them by previous generations of Americans, a legacy that is theirs to preserve and to build on.

Features

Because students learn best when they find a subject engaging, we have made a special effort to incorporate features that bring American history to life and make it memorable. **Chapter-opening vignettes** invite students into the narrative with vivid accounts of individuals or groups who embody each chapter's main themes. Vignettes new to this edition include Pocahontas's "rescue" of John Smith, Nat Turner's war on slavery, and Fannie Lou Hamer's civil rights struggles. **Two-tiered running heads** on every page remind students where the sections they read fall chronologically. At the close of each chapter, strengthened **conclusions** critically reexamine central ideas and provide a bridge to the next chapter, and **annotated chronologies** review the key events and developments explored in the chapter. We have enhanced the well-received **appendices** by extending our collection of reference materials in a new **Online Appendix** that contains such important documents as the Articles of Confederation, the Seneca Falls Resolution, the Confederate Constitution, and Martin Luther King, Jr.'s "I Have a Dream" speech. **Cross-references to the new Online Study Guide** in each chapter encourage mastery of visual and text material and development of critical-thinking skills. Additional text **cross-references to Online Bibliographies,** organized by chapter and topic, provide students with detailed suggestions for additional reading and research.

An enriched array of special features reinforces the narrative and offers teachers more points of departure for assignments and discussion. With the addition of sixteen new boxed features, this edition provides a wider variety of choices for sparking students' interest while helping them understand that history is both a body of knowledge

For FURTHER READING ABOUT THE TOPICS IN THIS CHAPTER, see the Online Bibliography at
www.bedfordstmartins.com/roarkcompact.

For ADDITIONAL FIRST-HAND ACCOUNTS OF THIS PERIOD, see pages 181–195 in Michael Johnson, ed., *Reading the American Past,* Second Edition, Volume I.

To ASSESS YOUR MASTERY OF THE MATERIAL IN THIS CHAPTER, see the Online Study Guide at
www.bedfordstmartins.com/roarkcompact.

and an ongoing process of investigation. The all-new **Promise of Technology** features examine the ramifications—positive and negative—of technological developments in American society and culture such as the cultivation of corn, the printing press, hydraulic mining, and air conditioning. **Documenting the American Promise** features (formerly "Texts in Historical Context") combine three or four primary documents that dramatize the human dimension of major events and controversies with interpretive commentary. New topics in this edition include "King Philip Considers Christianity," "The Destruction of the Tea," "Rockefeller and His Critics," and "The Emerging Cold War." Questions for Analysis and Debate now follow the documents to help students analyze and squeeze meaning from primary sources. Illustrated **Historical Questions** pose and interpret specific questions of continuing interest so as to demonstrate the depth and variety of possible answers, thereby countering the belief of many beginning students that historians simply gather facts and string them together into a chronological narrative. New Historical Questions in this edition include "Did Terrorists Sink the *Maine*?" and "Was Prohibition a Bad Joke?"

We take great pride as well in our full-color design and rich art program. We have preserved the **award-winning design** and added many new **illustrations** to make *The American Promise* a visual feast. In all, more than 350 images, many in full color and all large enough to study in detail, reinforce and extend the narrative. An illustration accompanies each chapter-opening vignette, providing a visual supplement to the narrative portrait that opens every chapter. All pictures are contemporaneous with the period of the chapter, with **comprehensive captions** that draw students into active engagement with the images and help

TOURISM AND THE LURE OF NATIVE TRADITION
This advertisement for vacationing in the mountainous Indian country of New Mexico implies the benefits of high altitude for health. But commerce in native crafts is also an objective. Others at the time headed to New Mexico to attain quite different benefits. Attracted by anthropologists studying native culture and a coterie of painters and writers who began an artists' colony near the ancient pueblo at Taos, disillusioned strivers and other refugees from the stresses of modern life hoped to find a spiritual inner wisdom within Pueblo culture that would reconnect them with nature and the past.
Private collection.
www.bedfordstmartins.com/roarkcompact SEE THE ONLINE STUDY GUIDE for more help in analyzing this image.

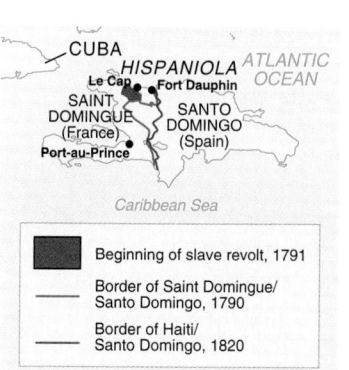

them unpack the layers of meaning. Full-page **chapter-opening artifacts** combine with many other illustrations of artifacts to emphasize the importance of material culture in the study of the past.

Finally, we have extended and expanded our highly regarded **map program** to offer the most effective set of maps available in a survey text. Each chapter offers, on average, three **full-size maps** showing major developments in a wide range of areas, from environmental and technological issues to political, social, cultural, and diplomatic matters. New maps reflect this edition's increased attention to Native American peoples and to a sustained continental perspective. Each chapter includes as well an average of two new **"spot maps,"** small, single-concept maps embedded in pertinent passages of the narrative to increase students' grasp of crucial issues. Unique to *The American Promise,* the spot maps highlight such topics as ancient California, Pontiac's rebellion, the Haitian revolution, the Vicksburg campaign, Pullman's company town, the Dust Bowl, the creation of Israel, the breakup of Yugoslavia, and the recent conflict in Afghanistan. In addition, **critical-thinking map exercises**—one per chapter—combine for an **embedded map workbook.**

Haitian Revolution, 1790–1804

made other major revisions in organization and coverage.

To mesh better with most course calendars and to provide a more focused narrative, we reduced the number of chapters from 32 to 31. We also shortened the text by an additional 5 percent from the First Compact Edition (making it 30 percent shorter than its parent, *The American Promise,* Second Edition), in the process highlighting a stronger thematic development. Specifically, coverage of ancient America now appears in a refashioned and richly illustrated chapter on ancient America, to show students how and why the discussion of this crucial but obscured history differs from the historical narrative that follows in the remainder of the book. Discussion of antebellum society has been reorganized and revised to ensure a smooth, unified narrative. Throughout the text we have incorporated the most important recent scholarship, as reflected in chapter bibliographies on the companion Web site (www.bedfordstmartins.com/roarkcompact).

To provide an even more dynamic and memorable narrative while reinforcing the text's central theme, we expanded the number of historical actors whose interpretations of "the American promise"—sometimes shared, often competing—drove historical change. More succinct coverage of politics also permitted us to expand discussion of cultural and social topics such as the diversity of West Africa, the experience of Native Americans, and Western history. We have also made an effort to better place American history in a global context. Discussions of early modern Europe's westward expansion and the Haitian revolution, for example, strengthen the text's balanced, braided international coverage. Revised conclusions focus on and extend the chapter's central ideas, contributing to our effort to provide the introductory classroom the most teachable and readable text available.

Textual Changes

A new edition of a textbook is cause for celebration, for it proudly announces the successful reception of the previous edition. But as authors, we found little time for complacency, for we welcomed this opportunity to reconsider the original text, to take stock of what worked and what could be improved. In addition to the many changes already mentioned to condense the text, we

Supplements

Developed with the guidance of the author team and thoroughly revised to reflect changes in the new edition, our comprehensive collection of print and electronic resources provides a host of practical learning and teaching aids. Cross-references in the textbook to the groundbreaking Online Study Guide and the primary-source reader reflect the tight integration of core text with supplements.

For Students

Reading the American Past: Selected Historical Documents, **Second Edition.** This highly regarded primary-source collection, edited by Michael Johnson (Johns Hopkins University), one of the authors of *The American Promise,* complements the textbook by offering 4 or 5 documents for each chapter. The new edition provides a host of compelling features while retaining its low cost and brevity: a rich selection of over 125 documents (one-quarter of them new to this edition), balancing accounts by well-known figures with the voices of ordinary people; a wide array of sources that vividly illustrate the diversity of materials with which historians work; and user-friendly editorial apparatus such as chapter introductions, headnotes, questions, and an Introduction for Students on the goals and methods of source analysis.

Online Study Guide www.bedfordstmartins.com/ roarkcompact. For each chapter, our free Online Study Guide offers an initial multiple-choice test that allows students to assess their comprehension of the material and a Recommended Study Plan that suggests specific exercises on the subject areas students still need to master. Two follow-up multiple-choice tests per chapter help students judge their command of the material. Additional exercises encourage students to think about chapter themes as well as help them develop skills of analysis. Password-protected reports for instructors allow them to monitor students' activity easily.

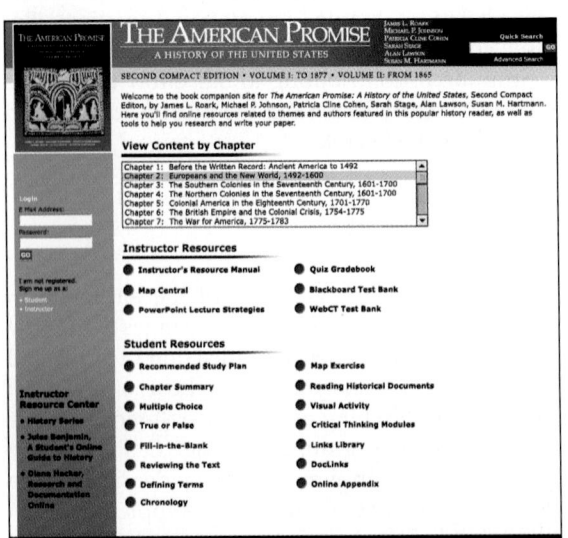

The Bedford Series in History and Culture. Over fifty American titles in this highly praised series combine first-rate scholarship, historical narrative, and important primary documents for undergraduate courses. Each book is brief, inexpensive, and focused on a specific topic or period. Package discounts are available.

Historians at Work Series. Brief enough for a single assignment yet substantive enough to provoke thoughtful discussion, each volume in this series combines the best thinking about an important historical issue with helpful learning aids. Selections by distinguished historians, each with a differing perspective, provide a unique structure within which to examine a single question. With headnotes and questions to guide their reading and the complete original footnotes, students are able to engage in discussion that captures the intellectual excitement of historical research and interpretation. Package discounts are available.

Links Library www.bedfordstmartins.com/historylinks. Links Library is a database of more than 350 carefully reviewed and annotated U.S. and Western history links searchable by historical topic and textbook chapter. Spanning history from ancient Mesopotamia to the present, the database contains diverse links to resources such as historical archaeology sites, primary documents collections, photograph and illustration galleries, map collections, secondary sources, and audio.

DocLinks www.bedfordstmartins.com/doclinks. DocLinks is a database of over 1000 annotated Web links to primary documents online for the study of U.S. and Western history. Documents in this database include speeches, legislation, U.S. Supreme Court decisions, essays, traveler's accounts, personal narratives and testimony, essays, e-books, manifestos, visual artifacts, songs, and poems. Documents are searchable by topic and date and are also indexed to the chapters of our major survey textbooks.

For Instructors

Instructor's Resource Manual. This popular manual by Sarah E. Gardner (Mercer University) offers extensive information for each chapter in the text-book: outlines of chapter themes and topics, lecture and discussion strategies, multiple-choice questions for quizzing, video and film resources, and advice on outside readings. In addition, the new edition offers suggestions on incorporating all the supplements for the Second Compact Edition of *The American Promise* into teaching plans; including Bedford series books relevant to each chapter; and assigning Using the Internet exercises that reinforce and extend the text. It also includes a wealth of practical suggestions for first-time teaching assistants, from suggestions on running discussion sections and designing assignments to advice on dealing with difficult students.

Online Instructor's Resource Manual www.bedfordstmartins.com/roarkcompact. The Online Instructor's Resource Manual combines all of the advantages of the print Instructor's Resource Manual along with links for Using the Internet exercises, annotated Web links for each chapter, PowerPoint slides for lectures, syllabus hosting, and the ability to track student work.

Videos. Available to all adopters of the text are two hours of video delivered in fifteen brief clips that allow instructors to intersperse their lectures with images and audio designed to engage students by giving voice to the history of early America. These segments are drawn from the award-winning telecourse "Shaping America," developed and distributed by the LeCroy Center for Educational Telecommunications, Dallas County Community College District. Bedford/St. Martin's is proud to announce that *The American Promise: To 1877*, Second Edition, has been selected for use in this distinguished distance learning program.

Computerized Test Bank CD-ROM for Windows or Macintosh. This thoroughly revised test bank by Valerie Hinton (Richland College) and Norman C. McLeod (Dixie State College) provides easy-to-use software to create and administer tests on paper or over a network. Instructors can generate exams and quizzes from the print test bank or write their own. A grade-management function helps keep track of student progress. It includes for each chapter in the text fifty multiple-choice questions, ten short-answer questions, four essay questions (all ranked as easy, medium, or difficult); an exercise in which students match important terms with definitions or examples; a chronology exercise; and a multipart map exercise. Also included are twenty-five black outline map quizzes. Answers for objective questions are provided.

Map Transparencies. Full-color transparencies of full-size maps from both the full and compact editions of *The American Promise* help instructors present the materials and teach students important map-reading skills.

Instructor Resources CD-ROM. This new CD-ROM offers all the maps and figures and numerous illustrations from the text in PowerPoint-ready files designed to enhance class presentations.

Using the Bedford Series in the U.S. History Survey www.bedfordstmartins.com/usingseries. This short guide by Scott Hovey (Boston University) gives practical suggestions for using more than sixty volumes from the Bedford Series in History and Culture and the Historians at Work Series with a core text in the survey classroom. The guide not only supplies links between the text and the supplements but also provides ideas for starting discussions focused on a single primary-source volume.

Map Central www.bedfordstmartins.com/mapcentral. Bedford/St. Martin's is proud to announce Map Central, a database of the more than 450 maps that appear in *The American Promise* and its other history survey texts. Designed to help instructors create more effective lecture presentations, Map Central is easily searchable by specific chapter or by keyword. Maps are in full color and downloadable for use in PowerPoint or other presentation software.

e-Content for Online Learning. e-Content for Online Learning helps instructors using *The American Promise*, Second Compact Edition, develop custom Web sites with WebCT, Blackboard, and other course-building systems.

Acknowledgments

We gratefully acknowledge all of the helpful suggestions that have come from those who have read and taught the previous editions of *The American Promise,* and we hope that our many classroom collaborators will see their influence in the Second Compact Edition. In particular, we wish to thank the talented scholars and teachers who gave generously of their time and knowledge to review this book; their critiques and suggestions have contributed greatly to the published work: Robert Allison, *Suffolk University;* Edward Baptist, *University of Miami;* Vernon Burton, *University of Illinois at Urbana-Champaign;* Manuel Callahan, *University of Texas;* Marvin Cann, *Lander University;* Robert Cormier, *Shrewsbury High School;* Dolores Davison Peterson, *Foothill College;* Alan C. Downs, *Georgia Southern University;* Frederick Fausz, *University of Missouri-St. Louis;* Richard M. Filipink, *SUNY College at Freedonia;* Randy Finley, *Georgia Perimeter College;* Ellen Fitzpatrick, *University of New Hampshire;* John M. Giggie, *University of Texas at San Antonio;* Valerie Hinton, *Richland College;* Tim Koerner, *Oakland Community College;* Jill Lepore, *Boston University;* Mike Light, *Grand Rapids Community College;* Barbara Loomis, *San Francisco State University;* Norman Love, *El Paso Community College;* Joanne Maypole, *Front Range Community College;* Tom Nierman, *University of Kansas;* Robert Olwell, *University of Texas at Austin;* Terry Perrin, *Austin Community College;* Nicolas W. Proctor, *Simpson College;* Peggy Renner, *Glendale Community College;* James Schick, *Pittsburgh State University;* Michael Searles, *Augusta State University;* Rebecca Shoemaker, *Indiana State University;* Rachel Standish, *Foothill College;* Richard M. Ugland, *The Ohio State University;* Elizabeth Van Beek, *San Jose State University;* Pamela West, *Jefferson State Community College;* Thomas Winn, *Austin Peay State University;* Molly M. Wood, *Wittenberg University;* Laura Woodward-Ney, *Idaho State University;* and William D. Young, *Maple Woods Community College.*

A project as complex as this requires the talents of many individuals. First, the authors would like to acknowledge our families for their support, forbearance, and toleration of our textbook responsibilities. Pembroke Herbert and Sandi Rygiel of Picture Research Consultants, Inc., contributed their imagination and research to make possible the extraordinary illustration program.

We would also like to thank the many people at Bedford/St. Martin's who have been crucial to this project. First we want to thank both Editor Heidi L. Hood, who coordinated the editorial process, and Editor Gretchen Boger, for their intelligence and commitment to excellence that guided every step of this revision. Thanks are also due to Editor Louise Townsend, whose accomplished editing of this and previous editions greatly improved our textbook. Special thanks also go to our friend, Executive Editor Elizabeth M. Welch, who contributed invaluably to past editions and advised on this revision. Brianna Germain, Rachel L. Siegel, and Elisabeth Stark helped with countless editorial tasks. Jane Knetzger, Director of Development for History, supported the efforts of the editorial team. We thank as well Patricia Rossi, Publisher for History and Communications, and Jenna Bookin Barry, Marketing Manager, for their tireless efforts in marketing the book. With great skill and professionalism, Project Manager Tina Samaha pulled all the pieces together with the assistance of Kerri Cardone. Managing Editor Elizabeth Schaaf, Assistant Managing Editor John Amburg, and Senior Production Supervisor Joe Ford oversaw production of the book. Our copy editor, Lisa Wehrle, improved our best efforts. Thanks also go to Associate Editor for New Media William J. Lombardo who guided the development of the companion Web site and supervised the editing of the book's supplements. New Media Production Coordinator Coleen O'Hanley helped transform the Companion Web site and other electronic supplements into reality. Director of New Media Denise Wydra provided support for these new media resources for history. Joan E. Feinberg, President, and Charles H. Christensen, former president, have taken a personal interest in *The American Promise* from the start and have guided all its editions through every stage of development.

ABOUT THE AUTHORS

James L. Roark

Born in Eunice, Louisiana, and raised in the West, James L. Roark received his B.A. from the University of California, Davis, in 1963 and his Ph.D. from Stanford University in 1973. His dissertation won the Allan Nevins Prize. He has taught at the University of Nigeria, Nsukka; the University of Nairobi, Kenya; the University of Missouri, St. Louis; and, since 1983, Emory University, where he is Samuel Candler Dobbs Professor of American History. In 1993, he received the Emory Williams Distinguished Teaching Award, and in 2001–2002 he was Pitt Professor of American Institutions at Cambridge University. He has written *Masters without Slaves: Southern Planters in the Civil War and Reconstruction* (1977). With Michael P. Johnson, he is author of *Black Masters: A Free Family of Color in the Old South* (1984) and editor of *No Chariot Let Down: Charleston's Free People of Color on the Eve of the Civil War* (1984). He has received research assistance from the American Philosophical Society, the National Endowment for the Humanities, and the Gilder Lehrman Institute of American History. Active in the Organization of American Historians and the Southern Historical Association, he is also a fellow of the Society of American Historians.

Michael P. Johnson

Born and raised in Ponca City, Oklahoma, Michael P. Johnson studied at Knox College in Galesburg, Illinois, where he received a B.A. in 1963, and at Stanford University in Palo Alto, California, earning a Ph.D. in 1973. He is currently professor of history at Johns Hopkins University in Baltimore, having previously taught at the University of California, Irvine; San Jose State University; and LeMoyne (now LeMoyne-Owen) College in Memphis. His publications include *Toward a Patriarchal Republic: The Secession of Georgia* (1977); *Black Masters: A Free Family of Color in the Old South* (1984); *No Chariot Let Down: Charleston's Free People of Color on the Eve of the Civil War* (1984); *Abraham Lincoln, Slavery, and the Civil War: Selected Speeches and Writings* (2001); and *Reading the American Past: Selected Historical Documents,* Second Edition, the documents reader for *The American Promise* (2002); and articles that have appeared in the *William and Mary Quarterly,* the *Journal of Southern History, Labor History,* the *New York Review of Books,* the *New Republic,* the *Nation,* and other journals. Johnson has been awarded research fellowships by the American Council of Learned Societies, the National Endowment for the Humanities, and the Center for Advanced Study in the Behavioral Sciences. He directed a National Endowment for the Humanities Summer Seminar for College Teachers and has been honored with the University of California, Irvine, Academic Senate Distinguished Teaching Award and the University of California, Irvine, Alumni Association Outstanding Teaching Award. He is an active member of the American Historical Association, the Organization of American Historians, and the Southern Historical Association.

Patricia Cline Cohen

Born in Ann Arbor, Michigan, and raised in Palo Alto, California, Patricia Cline Cohen earned a B.A. at the University of Chicago in 1968 and a Ph.D. at the University of California, Berkeley, in 1977. In 1976, she joined the history faculty at the University of California, Santa Barbara. Cohen has written *A Calculating People: The Spread of Numeracy in Early America* (1982; reissued 1999) and *The Murder of Helen Jewett: The Life and Death of a Prostitute in Nineteenth-Century New York* (1998). She has also published articles on quantitative literacy, mathematics education, prostitution, and murder in journals including the *Journal of Women's History, Radical History Review,* the *William and Mary Quarterly,* and the *NWSA Journal.* Her scholarly work has received support from the National Endowment for the Humanities, the National Humanities Center, the University of California President's Fellowship in the Humanities, the Mellon Foundation, the American Antiquarian Society, the Schlesinger Library, and the Newberry Library. She sits on the council for the Omohundro Institute of Early American History and Culture and on the advisory council of the Society for the History of the Early American Republic. She has served as chair of the Women's Studies Program and as acting dean of the humanities and fine arts at the

University of California, Santa Barbara. In 2001–2002 she was the Distinguished Senior Mellon Fellow at the American Antiquarian Society.

Sarah Stage

Sarah Stage was born in Davenport, Iowa, and received a B.A. from the University of Iowa in 1966 and a Ph.D. in American studies from Yale University in 1975. She has taught U.S. history for more than twenty-five years at Williams College and the University of California, Riverside. Currently she is professor of Women's Studies at Arizona State University West, in Phoenix. Her books include *Female Complaints: Lydia Pinkham and the Business of Women's Medicine* (1979) and *Rethinking Home Economics: Women and the History of a Profession* (1997), which is being translated for a Japanese edition. Among the fellowships she has received are the Rockefeller Foundation Humanities Fellowship, the American Association of University Women dissertation fellowship, a fellowship from the Charles Warren Center for the Study of History at Harvard University, and the University of California President's Fellowship in the Humanities. She is at work on a book entitled *Women and the Progressive Impulse in American Politics, 1890–1914.*

Alan Lawson

Born in Providence, Rhode Island, Alan Lawson received his B.A. from Brown University in 1955 and his M.A. from the University of Wisconsin in 1956. After Army service and experience as a high school teacher, he earned his Ph.D. from the University of Michigan in 1967. Since winning the Allan Nevins Prize for his dissertation, Lawson has served on the faculties of the University of California, Irvine; Smith College; and, currently, Boston College. He has written *The Failure of Independent Liberalism* (1971) and coedited *From Revolution to Republic* (1976). While completing the forthcoming *Ideas in Crisis: The New Deal and the Mobilization of Progressive Experience,* he has published book chapters and essays on political economy, the cultural legacy of the New Deal, multiculturalism, and the arts in public life. He has served as editor of the *Review of Education* and the *Intellectual History Newsletter* and contributed articles to those journals as well as to the *History of Education Quarterly.* He has been active in the field of American studies as director of the Boston College American Studies program and as a contributor to the *American Quarterly.* Under the auspices of the United States Information Agency, Lawson has been coordinator and lecturer for programs to instruct faculty from foreign nations in the state of American historical scholarship and teaching.

Susan M. Hartmann

Professor of history at Ohio State University, Susan M. Hartmann received her B.A. from Washington University in 1961 and her Ph.D. from the University of Missouri in 1966. After specializing in the political economy of the post–World War II period and publishing *Truman and the 80th Congress* (1971), she expanded her interests to the field of women's history, publishing many articles and three books: *The Home Front and Beyond: American Women in the 1940s* (1982); *From Margin to Mainstream: American Women and Politics since 1960* (1989); and *The Other Feminists: Activists in the Liberal Establishment* (1998). Her work has been supported by the Truman Library Institute, the Rockefeller Foundation, the National Endowment for the Humanities, and the American Council of Learned Societies. At Ohio State she has served as director of women's studies, and in 1995 she won the Exemplary Faculty Award in the College of Humanities. Hartmann has taught at the University of Missouri, St. Louis, and Boston University, and she has lectured on American history in Australia, Austria, France, Germany, Greece, Nepal, and New Zealand. She has served on award committees of the American Historical Association, the Organization of American Historians, the American Studies Association, and the National Women's Studies Association and currently is on the Board of Directors at the Truman Library Institute. Her current research is on gender and the transformation of politics since 1945.

THE
AMERICAN
PROMISE

A HISTORY OF THE UNITED STATES

Second Compact Edition

OLMEC RITUAL FIGURES

Ancient American artifacts sometimes portray human forms that probably bore a strong resemblance to the people for whom they were made. This astonishing group of Olmec men, crafted and buried between 900 and 600 B.C. in the ceremonial center at La Venta in what is now southern Mexico, is shown exactly as it was found when archaeologists excavated it in 1955. The men all exhibit cranial deformation, probably common among Olmecs of the era; it was created by wrapping tight bindings around the skulls of infants and children. These men seem to be engaged in an important ritual. The sandstone figure with his back to the upright stones, or celts, observes four men filing in front of him from his right, while eleven men of differing heights and distinctive physiognomies stand in a semicircle looking on. The significance of this ceremony is documented by its haunting artistry and careful burial, but exactly what the ceremony meant remains utterly mysterious, like so much else about ancient Americans.

Museo Nacional de Antropologia, Mexico City.

BEFORE THE WRITTEN RECORD: ANCIENT AMERICA

To 1492

I N AUGUST 1908, AFTER A VIOLENT RAINSTORM NEAR FOLSOM, NEW MEXICO, George McJunkin, the manager of the Crowfoot Ranch, rode out to mend fences and to look for missing cattle. An African American, McJunkin had been born a slave in Texas over fifty years earlier. After he became free at the end of the Civil War in 1865, McJunkin worked as a cowboy in Colorado and New Mexico, becoming the Crowfoot manager in 1891. As he surveyed the damage done by the recent storm, McJunkin noticed that the floodwater had exposed a deposit of stark white bones in the bank of a gulch called Wild Horse Arroyo. Curious, he dismounted and chipped away at the deposit until he uncovered an entire fossilized bone. Since the bone was considerably larger than the parched skeletons of range cattle and buffalo, McJunkin saved it, hoping someday to identify it.

In 1912, McJunkin met a white man named Carl Schwachheim, a blacksmith in Raton, New Mexico, who shared his curiosity about fossils, and the two men became friends. Ten years later, a few months after McJunkin's death, Schwachheim finally drove out to Wild Horse Arroyo, dug out several bones, and brought them back to Raton. But he could not identify animals that had such big bones.

In 1926, when Schwachheim delivered cattle to the stockyards in Denver, he took some of the old bones to the Denver Museum of Natural History and showed them to J. D. Figgins, a paleontologist who was an expert on fossils of ancient animals. Figgins immediately recognized the significance of the fossils and a few months later began an excavation of the Folsom site that revolutionized knowledge about the first Americans.

When Figgins began his dig at Folsom, archaeologists (individuals who study artifacts left by long-vanished peoples) believed that Native Americans had arrived relatively recently in the Western Hemisphere, probably no more than three or four thousand years earlier when, experts assumed, they had paddled small boats across the icy waters of the Bering Strait from what is now Siberia. At Folsom, Figgins learned that the bones McJunkin had first spotted belonged to twenty-three giant bison, a species known to have been extinct for at least 10,000 years. Far more startling, Figgins found nineteen flint projectile points (Folsom points, they have since been called) associated with the bones, proof that human beings had been alive at the same time as the giant bison. One flint point remained stuck between two ribs of a giant bison, just where a Stone Age hunter had plunged it more than 10,000

GEORGE MCJUNKIN
This photo shows McJunkin a few years after he discovered the Folsom site, but about fifteen years before anyone understood the significance of his find. He appears here in his work clothes on horseback, as he probably was when he made the discovery. The fossilized bones he discovered belonged to an extinct bison species that was much larger than modern bison; the horns of the ancient animal often spanned six feet, wide enough for McJunkin's horse to have stood sideways between the horns.

Eastern New Mexico University, Blackwater Draw Site, Portales, New Mexico 88130.

years earlier. No longer could anyone doubt that human beings had inhabited North America for at least ten millennia.

The Folsom discovery sparked other major finds of ancient artifacts that continue to this day. Since the 1930s, archaeologists have tried to reconstruct the history of ancient Americans, making connections between the hunters who killed giant bison with flint points, their descendants who built southwestern pueblos and eastern burial mounds, and *their* descendants who encountered the Europeans who arrived with Christopher Columbus in 1492. Although the story they have assembled is incomplete and controversial, nonetheless scholars have learned enough about ancient Americans to bring into focus who they were, where they came from, and some basic features of their history in the thousands of years before that moment in 1492 when some of them stood on the beach of a small island in the Caribbean and watched Columbus and his men row ashore.

Archaeology and History

Archaeologists and historians share the desire to learn about people who lived in the past, but they usually employ different methods to obtain information. Both archaeologists and historians study artifacts as clues to the activities and ideas of the humans who created them. They concentrate, however, on different kinds of artifacts. Archaeologists tend to focus on physical objects such as bones, stones, pots, baskets, jewelry, textiles, clothing, graves, and buildings. Historians direct their attention mostly to writings, which encompass personal and private jottings such as diary entries and love letters, official and public pronouncements such as laws and speeches, as well as an enormous variety of other documents such as court records, censuses, business ledgers, newspapers, books, and pamphlets. Although historians are interested in other artifacts and archaeologists do not neglect written sources if they exist, the characteristic concentration of historians on writings and archaeologists on other physical objects denotes a rough cultural and chronological boundary between the human beings studied by the two groups of scholars, a boundary marked by the use of writing.

A system of symbols that record spoken language, writing originated among ancient peoples in China, Egypt, and Central America about 8,000 years ago, within the most recent 2 percent of the 400 millennia that modern human beings (*Homo sapiens*) have existed. Writing came into use even later in most other places in the world. The ancient Americans who inhabited North America in 1492, for example, possessed many forms of symbolic representation, but not writing.

The people who lived during the millennia before writing were biologically nearly identical to people today. After all, their DNA was the template for ours. But they differed from us in many other ways, among them in not using writing to communicate across space and time. They certainly had a history, both individually and collectively. They moved across the face of the globe; they invented hundreds of spoken languages; they learned to survive and even to thrive in almost every natural environment; they chose and honored leaders; they traded, warred, and worshiped; and, above all, they learned from and taught each other, not just old ways but, little by little, surprising new ways. Nonetheless, much of what we would like to know about their history remains unknown because it took place before written history existed. It is this lack of written records that has prompted the misleading label of *prehistory* for this era. These ancient people spoke to each other, but, without writing, time forever muffled their words and thus their history.

Archaeologists specialize in learning about people whose history was not documented in writing. They study the millions of artifacts created by these people, trying to decipher what the objects can tell us about their lives. By also scrutinizing soil, geological strata, pollen, climate, and other environmental features, they attempt to reconstruct the outlines of the history of ancient peoples. But much of their history remains unknown and unknowable. The absence of written sources means that ancient human beings remain anonymous. No documents chronicle their births and deaths, comings and goings, victories and defeats. Despite these silences, archaeologists have learned to make ancient artifacts tell a great deal about the people who made them.

This introductory chapter relies on the work of archaeologists to sketch a brief overview of ancient America. Calling the long history of ancient Americans an introduction reflects our present-mindedness, an outgrowth of our desire to understand the origins and development of our own society over the last five centuries or so. Ancient Americans surely did not consider their history an introduction to a future that included us. They resided in North America for thousands of years before Europeans arrived. They created societies and cultures of amazing diversity and complexity. But because they did not use written records, their history cannot be reconstructed with the detail and certainty made possible by written documents. Nonetheless, their remarkable longevity and creativity make it far preferable to abbreviate and oversimplify their history than to ignore it.

The First Americans

Human beings existed elsewhere in the world long before they reached the Western Hemisphere. The basic reason for the prolonged absence of humans from the Western Hemisphere is that millions of years before human beings came into existence North and South America became detached from the gigantic continent scientists now call Pangaea. Beginning about 240 million years ago, powerful forces deep within the earth slowly pushed the continents apart to approximately their present positions (see Map 1.1). This process of continental drift encircled the land of the Western Hemisphere with large oceans and isolated it from the other continents, long before early human beings (*Homo erectus*) evolved in Africa about 2 million years ago. Only within the last 400,000 years did modern humans (*Homo sapiens*) evolve and migrate out of Africa and into Europe and Asia. For roughly 97 percent of the time *Homo sapiens* have existed, no one set foot in the Western Hemisphere.

Asian Origins

Two major developments made it possible for human beings to reach the Western Hemisphere. First, humans successfully adapted to the frigid environment near the Arctic Circle. Second, changes in the earth's climate reconnected North America to Asia.

By about 25,000 years ago, people had learned to use bone needles to sew animal skins into warm clothing that permitted humans to become permanent residents of extremely cold regions like northeastern Siberia. Today, the Bering Strait, a body of water about sixty miles wide, separates easternmost Siberia from westernmost Alaska. But during the last great global cold spell—the Wisconsin glaciation, which endured from about 80,000 years ago to about 10,000 years ago—snow piled up in glaciers that did not melt, causing the sea level

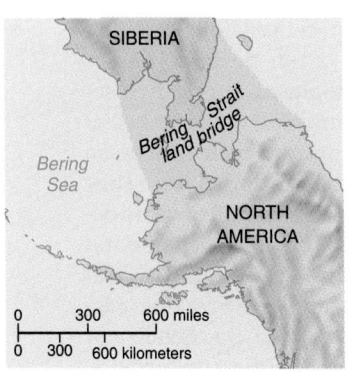

The Bering Strait

to drop as much as 350 feet below its current level. The seafloor that is now submerged 120 feet below the surface of the Bering Strait was then dry land, forming what is often called a "land bridge" between Asian Siberia and American Alaska. However, the exposed land was not a narrow bridge but a region about a thousand miles wide that scientists call Beringia.

Grasses and small shrubs covered Beringia and supported herds of mammoth, bison, and horses as well as numerous smaller animals. Siberian hunters presumably roamed into Beringia for thousands of years in search of game animals. Archaeologists speculate that hunters traveled in small bands of perhaps twenty-five people. How many such bands arrived in North America before water once again covered Beringia will never be known. When they arrived is hotly debated by experts. The first migrants probably arrived sometime after 15,000 years

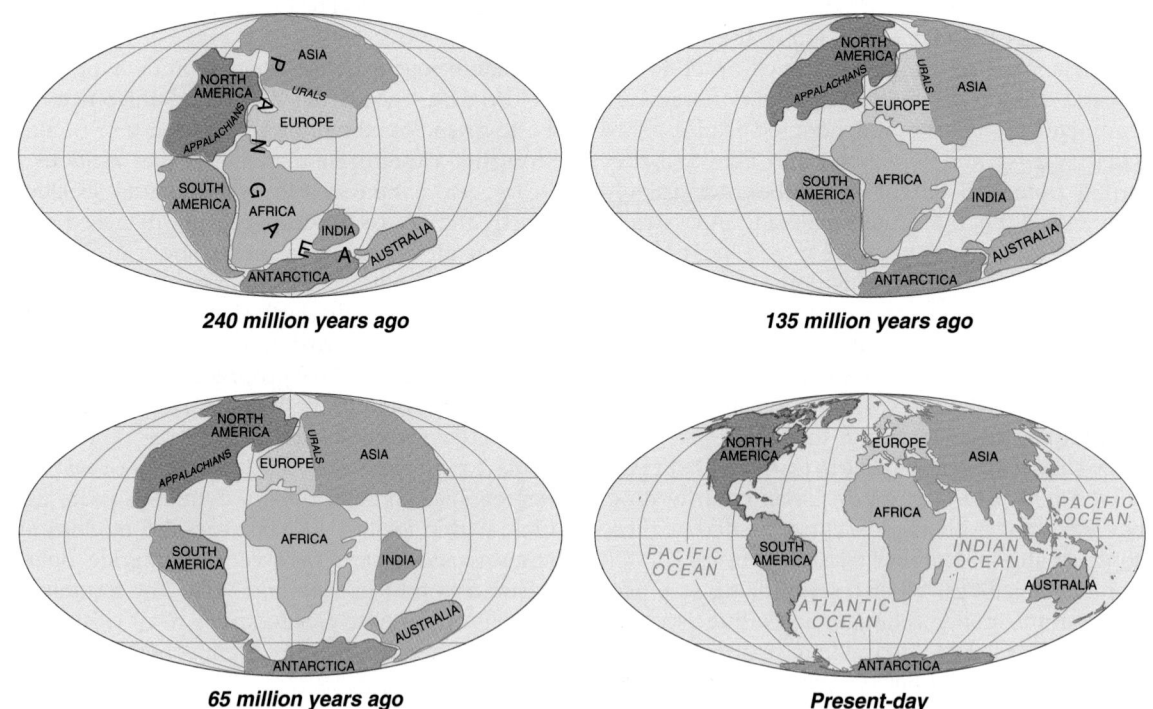

240 million years ago

135 million years ago

65 million years ago

Present-day

MAP 1.1

Continental Drift

Massive geological forces separated North and South America from other continents eons before human beings evolved in Africa in the last 1.5 million years. This continental drift explains why human life developed elsewhere on the planet for hundreds of thousands of years before the first person entered the Western Hemisphere during the last fifteen thousand years.

ago. Scattered and inconclusive evidence suggests that these first Americans may have arrived a few thousand years earlier.

Archaeologists refer to these first migrants and their descendants for the next few millennia as Paleo-Indians. Their Asian origins seem almost certain. Siberians hunted large game, and Beringia provided an attractive hunting ground that reached all the way to North America, a wide avenue to the Western Hemisphere that existed for no other humans at the time. Furthermore, Native Americans today still share certain obvious physical characteristics of Asians. Detailed analyses of Native American languages and of certain blood proteins provide additional compelling evidence of Asian origins.

Paleo-Indian Hunters

When humans first arrived in the Western Hemisphere, massive glaciers covered most of Canada. A narrow corridor not entirely obstructed by ice ran along the eastern side of the Canadian Rockies, and most archaeologists believe that Paleo-Indians migrated through it in pursuit of game. They may also have traveled along the coast in small boats, hopscotching from one desirable landing spot to another. At the southern edge of the glaciers, Paleo-Indians entered a hunters' paradise. North, Central, and South America teemed with wildlife that had never before confronted wily two-legged predators armed with razor-sharp spears. The abundance of game presumably made hunting relatively easy. Ample food permitted the Paleo-Indian population to grow. Within a thousand years or so, Paleo-Indians had reached the southern tip of South America and virtually everywhere else in the Western Hemisphere.

Paleo-Indians used a distinctively shaped spearhead known as a Clovis point, named for the place in New Mexico where it was first excavated. The discovery of Clovis points throughout North and Central America in sites dated between 11,500 and 11,000 years ago is powerful evidence that these nomadic hunters shared a common ancestry and way of life. The Paleo-Indians who used Clovis points to kill big animals probably also hunted smaller animals. But most of the artifacts that have survived from this era indicate that Paleo-Indians specialized in hunting big mammals. One mammoth kill supplied meat for weeks or, if dried, for months. The hide and bones could be used for clothing, shelter, and tools.

About 11,000 years ago Paleo-Indians confronted a major crisis. The big-game animals they hunted became extinct. Scientists are not completely certain why the extinction occurred, although the changing environment probably contributed to it. About this time the Wisconsin glacial period came to an end, glaciers melted, and sea levels rose. Large mammals presumably had difficulty adapting to the warmer climate. Many archaeologists also believe, however, that Paleo-Indian hunters were the major cause of the New World extinctions by killing animals more rapidly than these animals could reproduce.

Paleo-Indians adapted to the big-game extinctions by making at least two important changes in their way of life. First, hunters necessarily focused their attention on smaller animals. Second, Paleo-Indians devoted more energy to foraging, that is, to collecting wild plant foods such as roots, seeds, nuts, berries, and fruits. When Paleo-Indians made these changes, the apparent uniformity of the big-game-oriented Clovis culture* was replaced by great cultural diversity. Paleo-Indians adapted to the many natural environments throughout the hemisphere, ranging from icy tundra to steamy jungles.

Post-Clovis adaptations to local environments led to the astounding variety of Native American cultures that existed when Europeans arrived in 1492. By then, more than three hundred major tribes and hundreds of lesser groups inhabited North America alone. Hundreds more lived in Central and South America. These people spoke different languages, practiced different religions, lived in different dwellings, followed different subsistence strategies, and observed different rules of kinship and inheritance. Hundreds of other ancient American cultures had disappeared or transformed themselves as their members constantly adapted to changing environmental conditions. A full account of those changes and the cultural diversity they created is beyond the scope of this textbook. But we cannot ignore the most important changes and

---

*The word *culture* is used here to connote what is commonly called "way of life." It refers not only to how a group of people supplied themselves with food and shelter but also to family relationships, social groupings, religious ideas, and other features of their way of life. For most prehistoric cultures— as for the Clovis people—more is known about food and shelter because of the artifacts that have survived. Ancient Americans' ideas, assumptions, hopes, dreams, and fantasies were undoubtedly important, but we know very little about them.

adaptations made by ancient Americans during the last eleven millennia.

Archaic Hunters and Gatherers

Archaeologists use the term *Archaic* to describe the many different hunting and gathering cultures that descended from Paleo-Indians. *Archaic* also refers to the long period of time when those cultures dominated the history of ancient America, roughly from 8000 B.C. to somewhere between 2000 and 1000 B.C. Although the cultural and the chronological boundaries of the Archaic era are not sharply defined, the term *Archaic* usefully describes the important era in the history of ancient America that followed the Paleo-Indian big-game hunters and preceded the development of agriculture. It also denotes a hunter-gatherer way of life that persisted throughout most of North America well into the era of European colonization.

Like their Paleo-Indian ancestors, Archaic Indians hunted with spears; but they also took smaller game with traps, nets, and hooks. Unlike Paleo-Indians, most Archaic peoples used a variety of stone tools to prepare food from wild plants. A characteristic Archaic artifact is a grinding stone used to pulverize seeds into edible form. Most Archaic Indians migrated from place to place to harvest plants and hunt animals. They usually did not establish permanent villages, although they often returned to the same river valley or fertile meadow from year to year to take advantage of abundant food resources. In certain regions where resources were especially rich—such as California and the Pacific Northwest—permanent settlements developed. Many Archaic groups became highly proficient basket makers in order to collect and store plant food. Above all, Archaic folk did not depend on agriculture for food. Instead, they gathered wild plants and hunted wild animals. These general traits of Archaic peoples were expressed in distinctive ways in the major environmental regions of North America (Map 1.2).

FOLSOM POINT AT WILD HORSE ARROYO
In 1927, paleontologist J. D. Figgins found this spear point (subsequently named a Folsom point) at the site discovered by George McJunkin. Embedded between the fossilized ribs of a bison that had been extinct for 10,000 years, this point proved that ancient Americans had inhabited the hemisphere at least that long. The importance of this find led one paleontologist to hold up several Folsom points and proclaim, "In my hand I hold the answer to the antiquity of man in America." Although he exaggerated (since Folsom was only part of the answer), this discovery in Wild Horse Arroyo stimulated archaeologists to rethink the history of ancient Americans and to uncover fresh evidence of their many cultures.

Great Plains Bison Hunters

After the extinction of large game such as mammoths, hunters began to concentrate on huge herds of bison that grazed the grassy, arid plains stretching for hundreds of miles east of the Rocky Mountains. For almost a thousand years after the big-game extinctions, Archaic Indians hunted bison with Folsom points like those found at the site discovered by George McJunkin.

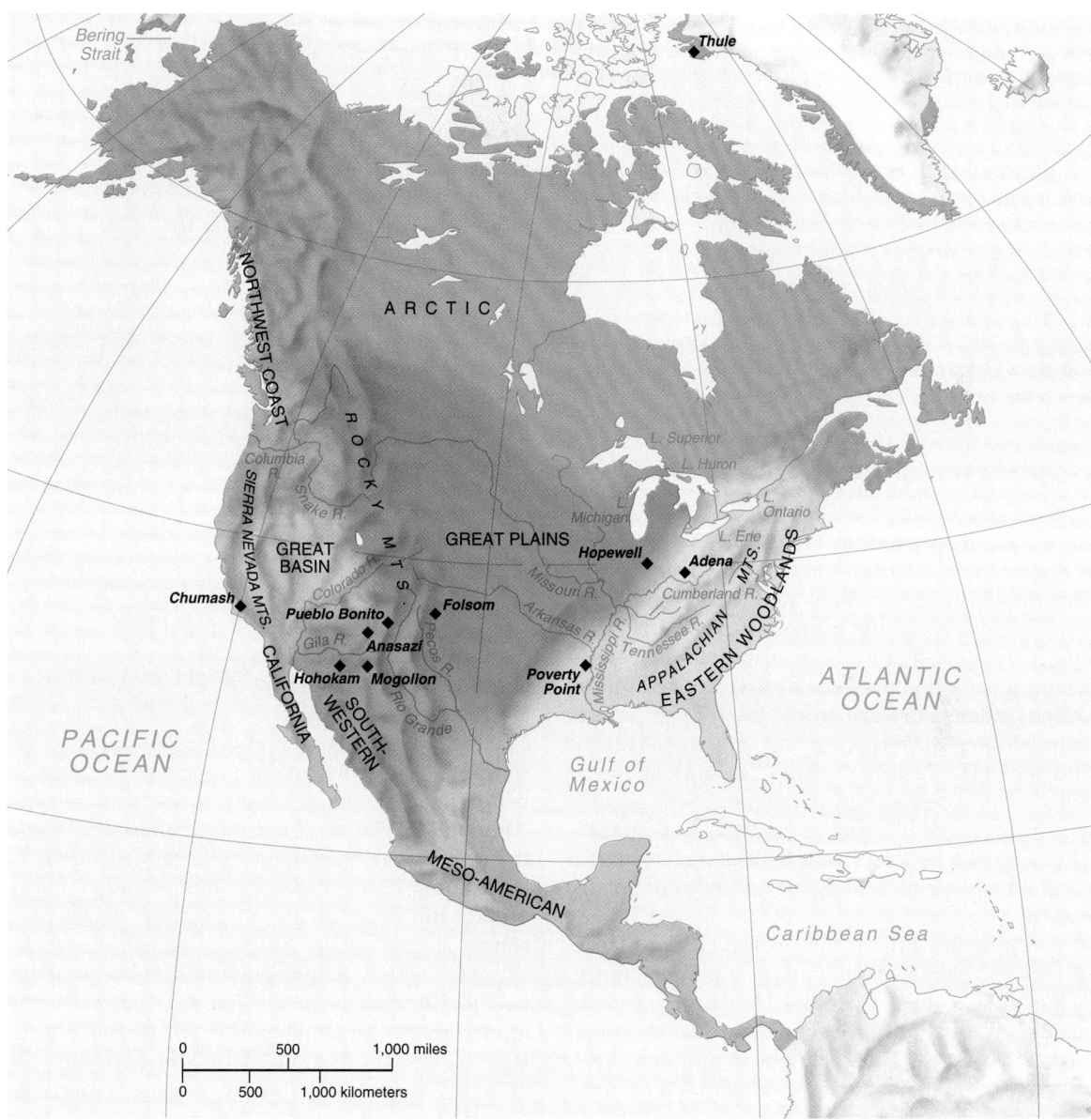

M A P 1 . 2

Native North American Cultures

Environmental conditions defined the boundaries of the broad zones of cultural similarity among ancient North Americans. Using the map, try to specify the crucial environmental features that set the boundaries of each cultural region. The topography indicated on Map 1.3, "Native North Americans about 1500," may be helpful.

Like their predecessors, Folsom hunters were nomads who moved constantly to maintain contact with their prey. Often two or three hunters from a band of several families would single out a few bison from a herd and creep up close enough to spear them. Bison hunters also developed trapping techniques that made it easier to kill large numbers of animals. At the original Folsom site, careful study of the bones McJunkin found suggests that early one winter hunters drove bison into the arroyo and speared twenty-three of them. At many other sites, hunters stampeded large numbers of bison over cliffs, killing some and injuring others, which could then be readily dispatched by waiting hunters.

Bows and arrows reached the Great Plains from the north by about A.D. 500 and largely replaced spears, which had been the hunters' weapon of choice for millennia. Bows permitted hunters to strike an animal from farther away, and arrows made it easy to shoot repeatedly. These new weapons did not otherwise alter the age-old techniques of bison hunting that had been developing since the Folsom era.

Great Basin Cultures

Archaic peoples in the Great Basin between the Rocky Mountains and the Sierra Nevada inhabited a region of great environmental diversity. Some Great Basin Indians lived along the shores of large marshes and lakes that formed during rainy periods. They ate fish of every available size and type, taking them with bone hooks as well as with nets. Other cultures survived in the foothills of mountains between the blistering heat in the desert floor and the cold, treeless mountain heights. Hunters killed deer, antelope, and sometimes bison, as well as smaller game like rabbits, rodents, and snakes. These broadly defined zones of habitation changed constantly depending largely on the amount of rainfall.

Despite the variety and occasional abundance of animals, plants were the most important source of food for Great Basin peoples. Unlike animal food, plant food could be collected in large quantities and stored in baskets for long periods to protect against shortages caused by the fickle rainfall. Piñon nuts became a dietary staple for many Great Basin peoples. By diversifying their food sources and migrating to favorable locations, Great Basin peoples adapted to environmental challenges and maintained their basic hunter-gatherer way of life until long after A.D. 1492.

Pacific Coast Cultures

The richness of the natural environment made California the most densely settled area in all of ancient North America. The abundant resources of both land and ocean offered such ample food that California groups remained hunters and gatherers for hundreds of years after Europeans arrived in the Western Hemisphere. The diversity of California's environment encouraged corresponding diversity among native peoples. By A.D. 1492, the mosaic of settlements in California included about five hundred separate tribes speaking some ninety languages, each with local dialects. No other region of comparable size in North America exhibited such cultural variety.

The Chumash, one of the many California cultures, emerged near Santa Barbara about 5,000 years ago. Comparatively plentiful food resources—especially acorns—permitted Chumash people to establish relatively permanent villages. Although few other California cultures achieved the population density and village settlements of the Chumash, all shared the hunter-gatherer way of life and reliance on acorns as a major food source.

Another rich natural environment lay along the Pacific Northwest coast. Like the Chumash, the Northwest peoples built more or less permanent villages. Abundant fish and marine life permitted the ancient Americans in this region to devote substantial time and energy to activities other than hunting and gathering. After about 5,500 years ago, they concentrated on catching large quantities of salmon, halibut, and other fish, which they dried to last throughout the year. With time free from the demands of food gathering, Northwest peoples developed sophisticated woodworking skills. They fashioned huge canoes, some big enough to hold fifty people, which they used to fish, hunt, and conduct warfare against neighboring tribes. They also carved totem poles with images of animals, ancestors, and supernatural beings to adorn their houses.

Ancient California

OZETTE WHALE EFFIGY
This carving of a whale fin decorated with hundreds of sea otter teeth was discovered along with thousands of other artifacts of daily life at Ozette, an ancient village on the tip of the Olympic Peninsula in present-day Washington that was inundated by a catastrophic mudslide about five hundred years ago. The fin illustrates the importance of whale hunting to the residents of Ozette, who set out in canoes carrying eight men armed with harpoons to catch and kill animals weighing twenty to thirty tons.
Makah Cultural and Resource Center.

Eastern Woodland Cultures

East of the Mississippi River, Archaic peoples adapted to a forest environment that included many local variants, such as the major river valleys of the Mississippi, Ohio, Tennessee, and Cumberland; the Great Lakes region; and the Atlantic coast (see Map 1.2). Throughout these diverse locales, Archaic peoples adopted basic survival strategies.

Deer were the most important prey of nearly all Woodland hunters. In addition to food, deer supplied hides and bones that were crafted into useful items such as clothing, weapons, needles, and other tools. Like Archaic peoples elsewhere, Woodland Indians gathered edible plants, seeds, and especially nuts. Hickory nuts were the most commonly gathered plant food, but pecans, walnuts, acorns, and hazelnuts were also collected. About 4000 B.C., some Woodland groups established more or less permanent settlements of 25 to 150 people, usually near a river or lake that offered a wide variety of plant and animal resources. The existence of semi-permanent settlements has permitted archaeologists to locate numerous Archaic burial sites that suggest the life expectancy at birth for these Woodland people was slightly over eighteen years.

Around 2000 B.C., the Woodland cultures incorporated two important features into their basic hunter-gatherer lifestyles: agriculture and pottery. Gourds and pumpkins that originated in Mexico spread to North America though trade and migration and began to be grown in parts of Missouri and Kentucky. After the introduction of these Mexican crops, Woodland peoples began to cultivate local species such as sunflowers. It is likely that they also grew tobacco, another import from South America, since stone pipes for smoking appeared by 1500 B.C. Corn, the most important plant food in Mexico, did not become a significant food crop until more than a thousand years later. These cultivated crops added to the quantity, variety, and predictability of Woodland food sources, but they did not fundamentally alter the hunter-gatherer way of life.

Techniques for making ceramic pots probably also originated in Mexico and may have been brought north by traders and migrants along with Mexican seeds. Pots were more durable than baskets for food preparation and storage, but they were also much heavier, probably an outgrowth of more permanent settlements. Neither pottery nor agriculture caused Woodland peoples to turn away from their basic hunter-gatherer cultures, which persisted in most areas to A.D. 1492 and beyond.

Agricultural Settlements and Chiefdoms

Among Eastern Woodland peoples and other Archaic cultures, agriculture supplemented rather than replaced hunter-gatherer subsistence strategies. Reliance on wild animals and plants required most Archaic groups to remain small and mobile. But in the centuries after 2000 B.C., distinctive southwestern cultures slowly came to rely on agriculture and to build permanent settlements. Later, around 500 B.C., Woodland peoples in the vast Mississippi valley began to construct burial mounds and other earthworks that suggest the existence of social and political hierarchies that archaeologists term chiefdoms. Although the hunter-gatherer lifestyle never entirely disappeared, the development of agricultural settlements and chiefdoms represented important innovations to the Archaic way of life.

Southwestern Cultures

Ancient Americans in Arizona, New Mexico, and southern portions of Utah and Colorado developed cultures characterized by agriculture and eventually by multiunit dwellings called pueblos. All southwestern peoples confronted the challenge of a dry climate and unpredictable fluctuations in rainfall that made the supply of wild plant food very unreliable. These ancient Americans probably adopted agriculture in response to this basic environmental condition.

Until about five thousand years ago, the population of the Southwest appears to have been extremely sparse. Sometime within a few centuries of 1500 B.C., southwestern hunters and gatherers began to cultivate their signature food crop, corn. Over the following centuries, corn became the basic cultivated food crop for Native American peoples throughout North America. The demands of corn cultivation encouraged southwestern hunter-gatherers to restrict their migratory habits in order to tend the crop. A vital consideration was access to water. Southwestern Indians became irrigation experts, conserving water from streams, springs, and rainfall and distributing it to thirsty crops.

Between about A.D. 200 and 900, small farming settlements appeared throughout southern New Mexico, marking the emergence of the Mogollon culture. Typically, a Mogollon settlement included about a dozen pit houses, made by digging out a

ANCIENT AGRICULTURE *Dropping seeds into holes punched in cleared ground by a pointed stick, this ancient American farmer sows a new crop while previously planted seeds— including the corn and beans immediately opposite him—bear fruit for harvest. Created by a sixteenth-century European artist, the drawing misrepresents who did the agricultural work in many ancient American cultures, namely women rather than men.* Art Resource, NY.

rounded pit about fifteen feet in diameter and a foot or two deep and then erecting poles to support a roof of branches or dirt. Larger villages usually had one or two bigger pit houses that may have been the predecessors of the circular kivas, the ceremonial rooms that became a characteristic of nearly all southwestern settlements. About A.D. 1000, Mogollon culture began to decline, for reasons that remain obscure.

About A.D. 500, people who appear to have emigrated from Mexico established the distinctive Hohokam culture in southern Arizona. Hohokam peoples made extensive use of irrigation to plant and harvest twice a year. Their comparatively high crop yields allowed the Hohokam population to grow and seek out more land to settle. Hohokam culture continued to be strongly influenced by Mexico. The people built sizable platform mounds and ball courts characteristic of cultures to the south. The Hohokam culture declined about A.D. 1400, for reasons that remain a mystery.

North of the Hohokam and Mogollon cultures, in a region that encompassed southern Utah and Colorado and northern Arizona and New Mexico, the Anasazi culture began to flourish during the

first century A.D. The early Anasazi built pit houses on mesa tops and used irrigation much like their neighbors to the south. Beginning around A.D. 1000 (again, it is not known why), the Anasazi began to move to large, multistory cliff dwellings whose spectacular ruins still exist at Mesa Verde, Colorado, and Canyon de Chelly, Arizona. Other Anasazi communities, like the one whose impressive ruins can be visited at Chaco Canyon, New Mexico, erected huge, stone-walled pueblos with enough rooms to house the entire population of the settlement. Pueblo Bonito at Chaco Canyon, for example, contained more than eight hundred rooms. Anasazi pueblos and cliff dwellings typically contained one or more kivas used for secret ceremonies, restricted to men, that sought to communicate with the supernatural world.

Around A.D. 1130, drought began to plague the region. The drought lasted for half a century and triggered the disappearance of Anasazi culture. By 1200, the large Anasazi pueblos had been abandoned. The prolonged drought may have intensified conflict among pueblos and rendered ineffective the agricultural methods that had been developed in earlier centuries. Some Anasazi

PUEBLO BONITO, CHACO CANYON
The ruins of Pueblo Bonito, the largest of many similar pueblos built centuries ago by the Anasazi in Chaco Canyon, New Mexico, can still be visited today. The numerous circular structures were kivas, underground ceremonial chambers that were originally covered with wooden roofs. What do the number, size, and arrangement of kivas at Pueblo Bonito suggest about the Anasazi who lived and visited there?
Richard Alexander Cooke III.

migrated toward regions with more reliable rainfall and settled in Hopi, Zuñi, and Acoma pueblos that their descendants in Arizona and New Mexico have occupied ever since.

Burial Mounds and Chiefdoms

No other ancient Americans created dwellings similar to pueblos, but around 500 B.C., Woodland cultures throughout the vast drainage of the Mississippi River began to build burial mounds. The size of the mounds, the labor and organization required to erect them, and the differences in the artifacts buried with certain individuals suggest the existence of a social and political hierarchy that archaeologists term a chiefdom.

Between about 500 and 100 B.C., Adena people built hundreds of burial mounds radiating from central Ohio (see Map 1.2). In the mounds, the Adena usually deposited a wide variety of grave goods, including spear points and stone pipes as well as decorative and ritualistic items such as thin sheets of mica (a glasslike mineral) crafted into naturalistic shapes. Once the body and grave goods were in place, dirt was piled into a mound one basketful at a time. Sometimes mounds were constructed all at once, but often they were built up over many years.

About 100 B.C., Adena culture evolved into the more elaborate Hopewell culture, which lasted about 500 years. It too was centered in Ohio but extended throughout the Ohio and Mississippi valleys. Hopewell people built larger mounds and filled them with more magnificent grave goods than had their Adena predecessors. Burial was probably reserved for the most important members of Hopewell groups. Most people were cremated.

Grave goods at Hopewell sites testify not only to the high quality of Hopewell crafts but also to the existence of a trade network ranging from Wyoming to Florida. After about A.D. 400, Hopewell culture declined, for reasons that are obscure. Some archaeologists believe that the bow and arrow and increasing reliance on agriculture may have made small settlements more self-sufficient and less dependent on the central authority of the chiefs responsible for the burial mounds.

Four hundred years later, another mound-building culture flourished. The Mississippian culture emerged in the floodplains of the major southeastern river systems about A.D. 800 and lasted until about 1500. Major Mississippian sites included huge mounds with platforms on top for ceremonies

WOODLAND EAGLE CARVING
This eagle effigy topped a post in a charnel house where Woodland Indians deposited the remains of their dead ancestors sometime between 1,500 and 1,000 years ago at a site in present-day Florida. The significance of the eagle is unknown; it may have represented the clan of the deceased in the charnel house.

Florida Museum of Natural History, photograph © 1985 The Detroit Institute of Arts.

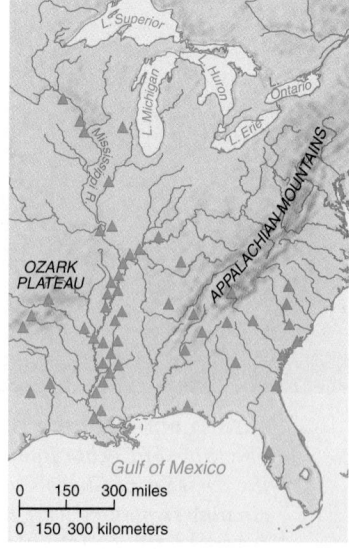

Major Mississippian Mounds, A.D. 800–1500

and for the residences of great chiefs. The largest Mississippian site was Cahokia, just across the Mississippi River from St. Louis, Missouri.

At Cahokia, more than one hundred mounds of different sizes and shapes were grouped around large open plazas. Monk's Mound, the largest, covered sixteen acres at its base and was one hundred feet tall. Dwellings at one time covered five square miles and may have housed as many as thirty thousand inhabitants, easily qualifying Cahokia as the largest settlement in North America. At Cahokia and other Mississippian sites, people evidently worshiped a sun god; perhaps the mounds were a way to elevate elites nearer to the sun.

One Cahokia burial mound suggests the authority a great chief exercised. One man—presumably the chief—was buried with the bodies of fifty-seven people who had evidently been killed at the time of burial. Such a mass sacrifice shows the power a Cahokian chief wielded and the obedience he commanded.

Cahokia and other Mississippian sites had dwindled by A.D. 1500. By the time of European contact, most of the descendants of Mississippian cultures lived in small dispersed villages supported by agriculture, hunting, and gathering.

Native Americans in 1492

By the time Europeans arrived, North American tribes had incorporated and adapted many of the cultural achievements of their ancestors. The rigors of the continent's natural environments required that they maintain time-tested adaptations.

Eastern Woodland peoples clustered into three major groups. Algonquian tribes inhabited the Atlantic seaboard, the Great Lakes region, and much of the upper Midwest (Map 1.3). The relatively mild climate along the Atlantic permitted the coastal Algonquians to grow corn and other crops as well as to hunt and fish. Around the Great Lakes and in northern New England, however, cool summers and severe winters made agriculture impractical. Instead, the Abenaki, Penobscot, Chippewa, and other tribes hunted and fished, using canoes both for transportation and for gathering wild rice.

Inland from the Algonquians were the territories of the Iroquoian tribes, centered in Pennsylvania and upstate New York, as well as the hilly upland regions of the Carolinas and Georgia. Several features distinguished Iroquoian tribes from their neighbors. First, their success in cultivating corn and other crops allowed them to build permanent settlements, usually consisting of several bark-covered longhouses up to one hundred feet long and housing five to ten families. Second, Iroquoian societies were thoroughly matriarchal. Property of all sorts, including land, children, and inheritance, belonged to women. Women headed family clans and even selected the chiefs (normally men) who governed tribes. Third, for purposes of war and diplomacy, the Seneca, Onondaga, Mohawk, Oneida, and Cayuga tribes formed the League of Five Nations, an Iroquoian confederation that remained powerful well into the eighteenth century.

Muskogean peoples spread throughout the Southeast, south of the Ohio River and east of the Mississippi. Including Creek, Choctaw, Chickasaw, and Natchez tribes, Muskogeans inhabited a bountiful natural environment that provided abundant food from hunting, gathering, and agriculture. Remnants of the Mississippian culture existed in the religious rites common among the Muskogean. They practiced a form of sun worship, and the Natchez even built temple mounds modeled after those of their Mississippian ancestors.

West of the Mississippi River, Great Plains peoples straddled the boundary between the Eastern Woodland and the western tribes. Many of the tribes had migrated to the plains within the century or two before 1500, forced westward by Iroquoian and Algonquian tribes. They were in the process of increasing their reliance on buffalo, although some tribes—especially the Mandan and Pawnee—were successful farmers, growing both corn and sunflowers. The Teton Sioux, Blackfeet, Comanche, Cheyenne, and Crow on the northern plains and the Apache and other nomadic tribes on the southern plains depended on buffalo. Tribes in the Great Basin region, such as the Comanche and Shoshone, also continued to follow earlier subsistence practices, as did Pacific coast cultures.

In the Southwest, descendants of the Mogollon, Hohokam, and Anasazi cultures lived in settled agricultural communities, many of them pueblos. However, a large number of warlike Athapascan tribes had invaded the area within the two hundred years before 1500. The Athapascans—principally Apache and Navajo—were skillful warriors who preyed on the sedentary pueblo Indians, reaping the fruits of agriculture without the work of farming.

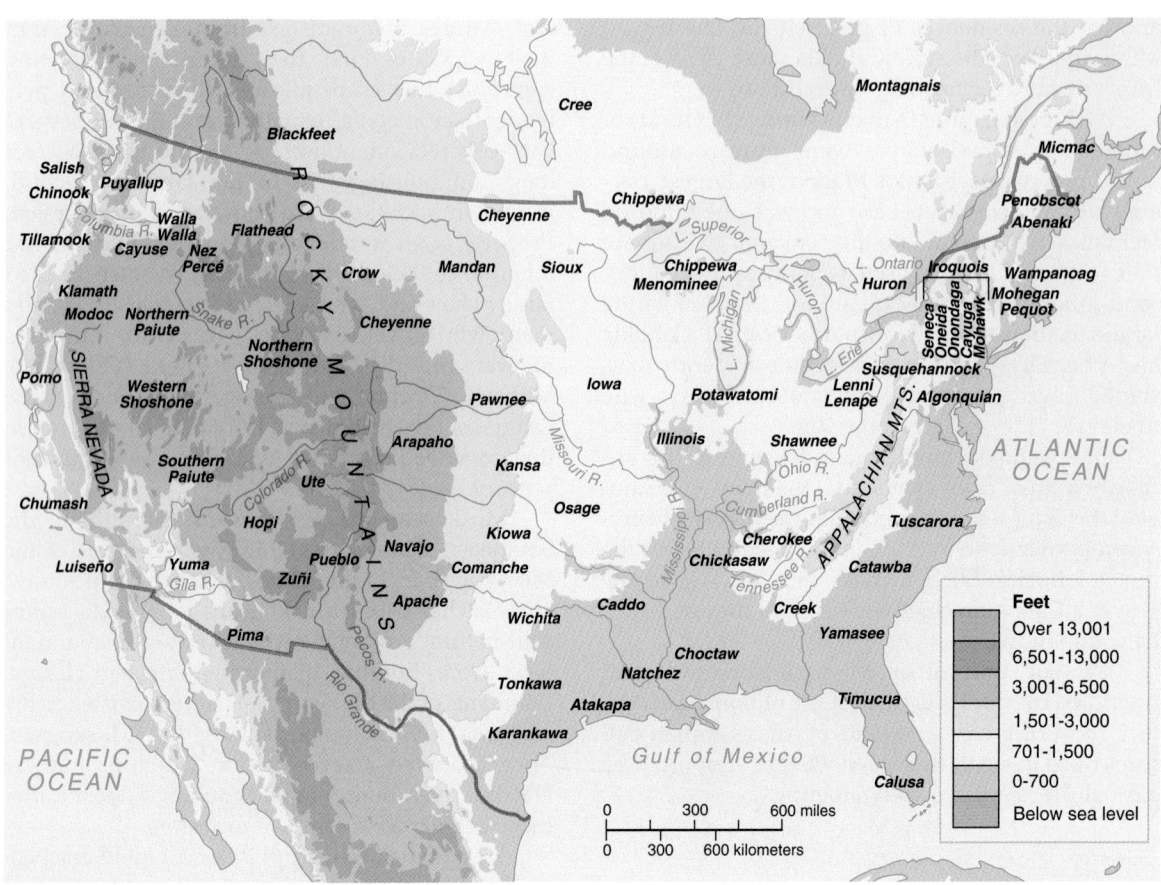

MAP 1.3

Native North Americans about 1500

Distinctive Native American peoples resided throughout the area that, centuries later, would become the United States. This map indicates the approximate location of some of the larger tribes about 1500. In the interest of legibility, many other peoples who inhabited North America at the time are omitted from the map.

By the time Columbus arrived, the comparatively small Native American settlements in North America supported a population estimated to be about four million, slightly less than the population of the British Isles at the time. All of them depended on hunting and gathering for a major portion of their food. Most of them also practiced agriculture, some far more than others. All of them used bows and arrows, as well as other weapons, for hunting and warfare. None of them employed writing, expressing themselves instead in many other ways. They made drawings on stones, wood, and animal skins; wove patterns in baskets and textiles; painted designs on pottery; and crafted beadwork, pipes, and other decorative items. They danced, sang, and

played music. They performed elaborate burial ceremonies and other religious rites.

Ancient Americans' rich and varied cultural resources did not include certain common features of life in late-fifteenth-century Europe: They did not use wheels; sailing ships were unknown; they had no large domesticated animals like horses, cows, or oxen; their use of metals was restricted to copper; and metallurgy did not exist in North America. However, the absence of these European conveniences was profoundly irrelevant to ancient North Americans. Their cultures had developed as adaptations to the natural environment local to each tribe. That great similarity underlay all the cultural diversity among native North Americans.

The Mexica:
A Meso-American Culture

By 1492, the indigenous population of the New World numbered roughly 80 million, about the same as the population of Europe. All but about 4 million of these people lived in Central and South America. Like their North American counterparts, they too lived in a natural environment of tremendous diversity. They too developed hundreds of cultures, far too numerous to catalog here. But among all the Central and South American cultures, the Mexica stood out. (Europeans often called these people Aztecs, a name the Mexica did not use.) Their empire stretched from coast to coast across central Mexico, encompassing as many as 25 million people. We know more about the fifteenth-century Mexica than about any other Native American society of the time, principally because of their written sources, massive monuments, and their Spanish conquerors' well-documented interest in subduing them. Their significance in the history of the New World after 1492 dictates a brief consideration of their culture and society.

The Mexica began their rise to prominence about A.D. 1325 when small bands settled on a marshy island in Lake Texcoco, the site of the future city of Tenochtitlán. Resourceful, courageous, and cold-blooded warriors, the Mexica often were hired as mercenaries by richer, more settled tribes. By 1430, the Mexica succeeded in asserting their dominance over their former allies and leading their own military campaigns in an ever-widening arc of empire building. Despite pockets of resistance, by 1500 the Mexica ruled an empire that covered more land than Spain and Portugal combined and contained almost three times as many people.

The empire exemplified the central values of Mexican society. The Mexica worshiped the war god Huitzilopochtli. Warriors held the most exalted positions in the Mexican social hierarchy, even above the priests who performed the sacred ceremonies that won Huitzilopochtli's favor. In the almost constant battles necessary to defend and extend the empire, young Mexican men exhibited the courage and daring that would allow them to rise in the carefully graduated ranks of warriors. The Mexica considered capturing prisoners the ultimate act of bravery. The captives usually were turned over to the priests, who sacrificed them to Huitzilopochtli

by cutting out their hearts. (See "Historical Question," page 18.)

The empire contributed far more to Mexican society than victims for sacrifice. At the most basic level, the empire was a military and political system for collecting tribute from subject peoples. The Mexica forced conquered tribes to pay tribute in goods, not money. Tribute redistributed to the

HUMAN SACRIFICE
Many ancient American peoples practiced human sacrifice as a sacred rite of communion with the gods. The Inca, a powerful people whose empire stretched down the west coast of South America, required each village to send one or two especially beautiful children to the capital, where they were honored in religious ceremonies and other festivities and then given an intoxicating drink and buried in a prepared tomb, where they died. This mummy was probably a child sacrificed in such a ritual about 500 years ago. Discovered in Chile at an altitude of about 20,000 feet, where the dry, intense cold preserved the body, the mummy was accompanied by a tiny female votive figure wrapped in finely woven cloth and capped with a bright feather headdress, a llama figurine, a bag of coca leaves, and other objects.
Loren McIntyre.

Why Did the Mexica Practice Human Sacrifice?

MEXICAN CEREMONIAL SKULL
This human skull, decorated by Mexican artisans with a mosaic of turquoise, jet, and shell, represented Tezcatlipoca, the Mexican deity who governed human fate. A handsome young man was selected for the great honor of impersonating Tezcatlipoca for eighteen months. The Mexican emperor gave the impersonator riches and privileges of all sorts, and even allowed him to rule Tenochtitlán for the last five days of his life. On the last day, the impersonator climbed the steps of a temple where priests cut out his heart and decapitated him. This skull from the Tezcatlipoca ceremony presumably belonged to one of the impersonators. The skull is said to have been a gift from the emperor Montezuma to Cortés, leader of the Spanish conquest of Mexico.
Copyright © The British Museum.

THE MEXICA PRACTICED HUMAN SACRIFICE on a scale unequaled in human history. That does not mean, of course, that they intentionally killed more people than any other society. Plenty of other societies, both before and since, have systematically killed other human beings. Only a partial accounting of the years from 1930 to 1945, for example, would include millions of Jews and others murdered by the Nazis, millions of Russians killed by the Soviet leader Joseph Stalin, hundreds of thousands of Chinese slaughtered by the Japanese, and hundreds of thousands of Japanese annihilated by the atomic bombs dropped by the United States on Hiroshima and Nagasaki. Warfare of any kind involves intentional sacrifice of human life. However, the human sacrifice practiced by the Mexica was different. For them, human sacrifice was an act of worship—in fact, the ultimate act of worship.

Looking back from our vantage point five hundred years later, we may find it difficult to understand why the Mexica accepted human sacrifice as a normal and reasonable activity. Yet it is perfectly clear that they did. Although the precise number of victims is unknown, experts estimate that roughly 20,000 people were sacrificed each year throughout the Mexican empire. Celebration of an important victory or the appointment of a new emperor often involved the sacrifice of hundreds, sometimes thousands.

Most of the victims were prisoners captured in battle or rendered in tribute. Nonetheless, ordinary Mexican citizens—especially young men, women, and children—were often sacrificed in religious rituals. Every eighteen months, for example, a greatly honored young man was sacrificed to Tezcatlipoca, the god of human fate. From time to time, all Mexica practiced sacrificial bloodletting, piercing themselves with stingray spines or cactus thorns to demonstrate their religious devotion. Both as symbol and reality, human sacrifice was an integral part of daily life in Mexican communities.

Mexica employed several different techniques of sacrifice, all supervised and carried out by priests. By far the most common sacrifice was performed at an altar on the top of a temple where a priest cut out the still-beating heart of a victim and offered it to the gods. The victim's head and limbs were then severed and the torso fed to wild animals kept in cages in and near the temple. The heads were displayed on large racks at the base of the temple, while the limbs were cooked and eaten in sacred rituals. It is likely that participation in this ritualistic cannibalism was restricted to a minority of Mexica, principally warriors, priests, and wealthier merchants. However, every Mexica participated in symbolic cannibalism by eating small cakes made of flour mixed with blood and shaped into human forms.

To us, these rituals may seem ghoulish and disgusting, as they certainly did to sixteenth-century Europeans who eventually witnessed them. Yet the Mexica devoted so much time, energy, and resources to such rituals that it is impossible to doubt their importance to them. But why was human sacrifice so important?

In recent times, some scholars have argued that the Mexica practiced human sacrifice and cannibalism to remedy protein deficiencies in their diet. However, the Mexica's diet contained many sources of protein, including turkeys, chickens, fish, turtles, and eggs as well as corn and beans. For most Mexica, dietary protein was adequate or better. Protein deficiency interprets human sacrifice as a solution to a problem that, evidently, did not actually exist.

Mexican religious beliefs offer a far more persuasive explanation for human sacrifice. Scholars know a good deal about Mexican religion because, in the years immediately following European conquest, Catholic priests studied Mexican religion in order to convert the people more readily to Christianity. These sources make clear that the Mexica inhabited a world suffused with the power of supernatural beings. A special deity oversaw nearly every important activity. Mexica believed that their gods communicated with human beings through omens, signs that the gods were either happy or displeased. In turn, the people communicated their own reverence for the gods by observing appropriate rituals. Bad omens such as an unexplained fire or a lightning bolt striking a temple meant that a god was angry and needed to be appeased with the proper rituals. Since almost every occurrence could be in-terpreted as an omen that revealed the will of a god, the routine events of daily life had a profound, supernatural dimension.

The Mexica's most powerful gods were Huitzilopochtli, the war god, and Quetzalcoatl, the god who gave sustenance to human beings. Mexica believed that these two gods had created the world, the sun, the moon, the first human beings, the whole array of lesser deities, and everything else in the universe. Since the moment of creation, the earth had passed through four different epochs, which Mexica called the Four Suns, each of which had ended in catastrophe. It fell to Quetzalcoatl and other potent deities to begin the Fifth Sun by recreating human beings and all the other features of the universe. After years of work, Quetzalcoatl and the other gods had accomplished everything except the creation of the sun. Finally, two gods agreed to sacrifice themselves by jumping into a fire. Thereby they became the sun and the moon, and other gods quickly followed them into the fire to keep the sun burning. But the sacrifice of the gods was sufficient only to ignite the sun. To maintain the light of the sun and keep it moving across the sky every day required human beings to follow the example of the gods and to feed the sun with human blood. Without the sacrificial blood, the world would go dark and time would stop. Mexica considered the Fifth Sun the final stage of the universe, which would end when cataclysmic earthquakes destroyed the earth and supernatural monsters ravaged human life. By feeding the sun with human sacrifices, Mexica believed they could delay that horrible final reckoning.

For the Mexica, human sacrifice was absolutely necessary for the maintenance of life on earth. Victims of sacrifice fulfilled the most sacred of duties. Through the sacrifice of their own lives they fed the sun and permitted others to live. The living demonstrated their respect and reverence for victims of sacrifice by eating their flesh. As one sixteenth-century Catholic priest explained, "The flesh of all those who died in sacrifice was held truly to be consecrated and blessed. It was eaten with reverence, ritual, and fastidiousness—as if it were something from heaven." From the Mexica's perspective, it was not wrong to engage in human sacrifice; it was wrong not to.

Mexica as much as one-third of the goods produced by conquered tribes. It included everything from candidates for human sacrifice to basic food products like corn and beans as well as exotic luxury items like gold, turquoise, and rare bird feathers.

Tribute reflected the fundamental relations of power and wealth that pervaded the Mexican empire. The relatively small nobility of Mexican warriors, supported by a still smaller priesthood, possessed the military and religious power to command the obedience of thousands of nonnoble Mexicans and of millions of other non-Mexicans in subjugated provinces. The Mexican elite exercised their power to obtain tribute and thereby to redistribute wealth from the conquered to the conquerors, from the commoners to the nobility, from the poor to the rich. This redistribution of wealth made possible the achievements of Mexican society that eventually amazed Europeans: the fabulous temples, markets, and gardens, not to mention the storehouses stuffed with gold and other treasures.

On the whole, the Mexica did not interfere much with the internal government of conquered regions. Instead, they usually permitted the traditional ruling elite to stay in power—so long as they paid tribute. For their efforts, the conquered provinces received very little from the Mexica, except immunity from punitive raids by the dreaded Mexican warriors. Subjugated communities felt exploited by the constant payment of tribute to the Mexica. By depending on military conquest and constant collection of tribute, the Mexica failed to create among their subjects a belief that Mexican domination was, at some level, legitimate and equitable. The high level of discontent among subject peoples constituted the soft, vulnerable underbelly of the Mexican empire. Instead of making friends for the Mexica, the empire created many bitter and resentful opponents, a fact Spanish intruders eventually exploited to conquer the Mexica.

SALADO RITUAL FIGURE
About A.D. 1350—more than a century before Columbus arrived in the New World—this figure was carefully wrapped in a reed mat with other items and stored in a cave in a mountainous region of New Mexico by people of the Salado culture, descendants of the Mimbres who had flourished three centuries earlier. The face of this figure is as close to a self-portrait of ancient Americans on the eve of their encounter with Europeans as we are ever likely to have. Adorned with vivid pigments, cotton string, bright feathers, and stones, the effigy testifies to the human complexity of all ancient Americans, a complexity visible in artifacts that have survived the millennia before the arrival of Europeans.
The Art Institute of Chicago.

Conclusion: The World of Ancient Americans

Ancient Americans shaped the history of human beings in the New World for more than twelve thousand years. They established continuous human habitation in the Western Hemisphere from the time the first big-game hunters crossed Beringia until 1492 and beyond. Much of their history remains irretrievably lost because they relied on oral rather than written communication. But much can be pieced together from artifacts they left behind, like the bones discovered at Folsom by George McJunkin. Ancient Americans achieved their success through resourceful adaptation to the hemisphere's many and ever-changing natural environments. They also adapted to social and cultural changes caused by human beings—such as marriages, deaths, political struggles, and warfare—but the sparse evidence that has survived renders those adaptations almost entirely unknowable. Their creativity and artistry are unmistakably documented in the artifacts they left behind at kill sites, camps, and burial mounds. Those artifacts sketch the only likenesses of ancient Americans we will ever have—blurred, shadowy images that are indisputably human but forever silent.

In the five centuries after 1492—just 4 percent of the time human beings have inhabited the Western Hemisphere—Europeans and their descendants began to shape and eventually to dominate Ameri-

can history. Native American peoples continued to influence major developments of American history after 1492. But the new wave of strangers that at first trickled and then flooded into the New World from Europe and Africa forever transformed the peoples and places of ancient America.

For further reading about the topics in this chapter, see the Online Bibliography at www.bedfordstmartins.com/roarkcompact.

For additional first-hand accounts of this period, see pages 1–8 in Michael Johnson, ed., *Reading the American Past,* Second Edition, Volume I.

To assess your mastery of the material in this chapter, see the Online Study Guide at www.bedfordstmartins.com/roarkcompact.

CHRONOLOGY

c. 80,000–10,000 B.C.	Wisconsin glaciation exposes Beringia, land bridge between Siberia and Alaska.
c. 13,000–10,000 B.C.	First humans arrive in North America.
c. 9500–9000 B.C.	Paleo-Indians in North and Central Americas use Clovis points to hunt big game.
c. 9000 B.C.	Mammoths and many other big-game prey of Paleo-Indians become extinct.
c. 8000–1000 B.C.	Archaic hunter-gatherer cultures dominate ancient America.
c. 5000 B.C.	Corn cultivation begins in Central and South Americas.
c. 2000 B.C.	Some Eastern Woodland people grow gourds and pumpkins and begin making pottery.
c. 1500 B.C.	Southwestern cultures begin corn cultivation. Stone pipes for tobacco smoking appear in Eastern Woodland.
c. 500 B.C.	Eastern Woodland cultures start to build burial mounds.
c. 500–100 B.C.	Adena culture develops in Ohio.
c. 300 B.C.	Some Eastern Woodland peoples begin to cultivate corn.
c. 100 B.C.–A.D. 400	Hopewell culture emerges in Ohio and Mississippi valleys.
c. A.D. 200–900	Mogollon culture emerges in New Mexico.
c. A.D. 500	Bows and arrows appear in North America south of Arctic. Pacific Northwest cultures denote wealth and status with elaborate wood carvings.
c. A.D. 500–1400	Hohokam culture develops in Arizona.
c. A.D. 800–1500	Mississippian culture flourishes in Southeast.
c. A.D. 1000–1150	Anasazi peoples build cliff dwellings at Mesa Verde, Colorado, and pueblos at Chaco Canyon, New Mexico.
c. A.D. 1325–1500	Mexica conquer neighboring peoples and establish Mexican empire.
A.D. 1492	Christopher Columbus arrives, beginning European conquest of New World.

TAINO ZEMI BASKET
This basket is an example of the effigies Tainos made to represent zemis, their deities. The effigy illustrates not only the artistry of the basket maker—probably a Taino woman— but also the basket maker's use of European mirrors in a sacred object. Crafted sometime between 1492 and about 1520, the effigy suggests that Tainos readily incorporated goods obtained through contacts with Europeans into their own traditional beliefs and practices.
Archìvio Fotogràfico del Museo Preistòrico Etnografico L. Pigorini, Rome.

EUROPEANS AND THE NEW WORLD

1492–1600

A HALF HOUR BEFORE SUNRISE ON AUGUST 3, 1492, Christopher Columbus commanded three ships to catch the tide out of a harbor in southern Spain and sail west. Just over two months later, in the predawn moonlight of October 12, 1492, Columbus glimpsed an island on the western horizon. At last, he believed, he had found what he had been looking for—the western end of a route across the Atlantic Ocean to Japan, China, and India. At daybreak, Columbus could see people on the shore who had spotted his ships. He rowed ashore and, as the curious islanders crowded around, he claimed possession of the land for Ferdinand and Isabella, king and queen of Spain, who had sponsored his voyage.

A day or two afterward, Columbus described that first encounter with the inhabitants of San Salvador in an extensive diary he kept during his voyage. He called these people Indians, assuming that their island lay somewhere in the East Indies near Japan or China. The Indians were not dressed in the finery Columbus expected. "All of them go around as naked as their mothers bore them; and the women also," he observed. Their skin color was "neither black nor white." This first encounter led Columbus to conclude, "They should be good and intelligent servants, for I see that they say very quickly everything that is said to them; and I believe that they would become Christians very easily, for it seemed to me that they had no religion."

The people Columbus called Indians called themselves Tainos, which to them meant "good" or "noble." They inhabited most of the Caribbean islands Columbus visited on his first voyage, as had their ancestors for more than two centuries. The Tainos were an agricultural people who grew cassava, a nutritious root, as well as sweet potatoes, corn, cotton, tobacco, and other crops. To fish and to travel from island to island, they built canoes from hollowed-out logs. The Tainos worshiped gods they called *zemis*, the spirits of ancestors and of natural objects like trees and stones. They made effigies of *zemis* and performed rituals to honor them. "It seemed to me that they were a people very poor in everything," Columbus wrote. But the Tainos mined gold in small quantities, enough to catch the eye of Columbus and his men.

What the Tainos thought about Spaniards we can only surmise, since they left no written documents. At first, Columbus believed that the Tainos thought he and his men came from heaven. After six weeks of contact, Columbus concluded that in fact he did not understand Tainos. Late in November 1492, he wrote that "the people of these lands do not understand me nor do I, nor anyone else that I have with me, them. And many times I understand one thing said by these Indians . . . for another, its contrary."

The confused communication between Europeans and Tainos suggests how different, how strange, each group seemed to the other. Columbus's perceptions of

CACIQUE'S CANOE
This sixteenth-century drawing of a large canoe carrying a cacique, or chief, and powered by twenty oarsmen probably resembles the canoes used by Tainos and the other native Americans who paddled out to visit the ships of Columbus and other European explorers. The influence of such European contacts may be reflected in the flags flying from the corners of the leafy awning that enthrones the cacique.
Art Resource, NY.

Tainos were shaped by European ideas, attitudes, and expectations, just as Tainos's perceptions of Europeans must have been colored by their own culture. Yet the word that Columbus coined for the Tainos—*Indians*, a word that originated in a colossal misunderstanding—hinted at the direction of the future. To Europeans, *Indians* came to mean all native inhabitants of the New World, the name they gave to the lands in the Western Hemisphere. After 1492, the perceptions, the cultures, and even the diseases of Europeans began to exert a transforming influence on the New World and its peoples.

Long before 1492, certain Europeans restlessly expanded the limits of the world known to them. Their efforts made possible Columbus's encounter with the Tainos. In turn, Columbus's landfall in the Caribbean changed the history not only of the Tainos, but also of Europe and the rest of the world. Beginning in 1492, the promise of the New World lured more and more Europeans to venture their lives and fortunes on the western shores of the Atlantic, a promise realized largely at the expense of New World peoples like Tainos.

Europe in the Age of Exploration

Historically, the East—not the West—attracted Europeans. Wealthy Europeans developed a taste for luxury goods from Asia and Africa, and merchants competed to satisfy that taste. As Europeans traded with the East and with one another, they acquired new information about the world they inhabited. A few people—sailors, merchants, aristocrats—took the risks of exploring beyond the limits of the world known to Europeans. Those risks were genuine and could be deadly. But sometimes they paid off in new information, new opportunities, and eventually in the discovery of a world entirely new to Europeans.

Mediterranean Trade and European Expansion

From the twelfth through the fifteenth centuries, spices, silk, carpets, ivory, gold, and other exotic goods traveled overland from Persia, Asia Minor,

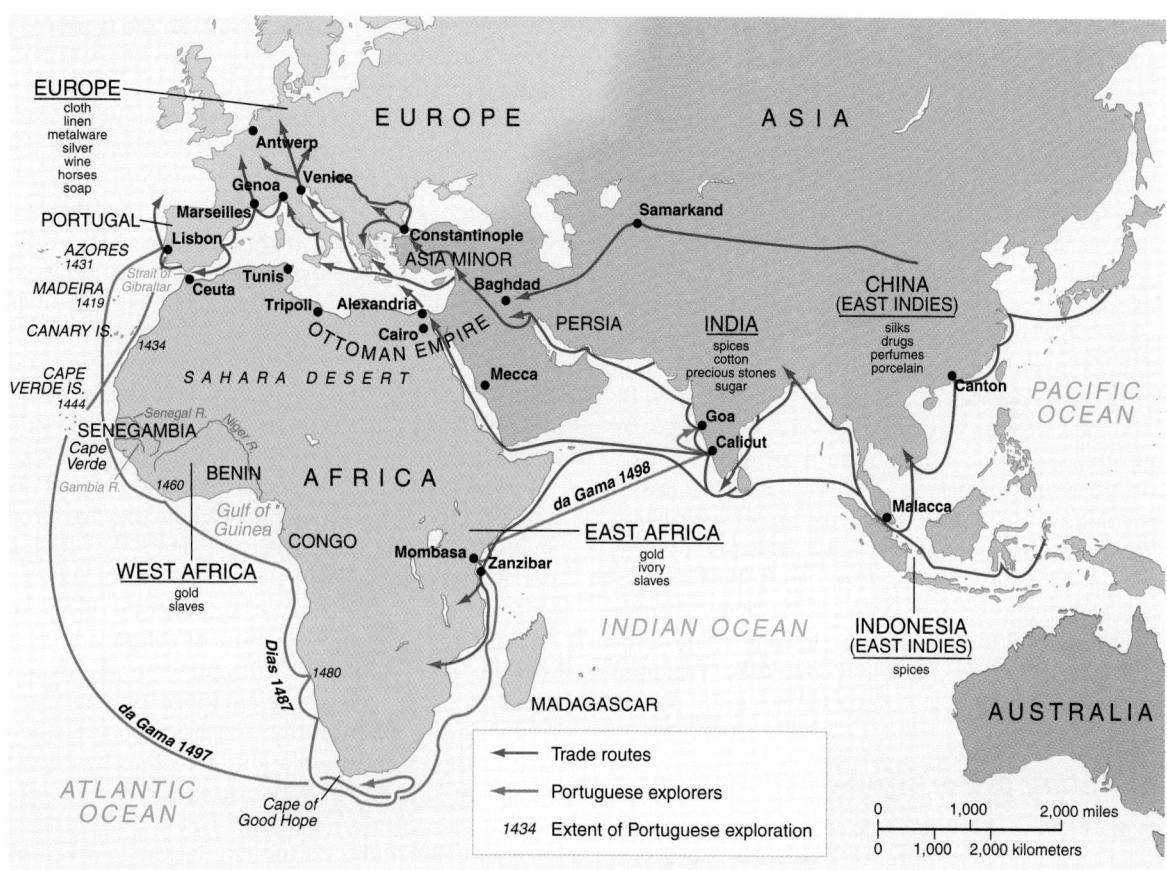

M AP 2.1

European Trade Routes and Portuguese Exploration in the Fifteenth Century
The strategic geographic position of Italian cities as a conduit for overland trade from
Asia was slowly undermined during the fifteenth century by Portuguese explorers who
hopscotched along the coast of Africa and eventually found a sea route that opened the
rich trade of the East to Portuguese merchants.

India, and Africa and then were funneled into continental Europe through Mediterranean trade routes (Map 2.1). Dominated primarily by the Italian cities of Venice, Genoa, and Pisa, this lucrative trade enriched Italian merchants and bankers. Instead of trying to displace the Italians, merchants in other European countries chose the safer alternative of trading with them. The vitality of the Mediterranean trade offered few incentives to look for alternatives. New routes to the East and the discovery of new lands were the stuff of fantasy.

Preconditions for turning fantasy into reality developed in fifteenth-century Europe. In the mid-

fourteenth century, Europeans suffered a catastrophic epidemic of bubonic plague. The Black Death, as it was called, killed about a third of the European population. Understandably, most Europeans perceived the world as a place of alarming risks where the delicate balance of health, harvests, and peace could quickly be tipped toward disaster by epidemics, famine, and violence. Curiously, the insecurity and uncertainty of fifteenth-century European life encouraged a few people to take greater chances, such as embarking on a dangerous sea voyage through uncharted waters to points unknown.

Monarchs who hoped to enlarge their realms and enrich their dynasties also had reasons to sponsor journeys of exploration. More territory meant more subjects who could pay more taxes, provide more soldiers, and participate in more commerce, magnifying monarchs' power and prestige. Explorers, both nobles and commoners like Columbus, sought to earn rewards and prestige in European society.

Scientific and technological advances also helped set the stage for exploration. The invention of movable type made printing easier and cheaper, stimulating diffusion of information, including news of discoveries, among literate Europeans. By 1400, the crucial navigational aids employed by maritime explorers like Columbus were already available: compasses; hourglasses, which allowed calculation of elapsed time, useful in estimating speed; and the astrolabe and the quadrant, devices for determining latitude. These and other technological advances were known to many people throughout fifteenth-century Europe. The Portuguese were the first to use them in a campaign to sail beyond the limits of the known world.

A Century of Portuguese Exploration

In many ways, Portugal was an unlikely candidate to take the lead in exploration. With less than 2 percent of the population of Christian Europe, the country devoted far more energy and wealth to the geographical exploration of the world between 1415 and 1460 than all the other countries of Europe combined.

Facing the Atlantic on the Iberian peninsula, the Portuguese lived on the fringes of the thriving Mediterranean trade. As a Christian kingdom, Portugal cooperated with Spain in the Reconquest, the centuries-long drive to expel Muslims from the Iberian peninsula. The religious zeal that propelled the Reconquest also justified expansion into what the Portuguese considered heathen lands.

The most influential advocate of Portuguese exploration was Prince Henry the Navigator, son of the Portuguese king. From 1415 until his death in 1460, Henry collected the latest information about sailing techniques and geography, supported new crusades against the Muslims, encouraged fresh sources of trade to fatten Portuguese pocketbooks, and pushed explorers to go farther still. African conquests also promised to wrest wheat fields from their Moroccan owners and to obtain gold, the currency of European trade.

Neither the Portuguese nor anybody else in Europe knew how big Africa was. At first, Portuguese mariners cautiously hugged the west coast of Africa, seldom venturing beyond sight of land. By 1434, they had reached the northern edge of the Sahara Desert, where strong westerly currents swept them out to sea. They soon learned how to ride those currents far away from the coast before sailing back toward land, a technique that allowed them to reach Cape Verde by 1444 (see Map 2.1). The Portuguese also developed sturdier ships called caravels that eventually allowed them to round Cape Verde. By 1480, Portuguese caravels sailed into and around the Gulf of Guinea and as far south as the Congo.

Fierce African resistance confined the Portuguese to coastal trading posts where they bartered successfully for gold, slaves, and ivory. Portuguese merchants learned that relatively peaceful trading posts on the coast were far more profitable than violent conquests and attempts at colonization inland. In the 1460s, the Portuguese used African slaves to develop sugar plantations on the Cape Verde Islands, inaugurating an association between African slaves and plantation labor that would be transplanted to the New World in the centuries to come.

About 1480, the Portuguese began a conscious search for a sea route to Asia. In 1488, Bartolomeu Dias sailed around the Cape of Good Hope at the southern tip of Africa and hurried back to Lisbon with the exciting news that it appeared to be possible to sail on to India and China. In 1498, after ten years of careful preparation, Vasco da Gama commanded the first Portuguese fleet to sail to India. Portugal quickly capitalized on the commercial potential of da Gama's new sea route. By the early sixteenth century, the Portuguese controlled a far-flung commercial empire in India, Indonesia, and China (collectively referred to as the East Indies). Their new sea route to the East eliminated overland travel and the numerous intermediate merchants and markups of the old Mediterranean trade routes controlled by the Italians.

Through its century of African explorations, Portugal broke the monopoly of the old Mediterranean trade with the East, dramatically expanded the known world, established a network of Portuguese outposts in Africa and Asia, and developed methods of sailing the high seas that Columbus employed on his revolutionary voyage west.

YORUBA QUEEN
This expressive terracotta head, discovered in Nigeria in 1957, was once part of a large sculpture of a Yoruba queen memorialized in a shrine built between 800 and 900 years ago, centuries before the arrival of Portuguese explorers.
The National Commission for Museums & Monuments & Life, Nigeria.

A Surprising New World in the Western Atlantic

In retrospect, the Portuguese seemed ideally qualified to venture across the Atlantic. They had pioneered the frontiers of seafaring, exploration, and geography for almost a century. However, the knowledge and experience gained in navigating around Africa made them cautious about the risks of trying to sail across the Atlantic. Most European experts believed it could not even be done. The European discovery of America required someone bold enough to believe that the experts were wrong and the risks were surmountable. That person was Christopher Columbus.

The Explorations of Columbus

Born in 1451 into the family of an obscure master weaver in Genoa, Italy, Columbus went to sea when he was about fourteen. By about 1476, he lived in Lisbon, venturing frequently to the Madeira Islands and at least twice sailing all the way to the coast of central Africa.

Like other educated Europeans, Columbus believed that the earth was a sphere and that theoretically it was possible to reach the East Indies by sailing west. Most Europeans believed, however, that the earth was simply too big for anyone to sail west from Europe to Asia. Sailors would die of thirst and starvation long before they reached Asia. Columbus rejected this conventional wisdom. With flawed calculations, he estimated that Asia lay about 2,500 miles from the westernmost boundary of the known world, a shorter distance than Portuguese ships routinely sailed between Lisbon and the Congo. Convinced by his erroneous calculations, Columbus became obsessed with a scheme to prove he was right.

In 1492, after years of unsuccessful lobbying for support from Portugal, England, and France, Columbus finally won financing for his journey from Spain's King Ferdinand and Queen Isabella. After barely three months of hurried preparation, Columbus and his small fleet—the *Niña* and *Pinta*, both caravels, and the *Santa María*, a larger merchant vessel—headed west. Six weeks after leaving the Canary Islands, where he stopped for supplies, Columbus landed on a tiny Caribbean island about three hundred miles north of the eastern tip of Cuba, which he named San Salvador.

Columbus and his men understood that they had made a momentous discovery. Yet they found it frustrating. Although the Tainos proved friendly, they did not have the riches Columbus expected to find in the East. For

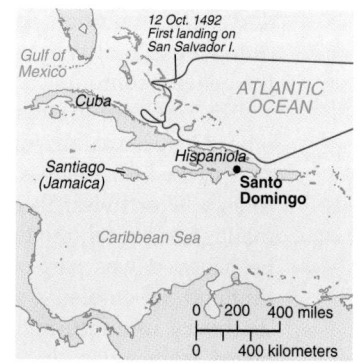

Columbus's First Voyage to the New World, 1492–1493

three months Columbus cruised from island to is-land, looking for the king of Japan. In mid-January 1493, he started back, taking seven Tainos with him. When he reached Isabella and Ferdinand, they were overjoyed by his news. With a voyage that had lasted barely eight months, Columbus appeared to have catapulted Spain from a secondary position in the race for a sea route to Asia into that of a serious challenger to Portugal (whose explorers had not yet sailed to India or China).

To protect their claims, the Spanish monarchs negotiated the Treaty of Tordesillas with Portugal in 1494, drawing an imaginary line eleven hundred miles west of the Canary Islands (Map 2.2). Land discovered west of the line belonged to Spain, while Portugal claimed land to the east.

Before Columbus died in 1506, he returned to the New World two more times without relinquishing his belief that the East Indies were there, someplace. Explorers continued to search for a passage to the East or some other source of profit. Before long, prospects of beating the Portuguese to Asia began to dim along with the hope of finding vast hoards of gold. Nonetheless, Columbus's discoveries forced sixteenth-century Europeans to think about the world in new ways. He proved that it was possible to sail from Europe to the western rim of the Atlantic and return to Europe. Most important, Columbus made clear that beyond the western shores of the Atlantic lay lands entirely unknown to Europeans.

The Geographic Revolution and the Columbian Exchange

Within thirty years of Columbus's initial discovery, Europeans' understanding of world geography underwent a revolution. But it took a generation of additional exploration before they could comprehend the general contours of what Columbus had found.

In 1497, King Henry VII of England sent another Genoese sailor, John Cabot, to look for a passage to the Indies across the North Atlantic, referred to as a "Northwest Passage" (see Map 2.2). Cabot managed to reach the tip of Newfoundland, which he believed was part of Asia. He hurried back to England, assembled a small fleet to follow up his discovery, and returned in 1498. But he was never heard from again. In 1499, a Spanish expedition landed on the northern coast of South America, accompanied by Amerigo Vespucci, an Italian businessman whose avocation was geography. In 1500,

Pedro Álvars Cabral commanded a Portuguese fleet bound for the Indian Ocean that accidentally made landfall on the coast of Brazil as it looped westward into the Atlantic.

By 1500, it was clear that several large chunks of land cluttered the western Atlantic. A few cartographers speculated that these chunks were connected to one another in a landmass that was not Asia. In 1507, Martin Waldseemüller, a German cartographer, published the first map that showed the New World separate from Asia; he named the land America, in honor of Amerigo Vespucci.

Two additional discoveries confirmed Waldseemüller's speculation. In 1513, Vasco Núñez de Balboa crossed the isthmus of Panama and reached the Pacific Ocean. Clearly, more water lay between the New World and Asia. How much water Ferdinand Magellan discovered when he led an expedition to circumnavigate the globe in 1519. Sponsored by King Charles I of Spain, Magellan's voyage took him first to the New World, around the southern tip of South America, and into the Pacific late in November 1520. Crossing the Pacific took almost four months. When he reached the Philippines, his crew had been decimated by extreme hunger and thirst. Magellan himself was killed by Philippine tribesmen. A remnant of his expedition continued into the Indian Ocean and managed to transport a cargo of spices back to Spain in 1522.

In most ways Magellan's voyage was a disaster. One ship and 18 men crawled back from an expedition that had begun with five ships and more than 250 men. But the geographic information it provided left no doubt that America was a continent separated from Asia by the enormous Pacific Ocean. The voyage made clear that Columbus was dead wrong about the identity of what he had discovered. It was possible to sail west to reach the East Indies, but that was a terrible way to go. After Magellan, most Europeans who sailed west had their sights set on the New World, not on Asia.

Columbus's arrival in the Caribbean anchored the western end of what might be imagined as a sea bridge spanning the Atlantic and connecting the New World to Europe. That sea bridge ended the age-old separation of the hemispheres and initiated the Columbian exchange, a transatlantic exchange of goods, people, and ideas that has continued ever since. Spaniards brought things that were novelties in the New World but commonplace in Europe, including Christianity, iron technology, sailing ships, firearms, wheeled vehicles, and horses and other

MAP 2.2

European Explorations in Sixteenth-Century America

This map illustrates the approximate routes of early European explorations of the New World.

READING THE MAP: Which countries were most actively exploring the New World? Which countries were exploring later than others?

CONNECTIONS: What were the motivations behind the explorations? What were the motivations for colonization?

www.bedfordstmartins.com/roarkcompact SEE THE ONLINE STUDY GUIDE for more help in analyzing this map.

COLUMBIAN EXCHANGE

The arrival of Columbus in the New World initiated an unending transatlantic exchange of goods, people, and ideas. Spaniards brought domesticated animals from the Old World, including horses, cattle, goats, chickens, cats, and sheep (left). The novelty of such animals is demonstrated by the Nahua words the Mexican people initially used to refer to these strange new beasts: for horses, they used the Nahua word for deer; a cow was "one with horns"; a goat was a "bearded one with horns"; a chicken was a "Spanish turkey hen"; a cat was a "little cougar"; a sheep was referred to with the word for cotton, linking the animal with its fibrous woolen coat. Spaniards brought many other alien items such as cannon, which the Mexica at first termed "fat fire trumpets," and guitars, which the Mexica called "rope drums." Spaniards also carried Old World microorganisms that caused devastating epidemics of smallpox, measles, and other diseases (center). Ancient American people, goods, and ideas made the return trip across the Atlantic. Columbus's sailors quickly learned to use Indian hammocks and became infected with syphilis in sexual encounters with Indian women; then they carried both hammocks and syphilis back to Europe. Smoking tobacco, like the cigar puffed by the ancient Mayan lord (right), became such a fashion in Europe that some came to believe, as a print of two men relaxing with their pipes was captioned, "Life Is Smoke." The strangeness of New World peoples and cultures also reinforced Europeans' notions of their own superiority. Although the Columbian exchange went in both directions, it was not a relationship of equality. Europeans seized and retained the upper hand.

The Bancroft Library; Arxiv Mas; Collection of Dr. Robicsek.

domesticated animals. Smuggled along unknowingly were also Old World microorganisms that caused epidemics of smallpox, measles, and other diseases that killed the vast majority of Indian peoples during the sixteenth century and continued to decimate survivors in later centuries. The catastrophic effects of European diseases made the Columbian exchange far from equal.

Ancient American goods, people, and ideas made the return trip across the Atlantic. Europeans were introduced to such vital New World crops as corn and potatoes as well as exotic items like pineapples, named for their resemblance to pinecones. Columbus's sailors became infected with syphilis in sexual encounters with New World women and then unwittingly carried the deadly parasite back to Europe. New World tobacco created a European rage for smoking that has yet to abate. But for almost a generation after 1492, this Columbian exchange did not reward Spaniards with the riches they longed to find.

Spanish Exploration and Conquest

During the sixteenth century, the New World helped Spain become the most powerful country in both Europe and the Americas. Initially, Spanish expeditions reconnoitered the Caribbean, scouted stretches of the Atlantic coast, and established settlements on the large islands of Hispaniola, Puerto Rico, Jamaica, and Cuba. Spaniards enslaved Caribbean tribes and put them to work growing crops and mining gold. But the profits from these early ventures barely covered the costs of maintaining the settlers. After almost thirty years of exploration, the promise of Columbus's discovery seemed illusory.

Soon after 1519, however, that promise was fulfilled, spectacularly. The mainland phase of exploration began in 1519 with Hernán Cortés's march into Mexico; by about 1545, Spanish conquests extended from northern Mexico to southern Chile, and New World riches filled Spanish treasure chests. Cortés's expedition served as the model for those to follow.

The Conquest of Mexico

Hernán Cortés, who would become the richest and most famous *conquistador* (conqueror), arrived in the New World in 1504, an obscure nineteen-year-old Spaniard seeking adventure and the chance to make a name for himself. He fought in the conquest of Cuba and elsewhere in the Caribbean. In 1519, the governor of Cuba authorized Cortés to organize an expedition to investigate rumors of a fabulously wealthy kingdom somewhere in the interior of the mainland. A charming, charismatic leader, Cortés quickly assembled a force of about six hundred men, loaded his ragtag army aboard eleven ships, and set out.

Cortés's confidence that he could talk his way out of most situations and fight his way out of the rest fortified the small band of Spaniards. Landing first on the Yucatán peninsula, Cortés had the good fortune to receive a gift from a Mayan chief: a young woman named Malinali who spoke both Mayan and Nahuatl, the language of most people in Mexico and Central America. Malinali, whom the Spaniards called Marina, soon learned Spanish and became Cortés's interpreter. Marina served as the essential conduit of communication between the Spaniards and the Indians. With her help, Cortés talked and fought with Indians along the Gulf coast of Mexico, trying to discover the location of the fabled kingdom.

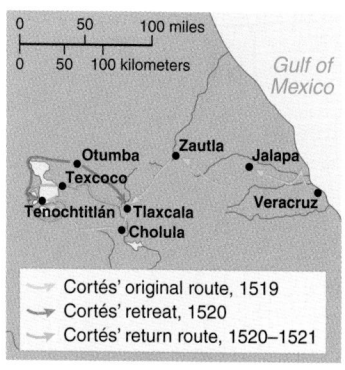

Cortés's Invasion of Tenochtitlán, 1519–1521

Leading about 350 men armed with swords, lances, and muskets, Cortés had to live off the land, making friends with the indigenous tribes when he could and killing them when he thought necessary. Montezuma, the Mexican emperor, received news of the intruders and sent scouts to try to obtain information about who they were and what they wanted. On November 8, 1519, when Cortés reached Tenochtitlán, the Mexican capital, Montezuma came out to meet him. After presenting Cortés with gifts, Montezuma welcomed the Spaniards to the royal palace and showered them with lavish hospitality. Quickly, Cortés took Montezuma hostage and held him under house arrest, hoping to make him a puppet through which the Spaniards could rule the Mexican empire. This uneasy peace existed for several months until, after a brutal massacre of many Mexican nobles by one of Cortés's subordinates, the population of Tenochtitlán revolted, murdered Montezuma, and mounted a ferocious assault on the Spaniards. On June 30, 1520, Cortés and about a hundred other Spaniards fought their way out of Tenochtitlán and retreated toward the coast about one hundred miles to Tlaxcala, a stronghold of bitter enemies of the Mexicans. The friendly Tlaxcalans—who had long resented the Mexicans' power—allowed Cortés to regroup, obtain reinforcements, and plan a strategy to conquer Tenochtitlán.

In the spring of 1521, Cortés mounted a complex campaign against the Mexican capital. The Spaniards and tens of thousands of Indian allies laid siege to the city. With a relentless, scorched-earth

MEXICAN COUNTERATTACK
*This postconquest painting by a sixteenth-century Mexican artist is one of a series de-
picting crucial battles in the Spaniards' ultimate defeat of the Mexica. Here Mexican
warriors attack the conquistadors, forcing the Spaniards to retreat from Tenochtitlán
and regroup for the final siege. The distinctive shields and costumes of the Mexicans
signified their military status, which was based on their battlefield prowess. The
Spaniards wear uniform battle armor. The painting contrasts the colorful individuality of the Mexican warriors with the massed, anonymous Spaniards who level cross-
bows and firearms against the Mexicans' wooden spears. The painting does not show
one of the Spaniards' deadliest weapons: steel swords.*
Oronoz.

strategy, Cortés finally defeated the last Mexican defenders on August 13, 1521. The great capital of the
Mexican empire "looked as if it had been ploughed
up," one of Cortés's soldiers remembered. A few
years later, one of the Mexica described the utter despair of the defeated:

> Broken spears lie in the roads;
> we have torn our hair in grief.
> The houses are roofless now, and their walls
> are red with blood. . . .
> We have pounded our hands in despair
> against the adobe walls,
> for our inheritance, our city, is lost and dead.

The Search for Other Mexicos

Lured by their insatiable appetite for gold, conquistadors quickly fanned out from Tenochtitlán in
search of other Mexicos. The most spectacular prize
fell to Francisco Pizarro, who conquered the Incan
empire in Peru. The Incas controlled a vast, complex region that contained more than nine million
people and stretched along the western coast of
South America for more than two thousand miles.
In 1532, Pizarro and his army of fewer than two
hundred men captured the Incan emperor
Atahualpa and held him hostage. As ransom, the
Incas gave Pizarro the largest treasure yet produced
by the conquests: gold and silver equivalent to half
a century's worth of precious-metal production in
Europe. With the ransom safely in their hands, the
Spaniards executed Atahualpa.

In 1539, Hernando de Soto, a seasoned conquistador who had taken part in the conquest of
Peru, set out to find another Peru in North America.
Landing in Florida, de Soto literally slashed his way
through much of southeastern North America for
three years, searching for the rich, majestic civilizations he thought were there. After many brutal battles and much hardship, de Soto became sick and
died in 1542, and his men turned back to Mexico,
disappointed.

Tales of the fabulous wealth of the mythical
Seven Cities of Cíbola also lured Francisco Vásquez
de Coronado to search the Southwest and Great

Plains of North America. In 1540, Coronado left northern Mexico with a large expedition including a priest who claimed to know the way to what he called "the greatest and best of the discoveries." Cíbola turned out to be a small Zuñi pueblo of about a hundred families. When the Zuñi shot arrows at the Spaniards, Coronado attacked the pueblo and routed the defenders after a hard battle. Convinced that the rich cities must lie somewhere over the horizon, Coronado kept moving all the way to central Kansas before deciding in 1542 that the rumors he had pursued were just that, nothing more.

Juan Rodríguez Cabrillo led an expedition in 1542 that sailed along the coast of California. Cabrillo died on Santa Catalina Island, offshore from present-day Los Angeles, but his men sailed on to the border of Oregon, where a ferocious storm forced them to turn back toward Mexico.

These probes into North America by de Soto, Coronado, and Cabrillo persuaded Spaniards that enormous territories stretched northward, yet their inhabitants had little to loot or exploit. After a generation of vigorous exploration, Spaniards concluded that there was only one Mexico and one Peru.

New Spain in the Sixteenth Century

For all practical purposes, Spain dominated the New World in the sixteenth century (Map 2.3). Portugal claimed the giant territory of Brazil under the Tordesillas treaty but was far more concerned with exploiting its hard-won trade with the East Indies than in colonizing the New World. England and France were absorbed in the affairs of Europe and largely lost interest in America until late in the century. In the decades after 1519, Spaniards created the distinctive colonial society of New Spain that gave other Europeans a striking illustration of how the New World could be made to serve the purposes of the Old.

The Spanish monarchy claimed ownership of most of the land in the Western Hemisphere and gave the conquistadors permission to explore and plunder. (See "Documenting the American Promise," page 36.) The crown took one-fifth, called the "royal fifth," of any loot confiscated by the conquerors and allowed the conquerors to divide the rest. In the end, most conquistadors received very little after the plunder was divided among Cortés and his favorite officers. After the conquest of Tenochtitlán, Cortés decided to compensate his disappointed,

battle-hardened men by giving them the towns the Spaniards had subdued.

The distribution of conquered towns institutionalized the system of *encomienda*, which empowered conquistadors to rule the Indians and the lands in and around their towns. The concept of encomienda was familiar to the Spaniards, who had used it to govern regions recaptured from the Muslims during the Reconquest. In New Spain, encomienda transferred to the Spanish *encomendero* (the man who "owned" the town) the tribute that the town had previously paid to the Mexican empire.

In theory, encomienda involved a reciprocal relationship between the encomendero and "his" Indians. In return for the tribute and labor of the Indians, the encomendero was supposed to encourage the Indians to convert to Christianity, to be responsible for their material well-being, and to guarantee order and justice in the town. Catholic missionaries labored earnestly to convert the Indians to Christianity. After baptizing tens of thousands of Indians, the missionaries discovered that the Indians continued to worship their own gods along with the Christian God. Most friars came to believe that the Indians were lesser beings inherently incapable of fully understanding the Christian faith.

In practice, encomenderos were far more interested in what the Indians could do for them than in what they or missionaries could do for the Indians. Encomenderos subjected Indians to chronic overwork, mistreatment, and abuse. Economically, however, encomienda recognized a fundamental reality of New Spain: The most important treasure the Spaniards could plunder from the New World was not gold, but uncompensated Indian labor. To exploit that labor, the hemisphere's richest natural resource, encomienda gave encomenderos the right to force Indians to work when, where, and how the Spaniards pleased.

Encomienda engendered two groups of influential critics. A few of the missionaries were horrified at the brutal mistreatment of the Indians. The cruelty of the encomenderos made it difficult for priests to persuade Indians of the tender mercies of the Spaniards' God. "What will [the Indians] think about the God of the Christians," Fray Bartolomé de Las Casas asked, when they see their friends "with their heads split, their hands amputated, their intestines torn open? . . . Would they want to come to Christ's sheepfold after their homes had been destroyed, their children imprisoned, their wives raped, their cities devastated, their maidens

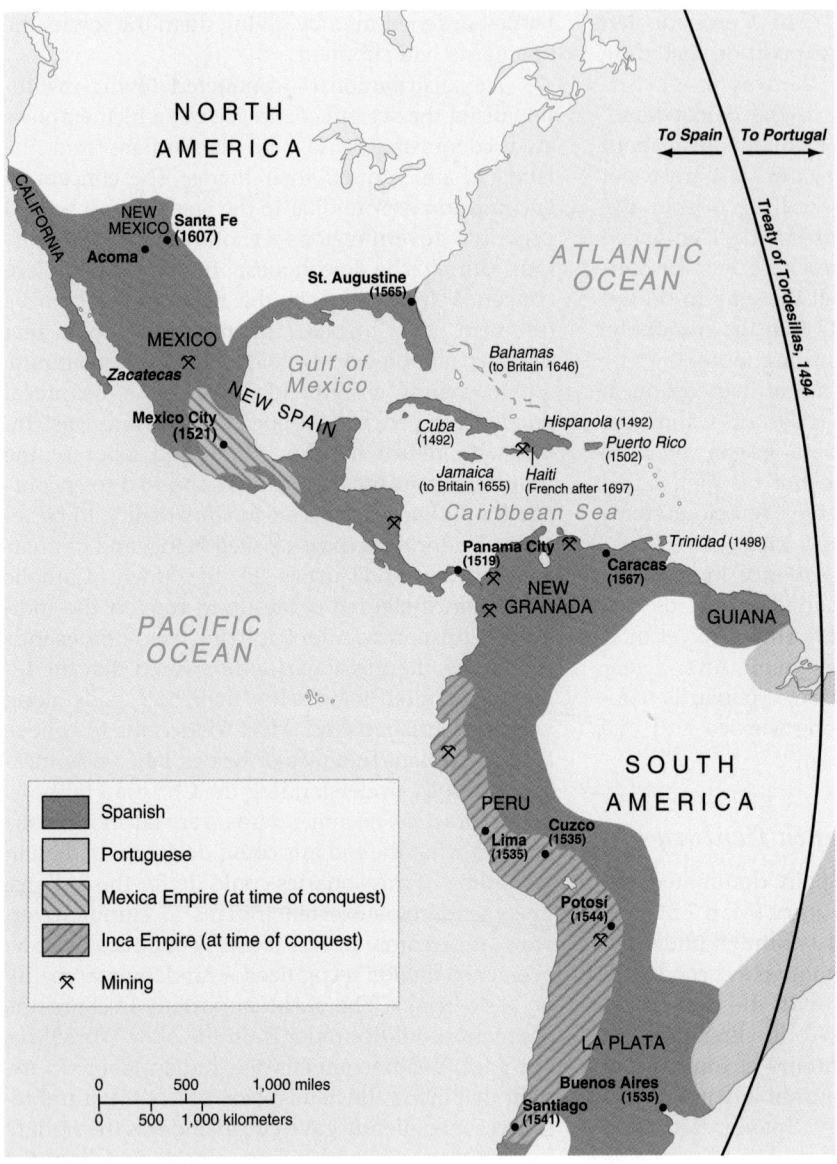

MAP 2.3

New Spain in the Sixteenth Century

Spanish control spread throughout Central and South America during the sixteenth century, with the important exception of Portuguese Brazil. North America, although claimed by Spain under the Treaty of Tordesillas, remained peripheral to Spain's New World empire.

deflowered, and their provinces laid waste?" Las Casas and other outspoken missionaries softened few hearts among the encomenderos, but they did win some sympathy for the Indians from the Spanish monarchy and royal bureaucracy.

One of the most important blows to encomienda was the imposition in 1549 of a reform called the *repartimiento*, which limited the labor an encomendero could command from his Indians to forty-five days per year from each adult male. The repartimiento, however, did not challenge the principle of forced labor, nor did it prevent encomenderos

from continuing to cheat, mistreat, and overwork their Indians. Slowly, as the old encomenderos died, repartimiento replaced encomienda as the basic system of exploiting Indian labor.

The practice of coerced labor in New Spain grew directly out of the Spaniards' assumption that they were superior to the Indians. As one missionary put it, the Indians "are incapable of learning. . . . The Indians are more stupid than asses and refuse to improve in anything." Therefore, most Spaniards assumed, Indians' labor should be organized by and for their conquerors.

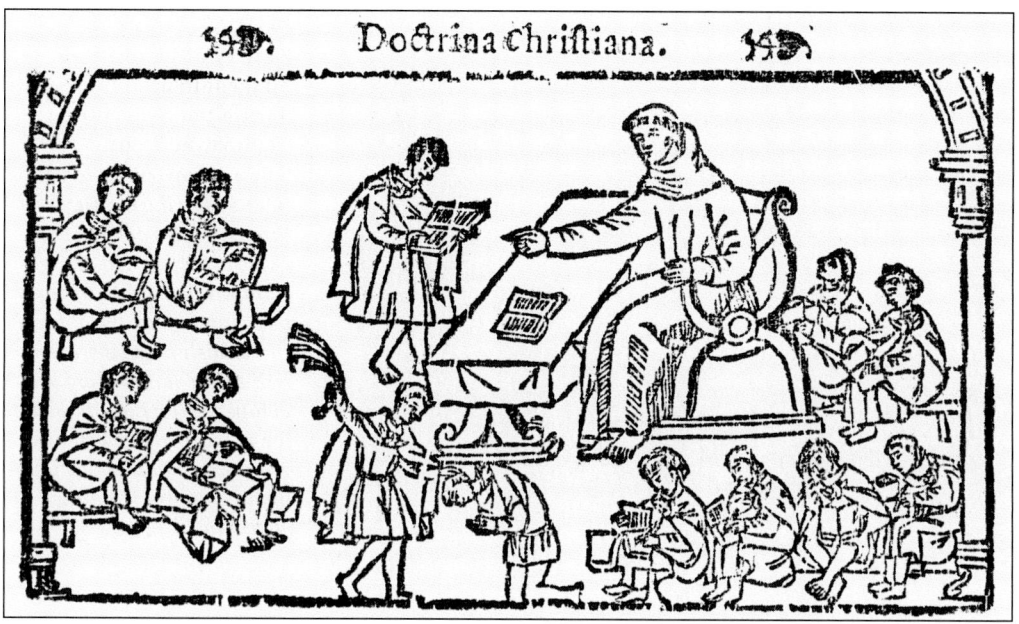

Doctrina Chriſtiana.

MISSION SCHOOL
This early-seventeenth-century woodcut depicts a mission school in New Spain. A monk instructs Indian children in Christian doctrine by leading them word by word through a printed book. The obedient students follow the monk's directions by pointing to the right passage in the book. A disobedient student is punished with a whipping administered by a fellow student at the monk's command. According to this woodcut, what lessons did mission school students learn in addition to Christian doctrine?
© Collection of the New-York Historical Society.

From the viewpoint of Spain, the single most important economic activity in New Spain after 1540 was silver mining. Spain imported more New World gold than silver in the early decades of the century, but that changed with the discovery of major silver deposits at Potosí, Bolivia, in 1545 and Zacatecas, Mexico, in 1546. As the mines swung into large-scale production during the 1540s, an ever-growing stream of silver flowed from New Spain to Spain (Figure 2.1). Overall, exports of precious metals from New Spain during the sixteenth century were worth about twenty-five times more than hides, the next most important export. The mines and their products were valuable principally for their contribution to the wealth of Spain, not to that of the colony.

During the century after 1492, about 225,000 Spaniards settled in the colonies. Virtually all of them were poor young men of common (nonnoble) lineage who came directly from Spain. Laborers and artisans made up the largest proportion, but sol-diers and sailors were also numerous. Throughout the sixteenth century, men vastly outnumbered women, although the proportion of women grew from about one in twenty before 1519 to nearly one in three by the 1580s. The gender and number of Spanish settlers shaped two fundamental features of the society of New Spain. First, despite the thousands of immigrants, Europeans never made up more than 1 or 2 percent of the total population. Although Spaniards ruled New Spain, the population was almost wholly Indian. Second, the shortage of Spanish women meant that a great deal of concubinage and intermarriage took place between Spanish men and Indian women.

The highest social status in New Spain was reserved for natives of Spain, *peninsulares* (people born on the Iberian peninsula). Below them but still within the elite were *creoles*, the children born in the New World to Spanish men and women. Below them on the social pyramid was a larger group of *mestizos*, the offspring of Spanish men and Indian

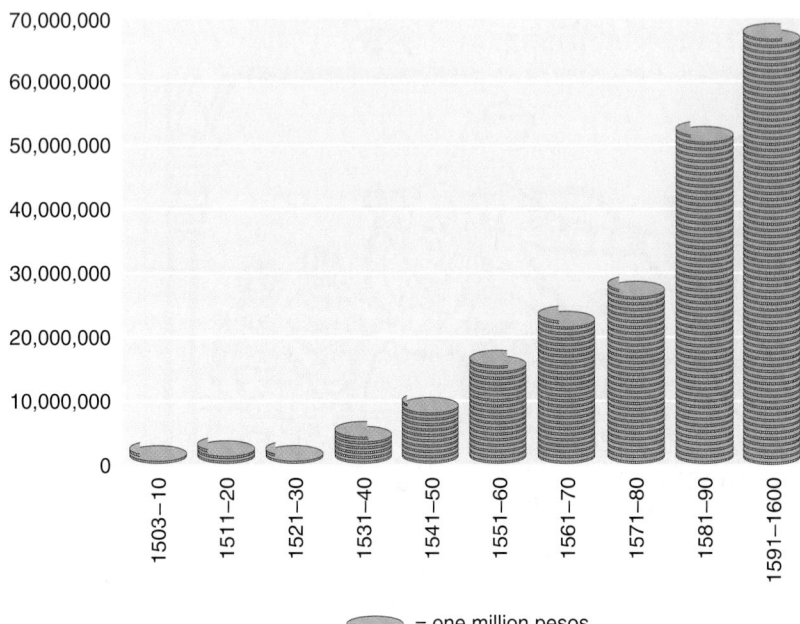

FIGURE 2.1

New World Gold and Silver Imported into Spain during the Sixteenth Century, in Pesos
Spain imported more gold than silver during the first three decades of the sixteenth century, but the total value of this treasure was quickly eclipsed during the 1530s and 1540s when rich silver mines were developed. Silver accounted for most of the enormous growth in Spain's precious-metal imports from the New World.

⬭ = one million pesos

women, who made up 4 or 5 percent of the population. So many of the mestizos were illegitimate that the term *mestizo* (from the Spanish word for "mixed") was almost synonymous with *bastard* in the sixteenth century. Some mestizos worked as artisans and labor overseers and lived well, and a few rose into the ranks of the elite, especially if their Indian ancestry was not obvious from their skin color. Most mestizos, however, were lumped with the Indians, the enormous bottom mass of the population.

The society of New Spain established the precedent for what would become a pronounced pattern in the European colonies of the New World: a society stratified sharply by social origin and race. All Europeans of whatever social origin considered themselves superior to the native Americans; in New Spain, they were a dominant minority in both power and status.

The Toll of Spanish Conquest and Colonization

By 1560, the major centers of Indian civilization had been conquered, their leaders overthrown, their religion held in contempt, and their people forced to work for the Spaniards. Profound demoralization pervaded Indian society. As a Mexican poet wrote:

Nothing but flowers and songs of sorrow
are left in Mexico . . .
where once we saw warriors and wise men. . . .
We are crushed to the ground;
we lie in ruins.
There is nothing but grief and suffering
in Mexico.

Adding to the culture shock of conquest and colonization was the deadly toll of European diseases. As conquest spread, Indians were struck by virulent epidemics of measles, smallpox, and respiratory illnesses, diseases unknown to them before the arrival of the Europeans. By 1570, only a half century after Cortés entered Tenochtitlán, the Indian population of New Spain had fallen to about 10 percent of what it had been when Columbus arrived. In little more than fifty years, nine out of ten Indians had succumbed to the severity of colonial policies and even more deadly European diseases. The destruction of the Indian population was a catastrophe unequaled in human history. A Mayan Indian recalled that when sickness struck his village, "Great was the stench of the dead. . . . The dogs and vultures devoured the bodies. The mortality was terrible. . . . So it was that we became orphans. . . . We were born to die!" For most Indians, New Spain was a graveyard.

Español con India.
Mestizo.

Mestizo con Españolo
Castizo.

Castizo con Española
Español.

Español con Mora
Mulato.

5

6

Mulato con Española
Morisco.

Morisco con Española
Chino.

7

Chino con India.
Salta atras.

Salta atras con Mulata.
Lobo.

For the Spaniards, Indian deaths meant that the most valuable resource of New Spain—Indian labor—dwindled rapidly. By the last quarter of the sixteenth century, Spanish colonists felt the pinch of a labor shortage. To help redress the need for laborers, the colonists began to import African slaves. In the years before 1550, only 15,000 slaves were imported from Africa. Even after Indian labor began to decline, the relatively high cost of African slaves kept imports low, approximately 36,000 from 1550 to the end of the century. During the sixteenth century, New Spain continued to rely primarily on a diminishing number of Indians.

Northern Outposts in Florida and New Mexico

After the explorations of de Soto, Coronado, and Cabrillo, officials in New Spain lost interest in North America. The monarchy claimed that Spain owned North America and insisted that a few North American settlements be established to give some tangible reality to its claims. Settlements in Florida would have the additional benefit of protecting Spanish ships from pirates and privateers who lurked along the southeastern coast, waiting for the Spanish treasure fleet sailing toward Spain.

In 1565, the Spanish king sent Pedro Menéndez de Avilés to create settlements along the Atlantic coast of North America. In early September, Menéndez founded St. Augustine in Florida, the first permanent European settlement within what became

---

MIXED RACES
Residents of New Spain maintained a lively interest in each person's racial lineage. These eighteenth-century paintings illustrate forms of racial mixture common in the sixteenth century. In the first painting, a Spanish man and an Indian woman have a mestizo son; in the fourth, a Spanish man and a woman of African descent have a mulatto son; in the fifth, a Spanish woman and a mulatto man have a morisco daughter. The many racial permutations of parents led residents of New Spain to develop an elaborate vocabulary of ancestry. The child of a morisco and a Spaniard was a chino; the child of a chino and an Indian was a salta abas; the child of a salta abas and a mulatto was a lobo; and so on. Can you detect hints of some of the meanings of racial categories in the clothing depicted in these paintings?
Bob Schalkwijk/INAH.

Justifying Conquest

*T*he immense riches Spain reaped from its New World empire came largely at the expense of Indians. A few individual Spaniards raised their voices against the brutal exploitation of Indians. Their criticisms prompted the Spanish monarchy to formulate an official justification of conquest that, in effect, blamed Indians for resisting Spanish dominion.

DOCUMENT 1. Montecino's 1511 Sermon

In 1511, a Dominican friar named Antón Montecino delivered a blistering sermon that astonished the Spaniards gathered in the church in Santo Domingo, headquarters of the Spanish Caribbean.

Your greed for gold is blind. Your pride, your lust, your anger, your envy, your sloth, all blind. . . . You are in mortal sin. And you are heading for damnation. . . . For you are destroying an innocent people. For they are God's people, these innocents, whom you destroyed. By what right do you make them die? Mining gold for you in your mines or working for you in your fields, by what right do you unleash enslaving wars upon them? They have lived in peace in this land before you came, in peace in their own homes. They did nothing to harm you to cause you to slaughter them wholesale. . . . Are you not under God's command to love them as you love yourselves? Are you out of your souls, out of your minds? Yes. And that will bring you to damnation.

SOURCE: Zvi Dor-Ner, *Columbus and the Age of Discovery* (New York: William Morrow, 1991), 220–21.

DOCUMENT 2. The *Requerimiento*

Montecino returned to Spain to bring the Indians' plight to the king's attention. In 1512 and 1513, King Ferdinand met with philosophers, theologians, and other advisers and concluded that the holy duty to spread the Christian faith justified conquest. To buttress this claim, the king had his advisers prepare the Requerimiento. *According to the* Requerimiento, *Indians who failed to welcome Spanish conquest and all its blessings deserved to die. Conquistadors were commanded to read the* Requerimiento *to Indians before any act of conquest. Beginning in 1514, they routinely did so, speaking in Spanish while other Spaniards brandishing unsheathed swords stood nearby.*

On the part of the King . . . [and] queen of [Spain], subduers of the barbarous nations, we their servants notify and make known to you, as best we can, that the Lord our God, living and eternal, created the heaven and the earth, and one man and one woman, of whom you and we, and all the men of the world, were and are descendants. . . .

God our lord gave charge to one man called St. Peter, that he should be lord and superior to all the men in the world, that all should obey him, and that he should be the head of the whole human race, wherever men should live . . . and he gave him the world for his kingdom and jurisdiction.

And he commanded him to place his seat in Rome, as the spot most fitting to rule the world from. . . . This man was called Pope, as if to say, Admirable Great Father and Governor of men. The men who lived in that time obeyed that St. Peter and took him for lord, king, and superior of the universe. So also they have regarded the others who after him have been elected to the pontificate, and so has it been continued even till now, and will continue till the end of the world.

One of these pontiffs, who succeeded that St. Peter as lord of the world . . . made donation of these islands and mainland to the aforesaid king and queen [of Spain] and to their successors. . . .

So their highnesses are kings and lords of these islands and mainland by virtue of this donation; and . . . almost all those to whom this has been notified, have received and served their highnesses, as lords and kings, in the way that subjects ought to do, with good will, without any resistance, immediately, without delay, when they were informed of the aforesaid facts. And also they received and obeyed the priests whom their highnesses sent to preach to them and to teach them our holy faith; and all these, of their own free will, without any reward or condition have become Christians, and are so, and the highnesses have joyfully and graciously received them, and they have also commanded them to be treated as their subjects and vassals; and you too are held and obliged to do the same. Wherefore, as best we can, we ask and require that you consider what we have said to you, and that you take the time that shall be necessary to understand and deliberate upon it, and that you acknowledge the Church as the ruler and superior of the whole world, and the high priest called Pope, and in his name the king and queen [of Spain] our lords, in his place, as superiors and lords and kings of these islands and this mainland by virtue of the said donation, and that you consent and permit that these religious fathers declare and preach to you. . . .

If you do so . . . we . . . shall receive you in all love and charity, and shall leave you your wives and your children and your lands free without servitude, that you may do with them and with yourselves freely what you like and think best, and they shall not compel you to turn to Christians unless you yourselves, when informed of the truth, should wish to be converted to our holy Catholic faith. . . . And besides this, their highnesses award you many privileges and exemptions and will grant you many benefits.

But if you do not do this or if you maliciously delay in doing it, I certify to you that with the help of God we shall forcefully enter into your country and shall make war against you in all ways and manners that we can, and shall subject you to the yoke and obedience of the Church and of their high-nesses; we shall take you and your wives and your children and shall make slaves of them, and as such shall sell and dispose of them as their highnesses may command; and we shall take away your goods and shall do to you all the harm and damage that we can, as to vassals who do not obey and refuse to receive their lord and resist and contradict him; and we protest that the deaths and losses which shall accrue from this are your fault, and not that of their highnesses, or ours, or of these soldiers who come with us.

Indians who heard the Requerimiento *could not understand Spanish, of course. No native documents survive to record the Indians' thoughts upon hearing the Spaniards' official justification for conquest, even when it was translated in a language they recognized. But one conquistador reported that when the* Requerimiento *was translated for two chiefs in Colombia, they responded that if the pope gave the king so much territory that belonged to other people, "the Pope must have been drunk."*

Source: Adapted from A. Helps and M. Oppenheim, eds., *The Spanish Conquest in America and Its Relation to the History of Slavery and to the Government of the Colonies,* 4 vols. (London and New York, 1900–1904), 1:264–67.

QUESTIONS FOR ANALYSIS AND DEBATE

1. How did the *Requerimiento* answer the criticisms of Montecino? According to the *Requerimiento,* why was conquest justified? What was the source of Indians' resistance to conquest?

2. What arguments might a critic like Montecino have used to respond to the *Requerimiento's* justification of conquest? What arguments might the Mexican leader Montezuma have made against those of the *Requerimiento?*

3. Was the *Requerimiento* a faithful expression or a cynical violation of Spaniards' Christian faith?

but the colony they established—like the search for a Northwest Passage—came to nothing.

English attempts to follow Spain's lead were slower but equally ill fated. Not until 1576, almost eighty years after John Cabot's voyages, did the English try again to find a Northwest Passage. This time Martin Frobisher sailed into the frigid waters of northern Canada; his sponsor was the Cathay Company, which hoped to open trade with China (see Map 2.2). Like many other explorers who preceded and followed him, Frobisher was mesmerized by the Spanish example and was sure he had found gold. But the tons of "ore" he hauled back to England proved worthless, the Cathay Company collapsed, and English interests shifted southward.

English attempts to establish North American settlements were no more fruitful than their search for a northern route to China. Sir Humphrey Gilbert led expeditions in 1578 and 1583 that made feeble efforts to found colonies in Newfoundland until Gilbert vanished at sea in 1583. Sir Walter Raleigh organized an expedition in 1585 to settle Roanoke Island off the coast of present-day North Carolina. The first group of explorers left no colonists on the island, but two years later Raleigh sent a contingent of more than one hundred settlers to Roanoke under John White's leadership. White returned to England for supplies and when he went back in 1590, the Roanoke colonists had disappeared, leaving only the word *Croatoan* (whose meaning is unknown) carved on a tree. The Roanoke colonists most likely died from a combination of natural causes and unfriendly Indians. By the end of the century, England had failed to secure a New World beachhead.

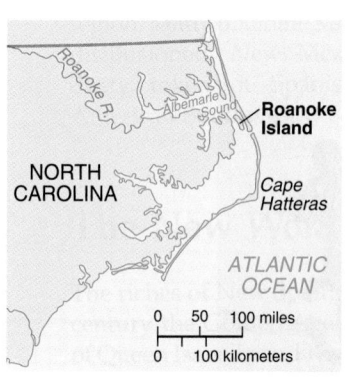

Roanoke Settlement, 1585–1590

Conclusion: The Promise of the New World for Europeans

The sixteenth century in the New World belonged to the Spaniards, who employed Columbus, and the Indians, who greeted him as he stepped ashore. Spaniards initiated the Columbian exchange between the New World and the Old that continues to this day. The exchange subjected native Americans to the ravages of European diseases and Spanish conquest. Spanish explorers, conquistadors, and colonists forced Indians to serve the interests of Spanish settlers and the Spanish monarchy. The exchange illustrated one of the most important lessons of the sixteenth century: After millions of years, the Atlantic no longer was an impermeable barrier separating the Eastern and Western Hemispheres. After the voyages of Columbus, European sailing ships regularly bridged the Atlantic and carried people, products, diseases, and ideas from one shore to the other.

No European monarch could forget the seductive lesson taught by Spain's example: The New World could vastly enrich the Old. Spain remained a New World power for almost four centuries, and its language, culture, and institutions left a permanent imprint. By the end of the sixteenth century, however, other European monarchies began to contest Spain's dominion in Europe and to make forays into the northern fringes of Spain's New World preserve. To reap some of the benefits the Spaniards enjoyed from their New World domain, the others had to learn a difficult lesson: how to deviate from Spain's example. That discovery lay ahead.

FOR FURTHER READING ABOUT THE TOPICS IN THIS CHAPTER, see the Online Bibliography at www.bedfordstmartins.com/roarkcompact.

FOR ADDITIONAL FIRST-HAND ACCOUNTS OF THIS PERIOD, see pages 9–26 in Michael Johnson, ed., *Reading the American Past,* Second Edition, Volume I.

TO ASSESS YOUR MASTERY OF THE MATERIAL IN THIS CHAPTER, see the Online Study Guide at www.bedfordstmartins.com/roarkcompact.

CHRONOLOGY

1415 Portuguese explorers begin forays along African coast.

1444 Portuguese explorers reach Cape Verde.

1451 Christopher Columbus born in Genoa, Italy.

1480 Portuguese ships reach Congo.

1488 Bartolomeu Dias rounds Cape of Good Hope.

1492 Columbus lands on Caribbean island that he names San Salvador.

1493 Columbus makes second voyage to the New World.

1494 Portugal and Spain negotiate the Treaty of Tordesillas to divide New World between them.

1497 John Cabot searches for Northwest Passage.

1498 Columbus makes third voyage to the New World and lands in Venezuela.

Vasco da Gama sails to India.

1500 Pedro Álvars Cabral makes landfall in Brazil.

1507 German mapmaker Martin Waldseemüller names New World *America*.

1513 Vasco Núñez de Balboa crosses isthmus of Panama.

1517 Protestant Reformation begins in Europe.

1519 Hernán Cortés leads expedition to find and conquer Mexico.

Ferdinand Magellan sets out to sail around the world.

Charles I of Spain becomes Holy Roman Emperor Charles V.

1521 Cortés conquers the Mexica at Tenochtitlán.

1532 Francisco Pizarro begins conquest of Peru.

1539 Hernando de Soto launches exploration of southeastern North America.

1540 Francisco Vásquez de Coronado starts to explore the Southwest and Great Plains of North America.

1542 Juan Rodríguez Cabrillo explores California coast.

1549 *Repartimiento* reforms begin to replace *encomienda*.

1565 Pedro Menéndez de Avilés establishes St. Augustine, Florida.

1576 Martin Frobisher sails into northern Canadian waters.

1578 Sir Humphrey Gilbert attempts to found colonies in Newfoundland.

1587 English colonists under Sir Walter Raleigh settle Roanoke Island.

1598 Juan de Oñate leads expedition into New Mexico.

TOBACCO JAR

This tobacco storage jar combines a product and place name from the southern colonies in North America with the fine craft of decorative ceramics designed for Europeans to use in their everyday lives. The jar illustrates the many ways tobacco grown in the New World influenced life beyond tobacco fields. Grown principally by servants and slaves, the tobacco stored in this jar would have been transported to port in barrels made by coopers, ferried across the Atlantic in ships—made by shipbuilders and equipped with sails, ropes, and specialized fittings made by skilled workingmen—and insured by financiers and insurance companies. Upon arrival on the eastern shores of the Atlantic, the tobacco barrels would have been off-loaded and opened, the tobacco chopped, ground, and flavored by tobacconists, who sold it in shops along with jars like the one pictured here to consumers avid for tobacco to smoke, sniff, or chew and for an attractive repository both to store their stimulant and to display their sophisticated taste. Most tobacco came from the Chesapeake region; the label "Carolina" was a brand name rather than an accurate indication of the origin of the tobacco.

Colonial Williamsburg Foundation.

THE SOUTHERN COLONIES IN THE SEVENTEENTH CENTURY

3

1601–1700

I N December 1607, barely six months after arriving at Jamestown with the first English colonists, Captain John Smith was captured by warriors of Powhatan, the supreme chief of about fourteen thousand Algonquian people who inhabited the coastal plain of present-day Virginia, near the Chesapeake Bay. According to Smith, Powhatan "feasted him after their best barbarous manner." Then, after the chief consulted with his men, "two great stones were brought before Powhatan: then as many [Indians] as could layd hands on [Smith], dragged him to [the stones], and thereon laid his head, and being ready with their clubs, to beate out his braines." At that moment, Pocahontas, Powhatan's eleven-year-old daughter, rushed forward and "got [Smith's] head in her armes, and laid her owne upon his to save him from death." Pocahontas, Smith wrote, "hazarded the beating out of her owne braines to save mine, and . . . so prevailed with her father, that I was safely conducted [back] to James towne."

This romantic story of an Indian maiden rescuing a white soldier and saving not only his life but also Jamestown and ultimately English colonization of North America has been enshrined in the writing of American history since 1624 when Smith published his *Generall Historie of Virginia* and has even been dramatized in a recent Disney movie. Historians believe that this episode actually happened more or less as Smith described it. But Smith did not understand why Pocahontas acted as she did. Many commentators have claimed that her love for Smith caused her to rebel against her father's authority.

On the contrary, when Pocahontas intervened to save Smith, she almost certainly was participating in an Algonquian ceremony that expressed Powhatan's supremacy and his ritualistic adoption of a subordinate chief, or *werowance*. Most likely, what Smith interpreted as Pocahontas's saving him from certain death was a ceremonial enactment of Powhatan's willingness to incorporate Smith and the white strangers at Jamestown into Powhatan's empire. The ceremony displayed Powhatan's power of life or death over a subordinate chief—Smith—and Powhatan's willingness to give protection to those who acknowledged his supremacy—in this case, the interlopers at Jamestown. By appearing to save Smith, Pocahontas was probably acting out Smith's new status as an adopted member of Powhatan's extended family. Rather than a rebellious, love-struck girl, Pocahontas was almost certainly a dutiful daughter playing the part prescribed for her by her father and her culture. It appears that Powhatan attempted to treat the tribe of white strangers at Jamestown as he did other tribes in his empire, an attempt that failed.

In 1613, after relations between Powhatan and the English colonists had deteriorated into bloody raids by both parties, Pocahontas was captured and held hostage at Jamestown. Within a year she converted to Christianity and married one of the colonists, a widower named John Rolfe. After giving birth to a son, Thomas, Pocahontas, her husband, and the new baby sailed for England in the spring of 1616. There, promoters of the Virginia colony dressed her as a proper Englishwoman and arranged for her to meet dignitaries.

Hearing that Pocahontas was in London, John Smith went to see her. According to Smith, Pocahontas said, "You did promise Powhatan what was yours should bee his, and he the like to you; you called him father, being in his land a stranger, and by the same reason so must I doe you." It seems likely, in other words, that Pocahontas understood what was happening to her in England as a counterpart to the ritual John Smith had experienced in Virginia back in 1607.

Pocahontas died in England in 1617. Her son, Thomas, ultimately returned to Virginia and by the time of the American Revolution his descendants numbered in the hundreds. But the world Thomas Rolfe and his descendants inhabited was shaped by a reversal of the power ritualized when his mother "saved" John Smith. By the end of the seventeenth century, native Americans were far from vanquished, but—unlike Powhatan—they no longer dominated the newcomers who had arrived in the Chesapeake with John Smith.

During the seventeenth century, the English colonists learned how to make a living growing tobacco, a crop native Americans had cultivated in small quantities for centuries. The new settlers, however, grew enormous crops of tobacco, far more than they could smoke, chew, or sniff themselves, and they exported most of it to England. Rather than incorporating Powhatan's people into their new society, the settlers appropriated lands surrounding the Chesapeake Bay that had supported ancient Americans for millennia and built new societies on the foundation of tobacco agriculture and transatlantic trade.

To produce large crop surpluses for export required hard labor and people who were willing—or could be forced—to do it. For the most part, native Americans refused to be conscripted into the colonists' fields. Instead, the settlers depended on the labor of family members, indentured servants, and, by the last third of the seventeenth century, African slaves. By the end of the century, the southern colonies had become sharply different both from the world dominated by Powhatan when the Jamestown settlers first arrived and from contemporary English society. In ways unimaginable to Powhatan, Pocahontas, or John Smith, the colonists paid homage to the international market and the English monarch by working mightily to make a good living growing crops for sale to the Old World.

POCAHONTAS IN ENGLAND
Shortly after Pocahontas and her husband John Rolfe arrived in England in 1616, an engraver made this portrait of her dressed in English clothing suitable for a princess. The portrait captures the dual novelty of England for Pocahontas and of Pocahontas for the English. Ornate, courtly clothing probably signified to English observers that Pocahontas was royalty and to Pocahontas that the English were accepting her as befitted the "Emperour" Powhatan's daughter. The mutability of Pocahontas's identity is displayed in the engraving's identification of her as "Matoaka alias Rebecca."
Library of Congress.

SECOTAN VILLAGE
This engraving, published in 1612, was copied from an original drawing John White made in 1585 when he visited the village of Secotan on the coast of North Carolina. The drawing provides a schematic view of daily life in the village, which may have resembled one of Powhatan's settlements. White noted on the original that the fire burning behind the line of crouching men was "the place of solemne prayer." The large building in the lower left was a tomb where the bodies of important leaders were kept. Dwellings lined a central space, where men and women ate. Corn is growing in the fields along the right side of the village. The engraver has included hunters shooting deer at the upper left; hunting was probably never so convenient—no such hunters or deer appear in White's original drawing. This portrait conveys the message that Secotan was orderly, settled, religious, harmonious, and peaceful (note the absence of fortifications), and very different from English villages.
Princeton University Libraries.

www.bedfordstmartins.com/roarkcompact
SEE THE ONLINE STUDY GUIDE for more help in analyzing this image.

An English Colony on the Chesapeake

By 1600, King James I eyed North America as a possible location for English colonies. In 1606, a number of "knightes, gentlemen, merchauntes, and other adventurers of our cittie of London" organized a joint stock company, the Virginia Company of London, and petitioned King James to grant them permission to establish a colony in North America. The king boldly granted the Virginia Company over six million acres and everything they might contain, in large measure because they were not his to grant. In effect, the charter was a royal license to poach on Spanish claims to the region and on Powhatan's chiefdom.

The adventurers in the Virginia Company hoped to found an empire that would strengthen England not only overseas but also at home. Jobless Englishmen would be put to work in the colony, producing goods that England currently had to import from other nations. They would also provide a ready market in the colony for English woolens.

But the main reason the Virginia Company was willing to risk its capital in Virginia was the fervent hope for quick profits. One way or another, Virginia promised to reward the adventurers. Or so they thought.

The Fragile Jamestown Settlement

In December 1606, the *Susan Constant*, *Discovery*, and *Godspeed* carried 144 Englishmen toward Virginia. They arrived at the mouth of the Chesapeake Bay on April 26, 1607. That night while the colonists rested onshore, one of them later recalled, a band of Indians "creeping upon all foure, from the Hills like Beares, with their Bowes in their mouthes," attacked and dangerously wounded two men. The attack gave the colonists an early warning that the North American wilderness was not quite the paradise described by the Virginia Company's publications in England. On May 14, they put ashore on a small peninsula in the midst of Powhatan's chiefdom. With the memory of their first night in America fresh in their minds, they quickly built a fort, the first building in the settlement they named Jamestown.

The Jamestown fort showed the colonists' awareness that native peoples were prepared to defend Virginia as their own. During May and June 1607, the settlers and Powhatan's warriors skirmished repeatedly. English muskets and cannon repelled Indian attacks on Jamestown, but the Indians' superior numbers and knowledge of the Virginia wilderness made it risky for the settlers to venture far beyond the peninsula. Late in June, Powhatan sensed a stalemate and made peace overtures.

The settlers soon confronted far more dangerous, invisible threats: disease and starvation. By September, fifty of the colonists had died. Powhatan's people came to the rescue of the weakened and distracted colonists. Early in September 1607, they began to bring corn to the colony for barter. When that was insufficient to keep the colonists fed, the settlers sent Captain John Smith to trade (and plunder) for corn with tribes upriver from Jamestown. His efforts managed to keep 38 of the original settlers alive until a fresh supply of food and 120 more colonists arrived from England in January 1608.

It is difficult to exaggerate the precarious state of the early Jamestown settlement. Although the Virginia Company sent hundreds of new settlers to Jamestown each year, few survived. During the "starving time" winter of 1609–1610, food was so short that one or two famished settlers resorted to eating their recently deceased neighbors.

Cooperation and Conflict between Natives and Newcomers

Native Americans stayed in contact with the English settlers, but maintained a cautious distance. The Virginia Company boasted that the settlers bought from the Indians "the pearles of earth [corn] and [sold] to them the pearles of heaven [Christianity]." In fact, few Indians converted to Christianity, and the English devoted scant effort to proselytizing. Marriage between Indian women and English men was also rare, despite the acute shortage of English women in Virginia in the early years. One of the few settlers who troubled to learn the Indians' language was John Smith. Powhatan's people regarded the English with suspicion, and for good reason. While the settlers often exhibited friendship toward the Indians, they did not hesitate to use their superior weapons to enforce English notions of proper Indian behavior.

The Indians retaliated against English violence, but for fifteen years they did not organize an all-out assault on the European intruders, probably for several reasons. Although the Indians felt no attraction to Christianity, they were impressed by the power of the settlers' God. One chief told John Smith that "he did believe that our God as much exceeded theirs as our guns did their bows and arrows." Powhatan probably concluded that these powerful strangers would make better allies than enemies. As allies, the English not only strengthened Powhatan's dominance over the tribes in the region; they also traded with his people, usually exchanging European goods for corn. Native Virginians had an insatiable desire for the settlers' iron and steel weapons and tools.

The trade that supplied Indians with European conveniences provided the English settlers with a prime necessity: food. But why did the settlers prove unable to feed themselves for more than a decade? First, as the staggering death rate suggests, many settlers were too sick to be productive members of the colony. Second, very few farmers came to Virginia in the early years. Instead, most of the newcomers were gentlemen and their servants, men who, in John Smith's words, "never did know what a day's work was." In the meantime, the colonists depended on the Indians' corn for food. (See "The Promise of Technology," page 50.)

Becaufe many doe defire to know the manner
of their Language, I haue inferted thefe few words.

KA katorawincs yowo. What call you this.

Nemarough, a man.

Crenepo, a woman.

Marowancheffo, a boy.

Yehawkans, Houfes.

Matchcores, Skins, or garments.

Mockafins, Shooes.

Tuffan, Beds. Pokatawer, Fire.

Attawp, A bow. Attonce, Arrowes.

Monacookes, Swords.

Aumouhhowgh, A Target.

Pawcuffacks, Gunnes.

Tomahacks, Axes.

Tockahacks, Pickaxes.

Pamefacks, Kniues.

Accowprets, Sheares.

Pawpecones, Pipes. Mattaßin, Copper

Vffawaffin, Iron, Braffe, Silver, or any white mettall. Muffes, Woods.

Attaffkuff, Leaues, weeds, or graffe.

Chepfin, Land. Shacquohocan. A ftone.

Wepenter, A cookold.

Suckahanna, Water. Noughmaff, Fifh.

Copotone, Sturgeon.

Weghfhaughes, Flefh.

Sawwehone, Bloud.

Netoppew, Friends.

Marrapough, Enemies.

Maskapow, the worft of the enemies.

Mawchick chammay, The beft of friends

Cafacunnakack, peya quagh acquintan vitafantafough, In how many daies will there come hither any more Englifh Ships.

Their Numbers.

Necut, 1. Ningh, 2. Nuff, 3. Yowgh, 4. Paranske, 5. Comotinch, 6. Toppawoff, 7 Nuffwafh, 8. Kekatawgh, 9. Kaskeke 10 They count no more but by tennes as followeth.

Cafe, how many.

Ninghfapooeksku, 20.

Nuffapooeksku, 30.

Yowghapooeksku, 40.

Parankeftaffapoocksku, 50.

Comatincktaffapooecksku, 60.

Nuffwafhtaffapooecksku, 70.

Kekataughtaffapooecksku, 90.

Necuttoughtyfinough, 100.

Necuttwevnquaough, 1000.

Rawcofowghs, Dayes.

Kefkowghes, Sunnes:

Toppquough. Nights.

Nepawwefhowghs, Moones.

Pawpaxfoughes, Yeares.

Pummahumps, Starres.

Ofies, Heavens.

Okees, Gods.

Quiyoughcofoughs, Pettie Gods, and their affinities.

Righcomoughes, Deaths.

Kekughes, Liues.

Mowchick woyawgh tawgh noeragh kaquere mecher, I am very hungry? what fhall I eate?

Yawnor nehiegh Powhatan, Where dwels Powhatan.

Mache, nehiegh yourowgh, Orapaks. Now he dwelsa great way hence at Orapaks.

Vittapitchewayne anpechitchs nehaw-per Werowacomoco, You lie, he ftaid ever at Werowacomoco.

Kator nehiegh mattagh neer vttapit-chewayne, Truely he is there I doe not lie.

Spaughtynere keragh werowance maw-marinough kekatë wawgh peyaquaugh. Run you then to the King Mawma-rynough and bid him come hither.

Vtteke, e peya weyack wighwhip, Get you gone, & come againe quickly.

Kekaten Pokahontas patiaquagh ningh tanks manotyens neer mowchick raw-renock audowgh, Bid Pokahontas bring hither two little Baskets, and I will giue her white Beads to make her a Chaine.   FINIS.

The persistence of the Virginia colony, precarious as it was, created difficulties for Powhatan's chiefdom. The steady contact between natives and newcomers spread European viruses among the Indians, who suffered deadly epidemics in 1608 and between 1617 and 1619. But from the Indians' view-point, the most important fact about the Virginia colony was that it was proving to be a permanent settlement.

Powhatan died in 1618, and his brother Opechancanough replaced him as supreme chief. In 1622, Opechancanough organized an all-out assault

Corn, the "Life-Giver"

Europeans first learned about corn from Columbus. As soon as he returned to Spain in 1493, he told the royal court about amazing things he had seen on his voyage to the other side of the Atlantic, including a plant he called *maize,* his version of *mahiz,* the Taino word for corn, which meant "life-giver." Ancient Americans had been growing corn for about seven thousand years. From its origin in central Mexico, corn had spread throughout the Western Hemisphere by the time Columbus arrived. Although the rest of the world had never seen or heard of corn, within a generation after 1493 travelers carried seeds throughout the Old World. By the early sixteenth century, corn seeds sprouted in Europe, the Middle East, Africa, India, and China.

Accustomed to growing wheat and eating foods derived from it, Europeans at first did not like corn. A few years before the settlers arrived in Jamestown, an English botanist expressed the common European view that "the barbarous Indians which know no better, are constrained to make a vertue of necessitie, and think [corn is] a good food; whereas we may easily judge that it nourisheth but little, and is of hard and evill digestion, a more convenient foode for swine than for man."

Early in the seventeenth century, English settlers in North America discovered that hunger quickly made a virtue of necessity. John Smith wrote that during the spring of 1609 Jamestown residents became so hungry that "they would have sould their soules" for a half-basket of Powhatan's corn. Before settlers could reliably subsist in the Chesapeake region, they had to learn the technology of corn.

From the perspective of the twenty-first century, it may seem odd to speak of the technology of corn. Today, we tend to think that technology refers only to machinery such as engines, computer chips, or airplanes. But technology also refers to a much broader range of human experience. *Webster's* defines technology as "the science of the application of knowledge to practical purposes." Nowadays, technological knowledge has found countless practical uses for corn as food, sweetener, and oil, as well as in such products as medicines, tires, batteries, and lipstick. The roots of these modern-day uses of corn stretch back to ancient Americans who first developed the technology of growing, processing, and consuming corn, a technology English settlers of North America sought to learn for the practical purpose of eating.

Corn needs help to grow. Bury an ear of corn in the soil and the seeds that sprout strangle each other in an overcrowded quest for light. But strip the husk from a ripe ear of corn, rub the seeds out of the cob, plant the separated seeds on a spring day in a spot with sufficient heat, light, and water, and during the summer each seed is capable of producting a stalk with two or more ears, each bearing hundreds of edible corn seeds. An awestruck English visitor described corn's "marveillous great increase; of a thousand, fifteene hundred and some two thousand fold."

To obtain this impressive yield, early-seventeenth-century European settlers throughout North America watched native Americans cultivate corn. "In place of ploughs" commonly used in England, one observer reported, "they use an instrument of hard wood, shaped like a spade" to break up the soil and prepare it for planting, work usually done by men. Then women used a stick to "make a hole [in the soil] wherein they put out four grains . . . and cover them." Another colonist acknowledged that native Americans were "our first instructors for the planting of their Indian Corne, by teaching us to cull out the finest seede, to observe the fittest season, to keepe distance for holes, and fit measure for hills, to worme it, and weede it; to prune it, and dresse it as occasion shall require." Jamestown's early settlers did not depend on chance observations of this planting technology. John Smith boasted that two hostages the colonists captured from Powhatan "taught us how to order and plant our fields" while they were held as "fettered prisoners."

Along with corn, Indians usually planted beans. "When they [beans] grow up they interlace with the corn . . . and they keep the ground very free from weeds," one newcomer noticed. Ancient Americans' association of beans with corn had a sound biochemical basis. Beans fixed nitrogen in the soil, a function corn roots cannot perform. Corn plants then absorbed the nitrogen to produce higher yields. Beans also made corn more nutritious. Beans contain niacin, an essential nutrient lacking in corn. Together, corn and beans provided the basic ingredients for a healthy diet.

As every popcorn eater knows, corn kernels are hard enough to crack a tooth. European settlers had no difficulty eating green or sweet corn, the immature form of ripening corn commonly consumed today as corn on the cob. But to obtain the nutritious interior of mature corn kernels without cracking their teeth they had to learn ancient American technology. For millennia native Americans had soaked or boiled corn kernels with wood ash or other alkaline material. The alkali softened and loosened the tough hull protecting the corn's nutrients. Treated in this way, corn kernels that otherwise were rock-hard could be separated from their hulls and readily mashed into dough for tortillas or mixed with beans or other foods in tasty stews. Early colonists copied this process to make softened corn foods they called samp, or hominy, or grits.

Since settlers were accustomed to wheat ground into a fine flour, they preferred cornmeal obtained by the much more laborious process of pulverizing corn kernels with a mortar and pestle or grinding them between stones, both processes familiar to native Americans. From cornmeal dough cooked on an iron griddle or baked in the coals of a cookfire, Europeans made corn bread, corn pone, hoecake, and johnnycake—English names for ancient American food.

Unlike wheat, many varieties of corn pop open when heated, an astonishing trait Columbus duly reported to his Spanish sponsors. Archaeologists speculate that ancient Americans first thought to cultivate corn when a few grains accidentally landed in a campfire and out popped a morsel of readily edible food. For millennia ancient Americans enjoyed popcorn, not least because it so easily avoided the need to soak, boil, or grind hard corn kernels. They also ground popped corn into a nu-

ANCIENT CORN POPPER
Long before movies and microwaves, ancient Americans munched popcorn. This corn popper comes from the Mochica culture, which thrived on the northern coast of Peru for about six hundred years after the birth of Christ. The Mochica presumably nestled the popper on a bed of coals with the opening facing up, placed corn inside, and covered the opening with a lid (not shown) while the kernels popped. The Mochica and other ancient Americans did not pop most of the corn they grew. Instead they ground it into corn meal which they incorporated in a wide variety of dishes, probably including ancient counterparts of modern tortillas.
The Field Museum #A112961c, Chicago. Photographer: Diane Alexander White.

tritious and portable powder that could be mixed with water and other foods for a satisfying meal. The New England minister Roger Williams wrote that he "made a good dinner and supper" with "a *spoonfull* of this *meale* and a *spoonfull* of water from the *Brooke*." Other colonists, too, learned the ancient technology of popcorn. Today, at the cineplex and on the couch, every American consumes about fifty quarts of popped corn each year, participating—usually unwittingly—in a technology that reaches back in unbroken continuity to a campfire in central Mexico about seven thousand years ago.

on the English settlers. Striking on March 22, the Indians killed 347 settlers, nearly a third of the English population. But the attack failed to dislodge the colonists. In the aftermath, the settlers unleashed a murderous campaign of Indian extermination that in a few years pushed Indians beyond the small circumference of white settlement. Before 1622, the settlers knew that the Indians, though dangerous, were necessary to keep the colony alive. After 1622, most colonists considered Indians their perpetual enemies.

From Private Company to Royal Government

The 1622 uprising came close to achieving Opechancanough's goal of pushing the colonists back into the Atlantic—so close that it prompted a royal investigation of affairs in Virginia. The investigators discovered that the appalling mortality among the colonists was caused by disease and mismanagement more than by Indian raids. In 1624, King James revoked the charter of the Virginia Company and made Virginia a royal colony, subject to the direction of the royal government rather than to the company's private investors, an arrangement that lasted until 1776.

The king now appointed the governor of Virginia and his council, but most other features of local government established under the Virginia Company remained intact. In 1619, for example, the company had inaugurated the House of Burgesses, an assembly of representatives (called burgesses) elected by the colony's inhabitants. (Historians do not know exactly which settlers were considered inhabitants and were thus qualified to vote.) Under the new royal government, laws passed by the burgesses had to be approved by the king's bureaucrats in England rather than by the company. Otherwise, the House of Burgesses continued as before, acquiring distinction as the oldest representative legislative assembly in the British colonies. Under the new royal government, all free adult men in Virginia could vote for the House of Burgesses, giving it a far broader and more representative constituency than the English House of Commons.

The demise of the Virginia Company marked the end of the first phase of colonization of the Chesapeake. From the first 105 adventurers in 1607, the population had grown to about 1,200 by 1624. Despite high mortality rates, new settlers still came. Their arrival and King James's willingness to take

over the struggling colony reflected a fundamental change in Virginia. After years of fruitless experimentation, it was becoming clear that English settlers could make a fortune in Virginia by growing tobacco.

A Tobacco Society

Tobacco never featured in the initial plans of the Virginia Company, but beginning in 1612, John Rolfe showed that it could be grown successfully in the

TOBACCO WRAPPER
This wrapper labeled a container of "Virginia Planters Best Tobacco." It shows a colonial planter supervising slaves who hold hoes used to chop weeds that robbed the leafy tobacco plants of nutrients and moisture. The planter enjoys a pipe in the shade of an umbrella held by a slave. Once the tobacco was harvested and dried, it was pressed tightly into barrels like those shown here for shipment overseas. How does the ad indicate the differences between the planter and the slaves?
Colonial Williamsburg Foundation.

0   20   40   60 miles

0   20   40   60 kilometers

Settled by 1650

Settled by 1700

PENNSYLVANIA

APPALACHIAN MTS.

MARYLAND

NEW JERSEY

Potomac R.

SHENANDOAH VALLEY

Shenandoah R.

BLUE RIDGE MTS.

DEL.

Delaware R.

Delaware Bay

FALL LINE

Annapolis (1648)

Rappahannock R.

St. Marys (1634)

VIRGINIA

Chesapeake Bay

James R.

Richmond (1644)

Williamsburg (1699)

Jamestown (1607)

Yorktown (1691)

ATLANTIC OCEAN

Norfolk (1682)

PIEDMONT

TIDEWATER

Roanoke R.

NORTH CAROLINA

MAP 3.1

The Chesapeake Colonies in the Seventeenth Century
The intimate association of land and water in the settlement of the Chesapeake in the seventeenth century is illustrated by this map. The fall line indicates the limit of navigable water, where rapids and falls prevented further upstream travel. Why was access to navigable water so important? Although Delaware had excellent access to navigable water, it was claimed and defended by the Dutch colony at New Amsterdam (discussed in chapter 4) rather than the English settlements in Virginia and Maryland shown on this map.

new colony. In 1617, when the first commercial shipment of tobacco to England sold for a high price, the same Virginia colonists who had difficulty growing enough corn to feed themselves quickly tried to learn how to grow as much tobacco as possible. In a sense, that first commercial cargo was a pivot on which Virginia turned from a colony of rather aimless adventurers into a society of dedicated planters.

Dedicated they were. In 1620, with fewer than a thousand colonists, Virginia shipped 60,000 pounds of tobacco to England. By 1700, tobacco exports from the Chesapeake region (encompassing Virginia and

Maryland) topped 35 million pounds, and more than 98,000 colonists lived in the region. Tobacco planters' endless need for labor attracted droves of indentured servants from England to work in tobacco fields and settle the Chesapeake (Map 3.1).

The requirements of tobacco agriculture shaped patterns of settlement, making the landscape of the English colonies in the Chesapeake quite different from that of rural England. English colonists professed the Protestant and Catholic faiths, but they governed their daily lives less by the dictates of religious doctrine than by the demands of tobacco cultivation.

A Servant Labor System

English settlers now were willing to work hard because they could expect to do much better in the Chesapeake than in England. A hired man would have to work two or three years in England to earn as much as he could in just one year in Chesapeake tobacco fields. Better still, in Virginia land was so abundant that even common laborers could buy one hundred acres of land for less than their annual wages—an impossibility in England. New settlers who paid their own transportation to the Chesapeake also received a grant of fifty acres of free land (a headright).

Headrights, cheap land, and high wages gave poor English folk powerful incentives to immigrate to the New World. Yet many potential immigrants could not scrape together the fare to cross the Atlantic. Their poverty and the colonists' crying need for labor formed the basic context for the creation of a servant labor system.

Today, people think of the colonial South as a slave society. The seventeenth-century Chesapeake, however, was fundamentally a servant society. Twenty Africans arrived in Virginia in 1619, but for the next fifty years, only a small number of slaves labored in Chesapeake tobacco fields. (Large numbers of slaves came in the eighteenth century, as chapter 5 explains.) About 80 percent of the immigrants to the Chesapeake during the seventeenth century were indentured servants. Along with tobacco, the servant labor system profoundly influenced nearly every feature of Chesapeake society.

To buy passage aboard a ship bound for the Chesapeake, an English immigrant had to come up with about £5, roughly a year's wages for an English servant or laborer. Lacking that much money, poor immigrants signed a contract called an indenture specifying that the holder of the indenture would pay for the immigrant's transportation to the Chesapeake. In return, the immigrant agreed to work for a period—usually four to seven years—without pay. During this period of indentured servitude, the immigrant received food and shelter from an employer in the colonies. When the indenture expired, the employer was required to give the former servant "freedom dues," usually three barrels of corn and a suit of clothes. In effect, indentures allowed poor immigrants to trade their most valuable asset—their ability to work—for a trip to the New World.

Most planters were willing to pay about twice the cost of transportation for the right to four to seven years of an indentured servant's labor. More servants meant more hands to grow more tobacco, and also more land. For every servant purchased, a planter received from the colonial government a headright of another fifty acres of land. But the high mortality rates in the Chesapeake meant that many servants died before serving out their indentures, reducing planters' gains.

For the most part, servants were simply poor young Englishmen seeking work. More than two-thirds of them were between fifteen and twenty-five when they came to the Chesapeake. Many were orphans. Most had no special training or skills, although the majority had some experience with agricultural work. "Hunger and fear of prisons bring to us onely such servants as have been brought up to no Art or Trade," a Virginia planter complained in 1662. A skilled craftsman could obtain a shorter indenture, but few risked coming to the colonies since their prospects were better at home.

Women were almost as rare as skilled craftsmen in the Chesapeake and more ardently desired. In the early days of the tobacco boom, the Virginia Company shipped young single women servants to the colony as prospective wives for male settlers willing to pay "120 weight [pounds] of the best leaf tobacco for each of them," in effect getting both a wife and a servant. The company reasoned that, as one official wrote in 1622, "the plantation can never flourish till families be planted, and the respect of wives and children fix the people on the soil." The company's efforts as a marriage broker proved no more successful than its other ventures. Men continued to outnumber women by a wide margin until late in the seventeenth century, since only one in four indentured servants was a woman.

Servant life was harsh by the standards of seventeenth-century England and even by the frontier standards of the Chesapeake. Severe laws were designed to keep servants in their place. Punishments for petty crimes like running away or stealing a pig stretched servitude far beyond the original terms of indenture. Just after midcentury, the Virginia legislature added at least three years to the servitude of most servants by requiring them to serve until they were twenty-four years old.

Women servants were subject to special restrictions and risks. They were prohibited from marrying until their servitude had expired. A servant

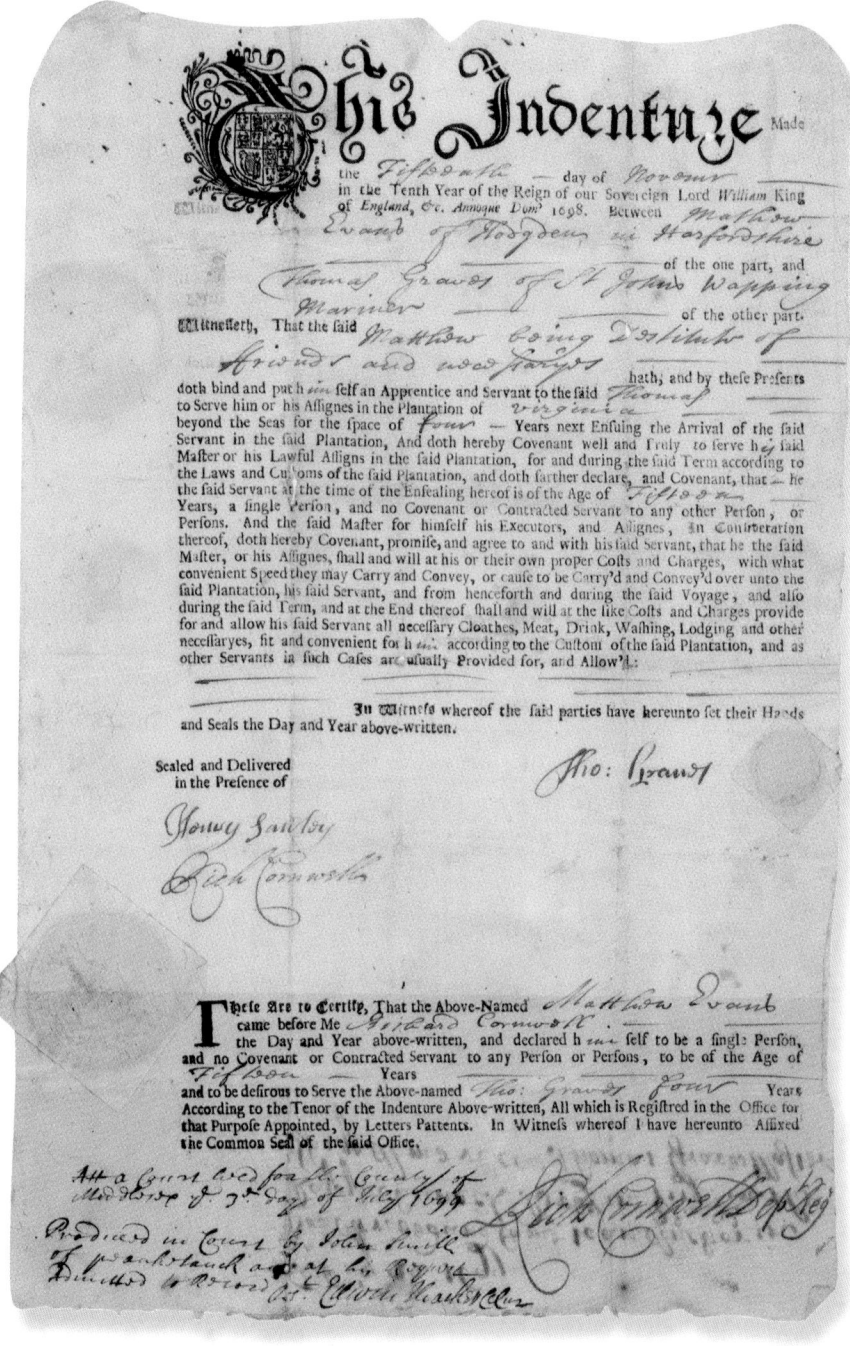

INDENTURE CONTRACT
*Indenture contracts were so
common that forms were
printed, leaving blank
spaces for the details. Here,
in mid-November 1698,
fifteen-year-old Mathew
Evans, a friendless boy
from Harfordshire, agreed
to serve mariner Thomas
Graves, or anybody to
whom Graves sold his
rights, for four years in
Virginia. The contract specified that Graves would
carry Evans to Virginia and
provide during the term of
the indenture, "all necessary Cloathes, Meat, Drink,
Washing, Lodging and
other necessaryes, fit and
convenient for him according to the Custom of the
said Plantation, as other
Servants in such Cases are
usually Provided for. . . ."*
The Library of Virginia.

woman, the law assumed, could not serve two masters at the same time: one who owned her indentured labor and another who was her husband.
However, the overwhelming predominance of men
in the Chesapeake population inevitably pressured
women to engage in sexual relations. As a rule, if a

woman servant gave birth to a child, she had to
serve two extra years and pay a fine.

Masters could not easily hire free men and
women because land was so readily available that
those who were free preferred to work for themselves on their own land. Furthermore, most

masters could not depend on much labor from family members. The preponderance of men meant that families were few, were started late, and thus had few children. And, until the 1680s and 1690s, slaves were expensive and hard to come by. Before then, masters who wanted to expand their labor force and grow more tobacco had few alternatives to buying indentured servants.

Cultivating Land and Faith

Villages and small towns dotted the rural landscape of seventeenth-century England, but in the Chesa-peake acres of wilderness were interrupted here and there by tobacco farms. Tobacco was such a labor-intensive crop that one field worker could tend only about two acres of the plants in a year (an acre is slightly smaller than a football field), plus a few more acres for food crops. A successful farmer needed a great deal more land, however, because tobacco quickly exhausted the fertility of the soil. Since each farmer cultivated only 5 or 10 percent of his land at any one time, a "settled" area comprised swatches of cultivated land surrounded by virgin forest. Arrangements for marketing tobacco also contributed to the dispersion of settlements.

TOBACCO PLANTATION
This print illustrates the tobacco harvest on a seventeenth-century plantation. Workers cut the mature plants and put the leaves in piles to wilt (left foreground and center background). After the leaves had dried somewhat, they were suspended from poles in a drying barn (right foreground), where they were seasoned before being packed in casks for shipping. Sometimes they were also dried in the fields (center background). The print suggests the labor demands of tobacco by showing twenty-two individuals, all but two of them actively at work with the crop. The one woman depicted (hand in hand with a man in the left foreground) may be on her way to work in the harvest, but it appears more likely that she and the man are overseeing the labor of their servants or employees.
From "About Tobacco," Lehman Brothers.

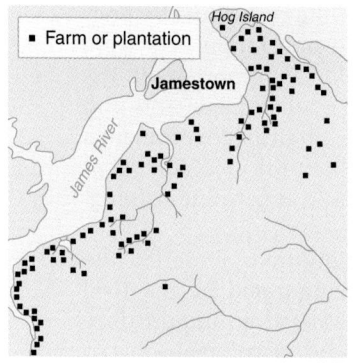

- Farm or plantation

Hog Island

Jamestown

James River

Settlement Patterns along the James River

Tobacco planters sought land that fronted a navigable river in order to minimize the work of transporting the heavy hogsheads of tobacco onto ships. A settled region thus resembled a lacework of farms stitched around waterways.

Most Chesapeake colonists were nominally Protestants. Attendance at Sunday services and conformity to the doctrines of the Church of England were required of all Englishmen and women. Certainly some colonists took their religion seriously. But on the whole, religion did not awaken the zeal of Chesapeake settlers, certainly not as it did the New England settlers in these same years (see chapter 4). Although the religion of the Chesapeake colonists was Anglican, their faith lay in the turbulent, competitive, high-stakes gamble of survival as tobacco planters.

The situation was similar in the Catholic colony of Maryland. In 1632, King Charles I granted his Catholic friend Lord Baltimore about six and a half million acres in the northern Chesapeake region. Lord Baltimore intended to create a refuge for Catholics, who suffered severe discrimination in England. He fitted out two ships, the *Ark* and the *Dove*, gathered about 150 settlers, and sent them to the new colony, where they arrived on March 25, 1634. However, the population of Maryland grew very slowly for the next twenty years, and most settlers were Protestants rather than Catholics. The religious turmoil of the Puritan Revolution in England (discussed in chapter 5) spilled across the Atlantic, creating conflict between Maryland's few Catholics—most of them wealthy and prominent—and the Protestant majority, most of them neither wealthy nor prominent. During the 1660s, Maryland began to attract settlers as readily as Virginia, mostly Protestants. Although Catholics and the Catholic faith continued to exert influence in Maryland, the colony's society, economy, politics, and culture became virtually indistinguishable from Virginia's. Both colonies shared a devotion to tobacco, the true faith of the Chesapeake.

The Evolution of Chesapeake Society

The system of indentured servitude sharpened inequality in Chesapeake society by the mid-seventeenth century, propelling social and political polarization that culminated in 1676 with Bacon's Rebellion. The rebellion ultimately prompted reforms that stabilized relations between elite planters and their lesser neighbors and paved the way for a social hierarchy based less overtly on land and wealth than on race. Amidst this social and political evolution, one thing did not change: the dedication of Chesapeake colonists to growing tobacco.

Social and Economic Polarization

The first half of the seventeenth century in the Chesapeake was the era of the yeoman planter— that is, a farmer who owned a small plot of land sufficient to support a family and tilled largely by family members and perhaps a few servants. A few elite planters had larger estates and commanded ten or more servants. But for the first several decades, few men lived long enough to accumulate a fortune sufficient to set them much apart from their neighbors. Until midcentury, the principal division in Chesapeake society was less between rich and poor planters than between free farmers and unfree servants. While these two groups contrasted sharply in their legal and economic status, their daily lives had many similarities. Servants looked forward to the time when their indentures would expire and they would become free and eventually own land. On the whole, a rough, frontier equality characterized free families in the Chesapeake until about 1650.

Three major developments splintered that equality during the third quarter of the century. First, as tobacco production increased, prices declined. Cheap tobacco reduced planters' profits and made it more difficult for freed servants to save enough to become landowners. Second, because the mortality rate dropped, more and more servants survived their indentures. As landless freemen became more numerous, they grew more discontent. Third, declining mortality also encouraged the formation of a planter elite. By living longer, the most successful planters compounded their success. The wealthiest planters also began to serve as merchants, marketing crops for their less successful neighbors, importing English goods for sale, and giving credit to hard-pressed customers.

By the 1670s, the social structure of the Chesapeake had become polarized. Landowners—the planter elite and the more numerous yeoman planters—clustered around one pole. Landless colonists, mainly freed servants, gathered at the other. Each group eyed the other with suspicion and mistrust. For the most part, planters saw landless freemen as a dangerous rabble rather than as fellow colonists with legitimate grievances.

Government Policies and Political Conflict

In general, government and politics amplified the distinctions in Chesapeake society. The most vital distinction separated servants and masters, and the colonial government enforced it with an iron fist. Poor men like William Tyler complained that "nether the Governor nor Counsell could or would doe any poore men right, but that they would shew favor to great men and wronge the poore." The poor had plenty of ammunition for such views. After 1640, no former servant ever served in either the governor's council or the House of Burgesses. Until 1670, all freemen could vote, and they routinely elected prosperous planters to the legislature. Most Chesapeake colonists, like most Europeans, assumed that the responsibilities of government were best borne by men of wealth and status.

In the 1660s and 1670s, colonial officials began to seek additional security as discontent mounted among the poor. Beginning in 1661, for example, Governor Berkeley did not call an election for the House of Burgesses for fifteen years. In 1670, the House of Burgesses limited voting rights to landowners and householders.

In 1660, the king himself began to tighten the royal government's control of trade and to collect substantial revenue from the Chesapeake. The Navigation Act passed that year required all tobacco and other colonial products to be sent only to English ports. The act supplemented laws of 1650 and 1651 that specified that colonial goods had to be transported in English ships with predominantly English crews. A 1663 law stipulated that all goods sent to the colonies must pass through English ports and be carried in English ships by English sailors. Together, these navigation acts were designed to funnel the colonial import trade exclusively into the hands of English merchants and shippers and reflected the English government's mercantilist assumptions about the colonies: What was good for England should determine colonial policy.

These mercantilist assumptions underlay the import duty on tobacco inaugurated by the 1660 Navigation Act. The law assessed an import duty of two pence on every pound of colonial tobacco brought into England, about the price a Chesapeake tobacco farmer received. The duty gave the king a major financial interest in the size of the tobacco crop.

Bacon's Rebellion

Colonists, like residents of European monarchies, accepted social hierarchy and inequality as long as they believed government officials ruled for the general good. When rulers violated that precept, ordinary people felt justified in rebelling. In 1676, Bacon's Rebellion erupted as a dispute over Indian policy. Before it was over, the rebellion convulsed Chesapeake politics and society, leaving in its wake death, destruction, and a legacy of hostility between the great planters and their poorer neighbors.

Opechancanough, the old chief who had led the Indian uprising of 1622 in Virginia, mounted another surprise attack in 1644 and killed about five hundred colonists in two days. During the next two years of bitter fighting, the colonists eventually gained the upper hand, capturing and murdering Opechancanough. The treaty that concluded the war established policies toward the Indians that the government tried to maintain for the next thirty years. The Indians relinquished all claims to land already settled by the English. Wilderness land beyond the fringe of English settlement was supposed to be reserved exclusively for Indian use. The government hoped to minimize contact between settlers and Indians and thereby maintain the peace.

Had the Chesapeake population remained constant, the policy might have worked. But the number of land-hungry colonists, especially poor, recently freed servants, continued to multiply. In their quest for land, they pushed beyond the treaty limits of English settlement and encroached steadily on Indian land. During the 1660s and 1670s, violence between colonists and Indians repeatedly flared along the advancing frontier. The government, headquartered in the tidewater region near the coast, far from the danger of Indian raids, took steps to calm the disputes and reestablish the peace. Frontier settlers thirsted for revenge against what their leader, Nathaniel Bacon, termed "the protected and Darling Indians." Bacon minced no words about his intention: "Our Design [is] not only to ruine and extirpate all Indians in Generall but all Manner of Trade and Commerce with them." Indians were not the only enemies Bacon and his men singled out. Bacon also urged colonists to "see what spounges have suckt up the Publique Treasure." He charged that "Grandees," or elite planters, operated the government for their private gain, a charge that made sense to many colonists. Bacon crystallized the grievances of the small planters and poor farmers against both the Indians and the colonial rulers in Jamestown.

Hoping to maintain the fragile peace on the frontier in 1676, Governor Berkeley pronounced Bacon a rebel, threatened to punish him for treason, and called for new elections of burgesses who, Berkeley believed, would endorse his get-tough policy. To Berkeley's surprise, the elections backfired. Almost all the old burgesses were voted out of office, their places taken by local leaders, including Bacon. The legislature was now in the hands of minor grandees who, like Bacon, chafed at the rule of the elite planters.

In June 1676, the new legislature passed a series of reform measures known as Bacon's Laws. Among other changes, the laws gave local settlers a voice in setting tax levies, forbade officeholders from demanding bribes or other extra fees for carrying out their duties, placed limits on holding multiple offices, and restored the vote to all freemen. Under pressure, Berkeley pardoned Bacon and authorized his campaign of Indian warfare. But elite planters soon convinced Berkeley that Bacon and his men were a greater threat than Indians.

When Bacon learned that Berkeley had once again branded him a traitor, he declared war against Berkeley and the other grandees. For three months, Bacon's forces fought the Indians and sacked the grandees' plantations. Berkeley's loyalists retaliated by plundering the homes of Bacon's supporters. The fighting continued until late October, when Bacon unexpectedly died, most likely from dysentery, and

several English ships arrived to bolster Berkeley's strength. With the rebellion crushed, Berkeley hanged several of Bacon's allies and destroyed farms that belonged to Bacon's supporters.

The rebellion did not dislodge the grandees from their positions of power. If anything, it strengthened their position. When the king learned of the turmoil in the Chesapeake and its devastating effect on tobacco exports and customs duties, he ordered an investigation. The royal officials replaced Berkeley with a governor more attentive to the king's interests, nullified Bacon's Laws, and instituted an export tax on every hogshead of tobacco as a way of paying the expenses of government without having to obtain the consent of the tight-fisted House of Burgesses. In a sense, the grandees of the Chesapeake were put in their place by still grander royal officials.

In the aftermath of Bacon's Rebellion, tensions between great planters and small farmers gradually lessened. By 1700, the new export duty on tobacco allowed the government to cut other taxes to just one-fourth what they had been in 1660, a move welcomed by all freemen. In the long run, however, the most important contribution to political stability was the declining importance of the servant labor system. During the 1680s and 1690s, fewer servants arrived in the Chesapeake, partly because of improving economic conditions in England. Accordingly, the number of poor, newly freed servants also declined, reducing the size of the lowest stratum of free society. In 1700, as many as one-third of the free colonists still worked as tenants on land owned by others, but the social and political distance between them and the great planters, enormous as it was, did not seem as profound as it had been in 1660. The main reason was that by 1700 the Chesapeake was in the midst of transition to a slave labor system that minimized the differences between poor farmers and rich planters and magnified the differences between whites and blacks.

Toward a Slave Labor System

Spaniards and Portuguese engaged in an extensive African slave trade in the sixteenth century, and they established slavery as a major form of coerced labor in the New World. In the seventeenth century,

British colonies in the West Indies followed the Spanish and Portuguese examples and developed sugar plantations with slave labor. In the British North American colonies, however, a slave labor system did not emerge until the last quarter of the seventeenth century. During the 1670s, settlers from Barbados brought slavery to the new English mainland colony of Carolina, where the imprint of the West Indies remained strong for decades. In Chesapeake tobacco fields at about the same time, slave labor began to replace servant labor, marking the transition toward a society of freedom for whites and slavery for Africans.

The West Indies: Sugar and Slavery

The most profitable part of the British New World empire in the seventeenth century lay in the Caribbean (Map 3.2). The tiny island of Barbados, colonized in the 1630s, was the jewel of the British West Indies. During the 1640s, Barbadian planters began to grow sugarcane, with such success that a colonial official proclaimed Barbados "the most flourishing Island in all those American parts, and I verily beleive in all the world for the production of sugar." Sugar commanded high prices in England, and planters rushed to grow as much as they could. By midcentury, annual sugar exports from the British Caribbean totaled about 150,000 pounds; by 1700, exports reached nearly 50 million pounds.

Sugar transformed Barbados and other West Indian islands. Poor farmers could not afford the expensive machinery that extracted and refined the sugarcane juice. Planters who had the necessary capital to grow sugar got rich. By 1680, the wealthiest Barbadian sugar planters were, on average, four times richer than tobacco grandees in the

SUGAR MILL
This seventeenth-century drawing of a Brazilian sugar mill highlights the heavy equipment needed to extract the juice from sugarcane. A vertical waterwheel turns a large horizontal gear that exerts force on the jaws of a press, which squeezes the cane. Workers constantly remove crushed cane from the press and replenish it with freshly harvested cane as it is unloaded from an oxcart. Note that except for the overseer (just to the right of the waterwheel), all of the workers are black, presumably slaves from Africa, as suggested by their clothing. All of the mill workers appear to be men, a hint of the predominance of men among newly imported African slaves.
Musées Royaux des Beaux-Arts de Belgique.

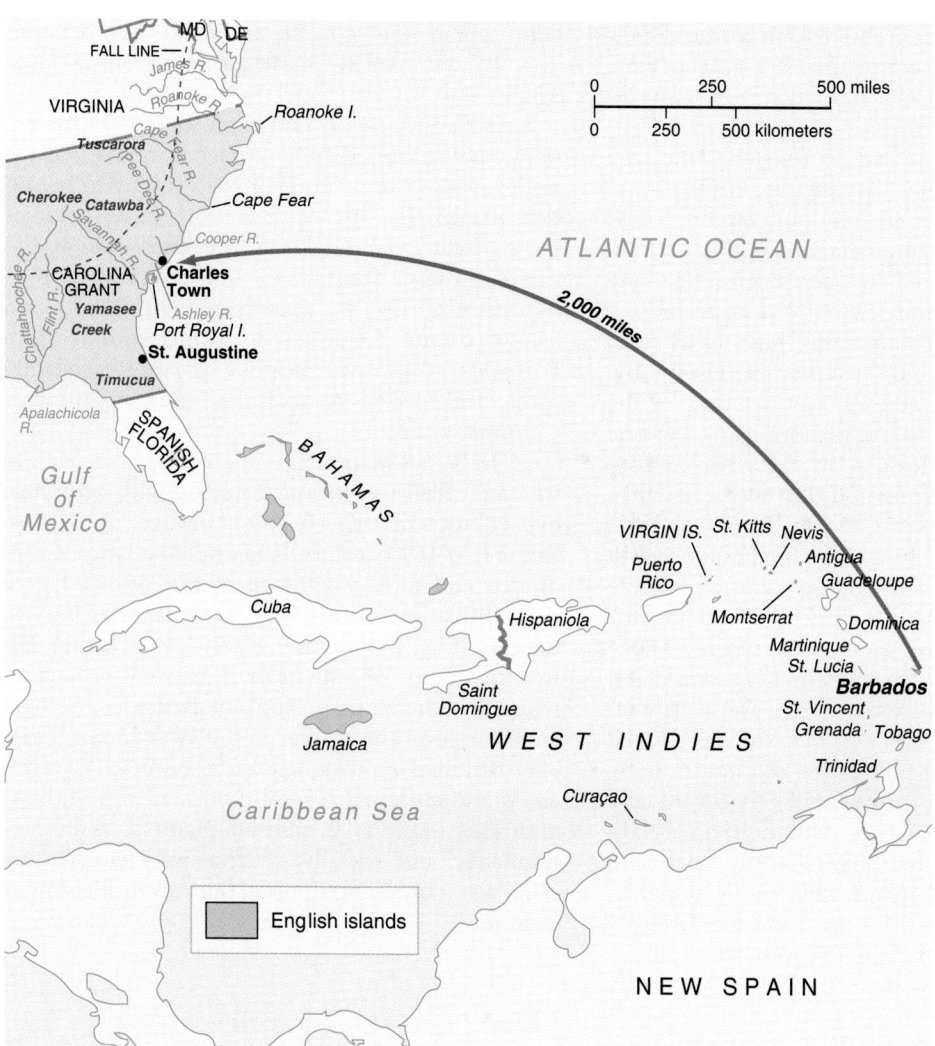

MAP 3.2

The West Indies and Carolina in the Seventeenth Century

Although Carolina was geographically closer to the Chesapeake colonies, it was cultur-
ally closer to the West Indies in the seventeenth century since its early settlers—both
blacks and whites—came from Barbados. South Carolina retained close ties to the West
Indies for more than a century, long after many of its subsequent settlers came from
England, Ireland, France, and elsewhere.

READING THE MAP: Locate English colonies in America and English holdings in the
Caribbean. Which European country controlled most of the mainland bordering the
Caribbean? Where was the closest mainland English territory?

CONNECTIONS: Why were colonists in Carolina so interested in Barbados? What goods
did they export? Describe the relationship between Carolina and Barbados in 1700.

www.bedfordstmartins.com/roarkcompact SEE THE ONLINE STUDY GUIDE for more help in
analyzing this map.

Chesapeake. The sugar grandees differed from their Chesapeake counterparts in another crucial way: The average sugar baron in Barbados in 1680 owned 115 slaves.

African slaves planted, cultivated, and harvested the sugarcane that made West Indian planters wealthy. Whites commonly assumed that people of African descent were degraded and inferior, and hence deserved bondage. Beginning in the 1640s, Barbadian planters purchased thousands of slaves to work their plantations, and the African population on the island mushroomed. During the 1650s, when blacks made up only 3 percent of the Chesapeake population, they had already become the majority on Barbados. By 1700, slaves constituted more than three-fourths of the island's population.

For slaves, work on a sugar plantation was a life sentence to brutal, unremitting labor. Slaves' life expectancy was short and their death rate high. Furthermore, since slave men outnumbered slave women two to one, the vast majority of slaves could not form a family and have children. These grim realities meant that in Barbados and elsewhere in the West Indies, the slave population did not grow by natural reproduction. Instead, planters continually purchased slaves from Africa. Although sugar plantations did not gain a foothold in North America in the seventeenth century, the West Indies nonetheless exerted a powerful influence on the development of slavery in the mainland colonies.

Carolina: A West Indian Frontier

The early settlers of what became South Carolina were immigrants from Barbados. In 1663, a Barbadian planter named John Colleton and a group of seven other men obtained a charter from King Charles II to establish a colony south of the Chesapeake and north of the Spanish territories in Florida. Colleton and his colleagues, known as the "proprietors," hoped to siphon settlers from Barbados and other colonies and encourage them to develop a profitable export crop comparable to West Indian sugar and Chesapeake tobacco. Following the Chesapeake example, the proprietors offered headrights of up to 150 acres of land for each settler. In 1670, they established the first permanent English beachhead in the colony, on the west bank of the Ashley River just across from the penin-

sula where the king's namesake city, Charles Towne (later spelled Charleston), was founded (see Map 3.2).

As the proprietors had planned, most of the settlers were from Barbados. In fact, Carolina was the only seventeenth-century English colony to be settled principally by colonists from other colonies rather than from England. The Barbadian immigrants brought their slaves with them. More than a fourth of the early settlers were black, and as the colony continued to attract settlers from Barbados, the black population multiplied. By 1700, blacks made up about half the population of Carolina.

The Carolinians experimented unsuccessfully to match their semitropical climate with profitable export crops of tobacco, cotton, indigo, and olives. In the mid-1690s, colonists identified a hardy strain of rice and took advantage of the knowledge of rice cultivation among their many African slaves, inaugurating a flourishing industry. During the first generation of settlement, however, Carolina remained an economic colony of Barbados. Settlers sold livestock and timber to the West Indies. They also exploited another "natural resource": They captured and enslaved several thousand local Indians and sold them to Caribbean planters. Both economically and socially, seventeenth-century Carolina was a frontier outpost of the West Indian sugar economy.

Slave Labor Emerges in the Chesapeake

By 1700, more than eight out of ten people in the southern colonies of British North America lived in the Chesapeake. Until the 1670s, almost all Chesapeake colonists were white people from England. In 1700, however, one out of eight people in the region was a black person from Africa. Although a few blacks had lived in the Chesapeake since the 1620s, the black population increased fivefold between 1670 and 1700 as hundreds of tobacco planters made the transition from servant to slave labor, purchasing slaves rather than servants to work in their tobacco fields. For planters, slaves had several obvious advantages over servants. Although slaves cost three to five times more than servants, slaves never became free. Since the mortality rate had declined by the 1680s, planters could reasonably expect slaves to live longer than a servant's period of indenture. Slaves also promised to be a perpetual labor force, since children of slave mothers inherited the status of slavery.

For planters, slaves had another important advantage over servants: They could be controlled politically. Bacon's Rebellion had demonstrated how disruptive former servants could be when their expectations were not met. A slave labor system promised to avoid the political problems caused by the servant labor system. Slavery kept discontented laborers in permanent servitude, and their color was a badge of their bondage.

The slave labor system polarized Chesapeake society along lines of race and status: All slaves were black and nearly all blacks were slaves; almost all free people were white and all whites were free or only temporarily bound in indentured servitude. Unlike Barbados, however, the Chesapeake retained a vast white majority. Among whites, huge differences of wealth and status still existed. In fact, the emerging slave labor system sharpened the economic differences among whites because only prosperous planters could afford to buy slaves. By 1700, more than three-quarters of white families had neither servants nor slaves. Nonetheless, poorer white farmers enjoyed the privileges of free status. Distinctions between slaves and free people made lesser white folk feel they had a genuine stake in the existence of slavery, even if they did not own a single slave. By emphasizing the privileges of freedom shared by all white people, the slave labor system reduced the tensions between poor folk and grandees that had plagued the Chesapeake region in the 1670s.

In contrast to Barbados, most slaves in the seventeenth-century Chesapeake colonies had frequent and close contact with white people. Slaves and white servants performed the same tasks on tobacco plantations, often working side by side in the fields. For slaves, work on a tobacco plantation was less onerous than on a sugar plantation. But slaves' constant exposure to white surveillance made Chesapeake slavery especially confining. Slaves took advantage of every opportunity to slip away from white supervision and seek out the company of other slaves, "going abroad" to visit slaves on neighboring plantations. More than once, slaves turned such seemingly innocent social pleasures to political ends, either to run away or to conspire to strike against their masters.

While slavery resolved the political unrest caused by the servant labor system, it created new political problems. By 1700, the bedrock political issue in the Chesapeake was keeping slaves in their place, at the business end of a hoe in a tobacco field. The Chesapeake was developing a slave labor system that stood midway, both geographically and socially, between the sugar plantations and black majority of Barbados to the south and the small farms and homogeneous villages that developed in seventeenth-century New England to the north.

Conclusion: The Growth of English Colonies Based on Export Crops and Slave Labor

By 1700, the colonies of Virginia, Maryland, and Carolina were firmly established. The staple crops they grew for export provided a livelihood for many, a fortune for a few, and valuable revenues for shippers, merchants, and the English monarchy. Their societies differed markedly from English society in most respects, yet the colonists considered themselves English people who happened to live in North America. They claimed the same rights and privileges as English men and women while they denied those rights and privileges to native Americans and African slaves.

The English colonies also differed from the sixteenth-century example of New Spain. Large quantities of gold and silver never materialized in the Chesapeake. The system of encomienda (see chapter 2) was never adopted because Indians were too few and too hostile and their communities too small and decentralized compared with those of the Mexica. Yet forms of coerced labor and racial distinction that developed in New Spain had North American counterparts, as English colonists employed servants and slaves and defined themselves as superior to Indians and Africans.

By 1700, the remnants of Powhatan's people still survived. As English settlement pushed north, west, and south of the Chesapeake Bay, the various Indian peoples were faced with the new colonial world that Powhatan and Pocahontas had encountered when John Smith and the first settlers arrived at Jamestown. By 1700, the many descendants of

Pocahontas's son, Thomas, as well as other colonists and native Americans, understood that the English had come to stay.

FOR FURTHER READING ABOUT THE TOPICS IN THIS CHAPTER, see the Online Bibliography at www.bedfordstmartins.com/roarkcompact.

FOR ADDITIONAL FIRST-HAND ACCOUNTS OF THIS PERIOD, see pages 27–42 in Michael Johnson, ed., *Reading the American Past,* Second Edition, Volume I.

TO ASSESS YOUR MASTERY OF THE MATERIAL IN THIS CHAPTER, see the Online Study Guide at www.bedfordstmartins.com/roarkcompact.

CHRONOLOGY

1606 Virginia Company of London receives royal charter to establish colony in North America.

1607 English colonists found Jamestown settlement; Pocahontas "rescues" John Smith.

1609 Starvation plagues Jamestown.

1612 John Rolfe begins to plant tobacco in Virginia.

1617 First commercial tobacco shipment leaves Virginia for England. Pocahontas dies in England.

1618 Powhatan dies and Opechancanough becomes supreme chief.

1619 First Africans arrive in Virginia. House of Burgesses begins to meet in Virginia.

1622 Opechancanough leads Indian uprising against Virginia colonists.

1624 Virginia becomes royal colony.

1632 King Charles I grants Lord Baltimore land for colony of Maryland.

1634 Colonists begin to arrive in Maryland.

1640s Barbados colonists begin to grow sugarcane with labor of African slaves.

1644 Opechancanough leads Indian uprising against Virginia colonists.

1660 Navigation Act requires colonial tobacco to be shipped to English ports and to be assessed customs tax.

1663 Carolina proprietors receive charter from King Charles II for Carolina colony.

1670 Charles Towne, South Carolina, founded.

1670–1700 Slave labor system emerges first in Carolina and more gradually in Chesapeake colonies.

1676 Bacon's Rebellion convulses Virginia.

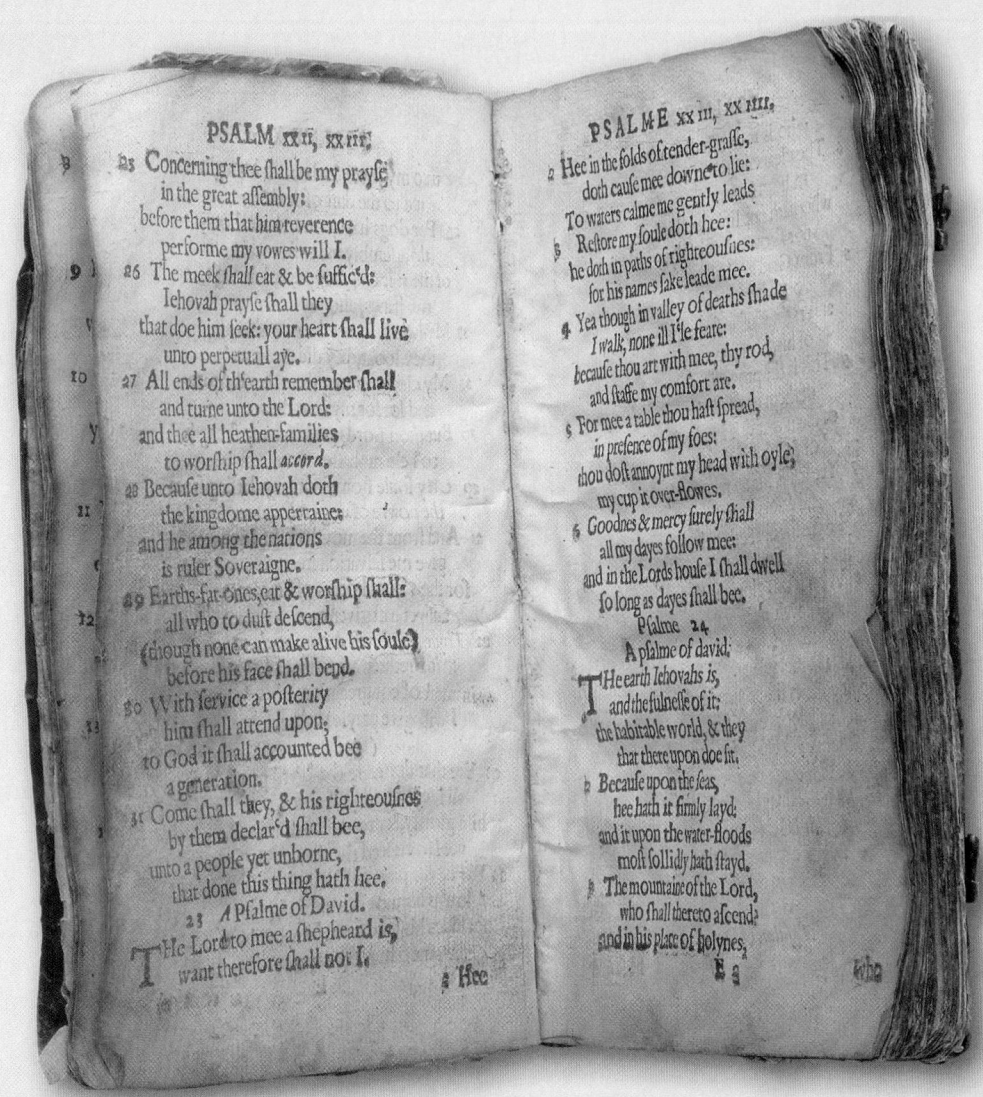

AMERICA'S FIRST BOOK

The first book printed in what is now the United States, this well-thumbed copy of **The Whole Booke of Psalmes Faithfully Translated into English Metre** *was published in Cambridge, Massachusetts, in 1640. Puritan services banned musical instruments and other diversions from God's holy word. Worshippers used this book and others to sing psalms, celebrating with a chorus of voices the wonders of God's Truth. The famous Twenty-third Psalm begins near the bottom of the left-hand page and concludes on the facing page. Read the psalm aloud to re-create the experience of seventeenth-century New England Puritan congregations.*

Library of Congress.

THE NORTHERN COLONIES IN THE SEVENTEENTH CENTURY

4

1601–1700

ANNE HUTCHINSON ARRIVED IN THE MASSACHUSETTS BAY COLONY in 1634 with her husband and family. She was a devout Puritan, steeped in Scripture and absorbed by sermons. A brilliant woman, Hutchinson had received an excellent education from her father in England. The mother of fourteen children, she served her neighbors as a skilled midwife. After she settled into her new home in Boston, women gathered there to hear her Thursday lectures on recent sermons, a proper female activity since, according to one minister, it "water[ed] the seeds *publikely* sowen." But as the months passed, the meetings increased to twice a week and the crowds grew to sixty or more women and men. One of those who attended praised Hutchinson as a "Woman that Preaches better Gospell then any of your black-coates that have been at the Ninneversity."

Hutchinson expounded on the sermons of John Cotton, her favorite minister. Cotton emphasized that individuals could be saved only by God's grace in choosing them to be members of the elect, a doctrine Cotton termed the "covenant of grace." Cotton contrasted this familiar Puritan tenet with the "covenant of works," the belief that one's behavior—one's works—could win God's favor and, ultimately, salvation. Cotton's sermons strongly hinted that many Puritans, even ministers, leaned toward this heretical covenant of works. Anne Hutchinson agreed. In her lectures to the groups assembled at her home, she amplified Cotton's somewhat muted message that the leaders of Massachusetts were repudiating the covenant of grace, the true basis of Puritan faith.

The meetings at Hutchinson's house alarmed her nearest neighbor, former governor John Winthrop, who believed that she was subverting the good order of the colony. In 1637, Winthrop had formal charges brought against Hutchinson and confronted her in court as her chief accuser. "You have stept out of your place," he said, "*you have rather bine a Husband than a Wife and a preacher than a Hearer; and a Magistrate than a Subject.*"

Winthrop and other Puritan elders referred to Hutchinson and her followers as "Antinomians," that is, people who opposed the law. Hutchinson's opponents charged that she believed that Christians could be saved by faith alone and that they therefore did not need to act according to God's law as set forth in the Bible and as interpreted by the colony's leaders. Hutchinson nimbly defended herself against this accusation. Yes, she believed that men and women were saved by faith alone; but no, she did not deny the need to obey God's law. "The Lord hath let me see which was the clear ministry and which the wrong," she said. Finally, her interrogators cornered her. How could she tell which was which? "By an immediate revelation," she replied, "by the voice of [God's] own spirit to my soul." Here was the crime Winthrop had been searching for, the erroneous view that God revealed his will directly to a believer instead of exclusively through the Bible, as every good Puritan knew.

In 1638, the Boston church formally excommunicated Hutchinson. The minister decreed, "I doe cast you out and . . . deliver you up to Satan that you may learne no more to blaspheme to seduce and to lye. . . . I command you . . . as a Leper to withdraw your selfe out of the Congregation." Banished, Hutchinson and her family moved first to Rhode Island and then to Long Island, where all but her ten-year-old daughter were killed by Indians.

Hutchinson's admission of divine revelation was a departure from standard Puritan belief. Yet by urging believers to search for evidence of God's grace, Puritanism encouraged the faithful to listen for a whisper from God. Puritanism combined rigid insistence on conformity to God's law and aching uncertainty about how to identify and act upon it. Despite the best efforts of Winthrop and other New England leaders to render God's instructions in no uncertain terms, Puritanism inspired believers like Anne Hutchinson to draw their own conclusions and stick to them.

During the seventeenth century, New England's Puritan zeal—exemplified by both Anne Hutchinson and her persecutors—cooled, and the goal of founding a holy New England faded. Late in the century, new "middle" colonies—New York, New Jersey, and Pennsylvania—were founded that featured greater religious and ethnic diversity than New England. Religion remained important throughout all the colonies, but it competed with a growing faith that the promise of a better life required less of the Puritans' intense focus on salvation and more attention to the mundane affairs of family, work, and trade.

By 1700, all the North American colonies had become more integrated into the English empire. Although located an ocean away from England, the colonists shipped North American wares east and off-loaded Old World goods on western shores. The continual exchange of products, people, and ideas was the lifeblood of empire that pulsed between England and the colonies, energizing both.

Puritan Origins: The English Reformation

The religious roots of the Puritans who founded New England reached back to the Protestant Reformation, which arose in Germany in 1517 (see chapter 2). The Reformation spread quickly to other countries, but the English church initially remained within the Catholic fold. King Henry VIII, who reigned from 1509 to 1547, understood that the Reformation offered him an opportunity to break with Rome and take control of the church in England. In 1534, Henry formally initiated the English Reformation. At his insistence, Parliament passed the Act of Supremacy, which outlawed the Catholic Church and proclaimed the king "the only supreme head on earth of the Church of England." The vast properties of the Catholic Church in England were now the king's, as was the privilege of appointing bishops and other members of the church hierarchy.

In the short run, the English Reformation allowed Henry VIII to achieve his political goal of controlling the church. In the long run, however, the English Reformation brought to England the political and religious turmoil that Henry had hoped to avoid. Henry himself sought no more than a halfway Reformation. Many English Catholics wanted no Reformation at all; they hoped to return the Church of England to the pope and to maintain Catholic doctrines and ceremonies. But many other English people insisted on a genuine, thoroughgoing Reformation; these people came to be called Puritans.

During the sixteenth century, Puritanism was less an organized movement than a set of ideas and religious principles that appealed strongly to many dissenting members of the Church of England. They sought to purify the Church of England by eliminating what they considered the offensive features of Catholicism. For example, they demanded that the church hierarchy be abolished and that ordinary Christians be given greater control over religious life. They wanted to do away with the rituals of Catholic worship and instead emphasize an individual's relationship with God developed through Bible study, prayer, and introspection. Although there were many varieties and degrees of Puritanism, all Puritans shared a desire to make the English church thoroughly Protestant.

You shall be led before Princes and rulers for my names sake.
Math, 10.

PERSECUTION OF ENGLISH PROTESTANTS
This sixteenth-century drawing shows the persecution of Protestants during the reign of Queen Mary, a staunch Catholic. Here Protestant prisoners are being marched to London to be tried for heresy. This pro-Protestant drawing emphasizes the severity of royal tyranny by depicting four well-armed guards, two of them mounted, escorting some fifteen prisoners, including at least five women. The women are roped together, but not because they appear to be menacing or likely to run away. The guards seem to be necessary less to maintain order among the prisoners than to prevent sympathetic citizens from rushing toward the marchers and freeing the prisoners. The drawing assumes that most citizens opposed the queen's persecution of Protestants. The Bible verse from the Book of Matthew underscored Protestants' fealty to Christ rather than to mere "Princes and rulers" like Queen Mary.
Folger Shakespeare Library.

The fate of Protestantism waxed and waned under the monarchs who succeeded Henry VIII, until the reign of his daughter, Elizabeth I (1558–1603). She reaffirmed the English Reformation and tried to position the English church between the extremes of Catholicism and Puritanism. By the time she died, many people in England looked on Protestantism as a defining feature of national identity. When her successor, James I, came to the throne, English Puritans petitioned for further reform of the Church of England. However, neither James I nor his son Charles I, who became king in 1625, was receptive to the ideas of Puritan reformers. James and Charles moved the Church of England away from Puritanism rather than toward it. They enforced conformity to the Church of England and punished dissenters, both ordinary Christians and ministers. In 1629, Charles I dissolved Parliament—where Puritans were well represented—and initiated aggressive anti-Puritan policies. Many Puritans despaired about continuing to defend their faith in England and began to make plans to emigrate. The largest number set out for America.

Puritans and the Settlement of New England

Puritans who emigrated aspired to escape the turmoil and persecution of England and to build a new, orderly society that resembled a Puritan version of England. Their faith shaped the colonies they established in virtually every way. Although many New England colonists were not Puritans, Puritanism remained a paramount influence in New England's religion, politics, and community life during the seventeenth century.

The Pilgrims and Plymouth Colony

One of the earliest groups to emigrate, known subsequently as Pilgrims, espoused a heresy known as separatism: They sought to withdraw and separate from the Church of England, actions that would be punished severely in England. Hoping that they might preserve their community in America, the Pilgrims obtained permission to settle in the extensive lands granted to the Virginia Company. To finance their journey, they formed a joint stock company with London investors. In August 1620, 102 settlers, mostly families, finally boarded the *Mayflower*. After eleven weeks at sea, all but one of them arrived at the outermost tip of Cape Cod, in present-day Massachusetts.

The Pilgrims realized immediately that they had landed far north of the Virginia grant and had no legal authority from the king to settle in the area. To provide order and security as well as a claim to legitimacy, they drew up the Mayflower Compact on the day they arrived. In signing the document, they agreed to "covenant and combine ourselves together into a civil Body Politick, for our better Ordering and Preservation"; the signers (all men) agreed to enact and obey necessary and just laws.

The Pilgrims soon settled at Plymouth and elected William Bradford their governor. That first winter "was most sad and lamentable," Bradford wrote later. "In two or three months' time half of [our] company died." In the spring, Indians rescued the floundering Plymouth settlement. First Samoset, then Squanto—both of whom understood English—befriended the settlers. Samoset arranged for the Pilgrims to meet and establish good relations

with Massasoit, the chief of the Wampanoags, whose territory included Plymouth. Squanto, Bradford recalled, "was a special instrument sent of God for their [the Pilgrims'] good. . . . He directed them how to set their corn, where to take fish, and to procure other commodities, and was also their pilot to bring them to unknown places." With Squanto's help and their own hard labor, the Pilgrims managed to store enough food to guarantee their survival through the coming winter, an occasion they celebrated in the fall of 1621 with a feast of thanksgiving attended by Massasoit and many of his warriors.

The colony's status remained precarious. But the Pilgrims lived quietly and simply, coexisting in relative peace with the Indians, paying Massasoit when settlers gradually encroached on Wampanoag territory. By 1630, Plymouth had become a permanent settlement, although it failed to attract many other English Puritans.

The Founding of Massachusetts Bay Colony

In 1629, shortly before Charles I dissolved Parliament, a group of Puritan merchants and country gentlemen obtained a royal charter for the Massachusetts Bay Company that provided the usual privileges granted to joint stock companies. It granted land for colonization that spanned the present-day states of Massachusetts, New Hampshire, Vermont, Maine, and upstate New York. In addition, the charter contained a unique provision that allowed the government of the company to be located in the colony rather than in England. With this royal permission, Puritans could exchange their position as a harassed minority in England for self-government in Massachusetts.

To lead the emigrants, the stockholders of the Massachusetts Bay Company elected John Winthrop, a prosperous lawyer and landowner, to serve as governor. In March 1630, eleven ships crammed with seven hundred passengers sailed for Massachusetts. Winthrop's fleet arrived in Massachusetts Bay in early June. Unlike the Pilgrims, Winthrop's Puritans aspired to reform the corrupt Church of England (rather than separate from it) by setting an example of godliness in the New World. Winthrop and a small group chose to settle on the peninsula that became Boston,

SEAL OF MASSACHUSETTS BAY COLONY
In 1629 the Massachusetts Bay Company designed this seal depicting an Indian man inviting English settlers to "Come Over And Help Us." Of course, such an invitation was never issued. Instead, the seal was an attempt to lend an aura of altruism to the Massachusetts Bay Company's colonization efforts. In English eyes, the Indian man obviously needed help. The only signs that he was more civilized than the pine trees flanking him were his girdle of leaves, his bow and arrow, and his miraculous use of English. In reality, colonists in Massachusetts and elsewhere were far less interested in helping Indians than in helping themselves. For the most part that suited Indians, since they did not want the colonists' "help."
Courtesy of Massachusetts Archives.

www.bedfordstmartins.com/roarkcompact SEE THE ON-LINE STUDY GUIDE for more help in analyzing this image.

and other settlers clustered at promising locations nearby (Map 4.1).

In a sermon to his companions aboard the *Arbella* while they were still at sea—probably the most famous sermon in American history—Winthrop explained the cosmic significance of their journey. The

Puritans had "entered into a covenant" with God to "work out our salvation under the power and purity of his holy ordinances," Winthrop proclaimed. The Puritans had to subordinate their individual interests to the common good. "We must be knit together in this work as one man," Winthrop declared. "We must delight in each other, make others' conditions our own, rejoice together, mourn together, labor and suffer together, always having before our eyes . . . our community as members of the same body." The stakes could not be higher, Winthrop told his listeners. "We must consider that we shall be as a city upon a hill. The eyes of all people are upon us."

That belief shaped seventeenth-century New England as profoundly as tobacco shaped the Chesapeake. The vision of a city on a hill announced the Puritans' fierce determination to keep their covenant and live according to God's laws, unlike the backsliders and compromisers who accommodated to the Church of England. Their determination to adhere strictly to God's plan charged nearly every feature of life in seventeenth-century New England with a distinctive, high-voltage piety.

The new colonists, as Winthrop's son John wrote later, had "all things to do, as in the beginning of the world." Unlike the early Chesapeake settlers, the first Massachusetts Bay colonists encountered few Indians because the local population had been almost entirely exterminated by an epidemic more than a decade earlier. Still, as in the Chesapeake, the colonists fell victim to deadly ailments. But each year from 1630 to 1640, ship after ship followed Winthrop's fleet. In all, more than twenty thousand new settlers came, their eyes fixed on the Puritans' city on a hill.

Often, when the Church of England cracked down on a Puritan minister in England, he and many of his followers uprooted and moved together to New England. By 1640, New England had one of the highest ratios of preachers to population in all of Christendom. A few ministers sought to carry the message of Christianity to Indians, accompanied by instructions about proper civilized (that is, English) behavior to replace what missionary John Eliot termed Indians' "unfixed, confused, and ungoverned . . . life, uncivilized and unsubdued to labor and order." (See "Documenting the American Promise," page 74.)

The occupations of the New England immigrants reflected the social origins of English Puritans. On the whole, the immigrants came from the middle ranks of English society. The vast majority

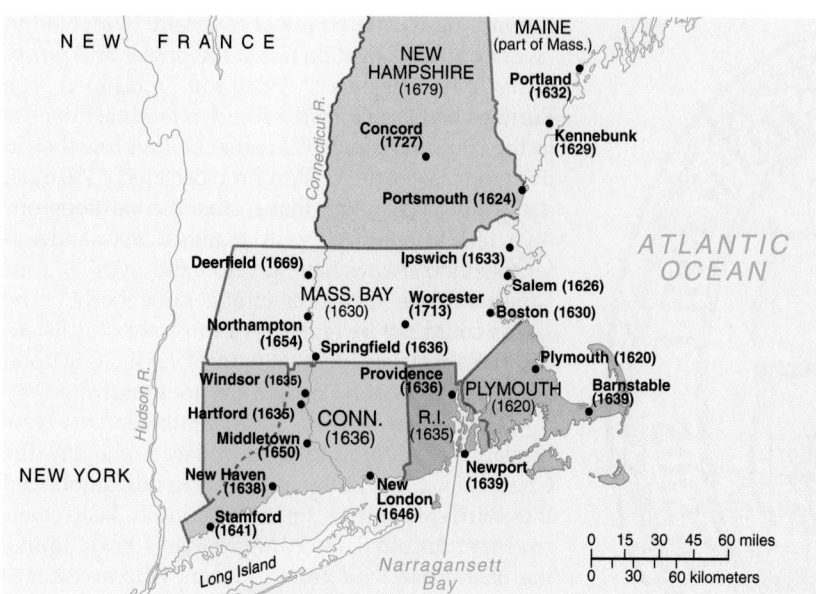

MAP 4.1
New England Colonies in the Seventeenth Century
New Englanders spread across the landscape town by town during the seventeenth century. (For the sake of legibility, only a few of the more important towns are shown on the map.) Why were towns so much more a feature of seventeenth-century New England than of the Chesapeake?

of immigrants were either farmers or tradesmen, including carpenters, tailors, and textile workers. Servants, whose numbers dominated the Chesapeake settlers, accounted for only about a fifth of those headed for New England.

In contrast to the Chesapeake, New England immigrants usually arrived as families. In fact, more Puritans came with family members than did any other group of immigrants in all of American history. These families were not democracies, of course. As Winthrop reminded the first settlers in his *Arbella* sermon, each family was a "little commonwealth" that mirrored the hierarchy among all God's creatures. Just as humankind was subordinate to God, so young people were subordinate to their elders, children to their parents, and wives to their husbands. The immigrants' family ties reinforced their religious beliefs with a form of government defined by the interlocking institutions of family, church, and community.

The Evolution of New England Society

The New England colonists, unlike their counterparts in the Chesapeake, settled in small towns, usually located on the coast or a river (see Map 4.1).

Church members' fervent piety, buttressed by the institutions of local government, enforced remarkable religious and social conformity in the small New England settlements. During the century, tensions within the Puritan faith and changes in New England communities splintered religious orthodoxy and weakened Puritan zeal. By 1700, however, Puritanism still maintained a distinctive influence in New England.

Church, Covenant, and Conformity

To Puritans, the church was composed of men and women who had entered a solemn covenant with one another and with God. Winthrop and three other men signed the original covenant of the first Boston church in 1630, agreeing to "Promisse, and bind our selves, to walke in all our wayes according to the Rule of the Gospell, and in all sincere Conformity to His holy Ordinaunces." A new member of the covenant also had to persuade existing members that she or he had fully experienced conversion. The fervent Puritans among the early colonists had little difficulty meeting the test of covenant membership. By 1635, the Boston church had added more than 250 names to the 4 original subscribers to the covenant.

Puritan views on church membership derived from John Calvin, a sixteenth-century Swiss Protes-

THE
World turn'd upfide down:
OR,
A briefe defcription of the ridiculous Fafhions
of thefe diftracted Times.

By T. J. a well-willer to King, Parliament and Kingdom.

London : Printed for John Smith. 1647.

THE PURITAN CHALLENGE TO THE STATUS QUO
*This title page of "The World Turn'd Upside Down,"
satirizes the Puritan notion that the contemporary
world was deeply flawed. Printed in London in
1647, the pamphlet refers to the "distracted Times"
of the Puritan Revolution in England. The drawing
ridicules criticisms of English society that were also
common among New England Puritans. The drawing
shows at least a dozen examples of the conventional
world of seventeenth-century England turned upside
down. Can you identify them? Puritans, of course,
would claim that the drawing had it wrong—that
instead the conventional world turned God's order
upside down. How might the drawing have been
different if a devout Puritan had drawn it?*
By permission of The British Library.

tant theologian. Calvin stressed the doctrine of pre-
destination, which held that before the creation of
the world, God exercised his divine grace and chose
a few human beings to receive eternal life. Only God
knew who these fortunate individuals—the "elect"
or "visible saints"—were. Nothing a person did
could change God's inscrutable choice.

Puritans, however, believed that if one were
among the elect, then one would surely act like it.
To a certain extent, one's sainthood would become
visible in one's behavior, especially if one were privileged to know God's Word as revealed in the Bible.
However, the connection between sainthood and
saintly behavior was far from firm. But the Puritans
thought that passing the demanding test of membership in one of their churches was a promising
clue that one was in fact among God's elect.

Members of Puritan churches ardently hoped
that they were visible saints and tried to act that
way. Their covenant bound them to help each other
attain this lofty goal and to discipline the entire
community by saintly standards. Church members
kept an eye on the behavior of everybody in town.
Infractions of morality, order, or propriety were reported to the elders, who summoned the wayward
to a church inquiry. Church members enforced a remarkable degree of righteous conformity in Puritan
communities.

Despite the central importance of religion,
churches had no direct role in the civil government
of New England communities. Puritans did not
want to emulate the Church of England, which they
considered a puppet of the king rather than an independent body that served the Lord. They were
determined to insulate New England churches from
the contaminating influence of the civil state and its
merely human laws. Although ministers were the
most highly respected figures in New England
towns, they were prohibited from holding government office.

Puritans had no qualms, however, about their
own beliefs influencing New England governments.
As much as possible, the Puritans tried to bring
public life into conformity with their view of God's
law. On the Sabbath, townsfolk could not work,
play, or travel. Fines were issued for Sabbath-
breaking activities such as playing a flute, smoking
a pipe, and visiting neighbors. Puritans mandated
other purifications of what they considered corrupt
English practices. They refused to celebrate either
Christmas or Easter, since the Bible did not mention
such rituals. They outlawed religious wedding ceremonies. They prohibited elaborate, colorful clothing and banned cards, dice, shuffleboard, and other
games of chance, as well as music and dancing. On
special occasions, Puritans proclaimed days of
fasting and humiliation, which, as one preacher
boasted, amounted to "so many Sabbaths more."

King Philip Considers Christianity

*B*eginning in 1646, Puritan minister John Eliot served as a missionary to New England's Indians, trying to teach both the doctrines of Christianity and the orthodoxies of proper English behavior. During his half-century tenure as the leader of the Puritan congregation in Roxbury, Massachusetts, Eliot studied the languages, customs, and beliefs of native Americans, hoping to help them along the path to Christian piety and to strengthen them against colonists' unscrupulous encroachment on Indian lands. The efforts of Eliot and other missionaries convinced some Indians to leave their own communities and settle in "praying towns" populated by native Americans who had agreed to live in conformity with English ways. Most Indians, however, did not move into praying towns or adopt the faith or manners of the colonists.

In Indian Dialogues, *a book published in 1671, Eliot illustrated the challenge he and other missionaries confronted as they tried to convince native Americans of the errors of their ways. Based upon his decades of missionary experience, Eliot created imaginary conversations between converted Indians and those who resisted Christianity. Eliot's invented conversations echoed arguments he and other missionaries had encountered repeatedly. The following selection from an imaginary dialogue between two praying Indians, Anthony and William, and King Philip (or Metacomet), the chief (or sachem) of the powerful Wampanoags, documents Eliot's perception of the attractions of Christianity and one Indian leader's doubts about it. These doubts ultimately prevailed when King Philip led the Wampanoags in an all-out attack against the settlers in 1675.*

Anthony. Sachem, we salute you in the Lord, and we declare unto you, that we are sent by the church, in the name of our Lord Jesus Christ, to call you, and beseech you to turn from your vain conversation unto God, to pray unto God, and to believe in Jesus Christ for the pardon of your sins, and for the salvation of your soul. . . . So we are come this day unto you, in the name of Jesus Christ, to call you to come unto the Lord, and serve him. [W]e hear that many of your people do desire to pray to God, only they depend on you. We pray you to consider that your love to your people should oblige you to do them all the good you can. . . . You will not only yourself turn from sin unto God . . . , but all your people will turn to God with you, so that you may say unto the Lord, oh Lord Jesus, behold here am I, and all the people which thou hast given me. We all come unto thy service, and promise to pray unto God so long as we live. . . . Oh how happy will all your people be. . . . It will be a joy to all the English magistrates, and ministers, and churches, and good people of the land, to hear that Philip and all his people are turned to God, and become praying Indians. . . .

Philip. Often have I heard of this great matter of praying unto God, and hitherto I have refused. . . . Mr. Eliot himself did come unto me. He was in this town, and did persuade me. But we were then in our sports, wherein I have much delighted, and in that temptation, I confess, I did neglect and despise the offer, and lost that opportunity. Since that time God hath afflicted and chastised me, and my heart doth begin to break. And I have some serious thoughts of accepting the offer, and turning to God, to become a praying Indian, I myself and all my people. But I have some great objections, which I cannot tell how to get over, which are still like great rocks in my way, over which I cannot climb. And if I should, I fear I shall fall down the precipice on the further side, and be spoiled and undone. By venturing to climb, I shall catch a deadly fall to me and my posterity.

The first objection that I have is this, because you praying Indians do reject your sachems, and refuse to pay them tribute, in so much that if any of my people turn to pray unto God, I do reckon that I have lost him. He will no longer own me for his sachem, nor pay me any tribute. And hence it will come to pass, that if I should pray to God, and all my people with me, I must become as a common man among them, and so lose all my power and authority over them. This is such a temptation as . . . I, nor any of the other great sachems, can tell how to get over. Were this temptation removed, the way would be more easy and open for me to turn praying Indian. I begin to have some good likance of the way, but I am loth to buy it at so dear a rate.

William. . . . I say, if any of the praying Indians should be disobedient (in lawful things) and refuse to pay tribute unto their sachems, it is not their religion and praying to God that teaches them so to do, but their corruptions. . . . I am sure the word of God commandeth all to be subject to the higher powers, and pay them tribute. . . . And therefore, beloved sachem, let not your heart fear that praying to God will alienate your people from you . . . for the more beneficent you are unto them, the more obligation you lay upon them. And what greater beneficence can you do unto them than to further them in religion, whereby they may be converted, pardoned, sanctified, and saved? . . .

Philip. I have another objection stronger than this, and that is, if I pray to God, then all my men that are willing to pray to God will (as you say) stick to me, and be true to me. But all such as love not and care not to pray to God, especially such as hate praying to God, all these will forsake me, yea will go and adjoin themselves unto other sachems that pray not to God. And so it will come to pass, that if I be a praying sachem, I shall be a poor and weak one, and easily trod upon by others, who are like to be more potent and numerous. And by this means my tribute will be small, and my people few, and I shall be a great loser by praying to God. In the way I am now, I am full and potent, but if I change my way and pray to God, I shall be empty and weak. . . .

William. . . . Suppose all your subjects that hate praying to God should leave you. What shall you lose by it? You are rid of such as by their sins vitiate others, and multiply transgression, and provoke the wrath of God against you and yours. But consider what you shall gain by praying to God . . . all the praying Indians will rejoice at it, and be your friends, and they are not a few. [And] you shall gain a more intimate love of the Governor, and Magistrates. . . . They will more honor, respect, and love you, than ever they did. [T]he Governor and Magistrates of the Massachusetts will own

you, and be fatherly and friendly to you. . . . Yea more, the King of England, and the great peers who . . . yearly send over means to encourage and promote our praying to God, they will take notice of you.

Philip. I perceive that in your praying to God, and in your churches, all are brought to an equality. Sachems and people they are all fellow brethren in your churches. Poor and rich are equally privileged. The vote of the lowest of the people hath as much weight as the vote of the sachem. Now I doubt [i.e., worry] that this way will lift up the heart of the poor to too much boldness, and debase the rulers to[o] low. This bringing all to an equality will bring all to a confusion. [T]here is yet another thing that I am much afraid of, and that is your church admonitions and excommunications. I hear that your sachems are under that yoke. I am a sinful man as well as others, but if I must be admonished by the church, who are my subjects, I know not how I shall like that. I doubt [i.e., worry] it will be a bitter pill, too hard for me to get down and swallow. . . . I feel your words sink into my heart and stick there. You speak arrows. . . . I desire to ponder and consider of these things. . . . I am willing they should still lie soaking in my heart and mind.

Source: John Eliot, *Indian Dialogues* (Cambridge, 1671), in Henry W. Bowden and James P. Ronda, eds., *John Eliot's Indian Dialogues: A Study in Cultural Interaction* (Westport, Conn., 1980), 120–31.

QUESTIONS FOR ANALYSIS AND DEBATE

1. To what degree is Eliot's dialogue a reliable guide to Philip's doubts about the wisdom of becoming a praying Indian?

2. According to Eliot, was Philip's religion a stumbling block to his acceptance of Christianity? What made Philip fear that he would "fall down the precipice"?

3. If Philip had written a dialogue proposing that Eliot convert to the Wampanoag way of life, what arguments might it have made?

NEW ENGLAND GREAT CHAIR
This throne-like chair belonged to Michael Metcalf, a teacher in seventeenth-century Dedham, Massachusetts. The oldest known piece of New England furniture inscribed with a date, 1652, the chair was made in Dedham specifically for Metcalf (note the initials flanking the date), who turned sixty-six in that year. Metcalf stored books, presumably including a Bible, in the enclosed compartment under the seat. No overstuffed recliner, the chair is suited less for a relaxing snooze than for alert concentration. The panels under the arms served to block chilly drafts. Otherwise, the chair shows few concessions to comfort or ease. The carved chair back—rigidly upright—displays motifs often found on Puritan tombstones. The grand austerity of the chair hints at the importance of serious Bible study and unflinching introspection in Puritan New England.
Dedham Historical Society/photo by Forrest Frazier.

Government by Puritans for Puritanism

It is only a slight exaggeration to say that seventeenth-century New England was governed by Puritans for Puritanism. The charter of the Massachusetts Bay Company empowered the company's stockholders, or freemen, to meet as a body known as the General Court and make the laws to govern the company's affairs. The colonists transformed this arrangement for running a joint stock company into a structure for governing the colony. In 1631, the General Court ruled that freemen must be male church members, hoping to ensure that godly men would decide government policies. When new settlers continued to be admitted as freemen, the number became too large for the group to meet conveniently. In 1634, the freemen in each town agreed to send two deputies to the General Court to act as the colony's legislative assembly.

All other men were classified as "inhabitants," and they had the right to vote, hold office, and participate fully in town government. A "town meeting," composed of all the town's inhabitants and freemen, chose the selectmen and other officials who administered local affairs. New England town meetings routinely practiced a level of popular participation in political life that was unprecedented elsewhere during the seventeenth century. Almost every adult man could speak out in town meetings and fortify his voice with a vote. However, all women—even church members—were prohibited from voting, and towns did not permit "contrary-minded" men to become or remain inhabitants. Although town meeting participants wrangled from time to time, widespread political participation tended to reinforce conformity to Puritan ideals.

One of the most important functions of New England government was land distribution. Settlers who desired to establish a new town entered a covenant and petitioned the General Court for a grant of land. The court granted town sites to suitably pious petitioners but did not allow settlement until the Indians who inhabited a grant agreed to relinquish their claim to the land, usually in exchange for manufactured goods. Having obtained their grant, town founders apportioned land among themselves and any newcomers they permitted to join them. Although there was a considerable difference between the largest and smallest family plots, most clustered in the middle range—roughly fifty to one hundred acres—giving New England a more equal distribution of land than the Chesapeake. Towns reserved some common land, which all inhabitants could use for grazing livestock and cutting wood, and saved the rest for new settlers and the descendants of the founders. The physical layout of the towns encouraged settlers to look inward toward their neighbors, multiplying the opportunities for godly vigilance.

The Splintering of Puritanism

Almost from the beginning, John Winthrop and other leaders had difficulty enforcing their views of Puritan orthodoxy. In England, persecution as a dissenting minority unified Puritan voices in opposition to the Church of England. But in New England, the promise of a godly society and the Puritans' emphasis on individual Bible study led New Englanders toward different visions of godliness. Puritan leaders, however, interpreted dissent as an error caused either by a misguided believer or by the malevolent power of Satan. Whatever the cause, errors could not be tolerated. As one Puritan minister proclaimed, "The Scripture saith . . . there is no Truth but one."

Among the immigrants who arrived in Massachusetts in 1630 was Roger Williams, a lively young minister who counted Winthrop and other Puritan elders among his friends. From the start, Williams needled the colony's leadership with his outspoken views that their church was fatally impure. Williams declared that the government of Massachusetts contaminated the purity of the church, which had to be kept absolutely separate from civil influence. For these opinions and others, Massachusetts banished Williams in 1635. He helped found the colony of Rhode Island, which became a refuge for dissenters from Puritan orthodoxies.

Strains within Puritanism exemplified by Williams and Anne Hutchinson caused it to splinter repeatedly during the seventeenth century. The prominent minister Thomas Hooker, for example, clashed with Winthrop and other leaders over the composition of the church. Hooker argued that men and women who lived godly lives should be admitted to church membership, even if they had not experienced conversion. This question, like most others in New England, had both religious and political dimensions, since only church members

could vote in Massachusetts. In 1636, Hooker led an exodus of more than eight hundred colonists from Massachusetts to the Connecticut River valley, where they founded Hartford and neighboring towns. In 1639, the towns adopted the Fundamental Orders of Connecticut, a quasi-constitution that could be altered by vote of the freemen, who did not have to be church members, though nearly all of them were. Other Puritan churches divided and subdivided throughout the seventeenth century as acrimony developed over doctrine and church government. These schisms arose from the ambiguities and tensions within Puritan belief. As the colonies matured, other tensions developed as well.

Religious Controversies and Economic Changes

A revolutionary transformation in the fortunes of Puritans in England had profound consequences in New England. Disputes between King Charles I and Parliament escalated in 1642 to civil war in England, known as the Puritan Revolution. The parliamentary forces led by the staunch Puritan Oliver Cromwell were victorious, executing Charles I in 1649 and proclaiming a Puritan Republic. From 1649 to 1660, England's rulers were not monarchs who suppressed Puritanism but believers who championed it. In a half century, English Puritans rose from a harassed group of religious dissenters to a dominant power in English government.

When the Puritan Revolution began, the stream of immigrants to New England dwindled to a trickle, creating hard times for the colonists. They could no longer consider themselves a city on a hill setting a godly example for humankind. English society was being reformed by Puritans in England, not New England. Furthermore, when immigrant ships became rare, the colonists faced sky-high prices for scarce English goods and few customers for their own colonial products. As they searched to find new products and markets, they established the enduring patterns of New England's economy.

New England's rocky soil and short growing season ruled out cultivating the southern colonies' crops of tobacco and rice that found a ready market in Atlantic ports. Exports that New Englanders could not get from the soil they took instead from the forest and the sea. During the first decade of settlement, colonists traded with Indians for animal pelts, which were in demand in Europe. By the

1640s, fur-bearing animals were scarce unless traders ventured far beyond the frontiers of English settlement. Trees from the seemingly limitless forests of New England proved a longer-lasting resource. Masts for ships and staves for barrels of Spanish wine and West Indian sugar were crafted from New England timber.

But the most important New England export was fish. During the religious and political turmoil of the 1640s, English ships withdrew from the rich North Atlantic fishing grounds and New England fishermen quickly took their place. Dried, salted codfish found markets in southern Europe and the West Indies. The fish trade also stimulated colonial shipbuilding and trained generations of fishermen, sailors, and merchants, creating a commercial network that endured for more than a century.

Although immigration came to a standstill in the 1640s, the population continued to boom, doubling every twenty years. In New England, almost everyone married and women often had eight or nine children. Long, cold winters prevented the warm-weather ailments of the southern colonies and reduced New England mortality. The descendants of the immigrants of the 1630s multiplied and remultiplied, boosting the New England population to roughly equal that of the southern colonies (Figure 4.1).

Under the pressures of steady population growth and integration into the Atlantic economy, the white-hot piety of the founders cooled during the last half of the seventeenth century. By the 1680s, women were the majority of full church members throughout New England. In some towns, only 15 percent of the adult men were members. Most alarming to Puritan leaders, the children of visible saints often failed to experience conversion and attain full church membership. The problem became urgent during the 1650s when the children of saints —people who had grown to adulthood in New England but who had not experienced conversion— began to have children themselves. These babies, the grandchildren of visible saints, could not receive the protection baptism afforded against the terrors of death because their parents were not converted.

Puritan churches debated what to do. In 1662, a synod of Massachusetts ministers reached a compromise known as the Halfway Covenant. The unconverted children of saints were permitted to become "halfway" church members. Like regular church members, they could baptize their infants. But unlike full church members, they could not par-

ticipate in communion or have the voting privileges of church membership. The Halfway Covenant generated a controversy that sputtered through Puritan churches for the remainder of the century. With the Halfway Covenant, Puritan churches came to terms with replacing the founders' burning zeal with what one called "luke-warm Indifferency."

Nonetheless, during the last half of the seventeenth century, New England communities continued to enforce piety with holy rigor. Beginning in 1656, small bands of Quakers began to arrive in Massachusetts. Quakers—or members of the Society of Friends, as they called themselves—believed that God spoke directly to each individual through an "inner light." Neither a preacher nor the Bible was necessary to discover God's Word. Furthermore, since all human beings were equal in God's eyes, Quakers refused to conform to mere temporal

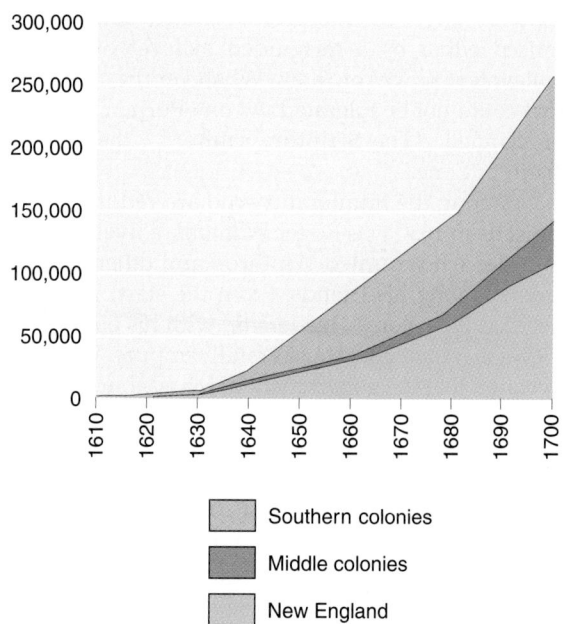

FIGURE 4.1

Population of British North American Colonies in the Seventeenth Century

The colonial population grew at a steadily accelerating rate during the seventeenth century. On the whole, New England and the southern colonies each comprised about half the total colonial population until after 1680, when the growth in Pennsylvania and New York contributed to a surge in the population of the middle colonies.

A NEW ENGLAND CHILD
This 1668 painting of young Alice Mason illustrates the drift away from the intense piety and plain dress of New England's founding generation. The elaborately decorated dress, especially the slashed sleeves, reflects the prosperity that some New Englanders had achieved by the 1660s, prosperity they displayed in their clothing and homes in ways the founders would have deemed profane.
Adams National Historic Site.

powers such as laws and governments, unless God requested otherwise. Quakers affronted Puritan doctrines of faith and social order. They refused to observe the Sabbath, for example, because they insisted that God did not set aside any special day for worship but instead expected the faithful to worship every day.

New England communities treated Quakers with ruthless severity. Some Quakers were branded on the face "with a red-hot iron with [an] H. for heresie." Several Quaker women were stripped to the waist, tied to the back of a cart, and whipped as they were paraded through towns. When Quakers refused to leave Massachusetts, the Boston magistrates sentenced two men and a woman to be hanged in 1659.

New Englanders' partial success in realizing the promise of a godly society ultimately undermined the intense appeal of Puritanism. In the pious communities of New England, leaders tried to eliminate sin. In the process, they diminished the sense of utter human depravity that was the wellspring of Puritanism. By 1700, New Englanders did not doubt that human beings sinned, but they were more concerned with the sins of others than with their own, as the Salem witch trials demonstrated. In 1692, more than one hundred individuals were accused of witchcraft, a capital crime, in the frenzied Salem proceedings. Most of the accused witches were middle-aged women who, their accusers charged, were in thrall to Satan who had caused misfortune to befall the accusers. Accusing vulnerable older women of witchcraft made it somewhat easier for their accusers to consider themselves saints who were victimized by evil witches, rather than sinners who were largely responsible for their own deviations from piety. The Salem court executed nineteen accused witches, signalling enduring belief in the supernatural origins of evil and gnawing doubt about the strength of New Englanders' faith.

The Founding of the Middle Colonies

The English colonies of New York, New Jersey, and Pennsylvania originated as proprietary colonies—that is, colonies granted by the crown to one or more proprietors, who then possessed both the land and extensive, almost monarchical, powers of government (see Map 4.2). Before the 1670s, few Europeans settled in any of these middle colonies. For the first two-thirds of the seventeenth century, the most important European outpost in the region north of the Chesapeake and south of New England was the relatively small Dutch colony of New Netherland. By 1700, however, the English monarchy had seized New Netherland, renamed it New York, and encouraged the creation of a Quaker colony led by William Penn.

From New Netherland to New York

In 1609, the Dutch East India Company dispatched Henry Hudson to search for a Northwest Passage to the Orient. Hudson sailed along the Atlantic coast and ventured up the large river that now bears his

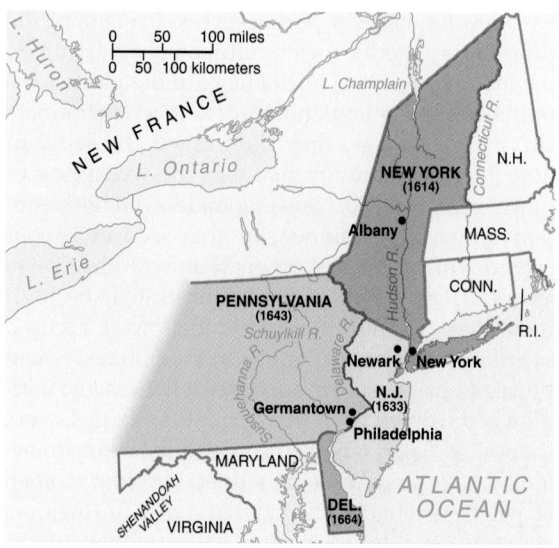

MAP 4.2

Middle Colonies in the Seventeenth Century

For the most part, the middle colonies in the seventeenth century were inhabited by settlers who clustered along the Hudson or Delaware River. The vast geographic extent of the colonies shown in this map represented land grants authorized in England but still inhabited by native Americans rather than settled by colonists.

name until it dwindled to a stream that obviously did not lead to China. A decade later, the Dutch government granted the West India Company—a group of Dutch merchants and shippers—exclusive rights to trade with the Western Hemisphere. In 1626, Peter Minuit, the resident director of the company, purchased Manhattan Island from the Manhate Indians for trade goods worth the equivalent of a dozen beaver pelts. New Amsterdam, the small settlement established at the southern tip of Manhattan Island, became the principal trading center in New Netherland and the colony's headquarters. Unlike the English colonies, New Netherland did not attract many European immigrants. Like New England and the Chesapeake colonies, New Netherland never realized the profits of its sponsors' dreams.

Although few in number, the New Netherlanders were remarkably diverse, especially compared with the homogeneous English settlers to the north and south. Religious dissenters and immigrants from Holland, Sweden, France, Germany, and else-

where made their way to the colony. A minister of the Dutch Reformed Church complained to his superiors in Holland that several groups of Jews had recently arrived, adding to the religious mixture of "Papists, Mennonites and Lutherans among the Dutch [and] many Puritans . . . and many other atheists . . . who conceal themselves under the name of Christians."

The West India Company struggled to govern the motley colonists. Peter Stuyvesant, governor from 1647 to 1664, tried to enforce conformity to the Dutch Reformed Church, but the company declared that "the consciences of men should be free and unshackled," making a virtue of New Netherland necessity. The company never permitted the colony's settlers to form a representative government. Instead, the company appointed government officials who set policies, including taxes, which many colonists deeply resented.

In 1664, New Netherland became New York. Charles II, who became king of England in 1660, gave his brother James, the Duke of York, an enormous grant of land that included New Netherland. Of course, the Dutch colony did not belong to the king of England. But that legal technicality did not impede the king or his brother. The duke quickly organized a small fleet of warships, which appeared off Manhattan Island in late summer 1664, and demanded that Stuyvesant surrender. With little choice, he did.

As the new proprietor of the colony, the Duke of York exercised almost the same unlimited authority over the colony as had the West India Company. The duke never set foot in New York, but his governors struggled to impose order on the unruly colonists. Like the Dutch, the duke permitted "all persons of what Religion soever, quietly to inhabit . . . provided they give no disturbance to the publique peace, nor doe molest or disquiet others in the free exercise of their religion." This policy of religious toleration was less an affirmation of liberty of conscience and more a recognition of the reality of the most heterogeneous colony in seventeenth-century North America.

New Jersey and Pennsylvania

The creation of New York led indirectly to the founding of two other middle colonies, New Jersey and Pennsylvania (Map 4.2). In 1664, the Duke of York subdivided his grant and gave the portion between the Hudson and Delaware Rivers to two of his friends. The proprietors of this new colony, New Jersey, soon discovered that Puritan and Dutch settlers already in the region stubbornly resisted the new government. The continuing strife persuaded one of the proprietors to sell his share to two Quakers. When the Quaker proprietors began to quarrel, they called in a prominent English Quaker, William Penn, to arbitrate their dispute. Penn eventually worked out a settlement that continued New Jersey's proprietary government but did little to end the conflict with the settlers. In the process, Penn became intensely interested in what he termed a "holy experiment" of establishing a genuinely Quaker colony in America.

The Quakers' concept of an open, generous God who made his love equally available to all people manifested itself in unusually egalitarian worship services and in social behavior that continually brought Quakers into conflict with the English government. Quaker leaders were ordinary men and women, not specially trained preachers. More than any other seventeenth-century sect, Quakers allowed women to assume positions of religious leadership. "In souls there is no sex," they said. Since all people were equal in the spiritual realm, Quakers considered social hierarchy false and evil. They called everyone "friend" and shook hands instead of curtsying or removing their hats—even when meeting the king. These customs enraged many non-Quakers and provoked innumerable beatings and worse. Penn was jailed four times for such offenses, once for nine months.

Despite his many run-ins with the government, Penn remained on good terms with Charles II, who granted him land to found a Quaker colony in America. Partly to rid England of the troublesome Quakers, in 1681 Charles made Penn the proprietor of 45,000 square miles for his new colony, called Pennsylvania.

WILLIAM PENN
This portrait of William Penn was drawn about a decade after the founding of Pennsylvania. At a time when extravagant clothing and fancy wigs proclaimed that their wearer was an important person, Penn is portrayed informally, lacking even a coat, his natural hair neat but undressed—all a reflection of his Quaker faith. Penn's full face and double chin show that his faith did not make him a stranger to the pleasures of the table. No hollow-cheeked ascetic or wild-eyed enthusiast, Penn appears sober and observant, as if sizing up the viewer and reserving judgment. The portrait captures the calm determination—anchored in his faith—that inspired Penn's hopes for his new colony.
Historical Society of Pennsylvania.

Toleration and Diversity in Pennsylvania

When Penn announced the creation of his colony, Quakers flocked to English ports in numbers exceeded only by the great Puritan migration to New England fifty years earlier. Between 1682 and 1685, nearly eight thousand immigrants arrived in Pennsylvania, most of them Quakers from England, Ireland, and Wales. They represented a cross section of the artisans, farmers, and laborers who predominated among English Quakers. Quaker missionaries also encouraged immigrants from the European continent, and many came, giving Pennsylvania greater ethnic diversity than any other English colony except New York. Pennsylvania prospered, and the capital city, Philadelphia, soon rivaled New York—though not yet Boston—as a center of commerce. By 1700, the city's five thousand inhabitants participated in a thriving trade exporting flour and other food products to the West Indies and importing textiles and manufactured goods.

Penn was determined to live in peace with the Indians who inhabited the region. His Indian policy expressed his Quaker ideals and contrasted sharply with the hostile policies of the other English colonies. Penn instructed his agents to obtain the Indians' consent by purchasing their land, respecting their claims, and dealing with them fairly.

Penn declared that the first principle of government was that every settler would "enjoy the free possession of his or her faith and exercise of worship towards God." Accordingly, Pennsylvania tolerated Protestant sects of all kinds as well as Roman Catholics. All voters and officeholders had to be Christians, but the government did not compel settlers to attend religious services, as in Massachusetts, or to pay taxes to maintain a state-supported church, as in Virginia.

Despite its toleration and diversity, Pennsylvania was as much a Quaker colony as New England was a stronghold of Puritanism. Penn had no hesitation about using civil government to enforce religious morality. The ethnic and religious diversity of Pennsylvania prevented strict enforcement of pious behavior, but Quaker expectations of godly order and sobriety set the tone of Pennsylvania society.

As proprietor, Penn had extensive powers, subject only to review by the king. He appointed a governor who maintained the proprietor's power to veto any laws passed by the colonial council, which was elected by property owners who possessed at least one hundred acres of land or who paid taxes. The council had the power to originate laws and administer all the affairs of government. A popularly elected assembly served as a check on the council; its members had the authority to reject or approve laws framed by the council.

Penn stressed that the exact form of government mattered less than the men who served in it. In Penn's eyes, "good men" staffed Pennsylvania's government because Quakers dominated elective and appointive offices. Quakers, of course, differed among themselves. Members of the assembly struggled to win the right to debate and amend laws, especially tax laws. They finally won the battle in 1701 when a new Charter of Privileges gave the proprietor the power to appoint the council and in turn stripped the council of all its former powers and gave them to the assembly, which became the only unicameral legislature in all the British colonies.

The Colonies and the British Empire

From the king's point of view, proprietary grants of faraway lands to which he had tenuous claims were a cheap way to reward friends. As the colonies grew, however, the grants became more valuable. After 1660, the king took initiatives to channel colonial trade through English hands and to consolidate royal authority over colonial governments. These initiatives defined the basic relationship between the colonies and England that endured until the American Revolution (Map 4.3).

Royal Regulation of Colonial Trade

English economic policies toward the colonies were designed to yield customs revenues for the monarchy and profitable business for English merchants and shippers. In addition, the policies were intended to divert the colonies' trade from England's enemies, the Dutch and the French.

The Navigation Acts of 1650, 1651, and 1660 set forth two fundamental regulations governing colonial trade. First, all colonial goods imported into England had to be transported in English ships using primarily English crews. Second, the Navigation Acts listed specific colonial products that could be shipped only to England or to other English colonies. The Staple Act of 1663 imposed a third regulation on colonial trade. It required all goods imported into the colonies to pass through England (see chapter 3).

By the end of the seventeenth century, colonial commerce was defined by regulations that subjected merchants and shippers to royal supervision and gave them access to markets throughout the British Empire. In addition, colonial commerce received protection from the British navy. By 1700, colonial goods (including those from the West Indies) accounted for one-fifth of all British imports and for two-thirds of all goods reexported from England to the continent. In turn, the colonies absorbed more than one-tenth of British exports. The commercial regulations gave economic value to England's proprietorship of American colonies.

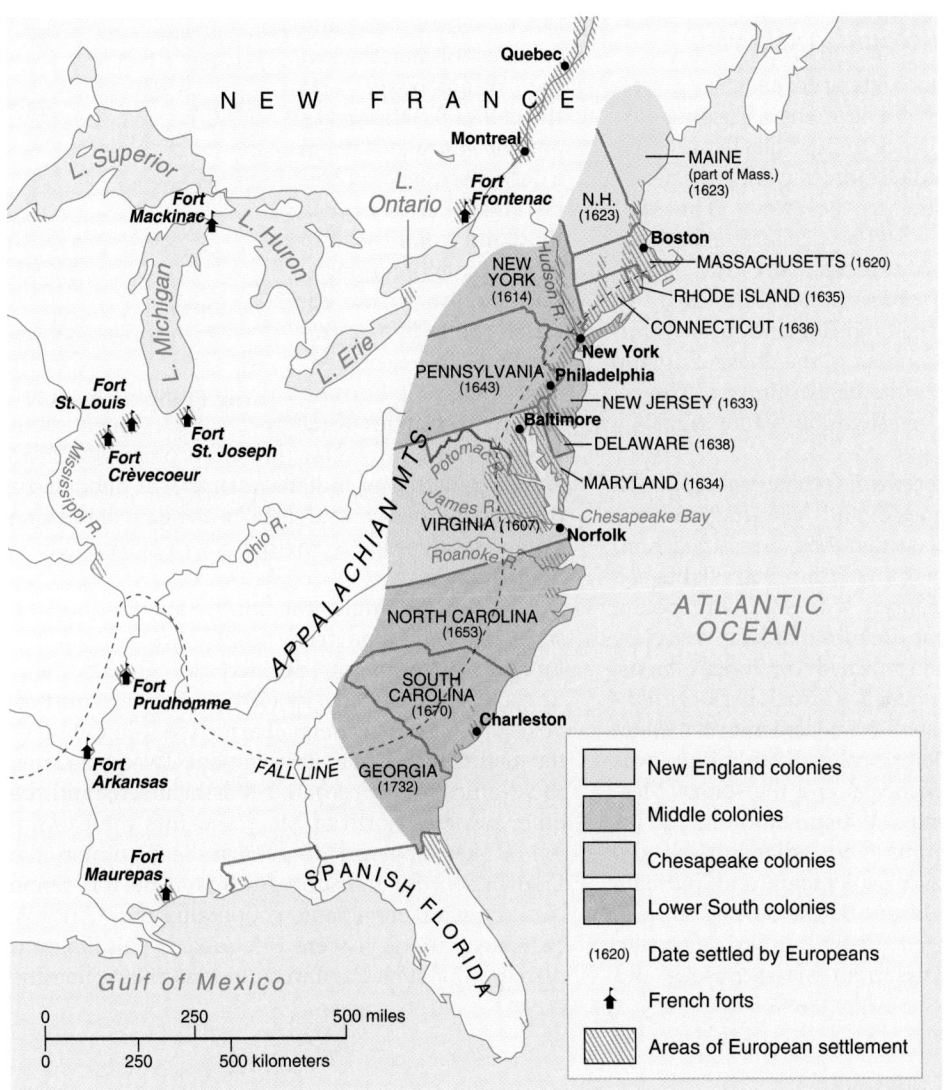

M A P 4 . 3

American Colonies at the End of the Seventeenth Century

By the end of the seventeenth century, settlers inhabited a narrow band of land that stretched more or less continuously from Boston to Norfolk, with pockets of settlement farther south. The colonies' claims to enormous tracts of land to the west were contested by native Americans as well as the ambitions of France and Spain.

READING THE MAP: What geographic feature acted as the boundary for colonial territorial claims? Which colonies were the most settled and which the least?

CONNECTIONS: The map divides the colonies into four regions; can you think of alternative organizations? On what criteria would they be based?

www.bedfordstmartins.com/roarkcompact SEE THE ONLINE STUDY GUIDE for more help in analyzing this map.

Consolidation of Royal Authority

The monarchy also took steps to exercise greater control over colonial governments. Virginia had been a royal colony since 1624; Maryland, South Carolina, and the middle colonies were proprietary colonies with close ties to the crown. The New England colonies possessed royal charters, but they had developed their own distinctively Puritan governments. Charles II, whose father, Charles I, had been executed by Puritans in England, took a particular interest in harnessing the New England colonies more firmly to the British Empire. The occasion was a royal investigation following King Philip's War.

In 1675, warfare between Indians and colonists erupted in the Chesapeake and New England. Although Massachusetts settlers had massacred hundreds of Pequot Indians in 1637, they had established relatively peaceful relations with the more potent Wampanoags. But in the decades that followed, New Englanders steadily encroached on Indian lands, and, in 1675, the Wampanoags struck back with attacks on settlements in western Massachusetts. Metacomet—whom the colonists called King Philip—was the chief of the Wampanoags and the son of Massasoit, who had befriended William Bradford and his original band of Pilgrims. The Indians utterly destroyed thirteen English settlements and partially burned another half dozen. By the spring of 1676, Indian warriors ranged freely within seventeen miles of Boston. Militias from Massachusetts and other New England colonies counterattacked the Wampanoags and their allies the Nipmucks and the Narragansetts in a deadly sequence of battles that killed over a thousand colonists and thousands more Indians. The colonists finally defeated the Indians, principally with a scorched-earth policy of burning their food supplies. King

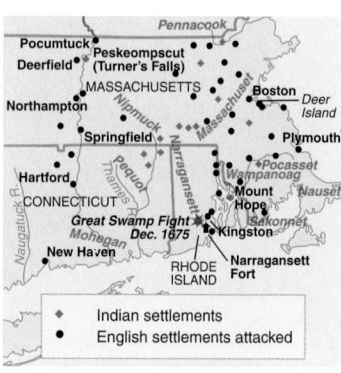

King Philip's War, 1675

Philip's War left the New England colonists with an enduring hatred of Indians, a large war debt, and a devastated frontier. And in 1676, an agent of the king arrived to investigate whether New England abided by English laws.

Not surprisingly, the king's agent found all sorts of deviations from English rules, and the English government decided to govern New England more directly. In 1684, an English court revoked the Massachusetts charter, the foundation of the distinctive Puritan government. Two years later, royal officials incorporated Massachusetts and the other colonies north of Maryland into the Dominion of New England. To govern the dominion, the English sent Sir Edmund Andros to Boston. Some New England merchants cooperated with Andros, but most colonists were offended by his flagrant disregard of such Puritan traditions as keeping the

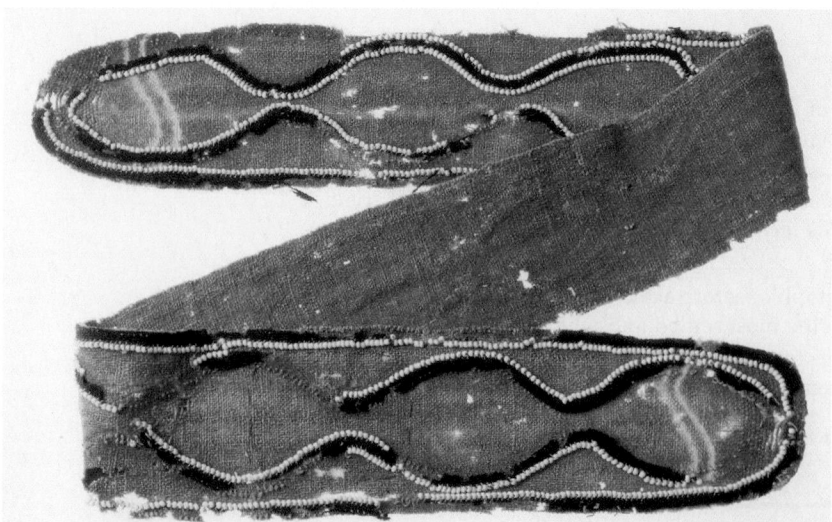

KING PHILIP'S SASH
This woolen sash belonged to Metacomet, or King Philip. Small white glass beads, obtained through trade with Europeans, embroider the sash in the shape of a serpent.
Peabody Museum, Harvard University.

Sabbath. Worst of all, the Dominion of New England invalidated all land titles, confronting every landowner in New England with the horrifying prospect of losing his or her land.

Events in England, however, permitted Massachusetts colonists to overthrow Andros and retain title to their property. When Charles II died in 1685, he was succeeded by his brother James II, a zealous Catholic. James's aggressive campaign to appoint Catholics to government posts engendered such unrest that in 1688 a group of Protestant noblemen invited the Dutch ruler William of Orange to claim the English throne. When William landed in England at the head of a large army, James fled to France and William became king in the bloodless Glorious Revolution, which reasserted Protestant influence in England and its empire. Rumors of the revolution raced across the Atlantic and emboldened colonial uprisings against royal authority in Massachusetts, New York, and Maryland.

In Boston, rebels reestablished the former charter government, destroying the Dominion of New England. New Yorkers under the leadership of Jacob Leisler followed the Massachusetts example. But when King William's governor of New York arrived in 1691, he executed Leisler for treason. In Maryland, the Protestant Association, led by John Coode, overthrew the colony's pro-Catholic government in 1689, fearing it would not recognize the new Protestant king. Coode's men ruled until the new royal governor arrived in 1692 and ended both Coode's rebellion and Lord Baltimore's proprietary government.

Much as they chafed under increasing royal control, the colonists still valued English protection from hostile neighbors. While the northern colonies were distracted by the Glorious Revolution, French forces from the fur trading regions along the Great Lakes and in Canada attacked villages in New England and New York. Known as King William's War, the conflict with the French was a colonial outgrowth of William's war against France in Europe. The war dragged on until 1697 and ended inconclusively in both Europe and the colonies. But it made clear to many colonists that along with English royal government came a welcome measure of military security.

In Massachusetts, John Winthrop's city on a hill became another royal colony in 1691, when a new charter was issued. Under the charter, the governor was appointed by the king rather than elected by the colonists' representatives. But perhaps the most unsettling change was the new qualification for voting. Possession of property replaced church membership as a prerequisite for voting in colony-wide elections. Wealth replaced God's grace as the defining characteristic of Massachusetts citizenship.

Conclusion: An English Model of Colonization in North America

By 1700, the diverse English colonies in North America had developed along lines quite different from the example New Spain had set in 1600. In the North American colonies, English immigrants and their descendants created societies of settlers, unlike the largely Indian societies in New Spain ruled by a tiny group of Spaniards. Although many settlers came to North America from other parts of Europe and a growing number of Africans arrived in bondage, English laws, habits, ideas, and language dominated all the colonies.

Economically, the English colonies thrived on agriculture and trade instead of mining silver and exploiting Indian labor as in New Spain. Southern colonies grew huge crops of tobacco and rice with the labor of indentured servants and slaves, while farmers in the middle colonies planted wheat and New England fishermen harvested the sea. Although servants and slaves could be found throughout the North American colonies, many settlers depended principally on the labor of family members. Relations between settlers and native Americans often exploded in bloody warfare, but Indians seldom served as an important source of labor for settlers, as they did in New Spain.

Protestantism prevailed in the North American settlements, relaxed in some colonies and straitlaced in others. The convictions of Puritanism that motivated John Winthrop and others to build a new England in the colonies became muted as the New England colonies matured and dissenters like Anne Hutchinson multiplied. Catholics, Quakers, Anglicans, Jews, and others settled in the middle and southern colonies, creating considerable religious toleration, especially in Pennsylvania and New York.

Politics and government differed from colony to colony, although the imprint of English institutions and practices existed everywhere. And everywhere, local settlers who were free adult white men had an extraordinary degree of political influence, far beyond that of colonists in New Spain or ordinary citizens in England. A new world of settlers that Columbus could not have imagined, that Powhatan only glimpsed, had been firmly established in English North America by 1700. During the next half century, that English colonial world would undergo surprising new developments built upon the achievements of the seventeenth century.

FOR FURTHER READING ABOUT THE TOPICS IN THIS CHAPTER, see the Online Bibliography at www.bedfordstmartins.com/roarkcompact.

FOR ADDITIONAL FIRST-HAND ACCOUNTS OF THIS PERIOD, see pages 43–59 in Michael Johnson, ed., *Reading the American Past*, Second Edition, Volume I.

TO ASSESS YOUR MASTERY OF THE MATERIAL IN THIS CHAPTER, see the Online Study Guide at www.bedfordstmartins.com/roarkcompact.

CHRONOLOGY

1534 Henry VIII breaks with Roman Catholic Church and initiates English Reformation.

1609 Henry Hudson searches for Northwest Passage for Dutch East India Company.

1620 English Puritans found Plymouth colony and elect William Bradford governor.

1626 Peter Minuit purchases Manhattan Island for Dutch West India Company and founds New Amsterdam.

1629 Massachusetts Bay Company receives royal charter for colony.

1630 John Winthrop leads Puritan settlers to Massachusetts Bay.

1635 Roger Williams, banished from Massachusetts, establishes Rhode Island colony.

1636 Thomas Hooker leaves Massachusetts and helps found Connecticut colony.

1637 Anne Hutchinson accused of Antinomianism; excommunicated from Boston church in 1638.

1642 Civil war inflames England, pitting Puritans against royalists.

1649 English Puritans win civil war and execute King Charles I.

1656 Quakers arrive in Massachusetts and are persecuted there.

1660 Monarchy restored in England; Charles II becomes king.

Navigation Act requires colonial goods to be shipped in English vessels through English ports.

1662 Many Puritan congregations adopt Halfway Covenant.

1663 Staple Act requires all colonial imports to come from England.

1664 English seize New Netherland colony from Dutch and rename it New York.

Duke of York subdivides his colony, creating new colony of New Jersey.

1675 Indians and colonists clash in King Philip's War.

1681 King Charles II grants William Penn charter for colony of Pennsylvania.

1686 Royal officials create Dominion of New England.

1688 James II overthrown by Glorious Revolution; William of Orange becomes king.

1691 Massachusetts becomes royal colony.

1692 Witch trials flourish at Salem, Massachusetts.

"DUMMY BOARD" OF PHYLLIS,
A NEW ENGLAND SLAVE

This life-size portrait of a slave woman named Phyllis, a mulatto who worked as a domestic servant for her owner, Elizabeth Hunt Wendell, was painted sometime before 1753. Known as a "dummy board," it was evidently propped against a wall or placed in a doorway or window to suggest that the residence was occupied and to discourage thieves. Phyllis is portrayed as a demure, well-groomed woman whose dress and demeanor suggest that she was capable, orderly, and efficient. Although tens of thousands of slaves were brought from Africa to the British North American colonies during the eighteenth century, it does not appear that Phyllis was one of them. Instead, she was probably born in the colonies of mixed black and white parentage. Like thousands of other slave women who labored in the homes of prosperous white families, Phyllis illustrates the integration of the mundane tasks of housekeeping with the shifting currents of transatlantic commerce.

Courtesy of the Society for the Preservation of New England Antiquities/photo by David Bohl.

COLONIAL AMERICA IN THE EIGHTEENTH CENTURY

5

1701–1770

EARLY ON A SUNDAY MORNING IN OCTOBER 1723, young Benjamin Franklin stepped from a wharf along the Delaware River onto the streets of Philadelphia. As he wrote later in his autobiography, "I was dirty from my Journey; my Pockets were stuff'd out with Shirts and Stockings; I knew no Soul, nor where to look for Lodging. I was fatigu'd with Travelling, Rowing and Want of Rest. I was very hungry."

Born in 1706, Benjamin Franklin grew up in Boston, where his father, Josiah, worked making soap and candles. The father of seventeen children, Josiah apprenticed each of his sons to learn a trade. At the age of twelve, Benjamin signed an indenture to serve for nine years as an apprentice to his brother James, a printer. In James's shop, Benjamin learned the printer's trade and had access to the latest books and pamphlets, which he read avidly. In 1721, James inaugurated the *New England Courant*, avowing to "expose the Vice and Follies of Persons of all Ranks and Degrees" with articles written "so that the meanest ploughman . . . may understand them."

Benjamin's responsibilities in the print shop grew quickly, but he chafed under his brother's supervision. "My Brother was passionate and had often beaten me," he remembered. Benjamin resolved "to assert my Freedom" and run away to New York, nearly three hundred miles from anyone he knew. When he could not find work, he wandered to the Delaware River and then talked his way aboard a small boat heading toward Philadelphia. After rowing half the night, Franklin arrived in the city and went straight to a bakery where he purchased "three great Puffy Rolls." Then he set off for the wharf, "with a Roll under each Arm," to wash down the bread with "a Draught of the River Water." After quenching his thirst, Franklin followed "many clean dress'd People . . . to the great Meeting House of the Quakers. . . . I sat down among them, and . . . I fell fast asleep, and continu'd so till the Meeting broke up."

Franklin's account of his life in Boston and his arrival in Philadelphia is probably the most well-known portrait of life in eighteenth-century America. It illustrates everyday experiences that Franklin shared with many other colonists: a large family; long hours of labor subject to the authority of a parent, relative, or employer; and a restless quest for escape from the ties that bound, for freedom. Franklin's account hints at other, less tangible trends: an ambition to make something of oneself in this world rather than worry too much about the hereafter; an eagerness to

PHILADELPHIA WHARF
This early-nineteenth-century drawing of the Arch Street wharf in Philadelphia approximates the world Benjamin Franklin entered when he stepped ashore in 1723. The wharf was a center of industrious activity; almost everyone depicted appears to be working. The pulse of Atlantic commerce propels casks of products from the deck of the small local sailboat (right) toward the hold of large oceangoing ships (center) bound for England and Europe. The small rowboat carrying four people (just to the right of the large ships) is probably similar to the boat Franklin rowed to the city. Coordinating the complicated comings and goings of people and goods that moved through the wharf required individuals who combined intelligence, energy, and discipline with efficiency, reliability, and trustworthiness—traits Franklin and other eighteenth-century colonists sought to cultivate.
Rare Book Department, The Free Library of Philadelphia.

subvert orthodox opinion by publishing dissenting views expressed in simple, clear language understandable by "the meanest ploughman"; a confidence that, with a valued skill and a few coins, a young man could make his way in the world, a confidence few young women could dare assert; and a slackening of religious fervor displayed, for example, in Franklin's quiet snooze—rather than rapt attention—during the Quaker meeting he wandered into on his first day in Philadelphia.

Franklin's story introduces some of the major changes that affected all the colonies in eighteenth-

century British North America. Social and economic changes tended to reinforce the differences among New England, the middle colonies, and the southern colonies, while important cultural and political developments tugged in the opposite direction, creating common experiences, aspirations, and identities. In 1776, when *E Pluribus Unum* (Latin meaning "From Many, One") was adopted as the motto for the Great Seal of the United States, the changes in eighteenth-century America that strengthened *Pluribus* also planted the seeds of *Unum.*

A Growing Population and Expanding Economy

The most important fact about eighteenth-century colonial America was its phenomenal population growth. In 1700, colonists numbered about 250,000; by 1770, they tallied well over 2 million. An index of the emerging significance of colonial America is that in 1700 there were 19 people in England for every American colonist, whereas by 1770 there were only 3. The eightfold growth of the colonial population signaled the maturation of a distinctive colonial society. That society was by no means homogeneous. Colonists of different ethnic groups, races, and religions lived in varied environments under thirteen different colonial governments, all of them part of the British Empire.

In general, the growth and diversity of the eighteenth-century colonial population derived from two sources: immigration and natural increase (that is, growth through reproduction). Natural increase contributed about three-fourths of the population growth, immigration about one-fourth. Immigration shifted the ethnic and racial balance among the colonists, making them by 1770 less English and less white than ever before. Fewer than 10 percent of eighteenth-century immigrants came from England; about 36 percent were Scots-Irish, mostly from northern Ireland; 33 percent arrived from Africa, almost all of them slaves; nearly 15 percent had left the many German-language principalities (the nation of Germany did not exist until 1871); and almost 10 percent came from Scotland. In 1670, more than 9 out of 10 colonists were of English ancestry, and only 1 out of 25 was of African ancestry. By 1770, only about half the colonists were of English descent, while more than 20 percent descended from Africans. By 1770, the people of the colonies had a distinctive colonial—rather than English—profile (Map 5.1).

The booming population of the colonies hints at a second major feature of eighteenth-century colonial society: an expanding economy. Today, societies with rapidly growing populations often have more people than they can adequately feed; or, put another way, they have a high ratio of people to land. In the eighteenth-century colonies, very different conditions prevailed.

In 1700, after almost a century of settlement, nearly all the colonists lived within fifty miles of

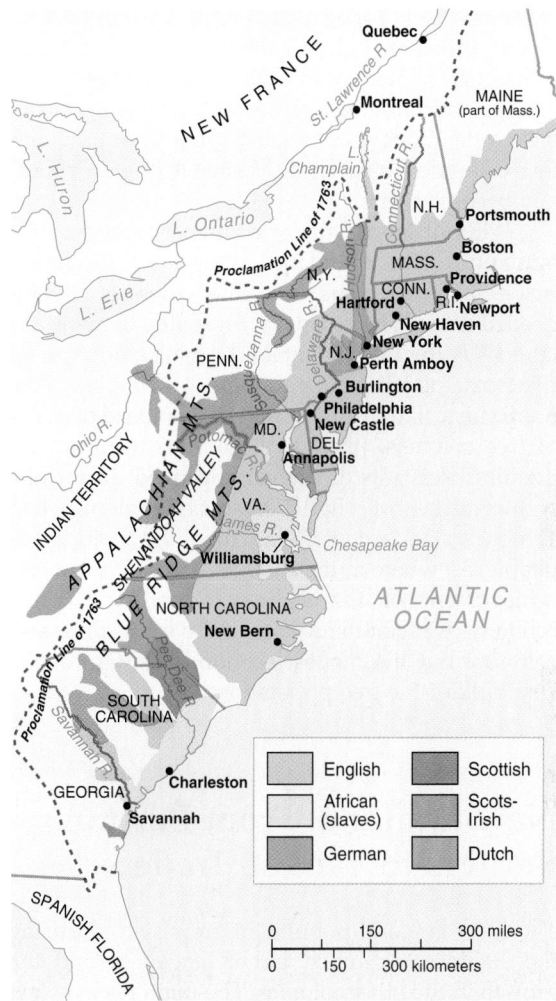

M A P 5.1

Europeans and Africans in the Eighteenth Century
This map illustrates regions where Africans and certain immigrant groups clustered. It is important to avoid misreading the map. Predominantly European regions, for example, also contained colonists from other places. Likewise, regions where African slaves resided in large numbers also included many whites, their masters among them. The map suggests the polyglot diversity of eighteenth-century colonial society.

the Atlantic coast, on the edge of a vast wilderness peopled by native Indians and a few trappers and traders. The almost limitless wilderness gave the colonies an extremely low ratio of people to land. Consequently, land was cheap. Land in the colonies commonly sold for a fraction of its price in the Old World, often for only a shilling an acre, at a time when a carpenter could earn three shillings a day. Along the frontiers of settlement, newcomers who lacked the money to buy land often lived as squatters on unoccupied land, hoping it might eventually become theirs.

Without labor, land was almost worthless for agriculture. The abundance of land in the colonies made labor precious, and the colonists always needed more. The colonists' insatiable demand for labor was the fundamental economic environment that sustained the mushrooming population. Economic historians estimate that the standard of living of free colonists (that is, those who were not indentured servants or slaves) improved during the eighteenth century: By 1770, most free colonists had a higher standard of living than the majority of people elsewhere in the Atlantic world. The unique achievement of the eighteenth-century colonial economy was not the wealth of the most successful colonists but the modest economic welfare of the vast bulk of the free population.

New England: From Puritan Settlers to Yankee Traders

The New England population grew sixfold during the eighteenth century, but it lagged behind the growth in the other colonies. The main reason New England failed to keep pace was that most immigrants chose other destinations because of New England's relatively densely settled land and because Puritan orthodoxy made these colonies comparatively inhospitable. As the population grew, many settlers in search of farmland dispersed from towns, and Puritan communities lost much of their cohesion. Nonetheless, networks of economic exchange laced New Englanders to Atlantic commerce. In many ways, trade became a faith that competed strongly with the traditions of Puritanism.

Natural Increase and Land Distribution

The New England population grew mostly by natural increase, much as it had during the seventeenth century. Nearly every adult woman married. Most married women had children and, thanks to the rel-

atively low mortality rate in New England, often many children. The burgeoning New England population pressed against a limited amount of land. The interior of New England was smaller than that of colonies farther south (see Map 5.1). Moreover, as the northernmost group of colonies, New England had a contested northern and western frontier. Powerful Indian tribes, especially the Iroquois and Mahicans, jealously guarded their territories.

In the seventeenth century, New Englanders practiced partible inheritance (that is, they subdivided land more or less equally among sons). By the eighteenth century, the original land allotments had to be further subdivided to accommodate grandsons and great-grandsons, causing many plots of land to become too small for subsistence. Sons who could not hope to inherit sufficient land to farm had to move away from the town where they were born.

During the eighteenth century, colonial governments in New England abandoned the seventeenth-century policy of granting land to towns. Needing revenue, the governments of both Connecticut and Massachusetts sold land directly to individuals, including speculators. Now money, rather than membership in a community bound by a church covenant, determined whether a person could obtain land. The new land policy eroded the seventeenth-century pattern of settlement. As colonists moved into western Massachusetts and Connecticut and north into present-day New Hampshire and Maine, they tended to settle on individual farms rather than in the towns and villages that characterized the seventeenth century. New Englanders still depended on their relatives and neighbors, but far more than in the seventeenth century, they regulated their behavior in newly settled areas by their own individual dictates.

Farms, Fish, and Trade

A New England farm was a place to get by, not to get rich. New England farmers grew food for their families, but their fields did not produce a huge marketable surplus. Instead of one big crop, farmers grew many small ones. If they had extra, they sold to or traded with neighbors. By 1770, New Englanders had only one-fourth as much wealth as free colonists in the southern colonies.

As consumers, New England farmers made up the foundation of a diversified commercial economy that linked remote farms to markets through-

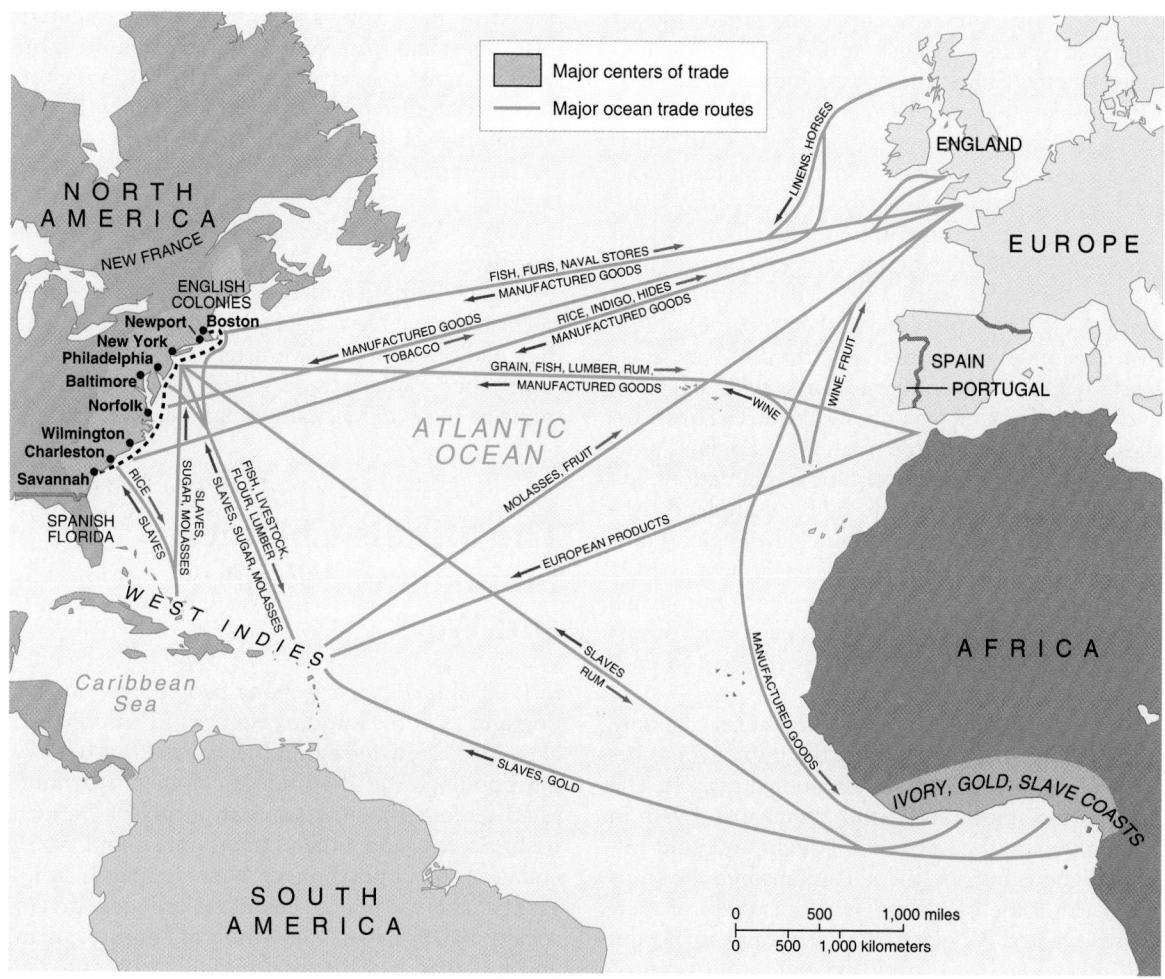

MAP 5.2
Atlantic Trade in the Eighteenth Century
This map illustrates the economic outlook of the colonies in the eighteenth century: that is, east toward the Atlantic world rather than west toward the interior of North America. The long distances involved in the Atlantic trade and the uncertainties of seaborne travel suggest the difficulties Britain experienced governing the colonies and regulating colonial commerce.

READING THE MAP: What were the major markets for trade coming out of Europe? What goods did the English colonies import and export?

CONNECTIONS: In what ways did the flow of raw materials from the colonies affect English industry? How did English colonial trade policies influence the Atlantic trade?

www.bedfordstmartins.com/roarkcompact SEE THE ONLINE STUDY GUIDE for more help in analyzing this map.

out the world. Merchants large and small stocked imported goods—English textiles, ceramics, and metal goods; Chinese tea; West Indian sugar; and Chesapeake tobacco. Farmers' needs for sturdy shoes, a warm coat, a sound cart, and a solid building supported local artisans. In the larger towns and especially in Boston, skilled tradesmen such as cabinetmakers and silversmiths could be found, along with printers like Benjamin Franklin's brother.

As they had since the seventeenth century, many New Englanders made their fortunes at sea. Fish accounted for more than a third of New England's eighteenth-century exports, with livestock and timber making up another third. The West Indies absorbed two-thirds of all New England's exports. Slaves on Caribbean sugar plantations ate dried, salted codfish caught by New England fishermen, filled barrels crafted from New England timber with molasses and refined sugar, and loaded them aboard ships bound ultimately for Europeans with a sweet tooth (see Map 5.2, page 93). Almost all the rest of New England's exports went to England and continental Europe.

Merchants dominated the commercial economy of New England and stood at the hub of trade between local folk and the international market. The largest and most successful merchants lived in Boston, where they not only bought and sold imported goods but also owned and insured the ships that carried the merchandise. The success of merchants created a polarization of wealth in Boston and other seaports during the eighteenth century. By 1770, the richest 5 percent of Bostonians owned about half the city's wealth; the poorest two-thirds of the population owned less than one-tenth.

Although the rich got richer, and everybody else had a smaller share of the total wealth, the incidence of genuine poverty did not change much. A Connecticut traveler wrote from England in 1764, "We in New England know nothing of poverty and want, we have no idea of the thing, how much better do our poor people live than 7/8 of the people on this much famed island."

The contrast with English poverty had meaning, since the overwhelming majority of New Englanders traced their ancestry to England, making the region more homogeneous than any other. The population of African ancestry (almost all slaves) in the region remained small. New Englanders had no hesitation about acquiring slaves, and many Puritan ministers owned one or two. In the Narragansett region of Rhode Island, numerous slaves were im-

ported by the colony's prominent slave traders to raise livestock. But New England's family farms were unsuited for slave labor. Instead, the region's slaves concentrated in towns, especially Boston, where most of them worked as domestic servants and laborers. Although the black population of New England grew to over fifteen thousand by 1770, it barely diluted the region's 97 percent white majority.

By 1770, the population, wealth, and commercial activity of New England differed from what they had been in 1700. Ministers still enjoyed high status, but Yankee traders had replaced Puritan saints as the symbolic New Englanders.

The Middle Colonies: Immigrants, Wheat, and Work

In 1700, almost twice as many people lived in New England as in the middle colonies of Pennsylvania, New York, New Jersey, and Delaware. But by 1770, the population of the middle colonies had multiplied tenfold—mainly from an influx of German, Irish, Scotch, and other immigrants—and nearly equaled the population of New England. Immigrants made the middle colonies a uniquely diverse society. By 1800, barely one-third of Pennsylvanians and less than half the total population of the middle colonies traced their ancestry to England.

German and Scots-Irish Immigrants

Germans made up the largest contingent of migrants from the European continent to the middle colonies. By 1770, about 85,000 Germans had arrived in the colonies. Their fellow colonists often referred to them as "Pennsylvania Dutch," an English corruption of *Deutsch*, the word the immigrants used to describe themselves.

Most German immigrants came from what is now southwestern Germany, although some hailed from German-speaking parts of Switzerland, Austria, and the Netherlands. Throughout Europe, peasants suffered from exploitation by landowners and governments, and they had few opportunities to improve their lives. Many German peasants, one observer noted, were "not as well off as cattle elsewhere." German immigrants included numerous artisans and a few merchants, but the great majority were farmers and laborers. Economically, they represented "middling" folk, neither the poorest (who could not afford the trip) nor the better off (who did not want to leave).

By the 1720s, Germans who had established themselves in the colonies wrote back to their friends and relatives, as one reported, "of the civil and religious liberties [and] privileges, and of all the goodness I have heard and seen." Such letters prompted still more Germans to pull up stakes and embark for America, to exchange the miserable certainties of their lives in Germany for the uncertain attractions of life in the colonies.

Similar motives propelled the Scots-Irish, who considerably outnumbered German immigrants. The term *Scots-Irish* was another misleading label coined in the colonies. Immigrants labeled Scots-Irish actually hailed from the north of Ireland, Scotland, and northern England. Some of the Scots-Irish were Irish natives who had no personal or ancestral connection whatever with Scotland.

Like the Germans, the Scots-Irish were Protestants, but with a difference. Most German immigrants worshiped in Lutheran or German Reformed churches; many others belonged to dissenting sects like the Mennonites, Moravians, and Amish, whose adherents sought relief from persecution they had suffered in Europe for their refusal to bear arms and to swear oaths, practices they shared with Quakers. In contrast, the Scots-Irish tended to be militant Presbyterians who seldom hesitated to bear arms or swear oaths. Like German settlers, however, Scots-Irish immigrants were clannish, residing when they could among relatives or neighbors from the old country.

In the eighteenth century, wave after wave of Scots-Irish immigrants arrived, beginning in 1717, cresting every twelve or fifteen years thereafter and culminating in a flood of immigration in the years just before the American Revolution. Deteriorating economic conditions in northern Ireland, Scotland, and England pushed many toward America. Most of the immigrants were farm laborers or tenant farmers fleeing droughts, crop failures, high food prices, or rising rents.

Both Scots-Irish and Germans probably heard the common saying that "Pennsylvania is heaven for farmers [and] paradise for artisans," but they almost certainly did not fully understand the risks of their decision to leave their native lands. Gottfried Mittelberger, a musician who traveled from Germany to Philadelphia in 1750, described the grueling passage to America commonly experienced by eighteenth-century emigrants. Mittelberger's trip from his home village in the interior to the port of Rotterdam took seven weeks and cost four times more than the trip from Rotterdam to Philadelphia. Nearly two-thirds of all German emigrants arrived at their port of departure with no money to stock up on extra provisions for the trip or even to buy a ticket. Likewise, they could not afford to go back home. Ship captains, aware of the hunger for labor in the colonies, eagerly signed up the penniless emigrants as "redemptioners," a variant of indentured servants. A captain would agree to provide transportation to Philadelphia, where redemptioners would obtain the money to pay for their passage from a friend or relative who was already in the colonies or, as most did, by selling themselves as servants. Impoverished Scots-Irish emigrants, especially the majority who traveled alone rather than with families, typically paid for their passage by contracting to become indentured servants before they sailed.

Unlike indentured servants, redemptioners negotiated independently with their purchasers about their period of servitude. Typically, a healthy adult redemptioner agreed to four years of labor. Indentured servants commonly served five, six, or seven years, as did weaker, younger, and less skilled redemptioners. Children ten years old or younger usually had to become indentured servants until they were twenty-one.

Pennsylvania: "The Best Poor [White] Man's Country"

New settlers, whether free or in servitude, poured into the middle colonies because they perceived unparalleled opportunities, particularly in Pennsylvania, "the best poor Man's Country in the World," as indentured servant William Moraley wrote in 1743. Although Moraley reported that "the Condition of bought Servants is very hard" and masters often failed to live up to their promise to provide decent food and clothing, opportunity abounded because there was more work to be done than workers to do it.

Most servants toiled in Philadelphia, New York City, or one of the smaller towns or villages. From the masters' viewpoint, servants were a bargain. A master could purchase five or six years of a servant's labor for approximately the wages a common laborer would earn in four months. Wage workers could walk away from their jobs when they pleased, and they did so often enough to be troublesome to employers. Servants, however, were legally bound to work for their masters until their terms expired.

A few black slaves worked in shops and homes in Philadelphia and New York City. After Benjamin Franklin became prosperous, he purchased five slaves. Since a slave cost at least three times as much as a servant, only affluent colonists could afford the long-term investment in slave labor. While the population of African ancestry (almost all slaves) in the middle colonies grew to over thirty thousand in 1770, it represented only about 7 percent of the total population, and in most of the region much less. The reason more slaves were not brought to the middle colonies was that farmers, the vast majority of the population, had little use for them. Most farms operated with family labor.

During the eighteenth century, most slaves came to the middle colonies and New England from the West Indies. Enough arrived to prompt colonial assemblies to pass slave codes that punished slaves much more severely than servants for the same transgressions. "For the least trespass," servant Moraley reported, slaves "undergo the severest Punishment." Even the few free African Americans did not escape whites' firm convictions about black inferiority and white supremacy. Whites' racism and blacks' lowly social status made African Americans scapegoats for European Americans' suspicions and anxieties. In 1741, when arson and several unexplained thefts plagued New York City, officials suspected a murderous slave conspiracy. On the basis of little more than evidence of slaves' "insolence" (that is, refusal to conform fully to whites' expectations of servile behavior), city authorities had thirteen slaves burned at the stake and eighteen others hanged.

Immigrants swarmed to the middle colonies because of the availability of land. The Penn family encouraged immigration to bring in potential buyers for their enormous tracts of land in Pennsylvania. From the beginning, Pennsylvania followed a policy of negotiating with Indian tribes to purchase additional land. This policy greatly reduced the violent frontier clashes evident elsewhere in the colonies. Few colonists drifted beyond the northern boundaries of Pennsylvania. The Iroquois dominated the lucrative fur trade of the St. Lawrence valley and eastern Great Lakes, and they had the po-

litical and military strength to defend their territory from colonial encroachment.

Since the cheapest land always lay at the margin of settlement, would-be farmers tended to migrate to promising areas just beyond already improved farms. From Philadelphia, settlers moved north along the Delaware River and west along the Schuylkill and Susquehanna Rivers. By midcentury, settlement had reached the eastern slopes of the Appalachian Mountains, and newcomers spilled down the fertile valley of the Shenandoah River into western Virginia and the Carolinas. Thousands of settlers migrated from the middle colonies through this back door to the South.

Farmers made the middle colonies the breadbasket of North America. They planted a wide variety of crops to feed their families, but they grew wheat in abundance. Flour milling was the number one industry and flour the number one export, constituting nearly three-fourths of all exports from the middle colonies. Pennsylvania flour fed residents in other colonies, in southern Europe, and, above all, in the West Indies.

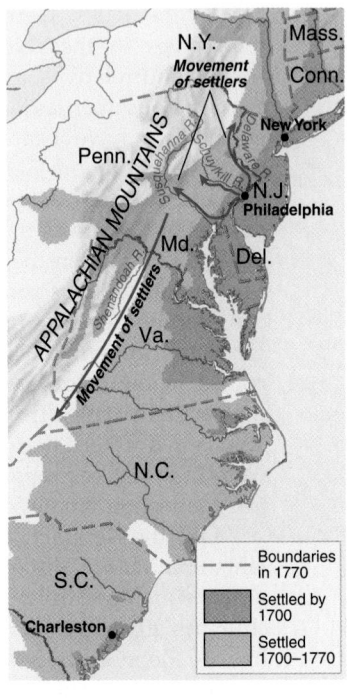

Patterns of Settlement, 1700–1770

The standard of living in rural Pennsylvania was probably higher than in any other agricultural region of the eighteenth-century world. The comparatively widespread prosperity of all the middle colonies permitted residents to indulge in a half-century shopping spree for English imports. The middle colonies' per capita consumption of imported goods from England more than doubled between 1720 and 1770, far outstripping the per capita consumption of English goods in New England and the southern colonies.

At the crossroads of trade in wheat exports and English imports stood Philadelphia. By 1776, Philadelphia had a larger population than any other city in the entire British Empire except London.

BETHLEHEM, PENNSYLVANIA

This view of the small community of Bethlehem, Pennsylvania, in 1757 dramatizes the profound transformation of the natural landscape in the eighteenth century by highly motivated human labor. Founded by Moravian immigrants in 1740, Bethlehem must have appeared at first like the dense woods on the upper left horizon. In fewer than twenty years, precisely laid-out orchards and fields had replaced forests and glades. Carefully penned livestock (lower center right) and fenced fields (lower left) kept the handiwork of farmers separate from the risks and disorders of untamed nature. Not only individual farmsteads (lower center) but impressive multistory brick town buildings (upper center) combined the bounty of the land with the delights of community life. Few eighteenth-century communities were as orderly as Bethlehem, but many effected a comparable transformation of the environment.

Miriam and Ira D. Walsh Division of Art, Prints, and Photographs, The New York Public Library. Astor, Lenox, and Tilden Foundations.

www.bedfordstmartins.com/roarkcompact SEE THE ONLINE STUDY GUIDE for more help in analyzing this image.

Merchants occupied the top stratum of Philadelphia society. In a city where only 2 percent of the residents owned enough property to qualify to vote, merchants built grand homes and dominated local government. Many of Philadelphia's wealthiest merchants were Quakers. Quaker traits of industry, thrift, honesty, and sobriety encouraged the accumulation of wealth.

The ranks of merchants reached downward to aspiring tradesmen like Benjamin Franklin. After he started to publish the *Pennsylvania Gazette* in 1728, Franklin opened a shop, run mostly by his wife, Deborah, that sold a little bit of everything: cheese, codfish, coffee, goose feathers, sealing wax, soap, and now and then a slave. In 1733, Franklin began to publish *Poor Richard's Almanack*, a calendar of weather predictions, astrological alignments, and pithy epigrams. Poor Richard preached the likelihood of long-term rewards for tireless labor. The *Almanack* sold thousands of copies, quickly becoming Franklin's most profitable product.

William Penn's Quaker utopia became a center of worldly affluence whose most famous citizen, Franklin, was neither a Quaker nor a utopian. Quakers remained influential, but Franklin spoke for most colonists with his aphorisms of work, discipline, and thrift that echoed Quaker rules for outward behavior. Franklin's maxims did not look to the Quakers' divine inner light for guidance. They depended instead on the spark of ambition and the glow of gain.

The Southern Colonies: Land of Slavery

Between 1700 and 1770, the population of the southern colonies of Virginia, Maryland, North Carolina, South Carolina, and Georgia grew almost ninefold. By 1770, about twice as many people lived in the South as in either the middle colonies or New England. As elsewhere, natural increase and immigration accounted for this rapid population growth. Many Scots-Irish and German immigrants funneled from the middle colonies into the southern backcountry. Other immigrants were indentured servants (mostly English and Scots-Irish) who followed their seventeenth-century predecessors. But slaves made the most striking contribution to the booming southern colonies, transforming the racial composition of the population and shaping the region's economy, society, and politics.

The Atlantic Slave Trade and the Growth of Slavery

The number of southerners of African ancestry (nearly all of them slaves) rocketed from just over 20,000 in 1700 to well over 400,000 in 1770. The black population increased nearly three times faster than the South's briskly growing white population. Consequently, the proportion of southerners who were black grew from 20 percent in 1700 to 40 percent in 1770. Slavery became the defining characteristic of the southern colonies during the eighteenth century.

Southern colonists clustered into two distinct geographic and agricultural zones. The colonies in the upper South, surrounding the Chesapeake Bay, specialized in growing tobacco, as they had since the early seventeenth century. Throughout the eighteenth century, nine out of ten southern whites and eight out of ten southern blacks lived in the Chesapeake region. The upper South retained a white majority during the eighteenth century.

In the lower South, a much smaller cluster of colonists inhabited the coastal region and specialized in the production of rice and indigo (a plant used to make blue dye). Lower South colonists made up only 5 percent of the total population of the southern colonies in 1700 but inched upward to 15 percent by 1770. South Carolina was the sole British colony along the South Atlantic coast until 1732, when Georgia was founded. (North Carolina, founded in 1711, was largely an extension of the Chesapeake region.) In contrast to every other British mainland colony, blacks in South Carolina outnumbered whites almost two to one; in some low country districts, the ratio of blacks to whites exceeded ten to one.

The enormous growth in the South's slave population occurred through natural increase and the flourishing Atlantic slave trade (see Map 5.3 and Table 5.1). Slave ships brought almost 300,000 Africans to British North America between 1619 and 1780. Of those Africans, 95 percent arrived in the South and 96 percent arrived during the eighteenth century. Unlike indentured servants or redemptioners, the Africans did not choose to come to the colonies. Most of them had been born into free families in villages located within a few hundred miles of the West African coast. Although they shared African origins, they came from many different African cultures, including Akan, Angolan, Asante, Bambara, Gambian, Igbo, Mandinga, and others. They spoke different languages, worshiped different deities, followed different rules of kinship, grew different crops, and recognized different rulers. The most important experience they had in common was enslavement. Captured in war, kidnapped, or sold into slavery by other Africans, they were brought to the coast, sold to African traders who assembled slaves for sale, and sold again to European or colonial slave traders or ship captains who bought them for shipment to the New World. Packed aboard a slave ship with two to three hundred or more other slaves, they were subjected to the infamous Middle Passage—the crossing of the Atlantic in the hold of a slave ship—and then sold yet again by the ship captain to a colonial slave merchant or to a southern planter.

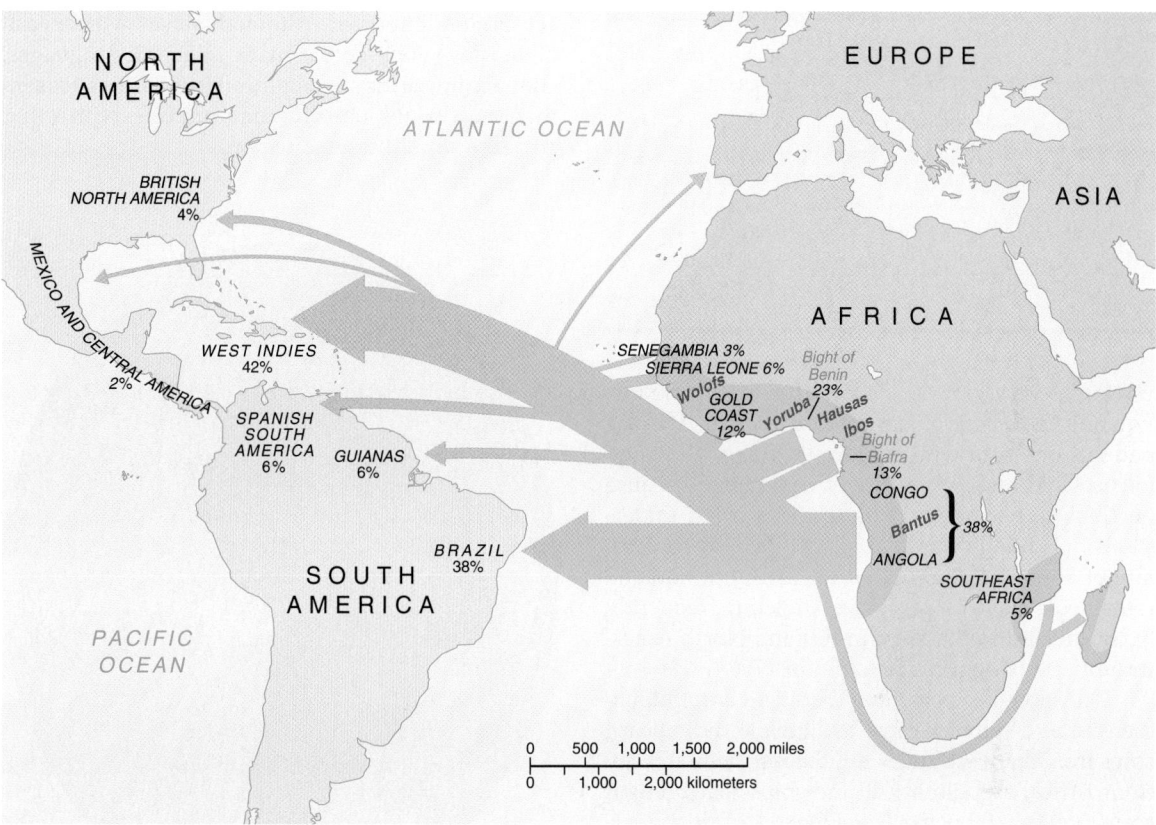

MAP 5.3

The Atlantic Slave Trade

Although the Atlantic slave trade endured from about 1450 to 1870, its heyday occurred during the eighteenth century, when more than six million African slaves were imported to the New World. Only a small fraction of the African slaves imported to the Western Hemisphere were taken to British North America; most went to sugar plantations in Brazil and the Caribbean. Why were so many more African slaves sent to the West Indies and Brazil than to British North America?

The voices of Africans who were swept up in the slave trade have been enveloped by a deafening historical silence, with one major exception. In 1789, Olaudah Equiano published *The Interesting Narrative*, an account of his own enslavement that hints at the stories that might have been told by the thousands of silenced Africans. Equiano was born in 1745 in the interior of what is now Nigeria. "I had never heard of white men or Europeans, nor of the sea," he recalled. One day when Equiano was eleven years old, two men and a woman, all Africans, broke into his home, seized him and his sister, and carried them off. The kidnappers soon separated Equiano from his sister, leaving him "in a state of distraction not to be described."

During the next six or seven months, Equiano was sold to several different African masters, each of whom moved him closer to the coast. When he arrived at the coast, a slave ship waited offshore. Equiano feared that he had "gotten into a world of bad spirits," that he was going to be killed and "eaten by those white men with horrible looks, red faces, and loose hair." Once the ship set sail, many slaves died from sickness, crowded together in suffocating heat fouled by filth of all descriptions. "The shrieks of the women and the groans of the dying rendered the whole a scene of horror almost inconceivable," Equiano recalled. Most of the slaves on the ship were sold in Barbados, but Equiano and other leftovers were shipped off to Virginia, where

TABLE 5.1
SLAVE IMPORTS, 1451–1870

Estimated Slave Imports to the
Western Hemisphere

1451–1600	275,000
1601–1700	1,341,000
1701–1810	6,100,000
1811–1870	1,900,000

slaves they imported. Although slaves within each of these regions spoke many different languages, enough linguistic and cultural similarities existed that they could usually communicate with other Africans from the same region.

Equiano "saw few or none of our native Africans and not one soul who could talk to me." Equiano felt isolated and "exceedingly miserable" because he "had no person to speak to that I could understand." He finally was sold to a white man, the captain of a tobacco ship bound for England. Equiano remained a slave for ten years, traveling frequently from England to the West Indies and North America until he bought his freedom in 1766.

Only about 15 percent of the slaves brought into the southern colonies came as Equiano did, aboard ships from the West Indies. All the rest came directly from Africa, and almost all the ships that brought them (roughly 90 percent) belonged to British merchants. Most slaves on board were young adults, men usually outnumbering women two to one. Children under the age of fourteen, like Equiano, were typically no more than 10 or 15 percent of a cargo. Mortality during the Middle Passage varied considerably from ship to ship. On average, about 15 percent of the slaves died, but sometimes half or more perished. The average mortality among the white crew of slave ships was often nearly as bad. In general, the longer the voyage, the larger the number of deaths.

Normally an individual planter purchased at any one time a relatively small number of newly arrived Africans, or "new Negroes," as they were called. Planters preferred to purchase small groups of slaves to permit the newcomers to be trained by the planters' other slaves. Planters' preferences for slaves from specific regions of Africa aided slaves' acculturation (or "seasoning," as it was called) to the routines of bondage in the southern colonies. Chesapeake planters preferred slaves from Senegambia, the Gold Coast, or—like Equiano—the Bight of Biafra, the origin of 40 percent of all Africans imported to the Chesapeake. South Carolina planters favored slaves from the central African Congo and Angola regions, the origin of about 40 percent of the African

OLAUDAH EQUIANO
This portrait of Olaudah Equiano was painted by an unknown English artist about 1780, when Equiano was in his mid-thirties, more than a decade after he had bought his freedom. The portrait evokes Equiano's successful acculturation to the customs of eighteenth-century England. His clothing and hairstyle reflect the fashions of respectable young Englishmen. In The Interesting Narrative, *Equiano explained that he had learned to speak and understand English while he was a slave. He wrote that he "looked upon [the English] . . . as men superior to us [Africans], and therefore I had the stronger desire to resemble them, to imbibe their spirit and imitate their manners; I therefore embraced every occasion of improvement, and every new thing that I observed I treasured up in my memory." Equiano's embrace of English culture did not cause him to forsake his African roots. He honored his dual identity by campaigning against slavery. His* **Narrative** *was one of the most important and powerful antislavery documents of the time.*
Olaudah Equiano: Royal Albert Memorial Museum, Exeter, Devon, UK/Bridgeman Art Library.

Negro's houses

a fire

Boys playing under that Rooff

a Woman with her Child on her back

y door

THE AFRICAN SLAVE TRADE

The African slave trade supplied the New World's demand for labor and Europe's voracious appetite for such New World products as sugar, tobacco, and rice with millions of enslaved Africans to work for their New World purchasers. African men, women, and children, like those pictured in this early-eighteenth-century engraving of a family residence in Sierra Leone, were kidnapped or captured in wars—typically by other Africans—and enslaved. Uprooted from their homes and kin, they were usually taken to coastal enclaves where African traders and European ship captains negotiated prices, made deals, and often branded the newly enslaved people. The significance of this diabolical collaboration between Europeans and their African trading partners is illustrated by the seventeenth-century Benin bronze box, which depicts a royal palace in Nigeria, whose slave trading and other activities are guarded by massive birds and two Portuguese soldiers. Jammed into the holds of slave ships, enslaved Africans made the dreaded Middle Passage to the New World. The model of a slave ship shown here was used in parliamentary debates by antislavery leaders in Britain to demonstrate the inhumanity of shipping people as if they were just so much tightly packed cargo. The model does not show another typical feature of slave ships: weapons. Slaves vastly outnumbered the crews aboard the ships, and crew members justifiably feared slave uprisings.

Museum für Volkerkunde, Berlin/Courtesy, Earl Gregg Swen Library, College of William and Mary, Williamsburg, Virginia/ Wilberforce House Museum, Hull City Museum, Art Gallery, and Archives, UK/Bridgeman Art Library.

Seasoning acclimated new Africans to the physical as well as the cultural environment of the southern colonies. Slaves who had just endured the Middle Passage were poorly nourished, weak, and sick. In this vulnerable state they encountered the alien diseases of North America without having developed a biological arsenal of acquired immunities. As many as 10 or 15 percent of newly arrived Africans, sometimes more, died during their first year in the southern colonies.

While newly enslaved Africans poured into the southern colonies, slave women made an even greater contribution to the growth of the black population by giving birth to slave babies, which caused the slave population to mushroom. Slave owners encouraged these births. Thomas Jefferson explained, "I consider the labor of a breeding [slave] woman as no object, that a [slave] child raised every 2 years is of more profit than the crop of the best laboring [slave] man." The high rate of natural increase in the southern colonies meant that by the 1740s the majority of southern slaves were native-born.

Slave Labor and African American Culture

Southern planters expected slaves to work from sunup to sundown and beyond. The conflict between the masters' desire for maximum labor and the slaves' reluctance to do more than necessary made the threat of physical punishment a constant for eighteenth-century slaves. Masters preferred black slaves over white indentured servants not just because slaves served for life, but also because colonial laws did not limit the force masters could use against slaves. As a traveler observed in 1740, "A new negro . . . will require more discipline than a young spaniel. . . . let a hundred men show him how to hoe, or drive a wheelbarrow; he'll still take the one by the bottom and the other by the wheel and . . . often die before [he] can be conquered." Slaves, the traveler noted, were not stupid or simply obstinate; despite the inevitable punishment, they resisted their masters' demands because of their "greatness of soul," their stubborn unwillingness to conform to their masters' definition of them as merely slaves.

Some slaves escalated their acts of resistance to direct physical confrontation with the master, mistress, or an overseer. But a hoe raised in anger, a punch in the face, or a desperate swipe with a knife led to swift and predictable retaliation by whites. Throughout the southern colonies, the balance of physical power rested securely in the hands of whites.

Rebellion occurred, however, at Stono, South Carolina, in 1739. Before dawn on a September Sunday, a group of about twenty slaves attacked a country store, killed the two storekeepers, confiscated the store's guns, ammunition, and powder, and set out toward Spanish Florida. Enticing other rebel slaves to join the march south, the group plundered and burned more than a half dozen plantations and killed more than twenty white men, women, and children. A mounted force of whites suppressed the rebellion. The Stono rebellion illustrated that eighteenth-century slaves had no chance of overturning slavery and very little chance of defending themselves in any bold strike for freedom. No other similar uprising occurred during the colonial period.

Slaves maneuvered constantly to protect themselves and to gain a measure of autonomy within the boundaries of slavery. In Chesapeake tobacco fields, most slaves were subject to close supervision by whites. In the lower South, the task system gave slaves some control over the pace of their work and some discretion in the use of the rest of their time. A task was typically defined as a certain area of ground to be planted, cultivated, and harvested or a specific job to be completed. A slave who completed the assigned task could use the remainder of the day to work in a garden, fish, hunt, spin, weave, sew, or cook.

Eighteenth-century slaves also planted the roots of African American lineages that branch out to the present. Historians are only beginning to explore the kin networks slaves built; much remains unknown. But it is clear that slaves valued family ties and that, as in West African societies, kinship structured slaves' relations with one another. Slave parents often gave a child the name of a grandparent, aunt, or uncle. In West Africa, kinship not only identified a person's place among living relatives; it also linked the person to ancestors among the dead and to descendants in the future. Newly imported African slaves usually arrived alone, like Equiano, without kin. Often slaves who had traversed the Middle Passage on the same ship adopted one another as "brothers" and "sisters." Likewise, as new Negroes were seasoned and incorporated into existing slave communities, established families often adopted them as "fictive" kin.

When possible, slaves expressed many other features of their West African origins in their lives on New World plantations. They gave their children African names such as Cudjo or Quash, Minda or Fuladi. They grew food crops familiar to them in Africa such as yams and okra. They constructed huts with mud walls and thatched roofs similar to African residences. They fashioned banjos, drums, and other musical instruments, held dances, and observed funeral rites that echoed African practices. In these and many other ways, slaves drew upon their African heritages to endow their personal lives with relationships and meanings that they controlled, as much as the oppressive circumstances of slavery permitted.

Tobacco, Rice, and Prosperity

Slaves' labor bestowed prosperity on their masters, British merchants, and the monarchy. The southern colonies supplied 90 percent of all North American exports to England. Rice exports from the lower South exploded from less than half a million pounds in 1700 to eighty million pounds in 1770, virtually all of it grown by slaves. Exports of indigo also boomed. Together, rice and indigo made up three-fourths of lower South exports, nearly two-thirds of them going to England and most of the rest to the West Indies, where sugar-growing slaves ate slave-grown rice. Tobacco was by far the most important export from British North America; by 1770, it represented almost one-third of all colonial exports and three-fourths of all Chesapeake exports. And under the provisions of the Navigation Acts (see chapter 4), nearly all of it went to England, where the monarchy collected a lucrative tax on each pound. British merchants then reexported more than 80 percent of the tobacco to the European continent, pocketing a nice markup for their troubles.

These products of slave labor made the southern colonies by far the richest in North America. The per capita wealth of free whites in the South was four times greater than that in New England and three times that in the middle colonies. At the top of the wealth pyramid stood the rice grandees of the lower South and the tobacco gentry of the Chesapeake. These elite families commonly resided on large estates adorned by handsome mansions and luxurious gardens, maintained and supported by slaves.

The vast differences in wealth among white southerners engendered envy and occasional ten-

PLANTATION MISTRESS
Enslaved Africans made possible the opulence of Mrs. Barnard Elliott, the wife of a wealthy South Carolina rice planter. Mrs. Elliott appears to be a discriminating consumer. Although she probably made most of her purchases in the best Charleston shops, her custom-made fashions would not have been out of place in the drawing rooms of the English gentry. Sensuous textiles, billowing lace-encrusted sleeves, a daring neckline, and dazzling jewels demonstrate Mrs. Elliott's cosmopolitan tastes despite her colonial residence. Her formal, almost regal pose evokes the enormous distance between the luxurious refinements of elite planters and workaday plantation realities. Contrast the appearance of Mrs. Elliott with that of her approximate contemporary, the New England household slave Phyllis (page 88).
The Gibbes Museum of Art, Carolina Art Association.

sion between rich and poor, but remarkably little open hostility. In private, the planter elite spoke disparagingly of humble whites, but in public they acknowledged their lesser neighbors as equals, at least in belonging to the superior—in their minds—white race. Looking upward, white yeomen and tenants (who owned neither land nor slaves) sensed the gentry's condescension and veiled contempt.

But they also appreciated the gentry for granting favors, upholding white supremacy, and keeping slaves in their place. While racial slavery made a few whites much richer than others, it also gave those who did not get rich a powerful reason to feel similar (in race) to those who were so different (in wealth).

The slaveholding gentry dominated the politics and economy of the southern colonies. In Virginia, only adult white men who owned at least one hundred acres of unimproved land or twenty-five acres of land with a house could vote. This property-holding requirement prevented about 40 percent of white men in Virginia from voting for representatives to the House of Burgesses. In South Carolina, only fifty acres of land were required to vote, and most adult white men qualified. But in both colonies, voters elected members of the gentry to serve in the colonial legislature. The gentry passed elected political offices from generation to generation, almost as if they were hereditary. Politically, the gentry built a self-perpetuating oligarchy—rule by the elite few—with the votes of their many humble neighbors.

The gentry also set the cultural standard in the southern colonies. They entertained lavishly, gambled regularly, and attended Anglican church services more for social than religious reasons. Above all they cultivated a life of leisurely pursuit of happiness. They did not condone idleness, however. Their many pleasures and responsibilities as plantation owners kept them busy. Thomas Jefferson, a phenomenally productive member of the gentry, recalled that his earliest childhood memory was of being carried on a pillow by a family slave—a powerful image of the slave hands beneath the gentry's leisure and achievement.

Unifying Experiences

While the societies of New England, the middle colonies, and the southern colonies became more sharply differentiated during the eighteenth century, colonists throughout British North America shared certain unifying experiences. The first was economic: The economies of all three regions had their roots in agriculture. But the tempo of commerce quickened during the eighteenth century. Colonists sold their distinctive products in markets that, in turn, offered to consumers throughout the colonies a more or less uniform array of goods. A second unifying experience was a decline in the importance of religion. Although some settlers called for a revival of religious intensity, for most people throughout the colonies religion mattered less, the affairs of the world more, than they did in the seventeenth century. Third, white inhabitants throughout North America became aware that they shared a distinctive identity as British colonists. Thirteen different governments presided over the North American colonies, but all of them answered to the British monarchy. Royal officials who expected loyalty from the colonists often had difficulty obtaining obedience. The North American colonists asserted their prerogatives as British subjects to defend their special colonial interests.

Commerce and Consumption

Eighteenth-century commerce whetted the appetite to consume. Colonial products spurred the development of mass markets throughout the Atlantic world (Figure 5.1). Huge increases in the supply of colonial tobacco and sugar brought the price of these small luxuries within reach of most free whites. Colonial goods brought into focus an important lesson of eighteenth-century commerce. Ordinary people, not just the wealthy elite, would buy the things that they desired in addition to what they absolutely needed. Even news, formerly restricted mostly to a few people through face-to-face conversations or private letters, became an object of public consumption through the innovation of newspapers. (See "The Promise of Technology," page 106.) With the appropriate stimulus, market demand seemed unlimited.

The Atlantic commerce that took colonial goods to markets in England brought objects of consumer desire back to the colonies. English merchants and manufacturers recognized that colonists made excellent customers, and the Navigation Acts gave English exporters privileged access to the colonial market. English exports to North America multiplied eightfold between 1700 and 1770, outpacing the rate of population growth after midcentury. When the colonists' eagerness to consume exceeded their ability to pay, English exporters willingly extended credit, and colonial debts soared.

Imported mirrors, silver plate, spices, bed and table linens, clocks, tea services, wigs, books, and more infiltrated parlors, kitchens, and bedrooms throughout the colonies. Despite the many

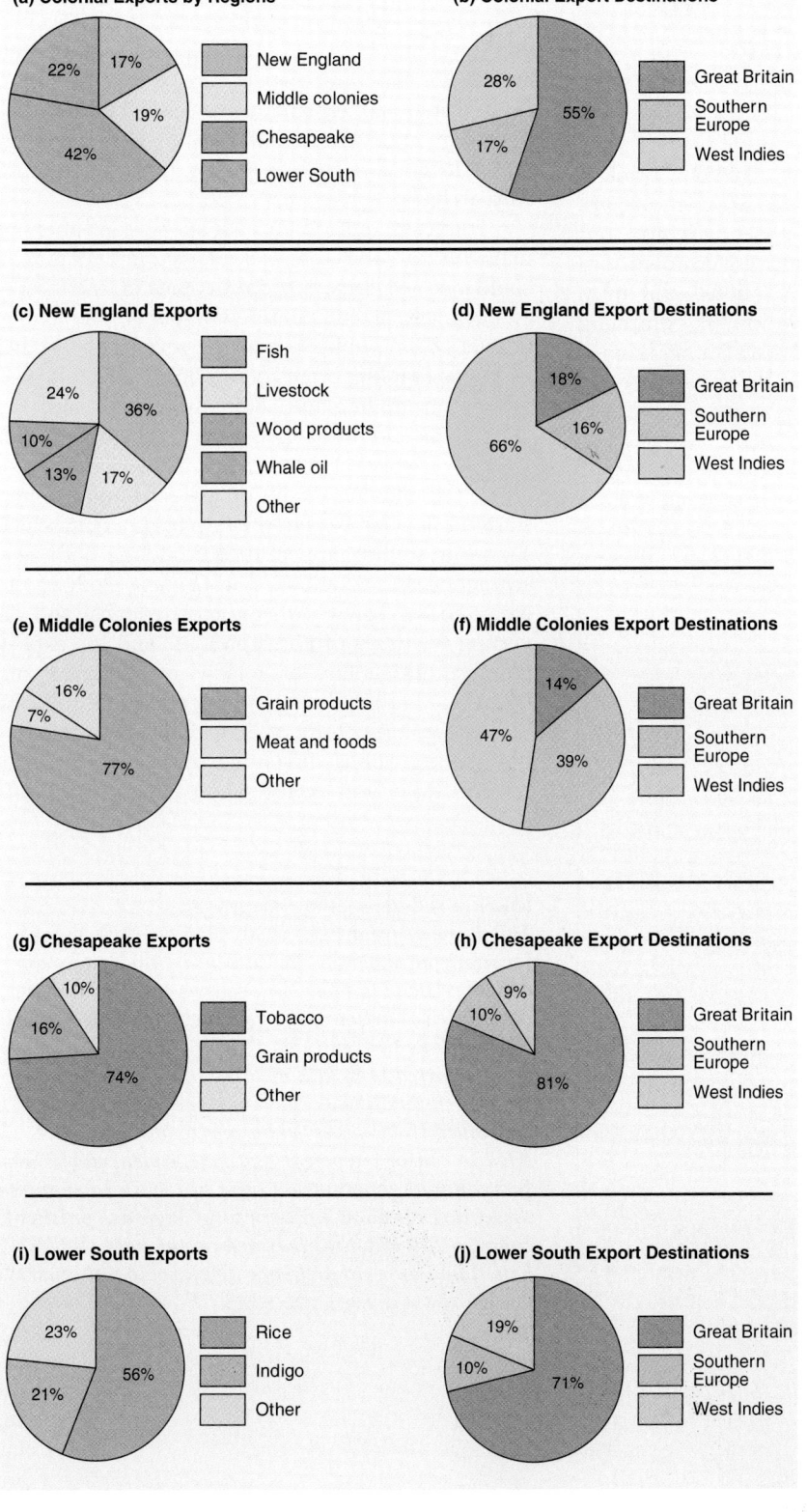

(a) Colonial Exports by Regions

17%
19%
42%
22%

New England
Middle colonies
Chesapeake
Lower South

(b) Colonial Export Destinations

28%
55%
17%

Great Britain
Southern Europe
West Indies

(c) New England Exports

24%
36%
10%
13%
17%

Fish
Livestock
Wood products
Whale oil
Other

(d) New England Export Destinations

18%
16%
66%

Great Britain
Southern Europe
West Indies

(e) Middle Colonies Exports

16%
7%
77%

Grain products
Meat and foods
Other

(f) Middle Colonies Export Destinations

14%
39%
47%

Great Britain
Southern Europe
West Indies

(g) Chesapeake Exports

10%
16%
74%

Tobacco
Grain products
Other

(h) Chesapeake Export Destinations

9%
10%
81%

Great Britain
Southern Europe
West Indies

(i) Lower South Exports

23%
56%
21%

Rice
Indigo
Other

(j) Lower South Export Destinations

19%
10%
71%

Great Britain
Southern Europe
West Indies

FIGURE 5.1

Colonial Exports, 1768–1772

These pie charts provide an overview of the colonial export economy in the 1760s. The first two show that almost two-thirds of colonial exports came from the South and that the majority of the colonies' exports went to Great Britain. The remaining charts illustrate the distinctive patterns of exports in each colonial region. Fish, livestock, and wood products were New England's most important exports; they were sent primarily to the West Indies, only a small fraction going to Great Britain. From the colonial breadbasket in the middle colonies, grain products made up three-fourths of all exports, most of which went to the West Indies or to southern Europe. The Chesapeake also exported some grain, but tobacco accounted for three-fourths of the region's export trade, nearly all of it bound for Great Britain as mandated by the Navigation Acts. Rice and indigo comprised three-fourths of the exports from the lower South, the bulk of which was sent to Great Britain. Taken together, these charts reveal Britain's economic interest in the exports of the North American colonies.

The Printing Press: "The Spring of Knowledge"

IN THE EIGHTEENTH CENTURY, colonial printers began to publish newspapers. Since the 1630s, colonial printers had used presses to churn out books, pamphlets, broadsides, government announcements, legal forms, invitations, and even promissory notes. The innovation of compiling newsworthy information and publishing it on a regular schedule began in 1704 with the appearance of the *Boston News-Letter*, which was usually printed on both sides of a single sheet of paper smaller than conventional typing paper. Each week the *News-Letter* contained reprints of articles that had appeared in English newspapers, along with a few tidbits of local news such as deaths, fires, storms, and ship arrivals.

For years, the audience for such information remained small; the editor complained in 1719 that he could not sell three hundred copies of each issue. Nonetheless, a competing newspaper, the *Boston Gazette*, began publication in that year. It was printed by James Franklin on his press (right), which he had brought from England. Both the *Gazette* and the *News-Letter* submitted their copy to the governor for official approval before the newspapers were printed. Frustrated by this official scrutiny, Franklin started a new paper, the *New England Courant*, which set out to thumb its nose at officialdom, both governmental and religious. The *Courant* pledged "to entertain the Town with the most comical and diverting Incidents of Humane Life" and to "expose the Vice and Follies of Persons of all Ranks and Degrees." Franklin's press—operated faithfully by his apprentice brother, Benjamin—broadcast to the reading public dissenting opinions previously confined to private conversations.

JOHN PETER ZENGER'S NEWSPAPER
This issue of John Peter Zenger's New-York Weekly Journal *contained on the third of its four pages an article criticizing New York's governor. For this and other critical articles, the governor had Zenger tried for seditious libel in 1735. The jury sided with Zenger and acquitted him, although the law favored the governor. Printers like Zenger throughout the colonies continued to be harassed by public officials who tried to censor irreverent and independent publishers. But colonial governments were too weak to suppress dissenting opinions for very long. Vigorous political commentary like that featured on the page shown here found an avid audience among colonial readers.*
Courtesy, American Antiquarian Society.

By 1740, more than a dozen newspapers were published in the colonies and their numbers continued to increase. The relatively high rates of literacy gave them a large reading audience. In the northern colonies, readers included well over half of adult men and nearly half of adult women. In the southern colonies, literacy rates among whites were slightly lower, but still considerably above those in Europe. Since whites tried to prevent slaves from learning to read, literacy rates remained low among southern blacks.

But the information printed by newspapers spread far beyond readers. Newspapers were often read aloud not just at home but in workshops, taverns, and courthouses. In these public places, people who could not read listened to the controversial ideas, partisan accusations, and salacious rumors that printers relished. An eighteenth-century poem illustrates the many connections between news and audiences cultivated by colonial newspapers:

JAMES FRANKLIN'S PRINTING PRESS
Newport Historical Society.

News'papers are the spring of knowledge,
The gen'ral source throughout the nation.
Of ev'ry modern conversation.
What would this mighty people do,
If there, alas! were nothing new?

A New-paper is like a feast,
Some dish there is for ev'ry guest;
Some large, some small, some strong, some tender,
For ev'ry stomach, stout or slender;
Those who roast beef and ale delight in,
Are pleas'd with trumpets, drums, and fighting;
For those who are more puny made,
Are arts and sciences, and trade;
For fanciful and am'rous blood,
We have a soft poetic food;
For witty and satyric folks,
High-season'd, acid, BITTER JOKES;
And when we strive to please the mob,
A jest, a quarrel, or a job.

If any gentleman wants a wife,
(A partner, as 'tis termed, for life)
An advertisement does the thing,
And quickly brings the pretty thing.

If you want health, consult our pages,
You shall be well, and live for ages. . . .

Our services you can't express,
The good we do you hardly guess;
There's not a want of human kind,
But we a remedy can find.

When newspapers employed the technology of printing to publish everything from political news to advertisements for a spouse, all kinds of information and ideas began to diffuse more readily beyond official channels and to help form public opinion. Eighteenth-century newspapers combined the old technology of printing with the new currents of commerce, dissent, and enlightenment, creating a novel awareness of the problems and possibilities of public life.

differences among the colonists, the consumption of English exports built a certain material uniformity across region, religion, class, and status, and even made the colonists look and feel more British. The rising tide of colonial consumption had other less visible but no less important consequences. Consumption presented women and men with a novel array of choices. In many respects the choices might appear trivial: whether to buy knives and forks, teacups, or a clock. But such small choices confronted eighteenth-century consumers with a big question: "What do you want?" As colonial consumers defined and expressed their desires with greater frequency during the eighteenth century, they became accustomed to thinking of themselves as individuals who had the power to make decisions that influenced the quality of their lives—attitudes of significance in the hierarchical world of eighteenth-century British North America.

Religion, Enlightenment, and Revival

Eighteenth-century colonists could choose from almost as many religions as consumer goods. Virtually all of the bewildering variety of religious denominations represented some form of Christianity, almost all of them Protestant. Slaves made up the largest group of non-Christians. A few slaves converted to Christianity in Africa or after they arrived in North America, but most continued to embrace elements of indigenous African religions. Roman Catholics concentrated in Maryland as they had since the seventeenth century, but even there they were outnumbered by Protestants.

The varieties of Protestant faith and practice ranged across an extremely broad spectrum. The thousands of immigrants in the middle colonies and the southern backcountry included militant Baptists and Presbyterians. Huguenots who had fled persecution in Catholic France peopled congregations in several cities. In New England, old-style Puritanism splintered into strands of Congregationalism that differed over fine points of theological doctrine. The Congregational Church was the official established church in New England, and all residents paid taxes for its support. Throughout the plantation South, and in urban centers like Charleston, New York, and Philadelphia, prominent colonists belonged to the Anglican Church. The Anglican Church in the South, like the Congregational Church in New

England, received support in the form of tax monies. But in both regions, dissenting faiths grew, and in most colonies adherents of other faiths won the right to worship publicly, although the established churches retained official sanction.

Many educated colonists became deists, looking for God's plan in nature more than in the Bible. Deists shared the ideas of eighteenth-century European Enlightenment thinkers. Representing a multifaceted intellectual movement that challenged many conventional ideas, Enlightenment thinkers tended to agree that science and reason could disclose God's laws in the natural order. In the colonies as well as in Europe, Enlightenment ideas encouraged people to study the world around them, to think for themselves, and to ask whether the disorderly appearance of things masked the principles of a deeper, more profound natural order. From New England towns to southern drawing rooms, individuals met to discuss such matters. Among the purposes of these discussions was to find ways to improve society. Franklin's interest in electricity, stoves, and eyeglasses exemplified the shift of focus among many eighteenth-century colonists from heaven to the here and now.

Most eighteenth-century colonists went to church seldom or not at all, although they probably considered themselves Christians. A minister in Charleston observed that on the Sabbath "the Taverns have more Visitants than the Churches." In the leading colonial cities, church members were a small minority of eligible adults, no more than 10 to 15 percent. Anglican parishes in the South rarely claimed more than one-fifth of eligible adults as members. In some regions of rural New England and the middle colonies, church membership embraced two-thirds of eligible adults, while in other areas only one-quarter of the residents belonged to a church. The dominant faith overall was religious indifference.

The spread of religious indifference, of deism, of denominational rivalry, and of comfortable backsliding profoundly concerned many Christians. To combat what one preacher called the "dead formality" of church services, some ministers set out to convert nonbelievers and to revive the piety of the faithful with a new style of preaching that appealed more to the heart than to the head. Historians have termed this wave of revivals the "Great Awakening." In Massachusetts during the mid-1730s, the fiery Puritan minister Jonathan Edwards

GEORGE WHITEFIELD
An anonymous artist portrayed George Whitefield preaching, emphasizing the power of his sermons to transport his audience to a revived awareness of divine spirituality. Light from above gleams off Whitefield's forehead. His crossed eyes and faraway gaze suggest that he spoke in a semihypnotic trance. Note the absence of a Bible at the pulpit. Rather than elaborating on God's word as revealed in Scripture, Whitefield speaks from his own inner awareness. The young woman bathed in light below his hands appears transfixed, her focus not on Whitefield but on some inner realm illuminated by his words. Her eyes and Whitefield's do not meet, yet the artist's use of light suggests that she and Whitefield see the same core of holy Truth. The other people in Whitefield's audience appear not to have achieved this state. They remain intent on Whitefield's words, failing so far to be ignited by the divine spark.
National Portrait Gallery, London.

reaped a harvest of souls by reemphasizing traditional Puritan doctrines of humanity's utter depravity and God's vengeful omnipotence.

The most famous revivalist in the eighteenth-century Atlantic world was George Whitefield. An Anglican, Whitefield preached well-worn messages of sin and salvation to large audiences in England using his spellbinding, unforgettable voice. Whitefield visited the North American colonies seven times, staying for more than three years during the mid-1740s and attracting tens of thousands, including Benjamin Franklin, to his sermons. His preach-

ing transported many in his audience to emotion-choked states of religious ecstasy. About one revival, he wrote, "Some of the people were as pale as death; others were wringing their hands; others lying on the ground; others sinking into the arms of their friends; and most lifting their eyes to heaven, and crying to God for mercy."

Whitefield's successful revivals spawned many lesser imitations. Itinerant preachers, many of them poorly educated, toured the colonial backcountry after midcentury, echoing Whitefield's medium and message as best they could. Educated and established ministers often regarded them with disgust. Bathsheba Kingsley, a member of Jonathan Edwards's flock, preached the revival message informally—as did an unprecedented number of other awakened women throughout the colonies—causing her congregation to brand her a "brawling woman" who had "gone quite *out* of her place." But the revivals nonetheless awakened and refreshed the spiritual energies of thousands of colonists struggling with the uncertainties and anxieties of eighteenth-century America. The conversions at revivals did not substantially boost the total number of church members, however. After the revivalists moved on, the routines and pressures of everyday existence reasserted their primacy in the lives of many converts. But revivals imparted an important message to colonists, both converted and unconverted. They communicated that every soul mattered, that men and women could choose to be saved, that individuals had the power to make a decision for everlasting life or death. Colonial revivals expressed in religious terms many of the same democratic and egalitarian values expressed in economic terms by colonists' patterns of consumption. One colonist noted the analogy by referring to itinerant revivalists as "Pedlars in divinity." Like consumption, revivals contributed to a set of common experiences that bridged colonial divides of faith, region, class, and status.

Bonds of Empire

The plurality of peoples, faiths, and communities that characterized the North American colonies arose from the somewhat haphazard policies of the eighteenth-century British Empire. Since the Puritan Revolution of the mid-seventeenth century, British monarchs had valued the colonies' contributions to trade and encouraged their growth and development. Unlike France—whose policy of excluding Protestants and foreigners kept the population of its territory tiny—Britain kept the door to its colonies open to anyone, and tens of thousands of non-British immigrants settled in the North American colonies and raised families. The open door did not extend to trade, however, as the seventeenth-century Navigation Acts restricted colonial trade to British ships and traders. These policies evolved because they served the interests of the monarchy and of influential groups in England and the colonies, but they

gave the colonists a common framework of political expectations and experiences.

At a minimum, British power defended the colonists from foreign enemies. Each colony organized a militia, and privateers sailed from every port to prey on foreign ships. But the British navy and army bore responsibility for colonial defense. Royal officials warily eyed the settlements of New France and New Spain for signs of threats to the colonies. Alone, neither New France nor Spanish Florida jeopardized British North America, but with Indian allies they became a potent force that kept colonists on their guard.

All along the ragged edge of settlement, colonists encountered Indians. Indians' impulse to defend their territory from colonial incursions warred with their desire for trade, which tugged them toward the settlers. The fur trade was the principal medium of exchange between the two groups.

HURON BONNET
This dazzling bonnet illustrates the trade between Native Americans and colonists. Beads of Venetian glass were one of the many items colonists imported from Europe to exchange for animal skins offered by Indian hunters and trappers. Native American women in turn incorporated these European beads into designs they had previously wrought with porcupine quills, shells, and bones. European needle and thread were also used to craft this bonnet. Native American artistry transformed these simple trade goods into a beautiful bonnet useful and valuable among the Huron, who lived near the Great Lakes.
Musée de l'Homme.

To trade for goods manufactured largely by the British, Indians trapped animals throughout the interior, and colonial traders competed for the furs. British officials monitored the trade to prevent French, Spanish, and Dutch competitors from deflecting the flow of hides toward their own markets. Indians took advantage of this competition to improve their own prospects, playing one trader off against another. And Indian tribes and confederacies competed for favored trading rights with one colony or another, a competition colonists encouraged.

The shifting alliances and complex dynamics of the fur trade struck a fragile balance along the frontier. The threat of violence from all sides was ever present, and the threat became reality often enough for all parties to be prepared for the worst. In the Yamasee War of 1715, Yamasee and Creek Indians— with French encouragement—mounted a coordinated attack against colonial settlements in South Carolina and inflicted heavy casualties. The Cherokees, traditional enemies of the Creeks, refused to join the attack. Instead, they protected their access to British trade goods by allying with the colonists and turning the tide of battle, thus triggering a murderous rampage of revenge by the colonists against the Creeks and Yamasees.

Relations between Indians and the colonists differed from colony to colony and from year to year. But the colonists' nagging perceptions of menace on the frontier kept them continually hoping for help from the British in keeping the Indians at bay and in maintaining the essential flow of trade. In 1754, the colonists' endemic competition with the French flared into the French and Indian War, which would inflame the frontier for years (see chapter 6). Before the 1760s, neither the colonists nor the British developed a coherent policy toward Indians. But both agreed that Indians made profitable trading partners, powerful allies, and deadly enemies.

British attempts to exercise political power in colonial governments met with success so long as British officials were on or very near the sea. Colonists acknowledged—although they did not always readily comply with—British authority to collect customs duties, inspect cargoes, and enforce trade regulations. But when royal officials tried to wield their authority on land, in the internal affairs of colonies, they invariably encountered colonial resistance. A governor appointed by the king in each of the nine royal colonies (Rhode Island and Con-necticut selected their own governors) or by the proprietors in Maryland and Pennsylvania headed the government of each colony. The British envisioned colonial governors as mini-monarchs able to exert influence in the colonies much as the king did in England. But colonial governors were not kings, and the colonies were not England.

Eighty percent of colonial governors had been born in England, not in the colonies. Some governors stayed in England, close to the source of royal patronage, and delegated the grubby details of colonial affairs to subordinates. Even the best-intentioned colonial governors had difficulty developing relations of trust and respect with influential colonists because their terms of office averaged just five years and could be terminated at any time. In obedience to England, colonial governors fought incessantly with the colonial assemblies. They battled over governors' vetoes of colonial legislation, removal of colonial judges, creation of new courts, dismissal of the representative assemblies, and other local issues. Some governors developed a working relationship with the assemblies. But during the eighteenth century, the assemblies gained the upper hand.

British policies did not clearly define the powers and responsibilities of colonial assemblies. In effect, the assemblies made many of their own rules and established a strong tradition of representative government analogous, in their eyes, to the English Parliament. Voters often returned the same representatives to the assemblies year after year, building continuity in power and leadership that far exceeded that of the governor. By 1720, colonial assemblies had won the power to initiate legislation, including tax laws and authorizations to spend public funds. Although all laws passed by the assemblies (except in Maryland, Rhode Island, and Connecticut) had to be approved by the governor and then by the Board of Trade in England, the difficulties in communication about complex subjects over long distances effectively ratified the assemblies' decisions.

The heated political struggles between royal governors and colonial assemblies that occurred throughout the eighteenth century taught colonists a common set of political lessons. They learned to employ traditionally British ideas of representative government to defend their own interests. They learned that power in the British colonies rarely belonged to the British government.

Conclusion: The Dual Identity of British North American Colonists

During the eighteenth century, a distinctive society emerged in British North America, a society that was both distinctively colonial and distinctively British. Tens of thousands of immigrants and slaves gave the colonies an unmistakably colonial complexion. People of different ethnicities and faiths sought their fortunes in the colonies, where land was cheap, labor was dear, and—as Benjamin Franklin preached—work promised to be rewarding. Indentured servants and redemptioners risked a temporary period of bondage for the potential reward of better opportunities than on the Atlantic's eastern shore. Slaves endured lifetime servitude that they neither chose nor desired but from which their masters greatly benefited.

Identifiably colonial products from New England, the middle colonies, and the southern colonies flowed across the Atlantic. Back came unquestionably British consumer goods along with fashions in ideas, faith, and politics. The bonds of the British Empire required colonists to think of themselves as British subjects and, at the same time, encouraged them to consider their status as colonists.

At midcentury, colonists could not imagine that their distinctively dual identity—as British and as colonists—would soon become a source of intense conflict. But by 1776, colonists in British North America had to choose whether they were British or American.

FOR FURTHER READING ABOUT THE TOPICS IN THIS CHAPTER, see the Online Bibliography at www.bedfordstmartins.com/roarkcompact.

FOR ADDITIONAL FIRST-HAND ACCOUNTS OF THIS PERIOD, see pages 60–77 in Michael Johnson, ed., *Reading the American Past*, Second Edition, Volume I.

TO ASSESS YOUR MASTERY OF THE MATERIAL IN THIS CHAPTER, see the Online Study Guide at www.bedfordstmartins.com/roarkcompact.

CHRONOLOGY

1711 North Carolina founded.

1715 Yamasee War pits South Carolina colonists against Yamasee and Creek Indians.

1717 Scots-Irish immigration to American colonies begins to increase.

1721 *New England Courant* begins publication.

1723 Benjamin Franklin arrives in Philadelphia.

1730s Jonathan Edwards leads New England religious awakening.

1732 Georgia founded.

1733 Benjamin Franklin begins to publish *Poor Richard's Almanack*.

1739 Slave insurrection occurs at Stono, South Carolina.

1740s George Whitefield preaches revival of religion throughout England and British North America.

Majority of southern slaves are born in colonies rather than in Africa.

1741 New York City officials suspect slave conspiracy and execute thirty-one slaves.

1745 Olaudah Equiano born in present-day Nigeria.

1750s Colonists begin to move down Shenandoah Valley from Pennsylvania into southern backcountry.

Colonists increasingly become indebted to English merchants.

1754 French and Indian War begins.

PATRICK HENRY'S MAP DESK

Patrick Henry's father, John Henry of Virginia, was both a county judge and a surveyor, and his son absorbed well the importance of both professions. Patrick studied law, and in 1763, he stunned a courtroom crowd by exclaiming that the king was a tyrant, for voiding an act of the Virginia House of Burgesses relating to ministers' salaries. Shocked onlookers muttered "treason," but the judge in the case—none other than John Henry—allowed his son's incendiary remark to stand. Two years later, Patrick's reputation for brilliant, unrestrained oratory was well established, and his county elected him to the House of Burgesses where he immediately created another sensation, skillfully maneuvering the burgesses into a startling repudiation of British power known as the Virginia Resolves. But Patrick Henry was not a reckless firebrand full-time. His father's surveying and mapmaking skills inclined him to attend to frontier real estate, the sure way to wealth in eighteenth-century Virginia. This map desk sat in Henry's law office. Its fold-out extensions provided support for the large maps required to represent Virginia's vast western land claims. Its light weight allowed Henry to move it near the window with the best light, depending on the time of day and year. Patrick Henry ultimately had seventeen children, fourteen of whom survived to adulthood. Through astute land purchases, he managed to establish each with a landed estate.

Courtesy of Scotchtown, photo by Katherine Wetzel.

THE BRITISH EMPIRE AND THE COLONIAL CRISIS

6

1754–1775

THOMAS HUTCHINSON WAS A FIFTH-GENERATION DESCENDANT of Anne Hutchinson, the woman of conscience who so rattled the Puritan town of Boston in the 1630s. Thomas Hutchinson likewise was a man of conscience, but there the resemblance to his famous ancestor ended. A Harvard-educated member of the Massachusetts elite, from a family of successful merchants, Hutchinson was also a measured and cautious man. "My temper does not incline to enthusiasm," he once wrote.

After serving two decades in the Massachusetts general assembly, Hutchinson was appointed lieutenant governor in 1758, as well as chief justice of the highest court in 1760. In 1771, with Boston politics a powder keg, he agreed to become the royal governor, knowing full well the risks. Despite his family's deep roots in American soil, Hutchinson remained steadfastly loyal to England. His love of order and tradition inclined him to unconditional support of the British Empire, but loyalty was a dangerous choice in Boston after 1765. Hutchinson faced agitated crowds during demonstrations over the Stamp Act, the Townshend duties, the Boston Massacre, and the Boston Tea Party, all landmark events on the road to the American Revolution. Privately, he lamented the stupidity of the British acts that provoked trouble, but his sense of duty required him to defend the king's policies, however misguided. Quickly, he became an inspiring villain to the emerging revolutionary movement. The man not inclined to enthusiasm unleashed popular enthusiasm all around him. He never appreciated that irony.

As early as anyone, Thomas Hutchinson recognized the difficulties of maintaining full rights and privileges for Americans so far from their supreme government, the king and Parliament in England. In 1769, soon after British troops had come to occupy Boston, he wrote privately to a friend in England, "There must be an abridgement of what are called English liberties. . . . I doubt whether it is possible to project a system of government in which a colony three thousand miles distant from the parent state shall enjoy all the liberty of the parent state." What he could not imagine was the possibility of giving up the parent state altogether and creating an independent government closer to home.

Thomas Hutchinson was a loyalist; in the 1750s, most English-speaking colonists were affectionately loyal to England. But the French and Indian War, which England and its colonies fought together as allies, shook that affection, and imperial policies in the decade following the war (1763–1773) shattered it completely. Over the course of that decade, serious questions about American liberties and rights were raised insistently and repeatedly, especially over the issues of taxation and representation. Many on the American side came to believe what

THOMAS HUTCHINSON
The only formal portrait of Thomas Hutchinson still in existence shows an assured young man in ruffles and hair ribbons. Decades of turmoil in Boston failed to puncture his self-confidence. Doubtless he sat for other portraits, as did all the Boston leaders in the 1760s to 1780s, but no other likeness has survived. Hutchinson was hated; any portrait that fell into his enemies' hands would probably have been mutilated.
Courtesy of the Massachusetts Historical Society ©.

Thomas Hutchinson could never credit, that a tyrannical Britain had embarked on a course to enslave the colonists by depriving them of their traditional English liberty. The opposite of liberty was slavery, a condition of unfreedom and of coercion. Political rhetoric about liberty, tyranny, and slavery heated up emotions during the many crises of the 1760s and 1770s. But this rhetoric turned out to be a two-edged sword. The call for an end to tyrannical slavery meant one thing when sounded by Boston merchants whose commercial shipping rights had been revoked; the same call meant something quite different when sounded by black Americans in 1775, locked in the bondage of perpetual slavery.

The French and Indian War, 1754–1763

For nearly half of the first fifty years of the eighteenth century, England was at war intermittently, with either France or Spain. Often the colonists in America experienced reverberations from these conflicts, most acutely along the French frontier in northern New England. In the 1750s, tensions mounted again, but this time over events originating in America. The conflict involved contested land in the Ohio valley, variously claimed by Virginians, by Pennsylvanians, by the French in Canada—and of course by the Indians living on that land. The result was the costly French and Indian War, which first brought the British and Americans together as allies but then began to split them over questions of war-related expenses.

French-English Rivalry in the Ohio Valley

In 1753, French soldiers advanced from Canada south into Indian territory in the Ohio valley, a region encompassing present-day western Pennsylvania and eastern Ohio. For more than a decade, the French had cultivated alliances with the Indian tribes there, cementing their relationship with trade and gifts. But in the late 1740s, aggressive Pennsylvania traders pushed into the Ohio valley and began to poach on their business, underselling French goods and threatening to reorient Indian loyalties. In response, the French began building a series of forts, hoping to create a western barrier to British-American expansion.

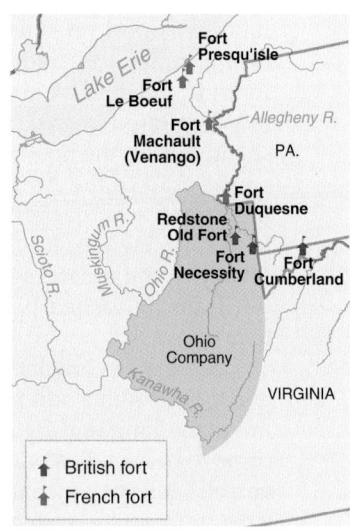

Ohio River Valley, 1753

The same region was also claimed by Virginia, and in 1747, a group of wealthy Virginians, including the brothers Lawrence and Augustine Washington, formed the Ohio Company and obtained a large land grant from the English king. The Virginians were interested in profits from the even-

T H E

J O U R N A L

O F

Major *George Wafhington,*

SENT BY THE

Hon. *ROBERT DINWIDDIE*, Efq;
His Majefty's Lieutenant-Governor, and
Commander in Chief of *VIRGINIA,*

T O   T H E

C O M M A N D A N T

OF THE

FRENCH FORCES

O N

O H I O.

To WHICH ARE ADDED, THE

GOVERNOR's LETTER,

AND A TRANSLATION OF THE

FRENCH OFFICER's ANSWER.

W I L L I A M S B U R G :

Printed by WILLIAM HUNTER. 1754

WASHINGTON'S JOURNAL, 1754
*When George Washington returned from his first
mission to the French, Governor Dinwiddie asked
him to write a full report of what he had seen of the
countryside, of the Indians, and of French troop
strength. Washington obliged, writing about 7,000
words in less than two days (about equivalent to a
25-page double-spaced typescript paper of today). He
coolly narrated scenes of personal danger: of traveling in deep snow and freezing temperatures, of
falling off a raft into an icy river, of being shot at by
a lone Indian. Dinwiddie printed Washington's report, along with his own letter and the French commander's defiant answer, in a 32-page pamphlet;
shortly thereafter it was reprinted in London. The
governor's aim was to inform Virginians and British
leaders about the French threat in the west. But the
pamphlet suited Washington's aims as well: at age
22, he was now known on both sides of the Atlantic
for resolute and rugged courage.*
Huntington Library.

tual resale of the land; the British government was
more interested in blocking the French. By 1753, the
enterprising Virginians had built a trading post near

present-day Pittsburgh. The royal governor of
Virginia, Robert Dinwiddie, himself a shareholder
in the Ohio Company, sent a messenger to warn the
French that they were trespassing on Virginia land.

The messenger on this dangerous mission was
George Washington, younger half-brother of the
Ohio Company leaders. Although he was only
twenty-one, Washington was an ambitious youth
whose imposing height (six feet two) and air of silent
competence convinced the governor he could do the
job. The middle child in a family of eight, Washington did not stand to inherit great wealth, so he
sought to gain public reputation and impress the
Virginia elite by volunteering for this perilous duty.

Washington returned from his mission with
crucial intelligence about French military plans. Impressed, Dinwiddie appointed the youth to lead a
small military force to chase off the adversaries.
Washington went west with several hundred soldiers and met bitter defeat by French troops. Thus
began the French and Indian War, as well as young
Washington's military career. By 1756, the war had
escalated to include a half dozen countries. In
Europe, it would be known as the Seven Years' War,
after it concluded in 1763. But for Americans, with
their two-year head start, it actually lasted nine
years.

The Albany Congress and Intercolonial Defense

To succeed in even a limited war, the British needed
help from the colonists as well as support, or at least
neutrality, from the Indians. Colonies from Virginia
northward were instructed to send delegates to a
meeting in Albany, New York. One goal of the
Albany Congress was to form an intercolonial
agency to coordinate the mutual defense of the
colonies. A second and perhaps more crucial goal
was to woo with gifts and promises selected tribes
of the powerful Iroquois Nation of western New
York.

In June 1754, twenty-four delegates from seven
colonies met in Albany, among them Benjamin
Franklin of Pennsylvania and Thomas Hutchinson
of Massachusetts. These two men, both rising political stars in their home colonies, coauthored a
document, the Albany Plan of Union, which proposed a unified but limited administration over all
the colonies. A president general, appointed by the
crown, together with a grand council, would have
powers only over defense and Indian affairs. The

Albany Plan humbly reaffirmed Parliament's authority; this was no bid for enlarged autonomy of the colonies.

To Franklin's surprise, not a single colony approved the Albany Plan. The Massachusetts assembly feared it was "a Design of gaining power over the Colonies," especially the power of taxation. Others objected that it would be impossible to agree on unified policies toward hundreds of quite different Indian tribes. Oddly enough, the British government never backed the Albany Plan either, which perplexed both Franklin and Hutchinson, who were earnestly trying to solidify British authority. Many years later, after the Revolution, Franklin wistfully reflected that if the Albany Plan "had been adopted and carried into Execution, the subsequent Separation of the Colonies from the Mother Country might not so soon have happened."

Representatives of the Iroquois League, embracing the Seneca, Mohawk, Onondaga, Cayuga, Oneida, and Tuscarora tribes, also attended the Albany Congress. They collected thirty wagon loads of gifts and made ambiguous promises to the colonists, but left without pledging to fight the French. The Iroquois preferred to stall and play off the English against the French, for their interests were best served by being on the winning side, which in 1754 looked to be the French.

The War and Its Consequences

By 1755, Washington's frontier skirmish had turned into a major mobilization of British and American troops against the French. At first, the British hoped for quick victory by throwing armies at the French in three strategic places. General Edward Braddock from England was to attack the French at Fort Duquesne in western Pennsylvania, accompanied by George Washington's Virginia militia. In Massachusetts, Governor William Shirley aimed his soldiers at Fort Niagara, critically located between Lakes Erie and Ontario. And finally, forces under William Johnson of New York moved north toward Lake Champlain to push the French back to Canada (Map 6.1).

Unfortunately for the British, the French were prepared to fight. In July 1755, General Braddock's army of 2,000 British and Virginian troops was ambushed by a combined French and Indian force a day short of their march to Fort Duquesne, leaving 976 killed or wounded. Washington was unhurt, though two horses in succession were shot from under him; Braddock was killed. Despite the humiliation of defeat, Washington's bravery in battle caused the governor to promote him to commander of the Virginia army. At age twenty-two, Washington was beginning to realize his ambitions.

News of Braddock's defeat alarmed the other two British armies, then hacking their way through dense New York forests, and they retreated from action. For the next two years, the British stumbled badly on the American front, with inadequate soldiers and supplies. But with the rise to power in 1757 of William Pitt in England, the war was turned around. Pitt's strategy of committing massive resources to all-out war resulted in a string of resounding successes, including the capture of Fort Duquesne in 1758 and Fort Niagara and Fort Ticonderoga in 1759. When the British navy advanced up the St. Lawrence River, the French cities of Montreal and Quebec were isolated from help. The decisive victory was the capture of the seemingly invincible fortress city of Quebec in September 1759 by the young British general James Wolfe.

The fall of Quebec broke the backbone of the French in North America. The victory was completed by the surrender of the French at Montreal in late 1760. American colonists rejoiced, but the war was not officially over yet. Battles continued in the Caribbean, where the French sugar islands Martinique and Guadeloupe fell to the English. After further fighting in Europe and India, France and Spain capitulated, and the Treaty of Paris was signed in 1763.

The triumph of victory was sweet but short-lived. The complex peace negotiations reorganized the map of North America but stopped short of providing the full spoils of victory to England. Canada was transferred to England, which eliminated the French threat from the north and west. But all French territory west of the Missississippi River,

---

MAP 6.1

European Areas of Influence and the French and Indian War, 1754–1763
In the mid-eighteenth century, France, England, and Spain claimed vast areas of North America, many of them already inhabited by various Indian peoples. The early flash points of the French and Indian War occurred in regions of disputed claims where the French had allied with powerful native groups—the Iroquois and the Algonquin—to put pressure on the westward-moving English.

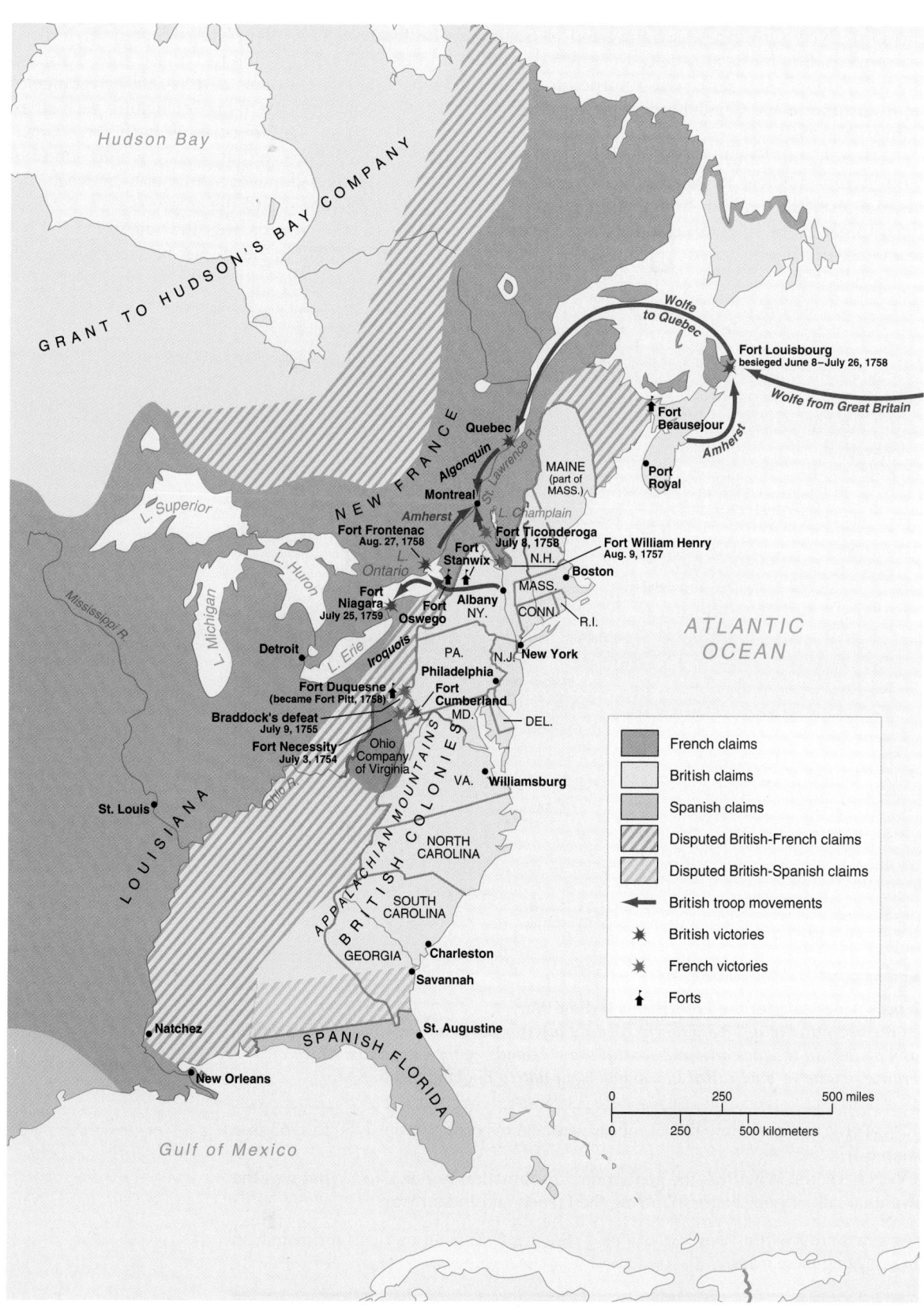

Hudson Bay

GRANT TO HUDSON'S BAY COMPANY

NEW FRANCE

L. Superior

L. Huron

L. Michigan

Mississippi R.

L. Ontario

L. Erie

Algonquin

Quebec

Montreal

Amherst

St. Lawrence R.

L. Champlain

Wolfe to Quebec

Wolfe from Great Britain

Amherst

Fort Louisbourg
besieged June 8–July 26, 1758

Fort Beausejour

Port Royal

MAINE
(part of MASS.)

Fort Frontenac
Aug. 27, 1758

Fort Stanwix

Fort Ticonderoga
July 8, 1758

Fort William Henry
Aug. 9, 1757

N.H.

Boston

MASS.

CONN.

R.I.

Fort Niagara
July 25, 1759

Fort Oswego

Albany
NY.

Iroquois

Detroit

PA.

N.J.   **New York**

Philadelphia

Fort Duquesne
(became Fort Pitt, 1758)

Fort Cumberland

MD.

DEL.

Braddock's defeat
July 9, 1755

Fort Necessity
July 3, 1754

Ohio
Company
of Virginia

Ohio R.

VA.   **Williamsburg**

St. Louis

LOUISIANA

APPALACHIAN MOUNTAINS

BRITISH COLONIES

NORTH
CAROLINA

SOUTH
CAROLINA

GEORGIA   **Charleston**

Savannah

Natchez

New Orleans

SPANISH FLORIDA

St. Augustine

ATLANTIC
OCEAN

Gulf of Mexico

	French claims
	British claims
	Spanish claims
	Disputed British-French claims
	Disputed British-Spanish claims
→	British troop movements
✳	British victories
✳	French victories
⚑	Forts

0   250   500 miles

0   250   500 kilometers

including New Orleans, was transferred to Spain as compensation for its assistance to France during the war. Stranger still, Cuba was returned to Spain, and Martinique and Guadeloupe were returned to France (Map 6.2).

In truth, the French islands in the Caribbean were hardly a threat to Americans, for they provided a profitable trade in smuggled molasses. The main threat to the safety of colonists came instead from Indians disheartened by England's victory.

The Treaty of Paris completely ignored the Indians and assigned their lands to English rule. With the French gone, the Indians had lost the advantage of having two opponents to play off against each other, and they now had to cope with the westward-moving Americans. Indian policy would soon become a serious bone of contention between the British government and the colonists.

England's version of the victory of 1763 awarded all credit to the mighty British army. In this

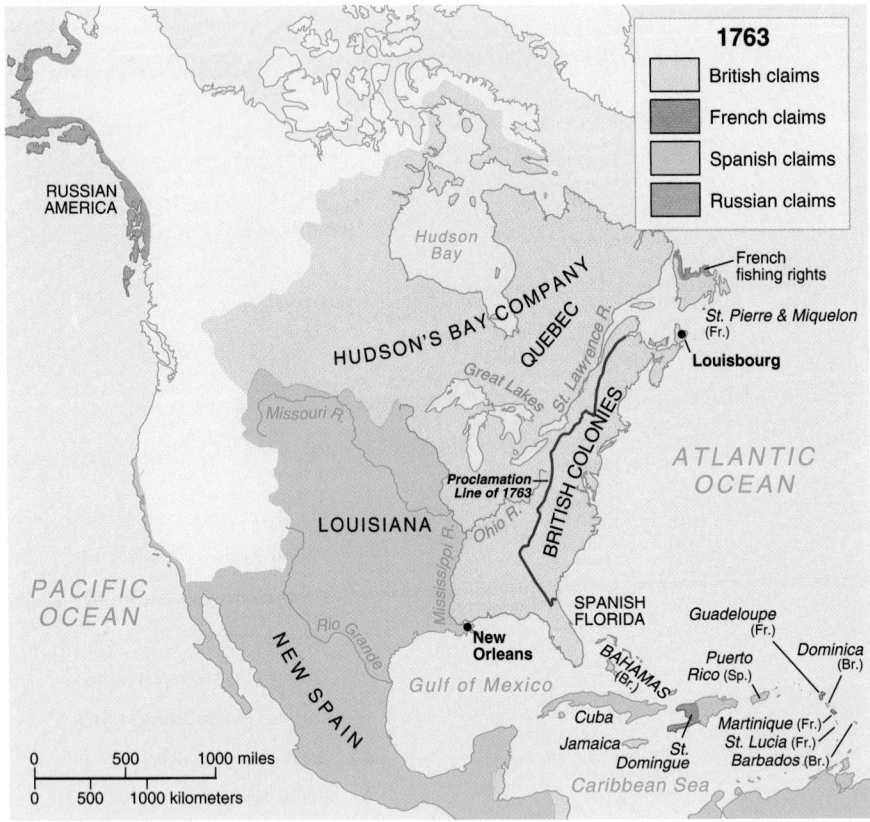

MAP 6.2
North America after the French and Indian War
In the peace treaty of 1763, France ceded its interior lands but retained fishing rights and islands in the far north and several sugar islands in the Caribbean. Much of France's claim to land called Louisiana went not to England but to Spain.

READING THE MAP: How did European land claims change from 1750 to 1763 (see Map 6.1)?

CONNECTIONS: What was the goal of the Proclamation Act of 1763? What was the eventual fate of Louisbourg following the French and Indian War?

www.bedfordstmartins.com/roarkcompact   SEE THE ONLINE STUDY GUIDE for more help in analyzing these maps.

version, ungrateful colonists had provided inadequate support for a war fought to save them from the French. In defiance of British law, colonists had engaged in smuggling, notably a lively trade in beaver pelts with French fur traders and an illegal molasses trade in the Caribbean. American traders, grumbled the British leaders, were really traitors. William Pitt was convinced that the illegal trade "principally, if not alone, enabled France to sustain and protract this long and expensive war."

Colonists read the lessons of the war differently. American provincial soldiers had turned out in force, they claimed, but the troops had been relegated to grunt work by arrogant British military leaders. General Braddock had foolishly bragged to Benjamin Franklin that "these savages may, indeed, be a formidable enemy to your raw American militia, but upon the king's regular and disciplined troops, sir, it is impossible they should make any impression." Braddock's defeat "gave us Americans," Franklin wrote, "the first suspicion that our exalted ideas of the prowess of British regulars had not been well founded."

The human costs of the war were also etched sharply in the minds of New England colonists, who had contributed most of the colonial troops. About one-third of all Massachusetts men between age fifteen and thirty had seen service. Many families lost loved ones, and this cost would not soon be forgotten. The enormous expense of the war caused by Pitt's no-holds-barred military strategy cast another huge shadow over the victory. By 1763, England's national debt, double what it had been when Pitt took office, posed a formidable challenge to the next decade of leadership in England. At the heart of the matter was disagreement about the relative responsibility the colonists should bear in helping to pay off that debt.

Tightening the Bonds of Empire

Throughout the 1760s, inconsistent leadership in England pursued a hodgepodge of policies toward the colonies. A new and inexperienced king gained the throne in 1760, and he spent the next ten years searching for a prime minister he could trust. Nearly half a dozen ministers in succession took their turns formulating policies designed to address one basic, underlying British reality: A huge war

debt needed to be serviced, and the colonists, as British subjects, should expect to pay. From the American side, however, these policies deeply violated what colonists perceived to be their rights and liberties as British subjects.

British Leadership and the Indian Question

In 1760, in the middle of the French and Indian War, George III, age twenty-two, came to the British throne, underprepared for his monarchical duties. The previous king, George II, was his grandfather;

MOHAWK WARRIOR
This rear view of a Mohawk warrior highlights clothes and body decoration: arm and ankle bracelets, earrings, a hair ornament, and body paint. The English watercolor artist includes an important element of frontal display—the warrior's tomahawk.
Musée du Nouveau Monde, Hotel Fleuriau, La Rochelle.

his father's death, when young George was thirteen, thrust the boy suddenly into the role of heir apparent. Timid and insecure, the new King George trusted only his tutor, the earl of Bute, a Scotsman who was an outsider to power circles in London. George III immediately installed Bute as head of his cabinet of ministers. Bute made blunders and did not last long, but in his short time in office he made one very significant decision—to keep a standing army in the colonies. In terms of money and political tension, this was a costly move.

The ostensible reason for keeping ten thousand British troops in America was to maintain the peace between the colonists and the Indians. This was not a misplaced concern. The defeat and withdrawal of the French from North America had left their Indian allies—who did not accept defeat—in suspension. Just three months after the Treaty of Paris was signed, Pontiac, chief of the Ottawa tribe in the northern Ohio region, attacked the British garrison near Detroit in late April 1763. Quickly, six more attacks on forts occurred; American settlements were also hit. Joining the Ottawa were tribes from western New York, the Ohio valley, and the Great Lakes region: the Chippewa, Huron, Potawatomi, Miami, Kickapoo, Mascouten, Wea, Shawnee, Mingo, Delaware, and Seneca tribes. By fall, these dozen tribes had captured every fort west of Detroit; more than four hundred British soldiers were dead, and another two thousand colonists had been killed or taken captive. Pontiac's uprising was quelled finally in December 1763 by the combined efforts of British and colonial soldiers, plus the realization that French aid to the Indians would not materialize. Pontiac later said to the British, "All my young men have buried their hatchets."

The potential for continued and costly wars with the Indians, so well illustrated by Pontiac's uprising, caused the British government to issue an order called the Proclamation Act of 1763, which forbade colonists to settle west of a line drawn from Canada to Georgia along the crest of the Appalachian Mountains. The line promised to protect

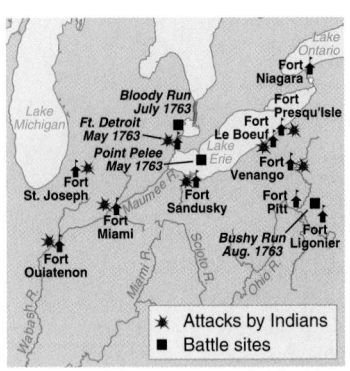

Pontiac's Rebellion, 1763

not only the Indians but also the lucrative fur trade, now in British rather than French hands. But the pressure of population growth meant that the proclamation line would be very difficult to enforce. Settlers had already moved west of the line, as had land speculators, such as those of Virginia's Ohio Company, who stood to lose opportunities for profitable resale of their claims. Bute's decision to leave a standing army in the colonies was thus a cause for concern for western settlers and eastern speculators alike.

Growing Resentment of British Authority

The mission of George Grenville, the king's next chief minister, was to tackle the problem of the war debt, which in 1763 amounted to £123 million, a shockingly high figure. To find increased revenue, Grenville first scrutinized the customs service, a division of the government responsible for monitoring the flow of ships and collecting duties on specified trade items in both England and America. Grenville found that customs officers' salaries cost the government four times what was collected in revenue. The shortfall was due in part to bribery and smuggling, and so Grenville began to insist on rigorous attention to paperwork and a strict accounting of collected duties.

The hardest duty for Grenville to enforce was the one imposed by the Molasses Act of 1733—a stiff tax of six pence per gallon on any molasses purchased from non-British sources. The purpose of the tax was to discourage trade with French Caribbean islands and redirect the molasses trade to British sugar islands. But it did not work: French molasses remained cheap and abundant because French planters on Martinique and Guadeloupe had no use for it. A by-product of sugar production, molasses was a key ingredient in making rum, a drink the French scorned. Rum-loving Americans were eager to buy French molasses, and they ignored the tax law for decades.

Grenville's ingenious solution to this problem was the Revenue Act of 1764, popularly dubbed the Sugar Act. It lowered the duty on French molasses to three pence, making it more attractive for shippers to obey the law, and at the same time raised penalties for smuggling. The act appeared to be in the tradition of navigation acts, meant to regulate trade, but Grenville's actual intent was to raise revenue. He was using an established form of law for new ends, and he was doing it by the novel means of lowering a duty.

The Sugar Act set out tougher enforcement policies. From now on, all British naval crews could act as impromptu customs officers, boarding suspicious ships and seizing cargoes found to be in violation. Smugglers caught without proper paperwork would be prosecuted, not in a friendly civil court with a local jury, but in a vice-admiralty court located in Halifax, Nova Scotia, where a single judge presided without a jury. The implication was that justice would be more sure and severe.

Grenville hoped that his tightening of the customs service and the lowered duties of the Sugar Act would reform American smugglers into law-abiding shippers and in turn generate income for the empire. Unfortunately, the decrease in duty was not sufficient to offset the attractions of smuggling. The vigilant customs officers made bribery harder to accomplish, and several ugly confrontations occurred in port cities. Reaction to the Sugar Act foreshadowed questions about England's right to tax Americans, but in 1764 objections to the act came principally from Americans in the shipping trades inconvenienced by the law.

From the British point of view, the 1763 Proclamation Act and the Sugar Act seemed to be reasonable efforts to administer the colonies. To the Americans, however, the British supervision appeared to be a disturbing intrusion into colonial practices.

The Stamp Act Crisis, 1765

By his second year in office, Grenville had made almost no dent in the national debt. Continued evasion prevented the Sugar Act from becoming the moneymaker he had hoped it would be. So in February 1765, he escalated his revenue program with the Stamp Act, which precipitated the first major conflict between England and the colonies over Parliament's right to tax.

Taxation and Consent

The Stamp Act imposed a tax on paper used for various colonial documents—newspapers, pamphlets, court documents, licenses, wills, ships' bills of lading—and required that a special stamp be affixed

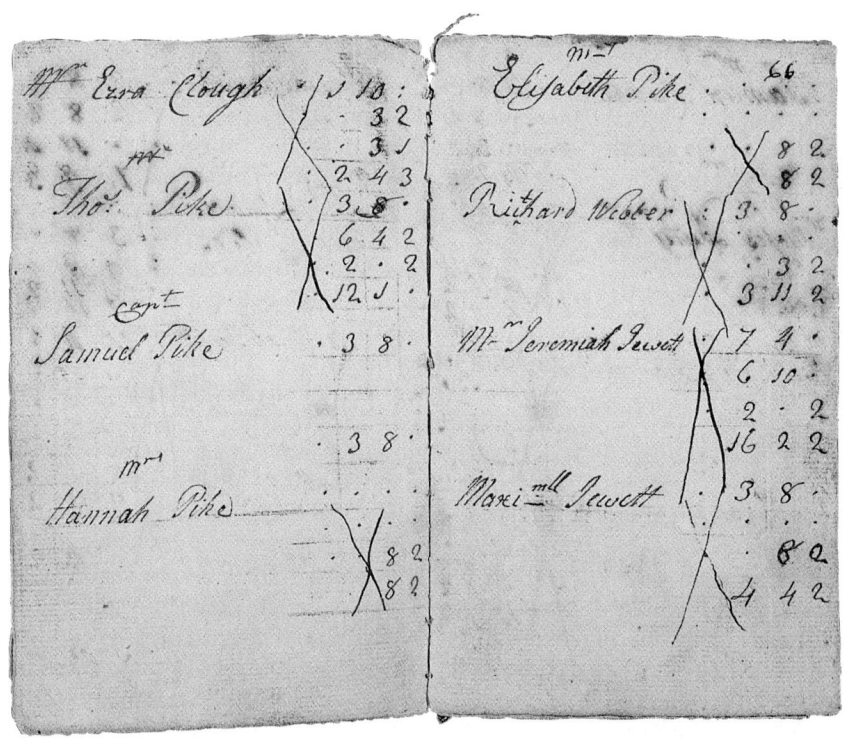

TAX ASSESSMENT BOOK *American colonists routinely paid property taxes to local authorities. This 1772 tax book from Rowley, Massachusetts, records amounts due in pounds, shillings, and pence. The several entries for each name indicate assessments on real estate, personal property, and a poll (per head) tax. Notice that two women identified as Mrs. owe taxes. Since married women by law owned no property, we can conclude that these were widows. What do you think the seven large X marks meant? Why might "Capt Samuel Pike" lack one?* Chicago Historical Society.

to the paper proving that the tax had been paid. While the Sugar Act regulated trade, the Stamp Act was designed plainly and simply to raise money. It affected nearly everyone who used any official paper, but it fell heaviest on the business and legal communities, whose repeated use of documents would now tax them the most.

Grenville was no fool; anticipating that the stamp tax would be unpopular—Thomas Hutchinson had forewarned him—he delegated the administration of the act to Americans, to avoid the problem of hostility to British enforcers. In each colony, local stamp distributors would be hired at a handsome salary of 8 percent of the revenue collected.

The colonists already paid taxes to support their local governments, but the taxing bodies were always the colonial assemblies, composed of elected representatives. English tradition held that taxation was a gift of the people to the king offered by the people's representatives. This view of taxes, as a freely given gift, preserved an essential concept of English political theory, the idea that citizens have the liberty to enjoy and use their property without fear of confiscation. The king could not simply demand money; only the House of Commons could grant it. Grenville quite agreed with the notion of taxation by consent, but he argued that the colonists were already "virtually" represented in Parliament; the House of Commons represented all British subjects, wherever they were. Colonial leaders emphatically rejected this British view, arguing that virtual representation could not withstand the stretch across the Atlantic. The stamp tax itself illustrated the problem, levied by a distant Parliament on unwilling colonies. "The MINISTER'S *virtual representation* in Support of the TAX on us is fantastical and frivolous," Maryland inhabitants complained.

Resistance Strategies and Crowd Politics

The Stamp Act was to take effect on November 1, 1765. News of its passage arrived in the colonies in April 1765, leaving colonial leaders seven months to contemplate a response. Colonial governors were unlikely to challenge the law, since most of them owed their office to the king. Instead, the colonial assemblies took the lead; eight of them held discussions on objections to the Stamp Act.

Virginia's assembly was the first to object to the Stamp Act. At the very end of the May 1765 session, when two-thirds of the members had already gone home, a twenty-nine-year-old lawyer and political newcomer named Patrick Henry presented a series of resolutions on the Stamp Act that were debated and passed, one by one. They came to be called the Virginia Resolves.

Henry's successive resolutions inched the assembly toward radical opposition to the Stamp Act. The first three resolutions stated the obvious: that Virginians were British citizens, that they enjoyed the same rights and privileges as Britons, and that self-taxation was one of those rights. The fourth resolution noted that Virginians had always taxed themselves, via their representatives in the House of Burgesses. The fifth took the radical leap, by pushing the other four unexceptional statements to one logical conclusion—that the Virginia assembly alone had the sole right to tax Virginians.

Two more fiery resolutions were debated, but majority support eroded as Henry pressed the logic of his case to the extreme. The sixth resolution denied legitimacy to any tax law originating outside Virginia, and a seventh boldly called anyone who disagreed with these propositions an enemy of Virginia. This was too much for the burgesses. They backed away from resolutions six and seven and later rescinded their vote on number five as well.

Their caution hardly mattered, however, because newspapers in other colonies printed all seven Virginia Resolves, creating the impression that a daring first challenge to the Stamp Act had taken place in Virginia. This made it easier for other assemblies to consider more radical questions, such as: By what authority could Parliament legislate for the colonies without also taxing them? No one disagreed, in 1765, that Parliament had legislative power over the colonists, who were, after all, British subjects. Several assemblies advanced the argument that there was a distinction between *external* taxes, imposed to regulate trade, and *internal* taxes, such as a stamp tax or a property tax, which could only be self-imposed.

Reaction to the Stamp Act ran far deeper than the politicians in assemblies. Every person whose livelihood required the use of official paper had to decide whether to comply with the act. Hence, local communities strategized their responses. Should they boycott all paper use? While this kept noncompliance within the law, it also was very inconvenient; if enough people ceased using stamped paper, the information network of newspapers, the legal system, and the world of trade might grind to a halt. Should they defy the law and conduct business as usual on unstamped paper, running the risk of fines or jail? A third strategy promised the surest success: to destroy the stamped paper or prevent its distribution at the source, before the law took effect, thus ensuring universal noncompliance.

The first organized resistance to the Stamp Act began in Boston, under the leadership of Samuel Adams, at forty-three a town politician with a history of opposition to then Lieutenant Governor Thomas Hutchinson. Unlike Hutchinson, Adams cared nothing for status, high office, or fine material goods. He was the Harvard-educated son of a Boston brewer, a man with shrewd political instincts and gift for organizing. He mobilized numbers of shopkeepers, master craftsmen, dockworkers, and laborers into a group of protestors who called themselves—and anyone who joined them—the Sons of Liberty.

The plan hatched by Samuel Adams and others called for a large street demonstration highlighting a ritualized mock execution, designed to convince Andrew Oliver, the stamp distributor, that his personal safety would best be served by resigning. With no stamp distributor, no stamps could be sold. On the morning of August 14, 1765, an effigy (stuffed dummy) of Oliver was found hanging from a tree. The royal governor of Massachusetts, Francis Bernard, took no action, in an effort to keep tensions under control. By evening, a large crowd of two to three thousand people paraded the effigy around town, using it as a prop in short plays demonstrating the dangers of selling stamps before beheading and burning it. The crowd also pulled down a small building on Oliver's dock, reported to be the future stamp office. The flesh-and-blood Oliver stayed in hiding; the next day he resigned his office in a well-publicized announcement.

There were lessons from the August 14 demonstration for everyone. Oliver learned that stamp distributors would be very unpopular people. Bernard and Hutchinson learned the limitations of their own powers to govern, with no police to call on. The demonstration's leaders learned that street action was very effective. And hundreds of laborers, sailors, and apprentices not only learned what the Stamp Act was all about but also gained pride in their ability to have a decisive impact on politics.

Twelve days later, a second crowd action, more properly termed a riot, showed just how well some of these lessons had been learned. On August 26, a crowd visited the houses of four detested officials.

SAMUEL ADAMS BY JOHN COPLEY
Samuel Adams consented to pose for Boston artist John Singleton Copley in 1770. The portrait highlights Adams's face, which projects a dramatic intensity and dominates the bulky body, subdued by dark clothes. Adams stares thoughtfully and silently at the viewer and points to important legal documents before him, including the Massachusetts charter of 1689. Wealthy merchant John Hancock commissioned the portrait, which hung in his house. Copley painted scores of Boston's leaders in the 1760s, both loyalists and patriots. He maintained neutrality until 1773, when his father-in-law became an official East India tea distributor. Copley's home was threatened by a crowd, and he left for England in 1774.
Deposited by the City of Boston, Museum of Fine Arts, Boston.

One was a customs officer and two others were officers of the admiralty courts, where smugglers were tried; the crowd broke windows and raided wine cellars. The fourth house was the finest dwelling in Massachusetts, owned by the stiff-necked Thomas Hutchinson. Rumors abounded that Hutchinson had urged Grenville to adopt the Stamp Act. In fact, he had done the opposite, but he refused to set the record straight, saying curtly, "I am not obliged to give an answer to all the questions that may be put me by every lawless person." The crowd attacked his house, and by daybreak only the exterior walls were standing.

The destruction of Hutchinson's house brought a temporary halt to crowd activities in Boston. The Boston town meeting issued a statement of sympathy; but a reward of £300 for the arrest and conviction of riot organizers failed to produce a single lead. The Sons of Liberty denied planning the event.

Essentially, the opponents of the Stamp Act in Boston had won the day; no one volunteered to replace Oliver as distributor. When November 1 arrived, the day the Stamp Act took effect, customs officers were unable to prevent ships from passing through the harbor without properly stamped clearance papers.

Liberty and Property

Boston's crowd actions of August sparked similar eruptions by groups calling themselves Sons of Liberty in virtually every colony, and stamp distributors everywhere hastened to resign. One Connecticut distributor was forced by a crowd to throw his hat and powdered wig in the air while shouting a cheer for "Liberty and property!" This man fared better than the stamp agent who was nearly buried alive by Sons of Liberty. Only when the thuds of dirt sounded on the coffin did he have a sudden change of heart, shouting out his resignation to the crowd above. In Charleston, South Carolina, the stamp distributor resigned after crowds burned effigies and chanted "Liberty! Liberty!"

Some colonial leaders, disturbed about the riots, hastened to mount a more moderate challenge to Parliamentary authority. Twenty-seven delegates representing nine colonial assemblies met in New York City in October 1765 as the Stamp Act Congress. For two weeks the men hammered out a petition about taxation addressed to the king and Parliament. Their statement closely resembled the first five Virginia Resolves, claiming taxes were "free gifts of the people" that only the people's representatives could give. They dismissed virtual representation: "The people of these colonies are not, and from their local circumstances, cannot be represented in the House of Commons." But the delegates also took great care to affirm their subordination to Parliament and monarch in deferential language. Nevertheless, the Stamp Act Congress, by the mere fact of its meeting, advanced a radical potential, the notion of intercolonial political action.

The rallying cry "Liberty and property" made perfect sense to many white Americans of all social ranks, who feared that the Stamp Act threatened their traditional right to liberty as British subjects. The opposite of liberty was slavery, the condition of being under the control of someone else. Civil society required some interference in perfect freedom in the form of laws, but Englishmen preserved liberty by making sure that only representative governments passed the laws. Up to 1765, Americans consented to accept Parliament as a body that in some way represented them, at least for purposes of legislation. But the right to own property was a special kind of liberty, requiring even stricter safeguards. This was why the tradition arose that only a representative body could tax British subjects.

To Americans, the Stamp Act violated this principle of liberty and property, and some Americans began to speak and write about a plot by British leaders to enslave them. A Maryland writer warned that if the colonies lost "the right of exemption from all taxes without their consent," that loss would "deprive them of every privilege distinguishing freemen from slaves." The opposite meanings of liberty and slavery were utterly clear to white Americans, but they stopped short of applying similar logic to the one million black Americans they held in bondage. Many blacks, however, could see the contradiction. When a crowd of Charleston blacks paraded with shouts of "Liberty!" just a few months after white Sons of Liberty had done the same, the town militia turned out to break up the demonstration.

Politicians and merchants in England reacted with alarm to the American demonstrations and petitions. Merchants particularly feared trade disruptions and pressured Parliament to repeal the Stamp Act. By late 1765, yet another new minister, the marquess of Rockingham, headed the king's cabinet. His dilemma was to find a dignified way to repeal the act that did not yield to the Americans' claim that Parliament could not tax them. The solution came in March 1766: The Stamp Act was repealed, but with it came the Declaratory Act, which asserted Parliament's right to legislate for the colonies "in all cases whatsoever." Perhaps the stamp tax had been inexpedient, but the power to tax—one prime case of a legislative power—was stoutly upheld.

The Townshend Acts and Economic Retaliation, 1767–1770

Rockingham did not last long as prime minister. By the summer of 1766, George III had persuaded William Pitt to resume that role. Pitt then appointed Charles Townshend to be chancellor of the exchequer, the chief financial minister. Townshend faced both the old war debt problem and the continuing cost of stationing the British army in America, and he turned again to taxation. But Townshend's knowledge of the developing political climate in the colonies was unfortunately limited; his simple idea to raise revenue turned into a major mistake.

The Townshend Duties

Townshend proposed new taxes in the old form of a navigation act. Officially called the Revenue Act of 1767, it established new duties on tea, glass, lead, paper, and painters' colors imported into the colonies, to be paid by the importer but passed on to consumers in the retail price. A year before, the duty on French molasses had been reduced from three pence down to one pence per gallon, and finally the Sugar Act was pulling in a tidy revenue of about £45,000 annually. So it was not unreasonable to suppose that duties on additional trade goods might also improve the cash flow. Townshend assumed that external taxes—that is, duties levied on the transatlantic trade—would be more acceptable to Americans than internal taxes, such as the stamp tax.

The Townshend duties were not especially burdensome, but the principle they embodied—taxation extracted through trade duties—looked different to the colonists now, in the wake of the Stamp Act crisis. If Americans once distinguished between external and internal taxes, that distinction was wiped out by an external tax meant only to raise money. John Dickinson, a Philadelphia lawyer, articulated this view in a series of articles titled *Letters from a Farmer in Pennsylvania*, widely reprinted in the winter of 1767–68. "We are taxed without our consent. . . . We are therefore—SLAVES," Dickinson wrote, calling for "a total denial of the power of Parliament to lay upon these colonies any 'tax' whatever."

A controversial provision of the Townshend duties directed that some of the revenue generated would be used to pay the salaries of royal governors. Before 1767, local assemblies set the salaries of their own officials, giving them significant influence over crown-appointed officeholders. Townshend wanted to strengthen the governors' position, as well as to curb the growing independence of the assemblies.

In New York, for example, the assembly had refused to enforce a British rule of 1765 called the Quartering Act, which directed the colonies to furnish shelter and provisions for the British army. The assembly argued that the Quartering Act was really a tax measure because it required New Yorkers to pay money by order of Parliament. Townshend came down hard on the New York assembly: He orchestrated a parliamentary order, the New York Suspending Act, which declared all the assembly's acts null and void until it met its obligations to the army. Both these measures—the new way to pay royal governors' salaries and the suspension of the governance functions of the New York assembly—struck a chill throughout the colonies. Many wondered if legislative government was at all secure.

The Massachusetts assembly took the lead in protesting the Townshend duties. Samuel Adams, now a member from Boston, argued that any form of parliamentary taxation was unjust because Americans were not represented in Parliament. The assembly circulated a letter with Adams's arguments to other colonial assemblies and urged their endorsement. As with the Stamp Act Congress of 1765, colonial assemblies were starting to coordinate their protests.

In response to Adams's letter, the new man in charge of colonial affairs in Britain, Lord Hillsborough, instructed the Massachusetts governor, Francis Bernard, to dissolve the assembly if it refused to rescind its statement. The assembly refused, by a vote of 92 to 17, and Governor Bernard carried out his instruction. In the summer of 1768, Boston was in an uproar.

Nonconsumption and the Daughters of Liberty

The Boston town meeting had already passed resolutions, termed "nonconsumption agreements," calling for a boycott of British-made goods. Dozens of other towns passed similar resolutions in 1767 and 1768. For example, prohibited purchases in the town of New Haven, Connecticut, included carriages, furniture, hats, clothing, shoes, lace, iron plate, clocks, jewelry, toys, textiles, malt liquors, and cheese. The idea was to encourage home manufacture of such items and to hurt trade with Britain, causing London merchants to pressure Parliament for repeal of the duties.

But nonconsumption agreements were very hard to enforce. With the Stamp Act, there was one hated item, a stamp, and a limited number of official distributors. In contrast, an agreement to boycott all British goods required serious personal sacrifice. Some merchants were wary of nonconsumption because it hurt their pocketbooks, and a few con-

EDENTON TEA LADIES
American women in many communities renounced British apparel and tea during the early 1770s. Women in Edenton, North Carolina, publicized their pledge and drew hostile fire in the form of a British cartoon. The cartoon's message is that brazen women who meddle in politics will undermine their femininity. Neglected babies, urinating dogs, wanton sexuality, and mean-looking women are some of the dire consequences, according to the artist. The cartoon works as humor for the British because of the gender inversions it predicts and because of the insult it poses to American men.
Library of Congress.

tinued to import in readiness for the end of nonconsumption (or to sell on the side to people choosing to ignore nonconsumption). In Boston, such merchants found themselves blacklisted in newspapers and broadsides.

A more direct blow to trade came from nonimportation agreements, but it proved even more difficult to get merchants to agree to these. There was always the risk that merchants in other colonies might continue to trade and thus receive handsome profits if neighboring colonies prohibited trade. Not until late 1768 could Boston merchants agree to suspend trade through a nonimportation agreement lasting from January 1, 1769, to January 1, 1770. Sixty signed the agreement. New York merchants soon followed suit, as did Philadelphia and Charleston merchants in 1769.

Doing without British products, either luxury goods or basics such as tea or textiles, no doubt was a hardship. But it also presented an opportunity, for many of the British products specified in nonconsumption agreements were household goods traditionally under the control of women. By 1769, male leaders in the patriot cause clearly understood that women's cooperation in nonconsumption and home manufacture was essential. The Townshend duties thus provided an unparalleled opportunity for developing and showcasing female patriotism. During the Stamp Act crisis, Sons of Liberty took to the streets in protest. During the difficulties of 1768–1769, the Daughters of Liberty emerged to give shape to a new idea—that women could play a role in public affairs.

Any woman could express affiliation with the colonial protest by boycotting goods and taking up home manufacture of items previously imported from England. Women in at least three towns met together to sign their own nonconsumption agreements. In Boston, over three hundred women signed a petition to abstain from tea, "sickness excepted." A nine-year-old girl visiting the royal governor's house in New Jersey took the tea she was offered, curtsied, and tossed the beverage out a nearby window. Homespun cloth also became a prominent symbol of patriotism, with dozens of towns organizing public "frolicks" or bees where women competed in spinning and weaving. Cloth making was no longer simply a family chore but a task invested with political content. A Connecticut girl who spun ten knots of wool in one day proclaimed in her journal that her work made her feel "Nationly." On the whole, the year of boycotts was a success. British imports fell by more than 40 percent, and British merchants felt the pinch.

Military Occupation and "Massacre" in Boston

By summer 1768, Boston's royal officials felt alarm. On August 15, a rollicking anniversary celebration of the Stamp Act demonstration of 1765 put crowds in the street and apprehension in the hearts of Governor Bernard and Lieutenant Governor Hutchinson. With no police force and no reasonable hope of controlling the town militia, Bernard concluded that he needed British soldiers to keep the peace.

In the fall, three thousand uniformed troops arrived to occupy Boston. The soldiers drilled conspicuously on the Common, played loud music on the Sabbath, and in general grated on the nerves of Bostonians. Although the situation was frequently tense, no major troubles occurred during that winter and through most of 1769. But as January 1 approached, marking the end of the nonimportation agreement, it was clear that some

merchants could no longer be kept in line. Thomas Hutchinson's two sons, for example, were both importers hostile to the boycott, and they had already ordered new goods from England. The early months of 1770 were thus bound to be a conflict-ridden period in Boston.

Serious troubles began in January. The Hutchinson sons' shop was visited by a crowd that smeared "Hillsborough paint," a potent mixture of human excrement and urine, on the door. In mid-February, a crowd surrounded the house of Ebenezer Richardson, a cranky, low-level customs official. When Richardson panicked and fired his musket to scare off the crowd, he accidentally killed a boy. The Sons of Liberty mounted a massive funeral procession to mark this first instance of violent death in the struggle with England.

For the next week, heightened tensions gripped Boston, and frequent brawls occurred. The climax came on Monday evening, March 5, 1770, when a small crowd taunted a soldier guarding the customs house. British Captain Thomas Preston sent a seven-man guard to join the lone sentry. Meanwhile, the hostile crowd grew, and the soldiers raised their

THE BLOODY MASSACRE PERPETRATED IN KING STREET, BOSTON, ON MARCH 5, 1770
This mass-produced engraving by Paul Revere sold for six pence per copy. In this patriot version, the soldiers fire on an unarmed crowd under orders of their captain. The tranquil dog is an artistic device to signal the crowd's peaceful intent; not even a deaf dog could actually hold that pose during the melee. Among the five killed was Crispus Attucks, a black sailor, but Revere shows only whites among the casualties.
Anne S. K. Brown Military Collection, Providence, R.I.

www.bedfordstmartins.com/ roarkcompact SEE THE ON-LINE STUDY GUIDE for more help in analyzing this image.

loaded muskets in defense. Onlookers threw snowballs and sticks, daring the soldiers to fire. Finally one of the soldiers, hit by some object, pulled his trigger. After a short pause, during which time someone yelled "Fire!" the other soldiers fired as well. Eleven men in the crowd were hit, five of them fatally.

The Boston Massacre, as it quickly became called, was over in minutes. In the immediate aftermath, Hutchinson (now acting governor after Bernard's recall to England) showed courage in confronting the crowd personally, from the balcony of the customs house. By daybreak of March 6, he ordered the removal of the regiments to an island in the harbor to prevent further bloodshed. Hutchinson also jailed Preston and the eight soldiers, as much for their own protection as to appease the townspeople, and promised they would be held for trial.

That trial came in the fall of 1770. The soldiers were defended by two young Boston attorneys, Samuel Adams's cousin John Adams and Josiah Quincy. Because Adams and Quincy had direct ties to the leadership of the Sons of Liberty, their decision to defend the British soldiers at first seems odd. But John Adams was deeply committed to the idea that even unpopular defendants deserve a fair trial. Samuel Adams respected his cousin's decision to take the case, for there was a tactical benefit as well. It showed that the Boston leadership was not lawless but could be seen as defenders of British liberty and law.

The five-day trial, with dozens of witnesses, resulted in acquittal for Preston and for all but two of the soldiers, who were convicted of manslaughter, branded on the thumbs and released. Nothing materialized in the trial to indicate a conspiracy or concerted plan, either by the British or by the leaders of the Sons of Liberty, to provoke trouble. To this day, the question of who was responsible for the Boston Massacre remains obscure.

The Tea Party and the Coercive Acts, 1770–1774

In the same week as the Boston Massacre, yet another new British prime minister, Frederick North, contemplated the decrease in trade caused by the Townshend duties and recommended repeal. A skillful politician, Lord North took office in 1770

and kept it for twelve years; at last King George had stability at the helm. North sought peace with the colonies and prosperity for British merchants, so all the Townshend duties were removed, except the tax on tea, a pointed reminder of Parliament's ultimate power. North hoped to cool tensions without sacrificing principles.

Those few Americans who could not abide the symbolism of the tea tax turned to smuggled Dutch tea. The renewal of trade and the return of cooperation between England and the colonies gave men like Thomas Hutchinson hope that the worst of the crisis was behind them. For nearly two years, peace seemed possible.

The Calm before the Storm

Repeal of the Townshend duties brought an end to nonimportation, despite the tax on tea. Trade boomed in 1770 and 1771. Moreover, the leaders of the popular movement seemed to be losing their power. Samuel Adams, for example, ran for a minor local office in Boston and lost to a conservative merchant.

In 1772, however, several incidents brought the conflict with England into focus again. One was the burning of the *Gaspée*, a Royal Navy ship chasing down suspected smugglers off the coast of Rhode Island. Although a royal investigating commission failed to arrest anyone, it announced that it would send suspects, if it found any, to England for trial on charges of high treason.

This decision seemed to fly in the face of the traditional English right to a trial by a jury of one's peers. When the news of the *Gaspée* investigation spread, it was greeted with disbelief in other colonies. Patrick Henry, Thomas Jefferson, and Richard Henry Lee from the Virginia House of Burgesses proposed that a network of standing committees be established to link the colonies and pass along alarming news. By mid-1773, every colonial assembly except Pennsylvania had a "committee of correspondence."

Another British action in 1772 further spread the communications network. Lord North proposed to pay the salaries of superior court justices out of the tea revenue, in a move parallel to Townshend's plan for royal governors. The Boston town meeting, alarmed that judges would now be in the pockets of their new paymasters, established a committee of correspondence and urged other towns to do likewise. The first vital message, circulated in

December 1772, attacked the judges' salary policy as the latest proof of a British plot to undermine traditional "liberties": unjust taxation, military occupation, massacre, now capped by the subversion of justice. By spring 1773, half the towns in Massachusetts had set up their own committees of correspondence, providing local forums for debate. These committees politicized ordinary townspeople and bypassed the official flow of power and information through the colony's royal government.

The third and final incident that irrevocably shattered the relative calm of the early 1770s was the Tea Act of 1773. Americans had been drinking moderate amounts of English tea and paying the tea duty without objection, but they were also smuggling large quantities of Dutch tea, cutting into the British East India Company's sales. So Lord North proposed special legislation giving favored status to the East India Company, allowing it to sell its tea through special government agents rather than through public auction to independent merchants. The hope was that the price of the East India tea, even with the duty, would then fall below that of the smuggled Dutch tea, motivating Americans to obey the law as well as boosting sales for the East India Company.

Tea in Boston Harbor

In the fall of 1773, news of the Tea Act reached the colonies. Parliamentary legislation to make tea inexpensive struck many colonists as an insidious plot to trick Americans into buying large quantities of the duued tea. The real goal, some argued, was the increased revenue, which would then be used to pay the royal governors and judges. The Tea Act

TOSSING THE TEA
This colored engraving appeared in an English book published in 1789, recounting the history of North America from its earliest settlement to "becoming united, free, and independent states." Men on the ship break into the chests and dump the contents; a few are depicted in Indian disguise, with feathers on their heads or topknots of hair. A large crowd on the shore looks on. The red rowboat is clearly stacked with tea chests, suggesting that some of the raiders were stealing rather than destroying the tea. However, the artist, perhaps careless, shows the rowboat heading toward the ship instead of away. This event was not dubbed the "Tea Party" until the 1830s when a later generation celebrated the illegal destruction of the tea and made heroes out of the few surviving participants, by then men in their eighties and nineties.
Library of Congress.

was thus a sudden and painful reminder of Parliament's claim to the power to tax and legislate for the colonies.

As with the Stamp Act and the Townshend duties, the colonists' strategy was crucial. Nonimportation was not a viable option, because the trade was too lucrative to expect colonial merchants to give it up willingly. Consumer boycotts of tea had proved ineffective since 1770, chiefly because it was impossible to distinguish between duticd tea (the object of the boycott) and smuggled tea (illegal but politically clean) once it was in the teapot. Like the Stamp Act, the Tea Act mandated special agents to handle the tea sales, and that requirement pointed to the solution for anti-tea activists. In every port city, revived Sons of Liberty pressured tea agents to resign.

The Boston Sons of Liberty were slower to act at first, but their action—more direct and illegal than anywhere else—ultimately provoked the most alarmed and alarming reprisals from England. Three ships bearing tea arrived in Boston in late November 1773. They cleared customs and unloaded their other cargoes, but not the tea. Sensing the extreme tension, the captains wished to return to England, but because the ships had already entered the harbor, they could not get clearance to leave without first paying the tea duty. On top of that, there was a twenty-day limit on the stay allowed in the harbor, by which time either the duty had to be paid or the tea would be confiscated and sold by the authorities. Governor Hutchinson refused to bend any rules.

For the full twenty days, pressure built in Boston. Daily mass meetings energized the citizenry not only from Boston but from surrounding towns, alerted by the committees of correspondence. On the final day, December 16, a large crowd gathered at Old South Church to hear Samuel Adams declare, "This meeting can do nothing more to save the country." This was a signal to adjourn to the harbor, where between 100 and 150 men, many dressed as Indians, dumped ninety thousand pounds of tea into the water while a crowd of two thousand watched. (See "Documenting the American Promise," page 134.)

The Coercive Acts

Lord North's response was swift and stern. Within three months he persuaded Parliament to issue the first of the Coercive Acts, a series of four laws meant to punish Massachusetts for the destruction of the tea. The laws were soon known as the Intolerable

Acts in America, along with a fifth one not aimed at Massachusetts alone, the Quebec Act.

The first, the Boston Port Act, closed Boston harbor to all shipping traffic as of June 1, 1774, for as long as the destroyed tea was not paid for. In effect, England was obliterating the commercial life of the city.

The second act, called the Massachusetts Government Act, altered the colony's charter (in itself an unprecedented step, underscoring Parliament's claim to supremacy over Massachusetts). The royal governor's powers were greatly augmented; the council became an appointive, not elective, body; and no town meeting beyond the annual spring election of town selectmen could be held unless the governor expressly permitted it. Not only Boston but every Massachusetts town felt the punitive sting.

The third of the Coercive Acts, the Impartial Administration of Justice Act, stipulated that any royal official accused of a capital crime—for example, Captain Preston and his soldiers at the Boston Massacre—would now be tried in a court in England. It did not matter that Preston in fact got a fair trial in Boston. What this act ominously suggested was that down the road, there might be more Captain Prestons and soldiers firing into crowds.

The fourth of the Coercive Acts was a new amendment to the 1765 Quartering Act, permitting military commanders to lodge soldiers wherever necessary, even in private households. For Boston this was no idle gesture, for in a related move Lord North appointed General Thomas Gage, commander of the Royal Army in New York, to be the new governor of Massachusetts. Thomas Hutchinson was out, relieved at long last of his duties, and military rule, including soldiers, returned once more to Boston.

The fifth Intolerable Act, the Quebec Act, had little to do with the first four but, ill-timed, it greatly fed the fear of Americans. It confirmed the continuation of French civil law, government form, and Catholicism for Quebec, all an affront to Protestant New Englanders denied their own representative government. The act also gave Quebec control of disputed lands (and hence control of the lucrative fur trade) throughout the Ohio valley, lands claimed variously by Virginia, Pennsylvania, and Connecticut.

The Coercive Acts spread alarm to all the colonies. If England could step on Massachusetts and change its charter, suspend government, inaugurate military rule, and on top of that give Ohio to Catholic Quebec, then what liberties were secure? Fearful royal governors in a half dozen colonies suspended sitting assemblies, adding to the sense of urgency; some suspended assemblies defiantly continued to meet in new locations. Via the committees of correspondence, the colonial leaders agreed to meet in Philadelphia in the fall of 1774 to respond to the crisis.

The First Continental Congress

Every colony except Georgia sent delegates to Philadelphia for the meeting of the First Continental Congress in September 1774. The gathering included the leading patriots, such as Samuel and John Adams from Massachusetts and George Washington and Patrick Henry from Virginia. A few colonies purposely sent men who were cool to provoking a crisis with England, like Pennsylvania's Joseph Galloway. Whatever their views, most of the delegates were the leading statesmen of their localities.

Two difficult tasks confronted the congress: The delegates wanted to agree on exactly what liberties they claimed as English subjects and what powers Parliament held over them, and they needed to make a unified response to the Coercive Acts. Some delegates wanted a total ban on trade with England, to force a repeal of the Coercive Acts, but others—especially those from southern colonies heavily dependent on the export of tobacco and rice—opposed halting trade. Samuel Adams and Patrick Henry were eager for a ringing denunciation of all parliamentary control, whereas the conservative Joseph Galloway proposed a plan (quickly defeated) to create a miniparliament in America to assist the British Parliament in ruling the colonies.

The congress met for seven weeks in Carpenter's Hall, Philadelphia, and produced a declaration of rights, couched in traditional language: "We ask only for peace, liberty and security. We wish no diminution of royal prerogatives, we demand no new rights." Yet the rights assumed already to exist were in fact radical, from England's point of view. Chief among them was the claim that Americans were not represented in Parliament and so each colonial government had the sole right to legislate for and tax its own people. The one slight concession to England was a carefully worded agreement that the colonists would "cheerfully consent" to trade regulations for the larger good of the empire—so long as trade regulation was not a covert means of raising revenue.

To put pressure on England, the delegates agreed to a staggered and limited boycott of trade—imports prohibited this year, exports the fol-lowing, and rice totally exempted, to keep South Carolinians happy. To enforce the boycott, they created the Continental Association, with chapters in each town, variously called committees of public safety or of inspection, to monitor all commerce and punish suspected violators of the boycott (sometimes with a bucket of tar and a bag of feathers). Its work done, the congress disbanded in October 1774, with agreement to reconvene the following May.

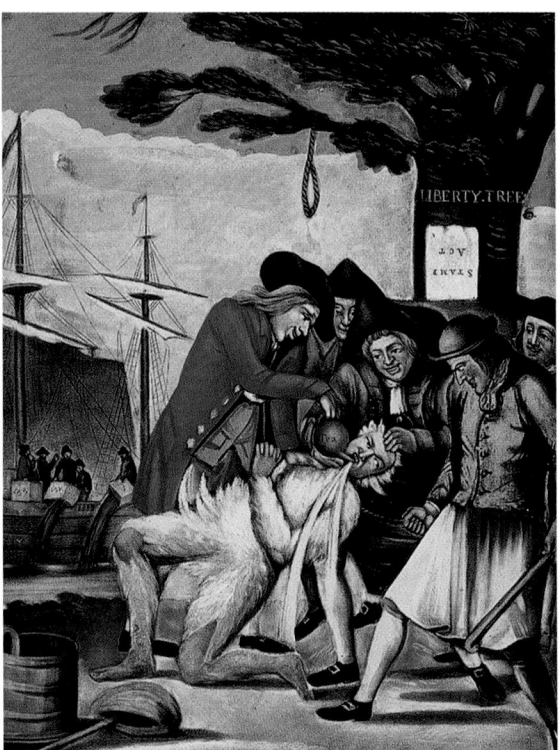

TAR AND FEATHERING CARTOON
In 1774, a Boston customs collector named John Malcolm felt the sting of pain at the hands of a Boston crowd which tarred and feathered him as punishment for extorting extra money from shippers. This ritualized humiliation involved stripping a man, painting him with tar, and dipping him in chicken feathers. Local committees of public safety often used threats of this treatment as a weapon to enforce boycotts; it happened far less often in actuality. This cartoon, of English origin, is hostile to Americans, who are shown with cruelly gleeful faces, forcing tea down Malcolm's throat. The Liberty Tree has become a gallows; posted to it is the Stamp Act, upside down, and the dumping of tea in the harbor is shown in the background.
Library of Congress.

The Destruction of the Tea

On the night of December 16, 1773, over a hundred men disguised as Indians threw 342 chests of tea into Boston harbor. Here are three accounts by participants close to the action.

DOCUMENT 1. Governor Hutchinson's Account, Published in 1828

In exile in England, Thomas Hutchinson wrote a long history of Massachusetts, which was first published in 1828, decades after his death. In narrating Boston events of the 1760s and 1770s, Hutchinson referred to himself in the third person, but his point of view was definitely weighted toward self-vindication. Here he describes the consequences of his final rejection of a demand by the town meeting that he permit the vessels to leave port without paying the tea tax.

It was not expected the governor would comply with the demand; and, before it was possible for the owner of the ship to return . . . with an answer, about fifty men had prepared themselves, and passed by the house where the people were assembled, to the wharf where the vessels lay, being covered with blankets, and making the appearance of Indians. The body of the people remained until they had received the governor's answer; and then, after it had been observed to them, that, every thing else in their power having been done, it now remained to proceed in the only way left . . . the meeting was declared to be dissolved, and the body of the people repaired to the wharf, and surrounded the immediate actors, as a guard and security, until they finished their work. In two or three hours, they hoisted out of the holds of the ships, three hundred and forty-two chests of tea, and emptied them into the sea. The governor was unjustly censured by many people in the province, and much abused by the pamphlet and newspaper writers in England, for refusing his pass, which, it was said, would have saved the property thus destroyed; but he would have been justly censured, if he had granted it. He was bound, as all the king's governors were, by oath, faithfully to observe the acts of trade. . . . His granting a pass to a vessel which had not cleared at the custom-house, would have been a direct violation of his oath, by making himself an accessory in the breach of those laws which he had sworn to observe. It was out of his power to have prevented this mischief, without the most imminent hazard of much greater mischief. The tea could have been secured in the town in no other way than by landing marines from the men of war, or bringing to town the regiment which was at the castle, to remove the guards from the ships, and to take their places. This would have brought on a greater convulsion than there was any danger of in 1770, and it would not have been possible . . . for so small a body of troops to have kept possession of the town. Such a measure the governor had no reason to suppose would have been approved of in England. He was not sure of support from any one person in authority. The house of representatives openly avowed principles which implied complete independency. The council, appointed by charter to be assisting to him, declared against any advice from which might be inferred an acknowledgment of the authority of parliament in imposing taxes. . . . There was not a justice of peace, sheriff, constable, or peace officer in the province, who would venture to take cognizance of any breach of law, against the general bent of the people.

SOURCE: Excerpt from "Governor Hutchinson's Account, 1828." In *The History of the Colony and Province of Massachusetts-Bay:* Volume II by Thomas Hutchinson, edited by Lawrence Shaw Mayo. Copyright © 1936 by the President and Fellows of Harvard College. Reprinted by permission of the publisher, Harvard University Press.

DOCUMENT 2. George Robert Twelves Hewes's Recollection, Transcribed in 1834

George Robert Twelves Hewes, a thirty-one-year-old Boston shoemaker, was first stirred to political action by witnessing the Boston Massacre. During the struggle over tea, he joined the "Indian" boarding party and found himself thrust into a leadership role, a singular moment of glory that he proudly recounted when he was in his nineties. As one of the last surviving participants of that famous event, he enjoyed enormous celebrity in the 1830s. His life came to symbolize the Revolution's power to lift up the common man and endow him with a sense of political significance.

The commander of the division to which I belonged, as soon as we were on board the ship, appointed me boatswain, and ordered me to go to the captain and demand of him the keys to the hatches and a dozen candles. I made the demand accordingly, and the captain promptly replied, and delivered the articles; but requested me at the same time to do no damage to the ship or rigging. We then were ordered by our commander to open the hatches, and take out all the chests of tea and throw them overboard, and we immediately proceeded to execute his orders; first cutting and splitting the chests with our tomahawks, so as thoroughly to expose them to the effects of the water. In about three hours from the time we went on board, we had thus broken and thrown overboard every tea chest to be found in the ship; while those in the other ships were disposing of the tea in the same way, at the same time. We were surrounded by British armed ships, but no attempt was made to resist us. We then quietly retired to our several places of residence, without having any conversation with each other, or taking any measures to discover who were our associates.

Source: [James Hawkes], *A Retrospect of the Boston Tea-Party, with a Memoir of George R. T. Hewes, a Survivor of the Little Band of Patriots Who Drowned the Tea in Boston Harbour in 1773* (New York, 1834), reprinted in Alfred F. Young, *The Shoemaker and the Tea Party: Memory and the American Revolution* (Boston: Beacon Press, 1999), 44.

Document 3: John Adams's Diary Entry of December 17, 1773

John Adams reveled in the bold destruction of the tea in his diary the day after the event. He also gave thought to the legal consequences that might follow, rehearsing the justifications that motivated "the People."

Last Night 3 Cargoes of Bohea Tea were emptied into the Sea. This Morning a Man of War sails.

This is the most magnificent Movement of all. There is a Dignity, a Majesty, a Sublimity, in this last Effort of the Patriots, that I greatly admire. . . . This Destruction of the Tea is so bold, so daring, so firm, intrepid and inflexible, and it must have so important Consequences, and so lasting, that I cant but consider it as an Epocha in History.

This however is but an Attack upon Property. Another similar Exertion of popular Power, may produce the destruction of Lives. Many Persons wish, that as many dead Carcasses were floating in the Harbour, as there are Chests of Tea:—a much less Number of Lives however would remove the Causes of all our Calamities.

The malicious Pleasure with which Hutchinson the Governor, the Consignees of the Tea, and the officers of the Customs, have stood and looked upon the distresses of the People, and their Struggles to get the Tea back to London, and at last the destruction of it, is amazing. Tis hard to believe Persons so hardened and abandoned.

What Measures will the Ministry take, in Consequence of this?—Will they resent it? will they dare to resent it? will they punish Us? How? By quartering Troops upon Us?—by annulling our Charter?—by laying on more duties? By restraining our Trade? By Sacrifice of Individuals, or how.

The Question is whether the Destruction of this Tea was necessary? I apprehend it was absolutely and indispensably so.—They could not send it back, the Governor, Admiral, and Collector and Comptroller would not suffer it. It was in their Power to have saved it—but in no other. It could not get by the Castle, the Men of War &c. Then there was no other Alternative but to destroy it or let it be landed. To let it be landed, would be giving up the Principle of Taxation by Parliamentary Authority, against which the Continent have struggled for 10 years, it was loosing all our labour for 10 years and subjecting ourselves and our Posterity forever to Egyptian Taskmasters—to Burthens, Indignities, to Ignominy, Reproach and Contempt, to Desolation and Oppression, to Poverty and Servitude.

Source: Excerpt from "John Adams' Diary Entry of December 17, 1773." In *The Adams Papers: Diary and Autobiography of John Adams*, Volume II 1771–1781, edited by L. H. Butterfield. Copyright © 1961 by the Massachusetts Historical Society. Reprinted by permission of the publisher, The Belknap Press of Harvard University Press.

QUESTIONS FOR ANALYSIS AND DEBATE

1. Does Thomas Hutchinson persuade you that he had no other option than to refuse to let the ship either leave or land? Why did he reject the use of troops to guard the tea?

2. How might men like Hewes be politicized by hacking open chests of tea?

3. John Adams says that Hutchinson took a malicious pleasure in forcing the tea crisis to its conclusion. Was he right or wrong in your judgment? Why?

4. What is at stake, for John Adams, in the showdown over tea, when he speaks of ten years of struggle by "the Continent" and of poverty and servitude to "Egyptian Taskmasters"? How does he feel about the possibility of deaths in the building struggle?

The committees of public safety, the committees of correspondence, the regrouped colonial assemblies, and the Continental Congresses were all functioning political bodies without any formal constitutional authority. British officials did not recognize them as legitimate, but many Americans who supported the patriot cause instantly accepted them. A key reason for the stability of such unauthorized bodies throughout the Revolutionary period was that they were composed of the same men, by and large, who had composed the official bodies now disbanded.

England's severe reaction to Boston's destruction of the tea finally succeeded in making many colonists from New Hampshire to Georgia realize that the problems of British rule went far beyond questions of taxation. The Coercive Acts infringed on liberty and denied self-government; they could not be ignored. With one colony subordinated to military rule now, and a British army at the ready in Boston, the threat of a general war was at the doorstep.

Domestic Insurrections, 1774–1775

Before the Second Continental Congress could meet, war broke out in Massachusetts. General Thomas Gage, military commander and new governor, at first thought he faced a domestic insurrection that needed only a show of force to quiet it. The rebels saw things differently: They were defending their homes and liberties against an intrusive power bent on enslaving them. To the south, a different and inverted version of the same story began to unfold, as thousands of enslaved black men and women seized an unprecedented opportunity to mount a different kind of insurrection, against planter-patriots who looked over their shoulders uneasily whenever they called out for liberty from the British.

Lexington and Concord

Over the winter of 1774–75 Americans pressed on with boycotts. Some hoped for the repeal of the Coercive Acts, while pessimists started accumulating arms and ammunition. In Massachusetts, gunpowder and shot were secretly stored, and militia units called minutemen prepared to respond on a minute's notice to any threat from the British in Boston.

Thomas Gage soon realized how desperate the British position was. The people, Gage wrote Lord North, were "numerous, worked up to a fury, and not a Boston rabble but the freeholders and farmers of the country." Gage requested twenty thousand reinforcements. He also strongly advised repeal of the Coercive Acts, but leaders in England could not admit failure. Instead, Gage was ordered in mid-April 1775 to arrest the troublemakers immediately, before the Americans got better organized.

Gage quickly planned a surprise attack on a suspected ammunition storage site at Concord, a village about eighteen miles west of Boston (Map 6.3). Near midnight on April 18, 1775, British soldiers moved west across the Charles River. Boston silversmith Paul Revere raced ahead to alert the minutemen. When the British soldiers got to Lexington, a village five miles east of Concord, they met with some seventy armed American men assembled on the village green. The British commander barked out, "Lay down your arms, you damned rebels and disperse." The militiamen hesitated and began to comply, turning to leave the green, but then someone—unknown —fired. In the next two minutes, more firing left eight Americans dead and ten wounded.

The British units then marched to Concord, any pretense of surprise gone. Three companies of minutemen nervously occupied the center of Concord but offered no challenge to the British troops as they searched in vain for the ammunition storage. Finally, at the Old North Bridge in Concord, shots were exchanged, killing two Americans and three British soldiers.

By now both sides were very apprehensive. The British had failed to find the expected arms storage, and the Americans had failed to stop their raid. As the British returned to Boston along a narrow road, militia units attacked from the sides in the bloodiest fighting of the day. In the end, 273 British soldiers were wounded or dead; the toll for the Americans stood at about 95. It was April 19, 1775, and the war had begun.

Another Rebellion against Slavery

News of the battles of Lexington and Concord spread rapidly. Within eight days, Virginians had heard of the fighting, and, as Thomas Jefferson reflected, "A phrenzy of revenge seems to have seized all ranks of people." The royal governor of Virginia,

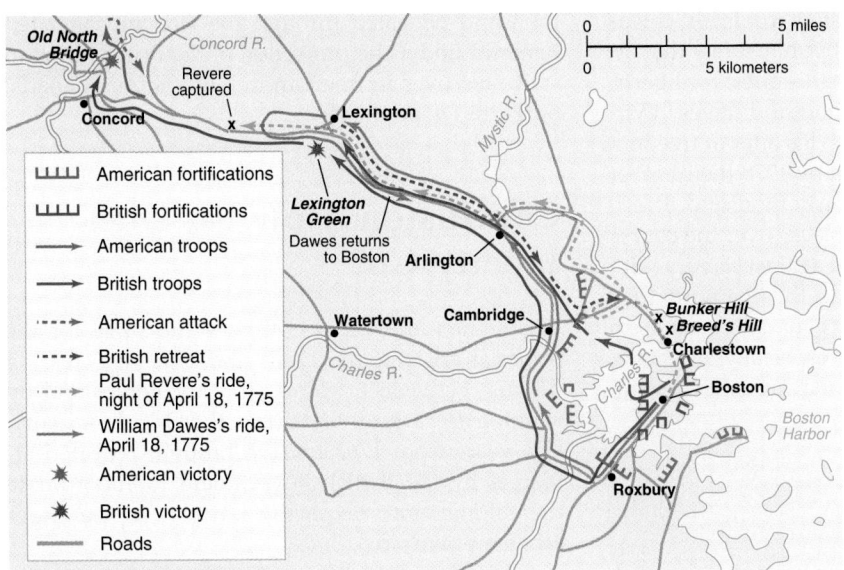

MAP 6.3

Lexington and Concord, April 1775

Under pressure from England, British forces at Boston staged a raid on a suspected rebel arms supply in Concord, Massachusetts, starting the first battle of the Revolutionary War.

Lord Dunmore, removed a large quantity of gunpowder from the Williamsburg powder house and put it on a ship in the dead of night, out of reach of any frenzied Virginians. Next, Dunmore threatened to arm the slaves, if necessary, to ward off attacks by colonists.

This was an effective threat; Dunmore understood full well how to produce panic among the planters. He did not act on it until November 1775, when he issued an official proclamation promising freedom to defecting, able-bodied slaves who would fight for the British. Dunmore's dilemma was that while he wanted to scare the planters, he had no intention of liberating all slaves or of starting a real slave rebellion. So his offer was limited to able-bodied men. Female, young, and elderly slaves were not welcome behind British lines, and many were sent back to face irate masters. Astute blacks noticed that Dunmore neglected to free his own slaves. A Virginia barber named Caesar declared that "he did not know any one foolish enough to believe him [Dunmore], for if he intended to do so, he ought first to set his own free."

In the northern colonies as well, slaves clearly recognized the evolving political struggle with England as an ideal moment to bid for freedom. A twenty-one-year-old Boston domestic slave employed biting sarcasm in a 1774 newspaper essay to call attention to the hypocrisy of local slave owners: "How well the Cry for Liberty, and the reverse Disposition for exercise of oppressive Power over others agree,—I humbly think it does not require the

Penetration of a Philosopher to Determine." This extraordinary young woman, Phillis Wheatley, had already gained international recognition through a book of poems, endorsed by Governor Thomas Hutchinson and Boston merchant John Hancock and published in London in 1773. Possibly neither man fully appreciated the irony of his endorsement, however, for Wheatley's poems spoke of "Fair Freedom" as the "Goddess long desir'd" by Africans enslaved in America. At the urging of his wife, Wheatley's master freed the young poet in 1775.

Wheatley's poetic ideas about freedom found concrete expression among other discontented groups. Some slaves in Boston petitioned Thomas Gage, promising to fight for the British if he would liberate them. Gage turned them down. In Ulster County, New York, along the Hudson River, two blacks were overheard discussing gunpowder, and thus a plot unraveled that involved at least twenty slaves in four villages discovered to have ammunition stashed away.

The numerical preponderance of black slaves in the southern colonies deepened white fears of rebellion. In Maryland, soon after the news of the Lexington battle arrived, slaves exhibited impatience with their status, in light of the revolutionary movement unfolding around them. One Maryland planter reported that "the insolence of the Negroes in this county is come to such a height, that we are under a necessity of disarming them. . . . We took about eighty guns, some bayonets, swords, etc." In North Carolina, a planned uprising was uncovered and scores of slaves were arrested; ironically, it was the revolutionary committee of public safety that ordered the whippings to punish this quest for liberty.

In 1775, probably several thousand slaves in Virginia took Lord Dunmore up on his offer of freedom for joining the British side, and by 1778 the number had escalated to as many as thirty thousand. Possibly eighty thousand southern blacks over the course of the Revolutionary War voted against slavery with their feet. Some failed to achieve the liberation they were seeking. The British army generally used them for menial labor; and disease, especially smallpox, devastated encampments of runaways. But several

thousand persisted through the war and later left America under the protection of the British army to start new lives in freedom in Nova Scotia, Canada, or Sierra Leone in Africa.

Conclusion: How Far Does Liberty Go?

The French and Indian War set the stage for the imperial crisis of the 1760s and 1770s by creating distrust between England and its colonies and by running up a huge deficit in the British treasury. The years from 1763 to 1775 brought repeated attempts by the British government to subordinate the colonies into taxpaying partners in the larger scheme of empire.

American resistance grew slowly but steadily over those years. In 1765, Thomas Hutchinson shared with Samuel Adams the belief that it was exceedingly unwise for England to assert a right to taxation, because Parliament did not adequately represent Americans. But by temperament and office, Hutchinson had to uphold British policy; Adams, in contrast, protested the policy and made political activists out of thousands in the process.

By 1775, events propelled many Americans to the conclusion that a concerted effort was afoot to deprive them of all their liberties, the most important of which were the right to self-taxation, the right to live free of an occupying army, and finally their right to self-rule. Hundreds of minutemen converged on Concord, prepared to die for these American liberties. April 19 marked the start of their rebellion.

Another rebellion under way in 1775 was doomed to be short-circuited. Black Americans who had experienced actual slavery now listened to shouts of "Liberty!" from white crowds and appropriated the language of revolution swirling around them that spoke to their deepest needs and hopes. Defiance of authority was indeed contagious.

The emerging leaders of the patriot cause were mindful of a delicate balance they felt they had to strike. To energize the American public about the crisis with England, they had to politicize masses of men—and eventually women too—and infuse them with a keen sense of their rights and liberties. But in so doing, they became fearful of the unintended consequences of teaching a vocabulary of rights and liberties. They worried that the rhetoric of enslavement might go too far.

LORD DUNMORE'S PROCLAMATION
In November 1775, Lord Dunmore of Virginia offered freedom to "all indented Servants, Negroes, or others (appertaining to Rebels)" who would help put down the rebellion. Dunmore issued multiple printed copies in broadside form from the safety of a ship anchored at Norfolk, Virginia.
Special Collections, University of Virginia, Alderman Library.

The question of how far the crisis could be stretched before something snapped was largely unexamined in 1765. Patriot leaders in that year wanted a correction, a restoration of an ancient liberty of self-taxation that Parliament seemed to be ignoring. But events from 1765 to 1775 convinced many that no return to the old ways was possible. A challenge to Parliament's right to tax had led, step by step, to a challenge to Parliament's right to legislate over the colonies in any matter. If Parliament's sovereignty was set aside, then who actually had authority over the American colonies? By 1775, with the outbreak of fighting and the specter of slave rebellions, American leaders turned to the king for the answer to that question.

FOR FURTHER READING ABOUT THE TOPICS IN THIS CHAPTER, see the Online Bibliography at www.bedfordstmartins.com/roarkcompact.

FOR ADDITIONAL FIRST-HAND ACCOUNTS OF THIS PERIOD, see pages 78–92 in Michael Johnson, ed., *Reading the American Past,* Second Edition, Volume I.

TO ASSESS YOUR MASTERY OF THE MATERIAL IN THIS CHAPTER, see the Online Study Guide at www.bedfordstmartins.com/roarkcompact.

CHRONOLOGY

1747 Ohio Company of Virginia formed.

1754 French and Indian War begins in America.

Albany Congress proposes Plan of Union and courts Iroquois support.

1755 General Edward Braddock defeated by French and Indians in Pennsylvania.

1757 William Pitt, prime minister in Britain, fully commits to war effort.

1759 Quebec falls to British.

1760 George III becomes British king.

1763 Treaty of Paris ends French and Indian War.

Pontiac's uprising provokes fear and destruction in western frontier settlements.

Proclamation Act of 1763 prohibits settlement west of Appalachians.

1764 The Revenue (Sugar) Act lowers tax on foreign molasses to promote compliance with trade duty.

1765 Stamp Act imposes tax on documents.

May. Patrick Henry sponsors Virginia Resolves.

August. Crowd actions in Boston inaugurate Sons of Liberty.

October. Stamp Act Congress meets in New York City.

1766 Stamp Act repealed; Declaratory Act asserts Parliament's control over colonies.

1767 Townshend duties reinstate revenue-raising taxes.

1768 **Fall.** British troops stationed in Boston.

1769 Year of nonimportation agreements; Daughters of Liberty appear.

1770 **March 5.** Boston Massacre.

Townshend duties repealed; Lord North comes to power.

1772 **June.** *Gaspée* attacked off Rhode Island.

Committees of correspondence formed.

1773 Tea Act lowers price of tea to encourage Americans to purchase legal rather than smuggled tea.

December 16. Destruction of tea in Boston harbor.

1774 Parliament passes Coercive Acts (Intolerable Acts): Boston Port Act, Massachusetts Government Act, Impartial Administration of Justice Act, a new amendment to the 1765 Quartering Act, and the Quebec Act.

September. First Continental Congress meets. Continental Association formed.

1775 **April 19.** Battles of Lexington and Concord.

Virginia's Lord Dunmore promises freedom to defecting slaves.

PAINTED DRUM

Drums were essential military equipment in eighteenth-century wars. Small to carry but loud in use, they provided a percussive beat that penetrated the din of the battlefield to signal troop advances, retreats, or other field movements. Drummers often stood right behind soldiers in firing formation, regulating the timing of each volley of shots. The eagle painted on this Revolutionary-era drum from Fort Ticonderoga in New York holds a banner inscribed "Sons of Liberty," a name adopted in 1765 to distinguish protesters of British policies toward the colonies.

Fort Ticonderoga Museum.

THE WAR FOR AMERICA
1775–1783

ABIGAIL ADAMS WAS IMPATIENT for American independence. While her husband, John, was away in Philadelphia as a member of the Second Continental Congress, Abigail tended house and farm in Braintree, Massachusetts, just south of British-occupied Boston. She had four young children to look after, and in addition to her female duties, such as cooking, sewing, and making soap, she also had to shoulder male duties in her husband's absence—hiring farm help, managing rental property, selling the crop. John wrote to her often, approving of the fine "Farmeress" who was conducting his business so well. She replied, conveying news of the family along with shrewd commentary on revolutionary politics. In December 1775, she chastised the congress for being too timid and urged that independence be declared. A few months later, she astutely observed to John that southern slave owners might shrink from a war in the name of liberty: "I have sometimes been ready to think that the passion for Liberty cannot be Equally strong in the Breasts of those who have been accustomed to deprive their fellow Creatures of theirs."

"I long to hear that you have declared an independency," she wrote in March 1776. "And by the way in the new Code of Laws which I suppose it will be necessary for you to make I desire you would Remember the Ladies, and be more generous and favourable to them than your ancestors." If Abigail was politically precocious in favoring independence and questioning slave owners' devotion to liberty, she was positively visionary in this extraordinary plea to her husband to "Remember the Ladies." "Do not put such unlimited power into the hands of the Husbands," she advised. "Remember all Men would be tyrants if they could." Abigail had put her finger on another form of tyranny that was rarely remarked on in her society: that of men over women. "If particular care and attention is not paid to the Ladies," she jokingly threatened, "we are determined to foment a Rebellion, and will not hold ourselves bound by any Laws in which we have no voice, or Representation."

John Adams dismissed his wife's provocative idea as a "saucy" suggestion: "As to your extraordinary Code of Laws, I cannot but Laugh." The Revolution had perhaps unleashed discontent among other dependent groups, he allowed; children, apprentices, students, Indians, and blacks had grown "disobedient" and "insolent." "But your Letter was the first Intimation that another Tribe more numerous and powerful than all the rest were grown discontented." Men were too smart to repeal their "Masculine Systems," John assured her, for otherwise they would find themselves living under a "despotism of the petticoat."

This clever exchange between husband and wife in 1776 says much about the cautious, limited radicalism of the American Revolution. Both John and Abigail Adams understood (Abigail probably far more than John) that ungluing the hierarchical bond between the king and his subjects potentially unglued other kinds of

ABIGAIL ADAMS

Abigail Smith Adams was twenty-two when she sat for this pastel portrait in 1766. A wife for two years and a mother for one, Adams exhibits a steady, intelligent gaze. Pearls and a lace collar anchor her femininity, while her facial expression projects a confidence and maturity not often credited to young women of the 1760s.

Courtesy of the Massachusetts Historical Society ©.

social inequalities. John was surely joking in listing the groups made unruly in the spirit of a challenge to authority, for children, apprentices, and students were hardly rebellious in the 1770s. But it would soon prove to be an uncomfortable joke, because Indians and blacks did take up the cause of their own liberty during the Revolution, and the great majority of them saw their liberty best served by joining the British side in the war.

Though Abigail Adams was impatient for independence, many other Americans feared separation from Britain. What kind of civilized country had no king? Who, if not Britain, would protect Americans from the French and Spanish? How could the colonies possibly win a war against the most powerful military machine on the globe? Rec-

onciliation, not independence, was favored by many.

Members of the Continental Congress, whether they were pro-independence like John Adams or more cautiously hoping for reconciliation, had their hands full in 1775 and 1776. The war had already begun, and it fell to the congress to raise an army, finance it, and explore diplomatic alliances with foreign countries. In part a classic war with professional armies and textbook battles, the Revolutionary War was also a civil war in America, at times even a brutal guerrilla war, of committed rebels versus loyalists.

In one glorious moment, the congress issued a ringing statement about how social hierarchy would be rearranged in America after submission to the king was undone. That was on July 4, 1776, when the Declaration of Independence asserted that "all men are created equal." But this striking phrase went completely unremarked in the two days of congressional debate spent tinkering with the language of the Declaration. The solvent to dissolve social inequalities in America was created at that moment, but none of the men at the congress, or even Abigail Adams up in Braintree, fully realized it at the time.

The Second Continental Congress

On May 10, 1775, nearly one month after the fighting at Lexington and Concord, the Second Continental Congress assembled in Philadelphia. The congress immediately set to work on two crucial and seemingly contradictory tasks: to raise and supply an army and to negotiate a reconciliation with England. But as the war progressed and hopes of reconciliation faded, delegates at the congress began to ponder the treasonous act of declaring independence.

Assuming Political and Military Authority

As with the First Continental Congress, the delegates to the second were well-established figures in their home colonies, but they still had to learn to know and trust each other; they did not always agree. The Adams cousins John and Samuel defined the radical end of the spectrum, favoring independence. John Dickinson of Pennsylvania, no longer the eager revolutionary who had dashed off *Letters from a Farmer* back in 1767, was now a moderate, seeking reconciliation with England. Benjamin Franklin, fresh off a ship from an eleven-year residence in England, was feared by some to be a British spy. Mutual suspicions flourished easily when the undertaking was so dangerous, opinions were so varied, and a misstep could spell disaster.

Most of the delegates were not yet prepared to break with England. Several legislatures instructed their delegates to oppose independence. Some felt that government without a monarchical element was unworkable, while others feared it might be suicidal to lose England's protection against the traditional enemies, France and Spain. Colonies that traded actively with England feared undermining their economies. Nor were the vast majority of ordinary Americans able to envision independence from the British monarchy. From the Stamp Act of 1765 to the Coercive Acts of 1774, the constitutional struggle with England had turned on the issue of parliamentary power. During that decade, almost no one had questioned the legitimacy of the monarchy.

The few men at the Continental Congress who did think that independence was desirable were, not surprisingly, from Massachusetts. Their colony had been stripped of civil government under the Coercive Acts and their capital was occupied by the British army. Even so, those men knew that it was premature to push for a break with England. John Adams wrote to Abigail in June 1775: "America is a great, unwieldy body. Its progress must be slow. It is like a large fleet sailing under convoy. The fleetest sailors must wait for the dullest and slowest."

As slow as the American colonies were in sailing toward political independence, they needed to take swift action to coordinate a military defense, for the Massachusetts countryside was under threat of further attack. Even the hesitant moderates in the congress agreed that a military buildup was necessary. Around the country, militia units from New York to Georgia collected arms and drilled on village greens in anticipation. On June 14, the congress voted to create the Continental army. Choosing the commander in chief offered an opportunity to demonstrate that this was no local war of a single rebellious colony. Congress bypassed Artemas Ward from Massachusetts, then already command-

ing the soldiers massed around Boston, and instead chose a southerner, George Washington. Washington's appointment sent the message to England that there was widespread commitment to war beyond New England.

Next the congress drew up a document titled "A Declaration of the Causes and Necessity of Taking Up Arms," which rehearsed familiar arguments about the tyranny of Parliament and the need to defend traditional English liberties. This declaration was first drafted by a young Virginia planter, Thomas Jefferson, a newcomer to the congress and a radical on the question of independence. The moderate John Dickinson, fearing that the declaration would offend England and rule out reconciliation, was allowed to rewrite it; however, he still left much of Jefferson's highly charged language about choosing "to die freemen rather than to live slaves." Even a man as reluctant for independence as Dickinson acknowledged the necessity of military defense against an invading army.

To pay for the military buildup, the congress authorized a currency issue of two million dollars. The Continental dollars were merely paper; they did not represent gold or silver, for the congress owned no precious metals. The delegates somewhat naively expected that the currency would be accepted as valuable on trust as it spread in the population through the hands of soldiers, farmers, munitions suppliers, and beyond.

In just two months, the Second Continental Congress had created an army, declared war, and issued its own currency. It had taken on the major functions of a legitimate government, both military and financial, without any legal basis for its authority, for it had not—and would not for a full year—declare independence from the authority of the king.

Pursuing Both War and Peace

Three days after the congress voted to raise the Continental army, one of the bloodiest battles of the Revolution occurred. The British commander in Boston, Thomas Gage, had recently received troop reinforcements, three talented generals (William Howe, John Burgoyne, and Henry Clinton), and new instructions to root out the rebels around Boston. But before Gage could take the offensive, the Americans fortified the hilly terrain of Charlestown, a peninsula just north of Boston, on the night of June 16, 1775.

The British generals could have nipped off the peninsula where it met the mainland, to box in the Americans. But General Howe insisted on a bold frontal assault, sending his 2,500 soldiers across the water and up the hill, in an intimidating but potentially costly attack. The American troops, 1,400 strong, held their fire until the British were about twenty yards away. At that distance, the musket volley was sure and deadly, and the British turned back. Twice more General Howe sent his men up the hill to receive the same blast of firepower; each time they had to step around the bodies felled in the previous attempts.

On the third assault, the British took the hill, mainly because the American ammunition supply gave out, and the defenders quickly retreated. The Battle of Bunker Hill was thus a British victory, but an expensive one. The dead numbered 226 on the British side, with more than 800 wounded; the Americans suffered 140 dead, 271 wounded, and 30 captured. As General Clinton later remarked, "It was a dear bought victory; another such would have ruined us."

Instead of pursuing the fleeing Americans, Howe pulled his army back to Boston, unwilling to risk more raids into the countryside. If the British had had any grasp of the basic instability of the American units gathered around Boston, they might have pushed westward and perhaps decisively defeated the core of the Continental army in its infancy. Instead they lingered in Boston, abandoning it without a fight nine months later. Howe used the time in Boston to inoculate his army against smallpox, because a new epidemic of the deadly disease was growing in port cities along the Atlantic. Inoculation worked by producing a light but real (and therefore risky) case of smallpox, followed by lifelong immunity. Howe's instinct here was right: from 1775 to 1782, the years coinciding with the American Revolution, some 130,000 people on the

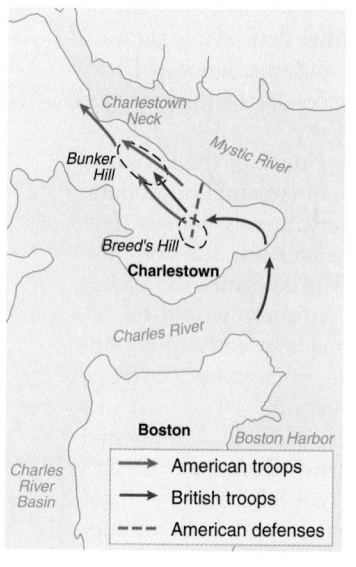

The Battle of Bunker Hill, 1775

American continent, most of them Indians, died of smallpox.

A week after Bunker Hill, when General Washington arrived to take charge of the new Continental army, he found enthusiastic but undisciplined troops. Sanitation was an unknown concept, drunkenness on duty was common, and soldiers came and went at will. The amazed general attributed the disarray to the New England custom of letting militia units elect their own officers, a custom he felt undermined deference. Washington quickly imposed more hierarchy and authority.

While military plans moved forward, the Second Continental Congress pursued its second, contradictory objective, reconciliation with England. Delegates from the middle colonies (Pennsylvania, Delaware, and New York) whose merchants depended on trade with England urged that channels for negotiation remain open. Congressional moderates led by John Dickinson engineered an appeal to the king, called the Olive Branch Petition, in July 1775. The petition affirmed loyalty to the monarchy and blamed all the troubles on the king's ministers and on Parliament. It proposed that the American colonial assemblies be recognized as individual parliaments, under the umbrella of the monarchy. By late fall 1775, however, reconciliation was out of the question. King George rejected the Olive Branch Petition and heatedly condemned the Americans, calling them rebels and traitors. It was thereafter hard to maintain the illusion that ministers and not the king himself were to blame for the conflict.

Thomas Paine and the Case for Independence

Pressure for independence mounted starting in January 1776, when a pamphlet titled *Common Sense* appeared in Philadelphia. Thomas Paine, its author, was an English artisan and coffeehouse intellectual who had come to America in the fall of 1774. He landed a job with the *Pennsylvania Magazine* and soon met delegates from the Second Continental Congress. With their encouragement, he wrote *Common Sense* to lay out a lively and compelling case for complete independence.

In simple yet forceful language, Paine elaborated on the absurdities of the British monarchy. Why should one man, by accident of birth, claim extensive power over others? he asked. A king might be foolish or wicked. "One of the strongest

RHODE ISLAND REGIMENT FLAG
In the absence of an official American flag, regiments often commissioned their own symbolic banners. Almost certainly the elaborate stitchery and even the design work of this Rhode Island artillery company flag came from female hands wielding needle and thread. There were thus dozens, not just one, "Betsy Ross," the legendary Philadelphia woman credited with designing the prototype of the stars and stripes. A popular 1770s flag-theme portrayed a coiled rattlesnake paired with the slogan "Don't Tread on Me." Such a flag conveyed a dire warning and a clear point of view about who had started the war in America: the rattler, uniquely American, was deadly only when aroused or provoked. This 1775 flag offers an unusual variant, using the more formal "do not" instead of "don't." The slogan endures today, showing up on state license plates and as lyrics in popular songs. Note as well another nearly familiar motto: "In God We Hope." It precedes by almost a century the Civil War–era origins of the modern-day motto on U.S. coinage, "In God We Trust."
Collection of Mr. and Mrs. Boleslaw Mastai.

natural proofs of the folly of hereditary right in kings," Paine wrote, "is that nature disapproves it; otherwise she would not so frequently turn it into ridicule by giving mankind an *ass for a lion.*" Calling the king of England an ass broke through the automatic deference most Americans still had for the monarchy. To replace monarchy, he advocated republican government, based on the consent of the people. Rulers, according to Paine, were only representatives of the people, and the best form of government relied on frequent elections to achieve the most direct democracy possible.

Paine's pamphlet sold more than 150,000 copies in a matter of weeks. Newspapers reprinted it; men read it aloud in taverns and coffeehouses; John Adams sent a copy to Abigail Adams, who passed it around to neighbors. Another of John Adams's correspondents wrote him in late February that many New Englanders desired an official declaration of independence. Middle and southern colonies, under no immediate threat of violence, remained cautious. But by May, all but four colonies were in favor of independence. Two of the holdouts were New York and South Carolina, both with large loyalist populations.

In early June, the Virginia delegation introduced a resolution calling for independence. The moderates still commanded enough support to postpone a vote on the measure until July, so they could go home and consult about this extreme step. In the meantime, the congress appointed a committee, with Thomas Jefferson and others, to draft a longer document setting out the case for independence.

On July 2, after intense politicking, all but one state voted for independence; New York abstained. The congress then turned to the document drafted by Thomas Jefferson and his committee. Jefferson began with a preamble that articulated philosophical principles about natural rights, equality, the right of revolution, and the consent of the governed as the only true basis for government. He then listed more than two dozen grievances against King George. The congress merely glanced at the political philosophy, finding nothing exceptional in it; the ideas about natural rights and the consent of the governed were seen as "self-evident truths," just as the document claimed. In itself, this absence of comment showed a remarkable transformation in political thinking since the end of the French and Indian War. The single phrase declaring the natural equality of "all men" was also passed over without comment; no one elaborated on its radical implications.

For two days, the congress wrangled over the list of grievances, especially the issue of slavery. Jefferson had included an impassioned statement blaming the king for slavery, which delegates from Georgia and South Carolina struck out. They had no intention of denouncing their labor system as an evil practice. But the congress let stand another of Jefferson's fervent grievances, blaming the king for mobilizing "the merciless Indian Savages" into bloody frontier warfare.

On July 4, the amendments to Jefferson's text were complete and the document was formally adopted. (See appendix, pages A-1–A-3.) Nearly a month later, on August 2, the delegates gathered to

DECLARATION OF INDEPENDENCE READ TO A CROWD
Printed copies of the Declaration of Independence (see appendix, pages A-1–A-3) were read aloud in public places throughout America in the week after July 4, 1776, often accompanied by carefully orchestrated celebrations.
Library of Congress.

www.bedfordstmartins.com/roarkcompact SEE THE ONLINE STUDY GUIDE for more help in analyzing this image.

sign the official parchment copy, handwritten by an exacting scribe. Four men, including John Dickinson, declined to sign; several others "signed with regret . . . and with many doubts," according to John Adams. The document was then printed, widely distributed, and read aloud in celebrations everywhere. A crowd in New York listened to a public reading of it and then toppled a lead statue of George III on horseback to melt it down for bullets. On July 15, the New York delegation switched from abstention to endorsement, making the vote on independence truly unanimous.

The First Year of War, 1775–1776

Both sides had cause to approach the war for America with uneasiness. The Americans, with only inexperienced and undertrained militias, opposed the mightiest military power in the world, and many thought it was foolhardy to expect victory. Further, pockets of loyalism remained strong; the country was not united. But the British faced serious obstacles as well. Their utter disdain for the fighting abilities of the Americans had to be reevaluated in light of their costly Bunker Hill victory. The logistics of supplying an army with food across three thousand miles of water were daunting. And since the British goal was to regain allegiance, not to destroy and conquer, the army was often constrained in its actions.

The American Military Forces

Americans claimed that the initial months of war were purely defensive, triggered by the British army's invasion. But quickly the war also became a rebellion, an overthrowing of long-established authority. As both defenders and rebels, Americans were generally highly motivated to fight, and the potential manpower that could be mobilized was in theory very great.

From the earliest decades of settlement, local defense in the colonies rested with a militia requiring participation from nearly every able-bodied man over age sixteen. When the main threat to public safety was the occasional Indian attack, the local militia made sense. But such attacks were now mostly limited to the frontier. Southern militias trained with potential slave rebellions in mind, but these too were rare. The annual muster day in most communities had evolved into a holiday of drinking, marching, and perhaps shooting practice with small fowling guns or muskets. (See "The Promise of Technology," page 148.)

Militias were best suited to limited engagements, when a local community was under immediate attack. But they were not appropriate for extended wars requiring military campaigns far from home. In forming the Continental army, the congress set enlistment at one year, but army leaders soon learned that that was not enough time to train soldiers and carry out campaigns. A three-year enlistment earned a new soldier a twenty-dollar bonus, while men who committed for the duration of the war were promised a postwar land grant of one hundred acres. To make this inducement effective, of course, recruits had to believe that the Americans would win. By early 1777, the army was the largest it would ever be.

Women also served in the Continental army. They were needed to do the daily cooking and washing, and after battle they nursed the wounded. The British army established a ratio of one woman to every ten men; in the Continental army, the ratio was set at one woman to fifteen men. Close to twenty thousand women served during the war, probably most of them wives of men in service. Children tagged along as well, and babies were born in the camps and on the road.

Black Americans were at first excluded from the Continental army, a rule that slave owner George

BLACK REVOLUTIONARY WAR SAILOR
Thousands of black men served on the patriot side as soldiers and sailors, usually at the rank of private or ordinary seaman. Their names are preserved in regiment records and crew lists; rarely, however, were their faces preserved. This 1780 portrait by an unknown artist shows an unnamed man, sword and scabbard at hand, dressed in military finery with a ship in view to establish his naval connection.
Collection of A. A. McBurney.

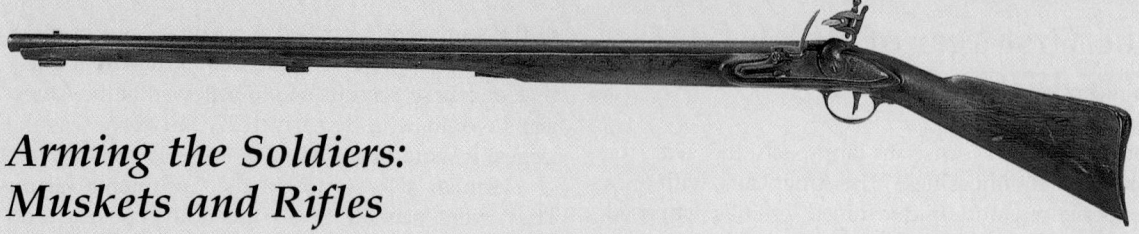

Arming the Soldiers: Muskets and Rifles

H OW COMBAT-READY WAS THE AMERICAN SIDE of the Revolutionary War? Were there adequate numbers of firearms along with men trained in their use? These are lively and important questions that have generated sharp debate among twenty-first-century historians and that speak to the question of the centrality and significance of guns in the founding days of the United States.

In theory, all towns in the colonies were expected to maintain a local militia, at the ready to protect their own communities. All able-bodied adult men were supposed to participate in annual training days, bringing their own guns, but in many communities, such "muster" or "train-band" days had been gradually transformed into festive town holidays. Male camaraderie as expressed in displays of parading and shooting competitions often took precedence over military drill and serious musket practice, an altogether understandable relaxation in coastal or northern towns not feeling any imminent threat of Indian attack or slave rebellion.

Guns were not the weapon of choice for procuring everyday food; table meat came mainly from domesticated animals slaughtered with large knives. But they were useful for the small-game hunting of ducks and wild turkeys, or raccoons and squirrels killed as farm pests. Americans used guns known as fowling pieces that fired shot (small pellets) to kill such game at close range. Households on the frontier would need larger guns for shooting deer, bears, or wolves; but residents of Lexington and Concord, not to mention Boston, rarely encountered bears.

Muskets firing one-ounce lead balls were the preferred weapon of eighteenth-century warfare. Muskets were a sixteenth-century invention, featuring by the mid-eighteenth century an improved flintlock ignition system in which the trigger released a spring-held cock that caused a hammer to strike a flint, a special rock that sparks easily. The

sparks set off a small charge in a priming pan leading directly to a larger explosion in the barrel. To load the gun, a soldier first put the it on half-cock, to prevent an accidental firing. He next put a small quantity of powder (carried in a powder horn) in the priming pan and closed it, poured more powder down the smooth gun barrel, dropped in the lead projectile, and then wadded paper down the barrel with a ramrod to hold the loose ball in place. He would then raise the gun to firing position, put it on full cock, and fire. The whole procedure took highly experienced shooters from 45 to 90 seconds.

The range of muskets extended only about 50 to 100 yards. They were notoriously inaccurate, owing to the poor fit between ball and barrel and

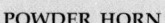

POWDER HORN
James Pike, a twenty-three-year-old New England militiaman, made and then personalized this powder horn, a hollow cow's horn capped on both ends with leather. The stopper was designed to be pulled off by the teeth, leaving the hands to hold the musket barrel and pour the powder. Pike's carvings suggest his motivation for fighting. Above his name he depicts a scene dated April 19, 1775, in which British soldiers, labeled "the Aggressors," fire through the Liberty Tree at "Provincials, Defending." Pike was not at Lexington or Concord; his first combat experience came two months later at the Battle of Bunker Hill, where he saw his brother killed and was himself wounded in the shoulder.
Chicago Historical Society.

to the considerable kick produced by firing, which interfered with aiming. Far more accurate were longer-barreled rifles, used in frontier regions where big-game hunting was more common. The interior of a rifle barrel carried spiral grooves that imparted spin to the ball as it traversed the barrel, stabilizing and lengthening its flight, and enabling expert marksmen to hit small targets at 150 or 200 yards. Yet military commanders much preferred muskets to rifles. Rifles took twice as long to load and fire, and their longer barrels made them unwieldy for soldiers on the march. Inaccurate muskets were quite deadly enough when fired in unison at 50 yards.

How many American men actually owned fowling pieces, muskets, or rifles? Evidence on this point is complicated and controversial. Probate inventories, many thousands of which exist in county courthouses, offer a partial answer. An inventory, taken soon after the owner's death, listed the contents of an estate in order to establish its value, both for inheritance purposes and for paying off the deceased person's creditors. Yet these sources are fraught with thorny problems that make them something less than an accurate indicator of possessions. For one thing, they are often not complete: If few inventories itemize clothing, can we conclude the decedents went nude? Clearly not. Further, they list possessions of a recently deceased person who owned property of interest to creditors and heirs, so they are biased by age (older), sex (male), and wealth (more). No doubt many men and women died without having their property inventoried at all.

Despite these and other complexities, scholars have worked with probate inventories as the best available source of information. Current careful studies based on this source yield estimates for the 1770s on overall gun ownership (including guns of

all kinds) that range from 40 to 50 percent of all probated estates, with significant regional variations.

A second way to assess gun ownership is to look at the arms procurement experiences of state legislatures and the Continental Congress as they geared up for war. Soldiers were requested to report for duty with muskets, gunpowder, and cartridges; when they were underarmed, their officers let superiors know. A New Hampshire captain complained of his unit's plight in June 1775: "We are in want of both arms and ammunition. There is but very little, or none worth mentioning—perhaps one pound of powder to twenty men, and not one-half our men have arms." A militia officer in Pennsylvania noted that men who owned high-quality muskets and rifles were often reluctant to report for duty with them unless assured they would be reimbursed in the event of loss of the valuable possession. A Prussian general, who volunteered his expertise to the Continental army, arrived at Valley Forge in 1778 and was shocked to find "muskets, carbines, fowling pieces, and rifles" all in the same company of troops. While this evidence points to an underarmed soldiery, the opposite evidence—militia captains who failed to register complaints—did not leave a paper trail for historians.

Certainly the Continental Congress understood that obtaining more muskets was essential to the war effort. Before 1774, American ironworks artisans imported British-made gunlocks, the central firing mechanism, and added the wooden stock and iron barrel to produce muskets. But the British Parliament, anticipating trouble, prohibited all gunlock and firearm exports to the colonies in October 1774. Congress turned to French and Dutch suppliers to purchase gunlocks, gunpowder, and finished muskets.

Muskets and even fowling pieces worked well enough for the Revolutionary War, where combatants on both sides were similarly armed and engaged in choreographed and synchronized firing at close range. Not until the fourth and fifth decades of the nineteenth century would the United States begin to manufacture firearms whose components were machine-tooled rather than handcrafted, leading to a faster and cheaper manufacturing process and more accurate and deadly weapons. With handguns like the Colt revolver and rifles like the Remington, both with repeat-fire capability, America entered an entirely new stage in gun history.

Washington made as commander in chief. But as manpower needs increased, the northern states began to welcome free blacks into service; even slaves could serve in some states, with their masters' permission. About five thousand black men served in the Revolutionary War on the rebel side, mostly from the northern states. Black Continental soldiers sometimes were segregated into separate units; two battalions from Rhode Island were entirely black. Just under three hundred blacks joined regiments from Connecticut. While some of these were draftees, others were clearly inspired by the ideals of freedom being voiced in a war against tyranny. For example, twenty-three blacks gave "Liberty," "Freedom," or "Freeman" as their surname at the time of enlistment.

Military service helped to politicize Americans during the early stages of the war. In early 1776, independence was a risky idea, potentially treasonous. But as the war heated up and recruiters demanded commitment, some Americans discovered that apathy had its dangers as well. Anyone who refused to serve ran the risk of being called a traitor to the cause. Military service established one's credentials as a patriot; it became a prime way of defining and demonstrating political allegiance.

The American army was at times raw and inexperienced and much of the time woefully undermanned. It never had the precision and discipline of European professional armies. But it was never as bad as the British continually assumed. The British were to learn that it was a serious mistake to underrate the enemy.

The British Strategy

The American strategy was relatively straightforward—to repulse and defeat an invading army. The British strategy was not nearly so clear. England wanted to put down a rebellion and restore monarchical power in the colonies, but the question was how to accomplish this. A decisive defeat of the Continental army was essential but not sufficient to end the rebellion, for the British would still have to contend with an armed and highly motivated insurgent population.

Furthermore, there was no single political nerve center whose capture would spell certain victory. The Continental Congress floated from place to place, staying just out of reach of the British. During the course of the war, the British captured and

for a time occupied every major port city—Boston, New York, Newport, Philadelphia, and Charleston—essential for receiving their constant caravan of supply ships. But capturing them brought no serious loss to the Americans, 95 percent of whom lived in the countryside.

England's delicate task was to restore the old governments, not to destroy an enemy country. Hence, the British generals were usually reluctant to ravage the countryside, confiscate food, or burn villages and towns. There were thirteen distinct political entities to capture, pacify, and then restore to the crown, and they were spread out in a long line from New Hampshire to Georgia. Clearly a large land army was required for the job. Without the willingness to seize food from the locals, such an army needed hundreds of supply ships that could keep several months' worth of food in storage. Another ingredient of the British strategy was the untested assumption that many Americans remained loyal to the king and would come to their aid. Without substantial numbers of loyal subjects, the plan to restore old royal governments made no sense.

The overall British plan was a divide-and-conquer approach, focusing first on New York, the state judged to harbor the greatest number of loyal subjects. New York offered a geographic advantage as well: Control of the Hudson River would allow the British to isolate those troublesome New Englanders. Armies could descend from Canada and move up from New York City along the Hudson River into western Massachusetts. Between a naval blockade on the eastern coast and army raids in the west, Massachusetts could be driven to surrender. New Jersey and Pennsylvania would fall in line, the British thought, due to loyalist strength. Virginia was a problem, like Massachusetts, but the British were confident that the Carolinas would help them isolate and subdue Virginia. Or so the British hoped.

Quebec, New York, and New Jersey

In late 1775, an American expedition was swiftly launched to capture the British cities Montreal and Quebec before British reinforcements could arrive. This offensive was a clear sign that the war was not purely a reaction to the invasion of Massachusetts. A force of New York Continentals commanded by General Richard Montgomery took Montreal easily in September 1775 and then advanced on Quebec.

Meanwhile, a second contingent of Continentals led by Colonel Benedict Arnold moved through Maine to Quebec, a punishing trek through freezing rain with woefully inadequate supplies; many men died. Arnold's determination to get to Quebec was heroic, but in human costs the campaign was a tragedy. Arnold and Montgomery jointly attacked Quebec in December but failed to take the city (Map 7.1). Worse yet, they encountered smallpox, which killed more men than had been felled by the British.

The main action of the first year of war came not in Canada, however, but in New York, so crucial to England. In August 1776, some 45,000 British troops (including 8,000 German mercenaries, called Hessians) landed south of New York City, under the command of General Howe. General Washington had anticipated that New York would be Howe's target and had moved his army, numbering about 20,000, south from Massachusetts. The Battle of Long Island, in late August 1776, pitted the well-trained British redcoats against a very green Continental army. Howe attacked, inflicting many casualties (1,500 dead and wounded) and spreading panic among the American soldiers, who fled under fire to the eastern edge of Long Island. Howe failed to press forward, however, perhaps remembering the costly victory of Bunker Hill, and in the meantime Washington evacuated his troops to Manhattan Island in the dead of a foggy night.

Washington knew it would be hard to hold Manhattan, so he further withdrew north to two critical forts on either side of the Hudson River. For two months, the armies engaged in limited skirmishing, but in November, Howe finally captured Fort Washington and Fort Lee, taking thousands of prisoners. Washington retreated quickly across New Jersey into Pennsylvania. Yet again, Howe unaccountably failed to press his advantage. Had he attacked Washington's army at Philadelphia, he probably would have taken the city. Instead he parked his German troops in winter quarters along the Delaware River. Perhaps he knew that many of the Continental soldiers' enlistment periods ended on December 31, so he felt confident that the Americans would not attack him. But he was wrong. On Christmas—a holiday Germans celebrated with much more spirit (and spirits) than did Americans—Washington recrossed the Delaware River at night with 2,400 men and made a quick capture of the unsuspecting German soldiers at Trenton. This impressive victory did much to restore the sagging morale of the patriot side. For the next two weeks, Washington remained on the offensive, capturing supplies in a clever attack on British units at Princeton on January 3. Soon he was safe in Morristown, in northern New Jersey, settled in for the winter, finally with time enough to administer mass smallpox inoculations and see the men through the abbrieviated course of the disease. Future recruits would also face inoculation.

All in all, in the first year of declared war, the rebellious Americans had a few isolated moments to feel proud of but also much to worry about. The very inexperienced Continental army had barely hung on in the New York campaign. Washington had shown exceptional daring as well as admirable restraint, but what really saved the Americans may have been the repeated reluctance of the British to follow through militarily when they had the advantage.

The Home Front

Battlefields alone did not determine the outcome of the war. Struggles on the home front were equally important. In 1776, each community contained small numbers of highly committed people on both sides and far larger numbers who were uncertain about whether independence was worth a war. The contest for the allegiance of the many neutrals thus was a major factor, and both persuasion and force were used. Revolutionaries who took control of local government often used it to punish loyalists and intimidate neutrals. On their side, loyalists worked to reestablish British authority. The struggle to secure political allegiance was complicated greatly by the wartime instability of the economy. The creative financing of the fledgling government brought hardships as well as opportunities, forcing Americans to confront new manifestations of virtue and corruption.

Patriotism at the Local Level

Committees of correspondence, of public safety, and of inspection dominated the political landscape in patriot communities. These committees took on more than customary local governance; they enforced boycotts, picked army draftees, and policed suspected traitors. They sometimes invaded homes to search for contraband goods.

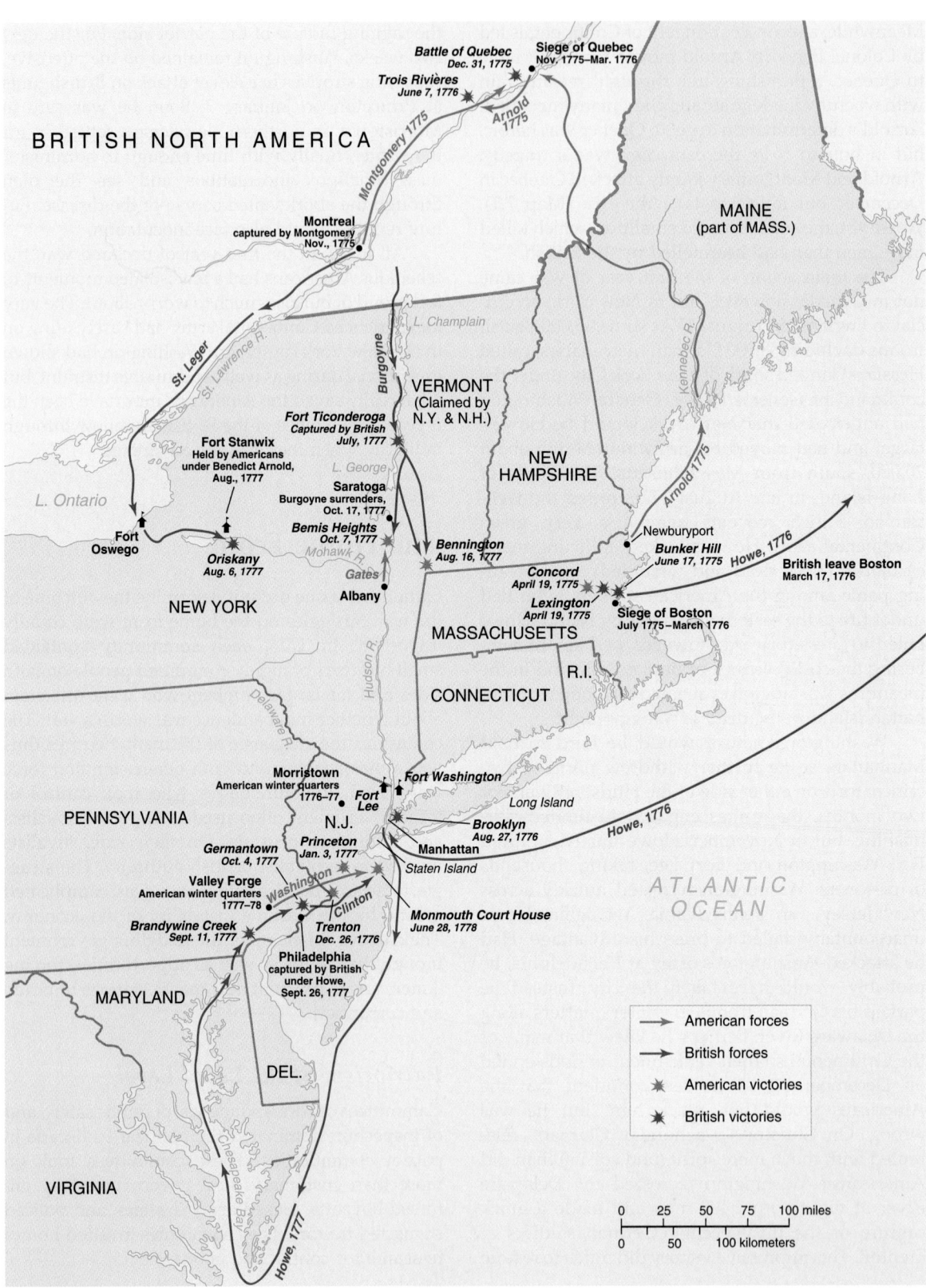

BRITISH NORTH AMERICA

Battle of Quebec
Dec. 31, 1775

Siege of Quebec
Nov. 1775–Mar. 1776

Trois Rivières
June 7, 1776

Arnold 1775

Montgomery 1775

MAINE
(part of MASS.)

Montreal
captured by Montgomery
Nov., 1775

L. Champlain

St. Leger

St. Lawrence R.

Burgoyne

VERMONT
(Claimed by
N.Y. & N.H.)

Kennebec R.

Fort Ticonderoga
Captured by British
July, 1777

NEW
HAMPSHIRE

Fort Stanwix
Held by Americans
under Benedict Arnold,
Aug., 1777

L. George

Arnold 1775

L. Ontario

Saratoga
Burgoyne surrenders,
Oct. 17, 1777

Bemis Heights
Oct. 7, 1777

Newburyport

Fort
Oswego

Oriskany
Aug. 6, 1777

Mohawk R.

Gates

Bennington
Aug. 16, 1777

Concord
April 19, 1775

Bunker Hill
June 17, 1775

Howe, 1776

British leave Boston
March 17, 1776

NEW YORK

Albany

Lexington
April 19, 1775

Siege of Boston
July 1775–March 1776

MASSACHUSETTS

Hudson R.

R.I.

CONNECTICUT

Delaware R.

Morristown
American winter quarters
1776–77

*Fort
Lee*

Fort Washington

Long Island

Howe, 1776

PENNSYLVANIA

N.J.

Germantown
Oct. 4, 1777

Princeton
Jan. 3, 1777

Brooklyn
Aug. 27, 1776

Manhattan

Valley Forge
American winter quarters
1777–78

Washington

Clinton

Staten Island

Monmouth Court House
June 28, 1778

ATLANTIC
OCEAN

Brandywine Creek
Sept. 11, 1777

Trenton
Dec. 26, 1776

Philadelphia
captured by British
under Howe,
Sept. 26, 1777

MARYLAND

DEL.

VIRGINIA

Chesapeake Bay

Howe, 1777

	American forces
	British forces
	American victories
	British victories

0   25   50   75   100 miles

0   50   100 kilometers

Loyalists were dismayed by what seemed to them to be arbitrary power taken on by patriots. A man in Westchester, New York, described his response to intrusions by committees: "Choose your committee or suffer it to be chosen by a half dozen fools in your neighborhood—open your doors to them—let them examine your tea-cannisters and molasses-jugs, and your wives' and daughters' petty coats—bow and cringe and tremble and quake—fall down and worship our sovereign lord the mob. . . . Should any pragmatical committee-gentleman come to my house and give himself airs, I shall show him the door, and if he does not soon take himself away, a good hickory cudgel shall teach him better manners." Oppressive or not, the local committees of safety and of inspection were rarely challenged. Their persuasive powers convinced many middle-of-the-road citizens that neutrality was not a comfortable option.

Another group new to political life—white women—increasingly demonstrated a capacity for patriotism at the local level as wartime hardships dramatically altered their work routines. Like Abigail Adams on her Braintree farm, many wives with husbands away on military or political service took on masculine duties. Their increased competence to tend farms and make business decisions encouraged some to assert competence in political matters as well. Eliza Wilkinson managed a plantation on the South Carolina coast and talked revolutionary politics with her women friends. "None were greater politicians than the several knots of ladies who met together," she remarked, alert to the unusual turn female conversations had taken. "We commenced perfect statesmen."

Women from prominent Philadelphia families went a step beyond political talk to action. In 1780, they formed the Ladies Association, going door to door collecting a substantial sum of money to help support the Continental soldiers. A published broadside, "The Sentiments of an American Woman," defended their female patriotism. "The time is arrived to display the same sentiments which animated us at the beginning of the Revolution, when we renounced the use of teas [and] when our republican and laborious hands spun the flax."

The Loyalists

Between 20 and 30 percent of the American population remained openly loyal to the British monarchy in 1776, and another 20 to 40 percent could be described as neutral. Such a large population base could have sustained the British Empire in America, if only the British army leaders had known how to use it (Map 7.2). In general, loyalists were people who still felt strong cultural and economic ties to the British Empire and who believed that American prosperity and stability depended on British rule and on a government anchored by monarchy and aristocracy. Perhaps most of all, they feared democratic tyranny. Like Abigail Adams, they understood that dissolving the automatic respect that subjects had for their king could lead to a society in which hierarchy came unglued. Adams welcomed this chance to identify tyranny in unequal power relations, as between men and women; loyalists feared it. Patriots seemed to them to be unscrupulous, violent, self-interested men who simply wanted power for themselves.

The most visible and dedicated loyalists (also called Tories by their enemies) were royal officials, not only top officeholders like Thomas Hutchinson in Massachusetts, but also local judges and customs officers. Wealthy merchants with commercial ties to England gravitated toward loyalism to maintain the trade protections of navigation acts and the British navy. Conservative urban lawyers admired the stability of British law and order. Some colonists were loyalists as a product of oppositional politics with leading patriot men. For example, backcountry farmers in the Carolinas tended to be loyalists out of resentment over the political and economic power of the lowlands gentry. And of course southern slaves had their own resentments against the white slave-owning class and looked to Britain for hope of freedom.

Many Indian tribes attempted to maintain neutrality at the start of the war, seeing it as a civil war between English and American brothers. But

---

MAP 7.1

The War in the North, 1775–1778
After the early battles in Massachusetts in 1775, rebel forces invaded Canada but failed to capture Quebec. A large British army landed in New York in August 1776, turning New Jersey into a continual site of battle in 1777 and 1778. Burgoyne arrived to secure Canada and made his attempt to pinch off New England along the Hudson River line, but he was stopped at Saratoga in 1777 in the key battle of the early war years.

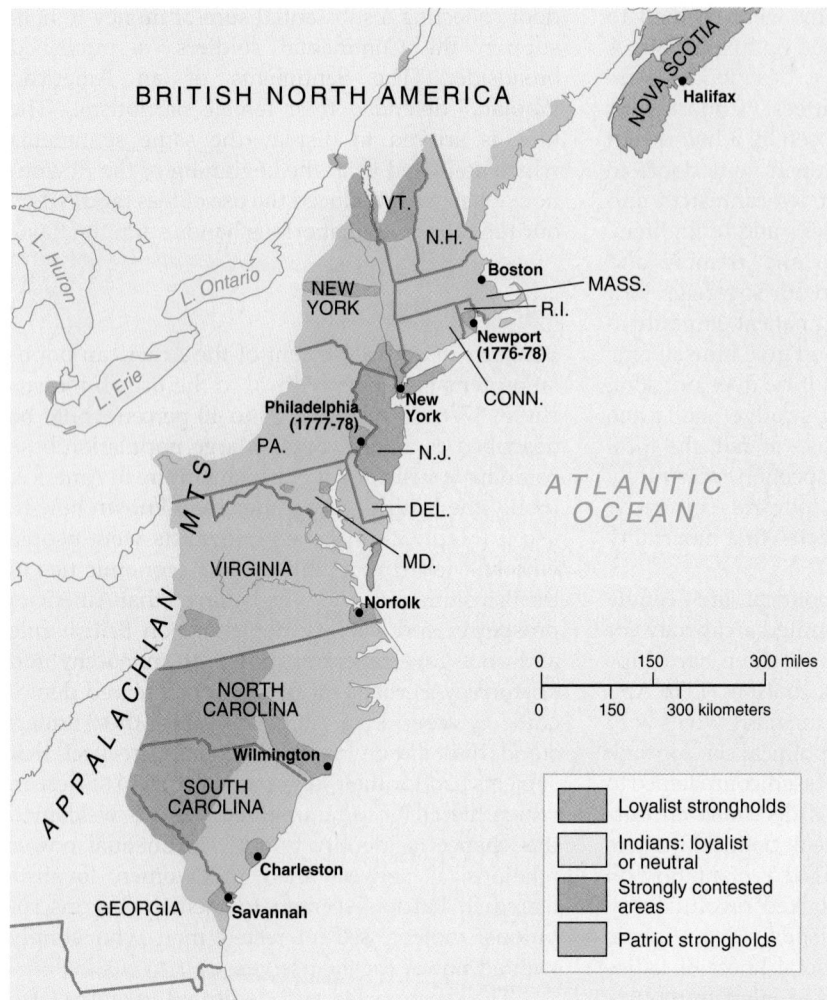

MAP 7.2

Loyalist Strength and Rebel Support
The exact number of loyalists can never be known. No one could have made an accurate count at the time; in addition, political allegiance often shifted with the winds. This map shows the pockets of loyalist strength on which the British relied—the lower Hudson valley and the Carolina Piedmont.

READING THE MAP: Which forces were stronger, those loyal to Britain or those rebelling? What areas were contested? If the contested areas ultimately sided with the British, how would the balance of power change?

CONNECTIONS: Who was more likely to be a loyalist, and why? How many loyalists left the United States, and where did they go?

www.bedfordstmartins.com/roarkcompact SEE THE ON-LINE STUDY GUIDE for more help in analyzing this map.

eventually most were drawn in, many taking the British side. The powerful Iroquois confederacy divided, with Mohawks, Cayugas, Senecas, and Onondagas lining up with the British, while the Oneidas and Tuscaroras aided the Americans. One young Mohawk leader, Thayendanegea (known to Americans as Joseph Brant), traveled to England in 1775 to complain to King George about how the colonists repeatedly deceived the Mohawks. "It is very hard when we have let the King's subjects have so much of our lands for so little value," he wrote, "they should want to cheat us in this manner of the small spots we have left for our women and children to live on. We are tired out in making complaints & getting no redress." Thayenda-

negea negotiated Indian support for the king in exchange for protection from encroaching settlers, under a revived implementation of the Proclamation Act of 1763.

Pockets of loyalism thus existed everywhere, in the middle colonies, in the backcountry of the southern colonies, and out beyond the Appalachian Mountains in Indian country. Even New England towns at the heart of turmoil, like Concord, Massachusetts, had a small and increasingly silenced core of loyalists who refused to countenance armed revolution.

The loyalists were most vocal between 1774 and 1776, when the possibility of a full-scale rebellion against England was still uncertain. Loyalists chal-

JOSEPH BRANT
The Mohawk leader Thayendanegea, called Joseph Brant by Americans, had been educated in English ways at Eleazar Wheelock's New England school (which became Dartmouth College in 1769). In 1775, the thirty-four-year-old Brant traveled to England with another warrior to negotiate Mohawk support for the British. While there, he had his portrait painted by English artist George Romney. Notice that Brant wears a metal gorget around his neck over his English shirt, along with Indian armbands, sash, and headdress. A gorget was a symbolic piece of armor, a shrunken version of a throatpiece from the feudal days of metal-clad knights. Many military men, both white and Indian, wore gorgets when they dressed formally for portraits — or for war.
National Gallery of Canada, Ottawa.

lenged the emerging patriot side using pamphlets, broadsides, and newspapers. In New York City in 1776, some loyalists even circulated a broadside titled "A Declaration of Dependence," in rebuttal to the congress's July 4 manifesto, denouncing this "most unnatural, unprovoked Rebellion that ever disgraced the annals of Time."

Who Is a Traitor?

In June 1775, the First Continental Congress passed a resolution declaring loyalists to be traitors. Over the next year, state laws defined as treason acts such as joining or provisioning the British army, saying or printing anything that undermined patriot morale, or discouraging men from enlisting in the Continental army. Punishments ranged from house arrest and suspension of voting privileges to confiscation of property and deportation. And sometimes self-appointed committees of Tory hunters bypassed the judicial niceties and terrorized loyalists, raiding their houses or tarring and feathering them.

A question rarely asked in the heat of the revolutionary moment was whether the wives of loyalists were traitors as well. When loyalist families fled the country, property held in the name of the family patriarch was then confiscated. But what if the wife stayed? One Connecticut woman brought witnesses to testify that she was "a steady and true and faithful friend to the American states in opposition to her husband, who has been of quite a different character." In such cases, the court typically allowed the woman to keep one-third of the property, the amount she was due if widowed, and confiscated the rest. But even when the wife fled with her husband, was she necessarily a traitor? If he insisted, was she not obligated to go? Such questions came up in several lawsuits after the Revolution, where descendants of refugee loyalists sued to regain property that had entered the family through the mother's inheritance. In one well-publicized Massachusetts case in 1805, the outcome confirmed the traditional view of women as political blank slates; the American son of loyalist refugee Anna Martin recovered her property on the grounds that she had no independent will to be a loyalist.

Tarring and feathering, property confiscation, deportation, terrorism—to the loyalists, such denials of liberty of conscience and of freedom to own private property proved that democratic tyranny was more to be feared than the monarchical variety. A Boston loyalist, Mather Byles, aptly expressed this point: "They call me a brainless Tory, but tell me . . . which is better—to be ruled by one tyrant three thousand miles away, or by three thousand tyrants not a mile away?" Byles was soon sentenced to deportation.

Throughout the war, probably 7,000 to 8,000 loyalists fled to England, while 28,000 found closer haven in Canada. But many chose to remain in the new United States and tried to swing with the changing political fortunes. In some instances, that proved difficult. In New Jersey, for example, 3,000 Jerseyites felt protected (or scared) enough by the occupying British army in 1776 to swear an oath of allegiance to the king. But then General Howe drew back to New York City, leaving them to the mercy of local patriot committees. British strategy depended on using loyalists to hold occupied territory, but the New Jersey experience showed just how poorly that strategy was carried out.

Financial Instability and Corruption

Wars cost money—for arms and ammunition, for food and uniforms, for soldiers' pay. The Continental Congress printed money, but within a few short years its value had deteriorated since the congress held no reserves of gold or silver to back the currency. In practice, the currency was worth only what a buyer and seller agreed it was worth. The dollar eventually bottomed out at one-fortieth of its face value; a loaf of bread that once sold for two and a half cents now sold for a dollar. States too were printing their own paper money to pay for wartime expenses, further complicating the economy.

Soon the congress had to resort to other means to procure supplies and labor. One method was to borrow hard money (coins, not paper) from wealthy men, who would get certificates of debt (also called public securities) promising repayment with interest. In effect, the wealthy men had bought government bonds. To pay soldiers, the congress offered land bounties, which amounted to a promise of a tangible form of wealth. Public securities and land bounties quickly became a form of negotiable currency. For example, a soldier with no cash might sell his land bounty certificate to get food for his family. These certificates also fluctuated in value, mainly depreciating.

Depreciating currency inevitably led to rising prices, as sellers compensated for the falling value of the money. The wartime economy of the late 1770s, with its unreliable currency and price inflation, was extremely demoralizing to Americans everywhere. So local committees of public safety in 1778 began to fix prices on goods such as flour, bread, and other essentials for short periods in an effort to impose some stability.

Inevitably, some Americans turned this unstable situation to their advantage. Money that fell fast in value needed to be spent quickly; being in debt was suddenly advantageous because the debt could be repaid weeks later in devalued currency. A brisk black market sprang up in prohibited luxury imports, such as tea, sugar, textiles, and wines. No matter that these items came from Britain. A New Hampshire delegate to the congress denounced the extravagance that flew in the face of the virtuous homespun association agreements of just a few years before: "We are a crooked and perverse generation, longing for the fineries and follies of those Egyptian task masters from whom we have so lately freed ourselves."

The Campaigns of 1777–1779: Highs and Lows

In early 1777, the Continental army had a bleak road ahead. Washington had shown considerable skill in avoiding outright defeat, but the minor victories in New Jersey lent only faint optimism to the American side. The British moved large numbers of soldiers into Quebec, readying their plan to isolate New England by controlling the Hudson River.

Burgoyne's Army and the Battle of Saratoga

In 1777, British General John Burgoyne assumed command of an army of 7,800 soldiers in Canada and began the northern squeeze on the Hudson River valley. His goal was to capture Albany, a town 150 miles north of New York City near the intersection of the Hudson and Mohawk Rivers (see Map 7.1). In addition to his soldiers, Burgoyne traveled with another 1,000 assorted "camp followers" (cooks, laundresses, musicians) and some 400 Indian warriors and scouts. This very large army did not travel light, requiring food supplies not only for 9,200 people but also for the more than 400 horses needed to haul heavy artillery. Burgoyne, who was nicknamed "Gentleman Johnny," also carted thirty trunks of personal belongings, including fine wines and elegant clothing.

Burgoyne first captured Fort Ticonderoga with ease. Some 3,000 American troops stationed there

DEATH OF JANE McCREA
This 1804 painting by John Vanderlyn memorializes the martyr legend of Jane Mc-Crea. McCrea lived with her patriot family in upstate New York, but in July 1777 she fled to join her fiancé, a loyalist fighting with Burgoyne's army. She was murdered en route, allegedly by Iroquois allies of the British. The American general Horatio Gates sent Burgoyne an accusatory letter. "The miserable fate of Miss McCrea was particularly aggravated by her being dressed to meet her promised husband," Gates wrote, "but she met her murderers employed by you." Gates skillfully used the story of the vulnerable, innocent maiden dressed in alluring clothes as propaganda to inspire his soldiers' drive for victory at Saratoga. Vanderlyn's work, and other similar pictorial representations, emphasized McCrea's helplessness and sexuality. Yet had McCrea been a man, her flight would have been traitorous. Why this different treatment of a woman?
Wadsworth Atheneum, Hartford.

spotted the approaching British and, low on food and supplies, abandoned the fort without a fight. The British continued to move south, but the large army moved slowly on primitive roads through heavily forested land.

The logical second step in isolating New England should have been to advance troops up the Hudson from New York City to meet Burgoyne. American surveillance indicated that General Howe in Manhattan was readying his men for a major move in August 1777. George Washington, watching from New Jersey, was astonished to see Howe's men sail south; Howe had decided to try to capture Philadelphia.

The third prong of British strategy involved troops moving east from the Great Lakes down the Mohawk River, aided by Mohawks and Senecas of Joseph Brant's Iroquois League. The British believed that the Palatine Germans living in the Mohawk valley were heavily loyalist, so they expected little trouble getting to Albany. But a hundred miles west of their goal they encountered American soldiers at Fort Stanwix, reinforced by Palatine Germans and Oneida Indians. The Seneca ambushed the Germans and their onetime allies the Oneida in a narrow ravine called Oriskany and inflicted heavy losses. But Fort Stanwix held back the British and Seneca and eventually sent them into retreat (see Map 7.1).

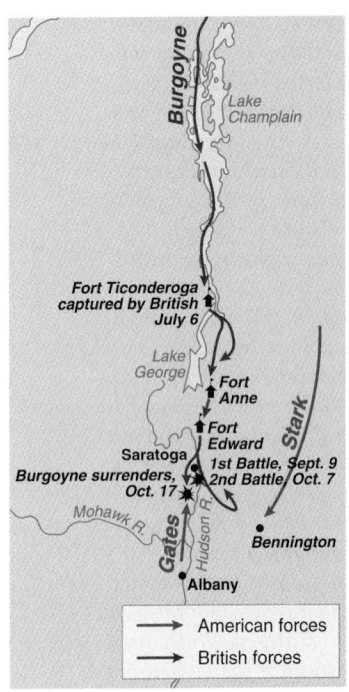

Battle of Saratoga, 1777

Burgoyne thus did not have the additional troops he expected. Camped at a small village called Saratoga, he was isolated with food supplies dwindling and men deserting. His adversary at Albany, General Horatio Gates, began moving 7,000 Continental soldiers toward him. Burgoyne decided to attack first, since every day his army weakened. The first Battle of Saratoga was a British victory, but an expensive one, leaving 600 dead and wounded redcoats. Only three weeks later, a second Battle of Saratoga cost the British another 600 men and most of their cannons. Burgoyne finally surrendered to the American forces on October 17, 1777.

General Howe, meanwhile, had succeeded in occupying Philadelphia in September 1777. Figuring that the Saratoga loss was balanced by the capture of Philadelphia, the British government proposed a negotiated settlement—not including independence—to end the war. But the American side refused.

Their optimism was not well founded, however, in the winter of 1777–78. Spirits ran high, but arms and food supplies ran precariously low. Washington moved his troops into winter quarters at Valley Forge, a day's march west of occupied Philadelphia. Quartered in drafty sheds, the men lacked blankets, boots, and stockings. Washington complained to the congress that nearly 3,000 of his men were "unfit for duty because they are bare foot and otherwise naked"; without blankets, large numbers were forced to "set up all Night by fires, instead of taking comfortable rest in a natural way." Food was also scarce. Local farms had produced adequate grain that year, but Washington was sure that the farmers were selling it to the British, who could pay with the king's silver.

The evidence of corruption indeed appeared abundant. Army suppliers too often provided defective food, clothing, and gunpowder. Washington's men unfolded a shipment of blankets only to discover that they were a quarter of their customary size. Teamsters who hauled barrels of preserved salted meat might drain out the brine to lighten their load and then refill the barrels later, allowing the meat to rot in transit. Selfishness and greed seemed to infect the American side. As one Continental officer said, "The people at home are destroying the Army by their conduct much faster than Howe and all his army can possibly do by fighting us."

The War in Indian Country

By 1779, it was clear that neutrality was not a viable option for the approximately 150,000 Indians living just west of the Appalachian Mountains. Despite the 1763 Proclamation Act, by 1778 something like 50,000 American settlers, many of them recent Scots-Irish immigrants to the colonies, had penetrated Indian country. The British maintained military outposts at Niagara and Detroit, but Fort Pitt was now an American garrison.

Even though the 1776 Declaration of Independence blamed the British for inciting "Savages," a significant group of Delaware and Shawnee Indians sought peace with the Americans—until 1778, when a series of murderous actions by frontier soldiers converted them to enemies. A Delaware leader named White Eyes negotiated a treaty with the Americans at Fort Pitt in mid-1778, pledging Indian support in the war in exchange for supplies and trade goods. But supplies and goods were not forthcoming, and escalating violence undermined the agreement. In one incident, American soldiers captured and killed friendly Shawnee chiefs Cornstalk and Red Hawk. A short time later, White Eyes himself was murdered by militiamen. Despite Indian professions of support, American military leaders repeatedly had trouble honoring distinctions between allied and enemy Indians.

Soon, isolated instances of violence escalated into anti-Indian campaigns. In North Carolina, militias attacked Cherokee settlements, destroying thirty-six villages and burning fields and livestock. To the north, Continental army troops carried out a planned campaign of terror and destruction against the Iroquois in western New York in late summer of 1779. Forty Indian towns met with total destruction; the soldiers looted and torched the dwellings, then burned cornfields and fruit orchards. Smallpox soon followed. The Delaware and Shawnee town of Coshocton, west of Fort Pitt, consisting of some two thousand inhabitants and still, amazingly, pro-American, was attacked and burned to the ground by militiamen in 1781. In these and other violent raids, Indians were driven into the hills, into starvation, and into the arms of the British at Detroit and Niagara, or into the arms of the Spanish west of the Mississippi River.

The French Alliance

On their own, the Americans could not have defeated England, and the western pressure from hostile Indians magnified their task. But essential help arrived as a result of the victory at Saratoga, which convinced the French to enter the war; a formal alliance was signed in February 1778. France recognized the United States as an independent nation and promised full military and commercial support throughout the war. The most crucial support was the French navy, which now could challenge England's transatlantic pipeline of supplies and troops.

Although France had been waiting for a promising American victory to justify a formal declaration of war, since 1776 the French had provided aid to the Americans in the form of cannons, muskets, gunpowder, and highly trained military advisors. Still, monarchical France was understandably cautious about endorsing a democratic revolution that attacked the principles of kingship. The main attraction of an alliance for France was simply the opportunity to defeat England, its archrival. A victory would also open pathways to trade and perhaps result in France acquiring the coveted British West Indies. Even American defeat was not a full disaster for France, if the war took many years and drained England of men and money.

The French support materialized slowly. The navy arrived off the coast of Virginia in July 1778 but then went south to the West Indies to defend the sugar islands. By 1781, the French proved indispensable to the American victory, but the first months of the alliance brought no dramatic victories, leading some Americans to grumble that the partnership would prove worthless.

The Southern Strategy and the End of the War

When France joined the war, some British officials wondered whether the fight was worth continuing. A troop commander, arguing for an immediate negotiated settlement, shrewdly observed that "we are far from an anticipated peace, because the bitterness of the rebels is too widespread, and in regions where we are masters the rebellious spirit is still in them. The land is too large, and there are too many people. The more land we win, the weaker our army gets in the field." The commander of the British navy argued for abandoning the war, and even Lord North, the prime minister, agreed. But the king was determined to crush the rebellion, and he encouraged a new strategy for victory. It was a brilliant but desperate plan.

Georgia and South Carolina

The new strategy abandoned New England and instead focused on the South, perhaps easier to recapture for the crown. The southern region had valuable crops—tobacco, rice, and indigo—worth keeping under the British flag. Further, the large slave population was a powerful destabilizing factor from which the British hoped to benefit. White southerners feared the instability of all-out war, which might unleash violence from slaves seizing the moment to claim freedom. Georgia and the Carolinas also looked promising for victory because of the large pockets of loyalists presumed to be militant. The British hoped to recapture the southern colonies one by one, restore the loyalists to power, and then move north to the more problematic middle colonies, saving prickly New England for last.

Georgia, the first target, fell at the end of December 1778 (Map 7.3). A small army of British soldiers occupied Savannah and Augusta, and a new royal governor and loyalist assembly were quickly installed. Taking Georgia was easy because the bulk of the Continental army was in New York and New Jersey, keeping an eye on General Henry Clinton, Howe's replacement as commander in chief, and the French were in the West Indies. The British in Georgia quickly organized twenty loyal militia units, and 1,400 Georgians swore an oath of allegiance to the king. So far, the plan looked as if it might work.

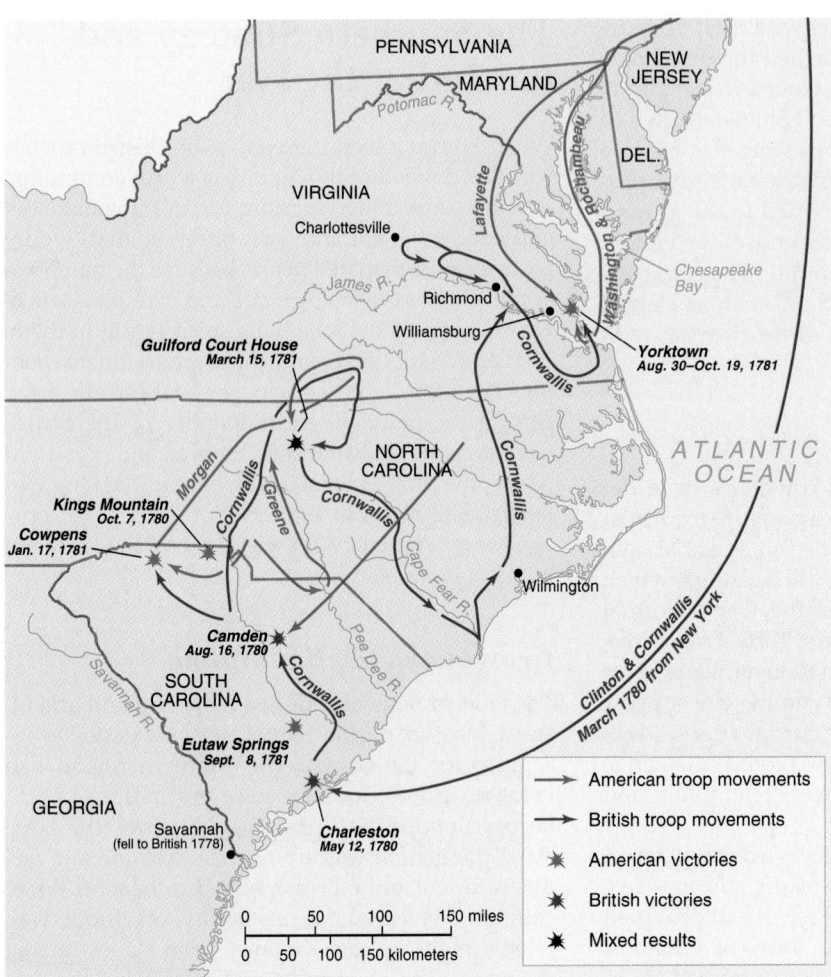

MAP 7.3

The War in the South, 1780–1781

After taking Charleston in May 1780, the British advanced into South Carolina and the foothill region of North Carolina, leaving a bloody civil war in their wake. When the American general Horatio Gates and his men fumbled and fled from the humiliating Battle of Camden, Gates was replaced by Generals Nathaniel Greene and Daniel Morgan, who pulled off major successes at Kings Mountain and Cowpens. The British general Cornwallis then moved north to invade Virginia, but was bottled up and finally overpowered at Yorktown in the fall of 1781. Yorktown was the last battle of the American Revolution.

The next target was South Carolina. General Clinton moved British troops south from New York, while the Continental army put ten regiments into Charleston to defend it. For five weeks in early 1780, the British laid siege to the city, which finally surrendered in mid-May 1780, sending 3,300 soldiers, a tremendous loss, into British captivity. Again, the king's new strategy seemed to be on target.

Clinton returned to New York, leaving the task of pacifying South Carolina to General Charles Cornwallis and 4,000 troops. The boldest of all the British generals in the war for America, Lord Cornwallis quickly moved into action. He chased out the remaining Continental army units and established military control of the province by midsummer 1780. He purged rebels from government office and disarmed potential rebel militias. The export of

South Carolina's main crop, rice, resumed, and, as in Georgia, pardons were offered to Carolinians who swore loyalty oaths to the crown and then proved their loyalty by taking up arms for the British.

In August 1780, the Continental army was ready to strike back at Cornwallis. General Gates, the hero of the Battle of Saratoga, arrived in South Carolina with more than 3,000 troops, some of them experienced army units and others green militiamen. They met Cornwallis's army at Camden, South Carolina, on August 16 (Map 7.3). Gates put the militiamen into the center of the battle, where a contagious panic gripped them at the sight of the approaching enemy cavalry. Men threw down unfired muskets and ran from the field of battle. When regiment leaders tried to regroup the next day, only

BENEDICT ARNOLD
This portrait shows Benedict Arnold in 1776, when he was the hero of the Quebec campaign. Probably the final straw for Arnold came when he failed to earn promotion, while men he considered inferior were elevated to higher rank.
Anne S. K. Brown Military Collection, Providence, R.I.

700 showed up, the rest dead, captured, or still in flight. Camden was a devastating defeat; prospects now seemed very grim for the Americans.

The new British strategy succeeded in 1780 partly because of improved information about American troop movements that was secretly furnished to the British by Benedict Arnold, the one-time American hero of several key battles. Arnold was a brilliant military talent but also a deeply insecure man who never felt he got his due, in either honor or financial reward. Sometime in 1779, he opened secret negotiations with General Clinton in New York, trading information for money and hinting he could deliver far more of value. When he was assigned the command of West Point, a new fort sixty miles north of New York City on the Hudson River, his plan crystallized. West Point controlled the Hudson; its easy capture by the British

might well have meant instant victory in the war.

Arnold's treasonous plot to sell a West Point victory to the British was foiled by the capture of the messenger between Arnold and Clinton. News of the Arnold treason created shock waves. Arnold represented all of the patriots' worst fears: greedy self-interest like that of the war profiteers, unprincipled abandonment of war aims like that of the turncoat Tories of the South, panic like that of the terrified soldiers with Gates at Camden. But instead of symbolizing all that was troubling about the American side of the war, the treachery of Arnold became celebrated in a kind of displacement of the anxieties of the moment. Vilifying Arnold allowed Americans to stake out a wide distance between themselves and dastardly conduct. It inspired a renewal of patriotism at a particularly low moment.

The Other Southern War: Guerrillas

Shock over Gates's defeat at Camden and Arnold's treason revitalized rebel support in western South Carolina, an area that Cornwallis had believed to be pacified and loyal. The backcountry of the South soon became the site of a guerrilla war. In hit-and-run attacks, both sides burned and ravaged not only opponents' property but the property of anyone claiming to be neutral. The loyalist militia units organized by the British were met by fierce rebel militia units who now figured they had little to lose. Guerrilla warfare soon spread to Georgia and North Carolina. In South Carolina, some six thousand men became active partisan fighters, and they entered into at least twenty-six engagements with loyalist units. Some of these were classic battles; but on other occasions the fighters were more like bandits than soldiers. Both sides committed murders and atrocities and plundered property, clear deviations from standard military practice.

The British southern strategy counted on sufficient loyalist strength to hold reconquered territory as the army moved north. The backcountry civil war proved this assumption false. The Americans won few major battles in the South, but they ultimately succeeded by harassing the British forces and thus preventing them from foraging for food. Cornwallis boldly moved the war into North Carolina in late 1780, not because he thought South Carolina was secure—it was not—but because the North Carolinians were supplying the South Carolina rebels with arms and men (see Map 7.3). But news of a brutal massacre of loyalist units in western South Carolina at Kings Mountain, at the hands of 1,400 frontier riflemen, sent him hurrying back. The British were stretched too thin to hold even two of their onetime colonies.

Surrender at Yorktown

In the early months of 1781, Cornwallis set out to try his North Carolina plan again; if successful, it would isolate South Carolina and Georgia. For months, he moved his army around the province, taking land but not holding it. So Cornwallis decided to push the war farther north, into Virginia. He captured Williamsburg, which had been the colony's old seat of royal government. He raided Charlottesville, where Virginia's revolutionary government was meeting, and seized members of the assembly. As late as the start of September, Cornwallis was not wrong to think he had the upper hand in Virginia.

What changed the picture dramatically was an infusion of French military support. A large French army under the command of the comte de Rochambeau had joined Washington in Rhode Island in mid-1780. News that a large fleet had sailed from France in the spring of 1781 set in motion Washington's plan to defeat the British. The fleet, commanded by the comte de Grasse, was bound for the Chesapeake Bay, so Washington and Rochambeau fixed their attention on Virginia. Bypassing New York (where Clinton had been expecting an attack), thousands of American and French soldiers headed south in August 1781.

By the time British ships arrived to defend the Chesapeake, the French had already taken control of it. A five-day naval battle in early September sent the British ships limping away and left the French in clear command of the Virginia and North Carolina coasts. This proved to be the decisive factor in ending the war, because it eliminated a water escape route for Cornwallis's land army, encamped at Yorktown, Virginia.

General Cornwallis and his 7,500 troops now faced a combined French and American army numbering over 16,000. For twelve days, the Americans and French bombarded the British fortifications at Yorktown; Cornwallis ran low on food and ammunition. An American observer keeping a diary noted that "the enemy, from want of forage, are killing off their horses in great numbers. Six or seven hundred of these valuable animals have been killed, and their carcasses are almost continually floating down the river." Realizing escape was impossible, Cornwallis signaled his intention to surrender. On October 19, 1781, he formally capitulated.

What had begun as a promising southern strategy by the British in 1778 had turned into a discouraging defeat by 1781. British attacks in the South energized American resistance, as did the timely exposure of Benedict Arnold's treason. The arrival of the French fleet sealed the fate of Cornwallis at

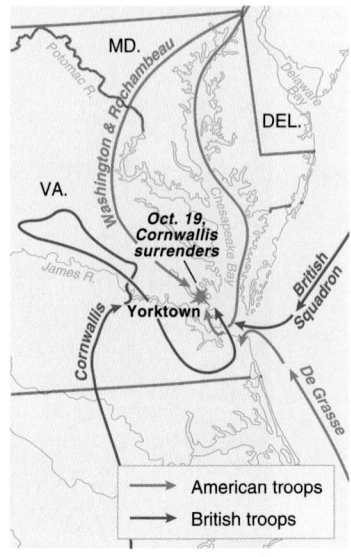

Siege of Yorktown, 1781

Yorktown, and the military war quickly came to a halt.

The Losers and the Winners

The surrender at Yorktown proved to be the end of the war, but it took some time for the principals to realize that. The peace treaty was nearly two years in the making, with both the American and the British armies still in the field, in case the treaty fell through. King George tenaciously clung to the idea of pursuing the war, but the sentiment for a formal peace was growing in Parliament. The war had become unpopular among the British citizenry in general, and support for it dwindled until finally the king had to realize it was over.

It took six months for the three American commissioners, Benjamin Franklin, John Adams, and John Jay of New York, to negotiate the three-way settlement in Paris, but at last, in November 1782, eighty-two articles of peace were agreed to. The first article went to the heart of the matter: "His Britannic Majesty acknowledges the said United States to be free Sovereign and independent States." Other articles described the boundaries of the new country and guaranteed that creditors on both sides could collect debts owed them in sterling money, a provision especially important to British merchants. England agreed to withdraw its troops quickly; more than a decade later, this promise would still not be fully kept. The final, official peace treaty—

the Treaty of Paris—was signed nearly a year later, on September 2, 1783.

As at the end of the French and Indian War, no article in this treaty recognized the Indians as players in the war. Indian lands were assigned to the victors as though they were uninhabited. Many Indian refugees had fled, some west into Missouri and Arkansas, others into Canada, and yet others into Spanish Florida. Their movements helped spread the deadly smallpox epidemic to the far ends of the continent. But significant numbers remained within the new United States, displaced from their ancestral homelands. For them, the peace of 1783 was only a temporary lull in a much longer war that would extend at least until 1795. As one delegation of Indians reported to the Spanish governor at St. Louis in 1784, the Revolutionary War was "the greatest blow that could have been dealt us, unless it had been our total destruction."

With the treaty finally signed, the British began their evacuation of New York, Charleston, and Savannah, a process complicated by the sheer numbers involved—soldiers, fearful loyalists, and runaway slaves by the thousands. In New York City, more than 27,000 soldiers and 30,000 loyalists sailed on hundreds of ships for England in late fall 1783. In a final act of mischief, on the November day when the last ships left, the losing side raised the British flag at the southern tip of Manhattan, cut away the ropes used to hoist it, and greased the flagpole.

Conclusion: Why the British Lost

The British began the war for America convinced that they could not lose. They had the strongest and best-trained army and navy in the world; they were familiar with the American landscape from the French and Indian War; they outnumbered their opponents in uniform; and they easily captured every port city of consequence in America. Probably one-fifth of the population was loyalist, and another two-fifths were undecided. Why, then, did they lose?

One continuing problem the British faced was the uncertainty of supplies. Unwilling to ravage the countryside, the army depended on a steady stream of supply ships from home. Insecurity about food helps explain the repeated reluctance of Howe and

Clinton to pursue the Continental army aggressively.

A second obstacle to British success was their continual misuse of loyalist energies. Any plan to repacify the colonies required the cooperation of the loyalists as well as new support from the many neutrals. But again and again, the British failed to back the loyalists, leaving them to the mercy of vengeful rebels. In the South, they allowed loyalist militias to engage in vicious guerrilla warfare that drove away potential converts among the rest of the population.

The French alliance looms large in any explanation of the British defeat. The artillery and ammunition the French supplied even before 1778 were critical necessities for the Continental army. In 1780, the French army brought a fresh infusion of troops to a war-weary America, and the French navy made the Yorktown victory possible. The major naval defeat in the Chesapeake, just before the Yorktown siege, dissolved the pro-war spirit in England and forced the king to admit it was over.

Finally, the British abdicated civil power in the colonies in 1775 and 1776, when royal officials were forced to flee to safety, and they never really regained it. For nearly seven years, of necessity the Americans created their own government structures, from the Continental Congress to local committees and militias. Staffed by many who before 1775 had been the political elites, these new government agencies had remarkably little trouble establishing their authority to rule. The basic British goal—to turn back the clock to imperial rule—receded into impossibility as the war dragged on.

The war for America had taken five and a half years to fight, from Lexington to Yorktown; negotiations and the evacuation took two more. It profoundly disrupted the lives of Americans everywhere. It was a war for independence from England, but it was more. It was a war that required men and women to think about politics and the legitimacy of authority. The precise disagreement with England about representation and political participation had profound implications for the kinds of governance the Americans would adopt, both in the moment of emergency, and in the longer run of the late 1770s and early 1780s when states began to write their constitutions. The rhetoric employed to justify the revolution against England put words like *liberty, tyranny, slavery, independence,* and *equality* into common usage. These words carried far deeper meanings than a mere complaint over taxation without representation. As Abigail Adams and others saw, the Revolution unleashed a dynamic of equality and liberty. That it was largely unintended and unwanted by the revolutionary leaders of 1776 made it all the more potent a force in American life in the decades to come.

For further reading about the topics in this chapter, see the Online Bibliography at

www.bedfordstmartins.com/roarkcompact.

For additional first-hand accounts of this period, see pages 93–112 in Michael Johnson, ed., *Reading the American Past*, Second Edition, Volume I.

To assess your mastery of the material in this chapter, see the Online Study Guide at

www.bedfordstmartins.com/roarkcompact.

CHRONOLOGY

1775 **May 10.** Second Continental Congress convenes in Philadelphia.

June 14. Continental Congress creates Continental army.

June 17. Battle of Bunker Hill won by the British, though at a great cost.

July. Congress offers Olive Branch Petition in attempt at reconciliation with king.

September. American army marches on Montreal and Quebec.

1776 **January.** Americans lose assault on Quebec.

Thomas Paine's *Common Sense* published.

March. British evacuate Boston.

July 4. Declaration of Independence adopted.

August 27. Battle of Long Island results in heavy American casualties.

September. British take Manhattan when American army retreats to Fort Washington and Fort Lee.

November. Americans retreat to Philadelphia.

Howe's troops capture Fort Washington and Fort Lee.

December 26. Washington surprises British and Hessians at Trenton.

1777 **January.** American army winters at Morristown, New Jersey.

July. Burgoyne takes Fort Ticonderoga for British.

August. Seneca ambush at Oriskany, but Americans hold Fort Stanwix against British attack.

September. Howe and the British occupy Philadelphia.

October 17. Burgoyne surrenders at Saratoga.

December. Washington leads army into winter quarters at Valley Forge, Pennsylvania.

1778 **February.** France enters war on American side.

July–August. French fleet threatens British occupation of New York and Newport, Rhode Island.

December. Savannah, Georgia, falls to British.

1779 **January–June.** Skirmishes in South Carolina and Georgia.

October. British evacuate Newport.

1780 Philadelphia Ladies Association raises money for soldiers.

March–May. British lay siege to Charleston, South Carolina.

July. Comte de Rochambeau and French army arrive at Newport.

August 16. Battle of Camden, South Carolina, dims hopes for Americans.

September–October. Benedict Arnold's treason exposed.

September–December. Guerrilla warfare starts in South Carolina and spreads to Georgia and North Carolina.

October 7. Battle of Kings Mountain, South Carolina, results in heavy loyalist casualties.

1781 **January 17.** Battle of Cowpens, South Carolina.

May–August. Cornwallis pushes army into Virginia, capturing Williamsburg.

August. Cornwallis occupies Yorktown, Virginia.

September 5. French fleet takes Chesapeake Bay.

September 28–October 19. Siege of Yorktown.

October 19. Cornwallis surrenders.

1783 Treaty of Paris ends war.

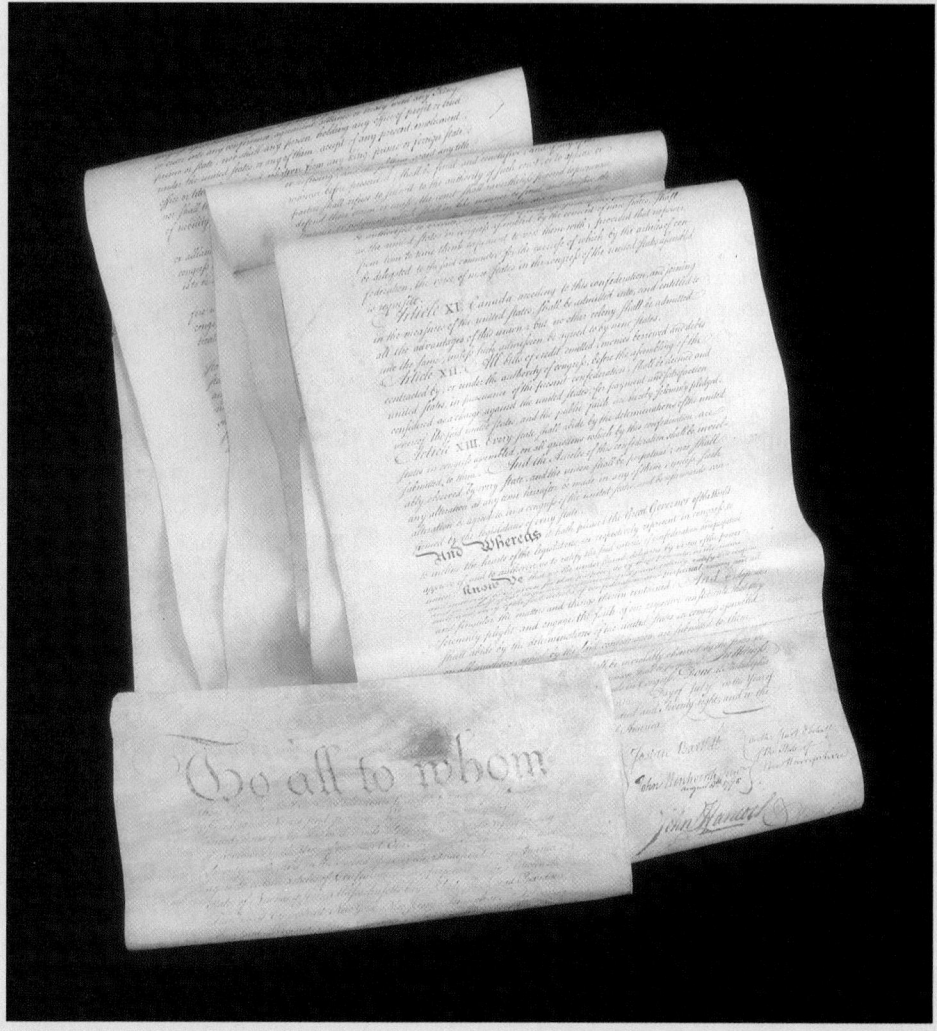

ARTICLES OF CONFEDERATION

The first written frame of government that bound together the thirteen rebelling provinces was called the Articles of Confederation. Delegates to the Second Continental Congress hammered out the plan over many months in 1776 and 1777, working on it when there was time free from the more pressing problems of pursuing the war. Once Congress agreed on it, the plan was printed and distributed to state legislatures for ratification, a process that took nearly five years because it required the assent of all thirteen. After ratification, in February 1781, this parchment copy became the official original version. As was often done with significant manuscript documents, the professional scribe wrote the opening words of the Articles in very large print, to proclaim the news. How does TO ALL TO WHOM *compare with such famous opening words as* IN CONGRESS, JULY 4, 1776—*the start of the Declaration of Independence—and later,* WE THE PEOPLE *for the U.S. Constitution, which replaced the Articles in 1788? Do you think* TO ALL TO WHOM *would have become a slogan or catchword had the Articles persisted as the country's sacred text? Why or why not?*

National Archives.

BUILDING A REPUBLIC

1775–1789

8

J AMES MADISON GRADUATED FROM PRINCETON COLLEGE in New Jersey in 1771, not knowing what to do next with his life. Certainly the twenty-year-old had an easy fallback position. As the firstborn son of a wealthy plantation master, he could return home to the foothills of Virginia and wait to inherit substantial land and a large force of slaves. But James was an intensely studious young man, uninterested in farming, and reluctant to leave the collegiate environment. Five years at boarding school had given him fluency in Greek, Latin, French, and mathematics, and three years at Princeton acquainted him with the great thinkers, both ancient and modern. Driven by a thirst for learning, young Madison slept only five hours a night, perhaps undermining his health. Protesting he was too ill to travel, he hung around Princeton six months after graduation.

In 1772, he returned home, still adrift. He swapped reading lists and ideas about political theory by letter with a Princeton classmate, prolonging his student life. While Madison struggled for direction, the powerful winds before the storm of the American Revolution swirled through the colonies; the youth's drifting would abruptly end. In May 1774, Madison traveled north to deliver his brother to boarding school and was in Philadelphia when the startling news broke that Britain had closed the port of Boston in retaliation for the destruction of the tea. Turbulent protests over the Coercive Acts turned him into a committed revolutionary.

Back in Virginia, Madison joined his father on the newly formed Committee of Public Safety. For a few days in early 1775, the twenty-four-year-old took up musket practice, but his continued poor health ruled out the soldier's life, and he quickly gave it up. His special contribution to the revolution lay along a different path. In spring 1776, Madison was elected to the Virginia Convention, an extralegal assembly replacing the defunct royal government. The convention's main task was to hammer out a state constitution featuring revolutionary goals such as frequent elections and a limited executive power. Madison, shy, self-effacing, and still learning the ropes, mostly stayed on the sidelines. Still, Virginia's elder statesmen noted the young man's logical, thoughtful contributions. When his county failed to return him to the assembly in the next election, he was appointed to the governor's council, where he spent two years gaining experience helping to manage a wartime government.

In early 1780, Madison represented Virginia in the Continental Congress. Not quite twenty-nine, unmarried, and supported by his father's money, Madison was free of the burdens that made distant political service difficult for so many others. Madison stayed in the North for three years, working with men like Alexander Hamilton of New York and Robert Morris of Pennsylvania as the congress wrestled with the chaotic economy and the ever-precarious war effort. In one crisis Madison's negotiating skills proved crucial: He broke the deadlock over the ratification of the Articles of Confederation by arranging for the cession of Virginia's western lands. More often, service in the congress proved frustrating to Madison because the confederation government seemed to lack essential powers.

Madison resumed a seat in the Virginia state assembly in 1784. But he did not retreat to a local point of view. He worked hard to bring about an all-state

JAMES MADISON BY CHARLES WILLSON PEALE
James Madison, a short and slight man, was often mistaken for being younger than he was. With natural hair (no wig) and smooth face, as shown here, he could pass for a youth of 20. This miniature portrait was made in 1783 when Madison was 32. That year he experienced his first serious romance, with a young woman who was just 16. She lived in his boarding house in Philadelphia, along with her father, a congressional delegate from New York. But the girl dropped him for another suitor. Madison waited eleven years to try romance again. New York congressman Aaron Burr introduced him to a Quaker widow named Dolley Payne Todd, who came from Virginia but lived in Philadelphia. Madison was 43 and Dolley was 26; they married four months after meeting.
Library of Congress.

convention in Philadelphia in the late spring of 1787, where he took the lead in steering the delegates to a complete rewrite of the structure of the national government, investing it with considerably greater powers. True to form, Madison spent the months before the convention in feverish study of the great thinkers he had read in college, searching out the best way to constitute a government on republican principles. His lifelong passion for scholarly study, seasoned by a dozen years of energetic political experience, paid off handsomely. The U.S. Constitution was the result.

By the end of the 1780s, James Madison had had his finger in every kind of political pie, on the local, state, confederation, and finally national level. He had transformed himself from a directionless and solitary youth into one of the leading political thinkers of the Revolutionary period. His personal history over the 1780s mirrored the path of the emerging United States.

The Articles of Confederation

For five years, from independence in 1776 until 1781, the Second Continental Congress continued to meet in Philadelphia and other cities. It existed without any formal constitutional basis, while its members groped to establish a government that embodied Revolutionary principles. With monarchy gone, where did sovereignty lie? What was the nature of representation? Who held the power of taxation? Who should vote; who should rule?

The initial answers to these questions took the form of a plan called the Articles of Confederation. The plan, however, proved to be surprisingly difficult to implement.

Congress, Confederation, and the Problem of Western Lands

Only after declaring independence did the Continental Congress turn its attention to the need for a written document that would specify what powers the congress had and by what authority it existed. There was widespread agreement on key government powers: pursuing war and peace, conducting foreign relations, regulating trade, and running a postal service. But there was serious disagreement about the powers of congress over the western boundaries of the states. Virginia and Connecticut, for example, had old colonial charters that located their boundaries along the Mississippi River. States without extensive land grants could not abide such grandiose claims.

For over a year, the congress tinkered with drafts of the Articles of Confederation, reaching agreement only in November 1777. The Articles defined the union as a loose confederation of states, characterized as "a firm league of friendship" existing mainly to foster a common defense. The structure of the government paralleled that of the existing Continental Congress. There was no national executive (that is, no president) and no national judiciary. The congress was composed of two to seven delegates from each state, selected annually by the state legislatures and prohibited from serving more than three years out of any six. The actual number of delegates was not critical, since each state delegation cast a single vote.

Routine decisions in the congress required a simple majority of seven states; for momentous powers, such as declaring war, nine states needed to agree. But to approve or amend the Articles required the unanimous consent both of the thirteen state delegations and of the thirteen state legislatures. The congressional delegates undoubtedly thought they were guaranteeing that no individual state could be railroaded by the other twelve in fundamental constitutional matters. But what this requirement really did was to hamstring the government. One state could—and did—hold the rest of the country hostage to its demands.

On the delicate question of deriving revenue to run the government, specifically to finance the war, the Articles provided an ingenious but ultimately troublesome solution. Each state was to contribute in proportion to the property value of the state's land. Large and populous states would give more than small or sparsely populated states. The actual taxes would be levied by the state legislatures, not by the congress, to preserve the Revolution's principle of taxation only by direct representation. However, no mechanism was created to compel states to contribute their fair share.

The lack of centralized authority in the confederation government was exactly what many state leaders wanted in the late 1770s. A league of states with rotating personnel, no executive branch, no power of taxation, and a requirement of unanimity for any major change seemed to be a good way to

avoid the potential tyranny of government. But right away, the inherent weaknesses of these features became apparent.

The requirement for unanimous approval, for example, stalled the acceptance of the Articles for five years. The key dispute involved the problem of lands west of the existing states and east of the Mississippi River. Five states, all lacking land claims, insisted that the congress control those lands as a national domain that would eventually constitute new states. The other eight states refused to yield their colonial-era claims and opposed giving congress power to alter boundaries (Map 8.1). In all the heated debate, few seemed to remember that those same western lands were inhabited by many thousands of Indians not party to the disputes.

The eight land-claiming states were ready to sign the Articles of Confederation in 1777. Rhode Island, Pennsylvania, and New Jersey eventually capitulated and signed, "not from a Conviction of the Equality and Justness of it," said a New Jersey delegate, "but merely from an absolute Necessity there was of complying to save the Continent." But Delaware and Maryland continued to hold out, insisting on a national domain policy. In 1779, the disputants finally compromised: Any land a state volunteered to relinquish would become the national domain. When congressmen James Madison and Thomas Jefferson ceded Virginia's huge land claim in 1781, the Articles were at last accepted by all states.

The western lands issue demonstrated that powerful interests divided the thirteen new states; the apparent unity of purpose inspired by fighting the war against England papered over sizable cracks in the new confederation.

Running the New Government

No fanfare greeted the long-awaited inauguration of the new government. The congress continued to sputter along, its problems far from solved by the signing of the Articles. Day-to-day activities were often hampered by the lack of a quorum. The Articles required representation from seven states to conduct business, with a minimum of two men from each state's delegation. But some days fewer than fourteen men in total showed up.

State legislatures were slow to select delegates; those appointed were often reluctant to attend, especially if they had wives and children at home,

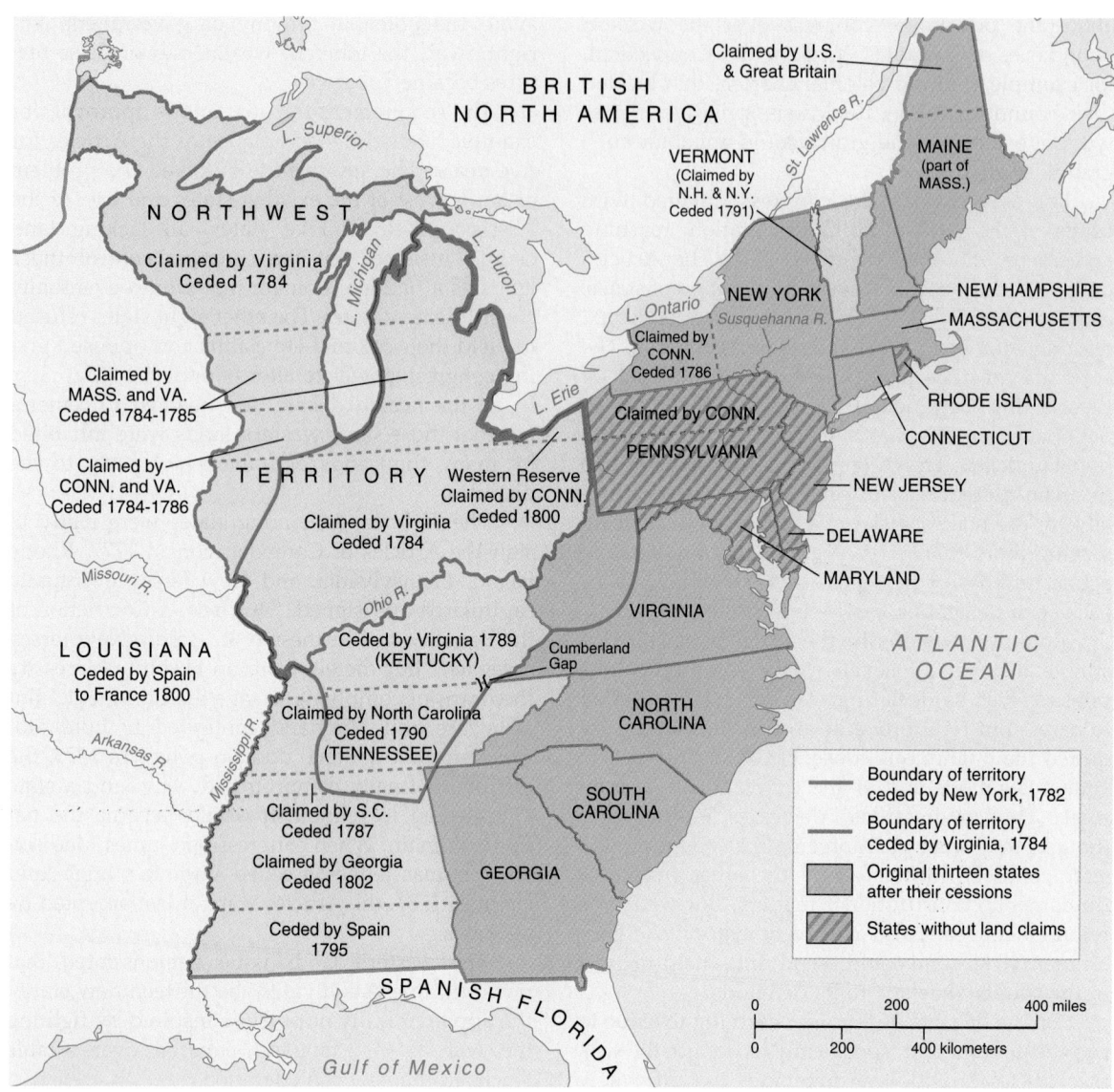

MAP 8.1

Cession of Western Lands, 1782–1802

The thirteen new states found it hard to ratify the Articles of Confederation without settling their conflicting land claims in the west, an area larger than the original states and occupied by Indian tribes. The five states objecting to the Articles' silence over western lands policy were Maryland, Delaware, New Jersey, Rhode Island, and Pennsylvania.

READING THE MAP: Which states had the largest claims on western territory? What disputed territory became the fourteenth state?

CONNECTIONS: In what context did the first dispute regarding western lands arise? How was it resolved? Does the map suggest a reason why Pennsylvania, a large state, joined the four much smaller states on this issue?

www.bedfordstmartins.com/roarkcompact SEE THE ONLINE STUDY GUIDE for more help in analyzing these maps.

and absenteeism was a constant problem. Consequently, some of the most effective and committed delegates were young bachelors like James Madison and men in their fifties and sixties whose families were grown, like Samuel Adams. Many active politicians preferred to devote their energies to their state governments, especially when the congress seemed deadlocked or, worse, irrelevant. Often, more exciting political work was going on at the state level, especially during the creative burst of state constitution writing in the late 1770s.

It also did not help that the congress had no permanent home. During the war, when the British army threatened Philadelphia, the congress relocated to small Pennsylvania towns like Lancaster and York and then to Baltimore. After hostilities ceased, the congress moved from Trenton to Princeton to Annapolis to New York City.

To address the difficulties of an inefficient congress, executive departments of war, finance, and foreign affairs were created to handle purely administrative functions. When the department heads were ambitious—as was Robert Morris, a wealthy Philadelphia merchant who served as superintendent of finance—they could exercise considerable executive power. The Articles of Confederation had deliberately refrained from setting up an executive branch, but a modest one was being invented by necessity.

The Sovereign States

In the first decade of independence, the states were sovereign and all-powerful. Relatively few functions, like that of declaring war and peace, had been transferred to the confederation government. Familiar and close to home, state governments claimed the allegiance of their citizens. As Americans discarded their English identity, they thought of themselves instead as Virginians or New Yorkers or Rhode Islanders. State government was thus the arena in which the Revolution's innovations would first be tried.

The State Constitutions

In May 1776, the congress in Philadelphia recommended that all the states draw up constitutions based on "the authority of the people." By 1778, ten

had done so, and two more (Connecticut and Rhode Island) adopted and updated their original colonial charters. Having been denied unwritten British liberties, Americans wanted written contracts that guaranteed basic principles.

A shared feature of all the state constitutions was the conviction that government ultimately rests on the consent of the governed. Political writers in the late 1770s embraced the concept of republicanism as the underpinning of the new governments. Republicanism meant more than just popular elections and representative institutions. For some, republicanism invoked a way of thinking about who leaders should be—ideally autonomous, virtuous citizens who placed civic values above private interests. For others, it suggested direct democracy, with nothing standing in the way of the will of the people. For all, it meant government that promoted the people's welfare.

Widespread agreement about the virtues of republicanism went hand in hand with the idea that republics could succeed only in relatively small units, so the people could make sure their interests were being served. Nearly every state continued the colonial practice of a two-chamber assembly but greatly augmented the powers of the lower house. Two states, Pennsylvania and Georgia, did away with the upper house altogether. Most states made their lower houses very responsive to popular majorities, with annual elections and guaranteed rotation in office. If a representative displeased his constituents, he could be out of office in a matter of months. Virtually all of the state constitutions severely limited the powers of the governor, and some restricted the governor's term to one year. Pennsylvania and Georgia abolished the office of governor altogether.

Six of the state constitutions included bills of rights, lists of basic individual liberties that governments could not abridge. Virginia debated and passed the first bill of rights in June 1776, and many of the other states borrowed from it. Its language bears a close resemblance to the wording of the Declaration of Independence, which Thomas Jefferson was composing that same June in Philadelphia: "That all men are by nature equally free and independent, and have certain inherent rights, of which, when they enter into a state of society, they cannot by any compact deprive or divest their posterity; namely, the enjoyment of life and liberty, with the means of acquiring and possessing property, and pursuing and obtaining happiness and safety." Along with these inherent rights went more specific rights to freedom of speech, freedom of the press, and trial by jury.

Who Are "the People"?

When the Continental Congress called for state constitutions based on "the authority of the people," and when the Virginia bill of rights granted "all men" certain rights, who was meant by "the people"? Who exactly were the citizens of this new country, and how far did the principle of democratic government extend? Different people answered these questions differently, but in the 1770s certain limits to full political participation by all Americans were widely agreed upon.

One limit was defined by property. In nearly every state, candidates for the highest offices—the governorship and membership in the upper house—needed to meet substantial property qualifications. In Maryland, for example, a candidate for governor had to be worth £5,000, quite a large sum of money. Voters in Maryland had to own fifty acres of land or £30. Only property owners were presumed to possess the necessary independence of mind and sense of community to make wise political choices. Are not propertyless men, asked John Adams, "too little acquainted with public affairs to form a right judgment, and too dependent upon other men to have a will of their own?"

Probably one-quarter to one-half of adult white males in all the states were disfranchised by property qualifications. Not all of them took their nonvoter status quietly. One Maryland man wondered what was so special about being worth £30: "Every poor man has a life, a personal liberty, and a right to his earnings; and is in danger of being injured by government in a variety of ways." Why then restrict such a man from voting for his representatives? Others pointed out that propertyless men were fighting and dying in the Revolutionary War; surely they were expressing an active concern about politics. Finally, a very few radical voices challenged the notion that owning property transformed men into good citizens. Perhaps it did the opposite: The richest men might well be greedy and selfish and therefore bad citizens.

But ideas like this were clearly outside the mainstream. The writers of the new constitutions, themselves men of property, viewed the Revolution as an effort to guarantee people the right to own property and to prevent unjust governments from appropriating it through taxation. John Adams urged the framers of the Massachusetts constitution not even to discuss the scope of suffrage but simply to adopt the traditional colonial property qualifications. If suffrage is brought up for debate, he warned, "there will be no end of it. New claims will arise; women will demand a vote; lads from twelve to twenty-one will think their rights not enough attended to; and every man who has not a farthing, will demand an equal voice with any other." Adams was astute enough to anticipate complaints about excluding women, youth, and poor men from political life, but it did not even occur to him to worry about another group: slaves.

Equality and Slavery

Restrictions on political participation did not mean that propertyless people enjoyed no civil rights and liberties. The various state bills of rights applied to all individuals who had, as the Virginia bill so carefully phrased it, "enter[ed] into a state of society." No matter how poor, a free person was entitled to life, liberty, property, and freedom of conscience. Unfree people, however, were another matter.

The author of the Virginia bill of rights was George Mason, a plantation owner with 118 slaves. When he penned the sentence "all men are by nature equally free and independent," he did not have his slaves in mind; he meant that Americans were the equals of the British and could not be denied the liberties of

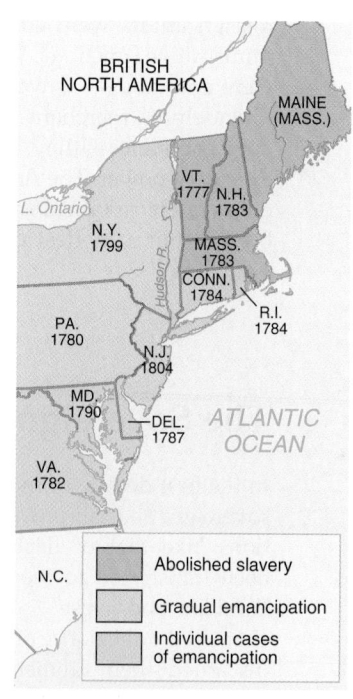

Legal Changes to Slavery, 1777–1804

British citizens. Other Virginia legislators, however, worried about misinterpretations, added the phrase specifying that rights belonged only to people who had entered civil society. As one wrote, with relief, "Slaves, not being constituent members of our society, could never pretend to any benefit from such a maxim."

One month later, the Declaration of Independence used essentially the same phrase about equality, this time without the modifying clause about entering society. Two state constitutions, for Pennsylvania and Massachusetts, also picked it up. In Massachusetts, one town suggested that the sentence on equality be reworded to read "All men, whites and blacks, are born free and equal." But the suggestion fell on deaf ears.

Nevertheless, after 1776, the ideals of the Revolution about natural equality and liberty began to erode the institution of slavery. Sometimes enslaved blacks led the challenge. In 1777, several Massachusetts slaves petitioned the state legislature, claiming a "natural & unalienable right to that freedom which the great Parent of the Universe hath bestowed equally on all mankind." They modestly asked for freedom for their children at age twenty-one and were turned down. In 1779, similar petitions in Connecticut and New Hampshire met with no success. Seven Massachusetts freemen, including the mariner brothers Paul and John Cuffe, refused to pay taxes for three years on the grounds that they could not vote and so were not represented. The Cuffe brothers landed in jail in 1780 for tax evasion, but their petition to the state legislature spurred the extension of suffrage to taxpaying free blacks in that state.

Another way to bring the issue before lawmakers was to sue in court. In 1781, a Massachusetts slave named Quok Walker charged his master with assault and battery, arguing he was a free man, under the state constitution's promise that "all men are born free and equal." Walker won and was set free; several similar cases followed, and by 1789 slavery had been effectively abolished by judicial decision in Massachusetts.

In other northern states, untold numbers of blacks simply ran away from owners and claimed their freedom, sometimes with the help of sympathetic whites. One estimate holds that more than half of young slave men in Philadelphia took flight in the 1780s. By 1790, free blacks outnumbered slaves in Pennsylvania by nearly a factor of two.

Pennsylvania was the first state to legislate an end to slavery by statute, in 1780. Yet the law provided for a very gradual emancipation: Only infants born to a slave mother on or after March 1, 1780, would be freed, and then not until age twenty-eight.

That meant that no current slave in Pennsylvania would gain freedom until 1808, and well into the nineteenth century some blacks would still be slaves. Rhode Island and Connecticut adopted gradual emancipation laws in 1784. In 1785, New York expanded the terms under which individual owners could free slaves, but only in 1799 did the state adopt a gradual emancipation law; New Jersey followed suit in 1804. These were the two northern states with the largest number of slaves: New York in 1800 with 20,000, and New Jersey, more than 12,000. In contrast, Pennsylvania had just 1,700. Gradual emancipation illustrates the tension between radical and conservative implications of republican ideology. Republican government protected people's liberties and property; yet slaves were both people and property. Gradual emancipation balanced the civil rights of blacks and the property rights of their owners by delaying the promise of freedom.

South of Pennsylvania, in Delaware, Maryland, and Virginia, where slavery was so important to the economy, general emancipation bills were rejected. All three states, however, eased legal restrictions and allowed individual acts of emancipation for adult slaves below the age of forty-five, under new manumission laws passed in the 1780s and 1790s. By 1790, close to 10,000 freed Virginia slaves had formed local free black communities complete with schools and churches.

In the deep South—the Carolinas and Georgia—freedom for slaves was unthinkable for whites. Yet more than 10,000 slaves from South Carolina achieved freedom in 1783 by leaving with the British army from Charleston, and another 6,000 set sail under the British flag from Savannah, Georgia. This was by far the largest emancipation of blacks in the entire country. Some went to Canada, some to England, and a small number to Sierra Leone, on the west coast of Africa. Additionally, many hundreds of ex-slaves took refuge with Seminole and Creek Indians, becoming permanent members of their communities in Spanish Florida and western Georgia.

Although emancipation affected fewer blacks in the North, simply because there were many fewer of them to begin with, its symbolic importance was enormous. Every state from Pennsylvania northward acknowledged that slavery was fundamentally inconsistent with revolutionary ideology; "all men are created equal" was beginning to acquire real force as a basic principle.

The Critical Period

From 1781 to 1786, a sense of crisis gripped some of the revolutionary leaders who feared the Articles of Confederation were too weak. But others defended the Articles as the best guarantee of individual liberty, because real governance occurred at the state level, closer to the people. Political theorizing about the proper relation among citizen, state, and confederation remained active and controversial throughout the decade as Americans confronted questions of finance, territorial expansion, and civil disorder.

Financial Chaos and Paper Money

Seven years of war produced a booming but chaotic economy in the 1780s. The confederation and the individual states had run up huge war debts, financed by printing paper money and borrowing from private sources. Some $400 to $500 million in paper currency had been injected into the economy, and prices and wages fluctuated wildly. Private debt and rapid expenditure flourished, and debtors' prisons became crowded. A serious postwar depression settled in by the mid-1780s and did not lift until the 1790s.

The confederation government was itself in a terrible financial fix. Continental dollars had lost almost all value: It took 146 of them to buy what a dollar had bought in 1775. Desperate times required desperate measures. The congress turned to Robert Morris, a merchant and newly reelected delegate from Pennsylvania, appointing him superintendent of finance. Six years earlier, the wealthy Morris had procured from Europe much-needed muskets for the army but had resigned from the congress in 1778 under suspicion that he had unfairly profited from his public service efforts; indeed, he had left public life many thousands of dollars richer than he had entered it. Nevertheless, the congress called on him from 1781 to 1784 to apply his considerable talent to the confederation's economic problems.

To augment the government's revenue, Morris first proposed a 5 percent import tax (called an *impost*). Since there was no authority in the Articles of Confederation for such a tax, Morris's plan required an amendment to the Articles approved unanimously by the thirteen states. But unanimous agreement was impossible. Rhode Island and New York, whose bustling ports provided ample state revenue, preferred to keep their money and simply refused to agree to the national impost.

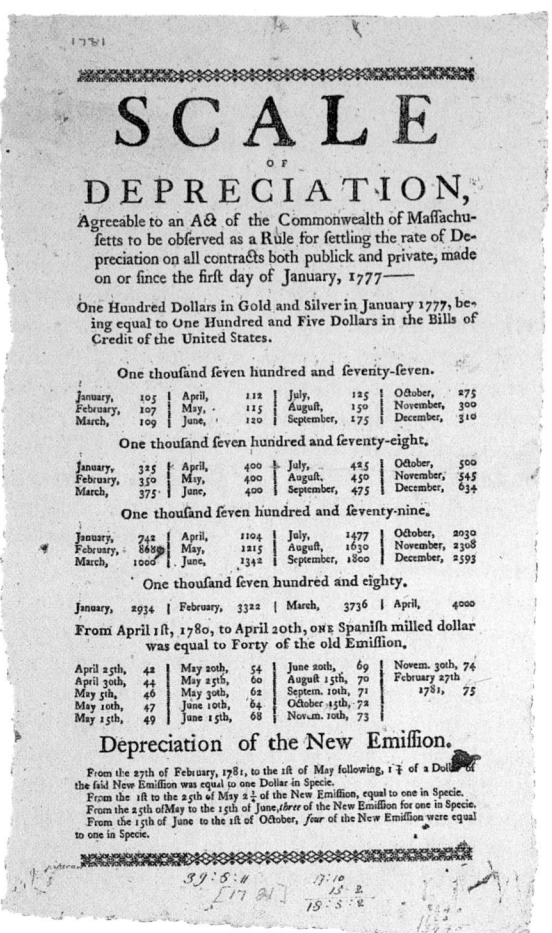

SCALE OF DEPRECIATION
This chart shows the monthly value of U.S. Continental dollars from January 1777 to February 1781, as stipulated by the government of Massachusetts. For example, in March 1780, it took 3,736 Continental dollars to equal the buying power of $100 in gold or silver based on values of the dollar in January 1777. By April 1780, the same value of hard money required $4,000 Continentals. Such a chart was needed when debtors and creditors settled accounts contracted at one time and paid off later in greatly depreciated dollars. How easy would you find it to keep your head above water in an economy with such fast currency depreciation? What level of arithmetic skills were required? chart-reading skills? Notice the hand-written figuring at the bottom of the chart. Do these arithmetic operations look familiar to you?
Courtesy, American Antiquarian Society.

Morris's next idea was the creation of the Bank of North America. This private bank would enjoy a special relationship with the confederation, holding the government's hard money as well as private deposits, and providing it with short-term loans. The bank's contribution to economic stability came in the form of banknotes, pieces of paper inscribed with a dollar value. Unlike paper money, banknotes were backed by hard money in the bank's vaults and thus would not depreciate. Morris hoped that the new banknotes would function like paper money without its drawbacks. Congress agreed and voted to approve the bank in 1781.

The Bank of North America, located in Philadelphia, had limited success curing the confederation's economic woes. In the short run, the bank supplied the government with a currency that held its value, but it issued so little that the impact was very small. When its charter expired in 1786, the Pennsylvania legislature refused to renew it.

If Morris could not resuscitate the economy in the 1780s, probably no one could have done it. Because the Articles of Confederation reserved most economic functions to the states, congress was helpless to tax trade, control inflation, or pay the mounting public debt. But the confederation had acquired one source of potential enormous wealth: the huge territory ceded by Virginia, which in 1784 became the national domain.

Land Ordinances and the Northwest Territory

The Continental Congress appointed Thomas Jefferson to draft a national domain policy. Jefferson proposed dividing the territory north of the Ohio River and east of the Mississippi—called the Northwest Territory—into ten new states, each divided into townships ten miles square. He advocated giving the land to settlers, rather than selling it, on the grounds that the improved lands would so enrich the country through future property taxes that there was no need to make the settlers pay twice. Jefferson's aim was to encourage rapid and democratic settlement of the land, to build a nation of freeholders (as opposed to renters), and to avoid speculative frenzy.

Jefferson also insisted that the new states have representative governments equal in status to those of the original states once they reached a certain population. This ensured that the new United States, so recently released from colonial dependency, would

THOMAS JEFFERSON BY JOHN TRUMBULL
This miniature shows Thomas Jefferson at age forty-five, during his years as a diplomat in Paris. The American artist John Trumbull visited France in 1788 and painted Jefferson's likeness in this five-by-four-inch format so he could later copy it into his planned large canvas depicting the signing of the Declaration of Independence. Jefferson requested three replicas of the miniature to bestow as gifts. One went to his daughter Martha, another to an American woman in London, and the third to Maria Cosway, a British artist with whom the widower Jefferson shared an intense infatuation during his stay in France. Jefferson never remarried, but a scandal over his private life erupted in 1802, when a journalist charged that he had fathered several children by his slave Sally Hemings. In 1998, a careful DNA study concluded that uniquely marked Jefferson Y-chromosomes were common to both Hemings's and Jefferson's descendants. The DNA evidence, when combined with historical evidence about Jefferson's whereabouts at the start of each of Hemings's six pregnancies, makes it extremely likely that Jefferson fathered some or perhaps all of her children. What cannot be known is the nature of the relationship between the two. Was it coerced or voluntary, or somewhere in between? In all his voluminous writings, Jefferson left no comment about Sally Hemings, and the record on her side is entirely mute. Monticello.

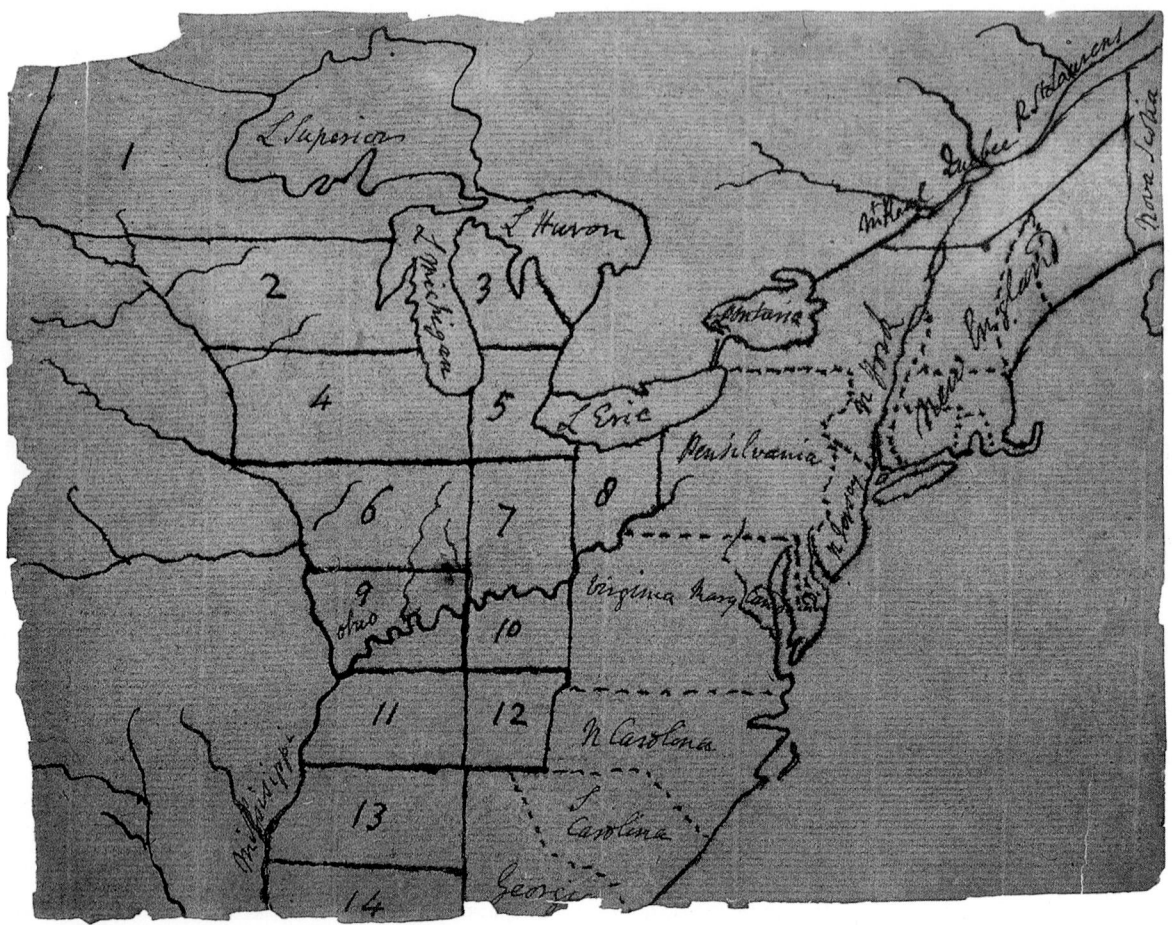

JEFFERSON'S MAP OF THE NORTHWEST TERRITORY
Thomas Jefferson sketched out borders for ten new states in his initial plan for the Northwest Territory in 1784. Straight lines and right angles held a strong appeal for him. But such regularity ignored inconvenient geographic features like rivers and even more inconvenient political features like Indian territorial claims, most unlikely to be ceded by treaty in orderly blocks. Jefferson also submitted ten distinctive names for the states. Number 9, for example, was Polypotamia, or "land of many rivers" in Greek.
William L. Clements Library.

www.bedfordstmartins.com/roarkcompact SEE THE ONLINE STUDY GUIDE for more help in analyzing this image.

not itself become a colonial power. Finally, Jefferson's draft prohibited slavery in the ten new states.

The congress adopted parts of Jefferson's plan in the Ordinance of 1784: the rectangular grid, the ten states, and the guarantee of self-government and eventual statehood. What the congress found too radical was the proposal to give away the land; the national domain was the confederation's only source of independent wealth. And the slavery prohibition failed by only one state's vote.

A year later, the congress reconsidered the land act and passed a new version, the Ordinance of 1785. The new plan called for walkable townships six miles square, each containing thirty-six sections; each section contained 640 acres, enough for four family farms. The 1785 ordinance reduced Jefferson's plan for ten rectangular states down to three to five states, with boundaries conforming to natural geographic features like the Great Lakes and major rivers instead of abstractly drawn survey lines. Land sales would occur by public auction, with minimum price one dollar an acre, but market forces could drive up the prices of the most desirable land. Two further restrictions applied: Land was sold in minimum parcels of 640 acres each, and payment had to be in hard money or in certificates of debt from Revolutionary days. This effectively meant that the land's first owners would be prosperous speculators.

Speculators usually held the land for resale rather than settling on it. Thus they avoided direct contact with the most serious obstacle to settlement: the dozens of Indian tribes that claimed the land as their own. Treaties signed at Fort Stanwix in 1784 and Fort McIntosh in 1785 coerced partial cessions of land from Iroquois, Delaware, Huron, and Miami tribes, but a united Indian meeting near Detroit in 1786 issued an ultimatum: No cession would be valid without unanimous consent. The Indians advised the United States to "prevent your surveyors and other people from coming upon our side of the Ohio river." For two more decades, violent Indian wars in Ohio and Indiana would continue to impede white settlement.

In 1787, a third land act, called the Northwest Ordinance, promised eventual self-government for a territory when the white male population reached five thousand, but it devised an interim plan for sparsely settled territories with a congressionally appointed governor. The other landmark feature of the 1787 act was a prohibition on slavery in the entire region, which this time passed without debate. A North-South sectionalism, based on slavery, was slowly taking shape.

Shays's Rebellion, 1786–1787

Without an impost amendment, the confederation turned to the states to contribute revenue voluntarily. Struggling with their own war debts, most state legislatures were reluctant to tax their constituents too heavily. Massachusetts, however, had a tough-minded, fiscally conservative legislature, dominated by the coastal commercial centers, which wanted to retire the state debt by raising taxes. Worse yet, it insisted that taxes be paid in hard money, not cheap paper. Farmers in the western half of the state found it difficult to comply, and by 1786 sheriffs frequently confiscated property and jailed tax delinquents.

However, the western farmers had learned from the American Revolution how to respond to

SILVER BOWL FOR ANTI-SHAYS GENERAL
The militia of Springfield in western Massachusetts presented its leader, General William Shepard, with this silver bowl to honor his victory over the insurgents in Shays's Rebellion. Presentational silver conveyed a double message. It announced gratitude and praise in engraved words, and it transmitted considerable monetary value in the silver itself. General Shepard could display his trophy on a shelf, use it as a punch bowl, will it to descendants to keep his famous moment alive in memory, or melt it down in hard times. Not only is Shepard's name commemorated on the silver; SHAYS *too appears in the last line, there for the ages to remember.*
Yale University Art Gallery, Mabel Brady Garvan Collection.

oppressive taxation. They called conventions to discuss their grievances and circulated petitions demanding tax reductions, paper money, and debt relief legislation. In the fall of 1786, about 2,500 armed men marched on the courthouses in three western Massachusetts counties. The leader of this tax revolt was a farmer and onetime captain in the Continental army, Daniel Shays.

The governor of Massachusetts, James Bowdoin, who had once organized protests against British taxes, now characterized the Shaysites as illegal rebels. Another former rebel, Samuel Adams, took the extreme position that "the man who dares rebel against the laws of a republic ought to suffer death." These aging revolutionaries had given little thought to the possibility that popular majorities, embodied in a state legislature, could seem to be oppressive, just as monarchs could. The Shaysites challenged the idea that popularly elected governments would always be fair and just.

In January 1787, Governor Bowdoin sent a volunteer army to quell the rebellion. When Shaysites numbering about 1,500 attacked a federal armory in Springfield, they were met with gunfire; 4 rebels were killed and another 20 wounded. The final and bloodless encounter came at Petersham, where the army surprised the rebels on a freezing morning and took 150 prisoners;

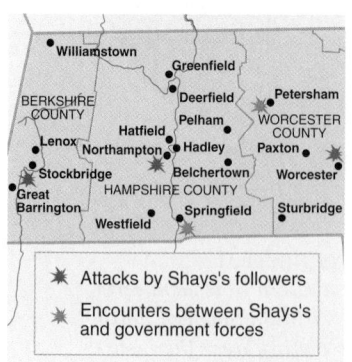

the others fled into the woods. Shays took off for Canada and other leaders left the state, but more than 1,000 dissidents were rounded up and jailed. No one was executed for rebellion, but the rebels were prohibited from ever again voting, holding public office, working as schoolmasters, or operating taverns. The first two prohibitions denied

Shays's Rebellion, 1786–1787

the men a political voice, and the second two denied them occupations in which they could instruct or influence others.

Shays's Rebellion caused leaders throughout the country to worry whether the confederation could handle problems of civil disorder. Perhaps there were similar "combustibles" in other states, awaiting the spark that would set off a dreadful political conflagration. New York lawyer and diplomat John Jay wrote to George Washington, "Our affairs seem to lead to some crisis, some revolution—something I cannot foresee or conjecture. I am uneasy and apprehensive; more so than during the war." Benjamin Franklin, in his eighties, shrewdly observed that in 1776 Americans had feared "an excess of power in the rulers," whereas now the problem was "a defect of obedience" in the subjects. To some, the sense of crisis in the confederation had greatly deepened.

The United States Constitution

Events in the fall of 1786 provoked an odd mixture of fear and hope that the government under the Articles of Confederation was losing its grip on power. A small circle of Virginians decided to try one last time to augment the powers granted to the government by the Articles. Their call for a meeting to discuss trade regulation led, more quickly than they could have imagined in 1786, to a total reworking of the national government.

From Annapolis to Philadelphia

The Virginians, led by James Madison, convinced the congress of the confederation government to allow a meeting of delegates at Annapolis, Maryland, in September 1786, to try again to revise the trade regulation powers of the Articles. But only five states participated. Like Madison, the dozen men who attended sensed an impending crisis, and they rescheduled the meeting for Philadelphia in May 1787. Congress reluctantly endorsed the Philadelphia meeting and tried to limit its scope to "the sole and express purpose of revising the Articles of Confederation." But at least one representative at the Annapolis meeting had far more ambitious plans. Alexander Hamilton of New York hoped the Philadelphia meeting would do whatever was necessary to strengthen the federal government.

Alexander Hamilton by character was suited for such bold steps. The illegitimate son of a poor mother in the West Indies, at age sixteen the bright lad greatly impressed an American trader, who sent him to New York City for a college education. Hamilton soon got swept up in the military enthusiasm of 1776 and by 1777 had joined George Washington's staff, serving at the general's side through much of the Revolution. After the war, he studied law, married into a New York mercantile family, and sat in the Continental Congress for two years. Despite his stigmatized and impoverished childhood, the aspiring Hamilton identified with the elite classes and their fear of democratic disorder.

The fifty-five men who assembled at Philadelphia in May 1787 to consider the shortcomings of the Articles of Confederation were generally those most concerned about weaknesses in the present government. Few attended who were opposed to revising the Articles. Patrick Henry, author of the Virginia Resolves in 1765 and more recently state governor, refused to go, saying he "smelled a rat." Two New York representatives left in dismay in the middle of the convention, leaving Hamilton as the sole New York delegate.

This gathering of white men included no artisans or day laborers or even farmers of middling wealth. Two-thirds of the delegates were lawyers. The majority had served in the confederation congress and knew its strengths and weaknesses; fully half had been officers in the Continental army. Seven men had been governors of their states and knew firsthand the frustrations of thwarted executive power. A few elder statesmen attended, such as

Benjamin Franklin and George Washington, but on the whole, the delegates were young, like Madison and Hamilton.

The Virginia and New Jersey Plans

The convention worked in secrecy, so the men could freely explore alternatives without fear that their honest opinions would come back to haunt them. The Virginia delegation first laid out a fifteen-point plan for a complete restructuring of the government. This Virginia Plan was a total repudiation of the principle of a confederation of states. Largely the work of Madison, the plan set out a three-branch government composed of a two-chamber legislature, a powerful executive, and a judiciary. It virtually eliminated the voices of the smaller states by pegging representation in both houses of the congress to population. The theory was that government operated directly on people, not on states. Among the breathtaking powers assigned to the congress were the rights to veto state legislation and to coerce states militarily to obey national laws. To prevent the congress from having absolute power, the executive and judiciary could jointly veto the actions of the congress.

In mid-June, delegates from New Jersey, Connecticut, Delaware, and New Hampshire, all small states, unveiled an alternative proposal. The New Jersey Plan, as it was called, resembled the existing Articles of Confederation in that it set out a single-house congress in which each state had one vote. Acknowledging the need for an executive, it created a plural presidency to be shared by three men elected by the congress from among its membership. Where it sharply departed from the existing government was in the sweeping powers it gave to the congress: the right to tax, to regulate trade, and to use force on unruly state governments. In favoring national power over states' rights, it aligned itself with the Virginia Plan. But the New Jersey Plan retained the confederation principle that the national government was to be an assembly of states, not of people.

For two weeks, delegates debated the two plans, focusing on the key issue of representation. The small-state delegates conceded that one house in a two-house legislature could be apportioned by population, but they would never agree that both houses could be. Madison was equally vehement about bypassing representation by state, which he viewed as the fundamental flaw in the Articles.

THE PENNSYLVANIA STATEHOUSE
The constitutional convention assembled at the Pennsylvania statehouse to sweat out the summer of 1787. Despite the heat, the delegates nailed the windows shut to eliminate the chance of being heard by eavesdroppers, so intent were they on secrecy. The statehouse, built in the 1740s to house the colony's assembly, accommodated the Continental Congress at various times in the 1770s and 1780s. The building is now called Independence Hall, in honor of the signing of the Declaration of Independence within its walls in 1776.
Historical Society of Pennsylvania.

The debate seemed deadlocked, and for a while the convention was "on the verge of dissolution, scarce held together by the strength of a hair," according to one delegate. Only in mid-July did the so-called Great Compromise break the logjam and produce the basic structural features of the emerging United States Constitution. Proponents of the competing plans agreed on a bicameral legislature; representation in the lower house, the House of Representatives, would be apportioned by population, and representation in the upper house, the Senate, would come from all the states equally. But instead of one vote per state in the upper house, as in the New Jersey Plan, the compromise provided two senators who voted independently. Plenty of fine-tuning followed, but the most difficult problem, representation, was solved.

Representation by population turned out to be an ambiguous concept once it was subjected to rigorous discussion. Who counted? Were slaves, for example, people or property? As people, they added weight to the southern delegations in the House of Representatives, but as property they added to the tax burdens of those states. What emerged was the compromise known as the three-fifths clause: All free persons plus "three-fifths of all other Persons" constituted the numerical base for the apportionment of representatives. Using "all other Persons" as a substitute for "slaves" indicates the discomfort delegates felt in acknowledging the existence of slavery in a republican document. But though slavery was nowhere named, nonetheless it was recognized, guaranteed, and thereby perpetuated by the U.S. Constitution.

Democracy versus Republicanism

The delegates in Philadelphia made a distinction between democracy and republicanism new to American political vocabulary. Pure democracy was now taken to be a dangerous thing. As a Massachusetts delegate put it, "the evils we experience flow from the excess of democracy." The delegates still favored republican institutions, but they created a government that gave direct voice to the people only in the House and that granted a check on that voice to the Senate, a body of men elected not by direct popular vote but by the state legislatures. Senators served for six years, with no limit on reelection; they were protected from the whims of democratic majorities, and their long terms fostered experience and maturity in office.

Similarly, the presidency evolved into a powerful office out of the reach of direct democracy. The delegates devised an electoral college whose only function was to elect the president and vice president. Each state's legislature would choose the electors, whose number was the sum of representatives and senators for the state, an interesting melding of the two principles of representation. The president thus would owe his office not to the Congress, the states, or the people, but to a temporary assemblage of distinguished citizens who could vote their own judgment on the candidates.

The framers had developed a far more complex form of federal government than that provided by the Articles of Confederation. To curb the excesses of democracy, they devised a government with limits and checks on all branches. They set forth a powerful president who could veto Congress but then gave Congress power to override presidential vetoes. They set up a national judiciary to settle disputes between states and citizens of different states.

They made each branch of government as independent from the other branches as they could, by basing election on different universes of voters—voting citizens, state legislators, the electoral college.

The convention carefully listed the powers of Congress and of the president. The president could initiate policy, propose legislation, and veto acts of Congress; he could command the military and direct foreign policy; and he could appoint the entire judiciary, subject to Senate approval. Congress held the purse strings: the power to levy taxes, to regulate trade, and to coin money and control the currency. States were expressly forbidden to issue paper money. Two further powers of Congress—to "provide for the common defence and general Welfare" of the country and "to make all laws which shall be necessary and proper" for carrying out its powers—provided elastic language that came closest to Madison's wish to grant sweeping powers to the new government.

The Constitution specified a mechanism for ratification that avoided the dilemma faced earlier by the confederation government: Nine states, not all thirteen, had to ratify it, and special ratifying conventions elected only for that purpose, not state legislatures, would make the crucial decision.

Ratification of the Constitution

Had a popular vote been taken on the Constitution in the fall of 1787, it would probably have been rejected. In the three most populous states—Virginia, Massachusetts, and New York—substantial majorities opposed a powerful new national government. North Carolina and Rhode Island refused to call ratifying conventions. Seven of the eight remaining states were easy victories for the Constitution, but securing the approval of the ninth proved difficult.

The Federalists

The proponents of the Constitution moved into action swiftly. To silence the criticism that they had gone beyond their charge (which indeed they had), they sent the document to the congress. Congress withheld explicit approval but resolved to send the Constitution to the states for their consideration. The pro-Constitution forces shrewdly secured an-

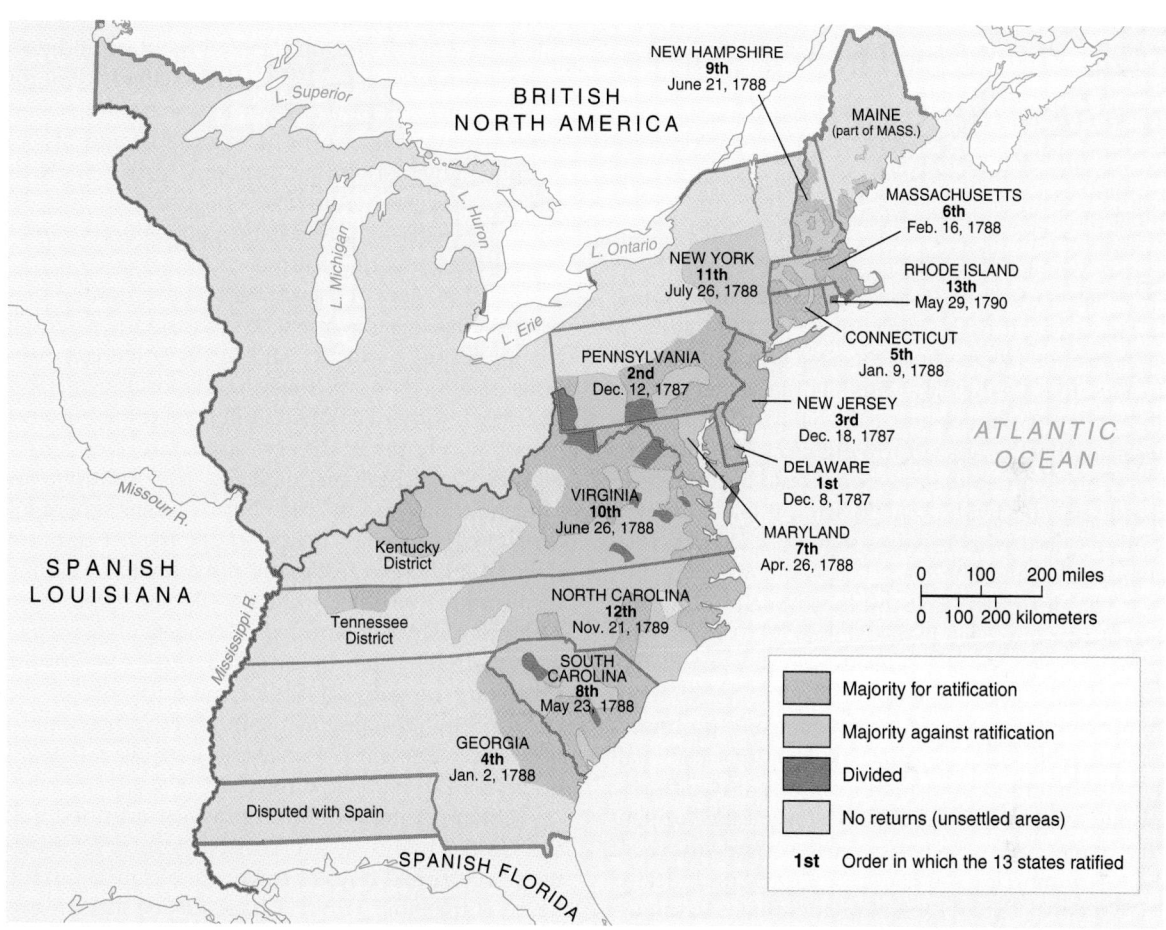

M A P 8 . 2
Ratification of the Constitution, 1788–1790
Populated areas cast votes for delegates to state ratification conventions. This map
shows Antifederalist strength generally concentrated in backcountry, noncoastal, and
nonurban areas, but with significant exceptions (for example, Rhode Island).

other advantage by calling themselves Federalists. By all logic, this label was more suitable for the backers of the confederation concept, since the Latin root of the word federal means "league." Their opponents became known as Antifederalists, a label that made them sound defensive and negative, lacking a program of their own.

The Federalists targeted the states most likely to ratify quickly, to gain momentum. Delaware provided a unanimous ratification by early December, before the Antifederalists had even begun to campaign. Pennsylvania, New Jersey, and Georgia followed within a month (Map 8.2). Delaware and New Jersey were small states surrounded by more powerful neighbors; a government that would regulate trade and set taxes according to population was an attractive proposition. Georgia sought the protection a stronger national government would afford against hostile Indians and Spanish Florida to the south.

Another three easy victories came in Connecticut, Maryland, and South Carolina. As in Pennsylvania, merchants, lawyers, and urban artisans in general favored the new Constitution, as did large landowners and slaveholders. This tendency for the established political elite to be Federalist enhanced the prospects of victory, for Federalists already had power disproportionate to their numbers.

Was the New United States a Christian Country?

R EBECCA SAMUEL, a Jewish resident of Virginia, conveyed her excitement about the new U.S. Constitution when she wrote her German parents in 1791 that finally "Jew and Gentile are as one" in the realm of politics and citizenship. Other voices were distinctly less approving. An Antifederalist pamphlet warned that the pope could become president; another feared that "a Turk, a Jew, a Roman Catholic, and what is worse than all, a Universalist, may be President."

The document that produced such wildly different readings was indeed remarkable in its handling of religion. The Constitution did not invoke Christianity as a state religion. It made no reference to an almighty being, and it specifically promised, in Article 6, section 3, that "no religious test shall ever be required as a qualification to any office or public trust under the United States." (See appendix, page A-8.) The six largest congregations of Jews—numbering about two thousand and located in Newport, New York, Philadelphia, Baltimore, Charleston, and Savannah—were delighted with this nearly unprecedented statement of political equality and wrote George Washington to express their hearty thanks.

But more than a few Christian leaders were stunned at the Constitution's near silence on religion. It seemed to represent a complete turnabout from the state constitutions of the 1770s and 1780s. A New Yorker warned that, "should the Citizens of America be as irreligious as her Constitution, we will have reason to tremble, lest the Governor of the universe . . . crush us to atoms." A delegate to North Carolina's ratifying convention played on anti-immigrant fears by predicting that the Constitution was "an invitation for Jews and pagans of every kind to come among us." A concerned Presbyterian minister asked Alexander Hamilton why religion was not in the Constitution, and Hamilton reportedly quipped, "Indeed, Doctor, we forgot it."

Measured against the practices of state governments, Hamilton's observation is hardly credible.

The men who wrote and debated the state and federal constitutions from 1775 to 1787 actively thought about principles of inclusion and exclusion when they defined citizenship, voting rights, and officeholding. They carefully considered property ownership, race, gender, and age in formulating rules about who could participate. And they also thought about religious qualifications.

Most leaders of the 1780s took for granted that Christianity was the one true faith and the essential foundation of morality. All but two state constitutions assumed the primacy of Protestantism, and one-third of them collected public taxes to support Christian churches. Every state but New York required a Christian oath as a condition for officeholding. Every member of Pennsylvania's legislature swore to "acknowledge the Scripture of the Old and New Testament to be given by divine inspiration." North Carolina's rule was even more restrictive, since it omitted Catholics: "No person who shall deny the being of God or the truth of the Protestant religion, or the divine authority of the Old or New Testaments" could hold office. South Carolina went much further and required that all voters had to be Protestants.

Other common political practices affirmed that the United States was a Christian country. Governors proclaimed days of public thanksgiving in the name of the Holy Trinity. Chaplains led legislatures in Christian prayer. Jurors and witnesses in court swore Christian oaths. New England states passed Sabbath laws prohibiting all work or travel on Sunday. Blasphemy laws punished people who cursed the Christian God or Jesus.

Close to half the state constitutions included the right to freedom of religion as an explicit guarantee. But freedom of religion meant only that difference would be tolerated; it did not guarantee political equality. How then did the U.S. Constitution come to be such a break from the immediate past? Had the framers really just forgotten about religion?

Not James Madison of Virginia. Madison arrived at the 1787 convention fresh from a hard-won victory in Virginia to establish religious liberty. At the end of 1786, he had finally secured passage of a bill written by Thomas Jefferson seven years earlier called the Virginia Statute of Religious Freedom. "All men shall be free to profess, and by argument to maintain, their opinions in matters of religion, and that the same shall in no wise diminish, enlarge,

TOURO SYNAGOGUE
A Jewish community inhabited the coastal shipping city of Newport, Rhode Island, as early as the 1650s. In 1759, the thriving group built a synagogue, the oldest Jewish house of worship still standing in the United States. The building blends a Georgian brick exterior with elements of Sephardic Jewish origin and is sited diagonally on its property so that worshipers face east, the direction of Jerusalem. President Washington visited Newport in 1790 and wrote to "the Hebrew Congregation" a few days later: "It is now no more that toleration is spoken of, as if it was by the indulgence of one class of people, that another enjoyed the exercise of their inherent natural rights."
Touro Synagogue/photo John T. Hopf.

or affect their civil capacities," the bill read. Madison had convinced both the Episcopalians and the Baptist dissenters, at war with each other over state support, that to grant either or both churches tax money would be to concede to the state the authority to endorse one religion—and by implication to crush another. The statute separated church from state to protect religion. Further, it went beyond mere toleration to guarantee that religious choice was independent of civil rights.

In Madison's judgment, it was best for the U.S. Constitution to say as little as possible about religion, especially since state laws reflected a variety of positions. When Antifederalists demanded a bill of rights, Madison drew up a list for the first Congress to consider. Two items dealt with religion, but only one was approved. One became part of the First Amendment: "Congress shall make no law respecting an establishment of religion, or prohibiting the free exercise thereof." In a stroke, Madison set religious worship and the privileging of any one church beyond Congress's power. Significantly, his second proposal failed to pass: "No State shall violate the equal rights of conscience." Evidently, the states wanted to be able to keep their Christian-only rules without federal interference. Different faiths would be tolerated—but not guaranteed equal standing. And the very same session of Congress proceeded to hire Christian chaplains and proclaim days of thanksgiving.

Gradually, states deleted restrictive laws, but as late as 1840 Jews still could not hold public office in four states. Into the twentieth century, some states maintained Sunday laws that forced business closings on the Christian Sabbath, working enormous hardship on those whose religion required Saturday closings. The guarantee of freedom of religion was embedded in state and federal founding documents in the 1770s and 1780s, but it has taken many years to fulfill Jefferson's vision of what true religious liberty means: the freedom for religious belief to be independent of civil status.

Antifederalists in these states tended to be rural, western, and noncommercial, men whose access to news was limited and whose participation in state government was tenuous.

Massachusetts was the only early state that gave the Federalists difficulty. The vote to select the ratification delegates was decidedly Antifederalist; Shays's Rebellion was of recent memory there. One rural delegate from Worcester County voiced widely shared suspicions: "These lawyers and men of learning and money men that talk so finely, and gloss over matters so smoothly, to make us poor illiterate people swallow down the pill, expect to get into Congress themselves; they expect to be the managers of the Constitution and get all the power and all the money into their own hands, and then they will swallow up all us little folks." Nevertheless, the Antifederalist lead was slowly eroded by a vigorous newspaper campaign. In the end, the Federalists won by a very slim margin and only with promises that amendments to the Constitution would be taken up in the first Congress.

By May 1788, eight states had ratified; only one more was needed. North Carolina and Rhode Island were hopeless for the Federalist cause, and New Hampshire seemed nearly as bleak. More worrisome was the failure to win over the largest and most important states, Virginia and New York.

The Antifederalists

Antifederalists were a composite group, united mainly in their desire to block the Constitution. Although much Antifederalist strength came from backcountry areas long suspicious of eastern elites, many Antifederalist leaders came from the same social background as Federalist leaders; economic class alone did not differentiate them. Antifederalism also drew strength in states already on sure economic footing, like New York, that could afford to remain independent. Probably the biggest appeal of antifederalism lay in the long-nurtured fear that distant power might infringe on people's liberties. The language of the earlier revolutionary movement was not easily forgotten.

For example, in the proposed House of Representatives, the only directly democratic element of the Constitution, one member represented some thirty thousand people. How could that member really know or communicate with 'his whole constituency, the Antifederalists wondered. In contrast,

one wrote, "The members of our state legislatures are annually elected—they are subject to instructions—they are chosen within small circles—they are sent but a small distance from their respective homes. Their conduct is constantly known to their constituents. They frequently see, and are seen, by the men whose servants they are."

The Antifederalists also worried that elected representatives would always be members of the elite. Such men "will be ignorant of the sentiments of the middling and much more of the lower class of citizens, strangers to their ability, unacquainted with their wants, difficulties, and distress," worried a Maryland man. None of this would be a problem under a confederation system, according to the Antifederalists, because real power would continue to reside in the state governments.

The Federalists generally agreed that the elite would be favored for election to the House of Representatives, not to mention the Senate and the presidency. That was precisely what they hoped. The Federalists wanted power to flow to intelligent, virtuous, public-spirited leaders like themselves. They did not envision a government constituted of every class of people. "Fools and knaves have voice enough in government already," argued a New York Federalist, without being guaranteed representation in proportion to the total population of fools. Alexander Hamilton claimed that mechanics and laborers preferred to have their social betters represent them. The Antifederalists challenged the notion that any class could be sufficiently selfless to rule disinterestedly for others. They feared that the Federalists were resurrecting rule by aristocracy.

Antifederalists fretted over many specific features of the Constitution. It prohibited state-issued paper money. It regulated the time and place of congressional elections, leading to fears that only one inconvenient polling place might be authorized, to disfranchise rural voters. The most widespread objection to the Constitution was its lack of any guarantees of individual liberties in a bill of rights, like those contained in many state constitutions.

Despite the Federalists' campaigns in the large states, it was a small state—New Hampshire—that provided the decisive ninth vote for ratification, on June 21, 1788. Federalists there succeeded in getting the convention postponed from February to June and in the interim conducted an intense and successful lobbying effort on specific delegates.

The Big Holdouts: Virginia and New York

Four states still remained outside the new union, and a glance at a map demonstrated the necessity of pressing the Federalist case in the two largest, Virginia and New York (see Map 8.2). Though Virginia was home to Madison and Washington, an influential Antifederalist group led by Patrick Henry and George Mason made the outcome uncertain. The Federalists finally but barely won ratification by proposing twenty specific amendments that the new government would promise to consider.

New York voters tended to Antifederalism out of a sense that a state so large and powerful need not relinquish so much authority to the new federal government. But New York was also home to some of the most persuasive Federalists. Starting in October 1787, Alexander Hamilton collaborated with James Madison and New York lawyer John Jay on a series of eighty-five essays on the political philosophy of the new Constitution, published in New York newspapers and later republished as *The Federalist*. The essays brilliantly set out the failures of the Articles of Confederation and offered an analysis of the complex nature of federalism. In one of the most compelling essays, number 10, Madison challenged the Antifederalists' heartfelt conviction that republican government had to be small scale. Madison argued that a large and diverse population was itself a guarantee of liberty. In a national government, no single faction could ever be large enough to subvert the freedom of other groups. "Extend the sphere, and you take in a greater variety of parties and interests; you make it less probable that a majority of the whole will have a common motive to invade the rights of other citizens," Madison asserted. He called it "a republican remedy for the diseases most incident to republican government."

At New York's ratifying convention, Antifederalists predominated, but impassioned debate and lobbying—plus the dramatic news of Virginia's ratification—finally tipped the balance to the Federalists. New York's ratification assured the solidity and legitimacy of the new government. It took another year and a half for the Antifederalists in North Carolina to come around. Fiercely independent Rhode Island held out until May 1790, and even then it ratified by only a two-vote margin.

In less than twelve months, the U.S. Constitution was both written and ratified. (See appendix, pages A-3–A-8.) An amazingly short time by twentieth-century standards, it is even more remarkable for the late eighteenth century, with its horse-powered transportation and hand-printed communications. The Federalists had faced a formidable task, but by building momentum and assuring a bill of rights, they did indeed carry the day.

Conclusion: The "Republican Remedy"

Thus ended one of the most intellectually tumultuous and creative decades in American history. Americans leaders experimented with ideas and drew up plans to embody their evolving and conflicting notions of how a society and a government ought to be formulated. While there was widespread agreement that government should derive its power and authority from the people, there was fierce disagreement over the degree of democracy—the amount of direct control of government by the people—that was truly workable in American society.

The decade began in 1776 with a confederation government that could barely be ratified because of its requirement of unanimity, but there was no reaching unanimity on the western lands, on the impost amendment, or on the proper way to respond to unfair taxation in a republican state. The new Constitution offered a different approach to these problems, by loosening the grip of impossible unanimity and by embracing the ideas of a heterogeneous public life and a carefully balanced government that together would prevent any one part of the public from tyrannizing another. The genius of James Madison was to anticipate that diversity of opinion was not only an unavoidable reality but a hidden strength of the new society beginning to take shape. This is what he meant in his tenth Federalist essay when he spoke of the "republican remedy" for the troubles most likely to befall a government where the people are the source of authority.

Despite Madison's optimism, political differences remained keen and worrisome to many. The Federalists still hoped for a society in which leaders of exceptional wisdom would discern the best path for public policy. They looked backward to a society of hierarchy, rank, and benevolent rule by an aristocracy of talent, but they created a government with forward-looking checks and balances as a guard against corruption, which they figured would most likely emanate from the people. The Antifederalists also looked backward, but to an old order of small-scale direct democracy and local control, where virtuous people kept a close eye on potentially corruptible rulers. Antifederalists feared a national government led by distant, self-interested leaders who needed to be held in check. In the 1790s, these two conceptions of republicanism and of leadership would be tested in real life.

FOR FURTHER READING ABOUT THE TOPICS IN THIS CHAPTER, see the Online Bibliography at www.bedfordstmartins.com/roarkcompact.

FOR ADDITIONAL FIRST-HAND ACCOUNTS OF THIS PERIOD, see pages 113–131 in Michael Johnson, ed., *Reading the American Past,* Second Edition, Volume I.

TO ASSESS YOUR MASTERY OF THE MATERIAL IN THIS CHAPTER, see the Online Study Guide at www.bedfordstmartins.com/roarkcompact.

CHRONOLOGY

1775 **May.** Second Continental Congress begins.

1776 Virginia adopts state bill of rights.

1777 **November.** Final draft of Articles of Confederation approved by congress and sent to states.

1778 State constitutions completed.

1780 Pennsylvania institutes gradual emancipation.

Cuffe brothers petition Massachusetts state legislature for extension of suffrage to tax-paying free blacks.

1781 Articles of Confederation ratified.

Creation of executive departments; Robert Morris appointed superintendent of finance.

Bank of North America formed.

Slave Quok Walker sues for freedom in Massachusetts.

1782 Virginia relaxes state manumission law.

1783 Treaty of Paris signed.

1784 Gradual emancipation laws passed in Rhode Island and Connecticut.

Treaty of Fort Stanwix cedes Iroquois land to confederation government.

1786 Bank of North America charter expires, not renewed.

Virginia adopts Statute of Religious Freedom.

Farmer Shays leads rebellion in western Massachusetts.

Annapolis meeting proposes convention to revise Articles of Confederation.

1787 Northwest Ordinance allows self-government and prohibits slavery in Northwest Territory.

Delaware provides manumission law.

May–September. Constitutional convention meets in Philadelphia.

1788 U.S. Constitution ratified.

1790 Maryland provides manumission law.

1799 Gradual emancipation in New York.

1804 Gradual emancipation in New Jersey.

WASHINGTON STANDS OUTSIDE OF TIME
    A French clockmaker and artist produced this piece
of Washington memorabilia after the death of the president. Washington's trim
figure, rendered in gilt bronze, sports a spiffy uniform complete with epaulets
on the shoulders. One gloved hand rests on a sword while the other holds a
rolled parchment, offered up in front of an eagle, the symbol of America's
strength. Below the eagle a familiar motto is inscribed: "E Pluribus Unum,"
or, "out of many, one," a reference to the political unity of the sovereign
states. Below the clock is another motto that quickly became a commonplace
one about Washington: "First in War, First in Peace, and First in the Hearts of
his Countrymen." In his lifetime and for years after, Washington attained
celebrity status, and Americans immortalized him in many souvenirs.

The Warner Collection of Gulf States Paper Corporation.

THE NEW NATION TAKES FORM

9

1789–1800

THE ELECTION OF GEORGE WASHINGTON in February 1789 was quick work. Seven months earlier, right after Virginia and New Hampshire ratified the Constitution, many July 4 orators and newspaper editors considered the Virginia planter as good as president, and the tallying of the unanimous votes by the electoral college became a mere formality. Washington was everyone's first choice. He perfectly embodied the republican ideal of disinterested, public-spirited leadership; indeed, he cultivated that image. At the end of the war, he had dramatically surrendered his sword to the Continental Congress, symbolizing the subservience of military power to the law.

Although somewhat reluctant, Washington ultimately accepted the presidency. He journeyed from Virginia to the capital, New York City, in six days, encountering cheering crowds, large triumphal arches, and military parades at many villages en route. In New York City, he rode a white horse down Broadway while a crowd of thirty thousand cheered. He took the oath of office at the newly built Federal Hall at Broad and Wall Streets; a cannon salute in the harbor signaled his inauguration.

The pageantry was a kind of hero worship for Washington as an individual. But the question, as yet unresolved, was whether the office of the presidency itself would be grandly heroic. The arches, the grand entry on a white horse, the gun salute—all were uneasy reminders of the trappings of monarchy. In its first month, Congress debated the proper form of address for the president, raising explicitly the issue of how kingly this new presidency was to be. Titles such as "His Highness, the President of the United States of America and Protector of Their Liberties" and "His Majesty, the President" were floated as possibilities, while Washington himself favored "His High Mightiness." Several former Antifederalists sitting in Congress held out for a less exalted title. The final version was simply "President of the United States of America," and the established form of address became "Mr. President," a subdued yet dignified title in a society where only property-owning adult white males could presume to be called "Mister."

Washington's genius in establishing the presidency lay in his capacity for implanting his own reputation for integrity into the office itself. He was not a particularly brilliant thinker, nor was he a shrewd political strategist. He was not even a very congenial man. In the political language of the day, he was virtuous. Washington was studiously aloof, resolute, and dignified, to the point of appearing wooden at times. He encouraged pomp and ceremony to create respect for the presidency, traveling with no fewer than six horses drawing his coach, hosting formal balls, and surrounding himself with servants in livery. He even held weekly levees, as European monarchs did, hour-long audiences granted to distinguished

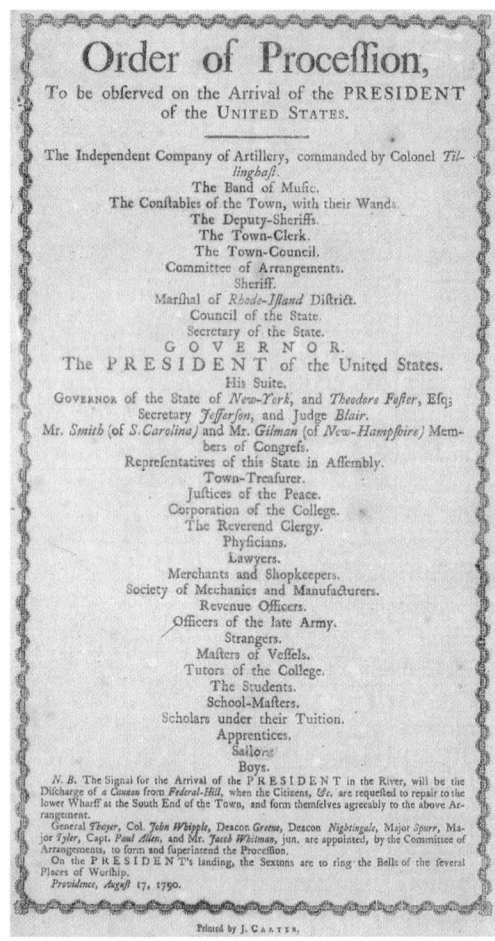

Order of Proceſſion,

To be obſerved on the Arrival of the PRESIDENT
of the UNITED STATES.

The Independent Company of Artillery, commanded by Colonel *Til-
linghaſt.*
The Band of Muſic.
The Conſtables of the Town, with their Wands.
The Deputy-Sheriffs.
The Town-Clerk.
The Town-Council.
Committee of Arrangements.
Sheriff.
Marſhal of *Rhode-Iſland* Diſtrict.
Council of the State.
Secretary of the State.
G O V E R N O R.
The P R E S I D E N T of the United States.
His Suite.
GOVERNOR of the State of *New-York,* and *Theodore Foſter,* Eſq;
Secretary *Jefferſon,* and Judge *Blair.*
Mr. *Smith* (of *S. Carolina)* and Mr. *Gilman* (of *New-Hampſhire)* Mem-
bers of Congreſs.
Repreſentatives of this State in Aſſembly.
Town-Treaſurer.
Juſtices of the Peace.
Corporation of the College.
The Reverend Clergy.
Phyſicians.
Lawyers.
Merchants and Shopkeepers.
Society of Mechanics and Manufacturers.
Revenue Officers.
Officers of the late Army.
Strangers.
Maſters of Veſſels.
Tutors of the College.
The Students.
School-Maſters.
Scholars under their Tuition.
Apprentices.
Sailors.
Boys.

N. B. The Signal for the Arrival of the P R E S I D E N T in the River, will be the
Diſcharge of a *Cannon* from *Federal-Hill,* when the Citizens, &c. are requeſted to repair to the
lower Wharff at the South End of the Town, and form themſelves agreeably to the above Ar-
rangement.
General *Thayer,* Col. *John Whipple,* Deacon *Greene,* Deacon *Nightingale,* Major *Spurr,* Ma-
jor *Tyler,* Capt. *Paul Allen,* and Mr. *Jacob Whitman,* jun. are appointed, by the Committee of
Arrangements, to form and ſuperintend the Proceſſion.
On the P R E S I D E N T's landing, the Sextons are to ring the Bells of the ſeveral
Places of Worſhip.
Providence, Auguſt 17, 1790.

Printed by J. CARTER.

ORDER OF PROCESSION
*When President Washington visited Providence,
Rhode Island, the town government prepared an
"Order of Procession" to inform citizens of their
exact place in the welcoming parade. Soldiers, a
band, and town officers preceded the honored guest,
whose immediate entourage included two governors, a cabinet member, a judge, and two members
of Congress. Next came town politicians, professors
in the local college (Brown), clergy, doctors,
lawyers, and merchants. Further along came masters of ships, tutors at Brown, college students,
and, bringing up the rear, apprentices, sailors, and
boys. Who was excluded from the procession? How
might merchants or sailors feel about their place in
line? Several such "orders of procession" exist for
other towns; were such elaborate rituals consistent
with a non-monarchical political system? In what
other ways might President Washington have
entered a town?*
The Huntington Library and Art Collections, San Marino, California.

visitors, at which Washington appeared attired in
black velvet, a feathered hat, and a polished sword.
The president and his guests bowed, avoiding the
egalitarian familiarity of handshakes. But he always
managed, perhaps just barely, to avoid the extreme
of royal splendor.

The thirteen American states had just come
through a difficult decade, swinging between a distrust of executive power on the one hand and a fear
of turbulent factional politics on the other. Washington's reputation for integrity boosted confidence
that executive power could be compatible with the
public good. And his strong pronouncements about
the evils of divisive factions raised hopes that at last
America was on a steady course.

National harmony proved elusive, however.
Political divisions emerged in the 1790s, despite the
best intentions. Even men who had worked together to ratify the Constitution found that the
process of implementing it exposed serious disagreement. Economic policy and foreign affairs
proved to be the two most significant fissures in
the political leadership of the 1790s. The disagreements were articulated around particular events
and policies, but at heart they arose out of opposing ideological stances about the nature of democracy and of leadership, and the limits of federal
power. By 1800, these divisions had begun to crystallize into political parties, the Federalists and the
Republicans.

The Search for Stability

Conventional wisdom today praises the development of a party system: Parties organize conflict, legitimize disagreement, and mediate among competing political strategies. Yet they were entirely
unanticipated by the writers of the Constitution. Instead, leaders in the early 1790s sought stability to
heal divisions of the 1780s. Veneration for President
Washington provided one powerful source of unity.
People trusted him to initiate the untested and perhaps elastic powers of the presidency. Congress
quickly agreed on passage of the Bill of Rights in
1791, which satisfied many Antifederalist critics.
And the private virtue of women was mobilized to
bolster the public virtue of male citizens; republicanism was forcing a rethinking of women's relation to the state.

Washington's Cabinet

Congress immediately set up departments of war, treasury, and state, leaving to Washington the selection of secretaries over each. The president picked talented and experienced individuals for each post, regardless of their deep philosophical differences. For the Department of War, he chose General Henry Knox, one-time secretary of war in the confederation government. For the Treasury—an especially tough job, in view of revenue conflicts during the confederation—Washington picked Alexander Hamilton of New York, known for his general brilliance and financial astuteness. To lead the Department of State, the foreign policy arm of the executive branch, Washington chose Thomas Jefferson, a master of the intricacy of diplomatic relations, who was then serving as minister to France.

In addition, for attorney general Washington picked Edmund Randolph, a Virginian who had attended the Constitutional Convention but had turned Antifederalist during ratification. For chief justice of the Supreme Court, Washington designated John Jay, the New York lawyer who vigorously defended the Constitution along with Madison and Hamilton in *The Federalist*.

Washington liked and trusted all these men, and by 1793, in his second term, he was meeting regularly with them, thereby establishing the precedent of a presidential cabinet. (Vice President John Adams did not join these meetings; his only official duty was to preside over the Senate, a job he found "a punishment" because he could not actually participate in legislative debates. He complained to his wife, Abigail, "My country has in its wisdom contrived for me the most insignificant office.") No one anticipated that two decades of party turbulence would emerge from the brilliant but explosive mix of Washington's first cabinet.

The Bill of Rights

Many Antifederalists had complained about the absence of guarantees of individual liberties and limitations to federal power in the Constitution, and seven states had ratified on the condition that a bill of rights be swiftly incorporated. Many state constitutions already protected freedom of speech, press, peaceable assembly, and the rights to petition and to have jury trials. In the final days of the 1787 Philadelphia convention, the delegates had decided an enumeration of

rights was unnecessary. But the complaint surfaced continually in the ratification process, and so in 1789, in response to Antifederalist criticisms, James Madison drew up a set of amendments.

Final agreement from both House and Senate on the first ten amendments to the Constitution, collectively known as the Bill of Rights, came in September 1789. Amendments 1–8 dealt with individual liberties, and 9 and 10 concerned the boundary between federal and state authority. (See the U.S. Constitution in the appendix, pages A-9–A-12.) The amendments had the immediate effect of cementing a sense of national unity. The process of state ratification took another two years, but there was no serious doubt about the outcome.

Still, not everyone was entirely satisfied. Some eighty proposed amendments had been submitted by state ratifying conventions. Proposals to change the structural details of the new government were never considered by Congress; Madison had no intention of reopening debates about the length of term for the president or the power to levy excise taxes.

Significantly, no one complained about one striking omission in the Bill of Rights: the right to vote. Only much later was voting seen as a fundamental liberty requiring protection by constitutional amendment—indeed, by four amendments. The 1788 Constitution deliberately left definition of voters to the states, which set differing property qualifications. Any uniform federal voting law would run the double risk of excluding some who could already vote in state elections or including too many new voters deemed undesirable in the more restrictive states.

Unlike most states, which routinely restricted voting to free, white males, New Jersey in 1776 enfranchised all free inhabitants worth over £50, thereby including free blacks as well as unmarried women who met the property requirement. (Married women owned no property, for by law their husbands held title to everything.) Little fanfare accompanied this radical shift, and some historians have inferred that the inclusion of blacks and unmarried women was accidental, the result of an unstated assumption that voters would be white and male. Yet other parts of the suffrage clause pertaining to residency and property were extensively debated when it was put in the state constitution, and no objections were raised at that time to its gender- and race-free language. Thus other historians have concluded that the law was intentionally inclusive. By 1790, a revised election law used the words *he* or *she* in reference to voters, thus making woman suffrage explicit. As one New Jersey legislator boasted, "Our Constitution gives this right to maids or widows black or white."

In 1790, only about 1,000 free black adults of both sexes lived in New Jersey, a state with a population of 184,000. The number of unmarried adult white women was probably also small and predominantly widows. Considering the property requirement, the voter bloc enfranchised under this law could not have been decisive in elections. Still, this highly unusual state of affairs lasted until 1807, when a new state law specifically disfranchised both blacks and women. Henceforth, independence of mind, that essential precondition of voting, was redefined to be sex- and race-specific.

The Republican Wife and Mother

The general exclusion of women from political activity did not mean they had no civic role or responsibility. A flood of periodical articles of the 1790s by both male and female writers reevaluated courtship, marriage, and motherhood in light of republican ideals. Tyrannical power in the ruler, whether king or husband, was now declared a thing of the past. Affection, not duty, bound wives to their husbands and citizens to their government. In republican marriages, the writers claimed, women had the capacity to reform the morals and manners of men. One male author promised women that "the solidity and stability of the liberties of your country rest with you; since Liberty is never sure, 'till Virtue reigns triumphant." By upholding public virtue, women bolstered political liberty.

Until the 1790s, public virtue was strictly a masculine quality. But another sort of virtue loomed in importance: sexual chastity, a private asset prized as a feminine quality. Essayists of the 1790s explicitly advised young women to use sexual virtue to produce more public virtue in men. "Love and courtship . . . invest a lady with more authority than in any other situation that falls to the lot of human beings," one male essayist proclaimed. If women spurned selfish suitors, they could promote good morals more than any social institution could, essayists promised.

Republican ideals also cast motherhood in a new light. Throughout the 1790s, advocates legitimized female education, still a controversial propo-

REPUBLICAN WOMANHOOD: JUDITH SARGENT MURRAY
The twenty-one-year-old in this portrait would become known eighteen years later as America's foremost public spokeswoman for the idea of woman's equality to man. Judith Sargent Murray wrote frequent essays for the **Massachusetts Magazine** *under the penname "Constantia." In one essay published in 1790, "On the Equality of the Sexes," she confidently asserted that women had "natural powers" of mind fully the equal of men's. Murray, the wife of a Universalist minister, wrote plays that were performed on the Boston stage, and in 1798 she published her collected "Constantia" essays in a book titled* **The Gleaner;** *George Washington and John Adams each bought a copy. Murray is the only woman of her era to keep an indexed letter book, containing copies of nearly two thousand of her own letters written over her lifetime.*
John Singleton Copley, Portrait of Mrs. John Stevens (Judith Sargent, later Mrs. John Murray), 1770–1772, oil on canvas, 50 x 40 inches, Terra Foundation for the Arts, Daniel J. Terra Art Acquisition Endowment Fund, 2000.6; Photograph courtesy of Terra Foundation for the Arts, Chicago.

sition, through the claim of significant maternal influence on the future male citizenry. Benjamin Rush, a Pennsylvania physician and educator, called for female education because "our ladies should be qualified . . . in instructing their sons in the principles of liberty and government." A series of essays by Judith Sargent Murray of Massachusetts favored education that would remake women into self-confident, competent, rational beings, poised to become the equals of men. But even Murray had to dress her advanced ideas in the cloak of republican motherhood, justifying female education in the context of family duty.

Although women's domestic obligations as wives and mothers were now infused with political meaning, traditional gender relations remained unaltered. The analogy between marriage and civil society worked precisely because of the self-subordination inherent in the term *virtue*. Men should put the public good first, before selfish desires, just as women must put their husbands and families first, before themselves. Women might gain literacy and knowledge, but only in the service of improved domestic duty.

Hamilton's Economic Policies

Compared to the severe economic instability of the 1780s, the 1790s seemed flush with opportunity and prosperity, as seen in increased agricultural trade, transportation, and banking improvements. The federal government moved from New York City to Philadelphia, a more central location. Alexander Hamilton, the secretary of the Treasury, proposed several pioneering yet controversial economic programs.

Agriculture, Transportation, and Banking

Dramatic increases in the international price of grain in the 1790s motivated American farmers to boost agricultural production and trade. Europe's rising population needed grain, and the Napoleonic Wars after 1793 compromised production there. From the Connecticut River valley to the Chesapeake, farmers responded by planting more wheat. The increase in overseas grain trade generated a host of new jobs in related areas as the number of millers, coopers, and ship and wagon builders expanded.

Cotton production also underwent a boom, spurred by market growth and a mechanical invention. Limited amounts of smooth-seed cotton had long been grown in the low-lying coastal areas of the South; but this variety of cotton did not prosper in the drier, inland regions. Green-seed cotton grew well inland, but it contained many rough seeds that adhered tenaciously to the cotton fibers, making it very labor-intensive to clean. In 1793, a Yale graduate named Eli Whitney, visiting a Georgia plantation, invented the cotton gin, a device to separate out the seeds. Use of the gin spurred cotton production, from 138,000 pounds in 1792 to 35 million in 1800. Most of it was shipped to English factories to be made into textiles.

A surge of road building helped propel the prosperous economy. Only one continuous and improved road existed before 1790, the Post Road running for sixteen hundred miles from Maine to Georgia near the coast. This was joined, in the 1790s, by the Lancaster Turnpike, the first private toll road in the nation, connecting Philadelphia with Lancaster. Soon another turnpike connected Boston with Albany and continued west. Private companies chartered by state governments financed and built these turnpikes, and collected fees from all vehicles. Further inland, a major road extended south-

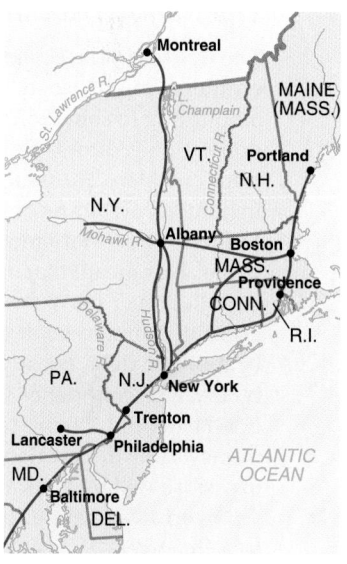

Major Roads in the 1790s

west down the Shenandoah Valley, while another road linked Richmond, Virginia, with the Tennessee towns of Knoxville and Nashville.

By 1800, a dense network of dirt, gravel, or plank roadways connected cities and towns in southern New England and the Middle Atlantic states, while isolated roadways and old Indian trails fanned out to the west. Commercial stage lines connected major eastern cities, offering four-day travel time between New York and Boston and an exhausting but speedy one-and-one-half-day trip between New York and Philadelphia. In 1790, only three stagecoach companies operated out of Boston, but by 1800 there were twenty-four. Transport of goods by roads was still expensive per mile, compared to water transport on navigable rivers or along the coast, but at least it was possible now.

A third development signalling economic resurgence was the growth of commercial banking. During the 1790s, the number of banks nationwide multiplied tenfold, from three to twenty-nine in 1800. Banks drew in money chiefly through the sale of stock. They then made loans in the form of banknotes, paper currency backed by the gold and silver paid in by stockholders. Because they issued two or three times as much money in banknotes as they held in hard money, banks were really creating new money for the economy.

The Public Debt and Taxes

The upturn in the economy suggested that the government might soon repay its wartime debts, amounting to some $52 million owed to foreign and domestic creditors. But Hamilton had a slightly different plan. He issued a *Report on Public Credit* in January 1790, recommending that the debt be funded—but not repaid immediately—at full value. This meant that old certificates of debt would be rolled over into new bonds, which earned interest until retired several years later. There would still be a public debt, but it would be secure, supported by citizens' confidence in the new government. The bonds would circulate, injecting new valuable money into the economy. "A national debt if not excessive will be to us a national blessing; it will be a powerfull cement of our union," Hamilton wrote to a financier.

A large part of the old debt had been bought up cheaply by speculators in the 1780s; these men would now have a direct financial stake in the new government, support that Hamilton regarded as essential to the country's stability. He was also providing those same men with more than $40 million released for new investment, a distinct improvement over the old depreciated bonds, which had circulated in daily transactions at a fraction of their face value.

If the *Report on Public Credit* had gone only this far, it would have been somewhat controversial. But Hamilton took a much bolder step by augmenting the debt with another $25 million still owed by state governments to individuals. All the states had obtained supplies during the war by issuing IOUs to farmers, merchants, and moneylenders. Some states, such as Virginia and New York, had paid off these debts entirely, while others, like Massachusetts, had partially paid them through

ALEXANDER HAMILTON BY JOHN TRUMBULL
Alexander Hamilton posed for this portrait in 1792, at age thirty-seven and at his height of power. Ever a prodigy, Hamilton at age nineteen became an indispensable wartime aide to George Washington. In his mid-twenties he gained admission to the bar after only three months of study. In 1789, he became Washington's youngest cabinet member.
Yale University Art Gallery.

heavy taxation of the inhabitants; about half the states had made little headway. Hamilton called for the federal government to assume these state debts and add them to the federal debt, in effect consolidating federal power over the states.

A national debt swollen to some $77 million required extra taxation to meet the interest payments. Hamilton did not propose raising import duties, in deference to the merchant class whose support he was seeking. Instead, he convinced Congress in 1791 to pass a 25 percent excise tax on whiskey, to be paid by the farmer when he brought his grain to the distillery. Members of Congress favored the tax, especially those from New England where the favorite drink was rum, an imported beverage already taxed under the import laws. A New Hampshire representative pointed out that the country would be "drinking down the national debt," an idea he evidently found acceptable.

Congressman James Madison objected to Hamilton's funding plan, fearing that windfall profits would go mainly to speculators who had bought the original IOUs at bargain prices. He also strenuously objected to assumption of all the states' debts. A large debt was dangerous, Madison warned, especially because it would lead to high taxation. But he lost the vote in Congress. Madison and Hamilton, so recently allies in writing *The Federalist*, were becoming opponents. Secretary of State Jefferson also was fearful of Hamilton's proposals. "No man is more ardently intent to see the public debt soon and sacredly paid off than I am. This exactly marks the difference between Colonel Hamilton's views and mine, that I would wish the debt paid tomorrow; he wishes it never to be paid, but always to be a thing where with to corrupt and manage the legislature."

The First Bank of the United States and the Report on Manufactures

The second and third major elements of Hamilton's economic plan were his proposal for a national Bank of the United States and his program to encourage domestic manufacturing. Believing that banks were the "nurseries of national wealth," Hamilton modeled his plan on the Bank of England, a private corporation that worked primarily for the public good. In Hamilton's plan, 20 percent of the bank's stock would be bought by the federal government. In effect, the bank would become the fiscal agent of the new government, holding and handling its revenues derived from import duties, land sales, and the whiskey excise tax. The other 80 percent of the bank's capital would come from private investors, who could buy stock in the bank with either hard money (silver or gold) or federal securities. By its size and the privilege of being the only national bank, the bank would help stabilize the economy by exerting prudent control over credit, interest rates, and the value of the currency.

Madison, concerned that the bank gave a handful of rich men undue influence over the economy, tried but failed to stop the plan in Congress. Jefferson advised Washington that the Constitution did not permit Congress to charter banks. Hamilton, however, argued that the Constitution listed certain powers to regulate commerce ending with a broad grant of the right "to make all laws

which shall be necessary and proper for carrying into execution the foregoing powers." Washington agreed with Hamilton and signed the Bank of the United States into law in February 1791, providing it with a charter to operate for twenty years. When the bank's privately held stock went on sale in New York City in July, it sold out in a few hours, touching off an immediate mania of speculation in resale. A discouraged Madison reported that "the Coffee House is an eternal buzz with the gamblers," some of them self-interested congressmen intent on "public plunder."

The third component of Hamilton's plan was issued in December 1791 in the *Report on Manufactures*, a proposal to encourage the production of American-made goods. Manufacturing was in its infancy in 1790, the result of years of dependence on British imports. Hamilton recognized that a balanced and self-reliant economy required the United States to produce its own cloth and iron products. His plan mobilized the new powers of the federal government to impose tariffs and grant subsidies to encourage the growth of local manufacturing. Hamilton had to be careful not to undercut his important merchant allies who traded with England and generated over half the government's income. A high tariff would either seriously dampen that trade or force merchants into smuggling. So Hamilton favored a moderate tariff, with extra bounties paid to American manufacturers to encourage production. The *Report on Manufactures* was the one Hamiltonian plan that was not approved by Congress.

The Whiskey Rebellion

Hamilton's excise tax on whiskey proved very unpopular with cash-short grain farmers and whiskey drinkers. In 1791, farmers in the western parts of Pennsylvania, Virginia, Maryland, and the Carolinas and throughout Kentucky conveyed to Congress their resentment of Hamilton's tax. Congress responded with modest modifications in the tax in 1792; but even so, discontent was rampant.

Simple evasion of the law was the most common response; the tax proved hard to collect. Crowds threatened to tar and feather federal tax collectors, while some distilleries underreported their production. With embarrassment, Hamilton admitted to Congress that the revenue was far less than anticipated. But rather than abandon the law, he tightened up the prosecution of tax evaders.

WHISKEY REBELLION "FIRE COPPER"
This forty-gallon "fire copper" produced Monongahela rye whiskey in the 1790s in western Pennsylvania. Mashed rye grain was mixed and heated with mash from a previously distilled brew. The distiller next added yeast and water and let the mixture ferment for several days. The mixture was then heated to 175 degrees, the boiling point of alcohol, in this three-foot copper vessel (called a "still"). Alcohol-laden vapor from the boiling brew cooled and condensed in a spiral copper tubing that dripped whiskey into a jug. High-proof, expensive whiskey required a second processing in the still to concentrate the vapors. The owner of this fire copper was James Miller, whose nephew Oliver Miller Jr. was one of the few fatalities in the Whiskey Rebellion.
Photo by Andrew Wagner. Courtesy of *American History* magazine.

In western Pennsylvania, Hamilton had one ally, a stubborn tax collector named John Neville who had refused to quit even after a group of spirited farmers had burned him in effigy. In May 1794, Neville filed charges against seventy-five farmers and distillers for tax evasion. In July, he and a federal marshal were ambushed in Allegheny County by a group of forty men, and then Neville's house was burned to the ground by a crowd estimated at five hundred. Seven thousand farmers staged a march on Pittsburgh to protest the hated tax.

In response, Washington nationalized the Pennsylvania militia, donned his old military garb, and set out, with Hamilton at his side urging him on, at the head of fifteen thousand soldiers. By the time the army arrived, in late September, the demonstrators had all gone home. No battles were fought, and no fire was exchanged. Twenty men were rounded up as rebels and charged with high trea-

son, but only two were convicted, and both were soon pardoned by Washington.

Had the government overreacted? Or was Hamilton right to think that the whiskey rioters posed a serious threat to the stability of the federal government? The long colonial tradition of crowd action to protest unfair practices had worked well when colonists had limited formal access to power. But in a republic, laws were passed by the supposed representatives of the people, not by tyrannical kings or distant parliaments. Burning effigies of stamp tax collectors in 1765 made sense as an effective contribution to the political process. Burning effigies of whiskey tax collectors in 1792 appeared to many to be an unlawful rejection of the will of the people as expressed through Congress.

The whiskey rebels, however, recognized oppressive taxes for what they were and felt entitled to resort to protest and demonstration. Representative government had not worked to their benefit. The Whiskey Rebellion was an early example of what would prove to be a long-term conflict: the tension between minority rights and majority rule.

Conflicts West, East, and South

Washington's second term began in 1793, with his unanimous reelection. But as the Whiskey Rebellion demonstrated, the widespread admiration for the individual man did not translate to complete domestic tranquility. While the whiskey rebels challenged federal leadership from within the country, disorder threatened the United States from external sources as well. To the west, a powerful confederation of Indian tribes in the Ohio country resisted white encroachment, resulting in a brutal war. At the same time, conflicts between the major European powers forced Americans to take sides and nearly thrust the country into another war, this time across the Atlantic. And to the south, a Caribbean slave rebellion raised fears of racial war imported to the United States.

To the West: The Indians

By the Treaty of Paris of 1783, England had given up all land east of the Mississippi River to the United States—but without consulting their one-time allies, the Indian tribes who inhabited 25,000 square miles of that territory. When they learned of the treaty terms, the Indians expressed astonishment. "They told me they never could believe that our king could pretend to cede to America what was not his own to give," the British commander at Fort Niagara wrote of the Iroquois. In southern Ohio, British Indian agents assured the Shawnees and Delawares that England had relinquished only political control to the United States but that Indians still had the right to occupy the land over the claims of American settlers. Such confusion and misrepresentation aggravated an already volatile situation.

A doubled American population, from two million in 1770 to nearly four million in 1790, created an insistent pressure for western land. Several thousand settlers a year moved down the Ohio River in the mid-1780s, some bound for Kentucky but many others eyeing the fresh forests and fields north of

the Ohio River. By the late 1780s, government land sales in eastern Ohio commenced (Map 9.1).

Even western Ohio was not safe from American incursions. Downriver, at the site of present-day Cincinnati, an outpost named Fort Washington was constructed in 1789 and put under the command of General Arthur St. Clair, who was also governor of the entire Northwest Territory. St. Clair's mission was to displace the Indians and clear the way for permanent American settlement in Ohio. He first tried peaceful tactics and got an assortment of Indians to sign a treaty yielding land near the Muskingum River in eastern Ohio. But these Indians were not chiefs authorized to undertake negotiations, so the dubious treaty did nothing to improve the chances for peace.

Bloody frontier raids and skirmishes between settlers and Indians led the United States to expand its military force. Finally, St. Clair took direct action. In the fall of 1791, more than two thousand men (and two hundred women camp followers) marched north from Fort Washington to engage in battle with Miami and Shawnee Indians. The Indians attacked first, at daybreak on November 4, at the headwaters of the Wabash River in western Ohio. The ferocious battle was a disaster for the Americans, 55 percent of whom were dead or wounded before noon; only three of the women escaped alive. It was the worst American defeat in the entire history of the U.S.-Indian wars. The Indians captured valuable weaponry, scalped and dismembered the dying, and pursued fleeing survivors for miles. The grisly tales of St. Clair's defeat became instantly infamous, increasing, if this were possible, the level of sheer terror that Americans brought to their confrontations with the Indians.

President Washington doubled the American military presence in Ohio and appointed a new commander, General Anthony Wayne of Pennsylvania, nicknamed "Mad Anthony" for his headstrong style of leadership. About the Ohio natives he wrote, "I have always been of the opinion that we never should have a permanent peace with those Indians until they were made to experience our superiority." With some 3,500 men, Wayne established two new military camps, Fort Greenville and Fort Recovery, deep in Indian territory in western Ohio.

Throughout 1794 Wayne's army engaged in skirmishes with the Shawnees and Delawares. The decisive action came in August 1794 at the Battle of Fallen Timbers, near the Maumee River where a recent severe rainstorm had felled many trees. The con-

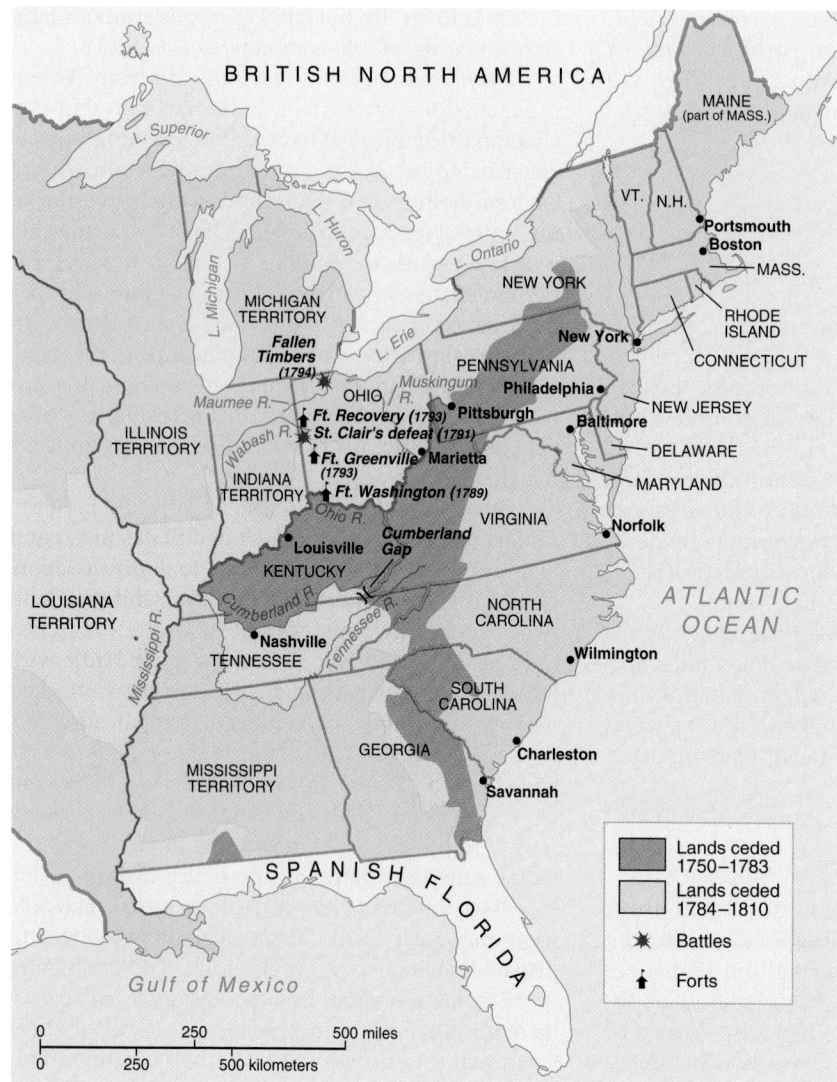

MAP 9.1

Western Expansion and Indian Land Cessions to 1810

By the first decade of the nineteenth century, the period of intense Indian wars had resulted in significant cessions of land to the U.S. government by treaty.

READING THE MAP: Locate the Appalachians. What line of 1763 ran along the mountains? What was that line's purpose, and how well was that purpose met?

CONNECTIONS: How much did the population of the United States grow between 1750 and 1790? How did this growth affect western settlement?

www.bedfordstmartins.com/ roarkcompact SEE THE ON-LINE STUDY GUIDE for more help in analyzing this map.

federated Indians—mainly Ottawas, Potawatomis, and Delawares, numbering around 800—first ambushed the Americans, but they were underarmed, many having only tomahawks. Wayne's well-disciplined troops made effective use of their guns and bayonets, and in just over an hour the Indians had retreated and scattered.

Fallen Timbers was a major defeat for the Indians. The Americans had destroyed cornfields and villages on the march north, and, with winter approaching, the Indians' confidence was sapped. They reentered negotiations in a much less powerful bargaining position. In 1795, about a thousand Indians representing nearly a dozen tribes met with

Wayne and other American emissaries to work out the Treaty of Greenville. The Americans offered $25,000 worth of treaty goods (calico shirts, axes, knives, blankets, kettles, mirrors, ribbons, thimbles, and abundant wine and liquor casks) and promised additional shipments every year. The government's idea was to create a dependency on American goods to keep the Indians friendly. In exchange, the Indians ceded most of Ohio to the Americans; only the northwest region of the territory was reserved solely for the Indians.

The treaty brought peace to the region, but it did not bring back a peaceful life to the Indians. The annual allowance from the United States too often

TREATY OF GREENVILLE, 1795
General Anthony Wayne meets with Chief Little Turtle of the Miamis and Chief Tarhe
the Crane of the Wyandots to sign the Treaty of Greenville in Ohio in 1795.
Chicago Historical Society.

came in the form of liquor. "More of us have died since the Treaty of Greenville than we lost by the years of war before, and it is all owing to the introduction of liquor among us," said Little Turtle, chief of the Miami people, in 1800. "This liquor that they introduce into our country is more to be feared than the gun and tomahawk."

Across the Atlantic: France and England

Since 1789, a violent revolution had been raging in France. At first, the general American reaction was positive, for it was flattering to think that the American Revolution had inspired imitation in France. Monarchy and privilege were overthrown in the name of republicanism; towns throughout America celebrated the victory of the French people with civic feasts and public festivities.

But news of the beheading of King Louis XVI quickly dampened the uncritical enthusiasm for everything French. Those who fondly remembered the excitement and risk of the American Revolution were still apt to regard France with optimism. However, the reluctant revolutionaries of the 1770s and 1780s, who had worried about excessive democracy and social upheaval in America, deplored the far greater violence occurring in the name of republicanism as France moved into the Reign of Terror.

Support for the French Revolution could remain a matter of personal conviction until 1793, when England and France went to war and French versus British loyalty became a critical foreign policy question. France had helped America substantially during the American Revolution, and the confederated government had signed an alliance in 1778 promising aid if France were ever under attack. Americans still optimistic about the eventual outcome of the French Revolution wanted to deliver on that promise now. But others, including those shaken by the guillotining of thousands of French people as well as those with strong commercial ties to England, sought ways to stay neutral.

In May 1793, President Washington issued a Neutrality Proclamation, with friendly assurances to both sides. But tensions at home flared in response to official neutrality. "The cause of France is the cause of man, and neutrality is desertion," wrote H. H. Brackenridge, a western Pennsylvanian, voicing the sentiments of thousands. Dozens of pro-French political clubs sprang up around the country, called Democratic or Republican Societies. The societies mobilized farmers and mechanics, issued circular letters, injected pro-French and anti-British feelings into local elections, and in general heightened popular participation and public interest in foreign policy. The activities of these societies disturbed Washington and Hamilton intensely, for they vented opposition to the policies of the president.

The Neutrality Proclamation was in theory a fine idea, in view of Washington's goal of staying out of European wars. Yet American ships continued to trade between the French West Indies and France, and in late 1793 and early 1794, the English expressed their displeasure by capturing more than three hundred of these vessels near the West Indies. At such a moment, even pro-British politicians like Hamilton agreed that it was necessary to deal firmly with England.

President Washington sent John Jay, the chief justice of the Supreme Court and a man of strong pro-British sentiments, to England to negotiate commercial relations and to secure compensation for the seizure of American ships. In addition, Jay was supposed to resolve several long-standing problems dating from the end of the Revolution. Southern planters wanted reimbursement for the slaves lured away by the British army during the war, and western settlers wanted England to vacate the western forts still occupied—twelve years after the end of the Revolution—for their strategic proximity to the Indian fur trade.

Jay returned from his diplomatic mission with a treaty that almost no one liked. First, the treaty made no direct provision for the captured ships or the lost property in slaves. Second, it granted the British eighteen more months to withdraw from the western forts while guaranteeing them continued rights in the fur trade. Finally, the Jay Treaty called for repayment with interest of the debts some American planters still owed to British firms dating from the Revolutionary War. In exchange for such generous terms, Jay secured some favorable commercial agreements for the United States, but even there the results were mixed. The treaty was widely regarded as exchanging the country's strong moral

bargaining power (the outrage over the seized ships) for an improved trading status beneficial to only a handful of merchants.

When newspapers published the terms of the treaty, powerful opposition emerged from Maine to Georgia. Nevertheless, the Jay Treaty passed the Senate in 1795 by a vote of twenty to ten. Some representatives in the House, led by Madison, tried to undermine the Senate's approval by insisting on a separate vote on the funding provisions of the treaty, on the grounds that the House controlled all money bills. Finally, in 1796, the House approved funds to implement the various commissions mandated by the treaty, but by only a three-vote margin. The cleavage of votes in both houses of Congress divided along the same lines as the Hamilton-Jefferson split on economic policy.

To the South: The Haitian Revolution

In addition to the Indian wars in Ohio and the European wars across the Atlantic, a third bloody conflict to the south polarized and even terrorized many Americans in the 1790s. The western third of the large Caribbean island of Hispaniola, just to the east of Cuba, became engulfed in revolution starting in 1791. The eastern portion of the island was a Spanish colony called Santo Domingo; the western part, in bloody conflagration, was the French

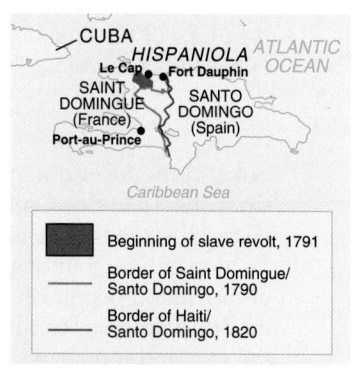

Haitian Revolution, 1790–1804

Saint Domingue. War raged there for over a decade, resulting in the birth of the Haitian Republic in 1804, distinguished as the first and only independent black state to arise out of a successful slave revolution.

The Haitian Revolution was a complex event involving many participants, including the diverse local population and, eventually, three European countries. Some 30,000 whites ruled the island in 1790, running sugar and coffee plantations with close to half a million slaves, two-thirds of them of African birth. The white French colonists were not the only plantation owners, however. About 28,000 free coloreds (*gens de couleur*) of mixed race also lived in Saint Domingue; they owned one-third of the island's plantations and nearly a quarter of the slave labor force. Despite their economic status, the free coloreds were barred from political power; but they aspired to it.

The French Revolution of 1789 was the immediate catalyst for rebellion in this already tense society. First, white colonists challenged the white royalist government in an effort to link Saint Domingue with the new revolutionary government in France. Next the free coloreds rebelled in 1791, demanding equal civil rights with the whites. No sooner was this revolt viciously suppressed than another part of the island exploded, this time involving thousands of slaves armed with machetes and torches who wreaked devastation and slaughter. In 1793, the civil war escalated to include French, Spanish, and British troops fighting the inhabitants and also each other. The slaves, led by Toussaint L'Ouverture in alliance with Spain, destroyed the northern regions of the island, leaving a thousand plantations in ruins and tens of thousands of people dead. Thousands of whites and free coloreds, along with some of their slaves, fled to Spanish Louisiana and southern cities of the United States.

White Americans followed the revolution in fascinated horror through newspapers and refugees' accounts. A few sympathized with the impulse for liberty, but many more shuddered at the violent atrocities. Many black American slaves also followed the revolution, for the amazing news of the success of a first-ever, massive revolution by slaves traveled quickly in this oral culture. Whites complained of behaviors that might prefigure plots and conspiracies, such as increased insolence and higher runaway rates among slaves.

The Haitian Revolution provoked naked fear in white Americans. Jefferson, agonizing over the contagion of liberty in 1797, wrote another Virginia slaveholder that "if something is not done, and soon done, we shall be the murderers of our own children . . . ; the revolutionary storm, now sweeping the globe, will be upon us, and happy if we make timely provision to give it an easy passage over our land. From the present state of things in Europe and America, the day which brings our combustion must be near at hand; and only a single spark is wanting to make that day to-morrow."

Federalists and Republicans

Political statesmen of the early 1790s had always believed that a division into political factions was a sign of failure, but this assumption was soon put to a severe test. In Washington's second term, consistent voting blocs first appeared in Congress on economic issues. By the time of the Jay Treaty, distinctive labels—Federalist and Republican—had come into use for rival politicians and rival newspapers. These words summarized conflicting ideologies and principles; they did not yet describe organized political parties. Washington's decision not to seek a third term opened the floodgates to serious partisan electioneering.

The Election of 1796

Washington struggled to appear to be above party politics, and in his farewell address of September 1796 he stressed the need to maintain a "unity of government" reflecting a unified body politic. He also urged the country to "steer clear of permanent alliances with any portion of the foreign world." The leading contenders for his position, John Adams of Massachusetts and Thomas Jefferson of Virginia, in theory agreed with him, but around them raged a party contest split along pro-English versus pro-French lines.

Adams and Jefferson were not adept politicians in the modern sense, skilled in the arts of persuasion and intrigue. Bruised by his conflicts with Hamilton, Jefferson had resigned as secretary of state in 1793 and retreated to Monticello, his home in Virginia. Adams's job as vice president kept him closer to the political action, but his personality often put people off. He was temperamental, thin-skinned, and quick to take offense.

The leading Federalists and Republicans informally caucused to choose candidates. The Federalists picked Thomas Pinckney of South Carolina to run with Adams; the Republicans settled on Aaron Burr of New York to pair with Jefferson. The Constitution did not anticipate parties and tickets. Instead, each electoral college voter could cast two votes for any two candidates, but on only one ballot; the top vote-getter became president and the next highest assumed the vice presidency. (This procedural flaw was corrected by the Twelfth Amendment, adopted in 1804.) With only one ballot, careful maneuvering was required to make sure the chief rivals for the presidency did not land in the top two spots.

Into that maneuverable moment stepped Alexander Hamilton. No longer in the cabinet, Hamilton had returned to his law practice in 1795, but he kept a firm hand on political developments. Hamilton did not trust Adams; he preferred Pinckney, and he tried to influence electors to throw their support to the South Carolinian. But his plan backfired: Adams was elected president with seventy-one electoral votes, and Jefferson came in second with sixty-eight and thus became vice president. Pinckney got fifty-nine votes, while Burr trailed with thirty.

Adams's inaugural speech pledged neutrality in foreign affairs and respect for the French people, which made Republicans hopeful. To please Feder-

alists, Adams retained three cabinet members from Washington's administration, the secretaries of state, treasury, and war. But the three were Hamilton loyalists, passing on Hamilton's judgments as their own to the unwitting Adams. Vice President Jefferson expected to work closely with his old friend Adams, but the Hamiltonian cabinet ruined the honeymoon. Jefferson's advice was spurned, and he withdrew from active counsel of the president.

The XYZ Affair

From the start, Adams's presidency was in crisis. France retaliated for the Jay Treaty by abandoning its 1778 alliance with the United States. French privateers—armed private vessels—started detaining American ships carrying British goods; by March 1797, more than three hundred American vessels had been seized. To avenge these insults, Federalists started murmuring openly about war with France. Adams preferred negotiations and dispatched a three-man commission to France in the fall of 1797. When the three arrived in Paris, French officials would not receive them. Finally the French minister of foreign affairs, Talleyrand, sent three French agents, unnamed and later known to the American public as X, Y, and Z, to the American commissioners with the recommendation that $250,000 might grease the wheels of diplomacy and that a $12 million loan to the French government would be the price of a peace treaty.

Americans reacted to the XYZ affair with shock and anger. Even staunch pro-French Republicans began to reevaluate their allegiance. The Federalist-dominated Congress appropriated money for an army of ten thousand soldiers. It repealed all prior treaties with France, and in 1798 twenty naval warships launched the United States into its first undeclared war, called the Quasi War by historians to underscore its uncertain legal status. The main scene of action was the Caribbean, where more than one hundred French privateers were captured.

But there was no homefront unification in this time of undeclared war; antagonism only intensified between Federalists and Republicans. Republican newspapers heaped abuse on Adams; Federalist newspapers celebrated over bonfires of rival papers, and one Federalist editor ominously declared that "he who is not for us is against us." Pro-French mobs roamed the capital city, and Adams, fearing for his personal safety, stocked weapons in his presidential quarters.

JOHN ADAMS BY JOHN TRUMBULL
In 1793, a year after the youthful Secretary of the Treasury Alexander Hamilton posed for him (see page 194), John Trumbull painted Vice President John Adams, then age fifty-eight. A friend once listed Adams's shortcomings as a politician: "He can't dance, drink, game, flatter, promise, dress, swear with gentlemen, and small talk and flirt with the ladies."
National Portrait Gallery, Smithsonian Institution/Art Resources, N.Y.

The Alien and Sedition Acts

If the United States had actually declared war on France, the pro-French Republicans could have been subject to laws of treason. But without a declared war, Federalists had to create another law to muffle opposition. In mid-1798, Congress hammered out a Sedition Act that mandated a heavy fine or a jail sentence for anyone engaged in conspiracies or revolts or convicted of speaking or writing anything that defamed the government.

Criticisms of government leaders were now criminal utterances. In all, twenty-five men, almost all newspaper editors, were charged with sedition; twelve were convicted. (See "Documenting the American Promise," page 204.)

Congress also passed two Alien Acts. The first extended the waiting period for an alien to achieve citizenship from five to fourteen years and required all aliens to register with the federal government. The second empowered the president in time of war to deport or imprison without trial any foreigner

CARTOON OF MATTHEW LYON FIGHT IN CONGRESS
The political tensions of 1798 were not merely intellectual. A February session in Congress degenerated from name-calling to a brawl. Roger Griswold, a Connecticut Federalist, called Matthew Lyon, a Vermont Republican, a coward. Lyon responded with some well-aimed spit, the first departure from the gentleman's code of honor. Griswold responded by raising his cane to Lyon, whereupon Lyon grabbed nearby fire tongs to beat back his assailant. Madison wrote to Jefferson that the two should have dueled: "No man ought to reproach another with cowardice, who is not ready to give proof of his own courage" by negotiating a duel, the honorable way to avenge insults. What is the picture on the wall of the House chambers?
Library of Congress.

www.bedfordstmartins.com/roarkcompact SEE THE ONLINE STUDY GUIDE for more help in analyzing this image.

The Crisis of 1798: Sedition

As President John Adams inched toward an unde-clared war on France, criticism of his foreign policy reached an all-time high. Newspaper editors and politicians favorable to France blasted him with such intemperate language that his supporters feared the country could be pushed to the brink of civil war. Federalists in Congress tried to muffle the opposition by criminalizing seditious words, believing it the only path to preserve the country. Republicans just redoubled their opposition.

DOCUMENT 1. Abigail Adams Complains of Sedition, 1798

Throughout the spring of 1798, a beleaguered Abigail Adams complained repeatedly in confidential letters to her sister Mary Cranch about the need for a sedition law to put a stop to the political criticisms of her husband, the president, by Benjamin Bache, pro-French editor of the Philadelphia Aurora.

(April 26): . . . Yet dairingly do the vile incendaries keep up in Baches paper the most wicked and base, voilent & caluminiating abuse—It was formerly considerd as leveld against the Government, but now it . . . insults the Majesty of the Sovereign People. But nothing will have an Effect untill congress pass a Sedition Bill. . . . (April 28): . . . we are now wonderfully popular except with Bache & Co who in his paper calls the President old, querilous, Bald, blind, cripled, Toothless Adams. (May 10): . . . This Bache is cursing & abusing daily. If that fellow . . . is not surpressd, we shall come to a civil war. (May 26): . . . I wish the Laws of our Country were competant to punish the stirer up of sedition, the writer and Printer of base and unfounded calumny. This would contribute as much to the Peace and harmony of our Country as any measure. . . . (June 19): . . . in any other Country Bache & all his papers would have been seazd and ought to be here, but congress are dilly dallying about passing a Bill enabling the President to seize suspisious persons, and their papers. (June 23): . . . I wish our Legislature would set the example & make a sedition act, to hold in order the base Newspaper calumniators. In this State, you could not get a verdict, if a prosecution was to be commenced.

SOURCE: Stewart Mitchell, ed., New Letters of Abigail Adams, 1788–1801 (Boston: Houghton Mifflin, 1947), 165, 167, 172, 179, 193, 196.

DOCUMENT 2. The Sedition Act of 1798

On July 14, 1798, the Congress approved a bill making sedition with malicious intent a crime.

SECTION 1. . . . if any persons shall unlawfully combine or conspire together, with intent to oppose any measure or measures of the government of the United States . . . , or to impede the operation of any law of the United States, or to intimidate or prevent any person holding . . . office in or under the government of the United States, from undertaking, performing or executing his trust or duty, and if any person or persons, with intent as aforesaid, shall counsel, advise or attempt to procure any insurrection, riot, unlawful assembly, or combination . . . , he or they shall be deemed guilty of a high misdemeanor, and on conviction . . . shall be punished by a fine not exceeding five thousand dollars, and by imprisonment during a term not less than six months nor exceeding five years. . . .

SEC. 2. . . . if any person shall write, print, utter or publish, or shall cause or procure to be written, printed, uttered or published . . . , any false, scandalous and malicious writing or writings against the government of the United States, or either house of the Congress of the United States, or the President of the United States, with intent to defame the said government . . . or to bring them . . . into contempt or disrepute; or to excite against them . . . the hatred of the good people of the United States . . . , or to aid, encourage or abet any hostile designs of any foreign nation against the United States . . . , then such person, being thereof convicted thereof . . . shall be punished by a fine not exceeding two thousand dollars, and by imprisonment not exceeding two years.

SOURCE: United States Statutes at Large; Containing the Laws and Concurrent Resolutions . . . and Proclamations, Treaties, International Agreements Other Than Treaties and Reorganized Plans (Washington: U.S. Government Printing Office, 1789–1845). Avalon Project, Yale Law School, 1996, <www.yale.edu/lawweb/avalon/statutes/sedact.htm>.

Document 3. Matthew Lyon Criticizes John Adams, 1798

Matthew Lyon, a member of Congress from Vermont, published this criticism of President Adams in a letter to the editor of Spooner's Vermont Journal *(July 31, 1798). It became the first of three counts against him in a sedition trial. Lyon drew a four-month sentence and a fine of $1,000. From jail he ran for reelection to Congress—and won.*

As to the Executive, when I shall see the efforts of that power bent on the promotion of the comfort, the happiness, and the accommodation of the people, that Executive shall have my zealous and uniform support. But when I see every consideration of the public welfare swallowed up in a continual grasp for power, in an unbounded thirst for ridiculous pomp, foolish adulation, or selfish avarice; when I shall behold men of real merit daily turned out of office for no other cause but independence of sentiment; when I shall see men of firmness, merit, years, abilities, and experience, discarded on their application for office, for fear they possess that independence; and men of meanness preferred for the ease with which they take up and advocate opinions, the consequence of which they know but little of; when I shall see the sacred name of religion employed as a State engine to make mankind hate and persecute one another, I shall not be their humble advocate.

SOURCE: Matthew Lyon, Letter in *Spooner's Vermont Journal,* July 31, 1798. Quoted in Aleine Austin, *Matthew Lyon: New Man of the Democratic Revolution, 1749–1822* (Pennsylvania State University Press, 1981), 108–109.

Document 4. James Bayard Defends the Law, 1799

James Bayard, a Federalist representative from Delaware, led the charge in the House to expel Matthew Lyon from his seat in Congress. Bayard argued that Lyon was guilty of subverting the government.

This Government . . . depends for its existence upon the good will of the people. That good will is maintained by their good opinion. But, how is that good opinion to be preserved, if wicked and unprincipled men, men of inordinate and desperate ambition, are allowed to state facts to the people which are not true, which they know at the time to be false, and which are stated with the criminal intention of bringing the Government into disrepute among the people? This was falsely and deceitfully stealing public opinion; it was a felony of the worst and most dangerous nature.

SOURCE: Annals of Congress (1799). Quoted in Richard Buel, *Securing the Revolution: Ideology in American Politics* (Ithaca, N.Y.: Cornell University Press, 1972), 256.

Document 5. The Virginia Resolution, December 24, 1798

James Madison drafted the Virginia Resolution and had a trusted ally present it to the Virginia legislature, which was dominated by Republicans. (Jefferson did the same for Kentucky.) The Virginia document denounces the Alien and Sedition Acts and declares that states have the right to "interpose" to stop unconstitutional actions by the federal government.

RESOLVED . . . That this assembly most solemnly declares a warm attachment to the Union of the States, to maintain which it pledges all its powers; and that for this end, it is their duty to watch over and oppose every infraction of those principles which constitute the only basis of that Union, because a faithful observance of them, can alone secure its existence and the public happiness.

That this Assembly doth explicitly and peremptorily declare, that it views the powers of the federal government, as resulting from the compact, to which the states are parties; as limited by the plain sense and intention of the instrument constituting the compact; as no further valid that they are authorized by the grants enumerated in that compact; and that in case of a deliberate, palpable, and dangerous exercise of other powers, not granted by the said compact, the states who are parties thereto, have the right, and are in duty bound, to interpose for arresting the progress of the evil, and for maintaining within their respective limits, the authorities, rights and liberties appertaining to them. . . .

That the General Assembly doth particularly protest against the palpable and alarming infractions of the Constitution, in the two late cases of the "Alien and Sedition Acts" . . . ; the first of which exercises a power no where delegated *(Continued)*

CHRONOLOGY

1789 George Washington inaugurated first president.

French Revolution begins.

First Congress meets in New York City.

1790 Alexander Hamilton's plans for funding the government—debts and assuming states' debts—approved.

Government moves from New York City to Philadelphia.

1791 Bill of Rights ratified by states.

Bank of the United States chartered by Congress.

General Arthur St. Clair's forces thoroughly defeated by Miami and Shawnee Indians in western Ohio.

Congress passes whiskey tax.

Haitian Revolution begins.

1793 Washington's second term begins.

Napoleonic Wars break out between France and England.

Washington issues Neutrality Proclamation over war between France and England.

Eli Whitney invents cotton gin.

1794 Farmers stage Whiskey Rebellion in western Pennsylvania.

Lancaster Turnpike, first private toll road, constructed.

General Anthony Wayne's forces defeat Shawnee and Delaware Indians at Battle of Fallen Timbers in western Ohio.

1795 Treaty of Greenville cedes most Indian land in Ohio to United States.

Senate approves Jay Treaty with England.

1796 John Adams elected president, Thomas Jefferson vice president.

1797 XYZ affair with France.

1798 Quasi War with France.

Alien and Sedition Acts passed by Congress.

Virginia and Kentucky Resolutions drafted by Jefferson and Madison.

1800 Jefferson elected president.

A JEFFERSON FAN

Ladies' fans became increasingly popular fashion accessories in the late eighteenth and early nineteenth centuries. This folding fan of vellum and carved ivory, made in the early 1800s, features a medallion portrait of President Thomas Jefferson. Carried by the ribbon on a woman's wrist, the fan could be flicked open to announce a partisan political statement. Fans and other handheld articles such as parasols and handkerchiefs expanded the repertoire of nonverbal expression for women, who by the custom and training of the time were expected to be less assertive than men in mixed-sex conversation. Many emotions and messages—from modesty, coyness, and flirtatiousness to anger, irritability, and boredom—could be communicated by the expert deployment of this delicate emblem of femininity.

Collection of David J. and Janice L. Frent.

REPUBLICAN ASCENDANCY 10

1800–1824

T HE NAME *TECUMSEH* translates to "the Shooting Star," a fitting name for the Shawnee chief who reached meteoric heights of fame among Indians during Thomas Jefferson's presidency. From Canada to Georgia and west to the Mississippi, Tecumseh was accounted a charismatic leader. White Americans, too, praised (and feared) him as a would-be Moses of the Indians. Graceful, eloquent, magnetic, astute: Tecumseh was all these things and more, a gifted natural leader, equal parts politician and warrior.

The Ohio country, where Tecumseh was born in 1768, had become home to some dozen Indian tribes, including the Shawnee, recently displaced from the South. Soon Ohio was ground zero in the struggle with the Big Knives, as the Shawnees called the Americans, producing perpetual conflict from the Revolution to the 1790s Indian wars. Tecumseh's childhood was marked by repeated violence and the loss of his father and two brothers in battle.

Tecumseh honed his warrior skills by ambushing pioneers flatboating down the Ohio. He fought at the Battle of Fallen Timbers, a major Indian defeat, but avoided the 1795 negotiations of the Treaty of Greenville, in which a half dozen dispirited tribes ceded much of Ohio to the Big Knives. With frustration he watched as seven further treaties between 1802 and 1805 whittled away more Indian land.

Some Indians, resigned and tired, looked for ways to accommodate to new realities, taking up farming, trade, and even intermarriage with the Big Knives. Others spent their treaty payments on deadly alcohol. Tecumseh's younger brother Tenskwatawa led an embittered life of idleness and drink. But Tecumseh rejected assimilation and inebriation, and embarked on a campaign to return his people to their ancient ways. Donning traditional animal-skin garb, he traveled around the Great Lakes area, persuading tribes to join his pan-Indian confederacy. The American territorial governor of Indiana, William Henry Harrison, reported, "For four years he has been in constant motion. You see him today on the Wabash, and in a short time hear of him on the shores of Lake Erie or Michigan, or on the banks of the Mississippi, and wherever he goes he makes an impression favorable to his purpose." In 1811, he toured the South, visiting tribes from Mississippi to Georgia.

Even his once-dissolute brother was born anew. After a near-death experience in 1805, Tenskwatawa miraculously revived and recounted a startling vision, a meeting with the Master of Life. Renaming himself the Prophet, Tenskwatawa urged Indians everywhere to return to tradition. He preached that the white Americans were children of the Evil Spirit, destined to be destroyed. Headquartered at a new village called Prophetstown, located in present-day Indiana along Tippecanoe Creek, Tecumseh and his brother pledged a potent blend of spiritual regeneration and political unity that attracted thousands of followers. Governor Harrison

TECUMSEH
Several portraits of Tecumseh exist, but they all present a different visage, and none of them enjoys a verified authenticity. This one perhaps comes closest: it is an engraving adapted from an earlier drawing that no longer exists, sketched by a French artist named Pierre Le Dru in a live sitting with the Indian leader. The engraver has given Tecumseh a British army officer's uniform, showing that Tecumseh fought on the British side in the War of 1812. Note the head covering and the medallion around the neck, marking Tecumseh's Indian identity.
Library of Congress.

admired and feared Tecumseh, calling him "one of those uncommon geniuses which spring up occasionally to produce revolutions." President Jefferson had great reason to worry about an organized Indian opposition, and more, its potential for a renewed alliance with the British in Canada.

Jefferson's first term in office was marked by notable successes, like the Louisiana Purchase and the Lewis and Clark expedition, but his second term was consumed by the threat of war with Britain and

France. Insults over shipping rights, the capture of vessels, and impressment of sailors escalated tensions. Jefferson tried to avoid war through trade embargoes against both countries, but this policy greatly alienated Federalist New England, whose economy depended on overseas trade. While New Englanders hoped to avoid a war, some western politicians in areas like Kentucky were actually eager for armed conflict with Britain, hoping it would provide an opportunity to seize extensive land not only from Indians confederated under Tecumseh but also from Canadians.

James Madison, Jefferson's successor, was not able to contain the opposing forces and deepening party strife. As had happened in the late 1790s, the country approached a crisis as it struggled to identify the real enemy, England or France. Congress finally declared war on England in 1812.

As expected, Tecumseh allied his confederacy with the British and delivered eight hundred warriors to augment British strength. Unfortunately for the Indians, the British concentrated on protecting Canada, not the Indians' country. Tecumseh died on Canadian soil at the Battle of the Thames in the fall of 1813, defending Canada against an army led by General William Henry Harrison. In the end, the War of 1812 settled little between the Americans and the British, but it was tragically conclusive for the Indians. No Tecumseh would emerge again east of the Mississippi.

Jefferson's Presidency

Thomas Jefferson called his election the "revolution of 1800." Certainly the turmoil in John Adams's last years in office suggested revolutionary potential, and the election itself, the first one decided in the House of Representatives, was highly suspenseful. Quite a different "revolution of 1800" nearly materialized, when a Virginia slave named Gabriel plotted rebellion, figuring it might succeed when white men were so badly divided. Gabriel was wrong, but his plot added greatly to the turbulence of the times.

Jefferson also radically transformed the presidency, away from the Federalists' vision of a powerful, even regal, executive branch to republican simplicity and limited government. Yet he found that circumstances sometimes required him to draw on the expansive powers of the presidency.

The Election of 1800

John Adams headed the Federalist ticket for reelection in 1800, even though he had angered many Federalists by his diplomatic overtures with France. New England Federalists supported him, but others from the middle and southern states hoped to ease him out in favor of his running mate, Charles Cotesworth Pinckney of South Carolina, through a careful manipulation of the electoral college votes. Alexander Hamilton went public with a contemptuous and abusive condemnation of Adams, so the surprise in the election tally was not that Adams lost but that the two Republican candidates tied each other, an outcome possible because of the single balloting to choose both president and vice president. Thomas Jefferson and his running mate, Senator Aaron Burr of New York, both got seventy-three votes. Burr, driven by ambition and vanity, declined to concede the presidency to Jefferson. So the election moved to the Federalist-dominated House of Representatives for decision.

In February 1801, the House met to choose. Each state delegation commanded one vote, and the winner needed nine votes. Some Federalists preferred Burr, believing his character flaws made him more susceptible to Federalist pressure. "His very selfishness prevents his entertaining any mischievous predilections for foreign nations," wrote one senator privately. But Hamilton, although no friend to Jefferson, recognized that the high-strung and arrogant Burr would be more dangerous in the presidency than Jefferson, with his hated but steady habits of republicanism. Jefferson was a fanatic and a "contemptible hypocrite" to Hamilton, but at least he was not corrupt. Jefferson had the votes of eight states on the first ballot; it took thirty-six more ballots and six days to get a ninth vote (and also a tenth) in his column. In the end, anti-Burr Federalist representatives in three states abstained from voting to allow Jefferson the victory without actually having to cast a ballot for him.

The election of 1800 demonstrated a remarkable feature of the new constitutional government. No matter how hard-fought the campaign, this election showed that leadership of the nation could shift from one group to a distinctly different one, in a peaceful transfer of power effected by ballots, not bullets.

Gabriel's Rebellion

As the country struggled over its white leadership, a twenty-four-year-old blacksmith named Gabriel plotted his own revolution of 1800 in Virginia. Gabriel, the slave of Thomas Prosser, recruited hundreds of co-conspirators from five counties. Inspired by the Haitian revolution, Gabriel and his followers planned to march on the state capitol at Richmond, set fires, capture an arsenal, and take the governor, James Monroe, hostage. Gabriel would spare Methodists and Quakers, known to hold antislavery views, and he also expected Indians and "the poor white people" of Richmond to join him. Taking seriously Federalist rhetoric about Republican Francophiles, Gabriel assumed that a pro-French (and thus liberty-loving) Republican Governor Monroe might prove sympathetic to their cause.

Gabriel's revolt never materialized. A massive thunderstorm scuttled it on the appointed day in August, and a few nervous slaves spilled the secret. Within days, scores of implicated conspirators were jailed and brought to trial. One jailed rebel compared himself to the most venerated icon of the early Republic: "I have nothing more to offer than what General Washington would have had to offer, had he been taken by the British and put to trial by them."

Such talk invoking the specter of a black George Washington worried James Monroe and Thomas Jefferson. Over September and October, twenty-seven black men were hanged for contemplating rebellion. Finally, Jefferson advised Monroe that the hangings had gone far enough and that deportation was a better alternative. "The world at large will forever condemn us if we indulge a principle of revenge," Jefferson wrote Monroe.

Gabriel's near-rebellion failed, but it scared Virginia politicians into a serious—but secret—effort to identify a site to which future troublesome slaves could be deported. In 1801, the Virginia legislature pressed the federal government for help, since deportation required cooperation with a foreign power. Jefferson was sympathetic to this effort, but he let the idea drop. Deporting insubordinate slaves to Sierra Leone in Africa or to some Spanish colony west of the Mississippi would perhaps reduce tensions in Virginia, but it might also encourage defiance because the eventual payoff was freedom.

The Jefferson Vision of Republican Simplicity

Jefferson sidestepped the problem of slavery and turned his attention to establishing a mode of governing that was a clear contrast to that of the Federalists. On inauguration day, held for the first time in the village of Washington, D.C., he dressed in everyday wear, to strike the tone of republican simplicity, and walked to the Senate chamber in the Capitol for the modest swearing-in ceremony. Once in office, he continued to emphasize unfussy frugality. He scaled back on Federalist building plans for Washington and cut the government budget. He wore plain clothes, appearing "neglected but not slovenly," according to one onlooker. He cultivated a casual style, wearing slippers to greet important guests, avoiding the formality of state dinner parties and liveried servants. Jefferson's studied carelessness was very deliberate.

Jefferson was no Antifederalist. He had supported the Constitution in 1788, although he had qualms about the unrestricted reelection allowed to the president. But events of the 1790s caused him to worry about the stretching of powers in the executive branch. Jefferson had watched with distrust as Hamilton led the Federalists to fund the public debt, establish a national bank, and secure commercial ties with England. The Hamiltonian program seemed to Jefferson to be promoting the interests of money-hungry speculators at the expense of the rest of the country. Jefferson was not at all anticommerce. But financial schemes that seemed merely to allow rich men to become richer, without enhancing the vast and natural productivity of America, were corrupt and worthless, he believed, and their promotion had no authority under the Constitution. In Jefferson's vision, the source of true liberty in America was the independent farmer, someone who owned and worked his land both for himself and for the market.

Jefferson set out to dismantle Federalist innovations. He reduced the size of the army by a third, leaving only three thousand soldiers, and cut back the navy from twenty-five to seven ships. Peacetime defense, he felt, should rest with "a well-disciplined militia," not a standing army. With the consent of Congress, he abolished all federal internal taxes

JEFFERSON'S RED WAISTCOAT
During his presidency, Jefferson often wore this red silk waistcoat as informal daywear. The garment had a velvet collar, woolen sleeves, and a thick lining made from recycled cotton and wool stockings. The thrifty Jefferson preferred to conserve firewood by wearing layers of warm clothes. A senator visiting in 1802 reported in dismay that the president was "dressed, or rather undressed, with an old brown coat, red waistcoat, old corduroy small clothes, much soiled, woolen hose, and slippers without heels." Another guest in 1804 found him in the red waistcoat, green velveteen breeches with pearl buttons, and "slippers down at the heels" which made him look like an ordinary farmer. Such colorful clothing in silk and velveteen carries dressy or feminine connotations in the twenty-first century, but not in 1800. Jefferson did dress up in silk stockings and clean linen for fancy dinner parties; and when he lived in Paris in the 1780s, he wore an elaborately embroidered silk waistcoat under a greatcoat trimmed with gold lace. But in the 1800s, he used his simple, colorful clothes to make a point about republican manners.
Courtesy Monticello, photo by Colonial Williamsburg.

based on population or on whiskey. (Just once, in 1798, the federal government had exacted a direct tax based on population, in a task as burdensome as taking a census.) Government revenue would now derive solely from customs duties and from the sale of western lands. This maneuver was of particular benefit to the South, where the three-fifths clause of the Constitution counted slaves for both representation and taxation. Now the South enjoyed its extra weight in the House of Representatives without the threat of extra taxes. By the end of his first term, Jefferson had deeply reduced Hamilton's cherished national debt.

A properly limited federal government, according to Jefferson, was responsible merely for running a postal system, maintaining the federal courts, staffing lighthouses, collecting customs duties, and conducting a census once every ten years. Government jobs were kept to a minimum. The president had just one private secretary, a young man named Meriwether Lewis, to help with his correspondence, and Jefferson paid him out of his own pocket. The Department of State employed only 8 people: Secretary James Madison, 6 clerks, and a messenger. The Treasury Department was by far the largest unit, with 73 revenue commissioners, auditors, and clerks and 2 watchmen. The entire payroll of the executive branch amounted to a mere 130 people in 1801.

The Judiciary and the Midnight Judges

There was one set of government workers not under Jefferson's control to appoint. His predecessor, John Adams, seized the short time between his election defeat and Jefferson's inauguration to appoint 217 Federalist men to various judicial, diplomatic, and military posts.

Most of this windfall of appointments came to Adams as a result of the Judiciary Act of 1801, passed in the final month of his presidency. The new law revised the original Judiciary Act of 1789, which had established a six-man Supreme Court and six circuit courts, each presided over by a Supreme Court justice. The new act authorized sixteen circuit courts, each headed by a new judge. A fast-acting Adams could appoint sixteen judges with lifetime tenure, plus dozens more state attorneys, marshals, and clerks for each court. The 1801 act also reduced the Supreme Court from six to five justices. Adams had recently appointed solidly Federalist Virginian

John Marshall to a vacant sixth seat, but once the Judiciary Act became law, a future president would not be able to fill the next empty seat.

Adams and Marshall worked feverishly in the last weeks of February to secure agreements from the new appointees. In view of the slowness of mail, achieving 217 acceptances was astonishing. The two men were still at work until 9 P.M. on the last night Adams was president, signing and delivering commissions to the new officeholders.

The appointment of "midnight judges" infuriated the Republicans. Jefferson, upon taking office, immediately canceled the appointments of the nontenured men. A few commissions had not yet been delivered and Jefferson refused to send them out. One of them was addressed to William Marbury, who soon decided to sue the new secretary of state, James Madison, for failure to make good on the appointment. This action gave rise to a landmark Supreme Court case, *Marbury v. Madison* decided in 1803. The Court, presided over by John Marshall, ruled that although Marbury's commission was valid and the new president should have delivered it, the Court could not compel him to do so. What made the case significant was little noted at the time: The Court found that the grounds of Marbury's suit, resting in the Judiciary Act of 1789, were in conflict with the Constitution. For the first time, the Court acted to disallow a law (part of the 1789 act) on the grounds that it was unconstitutional. John Marshall quietly established the concept of judicial review; the Supreme Court in effect assumed the legal authority to nullify acts judged in conflict with the Constitution.

The Promise of the West: The Louisiana Purchase and the Lewis and Clark Expedition

The reach of the *Marbury* decision went largely unnoticed in 1803 because the president and Congress were preoccupied with other major issues, among them the acquisition of the Louisiana Territory. Until the French and Indian War, France had claimed and partly settled this land west of the Mississippi River, only to lose it to Spain in the 1763 Treaty of Paris. Spain never sent adequate forces to control or settle the land, however; Spanish power remained precarious everywhere outside New Orleans. Meanwhile, American farming families were settling Kentucky and Tennessee, along rivers

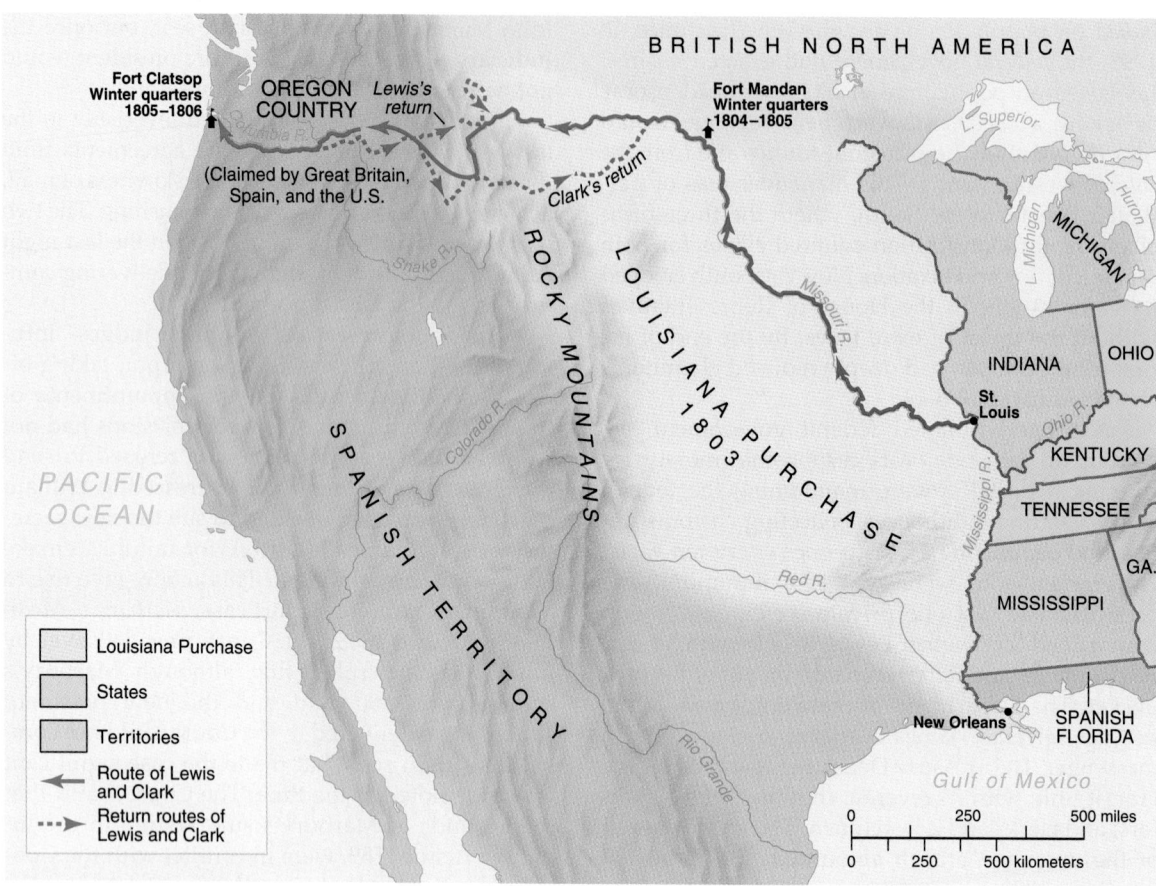

MAP 10.1

The Louisiana Purchase and the Lewis and Clark Expedition
Robert Livingston's bargain buy of 1803 far exceeded his initial assignment, to acquire just the city of New Orleans. Federalists of New England, worried that their own geographically based power in the federal government would someday be eclipsed by the West, voted against the purchase. The Indians who inhabited the vast region, unaware that their land had been sold, got their first look at Anglo-American and African American men when the Lewis and Clark expedition came exploring in 1804–1806.

emptying into the upper Mississippi, and for a time the Spanish allowed them to ship their agricultural produce downriver and even encouraged American settlements across the river, in an effort to augment the population. By 1801, Americans made up a sizable minority of the population around the lower Mississippi.

In 1802, rumors reached Jefferson that Spain had struck a secret bargain with France to hand over a large part of Spain's trans-Mississippi territory to Napoleon in exchange for a duchy in Italy. Spain had proved a weak western neighbor, but France was another story. Jefferson was sufficiently

alarmed that he instructed Robert R. Livingston, America's minister in France, to try to buy New Orleans. At first the French denied they owned the city, but when Livingston hinted that the United States might simply seize it if buying was not an option, the French negotiator suddenly asked him to name his price for the entire Louisiana Territory, from the Gulf of Mexico north to Canada. Livingston stalled, and the Frenchman made suggestions: $125 million? $60 million? Livingston shrewdly stalled some more, and within days the French sold the entire territory for the bargain price of $15 million (Map 10.1).

Jefferson and most of Congress were delighted with the outcome of the diplomatic mission. Still, Jefferson had some qualms about the Louisiana Purchase. The price was right, and the enormous territory fulfilled Jefferson's dream of abundant farmland for future generations. But by what authority in the Constitution could he justify the purchase? His frequent criticism of the Hamiltonian stretching of the Constitution came back to haunt him. His legal reasoning told him he needed a constitutional amendment to authorize the addition of territory; more expedient minds told him the treaty-making powers of the president were sufficient. Expediency won out. In late 1803, the American army took formal control of the Louisiana Territory, and the United States was now 828,000 square miles larger.

Even before the Louisiana Purchase, Jefferson had eyed the trans-Mississippi west with intense curiosity. In early 1803, he had arranged congressional funding for a secret scientific and military mission into Spanish and Indian territory. Jefferson appointed twenty-eight-year-old Meriwether Lewis, his personal secretary, to head the expedition, instructing him to investigate Indian cultures, to collect plant and animal specimens, and to chart the geography of the West. Congress had more traditional goals in mind: The expedition was to scout locations for military posts, open commercial agreements for the fur trade, and locate any possible waterway between the East and West Coasts.

For his co-leader, Lewis chose Kentuckian William Clark, a fellow veteran of the 1790s Indian wars. Together they handpicked a crew of forty-five, including expert rivermen, gunsmiths, hunters, interpreters, a cook, and a slave named York who belonged to Clark. The explorers left St. Louis in the spring of 1804, working their way northwest up the Missouri River. They camped for the winter at a Mandan village in what is now central North Dakota.

The following spring, the explorers headed west, aided by a French trapper accompanied by his wife, a sixteen-year-old Indian woman named Sacajawea, and their baby. Sacajawea's presence was to prove unexpectedly helpful. Indian tribes encountered en route withdrew their suspicion that the Americans were hostile because, as Lewis wrote in his journal, "no woman ever accompanies a war party of Indians in this quarter."

The Lewis and Clark expedition reached the Pacific Ocean at the mouth of the Columbia River in November 1805. When they returned home the following year, they were greeted as national heroes.

SACAJAWEA

Sacajawea is pictured here with her baby, as imagined by mid-nineteenth-century artist Edgar S. Paxson, who produced a series of paintings of grand moments on the Lewis and Clark expedition. The young Shoshone mother was also called Janey by the two explorers, who admired her courage and fortitude. Her baby, Jean Baptiste Charbonneau, was nicknamed Pompey. William Clark brought the boy to St. Louis when he was six years old to educate him. In the 1820s, the youth was taken to Germany by the prince of Württemberg; he returned six years later, fluent in German, French, Spanish, and English. Half Shoshone and half French, Charbonneau became a guide and interpreter for numerous trading expeditions throughout the West until his death in the 1860s.

Sacajawea oil painting by Edgar S. Paxson. The University of Montana Museum of Fine Arts Collection.

They had established favorable relations with dozens of Indian tribes; they had collected invaluable information on the peoples, soils, plants, animals, and geography of the West; and they had inspired a nation of restless explorers and solitary imitators.

Republicans in a Dangerous World

Foreign policy during Jefferson's two presidential terms was not as untroubled as his low-budget approach to the military would imply. From 1801 to 1805, the United States was drawn into belligerent exchanges off the north coast of Africa that featured hijacked ships and captured crews. His second term was dominated by the ongoing war between France and England, which continually threatened to involve the United States. As peaceful alternatives to war with a European superpower, the president experimented with economic sanctions and trade embargoes. Jefferson and his successors faced war threats not only across the Atlantic but also in the new northwest states, where Tecumseh's powerful Indian confederacy challenged the westward press of American settlement.

The Barbary Wars

For well over a century, four Arabic settlements on the Barbary coast—Morocco, Algiers, Tunis, and Tripoli—controlled shipping traffic through the Mediterranean by means of privateering. Swift vessels called *corsairs* overtook merchant ships, plundered the cargo, and captured the crew for ransom. Most European states spared their ships by paying tribute—an annual sum of money—to secure safe passage. When American ships flew under the British flag, up to 1776, they were protected. But once independent, the United States also began to pay tribute, by the mid-1790s, on the order of $50,000 to the leader of each state.

In 1801, the *pasha* (military head) of Tripoli demanded a large increase in his tribute. Jefferson had long thought such payments were extortion, and his response was to send four warships to Tripoli. A rallying slogan backed Jefferson: "Millions for defense, not one cent for tribute." Quickly, the pasha declared war on the United States.

From 1801 to 1803, American ships blockaded Tripoli and Tunis with only partial success and of-

fered escort protection to passing American merchant ships. Only a few skirmishes ensued. Then, in late 1803, the first major action by the United States floundered: the *USS Philadelphia*, a large frigate, ran aground near the Tripoli harbor. Its 300-man crew was captured, along with the ship, which greatly augmented Tripoli's naval strength.

Several months later, the Americans retaliated. Seventy men, led by twenty-five-year-old Lt. Stephen Decatur, sailed into the harbor after dark on a captured corsair with an Arabic-speaking pilot to fool harbor sentries. The corsair drew up to the *Philadelphia*, boarded it, set it on fire, and escaped. Decatur was an instant hero in America.

In summer of 1804, the U.S. forces attacked Tripoli, destroying enemy vessels, firing on the city, and also offering ransom for the captured *Philadelphia* sailors. The pasha resisted, holding out for more money, until he learned that fresh U.S. forces, aided by Egyptian and Turkish mercenaries, were headed toward Tripoli. The pasha then entered treaty negotiations, accepting $60,000 for the prisoners and agreeing to forgo tribute. One significant clause of the treaty stipulated that "no pretext arising from Religious Opinions" should interrupt good relations since the United States has "no character of enmity against the Laws, Religion or Tranquility of Musselmen" (that is, Muslims).

Although the tribute system with other Barbary states would not end until 1812, when frigates returned to the Mediterranean for further skirmishes, none of this affected the election of 1804, which proved an easy triumph for Jefferson. The Federalist candidate, Charles Cotesworth Pinckney of South Carolina, secured only 14 votes in the electoral college, in contrast to 162 for the president. Just months before the election, the Federalists had lost their shrewdest statesman: Alexander Hamilton, called by some "the brains of the Federalist Party," was tragically killed in a duel with Aaron Burr. (See "Historical Question," page 220.) Republicans would hold the presidency for another twenty years.

More Maritime Troubles: Impressment and Embargoes

When France and England resumed war in 1803, they each warned America not to aid the other. Britain acted on these threats in 1806, stopping American ships, inspecting cargoes for military aid to France, and seizing suspected deserters from the British navy, along with not a few Americans. Ultimately, 2,500 sailors were swept up—impressed—by the British. Jefferson and the American public were outraged.

One incident made the usually cautious Jefferson nearly belligerent. In June 1807, an American ship, the *Chesapeake*, harboring some British deserters, was ordered to stop by a British frigate, the *Leopard*. The *Chesapeake* refused, and the *Leopard* opened fire, killing three Americans—right at the mouth of Chesapeake Bay, well within U.S. territory. Before this incident, Jefferson had convinced Congress to pass non-importation laws banning a select list of British-made goods. But now Congress passed a total trade embargo, in December 1807. Although surely a drastic measure, the embargo was meant to forestall war. The goal was to make England suffer; and all foreign ports were banned, to discourage illegal trading through secondary ports. Jefferson was convinced that England needed America's agricultural products far more than America needed British goods.

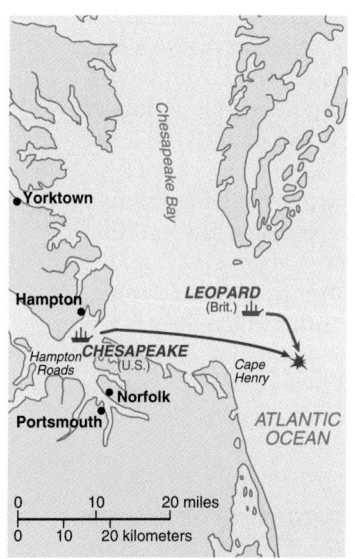

The *Chesapeake* Incident, June 22, 1807

The Embargo Act of 1807 was a total disaster. From 1790 to 1807, U.S. exports had increased fivefold; now commerce was at a standstill. In New England, the heart of the shipping industry, unemployment rose. Grain plummeted in value, river traffic halted, tobacco rotted in the South, and cotton went unpicked. Protest petitions flooded Washington. The federal government suffered too, for import duties were a significant source of revenue. Jefferson paid political costs as well. The Federalist Party, in danger of fading away after its weak showing in 1804, began to revive. Worse yet, England acquired grain from South America and seemed not to suffer particularly from American defiance.

In mid-1808, Jefferson indicated that he would not run for a third term. James Madison, Jefferson's

secretary of state, was the clear heir apparent. Disgruntled Republicans from hurting tobacco regions preferred James Monroe, a Virginia planter with experience as a diplomat to England, but Madison was the favorite among Republican caucuses. At this point, party politics, still held to be a bad thing, operated through informal caucuses that orchestrated state and local elections. The Federalist caucuses chose Charles Cotesworth Pinckney again to run against Madison. Pinckney did much better than in 1804; he received forty-seven electoral votes, nearly half Madison's total. Support for the Federalists remained centered in the New England states, but Republicans still held the balance of power nationwide.

The attacks on American ships continued, by the British and now the French. In 1809, Congress had softened the embargo by passing the Non-Intercourse Act, which prohibited trade only with England and France, opening up other trade routes to diminish the anguish of shippers, farmers, and planters. In 1810, the Non-Intercourse Act expired, and Congress replaced it with a law that permitted direct trade with either France or England, whichever first promised to stop harassing American ships. Napoleon seized the initiative and declared that France would comply. Madison too hastily accepted this offer, reopened trade with France, and notified England that he intended to reinstate the embargo in the spring of 1811 unless England rescinded its search-and-seizure policy.

Unfortunately for Madison, the duplicitous French leaders continued to seize American ships. Furthermore, the British made no move to stop impressments or to repeal trade restrictions, and Madison was forced to reactivate the embargo, much to the great displeasure of the New England shipping industry. In 1811, the country was seriously divided and in a deep quandary. To some, the United States was on the verge of war; but with France or England? To others, any war meant disaster for commerce.

A new Congress, elected in the fall of 1810, arrived in Washington in March 1811 as Madison's embargo took effect. Some of the new and much younger members were eager to avenge the insults from abroad. In particular, Henry Clay, thirty-four, from Kentucky, and John C. Calhoun, twenty-nine, from South Carolina, became the center of a group informally known as the War Hawks. Though called Republicans, these younger men had much more

How Could a Vice President Get Away with Murder?

ON JULY 11, 1804, the vice president of the United States, Aaron Burr, shot Alexander Hamilton, the architect of the Federalist Party, in a duel on a narrow ledge below the cliffs of Weehawken, New Jersey, across the Hudson River from New York City. The pistol blast tore through a rib, demolished Hamilton's liver, and splintered his spine. The forty-seven-year-old Hamilton died the next day, in agonizing pain.

How could it happen that a sitting vice president and a prominent political leader could put themselves at such risk? Why did men who made their living by the legal system go outside the law and turn to the centuries-old ritual of the duel? Here were two eminent attorneys, skilled in the legalistic negotiations meant to substitute for violent resolution of disputes, firing .54-caliber hair-trigger weapons at ten paces. Did anyone try to stop them? How did the public react? Was Hamilton's death a criminal act? How could Burr continue to fulfill his federal office, presiding over the U.S. Senate?

Burr challenged Hamilton in late June after learning about a newspaper report that Hamilton "looked upon Mr. Burr to be a dangerous man, and one who ought not be trusted with the reins of government." Burr knew that Hamilton had long held a very low opinion of him and had never hesitated to say so in private, but now his private disparagement had made its way into print. Compounding the insult were political consequences: Burr was sure that Hamilton's remark cost him election to the governorship of New York.

Quite possibly he was right. Knowing that Jefferson planned to dump him from the federal ticket in the 1804 election, Burr had chosen to run for New York's highest office. His opponent was an obscure Republican judge; Burr's success depended on the support of the old Federalist leadership in the state. Up to the eve of the election, he appeared to have it—until Hamilton's remark was circulated.

So on June 18, Burr challenged Hamilton to a duel if he did not disavow his comment. Over the next three weeks, the men exchanged several letters clarifying the nature of the insult that aggrieved Burr. Hamilton the lawyer evasively quibbled over words, causing Burr finally to rail against his focus on syntax and grammar. At heart, Hamilton could not deny the insult, nor could he spurn the challenge without injury to his reputation for integrity and bravery. Both Burr and Hamilton were locked in a highly ritualized procedure meant to uphold a gentleman's code of honor.

Each man had a trusted "second," in accord with the code of dueling, who helped frame and deliver the letters and finally assisted at the duel site. Only a handful of close friends knew of the challenge, and no one tried to stop it. Hamilton did not tell his wife. He wrote her a tender farewell letter the night before, to be opened in the event of his death. He knew full well the pain dueling brought to loved ones, for his nineteen-year-old son Philip had been killed in a duel three years earlier, at the same ledge at Weehawken, as a result of hotheaded words exchanged at a New York theater. Even when Hamilton's wife was called to her husband's deathbed, she was first told he had terrible spasms from an illness. Women were completely shut out of the masculine world of dueling.

AARON BURR BY JOHN VANDERLYN
Aaron Burr was fifty-three years old at the time of this portrait, painted in 1809 by the New York artist John Vanderlyn.
Collection of The New-York Historical Society.

News of Hamilton's death spread quickly in New York and then throughout the nation. On the day of the funeral, church bells tolled continuously and New York merchants shut down all business. Thousands joined the procession, and the city council declared a six-week mourning period. Burr fled to Philadelphia, fearing retribution by the crowd.

Northern newspapers expressed indignation over the illegal duel and the tragic death of so prominent a man. (Response in the South was more subdued. Dueling was fully accepted there as an extralegal remedy for insult, and Burr's grievance fit perfectly the sense of violated honor that legitimated duels. In addition, southerners had never been particularly fond of the Federalist Hamilton.) Many northern states had criminalized dueling recently, treating a challenge as a misdemeanor and a dueling death as a homicide. Even after death, the loser of an illegal duel could endure one final penalty—being buried without a coffin, having a stake driven through the body, being strung up in public until the body rotted, or, more horrible still for the time, being donated to medical students for dissection. Such prescribed mutilation of the dead showed that northern lawmakers themselves participated in the code of honor by using threats of postmortem humiliation to discourage dueling. Hamilton's body was spared such a fate. But two ministers in succession refused to administer Holy Communion to him in his dying hours because he was a duelist; finally, one relented.

The public demanded to know the reasons for the duel, so the seconds prepared the correspondence between the principals for publication. A coroner's jury in New York soon indicted Burr on misdemeanor charges for issuing a challenge; a grand jury in New Jersey indicted him for murder. By that time, Burr was a fugitive from justice hiding out with sympathetic friends in South Carolina.

But not for long. Amazingly, he returned to Washington, D.C., in November 1804 to resume presiding over sessions of the Senate, a role he continued to assume until his term ended in March 1805. Federalists snubbed him, but eleven Republican senators petitioned New Jersey to drop its indictment on the grounds that "civilized nations" do not treat dueling deaths as "common murders." New Jersey did not pursue the murder charge. Burr freely visited New Jersey and New York for three more decades, paying no penalty for killing Hamilton.

Few would doubt that Burr was a scoundrel, albeit a brilliant one. A few years later, he was in-

PISTOLS FROM THE BURR–HAMILTON DUEL
Alexander Hamilton's brother-in-law John B. Church purchased this pair of dueling pistols in London in 1797. Church used them once in a duel with Aaron Burr, occasioned by Church's calling Burr a scoundrel in public; neither man was hurt. Hamilton's son Philip had borrowed them for his own fatal duel, three years before. When Burr challenged Hamilton, the latter also turned to John Church for the weapons. The guns stayed in the Church family until 1930, when they were given to the Chase Manhattan Bank in New York City, chartered in 1799 as the Manhattan Company. (Burr, Church, and Hamilton all served on the bank's board of directors.) When the pistols were cleaned in 1874, a hidden hair trigger came to light. It could be cocked by moving the trigger forward one-eighth inch. It then required only a half-pound pull, instead of ten pounds, to fire the gun. Hamilton gained no advantage from the hair trigger, if he knew of it.
Courtesy of Chase Manhattan Archives.

dicted for treason against the U.S. government in a presumed plot to break off part of the United States and start his own country in the Southwest. (He dodged that bullet too, in a spectacular trial presided over by John Marshall, chief justice of the Supreme Court.) Hamilton certainly thought Burr a scoundrel, and when that opinion reached print, Burr had cause to defend his honor under the etiquette of dueling. The accuracy of Hamilton's charge was of absolutely no account. Dueling redressed questions of honor, not questions of fact.

Dueling continued to be a feature of southern society for many more decades, but in the North the custom became extremely rare by the 1820s, helped along by the disrepute of Hamilton's death and by the rise of a legalistic society that now preferred evidence, interrogation, and monetary judgments to avenge injury.

expansive ideas of the way the United States should meet the challenge of enemies abroad.

Indian Troubles in the West

In the atmosphere of indecision about European war, tensions mounted over difficulties with Indians. Northern tribes were already renewing ties with supportive British agents and fur traders in Canada, a potential source of food and weapons. If the United States embarked on war with England, there would be serious repercussions on the frontier.

Shifting demographics raised the stakes for both sides. The 1810 census counted some 230,000 Americans living in Ohio, only seven years after statehood. Another 40,000 Americans inhabited the territories of Indiana, Illinois, and Michigan. The Indian population of the entire region was much smaller, probably about 70,000, a number unknown (because uncounted) to the Americans but gauged by Tecumseh, based on his extensive travels.

Up to 1805, Indiana's territorial governor, William Henry Harrison, had negotiated a series of treaties in a divide-and-conquer strategy extracting Indian lands for paltry payments. But with the rise to power of Tecumseh and his brother Tenskwatawa, the Prophet, Harrison's strategy faltered. A fundamental part of Tecumseh's message was the assertion that all Indian lands were held in common by all the tribes: "No tribe has the right to sell, even to each other, much less to strangers. . . . Sell a country! Why not sell the air, the great sea, as well as the earth? Didn't the Great Spirit make them all for the use of his children?" Taking advantage of Tecumseh's absence on a recruiting trip, Harrison assembled leaders of the Potawatomi, Miami, and Delaware tribes to negotiate the Treaty of Fort Wayne in 1809. After promising (falsely) that this was the last cession of land the United States would seek, Harrison secured three million acres of land, at about two cents per acre.

When he returned, Tecumseh was furious with both Harrison and the tribal leaders. Leaving his brother in charge at Prophetstown on Tippecanoe Creek, the Shawnee chief left on a trip to seek alliances in the South. Harrison then decided to attack Prophetstown with one thousand men. The two-hour battle resulted in the deaths of sixty-two Americans and forty Indians before the Prophet's forces fled the town, which Harrison's men set on fire. The November 1811 Battle of Tippecanoe was heralded as a glorious victory for the Americans. But Tecumseh was now more ready than ever to make war on the Americans.

TENSKWATAWA

Tenskwatawa, the Shawnee Prophet, and his brother Tecumseh led the spiritual and political efforts of a number of Indian tribes to resist land-hungry Americans moving west in the decade before the War of 1812. The Prophet is shown in a portrait by George Catlin with beaded necklaces, metal arm- and wristbands, and earrings. Compare the metal gorget here with the one worn by Joseph Brant (page 155).

National Museum of American Art, Washington, D.C./Art Resource, New York.

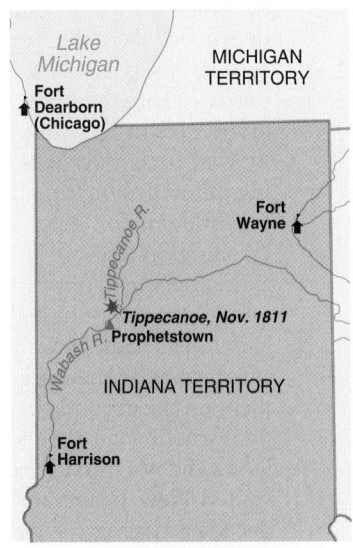

Battle of Tippecanoe, 1811

The War of 1812

The Indian conflicts in the Northwest Territory in 1811 soon merged into the wider conflict with England known as the War of 1812. The defeat at Tippecanoe propelled Tecumseh into an alliance with British military commanders stationed at outposts in lower Canada. If there had been doubt before about who would be the enemy, France or England, it was now abundantly clear, especially to westerners living near the frontier, that England should get the honor.

The War Begins

The several dozen young War Hawks new to Congress saluted Harrison's Tippecanoe victory and urged the country to war. Mostly lawyers by profession, they came from the West and South, and they welcomed a war with England both to legitimize attacks on the Indians and to bring an end to impressment. Many were also expansionists, looking to occupy Florida and threaten Canada. And they captured prominent posts in Congress from which to wield influence. Henry Clay was elected Speaker of the House, an extraordinary honor for a young newcomer. John C. Calhoun won a seat on the Foreign Relations Committee. The War Hawks approved major defense expenditures; the army, for example, quadrupled in size.

In June 1812, Congress declared war on Great Britain in a vote that divided on sectional lines: New England and some Middle Atlantic states opposed the war, while the South and West were strongly for it. Ironically, Great Britain had just announced it would stop the search and seizure of American ships. But the war momentum would not be slowed. The Foreign Relations Committee issued an elaborate justification titled *Report on the Causes and Reasons for War*, written mainly by Calhoun and containing extravagant language about Britain's "lust for power," "unbounded tyranny," and "mad ambition." These were fighting words, in a war that was in large measure about insult and honor.

The War Hawks proposed an invasion of Canada, confidently predicting victory in four weeks. Instead, the war lasted two and a half years, and Canada never fell. The northern invasion turned out to be a series of strategic blunders that revealed the grave unpreparedness of the United States for war. The combined British and Indian forces were unexpectedly powerful, and the United States made no attempt at the outset to create a naval presence on the Great Lakes. Detroit quickly fell, as did Fort Dearborn (site of the future Chicago). By the fall of 1812, the outlook was grim.

Worse, the New England states dragged their feet in raising troops, while New England merchants carried on illegal trade with Great Britain. Britain encouraged friendly overtures with New England, hoping to create dissention among the Americans. New Englanders drank India tea in Liverpool cups, while President Madison fumed in Washington about Federalist disloyalty.

The presidential election in 1812 solidified Federalist discontent with the war. Madison was opposed by DeWitt Clinton of New York, nominally Republican but able to attract the Federalist vote. He picked up all of New England's electoral votes, with the exception of Vermont's, and also took New York, New Jersey, and part of Maryland. Madison won in the electoral college, 128 to 89, but his margin of victory was considerably smaller than in 1808.

In late 1812 and early 1813, the tide began to turn in the Americans' favor. First came some reassuring victories at sea. Then Americans attacked York (now Toronto), the capital of Upper Canada, and burned it in April 1813. A few months later, Commodore Oliver Hazard Perry defeated the British fleet at the western end of Lake Erie. Emboldened, General Harrison drove an army into Canada from Detroit and in October 1813 defeated the British and Indians at the Battle of the Thames, where Tecumseh met his death.

Indians also met defeat in the South, where a general named Andrew Jackson led 2,500 Tennessee militiamen in an attack on Creek Indians, who were fighting in solidarity with Tecumseh's confederacy. At the Battle of Horseshoe Bend in March 1814, Jackson's militia killed more than 550 Indians, including women and children.

The British Offensives of 1814

In August 1814, British ships sailed into Chesapeake Bay throwing the capital into a panic. Families evacuated, banks hid their money, and government clerks carted away boxes of important papers. One State Department worker removed the Declaration of Independence to safety. Five thousand British troops entered the city and burned the president's house, the Capitol, a newspaper office, some dockyards, and a well-stocked arsenal. August 24 was a low moment for the American side.

A BOXING MATCH, or Another Bloody Nose for JOHN BULL.

WAR OF 1812: BOXING MATCH
A battle between the American ship Enterprise *and the British ship* Boxer *off the Maine coast sparked this wishful-thinking cartoon. A bare-knuckled James Madison has just punched King George III, blackened his eye, and made his nose bleed. The king begs "Mercy, mercy on me," and acknowledges "your [Madison's] superior skill." Madison asserts "we are an Enterpriseing Nation" capable of "equal force any day." This Madison clearly does not anticipate the humiliating burning of Washington in 1814.*
Courtesy, American Antiquarian Society.

Instead of trying to hold the city, the British headed north for Baltimore and attacked it on September 11, 1814. Here a fierce defense by the Maryland militia and a steady barrage of gunfire from Fort McHenry in the harbor kept them at bay. The firing continued until midnight, motivating Francis Scott Key to compose a poem he called "The Star-Spangled Banner" the next day. The British pulled back, unwilling to try to take the city.

September 1814 brought another powerful British offensive. Marching from Canada into New York State, the British seemed to have every advantage—trained soldiers, superior artillery, cavalry. But a series of mistakes cost them a naval skirmish at Plattsburgh on Lake Champlain. It also cost them their nerve and they retreated to Canada. This nonbattle was in fact a decisive military event, for British leaders in England, hearing of the retreat, concluded that incursions by land into the United States would be costly and difficult.

This point was confirmed when a large British army landed in lower Louisiana and encountered General Andrew Jackson and his militia just outside New Orleans, in early January 1815. Jackson's forces dramatically carried the day. The British suffered between two and three thousand casualties, the Americans less than eighty. Jackson became an instant hero, and the Battle of New Orleans was the most

glorious and decisive victory the Americans had experienced. Ironically, negotiators in Europe had already signed a peace agreement two weeks earlier.

The War Ends

The Treaty of Ghent, signed in December 1814, settled few of the surface issues that had led to war. Neither country could claim victory, and no land traded hands. Instead, the treaty reflected a mutual agreement to give up certain goals. The Americans yielded on impressment and gave up any claim to Canada; and the British agreed to evacuate western forts and abandoned aid to Indians. Nothing was said about shipping rights. The most concrete result was a plan for a commission to determine the exact boundary between the United States and Canada.

Antiwar New England Federalists did not feel triumph over the war's ambiguous conclusion. Instead they felt disgrace because of a meeting convened in Hartford, Connecticut, in December 1814. Politicians at the Hartford Convention discussed possible secession from the Union. They proposed amending the Constitution, to abolish the three-fifths clause as a basis of representation; to specify that congressional powers to pass embargoes, admit states, or declare war should require a two-thirds vote instead of a simple majority; and to limit the president to one term and prohibit successive presidents from the same state. The cumulative effect of these proposals would be to reduce the South's political power and break the lock of the Virginia dynasty on national office. New England wanted to assure that no one sectional party could again lead the country into war against the clear interests of another. Coming just as peace was achieved, however, the Hartford Convention suddenly looked very unpatriotic. The Federalist Party never recovered its grip, and within a few years its hold even in New England was reduced to a shadow.

No one really won the War of 1812. Americans celebrated as though they had, however, with parades and fireworks. The war gave rise to a new spirit of nationalism. The paranoia over British tyranny evident in the 1812 declaration of war was laid to rest, replaced by pride in a more equal relationship with the old mother country.

Perhaps the biggest winners in the War of 1812 were the young men, once called War Hawks, who took up the banner of the Republican Party and carried it in new, expansive directions. These younger politicians favored trade, western expansion, internal improvements, and the energetic development of new economic markets. The biggest losers of the war were the Indians. Tecumseh was dead, the Prophet discredited, the prospects of an Indian confederacy dashed, and the British protectors vanished.

Women's Status in the Early Republic

Unlike the American Revolution, the War of 1812 had little impact on the status of women. Developments in women's status in the early Republic came not as a result of wartime emergency but instead in incremental steps. As state legislatures and the courts grappled with the legal dependency of married white women in a country whose defining characteristic was independence, religious organizations struggled to redefine the role of women in church governance.

Women and the Law

The Anglo-American view of women, implanted in British common law, was that wives had no independent legal or political personhood. The legal doctrine of *feme covert* held that a wife's civic life

was completely subsumed by her husband's: A wife was obligated to obey her husband; her property was his; her domestic and sexual services were his; and even their children were legally his. Women had no right to keep their wages, to make contracts, or to sue or be sued.

State legislatures generally passed up the opportunity to rewrite the laws of domestic relations, even though they redrafted other British laws in light of republican principles. Lawyers never paused to defend, much less to challenge, the assumption that unequal power relations lay at the heart of marriage. The early Republic's conception of the "republican wife and mother" in no way altered the basic legal framework inherited from British law.

The one aspect of family law that changed in the early Republic was divorce. Before the Revolution, only New England jurisdictions had recognized a right to divorce, but by 1820, every state except South Carolina did so. Divorce was uncommon and difficult, however, and in many states could be obtained only by petition to the state's legislature, a daunting obstacle for many ordinary people. A mutual wish to terminate a marriage was never sufficient grounds for divorce. A New York judge affirmed that "it would be aiming a deadly blow at public morals to decree a dissolution of the marriage contract merely because the parties requested it. Divorces should never be allowed, except for the protection of the innocent party, and for the punishment of the guilty." States upheld the institution of marriage both to protect persons they thought of as naturally dependent (women and children) and to regulate the use and inheritance of property. Legal enforcement of marriage as an unequal relationship played a major role in maintaining gender inequality in the nineteenth century.

Single adult women could own and convey property, make contracts, initiate suits, and pay taxes. They could not vote (except in New Jersey until 1807), serve on juries, or practice law, so their civil status was limited. Single women's economic status was often limited as well, by custom as much as by law. Unless they had inherited adequate property or could live with married siblings, single adult women in the early Republic were very often poor.

None of the legal institutions that structured white gender relations applied to black slaves. As property themselves, slaves could not freely consent to any contractual obligations, including marriage. The protective features of state-sponsored unions were thus denied to black men and women in slavery, who were controlled by a more powerful authority, the slave owner. But this also meant that slave unions did not establish unequal power relations between partners, backed by the force of law, as did marriages among the free.

Women and Church Governance

In most Protestant denominations around 1800, white women made up the majority of congregants, as they had for some time. Yet the church hierarchy—ordained ministers and elders—was exclusively male, and the governance of most denominations rested in men's hands.

There were some exceptions, however. In Baptist congregations in New England, women served with men on church governance committees, where they decided admission of new members, voted on the hiring of ministers, and even debated doctrinal points. Quakers, too, had a history of recognizing women's spiritual talents. Quaker women who felt a special call were accorded the status of minister, which meant they were capable of leading and speaking in Quaker meetings.

Between 1790 and 1820, a small and highly unusual set of women emerged who actively engaged in open preaching. Most were from the Freewill Baptist groups centered in New England and upstate New York. Others were from small Methodist sects, and yet others rejected any formal religious affiliation. Probably fewer than a hundred such women existed, but several dozen traveled beyond their local communities, creating converts and controversy. They spoke from the heart, without prepared speeches, often exhibiting trances and claiming to exhort (counsel or warn) rather than to preach. But none of these women were ordained ministers, with official credentials to preach or perform baptisms.

Perhaps the most well-known exhorting woman was Jemima Wilkinson, who called herself the "Publick Universal Friend." After a near-death experience from high fever in 1776, Wilkinson proclaimed her body no longer female *or* male, but the incarnation of the "Spirit of Light." She dressed in men's clothes, wore her hair in a masculine style, shunned gender-specific pronouns, and preached openly in Rhode Island and Philadelphia. In the early nineteenth century, Wilkinson withdrew to a settlement called New Jerusalem in western New York with more than 250 followers.

WOMEN AND THE CHURCH: JEMIMA WILKINSON *Jemima Wilkinson, the "Publick Universal Friend," in an early woodcut, wears a clerical collar and body-obscuring robe, in keeping with the claim that the former Jemima was now a person without sex or gender. Her hair is pulled back tight on her head and curled at the neck in a masculine style of the 1790s.* Rhode Island Historical Society.

The decades from 1790 to the 1820s marked a period of unusual confusion, ferment, and creativity in American religion. New denominations blossomed, new styles of religiosity gripped adherents, and an extensive periodical press devoted to religion popularized all manner of theological and institutional innovations. In such a climate, the age-old tradition of gender subordination came into question here and there among the most radically democratic of the churches. But the presumption of male authority over women was deeply entrenched in American culture. Even denominations that had allowed women to participate in church governance began to pull back, and most churches reinstated patterns of hierarchy along gender lines.

Madison's Successors

With the elections of 1816 and 1820, Virginians continued their long hold on the presidency. In 1816, James Monroe beat Federalist Rufus King of New York by an electoral vote of 183 to 34. When Monroe was reelected in 1820 with all but one electoral vote, the national presence of the Federalists was fully eclipsed. The unanimity of the 1820 election did not reflect voter satisfaction with the status quo, however, for barely one-quarter of eligible voters bothered to vote.

Monroe's two terms were dubbed the "Era of Good Feelings" by a contemporary newspaper. Yet during Monroe's presidency, a major constitutional

A VIEW OF ST. LOUIS FROM AN ILLINOIS TOWN, 1835
Just fifteen years after the Missouri Compromise, St. Louis was already a booming city, having gotten its start in the eighteenth century as a French fur trading village. It was incorporated as a town in 1809 and chartered as a city in 1822. In this 1835 view, commercial buildings and steamships line the riverfront; a ferry on the Illinois shore prepares to transport travelers across the Mississippi River. Black laborers (in the foreground) handle loading tasks. The Illinois side is a free state; Missouri, where their ferry lands, is a slave state.
A View of St. Louis from an Illinois Town, 1835: Private collection.

www.bedfordstmartins.com/roarkcompact SEE THE ONLINE STUDY GUIDE for more help in analyzing this image.

crisis emerged over the admission of Missouri to the Union. Foreign policy questions animated sharp disagreements as well. The election of 1824 brought forth an abundance of candidates, all claiming to be Republicans. A one-party political system was put to the test of practical circumstances; it failed and then fractured.

The Missouri Compromise

In February 1819, Missouri applied for statehood. Since 1815, four other states had joined the Union (Indiana, Mississippi, Illinois, and Alabama). But Missouri posed a problem. Much of its area jutted up into the North, while its territorial population was already one-sixth slave. Missouri's unusual combination of geography and demography led a New York representative in Congress, James Tallmadge Jr., to propose two amendments to the statehood bill. The first stipulated that slaves born in Missouri after statehood would be free at age twenty-five, and the second declared that no new slaves could be imported into the state. Southerners in Congress loudly protested the amendments. Although gradual emancipation protected slave owners from immediate financial loss, in the long run it made Missouri a free state, tipping the national balance of power between free and slave states. Just as southern economic power rested on slave labor, southern political power drew extra strength from slaves, counted at three-fifths for purposes of representation. In 1820, the South had seventeen extra seats in the House of Representatives based on slave population.

Both of Tallmadge's amendments passed in the House, but with a close and sharply sectional vote of North against South (with a few northern Republicans taking the side of the South). The debate was ferocious, leading a Georgia representative to observe that the question had started "a fire which all the waters of the ocean could not extinguish. It can be extinguished only in blood." The Senate, with an even number of slave and free states, voted down the amendments, with some border states joining the proslavery line. Missouri statehood was postponed for the next congressional term.

In 1820, a compromise emerged in the Senate. Maine, once a part of Massachusetts, applied for statehood, which balanced Missouri as a slave state. To quiet northern fears about slavery reaching so far into the North, the Senate agreed that the southern boundary of Missouri, latitude 36° 30′, extended west would become the permanent line dividing slave from free (Map 10.2). The House also approved the compromise, thanks to expert deal brokering by Kentucky's Henry Clay, who earned the nickname the "Great Pacificator" for his superb negotiating skills.

President Monroe and Thomas Jefferson at first worried that the Missouri crisis would reinvigorate the Federalist Party as the party of the North. But even ex-Federalists agreed that the division of free versus slave states was too dangerous a fault line to let shape national politics. When new parties did develop in the 1830s, they took pains to bridge geography, each party developing a presence in both North and South. Monroe and Jefferson also worried about the future of slavery. Each understood slavery to be deeply problematic, but, as Jefferson said, "We have the wolf by the ears, and we can neither hold him, nor safely let him go. Justice is in one scale, and self-preservation in the other."

The Monroe Doctrine

New foreign policy challenges arose even as Congress struggled with the slavery issue. In 1816, American troops led by General Andrew Jackson invaded Spanish Florida in search of Seminole Indians harboring escaped slaves. Once there, Jackson declared himself the commander of northern Florida, demonstrating his power in 1818 by executing two British men who he claimed were dangerous enemies. In asserting rule over the territory, and surely in executing the two British subjects on Spanish land, Jackson had gone too far. Privately, President Monroe was distressed and pondered court-martialing Jackson, prevented only by Jackson's immense popularity as a war hero. Instead, John Quincy Adams, the secretary of state, negotiated with Spain the Adams-Onís Treaty, which delivered Florida to the United States in 1819. In exchange, the Americans agreed to abandon any claim to Texas or Cuba.

Spain at that moment was preoccupied with its colonies in South America. One after another—Chile, Colombia, Peru, and finally Mexico—declared itself independent in the early 1820s. To discourage Spain from reconquering its colonies, Monroe formulated a declaration of principles on South America, incorporated into his annual mes-

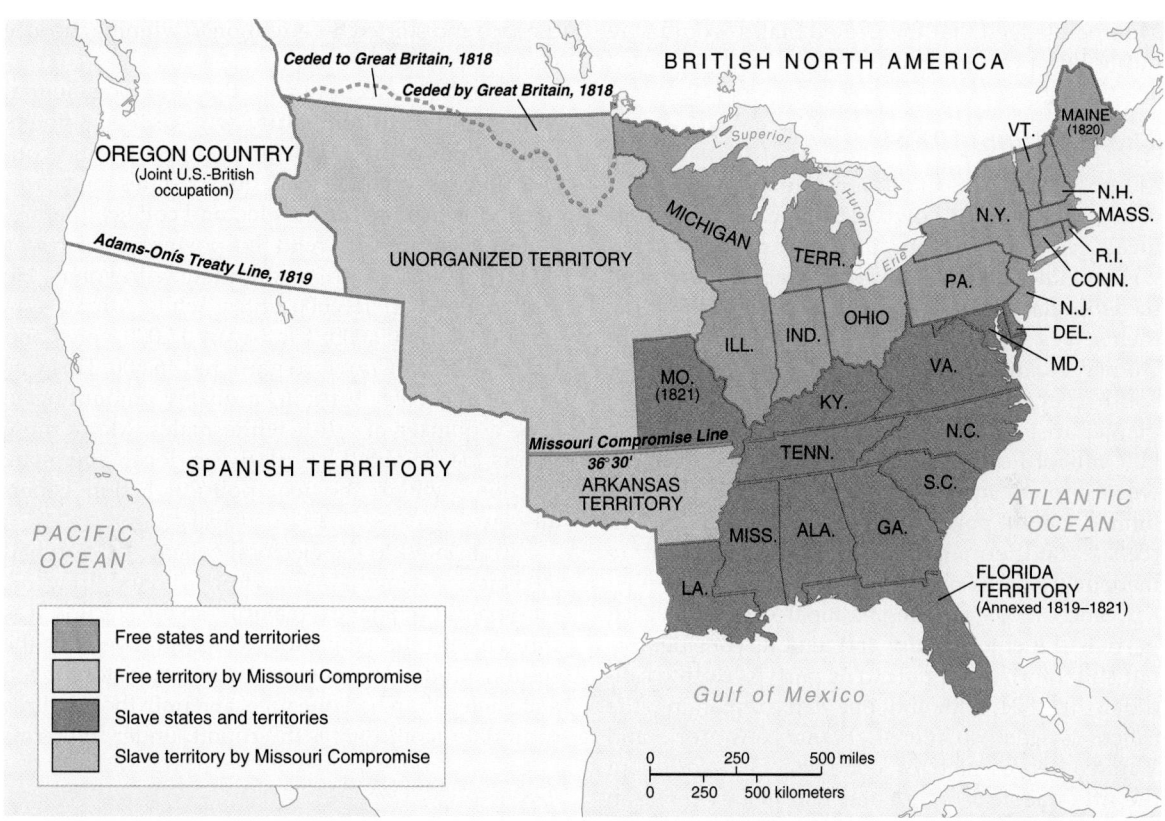

M A P   1 0 . 2
The Missouri Compromise, 1820
After a difficult battle in Congress, Missouri entered the Union in 1821 as part of a pack-age of compromises. Maine was admitted as a free state to balance slavery in Missouri; and a line drawn at latitude 36° 30′ put most of the rest of the Louisiana Territory off limits to slavery in the future.

READING THE MAP: How many free and how many slave states were there prior to the Missouri Compromise? What did the admission of Missouri as a slave state threaten to do?
CONNECTIONS: Who precipitated the crisis over Missouri, what did he propose, and where did the idea come from? Who proposed the Missouri Compromise, and who benefited from it?

www.bedfordstmartins.com/roarkcompact   SEE THE ONLINE STUDY GUIDE for more help in analyzing this map.

sage to Congress in December 1823, known in later years as the Monroe Doctrine. He warned that "the American Continents, by the free and independent condition which they have assumed and maintain, are henceforth not to be considered as subjects for future colonization by any European power." Any attempt to interfere in the Western Hemisphere would be regarded as "the manifestation of an un-friendly disposition towards the United States." In exchange for noninterference by Europeans,

Monroe pledged that the United States would stay out of European struggles.

The Election of 1824

Monroe's nonpartisan administration was the last of its kind, a fitting throwback to eighteenth-century ideals, led by the last president to wear a powdered wig and knee breeches. Monroe's cabinet contained men of sharply different philosophies, all calling themselves Republicans. Secretary of State John Quincy Adams represented the urban Northeast, South Carolinian John C. Calhoun spoke for the planter aristocracy as secretary of war, and William H. Crawford of Georgia, secretary of the treasury, was a proponent of Jeffersonian states' rights and limited federal power. Well before the end of Monroe's second term, these men and others began to maneuver for the presidency.

Since 1800, the congressional caucus of each party had met to identify and lend its considerable but still informal support to its party's leading candidate. In 1824, with only one party remaining, the caucus system splintered. Some New York and Virginia representatives endorsed Crawford, but the fifty-one-year-old planter had just suffered an incapacitating stroke.

Adams felt he had a claim on the office; since 1800, every president had once been secretary of state. Henry Clay, Speaker of the House, also was a declared candidate. A man of vast congressional experience, he had engaged in high-level diplomacy, having accompanied Adams to Ghent to negotiate the 1814 peace treaty with Britain. The Kentuckian put forth a set of policies he called the American System, a package of protective tariffs to promote manufacturing and federal expenditures for extensive internal improvements, many of them roads and canals in the western states. Calhoun, a lawyer as well as planter, was another serious contender, having served in Congress and in several cabinets. Like Clay, he favored internal improvements and protective tariffs, which he figured would gain him support in northern states.

The final candidate was an outsider: General Andrew Jackson of Tennessee. Jackson had much less national political experience than the others, having served one year in the House and two in the Senate. His fame rested mainly on his reputation as a military leader, but that was sufficient to gain him a huge following, much to the surprise of the experienced politicians. Calhoun soon dropped out of

the race and shifted his attention to winning the vice presidency.

The 1824 election was the first presidential contest in which popularity with ordinary voters could be measured. Recent changes in state constitutions gave voters in all but six states the power to choose electors for the electoral college. (Before, state legislatures had held this power.) Jackson was by far the most popular candidate with voters. He won more than 153,000 votes, while Adams was second with 109,000; Clay won 47,000 votes and the debilitated Crawford garnered 46,600. This was not a large voter turnout, probably amounting to only a quarter of adult white males. Many more voters participated regularly in local and state elections, where the real political action generally lay.

Translated to the electoral college, Jackson had 99 votes, Adams 84, Crawford 41, and Clay 37. Jackson did not have a majority, so the election was thrown into the House of Representatives, for the second (and last) time in American history. Each state delegation had one vote, and only the top three candidates could enter the runoff, under the terms

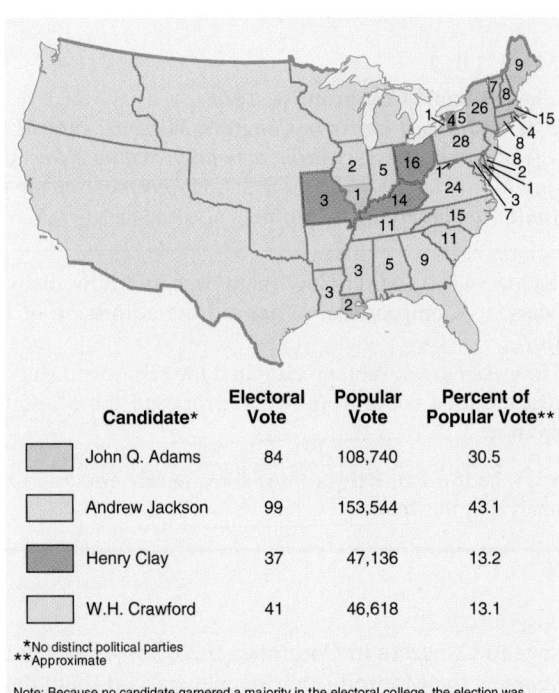

Candidate*	Electoral Vote	Popular Vote	Percent of Popular Vote**
John Q. Adams	84	108,740	30.5
Andrew Jackson	99	153,544	43.1
Henry Clay	37	47,136	13.2
W.H. Crawford	41	46,618	13.1

*No distinct political parties
**Approximate

Note: Because no candidate garnered a majority in the electoral college, the election was decided in the House of Representatives. Although Clay was eliminated from the running, as Speaker of the House he influenced the final decision in favor of Adams.

MAP 10.3

The Election of 1824

of the Twelfth Amendment to the Constitution, passed in 1804. Thus Henry Clay was out of the race and in a position now to throw his support to another candidate.

The election of 1824 came to be characterized as the "corrupt bargain" in the eyes of Jackson's supporters. Clay backed Adams, and Adams won by one vote in the House (Map 10.3). Clay's support made sense on several levels. Despite mutual dislike, he and Adams agreed on issues such as internal improvements, and Clay was uneasy with Jackson's volatile temperament and unstated political views and with Crawford's diminished capacity.

What made Clay's decision look unseemly was that immediately after the election, Adams offered to appoint Clay secretary of state—and Clay accepted. In the weeks before the vote in the House, rumors of such a deal were denied by Adams and Clay supporters, confident that two such archenemies could never cooperate. There probably was no actual bargain; Adams's subsequent cabinet appointments demonstrated his lack of political astuteness. But Andrew Jackson felt that the election had been stolen from him and wrote bitterly that "the Judas of the West has closed the contract and will receive the thirty pieces of silver."

The Adams Administration

John Quincy Adams, like his father, was a one-term president. His career had been built on diplomacy, not electoral politics, and his political horse sense was not well developed. His cabinet choices welcomed his opposition into his inner circle. He asked Crawford to stay on in the Treasury, and he retained an openly pro-Jackson postmaster general, even though that position controlled thousands of nationwide patronage appointments. Most amazingly, he asked Jackson to become secretary of war. With Calhoun as vice president (elected without opposition by the electoral college) and Clay at State, the whole argumentative crew would be thrust into the executive branch. Crawford and Jackson had the good sense to decline appointments.

Adams had lofty ideas for federal action during his presidency, and the plan he put before Congress was so sweeping that it took Henry Clay aback. Adams called for federally built roads, canals, and harbors. He proposed a national university in Washington as well as government-sponsored scientific research. He wanted to build observatories to advance astronomical knowledge

ELI TERRY'S PILLAR AND SCROLL CLOCK
Before the 1790s, sundials and church bells answered most timekeeping needs; clocks were objects of art, not utility. Connecticut clockmaker Eli Terry realized that affordable clocks might change all that. First he switched from brass to wood for the clock's internal movement, and then he designed machinery to mass-produce the parts, achieving the first successful system of "interchangeable parts" and turning out thousands of clocks a year. In 1814, Terry developed this inexpensive compact clock and sold tens of thousands over the next dozen years. Affordable clocks revolutionized timekeeping, enabling workers to arrive before the factory bell and travelers to make stagecoach and canal boat departure times. Employers could demand punctuality, a moral virtue made possible by the pervasiveness of clocks. For good or ill, clocks did not merely measure time; they helped speed up the pace of life.
American Clock & Watch Museum.

and to promote precision in timekeeping, and he backed a decimal-based system of weights and measures. In all these endeavors, Adams believed he was continuing the Jefferson and Madison legacy, using the powers of government to advance knowledge. But his opponents feared he was too Hamiltonian, using federal power inappropriately to advance commercial interests.

Whether he was more truly Federalist or Republican was a moot point, however. Lacking political skills, Adams was unable to implement much of his program. He scorned the idea of courting voters to gain support and the use of the patronage system to enhance his power. He often made appointments (to posts like customs house collectors) to placate enemies rather than reward friends. A story of a toast offered to the president may well have been mythical, but as humorous folklore it made the rounds during his term and came to summarize Adams's precarious hold on leadership. A dignitary raised a glass and pledged, "May he strike confusion to his foes . . . ," to which another voice scornfully chimed in, "as he has already done to his friends."

Conclusion: Republican Simplicity Becomes Complex

The nineteenth century opened with the Jeffersonian Republicans in power, trying to undo much of what Federalists created in the 1790s. But the Republican promise of a more simple government, limited in size, scope, and power, quickly gave way to the lure of the West. The sudden acquisition of the Louisiana Purchase promised land and opportunity to settlers but also complicated the country's political future with the issues central to the Missouri Compromise. Republican simplicity also gave way in the face of increasing antagonism both from foreign nations and from Indian nations, which Jefferson and his successor Madison met with a combination of embargoes, treaties, and military action. Battles with Indians blended into the major engagement with England, the War of 1812, a war mo-

tivated less by concrete economic or political issues than by questions of honor. Its conclusion at the Battle of New Orleans allowed Americans the illusion they had fought a second war of independence.

If the War of 1812 seemed a second war of independence for the whites, how much more so it was for the Indians, who lost both times. Tecumseh's vision of an unprecedentedly large confederacy of Indian tribes that would halt western expansion by white Americans was cut short by the war and by his death. Without British support, the Indians probably could not have successfully challenged for long the westward dynamic of American settlement. But British support came at a time when Canada was under attack, and the British put their own defense higher than their promises to help the Indians.

The war elevated to national prominence General Andrew Jackson, whose sudden popularity with voters in the 1824 election surprised traditional politicians and threw the one-party rule of Republicans into a tailspin. John Quincy Adams barely occupied his office in 1825 before the election campaign of 1828 was off and running. Appeals to the people—the mass of white male voters—would be the hallmark of all elections after 1824. It was a game Adams could not easily play.

The War of 1812 started another chain of events that would prove momentous in later decades. Jefferson's long embargo and Madison's wartime trade stoppages gave strong encouragement to American manufacturing, momentarily protected from competition with English factories. When peace resumed in 1815, the years of independent development burst forth into a period of sustained economic growth that continued nearly unabated into the mid-nineteenth century.

For further reading about the topics in this chapter, see the Online Bibliography at
www.bedfordstmartins.com/roarkcompact.

For additional first-hand accounts of this period, see pages 148–163 in Michael Johnson, ed., *Reading the American Past,* Second Edition, Volume I.

To assess your mastery of the material in this chapter, see the Online Study Guide at
www.bedfordstmartins.com/roarkcompact.

CHRONOLOGY

1789	Judiciary Act establishes six Supreme Court justices, who preside over six circuit courts.
1800	Thomas Jefferson and Aaron Burr tie in electoral college.
	Gabriel's slave rebellion fails in Virginia.
1801	Judiciary Act reduces Supreme Court justices to five and allows for sixteen circuit courts and circuit court judges.
	Jefferson elected president by House of Representatives.
1803	*Marbury v. Madison* declares part of Judiciary Act of 1789 unconstitutional.
	Embargoes on American shipping by England and France.
	Louisiana Territory purchased from France for $15 million.
1804	Jefferson reelected president.
	Burr-Hamilton duel ends in Hamilton's death.
1804–1806	Lewis and Clark expedition.
1807	**June.** *Chesapeake* attacked and searched by British in Chesapeake Bay.
	December. Embargo Act forbids any American ship from engaging in trade with any foreign port.
1808	James Madison elected president.
1809	Treaty of Fort Wayne with Indians in Indiana Territory.

	Non-Intercourse Act forbids American trade with England, France, and their colonies.
1811	Battle of Tippecanoe won by William Henry Harrison's troops.
1812	**June.** War declared on Great Britain.
	Madison reelected president.
1813	Death of Tecumseh at the Battle of the Thames.
1814	British attack Washington, D.C., burning several buildings.
	Treaty of Ghent ends War of 1812.
	Hartford Convention proposes constitutional amendments.
1815	Battle of New Orleans won by Andrew Jackson's forces.
1816	James Monroe elected president.
1819	Spain cedes Florida to United States in the Adams-Onis Treaty.
1820	Missouri Compromise admits Missouri as slave state and Maine as free state.
	Monroe reelected president.
1823	Monroe Doctrine asserts independence of Western Hemisphere from European intervention.
1824	"Corrupt bargain" election of John Quincy Adams.

SHIP'S FIGUREHEAD OF ANDREW JACKSON
*Carved in 1834 and affixed to the bow of the
revered navy frigate* Constitution, *this figurehead of Andrew Jackson symbolized national
pride by putting "the image of the most popular man of the West upon the favorite ship
of the East," according to the commodore
who commissioned it. But when Jackson
introduced a new, strict banking policy,
his popularity in the urban East quickly
plummeted. In Boston, where the* Constitution *was docked, protesters complained that
the figurehead of a tyrant corrupted their ship.
On the night of July 3, 1834, the eve of the national
holiday, a twenty-seven-year-old mariner and ardent
Whig stole on board and decapitated the figurehead,
sawing it through just below the ears. Jackson
deflected the insult with humor, declaring "I never did like that image!
Give the man a postmaster's job." The commodore, himself alert to symbolic actions,
wrapped the headless statue in a flag and sent it to New York City where woodworkers fashioned a new head in 1835. It was reattached to the ship in another port: Jackson's banking
policies still rankled in urban financial centers, and naval authorities did not want to risk a
second mutilation of the president's image. In 1990, the original head was recovered from a
private collector in France and restored to view in the museum that now owns the figurehead.*
Museum of the City of New York.

THE EXPANDING REPUBLIC

11

1815–1840

PRESIDENT ANDREW JACKSON WAS THE DOMINANT FIGURE of his age, yet his precarious childhood little foretold the fame, fortune, and influence he would enjoy in the years after 1815. Jackson was born in the Carolina backcountry in 1767. His Scots-Irish father had recently died, leaving a poor, struggling mother to support three small boys. During the Revolution, Andrew followed his brothers into the militia, where both died of disease, as did his mother. Orphaned at fourteen, Jackson drifted around, drinking, gambling, and brawling.

But at seventeen, his prospects improved. He studied under a lawyer for three years and then moved to Nashville, a frontier community full of opportunities for a young man of legal training and aggressive temperament. He became a public prosecutor, married into a leading family, and acquired land and slaves. When Tennessee became a state in 1796, Jackson, then twenty-nine, was elected to Congress for a single term.

Jackson captured national attention in 1815 by leading the victory at the Battle of New Orleans. Songs, broadsides, and an admiring biography set him up as the original self-made man, the parentless child magically responsible for his own destiny. Jackson seemed to have created himself, a gritty, forceful personality extracting opportunities from the dynamic, turbulent frontier.

Jackson was more than a man of action, however. He was also strong-willed, reckless, and quick to anger, impulsively challenging men to duels, sometimes on slight pretexts. In one legendary fight in 1806, Jackson deliberately let his opponent, an expert marksman, shoot first. The bullet hit him in a rib, but Jackson masked all sign of injury under a loose cloak and immobile face. He then took careful aim at the astonished man and killed him. Such steely courage chilled his political opponents.

Jackson's image as a tough frontier hero set him apart from the learned and privileged gentlemen from Virginia and Massachusetts who had monopolized the presidency up to 1828. When he lost the 1824 election to John Quincy Adams, an infuriated Jackson vowed to fight a rematch. He won in 1828 and again in 1832, capturing large majorities. His appeal stretched across the urban working classes of the East, frontier voters of the West, and slaveholders in the South, who all saw something of themselves in Jackson.

The confidence and even recklessness of Jackson's personality mirrored the new confidence of American society in the years after 1815. An entrepreneurial spirit gripped the country, producing a market revolution of unprecedented scale. Old social hierarchies eroded; ordinary men dreamed of moving high on the wheel of fortune, just as Jackson had done. Stunning advances in transportation and economic productivity fueled such dreams and propelled thousands to move west or to cities. Urban growth and technological change fostered the diffusion of a distinctive and vibrant public culture, spread through newspapers and the spoken word. The development of rapid print allowed popular opinions to coalesce and intensify; Jackson's sudden nationwide celebrity was a case in point.

Expanded communication transformed politics dramatically. Sharp disagreements over the best way to promote individual liberty, economic opportunity, and national prosperity in the new market economy defined key differences between Jackson and Adams and the parties they gave rise to in the 1830s. The process of party formation brought new habits of political participation and party loyalty to many thousands more adult white males. Religion became democratized as well: A nationwide evangelical revival brought its adherents the confidence that salvation and perfection were now available to all.

As president from 1828 to 1836, Jackson presided over all these changes, fighting some and supporting others in his vigorous and volatile way. As with his own stubborn personality, there was a dark underside to the confidence and expansiveness of American society. Steamboats blew up, banks and businesses periodically collapsed, alcoholism rates soared, Indians were killed or relocated farther west, and slavery continued to expand. The brash confidence that turned some people into rugged, self-promoting, Jackson-like individuals inspired others to think about the human costs of rapid economic expansion and thus about reforming society in dramatic ways. The common denominator was a faith that people and societies can shape their own destinies.

The Market Revolution

The return of peace in 1815 unleashed powerful forces that revolutionized the organization of the economy. Spectacular changes in transportation facilitated the movement of commodities, information, and people, while textile mills and other factories created many new jobs, especially for young unmarried women. Innovations in banking, legal practices, and tariff policies promoted swift economic growth.

This was not yet an industrial revolution, but a market revolution, fueled by traditional sources— water, wood, beasts of burden, and human muscle. What was new was the accelerated pace of economic activity and the scale of distribution of goods. Men and women were drawn out of old patterns of rural self-sufficiency into the wider realm of national market relations. At the same time, the nation's money supply enlarged considerably, leading to speculative investments in commerce, manufacturing, transportation, and land. The new nature and scale of production and consumption changed Americans' behavior, attitudes, and expectations.

Improvements in Transportation

Before 1815, transportation in the United States was slow and expensive; it cost as much to ship freight over thirty miles of domestic roads as it did to send the same cargo across the Atlantic Ocean. The fastest stagecoach trip from Boston to New York took an uncomfortable four days. But between 1815 and 1840, networks of roads, canals, steamboats, and finally railroads dramatically raised the speed and lowered the cost of travel (Map 11.1). Andrew Jackson spent weeks walking and riding west to Nashville in the 1790s along old Indian trails, but when he returned east in 1829, the new president traveled by steamboat and turnpike to Washington, D.C., in a matter of days.

Improved transportation moved goods and products into much wider markets. It moved people too, broadening the horizons of passengers on business and pleasure trips and providing means for youth to take up new employment in cities or factory towns. Transportation also facilitated the flow of political (and other) information, through a heavy traffic in newspapers, periodicals, and books.

Enhanced public transport was expensive and produced uneven economic benefits, so administrations from Jefferson to Monroe were reluctant to fund it with federal dollars. President John Quincy Adams adopted the pro-development view of Henry Clay's American System, pledging federal support for roads and canals, but Congress would not go along. Instead, private investors pooled resources and chartered stagecoach, canal, steamboat, and railroad companies, with significant aid from state governments in the form of subsidies and guarantees of monopoly rights. Turnpike and roadway mileage dramatically increased after 1815, reducing the cost of land shipment of goods. Stagecoach lines proliferated in an extensive network of passenger corridors dense in the populated East

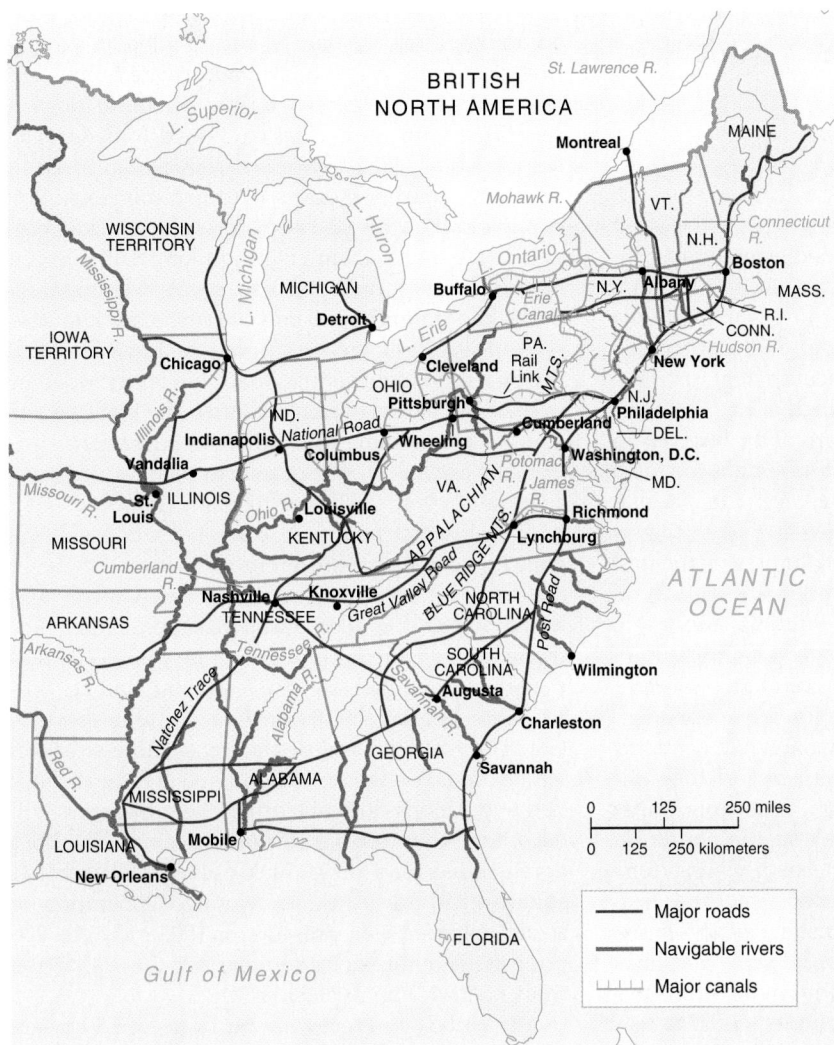

MAP 11.1

Routes of Transportation in 1840

The National Road, connecting Baltimore with the interior of Ohio, was the only federally sponsored roadway. Approved during Jefferson's presidency, it reached Ohio only in the 1830s. Its funding came from the sale of public lands in Ohio, the area that stood to benefit. Other roads and canals were the work of private companies operating under government charters. By 1840, transportation advances had cut travel times significantly. Goods and people could move from New York City to Buffalo, New York, in four days via the Erie Canal, a trip that took two weeks by road in 1800. A trip from New York to New Orleans that took four weeks in 1800 could now be accomplished in less than half that time on steamboats on the western rivers.

and fanning out to the Mississippi River. Travel time on main routes was cut in half; Boston to New York now took two days.

Water travel was similarly transformed. In 1807, Robert Fulton's steam-propelled boat, the *Clermont*, churned up the Hudson River from New York City to Albany, touching off a steamboat craze. In 1820, a dozen boats left New York City daily, and scores more operated on midwestern rivers and the Great Lakes. A voyager on one of the first steamboats to go down the Mississippi reported that the Chickasaw Indians called the vessel a "fire canoe" and considered it "an omen of evil." By the early 1830s, more than seven hundred steamboats were in operation on the Ohio and Mississippi Rivers. A

journey upriver from New Orleans to Louisville, Kentucky, took only one week. Such speed came with costs, however, of boiler explosions and terrible fatalities. (See "The Promise of Technology," page 238.)

Canals were another major innovation of the transportation revolution. These shallow highways of water provided passage for barges and boats, pulled by horses or mules along a towpath beside the canal. Travel speed was slow, under five miles per hour, but the economy came from increased loads: The low-friction water allowed one horse to pull a fifty-ton barge.

Pennsylvania in 1815 and New York in 1817 commenced major state-sponsored canal enterprises.

Early Steamboats

STEAMBOATS REVOLUTIONIZED TRAVEL in the early nineteenth century. The basic technology consisted of an engine, powered by the steam from a boiler heated by a wood-burning furnace. The steam first collected in a cylinder and then cooled and condensed to create a vacuum that drove a piston, which in turn propelled a paddlewheel mounted at the side or in the stern of the boat. From the 1780s to 1807, several inventors sought the ideal combination of engine size, boat size, and paddlewheel type. Robert Fulton's *Clermont* of 1807 was not the first American steamboat, but it was the first long-distance, commercially successful endeavor.

Two advantages marked Fulton's effort: He imported a superior British-made engine, a low-pressure model built with many precision parts, and he formed a partnership with New York businessman Robert R. Livingston. Livingston had acquired from the New York state legislature in 1798 the right to a twenty-year monopoly on all steam transportation on the Hudson River, on the condition that he produce a boat capable of traveling four miles per hour upriver. The *Clermont* met that test.

In 1811, Fulton and Livingston launched the first steamboat on the Mississippi River. Their low-pressure engine, operating at about two pounds per square inch of pressure in the cylinder, failed to maneuver against the river's shifting currents and many obstructions. A high-pressure steam engine developed by Delaware entrepreneur Oliver Evans proved far more suitable. Generating pressures from eighty to one hundred pounds per square inch, it required 30 percent more fuel, but wood was plentiful along western waterways. By the 1830s, there were many hundreds of boats on the Mississippi, the Ohio, and the lower Missouri Rivers, run by companies all competing to reduce travel time. An upriver trip from New Orleans to Louisville that took nearly a month in the 1810s took less than a week in the 1830s. The American traveling public fell in love with steamboats for their speed and power.

Steamboats offered luxury as well as speed. Boats often were floating palaces, providing swank accommodations to ladies and gentlemen paying first-class fares. A few boats had private cabins, but most often there were two large rooms, one for each sex, filled with chairs that converted to beds. (The separation of sexes answered an important need in addition to bodily modesty: Women travelers often expressed their disgust over the spit-drenched carpets in the men's cabin.) Dining rooms with elegant appointments served elaborate meals. Many steamboats had gambling rooms as well. Low-fare passengers, typically men, occupied the lower decks of the boats, taking sleeping space out in the open or in crowded berths in public rooms. The largest boats could accommodate four hundred passengers.

The fire and smoke of a steamboat proved awesome and even terrifying to many. An older gent making his first trip in 1836 wrote that "I went on board, and passing the fireroom, where they were just firing up, I stopped, with unfeigned horror, and asked myself if, indeed, I was prepared to die!" But many others were enthralled by the unprecedented power represented by the belching smoke. Impromptu boat racing became a popular sport. A German traveler identified a competitive streak in American passengers: "When two steamboats happen to get alongside each other, the passengers will encourage the captains to run a race. . . . The boilers intended for a pressure of only 100 pounds per square inch, are by the accelerated generation of steam, exposed to a pressure of 150, and even 200 pounds, and this goes sometimes so far, that the trials end with an explosion."

Steamboats in fact were far from safe. Between 1811 and 1851, accidents destroyed nearly a thousand boats, a third of all steam vessels built in that period. More than half the sinkings resulted from underwater debris which penetrated hulls. Fires, too, were fearsome hazards in wooden boats that commonly carried highly combustible cargoes, such as raw cotton in burlap bags. The development of sheet metal, which strengthened hulls and protected wooden surfaces near the smokestacks from sparks, was a major safety advance.

Boiler explosions were the most horrifying cause of accidents. By far the greatest loss of life came from scalding steam, flying wreckage, and the fire that would engulf a boat in a matter of minutes. In the 1830s alone, eighty-nine boiler explosions caused 861 deaths and many more injuries. The cause of explosion was often mysterious: Was it

THE *LEXINGTON* EXPLODES IN FLAMES ON LONG ISLAND SOUND, 1840
The **Lexington** *was six years old in 1840 and equipped with many extra safety features, such as a fire engine and pump. Three lifeboats contained enough room for only half the passengers; they were quickly swamped in the emergency and rendered useless. Only four people survived; many froze to death in the cold waters. Consider this lithograph as an object made for sale: Who would buy this kind of artistic production?*
Library of Congress.

excessive steam pressure or weak metal? Exactly how much pressure could plate iron fastened with rivets really withstand? Did a dangerous or explosive gas develop in the boiler when the water level fell too low? Or was it principally human error—reckless or drunk pilots (none of them licensed) or captains bent on breaking speed records?

And who was responsible for public safety? When the three-week-old *Moselle* blew up near Cincinnati in 1838, with the loss of 150 lives, a citizen's committee fixed blame on the twenty-eight-year-old captain, who had ordered the fires stoked with pitch and the safety valves shut to build up a bigger head of steam. "Such disasters have their foundation in the present mammoth evil of our country, an inordinate love of gain," said the committee. "We are not satisfied with getting rich, but we must get rich in a day. We are not satisfied with

traveling at a speed of ten miles an hour, but we must fly. Such is the effect of competition that everything must be done cheap; boiler iron must be cheap, traveling must be done cheap, freight must be cheap, yet everything must be speedy. A steamboat must establish a reputation of a few minutes 'swifter' in a hundred miles than others, before she can make fortunes fast enough to satisfy the owners."

In 1830, the federal government awarded a grant to the Franklin Institute of Philadelphia to study the causes of boiler explosions, but it was not until 1852 that public safety became a federal responsibility with passage of regulations by the U.S. Congress mandating steamboat inspections. After the Civil War, affordable sheet steel and the development of new welding techniques produced boilers that were much stronger and safer.

Pennsylvania's Schuylkill Canal stretched 108 miles west into the state when it was completed in 1826. It was overshadowed by the impressive Erie Canal in New York, finished in 1825, stretching 350 miles between Albany on the Hudson River and Buffalo on Lake Erie. The canal was a waterbridge linking the port of New York City with the entire Northwest Territory. Wheat and flour moved east, textiles and other goods moved west, and passengers went in both directions. By the 1830s, the cost of shipping by canal fell to less than a tenth of the cost of overland transport, and New York City quickly blossomed into the premier commercial city in the United States.

In the 1830s, private railroad companies began to give canals stiff competition, and by the mid-1840s the canal-building era was over. (However, use of the canals for freight continued well into the twentieth century.) The nation's first railroad, the Baltimore and Ohio, laid thirteen miles of track in 1829. During the 1830s, three thousand more miles of track materialized nationwide, the result of a speculative fever in railroad construction masterminded by bankers, locomotive manufacturers, and state legislators, who provided subsidies, charters, and land rights-of-way. Rail lines in the 1830s were generally short, on the order of twenty to one hundred miles; they were not yet an efficient distribution system for goods. But passengers flocked to experience the marvelous travel speeds of fifteen to twenty miles per hour, enduring the frightful noise and cascades of cinders that rained on them.

Factories, Workingwomen, and Wage Labor

Transportation advances promoted a rapid expansion of manufacturing after 1815. Teamsters and bargemen hauled consumer products like shoes, textiles, clocks, and books into nationwide distribution. Some of the gain in manufacturing, especially in the textile industry, came from the development of water-driven machinery, built near fast-coursing rivers. (The steam power harnessed for steamboats and railroads had limited application in industry until the 1840s.) But much of the new manufacturing involved only a reorganization of production, still using the power and skill of human hands. Both mechanized and manual manufacturing pulled young women into the labor market for the first time.

The earliest factory, built by British immigrant Samuel Slater in Pawtucket, Rhode Island, in the 1790s, featured a mechanical spinning machine that produced thread and yarn. By 1815, nearly 170 spinning mills dotted lower New England. Unlike English manufacturing cities, where entire families worked in low-wage, health-threatening factories, American factories targeted young women as employees, cheap to hire because of their limited employment options. Mill girls would retire to marriage, replaced by fresh recruits earning a beginner's wage.

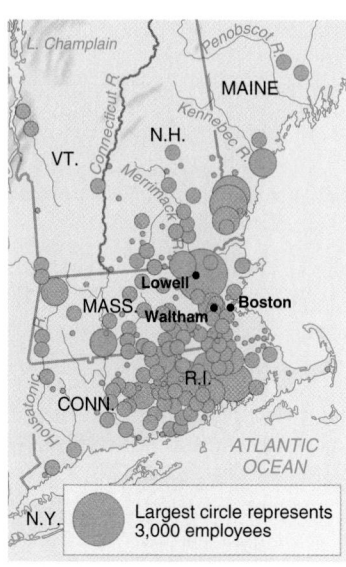

Cotton Textile Industry, 1839

In the 1820s, a group of Boston entrepreneurs founded the town of Lowell, on the Merrimack River, where all aspects of cloth production—carding, fulling, spinning, weaving, and dyeing—were centralized. By 1830, the eight mills in Lowell employed more than six thousand young women. A key innovation was the close moral supervision of the female workers, who lived in company-owned boardinghouses with housemothers, with four to six girls per bedroom. Typical mill workers were age sixteen to twenty-three; their pay averaged two to three dollars for a seventy-hour workweek, more than what a seamstress or domestic servant could earn but less than a young man's wages. The job consisted of tending noisy power looms in large rooms kept hot and humid, ideal for thread, but not for people.

Despite the discomforts, young women flocked to textile jobs. Animated by the same energy that moved Andrew Jackson westward—the faith that people can shape their own destinies—the mill workers left rural farms for factory towns in the hope of gaining more autonomy. They welcomed the unprecedented if still limited personal freedom of living in an all-female social space, away from parents and domestic tasks, and with pay in their pockets. In Lowell, the women could engage in evening self-improvement activities, like attending

MILL WORKER TENDING A POWER LOOM, 1850
This daguerreotype—the earliest form of photograph (see page 325)—shows a young woman weaver tending a power loom in a textile mill. Her main task was to replace the shuttle bobbin, a wooden cradle that held spooled yarn, when it was empty. She also had to be constantly alert for sudden breaks in the warp yarn, which then required a quick repair. In the 1830s, women weavers generally tended two machines at a time; in the 1840s, some companies increased the workload to four.
American Textile History Museum.

lectures, or writing for the company's newspaper, *The Lowell Offering.*

In the mid-1830s, worldwide changes in the cotton market impelled mill owners to speed up work and lower wages. The workers protested, emboldened by their communal living arrangements and by their relative independence from the job as temporary employees. In 1834 and again in 1836, hundreds of women at Lowell went out on strike. All over New England, female millworkers led strikes and formed unions. Women at a mill in Dover, New Hampshire, in 1834 denounced their owners for trying to turn them into "slaves": "However freely the epithet of 'factory slaves' may be bestowed upon us, we will never deserve it by a base and cringing submission to proud wealth or haughty insolence." Their assertiveness surprised many; but ultimately their easy replaceability undermined their bargaining power, and owners in the 1840s began to shift to immigrant families as their labor source.

Other manufacturing enterprises of the 1820s and 1830s, such as shoemaking, employed women in ever larger numbers. New modes of organizing the work allowed the manufacturers to step up production, control wastage and quality, and lower wages by subdividing the tasks and by hiring women, including wives. Male workers cut leather and made soles, while the stitching of the upper part of the shoe, called shoebinding, became women's work, performed at home so that it could mesh with domestic chores. Shoebinder wives could now contribute to family income, although their wages were much smaller than men's.

In the economically turbulent 1830s, the new shoe entrepreneurs cut shoebinder wages. Unlike the mill workers, women shoebinders worked in isolation, a serious hindrance to organized protest. In Lynn, Massachusetts, a major shoemaking center, women turned to other female networks, mainly churches, as sites for meetings and to religious newspapers as forums for communication. The Lynn shoebinders who demanded higher wages in 1834 built on a collective sense of themselves as women even though they did not share daily work lives. "Equal rights should be extended to all—to the weaker sex as well as the stronger," they wrote in a document forming the Female Society of Lynn. In the end, the Lynn shoebinders' protests failed to achieve wage increases. Isolated workers all over New England continued to accept low wages, and even in Lynn, many women shied away from organized protest, preferring to situate their work in the context of family duty (helping their menfolk to finish shoes) instead of market relations.

Bankers and Lawyers

Entrepreneurs like the Lowell factory owners relied on innovations in the banking system to finance their ventures. The number of state-chartered banks in the country more than doubled in the boom years 1814–1816, from fewer than 90 to 208; by 1830, there were 330, and hundreds more by 1840. Banks stimulated the economy both by making loans to merchants and manufacturers and by enlarging the money supply. Borrowers were issued loans in the form of banknotes, certificates unique to each bank. The borrowers then used the notes exactly like money, for all transactions. Neither federal nor state governments issued paper money, so banknotes became the currency of the country.

In theory, a note could always be traded in at the bank for its equivalent in gold or silver (in a transaction known as "specie payment"). A note from a solid local bank might be worth exactly what it was written for, but if the note came from a distant or questionable bank, its value would be discounted by a fraction. The money market of Jacksonian America definitely required knowledge and caution. Not surprisingly, counterfeiting flourished under these conditions.

Bankers exercised great power over the economy in deciding who would get loans and what the discount rates would be. The most powerful bankers sat on the board of directors for the second Bank of the United States, headquartered in Philadelphia. (The first Bank of the United States, chartered in 1791, had lapsed in 1811.) The second bank opened for business in 1816 under a twenty-year charter with eighteen branches throughout the country. The rechartering of this second bank would prove to be a major issue in Andrew Jackson's reelection campaign in 1832.

Accompanying the market revolution was a revolution in commercial law. In the decades after 1815, lawyers fashioned a legal system that advanced the interests of commercial activity and enhanced the prospects of private investment. Of particular significance was the changing practice of legal incorporation, the chartering of businesses by states. Earlier, charters were generally limited to businesses formed to serve the public good,

OFFICE SAFE
Financial records, ledgers, banknotes, and stock certificates required safekeeping in the stepped-up commercial world of the 1830s. This small office safe opened by key.
Eric Long/Smithsonian Institution.

such as to build a bridge. Under new state laws from 1811 on, corporations could be formed for any reasonable purpose; a key value of incorporation was legal protection for individual investors. In 1800, there were perhaps twenty corporations in the United States; by 1817, there were eighteen hundred.

Rising numbers of young men obtained legal training in the years after the War of 1812. By 1820, most representatives in the U.S. Congress were lawyers, and a similar wave of legal professionals moved into state politics. They rewrote commercial laws to promote the entreprenuerial marketplace, for example by defining employee strikes as illegal conspiracies. They wrote the laws of eminent domain, empowering states to buy land for roads and canals, even from unwilling sellers. They drafted legislation on contributory negligence, relieving employers from responsibility for workplace injuries. In such ways, entrepreneurial lawyers of the 1820s and 1830s created the legal foundation for an economy that gave priority to ambitious individuals interested in maximizing their own wealth.

Not everyone applauded these developments. Andrew Jackson, himself a skillful lawyer-turned-politician, spoke for a large and mistrustful segment of the population when he warned about the abuses of power "which the moneyed interest derives from a paper currency which they are able to control, from the multitude of corporations with exclusive privileges which they have succeeded in obtaining in the different states, and which are employed altogether for their benefit." Jacksonians believed that ending government-granted privileges was the way to maximize individual liberty and economic opportunity.

Booms and Busts

One aspect of the economy that the lawyer-politicians could not control was the threat of financial collapse. The boom years from 1815 to 1818 exhibited a volatility that resulted in the first sharp, large-scale economic downturn in U.S. history, a depression that Americans called a "panic"; the pattern was repeated in the 1830s. Rapidly rising consumer demand stimulated rising prices for goods, and speculative investment opportunities with high payoffs abounded—in bank stocks, western land sales, urban real estate, and commodities markets. Steep inflation made some people wealthy but created hardships for workers on fixed incomes.

When the bubble first burst in 1819, the overnight rich suddenly became the overnight poor. Some suspected that a precipitating cause of the panic of 1819 was the second Bank of the United States. For too long, the bank had neglected to exercise control over state banks, many of which had suspended specie payments—the exchange of gold or silver for banknotes—in their eagerness to make loans and expand the economic bubble. Then, in mid-1818, the Bank of the United States started to call in its loans and insisted that state banks do likewise. The contraction of the money supply created tremors throughout the economy, a foretaste of the catastrophe to come.

What made the crunch worse was a parallel financial crisis in Europe in the spring of 1819. Overseas prices of cotton, tobacco, and wheat plummeted by more than 50 percent. Now when the Bank

of the United States and state banks tried to call in their outstanding loans, debtors involved in the commodities trade could not pay. The number of business and personal bankruptcies skyrocketed. The intricate web of credit and debt relationships meant that almost everyone with even a toe in the new commercial economy was affected by the panic of 1819. Thousands of Americans lost their savings and property and unemployment estimates suggest that a half million people lost their jobs.

Recovery from the panic of 1819 took several years. Unemployment rates fell, but bitterness lingered, ready to be mobilized by politicians in the decades to come. The dangers of a system dependent on extensive credit were now clear: In one memorable, folksy formulation that circulated around 1820, a farmer was said to compare credit to "a man pissing in his breeches on a cold day to keep his arse warm—very comfortable at first but I dare say . . . you know how it feels afterwards."

By the mid-1820s, the booming economy was back on track, driven by increases in productivity and consumer demand for goods, an accelerating international trade, and a restless and calculating people moving goods, human labor, and investment capital in expanding circles of commerce. But an undercurrent of anxiety about rapid economic change continued to shape the political views of many Americans.

The Spread of Democracy

Just as the market revolution held out the promise, if not the reality, of economic opportunity for anyone who worked hard, the political transformation of the 1830s held out the promise of political opportunity for hundreds of thousands of new voters. Between 1828 and 1836, the years of Andrew Jackson's presidency, the second American party system took shape, although not until 1836 would the parties have distinct names and consistent programs that transcended the particular personalities running for office. Over those years, more men could and did vote, responding to new methods of arousing voter interest. In 1828, Jackson's charismatic personality defined his party. By 1836, both parties had institutionalized one of his most successful themes: that politicians had to appear to have the common touch in an era when popularity with voters drove the electoral process.

Popular Politics and Partisan Identity

The election of 1828 was the first presidential contest in which popular votes determined the outcome; in twenty-two out of twenty-four states, voters—and not state legislatures—now designated electors committed to a particular candidate. More than a million voters participated, three times the number in 1824 and nearly half the electorate, reflecting the high stakes voters perceived in the Adams-Jackson rematch. Throughout the 1830s, the number of voters rose to all-time highs. This increase resulted partly from relaxed voting restrictions; by the mid-1830s, all but three states allowed universal white male suffrage, without property qualifications. But the higher turnout also indicated increased political interest.

The 1828 election inaugurated new campaign styles as well. State-level candidates routinely gave speeches to woo the voters, appearing at rallies, picnics, and banquets. Adams and Jackson still declined such activities as too undignified; but Henry Clay of Kentucky, campaigning for Adams, earned the nickname the "Barbecue Orator." Campaign rhetoric, under the necessity to create popular appeal, became more informal and even blunt. The Jackson camp established many Hickory Clubs, trading on Jackson's popular nickname, "Old Hickory," from a common Tennessee tree suggesting resilience and toughness. (Jackson was the first presidential candidate to have an affectionate and widely used nickname.)

Partisan newspapers defined issues and publicized political personalities as never before. Party leaders judiciously dispensed subsidies and other favors to secure the loyalties of papers, even in remote towns and villages. In New York State, where party development was most advanced, a pro-Jackson group called the Bucktails controlled fifty weekly publications. Stories from the leading Jacksonian paper in Washington, D.C., would be reprinted two days later in a Boston or Cincinnati paper, as fast as the mail stage could carry them. Presidential campaigns were now coordinated in a national arena.

Parties declined to adopt official names in 1828, still honoring the fiction of Republican Party unity. Instead, they called themselves the Jackson party or the Adams party. By the 1832 election, labels began to appear; Adams's political heir, Henry Clay, rep-

resented the National Republicans, while Jackson's supporters called themselves Democratic Republicans. Both parties were still claiming the mantle of the Jefferson-to-Monroe heritage by keeping "Republican" in the name, but the National Republicans favored federal action to promote commercial development, while the Democratic Republicans promised to be responsive to the will of the majority. By 1834, a few state-level National Republicans shortened their name to the Whig Party, a term that was in common use by 1836, the same year that Jackson's party became simply the Democrats. Thus, Whig and Democrat crystallized as names only at the end of an eight-year evolution.

The Election of 1828 and the Character Issue

The campaign of 1828 was modern in more ways than just the drawn-out electioneering and the importance of popular votes. It was also the first national election in which scandal and character questions reigned supreme.

John Quincy Adams was vilified by his opponents as an elitist, bookish academic, perhaps even a monarchist. Critics pointed to Adams's White House billiard table and ivory chess set as symbols of his aristocratic degeneracy along with the "corrupt bargain" of 1824, the alleged election deal between Adams and Henry Clay. The Adams men returned fire with fire. They played on Jackson's fatherless childhood to portray him as the bastard son of a prostitute. Worse, the cloudy circumstances around his marriage to Rachel Donelson Robards in 1791 gave rise to the story that Jackson was a seducer and an adulterer, having married a woman whose divorce from her first husband was not entirely legal. Pro-Adams newspapers howled that Jackson was sinful and impulsive, while Adams was portrayed as pious, learned, and virtuous.

Editors in favor of Adams played up Jackson's notorious violent temper, evidenced by the many duels, brawls, and canings they could recount. Jackson men used the same stories to project the old man as a tough frontier hero who knew how to command obedience. As for learning, Jackson's rough frontier education gave him a "natural sense," wrote a Boston editor, which "can never be acquired by reading books—it can only be acquired, in perfection, by reading men."

These stories were not smoke screens to obscure the "real" issues in the election. They became real issues themselves because voters used them to comprehend the kind of public officer each man would make. Character issues conveyed in shorthand larger questions about morality, honor, and discipline; Jackson and Adams presented two radically different styles of masculinity.

Throughout the campaign, Jackson was vague on issues; he was famous for his support of a "judicious tariff," a position that could be endorsed by proponents of both higher and lower taxes on imports. His supporters were thus a diverse group who could be sure only that Jackson favored western expansion and more limited federal powers than Adams. As the incumbent, Adams stood by his record, mainly his promise to promote commerce through federal action, which brought him strength in New England and parts of New York.

Jackson won a sweeping victory, with 56 percent of the popular vote and 178 electoral votes, compared with Adams's 83 (Map 11.2). The victor took most of the South and West and carried Pennsylvania and New York as well. Jackson's vice president was John C. Calhoun, who had just served as vice president under Adams but had broken with Adams's policies.

After 1828, national politicians no longer deplored the existence of political parties. They were coming to see that parties mobilized and delivered voters, sharpened candidates' differences, and created party loyalty that surpassed loyalty to individual candidates and elections. Adams and Jackson clearly symbolized and defined for voters the competing ideas of the emerging parties: a moralistic, top-down party ready to make major decisions to promote economic growth competing against a contentious, energetic party ready to embrace liberty-loving individualism.

Jackson's Democratic Agenda

Before the inauguration in March 1829, Rachel Jackson died. The president, certain that the ugly campaign had hastened her death, went into deep mourning. His depression was worsened by constant pain from the 1806 bullet still lodged in his chest and by mercury poisoning from the medicines he took. Sixty-two years old, he carried only 140 pounds on his six-foot-one frame. His adversaries doubted he would make it to a second term. His supporters, however, went wild at the inauguration. Thousands cheered his ten-minute inaugural address, the shortest in history. An open reception at the White House turned into a near-riot as well-wishers jammed the premises, used windows as doors, stood on furniture for a better view of the great man, and broke thousands of dollars' worth of china and glasses.

During his presidency, Jackson continued to offer unprecedented hospitality to the public. Twenty spittoons newly installed in the East Room of the White House accommodated the spit of the throngs that arrived daily to see the president. Some were visitors and others were jobseekers. The courteous Jackson, committed to his image as the president of the "common man," held audience with unannounced visitors throughout his two terms.

Jackson's cabinet appointments marked a departure. Whereas past presidents had tried to lessen party conflict by including men of different factions in their cabinets, Jackson would have only Jackson loyalists, a political tactic followed by most later presidents. The most important position, secretary of state, he offered to Martin Van Buren, one of the shrewdest politicians of the day and newly elected governor of New York.

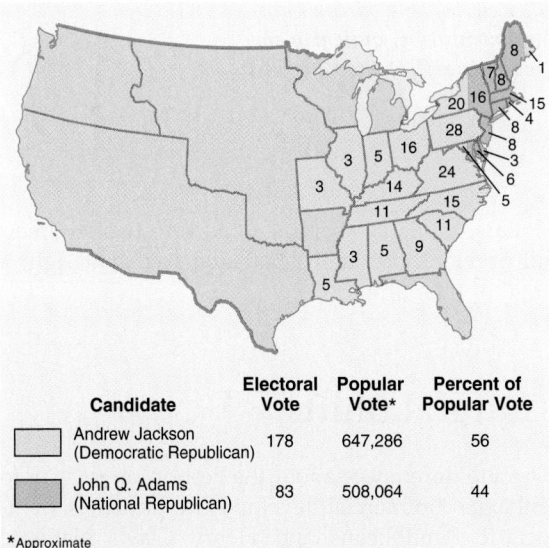

Candidate	Electoral Vote	Popular Vote*	Percent of Popular Vote
Andrew Jackson (Democratic Republican)	178	647,286	56
John Q. Adams (National Republican)	83	508,064	44

*Approximate

MAP 11.2
The Election of 1828

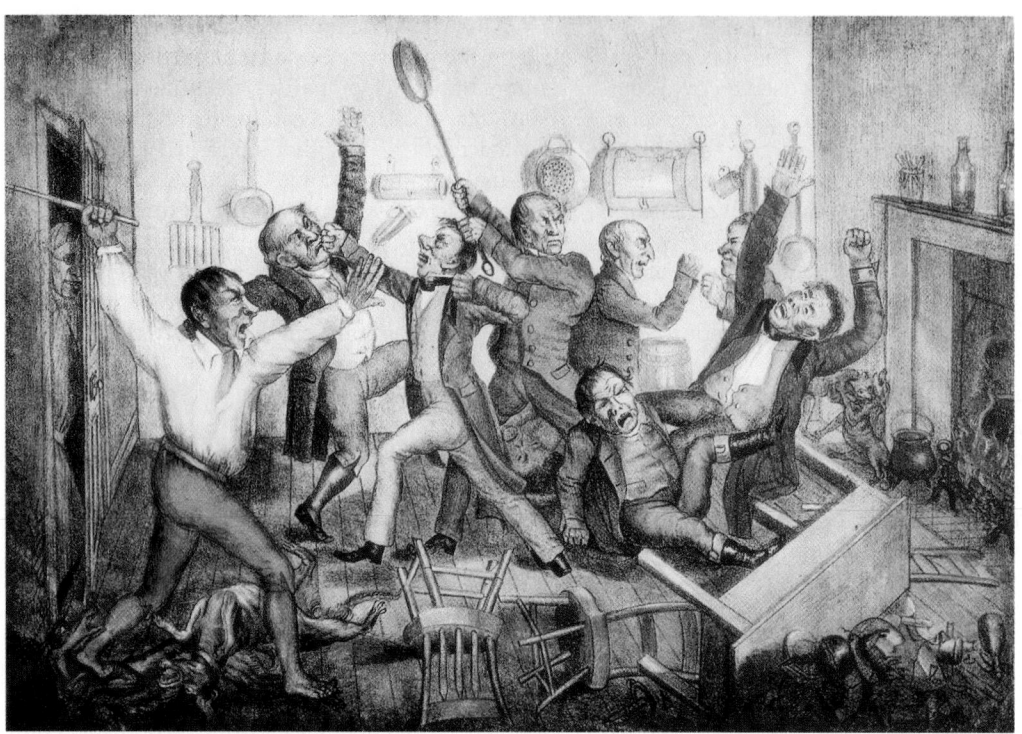

PRESIDENT JACKSON'S KITCHEN CABINET
Jackson's official cabinet, consisting of party loyalists who were heads of executive departments, did not inspire the president's trust and confidence. Instead, Jackson turned to a set of close friends, quickly dubbed the Kitchen Cabinet by the press, for advice, for patronage decisions, and even for the drafting of state papers. Several were newspapermen; one was an old Tennessee friend, William B. Lewis, who moved into the White House with Jackson. Martin Van Buren was also in this inner circle. This cartoon purports to show a meeting of the Kitchen Cabinet: raucous, argumentative, violently employing the tools of women's work. How does its pointed message reflect the new partisan politics of the time?
Granger Collection.

Jackson's agenda quickly emerged once he was in office. He favored a Jeffersonian limited federal government, fearing that intervention in the economy inevitably favored some groups at the expense of others. He therefore opposed federal support of transportation and grants of monopolies and charters that privileged wealthy investors. Like Jefferson, he anticipated rapid settlement of the country's interior, where land sales would spread economic democracy to settlers. Establishing a federal Indian policy thus had high priority. Unlike Jefferson, however, Jackson exercised full presidential powers over Congress. In 1830, he vetoed a highway project in Kentucky—Henry Clay's home state—that Congress voted to support with federal dollars. In all, Jackson used the veto twelve times; all previous presidents had exercised that right a total of nine times.

Cultural Shifts

Despite differences about the best or fairest way to enhance commercial development, Jackson's Democratic Republicans and Henry Clay's National Republicans shared enthusiasm for the outcome—a growing, booming economy. For increasing numbers of families, especially in the highly commercialized Northeast, the standard of living rose, consumption patterns changed, and the nature and location of work altered.

All of these changes had a direct impact on the roles and duties of men and women and on the training of youth for the economy of the future. New ideas about gender relations in a commercial economy surfaced in printed material and in public behavior. In Jacksonian America, a widely shared public culture came into being, originating within the new commercial classes and spreading rapidly through rising levels of literacy and an explosion of print.

The Family and Separate Spheres

The centerpiece of new ideas about gender relations held that husbands found their status and authority in the new world of work, leaving wives to tend the hearth and home. Sermons, advice books, periodicals, and novels reinforced the idea that men and women inhabited separate spheres with separate duties. "To woman it belongs . . . to elevate the intellectual character of her household [and] to kindle the fires of mental activity in childhood," wrote Mrs. A. J. Graves in a popular book titled *Advice to American Women*. For men, in contrast, "the absorbing passion for gain, and the pressing demands of business, engross their whole attention." In particular, the home, now the exclusive domain of women, was sentimentalized as the source of intimacy, love, and safety, a refuge from the cruel and competitive world of market relations.

Some new aspects of society gave substance to this formulation of separate spheres. Men's work, especially in the manufacturing, urban Northeast, was undergoing profound change after 1815. Increasingly, men's jobs brought cash to the household. Farmers and tradesmen sold products in a market, and bankers, bookkeepers, shoemakers, and canal diggers got pay envelopes. Furthermore, many men performed jobs outside of the home, at an office or store. For men who were not farmers, work indeed seemed newly disconnected from the home.

A woman's domestic role was more complicated than the cultural prescriptions indicated. Although the vast majority of married white women did not hold paying jobs, the home continued to be a site of time-consuming labor. But the advice books treated household tasks as loving familial duties; housework as work was thereby rendered invisible in an economy that evaluated work by how much

cash it generated. In reality, wives directly contributed to family income in many ways. Some took in boarders, while others engaged in outwork, earning pay for shoebinding, hatmaking, or needlework done at home. Wives in the poorer classes of society, including most free black wives, did not have the luxury of husbands earning adequate wages; for them, work as servants or laundresses helped augment family income.

The Education and Training of Youth

The market economy with its new expectations for men and women required fresh methods of training youth of both sexes. The generation that came of age in the 1820s and 1830s had opportunities for education and work unparalleled in previous eras, at least for children in the middling classes and above. Northern states adopted public schooling between 1790 and the 1820s, and within another decade southern states followed suit. The curriculum produced pupils who were able, by age twelve or fourteen, to read, write, and participate in marketplace calculations. Remarkably, girls usually received the same basic education as boys. Literacy rates for white females climbed dramatically, rivaling the rates for white males for the first time.

The fact that taxpayers paid for children's education created an incentive to seek an inexpensive teaching force. By the 1830s, northeastern school districts were replacing male teachers with young females. Like mill workers, teachers were in their late teens and regarded the work as temporary. In the 1840s, several states opened teacher training schools ("normal" schools) for women students. With the exception of Oberlin College in Ohio, no other colleges admitted women until after the Civil War, but a handful of private "female seminaries" established a rigorous curriculum that rivaled that of the best men's colleges. Two of the most prominent were the Troy Seminary in New York, founded by Emma Willard in 1821, and Mount Holyoke in Massachusetts, founded by Mary Lyon in 1837.

Male youths leaving public school faced two paths. A small percentage continued at private boys' academies (numbering in the several hundreds nationwide), and a far smaller number entered the country's two dozen colleges. More typically, boys left school at fourteen to apprentice to a specific trade or to seek business careers in entry-level clerkships, abundant in the growing urban centers.

WOMEN GRADUATES OF OBERLIN COLLEGE, CLASS OF 1855
*Oberlin College was founded in Ohio by evangelical and abolitionist activists in the
1830s; it admitted white and black men and women, although in the early years the
black students were all male and the women students were all white. Admission was
not exactly equal: The women entered a separate Ladies' Department. By 1855, as this
daguerreotype shows, black women had integrated the Ladies' Department. The two
older women with bonnets were the principal and a member of the board. The students
wear the latest fashion: dark taffeta dresses with sloping shoulders and tight bodice,
topped by detachable white lace collars. Hair fashions were similarly uniform for
women of all ages throughout the 1850s: a central part, hair dressed with oil and
lustrously coiled over the ears. Compare these women with the mill woman pictured on
page 241. What differences do you see?*
Oberlin College Archives, Oberlin, Ohio.

Young girls also headed for mill towns or for the
cities in unprecedented numbers, seeking work in
the expanding service sector as seamstresses and
domestic servants.

Changes in patterns of youth employment and
training meant that large numbers of youngsters in
the 1830s and later escaped the watchful eyes of
their families. Moralists fretted about the dangers
of unsupervised youth, and, following the lead of
the Lowell mill owners, some established apprentices' libraries and uplifting lecture series to keep
young people honorably occupied. Advice books
published by the hundreds instructed youth in the
virtues of hard work and delayed gratification.

Public Life, the Press, and Popular Amusements

Many new forms of inexpensive reading matter and
public entertainment competed with the moralistic
messages for youth. Innovations in printing technology as well as rising literacy rates created a brisk
market in the 1830s for publications appealing to
popular tastes: adventure and mystery pamphlets,
romance novels, and penny press newspapers. In
cities, theaters were nightly magnets for audiences
in the thousands.

In the 1790s, fewer than ninety newspapers,
each printing a few thousand copies per issue, pro-

vided news of current events. By 1830, there were eight hundred papers, sixty-five of them urban dailies, and in the 1830s the most successful of these, the new penny press papers, gained circulations of ten to twenty thousand copies daily. Such huge print runs were made possible by the development of steam-driven rotary presses with automatic paper feed devices replacing the old-style hand-presses. Six-cent papers covered politics, banking, and shipping news; the one-cent papers featured breezy political coverage, irreverent editorializing on current events, and crime reporting.

New York had three penny papers by 1835, and Philadelphia, Boston, and Baltimore each had one or two. Their influence extended throughout the nation, facilitated by a regular system of newspaper exchange via the postal system. Town and village papers reprinted the snappy political editorials and sensationalized crime stories, putting very undeferential ideas into the heads of readers new to politics.

Newspapers were not the only new medium for spreading a shared American culture. Starting in the 1820s, traveling lecturers crisscrossed the country, bringing entertainment and instruction to small-town audiences. Speakers gave dramatic readings of plays or poetry or lectured on history, current events, popular science, or controversial topics like advanced female education or anatomy and physiology. Theater also blossomed in the 1830s, providing urban Americans with their most common form of shared entertainment, featuring Shakespearean plays, melodramas, and the newly popular minstrelsy, a blackface musical comedy first performed in 1831 by white performers with blackened faces.

The popularity of theaters exemplified a general cultural turn toward the celebration of brilliant public speech. In this golden age of oration, actors, lawyers, politicians, and ministers could hold crowds spellbound for hours with their flawless elocution and elegant turns of phrase. Criminal trials, for example, were very short by modern standards, but the lawyers' closing arguments might consume many hours, with crowds of spectators hanging on every word. Senator Daniel Webster of Massachusetts was the acknowledged genius of political oration. At a Webster speech commemorating the Pilgrims' arrival, one man in a crowd of fifteen hundred recalled that "three or four times I thought my temples would burst with the gush of blood." Ministers with gifted tongues could in the space of an evening transform crowds of skeptics into

LURID COVER OF A CRIME PAMPHLET, NEW YORK
Cheap and easy printing in the early nineteenth century gave rise to new genres of popular reading matter, including a large pamphlet literature detailing horrific murder stories that invited readers to contemplate the nature of evil. This woodcut cover from 1836 promises to reveal the "interesting particulars" of the murder of Ellen Jewett, a New York City prostitute axed to death in her brothel bed. The pamphlet claims to constitute "an impressive warning" to youth about the tragedies of "dens of infamy." But the crude picture of the female corpse, with bare legs and breasts fully exposed, suggests that alternative, less moralistic readings of the same material were certainly possible for the purchasers.
William L. Clements Library.

believers. Skillful speakers demanded and generally got attentive listeners.

Democracy and Religion

An unprecedented revival of evangelical religion peaked in the early 1830s, after gathering three decades of momentum in states across the North and the upper South. Known as the Second Great Awakening, the outpouring of religious fervor changed the shape of American Protestantism. The heart of the evangelical message was that salvation was available to anyone willing to eradicate individual sin and accept faith in God's grace. Just as universal male suffrage allowed all white men to vote, democratized religion offered salvation to all who chose to embrace it.

Among the most serious adherents of evangelical Protestantism were men and women of the new mercantile classes whose self-discipline in pursuing market ambitions meshed well with the message of self-discipline in pursuit of spiritual perfection. Not content with individual perfection, many of these men and women sought to perfect society as well.

The Second Great Awakening

The earliest manifestations of fervent piety appeared in 1801 in Kentucky. A crowd of ten thousand people camped out on a hillside at Cane Ridge for a revival meeting that lasted several weeks. By the 1810s and 1820s, camp meetings had spread to the Atlantic seaboard states. The outdoor settings permitted huge attendance, which itself intensified the emotional impact of the experience. "For more than a half mile, I could see people on their knees before God in humble prayer," recalled one Cane Ridge worshiper.

The gatherings attracted women and men hungry for a more immediate access to spiritual peace, one not requiring years of soul-searching. One eyewitness at a revival reported that "some of the people were singing, others praying, some crying for mercy. . . . At one time I saw at least 500 swept down in a moment as if a battery of a thousand guns had been opened upon them, and then immediately followed shrieks and shouts that rent the very heavens."

From 1800 to 1820, church membership doubled in the United States, much of it among the

evangelical groups. Methodists, Baptists, and Presbyterians formed the core of the new movement, while Episcopalians, Congregationalists, Unitarians, Dutch Reformed, Lutherans, and Catholics maintained strong skepticism about the emotional enthusiasm. Women more than men were attracted to the evangelical movement, and wives and mothers typically recruited husbands and sons to join them.

The leading exemplar of the Second Great Awakening was a lawyer-turned-minister named Charles Grandison Finney. Finney lived in western New York, where the completion of the Erie Canal in 1825 fundamentally altered the social and economic landscape overnight. Towns swelled with new inhabitants who brought in remarkable prosperity along with other, less admirable activities, such as prostitution, drinking, and gaming. Finney saw New York canal towns as especially ripe for evangelical awakening. In Rochester, New York, he sustained a six-month revival through the winter of 1830–31, generating thousands of new converts.

Finney's message was directed primarily at women and men of the business classes, and, true to his training, he couched it in legal metaphors. "The world is divided into two great political parties," he announced—the party of Satan and the party of Jehovah. "Ministers should labor with sinners, as a lawyer does with a jury . . . ; and the sinner should weigh his arguments, and make up his mind as upon oath and for his life, and give a verdict upon the spot." Finney's sermons reached national distribution via the religious press. He argued that a reign of Christian perfection loomed, one that required a public-spirited outreach to the less than perfect to foster their salvation. Evangelicals promoted Sunday schools to bring piety to children; they battled to end mail delivery, stop public transport, and close shops on Sundays to honor the Sabbath. Many women formed missionary societies, which distributed millions of Bibles and religious tracts. Through such avenues, evangelical religion offered women expanded spheres of influence.

The Temperance Movement and the Campaign for Moral Reform

The evangelical disposition—a combination of faith, energy, self-discipline, and righteousness—animated vigorous campaigns to eliminate alcohol abuse and eradicate sexual sin. Millions of Americans took the temperance pledge to abstain

THE BROADWAY TABERNACLE.

CHARLES G. FINNEY'S BROADWAY TABERNACLE
The Reverend Charles G. Finney took his evangelical movement to New York City in the early 1830s, operating first out of a renovated theater. In 1836, the Broadway Tabernacle was built for his pastorate. In its use of space, the Tabernacle resembled a theater more than a traditional church, but in one respect it departed radically from one very theater-like tradition of churches—the custom of charging pew rents. In effect, most churches required worshipers to purchase their seats. In contrast, Finney insisted that all seats in his house were free, unreserved, and open to all.
Oberlin College Archives, Oberlin, Ohio.

www.bedfordstmartins.com/roarkcompact SEE THE ONLINE STUDY GUIDE for more help in analyzing this image.

from strong drink, and thousands became involved in efforts to end prostitution.

Alcohol consumption had risen steadily in the decades up to 1830, when the average person over age thirteen consumed an astonishing 9 gallons of hard liquor plus around 30 gallons of hard cider, beer, and wine per year. All classes imbibed. A lively saloon culture fostered masculine camaraderie among laborers along with extensive alcohol consumption, while in elite homes, the after-dinner whiskey or sherry was commonplace. Colleges before 1820 routinely served students a pint of ale with meals, and the army and navy included rum in the standard daily ration.

Organized opposition to drinking first surfaced in the 1810s among health and religious reformers. In 1826, Lyman Beecher, a Connecticut minister of an "awakened" church, founded the American Temperance Society, which held that drinking led to poverty, idleness, crime, and family violence.

Adopting the methods of evangelical ministers, temperance lecturers traveled the country expounding the damage of drink; by 1833, some six thousand local affiliates of the American Temperance Society boasted more than a million members. Middle-class drinking began a steep decline.

In 1836, the temperance leaders regrouped into a new society, the American Temperance Union, which demanded total abstinence of its adherents. The intensified war against alcohol moved beyond individual moral suasion into the realm of politics, as reformers sought to deny taverns liquor licenses. By 1845, temperance advocates had put an impressive dent in alcohol consumption, which had diminished to one-quarter of the per capita consumption of 1830. In 1851, Maine became the first state to ban entirely the manufacture and sale of all alcoholic beverages.

More controversial than temperance was a social movement called "moral reform," which first aimed at public morals in general but quickly narrowed to a campaign to eradicate sexual sin, especially prostitution. In 1833, a group of Finneyite women started the New York Female Moral Reform Society. Its members insisted that uncontrolled male sexual expression posed a serious threat to society in general and to women in particular. The society's nationally distributed newspaper, *The Advocate of Moral Reform*, was the first major woman-edited, woman-written, and woman-typeset paper in the country. In it they condemned men who visited brothels or who seduced innocent victims. Within five years, more than four thousand auxiliary groups of women members had sprung up, mostly in New England, New York, Pennsylvania, and Ohio.

In its analysis of the causes of licentiousness and its conviction that women had a duty to speak out about unspeakable things, the female Moral Reformers pushed the limits of what even the men in the evangelical movement could tolerate. Yet they did not regard themselves as radicals. They were simply pursuing the logic of a gender system that defined home protection and morality as women's special sphere and a religious conviction that called for the eradication of sin.

Organizing against Slavery

More radical still was the movement in the 1830s to abolish the sin of slavery. The only previous antislavery organization, the American Colonization Society, had been founded in 1817 by some Maryland and Virginia planters to promote gradual individual emancipation of slaves followed by colonization in Africa. By the early 1820s, several thousand exslaves had been transported to Liberia on the West African coast. But not surprisingly, newly freed men and women were often not eager to emigrate; their African roots were three or more generations in the past. Colonization was too moderate (and expensive) to have much impact on American slavery.

In 1831, an antislavery agitation developed in Boston, centered on William Lloyd Garrison, editor of the *Liberator*, a weekly newspaper. Garrison advocated immediate abolition: "On this subject, I do not wish to think, or speak, or write, with moderation. No! No! Tell a man whose house is on fire to give a moderate alarm; tell him to moderately rescue his wife from the hands of the ravisher; tell the mother to gradually extricate her babe from the fire into which it has fallen;—but urge me not to use moderation in a cause like the present."

Garrison's visibility built on several years of growing local antislavery sentiment. In 1829, a black printer named David Walker published *An Appeal to the Colored Citizens of the World*, which condemned racism, invoked the egalitarian language of the Declaration of Independence, and hinted at racial violence if whites did not change their prejudiced ways. And in 1831, a young black woman, Maria Stewart, delivered public lectures for black audiences in Boston on slavery and racial prejudice. While her arguments against slavery were welcomed, her voice—that of a woman—created problems. Few American-born women had yet engaged in public speaking beyond theatrical performances; Stewart was breaking a social taboo. She retired from the platform in 1833, but Garrison published her lectures, giving them wider circulation.

In 1832, Garrison supporters started the New England Anti-Slavery Society; Philadelphia and New York started similar groups in 1833. Soon there were a dozen antislavery newspapers, along with scores of antislavery lecturers spreading the word and inspiring the formation of new societies, which grew to number thirteen hundred by 1837. Confined to the North, their membership totaled a quarter of a million men and women.

However, many northerners were not prepared to embrace the abolitionist call for emancipation, immediate or gradual. They might oppose slavery as a blot on the country's ideals or as a rival to the free-labor system of the North, but at the same time most white northerners remained antiblack and

ABOLITIONIST PURSES
Female antislavery societies raised many thousands of dollars to support the abolitionist cause by selling handcrafted items at giant antislavery fairs. Toys, infant clothes, quilts, caps and collars, purses, needlebooks, wax flowers, inlaid boxes: The list was endless. Items were often emblazoned with abolitionist mottoes, such as "Let My People Go," "Liberty," and "Loose the Bonds of Wickedness." These pink silk drawstring bags were decorated with pictures of the hapless slave woman, an object of compassion. Dollars raised at these fairs supported the travels of abolitionist speakers as well as the publication and distribution of many antislavery books and articles.
The Daughters of the American Revolution Museum, Washington, D.C. Gift of Mrs. Erwin L. Broecker.

therefore antiabolition. From 1834 to 1838, there were more than a hundred eruptions of serious mob violence against abolitionists or free blacks. On one occasion, antislavery headquarters in Philadelphia and a black church and orphanage were burned to the ground; in another incident, Illinois abolitionist editor Elijah Lovejoy was killed by a rioting crowd attempting to destroy his printing press.

Women played a prominent role in abolition, just as they did in moral reform and evangelical religion. They formed women's auxiliaries and engaged in fundraising to support lecturers in the field. They circulated antislavery petitions, presented to the U.S. Congress with tens of thousands of signatures. Garrison particularly welcomed women's activity. When a southern plantation daughter named Angelina Grimké wrote him about her personal repugnance for slavery, Garrison published the letter in the *Liberator* and brought her overnight fame. Grimké and her older sister, Sarah,

now living in Philadelphia, quickly became lecturers for the antislavery movement and started a speaking tour to women's groups in Massachusetts in 1837. Grimké's powerful eyewitness speeches attracted men as well, causing the Congregational church leadership of Massachusetts to issue a warning to all its ministers not to let the Grimké sisters use their pulpits.

In the late 1830s, the cause of abolition divided the nation as no other issue did. Even among the abolitionists, significant divisions emerged. The Grimké sisters, radicalized by the public reaction to their speaking tour, began to write and speak about women's rights. They were opposed by moderate abolitionists who were unwilling to mix a new and controversial issue about women with their first cause, the rights of blacks. A few radical men, like Garrison, embraced women's rights fully, working to get women leadership positions in the national antislavery group.

The many men and women active in reform movements in the 1830s found their initial inspiration in evangelical Protestantism's dual message: Salvation was open to all and society needed to be perfected. Their activist mentality squared well with the interventionist tendencies of the party forming in opposition to Andrew Jackson's Democrats. On the whole, reformers gravitated to the Whig Party.

Jackson Defines the Democratic Party

In his eight years in office, Andrew Jackson worked to implement his vision of a politics of opportunity for all white men. He also greatly enhanced the power of the presidency. He favored rapid western land settlement, which led to conflict with Indian tribes. He had a dramatic confrontation with John C. Calhoun and South Carolina when that state tried to nullify the tariff of 1828. Disapproving of all government-granted privilege, Jackson challenged what he called the "monster" Bank of the United States and took it down to defeat. Jackson's legacy to his successor, Martin Van Buren, was a Democratic Party strong enough to withstand the passing of the powerful old man.

Indian Policy and the Trail of Tears

Improved transportation after 1815 greatly accelerated the westward flow of white settlers, and states containing Indian tribes rapidly joined the Union. But fundamental questions remained unresolved: What was the legal status of the quarter of a million Indians now resident in the United States? Were they subject to state and federal law?

From the 1790s to the 1820s, the federal government negotiated treaties with tribes on the assumption that the tribes were foreign nations. The Indians, though within state borders, asserted their sovereignty and communal rights to their land. Treaty making, however, proved a precarious practice. American negotiators found it hard to strike terms that whole tribes would accept, and all too often a few Indians with no legitimacy to speak for their tribes signed treaties ceding vast acreage.

Privately, Andrew Jackson thought it was "absurd" to call the Indians foreigners. In his view, they were subjects of the United States, entitled perhaps to keep small areas of their improved land but not their large hunting grounds. Jackson also did not think it feasible to promote assimilation of the Indians. From 1790 to the 1820s, various missionary associations had tried to "civilize" native peoples by converting them to Christianity, and presidents from Jefferson to Monroe had promoted assimilation as a peaceable alternative to warfare. In 1819, Congress authorized $10,000 a year for interdenominational missions to instruct Indians in religion, reading and writing, and agricultural practices. Missionaries also tried to get Indians to adopt white gender customs, but Indian women were reluctant to embrace practices that accorded them less power than their tribal system did. The general failure of assimilation moved Jackson to a more drastic policy.

In his first message to Congress in 1829, Jackson declared that Indians within U.S. borders could not remain independent and in sovereign control of tribal lands. Congress agreed and passed the Removal Act of 1830, appropriating $500,000 to relocate tribes west of the Mississippi River (Map 11.3).

For northern tribes, their numbers greatly diminished by years of war, gradual removal was already well under way. But not all the Indians went quietly. In 1832 in western Illinois, Black Hawk, a leader of the Sac and Fox Indians, resisted. Volunteer militias attacked and chased the Indians into southern Wisconsin, where, after several skirmishes and a deadly battle, Black Hawk was captured and more than nine hundred of his people massacred.

Southern tribes proved even more resistant to removal. The powerful Creek, Chickasaw, Choctaw, and Cherokee tribes, whose lands encompassed parts of North Carolina, Tennessee, and northern Georgia, Alabama, and Mississippi, at first refused to relocate. But their land attracted cotton-hungry white settlers, and a rumor of gold on Cherokee land in Georgia in 1829 only intensified the pressure.

Ironically, the seventeen thousand members of the Cherokee tribe had "assimilated" most successfully, spurred by dedicated missionaries living with them. More than two hundred Cherokees had intermarried with whites and had adopted white styles of housing, dress, and cotton agriculture, including the ownership of more than a thousand African American slaves. They had developed a

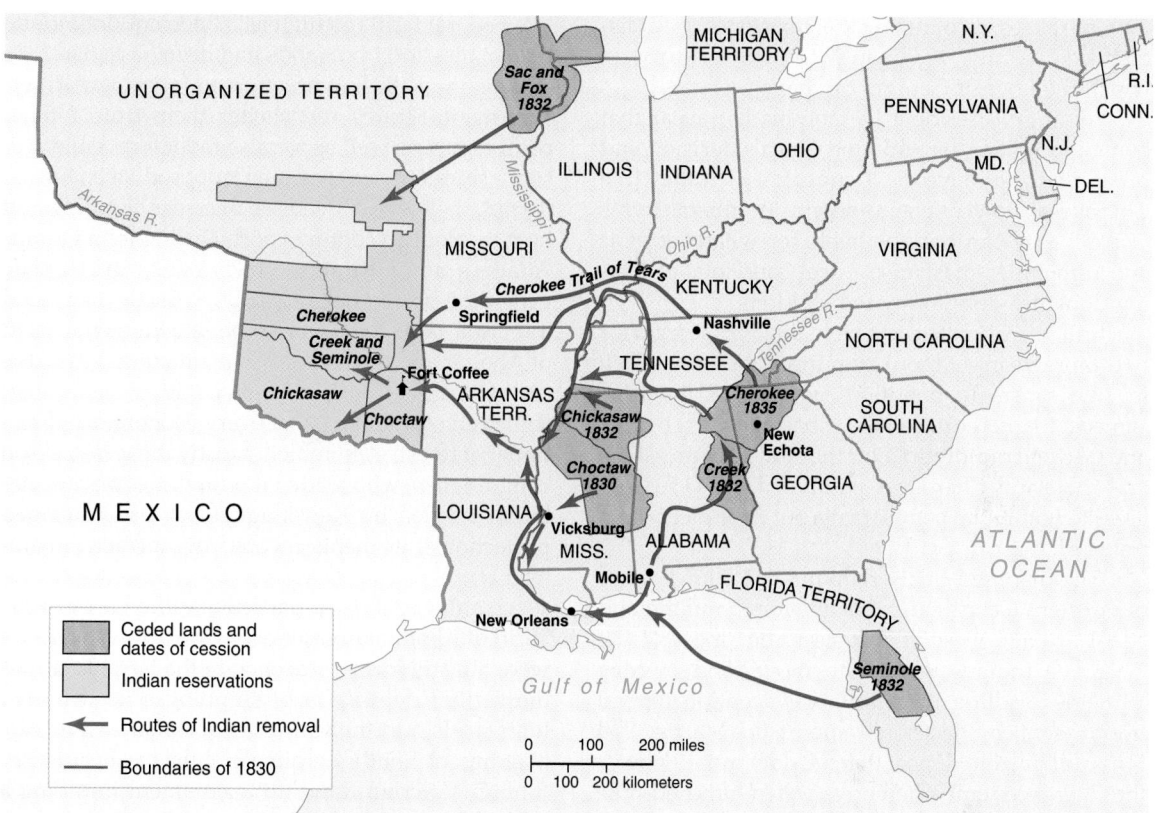

MAP 11.3

Indian Removal and the Trail of Tears

The federal government under President Andrew Jackson pursued a vigorous policy of Indian removal in the 1830s. Tribes were forcibly moved west to land known as the Indian Territory (in present-day Oklahoma). As many as a quarter of the Cherokee Indians died in 1838 on their route, known as the Trail of Tears.

READING THE MAP: From which states were most of the Native Americans removed? Through what states did the Trail of Tears go?

CONNECTIONS: Before Jackson's presidency, how did the federal government view Native Americans, and what policy initiatives were undertaken by the government and private groups? How did Jackson change the government's Native American policies?

www.bedfordstmartins.com/roarkcompact   SEE THE ONLINE STUDY GUIDE for more help in analyzing this map.

written alphabet and published a newspaper as well as Christian prayerbooks in their language, and by 1827 had a constitution directly modeled on that of the United States.

In 1831, after Georgia announced it would subject the Indians to state law, the Cherokee tribe responded by suing Georgia before the U.S. Supreme Court. Chief Justice John Marshall set aside the suit on technicalities but encouraged the Cherokees to seek further legal redress. When Georgia jailed two missionaries under an 1830 law forbidding missionary aid to Indians without state permission, the Cherokees brought suit again. In the 1832 case, *Worcester v. Georgia*, the Supreme Court found for the Cherokees, recognizing their existence as "a distinct community, occupying its own territory, in which the laws of Georgia can have no force."

An angry President Jackson made it clear that he would ignore the Supreme Court's decision and proceeded to enforce the Removal Act. "If they [the Cherokees] now refuse to accept the liberal terms offered, they can only be liable for whatever evils and difficulties may arise. I feel conscious of having done my duty to my red children."

Still, the Cherokee tribe remained in Georgia for two more years without significant violence. Then in 1835, a small, unauthorized part of the tribe signed a treaty ceding all the tribal lands to the state, and Georgia rapidly sold off the land to whites. Several thousand Cherokees petitioned the U.S. Congress to ignore the bogus treaty, but their pleas went unheard.

The disputed treaty relinquished a large piece of northern Georgia in exchange for $5 million and equal acreage west of Arkansas. But most of the Cherokee Indians refused to move, and in May 1838, the deadline for voluntary evacuation, federal troops sent by Jackson's successor, Martin Van Buren, arrived to deport them. Under armed guard, the Cherokees embarked on a twelve-hundred-mile journey that came to be called the Trail of Tears. Nearly a quarter of the Cherokees died en route, from hardship and starvation. They joined the thousands of Creek, Choctaw, and Chickasaw Indians also forcibly relocated to what is now Oklahoma.

In his farewell address to the nation in 1837, Jackson justified Indian removal with high-minded language about the benefit of the policy to the forlorn natives: "This unhappy race . . . are now placed in a situation where we may well hope that they will share in the blessings of civilization and be saved from the degradation and destruction to which they were rapidly hastening while they remained in the states."

The Tariff of Abominations and Nullification

Jackson's Indian policy happened to harmonize with the principle of states' rights: The president supported Georgia's right to ignore the Supreme Court decision in *Worcester v. Georgia*. But in another pressing question of states' rights, Jackson contested South Carolina's claim to ignore federal tariff policy.

Federal tariffs as high as 33 percent on imports like textiles and iron goods had been passed in 1816 and again in 1824, in an effort to favor new American manufactures and shelter them from foreign competition as well as to raise federal revenue. But some southern congressmen opposed steep tariffs, fearing they would decrease overseas shipping and hurt the South's cotton export. During John Quincy Adams's administration (1825–1829), tariff policy generated heated debate. In 1828, Congress passed a revised tariff that came to be known as the Tariff of Abominations. A bundle of conflicting duties, the set of tariffs—some as high as 50 percent—had something for and against every economic and sectional interest. Assembled mostly by pro-Jackson congressmen, who loaded it with duties on raw materials needed by New England, it also contained protectionist elements favored by northern manufacturers.

South Carolina in particular suffered from the Tariff of Abominations. Worldwide prices for cotton were already in sharp decline in the late 1820s, and the further depression of shipping caused by the high tariffs hurt the South's export market. In 1828, a group of South Carolina politicians headed by John C. Calhoun drew up a statement outlining a doctrine called "nullification." The Union, they argued, was a confederation of states that had yielded some but not all power to the federal government. When Congress overstepped its powers, states had the right to nullify Congress's acts; as precedents they pointed to the Virginia and Kentucky Resolutions of 1798, which had attempted to invalidate the Alien and Sedition Acts (see chapter 9). Congress had erred in using tariff policy as an instrument to benefit specific industries, the South Carolinians claimed; tariffs should be used only to raise revenue.

On assuming the presidency in 1829, Jackson ignored the South Carolina statement of nullification and shut out Calhoun, his new vice president, from influence or power. Tariff revisions in early 1832 brought little relief to the South. Sensing futility, Calhoun resigned from the vice presidency in 1832 and accepted election by the South Carolina legislature to a seat in the U.S. Senate, where he could better protect his state's antitariff stance. Strained to their limit, the South Carolina leaders took the radical step of declaring the federal tariffs to be null and void in their state as of February 1, 1833.

Finally, the constitutional crisis was out in the open. Opting for a dramatic confrontation, Jackson sent armed ships to Charleston's harbor and threatened to invade the state. He pushed through Congress a bill, called the Force Bill, defining the Carolina stance as treason and authorizing military action to collect federal tariffs.

At the same time, Congress moved quickly to pass a revised tariff more acceptable to the South. The conciliating Senator Henry Clay rallied support for a moderate bill that gradually reduced tariffs down to the 1816 level. Both the new tariff and the Force Bill were passed by Congress on March 1, 1833. South Carolina responded by withdrawing its nullification of the old tariff—and then nullifying the Force Bill. It was a symbolic gesture, since Jackson's show of muscle was no longer necessary. Both sides were satisfied with the immediate outcome. Federal power had prevailed over a dangerous assertion of states' rights; and South Carolina got the lower tariff it wanted.

Yet the question of federal power versus states' rights was far from settled. The implied threat behind nullification was secession, a position articulated in 1832 by some South Carolinians whose concerns went beyond tariff policy. The growing voice of antislavery activism in the North threatened the South's economic system. If and when a northern-dominated federal government decided to end slavery, the South Carolinians thought, the South must have the right to remove itself from the Union.

The Bank War and the Panic of 1837

President Jackson also did battle over the Bank of the United States. After riding out the panic of 1819, the bank finally prospered. It handled the federal government's deposits, extended credit and loans, and issued banknotes—by 1830 the most stable currency in the country. With twenty-nine branches, it benefited the whole nation. Jackson, however, did not find the bank's functions sufficiently valuable to offset his criticism of the concept of a national bank. In his first and second messages to Congress, in 1829 and 1830, Jackson claimed that the bank concentrated undue economic power in the hands of a few.

National Republican Senators Daniel Webster and Henry Clay decided to force the issue. They convinced the bank to apply for charter renewal in 1832, well before the fall election, even though the existing charter ran until 1836. They fully expected that Congress's renewal would force Jackson to follow through on his rhetoric with a veto. The unpopular veto would then cause Jackson to lose the election, while the bank would survive on an override vote from a new Congress swept into power in the anti-Jackson tide.

At first the plan seemed to work. The bank applied for recharter, Congress voted to renew, and Jackson, angry over being manipulated, issued his veto. But it was a brilliantly written veto, full of fierce language about privileges of the moneyed elite who oppress the democratic masses in order to enrich themselves. Jackson had translated the bank controversy into a language of class antagonism and egalitarian ideals that strongly resonated with many Americans. Old Hickory won the election easily over his National Republican opponent, Henry Clay, gaining 55 percent of the popular vote and a lopsided electoral college vote of 219 to 49. The Jackson party still controlled Congress, so no override was possible. The bank would cease to exist after 1836.

But Jackson wanted to destroy the bank sooner. Calling the bank a "monster," he had the federal deposits removed from its vaults and redeposited into "pet banks," Democratic-leaning institutions throughout the country; because of the high tariffs and high-volume sales of public lands, this government nest egg was quite sizable. In retaliation, the bank raised interest rates and called in loans; this action caused a minor recession in 1833 and actually enhanced Jackson's claim that the bank was too powerful for the good of the country.

Unleashed and unregulated, the economy went into high gear. Perhaps only a small part of the problem arose from irresponsible banking practices; just at this moment, an excess of silver from Mexican mines had made its way into American banks, giving bankers license to print ever more banknotes. Inflation soared from 1834 to 1837; prices of basic goods rose more than 50 percent. Many hundreds of new private banks were quickly chartered by the states, each bank issuing its own banknotes and setting interest rates as high as the market would bear. Entrepreneurs borrowed and invested money, much of it funneled into privately financed railroads and canals.

The market in western land sales heated up. In 1834, about 4.5 million acres of the public domain

FISTFIGHT BETWEEN OLD HICKORY AND BULLY NICK
This 1834 cartoon represents President Andrew Jackson squaring off to fight Nicholas Biddle, the director of the Bank of the United States. Pugilism as a semiprofessional sport gained great popularity in the 1830s; the joke here is that the aged Jackson and the aristocratic Biddle would strip to such revealing tight pants and engage in open combat. To Biddle's left are his seconds, Daniel Webster and Henry Clay; behind the president is his vice president, Martin Van Buren. Whiskey and port lubricate the action.
The Library Company of Philadelphia.

had been sold, the highest annual volume since the peak year 1819; by 1836, the total reached an astonishing 20 million acres. Some of this was southern land in Mississippi and Louisiana, which slave owners rushed to bring under cultivation, but much more was in the North, where land offices were deluged with buyers. The Jackson administration worried that the purchasers were overwhelmingly eastern capitalists, land speculators instead of self-reliant yeoman farmers who intended to settle on the land.

In one respect, the economy attained an admirable goal: The national debt disappeared, and, for the first and only time in American history, from 1835 to 1837, the government had a monetary surplus. But much of it consisted of questionable bank currencies—"bloated, diseased" currencies, in Jackson's vivid terminology.

Jackson decided to restrain the economy. In 1836, the Treasury Department issued the Specie Circular, an order that public land could be purchased only with hard money, federally coined gold and silver. In response, bankers started to reduce their loans, fearing a general contraction of the economy. Compounding the difficulty, the Bank of England also now insisted on hard-money payments for American loans, which had grown large in the years

since 1831 because of a trade imbalance. Failures in various crop markets, a downturn in cotton prices on the international market, and the silver glut, all unrelated to Jackson's fiscal policies, fed the growing economic crisis.

The familiar events of the panic of 1819 unfolded again, with terrifying rapidity. In April 1837, a wave of bank and business failures ensued, and the credit market tumbled like a house of cards. The Specie Circular was only one precipitating cause, but the Whig Party held it and Jackson responsible for the depression. For more than five years after the panic of 1837, the United States suffered from economic hard times.

Van Buren's One-Term Presidency

The election of 1836, which preceded the panic by six months, demonstrated the transformation of the Democrats from coalition to party. The personality of Jackson had stamped the elections of 1824, 1828, and 1832, but now the party apparatus was sufficiently developed to support itself. Local and state committees existed throughout the country. Democratic candidates ran in every state election, succeeding even in old Federalist states like Maine and New Hampshire. More than four hundred newspapers declared themselves Democratic. In 1836, the Democrats repeated an innovation begun in 1832, holding a national convention that nominated Vice President Martin Van Buren of New York for president. Van Buren's running mate was Richard M. Johnson, a slave owner from Kentucky whose principal claim to fame was the unverifiable boast that he had killed Shawnee chief Tecumseh in 1813.

Sophisticated party organization was Martin Van Buren's specialty. Nicknamed the "Little Magician" for his consummate political skills, the Dutch New Yorker had built his career by pioneering many of the loyalty-enhancing techniques the Democrats used in the 1830s. After serving as senator and then governor, he became Jackson's secretary of state in 1828. Four years later he replaced Calhoun as Jackson's running mate. His eight years in the volatile Jackson administration required the full measure of his political deftness, as he sought repeatedly to save Jackson both from his enemies and from his own obstinacy.

Van Buren was a backroom politician, not a popular public figure, and the Whigs hoped that he might be defeatable. In many states, Whigs had captured high office in 1834, shedding the awkward National Republican label and developing statewide organizations to rival those of the Democrats. However, no figure commanded nationwide support. The result was that three candidates opposed Van Buren in 1836, each with a solid regional base. Massachusetts Senator Daniel Webster could deliver New England; Tennessee Senator Hugh Lawson White attracted proslavery, pro-Jackson, but anti–Van Buren voters in the South; and the aging General William Henry Harrison of Indiana, memorable for his Indian war heroics in 1811, pulled in the western, anti-Indian vote. Not one of the three candidates could have won the presidency, but together they came close to denying Van Buren a majority vote. Their combined strength pulled many Whigs into office at the state level. In the end, Van Buren had 170 electoral votes, while the other three received a total of 113.

Van Buren took office in March 1837, and a month later the panic hit. The new president called a special session of Congress to consider creating an independent treasury system to fulfill some of the functions of the defunct Bank of the United States. Such a system, funded by government deposits, would deal only in hard money, forcing commercial banks to restrict their issuance of paper currency. Equally important, the new system would not make

loans and would thus avoid the danger of speculative meddling in the economy. In short, an independent treasury system could exert a powerful moderating influence on inflation and the credit market without itself being directly involved in the market. But Van Buren encountered strong resistance in Congress, even from Democrats. The treasury system finally won approval in 1840; by then, however, Van Buren's chances of a second term in office were virtually nil. The four years had proved to be tumultuous for the economy, with federal bank policy at a stalemate.

In 1840, the Whigs settled on William Henry Harrison, sixty-seven, to oppose Van Buren. The campaign drew on voter involvement as no other presidential campaign ever had. The Whigs borrowed tricks from the Democrats: Harrison was touted as a common man born in a log cabin, although a Virginia plantation was the real site. His Indian-fighting days, now thirty years behind him, were played up to give him a Jacksonian aura. Whigs staged festive rallies all over the country, drumming up mass appeal with candlelight parades and song shows. Women participated in Whig campaign rallies as never before. Some 78 percent of eligible voters cast ballots—the highest percentage ever in American history. Harrison took 53 percent of the popular vote and won a resounding 234 electoral college votes to Van Buren's 60. A Democratic editor lamented, "We have taught them how to conquer us!"

Conclusion: The Second American Party System

From 1828 to 1840, Andrew Jackson created and put his stamp on the newly emergent Democratic Party. Jackson's fame as an aggressive general, Indian fighter, champion of the common man, opponent of aristocracy, and defender of slavery and white privilege allowed him to pull together an unlikely but ultimately workable coalition of rural western farmers, urban laborers, pro-state bank commercial men, and wealthy southern slave owners. These groups embraced personal liberty, free competition, and egalitarian opportunity for all white men, compelling values embodied in the larger-than-life Old Hickory. Jacksonian Democrats accepted drinking and tolerated Sabbath violations, preferring not to legislate morality. They avoided debating the wisdom of slavery at all costs.

In contrast, the Whigs coalesced in the 1830s as the party of activist moralism and state-sponsored entrepreneurship. Wealthy merchants from Boston to Savannah who appreciated a national bank and protective tariffs tended to be Whigs, as did the evangelical middle classes. Personal liberty must be tempered by self-discipline and backed by government controls over moral issues, Whigs asserted, favoring laws that prohibited liquor sales or stagecoach travel on Sundays. Abolitionists tended to vote for Whigs, even though most Whig politicians shied away from antislavery ideas.

National politics in the 1830s were more heated and divisive than at any other time since the 1790s. The new party system of Democrats and Whigs cut far deeper into the electorate than had the previous system of Federalists and Republicans. Innovations in transportation and communication disseminated political information from the city to the backwoods, politicizing voters who now understood what they might gain or lose under the competing economic policies of the two parties. Politics acquired immediacy and excitement, causing four out of five white men to cast a ballot in 1840.

High rates of voter participation would continue into the 1840s and 1850s, because politics remained the arena where different choices about economic development and social change were contested. Unprecedented urban growth, westward expansion, and early industrialism marked those decades, sustaining the Jacksonian-Whig split in the electorate. But other new challenges not easily dealt with by those two parties—critiques of slavery, concerns for free labor, and an emerging protest against women's second-class citizenship—complicated the political scene of the 1840s, leading to third-party movements that splintered from the two parties of the 1830s. One of these third parties, called the Republican Party, would achieve dominance in 1860 with the election of an Illinois lawyer, Abraham Lincoln, to the presidency.

FOR FURTHER READING ABOUT THE TOPICS IN THIS CHAPTER, see the Online Bibliography at www.bedfordstmartins.com/roarkcompact.

FOR ADDITIONAL FIRST-HAND ACCOUNTS OF THIS PERIOD, see pages 164–180 in Michael Johnson, ed., *Reading the American Past*, Second Edition, Volume I.

TO ASSESS YOUR MASTERY OF THE MATERIAL IN THIS CHAPTER, see the Online Study Guide at www.bedfordstmartins.com/roarkcompact.

CHRONOLOGY

1807   Robert Fulton develops first commercially successful steamboat, *Clermont*.

1816   Second Bank of the United States chartered for twenty years.

Import tariff imposed on foreign textiles.

1817   American Colonization Society founded to promote gradual emancipation and removal of African Americans to Liberia.

1818   National Road links Baltimore and Wheeling, West Virginia.

1819   Economic collapse and panic nationwide.

1821   Boston business entrepreneurs start to build mills with power looms at Lowell, Massachusetts.

1824   Congress passes expanded tariff bill.

1825   Erie Canal spans 350 miles in New York State.

1826   Schuylkill Canal—108 miles long—opens in Pennsylvania.

1828   Tariff of Abominations passed.

Andrew Jackson elected president.

1829   David Walker's *An Appeal to the Colored Citizens of the World* published in Boston.

Baltimore and Ohio Railroad lays thirteen miles of track.

1830   Indian Removal Act appropriates money to relocate Indian tribes west of Mississippi River.

1831   William Lloyd Garrison begins publishing abolitionist newspaper *Liberator*.

Charles G. Finney stages evangelical revival in Rochester, New York.

Supreme Court allows Georgia to continue to subject Indians to state laws.

1832   Supreme Court in *Worcester v. Georgia* recognizes Cherokees as distinct community outside legal jurisdiction of Georgia.

Jackson vetoes Bank of the United States charter.

New England Anti-Slavery Society founded.

Andrew Jackson reelected president.

1833   Nullification crisis: South Carolina declares federal tariffs void in the state.

New York and Philadelphia Anti-Slavery Societies founded.

1834,   Female mill workers strike in
1836   Lowell, Massachusetts.

1836   Jackson issues Specie Circular.

Martin Van Buren elected president.

1837   Economic panic.

1838   Trail of Tears—Cherokees forced to relocate west.

William Henry Harrison elected president.

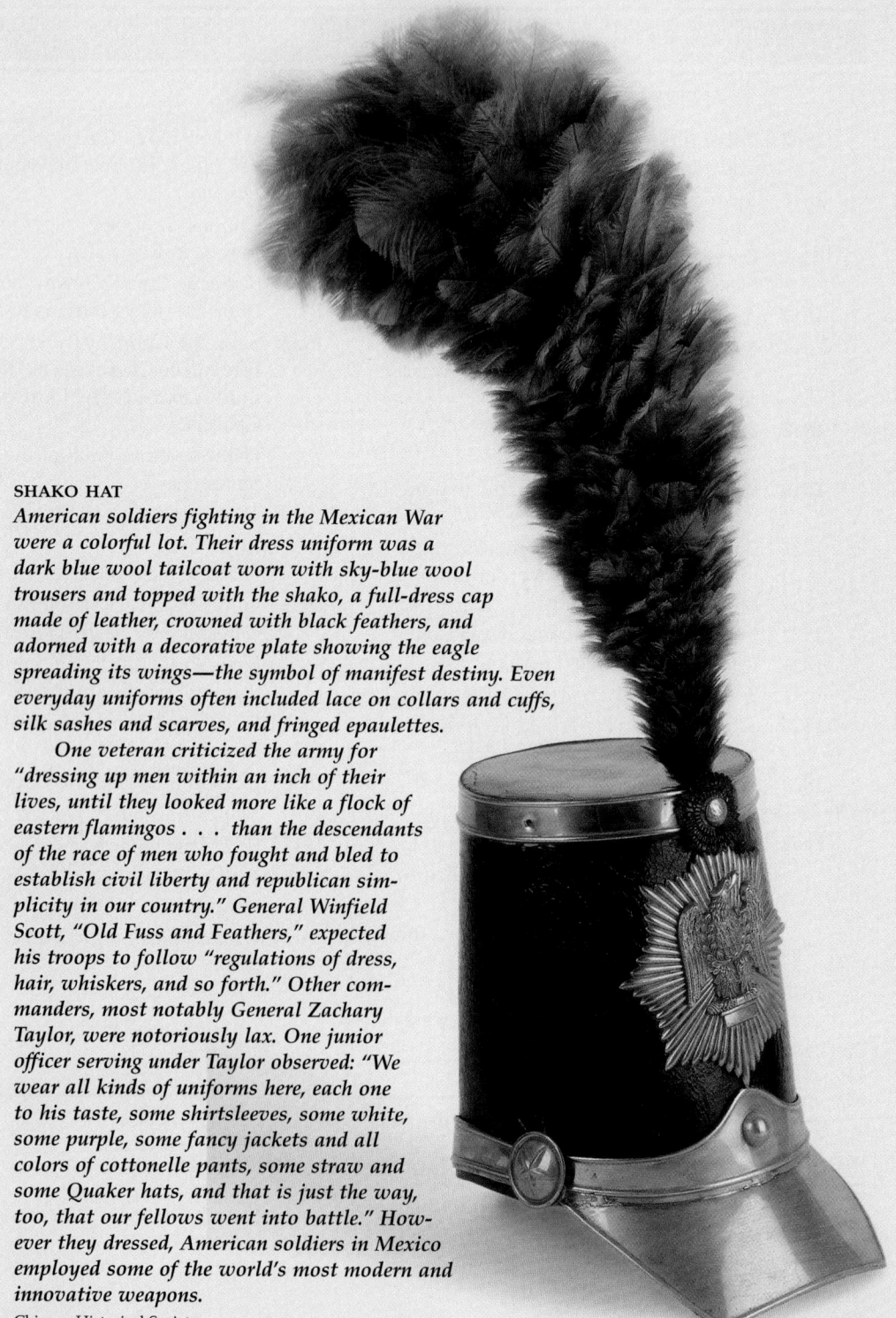

SHAKO HAT

American soldiers fighting in the Mexican War were a colorful lot. Their dress uniform was a dark blue wool tailcoat worn with sky-blue wool trousers and topped with the shako, a full-dress cap made of leather, crowned with black feathers, and adorned with a decorative plate showing the eagle spreading its wings—the symbol of manifest destiny. Even everyday uniforms often included lace on collars and cuffs, silk sashes and scarves, and fringed epaulettes.

One veteran criticized the army for "dressing up men within an inch of their lives, until they looked more like a flock of eastern flamingos . . . than the descendants of the race of men who fought and bled to establish civil liberty and republican simplicity in our country." General Winfield Scott, "Old Fuss and Feathers," expected his troops to follow "regulations of dress, hair, whiskers, and so forth." Other commanders, most notably General Zachary Taylor, were notoriously lax. One junior officer serving under Taylor observed: "We wear all kinds of uniforms here, each one to his taste, some shirtsleeves, some white, some purple, some fancy jackets and all colors of cottonelle pants, some straw and some Quaker hats, and that is just the way, too, that our fellows went into battle." However they dressed, American soldiers in Mexico employed some of the world's most modern and innovative weapons.

Chicago Historical Society.

THE FREE NORTH AND WEST

12

1840–1860

Eᴀʀʟʏ ɪɴ Nᴏᴠᴇᴍʙᴇʀ 1842, Abraham Lincoln and his new wife, Mary, moved into their first home in Springfield, Illinois, a rented room measuring eight by fourteen feet on the second floor of the Globe Tavern, the nicest place Abraham had ever lived. Mary Todd Lincoln had grown up in Lexington, Kentucky, attended by slaves in the elegant home of her father, a prosperous merchant, banker, and politician. The small, noisy room above the Globe Tavern was the worst place she had ever lived. Fewer than twenty years later, in March 1861, the Lincolns moved into what would prove to be their last home, the presidential mansion in Washington, D.C. Abraham Lincoln climbed from the Globe Tavern to the White House by relentless work, unslaked ambition, and immense talent, traits he had honed since boyhood.

Born in a Kentucky log cabin in 1809, Lincoln grew up on small, struggling farms. His father, Thomas, never learned to read and, Abraham explained, "never did more in the way of writing than to bunglingly sign his own name." Lincoln's mother, Nancy, could neither read nor write. In December 1816, Thomas Lincoln moved his young family out of Kentucky, crossing the Ohio River to the Indiana wilderness. They lived for two frozen months in a crude lean-to only partially enclosed by limbs and bushes while Thomas, a skilled carpenter, built a new cabin. There Abraham learned the arts of farming practiced by families throughout the nation. Although only eight years old, Abraham "had an axe put into his hands at once" and used it "almost constantly" for the next fifteen years, he recalled. When he could be spared from work, the boy attended school, less than a year in all. "There was absolutely nothing to excite ambition for education," Lincoln recollected. In contrast, Mary Todd, his future wife, received ten years of schooling in Lexington's best academies for young women.

By 1830, Thomas Lincoln decided to start over. The Lincolns moved two hundred miles west to central Illinois and built another log cabin. The next spring Thomas Lincoln moved again, and this time Abraham set out on his own, a "friendless, uneducated, penniless boy," as he described himself.

By dogged striving, Lincoln gained an education and the respect of his Illinois neighbors, although a steady income eluded him for years. He also received help from his father-in-law. Shortly after Lincoln married, Mary's father gave the young couple eighty acres of land and promised a yearly allowance of about $1,100 for six years, helping them to move out of their room above the Globe Tavern. Lincoln eventually built a thriving law practice in Springfield and served in the Illinois legislature and in Congress. His political activity and hard-driving ambition ultimately catapulted him into the White House.

ABRAHAM LINCOLN'S HAT
Abraham Lincoln wore this stovepipe hat, made of beaver pelt, during his years as president of the United States. Stovepipe hats were worn by established, respectable, middle-class men in the 1850s. Workingmen and farmers would have felt out of place wearing such a hat, except perhaps on special occasions like weddings or funerals. Growing up in Kentucky, Indiana, and Illinois, Lincoln may have seen stovepipe hats on the leading men of his community, but he probably never owned one until he became an aspiring Illinois lawyer and politician. Wearing such a hat was a mark that one had achieved a certain success in life, in Lincoln's case the enormous social distance he had traveled from his backwoods origins to the White House. But even as president he continued a backwoods practice he had begun as a young postmaster in New Salem, Illinois, using his hat as a place to store letters and papers. Lincoln's law partner William Herndon termed Lincoln's hat "an extraordinary receptacle [that] served as his desk and memorandum book."
Smithsonian Institution.

Like Lincoln, millions of Americans believed they could make something of themselves, whatever their origins, so long as they were willing to work. Individuals who refused to work—who were lazy, improvident, or foolish—had only themselves to blame if they failed. The promise of rewards from hard work spurred efforts that shaped the contours of America, pushing the boundaries of the nation south to the Rio Grande and west to the Pacific Ocean. That expansion—

economic, political, and geographic—also raised anew the question of slavery that Lincoln ultimately confronted as president.

Economic and Industrial Evolution

During the 1840s and 1850s, Lincoln and other Americans lived amidst profound economic transformation that had been under way since the start of the nineteenth century. By 1860, the nation's population numbered over 31 million and the total output of the American economy had multiplied twelvefold since 1800. Four fundamental changes in American society fueled this phenomenal economic growth.

First, Abraham Lincoln and millions of other Americans left farms behind, boosting the urban population, although farmers still made up 80 percent of the nation's population by 1860. A second major change was that a growing number of Americans worked in factories, by 1860 almost 20 percent of the labor force. This trend contributed to the nation's economic growth because, in general, factory workers were twice as productive (in output per unit of labor input) as agricultural workers. A third fundamental change—from water to steam as a source of energy—permitted factories to be more productive. During the 1830s, extensive mining began in Pennsylvania coal fields and massive quantities of coal became available for industrial fuel. Coal provided heat to power steam engines in factories, railroads, and ships.

This cascade of interrelated developments—steam, coal, factories, cities, railroads—had begun to transform the character of the American economy by the 1850s. Historians have often referred to this transformation as an industrial revolution. However, the profound changes in the American economy in these years did not cause a revolutionary discontinuity in the economy or society. The United States remained overwhelmingly agricultural. Old methods of production continued alongside the new. Before 1860, the American economy underwent a process that might best be termed "industrial evolution."

That evolution was made possible by a fourth fundamental development that propelled American economic growth. Agricultural productivity (defined as crop output per unit of labor input) nearly doubled during Lincoln's lifetime. This dramatic increase contributed more than any other single factor to the economic growth of the era. While cities, factories, and steam engines blossomed throughout the nation—especially in the North and West—the roots of American economic growth lay in agriculture.

Agriculture and Land Policy

The sheer physical labor required to convert unimproved land to cultivated fields limited agricultural productivity. Energy that might have gone to growing crops went instead to clearing land. But as farmers pushed westward, they encountered thinner forests and eventually the Midwest's comparatively treeless prairie, where they could spend less time with an ax and more time at the plow or hoe, significantly boosting agricultural productivity. Rich prairie soils also gave somewhat higher crop yields than eastern farms, and farmers migrated to the Midwest by the tens of thousands between 1830 and 1860.

Labor-saving improvements in farm implements also hiked agricultural productivity. The cast-iron plow in use since the 1820s proved too weak for the thick turf and dense soil of the midwestern prairie. In 1837, John Deere patented a strong, smooth steel plow that sliced through prairie soil so cleanly that farmers called it the "singing plow." Deere's company became the leading plow manufacturer in the Midwest, turning out more than ten thousand plows a year by the late 1850s. By 1860, the energy for plowing still came from two- and four-legged animals, but better plows permitted that energy to break more ground and plant more crops.

Improvements in wheat harvesting also multiplied farmers' productivity. In 1850, most farmers harvested wheat by hand, cutting two or three acres a day with back-breaking labor. Tinkerers throughout the nation tried to fashion a mechanical reaper that would make the wheat harvest easier and quicker. Cyrus McCormick and others experimented with designs until the late 1840s, when mechanical reapers began to appear in American wheat fields. A McCormick reaper that cost between $100 and $150 allowed a farmer to harvest up to twelve acres a day. By 1860, about eighty thousand reapers

had been sold. Although reapers represented the cutting edge of agricultural technology, they still had to be powered by a horse or an ox. Most farmers continued to cut their grain by hand. Reapers and improved plows, however, allowed more land to be brought into cultivation. Without access to fresh, uncultivated land, farmers could not have doubled the corn and wheat harvests between 1840 and 1860, as they did.

In the end, the agricultural productivity that fueled the nation's economy was an outgrowth of federal land policy. Up to 1860, the United States continued to be land rich and labor poor. During the nineteenth century, the nation became a great deal richer in land, acquiring more than a billion acres with the Louisiana Purchase and the annexation of Florida, Oregon, and vast territories following the Mexican War (discussed later in this chapter). The federal government made the land available for purchase to attract settlers and to generate revenues. Although federal land cost only $1.25 an acre, millions of Americans could not afford to pay $50 for a forty-acre farm. They squatted on unclaimed federal land and carved out a farm they neither rented nor owned. Many poor farmers never accumulated enough money to purchase the land on which they squatted, and eventually they moved elsewhere, often to squat again on unclaimed federal land.

In addition to aiding small farmers, government land policy enriched wily speculators who found ways to claim large tracts of the most desirable plots and sell them to settlers at a generous markup. Nonetheless, by making land available to millions of ordinary people, the federal government achieved the goal of attracting settlers to the new territories in the West, which in due course joined the Union as new states. Above all, federal land policy created the basic precondition for the increase in agricultural productivity that underlay the nation's impressive economic growth.

Manufacturing and Mechanization

Changes in manufacturing arose in the context of the nation's land-rich, labor-poor economy. England and other European countries had land-poor, labor-rich economies; there, meager opportunities in agriculture kept factory laborers plentiful and wages low. In the United States, geographical expansion and government land policies buoyed agriculture, keeping millions of people on the farm and thereby limiting the supply of workers for manufacturing and elevating wages. Because of this shortage of workers, manufacturers searched constantly for ways to save labor.

Mechanization marched forward as quickly as manufacturers could turn innovative ideas into workable combinations of gears, levers, screws, and pulleys. Outside the textile industry (see chapter 11), homegrown machines set the pace. The practice of manufacturing and then assembling interchangeable parts spread from gun making to other industries and became known as the "American system." Mechanization became so integral to American manufacturing that some machinists specialized in what was called the machine tool industry, namely making machines that made parts for other machines.

Manufacturing and agriculture meshed into a dynamic national economy. New England led the nation in manufacturing, shipping products like clocks, guns, and axes west and south, while commodities like wheat, pork, whiskey, tobacco, and cotton flowed north and east. Manufacturers specialized in producing for the gigantic domestic market rather than for export. U.S. manufacturers supported tariffs to minimize British competition, but their best protection from British competitors was to strive harder to please their American customers, the vast majority of whom were farmers.

Throughout American manufacturing, hand labor continued to be an essential component of production, despite the advances in mechanization. Even in heavily mechanized industries, factories remained fairly small, few having more than twenty or thirty employees. But the industrial evolution under way before 1860 would quicken later in the nineteenth century; railroads were a harbinger of that future.

Railroads: Breaking the Bonds of Nature

To a degree unequaled by any other industry, railroads incorporated the most advanced developments of the age. No wonder a Swedish visitor in 1849 noticed that American schoolboys constantly doodled sketches of locomotives, always smoking, always in motion. Railroads captured Americans'

imaginations in part because they seemed to break the bonds of nature. When canals and rivers froze in winter or became impassable during summer droughts, trains steamed ahead. When becalmed sailing ships went nowhere, locomotives kept on chugging, averaging over twenty miles an hour during the 1850s. Above all, railroads offered cities not blessed with canals or navigable rivers a way to compete for the trade of the countryside.

By 1850, trains steamed along nine thousand miles of track, almost two-thirds of it in New England and the Middle Atlantic states. By 1860, several railroads had crossed the Mississippi River to link frontier farmers to the nation's thirty thousand miles of track, approximately as much as in all the rest of the world combined (Map 12.1). This massive expansion of railroads helped the United States catapult into position as the world's second leading industrial power, behind Great Britain.

In addition to speeding transportation, railroads propelled growth of the iron and coal industries vital to railroad construction and operation. Railroads also stimulated the fledgling telegraph industry. In 1844, Samuel F. B. Morse persuasively demonstrated the potential of his telegraph by transmitting a series of dots and dashes that instantly conveyed an electronic message along forty miles of wire between Washington and Baltimore. By 1861, more than fifty thousand miles of wire stretched across the continent to the Pacific, often alongside railroad tracks. Telegraphy made railroads safer and more efficient, swiftly signaling whether tracks were clear.

Almost all railroads were built and owned by private corporations rather than by governments. Undergirding these private investments was massive government aid, especially federal land grants. Up to 1850, the federal government had granted a total of seven million acres of federal land to various turnpike, highway, and canal projects. In that year, Illinois Senator Stephen A. Douglas obtained congressional approval for a precedent-setting grant to railroads of six square miles of federal land for each mile of track constructed. Railroad companies quickly lined up congressional support for other lucrative land deals. By 1860, Congress had granted railroads more than twenty million acres of federal lands, establishing a generous policy that would last for decades.

The railroad boom of the 1850s was a signal of the growing industrial might of the American econ-

RAILROAD TRAVEL
In addition to carrying people and goods more quickly and reliably than ever before, railroads also brought many Americans face to face for the first time with machinery that was much larger and more powerful than any human being. This painting of a train leaving Rochester, New York, in 1852 contrasts the size and power of human beings and machines. The huge, lovingly portrayed, steam-belching locomotive is barely held back by some unseen brake against which the massive engine strains, ready to pull the long train through the columns of the station, out of the past and into the future. The people, in contrast, appear indistinct, passive, and dependent. Except for the two women and child in the foreground, the people face backward, and all of them avoid looking directly at the locomotive. The painting evokes the way the almost incomprehensible power of the railroads dwarfed human effort.
From the photographic collection of the Rochester Historical Society.

omy. But railroads, like other industries, succeeded because they served farms as well as cities. And older forms of transportation remained significant. By 1857, for example, trains carried about one-third of the mail; most of the rest still went by stagecoach or horseback. In 1860, most Americans were still far more familiar with horses than with iron horses.

The economy of the 1840s and 1850s linked muscles, animals, and farms to machines, steam, railroads, and cities. Abraham Lincoln split rails as a young man and defended railroad corporations as a successful attorney. His legendary upward

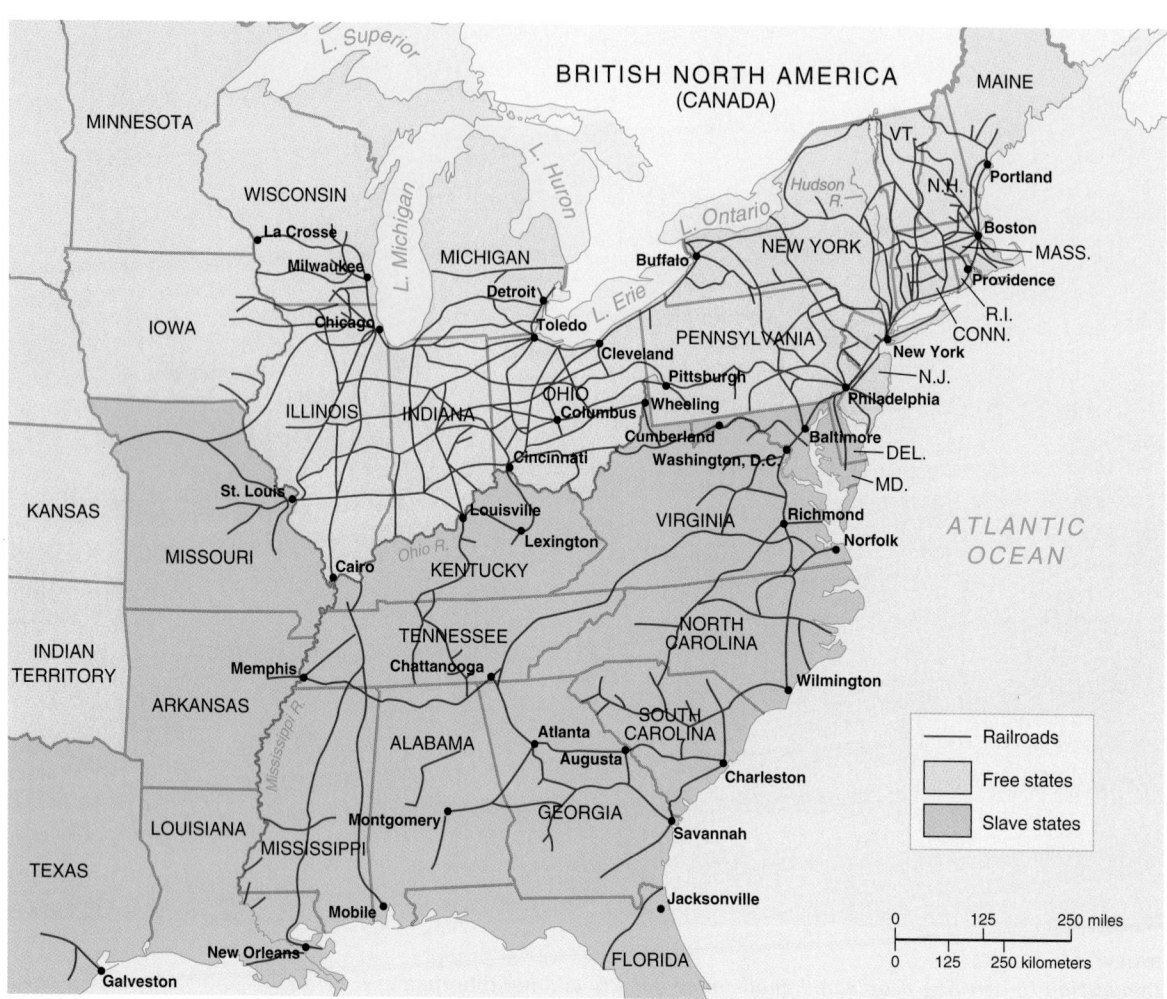

MAP 12.1

Railroads in 1860

Railroads were a crucial component of the revolutions in transportation and communications that transformed nineteenth-century America. The railroad system reflected the differences that had developed in the economies of the North and South.

mobility illustrated the direction of economic change and the opportunities that change offered to enterprising individuals.

Free Labor: Promise and Reality

The impressive economic performance did not reward all Americans equally. With few exceptions, women were excluded from the opportunities open to men. Tens of thousands of women worked as seamstresses, laundresses, domestic servants, factory hands, and teachers, but with little opportunity to aspire to more lucrative jobs. In the North and West, slavery was slowly eliminated in the half century after the American Revolution, but free African Americans there found themselves relegated, on the whole, to dead-end jobs as laborers and servants. This discrimination against women and free blacks did not trouble most white men. With certain notable exceptions, they considered it proper and just.

The Free-Labor Ideal: Freedom plus Labor

During the 1840s and 1850s, leaders throughout the North and West emphasized a set of ideas that seemed to explain why the changes under way in their society benefited some more than others. They referred again and again to the advantages of what they termed "free labor." (The word *free* referred to laborers who were not slaves; it did not mean laborers who worked for nothing.) By the 1850s, free-labor ideas described a social and economic ideal that accounted for both the successes and the shortcomings of the economy and society taking shape in the North and West.

Free-labor spokesmen celebrated hard work, self-reliance, and independence. They proclaimed that the door to success was open not just to those who inherited wealth or status but also to self-made men like Abraham Lincoln. Lincoln himself declared, "Free labor—the just and generous, and prosperous system, which opens the way for all— gives hope to all, and energy, and progress, and improvement of condition to all." The free-labor system permitted farmers and artisans to enjoy the products of their own labor and also benefited wage workers. Ultimately, the free-labor system made it possible for hired laborers to become independent property owners, proponents argued. "The prudent, penniless beginner in the world," Lincoln asserted, "labors for wages awhile, saves a surplus with which to buy tools or land, for himself; then labors on his own account another while, and at length hires another new beginner to help him." Wage labor was the first rung on the ladder toward self-employment and, eventually, to hiring others.

The free-labor ideal affirmed an egalitarian vision of human potential. Lincoln and other spokesmen stressed the importance of universal education to permit "heads and hands [to] cooperate as friends." Throughout the North and West, communities supported public schools to make the rudiments of learning available to young children. By 1860, many cities and towns boasted that up to 80 percent of children age seven to thirteen attended school, at least for a few days each year. In rural areas, where the labor of children was more difficult to spare, schools typically enrolled no more than half the school-age children. Lessons included more than arithmetic, penmanship, and a smattering of other subjects. Textbooks and teachers—most of whom were young women—drummed into students the virtues of the free-labor system: self-reliance, discipline, and, above all, hard work. "Remember that all the ignorance, degradation, and misery in the world is the result of indolence and vice," one textbook intoned. Free-labor ideology, whether in school or out, emphasized labor as much as freedom.

Economic Inequality

The free-labor ideal made sense to many Americans, especially in the North and West, because it seemed to describe their own experience. Lincoln frequently referred to his humble beginnings as a hired laborer and silently invited his listeners to consider how far he had come. In 1860, his wealth of $17,000 easily placed him in the top 5 percent of the population. Most Americans, however, measured success in far more modest terms. The average wealth of adult white men in the North in 1860 barely topped $2,000. Only about a quarter of American men possessed that much. Nearly 60 percent owned no land. It is difficult to estimate the wealth of adult white women since property possessed by married women was normally considered to belong to their husbands, but certainly women had less wealth than men. Free African Americans had still less; 90 percent were propertyless.

Free-labor spokesmen considered these economic inequalities a natural outgrowth of freedom, the inevitable result of some individuals being more able, more willing to work, and luckier. These inequalities suggest, however, the gap between the promise and the performance of the free-labor ideal in this era. Economic growth permitted many men to move from landless squatters to landowning farmers and from hired laborers to independent, self-employed producers. But many more Americans remained behind, landless and working for wages. Even those who realized their aspirations had a precarious hold on their independence; bad debts, crop failure, sickness, or death could quickly eliminate a family's gains.

Seeking out new opportunities in pursuit of free-labor ideals created restless social and geographic mobility. Commonly up to two-thirds of the residents of a rural area moved every decade, and the population turnover in cities was even greater. Such constant coming and going weakened community ties to neighbors and friends and threw individuals even more upon their own resources for help in times of trouble.

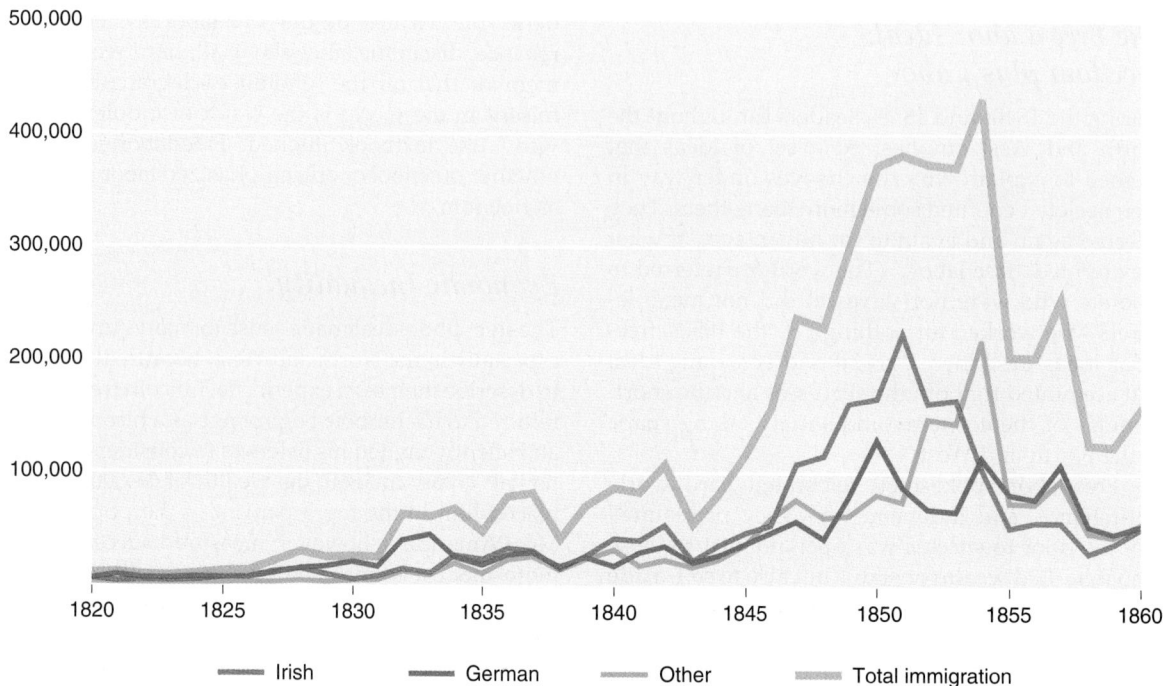

FIGURE 12.1
Antebellum Immigration, 1820–1860
After increasing gradually for several decades, immigration shot up in the mid-1840s.
Between 1848 and 1860, nearly 3.5 million immigrants entered the United States.

Immigrants and the Free-Labor Ladder

The risks and uncertainties of free labor did not deter millions of immigrants from entering the United States during the 1840s and 1850s. Almost four and a half million immigrants arrived between 1840 and 1860, six times more than had come during the previous two decades (Figure 12.1). The half million immigrants who came in 1854 accounted for nearly 2 percent of the entire population, a higher proportion than in any other single year of the nation's history. By 1860, foreign-born residents made up about one-eighth of the American population, a fraction that held steady well into the twentieth century.

Nearly three out of four of the immigrants who arrived between 1840 and 1860 came from either Germany or Ireland. The vast majority of the 1.4 million Germans who entered the United States during these years were skilled tradesmen and their families. They left Germany to escape deteriorating economic conditions and to seize opportunities offered by the expanding economy, where skilled artisans had little difficulty finding work. German butchers, bakers, beer makers, carpenters, shopkeepers, machinists, and others tended to congregate in cities, particularly in the Midwest. Roughly a quarter of German immigrants were farmers, most of whom scattered throughout the Midwest, although some settled in Texas. On the whole, German Americans settled into that middle stratum of sturdy independent producers celebrated by free-labor spokesmen; relatively few Germans occupied the bottom rung of the free-labor ladder as wage laborers or domestic servants.

Irish immigrants, in contrast, entered at the bottom of the free-labor ladder and had difficulty climbing up. Nearly 1.7 million Irish immigrants arrived between 1840 and 1860, nearly all of them desperately poor and often weakened by hunger and disease. Potato blight struck Ireland in 1845 and returned repeatedly in subsequent years, spreading a catastrophic famine throughout the island. Many of the lucky ones, half-starved, crowded into the holds of ships and set out for America, where they congregated in northeastern cities. As one immigrant group declared, "All we want is to get out of Ireland; we must be better anywhere than here."

Roughly three out of four Irish immigrants worked as laborers or domestic servants. Irish men dug canals, loaded ships, built railroad tracks, and took what other work they could find. Irish women hired out to cook, wash and iron, mind children, and clean house. Almost all Irish immigrants were Catholic, a fact that set them apart from the overwhelmingly Protestant native-born residents. Many natives regarded the Irish as hard-drinking, obstreperous, half-civilized folk. Such views lay behind the discrimination that often excluded Irish immigrants from better jobs. Job announcements commonly stated, "No Irish need apply." Despite such prejudices, native residents hired Irish immigrants because they accepted low pay and worked hard.

In America's labor-poor economy, Irish laborers could earn in one day wages that would require several weeks' work in Ireland, if work could be found there. In America, one immigrant explained in 1853, there was "plenty of work and plenty of wages plenty to eat and no land lords thats enough what more does a man want." But some immigrants wanted more, especially respect and decent working conditions. One immigrant complained that he was "a slave for the Americans as the generality of the Irish . . . are."

Such testimony illustrates that the free-labor system, whether for immigrants or native-born laborers, often did not live up to the optimistic vision outlined by Abraham Lincoln and others. Many wage laborers could not realistically aspire to become independent, self-sufficient property holders, despite the claims of free-labor proponents.

Reforming Self and Society

The emphasis on self-discipline and individual effort at the core of the free-labor ideal pervaded America in the 1840s and 1850s. Many Americans believed that insufficient self-control caused the most important social problems of the era. Evangelical Protestants struggled to control individuals' propensity to sin, and temperance advocates exhorted drinkers to control their urge for alcohol. In the midst of the worldly disruptions of geographic expansion and economic change, evangelicals brought more Americans than ever before into churches. Historians estimate that church members accounted for about one-third of the American population by midcentury. Most Americans remained outside churches, as did Abraham Lincoln. But the influence of evangelical religion reached far beyond those who belonged to churches. The evangelical temperament—a conviction of righteousness coupled with energy, self-discipline, and faith that the world could be improved—animated most reformers.

A few activists pointed out that certain fundamental injustices lay beyond the reach of self-control. Transcendentalists and utopians believed that perfection could be attained only by rejecting the competitive values of the larger society. Women's rights activists and abolitionists sought to reverse the subordination of women and to eliminate the enslavement of blacks by changing society. They confronted the daunting challenge of repudiating widespread assumptions about male supremacy and white supremacy and somehow subverting the entrenched institutions that reinforced those assumptions: the family and slavery.

The Pursuit of Perfection: Transcendentalists and Utopians

A group of New England writers that came to be known as transcendentalists believed that individuals should not conform to the materialistic world or to some abstract notion of religion. Instead, people should look within themselves for truth and guidance. The leading transcendentalist, Ralph Waldo Emerson—an essayist, poet, and lecturer—proclaimed that the power of the solitary individual was nearly limitless. Henry David Thoreau, Margaret Fuller, and other transcendentalists agreed with Emerson that "if the single man plant himself indomitably on his instincts, and there abide, the huge world will come round to him." In many ways, transcendentalism represented less an alternative to the values of mainstream society than an exaggerated form of the rampant individualism of the age.

ABOLITIONIST MEETING
This rare daguerreotype was made by Ezra Greenleaf Weld in August 1850 at an abolitionist meeting in Cazenovia, New York. Frederick Douglass, who had escaped from slavery in Maryland twelve years earlier, is seated on the platform next to the woman at the table. One of the nation's most brilliant and eloquent abolitionists, Douglass also supported equal rights for women. The man immediately behind Douglass gesturing with his outstretched arm is Gerrit Smith, a wealthy New Yorker and militant abolitionist whose funds supported many reform activities. Note the two black women in similar clothing on either side of Smith and the white woman next to Douglass. Most white Americans considered such voluntary racial proximity scandalous and promiscuous. What messages did abolitionists attempt to convey by attending such protest meetings?
Collection of the J. Paul Getty Museum, Malibu, Calif.

from the franchise. The pervasive racial discrimination both handicapped and energized black abolitionists. African American leaders organized campaigns against segregation, particularly in transportation and education. Their most notable success came in 1855 when Massachusetts integrated public schools. Elsewhere white supremacy continued unabated.

Outside the public spotlight, free African Americans in the North and West contributed to the antislavery cause by quietly aiding fugitive slaves. Harriet Tubman escaped from slavery in Maryland in 1849 and repeatedly risked her free-

dom and her life to return to the South to escort slaves to freedom. When the opportunity arose, free blacks in the North provided fugitive slaves with food, a safe place to rest, and a helping hand. This "underground railroad" ran mainly through black neighborhoods, black churches, and black homes, an outgrowth of the antislavery sentiment and opposition to white supremacy that unified virtually all African Americans in the North. While a few fortunate southern slaves rode the underground railroad to freedom in the North, millions of other Americans uprooted their families and headed west.

The Westward Movement

The 1840s ushered in an era of rapid westward movement. Until then, the overwhelming majority of Americans lived east of the Mississippi River. To the west, Native Americans inhabited the plains, prairies, and deserts to the rugged coasts of the Pacific. The British claimed Oregon Country, and the Mexican flag flew over the vast expanse of the Southwest. But by 1850, the boundaries of the United States stretched to the Pacific, and the nation had more than doubled its size. By 1860, the great migration had carried four million Americans west of the Mississippi River.

Thomas Jefferson, John Quincy Adams, and other government officials had helped clear the way for the march across the continent by aggressively acquiring territory in the east. The nation's revolution in transportation and communication, its swelling population, and its booming economy propelled the westward surge. But the emigrants themselves conquered the continent. Shock troops of the American empire, frontier settlers craving land took the soil and then lobbied their government to follow them with the flag. The human cost of westward expansion was high. Two centuries of Indian wars east of the Mississippi ended during the 1830s, but the old, fierce struggle between native inhabitant and invader continued for another half century in the West.

Manifest Destiny

Most Americans believed that the superiority of their institutions and white culture bestowed on them a God-given right to spread their civilization across the continent. They imagined the West as a howling wilderness, empty and undeveloped. If they recognized Indians and Mexicans at all, they dismissed them as primitive drags on progress who would have to be redeemed, shoved aside, or exterminated. The sense of uniqueness and mission was as old as the Puritans, but by the 1840s the conviction of superiority had been bolstered by the young nation's amazing success. The West needed the civilizing power of the hammer and plow, the ballot box and pulpit, that had transformed the East, most Americans believed.

In the summer of 1845, New York journalist John L. O'Sullivan coined the term *manifest destiny* as the latest justification for white settlers to take the land they coveted. O'Sullivan was an armchair expansionist, but he took second place to no one in his passion for conquest of the West. He called on Americans to resist any foreign power—British, French, or Mexican—that attempted to thwart "the fulfillment of our manifest destiny to overspread the continent allotted by Providence for the free development of our yearly multiplying millions [and] for the development of the great experiment of liberty and federative self-government entrusted to us." Almost overnight, the magic phrase "manifest destiny" swept the nation and provided an ideological shield for conquering the West.

As important as national pride and racial arrogance were to manifest destiny, economic gain made up its core. Land hunger drew hundreds of thousands of average Americans westward. Some politicians, moreover, had become convinced that national prosperity depended on capturing the rich trade of the Far East. To trade with Asia, the United States needed the Pacific ports that stretched from San Francisco to Puget Sound. No one was more eager to extend American trade in the Pacific than Missouri Senator Thomas Hart Benton. "The sun of civilization must shine across the sea: socially and commercially," he declared. The United States and Asia must "talk together, and trade together. Commerce is a great civilizer." In the 1840s, American economic expansion came wrapped in the rhetoric of uplift and civilization.

Oregon and the Overland Trail

Oregon Country, that vast region bounded on the west by the Pacific, on the east by the Rockies, on the south by the forty-second parallel, and on the north by Russian Alaska, caused the pulse of American expansionists to race (Map 12.2). But Americans were not alone in hungrily eyeing the Pacific Northwest. The British traced their interest—and their rights—to the voyage of Sir Francis Drake, who, they argued, discovered the Oregon coast in 1579. Americans matched the British assertion with historic claims of their own. Unable to agree on ownership, the United States and Great Britain decided in 1818 on a "joint occupation" that would leave Oregon "free and open" to settlement by both countries. A handful of American fur traders and "mountain men" roamed the region in the 1820s, but in the 1830s and 1840s expansionists made Oregon Country an early target of manifest destiny.

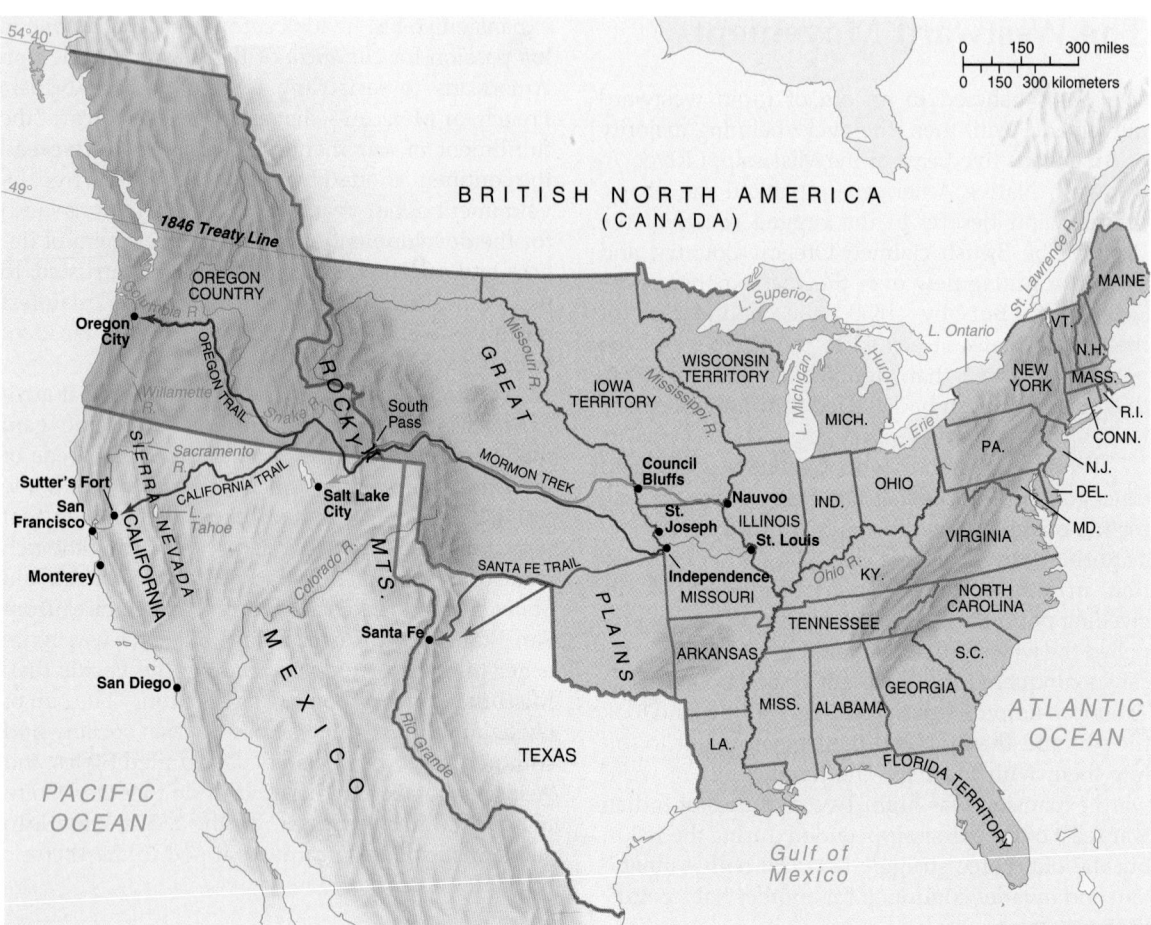

MAP 12.2
Trails to the West
In the 1830s, wagon trains began snaking their way to the Southwest and the Pacific coast. Deep ruts, some of which can still be seen today, soon marked the most popular routes.

By the late 1830s, settlers began to trickle along the Oregon Trail, following a path blazed by the mountain men (see Map 12.2). The first wagon trains hit the trail in 1841, and by 1843 about 1,000 emigrants a year set out from Independence, Missouri. By 1869, when the first transcontinental railroad was completed, something like 350,000 migrants had traveled west to the Pacific in wagon trains.

Emigrants encountered Plains Indians, whose cultures differed markedly from those of the Eastern Woodlands tribes. The quarter of a million Native Americans who populated the area between the Rocky Mountains and the Mississippi River defy

easy generalization. Some were farmers who lived peaceful, sedentary lives, but a majority of Plains Indians—the Sioux, Cheyenne, Shoshoni, and Arapaho of the Central Plains and the Kiowa, Wichita, Apache, and Comanche in the Southwest—were horse-mounted, nomadic, nonagricultural peoples whose warriors symbolized the "savage Indian" in the minds of whites.

Horses, which had been brought to the continent by Spaniards in the sixteenth century, permitted the Plains tribes to become highly mobile hunters of buffalo. In time they came to depend on buffalo for most of their food, clothing, shelter, and fuel. As they followed the huge herds over the plains, these peoples bumped into one another. Competition and warfare became a crucial component of their way of life. Young men were introduced to the art of war early, learning to ride ponies at breakneck speed while firing off arrows and, later, rifles with astounding accuracy. "A Comanche on his feet is out of his element," observed George Catlin, an artist of the West, "but the moment he lays his hands upon his horse, I doubt very much whether any people in the world can surpass [him]."

Plains Indians struck fear in the hearts of whites on the wagon trains. But Native Americans had far more to fear from whites. Indians killed fewer than four hundred emigrants on the trail between 1840 and 1860, while whites proved to be deadly to the Indians. Even though they were usually just passing through on their way to the Pacific slope, whites brought alcohol and disease, especially epidemics of smallpox, measles, cholera, and scarlet fever. Moreover, whites killed the buffalo, slaughtering hundreds of thousands for sport. Buffalo still numbered some twelve million in 1860, but the herds were shrinking rapidly, intensifying conflict among the Plains Indians.

As the number of wagon trains increased, emigrants insisted that the federal government provide them more protection. The government responded by constructing a chain of forts along the trail. More important, the United States adopted a new Indian policy of "concentration." To clear the way, the government rescinded the "permanent" buffer it had granted the Indians west of the ninety-fifth meridian, which was only two or three hundred miles west of the Mississippi River. Then, in 1851, it called the Plains tribes to a conference at Fort Laramie, Wyoming. Some ten thousand Dakota, Sioux, Arapaho, Cheyenne, Crow, and other Indians showed up, hopeful that something could be done

Plains Indians and Trails West in the 1840s and 1850s

to protect them from the ravages of the wagon trains. Instead, government negotiators persuaded the chiefs to sign agreements restricting their people to specific areas that whites promised they would never violate. This policy of isolation became the seedbed for the subsequent policy of reservations. But whites would not keep out of Indian territory, and Indians would not easily give up their traditional way of life. Competition meant warfare for decades to come.

Still, Indians threatened emigrants less than life on the trail did. The men, women, and children who headed west each spring could count on four to six months of grueling travel. With nearly two thousand miles to go and traveling no more than fifteen miles a day, the pioneers endured parching heat, drought, treacherous rivers, disease, physical and emotional exhaustion, and, if the snows closed the mountain passes before they got through, freezing and starvation. Women sometimes faced the dangers of trailside childbirth. It was said that one could walk from Missouri to the Pacific stepping only on the graves of those who had failed to make it.

Everyone experienced hardships on the trail, but no one felt the burden quite as much as the women who made the trip. Since husbands usually decided to pull up stakes and go west, many wives went involuntarily. One miserable woman, trying to keep her children dry in a rainstorm and to calm them as they listened to Indian shouts, wondered "what had possessed my husband, anyway, that he should have thought of bringing us away out through this God forsaken country." Men viewed the privation as a necessary step to land of their own and an independent life; women tended to judge it by the homes, kin, and friends they had left behind to take up what one called "this wild goose chase."

When men reached Oregon, they usually liked what they found. Oregon is "one of the greatest countries in the world," Richard R. Howard declared. From "the Cascade mountains to the Pacific, the whole country can be cultivated." When women reached Oregon, they found a wilderness. "I had all I could do to keep from asking George to turn around and bring me back home," one woman wrote to her mother in Missouri. Neighbors were few and far between, and the isolation weighed heavily. Moreover, things were in a "primitive state." One young wife set up housekeeping with her new husband with only one stew kettle and

WI-JUN-JON, AN ASSINIBOIN CHIEF
*Pennsylvania-born artist George Catlin, the painter of this 1845 dual portrait, was
present in the Assiniboin village when Wi-Jun-Jon returned from Washington, D.C.,
wearing the military uniform that President Andrew Jackson had presented to him. His
uniform and ceaseless boasting bred so much dislike and distrust that a young warrior
from a nearby tribe murdered him. Catlin was convinced that the western Indian
cultures he had begun observing in the 1830s would soon disappear, and he sought to
document Indian life through hundreds of paintings and prints.*
Library of Congress.

www.bedfordstmartins.com/roarkcompact   SEE THE ONLINE STUDY GUIDE for more help in
analyzing these images.

three knives. Necessity blurred the traditional division between men's and women's work. "I am maid
of all traids," one busy woman remarked in 1853.
Work seemed unending. "I am a very old woman,"
remarked twenty-nine-year-old Sarah Everett. "My
face is thin sunken and wrinkled, my hands bony

withered and hard." As one wife observed, "A
woman that can not endure almost as much as a
horse has no business here."

Despite the ordeal of the trail and the difficulties of starting from scratch, emigrants kept coming. By 1845, Oregon counted five thousand Amer-

PIONEER FAMILY ON THE TRAIL WEST
In 1860, W. G. Chamberlain photographed these unidentified travelers momentarily at rest by the Upper Arkansas River in Colorado. We do not know their fates, but we can hope that they fared better than the Sager family, Henry, Naomi, and their six daughters, who set out from St. Joseph, Missouri, in 1844. "Father," one of his daughters remembered, "was one of those restless men who are not content to remain in one place long at a time. [He] had been talking of going to Texas. But mother, hearing much said about the healthfulness of Oregon, preferred to go there." Still far from Oregon, Henry Sager died of fever, and twenty-six days later, Naomi died, leaving seven children, the last delivered on the trail. The Sager children, under the care of other families in the wagon train, pressed on. After traveling 2,000 miles in seven months, the migrants arrived in Oregon, where a couple named the Whitmans, whose daughter had drowned, adopted all of the Sager children.
Denver Public Library, Western History Division # F3226.

ican settlers. And from the beginning, they clamored for the protection of the U.S. government.

The Mormon Migration

Not every wagon train heading west was bound for the Pacific slope. One remarkable group of religious emigrants chose to settle in the heart of the arid West. Halting near the Great Salt Lake in what was

then Mexican territory, the Mormons deliberately chose the remote site as a refuge. After years of persecution in the East, they sought religious freedom and communal security in the West.

In 1830, Joseph Smith Jr., who was only twenty-four, published *The Book of Mormon* and founded the Church of Jesus Christ of Latter-Day Saints (the Mormons). A decade earlier, the upstate New York farm boy had begun to have visions and revelations that were followed, he said, by a visit from an angel who led him to golden tablets buried near his home. With the aid of magic stones, he translated the mysterious language on the tablets. What was revealed was *The Book of Mormon*. It told the story of an ancient Christian civilization in the New World and predicted the appearance of an American prophet who would reestablish Jesus Christ's undefiled kingdom in America. Converts, attracted to the promise of a pure faith in the midst of antebellum America's social turmoil and rampant materialism, flocked to the new church.

"Gentile" neighbors branded Mormons heretics and resented what they considered their religious self-righteousness and their sympathy toward abolitionists and Indians. Persecution drove Smith and his followers from New York to Ohio, then to Missouri, and finally in 1839 to Nauvoo, Illinois, where they built a prosperous community of fifteen thousand. But dissenters within the church accused Smith of advocating plural marriage (polygamy) and published an exposé of the practice. Non-Mormons caught wind of the controversy and eventually arrested Smith and his brother. On June 27, 1844, a mob stormed the jail and shot both men dead.

The embattled church turned to an extraordinary new leader, Brigham Young, who immediately began to plan the exodus of his people from Illinois. In 1846, traveling in 3,700 wagons, twelve thousand Mormons made their way to eastern Iowa and eventually to their new home beside the Great Salt Lake. Young described it as a barren waste, "the paradise of the lizard, the cricket and the rattlesnake." Within ten years, however, the Mormons developed an efficient irrigation system and made the desert bloom. They accomplished the feat through cooperative labor, not the individualistic and competitive enterprise common among most emigrants. Under the stern leadership of Young and other church leaders, the Mormons built a thriving community.

In 1850, only three years after its founding, Deseret, as the Mormons called their kingdom, became annexed to the United States as Utah Territory. But what focused the nation's attention on the Latter-Day Saints was the announcement by Brigham Young in 1852 that many Mormons practiced polygamy. Although only one Mormon man in five had more than one wife (Young had twenty-three), Young's public statement caused an outcry that forced the government to establish its authority in Utah. In 1857, twenty-five hundred U.S. troops in-

vaded Salt Lake City in what was known as the Mormon War. The bloodless occupation illustrates that most Americans viewed the Mormons as a threat to American morality, law, and institutions. The invasion did not dislodge the Mormon Church from its central place in Utah, however, and for years to come most Americans perceived the Mormon settlement as a strange, and suitably isolated, place.

The Mexican Borderlands

In the Mexican Southwest, westward-moving Anglo-American pioneers confronted northern-moving Spanish-speaking frontiersmen. On this frontier as elsewhere, cultures, interests, and aspirations collided. Since 1821, when Mexico won its independence from Spain, the Mexican flag had flown over the vast expanse that stretched from the Gulf of Mexico to the Pacific and from Oregon Country to Guatemala. Mexico's borders remained ill defined, and its northern provinces were sparsely populated. Moreover, severe problems plagued the young nation: civil wars, economic crises, quarrels between the Roman Catholic Church and the state, and devastating raids by the Comanche, Apache, and Kiowa. Mexico found it increasingly difficult to defend its borderlands, especially when faced with a northern neighbor that was convinced of its superiority and bent on territorial acquisition.

The American assault began quietly. In the 1820s, when Anglo-American trappers, traders, and settlers began drifting into Mexico's far northern provinces, they discovered that their newly independent neighbor was eager for American business. Santa Fe, a remote outpost in the province of New Mexico, became a magnet for American enterprise. American traders gathered each spring at Independence, Missouri, for the long trek southwest along the Santa Fe Trail (see Map 12.2). They crammed their wagons with inexpensive American manufactured goods and returned with Mexican silver, furs, and mules.

The Mexican province of Texas attracted a flood of Americans who had settlement, not long-distance trade, on their minds (Map 12.3). The Mexican government, which wanted to populate and develop its northern territory, granted the American Stephen F. Austin a huge tract of land, and in the 1820s he established a thriving settlement along the Brazos River. Land was cheap—only ten cents an acre—and thousands of farmers poured over the

MAP 12.3

Texas and Mexico in the 1830s

As Americans spilled into lightly populated and loosely governed northern Mexico, Texas and then other Mexican provinces became contested territory.

border. Most of the migrants were Southerners, who brought cotton and slaves with them. By 1835, the number of American settlers—free and slave—in Texas had reached thirty thousand, while the Tejano (Spanish-speaking) population was less than eight thousand. Most Anglo-American settlers were not Roman Catholic, did not speak Spanish, and cared little about assimilating into a culture that was so different from their own. In 1829, the Mexican government sought to arrest further immigration with an emancipation proclamation, which it hoped would make Texas less attractive. The settlers sidestepped the decree by calling their slaves servants, but settlers had other grievances, most significantly the puny voice they had in local government. General Antonio López de Santa Anna all but extinguished that voice when he seized political power and concentrated authority in Mexico City.

Faced with what they considered tyranny, the Texan settlers rebelled and declared the independent Republic of Texas. Santa Anna took the field and in February 1836 arrived at the outskirts of San Antonio with nearly 6,000 troops. The rebels, who included the Tennessee frontiersman Davy Crockett and the Louisiana adventurer Jim Bowie, as well

as a number of Tejanos, took refuge in the old Franciscan mission, the Alamo. Wave after wave of Mexicans crashed against the walls until the attackers finally broke through and killed all 187 defenders. A few weeks later in the small town of Goliad, Mexican forces surrounded and captured a garrison of 365 Texans. Following orders from Santa Anna, Mexican firing squads executed the men as pirates. But in April 1836 at San Jacinto, Santa Anna suffered a crushing defeat at the hands of forces under General Sam Houston. Texans had succeeded in establishing their Lone Star Republic, and the following year the United States recognized the independence of Texas from Mexico.

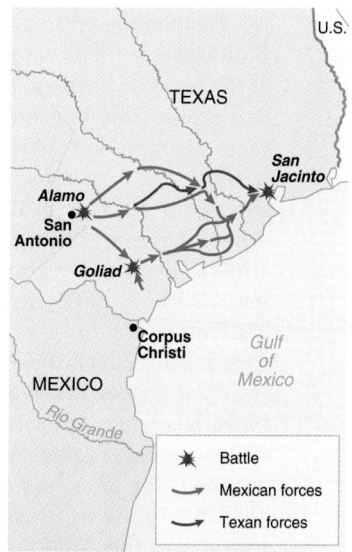

Texas War for Independence, 1836

The distant Mexican province of California also caught the eye of a few Anglo-Americans. Spain had first extended its influence into California in 1769, when it sent a naval expedition north from Mexico to San Francisco Bay in an effort to block Russian fur traders who were moving south along the Pacific Coast from their base in Alaska. The Spanish built garrisoned towns (*presidios*), but, more important, they constructed a string of twenty-one missions, spaced a day's journey apart, along the coast from San Diego to Sonoma. Junípero Serra and other Franciscan friars converted the Indians to Christianity and drew them into the life and often hard agricultural labor of the missions. In 1824, in an effort to increase Mexican migration to thinly settled California, the Mexican government granted *ranchos*—huge estates devoted to cattle raising—to new settlers. *Rancheros* ruled over near-feudal empires worked by Indians whose condition sometimes approached that of slaves. Not satisfied, *rancheros* coveted the vast lands controlled by the Franciscan missions. In 1834, they persuaded the government to confiscate the missions and make their lands available to new settlement, a development that accelerated the decline of California Indians. Devastated by disease, the Indians, who numbered approximately 300,000 when the Spanish arrived in 1769, declined to half that number by 1846.

Despite the efforts of the Mexican government, California in 1840 counted a population of only 7,000 Mexican settlers. Non-Mexican settlers numbered only 380, but among them were Americans who championed manifest destiny. Thomas O. Larkin, a prosperous merchant, John Marsh, a successful *ranchero* in the San Joaquin Valley, and others became boosters who sought to attract Americans from Oregon Country to California. The first overland party arrived in California in 1841. Thereafter, wagon after wagon followed the California Trail, which forked off from the Oregon Trail near the Snake River and led through the Sierra Nevada at Lake Tahoe (see Map 12.2). As the trickle of Americans became a river, Mexican officials grew alarmed, for as a New York newspaper put it in 1845, "Let the tide of emigration flow toward California and the American population will soon be sufficiently numerous to play the Texas game." Not all Americans in California wanted to play the "Texas game," but many dreamed of living again under the American flag.

The U.S. government made no secret of its desire to acquire California. In 1835, President Andrew Jackson tried to purchase it. In 1842, Commodore Thomas Catesby Jones, hearing a rumor that the United States and Mexico were at war, seized the port of Monterey and ran up the American flag. The red-faced officer promptly ran it down again when he learned of his error. But his actions left no doubt about Washington's intentions. In 1846, American settlers in the Sacramento Valley took matters into their own hands. Prodded by John C. Frémont, a former army captain and explorer who had arrived in December 1845 with a party of sixty buckskin-clad frontiersmen spoiling for a fight, the Californians raised an independence movement known as the Bear Flag Revolt. By then, James K. Polk, a champion of expansion, sat in the White House.

Expansion and the Mexican War

Although emigrants acted as the advanced guard of American empire, there was nothing automatic about the U.S. annexation of territory in the West. Acquiring territory required political action, and in the 1840s the difficult problems of Texas, Oregon, and the Mexican borderlands intruded into national politics. The politics of expansion became entangled with sectionalism and the slavery question and thrust the United States into dangerous diplomatic crises with Great Britain and Mexico.

Aggravation between Mexico and the United States escalated to open antagonism in 1845 when the United States annexed Texas. Absorbing territory still claimed by Mexico ruptured diplomatic relations between the two countries and set the stage for war. But it was President James K. Polk's insistence on having Mexico's other northern provinces that made war certain. The war was not as easy as Polk anticipated, but it ended in American victory and acquisition of a new American West.

The Politics of Expansion

The complicated issues of westward expansion and the nation's boundaries ended up on the desk of John Tyler when he became president in April 1841. The Whig William Henry Harrison had been elected president in 1840, but one month after he took office, he died. Tyler, nominally a Whig but actually a Democrat in his political convictions, spent much of his administration beating back the Whig Henry Clay's efforts to turn his party's American System —protective tariffs, a national bank, and internal improvements—into law.

But the issue that stirred John Tyler's blood, and that of much of the nation, was Texas. Texans had sought admission to the Union almost since their independence from Mexico in 1836, but Tyler, an ardent expansionist, understood that Texas was a dangerous issue. Any suggestion of adding another slave state to the Union brought many Northerners to a boil. Annexing Texas also risked precipitating war because Mexico had never relinquished its claim to its lost province.

Cold-shouldered by the United States, Texans explored Great Britain's interest in recognition. Britain was eager to keep Texas independent. In Britain's eyes, Texas provided a buffer against American expansion and a new market for English manufactured goods. American officials worried that Britain's real object was adding Texas to the British Empire. This volatile mix of threat, fear, and opportunity convinced Tyler to risk negotiations with Texas, and he worked vigorously to annex the republic before his term expired. His efforts pushed Texas and the slavery issue to the center of national politics.

In April 1844, after months of secret negotiations between Texas and the Tyler administration, the new secretary of state, John C. Calhoun, laid an annexation treaty before the Senate. But when Calhoun linked annexation to the defense of slavery, he doomed the treaty. Howls of protest erupted across the North. When the Senate soundly rejected the treaty, it appeared that Tyler had succeeded only in inflaming sectional conflict.

The issue of Texas had not died down by the 1844 elections. Henry Clay looked forward to receiving the Whig nomination and waging his campaign on the old Whig economic principles that Tyler had frustrated. But in an effort to appeal to northern voters, Clay came out against the immediate annexation of Texas. "Annexation and war with Mexico are identical," he declared. When news of Clay's statement reached Andrew Jackson at his plantation in Tennessee, he chuckled, "Clay [is] a dead political Duck." In Jackson's shrewd judgment, no man who opposed annexation could be elected president. But the Whig Party paid no attention and nominated Clay.

The Democrats chose James K. Polk of Tennessee. Polk was as strong for the annexation of Texas as Clay was against it. To make Texas annexation palatable to Northerners, the Democrats shrewdly yoked Texas to Oregon, thus tapping the desire for expansion in the free states of the North as well in the slave states of the South. The Democratic platform called for the "reannexation of Texas" and the "reoccupation of Oregon." The suggestion that the United States was merely reasserting its existing rights was poor history but good politics. According to the Democratic formula, Texas annexation did not give an advantage to slavery and the South. Linked to Oregon, Texas expanded America to the advantage of the entire nation.

During the campaign, Clay finally recognized the groundswell for expansion, and he waffled on Texas, hinting that he might accept annexation under certain circumstances. His retreat won little support in the South and only succeeded in alienating antislavery opinion in the North. James G. Birney, the candidate of the fledgling Liberty Party, picked up the votes of thousands of disillusioned Clay supporters. In the November election, Polk received 170 electoral votes and Clay 105. New York's 35 electoral votes proved critical to Clay's defeat. A shift of just one-third of Birney's 15,000 votes to Clay would have given him the state and the presidency.

The nation did not have to wait for Polk's inauguration to see results from his victory. One month after the election, President Tyler announced that the Democratic triumph provided a mandate for the annexation of Texas "promptly and immediately." In February 1845, after a fierce debate between antislavery and proslavery forces, Congress approved a joint resolution offering the Republic of Texas admission to the United States. Texas entered as the fifteenth slave state.

Tyler had delivered Texas, but Polk had promised Oregon, too. Westerners particularly demanded that the new president make good on the Democrats' campaign slogan—"Fifty-four Forty or Fight"—that is, all of Oregon, right up to Alaska (54°40′ being the southern latitude of Russian Alaska). But Polk was close to war with Mexico and could not afford a simultaneous war with Britain over its claims to Canada. After the initial bluster, therefore, Polk buried the Democrats' campaign promise and renewed an old offer to divide Oregon along the forty-ninth parallel. When Britain accepted the compromise, some cried betrayal, but most Americans celebrated the agreement that gave the nation an enormous territory peacefully. Besides, when the Senate finally approved the treaty in June 1846, the United States and Mexico were already at war.

The Mexican War, 1846–1848

From the day he entered the White House, Polk craved Mexico's remaining northern provinces: California and New Mexico, land that today makes up California, Nevada, and Utah, most of New Mexico and Arizona, and parts of Wyoming and Colorado. Polk hoped to buy the territory, but the Mexicans refused to sell off their country. A furious Polk concluded that it would take military force to realize the United States' manifest destiny.

Polk had already ordered General Zachary Taylor to march his 4,000-man Army of Occupation of Texas from its position on the Nueces River, the southern boundary of Texas according to the Mexicans, to the banks of the Rio Grande 150 miles south, the boundary claimed by Texans. The Mexican general in Matamoros viewed the American advance as aggression and ordered Taylor back to the Nueces. Taylor refused, and on April 25 Mexican cavalry attacked a party of American soldiers, killing or wounding 16 and capturing the rest. Even before news of the battle arrived in Washington, Polk had already obtained his cabinet's approval of a war message.

On May 11, 1846, the president told Congress, "Mexico has passed the boundary of the United States, has invaded our territory, and shed American blood upon American soil." Thus "war exists, and, notwithstanding all our efforts to avoid it, exists by the act of Mexico herself." Two days later, Congress passed a declaration of war and began raising an army. Despite years of saber rattling toward Mexico and Britain, the American army was pitifully small, only 7,400 soldiers. Faced with the nation's first foreign war, up against a Mexican army that numbered more than 30,000, Polk called for volunteers. Men rushed to the colors. Eventually, more than 112,000 white Americans (blacks were banned) joined the army to fight in Mexico.

Despite the outpouring of support, the war divided the nation. Northerners were not nearly as hot-blooded about the war as Southerners. North-

ern Whigs in particular loudly condemned the war as the unwarranted bullying of a weak nation by its greedy expansionist neighbor. On January 12, 1848, a gangly freshman Whig representative from Illinois rose from his back-row seat in the House of Representatives to deliver his first important speech in Congress. Before Abraham Lincoln sat down, he had questioned the president's intelligence, honesty, and sanity. President Polk simply ignored the upstart representative, but antislavery, antiwar Whigs kept up the attack throughout the conflict. In their effort to undercut national support, they labeled it "Mr. Polk's War."

Since most Americans backed the war, it was not really Polk's war, but the president acted as if it were. Although he had no military experience, he directed the war personally. Working eighteen hours a day, Polk established overall strategy and oversaw the details of military campaigns. He planned a short war in which American armies would occupy Mexico's northern provinces and defeat the Mexican army in a decisive battle or two, after which Mexico would sue for peace and the United States would keep the territory its armies occupied.

And, indeed, Polk's strategy seemed to work at first. In May 1846, Zachary Taylor's troops drove south from the Rio Grande and routed the Mexican army, first on the plain of Palo Alto and then in a palm-filled ravine known as Resaca de la Palma (Map 12.4). "Old Rough and Ready," as Taylor was affectionately known among his adoring troops, became an instant war hero. Polk rewarded Taylor for his victories by making him commander of the Mexican campaign.

A second prong of the campaign to occupy Mexico's northern provinces centered on Colonel Stephen Watts Kearny, who led a 1,700-man army from Missouri into New Mexico. Without firing a shot, American forces took Santa Fe in August 1846. Kearny promptly proclaimed New Mexico American territory and with 300 troops headed for California. Three months later, Kearny's army marched into San Diego and into a major Mexican rebellion against American rule. In January 1847, after several clashes, the American forces occupied Los Angeles. California and New Mexico were in American hands.

By then, Taylor had driven deep into the interior of Mexico. In September 1846, after a five-day siege and house-to-house fighting, he took the fortified city of Monterrey. With reinforcements and

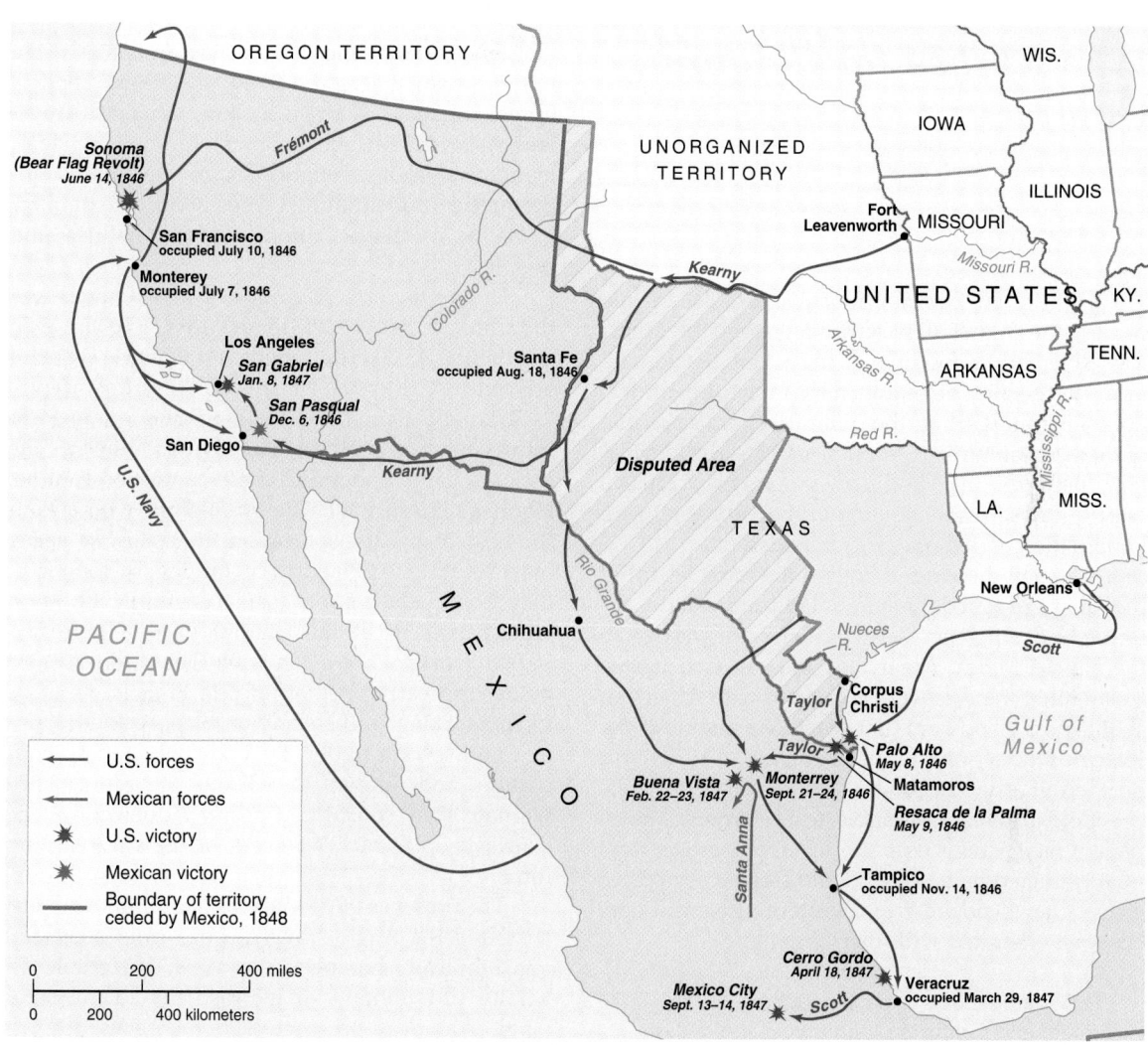

MAP 12.4
The Mexican War, 1846–1848
American and Mexican soldiers skirmished across much of northern Mexico, but the major battles took place between the Rio Grande and Mexico City.

fresh supplies, Taylor pushed his 5,000 troops southwest, where the Mexican hero of the Alamo, General Antonio López de Santa Anna, was concentrating a huge army of 21,000, which he hoped would strike a decisive blow against the invaders from the north.

In February 1847, Taylor's troops met Santa Anna's at Buena Vista. Superior American artillery and accurate musket fire won the day, but the Americans suffered heavy casualties, including Henry Clay Jr., the son of the man who had opposed Texas

annexation for fear it would precipitate war. But the Mexicans suffered even greater losses.

The series of uninterrupted victories in northern Mexico fed the American troops' sense of superiority and very nearly led to a feeling of invincibility. "No American force has ever thought of being defeated by any amount of Mexican troops," one soldier declared. The Americans worried about other hazards, however. "I can assure you that fighting is the least dangerous & arduous part of a soldier's life," one young man said. Of the 13,000

Who Rushed for California Gold?

ON A COLD JANUARY morning in 1848, while James Marshall was walking along the American River in the foothills of the Sierra Nevada, he detected the glint of yellow metal in the stream. The flakes he found set off the California gold rush, one of the wildest mining stampedes in the world's history. Between 1849 and 1852, more than 250,000 "forty-niners," as the would-be miners were known, descended on the Golden State.

Marshall discovered gold in the same year that the Treaty of Guadalupe Hidalgo transferred California and other northern provinces of Mexico to the United States. Americans did not find it surprising that the discovery coincided with American acquisition. "God kept that coast for a people of the Pilgrim blood," one minister intoned. "He would not permit any other to be fully developed there."

Gold proved irresistible to easterners. Newspapers went crazy with stories about prospectors who extracted half a pan of gold from every pan of gravel they scooped from western streams. Soon, cities reverberated with men singing:

Oh Susannah, don't you cry for me;
I'm gone to California with my wash-bowl on
    my knee.

Scores of ships sailed from East Coast ports, headed either around South America to San Francisco or across the Gulf of Mexico to Panama, where the passengers made their way by foot and canoe to the Pacific and waited for a ship to carry them north. Even larger numbers of gold seekers took riverboats to the Missouri River and then set out in wagons, on horseback, or by foot for the West.

But young men everywhere contracted gold fever. As stories of California gold circled the globe, Chinese and Germans, Mexicans and Irish, Australians and French, Chileans and Italians, and people of dozens of other nationalities set out to strike it rich. Louisa Knapp Clappe, wife of a minister and one of the few women in gold country, remarked that when she walked through Indian Bar, the little mining town where she lived, she heard English, French, Spanish, German, Italian, Kanaka (Hawaiian), Asian Indian, and American Indian languages. Hangtown, Hell's Delight, Gouge Eye, and a hundred other crude mining camps became temporary home to a diverse throng of nationalities and peoples.

One of the largest groups of new arrivals was the Chinese. Between 1848 and 1854, Chinese men numbering 45,000 (but almost no Chinese women) arrived in California. Most considered themselves "sojourners," temporary residents who planned to return home as soon as their savings allowed. The majority came under a Chinese-controlled contract labor system in which the immigrant worked out the cost of his transportation. In the early years, most became wage laborers in mining. By the 1860s, they dominated railroad construction in the West. Ninety percent of the Central Pacific Railroad's 10,000 workers were Chinese. The Chinese also made up nearly one-half of San Francisco's labor force, working in the shoe, tobacco, woolen, laundry, and sewing trades. By 1870, the Chinese population had grown to 63,200, including 4,500 women. They constituted nearly 10 percent of the state's people and 25 percent of its wage-earning force.

The presence of peoples from around the world shattered the Anglo-American dream of a racially and ethnically homogeneous West, but ethnic diversity did nothing to increase the tolerance of Anglo-American prospectors. In their eyes, no "foreigner" had a right to dig gold. In 1850, the California legislature passed the Foreign Miners' Tax Law, which levied high taxes on non-Americans to drive them from the gold fields, except as hired laborers working on claims owned by Americans. Stubborn foreign miners were sometimes hauled before "Judge Lynch." One of the earliest lynchings in the gold fields was of a Frenchman and a Chilean.

Anglo-Americans considered the Chinese devious and unassimilable. They also feared that hardworking, self-denying Chinese labor would undercut white labor and drive it from the country. As a consequence, the Chinese were segregated residentially and occupationally and made ineligible for citizenship. Along with blacks and Indians, Chinese were denied public education and the right to testify in court. In addition to exclusion, they suffered

from violence. Mobs drove them from Eureka, Truckee, and other mining towns.

American prospectors swamped the *Californios*, the Spanish and Mexican settlers who had lived in California for generations. On the eve of the American takeover, *Californios* included *rancheros*, professionals, merchants, artisans, and laborers. Raging prejudice and discriminatory laws increasingly pushed Hispanics into the ranks of unskilled labor. Americans took their land, even though the federal government had pledged to protect Mexican and Spanish land titles after the cession of 1848. Anglo forty-niners branded Spanish-speaking miners, even native-born *Californios*, "foreigners" and drove them from the diggings. Mariano Vallejo, a leading *Californio*, said of the forty-niners: "The good ones were few and the wicked many."

For Native Americans, the gold rush was a catastrophe. Numbering about 150,000 in 1848, the Indian population fell to 25,000 in 1856. *Californios* had exploited the native peoples, but the forty-niners wanted to eradicate them. Starvation, disease, and a declining birthrate took a heavy toll. Indians also fell victim to wholesale murder. "That a war of extermination will continue to be waged between the two races until the Indian race becomes extinct must

be expected," declared California governor Peter W. Burnett in 1851. Nineteenth-century historian Hubert Howe Bancroft described white behavior toward Indians during the gold rush as "one of the last human hunts of civilization, and the basest and most brutal of them all." To survive, Indians moved to the most remote areas of the state and tried to stay out of the way.

The forty-niners created dazzling wealth—in 1852, eighty-one million ounces of gold, nearly one-half of the world's production. But because Anglo-Americans made the rules, not everyone shared equally. And only a few prospectors—of whatever race and nationality—struck it rich. The era of the individual prospector panning in streams quickly gave way to corporate-owned deep-shaft mining. Most forty-niners eventually took up farming or worked for wages for the corporations that pushed them out. But because of gold, an avalanche of people had roared across California. Anglo-Americans were most numerous, and Anglo dominance developed early. But the gold rush also brought a rainbow of nationalities. Anglo-American ascendancy and ethnic and racial diversity in the West both count among the most significant legacies of the gold rush.

BATTLE OF PALO ALTO
The battle of Palo Alto, fought in May 1846 and captured here by lithographer Carl
Nebel, was the first full-scale battle the U.S. Army had fought since the War of 1812.
Here we see General Zachary Taylor astride Old Whitey, as he directs the action from
the right foreground. On the extreme right Colonel David Twiggs's infantry repulses
Anastasio Torrejon's cavalry. On the left smoke from the grass fire conceals 150 addi-
tional Mexican cavalrymen. Ferocious American artillery won the day. "The American
artillery," one Mexican reported, "much superior to ours, made terrible ravages in the
Mexican ranks. . . . The troops, drained by the needless deaths, pleaded to go before the
enemy's bayonets and die bravely in close range."
Amon Carter Museum of Western Art, Fort Worth, Texas.

American soldiers who died in Mexico (some 50,000 Mexicans died), only 2,000 fell to Mexican bullets and shells. Disease killed most of the others. Medicine was so primitive and conditions so harsh that army doctors could do little. As a Tennessee man observed, "nearly all who take sick die."

Victory in Mexico

Although Americans won battle after battle, President Polk's strategy misfired. Despite its loss of territory and men, Mexico determinedly refused to trade land for peace. One American soldier captured the Mexican mood: "They cannot submit to be deprived of California after the loss of Texas, and nothing but the conquest of their Capital will force them to such a humiliation." Polk had arrived at the same conclusion. Zachary Taylor had not proven decisive enough for Polk, and the president tapped another general to carry the war to Mexico City. While Taylor occupied the north, General Winfield Scott would land his army on the Gulf coast of Mexico and march 250 miles inland to the capital. Polk's plan entailed enormous risk; it meant that Scott would have to cut himself off from supplies on the coast and lead his men deep into enemy country against a numerically superior foe.

After months of careful planning and the skillful coordination of army and navy, an amphibious landing near Veracruz put 8,600 American troops ashore in five hours without the loss of a single life. After eighty-eight hours of furious shelling, Veracruz surrendered. Scott immediately began preparations for the march west. Transportation alone posed enormous problems. His army required 9,300 wagons and 17,000 pack mules, 500,000 bushels of oats and corn, and 100 pounds of blister ointment before it could begin the mountainous journey. In early April 1847, the army moved out, following the path that had been trodden more than three centuries earlier by Hernán Cortés.

Meanwhile, after the frightful defeat at Buena Vista, Santa Anna had returned to Mexico City. He rallied his ragged troops and marched them east to set a trap for Scott in the mountain pass at Cerro Gordo. But the Americans knifed through Mexican lines, almost capturing Santa Anna, who fled the field on foot. So complete was the victory that Scott gloated to Taylor, "Mexico no longer has an army." But ever resilient, Santa Anna again rallied the Mexican army. Some 30,000 troops took up defensive positions on the outskirts of Mexico City, where

MAP 12.5

Territorial Expansion by 1860
Less than a century after its founding, the United States had spread from the Atlantic seaboard to the Pacific Ocean. War, purchase, and diplomacy had gained a continent.

READING THE MAP: List the countries from which the United States acquired land. Which nation lost the most land because of U.S. expansion?
CONNECTIONS: Who coined the phrase "manifest destiny"? When? What does it mean? What areas targeted for expansion were debated during the presidential campaign of 1844?

www.bedfordstmartins.com/roarkcompact SEE THE ONLINE STUDY GUIDE for more help in analyzing this map.

they hurriedly began melting down church bells to cast new cannon.

In August, Scott began his assault on the Mexican capital. The fighting proved the most brutal of the war. Santa Anna backed his army into the city, fighting each step of the way. At the battle of Churubusco, the Mexicans took 4,000 casualties in a single day and the Americans more than 1,000. At the castle of Chapultepec, American troops scaled the walls and fought the Mexican defenders hand to hand. After Chapultepec, Santa Anna evacuated Mexico City, and on September 14, 1847, General Winfield Scott rode in triumphantly. The ancient capital of the Aztecs had fallen once again to an invading army.

With Mexico City in American hands, Polk sent Nicholas P. Trist, the chief clerk in the State Department, to Mexico to negotiate the peace. On February 2, 1848, Trist and Mexican officials signed the Treaty of Guadalupe Hidalgo. Mexico agreed to give up all claims to Texas above the Rio Grande and to cede the huge provinces of New Mexico and California to the United States. The United States agreed to pay Mexico $15 million and to assume $3.25 million in claims that American citizens had against Mexico. Some Americans clamored for all of Mexico, and others for less, but in March 1848 the Senate ratified the treaty by a vote of thirty-eight to fourteen. The last American soldiers left Mexico a few months later.

Less than three-quarters of a century after its founding, the United States had achieved its self-proclaimed manifest destiny to stretch from the Atlantic to the Pacific (Map 12.5, page 289). With the northern half of Mexico in American hands, California gold, which was discovered almost simultaneously with the transfer of territory, poured into American and not Mexican pockets. (See "Historical Question," page 286.) The war also reinforced the worst stereotypes Mexicans and Americans had of each other. A virulent anti-Yankee sentiment took root in Mexico, while deeply prejudiced views of Mexicans and Mexican culture flourished in the fertile soil of American victory. For Mexico, defeat meant national humiliation, but it also had a positive effect. It generated for the first time a genuine nationalism. In America, victory increased the sense of superiority that was already deeply ingrained.

Conclusion:
Free Labor, Free Men

In the 1840s, diplomacy and war handed the United States 1.2 million square miles and more than 1,000 miles of Pacific coastline. To most Americans, vast geographical expansion seemed to be the natural companion of a stunning economic transformation. A cluster of interrelated developments—steam power, railroads, and the growing mechanization of agriculture and manufacturing—resulted in greater productivity, a burst of output from farms and factories, and prosperity for many.

To Northerners, their industrial evolution confirmed the choice they had made to eliminate slavery and to promote free labor as the key to independence, equality, and prosperity. Millions of Northerners, like Abraham Lincoln, could point to personal experience as evidence of the practical truth of the free-labor ideal. But millions of others had different stories to tell. Rather than producing economic equality, the free-labor system saw wealth and poverty continue to rub shoulders. Instead of social independence, more than half of the nation's free-labor workforce toiled for someone else by 1860. Free-labor enthusiasts denied that the problems were built into the system. They argued that most social ills—including poverty and dependency—sprang from individual deficiencies. Consequently, reformers usually focused on the lack of self-control and discipline, on sin and alcohol. They denied that free labor meant exploitation. Slaves suffered, not free workers, they argued. White Southerners, on the other hand, pitied northern free workers, not slaves. By the 1840s, the nation was half slave and half free, and not even victory over Mexico could bridge the deepening differences between North and South.

FOR FURTHER READING ABOUT THE TOPICS IN THIS CHAPTER, see the Online Bibliography at
www.bedfordstmartins.com/roarkcompact.

FOR ADDITIONAL FIRST-HAND ACCOUNTS OF THIS PERIOD, see pages 181–195 in Michael Johnson, ed., *Reading the American Past,* Second Edition, Volume I.

TO ASSESS YOUR MASTERY OF THE MATERIAL IN THIS CHAPTER, see the Online Study Guide at
www.bedfordstmartins.com/roarkcompact.

CHRONOLOGY

1836 Texas declares independence from Mexico.

1837 John Deere patents his steel plow.

1840s Americans begin harnessing steam power to manufacturing.

Cyrus McCormick and others create practical mechanical reapers.

1841 First wagon trains set out for West on Oregon Trail.

Vice President John Tyler becomes president of the United States when William Henry Harrison dies in office after one month.

1844 Democrat James K. Polk elected president on platform calling for annexation of Texas and Oregon.

Samuel F. B. Morse invents telegraph.

1845 Term *manifest destiny* coined by New York journalist John L. O'Sullivan; used as justification for Anglo-American settlers to take land in West.

United States annexes Texas, which enters Union as slave state.

1846 Bear Flag Revolt, independence movement to secede from Mexico, takes place in California.

May 13. Congress declares war on Mexico.

United States and Great Britain agree to divide Oregon Country at forty-ninth parallel.

1847 Brigham Young leads advance party of Mormons to Great Salt Lake in Utah.

1848 Treaty of Guadalupe Hidalgo ends Mexican War. Mexico gives up all claims to Texas north of Rio Grande and cedes provinces of New Mexico and California to United States.

Oneida community organized in New York.

First women's rights convention in United States takes place at Seneca Falls, New York.

1849 California gold rush begins.

Harriet Tubman escapes from slavery in Maryland.

1850 Mormon community of Deseret annexed to United States as Utah Territory.

1851 Conference in Laramie, Wyoming, between U.S. government and Plains tribes marks beginning of government policy of forcing Indians onto reservations.

Massachusetts integrates public schools as result of campaigns led by African Americans.

CLAY JUG

This ceramic water cooler, made in about 1840, is attributed to Thomas Chandler, a famous potter of Edgefield District, South Carolina. The relatively fine clothes of the African American man and woman portrayed on the vessel suggest that they are house servants. On the wall of the home of Alexander Stephens in Crawfordsville, Georgia, an intriguing letter from Stephens states that two of his favorite slaves are getting married and orders the plantation manager to butcher a hog for their wedding. With its portrait of a couple, a hog, and a jug, it is possible that Stephens commissioned this cooler to commemorate the union.

Potters made vessels for use—they held water and food. Analysis of the form, decoration, and glazes of southern pottery suggests a blend of European, African, and Native American ceramic traditions. Some pottery went beyond the utilitarian and became art. The most renowned slave potter was another Edgefield man by the name of Dave, who skillfully fashioned huge vessels, inscribed poems on their surfaces, and proudly and boldly signed them, "Dave the potter." Although a slave, Dave self-consciously left his mark.

Collection of the High Museum of Art, Atlanta. Purchase in honor of Audrey Shilt, President of the Members Guild of the High Museum of Art, 1996–1997, with funds from the Decorative Arts Endowment & Acquisition Trust 1996.

THE SLAVE SOUTH
1820–1860

13

N AT TURNER WAS BORN A SLAVE IN SOUTHAMPTON COUNTY, VIRGINIA, on October 1, 1800. People in his neighborhood claimed that he had always been different. His parents had noticed special marks on his body, which they said were signs that he was "intended for some great purpose." His master said that he learned to read without being taught. As an adolescent, he adopted a severe lifestyle of Christian devotion and fasting. In his twenties, he received visits from the "Spirit," the same spirit, he believed, that had spoken to the ancient prophets. In time, Nat Turner began to interpret these things to mean that God had appointed him an instrument of divine vengeance for the sin of slaveholding.

In the early morning of August 22, 1831, he set out with six trusted friends— Hark, Henry, Sam, Nelson, Will, and Jack—to punish slave owners and free their suffering slaves. The first blow was that of Nat Turner's ax to the head of his master, Joseph Travis. The rebels killed all of the white men, women, and children they encountered in each household they attacked. By noon, they had visited eleven farms and slaughtered fifty-seven whites and, along the way, added fifty or sixty men to their army. Word spread quickly, however, and soon the militia and hundreds of local whites gathered. By the next day, whites had captured or killed all of the insurgents, except for Nat Turner, who successfully hid out for about ten weeks before being captured in nearby woods. Within a week, he was tried, convicted, and executed. By then, forty-five slaves had stood trial; twenty had been convicted and hanged and another ten had been transported from Virginia. Another hundred or more blacks—rebels and innocent bystanders—had been killed in the whites' frenzied counterattack against the insurrection.

Slave revolts were white Southerners' worst nightmare. Virginia's governor John Floyd asked how Turner with his band of "assassins and murderers" could have assaulted in their sleep the "unsuspecting and defenseless" citizens of "one of the fairest counties in the Commonwealth." Virginians prided themselves on having the "mildest" slavery in the South, but sixty black rebels on a rampage challenged the comforting theory of the contented slave. Nonetheless, whites found explanations that allowed them to feel more at ease. They placed the blame on outside agitators. In 1829, David Walker, a freeborn black man living in Boston, had published his *Appeal . . . to the Colored Citizens of the World*, an invitation to slaves to rise up in bloody rebellion, and copies had fallen into the hands of Virginia slaves. Moreover, on January 1, 1831, William Lloyd Garrison, the Massachusetts abolitionist, had published the first issue of his fiery newspaper, the *Liberator*. But white Virginians also dismissed the rebellion's leader, Nat Turner, as insane. "He is a complete fanatic, or plays his part admirably," wrote Thomas R. Gray, the lawyer who was assigned to defend Turner.

In the months following the insurrection, white Virginians debated the future of slavery in their state. While some expressed substantial doubts, the Virginia legislature reaffirmed the state's determination to beat back threats to white

NAT TURNER

There are no known contemporary images of Nat Turner. This imagined portrait comes from William Still's The Underground Railroad, *which was published in 1872. Meeting secretly at night deep in a forest and thus well out of earshot of whites, an intense Turner passionately tries to convince four other slaves to join him in rebellion. What do their faces reveal? What considerations do you suppose entered their calculations about whether to join Turner? Significantly perhaps, they are holding work tools, not arms.*
Library of Congress.

supremacy. Delegates passed a raft of laws strengthening the institution of slavery and further restricting free blacks. A thirty-year-old professor at the College of William and Mary, Thomas R. Dew, published a vigorous defense of slavery that became the bible of Southerners' proslavery arguments. More than ever, the nation was divided along the "Mason-Dixon line," the surveyors' mark that in colonial times had established the boundary between Maryland and Pennsylvania but half a century later divided the free North and slave South.

Black slavery increasingly dominated the South and shaped it into a distinctive region. In the decades after 1820, Southerners, like Northerners, raced westward, but they spread slavery, cotton, and plantations, whereas Northerners in contrast spread small farms and free labor. Geographic expansion meant that slavery became more vigorous and profitable than ever, embraced more people,

and increased the South's political power. Antebellum Southerners included diverse peoples who at times found themselves at odds with one another—not only slaves and free people, but also women and men; Indians, Africans, and Europeans; and aristocrats and common folk. Nevertheless, beneath this diversity of Southerners there was also forming a distinctively southern society and culture. The South became a slave society, and most white Southerners were proud of it.

The Growing Distinctiveness of the South

From the earliest settlements, inhabitants of southern colonies had shared a great deal with northern colonists. Most whites in both sections were British and Protestant, and they spoke a common language, even if a regional twang or drawl flavored their speech. They shared an exuberant pride in their victorious revolution against British rule. The creation of the new nation under the Constitution in 1789 forged strong political ties that bound all Americans. The beginnings of a national economy fostered economic interdependence and communication across regional boundaries. White Americans everywhere celebrated the achievements of the prosperous young nation, and they looked forward to its seemingly boundless future.

Despite these national similarities, Southerners and Northerners grew increasingly different. The French political observer Alexis de Tocqueville believed he knew why. "I could easily prove," he asserted in 1831, "that almost all the differences which may be noticed between the character of the Americans in the Southern and Northern states have originated in slavery." Slavery made the South different, and it was the differences between the North and the South, not the similarities, that came to shape antebellum American history.

Cotton Kingdom, Slave Empire

In the first half of the nineteenth century, legions of Americans migrated west, but in the South the surge westward was propelled by an insatiable hunger for more and better cotton land. Eager slaveholders seeking virgin acreage for new plantations, struggling farmers looking for patches of good land for small farms, herders and drovers pushing their hogs and cattle toward fresh pastures—anyone who was restless and ambitious felt the pull. Southerners relentlessly pushed westward, until by midcentury the South encompassed nearly a million square miles, much of it planted in cotton.

The South's climate and geography were ideally suited for the cultivation of cotton. Advancing Southerners encountered a variety of terrain, soil, and weather, but the cotton seeds they carried with them were very adaptable. By the 1830s, cotton fields stretched from southern Virginia to central Texas. Production soared, and by 1860 the South produced three-fourths of the world's supply. The South—especially that tier of states from South Carolina west to Texas known as the Lower South—had become the cotton kingdom (Map 13.1).

The cotton kingdom was also a slave empire. The South's cotton boom rested on the backs of slaves, who grew 75 percent of the crop on plantations, toiling in gangs in broad fields under the direct supervision of whites. As cotton agriculture expanded westward, whites shipped more than 300,000 slaves out of the old seaboard states. Some slaves accompanied masters who were leaving behind worn-out, eroded plantations, but at least two-thirds were victims of a brutal but thriving domestic slave trade. Traders advertised for slaves who were "hearty and well made" and marched black men, women, and children hundreds of miles to the new plantation regions of the Lower South. Cotton, slaves, and plantations moved west together.

The slave population grew enormously. Southern slaves numbered fewer than 700,000 in 1790, about 2 million in 1830, and about 4 million by 1860, an increase of almost 600 percent in seven decades. By 1860, the South contained more slaves than all the other slave societies in the New World combined. The extraordinary growth was not the result of the importation of slaves, which was outlawed in 1808. Instead the slave population grew through natural reproduction. By the nineteenth century, most slaves were black Southerners.

The South in Black and White

By 1860, one in every three Southerners was black (about 4 million blacks and 8 million whites). In the Lower South, the proportion was higher, for whites and blacks lived there in almost equal numbers. In Mississippi and South Carolina, blacks were the majority (Figure 13.1). The contrast with the North was striking: In 1860, only 1 Northerner in 76 was black (about 250,000 blacks to 19 million whites).

The presence of large numbers of African Americans had profound consequences for the South. Southern culture—language, food, music, religion, and even accents—was in part shaped by blacks. But the most direct consequence of the South's biracialism was the response it stimulated in the region's white majority. Southern whites were dedicated to white supremacy. Northern whites were, too, but they lived in a society in which blacks made up barely more than 1 percent of the population. Their commitment to white supremacy lacked the intensity and urgency increasingly felt by white Southerners. White Southerners lived among millions of blacks, whom they simultaneously despised and feared. They despised blacks because they considered them members of an inferior race, further degraded by their status as slaves. They feared blacks because they realized that slaves had every reason

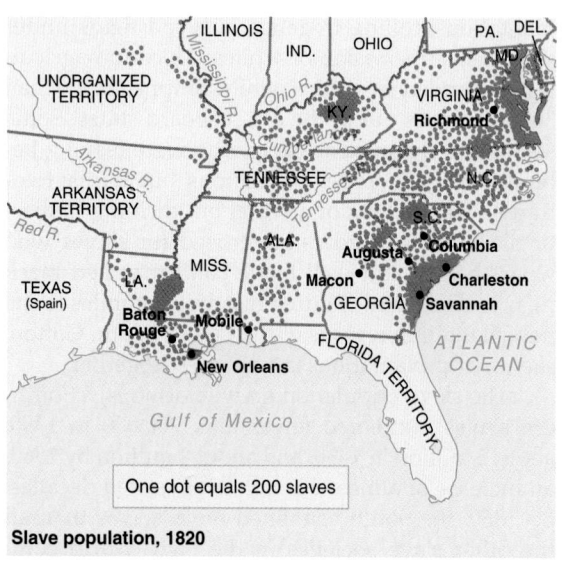

One dot equals 200 slaves

Slave population, 1820

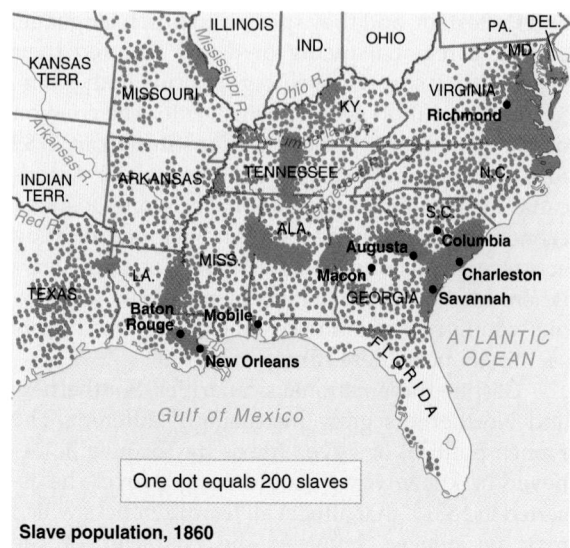

One dot equals 200 slaves

Slave population, 1860

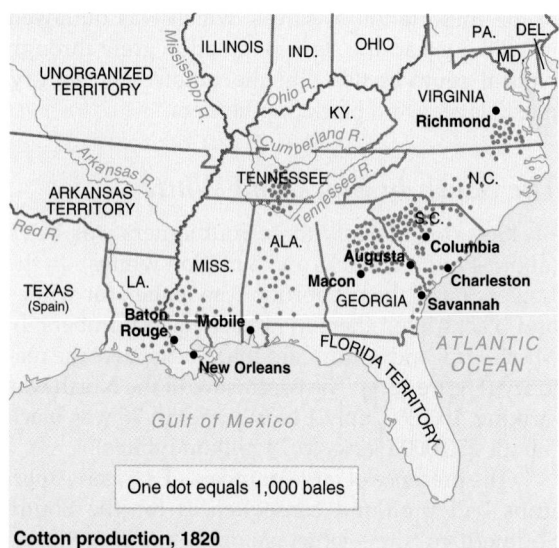

One dot equals 1,000 bales

Cotton production, 1820

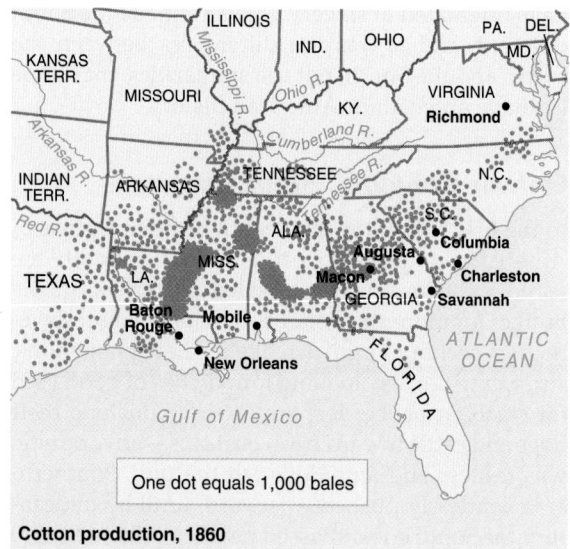

One dot equals 1,000 bales

Cotton production, 1860

Map 13.1

Cotton Kingdom, Slave Empire: 1820 and 1860

As the production of cotton soared, the slave population increased dramatically. Slaves continued to toil in tobacco and rice fields along the Atlantic seaboard, but increasingly they worked on cotton plantations in Alabama, Mississippi, and Louisiana.

Reading the map: Where was slavery most prevalent in 1820? In 1860? How did the spread of slavery compare with the spread of cotton?

Connections: How much of the world's cotton was produced in the American South in 1860? While most slaves worked in agriculture, how else were slaves employed?

www.bedfordstmartins.com/roarkcompact   See the Online Study Guide for more help in analyzing these maps.

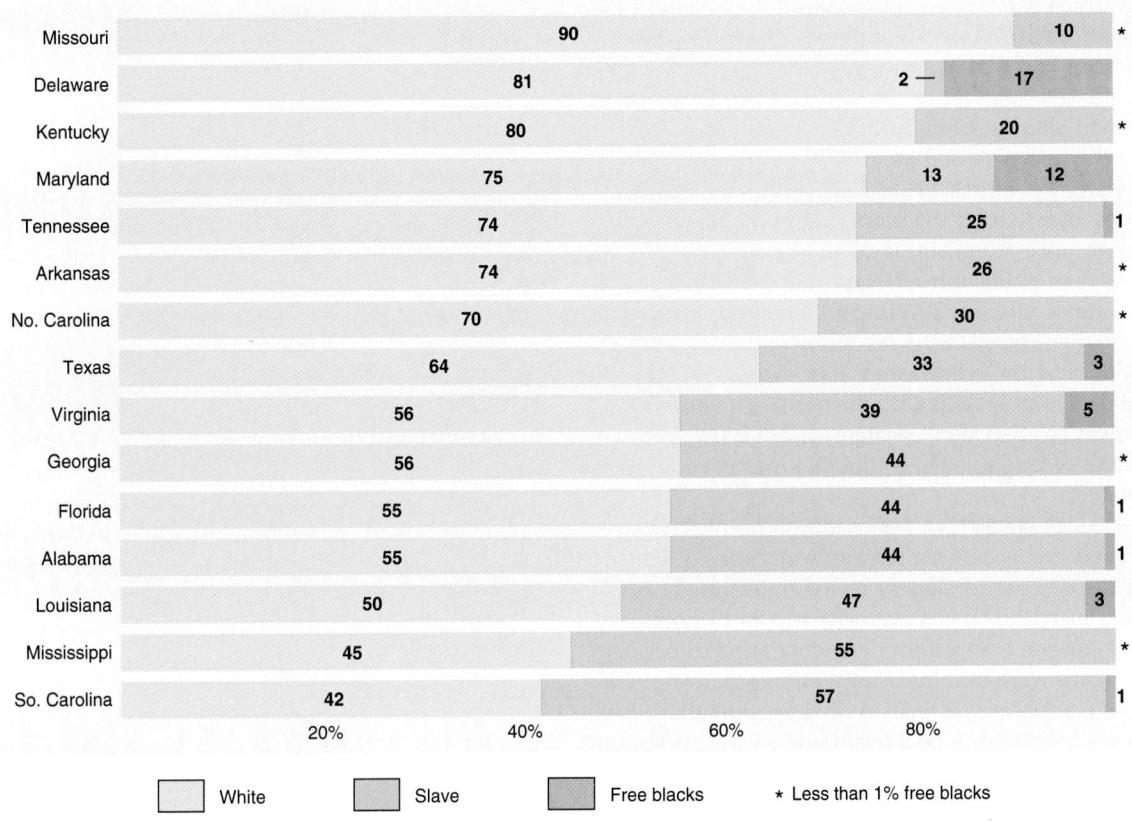

FIGURE 13.1

Black and White Population in the South, 1860
Blacks represented a much larger fraction of the population in the South than in the North, but considerable variation existed from state to state. Only one Missourian in ten, for example, was black, while Mississippi and South Carolina had black majorities. States in the Upper South were "whiter" than in the Lower South, despite the Upper South's greater number of free blacks.

to hate them and to seek to end their oppression, as Nat Turner had, by any means necessary.

Attacks on slavery after 1820—from blacks within and from abolitionists without—jolted southern slaveholders into a distressing awareness that they lived in a dangerous and fragile world. In response, southern leaders initiated fresh efforts to strengthen slavery. State legislatures constructed elaborate slave codes that required the total submission of slaves to their masters and to white society in general. As the Louisiana code stated, a slave "owes his master . . . a respect without bounds, and an absolute obedience." The laws underlined the authority of all whites, not just masters. Any white could "correct" slaves who did not stay "in their place."

Intellectuals joined legislators in the campaign to strengthen slavery. The South's academics, writers, and clergy constructed a proslavery argument that sought to unify the region's whites around slavery and provide ammunition for the emerging war of words with northern abolitionists. Under the intellectuals' tutelage, the white South gradually moved away from defending slavery as a "necessary evil"—the halfhearted argument popular in Jefferson's day—and toward a full-throated, aggressive defense of slavery as a "positive good."

Slavery's champions employed every imaginable defense. The law protected slavery, they observed, for slaves were legal property. And wasn't the security of property the bedrock of American liberty? History also endorsed slavery. Weren't the great civilizations—like those of the Hebrews, Greeks, and Romans—slave societies? They also argued that the Bible, properly interpreted, sanctioned slavery. Some proslavery spokesmen went on the offensive and attacked the economy and society of the North. George Fitzhugh of Virginia argued that behind the North's grand slogans—free labor, individualism, and egalitarianism—lay a heartless philosophy: "Every man for himself, and the devil take the hindmost." Gouging capitalists exploited wage workers unmercifully, Fitzhugh said, and he contrasted the vicious capitalist-laborer relationship with the humane relations that prevailed between masters and slaves because slaves were valuable capital that masters sought to protect.

Since slavery was a condition Southerners reserved exclusively for African Americans, the heart of the defense of slavery rested on claims of black inferiority. Black enslavement was both necessary and proper, antebellum defenders argued, because Africans were inferior beings. Rather than exploitative, slavery was a mass civilizing effort that lifted lowly blacks from barbarism and savagery, taught them disciplined work, and converted them to soul-saving Christianity. According to Virginian Thomas R. Dew, most slaves were grateful. "The slaves of a good master are his warmest, most constant, and most devoted friends," he declared.

Black slavery encouraged whites to unify around race rather than to divide by class. The grubbiest, most tobacco-stained white man could proudly proclaim his superiority to all blacks and his equality with the most refined southern patrician. Because slaves were not recognized as citizens in the South, Georgia attorney Thomas R. R. Cobb observed, every white Southerner "feels that he belongs to an elevated class. It matters not that he is no slaveholder; he is not of the inferior race; he is a freeborn citizen." Consequently, the "poorest meets the richest as an equal; sits at his table with him; salutes him as a neighbor; meets him in every public assembly, and stands on the same social platform." In the South, Cobb boasted, "there is no war of classes."

In reality, slavery did not create perfect harmony among whites or ease every strain along class lines. But by providing every antebellum white Southerner symbolic membership in the ruling class, racial slavery helped whites bridge differences in wealth, education, and culture. Slavery meant white dominance, white superiority, and white equality.

The Plantation Economy

Despite the importance of slavery in unifying white Southerners, only about one-quarter of the white population lived in slaveholding families. A majority of masters owned fewer than five. Only about 12 percent of slave owners owned twenty or more slaves, the number historians consider necessary to distinguish a planter from a farmer. Although hugely outnumbered, planters dominated the southern economy. In 1860, 52 percent of the South's slaves lived and worked on plantations. Plantation slaves produced more than 75 percent of the South's export crops, the backbone of the region's economy. Although slavery was dying elsewhere in the New World, slave plantations increased their domination of southern agriculture.

THE COTTON GIN
By the 1790s, the English had succeeded in mechanizing the manufacture of cotton cloth, but they were unable to get enough raw cotton. The South could grow cotton in unimaginable quantities, but cotton that was stuck to seeds was useless in English textile mills. In 1793, Eli Whitney, a Northerner who was living on a Savannah River plantation, built a simple device for separating the cotton from the seed. Widespread use of the cotton gin broke the bottleneck in the commercial production of cotton and eventually bound millions of African Americans to slavery.
Smithsonian Institution.

M A P 13.2

The Agricultural Economy of the South, 1860
Cotton dominated the South's agricultural economy, but the region grew a diversity of crops and was largely self-sufficient in foodstuffs.

The dominant cash crops of southern agriculture were the four major staples grown on plantations: tobacco, sugar, rice, and cotton (Map 13.2). Tobacco was the original plantation crop in North America, but by the nineteenth century tobacco had shifted westward from the Chesapeake to Tennessee and Kentucky. Large-scale sugar production began in 1795, when Étienne de Boré built a modern sugar mill in what is today New Orleans, and sugar plantations were confined almost entirely to Louisiana. Commercial rice production began in the seventeenth century, and like sugar, rice was confined to a small geographic area, a narrow strip stretching from the Carolinas into Georgia.

If tobacco, sugar, and rice were princes of plantation agriculture, cotton was king. Cotton became commercially significant after the advent of Eli Whitney's cotton gin in 1793, which allowed cotton to be prepared more quickly before being shipped to textile mills. By the early years of the nineteenth century, cotton had displaced tobacco and had begun to dominate the southern economy. It was grown almost everywhere in the South, by

small farmer and planter alike. Nonetheless, plantations produced three-quarters of the South's cotton. While hardscrabble farmer Jessup Snopes grew half a bale, Mississippian Frederick Stanton, who owned more than fifteen thousand prime acres, produced 3,054 bales of cotton worth $122,000 in 1859.

For major slaveholders, then, the Old South's economy was productive and profitable. Further, plantation slavery benefited the national economy. By 1840, cotton alone accounted for more than 60 percent of the nation's exports. Much of the profit from sales of cotton overseas returned to planters, but some went to northern middlemen who bought, sold, insured, warehoused, and shipped cotton to the mills in Great Britain and elsewhere. As they invested their profits in the burgeoning northern economy, industrial development received much-needed capital. Furthermore, planters provided an important market for northern textiles, agricultural tools, and other manufactured goods.

The economies of North and South steadily diverged. While the North developed a mixed economy—agriculture, commerce, and manufacturing—the South remained overwhelmingly agricultural. Since planters were earning healthy profits, they saw little reason to diversify. Year after year, they funneled the profits they earned from land and slaves back into more land and slaves.

With its capital flowing into agriculture, the Old South did not develop as many factories as did the North. By 1860, only 10 percent of the nation's industrial workers were in the South. And the region that produced 100 percent of the nation's cotton manufactured less than 7 percent of its cotton textiles.

Without significant economic diversification, the South developed fewer cities than the North. In 1860, it was the least urban region in the country. While nearly 37 percent of New England's population lived in cities, less than 12 percent of Southerners were urban dwellers. In fact, nine southern states had 5 percent or fewer of their people in cities.

Because the South had so few cities and industrial jobs, it attracted relatively small numbers of European immigrants. Seeking economic opportunity, not competition with slaves, immigrants steered well north of the South's slave-dominated, agricultural economy. In 1860, 13 percent of all Americans were foreign-born. But in nine of the fifteen slave states, only 2 percent or fewer were born abroad.

Not every Southerner celebrated the region's plantation economy. Critics railed against the excessive commitment to cotton and slaves and bemoaned the scarcity of factories. Diversification, reformers promised, would make the South not only economically independent but more prosperous as well. State governments encouraged economic diversification and development by helping to create banking systems that supplied credit for a wide range of projects, industrial as well as agricultural, and by building railroads.

But encouragement of a diversified economy had clear limits. State governments failed to create some of the essential services modern economies require. By midcentury, for example, no southern legislature had created a statewide public school system. Consequently, the South's illiteracy rate for whites topped 20 percent. Despite the flurry of railroad building, the South's mileage in 1860 was less than half that of the North. While railroads crisscrossed the North carrying manufactured goods as well as agricultural products, most railroads in the South were built primarily to export staple crops to port cities (see Map 12.1).

Northerners claimed that slavery was outmoded and doomed, but few Southerners perceived economic weakness in their region. In fact, the planters' pockets were never fuller than at the end of the antebellum period. Compared with Northerners, Southerners committed less of their capital to investment in industry, transportation, and public education. Planters' decisions to reinvest in staple agriculture ensured the momentum of the plantation economy and the social and political relationships that were rooted in it.

Masters, Mistresses, and the Big House

Nowhere was the contrast between northern and southern life more vivid than in the plantations of the South. Located on a patchwork of cleared fields and dense forests, a plantation typically included a "big house" and slave quarters. Scattered about were numerous outbuildings, each with a special function. Near the big house were the kitchen, storehouse, smokehouse (for curing and preserving meat), and hen coop. More distant were the barns, toolsheds, artisans' workshops, and overseer's house. Depending on the crop, there was a tobacco shed, a rice mill, a sugar refinery, or a cotton gin house.

The plantation was the home of masters, mistresses, and slaves. Slavery shaped the lives of all the plantation's inhabitants, but it affected each differently. A hierarchy of rigid roles and duties governed relationships. Presiding was the master, who ruled his wife, children, and slaves, none of whom had many legal rights and all of whom were des-

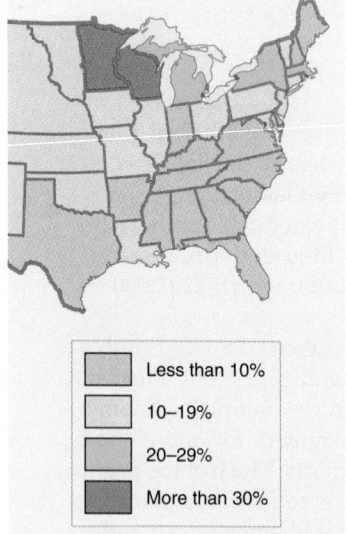

| Less than 10% |
| 10–19% |
| 20–29% |
| More than 30% |

Immigrants as a Percent of State Populations, 1860

ignated by the state as dependents under his dominion and protection.

Plantation Masters

While smaller planters supervised the labor of their slaves themselves, larger planters often hired overseers who went to the fields with the slaves, leaving planters free to concentrate on marketing, finance, and general plantation affairs. Planters also found time to escape to town to discuss the weather, to the courthouse and legislature to debate politics, and to the woods to hunt and fish.

Increasingly in the nineteenth century, planters characterized the master-slave relationship in terms of what historians have called "paternalism." The concept of paternalism denied that the form of slavery practiced in the South was brutal and exploitative. Instead, it defined slavery as a set of reciprocal obligations between masters and slaves. In exchange for the slaves' labor and obedience, masters provided basic care and necessary guidance. To northern claims that they were tyrants and exploiters, slaveholders responded that they were stewards and guardians. As owners of blacks, mas-

ters argued, they had the heavy responsibility of caring for a childlike, dependent people. In 1814, Thomas Jefferson captured the essence of the advancing ideal: "We should endeavor, with those whom fortune has thrown on our hands, to feed & clothe them well, protect them from ill usage, require such reasonable labor only as is performed voluntarily by freemen, and be led by no repugnancies to abdicate them, and our duties to them."

Paternalism was part propaganda and part self-delusion. But it was more. Indeed, there was some truth in the assertion that master-slave relationships in the South were unique. Unlike planters elsewhere in the New World, most southern planters lived year-round where their slaves worked, which meant that the relationship between master and slave was face to face, direct, and personal. In addition, after the close of the external slave trade in 1808, masters recognized slaves as assets to be maintained, and they realized that the expansion of the slave labor force could come only from natural reproduction.

One consequence of this paternalism and economic self-interest was a relative improvement in

SOUTHERN MAN WITH CHILDREN AND THEIR MAMMY
Obviously prosperous and projecting the aura of a man accustomed to giving orders and to being obeyed, this patriarch poses around 1848 with his young daughters and their nurse. The absent mother may have been dead, which might in part explain the inclusion of the slave woman in the family circle. But her presence also confirms her importance in the household. Fathers left the raising of children to mothers and nurses. However important, the black woman is clearly a servant, a status indicated by both her race and her attire.
Collection of the J. Paul Getty Museum, Malibu, Calif.

How Often Were Slaves Whipped?

A S IMPORTANT AS THIS QUESTION is to historians, and obviously was to slaves, we have very little reliable evidence on the frequency of whipping. We know from white sources that whipping was the prescribed method of physical punishment on most antebellum plantations. Masters' instructions to overseers authorized whippings and often set limits on the number of strokes an overseer could administer. Some planters allowed fifteen lashes, some fifty, and some one hundred. But slave owners' instructions, as revealing as they are, tell us more about the severity of beatings than their frequency.

Remembrances of former slaves confirm that whipping was widespread and frequent. In the 1930s, a government program gathered testimony from more than 2,300 elderly African Americans about their experiences as slaves. Their accounts offered grisly evidence of the cruelty of slavery. "You say how did our Master treat his slaves?" asked one woman. "Scandalous, they treated them just like dogs." She was herself whipped "till the blood dripped to the ground." A few slaves remembered kind masters and never personally felt the sting of the lash. Bert Strong was one such slave, but he also recalled hearing slaves on other farms "hollering when they get beat." He said, "They beat them till it a pity." Beatings occurred often, but how often?

A remarkably systematic record of whippings over a sustained period of time comes from the diary of Bennet H. Barrow, the master of Highland plantation in West Feliciana Parish, Louisiana. For a twenty-three-month period in 1840–1841, Barrow meticulously recorded every whipping he administered or ordered. On most large plantations, overseers handled the business of day-to-day management, but in 1838 Barrow concluded that overseers were "good for nothing" and "a perfect nuisance." He dismissed his white overseer and, assisted only by a black driver, began managing his own plantation.

What does the Barrow evidence show? In 1840, according to the federal census, Barrow owned 129 slaves. In the twenty-three-month period, Barrow recorded 160 whippings. That means that, on the average, a slave was whipped every four and a half days. Sixty of the 77 slaves who worked in the fields were whipped at least once. Most of the 17 field slaves who escaped being beaten were children and pregnant women. Eighty percent of male cotton pickers and 70 percent of the female cotton pickers were whipped at least once in this period. Dave Barley received eight floggings, more than any other Barrow slave, and Patience received six whippings, more than any other female slave.

In most instances, Barrow recorded not only the fact of a whipping but also its cause. All sorts of "misconduct," "rascallity," and "disorderly acts" made Barrow reach for his whip. The provocations included family quarrels in the slave quarters, impudence, running away, and failure to keep curfew. But nearly 80 percent of the acts he recorded were related to poor work. Barrow gave beatings for "not picking as well as he can," for picking "very trashy cotton," and for failing to pick the prescribed weight of cotton. One slave claimed to have lost his eyesight and for months refused to work until Barrow "gave him 25 cuts yesterday morning & ordered him to work Blind or not."

Whippings should not be mistaken for spankings. Some planters used whips that raised welts, caused blisters, and bruised. Others resorted to rawhide and cowhide whips that broke the skin, caused scarring, and sometimes permanently maimed. Occasionally, slaves were beaten to death. Whipping was not Barrow's only means of inflicting pain. His diary mentions confining slaves to a plantation jail, putting them in chains, shooting them, breaking a "sword cane" over one slave's head, having slaves mauled by dogs, placing them in stocks, "staking down" slaves for hours, "hand sawing" them, holding their heads under water, and a variety of punishments intending to ridicule and to shame, including making men wear women's clothing and do "women's work," such as the laundry. Still, Barrow's preferred instrument of punishment was the whip.

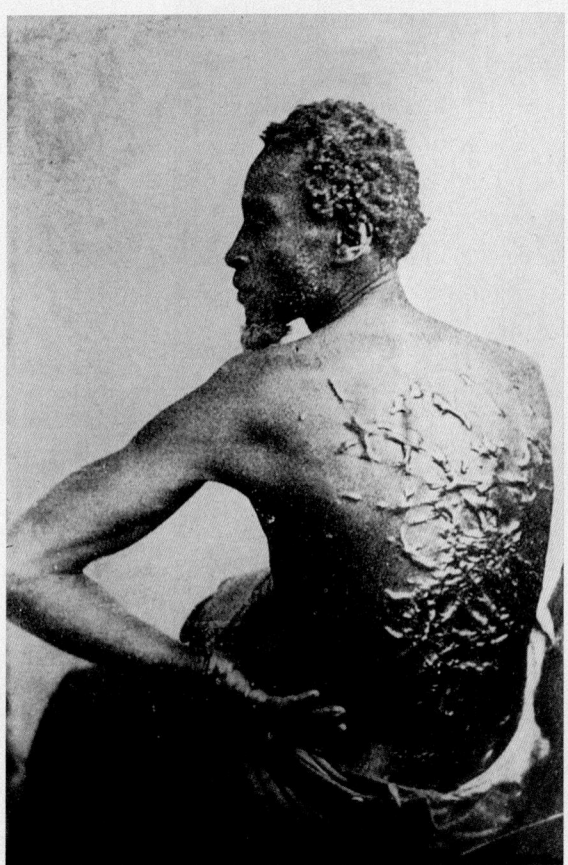

GORDON

This photograph of Gordon, a runaway slave from Baton Rouge, Louisiana, was taken on April 2, 1863, and sent home from the Civil War by Frederick W. Mercer, an assistant surgeon with the Forty-seventh Massachusetts Regiment. Mercer examined four hundred other runaways and found many "to be as badly lacerated." Masters claimed that they whipped only when they had to and only as hard as they had to, but slave testimony and photographic evidence refute their defense of slavery as a benign institution.
Courtesy of the Massachusetts Historical Society.

On the Barrow plantation, as on many others, whipping was public. Victims were often tied to a stake in the quarters, and the other slaves were made to watch. In a real sense the entire slave population on the plantation experienced a whipping every four and a half days. Even though some never felt the lash personally, all were familiar with its terror and agony.

Was whipping effective? Did it produce a hardworking, efficient, and conscientious labor force? Not according to Barrow's own record. No evidence indicates that whipping changed the slaves' behavior. What Barrow considered bad work continued. Unabated whipping is itself evidence of the failure of punishment to achieve the master's will. Slaves knew the rules. Yet they continued to act "badly." And they continued to suffer. It was a gruesome drama—the master seeking from his slaves hard labor and slaves denying their master what he most wanted, day after day.

Did Barrow whip with the same frequency as other planters? We simply do not know. As much as we would like to answer the question precisely, because of the lack of quantifiable evidence we will never know exactly how often whippings occurred. Still, the Barrow evidence allows us to speculate profitably on the frequency of whipping by large planters. We do know that Barrow did not consider himself a cruel man. He bitterly denounced his neighbor as "the most cruel Master i ever knew of" for castrating three of his slaves. Moreover, Barrow had dispensed with the overseers in part because of their "brutal feelings" toward slaves. Like most whites, he believed that the lash was essential to get work done. He used it no more than he believed absolutely necessary.

Most masters, including Barrow, tried to encourage work with promises of small gifts and brief holidays, but punishment was their most important motivator. We will never know if the typical slave was beaten once a year as on the Barrow plantation, but the admittedly scanty evidence suggests that on large plantations the whip fell on someone's back every few days.

And former slaves remembered. More than half a century after emancipation, their sharpest recollections usually involved punishment. They remembered the pain, the injustice, and their bitter resentment. They evaluated their former masters according to how frequently they reached for the whip. According to one former slave, "some was good and some was bad, and about the most of them was bad."

THE PRICE OF BLOOD
This 1868 painting by Thomas Satterwhite Noble depicts a transaction between a slave
trader and a rich planter. The trader nervously pretends to study the contract, while the
planter waits impatiently for the completion of the sale. The planter's mulatto son,
who is being sold, looks away. The children of white men and slave women were prop-
erty and could be sold by the father/master.
Morris Museum of Art, Augusta, Ga.

www.bedfordstmartins.com/roarkcompact SEE THE ONLINE STUDY GUIDE for more help in
analyzing this image.

Masters left the plantation when they pleased, but plantation mistresses needed chaperones to travel. When they could, they went to church, for their faith was important to them. But women spent most days on the plantation, where they often became lonely. In 1853, Mary Kendall wrote how much she enjoyed her sister's letter: "For about three weeks I did not have the pleasure of seeing one white female face, there being no white family except our own upon the plantation."

As members of slaveholding families, mistresses lived privileged lives. But they also had significant grounds for discontent, and a few independent-minded women protested. No feature of plantation life generated more rage and anguish among mistresses than miscegenation. Mary Boykin Chesnut of Camden, South Carolina, wrote in her diary, ". . . ours is a monstrous system, a wrong and iniquity. Like the patriarchs of old, our men live all in one house with their wives and their concubines; and the mulattos one sees in every family partly resemble the white children. Any lady is ready to tell you who is the father of all the mulatto children in everybody's household but her own. Those, she seems to think drop from the clouds."

But most planters' wives found ways to accept slavery. According to the southern ideal, the white man ruled over all in his household—wife, children, and slaves. Thus the mistress's world rested on slavery, just as the master's did.

Slaves and the Quarters

On most plantations, only a few hundred yards separated the big house and the slave quarters. The distance was short enough to assure whites easy access to the labor of blacks. Yet the distance was great enough to provide slaves with some privacy, despite increased paternalistic intrusion. Out of eyesight and earshot of the big house, slaves drew together and built lives of their own. They built families, worshiped God, and developed an African American community.

The rise of plantations still left a substantial minority of slaves living and working elsewhere. Most labored on small farms, where they wielded a hoe alongside another slave or two and perhaps their master. But by 1850, as many as half a million slaves (one in eight) did not work in agriculture at all. Some were employed in towns and cities as domestics, day laborers, bakers, barbers, tailors, and more. Others, far from urban centers, toiled as fishermen, lumbermen, railroad workers, and deckhands and stokers on riverboats. Slavery was a flexible labor system, and slaves could be found in virtually every skilled and unskilled occupation throughout the South, including the region's few factories. Nevertheless, a majority of slaves (52 percent) counted plantations as their homes and workplaces.

Work

All slaves who were capable of productive labor worked. Young children were introduced to the world of work as early as age five or six. Ex-slave Carrie Hudson recalled that children who were "knee high to a duck" were sent to the fields to carry water to thirsty workers or to protect ripening crops from hungry birds. Others helped in the slave nursery, caring for children even younger than themselves, or in the big house, where they swept floors or shooed flies in the dining room. When slave boys and girls reached the age of eleven or twelve, masters sent most of them to the fields, where they learned farmwork by laboring alongside their parents. After a lifetime of labor, old women left the fields to care for the small children and spin yarn and old men to mind livestock and clean stables.

The overwhelming majority of slaves in 1860 were field hands. Planters sometimes assigned men and women to separate gangs, the women working at lighter tasks and the men doing the heavy work of clearing and breaking the land. But women also did heavy work. "I had to work hard," Nancy Boudry remembered, "plow and go and split wood just like a man." The backbreaking labor and the monotonous year-round routines made for grim similarity. As one ex-slave observed, on the plantation the "history of one day is the history of every day."

A few slaves (only one or two in every ten) became house servants. And virtually all of those who did (nine of ten) were women. There, under the critical eye of the white mistress, they cooked, cleaned house, babysat, washed clothes, and did the dozens of other tasks the master and mistress required. House servants enjoyed certain advantages over field hands, such as somewhat less physically demanding work and better food, but working in the big house had significant drawbacks. House servants were constantly on call, with no time that was entirely their own. Since no servant could please constantly, most bore the brunt of white frustration and rage. Ex-slave Jacob Branch of Texas remembered, "My poor mama! Every washday old Missy give her a beating."

Even rarer than house servants were skilled artisans. In the cotton South, no more than one slave in twenty (almost all men) worked in a skilled trade. Most were blacksmiths and carpenters, but slaves also worked as masons, mechanics, millers, and shoemakers. Slave craftsmen took pride in their skills and often exhibited an independence of spirit that caused slaveholder James H. Hammond of South Carolina to declare in disgust that when a slave became a skilled artisan, "he is more than half freed."

Rarest of all slave occupations was that of slave driver. Probably no more than one male slave in a hundred worked in this capacity. These men were well named, for their primary task was driving other slaves to work harder in the fields. In some drivers' hands, the whip never rested. Ex-slave Jane Johnson of South Carolina called her driver the "meanest man, white or black, I ever see." But other drivers showed all the restraint they could. "Ole Gabe didn't like that whippin' business," West Turner of Virginia remembered. "When Marsa was there, he would lay it on 'cause he had to. But when old Marsa wasn't lookin', he never would beat them slaves."

Normally, slaves worked from sunup to sundown. Even with a break at noon for a meal

NANCY FORT, HOUSE SERVANT
This rare portrait of a slave woman at the turn of the nineteenth century depicts a strong and dignified person. Some who worked in domestic service took pride in their superior status and identified more with the master than with the slaves. "Honey, I wan't no common eve'day slave," one former servant recalled proudly. "I [helped] de white folks in de big house." But intense interaction with whites did not necessarily breed affection. Most domestic servants remained bound by ties of kinship and friendship, as well as by common oppression, to the slave quarters.
Courtesy of Georgia Department of Archives and History.

SLAVE CARPENTER
Haywood Dixon (1826–c. 1889) was a slave carpenter who worked in Greene County, North Carolina. In this 1854 daguerreotype, he is posed with a symbol of his craft, the carpenter's square. When work was slow on the home plantation, masters could hire out their skilled artisans to neighbors who needed a carpenter, blacksmith, or mason.
Collection of William L. Murphy.

and rest, it made for a long day. For slaves, Lewis Young recalled, "work, work, work, 'twas all they do."

Family, Religion, and Community

At night, when the labor was done, and all day Sundays and usually Saturday afternoons, slaves were left largely to themselves. Bone tired perhaps, they nonetheless used the time and space to develop and enjoy what mattered most: family, religion, and community.

In the quarters, slaves lived lives that their masters were hardly aware of. Temporarily leaving the master-slave relationship at their cabin doors, slaves became husbands and wives, mothers and fathers, sons and daughters, preachers and singers, storytellers and conjurers. Over the generations, they created a community and a culture of their own that buoyed them up during long hours in the fields and brought them joy and hope in the few hours they had to themselves.

One of the most important consequences of the slaves' limited autonomy was the preservation

SLAVE QUARTER, SOUTH CAROLINA

On large plantations, several score of African Americans lived in cabins that were often arranged along what slaves called "the street." The dwellings pictured in this image by Civil War photographer George N. Barnard of a South Carolina plantation were better built than the typical rickety, one-room, dirt-floored slave cabin. Although this photograph is almost certainly posed, it captures the inhabitants of the slave quarter—little children playing in the dirt, girls and women sitting on the steps talking and working at something, and older boys and men driving carts and wagons. During the daylight hours of the work week when most men and women labored in the fields, the quarter was largely empty. But at night and on Sundays, it was a busy place.
Collection of the New-York Historical Society.

and persistence of the family. Perhaps the most serious charge abolitionists leveled against slavery was that it wrecked black family life, a telling indictment in a society that put family at the heart of decent society. Slaveholders sometimes agreed that blacks had no family life, but they placed the blame on the slaves themselves, claim-ing that blacks chose to lead licentious, promiscuous lives.

Contrary to both abolitionists' and slaveholders' claims, the black family survived slavery. Indeed, family was the chief fact of life in the quarters. Owners sometimes encouraged the creation and maintenance of families, but slave family life grew primarily from slaves' own commitment. While no laws recognized slave marriage, and therefore no master or slave was legally obligated to honor the bond, plantation records show that slave marriages were often long-lasting. Young men and women in the slave quarters fell in love, married, and set up housekeeping in cabins of their own. The primary cause of the ending of slave marriages was death, just as it was in white families. But the second most frequent cause of the end of slave marriages was the sale of the husband or wife, something no white family ever had to fear. Precise figures are unavailable, but one scholar estimates that in the years 1820–1860, sales destroyed 300,000 slave marriages. Years after Moses Grandy was parted from his slave wife, he said, "I have never seen or heard of her from that day to this." And he added, "I loved her as I love my life."

Plantation records also reveal the importance of slave fathers. Not all fathers could live with their children—some men had been sold away and others had married women on neighboring plantations—but fathers were often present. Despite their inability to fulfill the traditional roles of provider and protector, slave fathers gained status by doing what they could to provide for their families: hunting, raising hogs, cultivating a garden, making furniture. Slaves held both their mothers and fathers in high esteem, grateful for the small bits of refuge their parents provided from the rigors of slavery when they were children.

Like families, religion also provided slaves with a refuge and a reason for living. Beginning about the time of the American Revolution, Protestant evangelical sects, particularly the Baptists and Methodists, began trying to convert slaves from their African beliefs. Evangelicals offered an emotional "religion of the heart" to which blacks (and many whites as well) responded enthusiastically. By the mid-nineteenth century, perhaps as many as one-quarter of all slaves claimed church membership, and many of the rest would not have objected to being called Christians.

Planters began promoting Christianity in the quarters because they came to see the slaves' salvation as part of their obligation and to believe that religion made slaves more obedient. Certainly, the Christianity that masters broadcast to slaves emphasized the meeker virtues. White preachers admonished their black congregants to love God and to obey their owners. Many slaves laughed up their sleeves at the message. "That old white preacher just was telling us slaves to be good to our masters," a Virginia ex-slave chuckled. "We ain't cared a bit about that stuff he was telling us 'cause we wanted to sing, pray, and serve God in our own way."

Meeting in their cabins or secretly in the woods, slaves created an African American Christianity that served their needs, not the masters'. Beginning in the 1830s, laws prohibited teaching slaves to read, but some slaves could read enough to struggle with the Bible. With the help of black preachers, they interpreted the Christian message themselves. Rather than obedience, their faith emphasized justice. Nat Turner felt himself to be an avenging angel who would punish whites and end bondage. More often, slaves believed that God kept score, and accounts of this world would be settled in the next. But the slaves' faith also spoke to their experiences in this world. In the Old Testament they discovered Moses, who delivered his people from slavery, and in the New Testament they found Jesus, who offered salvation to all and thereby established the equality of all people. Jesus' message of equality provided a potent antidote to the planters' claim that blacks were an inferior people whom God condemned to slavery and was a crucial buttress to the slaves' self-esteem.

Christianity did not entirely drive out traditional African beliefs. Even slaves who were Christians sometimes continued to believe that conjurers, witches, and spirits possessed the power to protect and defend. Moreover, their Christian music, preaching, and rituals showed the influence of Africa, as did much of the slaves' secular activities, such as wood carving, quilt making, and storytelling.

Resistance and Rebellion

Slaves did not suffer slavery passively. They were, as whites said, "troublesome property." Slaves understood that accommodation to what they could not change was the price of survival, but in a hundred ways they protested their bondage. Theoretically, the master was all-powerful and the slave powerless. But sustained by their culture, religion, and community, slaves engaged in day-to-day resistance against their enslavers.

The spectrum of slave resistance ranged from mild to extreme. Telling a pointed story by the fireside in a slave cabin was probably the mildest form of protest. But when the weak got the better of the strong, as they did in tales of Brer Rabbit and Brer

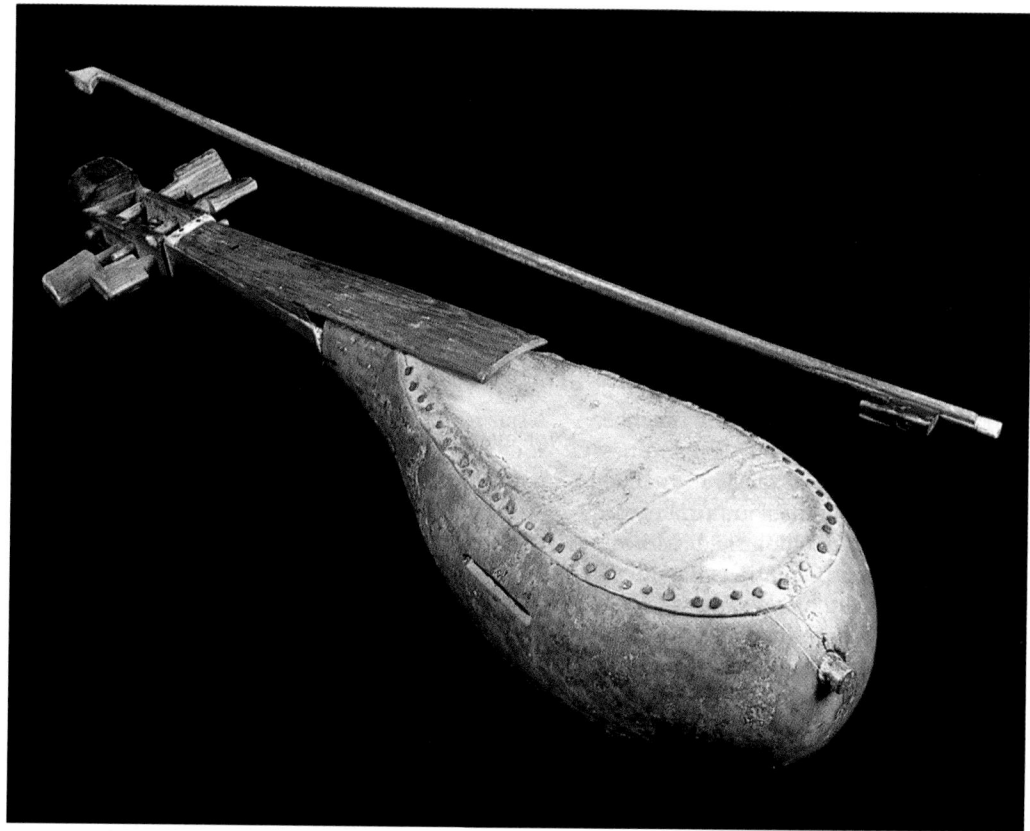

GOURD FIDDLE

Found in St. Mary's County, Maryland, this slave-made gourd fiddle is an example of the many musical instruments that African Americans crafted and played throughout the South. Henry Wright, an ex-slave from Georgia, remembered: "I made a fiddle out of a large sized gourd—a long wooden handle was used as a neck, and the hair from a horse's tail was used for the bow. The strings were made of catgut." A hybrid of African and European elements, this fiddle offers material evidence of the cultural transformation of African slaves. While Africans lost much in their forced journey to the Americas, Africa remained in their cultural memory. Black men and women drew on the traditions of their homeland and the South to create something new—an African American culture. Music, a crucial component of that sustaining culture, provided slaves with a creative outlet and relief from the rigors of slavery.

Smithsonian Institution/Aldo Tutino/Folio, Inc.

Fox (Brer is a contraction of Brother), listeners could enjoy the thrill of a vicarious victory over their masters. Protest in the fields was more active than that around firesides. Slaves were particularly inventive in resisting their master's demand that they work. They dragged their feet getting to the fields, put rocks in their cotton bags before putting them on the scale to be weighed, feigned illness, and pretended to be so thickheaded that they could not understand the simplest instruction. Slaves broke so many hoe handles that owners outfitted the hoes with oversized handles. Slaves so mistreated the work animals that masters switched from horses to mules, which could absorb more abuse. While slaves worked hard in the master's fields, they also sabotaged his interests.

Running away, a widespread form of protest, particularly angered masters. By escaping the plantation, runaways denied masters what they wanted most from their slaves—work. Sometimes runaways

The Culture of Southern Plain Folk

But not all nonslaveholding farmers were yeomen. Perhaps one in four farmers was landless. Landless farm families lived as tenants, renting rather than owning land. Other poor rural Southerners worked as unskilled day laborers, hunters, herders, and fisherman. Some landless whites barely made a go of it, but most were ambitious people scratching to survive and aspiring to climb into the yeomanry. Many succeeded, but in the 1850s upward mobility slowed. Rich planters expanded their operations, often driving the price of land beyond the reach of poor families. Despite these differences, poor rural Southerners shared some common cultural emphases with yeomen farmers.

Whether plain folk lived in the hills or in the flatlands, they did not usually associate "book learning" with the basic needs of life. A northern woman visiting the South in the 1850s observed, "Education is not extended to the masses here as at the North." Private academies charged fees that yeomen could not afford, and public schools were scarce. Although most people managed to pick up a basic knowledge of the "three R's," approximately one southern white man in five was illiterate in 1860, and the rate for white women was even higher. "People here prefer talking to reading," a Virginian remarked. Telling stories, reciting ballads, and singing hymns were important activities in yeoman folk culture.

Plain folk everywhere spent more hours in revival tents than in classrooms. By no means were all rural whites religious, but many were, and the most characteristic feature of their evangelical Christian faith was the revival. The greatest of the early nineteenth-century revivals occurred in 1801 at Cane Ridge, Kentucky, where some twenty thousand people gathered to listen to a host of evangelical preachers who spoke day and night for a week. Ministers sought to convert and save souls by bringing individuals to a personal conviction of sin. Revivalism crossed denominational lines; Baptists and Methodists adopted it wholeheartedly and by midcentury had become the South's largest religious groups. By emphasizing free choice and individual worth, the plain folk's religion was hopeful and affirming. Hymns and spirituals provided guides to right and wrong—praising modesty, condemning drinking and devilish activity like dancing. Above all, hymns spoke of eventual release from worldly sorrows and the assurance of eternal salvation.

The Politics of Slavery

Like every other significant feature of southern society, politics reflected slavery's power. Even after the South's politics became democratic in form for the white male population, political power remained unevenly distributed. The nonslaveholding white majority wielded less political power than their numbers indicated. The slaveholding white minority wielded more. Self-conscious, cohesive, and with a well-developed sense of class interest, slaveholders busied themselves with party politics, campaigns, and officeholding and made demands of state governments. As a result, they received significant benefits. But nonslaveholding whites were concerned mainly with preserving their liberties and keeping their taxes low. Collectively, they asked government for little of an economic nature, and they received little.

Slaveholders sometimes worried about nonslaveholders' loyalty to slavery, but since the eighteenth century, the mass of whites had accepted the planters' argument that the existing social order served all Southerners' interests. Slavery compensated every white man—no matter how poor—with membership in the South's white ruling class. It also provided the means by which nonslaveholders might someday advance into the ranks of the planters. White men in the South fought furiously about many things, but they agreed that they should take land from Indians, promote agriculture, uphold white supremacy, and defend slavery from its enemies.

The Democratization of the Political Arena

The political reforms that swept the nation in the first half of the nineteenth century reached deeply into the South. Southern politics became democratic politics—for white men. Southerners eliminated the wealth and property requirements that had once restricted political participation. Every state extended suffrage to all white males who were at least twenty-one years of age. Most southern states also removed the property requirements for holding state offices. In addition, increasing numbers of local and state officials—justices of the peace, judges, militia officers, and others—were chosen by the voters. To be sure, undemocratic features lingered. Plantation districts still wielded disproportionate power in several state legislatures. Nevertheless, southern politics increasingly took place within a democratic political structure.

White male suffrage ushered in an era of vigorous electoral competition. Eager voters rushed to the polls to exercise their new rights. In South Carolina, for example, in the 1810 election—the last election with voting restrictions in place—only 43 percent of white men cast ballots. In 1824, a remarkable 76 percent of white men voted. High turnouts became a hallmark of southern electoral politics.

As politics became aggressively democratic, it also grew fiercely partisan. From the 1830s to the 1850s, Whigs and Democrats battled for the electorate's favor. Whigs and Democrats both presented themselves as the plain white folk's best friend. All candidates declared their fervent commitment to republican equality and pledged to defend the people's liberty. Each party sought to portray the other as a collection of rich, snobbish, selfish men who had antidemocratic designs up their silk sleeves. Each, in turn, claimed for itself the mantle of humble "servant of the people."

The Whig and Democratic Parties sought to serve the people differently, however. Southern Whigs tended, as Whigs did elsewhere in the nation, to favor government intervention in the economy, and Democrats tended to oppose it. Whigs generally backed state support of banks, railroads, and corporations, arguing that government aid would stimulate the economy, enlarge opportunity, and thus increase the general welfare. Democrats emphasized the threat to individual liberty that government intervention posed, claiming that granting favors to special economic interests would result in concentrated power, which would in turn jeopardize the common man's opportunity and equality. Beginning with the panic of 1837, the parties clashed repeatedly on concrete economic and financial issues.

Planter Power

Whether Whig or Democrat, southern officeholders were likely to be slave owners. The power slaveholders exerted over slaves did not translate directly into political authority over whites, however. In the nineteenth century, political power could be won only at the ballot box, and almost everywhere nonslaveholders were in the majority. Yet year after year, proud and noisily egalitarian common men elected wealthy slaveholders (Table 13.1).

TABLE 13.1

SLAVEHOLDERS AND PLANTERS IN
LEGISLATURES, 1860

Legislature	Percent of Slaveholders	Percent of Planters*
Virginia	67.3	24.2
Maryland	53.4	19.3
North Carolina	85.8	36.6
Kentucky	60.6	8.4
Tennessee	66.0	14.0
Missouri	41.2	5.3
Arkansas	42.0	13.0
South Carolina	81.7	55.4
Georgia	71.6	29.0
Florida	55.4	20.0
Alabama	76.3	40.8
Mississippi	73.4	49.5
Louisiana	63.8	23.5
Texas	54.1	18.1

*Planters: Owned 20 or more slaves.

Source: Adapted from Ralph A. Wooster, *The People in Power: Courthouse and Statehouse in the Lower South, 1850–1860* (1969), 41; *Politicians, Planters, and Plain Folks: Courthouse and Statehouse in the Upper South* (1975), 40.

Courtesy of the University of Tennessee Press.

Over time, slaveholders increased their power in state legislatures. By 1860, the percentage of slave owners in state legislatures ranged from 41 percent in Missouri to nearly 86 percent in North Carolina. Legislators not only tended to own slaves—they often owned large numbers. The percentage of planters (individuals with twenty or more slaves) in southern legislatures in 1860 ranged from 5.3 percent in Missouri to 55.4 percent in South Carolina. In North Carolina, where only 3 percent of the state's white families belonged to the planter class, 36.6 percent of the legislature were planters. The democratization of politics in the nineteenth century meant that more ordinary citizens participated in elections, but yeomen and artisans remained rare sights in the halls of southern legislatures.

Upper-class dominance of southern politics reflected, in part, the strength of the rural folk culture, which valued tradition and stability. Since the colonial era, yeomen had looked to the upper class for political leadership. As democracy rose in the nineteenth century, notions of hierarchy and habits of deference declined, but planter status remained important in the South and the surest ticket to political advancement.

But tradition was not enough to ensure planter rule. Slaveholders had to persuade the white majority that what was good for slaveholders was also good for them. Slaveless white men proved to be receptive to the planters' argument. The South had, on the whole, done well by them. Most had farms of their own. They participated as equals in a democratic political system. They enjoyed an elevated social status, above all blacks and in theory equal to all other whites. As patriarchs, they commanded their households. As long as slavery existed, they could dream of joining the planter class, of rising above the drudgery of field labor. Slaveless white men found much to celebrate in the slave South.

Most slaveholders took pains to win the plain folk's trust and to nurture their respect. In the plantation districts especially, where slaveholders and nonslaveholders lived side by side, planters learned that flexing their economic muscle was a poor way to win the political allegiance of common men. Instead, they developed a lighter touch, fully attentive to their own interests but aware of the personal feelings of poorer whites. One South Carolinian told his wealthy neighbor that he had a bright political future because he never thought himself "too good to sit down & talk to a poor man."

Smart candidates found ways to convince wary yeomen of their democratic convictions and egalitarian sentiments, whether they were genuine or not. When young John A. Quitman ran for a seat in the Mississippi legislature, he amazed a boisterous crowd of small farmers at one campaign stop by not only entering but winning contests in jumping, boxing, wrestling, and sprinting. For his finale he outshot the area's champion marksman. Then, demonstrating his deft political touch, he gave his prize, a fat ox, to the defeated rifleman. The electorate showed its approval by sending Quitman to the state capital.

The massive representation of slaveholders ensured that southern legislatures would make every effort to preserve slavery. Georgia politics show how well the planters protected themselves in the political struggle. In 1850, about half of the state's revenues came from taxes on slave property, the characteristic form of planter wealth. However, the tax rate on slaves was trifling, only about one-fifth the rate on land. Moreover, planters benefited far more than other social groups from public spending: Financing railroads—which carried cotton to market—was the largest state expenditure. The legislature also established low tax rates on land, the characteristic form of yeoman wealth, which meant that the typical yeoman's annual tax bill was small. Still, relative to their wealth, large slaveholders paid less than did other whites. Relative to their numbers, they got more in return. A sympathetic slaveholding legislature protected planters' interests and gave the impression of protecting the small farmers' interests as well.

The South's elite protected slavery in other ways. In the 1830s, whites decided that slavery was too important to debate. "So interwoven is [slavery] with our interest, our manners, our climate and our very being," one man declared in 1833, "that no change can ever possibly be effected without a civil commotion from which the heart of a patriot must turn with horror." A "cotton curtain" descended along the Mason-Dixon line that ended free speech on the slavery question. Slavery's critics were dismissed from college faculties, driven from pulpits, and hounded from political life. Sometimes they fell victim to vigilantes and mob violence. One could defend slavery; one could even delicately suggest mild reforms. But no Southerner could safely call slavery evil or advocate its destruction.

In the antebellum South, therefore, the rise of the common man occurred alongside the continuing, even growing, power of the planter class. Rather than pitting slaveholders against nonslaveholders, elections remained an effective means of binding the region's whites together. Elections affirmed the sovereignty of white men, whether planter or plain folk, and the subordination of African Americans. Those twin themes played well among white women as well. Although unable to vote, white women supported equality for whites and slavery for blacks.

Conclusion: A Slave Society

Antebellum Americans came to see the South as fundamentally different from the rest of the nation. Rural and biracial, the South reflected the power of plantation slavery. Regional differences increased over time, not merely because the South became more and more dominated by slavery, but also because developments in the North rapidly propelled it in a very different direction.

In 1860, one-third of the South's population was enslaved. Bondage saddled blacks with enormous physical and spiritual burdens: hard labor, poor treatment, broken families, and, most important, the denial of freedom itself. Although degraded and exploited, they were not defeated. Out of African memories and New World realities, blacks created a life-affirming African American culture that sustained and strengthened them. Their families, religion, and community provided antidotes to white racist ideas and even to white power. Defined as property, they refused to be reduced to things. Perceived as inferior beings, they rejected the notion that they were natural slaves. Slaves engaged in a war of wills with masters who sought their labor while they sought to live dignified, autonomous lives.

Much more than racial slavery contributed to the South's distinctiveness and to the loyalty and regional identification of its whites. White Southerners felt strong attachments to local communities, to extended families, to personal, face-to-face relationships, to rural life, to evangelical Protestantism, and to codes of honor and chivalry, among other things. But slavery was crucial to the South's economy, society, and culture, as well as to its developing sectional consciousness. After the 1830s, the South was not merely a society with slaves; it was a slave society. Little disturbed the white consensus south of the Mason-Dixon line that racial slavery was necessary and just. By making all blacks a pariah class, all whites gained a measure of equality and harmony.

Racism did not erase stress along class lines. Nor did the other features of southern life that helped confine class tensions: the wide availability of land, rapid economic mobility, the democratic nature of political life, patriarchal power among white men, the shrewd behavior of slaveholders toward poorer whites, kinship ties between rich and poor, and rural traditions. Anxious slaveholders continued to worry that yeomen would defect from the proslavery consensus. But during the 1850s a far more ominous division emerged—that between the "slave states" and the "free states."

FOR FURTHER READING ABOUT THE TOPICS IN THIS CHAPTER, see the Online Bibliography at
www.bedfordstmartins.com/roarkcompact.

FOR ADDITIONAL FIRST-HAND ACCOUNTS OF THIS PERIOD, see pages 196–211 in Michael Johnson, ed., *Reading the American Past,* Second Edition, Volume I.

TO ASSESS YOUR MASTERY OF THE MATERIAL IN THIS CHAPTER, see the Online Study Guide at
www.bedfordstmartins.com/roarkcompact.

CHRONOLOGY

1808	External slave trade outlawed.		**1820–1860**	Cotton production soars from about 300,000 bales to nearly 5 million bales.
1810s–1850s	Suffrage gradually extended throughout South to white males over twenty-one years of age.		**1822**	Denmark Vesey executed for conspiring to lead a slave rebellion in South Carolina.
1820s–1830s	Southern legislatures enact slave codes to strengthen slavery.		**1831**	Nat Turner's slave rebellion occurs in Virginia.
	Southern legislatures enact laws to restrict growth of free black population and to limit freedom of free blacks.		**1860**	The slave population of the South surpasses 4 million, an increase of 600 percent in seven decades.
	Southern intellectuals begin to fashion systematic defense of slavery.			

JOHN BROWN'S PIKES

Scorning what he called "milk-and-water" abolitionists who only talked about slavery, John Brown favored "action!" In 1859 when he brought his abolitionist war to Virginia, he carried with him 950 pikes, handsome but deadly spears made by a Connecticut blacksmith, which he expected to put into the hands of rebelling slaves. Bloody pikes, he thought, would end slavery in America. But after Brown's failure at Harpers Ferry, townspeople sold many of the weapons as souvenirs.

Chicago Historical Society.

THE HOUSE DIVIDED

1846–1861

14

OTHER THAN TWENTY CHILDREN, John Brown did not have much to show for his life in 1859. Grizzled, gnarled, and fifty-nine years old, he had for decades lived like a nomad, hauling his large family back and forth across six states as he tried desperately to better himself. He turned his hand to farming, raising sheep, running a tannery, and selling wool, but failure followed failure. The world had given John Brown some hard licks, but it had not budged his conviction that slavery was wrong and ought to be destroyed. He had learned to hate slavery at his father's knee, and in the wake of the fighting that erupted over the issue in Kansas in the 1850s, his beliefs turned violent. On May 24, 1856, he led an eight-man antislavery posse in the midnight slaughter of five allegedly proslavery men at Pottawatomie, Kansas. He told Mahala Doyle, whose husband and two oldest sons he killed, that if a man stood between him and what he thought right, he would take that man's life as calmly as he would eat breakfast.

Kansans knew that John Brown and his men were the Pottawatomie killers, but Brown admitted nothing, slipped away from the territory, and reemerged in the East. More than ever, he was a man on fire for abolition. He spent thirty months begging money from New England abolitionists to support his vague plan for military operations against slavery. He captivated the genteel Easterners, particularly the Boston elite. They shared his antislavery convictions and were awed by his iron-willed determination and courage. They listened when the hypnotic-eyed Brown told them that God had touched him for a great purpose. Eventually, Brown received enough in gifts to gather a small band of antislavery warriors.

On the night of October 16, 1859, John Brown took his war against slavery into the South. With only twenty-one men, including five African Americans, he invaded Harpers Ferry, Virginia. Brown's band quickly seized the town's armory and rifle works, but the invaders were immediately surrounded, first by local militia and then by Colonel Robert E. Lee, who commanded the U.S. troops in the area. When Brown refused to surrender, federal soldiers charged with bayonets. Seventeen men, two of whom were slaves, lost their lives. Although a few of Brown's raiders escaped, federal forces killed ten (including two of his sons) and captured seven, among them Brown.

"When I strike, the bees will begin to swarm," Brown told Frederick Douglass a few months before the raid. As slaves rushed to Harpers Ferry, Brown planned to arm them with the pikes he carried with him and with weapons stolen from the armory. They would then fight a war of liberation. In reality, however, Brown had neglected to inform the slaves that he had arrived in Harpers Ferry, and the few who knew wanted nothing to do with the enterprise. "It was not a slave insurrection," Abraham Lincoln observed. "It was an attempt by white men to get up a revolt among slaves, in which the slaves refused to participate. In fact, it was so absurd that the slaves, with all their ignorance, saw plainly enough it could not succeed."

Southern supporters declared that popular sovereignty guaranteed that slavery would be unrestricted throughout the entire settlement period. Only at the very end, when settlers in the territory drew up a constitution and applied for statehood, could they decide the issue of slavery or freedom. By then, slavery would have sunk deep roots. As long as the matter of timing remained vague, popular sovereignty provided some Northerners and some Southerners with common ground.

When Congress ended its session in 1848, no plan had won a majority in both houses. Northerners who demanded no new slave territory anywhere, ever, and Southerners who demanded free entry for their slave property into all territories, or else, staked out their extreme positions. Unresolved in Congress, the territorial question naturally became an issue in the presidential election of 1848.

The Election of 1848

When President Polk—worn out, ailing, and unable to unite the Democratic Party—chose not to seek reelection, the Democratic convention nominated Lewis Cass of Michigan, the man most closely as-

GENERAL TAYLOR CIGAR CASE
This papier-mâché cigar case portrays General Zachary Taylor, Whig presidential candidate in 1848, in a colorful scene from the Mexican War. Shown as a dashing, elegant officer, Taylor was in fact a short, thickset, and roughly dressed Indian fighter who had spent his career commanding small frontier garrisons. The inscription reminds voters that Taylor was a victor in the first four battles fought in the war and directs attention away from the fact that in politics he was a rank amateur.
Collection of Janice L. and David J. Frent.

sociated with popular sovereignty, but in an effort to keep peace between the proslavery and antislavery factions within the party adopted a platform that avoided a firm position on slavery in the territories. The Whigs followed a different strategy in their effort to patch the fissure within their party over slavery. They nominated the Mexican War hero, General Zachary Taylor. The Whigs bet that selection of a military hero combined with total silence on the central issue facing the country would carry the day and thus declined to adopt a party platform. Taylor, who owned more than one hundred slaves on plantations in Mississippi and Louisiana, was hailed by Georgia politician Robert Toombs as a "Southern man, a slaveholder, a cotton planter."

Antislavery Whigs balked and looked for an alternative. The time seemed ripe for a major political realignment. Senator Charles Sumner called for "one grand Northern party of Freedom," and in the summer of 1848 antislavery Democrats and antislavery Whigs founded the Free-Soil Party. Nearly fifteen thousand noisy Free-Soilers gathered in Buffalo, New York, where they welded the factions together by nominating a Democrat, Martin Van Buren, for president and a Whig, Charles Francis Adams, for vice president. The platform boldly proclaimed, "Free soil, free speech, free labor, and free men."

The November election dashed the hopes of the Free-Soilers. Although they succeeded in making slavery the campaign's central issue, they did not carry a single state. The major parties went through contortions to present their candidates favorably in both the North and the South, and their evasions succeeded. Taylor won the all-important electoral vote, 163 to 127, carrying eight of the fifteen slave states and seven of the fifteen free states (Map 14.1). (Wisconsin had entered the Union earlier in 1848 as the fifteenth free state.) Northern voters proved they were not yet ready for Sumner's "one grand Northern party of Freedom," but the struggle over slavery in the territories had shaken the major parties badly.

Debate and Compromise

Zachary Taylor entered the White House in March 1849 and almost immediately shocked the nation. The southern slaveholder championed a free-soil solution to the problem of western land. He sent agents west to persuade settlers in California and

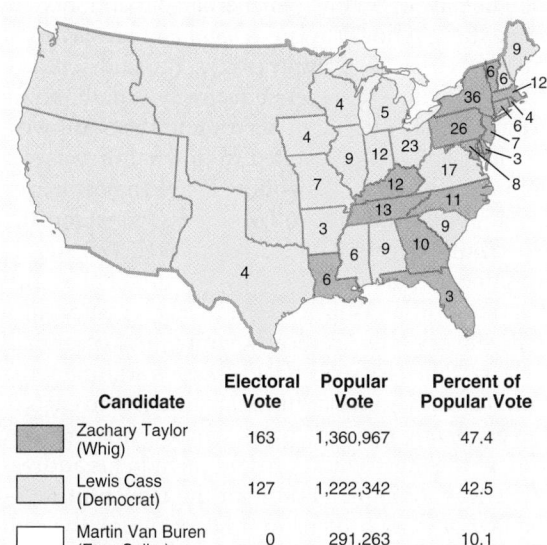

Candidate	Electoral Vote	Popular Vote	Percent of Popular Vote
Zachary Taylor (Whig)	163	1,360,967	47.4
Lewis Cass (Democrat)	127	1,222,342	42.5
Martin Van Buren (Free-Soiler)	0	291,263	10.1

MAP 14.1
The Election of 1848

New Mexico to frame constitutions and apply for admission to the Union as states. Predominately antislavery, the settlers began writing free-state constitutions. "For the first time," Mississippian Jefferson Davis lamented, "we are about permanently to destroy the balance of power between the sections."

When Congress convened in December 1849, anxious citizens packed the galleries, eager for the "Great Debate." They witnessed what proved to be one of the longest, most contentious, and most significant sessions in the history of Congress in which the territorial issue dominated. President Taylor urged Congress to admit California as a free state immediately and to admit New Mexico, which lagged behind, as soon as it applied. Southerners exploded. In their eyes, Taylor had betrayed his region. Southerners who would "consent to be thus degraded and enslaved," a North Carolinian declared, "ought to be whipped through their fields by their own negroes." Calhoun almost lost heart. "As things now stand," he said in February, the South "cannot with safety remain in the Union."

Into this rancorous scene stepped Henry Clay, recently returned to the Senate by his home state of Kentucky. His reputation preceded him: the "Great Pacificator," master of accommodation, architect of Union-saving compromises in the Missouri and nullification crises. "Mr. President," Clay declared

when he took the floor on January 29, 1850, "I hold in my hand a series of resolutions which I desire to submit to the consideration of this body. Taken together, in combination, they propose an amicable arrangement of all questions in controversy between the free and slave states, growing out of the subject of slavery." His comprehensive plan sought to balance the interests of the slave and free states. Admit California as a free state, he proposed, but organize the rest of the Southwest without restrictions on slavery. Require Texas to abandon its claim to parts of New Mexico, but compensate it by assuming its preannexation debt. Abolish the slave trade in Washington, D.C., but confirm slavery itself in the nation's capital. Reassert Congress's lack

JOHN C. CALHOUN
Hollow-cheeked and dark-eyed in this 1850 daguerreotype by Mathew Brady, Calhoun had only months to live. Still, his passion and indomitable will come through. British writer Harriet Martineau once described the champion of southern rights as "the cast-iron man who looks as if he had never been born and could never be extinguished."
National Portrait Gallery, Smithsonian Institution/Art Resource, N.Y.

of authority to interfere with the interstate slave trade. And enact a more effective fugitive slave law.

Antislavery advocates and "fire-eaters" (as radical southern secessionists were called) both savaged Clay's plan. Senator Salmon Chase of Ohio ridiculed it as "sentiment for the North, substance for the South." Senator Henry S. Foote of Mississippi denounced it as more offensive to the South than the speeches of abolitionists William Lloyd Garrison, Wendell Phillips, and Frederick Douglass combined. The most ominous response came from the mighty Calhoun, who concluded northern agitation on the slavery question had "snapped" many of the "cords which bind these states together in one common Union . . . and has greatly weakened all the others." The fragile political unity of North and South depended on continued equal representation in the Senate, which Clay's plan for a free California destroyed. Without equality, Calhoun declared, Southerners were defenseless and could not remain in the Union.

After Clay and Calhoun had spoken, it was time for the third member of the "great triumvirate," Daniel Webster of Massachusetts. Like Clay, Webster sought to build a constituency for compromise. Admitting that the South had complaints that required attention, he argued forcefully that secession from the Union would mean civil war. He appealed for an end to reckless proposals and, to the dismay of many Northerners, mentioned by name the Wilmot Proviso. A legal ban on slavery in the territories was unnecessary, he said, because rough climate and terrain effectively prohibited the expansion of cotton and slaves into the Southwest.

Free-soil forces recoiled from what they saw as Webster's desertion. Theodore Parker, a Boston clergyman and abolitionist, could only conclude that "the Southern men" must have offered Webster the presidency. Senator William H. Seward of New York responded that Webster's and Clay's compromise with slavery was "radically wrong and essentially vicious." He flatly rejected Calhoun's argument that Congress lacked constitutional authority to exclude slavery from the territories. In any case, Seward said, in the most sensational moment in his address, there was a "higher law than the Constitution"—the law of God—to ensure freedom in all the public domain. Claiming that God was a Free-Soiler did nothing to cool the superheated atmosphere of Washington.

In May, a Senate committee (with the tireless Clay at its head) reported a bill that joined Clay's resolutions into a single comprehensive package, known as the Omnibus Bill because it was a vehicle on which "every sort of passenger" could ride. Clay bet that a majority of Congress wanted compromise and that while the omnibus contained items individuals disliked, each would vote for the

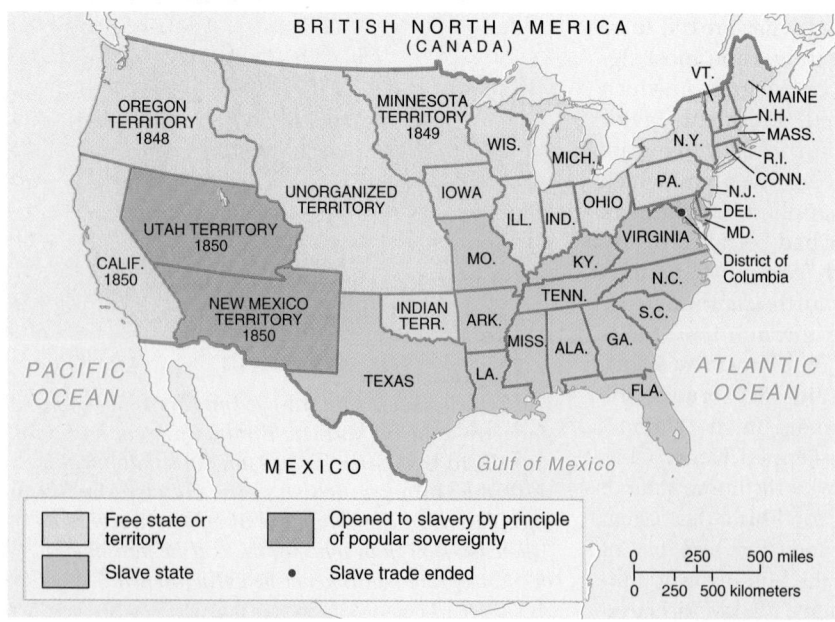

MAP 14.2

The Compromise of 1850
The patched-together sectional agreement was both clumsy and unstable. Few Americans—in either the North or the South— supported all five parts of the Compromise.

package to gain an overall settlement of sectional issues. But the omnibus strategy backfired. Free-Soilers, Conscience Whigs, and proslavery Southerners would support separate parts of Clay's bill, but they would not endorse the whole. After making seventy speeches to defend his plan, Clay saw it go down to defeat.

Fortunately for those who favored a settlement, Senator Stephen A. Douglas, a rising Democratic star from Illinois, stepped into Clay's shoes. Rejecting the omnibus strategy, he broke the bill into its various parts and skillfully ushered each through Congress. The agreement Douglas won in September 1850 was very much the one Clay had proposed in January. California entered the Union as a free state. New Mexico and Utah became territories in which the question of slavery would be decided by popular sovereignty. Texas accepted its present-day boundary with New Mexico and received $10 million from the federal government. Congress ended the slave trade in the District of Columbia yet enacted a more stringent fugitive slave law. In September, Millard Fillmore, who had become president upon the death of Zachary Taylor in July, signed each bill, collectively known as the Compromise of 1850, into law (Map 14.2).

Actually, the Compromise of 1850 was not a true compromise at all. Douglas's parliamentary skill, not a spirit of conciliation, led to legislative success. Only by nimbly allying a small group of true compromisers with larger blocs of Northerners and Southerners who voted along sectional lines did Douglas gain a majority for each separate measure. Nor was the Compromise the "final settlement," as President Fillmore announced.

The Sectional Balance Undone

The so-called final settlement of the Compromise of 1850 began to come apart almost immediately. The thread that unraveled the Compromise was not slavery in the Southwest, the crux of the disagreement, but runaway slaves in New England, a part of the settlement that had previously received relatively little attention. Rather than restore calm, the Compromise brought the horrors of slavery into the North.

Millions of Northerners who never saw a runaway slave nevertheless confronted slavery in the early 1850s. Harriet Beecher Stowe's *Uncle Tom's Cabin*, a novel that vividly depicted the brutality and heartlessness of the South's "peculiar institution," aroused passions so deep that many found goodwill toward white Southerners nearly impossible. But no popular uprising forced Congress to reopen the slavery controversy: Politicians did it themselves. Four years after Congress delicately stitched the sectional compromise together, it ripped the threads out. It once again posed the question of slavery in the territories, the deadliest of all sectional issues.

The Fugitive Slave Act

The Fugitive Slave Act proved the most explosive of the Compromise measures. The issue of runaways was as old as the Constitution, which contained a provision for the return of any "person held to service or labor in one state" who escaped to another. In 1793, a federal law gave muscle to the provision by authorizing slave owners to enter other states to recapture their slave property. Proclaiming the 1793 law a license to kidnap free blacks, northern states in the 1830s began passing "personal liberty laws" that provided fugitives with some protection. Some northern communities also formed vigilance committees to help runaways and to obstruct white Southerners who came north to reclaim them. Each year, a few hundred slaves escaped into free states and found friendly northern "conductors" who put them aboard the "underground railroad," which was not a railroad at all but a series of secret "stations" (hideouts) on the way to Canada.

Furious about northern interference, Southerners in 1850 insisted on the stricter fugitive slave law that was passed as part of the Compromise. To seize an alleged slave, a slaveholder or his agent simply had to appear before a commissioner and swear that the runaway was his. The commissioner earned ten dollars for every black returned to slavery but only five dollars for those set free. Most galling to Northerners, the law stipulated that all citizens were expected to assist officials in apprehending runaways. Theodore Parker, the clergyman and abolitionist, denounced the law as "a hateful statute of kidnappers" and headed a Boston vigilance committee that openly violated it. In February 1851, an angry crowd in Boston overpowered federal marshals and snatched a runaway named Shadrach from a courtroom, put him on the underground railroad, and whisked him off to Montreal, Canada.

To white Southerners, it seemed that fanatics of the "higher law" creed had whipped Northerners into a frenzy of massive resistance. Actually, the overwhelming majority of fugitives claimed before federal commissioners were reenslaved and shipped south peacefully. Spectacular rescues such as the one that saved Shadrach were rare. But brutal enforcement of the unpopular law had a radicalizing effect in the North, particularly in New England. And to Southerners it seemed that Northerners had betrayed the Compromise. As a Tennessee man warned in November 1850, "If the fugitive slave bill is not enforced in the north, the

moderate men of the South . . . will be overwhelmed by the 'fire-eaters.'"

Uncle Tom's Cabin

The spectacle of shackled African Americans being herded south seared the conscience of every Northerner who witnessed such a scene. But even more Northerners were turned against slavery by a fictional account, a novel. Harriet Beecher Stowe, a Northerner who had never seen a plantation, made the South's slaves into flesh-and-blood human beings almost more real than life.

A member of a famous clan of preachers, teachers, and reformers, Stowe despised the slave catch-

THEATER POSTER
During the 1850s, at least ten individuals, including Harriet Beecher Stowe herself, dramatized the novel **Uncle Tom's Cabin.** *These plays, known as "Tom Shows," drew crowds in America and Britain. Stowe's moral indictment of slavery translated well to the stage. Scenes of Eliza crossing the ice with bloodhounds in pursuit, the cruelty of Legree, and Little Eva borne to heaven on puffy clouds gripped the imagination of audiences and fueled the growing antislavery crusade.*
Smithsonian Institution.

www.bedfordstmartins.com/roarkcompact SEE THE ONLINE STUDY GUIDE for more help in analyzing this image.

ers and wrote to expose the sin of slavery. Published in 1852, her book *Uncle Tom's Cabin* became a blockbuster hit and sold 300,000 copies in its first year. Her characters leaped from the page. Here was the gentle slave Uncle Tom, a Christian saint who forgave those who beat him to death; the courageous slave Eliza, who fled with her child across the frozen Ohio River; and the fiendish overseer Simon Legree, whose Louisiana plantation was a nightmare of torture and death. Herself the mother of seven children, Stowe aimed her most powerful blows at slavery's destructive impact on the family. Her character Eliza succeeds in keeping her son from being sold away, but other mothers are not so fortunate. When told that her infant has been sold, Lucy drowns herself. Driven half mad by the sale of a son and daughter, Cassy decides "never again [to] let a child live to grow up!" She gives her third child an opiate and watches as "he slept to death."

Responses to *Uncle Tom's Cabin* depended on geography. In the North, common people and literary giants alike shed tears and sang its praises. The poet John Greenleaf Whittier sent "ten thousand thanks for thy immortal book," and poet Henry Wadsworth Longfellow judged it "one of the greatest triumphs recorded in literary history." What Northerners accepted as truth, Southerners denounced as slander. Virginian George F. Holmes proclaimed Stowe a member of the "Woman's Rights" and "Higher Law" schools and dismissed the novel as a work of "intense fanaticism." Unfortunately, he said, this "maze of misinterpretation" had filled those who knew nothing about slavery "with hatred for that institution and those who uphold it." Although it is impossible to measure precisely the impact of a novel on public opinion, *Uncle Tom's Cabin* clearly helped to crystallize northern sentiment against slavery and to confirm white Southerners' suspicion that they no longer had any sympathy in the free states.

Other writers—ex-slaves who knew life in slave cabins firsthand—also produced stinging indictments of slavery. Solomon Northup's compelling *Twelve Years a Slave* (1853) sold 27,000 copies in two years, and the powerful *Narrative of the Life of Frederick Douglass, as Told by Himself* (1845) eventually sold more than 30,000 copies. But no work touched the North's conscience like the novel by the woman who had never set foot on a plantation. A decade after its publication, when Stowe visited Abraham Lincoln at the White House, he reportedly said, "So you are the little woman who wrote the book that made this great war."

The Kansas-Nebraska Act

As national elections approached in 1852, Democrats and Whigs sought to close the sectional rifts that had opened within their parties. For their presidential nominee, the Democrats turned to Franklin Pierce of New Hampshire. Pierce's most valuable asset was his well-known sympathy with southern views on public issues. His leanings caused northern critics to include him among the "doughfaces," northern men malleable enough to champion southern causes. The Whigs were less successful in compromising differences. Adopting the formula that had proved successful in 1848, they chose another Mexican War hero, General Winfield Scott of Virginia. But the Whigs were hopeless divided and suffered a humiliating defeat. The Democrat Pierce carried twenty-seven states to Scott's four, 254 electoral votes to 42 (Table 14.1). In the afterglow of the

---

TABLE 14.1
THE ELECTION OF 1852

Candidate	Electoral Vote	Popular Vote	Percent of Popular Vote
Franklin Pierce (Democrat)	254	1,601,000	50.9
Winfield Scott (Whig)	42	1,385,000	44.1
John P. Hale (Free-Soil)	0	156,000	5.0

Compromise of 1850, the Free-Soil Party lost almost half of the voters who had turned to it in the tumultuous atmosphere of 1848.

Eager to leave the sectional controversy behind, the new president turned swiftly to foreign expansion. Manifest Destiny remained robust. Pierce's major objective was Cuba, which was owned by Spain and in which slavery flourished, but Pierce's clumsy diplomatic efforts galvanized antislavery Northerners, who blocked Cuba's acquisition. Pierce's fortunes improved in Mexico. In 1853, he sent diplomat James Gadsden, a former army officer and railroad company president, to negotiate a $15 million purchase of some 30,000 square miles of territory south of the Gila River in present-day Arizona and New Mexico. The Gadsden Purchase stemmed from the dream of a transcontinental railroad to California and Pierce's desire to build it through Mexican territory. The booming population of the Pacific coast made it obvious that the vast, loose-jointed republic needed a railroad to bind it together. Talk of a railroad ignited rivalries in cities from New Orleans to Chicago as they maneuvered to become the eastern terminus. Thus, the railroad became a sectional contest, which by the 1850s inevitably involved slavery.

No one played the railroad game more enthusiastically than Senator Stephen A. Douglas, who was an energetic spokesman for western economic development. He badly wanted the transcontinental railroad for Chicago and his home state, Illinois. His chairmanship of the Senate Committee on Territories provided him with an opportunity. Any railroad that ran west from Chicago would pass through a region that Congress in 1830 had designated a "permanent" Indian reserve. Douglas proposed giving this vast area between the Missouri River and the Rocky Mountains an Indian name, Nebraska, and then nullifying Indian titles and throwing the Indians out. Once the region achieved territorial status, whites could survey and sell the land, establish civil government, and build a railroad.

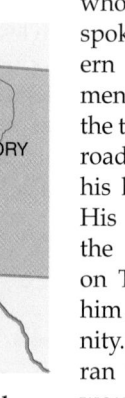

Gadsden Purchase of 1853

Nebraska lay within the Louisiana Purchase north of 36°30′, which, according to the Missouri Compromise of 1820, closed it to slavery. Since Douglas could not count on New England to back western economic development, he needed southern votes to pass his Nebraska legislation. But Southerners had no incentive to create another free territory or to help a northern city win the Pacific railroad. Southerners, however, would help to organize Nebraska—for a price: nothing less than the repeal of the Missouri Compromise. Southerners insisted that Congress organize Nebraska according to popular sovereignty, and that meant giving slavery a chance in the Nebraska Territory and reopening the dangerous issue of slavery expansion that Douglas himself had so ably helped to resolve only four years earlier.

In January 1854, Douglas introduced his bill to organize the Nebraska Territory, leaving to the settlers themselves the decision about slavery. At southern insistence, and even though he knew it would "raise a hell of a storm," Douglas added an explicit repeal of the Missouri Compromise. Indeed, the Nebraska bill raised a storm of controversy. Free-Soilers branded Douglas's plan "a gross violation of a sacred pledge" and an "atrocious plot" to transform free land into a "dreary region of despotism, inhabited by masters and slaves."

Douglas skillfully shepherded the explosive bill through Congress in May 1854. Nine-tenths of all southern members (Whigs and Democrats) and half of the northern Democrats cast votes in favor. Like Douglas, most northern Democrats believed that popular sovereignty would make Nebraska free territory. Ominously, however, half of the northern Democrats broke with their party and opposed the bill. In its final form, the Kansas-Nebraska Act divided the huge territory in two: Nebraska west of the free state of Iowa and Kansas west of the slave state of Missouri (Map 14.3).

The Realignment of the Party System

The Kansas-Nebraska Act marked a fateful escalation of the sectional conflict. Douglas's controversial measure had several consequences, none more crucial than the realignment of the nation's political parties. Since the rise of the Whigs in the early 1830s, Whigs and Democrats had or-

MAP 14.3

The Kansas-Nebraska Act, 1854
Americans hardly thought twice about dispossessing the Indians of lands guaranteed them by treaty, but many worried about the outcome of repealing the Missouri Compromise and opening up lands to slavery.

READING THE MAP: How many slave states and how many free states does the map show? Estimate the percentage of territory likely to be settled by slaveholders.
CONNECTIONS: Who would be more likely to support changes in government legislation to discontinue the Missouri Compromise, slaveholders or free-soil advocates? Why?

www.bedfordstmartins.com/roarkcompact   SEE THE ONLINE STUDY GUIDE for more help in analyzing this map.

ganized and channeled political conflict in the nation. This party system dampened sectionalism and strengthened the Union. To achieve national political power, Whigs and Democrats had to retain strength in both the North and the South. Strong northern and southern wings required that each party compromise and find positions acceptable to both wings.

The Kansas-Nebraska controversy shattered this conservative political system. In place of two national parties with bisectional strength, the mid-

1850s witnessed the development of one party heavily dominated by one section and another party entirely limited to the other section. Rather than "national" parties, the country had what one critic disdainfully called "geographic" parties. Parties now had the advantage of sharpening ideological and policy differences between the sections and no longer muffling moral issues, like slavery. But the new party system also thwarted political compromise and instead promoted political polarization and further jeopardized the Union.

The Old Parties: Whigs and Democrats

Distress signals could be heard from the Whig camp as early as the Mexican War, when members clashed over the future of slavery in annexed Mexican lands. But the disintegration of the party dated from 1849–1850, when southern Whigs watched in stunned amazement as Whig president Zachary Taylor sponsored a plan for a free California. And above the Mason-Dixon line, the strains of the slav- ery issue split northern Whigs. Anti-slavery Whigs gained a majority by 1852. The party could please the southern wing or the northern wing but not both. The Whigs' miserable showing in the election of 1852 made clear that they were no longer a strong national party. By 1856, after more than two decades of contesting the Democrats, they were hardly a party at all (Map 14.4).

The decline and eventual collapse of the Whig Party left the Democrats as the country's only na- tional party. Although the Democrats were not im-

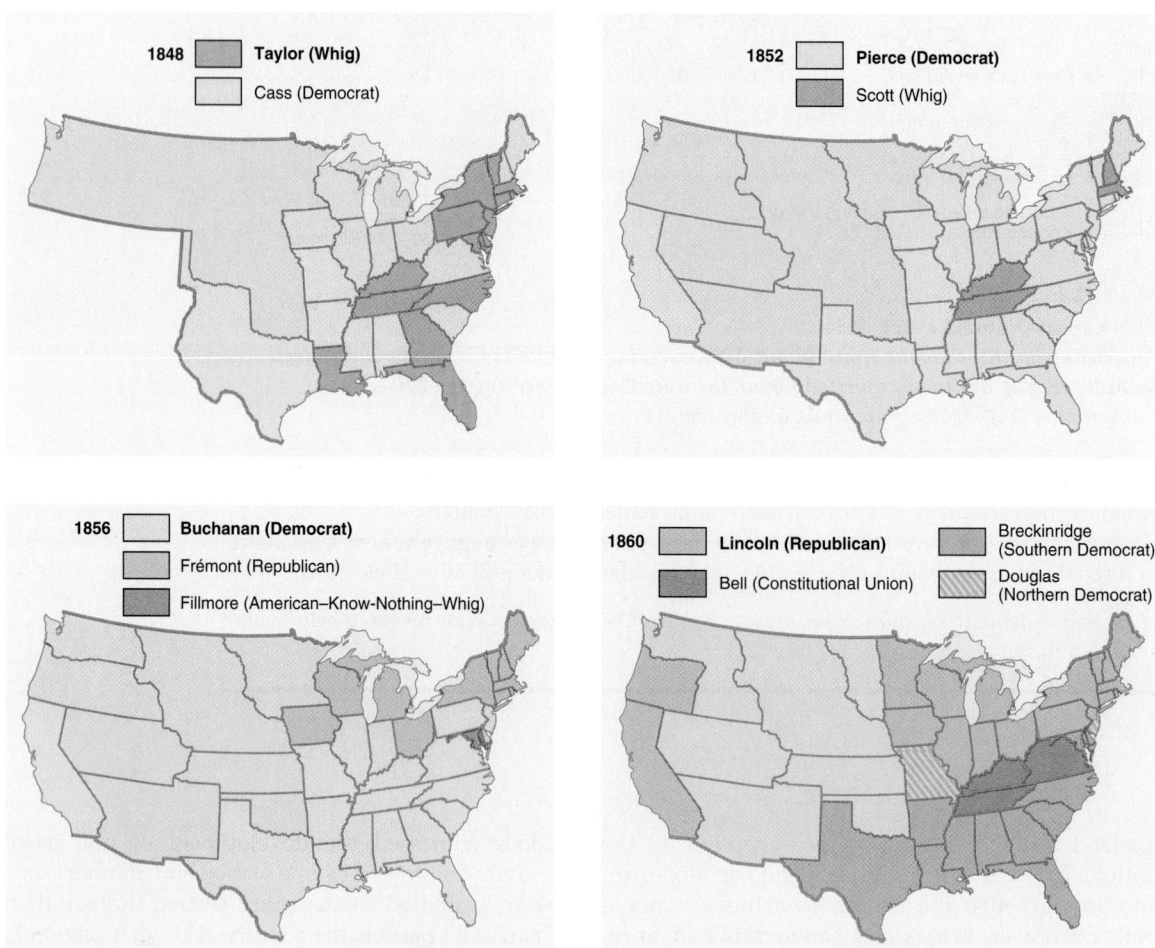

MAP 14.4

Political Realignment, 1848–1860

In 1848, slavery and sectionalism began hammering the country's party system. The Whig Party was an early casualty. By 1860, national parties—those that contended for votes in both the North and the South—had been replaced by regional parties.

mune to the disruptive pressures of the territorial question, they discovered in popular sovereignty a doctrine that many Democrats could support. But popular sovereignty very nearly undid the party as well. When Stephen Douglas applied the doctrine to that part of the Louisiana Purchase where slavery had been barred, he divided northern Democrats and destroyed the dominance of the Democratic Party in the free states. After 1854, the Democrats became a southern-dominated party.

Nevertheless, Democrats remained the dominant party throughout the 1850s. Gains in the South more than balanced losses in the North. During the decade, Democrats elected two presidents and won majorities in Congress in almost every election. But national power required that the party maintain a northern and a southern wing, which in turn required that they avoid the issue of the expansion of slavery.

The breakup of the Whigs and the disaffection of significant numbers of northern Democrats set many Americans politically adrift. As they searched for new political harbors, Americans found that the death of the old party system created a multitude of fresh political alternatives. The question was which party would attract the drifters.

The New Parties: Know-Nothings and Republicans

Dozens of new political organizations vied for voters' attention, but two emerged as true contenders. One grew out of the slavery controversy, a spontaneous coalition of indignant antislavery Northerners. The other arose from an entirely different split in American society, that between Roman Catholic immigrants and native Protestants.

The tidal wave of immigrants that broke over America in the decade from 1845 to 1855 produced a nasty backlash among Protestant Americans, who believed they were about to drown in a sea of Roman Catholics from Ireland and Germany (see Figure 12.1). When the immigrants entered American politics, they largely became Democrats because they perceived that party as more tolerant of newcomers than were the Whigs. But in the 1850s they met sharp political opposition when nativists (individuals who were anti-immigrant) began to organize, first into secret fraternal societies and then

into a political party. Recruits swore never to vote for either foreign-born or Roman Catholic candidates and not to reveal any information about the organization. When questioned, they said: "I know nothing." Officially, they were named the American Party, but most Americans called them Know-Nothings.

The Know-Nothings exploded onto the political stage in 1854 and 1855 with a series of dazzling successes. They captured state legislatures in the Northeast, West, and South and claimed dozens of seats in Congress. Their greatest triumph came in Massachusetts, a favorite destination for the Irish. Know-Nothings elected the Massachusetts governor, all of the state senators, all but two of the state representatives, and all of the congressmen. The American Party attracted both Democrats and Whigs, but with their party crumbling, more Whigs responded to the attraction. In 1855, an observer might reasonably have concluded that the Know-Nothings had emerged as the successor to the Whigs.

But Know-Nothings were not the only new party making noise. Among the new antislavery organizations provoked by the Kansas-Nebraska Act, one called itself Republican. Republicans attempted to unite under their banner all the dissidents and political orphans—Whigs, Free-Soilers, anti-Nebraska Democrats, even Know-Nothings—who opposed the extension of slavery into any territory of the United States.

The Republican creed tapped basic beliefs and values of the northern public. Slave labor and free labor, Republicans argued, had spawned two incompatible civilizations. In the South, they said, slavery degraded the dignity of white labor by associating work with blacks and servility. They argued slavery repressed every Southerner, except planter aristocrats. Those insatiable slave lords, whom antislavery Northerners called the Slave Power, now conspired to expand slavery, subvert liberty, and undermine the Constitution through the Democratic Party.

Only by restricting slavery to the South, Republicans believed, could free labor flourish elsewhere. The system of free labor respected the dignity of work and provided anyone willing to toil an opportunity for a decent living and for advancement. These powerful images attracted a wide range of Northerners to the Republican cause.

JOHN C. AND JESSIE BENTON FRÉMONT
The election of 1856 marked the first time a candidate's wife appeared on campaign items. Smart and ambitious, Jessie Benton Frémont made the breakthrough. Seen here on a silk ribbon with her husband, John C. Frémont, Republican Party presidential nominee, Jessie helped plan Frémont's campaign, coauthored his election biography, and drew northern women into political activity as never before. "What a shame that women can't vote!" declared abolitionist Lydia Maria Child. "We'd carry 'our Jessie' into the White House on our shoulders, wouldn't we." Critics of Jessie's violation of women's traditional sphere ridiculed both Frémonts. A man who met the couple in San Francisco pronounced her "the better man of the two." Jessie Frémont was, as Abraham Lincoln observed ambivalently, "quite a female politician."
Collection of Janice L. and David J. Frent.

The Election of 1856

By the mid-1850s, the Know-Nothings had emerged as the principal champion of nativism and the Republicans as the primary advocate of antislavery. But the election of 1856 revealed that the Republicans had emerged as the Democrats' main challenger, and slavery in the territories became the election's only issue. The Know-Nothings came apart when party leaders insisted on a platform that endorsed the Kansas-Nebraska Act, causing most Northerners to walk out. The Know-Nothings who remained nominated ex-president Millard Fillmore.

The Republicans, in contrast, adopted a platform that focused almost exclusively on "making every territory free." When they labeled slavery a "relic of barbarism," Republicans signaled that they had written off the South. For president, they nominated the dashing soldier and California adventurer John C. Frémont. Though a celebrated explorer, Frémont lacked political credentials. Political know-how resided in his wife, Jessie, who, as a daughter of Senator Thomas Hart Benton of Missouri, knew the political map as well as her husband knew western trails. Although careful to maintain a proper public image, the vivacious thirty-two-year-old mother and antislavery zealot helped draw ordinary women into electoral politics. (See "Documenting the American Promise," page 336.)

The Democrats, successful in 1852 in bridging sectional differences by nominating a northern man with southern principles, chose another "doughface," James Buchanan of Pennsylvania. The Democrats took refuge in the ambiguity of popular sovereignty and portrayed Republicans as extremists whose support for the Wilmot Proviso risked pushing the South out of the Union.

The Democratic strategy helped carry the day for Buchanan, but Frémont did astonishingly well. Buchanan won 174 electoral votes against Frémont's 114 and Fillmore's 8. Frémont carried all but five of the states north of the Mason-Dixon line. The election made clear that the Whigs had disintegrated, that the Know-Nothings would not ride nativism to national power, and that the Democrats were badly strained (see Map 14.4). But the big news was what the press called the "glorious defeat" of the Republicans. Despite being a brand-new party and purely sectional, Republicans challenged other parties for national power. Sectionalism had fashioned

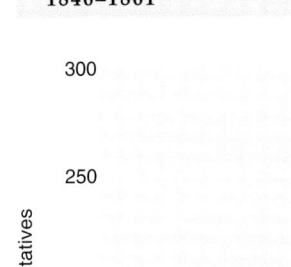
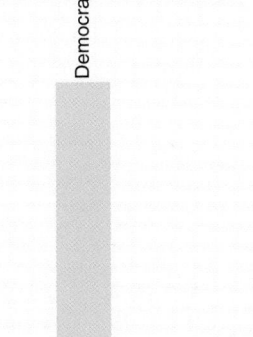

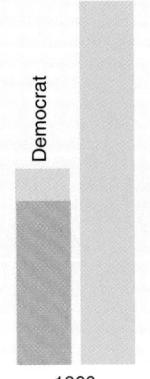

FIGURE **14.1**
Changing Political Landscape, 1848–1860
The polarization of American politics between the free states and slave states occurred in little more than a decade.

a new party system, one that spelled danger for the Republic (Figure 14.1).

Freedom under Siege

The "glorious defeat" of the Republicans meant that the second party in the new two-party system was entirely sectional. It felt no compelling need to compromise, to conciliate, to keep a southern wing happy. Indeed, the Republican Party organized around the premise that the slaveholding South provided a profound threat to "free soil, free labor, and free men."

Events in distant Kansas Territory provided the young Republican organization with an enormous boost. Kansas reeled with violence between proslavery and antislavery settlers, which Republicans argued was southern in origin. They claimed that the Kansas frontier offered a window onto southern

values and intentions. Republicans also pointed to the brutal beating by a Southerner of a respected northern senator on the floor of Congress. Even the Supreme Court, in the Republicans' view, reflected the South's drive toward tyranny and minority rule. Then, in 1858, the issues dividing North and South received an extraordinary airing in a senatorial contest in Illinois, when the nation's foremost Democrat debated a resourceful Republican.

"Bleeding Kansas"

Three days after the House of Representatives approved the Kansas-Nebraska Act, Senator William H. Seward of New York boldly challenged the South. "Come on then, Gentlemen of the Slave States," he cried, "since there is no escaping your challenge, I accept it in behalf of the cause of freedom. We will engage in competition for the virgin soil of Kansas, and God give the victory to the side which is stronger in numbers as it is in right."

Women's Politics

*A*lthough women could not vote before the Civil War, many women nevertheless participated in public political activity. Uncle Tom's Cabin, *Harriet Beecher Stowe's searing indictment of slavery, galvanized support for the Republican Party's campaign against the extension of slavery. The novel's moral power stemmed from its author's vivid description of how slavery assaulted cherished American institutions and values— Christian duty, female domesticity, and the family. Throughout her life, Jessie Benton Frémont sought to fulfill her domestic roles as wife and mother, even though she found them constraining. She also sought unabashedly to influence politics. She, like many other women, wrote to men of influence on behalf of her husband. "Do not suppose Sir, that I lightly interfere in a matter properly belonging to men," she began a letter to President James Polk in 1842, "but in the absence of Mr. Frémont I attend to his affairs at his request." During the 1850s, she became one of her husband's principal political analysts and advisers.*

DOCUMENT 1. Jessie Benton Frémont's Letter to Elizabeth Blair Lee, 1856

On October 20, 1856, Jessie Frémont offered a clear-eyed interpretation of the significance of the Republican Party's paper-thin but devastating loss in the October 14 Pennsylvania state election.

I heartily regret the defeat we have met and do not look for things to change for the better. The Democrats will follow up their advantage with the courage of success & our forces are unorganized and just now surprised and inactive. I wish the cause had triumphed. I do wish Mr. Frémont had been the one to administer the bitter dose of subjection to the South for he has the coolness & nerve to do it just as it needs to be done—without passion & without sympathy—as coldly as a surgeon over a hospital patient would he have cut off their

right hand Kansas from the old unhealthy southern body. . . . Tell your Father he must come to us for example & comfort in November for I don't think we will wear any but black feathers this year.

SOURCE: Pamela Herr and Mary Lee Spence, eds., *The Letters of Jessie Benton Frémont* (Urbana and Chicago: University of Illinois Press, 1993), 140.

DOCUMENT 2. Harriot K. Hunt's Letter "to . . . [the] Treasurer, and the Assessors, and other Authorities of the city of Boston, and the Citizens generally," 1852

Some activist women challenged the domesticity that Stowe and Frémont honored, however, arguing that women's equality depended on their liberation from tradition. These women not only attended women's rights conventions but also signed petitions asking legislators to change laws that discriminated against women and worked to put the ideas of equal rights into practice in their personal lives. Harriot K. Hunt protested having to pay taxes when she was prohibited from voting. A physician who had practiced medicine in Boston since 1835, Hunt had been refused admission to Harvard Medical School and finally received her medical degree in 1853 from the Female Medical College of Philadelphia.

Harriot K. Hunt, physician, a native and permanent resident of the city of Boston, and for many years a taxpayer therein, in making payment of her city taxes for the coming year, begs leave to protest against the injustice and inequality of levying taxes upon women, and at the same time refusing them any voice or vote in the imposition and expenditure of the same. The only classes of male persons required to pay taxes, and not at the same time allowed the privilege of voting, are aliens and minors. The objection in the case of aliens is their supposed want of interest in our institutions and knowledge of them. The objection in the case of minors, is the want of sufficient understanding. These objections can not apply to women, natives of the city, all of whose property interests are here, and who have accumulated, by their own sagacity and industry, the very property on which they are taxed. But this is not all; the alien, by going through the forms of nat-uralization, the minor on coming of age, obtain the right of voting; and so long as they continue to pay a mere poll-tax of a dollar and a half, they may con-tinue to exercise it, though so ignorant as not to be able to sign their names, or read the very votes they put into the ballot-boxes. Even drunkards, felons, idiots, and lunatics, if men, may still enjoy that right of voting to which no woman, however large the amount of taxes she pays, however respectable her character, or useful her life, can ever attain. Wherein, your remonstrant would inquire, is the justice, equality, or wisdom of this?

SOURCE: Elizabeth Cady Stanton, Susan B. Anthony, and Matilda Joslyn Gage, eds., *History of Woman Suffrage*, vol. 1 (New York: Fowler & Wells, 1881), 259.

DOCUMENT 3. Lucy Stone–Henry B. Blackwell Marriage Agreement, 1855

Marriage typically made women legally inferior to their husbands, but women's rights activists refashioned marriage vows to honor equality rather than subordina-tion. When women's rights leader Lucy Stone married Henry B. Blackwell in 1855, both signed the following statement.

While acknowledging our mutual affection by pub-licly assuming the relationship of husband and wife, yet in justice to ourselves and a great princi-ple, we deem it a duty to declare that this act on our part implies no sanction of, nor promise of volun-tary obedience to such of the present laws of marriage, as refuse to recognize the wife as an independent, rational being, while they confer upon the husband an injurious and unnatural superior-ity, investing him with legal powers which no hon-orable man would exercise, and which no man should possess. We protest especially against the laws which give to the husband:

1. The custody of the wife's person.
2. The exclusive control and guardianship of their children.
3. The sole ownership of her personal [property], and use of her real estate. . . .

4. The absolute right to the product of her in-dustry.
5. Also against laws which give to the widower so much larger and more permanent an inter-est in the property of his deceased wife, than they give to the widow in that of the deceased husband.
6. Finally, against the whole system by which "the legal existence of the wife is suspended during marriage," so that in most States, she neither has a legal part in the choice of her residence, nor can she make a will, nor sue or be sued in her own name, nor inherit property.

We believe that personal independence and equal human rights can never be forfeited, except for crime; that marriage should be an equal and per-manent partnership, and so recognized by law; that until it is so recognized, married partners should provide against the radical injustice of present laws, by every means in their power. . . .

Thus reverencing law, we enter our protest against rules and customs which are unworthy of the name, since they violate justice, the essence of law.

(signed) Henry B. Blackwell
Lucy Stone

SOURCE: Elizabeth Cady Stanton, Susan B. Anthony, and Matilda Joslyn Gage, eds., *History of Woman Suffrage,* vol. 1 (New York: Fowler & Wells, 1881), 260–61.

QUESTIONS FOR ANALYSIS AND DEBATE

1. Jessie Frémont did not interpret the Republican defeat in Pennsylvania in 1856 as a "glorious de-feat." Can you suggest possible reasons why she did not?
2. On what grounds, according to Harriot Hunt, should women be accorded the vote? Do you agree with her argument? Why or why not?
3. What legal disabilities for women was the mar-riage contract of Henry Blackstone and Lucy Stone designed to overcome?

THE DRED SCOTT FAMILY

*The **Dred Scott** case in 1857 not only produced a fierce political storm, but also fueled enormous curiosity about the family suing for freedom. The correspondent for the popular **Frank Leslie's Illustrated** met Dred Scott in St. Louis and reported: "We found him on examination to be a pure-blooded African, perhaps fifty years of age, with a shrewd, intelligent, good-natured face, of rather light frame, being not more than five feet six inches high." But as this illustration makes clear, Northerners wanted to see all of the Scotts: Harriet, who was a slave when Dred Scott married her in Wisconsin Territory in about 1836; daughter Eliza, who was born in 1838 on board a ship traveling in free territory north of Missouri; and daughter Lizzie, born after the Scotts returned to St. Louis.* Library of Congress.

knew no rest," observed his law partner William Herndon. At age twenty-six, he served his first term in the Illinois state legislature. Between 1847 and 1849, he enjoyed his only term in the House of Representatives, where he fired away at "Mr. Polk's War" and cast dozens of votes for free soil but otherwise served inconspicuously. When he returned to Springfield, he kept his eye fixed on public office.

But, like Whigs everywhere in the mid-1850s, Lincoln had no political home. His credo—opposition to "the extension of slavery"—made the Democrats an impossible choice. The Republicans made free soil their principal tenet, and in 1856 Lincoln joined the party. Convinced that slavery was a "monstrous injustice," a "great moral wrong," and an "unqualified evil to the negro, the white man, and the State," Lincoln condemned Douglas's Kansas-Nebraska Act of 1854 for giving slavery a new life. He accepted that the Constitution sanctioned slavery in those states where it existed, but he believed that the Founders planned to contain its spread. Penned in, Lincoln believed, plantation slavery would exhaust southern soil and in time Southerners would have no choice but to end slavery themselves. In Lincoln's eyes, by providing fresh land in the territories, Douglas put slavery "on the high road to extension and perpetuity."

Just as Lincoln staked out the middle ground on antislavery, he held what were, for his times, moderate racial views. Like a majority of Republicans, Lincoln defended black humanity without challenging white supremacy. He denounced slavery as immoral and believed that it should end, but he also viewed black equality as impractical and unachievable. "Negroes have natural rights . . . as other men have," he said, "although they cannot enjoy them here." Insurmountable white prejudice made it impossible to extend full citizenship and equality to blacks in America, he said. Freeing blacks and allowing them to remain in this country would lead to race war. In Lincoln's mind, social stability and black progress required that slavery end and that blacks leave the country.

Lincoln envisioned the western territories as "places for poor people to go to, and better their conditions." The "free labor system," he said, "opens the way for all—gives hope to all, and energy, and progress, and improvement of condition to all." In Lincoln's view, slavery's expansion threatened this freedom to succeed. He became persuaded that slaveholders formed an aggressive and dangerous conspiracy to nationalize slavery. The Kansas-Nebraska Act repealed the restriction on slavery's advance in the territories. The *Dred Scott* decision denied Congress the right to impose fresh restrictions. The next step, Lincoln warned, would be "another Supreme Court decision, declaring that the Constitution of the United States does not permit a State to exclude slavery from its limits." Unless its citizens woke up, he warned, the Supreme Court would make "Illinois a slave State."

In Lincoln's view, the nation could not "endure, permanently half slave and half free." Either opponents of slavery would arrest its spread and place it on the "course of ultimate extinction" or its advocates would push it forward until it became legal in "all the States, old as well as new—North as well as South." Lincoln's convictions that slavery was wrong, that Congress must stop its spread, and that it must be put on the road to extinction formed the core of the Republican ideology. By 1858, he had so impressed his fellow Republicans in Illinois that they put him forward to challenge the nation's premier Democrat, who was seeking reelection to the Senate.

The Lincoln-Douglas Debates

When Stephen Douglas learned that the Republican Abraham Lincoln would be his opponent for the Senate, he confided in a fellow Democrat: "He is the strong man of the party—full of wit, facts, dates—and the best stump speaker, with his droll ways and dry jokes, in the West. He is as honest as he is shrewd, and if I beat him my victory will be hardly won."

Not only did Douglas have to contend with a formidable foe, but he also carried the weight of a burden not of his own making. The previous year, the nation's economy experienced a sharp downturn. Prices plummeted, thousands of businesses failed, and unemployment rose. Although Illinois suffered less than the Northeast, Douglas had to go before the voters in 1858 as a member of the Democratic Party, whose policies stood accused of causing the "panic" of 1857.

Douglas's response to another crisis in 1857, however, helped shore up his standing with his constituents. Proslavery forces in Kansas met in the town of Lecompton, drafted a proslavery constitution, and applied for statehood. Everyone knew that free-soilers outnumbered proslavery settlers by at least two to one, but President Buchanan instructed Congress to admit Kansas as the sixteenth slave state. Republicans denounced

342 CHAPTER 14 • THE HOUSE DIVIDED

DISCUSSING THE NEWS
Newspapers permitted Midwesterners to keep up-to-date. Here a farmer takes a break from his task of cutting firewood to debate the latest news with his friends. He is so engrossed that he ignores the little girl tugging at his pants leg and trying to get him to notice the woman waving in the doorway. Men like these increasingly accepted Lincoln's portrait of the Republican Party as the guardian of the common people's liberty and economic opportunity. When Lincoln claimed that southern slaveholders threatened free labor and democracy, the midwestern farmers listened.

Copyright © 1971, The R. W. Norton Art Gallery, Shreveport, La. Used by permission. Painting by Arthur F. Tait.

the "Lecompton swindle." Douglas broke with the Democratic administration and came out against the proslavery constitution, not because it accepted slavery but because it violated the democratic requirement of popular sovereignty. Congress killed the Lecompton bill. (When Kansans reconsidered the Lecompton constitution in an honest election,

they rejected it six to one; Kansas entered the Union in 1861 as a free state.) In coming out against the constitution, Douglas declared his independence from the South and, he hoped, made himself acceptable at home.

A relative unknown and a decided underdog in the Illinois election, Lincoln challenged the incumbent Douglas to debate him face to face. Douglas agreed, and the two met in seven communities for what became a legendary series of debates. Thousands stood straining to see and hear, and Lincoln and Douglas showed the citizens of Illinois (and much of the nation because of widespread press coverage) the difference between an anti-Lecompton Democrat and a true Republican. They debated, often brilliantly, the central issue before the country: slavery and freedom.

Lincoln badgered Douglas with the question of whether he favored the spread of slavery. He tried to force Douglas into the damaging admission that the Supreme Court had repudiated his territorial solution, popular sovereignty. In the debate at Freeport, Illinois, Douglas admitted that settlers could not now pass legislation barring slavery, but he argued that they could ban slavery just as effectively by not passing protective laws. Without "appropriate police regulations and local legislation," such as those found in slave states, he explained, slavery could not live a day, an hour. Southerners condemned Douglas's "Freeport Doctrine" and charged him with trying to steal the victory they had gained with the *Dred Scott* decision. Lincoln chastised his opponent for his "don't care" attitude about slavery, for "blowing out the moral lights around us."

For his part, Douglas worked the racial issue. He called Lincoln an abolitionist and an egalitarian enamored with "our colored brethren." Put on the defensive, Lincoln came close to staking out positions on abolition and race that were as conservative as Douglas's. Lincoln reiterated his belief that slavery enjoyed constitutional protection where it existed. He also reaffirmed his faith in white rule: "I will say, then, that I am not, nor ever have been, in favor of bringing about in any way the social and political equality of the white and black race." But unlike Douglas, who told racist jokes and spit out racial epithets, Lincoln was no negrophobe. He always tried to steer the debate back to what he considered the true issue: the morality and future of slavery. "Slavery is wrong," Lincoln repeated, because "a man has the right to the fruits of his own labor."

As Douglas predicted, the election was hard-fought. It was also closely contested. In the nineteenth century, citizens voted for state legislators, who in turn selected the U.S. senator. Since Democrats won a slight majority in the legislature, the new legislature chose to return Douglas to the Senate. But the debates thrust Lincoln, the prairie Republican, into the national spotlight.

The Union Collapses

Lincoln's thesis that the "slavocracy" conspired to make slavery a national institution now seems exaggerated. But from the northern perspective, the Kansas-Nebraska Act, the Brooks-Sumner affair, the *Dred Scott* decision, and the Lecompton constitution seemed irrefutable evidence of the South's aggressiveness. Southerners, of course, saw things differently. They were the ones who were under siege and had grievances, they declared. Signs were everywhere, they argued, that the North planned to use its numerical advantage to attack slavery, and not just in the territories. Republicans had already proved themselves unwilling to be bound by the Constitution as interpreted by the Supreme Court in the *Dred Scott* decision. After John Brown attempted to incite a slave insurrection in Virginia in 1859, Southerners argued that Northerners had also proven themselves unwilling to be bound by Christian decency and reverence for life.

Threats of secession increasingly laced the sectional debate. Talk of leaving the Union had been heard for years, but until the final crisis, Southerners used secession as a ploy to gain concessions within the Union, not to destroy it. But the 1850s delivered powerful blows to Southerners' confidence that they could remain Americans and protect slavery. When the Republican Party won the White House in 1860, many Southerners concluded that they would have to leave.

The Aftermath of John Brown's Raid

If John Brown had been killed during his raid on Harpers Ferry in 1859, his impact on history would probably have been minor. But he lived, stood trial in Virginia for treason and conspiracy to incite slave insurrection, and on December 2, 1859, was hanged. In life, Brown was a ne'er-do-well, but he died with courage, dignity, and composure. He wrote his wife that he was "determined to make the utmost possible out of a defeat." Resolute and calm, he declared: "If it is deemed necessary that I should forfeit my life for the furtherance of the ends of justice, and mingle my blood further with the blood of

JOHN BROWN GOING TO HIS HANGING, HORACE PIPPIN, 1942
The grandparents of Horace Pippin, a Pennsylvania artist, had been slaves. His grand-mother had witnessed the hanging of John Brown, and here Pippin recalls the scene she so often described to him. He uses a muted palette to establish the bleak setting and to tell the grim story, but he manages to convey a striking intensity nevertheless. Tied and sitting erect on his coffin, Brown passes resolutely before the silent, staring white men. The black woman in the lower right corner is presumably Pippin's grandmother.

Romaire Bearden, a leading twentieth-century African American artist, recalled the place of John Brown in black memory: "Lincoln and John Brown were as much a part of the actuality of the Afro-American experience, as were the domino games and the hoe cakes for Sunday morning breakfast. I vividly recall the yearly commemorations for John Brown and see my grandfather reading Brown's last speech to the court, which was a regular part of the ceremony at Pittsburgh's Shiloh Baptist Church."

Pennsylvania Academy of Fine Arts. Lambert Fund Purchase, 1941.11.

. . . millions in this slave country whose rights are disregarded by wicked, cruel, and unjust enactments, I say, let it be done."

Some Northerners celebrated John Brown. Essayist Ralph Waldo Emerson dubbed him "that new saint" who "will make the gallows glorious like the cross." Writer Henry David Thoreau likened Brown to Christ and concluded, "he is an angel of light." Some abolitionists went beyond canonizing Brown to explicitly endorse his cause of slave rebellion. Abolitionist William Lloyd Garrison, who professed pacifism, announced, "I am prepared to say 'success to every slave insurrection at the South and in every country.'"

Generally, however, abolitionists did not condone violence, and northern opinion did not advocate bloody slave insurrection. Most Northerners believed that John Brown had acted lawlessly, with unwarranted violence. Lincoln spoke for the majority when he endorsed Brown's antislavery stance but concluded that noble ideals could not "excuse violence, bloodshed, and treason."

Lincoln's sober voice failed to still a gathering fury in the South. A Mississippian denounced the bloodthirsty fiend whose mission was "to incite slaves to murder helpless women and children." Southerners contemplated what they had in common with people who "regard John Brown as a martyr and a Christian hero, rather than a murderer and robber." Many whites in the South could no longer distinguish between Northerners who opposed slavery, like Lincoln, and those who were eager to see it washed away in a river of blood, like Brown. Georgia senator Robert Toombs announced solemnly that Southerners must "never permit this Federal government to pass into the traitorous hands of the black Republican party." At that moment, the presidential election was only months away.

Republican Victory in 1860

Anxieties provoked by John Brown's raid flared for months as southern whites feverishly searched for abolitionists and whipped, tarred and feathered, and sometimes hanged those they suspected. Moreover, other events in the eleven months between Brown's hanging and the presidential election heightened sectional hostility and estrangement. First, a southern business convention meeting in Nashville shocked the country (including many Southerners) by calling for the reopening of the African slave trade, closed since 1808 and considered an abomination everywhere in the Western world. Next, Chief Justice Taney provoked new indignation when the Supreme Court ruled northern personal liberty laws unconstitutional and reaffirmed the Fugitive Slave Act. Then, in February 1860, the normally routine business of electing a Speaker of the House threatened to turn bloody. After two months of acrimonious debate between Republicans and Democrats, one Congressman observed that the "only persons who do not have a re-

volver and a knife are those who have two revolvers." The House averted a shootout when a few Know-Nothings finally pitched in with the Republicans to elect an old Whig. Finally, Mississippian Jefferson Davis demanded that the Senate adopt a federal slave code for the territories, a goal of extreme proslavery Southerners for several years.

When Democrats converged on Charleston for their convention in April 1860, Southerners gave notice that they intended to make their extreme position on the territories binding doctrine. Southern fire-eaters denounced Stephen Douglas and demanded a platform that included federal protection of slavery in the territories. But northern Democrats knew that northern voters would not stomach a federal slave code. When two platforms—one with a federal slave code and one with popular sovereignty—came before the delegates, popular sovereignty won. Representatives from the entire lower South and Arkansas stomped out of the convention. The remaining delegates adjourned to meet a few weeks later in Baltimore, where they nominated Douglas for president and adopted a platform that advocated little beyond congressional noninterference in the territories.

When southern Democrats met, they nominated Vice President John C. Breckinridge of Kentucky for president and approved a platform with a federal slave code. But southern moderates refused to hand over their section to Breckinridge and the fire-eaters. Senator John J. Crittenden of Kentucky and others formed a new party that would provide voters a Unionist choice. Instead of adopting a platform, the new Constitutional Union Party merely approved a vague resolution pledging "to recognize no political principle other than the Constitution . . . the Union . . . and the Enforcement of the Laws." For president they picked former senator John Bell of Tennessee.

The Republicans smelled victory. Four years earlier they had enjoyed "glorious defeat" to a Democratic Party that had since broken up. Still, Republicans estimated that they needed to carry nearly all the free states to win. In 1856, they were essentially a one-idea party. In 1860, the Republicans expanded their platform beyond antislavery. They hoped that free homesteads, a protective tariff, a Pacific railroad, and a guarantee of immigrant political rights would provide an economic and social agenda broad enough to unify the North. While recommitting themselves to stopping the spread of slavery, they also denounced John Brown's raid as

ABRAHAM LINCOLN
Lincoln actively sought the Republican presidential nomination in 1860. When in New York City to give a political address, he had his photograph taken by Mathew Brady. "While I was there I was taken to one of the places where they get up such things," Lincoln explained, sounding more innocent than he was, "and I suppose they got my shadow, and can multiply copies indefinitely." Multiply they did. Copies of the dignified photograph of Lincoln soon replaced the less flattering drawings. Later, Lincoln credited his victory to his New York speech and to Mathew Brady.
The Lincoln Museum, Fort Wayne, Indiana. Photo: #0-17; drawing: #2024.

"among the gravest of crimes" and confirmed the security of slavery in the South.

Republicans cast about for a moderate candidate to go with their evenhanded platform. The foremost Republican, William H. Seward, had made enemies with his radical "higher law" doctrine and "irrepressible conflict" speech. Since bursting onto the national scene in 1858, Lincoln had demonstrated his clear purpose, good judgment, and solid Republican credentials. That, and his residence in Illinois, a crucial state, made him attractive to the party. Masterful maneuvering by Lincoln's managers converted his status as the second choice of

many delegates into a majority on the third ballot. Defeated by Douglas in a state contest less than two years earlier, Lincoln now stood ready to take him on for the presidency.

The election of 1860 was like none other in American politics. It took place in the midst of the nation's severest crisis. Moreover, four major candidates crowded the presidential field. Rather than a four-cornered contest, however, the election broke into two contests, each with two candidates. In the North, Lincoln faced Douglas, and in the South, Breckinridge confronted Bell. Southerners did not even permit Lincoln's name to appear on the ballot

1846–1861

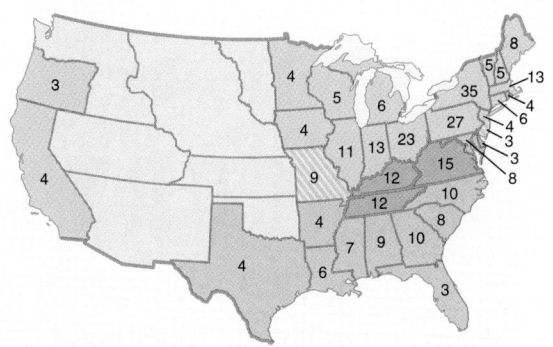

Candidate	Electoral Vote	Popular Vote	Percent of Popular Vote
Abraham Lincoln (Republican)	180	1,865,593	39.8
J.C. Breckinridge (Southern Democrat)	72	848,356	18.1
Stephen A. Douglas (Northern Democrat)	12	1,382,713	29.5
John Bell (Constitutional Union)	39	592,906	12.6

MAP 14.5

The Election of 1860

in ten of the fifteen slave states, so outrageous did they consider the Republican Party.

An unprecedented number of voters cast ballots on November 6, 1860. Approximately 82 percent of eligible northern men and nearly 70 percent of eligible southern men went to the polls. Lincoln swept all of the eighteen free states except New Jersey, which split its votes between him and Douglas. While Lincoln received only 39 percent of the popular vote, he won easily in the electoral balloting, gaining 180 votes, 28 more than he needed for victory. Lincoln did not win because his opposition was splintered. Even if the votes of his three opponents were combined, Lincoln would still have won. Ominously, however, Breckinridge, running on a southern-rights platform, won the entire Lower South plus Delaware, Maryland, and North Carolina. Two fully sectionalized parties swept their regions, but the northern one won the presidency (Map 14.5).

Secession Winter

Although Breckinridge had carried the South, a vote for "southern rights" was not necessarily a vote for secession. In fact, Breckinridge steadfastly denied that he was a secession candidate. Besides, slightly

more than half of the Southerners who voted cast ballots for Douglas and Bell, two stout defenders of the Union. During the winter of 1860–61, Southerners debated what to do.

Southern Unionists tried to calm the fears that Lincoln's election triggered. Let the dust settle, they pleaded. Extremists in both sections, they argued, had created the crisis. Alexander Stephens of Georgia eloquently defended the Union. He asked what Lincoln had done to justify something as extreme as secession. Had he not promised to respect slavery where it existed? In Stephens's judgment, the fire-eater cure would be worse than the Republican disease. Secession might lead to war, which would loosen the hinges of southern society, possibly even open the door to slave insurrection or a revolt by nonslaveholding whites. "Revolutions are much easier started than controlled," Stephens warned. "I consider slavery much more secure in the Union than out of it."

Secessionists emphasized the urgency of the moment and the dangers of delay. No Southerner should mistake Republican intentions, they argued. "Mr. Lincoln and his party assert that this doctrine of equality applies to the negro," Howell Cobb of Georgia asserted, "and necessarily there can exist no such thing as property in our equals." Lincoln's election without a single electoral vote from the South meant that Southerners were unable to defend themselves within the Union, they argued. Why wait, Cobb asked, for abolitionist emissaries to arrive? Secession would not result in war; the Union was a voluntary compact, and Lincoln would not coerce patriotism. If Northerners did resist with force, secessionists argued, the conflict would be brief, for one southern woodsman could whip five of Lincoln's greasy mechanics.

For all their differences, southern whites were generally united in their determination to defend slavery, to take slave property into the territories, and to squeeze from the North an admission that they were good and decent people. They disagreed about whether the mere presence of a Republican in the White House made it necessary to exercise what they considered a legitimate right to secede.

The debate about what to do was briefest in South Carolina. It seceded from the Union on December 20, 1860. By February 1861, the six other Deep South states marched in South Carolina's footsteps. Only South Carolinians voted overwhelmingly in favor of secession, however; elsewhere, the vote was close. In general, the nonslaveholding inhabitants of the pine barrens and mountain counties displayed the greatest attachment to the Union. Slaveholders spearheaded secession. On February 4, representatives from South Carolina, Georgia, Florida, Alabama, Mississippi, Louisiana, and Texas met in Montgomery, Alabama, where three days later they celebrated the birth of the Confederate States of America. Jefferson Davis became president and Alexander Stephens, who had spoken so eloquently about the dangers of revolution, became vice president.

Secession of the Lower South, Dec. 1860–Feb. 1861

Lincoln's election had split the Union. Now secession split the South. Seven slave states seceded during the winter, but eight did not. Citizens of the Upper South debated just as furiously whether the South could defend itself better inside or outside the Union, but they came down opposite the Lower South, at least for the moment. The fact was that the Upper South had a smaller stake in slavery. Just over half as many white families in the Upper South held slaves (21 percent) as did those in the Lower South (37 percent). Slaves represented twice as large a percentage of the population in the Lower South (48 percent) as in the Upper South (23 percent). Consequently, whites in the Upper South had fewer fears that Republican ascendancy meant economic catastrophe, racial war, and social chaos. Lincoln would need to do more than just be elected to provoke them into secession.

The nation had to wait until March 4, 1861, to see what Lincoln would do. (Presidents-elect waited four months to take office until 1933, when the Twentieth Amendment to the Constitution shifted the inauguration forward to January 20.) In his inaugural address, Lincoln began with reassurances to the South. He had "no lawful right" to interfere with slavery where it existed, he said again, adding for emphasis that he had "no inclination to do so." There would be "no invasion—no using of force against or among the people anywhere." In filling federal posts, he would not "force obnoxious strangers" on the South. Conciliatory toward Southerners, Lincoln proved inflexible about the Union.

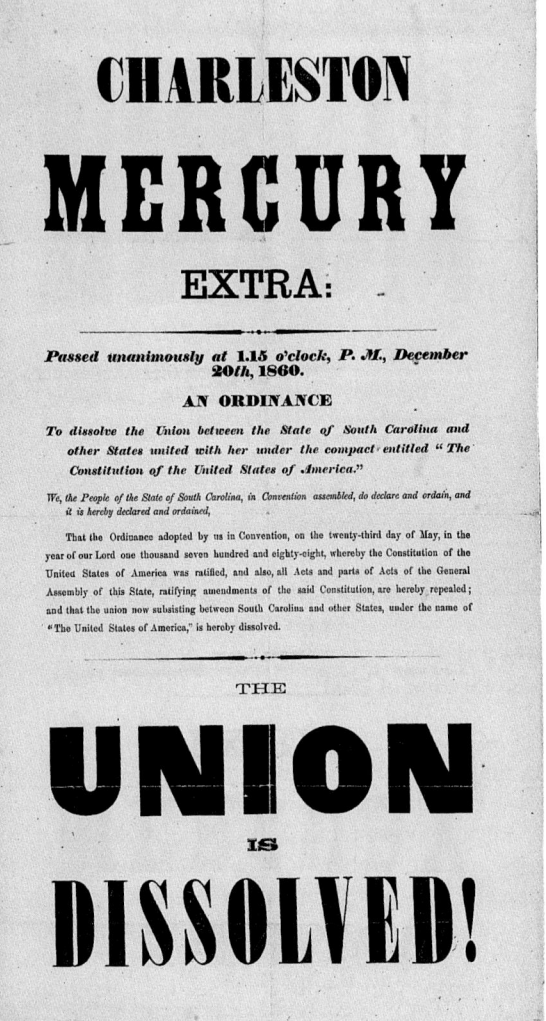

CHARLESTON
MERCURY
EXTRA:

Passed unanimously at 1.15 o'clock, P. M., December 20th, 1860.

AN ORDINANCE

To dissolve the Union between the State of South Carolina and other States united with her under the compact entitled "The Constitution of the United States of America."

We, the People of the State of South Carolina, in Convention assembled, do declare and ordain, and it is hereby declared and ordained,

That the Ordinance adopted by us in Convention, on the twenty-third day of May, in the year of our Lord one thousand seven hundred and eighty-eight, whereby the Constitution of the United States of America was ratified, and also, all Acts and parts of Acts of the General Assembly of this State, ratifying amendments of the said Constitution, are hereby repealed; and that the union now subsisting between South Carolina and other States, under the name of "The United States of America," is hereby dissolved.

THE
UNION
IS
DISSOLVED!

"THE UNION IS DISSOLVED!"
On December 20, 1860, the **Charleston Mercury** *put out this special edition of the paper to celebrate South Carolina's secession from the Union. Six weeks earlier, upon hearing the news that Lincoln had won the presidency, it had predicted as much. "The tea has been thrown overboard,"* *the* **Mercury** *announced. "The revolution of 1860 has been initiated."*
Chicago Historical Society.

The Union, he declared, is "perpetual." Secession was "anarchy" and "legally void." The Constitution required him to execute the law "in all the States." He would hold federal property, collect federal duties, and deliver the mails.

The decision for civil war or peace rested in the South's hands, Lincoln warned. "You can have no conflict, without being yourselves the aggressors. You have no oath registered in Heaven to destroy the government, while I shall have the most solemn one to 'preserve, protect, and defend' it." What Southerners in Charleston held in their hands at that very moment were the cords for firing the cannons that they aimed at the federal garrison at Fort Sumter.

Conclusion: The Failure of Compromise

As their economies, societies, and cultures diverged in the early nineteenth century, Northerners and Southerners increasingly expressed different concepts of the American promise. Their differences crystallized in 1846 when David Wilmot proposed banning slavery in any territory won in the Mexican War. "As if by magic," a Boston newspaper observed, "it brought to a head the great question that is about to divide the American people." During the extended crisis of the Union that stretched from 1846 to 1861, the nation's attention fixed on the expansion of slavery. From the beginning, though, both North-

erners and Southerners recognized that the controversy had less to do with the expansion of slavery than with the future of slavery in America.

For more than seventy years, imaginative statesmen had found compromises that accepted slavery and preserved the Union. Few Americans easily gave up the national experiment in republican democracy. But accommodation had limits. In 1859, John Brown had pushed white Southerners to the edge. Lincoln's election in 1860 convinced whites in the Deep South that slavery and the society they had built on it were at risk in the Union, and they seceded. In his inaugural, Lincoln pleaded, "We are not enemies but friends. We must not be enemies." By then, however, the Deep South had ceased to sing what he called "the chorus of the Union." It remained to be seen whether disunion would mean war.

FOR FURTHER READING ABOUT THE TOPICS IN THIS CHAPTER, see the Online Bibliography at

www.bedfordstmartins.com/roarkcompact.

FOR ADDITIONAL FIRST-HAND ACCOUNTS OF THIS PERIOD, see pages 212–223 in Michael Johnson, ed., *Reading the American Past,* Second Edition, Volume I.

TO ASSESS YOUR MASTERY OF THE MATERIAL IN THIS CHAPTER, see the Online Study Guide at

www.bedfordstmartins.com/roarkcompact.

CHRONOLOGY

1846 Wilmot Proviso proposes barring slavery from all lands acquired in Mexican War.

1847 John C. Calhoun challenges Wilmot Proviso on constitutional grounds, stating that Congress has no power to exclude slavery from territories.

Senator Lewis Cass offers compromise of "popular sovereignty," allowing people of territories to determine fate of slavery.

1848 Opponents of expansion of slavery found Free-Soil Party.

Whig candidate General Zachary Taylor elected president of United States, defeating Democrat Lewis Cass and Free-Soil candidate Martin Van Buren.

1850s Vigilance committees in North challenge and sometimes thwart Fugitive Slave Act.

1850 **July 9.** President Zachary Taylor dies; succeeded by Vice President Millard Fillmore.

Senator Henry Clay proposes Omnibus Bill to avert territorial crisis over slavery; bill ultimately defeated.

Senator Stephen Douglas's compromise bills (Compromise of 1850) pass Congress, signed into law by President Fillmore.

1852 Harriet Beecher Stowe's *Uncle Tom's Cabin* published in book form.

Democrat Franklin Pierce elected president of the United States, defeating Whig Winfield Scott.

1853 Gadsden Purchase adds 30,000 square miles of territory in present-day Arizona and New Mexico.

1854 American Party (Know-Nothings) emerges, advocating nativist positions.

Kansas-Nebraska Act opens the Kansas and Nebraska Territories to popular sovereignty.

Republican Party emerges on platform opposing extension of slavery in territories.

1856 Armed conflict between proslavery and antislavery forces erupts in Kansas.

Preston Brooks of South Carolina brutally assaults Charles Sumner of Massachusetts on Senate floor.

Democrat James Buchanan elected president of United States, defeating Republican John C. Frémont.

1857 *Dred Scott* decision declares that African Americans have no constitutional rights, that Congress cannot exclude slavery in the territories, and that the Missouri Compromise is unconstitutional.

Nation experiences economic downturn, panic of 1857.

1858 In Illinois senatorial campaign, Abraham Lincoln and Stephen A. Douglas debate slavery; Douglas defeats Lincoln for Senate seat.

1859 **October 16.** John Brown's attempt to foment slave uprising in Harpers Ferry, Virginia, further alienates South and moves nation toward war.

1860 Republican Abraham Lincoln elected president in four-way race that divides electorate along sectional lines.

December 20. South Carolina secedes from Union.

1861 Representatives of seven southern states, meeting in Montgomery, Alabama, form Confederate States of America.

DAGUERREOTYPE OF UNION DRUMMER BOY

The Civil War is often called a "brother's war." Families sometimes split and offered up soldiers for both the Union and the Confederate armies. But the war was also a children's war, as this daguerreotype of the twelve-year-old Johnny Clem, a Union drummer boy, reminds us. Clem ran away from his Ohio home when he was ten, joined the Twenty-second Michigan Regiment, and fought with it in all its major battles from Shiloh to Atlanta. He became a hero in the North when, during the retreat of Union soldiers at Chickamauga, he shot and wounded a Confederate officer with a sawed-off musket cut down to his small size. When he retired from the U.S. Army in 1915, Major General John L. Clem was the last federal soldier who had fought in the Civil War. Clem's face shows no trace of the horrors he had seen, but even children who stayed at home often experienced the heartbreak of youth destroyed and innocence lost.

Library of Congress.

THE CRUCIBLE OF WAR
1861–1865

IN 1838, A TWENTY-YEAR-OLD MARYLAND SLAVE by the name of Frederick Bailey fled north to freedom. The young runaway took a new name, Frederick Douglass, and might understandably have settled into obscurity, content just to avoid the slave catchers and to live quietly as a free man. Instead, he chose to wage war against slavery. In 1841, an agent for the Massachusetts Anti-Slavery Society observed that "the public have itching ears to hear a colored man speak, and particularly a slave." No fugitive slave stripped away the myth of the contented slave more eloquently than Frederick Douglass. In 1845, he published his immensely popular autobiography. In 1847, he began the *North Star,* an antislavery newspaper that reached thousands. Douglass's powerful denunciations of slavery and moving pleas for emancipation made him the most famous African American in the English-speaking world.

But after two decades of speaking and writing, Douglass feared that the country was no closer to ending slavery. In some ways the situation had grown worse. When Douglass fled slavery in 1838, two million Americans were in bondage. By 1860, the number of slaves had doubled to four million. Every step forward—the birth of the Republican Party, for instance—was followed by a giant step back, such as the *Dred Scott* decision. "How long! How long! O Lord God of Sabbath!" he cried at the end of the 1850s, "shall the crushed and bleeding bondsman wait?"

During the secession winter of 1860–61, Douglass found himself torn between hope and despair. Abraham Lincoln's election in November had revived his optimism. "The slaveholders know that the day of their power is over," Douglass exulted. But he realized that the Republican Party's free-soil principles fell short of abolition. Republicans opposed slavery's right to expand into the national territories, not slavery's right to exist in the South. Indeed, Douglass feared that the Republicans would become "the best protectors of slavery where it now is."

When news came from Charleston in April 1861 that Southerners had fired on the American flag, Douglass celebrated the outbreak of fighting. He realized that in going to war Lincoln was striking out against "treason and rebellion," but much earlier than most, he also understood that a war to save the Union would inevitably affect slavery. The South had initiated a "war for slavery," Douglass said, and it followed that a war to crush southern independence must become a war against slavery. Even though "the Government is not yet on the side of the oppressed, events mightier than the Government are bringing about that result," Douglass declared. "Friends of freedom!" he cried, "be up and doing;—now is your time." Few Northerners, certainly not Abraham Lincoln, agreed that the outbreak of fighting marked the beginning of the end of slavery. For eighteen months, Union soldiers fought solely to uphold the Constitution and preserve the nation. But in 1863, as Douglass foresaw, the northern war effort took on a dual purpose: to save the Union and to free the slaves.

FREDERICK DOUGLASS, 1852
Samuel J. Miller made this daguerreotype of Frederick Douglass in Akron, Ohio, a hotbed of abolitionism. Douglass self-consciously employed an aggressive posture and fiery expression to fashion his identity as a free man dead set on eradicating slavery. Fellow abolitionists understood that the "very look and bearing of Douglass are an irresistible logic against the oppression of his race."
Art Institute of Chicago.

Even if the Civil War had not touched slavery, the conflict still would have transformed America. As the world's first modern war, it mobilized entire populations, harnessed the productive capacities of entire economies, and enlisted millions of troops, with single battles fielding 200,000 soldiers and producing casualties in the tens of thousands. The carnage lasted four years and cost the nation an estimated 633,000 lives, nearly as many as in all of its other wars before and after combined. The war helped mold the modern American nation-state. The federal government emerged with new power and responsibility over national life. War furthered the emergence of a modern industrializing nation. But because the war to preserve the Union also became a war to destroy slavery, the northern victory had truly revolutionary meaning. Defeat and emancipation destroyed the slave society of the Old South and gave birth to a different society.

Years later, remembering the Civil War years, Douglass said, "It is something to couple one's name with great occasions." It was something—for millions of Americans. Whether they battled or defended the Confederacy, whether they labored behind the lines to produce goods for northern or southern soldiers, whether they kept the home fires burning for Yankees or rebels, all Americans experienced the crucible of war. But the war affected no group more than the four million African Americans who saw its beginning in 1861 as slaves and emerged in 1865 as free people.

"And the War Came"

New to high office, Abraham Lincoln faced the worst crisis in the history of the nation: the threat of disunion. Lincoln revealed his strategy on March 4, 1861, in his inaugural address, which he carefully crafted to combine firmness and conciliation. First, he sought to stop the contagion of secession. Eight of the fifteen slave states had said no to disunion, but they remained suspicious and skittish. Lincoln wanted to avoid any act that would push the Upper South (North Carolina, Virginia, Maryland, Delaware, Kentucky, Tennessee, Missouri, and Arkansas) into leaving. Second, he sought to buy time so that emotions could cool in the Deep South. By reassuring South Carolina, Georgia, Florida, Alabama, Mississippi, Louisiana, and Texas that slavery would not be abolished, he would provide Unionists there the opportunity to reassert themselves and to overturn the secession decision. Always, Lincoln expressed his uncompromising will to oppose secession and to uphold the Union.

His counterpart, Jefferson Davis, fully intended to establish the Confederate States of America as an independent republic. Neither man sought war. Both wanted to achieve their objectives peacefully. But as Lincoln later observed, "Both parties deprecated war, but one of them would make war rather than let the nation survive, and the other would accept war rather than let it perish. And the war came."

Attack on Fort Sumter

Although within newly seceded territory, Fort Sumter was occupied by Major Robert Anderson and some eighty U.S. soldiers. Sitting at the entrance to Charleston harbor, the fort became a hateful symbol of the nation Southerners had abandoned, and they wanted federal troops out. But Sumter was also a symbol to Northerners, a beacon affirming federal sovereignty in the seceded states.

The situation at Fort Sumter presented the new president with hard choices. Ordering the fort's evacuation would play well in the Upper South, whose edgy slave states threatened to bolt to the Confederacy if Lincoln resorted to military force. But yielding the fort would make it appear that Lincoln accepted the Confederacy's existence. Lincoln decided to hold Fort Sumter. But to do so, he had to provision it, for Anderson was running dangerously short of food. In the first week in April, Lincoln authorized a peaceful expedition to bring supplies, but not military reinforcements, to the fort. The president understood that he risked war, but his plan honored his inaugural promises to defend federal property and to avoid using military force unless first attacked. Masterfully, Lincoln had shifted the fateful decision of war or peace to Jefferson Davis.

On April 9, 1861, Jefferson Davis and his cabinet met to consider the situation in Charleston harbor. The territorial integrity of the Confederacy demanded the end of the federal presence, Davis argued. But his secretary of state, Robert Toombs of Georgia, pleaded against military action. "Mr. President," he declared, "at this time it is suicide, murder, and will lose us every friend at the North. You will wantonly strike a hornet's nest which extends from mountain to ocean, and legions now quiet will swarm out and sting us to death." Davis rejected Toombs's prophecy and sent word to the commander of Confederate troops in Charleston to take the fort before the relief expedition arrived. Thirty-three hours of bombardment on April 12 and 13 reduced the fort to rubble, but, miraculously, not a single Union soldier died. On April 14, with the fort ablaze, Major Anderson offered his surrender. The Confederates had Fort Sumter, but they also had war.

The response of the free states was thunderous. On April 15, Lincoln called for seventy-five thousand militia to serve for ninety days to put down the rebellion, and several times that number rushed to defend the flag. Democrats responded as fervently as Republicans. Stephen A. Douglas, the recently defeated Democratic candidate for president, pledged his support. "There are only two sides to the question," he told a massive crowd in Chicago. "Every man must be for the United States or against it. There can be no neutrals in this war, only patriots—or traitors." No one faced more acutely the dilemma of loyalty than the men and women of the Upper South.

The Upper South Chooses Sides

Many who had only months earlier rejected secession now embraced the Confederacy. To oppose southern independence was one thing; to fight fellow Southerners was another. Thousands felt betrayed, believing that Lincoln had promised to achieve a peaceful reunion by waiting patiently for Unionists to reassert themselves in the seceding states. One man furiously denounced the conflict as a "politician's war," conceding that "this is no time now to discuss the causes, but it is the duty of all who regard Southern institutions of value to side with the South, make common cause with the Confederate States and sink or swim with them."

One by one the states of the Upper South jumped off the fence. Within weeks, Virginia, Arkansas, North Carolina, and Tennessee had joined the Confederacy (Map 15.1). But in the border states of Delaware, Maryland, Kentucky, and Missouri, Unionism triumphed. Only in Delaware, though, where slaves accounted for less than 2 percent of the population, was the victory easy. In Maryland, Unionism needed a helping hand. Rather than allow the state to secede and make Washington, D.C., a federal island in a Confederate sea, Lincoln suspended the writ of habeas corpus, essentially setting aside normal constitutional guarantees such as trial before a jury of peers, and marched troops into Baltimore. Maryland's legislature, frightened by the federal invasion and aware of the strength of Union sentiment in the western counties, rejected secession.

The struggle turned violent in the West. In Missouri, Unionists won a narrow victory, but southern-sympathizing guerrilla bands roamed the

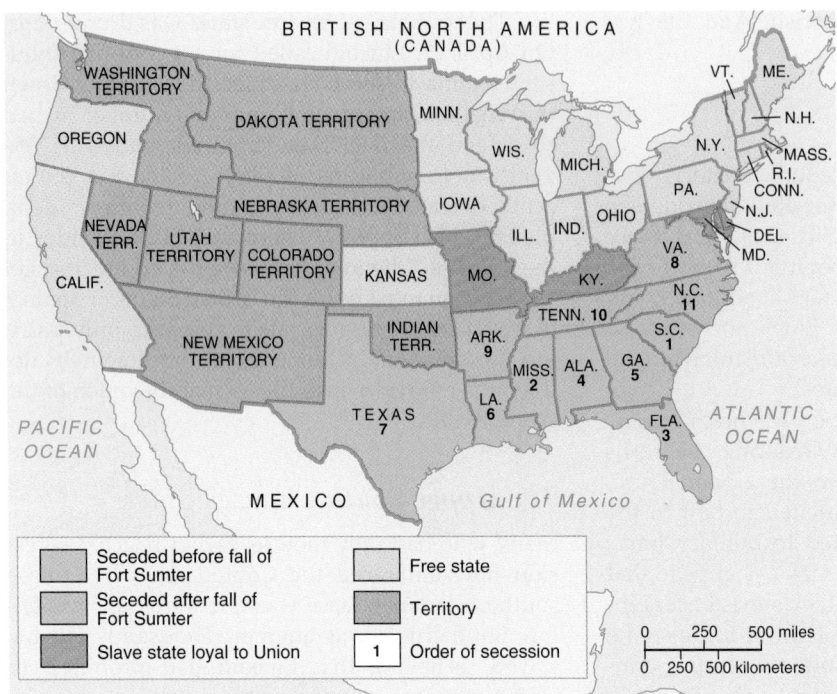

MAP 15.1

Secession, 1860–1861
After Lincoln's election, the fifteen slave states debated what to do. Seven states quickly left the Union, four left after the firing on Fort Sumter, and four refused to go.

state for the duration of the conflict, wreaking bloody havoc on civilians and soldiers alike. In Kentucky, as in Missouri, Unionists barely defeated secession and a prosouthern minority claimed that the state had severed its ties with the Union. The Confederacy, which located its capital in Richmond, Virginia, was not particularly fastidious in counting votes and eagerly made Missouri and Kentucky the twelfth and thirteenth Confederate states.

Throughout the border states, but especially in Kentucky, the Civil War was truly a "brother's war." Seven of Henry Clay's grandsons fought: four for the Confederacy and three for the Union. Lincoln understood that the border states—particularly Kentucky—not only contained indispensable resources, population, and wealth but also controlled major rivers and railroads. "I think to lose Kentucky is nearly the same as to lose the whole game," Lincoln said. "Kentucky gone, we can not hold Missouri, nor, as I think, Maryland. These all against us, . . . we would as well consent to separation at once."

In the end, only eleven of the fifteen slave states joined the Confederate States of America. Moreover, the four seceding Upper South states contained significant numbers of people who felt little affection for the Confederacy. Dissatisfaction was so rife in

the western counties of Virginia that in 1863 citizens there voted to create the separate state of West Virginia, loyal to the Union. Still, the acquisition of four new Confederate states greatly strengthened the cause of southern independence.

The Combatants

Although fierce struggle continued in the border states and in some areas within the seceding states, most whites in the South chose to defend the Confederacy. Only slaveholders had a direct economic stake in preserving slavery, but almost all white Southerners united in the defense of the institution. Moreover, Yankee "aggression" was no longer a secessionist's abstraction; it was real, and it was at their door. For Northerners, rebel "treason" threatened to destroy the best government on earth. The South's failure to accept the lawful election of a president and its firing on the nation's flag challenged the rule of law, the authority of the Constitution, and the ability of the people to govern themselves. Men rallied behind their separate battle flags, fully convinced that they were in the right and that God was on their side.

While both sides claimed the lion's share of virtue, no one could argue that the South's resources and forces equaled the North's. A glance at the census figures contradicted such a notion. Yankees took heart at their superior power, but the rebels believed they had advantages that nullified every northern strength. Both sides mobilized swiftly in the spring and summer of 1861, and each devised what it believed would be a winning military and diplomatic strategy.

How They Expected to Win

The balance sheet of northern and southern resources reveals enormous advantages for the Union (Figure 15.1). The twenty-three states remaining in the Union had a population of 22.3 million, while the eleven Confederate states had a population of only 9.1 million, of whom 3.67 million (40 percent) were slaves. The North's economic advantages were even more overwhelming. So mismatched were North and South that the question becomes why the South made war at all. Was not the South's cause lost before Confederates lobbed the first rounds at Fort Sumter? The answer quite simply is no. Southerners expected to win—and for some good reasons. They came very close to doing it.

Southerners believed that they would triumph because of their region's just cause, superior civilization, and unsurpassed character. Equating their position with that of the American patriots in 1776, Southerners saw themselves as a freedom-loving minority waging war against the encroachment of a tyrannical central government. Like the colonists, they bucked the military odds, but believed they could win. "Britain could not conquer three million," a Louisianan proclaimed, and "the world cannot conquer the South." How could anyone doubt the outcome of a contest between lean, hard, country-born rebel warriors defending family, property, and liberty, and soft, flabby, citified Yankee mechanics waging an unconstitutional war of aggression and subjugation?

The South's confidence also rested on its estimation of the economic clout of its principal crop, cotton. Southerners believed that northern prosperity depended on the South's cotton. It followed then that without cotton, New England textile mills

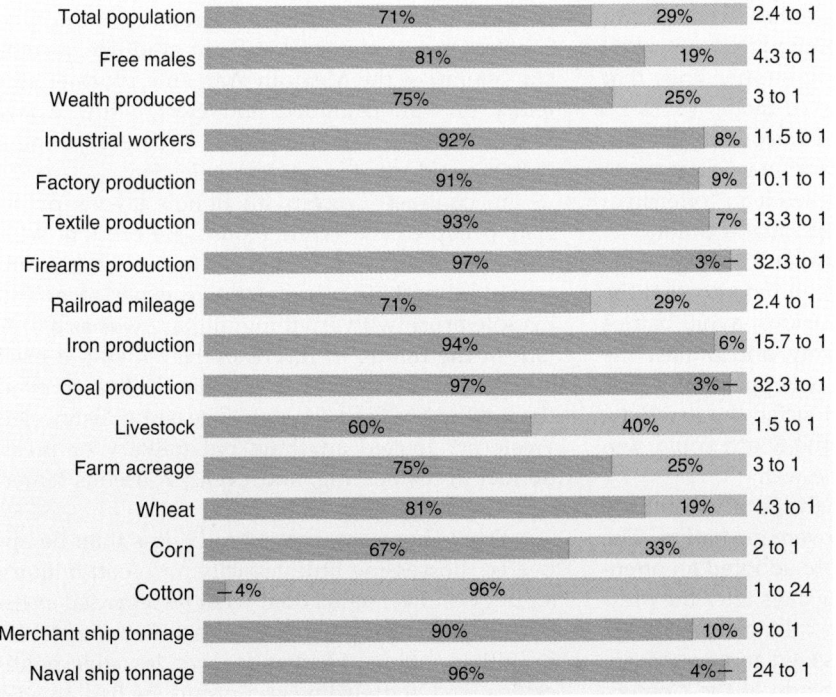

	Union	Confederacy	Ratio
Total population	71%	29%	2.4 to 1
Free males	81%	19%	4.3 to 1
Wealth produced	75%	25%	3 to 1
Industrial workers	92%	8%	11.5 to 1
Factory production	91%	9%	10.1 to 1
Textile production	93%	7%	13.3 to 1
Firearms production	97%	3%	32.3 to 1
Railroad mileage	71%	29%	2.4 to 1
Iron production	94%	6%	15.7 to 1
Coal production	97%	3%	32.3 to 1
Livestock	60%	40%	1.5 to 1
Farm acreage	75%	25%	3 to 1
Wheat	81%	19%	4.3 to 1
Corn	67%	33%	2 to 1
Cotton	4%	96%	1 to 24
Merchant ship tonnage	90%	10%	9 to 1
Naval ship tonnage	96%	4%	24 to 1

FIGURE 15.1
Resources of the Union and Confederacy
The Union's enormous statistical advantages failed to convince Confederates that their cause was doomed.

would stand idle. Without southern planters purchasing northern manufactured goods, northern factories would drown in their own surpluses. Without the foreign exchange earned by the overseas sales of cotton, the financial structure of the entire Yankee nation would collapse. One Virginian spoke for most Confederates when he declared that in the South's ability to "withhold the benefits of our trade, we hold a power over the North more powerful than a powerful army in the field."

King Cotton would also make Europe a powerful ally of the Confederacy, Southerners reasoned. After all, they said, England's economy (and to a lesser degree, France's) depended on cotton. Of the 900 million pounds of cotton England imported annually, more than 700 million came from the South. If the supply were interrupted, sheer economic need would make England (and perhaps France) a Confederate ally. And because the British navy ruled the seas, the North would find Britain a formidable foe.

Southerners' confidence may seem naive today, but even tough-minded European military observers picked the South to win. Offsetting the North's power was the South's expanse. The North, Europeans predicted, could not conquer the vast territory (750,000 square miles) from the Potomac to the Rio Grande, with its rugged terrain and bad roads. It would require raising a massive invading army, supplying it with huge quantities of provisions and arms, and protecting supply lines that would stretch farther than any in modern history.

Indeed, the South enjoyed major advantages, and the Confederacy devised a military strategy to exploit them. Jefferson Davis called it an "offensive-defensive" strategy. It recognized that a Union victory required the North to defeat and subjugate the South. A Confederate victory required only that the South stay at home, blunt invasions, avoid battles that risked annihilating its army, and outlast the northern will to fight. When an opportunity presented itself, the South would strike the invaders. Like the American colonists, the South could win independence by not losing the war.

If the North did nothing, the South would by default establish itself as a sovereign nation. The Lincoln administration therefore adopted an offensive strategy. On April 19, four days after the president issued the proclamation calling for a militia to put down the rebellion, he issued another proclamation declaring a naval blockade of the Confederacy. He sought to deny the Confederacy the use of its most valuable commodity—cotton. Without

the sale of cotton abroad, the South would have far fewer dollars to pay for war goods. Even before the North could mount an effective blockade, however, Jefferson Davis decided voluntarily to cease exporting cotton. He wanted to create a cotton "famine" that would enfeeble the northern economy and precipitate European intervention.

Southerners were not the only ones with illusions. Lincoln's call for 75,000 men for ninety days illustrates his failure to predict the magnitude and duration of the war. He was not alone. Most Americans thought of war in terms of their most recent experience, the Mexican War in the 1840s. In Mexico, fighting had taken place between relatively small armies, had cost relatively few lives, and had inflicted only light damage on the countryside. Americans on the eve of the Civil War could not know that four ghastly years of bloodletting lay ahead.

Lincoln and Davis Mobilize

Mobilization required effective political leadership, and at first glance it appeared that the South had the decided advantage. An aristocrat from a Mississippi planter family, Jefferson Davis brought to the Confederate presidency a distinguished political career, including experience in the U.S. Senate. He was also a West Point graduate, a combat veteran of the Mexican War, and a former secretary of war. Dignified and erect, with "a jaw sawed in steel," Davis appeared to be everything a nation could want in a wartime leader.

In contrast, Lincoln, an Illinois lawyer-politician, occupied the White House. He brought with him one lackluster term in the House of Representatives, almost no administrative experience, and his sole brush with anything military was as a captain in the militia in the Black Hawk War, a brief struggle in Illinois in 1832 in which whites expelled the last Indians from the state. The lanky, disheveled Westerner looked anything but military or presidential in his bearing, and even his friends feared that he was in over his head.

Davis, however, proved to be less than he appeared. Possessing little capacity for broad military strategy and yet vain about what he regarded as his own superior judgment, he intervened constantly in military affairs. He was an even less able political leader. Quarrelsome and proud, he had an acid tongue that made enemies the Confederacy could ill afford. The Confederacy's intimidating problems might have defeated an even more talented leader, however. For example, state sovereignty, which was enshrined in the Confederate constitution, made Davis's task of organizing a new nation and fighting a war difficult in the extreme.

In Lincoln, however, the North got far more than met the eye. He proved himself a master politician and a superb leader. He never allowed personal feelings to get in the way of his objectives. When forming his cabinet, for example, Lincoln shrewdly appointed representatives of every Republican faction, men who were often his chief rivals and critics. He made Salmon P. Chase secretary of the treasury, knowing that Chase had presidential ambitions. As secretary of state, he chose his chief opponent for the Republican nomination in 1860, William H. Seward, who mistakenly expected to twist Lincoln around his little finger and formulate policy himself. Despite his civilian background, Lincoln displayed an innate understanding of military strategy. In time, no one was more crucial in mapping the Union war plan. Further, Lincoln was an enormously eloquent man who reached out to the North's people, galvanizing them in defense of the nation he called "the last best hope of earth."

Guided by Lincoln and Davis, the North and South began gathering their armies. Southerners had the task of building almost everything from scratch, and Northerners had to mobilize their superior numbers and industrial resources for war. In 1861, the puny federal army numbered only 16,000 men. The navy was in better shape. Forty-two ships were in service, and a large merchant marine would in time provide more ships and sailors. Most of the officers and men were Northerners and loyal to the Union. The Confederate navy was never a match for the Union fleet, and thus the South pinned its hopes on its armies. Military companies sprang up everywhere.

From the beginning, the South exhibited more enthusiasm than ability to provide its soldiers with supplies and transportation. The Confederacy made prodigious efforts to build new factories to produce tents, blankets, shoes, and uniforms, but many soldiers slept in the open air without proper clothes and sometimes without shoes. Even when factories managed to produce what soldiers needed, southern railroads—constructed to connect plantations with ports—often could not deliver the goods. And with each year of the war, more railroads were captured, destroyed, or left in disrepair. Food production proved less of a problem, but food sometimes

rotted before it reached the soldiers. The one bright spot was the Confederacy's Ordnance Bureau, headed by Josiah Gorgas, a near miracle worker when it came to manufacturing gunpower, cannons, and rifles. In April 1864, Gorgas observed: "Where three years ago we were not making a gun, a pistol nor a sabre, no shot nor shell . . .—a pound of powder—we now make all these in quantities to meet the demands of our large armies."

Recruiting and supplying huge armies required enormous public spending. Before the war, the federal government's tiny income had come primarily from tariff duties and the sale of public lands. Massive wartime expenditures made new revenues imperative. At first, both the North and the South resorted to selling war bonds, which essentially were loans from patriotic citizens. In time, both sides began printing paper money. Inflation soared, but the South suffered more because it financed a greater part of its wartime costs through the printing press. Prices in the North rose by about 80 percent during the war, while in the South inflation topped 9,000 percent. Eventually, the Union and the Confederacy turned to taxes, but whereas the North raised one-fifth of its wartime revenue from taxes, the South raised only one-twentieth.

Within months of the bombardment of Fort Sumter, both sides had found men to fight and people to supply and support them. But the underlying strength of the northern economy gave the Union the decided advantage. With their military and industrial muscles beginning to ripple, Northerners became itchy for action. Northerners wanted an invasion that would once and for all smash the rebellion. Horace Greeley's *New York Tribune* began the chant: "Forward to Richmond! Forward to Richmond!"

The Battlefields, 1861–1862

During the first year and a half of the war, armies fought major campaigns in two theaters: in Virginia-Maryland in the East and in Tennessee-Kentucky in the West. With the rival capitals of Richmond and Washington, D.C., only ninety miles apart and each threatened more than once with capture, the eastern campaign was more dramatic and commanded public attention. But the battles in the West proved more decisive. And as Yankee and rebel armies pounded each other on land, their navies fought it out on the seas and their diplomats sought advantage in the corridors of power in Europe. All the while, casualty lists reached appalling lengths.

Stalemate in the Eastern Theater

As commander in chief, Lincoln appointed Mexican War veteran Irvin McDowell to be commanding general of the army assembling outside Washington. McDowell had no thought of taking his raw recruits into battle during the summer of 1861, but

Lincoln ordered McDowell to prepare his 30,000 greenhorn troops for an attack on the Confederate army gathered at Manassas, a railroad junction in Virginia about thirty miles southwest of Washington.

On July 21, the Union army forded Bull Run, a branch of the Potomac River, and engaged the southern forces effectively (Map 15.2). But fast-moving southern reinforcements blunted the Union attack and then counterattacked. What began as an orderly retreat turned into a panicky stampede.

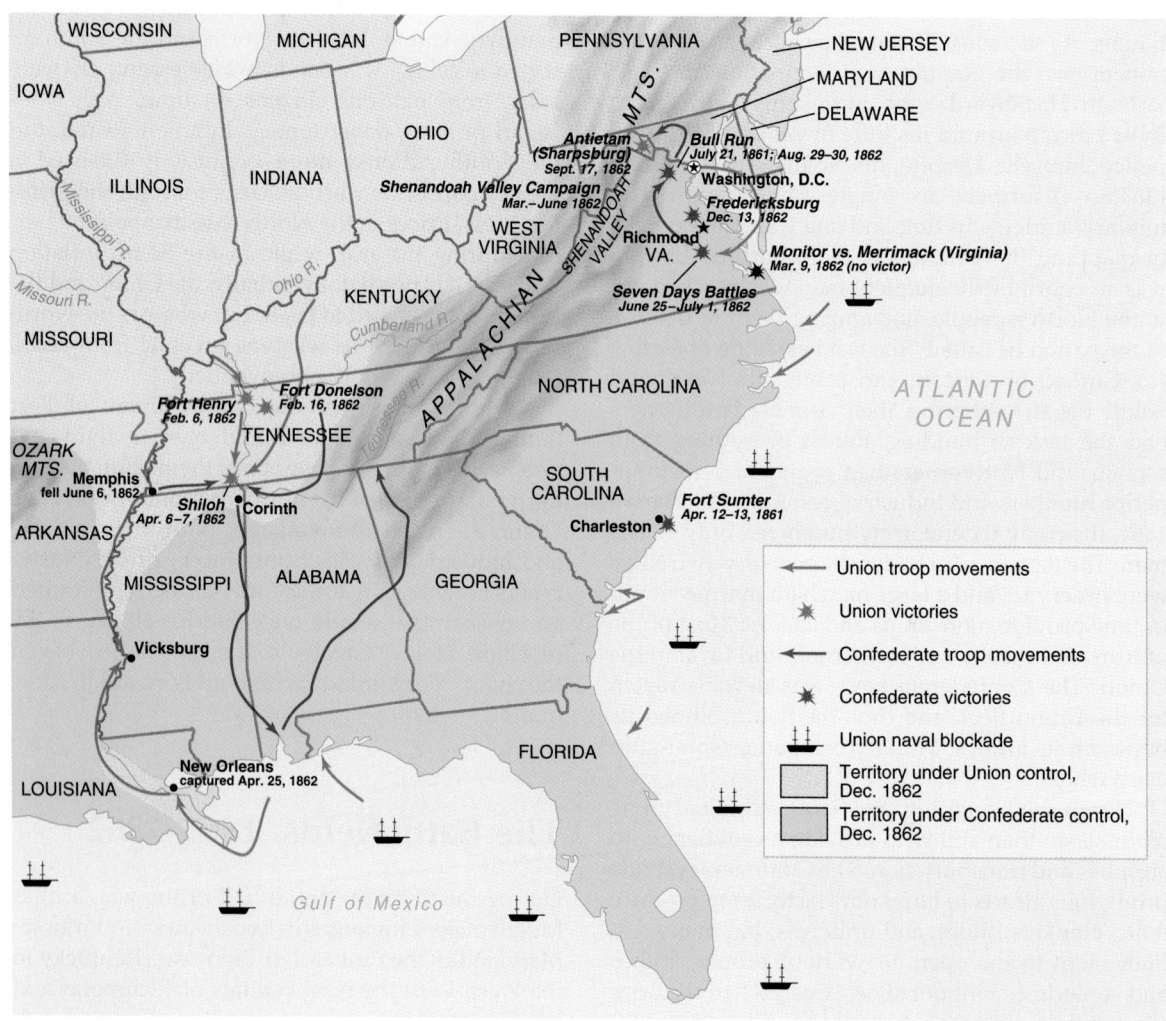

MAP 15.2

The Civil War, 1861–1862
While eyes focused on the eastern theater, especially the tiny geography between the two capitals of Washington and Richmond, strategic victories were being won by Union troops in the West.

Demoralized soldiers ran over shocked civilians as they raced back to Washington.

By Civil War standards, casualties at Bull Run (or Manassas, as Southerners called the battle) were light; the significance of the battle lay in the lessons Northerners and Southerners drew from it. For Southerners, it confirmed the superiority of rebel fighting men and the inevitability of Confederate nationhood. Manassas was "one of the decisive battles of the world," a Georgian proclaimed. It "has secured our independence." While victory elevated southern pride, defeat sobered Northerners. It was a major setback, admitted the *New York Tribune*, but "Let us go to work, then, with a will." Manassas taught Lincoln that victory would be neither quick nor easy. Within four days of the disaster, the president signed bills authorizing the enlistment of 1 million men for three years.

Lincoln also found a new general, replacing McDowell with the arrogant young George B. McClellan. Born in Philadelphia of well-to-do parents, educated in the best schools before graduating from West Point second in his class, the thirty-four-year-old McClellan believed that he was a great soldier and that Lincoln was a dunce, the "original Gorilla." A superb administrator and organizer, McClellan was brought to Washington as commander of the newly named Army of the Potomac. In the months following his appointment, McClellan energetically whipped his dispirited army into shape, yet was reluctant to send them into battle. McClellan, for all his energy, lacked decisiveness. Lincoln wanted a general who would advance, take risks, and fight, but McClellan went into winter quarters without budging from the Potomac. "If General McClellan does not want to use the army I would like to borrow it," Lincoln declared in frustration.

Finally, in the spring of 1862, McClellan launched his long-awaited offensive. He transported his highly polished army, now 130,000 strong, down the Chesapeake Bay to the mouth of the James River and began moving up the peninsula toward Richmond. McClellan took two and a half months to advance sixty-five miles. When he was within six miles of the Confederate capital, Confederate general Joseph Johnston hit him like a hammer. In the assault, Johnston was wounded and was replaced by Robert E. Lee of Virginia, a reluctant Confederate who would become the South's most celebrated general. Lee named his command the Army of Northern Virginia.

The contrast between Lee and McClellan could hardly have been greater. McClellan overflowed with conceit and braggadocio, while Lee was courteous and reserved. But on the battlefield, where McClellan grew timid and irresolute, Lee became audaciously, even recklessly, aggressive. And Lee had at his side in the peninsula campaign military men of real talent: General Thomas J. Jackson, nicknamed Stonewall for holding the line at Manassas, and James E. B. (Jeb) Stuart, the dashing twenty-nine-year-old cavalry commander who rode circles around Yankee troops. Lee's assault initiated the Seven Days Battle and began McClellan's backward march down the peninsula. By the time McClellan reached

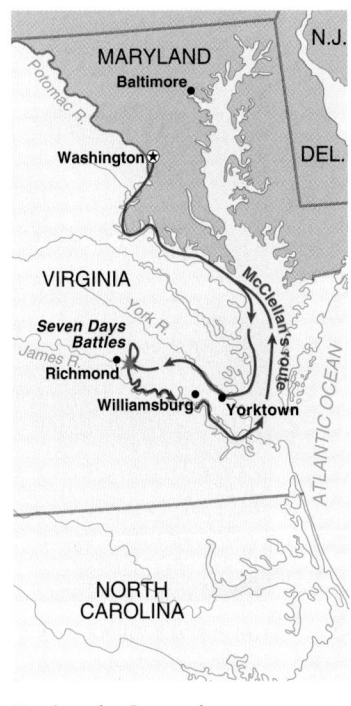

Peninsula Campaign, 1862

the water and the safety of the Union navy, 30,000 men from both sides had died or been wounded. Although Southerners suffered twice the casualties of Northerners, Lee had saved Richmond and achieved a strategic success. Lincoln wired McClellan to abandon the peninsula campaign and replaced him with General John Pope.

In August, just north of Richmond, Pope had his own rendezvous with Lee. At the Second Battle of Bull Run, Lee's smaller army battered Pope's forces and sent them scurrying back to Washington. Lincoln ordered Pope to Minnesota to pacify Indians and again put McClellan in command. Lincoln had not changed his mind about McClellan's capacity as a warrior. Instead, he reluctantly concluded, "If he can't fight himself, he excels in making others ready to fight."

Sensing that he had his enemy on the ropes, Lee sought to land the knockout punch. He pushed the Army of Northern Virginia across the Potomac and invaded Maryland. A victory on northern soil would dislodge Maryland from the Union, Lee reasoned, and might even cause Lincoln to sue for

THE BATTLE OF SAVAGE'S STATION, ROBERT KNOX SNEDEN, 1862
In 1862, thirty-year-old Robert Sneden joined the 40th New York Volunteers and soon found himself in Virginia, part of George McClellan's peninsula campaign. A gifted artist in water colors, as well as an eloquent writer, Sneden captures here an early Confederate assault in what became known as the Seven Days Battle. "The immense open space in front of Savage's [house] was densely thronged with wagon trains, artillery, caissons, ammunition trains, and moving troops," Sneden observed. The "storm of lead was continuous and deadly on the approaching lines of the Rebels. They bravely rushed up, however, to within twenty feet of our artillery, when bushels of grape and canister from the cannon laid them low in rows." Over the next three years, Sneden produced hundreds of vivid drawings and eventually thousands of pages of remembrance, providing one of the most complete accounts of a Union soldier's Civil War experience.
Virginia Historical Society.

peace. On September 17, 1862, McClellan's forces finally engaged Lee's army at Antietam Creek (see Map. 15.2). Earlier, a Union soldier had found a copy of Lee's orders to his army wrapped around some cigars dropped by a careless Confederate officer. McClellan had a clear picture of Lee's position, but his characteristic slowness meant that he missed a great opportunity to destroy the opposing army. Still, he did it severe damage. With "solid shot . . . cracking skulls like egg-shells," according to one observer, the armies went after each other. By nightfall the battlefield lay littered with 6,000 men dead or dying and 17,000 more wounded, making the Battle of Antietam the bloodiest day of the

war. Badly damaged and deeply disappointed, Lee turned back to Virginia. When McClellan, who had 33,000 fresh troops in reserve (more men than Lee had in his entire army), failed to renew the attack, Lincoln removed him from command of the Army of the Potomac and appointed General Ambrose Burnside.

Lee remained alert for an opportunity to punish his enemy, and in December, Burnside provided the Virginian a fresh chance. At Fredericksburg, Virginia, Burnside's 122,000 Union troops faced 78,500 Confederates dug in behind a stone wall on the heights above the Rappahannock River. Half a mile of open ground lay between the armies. A Confederate artillery officer predicted that "a chicken could not live on that field when we open on it." Yet Burnside ordered a frontal assault. Wave after wave of bluecoats crashed against impregnable defenses. When the guns finally ceased, the federals counted nearly 13,000 casualties while the Confederates suffered fewer than 5,000. It was one of the Union's worst defeats. At the end of 1862, the North seemed no nearer to ending the rebellion than it had been when the war began. Rather than checkmate, military struggle in the East had reached stalemate.

Union Victories in the Western Theater

While most eyes focused on the East, the decisive early encounters of the war took place between the Appalachian Mountains and the Ozarks. The West's rivers—the Mississippi, the Tennessee, and the Cumberland—became the keys to the military situation. Southerners looked northward along the rivers and spied Missouri and Kentucky, states they claimed but did not control. Looking southward, Northerners knew that by taking the Mississippi they would split Arkansas, Louisiana, and Texas from the Confederacy. And the Cumberland and Tennessee waterways penetrated Tennessee, one of the Confederacy's main producers of food, mules, and iron—all vital resources.

General Ulysses S. Grant became the key northern figure on the western battlefields. Although Grant had graduated from West Point, when war broke out he was a thirty-nine-year-old dry-goods clerk in Galena, Illinois. Gentle at home, he became pugnacious on the battlefield. "The art of war is simple," he said. "Find out where your enemy is, get at him as soon as you can and strike him as hard as you can, and keep moving on." Grant's philosophy of war as annihilation took a huge toll in human life, but it played to the North's strength: superior manpower. In time, the North fashioned victory from it. In his old uniform and slouch hat, with his tired, sad, nondescript face, Grant did not look much like a general. But Lincoln, who did not look much like a president, knew his worth.

In February 1862, operating in tandem with navy gunboats, Grant captured Fort Henry on the Tennessee River and Fort Donelson on the Cumberland (see Map 15.2). Defeat forced the Confederates to withdraw from all of Kentucky and most of Tennessee. Grant pushed after the retreating rebels until, on April 6, General Albert Sidney Johnston's army surprised him at Shiloh Church in Tennessee. Although his troops were badly mauled the first day, Grant remained cool and brought up reinforcements throughout the night. The next morning, the Union army counterattacked, driving the Confederates before it. The battle was terribly costly; there were 20,000 casualties, including the death of Johnston. Manassas had disabused Lincoln of the illusion of a short war; and, after Shiloh, Grant "gave up all idea of saving the Union except by complete conquest."

Although no one knew it at the time, Shiloh inflicted a mortal wound to the Confederacy's bid to control the Western theater. In short order, the Yankees captured the strategic town of Corinth, Mississippi, the river city of Memphis, and the South's largest city, New Orleans. By the end of 1862, most—but not all—of the Mississippi valley lay in Union hands.

War and Diplomacy in the Atlantic Theater

With a blockade fleet of only about three dozen ships at the beginning of the war and more than thirty-five hundred miles of southern coastline to patrol, the U.S. navy faced an impossible task. At first, rebel ships slipped in and out of port nearly at will. Taking on cargoes in the Caribbean, the sleek, fast blockade runners brought in vital supplies—guns and medicine—and also small quantities of luxury goods such as tea and liquor. But with the U.S. navy commissioning a new blockader almost weekly, the fleet eventually reached 150 ships on duty, and the Union navy dramatically improved its score.

Unable to build a conventional navy equal to the expanding federal fleet, the Confederates experimented with a radical new maritime design: the ironclad warship. At Norfolk, Virginia, they layered the wooden hull of the frigate *Merrimack* with two-inch-thick armor plate. Rechristened *Virginia*, it steamed out in March 1862 to engage the federal blockade. Within a few hours, it sank two large federal ships, killing at least 240 sailors. But when the *Virginia* returned the following morning to finish its work, it found the *Monitor*, a federal ironclad that had arrived from Brooklyn during the night. The *Monitor*, a ship of even more radical design than the *Virginia*, was topped by a revolving turret containing two eleven-inch guns. Although the two ships hurled shells at each other for two hours, neither could penetrate the other's armor and the duel ended in a draw (see Map 15.2).

The Confederacy never found a way to break the blockade. Each month the northern navy tightened its noose until by 1865 the Union fleet intercepted about half of the southern ships that attempted to break through. By 1863, the South had abandoned its embargo policy and desperately wanted to ship cotton to pay for imports it needed to fight the war. But the growing effectiveness of the federal blockade, a southern naval officer observed, "shut the Confederacy out from the world, deprived it of supplies, weakened its military and naval strength."

What they could not achieve on saltwater, Confederates sought through foreign policy. According to the theory of King Cotton, cotton-starved European nations had no choice but to break the blockade and recognize the Confederacy. Although European nations granted the Confederacy "belligerent" status, which enabled it to buy goods and build ships in European ports, none recognized Confederate nationhood, a bolder act that probably would have drawn them into war with the United States.

King Cotton diplomacy failed for several reasons. A bumper cotton crop in 1860 meant that the warehouses of British textile manufacturers bulged with surplus cotton throughout 1861. In 1862, when Europe began to feel the pinch of the cotton famine, manufacturers found new sources of cotton in Egypt and India. In addition, a brisk trade developed between the Union and Britain—British war materiel for American grain and flour—which helped offset the decline in textiles and encouraged Britain to remain neutral.

Europe's temptation to intervene disappeared for good in 1862. Union military successes on the rivers of the West made Britain and France think twice about linking their fates to the Confederacy. And in the fall of 1862, Lincoln announced a new policy that made an alliance with the Confederacy an alliance with slavery. The president finally acknowledged that it was impossible to fight for union without fighting against slavery.

Union *and* Freedom

For a year and a half, Lincoln insisted that emancipation was not a goal; the war he said was strictly to save the Union. But the war for union did become a war for African American freedom. Each

month the conflict dragged on, it became clearer that the Confederate war machine depended heavily on slavery. Rebel armies used slaves to build fortifications, haul materiel, tend horses, and perform camp chores. On the home front, slaves labored in ironworks and shipyards, and they grew the food that fed both soldiers and civilians. Slavery undergirded the Confederacy as certainly as it had the Old South. In the field among military commanders, in the halls of Congress, and in the White House, the truth gradually came into focus: To defeat the Confederacy, the North would have to destroy slavery. "I am a slow walker," Lincoln said, "but I never walk back."

From Slaves to Contraband

Personally, Lincoln detested human bondage, but as president he felt compelled to act prudently in the interests of the Union. He doubted his right under the Constitution to tamper with the "domestic institutions" of any state, even those in rebellion. An astute politician, Lincoln worked within the limits of public opinion, and in 1861 he believed those limits were tight. The issue of black freedom was particularly explosive in the loyal border states, where slaveholders threatened to jump into the arms of the Confederacy at even the hint of emancipation. Black freedom also attracted attention in the free states. The Democratic Party gave notice that emancipation would kill the bipartisan alliance and make the war strictly a Republican affair. Democrats were as ardent for union as Republicans, but they marched under the banner "The Constitution As It Is, the Union As It Was."

Moreover, many white Northerners were not about to risk their lives to satisfy abolitionist "fanaticism." "We Won't Fight to Free the Nigger," one popular banner read. They feared that emancipation would propel "two or three million semi-savages" northward, where they would crowd into white neighborhoods, compete for white jobs, and mix with white "sons and daughters." A surge of anti-emancipation, antiblack sentiment, then, threatened to dislodge the loyal slave states from the Union, alienate the Democratic Party, deplete the armies, and perhaps even spark race warfare.

Yet proponents of emancipation pressed Lincoln as relentlessly as the anti-emancipation forces. Abolitionists argued that by seceding, Southerners had forfeited their right to the protection of the Constitution. Lincoln could now—as the price

CONTRABANDS
*These refugees from slavery crossed the Rappahannock River in Virginia in August 1862
to seek the sanctuary of a federal army. Most slaves fled with little more than the
clothes on their backs, but not all escaped slavery empty-handed. The oxen, wagon, and
goods seen here could have been procured by a number of means—purchased during
slavery, "borrowed" from the former master, or gathered during flight. Refugees who
possessed draft animals and a wagon had much more economic opportunity than those
who had only their labor to sell.*
Library of Congress.

of treason—legally confiscate their property in slaves. When Lincoln refused, abolitionists scalded him. Frederick Douglass labeled Lincoln "the miserable tool of traitors and rebels."

The Republican-dominated Congress refused to leave slavery policy entirely in Lincoln's hands. In August 1861, Congress approved the Confiscation Act, which allowed the seizure of any slave who was employed directly by the Confederate military. The House and the Senate also fulfilled the free-soil dream of prohibiting slavery in the territories and abolished slavery in Washington, D.C. Democrats and border-state representatives voted against even these mild measures, but little by little, Congress displayed a stiffening of attitude as it cast about for a just and practical slavery policy.

But slaves, not politicians, became the most insistent force for emancipation. By escaping their masters by the tens of thousands and running away to Union lines, they forced slavery on the North's wartime agenda. Union officials could not ignore the flood of fugitives, and runaways precipitated a series of momentous decisions on the part of the military, Congress, and the president. Were the runaways now free, or were they still slaves who, according to the fugitive slave law, had to be returned to their masters? At first, most Yankee military commanders believed that administration policy required them to send the fugitives back. But Union armies needed laborers, and some officers accepted the runaways and put them to work. At Fort Monroe, Virginia, General Benjamin F. Butler not only refused to turn them over to their owners but also provided them with a new status. He called them "contraband of war," meaning "confiscated property." Congress established national policy in

March 1862 when it forbade the practice of returning fugitive slaves to their masters. Slaves were still not legally free, but there was a tilt toward emancipation.

Gradually, Lincoln's policy of noninterference with slavery crumbled. To calm Northerners' racial fears, which he considered the chief obstacle to Union acceptance of emancipation, Lincoln offered colonization, the deportation of African Americans from the United States to Haiti, Panama, or elsewhere. In the summer of 1862, he defended colonization to a delegation of black visitors to the White House. He told them that deep-seated racial prejudice made it impossible for blacks to achieve equality in this country. An African American from Philadelphia spoke for the group when he told the president, "This is our country as much as it is yours, and we will not leave it." Congress voted a small amount of money to underwrite colonization, but after one miserable experiment on a small island in the Caribbean, practical limitations and black opposition sank further efforts.

At the same time that Lincoln was developing his own initiatives, he snuffed out actions he believed jeopardized northern unity. He was particularly alert to Union commanders who tried to dictate slavery policy from the field. In August 1861, when John C. Frémont, commander of federal troops in Missouri, impetuously freed the slaves belonging to Missouri rebels, Lincoln forced the general to revoke his edict and then removed him from command. The following May, when General David Hunter issued a proclamation freeing the slaves in the southeast, Lincoln countermanded his order. Events moved so rapidly, however, that Lincoln found it impossible to control federal policy on slavery.

From Contraband to Free People

On August 22, 1862, Lincoln replied to an angry abolitionist who demanded that he go after slavery. "My paramount objective in this struggle is to save the Union," Lincoln said deliberately, "and is not either to save or destroy slavery. If I could save the Union without freeing any slave I would do it, and if I could save it by freeing all the slaves I would do it; and if I could save it by freeing some and leaving others alone I would also do that." At first glance, it seemed a restatement of his old position: that union was the North's sole objective. But what

marked it as a radical departure was Lincoln's refusal to say that slavery was safe. Instead, he said that he would emancipate every slave if it would preserve the Union.

By the summer of 1862, events were tumbling rapidly toward emancipation. On July 17, Congress adopted a second Confiscation Act. The first had confiscated slaves employed by the Confederate military; the second declared all slaves of rebel masters "forever free of their servitude." In theory, this breathtaking measure freed most of the slaves in the Confederacy, for slaveholders formed the backbone of the rebellion. Congress had traveled far since the war began. Lincoln had too. On July 21, the president informed his cabinet that he was ready "to take some definitive steps in respect to military action and slavery." The next day, he read a draft of a preliminary emancipation proclamation that promised to free all slaves in the seceding states on January 1, 1863.

Lincoln described emancipation as an "act of justice," but it was the lengthening casualty lists that finally brought him around. Emancipation, he declared, was "a military necessity, absolutely essential to the preservation of the Union." Only freeing the slaves would "strike at the heart of the rebellion." His cabinet favored Lincoln's plan but advised him to wait for a military victory before announcing it so that critics would not call it an act of desperation. Although Antietam was actually a draw, Lincoln called it a victory, and on September 22, five days after the battle, he served notice that if the rebel states did not lay down their arms and return to the Union by January 1, 1863, their slaves "shall be then, thenceforward, and forever free."

The limitations of the proclamation—it exempted the loyal border states and the Union-occupied areas of the Confederacy—caused some to ridicule the act. The *London Times* observed cynically, "Where he has no power Mr. Lincoln will set the negroes free, where he retains power he will consider them as slaves." But Lincoln had no power to free slaves in loyal states, and invading Union armies would liberate slaves in the Confederacy as they advanced.

By presenting emancipation as a "military necessity," Lincoln hoped he had disarmed his conservative critics. Emancipation would shorten the war and thus save lives. Instead, Democrats exploded with rage. They charged that the "shrieking and howling abolitionist faction" had captured the

White House and made it "a nigger war." The fall 1862 elections were only weeks away, and Democrats sought to make political hay out of Lincoln's action. They gained thirty-four congressional seats. When House Democrats proposed a resolution branding emancipation "a high crime against the Constitution," the Republicans, who maintained narrow majorities in both houses, beat it back. As promised, on New Year's Day, Lincoln issued the final Emancipation Proclamation. In addition to freeing the slaves in the states that were in rebellion, the edict also committed the federal government to the fullest use of African Americans to defeat the Confederate enemy.

War of Black Liberation

Even before Lincoln proclaimed freedom a Union war aim, African Americans in the North had volunteered to fight. But the War Department, doubtful of their abilities and fearful of white reaction to serving side by side with them, refused to make black men soldiers. Instead, the army employed black men as manual laborers; black women sometimes found employment as laundresses and cooks. The navy, however, from the outset accepted blacks as sailors. They usually served in noncombatant roles, but within months a few blacks served on gun crews.

BAND OF THE 107TH U.S. COLORED INFANTRY, ARLINGTON, VIRGINIA, 1865
Photographed carrying their music and over-the-shoulder instruments, the members of this military band represent only a tiny fraction of the African Americans who served in the federal military during the Civil War. The Lincoln administration was slow to accept black soldiers, in part because of lingering doubts about their ability to fight. Colonel Thomas W. Higginson, a white Massachusetts clergyman and abolitionist, commanded the First South Carolina Infantry, which was made up of former slaves. After his regiment's first skirmish with Confederate soldiers, Higginson celebrated his men's courage: "No officer in this regiment now doubts that the key to the successful prosecution of this war lies in the unlimited employment of black troops. . . . Instead of leaving their homes and families to fight they are fighting for their homes and families." After the spring of 1863 the federal government did all it could to maximize the number of black soldiers. Throughout the war, however, policy required that blacks serve under white commissioned officers, such as the man on the left of this photograph.
Library of Congress.

As the Union experienced manpower shortages, Northerners gradually and reluctantly turned to African Americans to fill blue uniforms. With the Militia Act of July 1862, Congress authorized enrolling blacks in "any military or naval service for which they may be found competent." Lingering resistance to black military service largely disappeared in 1863. After the Emancipation Proclamation, whites—like it or not—were fighting and dying for black freedom, and few were likely to insist that blacks remain out of harm's way behind the lines. Indeed, rather than resist black military participation, whites insisted that blacks share the danger, especially after March 1863, when Congress resorted to the draft to fill the Union army.

Black soldiers discovered that the military was far from color blind. The Union army established segregated black regiments, paid black soldiers $10 per month rather than the $13 it paid to whites, refused blacks the opportunity to become commissioned officers, punished blacks as if they were slaves, and assigned blacks to labor battalions rather than to combat units. But nothing deterred black recruits. When the war ended, 179,000 African American men had served in the Union forces, approximately 10 percent of the army total. An astounding 71 percent of black men ages eighteen to forty-five in the free states wore Union blue, a participation rate that was substantially higher than that of white men. More than 130,000 black soldiers came from the slave states, perhaps 100,000 of them ex-slaves.

In time, whites allowed blacks to put down their shovels and to shoulder rifles. At the battles of Port Hudson and Milliken's Bend on the Mississippi River and at Fort Wagner in Charleston harbor, black courage under fire finally dispelled notions that African Americans could not fight. More than 38,000 black soldiers died in the Civil War, a mortality rate that was higher than that of white troops. Blacks played a crucial role in the triumph of the Union and the destruction of slavery.

The South at War

During the secession winter of 1860–61, a Louisiana planter had declared confidently that the creation of the Confederate States of America would "guarantee order, security, tranquility, as well as liberty." Instead, by seceding Southerners brought on themselves a firestorm of unimaginable fury. Monstrous losses on the battlefields nearly bled the Confederacy to death. But white Southerners at the home front were also under attack.

The most surprising thrust came from their own government. Richmond's efforts to centralize power to fight the war effectively convinced many men and women that the Confederacy had betrayed them. Wartime economic changes hurt everyone, but some suffered more than others; by 1863, planters and yeomen who had stood together began to drift apart. Most disturbing of all, slaves became open participants in the destruction of slavery and the Confederacy.

Revolution from Above

When Jefferson Davis arrived in Richmond in 1861, he faced the gargantuan task of building an army and navy from scratch, supplying them from factories that were scarce and anemic, and paying for it all from a treasury that did not exist. As one Confederate general observed, Southerners were engaged in a total war "in which the whole population and the whole production . . . are to be put on a war footing, where every institution is to be made auxiliary to war." Building the army proved easiest. Hundreds of officers defected from the federal army, and hundreds of thousands of eager young rebels volunteered to join them. Very quickly, the Confederacy developed formidable striking power.

The Confederacy's economy and finances proved tougher. Because of the Union blockade, the government had no choice but to build an industrial sector itself. Government-owned clothing and shoe factories, mines, arsenals, and powder works "sprung up almost like magic," according to one Mississippian. In addition, the government harnessed private companies, such as the huge Tredegar Iron Works in Richmond, to the war effort. The financial task proved most difficult because Southerners had invested their capital in land and slaves, which were not easily tapped for the war. Richmond came up with a mix of bonds, taxes, and paper money to finance the war effort.

Despite its bold measures, however, the Davis administration failed to transform the slave-labor, staple-producing agricultural economy into a modern industrial one. The Confederacy manufactured much more than most people imagined possible, but it never produced all that the South needed. Each month, the gap between the North's and the South's production widened. Moreover, the flood of paper money coming from Richmond caused debilitating inflation. By 1863, Charlestonians paid ten times more for food than they had at the start of the war. By Christmas 1864, a Confederate soldier's monthly pay no longer bought a pair of socks.

Richmond's war-making effort meant that government intruded in unprecedented ways into the private lives of Confederate citizens. In April 1862, the Confederate Congress passed the first conscription (draft) law in American history. All able-bodied white males between the ages of eighteen and thirty-five (later seventeen and fifty) were liable to serve in the rebel army for three years. The Confederate government adopted a policy of impressment, which allowed officials to confiscate food, horses, wagons, or whatever they wanted from private citizens and to pay for them at below-market rates. After March 1863, the Confederacy also legally impressed slaves, employing them as government military laborers. In addition, Richmond took control of the South's railroads and shipping. The war necessitated much of the government's unprecedented behavior, but citizens found it arbitrary and inequitable. In time, Southerners named Jefferson Davis as the politician they hated most, after Lincoln.

Hardship Below

Richmond's centralizing efforts ran head-on into the South's traditional values of states' rights and unfettered individualism. The states lashed out at what Georgia governor Joseph E. Brown denounced as the "dangerous usurpation by Congress of the reserved right of the States." A tug-of-war between Richmond and the states ensued for control of money, supplies, and soldiers, with damaging consequences for the war effort. Individual citizens also remembered that Davis had promised to defend southern "liberty" against Republican "despotism."

Hardships were widespread, but they fell most heavily on the poor. Inflation, for example, threatened the poor with starvation. Salt—necessary for preserving meat—shot up from $2 to $60 a bag during the first year of the war. Flour that cost three or four cents a pound in 1861 cost thirty-five cents in 1863. The draft depopulated yeomen farms of men, leaving the women and children to grow what they ate. When farm wives succeeded in bringing in a harvest, government agents took 10 percent of it as a "tax-in-kind" on agriculture. Like inflation, shortages also afflicted the entire population, but the rich

MARIA ISABELLA ("BELLE") BOYD, SPY
Most white southern women, in addition to keeping their families fed and safe, served the Confederate cause by sewing uniforms, knitting socks, rolling bandages, and nursing the sick and wounded. But Belle Boyd became a spy. Only seventeen when the war broke out, she became in the words of a northern journalist "insanely devoted to the rebel cause." Her first act for the Confederacy came on July 3, 1861, when she shot a drunken federal soldier who barged into her Virginia home and insulted her mother. Her relations with occupying northern troops improved, and soon this compelling young woman was eavesdropping on officers' conversations and slipping messages to Confederate armies. Boyd's information handed Stonewall Jackson an easy victory at Front Royal, Virginia, in May 1862. "I thank you," the general wrote Boyd, " . . . for the immense service that you have rendered your country today." Imprisoned several times for spying, Boyd took up a theatrical career when the war ended.
Courtesy Warren Rifles Confederate Museum, Front Royal, Va.
Photo by Larry Sherer.

lost luxuries while the poor lost necessities. In the spring of 1863, bread riots broke out in a dozen cities and villages across the South. In Richmond, a mob of nearly a thousand hungry women broke into shops and took what they needed.

Severe deprivation had powerful consequences. One southern leader observed in November 1862, "Men cannot be expected to fight for the Government that permits their wives & children to starve." A few wealthy individuals shared their bounty, the Confederacy made some efforts at social welfare, and the states did even more, but every effort fell short. By some estimates, when the war ended, one-third of the soldiers had already gone home. A Mississippi deserter explained, "We are poor men and are willing to defend our country but our families [come] first."

The Confederacy also failed to persuade the suffering white majority that the war's burdens were being shared equally. Instead, yeomen saw a profound inequality of sacrifice. They called it "a rich man's war and a poor man's fight," and they had evidence. The original draft law permitted a man who had money to hire a substitute to take his place. Moreover, the "twenty-Negro law" exempted one white man on every plantation with twenty or more slaves. The government intended to provide protection for white women and to see that slaves tended the crops. But yeomen perceived rich men as evading military service. A slaveless Mississippian complained to his governor about stay-at-home planters who sent their slaves into the fields to grow cotton while in plain view "poor soldiers' wives are plowing with their own hands to make a subsistence for themselves and children—while their husbands are suffering, bleeding and dying for their country." In fact, most slaveholders went off to war, but the extreme suffering of common folk and the relative immunity of planters fueled class animosity.

The Richmond government hoped that the crucible of war would mold a region into a nation. Officials and others worked tirelessly to promote a vibrant southern nationalism that, as one Confederate politician said, would "excite in our citizens an ardent and enduring attachment to our Government and its institutions." Clergymen assured their congregations that God had blessed slavery and the new nation. Jefferson Davis asked citizens to observe national days of fasting and prayer. Patriotic songwriters, poets, authors, and artists extolled southern culture. But it proved difficult to create a

united slave republic in the midst of all-out war. Efforts to build consensus never succeeded in winning over thousands of die-hard Unionists. And friction between yeomen and planters increased rather than decreased. The war also threatened to rip the southern social fabric along its racial seam.

The Disintegration of Slavery

The legal destruction of slavery was the product of presidential proclamation, congressional legislation, and eventually constitutional amendment, but the practical destruction of slavery was the product of war, what Lincoln called war's "friction and abrasion." When the war ended in 1865, the institution had taken a heavy pounding, especially from within. More than 100,000 men fled bondage, took up arms, and attacked slavery directly. Other men and women stayed in the slave quarters, where they staked their claim to more freedom.

In dozens of ways, the war disrupted the routine, organization, and discipline of bondage. Almost immediately, it called the master away, leaving white women to assume managerial responsibilities. But plantation mistresses could not maintain traditional standards of slave discipline. No one could. Moreover, the government's impressment policy, extended to slaves, severed the personal relationship between masters and slaves. In addition, as military action increasingly sliced through the South's farms and plantations, some slaveholders fled, leaving behind their slaves. Many more took their slaves with them, but flight meant additional chaos and offered slaves new opportunities to resist bondage.

In large parts of the South, the balance of power between master and slave gradually shifted. Slaveholders complained about the slaves' "demoralization" and "betrayal." Slaves got to the fields late, worked indifferently, and quit early. Some slaveholders responded violently; most saw no alternative but to strike bargains—offering gifts or part of the crop—to keep slaves at home and at work. An Alabama woman reported that she "begged . . . what little is done." Changes in slave behavior shocked slaveholders. They had prided themselves on "knowing" their slaves, and they learned that they did not know them at all. When the war began, a North Carolina woman praised her slaves as "diligent and respectful." When it ended, she said, "As to the idea of a faithful servant, it is all a fiction." But whites' greatest fear—

CONFEDERATE SOLDIERS AND THEIR SLAVES
Soldiers of the Seventh Tennessee Cavalry pose with their slaves. Many slaveholders took "body servants" with them to war. These slaves cooked, washed, and cleaned for the white soldiers. In 1861, James H. Langhorne reported to his sister: "Peter . . . is charmed with being with me & 'being a soldier.' I gave him my old uniform overcoat & he says he is going to have his picture taken . . . to send to the servants." Do you think Peter was "puttin' on ol' massa" or just glad to be free of plantation labor?
Daguerreotype courtesy of Tom Farish. Photographed by Michael Latil.

www.bedfordstmartins.com/roarkcompact SEE THE ONLINE STUDY GUIDE for more help in analyzing this image.

black violence—rarely occurred. Instead, slaves undermined white mastery and expanded control over their own lives.

The North at War

Because rebel armies generally operated within the Confederate borders, the North remained largely untouched by fighting. But Northerners could not avoid being touched by war. Almost every family had a son, a husband, a brother in uniform. Moreover, this war—a total war—blurred the distinction between home front and battlefield. As in the South, men marched off to fight, but preserving the country, either Union or Confederacy, was also women's work. For civilians as well as soldiers, for women as well as men, war was transforming.

The need to build and fuel the Union war machine caused the northern economy to boom. The North sent nearly 2 million men into the military and still increased production in almost every area. But because the rewards and burdens of patriotism were not evenly distributed, the North experienced sharp, even violent, divisions. Workers confronted employers, whites confronted blacks, and Republicans confronted Democrats. Still, Northerners on the home front remained fervently attached to the ideals of free labor and the Union.

The Government and the Economy

When the war began, the United States had no national banking system, no national currency, and no federal income or excise taxes. But the secession of eleven slave states cut the Democrats' strength in Congress in half and destroyed their capacity to resist Republican programs to stimulate the economy. In May 1862, Congress approved the Homestead Act, which offered 160 acres of public land to settlers who would live and labor on it. In time, the Homestead Act resulted in more than a million new farms in the West. July 1862 saw passage of the Pacific Railroad Act, which provided massive federal assistance for the building of a transcontinental railroad. When completed in 1869, the railroad ran from Omaha to San Francisco. Congress also enacted a higher tariff to increase protection for manufacturers against foreign competition.

The Legal Tender Act of February 1862 created a national currency, paper money that Northerners called "greenbacks." With passage of the National Banking Act in February 1863, Congress created a system of national banks that by the 1870s had largely replaced the antebellum system of decentralized state banks. Congress also enacted a series of sweeping tax laws that encompassed everything from incomes to liquor to billiard tables. The Internal Revenue Act created the Bureau of Internal Revenue to collect taxes. By revolutionizing the country's banking, monetary, and tax structures, the Republicans generated enormous economic power.

Two additional initiatives had long-term consequences for agriculture and industry. Congress created a Department of Agriculture and passed the Land-Grant College Act (also known as the Morrill Act after its sponsor, Representative Justin Morrill of Vermont), which set aside public lands to support universities that emphasized "agriculture and mechanical arts." Republicans defended their wartime legislation by arguing that additional economic muscle meant increased military might. Initiatives from Washington immeasurably strengthened the North's effort to win the war, but they were also permanently changing the nation.

Women and Work on the Home Front

With more than a million farm men called to the military, farm women added men's chores to their own. "I met more women driving teams on the road and saw more at work in the fields than men," a visitor to Iowa reported in the fall of 1862. Rising production figures testified to their success in plowing, planting, and harvesting. Rapid mechanization assisted farm women in their new roles. Cyrus McCormick sold 165,000 of his reapers during the war years. The combination of high prices and increased production ensured that war and prosperity joined hands in the rural North.

While a few industries, such as textiles (which depended on southern cotton), declined during the war, many more grew. Huge profits prompted one Pennsylvania ironmaster to remark, "I am in no hurry for peace." With orders pouring in and a million nonfarm workers siphoned off into the military, unemployment declined and wages often rose. The boom proved friendlier to owners than to workers, however. Inflation and taxes cut so deeply that workers' standard of living actually fell.

As on the farm, women in cities stepped into jobs vacated by men, particularly in manufacturing, and also into essentially new occupations such as government civil service. Often they had no choice because they could not make ends meet on their husbands' army pay. Women made up about one-quarter of the manufacturing workforce when the war began and one-third when it ended. But as more women entered the workforce, employers cut wages. By 1864, fourteen-hour days earned New York seamstresses only an average of $1.54 per week. As Cincinnati seamstresses explained to Abraham Lincoln, their wages were not enough "to sustain life." Urban workers resorted increasingly to strikes to try to wrench decent salaries from their employers, but their protests rarely succeeded. Nevertheless, tough times failed to undermine the patriotism of most workers, who took pride in their contribution to northern victory.

Middle-class white women were supposed to be homebodies, and hundreds of thousands contributed to the war effort in traditional ways. Like many southern white women, they sewed, wrapped bandages, and sold homemade goods at local fairs to raise money to aid the soldiers. But other women expressed their patriotism in an untraditional way—as wartime nurses. Thousands of women on both sides defied prejudices about female delicacy

U.S. SANITARY COMMISSION, BRANDY STATION, VIRGINIA, 1863

The burden of caring for the millions of Union soldiers was more than the government could shoulder. Private initiative in the form of the U.S. Sanitary Commission brought additional medical attention to the Union wounded and boosted the comfort and morale of soldiers in the camps. Volunteers like these northern women standing in front of the Commission's headquarters in Brandy Station, Virginia, offered soldiers some of the comforts of home—clean socks, new blankets, and fresh fruit. Do you suppose that the freshly painted white picket fence surrounding their building had symbolic value? If so, what did it symbolize?

National Archives.

and volunteered to nurse the wounded. Many of the northern female volunteers worked through the U.S. Sanitary Commission, a civilian organization that bought and distributed clothing, food, and medicine and recruited doctors and nurses. Nursing meant working in the midst of unspeakable sights, sounds, and smells, but it often brought profound satisfaction. Katherine Wormeley of Rhode Island, who served three months as a volunteer nurse on a hospital ship in 1862, recorded in her diary, "We all know in our hearts that it is thorough enjoyment to be here—it is life."

Some volunteers went on to become paid military nurses. For example, Dorothea Dix, well known for her efforts to reform insane asylums, was named superintendent of female nurses; eventually, some three thousand women served under her. Most nurses worked in hospitals behind the battle lines, but some, like Clara Barton, who later founded the American Red Cross, worked in battlefield units. Women who served in the war went on to lead the postwar movement to establish training schools for female nurses.

Politics and Dissent

At first, the bustle of economic and military mobilization seemed to silence politics, with Democrats supporting the Union as fervently as Republicans. But bipartisan unity did not last. Within a year, Democrats were labeling the Republican administration a "reign of terror," and Republicans were calling Democrats the party of "Dixie, Davis, and the Devil." As bruising as the political struggle became, the North's two-party system actually strengthened government. In the Confederacy, which had no well-organized parties, political disagreement spiraled down into fruitless bickering, but in the Union, parties helped to discipline and legitimize political debate.

Nevertheless, Republican policy pushed the Democrats toward a dangerous alienation. Under Lincoln, the Republicans emancipated the slaves, subsidized private business, and expanded federal power at every turn. The Lincoln administration argued that the war required a loose interpretation of the Constitution, to which the Democrats countered, "The Constitution is as binding in war as in peace." In September 1862, in an effort to stifle opposition to the war, Lincoln placed under military arrest any person who discouraged enlistments, resisted the draft, or engaged in "disloyal" practices. Before the war ended, his administration had imprisoned nearly fourteen thousand individuals, most in the border states. The campaign fell short of a reign of terror, for the majority of the prisoners were not northern Democratic opponents but Confederate citizens, blockade runners, and citizens of foreign countries, and most of the arrested gained quick release. Still, the administration's heavy-handed tactics did suppress free speech.

When the Republican-dominated Congress enacted the draft law in March 1863, Democrats had another grievance. Grim news from the battlefields had dried up the stream of volunteers, and the North, like the South a year earlier, turned to military conscription to fill the ranks. The law required that all men between the ages of twenty and forty-five enroll and make themselves available for a lottery, which would decide who went to war. What poor men found particularly galling were provisions that allowed a draftee to hire a substitute or simply to pay a $300 fee and get out of his military obligation. As in the South, common folk could be heard chanting, "A rich man's war and a poor man's fight."

Linking the draft and emancipation, Democrats argued that Republicans employed an unconstitutional means (the draft) to achieve an unconstitutional end (emancipation). In the summer of 1863, antidraft, antiblack mobs went on rampages in northern cities. New York experienced an explosion of unprecedented proportions. Solidly Democratic Irish workingmen, crowded into stinking, disease-ridden tenements, gouged by inflation, enraged by the inequities of the draft, and dead set against fighting to free blacks, erupted in four days of rioting. By the time police and soldiers restored order, at least 105 people, most of them black, lay dead, and the Colored Orphan Asylum was a smoking ruin.

The riots stunned black Northerners, but the racist mobs failed to achieve their purpose: the subordination of African Americans. Free black leaders had lobbied aggressively for emancipation, and after Lincoln's proclamation they fanned out over the North agitating for equality. They won some small wartime successes. Illinois and Iowa overturned laws that excluded blacks from entering the states. Illinois and Ohio began permitting blacks to testify in court. But defeat was more common. Indiana, for example, continued to forbid blacks to vote, testify, and attend public schools, and additional blacks were not allowed to enter the state.

Grinding Out Victory, 1863–1865

In the early months of 1863, the Union's prospects looked bleak, while the Confederate cause stood at high tide. But in July 1863, the tide began to recede. The military man who was most responsible for seeing that it never rose again was Ulysses S. Grant.

Lifted from obscurity by brilliant successes in the West in 1862 and 1863, Grant became "the great man of the day," one man observed in July 1864, "perhaps of the age." Elevated to supreme command, Grant knit together a powerful war machine that integrated a sophisticated command structure, modern technology, and complex logistics and supply systems. But the arithmetic of this plain man remained unchanged: killing more of the enemy than he kills of you equaled "the complete overthrow of the rebellion."

The North ground out the victory, battle by bloody battle. The balance tipped in the Union's favor in 1863, but if the Confederacy was beaten, Southerners clearly did not know it. The fighting reached new levels of ferocity in the last two years of the war. As national elections approached in the fall of 1864, a discouraged Lincoln expected a war-weary North to make him a one-term president. Instead, northern voters declared their willingness to continue the war in the defense of the ideals of union and freedom.

Vicksburg and Gettysburg

Perched on the bluffs above the eastern bank of the Mississippi River, Vicksburg, Mississippi, bristled with cannon and dared Yankee ships to try to pass. This Confederate stronghold stood between Union forces and complete control of the river. Impenetrable terrain made it impossible to take the city from the north, and to get his army south of Vicksburg, Grant marched it down the swampy western bank of the Mississippi. Union forces crossed the Mississippi River, marched north more than one hundred miles, and attacked the city. When the Confederates beat back the assault, Grant began siege operations to starve out the enemy. Civilian inhabitants took to living in caves to escape incessant Union cannon bombardment, and to survive they soon began eating mules and rats.

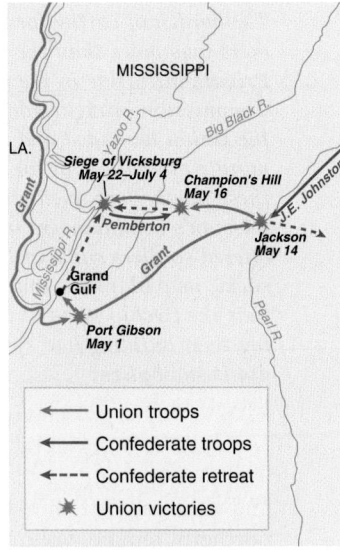

Vicksburg Campaign, 1863

Eventually, the siege succeeded. On July 4, 1863, nearly 30,000 rebels marched out of Vicksburg, stacked their arms, and surrendered unconditionally. A Yankee captain wrote home to his wife: "The backbone of the Rebellion is this day broken. The Confederacy is divided. . . . Vicksburg is ours. The Mississippi River is opened, and Gen. Grant is to be our next President."

On the same Fourth of July that a grateful nation received the news of Vicksburg, word arrived that Union forces had crushed General Lee at Gettysburg, Pennsylvania (Map 15.3). Lee's triumph two months earlier at Chancellorsville, Virginia, over Joseph "Fighting Joe" Hooker had revived his confidence, even though the battle cost him his favorite commander, the incomparable Stonewall Jackson, accidentally shot in the dark by his own troops. Lee wanted to relieve Virginia of the burden of the fighting, and he felt bold enough to think that he could deliver a morale-crunching defeat to the Yankees on their home turf.

In June, Lee's 75,000-man Army of Northern Virginia invaded Pennsylvania. On June 28, the Army of the Potomac, under its new commander, General George G. Meade, moved quickly to intercept it. Advanced units of both armies met at the small town of Gettysburg, where Union forces occupied the high ground. Three days of furious fighting, involving 165,000 soldiers, could not dislodge them from the ridges and hills. But Lee ached for a decisive victory, and on July 3 he ordered a major assault against the Union center on Cemetery Ridge. The open, rolling fields provided the dug-in Yankees with three-quarters of a mile of clear vision, and they raked the mile-wide line of Confederates with cannon and rifle fire. Time and again, the rebels closed ranks and raced on, until finally their momentum failed.

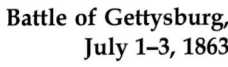

Battle of Gettysburg, July 1–3, 1863

Gettysburg cost Lee more than one-third of his army—28,000 casualties. "It's all my fault," he said. In a drenching rain on the night of July 4, 1863, he marched his battered army back to Virginia.

The twin disasters at Vicksburg and Gettysburg proved to be the turning point of the war. The Confederacy could not replace the nearly 60,000 soldiers who were captured, wounded, or killed. Lee never launched another major offensive north of the Mason-Dixon line. But it is hindsight that permits us to see the pair of battles as decisive. At the time, the Confederacy still controlled the heartland of the South, and Lee, back on the defensive in Virginia, still had a vicious sting. War-weariness threatened to erode the North's will to win before Union armies destroyed the Confederacy's ability to go on.

Grant Takes Command

In September 1863, Union general William Rosecrans placed his army in a dangerous situation in Chattanooga, Tennessee, where he had retreated after taking a whipping at the battle of Chickamauga (see Map 15.3). Rebels surrounded the disorganized bluecoats and threatened to starve them into submission. Ulysses S. Grant, whom Lincoln had made commander of all Union forces between the Mississippi River and the Appalachians, arrived in Chattanooga in October. Within weeks, he opened an effective supply line, broke the siege, and then (largely because troops disobeyed orders and charged wildly up Missionary Ridge) routed the Confederate army. The victory at Chattanooga had immense strategic value. It opened the door to Georgia. It also confirmed Lincoln's estimation of Grant. In March 1864, the president asked the commander to come east to become the general in chief of all Union armies.

In Washington, Grant implemented his grand strategy of a war of annihilation. He ordered a series of simultaneous assaults from Virginia to Louisiana. Two actions proved more significant than the others. In one, General William Tecumseh Sherman, whom Grant appointed his successor to command the western armies, plunged southeast toward Atlanta. In the other, Grant, who took control of the Army of the Potomac, went head-to-head with Lee for almost four straight weeks in Virginia.

Grant and Lee met in early May 1864 at the Wilderness, a dense tangle of scrub oaks and small

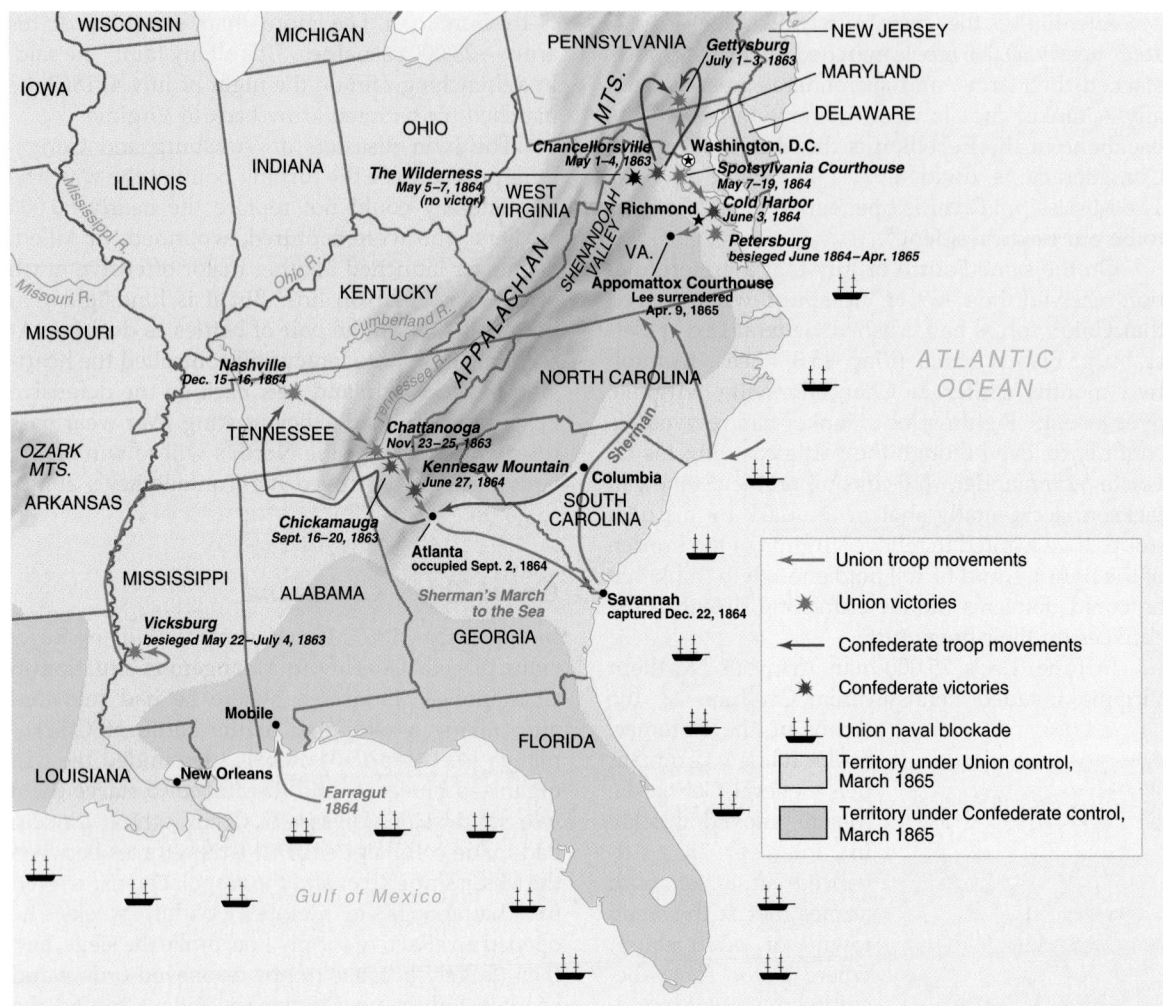

MAP 15.3

The Civil War, 1863–1865

Ulysses S. Grant's victory at Vicksburg divided the Confederacy at the Mississippi River. William Tecumseh Sherman's march from Chattanooga to Savannah divided it again. In northern Virginia, Robert E. Lee fought fiercely, but Grant's larger, better-supplied armies prevailed.

READING THE MAP: Describe the difference between Union and Confederate naval strength. Were the battles shown fought primarily in Union-controlled or Confederate-controlled territory?

CONNECTIONS: Did former slaves serve in the Civil War? If so, on which side(s)? Describe their efforts.

www.bedfordstmartins.com/roarkcompact   SEE THE ONLINE STUDY GUIDE for more help in analyzing this map.

pines that proved to be Lee's ally, for it helped off-set the Yankees' numerical superiority. Often unable to see more than ten paces, the armies pounded away at each other until approximately 18,000 Yankees and 11,000 rebels had fallen. But the savagery of the Wilderness did not compare with that at Spotsylvania Court House a few days later. Frenzied men fought hand to hand for eighteen hours in the rain. One veteran remembered men "piled upon each other in some places four layers deep, exhibiting every ghastly phase of mutilation." Spotsylvania cost Grant another 18,000 casualties and Lee 10,000. But the Yankee bulldog would not let go. Grant kept moving and tangled with Lee again at Cold Harbor, where he lost 13,000 additional troops to Lee's 5,000. (See "Historical Question," page 378.)

Twice as many Union soldiers as rebel soldiers died in the four weeks of fighting in Virginia in the spring of 1864. Yet Grant did not consider himself defeated. Since Lee had only half the number of troops, he lost proportionally as many men as Grant. Ever the mathematician of war, Grant knew that the South could not replace the losses. Moreover, the campaign had carried Grant to the outskirts of Petersburg, just south of the Confederate capital. Since most of the major railroad lines supplying Richmond ran through Petersburg, Lee had little choice but to defend the city. Grant abandoned the costly tactic of the frontal assault and began a siege that immobilized both armies and dragged on for nine months.

There was no pause in Sherman's invasion of Georgia. Grant had instructed Sherman to "get into the interior of the enemy's country as far as you can, inflicting all the damage you can against their War resources." In early May Sherman moved 100,000 men south against the 65,000 rebels in the rugged mountains of northern Georgia. Skillful maneuvering, constant skirmishing, and one pitched battle (Kennesaw Mountain) brought Sherman to Atlanta, which fell on September 1.

Sherman was only warming up. Intending to "make Georgia howl," he marched out of Atlanta on November 15 with 62,000 battle-hardened veterans, heading for Savannah, 285 miles away. Federal troops cut a swath from twenty-five to sixty miles wide. One veteran remembered, "[We] destroyed all we could not eat, stole their niggers, burned their cotton & gins, spilled their sorghum, burned & twisted their R. Roads and raised Hell generally." Sherman's "March to the Sea" aimed at

GRANT AT COLD HARBOR
Seated next to his chief of staff, John A. Rawlins, at his Cold Harbor, Virginia, headquarters, Ulysses S. Grant plots his next move against Robert E. Lee. On June 3, 1864, Grant ordered frontal assaults against entrenched Confederate forces, resulting in enormous Union losses. "I am disgusted with the generalship displayed," young Brigadier General Emory Upton exclaimed. "Our men have, in many cases, been foolishly and wantonly slaughtered." Years later, Grant said that he regretted the assault at Cold Harbor, but in 1864 he kept pushing toward Richmond.
Chicago Historical Society.

Why Did So Many Soldiers Die?

FROM 1861 TO 1865, Americans killed Americans on a scale that had never before been seen. Not until the First World War, a half century later, would the world match (and surpass) the killing fields at Shiloh, Antietam, and Gettysburg (Figure 15.2). Why were the Civil War totals so huge? Why did 260,000 rebel soldiers and 373,000 Union soldiers die?

The balance between the ability to kill and the ability to save lives had tipped disastrously toward death. The sheer size of the armies—some battles involved more than 200,000 soldiers—ensured that battlefields would turn red with blood. Moreover, armies fought with antiquated strategy. In the generals' eyes, the ideal soldier remained the veteran of Napoleonic warfare, a man trained to advance with his comrades in a compact, close-order formation. Theory also emphasized frontal assaults. In classrooms at West Point and on the high plains of Mexico in the 1840s, men who would one day be officers in rival armies learned that infantry advancing shoulder to shoulder, supported by artillery, carried the day.

But by the 1860s, modern technology had made such strategy appallingly deadly. Weapons with ri-

WOUNDED MEN AT SAVAGE'S STATION
Misery did not end when the cannon ceased firing. This heap of mangled humanity strewn on the ground was but a fraction of the cost of General George McClellan's campaign on the Virginia peninsula in 1862.
Library of Congress.

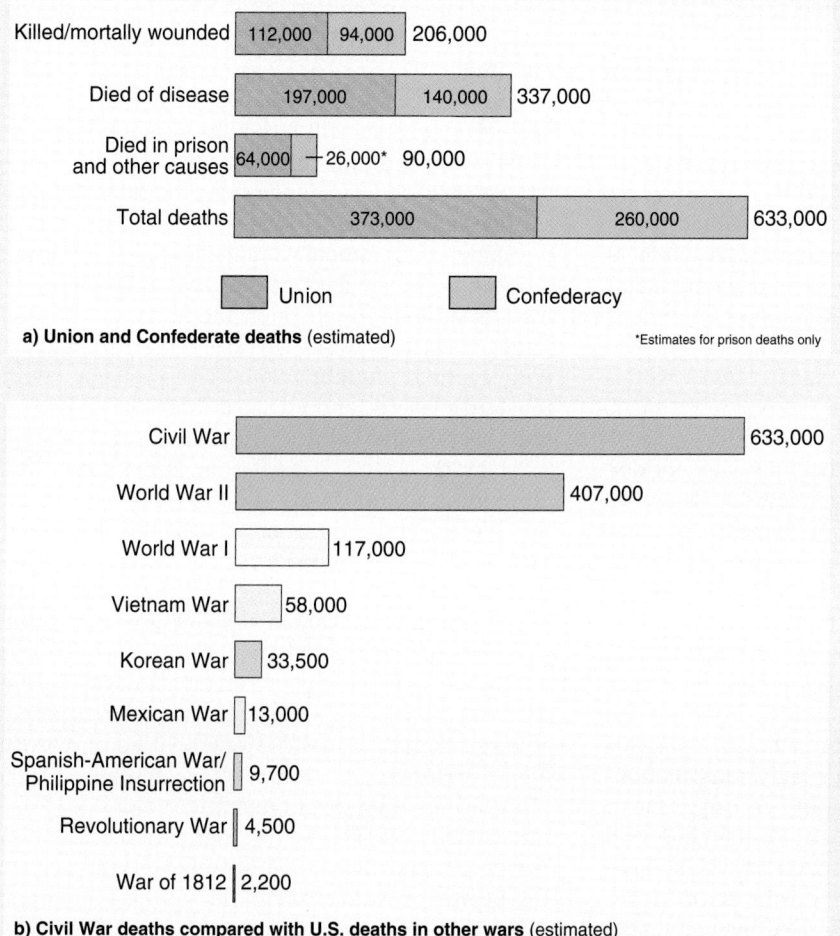

FIGURE 15.2
Civil War Deaths
The loss of life in the Civil War was almost equal to the losses in all other American wars.

Killed/mortally wounded: 112,000 | 94,000 | 206,000
Died of disease: 197,000 | 140,000 | 337,000
Died in prison and other causes: 64,000 — 26,000* | 90,000
Total deaths: 373,000 | 260,000 | 633,000

Union   Confederacy

a) Union and Confederate deaths (estimated)

*Estimates for prison deaths only

Civil War 633,000
World War II 407,000
World War I 117,000
Vietnam War 58,000
Korean War 33,500
Mexican War 13,000
Spanish-American War/Philippine Insurrection 9,700
Revolutionary War 4,500
War of 1812 2,200

b) Civil War deaths compared with U.S. deaths in other wars (estimated)

fled barrels (that is, with spiral grooves cut into the bore) were replacing old smoothbore muskets. Whereas muskets had an effective range of only about eighty yards, rifles propelled spinning bullets four times as far. The rifle's greater range and accuracy, along with cannons firing canisters filled with flesh-ripping, bone-breaking steel shot, made sitting ducks of charging infantry units and gave enormous advantage to entrenched defensive forces. As a result, battles took thousands of lives in a single day. On July 2, 1862, the morning after the battle at Malvern Hill in eastern Virginia, a Union officer surveyed the scene: "Over five thousand dead and wounded men were on the ground . . . enough were alive and moving to give to the field a singular crawling effect."

Soldiers who littered the battlefields often lay for hours, sometimes days, without water or care of any kind. When the war began, no one anticipated casualty lists with thousands of names. Union and Confederate medical departments could not cope with skirmishes, much less large-scale battles. They had no ambulance corps to lift the wounded from the scene. They had no field hospitals to deliver them to. At first, the Quartermaster Department, which was responsible for constructing Union hospitals, answered demands that it do something by saying: "Men need guns, not beds." It took the shock of massive casualties to compel reform. Although a lack of resources meant that the South lagged behind the North, both North and South gradually organized effective ambulance *(Continued)* corps, built hospitals, and hired trained surgeons and nurses.

Soldiers did not always count speedy transportation to a field hospital as a blessing, however. As one Union soldier said, "I had rather risk a battle than the Hospitals." Real danger lurked behind the lines. While the technology of killing had advanced to very high standards, medicine remained primitive. Physicians gained a reputation as butchers, and soldiers dreaded the operating table more than they did entrenched riflemen. Serious wounds to the leg or arm usually meant amputation, the best way doctors knew to save lives. After major battles, surgeons worked among piles of wounded men's limbs.

The wounded man's real enemy was not doctors' callousness, but rather medical ignorance. Physicians had almost no knowledge of the cause and transmission of disease or the benefits of antiseptics. Not aware of basic germ theory, they spread infection almost every time they operated. Doctors wore the same bloody smock for days and washed their hands and their scalpels and saws in buckets of dirty water. When they had difficulty threading their needles, they wet the thread with their own saliva. Soldiers often did not survive amputations, not because of the operation but because of the infection that inevitably followed. Of the Union soldiers whose legs were amputated above the knee, more than half died. A Union doctor discovered in 1864 that bromine (previously used in combination with other elements as a sedative) arrested gangrene, but the best most amputees could hope for was maggots, which ate dead flesh on the stump and thus inhibited the spread of infection. During the Civil War, nearly one of every five wounded rebel soldiers died, and one in every six Yankees. A

century later, in Vietnam, the proportion of deaths was one wounded American soldier in four hundred.

Soldiers who avoided battlefield wounds and hospital infections still faced sickness. Deadly diseases swept through crowded army camps, where latrines were often in dangerous proximity to water supplies. The principal killers were dysentery and typhoid, but pneumonia and malaria also cut down thousands of men. Doctors did what they could, but their treatments often only added to the misery. They prescribed doses of turpentine for patients with typhoid, fought respiratory problems with mustard plasters, and attacked intestinal disorders with blisters and sulfuric acid.

Dorothea Dix, Clara Barton, Juliet Ann Opie Hopkins, and thousands of other female nurses in the North and South improved the wounded men's odds and alleviated their misery. Civilian relief agencies, such as the U.S. Sanitary Commission and the Women's Relief Society of the Confederacy, promoted hygiene in army camps and made some headway. Nevertheless, as Figure 15.2 shows, disease killed nearly twice as many soldiers as did combat. Many who died of disease were prisoners of war. Approximately 30,000 Northerners died in Confederate prisons, and approximately 26,000 Southerners died in Union prisons. No northern prison, however, could equal the horror of Andersonville in southern Georgia. In August 1864, about 33,000 emaciated men lived in unspeakable conditions in a twenty-six-acre barren stockade with no shelter except what the prisoners were able to construct. More than 13,000 perished.

In the end, 633,000 northern and southern soldiers died, a staggering death toll.

destroying the will of the southern people. A few weeks earlier, General Philip H. Sheridan had tried as much in the Shenandoah Valley, complying with Grant's order to turn the valley into "a barren waste . . . so that crows flying over it for the balance of this season will have to carry their provender [food] with them." When Sherman's troops entered an undefended Savannah in the third week of December,

the general telegraphed Lincoln that he had "a Christmas gift" for him.

The Election of 1864

In the fall, white men in the Union states turned to the election of a president. Never before had a nation held general elections in the midst of war. "We can not have free government without elections," Lincoln explained, "and if the rebellion could force us to forgo or postpone a national election, it might fairly claim to have already conquered and ruined us."

Lincoln's determination to hold elections is especially noteworthy because the Democratic Party smelled victory. The Union war effort had stalled during the summer, and frustration had settled over the North. Rankled by inflation, the draft, the attack on civil liberties, and the commitment to blacks, Northerners appeared ready for a change. Lincoln himself concluded in the gloomy summer of 1864, "It seems exceedingly probable that this administration will not be re-elected."

Democrats were badly divided, however. "Peace" Democrats insisted on an armistice, while "war" Democrats supported the conflict but opposed Republican means of fighting it. They tried to paper over the chasm by nominating a war candidate, General George McClellan, but adopting a peace platform that demanded that "immediate efforts be made for a cessation of hostilities."

Lincoln was no shoo-in for renomination, much less reelection. Conservatives believed he had acted precipitously in emancipating the slaves, and radicals criticized him for moving too slowly to free them and for failing to champion black equality. But frightened by the strength of the peace Democrats, the Republican Party stuck with Lincoln. In an effort to reach out to the largest number of voters, however, the Republicans made two changes. First, they chose the new name the Union Party, making it easier for prowar Democrats to embrace Lincoln. Second, they chose a new vice presidential candidate, Andrew Johnson of Tennessee.

The capture of Atlanta in September turned the political tide in favor of the Republicans. Lincoln received 55 percent of the popular vote, but his electoral margin was a whopping 212 to McClellan's 21. The Republicans also stormed back in the congressional elections, gaining large margins over the Democrats in the Senate and the House. The Union Party bristled with factions, but they united for a resounding victory. The victory gave Lincoln a mandate to continue the war until slavery and the Confederacy were dead.

The Confederacy Collapses

Jefferson Davis found little to celebrate as the new year of 1865 dawned in Richmond. Military disaster littered the Confederate landscape. With the destruction of John B. Hood's army at Nashville in November, the interior of the Confederacy lay in Yankee hands (see Map 15.3). Sherman's troops, resting momentarily in Savannah, eyed South Carolina hungrily. Lee's army remained, but Grant had it pinned down in Petersburg just a few miles from Richmond. Southerners took out their frustration and bitterness on their president. Kinder than most, Alexander Stephens, vice president of the Confederacy, likened Davis to "my poor old blind and deaf dog."

In the final months of the war, more and more Confederates turned their backs on the rebellion. News from the battlefields made it difficult not to conclude that the Yankees had beaten them. Soldiers' wives begged their husbands to return home to keep their families from starving, and the stream of deserters became a flood. In most cases, they lost the will to continue not so much because they lost faith in southern independence but because they had been battered into submission. Despite all the divisions and conflicts within the Confederacy and the loss of heart in the final months, white Southerners had shown remarkable endurance for their cause. Half of the 900,000 Confederate soldiers had been killed or wounded, and ragged, hungry women and children had sacrificed for four years. Confederates had shown remarkable staying power through the bloodiest war then known to history.

The end came with a rush. On February 1, 1865, Sherman's troops stormed out of Savannah into South Carolina, the "cradle of the Confederacy." But before Sherman could push through North Carolina and arrive at the rear of Lee's army at Petersburg, Lee abandoned the city. Davis fled Richmond, and the capital city fell a few days later. Grant pursued Lee for one hundred miles, until Lee surrendered on April 9, 1865, in a farmhouse near the town of Appomattox Court House, Virginia. The beaten man arrived in an immaculate full-dress uniform, complete with sash and sword; the victor came in his usual mud-splattered private's outfit. Grant offered a generous peace. He allowed Lee's men to return home and to take their horses to help "put in a crop to carry themselves and their families through the next winter." With Lee gone, the remaining ragtag Confederate armies lost hope and gave up. After four years, the war was over.

The day after Lee's surrender, a brass band led a happy crowd of three thousand to the White House, where they pleaded with Lincoln for a speech. He begged off and asked the band to strike up "Dixie." He knew that the rebels had claimed the tune as their own, he said, but it was one of his favorites, and now he was taking it back. The crowd roared its approval, and the band played "Dixie," following it with "Yankee Doodle." No one was more relieved than Lincoln that the war was over, but his celebration was restrained. He told his cabinet that his postwar burdens would weigh almost as heavily as those of wartime. But Lincoln had other things on his mind when he attended Ford's Theatre on the evening of Good Friday, April 14, 1865. While he and his wife, Mary, enjoyed *Our American Cousin*, a British comedy, John Wilkes Booth, an actor with southern sympathies, slipped into the president's box and mortally wounded Lincoln with a single shot to his head. The man who had led the nation through the war would not lead it in its postwar search for a just peace.

Conclusion: The Second American Revolution

The Civil War had a profound effect on the nation and its people. It devastated the South. Three-fourths of southern white men of military age served in the army, and at least half of them were captured, wounded, or killed or died of disease. The war destroyed two-fifths of the South's livestock, wrecked half of the farm machinery, and blackened dozens of cities and towns. The immediate impact of the war on the North was more paradoxical. Putting down the slaveholders' rebellion cost the North a heavy price: 373,000 lives. But rather than devastating the land, war set the countryside and cities humming with business activity.

A transformed nation emerged from the crucible of war. Antebellum America was decentralized politically and loosely integrated economically. To bend the resources of the country to a Union victory, Congress enacted legislation that reshaped the nation's political and economic character. It adopted policies that established the sovereignty of the federal government and the dominance of industrial capitalism. Moreover, the common sacrifice of northern people to save the nation created an even fiercer national loyalty. The shift in power from South to North and the creation of a national government, a national economy, and a national spirit led one historian to call the American Civil War the "Second American Revolution."

RUINS OF RICHMOND

A Union soldier and a small boy in a Union cap contemplate the silence and devastation of Richmond, Virginia, the Confederacy's capital. On their way out of the city on the evening of April 2, 1865, Confederate demolition squads set fire to tobacco warehouses and ammunition dumps. Huge explosions tore holes in the city, and windswept fires destroyed much of what was left standing. As one Confederate observed, "The old war-scarred city seemed to prefer annihilation to conquest."
Library of Congress.

Most revolutionary of all, the war ended slavery. As Frederick Douglass had predicted, the South's war to preserve slavery killed it. Because that ancient labor and racial system was entangled in almost every aspect of southern life, slavery's uprooting would mean fundamental change. But the full meaning of abolition remained unclear in 1865. The task of determining the new economic, political, and social status of four million ex-slaves would be the principal task of the era known as Reconstruction.

FOR FURTHER READING ABOUT THE TOPICS IN THIS CHAPTER, see the Online Bibliography at

www.bedfordstmartins.com/roarkcompact.

FOR ADDITIONAL FIRST-HAND ACCOUNTS OF THIS PERIOD, see pages 224–241 in Michael Johnson, ed., *Reading the American Past*, Second Edition, Volume I.

TO ASSESS YOUR MASTERY OF THE MATERIAL IN THIS CHAPTER, see the Online Study Guide at

www.bedfordstmartins.com/roarkcompact.

CHRONOLOGY

1861 **April.** Union nurse Dorothea Dix named superintendent of female nurses.

April 12–13. Confederate forces attack Fort Sumter, South Carolina, the opening engagement of the Civil War.

April–May. Four Upper South states secede and join Confederacy.

July. Union forces routed at Manassas, Virginia, in first major clash of war.

August. Congress approves first Confiscation Act, which allows seizure of any slave employed by Confederate military.

1862 **February.** Legal Tender Act creates first national currency, called "greenbacks."

Union forces in West under General Ulysses S. Grant capture Fort Henry and Fort Donelson and drive Confederates from Kentucky and most of Tennessee.

April. Battle of Shiloh in Tennessee results in huge casualties and ends Confederate bid to control Mississippi Valley.

Confederate Congress passes first draft law in American history.

May. Homestead Act offers western land to those who would live and labor on it.

May–July. General George McClellan's Union forces defeated during peninsula campaign in Virginia.

July. Congress approves second Confiscation Act, freeing all slaves of rebel masters.

Congress passes Militia Act, authorizing enrollment of blacks in Union military.

September 17. Battle of Antietam stops Lee's advance into Maryland, but Confederate forces escape back to Virginia.

September 22. Lincoln announces preliminary emancipation proclamation.

1863 **January 1.** Emancipation Proclamation becomes law, freeing slaves in areas still in rebellion.

February. National Banking Act creates system of national banks.

March. Congress authorizes draft.

July. Vicksburg falls to Union forces under Grant, effectively cutting Confederacy in two along Mississippi River.

Battle of Gettysburg results in Confederate defeat and Lee's last offensive in North.

1864 **March.** Grant appointed general in chief of all Union forces.

May–June. Grant's forces engage Confederates in Virginia in bloodiest fighting of war, from Wilderness campaign to beginnings of siege of Petersburg.

September. Atlanta falls to Union forces under General William Tecumseh Sherman.

November. Lincoln reelected president.

December. Sherman occupies Savannah after scorched-earth campaign in Georgia.

1865 **April 9.** Lee surrenders to Grant at Appomattox Court House, Virginia, triggering the end of resistance.

April 14. Lincoln shot by John Wilkes Booth at Ford's Theatre in Washington. He dies on April 15, succeeded by Vice President Andrew Johnson.

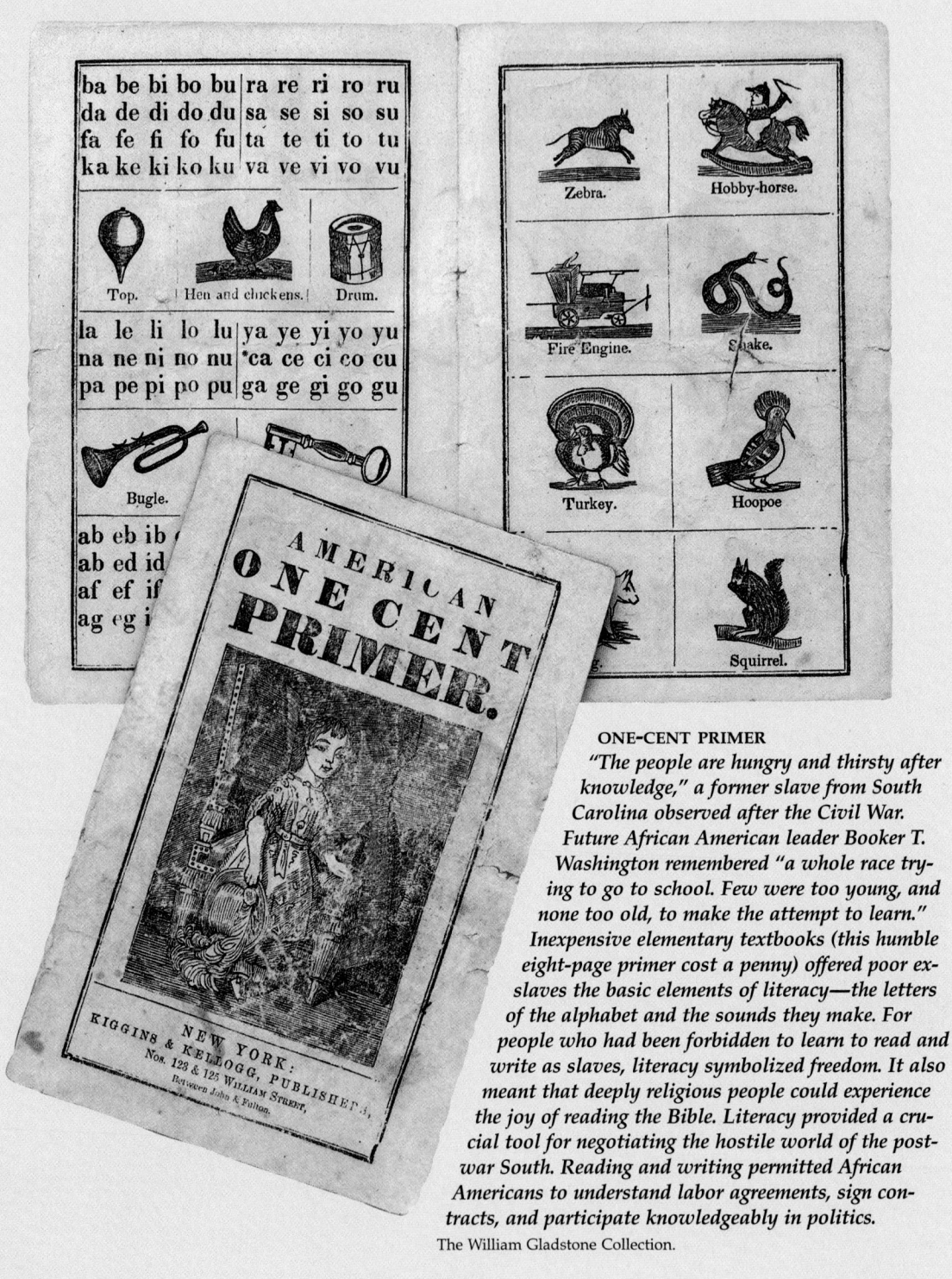

ba be bi bo bu | ra re ri ro ru
da de di do du | sa se si so su
fa fe fi fo fu | ta te ti to tu
ka ke ki ko ku | va ve vi vo vu

Top. | Hen and chickens. | Drum.

la le li lo lu | ya ye yi yo yu
na ne ni no nu | *ca ce ci co cu
pa pe pi po pu | ga ge gi go gu

Bugle.

ab eb ib
ab ed id
af ef if
ag eg i

Zebra. | Hobby-horse.

Fire Engine. | Snake.

Turkey. | Hoopoe

| Squirrel.

AMERICAN
ONE CENT
PRIMER.

NEW YORK:
KIGGINS & KELLOGG, PUBLISHERS,
Nos. 123 & 125 William Street,
Between John & Fulton.

ONE-CENT PRIMER

"The people are hungry and thirsty after knowledge," a former slave from South Carolina observed after the Civil War. Future African American leader Booker T. Washington remembered "a whole race trying to go to school. Few were too young, and none too old, to make the attempt to learn." Inexpensive elementary textbooks (this humble eight-page primer cost a penny) offered poor ex-slaves the basic elements of literacy—the letters of the alphabet and the sounds they make. For people who had been forbidden to learn to read and write as slaves, literacy symbolized freedom. It also meant that deeply religious people could experience the joy of reading the Bible. Literacy provided a crucial tool for negotiating the hostile world of the post-war South. Reading and writing permitted African Americans to understand labor agreements, sign contracts, and participate knowledgeably in politics.

The William Gladstone Collection.

RECONSTRUCTION
1863–1877

16

Y ORK DISAPPEARED ON YESTERDAY MORNING," David Golightly Harris noted in his journal on June 6, 1865. "I suppose that he has gone to the yankey. I wish they would give him a good whipping & hasten him back." York, a black field hand, had once belonged to Harris, a white slaveholder in Spartanburg District, South Carolina. When York disappeared, however, the war had been over for two months, and York was a free man. In Harris's mind, however, simply declaring York free did not make him so. In July, Harris noted that another field hand, Old Will, had left "to try to enjoy the freedom the Yankey's have promised the negroes." Two weeks later, black freedom still seemed in doubt. "There is much talk about freeing the negroes. Some are said already to have freed them," Harris declared. But Harris had not freed anyone. He did not inform his former slaves of their freedom until federal military authorities required him to. *"Freed the Negroes,"* he declared on August 16, four months after Appomattox.

Like many ex-slaveholders, Harris had trouble coming to grips with emancipation. "Family well, Horses well, Cattle well, Hogs well & everything else are well so far as I know, if it was not for the free negroes," Harris wrote on September 17. "On their account everything is turned upside down. So much so that we do not know what to do with our land, nor who to hire if we want it worked. . . . We are in the midst of troublesome times & do not know what will turn up." Harris had owned ten slaves, and now he faced what seemed to him an insoluble problem. He needed black labor to cultivate his farm, but like most whites he did not believe that blacks would work much when free. Some kind of compulsion would be needed. But slavery was gone, leaving the South upside down. Some white men in Harris's neighborhood sought to set it straight again. "In this district several negroes have been badly whipped & several have been hung by some unknown persons," he noted in November. "This has a tendency to keep them in their proper bounds & make them more humble." But the violence did not keep ex-slaves from acting like free people. On Christmas Day 1865, Harris recorded, "The negroes leave today to hunt themselves a new home while we will be left to wait upon ourselves."

Across the South, ex-masters predicted that emancipation would mean economic collapse and social anarchy. Carl Schurz, a Union general who undertook a fact-finding mission to the ex-Confederate states in the summer of 1865, encountered this dire prediction often enough to conclude that the Civil War was a "revolution but half accomplished." Northern victory had freed the slaves, but it had not changed former slaveholders' minds about the need for slavery. Left to themselves, Schurz believed, whites would "introduce some new system of forced labor, not perhaps exactly slavery in its old form but something similar to it." To defend their freedom, blacks would need federal protection, land of their own, and voting rights, Schurz concluded. Until whites "cut loose from the past, it will be a

BLACK WOMAN IN COTTON FIELDS, THOMASVILLE, GEORGIA
Few images of everyday black women during the era of Reconstruction survive. This photograph was taken in 1895, but it nevertheless goes to the heart of the labor struggle after the Civil War. As slaves, black women worked in the fields, and white landlords wanted them to continue working there after emancipation. Freedom allowed some women to escape field labor, but not this Georgian, who no doubt worked to survive. Despite her plight, the photograph reveals a strong person with a clear sense of who she is. Although worn to protect her head and body from the fierce heat, her intricately wrapped headdress dramatically expresses her individuality. However, what do her feet reveal about her life?
Vanishing Georgia Collection, Georgia Department of Archives and History, Atlanta, Georgia.

dangerous experiment to put Southern society upon its own legs." The end of the war did not mean the beginning of peace. Instead, the nation entered one of its most chaotic and conflicted eras—Reconstruction, an era that would define the status of the defeated South within the Union and the meaning of freedom for ex-slaves.

The status of the South and the nature of black freedom were determined by the political debate in the nation's capital and in the state legislatures and county seats of the South and through the active participation of blacks themselves. In the midst of the flux and chaos, a small band of crusading women sought to achieve gender equality. The years of reconstruction were characterized by struggle in which white Southerners eventually prevailed. Though they largely defined the "New South," it was a very different South from the one to which whites like David Golightly Harris wished to return.

Wartime Reconstruction

Reconstruction did not wait for the end of war. As the odds of a northern victory increased, thinking about reunification quickened. Immediately, a question arose: Who had authority to devise a plan for reconstructing the Union? Lincoln believed firmly that reconstruction was a matter of executive responsibility. Congress just as firmly asserted its jurisdiction. Fueling the argument about who had authority to set the terms of reconstruction were significant differences about the terms themselves. Lincoln's primary aim was the restoration of national unity, which he sought through a program of speedy, forgiving political reconciliation. Congress feared that the president's program amounted to restoring the old southern ruling class to power. It wanted greater assurances of white loyalty and greater guarantees of black rights.

In their eagerness to formulate a plan for political reunification, neither Lincoln nor Congress gave much attention to the South's land and labor problems. But the war rapidly eroded slavery and traditional plantation agriculture, and Yankee military commanders in the Union-occupied areas of the Confederacy had no choice but to oversee the emergence of a new labor system.

"To Bind Up the Nation's Wounds"

On March 4, 1865, President Abraham Lincoln delivered his second inaugural address. He surveyed the history of the long, deadly war and then looked ahead to peace. "With malice toward none; with charity for all; with firmness in the right, as God gives us to see the right," Lincoln said, "let us strive on to finish the work we are in; to bind up the nation's wounds . . . to do all which may achieve and cherish a just, and a lasting peace." Lincoln had contemplated reunion for nearly two years. Deep compassion for the enemy guided his thinking about peace. But kindness is not the key to understanding Lincoln's program. His reconstruction plan aimed primarily at shortening the war and ending slavery.

In his Proclamation of Amnesty and Reconstruction, issued in December 1863, Lincoln offered a full pardon to rebels willing to renounce secession and to accept the abolition of slavery. (Pardons were valuable because they restored all property, except slaves, and full political rights.) His offer excluded several groups of Confederates, such as high-ranking civilian and military officers. When only 10 percent of men who had been qualified voters in 1860 had taken an oath of allegiance, they could organize a new state government. Lincoln's plan did not require ex-rebels to extend social or political rights to ex-slaves, nor did it anticipate a program of long-term federal assistance to freedmen. Clearly, the president sought to restore the broken Union, not to reform it.

Lincoln's easy terms enraged abolitionists like Bostonian Wendell Phillips, who charged that the president "makes the negro's freedom a mere sham." He "is willing that the negro should be free but seeks nothing else for him," Phillips declared. Phillips and other northern radicals called instead for a thorough overhaul of southern society. Their ideas proved to be too drastic for most Republicans during the war years, but Congress agreed that Lincoln's plan was inadequate. In July 1864, Congress put forward a plan of its own.

Congressman Henry Winter Davis of Maryland and Senator Benjamin Wade of Ohio jointly sponsored a bill that threw out Lincoln's "10 percent plan" and demanded that at least half of the voters in a conquered rebel state take the oath of allegiance before reconstruction could begin. Moreover, the Wade-Davis bill banned ex-Confederates from participating in the drafting of new state constitutions. Finally, the bill guaranteed the equality of freedmen before the law. Congress's reconstruction would be neither as quick nor as forgiving as Lincoln's. Still, the Wade-Davis bill angered radicals because it did not include a provision for black suffrage. When Lincoln exercised his right not to sign the bill and let it die instead, Wade and Davis published a manifesto charging the president with usurpation of power. They warned Lincoln to confine himself to "his executive duties—to obey and execute, not make the laws—to suppress by arms armed rebellion, and leave political organization to Congress."

Undeterred, Lincoln continued to nurture the formation of loyal state governments under his own plan. Four states—Louisiana, Arkansas, Tennessee, and Virginia—fulfilled the president's requirements, but Congress refused to seat representatives from the "Lincoln states." In his last public address in April 1865, Lincoln defended his plan but for the first time expressed publicly his endorsement of suffrage for southern blacks, at least "the very intelligent, and . . . those who serve our cause as soldiers." The announcement demonstrated that Lincoln's thinking about reconstruction was still evolving. Four days later, he was dead.

Land and Labor

Of all the problems raised by emancipation, none proved more critical than the transition from slave to free labor. As federal armies proceeded to invade and occupy the Confederacy during the war, hundreds of thousands of slaves became free workers. Moreover, northern occupation meant that Union armies controlled vast territories where legal title to land had become unclear. The wartime Confiscation Acts punished "traitors" by taking away their property. What to do with federally occupied land and how to organize labor on it engaged former slaves, former slaveholders, Union military commanders, and federal government officials long before the war ended.

Occupying federal troops announced a new labor code. The code required planters to sign contracts with ex-slaves and to pay wages. It also obligated employers to provide food, housing, and medical care. It outlawed whipping, but it reserved to the army the right to discipline blacks who refused to work. The code required black laborers to enter into contracts, work diligently, and remain subordinate and obedient. Military leaders clearly had no intention of promoting a social or economic revolution. Instead, they sought to restore plantation agriculture with wage labor. The effort resulted in a hybrid system of "compulsory free labor" that satisfied no one. Depending on one's point of view, it either provided too little or too much of a break with the past.

Planters complained because the new system fell short of slavery. Blacks could not be "transformed by proclamation," a Louisiana sugar planter warned. Yet under the new system, blacks "are expected to perform their new obligations without coercion, & without the fear of punishment which is essential to stimulate the idle and correct the vicious." Without the right to whip, he argued, the new labor system did not have a chance.

African Americans found the new regime too reminiscent of slavery to be called "free labor." Of its many shortcomings, none disappointed exslaves more than the failure to provide them land of their own. "What's the use of being free if you don't own land enough to be buried in?" one man asked. Freedmen believed they had a moral right to land because they and their ancestors had worked it without compensation for more than two centuries. Moreover, several wartime developments led them to believe that the federal government planned to strengthen black freedom with landownership.

In January 1865, General William T. Sherman set aside part of the coast south of Charleston for black settlement. He devised the plan to relieve himself of the burden of thousands of impoverished blacks who trailed desperately after his army. By June 1865, some forty thousand freedmen sat on 400,000 acres of "Sherman land." In addition, in March 1865, Congress established the Bureau of Refugees, Freedmen, and Abandoned Lands. The Freedmen's Bureau, as it was called, distributed food and clothing to destitute Southerners and eased the transition of blacks from slaves to free persons. Congress also authorized the agency to divide abandoned and confiscated land into 40-acre plots, to rent them to freedmen, and eventually to sell them "with such title as the United States can convey." By June 1865, the bureau had situated nearly ten thousand black families on a half million acres that had been abandoned by fleeing planters. Hundreds of thousands of other ex-slaves eagerly anticipated farms of their own.

Despite the flurry of activity, wartime reconstruction had settled nothing. Two years of controversy had failed to produce agreement about whether the president or Congress had the authority to devise and direct policy or what proper policy should be. Clearly, the nation faced dilemmas almost as trying as those of the war.

The African American Quest for Autonomy

Ex-slaves never had any doubt about what they wanted freedom to mean. They had only to contemplate what they had been denied as slaves. (See "Documenting the American Promise," page 392.) Slaves had to remain on their plantations; freedom allowed blacks to go wherever they pleased. Thus, in the first heady weeks after emancipation, freedmen often abandoned their plantations just to see what was on the other side of the hill. Slaves had to be at work in the fields by dawn; freedom permitted blacks to taste the forbidden pleasure of sleeping through a sunrise. Freedmen also tested the etiquette of racial subordination. "Lizzie's maid passed me today when I was coming from church without speaking to me," huffed one plantation mistress.

To whites, it looked like pure anarchy. Without the discipline of slavery, they said, blacks had reverted to their natural condition: lazy, irresponsible, and wild. Actually, these former slaves were experimenting with freedom, but they could not long afford to roam the countryside, neglect work, and casually provoke whites. Soon, most were back on plantations, at work in the fields and kitchens.

But other items on ex-slaves' agenda of freedom endured. Freedmen did not easily give up their quest for economic independence. In addition, slavery had deliberately kept blacks illiterate, and freedmen emerged from slavery eager to read and write. Moreover, bondage had denied slaves secure family lives, and the restoration of their families became a persistent black aspiration. As a consequence, thousands of black men and women took to the roads in 1865 to look for relations who had been sold away. Couples who emerged from slavery with their marriages intact often rushed to northern military chaplains to legalize their unions.

Another hunger that freedom permitted African Americans to satisfy was independent worship. Under slavery, blacks had often prayed with whites in biracial churches. Intent on religious independence, blacks greeted freedom with a mass exodus from white churches. Some joined the newly established southern branches of all-black northern churches, such as the African Methodist Episcopal Church. Others formed black versions of the major southern denominations, Baptists and Methodists. Slaves had comprehended their tribulations through the lens of their deeply felt Christian faith, and freedmen continued to interpret the events of the Civil War and reconstruction as people of faith.

Presidential Reconstruction

Abraham Lincoln died on April 15, 1865, just hours after John Wilkes Booth had shot him at a Washington, D.C., theater. Chief Justice Salmon P. Chase immediately administered the oath of office to Vice President Andrew Johnson of Tennessee. Congress had adjourned in March, which meant that legislators were away from Washington when Lincoln was killed. They would not reconvene until December. Throughout the summer and fall, therefore, the "accidental president" made critical decisions about the future of the South. Like Lincoln, Johnson believed that responsibility for restoring the Union lay with the president. With dizzying speed, he drew up and executed a plan of reconstruction.

Congress returned to the capital in December to find that, as far as the president and former Confederates were concerned, reconstruction was over. To most Republicans, Johnson's modest demands of ex-rebels made a mockery of the sacrifice of Union soldiers. In an 1863 speech dedicating the cemetery at Gettysburg, Lincoln had spoken of the "great task remaining before us . . . that we here highly resolve that these dead shall not have died in vain— that this nation, under God, shall have a new birth of freedom." Instead, Johnson had acted as midwife to the rebirth of the Old South. He had achieved political reunification at the cost of black liberty. To let his program stand, Republican legislators said, would mean that the North's dead had indeed died in vain.

Johnson's Program of Reconciliation

Born in 1808 in Raleigh, North Carolina, Andrew Johnson was the son of poor, illiterate parents. Unable to afford to send her son to school, Johnson's widowed mother apprenticed him to a tailor. Self-educated and ambitious, he later worked as a tailor in Tennessee, accumulated a fortune in land, acquired five slaves, and built a career in politics championing the South's common white people and assailing its "illegitimate, swaggering, bastard, scrub aristocracy." The only senator from a Confederate state to remain loyal to the Union, Johnson held slaveholders responsible for secession. Less than two weeks before he became president, he made it clear what he would do to the rascals if he ever had the chance: "I would arrest them—I would try them—I would convict them and I would hang them."

In reality, however, Johnson was no friend of northern radicals. A southern Democrat all his life, Johnson occupied the White House only because the Republican Party in 1864 had needed to broaden its appeal to loyal, Union-supporting Democrats. Johnson favored traditional Democratic causes, vigorously defending states' rights (but not secession) and opposing Republican efforts to expand the power of the federal government.

Moreover, Johnson had been a steadfast defender of slavery. He had owned slaves until 1862, when Tennessee rebels, angry at his Unionism, confiscated them. He only grudgingly accepted emancipation. When he did, it was more because of his hatred for slaveholders than sympathy for slaves. "Damn the negroes," he said. "I am fighting those traitorous aristocrats, their masters." At a time when the nation faced its moment of truth regarding black Americans, the new president harbored unshakable racist convictions. Africans, Johnson said, were "inferior to the white man in point of intellect—better calculated in physical structure to undergo drudgery and hardship."

Johnson presented his plan of reconstruction as a continuation of Lincoln's plan, and in some ways it was. Like Lincoln, he stressed reconciliation between the Union and the defeated Confederacy and rapid restoration of civil government in the South. He offered to pardon most ex-rebels. Johnson recognized the state governments created by Lincoln and set out his own requirements for restoring the rebel states to the Union. All that the citizens of a state had to do was to renounce the right of secession, deny that the debts of the Confederacy were legal and binding, and ratify the Thirteenth Amendment abolishing slavery, which became part of the Constitution in December 1865. Johnson's plan ignored Lincoln's acceptance near the end of his life of some form of limited black voting.

The Meaning of Freedom

On New Year's Day 1863, President Abraham Lincoln issued the Emancipation Proclamation. It states that "all persons held as slaves" within the states still in rebellion "are, and henceforward shall be, free." Although it did not in and of itself free any slaves, it transformed the character of the war. Despite often intolerable conditions, black people focused on the possibilities of freedom.

DOCUMENT 1. Letter from John Q. A. Dennis to Edwin M. Stanton, July 26, 1864

John Q. A. Dennis, formerly a slave in Maryland, wrote to Secretary of War Edwin M. Stanton to ask his help in reuniting his family.

Boston

Dear Sir I am Glad that I have the Honour to Write you afew line I have been in troble for about four yars my Dear wife was taken from me Nov 19th 1859 and left me with three Children and I being a Slave At the time Could Not do Anny thing for the poor little Children for my master it was took me Carry me some forty mile from them So I Could Not do for them and the man that they live with half feed them and half Cloth them & beat them like dogs & when I was admitted to go to see them it use to brake my heart & Now I say again I am Glad to have the honour to write to you to see if you Can Do Anny thing for me or for my poor little Children I was keap in Slavy untell last Novr 1863. then the Good lord sent the Cornel borne [federal Colonel William Birney?] Down their in Marland in worsester Co So as I have been recently freed I have but letle to live on but I am Striveing Dear Sir but what I went too know of you Sir is it possible for me to go & take my Children from those men that keep them in Savery if it is possible will you pleas give me a permit from your hand then I think they would let them go. . . .

Hon sir will you please excuse my Miserable writeing & answer me as soon as you can I want get the little Children out of Slavery, I being Criple would like to know of you also if I Cant be permited to rase a Shool Down there & on what turm I Could be admited to Do so No more At present Dear Hon Sir

SOURCE: Excerpt from "Letter from John Q. A. Dennis to Edwin M. Stanton, July 26, 1864." In *Freedom: A Documentary History of Emancipation 1861–1867*, Series 1, Volume 1, The Destruction of Slavery, p. 386, by Ira Berlin, Joseph P. Reidy, and Leslie S. Rowland, eds. Copyright © 1985. Reprinted with the permission of Cambridge University Press.

DOCUMENT 2. Report from Reverend A. B. Randall, February 28, 1865

Freedom also prompted ex-slaves to seek legal marriages, which under slavery had been impossible. Writing from Little Rock, Arkansas, A. B. Randall, the white chaplain of a black regiment, in a report of February 1865 to the adjutant general of the Union army, affirmed the importance of marriage to freed slaves and emphasized their conviction that emancipation was just the first step toward full freedom.

Weddings, just now, are very popular, and abundant among the Colored People. They have just learned, of the Special Order No. 15. of Gen Thomas [Adjutant General Lorenzo Thomas] by which, they may not only be lawfully married, but have their Marriage Certificates, Recorded; in a book furnished by the Government. This is most desirable. . . . Those who were captured . . . at Ivy's Ford, on the 17th of January, by Col Brooks, had their Marriage Certificates, taken from them; and destroyed; and then were roundly cursed, for having such papers in their posession. I have married, during the month, at this Post; Twenty five couples; mostly, those, who have families; & have been living together for years. I try to dissuade single men, who are soldiers, from marrying, till their time of enlistment is out: as that course seems to me, to be most judicious.

The Colord People here, generally consider, this war not only; their exodus, from bondage; but the road, to Responsibility; Competency; and an honorable Citizenship—God grant that their hopes and expectations may be fully realized.

SOURCE: Excerpt from "Report from Reverend A. B. Randall, February 28, 1865." In *Freedom: A Documentary History of Emancipation 1861–1867*, Series 2, Volume 1, The Black Military Experience, p. 712, by Ira Berlin, Joseph P. Reidy, and Leslie S. Rowland, eds. Copyright © 1982. Reprinted with the permission of Cambridge University Press.

DOCUMENT 3. Petition "to the Union Convention of Tennessee Assembled in the Capitol at Nashville," January 9, 1865

Early efforts at political reconstruction prompted petitions from former slaves demanding civil and political rights. In January 1865, black Tennesseans petitioned a

convention of white Unionists debating the reorganization of state government.

We the undersigned petitioners, American citizens of African descent, natives and residents of Tennessee, and devoted friends of the great National cause, do most respectfully ask a patient hearing of your honorable body in regard to matters deeply affecting the future condition of our unfortunate and long suffering race.

First of all, however, we would say that words are too weak to tell how profoundly grateful we are to the Federal Government for the good work of freedom which it is gradually carrying forward; and for the Emancipation Proclamation which has set free all the slaves in some of the rebellious States, as well as many of the slaves in Tennessee. . . .

We claim freedom, as our natural right, and ask that in harmony and co-operation with the nation at large, you should cut up by the roots the system of slavery, which is not only a wrong to us, but the source of all the evil which at present afflicts the State. For slavery, corrupt itself, corrupted nearly all, also, around it, so that it has influenced nearly all the slave States to rebel against the Federal Government, in order to set up a government of pirates under which slavery might be perpetrated.

In the contest between the nation and slavery, our unfortunate people have sided, by instinct, with the former. We have little fortune to devote to the national cause, for a hard fate has hitherto forced us to live in poverty, but we do devote to its success, our hopes, our toils, our whole heart, our sacred honor, and our lives. We will work, pray, live, and, if need be, die for the Union, as cheerfully as ever a white patriot died for his country. The color of our skin does not lessen in the least degree, our love either for God or for the land of our birth. . . .

We know the burdens of citizenship, and are ready to bear them. We know the duties of the good citizen, and are ready to perform them cheerfully, and would ask to be put in a position in which we can discharge them more effectually. . . .

This is a democracy—a government of the people. It should aim to make every man, without regard to the color of his skin, the amount of his wealth, or the character of his religious faith, feel personally interested in its welfare. Every man who lives under the Government should feel that it is his property, his treasure, the bulwark and defence of himself and his family, his pearl of great price, which he must preserve, protect, and defend faithfully at all times, on all occasions, in every possible manner.

This is not a Democratic Government if a numerous, law-abiding, industrious, and useful class of citizens, born and bred on the soil, are to be treated as aliens and enemies, as an inferior degraded class, who must have no voice in the Government which they support, protect and defend, with all their heart, soul, mind, and body, both in peace and war. . . .

The possibility that the negro suffrage proposition may shock popular prejudice at first sight, is not a conclusive argument against its wisdom and policy. No proposition ever met with more furious or general opposition than the one to enlist colored soldiers in the United States army. The opponents of the measure exclaimed on all hands that the negro was a coward; that he would not fight; that one white man, with a whip in his hand could put to flight a regiment of them; that the experiment would end in the utter rout and ruin of the Federal army. Yet the colored man has fought so well, on almost every occasion, that the rebel government is prevented, only by its fears and distrust of being able to force him to fight for slavery as well as he fights against it, from putting half a million of negroes into its ranks.

The Government has asked the colored man to fight for its preservation and gladly has he done it. It can afford to trust him with a vote as safely as it trusted him with a bayonet.

SOURCE: Excerpt from "Petition to the Union Convention of Tennessee Assembled in the Capitol at Nashville, January 9, 1865." In *Freedom: A Documentary History of Emancipation 1861–1867*, Series 2, Volume 1, The Black Military Experience, p. 811-16, by Ira Berlin, Joseph P. Reidy, and Leslie S. Rowland, eds. Copyright © 1982. Reprinted with the permission of Cambridge University Press.

QUESTIONS FOR ANALYSIS AND DEBATE

1. How does John Q. A. Dennis interpret his responsibility as a father?
2. Why do you think ex-slaves wanted their marriages legalized?
3. Why, according to the Union Convention of Tennessee, did blacks deserve voting rights?

Johnson's eagerness to normalize relations with southern states and his lack of sympathy for blacks also led him to instruct military and government officials to return to pardoned ex-Confederates all confiscated and abandoned land, even if it was in the hands of freedmen. Reformers were shocked. They had expected the president's vendetta against planters to mean the permanent confiscation of the South's plantations and the distribution of the land to loyal freedmen. Instead, his instructions canceled the promising beginnings made by General Sherman and the Freedmen's Bureau to settle blacks on land of their own. As one freedman observed, "Things was hurt by Mr. Lincoln getting killed."

Southern Resistance and Black Codes

In the summer of 1865, delegates across the South gathered to draw up the new state constitutions required by Johnson's plan of reconstruction. While they had been defeated, clearly whites had not been subdued. Rather than take their medicine, delegates choked on even the president's mild requirements. Refusing to declare their secession ordinances null and void, the South Carolina and Georgia conventions merely "repudiated" their ordinances, preserving in principle their right to secede. In addition, South Carolina and Mississippi refused to repudiate their Confederate war debts. Finally, Mississippi rejected the Thirteenth Amendment outright, and Alabama rejected it in part. Despite these defiant acts, Johnson did not demand that Southerners comply with his lenient terms. By failing to draw a hard line, he rekindled southern resistance. White Southerners began to think that by standing up for themselves they—not victorious Northerners—would shape the transition from slavery to freedom. In the fall of 1865, newly elected southern legislators attempted to do just that.

State governments across the South adopted a series of laws known as the black codes. While emancipation had brought freedmen important rights that they had lacked as slaves—to own property, to make contracts, to marry legally, and to sue and be sued in court—the black codes made a travesty of freedom. They sought to keep blacks subordinate to whites by subjecting blacks to every sort of discrimination. Several states made it illegal for blacks to own a gun. Mississippi made insulting gestures and language by blacks a criminal offense. Blacks were barred from jury duty. Not a single southern state granted any black—no matter how educated, wealthy, or refined—the right to vote.

At the core of the black codes, however, lay the matter of labor. Faced with the death of slavery and the disintegration of plantations, legislators sought to hustle freedmen back into traditional tasks. South Carolina attempted to limit blacks to either farmwork or domestic service by requiring them to pay annual taxes of $10 to $100 to work in any other occupation. Mississippi declared that blacks who did not possess written evidence of employment could be declared vagrants and be subject to fines or involuntary plantation labor. Most states allowed judges to bind black children—orphans and others whose parents they deemed unable to support them—to white employers. Under these so-called apprenticeship laws, courts bound out thousands of black children to planter "guardians."

Johnson refused to intervene decisively. A staunch defender of states' rights, he believed that the citizens of every state, even those citizens who had attempted to destroy the Union, should be free to write their own constitutions and laws. Moreover, since Johnson was as eager as other white Southerners to restore white supremacy and black subordination, the black codes did not offend him.

But Johnson also followed the path he believed offered him the greatest political return. A conservative Tennessee Democrat at the head of a northern Republican Party, he began to look southward for political allies. By pardoning planters and Confederate officials, by acquiescing in the South's black codes, and by accepting the new southern governments even when they failed to satisfy his minimal demands, he won useful friends.

If Northerners had any doubts about the mood of the South, they evaporated in the elections of 1865. To represent them in Congress, white Southerners chose former Confederates, not loyal Unionists. Of the eighty senators and representatives they sent to Washington, fifteen had served in the Confederate army, ten of them as generals. Another sixteen had served in civil and judicial posts in the Confederacy. Nine others had served in the Confederate Congress. One—Alexander Stephens—had been vice president of the Confederacy. In December, this remarkable group arrived on the steps of the nation's Capitol building to be seated in Congress. As one Georgian later remarked: "It looked as though Richmond had moved to Washington."

Expansion of Black Rights and Federal Authority

Southerners had blundered monumentally. They had assumed that what Andrew Johnson was willing to accept, the northern public and Congress would accept as well. But southern intransigence compelled even moderate Republicans to conclude that ex-rebels were a "generation of vipers," still dangerous and untrustworthy.

The black codes in particular soured moderate Republicans on the South. The codes became a symbol of southern intentions not to accept the verdict

THE LOST CAUSE
While politicians in Washington, D.C., debated the future of the South, white Southerners were coming to grips with their emotions and history. They began to refer to their failure to secede from the Union as the "Lost Cause." They enshrined the memory of certain former Confederates, especially Robert E. Lee, whose nobility and courage represented the white South's image of itself. This quilt from about 1870, with Lee stitched in the center, illustrates how common whites incorporated the symbols of the Lost Cause into their daily lives. The maker of the quilt, a woman whose name is unknown, also included miniature Confederate flags and memorial ribbons.
Valentine Museum, Cook Collection.

of the battlefields, but instead to "restore all of slavery but its name." Northerners were hardly saints when it came to racial justice, but black freedom had become a hallowed war aim. "We tell the white men of Mississippi," the *Chicago Tribune* roared, "that the men of the North will convert the State of Mississippi into a frog pond before they will allow such laws to disgrace one foot of the soil in which the bones of our soldiers sleep and over which the flag of freedom waves."

Moderates represented the mainstream of the Republican Party and wanted only assurance that slavery and treason were dead. They did not champion black equality or the confiscation of plantations or black voting, as did the Radicals, a minority faction within the Republican Party. In December 1865, however, when Congress convened in Washington, it became clear that southern obstinacy had succeeded in forging unity (at least temporarily) among Republican factions. Exercising Congress's right to determine the qualifications of its members, Republicans refused to seat the southern representatives. Rather than accept Johnson's claim that the "work of restoration" was done, Congress challenged his executive power. Congressional Republicans enjoyed a three-to-one majority over the Democrats, and if they could agree on a program of reconstruction, they could easily pass legislation and even override presidential vetoes.

The moderates took the initiative. Senator Lyman Trumbull of Illinois declared that the president's policy of trusting southern whites proved that the ex-slave would "be tyrannized over, abused, and virtually reenslaved without some legislation by the nation for his protection." Early in 1866, the moderates produced two bills that strengthened the federal shield. The first, the Freedmen's Bureau bill, prolonged the life of the agency established by the previous Congress. Since the end of the war, it had distributed food, supervised labor contracts, and sponsored schools for freedmen. Arguing that the Constitution never contemplated a "system for the support of indigent persons," President Andrew Johnson vetoed the Freedmen's Bureau bill. Congress failed by a narrow margin to override the president's veto.

Johnson's shocking veto galvanized nearly unanimous Republican support for the moderates' second measure, the Civil Rights Act. Designed to nullify the black codes, it affirmed the rights of blacks to enjoy "full and equal benefit of all laws and proceedings for the security of person and property as is enjoyed by white citizens." The act boldly required the end of legal discrimination in state laws and represented an extraordinary expansion of black rights and federal authority. The president argued that the civil rights bill amounted to an "unconstitutional invasion of states' rights" and vetoed it. In essence, he denied that the federal government possessed authority to protect the civil rights of blacks.

The president did not have the final word. In April 1866, an incensed Republican Party again pushed a civil rights bill through Congress and overrode another presidential veto. In July, it sustained another Freedmen's Bureau Act. For the first time in American history, Congress had overridden presidential vetoes of major legislation. As a worried South Carolinian observed, Johnson had succeeded in uniting the Republicans and probably touched off "a fight this fall such as has never been seen."

Congressional Reconstruction

By the summer of 1866, President Andrew Johnson and Congress had dropped their gloves and stood toe to toe in a bare-knuckled contest unprecedented in American history. Moderate Republicans made a major effort to resolve the dilemma of reconstruction by amending the Constitution, but the obstinacy of Johnson and white Southerners pushed Republican moderates ever closer to the Radicals and to acceptance of additional federal intervention in the South. In time, white men in Congress debated whether to give the ballot to black men. Outside of Congress, blacks raised their voices on behalf of color-blind voting rights, while women argued to make voting sex-blind as well.

The Fourteenth Amendment and Escalating Violence

In April 1866, Republican moderates introduced the Fourteenth Amendment to the Constitution, Congress passed it in June, and two years later it gained the necessary ratification of three-fourths of the states. The most important provisions of this complex amendment made all native-born or naturalized persons American citizens and prohibited states from abridging the "privileges and immunities" of citizens, depriving them of "life, liberty, or property without due process of law," and denying them "equal protection of the laws." By making blacks national citizens, the amendment nullified the *Dred Scott* decision of 1857 and provided a national guarantee of equality before the law. In essence, it protected the rights of citizens against violation by their own state governments.

The Fourteenth Amendment also dealt with voting rights. Rather than explicitly granting the vote to blacks, as Radicals wanted, the amendment gave Congress the right to reduce the congressional representation of states that withheld suffrage from some of its adult male population. In other words, white Southerners could either allow their former slaves to vote or see their representation in Washington slashed.

Tennessee approved the Fourteenth Amendment in July, and Congress promptly welcomed its representatives and senators back. Had Johnson counseled other southern states to ratify this relatively mild amendment and warned them that they faced the fury of an outraged Republican Party if they refused, they might have listened. Instead, Johnson advised Southerners to reject the Fourteenth Amendment and to rely on him to trounce the Republicans in the fall congressional elections.

Johnson had decided to make the Fourteenth Amendment the overriding issue of the 1866 congressional elections and to gather its white opponents into a new conservative party, the National Union Party. In August, his supporters met in Philadelphia. Democrats came, but Republicans did not—Johnson failed to forge a new conservative party behind him.

The president's strategy had already suffered a setback two weeks earlier when whites in several southern cities went on rampages against blacks. It was less an outbreak of violence than an escalation of the violence that had never ceased. In New Orleans, a mob assaulted delegates to a black suffrage convention, and thirty-four blacks died. In Memphis, white mobs hurtled through the black sections of town and killed at least forty-six people. The slaughter shocked Northerners and renewed skepticism about Johnson's claim that southern whites could be trusted. "Who doubts that the Freedmen's Bureau ought to be abolished forthwith," a New Yorker observed sarcastically, "and the blacks remitted to the paternal care of their old masters, who 'understand the nigger, you know, a great deal better than the Yankees can.'"

MEMPHIS RIOTS, MAY 1866
On May 1, 1866, two carriages, one driven by a white man and the other by a black man, collided on a busy Memphis street. This minor incident spiraled into three days of bloody racial violence in which dozens of blacks and two whites died. Racial friction was common in postwar Memphis, and white newspapers routinely heaped abuse on black citizens. "Would to God they were back in Africa, or some other seaport town," the Memphis **Argus** *shouted two days before the riot erupted, "anywhere but here." South Memphis, pictured in this lithograph from* **Harper's Weekly,** *was a shantytown where the families of black soldiers stationed at nearby Fort Pickering lived. The army commander refused to send troops to protect soldiers' families and property, and white mobs ran wild.*
Library of Congress.

The 1866 election resulted in an overwhelming Republican victory in which the party retained its three-to-one congressional majority. Johnson had bet that Northerners would not support federal protection of black rights. But the Fourteenth Amendment was not radical enough to drive Republican voters into Johnson's camp, and the war was still fresh in northern minds. As one Republican explained, southern whites "with all their intelligence were traitors, the blacks with all their ignorance were loyal."

Radical Reconstruction and Military Rule

The elections of 1866 should have taught southern whites the folly of relying on Andrew Johnson as a guide through the thicket of reconstruction. But when Johnson continued to urge Southerners toward rejection of the Fourteenth Amendment, every southern state except Tennessee voted it down. In the void created by the South's rejection of the moderates' program, the Radicals seized the initiative.

Each act of defiance by southern whites had boosted the standing of the Radicals within the Republican Party. At the core was a small group of men who had cut their political teeth on the antebellum campaign against slavery, who had goaded Lincoln toward making the war a crusade for freedom, and who had carried into the postwar period the conviction that only federal power could protect the rights of the freedmen. Except for freedmen themselves, no one did more to make freedom the "mighty moral question of the age." Men like Senator Charles Sumner, that pompous but sincere

Massachusetts crusader, and Thaddeus Stevens, the caustic representative from Pennsylvania, did not speak with a single voice, but they united in calling for civil and political equality. They insisted on extending to ex-slaves the same opportunities that northern working people enjoyed under the free-labor system. The southern states were "like clay in the hands of the potter," Stevens declared in January 1867, and he called on Congress to begin reconstruction all over again.

In March 1867, moderates joined the Radicals to overturn the Johnson state governments and initiate military rule of the South. The Military Reconstruction Act (and three subsequent acts) divided the ten unreconstructed Confederate states into five military districts. Congress placed a Union general in charge of each district and instructed him to "suppress insurrection, disorder, and violence" and to begin political reform. After the military had completed voter registration, which would include black men and exclude all those barred by the Fourteenth Amendment from holding public office, voters would elect delegates to conventions that would draw up new state constitutions. Each constitution would guarantee black suffrage. When the voters of each state had approved the constitution and its legislature had ratified the Fourteenth Amendment, the state could submit its work to Congress. If Congress approved, the state's senators and representatives could be seated and political reunification would be accomplished.

Reconstruction Military Districts, 1867

Radicals proclaimed the provision for black suffrage "a prodigious triumph." The doggedness of the Radicals and of African Americans, along with the pigheadedness of Johnson and the white South, had swept the Republican Party far beyond the limited suffrage provisions of the Fourteenth Amendment. Republicans finally agreed with Sumner that only the voting power of ex-slaves could bring about a permanent revolution in the South. Indeed, suffrage provided blacks with a powerful instrument of change and self-protection. When combined with the disfranchisement of

thousands of ex-rebels, it promised to cripple any neo-Confederate resurgence and guarantee Republican governments in the South.

Despite its bold suffrage provision, the Military Reconstruction Act of 1867 disappointed those who advocated the confiscation and redistribution of southern plantations. Thaddeus Stevens believed that at bottom reconstruction was an economic problem. He agreed wholeheartedly with the ex-slave who said, "Give us our own land and we take care of ourselves, but without land, the old masters can hire us or starve us, as they please." But most Republicans believed they had already provided blacks with the critical tools: equal legal rights and the ballot. If blacks were to get forty acres, they would have to gain it themselves.

Declaring that he would rather sever his right arm than sign such a formula for "anarchy and chaos," Andrew Johnson vetoed the Military Reconstruction Act. Congress overrode his veto the very same day, dramatizing the shift in power from the executive to the legislative branch of government. With the passage of the Reconstruction Acts of 1867, congressional reconstruction was virtually completed. Congress had left white folks owning most of the South's land, but in a radical departure it had given black men the ballot. More than any other provision, black suffrage justifies the term "radical reconstruction." In 1867, the nation began an unprecedented experiment in interracial democracy—at least in the South, for Congress's plan did not touch the North. Soon the former Confederate states would become the primary theater for political struggle. But before the spotlight swung away from Washington, the president and Congress had one more scene to play.

Impeaching a President

Despite his defeats, Andrew Johnson had no intention of yielding control of reconstruction. In a dozen ways he sabotaged Congress's will and encouraged white belligerence and resistance. He issued a flood of pardons to undermine efforts at political and economic change. He waged war against the Freedmen's Bureau by removing officers who sympathized too fully with ex-slaves. And he replaced Union generals eager to enforce Congress's Reconstruction Acts with conservative men who were eager to defeat them. Johnson claimed that he was merely defending the "violated Constitution." At bottom, however, the president subverted congressional reconstruction to protect southern whites from what he considered the horrors of "Negro domination."

When Congress learned that overriding Johnson's vetoes did not ensure victory, it attempted to tie the president's hands. Congress required that all orders to field commanders pass through the General of the Army, Ulysses S. Grant, who Congress believed was sympathetic to southern freedmen, Unionists, and Republicans. It also enacted the Tenure of Office Act in 1867, which required the approval of the Senate for the removal of any government official who had been appointed with Senate consent. Congress intended that the Tenure of Office Act would protect Secretary of War Edwin M. Stanton, the last remaining friend of radical reconstruction in the cabinet. Some Republicans, however, believed that nothing less than removing Johnson from office could save reconstruction, and they initiated a crusade to impeach the president.

As long as Johnson refrained from breaking a law, however, impeachment languished. The Republicans got their chance in August 1867 when Johnson suspended Secretary of War Stanton from office. As required by the Tenure of Office Act, he requested the Senate to consent to dismissal. When the Senate balked, the president removed Stanton anyway. "Is the President crazy, or only drunk?" asked a dumbfounded Republican moderate. "I'm afraid his doings will make us all favor impeachment."

News of Johnson's open defiance of the law did indeed convince every Republican in the House to vote for a resolution impeaching the president. Chief Justice Salmon Chase presided over the Senate trial, which lasted from March until May 1868. Chase refused to allow Johnson's opponents to raise the broad issues of misuse of power and forced them to argue their case exclusively on the narrow legal grounds of Johnson's removal of Stanton. Johnson's lawyers argued that he had not committed a criminal offense, that the Tenure of Office Act was unconstitutional, and that in any case it did not apply to Stanton, who had been appointed by Lincoln. When the critical vote came, seven moderate Republicans broke with their party and joined the Democrats in voting not guilty. With thirty-five in favor and nineteen opposed, the impeachment forces fell one vote short of the two-thirds needed to convict.

Johnson survived, but he did not come through the ordeal unscathed. After his trial he called a truce, and for the remaining ten months of his term reconstruction proceeded unhindered by presidential interference.

The Fifteenth Amendment and Women's Demands

In February 1869, Republicans passed the Fifteenth Amendment to the Constitution. The amendment prohibited states from depriving any citizen of the right to vote because of "race, color, or previous condition of servitude." The Reconstruction Acts of 1867 had already required black suffrage in the South, but the Fifteenth Amendment extended black voting to the entire nation. Partisan advantage played an important role in the amendment's passage. Gains by northern Democrats in the 1868 elections worried Republicans, and black voters now represented the balance of power in several northern states. By giving ballots to northern blacks, Republicans could lessen their political vulnerability. As one Republican congressman observed, "Party expediency and exact justice coincide for once."

Some Republicans, however, found the final wording of the Fifteenth Amendment "lame and halting." Rather than absolutely guaranteeing the right to vote, the amendment merely prohibited exclusion on grounds of race. The distinction would prove to be significant. In time, inventive white Southerners would devise tests of literacy and property and other apparently nonracial measures that would effectively disfranchise blacks and yet not violate the Fifteenth Amendment. But an amendment that guaranteed the right to vote courted defeat in the North. Rising antiforeign sentiment—against the Chinese in California and against European immigrants in the Northeast—caused states to resist giving up control of suffrage requirements. In March 1870, after three-fourths of the states had ratified it, the Fifteenth Amendment became part of the Constitution. Republicans generally breathed a sigh of relief, confident that black suffrage had been "the last great point that remained to be settled of the issues of the war."

But the Republican Party's reappraisal of suffrage had ignored completely the small band of politicized and energized women who had emerged from the war demanding "the ballot for the two disenfranchised classes, negroes and women." Founding the Equal Rights Association in 1866, Susan B. Anthony and Elizabeth Cady

SUSAN B. ANTHONY
Like many outspoken suffragists, Anthony, depicted here in 1852, had begun her public career working on behalf of temperance and abolition. But she grew tired of laboring under the direction of male clergymen—"white orthodox little saints," she called them—who controlled the reform movements and who routinely dismissed the opinions of women. Anthony's continued passion for other causes—improving working conditions for labor, for example—led some conservatives to oppose women's political rights because they equated the suffragist cause with radicalism in general. Women could not easily overcome such views, and the long struggle for the vote eventually drew millions of women into public life.
Susan B. Anthony House, Inc.

Stanton lobbied for "a government by the people, and the whole people; for the people and the whole people." They felt betrayed when their old anti-slavery allies, who now occupied positions of national power, proved to be fickle and refused to work for their goals. "It was the Negro's hour," Frederick Douglass later explained. The Republican Party had to avoid anything that might jeopardize black gains, Charles Sumner declared. He suggested that woman suffrage could be "the great question of the future."

It was not the first time women's expectations had been dashed. The Fourteenth Amendment had provided for punishment of any state that excluded voters on the basis of race but not on the basis of sex. It had also introduced the word *male* into the Constitution when it referred to a citizen's right to vote. Stanton had predicted that "if that word 'male' be inserted, it will take us a century at least to get it out." The Fifteenth Amendment proved to be no less disappointing. Although women fought hard to include the word *sex*, the amendment denied states the right to forbid suffrage only on the basis of race. Stanton and Anthony condemned the Republicans' "negro first" strategy and concluded that woman "must not put her trust in man."

Although the Fifteenth Amendment left women with more work to do, northern Republicans declared victory and scratched the "Negro question" from the agenda of national politics. As the crusader for equality Wendell Phillips argued, the black man held "sufficient shield in his own hands. . . . Whatever he suffers will be largely now, and in future, his own fault." Reformers like Phillips had no idea of the violent struggles that lay ahead.

The Struggle in the South

While Northerners believed they had discharged their responsibilities with the Reconstruction Acts and the amendments to the Constitution, Southerners knew that the battle had just begun. Black suffrage and large-scale rebel disfranchisement that came with congressional reconstruction had destroyed traditional southern politics and established the foundation for the rise of the Republican Party in the South. Gathering together outsiders and outcasts, the southern Republicans won elections, wrote new state constitutions, and formed new state governments.

Challenging the established class for political control was dangerous business. Equally dangerous were the confrontations that took place on farms and plantations across the South. In the countryside, blacks sought to give practical, everyday meaning to their newly won legal and political equality. But ex-masters like David Golightly Harris and other whites had their own ideas about the social and economic arrangements that should replace slavery. Freedom remained contested territory, and Southerners fought pitched battles with one another to determine the contours of their postemancipation world.

Freedmen, Yankees, and Yeomen

African Americans made up the majority of southern Republicans. Freedmen realized that without the ballot they were almost powerless, and they threw themselves into the suffrage campaign. Southern black men gained voting rights in 1867, and within months virtually every eligible black man had registered to vote. Black women, like white women, remained disfranchised, but black women mobilized along with black men. They attended political rallies and parades and in the 1868 presidential election bravely wore buttons supporting the Republican candidate, General Ulysses S. Grant. Southern blacks did not have identical political priorities, but almost all voted Republican, and they united in their desire for education and equal treatment before the laws.

Northern whites who decided to make the South their home after the war were a second element of the South's Republican Party. Conservative white Southerners called any northern migrant a "carpetbagger," a man so poor that he could pack all his earthly belongings in a single carpet-sided suitcase and swoop southward like a buzzard to "fatten on our misfortunes." But most Northerners who moved south were restless, relatively well-educated young men, often former Union officers and Freedmen's Bureau agents who looked upon the South as they did the West—as a promising place to make a living. They expected that a South without slavery would prosper, and they wanted to be part of it. Northerners in the southern Republican Party consistently supported programs that encouraged vigorous economic development along the lines of the northern free-labor model.

Southern whites made up the third element of the Republican Party in the South. Approximately one out of four white Southerners voted Republican. The other three cursed those who did. They condemned southern-born white Republicans as traitors to their region and their race and called them "scalawags," a term for runty horses and low-down, good-for-nothing rascals. Yeoman farmers accounted for the vast majority of white Republicans in the South. Some were Unionists who

emerged from the war with bitter memories of Confederate persecution. Some small farmers also welcomed the Republican Party because it promised to end favoritism toward the interests of plantation owners. Yeomen usually supported initiatives for public schools and for expanding economic opportunity in the South.

The Republican Party in the South, then, was made up of freedmen, Yankees, and yeomen—an improbable coalition. The mix of races, regions, and classes inevitably meant friction as each group maneuvered to define the party. But reconstruction represents an extraordinary moment in American politics: Through the Republican Party, blacks and whites joined together to pursue political change. Formally, of course, only men participated in politics—casting ballots and holding offices—but women also played parts in the political struggle. Women joined in parades and rallies, attended stump speeches, and even campaigned.

Reconstruction politics was not for cowards. Any political act took courage. Most whites in the South condemned the entire political process as illegitimate and felt justified in doing whatever it took to stamp out Republicanism. Violence against blacks—the "white terror"—took brutal institutional form in 1866 with the formation of the Ku Klux Klan, a social club of Confederate veterans that quickly developed into a paramilitary organization armed against Republicans. The Klan went on a rampage of whipping, hanging, shooting, burning, and throat-cutting to defeat reconstruction and restore white supremacy. Rapid demobilization of the Union army after the war left only twenty thousand troops to patrol the entire South, a vast territory. Without effective military protection, southern Republicans had to take care of themselves.

Republican Rule

The Reconstruction Acts required southern states to draw up new constitutions before they could be readmitted to Congress. Beginning in the fall of 1867, states held elections for delegates to constitutional conventions. About 40 percent of the white electorate stayed home, either because they had been disfranchised or because they were boycotting politics. Republicans won three-fourths of the seats. About 15 percent of the Republican delegates were Northerners who had moved south, 25 percent were African Americans, and 60 percent were white

Southerners. As a British visitor observed, the elections reflected "the mighty revolution that had taken place in America." But Democrats described the conventions as zoos of "baboons, monkeys, mules . . . and other jackasses." In fact, the conventions brought together serious, purposeful men who hammered out the legal framework for a new order.

The reconstruction constitutions introduced two broad categories of changes in the South: those that reduced aristocratic privilege and increased democratic equality and those that expanded the state's responsibility for the general welfare. These forward-looking constitutions provided blueprints for a new South. But they stopped short of the specific reforms advocated by some southern Republicans. Despite the wishes of virtually every former slave, no southern constitution confiscated and redistributed land. And despite the prediction of Unionists that unless all former Confederates were banned from politics they would storm back and wreck reconstruction, no constitution disfranchised ex-rebels wholesale.

But Democrats were blind to the limits of the Republican program. In their eyes, they stared at wild revolution. According to Democrats, Republican victories initiated "black and tan" (ex-slave and mulatto) governments. But the claims of "Negro domination" had almost no validity. Four out of five Republican voters were black men, but more than four out of five Republican officeholders were white. Southerners sent fourteen black congressmen and two black senators to Washington, but only 6 percent of Southerners in Congress during reconstruction were black. With the exception of South Carolina, where blacks briefly held a majority in one house of the legislature, no state experienced "Negro rule," despite black majorities in the populations of three states.

In almost every state, voters ratified the new constitutions and swept Republicans into power. After they ratified the Fourteenth Amendment, the former Confederate states were readmitted to Congress. Southern Republicans then turned to a staggering array of problems. Wartime destruction still littered the landscape. The South's share of the nation's wealth had fallen from 30 percent to only 12 percent. Manufacturing limped along at a fraction of prewar levels, agricultural production remained anemic, and the region's railroads had hardly advanced from the devastated condition in which Sherman had left them. Without the efforts

CONGRESSMAN JOHN R. LYNCH
Although whites almost always maintained control of reconstruction politics, over six hundred blacks served in legislatures in the South. Ex-slaves made up the majority of the black legislators. The Union Army freed John R. Lynch of Mississippi, and he gained an education at a Natchez freedmen's school. Lynch achieved power at an extraordinary age. He was only twenty-four when he became speaker of Mississippi's House. In 1872, he joined six other African Americans in Congress in Washington, D.C., where in support of civil rights legislation he told stories from his personal experience of being forced to occupy railroad smoking cars with gamblers and drunks. After reconstruction ended, Lynch practiced law and fought for an honest history of reconstruction legislatures, which he argued were the "best governments those States ever had." Natchez photographer Henry C. Norman took this powerful photograph, probably in the early 1870s.
Collection of Thomas H. Gandy and Joan W. Gandy.

of the Freedmen's Bureau, black and white Southerners would have starved. Moreover, reactionary violence and racial harassment dogged Southerners who sought reform. In this desperate context,

Republicans struggled to breathe life into their new state governments.

Activity focused on three major areas. First, every state inaugurated a system of public education and began building schools and training teachers. Before the Civil War, whites had deliberately kept slaves illiterate, and planter-dominated governments rarely spent tax money to educate the children of yeomen. By 1875, half of Mississippi's and South Carolina's eligible children (the majority of whom were black) attended school. Despite underfunding and dilapidated facilities, literacy rates rose sharply. Although public schools were racially segregated, education remained for many blacks a tangible, deeply satisfying benefit of freedom and Republican rule.

Second, states attacked racial discrimination and defended civil rights. Republicans especially resisted efforts to segregate blacks from whites in public transportation. Mississippi levied fines of up to $1,000 and three years in jail for railroads, steamboats, hotels, and theaters that denied "full and equal rights" to all citizens. But passing color-blind laws was one thing; enforcing them was another. Segregation developed at white insistence despite the law and became a feature of southern life long before the end of reconstruction.

Third, Republican governments launched ambitious programs of economic development. They envisioned a South of diversified agriculture, roaring factories, and booming towns. Republican legislatures chartered scores of banks and industrial companies, appropriated funds to fix ruined levees and to drain swamps, and went on a railroad-building binge. These efforts fell far short of solving the South's economic troubles, however. Republican spending to stimulate economic growth also meant rising taxes and enormous debt that drained funds from schools and other programs.

The southern Republicans' record, then, was mixed. To their credit, the biracial Republican coalition had taken up an ambitious agenda to change the South under trying circumstances. Money was scarce, the Democrats kept up a constant drumbeat of harassment, and factionalism threatened the party from within. However, corruption infected Republican governments in the South. Public morality reached new lows everywhere in the nation after the Civil War, and the chaos and disruption of the postwar South proved fertile soil for bribery, fraud, and influence peddling. Despite all of its problems and shortcomings, however, the Republican Party made headway in its efforts to purge the South of aristocratic privilege and racist oppression.

White Landlords, Black Sharecroppers

In the countryside, clashes occurred daily between ex-slaves who wished to take control of the conditions of their own labor and ex-masters who wanted to reinstitute old ways. Except for having to put down the whip and pay subsistence wages, planters had not been required to offer many concessions to emancipation. Instead, they moved quickly to restore the antebellum world of work gangs, white overseers, field labor for black women and children, clustered cabins, minimal personal freedom, and even whipping whenever they could get away with it.

Ex-slaves resisted every effort to roll back the clock. Land of their own would do much to end planters' involvement in their personal lives. They wanted, for example, to make their own decisions about whether women and children would labor in the fields. Indeed, within months after the war, perhaps one-third of black women abandoned field labor, and hundreds of thousands of black children enrolled in school. But landownership proved to be beyond the reach of most blacks. Without land, ex-slaves would have little choice but to work on plantations.

Although they were forced to return to the planters' fields, freedmen resisted efforts to restore slavelike conditions. In his South Carolina neighborhood, David Golightly Harris discovered that few freedmen were "willing to hire by the day, month or year." Instead of working for wages, "the negroes all seem disposed to rent land." By rejecting wage labor, by striking, and by abandoning the most reactionary employers, blacks sought to force concessions. Out of this tug-of-war between white landlords and black laborers emerged a new system of southern agriculture.

Sharecropping was a compromise that offered both ex-masters and ex-slaves something but satisfied neither. Under the new system, planters divided their cotton plantations into small farms of twenty-five to thirty acres that freedmen rented, paying with a share of each year's crop, usually half. Sharecropping gave blacks more freedom than the system of wages and labor gangs and released them from the day-to-day supervision of whites. Black families abandoned the old slave quarters and scattered over plantations, building separate cabins on the patches of land they tilled (Map 16.1). Black families now decided who would work, for how long, and how hard. Still, most blacks remained dependent on the white landlord, who retained the power to expel them at the end of each season. For planters, sharecropping offered a way to resume agricultural production, but it did not allow them to reinstitute the unified plantation system or to administer what they considered necessary discipline.

Sharecropping also introduced a new figure—the country merchant—into the agricultural equation. While landlords supplied sharecroppers with land, mules, and tools, blacks also needed essential food and clothing on credit until they harvested their crops. Thousands of merchants at small cross-

roads stores sprang up to provide this service. Under an arrangement called a crop lien, local merchants advanced goods to sharecroppers in exchange for a lien, or claim, on the farmer's crop. Merchants sometimes charged exorbitant interest, as much as 60 percent, on the goods they sold. At "settling up time," after the landlord took half of the farmer's crop for rent, the merchant consulted his ledger. Often, the farmer's expenses exceeded the income from his half of the crop. Empty-handed, he was trapped and had no choice but to begin the cycle all over again.

An experiment at first, sharecropping spread quickly and soon dominated the cotton South. By 1870, the old gang system, direct white supervision, and clustered black living quarters were fading memories. Soon, sharecropping ensnared small white farmers as well as black farmers.

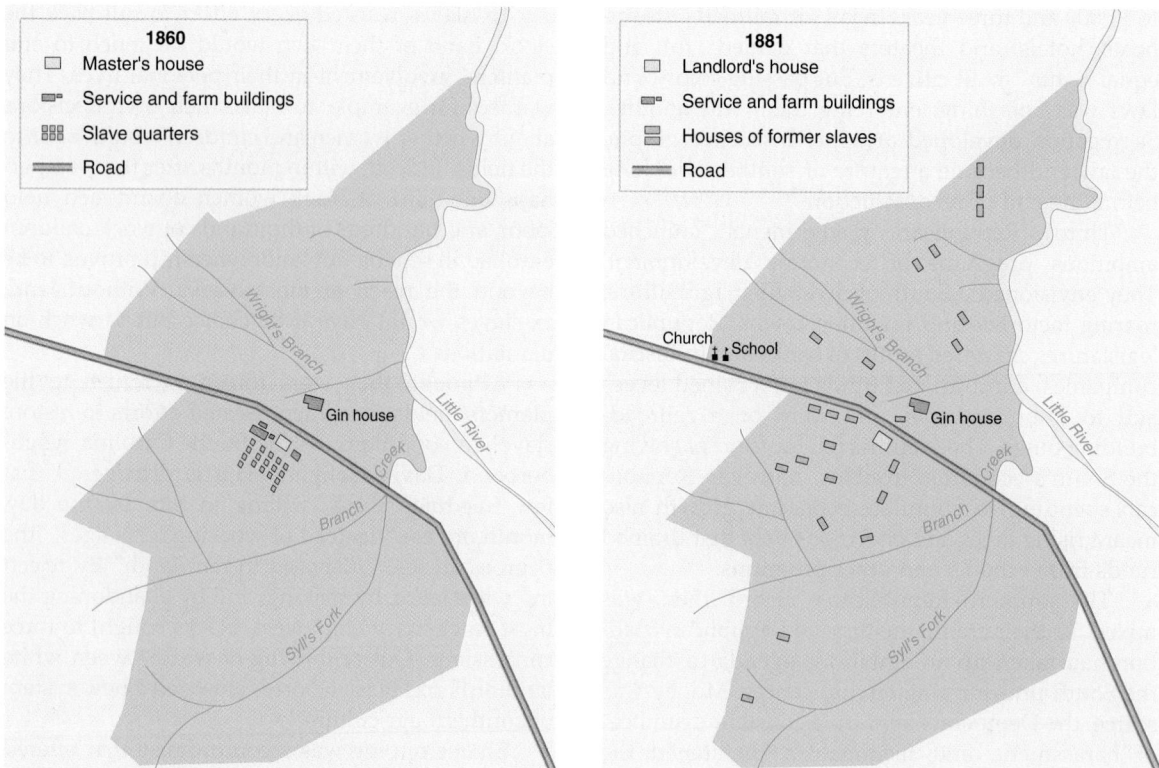

MAP 16.1

A Southern Plantation in 1860 and 1881
The maps of the Barrow plantation in Georgia illustrate some of the ways that ex-slaves expressed their freedom. Former slaves deserted the clustered living quarters behind the big house, scattered over the plantation, built new family cabins, and farmed rented land. These ex-slaves also worked together to build a school and a church.

Reconstruction Collapses

By 1870, after a decade of engagement with the public issues of war and reconstruction, Northerners wanted to turn to their own affairs and put "the southern problem" behind them. Increasingly, practical business-minded men came to the forefront of the Republican Party, replacing the band of reformers and idealists who had been prominent in the 1860s. While northern commitment to defend black freedom eroded, southern commitment to white supremacy intensified. Without northern protection, Republican state governments fell in the South. The election of 1876 both confirmed and completed the collapse of reconstruction.

Northern Resolve Withers

In 1868, Ulysses S. Grant, the general who beat Robert E. Lee, was elected president on the Republican ticket. Grant understood that most Northern-ers had grown weary of reconstruction. Northern businessmen who wanted to invest in the South had become convinced that recurrent federal intrusion was itself a major cause of instability in the region. A growing number of northern Republican leaders began to question the wisdom of their party's alliance with the South's lower classes—its small farmers and sharecroppers. Grant's secretary of the interior, Jacob D. Cox of Ohio, proposed allying with the "thinking and influential native southern-ers . . . the intelligent, well-to-do, and controlling class."

The talents Grant had demonstrated on the battlefield—decisiveness, clarity, and resolution—deserted him in the White House. He grew tentative, almost bewildered. Able advisers might have helped, but Grant surrounded himself with fumbling kinfolk and old cronies from his army days. He also made a string of dubious appointments that led to a series of damaging scandals. Charges of corruption tainted his vice president and brought

I BEG TO REPEAT THAT THESE FRAUDS ON THE GOVERNMENT SHALL BE PROBED TO THE VERY BOTTOM.

TAMMANY RING. CANAL RING. WHISKEY RING. INDIAN RING. PRESS RING. BELKNAP. FRAUD CLAIMS. STATE RING. BACK PAY GRAB. COUNTY RING. EMMA MINE. WHISKEY FRAUDS. BRIBERY. TOWN RING. WARD RING.

GRANT AND SCANDAL
This anti-Grant cartoon by the nation's most celebrated political cartoonist, Thomas Nast, shows the president falling headfirst into the barrel of fraud and corruption that tainted his administration. During Grant's eight years in the White House, many in his administration failed him. Sometimes duped, sometimes merely loyal, Grant stubbornly defended wrongdoers, even to the point of perjuring himself to keep an aide out of jail.

www.bedfordstmartins.com /roarkcompact SEE THE ONLINE STUDY GUIDE for more help in analyzing this image.

down his secretary of war and secretary of the navy as well as his private secretary. Grant's dogged loyalty to liars and cheats only compounded the damage. While never personally implicated in any scandal, Grant was aggravatingly naive and his administration filled with rot.

Anti-Grant Republicans grew increasingly disgusted, and in 1872 they bolted and launched the Liberal Party. The Liberals condemned the Grant regime of crude graft, tasteless materialism, and blatant anti-intellectualism. To clean up the mess, they proposed ending the spoils system, by which victorious parties rewarded loyal workers with public office, and replacing it with a nonpartisan civil service commission that would oversee competitive examinations for appointment to office. Moreover, they demanded that the government remove federal troops from the South and restore "home rule" (white control). Democrats especially liked the southern policy of the Liberals, and the Democratic Party endorsed the Liberal presidential candidate, Horace Greeley, the longtime editor of the *New York Tribune*. However, the nation still felt enormous affection for the man who had saved the Union, and in 1872 reelected Grant with 56 percent of the popular vote.

Northerners increasingly wanted to shift their attention from reconstruction to other issues, especially after the nation slipped into a devastating economic depression in 1873. More than eighteen thousand businesses collapsed, and more than a million workers lost their jobs. But the old issues of reconstruction would not go away. When southern Republicans pleaded for federal protection from Klan violence—the Klan had murdered hundreds of black and white Republicans during the 1868 election—Congress enacted three laws in 1870 and 1871 that were intended to break the back of white terrorism. The severest of the three, the Ku Klux Klan Act, made interference with voting rights a felony and authorized the use of the army to enforce it. Intrepid federal marshals arrested thousands of suspected Klansmen. While the government came close to destroying the Klan, it did not end terrorism against blacks. Congress also passed the Civil Rights Act of 1875, which boldly outlawed racial discrimination in transportation, public accommodations, and juries. But federal authorities did little to enforce the law, and segregated facilities remained the rule throughout the South.

In reality, the retreat from reconstruction had begun in 1868 with Grant's election. Grant genuinely wanted to see blacks' civil and political rights protected, but he felt uneasy about an open-ended commitment that seemed to ignore constitutional limitations on federal power. In May 1872, Congress restored the right of officeholding to all but three hundred ex-rebels. By the early 1870s, reform had lost its principal spokesmen to death or defeat at the polls. Many Republicans concluded that the quest for black equality was mistaken or hopelessly naive. In the minds of many, traditional white leaders offered the best hope for honesty, order, and prosperity in the South.

Underlying the North's abandonment of reconstruction was unyielding racial prejudice. During the war, Northerners had learned to accept black freedom, but deep-seated prejudice prevented many from equating freedom with equality. Even the actions they took on behalf of blacks often served partisan political advantage. Northerners generally supported Indiana Senator Thomas A. Hendricks's declaration that "this is a white man's Government, made by the white man for the white man."

The U.S. Supreme Court also did its part to undermine reconstruction. In the 1870s, a series of Court decisions significantly weakened the federal government's ability to protect black Southerners under the Fourteenth and Fifteenth Amendments. In the *Slaughterhouse* cases (1873), the Court distinguished between national and state citizenship and ruled that the Fourteenth Amendment protected only those rights that stemmed from the federal government, like voting in federal elections and interstate travel. Since the Court decided that most rights derived from the states, it sharply curtailed the federal government's authority to protect black citizens. Even more devastating, the *United States v. Cruikshank* ruling (1876) said that the reconstruction amendments gave Congress power to legislate only against discrimination by states, not by individuals. The "suppression of ordinary crime," such as assault, remained a state responsibility. The Supreme Court did not declare reconstruction unconstitutional, but it gradually undermined its legal foundation.

The mood of the North found political expression in the election of 1874, when for the first time in eighteen years the Democrats gained control of the House of Representatives. Reconstruction had come apart. Congress gradually abandoned it. President Grant grew increasingly unwilling to enforce it. The Supreme Court busily denied the constitutionality of significant parts of it. And the people sent unmistakable messages that they were tired of it. Rather than defend reconstruction from its southern enemies, Northerners steadily backed away from the challenge. After the early 1870s, southern blacks faced the forces of reaction largely on their own.

White Supremacy Triumphs

Republican governments in the South attracted more bitterness and hatred than any other political regimes in American history. In the eyes of the majority of whites, each day of Republican rule produced fresh insults: Black militiamen patrolled town streets, black laborers negotiated contracts with former masters, black maids stood up to former mistresses, black voters cast ballots, and black legislators enacted laws. The northern retreat from reconstruction permitted southern Democrats to harness this white rage to politics. Taking the name "Redeemers," they promised to replace "bayonet rule" (some federal troops continued to be stationed in the South) with "home rule." They branded Republican governments a carnival of extravagance, waste, and fraud and promised that honest, thrifty Democrats would supplant the irresponsible tax-and-spend Republicans. Above all, Redeemers swore to save southern civilization from a descent into African "barbarism" and "negro rule." As one man put it, "We must render this either a white man's government, or convert the land into a Negro man's cemetery."

By the early 1870s, Democrats understood that race was their most potent weapon. They adopted a two-pronged racial strategy to overthrow Republican governments. First, they sought to polarize the parties around color, and, second, they relentlessly intimidated black voters. They went about gathering all the South's white voters into the Democratic Party, leaving the Republicans to depend on blacks. The "straight-out" appeal to whites promised great advantage because whites made up a majority of the population in every southern state except Mississippi, South Carolina, and Louisiana.

Democrats employed several devices to dislodge whites from the Republican Party. First and foremost, they fanned the flames of racial prejudice. In South Carolina, a Democrat crowed that his party appealed to the "proud Caucasian race, whose sovereignty on earth God has proclaimed." Ostracism also proved effective. Local newspapers published the names of whites who kept company with blacks. So complete was the ostracism that one of its victims said, "No white man can live in the South in the future and act with any other than the Democratic party unless he is willing and prepared to live a life of social isolation."

In addition, Democrats exploited the small white farmer's severe economic plight by blaming it on Republican financial policy. Government spending soared during reconstruction, and small farmers saw their tax burden skyrocket. When cotton prices fell by nearly 50 percent in the 1870s, yeomen farmers without enough cash to pay their taxes lost their land. In 1871, Mississippi reported that one-seventh of the state's land—3.3 million acres—had been forfeited for nonpayment of taxes. The small farmer's economic distress had a racial dimension. Because few freedmen succeeded in acquiring land, they rarely paid taxes. From the perspective of the small white farmer, Republican rule meant not only that he was paying more taxes but that he was paying them to aid blacks. Democrats asked whether it was not time for hard-pressed yeomen to join the white man's party.

Democrats also turned to terrorism. "Night riders" targeted scalawags as well as blacks for murder and assassination. By the early 1870s, then, only a fraction of southern whites any longer professed allegiance to the party of Lincoln. Racial polarization became a reality as rich and poor whites united against southern Republicanism.

The second prong of Democratic strategy—intimidation of black voters—proved equally devastating. Antiblack political violence escalated to unprecedented levels. In 1873 in Louisiana, a clash between black militiamen and gun-toting whites killed two white men and an estimated seventy black men. Although the federal government indicted more than one hundred white men, local juries failed to convict a single one of them.

Even before adopting the all-out white supremacist tactics of the 1870s, Democrats had already captured Virginia, Tennessee, and North Carolina. The new campaign brought fresh gains. The Redeemers retook Georgia in 1871, Texas in 1873, and Arkansas and Alabama in 1874. In 1876, Mississippi fell. The story in Mississippi was one of open, unrelenting, and often savage intimidation of black voters and their few remaining white allies. As the state election approached in 1876, Governor Adelbert Ames appealed to Washington for federal troops to control the violence, only to hear from the attorney general that the "whole public are tired of these annual autumnal outbreaks in the South." Abandoned, Mississippi Republicans succumbed to the Democratic onslaught in the fall elections. By 1876, only three Republican state governments—in Florida, Louisiana, and South Carolina—survived (Map 16.2).

An Election and a Compromise

The centennial year of 1876 witnessed one of the most tumultuous elections in American history. Its chaos and confusion provided a fitting conclusion to the experiment known as Reconstruction. The election took place in November, but not until March 2 of the following year, at 4 A.M., did the nation know who would be inaugurated president on March 4. For four months the country suffered through a constitutional and political crisis. Sixteen years after Lincoln's election, Americans feared that a presidential contest would again precipitate civil war.

The Democrats had nominated New York's reform governor, Samuel J. Tilden, who immediately targeted the corruption of the Grant administration and the despotism of Republican reconstruction. The Republicans put forward a reformer of their

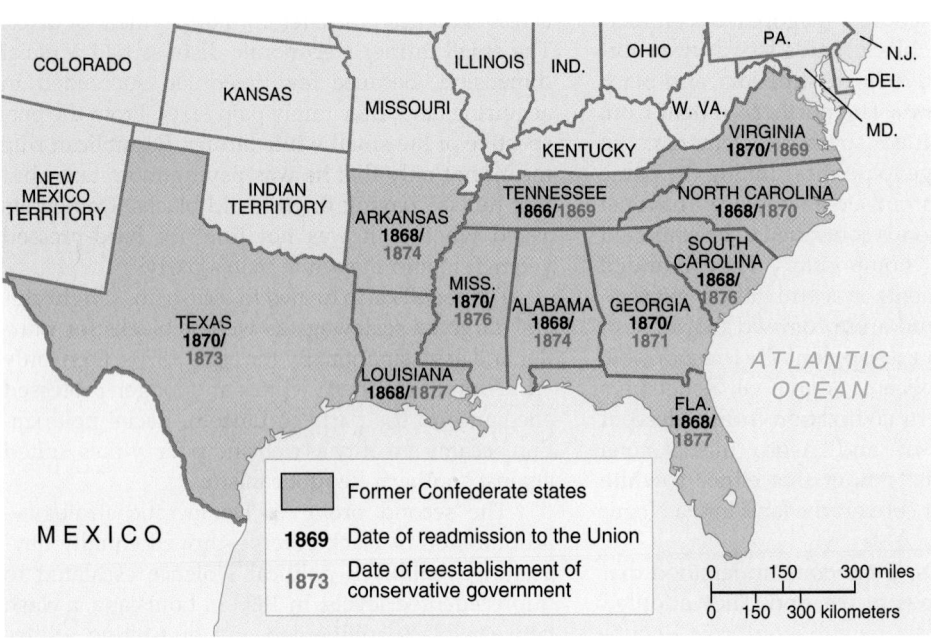

MAP 16.2

The Reconstruction of the South
Myth has it that Republican rule of the former Confederacy was not only harsh but long. In most states, however, conservative southern whites stormed back into power in only a matter of a few months or a very few years. By the election of 1876, Republican governments could be found in only three states. And they soon fell.

READING THE MAP: List in chronological order the readmission of former states to the Union. Which states reestablished conservative governments most quickly?

CONNECTIONS: What did the former Confederate states need to do in order to be readmitted to the Union? How did reestablished conservative governments react to reconstruction?

www.bedfordstmartins.com/roarkcompact SEE THE ONLINE STUDY GUIDE for more help in analyzing this map.

own, Rutherford B. Hayes, governor of Ohio. Privately, Hayes considered "bayonet rule" a mistake, but he concluded that waving the "bloody shirt," that is, reminding the voters that the Democrats were the "party of rebellion," remained the Republicans' best political strategy.

On election day, Tilden tallied 4,284,000 votes to Hayes's 4,036,000. Yet in the all-important electoral college, Tilden fell one vote short of the majority required for victory. However, the electoral votes of three states remained in doubt and thus were uncounted. Both Democrats and Republicans claimed the nineteen votes of South Carolina, Louisiana, and Florida, the only remaining Republican governments in the South. To win, Tilden needed only one of the contested votes. Hayes had to have all of them.

Congress had to decide who had actually won the elections in the three southern states and thus who would be president. The Constitution provided little guidance. Moreover, Democrats controlled the House, and Republicans the Senate. To break the deadlock, Congress created a special electoral commission to arbitrate the disputed returns. A cumbersome compromise, the commission was made up of five representatives (two Republicans, three Democrats), five senators (two Democrats, three Republicans), and five justices of the Supreme Court (two Republicans, two Democrats, and one justice who was considered an independent). But before the commission could meet, the Illinois legislature elected the independent justice to the Senate, and his place on the commission was filled with a Republican. The commissioners all voted the straight party line, giving every state to the Republican Hayes and putting him over the top in electoral votes (Map 16.3).

Some outraged Democrats vowed to resist Hayes's victory. But the impasse was broken when negotiations behind the scenes between Hayes's lieutenants and some moderate southern Democrats resulted in an informal understanding, known as the Compromise of 1877. In exchange for a Democratic promise not to block Hayes's inauguration and to deal fairly with the freedmen, Hayes vowed not to use the army to uphold the remaining Republican regimes. The South would also gain substantial federal subsidies for internal improvements. Two days later, the nation celebrated Hayes's peaceful inauguration.

Stubborn Tilden supporters bemoaned the "stolen election" and damned "His Fraudulency,"

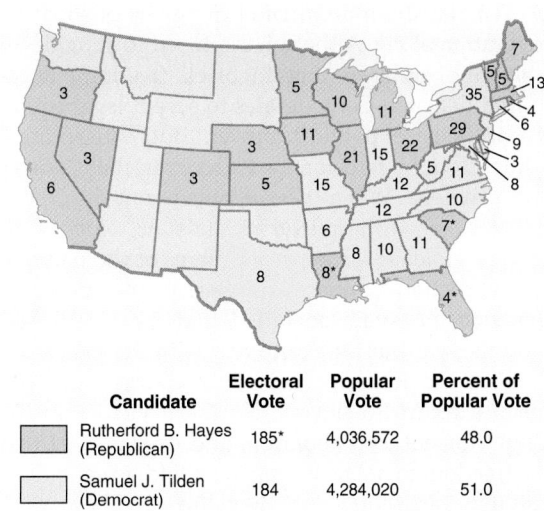

Candidate	Electoral Vote	Popular Vote	Percent of Popular Vote
Rutherford B. Hayes (Republican)	185*	4,036,572	48.0
Samuel J. Tilden (Democrat)	184	4,284,020	51.0

*19 electoral votes were disputed

MAP 16.3
The Election of 1876

Rutherford B. Hayes. Old-guard Radicals such as William Lloyd Garrison denounced Hayes's bargain as a "policy of compromise, of credulity, of weakness, of subserviency, of surrender." But the nation as a whole celebrated, for the Republic had weathered a grave crisis. The last three Republican state governments fell quickly once Hayes abandoned them and withdrew the army. Reconstruction had ended.

Conclusion: "A Revolution but Half-Accomplished"

In 1865, when General Carl Schurz visited the South, he discovered "a revolution but half accomplished." Defeat had not prepared the South for an easy transition from slavery to free labor, from white racial despotism to equal justice, and from white political monopoly to biracial democracy. Ex-masters like David Golightly Harris had trouble seeing former slaves like York and Old Will as free people. The old elite wanted to get "things back as near to slavery as possible," while ex-slaves and whites who had lacked power in the slave regime were eager to exploit the revolutionary implications of defeat and emancipation.

The northern-dominated Congress pushed the revolution along. Although it refused to provide an economic underpinning to black freedom, it required defeated Confederates to accept legal equality and share political power. But conservative whites fought ferociously to recover their power and privilege. When they regained control of politics, they used the power of the state, along with private violence, to wipe out many of the gains of reconstruction. So successful were the reactionaries that one observer concluded that the North had won the war but the South had won the peace.

But the Redeemer counterrevolution did not mean a return to slavery. Northern victory in the Civil War ensured abolition, and ex-slaves gained the freedom to not be whipped or sold, to send their children to school, to worship in their own churches, and to work independently on their own rented farms. The lives of impoverished sharecroppers overflowed with hardships, but even sharecropping provided more autonomy and economic welfare than bondage had. It was limited freedom, to be sure, but it was not slavery.

The Civil War and emancipation set in motion the most profound upheaval in the nation's history, and nothing whites did entirely erased its revolutionary impact. War destroyed the richest and largest slave society in the New World, and abolition overturned the social and economic order that had dominated the region for nearly two centuries. The world of masters and slaves succumbed to that of landlords and sharecroppers. In addition, for the first time sovereignty rested uncontested in the federal government. Moreover, the South returned to the Union, but as a junior partner. The victorious North now possessed the power to establish the nation's direction, and the new Republican leaders in the North set its compass toward the expansion of industrial capitalism.

Still, in one significant respect, the Civil War remained only a "half accomplished" revolution. As such, reconstruction represents a tragedy of enormous proportions. The nation did not fulfill the promises that it seemed to hold out to black Americans at war's end. The failure had enduring consequences. Almost a century after reconstruction, the nation would embark on what one observer called a "second reconstruction," another effort to fulfill nineteenth-century promises. The solid achievements of the Thirteenth, Fourteenth, and Fifteenth Amendments to the Constitution would provide a legal foundation for the renewed commitment. It is worth remembering, though, that it was only the failure of the first reconstruction that made a modern civil rights movement necessary.

FOR FURTHER READING ABOUT THE TOPICS IN THIS CHAPTER, see the Online Bibliography at

www.bedfordstmartins.com/roarkcompact.

FOR ADDITIONAL FIRST-HAND ACCOUNTS OF THIS PERIOD, see pages 242–256 in Michael Johnson, ed., *Reading the American Past,* Second Edition, Volume I, or pages 1–16 in Volume II.

TO ASSESS YOUR MASTERY OF THE MATERIAL IN THIS CHAPTER, see the Online Study Guide at

www.bedfordstmartins.com/roarkcompact.

1863–1877

CHRONOLOGY **411**

CHRONOLOGY

1863 **December.** Lincoln issues Proclamation of Amnesty and Reconstruction.

1864 **July.** Congress offers more stringent plan for reconstruction, Wade-Davis bill.

1865 **January.** General William T. Sherman sets aside land in South Carolina for black settlement.

March. Congress establishes Freedmen's Bureau.

March 4. Lincoln sworn in for second term as president of United States.

April 14. Lincoln shot, dies on April 15, succeeded by Vice President Andrew Johnson.

Fall. Southern legislatures enact discriminatory black codes.

December. Thirteenth Amendment abolishing slavery becomes part of U.S. Constitution.

1866 **April.** Congress approves Fourteenth Amendment making native-born blacks American citizens and guaranteeing all American citizens "equal protection of the laws." Amendment becomes part of Constitution in 1868.

April. Congress passes Civil Rights Act over President Johnson's veto.

May. Susan B. Anthony and Elizabeth Cady Stanton found Equal Rights Association to lobby for vote for women.

July. Congress extends Freedmen's Bureau over President Johnson's veto.

Summer. Ku Klux Klan founded in Tennessee.

November. Republicans triumph over Johnson's Democrats in congressional elections.

1867 **March.** Overriding Johnson's veto, Congress passes Military Reconstruction Act imposing military rule on South and requiring states to guarantee vote to black men.

1868 **March–May.** Senate impeachment trial of President Johnson results in acquittal.

November. Ulysses S. Grant elected president of the United States.

1869 **February.** Congress approves Fifteenth Amendment prohibiting racial discrimination in voting rights. Amendment becomes part of Constitution in 1870.

1871 **April.** Congress enacts Ku Klux Klan Act in effort to end white terrorism in South.

1872 **November.** President Grant reelected.

1873 Economic depression sets in for remainder of decade.

1874 **November.** Elections return Democratic majority to House of Representatives.

1875 **February.** Civil Rights Act of 1875 outlaws racial discrimination, but federal authorities do little to enforce law.

1877 **March.** Special congressional committee awards disputed electoral votes to Republican Rutherford B. Hayes, making him president of United States; Hayes agrees to pull military out of South.

KANSAS QUILT C. 1880S

This carefully hand-stitched quilt, made from pieces of leftover wool clothing and blankets, shows how a woman named Nancy Miller Grider responded creatively to the challenges of her life in Russell County, Kansas, in the 1880s. Historically, women have produced quilts as a visual language, to tell something about themselves by using materials at hand. The circular pattern in Grider's quilt may represent the spokes of a wheel—a fitting symbol not only of her own migration west but of the mass migrations taking place after the Civil War, when restless Americans on the move peopled the West and fed the growth of the big cities.

Collection of the Kentucky Quilt Project, photograph courtesy of the Kentucky Quilt Project, Inc., Louisville, Ky.

THE WEST AND THE CITY: AMERICANS ON THE MOVE

17

1870–1900

A Missouri homesteader remembered packing as the family pulled up stakes and headed west to Oklahoma:

> We were going to God's Country. Eighteen hundred and 90. . . . It was pretty hard to part with some of our things. We didn't have much but we had worked hard for everything we had. You had to work hard in that rocky country in Missouri. I was glad to be leaving it. We were going to God's Country. . . . We were going to a new land and get rich.

In the Dakotas an Oglala Sioux recalled moving with his family as a child:

> The snow was deep and it was very cold, and I remember sitting in another pony drag beside my father and mother, all wrapped up in fur. We were going away from where the soldiers were, and I do not know where we went, but it was west.

In the Midwest a young man turned his face to the city, leaving his hometown behind:

> He saw again in his mind's eye, as he tramped the road, a picture of the map on the wall of the railway station—the map with a picture of iron roads from all over the Middle West centering in a dark blotch in the corner. . . .
> "Chicago!" he said to himself.

And in Russia a young girl on her way to America bid good-bye to her village:

> I remember how the women crowded around mother . . . how, finally, the ringing of the signal bell set them all talking faster and louder than ever, in desperate efforts to give the last bits of advice, deliver the last messages, and, to their credit let it be said, to give the final, hearty, unfeigned good-bye kisses, hugs, and good wishes.

America in the nineteenth century witnessed a massive movement of peoples as men and women searched for jobs, land, and opportunity. In the last three decades of the century, this movement took many forms and went in many directions. The trek to the West continued apace as homesteaders, ranchers, and miners sought their fortunes. They in turn pushed Native Americans off the land and farther toward the sunset.

At the same time, the pull of the great industrial centers in the Northeast counterbalanced the westward migration. Farmers left the country to seek jobs in industrial centers like Chicago, New York, Pittsburgh, and Detroit. African Americans from the South began a migration to the northern cities, and Canadians crossed the border to work in the factories and mill towns of New England.

Fourteen million immigrants braved the Atlantic to come to America from Europe, creating the great migration that we think of as part of a worldwide westward movement. But the movement of immigrants was by no means limited to one direction. Immigrants from Mexico and Latin America journeyed to "El Norte." Canadians headed south. Asians voyaged east across the Pacific to work on the "gold mountain" of California. It is not an exaggeration to say that the decades surrounding the turn of the twentieth century witnessed a migration unmatched in the history of the world.

By the end of the nineteenth century, Americans on the move had peopled a continent and created the outlines of modern America. As industrial capitalism transformed the nation from a rural agrarian economy into an increasingly urban, industrial society, it changed life not just in the burgeoning cities but also on the plains of the Dakotas, in the mines of Colorado, in the cotton fields of the South, and on farms from New England to California. Iron rails and a national market economy inextricably linked the country and the city. The settlement of the West and the rise of the city occurred simultaneously and witnessed many of the same economic, social, and political manifestations—the rise of big business, growing ethnic and racial tensions, and the exploitation of labor and natural resources. It makes more sense to look at the West not as separate and unique, but as an important part of a nationwide transformation that took place in the last three decades of the nineteenth century.

RAILROAD LOCOMOTIVE
In the years following the Civil War, the locomotive replaced the covered wagon, enabling settlers to travel from Chicago or St. Louis to the West Coast in two days. By the 1890s, more than 72,000 miles of track stretched west of the Mississippi River. In this photograph, men and women hop aboard a locomotive to celebrate the completion of a section of track.
Library of Congress.

Western Land Fever

Americans by the hundreds of thousands packed up and moved, pinning their hopes and ambitions on the American West. In the three decades following 1870, this westward stream of migration swelled into a torrent, spilling across the prairies, moving on to the Pacific coast, and eventually flooding back onto the Great Plains. During this brief span of time, more land was settled than in all the previous history of the country. Between 1876 and 1900, eight new states entered the Union—Colorado, Montana, North and South Dakota, Washington, Idaho, Wyoming, and Utah—leaving only three territories—Oklahoma, New Mexico, and Arizona—in the continental United States.

Two factors stimulated the rapid settlement of the trans-Mississippi West. The Homestead Act of 1862 promised 160 acres free to any citizen or prospective citizen, male or female, who settled on the land for five years. And railroads opened up new areas and actively recruited settlers. In the 1870s, the promise of land lured thousands west across the plains in covered wagons, a hard journey that took many months and cost many lives. With the completion of a transcontinental railroad system in the 1880s, settlers could choose from four competing rail lines and make the trip in less than a week.

While the country was rich in land and resources, not all who wanted to own their own land were able to do so. A growing number of Americans found themselves dispossessed, forced to work for wages on land they would never own.

Moving West: Homesteaders and Speculators

Families who ventured west searching for "God's country" faced hardship, loneliness, and deprivation. To carve a farm from the raw prairie of Iowa, the plains of Nebraska, or the forests of the Pacific Northwest took more than fortitude and backbreaking toil. It took luck. Blizzards, tornadoes, grasshoppers, hailstorms, drought, prairie fires, accidental death, and disease were only a few of the catastrophes that could befall even the best farmer. Homesteaders on "free" land needed as much as a thousand dollars for a house, a team of farm animals, a well, fencing, and seed. Poor farmers, called "sodbusters," did without even these basics, living in dugouts carved in the land and using muscle instead of machinery.

"Father made a dugout and covered it with willows and grass," one Kansas girl recounted. When it rained, the dugout flooded and "we carried the water out in buckets, then waded around in the mud until it dried." Rain wasn't the only problem. "Sometimes the bull snakes would get in the roof and now and then one would lose his hold and fall down on the bed, then off on the floor. Mother would grab the hoe . . . and after the fight was over Mr. Bull Snake was dragged outside."

Despite the hardships, many farmers succeeded in building comfortable lives. But for others the opportunities of the West failed to materialize. Already by the 1870s, much of the best land had been taken, given to the railroads as land grants or to the states to finance education. Too often, homesteaders found that only the least desirable tracts were left—poorer lands, far from markets, transportation, and society. Land speculators took the lion's share of the remaining land. "There is plenty of land for sale in California," one migrant complained in 1870, but "the majority of the available lands are held by speculators, at prices far beyond the reach of a poor man."

The railroads were by far the biggest winners in the scramble for western land. To encourage railroad building in the decades after the Civil War, the federal government and the states gave public lands to the railroads. Together the land grants totaled approximately 180 million acres—an area almost one-tenth the size of the United States (Map 17.1). Farmers who went west to homestead often ended up buying land from the railroads or from the speculators and land companies that quickly followed the railroads into the new territories. Of the 2.5 million farms established on public lands between 1860 and 1900, homesteading accounted for only one in five; the vast majority of farmland sold for a profit.

As land for homesteading grew scarce on the prairie in the 1870s, farmers began to push farther westward, moving into western Kansas, Nebraska, and eastern Colorado—the land called the Great American Desert by settlers who had passed over it on their way to California and Oregon. Although many agricultural experts warned that the semiarid land (where less than twenty inches of rain fell annually) should be reserved for grazing, their words of caution were drowned out by the extravagant claims of western promoters. "Rain follows the plow" became the slogan of western boosters, who

MAP 17.1
Federal Land Grants to Railroads and the Development of the West, 1850–1900
Generous federal land grants meant that railroads could sell the desirable land next to the track at a profit or hold it for speculation. Railroads received more than 180 million acres, an area equal to the size of Texas. Note how the cattle trails connect with major railheads in Dodge City, Abilene, and Kansas City and to mines in Montana, Nevada, Colorado, and New Mexico.

insisted that cultivation would alter the climate of the region and bring more rainfall.

It would have been more accurate to say that drought followed the plow. Periodic droughts at roughly twenty-year intervals were a fact of life on the Great Plains. Plowed up, the dry topsoil blew away in the wind. A period of relatively good rainfall in the early 1880s encouraged farming, but a protracted drought in the late 1880s and early 1890s sent starving farmers reeling back from the plains. Hundreds of thousands retreated from western Kansas and Nebraska, some in wagons carrying the

slogan "In God we trusted, in Kansas we busted." A popular ballad bitterly summed up the plight of the worst off, those too poor to leave:

> But here I am stuck and here I must stay
> My money's all gone and I can't get away;
> There's nothing will make a man hard and profane
> Like starving to death on a government claim.

The fever for fertile land set off a series of spectacular land runs in Oklahoma. When the government took over two million acres of Indian territory

Areas Settled before 1862

and opened it to settlement in 1889, thousands rushed to grab a piece. Federal troops kept order as the homesteaders massed on the border. In one day, thousands staked their claims, and by nightfall Oklahoma boasted two tent cities with more than ten thousand residents. Four years later, in the last frenzied land rush on the Cherokee strip, several settlers were killed in the stampede, and nervous men guarded their claims with rifles. As public lands grew smaller, the hunger for land grew fiercer.

The Dispossessed: Tenants, Sharecroppers, and Migrants

Landownership proved an entirely elusive goal for many Americans—freed slaves, immigrants from Europe and Asia, and Mexicans on the Texas border. In the post–Civil War period, as agriculture became a big business tied to national and global markets, an increasing number of dispossessed laborers worked land that they would never own.

In the southern United States, the farmer labored under particularly heavy burdens. The Civil War wiped out much of the region's capital, which had been invested in slaves, and crippled the plantation economy. Although some freed people managed to move West, taking up land in Kansas, Texas, and Oklahoma, they were among the lucky few. Newly freed slaves rarely managed to obtain land of their own. Instead, they soon found themselves reduced to propertyless farm laborers. "The colored folks stayed with the old boss man and farmed and worked on the plantations," a black Alabama sharecropper observed bitterly. "They were still slaves, but they were free slaves."

Tenancy and sharecropping became a way of life for poor blacks and whites alike. The tenant rented land; the sharecropper worked someone else's land for a share of the proceeds. In the states of the old Confederacy, both money and credit were in short supply. In desperation, southern farmers turned for credit to country merchants, some of whom were former masters who opened stores on their plantations. Under an arrangement called crop lien, local merchants supplied goods to the farmers on credit; in return, the farmers put up their next year's crop as collateral. The merchants charged exorbitant interest, up to 60 percent, on the goods they sold—from cotton seed to a slab of bacon. At "settling up time," after the landlord took half the farmer's yield, the merchant consulted the debt ledger. Invariably, the farmer's expenses exceeded the income from his half of the cotton crop, and the cropper went home empty-handed, only to begin the cycle all over again.

In Texas, the coming of the railroads at the end of the nineteenth century made cattle ranching big business, undermining the free-range ranch culture. As early as the 1860s, the large ranchers had begun to enclose the open range with barbed-wire fences. As one old-timer observed, "Those persons, Mexicans and Americans, without land but who had cattle were put out of business by fencing." Fencing eliminated those cattle and sheep ranchers who had grazed their herds on the open range, and forced small-time landowners who could not afford to buy barbed wire or sink wells to sell out for the best price they could get.

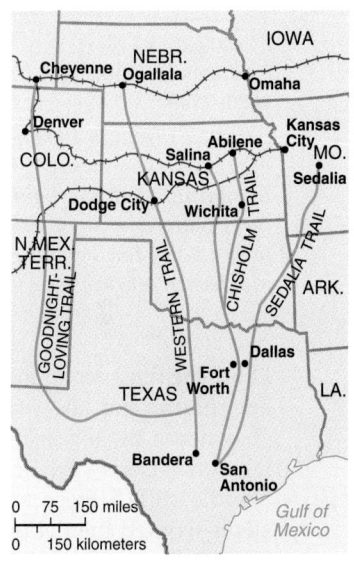

Cattle Trails, 1860–1890

The displaced ranchers, many of them Mexican, ended up as wageworkers on the huge spreads owned by Anglos or by European syndicates. After the heyday of cattle ranching ended in the late 1880s came the rise of cotton production in the southeastern regions of Texas. Ranchers turned their pastures into sharecroppers' plots and hired displaced cowboys, most of them Mexican, as seasonal laborers for as little as seventy-five cents a day. Within the space of ten years, ranch life in southern Texas gave way to a growing army of agricultural wageworkers.

In California, a pattern of land monopoly and large-scale farming fostered tenancy and migratory labor. By the 1870s, less than one percent of the population owned half the state's available agricultural

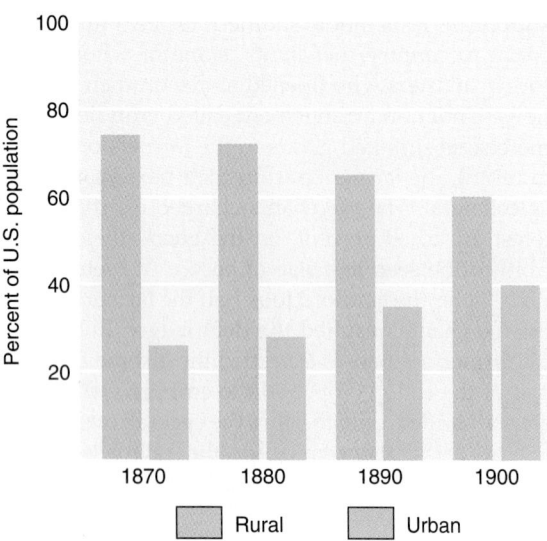

FIGURE 17.1
Changes in Rural and Urban Populations, 1870–1900
Between 1870 and 1900 not only did the number of urban dwellers increase, but the number of rural inhabitants fell. Mechanization made it possible to farm with fewer hands and fueled the exodus from farm to city throughout the second half of the nineteenth century.

land. The rigid economics of large-scale commercial agriculture and the seasonal nature of the crops spawned a ragged army of migratory agricultural laborers. Derisively labeled "blanket men" or "bindle stiffs," these homeless and landless transients worked the fields in the growing season and wintered in the flophouses of San Francisco. Wheat farming in California in the 1870s and 1880s exhausted the land and was replaced, with the introduction of irrigation, by fruit and sugar beet farming. Most of the California farm laborers were Chinese immigrants, until legislation prohibiting Chinese immigration in 1882 forced big growers to look to other groups, including Mexicans, Filipinos, and Japanese, for farm labor.

The Changing Face of Rural America

In the late nineteenth century, America's population remained overwhelmingly rural. The 1870 census showed that nearly 80 percent of the nation's

people lived on farms and in villages of less than eight thousand inhabitants. In 1900, the figure had dropped to 66 percent (Figure 17.1). But while the percentage of rural inhabitants fell, the number of farms grew. Rapid growth in the West increased the number of farms from 2 million in 1860 to over 5.7 million in 1900. Not all the nation's farmers lived in the West, though. The rural population spread evenly across the country, with rural inhabitants outnumbering city dwellers even in industrial states like Pennsylvania and New York as late as 1880.

Like all aspects of American life, farm life changed rapidly in the last decades of the nineteenth century. With the rise of industrialization and the growth of big cities, many farmers gave up their farms and moved to towns and cities. Those who stayed behind increasingly adopted new technologies, making farming less a way of life and more a business venture. In the states of the old Confederacy, the emphasis on a cotton cash-crop economy signaled a nationwide trend away from family farming and toward agribusiness.

The Colonial Economy of the New South

In the decades following the Civil War, the South struggled to regain its economic footing. The region's economy, devastated by the war and altered forever by the abolition of slavery, foundered at the same time the North experienced an unprecedented industrial boom. No wonder some Southerners called for a New South, modeled on the industrial North. Henry Grady, the ebullient young editor of the *Atlanta Constitution*, used his paper's substantial influence (it boasted the largest circulation of any weekly in the country) to extol the virtues of a new industrial South. Part bully, part booster, Grady exhorted the South to use its natural advantages— cheap labor and abundant natural resources—to go head to head in competition with northern industry.

Grady's message fell on receptive ears. Many Southerners, men and women, black and white, joined the national migration from farm to city, leaving the old plantations to molder and decay. With the end of military rule in 1877, the southern Democrats, who called themselves "Redeemers," regained political power in the southern states and enthusiastically embraced northern promoters who promised prosperity and profits.

Northern capital rushed south in the waning years of the 1870s as the country recovered from the hard times precipitated by the panic of 1873. The railroads came first, opening up the region for industrial development. Railroad mileage grew fourfold from 1865 to 1890 (see Map 17.1). The number of cotton spindles also soared, as textile mill owners abandoned New England in search of the cheap labor, low taxes, and proximity to raw materials promised in the South. By 1900, the South had become the nation's leading producer of cloth, and more than 100,000 Southerners, many of them women and children, had traded agricultural labor for work in textile mills.

The extractive industries, mining and lumber, also experienced a boom in the New South, often with devastating environmental and human costs. Coal from Appalachia could now be transported by rail to fuel the blast furnaces and factories of the nation. In the race to exploit the South's coal reserves, whole mountains were eaten up. Investors in the North and abroad, not Southerners, reaped the lion's share of the plunder. The miners themselves violently protested their poor wages and dangerous working conditions in a series of strikes that gave one county in Kentucky the name "Bloody" Harlan. In the lumber industry, the demand for southern wood led to untrammeled expansion. Twenty years of milling resulted in what one contemporary forestry expert called "probably the most rapid and reckless destruction of forests known in history."

The New South was proudest of its iron and steel industry, which grew up in the area surrounding Birmingham, Alabama. Soon the smokestack replaced the white-pillared plantation as the symbol of the South. Pennsylvania iron magnate Andrew Carnegie toured the region in 1889 and observed, "The South is Pennsylvania's most formidable industrial enemy." But as long as control of southern industry remained in the hands of northern investors, Pennsylvania had nothing to fear. Whatever the South's natural advantages, northern bankers and investors had no intention of letting the South beat the North at its own game. Elaborate mechanisms rigged the price of southern steel, inflating it, as one northern insider confessed "for the purpose of protecting the Pittsburgh mills and in turn the Pittsburgh steel users."

In only one industry did the South truly dominate—tobacco. Capitalizing on the invention of a machine for rolling cigarettes, the Duke family eventually dominated the industry with their American Tobacco Company. The new popularity of cigarettes, which replaced chewing tobacco among American's growing urban population, provided a booming market for the Dukes' "ready-made" cigarettes. Soon the company was selling 400,000 cigarettes a day.

In practical terms, the industrialized New South proved an illusion. Instead of thriving, the South found itself reduced to the status of an economic colony of the North. Just as today's colonial economies the world over feature cheap labor, extractive industries, and exported raw materials, so too did the economy of the New South. Similarly, the region experienced low wages, absentee ownership, and little control over policy or pricing—key determinants of colonial status.

Agriculture in the New South fared no better. Dependence on cotton increased rather than decreased in the postbellum period. Landlords and merchants alike demanded that sharecroppers grow more cotton, an easily marketable cash crop. Before the end of the nineteenth century, the South was producing nearly three times as much cotton as it had before the Civil War. Unfortunately, the South's vastly increased production, competing now with millions of bales from Egypt and India, coincided with a slowdown in world demand. Cotton prices plummeted. Further, relentless cotton cultivation exhausted the soil and eroded the countryside. Although a few merchants and landowners managed to hold on and even profit, the majority of Southerners succumbed to the numbing poverty that settled over the rural South. Dissatisfaction with this state of affairs would fuel the populist movement in the 1890s.

From the Family Farm toward Agribusiness

Despite the hardship of individual farmers, farming itself was thriving as an agricultural revolution transformed American farm life. New plows and reapers halved the time and labor cost of production and made it possible to farm vast tracts of land. Industrialization and urbanization provided farmers with expanding markets for their produce, and railroads carried farmers' crops to markets thousands of miles away. The diversified family farm of the past began to give way to specialized, commercial farming. Even before the opening of the twentieth century, American agriculture had entered the era of what would come to be called "agribusiness"—farming as a big business.

Business became the order of the day. Instead of extolling the virtues of the self-sufficient farmer, farm journals, agricultural societies, and educators pushed farmers to act more like businessmen, to specialize and to consolidate. Together they helped

MECHANICAL CORN PLANTER *The Farmer's Friend Manufacturing Company of Dayton, Ohio, advertised its lever and treadle corn planter in this colorful advertisement in the early 1880s. Mechanical planters came into use in the 1860s. Although the 1880 planter featured attachments for grain drilling and fertilizing, it appears designed to be drawn by farm animals. Steam-powered farm implements would soon replace animal power. Notice how the idealized, bucolic farm life pictured in the advertisement gets a dose of reality in the illustration of the company's impressive factory in Dayton.* Ohio Historical Society.

to create a striking new image of what constituted successful farming. "Farming for business, not for a living—this is the motif of the New Farmer," announced one agricultural writer. The message was clear: The job of the up-to-date farmer was to produce money, not just crops.

As farming moved onto the prairies and plains, mechanization took command. Steel plows, reapers, mowers, harrows, seed drills, combines, and threshers replaced human muscle on the farm. Horse-drawn implements gave way to steam-powered machinery. By 1880, a new harvester could reap and shock twenty acres of wheat in a day, and a single combine could do the work of twenty men. Machines enabled farmers to vastly increase their acreage. Two men with one machine could cultivate 250 acres of wheat. Production soared. Mechanization spurred the growth of huge wheat farms, some over 100,000 acres, in California and the Red River valley of North Dakota and Minnesota. The agricultural revolution meant that Americans raised more than four times the corn, five times the hay, and seven times the wheat and oats they had before the Civil War. Much of this new production went to feed people as far away as England and Germany. Like the cotton farmer in the South, northern grain and livestock farmers increasingly depended on foreign markets for their livelihood. A fall in commodity prices meant that a farmer's entire crop went to pay off debts. In periods of depression, many heavily mortgaged farmers lost their land to creditors. "By the time the World Gets their Liveing out of the

Farmer as we have to Feed the World," a Texas cotton farmer complained in the 1890s, "we the Farmer has nothing Left but a Bear Hard Liveing."

Since the days of Thomas Jefferson, farming had been linked with the highest ideals of a democratic society. Now agrarianism itself had been transformed. The farmer was no longer the self-sufficient yeoman, but a businessman on the one hand or a dispossessed wage laborer on the other, both tied to a global market. And even as farm production soared, industrial production outstripped it. More and more farmers left the fields for the factories. Now that the future seemed to lie with the cities, was democracy itself at risk? This question would ignite a farmers' revolt in the 1880s and dominate political debate in the 1890s.

The American West: A Clash of Cultures

In the movies, the American West is often portrayed in mythic terms as a picturesque landscape where strong-jawed heroes square off against villains. The good guys are always white, even their hats. Often the bad guys are red—Indians, the name Columbus mistakenly gave to Native Americans. In this masculine tableau, the setting is so timeless that it is easy to forget that the action takes place at roughly the same time that waves of new immigrants sailed past the Statue of Liberty, engineers built the Brooklyn Bridge, and men like John D. Rockefeller consolidated their empires in emerging industrial America. The mythical West exists away from all of this, out of time. Once the West is situated within its historical context, however, seen as a particular place at a particular time, reality supersedes myth, and the West appears to be not so different from the rest of the country. The problems and issues facing the nation at the beginning of the twentieth century—the growing power of corporations, ethnic and racial animosity, the exploitation of labor and of natural resources—all played themselves out under western skies.

The Peoples of the Great Plains and the Far West

"West" has always been a relative term. Until the gold rush of 1849 focused attention on California, the West for settlers lay beyond the Appalachians, east of the Mississippi in the lands drained by the Ohio River. But by 1870, "West" increasingly referred to the land across the Mississippi, from the Great Plains to the Pacific Ocean.

The West of the late nineteenth century was a polyglot place, as much so as the big cities of the East. An illustrator on his way to the California goldfields deftly depicted the mix: "The stranger as he ascends the mountains towards the mining towns . . . notices the contrast in the scenes around him to anything he ever saw before. Indians are met in groups. . . . Strings of Chinamen pass, and greet you in broken English. . . . Next comes a Negro, with a polite 'good morning, sar' or Chileno, Mexican, or Kanaka."

The parade of peoples who came to the West included immigrants from Europe, Asia, and Canada, not to mention New Englanders, Mormons, African Americans, Mexicans, Latinos, and numerous Indian tribes removed by the government. The sheer number of races that came together and mingled in the West produced a complex racism. One historian has noted, not entirely facetiously, that there were at least eight oppressed races in the West—Indians, Latinos, Chinese, Japanese, blacks, Mormons, strikers, and radicals. The Chinese suffered brutal treatment at the hands of employers and other laborers. Fearful of competition, workingmen rioted in the 1870s and fought to keep the Chinese out of the United States. African Americans who ventured out to the territories faced hostile settlers determined to keep the West "for whites only." And Native Americans, who once warred with one another, increasingly united to fight off white encroachment.

Hispanic peoples had lived in Texas and the Southwest since Juan de Oñate led his pioneer settlers up the Rio Grande in 1598 and had occupied the Pacific coast since San Diego was founded in 1769. Overnight they were reduced to a "minority" after the United States annexed Texas and took California in the Mexican War of the 1840s. Initially the Hispanic owners of large *ranchos* in California, New Mexico, and Texas, along with claimants of land grants from the Mexican and Spanish governments, greeted conquest as an economic opportunity—new markets for their livestock and buyers for their lands. But racial prejudice soon put an end to their optimism. *Californios*, granted American citizenship by the Treaty of Guadalupe Hidalgo (1848), soon found themselves discriminated against by whites who sought to keep them out of California's mines and commerce. Whites illegally squatted on rancho lands while protracted litigation over Spanish and Mexican land grants

Hydraulic Mining

INDIVIDUAL PROSPECTORS WHO MADE the first gold strikes in California in 1849 employed a simple process known as placer mining. "No capital is required to obtain this gold, as the laboring man wants nothing but his pick and shovel and tin pan with which to dig and wash the gravel." But when the easy pickings along the rivers and streams gave out, a good deal of gold still remained trapped in quartz or buried deep in the earth, extractable only by methods far beyond the means and capacity of the average prospector.

Soon technology and capital invaded the diggings. As early as 1853 a French Canadian sail maker, Antoine Chabot, hoping to avoid the cost and labor of digging a long feeder ditch to get water to his claim, stitched together heavy strips of canvas and made a 100-foot length of hose. Building on this invention, a Connecticut forty-niner named Edward Matteson marveled at the power of the new technology he called "hydraulicking." "Ten men who own a claim are enabled . . . by directing streams of water against the base of a high bank to cut away such an extent as to cause immense slides of earth which often bring with them large trees and heavy boulders." Tons of fallen earth "are carried away through the sluices with almost as much rapidity as if they were a bank of [melting] snow."

The speed and efficiency of hydraulic mining promised more gold in less time for less work. With water doing the labor formerly provided by pick and shovel, prospectors who came to the goldfields to make a fortune often ended up working for the big mines for four dollars a day, a decent wage for the time, but no way to get rich quick.

Hydraulic mining industrialized gold mining, introducing what amounted to a form of mass production that involved all the features of modern, capital-intensive industry: corporations trading shares on an international market, engineers installing large and expensive works and equipment, and wage laborers replacing prospectors. By the 1880s, the Army Corps of Engineers estimated that some $100 million had been spent to build California's hydraulic mining system. The results proved worth it for the mine owners. Hydraulic mining produced 90 percent of California's gold.

Eager to make a quick profit, the purveyors of this new technology gave little thought to its impact on the environment. Hydraulic mining used a prodigious amount of water—two large nozzles could shoot out 1.7 million gallons a day. These huge water cannons demolished entire mountains, devastating streambeds and creating heaps of rubble. Thomas Starr King, a young Unitarian minister visiting hydraulic mining operations near Nevada City, California, was appalled by the sight that greeted him. Huge nozzles blasted water, "tearing all the beauty out of the landscape and setting up 'the abomination of desolation' in its place." He grimly predicted, "If the hydraulic mining method is to be infinitely used, without restraint, upon all the surface that will yield a good return, then California of the future will be a waste more repulsive than any denounced in prophecy. . . ."

Angry farmers protested that hydraulic mines discharged tailings (debris) that filled channels and forced rivers out of their banks, causing devastating floods. Farms were swept away and cattle drowned. Millions of cubic yards of silt from the hydraulic tailings washed down and covered farms

HYDRAULIC MINING AND THE ENVIRONMENT
Hydraulic mining of California's gold ripped up the landscape, creating waterfalls, as seen in this picture. The pipes connected to the huge hoses, capable of washing away entire hills. The debris filled the rivers and led to devastating floods that wiped out entire farms.
California History Section, California State Library.

with a muddy sand—slickens—two to seven feet deep, destroying all hopes of vegetation. Orchards and fields disappeared each year under new layers of mining debris.

In 1875, farmers organized. But after four years of litigation, the California Supreme Court ruled in favor of the miners. Gold remained king in California. Not until the mid-1880s, when California's economy tilted from mining to agriculture and wheat became California's new gold, did farmers finally succeed in winning a court injunction against hydraulic mining. Renegade miners continued to use hydraulic methods until the 1890s, when more aggressive enforcement finally silenced the great hoses. The sounds of nature eventually returned to the California foothills and the rivers began to run clear.

forced the rancheros into court to fight for their land. Although the Supreme Court eventually validated most of their claims, it took so long that many had to sell their property to pay taxes and heavy legal debts. Today's city of Oakland, California, sits on what was once a 19,000-acre ranch owned by the Peralta family. Swindle, chicanery, and intimidation dispossessed scores of Hispanics. Many ended up segregated in urban *barrios* in their own homeland. In California, their population declined from 82 percent in 1850 to 19 percent by 1880. A similar fate befell Hispanic people in New Mexico and Texas. In these states, Hispanics remained the majority, but they became increasingly impoverished.

The Mormons, followers of Joseph Smith, the founder and prophet of the Church of Jesus Christ of Latter-Day Saints, fled west to avoid religious persecution. They believed that they had a divine right to the land, and their messianic militancy contributed to making them outcasts. Although they were not the only religious sect of this period to practice plural marriage, the Mormons' polygamy (men taking more than one wife) became a convenient point of attack for those who hated and feared the group. After Smith was killed by an Illinois mob in 1844, Brigham Young led the flock, which numbered more than 20,000, over the Rockies to the valley of the Great Salt Lake in Utah. The Utah land that they settled was a virtual desert, but the Mormons quickly set to work irrigating it. Lacking foreign or eastern capital to back them, they relied on cooperation and communalism. The church established and controlled water supplies, stores, insurance companies, and later factories and mining smelters. By 1882, the Mormons had built a thriving city of more than 150,000 residents in Salt Lake City. Not until 1896, however, when the church discontinued the traditional practice of polygamy, did Congress grant Utah statehood.

Prospectors and cowboys have a special place in the folklore of the West. Yet by the 1870s, both mining and cattle had become big business. The colorful prospector, with his pan and his burro, gave way to huge underground operations and quartz mines, which crushed rock to extract gold and base metals. (See "The Promise of Technology," page 422.) Corporate control of the industry replaced individual prospecting, and New York replaced San Francisco as the center of speculation in mining stock. On the range, the cowboy gave way to the cattle king. Cattle ranchers followed the railroads onto the plains, establishing between 1865

and 1885 a cattle kingdom from Texas to Wyoming. Severe blizzards in 1886–1887 decimated the herds. "A whole generation of cowmen," wrote one chronicler, "went dead broke." After the crash, cattle ranching, like mining, became largely a corporate business with distant boards of directors in the East.

The cowboy, that symbol of American independence, became, like the miner, a wage laborer. Though the cowboy was more colorful than his eastern counterparts in the factory, his life was no easier. Many cowboys were African Americans and Mexicans, although western literature chose to ignore that fact and portayed black cowboy Deadwood Dick as a white man. Like many other dissatisfied workers, cowboys organized labor unions in the 1880s and mounted strikes in both Texas and Wyoming.

The American West in the nineteenth century witnessed more than its share of bloodshed. Violence broke out between cattle ranchers and sheep ranchers, between ranchers and farmers, between strikers and bosses, between rival Indian groups, and between whites and Indians. At issue was who would control the vast resources of the emerging region. Each group claimed the public domain as its own, and each group was prepared to fight for it. In the ensuing struggle for preeminence, the biggest losers were those with the best claim to the land, the Americans who had been living on it since before Columbus or Coronado or de Soto arrived.

The Final Removal of the Indians

In the 1830s, President Andrew Jackson initiated the policy of Indian removal by pushing the Cherokee, Choctaw, Chickasaw, Creek, and Seminole tribes off their lands in the southern United States. Jackson's Indian removal forced thousands of men, women, and children to leave their homes in Georgia and Tennessee and walk hundreds of miles to lands across the Mississippi River. So many died of hunger, exhaustion, and disease along the way that the Cherokees called their path "the trail on which we cried." At the end of this trail of tears stood the Great Plains. Here, the government promised the Indians, they could remain "as long as grass shall grow."

But in the 1840s, Oregon land fever, the Mexican War, and the gold rush in California put an end to the promise. Settlers repeatedly trespassed onto Indian land and then were surprised when they encountered hostility. Indignantly, they demanded protection from the U.S. army. The result was thirty years of Indian wars that culminated in a final removal of the Indians.

The Indian wars on the plains lasted from 1861 until 1890. By the time they ended, only 250,000 Native Americans remained of the estimated 2.5 million who had lived on the continent when Columbus landed. To Americans filled with theories of racial superiority, the Indian constituted, in the words of a Colorado militia major, "an obstacle to civilization." Testifying before a congressional commission in 1864, the major

concluded that they "should be exterminated." The federal government, acting through the army, adopted a different policy, succinctly summed up by General William T. Sherman: "Rather remove all to a safe place and then reduce them to a helpless condition." The government herded the Indians into ever dwindling reservations where the U.S. Bureau of Indian Affairs, a badly managed, weak agency, often acting through corrupt agents, supposedly ministered to their needs (Map 17.2).

MAP 17.2

The Loss of Indian Lands, 1850–1890

By 1890, western Indians were isolated on small, scattered reservations. Native Americans struggled to retain their land in major battles, from the Santee uprising in Minnesota in 1862 to the massacre at Wounded Knee, South Dakota, in 1890.

INDIANS

Sevara, identified as a Ute chieftain, poses with three generations of his family in this photograph. Pictures like this one depict a way of life that by the end of the nineteenth century was already becoming extinct. Only in posed photographs carefully crafted for public consumption did the proud history of Native Americans seem able to survive.

From *The Birth of a Century,* KEA Publishing Services, Ltd.

On the plains, the Sioux, Cheyenne, Arapaho, Nez Perce, Comanche, Kiowa, Ute, Apache, and Navajo nations put up a determined resistance. The Indian wars involved violence and atrocities on both sides. In 1864 at Sand Creek, Colonel John M. Chivington, leader of the local Colorado militia, slaughtered an entire village of Cheyenne. An upright Methodist elder, Chivington watched as his men mutilated their hapless victims and later justified the killing of Indian children with the terse remark "Nits make lice." The city of Denver treated Chivington and his men as heroes, but after a congressional inquiry he was forced to resign his commission to avoid court-martial.

Two years later, the Cheyenne united with the Sioux and retaliated on the Bozeman Trail in Montana and Wyoming. Captain William Fetterman, who had boasted that with eighty men he could ride through the Sioux nation, was killed, along with all eighty-one of his troops. The Sioux's impressive victories led to a treaty in 1868, under which the government promised to give the Indians lands stretching from the Missouri River to the Black Hills in western South Dakota in return for their promise to stop fighting. The great chief Red Cloud led many of his people onto the new reser-

vation. But several young chiefs, among them Crazy Horse of the Oglala band and Sitting Bull of the Hunkpapa, refused to go. Crazy Horse said that he wanted no part of the "piecemeal penning" of his people. Renegade bands of Sioux continued to roam the plains, hunting buffalo.

The buffalo had a more dangerous enemy than the Indian—the railroad. To the Sioux and the Kiowa, the buffalo constituted a way of life; they were the source of food, fuel, and shelter and a central part of religion and ritual. To the railroads, the buffalo were a nuisance, at best a target for sport and a source of cheap meat for the workers. Buffalo hunters hired by the railroads decimated the great herds; sport hunters fired at random from railroad cars just for the thrill of it. In the heyday of buffalo hunting in the 1880s, hunters sold as many as fifty thousand hides at a time to tanneries in the East. In thirty years, more than sixty million animals were slaughtered. General Philip Sheridan applauded the hunters for "destroying the Indians' commissary." The army took credit for subduing the Indians, but their defeat came about more as a result of the decimation of the buffalo herds.

In 1876, rumors of gold in the Black Hills effectively nullified the government's promise to Red

Cloud. Miners began pouring into the area, and the Northern Pacific Railroad made plans to build tracks. Lt. Col. George Armstrong Custer fed the fever by trumpeting news of the first gold strikes. Under the leadership of Crazy Horse and Sitting Bull, the Sioux tribes massed to resist the incursion. In June, Custer led the two hundred men of the Seventh Cavalry into the largest group of Indians ever assembled in one place on the plains. At the Little Bighorn River in Montana Territory, four thousand Sioux warriors set upon them. No federal soldier lived to tell the story, but Crazy Horse, Sitting Bull, and others recounted the killing of Pahuska or Long Hair, as the Indians called the dashing Custer. Their victory was short-lived. In the next year, Crazy Horse was killed and Sitting Bull surrendered. Chief Joseph of the Nez Perce resisted removal and fled toward Canada. Just forty miles from freedom, federal troops caught up with his band. With his people cold and starving, the chief surrendered. His speech stands as an eloquent statement of the plight of the Indians: "I am tired of fighting. Our chiefs are killed. . . . It is cold and we have no blankets. The little children are freezing to death. My people, some of them, have run away to the hills, and have no blankets, no food; no one knows where they are—perhaps freezing to death. I want to have time to look for my children and see how many I can find. Maybe I shall find them among the dead. Hear me, my chiefs, I am tired; my heart is sick and sad. From where the sun now stands, I will fight no more forever."

The policy of rounding up Indians and herding them onto reservations gained momentum. After Custer's Last Stand, as the battle in 1876 came to be called, policy toward the Indians toughened. Even the most philanthropic Americans seemed convinced that the Indian way of life must go. Instead of remaining American Indians, they had to become Indian Americans. When Indians resisted, their children were taken off the reservations and sent to special schools to learn white ways—to play the piano, to farm, to act like white Americans.

In 1887, Congress passed the Dawes Act, breaking up the reservations and giving each Indian an allotment of land. Well-meaning philanthropists viewed the Dawes Act as a way to foster individualism among the Indians and to extend to them the rights of citizenship. The act, however, effectively reduced Indian lands from 138 million acres to a scant 48 million, making it, in the words of one critic, "a bill to despoil the Indians of their lands and to make them vagabonds on the face of the earth." The surplus land was then opened to white settlement, setting off the great land rushes in Oklahoma Territory.

Indian Resistance

Faced with the extinction of their entire way of life and means of livelihood, different groups of Indians responded in different ways. Outright violent resistance was perhaps best embodied in the Apaches of the Southwest, while nonviolent resistance was exemplified in the Ghost Dance religion, a movement that swept the Plains in the 1890s. Both met with the same brutal military repression.

The Apache tribes who roamed the Sonoran desert of southern Arizona and northern Mexico never combined as the Plains Indians had done so successfully at the Little Bighorn. Instead they operated in small raiding parties, perfecting a hit-and-run guerrilla warfare that terrorized white settlers and deviled the army in the 1870s and 1880s. General George Crook, a skilled Indian fighter, combined a policy of dogged pursuit with judicious diplomacy. Convinced that white troops could not fight the Apaches on their home ground, Crook relied on Indian scouts, recruiting nearly two hundred, to hunt down the Apaches. The Indians welcomed a release from the boredom of reservation life and joined up with Crook. Trained to a life of hunting, tracking, and raiding, even some Apaches proved willing to join Crook's scouts. Eventually Crook was able to persuade most of the renegades to surrender. By 1882, the Apaches had settled on the San Carlos reservation in Arizona territory.

Reservation life was particularly difficult for the nomadic Apaches. Geronimo, a recalcitrant chieftain, repeatedly led raiding parties of renegades off the reservation. These fierce warriors attacked ranches, killing the ranchers and stealing their cattle and horses. In the spring of 1885, Geronimo went on a ten-month rampage, moving from his sanctuary in the Sierra Madre to raid and burn ranches and towns on both sides of the Mexican border. General Crook caught up with Geronimo in the fall, only to have him slip away with a small band on the way back to the San Carlos reservation. Chagrined, Crook resigned his post. General Nelson Miles, Crook's replacement, determined to put an end to Geronimo once and for all by adopting a policy of hunt and destroy.

There were only thirty-three Apaches still at large, thirteen of them women, but they eluded Miles's troops for more than five months. Throughout the blistering summer, the Indians, constantly on the move, kept one step ahead of the army. In the end, this small band of Apaches fought two thousand soldiers to a stalemate. Miles, who believed in the superiority of white troops over any Indian, watched as his spit-and-polish cavalry, after months of tracking the elusive Apaches, became barely recognizable as soldiers. Lt. Leonard Wood, one of only two white soldiers who rode with the scouts to the end, discarded his horse and most of his clothes. Reduced to wearing nothing "but a pair of canton flannel drawers, and an old blue blouse, a pair of moccasins and a hat without a crown," Wood had trouble convincing one Indian party that he was actually a U.S. soldier.

Eventually the scouts tracked down Geronimo and his band. Caught between Mexican regulars and the American army, the chieftain agreed to march north with the soldiers and negotiate a settlement. "We have not slept for six months," Geronimo admitted, "and we are worn out." He met with General Miles to negotiate a peace, but, as in the past, the Indians did not get what they were promised.

Fewer than three dozen Apaches had been hostile when General Miles induced them to surrender, yet the government gathered up nearly five hundred Apaches and sent them as prisoners to Florida, including the scouts who had helped track Geronimo. By 1889, more than a quarter of the Indians had died, some by illness contracted in the damp, lowland climate and some by suicide. Their plight roused public opinion and eventually, in 1892, they were moved to Fort Sill in Oklahoma and later to New Mexico.

Geronimo lived to become something of a celebrity. He appeared at the St. Louis Exposition in 1904, where he sold pictures of himself for twenty-five cents apiece, and he rode in President Theodore Roosevelt's inaugural parade in 1905. In a newspaper interview he confessed, "I want to go to my old home before I die. . . . Want to go back to the mountains again. I asked the Great White Father to allow me to go back, but he said no." None of the Apaches were permitted to return to Arizona; when Geronimo died in 1909, he was buried in Oklahoma.

On the Plains many different tribes turned to a nonviolent form of resistance—a compelling new religion, the Ghost Dance. The Paiute shaman Wo-voka, drawing on a cult that had developed in the 1870s, combined elements of Christianity and traditional Indian religion to found the Ghost Dance religion in 1889. Wovoka claimed that he had received a vision in which the Great Spirit spoke through him to all Indians, urging them to unite and promising that whites would be destroyed in an apocalypse. The Indian warriors slain in battle would return to life, and buffalo once again would roam the land unimpeded.

This religion of despair with its message of hope spread like wildfire over the plains. It was danced in Idaho, Montana, Utah, Wyoming, Colorado, Nebraska, Kansas, the Dakotas, and Oklahoma Territory by tribes as diverse as the Arapaho, Cheyenne, Pawnee, and Shoshone. Various tribes developed different forms of the dance, but all dances were held in a circle. Often dancers went into hypnotic trances. Some danced until they dropped from exhaustion.

Ghost Dances were generally nonviolent, but among the Sioux, especially the Oglala, Blackfeet, and Hunkpapa, the dance took on a more militant flavor. Sioux disciples of the Ghost Dance religion taught that the wearing of white ghost shirts made Indians immune to the bullets of the soldiers. Their message frightened whites, who began to fear an uprising. "Indians are dancing in the snow and are wild and crazy," wrote the Bureau of Indian Affairs agent at the Pine Ridge reservation in South Dakota. Frantic, he pleaded for reinforcements. "We are at the mercy of these dancers. We need protection, and we need it now." President Benjamin Harrison dispatched several thousand federal troops to Sioux country to handle any outbreak.

In December 1889, when Sitting Bull sought permission to go to the Pine Ridge reservation to meet with Wovoka, the local Indian agent laid a trap for him, and Sitting Bull was shot. His people, fleeing the scene, were apprehended by the Seventh Cavalry, Custer's old regiment, near Wounded Knee Creek, South Dakota. As the Indians laid down their arms, a shot rang out and the army opened fire. In the ensuing melee, Indian warriors stormed the troops, killing more than thirty soldiers. But they were badly outgunned. Men, women, and children were mowed down in minutes by the army's brutally efficient Hotchkiss machine guns. More than two hundred Sioux lay dead or dying in the snow. Settler Jules Sandoz surveyed the scene the day after the massacre. "Here in ten minutes an entire community was as the buffalo that bleached on the plains," he wrote. "There was something loose in the world that hated joy and happiness as it hated brightness and color, reducing everything to drab agony and gray."

Although the massacre at Wounded Knee did not end the story of Native Americans, it did eliminate their way of life. The Indian population would gradually recover; the 2000 census showed 2.4 million native Americans. But their culture sustained a crushing blow. In the words of the visionary Black Elk, "The nation's hoop is broken and scattered. There is no center any longer, and the sacred tree is dead."

The West of the Imagination

Even as the Old West was dying, the myth of the West was being created. The dime novel, a precursor to today's paperback, capitalized on western heroes like Kit Carson, Wild Bill Hickok, Calamity Jane, and Deadwood Dick to entertain eastern readers seeking escapist fare. Published in the East and sometimes written by tenderfeet who had never ventured beyond the Hudson River, dime novels sold at a prodigious rate.

The prince of the dime novel heroes was Buffalo Bill, featured in more than two hundred titles. Born William F. Cody, the real-life Buffalo Bill had panned for gold, ridden for the Pony Express, scouted for the army, and earned his nickname hunting buffalo for the railroad. A masterful showman, he capitalized on his success and formed the touring Wild West Company in 1883. Part circus, part theater, the Wild West extravaganza featured exhibitions of riding, shooting, and roping and presented dramatic reenactments of great moments in western U.S. history. The star of the show was Annie Oakley. Dubbed "Little Miss Sure Shot," she delighted the crowd by shooting a dime out of her husband's hand. The centerpiece of Buffalo Bill's Wild West Show was the reenactment of Custer's Last Stand, in which Indians in war paint and bonnets massacred the hapless Custer and his men. At the end, Buffalo Bill galloped in with a cloud of dust and dramatically mouthed the words "Too late!"

The Wild West that Buffalo Bill presented indiscriminately mixed the authentic with the romantic until reality itself blurred in the popular mind. Cody had not been at the Little Bighorn, but some of the Indians in his troupe like Sitting Bull,

who toured with the show in 1885, had been there and knew their parts firsthand.

The rapid demise of the Wild West that Buffalo Bill enshrined in his show may perhaps best be comprehended if we juxtapose Cody with historian Frederick Jackson Turner. At the 1893 Columbian Exposition in Chicago, Turner addressed the American Historical Association on "The Significance of the Frontier in American History." The frontier, Turner posited, had shaped the character of Americans and the nation. Prompted by the U.S. Census Bureau's 1890 declaration that a clear frontier line no longer existed, Turner's message was elegiac. The sense of an old world passing that Turner summed up in his speech was perhaps nowhere better demonstrated than across the Chicago fairground in the spectacle of Buffalo Bill's Wild West Show performing to sellout crowds in the bleachers. The high drama of the struggle for the West by 1893 had become no more than a thrilling but harmless entertainment.

Yet the historical reality of the American West was every bit as dramatic as the fictions it sparked: By the 1890s, the American West had been transformed. More than seven-tenths of the farmland west of the Mississippi River was owned by investors who neither farmed nor ranched the land themselves. The shift from farming and ranching to agribusiness, not the disappearance of some magical frontier line, marked the end of an era in America. Far from being a mythic landscape out of place and time, the West was linked inextricably to the urban East by capital investment and iron rails that carried western goods to world markets.

The Rise of the City

Although much of the nation remained heavily rural, the last decades of the nineteenth century witnessed an urban explosion. Cities and towns grew more than twice as rapidly as the total population, far outstripping rural growth. Patterns of global migration contributed to the ascendancy of urban America. In the port cities, immigrants from southern and eastern Europe lived in dense ghettos where the English language was rarely heard. The word *slum* entered the American vocabulary during these years and with it a growing concern over the gap between the rich and the poor, a gap only widened by the changing social geography of the cities.

The Urban Explosion, a Global Migration

"We cannot all live in cities, yet nearly all seem determined to do so," New York editor Horace Greeley complained. The astonishing growth that occurred in the nation's cities between 1870 and 1900 came about not from the natural increase of the city population but from the internal and international movement of people. The percentage of people living in towns and cities leapt from 20 percent in 1870 to 33 percent by 1900. Growth in the urban population was actually divided about evenly between large and small cities. But the emergence of the modern metropolis marked the most dramatic demographic development of the period. The number of cities with more than 100,000 inhabitants jumped from eighteen in 1870 to thirty-eight by 1900. As the twentieth century began, the United States could boast three cities with more than a million inhabitants—New York, Chicago, and Philadelphia. Railroad growth stimulated much of this urban development. Cities like Reno, Butte, and Cheyenne sprang up along the tracks long before the surrounding countryside was settled. The transcontinental rail lines set off booms in Kansas City, Omaha, and Salt Lake City.

Urbanization went hand in hand with industrialization. As workers left the farm for the factory, the growth of the urban population fueled a constantly expanding market. In a process that economists call the multiplier effect, the growing market in turn stimulated greater and greater production, creating more jobs in an expanding spiral. The emergence of a mass consumer market enabled cities to become centers for wholesaling and retailing, not just manufacturing and industry. Chicago, with its mail order houses like Montgomery Ward and Sears, Roebuck, along with its great department stores, Marshall Field and Carson Pirie Scott, led the country as an urban marketing center.

The United States grew up in the country and moved to the city, or so it seemed by the twentieth century. Hundreds of thousands of farm boys and girls ran away to the city looking for jobs and adventure. But for at least one group, the move to the city promised something more. African Americans came north looking not just for economic opportunity. Restrictive laws that segregated blacks, called Jim Crow laws, became common throughout the South in the decades following reconstruction. Intimidation and lynching, justified by white South-

erners as necessary to "keep the Negro in his place," also became increasingly common throughout the South. "To die from the bite of frost is far more glorious than at the hands of a mob," proclaimed the *Defender,* Chicago's largest African American newspaper. By the 1890s, many blacks agreed. They moved North, settling for the most part in the growing cities. Racial discrimination and poverty limited blacks' options in the North, just as they had in the South. Yet by 1900, New York, Philadelphia, and Chicago contained the largest black communities in the nation. Although the greatest African American migration out of the South would occur during and after the end of World War I, the great exodus was already under way.

Rural migrants to the cities were by no means limited to American farmers and southern blacks.

IMMIGRANTS
Dressed in the clothing of the old country (cap and collarless shirt, apron and shawl), this immigrant couple carries their meager possessions, bedding in his bundle, food and utensils in her basket, and two umbrellas tied together. Note how the man gazes confidently, almost defiantly, into the camera, while the woman, looking miserable, averts her eyes. What do their postures tell about whose decision it was to come to America and about their hopes and apprehensions?
Wide World Photos, Inc.

Worldwide in scope, the movement from rural areas to industrial centers attracted to the United States more than fourteen million Europeans in the waning decades of the nineteenth century. That migration came in two distinct waves that have been called the old and the new immigration. Before 1880, the bulk of the new arrivals came from northern and western Europe, with the Germans, Irish, English, and Scandinavians making up approximately 85 percent of the newcomers.

After 1880, the pattern shifted, with more and more immigrant ships carrying passengers from southern and eastern Europe. Italians, Hungarians, eastern European Jews, Turks, Armenians, and Poles, Russians, and other Slavic peoples accounted for more than 80 percent of all the immigrants by 1896. Alongside the tide of new European immigrants streamed Japanese coming east from Asia, French Canadians flowing south to work in New England's mill towns, and Mexicans and other Latin Americans heading north to settle in California and the Southwest (Map 17.3).

In sheer numbers, the new immigration was unprecedented. In 1888 alone, more than half a million Europeans came to America, 75 percent landing in New York City. The Statue of Liberty, a gift from the people of France erected in 1886, stood sentinel in the harbor. A young Jewish girl named Emma Lazarus penned the verse at Liberty's base:

> Give me your tired, your poor,
> Your huddled masses yearning to breathe free,
> The wretched refuse of your teeming shore,
> Send these, the homeless, tempest-tost to me,
> I lift my lamp beside the golden door!

The tide of immigrants soon swamped the immigrant office at Castle Garden in lower Manhattan. An imposing new brick facility opened on Ellis Island in New York harbor in 1900. Able to handle 5,000 immigrants a day, it was already inadequate by the time it opened. In 1907, the peak year of immigration, more than a million immigrants passed through the gates at Ellis Island, and on a record day inspectors processed more than 11,700.

New Immigrants and the Call for Immigration Restriction

The new wave of immigration at the turn of the twentieth century resulted from a number of factors. Improved economic conditions in western Europe, as well as immigration to Australia and Canada, cut down on the flow of "old" immigrants to the United States. At the same time, a protracted economic depression in southern Italy, the religious persecution of Jews in eastern Europe, and a general desire to avoid conscription into the Russian army led many in southern and eastern Europe to move to the United States.

Economic factors in the United States also played a role. The need of America's industries for cheap, unskilled labor stimulated immigration during good times. In the depressions following the economic panics of 1873 and 1893, immigration slowed, only to pick up again when prosperity returned. Although the U.S. government did not offer direct inducements to immigrate, the steamship companies courted immigrants, who provided a highly profitable, self-loading cargo. Agents from the large lines traveled throughout Europe drumming up business. Colorful pamphlets and posters mingled fact with fantasy to advertise America as the land of promise.

Would-be immigrants eager for information about America relied on letters, advertisements, and word of mouth—sources that were not always dependable or truthful. Even photographs proved deceptive—American workers dressed in their Sunday best looked more prosperous than they actually were to the eyes of relatives in the old country, where only the very wealthy wore white collars or silk dresses. As one Italian immigrant recalled, "Everything emanating from America reached [Italy] as a distortion. . . . News was colored, success magnified, comforts and advantages exaggerated beyond all proportions." No wonder immigrants left for America believing "that if they were ever fortunate enough to reach America, they would fall into a pile of manure and get up brushing the diamonds out of their hair."

Where the old immigrants had spread out over the country, the new remained largely in the cities. By 1900, almost two-thirds of the country's immigrant population resided in cities, drawn by the availability of jobs in the nation's industrial centers at the same time poverty limited their ability to buy land in the West. Although nowhere did the foreign-born population outnumber the native-born population, taken together foreign immigrants and their American-born children did constitute a majority, particularly in nation's largest cities.

Not all the newcomers came to stay. Perhaps eight million, mostly young men, worked for a year or a season and then returned to their homelands. By 1900, almost 75 percent of the new immigrants were single young men. Intent on making money

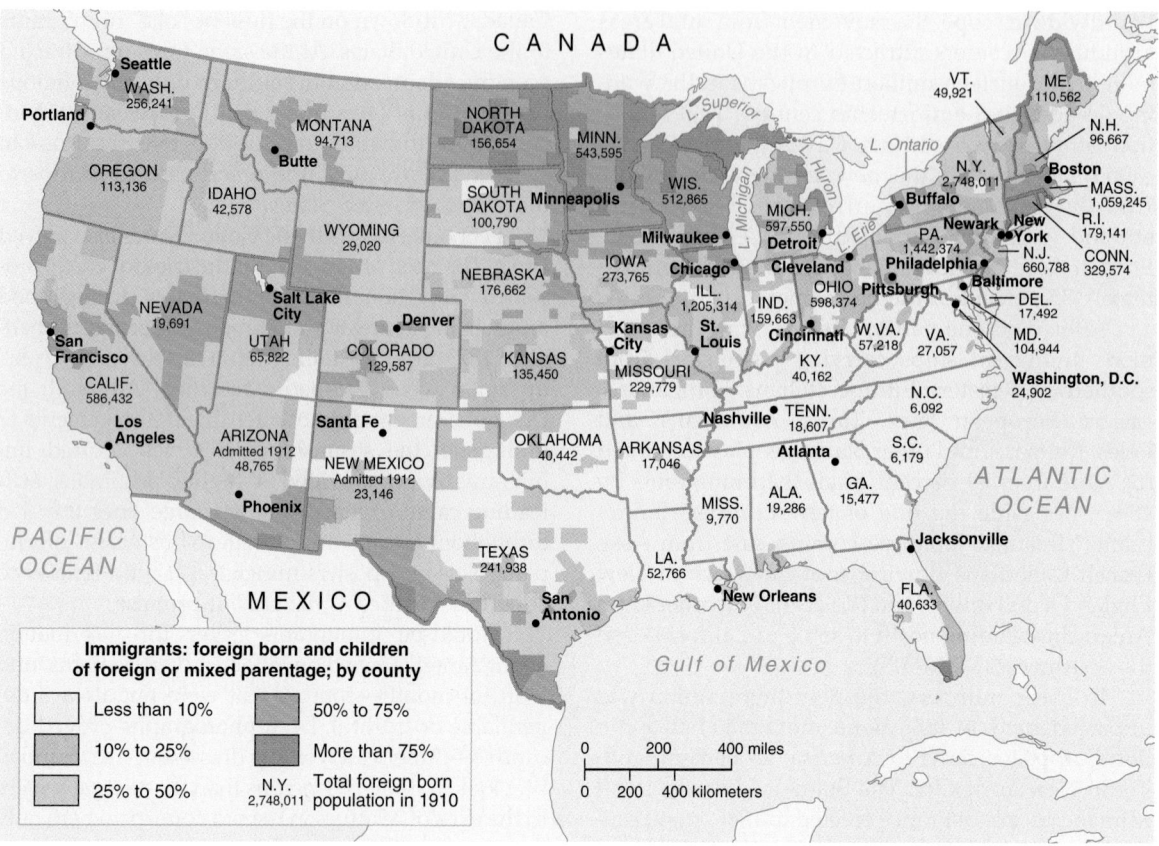

MAP 17.3

The Impact of Immigration to 1910

Immigration flowed in all directions—south from Canada, north from Mexico, east from Asia to the port cities of Seattle and San Francisco, and west from Europe to ports in Boston and New York.

READING THE MAP: What states have high percentages of immigrants? Which cities drew the most immigrants? Which cities the least?

CONNECTIONS: Why did most immigrants gravitate toward cities? Why do you think the South drew such a low percentage of immigrants?

www.bedfordstmartins.com/roarkcompact   SEE THE ONLINE STUDY GUIDE for more help in analyzing this map.

as quickly as possible, they were willing to accept conditions that other workers regarded as intolerable. They showed little interest in labor unions and organized only when the dream of returning home faded, as it did for millions who ultimately remained in the United States.

Jews from eastern Europe most often came with their families and came to stay. In the 1880s, a wave

of violent pogroms, or persecutions, in Russia and Poland led to the departure of more than a million Jews in the next two decades. They settled mostly in the port cities of the East. New York City's Lower East Side replicated the Jewish ghettos of eastern Europe, teeming with street peddlers and pushcarts.

To many Americans, the new immigrants from southern and eastern Europe seemed uneducated, backward, and outlandish in appearance—impossible to assimilate. "These people are not Americans," editorialized the popular journal *Public Opinion*, "they are the very scum and offal of Europe." Terence Powderly, head of the labor organization the Knights of Labor, complained that the newcomers "herded together like animals and lived like beasts." Convinced that the new immigrants were undesirable, groups began to call for measures to limit immigration.

Old-stock aristocrats such as Senator Henry Cabot Lodge of Massachusetts formed an unlikely alliance with organized labor to press for immigration restriction. A precedent for keeping out "undesirable" immigrants had been established in 1882, when labor agitation and racism in California led to passage of the Chinese Exclusion Act. On the East Coast, Lodge and his followers championed a literacy test, a device designed to limit immigration from Italy and eastern Europe by requiring immigrants to demonstrate the ability to read and write in their native language. Since the vast majority of Italian and Slavic peasants had no schooling, it was assumed that few would be able to pass the test. In 1896, Congress approved a literacy test for immigrants, but President Grover Cleveland promptly vetoed it. "It is said," the president reminded Congress, "that the quality of recent immigration is undesirable. The time is quite within recent memory when the same thing was said of immigrants, who, with their descendants, are now numbered among our best citizens." Cleveland's veto forestalled immigration restriction but did not stop the forces seeking to close the gates. They would continue to press for restriction until they achieved their goal in the 1920s.

The Social Geography of the City

In the 1870s, Cleveland, Ohio, was a small city, in both population and geographical area. Oil magnate John D. Rockefeller could, and often did, walk from his large brick house on Euclid Avenue to his office downtown. On his way, he passed the small homes of his clerks and other middle-class families. Behind these homes ran miles of alleys crowded with the dwellings of Cleveland's working class. Farther out, on the shores of Lake Erie, close to the factories and foundries, clustered the shanties of the city's poorest laborers.

Within two decades, the Cleveland that Rockefeller knew no longer existed. The coming of mass transit transformed the walking city. In its place emerged a central business district surrounded by concentric rings of residences graded by ethnicity and income. First the horsecar in the 1870s and then the electric streetcar in the 1880s made it possible to commute to work. City workers could enjoy single-family homes with lawns, gardens, and trees and still travel to work downtown for as little as five cents a day. By the early twentieth century, more than half of Cleveland's residents rode the streetcars to work. This pattern of development was repeated throughout the country as urban congestion and suburban sprawl forever altered the social geography of the city.

The city's poor, unable to afford even the few cents for trolley fare, crowded into the inner city or lived "back of the yards" near the factories where they worked. The term *slum* came into common use by the mid-nineteenth century, coinciding with the increased clustering of the poor in the least desirable areas of the city. This social segregation—rich and poor, ethnic and old-stock Americans—was one of the major social changes engendered by the rise of the industrial metropolis, and it occurred not only in Cleveland but in cities across the nation.

Race and ethnicity affected the way in which cities evolved. Newcomers to the burgeoning cities, whether Jews and Italians "just off the boat" or African Americans up from the South, sought out their kin and countryfolk and struggled to maintain their culture in distinct neighborhoods that often formed around the synagogue or church. Blacks typically experienced the greatest residential segregation, but every large city had its ethnic neighborhoods, its Little Italy, Chinatown, Bohemia Flats, or Germantown, where one could walk for blocks without hearing a word of English.

In 1890, a young police reporter named Jacob Riis took his notebook and his camera into the tenements of New York's Lower East Side; the result was the best-selling book *How the Other Half Lives*. Riis invited his audience into a Cherry Street tenement:

> Be careful please! The hall is dark and you might stumble over the children pitching pennies back there. . . . Close? Yes! What would you have? All the fresh air that ever enters these stairs comes from the hall door and it is forever slamming, and from the windows of dark bedrooms that in turn receive from the stairs their sole supply of the elements God meant to be free, but man deals out with such niggardly hand. . . .

HOW BOTH HALVES LIVED

The gap between the rich and poor documented so successfully in Jacob Riis's **How the Other Half Lives** *(1890) is underscored here by juxtaposing the photographs of two women. Riis took the photograph above left of a "scrub" or washer woman in one of the notorious Police Station lodging houses, the shelters of last resort for the city's poor. Notice how large and misshapen her hands are from her heavy work. To the right is Alice Vanderbilt as she appeared as "The Spirit of Electricity" at the Vanderbilt costume ball in 1883. Her gown, by the French designer Worth, was no doubt inspired by Thomas Edison's triumphant lighting of lower Manhattan six months earlier. Silk satin, velvet-trimmed with gilt metallic bullion and diamonds, the gown epitomized what political economist Thorstein Veblen would call "conspicuous consumption."*

Riis photograph courtesy of the Museum of the City of New York. Vanderbilt photograph courtesy of the Collection of the New-York Historical Society.

Here is a door. Listen! That short hacking cough, that tiny, helpless wail—what do they mean? They mean that the soiled bow of white you saw on the door downstairs will have another story to tell—Oh! a sadly familiar story—before the day is at an end. The child is dying with measles. With half a chance it might have lived; but it had none. That dark bedroom killed it.

As Riis discovered, poverty, crowding, dirt, and disease constituted the daily reality of New York's poor. Riis's book, like his photographs, presented a world of black and white. In reality, there were many layers to the population Riis labeled "the other half," distinctions furthered by ethnicity, religion, race, and gender. *How the Other Half Lives* must be read more as a social reformer's call to action than as an accurate portrayal.

Jacob Riis's audience shivered at his revelations about the "other half." But middle-class Americans worried equally about excesses of the wealthy and class antagonism fueled by the growing chasm between rich and poor. Many people shared Riis's view that "the real danger to society comes not only from the tenements, but from the ill-spent wealth which reared them."

The excesses of newly minted millionaires in the decades following the Civil War were nowhere more visible than in the lifestyle of the Vanderbilts. "Commodore" Cornelius Vanderbilt, the uncouth ferryman who built the New York Central Railroad, died in 1877, leaving his son $90 million. William Vanderbilt doubled that sum and his two sons proceeded to spend it on Fifth Avenue mansions and "cottages" in Newport, Rhode Island, which, with their marble and gold leaf, sought to rival the palaces of Europe. In 1883, Alva Vanderbilt (Mrs. William K. Vanderbilt I) launched herself in New York society by throwing a costume party so lavish that no one could resist an invitation. Dressed as a Venetian princess, the hostess greeted her twelve hundred guests. But her sister-in-law capped the evening, appearing in costume as that miraculous new invention, the electric light, resplendent in a white satin evening dress studded with diamonds. Many costumes cost as much as $1,500 apiece, three times the average yearly wage of a worker. The New York *World* speculated that the party cost over a quarter of a million dollars.

Such ostentatious displays of wealth became even more alarming when they were coupled with disdain for the general welfare of the people. When a reporter in 1882 asked William Vanderbilt whether he considered the public good in running his railroads, he shot back, "The public be damned." The fear that America had become a plutocracy—a society ruled by the rich—gained credence from the fact that the wealthiest one percent of the population owned more than half the real and personal property in the country (a century later, the top one percent controlled less than a quarter).

City Life and City Images

In America, private enterprise built the cities, competing fiercely for contracts and franchises from public officials. Boosters, builders, businessmen, planners, and politicians all had a hand in creating the modern city. With a few notable exceptions, such as Washington, D.C., there was no such thing as a comprehensive city plan. Cities simply mushroomed, formed by the dictates of private enterprise

and the exigencies of local politics. With the rise of the city came the need for public facilities, transportation, and services that would tax the imaginations of America's architects and engineers and set the scene for the rough-and-tumble story of big-city government, politics, and politicians.

Big-City Government and the "Bosses"

The physical growth of the cities required the expansion of public services and the creation of entirely new facilities: streets, subways, elevated trains, bridges, docks, parks, sewers, and public utilities. There was work to be done and money to be made. The professional politician—the colorful big-city boss—became a phenomenon of nineteenth-century urban growth. Although corrupt and often criminal, the boss saw to the building of the city and provided needed social services for the new residents. Yet not even the big-city boss could be said to rule the unruly city. The governing of America's cities resembled more a tug-of-war than boss rule.

The most notorious of all the city bosses was William Marcy Tweed of New York. At midcentury, Boss Tweed's Democratic Party machine held sway. A machine was really no more than a political party organized on the grassroots level. It existed to win elections and reward its followers with jobs on the city's payroll. New York's citywide Democratic organization, Tammany Hall, consisted of an army of party functionaries. At the bottom were the district captains. In return for votes, they provided services for their constituents, everything from a scuttle of coal in the winter to housing for an evicted family. At the top were the powerful ward bosses who distributed lucrative franchises for subways and streetcars. They formed a shadow government, more powerful than the city's elected officials. Tweed held the official title of alderman. But as a ward boss and chairman of the Tammany general committee, he wielded more power than the mayor. Through the use of bribery and graft, he held the Democratic Party together and ran the city.

The cost of Tweed's rule was staggering. The construction of New York City's courthouse, budgeted at $250,000, ended up costing the taxpayers $14 million. The inflated sum represented bribery, kickbacks, and the greasing of many palms. The excesses of the Tweed ring soon led to a clamor for reform and cries of "Throw the rascals out."

TAMMANY BANK
This cast-iron bank, a campaign novelty, is named after the New York City Democratic machine. It tells its political reform message graphically: When you put a penny into the politician's hand, he puts it in his pocket. Tammany Hall dominated city politics for more than a century, dispensing contracts and franchises worth millions of dollars. Some of those dollars invariably found their way into the pockets of Tammany politicians.
Collection of Janice L. and David J. Frent.

Cartoonist Thomas Nast pilloried Tweed in the pages of *Harper's Weekly.* His cartoons, easily understood even by those who could not read, did the boss more harm than hundreds of outraged editorials. Tweed fled to Europe in 1871 to avoid prosecution, but eventually he was tried and convicted and died in jail.

New York was not the only city to experience bossism and corruption. The British visitor James Bryce concluded in 1888, "There is no denying that the government of cities is the one conspicuous failure of the United States." More than 80 percent of the nation's thirty largest cities experienced some form of boss rule in the decades around the turn of the twentieth century.

Infighting among powerful ward bosses was more typical than domination by one big-city boss. "Czar" Martin Lomasney in Boston and Chicago's "Bathhouse" John Coughlin and Michael "Hinky Dink" Kenna exemplified the breed. Their colorful nicknames signaled their distance from respectable society and hinted at unsavory connections with an underworld of crime and vice. The power they wielded in their wards belied the charge that any single boss enjoyed hegemony in the big cities.

In the late nineteenth century, urban reformers and proponents of good government (derisively called "goo goos" by their rivals) challenged machine rule and sometimes succeeded in electing reform mayors. But the reformers rarely managed to stay in office for long. Their detractors called them "mornin' glories," observing that they "looked lovely in the mornin' and withered up in a short time."

The bosses enjoyed continued success over the reformers for one main reason: the help the urban political machine handed out to the cities' immigrants and poor. In return for votes, the machine provided legal aid, jobs, fuel, temporary shelter, and a host of small favors. The ability to combine philanthropy and politics was a hallmark of the urban boss. "What tells in holding your district is to go right down among the poor and help them in the different ways they need help," a Tammany ward boss observed. "It's philanthropy, but it's politics, too—mighty good politics." For the social services they received (and not because they were ignorant or undemocratic, as critics charged), the urban poor remained the bosses' staunchest allies.

Some reform mayors managed to achieve success and longevity. In cities where they sponsored public services and championed the working class, reformers proved as unbeatable as any boss. Hazen S. Pingree of Detroit exemplified the successful reform mayor. A businessman who went into politics in the 1890s, Pingree, like most good-government candidates, promised to root out dishonesty and inefficiency. He did, but he also tangled with business interests when he tried to lower streetcar fares and utility rates. When the depression of 1893 struck, Pingree emerged as a champion of the working class and the poor. He hired the unemployed to build schools, parks, and public baths. And he fought for and got public ownership of electric utilities. By providing needed services, he built a powerful political organization based on working-class support. Detroit's voters kept him in the mayor's office for four terms and then helped elect him governor twice.

While most good-government candidates harped on the Sunday closing of saloons and attacked vice and crime, Pingree demurred. "The most dangerous enemies to good government are not the saloons, the dives, the dens of iniquity and the criminals," but "the temptations which are offered to city officials when franchises are sought by wealthy corporations, or contracts are to be let for public works."

As Pingree shrewdly observed, not only the urban poor but the business class benefited from bossism and corruption. The boss could juggle tax assessments for property owners and provide lucrative franchises. Through the skillful orchestration of rewards, an astute political operator could exert powerful leverage and line up support for his party from a broad range of constituents, from the urban poor to wealthy industrialists. In 1902 when journalist Lincoln Steffens began "The Shame of the Cities," a series of articles exposing city corruption, he found that business leaders who fastidiously refused to mingle socially with the bosses nevertheless struck deals with them. "He is a self-righteous fraud, this big businessman," Steffens concluded. "I found him buying boodlers [bribers] in St. Louis, defending grafters in Minneapolis, originating corruption in Pittsburgh, sharing with bosses in Philadelphia, deploring reform in Chicago, and beating good government with corruption funds in New York."

The complexity of big-city government, apparent in the levels of corruption Steffens uncovered, pointed to one conclusion: For all the color and flamboyance of the big-city boss, he was simply one of many actors in the drama of municipal government. The successful boss was not an autocratic ruler but a power broker. Old-stock aristocrats, new professionals, saloon keepers, pushcart peddlers, and politicians all fought for their interests in the hurly-burly of city government. They didn't much like each other and they sometimes fought savagely. But they learned to live with one another. Compromise and accommodation—not boss rule—best characterized big-city government by the turn of the twentieth century.

Building Cities of Stone and Steel

"A town that crawled now stands erect," boasted an ironworker. "And we whose backs were bent above the [open] hearths know how it got its spine." Technology transformed the urban landscape in the late nineteenth and early twentieth centuries. Where once wooden buildings had stood rooted in the mire of unpaved streets, new cities of stone and steel sprang up. The skyscrapers and mighty bridges dominated the imagination and the urban landscape at the turn of the century. Less imposing, but no less significant, were the paved streets, the parks and public libraries, and the subways and sewers. In the late nineteenth century, Americans rushed to embrace new technology, making their cities the most modern in the world.

The Brooklyn Bridge opened in May 1883 and was quickly proclaimed "one of the wonders of the world." The world's longest suspension bridge soared over the East River in a single mile-long span connecting Brooklyn and Manhattan. Begun in 1869 during the days of Boss Tweed, the great bridge was the dream of builder John Roebling, who never lived to see it completed. His son, Washington Roebling, carried on the great work. The building of the Brooklyn Bridge called forth heroic effort. It took fourteen years and cost the lives of twenty men. Washington Roebling himself ended up an invalid, directing the completion of the bridge from his window in Brooklyn Heights through a telescope while his wife, Emily Warren Roebling, acted as site superintendent and general engineer of the project. When the bridge was dedicated in 1883, Roebling turned to his wife and said, "I want the world to know that you, too, are one of the Builders of the Bridge."

Skyscrapers as well as bridges changed the cityscape. Competition for space in Manhattan pushed the city up into the air even before the use of steel. The invention of Elisha Otis's elevator (called a "safety hoister") in the 1850s led to the construction of cast-iron buildings with elevators that carried passengers as high as ten stories. In 1890, the Pulitzer Building climbed to 349 feet, the tallest office building in the world. But until the advent of structural steel, no building in Manhattan topped the spire of Wall Street's Trinity Church.

Chicago, not New York, gave birth to the modern skyscraper. Rising from the ashes of the Great Fire of 1871, Chicago offered a generation of skilled architects and engineers the chance to experiment with new technologies. Commercial architecture became an art form at the hands of a skilled group of architects who together constituted the "Chicago school." Men of genius such as Louis Sullivan and John Wellborn Root gave Chicago some of the world's finest commercial buildings. Employing the dictum "form follows function," they built

PRICE 25¢

NEW YORK ILLUSTRATED

BROOKLYN BRIDGE
Arching 130 feet above the East River, the Brooklyn Bridge has proven not only aesthetically pleasing but remarkably functional for more than a century. A raised walkway allows pedestrians to enjoy their view above the traffic. John Roebling succeeded in his goal—to create "a great work of art" as well as "a successful specimen of advanced Bridge engineering."
Picture Research Consultants & Archives.

www.bedfordstmartins.com/roarkcompact   SEE THE ONLINE STUDY GUIDE for more help in analyzing this image.

startlingly modern structures. The massive commercial buildings, in Root's words, "carried out the ideas of modern business life, simplicity, breadth, dignity." A fitting symbol of modern America, the skyscraper expressed and exalted the domination of corporate power.

Alongside the skyscrapers rose new residential apartments for the rich and middle class. The "French flat" gained popularity in the 1880s as city dwellers overcame their distaste for multifamily housing (which carried the stigma of the tenement) and gave in to "flat fever." Fashionable new apartments, built for affluent tenants, boasted such

modern luxuries as electricity, telephones, central heating, elevators, and modern plumbing. The convenience of apartment living appealed particularly to women. "Housekeeping isn't fun," cried one New York woman. "Give us flats!" In 1883 alone, more than one thousand new apartments went up in Chicago.

Throughout the United States, municipal governments undertook public works on a scale unknown in European cities. They paved streets with asphalt, built sewers and water mains, replaced gas lamps with electric lights, ran trolley tracks on the old horsecar lines, and dug underground to build subways, tearing down the unsightly elevated tracks that had clogged the city streets. In San Francisco, Andrew Smith Hallidie mastered the city's hills, building a system of cable cars in 1873. Montgomery, Alabama, became the first city in the country to install a fully electrified streetcar system in 1886. Boston completed the nation's first subway system in 1897, and New York and Philadelphia soon followed.

Cities became more beautiful as planners created urban public parks. Much of the credit for America's public parks goes to one man—landscape architect Frederick Law Olmsted. Olmsted designed parks in cities from Atlanta, Brooklyn, and Hartford to Detroit, Chicago, and Louisville. The indefatigable Olmsted also laid out the grounds for the U.S. Capitol and planned an entire city, Riverside, Illinois. The Boston park system, a seven-mile ring of green that Olmsted called the city's "emerald necklace," was his most ambitious and successful project. But he is best remembered for the creation of New York's Central Park. He and his partner, Calvert Vaux, directed the planting of more than five million trees, shrubs, and vines to transform the eight hundred acres between 59th and 110th Streets into an oasis for urban dwellers. "We want a ground to which people may easily go after their day's work is done," he wrote, "where they may stroll for an hour, seeing, hearing, and feeling nothing of the bustle and jar of the streets."

American cities did not overlook the mind in their efforts at improvement. They created a comprehensive free public school system that educated everyone from the children of urban professionals to the sons and daughters of immigrants. The exploding urban population strained the system and led to crowded and inadequate facilities, but no one was turned away. In 1899, more than 544,000 pupils attended school in New York's five boroughs.

MOONLIGHT SKATING—CENTRAL PARK, THE TERRACE, AND LAKE
After the Civil War, Frederick Law Olmsted and Calvert Vaux put the finishing touches on
New York City's Central Park. As the centerpiece of the entire design, Bethesda terrace
stood with its central fountain dedicated as a monument to the Union navy's dead. Sculp-
tor Emma Stebbins designed Angel of the Waters, the graceful bronze figure that tops the
fountain. Vaux considered the grand terrace "the drawing room" of the park and by the
1870s it had become one of the most popular gathering places in the city. Shown here in an
1878 painting by John O'Brien Inman, Bethesda terrace shines in the moonlight as skaters
take a turn on the pond while bustled Victorian ladies converse with top-hatted gentlemen
on the shore in the foreground. The Angel of the Waters, with uplifted wings, can be
glimpsed in the center background.
Museum of the City of New York.

Schools in Boston, New York, Chicago, and Detroit as well as other cities and towns provided the only classrooms in the world where students could attend secondary school free of charge.

In addition to schools, the cities built libraries to educate their citizens. American cities in the late nineteenth century created the most extensive free public library system in the world. In 1895, the Boston Public Library opened its bronze doors under the inscription "Free to All." Designed in the style of a Renaissance palazzo, with more than 700,000 books on the shelves ready to be checked out, the library earned the description "a palace of

the people." Across the United States, other cities participated in the public library movement. Cincinnati, Detroit, St. Louis, Chicago, and Cleveland sponsored libraries in the 1870s. And in New York, Philadelphia, and Buffalo, the city stepped in with support when private libraries faltered in the 1890s.

Despite the Boston Public Library's legend "Free to All," the poor did not share equally in the advantages of city life. The parks, the libraries, and even the subways and sewers benefited some city dwellers more than others. Few library cards were held by Boston's laborers, who worked six days a week and found the library closed on Sunday. And in the 1890s, there was nothing central about New York's Central Park. It was a four-mile walk from the tenements of Hester Street to the park's entrance at 59th Street and Fifth Avenue. Cities spent more money on plumbing improvements for affluent apartment dwellers than on public baths and lodging houses for the down and out. Even the uniform subway fare, which enabled Boston and New York riders to travel anywhere in the system for five cents, worked to the advantage of the middle-class commuter and not the downtown poor. Then, as now, the comfortable majority, not the indigent minority, reaped a disproportionate share of the benefits in the nation's big cities.

Any story of the American city, it seems, must be a tale of two cities—or, given the cities' great diversity, a tale of many cities within each metropolis. At the turn of the twentieth century, a central paradox emerged: The enduring monuments of America's cities—the bridges, skyscrapers, parks, and libraries—stood as the undeniable achievements of the same system of municipal government that many reformers dismissed as boss ridden, criminal, and corrupt.

Conclusion: A Nation United

In the three decades between 1870 and 1900, the United States had filled out the map of the continent all the way to the Pacific Ocean as settlers pushed into the trans-Mississippi West, forcing the Native Americans onto reservations and establishing eight new states leaving three territories. A mass migration of peoples, global in scope, transformed both rural and urban life. As settlers moved out onto the plains, agriculture became increasingly commercial and mechanized, with huge farms totaling thousands of acres tilled by machine, not muscle. In urban America, mass transportation and the development of the skyscraper transformed the cityscape

at the same time that millions of new immigrants arrived on the shores. Municipal governments, straining to build the new cities, experienced the rough-and-tumble of machine politics as bosses and their constituents looked to profit from city growth and private enterprise fought for lucrative franchises and contracts.

During the second half of the nineteenth century in the American West and in the urban East, the nation confronted new problems that had replaced the old issues of slavery and sectionalism. The growing power of big business, the exploitation of labor and natural resources, and ethnic and racial tensions exacerbated by unparalleled immigration dominated the debates of the day. Urban industrialism challenged the American promise, which for decades had been dominated by Jeffersonian agrarian ideals. Could such a promise exist in the changing world of cities, tenements, immigrants, and huge corporations?

As the century ended, Americans had more questions than answers. But one thing was certain—the United States was united now in fact as well as name. An American contemplating a map of the nation in 1900 saw a spiderweb of railway tracks crisscrossing the continent, linking the burgeoning cities to the orange groves of California, the cotton fields of Texas, and the cattle ranches of Montana. No longer a set of isolated entities, by the twentieth century the farms, the villages and towns, the cities and the countryside of the United States were part of a vast network, linked to a global market and tied together by rails of steel.

FOR FURTHER READING ABOUT THE TOPICS IN THIS CHAPTER, see the Online Bibliography at
www.bedfordstmartins.com/roarkcompact.

FOR ADDITIONAL FIRST-HAND ACCOUNTS OF THIS PERIOD, see pages 17–36 in Michael Johnson, ed., *Reading the American Past*, Second Edition, Volume I.

TO ASSESS YOUR MASTERY OF THE MATERIAL IN THIS CHAPTER, see the Online Study Guide at
www.bedfordstmartins.com/roarkcompact.

CHRONOLOGY

1860–1900	Two and a half million farms established on public lands.
1862	Homestead Act promises 160 acres of western land to anyone who settles on land for five years.
1870	Eighty percent of population lives in rural areas, according to U.S. census.
1871	William Marcy Tweed's rule in New York ends.
	Fire ravages Chicago and leads to architectural innovation.
1873	Panic on Wall Street touches off nationwide economic depression.
1876	Custer's cavalry forces killed by Indians near Little Bighorn River in Montana Territory.
	Statehood granted to Colorado.
1880s	Immigration patterns shift as more people arrive from southern and eastern Europe.
1883	Buffalo Bill Cody begins to tour with his Wild West Company.
	Brooklyn Bridge opens.
1886	Statue of Liberty, a gift from France, dedicated in New York harbor.
	Severe blizzards in Dakotas devastate cattle ranching.
	Geronimo surrenders.
1887	Congress passes Dawes Act, breaking up Indian lands.
	Massive droughts defeat homesteaders on Great Plains.
1889	Rise of Ghost Dance religion.

	Sitting Bull killed by U.S. soldiers at Pine Ridge reservation.
	Government opens two million acres of former Indian territory in Oklahoma to settlement.
	Statehood granted to Montana, North Dakota, South Dakota, and Washington.
1890s	First wave of African American migration from South to North begins.
1890	Last remnant of Sioux surrenders, and army troops kill two hundred Indians at Wounded Knee, South Dakota.
	Jacob Riis's *How the Other Half Lives* published.
	Statehood granted to Idaho and Wyoming.
1893	Panic on Wall Street touches off major depression.
	Frenzied land rush takes place on Cherokee strip in Oklahoma Territory.
1895	Boston Public Library opens.
1896	Statehood granted to Utah.
1900	Ellis Island opens in New York harbor to process newly arrived immigrants.
	Census finds that 66 percent of population lives in rural areas, compared with 80 percent in 1870.
	Three cities—New York, Chicago, and Philadelphia—top one million inhabitants.

HAYES CAMPAIGN LANTERN, 1876

*Republicans employed this lantern in the cam-
paign of 1876. Designed for nighttime rallies, the
lantern featured paper transparencies that allowed
light to shine through the stars and illuminate the portrait
of candidate Rutherford B. Hayes. Marching men with lighted lanterns
held aloft must have made a dramatic scene in small towns across the country.
Nevertheless, Hayes did not win the popular vote and came to power in a contested
election that led Democrats to question his legitimacy and dub him "Rutherfraud."*

Collection of Janice L. and David J. Frent.

BUSINESS AND POLITICS IN THE GILDED AGE

18

1870–1895

ONE NIGHT AT DINNER, the humorist and author Mark Twain and his friend Charles Dudley Warner, editor of the *Hartford Courant*, teased their wives about the popular novels they read. Challenged to write something better, the two men set to work. Warner supplied the sentimental melodrama, while Twain "hurled in the facts." The result was a runaway best seller, uneven as fiction but offering a savage satire of the "get rich quick" era that forever after would be known by the book's title, *The Gilded Age* (1873).

Twain left no one unscathed in the novel—political hacks, Washington lobbyists, Wall Street financiers, small-town boosters, wildcat miners, and the "great putty-hearted public" that tolerated the plunder. The author had witnessed up close the corrupt partnership of business and politics in the administration of Ulysses S. Grant. Drawing on his experience, Twain described how a lobbyist could get an appropriation bill through Congress:

> Why the matter is simple enough. A Congressional appropriation costs money. Just reflect, for instance. A majority of the House Committee, say $10,000 apiece—$40,000; a majority of the Senate Committee, the same each—say $40,000; a little extra to one or two chairmen of one or two such committees, say $10,000 each—$20,000; and there's $100,000 of the money gone, to begin with. Then, seven male lobbyists, at $3,000 each—$21,000; one female lobbyist, $3,000; a high moral Congressman or Senator here and there—the high moral ones cost more, because they give tone to a measure—say ten of these at $3,000 each, is $30,000; then a lot of small fry country members who won't vote for anything whatever without pay—say twenty at $500 apiece, is $10,000 altogether; lot of jimcracks for Congressmen's wives and children—those go a long way—you can't spend too much money in that line—well, those things cost in a lump, say $10,000—along there somewhere;—and then comes your printed documents. . . . Oh, my dear sir, printing bills are destruction itself. Ours, so far amount to—let me see— . . . well, never mind the details, the total in clean numbers foots up $118,254.42 thus far!

The Gilded Age seemed to tarnish all who touched it. No one would learn that lesson better than Twain, who, even as he attacked it as an "era of incredible rottenness," fell prey to its enticements. Born Samuel Langhorne Clemens in a rough Mississippi river town, he first became a journeyman printer and then a riverboat pilot. Taking the pen name Mark Twain, he moved west and gained fame as a chronicler of Nevada's silver boom. In 1866 he came east to launch a career as an author, public speaker, and itinerant humorist. Twain played to packed houses, but his work was judged too vulgar for the genteel tastes of the time because he wrote about common people and used common language. *The Adventures of Huckleberry*

Finn, his masterpiece of American realistic fiction, was banned in Boston when it appeared in 1884.

Huck Finn's creator eventually stormed the citadels of polite society, hobnobbing with the wealthy and living in increasingly expensive and elegant style. He built an ornate Victorian mansion in Hartford, Connecticut, and maintained a townhouse off Fifth Avenue in New York City. Succumbing without much of a struggle to the money fever of his age, Twain plunged into one scheme after another in the hope of making millions. The Paige typesetting machine proved his downfall. This elaborate invention (it had more than eighteen thousand parts) promised to mechanize typesetting, replacing human labor with machine. The idea was a good one—German-born inventor Ottmar Mergenthaler soon successfully patented his own typesetting machine, the Linotype. But the Paige machine proved much too temperamental to be practical, and its investors lost out. By the 1890s, Twain faced bankruptcy. Only the help of Standard Oil millionaire Henry H. Rogers enabled him to begin his dogged climb out of debt.

Twain's tale was a common one in an age when the promise of wealth led as many to ruin as to riches. In the Gilded Age, great fortunes were made (and lost) with dizzying frequency. Wall Street panics, like those in 1873 and 1893, periodically interrupted the boom times and led to nationwide depressions. But with railroads to be built, cities demanding bridges, buildings, and mass transportation, and industry expanding on every level, the mood of the country remained buoyant. Hand in hand with the chances for riches went opportunities for graft and corruption. The interplay between business and politics, which Twain so deftly satirized in *The Gilded Age*, raised serious questions about the future of democracy.

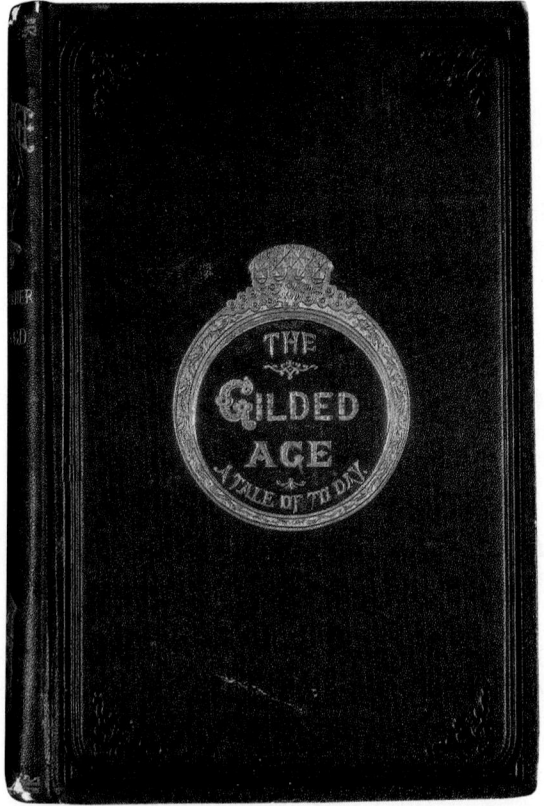

MARK TWAIN
Popular author Mark Twain (Samuel Langhorne Clemens) wrote acerbically about the excesses of the Gilded Age. No one knew the meretricious lure of the era better than Twain, who succumbed to a get-rich-quick scheme that left him virtually bankrupt.
Left: Beinecke Rare Book and Manuscript Library, Yale University. Right: Newberry Library.

The rise of industrialism in the United States and the interplay of business and politics strike the key themes in the Gilded Age, the period from the 1870s through the 1890s. In these three decades, the transition from a rural, agricultural economy to urban industrialism proved a deeply unsettling experience. The lives of America's workers as they navigated the transition are the focus of Chapter 19. This chapter highlights the businessmen and the politicians of the era. For perhaps nowhere were the hopes and fears that industrialism inspired better seen than in the public's attitude toward the great business moguls of the day, men like Jay Gould, Andrew Carnegie, John D. Rockefeller, and J. P. Morgan. These larger-than-life figures not only dominated business but also sparked the popular imagination as the heroes and villains in the high drama of industrialization. At no other period in U.S. history would the industrial giants and the businesses they built (and sometimes wrecked) loom so large in American life.

Old Industries Transformed, New Industries Born

In the years following the Civil War, the scale and scope of American industry expanded dramatically. Old industries became modern big businesses, while discovery and invention stimulated new industries such as oil and electric power. The rise of the railroad played the key role in the transformation of the American economy, creating a national market that enabled businesses to expand from a local to a nationwide scale.

The Railroads, America's First Big Business

In the decades following the Civil War, the United States built the greatest railroad network in the world and, in the process, created America's first big business. America's first transcontinental railroad system was completed in 1869 when the Union Pacific and Central Pacific tracks came together in Promontory Point, Utah, and a golden spike was driven to commemorate the occasion. Between 1870 and 1880, the amount of track laid in the country doubled, and it nearly doubled again in the following decade. By 1900, the country boasted over 193,000 miles of track, more than in all of Europe and Russia combined (Map 18.1).

To understand how the railroads developed and came to dominate American life, there is no better study than the career of Jay Gould, a man who came to personify the Gilded Age. Jason "Jay" Gould bought his first railroad before he was twenty-five years old. It was only sixty-two miles long, in bad repair, and on the brink of failure. But within two years, he had sold it at a profit of $130,000. Thus began the career of the man who would pioneer the development of America's railway system and become the era's most notorious speculator.

Gould, by his own account, knew little about railroads and cared less about their operation. Nevertheless, he became a master of corporate expansion, the architect of the vast railway systems that developed in the 1870s. The secretive Gould operated in the stock market like a shark, looking for vulnerable railroads, buying enough stock to take control, and threatening to undercut his competitors until they bought him out at a high profit. The railroads that fell into his hands fared badly and often went bankrupt; Gould's genius lay in cleverly buying and selling railroad stock, not in providing transportation.

The power and success Gould enjoyed underscored the haphazard development of the American railway system. The federal government held vast tracts of public land in the West, and Congress did not hesitate to give it away to promote railroad building. Over the years, the federal government granted the railroad builders a total of 180 million acres, an area larger than the state of Texas. But the lion's share of capital for the railroads came from private investors.

Lack of planning led to overbuilding. Already by the 1870s, the railroads competed fiercely for business on the eastern seaboard. A manufacturer who needed to get goods to the market and who was fortunate enough to be in an area served by a number of competing railroads could get a substantially reduced shipping rate in return for promising the chosen railroad steady business. Because railroad owners lost money through this kind of competition, they tried to set up agreements or "pools" to divide up territory and set rates. But these informal combinations invariably failed because they had no legal standing and because men like Jay Gould were intent on undercutting all competitors.

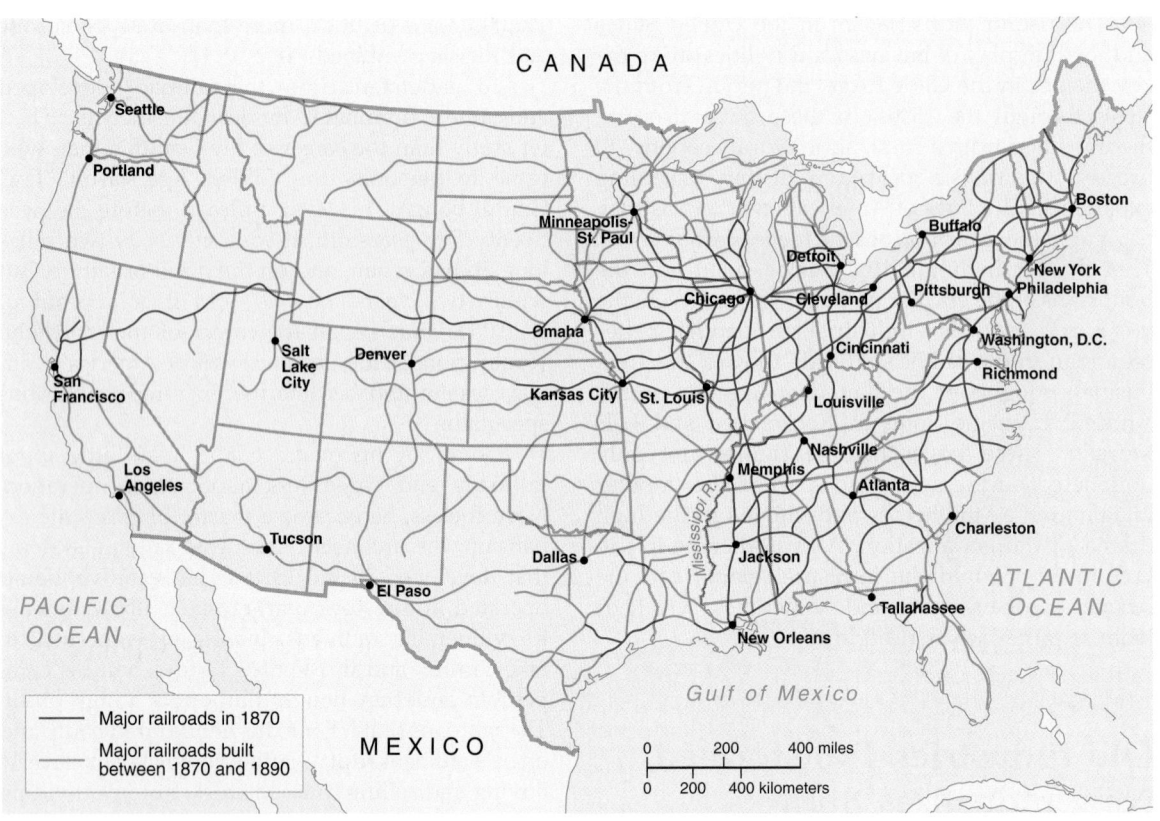

MAP 18.1

Railroad Expansion, 1870–1890

Railroad mileage nearly quadrupled between 1870 and 1890, with the greatest growth coming in the trans-Mississippi West. New transcontinental lines—the Great Northern, the Northern Pacific, the Southern Pacific, and the Atlantic and Pacific—were completed in the 1880s. Small feeder lines like the Oregon Short Line and the Atchison, Topeka, and Santa Fe fed into the great transcontinental systems, knitting the nation together.

READING THE MAP: Where were most of the railroad lines located in 1870? What cities were the major railroad centers? What was the endpoint of the only western route?

CONNECTIONS: Why were so many rails laid between 1870 and 1890? How did the railroads affect the nation's economy?

www.bedfordstmartins.com/roarkcompact SEE THE ONLINE STUDY GUIDE for more help in analyzing this map.

Not all the early railroad builders were as unscrupulous as Gould. James J. Hill built the Great Northern and built it well. Too late to benefit from land grants or subsidies, Hill had to plan carefully and calculate which areas would best be served by the railroad in order to maximize returns to his investors. As a result, the Great Northern was one of the few major railroads able to weather the hard times of the 1890s. In contrast, speculators like Daniel Drew and James Fisk, Gould's partners at the Erie Railroad, could more accurately be described as wreckers than as builders. They ruined the Erie by gambling with its stock to line their own pockets. In the West, the Big Four railroad

JAY GOULD AS A PIRATE
*In this 1885 political cartoon, Jay Gould is portrayed
as the pirate of Wall Street, sailing under the skull
and crossbones while afloat on the sea of speculation
in a raft of watered stock. "Out of His Reach" is the
Baltimore and Ohio stock he seeks to gain using the
hook of his monopoly of Western Union.*
Granger Collection.

builders—Collis P. Huntington, Richard Crocker, Leland Stanford, and Mark Hopkins—became so powerful that critics claimed the Southern Pacific held California in the grip of an "octopus."

The public's alarm at the control wielded by the new railroads provided a barometer of attitudes toward big business itself. When Jay Gould died in 1892, the press described him as "the world's richest man," estimating his fortune at over $100 million. His competitor "Commodore" Cornelius Vanderbilt, who built the New York Central Railroad, judged Gould "the smartest man in America." But to the public, who found in Gould a symbol of all that most troubled them about the rise of big business, he was, as he himself admitted shortly before his death, "the most hated man in America."

Andrew Carnegie and Vertical Integration

Railroad building led directly to the development of a second major industry—steel. The first railroads ran on iron rails, which cracked and broke with alarming frequency. Steel, both stronger and more flexible than iron, remained too expensive for use in rails until the 1850s, when an Englishman named Henry Bessemer developed a way to make steel more cheaply from iron ore. After the Civil War, with the discovery of rich iron deposits near the Great Lakes, the Bessemer process came into use in America. Andrew Carnegie, among the first to champion the new "King Steel," came to dominate the emerging industry.

If Jay Gould was the man Americans loved to hate, Andrew Carnegie was one of America's heroes. The infamy of the one man and the popularity of the other testified to the country's ambivalent reaction to industrialism. Carnegie, a Scottish immigrant, landed in New York in 1848 at the age of twelve. He rose from a job cleaning bobbins in a textile factory to become one of the richest men in America. Before he died, he gave away more than $300 million of his fortune, most notably to public libraries. His generosity, combined with his own rise from poverty, gave him a positive public image. But he had another side—that of a harsh taskmaster who made nearly inhuman demands on those who worked for him.

When Carnegie was still a teenager, his skill as a telegraph operator caught the attention of Tom Scott, superintendent of the Pennsylvania Railroad. Scott hired Carnegie, soon promoted him, and lent him the money for his first investments. A millionaire before he turned thirty, Carnegie struck out on his own to reshape the iron and steel industries. "My preference was always manufacturing," he wrote. "I wished to make something tangible." By applying the lessons of cost accounting and efficiency that he had learned from twelve years with the Pennsylvania Railroad, Carnegie turned steel into the nation's first manufacturing big business.

In Braddock, on the outskirts of Pittsburgh, Pennsylvania, in 1872 he built the most up-to-date Bessemer steel plant in the world and began turning out steel at a furious rate. At that time, steelmakers were able to produce about seventy tons a week. Within two decades, Carnegie's blast furnaces poured out an incredible ten thousand tons a week. He soon cut the cost of making rails by more than half. Carnegie's formula for success was simple: "Cut the prices, scoop the market, run the mills full; watch the costs and profits will take care of themselves." And they did. By 1900, Carnegie Steel earned $40 million a year.

To guarantee the lowest costs and the maximum output, Carnegie pioneered a system of business organization called vertical integration. All

ANDREW CARNEGIE
Andrew Carnegie, shown here in 1861, made a small fortune as a young man. In 1868, he totaled his assets. "Thirty three and an income of $50,000 per annum," he recorded. "Beyond this never earn—make no effort to increase fortune, but spend the surplus each year for benevolent [sic] purposes." Carnegie didn't stick to his plan. In 1872, he founded Carnegie Steel and went on to become one of the richest men in America, giving away an estimated $300 million to charitable causes before his death in 1919.
Carnegie Library.

aspects of the business were under Carnegie's control. From the mining of iron ore to its transport on the Great Lakes to the production of steel, vertical integration meant, in the words of one observer, that "from the moment these crude stuffs were dug out of the earth until they flowed in a stream of liquid steel in the ladles, there was never a price, profit, or royalty paid to any outsider."

The great productivity Carnegie encouraged came at a high price. He deliberately pitted his managers against one another, firing the losers and rewarding the winners with small shares in the

company. His workers achieved the high productivity Carnegie demanded by enduring long hours, low wages, and dangerous working conditions. Steelworkers toiled twelve hours a day in his plants, and when the shift changed every other week, they worked twenty-four hours straight.

Andrew Carnegie built Carnegie Steel into an industrial giant, the largest steel producer in the world. Carnegie's steel supported the elevated trains in New York and Chicago, formed the skeleton of the Washington Monument, supported the first steel bridge to span the Mississippi, and girded America's first skyscrapers. By 1900, Andrew Carnegie had become the best-known manufacturer in the world, and the age of iron had yielded to an age of steel.

Standard Oil and the Trust

Edwin Drake's discovery of oil in Pennsylvania in 1859 sent thousands rushing to the oil fields in search of "black gold." In the days before the automobile and gasoline, crude oil was refined into lubricating oil for machinery and kerosene for lamps, the major source of lighting in nineteenth-century houses before the advent of gas lamps or electric lighting. The amount of capital needed to buy or build an oil refinery in the 1860s and 1870s remained relatively low: less than $25,000, or roughly what it cost to lay one mile of railroad track. With investment cost so low, the story of the new petroleum industry was one of riotous competition among many small refineries. Ultimately, John D. Rockefeller, succeeded in controlling nine-tenths of the oil refining business.

Rockefeller grew up the son of a shrewd Yankee who peddled quack cures for cancer. At the age of twenty-five, he controlled the largest oil refinery in Cleveland. Like a growing number of business owners, Rockefeller abandoned partnership or single proprietorship to embrace the corporation as the business structure best suited to maximizing profit and minimizing personal liability. In 1870, he incorporated his oil business, founding the Standard Oil Company, the precursor of today's ExxonMobil Corporation.

As the largest refiner in Cleveland, Standard Oil demanded secret rebates, or refunds, from the railroads in exchange for its business. These rebates enabled Rockefeller to undercut his competitors. The railroads wanted his business so badly that they not only gave him rebates on his own shipping fares but also granted him a share of the rates paid by his competitors. As an official with the Pennsylvania Railroad later confessed, Rockefeller extracted such huge rebates that the railroad ended up paying Standard to transport its oil. Using this kind of leverage, Rockefeller pressured competing refiners to sell out or face ruin.

To gain legal standing for Standard Oil's secret deals, Rockefeller in 1882 pioneered a new form of corporate structure—the trust. The trust differed markedly from Carnegie's vertical approach in steel. Instead of attempting to control all aspects of the oil business, from the well to the consumer, Rockefeller moved horizontally to control only the refining process. Several trustees held stock in the various refineries "in trust" for Standard's stockholders. This elaborate stock swap allowed the trustees to coordinate policy between various refineries, ensuring that the companies could act in concert without running afoul of the law. The new enterprise, valued at $70 million, gave Rockefeller a virtual monopoly of the oil refining business with the unsuspecting public knowing nothing about it.

When the government threatened to outlaw the trust as a violation of free trade, Standard Oil changed its tactics and organized into a holding company. Instead of stockholders in competing companies acting through trustees to set prices and determine territories, the holding company simply combined competing companies under one central administration.

"WHAT A FUNNY LITTLE GOVERNMENT"
The power wielded by John D. Rockefeller and his Standard Oil Company is captured in this political cartoon that appeared in the January 22, 1900, issue of **The Verdict.** *Rockefeller is pictured holding the White House and the Treasury Department in the palm of his hand while in the background the U.S. Capitol has been converted into an oil refinery. Standard Oil epitomized the gigantic trusts that many feared threatened democracy in the Gilded Age.*
Collection of The New-York Historical Society.

www.bedfordstmartins.com/roarkcompact SEE THE ONLINE STUDY GUIDE for more help in analyzing this image.

Rockefeller began to integrate vertically, even as Standard Oil expanded horizontally. As the company's empire grew, central control became essential. Rockefeller ended the independence of the refinery operators and closed inefficient plants. Next he moved to control sources of crude oil and took charge of the transportation and marketing of petroleum products. By the 1890s, Standard Oil ruled more than 90 percent of the oil business, employed a hundred thousand people, and was the biggest, richest, most feared and admired business organization in the world.

Before he died in 1937, at the age of ninety-eight, Rockefeller had become the country's first billionaire. But despite his modest habits, his pious Baptist faith, and his many charitable gifts, he never shared in the public affection that Carnegie enjoyed. With its iron control of the market, its secret codes and spy system, and its ruthless suppression of competition, the company Rockefeller created earned the title "sovereign state of Standard Oil." To many Americans, Standard Oil came not only to symbolize all the disquieting forces reshaping America but also to pose a danger to democracy itself. (See "Documenting the American Promise," page 452.)

The Telephone and Electricity

Although Americans frequently disliked industrial giants like Rockefeller, they admired inventors. The second half of the nineteenth century was an age of invention, and men like Thomas Alva Edison and Alexander Graham Bell became folk heroes. But no matter how dramatic the inventors or the inventions themselves, the new electric and telephone industries they pioneered soon eclipsed their inventors and fell under the control of the bankers and the industrialists.

Alexander Graham Bell came to America from Scotland at the age of twenty-four with a passion to find a way to teach the deaf to speak; instead, he developed a way to transmit voice over wires—the telephone. American Bell, the company formed by the inventor in 1880, marketed the telephone under the skilled direction of a professional manager named Theodore N. Vail. Vail pioneered "long lines" or long-distance telephone service, creating American Telephone and Telegraph (AT&T) as a subsidiary. In 1900, AT&T became the parent company of the system as a whole, controlling

THE TELEPHONE IN THE HOME
The telephone achieved spectacular success, despite the daunting technical and marketing problems posed by a new technology that called for linking towns and cities by electrical wires to transmit voice. The number of phones soared from 310,000 in 1895 to over 1.5 million by 1900.
Corbis.

Western Electric, which manufactured and installed the equipment, and coordinating the Bell regional divisions. In practical terms, this complicated organizational structure meant that Americans could communicate not only locally but across the country as well, contributing greatly to speed and efficiency in business.

Thomas Alva Edison embodied the old-fashioned virtues of Yankee ingenuity and rugged individualism that Americans most admired. A self-educated dynamo, he worked twenty hours a day in his laboratory in Menlo Park, New Jersey, vowing to turn out "a minor invention every ten days and a big thing every six months or so." He almost made good on his promise. At the height of his career, he averaged a patent every eleven days and invented such "big things" as the phonograph, the motion picture camera, and the electric lightbulb.

Edison, in competition with George W. Westinghouse, went on to pioneer electricity as an energy source. By the turn of the twentieth century, electricity had become a part of American urban life. It powered trolley cars, subways, and factory machinery. It lighted homes, apartments, factories, and office buildings. In contrast, as late as the 1930s, only 10 percent of the nation's rural homes had electricity.

While Americans thrilled to the new electric cities, the day of the inventor quietly yielded to the heyday of the corporation. In 1892, the electric industry consolidated. Dropping the name of its

AN UNRESTRAINED DEMON.

FEARS OF ELECTRICITY
Electricity was by no means a technology easy to sell, as this 1889 cartoon shows. Innocent pedestrians are electrocuted by the wires, a woman swoons, presumably as a result of the buzzing current, a horse and driver have collapsed, and a policeman runs for help. The skull in the wires attached to the electric lightbulb warns that this new technology is deadly. Both an urban sophisticate in a top hat and a cowboy in boots have succumbed to the deadly wires. Edison had to develop an entirely new system of marketing that relied on skilled engineers to sell electric light and power.
The Granger Collection, New York.

Rockefeller and His Critics

No one inspired the nation's fear of industrial consolidation more than John D. Rockefeller, creator of the Standard Oil trust. To many Americans, Rockefeller and "the sovereign state of Standard Oil" came to represent a danger to democracy itself.

DOCUMENT 1. "The Smokeless Rebate" from Henry Demarest Lloyd's *Wealth v. Commonwealth*, 1894

As early as 1881, Henry Demarest Lloyd introduced Rockefeller to a national audience by attacking Standard Oil and its founder in "The Story of a Great Monopoly," published in the February issue of Atlantic Monthly. *The public eagerly snapped up the exposé—the issue went through six printings. Convinced that Standard Oil posed a threat to democracy, Lloyd embarked on a full-scale exposé of the company, published in 1894 under the title* Wealth v. Commonwealth. *To avoid charges of libel, Lloyd used no names, but his readers knew he referred to Rockefeller and Standard Oil when he charged that the "oil combination" controlled two U.S. senators and had "done everything with the Pennsylvania legislature except to refine it." Here Lloyd describes how Rockefeller used illegal railroad rebates to best his competitors.*

With searching intelligence, indomitable will, and a conscience which makes religion, patriotism, and the domestic virtues but subordinate paragraphs in a ritual of money worship, the mercantile mind flies its air-line to business supremacy. That entirely modern social arrangement—the private ownership of [railroads]—has introduced a new weapon into business warfare which means universal dominion to him who will use it with an iron hand.

This weapon is the rebate, smokeless, noiseless, invisible, of extraordinary range, and the deadliest gun known to commercial warfare. It is not a lawful weapon. . . . It has to be used secretly. All the rates he got were a secret between himself and the railroads. "It has never been otherwise," testified one of the oil combination. . . .

The smokeless rebate makes the secret of success in business to be not manufacture, but manu-

fracture—breaking down with a strong hand the true makers of things. To those who can get the rebate it makes no difference who does the digging, building, mining, making, producing the million forms of wealth they covet for themselves. They need only get control of the roads. . . . To succeed, ambitious men must make themselves refiners of freight raters, distillers of discriminations, owners not of lands, mines, and forests—not in the first place, at least—but of the railway officials through whose hands the produce must go to market. Builders, not of manufactories, but of privileges; inventors only of schemes . . . , contrivers, not of competition, but of ways to tax the property of their competitors into their pockets. They need not make money; they can take it from those who have made it.

SOURCE: Henry Demarest Lloyd, *Wealth v. Commonwealth* (Harper & Brothers, 1894), 474–75, 488.

DOCUMENT 2. Ida M. Tarbell, "The Oil War of 1872"

Editor and journalist Ida Minerva Tarbell, whose "History of the Standard Oil Company" ran for three years (1902–1905) in serial form in McClure's Magazine, *proved Rockefeller's most damaging critic. Tarbell grew up in the Pennsylvania oil region, and her father had owned one of the small refineries gobbled up by Standard Oil. Her devastatingly thorough history chronicled the underhanded methods Rockefeller employed to gain control of the oil refining industry. By the time she finished her story, Rockefeller slept with a loaded revolver by his bed in fear of would-be assassins.*

Here she portrays a critical chapter in the history of Standard Oil. In 1879, Rockefeller's first attempt to consolidate the oil industry through the use of illegal rebates had failed.

If Mr. Rockefeller had been an ordinary man the outburst of popular contempt and suspicion which suddenly poured on his head would have thwarted and crushed him. But he was no ordinary man. He had the powerful imagination to see what might be done with the oil business if it could be centered in his hands—the intelligence to analyze the problem into its elements and to find the key to control. He had the essential element to all great achievement, a steadfastness to a purpose once conceived which nothing can crush. The Oil Regions might rage, call him a conspirator and those who sold to him traitors; the railroads might withdraw their contacts and the legislature annul his charter; undisturbed and unresting he kept at this great purpose. . . .

He got a rebate. . . . How much less a rate than $1.25 Mr. Rockefeller had before the end of April the writer does not know. Of course the rate was secret and he probably understood now, as he had not two months before, how essential it was that he keep it secret. His task was more difficult now, for he had an enemy active, clamorous, contemptuous, whose suspicions had reached that acute point where they could believe nothing but evil of him—the producers and independents of the Oil Regions. It was utterly impossible that he should ever silence his enemy, for their points of view were diametrically opposed.

They believed in independent effort—every man for himself and fair play for all. They wanted competition, loved open fight. They considered that all business should be done openly—that railways were bound as public carriers to give equal rates—that any combination which favored one firm or one locality at the expense of another was unjust and illegal. . . .

Those theories which the body of oil men held as vital and fundamental Mr. Rockefeller and his associates either did not comprehend or were deaf to. This lack of comprehension by many men of what seems to other men to be the most obvious principles of justice is not rare. Many men who are widely known as good, share it. Mr. Rockefeller was "good." There was no more faithful Baptist in Cleveland than he. Every enterprise of that church he had supported liberally from youth. He gave to its poor. He visited its sick. He wept with its suffering. Moreover, he gave unostentatiously to many outside charities of whose worthiness he was satisfied. He was simple and frugal in his habits. He never went to the theater, never drank wine. He was a devoted husband, and he gave much time to the training of his children, seeking to develop in them his own habits of economy and of charity. Yet he was willing to strain every nerve to obtain for himself special and illegal privileges from the railroads which were bound to ruin every man in the oil business not sharing them with him. Religious emotion and sentiments of charity, propriety and self-denial seem to have taken the place in him of notions of justice and regard for the rights of others.

SOURCE: Ida M. Tarbell, "The Oil War of 1872," in Ellen F. Fitzpatrick, ed., *Muckraking: Three Landmark Articles* (Bedford Books of St. Martin's Press, 1994), 77–79.

DOCUMENT 3. Matthew Josephson, *The Robber Barons*, 1934

The historian Matthew Josephson, writing in 1934 in the trough of the depression, took a dim view of the great capitalists of the Gilded Age in his book The Robber Barons. *Noting that Rockefeller, Gould, and Morgan had avoided fighting in the Civil War by hiring substitutes, Josephson described them as follows.*

But besides the young men who marched to Bull Run, there were other young men of '61 whose instinctive sense of history proved to be unerring. Loving not the paths of glory they slunk away quickly bent upon business of their own. They were warlike enough and pitiless yet never risked their own skin: they fought without military rules or codes of honor or any tactics or weapons familiar to men: they were the strange, new mercenary soldiers of economic life. The plunder and trophies of victory would go neither to the soldier nor the statesman, but to these other young men of '61, who soon figured as "massive interests moving obscurely in the background" of wars. Hence these, rather than the military captains or tribunes are the subject of this history.

Josephson's portrait of the young John D. Rockefeller is a caricature of the bloodless miser:

In his first position, bookkeeper to a produce merchant at the Cleveland docks, when he was sixteen, he distinguished himself by his composed orderly habits. Very carefully he examined each item on each bill before he approved it for payment. Out of a salary which began at $15 a month and advanced ultimately to $50 a month, he saved $800 in three years, the lion's share of his total earnings! This was fantastic parsimony. . . .

He was given to secrecy; he loathed all display. When he married a few years afterward, he lost not a day from his business. His wife, Laura Spelman, proved an excellent mate. She encouraged his furtiveness, he relates, advising him always to be silent, to say as little as possible. His composure, his self-

(Continued)

possession was excessive. . . . He was a hard man to best in a trade, he rarely smiled and almost never laughed, save when he struck a good bargain. Then he might clap his hands with delight, or he might even, if the occasion warranted, throw up his hat, kick his heels, and hug his informer. One time he was so overjoyed at a favorable piece of news that he burst out: "I'm bound to be rich! Bound to be rich!"

SOURCE: Excerpt from *The Robber Barons: The Great American Capitalists, 1861-1901* by Matthew Josephson. Copyright © 1934 and renewed 1961 by Matthew Josephson. Reprinted by permission of Harcourt, Inc.

QUESTIONS FOR ANALYSIS AND DEBATE

1. Henry Demarest Lloyd and Ida Tarbell agree that Rockefeller gained control of the oil industry through illegal methods. What was his primary weapon, and how did it operate?

2. Compare Henry Demarest Lloyd's style to that of Ida Tarbell. Which is the more effective, and why? Do you think Tarbell is an impartial observer?

3. Rockefeller never responded to his critics. Although in private he referred to the author as "Miss Tarbarrel," he pointedly refused to respond, even to point out factual errors in her history. "If I step on that worm I will call attention to it," he said. "If I ignore it, it will disappear." Do you think Rockefeller's silence was a good strategy? Why or why not?

4. By the time Matthew Josephson wrote his unflattering portrait of Rockefeller in *The Robber Barons*, Rockefeller was long retired, Standard Oil had been broken up by an edict from the Supreme Court, and oil discoveries in Texas and Oklahoma had eclipsed the Oil Regions in Pennsylvania and Ohio. What do you think motivated Josephson's attack on the "robber barons" in 1934?

inventor, Edison General Electric became General Electric, a behemoth that soon dominated the market.

From Competition to Consolidation

Even as Rockefeller and Carnegie built their empires, the era of the industrial giant was coming to a close. Business increasingly developed into the anonymous corporate world of the twentieth century as the corporation became the dominant form of business organization and as corporate mergers restructured American industry.

Banks and financiers played a key role in this consolidation, so much so that individual entrepreneurship yielded to finance capitalism—investment sponsored by banks and bankers. During these years, a new social philosophy based on the theories of Charles Darwin helped to justify consolidation and to inhibit state or federal regulation of business. A conservative Supreme Court further proscribed attempts to control business by consistently declaring unconstitutional any legislation designed to regulate railroad rates or to outlaw trusts and monopolies.

J. P. Morgan and Finance Capitalism

The prominent business leaders of the late nineteenth century loathed competition and sought whenever possible to substitute consolidation and central control. None had a greater passion for order than John Pierpont Morgan, the Wall Street banker who became the architect of business consolidation. Aloof and silent, Morgan looked down on the climbers and the speculators with a haughtiness that led his rivals to call him "Jupiter," after the ruler of all the Roman gods. At the turn of the twentieth century, he exerted an influence so powerful that his critics charged that he controlled a vast "money trust."

Morgan acted as a power broker in the reorganization of the railroads and the creation of industrial giants like General Electric and U.S. Steel. When the railroads fell on hard times in the 1890s, Morgan, with his passion for order and his access to capital, took them in hand. He eliminated competition by creating what he called "a community of interest" among the managers he handpicked. By the time Morgan was finished reorganizing the railroads, seven major groups controlled two-thirds of the nation's track (Figure 18.1).

Banker control of the railroads rationalized, or coordinated, the industry. But peace came at a high

1870–1895

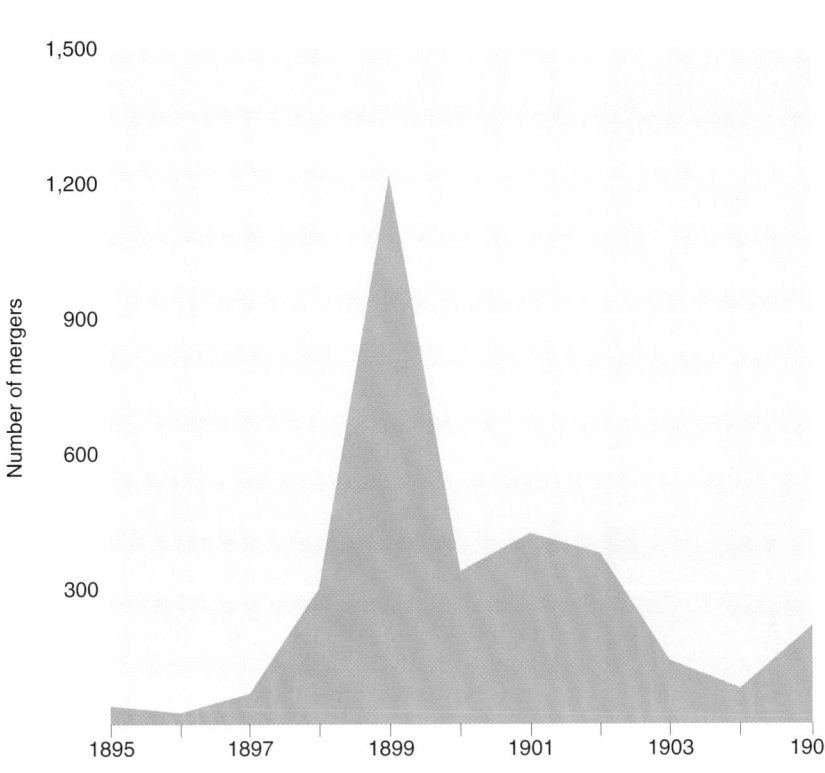

FIGURE 18.1
Merger Mania, 1895–1905
The depression that began with the panic of 1893 fueled a "merger mania," as businesses consolidated and reorganized, often at the prompting of finance capitalists like J. P. Morgan. The number of mergers peaked in 1899, but high rates of consolidation continued into the first decade of the twentieth century.

price. Morgan heavily "watered" the stock of the railroads, issuing new stock lavishly to keep old investors happy and to guarantee huge profits. J. P. Morgan & Co. made millions of dollars from commissions and from blocks of stock acquired through reorganization. The flagrant overcapitalization created by the watered stock hurt the railroads in the long run, saddling them with enormous debts. Equally harmful was the management style of the Morgan directors who ran the railroads. They were bankers, not railroad men, and they saw the railroads as little more than "a set of books." Their conservatism discouraged the continued technological and organizational innovation needed to run the railroads effectively.

In 1898, Morgan moved into the steel industry. His acquisition of Carnegie Steel exemplifies the passing of Carnegie's old entrepreneurial order and the rise of Morgan's new corporate system. Morgan supervised the mergers of several smaller steel companies, which soon moved from the manufacture of finished goods into steel production. Carnegie, who for decades had controlled the production of steel, countered by creating a new plant for the manufacture of finished products such as tubing, nails,

wire, and hoops. A pugnacious Carnegie cabled his partners in the summer of 1900: "Action essential: crisis has arrived . . . have no fear as to the result; victory certain."

The press trumpeted news of the impending fight between the feisty Scot and the haughty Wall Street banker, but what the papers called the "battle of the giants" in the end proved little more than the wily maneuvering of two businessmen so adept that even today it is difficult to say who won. For all his belligerence, the sixty-six-year-old Carnegie yearned to retire to Skibo Castle, his home in Scotland, and may well have invited Morgan's bid for power, knowing that only Morgan could command the capital to buy him out. Morgan, who disdained haggling, agreed to pay Carnegie's asking price, $480 million (the equivalent of about $9.6 billion, in today's currency). Carnegie's personal share alone amounted to more than $250 million.

Morgan quickly moved to pull together Carnegie's chief competitors to form a huge new steel corporation, United States Steel, known today as USX. Capitalized (some said grossly overcapitalized) at $1.4 billion, U.S. Steel was the largest corporation in the world. Yet for all its size, it did

J. P. MORGAN, PHOTOGRAPH BY EDWARD STEICHEN
Few photographs of J. P. Morgan exist. Morgan, who suffered from a skin condition that left him with a misshapen strawberry of a nose, rarely allowed his picture to be taken. But it was his eyes that people remembered—eyes so piercing that Edward Steichen, who took this photograph, observed that "meeting his gaze was a little like confronting the headlights of an express train."
George Eastman House. Reprinted with permission of Joanna T. Steichen.

not hold a monopoly in the steel industry. Significant small competitors such as Bethlehem Steel remained independent, creating a competitive system called an oligopoly, in which several large companies control production. Instead of competing head to head, the smaller firms simply followed the lead of giants like U.S. Steel in setting prices and dividing the market so that each company held a comfortable share. Although oligopoly did not entirely eliminate competition, it did effectively blunt it.

When J. P. Morgan died in 1913, his estate totaled $68 million, not counting an estimated $50 million in art treasures. Andrew Carnegie, who gave away more than $300 million before his death six years later, is said to have quipped, "And to think he

was not a rich man!" But Carnegie's gibe missed the mark. The quest for power, not wealth, characterized J. P. Morgan, and his power could best be measured not in the millions he owned, but in the billions he controlled. Morgan, during his lifetime, acted in place of a national bank and not until the creation of the Federal Reserve system was his power curtailed.

Social Darwinism and the Gospel of Wealth

John D. Rockefeller Jr., the son of the founder of Standard Oil, once remarked that the Standard Oil Company, like the American Beauty rose, resulted from "pruning the early buds that grew up around it." The elimination of smaller, inefficient units was, he said, "merely the working out of a law of nature and a law of God." The comparison of the business world to the natural world formed the backbone of a new theory of society based on the "law of evolution" formulated by British scientist Charles Darwin. In his monumental work *On the Origin of Species* (1859), Darwin theorized that in the struggle for survival, the process of adaptation to environment triggered a natural selection process among species that led to evolutionary progress. In the late nineteenth century, Herbert Spencer in Britain and William Graham Sumner in the United States developed a theory called social Darwinism. Crudely applying Darwin's teachings to human society, the social Darwinists concluded that progress came about as a result of relentless competition in which the strong survived and the weak died out.

In social terms, the doctrine of "survival of the fittest" had profound significance, as Sumner, a professor of political economy at Yale University, made clear in his 1883 book *What Social Classes Owe to Each Other.* "The drunkard in the gutter is just where he ought to be, according to the fitness and tendency of things," Sumner insisted. Any efforts by one class to aid another only tampered with the rigid laws of nature and slowed down evolution. Such a claim acted as a strong curb to reform at the same time that it glorified great wealth. In an age when men like Rockefeller and Carnegie amassed hundreds of millions of dollars while the average worker earned $500 a year, social Darwinism justified economic inequality.

Andrew Carnegie softened some of the harsher features of social Darwinism in his "Gospel of Wealth," published in 1889. The millionaire, Carnegie wrote, acted as a "mere trustee and agent for his poorer brethren, bringing to their service his superior wisdom, experience, and ability to administer, doing for them better than they could or would do for themselves." Carnegie preached philanthropy and urged the rich to "live unostentatious lives" and "administer surplus wealth for the good of the people." But although his Gospel of Wealth earned much praise, it won few converts. Most millionaires followed the lead of J. P. Morgan, who amassed private treasures in his marble library rather than distributing his wealth as Carnegie counseled.

Social Darwinism and the Gospel of Wealth suited an age in which the gross inequalities accompanying industrialization seemed to cry out for action. Assuaging the nation's conscience, social Darwinism made it possible to neglect the poor in the name of "race progress." When the poor were of a different race or ethnicity—as they so often were—social Darwinism smacked of racism. This ugly aspect was never far from social Darwinist ideology, which judged Anglo-Saxons superior to all other groups. Social Darwinism provided a perfect rationale for the status quo.

Laissez-Faire and the Courts

Business found a strong ally in the U.S. Supreme Court. During the 1880s and 1890s, the Court increasingly reinterpreted the Constitution to protect business from taxation, regulation, labor organization, and antitrust legislation. In a series of landmark decisions, the Court used the Fourteenth Amendment, originally intended to protect freed slaves from state laws violating their rights, to protect corporations. The Fourteenth Amendment declares that no state can "deprive any person of life, liberty, or property, without due process of law." By defining corporations as "persons" under the law, the Court determined that legislation designed to regulate corporations deprived them of "due process." Using this reasoning, the Court struck down state laws regulating railroad rates, declared income tax unconstitutional, and judged labor unions a "conspiracy in restraint of trade." The economic theory of laissez-faire (French for "let it alone") justified the notion that the government should not meddle in business by attempting to regulate it. However, when it came to economic assistance—tariffs, land grants, or subsidies—that was another matter, and laissez-faire did not seem to apply.

Faced with the host of economic and social dislocations caused by industrialism, the Court insisted on elevating the rights of property over the rights of people. According to Justice Stephen J. Field, the Constitution "allows no impediments to the acquisition of property." Field, born to a wealthy New England family, spoke with the bias of the privileged class to whom property rights were sacrosanct. Imbued with this ideology, the Court refused to impede corporate consolidation and did nothing to curb the excesses of corporate capitalism.

Party Politics in an Age of Enterprise

Why do the great industrialists like Rockefeller, Morgan, and Carnegie jump vividly from the pages of the past while the presidents of that period remain so pallid? The presidents from Rutherford B. Hayes (1877–1881) to William McKinley (1897–1901) are indeed forgotten men, largely because so little was expected of them. Until the 1890s, few Americans thought the president or the national government had any role in addressing the problems accompanying the industrial transformation of the nation. The dominant creed of laissez-faire, coupled with the dictates of social Darwinism, warned government to leave business alone. This crippling view of its rights and responsibilities in the economy and in society reduced the federal government to something of a sideshow. The real action took place elsewhere—in party politics on the local and state levels and in the centers of business and industry.

The power of the two major parties remained about equally divided from the 1870s into the 1890s. Although the Republicans captured the White House in four out of five elections, they rarely controlled the Congress. The Democrats, noted more for their local appeal than for their national unity, generally dominated the U.S. House of Representatives.

During this period, senators were not directly elected by the voters but were selected by state legislatures. In an era noted for its corruption, state legislatures frequently came under the influence of powerful business interests. Senators were often closely identified with business interests, as in the case of Nelson Aldrich, the powerful Republican from Rhode Island. Aldrich, whose daughter married John D. Rockefeller Jr., did not object to being called "the senator from Standard Oil."

Corruption and Party Strife

The political corruption and party factionalism that characterized the administration of Ulysses S. Grant (1869–1877) continued to trouble the nation in the 1880s. The spoils system—the awarding of jobs for political purposes—remained the driving force of party politics. The concept of ethics in government, precluding private individuals from getting rich from public office, remained an issue raised only among a small band of reformers during this period.

President Rutherford B. Hayes, whose disputed election in 1876 signaled the end of reconstruction in the South, proved to be a hardworking, well-informed executive who wanted peace, prosperity, and an end to party strife. Although he was ridiculed by the Democratic press as "Rutherfraud" and "His Fraudulency," Hayes was a figure of honesty and integrity who seemed well suited to his role as a national leader. But it was not an easy task.

Hayes headed a Republican party divided into factions led by strong party bosses who boasted that they could make or break a president. Fiery and dynamic leaders, they dominated national politics. Senator Roscoe Conkling of New York led the faction called the Stalwarts, who remained loyal to Grant. A master spoilsman, Conkling ridiculed civil service as "snivel service" and tried his best to get the Republicans to run Grant for a third term in 1880. Opposing him were the Half-Breeds, a faction led by Senator James G. Blaine of Maine. Blaine coveted the nomination for himself and worked to block Grant in 1880 and oust Hayes in 1884. A third faction, composed of prominent liberal Republicans called the Mugwumps, pressed for civil service but straddled the fence on other issues, leading one wit to remark "their mug [was] on one side and wump on the other."

President Hayes, despite his virtues, soon managed to alienate all factions in his party. He used federal patronage to build Republican strength by filling government jobs with, if not the best men, the best Republicans he could find. To the Stalwarts, who wanted more positions, his action constituted betrayal; to the Mugwumps, his appointments smacked too much of the spoils system. Hayes soon found himself a man without a party and announced that he would not seek reelection in 1880.

To avoid choosing among its factions the Republicans nominated a "dark-horse" candidate, Representative James A. Garfield from Ohio. To appease Conkling, they picked Stalwart Chester A. Arthur as the vice presidential candidate. The Democrats made an attempt to overcome sectionalism and establish a national party by selecting as their presidential standard-bearer the old Union general Winfield Scott Hancock. But as one observer noted, "It is a peculiarly constituted party which sends rebel brigadiers to Congress because of their rebellion, and which nominated a Union General as its candidate for president because of his loyalty." Although the popular vote was close, Garfield won 214 electoral votes to Hancock's 155.

Garfield's Assassination and Civil Service Reform

"My God," Garfield swore after only a few months in office, "what is there in this place that a man should ever want to get into it?" As the federal bureaucracy grew to nearly 150,000, thousands of office seekers swarmed to the nation's capital, each clamoring for a job. Garfield, like Hayes, faced the difficult task of remaining independent while pacifying the bosses and placating the reformers. The White House door stood open to all comers. Garfield took a fatalistic view. "Assassination," he told a friend, "can no more be guarded against than death by lightning, and it is best not to worry about either."

On July 2, 1881, less than four months after taking office, Garfield was shot in the back at a Washington, D.C., railroad station while catching a train. His assassin, Charles Guiteau, though clearly insane, was a disappointed office seeker who claimed to be motivated by political partisanship. He told the police officer who arrested him, "I did it; I will go to jail for it; Arthur is president, and I am a Stalwart (Conkling's faction)." Garfield lingered on through the hot summer while the nation held a long deathbed vigil. He died on September 19, 1881.

The press almost universally condemned Republican factionalism, if not for inspiring Guiteau, then for creating the political climate that produced him. Conkling's influence waned, as did his hopes for the White House. Attacks on the spoils system increased, and the public clamored for reform. But though Garfield's death crystallized the desire for civil service reform, the debate was long and hard.

Many of those who opposed reform recognized that civil service had built-in class and ethnic biases. At a time when few men had more than a grammar school education, written civil service examinations threatened to undo advances made by Irish Americans and turn government back over to an educated Yankee elite. One opponent argued, "George Washington could not have passed examination for a clerkship," observing that "in his will written by his own hand, he spells clothes, cloathes."

The legislation that established civil service reform—the Pendleton Act—passed in 1883, after more than a year of congressional debate and compromise. Both parties claimed credit for the act, which established a permanent Civil Service Commission of three members, appointed by the president. Some fourteen thousand jobs were placed under a merit system that required examinations for office and made it impossible to remove jobholders for political reasons. Half of the postal jobs and most of the customhouse jobs, the lion's share of the spoils system's bounty, passed to the control of the Civil Service Commission. The new law sought to prohibit federal jobholders from contributing to political campaigns, thus drying up a major source of the party bosses' revenue. Soon business interests replaced officeholders as the nation's chief political contributors. Ironically, civil service reform thus gave business an even greater influence in political life than it already had.

The Political Circus: The Campaign of 1884

With Conkling's downfall, James G. Blaine assumed leadership of the Republican Party and at long last captured the presidential nomination in 1884. A magnetic Irish American politician whose followers dubbed him the "Plumed Knight," Blaine inspired such devotion that his supporters were called Blainiacs. But to many reformers, Blaine personified corruption. Led by Carl Schurz, who insisted that Blaine "wallowed in spoils like a rhinoceros in an African pool," Republican reformers bolted the party and embraced the Democratic presidential candidate, the stolid Grover Cleveland, reform governor of New York. The burly, beer-drinking Cleveland distinguished himself from an entire generation of politicians by the simple motto "A public office is a public trust." First as mayor of Buffalo and later as governor of New York, he built a

solid reputation for honesty, economy, and administrative efficiency. He soon alienated the Tammany Hall political machine; but with reform in the air, the enemies he made only added to his appeal. The Democrats, who had not won the presidency since 1856, rushed to nominate him. In endorsing Cleveland, the Mugwumps announced that "the paramount issue this year is moral rather than political."

They would soon regret their words. The 1884 contest degenerated so far into nasty mudslinging that one disgusted journalist styled it "the vilest campaign ever waged." In July, Cleveland's hometown paper, the *Buffalo Telegraph*, dropped the bombshell that the bachelor candidate had fathered an illegitimate child in an affair with a widow named Maria Halpin. The crestfallen reformers tried to argue the difference between public and private morality. But robbed of their moral righteousness, they lost much of their enthusiasm. "Now I fear it has resolved itself into a choice of two evils," one weary reformer confessed.

At public rallies, Blaine's partisans taunted Cleveland, chanting:

Ma, ma, where's my pa?
Going to the White House
ha! ha! ha!

The stoic Cleveland accepted responsibility for the child, who may in fact have been fathered by his business partner. It is said Cleveland wished to spare his partner's reputation because he had fallen in love with the man's daughter. Silent but fuming, Cleveland waged his campaign in the traditional fashion—by staying home. Blaine broke precedent by making a national tour. On a last-minute stop in New York, the exhausted candidate overlooked a remark by a local clergyman that would cost him many votes. While introducing Blaine, the Reverend Samuel Burchard blasted the Democrats as the party of "Rum, Romanism, and Rebellion." An Associated Press correspondent hurriedly filed his story, crying, "If anything will elect Cleveland, these words will do it." By linking drinking and Catholicism, Burchard cast a slur on Irish Catholic voters, who had been counted on to desert the Democratic Party and support Blaine because of his Irish background.

With less than a week to go until the election, Blaine had no chance to recover from the negative publicity. He lost New York State by less than twelve hundred votes and with it the election. In the final tally, the Democrats ended twenty-five years of Republican rule, defeating Blaine by a scant 29,214 votes nationwide, but winning 219 electoral votes to 182 (Map 18.2). Cleveland's followers had the last word:

Hurrah for Maria! Hurrah for the kid!
I voted for Cleveland,
And Damned glad I did!

Economic Issues and Party Realignment

Four years later, in the election of 1888, fickle voters would turn Cleveland out, electing Republican Benjamin Harrison, the grandson of President William Henry Harrison. Then, in the only instance in America's history when a president who had once been defeated at the polls was returned to office, the voters brought Cleveland back in the election of 1892. What factors account for such a surprising turnaround? The strengths and weaknesses of the men themselves partially determined the outcome. The stubborn Cleveland, newly married to his partner's daughter, Frances Folsom, resented demands on his time and refused to campaign in 1888. Although he won more popular votes than Harrison, he lost the electoral college. Once in of-

fice, Harrison proved to be a cold and distant leader, prompting critics to call him "the human iceberg."

But issues as well as personalities increasingly swayed the voters. The 1880s witnessed a remarkable political realignment as a new set of economic concerns replaced appeals to Civil War sectional loyalties (a tactic called "waving the bloody shirt.") The tariff, federal regulation of the railroads and trusts, and the campaign for free silver restructured American politics.

The Tariff and the Politics of Protection

The concept of a protective tariff to raise the price of imported goods and stimulate American industry dated back to Alexander Hamilton in the founding days of the Republic. Congress enacted the first tariff following the War of 1812. The Republicans turned the tariff to political ends in 1861 by enacting a measure that simultaneously raised revenues for the Civil War and rewarded their industrial supporters who wanted protection from foreign competition. After the war, the Republicans continued to revise and enlarge the tariff at the prompting of northeastern industrialists. By the 1880s, the tariff posed a threat to prosperity. The huge surplus engendered by the tariff sat in the Treasury's vaults, depriving the country of money that might otherwise have been invested to create jobs and products, while the government argued about how (or even whether) to spend it.

To many Americans, particularly southern and midwestern farmers who sold their crops in a world market yet had to buy goods priced artificially high because of the protective tariff, the answer was simple: Reduce the tariff. Advocates of free trade and moderates agitated for tariff reform. But those who benefited from the tariff—industrialists like Andrew Carnegie who insisted that America's "infant industries" needed protection and westerners producing protected raw materials such as wool, hides, and lumber—firmly opposed lowering the tariff. Many workers, too, believed that the tariff protected American wage levels by giving American products a competitive edge over goods imported from other countries.

Blaine shrewdly recognized the potent political uses of the tariff in forging a new national alliance. "Fold up the bloody shirt and lay it away," he advised a colleague in 1880. "It's of no use to us. You want to shift the main issue to protection." By en-

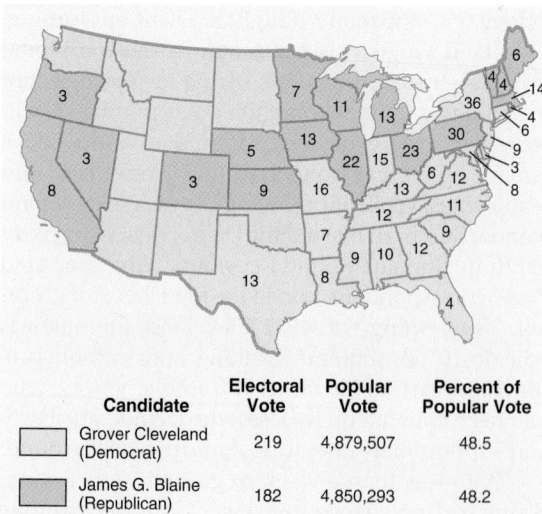

Candidate	Electoral Vote	Popular Vote	Percent of Popular Vote
Grover Cleveland (Democrat)	219	4,879,507	48.5
James G. Blaine (Republican)	182	4,850,293	48.2

MAP 18.2
The Election of 1884

couraging an alliance among industrialists, labor, and western producers of raw materials, groups who benefited from the tariff, Blaine hoped to solidify the North and West against the solidly Democratic South. Although the tactic failed for Blaine in the election of 1884, it worked for the Republicans four years later. Cleveland, who had straddled the tariff issue in the election of 1884, startled the nation in 1887 by calling for tariff reform. The Republicans countered by arguing that "tariff tinkering" would only unsettle prosperous industries, drive down wages, and shrink the farmers' home market. Benjamin Harrison, who supported the tariff, captured the White House in 1888, carrying all the northern and western states except Connecticut and New Jersey.

Back in office, the Republicans demonstrated their new commitment to economics over ideology by abandoning their support for freed slaves while currying favor with the new industrialists. Senator Henry Cabot Lodge's Force Bill, a federal election law to restore the vote to African Americans in the South, died in the same Republican Congress that passed the highest tariff in the nation's history in 1890. The new tariff, sponsored by Representative William McKinley of Ohio, stirred a hornet's nest of protest. The American people had elected Harrison to preserve protection, but not to enact a higher tariff.

Democrats condemned the McKinley tariff and labeled the Republican Congress that passed it the "Billion Dollar Congress" for its carnival of spending, depleting the nation's surplus by enacting a series of "pork barrel" programs shamelessly designed to bring federal money to legislators' own constituents. In the congressional election of 1890, angry voters swept the hapless Republicans, including tariff sponsor McKinley, out of office. Two years later, Harrison himself was defeated. Grover Cleveland, whose call for tariff revision had lost him the election in 1888, triumphantly returned to the White House vowing to lower the tariff. Such were the changes in the political winds whipped up by the tariff issue.

The Railroads, the Trusts, and the Federal Government

American voters may have divided on the tariff, but increasingly they agreed on the need for federal regulation of the railroads and federal legislation against the trusts. As early as the 1870s, angry farmers had organized to attack the railroads. The Patrons of Husbandry, or the Grange, founded in 1867 as a social and educational organization for farmers, soon became an independent political movement. By electing Grangers to state office, farmers made it possible for several midwestern states to pass laws regulating the railroads. At first the Supreme Court ruled in favor of regulation (*Munn v. Illinois*, 1877). But in 1886, the Court reversed itself, ruling that because railroads crossed state boundaries, they fell outside state jurisdiction (*Wabash v. Illinois*). With more than three-fourths of railroads crossing state lines, the Supreme Court's decision effectively quashed the states' attempts at railroad regulation.

Anger over the *Wabash* decision finally led to the first federal law regulating the railroads, the Interstate Commerce Act, passed in 1887 during Cleveland's first administration. The act established the nation's first federal regulatory agency, the Interstate Commerce Commission (ICC). In its early years, the ICC was never strong or sure enough to pose a serious threat to the railroads. It proved more important as a precedent than effective as a watchdog.

Concern over the growing power of the trusts led Congress to pass the Sherman Antitrust Act in 1890. The act outlawed pools and trusts, ruling that businesses could no longer enter into agreements to restrict competition. It did nothing to restrict huge holding companies like Standard Oil, however, and proved to be a weak sword against the trusts. In the decade after passing the Sherman Antitrust Act, the government successfully struck down only six trusts. However, the act was used four times against labor by outlawing unions as a "conspiracy in restraint of trade." Then, in 1895, the Supreme Court dealt the law a crippling blow in *United States v. E. C. Knight Company*. The decision in this case drastically narrowed the law by allowing the American Sugar Refining Company, which had bought out a number of other sugar companies (including E. C. Knight) and thus controlled 98 percent of the production of sugar, to continue its virtual monopoly on the grounds that "manufacture" did not constitute "trade."

Both the ICC and the Sherman Antitrust Act testified to the nation's concern about the big business's abuses of power and to a growing willingness to use federal measures to intervene on behalf of the public interest. Yet not until the twentieth century would more active presidents sharpen and use these weapons against the large corporations.

VOL. XLI. No. 1044. PUCK BUILDING, New York, March 10th, 1897. PRICE TEN CENTS.
Copyright, 1897, by Keppler & Schwarzmann.

Entered at N. Y. P. O. as Second-class Mail Matter.

C. J. Taylor

IN THE HANDS OF HIS PHILANTHROPIC FRIENDS.

**THE CORRUPTION OF GOVERNMENT
BY BIG BUSINESS**
In this **Puck** *cartoon, a gullible Uncle Sam is being
led by trusts and monopolies, satirically styled as
"his philanthropic friends." Concern over the power
of big business led in 1890 to the passage of the
Sherman Antitrust Act, the first attempt to regulate
business by making it illegal to restrict competition.*
Picture Research Consultants & Archives.

The Fight for Free Silver

The silver issue stirred passions like no other issue
of the day. On one side stood those who believed
that gold constituted the only honest money. Although other forms of currency circulated, notably
paper money like banknotes and greenbacks, the
government's support of the gold standard meant
that all currency could be redeemed for gold. Many
who supported the gold standard were eastern
creditors who did not wish to be paid in devalued
dollars. On the opposite side stood a coalition of sil-

ver barons and poor farmers. The mining interests,
who had seen the silver bonanza in the West drive
down the price of silver, wanted the government to
buy the metal and mint silver dollars to help jack
up the price. Farmers from the West and South who
had suffered economically during the 1870s and
1880s hoped that increasing the money supply with
silver dollars would give them some relief, enabling
them to pay off their debts with devalued dollars.

Advocates of silver pointed out that until 1873
the country had enjoyed a system of bimetallism,
with both silver and gold minted into coins. In that
year, at the behest of those who favored gold,
Congress voted to demonetize (stop buying and
minting) silver, an act advocates of bimetallism denounced as the "crime of '73." In 1878 and again in
1890, Congress took steps to appease advocates of
silver by passing legislation that required the government to buy silver and issue silver certificates.
While good for the mining interests, the laws did
little to promote the inflation desired by the farmers. Soon they began to call for "the free and unlimited coinage of silver," a plan whereby virtually
all the silver mined in the West would be minted
into coins circulated at the rate of sixteen ounces of
silver to one ounce of gold.

The silver issue crossed party lines, but the Democrats hoped to use it to achieve a union between
western and southern voters. Unfortunately for them,
Grover Cleveland, a conservative in money matters
and a strong supporter of the gold standard, sat in the
White House. Cleveland called a special session of
Congress in August 1893 and bullied the legislature
into repealing an act that had mandated the government to purchase silver. Repeal only divided the country. Angry farmers warned Cleveland not to travel
west of the Mississippi River if he valued his life.

The year 1893 marked a black time in the nation's economic history. In the spring a panic on
Wall Street touched off a deep economic depression
that would last for several years. In the winter of
1894–95, Cleveland walked the floor of the White
House, sleepless over the prospect that the United
States might go bankrupt. The Treasury's gold reserves had dipped so low that unless gold could be
purchased abroad, the unthinkable might happen—
the U.S. Treasury might not be able to meet its
obligations.

At this juncture J. P. Morgan stepped in and
suggested a plan whereby a private group of
bankers would purchase gold abroad and supply it

U.S. CURRENCY
While gold remained the nation's standard currency, silver supporters, including farmers and western mining interests, demanded the minting of silver coins and the issuance of silver certificates like those pictured on the right. In the center is a gold piece.
The American Numismatic Assn.; Picture Research Consultants & Archives.

to the Treasury. Cleveland knew only too well that such a scheme would touch off a thunder of protest from citizens and politicians already suspicious of the power the influential bankers wielded. Yet to save the gold standard, the president turned to Morgan for help. A storm of controversy erupted over the deal. The press claimed that Cleveland had lined his own pockets and rumored that Morgan had made $8.9 million on profits. Neither was true. Cleveland had not profited a penny, and Morgan made about $300,000 on the deal—far less than the millions his critics claimed.

Yet the passions stirred by Cleveland's action in 1895 cannot be dismissed lightly. Undoubtedly Morgan saved the gold reserves. But if President Cleveland's action managed to salvage the gold standard, it did not save the country. The winter of 1894–95 was one of the hardest in American history. People faced unemployment, cold, and hunger. It never occurred to Cleveland that his great faith in gold prolonged the depression, favored creditors over debtors, and caused immense hardship for millions of Americans.

Conclusion: Business Dominates an Era

The deal between J. P. Morgan and Grover Cleveland underscored a dangerous reality: The federal government was so weak that the solvency of the state depended upon a private banker. This lopsided power relationship signaled the dominance of business. Collusion and corruption marked the relationship between business and government on all levels in the Gilded Age. Mark Twain's satiric label has stood for more than a century as a fair representation of an era that spawned greed, corruption, and vulgarity on a grand scale, an era when speculator-industrialists like Jay Gould could not only build or wreck businesses to turn paper profits but also boast openly of buying politicians, who in turn lined their pockets at the public's expense.

Nevertheless, the era was not without its share of solid achievements. In these years, America made the leap into the industrial age. Factories and refineries turned out American steel and oil at unprecedented rates. Businessmen like Carnegie, Rockefeller, and Morgan developed new strategies to consolidate American industry. By the end of the nineteenth century, the country had achieved industrial maturity. No other era in the nation's history witnessed such a transformation.

America's workers shared little in the profits of the Gilded Age. The growing gap between the classes led many thoughtful people to wonder whether the nation could solve the problems accompanying industrialization and curb the power of the financiers and corporations. By the 1890s, the United States faced problems that were not only economic but also social and political—agrarian discontent, labor unrest, depression, and unemployment. It was in the midst of this unrest that President Cleveland reluctantly accepted Morgan's aid to bail out the country. No wonder in the grim winter of 1894–95, men and women talked of revolution, some of them in fear and some of them in anger.

FOR FURTHER READING ABOUT THE TOPICS IN THIS CHAPTER, see the Online Bibliography at www.bedfordstmartins.com/roarkcompact.

FOR ADDITIONAL FIRST-HAND ACCOUNTS OF THIS PERIOD, see pages 37–51 in Michael Johnson, ed., *Reading the American Past,* Second Edition, Volume II.

TO ASSESS YOUR MASTERY OF THE MATERIAL IN THIS CHAPTER, see the Online Study Guide at www.bedfordstmartins.com/roarkcompact.

CHRONOLOGY

1869 Completion of first transcontinental railroad.

1870 John D. Rockefeller incorporates Standard Oil Company in Cleveland.

1872 Andrew Carnegie builds nation's largest Bessemer process steel plant near Pittsburgh.

1873 U.S. government decides to stop minting silver dollars.

Panic on Wall Street leads to major economic depression.

Mark Twain and Charles Dudley Warner publish *The Gilded Age*.

1876 Alexander Graham Bell demonstrates telephone at Philadelphia Centennial Exposition.

1877 Rutherford B. Hayes sworn in as president of United States after disputed election.

U.S. Supreme Court upholds right of states to regulate railroads in *Munn v. Illinois*.

1879 Congress votes to resume gold standard.

Thomas Alva Edison perfects filament for incandescent lightbulb.

1880s Jay Gould becomes architect of a transcontinental railway system.

1880 Dark-horse Republican candidate James A. Garfield elected president of United States.

1881 President Garfield assassinated; Vice President Chester A. Arthur becomes president.

1882 Standard Oil develops the trust.

1883 Congress passes Pendleton Act, establishing civil service reform.

1884 Grover Cleveland wins presidency; first Democratic president since before the Civil War.

Mark Twain's *Adventures of Huckleberry Finn* published (and subsequently banned in Boston).

1886 In *Wabash* case, U.S. Supreme Court reverses itself and disallows state regulation of railroads that cross state lines.

1887 Congress passes Interstate Commerce Act, creating the first federal agency designed to regulate railroads.

1888 Benjamin Harrison elected president of United States.

1890 Congress passes McKinley tariff.

Congress passes Sherman Antitrust Act.

1893 Panic devastates financial markets and touches off national depression.

1895 J. P. Morgan bails out U.S. Treasury and saves country's gold reserves.

1901 J. P. Morgan buys out Carnegie Steel and creates U.S. Steel, first billion-dollar corporation in United States.

DINNER PAILS

The dinner pail or lunch working class, took many midday meal for workers bucket, the universal symbol of the sizes and shapes. Designed to carry a who did not have time to go home to eat, it might hold bread, leftovers, a sandwich, coffee, or whatever else fit easily into the container. Some cities such as Riverside, California, prohibited workers from carrying dinner pails on downtown streets. Presumably sidewalks were meant only for the middle class and well to do.

Anthracite Heritage Museum.

AMERICA'S WORKERS: LIFE AND LABOR

19

1870–1890

FOR TWO WEEKS DURING THE SUMMER OF 1877, the United States faced an insurrection greater than any since the Civil War. President Rutherford B. Hayes met daily with his cabinet to plan military strategy and sat up late into the night receiving reports from his generals. He dispatched federal troops to nine states, ordered warships to protect the nation's capital, and threatened to declare martial law. Not since the Confederates fired on Fort Sumter had the nation witnessed such an alarm. Who posed this threat to the Republic? Not former rebels or foreign armies, but American workers engaged in the first nationwide labor strike in the country's history.

Economic depression following the panic of 1873 had thrown as many as 3 million people out of work. Those who were lucky enough to keep their jobs watched as pay cuts eroded their wages until they could no longer feed their families. When the Baltimore and Ohio (B&O) Railroad announced a 10 percent wage reduction in the summer of 1877 at the same time it declared a 10 percent dividend to its stockholders, the brakemen in West Virginia, whose wages had already fallen from $70 to $30 a month, walked out on strike. One B&O worker described the hardship that had driven him to take such desperate action: "We eat our hard bread and tainted meat two days old on the sooty cars up the road, and when we come home, find our children gnawing bones and our wives complaining that they cannot even buy hominy and molasses for food."

The strike by brakemen in West Virginia touched off the Great Railroad Strike of 1877, a nationwide uprising that spread rapidly to Pittsburgh and Chicago, St. Louis and San Francisco (Map 19.1). Within a few days, nearly 100,000 railroad workers went out on strike. The spark of rebellion soon fired other workers to action. An estimated 500,000 laborers joined the striking train workers. Steelworkers, longshoremen, workers from all industries, often with their wives and children, made common cause with the railroad strikers. Violence erupted in Pittsburgh as the strikers clashed with state militia. When militiamen fired on the crowd, killing 20 people, angry workers retaliated by reducing an area two miles along the track to smoldering rubble, costing the railroad $2 million in damages. President Hayes, after hesitating briefly, called up federal troops. In three weeks it was over. "The strikes have been put down by force," Hayes noted in his diary on August 5. "But now for the real remedy. Can't something be done by education of the strikers, by judicious control of the capitalists, by wise general policy to end or diminish the evil? The railroad strikers, as a rule, are good men, sober, intelligent, and industrious."

The uprising of the workers in 1877 underscored the tensions produced by rapid industrialization and pointed to many grievances on the part of labor. The unprecedented industrial growth that occurred after the Civil War came about as

MAP 19.1
The Great Railroad Strike of 1877
Starting in West Virginia and Pennsylvania, the Great Railway Strike of 1877 spread as far north as Buffalo and as far west as San Francisco, bringing rail traffic to a standstill.

a result of the labor of millions of men, women, and children who toiled in workshops and factories, in sweatshops and mines, on the railroads and construction sites across America. Their stories provide a different perspective from that of the great industrialists and the politicians. Through their eyes it is possible to gauge how corporate capitalism transformed old work patterns and affected the social and cultural—as well as the economic and political—life of the United States.

America's New Industrial Workers

America's industrial growth in the years following the Civil War brought about a massive redistribution of population, as agricultural workers moved to the city and became recruits in the industrial labor force. Burgeoning industrial centers such as

Pittsburgh, Chicago, New York, and Detroit acted like giant magnets, attracting workers from the countryside. The movement from farms to industrial centers was not just American in scope. Farm boys and girls from western Pennsylvania who left for the mills of Pittsburgh were part of a global migration that included rural immigrants from Ireland, southern Italy, Russia, Japan, and China. As labor historian David Montgomery has pointed out, "The rural periphery of the nineteenth century industrial world became the primary source of supply for 'human machines.'"

Workers from the Rural Periphery

By the 1870s, the world could be seen as divided into three interlocking geographic regions (Map 19.2). At the center stood an industrial core bounded by Chicago and St. Louis in the west; Toronto, Glasgow, and Berlin in the north; Warsaw in the east; and Milan, Barcelona, Richmond, and Louisville in the south. Sur-

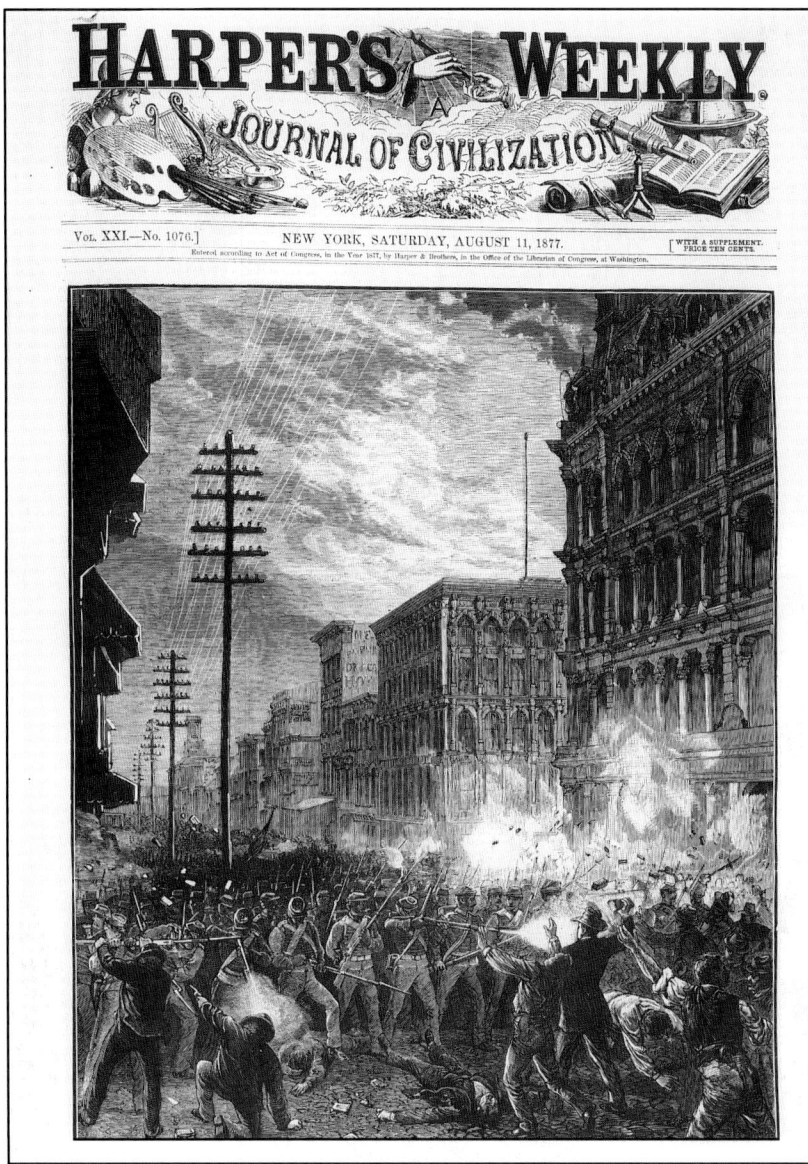

HARPER'S WEEKLY.
JOURNAL OF CIVILIZATION

Vol. XXI.—No. 1076.]   NEW YORK, SATURDAY, AUGUST 11, 1877.   [WITH A SUPPLEMENT.
PRICE TEN CENTS.

**THE GREAT RAILROAD
STRIKE**
*The August 11, 1877, cover
of* Harper's Weekly
*featured an illustration of
the great railroad strike
depicting the sixth
Maryland regiment firing
its way through Baltimore.
Notice the fixed bayonets
of the soldiers and the
brick-throwing strikers
fighting in close quarters.
Such scenes of violence
frightened many middle-
class Americans who
initially had sympathized
with the strikers. Public
opinion shifted as a result
of news coverage as many
blamed the strikers for the
bloodshed and damage to
property that accompanied
the strike.*
Harper's Weekly, August 11, 1877.

rounding the industrial core and its urban outposts lay a vast agricultural domain encompassing Canada, much of Scandinavia, Russia and Poland, Hungary, Greece, Italy and Sicily, southern Spain, the defeated Confederate states and the Great Plains of America, central and northern Mexico, the hinterlands of Canton, China, and later the southern islands of Japan. Capitalist development in the late nineteenth century shattered traditional patterns of economic activity in this rural periphery. As old patterns broke down, the rural areas exported, along with other raw materials, new recruits for the industrial labor force.

Beyond this second circle lay an even larger area including the Caribbean, Central and South America, the Middle East, Africa, India, and most of Asia. This third area too became increasingly tied to the industrial core in the late nineteenth century, but its peoples largely stayed put. They worked on the plantations and railroads, in the mines and ports as part of a huge export network managed by foreign powers that staked out spheres of influence and colonies, often with gunboats and soldiers.

Beginning in the 1870s, railroad expansion and low steamship fares gave the world's peoples a

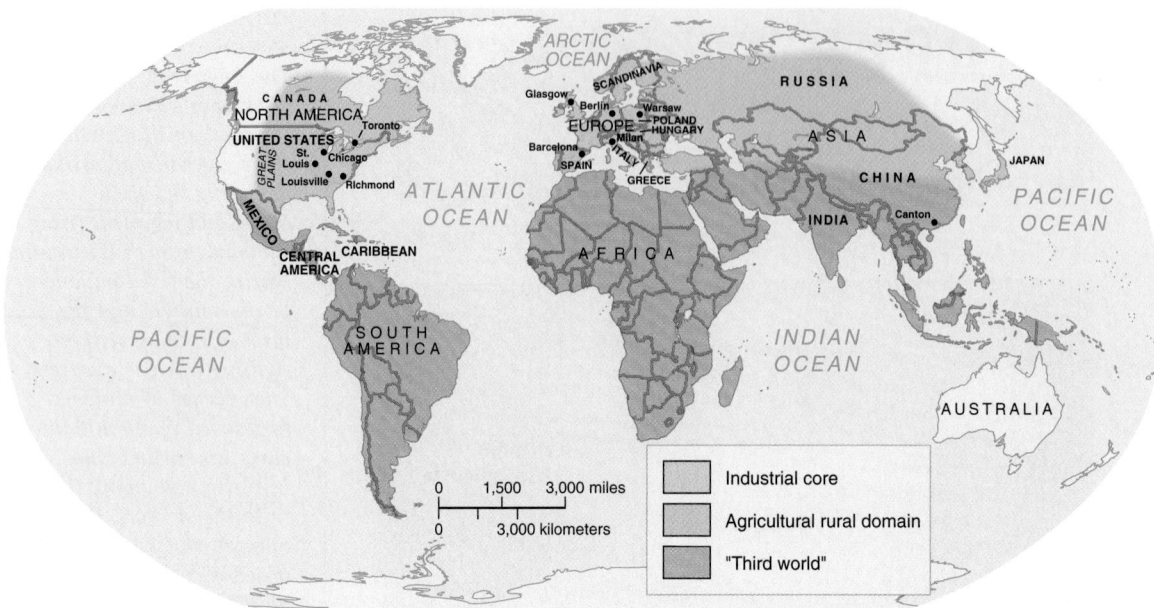

MAP 19.2

Economic Regions of the World
The global nature of the world economy at the turn of the twentieth century is indicated by three interlocking geographic regions. At the center was the industrial core—western Europe and the northeastern United States; the agricultural periphery (rural domain) supplied immigrant laborers to the industries in the core. Beyond these two regions lay a "third world" tied economically to the industrial core by colonialism.

READING THE MAP: What parts of the world did not belong to one of these three economic regions? Where did the United States fit in this economic division of the globe?

CONNECTIONS: What does this characterization of the United States say about its stage of economic development in the late nineteenth century? How would you characterize the areas outside the economic regions specified?

www.bedfordstmartins.com/roarkcompact SEE THE ONLINE STUDY GUIDE for more help in analyzing this map.

newfound mobility that enabled industrialists to draw on a worldwide population for cheap labor. When Andrew Carnegie opened his first steel mill in 1872, his superintendent hired workers he called "buckwheats"—young American boys just off the farm. By the 1890s, however, Carnegie's workforce was liberally sprinkled with other rural boys—Hungarians and Slavs who had migrated to the United States, willing to work for low wages. The ability to draw on cheap labor on a global scale helps explain why, in spite of the soaring demand for laborers after the Civil War, the wages of unskilled workers in the United States remained relatively stagnant. Their

pay fell dramatically during the depressions of 1873–1878 and 1893–1896, and did not regain 1872 levels before the end of the century.

Immigration, Ethnic Rivalry, and Racism

Ethnic diversity played a role in dividing skilled workers (those with a craft or specialized ability) from the unskilled (those who supplied muscle and brawn). As managers increasingly mechanized to replace skilled workers with lower-paid, unskilled labor, they drew on immigrants from southern and

VOL. 13 NO. 330   FEBRUARY 11, 1888.   PRICE 10 CENTS.

SUPPLY AND DEMAND—SHALL IMMIGRATION BE RESTRICTED?
EMPLOYER—"As long as I am plentifully supplied with Immigrant Labor, I shall be deaf to the demands of the native workingman."

THE COMPETITION OF CHEAP LABOR
Big business looks on approvingly as cheap immigrant labor outweighs American workers in this political cartoon published in the weekly **Judge** *in 1888. "As long as I am plentifully supplied with Immigrant Labor," says the portly manufacturer, "I shall be deaf to the demands of the native workingman." Cartoons like this one underscored organized labor's concern with the number of foreign workers entering the country in the 1880s—nearly eight million, twice the number of the previous decade. Organized labor argued that not only did the seemingly unlimited supply of immigrant laborers keep wages low, but that the new recruits, who knew nothing of labor's struggles, often took work as strikebreakers.*
Judge, February 11, 1888.

www.bedfordstmartins.com/roarkcompact SEE THE ON-LINE STUDY GUIDE for more help in analyzing this image.

eastern Europe—immigrants who came to the United States in the hope of bettering their lives. (See "Historical Question," page 472.) The skilled workers, mostly old immigrants from northern or western Europe, criticized the newcomers. As one Irish worker complained, "There should be a law . . . to

keep all the Italians from comin' in and takin' the bread out of the mouths of honest people."

The Irish worker's resentment of the new Italian immigrants brings into focus the impact of racism in the experience of America's immigrant laborers. Throughout the nineteenth century, members of the educated elite as well as workers viewed ethnic and even religious differences as racial characteristics—referring to the Polish "race" or the Jewish "race." Each wave of newcomers was seen as being somehow inferior to the established residents. The Irish who judged the Italians so harshly had themselves been seen as a subhuman species just a generation before. Immigrants not only brought their own religious and racial prejudices to the United States but also absorbed the popular prejudices of American culture. Social Darwinism, with its strongly racist overtones, decreed that whites stood at the top of the evolutionary ladder. But who was "white"? The social construction of race is nowhere more apparent than in the testimony of an Irish dockworker, who boasted that he hired only "white men" to load cargo, a category that he insisted excluded "Poles and Italians."

Racism took its most blatant form in the treatment of African Americans and Asians. Like other migrants from the rural periphery, African American men in the South, former slaves and the children of slaves, found work as human machines. The labor gang system used in many industries was most extreme and brutal in the South, where private employers contracted prison labor, mostly African Americans jailed for such minor crimes as vagrancy. Shackled together by chains as they worked under the watchful eyes of armed guards, these workers formed the bottom rung on labor's ladder. A Georgia man who escaped the brutal chain gang system remarked, "Call it slavery, peonage, or what not, the truth is we lived in a hell on earth."

On the West Coast, Asian immigrants became the scapegoats of the changing economy. Workers vigorously attacked the Chinese and later the Japanese as the "tools of corporate interest" recruited by the bosses to undercut wages and threaten "white society." The labor movement played a key role in excluding Asians from American life. Labor unions practiced exclusionary policies against both Chinese and Japanese workers and championed the 1882 Chinese Exclusion Act, which prohibited the immigration of Chinese to the United States.

From Rags to Riches: What Is "Making It" in America?

THE RAGS-TO-RICHES FABLES of novelists like Horatio Alger fueled the dreams of countless young people at the end of the nineteenth century. Alger's formulaic novels feature fatherless young men who through the right combination of "pluck and luck" move ahead in the world. Yet despite the myth, few Americans rose from rags to riches. Even Alger's heroes, like his popular *Ragged Dick*, more often traded rags for respectability, not for great wealth.

Without exception, Alger's characters came from old stock and were not the new immigrants who poured through the "golden door" into the United States at the turn of the century. What were *their* chances of success? Literature written by the new immigrants themselves tells different stories. Abraham Cahan's *The Rise of David Levinsky* (1917) describes the experience of an eastern European Jewish immigrant who, as the title indicates, rises to gain material success. But while the theme of success is distinctively American, the treatment is not. The author laments that Levinsky's "rise" is paralleled by a spiritual loss. "I cannot escape from my old self," Levinsky confesses at the end of the novel. "David, the poor lad swinging over a Talmud volume at the Preacher's Synagogue, seems to have more in common with my inner identity than David Levinsky the well-known cloak manufacturer." Having sacrificed all to material gain, Levinsky acknowledges, "At the height of my business success I feel that if I had my life to live over again I should never think of a business career."

Mike Gold tells a darker story of immigrant life in *Jews without Money* (1930), an autobiographical tale of the implacable economic forces that devastate Gold's fictional family and turn its young protagonist to communism. Gold's characters inhabit a world of grinding poverty and ignorance, a landscape so bleak that one character comes to doubt the existence of a benevolent God, asking plaintively, "Did God make bedbugs?" Determined

to "write a truthful book of Poverty," Gold pledged, "I will mention bedbugs":

> It wasn't a lack of cleanliness in our home. My mother was as clean as any German housewife; she slaved, she worked herself to the bone keeping us fresh and neat. The bedbugs were a torment to her. She doused the beds with kerosene, changed the sheets, sprayed the mattresses in an endless frantic war with the bedbugs. What was the use; nothing could help. It was Poverty; it was the Tenement.

Yet Gold's own success belied the grim economic determinism of his fiction. He made it out of the ghetto and into the world of literature and social activism.

Historians have been fascinated by the question of "making it" in America. Repeatedly they have attempted to measure economic and social mobility, from colonial times to the twentieth century. Looking at the lives of common folk, scholars have struggled to determine who made it, who did not, and why. Was America a land of boundless opportunity where the poor could rise? Or did the rich stay rich and the poor stay poor-to-middling, as pioneering studies of social mobility in the 1950s indicated?

By the 1960s, quantitative methods made possible by advances in computer technology promised to move history away from the "impressionistic," anecdotal evidence of fiction and memoirs and provide a statistical framework in which to measure success. But just what could historians measure with their new tools? Comparing Jewish and Italian immigrants in New York City at the turn of the century, one historian concluded that the Jews had done a better job of making it. By employing a table that categorized occupations, ranking them from professional, white-collar jobs to unskilled labor, the historian duly noted the movement from one category to another, concluding from his data that Jews moved more quickly than Italians into the white-collar class.

Studies of occupational mobility, however, contained major flaws. Census data, the staple of quantitative studies, provide information on occupation but not on income. Quantitative historians' decision to use occupational categories and not income as a yardstick of mobility in a country where money has been and continues to be the common measure of

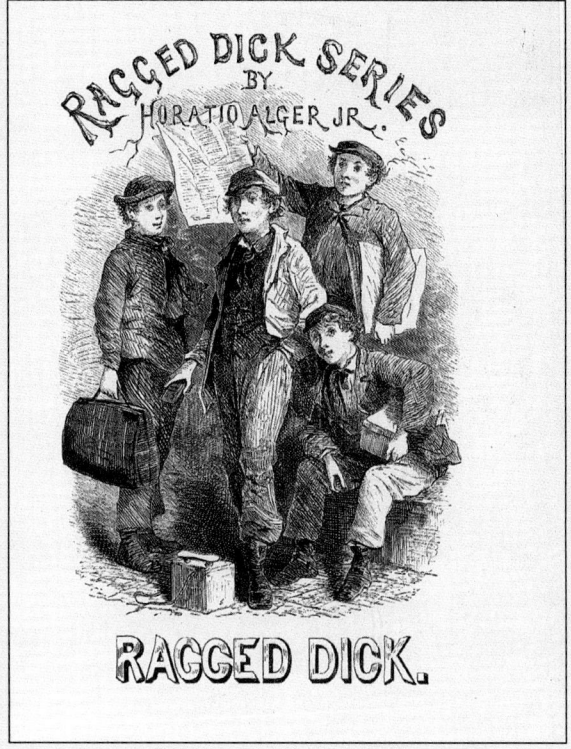

RAGS TO RICHES
Horatio Alger's novels like **Ragged Dick** *(1868) invariably end with the young hero on the road to success. Contrast Alger's cheerful message with the bathos of the 1900 song "No One Cares for Me," in which the young newsboy in his rags replicates Alger's hero. Instead of getting ahead, the newsboy is portrayed as a victim of cruel neglect. Which portrait is more accurate? Historians for decades have wrestled with the question of social mobility and success.*

Private collection; Picture Research Consultants & Archives.

success is misleading. Even occupational mobility proved difficult to measure accurately. For example, in the study cited, peddlers somewhat arbitrarily ranked at low-white-collar status because they were self-employed. Yet the pushcart peddler and the Italian street vendor could hardly be said to have enjoyed white-collar status in the larger society in which they moved. Students must look carefully at what historians measure, recognizing that occupational mobility may not equate with social mobility or economic success.

The larger questions remain: What is "making it" in America? How best can it be measured—in dollars and cents, job satisfaction, occupational status, comparison with the lives of one's parents or neighbors? And what of the immigrants them-

selves? How did they define it? If becoming a brick-layer spelled success to the Italian immigrant and his family, do studies of occupational mobility based on statisticians' categories and job rankings distort his lived reality? In dealing with the issue of "making it" in America, historians have increasingly come to recognize that each immigrant group had its own unique definition of success. Not all immigrants sought upward mobility, whether economic or occupational. Cultural factors, such as the value Italians placed on loyalty to the family, also played a key role. Ultimately, questions of success and mobility cannot easily be quantified, and they demand attention to the larger cultural context that shaped individual economic and occupational choices.

CHINESE RAILROAD WORKERS
Chinese workers like this section gang pictured at Promontory Point, Utah, in 1869 made up more than 80 percent of the workforce that built America's first transcontinental railroad. Charles Crocker of the Central Pacific hired them, reasoning that the race that built the Great Wall could build his road across the treacherous Sierra Nevada. Besides, the Chinese workers were a bargain: Crocker paid them $10 a month less than he paid his Irish section gangs.
Denver Public Library: Western History Collection, photo by J. B. Silvis.

At Work

Throughout the nineteenth century, America's industrial workers toiled in a variety of settings. Skilled craftsworkers and artisans still worked in small workshops or alone. But with the rise of corporate capitalism, large factories, mills, and mines increasingly dotted the landscape. Sweatshops and outwork, the contracting of piecework performed in the home, provided a different work experience from that of the factory operative (machine tender) or the industrial worker. Pick-and-shovel labor, whether on the railroads or in the building trades, constituted another kind of work. The best way to

get a sense of the diversity of workers and workplaces is to look at five distinct types of industrial work: common labor, skilled work, factory work, sweatshop labor, and mining.

America's Diverse Workers

Common laborers formed the backbone of the American labor force throughout the nineteenth century. They built the railroads and subways, tunneled under New York's East River to anchor the Brooklyn Bridge, and helped to lay the foundation of industrial America. In her book *China Men*, Maxine Hong Kingston tells the story of Ah Goong, one of the *gam saan haak* ("travelers to the gold mountain") who crossed the Pacific in 1863 and went to work for the Central Pacific Railroad. For less than a dollar a day, Ah Goong hung in a basket on the cliffs above the American River, setting black powder in crevices and firing the fuses to blast a path through the mountains. In 1869, when the railroad experimented with nitroglycerin, he sometimes risked his life to earn an extra dollar by going back into the tunnel to investigate when the temperamental nitro failed to explode. Working in the dark tunnel, Ah Goong toiled on eight-hour shifts seven days a week. When the railroad tried to increase the shift to ten hours, Ah Goong and ten thousand of his fellow workers went on strike in 1867. They demanded the same wages paid to the white, mostly Irish gangs, who earned $40 a month compared with Ah Goong's $30. Construction superintendent Charles Crocker broke the strike, but in the end he raised the wages of the Chinese workers to $35 a month. In 1869, when the Central Pacific reached Promontory Point, Utah, where it joined the Union Pacific to form the first transcontinental railroad, orators basked in the accomplishment of the "greatest monument of human labor," never mentioning the Chinese workers whose prodigious labor built the railroad.

At the opposite end of the economic ladder from common laborers were skilled craftsmen like iron puddler James J. Davis, a Welsh immigrant. When he was eleven years old, he went into the iron mills in Sharon, Pennsylvania, where his father was a puddler. Using brains along with brawn, puddlers took the melted pig iron in the heat of the furnace and, with long poles, formed the cooling metal into two-hundred-pound balls, relying on eye and intuition to make each ball uniform. Davis compared the task to baking bread: "I am like some frantic baker in the inferno kneading a batch of iron bread for the devil's breakfast. My spoon weighs twenty-five pounds, my porridge is pasty iron, and the heat of my kitchen is so great that if my body was not hardened to it, the ordeal would drop me in my tracks."

Possessing such a skill meant earning good wages, up to $7 a day, when there was work. But often no work could be found. Much industry and manufacturing in the nineteenth century remained seasonal; it was a rare worker who could count on year-round pay. In addition, two major depressions only twenty years apart, in 1873 and 1893, spelled unemployment and hardship for all workers. Pud-

dling jobs often passed from father to son, and although Davis earned the title of master puddler by the time he was sixteen, his father was not ready to turn over his hearth to his son, so in the hard times of the 1890s Davis tramped the countryside looking for work. In an era before unemployment insurance, workers' compensation, or old-age pensions, even the best worker could not guarantee security for his family. "The fear of ending in the poor-house is one of the terrors that dog a man through life," Davis confessed.

As the century wore on, employers attempted to limit workers' autonomy by replacing people with machinery, breaking down skilled work into ever smaller parts, and replacing skilled workers with unskilled factory operatives, often young women willing to work for low wages. The textile mills provide a classic example of mechanized factory labor in the nineteenth century. Mary, a weaver at the mills in Fall River, Massachusetts, told her story to the *Independent* magazine in 1903. She had gone to work in the 1880s at the age of twelve and had begun weaving at fourteen. Mechanization of the looms had reduced the job of the weaver to watching for breaks in the thread. "At first the noise is fierce, and you have to breathe the cotton all the time, but you get used to it," Mary told her interviewer. "When the bobbin flies out and a girl gets hurt, you can't hear her shout—not if she just screams, you can't. She's got to wait, 'till you see her. . . . Lots of us is deaf."

The majority of factory operatives in the textile mills were young, unmarried women like Mary who were paid by the piece rather than by the day or hour. Mary worked from six in the morning to six at night, six days a week, and took home about a dollar a day. The seasonal nature of the work also drove wages down. "Like as not your mill will 'shut down' three months," and "some weeks you only get two or three days' work," Mary recounted. After twenty years of working in the mill, Mary's family had not been able to scrape together enough money to buy a house: "We saved some, but something always comes."

Mechanization transformed the garment industry as well. With the introduction of the foot-pedaled sewing machine in the 1850s and the use of mechanical cloth-cutting knives in the 1870s, independent tailors were replaced with workers hired by contractors to sew pieces of cloth into clothing. Working in sweatshops, small rooms hired for the season, or even the contractor's own tenement, women and children formed an important segment of garment workers.

Sadie Frowne, a sixteen-year-old Polish Jew, went to work in a Brooklyn sweatshop in the 1890s. Frowne sewed for eleven hours a day in a room twenty feet long and fourteen feet wide containing fourteen machines. "The machines go like mad all day, because the faster you work the more money you get," she recalled. Paid by the piece, she earned about $4.50 a week and, by rigid economy, tried to save $2. Young and single, Frowne typified the woman wage earner in the late nineteenth century. In 1890, the average working woman was twenty-two, had been working since the age of fifteen, and working twelve hours a day, six days a week, and earning less than $6 a week. Discriminated against in the marketplace, where they earned less than men, and largely ignored by the labor unions, women generally worked only eight to ten years, until they married. These women formed a unique subculture. Their youth, high spirits, and cama-raderie made the hard, repetitive work they did bearable, and after hours they relished the "cheap amusements" of the day—the dance halls, social clubs, and amusement parks.

The most hazardous work and the worst working conditions in the nation existed in metal and coal mining, along with extractive industries such as lumbering. To look closely at conditions in the mines, mills, and forests, in the words of one historian, is to enter a "chamber of horrors." Ross Moudy, a miner in Cripple Creek, Colorado, recounted the dangers he faced in a chlorination mill. For nine or ten hours a day, he worked for $1.50 to $2, breathing sulfur dioxide or chlorine fumes and working in dust so thick that "one cannot see an object two feet away." He soon quit and went to work in a Cripple Creek gold mine. There, according to Moudy, "dangers do not seem so great to a practiced miner, who is used to climbing hundreds of feet on . . . braces put about six feet apart . . . and then walking the same distance on a couple of poles sometimes not larger than fence rails, where a misstep would mean a long drop." When a group of stockholders came to tour the mine, Moudy recounted how one man, white as a ghost after a near fall, told the miner beside him "that instead of being paid $3 per day they ought to have all the gold they could take out."

Miners died in explosions, cave-ins, and fires. New technology eliminated some dangers but often added others, for machinery could maim and kill.

In the hard-rock mines of the West in the 1870s, accidents annually disabled one out of every thirty miners and killed one in eighty. Moudy's biggest worry was the carbon dioxide that often filled the tunnels because of poor ventilation. "Many times," he confessed, "I have been carried out unconscious and not able to work for two or three days after." Those who avoided accidents still breathed air so dangerous that respiratory diseases eventually disabled them. After a year on the job, Moudy joined the union "because I saw it would help me to keep in work and for protection in case of accident or sickness." The union provided good sick benefits and hired nurses, "so if one is alone and sick he is sure to be taken care of." Moudy acknowledged that there were some "hotheads" in the union, the militant Western Federation of Miners. But he insisted that most union men "believe the change will come about gradually and not by revolution."

The Family Economy: Women and Children

Although real wages (pay measured in terms of buying power) rose by 15 percent between 1873 and 1893, workers did not share equally in the improvement. African American men, for example, continued to be paid at a much lower rate than white men, as did immigrant laborers and white women. And the protracted depressions following the panics of 1873 and 1893 undercut many workers' gains. In 1890, the average worker earned $500 a year. Many working-class families, whether native-born or immigrant, lived in poverty or near poverty; their economic survival depended on the contributions of all, regardless of sex or age. One statistician estimated that in 1900, as many as 64 percent of working-class families relied on income other than the husband's wages to make ends meet. The paid and unpaid work of women and children were thus essential for family survival and economic advancement.

Child labor had been common in the mines and textile mills since midcentury. As other industries mechanized in the 1880s and 1890s, factories hired children, girls as well as boys, who often could tend machines as efficiently as adults yet received wages considerably lower. One worker recalled his youth in the textile mills of Massachusetts: "When I began as a boy in the mill, I worked fifteen hours a day. I used to go in at a quarter past four in the morning and work until a quarter to eight at night, having thirty minutes for breakfast and the same for dinner, drinking tea after ringing out at night. . . . This I did for eleven years."

Attempts to abolish child labor began before the Civil War. By 1863, seven states had passed laws limiting the hours of child workers to forty-eight a week, but often the laws were not strictly enforced. Most southern states refused to regulate child labor, and children as young as six or seven years old continued to be widely employed in southern mills. In the nation's mines, particularly in Appalachia, young boys were recruited to pick out the slate and waste from coal as it passed along chutes. Suspended on wooden boards over the moving coal, these "breaker boys" engaged in dangerous, physically demanding work. A boy who slipped into the coal had little chance of surviving without serious injury. When a child labor committee investigated conditions in Pennsylvania, it found that more than ten thousand children were illegally employed in the coalfields. Child labor increased decade by decade, with the percentage of children under fifteen engaged in paid labor not dropping until after World War I. The 1900 census showed that 1,750,178 children ages ten to fifteen were employed, an increase of more than a million since 1870. Children in this age range constituted over 18 percent of the industrial labor force.

In the late nineteenth century, the number of women workers rose sharply, with their most common occupation changing slowly from domestic service to factory work and then to office work. In 1870, the census listed 1.5 million women working in nonagricultural occupations. By 1890, more than 3.7 million women earned wages, although they were paid less than men. Women's working patterns varied considerably according to race and ethnicity. White married women, even among the working class, rarely worked outside the home; in 1890, only 3 percent were employed. Nevertheless, married women found ways to contribute to the family economy. Families often took in boarders, which meant extra housework. In many Italian families, piecework such as making artificial flowers allowed married women to contribute to the family economy without leaving their homes. Black

"BREAKER BOYS"
Child labor in America's mines and mills was common at the turn of the century, despite state laws that attempted to restrict it. Here "breaker boys" in the 1890s take a rest from their twelve-hour day in the coal mines of Appalachia. Their unsmiling faces bear testimony to their hard and dangerous work. A committee investigating child labor found more than ten thousand children illegally employed in the Pennsylvania coalfields.
Brown Brothers.

women, married and unmarried, worked for wages outside their homes at a much higher rate than white women. The 1890 census showed that 25 percent of African American married women worked outside the home, often as domestics in the houses of white families.

Managers and White Collars

In the late nineteenth century, business expansion and consolidation led to a managerial revolution, creating a need for a new class of managers. As skilled workers saw their crafts replaced by mechanization, some moved into management positions. At the same time, new white-collar jobs in offices and department stores attracted a growing number of women workers.

The New Managerial Class

"The middle class is becoming a salaried class," a writer for the *Independent* magazine observed, "and is rapidly losing the economic and moral independence of former days." As large business organizations consolidated, corporate development separated management from ownership, and the job of directing the firm became the province of salaried managers and executives. The majority of these new middle managers were white men drawn from the 8 percent of Americans who held high school diplomas. In 1880, the middle managers at the Chicago, Burlington, and Quincy Railroad earned between $1,500 and $4,000 a year, while senior executives, generally recruited from the college-educated elite, took home $4,000 or more, and the company's general manager made $15,000 a year, approximately thirty times what the average worker earned.

Until late in the century, when engineering schools began to supply recruits, skilled workers trained on the job often moved from the shop floor to positions of considerable responsibility. The career of Captain William "Billy" Jones provides a glimpse of a skilled ironworker turned manager. Jones, the son of a Welsh immigrant, grew up in the heat of the blast furnaces, where he started working as an apprentice at the age of ten. During the Civil War, he served in the Union army and earned the rank of captain, a title he used for the rest of his life. When Andrew Carnegie opened his steelworks on the outskirts of Pittsburgh in 1872, he hired Jones

as his plant superintendent. By all accounts, Jones was the best steel man in the industry. "Good wages and good workmen" was his motto. Carnegie constantly tried to force down wages, but Jones fought for his men: In 1881, he succeeded in shortening the shift from twelve to eight hours a day by convincing Carnegie that shorter hours would reduce absenteeism and accidents. Jones himself demanded and received a "hell of a big salary." Carnegie paid him $25,000—the same salary as the president of the United States—a stupendous sum in 1881 and one that testified to the value the tightfisted Carnegie placed on his superintendent. Captain Jones did not have long to enjoy his newfound wealth. He died in 1889 when a blast furnace exploded, adding his name to the estimated 35,000 killed each year in industrial accidents.

"Typewriters" and Sales Clerks

As businesses became larger and more far-flung in the decades after the Civil War, the need for more elaborate and exact records as well as the greater volume of correspondence led to the hiring of more office workers. Mechanization soon transformed business as it had industry and manufacturing. The adding machine, the cash register, and the typewriter came into general use in the 1880s. Employers seeking literate workers soon turned to women. Educated men had many other career choices, while for middle-class, white women, secretarial work constituted one of the few areas where they could put their literacy to use for wages.

Sylvie Thygeson was typical of the young women who went to work as secretaries. Thygeson grew up in an Illinois prairie town. When her father died in 1884, she went to work as a country schoolteacher at the age of sixteen, immediately after graduating high school. Quickly learning that teaching school did not pay, she mastered typing and stenography and found work as a secretary to help support her family. According to her account, she made "a fabulous sum of money." Nevertheless, she gave up her job after a few years when she met and married her husband.

Called "typewriters," women workers like Thygeson were seen as indistinguishable from the machines they operated. Far from viewing their work as dehumanizing, women "typewriters" took pride in their work and relished the economic independence it afforded them. By the 1890s, secretarial work was the overwhelming choice of

CLERICAL WORKER
*A stenographer takes dictation in an 1890s office.
Note that the apron, a symbol of feminine
domesticity, has accompanied the woman into the
workplace. In the 1880s, with the utilization of the
typewriter, many women were able to put their literacy skills to use for wages in the nation's offices.*
Brown Brothers.

white, native-born women, who constituted over
90 percent of the female clerical force. Not only considered more genteel than factory work or domestic labor, office work also meant more money for
shorter hours. Boston's clerical workers made more
than $6 a week in 1883, compared with less than $5
for women working in manufacturing. For Sylvie
Thygeson and thousands of women like her, the
office provided a welcome addition to the options
available to women workers.

As a new consumer culture came to dominate
American life in the late nineteenth century, department stores offered another employment opportunity for women. Boasting ornate facades, large plate-
glass display windows, and marble and brass
fixtures, stores like Macy's in New York, Wanamaker's in Philadelphia, and Marshall Field in
Chicago stood as monuments to the material promise
of the era. Within these palaces of consumption, one
could find cash girls, stock clerks, and wrappers who
earned as little as $3 a week. At the top of the scale,
buyers like Belle Cushman of the fancy goods department at Macy's earned $25 a week, an unusually
high salary for a woman in the 1870s.

Typically, the gender segregation that kept
women's wages low in the office and the factory
also prevailed in the department stores. Male supervisors, called floorwalkers, commanded salaries
of $10 to $16 per week at a time when the typical
Macy's saleswoman received $5 to $6. In all stores,
saleswomen were subject to harsh and arbitrary discipline. Sitting was forbidden, and conversation
with other clerks led to instant dismissal. Yet white-
collar workers counted themselves a cut above factory workers, even when their pay envelopes did
not justify the sense of superiority.

At Home and at Play

The growth of American industrial capitalism not
only dramatically altered the workplace but also
transformed home and family life and gave rise to
new forms of commercialized leisure. Industrialization redefined the very concepts of work and
home. Increasingly, men went out to work for
wages, while most white married women stayed
home, either working in the home without pay—
cleaning, cooking, and rearing children—or supervising paid domestic servants who did the housework. The growing separation of workplace and

home led to a new ideology, one that sentimentalized the home and women's role in it.

Domesticity and "Domestics"

The separation of the workplace and the home that marked the shift to industrial society in the early nineteenth century redefined the home as a "haven in the heartless world," presided over by a wife and mother who made the household her "separate sphere." The cultural ideology that dictated woman's place to be in the home has been called the "cult of domesticity," a phrase used to prescribe an ideal of womanhood that dominated the period from 1820 to the end of the nineteenth century.

In the decades after the Civil War, the typical middle-class dwelling in which women were to find their place became more embellished architecturally and its interiors more cluttered. Possession of such a home, indeed of any home at all, marked the gulf between the working poor and the middle class. Home owners constituted only 36 percent of the U.S. housing population in 1900, compared with 68 percent today.

The cult of domesticity and the elaboration of the middle-class home in the nineteenth century led to a major change in patterns of hiring household help. The live-in servant, or domestic, replaced the hired girl in the North. (The South continued to rely on black female labor, first slave and later free.) In American cities by 1870, from 15 to 30 percent of all households included live-in domestic servants, more than 90 percent of whom were women.

By the mid-nineteenth century, native-born women increasingly took up other work and left domestic service to immigrants. The maid was so often Irish that "Bridget" became a generic term for female domestics. Domestic servants by all accounts resented their long hours and lack of privacy. Furthermore, going into service carried a social stigma. As one young woman observed, "If a girl goes into the kitchen she is sneered at and called 'the Bridget,' but if she goes behind the counter she is escorted by gentlemen." No wonder domestic service was the occupation of last resort, a "hard and lonely life" in the words of one servant girl.

For women of the white middle class, domestics were a boon, freeing them from household drudgery and giving them more time to spend with their children or to pursue club work or reform. Thus, while it supported the cult of domesticity, domestic service created for those women who could afford it opportunities that expanded their horizons outside the home.

SUNDAY DINNER
Sunday dinner at the home of the S. H. Fairfield family of Topeka, Kansas, is served by their African American domestic servant. Middle-class families as well as the wealthy relied on domestic help in the nineteenth century. Unlike white women, who rarely worked for wages after marriage, more than 25 percent of African American married women worked outside their homes, many as domestics. Often they had to leave their own homes and children and live in the homes of their white employers.
The Kansas State Historical Society, Topeka, Kansas.

Mill Towns and Company Towns

In the mill towns and company towns that sprang up across America, industrial capitalism redefined the concept of the home for the working class. Homestead, the Carnegie mill town outside Pittsburgh, grew up haphazardly. By 1892, eight thousand people lived in Homestead, transforming what had been a rural village into a bustling mill town that belied its pastoral name. As the Carnegie steelworks expanded, they encroached on the residential area, pushing the homes out of the flatlands along the Monongahela River. Workers moved into the hills and ravines. In an area called the Hollow, shanties hung precariously on the hillsides. These small, boxlike dwellings—many no larger than two rooms—housed the unskilled laborers from the mills.

Elsewhere, particularly in New England and the South, the company itself planned and built the town. The Amoskeag textile mill in Manchester, New Hampshire, was a self-contained world laid out according to a master plan conceived in the 1830s. Such planned communities rested on the notion of benevolent corporate paternalism. Viewing the workers as the "corporation's children," Amoskeag's owners sought to socialize their increasingly immigrant workforce to the patterns of industrial work and to instill loyalty to the company, curb labor unrest, and prevent unionization.

Perhaps the most famous company town in the United States was built by sleeping-car magnate George M. Pullman nine miles south of Chicago on the shores of Lake Calumet. In the wake of the Great Railroad Strike of 1877, Pullman determined to remove his plant and workers from the "snares of the great city." In 1880, he purchased forty-three hundred acres of bare prairie and built his model town as he built the Pullman Palace cars that made his fortune—to be orderly, clean, and with a patina of luxury. It was "to the employer's interest," he determined, "to see that his men are clean, contented, sober, educated, and happy."

When the first family moved in on January 1, 1881, the model town of Pullman boasted parks, artificial lakes, fountains, playgrounds, an auditorium, a library, a hotel, shops and markets, a men's club, and eighteen hundred units of housing. Noticeably absent was a saloon. One worker lamented that he frequently walked by and "looked at but dared not enter Pullman's hotel with its private bar." The intimidation the workers felt underscored a major flaw in Pullman's plan. In his eagerness to inculcate what he referred to as the "habits of respectability," Pullman consulted his own wishes and tastes rather than those of his workers.

Pullman intended the town to support itself and expected a 6 percent return on his investment. As a result, Pullman's rents ran 10 to 20 percent higher than housing costs in nearby communities. And a family in Pullman could not own its own home. George Pullman refused to "sell an acre under any circumstances" because as long as he controlled the town absolutely, he could evict troublemakers. Although observers were at first dazzled by its beauty and order, critics were soon comparing Pullman's model town to a "gilded cage" for workers. In 1884, the economist Richard T. Ely went to the heart of what concerned workers and critics alike: "The idea of Pullman is un-American. . . . It is benevolent, well wishing feudalism, which desires the happiness of the people, but in such way as shall please the authorities."

The autocracy that many feared in Pullman was realized both in textile mill towns south of the Mason-Dixon line and in mining towns in the West. "Practically speaking," a federal investigator traveling in the South observed, "the company owns everything and controls everything, and to a large extent controls everybody in the mill village." These largely nameless company towns, with their company-controlled stores, churches, schools, and houses, provide a classic example of social control over workers. Paid in company currency, or scrip, workers had no choice but to patronize the company store, where high prices led to a mounting spiral of debt that reduced the workers to virtual captives of the company. Otherwise facing the peonage

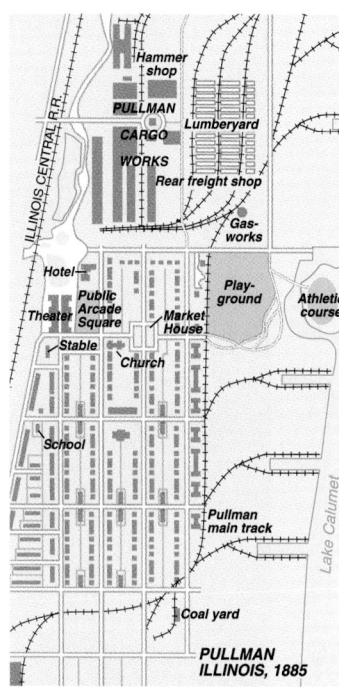

Pullman's Model Town
"Pullman's Company Town." NG MAPS/NGS Image Collection.

A PULLMAN CRAFTSWORKER
Pullman palace cars were known for their luxurious details. Here a painter working in the 1890s applies elaborate decoration to a Pullman car while in the foreground we see examples of carved doors and hand detailing. Pullman workers struck in 1894 (see page 497) to protest the company's efforts to undermine their status as craftsworkers and put them on piecework for lower wages.
Chicago Historical Society.

of sharecropping or tenancy, southern workers seeking industrial employment had little choice but to move to the towns owned by the mills. By 1890, 92 percent of southern textile workers' families lived in company towns.

In western mining towns, companies exerted control not only over the housing of the employees but over their religious and social lives as well. In Ludlow, a mining town in Colorado controlled by the Rockefeller family, the local minister was hired and supported by the company. Such ironfisted control was designed to prevent labor unions from gaining a foothold. Rockefeller hired spies to infiltrate the town, hang out at the local saloons, and report on any union activity.

The mill towns and company towns of America provide only the most dramatic examples of the ways in which industrialization and the rise of corporate capitalism changed the landscape of the United States and altered traditional patterns of work and home life. After the Civil War, communities where men and women of different classes knew and dealt with one another personally grew rare. In the face of increasing business consolidation and impersonality, traditional ideas about equal competition in the marketplace and the relative independence of employers and employees lost much of their hold.

Cheap Amusements

Growing class divisions manifested themselves in patterns of leisure as well as in work. The poor and working class took their leisure, when they had it, in the streets, the dance halls, the music houses, the ballparks, and the amusement arcades, which by the 1890s formed a familiar part of the landscape. Recreation varied according to ethnicity, religion, gender, and age. For many new immigrants, social life revolved around the family; weddings, baptisms, birthdays, and bar mitzvahs constituted the chief celebrations. Generally, older-stock American men spent more time away from home in neighborhood clubs, saloons, and fraternal orders than did their immigrant counterparts. German beer gardens, for example, included the whole family. But more often, men and women took their leisure separately, except during youth and courtship.

The growing anonymity of urban industrial society posed a challenge to traditional rituals of courtship. Adolescent working girls, immigrant and old stock, no longer met prospective husbands only through their families. Fleeing crowded tenements, the young sought each other's company in dance halls and other commercial retreats. Reformers worried that the dance halls served as a breeding ground for drunkenness and prostitution. In 1884, millionaire heiress Grace Dodge, determined to

1870–1890

CONEY ISLAND
Coney Island became a pleasure resort in the 1870s, but it was not until the turn of the century, with the development of elaborate amusement parks like Steeplechase, Luna, and Dreamland, that Coney Island came into its own as the capital of commercialized leisure. This official guide highlighted the beach, the vaudeville hall, and the midway with its rides and its risqué harem dancers. In the foreground a barker gesticulates and a hawker urges a young man in a straw hat to buy souvenir photographs for his companion.
Brooklyn Historical Society.

help young working women find respectability, set up a Working Girl's Club in New York City. Members contributed twenty-five cents a month to rent and furnish a comfortable club room where young women could relax and entertain. Designed as an alternative to dance halls and amusement resorts, the Working Girl's Club sought to replicate patterns of middle-class courtship, where the young met under the watchful eye of older adults. By 1885, branches had sprung up in Brooklyn, Philadelphia,

and Boston. But by far the majority of young working women seemed to prefer the pleasure (and danger) of the dance halls.

For men, baseball became a national pastime in the 1870s—then, as now, one force in urban life that was capable of uniting a city across class lines. Cincinnati mounted the first professional team, the Red Stockings, in 1869. Teams proliferated in cities across the nation, and Mark Twain hailed baseball as "the very symbol, the outward and visible expression, of the drive and push and rush and struggle of the raging, tearing, booming nineteenth century."

The increasing commercialization of entertainment in the late nineteenth century can best be seen at Coney Island. A two-mile stretch of sand close to Manhattan by trolley or steamship, Coney Island in the 1870s and 1880s attracted visitors to its beaches, dance pavilions, and penny arcades—all connected by its famous boardwalk. In the 1890s, Coney Island was transformed into the site of some of the largest and most elaborate amusement parks in the country. Promoter George Tilyou built Steeplechase Park in 1897, advertising "10 hours of fun for 10 cents." With its mechanical thrills and funhouse laughs, the amusement park encouraged behavior one schoolteacher aptly described as "everyone with the brakes off."

The Labor Movement

As industrialists like Andrew Carnegie invested heavily in new machinery that replaced skilled workers, the redefinition of labor as mere "machine tending" left the worker with a growing sense of individual helplessness that served as a spur to collective action. The Great Railroad Strike of 1877, as labor leader Samuel Gompers acknowledged, served as an alarm bell "that sounded a ringing message of hope to us all." The workers had learned the power of concerted action and would use it again in the future.

The Knights of Labor and the American Federation of Labor

The Knights of Labor, the first mass organization of America's working class, proved the chief beneficiary of labor's newfound consciousness. The Noble and Holy Order of the Knights of Labor had been founded in 1869 by Uriah Stephens, a Philadelphia garment cutter. A secret but peaceable society of workers, the knights envisioned a "universal brotherhood" of all laborers, from the common laborer to the master craftsman. Although the Knights played no active role in the 1877 strike, membership swelled as a result of the growing interest in unionism. In 1878, the organization dropped the trappings of secrecy and launched an ambitious campaign to organize workers regardless of skill, sex, race, or nationality.

Under the direction of Grand Master Workman Terence V. Powderly, the Knights of Labor became the dominant force in labor during the 1880s. The Knights advocated a kind of workers' democracy that embraced reforms including free land, income tax, public ownership of the railroads, equal pay for work by women, and the abolition of child labor. The Knights sought to remove class distinctions and encouraged local assemblies to welcome all comers, employees and employers alike. "I hate the word 'class' and would drive it from the English language if I could," Powderly stated. Only the "parasitic" members of society—gamblers, stockbrokers, lawyers, bankers, and liquor dealers—were denied membership.

In theory, the Knights of Labor opposed strikes. Powderly championed arbitration and preferred to use boycotts. But in practice, much of the organization's appeal came from the successful strike the Knights mounted in 1885 against three railroads controlled by Jay Gould. The Knights won a sweeping victory, including the revocation of a 15 percent pay cut. Despite the reservations of its leadership, the Knights of Labor was becoming a militant labor organization that excited passionate support from working people.

The Knights of Labor was not without rivals. Other trade unionists disliked the broad reform goals of the Knights and sought to focus on workplace issues. Samuel Gompers, a cigar maker born in London of Dutch Jewish ancestry, promoted what he called "pure and simple" unionism. Gompers founded the Organized Trades and Labor Unions in 1881 and reorganized it in 1886 into the American Federation of Labor (AFL), which coordinated the activities of craft unions throughout the United States. His plan was simple: Organize skilled craftworkers like machinists, locomotive engineers, and iron puddlers—those with the most bargaining power—and use strikes to gain immediate objectives such as higher pay and better working conditions. Gompers at first drew few converts. The AFL had only 138,000 members in 1886, compared with 730,000 for the Knights of Labor. But events soon brought down the Knights and enabled Gompers to take control of the labor movement.

Haymarket and the Specter of Labor Radicalism

While the AFL and the Knights of Labor competed for members, radical socialists and anarchists offered different visions of labor's true path. The radicals, many of whom were immigrants steeped in the tradition of European socialism, believed that reform was futile; they called instead for social revolution. Anarchists also wanted revolutionary change but envisioned a smaller role for the state than the socialists did. Both groups, sensitive to criticism that they preferred revolution in theory to improvements here and now, rallied around the popular issue of the eight-hour day.

Since the 1840s, labor had sought to end the twelve-hour workday, which was standard in industry and manufacturing. By the mid-1880s, it seemed clear to many workers that labor shared too little in the new prosperity of the decade, and pressure mounted for the eight-hour day. The radicals seized on the popular issue and launched major rallies in cities across the nation. Supporters of the movement set May 1, 1886, as the date for a nationwide general strike in support of the eight-hour day.

All factions of the nascent labor movement came together in Chicago on May Day, for what was billed as the largest demonstration in history in support of the eight-hour day. A group of radicals led by anarchist Albert Parsons, a Mayflower descendant, and August Spies, a German immigrant, spearheaded the eight-hour movement in Chicago. Chicago's Knights of Labor rallied to the cause even though Powderly and the union's leadership, worried by the increasing activism of the rank and file, refused to champion the movement for shorter hours.

Samuel Gompers was on hand, too, to lead the city's trade unionists, although he privately urged the AFL assemblies not to participate in a general strike. Gompers's skilled workers were labor's elite. Many still worked in small shops where negotiations between workers and employers took place in an environment tempered by personal relationships. Well dressed in their Prince Albert coats and starched shirts, they stood in sharp contrast to the dispossessed workers out on strike across town at

Chicago's huge McCormick reaper works. There, strikers watched helplessly as the company brought in strikebreakers to take their jobs and marched the scabs to work under the protection of the Chicago police and security guards supplied by the Pinkerton Detective Agency. Cyrus McCormick Jr., son of the inventor of the mechanical reaper, viewed labor organization as a threat to his power as well as to his profits; he was determined to smash the union.

During the May Day rally, 45,000 workers paraded peacefully down Michigan Avenue in support of the eight-hour day, many singing the song that had become the movement's anthem:

> We mean to make things over;
>   we're tired of toil for naught
> But bare enough to live on: never
>   an hour for thought.
> We want to feel the sunshine; we
>   want to smell the flowers;
> We're sure that God has willed it,
>   and we mean to have eight hours.
> We're summoning our forces from
>   shipyard, shop, and mill:
> Eight hours for work, eight hours for rest,
>   eight hours for what we will!

Trouble came two days later, when strikers attacked scabs outside the McCormick works and police opened fire, killing or wounding six men. Angry radicals rushed out a circular urging workers to "arm yourselves and appear in full force" at a rally in Haymarket Square. On the evening of May 4, the turnout at Haymarket was disappointing. No more than two or three thousand gathered in the drizzle to hear Spies, Parsons, and the other anarchist speakers. Mayor Carter Harrison, known as a friend of labor, mingled conspicuously in the crowd, pronounced the meeting peaceable, and went home to bed. A short time later, police captain John "Blackjack" Bonfield, who had made his reputation cracking skulls, marched his men into the crowd, by now fewer than three hundred people, and demanded that they disperse.

Suddenly, someone threw a bomb into the police ranks. After a moment of stunned silence, the police drew their revolvers. "Fire and kill all you can," shouted a police lieutenant. When the melee ended, seven policemen and an unknown number of civilians lay dead. An additional sixty policemen and thirty or forty civilians suffered injuries. News of the "Haymarket riot" provoked a nationwide

"THE CHICAGO RIOT"
Inflammatory pamphlets like this one published in the wake of the Haymarket affair presented a one-sided view of the incident and stirred public passion. The anarchist speakers were tried and convicted for the bombing, even though the identity and motivation of the bomb thrower remained undiscovered.
Chicago Historical Society.

convulsion of fear, followed by blind rage directed at anarchists, labor unions, strikers, immigrants, and the working class in general. The hysteria ran deepest in Chicago. The police rounded up Spies and the other Haymarket speakers and jailed hundreds of radicals. Parsons managed to escape but later turned himself in to stand trial with his fellows.

Eight men went on trial in Chicago, although witnesses could testify that none of them had thrown the bomb. It was clear from the start that the men were on trial for their ideas, not their actions. "Convict these men," cried State's Attorney Julius S. Grinnell, "make examples of them, hang them, and you save our institutions." Although the state could not link any of the defendants with the Haymarket bomb, the jury nevertheless found them all guilty. Four were executed, one committed suicide, and three received prison sentences. On the gallows, August Spies spoke for the Haymarket martyrs: "The time will come when our silence will be more powerful than the voices you throttle today."

In 1893, Governor John Peter Altgeld, after a thorough investigation, pardoned the three remaining Haymarket anarchists. He denounced the trial as a shameless travesty of justice and concluded that Captain Bonfield was "the man really responsible for the death of the police officers." The governor's action brought on a storm of protest and cost him his political career. But through the entire process, Altgeld never wavered. "If I decide they are innocent, I will pardon them," he promised, "even if I never hold office another day." He did, and he didn't.

The bomb blast at Haymarket had lasting repercussions. To commemorate the death of the Haymarket martyrs, labor would make May 1 an annual international celebration of the worker. But the Haymarket bomb, in the eyes of one observer, proved "a godsend to all enemies of the labor movement." It effectively scotched the eight-hour day and dealt a fatal blow to the Knights of Labor.

With the labor movement everywhere under attack, many workers severed their radical connections, and many skilled workers turned to the American Federation of Labor. Under the leadership of Samuel Gompers, the AFL soon became the dominant voice of American labor. Unlike the idealistic Knights of Labor, Gompers's AFL urged workers to focus on concrete gains—higher wages, shorter hours—and use strikes and boycotts judiciously to win its demands. Gompers's narrow economic strategy made sense at the time and enabled one segment of the workforce—the skilled— to organize effectively and achieve tangible gains. But the majority of unskilled workers remained largely untouched by the AFL's brand of "pure and simple" trade unionism.

Conclusion: The Workers' Struggle

Looking back at the impact on his life occasioned by industrialization, a Massachusetts machinist declared in the 1890s:

> The workers of Massachusetts have always been law and order men. We loved our country and respected the laws. For the last five years the times have been growing worse every year, until we have been brought down so far that we have not much farther to go. What do the Mechanics of Massachusetts say to each other? I will tell you: "We must have a change. Any thing is better than this. We cannot be worse off, no matter what the change is."

More than two decades after the Great Railroad Strike of 1877 workers still struggled for a better life—a life in which the independence eroded by industrialization could be countered by collective action and where workers could regain some control of the workplace. They had yet to achieve the shorter day and the higher wage that promised escape from a brutal life of toil. Yet they remained committed to their vision and their willingness to fight for it made them agents of social change, willing to risk their livelihood and sometimes even their lives in the struggle.

Their mounting anger and frustration would lead American workers and farmers to join forces in the 1890s and create a grassroots movement to fight for change under the banner of a new People's Party.

FOR FURTHER READING ABOUT THE TOPICS IN THIS CHAPTER, see the Online Bibliography at

www.bedfordstmartins.com/roarkcompact.

FOR ADDITIONAL FIRST-HAND ACCOUNTS OF THIS PERIOD, see pages 52–66 in Michael Johnson, ed., *Reading the American Past*, Second Edition, Volume II.

TO ASSESS YOUR MASTERY OF THE MATERIAL IN THIS CHAPTER, see the Online Study Guide at

www.bedfordstmartins.com/roarkcompact.

CHRONOLOGY

1869 Uriah Stephens founds Knights of Labor.

Cincinnati mounts first professional baseball team, the Red Stockings.

1870 Wage earners account for over half of those listed as employed in 1870 census.

1872 Andrew Carnegie opens his steel-works outside Pittsburgh.

1873 Panic on Wall Street touches off depression.

1877 Great Railroad Strike paralyzes nation.

1878 Knights of Labor campaigns to organize workers regardless of skill, sex, or race.

1880 George M. Pullman builds model town near Chicago.

1881 Samuel Gompers founds Organized Trades and Labor Unions.

1882 Chinese Exclusion Act prohibits immigration of Chinese to the United States.

1884 Grace Dodge organizes Working Girl's Club in New York City.

1886 Organized Trades and Labor Unions reorganized as the American Federation of Labor (AFL).

May 1. Massive rally in support of eight-hour workday takes place in Chicago.

May 4. Haymarket bombing results in widening fear of anarchy and a blow to the labor movement.

1890 Average worker earns $500 per year.

1893 Illinois Governor John Peter Altgeld pardons three remaining Haymarket anarchists.

Panic on Wall Street touches off major depression.

1897 Steeplechase amusement park opens on Coney Island.

FARMERS ALLIANCE SONGBOOK

In the 1880s, the Farmers Alliance recruited followers in the South and Midwest at the rate of 20,000 a month, using lectures, camp meetings, and even songs to educate and organize. Copies of this Farmers Alliance songbook sold by the hundreds—testimony to the growing movement. In the cover picture, an Alliance farmer shakes the hand of a blacksmith, who bears a not coincidental resemblance to Abraham Lincoln. The handshake symbolizes the willingness of the alliance to make common cause with laborers of every stripe, a message reiterated in the four corners with images of school, farm, factory, and ship.

Farmers' Alliance Songs, Elias Carr Papers, #160.53, East Carolina Manuscript Collection, J. Y. Joyner Library, East Carolina University, Greenville, North Carolina. Photo by Dewan Frentger.

FIGHTING FOR JUSTICE AND EMPIRE

20

1890–1900

S<small>T.</small> L<small>OUIS IN</small> F<small>EBRUARY</small> 1892 <small>PLAYED HOST</small> to one of the most striking political gatherings of the century. Thousands of farmers, laborers, reformers, and common people flocked to Missouri to attend a meeting that was, in the words of one reporter, "different from any other political meeting ever witnessed in St. Louis." The cigar-smoking politicians who generally worked the convention circuit were nowhere to be found. In their place were "mostly gray-haired, sunburned and roughly clothed men" assembled under a banner that proclaimed, "We do not ask for sympathy or pity. We ask for justice."

Exposition Music Hall presented a colorful spectacle. "The banners of the different states rose above the delegates throughout the hall, fluttering like the flags over an army encamped," wrote one reporter. Ignatius Donnelly, a fiery orator, attacked the money kings of Wall Street. Mary Elizabeth Lease, a veteran campaigner from Kansas known for exhorting farmers to "raise less corn and more hell," lent her powerful voice to the cause. Terence V. Powderly, head of the Knights of Labor, called on workers to join hands with farmers against the "nonproducing classes." And Frances Willard of the Woman's Christian Temperance Union argued against liquor and for woman suffrage. Between speeches the crowd sang labor songs like "Hurrah for the Toiler" and "All Hail the Power of Laboring Men."

In the course of the next few days, delegates hammered out a series of demands breathtaking in their scope. They tackled the tough questions of the day— the regulation of business, the need for banking and currency reform, the right of labor to organize and bargain collectively, and the role of the federal government in regulating business, curbing monopoly, and guaranteeing democracy. The convention ended its work amid a chorus of cheers. According to one eye witness, "Hats, paper, handkerchiefs, etc., were thrown into the air; wraps, umbrellas and parasols waved; cheer after cheer thundered and reverberated through the vast hall reaching the outside of the building where thousands who had been waiting the outcome joined in the applause till for blocks in every direction the exultation made the din indescribable."

What was all the shouting about? People were building a new political party, officially named the People's or Populist Party. Dissatisfied with the Democrats and Republicans, a broad coalition of groups came together in St. Louis to fight for change. They determined to reconvene in Omaha in July to nominate candidates for the upcoming presidential election.

The 1890s witnessed one of the most turbulent decades in U.S. history. Unrest, agitation, agrarian revolt, labor strikes, a severe financial panic and depression, and a war of expansion characterized the decade. While the major political parties continued to do business as usual, Americans flocked to organizations like the American Federation of Labor, the Farmers Alliance, and the Woman's Christian

PEOPLE'S PARTY BADGE, 1896
Delegates to the People's Party National Convention in St. Louis in 1896 sported ribbons like this one worn by a member of the Massachusetts delegation. As in 1896, the party's 1892 gathering in St. Louis had all the trappings of other political conventions, but the People's Party marked a new political alliance, as farmers, laborers, and reformers came together to fight for change.
Collection of Janice L. and David J. Frent.

Temperance Union and worked together to create new political alliances. The St. Louis gathering marked just one milestone on the road to a new politics. The People's Party challenged laissez-faire economics by insisting that the federal government play a more active role to ensure greater economic equity in industrial America. This challenge to the status quo would culminate in 1896 in one of the most hotly contested presidential elections in the nation's history. At the close of this tumultuous decade, the Spanish-American War helped to bring the United States together even as it raised questions about the country's new role on the world stage at the dawn of the twentieth century.

Women's Activism

"Do everything," Frances Willard urged her followers in 1881. The new president of the Woman's Christian Temperance Union (WCTU) meant what she said. The WCTU followed a trajectory that was common for women in the late nineteenth century. As women organized to deal with issues that touched their homes and families, they moved into politics, lending a new urgency to the cause of woman suffrage (the right to vote). Elizabeth Cady Stanton had advocated woman suffrage since the Woman's Rights Convention in Seneca Falls in 1848 and, together with Susan B. Anthony, she had formed the first independent women's movement in 1867 with the creation of the National Woman Suffrage Association. By the 1890s, Stanton and Anthony were coming to the end of their public careers, yet their goal still eluded them. For African American women, the intimidation and lynching of blacks in the South led to activism, as Ida B. Wells's antilynching campaign forcefully demonstrated.

The Woman's Christian Temperance Union and Woman Suffrage

Frances Willard, the visionary leader of the WCTU, spoke for a group that was left almost entirely out of the U.S. electoral process—women. In 1890, only one state, Wyoming, allowed women to vote. But lack of the franchise did not mean that women were apolitical. The WCTU demonstrates the breadth of women's political activity in the late nineteenth century.

Women supported the temperance movement (the movement to ban the sale of alcoholic beverages and eliminate drunkenness) because they felt particularly vulnerable. The drunken, abusive husband epitomized the evils of a nation in which women remained second-class citizens. The temperance movement provided women with a respectable outlet for their increasing resentment of women's inferior status and their growing recognition of women's capabilities.

Under the leadership of Frances Willard, the WCTU moved toward viewing alcoholism as a disease rather than a sin, and poverty as a cause rather than a result of drink. Accordingly, social action replaced prayer as women's answer to the threat of drunkenness. By 1896, twenty-five of the WCTU's departments dealt with nontemperance issues. Together with labor unions the WCTU pressed for better working conditions. One WCTU member described the condition of factory operatives in a textile mill. "It is dreadful to see those girls stripped almost to the skin, wearing only the kind of loose

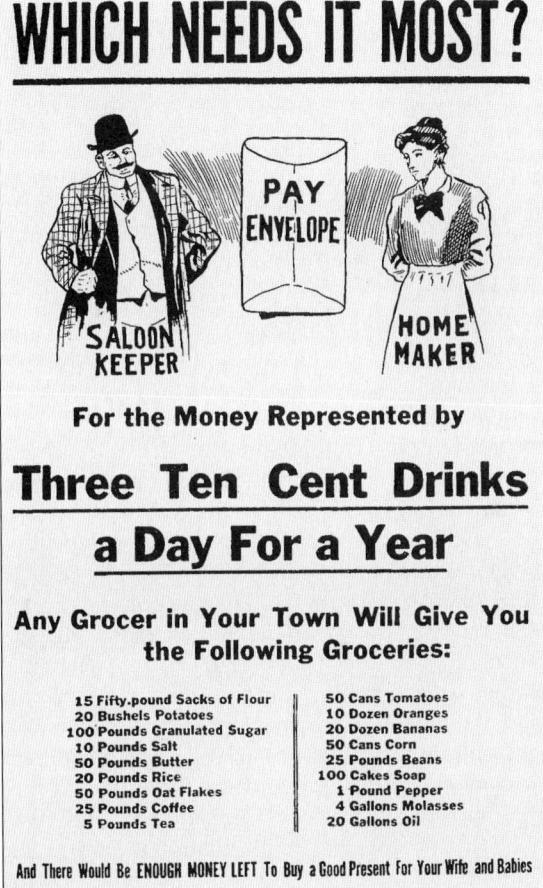

WHICH NEEDS IT MOST?

PAY ENVELOPE

SALOON KEEPER

HOME MAKER

For the Money Represented by

Three Ten Cent Drinks
a Day For a Year

Any Grocer in Your Town Will Give You the Following Groceries:

15 Fifty-pound Sacks of Flour	50 Cans Tomatoes
20 Bushels Potatoes	10 Dozen Oranges
100 Pounds Granulated Sugar	20 Dozen Bananas
10 Pounds Salt	50 Cans Corn
50 Pounds Butter	25 Pounds Beans
20 Pounds Rice	100 Cakes Soap
50 Pounds Oat Flakes	1 Pound Pepper
25 Pounds Coffee	4 Gallons Molasses
5 Pounds Tea	20 Gallons Oil

And There Would Be ENOUGH MONEY LEFT To Buy a Good Present For Your Wife and Babies

WCTU FLYER
This Woman's Christian Temperance Union flyer shows the wife pitted against the saloon keeper for her husband's pay. The economic consequences to the family of a drinker were a serious matter. At a time when the average worker made only $500 a year, the money spent on alcohol meant less to eat for the family. As the poster indicates, thirty cents a day for a year paid for a substantial amount of family staples. Beer and liquor lobbyists worked hard not only to counter the WCTU but to fight woman suffrage because they feared when women got the vote they would enact prohibition.
Culver Pictures.

wrapper, and running like racehorses from the beginning to the end of the day," she wrote in the *Union Signal*, the WCTU's monthly magazine. "The hard slavish work," she concluded, "is drawing the girls into the saloon."

Using "home protection" as her watchword, Willard capitalized on the cult of domesticity to move women into public life, arguing that they needed the vote to protect home and family. By the 1890s, the WCTU's grassroots network of local unions had spread to all but the most isolated rural areas of the country. Strong and rich, with over 150,000 dues-paying members, the WCTU was a formidable group.

Willard worked to create a broad reform coalition in the 1890s, embracing the Knights of Labor, the People's Party, and the Prohibition Party. Until her death in 1898, she led, if not a women's rights movement, then the first organized mass movement of women united around a women's issue. By 1900, women could claim a generation of experience in political action—speaking, lobbying, organizing, drafting legislation, and running private charitable institutions. As Willard observed, "All this work has tended more toward the liberation of women than it has toward the extinction of the saloon."

Unlike the WCTU, the organized movement for woman suffrage was small and relatively weak in the late nineteenth century. The women's rights movement had split in 1867 over whether the reconstruction amendments (Fourteenth and Fifteenth), which granted voting rights to African American men, should have extended the vote to women as well. By 1890 the split had healed and the newly united National American Woman Suffrage Association (NAWSA) launched campaigns on the state level to gain the vote for women. Suffragists won victories in Colorado in 1893 and Idaho in 1896. One more state joined the suffrage column when Utah entered the union in 1896. But women suffered a bitter defeat in a California referendum that same year. Although it would take almost three decades for all women to gain the vote, with the ratification of the Nineteenth Amendment in 1920, the unification of the two woman suffrage groups in 1890 signaled a new era in women's fight for the vote, just as Frances Willard's place on the platform in 1892 at the founding of the People's Party in St. Louis symbolized women's growing role in politics and reform.

Ida B. Wells and the Antilynching Campaign

While most white women focused on reforms designed to counter the impact of urban industrialism in the North, black women followed a different path. The majority of African Americans were neither urban nor industrial. As late as 1890, more than 90 percent of the black population remained in the South. As a result, African American women activists organized around issues that affected southern rural life. Foremost among their activities was the antilynching campaign mounted by Ida B. Wells.

In 1892, a white mob lynched a friend of Wells's whose successful grocery competed with a white-owned store. Wells concluded that lynching served "as an excuse to get rid of Negroes who were ac-

IDA B. WELLS
Ida B. Wells began her antilynching campaign at the age of thirty after the murder of a friend in 1892 led her to examine the extent of lynching in the South. She spread her message in lectures and pamphlets like this one distributed for fifteen cents. Wells brought the horror of lynching to a national and international audience and mobilized other African American women to take social action under the auspices of the National Association of Colored Women.
Manuscript, Archives and Rare Books Division, Schomburg Center for Research in Black Culture, The New York Public Library. Astor, Lenox and Tilden Foundations.

quiring wealth and property and thus keep the race terrorized." Determined to do something, she began systematically to collect data on lynching. In the decade between 1882 and 1892, she discovered lynching had risen in the South by an overwhelming 200 percent, with more than 241 people killed. The vast increase in lynchings testified to the retreat of the federal government following reconstruction and to white Southerners' determination to maintain supremacy through terrorism and intimidation.

At the time Wells began her antilynching campaign, she had already earned a reputation as an activist for African American rights. Born a slave in Holly Springs, Mississippi, in 1862, Wells grew up during reconstruction. Her parents were active in the struggle for Negro rights and provided their daughter with strong role models. Their deaths from yellow fever left Wells an orphan at the age of sixteen. She took over as head of the family, leaving Rust College to support her five siblings. Wells found work in the Memphis schools and became an active member of the local African Methodist Episcopal church. She also joined a local lyceum, or literary group. It was there that she began her career as a journalist, writing for the lyceum's journal, *Free Speech*, and in 1889 becoming its co-owner.

As the first salvo in her attack on lynching, Wells put to rest the "old threadbare lie that Negro men assault white women." As she pointed out, violations of black women by white men, which were much more frequent than black attacks on white women, went unnoticed and unpunished. Wells articulated lynching as a problem of race and gender, with the myth of black attacks on white southern womanhood masking the reality that mob violence had more to do with economics and the shifting social structure of the South than with rape. She demonstrated in a sophisticated way how the southern patriarchal system, having lost its control over blacks with the end of slavery, used its control over women to circumscribe the liberty of black men.

Wells's strong stance immediately resulted in reprisal. While she was traveling in the North, her office in Tennessee was ransacked and her printing equipment destroyed. Yet the warning that she would be killed on sight if she ever returned to Memphis only stiffened her resolve. As she wrote in her autobiography, *Crusade for Justice*, "Having lost my paper, had a price put on my life and been made an exile . . . , I felt that I owed it to myself and to my race to tell the whole truth now that I was where I could do so freely." Antilynching became a lifelong commitment that took Wells twice to Britain, where she placed lynching on the international agenda. As a reporter, first for the *New York Age* and later for the *Chicago Inter-Ocean*, she used every opportunity to hammer home her message.

Wells's activities mobilized other black women, including Victoria Earle Matthews and Maritcha Lyons, who were already engaged in social reform and self-improvement. They hosted a testimonial dinner for Wells in New York in 1892 that led to the organization of a black women's club, the Women's Loyal Union. The club became a spearhead for the creation of the National Association of Colored Women (NACW) in 1896. The organization's first president, Mary Church Terrell of Washington, D.C., urged her followers to "promote the welfare of our race, along all the lines that tend to its development and advancement." Taking as their motto "Lifting As We Climb," the women of the NACW shouldered the double burden of self-improvement and social reform. They attacked myriad issues, including health care, housing, education, and the promotion of a positive image of the Negro race. In their efforts, African American club women enjoyed little help from white women's clubs. At the insistence of its southern constituency, the General Federation of Women's Clubs remained largely segregated. The NACW played a critical role in Wells's antilynching campaign by lobbying for legislation that would make lynching a federal crime. Beginning in 1894 and continuing for decades, antilynching bills were introduced in Congress only to be defeated by southern opposition.

Lynching did not end during Ida B. Wells's lifetime, nor did antilynching legislation gain passage in Congress; but Wells's forceful voice brought the issue to national prominence. At her funeral in 1931, black leader W. E. B. Du Bois eulogized Wells as the woman who "began the awakening of the conscience of the nation."

The Farmers' Revolt and the Labor Wars

Farmers counted themselves among the most disaffected Americans in the country. Hard times in the 1880s and 1890s created a groundswell of agrarian revolt. Everywhere, the farmer seemed to be the victim of rules, such as the gold standard and the protective tariff, that worked to the advantage of big business. Angry farmers across the United States raised a chorus of protest. While the farmers united to fight for change, industrial laborers fought their own battles in a series of bloody strikes so fiercely waged on both sides that one historian has called them the "labor wars."

The Farmers Alliance and the Populist Movement

In the late nineteenth century, farm prices fell, decade after decade. Wheat that sold for a dollar a bushel in 1870 dropped to sixty cents in the 1890s. Cotton plummeted from fifteen cents to five cents a pound. Corn started at forty-five cents and fell to thirty cents a bushel by the 1890s. By 1894, in Kansas alone almost half the farms had fallen into the hands of the banks because poor farmers could not make enough money to pay their mortgages.

In the West, farmers rankled under a system in which railroads charged them exorbitant freight rates while granting rebates to large shippers (see Chapter 18). Also, the railroads' policy of charging higher rates for a short haul than for a long haul meant that large grain elevator companies could ship their wheat from Chicago to New York and across the ocean to England for less money than it cost a Dakota farmer to send a crop to mills in nearby Minneapolis. In the South, lack of currency and credit had driven farmers to the stopgap credit system of the crop lien (see Chapter 17). The combined southern states actually had less money in circulation than did the state of Massachusetts. At the heart of the problem stood a banking system that was rooted in the gold standard and dominated by eastern commercial banks, a railroad rate system capricious and unfair, and speculation that drove up the price of land.

Farm protest was not new. In the 1870s, farmers had supported the Grange and the Greenback Labor Party. But with the farmers' situation growing more desperate, the 1880s witnessed a spontaneous outbreak as farmers organized into alliances. The first group of farmers gathered at a Lampasas County farm in Texas and banded together into the Farmers Alliance to fight "landsharks and horse thieves." In frontier farmhouses in Texas, in log cabins in backwoods Arkansas, in the rural parishes of Louisiana, separate groups formed similar alliances for self-help.

As the movement grew, the farmers consolidated into two regional alliances, the Northwestern Farmers Alliance, which included the old Granger states of the Midwest, and the more radical Southern Farmers Alliance, which began in Texas but soon spread into Georgia and united with groups in Louisiana and Arkansas. By 1890, the Southern Alliance counted more than three million members. Determined to reach black farmers as well as whites, the Southern Alliance sponsored a separate National Colored Farmers Alliance that recruited more than a quarter of a million members.

At the same time, the Farmers Alliance broadened its base by reaching out to workers during the Great Southwestern Strike against Jay Gould's Texas and Pacific Railroad in 1886. The alliance insisted that the farmer, too, was a worker and that the labor question was a crucial issue for both the farmer and the wage laborer. The Southern Farmers Alliance rushed food and supplies to the strikers and issued a proclamation in support of the Knights of Labor, calling on farmers to boycott Gould's railroad.

At the heart of the alliance movement was a series of farmers' cooperatives. By "bulking" their cotton, that is, selling it together, farmers could negotiate a better price. And by setting up trade stores and exchanges, they sought to escape the grasp of the merchant/creditor. Soon alliances in a dozen states competed to pioneer new purchasing cooperatives. Through the cooperatives, the Farmers Alliance promised to change the way farmers lived. "We are going to get out of debt and be free and independent people once more," exulted one Georgia farmer. But the alliance failed in its attempt to replace the southern furnishing merchant with cooperative stores. Opposition by merchants, bankers, wholesalers, and manufacturers made it impossible for the cooperatives to get credit. The Texas exchange survived only one season. Farmers soon realized that the alliance cooperatives stood little chance of working unless fundamental changes were made in the American money and credit system.

As the cooperative movement died, what had begun as an organization for self-help moved toward direct political action. Texas farmers drafted a set of demands in 1886 and pressured political candidates to endorse them. These demands became the basis of a platform proposed by the Southern Alliance in 1890 calling for railroad regulation and control, laws against land speculation, and currency and credit reform. But it proved easier to get politicians to make promises than to follow through. Confounded by the failure of the Democrats and Re-publicans to break with commercial interests and support the farmer, the alliance moved, often reluctantly, in the direction of a third party.

At the start of the Farmers Alliance in 1877, leader C. W. Macune had insisted, "The Alliance is a strictly white man's nonpolitical, secret business association." But by 1892, it was none of those things. Although some southern leaders, like Macune, made it clear that they would never threaten the unity of the white vote in the South by leaving the Democratic Party, advocates of a third party carried the day at the convention of laborers, farmers, and common folk in St. Louis. There, the Farmers Alliance gave birth to the People's Party and launched the Populist movement.

The Populists mounted a critique of industrial society and a call for action. Convinced that the money and banking systems worked to the advantage of the wealthy few, they demanded economic democracy. To solve the farmers' credit problem, C. W. Macune hit on the ingenious idea of the subtreasury, a plan that would allow farmers to store nonperishable crops in government storehouses until the market was advantageous. At the same time, they would receive commodity credit from the federal government that would enable them to buy needed supplies and seed for the coming year's crops. The subtreasury became an article of faith in the South, where it promised to eliminate the crop lien system once and for all. Although Macune's idea would be enacted piecemeal in Progressive and New Deal legislation after the start of the twentieth century, conservatives in the 1890s dismissed it as far-fetched and communistic.

For the western farmer, the enemy was not the merchant but the speculator and the railroad. Populism promised land reform, championing a plan that would reclaim excessive lands granted or sold to railroads and foreign investors. The Populists' boldest proposal called for government ownership of the railroads and telegraphs to put an end to discriminatory rate practices. With the powerful railroads dominating politics and effectively nullifying the Interstate Commerce Act of 1887, Populists did not shrink from advocating what their opponents called state socialism.

Money joined transportation and land as the third major thrust of the Populist movement. Farmers in all sections rallied to the cry for cheaper currency, endorsing platform planks calling for free silver and greenbacks. To show their support for labor, Populists supported the eight-hour day and

ON THE WAY TO A POPULIST MEETING IN KANSAS
*Populism was more than a political movement; it was a culture unto itself. For farmers
in sparsely settled regions, the movement provided reassurance that they were not
alone, that others shared their problems, and that solutions could be found. When the
Populists called a meeting, wagons came from miles around, as in this gathering in
Dickinson County, Kansas.*
Kansas State Historical Society, Topeka, Kansas.

an end to contract labor. And to empower the common people, their platform called for the direct election of senators and electoral reforms including the secret ballot and the right to initiate legislation, to recall elected officials, and to submit issues to the people via referendum. More than just a response to hard times, Populism presented an alternative vision of what America could become.

The Homestead Lockout and Strike

By the 1890s labor, too, was in crisis. The year 1892 witnessed a decisive struggle as steelworkers in Pennsylvania squared off against Andrew Carnegie for the right to organize in the Homestead mills. At first glance it seemed ironic that Carnegie became the adversary in the workers' fight for the right to unionize. Andrew Carnegie was unique among industrialists as a self-styled friend of labor. In 1886 he had written, "The right of the workingmen to combine and to form trades unions is no less sacred

than the right of the manufacturer to enter into associations and conferences with his fellows." Yet six years later at Homestead, Carnegie set out to crush a union in one of labor's legendary confrontations.

As much as he cherished his liberal beliefs, Carnegie cherished his profits more. Labor unions had worked well for him during the years when he was building his empire. Labor strife at Homestead during the 1870s had enabled Carnegie to buy the plant from his competitors at cost and to take over the steel industry. And during the 1880s, strong national craft unions ensured that competing mills could not undercut his labor costs. But by the 1890s, Carnegie had beat out his competitors, and the only thing standing in the way of his control of the industry was the Amalgamated Association of Iron and Steel Workers, one of the largest and richest of the craft unions that made up the American Federation of Labor (AFL).

In 1892, when the Amalgamated attempted to renew its contract at Carnegie's Homestead mill, its leaders were told that since "the vast majority of our employees are Non union, the Firm has decided that the minority must give place to the majority." While it was true that only eight hundred skilled workers belonged to the elite Amalgamated, the union had long enjoyed the support of the plant's three thousand nonunion workers. Slavs, who did much of the unskilled work, made common cause with the Welsh, Scots, and Irish who belonged to the union. Never before had the Amalgamated been denied a contract.

As the situation built toward a showdown, Carnegie sailed to Scotland in the spring. No doubt aware of his hypocrisy, he preferred not to be directly involved in the union busting that lay on the horizon. He left Henry Clay Frick, the toughest antilabor man in the industry, in charge of the Homestead plant. By summer, a strike looked inevitable. Frick prepared by erecting a fifteen-foot fence around the plant and topping it with barbed wire. Workers aptly dubbed it "Fort Frick." To defend his fort, Frick hired 316 mercenaries from the Pinkerton Detective Agency at the rate of $5 per day, more than double the wage of the average Homestead worker.

On June 28, Frick locked the workers out of the mills. They immediately rallied to the support of the Amalgamated and declared a strike. Hugh O'Donnell, the young Irishman who led the union, vowed to prevent strikebreakers from entering the plant. On July 6 at four in the morning, a lookout spotted two barges moving up the Monongahela River in the fog. Frick was attempting to smuggle his Pinkertons into Homestead. Workers sounded the alarm, and within minutes a crowd of more than a thousand, hastily armed with rifles, hoes, and fence posts, rushed to the riverbank to meet the enemy. When the Pinkertons attempted to come ashore, gunfire broke out, and more than a dozen Pinkertons and some thirty strikers fell, killed or wounded. The Pinkertons retreated back onto the barges.

For twelve hours, the strikers (joined by their family members) threw everything they had at the barges. Finally, the Pinkertons hoisted a white flag and arranged with O'Donnell to surrender. With eight strikers dead or dying and scores wounded, the crowd, now numbering perhaps ten thousand, was in no mood for conciliation. As the hated "Pinks" came up the hill, they were forced to run a gauntlet of screaming, cursing men, women, and children. When a young guard dropped to his

LABOR TROUBLE AT HOMESTEAD
The nation's attention was riveted on the labor strife at Homestead in the summer of 1892. Frank Leslie's Illustrated Weekly *magazine ran a cover story on the violence Pinkerton agents faced from a crowd of men, women, and children armed with clubs, guns, and ax handles. The workers, who had been locked out by Henry Clay Frick, were enraged that Frick had hired the Pinkertons to bring in strikebreakers.*
The New York Society Library.

knees, weeping for mercy, a woman used her umbrella to poke out his eye. Only one Pinkerton had been killed in the siege on the barges, but in the grim rout that followed their surrender, three men died as a result of the beatings, and not one avoided injury.

The "battle of Fort Frick" ended in a dubious victory for the workers. They took control of the plant and elected a council to run the community. At first, public opinion favored their cause. Newspapers urged Frick to negotiate or submit to arbitration. A congressman castigated Carnegie for "skulking in his castle in Scotland," and the Populists, meeting in St. Louis, condemned the use of "hireling armies."

But the action of the strikers struck at the heart of the capitalist system, pitting the workers' right to their jobs against the rights of private property. Four days after the confrontation, the Pennsylvania governor, who sympathized with the workers, nonetheless yielded to pressure from Frick and ordered eight thousand National Guard troops into Homestead to protect Carnegie's mills. The strikers, thinking they had won the day, welcomed the troops with a brass band. But they soon understood the reality. The troops' ninety-five-day occupation not only protected Carnegie's property but also enabled Frick to reopen the mills using strikebreakers. "We have been deceived," one worker bitterly complained. "We have stood idly by and let the town be occupied by soldiers who come here, not as our protectors, but as the protectors of non-union men. . . . If we undertake to resist the seizure of our jobs, we will be shot down like dogs."

Then, in a misguided effort to ignite a general uprising, Alexander Berkman, a Russian immigrant and anarchist, attempted to assassinate Frick. Berkman bungled his attempt. Frick, shot twice, survived and showed considerable courage, allowing doctors to remove the bullets from his neck but refusing to leave his desk until the day's work was completed. "I do not think that I shall die," Frick remarked coolly, "but whether I do or not, the Company will pursue the same policy and it will win."

After the assassination attempt, public opinion turned against the workers. Berkman was quickly tried and sentenced to prison. Although the Amalgamated and the AFL denounced his action, the incident linked anarchism and unionism, already associated in the public mind as a result of the Haymarket bombing in 1886. Hugh O'Donnell later wrote that "the bullet from Berkman's pistol, failing in its foul intent, went straight through the heart of the Homestead strike."

In the end, the strike collapsed after four and a half months. The Homestead mill reopened in November and the men returned to work, except for the union leaders, who were blacklisted in every steel and iron mill in the country. With the owners firmly in charge, the mills reopened. The company slashed wages, reinstated the twelve-hour day, and eliminated five hundred jobs. The workers lapsed into a demoralized state.

In the drama of events surrounding Homestead, the significance of what occurred often remained obscured: The workers at Homestead had been taught a lesson. They would never again, in the words of the National Guard commander, "believe the works are their's [sic] quite as much as Carnegie's." It would take another forty-five years before steelworkers successfully unionized. In the meantime, Carnegie's production tripled, even in the midst of a depression. "Ashamed to tell you profits these days," Carnegie wrote a friend in 1899. And no wonder: Carnegie's profits had grown from $4 million in 1892 to $40 million in 1900.

Eugene V. Debs and the Pullman Strike

A year after the Homestead lockout, a major panic and depression hit the nation. A stock market crash on Wall Street in the spring of 1893 led to bitter hard times. The ranks of the unemployed swelled to three million, almost half of the working population. "A fearful crisis is upon us," wrote a labor publication. "Countless thousands of our fellow men are unemployed; men, women and children are suffering the pangs of hunger." Nowhere were workers more demoralized than in the model town of Pullman on the outskirts of Chicago (see Chapter 19). George M. Pullman, who made his millions by building Pullman Palace cars and leasing them to the railroads, prided himself on his enlightened approach to labor. But in 1893, Pullman's workers saw their pay sliced five times between May and December, with cuts totaling at least 28 percent.

At the same time, Pullman refused to lower the rents in his model town, insisting that "the renting of the dwellings and the employment of workmen at Pullman are in no way tied together." When workers went to the bank to cash their checks, the rent was taken out. One worker found that he had only forty-seven cents to live on for two weeks. When the bank teller asked him whether he wanted to apply it to his back rent, he retorted, "If Mr. Pullman needs that forty-seven cents worse than I do, let him have it." In the meantime, Pullman continued to pay his stockholders an 8 percent dividend, and the company accumulated a $25 million surplus.

At the heart of the labor problems at Pullman lay not only economic inequity but the company's attempt to control the work process, substituting piecework for day wages and undermining the skilled craftsworkers. The Pullman workers rebelled. During the spring of 1894, they flocked to the ranks of the American Railway Union (ARU), a new organization led by Eugene Victor Debs. The ARU, unlike the skilled craft unions of the AFL, pledged to organize all railway workers from the engineers down to the engine wipers.

George Pullman responded to his workers' grievances by firing three of the union's leaders the day after they led a delegation to protest wage cuts. Angry men and women walked off the job in disgust. What began as a spontaneous protest in May 1894 blossomed into a strike that involved more than 90 percent of Pullman's thirty-three hundred workers. "We do not know what the outcome will be, and in fact we do not much care," one worker confessed. "We do know that we are working for less wages than will maintain ourselves and families in the necessaries of life, and on that proposition we refuse to work any longer." Pullman countered by shutting down the plant.

In June, the Pullman strikers appealed to the ARU to come to their aid. Debs sympathized with the strikers, but he hesitated to commit his fledgling union to a major strike in the midst of a depression. He pleaded with the workers to find another solution. When Pullman adamantly refused to arbitrate, the ARU membership, brushing aside Debs's call for caution, voted to boycott all Pullman cars. Beginning on June 29, switchmen refused to handle any train that carried Pullman cars.

The conflict escalated quickly. The General Managers Association (GMA), a combination of managers from twenty-four different railroads, acted in concert to quash the boycott. Determined to kill the ARU, they recruited strikebreakers and fired all the protesting switchmen. Their tactics set off a chain reaction. Entire train crews walked off the job in a show of solidarity with the Pullman workers and the ARU. In a matter of days the boycott/strike spread to more than fifteen railroads and affected twenty-seven states and territories. By July 2, rail lines from New York to California lay paralyzed. Even the GMA was forced to concede that the railroads had been "fought to a standstill."

The strike remained surprisingly peaceful. Mobs stopped trains carrying Pullman cars and forced their crews to uncouple the cars and leave them on the sidings. But no major riots broke out, and no serious damage was done to railroad property. Debs, in a whirlwind of activity, fired off telegrams to all parts of the country advising his followers to avoid violence, to use no force to stop trains, and to respect law and order. But the nation's newspapers, fed press releases by the GMA, distorted and misrepresented the strike. Across the country, papers ran headlines like "Wild Riot in Chicago" and "Mob is in Control." Editors rushed to denounce "Dictator Debs."

In Washington, Attorney General Richard B. Olney, a lawyer with strong ties to the railroads, determined to put down the strike. When Illinois governor John Peter Altgeld refused to call out troops, Olney, acting in concert with the GMA, convinced President Grover Cleveland that federal troops should intervene to protect the mails. To further cripple the strike, two Chicago judges issued an injunction against the boycott so sweeping that it prohibited Debs from speaking in public. By issuing the injunction, the court in effect made the strike a crime punishable by jail sentence for contempt of court, a civil process that did not require trial by jury. Even the conservative Chicago *Tribune* judged the injunction "a menace to liberty . . . a weapon ever ready for the capitalist." Furious, Debs risked jail by refusing to honor it.

Olney's strategy worked. With the strikers violating a federal injunction and with the mails in jeopardy (the GMA made sure that Pullman cars were put on every mail train), Cleveland called out the army. On July 5, nearly eight thousand troops marched into Chicago. Violence immediately erupted. In one day, more than $340,000 worth of property was destroyed, twenty-five workers were shot, and more than sixty were wounded. In the face of bullets and bayonets, the strikers held firm. "Troops cannot move trains," Debs reminded the strikers, a fact that was borne out as the railroads remained paralyzed despite the military intervention. But if the army could not put down the strike, the injunction could and did. Debs was arrested and imprisoned for contempt of court. With its leader in jail, its headquarters raided and ransacked, and its members demoralized, the ARU was defeated along with the strike. Pullman reopened his factory, hiring new workers to replace many of the strikers and leaving sixteen hundred workers without jobs and without the means to relocate.

In the aftermath of the strike, a special commission investigated the events at Pullman, taking testimony from 107 witnesses, including workers and George M. Pullman himself. Stubborn and self-righteous, Pullman spoke for the business orthodoxy of his era, steadfastly affirming the right of business to safeguard its interests through confederacies like the GMA and at the same time denying labor's right to organize. "If we were to receive these men as representatives of the union," he stated, "they could probably force us to pay any wages which they saw fit."

From his jail cell, Eugene Debs reviewed the events of the Pullman strike. With the courts and the army ready to come to the aid of property, Debs realized, labor had little recourse. Strikes seemed futile, and unions remained helpless; workers must take control of the state itself. Debs went into jail a trade unionist and came out six months later a socialist. After a brief flirtation with Populism, he would go on to form the Socialist Party in 1900 and run for president on its ticket five times.

Depression Politics

The depression that began in the spring of 1893 and lasted for more than four years put nearly half of the labor force out of work. The human cost was staggering. "I Take my pen in hand to let you know that we are Starving to death," a Kansas farm woman wrote to the governor in 1894. The country swarmed with people looking for jobs. They rode the rails, slept in barns, begged for work, and, when they could not get work, begged for food.

The burden of feeding and sheltering the unemployed and their families fell to private charity, city government, and some of the stronger trade unions. The states and the federal government appropriated not a cent for aid. Following the harsh dictates of social Darwinism and laissez-faire, the majority of Americans believed that it was inappropriate for the government to intervene. But the scope of the depression made it impossible for local agencies to supply sufficient relief, and increasingly voices called on the federal government to take action.

Coxey's "Army"

Masses of unemployed Americans marched to Washington, D.C., in the spring of 1894 to call attention to their plight and to urge Congress to enact a public works program to end unemployment. From as far away as Seattle, San Francisco, Los Angeles, and Denver, hundreds joined the march. Jacob S. Coxey of Massilon, Ohio, led the most pub-

licized contingent. Coxey, a wealthy manufacturer, had a plan to end unemployment. He proposed that the government put the jobless to work building badly needed roads. His plan won the support of the AFL and the Populists.

Starting out from Ohio with one hundred men, Coxey's "army," as it was dubbed by journalists, swelled as it marched east through the spring snows of the Alleghenies. In Pennsylvania, Coxey recruited several hundred from the ranks of those left unemployed by the Homestead lockout. Called by Coxey the Commonweal of Christ, the army advanced to the tune of "Marching through Georgia":

> We are not tramps nor vagabonds,
>   that's shirking honest toil,
> But miners, clerks, skilled artisans,
>   and tillers of the soil
> Now forced to beg our brother worms
>   to give us leave to toil,
> While we are marching with Coxey.
> Hurrah! hurrah! for the unemployed's appeal
> Hurrah! hurrah! for the marching commonweal!

On May 1, Coxey's army arrived in Washington. Given permission to parade but forbidden to speak from the Capitol, Coxey defiantly marched his men onto the Capitol grounds. Police set upon the band, cracking heads and arresting Coxey and his lieutenants. Coxey went to jail for twenty days and was fined $5 for "walking on the grass."

Mass demonstrations of the unemployed served only to frighten comfortable Americans, who saw the specter of insurrection and rebellion everywhere in 1894. Those who had trembled for the safety of the Republic heaved a sigh of relief after Coxey's arrest, hoping that it would halt the march on Washington. But other armies of the unemployed, totaling possibly as many as five thousand people, were still on their way. Too poor to pay for railway tickets, they rode the rails as "freeloaders." The more daring contingents commandeered entire trains, stirring fears of revolution. Nervous midwestern governors put trains at the marchers' disposal to speed them quickly out of the state. Journalists who covered the march did little to quiet the nation's fears. They delighted in military terminology, dubbing the marchers "armies" and describing themselves as "war correspondents." Their writing gave to the episode a tone of urgency and heightened the sense of a nation imperiled.

COXEY'S ARMY
Coxey's army called itself a "petition in boots." Here a group of Coxeyites in coats, ties, and bowler hats march behind the American flag as onlookers join the curious crowd that greets the marchers as they pass. These well-dressed marchers hardly seem like a menacing army. But many feared Coxey and his followers, and the military rhetoric of the press only fueled their fears. Coxey dramatized the plight of millions of workers left unemployed in the wake of the panic of 1893.
Library of Congress.

By August, the leaderless, tattered armies dissolved. Although the "On to Washington" movement proved ineffective in forcing federal relief legislation, Coxey's army dramatized the plight of the unemployed and acted, in the words of one participant, as a "living, moving object lesson." Like the Populists, Coxey's army called into question the underlying values of the new industrial order and demonstrated how ordinary citizens turned to means outside the regular party system to influence politics in the 1890s.

The People's Party and the Election of 1896

Even before the depression of 1893 gave added impetus to their cause, the Populists had railed against the status quo. "We meet in the midst of a nation brought to the verge of moral, political, and material ruin," Ignatius Donnelly had declared in the preamble to the St. Louis platform in 1892.

Corruption dominates the ballot-box, the legislatures, the Congress, and touches even the ermine of the bench. . . . The fruits of the toil of millions are boldly stolen to build up colossal fortunes for a few. . . . From the same prolific womb of governmental injustice we breed the two great classes—tramps and millionaires.

The fiery rhetoric frightened many who saw in the People's Party a call not to reform but to revolution. Throughout the country, the press denounced the Populists as "cranks, lunatics, and idiots." When one righteous editor dismissed them as "calamity howlers," Populist Lorenzo Lewelling of Kansas shot back, "If that is so I want to continue to howl until those conditions are improved."

The People's Party had captured more than a million votes in the presidential election of 1892, a respectable showing for a new party. But sectional and racial animosities threatened party unity. More than their alliance with the Yankee North, it was the Populists' willingness to form common cause with black farmers that made them anathema in the white South. Tom Watson of Georgia had tackled the "Negro question" head-on in 1892. Realizing that race prejudice obscured the common interests of black and white farmers, Watson openly courted African Americans, appearing on platforms with black speakers and promising "to wipe out the color line." When angry Georgia whites threatened to lynch a black Populist preacher, Watson rallied two thousand guntoting Populists to the man's defense. The spectacle of white Georgians protecting a black man from lynching was symptomatic of the enormous changes Populism promised in the South.

As the election of 1896 approached, depression intensified cries for reform not only from the Populists but throughout the electorate. Depression worsened the tight money problem caused by the deflationary pressures of the gold standard. Once again, proponents of free silver (the coinage of silver in addition to gold) stirred rebellion in the ranks of both the Democratic and Republican Parties. When the Republicans nominated Ohio governor William McKinley on a platform pledging the preservation of the gold standard, western advocates of free silver walked out of the convention. Open rebellion also split the Democratic Party as vast segments in the West and South repudiated President Grover Cleveland because of his support for the gold standard. In South Carolina, Benjamin Tillman won his race for Congress by promising, "Send me to Washington and I'll stick my pitchfork into [Cleveland's] old ribs!"

The spirit of revolt animated the Democratic National Convention in Chicago in the summer of 1896. "Pitchfork Ben" Tillman set the tone by attacking the party's president, denouncing the Cleveland administration as "undemocratic and tyrannical." But the man of the hour was William Jennings Bryan of Nebraska, the thirty-six-year-old "boy orator from the Platte," who whipped the convention into a frenzy with his passionate call for free silver. In his keynote address, Bryan masterfully cataloged the grievances of farmers and laborers, closing his dramatic speech with the ringing exhortation "Do not crucify mankind upon a cross of gold." Pandemonium broke loose as delegates stampeded to nominate Bryan, the youngest candidate ever to run for the presidency.

The juggernaut of free silver rolled out of Chicago and on to St. Louis, where the People's Party met a week after the Democrats adjourned. Smelling victory, many western Populists urged the party to endorse Bryan. A note of warning came

GOLD ELEPHANT CAMPAIGN BUTTON, 1896
Mechanical elephant badges that opened to show portraits of William McKinley and his running mate, Garret Hobart, were popular campaign novelties in the election of 1896. The elephant, the mascot of the Republican Party, is gilded gold to indicate the party's support of the gold standard.
Collection of Janice L. and David J. Frent.

from Populists like Tom Watson, who denounced the Bryanites as opportunists and urged the Populists to steer clear of both major parties and stick to "the middle of the road." In the South, where Democrats had resorted to fraud and violence to steal elections from the Populists in 1892 and 1894, support for a Democratic ticket proved especially hard for Populists to swallow.

Populist delegates tried to remain true to their principles and their platform when they met in St. Louis in 1896. They voted to support all the planks of the 1892 platform, added to it a call for public works projects for the unemployed, and narrowly defeated a plank for woman suffrage. Only deceit and trickery enabled the fusionists (those who wished to join ranks with the Democrats) to carry the day. In an unorthodox turn of events, the convention selected the vice presidential candidate first. The nomination of Tom Watson undercut opposition to fusing with the Democrats. Bryan quickly wired the chairman of the convention, protesting that he would not drop his Democratic running mate or run on a Populist ticket with Watson. Mysteriously, his message never reached the convention floor. Watson's nomination paved the way for the selection of Bryan by a lopsided vote. The Populists did not know it, but their cheers for Bryan in St. Louis signaled not a chorus of victory, but the death knell of the People's Party.

Few contests in the nation's history have been as fiercely fought and as full of emotion as the presidential election of 1896. On one side stood Republican William McKinley, backed by the wealthy industrialist and party boss Marcus Alonzo Hanna. Hanna played on the business community's fears of free silver to raise more than $4 million for the Republican war chest, double that of any previous campaign. On the other side, William Jennings Bryan, with few assets beyond his silver tongue, struggled to make up in energy and eloquence what his party lacked in campaign funds. He set a new style for presidential campaigning, crisscrossing the country in a whirlwind tour, traveling more than eighteen thousand miles and delivering more than six hundred speeches in three months. According to his own reckoning, he visited twenty-seven states and spoke to more than five million Americans.

As election day approached, the silver states of the Rocky Mountains lined up solidly for Bryan. In Nevada, Idaho, and Colorado, miners and their bosses came together in the hope free silver would shore up the mining industry, which had seen the price of silver drop from $1.32 an ounce in the heyday of the Comstock Lode to a mere 87 cents in 1892. The Northeast stood solidly for McKinley. Much of the South, with the exception of the border states, abandoned the Populists and returned to the Democratic fold, leaving Tom Watson to lament that "[Populists] play Jonah while [Democrats] play the whale." The Midwest was in the balance. Bryan intensified his campaign in Illinois, Michigan, Ohio, and Indiana. But midwestern farmers could smell economic recovery and were less receptive to the blandishments of free silver than were voters farther west. In the cities, Democrats charged the Republicans with mass intimidation. "Men, vote as you please," the head of New Yorks's Steinway Piano Company reportedly announced on the eve of the election, "but if Bryan is elected tomorrow the whistle will not blow Wednesday morning."

Intimidation alone did not explain the failure of urban labor to rally to Bryan. Republicans repeatedly warned workers that if the Democrats won, the inflated silver dollar would be worth only fifty cents. However much farmers and laborers might insist that they were united as producers against the nonproducing bosses, it was equally true that inflation did not promise the boon to urban laborers that it did to western debtors.

On election day, four out of every five voters went to the polls, in an unprecedented turnout. In the critical midwestern states, as many as 95 percent of the eligible voters cast their ballots. In the end, the election outcome hinged on as few as one hundred to one thousand votes in several key states. Although McKinley won twenty-three states to Bryan's twenty-two, the electoral vote showed a lopsided 271–176 (Map 20.1).

The biggest losers in 1896 turned out to be the Populists. On the national level, they polled less than 300,000 votes, over a million less than in 1894. In the clamor to support Bryan, Populists in the South drifted back to the Democratic Party. The People's Party was crushed, and with it died the agrarian revolt.

But if Populism proved unsuccessful, it set the political agenda for the United States in the next decades, highlighting issues of social justice such as banking and currency reform, electoral reforms, and an enlarged role for the federal government in the economy. Meanwhile, as the decade ended, the bugle call to arms drowned out the trumpet of reform. The struggle for social justice gave way to a war for empire.

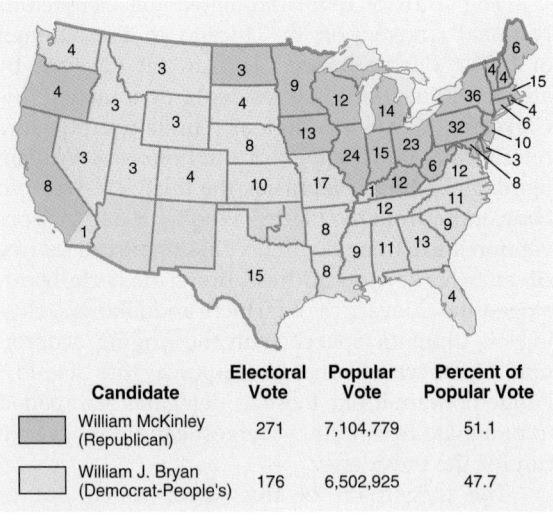

Candidate	Electoral Vote	Popular Vote	Percent of Popular Vote
William McKinley (Republican)	271	7,104,779	51.1
William J. Bryan (Democrat-People's)	176	6,502,925	47.7

M A P   2 0 . 1
The Election of 1896

The United States Looks Outward

In the last decade of the nineteenth century, American foreign policy consisted of two currents—isolation and expansion. The determination to remain aloof from European politics had been a hallmark of policy since President George Washington, in his farewell address, had warned Americans to "steer clear" of permanent alliances. Simultaneously, Americans believed in "manifest destiny"—the "obvious" right to expand the country from ocean to ocean and possibly on a continental scale, taking in Canada and Mexico. As the century ended, the United States moved away from isolation and prepared to take its place on the world stage.

Markets and Missionaries

The depression of the 1890s provided a powerful impetus to American commercial expansion. As markets weakened at home, American businesses looked abroad for profits. As early as 1890, Captain Alfred Thayer Mahan, leader of a growing group of American expansionists that included Henry Cabot Lodge, John Hay, and Theodore Roosevelt, prophesied, "Whether they will or not, Americans must now begin to look outward. The growing production of the country requires it." Although not all U.S. business leaders thought it advantageous to undertake adventures abroad, the logic of acquiring new markets to absorb the nation's growing capacity for production proved convincing to many. As the depression deepened, one diplomat warned that Americans "must turn [their] eyes abroad, or they will soon look inward upon discontent."

Exports of cloth, kerosene, flour, and steel already constituted a small but significant percentage of the profits of American business in the 1890s. And where American interests led, businessmen expected American power and influence to follow to protect their investments (Figure 20.1). Companies like Standard Oil actively sought to use the government as their agent, often putting foreign service employees on the payroll. "Our ambassadors and ministers and consuls," wrote John D. Rockefeller appreciatively, "have aided to push our way into new markets to the utmost corners of the world." Whether by "our" he meant the United States or Standard Oil remained ambiguous; in practice, the distinction was of little importance in late-nineteenth-century foreign policy.

In Hawaii, American sugar interests fomented a rebellion in 1893, toppling the increasingly anti-American Queen Liliuokalani. They pushed Congress to annex the islands, which would allow

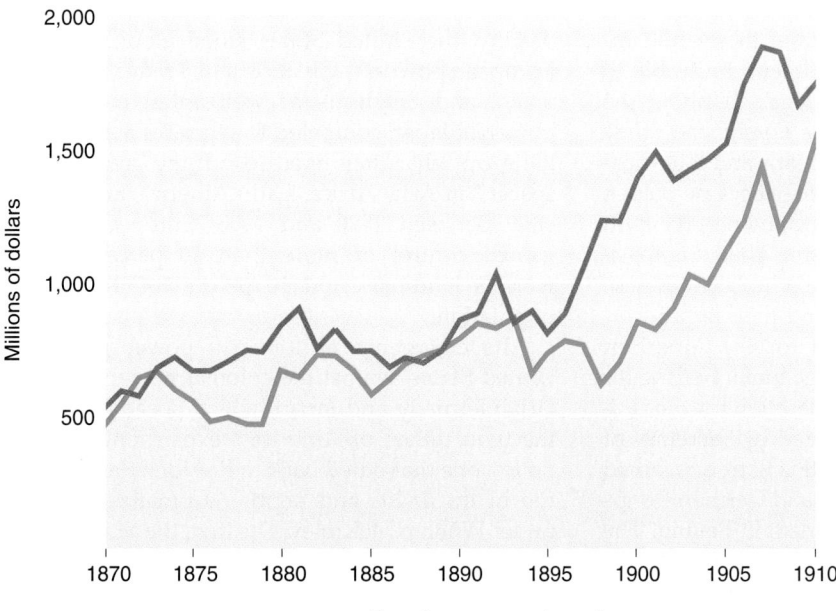

FIGURE 20.1
Expansion in U.S. Trade, 1870–1910

Between 1870 and 1910, American exports nearly tripled. Although imports rose, they were held in check by the high protective tariff championed by Republican presidents from Ulysses Grant to William Howard Taft. A decline in imports is particularly noticeable after passage of the prohibitive McKinley tariff in 1890.

planters to avoid the high tariff on sugar. When President Cleveland learned that Hawaiians opposed annexation, he withdrew the proposal from Congress. But expansionists continued to covet the islands and sought the first excuse to push through annexation.

However compelling the economic arguments about overseas markets proved, business interests alone did not account for the new expansionism that seized the nation during the 1890s. As Mahan confessed, "Even when material interests are the original exciting cause, it is the sentiment to which they give rise, the moral tone which emotion takes that constitutes the greater force." Much of that moral tone was set by American missionaries intent on spreading the gospel of Christianity to the "heathen." No area on the globe constituted a greater challenge than China. In 1858, the Tientsin treaty admitted foreign missionaries—Roman Catholics from France, Protestants from Britain, Germany, and the United States—to spread the gospel to the hinterlands.

Increased missionary activity and Western enterprise touched off a series of antiforeign uprisings in China that culminated in the Boxer Rebellion of 1900–1901. The Chinese resented the interference of missionaries in village life and the preference and protection they afforded their Christian converts. Opposition to foreign missionaries took the form of antiforeign secret societies, most notably the Boxers, whose Chinese name translated literally into "Righteous Harmonious Fist." No simple pugilists, the Boxers believed that through ritual they could induce a trance that would make them invincible to Western weapons. Under the slogan "Uphold the Ch'ing Dynasty, Exterminate the Foreigners," they began to terrorize Chinese Christians and later missionaries in northern China. As they became bolder, they attacked railroads and telegraph lines, the twin symbols of Western imperialism. Their rampage eventually led to the massacre of some 2,000 Chinese converts and 250 missionaries and their families.

The missionaries clamored for the American government to protect and avenge them. Fearing for their lives, they showed little toleration for the cautious diplomatic approach favored by Secretary of State John Hay. In the end, 2,500 U.S. troops joined an allied force including British and German troops sent to save the besieged foreigners in Beijing. The arrival of foreign troops chastened the imperial government, which adopted a tougher stance against the Boxers and a more accommodationist policy toward foreign missionaries.

In their fight against the Boxers, the missionaries saw no paradox in bringing Christianity to China at gunpoint. "It is worth any cost in money, worth any cost in bloodshed," argued one bishop, "if we can make millions of Chinese true and intelligent Christians." In truth, expansionists and missionaries worked hand in hand; trade and Christianity marched into China together. "Missionaries," admitted the American clergyman Charles Denby, "are the pioneers of trade and commerce. . . . The missionary, inspired by holy zeal, goes everywhere and by degrees foreign commerce and trade follow."

The moral tone of the age, set by social Darwinism with its emphasis on survival of the fittest and Anglo-Saxon racial superiority, proved ideally suited to imperialism. Congregational minister Josiah Strong revealed the mixture of racism and missionary zeal that fueled American adventurism abroad when he remarked, "It seems to me that God, with infinite wisdom and skill, is training the Anglo Saxon race for an hour sure to come in the world's future."

The Monroe Doctrine and the Open Door Policy

Throughout much of the last half of the nineteenth century, U.S. interest in foreign policy took a backseat to domestic developments. "Foreign relations," one historian has written, "were composed of incidents, not policies." Intent on its own manifest destiny, the United States stood aloof while the European powers—Great Britain, France, Germany, Spain, and Belgium—as well as an increasingly powerful Japan competed for empires abroad, gobbling up what they liked to call the great "empty spaces" in Asia, Africa, Latin America, and the Pacific. Between 1870 and 1900, European nations gained control of more than 20 percent of the world's landmass and 10 percent of the world's population.

Its emergence as a world power pitted the United States against the colonial powers, particularly Germany and Japan, which posed a threat to the twin pillars of America's expansionist foreign policy, one that dated back to President James Monroe in the 1820s and another formalized in 1900 under William McKinley. The first, the Monroe Doctrine, proclaimed the Western Hemisphere an American "sphere of influence" and warned European powers to keep their hands off or risk war. The second, the Open Door, dealt with Asia, an area cov-

THE OPEN DOOR
The trade advantage gained by the United States through the Open Door policy, enunci-
ated by Secretary of State John Hay in 1900, is portrayed graphically in this political car-
toon. Uncle Sam stands prominently in the "open door" while representatives of the other
great powers seek admittance to the "Flowery Kingdom" of China. Great Britain is sym-
bolized by the stocky figure of John Bull; czarist Russia is portrayed by the bearded figure
with the hat sporting the imperial double eagle. Other imperialist powers variously repre-
sented have yielded to Uncle Sam, who holds the golden key of "American Diplomacy"
while the Chinese beam with pleasure. In fact, the Open Door policy promised equal access
for all powers to the China trade, not U.S. preeminence as the cartoon implies.
Culver Pictures.

www.bedfordstmartins.com/roarkcompact SEE THE ONLINE STUDY GUIDE for more help in
analyzing this image.

eted by American merchants since the 1840s, the
heyday of clipper ships and the China trade. In the
1890s, China, weakened by years of warfare, looked
as if it might be partitioned into spheres of influence by England, Japan, Germany, France, and Russia. Concerned about the integrity of China and not
coincidentally American trade, Secretary of State
John Hay in 1899–1900 hastily wrote a series of
notes calling for an "open door" policy that would
ensure trade access to all and maintain the semblance of Chinese sovereignty. The notes—sent to
Britain, Germany, and Russia and later to France,
Japan, and Italy—were greeted by the major powers with polite evasions. Nevertheless, Hay skillfully managed to maneuver the powers into doing
his bidding and boldly announced in 1900 the Open
Door as international policy. By holding to this policy, the United States largely avoided the problems

of maintaining a far-flung colonial empire while also exerting and expanding its economic power (Map 20.2).

While demanding open access in Asia, closer to home the United States actively worked to buttress the Monroe Doctrine, with its assertion of American hegemony (domination) in the Western Hemisphere. In the 1880s, Republican secretary of state James G. Blaine promoted hemispheric peace and trade through Pan-American cooperation at the same time that he used American troops to inter-vene in Latin American border disputes. In 1895 Americans risked war with Great Britain to enforce the Monroe Doctrine. When a border dispute arose between Venezuela and British Guiana over lands where gold had been discovered, President Cleveland asserted the U.S. prerogative to step in and mediate, reducing Venezuela to the role of mere onlooker. At first, Britain refused to accept U.S. mediation and conflict seemed imminent. "Let the fight come if it must," wrote rising Republican neophyte Theodore Roosevelt, always itching to do battle. "I

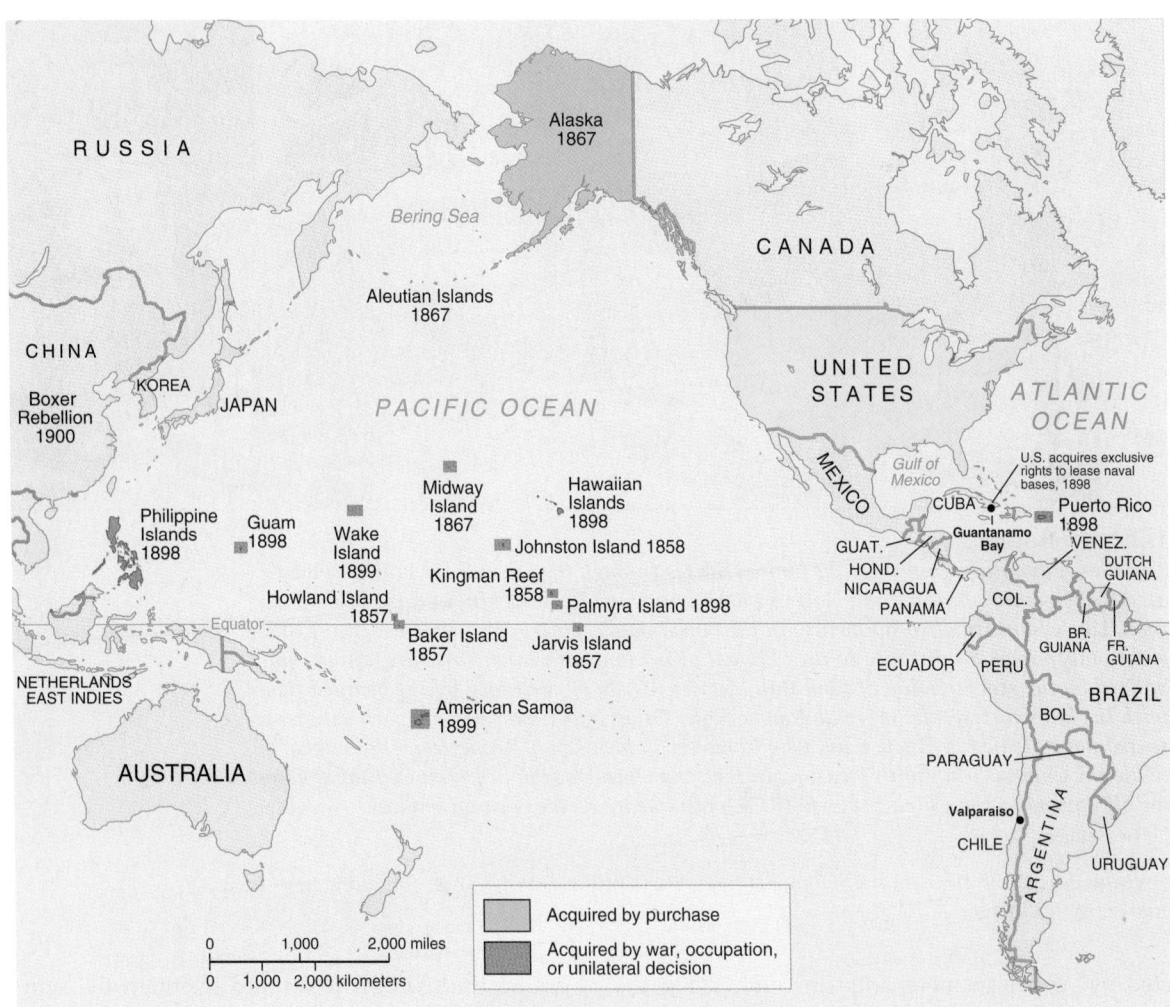

MAP 20.2

U.S. Territorial Expansion through 1900
The United States extended its interests abroad with a series of territorial acquisitions. Although Cuba was granted independence, the Platt Amendment kept the new nation firmly under U.S. control. In the wake of the Spanish-American War, the United States woke up to find that it held an empire extending halfway around the globe.

don't care whether our sea coast cities are bombarded or not." Seeing war with Britain as an opportunity to fulfill a long-held goal of extending manifest destiny to the North as well as to the West, Roosevelt promised that "we would take Canada." Cleveland, less bellicose than Roosevelt, wished only to see America's presence in the hemisphere respected and its solution for peace accepted. He was relieved when the British, who saw Germany as a greater threat and wished to avoid war in Latin America, accepted the terms of U.S. mediation.

In Central America, U.S. business triumphed in a bloodless takeover that saw French and British interests routed by behemoths like the United Fruit Company of Boston. United Fruit virtually dominated Costa Rica and Guatemala while an importer from New Orleans turned Honduras into a "banana republic" (a country dependent on U.S. trade). Thus, by 1895, the Venezuelan crisis signaled the extent to which the United States, through business as well as diplomacy, had successfully achieved hegemony in Latin America and the Caribbean, forcing even the British to concur with the secretary of state that "the infinite resources [of the United States] combined with its isolated position render it master of the situation and practically invulnerable as against any or all other powers."

War and Empire

The Spanish-American War, begun as a humanitarian effort to free Cuba from Spain's colonial grasp, ironically ended with the United States fighting a dirty guerrilla war with Filipino nationalists, who, like the Cubans, sought independence. Yet behind the contradiction stood the twin pillars of American foreign policy: The Monroe Doctrine made Spain's presence in Cuba unacceptable, while the determination to keep an open door in Asia rendered the Philippines a convenient stepping-stone to China.

"A Splendid Little War"

Looking back on the Spanish-American War of 1898, Secretary of State John Hay judged it "a splendid little war; begun with the highest motives, carried on with magnificent intelligence and spirit, favored by that fortune which loves the brave." At the close of a decade marred by bitter depression, social un-

rest, and political upheaval, the war offered Americans a chance to wave the flag and march in unison. War fever proved as infectious as the tune of a John Philip Sousa march. Few argued the merits of the conflict until it was over and the time came to divide the spoils.

The war began with moral outrage over the treatment of Cuban revolutionaries, who had launched a fight for independence against the Spanish colonial regime in 1895. In an attempt to isolate the guerrillas, Spanish general Valeriano Weyler herded Cubans into crowded and unsanitary concentration camps, where thousands died of hunger, disease, and exposure. Starvation soon spread to the cities. Tens of thousands of Cubans died, and countless others were left without food, clothing, or shelter. By 1898, fully a quarter of the island's population had perished in the revolution.

As the Cuban rebellion dragged on, pressure for American intervention mounted. Public outrage at Spain was fueled by American newspapers. A fierce circulation war raged in New York City between William Randolph Hearst's *Evening Journal* and Joseph Pulitzer's *World*. Their competition provoked what came to be called "yellow journalism," named for the color of ink Hearst used in a popular comic strip. This new style of journalism, which pandered to the public's appetite for violence and sensationalism, found in the Cuban war a wealth of dramatic copy. The papers fed the American people a daily diet of "Butcher" Weyler and Spanish atrocities. Hearst sent artist Frederic Remington to document the horror, and when Remington wired home, "There is no trouble here. There will be no war," Hearst shot back, "You furnish the pictures and I'll furnish the war."

American interests in Cuba were, in the words of the U.S. minister to Spain, more than "merely theoretical or sentimental." American business had more than $50 million invested in Cuban sugar, and American trade with Cuba, a brisk $100 million a year before the rebellion, had dropped to near zero. Nevertheless, the business community balked, wary of a war with Spain. When industrialist Mark Hanna, the Republican kingmaker and senator from Ohio, urged restraint, a hot-headed Theodore Roosevelt, appointed assistant secretary of the navy in 1897, exploded, "We will have this war for the freedom of Cuba, Senator Hanna, in spite of the timidity of commercial interests."

To expansionists like Roosevelt, more than Cuban independence was at stake. War with Spain

THE BIG TYPE WAR OF THE YELLOW KIDS.

YELLOW JOURNALISM
Newspaper publishers Joseph Pulitzer and William Randolph Hearst square off in "The Big Type War." As the cartoon indicates, Hearst insisted he had the better right to cover the Spanish-American War because he "bought and paid for it." In their 1890s circulation war, Hearst and Pulitzer not only used big type in sensational headlines, but employed color in new comic sections. Hearst's **Sunday American** *promised "eight pages of polychromatic effulgence that make the rainbow look like a lead pipe." Hearst also stole the era's most famous cartoon character, the "Yellow Kid," from Pulitzer after a bidding war for the cartoonist's talents. Soon all forms of sensational writing were labeled "yellow journalism."*
Library of Congress.

opened up the prospect of expansion into Asia as well, since Spain controlled not only Cuba and Puerto Rico but also Guam and the Philippine Islands. As assistant secretary of the navy, Roosevelt worked for preparedness whenever his boss's back was turned. During the summer of 1897, while Navy Secretary John D. Long was vacationing, Roosevelt audaciously ordered the U.S. fleet to Manila in the Philippines. In the event of conflict with Spain, he put the navy in a position to capture the islands and gain an entry point to China.

President McKinley slowly moved toward intervention. In a show of American force, he dispatched the armored cruiser *Maine* to Cuba. On the night of February 15, 1898, a mysterious explosion destroyed the *Maine*, killing 267 crew members. While the source of the explosion remained unclear, enraged Americans immediately blamed the Spanish government. (See "Historical Question," page 510.) Rallying to the cry "Remember the *Maine*," Congress declared war in April. In the surge of patriotism that followed, more than 235,000 men enlisted. War brought with it a unity of purpose and national harmony that ended a decade of internal strife. "In April, everywhere over this good fair land, flags were flying," wrote the Kansas editor William Allen White. "At the stations, crowds gathered to hurrah for the soldiers, and to throw hats into the air, and to unfurl flags."

They soon had something to cheer about. Five days after McKinley signed the war resolution, the U.S. navy, under Commodore George Dewey, destroyed the Spanish fleet in Manila Bay (Map 20.3). Dewey's stunning victory caught the nation by surprise. Although naval strategists had been orchestrating the move for some time, few Americans had ever heard of the Philippines. Even McKinley confessed that he could not immediately locate the archipelago on the map. He nevertheless recognized the Philippines as a convenient stepping-stone to China and dispatched U.S. troops to secure the islands.

The war in Cuba ended almost as quickly as it had begun. The first troops landed on June 22, and after a handful of battles the Spanish surrendered on July 17. The war lasted just long enough to elevate Theodore Roosevelt to the status of bona fide war hero. Roosevelt, sensitive to charges that he and his friends were no more than "armchair or parlor jingoes," resigned his navy post and formed the Rough Riders, a regiment composed about equally of Ivy League polo players and cowboys Roosevelt had met during his stint as a cattle rancher in the Dakotas in the 1880s. While the troops languished in Tampa awaiting their orders, Roosevelt and his men staged daily rodeos for the press, with the likes of New York blueblood William Tiffany busting broncs in competition with Dakota cowboy Jim "Dead Shot" Simpson. When the Rough Riders shipped out to Cuba, journalists fought for a berth with the colorful regiment. Roosevelt's charge up Kettle Hill and his role in the decisive battle of San Juan Hill made front-page news. Overnight, Roosevelt became the most famous man in America. By the time he sailed home from Cuba, a coalition of independent Republicans was already plotting his political future.

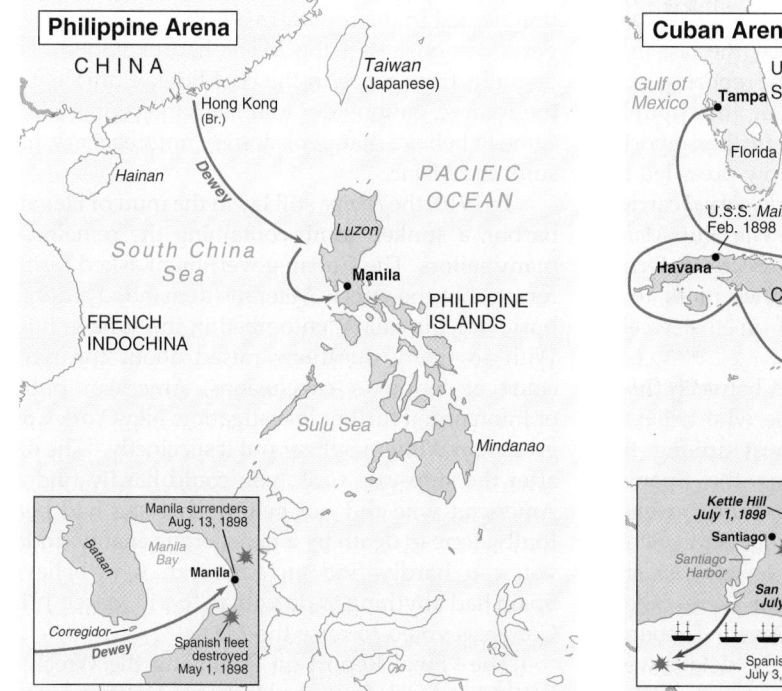
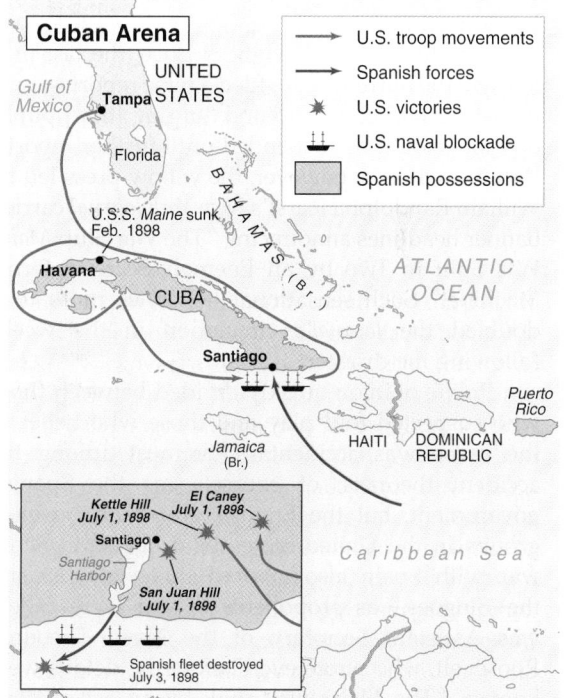

MAP 20.3

The Spanish-American War, 1898

The Spanish-American War of 1898 was fought in two theaters, the Philippine Islands and Cuba. Commodore George Dewey captured Manila without the loss of a single American sailor, five days after President William McKinley called for a declaration of war. The war lasted only a few months. Troops landed in Cuba in mid-June, and by mid-July they had taken Santiago and Havana and destroyed the Spanish fleet.

form in 1976, Rickover's report, entitled *How the Battleship* Maine *Was Destroyed*, became the accepted version of the event.

Today the pendulum has swung back. In an era of renewed terrorist attacks it is no surprise that a 1995 study of the *Maine* incident published by the Smithsonian Institution concludes that the battleship was sunk by zealot followers of General Weyler. "They had the opportunity, the means, and the motivation, and they blew up the *Maine* with a small low-strength mine they made themselves." According to this theory, the terrorists' homemade bomb burst the *Maine*'s hull and triggered a massive explosion in the ammunition magazines.

In looking at the now hundred-year-old history of controversy regarding the sinking of the *Maine*, only one thing seems certain: The "lessons" of the *Maine* have changed with the times and will no doubt continue to be drawn again as each new era questions history.

The Debate over American Imperialism

After a few brief campaigns in Cuba and Puerto Rico and Dewey's stunning naval victory in the Philippines, the American people woke up in possession of an empire that stretched halfway around the globe. Though Cuba escaped Spanish colonialism, the United States stopped short of granting the island the full autonomy it had promised. Contemptuous of the Cubans, whom General William Shafter, commander of U.S. troops, declared "no more fit for self-government than gun-powder is for hell," the U.S. government dictated a Cuban constitution that included the so-called Platt Amendment—a series of provisions that granted the United States the right to intervene to protect Cuba's "independence" as well as the power to oversee Cuban debt so that European creditors could not use it as an excuse for intervention. For good measure, the United States gave itself a ninety-nine-year lease on a naval base at Guantanamo. In return, it promised to implement an extensive sanitation program to clean up the island, not coincidentally to make it more attractive to American investors.

The formal Treaty of Paris ending the war with Spain also ceded to the United States control of Puerto Rico and Guam, former Spanish colonies. McKinley added Hawaii for good measure, annexing the islands in July 1898 and after brief hesitation the Philippines. America would soon feel the weight of what the British poet Rudyard Kipling called "the white man's burden" in the Philippines. Empire did not come cheap. When Spain balked, the United States agreed to pay an indemnity of $20 million for the islands. Nor was the cost measured in money alone. Filipino revolutionaries under Emilio Aguinaldo, who had greeted U.S. troops as liberators, bitterly fought the new masters. It would take seven years and four thousand American dead—almost ten times the number killed in Cuba—not to mention an estimated twenty thousand Filipino casualties, to defeat Aguinaldo and secure American control of the Philippines.

At home, a vocal minority composed largely of Democrats and former Populists resisted the country's foray into empire, judging it unwise, immoral, and unconstitutional. William Jennings Bryan, who had enlisted in the army along with Roosevelt but contracted typhoid fever and never saw action, came to the conclusion that American expansionism served only to distract the nation from its real problems at home. What did imperialism offer the ordinary American? Bryan asked. His answer: "Heavier taxes, Asiatic emigration and an opportunity to furnish more sons for the army." Mark Twain, lending his bitter eloquence to the cause of anti-imperialism, lamented that the United States had indeed become "yet another Civilized Power, with its banner of the Prince of Peace in one hand and its loot-basket and its butcher-knife in the other."

In the end the anti-imperialists would prove prophetic, and Hay's Open Door notes would demonstrate the principle that it was more effective for the United States to spread its influence abroad through economic power than by conquest. But in 1898, as the *Washington Post* trumpeted, "The taste of empire is in the mouth of the people," and Americans thrilled at the prospect of "an imperial policy,

THE BATTLE OF SAN JUAN HILL
This idealized 1898 lithograph portrays a highly romantic version of the Battle of San Juan Hill, far from the truth. The famous charge was much less glamorous than pictured here. Theodore Roosevelt, whose Rough Riders had taken nearby Kettle Hill, called to his men to charge the next line of Spanish trenches in the San Juan hills. But in the excitement of the battle, they didn't hear him and Roosevelt found himself charging virtually alone. He had to go back and rally the Rough Riders, who then charged the hill on foot. The illustration does get one thing right: Theodore Roosevelt led the charge wearing his spectacles. Roosevelt was so myopic he feared he might lose his glasses in battle and had Brooks Brothers, who custom-made his uniform, include a dozen pockets for extra eyeglasses.
Library of Congress.

the Republic renascent, taking her place with the armed nations."

Conclusion: Rallying around the Flag

A decade of domestic strife ended amid the blare of martial music and the waving of flags. The Spanish-American war effectively stifled the calls for social reform that had fueled the politics of the 1890s.

During that decade Americans offered competing visions of how the evils of urban industrialism and corporate capitalism might be mitigated. Women fought drunkenness and the conditions that fostered it, and mounted a suffrage movement to secure their basic political rights. Disaffected farmers facing hard times formed the Farmers Alliance to fight for their vision of economic democracy. Laborers staged bloody strikes to fight for control in the workplace. The Homestead lockout and the Pullman boycott brutally dramatized the power of property and the conservatism of the laissez-faire state. But workers' willingness to die in the streets of Chicago or at the Homestead works in their struggles eloquently testified to labor's growing unity and strength.

All in all, the 1890s witnessed more than its share of sound and fury—it was a decade of strife the likes of which the country would not see again for another seventy years. Although the 1890s ended on a harmonious note, with patriotic Americans rallying around the flag, it was not because the old grievances had been laid to rest. The People's Party, with its call for greater government involvement in the economy, expanded opportunities for direct democracy, and a more equitable balance of profits and power between the people and the big corporations, sounded the themes that would be taken up by a new generation of progressive reformers in the twentieth century.

FOR FURTHER READING ABOUT THE TOPICS IN THIS CHAPTER, see the Online Bibliography at

www.bedfordstmartins.com/roarkcompact.

FOR ADDITIONAL FIRST-HAND ACCOUNTS OF THIS PERIOD, see pages 67–85 in Michael Johnson, ed., *Reading the American Past*, Second Edition, Volume II.

TO ASSESS YOUR MASTERY OF THE MATERIAL IN THIS CHAPTER, see the Online Study Guide at

www.bedfordstmartins.com/roarkcompact.

CHRONOLOGY

1884 The Woman's Christian Temperance Union (WCTU), under Frances Willard, calls for woman suffrage (the "home protection ballot").

1890 National American Woman Suffrage Association (NAWSA) forms, electing Elizabeth Cady Stanton president.

Wyoming enters Union with woman suffrage.

1892 Ida B. Wells begins antilynching crusade.

People's Party (also known as Populist Party) founded in St. Louis.

Homestead lockout pits Carnegie steelworkers against hired Pinkertons.

Anarchist Alexander Berkman's attempt to assassinate Henry Clay Frick turns public opinion against Homestead workers.

The National Guard of Pennsylvania takes over the Homestead mills, ending the workers' strike.

People's Party wins more than one million votes.

1893 Severe economic depression touched off by panic on Wall Street.

President Grover Cleveland nixes attempt to annex Hawaii after Americans foment overthrow of Queen Liliuokalani.

1894 Coxey's "army" marches to Washington, D.C., to dramatize plight of unemployed.

Federal troops crush Pullman strike.

Union leader Eugene V. Debs jailed for violating court injunction.

1895 President Grover Cleveland risks war with Great Britain to defend Monroe Doctrine in border dispute between British Guiana and Venezuela.

1896 Democrats support William Jennings Bryan for president on free silver platform; People's Party also nominates Bryan but substitutes Populist Tom Watson as vice presidential nominee.

Republican William McKinley defeats Democrat William Jennings Bryan for presidency.

National Association of Colored Women (NACW) formed, with Mary Church Terrell as president.

1898 U.S. battleship *Maine* mysteriously explodes in Havana harbor.

Congress declares war on Spain.

Commodore George Dewey destroys Spanish fleet in Manila Bay, the Philippines.

U.S. troops defeat Spanish forces in Cuba.

Treaty of Paris ends Spanish-American War; under treaty, United States acquires Puerto Rico, Guam, and the Philippines.

United States annexes Hawaii.

Platt Amendment gives United States oversight of liberated Cuba.

1899 Secretary of State John Hay enunciates Open Door policy in China to guarantee trade access.

1900 Boxer Rebellion in China leads to deaths of more than 250 missionaries and their families.

PROGRESSIVE POSTER CONDEMNING CHILD LABOR

This poster attacks child labor, borrowing the convention of the business flow chart to portray graphically how industries employing children are "making human junk." Progressives' concern for the plight of poor children won them the label "the child savers." Although activists worked hard to enact federal legislation prohibiting child labor in 1916, the Supreme Court declared the law unconstitutional two years later on the grounds that Congress had no right to regulate manufacturing within states.

Library of Congress.

PROGRESSIVE REFORM FROM THE GRASS ROOTS TO THE WHITE HOUSE

21

1890–1916

I N THE SUMMER OF 1889, a young woman leased the upper floor of a dilapidated mansion on Chicago's West Side in the heart of a burgeoning immigrant population of Italians, Russian Jews, and Greeks. Watching the preparations at number 335, the neighbors scratched their heads, wondering why the well-dressed woman, who surely could afford a better house in a better neighborhood, chose to live on South Halsted Street. Yet the house built by Charles Hull precisely suited the needs of Jane Addams.

For Addams, personal action marked the first step in the search for solutions to the social problems fostered by urban industrialism. Her object was twofold: She wanted to help her immigrant neighbors and she wanted to offer an opportunity for educated women like herself to find meaningful work. As she later wrote in her autobiography, *Twenty Years at Hull-House* (1910), "I gradually became convinced that it would be a good thing to rent a house in a part of the city where many primitive and actual needs are found, in which young women who had been given over too exclusively to study might restore a balance of activity along traditional lines and learn of life from life itself." Addams's emphasis on the reciprocal relationship between the classes made Hull House different from other philanthropic enterprises. She wished to do things with, not just for, Chicago's poor.

In the next decade, Hull House expanded from one rented floor in the old brick mansion to some thirteen buildings that housed a remarkable variety of activities. The bathrooms in the basement were converted into public baths, a coffee shop and restaurant sold take-out food to working women too tired to cook after their long shifts, and a nursery and kindergarten provided care for neighborhood children. Hull House offered classes, lectures, art exhibits, musical instruction, and college extension courses. It boasted a gymnasium, a theater, a manual training workshop, a labor museum, and the first public playground in Chicago.

But Hull House was more than a group of buildings. From the first, it attracted an extraordinary set of reformers. Some stayed for decades, as did Julia Lathrop before she went to Washington, D.C., in 1912 to head the Children's Bureau. Others, like Gerard Swope, who later became president of the General Electric Company, came for only a short while. Most had jobs, paid room and board, and devoted time to research and reform. The people who lived at Hull House were among the first to investigate the problems of the city with scientific precision. Armed with statistics, they launched campaigns to improve housing, end child labor, fund playgrounds, mediate between labor and management, and lobby for protective legislation.

JANE ADDAMS
Jane Addams was twenty-nine years old when she founded Hull House on Halsted Street in Chicago. Her desire to live among the poor and her insistence that settlement house work provide benefits for educated women like herself as well as for the poor neighborhood residents separated her from the charity workers who had come before her and marked the distance from philanthropy to progressive reform.

The University of Illinois at Chicago, The University Library, Jane Addams Memorial Collection, JAMC neg. 103.

Addams quickly learned that it was impossible to deal with urban problems without becoming involved in political action. Her determination to get the garbage on Halstead Street picked up led her into municipal reform. After backing several unsuccessful electoral campaigns to unseat the corrupt political boss, Addams realized the boss was the symptom and not the cause of urban blight. Her struggle to better the condition of the urban poor led her not only to city hall but also to the state capitol and even further to Washington, D.C. A strong advocate of woman suffrage, she argued that city

women needed the ballot, not the broom, to keep their neighborhoods clean.

Under Jane Addams's leadership, Hull House, the premier settlement house in the United States, became a "spearhead for reform," part of a broader movement that contemporaries called the progressive movement. The transition from personal action to political activism that Addams personified became one of the hallmarks of this reform period, which lasted for almost three decades, from the 1890s to World War I.

What motivated comfortable, middle-class women and men to launch one of the major movements for social and political reform in U.S. history? There is no one answer because there is no single progressive profile. The progressives were a diverse group with a variety of goals. A sense of Christian mission inspired some. Others, frightened by the political tensions of the 1890s, feared social upheaval unless conditions were improved. Progressives shared a growing concern about the power of wealthy individuals and corporations, and a strong dislike of the trusts. But often they feared the new immigrants as well and sought to control and Americanize them. Along with moral fervor, a belief in technical expertise and scientific principles informed progressivism and made the cult of efficiency part and parcel of the movement. All of these elements—uplift and efficiency, social justice and social control—came together in the Progressive Era.

Grassroots Progressivism

Progressive reform began at the grassroots level and percolated upward into local, state, and eventually national politics as the reformers attacked the social problems fostered by urban industrialism. While reform flourished in many different settings across the country, the problems of urban America called forth the greatest efforts of the women and men who styled themselves progressives. In their zeal to "civilize the city," reformers founded settlement houses, professed a new Christian social gospel, and campaigned against vice and crime in the name of "social purity." Allying with the working class, they sought to better the lot of sweatshop garment workers and to end child labor. While their reform efforts often began on the local level, they just as often ended up being debated in state legislatures, in

Congress, and in the Oval Office. From Hull House to the White House, progressivism became a major political force in the first decade of the twentieth century.

Civilizing the City

Typically, progressives attacked the problems of the city on many fronts. The settlement house movement attempted to bridge the distance between the classes. The social gospel called for the churches to play a new role in social reformation. And the social purity movement campaigned to clean up vice, particularly prostitution.

The settlement house movement began in England and came to the United States in 1886 with the opening of the University Settlement House in New York City. Americans modified the settlement significantly, abandoning the strong religious overtones of the English movement. Settlement house workers quickly recognized that it would be divisive and counterproductive to promote Protestantism among their largely Catholic and Jewish neighbors. Another significant change from the English model was the substantial role of women, particularly college-educated women, who formed the backbone of the settlement house movement and helped it to grow from six settlements in 1891 to more than four hundred in 1911. Eager to use their knowledge, educated women found themselves blocked from medicine, law, and the clergy (fewer than fifteen hundred women practiced law in 1900, and women constituted only 6 percent of the medical profession). College-educated women like Jane Addams became a part of Hull House and other settlements to use their talents in the service of society. In the process, they created the new profession of social work.

The churches confronted the social problems raised in the cities by enunciating a new "social gospel," one that saw as its mission not simply to reform individuals but to reform society. On a basic level, the social gospel offered a powerful corrective to the gospel of wealth, as outlined by Andrew Carnegie, with its belief that riches somehow signaled divine favor. Washington Gladden, a prominent social gospel minister, challenged that view when he urged Congregationalists to turn down a gift from John D. Rockefeller, arguing that it was "tainted money." In place of the gospel of wealth, the clergy urged their congregations to put Christ's teachings to work in their daily lives. For Walter

Rauschenbusch, a Baptist minister working in New York's infamous Hell's Kitchen, the social gospel grew out of the depression of the 1890s that left hundreds of thousands of people unemployed. "They wore down our threshold and they wore away our hearts," he later wrote. "One could hear human virtue cracking and crumbling all around." In *Christianity and the Social Crisis* (1907), Rauschenbusch called for the church to play a new role in promoting social justice.

Ministers also played an active role in the social purity movement, the campaign to attack vice. To end the "social evil," as reformers euphemistically called prostitution, the social purity movement brought together ministers who wished to stamp out sin, doctors who were concerned about the spread of venereal disease, and women reformers who were determined to fight the double standard that made it acceptable for men to engage in premarital and extramarital sex but punished women who strayed. Together, they waged campaigns to close red-light districts in cities across the country and lobbied for the Mann Act, passed in 1910, which made it illegal to transport women across state lines for immoral purposes. On the state level, they struck at venereal disease by securing legislation to require a blood test for syphilis before marriage.

Attacks on alcohol went hand in hand with the push for social purity. The temperance campaign launched by the Woman's Christian Temperance Union (WCTU) heated up in the early twentieth century. The Anti-Saloon League, formed in 1895 under the leadership of Protestant clergy, campaigned for an end to the sale of liquor. Reformers pointed to the links connecting drink with prostitution, wife and child abuse, unemployment, and industrial accidents. The powerful liquor lobby fought back, spending liberally in election campaigns to defeat not only prohibition but also woman suffrage and, in the process, fueling the charge that liquor corrupted the political process.

An element of nativism (dislike of foreigners) ran through the move for prohibition. The Irish, the Italians, and the Germans were among the groups stigmatized by temperance reformers for their drinking. Progressives often failed to see the important role the tavern played in many ethnic communities. Unlike the American saloon, an almost exclusively male domain, the tavern or beer garden was often a family retreat. German Americans of all ages socialized at the beer garden after church on Sunday. Even though most workers toiled six days a week and had only Sunday for recreation and relaxation, progressives campaigned on the local level to enforce Sunday closings of taverns. To deny the working class access to alcohol, progressives pushed for state legislation to outlaw the liquor traffic; by 1912, seven states were "dry."

Progressives' efforts to civilize the city, whether by launching social settlements or campaigning against prostitution and alcohol, demonstrated their willingness to take action, their belief that environment, not heredity alone, determined human behavior, and their optimism that conditions could be corrected through government action without radically altering America's economy or institutions. All of these attitudes characterized the progressive movement.

Progressives and the Working Class

Day-to-day contact with their neighbors made settlement house workers particularly sympathetic to labor unions. When Mary Kenney O'Sullivan complained that her bookbinders' union met in a dirty, noisy saloon, Jane Addams invited the union to meet at Hull House. And during the Pullman strike in 1894, Hull House residents organized strike relief and lent their prestige and financial resources. "Hull-House has been so unionized," grumbled one Chicago businessman, "that it has lost its usefulness and become a detriment and harm to the community." But to the working class, the support of middle-class reformers marked a significant gain.

Attempts to forge a cross-class alliance became institutionalized in 1903 with the creation of the Women's Trade Union League (WTUL). The WTUL brought together women workers and middle-class "allies." Its goal was to organize working women into unions under the auspices of the American Federation of Labor (AFL). However, the AFL provided little more than lip service to the organization of women workers. As one working woman confided, "The men think that the girls should not get as good work as the men and should not make half as much money as a man." When it came to women, the AFL's main concern seemed to be to protect men from female competition. Samuel Gompers, president of the AFL, endorsed the principle of equal pay for equal work, shrewdly observing that it would help male workers more than women, since many employers hired women precisely because they could be paid less and otherwise would hire men. Given the AFL's attitude, it was not surprising that

the money and leadership to organize women came largely from wealthy allies in the WTUL.

The league's most notable success came in 1909 in the "uprising of twenty thousand." In November, hundreds of women employees of the Triangle Shirtwaist Company in New York City went on strike to protest low wages, dangerous and demeaning working conditions, and management's refusal to recognize their union, the International Ladies' Garment Workers Union (ILGWU). In support of the walkout, the ILGWU called for a general strike of all garment workers. An estimated twenty thousand workers, most of them teenage girls and many of them Jewish and Italian immigrants, went out on strike and stayed out through the winter, picketing in the bitter cold. By the time the strike ended in February 1910, the workers had won important demands in many shops. But they lost their bid to gain recognition for the ILGWU. The solidarity shown by the women proved to be the strike's greatest achievement. As Clara Lemlich, one of the strike's leaders, exclaimed, "They used to say that you couldn't even organize women. They wouldn't come to union meetings. They were 'temporary' workers. Well we showed them!"

The WTUL made enormous contributions to the success of the strike. The league provided volunteers for the picket lines, posted more than $29,000 in bail, protested police brutality, organized almost overnight a massive parade of ten thousand strikers, took part in the arbitration conference, arranged mass meetings, appealed for funds, and generated publicity for the strike. Under the leadership of the WTUL, women from every class of society, from J. P. Morgan's daughter Anne to socialists on New York's Lower East Side, joined the strikers in a dramatic demonstration of cross-class alliance.

For all its success, the uprising of twenty thousand failed fundamentally to change conditions for women workers. In 1911, a little over a year after the shirtwaist makers' strike ended, fire alarms sounded at the Triangle factory. The ramshackle building, full of lint and combustible cloth, went up in flames in minutes. A WTUL member described the scene below on the street: "Two young girls whom I knew to be working in the vicinity came rushing toward me, tears were running from their eyes and they were white and shaking as they caught me by the arm. 'Oh,' shrieked one of them, 'they are jumping. Jumping from ten stories up! They are going through the air like bundles of clothes.'"

The terrified Triangle workers had little choice but to jump. One door was blocked by flames, and the door to the fire escape had been locked to prevent the girls from sneaking out on breaks. Of 500 workers, 146 died and scores of others were injured. The owners of the Triangle firm were later tried for negligence, but they avoided conviction when authorities determined that the fire had been started by a careless smoker. The Triangle Shirtwaist Company reopened in another firetrap within a matter of weeks.

The Triangle fire tested severely the bonds of the cross-class alliance embodied in the WTUL. Its leaders experienced a growing sense of futility. It seemed not enough to organize and to strike, particularly when the AFL paid so little attention to women workers. Increasingly, the WTUL turned its efforts to lobbying for protective legislation—laws that would limit hours and regulate working conditions.

The principle of protective legislation won a major victory in 1908 when the U.S. Supreme Court,

in *Muller v. Oregon*, reversed its previous rulings and upheld an Oregon law that limited the hours women could work to ten a day. A mass of sociological evidence put together by Florence Kelley of the National Consumers League and Josephine Goldmark of the WTUL and presented by Goldmark's brother-in-law, lawyer Louis Brandeis, demonstrated the ill effects of long hours on the health and safety of women. The "Brandeis brief" convinced the Court that long hours endangered women and therefore the entire race. The Court's ruling set a precedent, but one that separated the well-being of women workers from that of men by arguing that women's reproductive role justified special treatment. Later generations of women fighting for equality would question the effectiveness of this strategy and argue that it ultimately closed good jobs to women. But the WTUL greeted protective legislation as a first stage in the attempt to ensure the safety not just of women but of all workers.

THE TRIANGLE SHIRTWAIST FACTORY FIRE
The **New York Herald** *carried the story of the fire at the Triangle Shirtwaist factory with bold headlines and a grim photo. A policeman stoops to identify the broken bodies of two of the workers who leapt to their death to escape the flames.*
The *New York Herald*, March 26, 1911.

www.bedfordstmartins.com/roarkcompact SEE THE ONLINE STUDY GUIDE for more help in analyzing this image.

The National Consumers League (NCL), like the WTUL, fostered cross-class alliance. Formed in 1899 and led by Florence Kelley, the NCL urged middle-class women to boycott stores to exert pressure for decent wages and working conditions for women employees, primarily saleswomen. But like the WTUL, the NCL turned increasingly to protective legislation to achieve its goals in the first decade of the twentieth century. These varied strands of progressive theory found practical application in state and local politics.

Progressive Politics at the Local and State Levels

The politicians who became premier progressives were generally the followers, not the leaders, in a movement that was already well advanced at the grassroots level. Yet they left their stamp on progressivism. Among the most preeminent progressive politicians were Thomas Lofton Johnson, who made Cleveland, Ohio, "the best governed city in America"; Robert La Follette, who turned Wisconsin into a laboratory for progressivism; and Hiram Johnson, who ended the domination of the Southern Pacific railroad in California politics.

Progressivism burst forth at every level in 1901, but nowhere more forcefully than in Cleveland, Ohio, where the voters elected Thomas Lofton Johnson mayor. Johnson, a self-made millionaire, had turned his back on business in 1899 and moved to Cleveland, where he determined to seek election as a reform mayor. A flamboyant man who craved power and acclaim, Johnson pledged during the campaign to reduce the streetcar fare from five cents to three cents. His election touched off a seven-year war between the mayor and the streetcar moguls. Johnson successfully championed municipal ownership of street railways and public utilities, a tactic that progressives called "gas and water socialism." The city bought the streetcar system and instituted the three-cent fare. Under Johnson's administration, Cleveland became, in the words of journalist Lincoln Steffens, the "best governed city in America."

In Wisconsin, Robert M. La Follette, who as a young congressional representative had supported William McKinley, abandoned Republican conservatism and converted to the progressive cause early in the 1900s. An astute politician, La Follette capitalized on the grassroots movement for reform to

THREE-CENT STREETCAR TOKEN
Tom Johnson, the reform mayor of Cleveland, Ohio, from 1901 to 1909, fought for a three-cent streetcar fare for more than seven years, winning the support of the working class and angering the business interests who ran the city's streetcars. To get his cheaper fare, Johnson finally instituted municipal ownership of the transit system. Johnson used a three-cent token in his reelection campaign in 1907.
The Western Reserve Historical Society, Cleveland, Ohio.

launch his long political career, first as governor (1901–1905) and later as senator (1906–1925). A graduate of the University of Wisconsin, La Follette brought scientists and professors into his administration and used the university, only a few blocks from the state house in Madison, as a resource in drafting legislation. As governor, he lowered railroad rates, raised railroad taxes, improved education, championed conservation, established factory regulation and workers' compensation, instituted the first direct primary in the country, and inaugurated the first state income tax. Under his leadership, Wisconsin earned the title "laboratory of democracy."

A fiery orator, "Fighting Bob" La Follette united his supporters around issues that transcended old party loyalties. This emphasis on reform rather than party loyalty became a characteristic of progressivism, which attracted followers from both major parties. Democrats like Tom Johnson and Republicans like Robert La Follette could lay equal claim to the label "progressive."

West of the Rockies, progressivism arrived somewhat later and found a champion in Hiram Johnson of California, who served as governor (1911–1917) and U.S. senator (1917–1945). Since the 1870s, California politics had been dominated by the Southern Pacific railroad, a corporation whose rapaciousness Frank Norris detailed in his novel *The Octopus* (1901). Hiram Johnson ran for governor in 1910 on the promise to "kick the Southern Pacific out of politics." With the support of the reform wing of the Republican Party, he handily won. Efficiency and rationalization became the watchwords of his new administration. Johnson promised to "return the government to the people"—to give them honest public service untarnished by corruption and corporate influence. As governor, he introduced the direct primary; supported the initiative, referendum, and recall (devices that allowed the voters direct say in legislative and judicial matters); strengthened the state's railroad commission; endorsed conservation; and signed into law employers liability.

A vigorous, compelling personality with a reputation for his towering temper, Hiram Johnson proved an able governor. In 1912, he could boast that by regulating the Southern Pacific railroad he had saved shippers more than $2 million. Who benefited from Johnson's progressivism? California's entrepreneurs—large farmers, independent oil producers, and other rising businessmen who could make money more easily once Johnson curtailed the influence of the Southern Pacific. These groups formed a primary constituency for California progressivism.

THEODORE ROOSEVELT
Described aptly by a contemporary observer as "a steam engine in trousers," Theodore Roosevelt at forty-two was the youngest president to occupy the White House. He brought to the office energy, intellect, and activism in equal measure. Roosevelt boasted that he used the presidency as a "bully pulpit"—a forum from which he advocated reforms ranging from trust-busting to simplified spelling.
Library of Congress.

Progressivism Finds a President: Theodore Roosevelt

On September 6, 1901, President William McKinley was shot twice by Leon Czolgosz, an anarchist, while attending the Pan American Exposition in Buffalo, New York. After lingering for a week, McKinley died on September 14. When news of his assassination reached his friend and political mentor Marcus Alonzo Hanna, Hanna is said to have growled, "Now that damned cowboy is president." Hanna was speaking of Vice President Theodore Roosevelt, the colorful hero of San Juan Hill, who had indeed punched cattle in the Dakotas in the 1880s.

At the age of forty-two, Roosevelt was the youngest man ever to move into the White House. A patrician by birth and an activist by temperament, Roosevelt brought to the job enormous talent and energy. By the time he graduated from Harvard, he was already an accomplished naturalist, an enthusiastic historian, and a naval strategist. He could have picked from any of these promising careers. Instead, he chose politics. He went from the New York state assembly at the age of twenty-three to the presidency in twenty years, with time out to be a cowboy in the Dakotas, police commissioner of New York City, and colonel of the Rough Riders.

The Square Deal

The "absolutely vital question" facing the country, Roosevelt wrote to a friend in 1901, was "whether or not the government has the power to control the trusts." The Sherman Antitrust Act of 1890 had been badly weakened by a conservative Supreme Court and by attorneys general more willing to use it against labor unions than against monopolies. To determine if the law had any teeth left, Roosevelt, in one of his first acts as president, ordered his attorney general to begin a secret antitrust investigation of the Northern Securities Company.

Five months later, in February 1902, Wall Street rocked with the news that the government had filed an antitrust suit against Northern Securities. As one newspaper editor sarcastically observed, "Wall Street is paralyzed at the thought that a President of the United States would sink so low as to try to enforce the law." An indignant J. P. Morgan demanded to know why he had not been consulted. "If we have done anything wrong," he told the president, "send your man to my man and they can fix it up." Roosevelt, amused, later noted that Morgan "could not help regarding me as a big rival operator." In a sense, that was just what Roosevelt intended. Roosevelt's thunderbolt put Wall Street on notice that the money men were dealing with a president who demanded to be treated as an equal and who was willing to use government as an instrument to control business. Perhaps sensing the new mood, the Supreme Court, in a significant turn-around, upheld the Sherman Act and called for the dissolution of Northern Securities in 1904.

"Hurrah for Teddy the Trustbuster," cheered the papers. Roosevelt went on to use the Sherman Act against forty-three trusts, including such giants as the American Tobacco Company, Du Pont, and Standard Oil. Always the moralist, he insisted on a "rule of reason." He would punish the "bad" trusts (those that broke the law) and leave the "good" ones alone. In practice, he preferred regulation to antitrust suits. In 1903, he pressured Congress to pass the Elkins Act, outlawing railroad rebates (money returned to a shipper to guarantee his business). And he created the new cabinet department of Commerce and Labor with a subsidiary Bureau of Corporations to act as a corporate watchdog.

In his handling of the anthracite coal strike in 1902, Roosevelt again demonstrated his willingness to assert the moral and political authority of the presidency, this time to mediate between labor and management. In May, more than fifty thousand coal miners in Pennsylvania went out on strike, demanding higher wages, shorter hours, and recognition of the United Mine Workers (UMW) union. "The miners don't suffer," scoffed George Baer, the mine operators' spokesman, "why they can't even speak English." Six eastern railroads owned over 70 percent of the anthracite mines. With the power of the railroads behind them, the mine owners refused to budge.

The strike dragged on through the summer and into the fall. Hoarding and profiteering drove up the price of coal from $2.50 to $6.00 a ton. Most American homes were heated with coal, and, with winter approaching, near riots broke out in big cities. In the face of mounting tension, Roosevelt issued a personal invitation to representatives from both sides to meet in Washington in October. At the meeting, Baer and the mine owners refused to talk to the union representatives, insulting both the president and the attorney general. Angered by the "wooden-headed obstinacy and stupidity" of management, Roosevelt threatened to seize the mines and run them with federal troops. It was a powerful bluff that called into question not only the supremacy of private property but also the rule of law. The specter of federal troops being used to operate the mines quickly brought management around. At the prompting of J. P. Morgan, the mine owners agreed to arbitration. In the end, the miners won a reduction in hours and a wage increase, but the owners succeeded in preventing formal recognition of the UMW.

Taken together, Roosevelt's actions in the Northern Securities case and the anthracite coal strike marked a dramatic departure from the tradition of William McKinley and the presidential passivity that had marked his predecessors in the years following the Civil War. Roosevelt demonstrated conclusively that government intended to act as a force independent of big business. Pleased with his role in the anthracite strike, Roosevelt announced that all he had tried to do was give labor and capital a "square deal."

The phrase became his slogan in the 1904 election campaign. To win the presidency in his own right, Roosevelt moved to wrest control of the Republican Party from Mark Hanna, the only man who stood between him and the nomination.

Roosevelt adroitly used patronage to win supporters so that even before Hanna died of typhoid fever in 1904, Roosevelt was the undisputed leader of the party. In the presidential election of 1904, Roosevelt swept into office with the largest popular majority—57.9 percent—any candidate had polled to that time

Roosevelt the Reformer

"Tomorrow I shall come into my office in my own right," Roosevelt is said to have remarked on the eve of his election. "Then watch out for me!" Roosevelt's stunning victory gave him a mandate for reform. He would need all the popularity and political savvy he could muster, however, to guide his reform measures through Congress, which was controlled by a staunchly conservative Republican "old guard" in the Senate. Roosevelt's pet project remained railroad regulation. The Elkins Act prohibiting rebates had not worked. No one could stop big shippers like Standard Oil from wringing concessions from the railroads. The Interstate Commerce Commission (ICC), created in 1887 to regulate the railroads, had been largely stripped of its powers by the Supreme Court. In the face of a widespread call for railroad reform, Roosevelt determined that the only solution lay in giving the ICC real power to set rates and prevent discriminatory practices. But the right to determine the price of goods or services was an age-old prerogative of private enterprise, and one that business had no intention of yielding to government.

To ensure passage of the Hepburn Railway Act, a bill increasing the power of the ICC, Roosevelt worked skillfully behind the scenes. To get the best bill possible, Roosevelt first worked with insurgent progressives and then, when they could not muster the needed votes, switched sides and succeeded in getting the old guard to accept a compromise. In its final form, the Hepburn Act, passed in May 1906, gave the ICC power to set rates subject to court review. Committed progressives like La Follette judged the bill a defeat for reform. Diehard conservatives branded it a "piece of populism." Both sides exaggerated. The bill left the courts too much power, and it failed to provide adequate means for the ICC to determine rates realistically, but its passage was a landmark in the evolution of federal control of private industry. For

THE JUNGLE
Novelist Upton Sinclair, a lifelong socialist, wrote **The Jungle** *to expose the evils of capitalism. But readers were more horrified by the unsanitary conditions he described in the meatpacking industry, where Sinclair's hapless hero encountered rats, filth, and diseased animals processed into potted beef. It was rumored that after reading the book, President Theodore Roosevelt could no longer stomach sausage for breakfast. The president immediately ordered a thorough study of conditions in the meatpacking industry. The public outcry surrounding* **The Jungle** *contributed to the enactment of pure food and drug legislation and federal meat inspection. Sinclair ruefully remarked, "I aimed at the public's heart, but I hit them in the stomach."*
By permission of the Houghton Library, Harvard University.

the first time, a government commission had the power to investigate private business records and to set rates.

Passage of the Hepburn Act marked the high point of Roosevelt's presidency. In a serious political blunder, Roosevelt had announced on the eve of his election in 1904 that he would not run again. By 1906, his term was starting to run out and his influence on Congress and his party was waning. Ironically, he had become a "lame duck" at the very moment he was not only enjoying his greatest public popularity but also wanted to press for more reform.

Always an apt reader of the public temper, Roosevelt witnessed a growing appetite for reform fed by the revelations of corporate and political wrongdoing that filled the papers and boosted the sales of popular periodicals. (See "The Promise of

Technology," page 528.) Roosevelt, who wielded publicity like a weapon in reform, counted many of the new investigative journalists like Jacob Riis among his friends. But sometimes he felt they went too far and warned them they should not be like the allegorical character in *Pilgrim's Progress* who was so busy raking up muck that he took no notice of higher things. Roosevelt's criticism gave the American vocabulary a new word: *muckraker.* Journalists soon appropriated the term and turned it into a badge of honor.

Muckraking, as Roosevelt was keenly aware, had been of enormous help in securing progressive legislation. The passage of the Pure Food and Drug legislation and the Meat Inspection Act provided powerful examples. In the spring of 1906, the publicity about poisons in patent medicines generated by the muckrakers goaded the Senate, with Roosevelt's backing, into passing a pure food and drug bill. Opponents in the House of Representatives hoped to keep it locked up in committee. There it would have died, were it not for publication of Upton Sinclair's novel *The Jungle* (1906), with its sensational account of the filthy conditions in the meatpacking industry. A massive public outcry led to the passage of a tough Pure Food and Drug Act and a bill mandating federal inspection of meat.

In the waning years of his administration, Roosevelt moved to the left, allying with the more progressive elements of the Republican Party. In speech after speech he attacked the "malefactors of great wealth." Styling himself a "radical," he claimed credit for leading the "ultra conservative" party of McKinley to a position of "progressive conservatism and conservative radicalism."

When a business panic developed in the fall of 1907, business interests quickly blamed the president. The panic of 1907 proved to be severe but short. As he had done in 1895, J. P. Morgan stepped in to avert disaster, this time switching funds from one bank to another to prop up weak institutions and keep them from failing. For his services, he claimed the Tennessee Coal and Iron Company, an independent steel business that had long been coveted by his U.S. Steel. Morgan dispatched his lieutenants to Washington, where they told Roosevelt that the sale of the company would aid the economy "but little benefit" U.S. Steel. Roosevelt, willing to take the word of a gentleman, tacitly agreed not to institute antitrust proceedings against U.S. Steel. As Roosevelt later learned, Morgan and his

ROOSEVELT AND MUIR IN YOSEMITE
In 1903, President Roosevelt took a camping trip to Yosemite, California, with John Muir, naturalist and founder of the Sierra Club. Roosevelt's experience as a rancher in the Dakotas made him the first president to have experienced firsthand the American West. As president, he acted vigorously to protect the beauty and resources of the West for posterity, using executive power to set aside more than a hundred million acres in government reserves and to create six national parks.

Theodore Roosevelt Collection, Harvard College Library.

men had been less than candid. The acquisition of Tennessee Coal and Iron for a price below market value greatly strengthened U.S. Steel and undercut the economy of the Southeast. The episode would come back to haunt Roosevelt, as it gave rise to the charge that he acted as a tool of the Morgan interests.

The charge of collusion between business and government underscored the extent to which business leaders like Morgan and his partner George W. Perkins found federal regulation preferable to unbridled competition or harsher state measures. During the Progressive Era, enlightened business leaders cooperated with government in the hope of avoiding antitrust prosecution. Roosevelt, convinced that regulation and not trust-busting was the best way to deal with big business, never acknowledged that, for all his strong rhetoric, his regulatory policies fostered an alliance between business and government. As Roosevelt's actions in the panic of 1907 demonstrated, despite his harsh attacks on the "malefactors of great wealth," the president remained indebted to Morgan, who still

functioned as the national bank and would continue to do so until the passage of the Federal Reserve Act six years later.

In at least one area, Roosevelt was well ahead of his time. Robert La Follette, who thought Roosevelt a lukewarm progressive and found much to criticize in his presidency, called Roosevelt's efforts in conservation of natural resources the president's "greatest work." When Roosevelt took office, some 45 million acres of land remained as government reserves. He more than tripled that number to 150 million acres, buying land and creating national parks and wildlife preserves by executive order. To conserve natural resources, he fought not only western cattle barons, lumber kings, and mining interests but also powerful leaders in Congress, including Speaker of the House Joseph Cannon, who was determined to spend "not one cent for scenery." Today, six national parks, sixteen national monuments, and fifty-one wildlife refuges created by Roosevelt stand as witnesses to his substantial accomplishments as a conservationist (Map 21.1).

M AP 21.1

National Parks and Forests

The national park system in the West began with Yellowstone in 1872, followed in the 1890s by Grand Canyon, Yosemite, Kings Canyon, and Sequoia. During his presidency, Theodore Roosevelt added six new parks—Crater Lake, Wind Cave, Petrified Forest, Lassen Volcanic, Mesa Verde, and Zion.

Flash Photography and the Birth of Photojournalism

THE CAMERA WAS NOT NEW at the turn of the twentieth century. Americans had eagerly imported the technology developed by Frenchman L. J. M. Daguerre to make portraits called daguerreotypes as early as the 1840s. By the 1880s, the invention of dry plates had simplified photography, and by the 1890s, Americans could purchase a Kodak camera marketed by George Eastman.

But for Jacob Riis, who wished to document the horrors of tenement life, photography was useless because it required daylight or careful studio lighting. Riis, a progressive reformer and journalist who covered the police beat for the New York *Tribune*, never thought of buying a camera. He could only rudely sketch the dim hovels, the criminal nightlife, and the windowless tenement rooms of New York. Then came the breakthrough. "One morning scanning my newspaper at the breakfast table," he wrote, "I put it down with an outcry. . . . There it was, the thing I had been looking for all these years. . . . A way had been discovered . . . to take pictures by flashlight. The darkest corner might be photographed that way."

The new technology involved a pistol lamp that fired magnesium cartridges to provide light for instantaneous photography. Armed with the new flash pistols, Riis and a band of amateur photographers soon set out to shine light in the dark corners of New York. "Our party carried terror wherever it went," Riis later recounted. "The spectacle of strange men invading a house in the mid-night hours armed with [flash] pistols which they shot off recklessly was hardly reassuring . . . and it was not to be wondered at if the tenants bolted through the windows and down fire-escapes."

Unhappy with the photographers he hired to follow him on his nighttime forays into the slums,

Riis determined to try his own hand at taking pictures and laid out $25 for his first photographic equipment in 1888. It consisted of a four-by-five-inch wooden box camera, glass plates, a tripod, a safety lantern, flash pistols, developing trays, and a printing frame. He soon replaced the pistols with a newer flash technology developed in 1887 that used magnesium powder blown through an alcohol flame. Riis carried a frying pan in which to ignite the powder, observing "It seemed more homelike."

Flash photography was dangerous. The pistol lamp cartridges contained highly explosive chemicals that could seriously burn the photographer. The newer technology employing magnesium powder was also risky. Riis once blew the flash into his own eyes and only his glasses saved him from being blinded. Nor was Riis the only one in peril. When he photographed the residents of a tenement on "Blind Man's Alley," he set the place on fire when he ignited the flash. He later claimed the tenement, nicknamed the "Dirty Spoon," was so filthy it wouldn't burn. He was able to douse the flames without his blind subjects ever realizing their danger.

Riis turned his photographs into slides that he used to illustrate his lectures on tenement life. They helped spread his message, but not until *Scribner's* magazine printed his story entitled "How the Other Half Lives" in December 1889 did he begin to develop a mass audience. The article, illustrated with line drawings of Riis's photographs, became the basis for his best-selling book of the same title published in 1890.

How the Other Half Lives made photographic history. It contained, along with Riis's text and the line drawings that had appeared in *Scribner's*, seventeen halftone prints of Riis's photographs. Riis's text and pictures shined the light on New York's darkest corners—vagrants in the filthy lodging houses; "street arabs," homeless boys who lived by their wits on the streets; the saloons and dives of lower New York; the evil smelling tenement yards; the stifling sweatshops. For the first time unposed action pictures taken with a flash documented social conditions. Riis's pioneering photojournalism shocked the nation and led not only to tenement reform, but also to the development of city playgrounds, neighborhood parks, and child labor laws.

JACOB RIIS AND BAXTER STREET COURT
Jacob Riis (inset), a Danish immigrant who knew the squalor of New York's lodging houses and slums from his early days in New York, vigorously campaigned for tenement reform. He warned slum landlords (some of them prominent in New York society) that their greed bred crime, disease, and, potentially, class warfare. Flash photography enabled Riis to show the dark alleys and tenements of New York. He took his camera into Baxter Street Court, then recorded these observations: "I counted the other day the little ones, up to ten years old in a . . . tenement that for a yard has a . . . space in the center with sides fourteen or fifteen feet long, just enough for a row of ill-smelling [water] closets . . . and a hydrant. . . . There was about as much light in the 'yard' as in the average cellar. . . . I counted one hundred twenty eight [children] in forty families."

National Portrait Gallery, Smithsonian Institution / Art Resources, N.Y.; Museum of the City of New York.

Roosevelt the Diplomat

Roosevelt took a keen interest in shaping foreign policy and actively worked to buttress the United States' newly won place among world leaders. A fierce proponent of America's interests abroad, he was convinced that Congress was inept in foreign affairs, and he relied on executive power to effect a vigorous foreign policy, sometimes stretching his powers beyond legal limits in his pursuit of American interests. A man who relished military discipline and viewed life as a constant conflict for supremacy, Roosevelt believed that the "civilized nations" should police the world and hold the "backward" countries in line. In his relations with the great European powers, he relied on military strength and diplomacy, a combination he aptly described with the aphorism "Speak softly but carry a big stick."

In the Caribbean, Roosevelt jealously guarded the Monroe Doctrine's American sphere of influence. In 1902, he risked war to keep Germany from intervening in Venezuela when that country's dictator borrowed money in Europe and could not pay it back. Roosevelt issued an ultimatum to the German Kaiser, warning him to stay out of Latin American affairs or face war with the United States. The matter was eventually settled by arbitration.

Roosevelt's proprietary attitude toward the hemisphere became evident in the infamous case of the Panama Canal. A firm advocate of naval power and an astute naval strategist, Roosevelt had long been a supporter of a canal connecting the Caribbean and the Pacific, enabling the navy to move

THE BIG STICK IN THE CARIBBEAN SEA

THEODORE ROOSEVELT AND THE BIG STICK
In this political cartoon from 1904, President Theodore Roosevelt, dressed in his Rough Rider uniform and carrying his "big stick," turns the Caribbean into a Yankee pond. His Roosevelt Corollary to the Monroe Doctrine did just that.
Granger Collection.

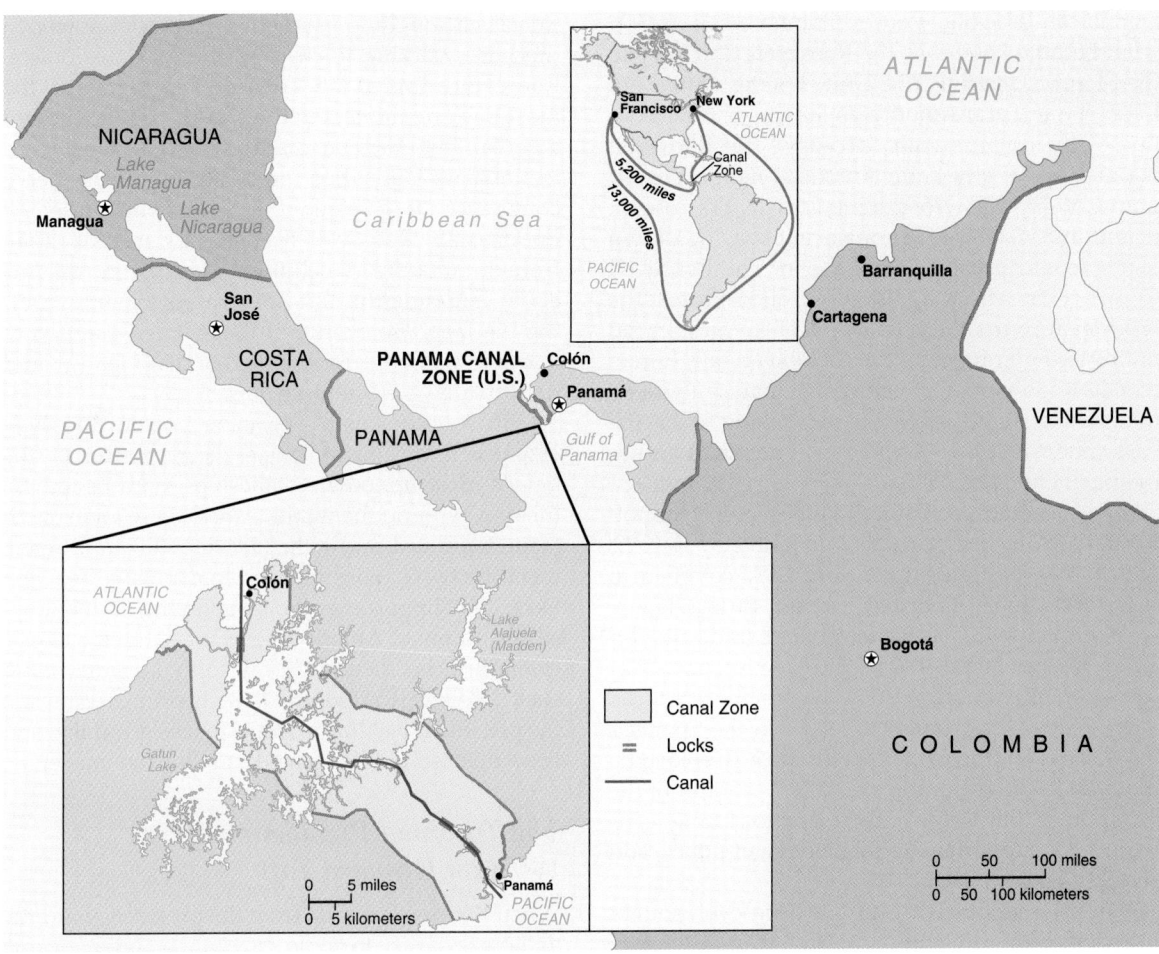

MAP 21.2

The Panama Canal, 1914

The Panama Canal, completed in 1914, bisected the isthmus in a series of massive locks and dams. As Theodore Roosevelt had planned, the canal greatly strengthened the navy by allowing ships to move from the Atlantic to the Pacific in a matter of days.

www.bedfordstmartins.com/roarkcompact SEE THE ONLINE STUDY GUIDE for more help in analyzing this map.

quickly from the Atlantic to the Pacific. Having decided upon a route through the Panamanian isthmus (the narrow strip of land connecting North and South America), then a part of Colombia, Roosevelt in 1902 offered the Colombian government a one-time sum of $10 million and an annual rent of $250,000. When the government in Bogotá refused to accept the offer, Roosevelt became incensed at what he called the "homicidal corruptionists" in Colombia for trying to "blackmail" the United States. The result was an uprising in Panama in 1903 arranged by New York investors. The U.S. government aided and protected

the "revolution" by placing the warship *Nashville* off the isthmus, and the State Department recognized the new government of Panama within twenty-four hours. The new Panamanian government promptly accepted the $10 million, and the building got under way (Map 21.2). The canal would take eleven years and $375 million to complete but would literally double the strength of the U.S. navy by allowing it to move quickly from Atlantic to Pacific.

In the wake of the Panama affair, the confrontation with Germany over Venezuela, and yet another default on a European debt, this time in the

Dominican Republic, Roosevelt announced in 1904 what became known as the Roosevelt Corollary to the Monroe Doctrine. The United States would not intervene in Latin America as long as nations conducted their affairs with "decency." But Roosevelt warned that if any Latin American nation proved guilty of "brutal wrongdoing," as in the case of defaulting on debts to European nations, the United States would insist on stepping in. The Roosevelt Corollary in effect made the United States the policeman of the Western Hemisphere and served notice to the European powers to keep out. Immediately Roosevelt put the corollary into practice by intervening in Costa Rica and taking over the customhouse in the Dominican Republic to ensure the payment of its debts.

In Asia, Roosevelt inherited the Open Door policy initiated by Secretary of State John Hay in 1899, which was designed to ensure U.S. commercial entry into China. As Britain, France, Russia, Japan, and Germany raced to secure Chinese trade and territory, Roosevelt was tempted to use force to enter the fray and gain economic or possibly territorial concessions. As a result of victory in the Spanish-American War, the United States already enjoyed a foothold in the region by virtue of its control of the Philippines. But Roosevelt realized that Americans would not support an aggressive Asian policy, and sensibly he held back.

In his relations with Europe, Roosevelt sought to establish the United States, fresh from its victory over Spain, as a rising force in world affairs. When tensions flared between France and Germany in Morocco in 1905, Roosevelt set up a conference in Algeciras, Spain, where he worked to maintain a balance of power to help neutralize German ambitions. His skillful mediation of the dispute gained him a reputation as an astute player on the world stage and demonstrated the United States' new presence in world affairs.

The Roosevelt Corollary in Action

Roosevelt earned the Nobel Peace Prize in 1906 for his role in negotiating an end to the Russo-Japanese War, which had broken out when the Japanese invaded Chinese Manchuria, threatening Russia's sphere of influence in the area. Once again,

Roosevelt sought to maintain a balance of power, in this case working to curb Japanese expansionism. Roosevelt admired the Japanese, judging them "the most dashing fighters in the world," but he did not want Japan to become too strong in Asia. He offered to mediate and thus presided over the peace conference at Portsmouth, New Hampshire. At Portsmouth, Roosevelt was able to prevent Japan from dominating Manchuria, but he had no qualms about initiating the Taft-Katsura agreement, granting the Japanese control of the sovereign nation of Korea in exchange for the pledge that Japan would not threaten the Philippines.

To counter Japan's growing power, Roosevelt dispatched the Great White Fleet, sixteen of the navy's most up-to-date battleships, on a "goodwill mission" around the world. American relations with Japan improved, and in the 1908 Root-Takahira agreement the two nations pledged to maintain the Open Door and support the status quo in the Pacific. Roosevelt's show of American force constituted a classic example of his dictum "Speak softly but carry a big stick." Political cartoonists delighted in caricaturing the president wielding a cudgel in foreign affairs, and the American public seemed to relish the image.

The Troubled Presidency of William Howard Taft

When Roosevelt retired from the presidency in 1909 at the age of fifty to go on safari and shoot big game in Africa, he turned the White House over to his handpicked successor, William Howard Taft, a lawyer who had served as governor general of the Philippines. In the presidential election of 1908, Taft soundly defeated the perennial Democratic candidate, William Jennings Bryan, who had come to be known as the "Great Commoner." But Taft's popular majority amounted to only half of Roosevelt's record win in 1904. On the eve of his inauguration, Taft showed little enthusiasm about his triumph and little zest for the future. In fact, the presidency for Taft proved an ordeal. As a symptom of his discomfort in office, his weight ballooned from an already hefty 297 pounds to over 350 pounds.

Any man would have found it difficult to follow in Roosevelt's footsteps, but Taft proved hopelessly ill suited to the task. A genial man with a talent for law, Taft had no experience in elective office, no feel for politics, no ability to compromise, and no nerve for controversy. His ambitious wife coveted the office and had urged him to seek it. He would have been better off listening to his mother, who warned,

WILLIAM HOWARD TAFT

William Howard Taft had little aptitude for politics. When Theodore Roosevelt tapped him as his successor in 1908, Taft had never held an elected office. A legalist by training and temperament, Taft moved congenially in the conservative circles of the Republican Party. His actions dismayed progressives and eventually led Roosevelt to challenge him for the presidency in 1912. The break with Roosevelt saddened and embittered Taft, who heartily disliked the presidency and was glad to leave it.

Library of Congress.

"Roosevelt is a good fighter and enjoys it, but the malice of politics would make you miserable."

Once in office, Taft proved a perfect tool in the hands of Republicans who yearned for a return to the days of McKinley. A lawyer by training and instinct, he believed that it was up to the courts, not the president, to arbitrate social issues. Roosevelt had carried presidential power to a new level, often castigating the judiciary and flouting the separation of powers. Taft the legalist found it difficult to condone such actions. Wary of the progressive insurgents in his own party and without Roosevelt to guide him, Taft relied increasingly on conservatives in the Republican Party. As a progressive senator

lamented, "Taft is a ponderous and amiable man completely surrounded by men who know exactly what they want."

Taft's troubles began on the eve of his inaugural when he called a special session of Congress to deal with the tariff. Roosevelt had been too politically astute to tackle the troublesome tariff issue, even though he knew that rates needed to be lowered. Taft, with his stubborn courage, blundered into the fray. The House of Representatives passed a modest downward revision and, to make up for lost revenue, imposed a small inheritance tax. Led by Senator Nelson Aldrich, the conservative Senate struck down the tax and added more than eight hundred crippling amendments to the tariff. The Payne-Aldrich bill that emerged actually raised the tariff. As if paralyzed, Taft neither fought for changes nor vetoed the measure. On a tour of the Midwest in 1909, he was greeted with jeers when he claimed, "I think the Payne bill is the best bill that the Republican Party ever passed." In the eyes of a growing number of Americans, his praise of the tariff made him either a fool or a liar.

Taft's legalism got him into hot water over conservation. He refused to endorse his predecessor's methods of bending the law to protect the wilderness. He undid Roosevelt's work to preserve waterpower sites when he learned that they had been improperly designated as ranger stations. And when Roosevelt's chief forester, Gifford Pinchot, publicly denounced Taft's secretary of the interior, Richard Ballinger, as a tool of western land-grabbers, Taft fired Pinchot, touching off a storm of controversy that damaged Taft and alienated Roosevelt.

Talk of substituting Roosevelt on the ticket in 1912 grew as Republican progressives became increasingly dissatisfied with Taft's policies. In June 1910, Roosevelt returned to New York, where he received a hero's welcome and attracted a stream of visitors and reporters seeking his advice and opinions. Hurt, Taft kept his distance. By late summer, Roosevelt had taken sides with the progressive insurgents in his party. "Taft is utterly hopeless as a leader," Roosevelt confided to his son as he set out on a speaking tour of the West. Reading the mood of the country, Roosevelt began to sound more and more like a candidate.

With the Republican Party divided, the Democrats swept the congressional elections of 1910. Branding the Payne-Aldrich tariff "the mother of trusts," they captured a majority in the House of Representatives and won several key governorships. The revitalized Democratic Party could look to new leaders, among them the progressive governor of New Jersey, Woodrow Wilson.

The new Democratic majority in the House, working with progressive Republicans in the Senate, achieved a number of key reforms, including legislation to regulate mine and railroad safety, to create a Children's Bureau in the Department of Labor, and to establish an eight-hour day for federal workers. Two significant constitutional amendments—the Sixteenth Amendment, which provided for a modest graduated income tax, and the Seventeenth Amendment, which called for the direct election of senators (formerly chosen by their state legislatures)—went to the states, where they would later win ratification in 1913. While Congress rode the high tide of progressive reform, Taft sat on the sidelines.

In foreign policy, too, Taft had a difficult time following in Roosevelt's footsteps. In the Caribbean he pursued a policy of "dollar diplomacy," championing commercial goals rather than the strategic aims that Roosevelt had advocated. He provoked anti-American feeling by attempting to force commercial treaties on Nicaragua and Honduras and by dispatching the U.S. marines to Nicaragua and the Dominican Republic in 1912.

In Asia, Taft's foreign policy proved equally inept. He openly avowed his intent to promote in China "active intervention to secure for . . . our capitalists opportunity for profitable investment." Lacking Roosevelt's understanding of power politics, Taft naively believed that he could substitute "dollars for bullets." He never recognized that an aggressive commercial policy could not exist without military might. As a result, dollar diplomacy was doomed to failure. Even Taft was forced to recognize its limits when revolution broke out in Mexico in 1911. Under pressure to protect American investment, which amounted to more than $4 billion, he mobilized troops along the

Taft's "Dollar Diplomacy"

border. But in the end, he relied on diplomatic pressure to salvage American interests.

Always a legalist at heart, Taft hoped to encourage world peace through the use of a world court and arbitration. He unsuccessfully sponsored a series of arbitration treaties that Roosevelt, who prized national honor more than international law, vehemently opposed. By 1910, Roosevelt had become a vocal critic of Taft's foreign policy, which he dismissed as "maudlin folly."

The final breach between Taft and Roosevelt came in 1911, when Taft's attorney general filed an antitrust suit against U.S. Steel. In its brief against the steel giant, the government cited Roosevelt's agreement with the Morgan interests in the 1907 acquisition of Tennessee Coal and Iron by U.S. Steel. The incident greatly embarrassed Roosevelt by making it clear that he either had been hoodwinked or had acted as a tool of Wall Street. Thoroughly enraged, Roosevelt first lambasted Taft's "archaic" antitrust policy and then began to hint that he might be persuaded to run for president again.

The Election of 1912

In February 1912, Roosevelt announced, "My hat is in the ring." But for all his popularity, Roosevelt no longer controlled the party machinery. Taft, with uncharacteristic strength, refused to step aside. As he bitterly told a journalist, "Even a rat in a corner will fight." Roosevelt took advantage of newly passed primary election laws and ran in thirteen states, winning 278 delegates to Taft's 48. But at the Chicago convention, Taft's bosses refused to seat the Roosevelt delegates. Fistfights broke out on the convention floor as Taft won renomination on the first ballot. Crying robbery, Roosevelt's supporters bolted the party.

Seven weeks later, in the same Chicago auditorium, a hastily organized Progressive Party met to nominate Roosevelt. Few Republican officeholders joined the new party, but the advance guard of progressivism turned out in full force. Amid a thunder of applause, Jane Addams seconded Roosevelt's nomination. Full of reforming zeal, the delegates chose Roosevelt and Hiram Johnson to head the new party and approved the most advanced platform since the Populists' in 1892. Planks called for woman suffrage, the direct election of senators, presidential primaries, conservation of natural resources, minimum wages for women, an end to child labor, workers' compensation, social security, and a federal income tax.

PASS PROSPERITY AROUND

BULL MOOSE POSTER
Accepting the nomination of the Progressive Party in 1912, Theodore Roosevelt exclaimed, "I feel as strong as a bull moose." Instantly the new party had a mascot and a nickname. The Bull Moose soon decorated party emblems, as in this poster where the animal is featured more prominently than Roosevelt or his vice presidential candidate, Hiram Johnson. The slogan "pass prosperity around" may refer to the party's platform, which pledged to tax the great fortunes of the day by ratifying the country's first graduated income tax.
Collection of Janice L. and David J. Frent.

Roosevelt arrived in Chicago to accept the nomination and announced that he felt "as strong as a bull moose," giving the new party a nickname and a mascot. But for all the excitement and the cheering, the new Progressive Party was doomed, and the candidate knew it. The people may have supported the party, but the politicians, even insurgents like La Follette, stayed within the Republican fold. "I am under no illusion about it," Roosevelt confessed to a friend. "It is a forlorn hope." But he had gone too far to turn back. He led the Bull Moose

Party into the fray, exhorting his followers in ringing biblical tones, "We shall not falter, we stand at Armageddon and do battle for the Lord."

The Democrats, delighted at the split in the Republican ranks, smelled victory for the first time since 1892. Their convention turned into a bitter fight for the nomination. After forty-six ballots Woodrow Wilson became the party's nominee. Wilson's career in politics was nothing short of astounding. After only eighteen months in office as governor of New Jersey, the former professor of political science and president of Princeton University found himself running for president of the United States.

Voters in 1912 could choose from three candidates, each of whom claimed to be a progressive. That the term could stretch to cover all three underscored some major disagreements in progressive thinking about the relation between business and government. Taft, for all his trust-busting, was generally conceded to be the candidate of the old guard. The real contest for the presidency was between Roosevelt and Wilson and the two political philosophies summed up in their campaign slogans: "The New Nationalism" and "The New Freedom."

Roosevelt's New Nationalism enunciated his belief in federal planning and regulation. He accepted big business as inevitable but demanded that government supervise it and act as "a steward of the people." Roosevelt called for an increase in the power of the federal government, a decrease in the power of the courts, and an active role for the president. As political theorist Herbert Croly pointed out in his influential book *The Promise of American Life* (1909), Roosevelt hoped to use the Hamiltonian means of a centralized federal government to further the Jeffersonian end of greater democracy.

Wilson, schooled in the Democratic principles of limited government and states' rights, set a markedly different course with his New Freedom. Tutored in economics by *Muller v. Oregon* lawyer Louis Brandeis, who railed against the "curse of bigness," Wilson promised to use antitrust legislation to get rid of big corporations and to give small businesses and farmers better opportunities in the marketplace.

Wilson and Roosevelt fought it out, but in the end only the energy and emotional enthusiasm of the Bull Moosers obscured the inevitable outcome of a race in which the Republican vote was split while the Democrats remained united. No candidate could claim a majority in the three-way race.

Wilson captured a bare 42 percent of the popular vote, polling fewer votes than Bryan had received when he lost to Taft in 1908. Roosevelt and his Bull Moose Party won 27 percent of the vote, an unprecedented tally for a new party. The incumbent Taft was in third with 23 percent. But in the electoral college, Wilson won a decisive 435, with 88 going to Roosevelt and only 8 to Taft. The real loser in 1912 was not Taft but the Bull Moose Party, which essentially collapsed after Roosevelt's defeat. It had always been, in the words of one astute observer, "a house divided against itself and already mortgaged."

Woodrow Wilson and Progressivism at High Tide

Born in Virginia and raised in Georgia, Woodrow Wilson became the first Southerner to be elected president since James K. Polk in 1844 and only the second Democrat to occupy the White House since reconstruction. Democrats who anticipated a wild celebration when Wilson took office soon had their hopes dashed. The son of a Presbyterian minister, Wilson was a teetotaler more given to scripture than to celebration. He called instead for a day of prayer.

This lean, ascetic man with an otherworldly gaze was, as one biographer conceded, a man whose "political convictions were never as fixed as his ambition." Although he owed his governorship to the Democratic machine, he quickly turned his back on the bosses and put New Jersey in the vanguard of progressivism. A year into his term, Wilson already had his eye on the presidency. Always able to equivocate, Wilson proved rarely able to compromise. He brought to the White House a gift for oratory, a stern will, and a set of fixed beliefs. His tendency to turn differences of opinion into personal hatreds would impair his leadership and damage his presidency. Fortunately for Wilson, he came to power with a Democratic Congress eager to do his bidding.

Although he opposed big government in his campaign, Wilson viewed himself as the only leader who could speak for the country. He was prepared to work on the base built by Roosevelt to strengthen presidential power, exerting leadership and working through his party in Congress to accomplish the Democratic agenda. Before he was finished, Wilson would preside over progressivism at high tide and see enacted not only the platform of the Democratic

FOR GOVERNOR

WOODROW WILSON

WOODROW WILSON
Woodrow Wilson's political career was meteoric, propelling him from the presidency of Princeton University to the presidency of the United States in three years. As governor of New Jersey from 1910 to 1912, Wilson turned against the Democratic machine that had backed him and made a reputation as a champion of progressive reform. Elected to the White House in 1912, he presided over the high tide of progressive reform.
Collection of Janice L. and David J. Frent.

Party but many of the humanitarian reforms championed by Roosevelt's Progressive Party as well.

Wilson's Reforms: Tariff, Banking, and the Trusts

In March 1913, Wilson became the first president since John Adams to go to Capitol Hill and speak directly to Congress, calling for tariff reform. "The object of the tariff," Wilson told Congress, "must be effective competition." Eager to topple the high tariff, the Democratic House of Representatives hastily passed the Underwood tariff, which lowered rates by 15 percent. To compensate for lost revenue, Congress approved a moderate income tax made possible by ratification of the Sixteenth Amendment a month earlier. In the Senate, lobbyists for industries quietly went to work to get the tariff raised, but Wilson rallied public opinion by attacking the "industrious and insidious lobby." In the harsh glare of publicity, the Senate passed the Underwood tariff, which earned praise as "the most honest tariff since the Civil War."

Wilson turned his attention next to banking. The panic of 1907 had dramatically testified to the failure of the banking system. Once again, a president had to turn to J. P. Morgan. But Morgan's legendary power was coming under close scrutiny. In 1913, Arsène Pujo, a Democratic senator from Louisiana, headed a committee to investigate the "money trust," calling J. P. Morgan himself to testify. The Pujo committee uncovered an alarming concentration of banking power. J. P. Morgan and Company and its affiliates held 341 directorships in 112 corporations, controlling assets of more than $22 billion. The sensational findings created a mandate for banking reform.

The Federal Reserve Act of 1913 was the most significant piece of domestic legislation in Wilson's presidency. It established a national banking system composed of twelve regional banks, privately controlled but regulated and supervised by a Federal Reserve Board appointed by the president. It gave the United States its first efficient banking and currency system and, at the same time, provided for a larger degree of government control over banking than had ever existed before. The new system made currency more elastic and credit adequate for the needs of business and agriculture. It did not, however, attempt to take control of the boom and bust cycles in the U.S. economy that would produce another major depression in the 1930s.

Flushed with success, Wilson tackled the trust issue. When Congress reconvened in January 1914, Wilson supported the Clayton bill to outlaw "unfair competition"—practices such as price discrimination and interlocking directorates (directors from one corporation sitting on the board of another). By spelling out which practices were unfair, Wilson hoped to guide business activity back to healthy competition without resorting to regulation. Despite a grandiose preamble that stated, "The labor of human beings is not a commodity or article of commerce," the Clayton Act did not succeed in improving labor's position. Although AFL president Samuel Gompers hailed the act as the "Magna Carta of labor," the conservative courts continued to issue injunctions and to use antitrust legislation against labor unions.

In the midst of the fight for the Clayton Act, Wilson, at the prompting of Louis Brandeis, threw his support behind the creation of the Federal Trade Commission (FTC), precisely the kind of federal regulatory agency that Roosevelt had advocated under his New Nationalism. The FTC, created in 1913, had not only wide investigatory powers but the authority to prosecute corporations for "unfair trade practices" and to enforce its judgments by issuing "cease and desist" orders. Along with the Clayton Act, Wilson's antitrust program worked to regulate rather than to break up big business.

By the fall of 1914, Wilson had exhausted the stock of ideas that made up the New Freedom. He alarmed progressives by declaring that the progressive movement had fulfilled its mission and that the country needed "a time of healing." Disgruntled progressives also disapproved of Wilson's conservative appointments. Having fought provisions in the Federal Reserve Act that would give bankers control, Wilson promptly named a banker, Paul Warburg, as the first chief of the Federal Reserve Board. Appointments to the new FTC also went to conservative businessmen. The progressive penchant for efficiency and expertise helps explain Wilson's choices. Believing that experts in the field could best understand the complex issues at stake, Wilson appointed bankers to oversee the banks and businessmen to regulate business.

Wilson, Reluctant Progressive

Progressives watched in dismay as Wilson repeatedly obstructed or obstinately refused to endorse further progressive reforms. He failed to support labor's demand for an end to injunctions. He twice threatened to veto legislation providing for farm credits on nonperishable crops. He refused to support child labor legislation or woman suffrage. Wilson justified his actions in the rhetoric of the New Freedom by claiming that his administration would condone "special privileges to none."

In the face of Wilson's obstinacy, reform might have ended in 1913 had not politics intruded. In the congressional elections of 1914, the Republican Party, no longer split by Roosevelt's Bull Moose faction, won substantial gains. Democratic strategists, with their eyes on the 1916 presidential race, recognized that Wilson needed to pick up support in the Midwest and the West by capturing votes from former Bull Moose progressives.

Wilson responded belatedly to this political pressure by championing reform in 1916. In a sharp about-face, he cultivated union labor, farmers, and social reformers. To please labor, he appointed Louis Brandeis to the Supreme Court. To woo farmers, he threw his support behind legislation to obtain rural credits. And he won support from advanced progressives such as Jane Addams by supporting workers' compensation and the Keating-Owen child labor law. When a railroad strike threatened in the months before the election, Wilson virtually ordered Congress to establish an eight-hour day at ten-hour pay on the railroads. He had moved a long way from his position in 1912 to embrace many of the social reforms championed by Theodore Roosevelt. As Wilson boasted, the Democrats had "opened their hearts to the demands of social justice" and had "come very near to carrying out the platform of the Progressive Party."

The Limits of Progressive Reform

While progressivism called for a more active role for the liberal state, at heart it was a movement that sought to preserve American institutions and stem the tide of more radical change. Its basic conservatism can be seen by comparing it to more radical movements of the era and by looking at the groups progressive reform left behind.

Radical Alternatives

The year 1900 witnessed the birth of the Social Democratic Party in America, later called simply the Socialist Party. Like the progressives, the socialists were middle class and native-born. They had broken with the older, more militant Socialist Labor Party precisely because of its dogmatic approach and im-

"WE WANT DEBS"
Eugene Victor Debs, shown wearing a bow tie in a train window, poses with Socialist Party campaign workers on a whistle-stop tour during the presidential campaign of 1912. Arguing that Roosevelt and Wilson were as alike as "Tweedledee and Tweedledum," Debs saw the Socialist Party as the only hope for the working class. Over a million voters agreed and cast their votes for him in 1912.
Brown Brothers; Collection of Janice L. and David J. Frent.

migrant constituency. The new group of socialists were eager to appeal to a broad mass of Americans.

The Socialist Party chose as its standard-bearer Eugene V. Debs, whose experience in the Pullman strike of 1894 convinced him that "there is no hope for the toiling masses of my countrymen, except by the pathways mapped out by Socialism." Debs's brand of socialism, which owed as much to the social gospel as to the theories of Karl Marx, advocated cooperation over competition and urged men and women to liberate themselves from "the barbarism of private ownership and wage slavery." Roosevelt labeled Debs a "mere inciter to murder and preacher of applied anarchy." Debs, for his part, pointed to the conservatism that underlay Roosevelt's fiery rhetoric. In the 1912 election, Debs indicted both old parties as "Tweedledee and Tweedledum," each dedicated to the preservation of capitalism and the continuation of the wage system. The Socialist Party alone, he argued, was the "revolutionary party of the working class." Debs would run for president five times, in every election (except 1916) from 1900 to 1920. His best showing came in 1912, when he polled 6 percent of the popular vote, capturing almost a million votes.

Farther to the left of the socialists stood the Industrial Workers of the World (IWW), nicknamed the Wobblies. In 1905, Debs, along with William Dudley "Big Bill" Haywood, created the IWW, "one big union" dedicated to organizing the most destitute segment of the workforce, the unskilled workers disdained by Samuel Gompers's AFL—western miners, migrant farmworkers, lumbermen, and immigrant textile workers. Haywood, a craggy-faced miner with one eye (he had lost the other in a childhood accident), was a charismatic leader and a proletarian intellectual. While Debs insisted that change could come from ballots, not bullets, the IWW unhesitatingly advocated direct action, sabotage, and the general strike—tactics designed to trigger a workers' uprising.

In contrast to political radicals like Debs and Haywood, Margaret Sanger, a nurse and social activist, promoted birth control as a movement for change. Sanger, the daughter of a radical Irish father and a mother who died at fifty after bearing eleven children, coined the term *birth control* in 1915 and launched a movement with broad social implications. Sanger and her followers saw birth control not only as a sexual and medical reform but also as a means to alter social and political power relationships and to alleviate human misery.

Although birth control became a public issue only in the early twentieth century, the birthrate in the United States had been falling consistently throughout the nineteenth century, with the average number of children per family falling from 7.0 in 1800 to 3.6 by 1900. The desire for family limitation was widespread, and, in this sense, birth control was nothing new. But the open advocacy of contraception, the use of artificial means to prevent pregnancy, seemed to many people both new and shocking. Theodore Roosevelt fulminated against birth control as "race suicide," warning that the "white" population was declining while immigrants and "undesirables" continued to breed.

Convinced that women needed to be able to control their pregnancies but unsure of the best methods to do so, Sanger traveled to Europe in 1913 to learn more about contraceptive techniques. On her return she promoted birth control in her newspaper, *The Woman Rebel*. Purity laws passed in the 1870s made it illegal to distribute both information on birth control and contraceptive devices, classing both as "obscene." The post office confiscated Sanger's magazine and brought charges against her. Facing arrest, she fled to Europe only to return in 1916 something of a national celebrity. In her absence, birth control had become linked with free speech and had been taken up as a liberal cause. Under public pressure, the government dropped the charges against Sanger, who undertook a nationwide tour to publicize the birth control cause.

Sanger then turned to direct action, opening the nation's first birth control clinic in the Brownsville section of Brooklyn, New York, in October 1916. Located in the heart of a Jewish and Italian immigrant neighborhood, the clinic attracted 464 clients in the nine days it was open. On the tenth day, police shut down the clinic and put Sanger in jail. By then she had become a national figure, and the cause she championed had gained legitimacy, if not legality. After World War I, the birth control movement would become much less radical as Sanger turned to doctors for support. But in its infancy, the movement that Sanger led was part of radical vision for reforming the world that made common cause with the socialists and the IWW in challenging the limits of progressive reform.

Progressivism for White Men Only

The day before President Woodrow Wilson's inauguration in March 1913, more than five thousand

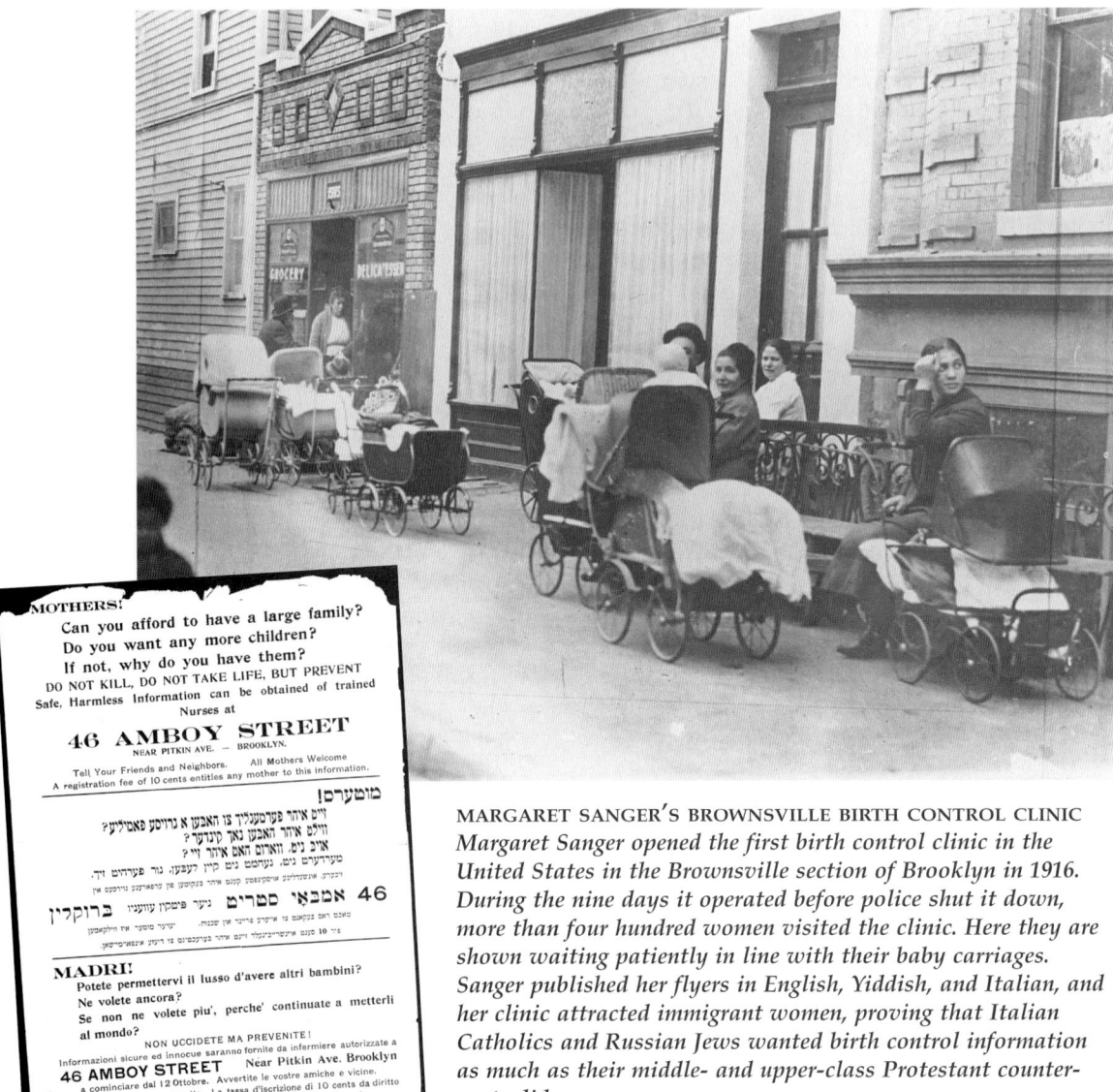

MARGARET SANGER'S BROWNSVILLE BIRTH CONTROL CLINIC
Margaret Sanger opened the first birth control clinic in the United States in the Brownsville section of Brooklyn in 1916. During the nine days it operated before police shut it down, more than four hundred women visited the clinic. Here they are shown waiting patiently in line with their baby carriages. Sanger published her flyers in English, Yiddish, and Italian, and her clinic attracted immigrant women, proving that Italian Catholics and Russian Jews wanted birth control information as much as their middle- and upper-class Protestant counterparts did.
Sophia Smith Collection, Smith College.

demonstrators marched in Washington to demand the vote for women. A rowdy crowd on hand to celebrate the Democrats' triumph heckled the marchers, as did the police. "If my wife were where you are," a burly cop told one suffragist, "I'd break her head." But for all the marching, Wilson, who didn't believe that a "lady" should vote, pointedly ignored woman suffrage in his inaugural address the next day.

The march served as a reminder that the political gains of progressivism were not spread equally in the population. When the twentieth century dawned, women still could not vote in most states.

Increasingly, however, woman suffrage had become an international movement. In Great Britain, Emmeline Pankhurst and her daughters Cristabel and Sylvia promoted a new, militant suffragism. They seized the spotlight in a series of marches, mass meetings, and acts of civil disobedience, which sometimes escalated into violence, riots, and arson.

Alice Paul, a Quaker social worker who had visited England and participated in suffrage activism there, returned to the United States in 1910 in time to plan the mass march on the eve of Wilson's inauguration and to lobby for a federal amendment to give women the vote. Paul's dramatic tactics alienated many in the National American Woman Suffrage Association (NAWSA). In 1916, she founded the militant National Woman's Party (NWP), which became the radical voice of the suffrage movement, advocating direct action and civil disobedience. Paul and her followers rejected the state-by-state strategy of the NAWSA and continued to press for a constitutional suffrage amendment, called by its supporters the Susan B. Anthony amendment.

The NAWSA, spurred by the actions of Paul and her followers, gained new direction when Carrie Chapman Catt became president in 1915. Catt revitalized the organization with a carefully crafted "winning plan" designed to achieve suffrage in six years. While Paul and her NWP held a six-month vigil outside the White House with banners that read "Mr. Wilson, What Will You Do for Woman Suffrage?" Catt led a centrally directed effort that worked on several levels. In states where women already voted, Catt lobbied for a federal amendment. Where state referenda could be won, she launched campaigns to maintain the suffrage momentum. Catt's strategy was to "keep so much 'suffrage noise' going all over the country that neither the enemy [n]or friends will discover where the real battle is." Catt's "winning plan" worked effectively, taking only four years instead of the six Catt had predicted.

World War I would provide the final impetus for woman suffrage. Paul and the NWP refused to work for the war, insisting "democracy should begin at home." In contrast, Catt seized the mantle of patriotism, arguing that there was no conflict between fighting for suffrage and aiding the war effort. It would take several more years before the Nineteenth Amendment became part of the U.S. Constitution, but when it was ratified in August 1920, the victory belonged both to Catt and to Paul, for without the militancy of the NWP, the NAWSA would not have seemed so moderate and respectable.

It was one of the great ironies of progressivism that, as it was practiced in the West and South, it viewed racism as reform. Anti-Asian bigotry in the West had led to a renewal of the Chinese Exclusion Act in 1902. As governor, Hiram Johnson at first stood against the strong anti-Asian prejudice of his state, but in 1913 he caved in to near unanimous pressure and signed the Alien Land Law preventing Japanese from purchasing land in California.

His support of the legislation amounted to little more than a cynical piece of demagoguery. As Johnson well knew, the law was largely symbolic— ineffectual in practice, since Japanese children born in the United States were citizens and property could be purchased in their names. Progressive politicians like Johnson, dedicated to democracy and opposed to special interests, proved willing to undermine their own principles to maintain their popularity.

South of the Mason-Dixon line, the progressives' racism targeted African Americans. Progressives preached the disfranchisement of black voters as a "reform." During the bitter electoral fights that had pitted Populists against Democrats in the 1890s, the party of white supremacy held its power by votes purchased or coerced from African Americans. Southern progressives proposed to "reform" the electoral system by eliminating black voters. Beginning in 1890 with Mississippi, Southern states curtailed the African American vote through devices like the poll tax (a fee required to vote) and the literacy test.

The Progressive Era also witnessed the rise of Jim Crow laws to segregate public facilities. (The name "Jim Crow" derived from a character in a popular minstrel song.) The new railroads precipitated segregation in the South where before it had rarely existed, at least on paper. Blacks were segregated in Jim Crow train coaches, even when they paid a first-class fare. Soon separate waiting rooms, separate bathrooms, and separate dining facilities sprang up across the South. In courtrooms in the state of Mississippi, blacks were even required to swear on a separate Bible.

In the face of this growing repression, Booker T. Washington, the preeminent black leader of the day, urged caution and restraint. A former slave, Washington opened the Tuskegee Institute in Alabama in 1881 to teach vocational skills to African Americans. Washington emphasized education and economic progress for his race and urged African Americans to put aside issues of political and social equality. In an 1895 speech in Atlanta, which came to be known as the "Atlanta Compromise," he stated, "In all things that are purely social we can be as separate as the fingers, yet one as the hand in all things essential to mutual progress." Washington's accommodationist policy appealed to whites in all sections, who elevated "the wizard of Tuskegee" to the role of national spokesman for African Americans.

The year after Washington proclaimed the Atlanta Compromise, the Supreme Court upheld the legality of racial segregation, affirming in *Plessy v. Ferguson* (1896) the constitutionality of the doctrine of "separate but equal." Blacks could be segregated in separate facilities, from schools to rest rooms, as long as the facilities were "equal." In actuality, facilities rarely were equal. In the North, where the growing tide of new immigrants led to a clamor for restrictive legislation, support for African American rights found few advocates. And with anti-Asian bigotry in the West, increasingly the doctrine of "white supremacy" found support in all sections of the country.

When Theodore Roosevelt invited Booker T. Washington to dine at the White House in 1901, a storm of racist criticism erupted. One southern editor fumed that the White House "had been painted black." But Roosevelt summoned Washington to talk politics and patronage, not African American rights. Busy tearing apart Mark Hanna's Republican machine and creating his own, Roosevelt wanted Washington's counsel in selecting black Republicans for party posts in the South. The president remained more interested in his own political fortunes than in those of African Americans.

DINNER GIVEN AT THE WHITE HOUSE BY PRESIDENT ROOSEVELT TO BOOKER T. WASHINGTON, OCTOBER 17th, 1901

BOOKER T. WASHINGTON AND THEODORE ROOSEVELT DINE AT THE WHITE HOUSE
When Theodore Roosevelt invited Booker T. Washington to the White House in 1901, he stirred up a hornet's nest of controversy that continued into the election of 1904. This Republican campaign piece gives the meeting a positive slant, with Roosevelt and Washington sitting under a portrait of Abraham Lincoln, a symbol of the party's historic commitment to African Americans. Democrats portrayed the meeting in a very different light; their campaign buttons pictured Washington with darker skin and implied that Roosevelt favored "race mingling."
Collection of Janice L. and David J. Frent.

When Woodrow Wilson came to power, he brought with him southern attitudes toward race and racial segregation. He allowed his postmaster general to segregate facilities, including drinking fountains and rest rooms, in the nation's capital. When critics attacked the policy, Wilson insisted that segregation was "in the interest of the Negro."

Faced with intolerance and open persecution, educated blacks in the North rebelled against the conservative leadership of Booker T. Washington. In *The Souls of Black Folk* (1903), Harvard graduate W. E. B. Du Bois attacked the "Tuskegee Machine," comparing Booker T. Washington to a political boss who used his influence to silence his critics and reward his followers. Du Bois founded the Niagara movement in 1905, calling for universal suffrage, civil rights, and leadership by a black intellectual elite. In 1909, the Niagara movement helped found the National Association for the Advancement of Colored People (NAACP), a coalition of blacks and whites that sought legal and political rights for African Americans through the courts. Like many progressive reform coalitions, the NAACP contained a diverse group—social workers, socialists, and black intellectuals. In the decades that followed, the NAACP came to represent the future for African Americans, while Booker T. Washington, who died in 1915, represented the past.

Conclusion: How Progressive Was Progressivism?

Progressivism was never a radical movement. Its goal remained the preservation of the existing system—by government intervention if necessary, but without uprooting any of the traditional American political, economic, or social institutions. As Theodore Roosevelt, the bellwether of the movement, insisted, "The only true conservative is the man who resolutely sets his face toward the future." Roosevelt was such a man, and progressivism

was such a movement. But while progressivism was not a radical movement, neither was it the stand pat support of the status quo advocated by the day's conservatives. Progressivism's willingness to use government to achieve a measure of social justice separated it from the conservatism of the old guard. The limitations of progressive reform should not obscure its very real achievements. The progressive movement brought significant gains as government moved away from laissez-faire to embrace a more active role designed to deal with the problems accompanying urban industrialism, to bring about greater social justice, and to achieve a better balance between business and government. Both Jane Addams and Theodore Roosevelt could lay equal claim to a movement that brought American politics into the twentieth century.

Progressivism contained many paradoxes. A diverse coalition of individuals and interests, the progressive movement began at the grass roots but left as its legacy a stronger presidency and an unprecedented federal involvement in the economy and social welfare. A movement that believed in social justice, progressivism often promoted social control. And while progressives called for greater democracy, they worshiped experts and efficiency.

But whatever its inconsistencies, progressivism attempted to deal with the problems posed by urban industrialism and, by increasing the power of the presidency and expanding the power of the government, helped to launch the liberal state of the twentieth century. War on a global scale would provide progressivism with yet another challenge even before it had completed its ambitious agenda.

FOR FURTHER READING ABOUT THE TOPICS IN THIS CHAPTER, see the Online Bibliography at

www.bedfordstmartins.com/roarkcompact.

FOR ADDITIONAL FIRST-HAND ACCOUNTS OF THIS PERIOD, see pages 86–101 in Michael Johnson, ed., *Reading the American Past*, Second Edition, Volume II.

TO ASSESS YOUR MASTERY OF THE MATERIAL IN THIS CHAPTER, see the Online Study Guide at

www.bedfordstmartins.com/roarkcompact.

CHRONOLOGY

1889 Jane Addams opens Hull House in Chicago.

1895 Booker T. Washington enunciates "Atlanta Compromise."

Anti-Saloon League founded by Protestant clergy.

1896 U.S. Supreme Court upholds doctrine of "separate but equal" in *Plessy v. Ferguson.*

1899 Florence Kelley launches the National Consumers League.

1900 Socialist Party founded with Eugene V. Debs as standard-bearer.

1901 Thomas Lofton Johnson elected mayor of Cleveland, Ohio.

Robert M. La Follette elected governor of Wisconsin.

Theodore Roosevelt succeeds to presidency following assassination of William McKinley.

1902 Roosevelt brings labor and management to bargaining table in anthracite coal strike.

U.S. government files antitrust lawsuit against Northern Securities Company.

1903 Women's Trade Union League (WTUL) founded.

Uprising in Panama leads to Panamanian independence; United States begins construction of Panama Canal.

W. E. B. Du Bois challenges Booker T. Washington in his book *The Souls of Black Folk.*

1904 Roosevelt wins presidential election in landslide.

Roosevelt Corollary to the Monroe Doctrine effectively makes United States "the policeman" of the Western Hemisphere.

1905 Industrial Workers of the World (IWW) founded by Big Bill Haywood.

W. E. B. Du Bois founds the Niagara movement.

Taft-Katsura Agreement gives Japan control over Korea.

1906 Pure Food and Drug Act and meat inspection legislation passed.

Congress passes Hepburn Act to regulate railroads and strengthen Interstate Commerce Commission.

Roosevelt receives Nobel Peace Prize for his role in mediating Russo-Japanese War.

1907 Panic on Wall Street.

Roosevelt signs "Gentlemen's Agreement" with Japan restricting immigration.

Walter Rauschenbusch publishes *Christianity and the Social Crisis.*

1908 Supreme Court upholds Oregon state law limiting women's working hours to ten a day (*Muller v. Oregon*).

Root-Takahira agreement regularizes relations between United States and Japan.

William Howard Taft elected president to succeed Theodore Roosevelt.

1909 "Uprising of twenty thousand" in New York City, a garment workers strike backed by the WTUL.

National Association for the Advancement of Colored People (NAACP) formed.

President Taft defends Payne-Aldrich tariff.

1910 Hiram Johnson elected governor of California.

Woodrow Wilson elected governor of New Jersey.

Wyoming enacts woman suffrage.

Jane Addams publishes *Twenty Years at Hull-House.*

1911 Triangle fire in New York City kills 146 workers.

Taft launches antitrust suit against U.S. Steel.

California votes for woman suffrage.

1912 President Taft sends marines into Nicaragua and the Dominican Republic.

Republicans nominate incumbent William Howard Taft.

Theodore Roosevelt runs for president on Progressive Party ticket.

Democrat Woodrow Wilson elected president, defeating Taft and Roosevelt.

Socialist Eugene V. Debs garners 6 percent of the vote.

Kansas, Oregon, and Arizona grant the vote to women.

1913 Suffragists march on eve of Wilson's inauguration to demand the vote.

Wilson signs legislation establishing Federal Trade Commission (FTC).

Sixteenth Amendment (income tax) and Seventeenth Amendment (direct election of senators) ratified.

1914 Congress passes Clayton Antitrust Act.

Panama Canal opens.

1915 Carrie Chapman Catt takes over leadership of national woman suffrage movement.

1916 Alice Paul launches National Woman's Party.

Margaret Sanger opens first U.S. birth control clinic in Brooklyn, New York.

Keating-Owen bill passed, outlawing child labor.

1918 Supreme Court strikes down child labor law.

WAR

Which Bird?

As viewed by Life

LIFE MAGAZINE COVER
This 1914 magazine cover provides a vivid visual demonstration of the early tendency of the American press to support U.S. entry into World War I. The image makes no bones about the way a viewer should answer the question posed below it. The American eagle in the center, wings spread and screaming for action, dominates the picture and makes the dove holding an olive branch appear pathetically weak. Considering the stereotyped knife-, gun-, and bomb-wielding foreigners lurking in the background, the sailor has understandably turned toward the eagle for inspiration to resist the enemies of democracy.
Picture Research Consultants & Archives.

WORLD WAR I: THE PROGRESSIVE CRUSADE AT HOME AND ABROAD

22

1914–1920

IN HIS 1914 NEW YEAR'S GREETING from the world's richest man, Andrew Carnegie proclaimed himself "strong in the faith that International Peace is soon to prevail." His optimism reflected confidence in the work of the forty-five peace societies that had arisen in America since 1900, capped by the Endowment for International Peace Carnegie created in 1910. Soon afterward he cheerfully assured students at St. Andrews University in Scotland that the safest career they could choose "is that of a soldier, who . . . marches from youth to age . . . in perfect safety."

So it was that Carnegie, vacationing at his castle in Scotland in the summer of 1914, serenely awaited word of a church peace conference in Germany. Having hailed German ruler, Kaiser Wilhelm II, as the "foremost apostle of peace in our time" for his willingness to consider arbitration of international disputes, Carnegie expected progress. Instead, the news that reached him confounded every hope. On the day the peace meeting was to convene, Germany declared war on Russia. Within days the other major powers in Europe took sides and touched off the most devastating conflict the world had ever known. Carnegie had planned to complete his autobiography with a tribute to "The Kaiser and World Peace." Now there was no happy ending. "What a change!" he wrote as he abandoned the project. "The world convulsed by war as never before! Men slaying each other like wild beasts."

Carnegie then left his beloved Scotland, never to return. The Old World had become, as an English friend wrote to him, "Hell at full blast." Like millions of others whose faith in rational and humane progress had been betrayed, Carnegie faced the dismaying question of why the masses, who had been counted on to understand their stake in peace, had turned ferociously to cheer for war.

Back in America, Carnegie hoped President Wilson might prove to be the hero he needed to replace the discredited Kaiser. Although Wilson was burdened with grief over the death of his wife, Ellen, on the day war broke out, he responded to the crisis with a firm policy that buoyed the spirits of Carnegie and other peace advocates with its promise to shield the nation from war while offering its democratic example and services to alleviate the conflict.

Wilson was convinced that the nation's only virtuous course was absolute neutrality. Even though his sympathies were with Great Britain and France, Wilson believed that blame for the war did not lie entirely with Germany and that the United States had no vital stake in a European power struggle. Wilson also had to consider that the United States was a nation of immigrants, millions of whom had only

CARNEGIE, THE PEACEMAKER
Andrew Carnegie hoped that his association with English and German leaders would help persuade them to a policy of peace. Here Carnegie (left) displays his ebullient confidence in 1913 as he takes the arm of British diplomat Lord Resdale to stroll near the headquarters of the Carnegie Endowment for International Peace in Washington. In turn, liberal leaders in England, like Resdale, and the kaiser in Germany hoped the richest man in the world would underwrite efforts to keep the increasingly dangerous armed standoff between their nations from exploding into war. As Carnegie and his allies saw it, reason and humaneness must transcend each separate national interest. The rulers of nation states, however, had doubts about how such a reversal of policy as usual could take place and fears about the weakness that would follow.
Library of Congress.

recently come from countries on both sides of the war. As he explained less than two weeks after the war started, the United States could offer "impartial mediation" and show the world the way to reconciliation and a healing peace. Wilson urged the American people to restrain their tendency to favor one side or the other and remain "impartial in thought as well as action."

Most Americans agreed with Wilson that the country should stay neutral, but they were less eager to use that neutrality to broker a peace. Essentially, the nation tried to distance itself from the conflict and just go about its business. But events were to prove that the Atlantic was no moat. Trade and travel eventually entangled the United States in the war's violence and blighted hopes for a peaceable, progressive world.

Woodrow Wilson and the World

Shortly after winning election to the presidency in 1912, Woodrow Wilson confided to a friend: "It would be an irony of fate if my administration had to deal chiefly with foreign affairs." Indeed, Wilson had based his life and career on local attachments, seldom venturing far from home and traveling abroad only on brief vacations. In his campaign for the presidency, Wilson spoke in passionate detail about domestic reform but hardly mentioned foreign affairs.

As a progressive moralist, however, Wilson could not let himself ignore the world. From the outset he acted on his conviction that the United States should set the example in international affairs by championing national self-determination, peaceful free trade, and political democracy. Presenting allegiance to democracy as a moral duty, Wilson concluded, "We dare not turn from the principle that morality and not expediency is the thing that must guide us."

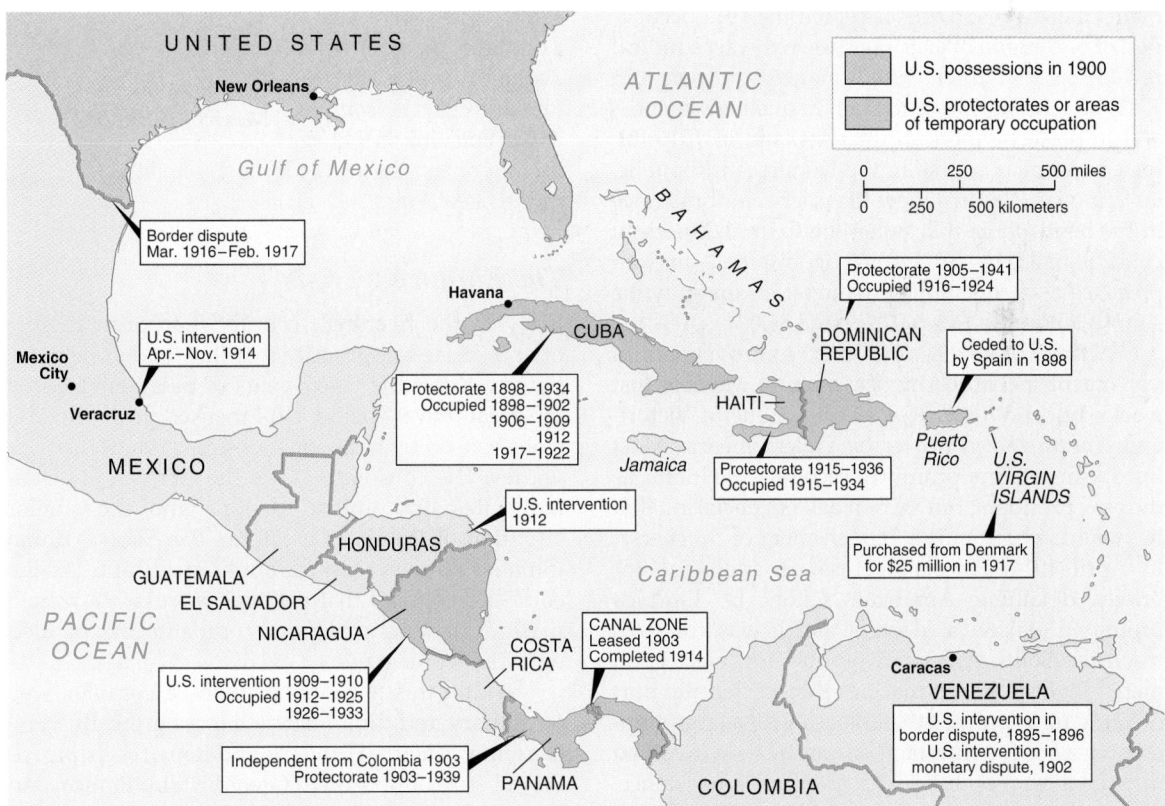

MAP 22.1

U.S. Involvement in Latin America and the Caribbean, 1895–1941

Victory against Spain in 1898 made Puerto Rico an American possession and Cuba a protectorate. America also gained control over the Panama Canal and was quick to protect expanding economic interests with military force to make sure that stable, if not necessarily democratic, governments prevailed.

Taming the Americas

When he came to office, Wilson sought to distinguish his foreign policy from that of his Republican predecessors. To Wilson, Theodore Roosevelt's "big stick" and William Howard Taft's "dollar diplomacy" appeared a crude flexing of military and economic muscle. To counter such arrogance, Wilson appointed William Jennings Bryan as secretary of state. A pacifist on religious grounds, Bryan immediately turned his attention to making agreements with thirty nations for the peaceful settlement of disputes.

But Wilson and Bryan, like Roosevelt and Taft, also believed that the Monroe Doctrine gave the United States special rights and responsibilities in the Western Hemisphere. The Wilson administration had the ambiguous goal, then, of encouraging justice and democracy in the Western Hemisphere while protecting and expanding American investments there. Wilson thus accepted the 1912 occupation of Nicaragua by U.S. marines to thwart a radical revolution that threatened American property. In 1915, he sent marines into Haiti to quell lawlessness and to protect American interests, and in 1916 followed a similar course in the Dominican Republic. So firm was Wilson's view of American dominance in the hemisphere that when the Central American court of justice issued a ruling against the American presence as a violation of national sovereignty, he simply ignored it (Map 22.1, page 549).

Wilson's most serious and controversial involvement in Latin America came in Mexico. Just weeks before Wilson was elected, General Victoriano Huerta seized power by violent means. Most European nations promptly recognized Huerta as the new president, but Wilson balked, declaring that he would not support a "government of butchers." In April 1914, Huerta's refusal to apologize for briefly detaining American sailors in Tampico prompted Wilson to declare that it was time "to teach the South American republics to elect good men!" Eight hundred marines then seized the port of Veracruz to prevent the unloading of a large shipment of arms for Huerta, who was by then involved in a civil war of his own. After brief resistance, Huerta fled to Spain, and the United States welcomed a more compliant government.

Wilson was not able to subdue Mexico that easily, however. A rebellion erupted among desperately poor farmers who believed that the new government, aided by American business interests, had betrayed the revolution's promise to help the common people. In January 1916, the rebel army,

commanded by Francisco, "Pancho" Villa, seized a train carrying gold to Texas from an American-owned mine deep within Mexico and killed the seventeen American engineers aboard. Another band of Villa's men crossed the border on March 9 for a predawn raid on Columbus, New Mexico, that cost several more lives and left the town in flames. Wilson promptly dispatched twelve thousand troops, led by General John J. Pershing, who years earlier had chased the Apache chief Geronimo through the same Mexican desert. This time the wily Villa avoided capture, and in January 1917 Wilson recalled Pershing so that he might prepare the army for the possibility of fighting in the Great War.

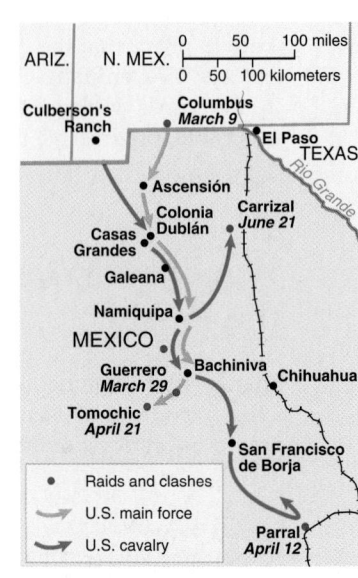

U.S. Intervention in Mexico, 1916–1917

The European Crisis

Early in the twentieth century, European leaders often proclaimed proudly that they had done away with war. But the many years of peace enjoyed by the great powers before 1914 masked profound tensions caused by nationalist desires and imperial rivalries. The consolidation of the German and Italian states into unified nations and the similar ambition of Russia to create a "Pan-Slavic" union initiated new rivalries throughout Europe. As the conviction spread that colonial possessions were a mark of national greatness, competition expanded onto the world stage.

Within this tense atmosphere, a complex web of military and diplomatic alliances grew. By 1914, Germany, Austria-Hungary, and Italy (the Triple Alliance) stood opposed to Great Britain, France, and Russia (the Triple Entente). In their effort to prevent war through a balance of power, the nations of Europe had actually magnified the possibility of conflict by creating national borders that were in effect trip wires between two heavily armed power blocs (Map 22.2).

The fatal sequence started in southeastern Europe, in the Balkans. On June 28, 1914, a Bosnian

"PANCHO" VILLA AND GENERAL PERSHING
Here in 1914, Mexican revolutionary Francisco "Pancho" Villa (center) and American general John J. Pershing (right) pose genially as allies in the struggle to overthrow the dictatorial ruler of Mexico, Victoriano Huerta. Soon afterward, Villa and Pershing would be adversaries. After a raid by Villa across the New Mexico border in 1915 to punish Americans for aiding Villa's revolutionary rivals, Pershing pursued Villa into Mexico.
Corbis-Bettmann.

Serb terrorist demonstrated Serbia's desire to extend its territory to the Adriatic Sea by killing Archduke Franz Ferdinand of Austria as he toured the Bosnian coastal city of Sarajevo, then part of the Austro-Hungarian Empire. Austria, holding Serbia to account for the assassination, declared war on that nation on July 28. The alliance system then swung into action. Russia, determined to protect its

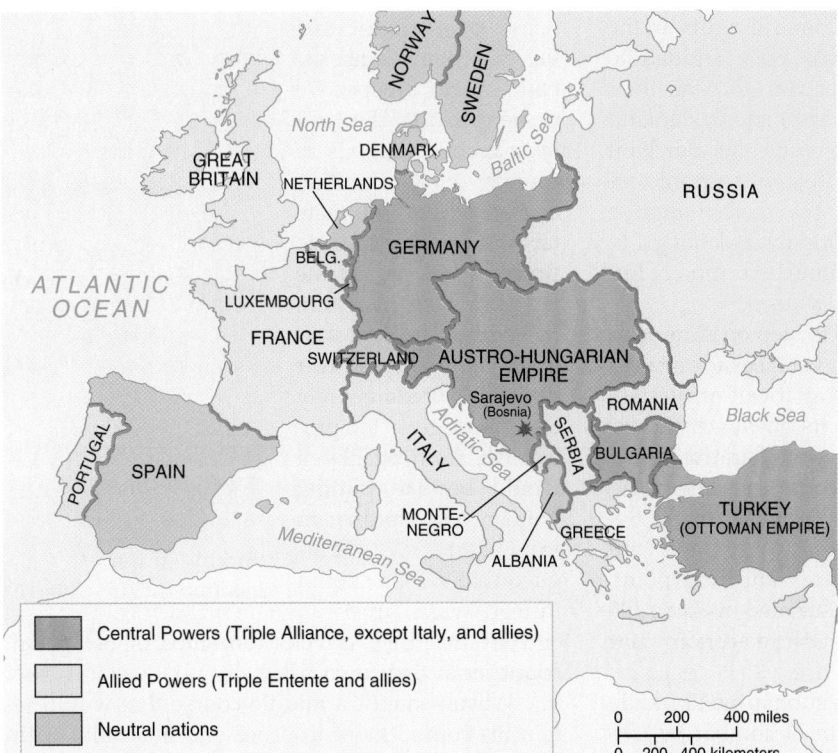

MAP 22.2
European Alliances after the Outbreak of World War I
With Germany and the Austro-Hungarian Empire wedged between their Entente rivals, and all parties fully armed, Europe was poised for war when the Archduke Franz Ferdinand of Austria was assassinated in Sarajevo in July 1914.

Slavic kin, announced that it would back the Serbs. Germany, feeling compelled to support Austria-Hungary, then declared war on Russia and on France. In response, Great Britain, upholding its pact with France, declared war on Germany. The conflict became a world war when Japan, seeing an opportunity to rid itself of imperialist competition in China, joined the Allied cause against Germany.

Recognizing how war would devastate the civilization he had served, England's foreign secretary, Edward Grey, said: "The lamps are going out all over Europe. We shall not see them lit again in our lifetime." But with the loyalty the doomed civilization had instilled in him, Grey assured Parliament that Great Britain would rally to the cause of war when it "realizes what is at stake, what the real issues are." The next day, the German imperial chancellor, Theobald von Bethmann Hollweg, insisted that Germany had grown strong "in the works of peace" and that "only in defense of a just cause shall our sword fly from its scabbard." But beyond vague assertions from each side that aggression must be halted and honor upheld, little was done to define "just cause."

The Ordeal of Neutrality

The United States had traditionally insisted on the broadest possible definition of neutral rights. In the American view, neutral nations were entitled to trade freely with all nations at war, to send their ships safely through the open seas, and to demand the safe passage of their citizens on the merchant and passenger ships of all belligerents. More was involved than principle. The year before Europe went to war, the American economy had started to slide into a recession that wartime disruption of European trade could drastically worsen.

Great Britain was the first to step on America's neutral rights by setting up a naval blockade against Germany. The United States vigorously protested, but Britain refused to give up its naval advantage. In the fall of 1914, the Wilson administration reluctantly accepted the British blockade, thus beginning the fateful process of alienation from Germany. Between 1914 and the spring of 1917, while trade with Germany dwindled toward the vanishing point, war-related exports to Britain escalated by some 300 percent, enough to pull the American economy out of its prewar slump.

Germany retaliated with a submarine blockade of British ports. This new form of combat by *Un-*

terseebooten, or U-boats, posed a disturbing threat to the traditional rules of war. Unlike surface warships that could harmlessly confiscate freighters or prevent them from entering a war zone, submarines relied on surprising and sinking their quarry. And once they sank a ship, the tiny, cramped U-boats could not possibly pick up the survivors. To much of the world, submarine warfare violated notions of how a "civilized" nation should behave. Nevertheless, in February 1915, the German high command declared the waters around Britain a war zone and warned that any ship in the area would be subject to attack.

Woodrow Wilson responded harshly, declaring that the United States would regard the loss of an American ship or the loss of American lives on ships of belligerent nations as "a flagrant violation of neutral rights" and would hold Germany to "strict accountability." What "strict accountability" meant was still unclear when Wilson received the shocking news of the sinking of the British passenger liner *Lusitania* off the coast of Ireland on May 7, 1915, with the loss of 1,198 lives, including 128 Americans.

American newspapers appeared with drawings of drowning women and children, and some editorial writers called for war. Most Americans, however, did not want to break relations with Germany. Some pointed out that the German embassy had warned prospective passengers that the *Lusitania* carried millions of rounds of ammunition and so was a legitimate target. Secretary of State Bryan, speaking for the peace movement within the administration, said that a ship carrying war materiel "should not rely on passengers to protect her from attack—it would be like putting women and children in front of an army." He argued that Wilson should instead warn American citizens that they traveled on ships of belligerent countries at their own risk.

Wilson sought a middle course that would retain his commitment to peace and neutrality with-

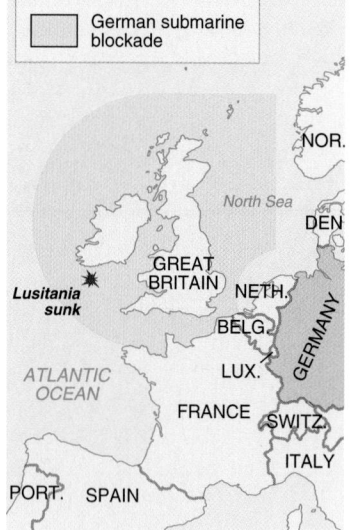

Sinking of the *Lusitania*, 1915

out condoning German attacks on passenger ships. On May 10, he distanced himself from the interventionists by declaring that "there is such a thing as a man being too proud to fight," for which former president Theodore Roosevelt raged at him as a "flub dub and mollycoddle" who should be too proud *not* to fight. But Wilson also rejected Bryan's position. Any further destruction of ships, Wilson warned, would be regarded as "deliberately unfriendly" and might lead the United States to break diplomatic relations with Germany. Wilson's insistence that Americans had the right to travel unharmed made Bryan realize that his pacifist hopes were doomed. When the secretary of state resigned, Wilson replaced him with Robert Lansing, a veteran State Department officer and a strong advocate of the Allied cause.

For a while after the *Lusitania* crisis, the tension subsided. Germany, anxious not to provoke the United States, apologized for civilian deaths and offered an indemnity. After the sinking of the English steamer *Sussex* in 1916, at the cost of two more American lives, the German government quickly acted to head off war by promising no more submarine attacks without warning and without provisions for the safety of civilians.

Wilson's efforts for peace were helpful in his bid for reelection in 1916. Still, controversies over neutrality, intervention in Mexico, and the government's role in regulating the economy made Wilson's chances uncertain. His opponent was the able associate justice of the Supreme Court Charles Evans Hughes, former governor of New York. The Democratic Party ran Wilson under the slogan "He kept us out of war," but Wilson shied away from the claim, protesting that "they talk of me as though I were a god. Any little German lieutenant can push us into the war at any time by some calculated outrage." Wilson did not disagree, however, when the Democrats argued that the Republican candidate was more likely to lead the nation into war. Ultimately, Wilson's case for neutrality appealed to the majority in favor of peace. Wilson won, but by only 600,000 popular and 23 electoral votes, leaving in doubt whether he spoke for a unified nation on foreign policy.

The United States Enters the War

The determination of each warring European nation to achieve peace on its own terms scuttled any chance for a negotiated peace. The Germans refused to specify their war aims, and the Allies made mediation difficult by announcing aims that would have broken up the Austro-Hungarian Empire and required the Germans to pay damages for the war. In early January 1917, the German military high command persuaded the head of state, Kaiser Wilhelm II, that the country could no longer afford to allow neutral shipping to reach Great Britain while the enemy blockade threatened to starve Germany, and decided to resume unrestricted submarine warfare at the end of the month. The German military understood that it risked war with the United States but gambled that Germany would achieve total victory before the United States could bring its armed might to bear.

When attacks on neutral shipping escalated, most of Wilson's advisers joined Theodore Roosevelt in calling for war, but Wilson, still hoping for a way out, would only sever diplomatic relations with Germany. Then, on February 25, 1917, British authorities informed Wilson of a secret telegram sent by the German foreign secretary, Arthur Zimmermann, to the German minister in Mexico. It promised that in the event of war between Germany and the United States, Germany would see that Mexico regained the territories in the Southwest it had lost in the Mexican War if Mexico would declare war against the United States. Wilson angrily responded to the Zimmermann telegram by asking Congress to approve a policy of "armed neutrality" that would allow merchant ships to fight back against any attackers. It was this wicked attempt to penetrate the Western Hemisphere, Wilson stated privately, that finally convinced him the war was, indeed, a defense of democracy against autocratic German aggression.

In mid-March, German submarines sank five American vessels in the sea lanes to Britain. After agonizing over the probable consequences, the president prevailed on Congress to issue a declaration of war on April 6. No longer too proud to fight, Wilson accused Germany of "warfare against mankind." Still, he insisted that the destruction of Germany was not the U.S. goal. Rather, the United States fought to make the world "safe for democracy" and to "vindicate the principles of peace and justice" in which a reconstructed Germany would find a democratic place.

Wilson did not overlook the tragic difference between those lofty aims and the brutal means chosen to achieve them. He spoke despairingly to a friend just prior to his appearance before Congress:

"Once lead this people into war, and they'll forget there ever was such a thing as tolerance."

The Crusade for Democracy

Despite Wilson's misgivings, progressives hoped that war would improve the quality of American life as well as free Europe from its bondage to tyranny and militarism. The American Expeditionary Force (AEF) that eventually carried two million troops to Europe, by far the largest military venture the United States had ever undertaken on foreign soil, was trained to be morally upright and knowledgeable about the civilization it was to save. Progressive enthusiasm also powered the mobilization of industrial and agricultural production. Moreover, labor shortages caused by workers leaving the workforce for military service provided new opportunities in the booming wartime economy.

The Call to Arms

On May 18, 1917, Wilson signed a sweeping Selective Service Act, authorizing a draft of all young men into the armed forces. Conscription soon transformed a tiny volunteer armed force of 80,000 men, spread thinly around the United States and in outposts from the Caribbean to China, into a vast army and navy. Although almost 350,000 inductees either failed to report or claimed conscientious objector status, the draft boards eventually inducted 2.8 million men into the armed services, in addition to the 2 million who volunteered.

Eventually, almost half of the 4.8 million U.S. armed forces served in Europe. In the training camps that transformed raw recruits into fighting men, medical examinations, along with recently developed sociological and psychological techniques, took the measure of American youth. The shocking news that almost 30 percent of those drafted were rejected on physical grounds acted as a stimulus to the public health and physical education movements. Secretary of War Newton D. Baker, whose outlook had been shaped by reform crusades as mayor of Cleveland, created a Commission on Training Camp Activities staffed by YMCA workers and veterans of the settlement house and playground movements. The Military Draft Act of 1917 prohibited prostitution and alcohol near training camps. Instead, military training was merged with games, singing, and college extension courses.

Baker described military camps in full progressive fervor as "national universities—training schools to which the flower of American youth is being sent" to provide them with an "invisible armor" of education, comradeship, and moral fitness.

Wilson's selection of General John J. Pershing to command the AEF recognized the need for hard professionalism in the lead, not the sort of romantic patriotism that had given amateurs like Theodore Roosevelt the chance to command combat troops in the Spanish-American War. Pershing had graduated from West Point in the 1880s and then seen combat in the Indian wars on the American plains and against the Spanish in Cuba, where his command of black troops had earned him the nickname "Black Jack." Pershing's impeccable military bearing and professional standing gave promise that he would carry out his duties with the level-headed efficiency required of modern war on a vast scale.

The Progressive Stake in the War

The idea of the war as an agent of social improvement fanned the old zeal and earnestness of the progressive movement. Believers in strong government realized that the Wilson administration would need to create agencies to mobilize the nation's resources and hoped they could be used to improve efficiency and raise the general standard of living. They hailed the choice of Bernard Baruch to head the central planning authority, the War Industries Board (WIB). At once a wealthy southern gentleman, a Jewish Wall Street stockbroker, and a reform Democrat, Baruch could speak to many constituencies. Shrewdly, he brought industrial management and labor together into a team that made the American soldier the most fully equipped in the world. Only in the vital area of weaponry did the quality of American workmanship lag behind that of the Europeans, who had long fielded large armies.

Herbert Hoover, a self-made millionaire engineer, gained similar acclaim as head of the Food Administration. Sober and tireless, he led remarkably successful "Hooverizing" campaigns for "wheatless" Mondays, "meatless" Tuesdays, and other means of conserving resources. Guaranteed high prices, the American heartland not only supplied the needs of U.S. citizens and armed forces but also became the breadbasket of America's allies. Even the First Family, including Wilson's new wife, Edith Galt, did its part with a White House "victory garden" and sheep on the White House lawn in place of the gardeners, who had moved on to new work in the war effort.

Buoyed by these developments, influential voices like those of philosopher-educator John Dewey and journalist-critic Walter Lippmann lined up support by most critics and intellectuals, many of them former pacifists. They viewed the war as a means of promoting progressive reform. Industrial leaders were also cheered that, in achieving feats of production and efficiency, wartime agencies helped corporate profits triple.

Reformers also had cause to celebrate the effect of the war on the labor front. Full mobilization meant high prices for farmers and plentiful jobs in the new war industries. Aware that increased industrial production required peaceful labor relations and the avoidance of strikes, the National War Labor Policies Board and other agencies enacted the eight-hour day, a living minimum wage, and collective bargaining rights in industries that had long resisted them. Wages rose sharply during the war, and the American Federation of Labor (AFL) saw its membership soar from 2.7 million to more than 5 million. After long insisting that health was a private matter, Congress bowed to the patriotic cause of providing death and disability insurance for the armed forces.

To raise the $33 billion it cost to wage the war (more than the federal government's total expenses from 1789 to 1917), imaginative fund-raising strategies were needed. Secretary of the Treasury William G. McAdoo, who happened to be Wilson's son-in-law, became the principal cheerleader for the purchase of war bonds, called Liberty Bonds.

The war also provided a huge boost to the stalled moral crusade to ban alcohol. Before the war, prohibitionists had campaigned fervently for a constitutional amendment to ban the manufacture and sale of alcoholic beverages, and by 1917, nineteen states had gone dry. Liquor's opponents could now cite the war as a reason for national prohibition, which would make the cause of democracy powerful and pure. At the same time, shutting down the distilleries would save millions of bushels of grain that could feed the United States and its allies. Prohibitionists added a patriotic twist by arguing that closing breweries with German names like Schlitz, Pabst, and Anheuser-Busch would deal a blow to Kaiser Wilhelm II and the German cause. Swept along by these arguments, Congress in December 1917 passed the Eighteenth Amendment, which banned the manufacture, transportation, and sale of alcohol; after swift ratification by all the states, the amendment went into effect on January 1, 1920.

The Advance to Woman Suffrage

War presented new opportunities for women. More than twenty thousand women served with the armed forces, a large number of them as nurses in France. In the private sector, long-standing barriers against hiring women fell when millions of working men became soldiers and few new immigrant

PICKETING THE WHITE HOUSE FOR THE VOTE
Facing the growing clamor for women's right to vote, Woodrow Wilson remarked that he could neither fault the case women made nor bring himself to accept it. Here Mrs. William L. Colt stands as one of many picketers at the White House gate bringing the faultless case to the president's own home. Under such direct pressure and in recognition of women's service in the defense industry and near the battlefields as nurses and Red Cross workers, Wilson finally pledged himself to support the Suffrage Amendment. As a southern gentleman who admired women as tamers of men's aggressive tendencies, Wilson also could hope that women's moderating influence would help achieve his aim that the Great War be the war to end all wars.
Corbis.

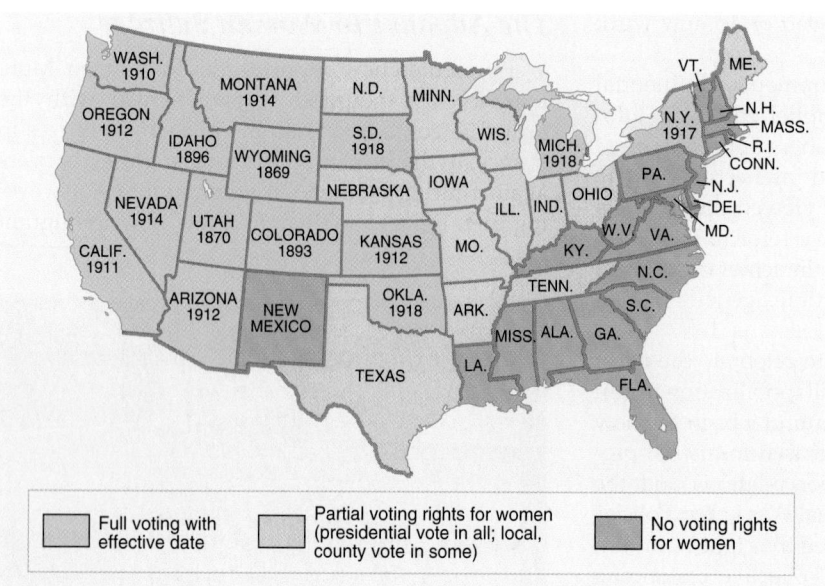

MAP 22.3

Women's Voting Rights before the Nineteenth Amendment

The long campaign for women's voting rights reversed the pioneer epic—rolling eastward from its first successes in the new democratic openness of the West toward the entrenched, male-dominated public life of the Northeast and the South.

READING THE MAP: What was the first state to grant woman suffrage? How many states extended full voting rights to women before the World War I years (1914–1918)? During World War I?

CONNECTIONS: Suffragists redirected their focus during World War I. What strategies did they use during the war? In which states was the struggle for woman suffrage fiercest, and why?

www.bedfordstmartins.com/roarkcompact   SEE THE ONLINE STUDY GUIDE for more help in analyzing this map.

workers found safe passage across the Atlantic. The new Women's Bureau of the Department of Labor along with the Women's Trade Union League (WTUL) helped open jobs to women, often against the opposition of the major trade organization, the AFL. For the first time, women in sizable numbers found work with the railroads and in defense plants as welders and heavy machine operators. Some gained entry to labor unions, whose members usually earned far higher wages than nonunion workers. "This is the women's age," exulted Margaret Dreier Robins, president of the WTUL. "At last . . . women are coming into the labor and festival of life on equal terms with men."

The war effort spurred women to victory in the political arena as well. Since the Seneca Falls con-

vention of 1848, where women voiced their first formal demand for the ballot, the struggle for woman suffrage had inched forward. Using a state-by-state approach, suffragists had achieved success in Wyoming in 1890 and in several other western states in the following years, but elsewhere they met defeat (Map 22.3).

By linking their crusade for a constitutional amendment to wartime emphasis on national unity and by adopting increasingly militant tactics, the crusaders for woman suffrage finally triumphed. Militant suffragists such as Alice Paul, the head of the new National Woman's Party, and women continuously picketing the White House made the suffrage campaign impossible to ignore. Finally, Woodrow Wilson gave his support to suffrage. It would be wrong, he conceded, not to reward the "partnership of suffering and sacrifice" with a "partnership of privilege and right." In 1919, Congress passed the Nineteenth Amendment, granting women the vote, and by 1920 it had been ratified by the required two-thirds of the states.

The "Great Migration" of African Americans

In 1900, thirty-five years after emancipation, African Americans had made little progress toward achieving full citizenship. Despite some migration to Northern cities since 1890, nine of every ten African Americans lived in the South, and disfranchisement, segregation, and violence dominated their lives. The majority of black men still toiled in agriculture, either mired in tenancy or working for wages of sixty cents a day. Black women worked in the homes of whites as domestics for $2 or less a week.

The First World War provided African Americans with the opportunity to escape cotton fields and kitchens. Blacks who were once welcome in the urban North only in personal service occupations now became unskilled and semiskilled industrial workers. Young black men, who made up the bulk of the migrants, found jobs in steel mills, shipyards, munitions plants, railroad yards, and mines. From 1915 to 1920, half a million blacks (approximately 10 percent of the South's black population) boarded trains bound for Philadelphia, Detroit, Cleveland, Chicago, St. Louis, and other industrial cities.

Blacks who joined the "great migration" were not just moving north. They were fleeing the South. Whole churches, almost entire communities, sometimes transplanted themselves to northern cities. By 1930, for example, Chicago claimed nearly forty thousand black Mississippians. One man, writing to a church congregation he'd left behind, announced proudly: "I just begin to feel like a man. . . . My children are going to the same school with the whites and I don't have to [h]umble to no one. I have registered—will vote the next election and there ain't any 'yes sir.'"

But the North was not yet the promised land. Whites, fearful of losing jobs and status, lashed out against the new migrants. In 1918, the nation witnessed ninety-six lynchings of blacks, some of them

AFRICAN AMERICANS MIGRATE NORTH *These newcomers to a northern city in 1912 pose in their best dress on the threshold of a changed life. Several factors combined to prompt almost 4.5 million African Americans to leave the South by midcentury. To the burden of racism was added the steady erosion of opportunities to make a living. In the 1920s, many rural blacks lost work when a boll weevil invasion reduced the cotton crop drastically. Subsequently, mechanization and government programs to support crop prices by reducing acreage drove many more people off the land.* Schomburg Center for Research in Black Culture, New York Public Library.

war veterans still in uniform. Race riots ripped two dozen northern cities. The worst occurred on a hot July night in 1917 when a mob of whites invaded a section of East St. Louis, Illinois, crowded with blacks who had been recruited to help break a strike. The mob murdered at least thirty-nine people and left most of the black district in flames.

African Americans in the military also experienced racial violence. The most disastrous episode occurred in August 1917 when a group of armed black soldiers went to Houston, Texas, to avenge incidents of harassment by the police. In the clash that followed, thirteen whites, including several policemen, and one black soldier were killed. With vengeful swiftness that denied any appeal to the War Department, a military court had thirteen of the black soldiers hanged and sentenced forty-one others to life imprisonment. (See "Historical Question," page 560.)

The Struggle over National Purpose

When Wilson finally did commit the nation to war, most peace advocates rallied around the flag. The Carnegie Endowment for International Peace, for example, adopted new stationery with the heading "Peace through Victory" and issued a resolution saying that "the most effectual means of promoting peace is to prosecute the war against the Imperial German Government." In a similar shift of view, several business and civic leaders who had been prewar advocates of peaceful means of settling disputes created the League to Enforce Peace in support of Wilson's insistence that military force had become the only means to peaceful ends.

Against the tide of that conversion from pacifism to patriotism, a handful of reformers remained true to the cause of peace. Soon after the guns began booming in 1914, a group of professional women, led by settlement house leader Jane Addams and economics professor Emily Greene Balch, convened to resist what Addams described as "the pathetic belief in the regenerative results of war." The Women's Peace Party that emerged in 1915 and its foreign affiliates in the Women's International League for Peace and Freedom (WILPF) led the struggle to persuade governments to negotiate peace and spare dissenters from harsh punishment. It was discouraging, unpopular work, and after America entered the conflict, advocates for peace were routinely labeled cowards and traitors, their efforts crushed by the steamroller of war enthusiasm.

Wilson's major strategy for fending off criticism of the war was to stir up patriotic fervor. In 1917, the president created the Committee on Public Information (CPI) under the direction of George Creel, a progressive journalist who thumped for the war like a cheerleader at the big game. He sent "Four-Minute Men," a squad of 75,000 volunteers, around the country to give brief pep talks and distribute millions of press releases that described successes on the battlefields and in the factories. Everywhere, posters, pamphlets, and cartoons depicted brave American soldiers and sailors defending freedom and democracy against the "evil Hun."

To help Creel's campaign, the film industry cranked out reels of melodrama about battle-line and home-front heroes and induced audiences to hiss at the German Kaiser as "the Beast of Berlin." Colleges and universities presented war propaganda in the guise of scholarship and added courses depicting the war as a culmination of the age-old struggle for civilization. When Professor James McKeen Cattell of Columbia University in New York urged that America should seek peace with Germany short of victory, university president Nicholas Murray Butler fired him on the grounds that "what had been folly is now treason."

A firestorm of anti-German passion swept the nation. Campaigns with the slogan "100% American" enlisted ordinary people to sniff out disloyalty. German, the most widely taught foreign language in 1914, virtually disappeared from the high school and college curriculum, and anger mounted against German-born Americans, including Karl Muck, conductor of the Boston Symphony Orchestra, and the renowned violinist Fritz Kreisler, who were driven from the concert stage. The rabid attempt to punish the enemy reached its extreme with the lynching of Robert Prager in Collinsville, Illinois. In the atmosphere of mob rule, it was enough that Prager was German-born and had socialist leanings, even though he had not opposed American participation in the war. In accord with the defense lawyer who praised what he called a "patriotic murder," the jury at the trial of the killers took only twenty-five minutes to acquit.

As hysteria increased, absurdity mingled with cruelty. In Montana, a school board barred a history text that had good things to say about medieval Germany. Menus across the nation changed German toast to French toast and sauerkraut to liberty cabbage. One vigilant citizen claimed to see a periscope in the Great Lakes, and on the dunes of

PROPAGANDA POSTER
All the primal fears of rape, invasion, and violence at the hands of a monster wielding the weapon of "KULTUR" are brought together in this 1916 scare poster. Germans so resented the dehumanizing portrait of themselves that in World War II, Nazi propagandists reproduced the poster with the warning that it had really been telling Americans to "destroy the German people."
Library of Congress.

www.bedfordstmartins.com/roarkcompact SEE THE ON-LINE STUDY GUIDE for more help in analyzing this image.

Cape Cod the fiancée of one of the war's leading critics was caught dancing and was held on suspicion of signaling to German submarines.

The Wilson administration's zeal in suppressing dissent contrasted sharply with its war aims of defending democracy. In the name of self-defense,

the Espionage Act (June 1917), the Trading with the Enemy Act (October 1917), and the Sedition Act (May 1918) gave the government sweeping powers to punish any opinion it considered "disloyal, profane, scurrilous, or abusive" of the American flag or uniform. When Postmaster General Albert Burleson blocked mailing privileges for publications he considered disloyal, a number of independent-minded journals were forced to close down, including the leading literary magazine *Seven Arts*. Of the fifteen hundred individuals eventually charged with sedition, all but a dozen had merely spoken words the government found objectionable. One of them was Eugene V. Debs, the leader of the Socialist Party, who was convicted under the Espionage Act for speeches condemning the war as a capitalist plot and was sent to the Atlanta penitentiary.

The president also hoped that national commitment to the war would subdue partisan politics. He could not legitimately repress his Republican rivals, however, and they found many opportunities to use the war as a weapon against the Democrats. The trick was to oppose Wilson's conduct of the war but not the war itself. For example, Republicans outshouted Wilson on the nation's need to mobilize for war but then complained that Wilson's War Industries Board was a tyrannical agency that crushed free enterprise. Such attacks appealed to widely diverse business, labor, and patriotic groups. With each month of the war, Republicans gathered power against the coalition of Democrats and progressives that had narrowly reelected Wilson in 1916.

Wilson erred when he attempted to make the off-year congressional elections of 1918 a referendum on his leadership. Instead, amid criticism of the White House for playing politics with the war, Republicans gained a narrow majority in both the House and the Senate. The end of Democratic control of Congress not only suspended any possibility of further domestic reform but also meant that the United States would advance toward military victory with authority divided between a Democratic presidency and a Republican Congress apt to contest Wilson's plans for international cooperation.

Over There

As the struggle over leadership and war aims unfolded at home, the AEF gathered strength in Europe. At the front, however, the AEF discovered a desperate situation. The three-year-old war had degenerated into a stalemate of armies dug

What Did the War Mean to African Americans?

WHEN THE UNITED STATES ENTERED the First World War, some black leaders remembered the crucial role of African American soldiers in the Civil War. They rejoiced that military service would again offer blacks a chance to prove their worth. Robert Moton, president of the nation's foremost black college, Tuskegee Institute, recollected clearly when that thought had come to him. He was sitting in the midst of "dignified bankers [and] merchants" gathered in the Waldorf-Astoria Hotel in New York City to promote the sale of Liberty Bonds. At that moment of patriotic inclusion, Moton "could not but feel that my people by their contribution, their loyalty, and their spirit . . . realized fully that they are heirs of America, and that as such they must be sharers of her struggles as well as partakers of her glory."

More surprising was the support for the war voiced by W. E. B. Du Bois. Known for his bold dissent against the white power structure, Du Bois shocked many readers with his editorial in the NAACP's journal *Crisis*, urging blacks to "close ranks" and "forget our special grievances" until after a unified nation had won the war. The enemy of the moment, Du Bois insisted, was German "military despotism." Unchecked, that despotism "spells death to the aspirations of Negroes and all darker races for equality, freedom, and democracy."

Although critics bitterly assailed Du Bois for not demanding equal treatment for blacks who fought for their country, African Americans generally followed his advice and closed ranks. On the first day of registration for military service, more than 700,000 black men signed in at their draft boards. By war's end, 370,000 blacks had been inducted, some 31 percent of the total number of blacks registered. The figure for whites was 26 percent.

During training, black recruits suffered the same prejudices that they had encountered in civilian life. Rigidly segregated, they were usually assigned to labor battalions. They faced crude abuse and miserable conditions. One base in Virginia that trained blacks as cargo handlers quartered troops in tents without floors or stoves and provided no changes of clothes, no blankets for the winter—not even facilities for bathing. Only several deaths from disease and exposure moved the authorities to make conditions barely tolerable.

When black soldiers began arriving in Europe, white commanders made a point of maintaining racial distinctions. A special report from the headquarters of the American commander, General John J. Pershing, advised the French that their failure to draw the color line threatened Franco-American relations. They should resist the urge, the report declared, to accept blacks as equals or to thank them for their efforts, for fear of "spoiling the Negroes."

Under such circumstances, German propagandists raised some painful questions. One leaflet distributed by the Germans to black troops reminded them that they lacked the rights that whites enjoyed and that they were segregated and often lynched. "Why, then, fight the Germans," the leaflet asked, "only for the benefit of the Wall Street robbers and to protect the millions they have loaned to the British, French, and Italians?" Why, indeed?

Black soldiers hoped to prove a point. While they worked at first mainly as laborers and stevedores, before long they had their chance to fight. In February 1918, General Pershing received an urgent call from the French for help in the Meuse-Argonne sector. Reluctant to lose command over the white troops he valued the most, he sent black soldiers—the 369th, 370th, 371st, and 372nd Regiments of the 92nd Division—to the front, where they were integrated into units of the French army. In the 191 days spent in battle—longer than the time spent by any other American outfit—the 369th Regiment won the most medals of any American combat unit, more than one hundred Croix de Guerre (crosses given by the French for gallantry in war) alone, and had no prisoners taken. In June 1918, the French high command paid its highest respect by asking the Americans to send all the black troops they could spare.

When the battle-scarred survivors of the 92nd Division returned home, they marched proudly past cheering crowds in Manhattan and Chicago. Black spokesmen proclaimed a new era for black Americans. In May 1919, Du Bois argued that it was time for African Americans to collect what was due them. "We return from fighting," Du Bois declared. "We return fighting. Make way for Democracy. We saved it in France, and by the Great Jehovah, we will save it in the U.S.A., or know the reason why."

Reasons soon presented themselves. Segregation remained entrenched, and its defenders con-

AFRICAN AMERICAN MACHINE GUN COMPANY
This company from the 370th Regiment of the Illinois National Guard, shown early in their training, exemplifies the proud determination of black soldiers to prove their worth in battle. Once in France, the 370th encountered resistance from American commanders reluctant to use combat-ready black troops for anything but hard labor behind the lines. When desperation in the face of a German offensive in the spring of 1918 gave them the chance to fight with French units, the 370th showed its mettle by receiving more medals for valor than any other unit in the American armed forces. Adding to the irony of black soldiers having to gain respect as Americans by serving with the French was the fact that the first black soldier from Lincoln's state of Illinois to fall in battle was a private named Robert E. Lee.
William Gladstone.

tinued to hold power in Congress and in the White House. Postwar recession left blacks worse off economically than before their wartime glory and also made them scapegoats for white resentments. Whites launched race riots against blacks in two dozen cities. The willingness of blacks to stand their ground showed a more determined self-esteem, but it also meant more suffering from escalating violence. Nor did the armed services continue to offer new opportunities. Until the late 1940s, after the next world war, the American military remained not only segregated but also almost devoid of black officers. Discrimination extended even beyond the ultimate sacrifice. When the organizers of a trip to France for parents of soldiers lost in the First World War announced that the boat would be segregated, black mothers felt honor-bound to decline the offer to visit the cemeteries where their sons lay.

It took decades for the nation to recognize the sacrifice and heroism of black soldiers in France. As one critic observed about the 92nd Division, "The example [they set] was so bright that most eyes closed against it." But in 1991, as the nation cheered U.S. success in the Persian Gulf War, Americans began to see the light. A Defense Department investigating team, though insisting it had found no evidence of discrimination in the fact that none of the 127 Medals of Honor awarded during World War I had gone to blacks, declared that the time had come to correct an "administrative oversight." For leading a charge on September 28, 1918, up a German-held hill that cost him and 40 percent of his company their lives, Corporal Freddie Stowers would receive the Medal of Honor—until then the only one attained by an African American in the world wars. The slain soldier's elderly sister, who had survived seventy-three years to accept the award for her hero brother, could take solace that recognition came under the command of General Colin Powell, the first black chairman of the Joint Chiefs of Staff.

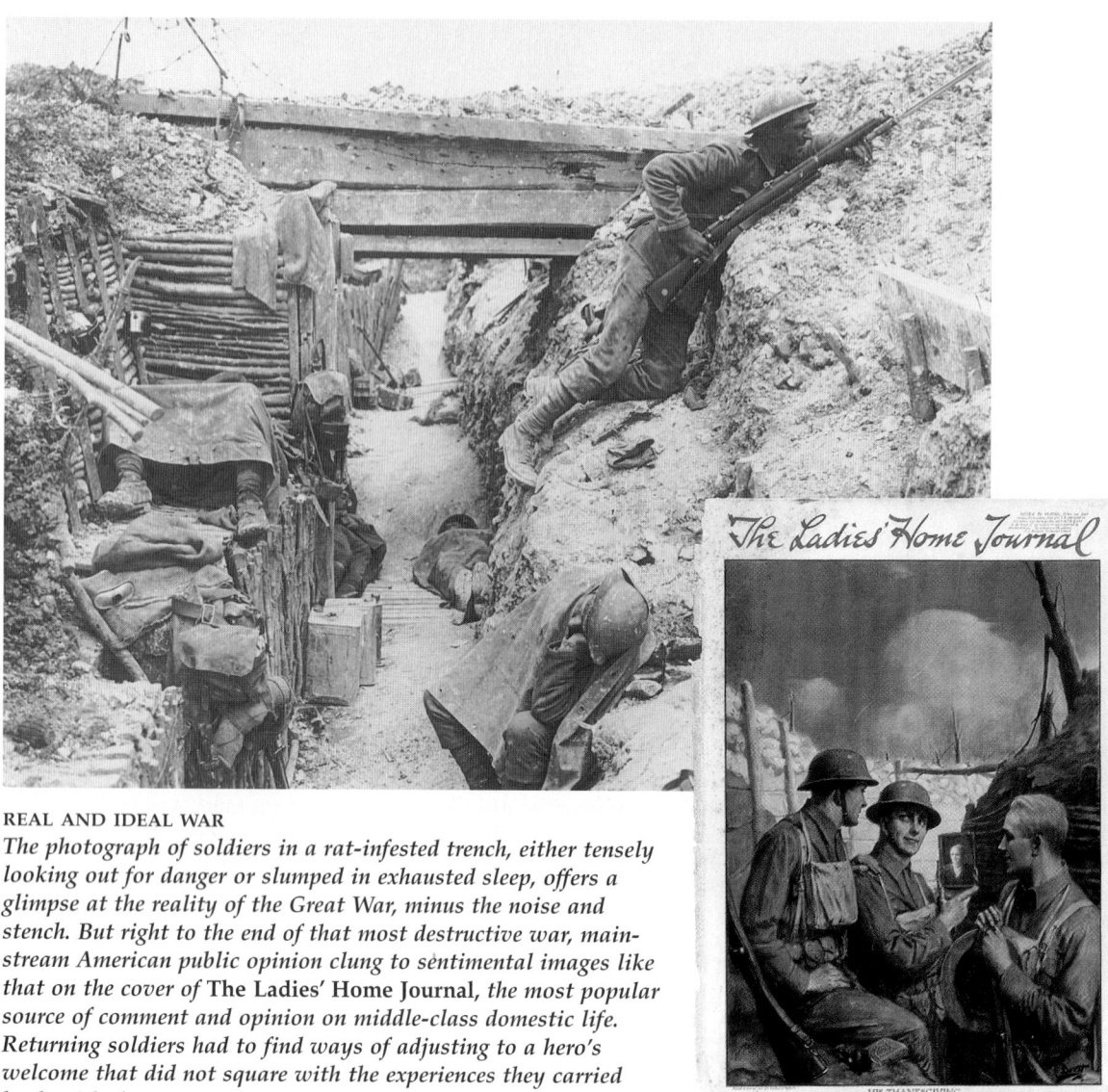

REAL AND IDEAL WAR
The photograph of soldiers in a rat-infested trench, either tensely looking out for danger or slumped in exhausted sleep, offers a glimpse at the reality of the Great War, minus the noise and stench. But right to the end of that most destructive war, mainstream American public opinion clung to sentimental images like that on the cover of **The Ladies' Home Journal,** *the most popular source of comment and opinion on middle-class domestic life. Returning soldiers had to find ways of adjusting to a hero's welcome that did not square with the experiences they carried back with them in memory.*
Imperial War Museum/Picture Research Consultants & Archives.

defensively into miles of trenches across France. Huddling in the mud among the bodies and rats, soldiers were separated from the enemy by only a few hundred yards of "no-man's-land." When ordered "over the top," troops raced desperately toward the enemy's trenches, merely to be entangled in barbed wire, enveloped in poison gas, and mowed down by machine guns. Only with tragic reluctance did commanders realize the impasse of modern warfare. They even resisted the lesson of the Battle of the Somme in 1916. After a futile three-

day assault in which French and British forces lost 600,000 (dead and wounded) and the Germans 500,000, the Allies had advanced their trenches only a few meaningless miles across devastated land.

To General Pershing, the tactics of stalemate violated the lessons that Civil War veterans had taught him at West Point and that he had put in practice in swift, mobile warfare on the American plains and in Cuba. His commitment was to what has been termed the "American way of war"— heavy frontal pressure through weight of numbers combined with swift surprise attacks on the flanks by infantry and cavalry. Pershing thus refused to allow his fresh new army to merge with French and British units in the trenches, despite the protests of the Allied commander in chief, General Ferdinand Foch. Pershing would save his soldiers for the moment when a series of lightning strikes might prove decisive.

In the best army fashion, then, American troops hurried to France, only to wait. They saw almost no combat in 1917, instead using most of their free time to explore places most could otherwise never have hoped to see. True to the crusader image, American officials allowed only uplifting tourism. Paris temptations were off-limits, and when French premier Georges Clemenceau offered to supply American troops with licensed prostitutes, the offer was declined with the half-serious remark that, if Wilson found out, he would stop the war.

Most of the sightseeing ended abruptly in March 1918 when the Germans launched a massive offensive aimed at French ports on the Atlantic. After six thousand cannons let loose the heaviest barrage in history, a million German soldiers smashed a hole forty miles deep into the French and British lines west of the Somme River at a cost of 250,000 casualties on each side. Paris became gripped by the greatest terror of the war when shells fired eighty miles away by "Big Bertha" cannons began falling on the city. More than a thousand civilians died, and a mood of defeatism began to settle in. Pershing, who believed the right moment for his crusaders had come, visited Foch to ask for the "great honor" of becoming "engaged in the greatest battle in history." Foch agreed to Pershing's terms of a separate American command and in May assigned a combined army and marine force to the central sector.

Once committed, the Americans remained true to their way of war. At Cantigny and then at Château-Thierry, the fresh but green Americans checked the German advance with a series of dashing assaults (Map 22.4). Then they headed toward the forest stronghold of Belleau Wood. The American force, with the Fifth and Sixth Marine Regiments in the lead, made its way against streams of refugees and retreating Allied soldiers who cried that the Germans had won: "La guerre est finie!" (The war is over!) But when a French officer commanded the marines to turn and retreat with them, the American commander replied sharply, "Retreat,

hell. We just got here." After charging through a wheat field against withering machine-gun fire, the marines plunged into a hand-to-hand forest battle of stalking and ambush. Victory came hard. On the single day of June 6, 1918, the marine spearhead lost 1,087 men, more than had been killed in the previous 143 years of marine corps history. In praise of the enemy's spirit, a German report noted that "the Americans' nerves are not yet worn out." Indeed, it was German morale that was on the verge of cracking.

In July 1918, the Allies launched a massive counteroffensive that would end the war. A quarter of a million American troops joined in the rout of German forces along the Marne River. In September, more than a million Americans took part in the assault that threw the Germans back from positions along the Meuse River. American forces drove toward the town of Sedan, where the French had lost a war to Germany in 1870 and whose capture was thus of great symbolic importance. In early November, the Allies overran stubborn German resistance around Sedan and sent the survivors trudging northward. Soon after, a revolt against the German government sent Kaiser Wilhelm II fleeing to Holland. On November 11, 1918, a delegation from the newly established German republic met with the French high command in a railroad car in Compiègne to sign an armistice that brought the fighting to an end.

The adventure of the AEF was brief, bloody, and victorious—just the right combination to fix vivid memories of a successful crusade. When Germany resumed unrestricted U-boat warfare in 1917, it had gambled that it could defeat Britain and France before the Americans could raise and train an army and ship it to France. The German military had miscalculated. Of the 2 million American troops in Europe, 1.3 million saw at least some action. By the end 112,000 soldiers of the AEF had perished, their deaths divided equally between wounds and disease. Another 230,000 Americans suffered casualties but survived, many of them with permanent physical and psychological disabilities. Only the Civil War, lasting for a much longer period, had been more costly in American lives. European nations suffered much greater losses, however: 2.2 million Germans, 1.9 million Russians, 1.4 million French, and 900,000 Britons. Where they had fought, the landscape was as blasted and barren as the moon.

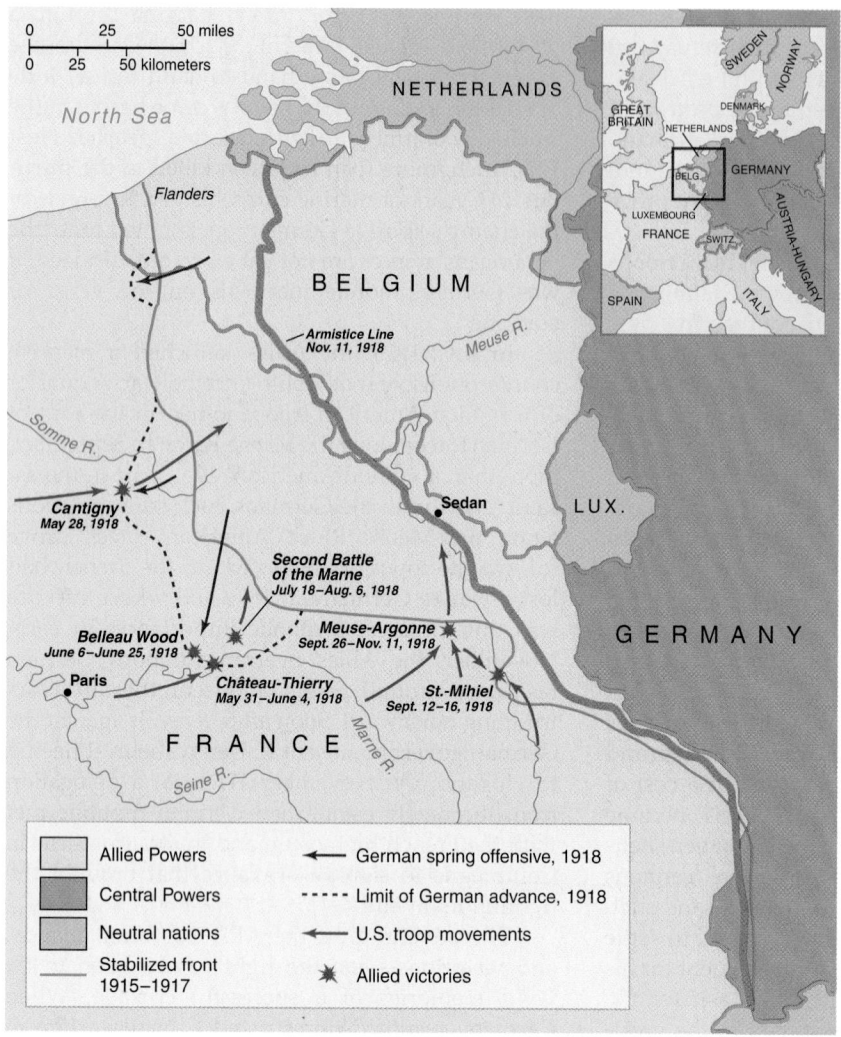

MAP 22.4
The American Expeditionary Force, 1917–1918
In the last year of the war, the AEF joined the French army on the western front to counterattack the final German offensive and pursue the retreating enemy until surrender.

A Compromised Peace

Wilson decided to reaffirm his noble war ideals by announcing his peace aims before the end of hostilities was in sight. He hoped the victorious Allies would rally around his generous ideas but soon discovered that his plan for international democracy did not receive ready acceptance. The leaders of England, France, and Italy understood that Wilson's principles jeopardized their own postwar plans for the acquisition of enemy territory, new colonial empires, and reparations. At home he also faced strong opposition from those who feared that his ardor for international cooperation would undermine American sovereignty.

Wilson's Fourteen Points

On January 8, 1918, ten months before the armistice in Europe, President Wilson delivered a speech to Congress that revealed his vision of a liberal peace. Wilson's famous Fourteen Points provided a blueprint for a new democratic world order. The first five points affirmed basic liberal ideals: "open covenants of peace, openly arrived at," that is, an end to secret treaties; freedom of the seas in war and peace; removal of economic barriers to free trade; reduction of weapons of war; and recognition of the rights of colonized peoples. The next eight points supported the right to self-determination of European peoples who had been dominated by Germany or its allies. Wilson's final point called for a "general association of nations"—a League of Nations—to provide "mutual guarantees of political independence and territorial integrity to great and small states alike." The insistence on a League of Nations reflected Wilson's lifelong dream of a "parliament of man." Only such an organization, he believed, could justify the war and secure peace. Wilson concluded his speech by pledging that the United States would welcome Germany into the family of "peace-loving nations," if it would renounce its militarism and imperialism.

The Fourteen Points roused popular enthusiasm in the United States and every Allied country. Armed with such public support, Wilson felt confident that he could prevail against undemocratic forces at the peace table. During the final year of the war, he pressured the Allies to accept the Fourteen Points as the basis of the settlement. But he also conveyed his willingness, if necessary, to speak over the heads of government leaders directly to the people and so expand his role as spokesman for American citizens to the grand role of champion of all the world's people. The Allies had won the war; Wilson would win the peace.

The Paris Peace Conference

Buoyed by his sense of mission, Wilson decided to attend the Paris peace conference in 1919 as head of the American delegation. The decision to leave the country at a time when his opponents were sharply contesting his leadership was risky enough, but his stubborn refusal to include prominent Republicans in the delegation proved foolhardy.

The peace venture began well. As Wilson's motorcade made its way from the port of Le Havre to Paris, huge crowds cheered the American president. After four terrible years of war, Europeans looked upon Wilson as someone who would create a safer, more decent world. However, when the peace conference convened at the magnificent palace Louis XIV had built at Versailles in the seventeenth century, Wilson encountered a very different reception. Representing the Allies were the decidedly unidealistic David Lloyd George of Britain, Georges Clemenceau of France, and Vittorio Orlando of Italy. To them, Wilson was a naive and impractical moralist whose desire to reconcile former foes within a new international democratic order showed that he understood little about hard European realities. The Allies wanted to fasten blame for the war on Germany, totally disarm it, and make it pay so

LEADERS OF THE PARIS PEACE CONFERENCE
The three leaders in charge of putting the world back together after the Great War—from left to right, David Lloyd George, prime minister of Great Britain; Georges Clemenceau, premier of France; and U.S. president Woodrow Wilson—show a confident stride in approaching the peace conference in the palace of Versailles. Clemenceau is caught here displaying his frequent inclination to offer animated instruction to Wilson, whom he considered naively idealistic. Indeed, in an unguarded moment, Clemenceau expressed his contempt for the entire United States as a country that was unique in having passed directly from barbarism to decadence without an intervening period of civilization. Walking silently alongside, Lloyd George maintains the poker face that helped keep his views carefully guarded throughout the conference.
Getty Images.

dearly that it would never threaten its neighbors again. The French, in particular, demanded retribution in the form of territory containing some of Germany's richest mineral resources.

Wilson was forced to make drastic compromises. In return for French moderation of territorial claims, Wilson agreed to support Article 231 of the peace treaty, assigning war guilt to Germany. Though saved from permanently losing Rhineland territory to the French, Germany was outraged at being singled out as the instigator of the war and saddled with more than $33 billion in damages. Many Germans felt that their nation had been stabbed in the back. After agreeing to an armistice on the belief that peace terms would be based on Wilson's generous Fourteen Points, they faced hardship and humiliation instead.

Wilson had better success in establishing the principle of self-determination. On that basis the conference redrew the map of Europe. Portions of the Austro-Hungarian Empire were ceded to Italy, Poland, and Romania, and the remainder was reassembled into Austria, Hungary, Czechoslovakia, and Yugoslavia—independent republics with boundaries determined according to concentrations of ethnic groups. More arbitrarily, the Ottoman Empire was carved up into small mandates (including Palestine) under the control of France and Great Britain, partly to satisfy Allied ambitions for influence in the Middle East and partly in accord with historical patterns of local sovereignty. Thus, with varying degrees of danger from ethnic and nationalist rivalries, each reconstructed nation faced the challenge of try-

ing to make a new democratic government work (Map 22.5).

Wilson hoped that self-determination would also be the fate of Germany's colonies in Asia and Africa. But the Allies would go no further than allowing the League of Nations they had created a mandate to administer them. Technically, the mandate system rejected imperialism. Yet it also denied self-determination to the former German colonies, even as the Allies retained their own colonial empires.

The cause of democratic equality suffered another setback when the peace conference refused to endorse Japan's proposal for a clause proclaiming the principle of racial equality. Wilson's belief in the superiority of whites, as well as his apprehension about how Americans would respond to such a declaration, led him to oppose the clause. To soothe hurt feelings, Wilson agreed to grant Japan a mandate over the Shantung Peninsula in northern China, which had formerly been controlled by Germany. The gesture mollified Japan's moderate leaders, but the military faction getting ready to take over the country used bitterness toward racist West-

MAP 22.5

Europe after World War I
The post–World War I settlement redrew boundaries to create new nations based on ethnic groupings. This left bitter peoples within defeated Germany and Russia who resolved to recover territory that the new arrangements took from their homelands.

ern colonialism to build support for expanding Japanese power throughout Asia.

Revolutionary upheaval also affected the dream of making the world safe for democracy. Most important was the revolution in Russia in March 1917, after terrible defeats in the war forced Czar Nicholas II to abdicate. Wilson, who was just then leading his country into war, greeted the Russian Revolution as confirmation that democracy would rise from the ashes of war's destruction. In reckless enthusiasm, he declared that Russia had always been "democratic at heart." A very different reality soon emerged, however. Marxist radicals calling themselves Bolsheviks seized control of the nation in November 1917 and made their leader, Vladimir Ilyich Lenin, ruler of the revolutionary state that came to be known as the Soviet Union. On December 15, 1917, Lenin concluded a separate peace with Germany. To make matters worse for Wilsonian idealists, Lenin insisted that the war was being fought not for democracy but to extend capitalist power. Outraged by what he considered the Bolsheviks' betrayal of the Russian Revolution and the war for democracy, Wilson reacted as he had to the Mexican revolution by refusing to recognize the new Russian government.

Respect for self-determination kept Wilson from agreeing with British leader Winston Churchill that "the Bolshevik infant should be strangled in its cradle" by direct military action. Nonetheless, in September 1918 the president did send fourteen thousand troops to Siberia to join British and French forces assisting a Russian army loyal to the czar that fought a losing battle to overthrow Lenin and annul the Bolshevik Revolution. American opinion divided significantly. A few observers believed that the war had created possibilities for suffering millions to overthrow the tyrants who had oppressed them. Most Americans, however, saw the outcome as evidence that the cause of democracy had fallen short and left the world full of radical menace.

To many Europeans and Americans whose hopes had been stirred by Wilson's lofty aims, the Versailles treaty came as a bitter disappointment. Wilson's admirers were shocked that the president dealt in compromise, like any other politician. But without Wilson's presence, the treaty that was signed on June 28, 1919, surely would have been more vindictive. Wilson returned home in July 1919 consoled that, despite his many frustrations, he had gained what he most wanted—creation of the League of Nations. His hopes rested on the belief

that the league could remedy the imperfections born of compromise and steer the world on a peaceful course.

The Fight for the Treaty

The tumultuous reception Wilson received when he arrived home persuaded him, probably correctly, that the American people supported the treaty. On July 10, 1919, the president submitted the treaty to the Senate, warning that failure to ratify it would "break the heart of the world." By then, news of the treaty's provisions had spread, and criticism was mounting, especially from Americans concerned that their countries of ethnic origin had not been given fair treatment. Even Wilson's supporters worried that the president's concessions at Versailles had jeopardized the treaty's capacity to provide a generous plan for rebuilding Europe and to guarantee the peace.

Some of the most potent critics were found in the Senate. Bolstered by a slight Republican majority in Congress, a group of Republican "irreconcilables," which included such powerful isolationist senators as Hiram Johnson of California and William Borah of Idaho, condemned the treaty for entangling the United States in world affairs. A larger group of Republicans did not object to U.S. participation in world politics but feared that membership in the League of Nations would jeopardize the nation's independence. No Republican, in any case, was eager to hand Wilson and the Democrats a foreign policy victory with the 1920 presidential election little more than a year away.

At the center of Republican opposition was Wilson's archenemy, Senator Henry Cabot Lodge of Massachusetts. Before Wilson had entered politics, Lodge, with his Ph.D. and historical publications, had become known as "the Scholar of the Senate." It rankled Lodge to be eclipsed by a rival of greater intellectual eminence who had also risen above him politically to become president. That injured pride tended to inflame Lodge's opposition to Wilson's Democratic reforms and to deepen Lodge's resentment at being left off the peace delegation. Lodge was no isolationist, however. Like his friend Theodore Roosevelt, who had died in January 1919, Lodge expected the United States' economic might and strong army and navy to propel the nation into a major role in world affairs. But Lodge insisted that membership in the League of Nations, which would require collective action to maintain peace,

The year 1919 witnessed nearly 3,600 strikes involving 4 million workers.

The most spectacular strike occurred in February 1919 in Seattle, where large numbers of metalworkers and shipbuilders had been put out of work by demobilization. When a coalition of the radical Industrial Workers of the World (IWW) and the moderate American Federation of Labor (AFL) called a general strike, the largest work stoppage in American history shut down the city for several days. Nationwide, elected officials and newspaper editorials echoed claims in the *Seattle Times* that the walkout was "a Bolshevik effort to start a revolution" engineered by "Seattle labor criminals." An effort to deport strike leaders failed because they were citizens, not aliens, but the suppression of the strike by Seattle's anti-union mayor, Ole Hanson, and widespread alarm about radicalism cost the AFL much of the support it had gained through the war and contributed to the destruction of the IWW soon afterward.

A strike by Boston policemen in the fall of 1919 brought out postwar hostility toward labor militancy in the public sector. Though they were paid less than pick-and-shovel laborers and had received no raise since before the war, the police won little public sympathy. Once the officers stopped walking their beats, looters sacked the city. After two days of near anarchy, only slightly tamed by a volunteer police force of Harvard students and recently discharged soldiers, Massachusetts governor Calvin Coolidge called in the National Guard to restore order. The public, yearning for peace and security in the wake of war, welcomed Coolidge's anti-union assurance that "there is no right to strike against the public safety by anybody, anywhere, any time."

Labor strife climaxed in the grim steel strike of 1919. Steelworkers had serious grievances, but for decades the industry had succeeded in beating back all their efforts to unionize. In 1919, however, the AFL, still led by its founding father, Samuel Gompers, decided it was time to try again in the face of the industry's plan to revert to seven-day weeks, twelve-hour days, and weekly wages of about $20. Having loyally backed the government's war effort, the AFL expected federal support for unionization. When Gompers began to recruit union members, however, he learned that he faced the steel barons alone. Following the refusal of U.S. Steel and Bethlehem Steel to negotiate, Gompers called for a strike; 350,000 workers in fifteen states walked out in September 1919.

The steel industry hired 30,000 strikebreakers (many of them African Americans) and turned public opinion against the strikers by portraying them as radicals bent on subverting the Republic. State and federal troops blocked union members from getting close enough to the steel mills to discourage scabs from crossing their picket line. In January 1920, after 18 workers had been killed, the strike collapsed. That devastating defeat initiated a sharp decline in the fortunes of the labor movement, a trend that would continue for almost twenty years.

The Red Scare

Suppression of labor strikes was one manifestation of a general fear of internal subversion that swept the nation in 1919. The "Red scare" of that time, which far outstripped the assault on civil liberties during the war, had homegrown causes in the postwar recession, labor unrest, and the difficulties of reintegrating millions of returning veterans. But unsettling events abroad also added to Americans' anxieties. Russian bolshevism became even more menacing in March 1919 when the new Soviet leaders created a worldwide association of Communist leaders it called the Third International in order to foment revolution in capitalist countries. The chance of a Communist revolution in the United States was zero, but a flurry of isolated terrorist acts in 1919, most notably thirty-eight bombs mailed to prominent Americans, made it seem to edgy Americans that revolutionaries were at the door. Although the post office intercepted all but one of the bombs, fear, anger, and uncertainty about the motives of terrorists led swiftly to a hunt for scapegoats. On the grounds that "there could be no nice distinctions drawn between the theoretical ideals of the radicals and their actual violations of our national laws," Attorney General A. Mitchell Palmer led an assault on alleged conspirators. Targeting men and women who harbored what Palmer considered ideas that could lead to violence, even though they may not have done anything illegal, the Justice Department sought to purge the supposed enemies of America.

In January 1920, Palmer ordered a series of raids that netted six thousand alleged subversives. Though the plans for revolution he expected to find did not turn up, and the three pistols he confiscated did not amount to a revolutionary armory, Palmer nevertheless ordered five hundred non-citizen suspects deported. His action came in the midst of a campaign against the most notorious radical alien, Russian-born Emma Goldman. Before the war, Goldman's passionate support of labor strikes, women's rights, and birth control had made her a leading symbol of outspoken disrespect for mainstream opinion. Finally, after a stay in prison for attacking military conscription, she was ordered deported by the fervent young director of the Radical Division of the Justice Department, J. Edgar Hoover. In December 1919, as Goldman and 250 others boarded a ship for exile in the Soviet Union, the defiant rebel turned on the gangplank to thumb her nose at a jeering crowd and disappeared onto the deck. Anticipating timid conformity in the next decade, one observer remarked, "With Prohibition coming in and Emma Goldman goin' out, 'twill be a dull country."

The effort to rid the country of alien radicals was matched by efforts to crush troublesome citizens. On Armistice Day, November 11, 1919, events reached their grimmest in Centralia, Washington, a rugged lumber town home to one of only two IWW halls left in the state. Intimidated by a menacing crowd gathered in front of the hall, nervous IWW members opened fire, killing three people. Three IWW members were arrested and later convicted of murder, but another, an ex-soldier, was carried off by a mob who castrated him and then, after hanging him from a bridge, riddled his body with bullets. His death was officially ruled a suicide. With that style of vigilante patriotism on the rise, combinations of law enforcement officials and private citizens in several cities and towns staged raids to rid themselves of so-called Reds.

Public institutions joined the attack on civil liberties. Local libraries removed dissenting books. Schools and colleges fired unorthodox teachers. Police shut down radical newspapers. State legislatures refused to seat elected representatives who professed socialist ideas, and in 1919, Congress removed its lone socialist representative, Victor Berger, on the grounds that he was a threat to national safety. That same year, the Supreme Court provided a formula for restricting free speech. In upholding the conviction of socialist Charles Schenck for publishing a pamphlet urging resistance to the draft during wartime (*Schenck v. United States*), Justice Oliver Wendell Holmes, writing for the Court, established a "clear and present danger" test. Such utterances as Schenck's during a time of national peril, Holmes wrote, were equivalent to shouting "Fire!" in a crowded theater. But the anal-

RED SCARE IMAGES
The bearded anarchist, sour radical, and alien draft dodger make up the usual cartoon cast of "reds" whom zealous patriots sought to drive out of American life. The aura of "American Legion" hanging over the city indicates the central role played by that veterans' organization in purging those who had opposed U.S. participation in the war and who in the Legion view posed a threat to basic American institutions. Comment from a dog about the radicals going away for their health wryly makes the point that American Legionnaires had shown a willingness to use violence against those they targeted.
Granger Collection.

ogy was false. Schenck's pamphlet echoed faintly in the open air, not in a crowded theater, and had little power to provoke a public firmly opposed to its message.

In time, the Red scare lost credibility. The lack of any real radical menace became clear after newspaper headlines carried Attorney General Palmer's warning that radicals were planning to celebrate the Bolshevik Revolution with a nationwide wave of violence on May 1, 1920. Officials responded by calling out state militia, fortifying public buildings and churches, mobilizing bomb squads, even putting machine-gun nests at major city intersections. When

May 1 came and went without a single disturbance, the public mood turned from fear to scorn, and Palmer, who had taken to calling himself the "Fighting Quaker," was jeered as the "Quaking Fighter."

Conclusion: Troubled Crusade

At home and abroad, the First World War was a traumatic experience that divided the American people. When Woodrow Wilson sought to keep the nation out of the conflict, he alienated those, like Theodore Roosevelt, who thought the United States should intervene to save the democratic Allies from the autocratic German aggressors. But when the country entered the war in 1917, those who had worked for the cause of peace and reform were conflicted. Most progressives and the major peace societies, like the Carnegie Endowment for International Peace, supported the war as a crusade that would insure lasting peace and so, in Wilson's words, "make the world safe for democracy." A critical minority, however, including pacifists who followed the lead of Jane Addams, socialists, and independent critics condemned America's entry as a futile effort to use war for peace and a sacrifice of youth and the working class on the battlefield for the personal glory and enrichment of the more privileged.

Though serving under idealistic banners, American soldiers and sailors encountered unprecedented horrors—submarines, poison gas, machine guns—and more than 100,000 died. Rather than redeeming their sacrifice, the peace that followed the armistice tarnished it. Few found consolation in the fact that the war thrust the nation into a position of international preeminence. At home, war brought prosperity, but rather than permanently improving working conditions, advancing public health, and spreading educational opportunity, the war threatened to undermine the progressive achievements of the previous two decades.

In 1920, a bruised and disillusioned society stumbled into a new decade. The era coming to an end had called on Americans to crusade and sacrifice. Now whoever could promise them peace, prosperity, and a good time would have the best chance to win their hearts.

FOR FURTHER READING ABOUT THE TOPICS IN THIS CHAPTER, see the Online Bibliography at
www.bedfordstmartins.com/roarkcompact.

FOR ADDITIONAL FIRST-HAND ACCOUNTS OF THIS PERIOD, see pages 108–128 in Michael Johnson, ed., *Reading the American Past,* Second Edition, Volume II.

TO ASSESS YOUR MASTERY OF THE MATERIAL IN THIS CHAPTER, see the Online Study Guide at
www.bedfordstmartins.com/roarkcompact.

CHRONOLOGY

1914 **April.** Attempting to impose democracy on Mexico, President Woodrow Wilson sends marines to occupy the port of Veracruz.

June 28. Archduke Franz Ferdinand of Austria assassinated in Bosnian city of Sarajevo, starting chain of events leading to World War I.

July 28. Austria declares war on Bosnia.

August 6. All-out conflict erupts when Germany declares war on

Russia and France. In response, Great Britain declares war on Russia.

1915 German submarine sinks British liner *Lusitania*, with loss of 1,198 lives, including 128 Americans.

Settlement house reformer Jane Addams helps form Women's Peace Party to seek peaceful resolution of war.

1916 General John J. Pershing leads military expedition into Mexico in pursuit of rebel leader Francisco "Pancho" Villa.

Wilson wins reelection by narrow margin.

1917 Intercepted telegram from German foreign secretary, Arthur Zimmermann, promising aid to Mexico for war against the United States prompts Wilson to ask Congress to approve "armed neutrality" policy.

April 6. Submarine attacks on American vessels convince Wilson to ask Congress for declaration of war on Germany.

Wilson creates Committee on Public Information to promote U.S. war aims.

Selective Service Act authorizes military draft that brings 2.8 million men into armed services; in addition, 2 million volunteer.

Espionage Act passed, first of three laws limiting First Amendment rights.

Resentment against blacks migrating northward in search of work ignites violent race riot in East St. Louis, Illinois.

August. Armed action by black soldiers against racial discrimination in Houston results in execution of thirteen of the soldiers and life sentences for forty-one more.

Bolshevik Revolution ends Russian participation in war when country arranges separate peace with Germany.

1918 **January 8.** President Wilson gives Fourteen Points speech, outlining his plan for peace.

May–June. American marines succeed in their first major combat with Germans at Cantigny and Château-Thierry.

September. American forces deployed to support Russian efforts to undo Bolshevik Revolution.

November 11. Armistice signed ending World War I.

1919 **January 18.** Paris peace conference begins, with President Wilson as head of U.S. delegation.

June 28. Versailles peace treaty signed.

September. Wilson undertakes speaking tour to rally support for ratification of Versailles treaty and League of Nations; ill health in Colorado ends the tour.

Postwar recession and end of wartime support for labor unions lead to wave of strikes.

1919–1920 Attorney General A. Mitchell Palmer leads effort, known as Red scare, to rid country of anarchists and aliens.

1920 **January 1.** Prohibition begins, following ratification of Eighteenth Amendment.

Steel strike ends without settlement, dealing organized labor its greatest blow.

Senate votes against ratification of Versailles peace treaty.

August 18. Nineteenth Amendment ratified, granting women the vote.

BOXING IN STYLE

*In the 1920s boxing enjoyed such acclaim that
lyrical sportswriter A. J. Liebling called it the
"sweet science." To capitalize on that golden era's
climactic rematch on September 27, 1927, between
heavyweight champion Gene Tunney and former
champion Jack Dempsey, the stylish New York
City department store Peck & Peck produced
this tie. Fighters and ties were not often associated, but in this case "Gentleman Gene" Tunney
had displayed a certain cultivated taste and
even made a news splash when he went to Yale
to read Shakespeare with the students. By
contrast, his opponent, Jack Dempsey, was a
brawler from the wrong side of the tracks.
The class and character contrast between
champion and challenger broadened the appeal
of the fight; but one cannot be sure how many up-
scale purchasers of this tie were glad when Gentleman Gene managed to beat the Manassa Mauler on a
disputed referee's call.*

Allentown Art Museum, Gift of Kate Fowler Merle-Smith, 1978.

FROM NEW ERA TO GREAT DEPRESSION

23

1920–1932

O N CHRISTMAS MORNING IN 1922, Federal Prisoner #9653 began his last day at the Atlanta penitentiary. The frail old man glanced at the crucifix on his cell wall as he changed into the cheap new suit the guard had brought. For Eugene Victor Debs, the leader and five-time presidential candidate of the Socialist Party, three long years in prison for opposition to World War I had come to an end when President Warren Harding granted him the pardon Woodrow Wilson had bitterly refused.

As he neared the main prison gate, Debs remembered, he heard behind him "what seemed a rumbling of the earth as if shaken by some violent explosion." Against every rule, the warden had allowed all twenty-three hundred inmates out of their cells to cheer the departure of the friend who had an uncanny hold on the hopes and feelings of downtrodden people. Many years later his cell mate, Sam Moore, cherished the recollection: "As miserable as I was I would defy fate with all its cruelty as long as Debs held my hand, and I was the most miserably happiest man on earth when I knew he was going home Christmas."

Debs's first stop was the White House, where his benefactor, President Harding, had invited him for a visit. The genial Harding bounded from behind his desk to shake Debs's hand, exclaiming, "Well, I have heard so damned much about you, Mr. Debs, that I am now very glad to meet you personally."

Then it was home to Terre Haute, Indiana, where a crowd estimated at twenty-five thousand lifted the old warrior from the train into the same horse-drawn wagon that had carried him back from his first imprisonment in 1895 for defying a federal injunction during the Pullman strike. When the parade arrived at the family home near the railroad tracks, Debs gave an impromptu speech from the porch, urging his cheering supporters to view his release as a step toward the ultimate victory of socialism and the working class.

It was a touching moment, but Debs's show of the old revolutionary fire would not be able to ignite a society very different from the one he envisioned. His Socialist Party had entered a drastic decline. Its membership down to 120,000 and nearly broke, the party would soon have to sell its headquarters in Chicago and move into an attic. There were few left to foresee the day when the working class would again yearn for a champion to rescue them from desperate hardship.

The New Era

Once Woodrow Wilson's leadership ended, the energy generated by the war flowed away from civic unity and toward private economic enterprise and personal creativity. In the midst of a freewheeling economy and a heightened sense of individual liberty, Secretary of Commerce Herbert Hoover was cheered for his announcement that America had entered a "New Era" of prosperity.

This declaration of newness on behalf of a revival of old free enterprise individualism was one of several factors that made the 1920s a time of contradiction and ambivalence. Stress between tradition and modern conditions was most often at issue. For the first time, according to the census of 1920, more Americans lived in urban than in rural areas, yet nostalgia idealized the farm and the small town. Although the nation prospered as a whole, the new wealth widened the gap between rich and poor. While millions admired the sophisticated new style, others condemned postwar society for its vulgar materialism. And the greatest outpouring of creative talent in the nation's history led to the irony of artists condemning the United States for being aesthetically barren.

The ambivalence of the 1920s finds expression in the competing myths and labels attached to the age. Some terms focus on the era's high-spirited energy: Roaring Twenties, Jazz Age, Flaming Youth, Age of the Flapper. Others echo the rising importance of money—Dollar Decade, Golden Twenties, Prosperity Decade—or reflect the sinister side of gangster profiteering—Lawless Decade. Still other references emphasize the lonely confusion of a Lost Generation. At the center of it all, President Calvin Coolidge spoke in praise of those in power when he declared, "The business of America is business." For the fortunes of the era rose, and then crashed, according to the values and ideology of the business community.

Postwar Politics and the Election of 1920

The economic chaos that accompanied the return to a peacetime economy made Americans yearn for security rather than for more progressive adventures. During the winter of 1920–21, the national unemployment rate hit 20 percent, the highest ever suffered up to that time. Farmers fared the worst, as their income fell and the bankruptcy rate increased tenfold.

Bedridden and paralyzed, President Wilson turned stubbornly from domestic troubles and insisted that the 1920 election would be a "solemn referendum" on the League of Nations. Dutifully, the Democratic nominees for president, James M. Cox, three-time governor of Ohio, and for vice president, the New York aristocrat Franklin Delano Roosevelt, campaigned on Wilson's international ideals.

The Republican Party chose a very different sort of candidate, handsome, gregarious Warren Gamaliel Harding, senator from Ohio. Unlike the strivers of his generation who left the countryside to make their fortunes in the city, Harding stayed home in Marion and became editor of the town newspaper. His subsequent rise in party politics was a tribute to his amiable ability to connect with grassroots sentiment rather than to any political commitment. Wanting to succeed in an atmosphere of goodwill, he developed an ability to land on the winning side of an argument without having to grapple with complex or controversial isues. On the two most heated domestic issues of the day— woman suffrage and prohibition—Harding showed little knowledge or conviction, but eventually he voted for them in a nod to public opinion.

Harding spun the winning formula in one of his campaign speeches by declaring that "America's present need is not heroics, but healing; not nostrums [questionable remedies] but normalcy." But what was "normalcy"? Harding explained: "By 'normalcy' I don't mean the old order but a regular steady order of things. I mean normal procedure, the natural way, without excess." The urbane *New York Times* understood the word's appeal, observing, "Mr. Harding is not writing for the super-fine weighers of verbs and adjectives but for the men and women who see in his expressions their own ideas."

Eager to put labor strife and the Red scare behind them, the voters responded by giving Harding the largest presidential victory ever: 60.5 percent of the popular vote and 76 percent of the electoral vote (Map 23.1). On his coattails rode Republican majorities in both houses of Congress. Once in the White House the Hardings threw open the gates, which had been closed since the declaration of war in 1917. Their welcome to throngs of visitors lifted the national pall and signified a new era of easygoing good cheer.

In accord with his promise to have a government run by the best minds, Harding chose some men of stature for his cabinet. Charles Evans

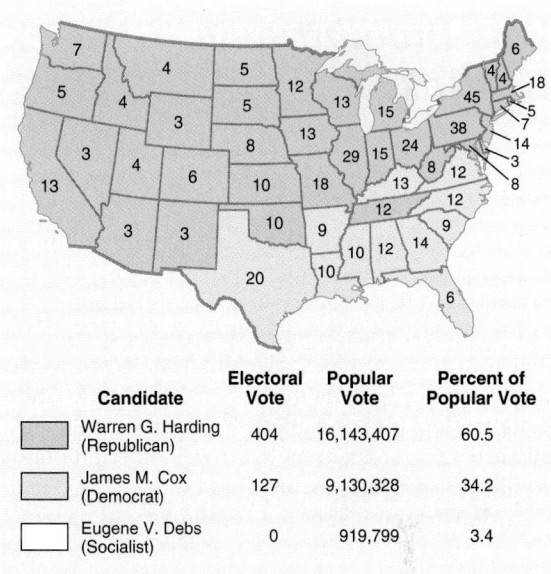

Candidate	Electoral Vote	Popular Vote	Percent of Popular Vote
Warren G. Harding (Republican)	404	16,143,407	60.5
James M. Cox (Democrat)	127	9,130,328	34.2
Eugene V. Debs (Socialist)	0	919,799	3.4

M A P   2 3 . 1
The Election of 1920

Hughes, former associate justice of the Supreme Court and Republican presidential candidate in 1916, became secretary of state; Herbert Hoover, the self-made millionaire and former head of the wartime Food Administration, was tapped for secretary of commerce; and the leading champion of scientific agriculture, Henry C. Wallace, took over as secretary of agriculture. But wealth also counted. Harding answered the call of conservatives to name Andrew Mellon, one of the richest men in America, secretary of the treasury. And then there was friendship. Loyally, Harding handed out jobs to acquaintances even though some of their qualifications were suspect. This curious combination of merit and cronyism made for a disjointed administration in which a few "best minds" debated national needs, while much lesser men looked for ways to advance their own interests.

Prohibition and Woman Suffrage

The appeal of normalcy showed in the public reaction to the last two great progressive achievements passed prior to Harding's inauguration: prohibition and woman suffrage. The Eighteenth Amendment, banning the sale of alcohol, succeeded in lowering its consumption but also suffered widespread disregard. (See "Historical Question," page 578.) The

Was Prohibition a Bad Joke?

GETTING HIGH HAS ALWAYS BEEN a part of human experience, so much so that the cultural psychologist R. K. Siegel has called intoxication "the fourth drive," after hunger, thirst, and sex. Fuel for that fourth drive has varied luxuriantly, from the caapi powder Indians in the Amazon jungle traditionally blew into one another's noses to the magic mushrooms a shaman on the frozen Siberian plains would eat so that he could pass on their essence in his urine for the rest of the community to drink.

In America, the intoxicant of choice has always been alcohol. Abundantly so. By the 1830s, the average adult was consuming a yearly total of fourteen gallons of hard liquor, mostly whiskey and rum. Alarm over what one historian has called the "alcoholic republic" soon produced two unique developments. First, the United States became the world's only society ever to outlaw its customary intoxicant. Second, to accomplish that feat, Americans passed the only constitutional amendment to be subsequently repealed.

Temperance campaigns in the nineteenth century anticipated the fate of the prohibition amendment in the twentieth century. Within an aura of general enthusiasm for reform, abstention from drink became respectable, even urgent, and by 1845 annual per capita consumption dropped to 1.8 gallons, the lowest level to that time. Yet even such sobering success could not contain the classic American insistence on free choice. Within a decade, many states repealed their laws against drinking and consumption began to climb, though not to the oceanic levels of the years before temperance consciousness-raising.

Prohibitionists rallied again at the end of the century in opposition to the thousands of saloons that were springing up alongside factories and immigrant quarters. Prominent dry champion Reverend Mark Matthews conveyed the moral intensity of the cause when he asserted that the saloon was "the most fiendish, corrupt and hell-soaked institution that ever crawled out of the slime of the eternal pit." To back up such extreme claims, the Anti-Saloon League (ASL) produced statistics and scientific studies of drunkenness, vividly touched up with horror stories of its destructive results. An irresistible coalition followed. Because saloons were mostly male preserves—awash with gambling and prostitution as well as beer—they tended to rouse strong resistance from advocates for women and children, who suffered most of the saloon's bad side effects. Out of their common concerns, women's rights activists and the ASL joined forces to battle for the prohibition amendment. Mobilization for

THE SALOON AND ITS CHILDREN
Here in 1910, in the Polish district of Chicago's South Side, children play in the dirt street in front of a saloon. This scene must have been quite typical, for the crowded city of Chicago had many saloons at the turn of the century but almost no playgrounds. Both children's advocates and supporters of the rising prohibition movement noticed the contrast and forged an alliance that helped empower Progressive campaigns for children's welfare and drive the prohibition amendment to victory.
Chicago Historical Society.

PROHIBITION ACTION
Prohibition agents sometimes liked to make sport of their work before appreciative audiences. The wastefulness of pouring nine hundred gallons of perfectly good wine down a drain in Los Angeles amuses some spectators and troubles others. Of course, those who had an interest in drinking despite the law could witness the disposal of bootleg wine and liquor serenely confident that more could easily be found.
Corbis.

World War I added a further boost in the army's insistence on soldiers remaining pure in spirit and free of drink. Hitching the profit motive to patriotism, many industrialists, including John D. Rockefeller and Henry Ford, took the advice of their efficiency experts that alcohol was the enemy of a productive workplace and thus of a successful war effort. With such broad support, the amendment was easily ratified in 1919.

Prohibition had a measure of success. F. Scott Fitzgerald famously misled his readers when he described the depression as a kind of hangover from the Jazz Age. In fact, at the start of the Jazz Age saloons disappeared from American street corners, and Americans emerged from prohibition drinking less than ever. The annual per capita consumption of alcoholic beverages declined from 2.60 gallons per capita just before prohibition to 0.97 gallons in 1934, the year after prohibition ended. Down as well were arrests for drunken disorder, along with alcohol-related deaths and psychoses.

Nonetheless, the "noble experiment," as Herbert Hoover called prohibition, was discredited. To skeptical critics, prohibition was a ridiculous violation of human nature by puritanical busybodies. H. L. Mencken, the leading journalistic cynic of the time and a devotee of German beer halls in his native Baltimore, made the most savage cut against the ideal of a sober republic. Given the depth of human depravity, he jeered, society would be safer if the people in it were drunk all the time.

An avalanche of other objections joined derision and rebelliousness in overthrowing prohibition. As gangsters moved into bootlegging and bodies began to pile up, the public became convinced that prohibition was more about crime than redemption. Believers in individual and states' rights joined the clamor by opposing the federal government's attempt to control private behavior; and even stalwart "drys" were inclined to think that prohibition was not such a noble experiment once it was taken up by the Ku Klux Klan as a justification for a brutal campaign against minorities. At the head of the parade to repeal the Eighteenth Amendment marched a group of practical businessmen. Although business leaders had originally supported prohibition as an aid to productivity, most concluded by 1930 that banning alcohol was more apt to produce an unruly lower class, angry over losing their saloons, than a dry and docile workforce.

The repeal of prohibition in 1933 set off a rush of profit seekers, including gangsters who converted their bootlegging empires into legitimate businesses. A heavy advertising campaign, along with story lines on radio and in the movies, promoted drinking and smoking as signs of sophistication and success. Making the old vices respectable and glamorous reversed the decline in drinking; by the 1970s, Americans had reached the pre-prohibition levels of consumption. By 1996, 52 percent of the population, or 111 million persons, used alcohol; of these, 32 million were part of the new binge-drinking trend and about 11 million were alcoholics. A quarter of the alcoholics followed another new trend by also abusing drugs. In the deranged mayhem that followed, over 100,000 people were killed in *(Continued)* alcohol- and drug-related incidents each year during the 1990s, mostly in traffic accidents.

Alarm over substance abuse in the latter part of the twentieth century led to sharply divided action. Memory of the prohibition fiasco prevented any serious consideration of outlawing alcohol use except by minors; rescue of the expanding number of alcoholics was left mainly to the self-help of Alcoholics Anonymous (AA), a group founded in 1935, just two years after prohibition ended. Other drugs, however, were strictly prohibited. In 1956, Congress passed the Narcotic Drug Control Act, mandating jail sentences for second offenses by drug dealers and making sale to minors a capital crime. Successive broadening and tightening of drug laws culminated in the Anti-Drug Abuse Acts of 1986 and 1988, which set mandatory minimum sentences for using as well as dealing controlled substances, and established the nation's first "drug czar" to coordinate several federal agencies into an all-out "war on drugs."

The results were the worst prohibitionists of any kind had ever experienced. Ten years after passage of the first Anti-Drug Abuse Act, the United States stood out in the world as the country with the largest proportion of its population in jail. The number of newly admitted prisoners, most of them in on drug charges, rose by 120 percent between 1986 and 1996, bringing the total incarcerated to a record one million, at an estimated increase in cost from $45.6 billion to $93.8 billion. By 2000, the number of persons behind bars in America for nonviolent drug offenses alone, a very disproportionate percentage of them black and Hispanic, exceeded the prison population of all European nations combined. To extend the reach of punitive measures against drugs even further, American foreign policy exerted strong pressure on supplier nations to take action against drug cartels, even to the point of triggering civil war. Yet, despite the crackdown and a corresponding wave of anti-drug propaganda, an estimated twenty-five million Americans continued to use hard drugs and double that number smoked marijuana.

The unwelcome ghost of the noble experiment has hovered confusingly around subsequent efforts to prohibit. The Eighteenth Amendment was repealed on the grounds that outlawing drink had been a spectacular failure that bred disrespect for the law. America today, however, has not seen fit to acknowledge an even greater defeat—greater because, unlike prohibition, the current war on drugs has not produced a decline in the use of forbidden substances. Perhaps the ironic lesson of the fight to repeal the Eighteenth Amendment is that the weapon of ridicule was all too successful. Looking around at today's active drug and alcohol scene, one can readily agree with the common perception that prohibition has been a joke. Not so easy to figure out, however, is whom the joke is on and who really has cause to laugh.

"speakeasy," a place where men (and, increasingly, women) drank publicly, became a common feature of the urban landscape. There bootleggers provided liquor smuggled from Canada or concocted in makeshift stills. Otherwise upright people discovered the thrill of breaking the law; one dealer, trading on common knowledge that whiskey still flowed in the White House, distributed cards advertising himself as the "President's Bootlegger."

Eventually, serious criminals took over most of the liquor trade. Al Capone became the era's most notorious gang lord by establishing a bootlegging empire in Chicago that reputedly grossed more than $60 million in a single year. The gang-war slayings that marked the struggle for control of the lucrative market prompted public cynicism that led finally to the repeal of Prohibition in 1933.

The Nineteenth Amendment, climaxing nearly a century of struggle to achieve political rights for women, finally provided women the chance to answer the question of how they would vote. The militant National Woman's Party wanted women to form a progressive reform bloc and fight for an Equal Rights Amendment, which the party put before Congress in 1923. The more moderate League of Women Voters had the less partisan aim of educating the new electorate on the issues. Activists in both groups expected women to reshape the political landscape, starting with passage of protective legislation for women and children that had long been high on their reform agenda.

But reality did not bear out expectations. Male domination and lack of experience in voting, especially among recent immigrants and Southerners,

s ,

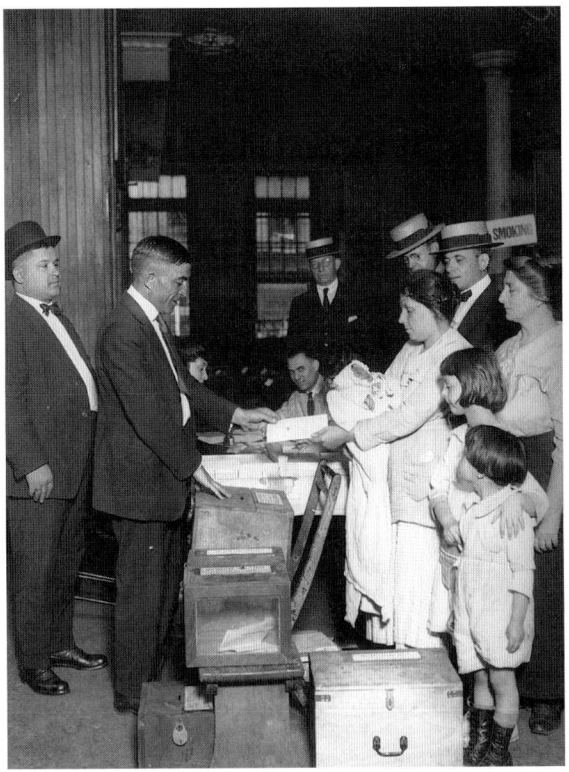

WOMEN VOTING IN NEW YORK CITY
Sharply attired New York City officials look wearily resigned or bemused as one of them hands ballots to two women voting for the first time in 1920. The contrast in appearance and demeanor of the two groups facing each other is strikingly reminiscent of photographs of apprehensive new immigrants applying for entry.
Corbis.

kept many women away from the polls or voting as their husbands instructed. Partly for those reasons, in 1920 and 1924, for the first time in American history, less than a majority of eligible voters cast ballots in the presidential elections. Those women who did vote showed no unified commitment to the goals of suffrage leaders.

It took a while for politicians to realize that they need not fear any female voting bloc. Assuming that women would have considerable political leverage, the new Congress passed the Sheppard-Towner Act in 1921, providing federal funds for maternal and infant health care. As understanding of the new voters' weak influence sank in, however, and the protests of doctors against "socialist" interference intensified, Congress ended the program in 1928.

Those women who stuck with a progressive agenda were forced to act within a network of private agencies and reform associations to advance the causes of birth control, protective legislation for the workplace, legal equality for minorities, and the end of child labor.

The United States Retreats from the World

Harding's desire for harmony equipped him well to preside over the country's retreat from international leadership. Only four months after his inauguration, he concluded peace treaties with Germany, Austria, and Hungary that removed the United States from supervision over their affairs. Harding's most ambitious foreign policy initiative was the Washington Disarmament Conference he convened in 1921 to establish a global balance of naval power. Through agreement on the proportional reduction of naval might among the major powers—Britain, France, Japan, Italy, and the United States—Harding gained popular acclaim for safeguarding the peace without the bother of joining the League of Nations.

Harding also had widespread support for limiting immigration. Alongside native-born Americans opposed to newcomers on racist and patriotic grounds stood union members, who feared competition for jobs. In full accord, Harding made it one of his first acts to sign a quota law. The act limited the number of immigrants to no more than 357,000 per year and gave each European nation a quota, based on 3 percent of the number of people from that country listed in the U.S. census of 1910. The law effectively reversed the trend toward immigration from southern and eastern Europe, which by 1914 had amounted to 75 percent of the yearly total. In 1923 Congress cut the quota in half and followed up the next year by excluding Asians and shifting the census standard back from 1910 to 1890, before the great influx of southern and eastern Europeans.

Antiforeign hysteria climaxed in the trial of two anarchist immigrants from Italy, Nicola Sacco and Bartolomeo Vanzetti. Arrested in 1920 for robbery and murder in South Braintree, Massachusetts, the men were sentenced to death by a judge who openly referred to them as "anarchist bastards." In response to doubts about the fairness of the verdict, the governor of Massachusetts named a review committee of establishment notables, including the presidents

AGITATING FOR SACCO AND VANZETTI
This image appeared in the anarchist journal that Bartolomeo Vanzetti's friend and fellow immigrant Aldino Felicani created to raise support for pardoning Sacco and Vanzetti. By writing in English under an Italian masthead, Felicani sought to make the two accused men symbols of both immigrant and working-class suffering. In the cartoon's dramatic version of events, capitalism's executioner, leaning on the electric chair like a sinister barber, summons working-class victims to their doom. In fact, deportation and mob violence were the typical weapons used against alien radicals and others deemed dangerously un-American.
L'Agitazione, *August 20, 1921.*

of Harvard University and the Massachusetts Institute of Technology. The panel found the trial judge guilty of a "grave breach of official decorum" but refused to recommend a motion for retrial.

For six years, critics who saw the verdict as an indication that the country was in the grip of a rich elite willing to exploit minorities and crush dissent tried vainly to save Sacco and Vanzetti from the electric chair. After the anarchists were executed on August 23, 1927, a crowd of fifty thousand mourners followed the coffins through the rain. Novelist John Dos Passos expressed their despair in the bitter words of a protester: "All right, all right, we are two nations."

A Business Government

By screening out the world, the Harding administration could concentrate on prosperity at home. Accordingly, Harding supported price supports for agriculture and the Fordney-McCumber tariff in 1922, which raised duties on imports to unprecedented heights. Harding's policies to boost American enterprise made him a very popular president, but ultimately the small-town congeniality and trusting ways that had made his career possible did him in. The affable Harding resisted admitting for as long as he could that certain of his friends were involved in law-breaking more serious than drinking bootleg booze. In the end, three of Harding's appointees would go to jail and others would be indicted. When Interior Secretary Albert Fall, the highest official caught up in the scandal, was convicted of accepting bribes of more than $400,000 for leasing oil reserves on public land in Teapot Dome, Wyoming, "Teapot Dome" entered the language permanently as a label for political corruption.

Harding set off on a trip to Alaska in the summer of 1923 to escape his troubles. Baffled about how to deal with "my God-damned friends," the president found no rest and his health declined. On August 2, 1923, a shocked nation learned of the fifty-eight-year-old Harding's sudden death from a heart attack. Harding himself was not involved in any financial wrongdoing, but only his death saved him from the further embarrassment of trying to do a job that was too big for him.

Vice President Calvin Coolidge was vacationing at his family's farmhouse in Plymouth Notch, Vermont, when he was wakened during the night with the news of Harding's death. The family gathered in the parlor where, by the flickering light of an oil lamp, Coolidge's father, a justice of the peace, swore his son in as president. This rustic drama had the intended effect of calming a nation confronting scandal, and the new president thereafter basked in the public's acceptance of him as a savior, wisely steeped in old-fashioned Yankee morality.

Coolidge's nomination for vice president in 1920 had resulted from the favorable publicity he received in 1919 when as governor of Massachusetts he had called out the National Guard to maintain order during the Boston police strike. A spare, solemn man—one critic thought he must have been "weaned on a pickle"—Coolidge once expressed his belief that "the man who builds a factory builds a temple, the man who works there worships there." In deference to sacrosanct free enterprise, Coolidge presided silently over the White House and discouraged others in his administration from taking initiatives. With his approval, Secretary of the Treasury Andrew Mellon focused on minimizing the role of government through tax cuts for corporations and wealthy individuals. Obligingly, Congress passed legislation that reduced its tax revenue by about half. Even the most active cabinet member, Secretary of Commerce Herbert Hoover, shied away from exerting governmental authority over the economy, preferring instead to encourage trade associations that would keep business honest and efficient through voluntary cooperation.

Coolidge found a staunch ally in the Supreme Court. For many years the Court had opposed federal regulation of hours, wages, and working conditions on the grounds that such legislation was the proper concern of the states. Early in the Coolidge years, the Court found ways to curtail state regulation of business as well. In 1923, the Court declared unconstitutional the District of Columbia's minimum-wage law for women, asserting that the law interfered with the freedom of employer and employee to make labor contracts. Soon afterward, the Court showed its partiality toward management by ruling against "closed shops," where only union members could be employed, while confirming the right of owners to form exclusive trade associations.

The election of 1924 confirmed the defeat of the progressive principle that the state should take a leading role in ensuring the general welfare. To oppose Coolidge, the Democrats nominated John W. Davis, a corporate lawyer whose conservative views differed little from Republican principles. Only the Progressive Party and its presidential nominee, Senator Robert La Follette of Wisconsin, offered a reform alternative. In the showdown, for which Republicans coined the slogan "Coolidge or Chaos," La Follette's fervent pledges to champion the progressive tradition of support for labor unions, regulation of business, and protection of civil liberties failed to rouse the public. The mostly silent Coolidge managed to capture more votes than his two opponents put together, and conservative Republicans strengthened their majorities in both houses of Congress. Apathy was the real winner, however: The percentage of eligible voters who bothered to go to the polls was the lowest ever.

Henry Ford and Assembly-Line Progress

With politics in eclipse, the most admired American in the 1920s was Henry Ford, the innovator of mass production who put America on wheels. Born in 1863 on a farm in Dearborn, Michigan, just outside Detroit, Ford soon rejected farmwork in favor of tinkering with machines. In 1893, he put together one of the first successful gasoline-driven carriages in the United States. Ten years later, with $28,000 from a few backers, Ford gathered twelve workers in a 250-by-50-foot shed and created the Ford Motor Company.

Ford's timing and location could not have been better. The growing nation had moved to its outer limits, leaving Americans, especially those west of the Mississippi, far from neighbors and services. With fewer than ten people to a square mile, the Midwest needed machinery to help its farmers make a living and to escape isolation. Ford's Detroit was well situated to meet these needs. Key materials for the automobile and the tractor—steel, oil, glass, and rubber—were manufactured nearby in Pennsylvania, Ohio, Indiana,

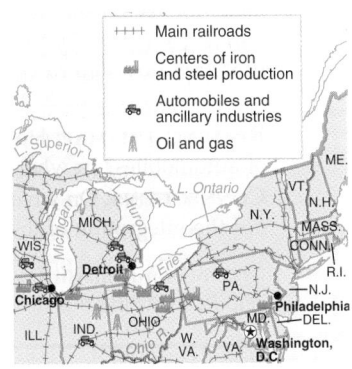

Detroit and the Automobile Industry in the 1920s

and Illinois and were easily transported by rail and the waterways of the Great Lakes. So great was the automobile industry's demand for materials that by 1929 one American in four found employment directly or indirectly in the industry. "Give us our daily bread" was no longer addressed to the Almighty, one commentator quipped, but to Detroit. Henry Ford's reward was dominance over the market. Throughout the rapid expansion of the automotive industry, the Ford Motor Company remained the industry leader, peaking in 1925 when it outsold all its rivals combined (Map 23.2).

The key to Ford's success in the factory was mass production. By installing a continuously

HEROES AND HEROINES

Within popular lore of the 1920s, two kinds of women looked up adoringly at two kinds of heroes. A wholesome image is seen at left on this 1927 cover of the **Popular Monthly Homecraft Magazine.** *Here the healthy outdoor girl type, smartly turned out in her raccoon coat and pennant, seems in flattering control of a naive college football hero. At the right, the pale, sensitive damsel Vilma Banky kneels imploringly before the hypnotic gaze of the movies' greatest heartthrob, Rudolph Valentino. The 1926 ad titillates with ambivalence. Is the pale heroine beseeching her kidnapper to release her? Or is she swooning with desire as the sheik begins to disrobe?*

Picture Research Consultants & Archives; Billy Rose Theatre Collection, The New York Public Library at Lincoln Center.

Jazz Age Ways

The nation's first licensed radio station, KDKA in Pittsburgh, began broadcasting in 1920, and soon American airwaves buzzed with news, sermons, soap operas, sports, comedy, and music. Americans isolated in the high plains laughed at the latest jokes from New York. For the first time, citizens were able to listen to the voices of political candidates without leaving home. Because they could now reach prospective customers in their own homes, adver-

tisers bankrolled the new medium's rapid growth. Between 1922 and 1929, the number of radio stations in the United States increased from 30 to 606. In those seven short years, homes with radios jumped from 60,000 to a staggering 10,250,000.

Radio added to the spread of popular music, especially jazz. The freer social atmosphere welcomed its energetic style and its suggestion of youthful freedom and sexual openness. Throughout the decade the majority white audience, with money too spend, preferred the jazz played by white bands in ballrooms and clubs. Black jazz—labelled "hot" to distinguish it from tamer white "sweet" jazz—had to make its way outside high-paying venues and recording studios. "What Did I Do to Be So Black and Blue?" Andy Razaf's blues anthem asked, while racist white bandleaders like Nick LaRocca derided claims that African Americans had much to do with creating jazz. It was away from the tourists—in urban speakeasies, at rent parties in Harlem, and in chicken shacks along the Chicago Black Belt "Stroll"—that hot jazz flourished. There black musicians, many of them exuberant about having escaped the segregationist South, displayed to other blacks the techniques and ideas that came to guide all jazz in the future. At the center of that burst of creativity was trumpeter Louis Armstrong, who refined the New Orleans band music of his youth into swing rhythms and invented a style of jazz singing uniquely expressive of African American joys and sorrows.

Jazz, white and black, provided the sensual surround for the rebellious mood of youth, who for the first time in the 1920s became a social class distinct in itself. As the traditional bonds of community, religion, and family loosened, the young felt less pressure to imitate their elders and more freedom to develop their own culture. An increasing number of college students helped the "rah-rah" style of college life become a fad, promoted in movies, songs, and advertisements. The collegiate set was the vanguard of the decade's "flaming youth."

Most stunning were the changes in the behavior of young women. In the 1920s, the "advanced" urban woman bared her knees, smoked cigarettes, drank in speakeasies, and generally played havoc with traditionally conservative notions of female behavior. The daring "flapper," as she was called, became the symbol of youthful revolt. As her contemporary and chronicler F. Scott Fitzgerald described her in his novel *This Side of Paradise* (1920), she was "lovely and expensive and about nineteen."

For all their spirit, rarely did the youth of the 1920s pose a threat to the status quo. Most young people, swept up in the new consumer culture, remained apathetic about social issues. Flaming youth rapidly cooled in office jobs and suburbs, and high-spirited flappers eventually settled down to become wives and mothers and employees. Yet even at home, women's lives reflected the changes of the new era. The greater availability of birth control allowed married people to remain passionate and yet have fewer children to raise. New home appliances also lightened the load, though not in most rural homes, which were beyond the reach of power lines.

For women who worked outside the home, the changing economy of the 1920s offered wider, but still limited, opportunity. Many factory jobs, such as those in the booming automobile industry, and most management positions remained male domains. Women continued to become teachers and nurses, but more often found work as poorly paid secretaries, typists, file clerks, and salesclerks. By 1930, nearly eleven million women were employed, constituting 24 percent of the workforce, compared with 18 percent in 1900.

Black Assertion and the Harlem Renaissance

Cheers for the black soldiers who marched up Broadway after the First World War soon faded, and grim days of race riots and hardship followed. Still, a sense of optimism remained strong among African Americans. In New York City, the key elements of hope and talent came together to form an exceptionally dynamic moment in black history. In the years before the war, black people in New York had moved uptown from their cramped confinement in Hell's Kitchen and San Juan Hill to the spacious heights of Harlem. A highly cosmopolitan population seeking freer opportunity included poor migrants from the South and a more sophisticated wave of immigrants from the West Indies. Within that turbulent mix, black artists and writers made Harlem a special place. Only with their guidance could a "New Negro," as critic and historian Alain Locke put it in a book by that name, rise from the ashes of a subjugated past and discover the race's true, creative identity.

That quest would prove more aggressive than it had been before the war. Disillusioned with mainstream politics, many poor urban blacks turned for new leadership to a Jamaican-born visionary named Marcus Garvey. Garvey urged African Americans to rediscover the heritage of Africa and to take pride in their own culture and achievements. In 1917, Garvey launched the Universal Negro Improvement Association (UNIA) to help African Americans gain economic and political independence entirely outside white society. By investing in their own ocean shipping company, the Black Star Line, Garvey's followers expressed the dual aim of financing their Back to Africa movement and providing the ships to carry themselves to their homeland.

Garvey's message drew enthusiastic crowds in Harlem and brought delegates from many countries to the UNIA convention of 1920. Garvey knew how to inspire followers; but he was a naive businessman, unprepared for the rough opposition he encountered. Sharp operators sold bad ships to the Black Star Line, and the federal government pinned

NOAH'S ARK
The Harlem Renaissance gained its principal visual expression at the hands of Kansas-born painter Aaron Douglas. When Douglas arrived in New York City in 1925, he quickly attracted the attention of W. E. B. Du Bois, who placed great importance on the arts as a carrier of the African American soul. At Du Bois's urging, Douglas sought ways of integrating the African cultural heritage with American experience. This depiction of an African Noah commanding the loading of the ark displays a technique that became closely associated with African American art: strong silhouetted figures awash in misty color, indicating a connection between Christian faith and the vital, colorful origins of black Americans in a distant, mythologized African past.
Fisk University Art Galleries, Nashville, Tennessee.

charges of illegal practices on Garvey and deported him to Jamaica in 1927. The issues Garvey raised about black identity, racial pride, and the search for equality persisted, however, and his legacy remains at the center of black nationalist thought.

Hope for the emergence of a New Negro was also roused by an artistic outpouring in the 1920s that came to be known as the Harlem Renaissance. The poet Langston Hughes summed up the movement's central theme of self-respect in verse that shouted: "I am a Negro—and beautiful." In his music and writing, James Weldon Johnson focused on the rural southern culture that migrants brought into the streets of Harlem. In 1903, he had written the Negro national anthem, "Lift Every Voice," and in 1927, in "God's Trombones," he expressed the wisdom and beauty of black folktales. Zora Neale Hurston, as an anthropology student at Barnard College, focused on those tales. Her masterpiece, a novel called *Their Eyes Were Watching God* (1937), explores the complex passions of people within a self-governing southern black community of the rare sort she had known as a child in Florida. Langston Hughes, Claude McKay, and Countee Cullen added poetry as a way of conveying the vitality of life in Harlem amid the indifference and hostility of white America. Harlem painters, led by Aaron Douglas, sought to adapt African art, from which European modernist artists had begun taking inspiration, to the concept of the New Negro. In bold, colorful scenes, Douglas combined biblical and African myths in ways that placed African Americans within a strong and unique tradition.

White patrons became an important means of support for the Harlem Renaissance. But for most whites, Harlem was an exotic dark continent just up the street where they could find a lively nightlife. The most famous spot was the Cotton Club, a gangster-owned outlet for bootleggers. There, black performers hired to entertain the strictly white audience had to enter by the delivery doors and make careful preparations not to need the rest rooms, which were for whites only. For all its vigor and optimism, the Harlem Renaissance existed as an isolated demonstration of achievement in a society not yet prepared to allow African American talent full opportunity to flourish.

The Lost Generation

For many white writers and artists who felt alienated from a society they found crude and materialistic, Europe seemed the place to seek their renaissance. Young and mostly college-educated, these expatriates, as they came to be called, felt embittered by the war and renounced the progressives and patriots who had promoted it as a crusade.

The American-born writer Gertrude Stein, long established in Paris, remarked famously as the young exiles gathered around her, "They are the lost generation." Most of the expatriates, however, believed to the contrary that they had finally found themselves. The cost of living in Paris was low, and the culture receptive to free expression. Far from the complications of home and steady work, the expatriates helped launch the most creative period in American art and literature in the twentieth century.

The novelist whose spare, clean style best exemplified the expatriate efforts to reduce art to a mirror of basic reality was Ernest Hemingway. Hemingway's experience in the war, where he was wounded, convinced him that the conventional world in which he was raised, with its Christian moralism and belief in progress, was bankrupt. His code of honor dismissed creeds, ideologies, and patriotism as pious attempts to cover up the fact that life is a losing battle with death. Hemingway's ideal of macho courage, "grace under pressure," guided a fateful journey to the inevitable (in his case, suicide). In his novel *The Sun Also Rises* (1926), Hemingway makes the point with unflinching directness. His main character, Jake Barnes, is impotent as the result of a war wound. Bereft of comforting beliefs or romantic prospects, Barnes sets out with friends on an aimless journey through France and Spain, the characters discovering little to sustain them except their own animal ability to appreciate sensual experience and endure suffering. Admirers of this exemplary work praised Hemingway's style because, in paring away unnecessary words, it seemed to express so perfectly a world stripped of illusions.

Writers who remained in America were often exiles in spirit who hoped that freedom from claims of duty and convention would help them explore the limits of creativity. Theater critic George Jean Nathan increased his fame when he proclaimed that "the great problems of the world—social, political, economic, and theological—do not concern me in the slightest." With similar scorn for conventional values, novelist Sinclair Lewis in *Main Street* (1920) and *Babbitt* (1922) satirized his native Midwest as a cultural wasteland. Humorists like James Thurber and Don Marquis created outlandish forms and characters to poke fun at taboos and inhibitions. And southern writers, led by William Faulkner, rallied against the South's reputation as a literary Sahara by exploring the dark undercurrents of that region's class and race heritage. But doubts about the new freedom surfaced as well. From the vantage of his own fame and wealth as chronicler of flaming youth, F. Scott Fitzgerald spoke with guilty brilliance in *This Side of Paradise* (1920) of a disillusioned generation "grown up to find all Gods dead, all wars fought, all faiths in man shaken."

Rural America and Resistance to Change

In 1920 the census reported that the majority of the population had shifted from the country to the city (Map 23.3). Included in that change were growing urban domination over political and cultural life and rising economic disparity. Between 1918 and 1921, while cities prospered, farm incomes and the value of farmland fell by 30 to 50 percent. Only large-scale farmers were able to afford the technological advances needed for prosperity. Others were hard pressed even to hold on to the agrarian ideal of self-reliant individualism. By the end of the decade, 40 percent of the nation's farmers had become landless, and 90 percent of rural homes had no indoor plumbing, gas, or electricity.

The Rebirth of the Ku Klux Klan

Some of those who felt forsaken by the modern world channeled their desperation into a revived Ku Klux Klan that first appeared in 1915. Although the new Klan rose once again in the South, where its predecessor had been created to curb the rights of blacks during reconstruction, it swiftly moved beyond the region. Imperial Grand Wizard Hiram Wesley Evans, a Texas dentist who styled himself as "the most average man in America," employed modern sales techniques to organize a network of klaverns (local societies) across the country. The Klan, Evans promised, would stoutly defend family, morality, and traditional values against the threat posed by blacks, immigrants, radicals, Catholics, and Jews.

The Klan offered a certain counterfeit dignity for those old-stock, Protestant, white Americans

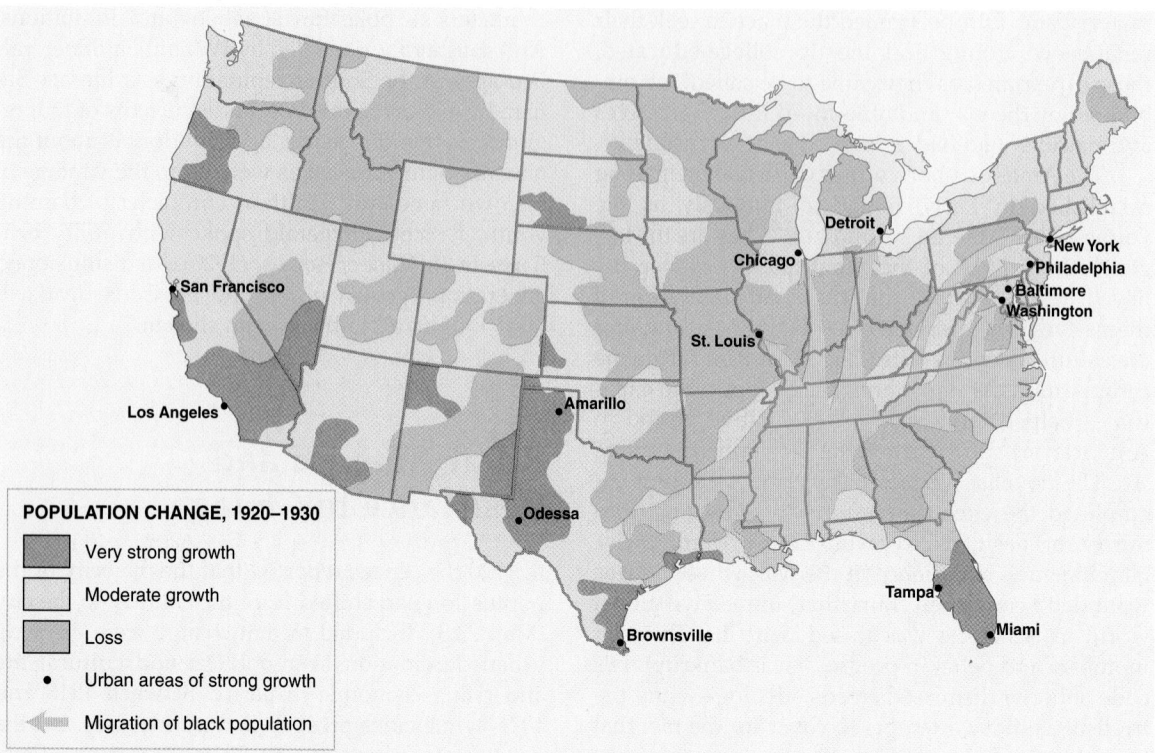

MAP 23.3

The Shift from Rural to Urban Population, 1920–1930

The movement of whites and Hispanics toward urban and agricultural opportunity made Florida, the West, and the Southwest the regions of fastest population growth. In contrast, large numbers of blacks left their traditional concentration in the South to find a better life in the North. Because almost all migrating blacks went from the countryside to cities in distant parts of the nation, while white and Hispanic migrants tended to move shorter distances toward familiar places, the population shift brought more drastic overall change to blacks than to whites and Hispanics.

who felt passed over by a changing society. So widespread was the sense of displacement that, at its peak, the Klan attracted some three to four million members. By the mid-1920s, it virtually controlled Indiana and influenced politics in Illinois, California, Oregon, Texas, Louisiana, Oklahoma, and Kansas. The Klan's secrecy, uniforms, and rituals helped counter a sense of insignificance for those outside the new world of giant corporations and large-scale farms. Like the Elks or the Odd Fellows, the Klan provided practical compensation in forging business contacts on the margins of society. At the same time, it appealed to the vengeful and brutal side of human nature, enabling its hooded members to intimidate blacks, Jews, and Catholics anonymously with little fear of consequences.

Eventually, social changes, along with lawless excess, brought the Klan down. Immigration restrictions eased the worry about invading foreigners, and sensational wrongdoing by Klan leaders cost it the support of radical moralists. Grand Dragon David Stephenson of Indiana, for example, went to jail for the kidnap and rape of a woman who subsequently committed suicide. Yet the social grievances and economic problems of the countryside and small towns remained, ready to be ignited by later protest movements.

THE LAW IS TOO SLOW
This stark depiction of a lynching by George Bel-
lows in 1923 appeared just as the revived Ku Klux
Klan was proclaiming itself the defender of tradi-
tional virtue in a sinful modern world. Bellows, an
athlete as well as an artist, had gained fame as a
realist and tough-minded radical before World War I
and continued until his death in 1925 to spur social
conscience even after doing so had gone out of
fashion.

The Scopes Trial

The clash between the old-time religion and the new spirit of science reached a dramatic climax in the Scopes trial in 1925. The confrontation occurred after several southern and border states passed legislation in the early 1920s against the teaching of Charles Darwin's theory of evolution in the public schools. Fundamentalist Protestants insisted that the Bible's creation story be taught as the literal truth. In answer to a clamor from scientists and civil liberties organizations for a challenge to the law, John Scopes, a young schoolteacher in Dayton, Tennessee, offered to test his state's ban on teaching

evolution. When Scopes was brought to trial in the summer of 1925, Clarence Darrow, a brilliant defense lawyer from Chicago, volunteered to defend him. Darrow, an avowed agnostic, took on state's attorney William Jennings Bryan, the symbol of rural America and a fervent fundamentalist.

The Scopes trial quickly degenerated into a media circus, despite the serious free inquiry issues it raised. The first trial to be covered live on radio, it attracted an avid nationwide audience. Reporters from big-city papers who converged on Dayton were largely hostile to Bryan, none more so than the cynical H. L. Mencken, who painted Bryan as a sort of Darwinian missing link ("a sweating anthropoid," a "gaping primate"). When, under relentless questioning by Darrow, Bryan declared on the witness stand that he did indeed believe the world was created in six days and that Jonah had lived in the belly of a whale, his humiliation in the eyes of most urban observers was complete. Although the Tennessee court upheld the law in defiance of modern intellectual consensus and punished Scopes with a $100 fine, Mencken had the last word in a merciless obituary for Bryan, who died just weeks after the trial ended. Portraying the "monkey trial" as a battle between the country and the city, Mencken flayed Bryan as a "charlatan, a mountebank, a zany without shame or dignity," motivated solely by "hatred of the city men who had laughed at him for so long."

As Mencken's acid prose indicated, Bryan's humiliation was not purely a victory of reason and science. It also reduced the esteem in which country people and their old values were held. The Ku Klux Klan revival and the Scopes trial dramatized and inflamed divisions between city and country, intellectuals and the unlettered, the privileged and the outcasts, the scoffers and the faithful.

Al Smith and the Election of 1928

Calvin Coolidge, who seemed a pillar of common sense and moral principle, added to the confusion by announcing in the summer of 1927 that he would not seek reelection. Who would now defuse the issues splitting the nation—prohibition, religious bigotry, and the clash between rural and urban values? Republicans chose Herbert Hoover, the energetic secretary of commerce who appeared best able to continue Coolidge's pro-business programs and bring conservative southern Democrats over to the

Republican side. The Democrats played into that strategy by nominating Governor Alfred E. Smith of New York City, the son of immigrant parents who was closely associated with the notorious Tammany Hall political machine and had actively championed the repeal of Prohibition.

Smith's greatest vulnerability in the heartland, however, was that he was the first Catholic to run for president. An editorial in the *Baptist and Commoner* was typical of many appeals to suspicious Protestants in arguing that the election of Smith "would be granting the Pope the right to dictate to this government what it should do." There would be edicts from the White House claiming that "Protestants are now living in adultery because they were not married by a priest." Are you willing, the editorial asked in its punch line, to accept a president who would tell us "our offspring are bastards"?

Hoover, who neatly combined the images of morality, efficiency, service, and prosperity, won the election by a landslide (Map 23.4). He received 58 percent of the vote, taking all but eight states, and gained 444 electoral votes to Smith's 87. The Republicans managed to retain the support of blacks and at the same time wrenched five states loose from the segregationist, formerly solid Democratic South. The only dark cloud over the Republican victory, not much noted at the time, was the party's reduced support in urban areas and among discontented farmers. The nation's largest cities voted Democratic in a striking reversal from 1924, indicating the rising strength of ethnic minorities, including Smith's fellow Catholics.

From the New Era to the Great Crash

At his inauguration in 1929, Herbert Hoover told the American people, "We in America today are nearer to the final triumph over poverty than ever before in the history of any land. The poorhouse is vanishing from among us." The nation had not yet reached that goal, he acknowledged, "but, given a chance to go forward with the policies of the last eight years, we shall soon with the help of God be in sight of the day when poverty will be banished from this nation." Those words came back to haunt Hoover, for in eight short months the Roaring Twenties came to a crashing halt. The prosperity Hoover touted collapsed with the stock market, and the nation fell into the most serious economic depression of all time. Hoover and his reputation were among the first casualties, along with the reverence for business that had been the hallmark of the New Era.

Herbert Hoover: The Great Engineer

It was one of the crueler ironies of the times that Herbert Hoover became president just before the depression struck. Coming into office in 1929, Hoover displayed credentials that seemed perfect for the president of a prosperous business civilization. He embodied the rags-to-riches ideal, having risen from poor orphaned beginnings to become one of the world's most successful mining engineers by the time he was thirty. His success in managing efforts to feed civilian victims of the fighting during World War I won him acclaim as "the Great Humanitarian" and led Woodrow Wilson to name him head of the Food Administration once the United States entered the war. During the 1920s, Hoover's reputation soared even higher when he used his position as secretary of commerce to become the most active and accomplished cabinet member.

Because he favored efficiency and growth, Hoover thought of himself as a progressive, but his

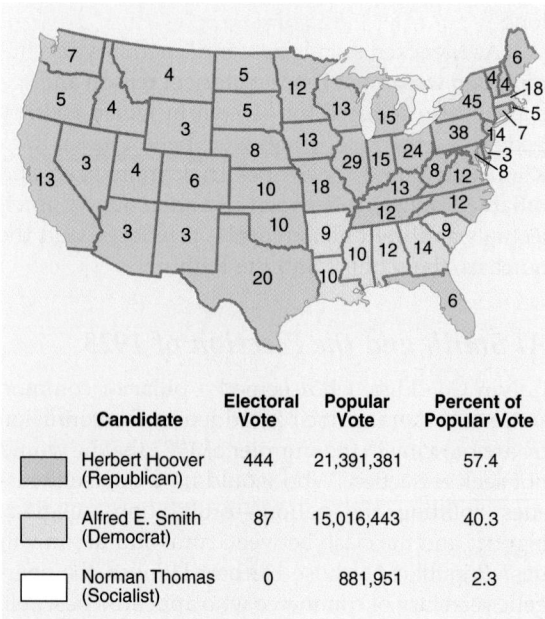

Candidate	Electoral Vote	Popular Vote	Percent of Popular Vote
Herbert Hoover (Republican)	444	21,391,381	57.4
Alfred E. Smith (Democrat)	87	15,016,443	40.3
Norman Thomas (Socialist)	0	881,951	2.3

MAP 23.4
The Election of 1928

VOTE FOR HERBERT HOOVER
and CHARLES CURTIS
for the Prosperity of your Country *and the Happiness and your home....*

HOOVER CAMPAIGN POSTER *Herbert Hoover's 1928 campaign poster neatly framed his major positions: middle-class prosperity in a house in the suburbs, complete with a car in every garage and, presumably, a chicken in every pot. To complete the display, smoking chimneys at a discreet distance remind voters that Hoover as secretary of commerce had promoted industry that made the suburban idyll possible.* Collection of Janice L. and David J. Frent.

reluctance to use the government to force change and ameliorate bad conditions distanced him from the reform spirit of prewar progressives. Having lived most of his adult life abroad, he had never even voted in a presidential election. Aware of his political limitations, Hoover confided to a friend: "I have no dread of the ordinary work of the presidency. What I do fear is the . . . exaggerated idea [that] I am a sort of superman, that no problem is beyond my capacity." He added prophetically, "If some unprecedented calamity should come upon the nation . . . I would be sacrificed to the unreasoning disappointment of a people who expected too much."

The Distorted Economy

In the spring of 1929, the United States basked in the sunshine of a fool's paradise. Although America had become the world's dominant economy, its leaders acted as though it were still a weak, developing country. American isolationism meant that European countries, devastated by the First World War, could not get the help they needed for full recovery. Rather than stepping in to help rebuild Europe's

shattered economy, the Harding and Coolidge administrations demanded that European nations repay their war loans. In addition, the United States enacted tariffs that kept other nations from selling their goods to Americans. Foreign nations thus had less money to buy American goods, which were pouring out in record abundance. In a move that could work only in the short run, the United States propped up its export trade by extending credit to its foreign customers. Debt piled onto debt in an absurd pyramid. By the end of the decade, the United States accounted for 40 percent of the world's economic production and had acquired most of the world's gold in return for its exports.

The economy also suffered from skewed wealth at home. Farmers continued to suffer from low prices and chronic indebtedness; the average income of families on the land amounted to only $240 per year during the 1920s, and 54 percent earned less than $1,000. Industrial workers, though enjoying a slight rise in wages during the decade, failed to keep up with productivity and corporate profits. Overall, nearly two-thirds of all American families lived on less than the $2,000 per year that economists estimated would "supply only basic necessities." In

struction Finance Corporation (RFC), a federal agency empowered to lend government funds to endangered banks, insurance companies, and railroads. It was a "trickle-down" theory: Pump money into the economy at the top, and in the long run the people at the bottom would benefit. But in the long run, as the great English economist of the day John Maynard Keynes pointed out, we are all dead. In the short run, what critics of the RFC called a "millionaires' dole" trickled very little down to the poor.

Life in the Depression

In 1930, the nation woke up to the realization that prosperity would not soon return. The trouble was too deep, the engine too cold to restart. Suffering on a massive scale set in, and despair settled over the land. Hollow-eyed men and women grew increasingly bewildered and angry in the face of cruel ambiguities. They saw unsellable agricultural sur-

pluses in the countryside and knew that their children were going to bed hungry. They saw factories standing idle and knew that they and millions of others were willing to work. The gap between the American people and leaders who failed to resolve these contradictions widened as the depression deepened. By 1932, America's economic problems had become a dangerous social crisis.

The Human Toll

Statistics provide a scaffolding for understanding the human dimension of the Great Depression. When Herbert Hoover took office in 1929, the American economy stood at its peak. When he left in 1933, it had reached its twentieth-century low (Figure 23.1). More than nine thousand banks had shut their doors, and depositors had lost more than $2.5 billion. In 1929, national income was $88 billion. By 1933, it had declined to $40 billion. In 1929, unemployment was 3.1 percent, one and a half million workers. By 1933, unemployment

Agricultural income —— Manufacturing income

FIGURE 23.1
Manufacturing and Agricultural Income, 1920–1940
After economic collapse, recovery in the 1930s began under New Deal auspices. Sharp declines in 1937–1938, when federal spending was reduced, indicated that restoring manufacturing and agricultural income still needed New Deal stimuli.

PRIVATE CAR

In the mid-1930s, LeConte Stewart, an artist who spent most of his life painting the landscapes of his native Utah, noticed a new sight. From his remote hillside above the Union Pacific railroad tracks, he witnessed a stream of tramps heading west. The sight of one young man jauntily braced in the doorway of a boxcar made Stewart think of the elegant private cars of millionaires that used to travel along those same tracks. Stewart entitled this painting **Private Car** *and achieved fame for his beautifully ironic depiction of a new wave of pioneers fleeing trouble.*

Private Car by LeConte Stewart. © by Intellectual Reserve, Inc. Courtesy of Museum of Church History and Art. Used by permission.

stood at 25 percent, twelve and a half million workers.

Jobless, homeless victims wandered in search of work, and the tramp, or hobo, became one of the most visible figures of the decade. Young men and women unable to land their first job made up about half of the million-strong army of hoboes. Riding the rails or hitchhiking, the vagabonds tended to move southward and westward, toward the sun and opportunities, they hoped, for seasonal agricultural work. Other unemployed men and women, less hopeful or sick, huddled in doorways—human "junk," as one writer put it. Scavengers haunted alleys behind restaurants and picked over garbage dumps in search of food. In describing what he

called the "American Earthquake," the writer Edmund Wilson told of an elderly woman who always took off her glasses to avoid seeing the maggots crawling over the garbage she ate. Starvation claimed its victims. Four New York City hospitals reported a total of ninety-five deaths from hunger in 1931. But enervating, rampant malnutrition posed the greater threat. The Children's Bureau announced that one of five schoolchildren did not get enough to eat.

Rural poverty was most acute. Landless tenant farmers and sharecroppers, mainly in the South, came to symbolize how poverty crushed the human spirit. In 1930, eight and a half million people, three million of them black, lived in tenant and sharecropping families—amounting to one-quarter of the total southern population. Often illiterate, usually without cash incomes, they crowded into two- and three-room cabins lacking screens or even doors, without plumbing, electricity, running water, or sanitary wells. They subsisted—just barely—on salt pork, cornmeal, molasses, beans, peas, and whatever they could hunt or fish. All the diseases of dietary and vitamin deficiencies wracked them. When economist John Maynard Keynes was asked whether anything like this degradation had existed before, he replied, "Yes, it was called the Dark Ages and it lasted four hundred years."

To meet this human catastrophe, the nation was equipped with the most limited welfare system in the Western world. There was no federal assistance, only a patchwork of voluntary institutions and pinchpenny state and local agencies. For a family of four without any income, the best the city of Philadelphia could do was provide $5.50 per week. That was not enough to live on, but still comparatively generous. New York City, where the greatest number of welfare cases gathered, provided only $2.39 per week; and Detroit, devastated when the bottom fell out of the auto industry, allotted 60 cents a week before the city ran out of money altogether.

The deepening crisis roused old fears and caused some Americans to look for scapegoats. Among the most thoroughly scapegoated were Mexican Americans. During the relatively prosperous years of the 1920s, cheap agricultural labor from Mexico flowed legally across the U.S. border, welcomed by the large farmers. In the 1930s, however, public opinion turned on the newcomers, decrying them as dangerous aliens who took jobs from Americans. Government officials, most prominently those in Los Angeles County, with support from the Department of Labor, targeted all Mexican residents for deportation, regardless of citizenship status. As many as half a million Mexicans and Mexican Americans were deported or fled to Mexico. Among them were children born in the United States, American citizens from the start who had never lived outside the country.

The depression deeply affected the American family. Young people postponed marriage; when they did marry, they produced so few children that demographers warned that, for the first time, the United States was on the verge of losing population. White women, who generally worked in low-paying service areas—as cooks, salesclerks, and secretaries—did not lose their jobs as often as men who worked in industry. Unemployed men resented women workers, yet necessity drove women into the marketplace during the depression. Overall, some 25 percent more women were employed for wages in 1940 than in 1930.

As women left the home to replace their husbands as breadwinners, families experienced stress. After a decade of rising consumption, smaller incomes led to significant belt tightening. Working women became increasingly decisive and self-reliant at the same time idle men fell prey to guilt and loss of self-esteem. Yet, though family violence, alcoholism, and suicide escalated, the divorce rate went down. The desperately poor could not afford the legal expense; instead, in dramatically rising numbers, men resorted to desertion.

Denial and Escape

In the midst of the mounting crisis, J. P. Morgan Jr., the living symbol of American capitalism, testified before a congressional committee where he defended the economic importance of preserving an elite. "If you destroy the leisure class," he lectured, "you destroy civilization." When pressed to define the "leisure class," Morgan responded that it included all those who could afford a maid—about twenty-five or thirty million people, he reckoned, until informed that there were only about two million servants in the entire country. Morgan's ignorance was typical of many from his class. Under scrutiny, those who had presided over the economic collapse and now sought to lead the nation back to prosperity showed how little they had troubled to learn about the society that had made them rich. It turned out, though, that Morgan had learned enough to avoid paying income tax from 1929 to 1932.

As the economy and the reputations of its leaders sank, Hoover became an object of scorn. Makeshift shantytowns that sprang up on the edges of America's cities were called "Hoovervilles." Newspapers used as cover by those sleeping on the streets were "Hoover blankets." An empty pocket turned inside out was a "Hoover flag," and jackrabbits caught for food were "Hoover hogs." Innumerable bitter jokes circulated about the president. One gibe asserted that Hoover was the world's greatest engineer: "In a little more than two years he has drained, ditched, and damned the United States." Another story told of Hoover asking Andrew Mellon for a nickel to call up a friend.

"BUT HE TOOK CREDIT FOR THIS!"
This angry cartoon in a traditionally Republican newspaper poses the key dilemma for Hoover's reelection campaign in 1932. How could Hoover, the "Great Engineer," lionized as the dynamic driver of the 1920s economic boom, now plead helplessness before what he considered the European causes of economic collapse? Stunned into silence by the accusing figure, who like a graveyard specter points the bony finger of doom, Hoover's spokesman can do nothing to counter the deepening sense that the great claims for guided prosperity in the 1920s had turned out to be empty.
Franklin D. Roosevelt Library.

"Here's a dime," Mellon is said to have replied, "call up all your friends."

Hoover's effort to set an example did not help. To express his confidence in prosperity, he favored formal dress and manners in the White House and for dinner, with or without guests, he was attended by a retinue of valets and waiters. No one was starving, he calmly assured the American people.

Not that his administration considered it the duty of the federal government to investigate the truth of that assertion. Walter Gifford, president of the American Telephone and Telegraph Company, appointed by Hoover to coordinate private relief efforts, acknowledged to a Senate subcommittee that he had made no attempt to compile figures on how many people were out of work and on relief. Exasperated, Senator Robert La Follette asked if Gifford had any impulse to know the facts. Gifford's response reflected how the nation's business leadership distanced itself from the problems of failure and poverty. "Well," said Gifford genially, "I will not say that I did not make any estimate for my own interest and amusement."

While the wealthy practiced denial, other Americans sought refuge from reality at the movies. Throughout the depression, between sixty and seventy-five million people (nearly two-thirds of the nation) managed to scrounge up enough change to fill the movie palaces every week. Box office successes typically blended nostalgia for the lost Golden Twenties with the hope that renewed prosperity lay just around the corner. The leading musicals in 1933, *Forty-Second Street* and *Gold Diggers*, each offered a variation on the old rags-to-riches story of the chorus girl who makes the most of her big break.

Grim conditions moved a few filmmakers to grapple with depression woes rather than escape them. Films such as King Vidor's *Our Daily Bread* (1932) and John Ford's *The Grapes of Wrath* (1940) expressed compassion for the down-and-out. Gangster films taught grim lessons about ill-gotten gains. Indeed, under the new production code of 1930, designed to protect public morals, all movies had to find some way to show that crime does not pay. *Public Enemy* (1931), the classic cautionary tale about the doom that awaits those who break the law found a particularly shocking way to do so when it ended with gangsters delivering the bullet-riddled body of a hoodlum to the doorstep of his saintly, long-suffering mother.

Despite Hollywood's efforts to keep Americans on the right side of the law, crime increased in the early 1930s. Away from the movie palaces, out in the countryside, the plight of people who had lost their farms to bank foreclosures led to the romantic idea that bank robbers were only getting back what banks had stolen from the poor. Woody Guthrie, the populist folk singer from Oklahoma, captured the public's tolerance for outlaws in his widely admired tribute to a murderous bank robber with a choirboy face, "The Ballad of Pretty Boy Floyd":

> Yes, as through this world I ramble,
> I see lots of funny men,
> Some will rob you with a six-gun,
> Some will rob you with a pen.
> But as through your life you'll travel,
> Wherever you may roam,
> You won't never see an outlaw drive
> A family from their home.

Working-Class Militancy

Although the nation's working people bore the brunt of the economic collapse, the labor movement, including the dominant American Federation of Labor (AFL), was slow to respond. Organized labor had been hobbled during the 1920s by court injunctions curtailing the right of unions to organize and strike. Early in the depression, William Green, head of the AFL, echoed Hoover when he argued that a dole would turn the worker into "a ward of the state." But by 1931, Green had turned militant. "I warn the people who are exploiting the workers," he shouted at the AFL's annual convention, "that they can drive them only so far before they will turn on them and destroy them. They are taking no account of the history of nations in which governments have been overturned. Revolutions grow out of the depths of hunger."

Like the labor leaders, the American people were slow to anger, then strong in protest. On the morning of March 7, 1932, several thousand unemployed autoworkers massed at the gates of Ford's River Rouge factory in Dearborn, Michigan, to demand work. Henry Ford sent out his private security forces, who told the demonstrators to disperse. The workers refused and began hurling rocks. The Ford army responded with tear gas and freezing water but quickly escalated to gunfire. When they stopped, four demonstrators were dead and dozens more wounded. An outraged public—forty thousand strong—turned out for the unemployed men's funerals, while editorials and protest rallies across the country denounced Ford's callous resort to violence.

Farmers, who desperately needed relief, mounted an uprising of their own soon afterward. When Congress refused to guarantee farm prices that would at least equal the cost of production, some three thousand farmers, led by the flamboyant Milo Reno, created the National Farmers' Holiday Association, so named because its members planned to force farmers to take a "holiday" from delivering produce to the public. Invoking the Boston Tea Party, Reno and his followers barricaded roads around Sioux City, Iowa, turned back farmers heading for market, and dumped thousands of gallons of milk in the ditches. Although the rebellion was short-lived and did not force a critical shortage of food, it raised general awareness of farm grievances. Farm militants had fuller material effect with what they called "penny sales." When farms

defaulted on their mortgages and were put up for auction, neighbors packed the auctions and, after warning others not to bid, bought the foreclosed property for a few pennies and returned it to the bankrupt owners. Under this kind of pressure, some states suspended debts or reduced mortgages.

In the vast agricultural holdings of California, resistance combined farmer and labor tactics. When landowners cut their already substandard wages to laborers in what one critic aptly called "factories in the fields," more than fifty thousand farmworkers, most of them Mexicans, went on strike. Surveying the strife mounting nationwide, John Simpson, president of the National Farmers Union, observed in 1933 that "the biggest and finest crop of revolutions you ever saw is sprouting all over the country right now."

Hard times also revived the left in America. When the crash struck, Eugene Debs was dead and so, for all purposes, was the Socialist Party. But the Great Depression—the massive failure of Western capitalism—brought socialism back to life and the Communist Party to its greatest size and influence in American history. Eventually, some 100,000 disillusioned Americans—workers, intellectuals, college students—joined the Communist Party in the belief that only an

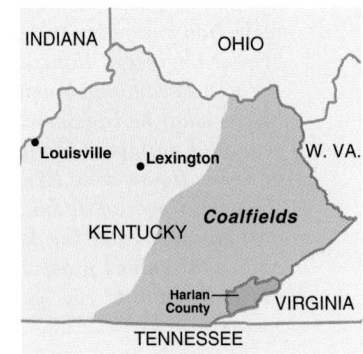

Harlan County Coal Strike, 1931

overthrow of the capitalist system could save the victims of depression. In 1931, the party, having increased membership in its National Miners Union from 100 to 25,000, carried its convictions into Harlan County, Kentucky, to support a strike by harshly oppressed coal miners. Newspapers and newsreels riveted the attention of the public with their graphic portrayal of the violence unleashed by mine owners' thugs against the strikers. Eventually, the miners were beaten down, but the Communist Party emerged from the coalfields with a reputation as the most dedicated and fearless champion of the union cause.

The left also led the fight against racism. While both major parties hesitated to challenge the system of segregation in the South, the Socialist Party, led by moral reformer Norman Thomas, sought to break down the system of sharecropping that left many African Americans in poverty and virtual servitude. The Communist Party took action as well. When nine young black men in Scottsboro, Alabama, were arrested on trumped-up rape charges, a team of lawyers sent by the party managed to save the defendants from the electric chair. The party also opposed the efforts of Alabama plantation owners to evict their black tenants. Although Communists were unable to force much change on the deeply entrenched southern way of life, their efforts briefly attracted new recruits to the party. From only about 50 black members in 1930, party totals rose to 10,000 by the end of the decade, before most of the converts returned to traditional reform movements rooted in constitutional rights and religious conviction.

The left often sparked action, but protests by workers and farmers occurred on a far greater scale. Breadlines, soup kitchens, foreclosures, unemployment, and cold despair drove patriotic men and women to question American capitalism. "I am as conservative as any man could be," a Wisconsin farmer explained, "but any economic system that has in its power to set me and my wife in the streets, at my age—what can I see but red?"

Conclusion: The Era of Boom and Bust

The decade of the 1920s was a time of extravagant expectation masking deep structural flaws. During those years living standards rose, economic opportunity increased, and an image of cultural and personal liberation prevailed. For many Americans at the time, however, none of the glamour had much meaning. Instead of plunging into speculation on Wall Street, seeking thrills at speakeasies, or escaping to Paris, the vast majority went ahead as before with the struggle to attain a decent existence.

After the stock market crash swept away the aura of high living, different images emerged to fix the depression in memory: apple sellers on Broadway; empty apartment buildings alongside cardboard shantytowns; mountains of oranges rotting in the California sun while guards with shotguns chased away the hungry. Sometimes the image came from sullen apathy flaming into revolt: a line of unemployed men in New York City suddenly charging hiring agents or destitute farmers invading a small town in Arkansas to loot the food stores at gunpoint.

Eugene Debs, the most beloved socialist and friend of the common man, took from his battles in and out of prison the lesson that human happiness is never found through a solitary search. "When I rise," he liked to say, "it will be *with* the ranks, and not *from* the ranks." In the first years of the depression, however, faith in any sort of rise waned as the laboring ranks receded into hardship. The businessmen who rallied around Herbert Hoover thus faced something more desperate, more radical, than the old call for working-class solidarity and progressive reform. On a night in June 1931, a man driving a large car on the outskirts of Gary, Indiana, got a taste of what that might be when a brick crashed through his windshield. "What's the big idea?" he shouted, as he slammed on his brakes. Out of the darkness came the reply: "All rich guys ought to be strung up." "Who are you?" the driver asked. "We're the fellows that'll do the stringing."

FOR FURTHER READING ABOUT THE TOPICS IN THIS CHAPTER, see the Online Bibliography at
www.bedfordstmartins.com/roarkcompact.

FOR ADDITIONAL FIRST-HAND ACCOUNTS OF THIS PERIOD, see pages 119–137 in Michael Johnson, ed., *Reading the American Past*, Second Edition, Volume II.

TO ASSESS YOUR MASTERY OF THE MATERIAL IN THIS CHAPTER, see the Online Study Guide at
www.bedfordstmartins.com/roarkcompact.

CHRONOLOGY

1920 Eighteenth Amendment, prohibiting sale of liquor, goes into effect.

Nineteenth Amendment, granting women the vote, ratified.

Station KDKA in Pittsburgh begins first regular commercial radio broadcasts.

Marcus Garvey hosts Universal Negro Improvement Association convention in Harlem.

Republican Warren G. Harding elected president.

1921 Sheppard-Towner Act, providing infant health care, passes in Congress.

1922 Fordney-McCumber Act sets protective tariffs at record heights.

New laws imposing quotas according to nationality end historical tradition of open immigration.

1923 Equal Rights Amendment introduced in Congress.

August. Harding dies in office, succeeded by Calvin Coolidge.

1924 Calvin Coolidge elected president.

1925 John Scopes convicted for violating Tennessee statute forbidding teaching of evolution.

Alain Locke expresses cultural aspirations of Harlem Renaissance in *The New Negro*.

1926 Ernest Hemingway's novel of expatriate Paris, *The Sun Also Rises*, published.

1927 Charles Lindbergh becomes America's most famous hero by flying alone across Atlantic.

Italian anarchist immigrants Nicola Sacco and Bartolomeo Vanzetti executed.

1928 Herbert Hoover defeats Alfred E. Smith in presidential election.

1929 Robert and Helen Lynd publish their study of an average American small city, *Middletown*.

October 24. Stock market collapses on Black Thursday.

1931 Nine black men arrested in Scottsboro, Alabama, ardently defended by Communist Party lawyers.

1932 Several thousand demonstrators at Ford plant protest unemployment; security forces fire on crowd, killing four.

National Farmers' Holiday Association blocks roads and pours milk on ground to protest falling prices.

SOUVENIR SEWING NEEDLE BOOK

Borrowing the current popular tune "Happy Days Are Here Again" as the theme song for Roosevelt's 1932 campaign was an inspired act of wishful thinking in those dark days. By 1936, conditions had improved enough that this souvenir needle book could celebrate "happiness restored" a bit more realistically. The major places where economic recovery was to be created—farm, factory, and office—are shown operating in full swing on the cover of this little container that held sewing needles. But in accord with the New Deal emphasis on security at home, the figure of domestic happiness looms largest in the center under the arch of prosperity.

Collection of Janice L. and David J. Frent.

THE NEW DEAL EXPERIMENT, 24

1932–1939

I N JULY 1932, A RAGGED, DUSTY CONTINGENT of some fifteen thousand World War I veterans, calling themselves the Bonus Expeditionary Army, marched into Washington, D.C., to request immediate payment of the bonus for their military service that they had been promised would be theirs in 1945. Destitute, they first camped in unfinished federal buildings just three blocks from the Capitol and then overflowed onto the mud flats along the Anacostia River.

President Herbert Hoover, angered by these raiders of the Treasury, urged Congress to vote against the bonus because its $2.4 billion cost was more than the government could afford. To strengthen that case, Hoover and his supporters vilified the bonus seekers. Though a study showed that 94 percent of the marchers had served in the armed forces, the administration claimed that many in the bonus army were not veterans at all. Compounding the slander, Hoover cited false reports that the march was a revolutionary menace because its leaders were Communists. In reality, most of the marchers believed in traditional values. They had come to Washington to regain their respectability, not to overthrow the government.

Refusing to confer with men whom he thought undeserving of recognition, Hoover resorted to force. With assurance from Army Chief of Staff Douglas MacArthur that the military would quickly get rid of the squatters and impress the public with the government's authority, Hoover watched from the Oval Office on the afternoon of July 28 as one thousand soldiers lobbed tear gas into the buildings occupied by the marchers. Then, in defiance of Hoover's orders to refrain from a direct attack, MacArthur commanded his troops to charge the nearby open-air encampment. In the rout that followed, several bonus marchers suffered bayonet wounds and one infant died of gas poisoning.

The following day, Franklin D. Roosevelt, Hoover's Democratic rival in the 1932 presidential campaign, read about the attack with "a feeling of horror." Were it up to him, Roosevelt declared, he would have taken coffee and doughnuts to the protesters and invited them to work on reforestation projects or settle on vacant federal land where they could farm and regain their independence. Like Hoover, Roosevelt thought the bonus payment was too expensive, but, unlike Hoover, he insisted that if people desperately needed help, the government should find a way to give it.

Almost a year later—after Roosevelt had been elected president—a second group of about three thousand veterans gathered in Washington to lobby for payment of the bonus. This time they were fed and housed in military barracks at

WASHINGTON BONUS MARCH
This watercolor is one of a series executed by twenty-four-year-old Lewis Rubenstein, who in 1932 traveled as an observer with the bonus marchers. Here he depicts the march in its early stages as a hopeful, somewhat theatrical adventure. The figure on the running board of the car, megaphone in hand, seems almost like a cheerleader encouraging the team as it advances on its goal—in this case the steps of the United States Capitol.
Janet Marqusee Fine Arts Ltd.

government expense while they petitioned Congress. Much to their enthusiastic surprise, Eleanor Roosevelt came striding through rain and mud to their camp to express her concern and join the men in singing favorite wartime songs. Franklin Roosevelt then received a delegation of the veterans at the White House. After genially recalling how they had all served together in the war, he reassured his visitors that, although he could not support the bonus, the government was prepared to rescue victims of the depression. In the end, twenty-six hundred of the marchers enrolled in the government's Civilian Conservation Corps, designed to put people to work conserving the nation's natural resources, rather than accepting government transportation home.

As the Second Bonus Army prepared to break camp, a reporter overheard remarks that brought into focus part of the meaning of Roosevelt's reform program, which he called the "New Deal." One bedraggled, rain-soaked veteran asked, "What is this bird Roosevelt up to?" Another shrugged and replied, "All I know is he's a hooman bein'."

Franklin D. Roosevelt: A Patrician in Government

The man elected president in 1932 was raised within the shelter of wealth and social prominence yet managed to establish an extraordinary relationship with the American people, especially the poor and dispossessed. In his twelve-year reign, Roosevelt experienced two of the nation's greatest crises—the Great Depression and World War II. His formidable political skills, along with his ability to convey sympathetic concern and to inspire confidence amidst trouble, enabled Roosevelt to emerge the dominant figure of his age.

The Growth of a Politician

Born in 1882, the only child of a family with substantial inherited wealth, Franklin Delano Roosevelt grew up in a safe and secure environment that steeped him in the values of Christian service. He absorbed early a belief, which never left him, that the privileged had a duty to look after the poor and weak. At the Groton School (a prestigious prep school in Massachusetts) and Harvard University, his beliefs were meshed with an education designed to prepare him for the leadership reserved for his elite social class.

After a brief career as a reform member of the New York state legislature from 1910 to 1912 and as assistant secretary of the navy in Woodrow Wilson's administration, Roosevelt was nominated by the Democrats for the vice presidency in 1920. Despite Republican Warren Harding's landslide win, Roosevelt's spirited campaigning convinced many that he had a golden future in politics.

Fate, however, had a grim detour in store. In the summer of 1921, Roosevelt became paralyzed from the waist down, a victim of the polio virus. He would never again walk unassisted, but with the help of his devoted wife, Eleanor, and his tireless aide, Louis Howe, he did regain his intense desire for an active political career. Going places to know people in their own setting had always been Roosevelt's personal and political style. After the polio attack, he reversed the tactic by finding ways to draw people to him through letters, phone calls, receptions, dinner parties, cruises, and the Warm Springs, Georgia, polio sanitarium that he founded. Roosevelt's uncomplaining adjustment to his disability convinced his uncle Frederick Delano that he was "twice-born," that his ordeal had raised him above his privileged youth to help him become a strong and compassionate person. Those closest to Roosevelt—Eleanor Roosevelt and Louis Howe chief among them—insisted that the illness did not transform him but merely shifted his focus. No longer able to distract himself in physical activity, he concentrated on the art of political strategy and the use of verbal and visual symbols.

Roosevelt's chance to return to political office came sooner than he expected. When New York governor Al Smith announced his presidential candidacy in 1928, he convinced Roosevelt to run for his vacated position and so help Smith capture the state's electoral votes. The tactic did not work for Smith, who was defeated by Herbert Hoover, but Roosevelt managed a narrow upset victory. As the newly elected governor, he proposed a balanced program of conservation and scientific farming in the countryside combined with improved social services and working conditions in the cities.

Then the 1929 stock market crash forced Roosevelt to take a different approach. His beliefs

that government's prime role was to respond to social need and that states could be laboratories for national policy allowed him to find democratic and humane ways of dealing with the crisis and impelled him to support the largest state relief program in the nation's history. He played down any appearance of radical change by naming his new relief initiative the Temporary Emergency Relief Act (TERA). Using words like *temporary* and *emergency* made it possible to reassure a fearful public that the new initiatives were set securely within the established traditions of democracy and capitalism.

Roosevelt's highly visible efforts to alleviate suffering and his argument that the nation should follow the example of World War I by mobilizing national resources to defeat the economic crisis gained him the gratitude of constituents and the attention of national politicians. In 1930, New Yorkers reelected him governor by a margin of 750,000 votes and assured his position as the Democratic Party's leading candidate in the 1932 presidential election. In an address to the New York legislature in August 1931, Roosevelt summed up his activist credo:

> The duty of the State toward the citizen is the duty of the servant to its master. . . . One of these duties of the State is that of caring for those of its citizens who find themselves the victims of such adverse circumstances as make them unable to obtain even the necessities for mere existence without the aid of others. . . . To these unfortunate citizens aid must be extended by governments, not as a matter of charity but as a matter of social duty. . . .

The Election of 1932

Roosevelt announced his candidacy for the presidency in January 1932. The Roosevelt name, his radiant personal charm, his earlier service in Washington, and his stature as a vice presidential candidate had made him a national figure before the 1929 crash. Afterward, his smashing reelection and leading role among governors in combating the depression earned him praise as the most active champion of recovery. In all respects, Roosevelt's record compared favorably with Hoover's dismal image as a last-ditch defender of the old order.

To supply his campaign with fresh ideas, Roosevelt assembled a group of experts on national issues that a journalist dubbed the "Brains Trust."

ROOSEVELT'S COMMON TOUCH
In his campaign for reelection as governor of New York in 1930, Franklin Roosevelt boosted his vote total by 700,000 over the slender margin of 25,000 by which he in 1928 he became the first Democratic candidate for governor to win the vote outside New York City. Sensing that his presentation of himself as a good neighbor was responsible for much of his popularity, Roosevelt arranged to have a friendly chat outside polls in his hometown of Hyde Park with working-class voter Ruben Appel. In this photograph, Appel seems unaware that Roosevelt's standing was itself a feat of stagecraft. His legs rendered useless by polio, Roosevelt could only remain upright by using the strength he had developed in his arms and shoulders to prop himself up on his cane. Rare photos like this and a taboo against showing Roosevelt in his wheelchair kept the public from thinking of Roosevelt as a cripple, unfit for office, or in many cases from even realizing he was disabled.
Franklin D. Roosevelt Library.

Led by Columbia University professor Rexford Tugwell and lawyer and economist Adolf Berle, the Brains Trust plied Roosevelt with passionate arguments in favor of government planning to introduce stability and fair play into the marketplace and a welfare state to aid the helpless and end poverty. Roosevelt needed all his impressive political skills to overcome his conservative rivals within the Democratic Party and enact any Brains Trust ideas. Appealing to the victimized masses, he identified himself with what he described as "the forgotten man at the bottom of the pyramid" and asserted a need for "bold, persistent experimentation." To win support from those who feared that change could make things worse, Roosevelt avoided any suggestion that he would tamper with established institutions.

Roosevelt's position drew fire from both wings of the party. On the right, Al Smith, the party's 1928 presidential candidate, attacked Roosevelt as a fomenter of class conflict, while progressives chided Roosevelt for his unwillingness to offer bold plans for redistributing wealth and regulating the economy. Still, Roosevelt narrowly won the nomination at the head of a peculiar new coalition. It lumped together his friends within the Democratic Party's eastern establishment, big-city machine bosses, old Wilsonian reformers, entrenched Southerners—many of them deeply conservative and racist—along with angry farmers, western ranchers, labor unions, and urban ethnic communities. To give that unwieldy coalition any degree of coherence, Roosevelt realized that he must establish a personal, symbolic presence as leader of the war against the depression. He also showed his awareness that he needed southern votes to enact any sort of reform program by selecting a Texan, Speaker of the House of Representatives John "Cactus Jack" Garner, to be his running mate.

Roosevelt broke with the precedent that the nominee should stay at home during the national convention and await word of the party's choice. Instead, he flew to the convention in Chicago to deliver his acceptance speech in person. The flight, he told the delegates, signified his intention to be bold and lead the party in the direction "of liberal thought, of planned action, of enlightened international outlook, and of the greatest good to the greatest number of our citizens." Roosevelt expressed his dual allegiance to the New Freedom of Woodrow Wilson and the Square Deal of Theodore Roosevelt by combining them into his program label: the New Deal.

Frustrated that his glib opponent was trying out a variety of positions rather than committing to only one, President Hoover, the Republican nominee, attacked Roosevelt as a "chameleon on plaid" and decried the New Deal as un-American collectivism of the sort that Communists and fascists used to subdue the masses. Hoover praised the tried-and-true virtues of self-reliance, as opposed to handouts and government controls. Many voters, however, heard Hoover's appeals for individual effort and sacrifice as coldhearted rhetoric that ignored their suffering. The president soon became the scapegoat for all ills, his very name a label for poverty. New York City's Parks Department officially designated as "Hoover Valley" a gully where derelicts huddled in Central Park. When home-run king Babe Ruth was criticized for requesting a salary higher than President Hoover's, the Babe shot back, "So what? I had a better year."

On election day, Hoover went down to utter defeat (Map 24.1). Roosevelt received 22.8 million votes, 57 percent of the total, to 15.8 million votes for Hoover. In the electoral college, Roosevelt's margin was even more lopsided, 472 to 59. Hitched to Roosevelt's star, Democrats swept into control of Congress for the first time since 1916. Democrats ruled the Senate by a margin of 59 to 36 and dominated the House by 313 to 117. Although Roosevelt had barely secured the Democrats' nomination, he won an overwhelming victory at the head of a fragmented party that had not elected a president with a majority of the votes since Franklin Pierce won in 1852.

The electoral switch from a landslide for Hoover and the Republicans in the 1928 election to a landslide for Roosevelt and the Democrats in 1932 was the greatest change in voter choice in the nation's history (Map 24.2). It began what political analysts have termed the "Roosevelt Revolution"—a fundamental realignment of voter allegiance that linked farmers, industrial laborers, white-collar workers, African Americans, immigrants, women, and intellectuals to the New Deal. The concept that had prevailed since the Civil War of weak central government deferring to economic free enterprise had been repudiated by a public eager to place its faith in a man who promised bold action.

The First New Deal in Action

At noon on March 4, 1933, Americans anxiously gathered around their radios to hear a serene and confident new president declare that the "only thing we have to fear is fear itself" and then promise "direct, vigorous action." The first months of Roosevelt's administration, called "the Hundred Days," were a blur of action that carried out that promise. The most immediate task was to offer relief to the destitute, including the 25 percent of the workforce that was unemployed. Their plight pointed toward a second need: the recovery of business and farming so that jobs would be available to all workers. And that goal led to the third challenge: reform of the system to guard against any future economic collapse.

The New Dealers

The New Deal represents the only moment in American history when a reform-minded president took office in bad times rather than good. Roosevelt's reform heroes—Andrew Jackson, Theodore Roosevelt, and Woodrow Wilson—had the advantage of serving during economic booms. Roosevelt con-

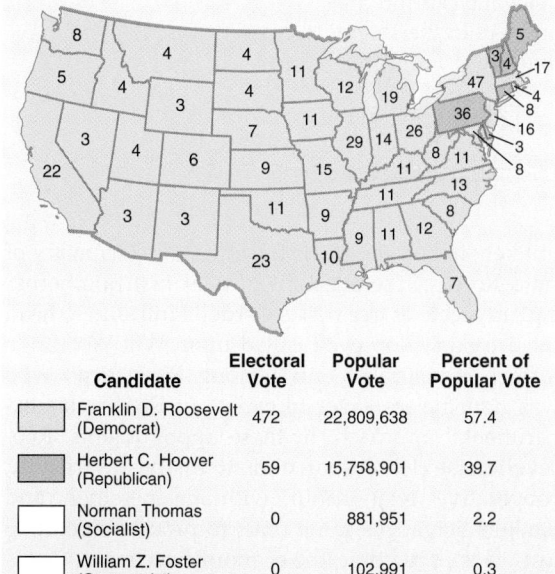

Candidate	Electoral Vote	Popular Vote	Percent of Popular Vote
Franklin D. Roosevelt (Democrat)	472	22,809,638	57.4
Herbert C. Hoover (Republican)	59	15,758,901	39.7
Norman Thomas (Socialist)	0	881,951	2.2
William Z. Foster (Communist)	0	102,991	0.3

MAP 24.1
The Election of 1932

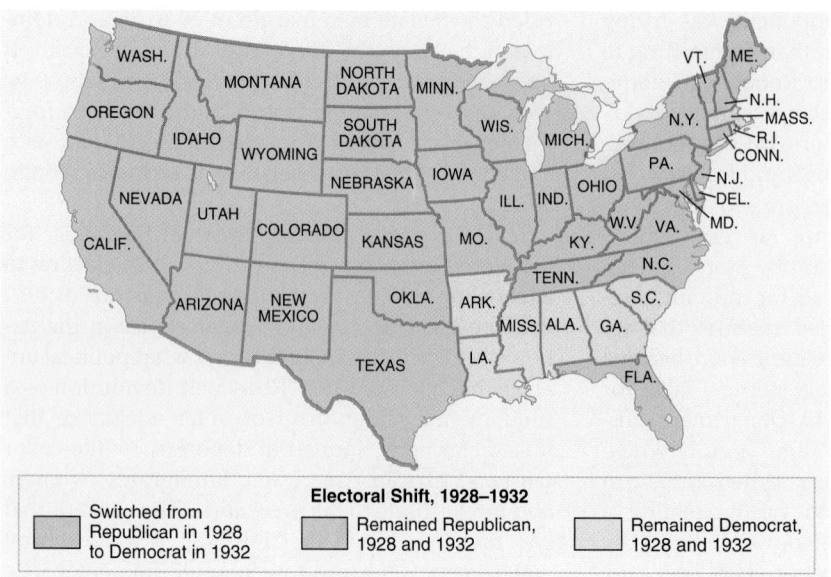

Electoral Shift, 1928–1932

Switched from
Republican in 1928
to Democrat in 1932

Remained Republican,
1928 and 1932

Remained Democrat,
1928 and 1932

MAP 24.2

Electoral Shift, 1928–1932

Democratic victory in 1932 signaled the rise of a New Deal coalition within which women and minorities, many of them new voters, made the Democrats the majority party for the first time in the twentieth century.

READING THE MAP: How many states voted Democratic in 1928? How many states voted Republican in 1932? How many states shifted from Republican to Democratic between 1928 and 1932?

CONNECTIONS: What did Franklin Roosevelt's campaign slogans call for, and what past programs did he cite as influences? What factions within the Democratic party opposed Roosevelt's candidacy in 1932, and why?

www.bedfordstmartins.com/roarkcompact SEE THE ONLINE STUDY GUIDE for more help in analyzing this map.

fronted the more daunting task of reversing an economic depression without violating the nation's allegiance to democracy and capitalism. Great numbers of reformers hurried to Washington in the spring of 1933, drawn by the combination of public desperation and the chance to serve under a president receptive to new ideas. "As for those first New Deal days," Gardiner C. Means, an economic adviser, recalled, "much of the excitement came from improvisation. Nothing was fully set in the minds of the people there. They were open to fresh ideas. Always."

In recognition of his sprawling party base, Roosevelt selected his cabinet and staff to represent important constituencies. He also chose advisers who would be loyal to him and who would be

unlikely to become rivals for power. For secretary of state, Roosevelt selected an old Wilsonian Southerner and advocate of free trade, Cordell Hull, and to head the Treasury, Roosevelt called upon Will Woodin, a former industrialist and lifelong Republican who was nonetheless eager to carry out Roosevelt's experimental approach. In these appointments, Roosevelt made clear his intention to establish a friendly, cooperative relationship with businessmen and bankers yet, at the same time, to proceed openly to test ways of rescuing the economic system.

For the heads of the Labor and Agriculture Departments, whose constituencies were more fully the forgotten and the hard-pressed, Roosevelt turned to reformers. He chose Frances Perkins to become the first female secretary of labor, much to the outrage of traditional labor leaders. Henry A. Wallace of Iowa, a voice for scientific experiment and government regulation of markets, was tapped to be secretary of agriculture.

For other, less central appointments, Roosevelt rounded out a cabinet and a set of advisers that represented virtually all sections of the country, both major parties, the Protestant, Catholic, and Jewish communities, and both sexes. Through it all, Roosevelt radiated good cheer and relished his task as the impresario of a great rescue operation and the restorer of public confidence. He wore out his assistants, picking their brains, prodding them to find fresh solutions. To communicate with the public, he began his practice of frequent news conferences, which brought him face to face with the press thirty times during the Hundred Days and at least once a week thereafter. His wide grin and infectious optimism made him the personal symbol of recovery, the emblem of hope for millions.

Banking and Finance Reform

The new administration first targeted the disaster engulfing America's banking system. Since 1930 more than five thousand banks, with $3.4 billion in assets, had gone under, and by the time Roosevelt was inaugurated on March 4, 1933, the nation's governors had suspended almost all banking opera-

tions within their states. On March 6, Roosevelt made good his inaugural pledge for "action now" by announcing a four-day "bank holiday" that converted emergency state action into federal policy. Three days later, Roosevelt sent Congress the Emergency Banking Act, which Congress passed in four hours (Table 24.1). Under the provisions of the bill, the secretary of the treasury could decide which banks were stable enough to reopen and could authorize the Reconstruction Finance Corporation (RFC) to supply funds for immediate circulation. Congress then created the Federal Deposit Insurance Corporation (FDIC) to insure bank customers against the loss of their deposits if their banks should fail.

The New Deal's more radical supporters were disappointed that Roosevelt did not nationalize the banks and make them a firm cornerstone for national planning. Instead, the private banking system was propped up with federal funds and subjected to federal regulation and oversight. Within a few days, most of the nation's major banks were able to reopen their doors, and they remained solvent through the remaining depression years.

On March 12, Roosevelt broadcast his first "fireside chat" to the nation, explaining why the banking legislation was needed and how it gave good reason for confidence. That radio talk, suggesting a cozy gathering of the nation at the family hearth to discuss how much spending money was left, was a

TABLE 24.1
MAJOR LEGISLATION OF THE NEW DEAL'S FIRST HUNDRED DAYS

Name of Act	Date Passed	Basic Provisions
Emergency Banking Act	March 9, 1933	Provided for reopening stable banks and authorizing RFC to supply funds
Civilian Conservation Corps Act	March 31, 1933	Provided jobs for unemployed youth
Agricultural Adjustment Act	May 12, 1933	Provided funds to pay farmers for not growing surplus crops
Federal Emergency Relief Act	May 12, 1933	Provided relief funds for the destitute
Tennessee Valley Authority Act	May 18, 1933	Set up authority for development of electric power and conservation
National Industrial Recovery Act	June 16, 1933	Specified cooperation among business, government, and labor in setting fair prices and working conditions
Glass-Steagall Banking Act	June 16, 1933	Created Federal Deposit Insurance Corporation (FDIC) to insure bank deposits

masterstroke. Roosevelt, speaking in cheerful, simple, fatherly terms, came through as a friendly savior echoing his inaugural address with his reassurance against fear. In the minds of a majority of Americans, the New Deal had established its competence and humaneness, and a glimmer of the nation's old optimism returned.

Turning to the stock market, whose scandals so vividly symbolized the 1920s, Roosevelt was eager to enact provisions that would end dubious practices such as the pyramiding of holding companies or profitable stock trading on the basis of insider information. At his insistence, Congress passed legislation in 1933 and 1934 that created the Securities and Exchange Commission (SEC) to license investment dealers, monitor all stock transactions, restrict margin buying, and require corporate officers to make full disclosures of their stock offerings and take responsibility for any claims they made about their companies.

Roosevelt named an abrasive and successful Wall Street trader, Joseph P. Kennedy, as chairman of the SEC. When critics opposed the choice of someone whose reputation had been clouded by shrewd stock manipulation, Roosevelt replied wickedly, "Set a thief to catch a thief." Kennedy proved to be tough enough to face down threats by brokers, some of them with things to hide, to boycott the exchange or even move it out of the country. Cleaned up and regulated, Wall Street soon regained the confidence of investors.

Relief and Conservation Programs

Having rescued the nation's financial structure, Roosevelt took on the plight of the unemployed, the landless, the disabled, and those who were too old or too young to work. The Federal Emergency Relief Administration (FERA) Act made good on the president's promise that he would not abandon Americans to hunger and homelessness. To win public support for this unprecedented federal initiative, FERA director Harry Hopkins sent reporters out to describe conditions. Firmly backed by a public aroused by the vivid reports, FERA supported from four to five million households each month and funded thousands of work projects for the unemployed. FERA also took the lead in providing vaccinations and immunizations for millions of unprotected poor people, helped build desperately needed flood protection systems, and funded literacy classes for the most ill-prepared citizens.

The most popular work relief program was the Civilian Conservation Corps (CCC), which offered unemployed young men a chance to perform useful outdoor work and reflected Roosevelt's long-standing enthusiasm for conservation and his preference for the country over the city. The three million young people who enlisted had good reason to agree with him. Typical was Blackie Gold, who remembered how as a child he had to "beg for coal, buy bread that's two, three days old" in order to help support his large family. In 1937 he joined the CCC and was able to send home $30 a month, while living a healthy outdoor life. By the end of the program in 1942, CCC workers had erected dams to stop soil erosion and tame rivers,

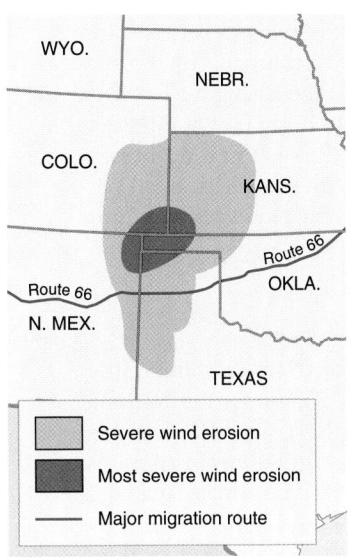

The Dust Bowl

and planted more than two billion new trees to replenish forest preserves and check dust storms in the Southwest. They also strung 83,000 miles of telephone wires, constructed 122,000 miles of minor roads and trails, and located 23,000 new water sources in the nation's wilderness. In the process, the CCC left a legacy of vast new recreation areas, along with the roads and communication that made them accessible to millions of people.

The most spectacular accomplishment of New Deal conservation efforts was the Tennessee Valley Authority (TVA), created in 1933 to build hydroelectric power dams along the Tennessee River to bring power and light to impoverished rural communities. The TVA plan included model towns for power station workers and new homes for farmers who would benefit from electricity and flood control. At the same time, the TVA sought to conserve the region's character through programs to encourage local crafts and other folkways (Map 24.3).

Following the Tennessee River across the state lines of Virginia, North Carolina, Tennessee, Georgia, Alabama, Mississippi, and Kentucky, the TVA set out to demonstrate that a partnership between the federal government and local residents could overcome traditional limitations of state boundaries and free enterprise to make efficient use of abundant resources and so break an ancient cycle of poverty. The TVA became the most ambitious example of New Deal enthusiasm for planning. But

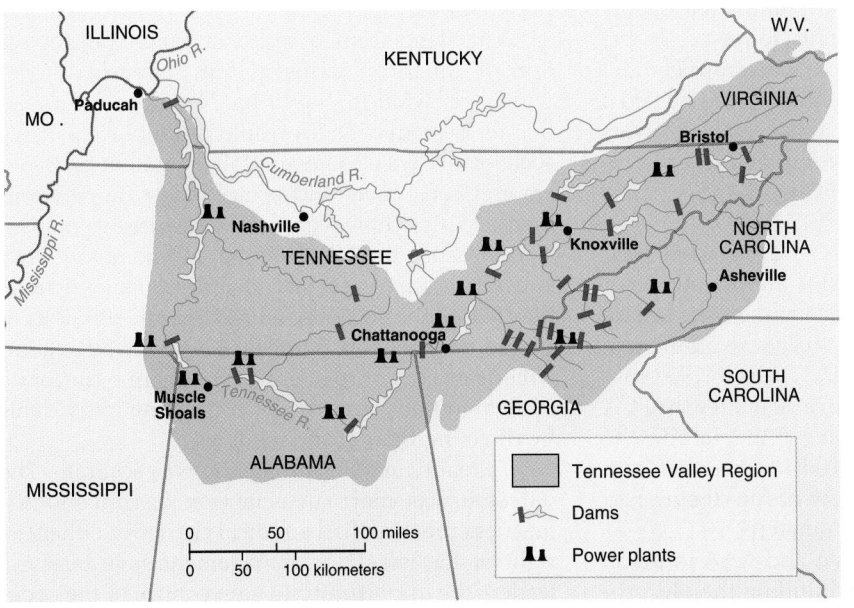

MAP 24.3

The Tennessee Valley Authority

The New Deal created the Tennessee Valley Authority to modernize a vast impoverished region with hydroelectric power dams and, at the same time, to reclaim eroded lands and preserve old folkways.

hampered by bitter resistance from competing private power companies, the TVA never fully realized its utopian ends. It did, however, succeed in bringing electric power, flood protection, and soil reclamation, and therefore sharply improved prosperity to the area it served.

Agricultural Initiatives

Farmers in the hard times after World War I tried to make up for low crop prices by increasing production, thus creating surpluses that drove prices still lower. In the 1920s, congressional bills to deal with the problem by dumping the surplus abroad were vetoed by presidents fearful that foreign countries would retaliate for the harm American surpluses would do to the efforts of their own farmers to earn a living. On the eve of the New Deal, a farm economist named M. L. Wilson devised a voluntary "domestic allotment plan," which would bring prosperity without surpluses by paying farmers to leave some of their land idle. In May, Congress enthusiastically incorporated Wilson's plan into the Agricultural Adjustment Act (AAA) and soon afterward passed companion legislation, the Farm Credit Act (FCA), to provide credit on mortgaged farm property to head off foreclosures that would drive debt-ridden farmers from their land.

The security provided by the AAA and FCA discouraged farm revolts and nudged prices upward. Overall results were mixed, however. In the corn, hog, and wheat region of the Midwest, farmers came together democratically, and a reasonably equitable distribution of benefits followed. In the South, local control meant that sharecroppers and tenant farmers on cotton plantations were denied a decent share of the benefits, while large growers reaped huge subsidies for putting land out of production—and tenants out of work. (See "The Promise of Technology," page 617.)

Nonetheless, the AAA and FCA guided agriculture toward prosperity. With almost all major crops limited, surpluses declined and gross farm income rose from $6.4 billion in 1932 to $8.5 billion in 1934. The trickle of 7,800 federal loans in 1932 rose to a flood of 287,881 in less than a year after the FCA was enacted in 1933. By the end of the decade, the federal government had financed 40 percent of farm mortgage debt, and the shadow of foreclosure had receded from most farmers' doorsteps.

After putting both the TVA and AAA in place, the administration turned to fulfilling the old pro-

gressive dream of extending electricity and all its modern benefits to rural America. When Roosevelt became president, about 90 percent of the country outside the cities and towns was without electricity. In May 1935, the New Deal created the Rural Electrification Administration (REA) to get around the reluctance of the private power industry to extend transmission lines into sparsely settled (and thus unprofitable) country. Encouraged by the successes of the AAA and TVA, the REA gave low-cost loans to farm cooperatives to bring power into their communities. By 1941, the REA succeeded in raising the number of farms with electricity to 40 percent. By 1950, nine out of every ten American farms were electrified.

Industrial Recovery

The New Deal's National Recovery Administration (NRA), established in June 1933 under the National Industrial Recovery Act (NIRA), was a far less successful experiment than the agricultural programs. The NRA's objective was to coordinate management, labor, and the federal government through a network of industrial codes that governed working conditions, prices, and trade practices. To secure worker rights, the NRA struck a bargain with business leaders to ease antitrust regulations in exchange for the right of labor to engage in collective bargaining. By the end of 1933, most industries were represented within the 541 NRA codes, and the Blue Eagle symbol displayed in store windows let the public know.

The stage seemed set for a major transformation of American industry, but opinions differed widely on what it should be. New Dealers hoped that the system of codes would produce a collective social conscience to ensure fair treatment of workers and consumers and protection of the environment. Critics, however, saw bureaucratic oppression. Because the NRA skirted antimonopoly laws and left industry subject to federal management, they feared the economy would become rigidly controlled from the top. Some even saw the NRA as an American version of Benito Mussolini's corporate fascism in Italy, a means for controlling individuals by directing their economic lives.

In reality, neither prediction was accurate. The outcome was more an extension of conventional business practice than a radical change to either the right or the left. Poor management gave business leaders the opportunity to gain control of the code-

Mechanized Cotton Picking Revolutionizes a Social System

I N 1935, TWO OF THE MOST IMPORTANT farm machines of the time, the Farmall tractor and the Rust cotton picker, cut through a sea of cotton, showing how mechanization could eliminate the backbreaking work of harvesting cotton by hand. Within ten years tractors would displace horses as the main means of doing heavy farm work, but success for mechanical cotton pickers was longer in coming. For a century and a half after the invention of the cotton gin in 1793 made cotton farming feasible, inventors tried to create a device that would make picking cotton as efficient as ginning it. The first patent for a crude mechanical picker was granted in 1850 and nearly two thousand more followed before John Rust in 1931 demonstrated a machine that could pick more bales of cotton in a day than the average farmer in the deep South grew in a year.

Ironically, though Southerners had realized their dream of mechanizing cotton picking, the machine was so efficient that it was ill suited to most southern cotton farms, whose yearly crop was relatively modest. Nor could most growers afford the machinery. By 1931, cotton prices had plunged from thirty-five cents a bale in 1919 to only six cents a bale.

In the next two decades, large farms using the new mechanical cotton picker became dominant and that change shifted most cotton growing to the West, where vast agricultural holdings were the rule. Displaced by the decline of King Cotton in the South, field hands like the woman shown above migrated in thousands to the North in search of new jobs.

Cotton picking machine: Mississippi State University Libraries.
Cotton picker: Courtesy of the Harvard University Art Museums.
Gift of Bernarda B. Shahn, Estate of Ben Shahn.

SKETCH FOR A FEDERAL ARTS PROGRAM MURAL
This sketch for a mural commissioned for Lenoir City, Tennessee, is typical of the Federal Arts Program's goal to memorialize significant moments of achievement in every region of the country. For rural folk, the sight of Rural Electrification Authority (REA) workers extending power lines was one of the more exciting symbols of the New Deal. When the REA came into existence in 1935, less than 10 percent of the nation outside the cities had electricity. By 1941, REA programs had increased that number to 40 percent; ten years later the figure had risen to 90 percent, and the gulf of silence and darkness between town and country was successfully bridged.
Public Buildings Service, General Services Administration.

writing mechanism, and they made sure the codes would first serve the interests of corporate profits rather than workers or the general welfare. By the mid-1930s, prospects for a rationally coordinated business system had faded.

Challenges to the New Deal

Since the New Deal sought economic recovery, New Dealers expected business leaders to come around eventually and welcome cooperative planning. But the administration was sorely disappointed. Business leaders never reconciled themselves to the administration's planning concept. One Republican senator derided the creator of the NRA as "Frankenstein" Roosevelt and declared that the Blue Eagle was really "the Soviet duck" in disguise. Meanwhile, critics on the left faulted the administration for not offering programs radical enough to meet the people's needs.

Resistance to Business Reform

Ironically, the business community kept up its criticism even though its situation improved more steadily during the depression than did that of most other social groups, including farmers and workers. The managerial elite remained mostly intact—despite some spectacular jailings, flights from prosecution, and suicides. So did the hierarchical corporate structure that had been developed during the boom years at the turn of the century. The greatest wounds business leaders suffered were to their confidence and pride. Fearful of regulation, taxes, and unions, they created stridently anti–New Deal public relations offices and sometimes deployed company spies to seek out disloyal workers. The rage of business leaders at their loss of public adoration and government favor fastened on Franklin Roosevelt.

By 1935, the two major business organizations, the National Association of Manufacturers and the Chamber of Commerce, had become openly anti–New Deal. But their critiques were mild compared with the all-out assault of the American Liberty League, founded in 1934. Prominent members of the league, including Al Smith, had once been leaders in the Democratic Party, but now they decried the New Deal as a betrayer of basic constitutional guarantees of freedom and individualism. To them, the AAA was a "trend toward fascist control of agriculture," relief programs marked "the end of democracy," and the NRA was a plunge into the "quicksand of visionary experimentation." Although the league's membership never exceeded 125,000, its well-financed publicity campaign led the way in widening the rift between Roosevelt and the business class.

Planners and labor leaders who favored more worker control attacked the New Deal from the other direction. In their view, the NRA had stifled enterprise by permitting monopolistic practices. They pointed out that industrial trade associations twisted codes to suit their aims, thwarted competition, and engaged in price gouging. Labor leaders especially resented the willingness of the NRA to allow companies to form their own unions, while blocking the organization of genuine grassroots unions that permitted workers to bargain on terms they chose for themselves.

In the midst of the crossfire, the Supreme Court in May 1935 declared that the NRA unconstitutionally conferred legislative power on an administrative agency and overstepped the limits of federal power to regulate interstate commerce. The NRA lingered briefly, but its codes lost their authority. In its failure, the NRA demonstrated both historic American resistance to economic planning and the refusal of the business community to yield its autonomy unless forced to do so.

Reaction against the New Deal Farm Program

The AAA weathered its battering by champions of the old order better than the NRA. Even though farmers were reluctant to abandon their freedom to increase production as a matter of pride and survival, the allotment checks for keeping land fallow and the higher prices for farm produce created loyalty among those with enough acreage to participate.

Protest stirred, however, among those with smaller farms who did not qualify for allotments. The Southern Farm Tenants Union argued passionately that the AAA was a device for enriching large farmers at the expense of smaller ones. By taking out of production the land on which tenants lived, owners could simultaneously qualify for government subsidies and be relieved of the need to provide for the dependent tenants. One black sharecropper found it simple enough to explain why only $75 a year from plantation subsidies made it down to her: "de landlord is landlord, de politicians is landlord, de judge is landlord, de shurf [sheriff] is landlord, ever'body is landlord, en we ain' got nothin'!"

The AAA's most potent critics, however, were agricultural processors and distributors. They were unhappy that the AAA reduced the volume of production—the only source of their profits—while they were required to pay for the very program that disadvantaged them. In 1936, the Supreme Court agreed with their contention that they were the victims of an illegal attempt to tax one group (processors and distributors) to enrich another (farmers). Down but not out, the AAA rebounded from the Supreme Court ruling by redesigning its allotment provisions with legislation that focused more on conservation measures the Court found acceptable.

Politics on the Fringes

The New Deal also faced challenges from a small but growing minority drawn to radical movements. Socialists and Communists accused the New Deal of mounting feeble resistance to business elites or, worse, rescuing capitalism from its self-inflicted crisis. Among those drawn to the left were many intellectuals and artists, who decided it was time to use their talents to advance the cause of radical change. Socialist author Upton Sinclair became the most prominent of the intellectuals who went directly into politics when he ran for governor of California in 1934. Rousing wide public support for his End Poverty in California plan to put the unemployed to work in idle factories, Sinclair lost by a narrow margin only because fraudulent charges that he was a Communist frightened many voters and caused Roosevelt to withdraw his support.

With that one exception, the left was never able to mount a serious electoral challenge. For all the doctrinaire talk of violent overthrow of the government by the proletariat, there was no real chance of that happening in a highly modern state where the authorities had great force to bring to bear against dissenters. Most Americans, with varying degrees of militancy, sought inclusion, not revolution, and fundamental entitlements, not radical novelties. Accordingly, homespun populist agitators preaching old-style religion and harping on birthrights, not socialist revolution, drew the biggest crowds looking for an alternative to the status quo.

The largest coalition of those feeling left out by the New Deal was led by a Catholic priest in Detroit named Charles Coughlin. Father Coughlin expressed his outrage at the depression in a series of radio broadcasts that drew a nationwide audience of forty million by 1930. The "Radio Priest" found villains in all the conventional places. He began by denouncing Communists as traditional foes of the church and soon added bankers and other "predatory capitalists," who, he increasingly insisted, were dominated by Jews. After first welcoming Roosevelt in 1932 as the nation's political savior, Coughlin soon turned against the administration for its failure to "drive the moneychangers from the temple." In 1935, Coughlin converted his grassroots coalition into the National Union for Social Justice, or the Union Party, and in 1936 called on other dissidents to join him in mounting an election challenge to Roosevelt. Drawing on the populist tradition, the Union Party favored an expanded money supply backed by silver so that the poor could be rescued from the "cross of gold" that William Jennings Bryan had so famously associated with business domination of the economy.

One of those who answered Father Coughlin's call was Dr. Francis Townsend, an elderly public health officer in Long Beach, California. Angered that his retired patients existed in misery in the golden land, Townsend in 1933 proposed the Old Age Revolving Pension, which would pay all persons over age sixty $200 a month on the condition that they spend the entire amount within thirty days and thereby stimulate the economy. Buoyed by the 90 percent of Long Beach voters who endorsed his petition to the federal government, Townsend organized pension clubs that attracted between 2 and 3.5 million paying members looking for security. When the major parties rebuffed his plan as impractical, Townsend merged his forces with Coughlin's Union Party in time for the 1936 election.

The most formidable of the rebellious populists came from another region ripe for protest. Huey Pierce Long, son of a backcountry farmer, had used his immense talents to become governor of Louisiana in 1928 and U.S. senator in 1932. Reaching out to the poor with brash rhetoric and country humor, he swept out of power a reactionary political machine that had kept Louisiana one of the poorest and most backward states. By delivering on his promises to build roads, schools, and hospitals and to provide jobs, Long shone as a beacon of hope to the dispossessed and a menace to the well-to-do. As a freshman senator, Long introduced a sweeping "soak the rich" tax bill that would outlaw personal incomes of more than $1 million and inheritances of more than $5 million. Swift rejection by the Senate triggered his long-range strategy of becoming president by mobilizing the vast numbers of low-income Americans into a Share Our Wealth protest movement. His opportunity never arrived, however. In 1935 he was gunned down in the Louisiana State House by the enraged son of a judge Long had removed from the bench.

BADGE FOR THE FORGOTTEN MAN
An emblem in the form of a police badge lent an air of authority to Huey Long's radical Share-Our-Wealth movement, while perhaps adding to the fear of the rich that much of their wealth would be taken into custody. More darkly, the motto proclaiming that the spirit and purpose of Huey Long would never die indicates Long's foreboding that he would be assassinated before his plans could bear fruit. He was right in fearing death, but not in supposing that success for Share Our Wealth would be his legacy.
Louisiana State University, Hill Memorial Library.

The populist challenge stirred the New Deal administration to solidify its winning coalition. An early test came in the 1934 congressional elections, normally a time when a seated president loses support. Roosevelt approached the elections as an opportunity to distance the New Deal from radical and crank causes on the right and left. In August, the president embarked on a national tour to support loyal Democratic candidates for whom an unusually high percentage of voters turned out to give New Dealers a landslide victory. Democrats increased their numbers in the House of Representatives from 310 to 319 out of 422; and in the Senate, the party gained 10 new seats to take a commanding two-thirds majority, the greatest margin ever achieved in that body.

The Second New Deal and the Rise of the Welfare State

Though Roosevelt had been "all but crowned by the people," as one journalist put it, the administration found the outlook at mid-decade troubling. The New Deal had begun with bold action to halt the economic decline and restore hope, yet a glance at almost any economic index—employment, production, or income—revealed how anemic the economy remained. The Hundred Days had spent itself, and major programs were faltering (AAA) or had been invalidated by the Supreme Court (NRA). With criticism of insufficient action intensifying on the right and the left, Roosevelt decided it was time for a departure.

In 1935, New Dealers surged ahead with a flurry of new policies, sometimes called the Second Hundred Days, that moved away from central economic planning toward provision for the special needs of various social groups. Out of the welter of legislative and executive action that made up the Second New Deal emerged the first elements of an American welfare state. Reformers who recognized that individuals were more often victims of economic forces beyond their control now looked to government as the legitimate, even sole, power able to improve the nation's economic health and guard its citizens' well-being.

Relief for the Unemployed

Decrying how unemployment wounded people by striking at "their self-respect, their self-confidence

and courage and determination," Roosevelt in May 1935 created the Works Progress Administration (WPA) to put the unemployed to work for the public benefit. State and municipal agencies were given the responsibility to propose needed projects; the WPA merely specified that the projects be useful, be undertaken in places where unemployment was high, and produce results that would bring revenues back to the Treasury as soon as possible.

By the time it ended in 1943, because the war effort absorbed the unemployed, the WPA had generated jobs costing $10 billion that provided an average of a year's worth of work for each of the thirteen million unemployed men and women put on the payroll. Construction amounted to about three-fourths of the total WPA projects, resulting in 572,000 miles of country roads, 40,000 buildings, 67,000 miles of city streets, 78,000 bridges, 8,000 parks, and 350 airports, along with a variety of smaller projects.

In a striking departure from the usual pick-and-shovel relief program, the WPA also allowed unemployed people in the arts to make use of their talents. After all, Roosevelt pointed out in endorsing the idea, artists "have to live . . . and surely there must be some public place where paintings are wanted." At its peak, the WPA employed some six thousand artists, musicians, actors, journalists, academics, poets, and novelists. The roster included towering figures such as novelist John Steinbeck and poet Conrad Aiken. WPA Theater brought sixty million people to its performances, and in the first fifteen months of the WPA Music Project, fifty million Americans heard concerts. As the program's most lasting reminder, paintings, sculptures, and prints came to grace America's courthouses, public buildings, and museums.

Empowering Labor

In 1934, a series of local uprisings, mostly by unskilled workers who had no unions to join, set in motion a labor revolution. Striking workers in Toledo, Minneapolis, and San Francisco, asserting their right to picket their employers, encountered ferocious opposition by police and the National Guard. Bloody battles in the streets and on the docks made plain the determination of militant new labor leaders to break the dominance that industrial management had achieved over workers during the 1920s.

After the violence of 1934 subsided, labor leaders focused on the National Labor Relations Act

MACBETH OPENS IN HARLEM
The New Deal Federal Theater Project, which began in 1935, had the good fortune of attracting as one of its directors a twenty-year-old genius named Orson Welles. Acting on news that Welles and an African American theater group had prepared a version of **Macbeth** *set in Haiti, an opening night crowd in 1938 mobbed the Lafayette theater in Harlem. As one reviewer put it, the play was "a classic stunt" that ensured the director's reputation and indicated new directions for the American theater.*
Library of Congress.

(NLRA), a bill sponsored by Senator Robert Wagner of New York that would create federal supervision of labor disputes. Justly considered a "Magna Carta for labor," the Wagner Act, as it came to be called, guaranteed workers the right to organize freely and created a National Labor Relations Board to oversee elections for union representation. If the majority of workers at a company voted for a union, the union became the sole bargaining agent for the entire workplace, and employers were required to negotiate with the duly elected union leaders.

Roosevelt was at first reluctant to have his NRA ideal of cooperative decision making replaced by adversarial collective bargaining, but he signed the Wagner Act into law in July 1935 as the best way available to protect the rights of workers and unions.

While the Wagner Act moved through Congress, unskilled workers, who had been largely unrepresented within organized labor, began to press for inclusion. Under the aggressive leadership of John L. Lewis, head of the United Mine Workers

(UMW), and Sidney Hillman, head of the Amalgamated Clothing Workers, a coalition of unskilled workers gathered in 1935 to form the Committee for Industrial Organization (CIO; later the Congress of Industrial Organizations). By mobilizing unskilled workers, the CIO greatly reduced the lordly power of industrialists and began to win significant concessions on wages and working conditions.

The achievements that flowed from the new militancy of labor and a sympathetic government were impressive. When Roosevelt took office in 1933, AFL membership stood at three million, down by half since the end of World War I. Once the Wagner Act took hold, unions expanded almost fivefold, to fourteen million members by the time of Roosevelt's death in 1945. Thirty percent of the workforce was then unionized, the highest union representation ever reached. Large numbers of unskilled assembly-line workers, many of them African Americans or immigrants, flocked to unions for the first time. A new left-wing militancy helped power union insurgency; and the exceptional courage and organizing skill of Communists and other radicals in the CIO earned them leadership roles in the campaign to organize the automobile and steel industries.

A campaign by the United Auto Workers (UAW) to unionize workers at General Motors climaxed in January 1937 when workers occupied the main assembly plant in Flint, Michigan, in a "sit-down" strike that reduced the plant's production of 15,000 cars a week to a mere 150. In desperation, General Motors obtained injunctions against the sit-down. But neither Roosevelt nor Michigan governor Frank Murphy would act. Although they did not approve of the strikers' illegal occupation of the plant, they were unwilling to end the strike by force. Stymied, General Motors signed an agreement that made the UAW the sole bargaining agent for all of the company's workers and prohibited the company from interfering with union activity. Having beaten the automobile industry's leading producer, the UAW expanded its campaign until, with the capitulation of Ford in 1941, the entire industry was unionized.

The CIO hoped to ride success in automobile plants to victory in the steel mills. But after unionizing the industry giant U.S. Steel, the CIO ran up against fanatic opposition from smaller steel firms, led by Bethlehem Steel's Tom Girdler. The climax came in May 1937 when a crowd of strikers gathered in a field outside Chicago to organize a picket line around Republic Steel. Without warning, police who had been sent there to keep order charged the crowd, firing their sidearms and wielding clubs, killing ten and injuring scores. The battered steelworkers then halted their organizing campaign. In steel and other major industries, such as the highly resistant southern textile mills, unions would have renewed success only after 1941, when the demands of military buildup gave workers greater bargaining power.

Social Security and Tax Reform

Standing alongside the Wagner Act and the WPA as a major New Deal accomplishment was the Social Security Act, designed to provide a supplementary income for aged and retired persons. Taking care of hard-hit elderly people during the depression had become almost as desperate a necessity as providing relief to the unemployed. The population over age sixty-five had doubled between 1870 and 1930 at the same time that work for the elderly declined. Of the tiny minority who worked, only 15 percent had pension plans, and insolvent corporations and banks often could not come up with funds during the depression to pay the meager pensions they had promised. Just eighteen states provided elderly assistance, which usually amounted to about a dollar a day for impoverished individuals. With the aggressive agitation of Dr. Townsend, Father Coughlin, and Huey Long rumbling ominously in the background, Roosevelt became the first president to advocate protection for the elderly, describing it as "our plain duty to provide for that security upon which [the general] welfare depends." In 1935, he appointed Frances Perkins to chair a committee that readied the Social Security Act for his signature in August of that year.

The struggle for Social Security brought out class differences in their starkest form. Support for the measure came from a coalition of advocate groups for the elderly and the poor, traditional progressives, leftists, social workers, labor unions, and educators. Arrayed against them were economic conservatives, including the Liberty League, the National Association of Manufacturers, the Chamber of Commerce, and the American Medical Association. Enact the Social Security system, these conservatives and their representatives in the Republican Party warned, and the government will gain a whip hand over private property, destroy initiative, and reduce proud individuals to spineless loafers.

Obvious need and the large New Deal majority in Congress carried the day. Yet the strong objections to federal involvement in matters traditionally left to individual and local charity persuaded the framers of Social Security to strike a balance among federal, state, and personal responsibility. The Social Security program therefore required that pensions for the elderly be funded by tax contributions from workers and their employers. It also created unemployment insurance, paid for by employers' contributions. In a bow to traditional local responsibility for public assistance, Social Security issued grants for the states to use to support dependent mothers and children, public health services, and the blind. A Supreme Court decision in 1937 upheld the right of Congress to require all citizens to pay for Social Security through their federal taxes and allowed the Social Security Act to be expanded to include benefits for dependent survivors of deceased recipients. As a result of this momentous change in public policy, the elderly began their journey from the lowest economic status to the highest, and the attachment of ordinary workers to the New Deal became even stronger.

Opposition to Social Security struck New Dealers as evidence that the rich had learned little from the depression. Roosevelt had long felt contempt for the moneyed elite and looked for a way to redistribute wealth that would, in a single stroke, weaken conservative opposition, advance the cause of social equity, and defuse populist challenges on the fringe. In June 1935, as the Social Security Act was being debated, Roosevelt delivered a message to Congress outlining comprehensive tax reform. Charging that large fortunes put "great and undesirable concentration of control in [the hands of] relatively few individuals," Roosevelt urged a graduated tax on corporations, a similar tax on holding company dividends used to shelter corporate income, an inheritance tax, and an increase in maximum personal income taxes from 63 to 79 percent. Against charges that higher taxes on the rich would dampen their initiative, Roosevelt contended that the new measures would instead stimulate competition. A progressive tax would make the wealthy work harder to retain their affluence and give ordinary Americans in small, innovative enterprises a better chance to succeed.

Congress endorsed Roosevelt's basic taxation principle by enacting a slightly progressive tax—one that taxed those with higher incomes at a higher rate—on undistributed corporate profits. From there, with the Revenue Act of 1937, Roosevelt moved to close loopholes that he considered outrageous. Threatening to name names of the wealthy who were not paying their fair share of taxes, Roosevelt persuaded Congress to eliminate a number of tax shelters, including such relics from the New Era as deductions for company yachts and country estates.

Broadening the New Deal Coalition

The largest groups that had been persistently excluded from economic and political benefits were women and African Americans. Their stories were strikingly parallel. Both received wages substantially lower than those of white men and owned only a tiny sliver of the nation's property. Though constitutionally entitled to vote since reconstruction, most African Americans had been disfranchised by intimidation and legal subterfuge. Women finally gained the vote as well, but they were only starting to exercise their electoral power in numbers comparable to those of men.

Eleanor Roosevelt was determined to use her position as First Lady to increase the influence of women and minorities. At her urging, President Roosevelt allowed the Democratic National Committee to create a Women's Division in 1933 to define women's issues and to screen candidates for administration positions. Headed by Molly Dewson, a former leader in the suffrage movement and the National Consumers League, the Women's Division created a talent pool of eighty thousand women from which the New Deal hired an unprecedented number for government positions.

Most remarkable was the entry of women into executive positions that had always been considered for men only. Frances Perkins became the first woman cabinet officer; Ruth Bryan Owen the first woman to hold an ambassadorial post; Florence Allen the first woman judge on a district court of appeals; Nellie Tayloe Ross the first woman director of the U.S. Mint; and Marion Glass Banister the first woman assistant secretary of the treasury. Alongside these breakthroughs, women gained prominent positions within relief and welfare programs. Under the broad WPA umbrella, Ellen Woodward headed Women's and Professional Projects, Hallie Flanagan directed the Federal Theater Project, and Hilda Smith organized Workers' Education. Women also played key roles in the Division of Labor Standards, the Children's Bureau, and the administra-

ELEANOR ROOSEVELT MEETING WOMEN REPORTERS
Even though about 80 percent of newspaper owners opposed the president and his wife,
both Franklin and Eleanor Roosevelt had close rapport with the working press. Making
the point that women had something important to contribute to public affairs and that
the First Lady could be more than simply a White House hostess, Eleanor Roosevelt
wrote a daily column, "My Day," and held regular news conferences to which only
women reporters were admitted. She used the occasions to reinvigorate the commitment
women had begun in the Progressive Era to education, equal rights, decent working con-
ditions, and child welfare.
Stock Montage.

tion of relief to the unemployed and destitute, both locally and in Washington.

These activities did not result, however, in equality between the sexes, either economically or politically. The efforts women made within the New Deal were largely devoted to improving conditions of children, the infirm, the unemployed, and others who lacked the ability to take care of themselves. Nonetheless, the experience of women in community organization and the design of welfare legislation established a foundation of skill and influence that buttressed future efforts to attain equal rights.

Eleanor Roosevelt also helped link the causes of gender and racial discrimination. One of her strongest allies was Mary McLeod Bethune, the founder of the Daytona Normal and Industrial Institute for Negro Women in Florida and a cofounder of the National Council on Negro Women in 1935. Bethune's accomplishments brought her to the attention of Eleanor Roosevelt and resulted in her appointment as the highest-ranking black official in the federal government as head of the Division of Negro Affairs in the National Youth Administration. Bethune used her position to guide a core group of black professionals and civil rights activists to posts within the New Deal. Nicknamed the "Black Cabinet," the group was the first sizable African American presence in the federal government. By mid-

MARY MCLEOD BETHUNE
At the urging of Eleanor Roosevelt, Mary McLeod Bethune, a southern educational and civil rights leader, became director of the National Youth Administration's Division of Negro Affairs. The first black woman to head a federal agency, Bethune used her position to promote social change. Here Bethune takes her mission to the streets to protest the Peoples Drug Store chain's discriminatory hiring practices in the nation's capital.
Moorland Spingarn Research Center, Howard University.

retaining their place on the land as owners or tenants. Moreover, to struggle against such deepening misery proved dangerous. After years of decline, lynching increased during the depression. In Alabama, the black "Scottsboro Boys" faced the death penalty in 1931 for a rape they did not commit (see Chapter 23), and radical black unionist Angelo Herndon narrowly escaped a Georgia chain gang for trying to organize black workers alongside white. Up north, a riot in 1935 that focused on white owned and staffed businesses in Harlem dramatized blacks' despair.

THE NEW DEAL RACE PROBLEM
Showing even the National Recovery Administration's mighty Blue Eagle stymied by racial discrimination, this cartoon bitingly mocks the motto of business participants in the NRA, "We do our part." The task of opening up opportunities for African Americans commensurate with their talents and training would remain up in the air as long as laws enforcing fair employment practices continued to be weak or unwritten.
Chicago Historical Society.

decade, their efforts helped open the way for inclusion of African Americans in New Deal relief programs to the point where about one-quarter of all blacks received some sort of federal assistance.

The conditions with which the Black Cabinet grappled were bleak in the extreme. At the outset of the New Deal, about half of urban blacks were out of work, twice the unemployment rate among whites. In the rural South, the majority of blacks had slim prospects of making a living or even

The New Deal response was cautious. Roosevelt believed that, to enact ambitious New Deal reforms, he was obliged to appease powerful conservative, segregationist, southern Democrats. Reflecting these political pressures, the major New Deal programs for economic recovery—the NRA, AAA, and WPA—failed in large measure to serve African Americans. Bitter critics charged that NRA stood for "Negro Run Around" or "Negroes Ruined Again." In the WPA, only eleven of more than ten thousand supervisors in the South were black.

Stymied by entrenched racism, New Dealers turned to coalition building with blacks. Off the record, Roosevelt spoke of a time when politics would be realigned into opposing conservative and progressive parties, with the Republicans and southern Democrats making up the former and the New Deal coalition the latter. Blacks played a key role in his conception. During Roosevelt's first presidential campaign, black journalist Robert Vann called on African Americans to "turn Lincoln's picture to the wall. That debt has been paid in full." In 1934, black voters noticeably shifted from the Republican to the Democratic Party, helping elect New Deal Democrats in numerous congressional and gubernatorial races.

By the end of Roosevelt's second term, however, African Americans still suffered severe handicaps. Most of the thirteen million black workers toiled at low-paying menial jobs. Infant mortality was half again as great as for whites, and life expectancy twelve years shorter. Making a mockery of the "separate but equal" doctrine, segregated black schools had less money and worse facilities than those of whites, and only 1 percent of black students earned college degrees. In southern states, where most blacks lived, there were no black police officers or judges and hardly any black lawyers, and lynching of blacks went unpunished. By mid-decade, little had happened to refute the grim witticism that, for African Americans, the United States was "the land of the tree and the home of the grave."

Hispanic Americans and Asian Americans had even fewer voters than women and blacks, and consequently less political clout. Mexican Americans, already at the economic margins, saw their wages in California's fields plummet to not much more than a dime an hour. Then, they had to face a new challenge from other victims of the depression. When persistent drought raised huge dust storms and turned large areas of the plains into a "dust bowl," hundreds of thousands of ruined farmers—

HISPANIC-AMERICAN ALLIANCE BANNER
Between 1910 and 1940, when refugees from the Mexican revolution poured across the American border, the Hispanic-American Alliance and other such organizations sought to protect Mexican Americans' rights against nativist fears and hostility. In the years between the world wars, many alliance banners such as this one flew in opposition to the deportation of Mexican aliens, an attempt in 1926 to bar Mexican Americans from city jobs in Los Angeles, and the disproportionately high use of the death penalty against Mexicans convicted of crimes. Throughout these and other trials, the alliance steadfastly emphasized the desire of Mexican Americans to receive permanent status in the United States.
The Oakland Museum.

called "Okies" or "Arkies" because most of them came from Oklahoma or Arkansas—moved westward and competed with Mexican Americans for scarce agricultural work. In addition, local administration of many New Deal programs meant that the treatment of minorities rested in the hands of established white leadership. When Hispanics and Indians were permitted to join government work

JOHN COLLIER MEETS WITH NAVAJO REPRESENTATIVES *Commissioner of Indian Affairs John Collier receives a Navajo delegation protesting restrictions in the Indian Reorganization Act of 1934. The Navajos display a blanket made from the wool of their own sheep to protest limits on the number of sheep they could raise. Collier had crafted the act to revive Native American society by granting tribes an independent land base and many self-governing powers. However, his attempt to make the reservations economically viable through conservation measures, including restrictions on grass-devouring sheep, roused resistance by Indians who chose traditional ways of using resources. The tension between federal benevolence and Indian views of their own way of life has remained a painful issue.* Wide World Photos, Inc.

projects, they often received lower pay than their white counterparts, and less aid when out of a job.

Asian Americans fared no better. Asian immigrants were still excluded from U.S. citizenship and in many states were not permitted to own land. Although more than half of Japanese Americans by 1930 had been born in the United States, they were still liable to discrimination. Even college-educated Asian Americans worked at family shops, restaurants, and laundries. As one frustrated young man said: "I am a fruitstand worker. I would much rather it were doctor or lawyer . . . but my aspirations [were] frustrated long ago by circumstances [and] I am only what I am, a professional carrot washer."

Native Americans, however, experienced a major change in their circumstances during the New Deal. Ever since the Dawes Act of 1887, the government had tried to solve the "Indian problem" by encouraging assimilation, that is, an end to a separate Indian identity. Because of the commitment of John Collier, commissioner of Indian affairs, that policy was mostly reversed in the Indian Reorganization Act of 1934. The act restored to Native Americans the right to own land communally. Though the change brought little immediate benefit and Indians remained the poorest of Americans, it did provide a foundation for economic and cultural resurgence a generation later.

The New Deal's Final Phase: From Victory to Deadlock

To speed up recovery, Roosevelt shifted the emphasis of the New Deal in the mid-1930s. Having failed to build a cooperative commonwealth out of all interest groups, Roosevelt decided in his second term to rely on the New Deal coalition to force reform on bitterly resisting business enemies. Support for the New Deal in the farm states and in the big cities had grown vast, spurred by the rise in the number of women and recent immigrants inspired by the New Deal to begin voting. Roosevelt even gained some unlikely allies on the left. Throughout Roosevelt's first term, socialists and Communists had denounced the slow pace of change and charged the New Deal with failing to serve the interests of the workers who produced the nation's wealth. But in 1935 the Soviet Union, worried about the threat of fascism in Europe, instructed Communists throughout the world to join hands in a "Popular Front" to advance the fortunes of the working class. With varying degrees of enthusiasm, radicals switched from opposition to the New Deal to support for its relief programs and encouragement of unions.

The president's business and conservative opponents reacted to the massing of New Deal force by intensifying their opposition to the welfare state. To Roosevelt, the situation seemed part of a central drama that had played out since the nation's beginning, pitting a Hamiltonian faction of wealth and privilege against the heirs of Jefferson who, like Roosevelt himself, favored shared wealth and equal opportunity.

The Election of 1936

Roosevelt believed that the presidential election of 1936 would be a test of his leadership and progressive ideals. Between 8.5 and 12.5 million workers were still unemployed, and most farmers remained poor. Opposition leaders took that as an indication that the American people were poised to vote against a failed experiment. From the Republican standpoint, the New Deal was undermining the individualized values that had made the country strong. On the left opponents insisted that the New Deal had missed its opportunity to displace capitalism with a socialized economy and would lose votes to radical candidates.

Republicans turned to the Kansas heartland to select Governor Alfred (Alf) Landon as their nominee for president. A moderate who had supported New Deal measures for conservation and farm relief and promised unions a fair deal, Landon stressed standard Republican proposals to achieve a balanced federal budget and to ease the perils of

illness and old age with old-fashioned neighborliness instead of Social Security.

Roosevelt put his faith in the growing coalition of New Deal supporters, who he believed shared his conviction that the New Deal was the nation's liberator from a long period of privilege and wealth for a few and "economic slavery" for the rest. At the end of the campaign, Roosevelt struck a defiant pose before a thunderous crowd at Madison Square Garden. Assailing his "old enemies—monopoly, speculation, reckless banking, class antagonism"— he proclaimed, "Never before in all our history have these forces been so united against one candidate as they stand today. They are unanimous in their hate for me—and I welcome their hatred." When the crowd's roar subsided, Roosevelt concluded: "I should like to have it said of my first Administration that in it the forces of selfishness and of lust for power met their match. I should like to have it said of my second Administration that in it these forces met their master."

Roosevelt triumphed spectacularly. His 60.8 percent majority and eleven million vote margin were the widest ever in a presidential race and won him every state except Maine and Vermont. Third parties—including the National Union for Social Justice, the Socialists, and the Communists—fell disastrously short of the support they had hoped for and never again posed a significant threat to the New Deal. Congressional results were equally lopsided, with Democrats outnumbering Republicans by more than three to one in both houses. And in the states, Democrats won twenty-six of thirty-three gubernatorial races, including the one in Landon's Kansas.

Roosevelt's triumph was a testimony to the New Deal coalition and aroused voter interest. Whereas the 1920s saw only about 45 percent of eligible voters at the polls in national elections, 57 percent of eligible voters turned out in 1936. Northern blacks gave Roosevelt 76 percent of their votes, allowing him to wrench the key states of Illinois, Michigan, and New Jersey away from the Republicans. In the nineteen northern cities where more than half the population was composed of first- and second-generation immigrants, the crisis and Democratic encouragement had greatly increased voting participation. Overwhelmingly, the new voters tilted toward the New Deal. Democratic votes increased by 205 percent over their total in 1932, while Republicans gained only 29 percent. Roosevelt also managed to retain the support of every traditionally Democratic southern state, delaying Hoover's dream of bringing the South into the Republican Party.

Court Packing

In the afterglow of his triumph, Roosevelt went on a cruise to ponder how to remove the remaining obstacles to New Deal reforms. He returned intent on targeting the Supreme Court. Laden with conservatives left over from the discredited Republican era, the Court had invalidated eleven New Deal measures as unwarranted interference with free enterprise; in more than 140 years before 1932, the Court had nullified only sixty laws. At that moment, Social Security, the Wagner Act, the Securities and Exchange Commission, and other New Deal innovations were moving toward an ominous rendezvous with the Court. Roosevelt concluded that he must do something to make sure the Court's "horse and buggy" notions did not nullify the popular will and demolish the New Deal.

Despite indications that more than two-thirds of Americans believed the Supreme Court should be free from political interference, Roosevelt proposed that one new justice be added to the Court for each existing judge who had already served for ten years and was over the age of seventy. In effect, the proposed law would give the president the power to overwhelm the elderly, conservative Republican justices by naming up to six New Dealers to the bench.

But the president had not reckoned with Americans' deeply rooted deference to the independent authority of the Supreme Court. Even New Deal supporters were disturbed by the "court-packing" scheme, and the implication that individuals over seventy had diminished mental capacity affronted many members of Congress who were past that age. Roosevelt deviously insisted that the bill was intended to improve the efficiency of an "overworked" Court; but it was plain that the real purpose was to make room for supporters of New Deal initiatives. Within a storm of public protest, whipped up by conservatives, the Senate sank the bill.

Although the Court reform plan failed, it apparently sounded the alarm for Supreme Court justices. After the furor abated, Chief Justice Charles Evans Hughes and fellow moderate Owen Roberts altered their views enough to keep the Court from invalidating the Wagner Act and Social Security.

Then the most resistant of the elderly justices—the "four horsemen of reaction," as New Dealer and future Supreme Court justice Felix Frankfurter called them—began to retire, and Roosevelt was eventually able to name eight justices—more than any other president. His choice of liberals to fill the vacancies on the Court ultimately ensured safe passage of New Deal laws through the shoals of judicial review. But Roosevelt's error in proposing his court-packing scheme had handed conservatives a crucial issue to use against the New Deal.

Reaction and Recession

No action by New Deal opponents was more damaging than the administration's self-inflicted wounds. Compounding the Court packing fiasco, Roosevelt accepted the view that the steady, though incomplete, economic recovery since 1933 had largely eliminated the depression crisis. He was persuaded that additional deficit spending designed to pump up the economy was no longer necessary. He also worried that inflation would reduce the value of savings and new investments the New Deal had tried to build up. Accordingly, he moved cautiously toward a balanced budget by cutting funds for relief projects, and at his urging the Federal Reserve raised interest rates to discourage borrowing on easy terms for unwise speculation.

Roosevelt's retrenchment soon backfired. Rather than merely preventing inflation, the reduction in deficit spending cooled down the economy drastically. Roosevelt's anxiety about inflation had failed to take into full consideration how far the economy had to go before it would reach inflationary levels. Even at the high-water mark of recovery in the summer of 1937, unemployment remained at about 14 percent, some seven million people in all. In the next few months, national income and production slipped backward so steeply that almost two-thirds of the economic gains since 1933 were lost by June 1938. Farm prices dropped 20 percent, and unemployment rose by more than two million.

This economic downturn hurt the New Deal politically. Conservatives argued that the recession proved New Deal measures had produced only an illusion of progress. Herbert Hoover had been right after all, they claimed. The way to weather the recession was to tax and spend less, thus boosting private spending and investment, and wait for the laws of the free enterprise system to restore prosperity.

Many New Dealers believed instead that the recession showed there was no going back to the orthodoxies of free enterprise. They insisted that the crash and the depression had demonstrated the shortcomings of an unregulated economy. They demanded that the administration revive federal spending and redouble efforts to stimulate the economy. In 1938, Congress heeded Roosevelt's plea to enact a massive new program of public works.

The New Deal's methods received support from new economic ideas advanced by the brilliant British economist John Maynard Keynes. In his influential work *The General Theory of Employment, Interest, and Money* (1936), Keynes made a sophisticated, theoretical argument in favor of practices that New Deal relief agencies had developed in an ad hoc, commonsense way. A nation's economy, Keynes declared, could not automatically reach its full potential in the complex, interdependent modern world. The depression had painfully illustrated that economic activity could become stalled at a level far short of a society's true potential. When that happened, only government intervention could pump enough money into the system to revive production, boost consumption, and restore prosperity.

Roosevelt never had the inclination or the time to follow his economic advisers into the thicket of Keynesian theory. But the recession scare of 1938 taught the president the Keynesian lesson that economic growth had to be carefully nurtured, not left to self-regulating market forces. Escape from the depression required a plan for large-scale spending to alleviate distress and stimulate economic growth.

The Last of the New Deal Reforms

From the moment he was sworn in, Roosevelt had tinkered with the small and antiquated office of the presidency. He believed that the powers of the presidency were inadequate, especially during emergencies such as the depression. He also wanted more power over the federal bureaucracy. Arguing the need for "efficiency," Roosevelt submitted an ambitious plan of executive reorganization to Congress in 1937. The bill failed, but in September 1939 Congress passed the Administrative Reorganization Act, which gave Roosevelt part of what he desired. With a Democratic majority in Congress, a now friendly Supreme Court, and the revival of deficit

spending, the newly empowered White House seemed to be in a good position to move ahead with a third New Deal.

Resistance was also on the rise, however. Conservatives argued that the New Deal had pressed its centralization too far and was bent on creating what later came to be known as "the imperial presidency." Even the New Deal's friends became weary of one emergency program after another, especially while economic recession still shadowed New Deal achievements. By the midpoint of Roosevelt's second term, restive members of Congress balked at new initiatives. Clearly, the New Deal was winding down, but enough energy remained for one last burst of reform.

The farm sector still had strong claims on New Deal attention in the face of drought, declining prices, and an impoverished class of landless hired hands. In 1937, the Agriculture Department created the Farm Security Administration (FSA) to provide housing and loans to help tenant farmers become independent. But the FSA was starved for funds and ran up against the major farm organizations, which were intent on serving the interests of the large farms. With only minor successes to show, the FSA petered out in the early 1940s. For those who owned farms, the New Deal completed its efforts to establish a secure plateau of prosperity with the Agricultural Adjustment Act (AAA) of February 1938. The plan combined production quotas on five staple crops—cotton, tobacco, wheat, corn, and rice—with storage loans through its Commodity Credit Corporation to moderate price swings by regulating supply. The most prosperous farmers benefited most, but the act's Federal Surplus Commodities Corporation added an element of charity by issuing food stamps so that the poor could purchase surplus food. Through that balance, the AAA of 1938 brought stability to American agriculture and ample food to the table.

Advocates for the urban underclass also had modest luck gaining attention after decades of neglect. New York senator Robert Wagner convinced Congress to pass the National Housing Act in September 1937. By 1941, some 160,000 residences had been made available at rates affordable for those below the poverty line. The project did not come close to meeting the need for affordable housing, but for the first time the federal government took an active role in providing decent urban housing.

the Roosevelt administration would have to turn from the symbolic New Deal war at home to test its strength in a shooting war against the enemies of democracy abroad.

FOR FURTHER READING ABOUT THE TOPICS IN THIS CHAPTER, see the Online Bibliography at
www.bedfordstmartins.com/roarkcompact.

FOR ADDITIONAL FIRST-HAND ACCOUNTS OF THIS PERIOD, see pages 148–165 in Michael Johnson, ed., *Reading the American Past,* Second Edition, Volume II.

TO ASSESS YOUR MASTERY OF THE MATERIAL IN THIS CHAPTER, see the Online Study Guide at
www.bedfordstmartins.com/roarkcompact.

CHRONOLOGY

1932 The Bonus Expeditionary Army marches on Washington and is routed by federal troops.

1933 Franklin D. Roosevelt assumes presidency.

March–June. New Deal established through passage of reform legislation of the Hundred Days.

Roosevelt closes nation's banks for four-day "holiday" to allow time to stabilize banking system.

The Federal Emergency Relief Administration (FERA) provides relief for unemployed.

1934 Securities and Exchange Commission licenses and regulates stock exchanges.

Upton Sinclair loses bid for governor of California and chance to enact his End Poverty in California work relief program.

Wealthy conservatives of American Liberty League oppose New Deal.

Dr. Francis Townsend devises Old Age Revolving Pension scheme to provide money to impoverished elderly.

Congress adopts Indian Reorganization Act.

1935 Louisiana senator Huey Long assassinated.

As part of Second Hundred Days, legislation creates Works Progress Administration (WPA).

Congress passes Wagner Act to guarantee workers the right to organize unions and bargain collectively.

Committee for Industrial Organization (CIO) founded to provide union representation for unskilled workers.

Social Security Act provides supplementary income for aged and retired persons.

"Radio Priest" Father Charles Coughlin begins National Union for Social Justice.

1936 John Maynard Keynes publishes *The General Theory of Employment, Interest, and Money*, providing theoretical justification for government deficit financing.

Franklin Roosevelt reelected by a landslide over Republican Alfred Landon.

1937 CIO stages successful sit-down strike at General Motors plant in Flint, Michigan. Roosevelt's "Court-packing" legislation defeated in Senate.

1937–1938 Economic recession slows recovery from depression.

1938 Second Agricultural Adjustment Act and Fair Labor Standards Act bring New Deal legislation to an end.

Congress rejects administration's antilynching bill.

1939 Administrative Reorganization Act enlarges scope and power of presidency.

GOD BLESS AMERICA

MEMENTO OF WAR
To mark the seriousness of going to war, servicemen and their families often mounted photos in special settings, such as this painted-on-glass frame. Symbols of God and country sum up patriotic devotion to a just cause. And in the midst of these ritualized sentiments, as if looking back through a window draped in his honor, an unknown sailor seems about to tell us something more.
Private collection.

THE SECOND WORLD WAR 25

1939–1945

EXCITED ABOUT SEEING AMERICA'S MOST FAMOUS HERO IN PERSON, a noisy crowd of eight thousand jostled into the America First rally in Des Moines, Iowa, on the evening of September 1, 1941, to hear Charles Lindbergh. A private man who had always resisted his celebrity, Lindbergh dreaded the event. Only a compelling sense of duty convinced him that he must suffer the spotlight to take a stand against Roosevelt administration policies of aiding Britain's defense against Nazism that threatened to drag the United States into another foreign war.

Lindbergh's speech was sponsored by the America First Committee (AFC), organized in the fall of 1940 to maintain American neutrality, supposedly safely protected by two oceans against wars raging in Europe and Asia. The AFC's youthful organizers attracted many supporters, including two draft-age future presidents, Gerald Ford and John Kennedy. Most Americans, however, wavered between the isolationism of the AFC and those, like Franklin Roosevelt, who believed American security and the cause Democracy depended on Britain's survival. In its effort to keep the AFC from persuading Congress to forbid aid to Britain, the Roosevelt administration sought to counter Lindbergh's hero status. Secretary of the Interior Harold Ickes referred to him in the anxious summer of 1941 as "America's No. 1 Nazi fellow traveler." A year earlier, Roosevelt had gone even further. "I am absolutely convinced," he told Secretary of the Treasury Henry Morgenthau, "that Lindbergh is a Nazi."

Yet the man who had been the first to fly the Atlantic alone still had such a strong hold on the American imagination that the crowd in Des Moines settled down immediately when he stepped onto the stage, straight and tall, remaining at thirty-nine the godlike young aviator. In his clear, earnest voice, Lindbergh declared that war would needlessly take the lives of the nation's best young men and bleed precious resources. He then charged that "the three most important groups who have been pressing this country toward war are the British, the Jewish, and the Roosevelt administration." Lindbergh received a standing ovation. Elsewhere, however, the effect of placing blame on the victims of Nazism for appealing for help was chilling. As criticism mounted that he was anti-Semitic, if not pro-Nazi, Lindbergh lost his hold on the public, and even close associates backed away. By the time the United States entered the war in December 1941, the "Lone Eagle" was alone again.

In 1940–1941, millions of Americans shared Lindbergh's concerns about the destructiveness of war, but few questioned the Allied cause. Torn between abhorrence of Nazism and a desire not to be drawn into another world war, most people accepted Roosevelt's support for Britain's last-ditch defense against tyranny. Only when the United States was attacked, however, did the citizenry throw itself

The Onset of War

Events had not spiraled far enough into disaster by the start of Roosevelt's second term to convince the public that noninvolvement would have to give way to an active role in foreign affairs, backed up by expanded armed forces. To be sure, the saber-rattling rhetoric and aggression of fascist dictators had alerted some observers to the danger. But troubles in China, Ethiopia, and Spain seemed too remote and minor to bring most Americans around to the view that it was time to take a stand.

Nazi Aggression and War in Europe

Under the spell of neutrality, Americans watched impotently as Adolf Hitler continued his campaign to dominate Europe. In the name of uniting all German peoples, Hitler in 1938 bullied Austria into accepting incorporation—*Anschluss*—into the Nazi Third Reich. He then turned his attention to the German-speaking Sudetenland, granted to Czechoslovakia by the Versailles treaty. Although the Czechs were prepared to fight rather than surrender territory, the British and French wanted peace and sought to strike a deal with Hitler. British prime minister Neville Chamberlain went to confer with the German ruler in Munich, offering terms of "appeasement," as he called it, that would turn over the Sudetenland to Germany in exchange for Germany's leaving the rest of Czechoslovakia alone. On September 29, 1938, Hitler accepted the offer, solemnly promising that he would make no more territorial claims in Europe. Chamberlain returned home convinced that he had obtained "peace in our time." But in March 1939, Hitler marched the German army into weakened Czechoslovakia and took over the entire country without firing a shot (Map 25.1).

Hardly pausing for breath, Hitler in April demanded that Poland return the German territory it had been awarded after World War I. Britain and France finally recognized that the policy of appeasement was a failure. They assured Poland that they would go to its aid if Hitler attacked. Hitler then offered Soviet Premier Joseph Stalin concessions to prevent the Soviet Union from joining Germany's adversaries in the West. Despite deep enmity between Nazi Germany and the communist Soviet Union, the two powers shocked the world by signing a Nazi-Soviet treaty of nonaggression in August 1939.

With the way open, Hitler exhorted his generals to "close your hearts to pity! Act brutally!" So bidden, at dawn on September 1, 1939, the German army crossed the Polish border. France and Britain then kept their word by declaring war. The greatest conflict in history had begun.

From Neutrality to the Arsenal of Democracy

When war erupted, Roosevelt issued an official proclamation of American neutrality. But unlike Woodrow Wilson, he did not ask Americans to be impartial in thought as well as deed. Roosevelt's immediate objective was to persuade Congress to repeal the arms embargo mandated by the neutrality legislation so France and Britain could obtain weapons to resist Nazi evil. The president's request provoked Charles Lindbergh and his allies in the Senate to protest that the war was a European matter the United States should stay out of. But Congress finally consented to extend neutrality legislation and adopt a cash-and-carry policy for arms sales, as well as for nonmilitary goods, which meant that Allied, not American, ships would run the risk of transporting war goods through the German submarine blockade.

After Hitler's armies overran Poland, they paused; but the lull was shattered in the spring of 1940 by a series of Nazi hammer blows. In a lightning-fast attack called a *blitzkrieg*, German dive-bombers and tanks smashed through Denmark, Norway, Belgium, and Holland and into northern France. The French made the fatal mistake of believing that they could hold out behind the Maginot Line, a massive concrete fortification that stretched from the Swiss border to the forested Ardennes region on the edge of Belgium (see Map 25.1). Reality struck in early summer when Mussolini's armies invaded France from the south, while Hitler's blitzkrieg flanked the Maginot Line in the north.

British forces in the north were then trapped by the swift German advance and forced to retreat to the port of Dunkirk, from which they were narrowly rescued by a heroic sealift that used every boat able to make it across the English Channel. Less than three weeks later, reeling from a German sweep southward, the French surrendered the largest army in the world and signed an armistice that placed three-fifths of the country under German control.

M A P 25.1

Axis Aggression through 1941

For different reasons, Hitler and Mussolini launched a series of surprise military strikes. Mussolini sought to recreate the Roman Empire in the Mediterranean. Hitler struck to reclaim German territories occupied by France after World War I and to annex Austria. When the German dictator then began his campaign to rule over "inferior" peoples beyond Germany's border by attacking Poland, World War II broke out.

With the possibility of a German invasion across the Channel now looming, Parliament turned the appeaser Neville Chamberlain out of office and welcomed as prime minister the defiant Winston Churchill. Churchill had watched from the sidelines with mounting fury as Chamberlain kowtowed to Hitler. When the Germans attacked Britain itself, Churchill was ready with a vengeance to take over the last-ditch defense of the nation. His oratorical genius shone through the intensive German bombing campaign against English cities in the summer and fall of 1940. By the time the Royal Air Force won the Battle of Britain in November, ridding the skies of German bombers, Churchill had become the symbol of indomitable British resistance.

Roosevelt strove for a comparable role as leader and symbol by inspiring the American public to rise above its isolationist fears. In the spring of 1940, the president prevailed on Kansas journalist William Allen White to form the Committee to Defend America by Aiding the Allies for a nationwide campaign to generate public support for Roosevelt's policy of providing all aid to the Allies short of war. Noninterventionists organized in response.

In the midst of the vital debate about American foreign policy, the presidential election of 1940 unfolded. Having decided to run for an unprecedented third term rather than step aside in the time of crisis, Roosevelt looked forward to a campaign pitting the reformist, internationalist thrust of the New Deal against Republican isolationism and business conservatism. Instead he faced Wendell Willkie, a former Democrat who supported most of the New Deal domestic program and generally agreed with Roosevelt's foreign policy. Realizing that he trailed Roosevelt badly, Willkie veered from internationalism and attacked Roosevelt as a warmonger, forcing the president to declare, "Your boys are not going to be sent into any foreign wars." Even with mixed messages about opposing fascist aggression and staying out of war, Roosevelt claimed a comfortable victory, although his margin was smaller than in 1936.

The president interpreted his victory as a mandate to continue to support Britain in every way short of war. By then, the British were in desperate straits; their treasury exhausted, they could no longer pay cash for weapons. To head off the catastrophic end of American aid, Roosevelt held a fireside chat with the American people on December 16, 1940, to explain that only the British stood between the United States and Nazi barbarism. "We must be the great arsenal of democracy," he declared. As for how the British would pay, he offered the homey example of a man who lent his neighbor a garden hose when his house caught on fire: "I don't say to him . . . 'you have to pay me $15 for it.' I don't want $15—I want my garden hose back after the fire is over."

Buoyed by favorable public response, Congress approved the Lend-Lease Act in March 1941, which allowed the British to obtain armaments from the United States so long as they returned them or their equivalent after the war was over. In reality, Lend-Lease was a charade to retain the semblance of neutrality. As one observer noted, "Lending war materiel is a little like lending chewing gum. You don't

want it back." With Lend-Lease, the United States entered into full-fledged economic warfare against Germany. Moreover, since Britain could not sustain its shipping in the face of losses to German submarines, the United States inevitably would need to build and protect a vast merchant fleet. It was only a matter of time before an armed attack occurred of the sort that had precipitated World War I.

The predictable series of events began on June 11, 1941, when a German U-boat (submarine) sank the American freighter *Robin Moor* off the coast of Africa. Several months later, an American destroyer and a German submarine engaged in a firefight. Roosevelt issued a "shoot on sight" policy for American escort vessels. In August, Roosevelt and Churchill cemented their relationship when they met on shipboard near Newfoundland to devise an Atlantic Charter. Echoing Woodrow Wilson's creed, the charter called for the right of nations to choose their own forms of government, freedom of the seas, and postwar disarmament.

As danger in the Atlantic mounted, Hitler took a terrible gamble by launching a massive invasion of the Soviet Union on June 22, 1941. Until that violent rupture of the Nazi-Soviet pact, Americans generally thought little better of the Communists than they did of the Nazis. But the brutal facts of war called for drastic change. Churchill bluntly welcomed his old archenemy Joseph Stalin to the cause by stating that he would not hesitate to deal with the devil if Hitler invaded hell. Roosevelt stressed the importance of Russia's entrance in diverting German forces away from the hard-pressed British and quickly persuaded Congress to extend Lend-Lease to the Russians.

War Comes to America

Despite America's primary concern with Europe, the expansion of the Japanese empire made the danger of war for the United States most immediate in Asia. The rising tide of Japanese imperialism clashed with U.S. aspirations and commitments, especially in China. The island-bound Japanese coveted raw material and markets, and their weak neighbor China was the natural place to turn. The military invasion of Manchuria in 1931 proved to be the opening salvo of continuing Japanese aggression in China (Map 25.2). Each act of territorial conquest received a stern rebuke from the Roosevelt administration, but toothless proclamations did little to deter the Japanese. Appealing to bitterness

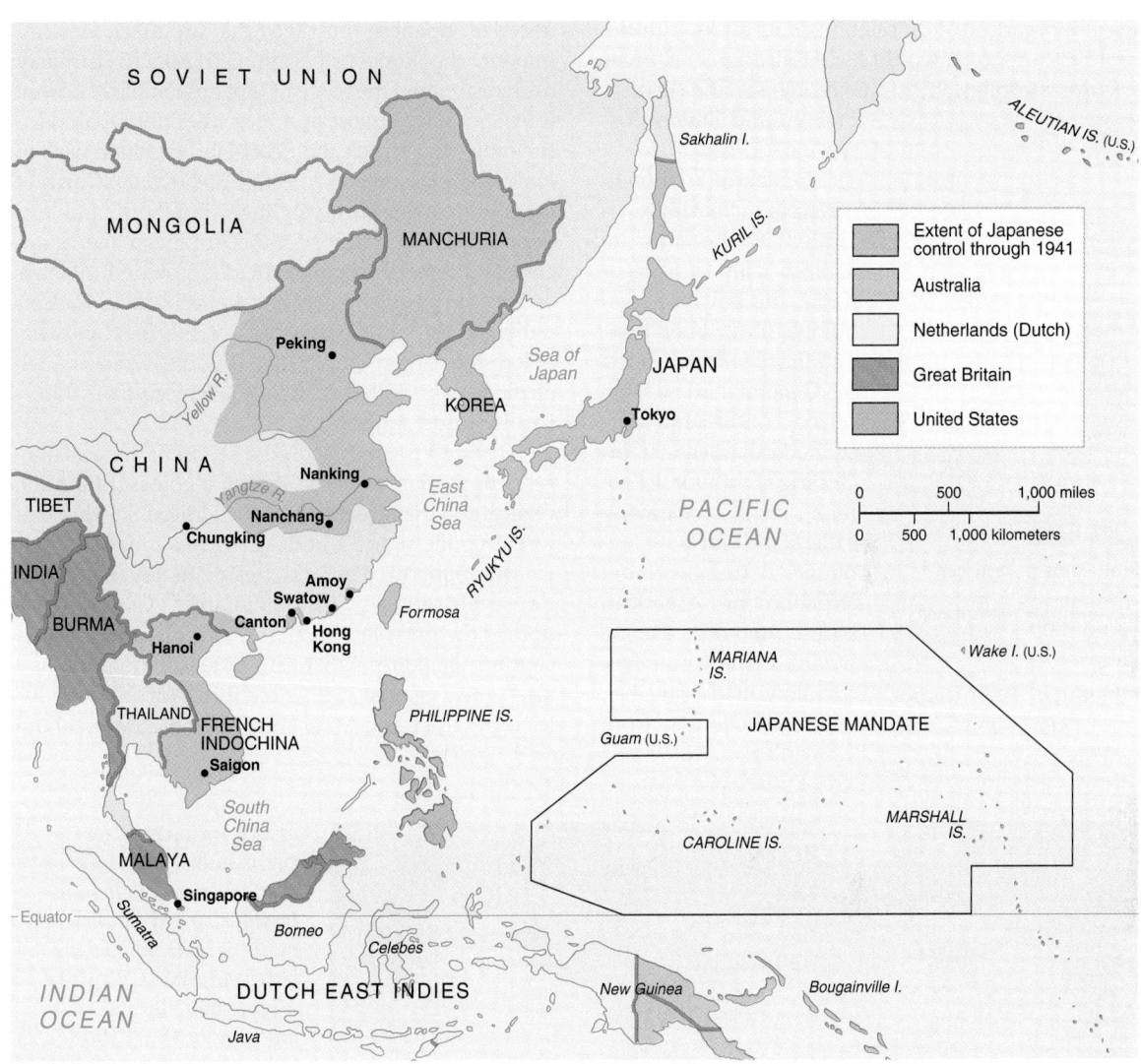

MAP 25.2

Japanese Aggression through 1941

Beginning with the invasion of Manchuria in 1931, Japan sought to force its imperialist control over most of East Asia. Japanese aggression was driven by the need for raw materials for the country's expanding industries and by the military government's devotion to martial honor.

in the region against white colonialism, the Japanese marched forward under the banner "Asia for the Asians," which really meant China for the Japanese.

In 1940, Japan signed the Tripartite Pact, a defensive alliance with Germany and Italy. It also obtained from the Vichy government (the German puppet regime in France) the right to build airfields and station troops in northern Indochina. In 1941,

U.S. naval intelligence cracked the Japanese code and learned that Tokyo had set its sights on the resource-rich Dutch East Indies (the archipelago stretching from Sumatra to New Guinea). In response, the Roosevelt administration announced a complete trade embargo, which denied Japan access to essential oil and scrap iron. Roosevelt had given Japan a choice: Japan would either have to halt its aggression and restore relations and trade with the United States, or it would have to find new sources of vital supplies, most likely by seizing British, French, and Dutch possessions in East Asia.

Japanese nationalists were increasingly offended by the pressure against Japan's economic and territorial ambitions. In October 1941, a military clique headed by General Hideki Tojo seized control and persuaded other leaders, including Emperor Hirohito, who originally called the idea "harebrained," that swift destruction of American bases in the Pacific would leave Japan free to follow its destiny. Despite knowledge from

decoded Japanese messages that an attack was imminent, the Roosevelt administration disastrously underestimated the reach of Japanese military power. Consequently, American forces were unprepared for the blow that struck the Pearl Harbor naval base in Hawaii on December 7, 1941. At dawn, a swarm of Japanese carrier-borne fighters, bombers, and torpedo planes found most of the American fleet at anchor and American planes neatly crowded together at Hickam Field. In two hours, the raiders sank or damaged all eight battleships of the fleet and disabled ten other ships. The bombs wrecked 340 airplanes and killed or wounded more than thirty-five hundred Americans.

Though the raid scored a stunning tactical success, in the larger sense it was a colossal blunder. Overnight, disagreement in the United States about foreign policy ended, and Americans united in their commitment to war and desire to revenge what Roosevelt called a "day of infamy." Congress endorsed the president's call for war unanimously, except for Quaker pacifist Jeannette Rankin, who had also voted against U.S. entry into World War I. Although Hitler and Mussolini had not known about

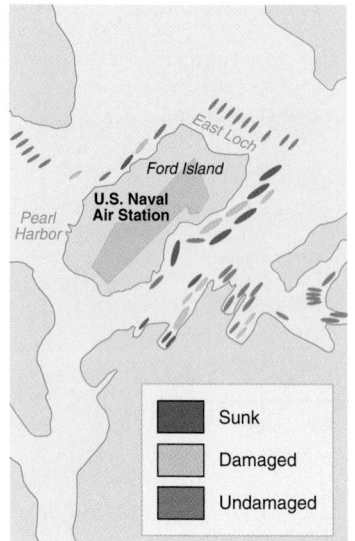

Bombing of Pearl Harbor, December 7, 1941

PEARL HARBOR, DECEMBER 7, 1941
A rescue fireboat is hopelessly dwarfed by the enormous catastrophe of the battleship **West Virginia** *aflame and sinking at its mooring in Pearl Harbor. With the dramatic force of a vast seascape painting, this photograph was widely reproduced as a graphic indication of how great a crime the Japanese had committed.*
U.S. Army.

the Japanese attack in advance, Germany and Italy declared war against America on December 11.

The Global Challenge

Never had the United States faced such a desperate military situation or so staggering a task as it did in 1941. Hitler and his armies had conquered most of Europe, and the Japanese military machine was slicing through the Pacific with amazing speed. From the beginning, American concern had centered on saving Britain and the Soviet Union from defeat so that the United States would not have to face Hitler alone. Before turning to Hitler, however, the United States and its allies would have to stop the Japanese advance through the Pacific.

Turning the Tide in the Pacific

Following Pearl Harbor, Japan's leading military genius, Admiral Isoroku Yamamoto, ordered an all-out offensive in the Pacific on the belief that, if his forces did not win quickly, Japan would lose the war to America's far greater manpower and resources. Swiftly, the Japanese attacked American airfields in the Philippines and captured the American outposts of Guam and Wake Island. Singapore, the great British naval base in Malaya, surrendered in February 1942, and most of Burma had fallen by March. All that stood in the way of Japan's total domination of the southwestern Pacific was the Philippine Islands.

Under intense attack, General Douglas MacArthur, who commanded the Philippine defenses, retreated to fortifications on the Bataan Peninsula across the harbor from Manila. In March, MacArthur escaped to Australian command headquarters, leaving General Jonathan Wainwright to hold out as long as possible. When Wainwright surrendered the Corregidor fortress in May, Japanese soldiers marched the starved and ill survivors sixty-five miles to a concentration camp. Hundreds of Americans and as many as ten thousand Filipinos died en route. Of those who survived the Bataan Death March, sixteen thousand died within weeks from disease and mistreatment in the brutal prison camp. By summer 1942, the Japanese war machine had also conquered the oil-rich Dutch East Indies and was poised to strike at Australia and New Zealand (see Map 25.4, page 663).

Americans had learned that the soldiers of the Rising Sun were tough, fearless, and prepared to fight to the death for honor and the emperor. At sea, the Japanese had larger, faster, heavier armored ships than the United States, with bigger guns and more accurate torpedoes. And the four different kinds of airplanes that rained bombs and bullets on Pearl Harbor outperformed anything the Americans could send up against them.

The string of unbroken Japanese victories even caused Americans at home to worry about their own safety. A false report that Japanese fighter planes had been spotted near Los Angeles set off an antiaircraft barrage and inspired the commander of West Coast defenses to announce that "death and destruction [from enemy planes] are likely to come at any moment." Antiaircraft guns appeared up and down the Pacific coast. In Hawaii, still shaken from the attack on Pearl Harbor, one vigilant citizen advised the authorities that he had spotted a dog on the beach "barking in Morse code to Japanese subs offshore." Americans needed some sort of success to take the edge off panic.

In the spring of 1942, U.S. forces launched a two-pronged offensive that the Americans hoped would stop and then reverse the Japanese advance. Forces led by General MacArthur moved north from Australia to invade the Philippines, while Admiral Chester W. Nimitz sailed west from Hawaii to retake the Japanese-held islands in the mid-Pacific. Success was not long in coming. On May 7, 1942, in the Coral Sea just north of Australia, an American fleet and carrier-based planes stopped the Japanese armada that was sailing around the coast of New Guinea.

The Battle of the Coral Sea was a prelude to an even more significant encounter. Learning that the Japanese were sending an invasion force against Midway Island, an outpost guarding the Hawaiian Islands, Admiral Nimitz moved his carriers and cruisers into the Central Pacific. In a wild melee that raged from June 3 to June 6, American planes sank four Japanese carriers, a heavy cruiser, and two destroyers, while the American armada lost only one carrier and a destroyer. The Battle of the Coral Sea and the Battle of Midway marked the turning of the tide against Japanese power in the Pacific.

The Campaign in Europe

With the Japanese offensive in the Pacific halted, American attention focused on defeating Germany.

In the dark months after Pearl Harbor, the war news from Europe was as depressing as that from the Pacific. Hitler's army had driven deep into the Soviet Union and was preparing for an invasion of Britain. As in World War I, the Germans attempted to starve the British into submission by destroying their seaborne lifeline. Advances in technology made German U-boats so much more effective than in World War I that at first they sank ships faster than new ones could be built. Moreover, because Americans did not institute blackouts until the spring of 1942, U-boats near the Atlantic coast could spot merchant targets at night almost as easily as during the day. Using only six U-boats, the Germans sank eighty-two ships off the American East Coast and more than two hundred additional ships in the waters around Bermuda and the Caribbean islands. The toll eventually reached 4,786 merchant ships, nearly double the number in World War I, and almost 200 warships. The human cost was forty thousand Allied seamen and almost as many Germans who perished in their 781 stricken U-boats.

Until 1943, the war in the Atlantic remained in doubt. Then newly invented radar detectors and production of sufficient destroyer escorts for merchant vessels made the U-boats easy prey and allowed the United States to move massive amounts of supplies to England and to the Soviet ports. The battle of the Atlantic had been won.

The big question then was when and where to open a second front against the Nazis. Stalin, desperate to keep German divisions away from his bloody doorstep, strongly urged an immediate and massive invasion of France across the English Channel. But Churchill favored something smaller, perhaps a Mediterranean target such as Europe's "soft underbelly," the Balkans. Roosevelt worried about a plan that would merely "peck on the periphery" but ultimately backed an invasion of North Africa as a first step. Since the rapidly expanding U.S. military force was clearly the vital element in any western front, Roosevelt's wishes prevailed.

The strategy targeted the one area where the Allies were having some success against the Germans. In October 1942, at El-Alamein in Egypt, the British halted General Erwin Rommel's drive to capture the Suez Canal. A few weeks later, an American army under the supreme commander of American forces in Europe, General Dwight D. Eisenhower, landed in French Morocco. The addition of American armored forces, led by General George Patton, the ablest U.S. tank commander, enabled the Allied armies in May 1943 to close the jaws of a gigantic vise on the last enemy troops in North Africa. With some 350,000 German and Italian soldiers soon dead or captured, the Mediterranean was safe for Allied shipping and Italy was open to invasion (see Map 25.3).

As the North African campaign unfolded, Roosevelt arrived at the Moroccan city of Casablanca in January 1943 to confer with his fellow Allied leaders, Winston Churchill and General Charles de Gaulle, the leader of the Free French government in exile. Stalin, preoccupied with the desperate defense of Stalingrad, was an absent but watchful partner. Bluntly, the Allied leaders announced that they would insist on "unconditional surrender." Of equal importance was their judgment that more time was needed for the buildup of enough forces in England to launch a successful cross-channel invasion of France. A strike against Italy in the meantime would capitalize on success in North Africa, a decision that meant the Soviet Union would continue to absorb the brunt of the Nazi attack for another year.

On July 10, 1943, a combined American and British amphibious operation, the largest in history, landed 160,000 troops in Sicily. The badly equipped Italian defenders, with little will to fight after the disastrous North African campaign, quickly withdrew to the mainland. When Sicily fell, the Fascist Grand Council expelled Mussolini from power, marking the end of Italian fascism. Almost immediately after the Allies invaded the mainland, the Italian government surrendered unconditionally. The Germans responded by rushing additional divisions into the country and seizing control of Rome, at which point the military campaign in Italy became a war of liberation from German occupation.

Success came hard against the occupiers, who waited in sophisticated fortifications atop the mountainous Italian terrain. Not until June 1944, after a long and bloody campaign, did massive firepower finally breach the German lines and enable Allied forces to liberate Rome. From that time until the end of the war, the Allies struggled against German mountain defenses in northern Italy. The Italian campaign, which fell frustratingly below total victory, was the costliest of the war to the American infantry and did not satisfy the demand of an increasingly embittered Stalin for a second front. It did, however, manage to tie up twenty-five German divisions that might otherwise have been used against either the Russians or a second front in France.

The War at Home

World War II brought no physical destruction to the United States mainland; no one starved, and no civilians lost their lives in the fighting. However, a war as vast and as long as World War II was bound to disrupt the traditional social patterns it sought to defend. Total war meant that millions of troops went to unheard-of places to face unimaginable dangers. Conversion of the economy to war purposes also drew millions of civilians away from their roots to seize opportunities they never had before in places where they never expected to live.

From Reform to Recovery

There is partial truth in the observation that Adolf Hitler was more responsible for ending the depression in the United States than was Franklin Roosevelt. In 1939, the federal budget was $9 billion; by 1945, at the end of total mobilization for war, it had grown to $100 billion. Within months after Pearl Harbor, unemployment, which in 1940 had stood at 14.6 percent of the nation's workforce, had virtually disappeared. Industrial cities boomed with orders for war materiel, enough not only to give work to urban dwellers but also to draw displaced farm laborers into the cities, where they enjoyed a modest prosperity far beyond anything they had known.

There was no longer much talk about social reform, however. As Roosevelt remarked, he had given up being "Dr. New Deal" in order to become "Dr. Win the War." In the spirit of victory at all costs, the administration oversaw a miracle of production. Called to Washington by a president they had mostly opposed, "dollar-a-year" businessmen (so called because they served without pay) headed the rapidly multiplying war production agencies. Organized labor was asked to make the more difficult sacrifice of agreeing not to strike. Even though continuing depression misery had moved 2.3 million workers to go out on strike during 1941, the major unions agreed to the pledge. Only a relative few brief work stoppages and the notable exception of

the United Mine Workers, who followed their irascible leader, John L. Lewis, out of the mines in 1943, marred the no strike agreement.

With a steady workforce, swelled by the millions of workers who had been unemployed before the war, results were prodigious. The United States produced 275,000 airplanes during the war and by 1945 was launching a new ship every twenty-four hours. The arsenal of democracy not only equipped its own gigantic armed forces but also supplied its allies in Europe and Asia with a large part of what they required. By 1942, American production equaled that of Germany, Italy, and Japan combined; by 1944, it stood at double their production. Confirmation that the depression was over came when business profit margins in 1943 soared well beyond those of 1929.

The nation's economic expansion was powered by the mobilization of its citizens. Draft boards registered 31 million men, of whom 10 million were inducted into service. In addition, more than 5 million men and women volunteered. When the war ended, 10,400,000 had served in the army, 3,900,000 in the navy, 600,000 in the marines, and 240,000 in the coast guard.

The war boom also accelerated the transformation of agriculture that the New Deal had begun. Family farms declined and tenant farmers virtually disappeared, many of them transplanted to urban centers of war production. Traditional patterns of rural black life underwent especially dramatic change. By 1950, the official census showed that only 115,000 African Americans remained on the land out of a total of 1,406,000 who had lived on farms when the war started. For the large farms that remained, the task of feeding both Americans and Allies meant an increase of production by 25 percent each year of the war.

The industrial sector broadened and prospered as well. With more than 15 million adults in the military, new workers—the old, the young, and especially women—were brought into the labor force. The cost of living increased by 30 percent from 1941 to 1945; but a 70 percent rise in weekly earnings of workers employed in manufacturing greatly outpaced inflation. Finding much to spend the new money on was another matter. Conversion of industrial plants to war purposes meant that automobiles, washing machines, refrigerators, and numerous other consumer items were no longer being manufactured. Many other civilian goods—

PITCHING IN AT HOME
This poster adapts the standard children's book illustration style of the period to the war effort. White and middle class all, mother and children collect old golf clubs, cocktail shakers, and trophies—which dad, away at war, will never miss—to recycle these symbols of the American way of life into armament for defense.
Chicago Historical Society.

automobile tires, gasoline, shoes, meat—were rationed because they were hard to obtain from war zones or were needed in large quantities for the military.

Political Crosscurrents

Inconveniences and dislocations notwithstanding, Americans on the home front rallied around the war effort in unprecedented unity. There were hardly any vigilante attacks on Americans suspected of being unpatriotic, because dissenters were so few.

Despite the consensus on war aims, however, the Roosevelt administration struggled to hold its governing coalition together. Resentment over price controls and shortages of rationed goods, white indignation over blacks leaving their subordinate place on southern farms, and dismay that the war was not going well provoked discontent with the Democratic administration. Moreover, in the congressional elections of 1942, many working-class soldiers and defense workers away at war were unable to cast their usual Democratic votes. Low voter turnout thus helped Republicans to gain seats in the House and Senate.

Republican opponents saw the war years as an opportunity to roll back New Deal reforms in favor of traditional American free enterprise. A conservative coalition of Republicans and southern Democrats succeeded in abolishing several New Deal agencies in 1942 and 1943, including the Work Projects Administration and the Civilian Conservation Corps. But the Democratic administration did not sit idly by while Republicans mounted a threat to their congressional majority. By persuading states to ease residency requirements and Congress to guarantee absentee ballots for servicemen, they arranged to bring scattered members of the New Deal coalition back to the voting booth.

Franklin Roosevelt, though exhausted and gravely ill, decided to run for a fourth term in 1944 (breaking the record he had already set by running for a third) rather than turn the uncompleted war effort over to a new leader. "All that is within me cries out to go back to my home on the Hudson River," he declared. "But as a good soldier . . . I will accept and serve." Convinced that many Americans had soured on liberal reform, Roosevelt replaced Vice President Henry Wallace, an outspoken progressive, with a more politically viable running mate, Senator Harry S. Truman of Missouri. A reliable party man from a border state, Truman seemed likely to satisfy urban Democratic leaders while not posing a threat to Southerners who were nervous about challenges to segregation.

The Republicans, confident of a strong conservative upsurge, nominated the governor of New York, Thomas E. Dewey, who had made his reputation as a tough crime fighter. Roosevelt's failing health limited his ability to campaign and alarmed many observers. In the final reckoning, though, that weakness was outweighed by the unwillingness of the American people to change presidents at the height of a foreign war or to accept Dewey's recycling of Herbert Hoover's argument that the New Deal was a creeping socialist menace. At only 53.5 percent of the popular vote, Roosevelt's victory was his narrowest; but it virtually assured that, if he lived, he would remain commander in chief throughout the war.

Women, Family, and the War

With war mobilization in full swing and men leaving for the armed forces, women by the millions found work in the defense industry. By 1944, some eighteen million women held full-time jobs, 50 percent more than in 1939. *Chicago Daily News* columnist Mike Royko remembered: "My sister became Rosie the Riveter. She put a bandanna on her head every day and went down to this organ company that had been converted to war work. . . . There was a sense of mission about it. Her husband was Over There." Along with the mission came an amazing rise in pay to an average of $31 weekly. In the patriotic euphoria, it was understandable that few complained that men received $54 for comparable work.

Alongside women in the civilian workforce stood 350,000 women who joined the Nurse's Corps and the newly created military units the Women's Army Corps (WACs), the navy's Women Accepted for Volunteer Emergency Service (Waves), the coast guard's Semper Paratus (SPARs), and the Women's Marine Corps. Women also served in the Women Air Service Pilots (WASPs). While barred from combat duty, women worked at nearly every noncombatant assignment.

Despite the war's dynamic social changes, most women remained at home or worked only part-time. With men no longer unemployed and wages up, family survival depended less on women's earning money. Not all trends pointed in the direction of middle-class stability, however. The absence of millions of able-bodied young men left many families without a father in the house; other family groups traveled from one to another of the seedy fringe settlements near military bases and defense. A desire to make the most of the moment in the face of an uncertain future prompted a rise in the number of marriages and births, but also of illegitimacy and divorce. In many cases, children compensated for the absence of fathers by helping at home and doing their part for the war effort. Girl and boy scouts collected metal and wastepaper, and older teenagers took jobs formerly reserved for adults.

FEMALE DEFENSE WORKER
The war effort brought persons and activities together in unlikely ways, leading to unexpected outcomes. In this photo, the army magazine Yank *sought to boost morale by presenting a defense worker as pinup girl. No one could know that the young propeller technician, nineteen-year-old Norma Jean Baker Dougherty, would later remake herself as the most glamorous of movie stars, Marilyn Monroe.*
David Conover Images © Norma Jean Enterprises, a division of 733548 Ontario Limited.

But new responsibilities and opportunities were countered by disruptive problems. Children in the workplace faced the same hardships that caused resistance to child labor in previous times. The absence of older men also meant that young people had less guidance than usual, and juvenile delinquency, especially among girls, increased accordingly. The yearning for war's end included a desire for stability at home as well as abroad.

Prejudice and the War

Fighting against Nazism and its ideology of Aryan racial supremacy forced Americans to examine prejudice in their own society. In a letter to the Southern Negro Youth Congress, Roosevelt declared that blacks were in the war "not only to defend America but . . . to establish a universal freedom under which a new basis of security and prosperity can be established for all—regardless of station, race, or creed." The *Pittsburgh Courier*, a leading black newspaper, rejoiced that, though "war may be hell for some," it appeared ready to "open up the portals of heaven for us."

Others sought to enter those portals as well. More than 13,000 Chinese Americans and more than 25,000 Native Americans fought in the armed forces. Mexican Americans feared that for them the war would mean deportation; instead, more than 200,000 laborers were imported from Mexico to cultivate American crops in the federal government's *bracero* program. In addition, 500,000 Mexican Americans served in the U.S. armed forces.

In an attempt to root old prejudicial patterns out of the war effort, black organizations sent a barrage of petitions to Congress and the White House demanding that the federal government require companies receiving defense contracts to integrate their workforces. A. Philip Randolph, head of the almost completely black Brotherhood of Sleeping Car Porters, promised that 100,000 marchers would descend on Washington if the president did not eliminate discrimination in defense industries. The president decided he had less to lose by offending old southern and union allies and issued Executive Order 8802, authorizing a Committee on Fair Employment Practices to investigate and prevent race discrimination in employment. Civil rights champions hailed the act as the first direct presidential intervention on behalf of black civil rights, and Randolph triumphantly called off the march.

Actual progress developed slowly. The five and a half million blacks who flooded into industrial cities during the 1940s, making African Americans a predominantly urban population for the first time, discovered that industry policies barred them from many skilled jobs. At least eighteen major unions, including such vital participants in the defense industry as the machinists, ironworkers, shipbuilders, and railway workers, had explicit bans against black membership. In time, however, severe labor shortages and government pressure opened up defense plants to African American workers. Black unemployment dropped by about 80 percent during the war, and the percentage of blacks in the defense industry doubled to a level almost equal to the percentage of blacks in the general population. Though

equality of pay was still a distant hope, by the end of the war the average income of black families had risen to half that of white families.

With migration and progress went racial antagonism, which boiled over in the hot summer of 1943 when 242 racial outbreaks in forty-seven different cities far surpassed the 26 riots in the Red scare year of 1919. In Los Angeles, hundreds of white servicemen, claiming they were punishing draft dodgers, chased and beat young Chicano men who dressed in distinctive broad-shouldered, peg-legged "zoot" suits. Worst of all were two days of mayhem in Detroit. Conflict between whites and blacks at a city park ignited a race war that saw whites smash their way with clubs through black neighborhoods and blacks retaliate by destroying and looting white-owned businesses. In the end, scores of persons suffered injury and thirty-four died, twenty-five of them African Americans.

Out of the depths of violence came the stimulus for promising new strategies. The National As-

DOUBLE V BUTTON
The Double V became African Americans' special version of the official "V for victory" symbol. Thousands of these buttons were worn as a reminder that both the Axis powers and racial discrimination should surrender unconditionally.
Private collection.

www.bedfordstmartins.com/roarkcompact   SEE THE ONLINE STUDY GUIDE for more help in analyzing this image.

sociation for the Advancement of Colored People (NAACP) launched the "Double V" campaign—victory abroad, victory at home—and intensified legal challenges to segregation. In 1942, civil rights activists who wanted more direct confrontations founded a new organization, the Congress of Racial Equality (CORE), that organized picketing and sit-ins against Jim Crow restaurants and theaters and would achieve significant results after the war.

The military was no more free of discrimination than was the home front. Secretary of War Henry Stimson opposed any change in the segregation of blacks and whites into separate units, declaring that the military effort should not serve as a "sociological laboratory." In 1942, Stimson fumed in his diary about black reformers' claims, which he deemed absurdly presumptuous: "What these foolish leaders of the colored race are seeking is at bottom social equality." Denied equality, blacks joined anyway, and by the end of the war nearly one million African American men and women had served. Segregation loosened as the war progressed. Blacks were trained as pilots for the first time, served on warships with white sailors, and saw extensive combat duty in the ground war in Europe and the Pacific. Yet military facilities remained segregated, and the Red Cross even segregated by race the blood it supplied to treat battlefield casualties. Perhaps nothing more poignantly captured the reality of wartime race relations than the moment when Lloyd Brown, a black soldier caught in the dusty heat of a Kansas summer day, gazed past the restaurant owner denying him entry and saw a row of German prisoners of war enjoying their lunch at the counter.

World War II did not witness a repetition of the hysteria and viciousness that had characterized the home front during World War I. With almost no dissent against the war, Roosevelt felt no need to engage in a high-powered propaganda campaign such as Wilson had unleashed in 1917. This time, the government took control of the media not to stir passions against the enemy, but to suppress bad news from the war effort. Americans did worry about espionage, however. Walls were plastered with slogans such as "Loose lips sink ships" and "Enemy agents are always near; if you don't talk, they won't hear."

There was one major exception to the atmosphere of tolerance—the drastic violation of the rights of Japanese Americans, the only minority group to lose ground during the war. From the time of their first entry into the country in significant numbers in the 1890s, mainly to settle on the West Coast, the Japanese had encountered hostility as economic competitors in small businesses and farming, intruding in a "white man's country." In 1924 federal law established that Japanese immigrants were "aliens ineligible to citizenship," and the *Los Angeles Times* broadcast the popular view that all Japanese Americans were a threat because they would multiply endlessly and outcompete "real" Americans. Any recognition that the actual role of most Japanese was to provide cheap food—exactly what white workers, managers, and homemakers should have hailed—was swallowed up in the storm of hatred that followed the attack on Pearl Harbor. (See "Documenting the American Promise," page 654.)

Even though a military survey concluded that Japanese Americans posed no danger, President Roosevelt on February 19, 1942, gave racism the force of law in an executive order authorizing the roundup of all Americans of Japanese descent. Allowed little time to secure or sell their assets, the victims (most of whom were American citizens) lost jobs and property. Not a single case of subversion or sabotage was ever uncovered, yet Japanese Americans were sent to "relocation centers"—basically makeshift prison camps—in remote areas where they were penned in by barbed wire and armed guards for more than three years. Not until 1988 did Congress award modest reparations to Japanese Americans for their wartime losses.

War posed challenges for homosexual Americans in some ways comparable to those faced by other marginalized groups. The view that gays were a threat to good order and were apt to crack under stress had long dominated military thinking. After uncovering gay activity in World War I, the military tightened its psychological screening process and specified criminal penalties. However, authorities showed little inclination to pursue gays in the period between the world wars when the military shrank to a small volunteer force. A few men did serve time in prison for sodomy, but psychological screening was seldom used by officers ill equipped to understand it. Essentially, those in charge followed what would later become an official policy of "Don't ask, don't tell."

Once the Selective Service Act of 1940 began bringing vast numbers of recruits into the armed forces, Secretary of War Henry Stimson reminded all commanding generals that they were expected

Japanese Internment

*A*ngrily determined that the bombing of Pearl Harbor would not be followed by more sneak attacks, military and political leaders on the West Coast targeted persons of Japanese descent—alien and citizen alike—as potential saboteurs.

DOCUMENT 1. Final Recommendations of the Commanding General, Western Defense Command and Fourth Army, Submitted to the Secretary of War

Early in 1942, General John DeWitt, commander of the Western Defense Command, persuaded President Franklin Roosevelt to issue an executive order authorizing the removal of the Japanese living in the United States. Subsequently, some 110,000 Japanese Americans were confined to relocation camps in remote areas, surrounded by barbed wire and armed guards. DeWitt's recommendation expressed concern for military security within racist conceptions long used to curb Asian immigration. Belying DeWitt's notion that all Japanese were the same, response on the part of detainees varied widely, from incomprehension, to resistance in the courts, to reassessment of their Japanese ancestry. In later years, after official government apology for the incident and monetary redress, the experience was remembered as a profound test of identity and assimilation.

February 14, 1942
Memorandum for the Secretary of War.
Subject: Evacuation of Japanese and Other Subversive Persons from the Pacific Coast.
1. In presenting a recommendation for the evacuation of Japanese and other subversive persons from the Pacific Coast, the following facts have been considered:
a. Mission of the Western Defense Command and Fourth Army.
(1) Defense of the Pacific Coast of the Western Defense Command, as extended, against attacks by sea, land, or air;

(2) Local protection of establishment and communications vital to the National Defense for which adequate defense cannot be provided by local civilian authorities.
b. Brief Estimate of the Situation.
(1) . . . The following are possible and probable enemy activities: . . .
(a) Naval attack on shipping on coastal waters;
(b) Naval attack on coastal cities and vital installations;
(c) Air raids on vital installations, particularly within two hundred miles of the coast;
(d) Sabotage of vital installations throughout the Western Defense Command.
Hostile Naval and air raids will be assisted by enemy agents signaling from the coastline and the vicinity thereof; and by supplying and otherwise assisting enemy vessels and by sabotage.
. . . The Japanese race is an enemy race and while many second and third generation Japanese born on United States soil, possessed of United States citizenship, have become "Americanized," the racial strains are undiluted. To conclude otherwise is to expect that children born of white parents on Japanese soil sever all racial affinity and become loyal Japanese subjects, ready to fight and, if necessary, to die for Japan in a war against the nation of their parents. . . .
It, therefore, follows that along the vital Pacific Coast over 112,000 potential enemies, of Japanese extraction, are at large today. There are indications that these are organized and ready for concerted action at a favorable opportunity. The very fact that no sabotage has taken place to date is a disturbing and confirming indication that such action will be taken.

SOURCE: *Final Recommendations*, report by General John Lesesne DeWitt to the United States Secretary of War, February 14, 1942.

DOCUMENT 2. An Oral History of Life in the Japanese American Detention Camps

Imprisoned in bleak surroundings far from home, Japanese internees were prey to despair and bitterness. Looking back after forty years, Kazue Yamane recalled her confinement as a disturbing and baffling experience.

In April 1942, my husband and I and our two children left for camp, and my mother-in-law and father-in-law came about a month later. I wasn't afraid, but I kept asking in my mind, how could they? This is impossible. Even today I still think it was a nightmarish thing. I cannot reconcile myself to the fact that I had to go, that I was interned, that I was segregated, that I was taken away, even though it goes back forty years. . . .

I was separated from my husband; he went to the Santa Fe, New Mexico, camp. All our letters were censored; all our letters were cut in parts and all that. So we were not too sure what messages was getting through and not getting through, but I do know that I informed him many times of his mother's condition. He should have been allowed to come back to see her, because I thought she wouldn't live too long, but they never did allow him to come back, even for her funeral. They did not allow that. I learned that a lot of the messages didn't get to him; they were crossed out. I now have those letters with me.

In 1944 I was left with his parents and our kids. But I had no time to think of what was going to happen because my child was always sick and I had been quite sick. . . .

My son knew what was going on, and he too had many times asked me why . . . you know, why? why? Of course, I had no explanation why this was happening to us.

Source: Excerpt from "An Oral History of Life in the Japanese American Detention Camps." In *And Justice for All*, by John Tateishi. Copyright © 1999 by John Tateishi. Reprinted by permission of the University of Washington Press.

Document 3. The Kikuchi Diary

Forcibly removed from the tension between his life as a student at the University of California at Berkeley and his unassimilated family, Charles Kikuchi sought in his prison camp diary to make sense of the internment and to judge where it would lead.

December 7, 1941, Berkeley, California
Pearl Harbor. We are at war! Jesus Christ, the Japs bombed Hawaii and the entire fleet has been sunk. I just can't believe it. I don't know what in the hell is going to happen to us, but we will all be called into the Army right away.

. . . The next five years will determine the future of the Nisei [Japanese American citizens]. They are now at the crossroads. Will they be able to take it or will they go under? If we are ever going to prove our Americanism, this is the time. The Anti-Jap feeling is bound to rise to hysterical heights, and it is most likely that the Nisei will be included as Japs. I wanted to go to San Francisco tonight, but Pierre says I am crazy. He says it's best we stick on campus. In any event, we can't remain on the fence, and a positive approach must be taken if we are to have a place in fulfilling the Promise of America. I think the U.S. is in danger of going Fascist too, or maybe Socialist. . . .

I don't know what to think or do. Everybody is in a daze.

April 30, 1942, Berkeley
Today is the day that we are going to get kicked out of Berkeley. It certainly is degrading. . . .

I'm supposed to see my family at Tanforan as Jack told me to give the same family number. I wonder how it is going to be living with them as I haven't done this for years and years? I should have gone over to San Francisco and evacuated with them, but I had a last final to take. I understand that we are going to live in the horse stalls. I hope that the Army has the courtesy to remove the manure first. . . .

July 14, 1942
Marie, Ann, Mitch, Jimmy, Jack, and myself got into a long discussion about how much democracy meant to us as individuals. Mitch says that he would even go in the army and die for it, in spite of the fact that he knew he would be kept down. Marie said that although democracy was not perfect, it was the only system that offered any hope for a future, if we could fulfill its destinies. Jack was a little more skeptical. He even suggested that we [could] be in such grave danger that we would then realize that we were losing something. Where this point was he could not say. I said that this was what happened in France and they lost all. Jimmy suggested that the colored races of the world had reason to feel despair and mistrust the white man because of the past experiences. . . .

In reviewing the four months here, the chief value I got out of this forced evacuation was the strengthening of the family bonds. I never knew my family before this and this was the first chance that I have had to really get acquainted. (*Continued*)

DOCUMENT 4. Internment Poems

For some Japanese Americans who endured confinement in the desert, only artistic expression could convey their experience adequately. When poet and teacher Toyo Kawakami arrived at the internment camp in Topaz, Utah, she pondered her fate in "Barracks Home." Many years later, she visited Topaz again and distilled the experience in "Camp Memories."

"Barracks Home"
The floor is carpeted with dust, wind-borne
Dry alkali, patterned by insect feet.
What peace can such a place as this impart?
We can but sense, bewildered and forlorn,
That time, disrupted by the war from neat
Routines, must now adjust within the heart.

"Camp Memories"
I have dredged up
Hard fragments lost
I thought, in years

Of whirlwind dust.
Exposed to light,
Silently rough
And broken shards
Confront belief.

QUESTIONS FOR ANALYSIS AND DEBATE

1. What explains General DeWitt's insistence on evacuating the Japanese after he received the report of military investigators that no acts of sabotage had occurred?
2. In what ways are the poems of Toyo Kawakami similar to the oral history of life in the camps and the Kikuchi diary? How are they different?
3. Despite the internment of their families and friends in concentration camps, the Japanese American army unit in Italy earned the largest number of citations for combat heroism of any army group. How can this be explained?

to prosecute cases of sodomy. Ironically, though, the need to build a huge fighting force made those in charge reluctant to depart from the old policy of looking the other way. And because screening procedures had been set up with only men in mind, lesbians volunteering for the newly formed women's branches of service seldom encountered any effort to exclude them.

Thus allowed to serve, gay Americans found the war to be a special sort of transforming experience. Like other beleaguered minorities, gays sought to demonstrate their worth under fire. "I was superpatriotic," a combat veteran recalled. "And being a homosexual, I had that constant compelling need to prove how virile I was." Another gay veteran, a survivor of the brutal Iwo Jima campaign, had a more basic reaction: In the midst of life-or-death realities, "who in the hell is going to worry about this shit?"

After the war, gay veterans tended to cluster in large cities where their sense of mutual interests and loyalty shaped their communities. Toughened by the military ordeal and angry that they had been part of a successful war against oppression, including the Nazi policy of exterminating homosexuals, while remaining oppressed themselves, veterans led the way in promoting the gay liberation movement. In 1950, a group of gay veterans formed the Mattachine Society to combat discrimination, and five years later lesbians in San Francisco followed their example by founding the Daughters of Bilitis. These efforts provided the impetus for gay activism to become part of a broad front of civil rights insurgency.

FBI SEARCHING JAPANESE AMERICAN HOME
When President Roosevelt informed military commanders that they might "from time to time" remove persons deemed dangerous, he had reason to suspect that virtually all Japanese Americans would be affected. An army "expert" on Asian culture had already advised the War Department that, "as you cannot . . . penetrate the Oriental thinking . . . the easiest course is to remove them all from the West Coast and place them . . . under guard." Intent on getting to the bottom of one Japanese American family's allegiance, an FBI agent in 1942 scrutinizes a picture album, while family members whose home has been invaded look on helplessly.
Department of Special Collections, Charles E. Young Research Library, Los Angeles *Daily News* Photographic Archive, UCLA.

Reaction to the Holocaust

Throughout the 1930s, Spanish Loyalists fleeing Franco, opponents of Mussolini, and, most numerous, the targets of Hitler's maniacal racism clamored for asylum. As Hitler expanded his campaign to "purify" Germany, Jews, gypsies, religious dissenters, homosexuals, avant-garde artists, and others came under increasing pressure to flee or risk extermination. As American resolve against totalitarian oppression stiffened, a desperate contest arose between those who would rescue the victims of persecution and those who would bar the gate.

Roosevelt sympathized with the pleas for help, but only if action did not jeopardize his foreign policy or his hold on the electorate. After the German army took over Austria in March 1938, crowds of Jews besieged the American embassy in Vienna, seeking immigration visas. Roosevelt tried to raise the annual quota, which allowed only fourteen hundred Austrians into the country, but Congress, trying to keep out of war and mindful of polls showing that 82 percent of Americans were against admitting Jewish exiles, refused the request. Roosevelt then sought to persuade countries in Latin America and Africa to accept refugees. None would agree. In a last attempt before war broke out, friends of the refugees introduced legislation in Congress in 1939 that would grant asylum to twenty thousand German refugee children, most of them

Jewish. Both anti-Semitism and isolationism were undoubtedly factors in the defeat of the bill, for the following year refugee English children who were not predominantly Jewish gained entry without delay.

In 1942, word leaked out that Hitler was implementing a "final solution": Jews and other "undesirables" were being sent to concentration camps in remote areas; old people, children, and others deemed too weak to work were gassed and cremated while the able-bodied were put to work until lack of food and harsh conditions killed them. Even then skeptical U.S. State Department officials stood firmly in the way. Only 152,000 Jews had managed to gain refuge in the United

The Holocaust, 1933–1945

Principal German
• concentration and
extermination camp

States prior to America's entry into the war; thereafter, the numbers dropped steadily to a mere 2,400 in 1944. Those trapped in Europe could only wait for rescue by Allied armies.

Fear of adverse reaction also prevented action. The Office of War Information worried that charging the Germans with crimes against humanity would incite them to greater resistance that would prolong the war. Also, because officials could not provide eyewitness proof that the camps really existed to sway public opinion, they chose to stall further action until victorious troops could verify their existence. In fact, without this conclusive evidence, many top officials found the truth incomprehensible and clung to the rationalization that the nightmare could not be real.

The nightmare was real, however. When Russian troops arrived at Auschwitz in Poland in February 1945, they found only a handful of emaciated prisoners, some too weak to survive their liberation. Skeletal corpses, some half burned, lay around them; nearby were ponds and pits filled with the ashes of those who had perished. The Russians discovered sheds filled with loot stripped from the dead—clothing, gold fillings, false teeth, even cloth made from human hair. At last, the truth

THE DEAD AT BUCHENWALD
In this stark moment, all distance between official Washington and the Holocaust is breached. Soldiers and civilians pause somberly in the background of the Buchenwald concentration camp as Senator Alben Barkley of Kentucky, stooped in sadness, contemplates some of the victims of the Nazis' attempt to carry out their "final solution." Soon afterward Germans in the area, who had claimed not to know of the camp's existence, were forced to witness the scene and then bury the dead.

Pentagon, U.S. Army Signal Corps.

about Nazi atrocities breached the wall of denial. But by then it was too late; Nazi extermination had reached its final toll of nine million victims.

Military Victory: 1943–1945

By early 1943, the defensive phase of the war was over. Having halted enemy advances, the Allies faced the daunting task of driving the Axis back and finally defeating Germany and Japan on their home territory. Stalin's anger over the reluctance of the United States and Britain to relieve the Soviet Union from the brunt of Hitler's attack by opening a second front in France strained the alliance. By the time the invasion of Normandy occurred, the Soviet Union had already broken German power in the east. Simultaneously in the Pacific, the United States, alongside Australia and New Zealand, unleashed its final victorious drive toward the Japanese mainland.

From Normandy to Berlin

In November 1943, as the Italian campaign slogged on at its cold, muddy pace, Churchill, Roosevelt, and Stalin held meetings in Teheran, Iran, and Cairo, Egypt, to plan the final assault on Hitler. Stalin finally succeeded in getting Roosevelt and Churchill to commit the enormous forces that had been training in England for two years to an invasion of Europe in May 1944. General Dwight D. Eisenhower, with his great tact and organizing skills, became Supreme Commander of the Allied forces—American, British, and Free French—while General Sir Bernard Montgomery, the hero of victory in North Africa, took charge of the landing itself.

German forces, directed by the master tactician General Erwin Rommel, fortified the cliffs and mined the beaches of northwestern France. Yet, as Rommel realized more clearly than Hitler, the huge deployment of German armies in the east trying to contain the massive Soviet offensive in the spring of 1943 left too few troops to stop the three million Allied soldiers waiting in England. Even more of a handicap was Rommel's inability to control the air. On the eve of invasion, the Luftwaffe (German air force) had only three hundred fighter planes to face twelve thousand Allied aircraft.

False radio signals, invented armies, and diversionary air sorties encouraged the Germans to expect an invasion at the Pas de Calais area, where the English Channel is narrowest. The actual site was miles to the south on the beaches of Normandy (Map 25.3). First came raging air and naval attacks, then the dropping of paratroopers behind the German lines, and finally at 7:30 a.m. on June 6, 1944, referred to in military parlance as "D Day," seaborne soldiers hit the beaches. For a perilous few hours, rough seas and fortified machine guns stopped the assault in a chaos of overturned tanks, drowning men, and frantic attempts by those who made it ashore to find cover. But paratroopers coming up behind the German line and rangers scaling the cliffs to knock out enemy gun emplacements finally secured the beachhead.

Within a week, Allied forces had broken out of the Normandy pocket and begun their massive sweep toward Germany. On August 25, the Allies liberated Paris from four years of Nazi occupation. Two months later, they made their first foray into Germany to capture the city of Aachen. Hitler then took a mad gamble as the giant pincers of the Allied and Soviet armies closed on German headquarters in Berlin. In December 1944, he ordered a counterattack through Belgium to recapture Antwerp and deny the Allies their major supply port. Massive German forces drove fifty-five miles into Allied lines in what was known as the Battle of the Bulge before being stopped at Bastogne with a disastrous loss of eighty-two thousand men and hundreds of tanks. By committing so many of his reserves to the Bulge, Hitler left the remnant of his army, facing the Russians, close to collapse.

In February 1945, with the end in sight, Churchill, Stalin, and a seriously ill Roosevelt met secretly at the Russian Black Sea resort town of Yalta to discuss the structure of the postwar world. Although his stamina and mental alertness flickered, Roosevelt still managed to secure a major share of what he sought. The Soviets agreed to a declaration of self-determination for the countries their armies occupied in Eastern Europe. Chiang Kai-shek would receive Allied support as leader of China in the war against Japan. And the Soviet Union would have a say in the governance of Korea and Manchuria in exchange for entering the war against Japan after the defeat of Germany.

The "Big Three" also agreed on the creation of a new international organization, the United Nations (UN). All countries would have a place in the organization's General Assembly, but the Security Council would ultimately wield decisive power.

M A P 25.3

The European Theater of World War II, 1942–1945

Russian reversal of the German offensive by breaking the sieges of Stalingrad and Leningrad, combined with Allied landings in North Africa and Normandy, placed Germany in a closing vise of armies from all sides.

READING THE MAP: By 1942, what nations or parts of nations in Europe were under Axis control? What nations had been absorbed before the war? What nations remained neutral, and what nations were members of the Allies?

CONNECTIONS: What were the three fronts in the European theater? When did the Allies initiate actions in each of them, and why did Churchill, Stalin, and Roosevelt disagree on the timing of the opening of these fronts?

D DAY INVASION
"Taxi to Hell—and Back" is what Robert Sargent called his photograph of the D Day invasion of Normandy on June 6, 1944. Amid a dense thicket of landing craft, men and equipment lucky enough to have made it through rough seas and enemy fire struggle onto the beach to open a second front in Europe. After this brief moment of safe passage, the majority of this first wave of soldiers would be cut down by withering enemy fire from the high cliffs beyond the beach.
Library of Congress.

The Security Council would be composed of temporary members and of permanent representatives from China, France, Great Britain, the Soviet Union, and the United States, each of which would retain the veto.

American response to the creation of the UN was startlingly different from the nation's refusal to join the League of Nations in 1919. Internationalism triumphed when Republican senator Arthur Vandenberg of Michigan, who had long been a staunch isolationist, declared that it was his mission to "end the miserable notion that the Republican Party will return to its foxhole when the last shot in this war has been fired and will blindly let the world rot in its own anarchy." The Senate ratified the United Nations charter in July by a vote of 89 to 2.

Following the Yalta agreement, the Allies began the final assault on Hitler. While American forces pounded Germany from the west, the Soviets, having swept through Poland, arrived at the outskirts of Berlin in April 1945. Hitler, who had descended into his underground bunker on January 16, signaled the end of Nazism by committing suicide on April 30. On May 7, a provisional German government surrendered unconditionally.

Franklin Roosevelt did not live to witness the end of the Nazi horror. On April 12, while resting in Warm Springs, Georgia, the president suffered a fatal stroke. Americans grieved publicly for the man who had led them through more than twelve years of depression and world war, and they worried aloud about his successor. Vice President Harry Truman's

YALTA CONFERENCE
*In February 1945, President Roosevelt and British prime minister Winston Churchill met
with Russian leader Joseph Stalin at the Black Sea resort of Yalta to plan the postwar
reconstruction of Europe. Roosevelt, near the end of his life, and Churchill, soon to suffer reelection defeat, look weary next to the resolute "Man of Steel." Controversy would
later arise over whether a stronger stand by the American and British leaders could
have prevented the Soviet Union from imposing communist rule on eastern Europe.*
U.S. Army.

colleagues in Congress generally believed he would
be little more than a caretaker, and the new leader
seemed to agree. When a reporter called him "Mr.
President," he replied uneasily, "I wish you didn't
have to call me that." To other reporters he pleaded,
"Boys, if newspapermen pray, pray for me now."
Truman showed himself to be tough-minded and a
quick learner, however, with a knowledge of history
deeper than that of almost any previous president.
It soon became clear that he would not hesitate to
make hard decisions.

The Defeat of Japan

Japan had intended to use its navy to shield a vast
economic empire in China and Southeast Asia. Instead, after battle losses in 1942, it had to fend off
aroused Allied forces while also trying to quell renewed resistance on the Asian mainland. In China
the Japanese army, despite many victories, was unable to finish off Chiang Kai-shek. To the west Japan
had advanced almost to India, but in 1943 British
and American forces, along with Indian and Chinese troops, launched a counterthrust through
Burma and into China. The most decisive action,
however, came in the Pacific, where the Allies
moved slowly and painfully, island by island, toward the Japanese homeland (Map 25.4).

In August 1942, the island campaign began
when the First Marine Division landed on Guadalcanal, where the Japanese were constructing an air-
field. For the next six months, a savage battle raged

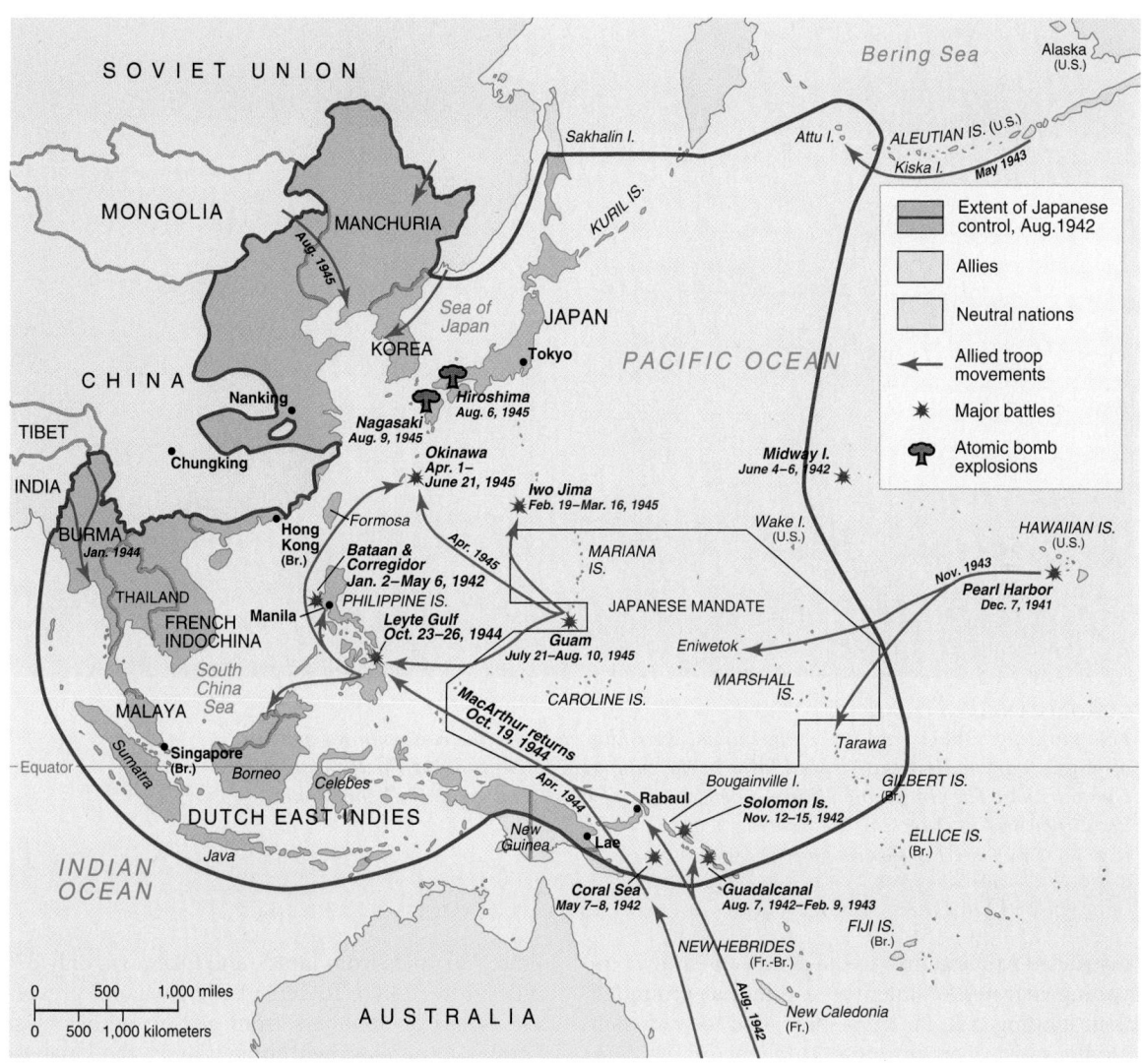

MAP 25.4

The Pacific Theater of World War II, 1941–1945
*To drive the Japanese from their far-flung empire, the Allies launched two combined
naval and military offensives—one to recapture the Philippines and then attack Japanese forces in China, the other to hop from island to island in the Central Pacific
toward the Japanese mainland.*

for control of the strategic area. Finally, during the
night of February 7, 1943, Japanese forces withdrew
after terrible losses on both sides that indicated just
how costly the long march to Japan would be.

In mid-1943, American, Australian, and New
Zealand forces launched offensives that penetrated
the outer perimeter of Japanese defenses. Bloody
campaigns in New Guinea and the Solomon Islands

gradually secured the South Pacific. In the Central
Pacific, amphibious forces, borne by the greatest
fleet in history, took the Gilbert and Marshall Islands, which served eventually as forward positions
for launching the decisive air and ground assaults
on the Japanese home islands.

As the Allied offensive pressed on, resistance
grew fiercer from Japanese soldiers who had been

GUADALCANAL: *GHOST TRAIL*
This painting, **Ghost Trail** *by combat artist Kerr Eby, captures the eerie, murky quality of jungle warfare first experienced fully in the campaign to capture the Pacific island of Guadalcanal. The troops blend into a dense maze of black and green that compounds the difficulties of detecting the hidden enemy.*
Navy Art Collection/Gift of Abbott Laboratories.

instructed to stand firm to the death. At Tarawa, invading marines, stymied by a tide that grounded their landing craft far from shore, had to wade half a mile, waist-deep, through brutal enemy fire. Survivors of that barrage then faced fortified emplacements manned by well-armed troops who had no intention of retreating. Within three days, the marines had suffered one thousand dead and another two thousand wounded—all to take a barren coral island not three square miles. Only seventeen of the three thousand Japanese defenders were left alive to surrender. Thereafter, island-to-island warfare took on an awful sameness of rooting the enemy out of bunkers and caves with explosives and flame-throwers.

Both land and sea war climaxed in the fall of 1944 with the invasion of the Philippines and the battle for Leyte Gulf. The greatest naval encounter in history cost the Japanese practically their entire fleet. Before the Philippines were retaken, Allied forces captured two vital island strongholds—Iwo

Jima, 750 miles from Japan, and Okinawa, only 370 miles from Tokyo. To defend Okinawa and prevent the American invaders from getting within close bombing range of their home islands, the Japanese called on thousands of suicide pilots, known as *kamikaze* ("divine wind"). Their mission was to crash bomb-laden planes into Allied ships and thus, it was hoped, make the landing forces turn back. The *kamikaze* made life harrowing for the American fleet but did not deter it. Rather, the suicide gesture destroyed the last vestige of the Japanese air force. By June 1945, the Japanese were virtually defenseless on sea and in the air.

Atomic Warfare

The race to develop an atomic bomb began in 1942 after refugee scientists warned that the Nazis were working to convert nuclear energy into a superbomb. The Roosevelt administration quickly authorized the top-secret Manhattan Project to develop the bomb before the Germans did. In thirty-seven locations across the country, coordinated by leading theorists at Los Alamos, New Mexico, 100,000 persons worked at top speed to win the race.

Germany surrendered before it produced a bomb and before the United States was ready to test its own. Then, just before dawn on July 16, 1945, a test explosion lit up the sky in an isolated corner of the Alamogordo Air Base near Los Alamos. None of the project scientists had guessed that the force of the bomb would be greater than a few hundred tons of TNT. Nor was anyone prepared for a flash of multicolored light more brilliant than ever seen before or the vast fireball and mushroom-shaped cloud of dust and debris that rose eight miles into the upper atmosphere.

A delegation of scientists and officials, troubled by the power they had unleashed, proposed a pub-lic demonstration of the bomb's doomsday force to persuade Japan to surrender. With Japanese forces incapable of offensive action and Japan totally blockaded, test proponents argued that the United States could afford to wait until the point of the demonstration sank in. The Japanese government had already sent emissaries to see if a negotiated peace could be reached. The sticking point was that the Japanese wanted to retain their emperor, while the American government remained committed to unconditional surrender.

In the end, all reluctance to unleash the atomic monster on populated targets yielded to other urgent considerations. When President Truman heard about the bomb test, he was involved in hard bargaining with the Soviets in Potsdam, Germany, about how to reorganize the postwar world. Truman showed his distrust of the Russians by keep-

HIROSHIMA BOMBING
This rare shot taken by a news photographer in Hiroshima immediately after the atomic bomb exploded on August 6, 1945, suggests the shock and incomprehension that survivors would describe as their first reaction. Three days later another atomic bomb created similar devastation in Nagasaki.
UN photo.

ing the news of the test secret. Then he adjusted his strategy to take advantage of the new weapon. Clearly, the bomb made it unnecessary to call on the Russian promise to hasten victory by declaring war on Japan. Rather, a surprise use of the new super-weapon might end the conflict before the Soviet Union could attack the Japanese in Korea and Manchuria. Perhaps, also, the bomb's devastation would convince the Soviets that they could not safely challenge American leadership after the war ended.

A more basic motive was to save American lives. As Truman pondered his options, Americans were preparing for Operation Downfall—the invasion of the Japanese home island. Experience with Japanese soldiers who fought to the death filled American military and civilian leaders with dread. Intelligence reports indicated that more than two million Japanese army troops were available for a last-ditch defense of their homeland. Behind them were twenty-eight million men, women, and boys of the civilian militia, armed with sharpened bamboo stakes, farm implements, and any other weapons they could muster.

Truman, who had been a commander of combat troops on the ground in World War I, was keenly sympathetic to the ordeal facing an invading army. He saw no reason not to use a weapon of war, even a terribly destructive one, if it would save American lives. But first he issued an ultimatum that Japan must surrender unconditionally or face utter ruin. When the Japanese failed to respond by the deadline, Truman turned to his advisory committee's recommendation that, to shock the Japanese into surrender, the bomb must be dropped without warning on cities that had not already been heavily damaged. On August 6, a single B-29, the *Enola Gay*, droned over Hiroshima and released one of the three operational atomic bombs the Americans possessed. As the plane banked sharply away, crew members could see behind them the mushroom cloud that signified the obliteration of the city and the death of seventy-eight thousand inhabitants. Three days later, a second atomic bomb devastated Nagasaki with at least forty thousand deaths.

At last, in the midst of ruin, a peace faction took control of the Japanese government, and with assurance that the emperor could retain his throne under Allied control, Japan surrendered on August 14. When Hirohito broadcast the news over the radio—the first words that the public had ever heard the emperor utter—his subjects obediently laid down their arms and stood quietly by as the giant battleship *Missouri* sailed into Tokyo harbor for the formal signing of surrender on September 2, 1945.

Conclusion: Victory and Uncertainty

For Americans, the attack on Pearl Harbor was just the first shock of a war whose scope and violence were unprecedented. An estimated 35 million died, evenly divided between military and civilian losses. Approximately 400,000 Americans lost their lives in military service; the Soviet Union lost more in the battle of Stalingrad alone and eventually suffered nearly 20 million civilian and military deaths.

Out of war's carnage arose misgivings about human nature. The Holocaust demonstrated cruelty beyond what many had imagined possible, and the atomic bomb added alarm over the destructive powers of science and technology. Charles Lindbergh, who had been vilified for questioning America's intervention, found much to reinforce his foreboding during his service in both theaters of war. Just days after Germany's surrender, an assignment to study German jet planes caused Lindbergh to pass through a liberated death camp at Nordhausen. Gaunt survivors and the furnaces designed to cremate them forced memories of the savage Pacific campaign back on Lindbergh: Japanese prisoners machine-gunned on an airstrip, others pushed out of transport planes supposed to take them to safe captivity, shin bones cut for letter openers. Committing atrocities, he realized at that moment, "is not a thing confined to any nation or to any people. . . . It is not the Germans alone, or the Japs, but the men of all nations to whom this war has brought shame and degradation."

Nevertheless, most Americans emerged from the conflict convinced that they had won a "good war" against totalitarian evil. The Allies had saved Asia and Europe from enslavement and thwarted the Nazi attempt to murder those its insane racial theories deemed unfit. To secure human rights and protect the world against future wars the Roosevelt administration had taken the lead in creating the United Nations. Economically there was also the good news that war had brought America out of the Depression. Unemployment was negligible, and the gross national product had soared to four times what it had been when Roosevelt was elected president in 1932. The remaining challenge was to create a stable prosperity and reintegrate the millions of men and women who were returning from the fighting.

Postwar challenges abroad, where the destructive force of war had been directly felt, were grimmer. Reconstructing shattered lives and nations took place within political turmoil, and the United States and Western Europe soon found themselves at odds with Russian seizure of control over Eastern Europe and a Communist revolution against the government in China that had been a partner in the war against Japan. Efforts by Britain and France to maintain their colonial empires also roused resistance from national forces seeking liberation. Under these circumstances, the confidence bred of winning the good war began to give way to the anxious uncertainties of what came to be called the cold war.

FOR FURTHER READING ABOUT THE TOPICS IN THIS CHAPTER, see the Online Bibliography at www.bedfordstmartins.com/roarkcompact.

FOR ADDITIONAL FIRST-HAND ACCOUNTS OF THIS PERIOD, see pages 166–185 in Michael Johnson, ed., *Reading the American Past,* Second Edition, Volume II.

TO ASSESS YOUR MASTERY OF THE MATERIAL IN THIS CHAPTER, see the Online Study Guide at www.bedfordstmartins.com/roarkcompact.

CHRONOLOGY

1933 Adolf Hitler becomes chancellor of Germany.

United States formally recognizes Soviet Union.

1935– Congress seeks to shield America
1937 from world conflicts with neutrality acts.

1936 Nazi Germany occupies Rhineland.

Mussolini's fascist Italian regime conquers Ethiopia.

Civil war breaks out in Spain.

1937 Japanese troops capture Nanking.

Roosevelt delivers speech urging "quarantine" against aggressor nations.

1938 Hitler annexes Austria.

British prime minister Neville Chamberlain meets with Hitler in Munich and agrees to German seizure of Sudetenland in Czechoslovakia.

1939 German troops occupy remainder of Czechoslovakia without resistance.

Nazi Germany and Soviet Union sign nonaggression pact.

September 1. Germany's attack on Poland begins World War II.

United States and Great Britain conclude cash-and-carry agreement for arms sales.

1940 **May–June.** British troops evacuated at Dunkirk, France.

June. German occupation of France begins.

Isolationists, including Charles Lindbergh, create America First Committee.

Roosevelt wins reelection against Wendell Willkie.

1941 Lend-Lease Act enables Britain to obtain war materiel from United States on credit.

June. Germany invades Soviet Union.

August. Atlantic Charter devised by Roosevelt and Allies to guarantee

human and international freedoms after war.

December 7. Japanese launch surprise attack on Pearl Harbor; United States declares war on Japan.

1942 Japan captures Philippines.

Civil rights activists found Congress of Racial Equality (CORE).

U.S. navy scores its first major victories in Battle of Coral Sea and at Midway.

Roosevelt authorizes top-secret Manhattan Project.

November. U.S. forces invade North Africa.

Roosevelt authorizes internment of Japanese Americans.

1943 Allied leaders agree that war will end only with unconditional surrender of Axis forces.

"Zoot suit" riots occur in Los Angeles.

U.S. forces invade Sicily.

1944 **June 6.** Combined Allied army stages successful D Day landing at Normandy.

Roosevelt wins reelection against Thomas E. Dewey.

1945 The Allies meet at Yalta to plan reconstruction of Europe after defeat of Germany.

April 12. Franklin Roosevelt dies, and Harry Truman becomes president.

Delegates from fifty nations, meeting in San Francisco, approve charter of United Nations.

April 30. Hitler commits suicide.

May 7. Germany surrenders.

August 6. United States drops atomic bomb on Hiroshima.

August 9. United States drops atomic bomb on Nagasaki.

August 14. Japan surrenders, ending World War II.

COLD WAR COMIC BOOK
Americans barely had time to celebrate the Allied victory in World War II when they perceived a new threat, that posed by the Soviet Union. Fear of communism dominated much of postwar American life and politics, even invading the realm of popular culture. Four million copies of this comic book, published by a religious organization in 1947, painted a terrifying picture of what would happen to Americans if the Soviets took over the country. Such takeover stories appeared in movies, cartoons, and magazines as well as in other comic books.

Collection of Charles H. Christensen.

COLD WAR POLITICS IN THE TRUMAN YEARS

26

1945–1953

O N NOVEMBER 5, 1946, President Harry S. Truman, his wife, and his daughter boarded the train back to Washington from Truman's hometown, Independence, Missouri, where they had gone to vote in the congressional elections. During the campaigns, Republicans had blasted Truman as incapable of dealing with economic problems and the threat of communism. The president's approval rating had sunk to a mere 32 percent. Many Democratic candidates had avoided mentioning his name and instead used recordings of the late Franklin Roosevelt's voice to stir voters. Playing poker with reporters on the train as the returns came in, Truman appeared unconcerned. But the results were devastating: The Republicans had captured both the House and the Senate by substantial majorities.

When Truman arrived in Washington at the lowest point of his presidency, only one member of his administration showed up to greet him, Undersecretary of State Dean Acheson. Acheson's gesture signaled a developing relationship of central importance to the two men and to postwar history. The fifty-three-year-old Acheson shared most of Truman's political principles, though their backgrounds differed sharply. Acheson had enjoyed an upper-class education at a private prep school, Yale University, and Harvard Law School. After clerking for Supreme Court Justice Louis Brandeis, he earned a comfortable living as a corporate lawyer. In contrast, Truman, the son of a Missouri farmer, had not attended college and had failed in a business venture before entering local politics in the 1920s.

Despite his wealth and privilege, Acheson supported much of the New Deal and staunchly defended organized labor. He spoke out against isolationism in the 1930s, and in 1941 he accepted President Roosevelt's offer of a job at the State Department. Shortly after Truman became president, the supremely confident Acheson wrote privately about shortcomings in Truman's "judgment and wisdom that the limitations of his experience produce," but he also believed that the fledgling president "will learn fast and will inspire confidence." In June 1947, Acheson left the State Department, but Truman lured him back in 1949 to be secretary of state during the president's second term. Acheson appreciated Truman's willingness to make tough decisions and admiringly noted that Truman's "ego never came between him and his job." Truman cherished Acheson's abiding loyalty, calling him "my good right hand."

Truman needed all the help he could get. The "accidental president" lacked the charisma, experience, and political skills with which Roosevelt had transformed both foreign and domestic policy, won four presidential elections, and forged a Democratic Party coalition that dominated national politics. Initially criticized and abandoned by many Roosevelt loyalists, Truman faced a resurgent Republican Party

DEAN ACHESON
No individual had more to do with transforming America's role in the world after World War II than Dean Acheson, President Truman's closest foreign policy adviser. Acheson, shown here with Truman in 1945, criticized those who saw the cold war in black-and-white terms and communism as an evil that the United States could expel from the earth. Rather, he advocated that American leaders learn "to limit objectives, to get ourselves away from the search for the absolute, to find out what is within our powers."
Harry S. Truman Library.

as well as revolts from within his own party. Besides solving domestic problems left over from the New Deal—how to sustain economic growth and avoid another depression without the war to fuel the economy—Truman had to redefine the nation's foreign policy goals in a new international context.

Dean Acheson was instrumental in forging that foreign policy. As early as 1946, Acheson became convinced that the Soviet Union posed a major threat to U.S. security. With other officials, he helped to shape a policy designed to contain and thwart Soviet power wherever it threatened to spread. By 1947, a new term had been coined to describe the intense rivalry between the superpowers—the "cold war." The containment policy worked in Western Europe, but communism spread in Asia, and at home a wave of anti-Communist hysteria erupted that harmed many Americans and stifled dissent and debate about U.S. policies.

As the preeminent foreign policy official, Acheson too reaped abuse from Republicans for being "soft on communism." At the height of the anti-Communist frenzy, Acheson received so much

hate mail that guards were posted at his house. Yet he kept both his job and his sense of humor. When cab drivers asked him, "Aren't you Dean Acheson?" he would reply, "Yes. Do I have to get out?"

From the Grand Alliance to Containment

With victory over Japan in August 1945, Americans besieged the government for the return of their loved ones. Baby booties arrived at the White House with a note, "Please send my daddy home." Americans looked forward to the end of international crises and the dismantling of the large military establishment. They expected the Allies, led by the United States and working within the United Nations, to cooperate in the management of international peace. Postwar realities quickly dashed these expectations. A dangerous new threat seemed to arise as the wartime alliance forged by the United States, Great Britain, and the Soviet Union crumbled, and the United States began to develop the military and diplomatic means to contain the spread of Soviet power around the globe.

The Cold War Begins

"The guys who came out of World War II were idealistic," reported Harold Russell, a young paratrooper who lost both hands in a training accident. "We felt the day had come when the wars were all over." Public opinion polls echoed the veterans' confidence in the promise of peace. But political leaders were less optimistic, especially Winston Churchill, who had always distrusted the Soviets. Once the Allies had overcome a common enemy, the prewar mistrust and antagonism between the Soviet Union and the West resurfaced over their very different visions of the postwar world.

The Western Allies' delay in opening a second front in Western Europe aroused Soviet suspicions during the war. The Soviet Union made supreme wartime sacrifices, losing more than twenty million citizens and vast portions of its agricultural and industrial capacity. At the war's end, Soviet leader Joseph Stalin wanted to make Germany pay for the rebuilding of the Soviet economy and to expand Soviet influence in the world. Above all, he wanted governments friendly to the Soviet Union on its borders in Eastern Europe, especially in Poland, through which Germany had attacked the Soviet Union twice within twenty-five years.

In contrast, enemy fire had never touched the mainland of the United States, and its 405,000 dead amounted to just 2 percent of the Soviet loss. With a vastly expanded productive capacity, a monopoly on atomic weapons, and supreme confidence in American institutions, the United States emerged from the war the most powerful nation on the planet.

Worried about a return of the depression, U.S. officials believed that a healthy economy depended on opportunities abroad. The United States needed access to raw materials, markets for its goods, and security for American investments overseas. These needs could be met best in countries with economic and political systems resembling its own, not in those where government controls interfered with the free flow of products and dollars. As Truman put it in 1947, "The American system can survive in America only if it becomes a world system." At the same time, Americans downplayed the economic self-interest and regarded their foreign pol-

icy as the means to preserve national security and bring freedom, democracy, and capitalism to the rest of the world. Laura Briggs spoke for many Americans who believed "it was our destiny to prove that we were the children of God and that our way was right for the world."

The man with ultimate responsibility for U.S. policy came to the White House with little experience in international affairs. Truman hoped to maintain Soviet-American cooperation, but, confident that America's nuclear monopoly gave him the advantage, he demanded that the Soviet Union comply with U.S. plans for the postwar world and restrain its expansionist impulses.

Soviet and American interests clashed first in Eastern Europe. Stalin insisted that the Allies' wartime agreements gave him a free hand in the countries defeated or liberated by the Red Army, just as the United States was unilaterally reconstructing governments in Italy and Japan. The Soviet dictator used harsh methods to install Communist governments in neighboring Poland and Bulgaria. Elsewhere, the Soviets initially tolerated non-Communist governments in Hungary and Czechoslovakia. And in the spring of 1946, Stalin responded to pressure from the West and removed troops from Iran on the Soviet Union's southwest border, allowing United States access to rich oilfields there.

Stalin considered U.S. officials hypocritical in demanding democratic elections in Eastern Europe while supporting dictatorships friendly to U.S. interests in Cuba and other Latin American countries. The United States clung to its own sphere of influence while adamantly denying one to the Soviets. But the Western allies were unwilling to match tough words with military force; and their sharp protests failed to prevent the Soviet Union from establishing satellite countries in most of Eastern Europe.

In 1946, the wartime Allies contended over Germany's future. American policymakers wanted to strip the nation of its military capacity, but they also desired a rapid industrial revival in Germany to foster European economic recovery and thus America's own long-term prosperity. By contrast, the Soviet Union wanted Germany weak militarily and economically, and it sought heavy reparations that could be used to rebuild the Soviet economy. Unable to settle their differences, the Allies divided Germany. The Soviet Union installed a puppet Communist government in the eastern section,

MAP 26.1
The Division of Europe after World War II
The "iron curtain," a term coined by Winston Churchill to refer to the Soviet grip on Eastern and central Europe, divided Europe for nearly fifty years. Communist governments controlled the countries along the Soviet Union's western border. The only exception was Finland, which remained neutral.

READING THE MAP: Is the division of Europe between NATO, Communist, and neutral countries about equal? Does the map of Berlin portray Soviet rule as monolithic?
CONNECTIONS: When was NATO founded, and what is its purpose? How did the post-war division of Europe compare with the wartime alliances?

www.bedfordstmartins.com/roarkcompact SEE THE ONLINE STUDY GUIDE for more help in analyzing this map.

and in December 1946, Britain, France, and the United States unified their occupation zones and began the process that established the Federal Republic of Germany—West Germany—in 1949 (Map 26.1).

The war of words escalated early in 1946. Boasting of the superiority of the Soviet system, Stalin told a Moscow audience in February that capitalist economies inevitably produced war. One month later, Truman traveled with Winston Churchill to

Fulton, Missouri, where the former prime minister denounced Soviet suppression of the popular will in Eastern and central Europe. "From Stettin in the Baltic to Trieste in the Adriatic, an iron curtain has descended across the continent," Churchill said. Although Truman did not officially endorse Churchill's iron curtain speech, his presence implied agreement with the idea of joint British-American strength to combat Soviet aggression. Stalin regarded the speech as "a call to war against the USSR." (See "Documenting the American Promise," page 676.)

In February 1946, career diplomat George F. Kennan, who had served in U.S. embassies in Eastern Europe and Moscow, wrote a comprehensive rationale for hard-line foreign policy. He downplayed the influence of Communist ideology in Soviet policy but noted the Soviets' insecurity and their need to maintain authority at home. These circumstances, Kennan argued, made it impossible to negotiate with Stalin, a conclusion shared by Secretary of State James F. Byrnes, Undersecretary Acheson, and other key Truman advisers.

Kennan predicted that the Soviet Union would try to expand its influence worldwide but would retreat "in the face of superior force." Therefore, the United States should respond with "unalterable counterforce," making Russia "face frustration indefinitely," an approach that came to be called containment. Kennan expected that containment would eventually end in "either the breakup or the gradual mellowing of Soviet power." This message reached a larger audience when, as "Mr. X," Kennan published an article in *Foreign Affairs* magazine in July 1947. Kennan later displayed dismay at the use of his ideas to justify what he considered an indiscriminate American response wherever communism seemed likely to succeed.

Not all public figures accepted the toughening line. In an election campaign speech in September 1946, Secretary of Commerce Henry A. Wallace, Truman's predecessor as vice president, urged greater understanding of the Soviets' concerns about their nation's security, insisting that "we have no more business in the political affairs of Eastern Europe than Russia has in the political affairs of Latin America." (See "Documenting the American Promise," page 676.) State Department officials were furious. When Wallace refused to be muzzled on foreign policy topics, Truman fired him.

The Truman Doctrine and the Marshall Plan

In 1947, the United States moved from tough words to action, implementing the doctrine of containment that would guide foreign policy for the next four decades. It was not an easy transition; despite public approval of a verbal hard line, Americans wanted to keep their soldiers and tax dollars at home. In addition to selling containment to the public, Truman had to gain the support of a Republican-controlled Congress, which included a forceful bloc, led by Ohio senator Robert A. Taft, opposed to a strong U.S. presence in Europe.

Crises in two Mediterranean countries triggered the implementation of containment. In February 1947, Britain informed the United States that its crippled economy could no longer sustain military assistance to Greece and Turkey. Turkey was trying to resist Soviet pressures, and the monarchist government in Greece faced a challenge from internal leftists. Truman promptly sought congressional authority to send military and economic missions, along with $400 million in aid, to the two countries. At a meeting that Truman called with congressional leaders, Undersecretary of State Acheson predicted that if Greece and Turkey fell, communism would soon consume three-fourths of the planet. After a stunned silence, Michigan senator Arthur Vandenberg, the Republican foreign policy leader and a recent convert from isolationism, warned that to get approval Truman would have to "scare hell out of the country."

Truman did just that. Outlining what would later be called the domino theory, he warned that if Greece fell to the rebels, "confusion and disorder might well spread throughout the entire Middle East . . . and would have a profound effect upon . . . Europe." Failure to step in, he said, "may endanger the peace of the world—and shall surely endanger the welfare of the nation." According to what came to be called the Truman Doctrine, the United States must not just resist Soviet military power but must "support free peoples who are resisting attempted subjugation by armed minorities or by outside pressures." Congressional authorization of aid for Greece and Turkey did not entail formal acceptance of the Truman Doctrine. Yet the assumption that American security depended on rescuing any anti-Communist government from internal rebels or outside pressure became the

The Emerging Cold War

*A*lthough antagonism between the Soviet Union and the West stretched back to the Russian Revolution of 1917, the United States, the Soviet Union, Britain, and other powers had cooperated to win World War II and managed to reach compromises at the Yalta and Potsdam summits in 1945. Early in 1946, however, officials in both the Soviet Union and the West publicly expressed distrust and attributed hostile motivations to each other. Within the United States, disagreement developed about how to deal with the Soviet Union.

Document 1. Joseph Stalin Addresses an Election Rally in Moscow, February 9, 1946

At an election rally in early 1946 ("election" in name only since there was just one Communist Party candidate for each position), Premier Joseph Stalin called on the Soviet people to support his program for economic development and postwar recovery. Although Stalin did not address cold war issues, leaders in the West viewed his comments about communism and capitalism, as well as his boasts about the strength of the Red Army, as a threat to peace.

It would be incorrect to think that the [Second World] war arose accidentally or as the result of the fault of some of the statesmen. Although these faults did exist, the war arose in reality as the inevitable result of the development of the world economic and political forces on the basis of monopoly capitalism.

Our Marxists declare that the capitalist system of world economy conceals elements of crisis and war, that the development of world capitalism does not follow a steady and even course forward, but proceeds through crises and catastrophes. The uneven development of the capitalist countries leads in time to sharp disturbances in their relations and the group of countries which consider themselves inadequately provided with raw materials and export markets try usually to change this situation and to change the position in their favor by means of armed force. As a result of these factors, the capitalist world is split into two hostile camps and war follows. . . .

Now victory [in World War II] means, first of all, that our Soviet social system has won, that the Soviet social system has successfully stood the test in the fire of war and has proved its complete vitality. . . .

The war has shown that the Soviet social system is a truly popular system, issued from the depths of the people and enjoying its mighty support. . . . The Soviet social system has proved to be more capable of life and more stable than a non-Soviet social system. . . .

Our victory implies that it was the Soviet armed forces that won. . . . The Red Army heroically withstood all the adversities of the war, routed completely the armies of our enemies and emerged victoriously from the war. This is recognized by everybody—friend and foe.

Now a few words on the plans for the work of the Communist party in the near future. . . . The fundamental task of the new Five-Year Plan consists in restoring the areas of the country which have suffered, restoring the prewar level in industry and agriculture, and then exceeding this level.

Apart from the fact that in the very near future the rationing system will be abolished, special attention will be focused on expanding the production of goods for mass consumption, on raising the standard of life of the working people by consistent and systematic reduction of the costs of all goods, and on wide scale construction of all kinds of scientific research institutes to enable science to develop its forces. I have no doubt that if we render the necessary assistance to our scientists they will be able not only to overtake but also in the very near future to surpass the achievements of science outside the boundaries of our country. [Stalin then announced goals for production of key materials.] Only under such conditions will our country be insured against any eventuality.

SOURCE: Excerpts from Joseph Stalin, Vital Speeches of the Day, February 9 (1946). Reprinted with permission.

Document 2. Winston Churchill Delivers His "Iron Curtain" Speech at Westminster College, in Fulton, Missouri, March 5, 1946

Winston Churchill, former prime minister of Britain, stated that he spoke for himself alone, but President Harry Truman's presence on the platform at Westmin-

ster College suggested his approval of Churchill's assessment of Soviet actions. After reading Churchill's words, Stalin justified Soviet action in Eastern Europe as the means to "ensure its security," drew parallels between Hitler and Churchill, and called Churchill's words "a call to war with the Soviet Union."

The United States stands at this time at the pinnacle of world power. It is a solemn moment for the American democracy. With primacy in power is also joined an awe-inspiring accountability to the future. [Churchill spoke of the need to support the United Nations.]

It would nevertheless be wrong and imprudent to intrust the secret knowledge or experience of the atomic bomb, which the United States, Great Britain and Canada now share, to the world organization, while it is still in its infancy. It would be criminal madness to cast it adrift in this still agitated and un-united world. No one in any country has slept less well . . . because this knowledge and the method and the raw materials to apply it are at present largely retained in American hands. I do not believe we should all have slept so soundly had the positions been reversed and some Communist or neo-Fascist state monopolized, for the time being, these dread agencies. The fear of them alone might easily have been used to enforce totalitarian systems upon the free democratic world. . . . God has willed that this shall not be, and we have at least a breathing space before this period has to be encountered, and even then, if no effort is spared, we should still possess so formidable superiority as to impose effective deterrents upon its employment or threat of employment by others. . . .

A shadow has fallen upon the scenes so lately lighted by the Allied victory. Nobody knows what Soviet Russia and its Communist international organization intends to do in the immediate future, or what are the limits, if any, to their expansive and proselytizing tendencies. I have a strong admiration and regard for the valiant Russian people and for my war-time comrade, Marshal Stalin. . . . We understand the Russians need to be secure on her western frontiers from all renewal of German aggression. . . . It is my duty, however, to place before you certain facts. . . .

From Stettin in the Baltic to Trieste in the Adriatic, an iron curtain has descended across the Continent. Behind that line lie all the capitals of the an-cient states of central and eastern Europe. Warsaw, Berlin, Prague, Vienna, Budapest, Belgrade, Bucharest and Sofia, all these famous cities and the populations around them lie in the Soviet sphere and all are subject in one form or another, not only to Soviet influence but to a very high and increasing measure of control from Moscow. . . . The Communist parties, which were very small in all these eastern states of Europe, have been raised to pre-eminence and power far beyond their numbers and are seeking everywhere to obtain totalitarian control. Police governments are prevailing in nearly every case, and so far, except in Czechoslovakia, there is no true democracy. . . .

In front of the iron curtain which lies across Europe are other causes for anxiety. . . . In a great number of countries, far from the Russian frontiers and throughout the world, Communist fifth columns are established and work in complete unity and absolute obedience to the directions they receive from the Communist center.

I do not believe that Soviet Russia desires war. What they desire is the fruits of war and the indefinite expansion of their power and doctrines. . . . Our difficulties and dangers will not be removed by closing our eyes to them. They will not be removed by mere waiting to see what happens; nor will they be relieved by a policy of appeasement. . . . From what I have seen of our Russian friends and allies during the war, I am convinced that there is nothing they admire so much as strength, and there is nothing for which they have less respect than for military weakness.

SOURCE: Excerpts from Winston Churchill, Vital Speeches of the Day, March 5 (1946). Reprinted with permission.

DOCUMENT 3. Henry A. Wallace Addresses an Election Rally at Madison Square Garden, New York, September 12, 1946

Throughout 1946, Henry A. Wallace, Franklin D. Roosevelt's vice president from 1941 to 1945, and Harry S. Truman's secretary of commerce, urged the president to take a more conciliatory approach toward the Soviet Union, a position reflected in a speech Wallace gave to a rally of leftist and other liberal groups in New York City. Compared with the more pro-Soviet ones given that night, Wallace's speech was moderate and drew criticism from the U.S. Communist Party's newspaper. (Continued)

Nevertheless, Wallace's words in the context in which he delivered them seemed to the president to undermine his foreign policy. One week later, Truman asked for Wallace's resignation.

Tonight I want to talk about peace—and how to get peace. Never have the common people of all lands so longed for peace. Yet, never in a time of comparative peace have they feared war so much. . . .

During the past year or so, the significance of peace has been increased immeasurably by the atomic bomb, guided missiles and airplanes which soon will travel as fast as sound. . . . We cannot rest in the assurance that we invented the atom bomb—and therefore that this agent of destruction will work best for us. He who trusts in the atom bomb will sooner or later perish by the atom bomb—or something worse. . . .

To prevent war and insure our survival in a stable world, it is essential that we look abroad through our own American eyes and not through the eyes of either the British Foreign Office or a pro-British or anti-Russian press. . . . We must not let British balance-of-power manipulations determine whether and when the United States gets into war. . . .

To achieve lasting peace, we must study in detail just how the Russian character was formed—by invasions of Tartars, Mongols, Germans, Poles, Swedes, and French; by the czarist rule based on ignorance, fear and force; by the intervention of the British, French and Americans in Russian affairs from 1919 to 1921; by the geography of the huge Russian land mass situated strategically between Europe and Asia; and by the vitality derived from the rich Russian soil and the strenuous Russian climate. Add to all this the tremendous emotional power which Marxism and Leninism gives to the Russian leaders—and then we can realize that we are reckoning with a force which cannot be handled successfully by a "Get tough with Russia" policy. "Getting tough" never bought anything real and lasting—whether for schoolyard bullies or businessmen or world powers. The tougher we get, the tougher the Russians will get. . . .

We most earnestly want peace with Russia—but we want to be met half way. We want cooperation. And I believe that we can get cooperation once Russia understands that our primary objective is neither saving the British Empire nor purchasing oil in the Near East with the lives of American soldiers. . . .

On our part we should recognize that we have no more business in the *political* affairs of Eastern Europe than Russia has in the *political* affairs of

cornerstone of U.S. foreign policy from 1947 until the end of the 1980s.

Aid to Greece and Turkey was a prelude to a much larger program for Europe. In May 1947, Dean Acheson described a war-ravaged Western Europe, with "factories destroyed, fields impoverished, transportation systems wrecked, populations scattered and on the borderline of starvation." American citizens were sending generous amounts of private aid, but Europe needed large-scale assistance. It was "a matter of national self-interest," Acheson argued, for the United States to provide aid. Only economic recovery could halt the growth of socialist and Communist parties in France and Italy and confine Soviet influence to Eastern Europe.

In March 1948, Congress approved the European Recovery Program—more commonly known as the Marshall Plan, after retired general George C. Marshall, then serving as secretary of state—and over the next five years the United States spent $13 billion to restore the economies of Western Europe. The Marshall Plan helped the U.S. economy, because the European nations spent most of the dollars to buy American products carried on American ships, and Europe's economic recovery expanded the realm of raw materials, markets, and investment opportunities available to American capitalists.

While Congress debated the Marshall Plan, in February 1948 the Soviets staged a brutal coup against the government of Czechoslovakia and installed a Communist regime. Next, Soviet leaders threatened Western access to Berlin. The former capital of Germany lay within Soviet-controlled East Germany, but all four Allies jointly occupied Berlin, dividing it into separate administrative units. As the

Latin America, Western Europe and the United States. . . . The Russians have no more business in stirring up native communists to political activity in Western Europe, Latin America and the United States than we have in interfering in the politics of Eastern Europe and Russia. We know what Russia is up to in Eastern Europe, for example, and Russia knows what we are up to. We cannot permit the door to be closed against our trade in Eastern Europe any more than we can in China. But at the same time we have to recognize that the Balkans are closer to Russia than to us—and that Russia cannot permit either England or the United States to dominate the politics of that area. . . .

Russian ideas of social-economic justice are going to govern nearly a third of the world. Our ideas of free enterprise democracy will govern much of the rest. The two ideas will endeavor to prove which can deliver the most satisfaction to the common man in their respective areas of political dominance. . . . Under friendly peaceful competition the Russian world and the American world will gradually become more alike. The Russians will be forced to grant more and more of the personal freedoms; and we shall become more and more absorbed with the problems of social-economic justice.

Source: Excerpts from Henry A. Wallace, Vital Speeches of the Day, September 12 (1946). Reprinted with permission.

QUESTIONS FOR ANALYSIS AND DEBATE

1. What lessons do these three leaders draw from World War II? What do they see as the most critical steps to preventing another war?

2. How do these three men describe the political and economic system of the Soviet Union? What differences do they see between the systems of the Soviet Union on the one hand and the United States and Western Europe on the other? How do they differ in their predictions about these systems in the future?

3. What motives do these three men ascribe to Soviet actions? How do Churchill and Wallace differ in their proposals for the Western response to the Soviet Union?

4. Which leader do you think was most optimistic about the prospects for good relationships between Russia and the West? Which was most correct? Why?

Western Allies moved to organize West Germany as a separate nation, the Soviets retaliated by blocking roads and rail lines that connected West Germany to the Western-held sections of Berlin, cutting off food, fuel, and other essentials to two million inhabitants.

"We stay in Berlin, period," Truman insisted. Yet he wanted to avoid a confrontation with Soviet troops. So over fifteen months, U.S. and British pilots airlifted 2.3 million tons of goods to sustain the West Berliners. Stalin hesitated to shoot down

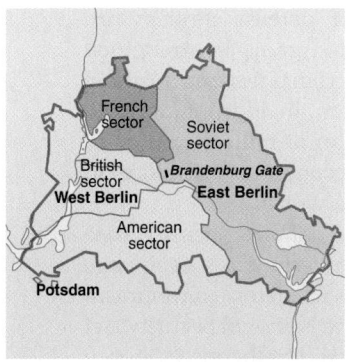

Berlin Divided, 1948

these cargo planes, and in 1949 he lifted the blockade. The city was then divided into East Berlin, under Soviet control, and West Berlin, which became part of West Germany. For many Americans, the Berlin airlift confirmed the wisdom of containment: When challenged, the Russians backed down, as Kennan had predicted.

Creating a National Security State

The new policy of containment quickly acquired a military capacity to back it up. During the Truman years, the United States fashioned a five-pronged defense strategy: (1) development of atomic weapons, (2) strengthening traditional military power, (3) military alliances with other nations, (4) military and economic aid to friendly nations, and

THE MARSHALL PLAN
*World War II not only devastated European nations'
economies, but also deprived them of raw materials
and profits formerly obtained from their colonies in
South and Southeast Asia; in addition, Soviet control of Eastern Europe closed that former avenue of
trade. Consequently, Marshall Plan aid was critical
for European countries to purchase the raw materials, capital goods, and technology required to rebuild their economies. While economic stabilization
stood at the center of European assistance, it also
reflected the generosity and compassion of ordinary
Americans. The human side of assistance is expressed in the joy on the face of this Austrian boy
who has just received a new pair of shoes from Red
Cross volunteers.*
American Red Cross.

(5) an espionage network and secret means to subvert Communist expansion.

In September 1949, the United States lost its nuclear monopoly when officials confirmed that the
Soviets had detonated an atomic bomb. Within
months, Truman approved development of an even
deadlier weapon, a hydrogen bomb based on a
thermonuclear explosion equivalent to five hundred atomic bombs. By 1954, the United States had
the capacity to deliver the "super bomb," but its advantage was brief. In November 1955, the Soviets
exploded their own hydrogen bomb.

From the 1950s through the 1980s, "deterrence"
formed the basis of American nuclear strategy. To
deter the Soviet Union from attacking, the United
States strived to maintain a more powerful nuclear
force than the Soviets. Because the Russians pursued a similar policy, the superpowers became
locked in an ever-escalating race for nuclear dominance. Albert Einstein, whose mathematical discoveries had laid the foundations for nuclear
weapons, commented grimly on the enormous destructive force now possessed by the superpowers.
The war that came after World War III, he said,
would be fought with stones.

The United States also beefed up its conventional military power to deter Soviet threats that
might not warrant nuclear retaliation. To streamline
defense planning, Congress passed the National Security Act in 1947, uniting the military branches
under a single secretary of defense and creating the
National Security Council (NSC) to advise the president. As the Berlin crisis simmered in 1948, Congress stepped up military appropriations and enacted a peacetime draft. Congress also granted
permanent status to the women's military branches.
With about 1.5 million men and women in uniform
in 1950, the military strength of the United States
had quadrupled since the 1930s.

Collective security, the third prong of postwar
military strategy and the sharpest break from America's past, also developed during the Berlin showdown. In June 1948, the Senate approved the general
principle of regional military alliances. One year
later, the United States joined Canada and Western
European nations in its first peacetime military alliance, the North Atlantic Treaty Organization
(NATO), designed to counter a Soviet threat to
Western Europe (see Map 26.1). For the first time in
its history, the United States pledged to go to war
should one of its allies be attacked.

The fourth element of defense strategy involved foreign assistance programs to strengthen
friendly countries, such as aid to Greece and Turkey
in 1947 and the Marshall Plan. In addition, in 1949,
Congress approved $1 billion of military aid to its
NATO allies and began economic assistance to
nations in other parts of the world.

The fifth element of the national security state
was development of the government's espionage
capacities and the means to deter communism
through covert activities. The National Security Act
of 1947 created the Central Intelligence Agency
(CIA) to gather information and to perform any

"functions and duties related to intelligence affecting the national security" that the NSC might authorize. Eventually, CIA agents conducted secret operations that toppled legitimate foreign governments and violated the rights of U.S. citizens. In many respects, the CIA was virtually unaccountable to Congress or the public.

By 1950, the United States had abandoned age-old tenets of foreign policy. Isolationism and neutrality were replaced with a regional military alliance and economic and military efforts to control events far beyond U.S. borders. Short of war, the United States could not stop the descent of the iron curtain, but it aggressively and successfully promoted economic recovery and a military shield for the rest of Europe.

Superpower Rivalry around the Globe

Efforts to implement containment were not confined to Europe. In Africa, Asia, and the Middle East, World War II furthered a tide of national liberation movements against war-weakened imperial powers. Between 1945 and 1960, forty countries, with more than a quarter of the world's people, won their independence. These nations came to be referred to collectively, along with Latin America, as the third world, a term denoting countries outside the Western (first world) and Soviet (second world) orbits that had not yet developed industrial economies. Like Woodrow Wilson during World War I, Roosevelt and Truman promoted the ideal of

THE CHINESE COMMUNIST MOVEMENT
The leaders of the young Communist movement in China in 1937 exude confidence as they stand in a doorway to one of the cave dwellings where they lived and worked in Yan'an, in Northwest China. Bo Gu (right) died in a plane crash in 1946, but Zhou Enlai (left) and Mao Zedong (center) led the revolutionary forces to victory and the establishment of the People's Republic of China in 1949.
Peabody Museum, Harvard University.

self-determination: The United States granted independence to its own dominion, the Philippines, in 1946; applauded the British withdrawal from India; and encouraged France to relinquish its empire in Indochina. At the same time, both the United States and the Soviet Union cultivated governments in emerging nations that were friendly to their own interests.

Leaders of many liberation movements, impressed with the rapid economic growth of Russia, adopted socialist or Communist ideas, although few had formal ties with the Soviet Union. But American leaders insisted on viewing these movements as a threatening extension of Soviet power. Seeking to hold communism at bay by fostering economic development and political stability, in 1949 the Truman administration initiated the Point IV Program, providing technical aid to developing nations. Reflecting the Truman administration's cold war priorities, the modest amounts of such aid contrasted sharply with the huge sums provided to Europe.

In Asia, civil war raged in China, where the Communists, led by Mao Zedong (Mao Tse-tung), fought the official Nationalist government under Chiang Kai-shek. While the Communists gained support among the peasants for their land reforms and valiant stand against the Japanese, Chiang's corrupt government and poor management of the war against Japan alienated much of the population. The so-called China bloc, a lobby that included Republican members of Congress and religious groups with missionary ties to China, pressured the Truman administration to save that nation from the Communists. Failing in its effort to promote negotiations between Chiang and Mao, the United States provided almost $3 billion in aid to the Nationalists during the civil war. Yet Truman and his advisers believed that to divert further resources from Europe to China would be futile, given the ineptness of Chiang's government.

In October 1949, Mao established the People's Republic of China (PRC), and the Nationalists fled to the island of Taiwan. The United States refused to recognize the existence of the PRC, blocked its admission to the United Nations, and sent aid to the Nationalist government in Taiwan. Nothing less than a massive U.S. military commitment could have stopped the Chinese Communists, but some Republicans cried that Truman and "the pro-Communists in the State Department" had "lost" China. Thus, China became a political al-

batross for the Democrats, who resolved never again to be vulnerable to charges of being soft on communism.

As it became clear that China would not be a stable capitalist ally in Asia, the administration reconsidered its plans for postwar Japan. Initially, the U.S. military occupation had aimed to reform the Japanese government, purge militarists from official positions, and decentralize the economy. But by 1948, U.S. policy had shifted to concentrate on economic recovery. The new goals were to help Japan rapidly reindustrialize and secure access to markets and natural resources in Asia, and in a short time the Japanese economy was flourishing. American soldiers remained on military bases in Japan, but the official occupation ended when the two nations signed a peace treaty and a mutual security pact in September 1951. Like West Germany, Japan now sat squarely within the American orbit, ready to serve as an economic hub in a vital area.

The one area where cold war considerations did not control American policy was Palestine. In 1943, then senator Harry Truman spoke passionately about Nazi Germany's systematic extermination of Jews, asserting, "This is not a Jewish problem, it is an American problem— and we must . . . face it squarely and honorably." As president, he had the opportunity to make good on his words. Jews had been migrating to Palestine since the nineteenth century, resulting in tension and hostilities between Palestinian Arabs and Jews. After World War II, as hundreds of thousands of European Jews sought refuge in Palestine, fighting devolved into brutal terrorism on both sides. Truman's foreign policy experts saw American-Arab friendship as a critical barrier against Soviet influence in the Middle East and a means to secure

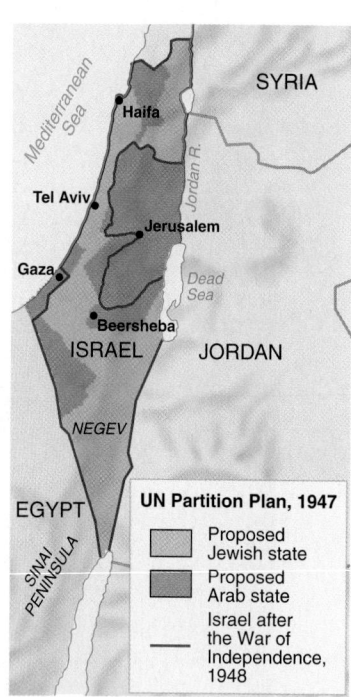

The Partition of Palestine and the Creation of Israel, 1947–1948

access to Arabian oil. Uncharacteristically defying his advisers, the president responded instead to pressure from Jewish organizations, his moral commitment to Holocaust survivors, and his interest in the American Jewish vote for the 1948 elections. After Arabs rejected a UN partition plan that would have separated Palestinians and placed some under Jewish authority, Jews declared the state of Israel in May 1948. Truman quickly recognized the new country and made its defense the cornerstone of U.S. policy in the Middle East.

Truman and the Fair Deal at Home

Referring to the Civil War general who coined the phrase "War is hell," Truman said in December 1945, "Sherman was wrong. I'm telling you I find peace is hell." Challenged by crises abroad, Truman also faced shortages, strikes, inflation, and other problems attending the reconversion of the economy to peacetime production. At the same time, he tried to expand New Deal reform, with his own "Fair Deal" agenda, which proposed initiatives in civil rights, housing, education, and health care. The most he was able to achieve, however, was consolidation of liberal programs already in place.

Reconversion and the Postwar Economic Boom

Despite deprivations during World War II, most Americans had enjoyed a higher standard of living than ever before. Economic experts as well as ordinary citizens worried about both sustaining that standard and providing jobs for millions of returning soldiers. Truman wasted no time unveiling his plan, asking Congress to enact a twenty-one-point program of social and economic reforms. "Not even President Roosevelt ever asked for as much at one sitting," exploded Republican leader Joseph W. Martin Jr.

Congress approved only one of Truman's key proposals—full-employment legislation—and even that was watered down. The Employment Act of 1946 invested the federal government with responsibility "to promote maximum employment, production, and purchasing power," thereby formalizing what had been implicit in Roosevelt's actions to counter the depression—government's responsibil-

ity for maintaining a healthy economy. The law created a Council of Economic Advisers to assist the president, but it authorized no new powers to translate the government's obligation into effective action.

Inflation turned out to be the most severe problem in the early postwar years. Unable to buy civilian goods during the war, in 1945 consumers had $30 billion of savings that they now itched to spend. But shortages of meat, automobiles, housing, and a host of other items persisted. Until industry could convert fully to civilian production and make more goods available, consumer demand could only drive up prices. The consumer price index—an official measure of the rate of inflation—shot up by 18 percent in 1946.

Labor relations were another thorn in Truman's side. Organized labor survived the war stronger than ever, its 14.5 million members making up 35 percent of the civilian workforce. "The workers felt they were in a good bargaining position," Henry Fiering recalled, "so they went after some more things." Union members feared erosion of wartime gains. With wages frozen during the war, the rising incomes enjoyed by working-class families had come largely from the availability of higher-paying jobs and the chance to work longer hours than before. The end of overtime meant a 30 percent cut in take-home pay for most workers.

Women who had flocked into wartime jobs also saw their earnings decline. Some were ready to return to their homes, but polls indicated that as many as 68 to 85 percent wanted to keep their jobs. Most who remained in the workforce had to settle for relatively low-paying jobs in light industry or the service sector. Displaced from her shipyard work, Marie Schreiber found work as a cashier. "You were back to women's wages, you know . . . practically in half," she recalled.

Unions, while paying scant attention to the problems of women workers, fought to preserve labor's wartime gains. More strikes took place in 1946 than at any other time in U.S. history, with five million workers disrupting production in virtually every major industry. Although most Americans approved of unions in principle, they became fed up with labor stoppages, blamed unions for rising prices and shortages of consumer goods, and called for more government restrictions on organized labor. Truman shared the public's exasperation, although, in a letter to his mother in October 1945, he spread the blame around: "The Congress [is]

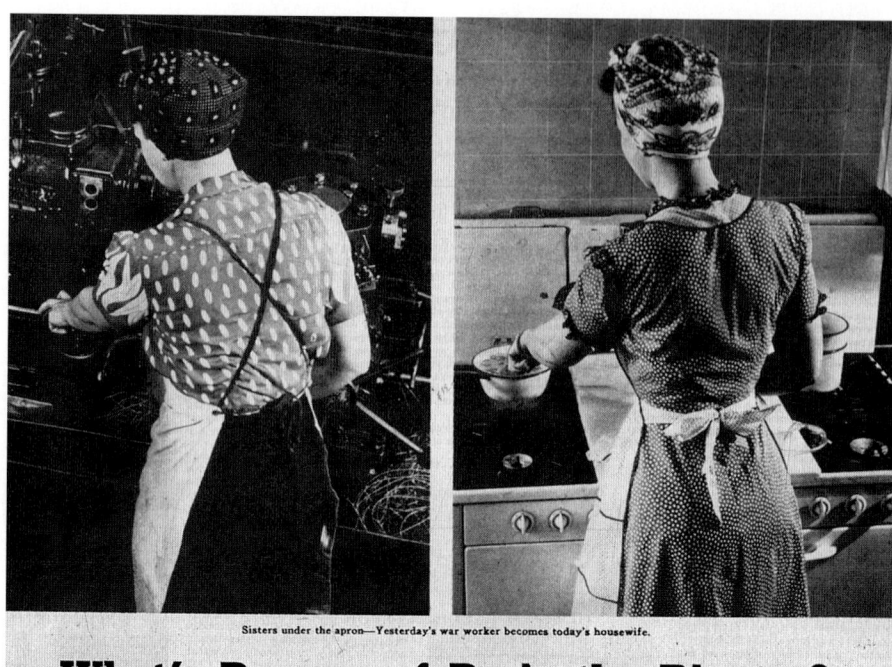

Sisters under the apron—Yesterday's war worker becomes today's housewife.

What's Become of Rosie the Riveter?

WOMEN'S POSTWAR FUTURE
This photograph headed a **New York Times Magazine** *article in June 1946. While the article supported women's right to work and to equal pay, it also assumed that women would all but vanish from heavy manufacturing. The company newsletter at Kaiser shipyards was more direct, proclaiming, "The Kitchen—Women's Big Post-War Goal." Because most of the media assumed that women would or should leave their war jobs, those who needed jobs struggled. Two women who worked at a Memphis Ford plant insisted, "Women didn't stop eating when the war stopped."*
Ellen Kaiper.

balking, labor has gone crazy, and management isn't far from insane in selfishness." In May 1946, after coal miners rejected government recommendations for a settlement, Truman placed the mines under federal control. When the massive wave of strikes subsided at the end of 1946, workers had won wage increases of about 20 percent, but the loss of overtime along with rising prices left their purchasing power only slightly higher than in 1942.

"The conversion period was not as traumatic as everybody was afraid it was going to be," Henry Fiering remembered. By 1947, the nation had survived the strains of reconversion and avoided a postwar depression. Wartime profits enabled businesses to invest in new plants and equipment. Consumers used their wartime savings to buy the houses, cars, and appliances that had lain beyond

their reach during the depression and war. Both defense spending and the $38 billion in grants and loans that enabled war-torn countries to purchase American products also stimulated the economy. A soaring birthrate, 25 percent higher in 1949 than in 1940, further sustained consumer demand. The United States entered into a remarkable economic boom that lasted through the 1960s and flooded the American people with new consumer goods. (See Chapter 27.)

The nation's gratitude to its returning warriors provided yet another economic boost. Under the Servicemen's Readjustment Act (the GI Bill), passed in 1944, 16 million veterans could receive job training and education; claim unemployment compensation while they looked for jobs; and take out low-interest loans to purchase homes, farms, and small businesses.

By 1948, some 1.3 million veterans had bought houses with government loans, and by 1956 veterans had used $14.5 million in educational benefits. Helping 2.2 million ex-soldiers attend college, the subsidies sparked a boom in higher education. A drugstore clerk before his military service, Don Condren used the GI Bill to get an engineering degree and to buy his first house. "I think the GI Bill gave the whole country an upward boost economically," he said.

Yet prosperity was not universal. The real gains came during the war, and while wages and salaries increased by 23 percent from 1945 to 1950, prices went up by 36.2 percent. A recession in 1949 threw 7 percent of the labor force out of work; it abated only when the Korean War sparked economic recovery. Moreover, the one-third of all Americans who lived in poverty failed to receive any significant benefits from the return to peacetime production.

Black Protest and the Politics of Civil Rights

"I spent four years in the army to free a bunch of Frenchmen and Dutchmen," an African American corporal declared, "and I'm hanged if I'm going to let the Alabama version of the Germans kick me around when I get home." Black men and women filled 16 percent of military positions in World War II; they as well as civilians resolved that the return to peace would not be a return to the racial injustices of prewar America. Black political clout had grown with the migration of two million African Americans to northern and western cities, where they could vote and make a difference. Even in the South, the proportion of blacks who were able to vote inched up from 2 percent to 12 percent in the 1940s. Pursuing civil rights through the courts and Congress, the National Association for the Advancement of Colored People (NAACP) counted half a million members.

In the postwar years, individual African Americans broke through the color barrier, achieving several "firsts." Jackie Robinson integrated major league baseball when he played second base for the Brooklyn Dodgers in 1947, braving abuse from fans and players to win the Rookie of the Year Award. In 1950, Ralph J. Bunche won the Nobel Peace Prize for his contributions to the United Nations, and Gwendolyn Brooks earned the Pulitzer Prize for poetry.

JACKIE ROBINSON
John Roosevelt Robinson slides into home in a game against the Philadelphia Phillies in 1952. Before becoming the first African American to play major league baseball in 1947, Robinson had excelled in track as well as baseball at UCLA and had been an army officer in World War II. Even his brilliant play for the Brooklyn Dodgers did not save him from fans' and players' racist taunts or exclusion from restaurants and hotels that catered to his white teammates. Having paved the way for other black players, Robinson competed until 1956.
The Michael Barson Collection/Past Perfect.

Still, in most respects little had changed, especially in the South, where violence greeted African Americans' attempts to assert their rights. Armed white men turned back Medgar Evers (who would become a key civil rights leader in the 1960s) and four other veterans trying to vote in Mississippi. A mob lynched Isaac Nixon for voting in Georgia, and an all-white jury acquitted the men accused of his murder. Governors, U.S. senators, and other southern politicians routinely intimidated potential black voters with threats of economic retaliation and violence.

"My very stomach turned over when I learned that Negro soldiers just back from overseas were being dumped out of army trucks in Mississippi and beaten," wrote Truman, shaken by the violence and pressed to act by civil rights leaders and liberals. Wrestling with the Democrats' need for northern black and liberal votes as well as white southern votes, Truman acted more boldly on civil rights than had any previous president. In 1946, he created a Committee on Civil Rights, asking Congress in February 1948 to enact the committee's recommendations. The first president to address the NAACP, Truman asserted that all Americans should have equal rights to housing, education, employment, and the

ballot. As with much of his domestic program, the president failed to follow up aggressively on his bold words. In the throes of the 1948 election campaign and pressured by civil rights activists, Truman did issue an executive order to desegregate the armed services. But he allowed it to lie unimplemented until demands of the Korean War forced the military's hand.

Although a large gap loomed between what Truman said about civil rights and what his government accomplished, desegregation of the military and the administration's support of civil rights cases in the Supreme Court contributed to far-reaching changes. Breaking sharply with the past, Truman used his office to set a moral agenda for the nation's longest unfulfilled promise.

The Fair Deal Flounders

Republicans capitalized on public frustrations with economic reconversion in the 1946 congressional elections. They accused the administration of "confusion, corruption, and communism" and jeered, "To Err Is Truman." Capturing Congress for the first time in fourteen years, Republicans looked eagerly to the 1948 presidential campaign. Railing against New Deal "radicalism," Republicans in the Eightieth Congress weakened some reform programs and enacted tax cuts favoring higher income groups over Truman's veto.

Organized labor took the most severe attack, when Congress passed the Taft-Hartley Act over Truman's veto in 1947. Called a "slave labor" law and "Tuff-Heartless" by unions, Taft-Hartley imposed heavy restrictions on organizing workers. States could now pass "right-to-work" laws banning the practice of requiring all workers to join a union once a majority had voted for it. The law also compelled union leaders to swear that they were not Communists and to make public annual financial reports. Taft-Hartley maintained the New Deal principle of government protection for collective bargaining, but it put the government more squarely between labor and management and between unions and individual workers.

As the 1948 elections approached, Truman faced not only a resurgent Republican Party headed by its nominee Thomas E. Dewey, but also two revolts within his own party. On the left, Henry Wallace, whose foreign policy views had cost him his cabinet seat, led a new Progressive Party. On the right, South Carolina governor J. Strom Thurmond

SEGREGATION
Signs like this were a normal feature of life in the South from the late nineteenth century until the 1960s. State and local laws mandated segregation in every aspect of life, literally from the cradle to the grave. African Americans could not use white hospitals, cemeteries, schools, libraries, swimming pools, playgrounds, restrooms, or drinking fountains. They were relegated to balconies in movie theaters and kept apart from whites in all public meetings.
Martin Magner/Courtesy, Center for Creative Photography, The University of Arizona.

TRUMAN'S WHISTLE-STOP CAMPAIGN
Harry Truman rallies a crowd from his campaign train at a stop in Bridgeport, Pennsylvania, in October 1948. His campaign theme song, "I'm Just Wild about Harry," was borrowed, with the words slightly changed, from the 1921 musical **Shuffle Along.** *This was the last presidential election in which the pollsters predicted the wrong winner. They stopped taking polls in mid-October, after which many voters apparently changed their minds. One commentator praised the American citizenry, who "couldn't be ticketed by the polls, knew its own mind and had picked the rather unlikely but courageous figure of Truman to carry on its banner." In what ways have presidential campaigns changed since Harry Truman's time?*
Photo: Truman Library; Sheet music: Collection of Janice L. and David J. Frent.

headed the States' Rights Party—the Dixiecrats— formed by southern Democrats who walked out of the 1948 Democratic Party convention when it passed a liberal civil rights plank.

Virtually alone in believing he could win, Truman crisscrossed the country by train, answering supporters' cries of "Give 'em hell, Harry." So bleak were Truman's prospects that the confident Dewey ran a low-key campaign and, on election night, the *Chicago Daily Tribune* printed its next day's issue with the headline DEWEY DEFEATS TRUMAN. But Truman took 303 electoral votes to Dewey's 189, as his

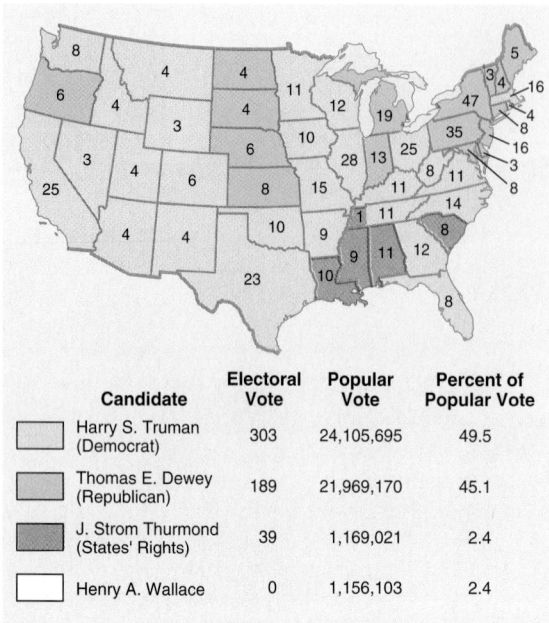

MAP 26.2
The Election of 1948

Candidate	Electoral Vote	Popular Vote	Percent of Popular Vote
Harry S. Truman (Democrat)	303	24,105,695	49.5
Thomas E. Dewey (Republican)	189	21,969,170	45.1
J. Strom Thurmond (States' Rights)	39	1,169,021	2.4
Henry A. Wallace	0	1,156,103	2.4

party regained control of Congress (Map 26.2). In addition to reflecting popular support for his foreign policy, Truman's unexpected victory attested to his skills as a campaigner, the enduring popularity of New Deal reform, and the booming economy.

Yet victory did not result in enactment of Truman's Fair Deal. Congress made modest improvements in Social Security and raised the minimum wage, but it passed only one significant reform measure. The Housing Act of 1949 authorized 350,000 units of government-constructed housing over the next fifteen years. Although it fell far short of actual need, the legislation represented a landmark commitment by the government to address the housing needs of the poor.

With southern Democrats often joining the Republicans, Congress rejected Truman's civil rights measures and proposals for a federal health care program, federal aid to education, and a new agriculture program to benefit small farmers and consumers. His efforts to revise immigration policy produced the McCarran-Walter Act of 1952, ending the outright ban on immigration and citizenship for Japanese and other Asians. But the law also authorized the government to bar immigration of suspected Communists and homosexuals and main-

tained the discriminatory quota system established in the 1920s.

Although he blamed political opponents for defeating his Fair Deal, in fact Truman chose to devote much more energy to foreign policy than to his domestic proposals. Moreover, by late 1950, the Korean War embroiled Truman in controversy, diverted his attention from domestic affairs, and depleted his power as a legislative leader.

The Domestic Chill: A Second Red Scare

Truman's domestic program also suffered from a wave of anti-Communist hysteria that weakened left and liberal forces. Both "red-baiting" (attempts to discredit individuals or ideas by associating them with Communists) and official retaliation against leftist critics of the government had flourished during the Red scare at the end of World War I. A second Red scare convulsed the nation after World War II, born of partisan political maneuvering, collapse of the Soviet-American alliance, setbacks in U.S. foreign policy, and disclosures of Soviet espionage.

Republicans jumped on Cold War setbacks, such as the Communist triumph in China, to accuse Democrats of fostering internal subversion. Wisconsin senator Joseph R. McCarthy, the leading anti-Communist, charged, "The Communists within our borders have been more responsible for the success of Communism abroad than Soviet Russia." Revelations of Soviet espionage furnished some credibility to such charges. For example, a number of ex-Communists, including Whittaker Chambers and Elizabeth Bentley, testified that they and others had provided secret documents to the Soviets. In 1950, a British physicist working on the atomic bomb project, confessed that he was a spy and implicated several Americans, including a couple, Ethel and Julius Rosenberg. The Rosenbergs pleaded innocent but were convicted of conspiracy to commit espionage and electrocuted in 1953.

Records opened in the 1990s showed that the Soviet Union did receive secret documents from Americans, but such information may have, at most, sped up Soviet development of nuclear weapons. At the peak of the hysteria, the U.S. Communist Party counted only about twenty thousand members, some of them FBI agents. The vast majority of individuals prosecuted in the Red scare were guilty of nothing more than having joined the Communist

Party, associated with Communists, or supported radical causes. And most of the charges involved activities that took place long before the cold war had made the Soviet Union an enemy. Red-hunters cared little for such distinctions, however. For more than ten years following World War II, congressional committees and a host of other official bodies ordered citizens to testify about their past and present political associations. If they refused, anti-Communists charged that silence was tantamount to confession, and these "unfriendly witnesses" lost their jobs and suffered public ostracism.

Senator McCarthy's influence was so great that "McCarthyism" became a term synonymous with

the anti-Communist crusade. Attacking individuals recklessly, in 1950 McCarthy claimed to have a list of 205 "known Communists" employed in the State Department. He charged Dean Acheson, "a pompous diplomat in striped pants, with a phony British accent," with saying that Jesus Christ "endorsed communism, high treason, and betrayal of a sacred trust." Even though most of his charges were absurd—such as the allegation that retired general George C. Marshall belonged to a Communist conspiracy—the press covered McCarthy avidly.

Not all Republicans joined McCarthy, nor did the party have a monopoly on the politics of anti-communism. In March 1947, President Truman issued Executive Order 9835 requiring investigation of every federal employee. In effect, Truman's "loyalty program" violated the principles of American justice by allowing anonymous informers to make charges and placing the burden of proof on the accused. More than two thousand civil service employees lost their jobs and another ten thousand resigned while the program continued into the mid-1950s. "A nightmare from which there [was] no awakening" was how State Department employee Esther Brunauer described it when she and her husband, a chemist in the navy, both lost their jobs. Years later, Truman admitted that the loyalty program had been a mistake.

The administration also went directly after the Communist Party, prosecuting its leaders under the Smith Act, passed in 1940, which made it a crime to "advocate the overthrow and destruction of the Government of the United States by force and violence." Although civil libertarians argued that the verdicts violated First Amendment rights to freedom of speech, press, and association, the Supreme Court ruled in 1951 (*Dennis v. United States*) that the Communist threat overrode constitutional guarantees.

The domestic cold war spread beyond the nation's capital. State and local governments undertook investigations, demanded loyalty oaths, fired individuals suspected of disloyalty, banned books from public libraries, and more. In addition, a 1950 Senate report claimed that homosexuals' "moral turpitude" and their susceptibility to blackmail made them unfit for government jobs. Fired from civil service jobs and drummed out of the military, gay men and women also underwent surveillance and harassment at the hands of the FBI and local police forces. Rutgers, Harvard, Michigan, and

SENATOR JOSEPH R. McCARTHY
In March 1950, McCarthy reads letters responding to his claim to have a list of 205 Communists in the State Department. Although McCarthy made his reputation from anticommunism, he seized that issue more from the need to have a campaign platform in 1950 than from genuine concern grounded in real evidence. McCarthy had loved politics from his high school days in Appleton, Wisconsin, and easily distorted the truth to promote his political ambitions.
World Wide Photos, Inc.

other universities dismissed professors, and public school teachers lost their jobs in New York, Philadelphia, Los Angeles, and elsewhere. The House Un-American Activities Committee (HUAC) took on the movie industry in 1947. When ten writers and directors refused to testify, they went to prison and later were blacklisted from Hollywood jobs. Because the Communist Party had helped organize unions and championed racial justice, labor and civil rights activists, too, fell prey to McCarthyism.

McCarthyism caused untold economic and psychological harm to individuals innocent of breaking any law. Thousands of people found themselves humiliated and discredited, hounded from their jobs, even in some cases put behind prison bars. The anti-Communist crusade violated fundamental constitutional rights of freedom of speech and association, stifled expression of dissenting ideas, and removed unpopular causes from public contemplation.

The Cold War Becomes Hot: Korea

The cold war erupted into a shooting war in June 1950, when troops from Communist North Korea invaded South Korea. For the first time, Americans went into battle to implement containment. Confirming the global reach of the Truman Doctrine, U.S. involvement in Korea also marked the militarization of American foreign policy. The United States, in concert with the United Nations, ultimately held the line in Korea, but at a great cost in lives, dollars, and domestic unity.

Korea and the Military Implementation of Containment

The war grew out of the artificial division of Korea after World War II. Having expelled the Japanese, who had controlled Korea since 1904, the United States and the Soviet Union divided Korea at the thirty-eighth parallel into two occupation zones (Map 26.3). The Soviets supported the Korean Communist Party in the north, while the United States backed the Korean Democratic Party in the south. With Moscow and Washington unable to agree on a unification plan, in July 1948 the United Nations sponsored elections in South Korea. The American-favored candidate, Korean nationalist Syngman

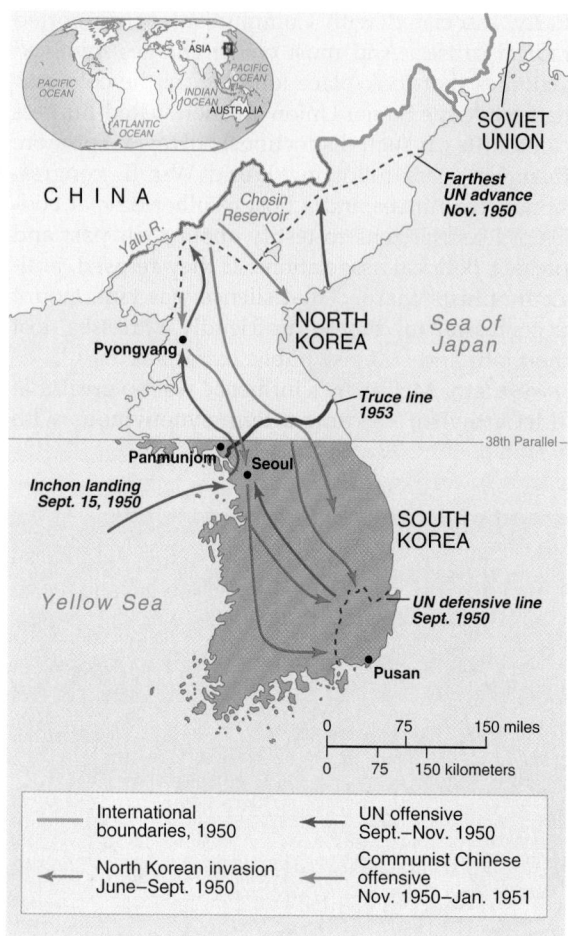

MAP 26.3

The Korean War, 1950–1953

After each side had plunged deep into its enemy's territory, the Korean War ended in 1953 with the dividing line between North and South Korea being nearly the same as it had been before the war.

Rhee was elected president, and the United States withdrew most of its troops. In the fall of 1948, the Soviets established the People's Republic of North Korea and also withdrew. U.S. Defense and State Department officials did not consider Korea to be of vital strategic interest, and many doubted that Rhee's repressive government could sustain popular support. But because Rhee was staunchly anti-Communist, Truman authorized a small amount of economic and military aid to South Korea.

Skirmishes between North and South Korean troops had occurred since 1948, with both sides crossing the thirty-eighth parallel. In June 1950, however, ninety thousand North Koreans swept into South Korea. Truman's advisers immediately assumed that either the Soviet Union, China, or both had instigated the attack. Revelations by former Soviet officials decades later indicated only that the Kremlin had acquiesced in North Korean plans.

On June 30, six days after learning of the attack, Truman decided to commit ground troops, believing that Korea was "the Greece of the Far East" and that the United States must "put up a fight [against communism] right now." Because the Soviet Union was boycotting the UN Security Council for its refusal to seat a delegate from the People's Republic of China, the U.S. representative was able to obtain UN sponsorship of a collective effort to repel the attack. Authorized to appoint a commander for the UN force, Truman named General Douglas MacArthur, hero of the American World War II victory in the Pacific and head of the postwar occupation of Japan.

Sixteen nations, including many NATO allies, sent troops to Korea, but the United States furnished most of the personnel and weapons, deploying almost 1.8 million troops and essentially dictating military strategy. By failing to ask Congress for a declaration of war, Truman violated at least the spirit if not the letter of the Constitution. Moreover, although Congress authorized the mobilization of troops and appropriated funds to fight the war, the president's political opponents called it "Truman's war" when the military situation worsened.

The first American soldiers rushed to Korea unprepared and ill equipped. The North Koreans took the capital of Seoul and drove deep into the south between June and September, forcing UN troops to retreat south to Pusan. Then, in September, General MacArthur launched a bold counteroffensive at Inchon, 180 miles behind the North Korean lines. By mid-October, UN forces had pushed the North Koreans back to the thirty-eighth parallel. Now came the momentous decision of whether to invade North Korea and seek to unify Korea under UN supervision.

From Containment to Rollback to Containment

"Troops could not be expected . . . to march up to a surveyor's line and stop," remarked Dean Acheson, now secretary of state, reflecting sentiment among the public and most government officials to transform the military objective from containment to elimination of the enemy and unification of Korea. With UN approval, on September 27, 1950, Truman ordered MacArthur to move beyond the thirty-eighth parallel if necessary to destroy North Korean forces. Concerned about possible intervention by China and the Soviet Union, Truman directed the general to keep UN troops away from the Korean-Chinese border. Yet MacArthur sent UN forces to within forty miles of China, whereupon more than 150,000 Chinese troops crossed the Yalu River into Korea. With Chinese help, by December 1950, the North Koreans had recaptured Seoul. It took three months of grueling battle for UN forces to work their way back to the thirty-eighth parallel. At that point, Truman decided to seek a negotiated settlement.

When the goal of the war reverted to containment, MacArthur was furious. To him, a holding action against communism represented defeat. Truman and his advisers, however, adamantly opposed a wider war in Asia. According to General Omar Bradley, chairman of the Joint Chiefs of Staff, MacArthur wanted to wage "the wrong war, at the wrong place, at the wrong time, with the wrong enemy."

MacArthur took his case public, in effect challenging the president's authority to make foreign policy and violating the principle of civilian control over the military. Fed up with MacArthur's insubordination, Truman fired him in April 1951. Many Americans, however, sided with MacArthur and castigated Truman. "Quite an explosion. . . . Letters of abuse by the dozens," Truman recorded in his diary. The general came home to a hero's welcome, and more than seven million people lined the streets for his triumphant parade in New York City. Baseball fans booed Truman when he appeared at Griffith Stadium on opening day.

The adulation of MacArthur reflected American frustrations with containment. Why should Americans die simply to preserve the status quo rather than destroy the enemy once and for all? Taking MacArthur's perspective enabled Americans to hold on to their belief that the United States was all-powerful and to pin the Korean stalemate on the government's ineptitude or willingness to shelter subversives. Moreover, Truman's earlier success in "scaring the hell" out of the American people over the threat of communism in the Mediterranean came back to haunt him. If communism was so evil,

1953 and remained above $40 billion thereafter. By 1953, defense spending claimed 60 percent of the federal budget, and the size of the armed forces had tripled.

To General Matthew Ridgway, who succeeded MacArthur as commander of the UN forces, Korea taught the lesson that U.S. forces should never again fight a land war in Asia. Eisenhower concurred. Nevertheless, the Korean War induced the Truman administration to expand its role in Asia by increasing aid to the French, who were fighting to hang on to their colonial empire in Indochina. As U.S. marines retreated from a battle against Chinese soldiers in 1950, they sang, prophetically, "We're Harry's police force on call, / So put back your pack on, / The next step is Saigon, / Cheer up, me lads, bless 'em all."

Conclusion: The Cold War's Costs and Consequences

Dean Acheson titled his memoir about the Truman years *Present at the Creation*, aptly capturing the magnitude of change that marked the aftermath of World War II. More than any development in the postwar world, the cold war defined American politics and society for decades to come. Truman's decision to oppose communism throughout the world marked the most momentous foreign policy initiative in the nation's history. It transformed the federal government, shifting its priorities from domestic to external affairs, greatly expanding its budget, and substantially increasing the power of the president. The nuclear arms race attending the cold war put the people of the world at risk, consumed resources that might have been used to improve liv-

ing standards, and skewed the economy toward dependence on military projects. While debate about who was responsible for the cold war and whether it could have been avoided persisted, no one could doubt its impact on American society or the world.

In sharp contrast to foreign policy, the domestic policies of the postwar years reflected continuity with the past. Preoccupied with foreign policy, Truman failed to mobilize support for his ambition to assist the disadvantaged with new initiatives in education, health, agriculture, and civil rights, but he successfully defended most New Deal reforms. The boost to industry from cold war spending and the reconstruction of Western Europe and Japan contributed to an economic boom that lifted the standard of living for a majority of Americans.

The anti-Communist hysteria that grew out of the cold war contributed to the domestic status quo by silencing the left, stifling debate, and narrowing the range of acceptable ideas. Partisan politics and the Truman administration's constant rhetoric about the Communist menace fueled McCarthyism, but the obsession with subversion also fed on popular frustrations over the failure of containment to produce clear-cut victories. Convulsing the nation in bitter disunity, McCarthyism reflected a loss of confidence in American power. It would be a major challenge of the next administration to restore that unity and confidence.

FOR FURTHER READING ABOUT THE TOPICS IN THIS CHAPTER, see the Online Bibliography at www.bedfordstmartins.com/roarkcompact.

FOR ADDITIONAL FIRST-HAND ACCOUNTS OF THIS PERIOD, see pages 172–188 in Michael Johnson, ed., *Reading the American Past*, Second Edition, Volume II.

TO ASSESS YOUR MASTERY OF THE MATERIAL IN THIS CHAPTER, see the Online Study Guide at www.bedfordstmartins.com/roarkcompact.

CHRONOLOGY

1945 Harry S. Truman becomes president of United States upon death of Franklin D. Roosevelt.

1946 Postwar labor unrest erupts throughout United States.

Truman creates Committee on Civil Rights.

United States grants independence to Philippines.

Congress passes Employment Act signifying government's responsibility for healthy economy.

Congressional elections result in Republican control of 80th Congress.

1947 George F. Kennan's article on policy of containment appears in *Foreign Affairs*.

National Security Act of 1947 unifies military services under secretary of defense and creates National Security Council (NSC) and Central Intelligence Agency (CIA).

Truman asks Congress for aid to Greece and Turkey to counter communism and announces Truman Doctrine.

Truman establishes by executive order federal employees loyalty and security program designed to eliminate Communists and their sympathizers from the government.

1948 Congress approves Marshall Plan, providing massive aid to stimulate European recovery.

Congress makes women permanent part of armed services.

Truman issues executive order to desegregate armed services.

United States recognizes state of Israel.

Truman defeats Thomas E. Dewey to win full term as president.

1948–1949 Soviets block access to West Berlin, setting off Berlin crisis and fifteen-month Western airlift.

1949 Communists under Mao Zedong win Chinese civil war and take over mainland China; Nationalists under Chiang Kai-shek retreat to Taiwan.

The North Atlantic Treaty Organization (NATO) organizes to counter Soviet threat to Western Europe.

Truman administration initiates Point IV technical aid program to third world nations.

Soviet Union explodes atomic bomb.

1950 Senator Joseph McCarthy begins campaign against alleged Communists in United States, giving his name to period of anti-Communist hysteria.

Truman approves development of hydrogen bomb.

United States sends troops to South Korea to repel North Korean assault.

1951 Truman relieves General Douglas MacArthur of command in Korea for insubordination.

United States ends postwar occupation of Japan; the two nations sign peace treaty and mutual security pact.

1952 Republican Dwight D. Eisenhower elected president of United States.

1953 Armistice signed in Korean War.

1956 CADILLAC CONVERTIBLE

The automobile reflected both corporate and family prosperity in the 1950s. This car was manufactured by General Motors, the biggest and richest corporation in the world and the first to sell a billion dollars' worth of products. Costing about $5,000, the Cadillac was GM's top-of-the-line car, one of the first purchases the McDonald brothers made when they struck it rich with their hamburger stand in California. Even the cheaper models that average Americans could afford featured the gas-guzzling size and space-age style of this Cadillac.

Ron Kimball Photography.

THE POLITICS AND CULTURE OF ABUNDANCE

27

1952–1960

T RAILED BY REPORTERS, U.S. vice president Richard M. Nixon led Soviet premier Nikita Khrushchev through the American National Exhibition in Moscow in July 1959. The display of American consumer goods followed an exhibition of Soviet products in New York, part of a cultural exchange between the two superpowers that reflected a slight thaw in the cold war. Both Khrushchev and Nixon seized on the propaganda potential of the moment. As they made their way through the display, their verbal sparring turned into a slugfest of words and gestures that reporters dubbed "the kitchen debate."

Showing off a new color television set, Nixon told Khrushchev that the Soviet Union "may be ahead of us . . . in the thrust of your rockets for . . . outer space," but the United States outstripped the Soviets in consumer goods. "Any steelworker could buy this house," Nixon boasted, as they walked through a six-room ranch-style model. Khrushchev retorted that in the Soviet Union, "you are entitled to housing," whereas in the United States the poor were reduced to sleeping on the pavement.

While the two men inspected appliances in the model kitchen, Nixon declared, "These are designed to make things easier for our women." Khrushchev responded that his country did not have "the capitalist attitude toward women" and appreciated women's contributions to the economy, not their domesticity. The Soviet leader found many of the items on display interesting, he said, but he added that "they are not needed in life. . . . They are merely gadgets." In reply, Nixon insisted, "Isn't it far better to be talking about washing machines than machines of war?" Khrushchev agreed, yet he affirmed the persistence of cold war tensions when he later blustered, "We too are giants. You want to threaten—we will answer threats with threats."

The Eisenhower administration in fact had begun with threats to the Soviet Union. Republican campaigners vowed to roll back communism and liberate "enslaved" peoples under Soviet rule. In practice, however, Eisenhower settled for a containment policy much like that of his predecessor, Harry S. Truman, though Eisenhower relied more on nuclear weapons and the Central Intelligence Agency (CIA). Yet, as Nixon's visit to Moscow demonstrated, Eisenhower took advantage of political changes in the Soviet Union to reduce tensions in Soviet-American relations.

Continuity with the Truman administration also characterized domestic policy. A majority of Americans enjoyed prosperity under the immensely popular

THE KITCHEN DEBATE
Soviet Premier Nikita Khrushchev (left) and Vice President Richard M. Nixon (center)
debate the relative merits of their nations' economies at the American National
Exhibition held in Moscow in 1959.
Howard Sochurek/TimePix.

president and seemed content with his "moderate Republicanism." Cold war weapons production spurred the economy, and most Americans could afford the products on display in Moscow, resulting in a dominant consumer culture that celebrated the family and traditional gender roles.

African Americans mounted a strong challenge to tradition in the 1950s. Reacting against segregation and disfranchisement, they developed the institutions, leadership, and strategies to mount a civil rights movement of unprecedented size and power.

Eisenhower and the Politics of the "Middle Way"

Moderation was the guiding principle of Eisenhower's domestic agenda and leadership style. Favoring in 1953 a "middle way between untrammeled freedom of the individual and the demands

for the welfare of the whole Nation," he pledged that his administration would "avoid government by bureaucracy as carefully as it avoids neglect of the helpless." Claiming that Democrats appealed to divisive class interests, Eisenhower presented himself as a leader above partisan politics and interest groups who would govern by compromise and consensus. Nicknamed "Ike" by his friends and the public, the confident war hero remained popular throughout his presidency.

The President and McCarthy

The new president attempted to distance himself from the anti-Communist fervor that had plagued the Truman administration. Eisenhower shared Senator Joseph McCarthy's goal of eliminating communism from American life, and though he deplored McCarthy's methods, he made little effort to silence him. Eisenhower feared that denouncing McCarthy would alienate powerful old-guard Republicans in

Congress. Even under a Republican administration, McCarthy continued his allegations of Communists in the government. The purge continued, and thousands of federal employees lost their jobs.

McCarthy ultimately destroyed himself. With the end of the Korean War, popular frustrations over containment abated, and the anti-Communist hysteria subsided. Yet in 1954 McCarthy turned against the army. As he hurled reckless charges of communism during weeks of televised hearings, public opinion turned against him. "Have you left no sense of decency?" demanded the army's lawyer. A Senate vote to condemn him in December 1954 marked the end of his influence.

Moderate Republicanism

After the Democrats regained control of Congress in 1954, Eisenhower presided over a divided government. Thus, the moderate Republicanism of his administration (1953–1961) was shaped not just by Eisenhower's determination to limit the growth of the federal government but also by a Democratic majority in Congress that maintained the course charted by the New Deal and Fair Deal.

Eisenhower claimed to be above interest-group politics, yet he turned for advice almost exclusively to business leaders and chose wealthy executives and attorneys for his cabinet. When he appointed Martin Durkin, president of the plumbers union, as secretary of labor, a liberal journal quipped that Eisenhower had "picked a cabinet of eight millionaires and one plumber." Eisenhower also sought advice from his "gang," a group of wealthy businessmen with whom he socialized.

Eisenhower shared the conservative old-guard Republicans' conviction that government was best left to the states and economic decisions to private business. "If all Americans want is security, they can go to prison," Eisenhower commented about social welfare in 1949. Yet, although liberals scorned the president's conservatism by calling him "Eisenhoover," the welfare state actually grew during his administration, and the federal government took on new projects. The "middle way" applied the brakes but did not reduce federal responsibility for economic development and assistance to poor Americans.

In 1954, Eisenhower signed laws expanding Social Security and continuing the federal govern-

POLIO VACCINE DISTRIBUTION IN THE SOUTH
In 1954, American children lined up to be inoculated with the new vaccine to prevent polio. But as this scene from Blytheville, Arkansas, shows, children waiting to receive the vaccine stood in strictly segregated lines.
Charles Bell, *Memphis Commercial Appeal.*

ment's role in financing public housing. He enlarged the government by obtaining congressional approval for a Department of Health, Education, and Welfare. And when the spread of polio neared epidemic proportions in the 1950s, Eisenhower obtained funds from Congress to distribute a vaccine, even though conservatives preferred that states assume that responsibility.

Eisenhower's greatest domestic initiative was the Interstate Highway and Defense System Act of 1956. Promoted as essential to the nation's cold war defense strategy and an impetus to economic growth, the act authorized construction of a national highway system, with the federal government paying most of the costs through increased fuel and vehicle taxes. Millions of Americans benefited from the greater ease of travel and improved transportation of goods, and the new highways also spurred growth in the fast-food and motel industries as well as the development of shopping malls. The most substantial gains went to the trucking, construction, and automobile industries, which had lobbied hard for the law. The monumental highway project eventually exacted severe costs, unforeseen at the time, in the form of air pollution, energy consumption, declining mass transportation, and decay in central cities.

In other areas, Eisenhower restrained the federal government in favor of state governments and private enterprise. His large tax cuts, for example, favored business and the wealthy, and he stubbornly resisted a larger federal role in health care, education, and civil rights. Moreover, whereas Democrats sought to keep nuclear power in government hands, Eisenhower signed legislation authorizing the private manufacture and sale of nuclear power. Workers broke ground at Shippingport, Pennsylvania, for the first commercial nuclear power plant in 1954.

The 1956 Election and the Second Term

With the nation at peace and the economy booming, Eisenhower easily defeated Adlai Stevenson in 1956, losing only seven states. But two years later, the Democrats all but wiped out the Republican party, gaining a 64–34 majority in the Senate and a 282–135 advantage in the House. Though Ike captured voters' hearts, a majority of them remained wedded to the programs and policies of the Democrats.

In part because of the Democratic resurgence, Eisenhower faced more serious leadership challenges in his second term. The economy plunged into a recession, and unemployment rose to 7 percent. Eisenhower fought with Congress over the budget and vetoed bills providing for expanded public works projects, a high level of price supports for farmers, and housing and urban development.

In the end, the first Republican administration after the New Deal left the size and functions of the federal government intact, though it tipped policy somewhat more in favor of corporate interests. Unparalleled prosperity graced the Eisenhower years, and inflation was kept low. The late-1957 recession was one of two in the 1950s, but the economy recovered without putting to a test the president's aversion to substantial federal intervention.

Liberation Rhetoric and the Practice of Containment

At his 1953 inauguration, Eisenhower warned that "forces of good and evil are massed and armed and opposed as rarely before in history." Like Truman, he saw communism as a threat to the nation's security and economic interests. Eisenhower's foreign policy differed from Truman's, though, in three areas: its rhetoric, its means, and—after Stalin's death in 1953—its movement toward accommodation with the Soviet Union.

The "New Look" in Foreign Policy

Reflecting Americans' confidence in technology and opposition to a large peacetime army, Eisenhower's defense strategy concentrated U.S. military strength in nuclear weapons and planes and missiles to deliver them. By 1955, one U.S. bomber carried more force than all the explosives ever detonated in the history of humankind. Instead of spending huge amounts for large ground forces of its own, the United States would give friendly nations American weapons and back them up with an ominous nuclear arsenal.

This was Eisenhower's "New Look" in foreign policy. Air power and nuclear weapons provided, in Secretary of State John Foster Dulles's words, a "maximum deterrent at bearable cost" or, as Defense Secretary Charles Wilson put it, a "bigger bang for the buck," enabling the administration to meet its

Newsweek

THE GREAT ENCOUNTER } 'We Are Talking About the Human Race'
— President Eisenhower

Special Section

25¢
SEPTEMBER 21, 1959

THE NUCLEAR ARMS RACE
This Newsweek *cover of Soviet leader Nikita Khrushchev and President Dwight D. Eisenhower balanced on the head of a nuclear missile suggests the precarious world created by the nuclear arms race. The table on which the two men sit refers to the arms limitation negotiations under way when the magazine came off the press in 1959.*

goals of cutting taxes and balancing the budget. Dulles believed that America's willingness to "go to the brink" of war with its intimidating nuclear superiority would block Soviet efforts to expand.

Nuclear weapons could not stop a Soviet nuclear attack, but, in response to one, they could inflict enormous destruction on the U.S.S.R. The certainty of "massive retaliation" was meant to deter the Soviets from launching an attack. Because the Soviet Union could respond similarly to an American first strike, this delicately balanced nuclear standoff became known as mutually assured destruction, or MAD. Winston Churchill called it a "mutual balance of terror."

Nuclear weapons were useless, however, in rolling back the iron curtain, because they would destroy the very peoples that the United States promised to liberate. When a revolt against the Soviet-controlled government began in Hungary in 1956, such promises of liberation proved to be empty rhetoric. Unwilling to risk U.S. soldiers and possible nuclear war, Eisenhower rebuffed the Hungarian Freedom Fighters' pleas for help. Soviet troops soon suppressed the insurrection, killing thirty thousand Hungarians.

Applying Containment to Vietnam

A major challenge to the containment policy came in Southeast Asia, where in 1945 a nationalist coalition called the Vietminh, led by Ho Chi Minh, had proclaimed Vietnam's independence from France. When France fought to maintain its colony, Ho fought back, and the area plunged into war. (See Map 29.2 in Chapter 29.) Because Ho declared himself a Communist, the Truman administration had quietly begun to provide aid to the French.

Eisenhower viewed communism in Vietnam much as Truman had regarded it in Greece and Turkey. "You have a row of dominoes," Eisenhower said, and "you knock over the first one, and what will happen to the last one is the certainty that it will go over very quickly." A communist victory in Southeast Asia, he warned, could trigger the fall of Japan, Taiwan, and the Philippines. By 1954, the United States was contributing 75 percent of the cost of France's war, but Eisenhower resisted a larger role. When the French asked for troops and airplanes from the United States in order to avert almost certain defeat at Dien Bien Phu, Eisenhower firmly said no. Conscious of U.S. losses in the Korean War, he would not commit troops to another ground war in Asia.

Dien Bien Phu fell in May 1954 and with it the French colony of Vietnam. Two months later in Geneva, France signed a truce. The Geneva accords drew a temporary line across the seventeenth parallel of Vietnam and prohibited both the Vietminh in the north and the puppet government established in the south by the French from joining a military alliance or permitting foreign bases on their soil. Within two years, the Vietnamese people were to vote in elections for a unified government. The United States promised to support free elections but did not sign the accords.

The French defeat in Vietnam prompted Eisenhower to prop up the dominoes with a new alliance.

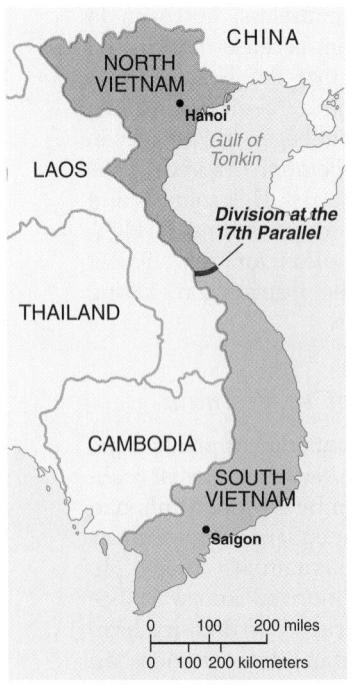

Geneva Accords of 1954

In September 1954, the United States joined with Britain, France, Australia, New Zealand, Thailand, Pakistan, and the Philippines in the Southeast Asia Treaty Organization (SEATO), committed to the defense of Cambodia, Laos, and South Vietnam. The ink was barely dry on the treaty when the United States began to send weapons and military advisers to South Vietnam and put the CIA to work at destabilizing North Vietnam. Fearing that the popular vote mandated by the Geneva accords would result in a Communist victory, the United States supported South Vietnamese prime minister Ngo Dinh Diem's refusal to hold the election.

Between 1955 and 1961, the United States provided $800 million to the South Vietnamese army (ARVN). Yet even with U.S. dollars, the ARVN was grossly unprepared for the guerrilla warfare that began in the late 1950s. In 1959, Ho Chi Minh's government in Hanoi began sending military assistance to Vietminh rebels in the south, who stepped up their guerrilla attacks on the Diem government. The insurgents gained control over villages not only through sheer military power but also because peasants were outraged by Diem's repressive regime. Unwilling to abandon containment, Eisenhower handed over the deteriorating situation—along with a firm commitment to defend South Vietnam against communism—to his successor.

Interventions in Latin America and the Middle East

While buttressing friendly governments in Asia, the Eisenhower administration also worked to topple unfriendly ones in Latin America and the Middle East. The CIA became an important arm of foreign policy in the 1950s, as Eisenhower relied on behind-the-scenes efforts and covert activities against un-

friendly governments. Increasingly, the administration conducted foreign policy behind the back of Congress.

The Eisenhower administration employed clandestine activities in Guatemala, where the government was not Communist or Soviet-controlled, but accepted support from the local Communist Party and threatened U.S. economic interests. (See Map 29.1 in Chapter 29.) In 1954, Eisenhower authorized the CIA to stage a coup, which displaced the popularly elected government of Jacobo Arbenz with a military dictatorship.

"We're going to take care of Castro just like we took care of Arbenz," promised a CIA agent when Cubans' desire for political and economic auton-

FIDEL CASTRO TRIUMPHS IN CUBA
Fidel Castro came from a privileged family and attended law school at the University of Havana, but he spent his youth working for the overthrow of Cuban dictator Fulgencio Batista. After leading an assault on Batista's soldiers in 1953, he spent two years in prison and then slowly built up an army of guerrilla fighters. He is shown here in his triumphal entrance into Havana in January 1959.
TimePix.

omy erupted in 1959. American companies had long controlled major Cuban resources—especially sugar, tobacco, and mines—and decisions made in Washington directly influenced the lives and livelihoods of the Cuban people. An uprising in 1959 led by Fidel Castro drove out the U.S.-supported dictator Fulgencio Batista and led the CIA to warn Eisenhower that "Communists and other extreme radicals appear to have penetrated the Castro movement." When the United States denied Castro's requests for loans, he turned for help to the Soviet Union. And when U.S. companies refused Castro's offer to purchase them at their assessed value, he began to nationalize their property. Many anti-Castro Cubans fled to the United States and reported his atrocities, including the execution of hundreds of Batista's supporters. Before leaving office, Eisenhower broke off diplomatic relations with Cuba and authorized the CIA to train Cuban exiles for an invasion.

In the Middle East, as in Guatemala, the CIA intervened to support an unpopular dictatorship and help American corporations. (See Map 31.1 in Chapter 31.) In 1951, the left-leaning prime minister of Iran, Mohammed Mossadegh, had nationalized oil fields and refineries, thereby threatening Western oil interests. While accepting support from the Iranian Communist Party, Mossadegh also challenged the power of the shah, Mohammad Reza Pahlavi, Iran's hereditary leader, who favored foreign oil interests and the Iranian wealthy classes.

For all of these reasons, Eisenhower authorized CIA agents to instigate a coup by bribing army officers and paying Iranians to demonstrate against the government. In August 1953, army officers took Mossadegh prisoner and reestablished the shah's power. Iran renegotiated oil concessions, giving U.S. companies a 40 percent share. Although the intervention worked in the short run, Americans in the 1970s and 1980s would feel the full fury of Iranian opposition to the repressive government that the United States had helped to reinstall.

Elsewhere in the Middle East, the Eisenhower administration shifted from Truman's all-out support for Israel to fostering friendships with Arab nations. Hindering such efforts, however, were U.S. demands that smaller nations take the American side in the cold war, when those nations preferred neutrality and the opportunity for assistance from both Western and Communist nations. In 1955,

Secretary of State Dulles began talks with Egypt about American support to build the Aswan Dam on the Nile River. But in 1956, Egypt's leader, Gamal Abdel Nasser, sought arms from Communist Czechoslovakia, formed a military alliance with other Arab nations, and recognized the People's Republic of China.

Unwilling to tolerate such independence, Dulles called off the deal for the dam. On July 26, 1956, Nasser responded by seizing the Suez Canal, then owned by Britain and France. Taking the canal advanced Nasser's prestige and power because it coincided with nationalist aspirations in the Arab world, and revenue from the canal could provide capital for constructing the dam. In response to the seizure, Israel, whose forces had been skirmishing with Egyptian troops along their common border since 1948, attacked Egypt, with military help from Britain and France.

Eisenhower opposed the intervention, recognizing that the Egyptians had claimed their own territory and believing that Nasser "embodie[d] the emotional demands of the people . . . for independence." He cut off oil to Britain and France while calling on the United Nations to arrange a truce. Lacking U.S. support, the French and British soon pulled back, forcing Israel to retreat from territory it had captured in the Sinai Desert region of Egypt.

Although staying out of the Suez crisis, Eisenhower made clear that the United States would actively combat communism in the Middle East. In March 1957, Congress passed a joint resolution approving economic and military aid to any Middle Eastern nation "requesting assistance against armed aggression from any country controlled by international communism." The president invoked this "Eisenhower Doctrine" to send aid to Jordan in 1957 and troops to Lebanon

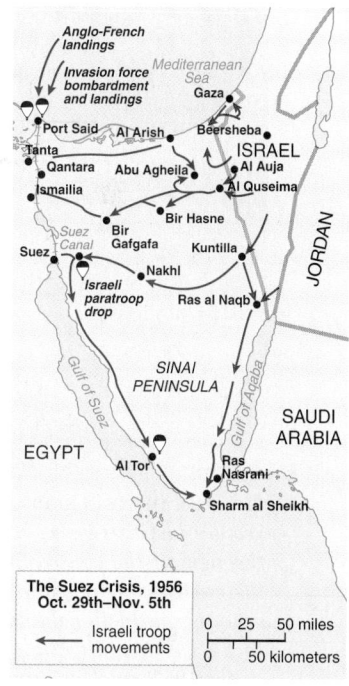

The Suez Crisis, 1956

in 1958 to counter anti-Western pressures on those governments.

The Nuclear Arms Race

A number of events encouraged Eisenhower to seek reduction of superpower tensions and accommodation with the Soviet Union. After Stalin's death in 1953, a more moderate leadership under Nikita Khrushchev emerged. The Soviet Union signed a peace treaty with Austria guaranteeing Austrian neutrality and removed its troops. Like Eisenhower,

who remarked privately that the arms race would lead "at worst to atomic warfare, at best to robbing every people and nation on earth of the fruits of their own toil," Khrushchev worried about the domestic costs of the cold war and wanted to reduce defense spending and the threat of nuclear devastation.

Eisenhower and Khrushchev met in Geneva in 1955 at the first summit conference since the end of World War II. Though it produced no significant agreements, the meeting symbolized a lessening of tensions—in Eisenhower's words, "a new spirit of conciliation and cooperation." In 1959, Khrushchev

THE AGE OF NUCLEAR ANXIETY
Within just five years after World War II, governments throughout the United States were educating the public about the nuclear threat and planning for a possible attack. As schools routinely held drills to prepare for possible Soviet attacks, children directly experienced the anxiety and insecurity of the 1950s nuclear arms race. This pamphlet about how to survive an atomic attack was published by the federal government and distributed to the general public. How effective do you think the strategy pictured here would have been in the event of a nuclear attack?
Archive Photos; Lynn Historical Society.

www.bedfordstmartins.com/roarkcompact SEE THE ONLINE STUDY GUIDE for more help in analyzing this image.

visited the United States, and Nixon went to the Soviet Union, where he engaged in the famous kitchen debate. By 1960, the two sides were within reach of a ban on nuclear testing, and Khrushchev and Eisenhower agreed to meet again in Paris in May.

To avoid jeopardizing the summit, Eisenhower decided to cancel espionage flights over the Soviet Union, but his order came one day too late. On May 1, 1960, Soviet gunners shot down a U-2 spy plane over Soviet territory. The State Department first denied that U.S. planes had been violating Soviet air space, but then the Soviets produced the pilot and the photos taken on his flight. Eisenhower met with Khrushchev briefly in Paris, but the U-2 incident dashed all prospects for a nuclear arms agreement.

Eisenhower's "more bang for the buck" defense budget enormously increased the U.S. nuclear capacity, more than quadrupling the stockpile of nuclear weapons. By the time he left office in 1961, the United States had installed seventy-two intercontinental ballistic missiles (ICBMs) in the United States and Britain and was prepared to deploy more in Italy and Turkey. The first Polaris submarine carrying nuclear missiles was launched in November 1960.

In August 1957, the Soviets test-fired their first ICBM and two months later beat the U.S. into space by launching *Sputnik*, the first artificial satellite to circle the planet. Senate majority leader Lyndon Johnson called the Soviet success a scientific Pearl Harbor, and other leaders warned that the United States lagged behind not only in missile development and space exploration but also in science and education. The United States finally launched its first satellite in January 1958.

Eisenhower insisted that the United States possessed nuclear superiority, but in 1957 he could not reveal the evidence for his confidence, the top-secret U-2 surveillance of the Soviet Union. He tried to diminish public panic, establishing the National Aeronautics and Space Administration (NASA) in July 1958 and approving a gigantic budget increase for space research and development. In addition, he signed the National Defense Education Act, providing loans and scholarships for students in math, foreign languages, and science.

As he left office, Eisenhower warned about the growing influence of the "military-industrial complex" in American government and life. To contain the defense budget, Eisenhower had struggled against persistent pressures from defense contractors who, in tandem with the military, sought more dollars for newer, more powerful weapons systems.

In his farewell address, he warned that the "conjunction of an immense military establishment and a large arms industry . . . exercised a total influence . . . in every city, every state house, every office of the federal government." The cold war had created a warfare state.

New Work and Living Patterns in an Economy of Abundance

American military spending helped stimulate domestic prosperity. Economic productivity increased enormously in the 1950s, a multitude of new items came on the market, consumption became the order of the day, and millions of Americans enjoyed new homes in the suburbs. Young people stayed in school longer, and higher education became the norm for the middle class. Although every section of the nation enjoyed the new prosperity, the West and Southwest especially boomed in production, commerce, and population.

Work itself changed: Fewer people labored on farms; service sector employment overtook manufacturing jobs; and women's employment grew. These economic shifts disadvantaged some Americans, and some forty million people—20 percent of the population—lived in poverty. Most Americans, however, enjoyed a higher standard of living, leading the economist John Kenneth Galbraith to call the United States "the affluent society."

Technology Transforms Agriculture and Industry

Between 1940 and 1960, the output of American farms mushroomed, while the number of farmworkers declined by nearly one-third. Farmers achieved nearly miraculous productivity through greater crop specialization, more intensive use of fertilizers, and, above all, mechanization. Tractors, mechanical pickers, and other machines increasingly substituted for human and animal power. A single mechanical cotton picker replaced fifty people and cut the cost of harvesting a bale of cotton from forty dollars to five dollars.

The decline of family farms and the growth of large commercial farming, or "agribusiness," were both causes and consequences of mechanization. Larger farmers benefited handsomely from federal price supports begun in the New Deal, and they could afford technological improvements, whereas smaller producers lacked capital to invest in the machinery necessary to compete. Consequently, average farm size more than doubled between 1940 and 1964, while the farm population sunk from thirty million to thirteen million, and the number of farms fell by more than 40 percent.

Many small farmers who hung on constituted a core of rural poverty often overlooked in the celebration of affluence. Southern landowners replaced sharecroppers with machines, forcing them off the land. Hundreds of thousands of African Americans joined an exodus to cities, where racial

MECHANIZING AGRICULTURE
This farm equipment ad reflects the growing application of technology to agriculture. Ever more elaborate machinery created a long-term trend in which family farms were overtaken by agribusiness. Giant farms employed the latest technology and thus reduced the need for human labor. Between 1945 and 1960, the nation's population living on farms shrank from 17.5 to 8.7 percent.

John Deere Company.

discrimination and a lack of jobs for which they could qualify mired many in urban poverty. A Mississippi woman whose family had worked on a plantation since slavery reported that most of her relatives headed for Chicago when they heard that "it was going to be machines now that harvest the crops." Worrying that "it might be worse up there," she agonized, "I'm afraid to leave and I'm afraid to stay, and whichever I do, I think it might be real bad for my boys and girls."

Alongside the 20 percent poverty rate, economists claimed that 60 percent of Americans enjoyed middle-class incomes in 1960. Between 1950 and 1960, the gross national product (the value of all goods and services produced during a year) as well as median family income grew by 25 percent in constant dollars. By the late 1950s, four of every five families owned television sets and washing machines, nearly all had refrigerators, and the majority owned at least one car.

Several forces spurred this unparalleled abundance. Even with Eisenhower's conservative fiscal policies, government spending reached $80 billion annually and created new jobs. A population surge—from 152 million in 1950 to 180 million in 1960—expanded demand for products and boosted industries ranging from baby goods to music. Consumer borrowing also fueled the economic boom, as people increasingly bought houses, cars, and appliances on installment plans.

As in agriculture, new technology increased industrial production. Between 1945 and 1960, for example, the automobile industry cut in half the number of labor-hours needed to manufacture a car. Technology also transformed such industries as electronics, chemicals, and air transportation and promoted the growth of television, plastics, computers, and other newer industries. American businesses enjoyed access to cheap oil, and the nation's dominance in the international economy guaranteed ample markets abroad and little foreign competition.

Labor unions enjoyed their greatest success during the 1950s, and real earnings for production workers shot up 40 percent. The merger in 1955 of the American Federation of Labor (AFL) and the Congress of Industrial Organizations (CIO) lessened internal conflicts and improved labor's bargaining position. As one worker put it, "We saw continual improvement in wages, fringe benefits like holidays, vacation, medical plans . . . all sorts of things that provided more security for people." Such benefits became a staple of most union contracts, though workers in heavy industries such as steel and automobiles did much better than those in food processing, garment making, and other light manufacturing. Unlike most industrial nations, where government provided most of the benefits, the United States developed a mixed system in which company-funded programs won by unions through collective bargaining played a larger role. This system resulted in wide disparities among workers, severely disadvantaging those not represented by unions.

While the absolute number of organized workers continued to increase, union membership peaked at 27.1 percent of the labor force in 1957. Technological advances chipped away at jobs in heavy industry, reducing the number of workers in the steel, copper, and aluminum industries by 17 percent. Moreover, the economy as a whole was shifting from production to service. Instead of making products, more and more workers distributed goods, performed services, kept records, provided education, or carried out government work. Unions made some headway in these fields, but most service industries resisted unionization, and many of the workers—such as janitors, food servers, and domestics—performed hard manual labor for low wages.

The growing clerical and service occupations swelled the demand for female workers. By the end of the 1950s, 35 percent of all women over age sixteen worked outside the home—twice as many as in 1940—and women held more than one-third of all jobs. Moreover, the largest increases in employment occurred for married women, who hoped to secure some of the new abundance for their families. As one woman remarked, "My Joe can't put five kids through college . . . and the washer had to be replaced, and Ann was ashamed to bring friends home because the living room furniture was such a mess, so I went to work."

Women entered a sharply segregated workplace. The vast majority worked in clerical jobs, light manufacturing, domestic service, teaching, and nursing, and because these were female occupations, wages were relatively low. In 1960, the average full-time female worker earned just 60 percent of the average male worker's wages. At the bottom of the employment ladder, black women took home only 42 percent of what white men earned.

Burgeoning Suburbs and Declining Cities

Although suburbs had existed since the nineteenth century, nothing symbolized the affluent society more than their tremendous expansion in the 1950s:

Eleven million of the thirteen million new homes were built in the suburbs, and by 1960, one in four Americans lived there. The suburbs were accessible to families with modest incomes. Builder William J. Levitt modified the factory assembly-line process, planning nearly identical units so that individual construction workers could move from house to house and perform the same single operation in each, such as caulking windows or installing bathtubs. In 1949, families could purchase these mass-produced houses in his 17,000-home development called Levittown, on Long Island, New York, for just under $8,000. Developments similar to Levittown, as well as more luxurious ones, quickly went up throughout the country.

While private industry built the suburbs, the government supported home ownership with low-interest mortgage guarantees through the Federal Housing Administration and the Veterans Administration. A veteran could buy a house in Levittown with payments of just $58 per month for twenty-five years. Moreover, thousands of interstate highway miles ran through urban areas, indirectly subsidizing suburban development. Without the automobile and the freeway, the suburban explosion could not have occurred.

Suburban culture was not without detractors. Social critic Lewis Mumford blasted the suburbs as "a multitude of uniform, unidentifiable houses, lined up inflexibly, at uniform distances, on uniform roads, in a treeless communal wasteland, inhabited by people of the same class, the same income, the same age group." The growing suburbs did contribute to a more polarized society, especially along racial lines. Each Levittown homeowner signed a contract pledging that "no dwelling shall be used or occupied by members of other than the Caucasian race." Although the Supreme Court declared such covenants unenforceable in 1948, suburban America remained dramatically segregated.

As white residents joined the suburban migration, blacks moved to cities in search of economic opportunity, increasing their numbers in most cities by 50 percent during the 1950s. Black migrants to the north and east, however, came to cities that were already in decline, losing not only population but also commerce and industry to the suburbs or to southern and western states. New business facilities began to ring central cities, and shoppers gradually chose suburban malls over downtown department stores. Many of the new jobs lay beyond the reach of the recent black arrivals to the inner cities.

AN AFRICAN AMERICAN SUBURB
*The pioneer of mass-produced suburban housing, William J. Levitt, reflected the racism
that kept blacks out of suburbia when he said, "We can solve a housing problem, or
we can try and solve a racial problem but we cannot combine the two." These African
Americans developed their own suburb, a planned community for middle-class blacks
in Richmond, California, which welcomed the first families in 1950.*
Courtesy Richmond Public Library.

The Democratization of Higher Education

Affluence spectacularly transformed higher education. Between 1940 and 1960, enrollments leaped from 1.5 million to 3.6 million; and more than 40 percent of young Americans attended college by the mid-1960s, in contrast to 15 percent in the 1940s. More families could afford to keep their children in school longer, and the federal government subsidized the education of more than two million World War II and Korean War veterans. The cold war also sent millions of federal dollars to universities for defense-related research. Total tax dollars spent for higher education more than doubled from 1950 to 1960, as state governments vastly expanded the number of four-year colleges and universities, and municipalities began to build two-year junior or community colleges.

The GI Bill made college possible for thousands of African Americans, the majority of whom attended black institutions. College enrollments of blacks surged from 37,000 in 1941 to 90,000 in 1961. Yet African Americans constituted only about 5 percent of all college students, less than half their percentage in the general population. Unlike their white counterparts, among whom women received just 33 percent of college degrees in 1960, black men and women attended college in nearly equal numbers.

The Rise of the Sun Belt

The nation seemed to be tipped westward, quipped architect Frank Lloyd Wright: Everything not bolted down was sliding toward California. No regions experienced the postwar economic and population booms more intensely than the West and Southwest. With its inhabitants more than doubling after World War II, California overtook New York as the most populous state in 1962. A warm climate and a pleas-

ant natural environment drew new residents to the West and Southwest, but no magnet proved stronger than the promise of economic opportunity (Map 27.1).

As railroads had fueled western growth in the nineteenth century, the automobile and airplane spurred the post–World War II surge, providing efficient transportation for people and products. The technology of air-conditioning made possible industrial development in the so-called Sun Belt,

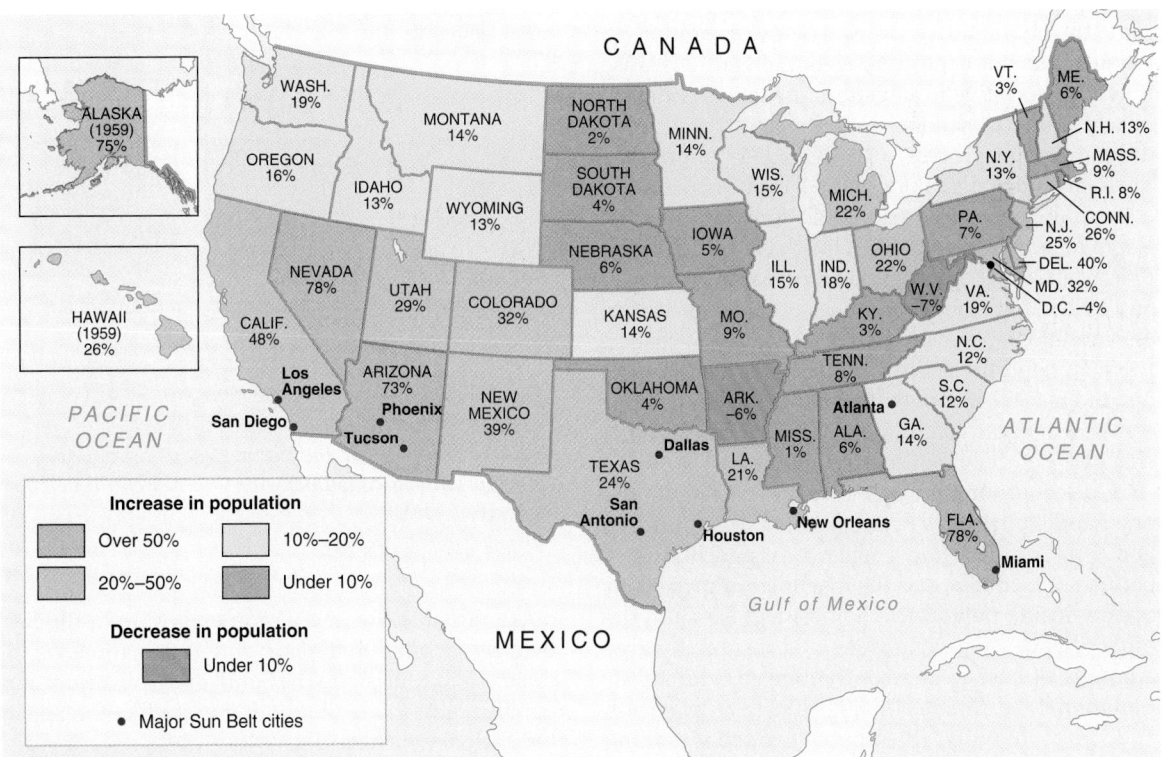

MAP 27.1

The Rise of the Sun Belt, 1940–1980

The growth of defense industries, a nonunionized labor force, and the spread of air-conditioning all helped spur economic development and population growth, which made the Sun Belt the fastest-growing region of the nation between 1940 and 1980.

READING THE MAP: What states experienced an over 20 percent growth in population? What states experienced the largest population growth?

CONNECTIONS: What stimulated the population boom in the Southwest? What role did the cold war play in this boom? What role did African Americans play in the western population boom?

www.bedfordstmartins.com/roarkcompact SEE THE ONLINE STUDY GUIDE for more help in analyzing this map.

Air-Conditioning

AIR-CONDITIONING DEVELOPED PRIMARILY in response to the needs of industry. In 1902, Willis Haviland Carrier, an American engineer who formulated basic theories of air-conditioning, designed the first system to control temperature and humidity and installed it in a Brooklyn printing plant. In 1915, he founded the Carrier Corporation to manufacture air-conditioning equipment. Because fibers are sensitive to moisture, the textile industry provided an early and important market for air-conditioning. The process also helped to popularize movie theaters by making them a cool as well as an entertaining retreat during hot summer months. Room air conditioners began to appear in the 1930s. This 1950 Carrier ad promoted the clean air in homes and offices that would come with purchase of a room air conditioner. Fewer than a million homes had room air conditioners in 1950, but nearly eight million did in 1960, and more than half of all homes had some form of air conditioning by 1975, as its status changed from a luxury to a necessity.

Air-conditioning was a mixed blessing. On the one hand, companies no longer had to shut down and send workers home when heat and humidity became unbearable, and the machines improved air quality inside businesses, homes, and cars. On the other hand, air conditioners consumed large amounts of energy and contributed to outdoor air pollution. Like other technologies such as television and, more recently, the Internet, air-conditioning had an isolating effect as people deserted front porches and backyards for closed-up houses and thus curtailed their interactions with neighbors. Perhaps its greatest impact on the nation was to

"THAT'S MODERN AIR CONTROL!"
Ads like this one for the Carrier room air conditioner promised consumers that homes could be cool as well as clean.
Courtesy Carrier Corporation.

make possible the population explosion in the Sun Belt. By facilitating the movement of commerce, industry, and tourism to the South and Southwest, air-conditioning made that region more like the rest of the nation. One historian of the South, referring disparagingly to the transformation worked by air-conditioning on that region, proclaimed that "[General Electric] has proved a more devastating invader than even General Sherman."

which stretched from Florida to California. Crucial to the region's population explosion, air-conditioning cooled nearly eight million Sun Belt homes by 1960. (See "The Promise of Technology," above.)

The aerospace industry boomed in Seattle–Tacoma, Los Angeles, Tucson, and Dallas–Fort

Worth, and military bases helped underwrite prosperity in such cities as San Diego and San Antonio. The Sun Belt captured the lion's share of cold war spending for research and production of bombers and missiles, leading some to call it the "Gun Belt." In California alone, the federal government spent

ROUNDING UP UNDOCUMENTED MIGRANTS
Not all Mexican Americans who wanted to work in the United States were accommodated by the **bracero** *program. In 1953, Los Angeles police arrested these men who did not have legal documents and were hiding in a freight train. Americans used the crude term* **wetback** *to refer to illegal immigrants because many of them swam across the Rio Grande, at the border between the United States and Mexico.*
Corbis-Bettmann.

more than $100 billion for defense between 1945 and 1965. By the 1960s, nearly one of every three California workers held a defense-related job.

The high-technology basis of postwar economic development drew well-educated, highly skilled workers to the West. But the economic promise also attracted the poor. "We see opportunity all around us here. . . . We smell freedom here, and maybe soon we can taste it," commented a black mother in California. Between 1945 and 1960, more than one-third of the African Americans who left the South moved west.

The Mexican American population also grew, especially in California and Texas. To supply California's vast agribusiness industry, the government continued the *bracero* program begun during World War II. Until the program ended in 1964, more than a hundred thousand Mexicans entered the United States each year to labor in the fields—and many of them stayed, legally or illegally. But while the government encouraged the use of Mexican labor, it reflected white Americans' opposition to permanent Mexican immigration, launching in 1954 a series of raids called "Operation Wetback." Designed to ferret out and deport illegal immigrants, the operation made U.S. citizens of Mexican descent feel unwelcome and threatened them with incidents of mistaken identity.

Native Americans suffered under a new government policy in 1953, called "termination," aimed to eliminate their reservations and do away with tribal sovereignty. Termination fit well with Eisenhower's preference for a limited federal government, but it proved devastating for Native Americans. Before the policy was abandoned in the 1960s, 170,000 Indians moved from their reservations to cities, where, like many black migrants from the South, they typically exchanged rural for urban poverty. Many lost their cultural identity as well. As one woman reported, "I talked to my children . . . about the ways of the Ojibway people. . . . They listened, but I had a feeling that they listened the same as when I read a story about the Bobbsey twins or Marco Polo. I was speaking of another people, removed from them."

Free of the discrimination faced by minorities, white Americans reaped the fullest fruits of prosperity in the West. In April 1950, California developers advertised the opening of Lakewood, a large housing development in Los Angeles County. On the first day of sales, thirty thousand people lined up to purchase tract houses for $8,000 to $10,000. Many of the new home owners were veterans, blue-collar and lower-level white-collar workers whose defense-based jobs at McDonnell Douglas and other aerospace corporations or at the Long Beach naval base enabled them to fulfill the American dream of the 1950s. A huge shopping mall, Lakewood Center, offered myriad products of the consumer culture. And California's higher education plan allowed their children access to community colleges, four campuses of California State University, and two campuses of the University of California system—all within easy reach of Lakewood.

The Culture of Abundance

With increased prosperity in the 1950s, more people married and the birthrate soared. Religious observance quickened even as Americans sought satisfaction in material possessions. Television entered the homes of most Americans, helping to promote a consumer culture. Dominant values favored family life and traditional gender roles, consumption, and conformity. Undercurrents of rebellion, especially among youth, defied some of the dominant norms but did not greatly disrupt the complacency of the 1950s.

The Revival of Domesticity and Religion

Married women took jobs in unprecedented numbers, yet a dominant ideology celebrated traditional family life and conventional gender roles. Even though more than one-third of mothers with school-age children left the home for work, the family ideal defined by popular culture and public figures persisted: a male breadwinner, a full-time homemaker, and three or four children in a new suburban home. One government official saw women's role in cold war terms, charging that the Soviet Union viewed women "first as a source of manpower, second as a mother," and insisting that "the highest calling of a woman's sex is the home." *Life* magazine echoed the sentiment: "Of all the accomplishments of the American woman, the one she brings off with the most spectacular success is having babies."

Writer and feminist Betty Friedan gave a name to the idealization of women's domestic roles in her book *The Feminine Mystique*, published in 1963. Friedan criticized advertisers, social scientists, educators, women's magazines, and public officials for pressuring women to seek fulfillment in serving others. According to the feminine mystique that they promulgated, biological differences fitted men and women for entirely different roles in life. The ideal woman kept a spotless house, raised perfect children, served her husband's career, and provided him emotional and sexual satisfaction. Not many women then directly challenged the feminine mystique, but Edith Stern, a college-educated writer maintained that "many arguments about the joys of housewifery have been advanced, largely by those who have never had to work at it," while she deplored the "incalculable skilled services" that were "buried in the homemade cakes the family loves and sunk in the suds of the week's wash."

Although the glorification of domesticity clashed with married women's increasing participation in the labor force, the lives of many Americans did embody the family ideal. Postwar prosperity enabled people to marry earlier and to have more children. Whereas its general trend over the twentieth century was downward, the American birthrate soared during the period 1945 to 1965, reaching a peak in 1957 with 4.3 million births and producing the "baby boom" generation. (See appendix, page A-31.) The norms for childrearing were more demanding than ever before. Dr. Benjamin Spock's best-selling *Common Sense Book of Baby and Child Care* (1946) advocated a permissive approach instead of the traditional emphasis on strictness and rigid schedules, an approach requiring mothers' fulltime involvement. Experts also urged that fathers cultivate family "togetherness" and spend more time with their children.

Along with a renewed emphasis on family life, the 1950s witnessed a surge of interest in religion. By 1960, about 63 percent of Americans belonged to churches and synagogues, up from 50 percent in 1940. Polls reported that 95 percent of all Americans believed in God. Evangelism took on new life, most notably in the nationwide crusades of Baptist minister Billy Graham, whose powerful oratory moved mass audiences to accept Christ. Congress linked religion more closely to the state by adding "under God" to the pledge of allegiance in 1954 and by requiring in 1955 that "In God We Trust" be printed on all currency.

Some critics suggested that in their renewed interest in religion Americans were seeking peace of mind from cold war anxieties and the threat of nuclear annihilation. Others questioned the depth of the religious revival, attributing the growth in church membership to a desire for conformity and

a need for social outlets. One commentator, for example, noted that 53 percent of Americans could not name any book of the New Testament.

Television Transforms Culture and Politics

Just as family life and religion offered a respite from cold war anxieties, so too did the new medium of television. In 1950, fewer than 10 percent of American homes boasted a television set, but by 1960 about 87 percent of all households owned one. On average, Americans spent more than five hours each day in front of the screen.

Especially popular were situation comedies, which projected the family ideal and the feminine mystique into millions of homes. On TV, married women did not work outside the home and deferred to their husbands, though they often got the upper hand through subtle manipulation. In the most popular television show of the early 1950s, *I Love Lucy*, the husband-and-wife team of Lucille Ball and Desi Arnaz played the couple Lucy and Ricky Ricardo. In step with the trends, they moved from an apartment in the city to a house in suburbia. Ricky would not let Lucy get a job, and many plots depicted her zany attempts to thwart his objections.

Television began to affect politics in the 1950s. Richard Nixon's "Checkers speech" reached a nationwide audience and kept him on the Republican ticket in 1952. Senator McCarthy's reckless attacks on army members televised nationwide contributed to his downfall. Eisenhower's 1952 presidential campaign used TV ads for the first time, and by 1960, television played a key role in election campaigns. Reflecting on his narrow victory in 1960, President-elect John F. Kennedy remarked, "We wouldn't have had a prayer without that gadget."

Television transformed politics in other ways. Money became a much larger force in elections, because candidates needed to raise huge sums for expensive TV spots. The ability to appeal directly to voters in their living rooms encouraged candidates to build their own campaign organizations, relying less on political parties. The declining strength of parties and the growing power of money in elections were not new trends, but television did much to accelerate them.

JACKSON POLLOCK
The leading artist in the post–World War II revolution in painting, Jackson Pollock, illustrates his technique of pouring and splattering paint onto the canvas. He worked with the canvas on the floor because, he said, "I feel nearer, more a part of the painting. . . . I can walk around it, work from the four sides and be literally 'in' the painting."
Jackson Pollock, 1950 photograph by Hans Namuth, © 1991 Hans Namuth Estate. Courtesty, Center for Creative Photography, The University of Arizona.

Developments in the visual arts also showed the 1950s to be more than a decade of bland conventionality. An artistic revolution that flowered in New York City, known as "action painting," "abstract expressionism," or the "New York school," rejected the idea that painting should represent recognizable forms. Jackson Pollock and other abstract expressionists poured, dripped, and threw paint on canvases or substituted sticks and other implements for brushes. Their work emphasized energy and spontaneity, and it so captivated and redirected the Western art world that New York replaced Paris as its center.

Emergence of a Civil Rights Movement

African Americans conducted the most dramatic challenge to the status quo of the 1950s as they sought to break the chains that had replaced the literal bonds of slavery. Every southern state mandated rigid segregation in public settings from hospitals and schools to drinking fountains and rest rooms. Southern voting laws and practices disfranchised the vast majority of African Americans; employment discrimination kept them at the bottom of the economic ladder.

Although black protest was as old as American racism, in the 1950s that protest developed into a grassroots movement that attracted national attention and the support of white liberals. The Supreme Court delivered significant institutional reforms, but blacks themselves directed the most important changes. Ordinary African Americans in substantial numbers sought their own liberation, building a movement that would transform race relations in the United States.

African Americans Challenge the Supreme Court and the President

A number of factors spurred black protest in the 1950s. Between 1940 and 1960, more than three million African Americans moved from the South into areas where they could vote and exert pressure on politicians. Moreover, the cold war raised white leaders' concern that its dismal state of race relations handicapped the United States in competing with the Soviet Union. In the South, African Americans controlled resources essential to a movement, such as black churches and colleges, which developed leadership skills and provided a mass base and organizational network.

The legal strategy of the major civil rights organization, the National Association for the Advancement of Colored People (NAACP), reached its crowning achievement with the Supreme Court decision in *Brown v. Board of Education* in 1954. *Brown* was actually a consolidation of five separate suits that reflected the growing determination of black Americans to fight for their rights. Oliver Brown, a welder in Topeka, Kansas, filed suit because his eight-year-old daughter had to pass by a white school just seven blocks from their home to attend a black school more than a mile away. Another of

SCHOOL INTEGRATION
In 1964, the popular artist Norman Rockwell painted **The Problem We All Live With,**
based on the experience of Ruby Bridges during the 1962 integration of the New Orleans
public schools. He hoped through this painting to get people to realize what America
was doing to its children. How do the composition of the scene and the characteristics
of the people indicate Rockwell's intentions?
Norman Rockwell Family Trust and Curtis Archives.

the suits grew out of a strike initiated by Virginia teenagers to protest the inadequate schools set up for blacks. The lead lawyer for the NAACP, future Supreme Court Justice Thurgood Marshall, urged the Court to overturn the precedent established in *Plessy v. Ferguson* (1896), which had enshrined "separate but equal" as the law of the land. A unanimous Court, headed by Chief Justice Earl Warren, declared, "Separate educational facilities are inherently unequal" and thus violated the Fourteenth Amendment.

It was one thing to issue a decision, another matter entirely to see it enforced. The Court called for desegregation "with all deliberate speed," but established no deadlines or guidelines. Ultimate responsibility for enforcement lay with President Eisenhower, but he refused to endorse *Brown*. Reflecting his own racial prejudice, preference for a

limited federal government, and leadership style that favored consensus and gradual progress, he would not urge the South to comply. Such inaction fortified southern resistance to school desegregation and contributed to the gravest constitutional crisis since the Civil War.

The crisis came in Little Rock, Arkansas, in September 1957. Local officials dutifully prepared for the integration of Central High School, but Governor Orval Faubus sent National Guard troops to block the enrollment of nine black students, claiming that their presence would cause public disorder. Later, Faubus agreed to allow the black students to enter, but he withdrew the National Guard, leaving the students to face an angry mob of whites. As television cameras transmitted the ugly scene across the nation, Eisenhower was forced to send regular army troops to take federal control of the Arkansas

National Guard, the first federal military intervention in the South since Reconstruction.

Escorted by paratroopers, the black students stayed in school, and Eisenhower withdrew the army in November. Other southern cities avoided integration by closing public schools and using tax dollars to support private, white-only schools. In 1961—nearly seven years after *Brown*—only 6.4 percent of southern black students attended integrated schools.

Eisenhower did order the integration of public facilities in Washington, D.C., and on military bases, and he supported the first federal civil rights legislation since Reconstruction. The Civil Rights Acts of 1957 and 1960, though, represented only marginal improvements for blacks. Baseball star Jackie Robinson spoke for many African Americans when he wired Eisenhower, "We disagree that half a loaf is better than none. Have waited this long for bill with meaning—can wait a little longer."

Montgomery and Mass Protest

From slave revolts and individual acts of defiance through the legal and lobbying efforts of the NAACP, black protest had a long tradition in American society. What set the civil rights movement of the 1950s and 1960s apart were the many people involved, their willingness to confront white institutions directly, and the use of nonviolence and passive resistance to bring about change. The Congress of Racial Equality (CORE) and other groups had experimented with these tactics in the 1940s, and African Americans had boycotted the segregated bus system in Baton Rouge, Louisiana, in 1953, but the first sustained protest to claim national attention began in Montgomery, Alabama, on December 1, 1955.

On that day police arrested a black woman, Rosa Parks, for violating a local segregation ordinance by refusing to give up her seat on a city bus to a white man. Parks had long been active in the local NAACP, headed by E. D. Nixon, who was also president of the local Brotherhood of Sleeping Car Porters. They and others had already talked about challenging bus segregation. A possible boycott had engaged another group, the Women's Political Council (WPC), composed of black professional women and led by Jo Ann Robinson, an English professor at Alabama State College who had been humiliated by a bus driver when she had inadvertently sat in the white section. Such local individuals and organizations, long committed to improving conditions for African Americans, laid critical foundations for the black freedom struggle throughout the South.

MONTGOMERY CIVIL RIGHTS LEADERS
During the Montgomery bus boycott, local white officials harassed African Americans with arrests and lawsuits. Here Rosa Parks, one of ninety-two defendants, ascends the steps of the Montgomery County courthouse in March 1956, accompanied by longtime civil rights leader E. D. Nixon. He felt that Parks would be a perfect plaintiff in a suit against segregation, and Parks agreed. "The white people couldn't say that there was anything I had done to deserve such treatment except to be born black."
Wide World Photos.

WPC leaders immediately mobilized teachers and students to distribute flyers calling for Montgomery blacks to stay off the busses. E. D. Nixon called a mass meeting for December 5 at the Holt Street Baptist Church, where so many gathered that a crowd of people stretched for blocks outside. Those assembled founded the Montgomery Improvement Association (MIA) to organize a bus boycott among the African American community. The MIA ran a system of volunteer car pools and marshaled more than 90 percent of the black community to sustain the year-long boycott. It held mass meetings to keep up the spirits of those who had to depend on the car pool to get to work and back, brave bad weather on foot to keep a job or get to the grocery store, or face harassment from policemen. Jo Ann Robinson, though a cautious driver, got seventeen traffic tickets in the space of two months.

Elected to head the MIA was Martin Luther King Jr., a newcomer to Montgomery and pastor at the Dexter Avenue Baptist Church. At only twenty-six, King had a doctorate in theology from Boston University. A captivating speaker before blacks who gathered regularly at churches throughout the boycott, King inspired their courage and commitment by linking racial justice to the redeeming power of Christian love. He promised, "If you will protest courageously and yet with dignity and Christian love . . . historians will have to pause and say, 'There lived a great people—a black people—who injected a new meaning and dignity into the veins of civilization.' This is our challenge and our overwhelming responsibility."

Montgomery blacks summoned their courage and determination in abundance. They walked miles to get to work, contributed their meager financial resources, and stood up with dignity to legal, economic, and physical intimidation. One older woman insisted, "I'm not walking for myself, I'm walking for my children and my grandchildren." Authorities arrested several leaders, and whites firebombed King's house. Yet the movement persisted, and in November 1956, the Supreme Court finally declared unconstitutional Alabama's laws requiring bus segregation. Although the Montgomery movement's victory came from Washington rather than the local power structure, it had demonstrated that blacks could sustain a lengthy protest and would not be intimidated.

In January 1957, black clergy from across the South met to coordinate local protests against segregation and to secure the ballot for blacks. They founded the Southern Christian Leadership Conference (SCLC) and chose King to head it. Although dominated by ministers, the SCLC owed much of its success to Ella Baker, a seasoned activist who came from New York to set up and run its office.

King's face on the cover of *Time* magazine in February 1957 marked his rapid rise to national and international fame. He crisscrossed the nation and the world, speaking to large audiences, raising funds, and meeting with other activists. In June 1958, Eisenhower extended his first invitation to black leaders, and King and three others met with the president. Meanwhile, in the late 1950s, the SCLC, NAACP, and CORE developed centers in several southern cities, paving the way for a mass movement that would revolutionize the racial system of the South.

Conclusion: Peace, Prosperity, and Unmet Challenges

At the American National Exhibition in Moscow in 1959, the consumer goods that Nixon proudly displayed to Khrushchev and the cold war competition that crackled through their conversation reflected two dominant themes of the 1950s: the prosperity of the U.S. economy and the superpowers' success in keeping cold war competition within the bounds of peace. The tremendous economic growth of the 1950s, which raised the standard of living for most Americans, resulted in part from the cold war: One of every ten American jobs depended directly on defense spending.

Affluence helped to change the very landscape of the United States. Suburban housing developments sprang up, interstate highways began to divide cities and connect the country, farms declined in number but grew in size, and population and industry moved south and west. Daily habits and even values of ordinary people changed as the economy became more service-oriented and the opportunity to buy a host of new products intensified the growth of a culture based on consumption. The general prosperity and seeming conformity, however, masked a number of developments and problems that Americans would face head-on in later years: rising resistance to an unjust racial system, a 20 percent poverty rate, the movement of married women into the labor force, and the development of a self-conscious youth generation.

Although the federal government's defense spending and housing, highway, and education subsidies played a large role in the economic boom, in general Eisenhower tried to curb domestic programs and let private enterprise have its way. His administration maintained the welfare state inherited from the Democrats but opposed further reforms. In global affairs, Eisenhower exercised restraint on large issues, recognizing the limits of U.S. power. In the name of deterrence, he promoted development of more destructive atomic weapons, but he resisted pressures for even larger defense budgets. Still, Eisenhower took from Truman the assumption that the United States must fight communism everywhere, and when movements in Iran, Guatemala, Cuba, and Vietnam seemed too radical, too friendly to communism, or too inimical to American economic interests, he tried to undermine them, often with secret operations.

Thus, although Eisenhower presided over eight years of peace and prosperity, his foreign policy inspired anti-Americanism, established dangerous precedents for the expansion of executive power, and forged commitments that future generations would deem unwise. As Eisenhower's successors took on the struggle against communism and grappled with the domestic challenges of race, poverty, and urban decay that he had avoided, the tranquillity and consensus of the 1950s would give way to the turbulence and conflict of the 1960s.

For further reading about the topics in this chapter, see the Online Bibliography at

www.bedfordstmartins.com/roarkcompact.

For additional first-hand accounts of this period, see pages 189–203 in Michael Johnson, ed., *Reading the American Past,* Second Edition, Volume II.

To assess your mastery of the material in this chapter, see the Online Study Guide at

www.bedfordstmartins.com/roarkcompact.

CHRONOLOGY

1952 Dwight D. Eisenhower elected president of United States.

I Love Lucy becomes number one television show.

1953 Government begins policy of termination of special status of American Indians and relocates thousands off reservations.

CIA engineers coup against government of Mohammed Mossadegh in Iran.

1954 CIA stages coup against government of Jacobo Arbenz in Guatemala.

France signs Geneva Accords, withdrawing from Vietnam.

United States organizes Southeast Asia Treaty Organization (SEATO) in wake of French defeat in Vietnam; Eisenhower administration begins aid program to government of South Vietnam.

Government launches Operation Wetback, a series of raids designed to seek out and deport illegal immigrants.

Ground broken in Pennsylvania for first commercial nuclear power plant.

U.S. Supreme Court declares segregation in public schools unconstitutional in *Brown v. Board of Education*.

Senate condemns Senator Joseph McCarthy.

1955 Eisenhower and Khrushchev meet in Geneva for first superpower summit since end of World War II.

1955– Montgomery, Alabama, bus boycott
1956 by African Americans focuses national attention on civil rights.

1956 Interstate Highway and Defense System Act involves federal government in road-building activities previously done by state and local governments.

Eisenhower reelected by landslide to second term.

Allen Ginsberg publishes poem *Howl*, expressing rebelliousness of Beat generation.

1957 Southern Christian Leadership Conference (SCLC) organizes and elects Martin Luther King Jr. its president.

Soviets launch *Sputnik*, first satellite to orbit Earth.

Labor union membership peaks at 27.1 percent of labor force.

1958 United States and Soviet Union suspend nuclear testing in atmosphere.

Eisenhower establishes the National Aeronautics and Space Administration (NASA).

1958– U.S. nuclear weapons stockpile
1960 triples in size.

1959 American National Exhibition in Moscow is scene of "kitchen debate" between Nixon and Khrushchev.

1960 Soviets shoot down U.S. U-2 spy plane, causing rift in U.S.-Soviet relations.

Women represent one-third of labor force; 35 percent of women work outside the home.

One-quarter of Americans live in suburbs.

"COUNTRY JOE" McDONALD'S GUITAR
Music was an omnipresent element of protest movements in the 1960s. Civil rights demonstrators sang "We Shall Overcome," antiwar rallies featured folk singers, and hippies turned on to acid rock. The guitar was the central musical instrument for each kind of music: traditional African American, folk, and rock. This wooden acoustic guitar belonged to "Country Joe" McDonald, who started his band, Country Joe and the Fish, at a draft protest in Oakland, California, in 1965. The band was one of many that originated in the San Francisco Bay area, but its popularity soon spread across the country.
The Oakland Museum of California.

A DECADE OF REBELLION AND REFORM

28

1960–1968

O N AUGUST 31, 1962, Fannie Lou Hamer boarded a bus carrying eighteen African Americans from Ruleville, Mississippi, to the county seat in Indianola, where they intended to register to vote. Blacks made up more than 60 percent of Sunflower County's population but only 1.2 percent of registered voters. Before young civil rights activists arrived in Ruleville to start a voter registration drive, Hamer recalled, "I didn't know that a Negro could register and vote." Her forty-five years of poverty, exploitation, and political disfranchisement typified the lives of most blacks in the rural south. The daughter of sharecroppers, Hamer began work in the cotton fields at age six, attending school in a one-room shack only from December to March, and only until she was twelve. In her late twenties, she married Perry Hamer and moved onto the plantation where he sharecropped. She worked in the fields, did domestic work for the plantation owner, and recorded the cotton sharecroppers brought in to be weighed.

At Indianola, Hamer and her companions defied a hostile, white, gun-carrying crowd to enter the county courthouse. Using a common practice to keep blacks from voting, the registrar gave Hamer a test requiring interpretation of an obscure section of the state constitution. Hamer's schooling had not included Mississippi's constitution; she, predictably, failed the test but resolved to try again. When she arrived home, her plantation-owner boss ordered her to withdraw her registration application or leave his land. Refusing to back down, Hamer left the plantation. Ten days later, sixteen bullets flew into the home of friends who housed her. Refusing to be intimidated, she tried again to register (and succeeded on the third attempt), attended a civil rights leadership training conference, and began to mobilize others to vote. In 1963, she and other activists were arrested in Winona, Mississippi, and beaten so brutally that Hamer went from the jail to the hospital, refusing to see her family, except for one sister, who could not recognize her battered face.

Fannie Lou Hamer's courage and determination made her a prominent figure in a movement that shook the nation's conscience, raised hopes for change, provided a model of protest for other groups, and transformed national policy. Although the federal government often tried to curb civil rights activists, the two Democratic presidents of the 1960s favored a progressive government and—helped by a prosperous economy—put solving social and economic problems high on the national agenda. After John F. Kennedy was assassinated in November 1963, Lyndon B. Johnson launched the Great Society—a multitude of efforts to promote racial justice, education, medical care, urban development, and environmental and economic health. Those who struggled for racial justice lost property, personal

MISSISSIPPI FREEDOM DEMOCRATIC PARTY RALLY
Fannie Lou Hamer (left foreground) and other activists sing at a rally outside the Democratic National Convention hall in 1964, supporting the Mississippi Freedom Democratic Party (MFDP) in its challenge to the all-white delegation sent by the regular Mississippi Democratic Party. Next to Hamer is Eleanor Holmes Norton, a civil rights lawyer, and Ella Baker (far right), who helped organize the Southern Christian Leadership Conference and later managed MFDP headquarters in Washington, D.C.
Matt Herron.

safety, and sometimes their lives, but by the end of the decade, law had caught up with the American ideal of equality.

Yet legal change did not go far enough. Although Congress passed watershed legislation and the Supreme Court issued pathbreaking civil rights decisions, the law affected little the deplorable economic conditions of African Americans, on which Hamer and others increasingly focused after 1965. Nor was the political establishment a consistently reliable ally, as Hamer found out in 1964 when President Johnson and his allies rebuffed black Mississippi Democrats' efforts to be represented at the Democratic National Convention. "We followed all the laws that the white people themselves made," she said, only to find that "the white man is not going to give up his power to us. . . .

We have to take for ourselves." By 1966, a minority of African American activists were demanding black power; the movement soon splintered, and white support sharply declined. Radicals who formed what came to be called the New Left scorned the Great Society for failing to strike at the roots of injustice in America's political and economic system. Conservatives protested that it went too far and condemned the challenge to American values and institutions mounted by blacks, students, and others.

Although disillusioned and often frustrated, Fannie Lou Hamer remained an activist until her death in 1977, mingling with new social movements stimulated by the black freedom struggle. In 1969, she supported Mississippi Valley State College students' demands for black studies courses and a greater voice in campus decisions. In 1972, she attended the founding conference of the National Women's Political Caucus, established to achieve greater representation for women in government.

Feminists and other groups, including ethnic minorities, environmentalists, gays and lesbians, benefited and borrowed from the ideas, tactics, and policy precedents of the civil rights movement. All of these movements aroused the moral sensibility of the nation and contributed to the greatest efforts to reconcile America's promise with reality since the New Deal.

Kennedy and the New Frontier

At the Democratic National Convention in 1960, John F. Kennedy announced that the United States stood "on the edge of a New Frontier . . . of unfulfilled hopes and threats," and he promised to confront "unsolved problems of peace and war, unconquered pockets of ignorance and prejudice, unanswered questions of poverty and surplus." Once in office, Kennedy instituted an aggressive foreign policy, but not until his final months did grassroots pressures spur him to launch a substantial assault on prejudice and poverty. Before his efforts reached fruition, an assassin took his life.

The Style and Substance of the New Frontier

John F. Kennedy grew up in privilege, the child of an Irish Catholic businessman who served in Franklin D. Roosevelt's administration and nourished political ambitions for his sons. Helped by a distinguished World War II navy record, Kennedy won election to the House of Representatives in 1946 and the Senate in 1952. Using his family's fortunes, the Massachusetts senator built a powerful political machine to win the Democratic presidential nomination in 1960.

His overwhelming financial advantage, handsome appearance, and dynamic style enabled Kennedy to woo liberals put off by his undistinguished record in Congress and to win a series of state primaries. A critical victory in heavily Protestant West Virginia muted the question of his Catholicism, an issue that had doomed Al Smith in 1928. After winning the Democratic nomination, Kennedy stunned nearly everyone by choosing Lyndon B. Johnson of Texas as his running mate. Although ticket balancing was a time-honored tradition, liberals detested the choice of a man whom they viewed as a typical southern conservative. The party platform, however, embodied liberal priorities, including the strongest civil rights plank the Democrats had ever endorsed.

The Republicans nominated Vice President Richard M. Nixon, who campaigned on his experience in the Eisenhower White House. With Nixon merely defending Eisenhower's policies, Kennedy seemed more dynamic, promising to strengthen America in the cold war, expand the welfare state, and jump-start the economy. The two candidates actually differed little, however, on defense and foreign policy questions.

Kennedy won the excruciatingly close election, helped by African American voters. Nixon gained 52 percent of the white vote, but the black preference for Kennedy contributed to his 120,000-vote margin overall and close victories in such key states as Illinois and Michigan. In addition, Lyndon Johnson helped the ticket carry most of the South; and a rise in unemployment in 1960 also favored the Democrats. Kennedy benefited too from the nation's first televised presidential debates, appearing cool, confident, and in command of the issues, beside a nervous, sweaty, and pale Nixon.

The Kennedy administration projected energy, idealism, and glamour. The first president to hold live televised press conferences, Kennedy charmed the press corps and the people with his grace, vigor, and self-mocking wit. In his private life, however, Kennedy had affairs with several women, recklessly exposing himself to blackmail and risking the dignity of his office. Journalists turned a blind eye, instead projecting warm images of an energetic, youthful president with his chic and cultured wife, Jacqueline.

A number of Kennedy's subcabinet and White House staff appointments shared the President's youth, Ivy League education, and competitiveness. Exuding confidence and eager to apply technology to problem solving, they welcomed danger and risk—characteristics that sometimes contributed to foreign policy crises under both Kennedy and Johnson. But they were not well schooled in practical politics. Longtime Speaker of the House Sam Rayburn said of them, "I'd feel a whole lot better . . . if just one of them had run for sheriff once."

At his inauguration, Kennedy called on Americans to cast off complacency and self-indulgence and serve the common good, imploring, "ask not what your country can do for you—ask what you can do for your country." He declared that a "new generation" was assuming leadership and described the cold war in a tone of crisis, emphasizing America's "role of defending freedom in its hour of maximum danger." Though Kennedy's idealism inspired many, especially the young, to replace self-interest with service to a larger cause, his address gave domestic problems short shrift and he failed to redeem campaign promises to expand the welfare state. Nor did he assume leadership on behalf of racial justice until late in his term, when civil rights activists gave him no choice.

Kennedy did win support for a $2 billion slum clearance and urban renewal program; the Area Redevelopment Act of 1961, offering incentives to businesses to locate in depressed areas; and the Manpower Development and Training Act of 1962, which provided training for the unemployed. But two key items on the Democratic agenda since the Truman administration, federal aid to education and health care for the elderly, got nowhere.

Two actions relating to women's rights had important long-term ramifications. In 1961, Assistant Secretary of Labor Esther Peterson persuaded Kennedy to strengthen his support among women by appointing a President's Commission on the Status of Women. Chaired by Eleanor Roosevelt, the commission reported its findings in October 1963, eight months after Betty Friedan attacked sex discrimination in *The Feminine Mystique*. Although not challenging women's traditional roles, the commission reported widespread discrimination against women and recommended remedies. Spawning state counterparts, the president's commission created networks of motivated women eager for action, who would launch a grassroots women's movement a few years later.

The president's commission highlighted a practice that women's organizations and labor unions had sought to eliminate for two decades: the age-old custom of paying women less than men for the same work. They achieved their goal when Kennedy signed the Equal Pay Act in June 1963, making wage disparities based solely on gender illegal. Within a few years, women began to win pay increases and back pay worth millions of dollars.

Poverty had gained Kennedy's attention in 1960, when he campaigned in Appalachia for the votes of the rural poor. In 1962, he read *The Other*

America, Michael Harrington's devastating account of the wretched conditions endured by more than one in every five Americans. "A rising tide lifts all boats" expressed Kennedy's belief that economic growth could eradicate poverty and solve most social problems. He also focused on growth to make the nation more competitive with the Soviet Union. Key economic advisers argued that infusing money into the economy by reducing taxes would increase demand, boost production, and decrease unemployment. To that end, Kennedy asked Congress to pass an enormous tax cut in 1963. This use of fiscal policy to stimulate the economy even when there was no recession gained the name "the new economics."

Kennedy did not live to see approval of his bill. Passed in February 1964, the law contributed to the greatest economic boom since World War II. Unemployment dropped to 4.1 percent, and the gross national product shot up by 7 to 9 percent annually between 1964 and 1966. Some liberal critics of the tax cut, however, maintained that economic growth alone would not eliminate poverty, arguing instead for increased spending on social programs.

The summer of 1963 marked a turning point in Kennedy's attitude toward domestic problems. In addition to his tax cut initiative, he asked aides to plan an attack on poverty and issued a dramatic call for a comprehensive civil rights bill. Whether he could have achieved these breakthroughs was left unanswered by his assassination on November 22, 1963.

Assassination of a President

The murder of the president shocked Americans as had no other event since the end of World War II. Within minutes of the shooting—which occurred as the Kennedy motorcade passed through Dallas, Texas—radio and television broadcast the unfolding horror to the nation. Millions watched the return of *Air Force One* to Washington bearing the president's coffin, his widow in her bloodstained suit, and the new president, Lyndon Baines Johnson, who had already taken the oath of office.

Stunned Americans struggled with what had happened and why. Soon after the assassination, police arrested Lee Harvey Oswald and concluded that he had fired the shots from a nearby building. Two days later, as a television audience watched Oswald being transferred from one jail to another, a local nightclub operator, Jack Ruby, killed him.

JOHN F. KENNEDY'S FUNERAL
For a few days following November 22, 1963, normal life stopped in the United States. Schools and businesses were closed, while tens of thousands of Americans traveled to Washington, D.C., to file past Kennedy's coffin in the rotunda of the Capitol. The relatively new medium of television unified the nation, as it allowed millions of viewers to experience every moment of that long, terrible weekend, culminating in the funeral procession, shown here. The president's widow, Jacqueline Kennedy, is escorted in the procession by the president's brothers Robert (left) and Edward (right).
© Henri Dauman NYC.

Suspicions arose that Ruby murdered Oswald to cover up a conspiracy by ultraconservative Texans who hated Kennedy, or by Communists who supported Castro's Cuba. To get at the truth, President Johnson appointed a commission headed by Chief Justice Earl Warren, which concluded in September 1964 that both Oswald and Ruby had acted alone. Although several experts pointed to errors and omissions in the report, and some contested the lone-killer explanation, most scholars agreed with the general conclusions of the Warren Commission.

Debate also continued over how to assess Kennedy's domestic record. It had been unremarkable in his first two years, but his initiatives on taxes, civil rights, and poverty in 1963 suggested an important shift. Whether Kennedy could have persuaded Congress to enact his proposals cannot be known. In the words of journalist James Reston,

"What was killed was not only the president but the promise. . . . He never reached his meridian: We saw him only as a rising sun."

Liberalism at High Tide: Johnson and the Great Society

Within six months of becoming president, Lyndon Johnson found a theme for his administration. In May 1964, he announced the goal of a "Great Society, [which] rests on abundance and liberty for all. It demands an end to poverty and racial injustice." In pursuing that Great Society, Johnson won from Congress three civil rights acts and a host of laws dealing with poverty, education, medical care, housing, consumer protection, the environment, and more. While not achieving all of Johnson's goals, the legislation of the 1960s represented the high tide of liberalism in the last half of the twentieth century.

Fulfilling the Kennedy Promise

Lyndon Johnson assumed the presidency with a wealth of political experience. A self-made man from the Texas hill country, he had won election to the House of Representatives in 1937 and to the Sen-

THE "JOHNSON TREATMENT"
Abe Fortas was a distinguished lawyer who had argued one of the major criminal rights cases, **Gideon v. Wainwright** *(1963), before the Supreme Court and who was a close friend and adviser to President Lyndon Johnson. This photograph of the president and Fortas taken in July 1965 illustrates how Johnson used his body as well as his voice to bend people to his will.*
Yoichi R. Okamoto/LBJ Library Collection.

ate in 1948. By 1955, he had secured the top post of Senate majority leader, which he used brilliantly to forge a Democratic consensus on the Civil Rights Acts of 1957 and 1960 and other programs.

Johnson's coarse wit, extreme vanity, and Texas accent put off many who preferred the sophisticated Kennedy style. Lacking his predecessor's eloquence, Johnson excelled behind the scenes, where he could entice or threaten legislators into support of his objectives. The famous "Johnson treatment" became legendary. In his ability to achieve his overriding goal of consensus—and in the means to which he was willing to resort—he had few peers in American history.

Mobilizing emotions aroused by the assassination, he asked Congress to act so that "John Fitzgerald Kennedy did not live or die in vain." By trimming the federal budget and promising government frugality, he won over fiscal conservatives and signed Kennedy's tax cut bill in February 1964. Still more revolutionary was the Civil Rights Act of July 1964, the strongest such measure since Reconstruction, and one which required every ounce of Johnson's political skills to win sufficient votes from Republicans and southern Democrats.

Fast on the heels of the Civil Rights Act came a response to Johnson's call for "an unconditional war on poverty." The Economic Opportunity Act of 1964 authorized ten programs under a newly created Office of Economic Opportunity, allocating $800 million for the first year (about 1 percent of the federal budget). Many provisions targeted impoverished youth—from Head Start, a preschool program to work-study grants for college students and a Job Corps providing job training. There were also loans to businesses willing to hire the long-term unemployed; aid to small farmers; and the Volunteers in Service to America (VISTA) program, which paid modest wages to volunteers working with the disadvantaged. A legal services program provided lawyers for the poor, leading to lawsuits that enforced their rights to welfare programs.

The most novel and controversial part of the law, the Community Action Program (CAP), required "maximum feasible participation" of the poor themselves in antipoverty programs. Unlike other aspects of the war on poverty, this provision challenged the system itself. Poor people began to organize community action programs to take control of their neighborhoods and to reform welfare agencies, school boards, police departments, housing authorities, and the like. When mayors complained that activists were attacking local governments and "fostering class struggle," Johnson directed antipoverty officials to back off from genuine representation for the poor. Although CAP failed to live up to its promise, for the first time people usually excluded from government gained an opportunity to act on their own behalf and to develop leadership skills.

Completing the Great Society Agenda

Having steered the nation through the assassination trauma and established his capacity for national leadership, Johnson projected stability and security. With the economy booming, few voters proved willing to risk the dramatic change promised by his Republican opponent in the 1964 election, Barry M. Goldwater. His nomination reflecting the growth of the right wing in the GOP, the Arizona senator attacked the welfare state and suggested using nuclear weapons if necessary to crush communism in Vietnam. Although Goldwater captured five Southern states, Johnson achieved a record-breaking landslide of 61 percent of the popular vote. On his coattails came resounding Democratic majorities in the House (295–140) and Senate (68–32).

"I want to see a whole bunch of coonskins on the wall," Johnson told his aides, using a hunting analogy to stress his ambitious legislative goals. In the sheer amount and breadth of new laws, Johnson succeeded mightily, persuading Congress to act on discrimination, poverty, education, medical care, housing, consumer and environmental protections, and more. Public opinion polls gave unusually high marks to both the president and Congress. Reporters called the legislation of the Eighty-ninth Congress (1965–1966) "a political miracle."

The Economic Opportunity Act of 1964 was just the opening shot in the war on poverty. Congress increased the program's funding in 1965 to $2 billion and passed two new initiatives—the Appalachian Regional Development Act and the Public Works and Economic Development Act. Targeting depressed regions bypassed by the general economic boom, these measures—like the tax cut of 1964—sought to help the poor indirectly by stimulating economic growth and providing jobs through road building and other public works projects.

A second approach endeavored to equip the poor with the skills necessary to find jobs. The largest assault on poverty through education was

the Elementary and Secondary Education Act of 1965, which for the first time authorized federal funds to aid school districts. The law allocated funds based on the number of poor children districts educated and provided equipment and supplies to private and parochial schools to be used for poor children. That same year Congress passed the Higher Education Act, vastly expanding federal assistance to colleges and universities for buildings, programs, scholarships, and low-interest student loans.

Other antipoverty efforts provided direct aid, like a new food stamp program that gave poor people greater choice in obtaining food. Rent supplements also allowed some poor families more options, enabling them to avoid public housing projects. In addition, with the Model Cities Act, Congress authorized more than $1 billion to improve conditions in the nation's slums.

The federal government's responsibility for health care grew even more. Trimming down Truman's proposed plan for government-sponsored universal care, Johnson focused on the elderly, who constituted a large portion of the nation's poor. Congress responded with the Medicare program, providing the elderly with universal compulsory medical insurance financed largely through Social Security taxes. A separate program, Medicaid, authorized federal grants to supplement state-paid medical care for poor people under sixty-five.

Pressured by the black freedom struggle, Johnson got Congress to pass the Voting Rights Act of 1965, which banned literacy tests, like the one that stymied Fannie Lou Hamer, and authorized federal intervention to ensure African Americans' access to the voting booth. Another form of discrimination fell with the Immigration and Nationality Act of 1965, which abolished the fifty-year-old quotas based on national origins that were biased against immigrants from areas outside northern and western Europe. It did, however, maintain caps on the number of immigrants and for the first time limited those from the Western Hemisphere.

Benefits of the Great Society reached well beyond the poverty-stricken. A growing consumer movement led by liberal activist Ralph Nader and others won legislation to make automobiles safer and to raise standards for the food, drug, and cosmetics industries. In 1965, Johnson became the first president to send Congress a special message on the environment, obtaining measures to control water and air pollution and to preserve the natural beauty of the American landscape. The National Arts and Humanities Act of 1965 funded artists, musicians, writers, and scholars and brought their work to public audiences.

The flood of reform legislation dwindled to a trickle after 1966, when midterm elections reduced the Democrats' huge majorities in Congress, and a backlash against government programs arose. Even though most poor people were white, whites tended to associate antipoverty programs with African Americans and expressed their opposition with buttons reading "I fight poverty—I work." The Vietnam War dealt the largest blow to reform, diverting the president's attention from domestic affairs and spawning an antiwar movement that crippled his leadership. Even more damaging, the war's cost sky-rocketed, increasing the federal deficit, and exerting inflationary pressures on the economy.

Against these odds, in 1968 Johnson pried out of Congress one more civil rights law, which banned discrimination in housing, and he secured a new housing program. The National Housing Act of 1968 authorized an enormous increase in construction of low-income housing—1.7 million units over three years—and, by leaving construction and ownership in private hands, a new way of providing it. Government-guaranteed low-interest loans spurred developers to build housing for the needy and enabled poor people to purchase those houses.

Assessing the War on Poverty

Measured by statistics, the reduction in poverty in the 1960s was notable. The number of impoverished Americans fell from forty million in 1959 to twenty-five million in 1968, from over 20 percent of the population to around 13 percent (Figure 28.1). Attitudes shifted too, as more people saw poverty arising from economic and social conditions rather than from individuals' shortcomings. Especially through the community action programs, poor people gained more control of their circumstances and a sense of their right to a fairer share of America's bounty.

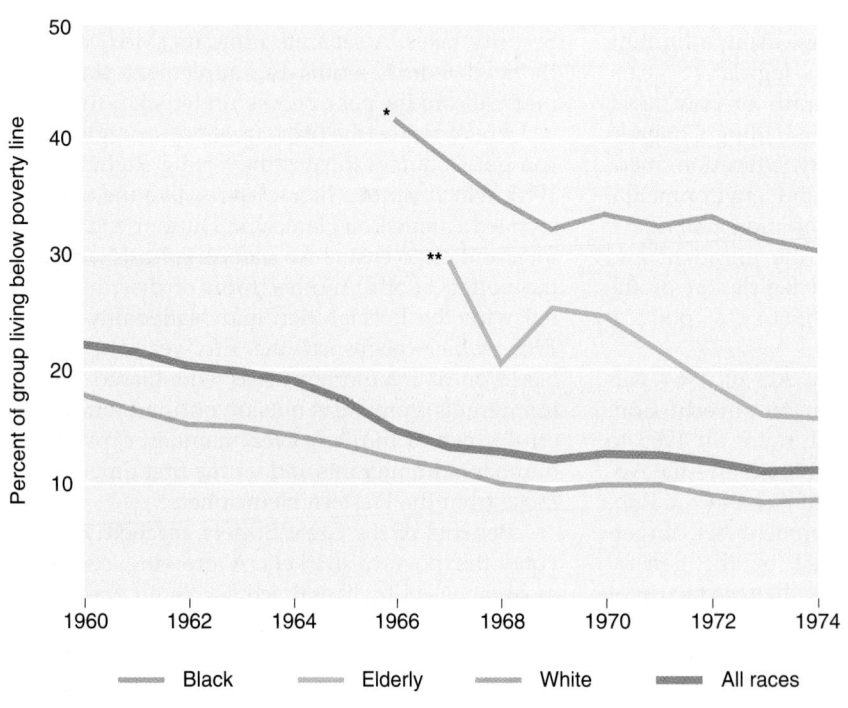

**FIGURE 28.1
Poverty in the United States, 1960–1974**

The short-term effects of economic growth and the Great Society's attack on poverty are seen here. Which groups experienced the sharpest decline in poverty, and what might account for the differences?

*Statistics on blacks for years 1960–1965 not available.
**Statistics on the elderly for years 1960–1966 not available.

Certain groups fared much better than others, however. Large numbers of the aged and members of male-headed families rose out of poverty, while the plight of female-headed families actually worsened. Although African American family income grew from 54 percent of white family income to 61 percent, whites escaped poverty at a faster rate than blacks, who constituted one-third of the poor population at decade's end. Moreover, despite large increases in subsidies for food stamps, housing, medical care, and Aid to Families with Dependent Children (AFDC), a program launched by the New Deal, no significant redistribution of income resulted. The poorest 20 percent of the population received 5.1 percent of total national income in 1964 and 5.4 percent in 1974.

Conservatives charged that Great Society programs discouraged initiative by giving the poor "handouts." Critics on the left claimed that the emphasis on training and education placed the responsibility for poverty on the poor themselves rather than on an economic system that had failed them. Most training programs prepared graduates for low-level jobs and could not guarantee employment. Surveys in 1966 and 1967, for example, found 28 percent of Job Corps graduates unemployed six months after finishing their training.

Who reaped the greatest benefits from Great Society programs? Critics noted that most of the funds for economically depressed areas built highways and thus helped the construction industry. Real estate developers, investors, and moderate-income families benefited most from the National Housing Act of 1968. Observing that in slum clearance programs, commercial development and high-income housing often displaced poor families, blacks called urban renewal "Negro removal." Physicians' fees and hospital costs soared after enactment of Medicare and Medicaid.

Some critics of the War on Poverty argued that ending poverty required a major redistribution of income—raising taxes and using those funds in the public sector to create jobs, overhaul social welfare systems, and rebuild slums. Great Society programs did invest more heavily in the public sector, but to wage the war on poverty Johnson relied on economic growth rather than new taxes on the rich or middle class to increase revenues. Determined to avoid conflict, Johnson would not take from the advantaged to provide for the poor. Economic prosperity allowed spending for the poor to rise and sig-

nificantly improved the lives of millions, but that spending never approached the amounts necessary to claim victory in the War on Poverty.

The Second Reconstruction

Unlike many Great Society reforms, which failed to live up to their promise and provoked widespread criticism, the civil rights movement effected a revolution in the legal status of African Americans that won widespread acceptance. The first Reconstruction in the aftermath of the Civil War had ended slavery and written racial equality into the Constitution; the second Reconstruction a century later made that constitutional guarantee a reality. That accomplishment depended heavily on the courage and determination of black people themselves. In the words of Sheyann Webb, one of the thousands of marchers in the 1965 Selma, Alabama, campaign for voting rights, "We were just people, ordinary people, and we did it."

The Flowering of the Black Freedom Struggle

The Montgomery bus boycott of 1956–1957 had given racial issues national visibility, produced a leader in Martin Luther King Jr., and demonstrated the effectiveness of mass organization. In the 1960s, protest underwent a major change, mobilizing blacks into direct and personal confrontation with the people and institutions that segregated and discriminated against them: lunch counters, department stores, public parks and libraries, buses and depots, and voting registrars.

Massive direct action began in February 1960, when four African American students at North Carolina A&T College in Greensboro sat at the whites-only Woolworth's lunch counter and requested service. Within days, hundreds of young people joined their demonstration, and others launched sit-ins in thirty-one cities in eight southern states. In April, Ella Baker, executive secretary of the Southern Christian Leadership Conference (SCLC), called activists together from campuses across the South. Choosing independence from the older civil rights organizations, they founded the Student Nonviolent Coordinating Committee (SNCC, pronounced "snick"), creating a decentralized, nonhierarchical structure that encouraged leadership and decision making at the grassroots level.

Although rejecting organizational patterns of the older groups, SNCC initially embraced civil disobedience and the nonviolence principles of Martin Luther King Jr. While directly confronting their oppressors, students would stand up for their rights, but they would not practice self-defense if attacked. At SNCC's founding conference, minister James Lawson defined a strategy for blacks that he believed could change the hearts of their antagonists: "We affirm . . . nonviolence as a foundation of our purpose, the presupposition of our faith, and the manner of our action." With its appeal to human conscience, "nonviolence nurtures the atmosphere in which reconciliation and justice become actual possibilities."

The activists' optimism and commitment to nonviolence soon met severe testing. Although some cities quietly met student demands, more typically authorities and local citizens reacted with violence. Hostile whites poured food over demonstrators, burned them with cigarettes, called them "niggers," and pelted them with rocks. Local police went after protesters with dogs, clubs, fire hoses, and tear gas; they arrested more than 3,600 civil rights demonstrators in the year following the Greensboro sit-in.

In May 1961, the Congress of Racial Equality (CORE) organized Freedom Rides to integrate interstate transportation in the South. Six whites and seven blacks boarded two buses in Washington, D.C., bound for New Orleans. They crossed the color line unharmed in Virginia and North Carolina, but in Alabama white hoodlums bombed a bus and beat the riders with baseball bats. When some Freedom Riders turned back, SNCC members took their places. After a huge mob attacked the activists in Montgomery, Attorney General Robert Kennedy dispatched federal marshals to restore order. But when the buses reached Jackson, Mississippi, the Freedom Riders were promptly arrested, and several hundred spent part of the summer in Mississippi jails.

Encouraged by Kennedy administration officials who viewed voter registration as less controversial than civil disobedience (and more likely to benefit the Democratic Party), SNCC and other groups began a Voter Education Project in the summer of 1961. Seeking to register black voters in the Deep South, they too met violence. Whites bombed black churches, threw tenant farmers out of their homes, and beat and jailed activists like Fannie Lou Hamer. In June 1963, a white man gunned down Mississippi NAACP leader Medgar Evers in front of his house in Jackson; the murderer eluded conviction until the 1990s.

Television revealed to the world the brutality of southern resistance to racial equality in April 1963, when Martin Luther King Jr. launched a campaign in Birmingham, Alabama, to integrate public facilities and open jobs to African Americans. The city's police chief, Eugene "Bull" Connor, responded with police dogs, electric cattle prods, and high-pressure hoses. Hundreds of demonstrators, including school-age children, went to jail, and firebombs exploded at King's motel and his brother's house. Four months later, a bomb killed four black children attending Sunday school in Birmingham.

The largest demonstration drew 250,000 blacks and whites to the nation's capital in August 1963, where King put his indelible stamp on the day. Speaking from the Lincoln Memorial and moved by the intense emotions of the crowd, King drew on all the passion and skills that made him the greatest orator of his day. His words came from the Bible, Negro spirituals, and the nation's patriotic anthems. "I have a dream," he repeated again and again, that "the sons of former slaves and the sons of former slave owners will be able to sit down together at the table of brotherhood." With the crowd roaring in support, he imagined the day "when all of God's children . . . will be able to join hands and sing . . . 'Free at last, free at last; thank God Almighty, we are free at last.'"

Yet the euphoria of the March on Washington quickly faded as activists returned to continued violence in the South. In 1964, the Mississippi Freedom Summer Project mobilized more than a thousand northern college students to conduct a voter education registration drive. Resistance was fierce.

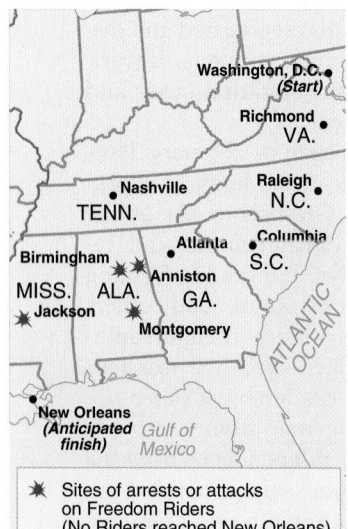

Sites of arrests or attacks on Freedom Riders (No Riders reached New Orleans)

Civil Rights Freedom Rides, May 1961

LUNCH COUNTER SIT-IN
John Salter Jr., a professor at Tougaloo College, and students Joan Trumpauer and Anne Moody take part in a 1963 sit-in at the Woolworth's lunch counter in Jackson, Mississippi. Shortly before this photograph was taken, whites had thrown two students to the floor and police had arrested one student. Salter was spattered with mustard and ketchup. Moody would publish a popular book in 1968 about her experiences in the black freedom struggle, **Coming of Age in Mississippi.**
State Historical Society of Wisconsin.

www.bedfordstmartins.com/roarkcompact SEE THE ONLINE STUDY GUIDE for more help in assessing this image.

By the end of the summer, only twelve hundred new voters had been allowed to register; whites had killed several activists, beaten eighty, arrested more than a thousand, and burned thirty-five black churches. Less apparent resistance came from the federal government itself, as the FBI spied on King and other leaders and expanded its activities to "expose, disrupt, misdirect, discredit, or otherwise neutralize" black protest.

Still the movement persisted. In March 1965, Alabama troopers used such fierce force to turn back a fifty-four-mile march from Selma to the state capitol in Montgomery that the incident earned the name "Bloody Sunday." After several days, President Johnson called up the Alabama National Guard to protect the marchers. Before the Selma campaign was over, whites had killed three demonstrators. Battered and hospitalized on Bloody Sunday, John Lewis, chairman of the SNCC (and later, a congressman), managed to make the final march to the capitol, which he counted as one of the most meaningful events in his life: "In October of that year the Voting Rights bill was passed and we all felt we'd had a part in it."

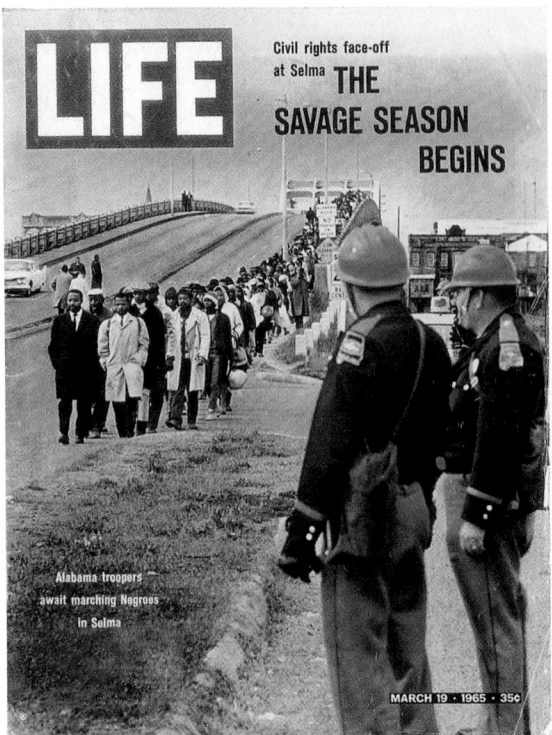

THE SELMA MARCH FOR VOTING RIGHTS
*In 1963, the Student Nonviolent Coordinating Com-
mittee (SNCC) began a campaign for voting rights in
Selma, Alabama, where white officials had registered
only 335 of the 15,000 African Americans of voting
age. As often happened, after younger activists had
gotten things started, Martin Luther King Jr. came to
Selma in January 1965. He planned a fifty-four-mile
march from Selma to Montgomery, the state capital,
to insist that blacks be registered, but, warned of a
serious threat on his life, King did not lead the
march. Here John Lewis of SNCC and Hosea
Williams of the Southern Christian Leadership
Conference head the line of marchers just before,
as Lewis recalled, "They came at us like a human
wave, a blur of blue uniforms, billy clubs, bullwhips
and tear gas," beating him to the ground. Looking at
the words as well as the photo on Life's cover, how
did this popular magazine choose to portray the
civil rights movement? What alternative visuals
might have been on the cover?*
Life magazine © 1965 Time, Inc.

The Response in Washington

Civil rights leaders would have to wear sneakers,
Lyndon Johnson said, if they were going to keep up
with him. But both Kennedy and Johnson acted
more in response to the black freedom struggle than
on their own initiative, moving only when events
gave them little choice. Kennedy sent federal
marshals to Montgomery to protect the Freedom
Riders, dispatched federal troops to enable air force
veteran James H. Meredith to enroll in the all-white
University of Mississippi in 1962, and called up the
Alabama National Guard during the Birmingham
demonstrations in May 1963. But, well aware of the
political costs of deploying federal force, Kennedy
told activists pleading for more federal protection
that law enforcement was a local matter.

In June 1963, Kennedy finally made good on his
promise to seek legislation to enforce voting rights
and equal access to public schools and accommodations. Pointing to the injustice suffered by blacks,
Kennedy asked white Americans, "Who among us
would then be content with the counsels of patience
and delay?" Johnson took up Kennedy's commitment with passion, assisted by a number of factors.
Television conveyed scenes of violence against
peaceful demonstrators that appalled many viewers across the nation. The resulting public support,
the "Johnson treatment," and the president's ability
to turn the measure into a memorial to the martyred
Kennedy all produced the most important civil
rights law since Reconstruction.

The Civil Rights Act of 1964 guaranteed access
for all Americans to public accommodations, public education, employment, and voting, thus sounding the death knell for the South's system of segregation and discrimination. Title VII of the measure,
banning discrimination in employment, also attacked racial inequality outside the South. In addition, Title VII outlawed sex discrimination in employment. Introduced by a conservative southerner
in hopes of defeating the entire bill, the sex provision nonetheless had the support of some women's
rights advocates. Because Title VII applied not just
to wages but to every aspect of employment, including hiring and promotion, it represented a giant
step toward equal employment opportunity for
white women as well as racial minorities.

Responding to black voter registration drives in
the South, Johnson soon demanded a law that
would remove "every remaining obstacle to the
right and the opportunity to vote." In August
1965, he signed the Voting Rights Act, which
empowered the federal government to act directly to enable African Americans to register and
vote. A major transformation began in southern
politics. (See Map 28.1 and "Historical Question,"
page 736.)

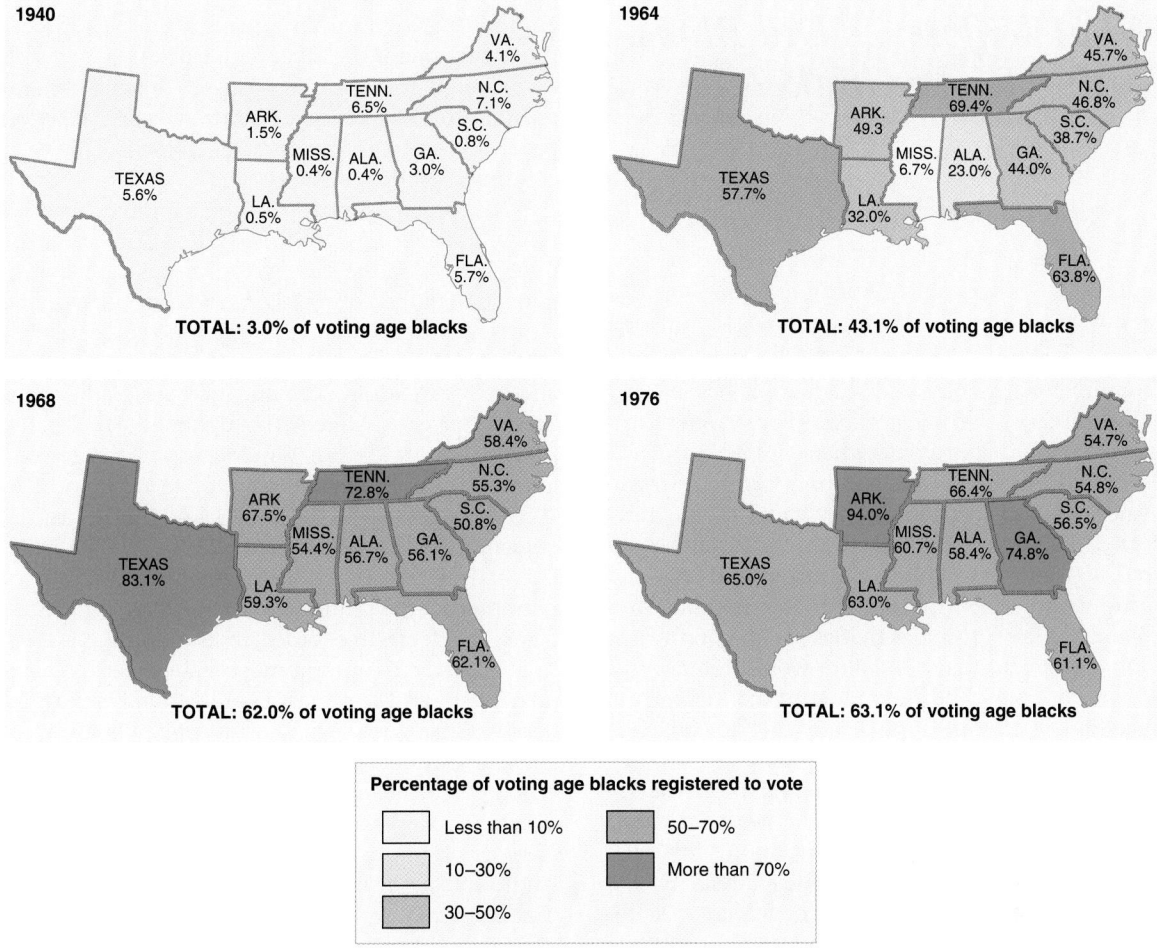

1940

VA.
4.1%

TENN.
6.5%

N.C.
7.1%

ARK.
1.5%

S.C.
0.8%

MISS.
0.4%

ALA.
0.4%

GA.
3.0%

TEXAS
5.6%

LA.
0.5%

FLA.
5.7%

TOTAL: 3.0% of voting age blacks

1964

VA.
45.7%

TENN.
69.4%

N.C.
46.8%

ARK.
49.3

S.C.
38.7%

MISS.
6.7%

ALA.
23.0%

GA.
44.0%

TEXAS
57.7%

LA.
32.0%

FLA.
63.8%

TOTAL: 43.1% of voting age blacks

1968

VA.
58.4%

TENN.
72.8%

N.C.
55.3%

ARK
67.5%

S.C.
50.8%

MISS.
54.4%

ALA.
56.7%

GA.
56.1%

TEXAS
83.1%

LA.
59.3%

FLA
62.1%

TOTAL: 62.0% of voting age blacks

1976

VA.
54.7%

TENN.
66.4%

N.C.
54.8%

ARK.
94.0%

S.C.
56.5%

MISS.
60.7%

ALA.
58.4%

GA.
74.8%

TEXAS
65.0%

LA.
63.0%

FLA.
61.1%

TOTAL: 63.1% of voting age blacks

Percentage of voting age blacks registered to vote

Less than 10%   50–70%

10–30%   More than 70%

30–50%

MAP 28.1

The Rise of the African American Vote, 1940–1976

Voting rates of southern blacks increased gradually in the 1940s and 1950s but shot up dramatically in the Deep South after the Voting Rights Act of 1965 provided for federal agents to enforce African Americans' right to vote.

READING THE MAP: When did the biggest change in African American voter registration occur in the South? Which states had the highest and which had the lowest voter registration rates in 1968?

CONNECTIONS: What role did African American voters play in the 1960 election? What were the targets of three major voting drives in the 1960s?

www.bedfordstmartins.com/roarkcompact   SEE THE ONLINE STUDY GUIDE for more help in analyzing this map.

Two more measures completed Johnson's civil rights record. The Civil Rights Act of 1968 banned racial discrimination in housing and jury selection and provided for federal intervention when states failed to protect civil rights workers from violence.

In addition, Johnson used his presidential authority in September 1965 to issue Executive Order 11246, which not only banned discrimination by employers holding government contracts (affecting about one-third of the labor force) but also

What Difference Did Black Voting Rights Make?

BORN TO POOR BLACK SHARECROPPERS in the Mississippi Delta, Unita Blackwell hearkened in church one Sunday in 1964 when a SNCC worker talked about voter registration. The very next day she went to the courthouse where, as had happened to Fannie Lou Hamer and hundreds of other African Americans, officials refused her application. Undeterred, she succeeded on the third try, threw herself into activism as a SNCC organizer, and saw her share of jail cells. In fact, she and her husband planned their protest activities so that only one would risk arrest and the other would remain free to care for their child. A founder of the Mississippi Freedom Democratic Party, established to challenge the all-white state organization, Blackwell saw the challenge fall to compromise at the 1964 Democratic National Convention. But four years later, she participated in the national convention with Mississippi's reconfigured biracial delegation. Subsequently, she served as vice chair of the state Democratic Party and on the Democratic National Committee. When her small town of Mayersville incorporated in 1976, Blackwell won election as its first mayor and the first black female mayor in Mississippi.

Blackwell's career is but one measure of the transformations generated by African Americans' struggle for the most basic right of citizenship. Their determination to register to vote and the resulting resistance and violence of southern whites created a crisis that the federal government could not ignore. Its response—the Voting Rights Act of 1965 and subsequent extensions—suspended the literacy tests that had been used to disqualify blacks but not whites and brought electoral operations in most southern states under federal supervision. The law required the Justice Department to approve in advance any changes in state procedures that might disadvantage black voters, and it empowered the attorney general to send federal agents to observe registration and election processes and even to register voters in areas of continued white resistance.

"Legislation is not self-implementing," warned NAACP leader Roy Wilkins. "There is work to be done." As was the case with its passage, implementation of the Voting Rights Act depended on the efforts of African Americans themselves. More than two hundred voter registration drives between 1966 and 1968 paid off in dramatic increases in the numbers of blacks registered. Throughout the South, the proportion of African Americans on voter rolls jumped from 43 percent in 1964 to 62 percent in 1968. In Mississippi, the total leaped from just 6.7 percent in 1964 to 68 percent in 1968.

African Americans also gained political offices in unprecedented numbers. Fewer than two dozen blacks held elective office in the South in 1964. In 1970, they claimed almost 500 elected government posts, and two years later the number reached nearly 1,200. Just seven years after whites bludgeoned civil rights activists during the Selma voting drive, black candidates won half of the ten seats on Selma's city council. With the victories of Barbara Jordan from Houston, Texas, and Andrew Young from Atlanta, Georgia, in 1972, the former Confederacy sent its first African Americans to the House of Representatives since Reconstruction.

Black electoral success was not limited to the South. Across the nation, African Americans held 1,500 elected positions in 1970, and by 1990 that number exceeded 7,000. The greatest progress came at the local level. The number of black city council members vaulted from 552 in 1970 to nearly 3,000 in 1989, and the number of black mayors grew sixfold, to more than 300, in the 1990s. The total of black representatives in Congress inched up from 10 in 1970 to 25 in 1990 and to 37 in the 1996 elections.

Electoral success translated into tangible benefits. When black officials took office, their constituents saw improvements in public facilities, police protection, roads, trash collection, and other

REGISTERING TO VOTE
Two civil rights volunteers during the 1964 Mississippi Freedom Summer campaign help a couple fill out voter registration forms. The form included a question asking the applicant to interpret a portion of the state's constitution, one of the ways white officials kept African Americans from voting in southern states before passage of the Voting Rights Act in 1965.
Charles Moore/Black Star.

basic services. Referring to Unita Blackwell's accomplishments as mayor, a Mayersville resident noted, "She brought in the water tower. Mostly it was pumps then. . . . Sewage, too. There wasn't nothing but those little old outdoor houses." Another constituent pointed to "old folks' houses. And paved streets. I grew up here when they wasn't

paved." Black local officials also awarded more government jobs to African Americans and contracts to minority businesses. Elected mayor of Atlanta in 1973, Maynard Jackson appointed a black police chief and increased blacks' share of city jobs from 42 to 51 percent.

Most black officials had far less power than Jackson, but even when they were outnumbered by whites, they could at least introduce issues of concern to blacks that whites had ignored, and they gained access to information about behind-the-scenes government. An African American serving on a city council in Florida pointed out that "no matter what happened, [my white colleagues] knew I was listening to everything that went on." Activist Fannie Lou Hamer noted the psychological benefits of electoral progress. When blacks had no political voice, she recalled, "some white folks would drive past your house in a pickup truck with guns hanging up on the back and give you hate stares. . . . Those same people now call me Mrs. Hamer."

Yet increased political power did not guarantee African Americans economic equality or even material security. Their minority status in the population and their residential dispersion, combined with many whites' disinclination to vote for blacks, meant that even by 1990 African Americans occupied fewer than 2 percent of all elected positions in the nation. As African Americans looked to increase their political force and shape policy to meet their needs, they sought to revive grassroots activism and form coalitions with other racial and ethnic groups. In addition, they considered a number of electoral strategies to solidify black and minority strength in a majoritarian system: reducing the number of at-large elections, which dilute minorities' power, and increasing the number of single-member district systems; monitoring electoral redistricting to ensure as many black-majority districts as possible; and supporting proportionate or cumulative voting.

Despite the limited reach of black enfranchisement, most experts nonetheless view the voting rights revolution as the most successful of all civil rights initiatives. As Unita Blackwell put it, "We didn't have nothing, and we changed the whole world with nothing. We changed a whole outlook."

required them to take affirmative action to ensure equal opportunity. Extended to cover women in 1967, the controversial affirmative action program was called "reverse discrimination" by many people who incorrectly thought that affirmative action required rigid quotas and employing unqualified candidates. In fact, the order required employers to counter the effects of centuries of oppression by acting forcefully to align their labor force with the available pool of qualified candidates. Within a few years, most large businesses came to see affirmative action as a good employment practice.

Black Nationalism and the End of the Civil Rights Coalition

By 1966, civil rights activism was undergoing dramatic changes. Black protest extended from the South to the entire nation, demanded not just legal equality but also economic justice, and no longer held nonviolence as its basic principle. None of these developments was entirely new. For example, some African Americans had armed themselves in self-defense since Reconstruction, and even in the 1950s and early 1960s many activists doubted that demonstrators' passive suffering in the face of violence would change the hearts of racists. Still, the black freedom struggle began to show a different face, one more threatening to the white majority.

In part the new emphases resulted from earlier successes, as legal oppression receded only to reveal other injustices more subtle but no less pervasive. Integration and legal equality did little to improve the material conditions of blacks; and black rage at oppressive conditions erupted in waves of urban riots across the country every summer from 1964 to 1968. The Watts district of Los Angeles in 1965, Newark and Detroit in 1967, and the nation's capital in 1968 saw the most destruction, but hundreds of cities erupted in violence, usually after an incident between white police and local blacks. Rioting in Detroit resulted in 43 deaths, 7,000 arrests, 1,300 destroyed buildings, and 2,700 looted shops. "Our nation is moving toward two societies, one black, one white—separate and unequal," warned a commission investigating the turmoil, but little was done about the basic conditions from which riots sprang.

King himself expanded the scope of the struggle. In 1965, the SCLC mounted a drive for better jobs, schools, and housing in Chicago. King planned

a Poor People's March to Washington in 1968 to seek more adequate funding of the antipoverty program. Similarly, following her drive for voter registration, Fannie Lou Hamer channeled much of her energy into projects to ameliorate poverty in Mississippi.

In the North, a powerful new challenge to the ethos of nonviolence arose. Malcolm Little grew up in poverty and went to prison at the age of twenty-one for attempted burglary. There he educated himself, joined the Nation of Islam, whose adherents called themselves Black Muslims, and changed his name to Malcolm X, to symbolize the African identity stripped from his ancestors. Released from jail in 1952, he went to work for the Nation of Islam, which drew on a long African American tradition of nationalism. Malcolm X attracted a large following, especially in urban ghettos, calling for black pride and autonomy, separation from the "corrupt [white] society," and self-defense against white violence. In 1964, he left the Nation, began to cultivate a wider constituency, and expressed an openness to working with whites. At a Harlem rally in February 1965, three Black Muslims shot and killed him.

The ideas espoused by Malcolm X resonated among younger activists. At a June 1966 rally in Greenwood, Mississippi, SNCC chairman Stokely Carmichael gave those principles a new name. "We want black power," he shouted again and again. "Black power" quickly became the rallying cry in SNCC and CORE. Though embraced fully by only a minority of African Americans, the black power movement rivetted national attention in the late 1960s.

Calling integration "a subterfuge for the maintenance of white supremacy," Carmichael rejected assimilation because it implied the superiority of white institutions and values. African Americans were encouraged to develop independent businesses, control their own schools and communities, and form all-black political organizations, such as the Black Panther Party, founded in Oakland, California, in 1966. The phrase "Black is beautiful" emphasized pride in African American culture and connections to blacks around the planet.

To black power advocates, nonviolence only brought more beatings and killings. Malcolm X had once said, "If someone puts a hand on you, send him to the cemetery." Carmichael agreed: "Black people should and must fight back." The press paid an inordinate amount of attention to black radicals, and the black power movement contributed to a severe white backlash. Although the urban riots of the mid-1960s erupted spontaneously, triggered by specific incidents, horrified whites blamed them on black power militants. By 1966, a full 85 percent of the white population thought that blacks were pressing for too much too quickly, up from 34 percent two years earlier.

King agreed with black power advocates on the need for "a radical reconstruction of society," but he clung to nonviolence and integration as the means to this end. In 1968, the thirty-nine-year-old leader went to Memphis to support a strike of municipal garbage workers. There, on April 4, King was shot and killed. James Earl Ray, an escaped white convict, confessed to the murder but later recanted, insisting that he was a scapegoat for a wider conspiracy.

Although they made the headlines, black power organizations failed to capture the massive support that African Americans gave King and other earlier leaders. Black militants were harassed by the FBI, jailed, and sometimes killed by the police, some of whom were also killed. Black nationalism's emphasis on racial pride and culture and its critique of American institutions, however, resonated broadly and helped to shape the protest of other groups.

A Multitude of Movements

The civil rights movement's undeniable moral claims helped to make protest respectable, while its impact on public opinion and government policy encouraged other groups with grievances. Native Americans, Latinos, college students, women, and others drew on the black freedom struggle for inspiration and models of activism. These groups engaged in direct-action protests, expressed their own cultural nationalism, and challenged dominant institutions and values.

Native American Protest

Protest was not new to the group of Americans with the oldest grievances, but Native American activism took on fresh militancy and goals in the 1960s. The cry "red power" reflected the influence of black radicalism on Native Americans who rejected the goal

AMERICAN INDIANS OCCUPY ALCATRAZ
In November 1969, 150 Native Americans occupied Alcatraz Island in San Francisco Bay, the site of a federal prison. Part of the Red Power movement, they were there, as one activist explained, to protest "extermination of our cultures . . . the chronic and cyclical poverty of reservations and the relocation of that poverty into Red Ghettoes in the cities." The protesters, whose demand for "Land, Peace, and Freedom" appears on the water tower, offered to pay the government beads and cloth for the island in the amount that Dutch colonists had paid American Indians for Manhattan Island in 1626.
Ralph Crane/TimePix.

of assimilation. As one Indian put it, the civil rights struggle led by King "was within the System, and the System had nothing to do with Indians." Rather, American Indians sought tribal sovereignty and just treatment as independent nations.

Native Americans demonstrated and occupied land and public buildings, claiming rights to natural resources and territory that they had owned collectively before European settlement. For example, in 1963 Northwest Indians mounted "fish-ins" to enforce century-old treaty rights. A new, more militant generation participated in these demonstrations through the National Indian Youth Council, founded in 1961. In the most dramatic action, Indians seized Alcatraz Island in San Francisco Bay in 1969, using it as a cultural center until the federal government ran them out in 1971.

In Minneapolis in 1968, two Chippewa, Dennis Banks and George Mitchell, founded the American Indian Movement (AIM) to deal with problems in cities, where about 300,000 Indians lived. Many of these, moved to urban areas by relocation programs of the 1950s, found only unemployment, poverty, and alienation from their traditions. AIM sought to protect Indians from police harassment, secure antipoverty funds, and establish "survival schools" to teach Indian history and values. The new movement's appeal quickly spread beyond urban areas. AIM members did not have "that hangdog reservation look I was used to," Mary Crow Dog wrote, and their visit to her South Dakota reservation "loosened a sort of earthquake inside me."

Native American protest gained attention from the Bureau of Indian Affairs, legislation to meet educational and health needs, and government decisions recognizing Indian rights to ancestral lands. Taos Indians, for example, regained territory in New Mexico, and the government paid the Sioux more than $100 million for lands taken in the nineteenth century. Native Americans recovered a measure of identity and pride, greater respect for and protection of their culture, and, in the words of President Johnson, recognition of "the right of the First Americans to remain Indians while exercising their rights as Americans."

Latino Struggles for Justice

The fastest-growing minority group in the 1960s were Latinos, or Hispanic Americans, an extraordinarily varied population comprised of people of Mexican, Puerto Rican, Caribbean, and other Latin American origins. (The term *Latino* stresses their common bonds as a minority group in the United States, while the less political term *Hispanic* also includes those with origins in Spain.) People of Puerto Rican and Caribbean descent tended to live in East Coast cities, but more than half of the Latino population of the United States—some six million Mexican Americans—lived in California, Texas, Arizona, New Mexico, and Colorado. In addition, thousands illegally crossed the two-thousand-mile border between Mexico and the United States in search of economic opportunity.

Mexican Americans had always organized to push for political power and economic rights. In 1929, for example, middle-class Mexican Americans formed the League of United Latin American Citizens (LULAC), which provided aid to newer immigrants and, like the NAACP, fought segregation and discrimination through litigation. In the 1960s, however, young Mexican Americans, like African Americans and Native Americans, increasingly rejected traditional politics in favor of direct action. One symbol of this generational challenge was the adoption of the term *Chicano* (from the Spanish word for Mexican, *mejicano*) by young activists.

Chicano protest drew national attention to California, where Cesar Chavez and Dolores Huerta organized a movement to improve the wretched conditions of migrant agricultural workers. As a child moving from farm to farm with his family, often crowded in soggy tents or tarpaper cabins, exploited by labor contractors, Chavez had to change schools frequently and stopped after the eighth grade. He encountered indifference and discrimination in the educational system, where Spanish was forbidden. One teacher, he recalled, "hung a sign on me that said, 'I am a clown, I speak Spanish.'" After serving in the navy during World War II and starting a family, Chavez began to organize voter registration drives among Mexican Americans and to study labor history and the ideas of Catholic reformers and Mahatma Gandhi.

In contrast to Chavez, Dolores Huerta grew up in an integrated urban neighborhood and avoided the farmworkers' grinding poverty and exploitation, but she witnessed subtle forms of discrimination. Once, for example, a high school teacher challenged her authorship of an essay because it was so well written. After completing community college and starting a family, at the age of twenty-five she met Chavez and soon they both determined that a union was the key to improving the lives of farmworkers. Together they founded the United Farm Workers (UFW) in 1962, which Chavez headed until his death in 1993. UFW

**CESAR CHAVEZ IN THE
VINEYARDS**
*Cesar Chavez, whose
grandfather had migrated
to the United States in the
nineteenth century, experienced the plight of farm-
workers when his family
lost its business and farm
in Arizona during the de-
pression. Here he meets
with grape pickers in California during the national
grape boycott of 1965. The
boycott's proclamation
listed these aims: "just
wages, humane working
conditions, protection from
the misuse of pesticides,
and the fundamental right
of collective bargaining." In
1999, California made the
date of Chavez's birth a
state holiday.*
Arthur Schatz/TimePix.

marches and strikes gained widespread support,
and a national boycott of California grapes helped
the union win a wage increase for the workers
in 1970. Although the UFW struggled and lost
membership, it helped politicize Mexican Americans and improved the lives of thousands of farm
workers.

Chicanos mobilized elsewhere to end discrimination in employment and education, gain political
power, and combat police brutality. In Southwestern cities in 1968, high school students launched a
wave of strikes, called "Blow Outs," to protest
racism in the public schools. In Denver, Colorado,
Rodolfo "Corky" Gonzales set up "freedom
schools," where Chicano children studied Spanish
and Mexican American history and chanted,
"Chicano power." The nationalist strains of Chicano

protest were evident in La Raza Unida (the United
Race), a political party founded by José Angel
Gutierrez in Texas and based on cultural pride and
brotherhood. With blacks and Native Americans,
Chicanos continued to be overrepresented among
the poor but gradually won more political offices,
more effective enforcement of antidiscrimination
legislation, and greater respect for their culture.

Student Rebellion and the New Left

Connections between the black freedom struggle
and other protest movements were direct and immediate, as white civil rights activists also launched
student protests, the antiwar movement, and the
new feminist movement. Challenging establishment institutions and traditional values, these

movements, along with those of racial and ethnic minorities, formed part of a reinvigorated political left and left their marks on higher education, the family, the national government, and other key institutions.

The central organization of white student protest was Students for a Democratic Society (SDS), formed in 1960 by a remnant of an older socialist-oriented student organization. In 1962, some sixty members met in Port Huron, Michigan, to draft a statement of purpose. "We are people of this generation, bred in at least modest comfort, housed now in universities, looking uncomfortably at the world we inherit," the statement began. The idealistic students criticized the complacency of their elders, the remoteness of decision makers from the people, and the powerlessness and alienation generated in a society run by impersonal bureaucratic institutions. SDS aimed to mobilize a "New Left," around the goals of civil rights, peace, and universal economic security. It remained small until 1965, but other forms of student activism soon followed.

The first large-scale white student protest arose in the free speech movement at the University of California, Berkeley, in 1964, when university officials banned student organizations from setting up tables to recruit support for various causes. Led by whites back from civil rights work in the South, the students claimed the right to freedom of expression and political action. They occupied the administration building, and more than seven hundred were arrested before the California Board of Regents overturned the new restrictions.

Hundreds of student rebellions followed on campuses across the country. Opposition to the Vietnam War activated the largest number of students, who held rallies and took over buildings to protest universities' links to the war. But they also demanded curricular reforms, more financial aid for minority and poor students, independence from paternalistic rules, and a larger voice in campus decision making.

The Counterculture

Growing up alongside and often overlapping the New Left and student movements was a rebellion known as the counterculture, which drew on the ideas of the Beats of the 1950s. The counterculture followers sought personal rather than political

change. Cultural radicals, or "hippies," as they were called, rejected many mainstream values, such as the work ethic, materialism, rationality, order, and sexual control. "Do your own thing" became their motto. Hippies stood out with their long hair and wildly colorful clothing. The Haight-Ashbury district of San Francisco harbored the most famous hippie community, but thousands of others established communes in cities or on farms, where they renounced private property and shared

FEMINISTS PICKET THE MISS AMERICA PAGEANT
This picketer was among the feminists who demonstrated at the Miss America pageant at Atlantic City, New Jersey, in 1968 in protest against society's exaggerated emphasis on women's appearance and its rigid beauty standards. They set up a "freedom trash can" and invited women to throw away their "bras, girdles, curlers, false eyelashes, wigs, and **Cosmopolitan,** *which they called "objects of female torture." They also crowned a sheep Miss America. Why?*
Chicago Historical Society.

everything, often including sex partners. They sought to discard inhibitions and elevate their senses with illegal drugs such as marijuana and LSD.

Rock music defined both the counterculture and the political left. English groups such as the Beatles and the Rolling Stones and homegrown products like Bob Dylan, Janis Joplin, the Jefferson Airplane, and Jerry Garcia's Grateful Dead took American youth by storm. Music during the 1960s often carried insurgent political and social messages. Despairing of the violence around the world and the threat of nuclear annihilation, "Eve of Destruction," a top hit of 1965, reminded young men, "You're old enough to kill but not for votin'." Other popular songs derided authority, touted drug use and sexual freedom, and called for peace, love, and revolution.

Many elements of the counterculture—from rock music to jeans and long hair—filtered into the mainstream. Sex outside marriage and tolerant attitudes about sexual morality spawned what came to be called a "sexual revolution." Self-fulfillment became a dominant concern of many Americans, and questioning of authority became much more widespread. The hippies faded away in the early 1970s, but their legacy continued to influence American society.

Beginnings of a Feminist Movement

A new women's movement grew out of both the civil rights struggle and the New Left. By piggybacking onto civil rights measures, white feminists gained the ban against sex discrimination in the Civil Rights Act of 1964 and the extension of affirmative action to women. Their expectations raised by these new policies, feminists grew impatient when the government moved slowly to enforce them. Deciding that they needed a "civil rights organization for women," Betty Friedan and others founded the National Organization for Women (NOW) in 1966.

Simultaneously, a more radical feminism grew among women in the black freedom struggle and the New Left. In 1964, two white women in SNCC, Mary King and Casey Hayden, pointed to the contradiction between the ideal of equality and women's actual status, and in 1965 they began circulating their ideas to other New Left women. King and Hayden argued that, like blacks, women were subject to a "caste system . . . forcing them to

work around or outside hierarchical structures of power which may exclude them" and were also subordinated in personal relations. Their ideas resonated with white activist women, but most male radicals reacted with indifference or ridicule. Ignored or trivialized, women began to walk out of male-dominated political meetings, and by 1967 they had created an independent women's liberation movement composed of groups across the nation. Their demonstrations began to gain public attention, especially when dozens of women picketed the Miss America beauty pageant in 1968, protesting against being forced "to compete for male approval [and] enslaved by ludicrous 'beauty' standards." Activism by radicals and more moderate feminists surged into a mass movement that dramatically changed public policy and popular attitudes in the 1970s.

The Judicial Revolution

The Supreme Court under Chief Justice Earl Warren (presiding from 1953 to 1969) spearheaded another form of change. In expanding the Constitution's promise of equality and individual rights, the Court's decisions shifted power from the states to the judicial branch of the federal government—that is, to the Supreme Court—and supported an activist government to prevent injustice and discrimination.

Civil Rights and Criminal Justice

Enlarging the rights of disadvantaged groups and accused criminals, Supreme Court decisions in the Warren era overturned judicial precedents and often moved ahead of public opinion. Following the pathbreaking *Brown* school desegregation decision of 1954, the Court ruled against all-white public facilities and struck down educational plans devised by southern states to avoid integration. The Court also upheld the rights of freedom of assembly and speech, thereby enabling the black freedom struggle to continue sit-ins, mass marches, and other tactics critical to its success.

Chief Justice Warren considered *Baker v. Carr* (1963) his most important decision. The case grew out of a complaint that Tennessee electoral districts were so inequitably drawn that sparsely populated rural districts had far more representatives than densely populated urban areas. Using the Fourteenth Amendment guarantee of "equal protection of the laws," the Court in *Baker* and companion cases established the principle of "one person, one vote" both for state legislatures and for the House of Representatives. Requiring most states to redraw electoral districts, the rulings helped to make state legislatures more responsive to metropolitan interests.

The egalitarian thrust of the Warren Court also touched the criminal justice system. Between 1957 and 1967, the Court overturned a series of convictions on the grounds that the accused had been deprived of "life, liberty, or property, without due process of law," a denial of their Fourteenth Amendment rights. Furthermore, the Court decided that states as well as the federal government were subject to the Bill of Rights, with rulings that transformed law enforcement practices and the treatment of individuals accused of crime. In *Gideon v. Wainwright* (1963), the Court ruled that when accused criminals could not afford to hire lawyers, states must provide them without charge. In *Escobedo v. Illinois* (1964), the justices extended the right to counsel to the period when suspects are being questioned by police officers. Two years later, in *Miranda v. Arizona*, the Court ruled that officers must inform suspects of their rights upon arrest; and it overturned convictions based on evidence obtained by unlawful arrest, by electronic surveillance, or without a search warrant.

Critics accused the Supreme Court of obstructing law enforcement and letting criminals go free. Liberals, however, argued that these rulings promoted equal treatment in the criminal justice system: The wealthy always had access to legal counsel, and practiced criminals were well aware of their right to remain silent. The beneficiaries of the decisions were the poor and the ignorant, as well as the general population, whose right to privacy was strengthened by the Court's stricter guidelines for admissible evidence.

Dissent and Religious Issues

The Warren Court also strengthened protections for people suspected of being Communists or subversives, setting limits, for example, on government officials who investigated and prosecuted them. Like the criminal justice cases, these rulings guaranteed the rights of people on the margins of American society and aroused opposition.

The Court's decisions on prayer and Bible reading in public schools provoked even greater outrage. In *Abington School District v. Schempp* (1963), it overturned a Pennsylvania law requiring Bible reading and prayer in the schools as a violation of the First Amendment principle of separation of church and state. Later decisions ruled out official prayer in public schools even if students were not required to participate. Even though these decisions left students perfectly free to pray on their own, an infuriated Alabama legislator cried, "They put Negroes in the schools and now they've driven God out." The Court's supporters, however, declared that the religion cases protected the rights of non-Christians and atheists.

Two or three justices who believed that the Court was overstepping its authority often issued sharp dissents. Outside the Court, opponents worked to pass laws or constitutional amendments that would upset despised decisions, and billboards demanded, "Impeach Earl Warren." Nonetheless, the Court's major decisions withstood Warren's retirement in 1969 and the test of time.

Conclusion: Achievements and Limitations of 1960s Liberalism

Senate majority leader Mike Mansfield was not alone in concluding that Lyndon Johnson "has done more than FDR ever did, or ever thought of doing." Yet opposition to his leadership grew so strong by 1968 that Johnson abandoned hopes for reelection. As his liberal vision lay in ruins, he asked, "How was it possible that all these people could be so ungrateful to me after I have given them so much?"

Fannie Lou Hamer could have provided a number of reasons. Support from the federal government was minimal when local officials arrested and beat her and others trying to organize Mississippi blacks. Hamer felt betrayed when President Johnson and his aides refused to support the Mississippi Freedom Democratic Party (MFDP) in its struggle for representation at the 1964 Democratic National Convention. "We learned the hard way that even though we had all the law and all the righteousness on our side—that white man is not going to give up his power to us," Hamer concluded.

Hamer's efforts to use Johnson's antipoverty

programs to help poor blacks in Mississippi eventually ended in failure. Internal problems hampered her projects, but they also reflected some of the more general shortcomings of the War on Poverty. Inadequately planned and funded, many antipoverty programs ended up benefiting industry and the nonpoor as much as or more than the impoverished. Because Johnson refused to ask for sacrifices from prosperous Americans, the Great Society never approached the redistribution of wealth and resources that would have been necessary for the elimination of poverty.

Black aspirations exceeded white Americans' commitment to genuine equality. It was easy for northerners to be sympathetic when the civil rights movement focused on crude and blatant forms of racism in the South. But when it attacked the subtler racism that existed throughout the nation and sought equality in fact as well as in rights, the black freedom struggle confronted a powerful backlash. By the end of the 1960s, the revolution in the legal status of African Americans was complete, but the black freedom struggle had lost much of its momentum, and African Americans remained at the bottom of the economic ladder.

Such shortcomings contributed to a rising challenge to liberalism from the New Left. Radicalized by the black freedom struggle, a small but vocal minority of Americans criticized the Great Society and questioned whether real reform could be achieved within the framework of traditional American institutions and values. Young radicals launched direct confrontations with the government and universities that, together with racial conflict, escalated into political discord and social disorder not seen since the union wars of the 1930s. The war in Vietnam polarized American society as much as did racial issues or the behavior of young people, and Johnson's conduct of the war undermined faith in his leadership. The war starved the Great Society, devouring revenues that might have been used for social reform and eclipsing the substantial progress that had actually been achieved.

FOR FURTHER READING ABOUT THE TOPICS IN THIS CHAPTER, see the Online Bibliography at
www.bedfordstmartins.com/roarkcompact.

FOR ADDITIONAL FIRST-HAND ACCOUNTS OF THIS PERIOD, see pages 204–220 in Michael Johnson, ed., *Reading the American Past,* Second Edition, Volume II.

TO ASSESS YOUR MASTERY OF THE MATERIAL IN THIS CHAPTER, see the Online Study Guide at
www.bedfordstmartins.com/roarkcompact.

FATIGUE HAT WITH BUTTONS
The button on this fatigue hat of a veteran who had served two tours of duty demonstrates veterans' response to the many Americans who just wanted to forget the war that the United States had failed to win. Because their war was so different from other American wars, Vietnam veterans often returned home to hostility or indifference. The POW-MIA pin refers to prisoners of war and those missing in action.
Nancy Gewitz/Antique Textile Resource/Picture Research Consultants & Archives.

VIETNAM AND THE LIMITS OF POWER

29

1961–1975

As Charles Anderson's plane prepared to land, the pilot announced, "Gentlemen, we'll be touching down in Da Nang, Vietnam, in about ten minutes. . . . Fasten your seat belts, please. On behalf of the entire crew and staff, I'd like to say we've enjoyed having you with us . . . and we hope to see all of you again next year on your way home. Goodbye and good luck." Like most soldiers after 1966, Charles Anderson went to war on a commercial jetliner, complete with stewardesses (as they were called then) in miniskirts.

Military personnel traveling to battle like business executives or tourists only hints at how different the Vietnam War was from America's previous wars. Marine infantry officer Philip Caputo landed at Da Nang in March 1965 confident that the enemy "would be quickly beaten and that we were doing something altogether noble and good." But in just a few months, "what had begun as an adventurous expedition had turned into an exhausting, indecisive war of attrition in which we fought for no other cause than our own survival."

Another soldier discovered even more quickly that "something was wrong." Wondering why the bus taking him from the air base to the compound had wire mesh over the windows, he was told, "The gooks will throw grenades through the windows." Soldiers in Vietnam initially used the racist word *gook* to refer to the enemy—the North Vietnamese or their supporters in the south—but it quickly became a term used for any Vietnamese. "From one day to the next, you could see for yourself changes coming over guys on our side—decent fellows, who wouldn't dream of calling an Oriental a 'gook' back home," reported one American. The problem was that "they couldn't tell who was their friend and who wasn't. Day after day, out on patrol we'd come to . . . a shabby village, and the elders would welcome us and the children come running with smiles on their faces, waiting for the candy we'd give them. But . . . just as we were leaving the village behind, the enemy would open up on us, and there was bitterness among us that the villagers hadn't given us warning."

Americans' horrifying and bewildering experiences in Vietnam grew out of cold war commitments made in the 1940s and 1950s by Presidents Harry S. Truman and Dwight D. Eisenhower. John F. Kennedy wholeheartedly took on those commitments, promising more flexible and vigorous efforts to thwart communism. In the most memorable words of his 1961 inauguration, he declared, "Let every nation know, whether it wishes us well or ill, that we shall pay any price, bear any burden, meet any hardship, support any friend, oppose any foe to assure the survival and the success of liberty."

Vietnam became the foremost test of Kennedy's pledge. He sent increasing amounts of American arms and personnel to sustain the South Vietnamese gov-

FIGHTING THE CLIMATE AND GEOGRAPHY
Steamy tropical conditions and inhospitable terrain were among the nonhuman enemies
U.S. troops faced in Vietnam. Soldiers like this one making his way under fire through a
rice paddy in 1966 were soaked for weeks on end. Veteran Philip Caputo wrote about
"being pounded numb by ceaseless rain" during the monsoon; "at night we squatted in
muddy holes, picked off the leeches that sucked on our veins."
Henri Gilles Huet/World Wide Photos, Inc.

ernment, and Lyndon B. Johnson dramatically escalated that commitment. By 1965, the civil war in Vietnam had become America's war, with 543,000 military personnel serving there at peak strength in 1968 and more than 3 million total throughout the war's duration. Yet this massive intervention not only failed to defeat North Vietnam but also added a new burden to the costs of fighting the cold war—intense discord at home. The Vietnam War cost President Johnson another term in office and contributed to the political demise of his Republican successor, Richard M. Nixon. Some Americans lauded the U.S. goal in Vietnam and decried only the nation's unwillingness to pursue it effectively. Others believed that preserving a non-Communist South Vietnam was neither in the best interests of the United States nor within its capacity or moral right to achieve.

None could deny the war's enormous costs. "The promises of the Great Society have been shot down on the battlefield of Vietnam," said Martin Luther King Jr. In addition to derailing domestic reform, the war exacted a heavy toll in American lives and dollars, kindled internal conflict, and led to the violation of the rights of antiwar protesters. With the exception of the African American freedom struggle, no other post–World War II event affected the nation so deeply.

New Frontiers in Foreign Policy

John F. Kennedy moved quickly to fulfill his promise to pursue containment with a more aggressive yet more flexible foreign policy, working with his like-minded secretary of defense, Robert S. McNamara, to expand the nation's ability to wage nuclear, conventional, or guerrilla warfare. To ensure U.S. superiority over the Soviet Union in every domain, Kennedy accelerated the nation's space exploration program and increased attention to the third world. In his unflinching determination to halt communism, Kennedy took the United States to the brink of nuclear war during the 1962 Cuban missile crisis. Less dramatically, but no less tenaciously, Kennedy stepped up American arms and personnel to save the government of South Vietnam from Communist insurgents.

Meeting the "Hour of Maximum Danger"

Kennedy and other Democrats criticized the Eisenhower administration for relying too heavily on nuclear weapons, thereby denying the nation a "flexible response" to Communist expansion. They also charged that limits on defense spending had allowed the United States to fall behind even in nuclear capability. In January 1961, Kennedy warned that the nation faced a grave peril: "Each day the

crises multiply. . . . Each day we draw nearer the hour of maximum danger."

Although the president exaggerated the actual threat to national security, several developments in 1961 heightened the sense of crisis and provided rationalization for a military buildup. In a speech made shortly before Kennedy's inauguration, Soviet premier Nikita Khrushchev had encouraged "wars of national liberation," thereby aligning the Soviet Union with independence movements (usually anti-Western) in the third world. Khrushchev wanted to bolster Soviet leadership of the Communist world against challenges by the People's Republic of China, and to shore up his political position at home by projecting forcefulness abroad. U.S. officials, however, saw in his words a threat to the status quo of containment.

Fidel Castro's revolution had already moved Cuba—just ninety miles from the United States—into the Soviet orbit; and under Eisenhower, the

HUMANS REACH THE MOON
In July 1969, less than a decade after President John F. Kennedy announced the goal of "landing a man on the moon and returning him safely to earth," the space capsule Apollo 11 carried astronauts Edwin E. Aldrin Jr. and Neil A. Armstrong to the moon. As millions of people watched on television, Armstrong became the first human to step on the moon's surface, saying, "That's one small step for a man, one giant leap for mankind." Armstrong and Aldrin collected rock samples and conducted scientific experiments. Other missions to the moon followed. In this 1971 photograph of the Apollo 15 mission, astronaut James B. Irwin salutes near the lunar module and lunar roving vehicle.
NASA/Johnson Space Center.

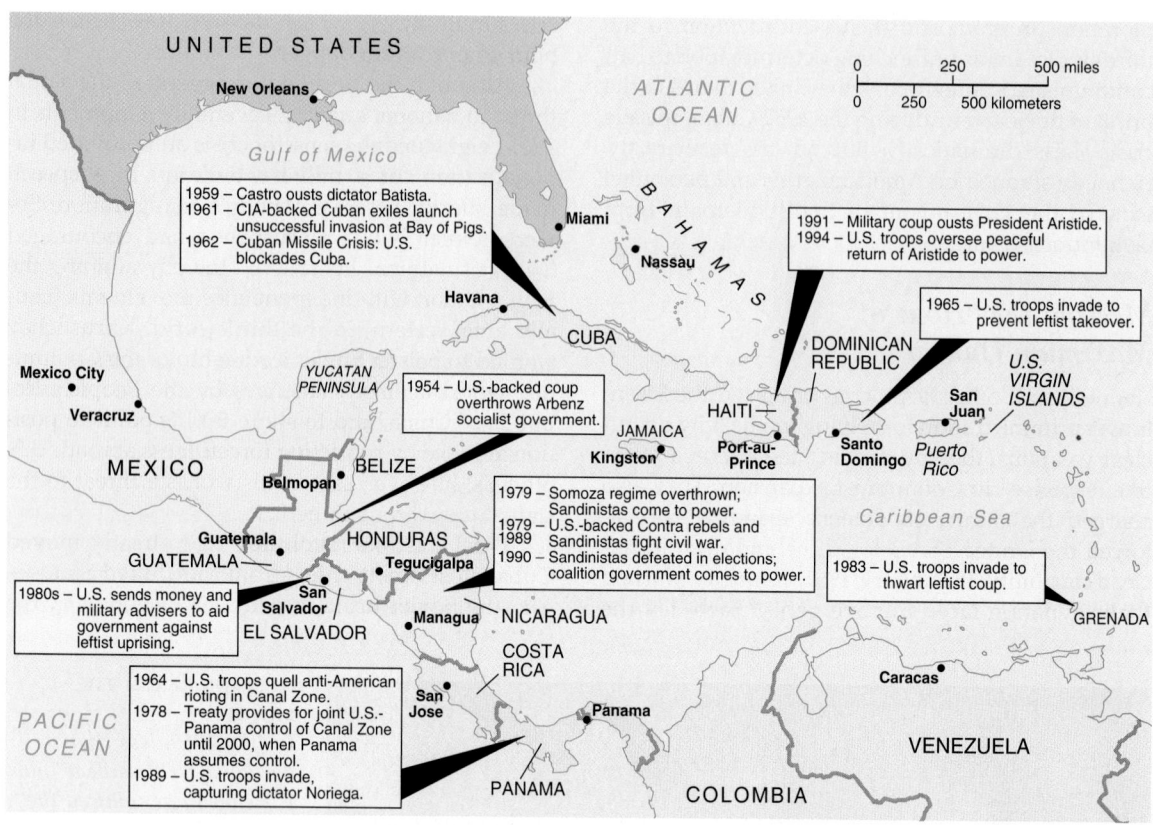

MAP 29.1

U.S. Involvement in Latin America and the Caribbean, 1954–1996
*During the cold war, the United States frequently intervened in Central American and
Caribbean countries to suppress Communist or leftist movements.*

CIA had been planning an invasion by anti-Castro exiles. Kennedy ordered the invasion to proceed even though his military advisers gave it only a fair chance of success. To do otherwise, the president believed, would create an appearance of weakness.

On April 17, 1961, about thirteen hundred anti-Castro exiles, who had been trained and armed by the CIA, landed at the Bay of Pigs on the south shore of Cuba (see Map 29.1). Contrary to expectations, no popular uprising materialized to support the anti-Castro brigade. Kennedy refused to supply direct military support, and the invaders quickly fell to Castro's forces. The disaster was humiliating for Kennedy and the United States, posing a stark contrast to Kennedy's inaugural promise of a new, more effective foreign policy. The attempted armed interference in another nation compromised the moral authority of the United States, evoked memories of

Yankee imperialism among Latin American countries, and aligned Cuba even more closely with the Soviet Union.

Shortly before the Bay of Pigs invasion, the United States had suffered a psychological blow when a Soviet astronaut became the first human to orbit the earth. In May 1961, Kennedy called for a huge new commitment to the space race. "If we are to win the battle that is now going on around the world between freedom and tyranny," the United States must "take a clearly leading role in space achievement." His goal: an American on the moon within six to eight years. Congress authorized the Apollo program and boosted appropriations for space exploration. In 1962, John H. Glenn orbited the earth, and in 1969, the United States surpassed the Soviet Union when Neil A. Armstrong and Edwin E. "Buzz" Aldrin Jr. became the first humans to set foot on the moon.

Early in his presidency, Kennedy sought a meeting with Khrushchev, "to show him that we can be as tough as he is." The two met in June 1961, in Vienna, Austria, but contrary to Kennedy's expectations, Khrushchev was belligerent and threatening and shook the president's confidence. The stunned president reported to a journalist, "He just beat [the] hell out of me. . . . If he thinks I'm inexperienced and have no guts . . . we won't get anywhere with him." Khrushchev demanded an agreement recognizing the existence of two Germanys; otherwise, he warned, the Soviets would sign a separate treaty with East Germany, a move that would threaten America's occupation rights in West Berlin and its access to the city, which lay some one hundred miles within East Germany. Kennedy responded by substantially increasing U.S. military forces in Europe.

The massive exodus of East Germans into West Berlin, which had begun shortly after Berlin was partitioned following World War II, caused the Communists major embarrassment. To stop this flow of escapees from behind the iron curtain, on August 13, 1961, East Germany shocked the world by erecting the Berlin Wall. Khrushchev backed off from his threats, but not until 1972 did the superpowers recognize East and West Germany as separate nations and guarantee Western access to West Berlin.

Kennedy used the Berlin crisis to add $3.2 billion to the defense budget and to expand the military by 300,000 troops. When the Soviet Union terminated its three-year moratorium on nuclear testing, the United States followed suit and vigorously developed new weapons and delivery systems.

New Approaches to the Third World

Kennedy administration officials sought fresh approaches to the independence movements that had convulsed the world since the end of World War II. The president publicly supported third world democratic and nationalist aspirations, believing that the United States could win over developing nations by helping to fulfill hopes for independence and democracy. To that end, Kennedy created the Alliance for Progress, promising $20 billion in aid for Latin America over the next decade. Like the Marshall Plan, the Alliance for Progress was designed to thwart communism and hold nations within the American sphere by fostering economic development. Likewise, the new Agency for International Development (AID) emphasized economic aid over military aid in foreign assistance programs.

In 1961 Kennedy launched his most dramatic third world initiative: the Peace Corps. Exemplifying the personal sacrifice summoned by Kennedy in his inaugural address, the program attracted idealistic volunteers, such as one who expressed his discomfort at having been "born between clean sheets when others were issued into the dust with a birthright of hunger." After studying a country's language and culture, Peace Corps volunteers went to work directly with its people, opening schools, providing basic health care, and assisting with agriculture, nutrition, and small economic enterprises. By the mid-1970s, more than 60,000 volunteers had fanned out around the globe, serving two-year stints in Latin America, Africa, and Asia.

Nevertheless, Kennedy's foreign aid initiatives fell far short of their objectives. Though generally welcomed, Peace Corps projects numbered too few to make a dent in the poverty and suffering in third world countries. By 1969, the United States had provided only half of the $20 billion promised to the Alliance for Progress, and much of that funded military projects or was skimmed off by corrupt ruling elites. In addition, a soaring birthrate in Latin America counteracted economic gains, and these nations increasingly bore heavy foreign debt.

Kennedy also reverted to direct military means to bring political stability to the third world. Although he supported popular movements' efforts to gain independence and better living conditions, he drew the line at uprisings that appeared to have Communist connections or goals. Even though a growing split between the Soviet Union and Communist China suggested otherwise, Kennedy clung to the basic cold war tenet: that communism was a monolithic force and had to be contained, no matter what form it took.

To that end, he promoted counterinsurgency forces to put down insurrections that smacked of communism. The showcase of the administration's counterinsurgency strategy was an elite military corps trained to wage guerrilla warfare. Called "special forces," the corps had been established under Eisenhower to aid groups sympathetic to the United States and opposed to Communist-leaning national liberation movements. Kennedy rapidly expanded the special forces, called them the Green Berets (after their official headgear), and equipped them with the latest technology.

The Arms Race and the Nuclear Brink

The final piece of Kennedy's defense strategy was to strengthen American nuclear superiority over the Soviet Union. This drive for nuclear dominance increased the number of U.S. nuclear weapons based in Europe from 2,500 to 7,200 and multiplied fivefold the supply of intercontinental ballistic missiles (ICBMs). Concerned that this buildup would enable the United States to launch a first strike and wipe out Soviet missile sites before the Soviets could respond, the Kremlin stepped up its own ICBM program. Thus began the most intense arms race in history.

The superpowers came perilously close to using their weapons of terror in 1962, when Khrushchev decided to install nuclear missiles in Cuba. On October 16, the CIA showed Kennedy aerial photographs of launching sites under construction in Cuba for missiles with ranges of 1,000 and 2,200 miles. Considering this an intolerable threat to the United States, the president met daily in secret with a small group of advisers to manage the ensuing thirteen-day Cuban missile crisis. On October 22, he told a television audience that he had placed the military on full alert and was imposing a "strict quarantine on all offensive military equipment" headed from the Soviet Union to Cuba. The U.S. navy would turn back any Soviet vessel suspected of carrying offensive missiles to Cuba. (Only later did the United States find out that offensive missiles were already in Cuba.) Kennedy warned Khrushchev that any attack launched from Cuba would trigger a full nuclear assault against the Soviet Union.

To Kennedy, projecting the appearance of toughness was paramount. According to his speechwriter, Theodore Sorensen, although the missiles

Cuban Missile Crisis, 1962

U.S. blockade zone

Range of Soviet missiles

Soviet missile and jet bomber bases

did not "alter the strategic balance in fact . . . that balance would have been substantially altered in appearance; and in matters of national will and world leadership such appearances contribute to reality." But if Kennedy was willing to risk nuclear war for appearances, he also exercised caution. He refused advice from the military to bomb the missile sites and instead ordered the quarantine to allow time for negotiations. On October 24, some of the Russian ships carrying nuclear warheads toward Cuba suddenly turned back. Kennedy matched Khrushchev's restraint. When one ship crossed the blockade line, he ordered the navy to follow it rather than attempt to stop it. "We don't want to push him [Khrushchev] to a precipitous action," he said.

While Americans experienced the cold war's most fearful days, Kennedy and Khrushchev exchanged offers and counteroffers. Finally, the Soviets removed the missiles and pledged not to introduce new offensive weapons into Cuba. The United States promised not to invade the island. Secretly, Kennedy also agreed to remove U.S. missiles based in Turkey and aimed at the Soviet Union.

In miscalculating Kennedy's resolution, the Soviets lost ground in their contest with China for the allegiance of third world countries, and the missile crisis contributed to Khrushchev's fall from power two years later. Kennedy emerged triumphant. The image of an inexperienced president fumbling the Bay of Pigs invasion and being bullied by Khrushchev in Vienna gave way to that of a brilliant leader combining firmness with restraint, bearing the United States through its "hour of maximum danger."

After the Cuban missile crisis, Kennedy acted to prevent future confrontations. He and Khrushchev installed a special telephone "hot line" to speed top-level communication at critical moments. In a major speech at American University in June 1963, Kennedy called for a reexamination of cold war assumptions, asking Americans "not to see conflict as inevitable." Acknowledging the superpowers' immense differences, Kennedy stressed their similarities: "We all inhabit this small planet. We all breathe the same air. We all cherish our children's future and we are all mortal."

Responding to pressures from scientists and other Americans alarmed by the dangers of nuclear weapons, Kennedy also called for an end to "a vicious cycle" in which "new weapons beget counterweapons." In August 1963, the United States, the

Soviet Union, and Great Britain signed a limited test ban treaty. Because France and China refused to sign, the agreement failed to stop the proliferation of nuclear weapons. Nonetheless, it reduced the threat of radioactive fallout from nuclear testing and raised hopes for superpower accord on other issues.

Venturing into a Quagmire in Vietnam

The new approach that Kennedy outlined at American University did not mean abandoning South Vietnam to communism. He had criticized the idea of "a Pax Americana enforced on the world by American weapons of war," but he increased the flow of those weapons into South Vietnam. His early foreign policy setbacks suggested the need to make a strong stand somewhere, and he also remembered the political blows to the Democratic Party when China was "lost" in 1949.

Kennedy's strong anticommunism, his interpretation of the lessons of history, and his commitment to an activist foreign policy prepared him to take a stand in Vietnam. The new counterinsurgency program provided the means. Kennedy's key military adviser, General Maxwell Taylor, thought that Vietnam would be a good testing ground for the Green Berets. Holding firm in Vietnam would show the Soviets that wars of national liberation were "costly, dangerous, and doomed to failure."

Two major problems, however, undercut Taylor's analysis. First, the South Vietnamese insurgents—called Vietcong, short for *Vietnam Cong-san* ("Vietnamese Communists"), by the Americans—were an indigenous force whose initiative came from within, not from the Soviet Union or China. Even Ho Chi Minh's Communist government in North Vietnam did not supply weapons or soldiers to the rebels in the south until 1959, after those rebels had initiated guerrilla activities against the South Vietnamese government on their own. Because the Saigon government refused to hold the elections promised in the Geneva accords and was determined to exterminate its opponents, the rebels saw no choice but to take up arms.

The second problem lay in the South Vietnamese government and army (the Army of the Republic of Vietnam, or ARVN), which proved to be ineffective at containing communism. Ngo Dinh Diem, South Vietnamese premier from 1954 to 1963,

chose self-serving military leaders merely for their personal loyalty. The government's corruption and repression of opponents alienated many South Vietnamese, not just the Communists.

Intervention by North Vietnam made matters worse. In 1960, the Hanoi government established the National Liberation Front (NLF), composed of South Vietnamese rebels but directed by the northern army. In addition, Hanoi constructed a network of infiltration routes (called the "Ho Chi Minh Trail") in neighboring Laos and Cambodia, through which it sent people and supplies to help liberate the south (see Map 29.2). Violence escalated between 1960 and 1963, bringing the Saigon government close to collapse.

When Kennedy took office, more than $1 billion of aid and seven hundred U.S. military advisers had failed to stabilize South Vietnam. He resisted pressure from some advisers for an all-out effort, but he began to escalate the American commitment. By spring 1963, military aid doubled, and nine thousand Americans served in Vietnam as military advisers, who occasionally participated in actual combat. Although the United States extracted new promises of reform from Diem, the South Vietnamese government never made good on them.

Administration officials assumed that military technology and sheer power could stem the Communist tide in South Vietnam. Yet advanced weapons were ill suited to a guerrilla-type war and harmed the very people they were intended to save. Thousands of peasants were uprooted and resettled in "strategic hamlets," supposedly secure from the Communists. Those left in the countryside fell victim to bombs—containing the highly flammable substance napalm—dropped by the U.S.-backed ARVN in an effort to quell the Vietcong. In January 1962, U.S. planes began to spray herbicides to destroy the Vietcong's jungle hideouts and food supply.

South Vietnamese military leaders effected a coup on November 2, 1963, brutally executing Premier Diem and his brother who headed the secret police. Although shocked by the killings, Kennedy indicated no change in policy. In a speech to be given on the day he was assassinated, Kennedy called Americans to their responsibilities as "the watchmen on the walls of world freedom." Referring specifically to Southeast Asia, his undelivered speech warned, "We dare not weary of the task." At his death, sixteen thousand Americans had served in Vietnam and one hundred had died there.

Lyndon Johnson's War against Communism

The cold war assumptions that shaped Kennedy's foreign policy underlay the new president's approach to Southeast Asia and Latin America as well. Retaining Kennedy's key advisers, Lyndon Johnson continued his massive buildup of nuclear weapons and conventional and counterinsurgency forces. In 1965, when the South Vietnamese government approached collapse, Johnson made the fateful decisions to order U.S. troops into combat and initiate sustained bombing of the north. That same year, Johnson sent U.S. marines to the Dominican Republic to crush a leftist rebellion.

Toward an All-Out Commitment in Vietnam

Having sent more military advisers, weapons, and economic aid to South Vietnam during his first year as president, in August 1964, Lyndon Johnson seized an opportunity to increase the pressure on North Vietnam. American ships routinely engaged in espionage in the Gulf of Tonkin off the coast of North Vietnam and two U.S. destroyers reported that North Vietnamese gunboats had fired on them on August 2 and 4 (Map 29.2). Johnson quickly ordered air strikes on North Vietnamese torpedo bases and oil storage facilities, and sought authority to take "all necessary measures to repel any armed attacks against the forces of the United States and to prevent further aggression." His portrayal of the situation was at best misleading, revealing neither the uncertainty about whether the second attack had even occurred nor the provocative U.S. actions (staging covert raids and operating close to the North Vietnamese coast). Congress supported Johnson's plan by passing the Gulf of Tonkin Resolution on August 7, 1964, with just two senators voting no.

Johnson's tough stance just two months before the 1964 elections helped counter the charges made by his opponent, Barry Goldwater, that he was "soft on communism." Yet the president also presented himself as the peace candidate. When Goldwater proposed massive bombing of North Vietnam, Johnson assured Americans that "we are not going to send American boys nine or ten thousand miles away from home to do what Asian boys ought to be doing for themselves."

Soon after winning reelection, however, Johnson did widen the war. He rejected peace overtures from North Vietnam, which insisted on American withdrawal and a coalition government in South Vietnam as steps toward ultimate unification of the country. Instead he accepted the advice of Secretary of Defense Robert S. McNamara and other officials to begin a bombing campaign against the north. Operation Rolling Thunder, a strategy of gradually intensified bombing of North Vietnam, began in February 1965. Less than a month later, the first U.S. combat troops landed near Da Nang, South Vietnam. In July, Johnson shifted U.S. troops from defensive to offensive operations and authorized the dispatch of fifty thousand more soldiers. Those decisions, whose import was downplayed for Congress and the public, marked a critical turning point. Now it was genuinely America's war.

Preventing Another Castro in Latin America

Closer to home, Johnson faced perpetual problems in Latin America, despite the efforts of the Alliance for Progress. Thirteen times during the 1960s, military coups toppled Latin American governments, and local insurgencies grew apace. The administration's response to such turmoil varied from case to case but centered on the determination to prevent any more Castro-type revolutions.

In 1964, riots erupted in the Panama Canal Zone, which the United States had seized and made a U.S. territory early in the century. Instigated by Panamanian nationalists, the riots left four U.S. soldiers and more than twenty Panamanians dead. Johnson sent troops to quell the disturbance, but he also initiated negotiations that eventually led to Panamanian authority over the canal in 2000.

Meanwhile, Johnson's Latin American policy generated new cries of "Yankee imperialism." In 1961, voters in the Dominican Republic ousted a long-standing dictator and elected a constitutional government headed by Juan Bosch, who was overthrown by a military coup two years later. In 1965, when Bosch supporters rallied in an uprising against the military government, Johnson sent more than twenty thousand soldiers to take control of the island. After a truce was arranged, Dominicans voted in a constitutional government under a moderate rightist in 1966.

Yet this first outright show of Yankee force in Latin America in forty years damaged the adminis-

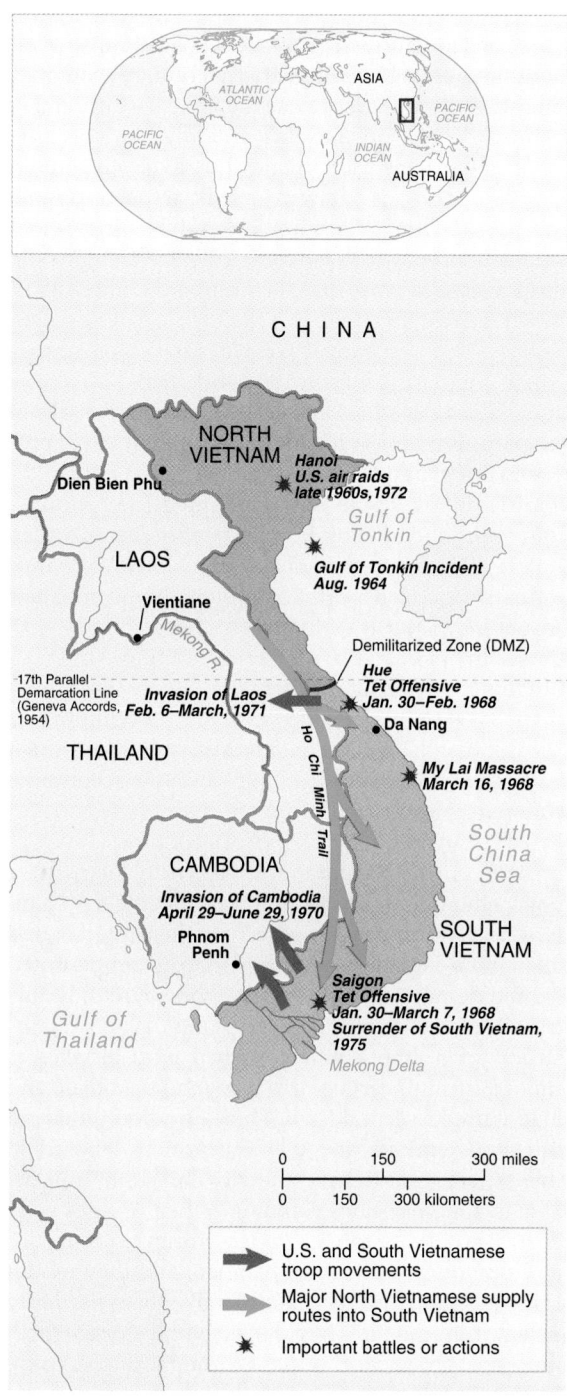

MAP 29.2

The Vietnam War, 1964–1975

The United States sent 2.6 million soldiers to Vietnam and spent more than $150 billion on the longest war in American history, but it was unable to prevent the unification of Vietnam under a Communist government.

READING THE MAP: What accord divided Vietnam into two nations? When was it signed, and where was the line of division drawn? Through what countries did the Ho Chi Minh Trail go?

CONNECTIONS: What was the Gulf of Tonkin incident, and how did the United States respond? What was the Tet Offensive, and how did it affect the war?

www.bedfordstmartins.com/roarkcompact SEE THE ON-LINE STUDY GUIDE for more help in analyzing this map.

Boschists from returning to power. Moreover, the president had not consulted the Dominicans or the Organization of American States (OAS), to which the United States had pledged to respect national sovereignty in Latin America.

The Americanized War

The apparent success in the Dominican Republic no doubt encouraged the president to press on in Vietnam. From Operation Rolling Thunder in 1965 to early 1968, the United States gradually escalated attacks against the North Vietnamese and their Vietcong allies, endeavoring to break their will while avoiding intervention by the Chinese, as they had done in Korea. Johnson himself scrutinized military plans, boasting, "They can't even bomb an outhouse without my approval."

Over the course of the war, U.S. pilots dropped 3.2 million tons of explosives, more than the United States had launched in all of World War II. Claiming monthly death tolls of more than two thousand North Vietnamese, the intensive bombing nonetheless failed to dampen the Hanoi government's commitment. (See "Historical Question," page 758.) In the south, the United States rained down more than twice the tonnage of bombs dropped on North Vietnam. Because there was no battlefront as in previous wars, military officials calculated progress not in territory seized, but in "body counts" and "kill

tration at home and abroad. Although the administration had justified intervention on the grounds that Communists were among the rebels, it quickly became clear that they had played no significant role, and U.S. intervention kept the reform-oriented

Why Couldn't the United States Bomb Its Way to Victory in Vietnam?

WORLD WAR II DEMONSTRATED the critical importance of airpower in modern war. According to the official U.S. study of strategic bombing during World War II, "No nation can long survive the free exploitation of air weapons over its homeland." In the Vietnam War, U.S. planes delivered even more explosives than they had in World War II. Why, then, did strategic bombing not bring victory in Vietnam?

"Our airpower did not fail us; it was the decision makers," asserted Admiral U.S. Grant Sharp, World War II veteran and commander in chief of the Pacific Command during the Vietnam War. Military officials welcomed President Johnson's order to begin bombing North Vietnam in February 1965 as a means to destroy the north's capacity and will to support the Communist insurgents in South Vietnam. But they chafed at Johnson's strategy of gradual escalation and the restrictions he imposed on Operation Rolling Thunder, the three-and-a-half-year bombing campaign. Military officials believed that the United States should have begun Operation Rolling Thunder with all-out massive bombing and continued until the devastation brought North Vietnam to its knees. Instead, they charged, civilian decision makers compelled the military to fight with one hand tied behind its back. Their arguments echoed General Douglas MacArthur's criticism of Truman's policy during the Korean War—though these officials did not repeat MacArthur's insubordination.

Unlike military officials, who could single-mindedly focus on defeating the enemy, the president needed to balance military objectives against political considerations and found compelling reasons to limit the application of airpower. Recalling the Korean War, Johnson noted that "China is there on the [North Vietnamese] border with 700 million men," and he studiously avoided action that might provoke intervention by the Chinese, who now possessed nuclear weapons. Johnson's strategy also aimed to keep the Soviet Union out of the war, to avoid inflaming antiwar sentiment at home, and to avert international criticism of the United States.

Consequently, the president would not permit bombing of areas where high civilian casualties might result and areas near the Chinese border. He banned strikes on airfields and missile sites that were under construction and thus likely to contain Chinese or Soviet advisers, and he refused to mine North Vietnam's harbors, through which Soviet ships imported goods to North Vietnam. But Johnson did escalate the pressure, increasing the intensity of the bombing fourfold by 1968. In all, Operation Rolling Thunder rained 643,000 tons of bombs on North Vietnam between 1965 and 1968.

Military leaders agreed with Johnson's desire to spare civilians. The Joint Chiefs of Staff never proposed, for example, strikes against a system of dikes and dams that could have disrupted food production and flooded Hanoi under twenty feet of water. Rather, they focused on destroying North Vietnam's industry and transportation system. Noncombatant casualties in North Vietnam contrasted sharply with those in World War II, when Anglo-American bombing of Dresden, Germany, alone took more than 35,000 civilian lives and the firebombing of Japan caused 330,000 civilian deaths. In three and a half years, Operation Rolling Thunder's bombing claimed an estimated 52,000 civilian lives.

The relatively low level of economic development in North Vietnam and the North Vietnamese government's ability to mobilize its citizens counteracted the military superiority of the United States. Sheer man-, woman-, and child-power compensated for the demolition of transportation sources, industry sites, and electric power plants. When bombs struck a rail line, civilians rushed with bicycles to unload a train's cargo, carry it beyond the break, and load it onto a second train. Three hundred thousand full-time workers and 200,000 farmers labored in their spare time to keep the Ho Chi Minh Trail usable in spite of heavy bombing. When bridges were destroyed, the North Vietnamese resorted to ferries and pontoons made from bamboo, and they rebuilt bridges slightly underwater to make them harder to detect from the air. They dispersed oil storage facilities and production centers throughout the countryside, and when bombs knocked out electric power plants, the Vietnamese turned to more than two thousand portable generators and used oil lamps and candles in their homes.

North Vietnam's military needs were relatively small, and officials found ample means to meet them. In 1967, North Vietnam had only about 55,000

THE B-52 BOMBER
After 1965, B-52 bombers constantly filled the skies over Vietnam, and at times over Laos and Cambodia. Designed originally to deliver nuclear bombs, a single B-52 carried thirty tons of explosives. A mission of six planes could destroy an area one-half mile wide by three miles long. The B-52 flew too high to be heard on the ground, but its bombs hit with such force that they could kill people in underground shelters.
Co Rentmeester, *Life* magazine
© 1972 *Time* magazine.

soldiers in South Vietnam, and because they waged a guerrilla war with only sporadic fighting, the insurgents in the south did not require huge amounts of supplies. Even after communist forces in the south increased, the total nonfood needs of these soldiers were estimated at just one-fifth of what a single U.S. division required. What U.S. bombs destroyed, the North Vietnamese replaced with Chinese and Soviet imports. China provided 600,000 tons of rice in 1967 alone, and it supplied small arms and ammunition, vehicles, and other goods throughout the war. Competing with China for influence in North Vietnam and favor in the third world, the Soviets contributed tanks, fighter planes, surface-to-air missiles, and other sophisticated weapons. An estimated $2 billion of foreign aid substantially curtailed the effect of Operation Rolling Thunder, and the Soviet-installed modern defense systems made the bombing more difficult and dangerous for U.S. pilots.

In July 1969, Seventh Air Force commander General William W. Momyer commented on Operation Rolling Thunder to the retiring air force chief of staff, "We had the force, skill, and intelligence, but our civilian betters wouldn't turn us loose." Johnson refused to turn the military loose because in addition to the goal he shared with the military—breaking Hanoi's ability to support insurgency in the south—he also wanted to keep China and the Soviet Union (and nuclear weapons) out of the war and to contain domestic and international criticism of U.S. policy. Whether a more devastating air war would have provoked Chinese or Soviet intervention can never be known.

Nor can we know whether all-out bombing of the north could have guaranteed an independent non-Communist government in the south. We do know that Johnson's military advisers imposed their own restraints, never recommending the wholesale attacks on civilians that took place in World War II. Short of decimating the civilian population, it is questionable whether more intense bombing could have completely halted North Vietnamese support for the Vietcong, given the nature of the North Vietnamese economy, the determination and ingenuity of its people, and the plentiful assistance from China and the Soviet Union. Whether the strategic bombing that worked so well in a world war against major industrial powers could be effective in a third world guerrilla war remained in doubt after the Vietnam War.

ratios"—the number of enemies killed relative to the cost in American and ARVN lives.

General William Westmoreland's strategy of attrition was designed to search out and kill the Vietcong and North Vietnamese regular army, but American soldiers did not always distinguish between military combatants and civilians. Lieutenant Philip Caputo reported that the operating rule was "if it's dead and Vietnamese, it's VC [Vietcong]." A helicopter pilot summed up the attrition strategy when, after a brutal battle, his comrade asked, "What did we win? We don't have any more real estate, no new villages are under American control, and it took everything we had to stop them." The pilot responded, "More of them got killed than us. It's that simple."

In contrast to World War II, when the average soldier was twenty-six years old, teenagers fought the Vietnam War. Until the Twenty-sixth Amendment reduced the voting age from twenty-one to eighteen in 1971, most soldiers, whose average age was nineteen, could not even vote for the officials who sent them to war. Men of all classes had fought World War II, but Vietnam was the war of the poor and working class, who constituted about 80 percent of the troops. More privileged youth found ways to avoid the draft, usually through college deferments. Early in the war, African Americans constituted 31 percent of combat troops, often choosing the military over the meager opportunities in the civilian economy. Thus, death rates among black soldiers were disproportionately high until 1966, when the military adjusted personnel assignments to produce a more racially balanced distribution of sacrifice.

The young American troops faced extremely difficult conditions. Soldiers fought in thick jungles and swamps filled with leeches, in oppressive heat, rain, and humidity. Lt. Caputo remembered "weeks of expectant waiting and, at random intervals, conducting vicious manhunts through jungles and swamps where snipers harassed us constantly and booby traps cut us down one by one." The U.S. military inflicted great losses on the enemy, estimated at more than 200,000 by the end of 1967. Yet it could claim no more than a stalemate.

One obstacle was the South Vietnamese government. After a series of coups and short-lived regimes, in 1965 Air Marshal Nguyen Cao Ky became prime minister, but his government failed to rally popular support. Graft and corruption continued to flourish. In the intensified fighting and inability to distinguish friend from foe, thousands of South Vietnamese civilians were killed and wounded, their farms and villages bombed and burned. By 1968, five million people, nearly 30 percent of the population, had become refugees. Huge infusions of American dollars and goods produced rampant inflation, hurt local industries, and increased dependence on foreign aid.

Johnson's Americanization of the war resulted from decisions that flowed logically from the commitments of three presidents before him. All the same, 1965 marked a critical turning point: The rationale for involvement in the war shifted from the need to contain communism in Southeast Asia to the need to prove to the world the ability of the United States to make good on its commitments.

A Nation Polarized

Soon President Johnson was fighting a war on two fronts. Domestic opposition to the war grew significantly after 1965, and the United States experienced internal conflict unparalleled since the Civil War. Television brought the carnage of Vietnam into American homes day after day, making it the first "living-room war." Torn between his domestic critics and the military's clamor for more troops, in March 1968 Johnson announced restrictions on the bombing, a new effort at negotiations, and his decision not to pursue reelection. Throughout 1968, demonstrations, violence, and assassinations convulsed the nation. Vietnam took center stage in the election, and voters narrowly favored the Republican candidate, former vice president Richard Nixon, who promised to "bring Americans together again" and to achieve "peace with honor."

The Widening War at Home

Before 1965, American actions in Vietnam evoked little domestic criticism. But Johnson's authorization of Operation Rolling Thunder sparked a mass movement against the war. In April 1965, Students for a Democratic Society (SDS) recruited twenty thousand people for the first major protest, a rally in Washington, D.C., and SDS chapters sprang up on more than three hundred college campuses across the country. Thousands of young people joined campus protests against Reserve Officers Training Corps (ROTC) programs, CIA recruiters,

AFRICAN AMERICAN ANTIWAR PROTEST
The first expression of African American opposition to the war in Vietnam occurred in Mississippi in July 1965 when a group of civil rights workers called for draft resistance. Blacks should not fight for freedom in Vietnam "until all the Negro People are free in Mississippi," and they should not "risk our lives and kill other Colored People in Santo Domingo and Viet Nam." This protester on the West Coast in April 1967 expresses similar sentiments. How might African American soldiers have responded to the civil rights activists' calls for draft resistance?
Robert LeBeck/Black Star.

manufacturers of war materials, and university departments that conducted research for the Department of Defense. A new draft policy in 1967, which ended deferments for postgraduate education, upped male students' stake in ending the war. In the spring of 1968, as many as one million college and high school students participated in a nationwide strike.

Antiwar sentiment also entered society's mainstream. The *New York Times* began questioning ad-ministration policy in 1965, and by 1968 media critics included the *Wall Street Journal, Life* magazine, and popular TV journalist Walter Cronkite. Clergy, businesspeople, scientists, and physicians formed their own groups to pressure Johnson to stop the bombing and start negotiations. Though most of organized labor supported the president, some union members joined the peace movement. Increasing numbers of prominent Democratic senators, including J. William Fulbright, George McGovern, and majority leader Mike Mansfield, urged Johnson to substitute negotiation for force.

Opposition to the war took diverse forms: letter-writing campaigns to officials, teach-ins on college campuses, mass marches, student strikes, withholding of federal taxes, draft card burnings, and civil disobedience. Although the peace movement never claimed a majority of the population, it focused media attention on the war and severely limited the administration's options. The twenty-year-old consensus about cold war foreign policy had broken down.

Many would not fight in the war. The World Boxing Association stripped Muhammad Ali of his world heavyweight title when he refused to serve in what he called a "white man's war." More than 170,000 men who opposed the war on moral or religious grounds gained conscientious objector status and performed nonmilitary duties at home or in Vietnam. About 60,000 fled the country to escape the draft, and more than 200,000 were accused of failing to register or committing other draft offenses.

Opponents of the war held far from unanimous views. Some condemned the war on moral grounds, insisting that their country had no right to interfere in another country and stressing the suffering of the Vietnamese people. Their goal was total withdrawal. As American intervention escalated with no tangible results, a larger segment of antiwar sentiment reflected practical considerations—that the war could not be won or that the cost would be too great to bear. Not demanding withdrawal, those activists wanted Johnson to stop bombing North Vietnam and seek negotiations.

The antiwar movement outraged millions of Americans who supported the war. Some members of the generation who had fought against Hitler could not understand younger men's refusal to support the government. Working-class people were no more pro-war than other groups, but they were especially conscious of the class dimensions of

PRO-WAR DEMONSTRATORS
Advocates as well as opponents of the war in Vietnam took to the streets, as these New Yorkers did in support of the U.S. invasion of Cambodia in May 1970. Construction workers—called "hard hats"—and other union members marched with American flags and posters championing President Nixon's policies and blasting New York mayor John Lindsay for his antiwar position. Following the demonstration, sympathetic union leaders presented Nixon with an honorary hard hat.
Paul Fusco/Magnum Photos, Inc.

www.bedfordstmartins.com/
roarkcompact SEE THE ONLINE
STUDY GUIDE for more help in
analyzing this image.

the war and the public opposition to it. A firefighter whose son had died in Vietnam said bitterly, "It's people like us who give up our sons for the country. The businesspeople, they run the country and make money from it. The college types . . . go to Washington and tell the government what to do. . . . But their sons don't end up in the swamps over there, in Vietnam."

President Johnson tried a number of means to silence critics. To avoid focusing attention on the war's burdens, he eschewed price and wage controls, imposed in other wars to control inflation, and delayed asking for a tax increase to pay for the war. Congress passed a 10 percent surcharge on federal income taxes in June 1968, after Johnson promised to cut domestic spending. The Great Society programs suffered, but the surcharge failed to reverse the inflationary surge.

The president agonized over casualty reports and felt personally wounded when protesters chanted outside the White House, "Hey, hey, LBJ, how many kids have you killed today?" Reacting harshly to antiwar sentiment, he attempted to mislead the public about the war's progress, tried to discredit opponents by labeling them "nervous Nellies" or Communists, and ordered the CIA to spy on peace advocates. Without the president's specific authorization, the FBI infiltrated the peace movement, disrupted its work, and spread false information about activists. However, even the resort to illegal measures failed to subdue the opposition.

1968: Year of Upheaval

By late 1967—two years after the Americanization of the war—public impatience and frustration had intensified. On one side were the "hawks," who charged that the United States was fighting with one hand tied behind its back and called for the government to apply more power against North Vietnam. The "doves" wanted de-escalation or withdrawal. Most people were torn between weariness of the war and worry about abandoning the American commitment. As one woman said to a pollster, "I want to get out but I don't want to give up."

Grave doubts about the war penetrated the administration itself in 1967. Secretary of Defense Robert McNamara, a principal architect of U.S. involvement, now doubted that the war was winnable. And he feared for the image of the United States, "the world's greatest superpower killing or seriously injuring 1,000 noncombatants a week, while trying to pound a tiny, backward nation into submission on an issue whose merits are hotly disputed." McNamara kept those views to himself until thirty years later, but in early 1968 he left the administration.

The critical turning point came with the Tet Offensive, which began on January 30, 1968. Just a few weeks after General Westmoreland had reported that "the enemy has been driven away from the population centers [and] has been compelled to disperse," the North Vietnamese and Vietcong attacked key cities and every major American base in South Vietnam. This was the biggest surprise of the war, and not simply because both sides had customarily observed a truce during the Vietnamese new year holiday (called Tet). The offensive displayed the Communists' vitality and refusal to be intimidated by the presence of half a million American soldiers. Militarily, the enemy suffered a defeat, losing more than thirty thousand men, ten times as many as ARVN and U.S. forces. Psychologically, however, Tet was devastating to the United States.

The Tet Offensive underscored the credibility gap between official statements and the war's actual progress. The attacks created a million more South Vietnamese refugees as well as widespread destruction, especially in the ancient city of Hue, whose archeological treasures were reduced to rubble. Explaining how he had defended a village, a U.S. army official said, "We had to destroy the town to save it." The statement epitomized for more and more Americans the brutality and senselessness of the war.

In the aftermath of Tet, Johnson considered a request from Westmoreland for 200,000 more troops. He conferred with advisers in the Defense Department and an unofficial group of foreign policy experts, dubbed the "Wise Men," who had been key architects of cold war policies since World War II. Dean Acheson, secretary of state under Truman, summarized their conclusion: "We can no longer do the job we set out to do in the time we have left and we must begin to take steps to disengage."

On March 31, 1968, Lyndon Johnson announced in a televised speech that the United States would reduce its bombing of North Vietnam and that he was prepared to begin peace talks with its leaders. Then he stunned his audience by concluding that he would not run for reelection. The announcement marked the end of the gradual escalation that had begun in 1965. What followed was a shift from "Americanization" to "Vietnamization" of the war,

but it was a shift in strategy, not in policy. The United States maintained its goal of a non-Communist South Vietnam; it simply aimed to reach that goal by relying more heavily on the South Vietnamese.

Negotiations began in Paris in May 1968. But the United States would not agree to recognition of the Hanoi government's National Liberation Front, a coalition government, and American withdrawal. The North Vietnamese would agree to nothing less. Although the talks continued, so did the fighting.

Meanwhile, violence escalated at home. In June, two months after the murder of Martin Luther King Jr. and the ensuing riots, another assassination shook the nation. Running for the Democratic presidential nomination, Senator Robert F. Kennedy, the late president's brother, had just celebrated his triumph in the California primary when he was shot by a Palestinian Arab refugee, Sirhan B. Sirhan, who was outraged by Kennedy's support for Israel.

Spring 1968 also saw campus demonstrations intensify around the world as well as in the United States, where some two hundred protests occurred before summer. In the bloodiest action, students took over buildings at Columbia University in New York City, demanding that the university stop uprooting African Americans in the neighboring community, do more to meet black students' needs, stop research for the Department of Defense, and grant amnesty to student demonstrators. When negotiations failed, university officials called in the city police, who cleared the buildings, injuring more than one hundred demonstrators and arresting more than seven hundred others. An ensuing student strike prematurely ended the academic year.

In August, protesters battled the police in Chicago, where the Democratic Party had convened to nominate its presidential ticket. Several thousand demonstrators came to the city, some to support the peace candidate Eugene McCarthy, others to act more aggressively. Many of the latter had been mobilized by the Youth International Party (Yippies), which urged students to demonstrate their hatred of the establishment by provoking the police to violence and creating chaos in the backyard of the Democratic convention.

Chicago's leading Democrat, mayor Richard J. Daley, issued a ban on rallies and marches, ordered a curfew, and mobilized thousands of police. On August 25, demonstrators responded to police orders to disperse with insults and jeers, whereupon police attacked protesters with tear gas and clubs. Street battles continued for three days, culminating in what an official commission later termed a "police riot" on the night of August 28. Taunted by the crowd, the police used mace and nightsticks, clubbing not only those who had come to provoke violence but also reporters, peaceful demonstrators, and convention delegates.

The bloodshed in Chicago and upheaval across the country had little effect on the outcome of either major party's convention. Peace Democrats lost the presidential nomination, as Vice President Hubert H. Humphrey trounced Eugene McCarthy by nearly three to one. McCarthy's refusal to share the podium with Humphrey as the convention ended illustrated the bitter split within the party. In contrast, the Republican convention peacefully nominated former vice president Richard Nixon on the first ballot. For his running mate, Nixon chose Maryland governor Spiro T. Agnew, hoping to gather southern support while not alienating northern and western voters.

For the first time in nearly fifty years, a strong third party entered the electoral scene. Staunch segregationist former Alabama governor George C. Wallace ran on the ticket of the American Independent Party. Wallace appealed to Americans nationwide who believed that civil rights and antipoverty programs benefited the undeserving at their expense and who were outraged by assaults on traditional values by students and others. Nixon guardedly played on resentments that fueled the Wallace campaign, appealing to "the forgotten Americans, the non-shouters, the non-demonstrators."

Few differences separated the two major-party candidates on the central issue of Vietnam. Nixon promised to "bring an honorable end" to the war but did not indicate how he would do it. Humphrey had strong reservations about U.S. policy in Vietnam, yet as vice president he wanted to avoid a break with Johnson. Finally Johnson boosted Humphrey's campaign when he announced a halt to the bombing of North Vietnam. By election eve, Nixon and Humphrey were neck-and-neck.

With nearly ten million votes (13 percent of the total), the American Independent Party produced the strongest third-party finish since 1924. Nixon edged out Humphrey by just half a million popular votes, prevailing more strongly in the electoral college, with 301 votes to Humphrey's 191 and Wallace's 46. The Democrats lost a few seats in Congress but kept control of both the House and the Senate.

The 1968 elections revealed deep cracks in the coalition that had, with the exception of the Eisenhower years, kept the Democrats in power for thirty years. The Democrats' policies on race moved most of the former "Solid South" behind Nixon or Wallace, breaking a century of Democratic Party ascendance in that region. Large numbers of blue-collar workers broke union ranks to vote for Wallace or Nixon, along with other groups associating the Democrats with racial turmoil, inflation, antiwar protesters, changing sexual mores, urban riots, and America's impotence in Vietnam. These resentments continued to simmer, later to be mobilized into a resurging right in American politics.

Nixon's Failed Search for Peace with Honor

"I'm not going to end up like LBJ, holed up in the White House afraid to show my face on the street," the new president asserted. "I'm going to stop that war. Fast." Although he began a gradual withdrawal of U.S. ground troops, Nixon was no more willing than Johnson to allow South Vietnam to fall to the Communists. Neither was he more able to prevent it, despite expanding military operations into Cambodia and Laos and sporadically but ferociously bombing North Vietnam. In January 1973, the administration concluded a truce that ended the direct involvement of the United States and led to total victory for the North Vietnamese in April 1975.

Vietnamization and Negotiations

Nixon's most important adviser was national security assistant Henry A. Kissinger, a German-born refugee from Hitler's Holocaust and a Harvard professor of international relations. Nixon and Kissinger embraced the overriding goal of the three preceding administrations: a non-Communist South Vietnam. By 1969, however, that goal had become almost incidental to the larger objective of maintaining American credibility. Regardless of the wisdom of the initial intervention, Kissenger asserted, "the commitment of five hundred thousand Americans has settled the importance of Vietnam. For what is involved now is confidence in American promises."

From 1969 to 1972, Nixon and Kissinger pursued a four-pronged approach. First, they tried to strengthen the South Vietnamese military and government. Second, to disarm the antiwar movement at home, Nixon gradually replaced U.S. forces with South Vietnamese soldiers and American technology and bombs. Third, Nixon and Kissinger negotiated with both North Vietnam and the Soviet Union. Fourth, they applied enormous firepower to persuade Hanoi to accept American terms at the bargaining table.

As part of the Vietnamization of the war, ARVN forces grew to over one million, supported with the latest American equipment and training. The South Vietnamese air force became the fourth largest in the world. U.S. advisers and funds also promoted land reform, village elections, and the building of schools, hospitals, and transportation facilities.

The other side of Vietnamization was the withdrawal of U.S. forces. The number of GIs decreased from 543,000 in 1968 to 140,000 by the end of 1971. Despite reduced draft calls and casualties (from nearly 800 deaths a month in 1969 to 352 in 1970), more than 20,000 Americans perished in Vietnam during the last four years of the war. Having been exposed to the antiwar movement at home, many of the remaining soldiers had less faith in the war than their predecessors had. In addition to mounting racial tensions among soldiers, more incidents of "fragging" (attacks on officers by enlisted men) occurred than in any previous wars, and many soldiers sought escape in illegal drugs.

Nixon and Kissinger also endeavored to link Soviet interest in expanded trade and arms reductions with U.S. goals in Vietnam. However, their breakthroughs in summit diplomacy with the Soviet Union and China (discussed in Chapter 31) failed to change the course of the war. Nor did intensification of bombing achieve its objective. Echoing Johnson, Kissinger believed that a "fourth-rate power like North Vietnam" had to have a "breaking point," but the hundreds of thousands of tons of bombs delivered by U.S. pilots failed to find it. Fierce application of American power bought time, but little else. (See "Historical Question," page 758.)

Nixon's War

In the spring of 1969, Nixon began a ferocious air war in Cambodia, carefully hiding it from Congress and the public for more than a year. Seeking to knock out North Vietnamese sanctuaries in Cambodia, the campaign dropped more than 100,000 tons of bombs but succeeded only in sending the North Vietnamese to other hiding places. To sup-

port a new, pro-Western Cambodian government installed through a military coup in 1970 and "to show the enemy that we were still serious about our commitment in Vietnam," in April 1970 Nixon ordered a joint U.S.-ARVN invasion of Cambodia.

That order made Vietnam "Nixon's war" and provoked outrage at home. Nixon made a belligerent speech defending his move and emphasizing the importance of U.S. credibility: "If when the chips are down, the world's most powerful nation acts like a pitiful helpless giant, the forces of totalitarianism and anarchy will threaten free nations" everywhere. "This will make the students puke," a cabinet member said when he read Nixon's speech. They did more. More than 100,000 people protested in Washington, and students demonstrated and boycotted classes on hundreds of campuses. At a peaceful rally on May 4, 1970, at Kent State University in Ohio, nervous National Guard troops fired at students, killing four and wounding ten others. "They're starting to treat their own children like they treat us," commented a black woman in Harlem. In a confrontation at Jackson State College in Mississippi on May 14, police shot into a dormitory, killing two black students. In August, police used tear gas and clubs against protesters at a Chicano antiwar rally in Los Angeles.

Upon learning of the bombing and invasion of Cambodia, furious legislators attempted to curb the president. The Senate voted to terminate the Gulf of Tonkin Resolution, which had given the president virtually a blank check in Vietnam, and to cut off funds for the Cambodian operation. The House of Representatives refused to go along, but Congress was clearly becoming an obstacle to the Nixon administration's plans. By the end of June, Nixon pulled out all U.S. soldiers from Cambodia.

In 1971, Vietnam veterans themselves became a visible part of the peace movement, the first men in U.S. history to oppose a war in which they had fought. Veterans held a public investigation of "war crimes" in Vietnam, rallied in front of the Capitol, and cast away their war medals. In May 1971, veterans numbered among the forty thousand protesters who engaged in civil disobedience in an effort to shut down Washington. Officials made more than twelve thousand arrests, which courts later ruled violations of protesters' rights.

After the spring of 1971, there were fewer massive antiwar demonstrations, but protest continued. Public attention focused on the court-martial of Lieutenant William Calley, which began in November 1970 and resulted in his conviction. During the trial, Americans learned that Calley's company had massacred more than four hundred civilians in the hamlet of My Lai in March 1968. Among those murdered were children and women, an atrocity that the military had covered up for more than a year.

Administration policy suffered another blow in June 1971 with publication of the *Pentagon Papers*, a secret government study critical of U.S. policy in Vietnam. Daniel Ellsberg, once a civilian adviser in Vietnam and an aide to Henry Kissinger, had worked on the study. Frustrated in his attempts to persuade officials of the war's futility, Ellsberg copied the papers and gave them to the *New York Times*. Administration efforts to prevent their publication were defeated by the Supreme Court as a violation of freedom of the press. The *Pentagon Papers* heightened disillusionment with the war by

casting doubts on the government's credibility. More than 60 percent of respondents to a public opinion poll in 1971 considered it a mistake to have sent American troops to Vietnam; 58 percent believed the war to be immoral.

The Peace Accords and the Fall of Saigon

Nixon and Kissinger continued to combine military force and negotiation. In March 1972, responding to a strong North Vietnamese offensive, the United States resumed sustained bombing of the north, mined Haiphong and other harbors for the first time, and announced a naval blockade. With peace talks stalled, in December Nixon ordered the most devastating bombing of North Vietnam yet: In twelve days, U.S. planes dropped more bombs than they had in all of 1969–1971.

MY LAI MASSACRE
When U.S. forces attacked the village of My Lai in March 1968, they believed that it was a Vietcong stronghold and expected a fierce fight. Even though they encountered no enemy forces, the men of Charlie Company systematically killed every inhabitant, nearly all of whom were old men, women, and children. Estimates put the death toll at more than 400 villagers. Twelve officers and enlisted men were charged with murder or assault to commit murder, but only one, First Lieutenant William Calley, was convicted. Though he was convicted of premeditated murder, Calley was paroled after serving less than four years in prison. This photograph of murdered villagers was taken by an army photographer.
Ron Haeberle, *Life* magazine © Time, Inc.

On January 27, 1973, representatives of the United States, North Vietnam, the South Vietnamese government, and the Vietcong (now called the People's Revolutionary Government) signed a formal accord in Paris. The agreement required removal of all U.S. troops and military advisers but allowed North Vietnamese forces to remain. Both sides agreed to return prisoners of war. The South Vietnamese government continued in power, and the peace treaty allowed the United States a face-saving withdrawal, but it was doubtful that South Vietnam would remain non-Communist for long.

Fighting resumed immediately among the Vietnamese. Nixon's efforts to support the South Vietnamese government, and indeed his ability to govern at all, were increasingly eroded by what came to be known as the Watergate scandals (discussed in Chapter 30). In 1975, North Vietnam launched a new offensive in South Vietnam, and on May 1, occupied Saigon and renamed it Ho Chi Minh City to honor the Communist leader.

Confusion, humiliation, and tragedy marked the hasty evacuation of Americans and their South Vietnamese allies. The United States got its own citizens out, along with 150,000 South Vietnamese, but it lacked sufficient transport and time to evacuate all those who wanted to leave. U.S. marines beat back desperate Vietnamese trying to escape through the U.S. embassy. Some South Vietnamese troops, frightened and angry at being left behind, fired on departing Americans.

The Legacy of Defeat

It took Nixon four years to end the war. During that time, the conflict expanded into Cambodia and Laos, Southeast Asia endured massive bombing campaigns, and the Vietnam War became genuinely bipartisan. But, although increasing numbers of legislators criticized the war, Congress never denied the funds to fight it.

Only after the peace accords did the legislative branch stiffen its constitutional authority over the making of war. In November 1973, Congress passed the War Powers Act requiring the president to report to Congress within forty-eight hours of deploying military forces abroad. If Congress failed to endorse the president's action within sixty days, the troops would have to be withdrawn.

The dire predictions of three presidents that a Communist victory in South Vietnam would set the dominoes cascading did not materialize. Although Vietnam, Laos, and Cambodia all fell within the Communist camp in the spring of 1975, Thailand, Burma, Malaysia, and the rest of Southeast Asia did not. When China and Vietnam reverted to their historically hostile relationship, the myth of a monolithic Communist power overrunning Asia evaporated.

While most Americans wanted simply to forget defeat in Vietnam, veterans and those who lost loved ones could not so easily put the war behind them. The nation had always honored its soldiers' sacrifices, but three unique elements of the Vietnam War denied veterans the traditional homecoming: its lack of strong support at home, its character as a guerrilla war, and its ultimate failure. As one veteran remarked, "The left hated us for killing, and the right hated us for not killing enough."

Because the Vietnam War was in large part a civil, guerrilla war, combat was especially brutal. The terrors of conventional warfare were multiplied, and so were the opportunities and motivations to commit atrocities. The massacre at My Lai was only the most publicized war crime. To demonstrate the immorality of the war, peace advocates stressed the atrocities, contributing to an image of the Vietnam War veteran as dehumanized and violent and thus deserving of public hostility or indifference.

Veterans largely expressed two kinds of reactions to the defeat. Many regarded the commitment as an honorable one and felt betrayed by the government for not letting them and their now-dead comrades win the war. Others blamed the government for sacrificing the nation's youth in an immoral or useless war. These soldiers best expressed their sense of the war's futility in the slang term they used for a comrade's death: He was "wasted."

"We would not return to cheering crowds, parades, and the pealing of great cathedral bells," wrote Philip Caputo. Most veterans came home to public neglect, while some faced harassment from antiwar activists who did not distinguish the war from the warriors. A veteran remembered the "feelings of rejection and scorn that a bunch of depressed and confused young men experienced when they returned home from doing what their country told them to do." Government benefits were less generous to Vietnam War veterans than they had been to World War II and Korean War soldiers. Much more than World War II, the Vietnam War was a men's war, and the 11,500 women who had served felt even more isolated and ignored by the government,

the public, and veterans' groups. Yet two-thirds of Vietnam veterans said that they would serve again, and most veterans readjusted well to civilian life under difficult circumstances.

Nonetheless, the Veterans Administration (VA) estimated that nearly one-sixth of the three million veterans suffered from posttraumatic stress disorder, with its symptoms of fear, recurring nightmares, feelings of guilt and shame, violence, drug and alcohol abuse, and suicidal tendencies. More than fifteen years after the war's end, veterans remained on long waiting lists for treatment.

In the late 1970s, many of those who had served in Vietnam began to display a different set of symptoms: They produced deformed children and fell ill themselves with cancer, severe skin disorders, and other ailments. Veterans claimed a link between these illnesses and Agent Orange, an herbicide that contained the deadly poison dioxin, which the mil-

itary had sprayed by the millions of gallons over Vietnam. Scientists disagreed about the chemical's effects, and not until 1991 did Congress provide assistance to veterans with diseases linked to Agent Orange.

The government's new position on Agent Orange coincided with a shift in the climate surrounding Vietnam War veterans. "It wasn't until the early 1980s," one veteran observed, "that it became 'all right' to be a combat veteran." The Vietnam War began to enter the realm of popular culture with novels, TV shows, and hit movies depicting a broad range of military experience—from soldiers reduced to brutality to men and women serving with courage and integrity.

The incorporation of the Vietnam War into the collective experience was symbolized most dramatically in the Vietnam Veterans Memorial unveiled in Washington, D.C., in November 1982. The black,

V-shaped wall inscribed with the names of 58,000 men and women lost to the war became the second most visited site in the capital. In an article describing the memorial's dedication, a Vietnam combat veteran spoke to and for his former comrades: "Welcome home. The war is over."

Conclusion: An Unwinnable War

Vietnam was America's longest war. The United States spent $150 billion and sent 2.6 million of its young men and women to Vietnam. Of those, 58,000 never returned, and 150,000 suffered serious injury. The war shattered consensus at home and contributed to the most severe internal disorder in a century. It increased presidential power at the expense of congressional authority and public accountability and led to the downfall of two presidents.

The Vietnam War was a logical extension of the nation's post–World War II commitment to contain communism everywhere on the planet, a commitment begun when the United States had enjoyed an extraordinary margin of power, largely because World War II had so ravaged the other major nations. As other nations recovered, the United States lost its temporary advantage. Defeat in Vietnam did not make the United States the "pitiful helpless giant" predicted by Nixon, but it did suggest the relative decline of U.S. power and the impossibility of containment on a global scale.

One of the constraints on U.S. power was the tenacity of revolutionary movements that were determined to achieve national independence. Marine Lieutenant Philip Caputo recalled the surprise at discovering "that the men we had scorned as peasant guerrillas were, in fact, a lethal, determined enemy." U.S. officials badly underestimated the sacrifices that the enemy was willing to make to achieve national liberation. Policymakers overestimated the effectiveness of American technological superiority, and they failed to realize how easily the United States could be perceived as a colonial intruder, no more welcome than the French had been.

A second constraint on Eisenhower, Kennedy, Johnson, and Nixon was their resolve to avoid a major confrontation with the Soviet Union or China. For Johnson, who conducted the largest escalation of the war, caution was especially critical so as not to provoke direct intervention by the Communist superpowers. After China exploded its first atomic bomb in 1964, the potential heightened for the Vietnam conflict to escalate into worldwide disaster.

Third, in Vietnam the United States faced the problem of containment by means of an extremely weak ally. The South Vietnamese government never won the support of its people, and the intense devastation and suffering the war brought to civilians only made things worse. Short of taking over the South Vietnamese government and military, the United States could do little to strengthen South Vietnam's ability to resist communism.

Finally, domestic opposition to the war constrained the options of Johnson and Nixon. From its origin in 1965, the antiwar movement grew to include significant portions of mainstream America by 1968. As the war dragged on, with increasing American casualties and growing evidence of the damage being inflicted on innocent Vietnamese, more and more civilians wearied of the conflict. Even some who had fought the war joined the movement, including Philip Caputo, who sent his campaign ribbons and a bitter letter of protest to the White House. By 1968, distinguished experts who had fashioned and implemented the containment policy recognized that erosion of support for the war made its continuation untenable. Five years later Nixon and Kissinger bowed to the resolution of the enemy and the limitations of U.S. power. As the war wound down, passions surrounding it contributed to a rising conservative movement that would substantially alter the post–World War II political order.

FOR FURTHER READING ABOUT THE TOPICS IN THIS CHAPTER, see the Online Bibliography at
www.bedfordstmartins.com/roarkcompact.

FOR ADDITIONAL FIRST-HAND ACCOUNTS OF THIS PERIOD, see pages 221–237 in Michael Johnson, ed., *Reading the American Past*, Second Edition, Volume II.

TO ASSESS YOUR MASTERY OF THE MATERIAL IN THIS CHAPTER, see the Online Study Guide at
www.bedfordstmartins.com/roarkcompact.

CHRONOLOGY

1961 CIA-backed Cuban exiles launch unsuccessful invasion of Cuba at Bay of Pigs.

Berlin Wall erected, dividing East and West Berlin.

Kennedy administration increases military aid and military advisers in South Vietnam.

Kennedy administration creates Alliance for Progress and Peace Corps.

1962 Cuban missile crisis results in Soviet removal of missiles in Cuba.

1963 Limited nuclear test-ban treaty signed by United States and Soviet Union.

South Vietnamese military overthrows President Ngo Dinh Diem.

1964 U.S. troops quell anti-American rioting in Panama Canal Zone.

President Johnson uses Gulf of Tonkin incident to get congressional resolution of support for escalating the war.

1965 First major protest demonstration in Washington, D.C., against Vietnam War attracts twenty thousand people.

Johnson administration initiates Operation Rolling Thunder, intensified bombing of North Vietnam.

Johnson orders increase in number of U.S. troops in Vietnam; peak is 543,000 in 1968.

U.S. troops invade Dominican Republic to prevent leftist government from taking power.

1968 Hundreds of thousands of Americans demonstrate against war.

Vietnamese Communists' Tet Offensive leads Johnson administration to reverse its policy in Vietnam and seek negotiated settlement.

In wake of Tet Offensive, President Johnson decides not to seek second term.

Richard Nixon elected president.

1969 Nixon orders secret bombing of Cambodia.

1970 Nixon orders joint U.S.–South Vietnamese invasion of Cambodia.

Students killed by national guard members and police during campus protests at Kent State and Jackson State.

1971 *New York Times* publishes *Pentagon Papers*, a secret government study critical of U.S. policy in Vietnam.

1973 The Paris accords between the United States, North and South Vietnam, and Vietcong bring formal end to U.S. role in Vietnam.

Congress enacts War Powers Act, limiting president's ability to send Americans to war without congressional consent.

1975 North Vietnam launches final offensive and takes over all of South Vietnam, ending war in Vietnam.

THE ECONOMICS AND POLITICS OF CONFIDENCE
This sculpture of a bull sits on Wall Street, in the southern section of Manhattan and the
financial heart of the United States, where the New York Stock Exchange, investment
banks, the Federal Reserve Bank, and other financial institutions are located. In contrast
to the bear, which symbolizes a declining stock market, the bull stands for investors' confi-
dence that stock prices will continue to rise, as they did so remarkably in the 1980s and
1990s. President Ronald Reagan's ability to inspire the American people's confidence in
their nation as well as its economy helped enormously in his drive to reverse the liberal
direction that national politics had taken in the 1960s.
Gary Gabino/Sipa Press.

RETREAT FROM LIBERALISM 30

1968–2000

FRANKLIN DELANO REAGAN headlined the *New York Times* editorial on Ronald Wilson Reagan's acceptance speech at the 1980 Republican convention. The presidential nominee had repeatedly quoted Roosevelt, all the while promising to reduce drastically the federal government's role in American life. Once in the White House, Reagan promptly rehung a portrait of President Calvin Coolidge—that staunch Republican believer in big business—but he continued to grasp the mantle of Roosevelt even as his policies formed the antithesis of New Deal liberalism.

Reagan genuinely admired Roosevelt's dynamism and his optimism about the nation's future; but his invocation of Franklin Roosevelt also aimed at his political goal—to appeal to traditional Democrats. In 1968, Richard Nixon had capitalized on the disaffection of Democrats that grew out of the turmoil of the 1960s, and he won reelection in a landslide victory in 1972. But just two years later he resigned the office in disgrace. His successor, Gerald Ford, occupied the Oval Office for little more than two years, losing to Democrat Jimmy Carter in the 1976 election. After a single term, Carter, too, was voted out of office. This rapid turnover in the presidency reflected in part a widespread loss of trust and confidence in government, expressed cynically by some Americans whose bumper stickers exhorted, "Don't vote. . . . It only encourages them." Voter turnout declined to just 52.3 percent in 1980, as polls revealed a drop from 56 to 29 percent in citizens' belief that government would "do what is right most of the time."

Nixon's moral failings and Ford's and Carter's weak leadership contributed to the demise of all three, but changes in the institutions of politics and government along with new domestic and foreign challenges created obstacles that might well have defeated more talented politicians. In reaction to the expansion of presidential power by Johnson and Nixon, Congress reasserted its authority, but at the expense of undercutting the position of congressional party leaders. Political parties further lost influence as primary elections replaced conventions in the nomination of candidates and as elected officials depended less on party support and more on campaign funds from interest groups. This fragmented leadership in turn confronted critical economic problems as rising unemployment, declining productivity, and spiraling inflation replaced the rapid economic growth of the 1960s. Two social movements—feminism and environmentalism—gained key policy objectives during the 1970s, but public opinion along with a growing conservative movement reflected a more general loss of faith in government to solve social problems.

While restoring national optimism and presiding over an economic upturn, Reagan also sought a revolution in domestic policy as striking as Roosevelt's in extent—though opposite in kind—and a new national political alignment as dominant and lasting as Roosevelt's New Deal coalition. He cultivated groups upset with social changes evident since the 1960s and pursued policies to limit government's role in regulating the economy and providing for the disadvantaged. His vice president George H. Bush maintained the Republican hold on the White House for four more years but lost to Democrat William Jefferson Clinton in 1992.

Even though Reagan and Bush failed to achieve for the Republican Party the dominance enjoyed by the Democrats for three decades or policy changes as dramatic as those of the New Deal, they did help push the entire political spectrum to the right. Their successor, Bill Clinton, presented himself as a "New Democrat" in contrast to the liberalism of the party in the 1960s. The Republicans' control of Congress and Clinton's own political and personal flaws limited his administration's accomplishments. Above all, his record reflected the Democratic Party's retreat from the liberalism of the 1960s, a development that began with Jimmy Carter and that Clinton captured in 1996, when, echoing Ronald Reagan, he asserted, "The era of big government is over." And when the 2000 elections delivered the White House to George W. Bush, son of the former president, and produced a closely divided Congress, national politics seemed likely to remain on center ground.

Conservative Politics and Liberal Programs in the Nixon Administration

Richard Nixon took his victory in 1968 as evidence that most Americans were fed up with social protest and government efforts to expand individual rights and to provide for the disadvantaged. He continued to appeal to those frustrations, and the pace of reform slackened during his administration. Yet Nixon had won the Republican nomination as a centrist, and two newer reform movements—feminism and environmentalism—exerted pressures that he could not ignore. In contrast to his public rhetoric, his administration's legislative record incorporated the very government activism that the president's speeches decried. Nixon's political expediency, a Democratic Congress representing a broad spectrum of political positions, the president's eye on his place in history, and serious economic problems all helped to sustain many of the reforms of the 1960s and even expand the government's role.

Nixon's "Southern Strategy" and Race Relations

Nixon's 1968 campaign had exploited antipathy to black protest and new civil rights policies in order to woo white southerners away from the Democratic Party. This "southern strategy" helped Nixon capture the presidency, and Republicans hoped to use it to make further inroads into traditional Democratic strongholds in the 1972 election.

Yet the Nixon administration had to answer to the courts and Congress. In 1968, fourteen years after the *Brown* decision, school desegregation had barely touched the South: Two-thirds of African American children did not have a single white schoolmate. Like Eisenhower, Nixon did not want to use federal power to compel integration, but when the Supreme Court overruled efforts by the Justice Department to delay court-ordered desegregation, the administration was compelled to enforce the law. By the time Nixon left office, fewer than one in ten southern black children attended totally segregated schools.

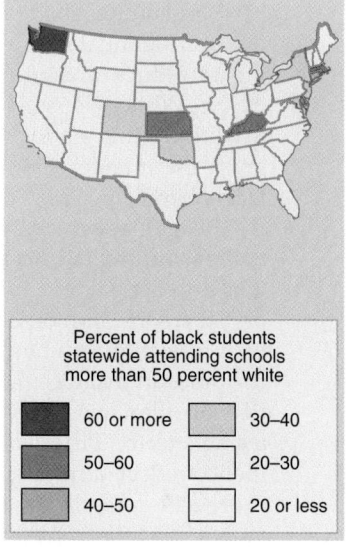

Percent of black students statewide attending schools more than 50 percent white

- 60 or more
- 50–60
- 40–50
- 30–40
- 20–30
- 20 or less

Integration of Public Schools, 1968

School segregation was widespread also in northern and western cities, where residential patterns left half of all African American children attending virtually all-black schools. When the courts began to order transfer of students between schools in white and black neighborhoods to achieve desegregation, busing became one of the most inflammatory civil rights issues.

Outrage over busing erupted in Boston in 1974 when black students began to attend the formerly all-white South Boston High School. Virtually all the white students boycotted classes while angry white crowds threw rocks at black students disembarking from buses. The whites most affected came from working-class families, who remained in cities abandoned by more affluent whites and whose children were usually the ones riding buses to predominantly black schools where overcrowding

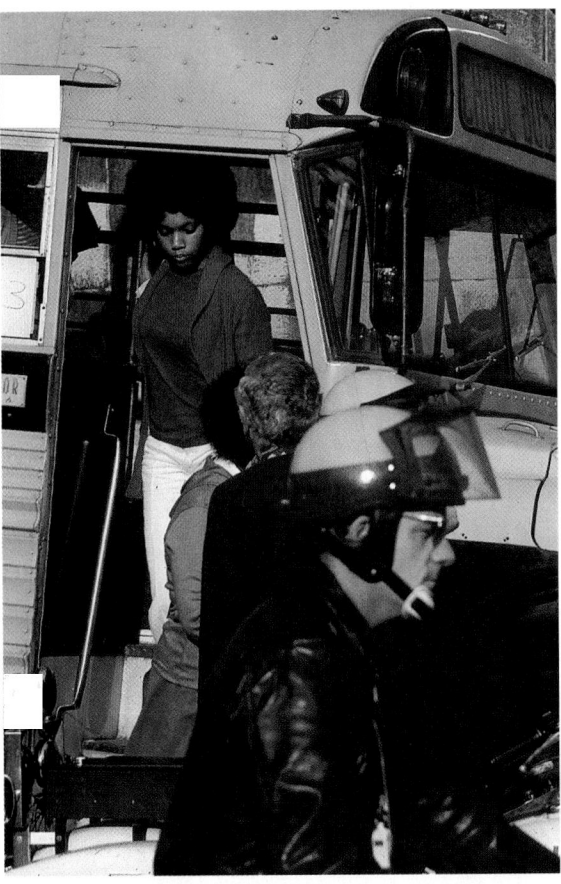

SCHOOL BUSING
Controversy over busing as a means to integrate public schools erupted in Boston when the school year started in autumn 1974. Opposition was especially high in white ethnic neighborhoods like South Boston, whose residents resented liberal judges from the suburbs assigning them the burden of integration. Clashes between blacks and whites in South Boston prompted authorities to dispatch police to protect black students.
Ira Wyman.

and deficient facilities often meant inferior education. African Americans themselves were divided over the desirability of busing children across district lines. Nixon failed to persuade Congress to end court-ordered busing, but after he had appointed four new justices, the Supreme Court moved in the president's direction in 1974. In a five-to-four decision concerning the Detroit public schools (*Milliken v. Bradley*), the Court imposed strict limits on the use of busing to achieve racial balance.

Despite Nixon's conservative rhetoric and practice, his administration did take some steps against discrimination, requiring contractors and unions to employ more minority workers on federally funded construction projects and awarding more government contracts and loans to minority businesses. Congress took the initiative in other areas. In 1970, it extended the Voting Rights Act of 1965 by five years; and in 1972, Congress strengthened the Civil Rights Act of 1964 by enlarging the authority of the Equal Employment Opportunity Commission, the act's enforcement agency.

Nixon believed that the Supreme Court under Chief Justice Earl Warren had been "unprecedentedly politically active . . . too often using their interpretation of the law to remake American society according to their own social, political, and ideological precepts." Through his appointments, Nixon planned both to reverse the Court's direction and to implement his southern strategy. When Warren resigned in June 1969, Nixon replaced him with Warren E. Burger, a federal appeals court judge, who was seen as a more conservative, strict constructionist—one who would more narrowly interpret the Constitution and limit government intervention to protect individual rights.

When Nixon tried to appoint two conservative southern judges, however, the Senate forced him to settle on more moderate candidates. The Burger Court proved more sympathetic to the president's agenda, restricting somewhat the protections of individual rights established by the Warren Court, limiting, for example the range of affirmative action in *Regents of the University of California v. Bakke* (1978). Yet that decision did sanction affirmative action programs to attack the results of past discrimination as long as strict quotas or racial classifications were not involved. In this and other cases it continued to uphold liberal programs of the 1960s.

The New Feminism

New social movements also contributed to the persistence of an activist federal government. On August 26, 1970, fifty years after women won the right to vote, tens of thousands of women across the country took to the streets. They carried signs reading "Sisterhood Is Powerful" and "Don't Cook Dinner—Starve a Rat Today." Some of the banners proclaimed, "The Women of Vietnam Are Our Sisters," and others demanded racial justice. But this time, women placed their own liberation at the forefront.

Organized largely by chapters of the National Organization for Women (NOW), the protest reflected diverse strands of a movement that in the 1970s spawned hundreds of new groups throughout the nation. Participants included radical women in jeans and conservatively dressed suburbanites, peace activists and politicians, and a sprinkling of women of color. Three demands were prominent: equality for women in employment and education; child care centers throughout the nation; and women's control over reproduction, including the right to abortion.

Although NOW elected a black president, Aileen Hernandez, in 1970, white middle-class women predominated in the new feminism's na-

tional leadership and much of its constituency. They were criticized for their frequent indifference to the concerns of women who were unlike themselves, yet support for feminism was exceedingly multifaceted. Most African American women worked through their own groups such as the older National Council of Negro Women and the National Black Feminist Organization, founded in 1973. Similarly, in the early 1970s American Indian women and Mexican American women founded national organizations, and Asian American women formed their own local movements. Blue-collar women or-

TITLE IX AND WOMEN'S SPORTS
The women's swim team of Brown University practice under a sign designating the "respect" women's intercollegiate athletics have won since the passage of Title IX in 1972, which banned gender discrimination in education. Nearly the entire male sports establishment opposed the law, fearing diminished funding for football and other men's sports. Reflecting this opposition, few enforcement efforts were made during the Reagan and Bush administrations, causing women to file lawsuits against several colleges and universities. In the landmark case **Amy Brown et al. v. Brown University,** *decided in 1997, the U.S. Supreme Court let stand a lower-court decision that Brown University violated Title IX when it eliminated women's gymnastics and volleyball in 1991. Women's athletics flourished, with the number of participants quadrupling from 31,000 in 1972 to more than 150,000 in 2002. Although the American public tends to think of athletics when they hear the term, Title IX applies to every aspect of education and has promoted greater equity in admissions, scholarships, housing, and more.*
Irene Perlman.

ganized the National Coalition of Labor Union Women in 1974. Lesbians established collectives throughout the country as well as their own caucuses in organizations such as NOW. Women founded a host of other groups that focused on single issues such as health, abortion rights, education, and violence against women.

Common threads underlay the great diversity of organizations, issues, and activities. Above all, feminism represented the belief that women were barred from, unequally treated in, or poorly served by the male-dominated public arena, encompassing politics, medicine, law, education, and religion. Feminists also sought equality in the private sphere, challenging traditional norms that identified women primarily as wives and mothers or sex objects.

The women's movement was an effect more than a cause of women's rising employment, but feminism lifted female aspirations and helped lower barriers to jobs and offices historically monopolized by men. Women made some inroads into skilled crafts and management positions. Between 1970 and 2000, their share of law degrees shot up from 5 percent to nearly 50 percent, and their proportion of medical degrees from less than 10 percent to more than 35 percent. Women gained political offices very slowly; yet by the 1990s, women constituted more than 10 percent of Congress, and more than 20 percent of all state executives and legislators.

Feminist activism produced the most sweeping changes in laws and policies concerning women since they had won the right to vote in 1920. In 1972, Congress passed Title IX of the Education Amendments Act, banning sex discrimination in all aspects of education, such as admissions, athletics, and faculty hiring. Congress also outlawed sex discrimination in the granting of loans in 1974, opened U.S. military academies to women in 1976, and prohibited discrimination against pregnant workers in 1978. The Burger Court struck down laws that treated men and women differently in Social Security, welfare and military benefits, and workers' compensation.

At the state and local levels, radical feminists won laws forcing police departments and the legal system to treat rape victims more justly and humanely. Activists set up shelters for battered women and their children, and they won state laws ensuring greater protection for victims of domestic violence and more effective prosecution of offenders. Feminists pressured state legislatures to end restric-

tions on abortion, and many testified publicly about their own illegal abortions. In 1973, the Supreme Court issued the landmark *Roe v. Wade* decision, ruling that the Constitution protects the right to abortion, which states cannot prohibit in the early stages of pregnancy. However, later decisions allowed state governments to impose restrictions on that right, such as denying coverage under Medicaid and other government-financed health programs, thereby making it harder for poor women to obtain abortions.

Public opinion polls registered majority support for most feminist goals, yet by the mid-1970s feminism faced a strong countermovement focused on defeating an Equal Rights Amendment to the Constitution that would outlaw differential treatment of men and women under all state and federal laws. Most states rushed to ratify the amendment, yet by 1973 a powerful opposition developed, led by Phyllis Schlafly, a conservative activist in the Republican party. Schlafly mobilized a highly effective host of women at the grassroots level who believed that traditional gender roles were God-given and feared that feminism would devalue their own roles as wives and mothers. These women, marching on state capitols, persuaded some male legislators to block ratification. When the time limit ran out in 1982, only thirty-five states had ratified the amendment, three short of the necessary three-fourths majority (Map 30.1).

Opposition to the right to abortion was even more intense. Many Americans believed that human life begins with conception, and they equated abortion with murder. The Catholic Church and other religious organizations provided institutional support for their protest. Right-wing politicians and their supporters constituted another segment of the right-to-life movement. Like ERA opponents, the right-to-life movement mobilized thousands of women who believed that abortion devalued motherhood and saw feminism as a threat to their traditional roles.

Feminists faced a host of other challenges. Despite some inroads into male-dominated occupations, most women still worked in low-paying traditionally female jobs. Employed women continued to bear primary responsibility for their homes and families, thereby working a "double day." As the number of female-headed families doubled from 10 percent to 20 percent of all American families by the end of the century, the situation of working mothers became even more critical.

MAP 30.1

The Fight for the Equal Rights Amendment

Many states that failed to ratify the Equal Rights Amendment had previously refused to ratify the woman suffrage amendment (or ratified it decades later, as did North Carolina in 1971).

READING THE MAP: How many states ratified the amendment, and how many did not? Did any regions overwhelmingly support or oppose the ERA?

CONNECTIONS: What was the goal of the ERA? Who were its opponents, and what were their main points of opposition?

www.bedfordstmartins.com/roarkcompact SEE THE ONLINE STUDY GUIDE for more help in analyzing this map.

A New Movement to Save the Environment

Feminists were not alone in forcing attention on a new set of issues. In April 1970, millions of Americans observed the first Earth Day to protest the ravaging effects of industrial development on the environment. In Wisconsin, students distributed flyers on recycling, and a group of Detroit women picketed a steel plant that polluted a river with industrial waste. Girl Scouts cleaned garbage from the Potomac River, African Americans in St. Louis dramatized the effects of poisons in lead paint, students in Michigan smashed a Ford to protest auto emissions, and all over the country people planted trees. Inheriting their concern for the natural world from the decades-old conservation movement, the new environmentalists had a far broader agenda. Even more important than preserving portions of nature for aesthetic and recreational purposes was protecting human beings, wildlife, and plants from the devastating side effects of industrial development and economic growth—polluted air and water and the spread of deadly chemicals.

Biologist Rachel Carson had first drawn national attention to environmental concerns in 1962 with her best-seller *Silent Spring*, which described the harmful effects of toxic chemicals, particularly the pesticide DDT. Older conservation organizations like the Sierra Club and the Wilderness Society expanded their agendas, and a host of new organizations arose. In 1971, environmentalists founded Greenpeace, which protested nuclear testing around the world and campaigned to save marine life and tropical rain forests. Even more militant was Earth First!, created in 1980 and committed to direct action and sabotage of projects injurious to the environment.

Although President Nixon asserted that the nation must begin "reclaiming the purity of its air, its waters, our living environment," he generally favored economic growth over environmental considerations. He vetoed anti–water-pollution legisla-

tion, forcing an override from Congress, and, disregarding environmentalists' objections, pushed Congress to authorize construction of a 789-mile-long pipeline to carry oil across Alaska. Yet in other respects the Nixon administration proved more friendly to the environmental movement. In 1970, Nixon established the Environmental Protection Agency (EPA) to enforce clean air and water policies and regulate pesticides. He also signed the Occupational Safety and Health Act (OSHA), which safeguarded workers against workplace accidents and disease. The strongest measure supported by the Nixon administration was the Clean Air Act of

EARTH DAY
Because of its association with nature and the earth, green was the color of the environmental movement, and environmentalists called themselves "greens." These activists leave no doubt about their affiliation at an Earth Day celebration in New York City in April 1970. The button, a takeoff on the antiwar slogan "Give Peace a Chance," reflects the continuing impact of the antiwar movement.
Dennis Stock/Magnum Photos, Inc.

www.bedfordstmartins.com/roarkcompact   SEE THE ONLINE STUDY GUIDE for more help in analyzing this image.

1970, which set national standards for air quality and restricted factory and automobile emissions. Twenty years after enactment, no major city met the new standards, but even with lenient enforcement, the Clean Air Act cut air pollutants by one-third, despite population and economic growth.

Warning of radiation leakage, potential accidents, and the hazards of nuclear wastes, environmentalists also targeted nuclear power plants, which by 1977 produced about 11 percent of the country's electricity. The perils of nuclear energy came into dramatic focus in March 1979, when an accident occurred at the Three Mile Island nuclear facility near Harrisburg, Pennsylvania, and technicians worked for days to prevent a meltdown of the reactor core. Popular opposition and the great expense of building nuclear plants stalled further development of the nuclear power industry; but antinuclear activism endured as a part of the environmental movement, especially after the explosion of a nuclear reactor and the spread of deadly radiation in Chernobyl, Ukraine, in 1986.

Extending the Welfare State and Economic Regulation

Richard Nixon objected to much of Lyndon Johnson's Great Society, insisting that "government must learn to take less from people so people can do more for themselves." He appealed to those he labeled "middle America," resentful of government's apparent disregard for their interests while favoring individuals who they felt lacked the discipline to help themselves. Thus, Nixon blocked initiatives from the Democrat-controlled Congress, such as a 1971 child care bill, objecting both to the program's $2 billion cost and to its "family-weakening implications."

Yet under Nixon, government assistance programs actually grew. For one thing, Congress resisted many of his attacks on antipoverty programs, refusing, for example, to eliminate the Office of Economic Opportunity. Key programs such as Medicare and Medicaid, Head Start, Legal Services, and job training remained intact. Indeed, the federal budget for social services exceeded defense spending for the first time since World War II. Social Security benefits—now required to rise with the cost of living—increased; subsidies for low-income housing tripled; and a new billion-dollar program provided Pell grants (named for the bill's sponsor)

for low-income students to attend college. In response to growing public concern about undernourishment, Nixon supported a huge expansion of the food stamp program, which benefited 12.5 million recipients.

Nixon also acted contrary to his rhetoric against a growing federal bureaucracy in expanding government controls over the economy. Political pressures impelled him to approve new environmental controls, while economic crises and energy shortages induced him to increase the federal government's power in the marketplace.

Throughout the post–World War II economic boom, the nation's abundant oil deposits and access to cheap Middle Eastern oil had encouraged the building of large cars and glass-enclosed skyscrapers with no concern for fuel efficiency. The traditional American assumption that energy resources were boundless and the resulting wasteful practices meant that by the 1970s the United States, with just 6 percent of the world's population, consumed one-third of its fuel resources.

In the fall of 1973, the United States faced its first energy crisis when Arab nations, furious at the nation's support of Israel during the Yom Kippur War, cut off oil shipments to the United States. As oil supplies fell in the winter of 1973–74, long lines formed at gas stations, where prices had nearly doubled, many homes were cold, and some schools closed. In response, Nixon authorized temporary emergency measures allocating petroleum and establishing a national fifty-five-mile-per-hour speed limit to save gasoline. By the spring of 1974, the crisis had eased, but the United States had yet to come to grips with its seemingly unquenchable demand for fuel and its dependence on foreign oil.

Soaring energy prices contributed to severe economic problems. By 1969, inflation had risen to 7 percent, an enormous increase to Americans used to rates of about 2 percent. By 1970, unemployment also became a serious problem. This unprecedented combination of a stagnant economy and inflation was dubbed "stagflation." Domestic troubles were compounded by the decline of American dominance in the international economy. Having fully recovered from World War II, the economies of Japan and Western Europe grew faster than that of the United States in the 1970s. Foreign cars, electronic equipment, and other products competed favorably with American goods throughout the world. In 1971, for the first time in decades, the United States imported more than it exported. Because the amount of dollars in foreign hands exceeded U.S. gold reserves, the nation could no longer back up its currency with gold.

The president's response to these economic problems diverged from conventional Republican doctrine. With an eye to the 1972 election, Nixon announced a "New Economic Policy" in August 1971. He abandoned the convertibility of dollars into gold, devalued the dollar to make American goods cheaper in foreign markets and thus increase exports, and imposed a 10 percent surcharge on most imports. Nixon also froze wages and prices, thus enabling the government to stimulate the economy without fueling more inflation. In the short run, these policies worked. Exports surged ahead of imports, inflation subsided, unemployment fell below 5 percent, and Nixon was resoundingly reelected in 1972. Yet the New Economic Policy treated the economy only superficially. The lifting of price and wage controls in 1973, the Arab oil embargo, and rising food prices sent the consumer price index soaring by 11 percent by 1974. Unemployment also crept back up, and Nixon's successor inherited the most severe economic crisis since the depression of the 1930s.

Constitutional Crisis and Restoration

Less than two years after his landslide victory in the 1972 election, Richard Nixon abandoned the presidency in disgrace. His abuse of power and efforts to cover up crimes committed by subordinates betrayed the public trust and forced the first presidential resignation in history. Nixon's handpicked successor, Gerald Ford, helped to restore confidence in the presidency, but he faced even more severe economic problems and lost the presidency in 1976 to Democrat Jimmy Carter.

From Triumph to Disgrace: Watergate

Nixon's most spectacular foreign policy initiatives, détente with the Soviet Union and the opening of relations with China (see Chapter 31), heightened his prospects for reelection in 1972. Although the war in Vietnam continued, antiwar protests diminished with the decrease in American ground forces

and casualties. Nixon's New Economic Policy had temporarily checked inflation and unemployment, and his attacks on busing and antiwar protesters had appealed to the right, positioning him favorably for the 1972 election.

The Democrats nominated Senator George S. McGovern of South Dakota, who had defeated a large field of contenders, including New York Representative Shirley Chisholm, the first African American politician to make a serious bid for the presidency. On the right, Governor George Wallace of Alabama won a series of southern primaries as well as those in Michigan and Maryland, but his campaign was cut short when a deranged man shot him, leaving Wallace paralyzed below the waist. McGovern struggled from the outset, portrayed by Republicans as a left extremist, alienating more conservative Democrats with his call for immediate withdrawal from Vietnam and pledge to cut $30 billion from the Pentagon's budget.

Nixon received 60.7 percent of the popular vote, carrying every state except Massachusetts in a landslide victory second only to Johnson's in 1964. Although the Democrats maintained control of Congress, Nixon won a majority of votes among southerners, Catholics, urbanites, and blue-collar workers, all traditionally strong supporters of the Democratic Party. The president had little time to savor his triumph, however, as revelations began to emerge about crimes and misdemeanors that had been committed to ensure the victory.

During the early morning hours of June 17, 1972, five men working for Nixon's reelection campaign crept into Democratic Party headquarters in the Watergate complex in Washington. Intending to repair a bugging device installed in an earlier break-in, they were discovered and arrested on the scene. In trying to cover up the connection between those arrested and administration officials, Nixon and his aides set in motion the most serious constitutional crisis since the Civil War, which reporters dubbed "Watergate."

Over the next two years, Americans learned that Nixon and his associates had engaged in a host of other abuses, such as accepting illegal campaign contributions, using so-called dirty tricks to sabotage Democratic candidates, and unlawfully attempting to silence critics of the Vietnam War. Nixon was not the first president to lie to the public or to misuse power. Every president since Roosevelt had enlarged the powers of the presidency, justifying his actions as necessary to protect national

NIXON RESIGNS

Flanked by his wife, daughter, and son-in-law, Richard Nixon becomes the first president in American history to resign the presidency. In this televised speech on August 8, 1974, Nixon did not admit guilt, even though tapes of his conversations indicated that he had obstructed justice, abused his power, and lied. He referred only to mistakes he had made while trying to govern "in the best interest of the nation." In the decades after his resignation, he gradually rehabilitated his reputation and became an elder statesman and foreign-policy adviser. All the living presidents attended his funeral in 1994.
Harry Benson Ltd.

security. This expansion of executive powers, often called the "imperial presidency," weakened some of the traditional checks and balances on the executive branch and opened the door to abuses.

Nixon's self-righteousness, insecurity, and tendency to see opposition to his policies as a conspiracy against him encouraged him to employ the vast powers of the executive against his enemies. Faced with a grand jury investigation, a Senate inquiry, and press reports implicating his former attorney general John Mitchell and several aides, Nixon decided to act.

In April 1973, Nixon accepted official responsibility for Watergate but denied any personal knowledge of the break-in or of a cover-up. He also an-

nounced the resignations of three White House aides and Attorney General Richard Kleindienst. In May, he authorized the appointment of an independent special prosecutor, Archibald Cox, to conduct an investigation. Meanwhile, sensational revelations exploded in the Senate investigating committee, headed by Democrat Samuel J. Ervin of North Carolina. Counsel to the President John Dean described projects to harass "enemies" through tax audits and other illegal means and asserted that the president had long known of efforts to cover up the Watergate burglary. The most damaging blow struck when a White House aide disclosed that all conversations in the Oval Office were taped. Both Cox and the Ervin committee immediately asked for tapes related to Watergate. When Nixon refused, citing executive privilege and separation of powers, Cox and Ervin took their case to federal district court.

At the same time, more disclosures revealed Nixon's misuse of federal funds and tax evasion. In August 1973, Vice President Spiro Agnew was compelled to resign after an investigation revealed that he had taken bribes as governor of Maryland. Although Nixon's choice of House minority leader Gerald Ford of Michigan to succeed Agnew won widespread approval, the vice president's resignation further tarnished the administration.

On October 19, 1973, Nixon ordered special prosecutor Cox to cease his efforts to obtain the Oval Office tapes. When Cox refused, Nixon ordered Attorney General Elliot Richardson to fire Cox. Richardson instead resigned, as did the next man in line at the Justice Department. Finally, the solicitor general, Robert Bork, agreed to carry out the president's order. The press called the series of dismissals and resignations the "Saturday night massacre," 250,000 telegrams condemning Nixon's action flooded the White House, and his popular support plummeted to 27 percent.

In February 1974, the House of Representatives voted to begin an impeachment investigation. In April, Nixon began to release edited transcripts of the tapes. As the public read passages sprinkled with "expletive deleted," the House Republican leader Hugh Scott abandoned his support of the president, calling the transcripts a "deplorable, shabby, disgusting, and immoral performance by all." The transcripts included Nixon's orders to Mitchell and Dean in March 1973: "I don't give a shit what happens. I want you all to stonewall it, let them plead the Fifth Amendment, cover up or anything else, if it'll save it—save the plan."

In July 1974, the House Judiciary Committee began debate over specific charges for impeachment: (1) obstruction of justice, (2) abuse of power, (3) contempt of Congress, (4) unconstitutional waging of war by the secret bombing of Cambodia, and (5) tax evasion and the selling of political favors. While the last two counts failed to get a majority, the committee voted to take the first three charges to the House, where a vote of impeachment seemed certain. On July 24, a unanimous Supreme Court ordered Nixon to hand over the remaining tapes. Transcripts of tapes released August 5 revealed that just six days after the break-in Nixon and aides had discussed manipulating the CIA to hinder the FBI's investigation of the burglary. This was sufficient evidence to seal his fate.

On August 8, 1974, Nixon announced his resignation to a national television audience. Acknowledging some incorrect judgments, he insisted that he had always tried to do what was best for the nation. The next morning, Nixon ended a rambling, emotional farewell to his staff with some advice: "Always give your best, never get discouraged, never get petty; always remember, others may hate you, but those who hate you don't win unless you hate them, and then you destroy yourself." Had he practiced that advice, he might have saved his presidency.

Backlash: The Ford Interregnum

Gerald R. Ford, who had represented Michigan in the House of Representatives since 1948, had built a reputation as a conservative party loyalist who treated opponents with respect. Not a brilliant thinker, Ford was known for his integrity, humility, and dedication to public office. Most of official Washington and the American public looked favorably on his succession as president.

Upon taking office, Ford announced, "Our long nightmare is over," but he shocked many Americans when he ended the particular nightmare of the former president. On September 8, 1974, Ford granted Nixon a pardon "for all offenses against the United States which he . . . has committed or may have committed or taken part in" during his presidency. It was the most generous presidential pardon ever issued, saving Nixon from nearly certain indictment and trial. It also provoked a tremendous outcry from Congress and the public. Capitalizing on revulsion over Watergate and the pardon, Democrats made impressive gains in the November congressional elections.

With the Democrats in control, Congress sought to guard against the types of abuses revealed in the Watergate investigations. The Federal Election Campaign Act of 1974, for example, established public financing of presidential campaigns, though it failed to stop the ever larger campaign chests that candidates found ways to solicit from interest groups, corporations, labor unions, and wealthy individuals. In 1978, Congress passed an independent counsel law establishing a nonpartisan procedure for the appointment of special prosecutors who could not be fired. The law was used to investigate potential criminal actions by Presidents Reagan and

Clinton as well as more than a dozen lesser officials before it expired in 1998.

Special investigating committees in Congress discovered a host of illegal FBI and CIA activities stretching back to the 1950s. Both agencies had harassed political dissenters, and the CIA had also made plans to assassinate Fidel Castro and other foreign leaders. In response to these revelations, Ford established new controls on covert operations and Congress created permanent committees to oversee the intelligence agencies. Yet these measures did little to diminish the public cynicism and lack of trust in government that had been developing since the Johnson years.

Ford carried a number of burdens into the 1976 presidential race. Underlying weaknesses in the U.S. economy remained: a low growth rate, high unemployment, a foreign trade deficit, and high energy prices tied to dependence on oil from abroad. Ford also faced a major challenge from the Republican right, as California governor Ronald Reagan came close to capturing the nomination.

The Democrats nominated James Earl "Jimmy" Carter Jr., former state senator and governor of Georgia. Highly intelligent and well-prepared on the issues, the soft-spoken Carter stressed his small-town roots, deep religious commitment, and distance from the suspect national government. Although Carter selected liberal senator Walter F. Mondale of Minnesota as his running mate and accepted a platform compatible with traditional Democratic principles, his nomination nonetheless represented a decided rightward turn in the party.

Carter benefited from the Watergate backlash, the country's economic problems, and his ability to attract votes from the traditional Democratic coalition of blacks, southerners, organized labor, and ethnic groups. Yet, although Democrats retained substantial margins in Congress, Carter received just 49.9 percent of the popular vote to Ford's 47.9 percent

The "Outsider" Presidency of Jimmy Carter

Jimmy Carter promised "to help the poor and aged, to improve education, and to provide jobs" but at the same time "not to waste money." He wanted a government that would help those in need, but one that also was efficient and prudent in its spending. When these aims conflicted, especially when inflation threatened economic stability, Carter's commitment to reform took second place. Liberal Dem-

ocrats accused him of deserting the Democratic reform tradition that stretched back to Franklin Roosevelt.

Although Carter's outsider status helped him win the presidency, it left him without strong ties to party insiders or prominent legislators. Moreover, his comprehensive proposals went against the congressional tendency to tackle problems with a piecemeal, incremental approach. Legislators complained of inadequate consultation and Carter's tendency to flood them with a mass of unprioritized proposals.

Even a president without these liabilities might not have done much better than Carter, as Congress itself diminished the ability of party leaders to deliver a united front. While it flexed its muscles in response to Watergate and abuses of presidential power, Congress reduced the power of committee chairs, weakened party control over legislators, and decentralized the decision-making process. In addition, because primary elections rather than party conventions now controlled the nominating process, candidates depended less on party support and more on campaign funds from interest groups, which they used to appeal directly to voters through television.

The Carter administration did little better with the formidable problems that had plagued the Nixon and Ford administrations—unemployment, inflation, and slow economic growth. With new tax cuts and federal spending, unemployment receded somewhat, but in 1978 rising inflation impelled Carter to curtail federal spending and the Federal Reserve Board to increase interest rates and tighten the money supply. These policies not only failed to halt inflation, which surpassed 13 percent in 1980, but also contributed to rising unemployment, reversing gains made in Carter's first two years.

Nor did Carter achieve much progress on traditional Democratic issues. Responding to feminist pressures, Carter appointed three women at cabinet-level rank, and he far surpassed his predecessors in appointing women and members of minority groups to federal judgeships and high government positions. And his wife Rosalynn played a larger political role than any First Lady since Eleanor Roosevelt. Yet, Carter's commitment to holding down the federal budget frustrated Democrats pushing for comprehensive welfare reform and a national health insurance program. To ensure solvency in Social Security, Carter and Congress agreed to raise employer and employee contribu-

CARTER RECEIVES CIVIL RIGHTS AND PEACE AWARD
From left, Martin Luther King Sr., Rosalynn Carter, Andrew Young, Coretta Scott King, and Jimmy Carter join hands and sing in 1979 in the Ebenezer Baptist Church in Atlanta, which was the elder King's congregation. Carter was there to receive the Martin Luther King Non-Violent Peace Award for his role in the Camp David accords between Israel and Egypt and his efforts to promote civil rights at home.
Jimmy Carter Presidential Library.

tions, but this also increased the tax burden of lower- and middle-income Americans.

In contrast, corporations and wealthy individuals gained from new legislation. A sharp cut in the capital gains tax benefited high-income individuals. When the Chrysler Corporation approached bankruptcy in 1979, Congress provided $1.5 billion worth of loan guarantees to ensure its survival. The government also reduced controls in several industries, deregulating airlines in 1978 and the banking, trucking, and railroad industries in 1980.

Designating the energy issue "the moral equivalent of war," Carter fought for a comprehensive program, but his goal fell victim to his poor relationship with Congress and to competing demands among energy producers and consumers. In 1979, declines in oil production abroad created the most severe energy shortage yet. Congress eventually authorized energy measures to limit consumption and decrease dependency on foreign oil. Still, they fell short of Carter's initial proposal and failed to curb Americans' sinking confidence in his leadership.

The Conservative Resurgence

Ronald Reagan's defeat of Carter for the presidency in 1980 marked the most important turning point in politics since Franklin D. Roosevelt's victory in 1932. Eisenhower and Nixon had campaigned as middle-of-the-road Republicans, but Reagan's victory established conservatism's dominance in the Republican Party. Since the 1930s, the Democratic Party had defined the major issues; in the 1980s, the Republicans assumed that initiative, while the Democrats moved toward the right in their search for voter support.

An extraordinarily adept politician, Reagan appealed to a wide spectrum of conservative groups and sentiments: free-market advocates, militant anti-Communists, fundamentalist Christians, and white working-class Democrats disenchanted with the Great Society and suffering from the high inflation and unemployment rates of the last years of the

Carter administration. On the domestic front, the Reagan administration left its most important mark on the economy: victory over inflation, deregulation of industry, a moratorium on social spending, enormous tax cuts, and a staggering budget deficit.

Reagan and the Spectrum of Conservatism

The oldest candidate ever nominated for the presidency, Ronald Reagan was born in Tampico, Illinois, in 1911. After attending Eureka, a small religious college, he worked as a sportscaster before becoming a movie actor and, later, president of the Screen Actors Guild. He initially shared the politics of his staunchly Democratic father but moved to the right in the 1940s and 1950s. Reagan's political career took off when he was elected governor of California in 1966. A conservative, as governor he displayed considerable flexibility, approving a major tax increase, a strong water pollution bill, and a liberal abortion law. Displaying similar flexibility in his 1980 presidential campaign, he softened earlier attacks on issues like Social Security and chose moderate Republican George H. Bush as his running mate.

The poor state of the economy and the country's declining international stature—symbolized by the dozens of Americans held hostage in Iran (see Chapter 31)—provided ample weapons for Reagan's campaign. Repeatedly Reagan reminded voters of the "misery index"—the combined rates of unemployment and inflation—and asked, "Are you better off now than you were four years ago?" Reagan promised to "take government off the backs of the people" and to restore Americans' morale and other nations' respect. A narrow majority of voters, 51 percent, responded to Reagan's upbeat message. Carter won just 41 percent of the vote, and 7 percent went to independent candidate, moderate John R. Anderson. The Republicans also picked up thirty-three new seats in the House and won control of the Senate.

With the election of 1980, conservatism gained greater ascendancy in American political culture than at any time since the 1920s. Reagan clearly benefited from a lingering backlash against the upheavals associated with the 1960s—the civil rights revolution, the reforms of the Johnson era, the antiwar movement, feminism, the new sexual permissiveness, and a liberal Supreme Court. Much

RONALD REAGAN NOMINATED FOR PRESIDENT
Nancy and Ronald Reagan respond to cheers at the Republican National Convention where he was nominated for president in the summer of 1980. Reagan became one of the most popular presidents of the twentieth century, though his wife did not always share his high ratings from the American people.
Lester Sloan/Woodfin Camp & Associates.

of Reagan's support came from religious conservatives, who constituted a relatively new phenomenon known as the New Right. During the 1970s, evangelical and fundamentalist Christianity claimed thousands of new adherents and made adept use of sophisticated mass-mailing techniques and the "electronic ministry." Evangelical ministers such as Jim Bakker and Pat Robertson preached to huge television audiences, attacking feminism, abortion, homosexuality, and pornography and calling for restoration of old-fashioned "family values." They wanted prayer back in and sex education out of the schools.

Conservatives created a raft of political organizations, such as the Moral Majority, founded by minister Jerry Falwell in 1979, and the Christian Coalition, which Pat Robertson formed in 1989. Within a few years, the Christian Coalition claimed 1.6 million members and control of the Republican Party in more than a dozen states. The instruments of more traditional conservatives—those who advocated limited government at home and militant anticommunism abroad—likewise flourished. These included publications such as the *National Review*, edited by William F. Buckley Jr., and think tanks such as the American Enterprise Institute and the Heritage Foundation, which supported experts who developed new policy approaches.

Reagan embraced the full spectrum of conservatism. He avowed agreement on abortion, school prayer, and other New Right issues, yet he was careful not to alienate the more traditional conservatives by pushing hard on so-called moral issues. Rather, Reagan's major achievements lay in areas most important to traditional conservatives—strengthening the nation's anti-Communist posture and reducing taxes and government restraints on free enterprise. "In the present crisis," Reagan argued, "government is not the solution to our problem, government is the problem."

Reagan's admirers, however, stretched far beyond conservatives. The extraordinarily popular president was liked even by Americans who opposed his policies and even when he made glaring mistakes. At one meeting, he failed to recognize his own secretary of housing and urban development, calling him "Mr. Mayor." On another occasion he proclaimed that vegetation caused 90 percent of all air pollution. He made so many misstatements that aides tried to keep him away from reporters.

Democratic Representative Patricia Schroeder tagged Reagan the "Teflon President" because none of his administration's mistakes, even his own errors and falsehoods, seemed to stick to him. His confidence and easygoing humor were a large part of his appeal, and, ignoring darker aspects of the nation's past, he presented a version of history that Americans could feel good about. Listeners understood Reagan's declaration that it was "morning in America" as a promise that the best was yet to come for the nation. He also gained public sympathy after being shot by a would-be assassin in March 1981. Just before surgery for removal of the bullet, Reagan joked to physicians, "I hope you're Republi-

cans." So great was Reagan's appeal that his popularity withstood serious charges of executive branch misconduct in foreign policy in his second term (see Chapter 31).

Unleashing Free Enterprise

Reagan's first objective was a massive tax cut. Although tax reduction, especially with a large budget deficit, contradicted traditional Republican economic doctrine, Reagan relied on a new theory called supply-side economics, which held that cutting taxes would actually increase revenue. In this view, lower taxes would enable businesses to expand and individuals would work harder because they could keep more of their earnings. Tax reduction would increase the production of goods and services, or supply, which in turn would boost demand. To allay worries about the budget deficit, Reagan promised to cut federal expenditures, a position fully compatible with his antigovernment views.

In the summer of 1981, Congress passed the largest tax reduction in U.S. history, cutting individual taxes on the lowest incomes from 14 to 11 percent and on the highest from 70 to 50 percent. Corporations also received tax breaks, and taxes on capital gains, gifts, and inheritances fell. A second measure, the Tax Reform Act of 1986, reduced taxes even further, lowering the maximum tax on individual incomes to 28 percent and on business to 35 percent. The entire tax structure became more regressive—that is, affluent Americans saved far more on their tax bills than did the average taxpayer, and the distribution of wealth was further skewed in favor of the rich.

"Hack, chop, crunch!" were *Time* magazine's words for the administration's efforts to free private enterprise from government restraints. Carter had confined deregulation to particular industries while increasing regulation in such areas as health, safety, and environmental protection. The Reagan administration, by contrast, pursued across-the-board deregulation. It declined to enforce the Sherman Antitrust Act—the law designed to reduce monopoly and promote competition—against an unprecedented number of business mergers and takeovers. Reagan also loosened restraints on business imposed by employee health and safety measures and weakened organized labor. When thirteen thousand members of the Professional Air Traffic Controllers

June 29, 1981 / $1.25

Newsweek

Watt's Land Rush
Digging Up the Last Frontier?

Interior Secretary
James Watt

CONTROVERSY OVER THE ENVIRONMENT
*Secretary of the Interior James Watt joined the
Reagan cabinet committed to dismantling much of
the environmental regulation of the previous two
decades. His efforts drew considerable opposition,
and he failed to turn back the clock substantially. In
1983, President Reagan appointed a more moderate
replacement. What exactly does this* **Newsweek**
*cover suggest that Watt wants to do to the environ-
ment?*

Illustration by Wilson McLean. Reprinted with permission of the
artist and *Newsweek* magazine.

Organization (PATCO) struck in 1981, Reagan fired
them, destroying their union.

Blaming environmental laws for the nation's
sluggish economic growth, Reagan targeted them
too for deregulation. His administration released
federal lands to private exploitation and eased enforcement of air and water pollution measures. Popular support for environmental protection blocked
complete realization of Reagan's deregulatory
goals, and over presidential vetoes Congress enacted clean water legislation and a bill establishing
the Superfund for cleanup of hazardous waste sites.

Deregulation of the banking industry, supported by Democrats and Republicans alike, created
a crisis in the savings and loan industry. Some of
the newly deregulated savings and loan institutions
(S&Ls) extended enormous loans to real estate
developers and invested in other high-yield but
risky ventures. S&L owners reaped lavish profits,
and their depositors enjoyed high interest rates. But
when real estate values began to plunge, hundreds
of S&Ls went bankrupt. After Congress voted to bail
out the S&L industry in 1989, the burden of the
largest financial scandal in U.S. history fell on
American taxpayers.

The S&L crisis deepened the federal budget
deficit, which soared during the 1980s despite Reagan's pledge to pare federal spending. When the administration cut funds for food stamps, job training,
aid to low-income students, health services, and
other welfare programs, hundreds of thousands of
people lost benefits, and those with incomes just
around the poverty line were hardest hit. Increases
in defense spending, however, far exceeded the
budget cuts, and the deficit continued to climb: from
$74 billion when Carter left office in 1981 to a high
of $220 billion in 1986. Under Reagan, the nation's
debt grew from $834 billion to $2.3 trillion, and interest on the debt consumed one-seventh of all federal expenditures.

It took the severest recession since the 1930s to
squeeze inflation out of the U.S. economy. Beginning in 1981, unemployment rose sharply, approaching 11 percent late in 1982. Record numbers
of banks and businesses closed, and twelve million
workers could not find jobs. The threat of unemployment further undermined organized labor,
forcing unions to make concessions that management insisted were necessary for industry's survival. The economy recovered in 1983 and entered
an unprecedented period of growth, yet unemployment never fell below 5 percent during the
decade.

The economic upswing and Reagan's own popularity posed a formidable challenge for the Democrats in the 1984 election. Walter F. Mondale, vice
president under Carter, won the Democratic nomination. Although he electrified the Democratic National Convention by choosing as his running mate
New York Representative Geraldine A. Ferraro, the
first woman on a major party ticket, it failed to save
the Democrats from a humiliating defeat. Reagan
charged his opponents with concentrating on Amer-

ica's failures, while he emphasized success and possibility. Democrats, he claimed, "see an America where every day is April 15th [the due date for income tax returns] . . . we see an America where every day is the Fourth of July."

Voters responded to the president's vision and to the economic comeback, giving him a landslide 59 percent of the vote. Winning only the state of Minnesota, the Democrats pondered how to stem the exodus of longtime loyalists—particularly southern white males—to the Republican Party. Stung by Republican charges that the Democratic Party was captive to "special interests" such as labor, women, and minorities, some Democratic leaders urged that the party shift more toward the right.

Maintaining the Reagan Legacy: The Bush Administration

No longer burdened with Reagan's immense popularity, the Democrats did better in the 1988 election, but not enough to deny the White House to Reagan's vice president, George Herbert Walker Bush. The son of a wealthy New England senator, Bush fought in World War II, earned a Yale degree, and then settled in Texas to make his own way in the oil industry and politics. He served in Congress during the 1960s and headed the CIA during the Nixon-Ford years.

Michael Dukakis, governor of Massachusetts, won the Democratic Party nomination after defeating a number of candidates. An important contender was the Reverend Jesse Jackson, who had fought civil rights battles alongside Martin Luther King Jr., and whose Rainbow Coalition campaign centered on the needs of minorities, women, working-class families, and the poor. Jackson won several primaries and gathered seven million votes, one-third of them from whites, but in the end, his race, lack of experience in public office, and position on the left wing of the Democratic Party proved to be insuperable obstacles. Half the eligible voters stayed home on election day, indicating the electorate's general disgust with a campaign that favored vitriolic attacks over serious debate. Fifty-four percent of voters were satisfied with the Republican record on peace and prosperity, but the Democrats gained seats in the House and Senate.

President Bush saw himself primarily as guardian of the Reagan legacy. He promised "a kinder, gentler nation" and was more inclined than Reagan to approve government activity in the private sphere. For example, he signed the Clean Air Act of 1990, the strongest, most comprehensive environmental law in history; it required power plants to cut sulfur dioxide emissions by more than half by the year 2000 and oil companies to develop cleaner-burning gasoline. Some forty million Americans reaped the benefits of another regulatory measure, the 1991 Americans with Disabilities Act, which banned job discrimination against the disabled and required that private businesses, public accommodations, and transportation be made handicapped-accessible.

Still, "If you're looking for George Bush's domestic program, and many people are, this is it: the veto pen," charged Democratic House majority leader Richard Gephardt in 1991. Bush blocked Congress thirty-six times, vetoing bills that lifted abortion restrictions, extended unemployment benefits, raised taxes, mandated family and medical leave for workers, and reformed campaign financing. By the end of his term, press reports were filled with the words *stalemate*, *gridlock*, and *divided government*.

Continuing a trend begun during the Reagan administration, states tried to compensate for this paralysis, becoming more innovative than Washington. "Our federal politics are gridlocked, and governors have become the ones who have to have the courage to put their necks out," said a spokesperson for governors. States passed bills to block corporate takeovers, establish parental leave policies, require equal pay for jobs of equal worth, improve food labeling, and protect the environment. Beginning in the 1980s, a few states began to pass measures guaranteeing gay and lesbian rights.

The president and Congress broke the deadlock in response to the budget deficit inherited from the Reagan administration. Bush reluctantly abandoned his "no new taxes" pledge and agreed to modest tax increases for high-income Americans and higher levies on gasoline, cigarettes, alcohol, and luxury items. Although the budget agreement brought in new revenues and Congress limited spending, three years later the deficit soared even higher, boosted by rising costs in entitlement programs such as Social Security and Medicare-Medicaid as well as by spending on unforeseen emergencies of war and natural disasters. The new taxes affected only slightly the massive tax reductions of the early 1980s, leaving intact a key element of Reagan's legacy.

The Conservative Shift in the Federal Courts

Since the 1950s and Earl Warren's tenure as chief justice, proponents of government intervention to secure minority rights and social justice had counted on the federal judiciary. Yet in the 1980s, liberals saw their allies slipping away as conservative justices increasingly populated the Supreme Court and the lower federal courts. With the opportunity to appoint more than 380 federal court judges and five new Supreme Court justices, Presidents Reagan and Bush followed Nixon's example and sought candidates who would uphold the doctrine of strict construction.

Reagan used his first opportunity in 1981 to appoint the first woman to the Supreme Court, moderate conservative Sandra Day O'Connor. His next two appointments, Antonin Scalia and Anthony M. Kennedy, tipped the balance further to the right. Bush first nominated moderate federal appeals judge David Souter; but in 1991, when he had to replace Justice Thurgood Marshall, the only African American on the Court, he set off a national controversy. The spark was his selection of Clarence Thomas, a conservative black appeals judge, who had opposed affirmative action as head of the Equal Employment Opportunity Commission (EEOC) under Reagan. Charging that Thomas would not protect minority rights, the National Association for the Advancement of Colored People (NAACP) and other liberal organizations fought the nomination. Then Anita Hill, a law professor and former EEOC employee, stunned the nation by accusing Thomas of sexual harassment. Despite nationally televised hearings on the harassment charges, the Senate voted narrowly to confirm him. Although the hearings sensitized the public to sexual harassment and gave the women's movement a boost, Thomas's appointment solidified the conservative shift on the Supreme Court.

The Democrats' victory in the 1992 election gave President Bill Clinton the opportunity to put his own stamp on the federal courts. Whereas Reagan and Bush had appointed very few women or minorities, Clinton made diversity a key objective. Of his first 129 judicial appointments, nearly one-third were women, 31 were black, and 11 were Hispanic. In June 1993, he appointed the second woman to the Supreme Court, Ruth Bader Ginsburg, a feminist who had won key women's rights rulings from the Supreme Court before becoming a federal appeals court judge in 1980.

Because of its tradition of respecting precedent, the Court did not execute an abrupt about-face in the 1980s and 1990s. It upheld important antidiscrimination policies, ruled that sexual harassment in the workplace constituted sex discrimination, and sustained certain rights to welfare benefits. Yet it allowed states to further restrict abortion, narrowed application of the Americans with Disabilities Act, and whittled away at legal safeguards around the death sentence. In a series of cases in 1999, Reagan and Bush appointees constituted a five-to-four majority that limited federal authority in favor of state sovereignty.

Winners and Losers in a Flourishing Economy

After 1983, the economy entered a period of unprecedented expansion, halted only temporarily by a recession in the early 1990s. Although most Americans benefited from the prosperity, the better-off gained most while poverty increased. In keeping with conservative philosophy, Reagan and Bush avoided substantial government efforts to reverse this growing income inequality (which their tax policies encouraged); and they tried to limit federal protections of civil rights, breaking sharply with the national commitment to equal opportunity undertaken in the 1960s. Despite the more conservative climate, the women's movement and the newer gay and lesbian rights movement achieved piecemeal policy reforms. As American society became increasingly diverse and the economy surged, the economic and political status of minority groups improved, but people of color continued to lag behind whites in opportunity, income, and political influence.

The Prosperous 1980s

After the recession of 1981–1982, the economy took off, bringing great fortunes to some as popular culture celebrated making money and displaying wealth. Books by business wizards topped bestseller lists, the press described lavish parties costing millions of dollars, and popular magazines featured such articles as, "They're Like Us, Except They're Rich." College students told poll takers that their primary ambition was to make money.

HOMELESSNESS
The increased presence of homeless people in cities across the nation challenged the
view of the 1980s as a decade of prosperity. Hundreds of homeless people could be
found on the sidewalks of the nation's capital every night. In November 1987, during
the first snow of the season, a homeless man sleeps in Lafayette Square across from
the White House. What might the location of this homeless man suggest to viewers
of the photograph?
Corbis-Bettmann.

Participating conspicuously in the affluence of the 1980s were members of the baby boom generation known popularly as "yuppies," short for "young urban professionals." These mostly white, well-educated young men and women tended to live in urban condominiums and to pursue fast-track careers; in their leisure time, they consumed lavishly—fancy cars, gourmet food, expensive vacations, and electronic gadgets. Though definitely a minority, they established consumption standards that many tried to emulate.

Problems remained, even in an abundant economy. The steel, automobile, and electronics industries were surpassed by those of Germany and Japan; Americans bought more Volkswagens and Hondas and fewer Fords and Chevrolets. With Americans purchasing more foreign-made goods than domestic producers were able to sell abroad, the nation's trade deficit (the difference between imports and exports) soared to $126 billion by 1988.

International competition forced the collapse of some older companies, while others moved factories and jobs abroad to be closer to foreign markets or to benefit from the low wage standards of such countries as Mexico and Korea. The growth of service industries created new jobs at home, but former blue-collar workers forced to take them found their wages substantially lower. When David Ramos was laid off in 1982 from his $12.75-an-hour job in a steel plant, his wages fell to just $5 an hour as a security guard, forcing his family to rely on food stamps. Overall, the number of full-time workers earning wages below the poverty level ($12,195 for a family of four in 1990) rose sharply from 12 to 18 percent of all workers in the 1980s.

The weakening of organized labor combined with the decline in manufacturing to erode the position of blue-collar workers like David Ramos. Increasingly, a second income was needed to stave off economic decline. By 1990, nearly 60 percent of married women with young children worked outside the home. Yet even with two incomes, fewer young families could purchase their first home. The average $10,000 disparity between male and female annual earnings made things even harder for the nearly 20 percent of female-headed families. One mother of two, divorced from an abusive husband, supplemented her paycheck by selling her blood and accepting help from her church.

President Reagan insisted that a booming economy would benefit everyone. Average personal income did rise during his tenure, but the trend toward greater economic inequality that had begun in the 1970s intensified in the 1980s, in part because of the new tax policies. The rich got richer, a portion of the middle class did well, and the poor got poorer. Personal income shot up sharply for the wealthiest 20 percent of Americans while it fell for the poorest by 9.8 percent between 1979 and 1987. No longer could all Americans expect, as they had in the two decades following World War II, that their children would do better than they had done (Figure 30.1).

Poverty statistics, too, revealed a reversal of the trend toward greater equality. Between 1980 and 1988, poor people increased from 11.7 to 13.5 percent of total U.S. population—the highest poverty rate in the industrialized world. A relatively low poverty rate among the elderly testified to the lasting success of Social Security and Medicare. Less fortunate were large segments of other groups that the economic boom had bypassed: racial minorities, female-headed families, and children. One child in every five lived in poverty.

Even before the 1990 recession, affluent urbanites walked past numerous men and women sleeping in subway stations, on grates over steam vents, and on park benches. Experts debated the total number of homeless Americans—estimates ranged from 350,000 upwards—but no one doubted that homelessness had increased. Women and children constituted the fastest-growing population without shelter. Those without homes included the victims of long-term unemployment, erosion of welfare benefits, and slum clearance as well as individuals suffering from mental illness, drug abuse, and alcoholism.

Setbacks and Gains for the Women's Movement

One of the marks of the conservative resurgence in the 1980s was its capture of the Republican Party's position on women's rights, giving that party an explicitly antifeminist tone as it opposed both the Equal Rights Amendment and women's right to abortion. Republicans did express concerns about the "gender gap"—women's tendency throughout the 1980s to vote for liberal and Democratic candidates in larger numbers than men did. Reagan appointed three women to cabinet posts and the first woman to the Supreme Court. But these actions accompanied a general decline in the number of women and minorities in high-level positions. And with higher poverty rates than men, women suffered most from budget cuts in social programs.

In this more hostile political environment, the women's movement continued to defend abortion rights and antidiscrimination measures, but it focused more on women's economic and family problems, solutions to which lay beyond simple antidiscrimination policies. This new agenda recognized the needs of less advantaged women and acknowledged the disproportionate share of women and children among the poor, a development that some termed "the feminization of poverty." It was also clear that despite the much

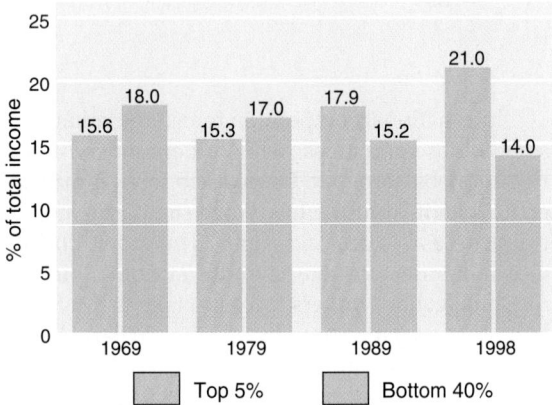

FIGURE 30.1
The Growth of Inequality: Changes in Family Income, 1969–1998

For three decades after World War II, income increased for all groups on the economic ladder; but after 1979, income of the poorest families actually declined, while it grew substantially for the richest 20 percent of the population.

Copyright © 1989 by the New York Times Co. Reprinted by permission.

CONFRONTATIONS OVER ABORTION
Failing to win a constitutional amendment banning abortion, in the late 1970s and 1980s some groups in the right-to-life movement adopted more militant tactics, picketing abortion clinics, yelling at patients and employees, and trying to block entrance into clinics. The pro-choice activists shown here defend clinic access and the right to abortion.

Paul S. Howell/Gamma Liaison.

publicized entrance of some women into formerly male fields, the majority still worked in traditionally female, low-paying jobs.

Feminists found some common ground with the Reagan administration in two measures that addressed women's economic distress. The Child Support Enforcement Amendments helped single and divorced mothers to collect court-ordered child support payments from absent parents. The Retirement Equity Act of 1984 benefited divorced and older women by strengthening their claims to their husbands' pensions and enabling women to qualify more easily for private retirement pensions.

Feminists fought successfully to retain women's right to abortion, but they hit a stone wall in their efforts to improve day care services and promote pay equity—that is, equal pay for traditionally female jobs that were comparable in worth to jobs performed primarily by men. Like other pressure groups, the women's movement pursued locally what it failed to achieve at the federal level. The pay equity movement took hold in several states, and many states strengthened their laws against rape. States also increased funding for domestic violence programs and stepped up efforts to protect victims and prosecute abusers.

The Democratic administration of Bill Clinton ameliorated policies enacted under Reagan and Bush and advanced measures that they had blocked. For example, Clinton used his executive authority to ease some of the restrictions on abortion. The Family and Medical Leave Act, passed in 1993, enabled workers in larger companies to take time off for childbirth, adoption, family medical emergencies, or to care for aging parents. And the Violence Against Women Act of 1994 authorized $1.6 billion for combating rape and domestic violence.

Clinton also increased the presence of women in government. In addition to his judicial appointments, he named women to six of twenty-three key executive posts. Janet Reno became the first female attorney general, and Madeleine K. Albright the first female secretary of state. Using sophisticated fundraising and electioneering techniques, feminists helped elect more women to political office. By the end of the century, women had made their marks as governors of Connecticut, Kentucky, Vermont, Nebraska, New Hampshire, and New Jersey; and they had served as mayors of several large cities, including Jane Byrne of Chicago and Dianne Feinstein of San Francisco. Women continued to inch their way into Congress, holding seventy-two seats, or 13.5 percent of the total, in 2001. One of those women was Hillary Rodham Clinton, the new senator from New York and first First Lady to run for political office.

Minorities' Struggles and Successes

At the end of the twentieth century, the overwhelming predominance of European Americans in American society was giving way to an increasingly diverse population. African Americans constituted about 13 percent of the population, Hispanic Americans more than 11 percent, and Asian Americans and Pacific Islanders 4 percent. Demographers predicted that by the middle of the twenty-first century whites would constitute just a little over half of the population; the fastest growing groups, Latinos and Asian Americans, were projected at 24 and 9 percent respectively. Propelling this growing variety was a new wave of immigrants, the vast majority of whom came from Asia or Latin America (Figure 30.2).

The racial composition of the new immigration revived the century-old wariness of the native-born toward recent arrivals. Pressure for more restrictive policies stemmed from beliefs (generally unfounded) that immigrants took jobs from the native-born and fears that immigrants would erode the dominant culture and language. Americans expressed particular hostility to immigrants who entered the country illegally. Primarily Latin Americans fleeing civil war and economic deprivation, illegal immigrants were estimated to number at least three million. To stem this tide, Congress passed the Immigration Reform and Control Act of

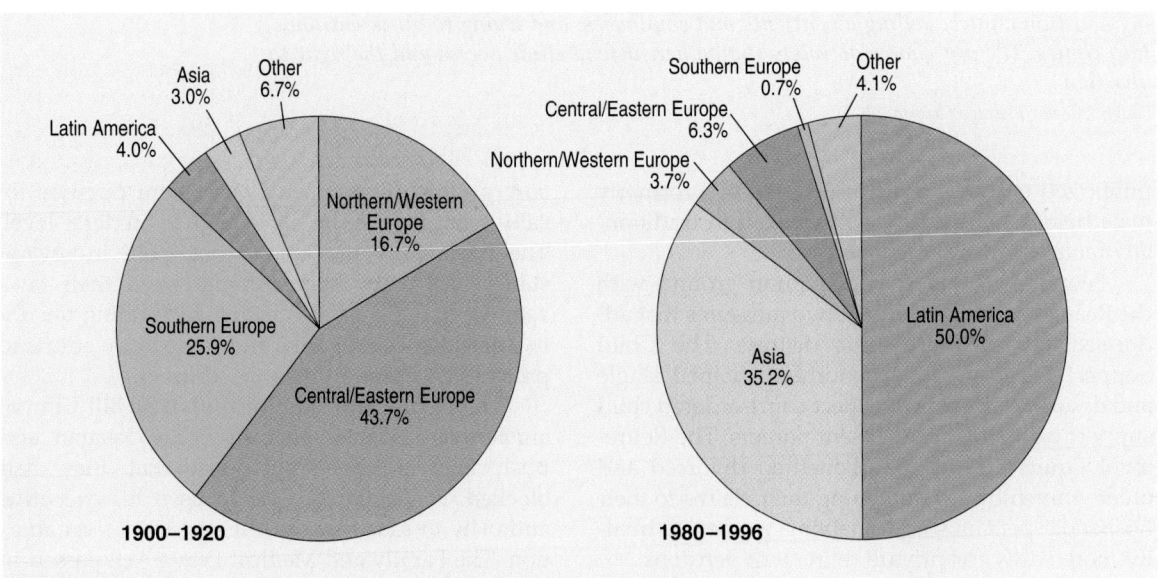

FIGURE 30.2
The Changing Profile of Immigration, 1900–1920 and 1980–1996
The United States received its largest number of immigrants during the opening and closing decades of the twentieth century, but the cultures and countries of origin of the new arrivals shifted dramatically between the two periods.

1986, which penalized employers who hired undocumented aliens but also granted amnesty to illegal immigrants who could prove residence before 1982. Some two million people took advantage of this provision. In California, with large numbers of illegal immigrants, voters passed an initiative denying public schooling to their children. Nor were legal immigrants immune from nativist policy. In 1996, Congress denied food stamps, Medicaid, and other benefits to those who had not become citizens.

Although more minorities than ever attained middle-class status, in general people of color remained low on the economic ladder, and their situation worsened in the 1980s and 1990s as the gap between rich and poor widened. In 1995, when the median income for white families surpassed $34,000, it stood at less than $25,000 for African American and Hispanic American households. Even in families where both parents had jobs, the median income for white families was $10,000 more than that of black families. In 1999, poverty afflicted about 23 percent of blacks and Latinos and 25 percent of American Indians, double the overall poverty rate of 11.8 percent.

The media hailed Asian Americans as "America's Super Minority" but failed to note vast differences within that group. More than 60 percent of immigrants from India, for example, came with college degrees, while just 20 percent of those from Vietnam did. Overall, median family income for Asian Americans surpassed that of whites, but only because Asian families had more wage earners. Even though a larger percentage of Asian Americans had completed college than whites, they had less per capita income and experienced greater poverty. Poor Chinese American women in the New York garment industry endured wages and working conditions resembling those of the early-twentieth-century sweatshops.

Minorities edged slowly into the corridors of political power. At the end of the 1980s, more than seven thousand blacks held public office, an increase of nearly 50 percent from 1980. The most impressive gains occurred in city government, where black mayors presided over Atlanta, Chicago, Los Angeles, Philadelphia, Seattle, and other large cities. The election of David Dinkins as mayor of New York City in 1989 epitomized the rise of black leaders even in cities with predominantly white electorates.

Jesse Jackson's presidential campaigns in 1984 and 1988 inspired African Americans and demonstrated white willingness to support a minority candidate. In 1989, Democrat L. Douglas Wilder of Virginia became the first black governor since Reconstruction, joining the only Hispanic governor, Republican Bob Martinez of Florida. Minorities remained underrepresented in national politics, however. When the 107th Congress convened in January 2001, two Asian Americans and one American Indian were the only ethnic minorities in the Senate. Thirty-six African Americans served in the 435-member House of Representatives, along with nineteen Hispanics and four Asian Americans.

The Gay and Lesbian Rights Movement

Influenced by minority struggles, the New Left, the counterculture, and feminism, gay men and lesbians began to claim equal rights and to express pride in their sexual identities. Although an organization for homosexual rights had existed as early as 1924, not until the 1980s did a national mass movement emerge. It grew out of the social upheaval of the 1960s, symbolized by the Stonewall riot of 1969, when gay men and lesbians fought back against a police raid on the Stonewall Inn, a gay bar in New York City's Greenwich Village.

The acquired immune deficiency syndrome (AIDS) epidemic further mobilized the gay and lesbian rights movement in the 1980s, because initially male homosexuals were disproportionately afflicted. As the disease swept through communities of gay men in New York, San Francisco, and elsewhere, gay men and lesbians organized to promote public funding for AIDS education, prevention, and treatment.

The gay and lesbian rights movement helped thousands of closeted homosexuals experience the relief of "coming out." Their visibility helped to increase awareness (if not always acceptance) of homosexuality among the larger population. Activists organized gay rights and gay pride marches throughout the country and began to win local victories, gaining some protections against discrimination. (See "Documenting the American Promise," page 796.) Beginning with the election of Elaine Noble to the Massachusetts legislature in 1974, several openly gay politicians won offices from mayor to member of Congress. The Democrats began to include gay rights in their party platforms.

Protecting Gay and Lesbian Rights

*S*ince the 1970s, the gay and lesbian rights movement has worked for passage of laws and ordinances to protect homosexuals from discrimination. In 1982, Wisconsin became the first state to ban discrimination on the basis of sexual orientation, following the lead of several cities throughout the United States that passed gay rights ordinances in the 1970s. By the mid-1990s, nine states and more than eighty cities had such legislation on the books. These measures ignited controversy that surrounded the issue into the twenty-first century.

DOCUMENT 1. Ordinance of the City of Minneapolis, 1974

In 1974, the city council of Minneapolis amended its civil rights ordinance to cover discrimination based on sexual preference. The law provided a rationale for banning discrimination and, unlike some laws focusing exclusively on employment, encompassed a broad range of activities.

It is determined that discriminatory practices based on race, color, creed, religion, national origin, sex or affectional or sexual preference, with respect to employment, labor union membership, housing accommodations, property rights, education, public accommodations, and public services, or any of them, tend to create and intensify conditions of poverty, ill health, unrest, civil disobedience, lawlessness, and vice and adversely affect the public health, safety, order, convenience, and general welfare; such discriminatory practices threaten the rights, privileges, and opportunities of all inhabitants of the city and such rights, privileges, and opportunities are hereby to be declared civil rights, and the adoption of this Chapter is deemed to be an exercise of the policy power of the City to protect such rights.

SOURCE: Norman Dorsen and Aryeh Neier, eds., *The Rights of Gay People: The Basic ACLU Guide to a Gay Person's Rights* (New York: E. P. Dutton, 1992), 251.

DOCUMENT 2. Letter to the Editor of the *New York Times* from Paul Moore, November 23, 1981

Paul Moore, Episcopal bishop of New York, made a religious argument for gay rights in his letter to the editor of the New York Times.

I quote our diocesan resolution: "Whereas this Convention, without making any judgment on the morality of homosexuality, agrees that homosexuals are entitled to full civil rights. Now therefore be it resolved this Convention supports laws guaranteeing homosexuals all civil rights guaranteed to other citizens."

The Bible stands for justice and compassion for all of God's children. To deny civil rights to anyone for something he or she cannot help is against the clear commandment of justice and love, which is the message of the word of God.

As a New Yorker I find it incredible that this great city, populated by more gay persons than any other city in the world, still denies them basic human rights. They make an enormous contribution to the commercial, artistic, and religious life of our city.

SOURCE: Paul Moore, letter to the editor, *New York Times*, December 8, 1981. Reprinted with permission.

DOCUMENT 3. Vatican Congregation for the Doctrine of the Faith, August 6, 1992

The following statement from the Roman Catholic Church reflects the views of many religious groups that take positions against gay rights.

"Sexual orientation" does not constitute a quality comparable to race, ethnic background, etc., in respect to nondiscrimination. Unlike these, homosexual orientation is an objective disorder and evokes moral concern.

There are areas in which it is not unjust discrimination to take sexual orientation into account, for example, in the placement of children for adoption or foster care, in employment of teachers or athletic coaches, and in military recruitment.

SOURCE: Vatican Congregation for the Doctrine of the Faith, *Origins*, August 6, 1992.

DOCUMENT 4. Testimony of Charles Cochrane Jr. before the House Subcommittee on Employment Opportunities of the Committee on Education and Labor, January 27, 1982

Although the U.S. Congress has never enacted legislation banning discrimination on the basis of sexual orientation, it has considered a number of bills for that pur-

pose. Charles Cochrane Jr., an army veteran and police sergeant, testified on behalf of such a bill in 1982.

I am very proud of being a New York City policeman. And I am equally proud of being gay. I have always been gay.

I have been out of the closet for 4 years. November 6 was my anniversary. It took me 34 years to muster enough courage to declare myself openly.

We gays are loathed by some, pitied by others, and misunderstood by most. We are not cruel, wicked, cursed, sick, or possessed by demons. We are artists, business people, police officers, and clergymen. We are scientists, truck drivers, politicians; we work in every field. We are loving human beings who are in some ways different. . . .

During the early years of my association with the New York City Police Department a great deal of energy did go into guarding and concealing my innermost feelings. I believed that I would be subjected to ridicule and harassment were my colleagues to learn of my sexual orientation. Happily, when I actually began to integrate the various aspects of my total self, those who knew me did not reject me.

Then what need is there for such legislation as H.R. 1454? The crying need of others, still trapped in their closets, who must be protected, who must be reassured that honesty about themselves and their lives will not cost them their homes or their jobs. . . .

The bill before you will not act as a proselytizing agent in matters of sexual orientation or preference. It will not include affirmative action provisions. Passage of this bill will protect the inherent human rights of all people of the United States, while in no way diminishing the rights of those who do not see the need for such legislation. Finally, it will signify, quite clearly, recognition and compassion for a group which is often maligned without justification.

SOURCE: U.S. House Subcommittee on Employment Opportunities of the Committee on Education and Labor, Hearing on H.R. 1454, 97th Cong., 2nd sess., 1982, 54–56.

DOCUMENT 5. Carl F. Horowitz, "Homosexuality's Legal Revolution," May 1991

Carl Horowitz, a policy analyst at a conservative think tank, the Heritage Foundation, expresses arguments of those opposed to government protection of homosexual rights.

Homosexual activists have all but completed their campaign to persuade the nation's educational establishment that homosexuality is normal "alternative" behavior, and thus any adverse reaction to it is akin to a phobia, such as fear of heights, or an ethnic prejudice, such as anti-Semitism.

The movement now stands on the verge of fully realizing its use of law to . . . intimidate heterosexuals uncomfortable about coming into contact with it. . . .

The movement seeks to win sinecures through the state, and over any objections by "homophobic" opposition. With a cloud of a heavy fine or even a jail sentence hanging over a mortgage lender, a rental agent, or a job interviewer who might be discomforted by them, homosexuals under these laws can win employment, credit, housing, and other economic entitlements. Heterosexuals would have no right to discriminate against homosexuals, but apparently, not vice versa. . . .

These laws will create market bottlenecks. Heterosexuals and even "closeted" homosexuals will be at a competitive disadvantage for jobs and housing. . . .

The new legalism will increase heterosexual anger—and even violence—toward homosexuals.

SOURCE: Carl F. Horowitz, "Homosexuality's Legal Revolution," *Freeman*, May 1991. Reprinted with permission.

QUESTIONS FOR ANALYSIS AND DEBATE

1. According to these documents, how would heterosexuals be affected by laws protecting gay and lesbian rights?

2. Which of these documents suggest that the civil rights movement influenced the authors' views on homosexual rights?

3. What do you think is the strongest argument for government protection of homosexual rights? What do you think is the strongest argument against government protection?

AIDS QUILT
An enormous quilt dedicated to AIDS victims spreads across the Washington Mall in October 1989. Composed of patches made by individuals who lost loved ones to the fatal epidemic, the quilt was exhibited throughout the country before its arrival in the nation's capital. The quilt helped to raise money for research on and treatment of AIDS, promoted recognition of the disease, and offered a way for the bereaved to mourn and receive comfort. New AIDS quilt projects quickly followed.
Lee Snider/Image Works.

Popular attitudes about homosexuality moved toward greater tolerance but remained complex. For example, in a 1998 poll, 84 percent supported equal job opportunities for gays and lesbians, but 59 percent thought homosexuality was morally wrong. These diverse attitudes were reflected in uneven changes in policies. In some states and cities, lesbians and gay men won protections that were enjoyed by heterosexual citizens. Dozens of cities banned job discrimination against ho-

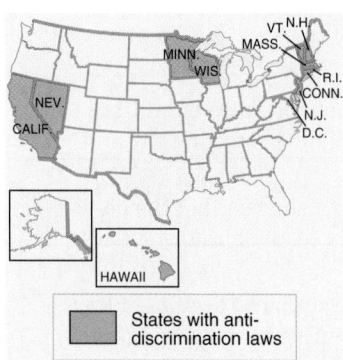

Antidiscrimination Laws for Gays and Lesbians, 2000

mosexuals, and beginning with Wisconsin in 1982, eleven states made sexual orientation a protected category under civil rights laws. Nearly one hundred cities and many large corporations began to offer health insurance and other benefits to domestic partners. After the Vermont Supreme Court ruled that gay couples were unconstitutionally discriminated against, the Vermont legislature created the category of "civil unions" for same-sex couples that would entitle them to rights available to married couples in areas such as inheritance, taxes, and medical decisions.

Such initiatives found less support at the national level. For example, in 1993 opposition from military leaders, enlisted men, and key legislators caused Clinton to back away from his campaign promise to lift the ban on homosexuals in the military. Instead, he announced the so-called don't ask, don't tell policy, forbidding officials from asking military personnel about their sexuality, but allowing dismissal of men and women who said they were gay or engaged in homosexual behavior. What began as an effort to promote tolerance ended in a 67 percent jump in discharges of homosexuals. In 1996, Clinton also signed the Defense of Marriage Act, prohibiting the federal government from recognizing state-licensed marriages between same-sex couples. And in 2000, the Supreme Court ruled five to four that it was constitutional under the First Amendment right of freedom of association for the Boy Scouts to exclude gay members.

Even as popular TV shows and movies increasingly featured gay men and lesbians, most remained vulnerable to intolerance and sometimes violence. The New Right targeted gays and lesbians as symbols of national immorality and succeeded in overturning some homosexual rights measures, which in any case lagged far behind the civil rights guarantees that racial minorities and women had achieved.

Battling for the Center Ground: The Clinton Years

After more than two decades during which Democrats occupied the White House for only four years, Bill Clinton believed that to win back voters his party had to move away from liberalism and toward the center of the political spectrum. This meant paying less attention to the needs of the poor and more to those of middle-class Americans, restraining federal programs and budgets, being tough on crime, and emphasizing religion and traditional family values. Yet Clinton did not completely abandon the principles that had guided the party in the 1960s. He signed some measures benefiting the working poor, delivered incremental reforms to feminists, environmentalists, and other groups, and spoke out in favor of affirmative action and gay rights.

The Clinton administration ended its eight years with a surplus in the federal budget and the longest economic boom in history. Although various factors generated the prosperity, many Americans identified Clinton with the buoyant economy and returned him to office for a second term. A majority continued to support him even when his reckless sexual behavior disgraced the presidency and resulted in Clinton's impeachment. Although the Senate did not find sufficient cause to remove him from office, the fallout from the scandal helped the Republicans capture the presidency in the bitterly contested election of 2000.

The 1992 Election and the Promise of Change

Because President Bush's chances for reelection had looked so golden in 1991, the most prominent Democrats opted out of the race. That, however, did not deter William Jefferson "Bill" Clinton, who at age forty-five had served as governor of Arkansas for twelve years. Like Jimmy Carter in 1976 and Michael Dukakis in 1988, Clinton and his running mate, Albert Gore Jr., presented themselves as "New Democrats." Both belonged to the Democratic Leadership Council, which Clinton had helped found in 1985 to rid the party of its liberal image. Clinton deliberately distanced himself from Jesse Jackson and his Rainbow Coalition and appealed to voters who believed that some Americans were getting a free ride at their expense. "We're going to put an end to welfare as we know it," Clinton claimed. Disavowing the "tax and spend" label that Republicans pinned on his party, he promised a tax cut for the middle class and vowed to reinvigorate government and the economy.

The popularity of a third candidate revealed Americans' frustrations with government. In announcing his candidacy on the popular TV talk show *Larry King Live*, self-made Texas billionaire H. Ross Perot set the tone of his unconventional campaign. Although he gave no press conferences, he had plenty of money and attracted a sizable grassroots movement with his down-to-earth personality and appeals to voters' disgust with Washington. Perot's candidacy hurt the president more than it hurt Clinton, and it established the federal budget deficit as a key campaign issue.

Americans gave Clinton 43 percent of their votes, Bush 38 percent, and Perot 19 percent—the strongest third-party finish since Theodore Roosevelt's Progressive Party candidacy in 1912. The Democrats barely maintained their majority in Congress. Although casting two-thirds of their votes against Bush demonstrated a mandate for change, voters formed no majority around a particular direction that change should take.

Some Americans worried about the growing federal debt, which reached $4.4 trillion in 1993. Yet

CLINTON AND GORE ON TOUR
The gregarious Bill Clinton excelled at political campaigning. During the 1992 presidential election campaign, he and his wife, Hillary—accompanied by running mate Al Gore and his wife, Tipper—went out on several bus tours as a way of demonstrating the Democrats' connection to ordinary people. Not far from this campaign stop in Sylvester, Georgia, the bus caravan passed by a hand-made sign that read "Bubbas for Clinton/Gore."
Copyright © Ira Wyman/Sygma.

most opposed higher taxes and did not want to give up the government benefits they enjoyed. As businesses tried to trim budgets and become more competitive, victims of corporate restructuring worried about finding new jobs. An inadequate health care system and rising crime rates constituted other major concerns, but required more federal spending or intrusion than most Americans seemed willing to accept.

Clinton wanted to restore confidence in government as a force for good but avoid alienating antigovernment voters by proposing new large federal programs, and in any case, the budget deficit precluded such spending. Just as Clinton was short on cash for using government in positive ways, he also lacked political capital, for the Republicans controlled Congress all but his first two years in office. Further, the end of the cold war deprived Clinton of a national agenda around which to unite Americans and prevented him from justifying domestic reform as a means to combat communism abroad.

Still, the popular mandate for change allowed the New Democrat president to exert some federal authority to solve national problems. Using his executive powers to reverse Reagan and Bush policies, Clinton eased restrictions on abortion and paved the way for import of the French abortion pill, RU-486. He signed several bills that Republicans had previously blocked, including gun control legislation, the family and medical leave measure, and a $30 billion anticrime program. Further, he approved measures to increase the minimum wage,

improve college students' access to federal loans, and establish Americorps, a program enabling students to pay for their education with community service. Most significantly, to ensure that no full-time worker should live in poverty, Clinton pushed through a substantial increase in the Earned Income Tax Credit for low wage earners. This gave tax reductions to people who worked full-time at meager wages or, if they paid no taxes, a government subsidy to lift their family income above the poverty line. By 2000, fifteen million low-income families were benefiting from the Earned Income Tax Credit.

The booming economy undergirded Clinton's popularity through the 1990s. Economic expansion, along with budget cuts, tax increases, and declining unemployment, reduced the federal budget deficit by about half between 1992 and 1996 and in 1998 produced the first surplus since 1969. Even with the largest tax cut since 1981, a 1997 law reducing levies on estates and capital gains and providing tax credits for families with children and for higher education, the surplus grew. The seemingly inexorable growth of government debt had turned around.

Clinton stumbled badly, however, over an ambitious health care reform plan, which had two key objectives: to help 39 million Americans without health insurance by providing universal coverage and to curb steeply rising medical costs. Under the direction of First Lady Hillary Rodham Clinton, the administration presented a complex bill that much of the health care industry charged would mean higher taxes and government interference in health care decisions. Although the bill failed, private industry made strides in curtailing costs—at patients' expense, some argued. Congress enacted piecemeal reform by enabling workers who changed jobs to retain health insurance and by establishing a new health care program for 5 million uninsured children. Yet the number of Americans without health insurance surpassed 40 million, about 15 percent of the population, in 2000.

Clinton Courts the Right

If parts of Clinton's agenda sustained the traditional Democratic reliance on government to help the disadvantaged, his presidency in general moved the party to the right. The 1994 elections swept away the Democratic majorities in both houses of Congress and contributed to Clinton's embrace of Republican issues such as welfare reform and downsizing government. Led by Representative Newt Gingrich of Georgia, Republicans considered the 1994 elections a mandate for their "contract with America," a conservative platform that included drastic contraction of the federal government, deep tax cuts, and a constitutional amendment to ban abortions. Opposition from Democrats and more moderate Republicans stymied most of the contract pledges, but Gingrich succeeded in moving the debate to the right.

Far from Washington, a more extreme antigovernment movement emerged in the form of grassroots armed militias claiming the need to defend themselves from government tyranny. Anticipating government repression, they stockpiled, according to one militia leader, "the four Bs: Bibles, bullets, beans, and bandages" and embraced a variety of sentiments, including opposition to taxes and the United Nations, and white Christian supremacy. Their ranks grew with passage of gun control legislation and after government agents stormed the headquarters of an armed religious cult in Waco, Texas, resulting in more than eighty deaths. On the second anniversary of that event, April 19, 1995, in the worst terrorist attack in the nation's history up to then, a bomb leveled a federal building in Oklahoma City, taking 169 lives. Authorities quickly arrested two militia members, who were tried and convicted in 1997.

Clinton's determination to cast himself as a centrist was nowhere more apparent than in his handling of welfare reform. Since Lyndon Johnson's war on poverty in the 1960s, public sentiment had shifted. Instead of blaming poverty on a shortage

of adequate jobs, poor education, and other external circumstances, more people were inclined to blame the poor themselves and government welfare, which they charged kept people in cycles of dependency. Nearly everyone considered work better than welfare but disagreed about whether the economy could provide sufficient jobs at decent wages and how much government assistance poor people needed in the transition from welfare to work. Most estimates showed that it cost less to support a family on welfare than to provide job training, child care, and other supports necessary for that transition.

Clinton vetoed two measures on welfare reform, thereby forcing a less punitive bill, which he signed as the 1996 election approached. The Personal Responsibility and Work Opportunity Reconciliation Act abolished Aid to Families with Dependent Children (AFDC) and with it the nation's pledge to provide a minimum level of subsistence for all its children. In place of AFDC, the law authorized grants to the states along with two-year limits on welfare payments whether the recipient could find a job or not. The law set a lifetime limit of aid at five years, barred legal immigrants who had not become citizens from food stamps and other benefits, and allowed states to stop Medicaid to legal immigrants.

A "moment of shame," cried Marian Wright Edelman, president of the Children's Defense Fund, when Clinton signed the bill. State and local officials across the country scrambled to understand the law and how to implement it. "We certainly endorse the overall direction toward work," a Minnesota official said, while expressing grave concern about how the law would operate. "A child could very well have to go to foster care," predicted a Louisiana social worker. Critics proved wrong in their most severe predictions. By 2000, welfare rolls had been cut nearly in half, while the poverty rate fell to 11.4 percent, its lowest in more than two decades. That did not mean, however, that all former welfare recipients were now self-supporting. Forty percent of former welfare mothers were not working regularly after being cut from the rolls, and those with jobs earned on average only about $12,000 a year. The strong economy along with the earned income tax credit and other forms of assistance to the working poor made it possible to reduce welfare rolls without catastrophic results.

Clinton claimed that the new law meant that "welfare will no longer be a political issue," and his signature on it denied the Republicans a partisan issue. In the 1996 election campaign, the president ran as a moderate who would save the country from extremist Republicans. In fact, the Republican Party also moved to the center, passing over a field of conservatives to nominate Kansan Robert Dole, a World War II hero and former Senate majority leader who had served in Washington for more than two decades.

Whether out of satisfaction with a favorable economy or boredom with the candidates, about half of the electorate stayed home. Fifty percent of voters chose Clinton, while 41 percent favored Dole, and 9 percent Perot, who ran again as a third-party candidate. The largest gender gap to date appeared in the election: Women gave 54 percent of their votes to Clinton and 38 percent to Dole, while men split their votes nearly evenly. Although Clinton won reelection with room to spare, voters sent a Republican majority back to Congress.

Impeaching the President

Clinton's ability to undercut the Republicans and capture the middle ground of the electorate, along with the nation's economic successes, enabled the self-proclaimed "comeback kid" to survive scandals and an impeachment trial in 1998. Early in the first Clinton administration, charges of illegalities related to firings of White House staff, political use of FBI records, and the Clintons' involvement in a real estate deal in Arkansas, nicknamed "Whitewater," led to an official investigation by an independent prosecutor. Clinton also faced a sexual harassment lawsuit filed in 1994 by Arkansas state employee Paula Corbin Jones, who asserted that in 1991 the Arkansas governor had made unwanted sexual advances. A federal court threw out Jones's suit in April 1998, but Clinton's amorous relationships continued to threaten his presidency.

In January 1998, independent prosecutor Kenneth Starr, who had taken over the Whitewater probe in 1994, began to investigate the most inflammatory charge—that Clinton had had sexual relations with a twenty-one-year-old White House intern, Monica Lewinsky, and then lied about it to a federal grand jury. Clinton first vehemently denied the charge but subsequently bowed to the mounting evidence against him. Starr took his case for impeachment to the House of Representatives, which in December 1998 voted, mostly along party lines, to impeach the president on two counts, perjury and obstruction of justice. Clinton became the second president—after Andrew Johnson, in 1868—to be impeached by the House and tried by the Senate.

Most Americans believed that the president had acted recklessly and inappropriately with Lewinsky, yet they continued to approve his presidency and to oppose impeachment. Some saw Starr as a fanatic invading individuals' privacy; most people separated what they considered the president's private actions from his public duties. One man said, "Let him get a divorce from his wife. Don't take him out of office and disrupt the country." Those favoring impeachment insisted that the president was not above the law, that he must set a

CLINTON'S IMPEACHMENT *This cartoon expresses the consternation of Republicans when President Clinton's approval ratings remained high despite the revelation of his affair with Monica Lewinsky and his subsequent impeachment. Many Americans, although not condoning the president's behavior, separated what they considered his private actions from his public duties and criticized prosecutor Kenneth Starr and the Republicans for not doing the same.*

high moral standard for the nation, and that lying to a grand jury, even over a private matter, was a serious offense.

The Senate conducted the impeachment trial with much less partisanship than that displayed in the House. A number of senators believed that Clinton had committed perjury and obstruction of justice but did not find those actions to constitute the high crimes and misdemeanors required by the Constitution for his removal. With a two-thirds majority needed for that result, the Senate voted 45 to 55 (with 10 Republicans supporting the president) on the perjury count and 50 to 50 (with 5 Republicans joining the Democrats) on the obstruction of justice count. A majority of senators seemed to agree with Clinton's advocate, former Democratic Senator Dale Bumpers of Arkansas, who found the president's behavior "indefensible, outrageous, unforgivable, shameless," but insufficient to warrant his removal from office.

The investigation that triggered events leading up to impeachment culminated in 2000 with the independent counsel's finding of insufficient evidence that the Clintons disobeyed the law in the Whitewater land deals. The investigation had lasted six years and cost almost $60 million of federal funds. In the face of widespread dissatisfaction with Whitewater and other investigations by special prosecutors, Congress let the independent counsel act expire in 1998.

The Booming Economy of the 1990s

Clinton's ability to weather the impeachment crisis drew incalculable help from the prosperous economy. In 1991 began the longest period of economic growth in U.S. history. During his presidency, the gross domestic product grew by more than one-third, thirteen million new jobs were created, unemployment reached its lowest point in twenty-five years, inflation remained in check, and the stock market soared.

Clinton eagerly took credit for the thriving economy, and his policies did contribute to the boom. He made deficit reduction a priority, and in exchange the Federal Reserve Board and bond market traders lowered interest rates, which in turn encouraged economic expansion by making money easier to borrow. Businesses prospered also because they had squeezed down their costs through restructuring and laying off workers. Economic problems in Europe and Asia helped American firms become more competitive in the international market.

Above all, the computer revolution and the application of information technology to the production and distribution of goods and services tremendously boosted productivity. By the end of the century, half the workforce used computers in their jobs.

People at all income levels benefited from the economic boom, but it had uneven effects. In contrast to the economic expansion of the 1950s and 1960s, the gaps between rich and poor and between rich and middle class that had been growing since the 1970s failed to narrow. (See Figure 30.1.) This persistence of inequality in a rising economy was linked in part to what fueled the boom, the growing use of information technology. That and the movement of manufacturing jobs abroad increased demand for highly skilled workers and lessened opportunities and wages for those not trained in the requisite skills. In addition, deregulation, globalization, and the continuing decline of unions hurt lower-skilled workers; and the national minimum wage failed to keep up with inflation.

The Election of 2000

Even with the flourishing economy, Democratic candidate Vice President Albert Gore failed to retain the White House for his party in the election of 2000. His choice of running mate, Connecticut Senator Joseph Lieberman, the first Jew to run on a major party ticket, was popular, and public opinion polls indicated that a majority of Americans agreed with the Democratic nominees on most issues. Yet Gore appeared stiff and aloof to many voters, too willing to change his positions to gain political advantage, and too inclined to shade the truth.

Texas governor George W. Bush emerged as the Republican nominee from a series of hard-fought primaries, financed with the most money ever raised in a presidential campaign. The oldest son of former president George H. Bush had attended Yale and Harvard and then worked in the oil industry in Texas and as managing partner of the Texas Rangers baseball team. In 1994, Texans elected him governor. Criticized for his lack of Washington and international experience and his unfamiliarity with certain policy issues, Bush chose for his running mate a seasoned official, Richard B. Cheney, who had served in the Nixon, Ford, and first Bush administrations.

Both candidates ran cautious campaigns, accommodating their positions to what polls indicated that voters wanted. Bush's strategy mirrored that of Clinton in 1992. Calling himself a "compassionate conservative," he separated himself from the extreme right wing of his party and tried to coopt Democratic issues such as education. Like Republicans before him, he promised a substantial tax cut and charged that Gore represented the party of big government.

Many observers predicted that the amazingly strong economy would give Gore the edge in the close race, and he did surpass Bush by more than one-half million votes. Once the polls closed, it became clear that whoever won Florida's twenty-five electoral college votes would win the election. Bush's margin was so tiny there, where his brother served as governor, that it prompted an automatic recount of the votes, which eventually gave Bush an edge of 537 votes.

Meanwhile the Democrats asked for hand-counting of Florida ballots in several heavily Democratic counties where machine errors may have left hundreds of votes unrecorded. The Republicans, in turn, went to court to try to stop the hand counts.

As the dispute unfolded, Americans discovered that counties used different voting systems and that some systems were more prone to error. Punch-card ballots were most unreliable, and they were used more in counties with large numbers of minority and poor voters.

The outcome of the 2000 election hung in the balance for more than a month as the court cases went all the way up to the Supreme Court. Finally, a bitterly divided Supreme Court ruled five to four against further recounts of the Florida vote, and Gore conceded the presidency to Bush on December 13, 2000. For the first time since 1888, a president who failed to win the popular vote took office (Map 30.2). For that reason and because Republicans held a mere five-vote margin in the House of Representatives and the Senate was evenly divided, national politics seemed likely to remain on center ground and hotly contested during the first administration of the twenty-first century.

Conclusion: Reversing the Course of Government

"Ours was the first revolution in the history of mankind that truly reversed the course of government," boasted Ronald Reagan in his Farewell Address in 1989. Although the word *revolution* exaggerated the change, his administration did mark the reversal of the expanding federal budgets, programs, and regulations that had taken off in the 1930s. Incongruously, Reagan admired and emulated Franklin Delano Roosevelt, who had launched that expansion, but he used his comparable skills as "the Great Communicator" to cultivate antigovernment sentiment and undo the liberal assumptions of the New Deal.

Hostility toward and distrust of the federal government grew along with the backlash against the reforms of the 1960s and the conduct of the Vietnam War. Watergate and other misdeeds of the Nixon administration further disillusioned Americans. Presidents Ford and Carter restored morality to the White House, but neither could solve the gravest economic problems since the Great Depression—a low rate of economic growth, stagflation, and an increasing trade deficit. Even the Democrat Carter gave higher priority to fiscal austerity than to social reform, and he began the government's retreat from regulation of key industries.

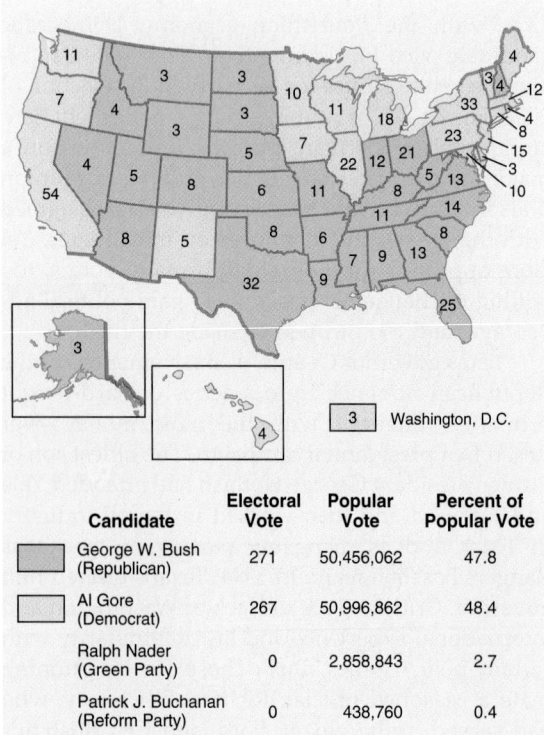

Candidate	Electoral Vote	Popular Vote	Percent of Popular Vote
George W. Bush (Republican)	271	50,456,062	47.8
Al Gore (Democrat)	267	50,996,862	48.4
Ralph Nader (Green Party)	0	2,858,843	2.7
Patrick J. Buchanan (Reform Party)	0	438,760	0.4

MAP 30.2

The Election of 2000

THE STABILITY OF AMERICAN CONSTITUTIONALISM
A week after the Supreme Court stopped the recounting of votes in Florida and Gore conceded the presidency to Bush, the two met in Washington, D.C., at the vice president's residence. Their public handshake in the snow symbolized Americans' willingness to abide by the rules governing their political institutions even when the electoral process was flawed and bitterly contested.
Wide World Photos, Inc.

During the Reagan-Bush years, as a new conservative movement flourished, the United States turned explicitly away from the assumptions that had shaped domestic policy since the New Deal. Republican presidents Eisenhower and Nixon had attempted to curb the role of the federal government, but no president before Ronald Reagan had so castigated its activities. His tax cuts, combined with hefty increases in defense spending, created a federal deficit crisis that justified cuts in social welfare spending and made new federal initiatives unthinkable. Many Americans continued to approve of specific federal programs at the end of the Reagan-Bush years, but public sentiment about the government in general had undergone a U-turn

from the Roosevelt era. Instead of seeing the government as a helpful and problem-solving institution, they believed it was not only ineffective at solving national problems but often made things worse. As conservative presidents appointed new Supreme Court justices, that body also retreated from its earlier liberalism, in which it had upheld the government's authority to protect individual rights and regulate the economy.

When the Democrats regained the White House in 1992, it was clear that the political spectrum had shifted to the right. The Clinton administration accomplished some reforms that used federal authority to solve national problems, but overall Clinton pursued a centrist strategy both in rhetoric and practice. In the 2000 elections for president and Congress, the American electorate split its vote so evenly that the new administration of Republican George W. Bush seemed bound to continue the politics of the center.

With his optimistic rhetoric, Ronald Reagan had also lifted the confidence of Americans about their nation and its promise. The sense of American greatness, which had suffered with the economic and foreign policy blows of the 1970s (see Chapter 31), gained further strength when the United States achieved unparalleled prosperity in the 1990s and stood as the world's only superpower. Yet a huge gap between rich and poor did not budge, and more than one in ten individuals continued to live in poverty. Children were disproportionately poor, as were members of minority groups, many of whom were part of the surge of immigrants that began in the 1970s. That new immigration both propelled the diversifying of American society that would stretch into the twenty-first century and reflected the process of globalization that changed American lives in manifold ways.

FOR FURTHER READING ABOUT THE TOPICS IN THIS CHAPTER, see the Online Bibliography at
www.bedfordstmartins.com/roarkcompact.

FOR ADDITIONAL FIRST-HAND ACCOUNTS OF THIS PERIOD, see pages 238–258 in Michael Johnson, ed., *Reading the American Past,* Second Edition, Volume II.

TO ASSESS YOUR MASTERY OF THE MATERIAL IN THIS CHAPTER, see the Online Study Guide at
www.bedfordstmartins.com/roarkcompact.

CHRONOLOGY

1968 Richard Nixon elected president of United States.

1969 Warren E. Burger appointed chief justice of U.S. Supreme Court by Nixon.

1970 Earth Day demonstrations held to support environmental goals.

Congress passes Occupational Safety and Health Act.

Environmental Protection Agency established by Nixon.

Native American Women's Association founded.

Women's movement stages demonstrations nationwide on August 26.

1971 First national Mexican American women's conference held.

Nixon announces abandonment of gold standard in his New Economic Policy.

Nixon vetoes comprehensive child care bill.

1972 Congress passes Title IX of Education Amendments Act, banning sex discrimination in education.

Nixon campaign aides apprehended breaking into Democratic Party headquarters in Watergate apartment complex in Washington, D.C.

Richard Nixon reelected president in landslide.

1973 National Black Feminist Organization founded.

In *Roe v. Wade*, Supreme Court rules that abortion is constitutionally protected.

1974 Nixon resigns as president in face of certain impeachment by House of Representatives over his role in Watergate affair; Gerald Ford becomes president of United States.

Ford pardons Nixon of any crimes he may have committed while president.

Supreme Court imposes some limitations on use of busing to achieve racial integration in schools.

1976 Jimmy Carter elected president of United States.

1978 In *Bakke*, Supreme Court rules against racial quotas and "reverse" discrimination.

Congress passes law banning discrimination against pregnant women.

1979–1980 Congress enacts measures to conserve energy and increase its production.

1980 Ronald Reagan elected president of United States, defeating incumbent Jimmy Carter.

1981 Researchers identify cause of AIDS epidemic as virus.

Congress passes Economic Recovery Tax Act advocated by Reagan, largest tax cut in U.S. history.

Reagan appoints Sandra Day O'Connor first female justice to U.S. Supreme Court.

1982 Banking industry deregulated.

1984 Ronald Reagan reelected president.

1988 Vice President George Bush elected forty-first president of United States.

1990 Bush and Congress agree to tax increase because of mounting federal deficit.

1991 Bush's nominee Clarence Thomas becomes second African American to sit on U.S. Supreme Court.

Congress passes Americans with Disabilities Act.

1992 Bill Clinton elected forty-second president of the United States.

1993 Janet Reno appointed first female attorney general in U.S. history.

Ruth Bader Ginsburg appointed second woman to U.S. Supreme Court.

Clinton announces "don't ask, don't tell" policy for gays in military.

Gun control and anticrime bills passed.

Clinton signs Family and Medical Leave Act, enabling many workers to take time off for childbirth, adoption, or family medical emergencies.

1994   Republicans recapture both House and Senate in congressional elections.

Representative Newt Gingrich declares 1994 elections a mandate for Republicans' conservative "contract with America."

1995   Bomb destroys federal building in Oklahoma City, claiming 169 lives;

two militia members convicted in 1997.

1996   Clinton signs Personal Responsibility and Work Opportunity Reconciliation Act, ending the federal welfare program begun in 1930s.

Clinton reelected president.

1997   Clinton signs largest tax cut since 1981.

1998   Federal budget shows surplus for first time since 1969.

House of Representatives votes to impeach President Clinton for perjury and obstruction of justice.

1999   Senate fails to approve articles of impeachment.

2000   George W. Bush elected forty-third president of the United States.

A SHRINKING WORLD

The cellular telephone is one of the new technologies contributing to the process of globalization that intensified with the end of the cold war in 1990. Connecting users to conventional telephone networks through microwave radio frequencies, wireless phones began to be used in Tokyo in 1979, and the first American system began in 1983. By the end of the century hundreds of millions of people used cell phones around the world, not only to call friends and business associates but also to connect to the Internet and send and receive e-mail. Cellular systems have improved communication for people in countries that lack a good wire-based telephone system, facilitating commerce as well as connecting far-flung family members and other individuals. Terrorists who struck the World Trade Center towers and the Pentagon on September 11, 2001, used mobile devices to coordinate the attacks, and many victims of the terror spoke their last words to loved ones over cell phones. Wireless phones decorated with the American flag became popular expressions of patriotism in the United States following the September 11 attacks on the world's lone superpower in the post–cold war world.

Kit Hinricks/Pentagon Design.

THE END OF THE COLD WAR AND THE CHALLENGES OF GLOBALIZATION

31

1975–2003

I N NOVEMBER 1999, TENS OF THOUSANDS OF AMERICANS went to Seattle, Washington, to protest U.S. government policy. Most marched peacefully and attended rallies. Hundreds of activists, however, practiced civil disobedience, blocking traffic to prevent officials from reaching their meeting halls. Some smashed windows, spray-painted graffiti, and set fires. Police in riot gear aimed tear gas and rubber bullets at those who refused to move and arrested more than six hundred people. Seattle's mayor declared a civil emergency and asked the governor to dispatch the National Guard. Although the vast majority of the protesters acted lawfully, such civil strife had not occurred in the United States since the antiwar demonstrations of the 1960s and 1970s.

The outward resemblances to anti–Vietnam War demonstrations, however, overlay acute differences demonstrating how much the world had changed by the 1990s. Controversy about Vietnam dealt with political and military issues; by contrast, the Seattle protests focused on economic and environmental questions. In fact, the demonstrators were in Seattle because an international economic body, the World Trade Organization (WTO), was meeting there. In 1995, the WTO replaced the General Agreement on Tariffs and Trade (GATT), which had been established in 1948 to liberalize trading policies and practices among 23 nations; having grown to 135 members, the WTO continued the GATT's work and also mediated trade disputes. The WTO's critics charged it with promoting a global economy that undercut standards and wages for workers, destroyed the environment, and devastated poorer, developing nations; others, who reflected an older isolationist tradition, objected to diluting American autonomy in economic decision making.

The Seattle protesters covered a broader political spectrum and differed in significant ways from the opponents of the Vietnam War. Young radicals appeared in both movements, but in Seattle they joined with steelworkers and other labor union members—the hard-hat workers who had largely supported government policy in Vietnam. Invisible in anti–Vietnam War activism, environmentalists were prominent in Seattle; some dressed as sea turtles, an endangered species, to symbolize the WTO's failure to uphold environmental standards. Reflecting new alliances, one protest sign read "Teamsters and Turtles—Together at Last." These and other activists representing human rights groups and the concerns of developing nations and consumers gained considerable attention. California state senator Tom Hayden, the former student radical leader from the 1960s, proclaimed, "A week ago no one even knew what the WTO was. Now these protests have made WTO a household word."

The Seattle demonstrations reflected massive changes that ended the cold war and transformed the world. Yet as late as 1990, few anticipated the imminent dissolution of the Soviet Union. In the 1970s, President Richard Nixon pursued less hostile relationships with both the Soviet Union and China, while practicing unrelenting opposition to communism in the third world. In the 1980s, President Ronald Reagan voiced the most anti-Soviet rhetoric since the days of John Foster Dulles and oversaw the nation's largest military buildup in peacetime, although relations with the Soviet Union improved near the end of his presidency.

Eastern Europe broke free from Communist control in 1989, and the Soviet Union disintegrated in 1991. With the end of the cold war—the obsession of U.S. foreign policy for forty-five years—the nation's leaders searched for a new strategy in an era no longer defined by containment of communism. As the lone superpower, the United States deployed both military and diplomatic power during episodes of instability in Latin America, the Middle East, eastern Europe, and Africa. And, as the demonstrations in Seattle reflected, the United States held sway in an increasingly interconnected global economy. But in September 2001, deadly terrorist attacks on New York City, the nation's economic center, and on Washington, D.C., its political and military core, exposed American vulnerability to new international threats.

New Opportunities and Dangers in a Multipolar World

His imagination captivated by opportunities in a changing world, Richard M. Nixon hoped to make his mark on history using his broad understanding of international relations. Diverging from Republican orthodoxy, his dramatic overtures to the Soviet Union and China reduced decades-old hostilities. Yet, anticommunism remained central to American policy, especially in Nixon's approach to less developed parts of the world.

Détente (French for "loosening") faltered under Nixon's successors, Presidents Ford and Carter, and Soviet-American relations deteriorated. Carter built on Nixon's initiatives by establishing normal diplomatic relations with China. In addition, he pushed through treaties ending U.S. control over the Panama Canal, and he helped negotiate a peace treaty between Israel and Egypt. But Middle East tensions eased only slightly, and in 1979 a crisis with an intensely anti-American government in Iran displayed an international force that would shake the nation two decades later.

Moving toward Détente with the Soviet Union and China

Nixon saw the increasing Soviet-Chinese discord and the growing power of Europe and Japan as indications that the "rigid and bipolar world of the 1940s and 1950s" was giving way to "the fluidity of a new era of multilateral diplomacy." With his chief foreign policy adviser, Henry Kissinger, he, often secretly, exploited the deterioration in Soviet-Chinese relations that had begun in the early 1960s. If these two nations checked each other's power, Nixon believed, their threat to the United States would lessen; thus Soviet-Chinese hostility "served our purpose best if we maintained closer relations with each side than they did with each other."

In February 1972, he became the nation's first president to set foot on Chinese soil—an astonishing act by a man who had climbed the political ladder as a fervent anti-Communist. Recognizing that his anti-Communist credentials were what enabled him to conduct this shift in U.S.-Chinese relations with no significant objections at home, Nixon remarked to Chinese leader Mao Zedong, "Those on the right can do what those on the left only talk about." Although the act was largely symbolic, cultural and scientific exchanges followed, and American manufacturers began to find markets in China—small steps in the process of globalization that would take giant strides in the 1990s.

As Nixon and Kissinger hoped, the warming of U.S.-Chinese relations increased Soviet responsiveness to their strategy of détente, their term for easing conflict with the Soviet Union. Détente did not mean abandoning containment but instead focusing on arms control, trade, and other issues of common concern. Containment would be achieved not only by military threat but also by ensuring that Russian and Chinese stakes in a stable international order would restrain them from precipitating crises. Nixon's goal was "a stronger healthy United States,

PROTESTS AGAINST THE WTO
Environmentalists and animal protection advocates were among the varied groups demonstrating against the World Trade Organization when it attempted to meet in Seattle, Washington, in November 1999. These activists dressed as sea turtles to protest WTO agreements permitting economic actions that they believed threatened the survival of the animals.
Wide World Photos, Inc.

Europe, Soviet Union, China, Japan, each balancing the other."

In May 1972, three months after his trip to China, Nixon visited Moscow, signing several agreements on trade and cooperation in science and space. Most significantly, Soviet and U.S. leaders concluded arms limitation treaties that had grown out of the Strategic Arms Limitation Talks (SALT) begun in 1969. Both sides agreed to limit antiballistic missile systems (ABMs) to two each. Giving up pursuit of a defense against nuclear weapons was a critical move, because it meant that neither nation could become so secure against a nuclear attack that it would risk a first strike.

Gerald Ford, who took over as president when Nixon resigned in 1974, failed to sustain widespread support of détente. The secrecy of the Nixon-Kissinger initiatives had alienated legislators, and

some Democrats charged that détente ignored Soviet violations of human rights. Members of both parties worried that Soviet strength was overtaking that of the United States. In response, Congress derailed trade agreements with the Soviet Union, refusing economic favors unless the Soviets stopped their harsh treatment of internal dissidents and Jews.

Further negotiations on limiting strategic arms went nowhere, but U.S., Soviet, and European leaders signed a historic agreement in 1975 in Helsinki, Finland, formally recognizing the existing post–World War II boundaries in Europe. In agreeing to the Helsinki accords, the United States accepted the Soviets' domination over their satellite countries in eastern Europe—a condition to which it had objected so bitterly thirty years earlier as the cold war began.

Shoring Up Anticommunism in the Third World

Nixon promised in 1973, "The time has passed when America will make every other nation's conflict our own . . . or presume to tell the people of other nations how to manage their own affairs." Yet even while applying practical politics to U.S. relations with China and the Soviet Union, in Vietnam and elsewhere he continued to equate Marxism with a threat to U.S. interests and actively resisted social revolutions that might lead to communism.

The Nixon administration found such a threat in Salvador Allende, a self-proclaimed Marxist who was elected president of Chile in 1970. Since 1964, the Central Intelligence Agency (CIA) and U.S. corporations concerned about nationalization of their Chilean properties had assisted Allende's opponents. When Allende won the election, the United States tried to destabilize his government with political and economic pressure. In 1973, with the help of the CIA, the Chilean military engineered a coup, killed Allende, and established a brutal dictatorship under General Augusto Pinochet, who twenty-five years later was found guilty of torture, murder, and terrorism by an international court.

In other parts of the world, too, the Nixon administration stood by repressive governments. It eased pressures on white minority governments that tyrannized blacks in southern Africa, believing that, as a National Security Council (NSC) memorandum put it, the "whites are here to stay. . . . There is no hope for the blacks to gain the political rights they seek through violence, which will lead only to chaos and increased opportunities for Communists." In the Middle East, the United States supported the harsh regime of the shah of Iran—whom the CIA had helped regain power in 1953—because it considered Iran a stable anti-Communist ally with enormous petroleum reserves. Nixon secretly began massive arms shipments to the shah in 1972, cementing a relationship that would ignite a new crisis when the shah was overthrown in 1979.

Like his predecessors, Nixon pursued a delicate balance between defending Israel's security and seeking the goodwill of Arab nations strategically and economically important to the United States. Conflict between Israel and the Arab nations had escalated into the all-out Six-Day War in 1967, when Israel won a stunning victory over Egyptian, Syrian, and Jordanian forces, seizing territory that amounted to twice its original size. Israeli forces took control of the Sinai Peninsula and Gaza Strip from Egypt, the Golan Heights from Syria, and the West Bank from Jordan, which included the Arab sector of Jerusalem, a city sacred to Jews, Christians, and Muslims alike (Map 31.1).

That decisive victory did not quell Middle Eastern turmoil. In October 1973, on the Jewish holiday Yom Kippur, Egypt and Syria surprised Israel with a full-scale attack. When the Nixon administration sided with Israel, the Arab nations retaliated with an oil embargo. After Israel repulsed the attack, Kissinger attempted to mediate between Israel and Arab nations, efforts that continued for the next three decades with only limited success. The Arab countries refused to recognize Israel's right to exist; Israel would not withdraw from the territories occupied during the Six-Day War and in fact began to settle Israelis there; and no solution could be found for the Palestinian refugees who had been displaced by the creation of Israel in the late 1940s. The simmering conflict contributed to anti-American sentiment among Arabs who viewed the United States as Israel's supporter.

Carter Promotes Human Rights

Campaigning for president in 1976, Jimmy Carter charged his predecessors' foreign policy with violating the nation's principles of freedom and human dignity. "We've seen a loss of morality . . . and we're ashamed of what our government is as we deal with other nations around the world," he said. The cynical support of dictators, the secret diplomacy, the interference in the internal affairs of other countries, and the excessive reliance on military solutions—Carter promised to reverse them all.

Human rights formed the cornerstone of his approach. Administration officials chastised governments that denied their citizens basic political and civil rights. They also applied economic pressure, denying aid or trading privileges to such nations as Argentina, Chile, and El Salvador, and the white minority governments of Rhodesia and South Africa, which blatantly violated the rights of their black majorities. Yet glaring inconsistencies appeared in the human rights policy. Carter's establishment of formal diplomatic relations with the People's Republic of China trumped concern over democratic rights for the Chinese people. Moreover, the administration invoked no sanctions against repressive governments in Iran, South Korea, and the

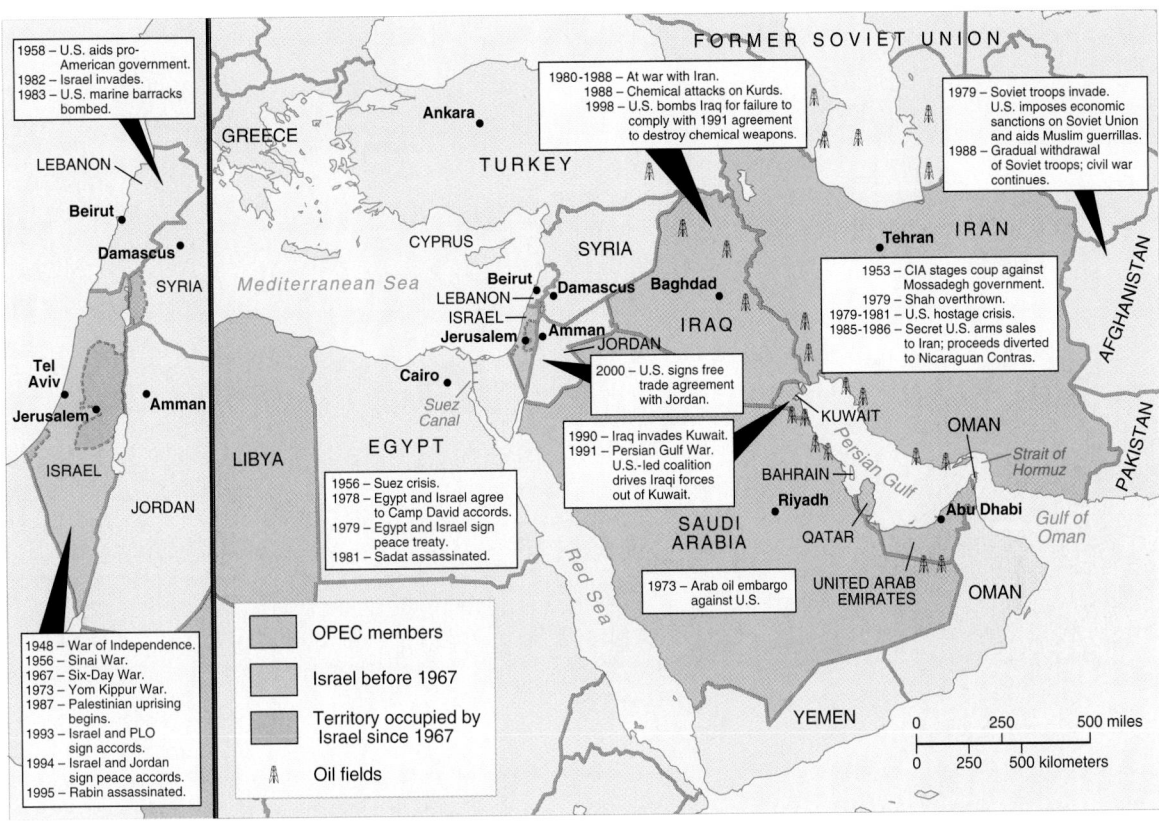

M AP 31.1

The Middle East, 1948–2002

U.S. determination to preserve access to the rich oil reserves of the Middle East and its commitment to the security of Israel were the fundamental—and sometimes conflicting—principles of U.S. foreign policy in that region.

Philippines, thus sacrificing human rights ideals to strategic and security considerations.

Cold war considerations vied with human rights concerns in Carter's approach to Nicaragua, which had been ruled since 1936 by the corrupt and viciously oppressive Somoza regime. U.S. officials complained about the dictatorship's excesses and invoked some economic sanctions, but when civil war erupted, their greatest concern was to contain Communist influence in the anti-Somoza movement. Officials were particularly uneasy about the Sandinistas, a leading element in the opposition with ties to Cuba. Nonetheless, when the Somoza regime fell in 1979 and Sandinista leader Daniel Ortega assumed power, Carter extended recognition and economic aid to the new government. His critics attacked Carter for pressuring the Somoza regime on human rights and recognizing the Ortega

government, demanding instead the more typical test for U.S. support during the cold war years—whether a country was anti-Communist and friendly to American interests, not how it treated its citizens.

Applying moral principles to relations with Panama, Carter sped up negotiations over control of the Panama Canal—the most conspicuous symbol of Yankee imperialism. In 1977, the United States and Panama signed treaties providing for joint control of the canal until 2000, when Panama would take over. Although treaty supporters viewed the agreement as recompense for the blatant use of U.S. power to obtain the canal in 1903, angry opponents insisted on retaining this vital waterway. "We bought it, we paid for it, it's ours," claimed Ronald Reagan during the presidential primaries of 1976. Only after the Carter administration undertook a

AMERICAN HOSTAGES IN IRAN
Iranian militants display one of the hostages they took when they occupied the American embassy in Teheran on November 4, 1979. Until the hostages were released in January 1981, Americans regularly watched TV images of the American captives being paraded before angry Iranian crowds. The bound, blindfolded hostages served as humiliating symbols of the limitations of American power.
Ph. Ledru/Sygma.

massive campaign to rally support did the Senate ratify the treaties by the narrowest margins.

Seeking to apply his moral authority to peace in the Middle East, Carter seized on the courage of Egyptian president Anwar Sadat, the first Arab leader to risk his political career by talking directly with Israeli officials. When initial discussions between Sadat and Israeli prime minister Menachem Begin faltered, Carter invited them to the presidential retreat at Camp David, Maryland, and spent thirteen days there mediating between the two. The Camp David accords led to an agreement that Begin and Sadat signed at the White House in March 1979: Egypt became the first Arab state to recognize Israel,

and Israel agreed to gradual withdrawal from the Sinai Peninsula, territory that it had seized in the 1967 war (see Map 31.1). Although the issues of Palestinian self-determination in other Israeli-occupied territories—the West Bank and Gaza—and the plight of Palestinian refugees remained unresolved, the first meaningful steps toward peace in the Middle East had been taken.

The Cold War Intensifies

Carter was unable to duplicate his success with the Panama treaties and the Egypt-Israel accord elsewhere. During his last two years in office, U.S.-

Soviet relations deteriorated, and the administration began a sizable military buildup. Preferring to pursue national security through nonmilitary means, Carter initially sought accommodation with the Soviet Union. But in 1979, he abandoned efforts to obtain Senate ratification of a new strategic arms limitation treaty and authorized development of intermediate-range missiles to be deployed in western Europe and an enormous new missile system for the United States.

The military buildup followed the Soviet Union's invasion of its neighbor Afghanistan, whose recently installed pro-Soviet government was threatened by Muslim opposition (see Map 31.1). Carter also imposed economic sanctions on the Soviet Union, barred U.S. participation in the 1980 Olympic Games in Moscow, and obtained legislation requiring all nineteen-year-old men to register for the draft.

The president claimed that Soviet actions jeopardized oil supplies from the Middle East and announced his own "Carter Doctrine," threatening the use of any means necessary to prevent an outside force from gaining control of the Persian Gulf. His human rights policy fell by the wayside as the United States stepped up aid to Afghanistan's neighbor, Pakistan, then under a military dictatorship. Finally, Carter called for hefty increases in defense spending over the next five years.

Events in Iran fueled this reversion to a hardline, militaristic approach. All the U.S. arms and aid had not enabled the shah to suppress increasing numbers of Iranian dissidents who still resented the CIA's role in the overthrow of the Mossadegh government in 1953 and condemned the shah's savage attempts to silence opposition. In 1979, a revolution forced the shah out of Iran and gave Ayatollah Ruholla Khomeini and other Shiite Islamic fundamentalists control of the government. These forces were intensely hostile to the United States, which they blamed for supporting the shah's brutalities and undermining the religious foundations of their country.

When Carter permitted the shah to enter the United States for medical treatment, anti-American demonstrations escalated in Teheran. On November 4, 1979, a crowd broke into the U.S. embassy and seized more than sixty Americans, demanding that the shah be returned for trial. When Khomeini supported the captors, Carter froze Iranian assets in U.S. banks and placed an embargo on Iranian oil. He sent a small military operation into Iran in April 1980, but the rescue mission failed and the hostages remained prisoners until the day he left office in January 1981.

The aborted mission fed Americans' feelings of impotence, simmering since the nation's defeat in Vietnam. Those frustrations in turn produced support for a more militaristic foreign policy. Opposition to Soviet-American détente, combined with the Soviet invasion of Afghanistan, nullified the thaw in relations that Nixon and Kissinger had begun.

Ronald Reagan Confronts an "Evil Empire"

Running for president in 1980, Ronald Reagan capitalized on the Soviet invasion of Afghanistan and the Iranian hostage crisis, accusing Carter of weakening the military and losing the confidence of the nation's allies and its enemies' respect. As president, he accelerated the arms buildup begun by Carter and harshly censured the Soviet Union, calling it "an evil empire." Yet despite the new aggressiveness—or, as some have argued, because of it—Reagan presided over the most impressive improvement in superpower relations since the shattering of the World War II alliance. On the periphery of the cold war, however, Reagan practiced militant anticommunism, authorizing aid to anti-leftist movements in Asia, Africa, and Central America and dispatching troops to both the Middle East and the Caribbean.

Militarization and Interventions Abroad

Reagan sought to expand the military with new bombers and missiles, an enhanced nuclear force in Europe, a larger navy, and a rapid-deployment force. Despite the growing budget deficit, Congress approved most of these programs, and military expenditures shot up by one-third in the first half of the 1980s. Throughout Reagan's presidency, defense spending averaged $216 billion a year, up from $158 billion in the Carter years and higher even than in the Vietnam era.

Justifying the buildup as a means to negotiate with the Soviets from a position of strength, Reagan provoked an outburst of calls to halt the arms race. A rally demanding a freeze on additional nuclear weapons drew 700,000 people in New York City in 1982. Hundreds of thousands of Europeans demonstrated across the continent, stimulated by fears of

THE NUCLEAR FREEZE CAMPAIGN
*An active movement in the United States and Europe worked to limit nuclear weapons
and diminish the threat of nuclear destruction in the early 1980s. In 1982, half a million
antinuclear protesters marched and rallied in New York City.*
Corbis-Bettmann.

new U.S. missiles scheduled for deployment in North Atlantic Treaty Organization (NATO) countries in 1983.

Reagan startled many of his own advisers in March 1983 by announcing plans for research on the Strategic Defense Initiative (SDI). Immediately dubbed "Star Wars" by critics who doubted its feasibility, the project would deploy lasers in space to destroy enemy missiles before they could reach their targets. Reagan conceded that SDI could appear as "an aggressive policy" allowing the United States to strike first and not fear retaliation. The Soviets reacted angrily because SDI development violated the 1972 ABM treaty and would require the Soviets to invest huge sums in their own Star Wars technology. SDI research continued even after the end of the cold war, but with no workable results despite more than $60 billion in funding.

The U.S. military buildup placed the Soviets on the defensive, but it did not guarantee American security. Although Iran released the American hostages, terrorism continued to threaten the United States. In October 1983, an Islamic extremist drove a bomb-filled truck into a marine barracks in Lebanon, killing 241 Americans (see Map 31.1). Faced with other incidents of murder, kidnapping, and hijacking by various Middle Eastern extremist groups, Reagan refused to negotiate, insisting that to bargain with terrorists would only encourage more assaults.

The Reagan administration sought to contain leftist movements close to home and across the globe. In 1983, U.S. troops invaded Grenada, a small island nation in the Caribbean that had succumbed to a left-wing coup. In Asia, the United States moved more quietly, aiding the Afghan rebels' war against Afghanistan's Soviet-backed government. In the African nation of Angola, the United States armed rebel forces against the Soviet- and Cuban-backed government. Reagan also sided with the South African government that was brutally suppressing black protest against apartheid. In 1985, Congress had to override Reagan's veto in order to impose economic sanctions against South Africa.

Administration officials were most fearful of left-wing movements in Central America that, according to Reagan, threatened to "destabilize the entire region from the Panama Canal to Mexico." When a leftist uprising occurred in 1981 in El Salvador, the United States sent money and military advisers to prop up the government, even though it had committed murderous human rights violations and opposed social reform.

In neighboring Nicaragua, where Reagan aimed to unseat the left-wing Sandinistas, the administration aided the Contras (literally, "opposers"), a coalition of armed opposition to the Sandinistas that included many individuals from the ousted regime. Fearing another Vietnam, many Americans opposed aligning the United States with reactionary forces not supported by the majority of Nicaraguans. Congress repeatedly instructed the president to stop aid to the Contras or limit it to nonmilitary purposes.

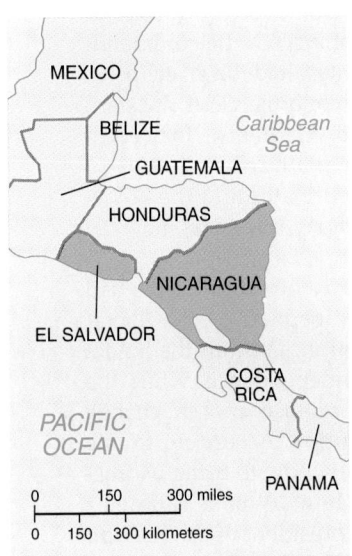

El Salvador and Nicaragua

Deliberately violating congressional will, the administration secretly provided weapons and training to the Contras. The CIA directed assaults on economic targets and helped to mine Nicaraguan harbors in 1984. Through legal and illegal means, the Reagan administration sustained the Contras and helped wreck the Nicaraguan economy, thereby undermining support for the Sandinista government. After nine years of civil war, its president agreed to a political settlement, and when defeated by a coalition of all the opposition groups, he stepped aside.

The Iran-Contra Scandal

Secret aid to the Contras was part of a larger project that came to be known as the Iran-Contra scandal. It began in 1985, when heads of the NSC, NSC aide Marine Lieutenant Colonel Oliver North, and CIA Director William Casey arranged to sell arms to Iran, then at war with neighboring Iraq. In exchange, Iranians were to pressure Muslim terrorists to release seven American hostages being held in Lebanon (see Map 31.1). Funds from the arms sales were then channeled through Swiss bank accounts to aid the Nicaraguan Contras. Over the objections of Secretary of State George Shultz and Defense Secretary Caspar Weinberger, Reagan approved the arms sales, but the three subsequently denied knowing that the proceeds were diverted to the Contras.

When news of the affair surfaced in November 1986, the Reagan administration faced serious charges. The president who had pledged never to bargain with terrorists had allowed his aides to do so, violating U.S. neutrality in the Iran-Iraq War. Even worse, the administration had defied Congress's express ban on military aid for the Contras. Although North and others destroyed incriminating documents, enough remained to demonstrate the culpability of seven individuals. Brought to trial by an independent prosecutor appointed by Reagan, all pleaded guilty or were convicted of lying to Congress and destroying evidence. North's felony conviction was later overturned on a technicality, and President George Bush pardoned the other six officials in December 1992. The independent prosecutor's final report, issued in 1994, found no evidence that Reagan had broken the law; but it concluded that both Reagan and Vice President Bush had known about the diversion of funds to the Contras and that Reagan had "knowingly participated or at least acquiesced" in covering up the scandal—the most serious case of executive branch misconduct since Watergate.

A Thaw in Soviet-American Relations

Reagan weathered Iran-Contra in part because Americans applauded a momentous thaw in the cold war. The new Soviet-American accord depended on Reagan's flexibility and an innovative Soviet head of state who recognized that his country's domestic problems demanded a relaxation of cold war antagonism. Mikhail Gorbachev assumed power in 1985 determined to revitalize an inefficient Soviet economy incapable of delivering basic consumer goods. Hoping to stimulate production and streamline distribution, Gorbachev introduced some elements of free enterprise and proclaimed a new era of *glasnost* (greater freedom of expression), eventually allowing new political parties, contested elections, and challenges to Communist rule.

Concerns about immense defense budgets moved both Reagan and Gorbachev to the negotiating table. Enormous military expenditures stood between the Soviet premier and his goal of economic revival. With Congress increasingly criticizing the arms race and popular support for arms reductions, Reagan made disarmament a major goal in his last years in office and readily responded when Gorbachev took the initiative.

A positive personal chemistry developed between Reagan and Gorbachev, who met four times between 1985 and 1988. By December 1987, the superpowers had completed an intermediate-range nuclear forces (INF) agreement, eliminating all short- and medium-range missiles from Europe and providing for on-site inspection for the first time. George H. W. Bush, Reagan's successor, achieved another breakthrough in June 1990, with a strategic arms reduction treaty (START) that cut about 30 percent of each superpower's nuclear arsenal.

In 1988, Gorbachev further reduced tensions by announcing a gradual withdrawal from Afghanistan, which had become the Soviet equivalent of America's Vietnam. In Africa, the Soviet Union, the United States, and Cuba agreed on a political settlement for the civil war in Angola. And in the Middle East, both superpowers supported a cease-fire and peace talks in the eight-year war between Iran and Iraq.

Defining American Interests in a Post-Cold War World

Global shifts of the magnitude that transformed the world between 1989 and 1991 usually occurred in the context of tremendous warfare. In contrast, the eastern bloc nations threw out their Communist rulers, and then in 1991, the Soviet Union fell apart, with very little bloodshed. Although U.S. leaders failed to develop guiding principles of foreign policy that would replace containment of communism, they did not hesitate to act in the transformed world. President George H. W. Bush deployed military power in Latin America and the Middle East; his successor, Bill Clinton, sent troops to Somalia, Haiti, the Middle East, and eastern Europe; and President George W. Bush declared a world-wide war on terrorism.

The End of the Cold War

The forces of change that Gorbachev had encouraged swept through eastern Europe in 1989, where popular uprisings demanded an end to state repression, official corruption, and economic bureaucracies unable to deliver an acceptable standard of living. Communist governments toppled like dominoes (Map 31.2). East Germany opened its border with West Germany, and on November 12, 1989, ecstatic Germans danced on the Berlin Wall and began to demolish that dominant symbol of the cold war.

Unification of East and West Germany into one nation sped to completion in 1990. The Warsaw Pact dissolved, and three former iron curtain countries—the Czech Republic, Hungary, and Poland—joined NATO in 1999. Although U.S. military forces remained in Europe as part of NATO, the commanding role of the United States had been eclipsed. The same was true of its economic clout: Western Europe, including unified Germany, formed a common economic market in 1992. The destiny of Europe, to which the United States and the Soviet Union had held the key for forty-five years, now lay in European hands.

By the end of 1991, Gorbachev's initiatives had brought his own downfall. Inspired by the liberation of eastern Europe, republics within the Soviet Union sought their own independence, while the Moscow government's efforts at economic change brought widespread destitution. According to one Muscovite, "Gorbachev knew how to bring us freedom but he did not know how to make sausage." In December, Boris Yeltsin, president of the Russian Republic, announced that Russia and eleven other republics had formed a new entity, the Commonwealth of Independent States (CIS), and other former Soviet states declared independence. With nothing left to govern, Gorbachev resigned.

The United States officially recognized Russia, but the breakup of the Soviet Union brought its own dangers. "The post–cold war world is decidedly not postnuclear," declared President Clinton's secretary of defense, Les Aspin. The breakdown of the Soviet Union meant that four countries with nuclear weapons—Russia, Ukraine, Belarus, and Kazakhstan—now stood in place of one, in addition to the United States, Britain, France, China, India, Israel, Pakistan, and possibly North Korea, still under a Communist dictatorship. In 1996, leaders of the nuclear powers signed a comprehensive test ban

FALL OF THE BERLIN WALL
*After 1961, the Berlin Wall stood as the prime symbol of the cold war and the iron grip
of communism over eastern Europe and the Soviet Union. More than four hundred easterners were killed trying to flee. After Communist authorities opened the wall on November 9, 1989, permitting free travel between the east and west, Berliners from both
sides gathered at the wall to celebrate.*
Eric Bouvet/Gamma Liaison.

www.bedfordstmartins.com/roarkcompact   SEE THE ONLINE STUDY GUIDE for more help in
analyzing this image.

treaty. Yet India and Pakistan, hostile neighbors, refused to sign the pact, and both exploded atomic
devices in May 1998. Moreover, the Republican-
controlled Senate defeated ratification of the treaty
in October 1999, the first rejection of a major international agreement since the Senate repudiated the
Versailles treaty in 1919. A decade of progress on
nuclear weapons control halted.

The Gulf War, 1991

Former cold war enemies cooperated when, in August 1990, Iraq invaded and occupied the small, oil-
rich country of Kuwait (see Map 31.1). With an enormous debt from ten years of war against Iran, Iraqi
president Saddam Hussein sought control of
Kuwaiti oil. Within days of invading Kuwait, Iraqi
troops moved toward the Saudi Arabian border,
threatening the world's largest oil reserves.

President Bush reacted quickly. Although he invoked principles of national self-determination and
international law, the need to maintain access to oil
primarily determined the U.S. response. With the
consent of Saudi Arabia, Bush ordered Operation
Desert Shield, a massive mobilization of land, air,
and naval forces, and assembled more than thirty
nations in an international coalition to repel Iraqi
aggression.

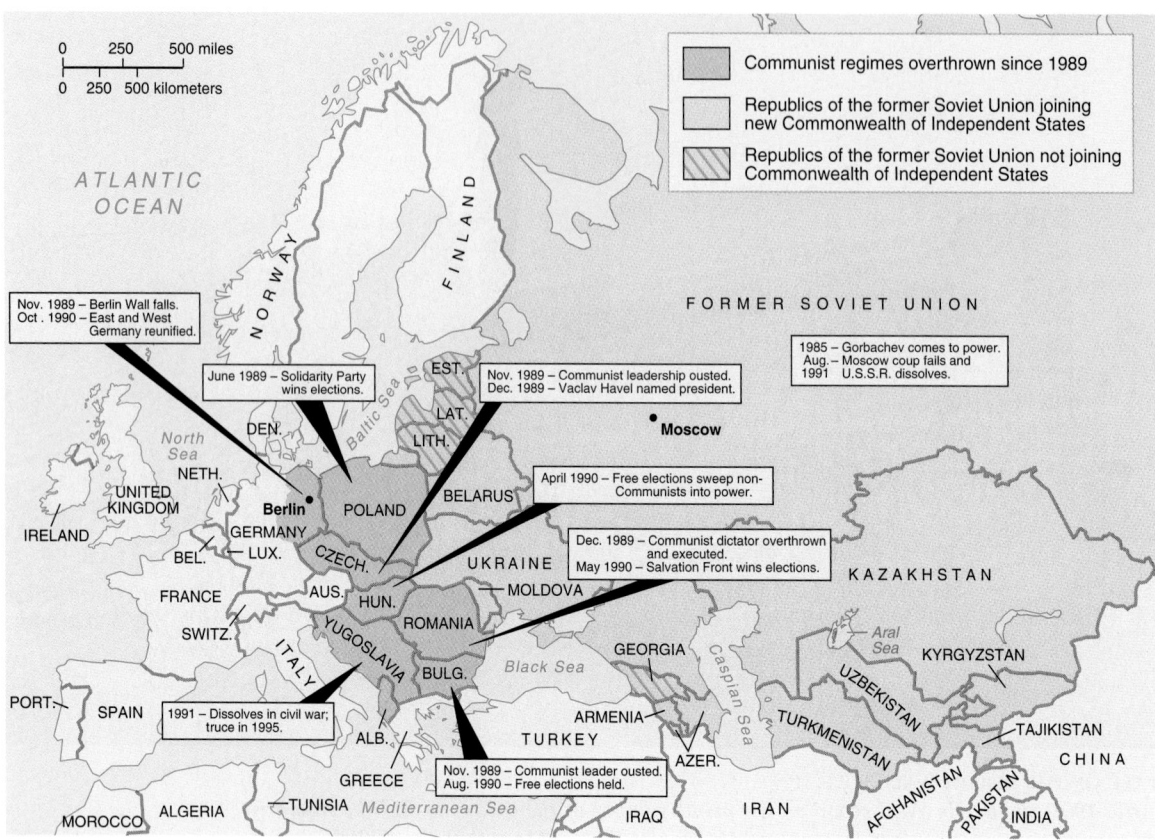

MAP 31.2
Events in Eastern Europe, 1989–2002
The overthrow of Communist governments throughout eastern and central Europe and the splintering of the Soviet Union into more than a dozen separate nations were the most momentous changes in world history since World War II.

READING THE MAP: Which country was the first to overthrow its Communist government? Which was the last? In which nations did elections usher in change in government?

CONNECTIONS: What problems did Mikhail Gorbachev try to solve, and how did he try to solve them? What policy launched by Ronald Reagan contributed to Soviet dilemmas? Did it create any problems in the United States?

www.bedfordstmartins.com/roarkcompact   SEE THE ONLINE STUDY GUIDE for more help in analyzing this map.

Reflecting the end of superpower conflict in the Middle East, the Soviet Union joined the United States in condemning Hussein and cut off arms shipments to Iraq. The United Nations (UN) declared an embargo on Iraqi oil and authorized the use of force if Iraq did not withdraw from Kuwait by January 15, 1991. By early January, the United States had deployed 400,000 soldiers to Saudi Arabia, joined by 265,000 troops from European na-

tions, Egypt, Syria, and several other Arab states. Although considerable public and legislative sentiment favored waiting to see whether the embargo would force Hussein to back down, Congress authorized the use of military force against Iraq by margins of five votes in the Senate and sixty-seven in the House.

On January 17, 1991, Operation Desert Shield became Operation Desert Storm, when the U.S.-led coalition began a forty-day air war against Iraq, bombing military targets, power plants, oil refineries, and transportation networks. Having severely crippled Iraq, the coalition launched a massive ground assault on February 23, and within one hundred hours Hussein announced that he would withdraw from Kuwait (Map 31.1).

"By God, we've kicked the Vietnam syndrome once and for all," President Bush exulted on March 1. Most Americans found no moral ambiguity in the Persian Gulf War and took pride in the display of military competence. In contrast to the loss of 50,000 American lives in Vietnam, 270 U.S. servicemen and women lost their lives in Desert Storm. The United States stood at the apex of global leadership, steering a coalition in which Arab nations fought beside their former colonial rulers.

THE GULF WAR
These soldiers from the Twenty-fourth Infantry arrived in Saudi Arabia in August 1990 as part of the U.S.-led effort to drive Iraq out of Kuwait. For the first time women served in combat-support positions, with more than 33,000 stationed throughout the Gulf; 11 died and 2 were held as prisoners of war. Among their duties, women piloted planes and helicopters, directed artillery, and fought fires.
Corbis-Bettmann.

Yet victory did not bring stability to the Middle East. Israel, which had endured Iraqi missile attacks, was more secure, but the Israeli-Palestinian conflict remained intractable. Despite military losses, Hussein remained in power and sought to develop chemical and nuclear weapons of mass destruction, while Iraqi citizens suffered malnutrition, disease, and death caused by the continuing embargo.

Deploying American Power

The Gulf War demonstrated the dominance of United States leadership in world affairs. How and where American power would be applied in a post–cold war world of some 190 nations remained to be determined. Although the international context had shifted, the nation still faced fundamental challenges to its secure place in the world: the continuing threat of nuclear peril, the need to safeguard its global economic interests, and a relatively new danger—terrorism carried out by Islamic political extremists.

Both before and after the Gulf War, the United States inconsistently used its diplomatic and military power in a variety of situations. Guided largely by humanitarian concern, in December 1992 President Bush attached U.S. forces to a UN operation in the small African country of Somalia, where famine and civil war raged. In 1993, President Clinton allowed the humanitarian mission to turn into "nation building," an effort to restore stability. Eighteen U.S. soldiers were killed in the process, and an outcry at home suggested that most Americans would not sacrifice lives when no vital economic or political interests seemed threatened. For example, the UN and the United States stood by when more than half a million people were massacred in a brutal civil war in the central African nation of Rwanda in 1994.

The United States was less restrained when turmoil threatened Latin America and Europe. In 1989, President Bush ordered 25,000 troops into Panama to capture General Manuel Noriega, who had amassed a fortune from illegal drugs, while torturing and killing his domestic opposition, and who was indicted for drug trafficking by a Miami, Florida, grand jury. U.S. forces quickly overcame Noriega's troops, at the cost of twenty-three Americans and hundreds of Panamanians, many of them civilians. This resort to military intervention revived the image of Yankee imperialism.

A UN-authorized intervention of U.S. troops in Haiti in 1994 received a warmer welcome. When a military coup overthrew their democratically elected president, thousands of Haitians tried to escape their island's poverty and political violence, many on flimsy boats heading for Florida. With anti-immigrant sentiment already high in the nation, President Clinton was pressed hard to stop the refugee flow. (See "Historical Question," page 826.) In September 1994, hours before 20,000 troops were to invade Haiti, the military leaders promised to step down, and U.S. forces peacefully landed and began disarming Haitian troops. Initially a huge success, U.S. policy would continue to be tested as Haiti faced grave economic and political challenges.

In eastern Europe, the collapse of communism ignited the most severe crisis on the continent since the 1940s. During the cold war, the Communist government of Yugoslavia, a federation of six republics, had held ethnic tensions in check, and many Muslims, Croats, and Serbs had grown accustomed to living and working together. After the Communists were swept out in 1989, Yugoslavia splintered into separate states and fell into civil war as ruthless leaders exploited ethnic differences to bolster their power. The Serbs' aggression against the Bosnian Muslims horrified much of the world.

As reports of terror, rape, and torture in Bosnia worsened, American leaders worried about the image of the world's strongest nation unwilling to use its power to stop the violence. In November 1995, the United States brought the leaders of Serbia, Croatia, and Bosnia to Dayton, Ohio, where they hammered out a peace treaty. President Clinton then agreed to send 20,000 American troops to Bosnia as part of a NATO peacekeeping mission.

In 1998, new fighting broke out in the southern Serbian province of Kosovo, where ethnic Albanians, who constituted 90 percent of the population, were making a bid for inde-

Reconfiguration of Yugoslavia, 1991–1992

pendence. The Serbian army brutally retaliated, driving out one-third of Kosovo's 1.8 million Albanian Muslims. When Serbian president Slobodan Milosevic refused to agree to a peace settlement in 1999, NATO launched a bombing attack on Serbian military and government targets, carried out largely by U.S. pilots and planes. Three months of bombing forced Serbia to agree to a settlement. Although the situation in Kosovo remained unstable politically and economically, Serbians voted Milosevic out of office in October 2000, and he was brought before an international tribunal in 2002 for genocide.

President Clinton was less hesitant to deploy American power when he could send missiles rather than men and women; and he also proved willing to act without international support or UN sanction. In August 1998, bombs exploded in U.S. embassies in Kenya and Tanzania, killing 12 Americans and more than 250 Africans. In response, Clinton ordered missile attacks on terrorist training camps in Afghanistan controlled by Osama bin Laden, a Saudi-born millionaire who financed an Islamic-extremist terrorist network and directed the embassy bombings.

A few months later, in December 1998, Clinton launched air strikes against Iraqi military installations. At the end of the Gulf War in 1991, President Hussein had agreed to eliminate Iraq's chemical, germ, and nuclear weapons and to allow UN inspections. But he resisted compliance with the agreement and tried to block inspection officials, prompting the U.S. attacks. Whereas Bush had acted in the Gulf War with the support of an international force that included Arab states, Clinton acted unilaterally and in the face of Arab opposition.

Using diplomatic rather than military power, Clinton continued the decades-long efforts to ameliorate the Israeli-Palestinian conflict. In 1993, Yasir Arafat, head of the Palestine Liberation Organization (PLO), and Yitzhak Rabin, Israeli prime minister, recognized for the first time existence of the other's state and agreed to Israeli withdrawal from the Gaza Strip and Jericho, and to Palestinian self-government in those territories. Less than a year later, in July 1994, Clinton presided over another turning point as Rabin and King Hussein of Jordan signed a declaration of peace. Although these constituted momentous steps, negotiations over control of Jerusalem, the fate of Palestinian refugees, and the presence of more than 200,000 Israeli settlers living among 3 million Palestinians determined to es-

1975–2003

tablish their own state in the West Bank and Gaza Strip broke down in 2000, and violence between Israelis and Palestinians consumed the area.

American Efforts to Shape Globalization

Unlike his six predecessors, whose international meetings had focused on arms control and national security, President Bill Clinton traveled to summits where leaders more typically discussed trade policies and other economic issues. As the United States emerged from the cold war as the only military superpower, it also dominated the world economy.

From that position, American leaders tried to shape the tremendous economic transformations occurring in a process that came to be called globalization.

As the tumult around the 1999 WTO meeting in Seattle demonstrated, both gains and losses attended the growing integration and interdependence of national citizens and economies. The liberalization of international trade produced unprecedented products and profits for some, but it brought economic insecurity and environmental damage to others. And with the greater ease of travel and communication around the globe, individuals and nations became more at risk from terrorist violence, a vulnerability that Americans experienced firsthand on September 11, 2001.

THE INTERNET LINKS THE WORLD
By the end of the twentieth century, even the poorest countries had some access to the Internet, the network that links millions of computers throughout the world. The Internet and the World Wide Web, which contains billions of documents connected to each other by hyperlinks, were central to what journalist Thomas Friedman called "the democratization of information." President Bill Clinton displayed his fervent faith in the promise of technology to encourage democracy, claiming that, "when over 100 million people in China can get on the Net, it will be impossible to maintain a closed political and economic society." These Buddhist monks stand outside an Internet cafe in the Cambodian capital of Phnom Penh in December 2000.
© AFP/Corbis.

Debates over Globalization

The process of globalization had begun in the fifteenth century, when Europeans began to trade with and populate other parts of the world. Between the U.S. Civil War and World War I, the flow of products, capital, and labor crossed national boundaries in especially large quantities. What distinguished the globalization at the end of the twentieth century was its scope and intensity: The Internet, cell phones, and other new communications technology connected nations, corporations, and individuals— nearly the entire planet—with much greater speed and much less cost than at any previous time.

Debates over globalization in the United States and elsewhere concerned which trade barriers to eliminate, how fast, and under what conditions. In a world economy characterized by laissez-faire capitalism, who would protect workers' health and security, human rights, and the environment?

Those who wanted to slow the growth of free trade pointed to how quickly, in an integrated global economy, economic disasters could move from country to country. Exactly that happened in 1997 when a banking crisis, caused in part by international investors and currency speculators, began in Thailand and spread throughout Asia, threatening American investments there. Unlike in single nations, where governments could step in to counter economic downslides, the global marketplace was beyond any one organization's or person's control.

Labor unions emphasized the flight of factory jobs to developing nations, as corporate executives sought cheaper labor to lower production costs. For example, General Motors, one of the nation's largest manufacturers, produced its Pontiac Le Mans in South Korea, with parts manufactured in Japan, Germany, Taiwan, Singapore, Britain, Ireland, and Barbados. Critics linked globalization to the weakening of unions, the erosion of the safety net provided for workers since the 1930s, and the growing gap between rich and poor in the United States. Demanding "fair trade" rather than simply free trade, they wanted trade treaties requiring other countries to enforce decent wage and labor standards. Environmentalists similarly wanted countries seeking increased trade with the United States to adopt measures that would eliminate or reduce pollution and prevent the destruction of endangered species.

Globalization controversies often centered on relationships between the United States, which dominated the world's industrial core, and the developing nations on the periphery, whose cheap labor and lax environmental standards attracted investment. United Students Against Sweatshops, for example, attacked the international conglomerate Nike, which paid Chinese workers $1.50 per pair to produce shoes that sold for more than $100 in the United States. Yet many leaders of developing nations wanted foreign investment and manufacturing jobs for their workers, insisting that wages deemed pitiful by American standards offered people in poor nations a much better living than they could otherwise obtain.

The demonstrations in Seattle, and the protests that followed in Washington, D.C., Prague, capital of the Czech Republic, and Genoa, Italy, targeted international financial institutions like the WTO and the International Monetary Fund (IMF). Protesters charged that the WTO and IMF forced devastating regulations on developing nations, which had little voice in trade policy decisions. For example, the IMF often required poor nations to privatize state industries, deregulate their economies, and cut government spending for social welfare in order to obtain loans. While globalization's cheerleaders argued that in the long run everyone would benefit, critics focused on the short-term victims and destruction of traditional cultures that accompanied economic modernization.

Liberalizing Foreign Trade

Building on steps taken by Presidents Reagan and Bush, Bill Clinton sought new measures to ease restrictions on international commerce. In November 1993, Congress approved the North American Free Trade Agreement (NAFTA), which eliminated all tariffs and trade barriers among the United States, Canada, and Mexico. Organized labor and other groups, fearing loss of jobs and industries to Mexico, lobbied vigorously against NAFTA. But proponents argued that all three trading partners would benefit from greater export opportunities, creation of more jobs in the long run, and global clout. With 360 million people and a $6 billion economy, the NAFTA trio constituted the largest trading bloc in the world. A year later, the Senate ratified the General Agreement on Tariffs and Trade (GATT), joining more than one hundred nations. GATT established the WTO to enforce provisions of the treaty, which included substantial tariff reductions and elimination of import quotas.

The China trade bill of 2000, which added China to the vast majority of countries that enjoyed normal trade relations with the United States, aroused another controversy over free trade. Despite the potential for opening large markets to American producers, conservatives attacked the deal with Communist China as "selling out the very moral and spiritual principles that made America great," while liberals expressed concerns about Chinese labor standards and human rights violations. In contrast, supporters of the bill argued that increased trade would promote human rights and humane working conditions. Clinton himself advocated trade not just for its economic benefits but as a means of promoting international peace and security. Opening China to outside competition, he asserted, would "speed the information revolution there . . . speed the demise of China's huge state

industries . . . spur the enterprise of private-sector involvement . . . and diminish the role of government in people's daily lives." Although advocates of globalization prevailed on NAFTA, GATT, and the China bill, in 2000 opponents won an executive order from President Clinton requiring an environmental impact review before the signing of any trade agreement.

The Internationalization of the United States

Globalization was typically associated with the expansion of American enterprise and culture to—or its imposition on—other countries, yet the United States itself experienced the dynamic forces creating a global economy. Already in the 1980s, Japanese, European, and Middle Eastern investors had

THE NEW IMMIGRATION
These employees at UroGenesys, Inc., in Santa Monica, California, provide one example of America's increasingly diverse workforce at the start of the twenty-first century, the result of the largest immigration rates in a hundred years and of the economy's increasing need for a technologically skilled workforce. This biotechnology company conducts research aimed at discovering and developing therapeutic and diagnostic products for urological cancers, especially prostate cancer.
Courtesy UroGenesys. Photo by Deidre Davidson.

Still a Promised Land?

"THE UNITED STATES IS OUR LAND. . . . We intend to maintain it so. The day of unalloyed welcome to all peoples, the day of indiscriminate acceptance of all races, has definitely ended." So spoke Washington senator Albert Johnson in 1924, just after Congress severely limited immigration with passage of the National Origins Act, which Johnson had sponsored. Thereafter, immigration, which had forcefully shaped American society since its beginning, ebbed for several decades as the restrictive law combined with the Great Depression and World War II to discourage potential newcomers. In fact, during the worst years of the depression, more people abandoned the United States than chose to migrate there. Yet the immigration question had not been finally settled. By the 1980s, large numbers of immigrants once more were entering the United States, reigniting old debates about whether Americans should share their promise of political freedom and economic opportunity with people from other lands.

What reopened the door to immigration after World War II? Economic considerations always loomed large in prompting migration to the United States and in determining how welcome immigrants would be: The twenty-five-year economic boom that followed World War II exerted a positive force on both ends. In fact, until 1964 the U.S. government actively encouraged the temporary migration of Mexicans by continuing the so-called *bracero* program begun during World War II to fill a shortage of agricultural workers. Hundreds of thousands of Mexicans established social networks in the United States and grew accustomed to crossing the border for jobs, even when the jobs were backbreaking and low-paying by U.S. standards. When the *bracero* program ended, many Mexicans continued to come north for work, with or without legal authorization.

In addition to a prosperous economy, a growing tolerance toward people of different races and ethnic groups in the decades following World War II contributed to the increase in immigration. Like the key civil rights laws passed around the same time, the Immigration Act of 1965 reflected a belief that people should be treated as individuals rather than as members of a particular group. The new immigration law ended the national quotas that were so insulting to non–Western European groups, although it for the first time placed limits on newcomers from the Western Hemisphere. It made possible a tremendous rise in the volume of immigration and facilitated a huge increase in migrants from Asia and Latin America, a result that the law's sponsors did not anticipate.

The 1965 law set an annual ceiling of 270,000, but the actual volume was much higher. Besides those who came illegally, hundreds of thousands fell into special categories that gained them legal admission above and beyond the limit. In 1986, for example, the United States admitted 335,000 immigrants over the ceiling; about two-thirds of these were children, spouses, or parents of U.S. citizens, and the rest were political refugees and asylum seekers. Migration chains were thus established by which, once newcomers became citizens, their sisters, brothers, and adult children received special preference, while even closer relatives gained entry without regard to the limit.

The new immigration waves also grew directly from foreign policy after World War II. The cold war spread U.S. military and other personnel throughout the world, enabling foreigners to learn about the United States and make personal contacts with Americans. Once the cold war identified communism as an unmitigated evil, the United States could hardly refuse asylum to its enemy's victims. In the twenty-five years following Fidel Castro's revolution

purchased American stocks and bonds, real estate, and corporations, such as Firestone, Brooks Brothers, and 20th Century-Fox. Local communities welcomed foreign capital, and several states went to great lengths to encourage foreign automakers to establish plants within their boundaries. American nonunion workers began to produce Hondas in Marysville, Ohio, and BMWs in Spartanburg, South Carolina.

Globalization was transforming not just the economy but American society as well, as the United States experienced a tremendous surge of

in 1959, for example, more than 800,000 Cubans fled to the United States. The Vietnam War and its aftermath brought more than 600,000 Vietnamese, Laotians, and Cambodians in the decade following 1974.

Not all refugees entered the United States so easily, for refugee policy bore a distinct anti-Communist bias. Haitians, Salvadorans, and others fleeing right-wing dictatorships were frequently turned back or, having reached the United States, were denied asylum and deported. "Why let Poles stay but not Salvadorans?" demanded one advocate for these refugees, pointing out the more favorable treatment given to immigrants from Communist countries.

Even though U.S. policy failed to accommodate all who wanted to immigrate, by the 1980s immigration was once more a major force in American society. During that decade, the six million legal and estimated two million undocumented immigrants accounted for more than one-third of total population growth. Seventy-five percent of the immigrants settled in just seven states, with California, New York, Texas, and Florida receiving the most. After the 1990 census, California won five additional seats in the House of Representatives solely on the basis of immigrant additions to the population. A 1983 *Time* magazine article called Los Angeles "the new Ellis Island" because of its large Asian and Hispanic populations.

The higher volume of immigration, its third world sources, and the economy's recession combined to reactivate nativist sentiment in the 1980s. Increasingly, Americans saw immigrants as taking jobs from the native-born and acting as a drain on schools, health care, police, and other services; and Congress sought to reduce illegal immigration with the Immigration Reform and Control Act of 1986. In the 1990s, anti-immigrant sentiment grew especially strong in California, then reeling from an economic slump owing to the downsizing of defense production. That state took in more than one-third

of the nation's immigrants in the 1980s and an estimated one-half of the undocumented ones. Congress reflected national anti-immigrant feelings by restricting health care, food stamps, and other benefits to immigrants in the welfare reform legislation of 1996.

Greatest hostility focused on people who entered without legal documentation, a phenomenon that the 1986 law penalizing employers of such people had not significantly curtailed. Some states, including California, Florida, and New Jersey, filed lawsuits charging the federal government with failure to stop the flow of illegal immigration and suing for the costs it added to state budgets. In 1994, California voters passed a referendum that barred the children of illegal immigrants from attending public schools, although the courts later ruled it unconstitutional.

Economic and political crises elsewhere and the continuing appeal of the United States meant that high levels of immigration—legal and illegal—persisted into the twenty-first century. Anti-immigrant sentiment diminished somewhat as jobs became plentiful during the spectacular economic boom at the end of the twentieth century. The chief executive of a semiconductor firm who filled more than one-third of his administrative and engineering positions with immigrants, lashed out at restrictionist legislators: "They want to send back the first-round draft choices of the intellectual world so that they can compete against us in their homelands." With employers especially desperate for skilled workers, former opponents of immigration pressured the government to relax restrictions, and politicians of both parties recognized the risks of immigrant bashing given the rapidly rising population of Latino voters. America entered the twenty-first century as it had the twentieth, with a rapidly diversifying society, continuing to make itself, as sociologist Nathan Glazer put it, a "permanently unfinished country."

immigration in the late twentieth century. Five million new immigrants arrived in the 1980s, more than in any decade in the twentieth century but the first, and exhibiting a striking difference in country of origin. While 85 percent of the previous immigrants had come from Europe, by the 1980s almost half

were Asians, and nearly 40 percent came from Latin America and the Caribbean. The flow of newcomers continued in the 1990s, as the Asian and Pacific Islander population grew by 43 percent to nearly 11 million, and the number of Latinos increased by 39 percent to 31 million. In 2000, immigrants made up more than 9 percent of the population. (See "Historical Question," page 826, and appendix, page A-31.)

The new immigration was again making America an international, interracial society, and not just along the coasts. American culture reflected growing diversity: Salsa became a popular condiment, sushi bars appeared in midwestern cities, cable TV companies added Spanish-speaking stations, and a truly international sport, soccer, soared in popularity. Mixed marriages displayed a growing fusion of cultures, recognized by the Census Bureau in 2000 when it let Americans check more than one racial category on their forms. Demographers predicted that by 2050 the American population would be just over 50 percent white, 16 percent black, 24 percent Hispanic, and 9 percent Asian.

Like their predecessors a hundred years earlier, the majority of post-1965 immigrants were unskilled. They took the lowest-paying jobs, providing household help, yard work, child and elder care, and cleaning services. Yet a significant number were highly skilled workers, sought after by burgeoning high-tech industries. For example, in 1999 about one-third of the scientists and engineers who worked in California's Silicon Valley had been born abroad. One small thirty-one-person biotech company seeking cures for prostate diseases employed two Vietnamese, two Canadians, one Pole, two Lebanese, three Chinese, one Korean, one Indian, one Israeli, one Scot, one English, and two Latinos—all scientists except one Vietnamese administrator. Emphasizing the multicultural uniqueness of American society at the turn of the twenty-first century, the company's owner boasted, "I cannot think of another country in the world where you could so easily put such a team together."

The Globalization of Terrorism

Immigrants and citizens from sixty nations shared the fate of more than two thousand Americans killed on the morning of September 11, 2001, when U.S. civilian airplanes crashed into the twin towers of the World Trade Center in lower Manhattan and the Pentagon in Washington, D.C. In the most deadly and shocking devastation ever launched on American soil, nineteen members of Osama bin Laden's Al Qaeda international terrorist organization had hijacked four planes and flown three of them into the buildings, the fourth crashing in a field in Pennsylvania. The nation, indeed, the world,

was stunned. As one commentator observed in the days immediately following the events, "It took hours to comprehend their magnitude; it is taking days for the defensive numbness they induced to wear off; it will take months—or years—to measure their impact and meaning."

The attacks, organized from Osama bin Laden's sanctuaries in Afghanistan, where the radical Muslim Taliban government had taken control after the Soviet departure, related to globalization in several ways. The spread of Western goods, culture, and values into the Muslim world, along with the Gulf War against Iraq and stationing of American troops in Saudi Arabia, enraged Islamic extremists. Acting on a distorted interpretation of one of the world's great religions, bin Laden sought to rid the Middle East of Western influence and install puritanical Muslim control. High levels of poverty unattended to by undemocratic and corrupt governments provided bin Laden a pool of disaffected young Muslims, who saw the United States as the evil source of their misery and the supporter of Israel's oppression of Palestinian Muslims. The technological advances accompanying globalization and the increased mobility of people facilitated bin Laden's worldwide coordination of his Al Qaeda network and eased the hijackers' entrance into and activities in the United States.

President George W. Bush sought a global alliance against terrorism and won at least verbal support from most governments. On October 11, the United States and Britain began bombing Afghanistan, and American special forces aided the Northern Alliance, the Taliban government's main opposition. By December the Taliban were routed, but bin Laden had not been captured and numerous Al Qaeda forces had escaped or remained in hiding throughout the world.

The United States remained vulnerable to random murder of its citizens and faced a host of challenges. Eliminating the underlying sources of terrorism would be infinitely more difficult than conquering the Taliban. European allies expressed alarm at the Bush administration's unilateral decision making and threats of military action against Iraq

Afghanistan

THE "TRIBUTE IN LIGHT"
These twin pillars of light, projected by eighty-eight searchlights in the place where the World Trade Center twin towers had stood, soared as a monument to the victims of the terrorist attacks of September 11, 2001. Sharon Weicman, who worked as a volunteer for a month on the site of the destruction, was drawn by the illumination, remarking, "The closer I got, the more at peace I felt." Turned on at the six-month anniversary of the attack, the "Tribute in Light" was dimmed one month later.
Daniel Derella/AP/Wide World Photos.

and other nations. At home, the balance between liberty and security tilted, as authorities arrested hundreds of Arabs and Muslims, holding more than three hundred on immigration violations for months, even though they had not been charged with any crimes related to the attacks. As one former security official put it, "It's civil liberties ver-

sus getting the bad guys." Or, as another official stated, more diplomatically: "It doesn't mean we're going to profile Arabs, but we are going to look at people who come from a certain culture with a certain background." Large expenditures for domestic security and the Afghan war helped create a budget deficit, and the destruction wrought by foreign nationals within U.S. borders revived anti-immigrant sentiment and suspicions of anyone appearing to be Middle Eastern or practicing Islam.

Conclusion: Challenges of the New Millennium

Despite the differences between the protesters of the 1960s and those who demonstrated against the globalizing economy in 1999, both groups belonged to a deep-rooted reform tradition that sought to realize the American promise of justice and human well-being. The demonstrators in Seattle sought internationally what the populists and progressives, the New Deal reformers, and many activists of the 1960s had sought for the domestic population— protection of individual rights, curbs on laissez-faire capitalism, and assistance for victims of rapid economic change. Yet, the global focus of reformers at the dawn of the twenty-first century did not mean that universal justice and material security had been achieved at home or that the nation had settled the question of what role the government should play in meeting those challenges.

In a population so greatly derived from people fleeing oppressive governments, Americans had debated for more than two centuries what the government could or should do, and what was best left to private enterprise, families, churches, and other voluntary institutions. Far more than other democracies, the United States had taken the path of private rather than public obligation, individual rather than collective solutions. In the twentieth century, Americans had significantly enlarged the federal government's powers and responsibilities, but the last three decades of the twentieth century had seen a decline of trust in government's ability to improve peoples' lives, even as a poverty rate of 20 percent among children and a growing gap between rich and poor accompanied the economic boom of the 1990s.

Americans for two centuries had also struggled over how their nation should act in the world. That question became particularly acute when the ending of the cold war eliminated containment of communism as the linchpin of foreign policy, yet no consensus formed around what constituted U.S. interests in the world and how those interests should be secured. Unlike their counterparts at the end of the nineteenth century, Americans displayed little taste for foreign adventures, nor did a majority want their tax dollars used abroad. Yet as it entered the twenty-first century, the United States became ever more deeply embedded in the global economy as products, information, and people crossed borders with amazing speed and frequency. And that very globalization contributed to international instability and the threat of deadly terrorism to a nation unaccustomed to foreign perils within its own borders. How it would maintain domestic security and exercise its economic and military power on a rapidly changing planet constituted its greatest ongoing challenge.

FOR FURTHER READING ABOUT THE TOPICS IN THIS CHAPTER, see the Online Bibliography at

www.bedfordstmartins.com/roarkcompact.

FOR ADDITIONAL FIRST-HAND ACCOUNTS OF THIS PERIOD, see pages 259–274 in Michael Johnson, ed., *Reading the American Past*, Second Edition, Volume II.

TO ASSESS YOUR MASTERY OF THE MATERIAL IN THIS CHAPTER, see the Online Study Guide at

www.bedfordstmartins.com/roarkcompact.

CHRONOLOGY

1972 Nixon becomes first U.S. president to visit China.

Nixon visits Moscow to sign arms limitation treaties with Soviets.

1973 Arab oil embargo in retaliation for U.S. support of Israel creates energy crisis in United States.

1976 Jimmy Carter elected thirty-ninth president of the United States.

1978 Carter helps negotiate peace agreement between Israel and Egypt (Camp David accords).

1979 **November 4.** Beginning of hostage crisis in Iran.

1980 **April.** Attempt to free U.S. hostages in Iran fails.

Ronald Reagan elected fortieth president of the United States.

1982 United States invades Grenada and topples its Marxist government.

1983 U.S. involvement in Lebanon terminated after bombing of Marine barracks and deaths of 241 Americans.

Reagan announces plans for Strategic Defense Initiative ("Star Wars").

1986 Iran-Contra scandal shakes Reagan administration.

1987 Soviet leader Mikhail Gorbachev visits Washington to sign INF agreement.

1988 George H. W. Bush elected forty-first president of the United States.

1989 Communism collapses in eastern Europe; Berlin Wall falls.

United States invades Panama and arrests dictator Manuel Noriega, who is jailed in United States.

1991 United States commits more than 400,000 in troops to oust Iraqi army from Kuwait in Persian Gulf War.

1993 Israeli prime minister Yitzhak Rabin and PLO leader Yasir Arafat sign peace accords.

Eighteen U.S. soldiers are killed in Somalia.

Congress approves North American Free Trade Agreement (NAFTA).

1994 U.S. troops oversee peaceful return of Haitian president Jean-Bertrand Aristide to power.

Senate ratifies General Agreement on Tariffs and Trade (GATT).

1995 U.S. leaders broker peace accords among Serbia, Croatia, and Bosnia in Dayton, Ohio, temporarily ending civil war in former Yugoslavia.

1996 Leaders of nuclear powers sign comprehensive test ban treaty at United Nations.

1998 United States bombs terrorist sites in Afghanistan and Sudan.

United States bombs Iraq for failure to comply with its 1991 agreement to destroy its weapons of mass destruction.

1999 United States, with NATO, bombs Serbia for more than two months to force an end to Serbian atrocities against ethnic Albanians in Kosovo.

Protesters disrupt meeting of the World Trade Organization in Seattle.

2000 Congress approves China trade bill, normalizing trade relations.

2001 **September 11.** Terrorists fly airplanes into the two World Trade Center buildings in New York and the Pentagon in Washington, D.C., killing nearly three thousand people.

APPENDIX I. DOCUMENTS

For additional documents see the Online Appendix at
www.bedfordstmartins.com/roarkcompact.

THE DECLARATION OF INDEPENDENCE

In Congress, July 4, 1776,

THE UNANIMOUS DECLARATION OF THE
THIRTEEN UNITED STATES OF AMERICA

When in the course of human events, it becomes necessary for one people to dissolve the political bands which have connected them with another, and to assume, among the powers of the earth, the separate and equal station to which the laws of nature and of nature's God entitle them, a decent respect to the opinions of mankind requires that they should declare the causes which impel them to the separation.

We hold these truths to be self-evident, that all men are created equal; that they are endowed by their Creator with certain unalienable rights; that among these, are life, liberty, and the pursuit of happiness. That, to secure these rights, governments are instituted among men, deriving their just powers from the consent of the governed; that, whenever any form of government becomes destructive of these ends, it is the right of the people to alter or to abolish it, and to institute a new government, laying its foundation on such principles, and organizing its powers in such form, as to them shall seem most likely to effect their safety and happiness. Prudence, indeed, will dictate that governments long established, should not be changed for light and transient causes; and, accordingly, all experience hath shown, that mankind are more disposed to suffer, while evils are sufferable, than to right themselves by abolishing the forms to which they are accustomed. But, when a long train of abuses and usurpations, pursuing invariably the same object, evinces a design to reduce them under absolute despotism, it is their right, it is their duty, to throw off such government and to provide new guards for their future security. Such has been the patient sufferance of these colonies, and such is now the necessity which constrains them to alter their former systems of government. The history of the present King of Great Britain is a history of repeated injuries and usurpations, all having, in direct object, the establishment of an absolute tyranny over these States. To prove this, let facts be submitted to a candid world:

He has refused his assent to laws the most wholesome and necessary for the public good.

He has forbidden his governors to pass laws of immediate and pressing importance, unless suspended in their operation till his assent should be obtained; and, when so suspended, he has utterly neglected to attend to them.

He has refused to pass other laws for the accommodation of large districts of people, unless those people would relinquish the right of representation in the legislature; a right inestimable to them, and formidable to tyrants only.

He has called together legislative bodies at places unusual, uncomfortable, and distant from the depository of their public records, for the sole purpose of fatiguing them into compliance with his measures.

He has dissolved representative houses repeatedly for opposing, with manly firmness, his invasions on the rights of the people.

He has refused, for a long time after such dissolutions, to cause others to be elected; whereby the legislative powers, incapable of annihilation, have returned to the people at large for their exercise; the state remaining in the mean-time exposed to all the danger of invasion from without, and convulsions within.

He has endeavoured to prevent the population of these States; for that purpose, obstructing the laws for naturalization of foreigners, refusing to pass others to encourage their migration hither, and raising the conditions of new appropriations of lands.

He has obstructed the administration of justice, by refusing his assent to laws for establishing judiciary powers.

He has made judges dependent on his will alone, for the tenure of their offices, and the amount and payment of their salaries.

He has erected a multitude of new offices, and sent hither swarms of officers to harass our people, and eat out their substance.

He has kept among us, in times of peace, standing armies, without the consent of our legislature.

He has affected to render the military independent of, and superior to, the civil power.

He has combined, with others, to subject us to a jurisdiction foreign to our Constitution, and unacknowledged by our laws; giving his assent to their acts of pretended legislation:

For quartering large bodies of armed troops among us:

For protecting them by a mock trial, from punishment, for any murders which they should commit on the inhabitants of these States:

For cutting off our trade with all parts of the world:

For imposing taxes on us without our consent:

For depriving us, in many cases, of the benefit of trial by jury:

For transporting us beyond seas to be tried for pretended offences:

For abolishing the free system of English laws in a neighboring province, establishing therein an arbitrary government, and enlarging its boundaries, so as to render it at once an example and fit instrument for introducing the same absolute rule into these colonies:

For taking away our charters, abolishing our most valuable laws, and altering, fundamentally, the powers of our governments:

For suspending our own legislatures, and declaring themselves invested with power to legislate for us in all cases whatsoever.

He has abdicated government here, by declaring us out of his protection, and waging war against us.

He has plundered our seas, ravaged our coasts, burnt our towns, and destroyed the lives of our people.

He is, at this time, transporting large armies of foreign mercenaries to complete the works of death, desolation, and tyranny, already begun, with circumstances of cruelty and perfidy scarcely paralleled in the most barbarous ages, and totally unworthy the head of a civilized nation.

He has constrained our fellow citizens, taken captive on the high seas, to bear arms against their country, to become the executioners of their friends, and brethren, or to fall themselves by their hands.

He has excited domestic insurrections amongst us, and has endeavored to bring on the inhabitants of our frontiers, the merciless Indian savages, whose known rule of warfare is an undistinguished destruction of all ages, sexes, and conditions.

In every stage of these oppressions, we have petitioned for redress; in the most humble terms; our repeated petitions have been answered only by repeated injury. A prince, whose character is thus marked by every act which may define a tyrant, is unfit to be the ruler of a free people.

Nor have we been wanting in attention to our British brethren. We have warned them, from time to time, of attempts made by their legislature to extend an unwarrantable jurisdiction over us. We have reminded them of the circumstances of our emigration and settlement here. We have appealed to their native justice and magnanimity, and we have conjured them, by the ties of our common kindred, to disavow these usurpations, which would inevitably interrupt our connections and correspondence. They, too, have been deaf to the voice of justice and consanguinity. We must, therefore, acquiesce in the necessity which denounces our separation, and hold them as we hold the rest of mankind, enemies in war, in peace, friends.

We, therefore, the representatives of the United States of America, in general Congress assembled, appealing to the Supreme Judge of the world for the rectitude of our intentions, do, in the name, and by authority of the good people of these colonies, solemnly publish and declare, that these united colonies are, and of right ought to be, free and independent states: that they are absolved from all allegiance to the British Crown, and that all political connection between them and the state of Great Britain is, and ought to be, totally dissolved; and that, as free and independent states, they have full power to levy war, conclude peace, contract alliances, establish commerce, and to do all other acts and things which independent states may of right do. And, for the support of this declaration, with a firm reliance on the protection of Divine Providence, we mutually pledge to each other our lives, our fortunes, and our sacred honor.

The foregoing Declaration was, by order of Congress, engrossed, and signed by the following members:

JOHN HANCOCK

New Hampshire
Josiah Bartlett
William Whipple
Matthew Thornton

Massachusetts Bay
Samuel Adams
John Adams
Robert Treat Paine
Elbridge Gerry

Rhode Island
Stephen Hopkins
William Ellery

Connecticut
Roger Sherman
Samuel Huntington
William Williams
Oliver Wolcott

New York
William Floyd
Phillip Livingston
Francis Lewis
Lewis Morris

New Jersey
Richard Stockton
John Witherspoon
Francis Hopkinson
John Hart
Abraham Clark

Pennsylvania
Robert Morris
Benjamin Rush
Benjamin Franklin
John Morton
George Clymer
James Smith
George Taylor
James Wilson
George Ross

Delaware	North Carolina	Virginia	Georgia
Caesar Rodney	William Hooper	George Wythe	Button Gwinnett
George Read	Joseph Hewes	Richard Henry Lee	Lyman Hall
Thomas M'Kean	John Penn	Thomas Jefferson	George Walton
		Benjamin Harrison	
Maryland	**South Carolina**	Thomas Nelson, Jr.	
Samuel Chase	Edward Rutledge	Francis Lightfoot Lee	
William Paca	Thomas Heyward, Jr.	Carter Braxton	
Thomas Stone	Thomas Lynch, Jr.		
Charles Carroll,	Arthur Middleton		
of Carrollton			

Resolved, That copies of the Declaration be sent to the several assemblies, conventions, and committees, or councils of safety, and to the several commanding officers of the continental troops; that it be proclaimed in each of the United States, at the head of the army.

THE CONSTITUTION OF THE UNITED STATES*

Agreed to by Philadelphia Convention, September 17, 1787. Implemented March 4, 1789.

Preamble

We the people of the United States, in order to form a more perfect union, establish justice, insure domestic tranquility, provide for the common defense, promote the general welfare, and secure the blessings of liberty to ourselves and our posterity, do ordain and establish this Constitution for the United States of America.

Article I

Section 1   All legislative powers herein granted shall be vested in a Congress of the United States, which shall consist of a Senate and a House of Representatives.

Section 2   The House of Representatives shall be composed of members chosen every second year by the people of the several States, and the electors in each State shall have the qualifications requisite for electors of the most numerous branch of the State Legislature.

No person shall be a Representative who shall not have attained to the age of twenty-five years, and been seven years a citizen of the United States, and who shall not, when elected, be an inhabitant of that State in which he shall be chosen.

Representatives and direct taxes shall be apportioned among the several States which may be included within this Union, according to their respective numbers, *which shall be determined by adding to the whole number of free persons, including those bound to service for a term of years and excluding Indians not taxed, three-fifths of all other persons.* The actual enumeration shall be made within three years after the first meeting of the Congress of the United States, and within every subsequent term of ten years, in such manner as they shall by law direct. The number of Representatives shall not exceed one for every thirty thousand, but each State shall have at least one Representative; *and until such enumeration shall be made, the State of New Hampshire shall be entitled to choose three, Massachusetts eight, Rhode Island and Providence Plantations one, Connecticut five, New York six, New Jersey four, Pennsylvania eight, Delaware one, Maryland six, Virginia ten, North Carolina five, South Carolina five, and Georgia three.*

When vacancies happen in the representation from any State, the Executive authority thereof shall issue writs of election to fill such vacancies.

The House of Representatives shall choose their Speaker and other officers; and shall have the sole power of impeachment.

---

*Passages no longer in effect are in italic type.

Section 3 The Senate of the United States shall be composed of two Senators from each State, *chosen by the legislature thereof,* for six years; and each Senator shall have one vote.

Immediately after they shall be assembled in consequence of the first election, they shall be divided as equally as may be into three classes. The seats of the Senators of the first class shall be vacated at the expiration of the second year, of the second class at the expiration of the fourth year, and of the third class at the expiration of the sixth year, so that one-third may be chosen every second year; *and if vacancies happen by resignation or otherwise, during the recess of the legislature of any State, the Executive thereof may make temporary appointments until the next meeting of the legislature, which shall then fill such vacancies.*

No person shall be a Senator who shall not have attained to the age of thirty years, and been nine years a citizen of the United States, and who shall not, when elected, be an inhabitant of that State for which he shall be chosen.

The Vice-President of the United States shall be President of the Senate, but shall have no vote, unless they be equally divided.

The Senate shall choose their other officers, and also a President *pro tempore,* in the absence of the Vice-President, or when he shall exercise the office of President of the United States.

The Senate shall have the sole power to try all impeachments. When sitting for that purpose, they shall be on oath or affirmation. When the President of the United States is tried, the Chief Justice shall preside: and no person shall be convicted without the concurrence of two-thirds of the members present.

Judgment in cases of impeachment shall not extend further than to removal from the office, and disqualification to hold and enjoy any office of honor, trust or profit under the United States: but the party convicted shall nevertheless be liable and subject to indictment, trial, judgment and punishment, according to law.

Section 4 The times, places and manner of holding elections for Senators and Representatives shall be prescribed in each State by the legislature thereof; but the Congress may at any time by law make or alter such regulations, except as to the places of choosing Senators.

The Congress shall assemble at least once in every year, and such meeting *shall be on the first Monday in December, unless they shall by law appoint a different day.*

Section 5 Each house shall be the judge of the elections, returns and qualifications of its own members, and a majority of each shall constitute a quorum to do business; but a smaller number may adjourn from day to day, and may be authorized to compel the attendance of absent members, in such manner, and under such penalties, as each house may provide.

Each house may determine the rules of its proceedings, punish its members for disorderly behavior, and with the concurrence of two-thirds, expel a member.

Each house shall keep a journal of its proceedings, and from time to time publish the same, excepting such parts as may in their judgment require secrecy; and the yeas and nays of the members of either house on any question shall, at the desire of one-fifth of those present, be entered on the journal.

Neither house, during the session of Congress, shall, without the consent of the other, adjourn for more than three days, nor to any other place than that in which the two houses shall be sitting.

Section 6 The Senators and Representatives shall receive a compensation for their services, to be ascertained by law and paid out of the treasury of the United States. They shall in all cases except treason, felony and breach of the peace, be privileged from arrest during their attendance at the session of their respective houses, and in going to and returning from the same; and for any speech or debate in either house, they shall not be questioned in any other place.

No Senator or Representative shall, during the time for which he was elected, be appointed to any civil office under the authority of the United States, which shall have been created, or the emoluments whereof shall have been increased, during such time; and no person holding any office under the United States shall be a member of either house during his continuance in office.

Section 7 All bills for raising revenue shall originate in the House of Representatives; but the Senate may propose or concur with amendments as on other bills.

Every bill which shall have passed the House of Representatives and the Senate, shall, before it become a law, be presented to the President of the United States; if he approve he shall sign it, but if not he shall return it with objections to that house in which it shall have originated, who shall enter the objections at large on their journal, and proceed to reconsider it. If after such reconsideration two-thirds of that house shall agree to pass the bill, it shall be sent, together with the objections, to the other house, by which it shall likewise be reconsidered, and, if approved by two-thirds of that house, it shall become a law. But in all such cases the votes of both houses shall be determined by yeas and nays, and the names of the persons voting for and against the bill shall be entered on the journal of each house respectively. If any bill shall not be re-

THE CONSTITUTION OF THE UNITED STATES

turned by the President within ten days (Sundays excepted) after it shall have been presented to him, the same shall be a law, in like manner as if he had signed it, unless the Congress by their adjournment prevent its return, in which case it shall not be a law.

Every order, resolution, or vote to which the concurrence of the Senate and House of Representatives may be necessary (except on a question of adjournment) shall be presented to the President of the United States; and before the same shall take effect, shall be approved by him, or being disapproved by him, shall be repassed by two-thirds of the Senate and House of Representatives, according to the rules and limitations prescribed in the case of a bill.

Section 8   The Congress shall have power

To lay and collect taxes, duties, imposts, and excises, to pay the debts and provide for the common defense and general welfare of the United States; but all duties, imposts and excises shall be uniform throughout the United States;

To borrow money on the credit of the United States;

To regulate commerce with foreign nations, and among the several States, and with the Indian tribes;

To establish an uniform rule of naturalization, and uniform laws on the subject of bankruptcies throughout the United States;

To coin money, regulate the value thereof, and of foreign coin, and fix the standard of weights and measures;

To provide for the punishment of counterfeiting the securities and current coin of the United States;

To establish post offices and post roads;

To promote the progress of science and useful arts by securing for limited times to authors and inventors the exclusive right to their respective writings and discoveries;

To constitute tribunals inferior to the Supreme Court;

To define and punish piracies and felonies committed on the high seas and offences against the law of nations;

To declare war, grant letters of marque and reprisal, and make rules concerning captures on land and water;

To raise and support armies, but no appropriation of money to that use shall be for a longer term than two years;

To provide and maintain a navy;

To make rules for the government and regulation of the land and naval forces;

To provide for calling forth the militia to execute the laws of the Union, suppress insurrections and repel invasions;

To provide for organizing, arming, and disciplining the militia, and for governing such part of them as may be employed in the service of the United States, reserving to the States respectively the appointment of the officers, and the authority of training the militia according to the discipline prescribed by Congress;

To exercise exclusive legislation in all cases whatsoever, over such district (not exceeding ten miles square) as may, by cession of particular States, and the acceptance of Congress, become the seat of the government of the United States, and to exercise like authority over all places purchased by the consent of the legislature of the State, in which the same shall be, for erection of forts, magazines, arsenals, dock-yards, and other needful buildings;—and

To make all laws which shall be necessary and proper for carrying into execution the foregoing powers, and all other powers vested by this Constitution in the government of the United States, or in any department or officer thereof.

Section 9   *The migration or importation of such persons as any of the States now existing shall think proper to admit shall not be prohibited by the Congress prior to the year one thousand eight hundred and eight; but a tax or duty may be imposed on such importation, not exceeding ten dollars for each person.*

The privilege of the writ of habeas corpus shall not be suspended, unless when in cases of rebellion or invasion the public safety may require it.

No bill of attainder or ex post facto law shall be passed.

No capitation, or other direct, tax shall be laid, unless in proportion to the census or enumeration herein before directed to be taken.

No tax or duty shall be laid on articles exported from any State.

No preference shall be given by any regulation of commerce or revenue to the ports of one State over those of another; nor shall vessels bound to, or from, one State be obliged to enter, clear, or pay duties in another.

No money shall be drawn from the treasury, but in consequence of appropriations made by law; and a regular statement and account of the receipts and expenditures of all public money shall be published from time to time.

No title of nobility shall be granted by the United States: and no person holding any office of profit or trust under them, shall, without the consent of the Congress, accept of any present, emolument, office, or title, of any kind whatever, from any king, prince, or foreign state.

Section 10   No State shall enter into any treaty, alliance, or confederation; grant letters of marque and reprisal; coin money; emit bills of credit; make anything but gold and silver coin a tender in payment of debts; pass any bill of attainder, ex post facto law, or law impairing the obligation of contracts, or grant any title of nobility.

No State shall, without the consent of Congress, lay any imposts or duties on imports or exports, except what may be absolutely necessary for executing its inspection laws: and the net produce of all duties and imposts, laid by any State on imports or exports, shall be for the use of the treasury of the United States; and all such laws shall be subject to the revision and control of the Congress.

No State shall, without the consent of Congress, lay any duty of tonnage, keep troops, or ships of war in time of peace, enter into any agreement or compact with another State, or with a foreign power, or engage in war, unless actually invaded, or in such imminent danger as will not admit of delay.

Article II

Section 1 The executive power shall be vested in a President of the United States of America. He shall hold his office during the term of four years, and, together with the Vice-President, chosen for the same term, be elected as follows:

Each State shall appoint, in such manner as the legislature thereof may direct, a number of electors, equal to the whole number of Senators and Representatives to which the State may be entitled in the Congress; but no Senator or Representative, or person holding an office of trust or profit under the United States, shall be appointed an elector.

The electors shall meet in their respective States, and vote by ballot for two persons, of whom one at least shall not be an inhabitant of the same State with themselves. And they shall make a list of all the persons voted for, and of the number of votes for each; which list they shall sign and certify, and transmit sealed to the seat of government of the United States, directed to the President of the Senate. The President of the Senate shall, in the presence of the Senate and House of Representatives, open all the certificates, and the votes shall then be counted. The person having the greatest number of votes shall be the President, if such number be a majority of the whole number of electors appointed; and if there be more than one who have such majority, and have an equal number of votes, then the House of Representatives shall immediately choose by ballot one of them for President; and if no person have a majority, then from the five highest on the list said house shall in like manner choose the President. But in choosing the President the votes shall be taken by States, the representation from each State having one vote; a quorum for this purpose shall consist of a member or members from two-thirds of the States, and a majority of all the States shall be necessary to a choice. In every case,

after the choice of the President, the person having the greatest number of votes of the electors shall be the Vice-President. But if there should remain two or more who have equal votes, the Senate shall choose from them by ballot the Vice-President.

The Congress may determine the time of choosing the electors, and the day on which they shall give their votes; which day shall be the same throughout the United States.

No person except a natural-born citizen, *or a citizen of the United States at the time of the adoption of this Constitution,* shall be eligible to the office of President; neither shall any person be eligible to that office who shall not have attained to the age of thirty-five years, and been fourteen years a resident within the United States.

In cases of the removal of the President from office or of his death, resignation, or inability to discharge the powers and duties of the said office, the same shall devolve on the Vice-President, and the Congress may by law provide for the case of removal, death, resignation, or inability, both of the President and Vice-President, declaring what officer shall then act as President, and such officer shall act accordingly, until the disability be removed, or a President shall be elected.

The President shall, at stated times, receive for his services a compensation, which shall neither be increased nor diminished during the period for which he shall have been elected, and he shall not receive within that period any other emolument from the United States, or any of them.

Before he enter on the execution of his office, he shall take the following oath or affirmation:—"I do solemnly swear (or affirm) that I will faithfully execute the office of the President of the United States, and will to the best of my ability preserve, protect and defend the Constitution of the United States."

Section 2 The President shall be commander in chief of the army and navy of the United States, and of the militia of the several States, when called into the actual service of the United States; he may require the opinion, in writing, of the principal officer in each of the executive departments, upon any subject relating to the duties of their respective offices, and he shall have power to grant reprieves and pardons for offenses against the United States, except in cases of impeachment.

He shall have power, by and with the advice and consent of the Senate, to make treaties, provided two-thirds of the Senators present concur; and he shall nominate, and by and with the advice and consent of the Senate, shall appoint ambassadors, other public ministers and consuls, judges of the Supreme Court,

THE CONSTITUTION OF THE UNITED STATES

and all other officers of the United States, whose appointments are not herein otherwise provided for, and which shall be established by law: but Congress may by law vest the appointment of such inferior officers, as they think proper, in the President alone, in the courts of law, or in the heads of departments.

The President shall have power to fill up all vacancies that may happen during the recess of the Senate, by granting commissions which shall expire at the end of their next session.

Section 3   He shall from time to time give to the Congress information of the state of the Union, and recommend to their consideration such measures as he shall judge necessary and expedient; he may, on extraordinary occasions, convene both houses, or either of them, and in case of disagreement between them, with respect to the time of adjournment, he may adjourn them to such time as he shall think proper; he shall receive ambassadors and other public ministers; he shall take care that the laws be faithfully executed, and shall commission all the officers of the United States.

Section 4   The President, Vice-President and all civil officers of the United States shall be removed from office on impeachment for, and on conviction of, treason, bribery, or other high crimes and misdemeanors.

Article III

Section 1   The judicial power of the United States shall be vested in one Supreme Court, and in such inferior courts as the Congress may from time to time ordain and establish. The judges, both of the Supreme and inferior courts, shall hold their offices during good behavior, and shall, at stated times, receive for their services a compensation which shall not be diminished during their continuance in office.

Section 2   The judicial power shall extend to all cases, in law and equity, arising under this Constitution, the laws of the United States, and treaties made, or which shall be made, under their authority;—to all cases affecting ambassadors, other public ministers and consuls;—to all cases of admiralty and maritime jurisdiction;—to controversies to which the United States shall be a party;—to controversies between two or more States;—*between a State and citizens of another State*;—between citizens of different States;—between citizens of the same State claiming lands under grants of different States, and between a State, or the citizens thereof, and foreign states, citizens or subjects.

In all cases affecting ambassadors, other public ministers and consuls, and those in which a State shall

be party, the Supreme Court shall have original jurisdiction. In all the other cases before mentioned, the Supreme Court shall have appellate jurisdiction, both as to law and fact, with such exceptions, and under such regulations, as the Congress shall make.

The trial of all crimes, except in cases of impeachment, shall be by jury; and such trial shall be held in the State where said crimes shall have been committed; but when not committed within any State, the trial shall be at such place or places as the Congress may by Law have directed.

Section 3   Treason against the United States shall consist only in levying war against them, or in adhering to their enemies, giving them aid and comfort. No person shall be convicted of treason unless on the testimony of two witnesses to the same overt act, or on confession in open court.

The Congress shall have power to declare the punishment of treason, but no attainder of treason shall work corruption of blood, or forfeiture except during the life of the person attainted.

Article IV

Section 1   Full faith and credit shall be given in each State to the public acts, records, and judicial proceedings of every other State. And the Congress may by general laws prescribe the manner in which such acts, records, and proceedings shall be proved, and the effect thereof.

Section 2   The citizens of each State shall be entitled to all privileges and immunities of citizens in the several States.

A person charged in any State with treason, felony, or other crime, who shall flee from justice, and be found in another State, shall on demand of the executive authority of the State from which he fled, be delivered up, to be removed to the State having jurisdiction of the crime.

No Person held to service or labor in one State, under the laws thereof, escaping into another, shall, in consequence of any law or regulation therein, be discharged from such service or labor, but shall be delivered up on claim of the party to whom such service or labor may be due.

Section 3   New States may be admitted by the Congress into this Union; but no new State shall be formed or erected within the jurisdiction of any other State; nor any State be formed by the junction of two or more States, or parts of States, without the consent of the legislatures of the States concerned as well as of the Congress.

The Congress shall have power to dispose of and make all needful rules and regulations respecting the territory or other property belonging to the United States; and nothing in this Constitution shall be so construed as to prejudice any claims of the United States, or of any particular State.

Section 4 The United States shall guarantee to every State in this Union a republican form of government, and shall protect each of them against invasion; and on application of the legislature, or of the executive (when the legislature cannot be convened), against domestic violence.

Article V

The Congress, whenever two-thirds of both houses shall deem it necessary, shall propose amendments to this Constitution, or, on the application of the legislatures of two-thirds of the several States, shall call a convention for proposing amendments, which, in either case, shall be valid to all intents and purposes, as part of this Constitution, when ratified by the legislatures of three-fourths of the several States, or by conventions in three-fourths thereof, as the one or the other mode of ratification may be proposed by the Congress; provided *that no amendments which may be made prior to the year one thousand eight hundred and eight shall in any manner affect the first and fourth clauses in the ninth section of the first article*; and that no State, without its consent, shall be deprived of its equal suffrage in the Senate.

Article VI

All debts contracted and engagements entered into, before the adoption of this Constitution, shall be as valid against the United States under this Constitution, as under the Confederation.

This Constitution, and the laws of the United States which shall be made in pursuance thereof; and all treaties made, or which shall be made, under the authority of the United States, shall be the supreme law of the land; and the judges in every State shall be bound thereby, anything in the Constitution or laws of any State to the contrary notwithstanding.

The Senators and Representatives before mentioned, and the members of the several State legislatures, and all executive and judicial officers, both of the United States and of the several States, shall be bound by oath or affirmation to support this Constitution; but no religious test shall ever be required as a qualification to any office or public trust under the United States.

Article VII

The ratification of the conventions of nine States shall be sufficient for the establishment of this Constitution between the States so ratifying the same.

Done in convention by the unanimous consent of the States present, the seventeenth day of September in the year of our Lord one thousand seven hundred and eighty-seven and of the Independence of the United States of America the twelfth. In witness whereof we have hereunto subscribed our names.

GEORGE WASHINGTON
PRESIDENT AND DEPUTY FROM VIRGINIA

New Hampshire
John Langdon
Nicholas Gilman

Massachusetts
Nathaniel Gorham
Rufus King

Connecticut
William Samuel
  Johnson
Roger Sherman

New York
Alexander Hamilton

New Jersey
William Livingston
David Brearley
William Paterson
Jonathan Dayton

Pennsylvania
Benjamin Franklin
Thomas Mifflin
Robert Morris
George Clymer
Thomas FitzSimons
Jared Ingersoll
James Wilson
Gouverneur Morris

Delaware
George Read
Gunning Bedford, Jr.
John Dickinson
Richard Bassett
Jacob Broom

Maryland
James McHenry
Daniel of
  St. Thomas Jenifer
Daniel Carroll

Virginia
John Blair
James Madison, Jr.

North Carolina
William Blount
Richard Dobbs
  Spaight
Hugh Williamson

South Carolina
John Rutledge
Charles Cotesworth
  Pinckney
Charles Pinckney
Pierce Butler

Georgia
William Few
Abraham Baldwin

AMENDMENTS TO THE CONSTITUTION WITH ANNOTATIONS
(Including the six unratified amendments)

IN THEIR EFFORT TO GAIN Antifederalists' support for the Constitution, Federalists frequently pointed to the inclusion of Article 5, which provides an orderly method of amending the Constitution. In contrast, the Articles of Confederation, which were universally recognized as seriously flawed, offered no means of amendment. For their part, Antifederalists argued that the amendment process was so "intricate" that one might as easily roll "sixes an hundred times in succession" as change the Constitution.

The system for amendment laid out in the Constitution requires that two-thirds of both houses of Congress agree to a proposed amendment, which must then be ratified by three-quarters of the legislatures of the states. Alternatively, an amendment may be proposed by a convention called by the legislatures of two-thirds of the states. Since 1789, members of Congress have proposed thousands of amendments. Besides the seventeen amendments added since 1789, only the six "unratified" ones included here were approved by two-thirds of both houses and sent to the states for ratification.

Among the many amendments that never made it out of Congress have been proposals to declare dueling, divorce, and interracial marriage unconstitutional as well as proposals to establish a national university, to acknowledge the sovereignty of Jesus Christ, and to prohibit any person from possessing wealth in excess of ten million dollars.[1]

Among the issues facing Americans today that might lead to constitutional amendment are efforts to balance the federal budget, to limit the number of terms elected officials may serve, to limit access to or prohibit abortion, to establish English as the official language of the United States, and to prohibit flag burning. None of these proposed amendments has yet garnered enough support in Congress to be sent to the states for ratification.

Although the first ten amendments to the Constitution are commonly known as the Bill of Rights, only Amendments 1–8 actually provide guarantees of individual rights. Amendments 9 and 10 deal with the structure of power within the constitutional system. The Bill of Rights was promised to appease Antifederalists who refused to ratify the Constitution without guarantees of individual liberties and limitations to federal power. After studying more than two hundred amendments recommended by the ratifying conventions of the states, Federalist James Madison presented a list of seventeen to Congress, which used Madison's list as the foundation for the twelve amendments that were sent to the states for ratification. Ten of the twelve were adopted in 1791. The first on the list of twelve, known as the Reapportionment Amendment, was never adopted (see page A-12). The second proposed amendment was adopted in 1992 as Amendment 27 (see page A-21).

Amendment I

Congress shall make no law respecting an establishment of religion, or prohibiting the free exercise thereof; or abridging the freedom of speech, or of the press; or the right of the people peaceably to assemble, and to petition the government for a redress of grievances.

◆ ◆ ◆

The First Amendment is a potent symbol for many Americans. Most are well aware of their rights to free speech, freedom of the press, and freedom of religion and their rights to assemble and to petition, even if they cannot cite the exact words of this amendment.

The First Amendment guarantee of freedom of religion has two clauses: the "free exercise clause," which allows individuals to practice or not practice any religion, and the "establishment clause," which prevents the federal government from discriminating against or favoring any particular religion. This clause was designed to create what Thomas Jefferson referred to as "a wall of separation between church and state." In the 1960s, the Supreme Court ruled that the First Amendment prohibits prayer (see Engel v. Vitale, *online) and Bible reading in public schools.*

Although the rights to free speech and freedom of the press are established in the First Amendment, it was not until the twentieth century that the Supreme Court began to explore the full meaning of these guarantees. In 1919, the Court ruled in Schenck v. United States *(online) that the government could suppress free expression only where it could cite a "clear and present danger." In a decision that continues to raise controversies, the Court ruled in 1990, in* Texas v. Johnson, *that flag burning is a form of symbolic speech protected by the First Amendment.*

[1]Richard B. Bernstein, *Amending America* (New York: Times Books, 1993), 177–81.

Amendment II

A well-regulated militia being necessary to the security of a free State, the right of the people to keep and bear arms shall not be infringed.

◆◆◆

Fear of a standing army under the control of a hostile government made the Second Amendment an important part of the Bill of Rights. Advocates of gun ownership claim that the amendment prevents the government from regulating firearms. Proponents of gun control argue that the amendment is designed only to protect the right of the states to maintain militia units.

In 1939, the Supreme Court ruled in United States v. Miller *that the Second Amendment did not protect the right of an individual to own a sawed-off shotgun, which it argued was not ordinary militia equipment. Since then, the Supreme Court has refused to hear Second Amendment cases, while lower courts have upheld firearms regulations. Several justices currently on the bench seem to favor a narrow interpretation of the Second Amendment, which would allow gun control legislation. The controversy over the impact of the Second Amendment on gun owners and gun control legislation will certainly continue.*

Amendment III

No soldier shall, in time of peace, be quartered in any house without the consent of the owner, nor in time of war, but in a manner to be prescribed by law.

◆◆◆

The Third Amendment was extremely important to the framers of the Constitution, but today it is nearly forgotten. American colonists were especially outraged that they were forced to quarter British troops in the years before and during the American Revolution. The philosophy of the Third Amendment has been viewed by some justices and scholars as the foundation of the modern constitutional right to privacy. One example of this can be found in Justice William O. Douglas's opinion in Griswold v. Connecticut *(online).*

Amendment IV

The right of the people to be secure in their persons, houses, papers, and effects, against unreasonable searches and seizures, shall not be violated, and no warrants shall issue but upon probable cause, supported by oath or affirmation, and particularly describing the place to be searched, and the persons or things to be seized.

◆◆◆

In the years before the Revolution, the houses, barns, stores, and warehouses of American colonists were ransacked by British authorities under "writs of assistance" or general warrants. The British, thus empowered, searched for seditious material or smuggled goods that could then be used as evidence against colonists who were charged with a crime only after the items were found.

The first part of the Fourth Amendment protects citizens from "unreasonable" searches and seizures. The Supreme Court has interpreted this protection as well as the words search *and* seizure *in different ways at different times. At one time, the Court did not recognize electronic eavesdropping as a form of search and seizure, though it does today. At times, an "unreasonable" search has been almost any search carried out without a warrant, but in the two decades before 1969 the Court sometimes sanctioned warrantless searches that it considered reasonable based on "the total atmosphere of the case."*

The second part of the Fourth Amendment defines the procedure for issuing a search warrant and states the requirement of "probable cause," which is generally viewed as evidence indicating that a suspect has committed an offense.

The Fourth Amendment has been controversial because the Court has sometimes excluded evidence that has been seized in violation of constitutional standards. The justification is that excluding such evidence deters violations of the amendment, but doing so may allow a guilty person to escape punishment.

Amendment V

No person shall be held to answer for a capital, or otherwise infamous crime, unless on a presentment or indictment of a grand jury, except in cases arising in the land or naval forces, or in the militia, when in actual service in time of war or public danger; nor shall any person be subject for the same offence to be twice put in jeopardy of life or limb; nor shall be compelled in any criminal case to be a witness against himself, nor be deprived of life, liberty, or property, without due process of law; nor shall private property be taken for public use without just compensation.

◆◆◆

The Fifth Amendment protects people against government authority in the prosecution of criminal offenses. It prohibits the state, first, from charging a person with a serious crime without a grand jury hearing to decide whether there is sufficient evidence to support the charge and, second, from charging a person with the same crime twice. The best-known aspect of the Fifth Amendment is that it prevents a person from being "compelled . . . to be a witness against himself." The last clause, the "takings clause," limits the power of the government to seize property.

Although invoking the Fifth Amendment is popularly viewed as a confession of guilt, a person may be innocent yet still fear prosecution. For example, during the Red-baiting era of the late 1940s and 1950s, many people who had participated in legal activities that were associated with the Communist Party claimed the Fifth Amendment privilege rather than testify before the House Un-American Activities Committee because the mood of the times cast those activities in a negative light. Since "taking the Fifth" was viewed as an admission of guilt, those people often lost their jobs or became unemployable. (See Chapter 26.) Nonetheless, the right to protect oneself against self-incrimination plays an important role in guarding against the collective power of the state.

Amendment VI

In all criminal prosecutions, the accused shall enjoy the right to a speedy and public trial, by an impartial jury of the State and district wherein the crime shall have been committed, which district shall have been previously ascertained by law, and to be informed of the nature and cause of the accusation; to be confronted with the witnesses against him; to have compulsory process for obtaining witnesses in his favor, and to have the assistance of counsel for his defence.

The original Constitution put few limits on the government's power to investigate, prosecute, and punish crime. This process was of great concern to the early Americans, however, and of the twenty-eight rights specified in the first eight amendments, fifteen have to do with it. Seven rights are specified in the Sixth Amendment. These include the right to a speedy trial, a public trial, a jury trial, a notice of accusation, confrontation by opposing witnesses, testimony by favorable witnesses, and the assistance of counsel.

Although this amendment originally guaranteed these rights only in cases involving the federal government, the adoption of the Fourteenth Amendment began a process of applying the protections of the Bill of Rights to the states through court cases such as Gideon v. Wainwright *(online).*

Amendment VII

In suits at common law, where the value in controversy shall exceed twenty dollars, the right of trial by jury shall be preserved, and no fact tried by a jury shall be otherwise reexamined in any court of the United States, than according to the rules of the common law.

This amendment guarantees people the same right to a trial by jury as was guaranteed by English common law in 1791.

Under common law, in civil trials (those involving money damages) the role of the judge was to settle questions of law and that of the jury was to settle questions of fact. The amendment does not specify the size of the jury or its role in a trial, however. The Supreme Court has generally held that those issues be determined by English common law of 1791, which stated that a jury consists of twelve people, that a trial must be conducted before a judge who instructs the jury on the law and advises it on facts, and that a verdict must be unanimous.

Amendment VIII

Excessive bail shall not be required, nor excessive fines imposed, nor cruel and unusual punishments inflicted.

The language used to guarantee the three rights in this amendment was inspired by the English Bill of Rights of 1689. The Supreme Court has not had a lot to say about "excessive fines." In recent years it has agreed that despite the provision against "excessive bail," persons who are believed to be dangerous to others can be held without bail even before they have been convicted.

Although opponents of the death penalty have not succeeded in using the Eighth Amendment to achieve the end of capital punishment, the clause regarding "cruel and unusual punishments" has been used to prohibit capital punishment in certain cases (see Furman v. Georgia, *online) and to require improved conditions in prisons.*

Amendment IX

The enumeration in the Constitution, of certain rights, shall not be construed to deny or disparage others retained by the people.

Some Federalists feared that inclusion of the Bill of Rights in the Constitution would allow later generations of interpreters to claim that the people had surrendered any rights not specifically enumerated there. To guard against this, Madison added language that became the Ninth Amendment. Interest in this heretofore largely ignored amendment revived in 1965 when it was used in a concurring opinion in Griswold v. Connecticut *(online). While Justice William O. Douglas called on the Third Amendment to support the right to privacy in deciding that case, Justice Arthur Goldberg, in the concurring opinion, argued that the right to privacy regarding contraception was an unenumerated right that was protected by the Ninth Amendment.*

In 1980, the Court ruled that the right of the press to attend a public trial was protected by the Ninth Amendment. While some scholars argue that modern judges cannot identify the unenumerated rights that the framers were trying to protect, others argue that the Ninth Amendment should be read as providing a constitutional "presumption of liberty" that allows people to act in any way that does not violate the rights of others.

Amendment X

The powers not delegated to the United States by the Constitution, nor prohibited by it to the States, are reserved to the States respectively, or to the people.

The Antifederalists were especially eager to see a "reserved powers clause" explicitly guaranteeing the states control over their internal affairs. Not surprisingly, the Tenth Amendment has been a frequent battleground in the struggle over states' rights and federal supremacy. Prior to the Civil War, the Democratic Republican Party and Jacksonian Democrats invoked the Tenth Amendment to prohibit the federal government from making decisions about whether people in individual states could own slaves. The Tenth Amendment was virtually suspended during Reconstruction following the Civil War. In 1883, however, the Supreme Court declared the Civil Rights Act of 1875 unconstitutional on the grounds that it violated the Tenth Amendment. Business interests also called on the amendment to block efforts at federal regulation.

The Court was inconsistent over the next several decades as it attempted to resolve the tension between the restrictions of the Tenth Amendment and the powers the Constitution granted to Congress to regulate interstate commerce and levy taxes. The Court upheld the Pure Food and Drug Act (1906), the Meat Inspection Acts (1906 and 1907), and the White Slave Traffic Act (1910), all of which affected the states, but struck down an act prohibiting interstate shipment of goods produced through child labor. Between 1934 and 1935, a number of New Deal programs created by Franklin D. Roosevelt were declared unconstitutional on the grounds that they violated the Tenth Amendment. (See Chapter 24.) As Roosevelt appointees changed the composition of the Court, the Tenth Amendment was declared to have no substantive meaning. Generally, the amendment is held to protect the rights of states to regulate internal matters such as local government, education, commerce, labor, and business, as well as matters involving families such as marriage, divorce, and inheritance within the state.

Unratified Amendment
Reapportionment Amendment (proposed by Congress September 25, 1789, along with the Bill of Rights)

After the first enumeration required by the first article of the Constitution, there shall be one Representative for every thirty thousand, until the number shall amount to one hundred, after which the proportion shall be so regulated by Congress, that there shall be not less than one hundred Representatives, nor less than one Representative for every forty thousand persons, until the number of Representatives shall amount to two hundred; after which the proportion shall be so regulated by Congress, that there shall not be less than two hundred Representatives, nor more than one Representative for every fifty thousand persons.

If the Reapportionment Amendment had passed and remained in effect, the House of Representatives today would have more than 5,000 members rather than 435.

Amendment XI
[Adopted 1798]

The judicial power of the United States shall not be construed to extend to any suit in law or equity, commenced or prosecuted against one of the United States by citizens of another State, or by citizens or subjects of any foreign state.

In 1793, the Supreme Court ruled in favor of Alexander Chisholm, executor of the estate of a deceased South Carolina merchant. Chisholm was suing the state of Georgia because the merchant had never been paid for provisions he had supplied during the Revolution. Many regarded this Court decision as an error that violated the intent of the Constitution.

Antifederalists had long feared a federal court system with the power to overrule a state court. When the Constitution was being drafted, Federalists had assured worried Antifederalists that section 2 of Article 3, which allows federal courts to hear cases "between a State and citizens of another State," did not mean that the federal courts were authorized to hear suits against a state by citizens of another state or a foreign country. Antifederalists and many other Americans feared a powerful federal court system because they worried that it would become like the British courts of this period, which were accountable only to the monarch. Furthermore, Chisholm v. Georgia prompted a series of suits against state governments by creditors and suppliers who had made loans during the war.

In addition, state legislators and Congress feared that the shaky economies of the new states, as well as the country as a whole, would be destroyed, especially if Loyalists who had fled to other countries sought reimbursement for land and property that had been seized. The day after the Supreme Court announced its decision, a resolution proposing the Eleventh Amendment, which overturned the decision in Chisholm v. Georgia, was introduced in the U.S. Senate.

AMENDMENTS TO THE CONSTITUTION WITH ANNOTATIONS

Amendment XII
[Adopted 1804]

The electors shall meet in their respective States, and vote by ballot for President and Vice-President, one of whom, at least, shall not be an inhabitant of the same State with themselves; they shall name in their ballots the person voted for as President, and in distinct ballots the person voted for as Vice-President, and they shall make distinct lists of all persons voted for as President, and of all persons voted for as Vice-President, and of the number of votes for each, which lists they shall sign and certify, and transmit sealed to the seat of government of the United States, directed to the President of the Senate;—the President of the Senate shall, in the presence of the Senate and House of Representatives, open all the certificates and the votes shall then be counted;—the person having the greatest number of votes for President shall be the President, if such number be a majority of the whole number of electors appointed; and if no person have such majority, then from the persons having the highest numbers not exceeding three on the list of those voted for as President, the House of Representatives shall choose immediately, by ballot, the President. But in choosing the President, the votes shall be taken by States, the representation from each State having one vote; a quorum for this purpose shall consist of a member or members from two-thirds of the States, and a majority of all the States shall be necessary to a choice. And if the House of Representatives shall not choose a President whenever the right of choice shall devolve upon them, before *the fourth day of March* next following, then the Vice-President shall act as President, as in the case of the death or other constitutional disability of the President.

The person having the greatest number of votes as Vice-President shall be the Vice-President, if such number be a majority of the whole number of electors appointed; and if no person have a majority, then from the two highest numbers on the list the Senate shall choose the Vice-President; a quorum for the purpose shall consist of two-thirds of the whole number of Senators, and a majority of the whole number shall be necessary to a choice. But no person constitutionally ineligible to the office of President shall be eligible to that of Vice-President of the United States.

◆◆◆

The framers of the Constitution disliked political parties and assumed that none would ever form. Under the original system, electors chosen by the states would each vote for two candidates. The candidate who won the most votes would become president, while the person who won the second-highest number of votes would become vice president. Rivalries between Federalists and Antifederalists led to the formation of political parties, however, even before

George Washington had left office. Though Washington was elected unanimously in 1789 and 1792, the elections of 1796 and 1800 were procedural disasters because of party maneuvering (see Chapters 9 and 10). In 1796, Federalist John Adams was chosen as president, and his great rival, the Antifederalist Thomas Jefferson (whose party was called the Republican Party), became his vice president. In 1800, all the electors cast their two votes as one of two party blocs. Jefferson and his fellow Republican nominee, Aaron Burr, were tied with seventy-three votes each. The contest went to the House of Representatives, which finally elected Jefferson after thirty-six ballots. The Twelfth Amendment prevents these problems by requiring electors to vote separately for the president and vice president.

Unratified Amendment
Titles of Nobility Amendment
(proposed by Congress May 1, 1810)

If any citizen of the United States shall accept, claim, receive or retain any title of nobility or honor or shall, without the consent of Congress, accept and retain any present, pension, office or emolument of any kind whatever, from any emperor, king, prince or foreign power, such person shall cease to be a citizen of the United States, and shall be incapable of holding any office of trust or profit under them, or either of them.

This amendment would have extended Article 1, section 9, clause 8 of the Constitution, which prevents the awarding of titles by the United States and the acceptance of such awards from foreign powers without congressional consent. Historians speculate that general nervousness about the power of the Emperor Napoleon, who was at that time extending France's empire throughout Europe, may have prompted the proposal. Though it fell one vote short of ratification, Congress and the American people thought the proposal had been ratified and it was included in many nineteenth-century editions of the Constitution.

The Civil War and Reconstruction Amendments (Thirteenth, Fourteenth, and Fifteenth Amendments)

In the four months between the election of Abraham Lincoln and his inauguration, more than two hundred proposed constitutional amendments were presented to Congress as part of a desperate attempt to hold the rapidly dissolving Union together. Most of these were efforts to appease the southern states by protecting the right to own slaves or by disfranchising African Americans through constitutional amendment. None were able to win the votes required from Congress to send them to the states. The relatively innocuous Corwin Amendment seemed to be the only hope for preserving the Union by amending the Constitution.

The northern victors in the Civil War tried to restructure the Constitution just as the war had restructured the nation. Yet they were often divided in their goals. Some wanted to end slavery; others hoped for social and economic equality regardless of race; others hoped that extending the power of the ballot box to former slaves would help create a new political order. The debates over the Thirteenth, Fourteenth, and Fifteenth Amendments were bitter. Few of those who fought for these changes were satisfied with the amendments themselves; fewer still were satisfied with their interpretation. Although the amendments put an end to the legal status of slavery, it took nearly a hundred years after the amendments' passage before most of the descendants of former slaves could begin to experience the economic, social, and political equality the amendments had been intended to provide.

Unratified Amendment
Corwin Amendment (proposed by Congress March 2, 1861)

No amendment shall be made to the Constitution which will authorize or give to Congress the power to abolish or interfere, within any State, with the domestic institutions thereof, including that of persons held to labor or service by the laws of said State.

Following the election of Abraham Lincoln, Congress scrambled to try to prevent the secession of the slave-holding states. House member Thomas Corwin of Ohio proposed the "unamendable" amendment in the hope that by protecting slavery where it existed, Congress would keep the southern states in the Union. Lincoln indicated his support for the proposed amendment in his first inaugural address. Only Ohio and Maryland ratified the Corwin Amendment before it was forgotten.

Amendment XIII
[Adopted 1865]

Section 1 Neither slavery nor involuntary servitude, except as a punishment for crime whereof the party shall have been duly convicted, shall exist within the United States, or any place subject to their jurisdiction.

Section 2 Congress shall have power to enforce this article by appropriate legislation.

Although President Lincoln had abolished slavery in the Confederacy with the Emancipation Proclamation of 1863, abolitionists wanted to rid the entire country of slavery. The Thirteenth Amendment did this in a clear and straightforward manner. In February 1865, when the proposal was approved by the House, the gallery of the House was newly opened to black Americans who had a chance at last to see their government at work. Passage of the proposal was greeted by wild cheers from the gallery as well as tears on the House floor, where congressional representatives openly embraced one another.

The problem of ratification remained, however. The Union position was that the Confederate states were part of the country of thirty-six states. Therefore, twenty-seven states were needed to ratify the amendment. When Kentucky and Delaware rejected it, backers realized that without approval from at least four former Confederate states, the amendment would fail. Lincoln's successor, President Andrew Johnson, made ratification of the Thirteenth Amendment a condition for southern states to rejoin the Union. Under those terms, all the former Confederate states except Mississippi accepted the Thirteenth Amendment, and by the end of 1865 the amendment had become part of the Constitution and slavery had been prohibited in the United States.

Amendment XIV
[Adopted 1868]

Section 1 All persons born or naturalized in the United States, and subject to the jurisdiction thereof, are citizens of the United States and of the State wherein they reside. No State shall make or enforce any law which shall abridge the privileges or immunities of citizens of the United States; nor shall any State deprive any person of life, liberty, or property, without due process of law; nor deny to any person within its jurisdiction the equal protection of the laws.

Section 2 Representatives shall be appointed among the several States according to their respective numbers, counting the whole number of persons in each State, excluding Indians not taxed. But when the right to vote at any election for the choice of Electors for President and Vice-President of the United States, Representatives in Congress, the executive and judicial officers of a State, or the members of the legislature thereof, is denied to any of the male inhabitants of such State, being twenty-one years of age and citizens of the United States, or in any way abridged, except for participation in rebellion, or other crime, the basis of representation therein shall be reduced in the proportion which the number of such male citizens shall bear to the whole number of male citizens twenty-one years of age in such State.

Section 3 No person shall be a Senator or Representative in Congress, or Elector of President and Vice-President, or hold any office, civil or military, under the United States, or under any State, who, having previously taken an oath, as a member of Congress, or as an officer of the United States, or as a member of any State legislature, or as an executive or judicial officer of any State, to support the Constitution of the United States, shall have engaged in insurrection or rebellion against the same, or given aid or comfort to the enemies thereof. Congress may, by a vote of two-thirds of each house, remove such disability.

Section 4 The validity of the public debt of the United States, authorized by law, including debts incurred for payment of pensions and bounties for services in suppressing insurrection or rebellion, shall not be questioned. But neither the United States nor any State shall assume or pay any debt or obligation incurred in aid of insurrection or rebellion against the United States, or any claim for the loss or emancipation of any slave; but all such debts, obligations, and claims shall be held illegal and void.

Section 5 The Congress shall have power to enforce, by appropriate legislation, the provisions of this article.

◆◆◆

Without Lincoln's leadership in the reconstruction of the nation following the Civil War, it soon became clear that the Thirteenth Amendment needed additional constitutional support. Less than a year after Lincoln's assassination, Andrew Johnson was ready to bring the former Confederate states back into the Union with few changes in their governments or politics. Anxious Republicans drafted the Fourteenth Amendment to prevent that from happening. The most important provisions of this complex amendment made all native-born or naturalized persons American citizens and prohibited states from abridging the "privileges or immunities" of citizens; depriving them of "life, liberty, or property, without due process of law"; and denying them "equal protection of the laws." In essence, it made all ex-slaves citizens and protected the rights of all citizens against violation by their own state governments.

As occurred in the case of the Thirteenth Amendment, former Confederate states were forced to ratify the amendment as a condition of representation in the House and the Senate. The intentions of the Fourteenth Amendment, and how those intentions should be enforced, have been the most debated point of constitutional history. The terms due process *and* equal protection *have been especially troublesome. Was the amendment designed to outlaw racial segregation? Or was the goal simply to prevent the leaders of the rebellious South from gaining political power?*

The framers of the Fourteenth Amendment hoped Article 2 would produce black voters who would increase the power of the Republican Party. The federal government, however, never used its power to punish states for denying blacks their right to vote. Although the Fourteenth Amendment had an immediate impact in giving black Americans citizenship, it did nothing to protect blacks from the vengeance of whites once Reconstruction ended. In the late nineteenth and early twentieth centuries, section 1 of the Fourteenth Amendment was often used to protect business interests and strike down laws protecting workers on the grounds that the rights of "persons," that is, corporations, were protected by "due process." More recently, the Fourteenth Amendment has been used to justify school desegregation and affirmative action programs, as well as to dismantle such programs.

Amendment XV
[Adopted 1870]

Section 1 The right of citizens of the United States to vote shall not be denied or abridged by the United States or by any State on account of race, color, or previous condition of servitude.

Section 2 The Congress shall have power to enforce this article by appropriate legislation.

◆◆◆

The Fifteenth Amendment was the last major piece of Reconstruction legislation. While earlier Reconstruction acts had already required black suffrage in the South, the Fifteenth Amendment extended black voting rights to the entire nation. Some Republicans felt morally obligated to do away with the double standard between North and South since many northern states had stubbornly refused to enfranchise blacks. Others believed that the freedman's ballot required the extra protection of a constitutional amendment to shield it from white counterattack. But partisan advantage also played an important role in the amendment's passage, since Republicans hoped that by giving the ballot to northern blacks, they could lessen their political vulnerability.

Many women's rights advocates had fought for the amendment. They had felt betrayed by the inclusion of the word male *in section 2 of the Fourteenth Amendment and were further angered when the proposed Fifteenth Amendment failed to prohibit denial of the right to vote on the grounds of sex as well as "race, color, or previous condition of servitude." In this amendment, for the first time, the federal government claimed the power to regulate the franchise, or vote. It was also the first time the Constitution placed limits on the power of the states to regulate access to the franchise. Although ratified in 1870, however, the amendment was not enforced until the twentieth century.*

The Progressive Amendments (Sixteenth–Nineteenth Amendments)

No amendments were added to the Constitution between the Civil War and the Progressive Era. America was changing, however, in fundamental ways. The rapid industrialization of the United States after the Civil War led to many social and economic problems. Hundreds of amendments were proposed, but none received enough support in Congress to be sent to the states. Some scholars believe that regional differences and rivalries were so strong during this period that it was almost impossible to gain a consensus on a constitutional amendment. During the Progressive Era, however, the Constitution was amended four times in seven years.

Amendment XVI
[Adopted 1913]

The Congress shall have power to lay and collect taxes on incomes, from whatever source derived, without apportionment among the several States, and without regard to any census or enumeration.

Until passage of the Sixteenth Amendment, most of the money used to run the federal government came from customs duties and taxes on specific items, such as liquor. During the Civil War, the federal government taxed incomes as an emergency measure. Pressure to enact an income tax came from those who were concerned about the growing gap between rich and poor in the United States. The Populist Party began campaigning for a graduated income tax in 1892, and support continued to grow. By 1909, thirty-three proposed income tax amendments had been presented in Congress, but lobbying by corporate and other special interests had defeated them all. In June 1909, the growing pressure for an income tax, which had been endorsed by Presidents Roosevelt and Taft, finally pushed an amendment through the Senate. The required thirty-six states had ratified the amendment by February 1913.

Amendment XVII
[Adopted 1913]

Section 1   The Senate of the United States shall be composed of two Senators from each State, elected by the people thereof, for six years; and each Senator shall have one vote. The electors in each State shall have the qualifications requisite for electors of [voters for] the most numerous branch of the State legislatures.

Section 2   When vacancies happen in the representation of any State in the Senate, the executive authority of such State shall issue writs of election to fill such vacancies: Provided, that the Legislature of any State may empower the executive thereof to make temporary appointments until the people fill the vacancies by election as the Legislature may direct.

Section 3   This amendment shall not be so construed as to affect the election or term of any Senator chosen before it becomes valid as part of the Constitution.

The framers of the Constitution saw the members of the House as the representatives of the people and the members of the Senate as the representatives of the states. Originally senators were to be chosen by the state legislators. According to reform advocates, however, the growth of private industry and transportation conglomerates during the Gilded Age had created a network of corruption in which wealth and power were exchanged for influence and votes in the Senate. Senator Nelson Aldrich, who represented Rhode Island in the late nineteenth and early twentieth centuries, for example, was known as "the senator from Standard Oil" because of his open support of special business interests.

Efforts to amend the Constitution to allow direct election of senators had begun in 1826, but since any proposal had to be approved by the Senate, reform seemed impossible. Progressives tried to gain influence in the Senate by instituting party caucuses and primary elections, which gave citizens the chance to express their choice of a senator who could then be officially elected by the state legislature. By 1910, fourteen of the country's thirty senators received popular votes through a state primary before the state legislature made its selection. Despairing of getting a proposal through the Senate, supporters of a direct-election amendment had begun in 1893 to seek a convention of representatives from two-thirds of the states to propose an amendment that could then be ratified. By 1905, thirty-one of forty-five states had endorsed such an amendment. Finally, in 1911, despite extraordinary opposition, a proposed amendment passed the Senate; by 1913, it had been ratified.

Amendment XVIII
[Adopted 1919; Repealed 1933 by Amendment XXI]

Section 1   After one year from the ratification of this article the manufacture, sale, or transportation of intoxicating liquors within, the importation thereof into, or the exportation thereof from the United States and all territory subject to the jurisdiction thereof, for beverage purposes, is hereby prohibited.

Section 2   The Congress and the several States shall have concurrent power to enforce this article by appropriate legislation.

Section 3 This article shall be inoperative unless it shall have been ratified as an amendment to the Constitution by the legislatures of the several States, as provided by the Constitution, within seven years from the date of the submission thereof to the States by the Congress.

The Prohibition Party, formed in 1869, began calling for a constitutional amendment to outlaw alcoholic beverages in 1872. A prohibition amendment was first proposed in the Senate in 1876 and was revived eighteen times before 1913. Between 1913 and 1919, another thirty-nine attempts were made to prohibit liquor in the United States through a constitutional amendment. Prohibition became a key element of the Progressive agenda as reformers linked alcohol and drunkenness to numerous social problems, including the corruption of immigrant voters. While opponents of such an amendment argued that it was undemocratic, supporters claimed that their efforts had widespread public support. The admission of twelve "dry" western states to the Union in the early twentieth century and the spirit of sacrifice during World War I laid the groundwork for passage and ratification of the Eighteenth Amendment in 1919. Opponents added a time limit to the amendment in the hope that they could thus block ratification, but this effort failed. (See also Amendment XXI.)

Amendment XIX
[Adopted 1920]

Section 1 The right of citizens of the United States to vote shall not be denied or abridged by the United States or by any State on account of sex.

Section 2 Congress shall have the power to enforce this article by appropriate legislation.

Advocates of women's rights tried and failed to link woman suffrage to the Fourteenth and Fifteenth Amendments. Nonetheless, the effort for woman suffrage continued. Between 1878 and 1912, at least one and sometimes as many as four proposed amendments were introduced in Congress each year to grant women the right to vote. While over time women won very limited voting rights in some states, at both the state and federal levels opposition to an amendment for woman suffrage remained very strong. President Woodrow Wilson and other officials felt that the federal government should not interfere with the power of the states in this matter. Others worried that granting suffrage to women would encourage ethnic minorities to exercise their own right to vote. And many were concerned that giving women the vote would result in their abandoning traditional gender roles. In 1919, fol-

lowing a protracted and often bitter campaign of protest in which women went on hunger strikes and chained themselves to fences, an amendment was introduced with the backing of President Wilson. It narrowly passed the Senate (after efforts to limit the suffrage to white women failed) and was adopted in 1920 after Tennessee became the thirty-sixth state to ratify it.

Unratified Amendment
Child Labor Amendment
(proposed by Congress June 2, 1924)

Section 1 The Congress shall have power to limit, regulate, and prohibit the labor of persons under eighteen years of age.

Section 2 The power of the several States is unimpaired by this article except that the operation of State laws shall be suspended to the extent necessary to give effect to legislation enacted by Congress.

Throughout the late nineteenth and early twentieth centuries, alarm over the condition of child workers grew. Opponents of child labor argued that children worked in dangerous and unhealthy conditions, that they took jobs from adult workers, that they depressed wages in certain industries, and that states that allowed child labor had an economic advantage over those that did not. Defenders of child labor claimed that children provided needed income in many families, that working at a young age developed character, and that the effort to prohibit the practice constituted an invasion of family privacy.

In 1916, Congress passed a law that made it illegal to sell goods made by children through interstate commerce. The Supreme Court, however, ruled that the law violated the limits on the power of Congress to regulate interstate commerce. Congress then tried to penalize industries that used child labor by taxing such goods. This measure was also thrown out by the courts. In response, reformers set out to amend the Constitution. The proposed amendment was ratified by twenty-eight states, but by 1925, thirteen states had rejected it. Passage of the Fair Labor Standards Act in 1938, which was upheld by the Supreme Court in 1941, made the amendment irrelevant.

Amendment XX
[Adopted 1933]

Section 1 The terms of the President and Vice-President shall end at noon on the 20th day of January, and the terms of Senators and Representatives at noon on the 3rd day of January, of the years in which such terms would have ended if this article had not been ratified; and the terms of their successors shall then begin.

Section 2 The Congress shall assemble at least once in every year, and such meeting shall begin at noon on the 3rd day of January, unless they shall by law appoint a different day.

Section 3 If, at the time fixed for the beginning of the term of the President, the President-elect shall have died, the Vice-President-elect shall become President. If a President shall not have been chosen before the time fixed for the beginning of his term, or if the President-elect shall have failed to qualify, then the Vice-President-elect shall act as President until a President shall have qualified; and the Congress may by law provide for the case wherein neither a President-elect nor a Vice-President-elect shall have qualified, declaring who shall then act as President, or the manner in which one who is to act shall be selected, and such person shall act accordingly until a President or Vice-President shall have qualified.

Section 4 The Congress may by law provide for the case of the death of any of the persons from whom the House of Representatives may choose a President whenever the right of choice shall have devolved upon them, and for the case of the death of any of the persons from whom the Senate may choose a Vice-President whenever the right of choice shall have devolved upon them.

Section 5 Sections 1 and 2 shall take effect on the 15th day of October following the ratification of this article.

Section 6 This article shall be inoperative unless it shall have been ratified as an amendment to the Constitution by the Legislatures of three-fourths of the several States within seven years from the date of its submission.

Until 1933, presidents took office on March 4. Since elections are held in early November and electoral votes are counted in mid-December, this meant that more than three months passed between the time a new president was elected and when he took office. Moving the inauguration to January shortened the transition period and allowed Congress to begin its term closer to the time of the president's inauguration. Although this seems like a minor change, an amendment was required because the Constitution specifies terms of office. This amendment also deals with questions of succession in the event that a president- or vice president-elect dies before assuming office. Section 3 also clarifies a method for resolving a deadlock in the electoral college.

Amendment XXI
[Adopted 1933]

Section 1 The eighteenth article of amendment to the Constitution of the United States is hereby repealed.

Section 2 The transportation or importation into any State, Territory, or Possession of the United States for delivery or use therein of intoxicating liquors, in violation of the laws thereof, is hereby prohibited.

Section 3 This article shall be inoperative unless it shall have been ratified as an amendment to the Constitution by conventions in the several States, as provided in the Constitution, within seven years from the date of the submission thereof to the States by the Congress.

Widespread violation of the Volstead Act, the law enacted to enforce prohibition, made the United States a nation of lawbreakers. Prohibition caused more problems than it solved by encouraging crime, bribery, and corruption. Further, a coalition of liquor and beer manufacturers, personal liberty advocates, and constitutional scholars joined forces to challenge the amendment. By 1929, thirty proposed repeal amendments had been introduced in Congress, and the Democratic Party made repeal part of its platform in the 1932 presidential campaign. The Twenty-First Amendment was proposed in February 1933 and ratified less than a year later. The failure of the effort to enforce prohibition through a constitutional amendment has often been cited by opponents to subsequent efforts to shape public virtue and private morality.

Amendment XXII
[Adopted 1951]

Section 1 No person shall be elected to the office of the President more than twice, and no person who has held the office of President, or acted as President, for more than two years of a term to which some other person was elected President shall be elected to the office of President more than once. But this article shall not apply to any person holding the office of President when this Article was proposed by the Congress, and shall not prevent any person who may be holding the office of President, or acting as President, during the term within which this Article becomes operative from holding the office of President or acting as President during the remainder of such term.

Section 2 This article shall be inoperative unless it shall have been ratified as an amendment to the Constitution by the legislatures of three-fourths of the several States within seven years from the date of its submission to the States by the Congress.

George Washington's refusal to seek a third term of office set a precedent that stood until 1912, when former President Theodore Roosevelt sought, without success, another term as an independent candidate. Democrat Franklin Roosevelt was the only president to seek and win a fourth term, though he did so amid great controversy. Roosevelt died in April 1945, a few months after the beginning of his fourth term. In 1946, Republicans won control of the House and the Senate, and early in 1947 a proposal for an amendment to limit future presidents to two four-year terms was offered to the states for ratification. Democratic critics of the Twenty-Second Amendment charged that it was a partisan posthumous jab at Roosevelt.

Since the Twenty-Second Amendment was adopted, however, the only presidents who might have been able to seek a third term, had it not existed, were Republicans Dwight Eisenhower and Ronald Reagan, and Democrat Bill Clinton. Since 1826, Congress has entertained 160 proposed amendments to limit the president to one six-year term. Such amendments have been backed by fifteen presidents, including Gerald Ford and Jimmy Carter.

Amendment XXIII
[Adopted 1961]

Section 1   The District constituting the seat of Government of the United States shall appoint in such manner as the Congress may direct: A number of electors of President and Vice-President equal to the whole number of Senators and Representatives in Congress to which the District would be entitled if it were a State, but in no event more than the least populous State; they shall be in addition to those appointed by the States, but they shall be considered for the purposes of the election of President and Vice-President, to be electors appointed by a State; and they shall meet in the District and perform such duties as provided by the twelfth article of amendment.

Section 2   The Congress shall have the power to enforce this article by appropriate legislation.

When Washington, D.C., was established as a federal district, no one expected that a significant number of people would make it their permanent and primary residence. A proposal to allow citizens of the district to vote in presidential elections was approved by Congress in June 1960 and was ratified on March 29, 1961.

Amendment XXIV
[Adopted 1964]

Section 1   The right of citizens of the United States to vote in any primary or other election for President or Vice-President, for electors for President or Vice-President, or for Senator or Representative in Congress, shall not be denied or abridged by the United States or any State by reason of failure to pay any poll tax or other tax.

Section 2   The Congress shall have the power to enforce this article by appropriate legislation.

In the colonial and Revolutionary eras, financial independence was seen as necessary to political independence, and the poll tax was used as a requirement for voting. By the twentieth century, however, the poll tax was used mostly to bar poor people, especially southern blacks, from voting. While conservatives complained that the amendment interfered with states' rights, liberals thought that the amendment did not go far enough because it barred the poll tax only in national elections and not in state or local elections. The amendment was ratified in 1964, however, and two years later, the Supreme Court ruled that poll taxes in state and local elections also violated the equal protection clause of the Fourteenth Amendment.

Amendment XXV
[Adopted 1967]

Section 1   In case of the removal of the President from office or of his death or resignation, the Vice-President shall become President.

Section 2   Whenever there is a vacancy in the office of the Vice-President, the President shall nominate a Vice-President who shall take office upon confirmation by a majority vote of both Houses of Congress.

Section 3   Whenever the President transmits to the President pro tempore of the Senate and the Speaker of the House of Representatives his written declaration that he is unable to discharge the powers and duties of his office, and until he transmits to them a written declaration to the contrary, such powers and duties shall be discharged by the Vice-President as Acting President.

Section 4   Whenever the Vice-President and a majority of either the principal officers of the executive departments or of such other body as Congress may by law provide, transmit to the President pro tempore of the Senate and the Speaker of the House of Representatives their written declaration that the President is unable to discharge the powers and duties of his office, the Vice-President shall immediately assume the powers and duties of the office as Acting President.

Thereafter, when the President transmits to the President pro tempore of the Senate and the Speaker of the House of Representatives his written declaration that no inability exists, he shall resume the powers and duties of his office unless the Vice-President and a majority of either the principal officers of the executive department[s] or of such other body as Congress may by law provide, transmit within four days to the President pro tempore of the Senate and the Speaker of the House of Representatives their written declaration that the President is unable to discharge the powers and duties of his office. Thereupon Congress shall decide the issue, assembling within forty-eight hours for that purpose if not in session. If the Congress, within twenty-one days after receipt of the latter written declaration, or, if Congress is not in session, within twenty-one days after Congress is required to assemble, determines by two-thirds vote of both Houses that the President is unable to discharge the powers and duties of his office, the Vice-President shall continue to discharge the same as Acting President; otherwise, the President shall resume the powers and duties of his office.

◆◆◆

The framers of the Constitution established the office of vice president because someone was needed to preside over the Senate. The first president to die in office was William Henry Harrison, in 1841. Vice President John Tyler had himself sworn in as president, setting a precedent that was followed when seven later presidents died in office. The assassination of President James A. Garfield in 1881 posed a new problem, however. After he was shot, the president was incapacitated for two months before he died; he was unable to lead the country, while his vice president, Chester A. Arthur, was unable to assume leadership. Efforts to resolve questions of succession in the event of a presidential disability thus began with the death of Garfield.

In 1963, the assassination of President John F. Kennedy galvanized Congress to action. Vice President Lyndon Johnson was a chain smoker with a history of heart trouble. According to the 1947 Presidential Succession Act, the two men who stood in line to succeed him were the seventy-two-year-old Speaker of the House and the eighty-six-year-old president of the Senate. There were serious concerns that any of these men might become incapacitated while serving as chief executive. The first time the Twenty-Fifth Amendment was used, however, was not in the case of presidential death or illness, but during the Watergate crisis. When Vice President Spiro T. Agnew was forced to resign following allegations of bribery and tax violations,

President Richard M. Nixon appointed House Minority Leader Gerald R. Ford vice president. Ford became president following Nixon's resignation eight months later and named Nelson A. Rockefeller as his vice president. Thus, for more than two years, the two highest offices in the country were held by people who had not been elected to them.

Amendment XXVI
[Adopted 1971]

Section 1   The right of citizens of the United States, who are eighteen years of age or older, to vote shall not be denied or abridged by the United States or by any State on account of age.

Section 2   The Congress shall have power to enforce this article by appropriate legislation.

Efforts to lower the voting age from twenty-one to eighteen began during World War II. Recognizing that those who were old enough to fight a war should have some say in the government policies that involved them in the war, Presidents Eisenhower, Johnson, and Nixon endorsed the idea. In 1970, the combined pressure of the antiwar movement and the demographic pressure of the baby boom generation led to a Voting Rights Act lowering the voting age in federal, state, and local elections.

In Oregon v. Mitchell (1970), the state of Oregon challenged the right of Congress to determine the age at which people could vote in state or local elections. The Supreme Court agreed with Oregon. Since the Voting Rights Act was ruled unconstitutional, the Constitution had to be amended to allow passage of a law that would lower the voting age. The amendment was ratified in a little more than three months, making it the most rapidly ratified amendment in U.S. history.

Unratified Amendment
Equal Rights Amendment (proposed by Congress March 22, 1972; seven-year deadline for ratification extended June 30, 1982)

Section 1   Equality of rights under the law shall not be denied or abridged by the United States or by any State on account of sex.

Section 2   The Congress shall have the power to enforce, by appropriate legislation, the provisions of this article.

Section 3   This amendment shall take effect two years after the date of ratification.

◆ ◆ ◆

In 1923, soon after women had won the right to vote, Alice Paul, a leading activist in the woman suffrage movement, proposed an amendment requiring equal treatment of men and women. Opponents of the proposal argued that such an amendment would invalidate laws that protected women and would make women subject to the military draft. After the 1964 Civil Rights Act was adopted, protective workplace legislation was removed anyway.

The renewal of the women's movement, as a by-product of the civil rights and antiwar movements, led to a revival of the Equal Rights Amendment (ERA) in Congress. Disagreements over language held up congressional passage of the proposed amendment, but on March 22, 1972, the Senate approved the ERA by a vote of eighty-four to eight, and it was sent to the states. Six states ratified the amendment within two days, and by the middle of 1973 the amendment seemed well on its way to adoption, with thirty of the needed thirty-eight states having ratified it. In the mid-1970s, however, a powerful "Stop ERA" campaign developed. The campaign portrayed the ERA as a threat to "family values" and traditional relationships between men and women. Although thirty-five states ultimately ratified the ERA, five of those state legislatures voted to rescind ratification, and the amendment was never adopted.

Unratified Amendment
D.C. Statehood Amendment (proposed by Congress August 22, 1978)

Section 1 For purposes of representation in the Congress, election of the President and Vice President, and article V of this Constitution, the District constituting the seat of government of the United States shall be treated as though it were a State.

Section 2 The exercise of the rights and powers conferred under this article shall be by the people of the District constituting the seat of government, and as shall be provided by Congress.

Section 3 The twenty-third article of amendment to the Constitution of the United States is hereby repealed.

Section 4 This article shall be inoperative, unless it shall have been ratified as an amendment to the Constitution by the legislatures of three-fourths of the several states within seven years from the date of its submission.

◆ ◆ ◆

The 1961 ratification of the Twenty-Third Amendment, giving residents of the District of Columbia the right to

vote for a president and vice president, inspired an effort to give residents of the district full voting rights. In 1966, President Lyndon Johnson appointed a mayor and city council; in 1971, D.C. residents were allowed to name a nonvoting delegate to the House; and in 1981, residents were allowed to elect the mayor and city council. Congress retained the right to overrule laws that might affect commuters, the height of federal buildings, and selection of judges and prosecutors. The district's nonvoting delegate to Congress, Walter Fauntroy, lobbied fiercely for a congressional amendment granting statehood to the district. In 1978, a proposed amendment was approved and sent to the states. A number of states quickly ratified the amendment, but, like the ERA, the D.C. Statehood Amendment ran into trouble. Opponents argued that section 2 created a separate category of "nominal" statehood. They argued that the federal district should be eliminated and that the territory should be reabsorbed into the state of Maryland. Although these theoretical arguments were strong, some scholars believe that racist attitudes toward the predominantly black population of the city was also a factor leading to the defeat of the amendment.

Amendment XXVII
[Adopted 1992]

No law, varying the compensation for the services of the Senators and Representatives, shall take effect, until an election of Representatives shall have intervened.

◆ ◆ ◆

While the Twenty-Sixth Amendment was the most rapidly ratified amendment in U.S. history, the Twenty-Seventh Amendment had the longest journey to ratification. First proposed by James Madison in 1789 as part of the package that included the Bill of Rights, this amendment had been ratified by only six states by 1791. In 1873, however, it was ratified by Ohio to protest a massive retroactive salary increase by the federal government. Unlike later proposed amendments, this one came with no time limit on ratification. In the early 1980s, Gregory D. Watson, a University of Texas economics major, discovered the "lost" amendment and began a single-handed campaign to get state legislators to introduce it for ratification. In 1983, it was accepted by Maine. In 1984, it passed the Colorado legislature. Ratifications trickled in slowly until May 1992, when Michigan and New Jersey became the thirty-eighth and thirty-ninth states, respectively, to ratify. This amendment prevents members of Congress from raising their own salaries without giving voters a chance to vote them out of office before they can benefit from the raises.

APPENDIX II. FACTS AND FIGURES: GOVERNMENT, ECONOMY, AND DEMOGRAPHICS

For additional facts and figures see the Online Appendix at
www.bedfordstmartins.com/roarkcompact.

PRESIDENTIAL ELECTIONS

Year	Candidates	Parties	Popular Vote	Percentage of Popular Vote	Electoral Vote	Percentage of Voter Participation
1789	**GEORGE WASHINGTON (Va.)***				69	
	John Adams				34	
	Others				35	
1792	**GEORGE WASHINGTON (Va.)**				132	
	John Adams				77	
	George Clinton				50	
	Others				5	
1796	**JOHN ADAMS (Mass.)**	Federalist			71	
	Thomas Jefferson	Democratic-Republican			68	
	Thomas Pinckney	Federalist			59	
	Aaron Burr	Dem.-Rep.			30	
	Others				48	
1800	**THOMAS JEFFERSON (Va.)**	Dem.-Rep.			73	
	Aaron Burr	Dem.-Rep.			73	
	John Adams	Federalist			65	
	C. C. Pinckney	Federalist			64	
	John Jay	Federalist			1	
1804	**THOMAS JEFFERSON (Va.)**	Dem.-Rep.			162	
	C. C. Pinckney	Federalist			14	
1808	**JAMES MADISON (Va.)**	Dem.-Rep.			122	
	C. C. Pinckney	Federalist			47	
	George Clinton	Dem.-Rep.			6	
1812	**JAMES MADISON (Va.)**	Dem.-Rep.			128	
	De Witt Clinton	Federalist			89	
1816	**JAMES MONROE (Va.)**	Dem.-Rep.			183	
	Rufus King	Federalist			34	
1820	**JAMES MONROE (Va.)**	Dem.-Rep.			231	
	John Quincy Adams	Dem.-Rep.			1	

*State of residence when elected president.

PRESIDENTIAL ELECTIONS

Year	Candidates	Parties	Popular Vote	Percentage of Popular Vote	Electoral Vote	Percentage of Voter Participation
1824	**JOHN Q. ADAMS (Mass.)**	Dem.-Rep.	108,740	30.5	84	26.9
	Andrew Jackson	Dem.-Rep.	153,544	43.1	99	
	William H. Crawford	Dem.-Rep.	46,618	13.1	41	
	Henry Clay	Dem.-Rep.	47,136	13.2	37	
1828	**ANDREW JACKSON (Tenn.)**	Democratic	647,286	56.0	178	57.6
	John Quincy Adams	National Republican	508,064	44.0	83	
1832	**ANDREW JACKSON (Tenn.)**	Democratic	687,502	55.0	219	55.4
	Henry Clay	National Republican	530,189	42.4	49	
	John Floyd	Independent			11	
	William Wirt	Anti-Mason	33,108	2.6	7	
1836	**MARTIN VAN BUREN (N.Y.)**	Democratic	765,483	50.9	170	57.8
	W. H. Harrison	Whig			73	
	Hugh L. White	Whig	739,795	49.1	26	
	Daniel Webster	Whig			14	
	W. P. Magnum	Independent			11	
1840	**WILLIAM H. HARRISON (Ohio)**	Whig	1,274,624	53.1	234	80.2
	Martin Van Buren	Democratic	1,127,781	46.9	60	
	J. G. Birney	Liberty	7,069		—	
1844	**JAMES K. POLK (Tenn.)**	Democratic	1,338,464	49.6	170	78.9
	Henry Clay	Whig	1,300,097	48.1	105	
	J. G. Birney	Liberty	62,300	2.3	—	
1848	**ZACHARY TAYLOR (La.)**	Whig	1,360,967	47.4	163	72.7
	Lewis Cass	Democratic	1,222,342	42.5	127	
	Martin Van Buren	Free-Soil	291,263	10.1	—	
1852	**FRANKLIN PIERCE (N.H.)**	Democratic	1,601,117	50.9	254	69.6
	Winfield Scott	Whig	1,385,453	44.1	42	
	John P. Hale	Free-Soil	155,825	5.0	—	
1856	**JAMES BUCHANAN (Pa.)**	Democratic	1,832,995	45.3	174	78.9
	John C. Frémont	Republican	1,339,932	33.1	114	
	Millard Fillmore	American	871,731	21.6	8	
1860	**ABRAHAM LINCOLN (Ill.)**	Republican	1,865,593	39.8	180	81.2
	Stephen A. Douglas	Democratic	1,382,713	29.5	12	
	John C. Breckinridge	Democratic	848,356	18.1	72	
	John Bell	Union	592,906	12.6	39	
1864	**ABRAHAM LINCOLN (Ill.)**	Republican	2,206,938	55.0	212	73.8
	George B. McClellan	Democratic	1,803,787	45.0	21	
1868	**ULYSSES S. GRANT (Ill.)**	Republican	3,012,833	52.7	214	78.1
	Horatio Seymour	Democratic	2,703,249	47.3	80	
1872	**ULYSSES S. GRANT (Ill.)**	Republican	3,597,132	55.6	286	71.3
	Horace Greeley	Democratic; Liberal Republican	2,834,125	43.9	66	
1876	**RUTHERFORD B. HAYES (Ohio)**	Republican	4,036,572	48.0	185	81.8
	Samuel J. Tilden	Democratic	4,284,020	51.0	184	
1880	**JAMES A. GARFIELD (Ohio)**	Republican	4,454,416	48.5	214	79.4
	Winfield S. Hancock	Democratic	4,444,952	48.1	155	

Year	Candidates	Parties	Popular Vote	Percentage of Popular Vote	Electoral Vote	Percentage of Voter Participation
1884	**GROVER CLEVELAND (N.Y.)**	Democratic	4,879,507	48.5	219	77.5
	James G. Blaine	Republican	4,850,293	48.2	182	
1888	**BENJAMIN HARRISON (Ind.)**	Republican	5,439,853	47.9	233	79.3
	Grover Cleveland	Democratic	5,540,309	48.6	168	
1892	**GROVER CLEVELAND (N.Y.)**	Democratic	5,555,426	46.1	277	74.7
	Benjamin Harrison	Republican	5,182,690	43.0	145	
	James B. Weaver	People's	1,029,846	8.5	22	
1896	**WILLIAM McKINLEY (Ohio)**	Republican	7,104,779	51.1	271	79.3
	William J. Bryan	Democratic-People's	6,502,925	47.7	176	
1900	**WILLIAM McKINLEY (Ohio)**	Republican	7,207,923	51.7	292	73.2
	William J. Bryan	Dem.-Populist	6,358,133	45.5	155	
1904	**THEODORE ROOSEVELT (N.Y.)**	Republican	7,623,486	57.9	336	65.2
	Alton B. Parker	Democratic	5,077,911	37.6	140	
	Eugene V. Debs	Socialist	402,283	3.0	—	
1908	**WILLIAM H. TAFT (Ohio)**	Republican	7,678,908	51.6	321	65.4
	William J. Bryan	Democratic	6,409,104	43.1	162	
	Eugene V. Debs	Socialist	420,793	2.8	—	
1912	**WOODROW WILSON (N.J.)**	Democratic	6,293,454	41.9	435	58.8
	Theodore Roosevelt	Progressive	4,119,538	27.4	88	
	William H. Taft	Republican	3,484,980	23.2	8	
	Eugene V. Debs	Socialist	900,672	6.1	—	
1916	**WOODROW WILSON (N.J.)**	Democratic	9,129,606	49.4	277	61.6
	Charles E. Hughes	Republican	8,538,221	46.2	254	
	A. L. Benson	Socialist	585,113	3.2	—	
1920	**WARREN G. HARDING (Ohio)**	Republican	16,143,407	60.5	404	49.2
	James M. Cox	Democratic	9,130,328	34.2	127	
	Eugene V. Debs	Socialist	919,799	3.4	—	
1924	**CALVIN COOLIDGE (Mass.)**	Republican	15,725,016	54.0	382	48.9
	John W. Davis	Democratic	8,386,503	28.8	136	
	Robert M. LaFollette	Progressive	4,822,856	16.6	13	
1928	**HERBERT HOOVER (Calif.)**	Republican	21,391,381	58.2	444	56.9
	Alfred E. Smith	Democratic	15,016,443	40.9	87	
	Norman Thomas	Socialist	267,835	0.7	—	
1932	**FRANKLIN D. ROOSEVELT (N.Y.)**	Democratic	22,809,638	57.4	472	56.9
	Herbert Hoover	Republican	15,758,901	39.7	59	
	Norman Thomas	Socialist	881,951	2.2	—	
1936	**FRANKLIN D. ROOSEVELT (N.Y.)**	Democratic	27,751,597	60.8	523	61.0
	Alfred M. Landon	Republican	16,679,583	36.5	8	
	William Lemke	Union	882,479	1.9	—	
1940	**FRANKLIN D. ROOSEVELT (N.Y.)**	Democratic	27,244,160	54.8	449	62.5
	Wendell Willkie	Republican	22,305,198	44.8	82	
1944	**FRANKLIN D. ROOSEVELT (N.Y.)**	Democratic	25,602,504	53.5	432	55.9
	Thomas E. Dewey	Republican	22,006,285	46.0	99	
1948	**HARRY S. TRUMAN (Mo.)**	Democratic	24,105,695	49.5	303	53.0
	Thomas E. Dewey	Republican	21,969,170	45.1	189	
	J. Strom Thurmond	State-Rights Democratic	1,169,021	2.4	38	
	Henry A. Wallace	Progressive	1,156,103	2.4	—	

PRESIDENTIAL ELECTIONS

Year	Candidates	Parties	Popular Vote	Percentage of Popular Vote	Electoral Vote	Percentage of Voter Participation
1952	**DWIGHT D. EISENHOWER (N.Y.)**	Republican	33,936,252	55.1	442	63.3
	Adlai Stevenson	Democratic	27,314,992	44.4	89	
1956	**DWIGHT D. EISENHOWER (N.Y.)**	Republican	35,575,420	57.6	457	60.6
	Adlai Stevenson	Democratic	26,033,066	42.1	73	
	Other	—	—		1	
1960	**JOHN F. KENNEDY (Mass.)**	Democratic	34,227,096	49.9	303	62.8
	Richard M. Nixon	Republican	34,108,546	49.6	219	
	Other	—	—		15	
1964	**LYNDON B. JOHNSON (Texas)**	Democratic	43,126,506	61.1	486	61.7
	Barry M. Goldwater	Republican	27,176,799	38.5	52	
1968	**RICHARD M. NIXON (N.Y.)**	Republican	31,770,237	43.4	301	60.9
	Hubert H. Humphrey	Democratic	31,270,533	42.7	191	
	George Wallace	American Indep.	9,906,141	13.5	46	
1972	**RICHARD M. NIXON (N.Y.)**	Republican	47,169,911	60.7	520	55.2
	George S. McGovern	Democratic	29,170,383	37.5	17	
	Other	—	—		1	
1976	**JIMMY CARTER (Ga.)**	Democratic	40,828,587	50.0	297	53.5
	Gerald R. Ford	Republican	39,147,613	47.9	241	
	Other	—	1,575,459	2.1	—	
1980	**RONALD REAGAN (Calif.)**	Republican	43,901,812	50.7	489	54.0
	Jimmy Carter	Democratic	35,483,820	41.0	49	
	John B. Anderson	Independent	5,719,722	6.6	—	
	Ed Clark	Libertarian	921,188	1.1	—	
1984	**RONALD REAGAN (Calif.)**	Republican	54,455,075	59.0	525	53.1
	Walter Mondale	Democratic	37,577,185	41.0	13	
1988	**GEORGE BUSH (Texas)**	Republican	47,946,422	54.0	426	50.2
	Michael S. Dukakis	Democratic	41,016,429	46.0	112	
1992	**WILLIAM J. CLINTON (Ark.)**	Democratic	44,908,254	42.3	370	55.9
	George Bush	Republican	39,102,282	37.4	168	
	H. Ross Perot	Independent	19,721,433	18.9	—	
1996	**WILLIAM J. CLINTON (Ark.)**	Democratic	47,401,185	49.2	379	49.0
	Robert Dole	Republican	39,197,469	40.7	159	
	H. Ross Perot	Independent	8,085,294	8.4	—	
2000	**GEORGE W. BUSH (Texas)**	Republican	50,456,062	47.8	271	51.2
	Al Gore	Democratic	50,996,862	48.4	267	
	Ralph Nader	Green Party	2,858,843	2.7	—	
	Patrick J. Buchanan	—	438,760	.4	—	

PRESIDENTS, VICE PRESIDENTS, AND SECRETARIES OF STATE

The Washington Administration (1789–1797)
Vice President	John Adams	1789–1797
Secretary of State	Thomas Jefferson	1789–1793
	Edmund Randolph	1794–1795
	Timothy Pickering	1795–1797

The John Adams Administration (1797–1801)
Vice President	Thomas Jefferson	1797–1801
Secretary of State	Timothy Pickering	1797–1800
	John Marshall	1800–1801

The Jefferson Administration (1801–1809)
Vice President	Aaron Burr	1801–1805
	George Clinton	1805–1809
Secretary of State	James Madison	1801–1809

The Madison Administration (1809–1817)
Vice President	George Clinton	1809–1813
	Elbridge Gerry	1813–1817
Secretary of State	Robert Smith	1809–1811
	James Monroe	1811–1817

The Monroe Administration (1817–1825)
Vice President	Daniel Tompkins	1817–1825
Secretary of State	John Quincy Adams	1817–1825

The John Quincy Adams Administration (1825–1829)
Vice President	John C. Calhoun	1825–1829
Secretary of State	Henry Clay	1825–1829

The Jackson Administration (1829–1837)
Vice President	John C. Calhoun	1829–1833
	Martin Van Buren	1833–1837
Secretary of State	Martin Van Buren	1829–1831
	Edward Livingston	1831–1833
	Louis McLane	1833–1834
	John Forsyth	1834–1837

The Van Buren Administration (1837–1841)
Vice President	Richard M. Johnson	1837–1841
Secretary of State	John Forsyth	1837–1841

The William Harrison Administration (1841)
Vice President	John Tyler	1841
Secretary of State	Daniel Webster	1841

The Tyler Administration (1841–1845)
Vice President	None	
Secretary of State	Daniel Webster	1841–1843
	Hugh S. Legaré	1843
	Abel P. Upshur	1843–1844
	John C. Calhoun	1844–1845

The Polk Administration (1845–1849)
Vice President	George M. Dallas	1845–1849
Secretary of State	James Buchanan	1845–1849

The Taylor Administration (1849–1850)
Vice President	Millard Fillmore	1849–1850
Secretary of State	John M. Clayton	1849–1850

The Fillmore Administration (1850–1853)
Vice President	None	
Secretary of State	Daniel Webster	1850–1852
	Edward Everett	1852–1853

The Pierce Administration (1853–1857)
Vice President	William R. King	1853–1857
Secretary of State	William L. Marcy	1853–1857

The Buchanan Administration (1857–1861)
Vice President	John C. Breckinridge	1857–1861
Secretary of State	Lewis Cass	1857–1860
	Jeremiah S. Black	1860–1861

The Lincoln Administration (1861–1865)
Vice President	Hannibal Hamlin	1861–1865
	Andrew Johnson	1865
Secretary of State	William H. Seward	1861–1865

The Andrew Johnson Administration (1865–1869)
Vice President	None	
Secretary of State	William H. Seward	1865–1869

PRESIDENTS, VICE PRESIDENTS, AND SECRETARIES OF STATE

The Grant Administration (1869–1877)

Vice President	Schuyler Colfax	1869–1873
	Henry Wilson	1873–1877
Secretary of State	Elihu B. Washburne	1869
	Hamilton Fish	1869–1877

The Hayes Administration (1877–1881)

Vice President	William A. Wheeler	1877–1881
Secretary of State	William M. Evarts	1877–1881

The Garfield Administration (1881)

Vice President	Chester A. Arthur	1881
Secretary of State	James G. Blaine	1881

The Arthur Administration (1881–1885)

Vice President	None	
Secretary of State	F. T. Frelinghuysen	1881–1885

The Cleveland Administration (1885–1889)

Vice President	Thomas A. Hendricks	1885–1889
Secretary of State	Thomas F. Bayard	1885–1889

The Benjamin Harrison Administration (1889–1893)

Vice President	Levi P. Morton	1889–1893
Secretary of State	James G. Blaine	1889–1892
	John W. Foster	1892–1893

The Cleveland Administration (1893–1897)

Vice President	Adlai E. Stevenson	1893–1897
Secretary of State	Walter Q. Gresham	1893–1895
	Richard Olney	1895–1897

The McKinley Administration (1897–1901)

Vice President	Garret A. Hobart	1897–1901
	Theodore Roosevelt	1901
Secretary of State	John Sherman	1897–1898
	William R. Day	1898
	John Hay	1898–1901

The Theodore Roosevelt Administration (1901–1909)

Vice President	Charles Fairbanks	1905–1909
Secretary of State	John Hay	1901–1905
	Elihu Root	1905–1909
	Robert Bacon	1909

The Taft Administration (1909–1913)

Vice President	James S. Sherman	1909–1913
Secretary of State	Philander C. Knox	1909–1913

The Wilson Administration (1913–1921)

Vice President	Thomas R. Marshall	1913–1921
Secretary of State	William J. Bryan	1913–1915
	Robert Lansing	1915–1920
	Bainbridge Colby	1920–1921

The Harding Administration (1921–1923)

Vice President	Calvin Coolidge	1921–1923
Secretary of State	Charles E. Hughes	1921–1923

The Coolidge Administration (1923–1929)

Vice President	Charles G. Dawes	1925–1929
Secretary of State	Charles E. Hughes	1923–1925
	Frank B. Kellogg	1925–1929

The Hoover Administration (1929–1933)

Vice President	Charles Curtis	1929–1933
Secretary of State	Henry L. Stimson	1929–1933

The Franklin D. Roosevelt Administration (1933–1945)

Vice President	John Nance Garner	1933–1941
	Henry A. Wallace	1941–1945
	Harry S. Truman	1945
Secretary of State	Cordell Hull	1933–1944
	Edward R. Stettinius Jr.	1944–1945

The Truman Administration (1945–1953)

Vice President	Alben W. Barkley	1949–1953
Secretary of State	Edward R. Stettinius Jr.	1945
	James F. Byrnes	1945–1947
	George C. Marshall	1947–1949
	Dean G. Acheson	1949–1953

The Eisenhower Administration (1953–1961)

Vice President	Richard M. Nixon	1953–1961
Secretary of State	John Foster Dulles	1953–1959
	Christian A. Herter	1959–1961

The Kennedy Administration (1961–1963)

Vice President	Lyndon B. Johnson	1961–1963
Secretary of State	Dean Rusk	1961–1963

The Lyndon Johnson Administration (1963–1969)

Vice President	Hubert H. Humphrey	1965–1969
Secretary of State	Dean Rusk	1963–1969

The Nixon Administration (1969–1974)

Vice President	Spiro T. Agnew	1969–1973
	Gerald R. Ford	1973–1974
Secretary of State	William P. Rogers	1969–1973
	Henry A. Kissinger	1973–1974

The Ford Administration (1974–1977)

Vice President	Nelson A. Rockefeller	1974–1977
Secretary of State	Henry A. Kissinger	1974–1977

The Carter Administration (1977–1981)

Vice President	Walter F. Mondale	1977–1981
Secretary of State	Cyrus R. Vance	1977–1980
	Edmund Muskie	1980–1981

The Reagan Administration (1981–1989)

Vice President	George H. W. Bush	1981–1989
Secretary of State	Alexander M. Haig	1981–1982
	George P. Shultz	1982–1989

The George H. W. Bush Administration (1989–1993)

Vice President	J. Danforth Quayle	1989–1993
Secretary of State	James A. Baker III	1989–1992
	Lawrence S. Eagleburger	1992–1993

The Clinton Administration (1993–2001)

Vice President	Albert Gore	1993–2001
Secretary of State	Warren M. Christopher	1993–1997
	Madeleine K. Albright	1997–2001

The George W. Bush Administration (2001–)

Vice President	Dick Cheney	2001–
Secretary of State	Colin Powell	2001–

SUPREME COURT JUSTICES

Name	Service	Appointed by	Name	Service	Appointed by
John Jay*	1789–1795	Washington	Henry B. Livingston	1806–1823	Jefferson
James Wilson	1789–1798	Washington	Thomas Todd	1807–1826	Jefferson
John Blair	1789–1796	Washington	Gabriel Duval	1811–1836	Madison
John Rutledge	1790–1791	Washington	Joseph Story	1811–1845	Madison
William Cushing	1790–1810	Washington	Smith Thompson	1823–1843	Monroe
James Iredell	1790–1799	Washington	Robert Trimble	1826–1828	J. Q. Adams
Thomas Johnson	1791–1793	Washington	John McLean	1829–1861	Jackson
William Paterson	1793–1806	Washington	Henry Baldwin	1830–1844	Jackson
John Rutledge†	1795	Washington	James M. Wayne	1835–1867	Jackson
Samuel Chase	1796–1811	Washington	**Roger B. Taney**	1836–1864	Jackson
Oliver Ellsworth	1796–1799	Washington	Philip P. Barbour	1836–1841	Jackson
Bushrod Washington	1798–1829	J. Adams	John Catron	1837–1865	Van Buren
Alfred Moore	1799–1804	J. Adams	John McKinley	1837–1852	Van Buren
John Marshall	1801–1835	J. Adams	Peter V. Daniel	1841–1860	Van Buren
William Johnson	1804–1834	Jefferson	Samuel Nelson	1845–1872	Tyler
			Levi Woodbury	1845–1851	Polk
			Robert C. Grier	1846–1870	Polk
			Benjamin R. Curtis	1851–1857	Fillmore
			John A. Campbell	1853–1861	Pierce

*Chief Justices appear in bold type.
†Acting Chief Justice; Senate refused to confirm appointment.

SUPREME COURT JUSTICES

Name	Service	Appointed by	Name	Service	Appointed by
Nathan Clifford	1858–1881	Buchanan	Owen J. Roberts	1930–1945	Hoover
Noah H. Swayne	1862–1881	Lincoln	Benjamin N. Cardozo	1932–1938	Hoover
Samuel F. Miller	1862–1890	Lincoln	Hugo L. Black	1937–1971	F. Roosevelt
David Davis	1862–1877	Lincoln	Stanley F. Reed	1938–1957	F. Roosevelt
Stephen J. Field	1863–1897	Lincoln	Felix Frankfurter	1939–1962	F. Roosevelt
Salmon P. Chase	1864–1873	Lincoln	William O. Douglas	1939–1975	F. Roosevelt
William Strong	1870–1880	Grant	Frank Murphy	1940–1949	F. Roosevelt
Joseph P. Bradley	1870–1892	Grant	**Harlan F. Stone**	1941–1946	F. Roosevelt
Ward Hunt	1873–1882	Grant	James F. Byrnes	1941–1942	F. Roosevelt
Morrison R. Waite	1874–1888	Grant	Robert H. Jackson	1941–1954	F. Roosevelt
John M. Harlan	1877–1911	Hayes	Wiley B. Rutledge	1943–1949	F. Roosevelt
William B. Woods	1880–1887	Hayes	Harold H. Burton	1945–1958	Truman
Stanley Matthews	1881–1889	Garfield	**Frederick M. Vinson**	1946–1953	Truman
Horace Gray	1882–1902	Arthur	Tom C. Clark	1949–1967	Truman
Samuel Blatchford	1882–1893	Arthur	Sherman Minton	1949–1956	Truman
Lucious Q. C. Lamar	1888–1893	Cleveland	**Earl Warren**	1953–1969	Eisenhower
Melville W. Fuller	1888–1910	Cleveland	John Marshall Harlan	1955–1971	Eisenhower
David J. Brewer	1889–1910	B. Harrison	William J. Brennan Jr.	1956–1990	Eisenhower
Henry B. Brown	1890–1906	B. Harrison	Charles E. Whittaker	1957–1962	Eisenhower
George Shiras	1892–1903	B. Harrison	Potter Stewart	1958–1981	Eisenhower
Howell E. Jackson	1893–1895	B. Harrison	Byron R. White	1962–1993	Kennedy
Edward D. White	1894–1910	Cleveland	Arthur J. Goldberg	1962–1965	Kennedy
Rufus W. Peckham	1896–1909	Cleveland	Abe Fortas	1965–1969	L. Johnson
Joseph McKenna	1898–1925	McKinley	Thurgood Marshall	1967–1991	L. Johnson
Oliver W. Holmes	1902–1932	T. Roosevelt	**Warren E. Burger**	1969–1986	Nixon
William R. Day	1903–1922	T. Roosevelt	Harry A. Blackmun	1970–1994	Nixon
William H. Moody	1906–1910	T. Roosevelt	Lewis F. Powell Jr.	1972–1988	Nixon
Horace H. Lurton	1910–1914	Taft	William H. Rehnquist	1972–1986	Nixon
Charles E. Hughes	1910–1916	Taft	John Paul Stevens	1975–	Ford
Willis Van Devanter	1910–1937	Taft	Sandra Day O'Connor	1981–	Reagan
Joseph R. Lamar	1911–1916	Taft	**William H. Rehnquist**	1986–	Reagan
Edward D. White	1910–1921	Taft	Antonin Scalia	1986–	Reagan
Mahlon Pitney	1912–1922	Taft	Anthony M. Kennedy	1988–	Reagan
James C. McReynolds	1914–1941	Wilson	David H. Souter	1990–	Bush
Louis D. Brandeis	1916–1939	Wilson	Clarence Thomas	1991–	Bush
John H. Clarke	1916–1922	Wilson	Ruth Bader Ginsburg	1993–	Clinton
William H. Taft	1921–1930	Harding	Stephen Breyer	1994–	Clinton
George Sutherland	1922–1938	Harding			
Pierce Butler	1923–1939	Harding			
Edward T. Sanford	1923–1930	Harding			
Harlan F. Stone	1925–1941	Coolidge			
Charles E. Hughes	1930–1941	Hoover			

Federal Spending and the Economy, 1790–1998

Year	Gross National Product (in billions)	Foreign Trade (in millions) Exports	Imports	Federal Budget (in billions)	Federal Surplus/Deficit (in billions)	Federal Debt (in billions)
1790	NA	20	23	0.004	0.00015	0.076
1800	NA	71	91	0.011	0.0006	0.083
1810	NA	67	85	0.008	0.0012	0.053
1820	NA	70	74	0.018	−0.0004	0.091
1830	NA	74	71	0.015	0.100	0.049
1840	NA	132	107	0.024	−0.005	0.004
1850	NA	152	178	0.040	0.004	0.064
1860	NA	400	362	0.063	−0.01	0.065
1870	7.4	451	462	0.310	0.10	2.4
1880	11.2	853	761	0.268	0.07	2.1
1890	13.1	910	823	0.318	0.09	1.2
1900	18.7	1,499	930	0.521	0.05	1.2
1910	35.3	1,919	1,646	0.694	−0.02	1.1
1920	91.5	8,664	5,784	6.357	0.3	24.3
1930	90.4	4,013	3,500	3.320	0.7	16.3
1940	99.7	4,030	7,433	9.6	−2.7	43.0
1950	284.8	10,816	9,125	43.1	−2.2	257.4
1960	503.7	19,600	15,046	92.2	0.3	286.3
1970	977.1	42,700	40,189	195.6	−2.8	371.0
1980	2,631.7	220,600	244,871	590.9	−73.8	907.7
1990	5,764.9	393,600	495,300	1,253.2	−221.2	3,266.1
1998	8,490.5	682,100	911,900	1,652.5	69.2	5,555.5

Source: Historical Statistics of the U.S., Colonial Times to 1970 (1975), Statistical Abstract of the U.S., 1996 (1996), and Statistical Abstract of the U.S., 1999 (1999).

Population Growth, 1630–2000

Year	Population	Percent Increase	Year	Population	Percent Increase
1630	4,600	—	1820	9,638,453	33.1
1640	26,600	473.3	1830	12,866,020	33.5
1650	50,400	89.1	1840	17,069,453	32.7
1660	75,100	49.0	1850	23,191,876	35.9
1670	111,900	49.1	1860	31,443,321	35.6
1680	151,500	35.4	1870	39,818,449	26.6
1690	210,400	38.9	1880	50,155,783	26.0
1700	250,900	19.3	1890	62,947,714	25.5
1710	331,700	32.2	1900	75,994,575	20.7
1720	466,200	40.5	1910	91,972,266	21.0
1730	629,400	35.0	1920	105,710,620	14.9
1740	905,600	43.9	1930	122,775,046	16.1
1750	1,170,800	30.0	1940	131,669,275	7.2
1760	1,593,600	36.1	1950	150,697,361	14.5
1770	2,148,100	34.8	1960	179,323,175	19.0
1780	2,780,400	29.4	1970	203,302,031	13.4
1790	3,929,214	41.3	1980	226,542,199	11.4
1800	5,308,483	35.1	1990	248,718,301	9.8
1810	7,239,881	36.4	2000	281,421,906	11.0

Source: Historical Statistics of the U.S. (1960), Historical Statistics of the U.S., Colonial Times to 1970 (1975), Statistical Abstract of the U.S., 1996 (1996), and United States Census, 2000 (2000).

THE AMERICAN ECONOMY

Birthrate, 1820–2000

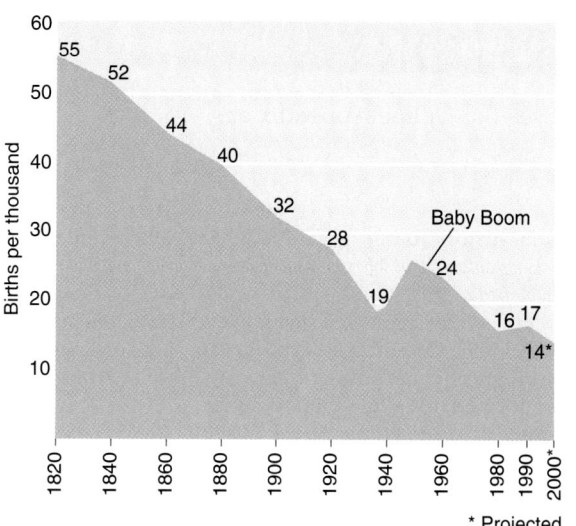

Source: Data from *Historical Statistics of the U.S., Colonial Times to 1970* (1975) and *Statistical Abstract of the U.S., 1996* (1996).

Life Expectancy, 1900–2000

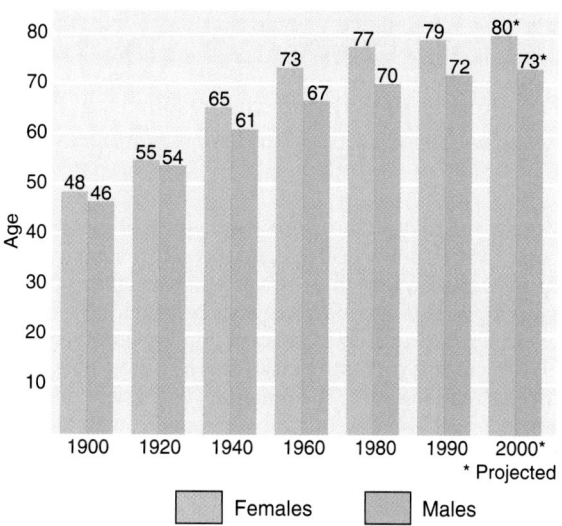

Source: *Historical Statistics of the U.S., Colonial Times to 1970* (1975) and *Statistical Abstract of the U.S., 1996* (1996).

Major Trends in Immigration, 1820–1998

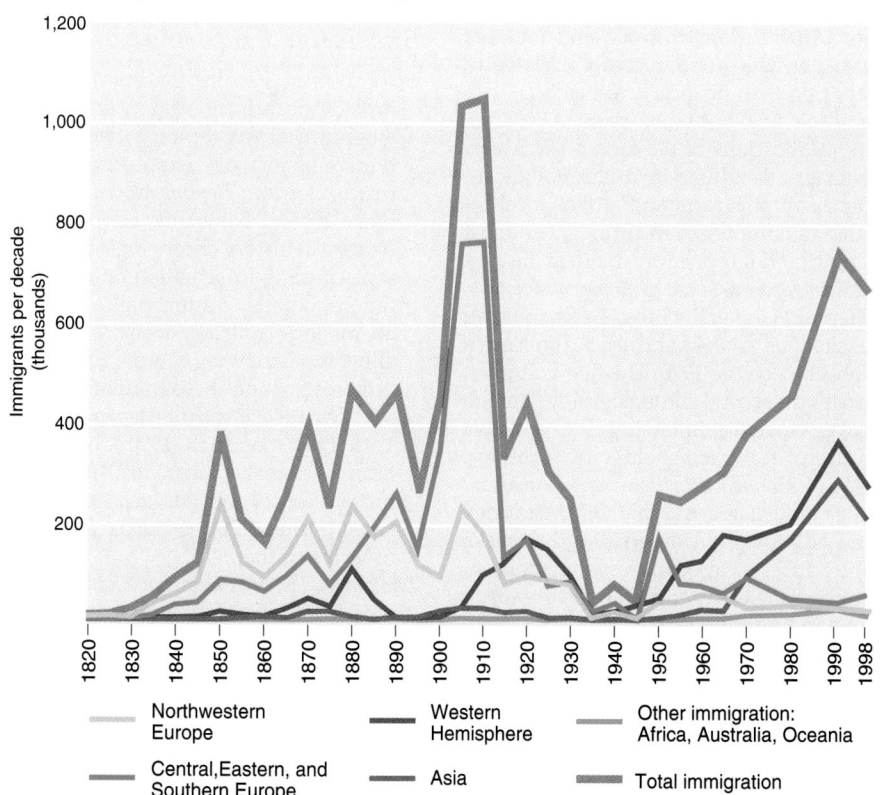

Source: *Historical Statistics of the U.S., Colonial Times to 1970* (1975) and *Statistical Abstract of the U.S., 1999* (1999).

Appendix III. RESEARCH RESOURCES IN U.S. HISTORY

For direct links to the internet resources in this appendix see the Online Appendix at www.bedfordstmartins.com/roarkcompact.

WHILE DOING RESEARCH IN HISTORY, you will use the library to track down primary and secondary sources and to answer questions that arise as you learn more about your topic. This appendix suggests helpful indexes, references, periodicals, and sources of primary documents. It also offers an overview of electronic resources available through the Internet. The materials listed here are not carried at all libraries, but they will give you an idea of the range of sources available. Remember, too, that librarians are an extremely helpful resource. They can direct you to useful materials throughout your research process.

Bibliographies and Indexes

American Historical Association Guide to Historical Literature. 3rd ed. New York: Oxford University Press, 1995. Offers 27,000 citations to important historical literature, arranged in forty-eight sections covering theory, international history, and regional history. An indispensable guide recently updated to include current trends in historical research.

American History and Life. Santa Barbara: ABC-Clio, 1964–. Covers publications of all sorts on U.S. and Canadian history and culture in a chronological/regional format, with abstracts and alphabetical indexes. Available in computerized format. The most complete ongoing bibliography for American history.

Freidel, Frank Burt. *Harvard Guide to American History.* Cambridge: Harvard University Press, Belknap Press, 1974. Provides citations to books and articles on American history published before 1970. The first volume is arranged topically, the second chronologically. Though it does not cover current scholarship, it is a classic and remains useful for tracing older publications.

Prucha, Francis Paul. *Handbook for Research in American History: A Guide to Bibliographies and Other Reference Works.* 2nd rev. ed. Lincoln: University of Nebraska Press, 1994. Introduces a variety of research tools, including electronic ones. A good source to consult when planning an in-depth research project.

General Overviews

Dictionary of American Biography. New York: Scribner's, 1928–1937, with supplements. Gives substantial biographies of prominent Americans in history.

Dictionary of American History. New York: Scribner's, 1976. An encyclopedia of terms, places, and concepts in U.S. history; other more specialized sets include the *Encyclopedia of North American Colonies* and the *Encyclopedia of the Confederacy.*

Dictionary of Concepts in History. New York: Greenwood, 1986. Contains essays defining concepts in historiography and describing how the concepts were formed; excellent bibliographies.

Encyclopedia of American Social History. New York: Scribner's, 1993. Surveys topics such as religion, class, gender, race, popular culture, regionalism, and everyday life from pre-Columbian to modern times.

Encyclopedia of the United States in the Twentieth Century. New York: Scribner's, 1996. An ambitious overview of American cultural, social, and intellectual history in broad articles arranged topically. Each article is followed by a thorough and very useful bibliography for further research.

Specialized Information

Black Women in America: An Historical Encyclopedia. Brooklyn: Carlson, 1993. A scholarly compilation of biographical and topical articles that constitute a definitive history of African American women.

Carruth, Gordon. *The Encyclopedia of American Facts and Dates.* 10th ed. New York: HarperCollins, 1997. Covers American history chronologically from 986 to the present, offering information on treaties, battles, explorations, popular culture, philosophy, literature, and so on, mixing significant events with telling trivia. Tables allow for reviewing a year from a variety of angles. A thorough index helps pinpoint specific facts in time.

Cook, Chris. *Dictionary of Historical Terms.* 2nd ed. New York: Peter Bendrick, 1990. Covers a wide variety of terms—events, places, institutions, and topics—in history for all periods and places in a remarkably small package. A good place for quick identification of terms in the field.

Dictionary of Afro-American Slavery. New York: Greenwood, 1985. Surveys important people, events, and topics, with useful bibliographies; similar works include *Dictionary of the Vietnam War*, *Historical Dictionary of the New Deal*, and *Historical Dictionary of the Progressive Era.*

Knappman-Frost, Elizabeth. *The ABC-Clio Companion to Women's Progress in America.* Santa Barbara: ABC-Clio, 1994. Covers American women who were notable for their time as well as topics and organizations that have been significant in women's quest for equality. Each article is brief; there are a chronology and a bibliography at the back of the book.

United States Bureau of the Census. *Historical Statistics of the United States, Colonial Times to 1970*. Washington, D.C.: Government Printing Office, 1975. Offers vital statistics, economic figures, and social data for the United States. An index at the back helps locate tables by subject. For statistics since 1970, consult the annual *Statistical Abstract of the United States*.

Primary Resources

There are many routes to finding contemporary material for historical research. You may search your library catalog using the name of a prominent historical figure as an author; you may also find anthologies covering particular themes or periods in history. Consider also the following special materials for your research.

THE PRESS

American Periodical Series, 1741–1900. Ann Arbor: University Microfilms, 1946–1979. Microfilm collection of periodicals from the colonial period to the turn of the century. An index identifies periodicals that focused on particular topics.

Herstory Microfilm Collection. Berkeley: Women's History Research Center, 1973. A microfilm collection of alternative feminist periodicals published between 1960 and 1980. Offers an interesting documentary history of the women's movement.

New York Times. New York: New York Times, 1851–. Many libraries have this newspaper on microfilm going back to its beginning in 1851. An index is available to locate specific dates and pages of news stories; it also provides detailed chronologies of events as they were reported in the news.

Readers' Guide to Periodical Literature. New York: Wilson, 1900–. This index to popular magazines started in 1900; an earlier index, *Poole's Index to Periodical Literature*, covers 1802–1906, though it does not provide such thorough indexing.

DIARIES, PAMPHLETS, BOOKS

The American Culture Series. Ann Arbor: University Microfilms, 1941–1974. A microfilm set, with a useful index, featuring books and pamphlets published between 1493 and 1875.

American Women's Diaries. New Canaan: Readex, 1984–. A collection of reproductions of women's diaries. There are different series for different regions of the country.

The March of America Facsimile Series. Ann Arbor: University Microfilms, 1966. A collection of more than ninety facsimiles of travel accounts to the New World published in English or English translation from the fifteenth through the nineteenth century.

Women in America from Colonial Times to the Twentieth Century. New York: Arno, 1974. A collection of reprints of dozens of books written by women describing women's lives and experiences in their own words.

GOVERNMENT DOCUMENTS

Congressional Record. Washington, D.C.: Government Printing Office, 1874–. Covers daily debates and proceedings of Congress. Earlier series were called *Debates and Proceedings in the Congress of the United States* and *The Congressional Globe*.

Foreign Relations of the United States. Washington, D.C.: Department of State, 1861–. A collection of documents from 1861, including diplomatic papers, correspondence, and memoranda, that provides a documentary record of U.S. foreign policy.

Public Papers of the Presidents. Washington, D.C.: Office of the Federal Register, 1957–. Includes major documents issued by the executive branch from the Hoover administration to the present.

Serial Set. Washington, D.C.: Government Printing Office, 1789–1969. A huge collection of congressional documents, available in many libraries on microfiche, with a useful index.

LOCAL HISTORY COLLECTIONS

State and county historical societies often house a wealth of historical documents; consider their resources when planning your research—you may find yourself working with material that no one else has analyzed before.

Internet Resources

The Internet has been a useful place for scholars to communicate and publish information in recent years. Electronic discussion lists, electronic journals, and primary texts are among the resources available for historians. The following sources are good places to find historical information. You can also search the World Wide Web using any of a number of search engines. However, bear in mind that there is no board of editors screening Internet sites for accuracy or usefulness, and the search engines generally rely on free-text searches rather than subject headings. Be critical of all of your sources, particularly those found on the Internet. Note that when this book went to press, the sites listed below were active and maintained.

American Memory: Historical Collections for the National Digital Library Program. <http://rs6.loc.gov/amhome.html> An Internet site that features digitized primary source materials from the Library of Congress, among them African American pamphlets, Civil War photographs, documents from the Continental Congress and the Constitutional Convention of 1774–1790, materials on woman suffrage, and oral histories.

Supreme Court Collection. <http://supct.law.cornell.edu/supct> This database can be used to search for information on various Supreme Court cases. Although the site primarily covers cases that occurred after 1990, there is information on some earlier historic cases. The justices' opinions, as originally written, are also included.

Directory of Scholarly and Professional E-Conferences. <http://kovacs.com/directory> A good place to find out what electronic conversations are going on in a scholarly discipline. Includes a good search facility and instructions on how to connect to e-mail discussion lists, newsgroups, and interactive chat sites with academic content. Once identified, these conferences are good places to raise questions, find out what controversies are currently stirring the profession, and even find out about grants and jobs.

Douglass Archives of American Public Address. <http://douglassarchives.org> An electronic archive of American speeches and documents by a variety of people from Jane Addams to Jonathan Edwards to Theodore Roosevelt.

Historical Text Archive. <http://historicaltextarchive.com> A Web interface for the oldest and largest Internet site for historical documents. Includes sections on Native American, African American, and U.S. history, in which can be found texts of the Declaration of Independence, the U.S. Constitution, the Constitution of Iroquois Nations, World War II surrender documents, photograph collections, and a great deal more. These can be used online or saved as files.

History Links from Yahoo! <http://dir.yahoo.com/Arts/Humanities/History> A categorically arranged and frequently updated site list for all types of history. Some of the sources are more useful than others, but this can be a helpful gateway to some good information.

Index of Civil War Information on the Internet. <http://www.cwc.lsu.edu/cwc/civlink.htm> Compiled by the United States Civil War Center, this index lists everything from diaries to historic battlefields to reenactments.

Index of Native American Resources on the Internet. <http://www.hanksville.org/NAresources> A vast index of Native American resources organized by category. Within the history category, links are organized under subcategories: oral history, written history, geographical areas, timelines, and photographs and photographic archives. A central place to come in the search for information on Native American history.

WWW-VL History Index. <http://www.ukans.edu/history/VL> A vast list of more than 1,700 links to sites of interest to historians, arranged alphabetically by general topic. Some links are to sources for general reference information, but most are on historical topics. A good place to start an exploration of Internet resources.

Internet Resources for Students of Afro-American History and Culture. <http://www.libraries.rutgers.edu/rul/rr_gateway/research_guides/history/afrores.shtml> A good place to begin research on topics in African American history. The site is indexed and linked to a wide variety of sources, including primary documents, text collections, and archival sources on African American history. Individual documents such as slave narratives and petitions, the Fugitive Slave Acts, and speeches by W. E. B. Du Bois, Booker T. Washington, and Martin Luther King Jr. are categorized by century.

The Martin Luther King Jr. Papers Project. <http://www.stanford.edu/group/King> Organized by Stanford University, this site gives information about Martin Luther King Jr. and offers some of his writings.

NativeWeb. <http://www.nativeweb.org> One of the best-organized and most-accessible sites available on Native American issues, *NativeWeb* combines an events calendar and message board with history, statistics, a list of news sources, archives, new and updated related sites each week, and documents. The text is indexed and can be searched by subject, nation, and geographic region.

Perry-Castañeda Library Map Collection. <http://www.lib.utexas.edu/maps/index.html> The University of Texas at Austin library has put over seven hundred United States maps on the Web for viewing by students and professors alike.

Smithsonian Institution. <http://www.si.edu> Organized by subject, such as military history or Hispanic/Latino American resources, this site offers selected links to sites hosted by Smithsonian Institution museums and organizations. Content includes graphics of museum pieces and relevant textual information, book suggestions, maps, and links.

United States History Index. <http://www.ukans.edu history/VL/USA> Maintained by a history professor and arranged by subject, such as women's history, labor history, and agricultural history, this index provides links to a variety of other sites. Although the list is extensive, it does not include a synopsis of each site, which makes finding specific information a time-consuming process.

United States Holocaust Memorial Museum. <http://www.ushmm.org> This site contains information about the Holocaust Museum in Washington, D.C., in particular and the Holocaust in general, and it lists links to related sites.

Women's History Resources. <http://www.mcps.k12.md.us/curriculum/socialstd/Women_Bookmarks.html> An extensive listing of women's history sources available on the Internet. The site indexes resources on subjects as diverse as woman suffrage, women in the workplace, and celebrated women writers. Some of the links are to equally vast indexes, providing an overwhelming wealth of information.

INDEX

A note about the index:

Names of individuals appear in boldface; biographical dates are included for major historical figures.

Letters in parentheses following pages refer to:
(i)   illustrations, including photographs and artifacts, as well as information in picture captions
(f)   figures, including charts and graphs
(m)   maps
(b)   boxed features (such as "Historical Question")

Fulton, Robert (1765–1815), 237, 238

Fundamentalist Protestants, 593, 785, 786

Fundamental Orders of Connecticut, 77

Fur trade, 96, 110–111, 121, 122, 132

Gabriel's rebellion (1800), 213–214

Gadsden, James, 330

Gadsden Purchase (1853), 330, 330(m)

Gage, Thomas (1721–1787), 132, 136, 137, 143

Galloway, Joseph, 133

Galt, Edith, 554

Gama, Vasco de (c. 1460–1524), 26

Garfield, James A. (1831–1881), 458

Garment industry, 475–476

Garner, John "Cactus Jack," 610

Garnet, Henry Highland, 273

Garrison, William Lloyd (1805–1879), 252, 293, 345

Garvey, Marcus (1887–1940), 589–590

Gaspée (ship), burning of (1772), 130

Gates, Horatio (c. 1728–1806), 157(i), 160, 160(m)

GATT (General Agreement on Tariffs and Trade), 809, 824

Gays and lesbians, 688, 689
in the 1980s and 1990s, 795, 796–797(b), 798–799
antidiscrimination laws for, 796–797(b)
during World War II, 653, 656

Geisel, Theodor Seuss (Dr. Seuss), 640(i)

Gender discrimination. See Sex discrimination

Gender relations. See also Women
in 1790s, 192–193
1815–1840, 247
Abigail Adams on, 141
courtship in 1880s–1890s, 482–483
in the early Republic, 225
westward expansion and, 277–278

General Agreement on Tariffs and Trade (GATT), 809, 824

General Court (Massachusetts Bay Colony), 76

General Electric, 454

General Managers Association (GMA), 498

General Motors, 623, 696(i)

Geneva, summit conference in (1955), 704

Gentry, in southern colonies, 103–104

Geography, revolution in, 28

George III, king of England
(r. 1760–1820), 121–122, 127, 146, 154, 159, 162

Georgia, 15, 146, 173, 615
during Civil War, 377
Indians in, 254–256
in late 1770s, 171
ratification of the U.S. Constitution and, 181
reconstruction and, 394, 407
during Revolutionary War, 159
secession of, 394

Gephardt, Richard, 789

German mercenaries (Hessians), 151

Germans (German immigrants), 91, 94–95, 270
Palatine, 157
during World War I, 558

Germany, 507, 530, 532
in the 1930s, 638–641
reunification of (1990), 818
World War I and, 550, 552, 553, 559(i), 563, 565–566
after World War II, 673–674
World War II and, 642, 643–645, 647–649, 659–662, 660(m)
Holocaust, 657–659, 658(i), 658(m)

Geronimo (Apache chief), 427–428

Gettysburg (Pennsylvania), battle of (1863), 375, 375(m)

Ghent, Treaty of (1814), 224

Ghost Dance religion, 427, 428

GI Bill, 684, 685, 708

Gideon v. Wainwright (1963), 728(i), 744

Gifford, Walter, 601

Gilbert, Sir Humphrey, 42

Gilded Age (1870–1895), 443–463

Gilded Age, The (Twain and Warner), 443, 444

Gingrich, Newt, 801

Ginsberg, Allen, 715

Ginsburg, Ruth Bader, 790

Girdler, Tom, 623

Gladden, Washington, 519

Glenn, John H., 752

Globalization (global economy)
American efforts to shape, 823–829
debates over, 824
geographic regions (early twentieth century), 468–470, 470(m)
internationalization of the United States and, 825–828
protests against, 809–810

Glorious Revolution (England), 85

God(s) (deities)
Mexica, 17–19
Native American, 33
Puritan covenant with, 72, 78
Quakers' view of, 78–79, 81
Taino, 22(i), 23

Gold and gold mining, 35, 36(i), 38, 423, 426, 595
California gold rush (1849–1852), 286–287(b)
hydraulic mining, 422–423

Gold, Mike, 472

Gold Diggers (movie), 601

Goldman, Emma (1869–1940), 571

Goldmark, Josephine, 521

Gold rush, California (1849–1852), 286–287(b)

Gold standard, 462, 463, 501

Goldwater, Barry M. (1909–1998), 729, 756

Goliad (Texas), 281

Gompers, Samuel (1850–1924), 483, 484, 486
Clayton Act (1914) and, 537
steelworkers strike and (1919), 570
women workers and, 520–521

Gonzales, Rodolfo "Corky," 741

Good-government movement, 436–437

Good neighbor policy, 639–640

Gorbachev, Mikhail (b. 1931), 817, 818

Gore, Albert, Jr. (b. 1948), 799, 803–805, 805(i)

Gorgas, Josiah, 359

Gospel of Wealth, 456–457

Gould, Jay (1836–1892), 445, 447, 447(i), 484, 494

Gourd fiddle, 311(i)

Government
    under Articles of Confederation,
        169
    big-city (1870–1900), 435–437
    colonial. *See also* Legislatures,
        colonial
        in Pennsylvania, 82
        Puritans and, 76–77
        royal (British) authority, 84–85,
            111
    Governors, colonial, 111
Grady, Henry, 418
Graham, Billy (b. 1918), 712, 713(i),
    715
Grange, the (Patrons of Hus-
    bandry), 461, 493
Grange, Red, 587
Grant, Ulysses S. (1822–1885), 401,
    458
    1868 election and, 405
    1872 election and, 406
    in Civil War, 363, 374, 375, 376(i),
        377, 377(i), 380, 381
    as president, 405–406, 405(i)
    reconstruction and, 399
Grapes of Wrath, The (movie), 601
Grasse, Comte de, 162
Graves, A. J., 247
Gray, Thomas R., 293
Great Awakening, 108–109
Great Basin cultures, 10
Great Britain. *See also* England
    Civil War and, 358, 364
    colonial policies. *See also* Tariffs
        and duties, colonial period
        1700s–1750s, 110, 111
        1760s, 121–130
        Coercive Acts (1774), 132–133
        Proclamation Act of 1763, 122
        resentment of British authority,
            122–123
        Stamp Act (1765), 115, 123–126
        Townshend duties (Revenue
            Act of 1767), 127
    Embargo Act of 1807 and, 219
    French and Indian War
        (1754–1763) and. *See* French
        and Indian War
    impressment of sailors by
        (1807–1812), 218–219
    Jefferson administration and,
        219
    Monroe Doctrine and, 506–507
    Oregon and, 275, 283–284

Revolutionary War and. *See* Revo-
    lutionary War
seizure of American ships by
    (1790s), 200
Texas and, 283
trade. *See* Trade, colonial period
War of 1812, 223–225, 224(i)
woman suffrage in, 540
World War I and, 550, 552, 553,
    563
World War II and, 642, 644, 648
Great Compromise, 179
Great Crash of 1929, 596–597
Great Depression (1930s), 598–603.
    See also New Deal
    denial and escape as response to,
        600–601
    human toll of, 598–600
    working-class militancy and,
        602–603
Great Gatsby, The (Fitzgerald), 596
Great Northern Railroad, 446
Great Plains, 32–33, 421, 424
Great Plains peoples, 8–10, 15
Great Railroad Strike (1877),
    467–468, 468(m), 469(i)
Great Society programs, 727,
    729–730, 762
Great Southwestern Strike (1886),
    494
Great White Fleet (1907–1909), 532
Greece, 675, 678
Greeley, Horace (1811–1872), 359,
    406, 430
Green, William, 602
Greenback Labor Party, 493
Greenbacks, 372
Green Berets, 753, 755
Greene, Nathaniel, 160(m)
Greenpeace, 779
Greenville, Treaty of (1795), 198
Grenada, 1983 invasion of, 816
Grenville, George (1712–1770),
    122–124
Grey, Edward, 552
Grider, Nancy Miller, 412(i)
Grimké, Angelina (1805–1879),
    253
Grimké, Sarah (1792–1873), 253
Grinnell, Julius S., 485–486
Griswold, Roger, 203(i)
Guadalupe Hidalgo, Treaty of
    (1848), 286, 290
Guadeloupe, 118, 120, 122

Guam, 508, 512, 647
Guerrilla warfare, in Revolutionary
    War, 161–162
Guiteau, Charles, 458
Gulf of Tonkin Resolution (1964),
    756, 765
Gulf War (1991), 819–821, 821(i)
Gun ownership, during Revolution-
    ary War, 149
Guthrie, Woody, 601
Gutierrez, José Angel, 741

Haight-Ashbury district (San Fran-
    cisco), 742–743
Haiti, 550, 639
    1994 intervention in, 822
Haitian Revolution (1790–1804),
    200–201, 200(m), 213
Halfway Covenant, 78
Hallidie, Andrew Smith, 438
Hamer, Fannie Lou (1917–1977),
    723, 724, 724(i), 738
Hamilton, Alexander (1755–1804),
    167, 178, 184, 194(i)
    1796 election and, 202
    1800 election and, 213
    duel with Burr (1804), 218,
        220–221(b), 221(i)
    The Federalist essays, 185
    Jefferson as president and, 214
    ratification of the U.S. Constitu-
        tion and, 185
    on religion, 182
    as secretary of the Treasury, 191,
        193–197
Hancock, John (1737–1793), 125(i),
    137
Hancock, Winfield Scott
    (1824–1886), 458
Hanna, Marcus Alonzo (Mark)
    (1837–1904), 502, 507, 523,
    524
Harding, Warren Gamaliel
    (1865–1923), 575, 577, 581,
    582
Harlan County (Kentucky) strike
    (1931), 602, 602(m)
Harlem Renaissance, 590, 590(i)
Harpers Ferry (Virginia), raid on
    (1859), 321
    aftermath of, 343–346
Harrington, Michael, 726
Harris, David Golightly, 387, 400,
    403

WASHINGTON
Olympia Seattle
▲ Mt. Rainier
(14,410 ft.; 4,392 m)
Mt. St. Helens
(8,366 ft.; 2,550 m) ▲
Portland
Salem
Eugene
OREGON

COAST RANGES
CASCADE MTS.
Columbia River

Helena
MONTANA
Missouri River
Yellowstone River
Billings

NORTH DAKOTA
Bismarck

Boise
IDAHO
Snake River

WYOMING

ROCKY

SOUTH DAKOTA
Pierre
GREAT
BLACK HILLS
NEBRASKA

Carson City
Sacramento
San Francisco Oakland
San Jose
SIERRA NEVADA
Sacramento River

GREAT
SALT
Lake
Great Salt Lake
Salt Lake City

GREAT
BASIN
NEVADA
UTAH

COLORADO
Cheyenne
Denver
Mt. Elbert
(14,433 ft.; 4,399 m) ▲
Pikes Peak
(14,110 ft.; 4,301 m) ▲
Colorado Springs
Arkansas River

PLAINS
KANS

PACIFIC OCEAN

Fresno
San Joaquin River
▲ Mt. Whitney
(14,494ft.; 4,418 m)
CALIFORNIA

Las Vegas

Los Angeles

San Diego

N
W   E
S

0   150   300 miles
0   150   300 kilometers

ARIZONA

Phoenix

MOUNTAINS

Santa Fe
Albuquerque
NEW MEXICO

Tucson

Pecos River
Rio Grande

Lubbock

San Anto

Colorado River

TEXAS

El Paso

MEXICO

ARCTIC OCEAN
RUSSIA
BROOKS RANGE
ALASKA
Mt. McKinley
(20,320 ft.; 6,194 m) ▲
ALASKA RANGE
Yukon River
CANADA
Anchorage
Bering Sea
Gulf of Alaska
Juneau
ALEUTIAN ISLANDS

0   250   500 miles
0   250   500 kilometers

Kauai
Niihau
Honolulu Oahu
HAWAII
Molokai
Lanai   Maui
Kahoolawe
PACIFIC OCEAN
Hawaii

0   50   100 miles
0   50   100 kilometers

PINOLE VALLEY HIGH SCHOOL

BOOK NUMBER

STUDENT	Date Rec'd	Condition	Issued By	Date Returned
Victor Faria	5-05	New	Behonek)	
MORGAN Spiller		New		

PRENTICE HALL
LITERATURE

Timeless Voices, Timeless Themes

GOLD LEVEL

Prentice
Hall

Upper Saddle River, New Jersey

Glenview, Illinois

Needham, Massachusetts

ISBN 0-13-054805-7

6 7 8 9 10   08 07 06 05 04

PRENTICE HALL
LITERATURE
Timeless Voices, Timeless Themes

Copper

Bronze

Silver

Gold

Platinum

The American Experience

The British Tradition

Cover: *The Fog Warning,* 1885, oil on canvas, Winslow Homer, Courtesy, Museum of Fine Arts, Boston.

ACKNOWLEDGMENTS

Grateful acknowledgment is made to the following for copyrighted material:

The Estate of Margaret Walker Alexander and the University of Georgia Press "Memory" from *For My People* by Margaret Walker. Copyright 1942 Yale University Press. Used by permission of the University of Georgia Press.

American Library Association From "Books and Bytes: Digital Connections. Passing Time in Times Past" by Virginia A. Walker, from *Book Links (Connecting Books, Libraries, and Classrooms),* May 1999, Volume 8, No. 5. used by permission. Copyright © 1999 by the American Library Association. Used by permission.

Arcade Publishing, Inc. "Make up your mind snail!" reprinted from *Haiku: This Other World,* by Richard Wright. Published by Arcade Publishing, New York, New York. Copyright © 1998 by Ellen Wright. Used by permission.

Arte Público Press "The Harvest" by Tomás Rivera is reprinted with permission from the publisher of *La Cosecha* (Houston: Arte Público Press—University of Houston, 1989).

Atlantic Monthly Press Book jacket copy for *In These Girls, Hope Is a Muscle,* book written by Madeleine Blais, copyright 1995 by Madeleine Blais. Reprinted by permission of Atlantic Monthly Press.

Bantam Books, A Division of Random House, Inc. "One Ordinary Day, With Peanuts," excerpts from *Just*

an Ordinary Day: The Uncollected Stories by Shirley Jackson. Copyright © 1997 by The Estate of Shirley Jackson. Used by permission of Bantam Books, a division of Random House, Inc.

Susan Bergholz Literary Services From "A Celebration of Grandfathers." Copyright © 1983 by Rudolfo Anaya. First published in *New Mexico Magazine,* March 1983. "Julia Alvarez's Aha Moment" by Julia Alvarez. Copyright © 2000 by Julia Alvarez. First published in *O, The Oprah Magazine* 1, No. 5 (November 2000). "Woman's Work" from *Homecoming* by Julia Alvarez. Copyright © 1984, 1996 by Julia Alvarez. Published by Plume, an imprint of Dutton Signet, a division of Penguin Books USA, Inc.; originally published by Grove Press. Reprinted by permission of Susan Bergholz Literary Services, New York. All rights reserved.

Brandt & Hochman Literary Agents, Inc. "The Most Dangerous Game" by Richard Connell. Copyright, 1924 by Richard Connell. Copyright renewed © 1952 by Louise Fox Connell. "Sonata for Harp and Bicycle" from *The Green Flash* by Joan Aiken. Copyright © 1957, 1958, 1959, 1960, 1965, 1968, 1969, 1971 by Joan Aiken. Reprinted by permission of Brandt & Hochman Literary Agents, Inc.

(Acknowledgments continue on page R43, which constitutes an extension of this copyright page.)

CONTRIBUTING AUTHORS

The contributing authors guided the direction and philosophy of *Prentice Hall Literature: Timeless Voices, Timeless Themes*. Working with the development team, they helped to build the pedagogical integrity of the program and to ensure its relevance for today's teachers and students.

Kate Kinsella

Kate Kinsella, Ed.D., is a faculty member in the Department of Secondary Education at San Francisco State University. A specialist in second-language acquisition and adolescent reading and writing, she teaches coursework addressing language and literacy development across the secondary curricula. She has taught high-school ESL and directed SFSU's *Intensive English Program* for first-generation bilingual college students. She maintains secondary classroom involvement by teaching an academic literacy class for second-language learners through the University's *Step to College* partnership program. A former Fulbright lecturer and perennial institute leader for TESOL, the California Reading Association, and the California League of Middle Schools, Dr. Kinsella provides professional development nationally on topics ranging from learning-style enhancement to second-language reading. Her scholarship has been published in journals such as the *TESOL Journal,* the *CATESOL Journal,* and the *Social Studies Review.* Dr. Kinsella earned her M.A. in TESOL from San Francisco State University and her Ed.D. in Second Language Acquisition from the University of San Francisco.

Kevin Feldman

Kevin Feldman, Ed.D., is the Director of Reading and Early Intervention with the Sonoma County Office of Education (SCOE). His career in education spans thirty-one years. As the Director of Reading and Early Intervention for SCOE, he develops, organizes, and monitors programs related to K–12 literacy and prevention of reading difficulties. He also serves as a Leadership Team Consultant to the California Reading and Literature Project and assists in the development and implementation of K–12 programs throughout California. Dr. Feldman earned his undergraduate degree in Psychology from Washington State University and has a Master's degree in Special Education, Learning Disabilities, and Instructional Design from U.C. Riverside. He earned his Ed.D. in Curriculum and Instruction from the University of San Francisco.

Colleen Shea Stump

Colleen Shea Stump, Ph.D., is a Special Education supervisor in the area of Resource and Inclusion for Seattle Public Schools. She served as a professor and chairperson for the Department of Special Education at San Francisco State University. She continues as a lead consultant in the area of collaboration for the California State Improvement Grant and travels the state of California providing professional development training in the areas of collaboration, content literacy instruction, and inclusive instruction. Dr. Stump earned her doctorate at the University of Washington, her M.A. in Special Education from the University of New Mexico, and her B.S. in Elementary Education from the University of Wisconsin–Eau Claire.

Joyce Armstrong Carroll

In her forty-year career, Joyce Armstrong Carroll, Ed.D., has taught on every grade level from primary to graduate school. In the past twenty years, she has trained teachers in the teaching of writing. A nationally known consultant, she has served as president of TCTE and on NCTE's Commission on Composition. More than fifty of her articles have appeared in journals such as *Curriculum Review, English Journal, Media & Methods, Southwest Philosophical Studies, English in Texas,* and the *Florida English Journal.* With Edward E. Wilson, Dr. Carroll co-authored *Acts of Teaching: How to Teach Writing* and co-edited *Poetry After Lunch: Poetry to Read Aloud.* She co-directs the New Jersey Writing Project in Texas.

Edward E. Wilson

A former editor of *English in Texas,* Edward E. Wilson has served as a high-school English teacher and a writing consultant in school districts nationwide. Wilson has served on both the Texas Teacher Professional Practices Commission and NCTE's Commission on Composition. Wilson's poetry appears in Paul Janeczko's anthology *The Music of What Happens.* With Dr. Carroll, he co-wrote *Acts of Teaching: How to Teach Writing* and co-edited *Poetry After Lunch: Poetry to Read Aloud.* Wilson co-directs the New Jersey Writing Project in Texas.

CALIFORNIA PROGRAM ADVISORS

The California program advisors provided ongoing input throughout the development of *Prentice Hall Literature: Timeless Voices, Timeless Themes*. Their valuable insights ensure that the perspectives of the teachers throughout California are represented within this literature series.

Dawn Akuna
Teacher of Reading
Harriet Eddy Middle
  School
Elk Grove, CA

Kathy Allen
English Language Arts
  Teacher
Palos Verdes
  Intermediate School
Palos Verdes, CA

Maxine K. Bigler
Associate Director,
  Region II, Migrant
  Education, Butte
  County Office of
  Education
Chico, CA

Cathy Cirimele
Teacher of English
Bullard High School
Fresno, CA

Jesse L. Culbert
English Teacher
Willowbrook Middle
  School
Compton, CA

Terry Day
English and Speech
  Teacher
Downey High School
Modesto, CA

Yvonne Divans-Hutchinson
Language Arts Teacher
King/Drew Magnet High
  School of Medicine
  and Science
Los Angeles, CA

Diane Erickson
Teacher of English
Oxford Academy
Cypress, CA

Cynthia Hardy Gayle
Assistant Principal
Rancho del Rey Middle
  School
Chula Vista, CA

Joe Glover
Language Arts/ELD
  Teacher
Mesa Intermediate
  School
Palmdale, CA

Jeannette Hampton
Literacy Coordinator
  for Sacramento City
  USD, Retired
Fern Bacon Basic
  Middle School
Sacramento, CA

Carleen Hemric
Language Arts Teacher
Pershing Middle School
San Diego, CA

Kimberly Wise Johnson, M.Ed.
English Teacher
Arcade Fundamental
  Middle School
Sacramento, CA

Keith R. Jones
English/Social Studies
  Teacher
Elmhurst Middle School
Oakland, CA

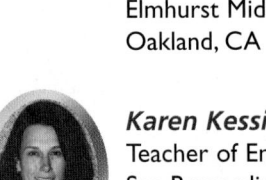
Karen Kessinger
Teacher of English
San Bernardino High
  School
San Bernardino, CA

Gail Catherine Kidd
Language Arts Teacher
Center Middle School
Azusa, CA

Alan J. Leonard
English Instructor,
  Retired
Anaheim, CA

Catherine C. Linn, Ph.D.
Teacher of Literature
  and Writing
Palm Springs High
  School
Palm Springs, CA

Karen Lopez
English Teacher
William S. Hart High
  School
Newhall, CA

Robert Lopez
ELL Instructor
Gage Middle School
Huntington Park, CA

Celia Monge Mana
Language Arts Teacher
Horace Mann Middle
  School
San Francisco, CA

Kathleen Marshall
English Teacher
Stagg High School
Stockton, CA

Peggy P. Moore
Middle School Educator,
  Retired
Bayshore School
  District
Daly City, CA

Akiko Morimoto
Language Arts Teacher
Washington Middle
  School
Vista, CA

Dewhanne Nyivih
Former English Teacher
Marshall Fundamental
  High School
Pasadena, CA

Judith L. O'Brien
Language Arts
  Instructor
Walter Stiern Middle
  School
Bakersfield, CA

Ann Okamura
Teacher of English
Laguna Creek High
  School
Elk Grove, CA

Judy Plouff
Language Arts/Social
  Studies Teacher
Sherman Oaks Center
  for Enriched Studies
Reseda, CA

Jan Reed
English Curriculum
  Specialist, Retired
Garden Grove USD
Garden Grove, CA

Marian Reimann
Assistant Principal,
  Curriculum and
  Instruction
Sutter Middle School
Winnetka, CA

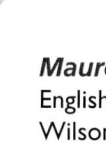

Lynne Richter
Teacher of English
Fulton Middle School
Van Nuys, CA

Maureen Rippee
English Instructor
Wilson High School
Long Beach, CA

Meredith Ritner
Language Arts Teacher
Alieso Viejo Middle
  School
Alieso Viejo, CA

Sharon Schiesl
Language Arts Teacher
Mendez Fundamental
  Intermediate School
Santa Ana, CA

Carol J. Schowalter
Language Arts Teacher
El Roble Middle School
Claremont, CA

Cheryl Spivak
Language Arts/Reading
  Intervention Teacher
Portola Middle School
Tarzana, CA

Peggy Todd Stover
Teacher of English
Independence High
  School
San Jose, CA

Michael C. Sullivan
Language Arts Teacher
Pacifica High School
Garden Grove, CA

Sandra Sullivan
Language Arts Teacher
Garden Grove High
  School
Garden Grove, CA

Vanna Turner
Language Arts Teacher
Albert Einstein Middle
  School
Sacramento, CA

Linda Valdez
English Teacher
Camarillo High School
Camarillo, CA

Sonia Wilson
English Teacher
Steve Garvey Junior
  High School
Lindsay, CA

Mary Jo Wynne
Language Arts/Social
  Studies Teacher
Assumption of the
  Blessed Virgin Mary
  School
Pasadena, CA

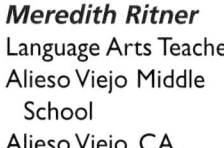

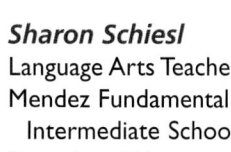

CALIFORNIA GRADE 9 LANGUAGE ARTS STANDARDS

Here is a complete list of the Standards so that you can know what you're expected to learn this year.

READING

1.0 WORD ANALYSIS, FLUENCY, AND SYSTEMATIC VOCABULARY DEVELOPMENT: In this strand of standards, you will use your prior knowledge of word origins to learn the meanings of new words and to use these words correctly.

Vocabulary and Concept Development

1.1 Identify and use the literal and figurative meanings of words and understand word derivations.

Many English words have both literal and figurative meanings. In the 9th grade, you will learn to recognize both kinds of meanings and use them appropriately. You will also develop a deeper understanding of language by learning about the sources, or derivations, of words.	*Example:* **Figurative meaning** "What did we say to each other that now we are as the deer who walk in single file . . ." 　　　—from "Simile," by N. Scott Momaday

1.2 Distinguish between the denotative and connotative meanings of words and interpret the connotative power of words.

Each word has an explicit definition, or denotation; the connotation of a word suggests other, less explicit meanings, or ideas that are associated with the word. You will recognize denotations and connotations, and understand how connotations add to language.	*Example:* **Connotative meaning** "We do not ride on the railroad; it rides upon us." 　　　—from *Walden,* by Henry David Thoreau

1.3 Identify Greek, Roman, and Norse mythology and use the knowledge to understand the origin and meaning of new words (e.g., the word *narcissistic* drawn from the myth of Narcissus and Echo).

Many English words have their origins in classical and other ancient languages. Knowing this mythology can help us understand where the new English words we encounter come from and what they mean.	*Example:* **Greek mythology** **Music:** Drawn from the myth of the Muses, literally "the art of the Muse"

2.0 **READING COMPREHENSION (FOCUS ON INFORMATIONAL MATERIALS):** In this strand, you will study grade-level materials and examine the positions they take on various issues, the arguments they present, and the different ways they are organized. You will also begin working towards the goal of reading two million words a year from a variety of sources.

Structural Features of Informational Materials

2.1 Analyze the structure and format of functional workplace documents, including the graphics and headers, and explain how authors use the features to achieve their purposes.

You will study the kinds of documents used in the workplace, such as reports and memoranda. You will learn why these documents are written and how they use such features as graphics and headers, or labels that tell the reader about the purpose of a block of text.

2.2 Prepare a bibliography of reference materials for a report using a variety of consumer, workplace, and public documents.

A bibliography is a list of information about the sources you use for references in an essay or report. You will prepare and write a bibliography for a report using consumer, workplace, and public documents as sources.	*Example:* **Automobile safety** Network of Employers for Traffic Safety. "Road readiness: NETS 1998 planner." Washington: The Network, 1997.

Comprehension and Analysis of Grade-Level-Appropriate Text

2.3 Generate relevant questions about readings on issues that can be researched.

When you research an issue, you can get more out of readings by asking questions about how the text relates to the issue. You will learn how to think of relevant questions to ask yourself as you research.	*Example:* How have United States companies worked with the government to improve automobile safety?

2.4 Synthesize the content from several sources or works by a single author dealing with a single issue; paraphrase the ideas and connect them to other sources and related topics to demonstrate comprehension.

Another important research skill is synthesizing, or bringing together ideas from a number of different sources. You will synthesize ideas from different texts by the same author by paraphrasing the ideas and connecting them to similar topics.	*Example:* "Overcrowded schools undermine student performance." —from "Standing in the Way," by Bob Herbert ". . . class size reduction in the early grades has many benefits, including higher pupil achievement . . ." —from "Fewer Students, Greater Gains," by Bob Herbert **Synthesis:** Smaller classes would improve student performance.

2.5 Extend ideas presented in primary or secondary sources through original analysis, evaluation, and elaboration.

You will learn how to take the ideas you find in primary and secondary sources and develop them further on your own by examining them, deciding how valuable they are, and working out their details.

Example:
"Let every man make known what kind of government would command his respect, and that will be one step toward obtaining it."
—from "Civil Disobedience,"
by Henry David Thoreau
Thoreau wrote in 1849 that all citizens should speak out about what they think government should be, which is the first step in making government better.

2.6 Demonstrate use of sophisticated learning tools by following technical directions (e.g., those found with graphic calculators and specialized software programs and in access guides to World Wide Web sites on the Internet).

Technical direction—such as the instruction manuals included with graphic calculators or computer software, or the access guides you might find on the Internet—are a sophisticated type of writing that you will show you can understand and use.

Expository Critique

2.7 Critique the logic of functional documents by examining the sequence of information and procedures in anticipation of possible reader misunderstandings.

In documents that present a sequence of instructions or steps, the order in which the information appears can be very confusing to a reader. You will examine these functional documents and decide if the information is presented in a logical order.

Example: Illogical order
1. Turn the main switch to the "on" position to start the projector.
2. Thread the film through the lamp housing to the take-up reel before starting the projector.

2.8 Evaluate the credibility of an author's argument or defense of a claim by critiquing the relationship between generalizations and evidence, the comprehensiveness of evidence, and the way in which the author's intent affects the structure and tone of the text (e.g., in professional journals, editorials, political speeches, primary source material).

In many informational texts, authors make claims or arguments. You will decide how credible or convincing these arguments are by examining the generalizations the authors make and the evidence used to support them, as well as the way the text has been shaped by the author's purpose.

Example:
"The prime myth about the British monarchy is that it is not political. It is intensely and variously political, a huge political fact, . . . a definer of the national image, a load on the national psyche, the focus of feeling and opinion that is itself politically potent."
—from "Blair and the Queen," by Hugo Young, *The Guardian*

3.0   **LITERARY RESPONSE AND ANALYSIS:** In this group of standards, you will read important literary works that are connected to the subjects you will study in history and social science classes. You will respond to these works and examine them in detail, looking for themes and patterns that appear in many different literary works.

Structural Features of Literature

3.1   Articulate the relationship between the expressed purposes and the characteristics of different forms of dramatic literature (e.g., comedy, tragedy, drama, dramatic monologue).

One of the focuses of your reading in the 9th grade will be dramatic literature, such as comedies, tragedies, dramas, and monologues or long speeches. You will explain how the different types of dramatic literature are shaped by their purposes.	*Example*: **Comedy**
	 purpose: to entertain via humor
	 TONY: What was it about [me] that first took your girlish heart?
	 ALICE: The back of your head.
	   —from *You Can't Take it with You,*
	   Moss Hart and George S. Kaufman

3.2   Compare and contrast the presentation of a similar theme or topic across genres to explain how the selection of genre shapes the theme or topic.

A genre is any particular type of literature. You will follow one theme or topic through literary works from different genres, and explain how the theme or topic is affected by each genre.

Narrative Analysis of Grade-Level-Appropriate Text

3.3   Analyze interactions between main and subordinate characters in a literary text (e.g., internal and external conflicts, motivations, relationships, influences) and explain the way those interactions affect the plot.

The plot of a literary work is often affected by the way the main characters interact with less important characters. You will examine those interactions—including conflicts between and within characters, the motives behind characters' actions, and the relationships between characters—and explain how they affect the plot.	*Example*: **External conflict**
	 "Imagine my surprise, nay, my consternation, when, without moving from his privacy, Bartleby, in a singularly mild, firm voice, replied, 'I would prefer not to.'"
	   —from "Bartleby, The Scrivener,"
	   by Herman Melville

3.4   Determine characters' traits by what the characters say about themselves in narration, dialogue, dramatic monologue, and soliloquy.

Sometimes, literary characters talk about themselves as they narrate stories, speak to other characters, or—in dramatic literature—speak directly to the audience. From these examples, you will learn about the qualities characters have.	*Example*: **Dialogue**
	 WILLY: I know it when I walk in. They seem to laugh at me.
	 LINDA: Why? Why would they laugh at you? Don't talk that way, Willy.
	   —from *Death of a Salesman,*
	   by Arthur Miller

3.5   Compare works that express a universal theme and provide evidence to support the ideas expressed in each work.

A universal theme is a central message or idea about life that is expressed by works of literature from many different times and cultures. You will compare different literary works that express the same universal theme, and find examples in each work to support this theme.

Example: **Peace**
"Peace is not an absence of war, it is a virtue, a state of mind, a disposition for benevolence . . ."
　　—Baruch Spinoza
"Is life so dear, or peace so sweet, as to be purchased at the price of chains of slavery?"
　　—from "Speech in the Virginia Convention," by Patrick Henry

3.6   Analyze and trace an author's development of time and sequence, including the use of complex literary devices (e.g., foreshadowing, flashbacks).

You will study how an author creates a sense of the past and the future, and of time passing, in a literary work. The literary devices authors use to achieve this include foreshadowing and flashbacks.

Example: **Flashback**
"The rest of our family, however, felt the full impact of Hitler's anti-Jewish laws [in 1938], so life was filled with anxiety."
　　—from *The Diary of a Young Girl*, by Anne Frank

3.7   Recognize and understand the significance of various literary devices, including figurative language, imagery, allegory, and symbolism, and explain their appeal.

Literary devices are special ways that authors use language to create effects and convey meaning. You will learn about such devices—including figurative or non-literal language, the use of images that appeal to the senses, and the use of elements of a story to symbolize themes or ideas—and explain how they affect a reader.

Example: **Figurative language**
"The story of Wing Biddlebaum is a story of hands. Their restless activity, like unto the beating of the wings of an imprisoned bird, had given him his name."
　　—from "Hands," by Sherwood Anderson

3.8   Interpret and evaluate the impact of ambiguities, subtleties, contradictions, ironies, and incongruities in a text.

Not all works of literature are simple and straightforward. Many have ambiguous or uncertain meanings. They may be very subtle; their elements may seem to contradict one another; their conflicts might be resolved in ironic ways; or they may contain moments that seem puzzling and out of place.

3.9   Explain how voice, persona, and the choice of a narrator affect characterization and the tone, plot, and credibility of a text.

A narrator is the person who tells the story of a literary work; persona and voice describe the qualities of the narrator's voice. You will explain how the decisions an author makes about voice, persona, and narrator affect the tone and plot and credibility of a work.

Example:
"We did not say she was crazy then. We believed she had to do that."
　　—from "A Rose for Emily," by William Faulkner

3.10 Identify and describe the function of dialogue, scene designs, soliloquies, asides, and character foils in dramatic literature.

Dramatic literature includes special types of language, including dialogue between characters, soliloquies a main character might deliver, or asides a character might make to the audience. Drama also features secondary characters who serve as foils for the main characters, as well as set designs.

Example: **Soliloquy**
"Oh, that this too too solid flesh would melt, Thaw, and resolve itself into a dew!"
—from *Hamlet*, by William Shakespeare

Literary Criticism

3.11 Evaluate the aesthetic qualities of style, including the impact of diction and figurative language on tone, mood, and theme, using the terminology of literary criticism. (Aesthetic approach)

In the aesthetic approach to literature, you will use appropriate language to evaluate the style of literary works—including how the choice of words and use of figurative language in a work affect its tone, mood, and themes.

Example:
"No, no, go not to Lethe, neither twist / Wolf's-bane tight-rooted, for its poisonous wine."
—from "Ode on Melancholy," by John Keats

3.12 Analyze the way in which a work of literature is related to the themes and issues of its historical period. (Historical approach)

In the historical approach to literature, you will look closely at a literary work and figure out how its themes and the issues it addresses are connected to the historical period in which it was written.

Example:
"The problem of the twentieth century is the problem of the color line."
—from "To the Nations of the World," by W.E.B. Du Bois

WRITING

1.0 **WRITING STRATEGIES:** In this set of standards, you will write essays that present clear and understandable perspectives and well-constructed, tightly reasoned arguments. Your essays will hold together, stay focused on their topics, and show that you understand your readers and your purpose. You will move through the different steps of the writing process at an appropriate pace.

Organization and Focus

1.1 Establish a controlling impression or coherent thesis that conveys a clear and distinctive perspective on the subject and maintain a consistent tone and focus throughout the piece of writing.

The writing you will do in the 9th grade will establish an impression of the subject or a thesis that clearly presents your original perspective. Your writing will stay focused on the impression or thesis and keep the same tone from beginning to end.

Example: **Thesis**
High schools should expand varsity sports programs because sports are an important part of the educational experience.

1.2   Use precise language, action verbs, sensory details, appropriate modifiers, and the active rather than the passive voice.

In your writing, you will use language that is clear and specific, including verbs that describe actions and the active instead of the passive voice, and details that appeal to the senses.	***Example*: Sensory details** "The play area was bordered by wood-slat benches where old-country people sat cracking roasted watermelon seeds . . ." —from *The Joy Luck CLub*, by Amy Tan

Research and Technology

1.3   Use clear research questions and suitable research methods (e.g., library, electronic media, personal interview) to elicit and present evidence from primary and secondary sources.

To find evidence in primary and secondary sources, you will use clear research questions and such research methods as library research, electronic media, and personal interviews.	***Example*: Research question** How did the lives of women in the western United States in the nineteenth century differ from the lives of women who lived in the East in the same time period?

1.4   Develop the main ideas within the body of the composition through supporting evidence (e.g., scenarios, commonly held beliefs, hypotheses, definitions).

Your essays will have main ideas that you will develop by supporting them with such evidence as scenarios, beliefs that many people share, hypotheses or theories, and definitions of important terms and concepts.	***Example*: Commonly held belief** The common agreement that education is the key to a better life reaches as far back as Aristotle, who wrote, "Education is the best provision for old age."

1.5   Synthesize information from multiple sources and identify complexities and discrepancies in the information and the different perspectives found in each medium (e.g., almanacs, microfiche, news sources, in-depth field studies, speeches, journals, technical documents).

As you conduct your research, you will find information in many different sources, including almanacs, microfiche, news sources, in-depth field studies, journals, and technical documents. To get a full understanding of the topic, you will combine all of the information, taking note of different perspectives they offer.

1.6   Integrate quotations and citations into a written text while maintaining the flow of ideas.

In your research essays, you will fully integrate exact quotes into your writing and include the correct citations, while keeping your essay's ideas flowing smoothly.	***Example*:** "Kate Chopin, *The Atlantic* concluded, was 'a genuine and delightful addition to the ranks of our storytellers.' " —from *Kate Chopin*, by Emily Toth

1.7 Use appropriate conventions for documentation in the text, notes, and bibliographies by adhering to those in style manuals (e.g., Modern Language Association Handbook, The Chicago Manual of Style).

It is very important to document the information you borrow from your sources. The correct methods of documentation of all types can be found in style manuals, like *The Modern Language Association Handbook* and the *Chicago Manual of Style*.

Example: **Bibliography (MLA style)**
Mount, Charles Merrill. *Monet: A Biography.* New York: Simon and Schuster, 1966.

1.8 Design and publish documents by using advanced publishing software and graphic programs.

You will use advanced computer desktop publishing programs for creating graphics to design and create—or publish—documents.

Evaluation and Revision

1.9 Revise writing to improve the logic and coherence of the organization and controlling perspective, the precision of word choice, and the tone by taking into consideration the audience, purpose, and formality of the context.

Revising is an important part of the writing process. As you revise, strengthen the organization and overall perspective of your writing by improving logic and coherence. You will also make your word choice more precise and make your tone more appropriate for your audience, purpose, and context.

Example: **Precision of word choice, formality**
Original: Back in the 1850's and later, things changed a lot for lots of women, especially in New England.
Revised: During the second half of the nineteenth century, the lives of many New England women changed dramatically.

2.0 **WRITING APPLICATIONS (GENRES AND THEIR CHARACTERISTICS):** In this string of standards, you will combine what you have learned writing narratives, expository essays, persuasive essays, and descriptive texts, and use this knowledge to write texts of at least 1,500 words each. Your writing will show that you have mastered standard American English as well as the research, organization, and drafting skills and strategies taught in the previous strand of 9th grade standards.

2.1   Write biographical or autobiographical narratives or short stories: a) Relate a sequence of events and communicate the significance of the events to the audience; b) Locate scenes and incidents in specific places; c) Describe with concrete sensory details the sights, sounds, and smells of a scene and the specific actions, movements, gestures, and feelings of the characters; use interior monologue to depict the characters' feelings; d) Pace the presentation of actions to accommodate changes in time and mood; e) Make effective use of descriptions of appearance, images, shifting perspectives, and sensory details.

In the 9th grade, you will master the writing of biographical or autobiographical narratives or short stories. You will demonstrate the skills of: sequencing events; describing details of place, characterization, and mood; pacing; and shifting perspectives within your narrative.

Example: **Autobiographical narrative**

"That is why, walking across a school campus on this particular December morning, I keep searching the sky. As if I expected to see, rather like hearts, a lost pair of kites hurrying toward heaven."

—from "A Christmas Memory," by Truman Capote

2.2   Write responses to literature: a) Demonstrate a comprehensive grasp of the significant ideas of literary works; b) Support important ideas and viewpoints through accurate and detailed references to the text or to other works; c) Demonstrate awareness of the author's use of stylistic devices and an appreciation of the effects created; d) Identify and assess the impact of perceived ambiguities, nuances, and complexities within the text.

Effective responses to literature show that you understand the important ideas of the literary works you read; support your ideas with accurate and detailed references to literary works; acknowledge the effects the author achieves with stylistic devices; and critique the works' ambiguities, nuances, and complexities.

Example: **Response to literature**

"*Hamlet*, like the sonnets, is full of some stuff that the writer could not drag to light, contemplate, or manipulate into art. And when we search for this feeling, we find it, as in the sonnets, very difficult to localize."

—from "Hamlet," by T. S. Eliot

2.3   Write expository compositions, including analytical essays and research reports: a) Marshal evidence in support of a thesis and related claims, including information on all relevant perspectives; b) Convey information and ideas from primary and secondary sources accurately and coherently; c) Make distinctions between the relative value and significance of specific data, facts, and ideas; d) Include visual aids by employing appropriate technology to organize and record information on charts, maps, and graphs; e) Anticipate and address readers' potential misunderstandings, biases, and expectations; f) Use technical terms and notations accurately.

In expository compositions, including analytical essays and research reports, you will support your theses and claims with relevant, accurate information; show an understanding of the value of each fact and idea; and strive for clarity by using charts, graphs, and correct terms and notations.

2.4 Write persuasive compositions: a) Structure ideas and arguments in a sustained and logical fashion; b) Use specific rhetorical devices to support assertions (e.g., appeal to logic through reasoning; appeal to emotion or ethical belief; relate a personal anecdote, case study, or analogy); c) Clarify and defend positions with precise and relevant evidence, including facts, expert opinions, quotations, and expressions of commonly accepted beliefs and logical reasoning; d) Address readers' concerns, counterclaims, biases, and expectations.

Persuasive compositions feature logically structured ideas and arguments. You will support your argument with rhetorical devices that persuade your readers by appealing to their logic, emotions, and beliefs; defend your position clearly with logical reasoning and precise, relevant evidence; and address expectations or disagreements your readers might have.

Example:
"One may well ask: 'How can you advocate breaking some laws and obeying others?' The answer lies in the fact that there are two types of laws: just and unjust."
—from "Letter from Birmingham Jail," by Martin Luther King, Jr.

2.5 Write business letters: a) Provide clear and purposeful information and address the intended audience appropriately; b) Use appropriate vocabulary, tone, and style to take into account the nature of the relationship with, and the knowledge and interests of, the recipients; c) Highlight central ideas or images; d) Follow a conventional style with page formats, fonts, and spacing that contribute to the documents' readability and impact.

You will learn how to write business letters that provide clear, purposeful information and appropriately address your intended audience. Your writing will reflect suitable vocabulary and tone, focus on a central idea, and follow a standard business style for readability.

Example: Application
I am writing to apply for an internship with your company. My resume and two letters of recommendation are enclosed.

2.6 Write technical documents (e.g., a manual on rules of behavior for conflict resolution, procedures for conducting a meeting, minutes of a meeting): a) Report information and convey ideas logically and correctly; b) Offer detailed and accurate specifications; c) Include scenarios, definitions, and examples to aid comprehension (e.g., troubleshooting guide); d) Anticipate readers' problems, mistakes, and misunderstandings.

In 9th grade, you will write technical documents, like minutes of meetings, that report accurate information and ideas, include definitions and examples, and anticipate any problems readers may encounter.

Example: Minutes of a meeting

Old Business
• <u>October Meeting Minutes:</u> Minutes of last month's meeting were read.

WRITTEN AND ORAL ENGLISH LANGUAGE CONVENTIONS

1.0 **WRITTEN AND ORAL ENGLISH LANGUAGE CONVENTIONS:** In this strand of standards, you will master the conventions of standard English for writing and speaking.

Grammar and Mechanics of Writing

1.1 Identify and correctly use clauses (e.g., main and subordinate), phrases (e.g., gerund, infinitive, and participial), and mechanics of punctuation (e.g., semicolons, colons, ellipses, hyphens).

In the 9th grade, you will show that you recognize and can correctly use clauses and the different types of phrases, as well as such punctuation marks as semicolons, colons, ellipses, and hyphens.	***Example:*** **Clauses** "The translucent walls of childhood no longer close them in, for suddenly they discover the wide gateways and the gates ready to swing open at a touch of a hand." —from *Family*, by Margaret Mead

1.2 Understand sentence construction (e.g., parallel structure, subordination, proper placement of modifiers) and proper English usage (e.g., consistency of verb tenses).

Sentences can be put together using several different strategies, including parallel structure and subordination. You will master these aspects of sentence construction, the proper placement of modifiers, and such English usage conventions as consistent verb tenses.	***Example:*** **Parallel structure, consistency of verb tenses** ". . . we shall fight in the fields and in the streets, we shall fight in the hills; we shall never surrender." —from "Speech on Dunkirk," by Winston Churchill

1.3 Demonstrate an understanding of proper English usage and control of grammar, paragraph and sentence structure, diction, and syntax.

You will also show that you understand English usage, grammar, diction, and syntax, as well as effective sentence and paragraph structures.

Manuscript Form

1.4 Produce legible work that shows accurate spelling and correct use of the conventions of punctuation and capitalization.

At this grade level, the written work you present in class should be legible, including accurate spelling and correct punctuation and grammar.

1.5 Reflect appropriate manuscript requirements, including title page presentation, pagination, spacing and margins, and integration of source and support material (e.g., in-text citation, use of direct quotations, paraphrasing) with appropriate citations.

Your work should also follow appropriate rules for manuscripts, which may include requirements for a title page, page numbering and margins, line spacing, and the use and citing of material borrowed from sources.	***Example:*** **Integration of source (MLA)** In "Barn Burning," an illiterate boy reads the labels of cans with "his stomach . . . from the scarlet devils and the silver curve of fish" (Faulkner 3).

LISTENING AND SPEAKING

1.0   **LISTENING AND SPEAKING STRATEGIES:** In this group of standards, you will make skillful decisions about speaking, such as tailoring your gestures, tone, and vocabulary to suit your audience. Also, you will deliver focused and coherent presentations that clearly convey solid reasoning and your own perspective on the topic.

Comprehension

1.1   **Formulate judgments about the ideas under discussion and support those judgments with convincing evidence.**

In the 9th grade, you will show that you understand ideas being discussed by forming judgments about them and supporting your judgments with convincing evidence.

Example: **Forming judgments**
"[*The Jungle*] is remembered as a stomach-turning exposé of unsanitary conditions and deceitful practices in the meat-packing industry . . . and it contributed enormously to the landmark passage of the Pure Food and Drug Act of 1906."
—from "Introduction to *The Jungle*," by Morris Dickstein

1.2   **Compare and contrast the ways in which media genres (e.g., televised news, newsmagazines, documentaries, online information) cover the same event.**

You will also demonstrate your comprehension of news coverage by comparing and contrasting the way different news media—including television news, newsmagazines, documentaries, and online news sources—report on the same event.

Organization and Delivery of Oral Communication

1.3   **Choose logical patterns of organization (e.g., chronological, topical, cause and effect) to inform and to persuade, by soliciting agreement or action, or to unite audiences behind a common belief or cause.**

At this grade level, you will make oral presentations that inform, persuade, or unite your audience behind one cause or belief. Your presentations will be logically organized, using chronological, topical, and cause-and-effect patterns.

Example: **Speech to unite**
"I shall see our young braves and our chiefs sitting in the houses of law and government, ruling and being ruled by the knowledge and freedoms of *our* great land."
—from "There Is a Longing," by Chief Dan George

1.4   **Choose appropriate techniques for developing the introduction and conclusion (e.g., by using literary quotations, anecdotes, and references to authoritative sources).**

You will develop the introductions and conclusions of your presentations by using appropriate strategies, such as literary quotations, anecdotes, and references to sources.

Example: **Conclusion**
Therefore, if anyone suggests it is a bad idea to get involved in local government, remember Walt Whitman's words: "Political democracy . . . supplies a training school for making first-class men."

1.5 Recognize and use elements of classical speech forms (e.g., introduction, first and second transitions, body, conclusion) in formulating rational arguments and applying the art of persuasion and debate.

Classical speech form includes such elements as the introduction, transitions, the body, and the conclusion. You will recognize these elements, use them to develop rational arguments, and apply them persuasively in debate.

Example: **Introduction**
". . . now standing upon the soil which once was, and now ought to be, the property of this tribe, . . . I would shake you by the hand, and ask you to listen, for a little while, to what I have to say."
— from "Quinney's Speech," by John Wannuaucon Quinney

1.6 Present and advance a clear thesis statement and choose appropriate types of proof (e.g., statistics, testimony, specific instances) that meet standard tests for evidence, including credibility, validity, and relevance.

Your presentations will present clear thesis statements and support them with credible, valid, relevant types of proof, including statistics, testimony from experts, and specific examples.

Example: **Thesis**
"The history of the present king of Great Britain is a history of repeated injuries . . . To prove this, let facts be submitted to a candid world."
— from The Declaration of Independence, by Thomas Jefferson

1.7 Use props, visual aids, graphs, and electronic media to enhance the appeal and accuracy of presentations.

You will make your presentations more appealing and accurate by using props, visual aids like graphs, and electronic media.

Example: **Graphs**

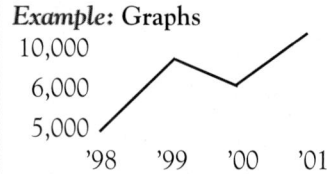

1.8 Produce concise notes for extemporaneous delivery.

At this grade level, you will be expected to deliver oral communications without preparation. You will learn to take concise notes that will help you make these extemporaneous presentations.

Example: **Notes**
1) Introduce topic: Causes of the Civil War
2) List major causes
    A) Conflict over slavery
    B) Industrial North vs. Agricultural South

1.9 Analyze the occasion and the interests of the audience and choose effective verbal and nonverbal techniques (e.g., voice, gestures, eye contact) for presentations.

To make your presentations more effective, you will use techniques—including voice, gestures, and eye contact—that are appropriate for the occasion and your audience.

Example:
For her Speech to the Commonwealth, Britain's Queen Elizabeth elected to wear her formal robes and crown of state to commemorate the annual occasion and the dignitaries in attendance.

Analysis and Evaluation of Oral and Media Communications

1.10 Analyze historically significant speeches (e.g., Abraham Lincoln's "Gettysburg Address," Martin Luther King, Jr.'s "I Have a Dream") to find the rhetorical devices and features that make them memorable.

At this grade level, you will examine and evaluate historic speeches such as Abraham Lincoln's "Gettysburg Address" and Martin Luther King, Jr.'s "I Have a Dream," in order to find out what makes them memorable.

Example: **Rhetorical device: repetition**
". . . that the government of the people, by the people, for the people, shall not perish from the earth."
—from "The Gettysburg Address," by Abraham Lincoln

1.11 Assess how language and delivery affect the mood and tone of the oral communication and make an impact on the audience.

You will also consider the language and delivery of oral communication, evaluating how they make an impact on the audience by affecting mood and tone.

1.12 Evaluate the clarity, quality, effectiveness, and general coherence of a speaker's important points, arguments, evidence, organization of ideas, delivery, diction, and syntax.

You will listen closely to a speaker's argument and evaluate its clarity, quality, effectiveness, and general coherence, paying close attention to the organization of ideas, major points, evidence, delivery, diction, and syntax.

Example: **Clarity of important points**
"If a free society cannot help the many who are poor, it cannot save the few who are rich."
—from "Inaugural Address," by John F. Kennedy

1.13 Analyze the types of arguments used by the speaker, including argument by causation, analogy, authority, emotion, and logic.

You will also analyze the types of argument the speaker uses, including such strategies as cause and effect, making analogies, relying on authorities, appealing to emotions, and the use of logic.

Example: **Argument by emotion**
"I see one-third of a nation ill-housed, ill-clad, ill-nourished."
—from "Second Inaugural Address," by Franklin D. Roosevelt

1.14 Identify the aesthetic effects of a media presentation and evaluate the techniques used to create them (e.g., compare Shakespeare's Henry V with Kenneth Branagh's 1990 film version).

Finally, you will study and evaluate the aesthetic effects media can achieve by comparing how the same presentation changes in different media—for example, by evaluating the effects the medium of film has on a play.

2.0 **SPEAKING APPLICATIONS (GENRES AND THEIR CHARACTERISTICS):** In this set of standards, you will focus on delivering both formal, planned presentations and on-the-spot, unprepared presentations that use traditional rhetorical strategies, such as narration, exposition, persuasion, and description. You will speak with a mastery of standard American English, making use of the skills mastered in the previous group of standards.

2.1 Deliver narrative presentations: a) Narrate a sequence of events and communicate their significance to the audience; b) Locate scenes and incidents in specific places; c) Describe with concrete sensory details the sights, sounds, and smells of a scene and the specific actions, movements, gestures, and feelings of characters; d) Pace the presentation of actions to accommodate time or mood changes.

In grade 9, you will master the narrative presentation, both fictional and autobiographical. You will add in such elements as a standard plot line, character development, concrete details that appeal to the senses, pacing that changes with the time and mood of your narrative, and other elements of story-writing.

Example: **Feelings of a character**
"I hoped then that life might offer me the opportunity to serve my people and make my own humble contribution to their freedom struggle."
—from "I Am Prepared to Die," by Nelson Mandela

2.2 Deliver expository presentations: a) Marshal evidence in support of a thesis and related claims, including information on all relevant perspectives; b) Convey information and ideas from primary and secondary sources accurately and coherently; c) Make distinctions between the relative value and significance of specific data, facts, and ideas; d) Include visual aids by employing appropriate technology to organize and display information on charts, maps, and graphs; e) Anticipate and address the listener's potential misunderstandings, biases, and expectations; f) Use technical terms and notations accurately.

At this grade level, you will deliver expository presentations that present clear theses that are supported with well-organized evidence drawn from every relevant perspective. In addition, you will include informative visual aids, address any problems or expectations your listeners might have, and use all terms correctly.

Example: **Marshalling evidence**
Carbon dioxide is a major contributor to global warming trends. Michael D. Lemonick states, in his article "Life in the Greenhouse," that "humans have increased the concentration of carbon dioxide, the most abundant heat-trapping gas in the atmosphere, to 30% above the pre-industrial levels . . ."

2.3 Apply appropriate interviewing techniques: a) Prepare and ask relevant questions; b) Make notes of responses; c) Use language that conveys maturity, sensitivity, and respect; d) Respond correctly and effectively to questions; e) Demonstrate knowledge of the subject or organization; f) Compile and report responses; g) Evaluate the effectiveness of the interview.

In grade 9, you will learn how to conduct interviews appropriately. You will prepare relevant questions that demonstrate your knowledge of the subject and ask them using mature, sensitive, and respectful language. You will learn how to effectively use your notes to report on the responses and evaluate the interview.

Example: **Ask relevant questions**
"A character in *Things Fall Apart* remarks that the white man 'has put a knife on the things that held us together, and we have fallen apart.' Are those things still severed, or have the wounds begun to heal?"
—from "An African Voice: Interview with Chinua Achebe," by Katie Bacon

2.4 Deliver oral responses to literature: a) Advance a judgment demonstrating a comprehensive grasp of the significant ideas of works or passages (i.e., make and support warranted assertions about the text); b) Support important ideas and viewpoints through accurate and detailed references to the text or to other works; c) Demonstrate awareness of the author's use of stylistic devices and an appreciation of the effects created; d) Identify and assess the impact of perceived ambiguities, nuances, and complexities within the text.

In grade 9, you will learn how to state clearly your thoughts and opinions on a literary work, and support them with the best possible evidence from the text and other texts that deal with your thesis. You will show that you understand the effects the author achieves with stylistic devices; you will also identify and evaluate the works' ambiguities, nuances, and complexities.

Example: **Reference to literary work**
"I am thinking now of what I rate the best one [literary work from the late 1950s]: Salinger's *Catcher in the Rye*, perhaps because this one expresses so completely what I have tried to say: a youth, father to what will, must someday be a man . . ."
—from *Faulkner in the University,* by William Faulkner

2.5 Deliver persuasive arguments (including evaluation and analysis of problems and solutions and causes and effects): a) Structure ideas and arguments in a coherent, logical fashion. b) Use rhetorical devices to support assertions (e.g., by appeal to logic through reasoning; by appeal to emotion or ethical belief; by use of personal anecdote, case study, or analogy). c) Clarify and defend positions with precise and relevant evidence, including facts, expert opinions, quotations, expressions of commonly accepted beliefs, and logical reasoning. d) Anticipate and address the listener's concerns and counterarguments.

In grade 9, you will learn how to construct oral presentations that will help you convince an audience of your position. You will learn how to support your assertions with the best possible evidence, and use verbal and nonverbal strategies to emphasize your message. You will learn how to defend your position clearly with logical reasoning and precise, relevant evidence.

Example: **Rhetorical devices, logic**
"We aren't engaged in any negative protest and in any negative argument with anybody. We are saying that we are determined to be men. We are determined to be people."
—from "I've Been to the Mountaintop," by Martin Luther King, Jr.

2.6 Deliver descriptive presentations: a) Establish clearly the speaker's point of view on the subject of the presentation; b) Establish clearly the speaker's relationship with that subject (e.g., dispassionate observation, personal involvement); c) Use effective, factual descriptions of appearance, concrete images, shifting perspectives and vantage points, and sensory details.

Finally, you will deliver descriptive presentations in which you establish a clear point of view on the subject, clarifying how close to or distant from it you are, describing images and appearances, and shifting perspectives and points of view.

Example: **Description, sensory details**
". . . on a little hill, in a lonely cabin, overspread by the forest oak, I first drew my breath . . ."
—from "An Address to the Whites," by Elias Boudinot

CONTENTS IN BRIEF

Learn About Literature

Themes in Literature

Literary Genres

Resources

Handbooks

Indexes

UNIT 1

THEME: *Spine Tinglers*

Comparing Literary Works

SKILLS WORKSHOPS

THEME: *Challenges and Choices*

UNIT 3

THEME: *Moments of Discovery*

SKILLS WORKSHOPS

UNIT 4

THEME: *The Lighter Side*

UNIT 5

THEME: *Visions of the Future*

SKILLS WORKSHOPS

UNIT 6

GENRE: *Short Stories*

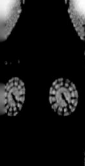

UNIT 7

Genre: *Nonfiction*

Skills Workshops

UNIT 9

GENRE: *Poetry*

(Continued on page xvi.)

UNIT 9

GENRE: *Poetry* (continued)

SKILLS WORKSHOPS

UNIT 10 GENRE: *The Epic*

SKILLS WORKSHOPS

COMPLETE CONTENTS BY GENRE

COMPARING LITERARY WORKS

HOW TO READ LITERATURE

WRITING WORKSHOPS

LISTENING AND SPEAKING WORKSHOPS

ASSESSMENT WORKSHOPS

Learn About Literature

Forms of Literature

Short Story • Nonfiction • Drama • Poetry • Folk Literature

Just as there are different styles of music, such as classical or rock, so too are there different forms of literature. Each is called a genre and has its own distinct characteristics. These pages present a brief explanation and an example of each genre. They will help you understand and appreciate the literature when you read these various works in their entirety.

Short Story

A **short story** is a brief work of fiction. In most short stories, one main character faces a conflict that is resolved in the plot. In addition, a short story usually conveys a theme, or message about life. Good craftsmanship goes into the writing of a good story, which must accomplish its purpose in relatively few words.

● **What do you learn about a character's conflict in this story's opening?**

> She was one of those pretty, charming young women who are born, as if by an error of Fate, into a petty official's family. She had no dowry, no hopes, not the slightest chance of being appreciated, understood, loved, and married by a rich and distinguished man; so she slipped into marriage with a minor civil servant at the Ministry of Education.
>
> FROM "THE NECKLACE," GUY DE MAUPASSANT, P. 608

Nonfiction

Nonfiction is writing that tells about real people, places, objects, events, and ideas. Many of the nonfiction articles in this book are either essays or biographical or autobiographical sketches. All discuss the real world as opposed to an imaginary one. The author of a nonfiction article may wish to convey and explain information, convince readers to accept a particular idea or opinion, or simply entertain and amuse readers.

● **Based on its opening, what do you sense is the author's purpose in this nonfiction article?**

> The essence of childhood, of course, is play, which my friends and I did endlessly on streets that we reluctantly shared with traffic. As a daring receiver in touch football, I spent many happy years running up and down those asphalt fields, hoping that a football would hit me before a Chevrolet did.
>
> FROM "GO DEEP TO THE SEWER," BILL COSBY, P. 368

> *"In the midst of any adventure, a born writer has a desire to hurry home and put it into words."*
>
> —Maxine Hong Kingston

Drama

Drama is written to be performed by actors. The script is made up of dialogue and monologue—the words the actors say—and stage directions, which comment on how and where the action occurs.

● **How does the appearance of this dramatic text differ from the appearance of a short story?**

> **HORACE.** That's a pretty piece.
> **MARY CATHERINE.** Yes, it is.
> [*A pause. They dance again.* HORACE *stops.*]
> **HORACE.** I'm ready to go if you are, Mary Catherine.
> **MARY CATHERINE.** I'm ready. [*They start out.*] Scared?
>
> FROM "THE DANCERS," HORTON FOOTE, P. 734

Poetry

Poetry is literature that appears in verse form. It often has a regular rhythm and, sometimes, a rhyme scheme. Some poems tell a story, while other poems present a single image or express a single emotion or thought. Most poems use concise, musical, and emotionally charged language to convey an idea.

● **How do the lines of poetry below differ in form from the prose paragraphs on the facing page?**

> Some say the world will end in fire,
> Some say in ice.
> From what I've tasted of desire
> I hold with those who favor fire.
>
> FROM "FIRE AND ICE," ROBERT FROST, P. 472

Folk Literature

Folk literature is the unwritten lore of a specific people or culture, passed down through the generations by word of mouth until, at some point, it is put into writing. Folk literature includes myths, folk tales, fairy tales, legends, and fables. Such stories express the hopes, fears, loves, dreams, and values of the people who tell them and pass them on.

● **What does the beginning of this myth indicate about the values of people in ancient Greece?**

> King Acrisius of Argos had only one child, a daughter, Danaë. She was beautiful above all the other women of the land, but this was small comfort to the King for not having a son.
>
> FROM "PERSEUS," EDITH HAMILTON, P. 214

Short Stories

Plot • Characters • Setting • Point of View • Theme

Short stories invite you to travel to fictional places, meet interesting and unusual people, and get involved with the problems they face. This book presents a variety of short stories. No two are exactly the same, although all the stories share certain characteristics and follow a prescribed structure.

Plot

The **plot** of a short story is its sequence of events. It involves both characters and a problem, or conflict. The plot begins with an exposition that introduces the characters, setting, and basic story. The action rises as characters try to resolve the problem. Tension increases as events lead to a climax, or high point of interest or suspense. The climax is followed by falling action, leading to the resolution of the conflict.

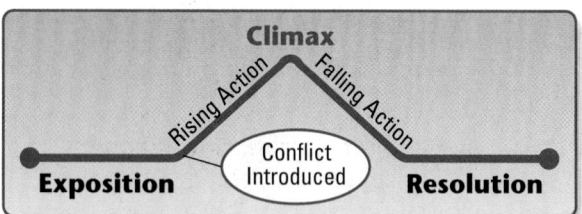

● **Which plot details do you learn from the opening sentence of this short story?**

I had called upon my friend, Mr. Sherlock Holmes, one day in the autumn of last year and found him in deep conversation with a very stout, florid-faced, elderly gentleman with fiery red hair.

FROM "THE RED-HEADED LEAGUE," SIR ARTHUR CONAN DOYLE, P. 96

Characters

The **characters** in a short story are the people or animals who participate in the action. Writers can develop characters in a variety of ways. Details about characters are revealed through their physical description and their words and actions. In addition, writers reveal characters through their interaction with other characters in the story.

● **What do the details in the following passage tell you about Nat's character?**

Nat Hocken, because of a wartime disability, had a pension and did not work full-time at the farm. He worked three days a week, and they gave him the lighter jobs: hedging, thatching, repairs to the farm buildings.

Although he was married, with children, his was a solitary disposition; he liked best to work alone. It pleased him when he was given a bank to build up, or a gate to mend at the far end of the peninsula, where the sea surrounded the farmland on either side. Then, at midday, he would pause and eat the pasty that his wife had baked for him, and, sitting on the cliff's edge, watch the birds.

FROM "THE BIRDS," DAPHNE DU MAURIER, P. 50

> "They ghosted you up a swell story . . ." —Langston Hughes

Setting

The **setting** of a story is the time and place of the action. Time can include not only the historical period—past, present, or future—but also a specific year, season, or time of day. Place may involve not only the geographical place—a region, country, state, or town—but also the social, economic, or cultural environment.

In some stories, setting serves as a decorative but nonessential background. In contrast, the setting of other stories may drive the action by providing a problem that the characters must face and overcome.

● **Which details in this passage help you to identify the setting of the story?**

I belong in Cleveland, Ohio. One winter's night, two years ago, I reached home just after dark, in a driving snowstorm, and the first thing I heard when I entered the house was that my dearest boyhood friend and schoolmate, John B. Hackett, had died the day before, and that his last utterance had been a desire that I would take his remains home to his poor old father and mother in Wisconsin. I was greatly shocked and grieved, but there was no time to waste in emotions; I must start at once.

FROM "THE INVALID'S STORY," MARK TWAIN, P. 596

Point of View

The **point of view** in a story is the vantage point from which the story is told. In *first-person narration*, the storyteller is a character in the action. In *third-person narration*, the story-teller reports events, taking no direct part in the action.

● **Which clues in this sentence indicate the point of view of this short story?**

I was six when my mother taught me the art of invisible strength.

FROM "RULES OF THE GAME," AMY TAN, P. 262

Theme

The **theme** of a short story is the central message or insight into life revealed through the work. In some stories, the theme may be stated directly. In most stories, however, the theme is only implied. You must use the story's events to help you draw conclusions about its theme.

● **Based on the following passage, what might be the theme of this story?**

He also felt the warmth of the earth. He sensed he was inside someone. Then he understood what Don Trine was doing. He was not crazy, he simply liked to feel the earth when it was sleeping.

FROM "THE HARVEST," TOMÁS RIVERA, P. 616

Nonfiction

Autobiography • Biography • Essay • Informational Text

Nonfiction is prose writing that presents and explains ideas or that tells about real people. Among nonfiction forms are essays, newspaper and magazine articles, journals, travelogues, biographies, and autobiographies. In this book, you will read several kinds of nonfiction and have the opportunity to explore the similarities and differences among them.

Autobiography

An **autobiography** is a form of non-fiction in which a person relates his or her own life story. It may tell about the person's whole life or only part of it. The author's purpose may be to explain his or her values, to teach lessons about life, to entertain or amuse readers, or any combination of these.

● What does this passage from Rosa Parks's autobiography suggest about her purpose for writing?

> As I sat there, I tried not to think about what might happen. I knew that anything was possible. I could be manhandled or beaten. I could be arrested. People have asked me if it occurred to me then that I could be the test case the NAACP had been looking for. I did not think about that at all. In fact if I had let myself think too deeply about what might happen to me, I might have gotten off the bus. But I chose to remain.
>
> FROM ROSA PARKS: MY STORY, ROSA PARKS, P. 168

Biography

A **biography** is a form of nonfiction in which a writer tells the life story of another person. Biographies have been written about many famous people, historical and contemporary, but they can also be written about "ordinary" people. As with an autobiography, a biography is factual and may be written to express a person's values, to teach lessons about life, or to entertain or inspire readers. A biography usually emphasizes the causes and effects of a person's actions.

● Why might a writer have included the information presented here in a biography of Arthur Ashe?

> He once described his life as "a succession of fortunate circumstances." He was in his twenties then. More than half of his life was behind him. His memory of his mother was confined to a single image: in a blue corduroy bathrobe she stood in a doorway looking out on the courts and playing fields surrounding their house, which stood in the center of a Richmond playground. Weakened by illness, she was taken to a hospital that day, and died at the age of twenty-seven. He was six.
>
> FROM "ARTHUR ASHE REMEMBERED," JOHN MCPHEE, P. 682

> "It has always seemed to me that truth is not just 'stranger than fiction,' but also more interesting."
> —Jim Haskins

Essay

An **essay** is a short nonfiction work about a particular subject. It presents a main idea and supports it with examples, facts, statistics, or anecdotes.

- A *narrative essay* tells a true story.
- An *expository essay* gives information, discusses ideas, or explains a process.
- A *persuasive essay* tries to convince readers to do something or to accept the writer's point of view.
- A *reflective essay* presents the writer's reflections or thoughts on a topic of personal importance.

○ **What does this opening from an essay suggest about its main idea?**

It has taken me a good number of years to come to any measure of respect for summer. I was, being May-born, literally an "infant of the spring" and, during the later childhood years, tended, for some reason or other, to rather worship the cold aloofness of winter. . . . For the longest kind of time I simply thought that *summer* was a mistake.

FROM "ON SUMMER," LORRAINE HANSBERRY, P. **656**

Informational Text

Informational text is writing that provides the knowledge to guide and educate you. Informational texts include magazine and newspaper articles on current topics, as well as instructional manuals and textbooks.

○ **Based on this lead paragraph from a newspaper article, how might you expect the text to educate or enlighten you?**

San Francisco—In dim light they appear to be sleeping, but they've been dead up to 4,000 years: more than 100 astoundingly well-preserved mummies unearthed in a Chinese desert, whose inexplicably blond hair and white skin could topple dogmas about early human history.

FROM "CAUCASIAN MUMMIES MYSTIFY CHINESE," KEAY DAVIDSON, P. **132**

Drama

*Types of Plays • Dialogue and Monologue •
Stage Directions • Plot and Conflict*

Drama consists of writing that is intended to be performed by actors for an audience. The script combines dialogue—the words the actors say—with stage directions—the author's comments on how and where the actors should move and speak. As you read drama, you "set the stage" in your own mind, using your imagination to visualize the scenery, lighting, costumes, and actors.

Types of Plays

Not all plays are the same in their tone, style, or message. A **comedy** is a humorous play with a happy ending. A **tragedy** is a play in which a hero suffers a major downfall. A **drama** is a serious play, although the consequences are not necessarily as dire as those in a tragedy.

● **From what type of play do you think the following passage comes? Why?**

> BENVOLIO.
>
> O noble Prince, I can discover all
> The unlucky manage of this fatal
>   brawl.
> There lies the man, slain by young
>   Romeo,
> That slew thy kinsman, brave
>   Mercutio.
>
> FROM THE TRAGEDY OF ROMEO AND JULIET,
> WILLIAM SHAKESPEARE, P. 770

Dialogue and Monologue

The action of a play is conveyed mainly through **dialogue**—the conversations between two or more characters. A **monologue** is a lengthy speech that one character addresses to others on stage. Both dialogue and monologue reveal character traits and advance the story action in drama.

● **What do you learn about the speakers in this brief piece of dialogue?**

> MARY CATHERINE. I love to dance.
>
> HORACE. Well . . . I don't dance too well.
>
> MARY CATHERINE. There's nothing to it but confidence.
>
> HORACE. That's what my sister says. . . .
>
> MARY CATHERINE. I didn't learn for the longest kind of time for lack of confidence and then Emily gave me a long lecture about it and I got confidence and went ahead and learned. Would you like to come in for a while?
>
> HORACE. Well . . . if it's all right with you. . . .
>
> MARY CATHERINE. I'd be glad to have you.
>
> HORACE. Thank you.
>
> FROM THE DANCERS, HORTON FOOTE, P. 734

Upstage Right	Upstage Center	Upstage Left
Right	Center	Left
Downstage Right	Downstage Center	Downstage Left

Stage Directions

Stage directions are the instructions for performing the play and the descriptions of settings, characters, and actions. When you read dramatic literature, the stage directions can help you visualize the play. Using a staging chart like the one shown above, you can imagine where the scenery is and how the actors move by following the indications of downstage, upstage, left, and right.

⬤ **What information in these stage directions helps you visualize the setting of the play?**

[*Scene: The stage is divided into four acting areas: downstage left is the living room of* INEZ *and* HERMAN STANLEY. *Downstage right is part of a small-town drugstore. Upstage right is the living room of* ELIZABETH CREWS. *Upstage left, the yard and living room of* MARY CATHERINE DAVIS.]

FROM <u>THE DANCERS</u>, HORTON FOOTE, P. 734

Plot and Conflict

A play, much like a short story, contains a **plot,** or series of events, involving a **conflict,** or problem, that one or more characters face. The conflict is introduced early in the play, perhaps in its opening scene. Tension builds to the climax, and by the final scene of the play, the conflict has been resolved, either happily or unhappily, for the main characters.

⬤ **What kind of conflict is indicated in this dialogue?**

EMILY. I don't feel good . . . . [*She begins to cry.*] Oh, Mother, I don't want to go to the dance tonight. Please, ma'm, don't make me. I'll do anything in this world for you if you promise me . . .

ELIZABETH. Emily. This is all settled. You are going to that dance. Do you understand me? You are going to that dance. That sweet, nice brother of Inez Stanley's will be here any minute. . . .

FROM <u>THE DANCERS</u>, HORTON FOOTE, P. 734

Poetry

Types of Poetry • Poetic Form • Figurative Language • Rhyme and Rhythm

Poetry is writing that combines language, images, and sounds to create a special emotional effect. A poem's sound and structure are different from those of prose, the writing you find in short stories and nonfiction. Poetry is arranged in lines and stanzas, and its language is more visual and musical than prose. A story speaks to readers, but a poem sings to them.

Types of Poetry

There are many different types of poems. A **narrative poem,** like a short story, tells a story that includes a plot, characters, and a setting. A **lyric poem** expresses the observations and feelings of a speaker in a musical way. A **dramatic poem** uses the techniques of drama in the form of a monologue for one speaker or dramatic dialogue for two or more speakers.

 **Which details in this passage help you to recognize it comes from a lyric poem?**

I like hot days, hot days
Sweat is what you got days
Bugs buzzin from cousin to cousin
Juices dripping
Running and ripping
Catch the one you love days
FROM "SUMMER," WALTER DEAN MYERS,
P. 927

Poetic Form

Poetic form refers to the way the lines of a poem are shaped and arranged. Often, a poet groups lines into formal units called *stanzas*. A stanza may have any number of lines. Poetic form affects the way the poem is read aloud and, to a degree, the message that the poem conveys.

 **Why do you think the last lines of this poem have been set apart?**

Harlem

What happens to a dream deferred?

    Does it dry up
    like a raisin in the sun?
    Or fester like a sore——
    And then run?
    Does it stink like rotten meat?
    Or crust and sugar over——
    like a syrupy sweet?

    Maybe it just sags
    like a heavy load.

Or does it explode?
"DREAM DEFERRED," LANGSTON HUGHES, P. 904

> "To have great poetry, there must be great audiences, too."
> —Walt Whitman

Figurative Language

Figurative language is writing or speech that is not meant to be taken literally. It is often used to create vivid impressions by setting up fresh comparisons between dissimilar things.

In a **simile,** *like* or *as* is used to compare two basically different things. For example, the simile "I wandered lonely as a cloud" compares the speaker to a cloud and emphasizes the speaker's aimlessness.

In contrast to a simile, a **metaphor** states a comparison of two things directly. In the metaphor "if dreams die / Life is a broken-winged bird," the poet compares life to an injured bird and shows the effect of losing hope.

In **personification,** a nonhuman subject is given human characteristics. In the lines "Let the rain kiss you. / Let the rain sing you a lullaby," the poet personifies the rain, making it seem vital and alive.

● **What comparisons do you find in these lines of poetry?**

Continuous as the stars that shine
And twinkle on the milky way,
They stretched in never-ending line
Along the margin of a bay:
Ten thousand saw I at a glance,
Tossing their heads in sprightly dance.
FROM "I WANDERED LONELY AS A CLOUD,"
WILLIAM WORDSWORTH, P. 896

Rhythm and Rhyme

In addition to poetic conventions like figurative language and stanza structure, the elements of rhythm and rhyme give poetry its musical qualities.

Rhythm in a poem is the pattern of stressed (´) and unstressed (ˇ) syllables in each line. Notice the regular rhythm in this line:

Once upon a midnight dreary . . .

Rhyme in a poem is the repetition of sounds at the ends of words. For example:

Once upon a midnight <u>dreary</u>,
While I pondered, weak and <u>weary</u> . . .

● **What rhythm and rhyme do you find in these lines of poetry?**

Two roads diverged in a yellow wood,
And sorry I could not travel both
And be one traveler, long I stood
And looked down one as far as I could
To where it bent in the undergrowth;
FROM "THE ROAD NOT TAKEN," ROBERT FROST,
P. 188

Folk Literature

Myth • Folk Tale • Tall Tale • Epic

Not all stories were written down when they were first told. Folk literature comes from generations of peoples or cultures that passed down their favorite tales orally before ever recording them. Folk literature includes myths, folk tales, tall tales, and epics. Like a favorite family recipe, folk literature holds special enjoyment for all those who know it and pass it on.

Myth

A **myth** is a fictional tale that explains the actions of gods or the causes of natural phenomena. It involves supernatural elements and has little historical truth to it. Among the most familiar myths today are those of the ancient Greeks and Romans.

Myths have several purposes. They serve as a cultural history, explaining natural phenomena such as oceans and mountains. They also reinforce a culture's values. Finally, they are a source of entertainment.

● **Which details in this passage indicate that it is from a myth?**

King Acrisius of Argos had only one child, a daughter, Danaë. She was beautiful above all the other women of the land, but this was small comfort to the King for not having a son. He journeyed to Delphi to ask the god if there was any hope that some day he would be the father of a boy. The priestess told him no, and added what was far worse: that his daughter would have a son who would kill him.

FROM "PERSEUS," EDITH HAMILTON, P. 214

Folk Tale

A **folk tale** is a story composed orally and then passed from person to person by word of mouth. As part of an oral tradition, folk tales originated among people who could neither read nor write. They entertained one another by telling stories aloud, often about heroes, adventure, magic, or romance. Like mythology, folk tales also help reinforce a culture's values and explain the natural world.

● **This passage comes from an African folk tale. Which elements make it an appealing story to hear?**

Once, not far from the city of Accra on the Gulf of Guinea, a country man went out to his garden to dig up some yams to take to market. While he was digging, one of the yams said to him, "Well, at last you're here. You never weeded me, but now you come around with your digging stick. Go away and leave me alone!"

FROM "TALK," HAROLD COURLANDER AND GEORGE HERZOG, P. 412

Tall Tale

A **tall tale** is a kind of humorous story in which characters possess superhuman abilities and impossible happenings occur. Tall tales were common on the American frontier, when characters like Paul Bunyan and Febold Feboldson were favorites. Tall tales are told in common, everyday speech and employ some realistic detail in addition to exaggeration.

● Which details from this passage indicate that it is from a tall tale?

... The sun shone on his cornfield until the corn began to pop, while the rain washed the syrup out of his sugar cane.

Now the cane field was on a hill and the cornfield was in a valley. The syrup flowed downhill into the popped corn and rolled it into great balls. Bergstrom says some of them were hundreds of feet high and looked like big tennis balls from a distance. You never see any of them now, because the grasshoppers ate them all up in one day, July 21, 1874.

FROM "FEBOLD FEBOLDSON," PAUL R. BEATH, IN <u>WRITERS OF THE AMERICAN MIDWEST</u>, PRENTICE HALL LITERATURE LIBRARY, P. 23

Epic

An **epic** is a long narrative poem about the deeds of gods or heroes in war or travel. An epic is written in ornate, poetic language. It incorporates myth, legend, and history and often includes the intervention of the gods in human affairs.

In an epic, the poet begins by announcing the subject and asking a Muse, one of the nine goddesses of the arts, literature, and sciences, to help.

Homer's epic *Odyssey* (p. 980) tells the story of the Greek hero Odysseus, the king of Ithaca.

● Which characteristics of an epic do you find in this opening verse of Homer's *Odyssey*?

Sing in me, Muse, and through me
    tell the story
of that man skilled in the ways of
    contending,
the wanderer, harried for years on end,
after he plundered the stronghold
of the proud height of Troy.

FROM THE <u>ODYSSEY</u>, HOMER, P. 980

UNIT 1

Spine Tinglers

The Storm, 1893, Edvard Munch, ©1997 The Museum of Modern Art, New York

Exploring the Theme

Turn the page to enter a world of suspense and mystery. Here, extraordinary events are commonplace, and desperate acts or unexplained phenomena can change the course of a life forever. Experience these stories, poems, and essays—if you dare! Your heart will race, your fists will clench, and your spine will tingle.

In "The Cask of Amontillado," a man is driven to cold-blooded, methodical murder for reasons known only to himself. Follow the condemned man as he is unknowingly led to a terrifying end. Scream out a warning to him if you choose, but he is not likely to hear you. His fate has already been decided by others more powerful.

▲ **Critical Viewing** Which details in this painting create a sense of mystery or suspense? [**Analyze**]

Why Read Literature?

Whenever you read a work of suspense, you have a purpose, or reason. You might just want to experience the feeling of a good scare, but you may have other reasons for reading as well. Preview these three purposes you might set before reading works in this unit.

1 Read for the Love of Literature

Edgar Allan Poe was obsessed with the fear of being buried alive. Poe conveyed this horror so imaginatively in his stories that he inspired one Russian reader to patent his own device. The mechanism enabled the "deceased" to signal those above ground that they had acted a little too hastily. You may understand why someone would go to such lengths when you read **"The Cask of Amontillado,"** page 6.

What happens when the hunter becomes the hunted? That is the ominous question Richard Connell seeks to answer in a frightening story about a different kind of hunt. You may not be able to resist rushing to the end to learn what happens in **"The Most Dangerous Game,"** page 18.

2 Read to Be Entertained

Sometimes the most unexpected events happen at the end of a close contest when the entire game is on the line. Find out what happens when it all comes down to the final man in Ernest Thayer's **"Casey at the Bat,"** page 42.

If you have ever heard footsteps echoing loudly on an empty street at night or imagined a lurking shadow behind every tree, you will sympathize with the spooked horseman in Walter de la Mare's **"The Listeners,"** page 122.

3 Read for Information

The discovery of 100 Caucasian mummies in a remote region of China challenges established beliefs about ancient Chinese history. Learn more about these mysterious mummies by reading Keay Davidson's article **"Caucasian Mummies Mystify Chinese,"** page 132.

 Take It to the Net

Visit the Web site for online instruction and activities related to each selection in this unit.
www.phschool.com

How to Read Literature

Use Literal Comprehension Strategies

Your first goal in reading is to understand what the writer is saying. This task becomes more difficult when writers use unfamiliar words or construct sentences that do not make sense when you first read them. You can use the following literal comprehension strategies to help clear up confusion.

1. Break down long sentences.

- Read sentences in meaningful groups of words, not word by word.
- Figure out the subject of the sentence. Then, determine what the sentence is saying about that subject.
- Rearrange the sentence if you are confused by word order, as the example at right demonstrates.

2. Use context clues.

Context refers to the words, phrases, sentences, and ideas that surround a word. Use clues contained in the context to help determine the meaning of unfamiliar words or phrases. Look at this sample passage:

> "I wanted the ideal animal to hunt," explained the general. "So I said: 'What are the attributes of an ideal *quarry*?'"
>
> —from "The Most Dangerous Game"

If the word *quarry* is unfamiliar, you could determine its meaning by looking at the previous sentence and noticing how the word *ideal* is repeated. The general is looking for the *ideal* animal to hunt, so you can conclude that *quarry* probably means a hunted animal.

Breaking Down Sentences

Poe's sentence: The thousand injuries of Fortunato I had borne as best I could, but when he ventured upon insult I vowed revenge.

Rearranged sentence: I had borne the thousand injuries of Fortunato as best I could, but I vowed revenge when he ventured upon insult.

3. Summarize.

Summarizing involves picking out key events, describing them briefly in your own words, and then placing them in order of occurrence to concisely report the action or main idea of a selection. Prepare a summary to serve these purposes:

- Make sure you understand what happens in a story as you read.
- Remind yourself of basic plot events later on.

4. Predict.

Predicting, or making guesses about what will happen later in a selection, keeps you actively involved in a story. Use prediction to avoid missing important details and to check your understanding of what you have read.

As you read this unit's selections, apply these strategies to increase your understanding of the text.

Prepare to Read

The Cask of Amontillado

 Take It to the Net

Visit www.phschool.com for interactive activities and instruction related to "The Cask of Amontillado," including

- background
- graphic organizers
- literary elements
- reading strategies

Preview

Connecting to the Literature

Often, it does not take much to spark a desire for revenge. It can start with a simple insult or an unresolved dispute. You encounter these situations in books, movies, television shows, and in real life. Sometimes, as in this story, a quest for revenge can get out of hand.

Background

Much of the action in this story takes place in catacombs. These long passageways and side tunnels stretch out like cities of the dead. In past centuries, many wealthy European families held funerals in catacombs beneath the family manor. The dead were then laid to rest, surrounded by the bones of their ancestors. The most extensive known catacombs are found outside Rome.

Literary Analysis

Mood

The **mood** of a work of literature is the primary feeling that the reader experiences while reading it. In "The Cask of Amontillado," Edgar Allan Poe carefully chooses words and details to create a mood of eerie suspense. In this example, notice how the italicized words affect the mood.

> We passed through a *range of low arches, descended,* passed on, and *descending* again, arrived at a *deep crypt,* in which the *foulness* of the air caused our flambeaux rather to *glow* than flame.

As the story unfolds, see how quickly the mood changes.

Connecting Literary Elements

A **description** is a portrait painted in words of a person, place, or object. In "The Cask of Amontillado," description creates the eerie mood. For example, details such as *drops of moisture* that *trickle among the bones* help readers picture the scene and sense the mood. Take note of dark descriptions that contribute to the mood.

Instruction with this selection addresses these standards:

R 1.1*, 3.6*
W 1.8, 2.1*
WOLC 1.3*
LS 1.9

* Standards tested on HS Exit Exam. For complete standards, see p. CA 4.

Reading Strategy

Breaking Down Confusing Sentences

When you approach Poe's writing, you may need to **break down confusing sentences**. To do this:

- Read sentences in meaningful sections, not word by word.
- Figure out the subject—who or what the sentence is about. Then, determine what the sentence is saying about that subject.
- Rearrange, change, or take out words to make the sentence clearer.

If you come to a difficult sentence while you are reading, use a chart like this one to break the sentence into sections and clarify information about the subjects. The example on the right breaks down the first sentence in the story.

Subject	Information About the Subject
I (narrator)	had borne the thousand injuries of Fortunato
he (Fortunato)	ventured upon insult
I (narrator)	vowed revenge

Vocabulary Development

precluded (prē klōōd´ id) *v.* prevented; made impossible in advance (p. 7)

retribution (re´ trə byōō´ shən) *n.* payback; punishment for a misdeed (p. 7)

accosted (ə kôst´ id) *v.* greeted, especially in an aggressive way (p. 7)

afflicted (ə flikt´ id) *v.* suffering or sickened (p. 8)

explicit (eks plis´ it) *adj.* clearly stated (p. 8)

recoiling (ri koil´ in) *v.* staggering back (p. 10)

termination (tʉr´ mə nā´ shən) *n.* end (p. 10)

subsided (səb sīd´ id) *v.* settled down; became less active or intense (p. 11)

The Cask of Amontillado[1]

Edgar Allan Poe

▲ **Critical Viewing** How does this costume compare with your image of the costume worn by Fortunato? **[Compare and Contrast]**

The thousand injuries of Fortunato I had borne as I best could, but when he ventured upon insult I vowed revenge. You, who so well know the nature of my soul, will not suppose, however, that I gave utterance to a threat. At *length* I would be avenged; this was a point definitely settled—but the very definitiveness with which it was resolved <u>precluded</u> the idea of risk. I must not only punish but punish with impunity.[2] A wrong is unredressed when <u>retribution</u> overtakes its redresser. It is equally unredressed when the avenger fails to make himself felt as such to him who has done the wrong.

It must be understood that neither by word nor deed had I given Fortunato cause to doubt my good will. I continued, as was my wont, to smile in his face, and he did not perceive that my smile *now* was at the thought of his immolation.[3]

He had a weak point—this Fortunato—although in other regards he was a man to be respected and even feared. He prided himself on his connoisseurship[4] in wine. Few Italians have the true virtuoso[5] spirit. For the most part their enthusiasm is adopted to suit the time and opportunity, to practice imposture upon the British and Austrian millionaires. In painting and gemmary, Fortunato, like his country-men, was a quack, but in the matter of old wines he was sincere. In this respect I did not differ from him materially; I was skillful in the Italian vintages myself, and bought largely whenever I could.

It was about dusk, one evening during the supreme madness of the carnival season, that I encountered my friend. He <u>accosted</u> me with excessive warmth, for he had been drinking much. The man wore motley.[6] He had on a tight-fitting parti-striped dress, and his head was surmounted by the conical cap and bells. I was so pleased to see him that I thought I should never have done wringing his hand.

I said to him, "My dear Fortunato, you are luckily met. How remarkably well you are looking today. But I have received a pipe[7] of what passes for Amontillado, and I have my doubts."

"How?" said he. "Amontillado? A pipe? Impossible! And in the mid-dle of the carnival!"

"I have my doubts," I replied: "and I was silly enough to pay the full Amontillado price without consulting you in the matter. You were not to be found, and I was fearful of losing a bargain."

"Amontillado!"

"I have my doubts."

"Amontillado!"

"And I must satisfy them."

"Amontillado!"

---

1. **Amontillado** (ə män′ tə ya′ dō) *n.* a pale, dry sherry.
2. **impunity** (im pyo͞o′ ni tē) *n.* freedom from consequences.
3. **immolation** (im′ ə lā′ shən) *n.* destruction.
4. **connoisseurship** (kän′ ə sur′ ship) *n.* expert judgment.
5. **virtuoso** (vur′ cho͞o ō′ sō) *adj.* masterly skill in a particular field.
6. **motley** (mät′ lē) *n.* a clown's multicolored costume.
7. **pipe** (pīp) *n.* large barrel, holding approximately 126 gallons.

precluded (prē klo͞od′ id) *v.* prevented; made impossible in advance

retribution (re trə byo͞o′ shən) *n.* payback; punishment for a misdeed

accosted (ə kôst′ id) *v.* greeted, especially in a forward or aggressive way

Reading Check

Why does the speaker vow revenge on Fortunato?

"As you are engaged, I am on my way to Luchesi. If any one has a critical turn it is he. He will tell me—"

"Luchesi cannot tell Amontillado from sherry."

"And yet some fools will have it that his taste is a match for your own."

"Come, let us go."

"Whither?"

"To your vaults."

"My friend, no; I will not impose upon your good nature. I perceive you have an engagement. Luchesi—"

"I have no engagement—come."

"My friend, no. It is not the engagement, but the severe cold with which I perceive you are <u>afflicted</u>. The vaults are insufferably damp. They are encrusted with niter."

"Let us go, nevertheless. The cold is merely nothing. Amontillado! You have been imposed upon. And as for Luchesi, he cannot distinguish sherry from Amontillado."

Thus speaking, Fortunato possessed himself of my arm; and putting on a mask of black silk and drawing a *roquelaure*[8] closely about my person, I suffered him to hurry me to my palazzo.

There were no attendants at home; they had absconded to make merry in honor of the time. I had told them that I should not return until the morning, and had given them <u>explicit</u> orders not to stir from the house. These orders were sufficient, I well knew, to insure their immediate disappearance, one and all, as soon as my back was turned.

I took from their sconces two flambeaux, and giving one to Fortunato, bowed him through several suites of rooms to the archway that led into the vaults. I passed down a long and winding staircase, requesting him to be cautious as he followed. We came at length to the foot of the descent, and stood together upon the damp ground of the catacombs of the Montresors.

The gait of my friend was unsteady, and the bells upon his cap jingled as he strode.

"The pipe," he said.

"It is farther on," said I; "but observe the white webwork which gleams from these cavern walls."

He turned towards me, and looked into my eyes with two filmy orbs that distilled the rheum of intoxication.

"Niter?" he asked, at length.

"Niter," I replied. "How long have you had that cough?"

"Ugh! ugh! ugh!—ugh! ugh! ugh!—ugh! ugh! ugh!—ugh! ugh! ugh!—ugh! ugh! ugh!"

My poor friend found it impossible to reply for many minutes.

"It is nothing," he said, at last.

"Come," I said, with decision, "we will go back; your health is precious. You are rich, respected, admired, beloved; you are happy, as once I was.

---

afflicted (ə flikt´ id) v. suffering or sickened

explicit (eks plis´ it) adj. clearly stated

Literary Analysis
Mood How does Fortunato's cough add to the eerie mood?

---

8. *roquelaure* (räk´ ə lôr) n. knee-length cloak.

You are a man to be missed. For me it is no matter. We will go back; you will be ill, and I cannot be responsible. Besides, there is Luchesi—"

"Enough," he said; "the cough is a mere nothing; it will not kill me. I shall not die of a cough."

"True—true," I replied; "and, indeed, I had no intention of alarming you unnecessarily—but you should use all proper caution. A draft of this Medoc will defend us from the damps."

Here I knocked off the neck of a bottle which I drew from a long row of its fellows that lay upon the mold.

"Drink," I said, presenting him the wine.

He raised it to his lips with a leer. He paused and nodded to me familiarly, while his bells jingled.

"I drink," he said "to the buried that repose around us."

"And I to your long life."

He again took my arm, and we proceeded.

"These vaults," he said, "are extensive."

"The Montresors," I replied, "were a great and numerous family."

"I forget your arms."

"A huge human foot d'or, in a field azure; the foot crushes a serpent rampant whose fangs are imbedded in the heel."

"And the motto?"

"Nemo me impune lacessit."[9]

"Good!" he said.

The wine sparkled in his eyes and the bells jingled. My own fancy grew warm with the Medoc. We had passed through long walls of piled skeletons, with casks and puncheons[10] intermingling, into the inmost recesses of the catacombs. I paused again, and this time I made bold to seize Fortunato by an arm above the elbow.

"The niter!" I said; "see, it increases. It hangs like moss upon the vaults. We are below the river's bed. The drops of moisture trickle among the bones. Come, we will go back ere it is too late. Your cough—"

"It is nothing," he said; "let us go on. But first, another draft of the Medoc."

I broke and reached him a flagon of De Grâve. He emptied it at a breath. His eyes flashed with a fierce light. He laughed and threw the bottle upwards with a gesticulation I did not understand.

I looked at him in surprise. He repeated the movement—a grotesque one.

▲ Critical Viewing
Which details of this photograph reflect the mood of the story? **[Connect]**

✓ Reading Check
Where is Montresor bringing Fortunato?

---

9. *Nemo me impune lacessit* Latin for "No one attacks me with impunity."
10. puncheons (pun´ chənz) *n.* large barrels.

"You do not comprehend?" he said.

"Not I," I replied.

"Then you are not of the brotherhood."

"How?"

"You are not of the masons."[11]

"Yes, yes," I said; "yes, yes."

"You? Impossible! A mason?"

"A mason," I replied.

"A sign," he said, "a sign."

"It is this," I answered, producing from beneath the folds of my *roquelaure* a trowel.

"You jest," he exclaimed, recoiling a few paces. "But let us proceed to the Amontillado."

"Be it so," I said, replacing the tool beneath the cloak and again offering him my arm. He leaned upon it heavily. We continued our route in search of the Amontillado. We passed through a range of low arches, descended, passed on, and descending again, arrived at a deep crypt, in which the foulness of the air caused our flambeaux rather to glow than flame.

At the most remote end of the crypt there appeared another less spacious. Its walls had been lined with human remains, piled to the vault overhead, in the fashion of the great catacombs of Paris. Three sides of this interior crypt were still ornamented in this manner. From the fourth side the bones had been thrown down, and lay promiscuously upon the earth, forming at one point a mound of some size. Within the wall thus exposed by the displacing of the bones, we perceived a still interior crypt or recess, in depth about four feet, in width three, in height six or seven. It seemed to have been constructed for no especial use within itself, but formed merely the *interval* between two of the colossal supports of the roof of the catacombs, and was backed by one of their circumscribing walls of solid granite.

It was in vain that Fortunato, uplifting his dull torch, endeavored to pry into the depth of the recess. Its termination the feeble light did not enable us to see.

"Proceed," I said: "herein is the Amontillado. As for Luchesi—"

"He is an ignoramus," interrupted my friend, as he stepped unsteadily forward, while I followed immediately at his heels. In an instant he had reached the extremity of the niche, and finding his progress arrested by the rock, stood stupidly bewildered. A moment more and I had fettered him to the granite. In its surface were two iron staples, distant from each other about two feet, horizontally. From one of these depended a short chain, from the other a padlock. Throwing the links about his waist, it was but the work of a few seconds to secure it. He was too much astounded to resist. Withdrawing the key I stepped back from the recess.

"Pass your hand," I said, "over the wall; you cannot help feeling the

---

11. masons the Freemasons, an international secret society.

niter. Indeed, it is *very* damp. Once more let me *implore* you to return. No? Then I must positively leave you. But I must first render you all the little attentions in my power."

"The Amontillado!" ejaculated my friend, not yet recovered from his astonishment.

"True," I replied; "the Amontillado."

As I said these words I busied myself among the pile of bones of which I have before spoken. Throwing them aside, I soon uncovered a quantity of building stone and mortar. With these materials and with the aid of my trowel, I began vigorously to wall up the entrance of the niche.

I had scarcely laid the first tier of the masonry when I discovered that the intoxication of Fortunato had in a great measure worn off. The earliest indication I had of this was a low moaning cry from the depth of the recess. It was *not* the cry of a drunken man. There was then a long and obstinate silence. I laid the second tier, and the third, and the fourth; and then I heard the furious vibrations of the chain. The noise lasted for several minutes, during which, that I might hearken to it with the more satisfaction, I ceased my labors and sat down upon the bones. When at last the clanking <u>subsided</u>, I resumed the trowel, and finished without interruption the fifth, the sixth, and the seventh tier. The wall was now nearly upon a level with my breast. I again paused, and holding the flambeaux over the masonwork, threw a few feeble rays upon the figure within.

A succession of loud and shrill screams, bursting suddenly from the throat of the chained form, seemed to thrust me violently back. For a brief moment I hesitated, I trembled. Unsheathing my rapier, I began to grope with it about the recess; but the thought of an instant reassured me. I placed my hand upon the solid fabric of the catacombs, and felt satisfied. I reapproached the wall; I replied to the yells of him who clamored. I reechoed, I aided, I surpassed them in volume and in strength. I did this, and the clamorer grew still.

It was now midnight, and my task was drawing to a close. I had completed the eighth, the ninth, and the tenth tier. I had finished a portion of the last and the eleventh; there remained but a single stone to be fitted and plastered in. I struggled with its weight; I placed it partially in its destined position. But now there came from out the niche a low laugh that erected the hairs upon my head. It was succeeded by a sad voice, which I had difficulty in recognizing as that of the noble Fortunato. The voice said—

▲ **Critical Viewing**
Explain how the context of a story might make a festive mask such as this one appear sinister. **[Interpret]**

subsided (səb sīd´ id) v. settled down; became less active or intense

✔**Reading Check**

What has Montresor done to Fortunato?

The Cask of Amontillado ◆ 11

"Ha! ha! ha!—he! he! he!—a very good joke, indeed—an excellent jest. We will have many a rich laugh about it at the palazzo—he! he! he!—over our wine—he! he! he!"

"The Amontillado!" I said.

"He! he! he!—he! he! he!—yes, the Amontillado. But is it not getting late? Will not they be awaiting us at the palazzo, the Lady Fortunato and the rest? Let us be gone."

"Yes," I said, "let us be gone."

"*For the love of God, Montresor!*"

"Yes," I said, "for the love of God!"

But to these words I hearkened in vain for a reply. I grew impatient. I called aloud—

"Fortunato!"

No answer. I called again—

"Fortunato!"

No answer still. I thrust a torch through the remaining aperture and let it fall within. There came forth in return only a jingling of the bells. My heart grew sick; it was the dampness of the catacombs that made it so. I hastened to make an end of my labor. I forced the last stone into its position; I plastered it up. Against the new masonry I reerected the old rampart of bones. For the half of a century no mortal has disturbed them. *In pace requiescat!*[12]

---

12. *In pace requiescat!*   Latin for "May he rest in peace!"

Review and Assess

Thinking About the Selection

1. **Respond:** At what point in the story do you find Montresor most disturbing? Explain.

2. **(a) Recall:** How does Montresor describe Fortunato's actions and attitudes early in the story? **(b) Analyze Causes and Effects:** Which character traits make Fortunato such an easy prey for Montresor?

3. **(a) Recall:** What specific steps does Montresor take to ensure that his plan works? **(b) Interpret:** Why does Montresor keep urging Fortunato to turn back?

4. **(a) Recall:** Why does Montresor hate Fortunato?
   (b) Support: Why does Montresor feel he has the right to take justice into his own hands?

5. **Evaluate:** Montresor acts as judge and executioner in this story. Explain whether you think individuals are ever justified in taking justice into their own hands.

Edgar Allan Poe

(1809–1849)

One of the first great American storytellers, Edgar Allan Poe blazed the trail for writers like Stephen King.

Poe's amazing but dark imagination may have had its roots in his troubled childhood, for he was orphaned by the age of three. Trouble plagued Poe in his adult life, too. He had to leave the University of Virginia when John Allan, his foster father, refused to pay the gambling debts that Poe had amassed. Later, Poe's dismissal from West Point caused Allan to disown him.

Poe found some happiness when he married Virginia Clemm. After she died of tuberculosis in 1847, however, Poe became increasingly antisocial. In 1849, he was discovered in a delirious condition in a Baltimore street. Three days later, he was dead at the age of forty.

Review and Assess

Literary Analysis

Mood

1. Name at least three images that contribute to the story's eerie **mood**.
2. (a) Describe the mood of the scene in which Montresor first tells Fortunato about the Amontillado. (b) How does the mood change as the story unfolds?
3. How does Montresor's response to Fortunato's screams add to the mood as the story reaches its high point?

Connecting Literary Elements

4. Which **descriptions** of Fortunato shape your impression of him the most? Explain.
5. Using a chart like the one below, show how the descriptions of the catacombs contribute to the mood.

Description of Catacomb	Mood Created

Reading Strategy

Breaking Down Confusing Sentences

6. To **break down** the following sentence, make a flowchart like the one below to show the three things that Montresor does after Fortunato grabs his arm.

   "Thus speaking, Fortunato possessed himself of my arm; and putting on a mask of black silk and drawing a *roquelaure* closely about my person, I suffered him to hurry me to my palazzo."

7. Break down this sentence to explain what has happened: "A moment more and I had fettered him to the granite."

Extend Understanding

8. **Career Connection:** If you were a lawyer, what evidence would you use to prove Montresor's guilt?

Quick Review

Mood is the feeling that a piece of literature creates in the reader.

A **description** is a portrait in words of a person, place, or object.

To **break down** a confusing sentence, rearrange, change, or take out words in order to identify its subject and what is being said about that subject.

 Take It to the Net
www.phschool.com
Take the interactive self-test online to check your understanding of the selection.

Integrate Language Skills

Vocabulary Development Lesson

Word Analysis: Latin Prefix *pre-*

The Latin prefix *pre-*, as found in *precluded*, means "before" or "in advance." Identify the word from the list below that best fits each definition.

preview   precaution   prejudice

1. To see in advance
2. Judgment without sufficient facts
3. Care taken in advance

Spelling Strategy

When you add an ending that begins with a vowel to a word that ends in a silent *e*, the *e* is usually dropped. For example, when adding *-ing* to the word *subside*, drop the silent *e* to form *subsiding*. Write the word formed by adding the ending to each word below.

1. smile + *-ing*   3. believe + *-able*
2. jingle + *-ed*   4. face + *-ing*

Concept Development: Antonyms

Identify the antonym, or opposite, of the first word.

1. precluded: (a) prevented, (b) aided, (c) started
2. retribution: (a) reward, (b) disaster, (c) assignment
3. accosted: (a) sought, (b) retreated, (c) discovered
4. subsided: (a) increased, (b) created, (c) challenged
5. afflicted: (a) weary, (b) skeptical, (c) blessed
6. explicit: (a) unnecessary, (b) vague, (c) impatient
7. recoiling: (a) unfastening, (b) releasing, (c) advancing
8. termination: (a) height, (b) beginning, (c) extension

Grammar Lesson

Common Nouns and Proper Nouns

A **common noun** names any one of a class of people, places, or things—for example, *man*, *city*, or *month*. A **proper noun** names a specific person, place, or thing and always begins with a capital letter—for example, *William*, *Los Angeles*, or *September*.

In the following excerpt from "The Cask of Amontillado," the common nouns are underlined, and the proper noun is in boldface.

> **Example:** I paused again, and this <u>time</u> I made bold to seize **Fortunato** by an <u>arm</u> above the <u>elbow</u>.

Practice Copy each sentence below. Draw one line under each common noun and two lines under each proper noun.

1. Edgar Allan Poe wrote the story.
2. A modern writer might set the story in New Orleans.
3. Mardi Gras, held in February or March, is a wild celebration.
4. Montresor led him through the catacombs.
5. It would be difficult to find Montresor in the French Quarter.

Writing Application Write a paragraph about a scene from the story. Use at least three common nouns and three proper nouns.

WG Prentice Hall Writing and Grammar Connection: Chapter 16, Section 1

Writing Lesson

Description of a Set

Imagine that "The Cask of Amontillado" is being made into a movie. Choose a scene from the story. Use your imagination to expand upon Poe's description as you prepare a vivid, precise description of a set design for that scene.

Prewriting Review the scene you have chosen and picture it in your mind. Jot down precise details of sight, sound, smell, taste, and texture.

Model: Gathering Precise Details

Scene: Montresor meets Fortunato.

Poe: "It was about dusk, one evening during the
             supreme madness of the carnival season, . . ."

Set Details: rough cobblestone street, lit by flickering torches
             distant sound of singing; people in costumes

> Precise details, such as *rough cobblestones* and *flickering torches*, will help the audience "see" the scene.

Drafting Organize your set description by describing it spatially, moving from left to right or from the foreground to the background. Refer to your notes, and include the specific elements of the set.

Revising Read your draft aloud to a classmate. Add or change any details that you feel will help readers see your set more clearly.

Prentice Hall Writing and Grammar Connection: Chapter 6, Section 2

Extension Activities

Listening and Speaking Retell part of "The Cask of Amontillado" from Fortunato's perspective. Include the following in your **retelling:**

- Fortunato's thoughts about Montresor in the beginning and at the end of the story
- Fortunato's feelings about the situation

Present your retelling to your class, using tones and gestures you think Fortunato would use. After your retelling, ask your classmates for feedback.

Research and Technology In a group, create a **storyboard** outlining the main events of the plot for a movie version of "The Cask of Amontillado." Draw each important scene in comic-book style. For each frame, write a brief description of the action. Include Poe's main events and any important events that you add. Use graphics software to help create the storyboard scenes. **[Group Activity]**

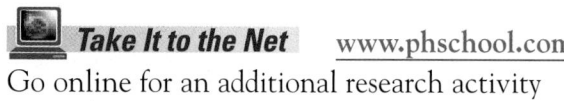 **Take It to the Net** www.phschool.com

Go online for an additional research activity using the Internet.

Prepare to Read

The Most Dangerous Game

 Take It to the Net

Visit www.phschool.com for interactive activities and instruction related to "The Most Dangerous Game," including

- background
- graphic organizers
- literary elements
- reading strategies

Preview

Connecting to the Literature

Some competitions can be friendly, while others can be fierce. If one side takes the competition more seriously than the other, the situation can become unpleasant, or even dangerous. In "The Most Dangerous Game," a competition becomes a life-or-death situation.

Background

The main characters in this story enjoy hunting big game—large animals, such as lions or bears—for sport. For hunting enthusiasts, big-game hunting is the ultimate test of skill. In recent times, however, this sport has become controversial as populations of big-game animals have dwindled or have even become endangered.

Literary Analysis

Suspense

Suspense is the reader's feeling of curiosity, uncertainty, or even anxiety about the outcome of events in a story. Writers can create suspense by putting characters into tense or risky situations. In this example from the story, the uncertainty of the situation helps to create suspense.

> For a seemingly endless time he fought the sea. He began to count his strokes; he could do possibly a hundred more and then—

As you read, pay attention to events and details that create suspense.

Connecting Literary Elements

Conflict plays a key role in establishing suspense. A **conflict** is a struggle between opposing forces, setting one character against another character, a character against nature, or a character against himself or herself. In "The Most Dangerous Game," suspense grows as the conflict between the story's two main characters intensifies.

Reading Strategy

Using Context Clues

As you read, use **context clues** to figure out the approximate meaning of an unfamiliar word.

- Look at the words, phrases, and sentences that surround the unfamiliar word. These "surroundings" are the context. In particular, look for words or details that might describe or rename the word.
- Once you find clue words, create a definition that makes sense to you. Reread your sentence using your new definition in place of the difficult word to see whether the sentence now makes more sense.

Use a chart like this to gather context clues and figure out meanings.

CALIFORNIA STANDARDS

Instruction with
this selection
addresses these standards:

R 1.1*, 3.6*
W 1.5*, 2.6
WOLC 1.3*
LS 1.7

* Standards tested on
HS Exit Exam. For complete
standards, see p. CA 4.

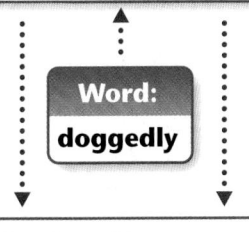

Clues: using slow, deliberate strokes

swimming for a seemingly endless time

Word: doggedly

Meaning: with determination

Vocabulary Development

palpable (pal′ pə bəl) *adj.* able to be touched or felt (p. 19)

indolently (in′ də lənt lē) *adv.* lazily; idly (p. 20)

bizarre (bi zär′) *adj.* odd in appearance (p. 23)

naive (nä ēv′) *adj.* unsophisticated (p. 27)

scruples (scrōō′ pəlz) *n.* misgivings about something one feels is wrong (p. 27)

blandly (bland′ lē) *adv.* in a mild and soothing manner (p. 28)

grotesque (grō tesk′) *adj.* having a strange, bizarre design (p. 29)

futile (fyōōt′ ′l) *adj.* hopeless (p. 31)

▲ **Critical Viewing** How does this painting create a feeling of suspense? **[Analyze]**

The Most Dangerous Game

Richard Connell

"Off there to the right—somewhere—is a large island," said Whitney. "It's rather a mystery—"

"What island is it?" Rainsford asked.

"The old charts call it 'Ship-Trap Island,' " Whitney replied. "A suggestive name, isn't it? Sailors have a curious dread of the place. I don't know why. Some superstition—"

"Can't see it," remarked Rainsford, trying to peer through the dank tropical night that was palpable as it pressed its thick warm blackness in upon the yacht.

"You've good eyes," said Whitney, with a laugh, "and I've seen you pick off a moose moving in the brown fall bush at four hundred yards, but even you can't see four miles or so through a moonless Caribbean[1] night."

"Not four yards," admitted Rainsford. "Ugh! It's like moist black velvet."

"It will be light in Rio," promised Whitney. "We should make it in a few days. I hope the jaguar guns have come from Purdey's. We should have some good hunting up the Amazon.[2] Great sport, hunting."

"The best sport in the world," agreed Rainsford.

"For the hunter," amended Whitney. "Not for the jaguar."

"Don't talk rot, Whitney," said Rainsford. "You're a big-game hunter, not a philosopher. Who cares how a jaguar feels?"

palpable (pal´ pə bəl) *adj.* able to be touched or felt

✔**Reading Check**

How do sailors feel about the mysterious "ship-trap island"?

---

1. **Caribbean** (kar´ ə bē´ ən) the Caribbean Sea, a part of the Atlantic Ocean, bounded by South America, Central America, and the West Indies.
2. **Amazon** (am´ ə zän´) large river in South America.

himself upward, hand over hand. Gasping, his hands raw, he reached a flat place at the top. Dense jungle came down to the very edge of the cliffs. What perils that tangle of trees and underbrush might hold for him did not concern Rainsford just then. All he knew was that he was safe from his enemy, the sea, and that utter weariness was on him. He flung himself down at the jungle edge and tumbled headlong into the deepest sleep of his life.

When he opened his eyes he knew from the position of the sun that it was late in the afternoon. Sleep had given him new vigor; a sharp hunger was picking at him. He looked about him, almost cheerfully.

"Where there are pistol shots, there are men. Where there are men, there is food," he thought. But what kind of men, he wondered, in so forbidding a place? An unbroken front of snarled and ragged jungle fringed the shore.

He saw no sign of a trail through the closely knit web of weeds and trees; it was easier to go along the shore, and Rainsford floundered along by the water. Not far from where he had landed, he stopped.

Some wounded thing, by the evidence a large animal, had thrashed about in the underbrush; the jungle weeds were crushed down and the moss was lacerated; one patch of weeds was stained crimson. A small, glittering object not far away caught Rainsford's eye and he picked it up. It was an empty cartridge.

"A twenty-two," he remarked. "That's odd. It must have been a fairly large animal too. The hunter had his nerve with him to tackle it with a light gun. It's clear that the brute put up a fight. I suppose the first three shots I heard was when the hunter flushed his quarry[3] and wounded it. The last shot was when he trailed it here and finished it."

He examined the ground closely and found what he had hoped to find—the print of hunting boots. They pointed along the cliff in the direction he had been going. Eagerly he hurried along, now slipping on a rotten log or a loose stone, but making headway; night was beginning to settle down on the island.

Bleak darkness was blacking out the sea and jungle when Rainsford sighted the lights. He came upon them as he turned a crook in the coast line, and his first thought was that he had come upon a village, for there were many lights. But as he forged along he saw to his great astonishment that all the lights were in one enormous building—a lofty structure with pointed towers plunging upward into the gloom. His eyes made out the shadowy outlines of a palatial château;[4] it was set on a high bluff, and on three sides of it cliffs dived down to where the sea licked greedy lips in the shadows.

"Mirage," thought Rainsford. But it was no mirage, he found, when he

▲ **Critical Viewing**
What does this picture suggest about Rainsford's struggle to climb out of the water and on to land? **[Analyze]**

Literary Analysis
Conflict and Suspense
Which details of Rainsford's struggle build suspense?

---

3. **flushed his quarry** (kwôr′ ē) drove his prey into the open.
4. **palatial château** (pə lā′ shəl sha tō′) a mansion as luxurious as a palace.

opened the tall spiked iron gate. The stone steps were real enough; the massive door with a leering gargoyle[5] for a knocker was real enough; yet about it all hung an air of unreality.

He lifted the knocker, and it creaked up stiffly, as if it had never before been used. He let it fall, and it startled him with its booming loudness. He thought he heard steps within; the door remained closed. Again Rainsford lifted the heavy knocker, and let it fall. The door opened then, opened as suddenly as if it were on a spring, and Rainsford stood blinking in the river of glaring gold light that poured out. The first thing Rainsford's eyes discerned was the largest man Rainsford had ever seen—a gigantic creature, solidly made and black-bearded to the waist. In his hand the man held a long-barreled revolver, and he was pointing it straight at Rainsford's heart.

Out of the snarl of beard two small eyes regarded Rainsford.

"Don't be alarmed," said Rainsford, with a smile which he hoped was disarming. "I'm no robber. I fell off a yacht. My name is Sanger Rainsford of New York City."

The menacing look in the eyes did not change. The revolver pointed as rigidly as if the giant were a statue. He gave no sign that he understood Rainsford's words, or that he had even heard them. He was dressed in uniform, a black uniform trimmed with gray astrakhan.[6]

"I'm Sanger Rainsford of New York," Rainsford began again. "I fell off a yacht. I am hungry."

The man's only answer was to raise with his thumb the hammer of his revolver. Then Rainsford saw the man's free hand go to his forehead in a military salute, and he saw him click his heels together and stand at attention. Another man was coming down the broad marble steps, an erect, slender man in evening clothes. He advanced to Rainsford and held out his hand.

In a cultivated voice marked by a slight accent that gave it added precision and deliberateness, he said: "It is a very great pleasure and honor to welcome Mr. Sanger Rainsford, the celebrated hunter, to my home."

Automatically Rainsford shook the man's hand.

"I've read your book about hunting snow leopards in Tibet, you see," explained the man. "I am General Zaroff."

Rainsford's first impression was that the man was singularly handsome; his second was that there was an original, almost bizarre quality about the general's face. He was a tall man past middle age, for his hair was a vivid white; but his thick eyebrows and pointed military mustache were as black as the night from which Rainsford had come. His eyes, too, were black and very bright. He had high cheek bones, a sharp-cut nose, a spare, dark face, the face of a man used to giving orders, the face of an aristocrat. Turning to the giant in uniform, the general made a sign. The giant put away his pistol, saluted, withdrew.

"Ivan is an incredibly strong fellow," remarked the general, "but he

---

5. **gargoyle** (gär´ goil) *n.* strange and distorted animal form projecting from a building.
6. **astrakhan** (as´ trə kan´) *n.* loosely curled fur made from the skins of young lambs.

Reading Strategy
Using Context Clues
Which context clues can you use to determine the meaning of *discerned*?

bizarre (bi zär´) *adj.* odd in appearance

**Reading Check**

What does Rainsford find when he finally makes it to the island?

has the misfortune to be deaf and dumb. A simple fellow, but, I'm afraid, like all his race, a bit of a savage."

"Is he Russian?"

"He is a Cossack,"[7] said the general, and his smile showed red lips and pointed teeth. "So am I."

"Come," he said, "we shouldn't be chatting here. We can talk later. Now you want clothes, food, rest. You shall have them. This is a most restful spot."

Ivan had reappeared, and the general spoke to him with lips that moved but gave forth no sound.

"Follow Ivan, if you please, Mr. Rainsford," said the general. "I was about to have my dinner when you came. I'll wait for you. You'll find that my clothes will fit you, I think."

It was to a huge, beam-ceilinged bedroom with a canopied bed big enough for six men that Rainsford followed the silent giant. Ivan laid out an evening suit, and Rainsford, as he put it on, noticed that it came from a London tailor who ordinarily cut and sewed for none below the rank of duke.

The dining room to which Ivan conducted him was in many ways remarkable. There was a medieval magnificence about it; it suggested a baronial hall of feudal times with its oaken panels, its high ceiling, its vast refectory table where twoscore men could sit down to eat. About the hall were the mounted heads of many animals—lions, tigers, elephants, moose, bears; larger or more perfect specimens Rainsford had never seen. At the great table the general was sitting, alone.

"You'll have a cocktail, Mr. Rainsford," he suggested. The cocktail was surpassingly good; and, Rainsford noted, the table appointments were of the finest—the linen, the crystal, the silver, the china.

They were eating *borsch*, the rich, red soup with whipped cream so dear to Russian palates. Half apologetically General Zaroff said: "We do our best to preserve the amenities of civilization here. Please forgive any lapses. We are well off the beaten track, you know. Do you think the champagne has suffered from its long ocean trip?"

"Not in the least," declared Rainsford. He was finding the general a most thoughtful and affable host, a true cosmopolite.[8] But there was one small trait of the general's that made Rainsford uncomfortable. Whenever he looked up from his plate he found the general studying him, appraising him narrowly.

"Perhaps," said General Zaroff, "you were surprised that I recognized your name. You see, I read all books on hunting published in English, French, and Russian. I have but one passion in my life, Mr. Rainsford, and it is the hunt."

"You have some wonderful heads here," said Rainsford as he ate a particularly well cooked filet mignon. "That Cape buffalo is the largest I ever saw."

"Oh, that fellow. Yes, he was a monster."

---

7. **Cossack** (käs´ ak) member of a people from southern Russia, famous for their fierceness.
8. **cosmopolite** (käz mäp´ ə lit´) *n.* person at home in all parts of the world.

Literary Analysis
Suspense What is your impression of the general? Can he be trusted?

Reading Strategy
Using Context Clues Which context clues suggest the approximate meaning of *amenities*?

"Did he charge you?"

"Hurled me against a tree," said the general. "Fractured my skull. But I got the brute."

"I've always thought," said Rainsford, "that the Cape buffalo is the most dangerous of all big game."

For a moment the general did not reply; he was smiling his curious red-lipped smile. Then he said slowly: "No. You are wrong, sir. The Cape buffalo is not the most dangerous big game." He sipped his wine. "Here in my preserve on this island," he said in the same slow tone, "I hunt more dangerous game."

Rainsford expressed his surprise. "Is there big game on this island?"

The general nodded. "The biggest."

"Really?"

"Oh, it isn't here naturally, of course. I have to stock the island."

"What have you imported, general?" Rainsford asked. "Tigers?"

The general smiled. "No," he said. "Hunting tigers ceased to interest me some years ago. I exhausted their possibilities, you see. No thrill left in tigers, no real danger. I live for danger, Mr. Rainsford."

The general took from his pocket a gold cigarette case and offered his guest a long black cigarette with a silver tip; it was perfumed and gave off a smell like incense.

"We will have some capital hunting, you and I," said the general. "I shall be most glad to have your society."

"But what game—" began Rainsford.

"I'll tell you," said the general. "You will be amused, I know. I think I may say, in all modesty, that I have done a rare thing. I have invented a new sensation. May I pour you another glass of port, Mr. Rainsford?"

"Thank you, general."

The general filled both glasses, and said: "God makes some men poets. Some He makes kings, some beggars. Me He made a hunter. My hand was made for the trigger, my father said. He was a very rich man with a quarter of a million acres in the Crimea,[9] and he was an ardent sportsman. When I was only five years old he gave me a little gun, specially made in Moscow for me, to shoot sparrows with. When I shot some of his prize turkeys with it, he did not punish me; he complimented me on my marksmanship. I killed my first bear in the Caucasus[10] when I was ten. My whole life has been one prolonged hunt. I went into the army—it was expected of noblemen's sons—and for a time commanded a division of Cossack cavalry, but my real interest was always the hunt. I have hunted every kind of game in every land. It would be impossible for me to tell you how many animals I have killed."

The general puffed at his cigarette.

"After the debacle[11] in Russia I left the country, for it was imprudent for an officer of the Czar to stay there. Many noble Russians lost

---

9. **Crimea** (krī mē′ ə) region in southwestern Russia on the Black Sea.
10. **Caucasus** (kô′ kə səs) mountain range in southern Russia.
11. **debacle** (di bäk′ əl) *n.* bad defeat—Zaroff is referring to the Russian Revolution of 1917, a defeat for upper-class Russians like himself.

Literary Analysis
Suspense How does this discussion about the biggest game create suspense?

**Reading Check**

Why has Zaroff lost interest in hunting tigers?

everything. I, luckily, had invested heavily in American securities, so I shall never have to open a tea room in Monte Carlo or drive a taxi in Paris. Naturally, I continued to hunt—grizzlies in your Rockies, crocodiles in the Ganges, rhinoceroses in East Africa. It was in Africa that the Cape buffalo hit me and laid me up for six months. As soon as I recovered I started for the Amazon to hunt jaguars, for I had heard they were unusually cunning. They weren't." The Cossack◆ sighed. "They were no match at all for a hunter with his wits about him, and a high-powered rifle. I was bitterly disappointed. I was lying in my tent with a splitting headache one night when a terrible thought pushed its way into my mind. Hunting was beginning to bore me! And hunting, remember, had been my life. I have heard that in America business men often go to pieces when they give up the business that has been their life."

"Yes, that's so," said Rainsford.

The general smiled. "I had no wish to go to pieces," he said. "I must do something. Now, mine is an analytical mind, Mr. Rainsford. Doubtless that is why I enjoy the problems of the chase."

"No doubt, General Zaroff."

"So," continued the general, "I asked myself why the hunt no longer fascinated me. You are much younger than I am, Mr. Rainsford, and have not hunted as much, but you perhaps can guess the answer."

"What was it?"

"Simply this: hunting had ceased to be what you call 'a sporting proposition.' It had become too easy. I always got my quarry. Always. There is no greater bore than perfection."

The general lit a fresh cigarette.

"No animal had a chance with me any more. That is no boast; it is a mathematical certainty. The animal had nothing but his legs and his instinct. Instinct is no match for reason. When I thought of this it was a tragic moment for me, I can tell you."

Rainsford leaned across the table, absorbed in what his host was saying.

"It came to me as an inspiration what I must do," the general went on.

"And that was?"

The general smiled the quiet smile of one who has faced an obstacle and surmounted it with success. "I had to invent a new animal to hunt," he said.

"A new animal? You're joking."

"Not at all," said the general. "I never joke about hunting. I needed a new animal. I found one. So I bought this island, built this house, and here I do my hunting. The island is perfect for my purpose—there are jungles with a maze of trails in them, hills, swamps—"

Literature in context History Connection

◆ **Cossack**

Zaroff was a Cossack, a member of a special Russian military unit that enjoyed an elite and privileged status. As a result, these soldiers were fiercely independent. When the czar—the ruler of Russia—was overthrown in the Russian Revolution of 1917, Cossacks like Zaroff were banished, executed, or forced into exile. As a Cossack, Zaroff is unwilling to acknowledge that the rules of ordinary people apply to him.

Czar Nicholas II, overthrown in the Russian Revolution of 1917

Literary Analysis

Suspense What do you think Zaroff is going to identify as the "most dangerous game"? Explain.

"But the animal, General Zaroff?"

"Oh," said the general, "it supplies me with the most exciting hunting in the world. No other hunting compares with it for an instant. Every day I hunt, and I never grow bored now, for I have a quarry with which I can match my wits."

Rainsford's bewilderment showed in his face.

"I wanted the ideal animal to hunt," explained the general. "So I said: 'What are the attributes of an ideal quarry?' And the answer was, of course: 'It must have courage, cunning, and, above all, it must be able to reason.' "

"But no animal can reason," objected Rainsford.

"My dear fellow," said the general, "there is one that can."

"But you can't mean—" gasped Rainsford.

"And why not?"

"I can't believe you are serious, General Zaroff. This is a grisly joke."

"Why should I not be serious? I am speaking of hunting."

"Hunting? General Zaroff, what you speak of is murder."

The general laughed with entire good nature. He regarded Rainsford quizzically. "I refuse to believe that so modern and civilized a young man as you seem to be harbors romantic ideas about the value of human life. Surely your experiences in the war—"

"Did not make me condone cold-blooded murder," finished Rainsford stiffly.

Laughter shook the general. "How extraordinarily droll you are!" he said. "One does not expect nowadays to find a young man of the educated class, even in America, with such a <u>naive</u>, and, if I may say so, mid-Victorian point of view.[12] It's like finding a snuff-box in a limousine. Ah, well, doubtless you had Puritan ancestors. So many Americans appear to have had. I'll wager you'll forget your notions when you go hunting with me. You've a genuine new thrill in store for you, Mr. Rainsford."

"Thank you, I'm a hunter, not a murderer."

"Dear me," said the general, quite unruffled, "again that unpleasant word. But I think I can show you that your <u>scruples</u> are quite ill founded."

"Yes?"

"Life is for the strong, to be lived by the strong, and, if need be, taken by the strong. The weak of the world were put here to give the strong pleasure. I am strong. Why should I not use my gift? If I wish to hunt, why should I not? I hunt the scum of the earth—sailors from tramp ships—lascars,[13] blacks, Chinese, whites, mongrels—a thoroughbred horse or hound is worth more than a score of them."

"But they are men," said Rainsford hotly.

"Precisely," said the general. "That is why I use them. It gives me pleasure. They can reason, after a fashion. So they are dangerous."

"But where do you get them?"

---

naive (nä ēv´) *adj.* unsophisticated

scruples (scroo´ pəlz) *n.* misgivings about something one feels is wrong

**Reading Check**

What kind of animal does Zaroff hunt?

---

12. **mid-Victorian point of view** a point of view emphasizing proper behavior and associated with the time of Queen Victoria of England (1819–1901).
13. **lascars** (las´ kərz) *n.* Oriental sailors, especially natives of India.

The general's left eyelid fluttered down in a wink. "This island is called Ship-Trap," he answered. "Sometimes an angry god of the high seas sends them to me. Sometimes, when Providence is not so kind, I help Providence a bit. Come to the window with me."

Rainsford went to the window and looked out toward the sea.

"Watch! Out there!" exclaimed the general, pointing into the night. Rainsford's eyes saw only blackness, and then, as the general pressed a button, far out to sea Rainsford saw the flash of lights.

The general chuckled. "They indicate a channel," he said, "where there's none: giant rocks with razor edges crouch like a sea monster with wide-open jaws. They can crush a ship as easily as I crush this nut." He dropped a walnut on the hardwood floor and brought his heel grinding down on it. "Oh, yes," he said, casually, as if in answer to a question, "I have electricity. We try to be civilized here."

▲ **Critical Viewing**
What might it be like to hunt in an environment such as the one pictured here? **[Speculate]**

"Civilized? And you shoot down men?"

A trace of anger was in the general's black eyes, but it was there for but a second, and he said, in his most pleasant manner: "Dear me, what a righteous young man you are! I assure you I do not do the thing you suggest. That would be barbarous. I treat these visitors with every consideration. They get plenty of good food and exercise. They get into splendid physical condition. You shall see for yourself tomorrow."

"What do you mean?"

"We'll visit my training school," smiled the general. "It's in the cellar. I have about a dozen pupils down there now. They're from the Spanish bark San Lucar that had the bad luck to go on the rocks out there. A very inferior lot, I regret to say. Poor specimens and more accustomed to the deck than to the jungle."

He raised his hand, and Ivan, who served as waiter, brought thick Turkish coffee. Rainsford, with an effort, held his tongue in check.

"It's a game, you see," pursued the general <u>blandly</u>. "I suggest to one of them that we go hunting. I give him a supply of food and an excellent hunting knife. I give him three hours' start. I am to follow, armed only with a pistol of the smallest caliber and range. If my quarry eludes me for three whole days, he wins the game. If I find him"—the general smiled—"he loses."

"Suppose he refuses to be hunted?"

"Oh," said the general, "I give him his option, of course. He need not play the game if he doesn't wish to. If he does not wish to hunt, I turn

blandly (bland´ lē) *adv.* in a mild and soothing manner

him over to Ivan. Ivan once had the honor of serving as official knouter[14] to the Great White Czar, and he has his own ideas of sport. Invariably, Mr. Rainsford, invariably they choose the hunt."

"And if they win?"

The smile on the general's face widened. "To date I have not lost," he said.

Then he added, hastily: "I don't wish you to think me a braggart, Mr. Rainsford. Many of them afford only the most elementary sort of problem. Occasionally I strike a tartar.[15] One almost did win. I eventually had to use the dogs."

"The dogs?"

"This way, please. I'll show you."

The general steered Rainsford to a window. The lights from the windows sent a flickering illumination that made <u>grotesque</u> patterns on the courtyard below, and Rainsford could see moving about there a dozen or so huge black shapes; as they turned toward him, their eyes glittered greenly.

grotesque (grō tesk') *adj.* having a strange, bizarre design

"A rather good lot, I think," observed the general. "They are let out at seven every night. If anyone should try to get into my house—or out of it—something extremely regrettable would occur to him." He hummed a snatch of song from the Folies Bergère.[16]

"And now," said the general, "I want to show you my new collection of heads. Will you come with me to the library?"

"I hope," said Rainsford, "that you will excuse me tonight, General Zaroff. I'm really not feeling at all well."

"Ah, indeed?" the general inquired solicitously. "Well, I suppose that's only natural, after your long swim. You need a good, restful night's sleep. Tomorrow you'll feel like a new man, I'll wager. Then we'll hunt, eh? I've one rather promising prospect—"

Rainsford was hurrying from the room.

"Sorry you can't go with me tonight," called the general. "I expect rather fair sport—a big, strong black. He looks resourceful—Well good night, Mr. Rainsford; I hope you have a good night's rest."

The bed was good, and the pajamas of the softest silk, and he was tired in every fiber of his being, but nevertheless Rainsford could not quiet his brain with the opiate of sleep. He lay, eyes wide open. Once he thought he heard stealthy steps in the corridor outside his room. He sought to throw open the door; it would not open. He went to the window and looked out. His room was high up in one of the towers. The lights of the château were out now, and it was dark and silent, but there was a fragment of sallow moon, and by its wan light he could see, dimly, the courtyard; there, weaving in and out in the pattern of shadow, were black, noiseless forms; the hounds heard him at the window and looked up, expectantly, with their green eyes. Rainsford went back to the bed

---

14. **knouter** (nout´ ər) *n.* someone who beats criminals with a leather whip, or knout.
15. **tartar** (tär´ tər) *n.* stubborn, violent person.
16. **Folies Bergère** (fô´ lē ber zher´) musical theater in Paris.

**Reading Check**

Explain the game that Zaroff plays.

and lay down. By many methods he tried to put himself to sleep. He had achieved a doze when, just as morning began to come, he heard, far off in the jungle, the faint report of a pistol.

General Zaroff did not appear until luncheon. He was dressed faultlessly in the tweeds of a country squire. He was solicitous about the state of Rainsford's health.

"As for me," sighed the general, "I do not feel so well. I am worried, Mr. Rainsford. Last night I detected traces of my old complaint."

To Rainsford's questioning glance the general said: "Ennui. Boredom."

Then, taking a second helping of crêpes suzette, the general explained: "The hunting was not good last night. The fellow lost his head. He made a straight trail that offered no problems at all. That's the trouble with these sailors; they have dull brains to begin with, and they do not know how to get about in the woods. They do excessively stupid and obvious things. It's most annoying. Will you have another glass of Chablis, Mr. Rainsford?"

"General," said Rainsford firmly, "I wish to leave this island at once."

The general raised his thickets of eyebrows; he seemed hurt. "But, my dear fellow," the general protested, "you've only just come. You've had no hunting—"

"I wish to go today," said Rainsford. He saw the dead black eyes of the general on him, studying him. General Zaroff's face suddenly brightened.

He filled Rainsford's glass with venerable Chablis from a dusty bottle.

"Tonight," said the general, "we will hunt—you and I."

Rainsford shook his head. "No, general," he said. "I will not hunt."

The general shrugged his shoulders and delicately ate a hothouse grape. "As you wish, my friend," he said. "The choice rests entirely with you. But may I not venture to suggest that you will find my idea of sport more diverting than Ivan's?"

He nodded toward the corner to where the giant stood, scowling, his thick arms crossed on his hogshead of chest.

"You don't mean—" cried Rainsford.

"My dear fellow," said the general, "have I not told you I always mean what I say about hunting? This is really an inspiration. I drink to a foeman worthy of my steel—at last."

The general raised his glass, but Rainsford sat staring at him.

"You'll find this game worth playing," the general said enthusiastically. "Your brain against mine. Your woodcraft against mine. Your strength and stamina against mine. Outdoor chess! And the stake is not without value, eh?"

"And if I win—" began Rainsford huskily.

"I'll cheerfully acknowledge myself defeated if I do not find you by midnight of the third day," said General Zaroff. "My sloop will place you on the mainland near a town."

The general read what Rainsford was thinking.

"Oh, you can trust me," said the Cossack. "I will give you my word as

▲ **Critical Viewing**
How does Rainsford's room, high in a tower, add to the suspense of the story? **[Connect]**

Literary Analysis
Suspense and Conflict
Why does this conflict between Rainsford and Zaroff escalate the suspense?

a gentleman and a sportsman. Of course you, in turn, must agree to say nothing of your visit here."

"I'll agree to nothing of the kind," said Rainsford.

"Oh," said the general, "in that case— But why discuss that now? Three days hence we can discuss it over a bottle of Veuve Cliquot, unless—"

The general sipped his wine.

Then a businesslike air animated him. "Ivan," he said to Rainsford, "will supply you with hunting clothes, food, a knife. I suggest you wear moccasins; they leave a poorer trail. I suggest too that you avoid the big swamp in the southeast corner of the island. We call it Death Swamp. There's quicksand there. One foolish fellow tried it. The deplorable part of it was that Lazarus followed him. You can imagine my feelings, Mr. Rainsford. I loved Lazarus; he was the finest hound in my pack. Well, I must beg you to excuse me now. I always take a siesta after lunch. You'll hardly have time for a nap, I fear. You'll want to start, no doubt. I shall not follow till dusk. Hunting at night is so much more exciting than by day, don't you think? Au revoir,[17] Mr. Rainsford, au revoir."

General Zaroff, with a deep, courtly bow, strolled from the room.

From another door came Ivan. Under one arm he carried khaki hunting clothes, a haversack of food, a leather sheath containing a long-bladed hunting knife; his right hand rested on a cocked revolver thrust in the crimson sash about his waist. . . .

Reading Strategy
Using Context Clues
Which clues help you determine the meaning of *hence*?

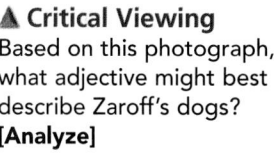

▲ **Critical Viewing**
Based on this photograph, what adjective might best describe Zaroff's dogs? **[Analyze]**

Rainsford had fought his way through the bush for two hours. "I must keep my nerve. I must keep my nerve," he said through tight teeth.

He had not been entirely clear-headed when the château gates snapped shut behind him.

His whole idea at first was to put distance between himself and General Zaroff, and, to this end, he had plunged along, spurred on by the sharp rowels of something very like panic. Now he had got a grip on himself, had stopped, and was taking stock of himself and the situation.

He saw that straight flight was <u>futile</u>; inevitably it would bring him face to face with the sea. He was in a picture with a frame of water, and his operations, clearly, must take place within that frame.

"I'll give him a trail to follow," muttered Rainsford, and he struck off from the rude paths he had been following into the trackless wilderness. He executed a series of intricate loops; he doubled on his trail again and again, recalling all the lore of the fox hunt, and all the dodges of the fox. Night found him leg-weary, with his hands and face lashed by the branches, on a thickly wooded ridge. He knew it would be insane to blunder on through the dark, even if he had the strength. His need for rest was imperative and he thought: "I have played the fox, now I must

futile (fyo͞ot′ əl) *adj.* useless; hopeless

Reading Check
What is Rainsford's initial strategy?

---

17. au revoir (ō′ rə vwär′) French for "until we meet again."

play the cat of the fable." A big tree with a thick trunk and outspread branches was nearby, and, taking care to leave not the slightest mark, he climbed up into the crotch, and stretching out on one of the broad limbs, after a fashion, rested. Rest brought him new confidence and almost a feeling of security. Even so zealous a hunter as General Zaroff could not trace him there, he told himself; only the devil himself could follow that complicated trail through the jungle after dark. But, perhaps, the general was a devil—

An apprehensive night crawled slowly by like a wounded snake, and sleep did not visit Rainsford, although the silence of a dead world was on the jungle. Toward morning when a dingy gray was varnishing the sky, the cry of some startled bird focused Rainsford's attention in that direction. Something was coming through the bush, coming slowly, carefully, coming by the same winding way Rainsford had come. He flattened himself down on the limb, and through a screen of leaves almost as thick as tapestry, he watched. The thing that was approaching was a man.

It was General Zaroff. He made his way along with his eyes fixed in utmost concentration on the ground before him. He paused, almost beneath the tree, dropped to his knees and studied the ground. Rainsford's impulse was to hurl himself down like a panther, but he saw the general's right hand held something metallic—a small automatic pistol.

The hunter shook his head several times, as if he were puzzled. Then he straightened up and took from his case one of his black cigarettes; its pungent incense-like smoke floated up to Rainsford's nostrils.

Rainsford held his breath. The general's eyes had left the ground and were traveling inch by inch up the tree. Rainsford froze there, every muscle tensed for a spring. But the sharp eyes of the hunter stopped before they reached the limb where Rainsford lay; a smile spread over his brown face. Very deliberately he blew a smoke ring into the air; then he turned his back on the tree and walked carelessly away, back along the trail he had come. The swish of the underbrush against his hunting boots grew fainter and fainter.

The pent-up air burst hotly from Rainsford's lungs. His first thought made him feel sick and numb. The general could follow a trail through the woods at night; he could follow an extremely difficult trail; he must have uncanny powers; only by the merest chance had the Cossack failed to see his quarry.

Rainsford's second thought was even more terrible. It sent a shudder of cold horror through his whole being. Why had the general smiled? Why had he turned back?

Rainsford did not want to believe what his reason told him was true, but the truth was as evident as the sun that had by now pushed through the morning mists. The general was playing with him! The general was saving him for another day's sport! The Cossack was the cat; he was the mouse. Then it was that Rainsford knew the full meaning of terror.

"I will not lose my nerve. I will not."

Literary Analysis
Suspense Which words in this paragraph help create suspense?

Literary Analysis
Suspense and Conflict How are the conflict and suspense intensified at this point?

He slid down from the tree, and struck off again into the woods. His face was set and he forced the machinery of his mind to function. Three hundred yards from his hiding place he stopped where a huge dead tree leaned precariously on a smaller, living one. Throwing off his sack of food, Rainsford took his knife from its sheath and began to work with all his energy.

The job was finished at last, and he threw himself down behind a fallen log a hundred feet away. He did not have to wait long. The cat was coming again to play with the mouse.

Following the trail with the sureness of a bloodhound, came General Zaroff. Nothing escaped those searching black eyes, no crushed blade of grass, no bent twig, no mark, no matter how faint, in the moss. So intent was the Cossack on his stalking that he was upon the thing Rainsford had made before he saw it. His foot touched the protruding bough that was the trigger. Even as he touched it, the general sensed his danger and leaped back with the agility of an ape. But he was not quite quick enough; the dead tree, delicately adjusted to rest on the cut living one, crashed down and struck the general a glancing blow on the shoulder as it fell; but for his alertness, he must have been smashed beneath it. He staggered, but he did not fall; nor did he drop his revolver. He stood there, rubbing his injured shoulder, and Rainsford, with fear again gripping his heart, heard the general's mocking laugh ring through the jungle.

"Rainsford," called the general, "if you are within the sound of my voice, as I suppose you are, let me congratulate you. Not many men know how to make a Malay man-catcher. Luckily, for me, I too have hunted in Malacca. You are proving interesting, Mr. Rainsford. I am going now to have my wound dressed; it's only a slight one. But I shall be back. I shall be back."

When the general, nursing his bruised shoulder, had gone, Rainsford took up his flight again. It was flight now, a desperate, hopeless flight, that carried him on for some hours. Dusk came, then darkness, and still he pressed on. The ground grew softer under his moccasins; the vegetation grew ranker, denser; insects bit him savagely. Then, as he stepped forward, his foot sank into the ooze. He tried to wrench it back, but the muck sucked viciously at his foot as if it were a giant leech. With a violent effort, he tore his foot loose. He knew where he was now. Death Swamp and its quicksand.

His hands were tight closed as if his nerve were something tangible that someone in the darkness was trying to tear from his grip. The softness of the earth had given him an idea. He stepped back from the quicksand a dozen feet or so, and, like some huge prehistoric beaver, he began to dig.

Rainsford had dug himself in in France◆ when a second's delay meant death. That had been a placid pastime compared to his digging now.

Literature in context Social Studies Connection

◆ *WWI Trenches*

When Rainsford "digs himself in," he is drawing on his experience as a soldier. In World War I, soldiers protected themselves from their enemies by digging deep trenches. The soldiers then lived in the trenches and took turns charging the enemy's trenches in the face of machine-gun fire. Imagine the fear Rainsford must feel if his experience as a soldier is considered "a placid pastime compared to his digging now."

Canadian Troops Leave the Trenches, World War I

✓**Reading Check**

What does Rainsford build in an effort to save himself?

The pit grew deeper; when it was above his shoulders, he climbed out and from some hard saplings cut stakes and sharpened them to a fine point. These stakes he planted in the bottom of the pit with the points sticking up. With flying fingers he wove a rough carpet of weeds and branches and with it he covered the mouth of the pit. Then, wet with sweat and aching with tiredness, he crouched behind the stump of a lightning-charred tree.

He knew his pursuer was coming; he heard the padding sound of feet on the soft earth, and the night breeze brought him the perfume of the general's cigarette. It seemed to Rainsford that the general was coming with unusual swiftness; he was not feeling his way along, foot by foot. Rainsford, crouching there, could not see the general, nor could he see the pit. He lived a year in a minute. Then he felt an impulse to cry aloud with joy, for he heard the sharp crackle of the breaking branches as the cover of the pit gave way; he heard the sharp scream of pain as the pointed stakes found their mark. He leaped up from his place of concealment. Then he cowered back. Three feet from the pit a man was standing, with an electric torch in his hand.

"You've done well, Rainsford," the voice of the general called. "Your Burmese tiger pit has claimed one of my best dogs. Again you score. I think, Mr. Rainsford, I'll see what you can do against my whole pack. I'm going home for a rest now. Thank you for a most amusing evening."

At daybreak Rainsford, lying near the swamp, was awakened by a sound that made him know that he had new things to learn about fear.

Literary Analysis
Suspense How does Rainsford feel after his efforts? How does this passage make you, the reader, feel?

◀ **Critical Viewing**
Imagine Rainsford at the edge of the cliff. What would result from his leaping into the crashing waves? **[Speculate]**

It was a distant sound, faint and wavering, but he knew it. It was the baying of a pack of hounds.

Rainsford knew he could do one of two things. He could stay where he was and wait. That was suicide. He could flee. That was postponing the inevitable. For a moment he stood there, thinking. An idea that held a wild chance came to him, and, tightening his belt, he headed away from the swamp.

The baying of the hounds drew nearer, then still nearer, nearer, ever nearer. On a ridge Rainsford climbed a tree. Down a watercourse, not a quarter of a mile away, he could see the bush moving. Straining his eyes, he saw the lean figure of General Zaroff; just ahead of him Rainsford made out another figure whose wide shoulders surged through the tall jungle weeds; it was the giant Ivan, and he seemed pulled forward by some unseen force; Rainsford knew that Ivan must be holding the pack in leash.

They would be on him any minute now. His mind worked frantically. He thought of a native trick he had learned in Uganda. He slid down the tree. He caught hold of a springy young sapling and to it he fastened his hunting knife, with the blade pointing down the trail; with a bit of wild grapevine he tied back the sapling. Then he ran for his life. The hounds raised their voices as they hit the fresh scent. Rainsford knew now how an animal at bay feels.

He had to stop to get his breath. The baying of the hounds stopped abruptly, and Rainsford's heart stopped too. They must have reached the knife.

He shinnied excitedly up a tree and looked back. His pursuers had stopped. But the hope that was in Rainsford's brain when he climbed died, for he saw in the shallow valley that General Zaroff was still on his feet. But Ivan was not. The knife, driven by the recoil of the springing tree, had not wholly failed.

"Nerve, nerve, nerve!" he panted, as he dashed along. A blue gap showed between the trees dead ahead. Ever nearer drew the hounds. Rainsford forced himself on toward that gap. He reached it. It was the shore of the sea. Across a cove he could see the gloomy gray stone of the château. Twenty feet below him the sea rumbled and hissed. Rainsford hesitated. He heard the hounds. Then he leaped far out into the sea. . . .

When the general and his pack reached the place by the sea, the Cossack stopped. For some minutes he stood regarding the blue-green expanse of water. He shrugged his shoulders. Then he sat down, took a drink of brandy from a silver flask, lit a perfumed cigarette, and hummed a bit from *Madame Butterfly*.[18]

General Zaroff had an exceedingly good dinner in his great paneled dining hall that evening. With it he had a bottle of Pol Roger and half a bottle of Chambertin. Two slight annoyances kept him from perfect enjoyment. One was the thought that it would be difficult to replace Ivan; the other was that his quarry had escaped him; of course the

---

18. *Madame Butterfly* an opera by Giacomo Puccini.

Literary Analysis
Suspense How does this peaceful scene add to the suspense?

✔**Reading Check**
What happens to Ivan during the hunt?

American hadn't played the game—so thought the general as he tasted his after-dinner liqueur. In his library he read, to soothe himself, from the works of Marcus Aurelius.[19] At ten he went up to his bedroom. He was deliciously tired, he said to himself, as he locked himself in. There was a little moonlight, so, before turning on his light, he went to the window and looked down at the courtyard. He could see the great hounds, and he called: "Better luck another time," to them. Then he switched on the light.

A man, who had been hiding in the curtain of the bed, was standing there.

"Rainsford!" screamed the general. "How in God's name did you get here?"

"Swam," said Rainsford. "I found it quicker than walking through the jungle."

The general sucked in his breath and smiled. "I congratulate you," he said. "You have won the game."

Rainsford did not smile. "I am still a beast at bay," he said, in a low, hoarse voice. "Get ready, General Zaroff."

The general made one of his deepest bows. "I see," he said. "Splendid! One of us is to furnish a repast for the hounds. The other will sleep in this very excellent bed. On guard, Rainsford. . . ."

He had never slept in a better bed, Rainsford decided.

---

19. **Marcus Aurelius** (ô rē´ lē əs) Roman emperor and philosopher (A.D. 121–180).

Review and Assess

Thinking About the Selection

1. **Respond:** What do you admire or dislike about Rainsford?

2. **(a) Recall:** What, according to Zaroff, is the most dangerous game? **(b) Analyze:** Based on his attitude, would you call Zaroff "civilized"? Why or why not?

3. **(a) Recall:** Early in the story, what do you learn about Rainsford's views on hunting? **(b) Compare and Contrast:** How does Rainsford's attitude toward hunting compare with Zaroff's?

4. **(a) Recall:** What happens at the end of the story? **(b) Infer:** In the last scene of the story, why does Rainsford say "I am still a beast at bay"?

5. **Draw Conclusions:** How do you think the hunting experience with Zaroff changed Rainsford?

6. **(a) Analyze:** What words would you use to describe Zaroff's character? **(b) Apply:** Do you think people like Zaroff exist in real life? Explain.

Richard Connell

(1893–1949)

Richard Connell seemed destined to become a writer: He was a sports reporter at the age of ten! By the time he was sixteen, Connell was editing his father's newspaper in Poughkeepsie, New York. He stayed involved in journalism at Harvard University, where he was an editor for the *Daily Crimson.* During World War I, Connell edited his division's newspaper and reported on wartime events.

In 1924, Connell published the story you have just read. A year later, he settled in Beverly Hills, California. The film version of "The Most Dangerous Game" was released in 1932 and has inspired many other adventure movies. Connell's success as a movie screenwriter continued for the rest of his life, and he received two Academy Award nominations for his work.

Review and Assess

Literary Analysis

Suspense

1. (a) Find three details that provide early clues about Zaroff's hobby. (b) How do these clues create **suspense**?

2. Using a chart like the one below, show how the details of Rainford's first night build a sense of dread.

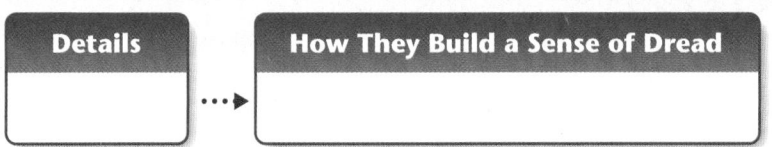

Details		How They Build a Sense of Dread
	...▶	

3. In your opinion, what are the three most suspenseful events in the story? Why?

Connecting Literary Elements

4. Early in the story, Rainsford says, "The world is made up of two classes—the hunters and the huntees." How does his **conflict** with Zaroff help Rainsford understand this expression in a new way?

5. In addition to conflicts between characters, stories may include conflicts between a character and nature and internal conflicts within a character. Use a chart like this one to explain each conflict.

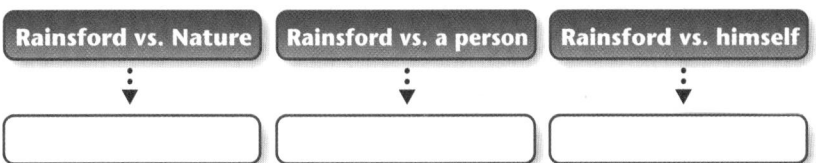

Rainsford vs. Nature	Rainsford vs. a person	Rainsford vs. himself
⋮	⋮	⋮
▼	▼	▼

Reading Strategy

Using Context Clues

6. For each passage from the story, give an approximate meaning for the italicized word and explain which **context clues** helped you.
   (a) He heard [the sound] again; then it was cut short by another noise, crisp, *staccato*. "Pistol shot," muttered Rainsford, swimming on. (b) To Rainsford's questioning glance the general said: "*Ennui*. Boredom."

Extend Understanding

7. **Career Connection:** What careers, other than hunter, would be suited to someone with Rainsford's skills and attitudes? Why?

Integrate Language Skills

Vocabulary Development Lesson

Word Analysis: Forms of *scruples*

The noun *scruples* refers to the uncomfortable feeling one has about doing something one thinks is wrong. By adding the suffix *-ous*, you form *scrupulous*, which means "having scruples."

Use *scruples*, *scrupulous*, and *unscrupulous* in a paragraph.

Spelling Strategy

The suffixes *-able* and *-ible* have the same meaning but slightly different spellings. The suffix *-able*, as in *palpable*, is more common, but *-ible*, as in *tangible*, sometimes applies.

Review each item below. Write *Correct* if the spelling is correct. If the spelling is incorrect, write the correct spelling.

1. terrable   3. regrettible
2. unquenchable   4. impossable

Fluency: Clarify Word Meaning

Complete each item with a vocabulary word from the list on page 17.

1. The farmer was ___?___ about city life.
2. "Surrender now," commanded the conqueror. "Resistance is ___?___."
3. The silence was so ___?___ that you could cut it with a knife.
4. He lounged on the couch ___?___.
5. They met under rather ___?___ circumstances: a camel auction.
6. With its fans and twisted features, the mask was amazingly ___?___.
7. The officer phrased his sentences ___?___ to avoid making people angry.
8. She had her ___?___ and would not give in to peer pressure.

Grammar Lesson

Pronouns and Antecedents

Pronouns are words that stand for nouns or for words that take the place of nouns. **Antecedents** are the words for which pronouns stand. Some of the most common pronouns are *I/me/my/mine*, *you/your/yours*, *he/him/his*, *she/her/hers*, *we/us/our/ours*, and *they/them/their/theirs*.

In these examples, the pronouns are set in italics; the antecedents are underlined.

> **Examples:** <u>Rainsford</u> feared for *his* life.
>
> Zaroff's <u>dogs</u> used *their* sense of smell.
>
> The <u>jungle</u> is a unique place with *its* wild animals and dense trees.

Practice Copy these sentences. Underline each pronoun and circle its antecedent.

1. One superstitious sailor can taint the whole company with his fear.
2. Rainsford remembered the shots. They had come from the right.
3. Follow Ivan, if you please, Mr. Rainsford. . . .
4. The general said, "I was about to have my dinner."
5. He had never slept better, Rainsford decided.

Writing Application Write sentences that include pronouns by using *Rainsford* and *jungle* as the antecedents.

 Prentice Hall Writing and Grammar Connection: Chapter 16, Section 2

Writing Lesson

Survival Manual

Rainsford triumphs because he has the knowledge he needs to survive. Think about Rainsford's situation, and create a set of detailed instructions on how to survive a ruthless pursuer that you think Rainsford would write.

Prewriting   Review the story and note the techniques Rainsford uses. Make a list of questions readers might have about techniques. Then, arrange your notes into a logical order.

Model: Anticipating Readers' Questions

What materials would I need if I were building a trap?

Could I build a trap if I didn't have tools? How?

How large or deep should the trap be?

> A list of potential trouble spots can help a writer plan an effective guide.

Drafting   Using your questions and answers, write a first draft of Rainsford's survival manual. Give precise measurements or other specifications, define terms, and provide examples when necessary.

Revising   To improve your draft, try to follow the instructions. For example, if you have described how to create a trap, try drawing the trap based on your instructions. Add any details necessary to ensure that your readers can follow the directions.

*W*G *Prentice Hall Writing and Grammar Connection: Chapter 11, Section 2*

Extension Activities

Listening and Speaking With a group of classmates, put Rainsford on trial for killing Zaroff. These tips will help you plan a **video trial:**

- Plan arguments for both the prosecution and the defense.
- Have the two sides use props or diagrams to make their arguments accurate and persuasive.

Videotape your trial and show it to the rest of your class. After classmates see the video, discuss the effect of this form of media on viewers' perceptions of the trial. **[Group Activity]**

Research and Technology Hunting has threatened the population of many big-game species. Create a **database** of information about two or three big-game species, such as moose, jaguar, lion, tiger, elephant, crocodile, grizzly bear, or Cape buffalo. Use the database to help prepare a presentation about these species and their status today.

 Take It to the Net   www.phschool.com

Go online for an additional research activity using the Internet.

Prepare to Read

Casey at the Bat

Baseball Players Practicing, 1875, Thomas Eakins Museum of Art, Rhode Island School of Design

 Take It to the Net

Visit www.phschool.com for interactive activities and instruction related to "Casey at the Bat," including

- background
- graphic organizers
- literary elements
- reading strategies

Preview

Connecting to the Literature

Sporting events can really keep you on the edge of your seat! An athlete can break a world record, or a losing team can charge to victory at the last minute. This poem may remind you of nail-biting moments you have experienced while either watching or playing a sport.

Background

In most cases, a baseball game does not end until all innings have been played and one team has scored the most runs. As a result, a team that is behind always has the chance for a comeback as long as players keep getting base hits and avoid making the final out. "Casey at the Bat" captures the hopes of a team that is behind by two runs as they go to bat for a final time.

Literary Analysis

Climax and Anticlimax

The **climax** of a story, or any type of narrative, is its biggest moment. During the climax, you can expect the following:

- The action of the story is at its peak.
- The feelings of the readers are at their most intense.

At the climax, you know that you are about to discover how the story's main problem or struggle will turn out.

If the action starts in a grand manner but the outcome is trivial or disappointing, the story has an anticlimax, too. An **anticlimax** is the point at which you learn that the story has not turned out the way you had expected. As you read "Casey at the Bat," notice how the story builds to its climax, and decide whether or not the story has an anticlimax.

Connecting Literary Elements

The climax is a key element in a story—whether that story is told in a movie, a novel, a short story, or a narrative poem. "Casey at the Bat" is an example of a **narrative poem,** a poem that tells a story. Like other stories, a narrative poem has a sequence of events and characters whose lives are set in a specific time and place.

Reading Strategy

Summarizing

Summarizing sections of a poem or story can help you better understand what you are reading. Follow these steps as you summarize:

- State the main points and details of a passage briefly and in your own words.
- Notice important story details and fit them into your picture of what is happening.
- Use your own language and style to express that information.

Use a chart like the one shown here to help you summarize.

Vocabulary Development

pallor (pal´ ər) n. paleness (p. 43)

wreathed (rēthd) v. curled around (p. 43)

writhing (rīth´ iŋ) v. twisting; turning (p. 43)

tumult (too¯´ mult) n. noisy commotion (p. 44)

Instruction with this selection addresses these standards:

R 1.1*, 3.7*
W 1.5*, 2.3*
WOLC 1.3*
LS 1.9, 2.3

* Standards tested on HS Exit Exam. For complete standards, see p. CA 4.

Main Points

- a baseball game
- one team is losing
- fans are watching

Details

Mudville: the home-team fans are worried

Summary

"In the last inning of its game, Mudville is losing. There are two outs against them, and the fans are worried."

Casey at the Bat

Ernest Lawrence Thayer

Baseball Players Practicing, 1875, Thomas Eakins Museum of Art, Rhode Island School of Design

▲ **Critical Viewing** Compare and contrast the stance and attitude of the batter in this painting with Casey's stance and attitude. **[Compare and Contrast]**

It looked extremely rocky for the Mudville nine that day;
The score stood two to four, with but an inning left to play.
So, when Cooney died at second, and Burrows did the same,
A <u>pallor</u> <u>wreathed</u> the features of the patrons of the game.

pallor (pal′ ər) *n.* paleness

wreathed (rēth̄d) *v.* curled around

5   A straggling few got up to go, leaving there the rest,
With that hope which springs eternal within the human breast.
For they thought: "If only Casey would get a whack at that,"
They'd put even money now, with Casey at the bat.

But Flynn preceded Casey, and likewise so did Blake,
10   And the former was a pudd'n, and the latter was a fake.
So on that stricken multitude a deathlike silence sat;
For there seemed but little chance of Casey's getting to the bat.

But Flynn let drive a "single," to the wonderment of all.
And the much-despised Blakey "tore the cover off the ball."
15   And when the dust had lifted, and they saw what had occurred,
There was Blakey safe at second, and Flynn a-huggin' third.

Literary Analysis
Climax and Anticlimax
What expectation for Casey do the successes of Flynn and Blake create?

Then from the gladdened multitude went up a joyous yell—
It rumbled in the mountaintops, it rattled in the dell;[1]
It struck upon the hillside and rebounded on the flat;
20   For Casey, mighty Casey, was advancing to the bat.

There was ease in Casey's manner as he stepped into his place,
There was pride in Casey's bearing and a smile on Casey's face;
And when responding to the cheers he lightly doffed[2] his hat,
No stranger in the crowd could doubt 'twas Casey at the bat.

25   Ten thousand eyes were on him as he rubbed his hands with dirt,
Five thousand tongues applauded when he wiped them on his shirt;
Then when the <u>writhing</u> pitcher ground the ball into his hip,
Defiance glanced in Casey's eye, a sneer curled Casey's lip.

writhing (rīth̄′ iŋ) *v.* twisting; turning

And now the leather-covered sphere came hurtling through the air,
30   And Casey stood a-watching it in haughty grandeur there.
Close by the sturdy batsman the ball unheeded sped;
"That ain't my style," said Casey. "Strike one," the umpire said.

From the benches, black with people, there went up a muffled roar,
Like the beating of the storm waves on the stern and distant shore.
35   "Kill him! kill the umpire!" shouted someone on the stand;
And it's likely they'd have killed him had not Casey raised his hand.

✔Reading Check

What happens when the first ball is thrown to Casey?

---

1. **dell** (del) *n.* small, secluded valley.
2. **doffed** (däft) *v.* lifted.

With a smile of Christian charity great Casey's visage[3] shone;
He stilled the rising <u>tumult</u>, he made the game go on;
He signaled to the pitcher, and once more the spheroid flew;
40   But Casey still ignored it, and the umpire said, "Strike two."

"Fraud!" cried the maddened thousands, and the echo answered
    "Fraud!"
But one scornful look from Casey and the audience was awed;
They saw his face grow stern and cold, they saw his muscles strain,
And they knew that Casey wouldn't let the ball go by again.

45   The sneer is gone from Casey's lips, his teeth are clenched in hate.
He pounds with cruel vengeance his bat upon the plate:
And now the pitcher holds the ball, and now he lets it go,
And now the air is shattered by the force of Casey's blow.

Oh, somewhere in this favored land the sun is shining bright,
50   The band is playing somewhere, and somewhere hearts are light:
And somewhere men are laughing, and somewhere children shout,
But there is no joy in Mudville: Mighty Casey has struck out.

tumult (too´ mult) *n.* noisy commotion

Reading Strategy
Summarizing State the main points and details of these two stanzas briefly and in your own words.

---

3. visage (viz´ ij) *n.* face.

Review and Assess

Thinking About the Selection

1. **Respond:** Did you expect the poem to end the way it did? Why or why not?

2. **(a) Recall:** What happens in the first two stanzas? **(b) Analyze Causes and Effects:** How does the first part of the poem make you want to keep reading?

3. **(a) Recall:** Describe Casey, citing details of his appearance and actions. **(b) Infer:** What type of player would you say Casey is? Why?

4. **(a) Recall:** How is Casey described before the last pitch? **(b) Draw Conclusions:** How might Casey's attitude have affected his game?

5. **(a) Recall:** What is the outcome of Casey's turn at bat? **(b) Speculate:** Based on what you know about Casey, what do you think was his reaction? Why?

6. **(a) Analyze:** Why do you think this poem—written more than a century ago—has remained one of the most popular sports poems to this day? **(b) Evaluate:** Do you think the poem deserves this status? Why or why not?

Ernest Lawrence Thayer

(1863–1940)

It is not surprising that "Casey at the Bat" reads like a sports story in verse. The poet, Ernest Lawrence Thayer, spent many years working as a newspaper reporter. Thayer began his reporting career working on *The Lampoon*, Harvard University's humor magazine. He later worked at newspapers in New York and California.

"Casey at the Bat" first appeared in the *San Francisco Examiner* on June 3, 1888, under Thayer's pen name, Phin. The poem became such a favorite that in 1953 it inspired an operetta called *The Mighty Casey*.

Review and Assess

Literary Analysis

Climax and Anticlimax
1. What problem or struggle sets the stage for the **climax**?
2. Which lines of the poem present the climax itself? Explain.
3. Is the outcome of the poem an **anticlimax**? Why or why not?

Connecting Literary Elements
4. Complete a chart like this one to show that "Casey at the Bat" has the three major elements of a **narrative poem**.

Characters	Time and Place	Sequence of Events

5. To which elements in the chart did Thayer give the most attention? Explain.
6. (a) How would "Casey at the Bat" be different if it were written as a short story or play? (b) Would the story be as effective if it were not told in the form of a poem?

Reading Strategy

Summarizing
7. What information is left out of the following summary of lines 5–8? "Some fans left, but most stayed because they were hopeful."
8. Use a chart like this one to explain what happened at the beginning, middle, and end of the poem. Then, in three sentences, summarize the entire poem.

Beginning	Middle	End
Summary:		

Extend Understanding
9. **Sports Connection:** How might defeat add to a player's popularity?

Quick Review

The **climax** of a narrative is its moment of peak action and greatest intensity. An **anticlimax** occurs when the outcome is trivial or disappointing when compared to the reader's expectations.

A **narrative poem** is a poem that tells a story.

When you **summarize** a passage, you briefly state its main points and details in your own words.

 **Take It to the Net**
www.phschool.com
Take the interactive self-test online to check your understanding of the selection.

Integrate Language Skills

Vocabulary Development Lesson

Word Analysis: Forms of *tumult*

Learning other forms of a word can expand your vocabulary. *Tumult*, a noun, is changed into an adjective, *tumultuous*, by adding the suffix *-ous*. You may already know that the adjective *tumultuous* means "wild and noisy." If so, when you come across the noun *tumult* in "Casey at the Bat," you will be able to figure out that it means "a noisy commotion."

On your paper, complete each sentence with one of the following words.

tumult   tumultuous   tumultuously

1. Her supporters gave the senator a _____?_____ greeting following her speech.
2. An explosion caused a _____?_____ downtown.
3. The crowd responded _____?_____ when he struck out.

Fluency: Words in Sentences

For each item below, write a sentence that uses a word from the vocabulary list on page 41.

1. Write the first sentence of a news article describing a noisy demonstration in the city.
2. Describe the way a snake moves.
3. Explain why you think that your friend may not be feeling well today.
4. Tell about an old house that has ivy growing around its pillars.

Spelling Strategy

When you add the suffix *-ous* to a word, you may need to make additional spelling changes. For example, when you add *-ous* to *tumult*, you add a *u* before the suffix to form *tumultuous*.

Write the adjective form of each noun below.

1. glory   2. tempest   3. religion

Grammar Lesson

Possessive Nouns

A **possessive noun** is used to show ownership. It serves as an adjective by modifying another noun.

In these lines, the possessive nouns are set in italics. Notice that, in the first example, the underlined word that is "owned" is not a physical object but an aspect of Casey's personality.

Examples:	There was ease in *Casey's* <u>manner</u> as he stepped into his place, . . .
	The *team's* <u>defeat</u> was discouraging.
	The *player's* <u>fans</u> roared loudly.

Practice List the five possessive nouns in the following paragraph, as well as the word that is "owned" by each one.

Casey's face broke into a grin when he connected with the ball. Every fan's eyes followed the ball as it flew over the pitcher's head. The ball reached the top of its arc and then fell—right toward an outfielder's glove. It took only a moment's work to catch the ball and declare Casey "out."

Writing Application For each noun below, write a sentence using it as a possessive noun.

1. catcher   2. coach   3. fan

 Prentice Hall Writing and Grammar Connection: Chapter 29, Section 6

Writing Lesson

Sportscast

Like "Casey at the Bat," a good sportscast uses vivid and lively language. Vivid language captures the thrills and disappointments of a sports event. Write a sportscast about Casey's experience that hooks your audience and tells a good story.

Prewriting Create a list of the vivid verbs—action words with a punch—that describe Casey's experience. For example, list ways that Casey might swing the bat or ways the pitcher might throw the ball to Casey.

Drafting As you draft, picture the game in your mind. Make sure the verbs you choose are appropriate for describing a baseball game.

Revising Reread your draft. Using this model as an example, circle the verbs in your draft and decide whether more lively action words would make your writing sparkle.

Model: Revising to Include Vivid Verbs

raced
Ana Moreno ran down the court, the Panthers in hot pursuit.

spotted   *slipped*
She saw a teammate's signal and gave Keisha Washington the

bagged
ball. Washington's play got the victory.

> Vivid verbs make the action in these sentences more exciting and easier to visualize.

WG *Prentice Hall Writing and Grammar Connection: Chapter 4, Section 4*

Extension Activities

Listening and Speaking With a partner, role-play a **sports interview** with Casey. Follow these suggestions as you plan:

- Identify your audience and list the questions that would interest them.
- Practice verbal strategies, such as changing the pitch and tone of your voice. For example, if Casey is upset about the recent loss, he should sound disappointed or angry.

Role-play your interview in front of your class, and ask classmates to evaluate your work. **[Group Activity]**

Research and Technology In "Casey at the Bat," the fans have very high expectations of Casey, Mudville's famous player. Write a **research report** comparing a famous baseball player in history to a famous present-day baseball player. Use library resources such as the Internet, newspapers, and books to research the experiences of each player. In your report, compare their lifestyles and successes.

Take It to the Net www.phschool.com
Go online for an additional research activity using the Internet.

Prepare to Read

The Birds

 Take It to the Net

Visit www.phschool.com
for interactive activities
and instruction related to
"The Birds," including

- background
- graphic organizers
- literary elements
- reading strategies

Preview

Connecting to the Literature

You step outside and the sky is dark and threatening. Low rumbles of thunder are becoming louder. You look at the threatening scene and fear makes your blood run cold. Daphne du Maurier's "The Birds" will probably evoke these same eerie feelings as you read about nature itself brooding and eventually striking out.

Background

Imagine sitting in a dark movie theater, watching images of flocks of birds descending upon average people in an unsuspecting town. This is what it was like to see *The Birds*, which filmmaker Alfred Hitchcock adapted from this story. After reading "The Birds," you will probably see why Hitchcock decided to adapt the story into his frightening film.

Literary Analysis

Foreshadowing

As its name suggests, **foreshadowing** is the author's use of clues to hint at future events. In this passage from "The Birds," for instance, du Maurier hints at danger to come.

> The birds had been more restless than ever this fall of the year.

Keep an eye out for other examples of foreshadowing as you read; in particular, watch for details that seem unusual or disturbing.

Connecting Literary Elements

Imagery is language that a writer uses to create word pictures for the reader. These pictures, or images, are created by details of sight, sound, taste, touch, smell, or movement. In "The Birds," vivid images help bring the scenes to life. They also call attention to details—and help you discover the foreshadowing clues that du Maurier provides.

Reading Strategy

Predicting

Predicting, or making guesses about what will happen before a story ends, can often help you check your understanding of a story.

- To make a prediction, start by looking for small but unusual details. These details might be minor events that catch your attention but that the characters in the story seem to ignore.
- Ask yourself what would happen if the detail were to become more important. In "The Birds," for example, think about what would happen if a disturbing detail were multiplied many times.
- Note your predictions, but be prepared to revise your guesses as the story develops.

Use a chart to help you record your predictions. The chart shown here presents a small but unusual detail from "The Birds."

CALIFORNIA STANDARDS

Instruction with this selection addresses these standards:

R 1.1*, 3.6*
W 1.1*, 1.3*
WOLC 1.3*
LS 1.8

* Standards tested on HS Exit Exam. For complete standards, see p. CA 4.

Unusual Detail

Nat enjoys working alone.

Magnified Detail

When trouble comes, Nat will have to stand against it alone.

Prediction

Vocabulary Development

placid (plas′ id) *adj.* calm (p. 51)

garish (gar′ ish) *adj.* too bright (p. 54)

recounted (ri kount′ ed) *v.* told in detail; narrated (p. 61)

sullen (sul′ ən) *adj.* gloomy (p. 62)

furtively (fur′ tiv lē) *adv.* stealthily, so as to avoid being heard (p. 67)

imperative (im per′ ə tiv) *adj.* urgent; absolutely necessary (p. 69)

reconnaissance (ri kän′ ə səns) *adj.* exploratory in nature, as when observing to seek information (p. 70)

fretful (fret′ fəl) *adj.* irritable and discontented (p. 77)

The Birds

Daphne du Maurier

Attack of the Birds, 1994, Lev Tabenkin, Maya Polsky Gallery

▲ **Critical Viewing** Based on this painting, what do you think might happen in this story? **[Predict]**

n December the third the wind changed overnight and it was winter. Until then the autumn had been mellow, soft. The leaves had lingered on the trees, golden-red, and the hedgerows were still green. The earth was rich where the plow had turned it.

Nat Hocken, because of a wartime disability, had a pension and did not work full-time at the farm. He worked three days a week, and they gave him the lighter jobs: hedging, thatching, repairs to the farm buildings.

Although he was married, with children, his was a solitary disposition; he liked best to work alone. It pleased him when he was given a bank to build up, or a gate to mend at the far end of the peninsula, where the sea surrounded the farmland on either side. Then, at midday, he would pause and eat the pasty[1] that his wife had baked for him, and, sitting on the cliff's edge, watch the birds. Autumn was best for this, better than spring. In spring the birds flew inland, purposeful, intent; they knew where they were bound; the rhythm and ritual of their life brooked no delay. In autumn those that had not migrated overseas but remained to pass the winter were caught up in the same driving urge, but because migration was denied them followed a pattern of their own. Great flocks of them came to the peninsula, restless, uneasy, spending themselves in motion; now wheeling, circling in the sky, now settling to feed on the rich new-turned soil, but even when they fed it was as though they did so without hunger, without desire. Restlessness drove them to the skies again.

Black and white, jackdaw and gull, mingled in strange partnership, seeking some sort of liberation, never satisfied, never still. Flocks of starlings, rustling like silk, flew to fresh pasture, driven by the same necessity of movement, and the smaller birds, the finches and the larks, scattered from tree to hedge as if compelled.

Nat watched them, and he watched the sea birds too. Down in the bay they waited for the tide. They had more patience. Oyster catchers, redshank, sanderling, and curlew watched by the water's edge; as the slow sea sucked at the shore and then withdrew, leaving the strip of seaweed bare and the shingle churned, the sea birds raced and ran upon the beaches. Then that same impulse to flight seized upon them too. Crying, whistling, calling, they skimmed the <u>placid</u> sea and left the shore. Make haste, make speed, hurry and begone; yet where, and to what purpose? The restless urge of autumn, unsatisfying, sad, had put a spell upon them and they must flock, and wheel, and cry; they must spill themselves of motion before winter came.

"Perhaps," thought Nat, munching his pasty by the cliff's edge, "a message comes to the birds in autumn, like a warning. Winter is coming. Many of them perish. And like the people who, apprehensive of death before their time, drive themselves to work or folly, the birds do likewise."

---

1. pasty (pas´ tē) *n.* a meat pie.

Reading Strategy
Predicting How could this scene of "strange partnership" hint at a danger later on?

placid (plas´ id) *adj.* calm

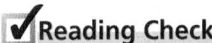**Reading Check**
What happens to the birds that do not migrate?

The birds had been more restless than ever this fall of the year, the agitation more marked because the days were still. As the tractor traced its path up and down the western hills, the figure of the farmer silhouetted on the driving seat, the whole machine and the man upon it would be lost momentarily in the great cloud of wheeling, crying birds. There were many more than usual; Nat was sure of this.

Always, in autumn, they followed the plow, but not in great flocks like these, nor with such clamor.

Nat remarked upon it when hedging was finished for the day. "Yes," said the farmer, "there are more birds about than usual; I've noticed it too. And daring, some of them, taking no notice of the tractor. One or two gulls came so close to my head this afternoon I thought they'd knock my cap off! As it was, I could scarcely see what I was doing, when they were overhead and I had the sun in my eyes. I have a notion the weather will change. It will be a hard winter. That's why the birds are restless."

Nat, tramping home across the fields and down the lane to his cottage, saw the birds still flocking over the western hills, in the last glow of the sun. No wind, and the gray sea calm and full. Campion in bloom yet in the hedges, and the air mild. The farmer was right, though, and it was that night the weather turned. Nat's bedroom faced east. He woke just after two and heard the wind in the chimney. Not the storm and bluster of a sou' westerly gale, bringing the rain, but east wind, cold and dry. It sounded hollow in the chimney, and a loose slate rattled on the roof. Nat listened, and he could hear the sea roaring in the bay. Even the air in the small bedroom had turned chill: a draft came under the skirting of the door, blowing upon the bed. Nat drew the blanket round him, leaned closer to the back of his sleeping wife, and stayed wakeful, watchful, aware of misgiving without cause.

Then he heard the tapping on the window. There was no creeper on the cottage walls to break loose and scratch upon the pane. He listened, and the tapping continued until, irritated by the sound, Nat got out of bed and went to the window. He opened it, and as he did so something brushed his hand, jabbing at his knuckles, grazing the skin. Then he saw the flutter of the wings and it was gone, over the roof, behind the cottage.

It was a bird; what kind of bird he could not tell. The wind must have driven it to shelter on the sill.

He shut the window and went back to bed, but, feeling his knuckles wet, put his mouth to the scratch. The bird had drawn blood. Frightened, he supposed, and bewildered, the bird, seeking shelter, had stabbed at him in the darkness. Once more he settled himself to sleep.

Literary Analysis
Foreshadowing What might the birds' restlessness and large numbers foreshadow?

Literary Analysis
Foreshadowing and Imagery What image of the wind does this description generate, and what might it foreshadow about the next day?

Presently the tapping came again, this time more forceful, more insistent, and now his wife woke at the sound and, turning in the bed, said to him, "See to the window, Nat, it's rattling."

"I've already seen to it," he told her; "there's some bird there trying to get in. Can't you hear the wind? It's blowing from the east, driving the birds to shelter."

"Send them away," she said, "I can't sleep with that noise."

He went to the window for the second time, and now when he opened it there was not one bird upon the sill but half a dozen; they flew straight into his face, attacking him.

He shouted, striking out at them with his arms, scattering them; like the first one, they flew over the roof and disappeared. Quickly he let the window fall and latched it.

"Did you hear that?" he said. "They went for me. Tried to peck my eyes." He stood by the window, peering into the darkness, and could see nothing. His wife, heavy with sleep, murmured from the bed.

"I'm not making it up," he said, angry at her suggestion. "I tell you the birds were on the sill, trying to get into the room."

Suddenly a frightened cry came from the room across the passage where the children slept.

"It's Jill," said his wife, roused at the sound, sitting up in bed. "Go to her, see what's the matter."

Nat lit the candle, but when he opened the bedroom door to cross the passage the draft blew out the flame.

There came a second cry of terror, this time from both children, and stumbling into their room, he felt the beating of wings about him in the darkness. The window was wide open. Through it came the birds, hitting first the ceiling and the walls, then swerving in mid-flight, turning to the children in their beds.

"It's all right, I'm here," shouted Nat, and the children flung themselves, screaming, upon him, while in the darkness the birds rose and dived and came for him again.

"What is it, Nat, what's happened?" his wife called from the further bedroom, and swiftly he pushed the children through the door to the passage and shut it upon them, so that he was alone now in their bedroom with the birds.

He seized a blanket from the nearest bed and, using it as a weapon, flung it to right and left about him in the air. He felt the thud of bodies, heard the fluttering of wings, but they were not yet defeated, for again and again they returned to the assault, jabbing his hands, his head, the little stabbing beaks sharp as pointed forks. The blanket became a weapon of defense; he wound it about his

Reading Strategy
Predicting Based on this detail and others, predict what will happen in the children's room.

✔**Reading Check**

What happens in the children's room?

head, and then in greater darkness beat at the birds with his bare hands. He dared not stumble to the door and open it, lest in doing so the birds should follow him.

How long he fought with them in the darkness he could not tell, but at last the beating of the wings about him lessened and then withdrew, and through the density of the blanket he was aware of light. He waited, listened; there was no sound except the fretful crying of one of the children from the bedroom beyond. The fluttering, the whirring of the wings had ceased.

He took the blanket from his head and stared about him. The cold gray morning light exposed the room. Dawn and the open window had called the living birds; the dead lay on the floor. Nat gazed at the little corpses, shocked and horrified. They were all small birds, none of any size; there must have been fifty of them lying there upon the floor. There were robins, finches, sparrows, blue tits, larks, and bramblings, birds that by nature's law kept to their own flock and their own territory, and now, joining one with another in their urge for battle, had destroyed themselves against the bedroom walls or in the strife had been destroyed by him. Some had lost feathers in the fight; others had blood, his blood, upon their beaks.

Sickened, Nat went to the window and stared out across his patch of garden to the fields.

It was bitter cold, and the ground had all the hard black look of frost. Not white frost, to shine in the morning sun, but the black frost that the east wind brings. The sea, fiercer now with the turning tide, white-capped and steep, broke harshly in the bay. Of the birds there was no sign. Not a sparrow chattered in the hedge beyond the garden gate, no early missel-thrush or blackbird pecked on the grass for worms. There was no sound at all but the east wind and the sea.

Nat shut the window and the door of the small bedroom, and went back across the passage to his own. His wife sat up in bed, one child asleep beside her, the smaller in her arms, his face bandaged. The curtains were tightly drawn across the window, the candles lit. Her face looked <u>garish</u> in the yellow light. She shook her head for silence.

"He's sleeping now," she whispered, "but only just. Something must have cut him, there was blood at the corner of his eyes. Jill said it was the birds. She said she woke up, and the birds were in the room."

His wife looked up at Nat, searching his face for confirmation. She looked terrified, bewildered, and he did not want her to know that he was also shaken, dazed almost, by the events of the past few hours.

"There are birds in there," he said, "dead birds, nearly fifty of them. Robins, wrens, all the little birds from hereabouts. It's as though a madness seized them, with the east wind." He sat down on the bed beside his wife and held her hand. "It's the weather," he said, "it must be that, it's the hard weather. They aren't the birds, maybe, from here around. They've been driven down from upcountry."

"But, Nat," whispered his wife, "it's only this night that the weather

Literary Analysis
Foreshadowing and Imagery What might the imagery of this description foreshadow?

garish (gar´ ish) *adj.* too bright

turned. There's been no snow to drive them. And they can't be hungry yet. There's food for them out there in the fields."

"It's the weather," repeated Nat. "I tell you, it's the weather."

His face, too, was drawn and tired, like hers. They stared at one another for a while without speaking.

"I'll go downstairs and make a cup of tea," he said.

The sight of the kitchen reassured him. The cups and saucers, neatly stacked upon the dresser, the table and chairs, his wife's roll of knitting on her basket chair, the children's toys in a corner cupboard.

He knelt down, raked out the old embers, and relit the fire. The glowing sticks brought normality, the steaming kettle and the brown teapot comfort and security. He drank his tea, carried a cup up to his wife. Then he washed in the scullery,² and, putting on his boots, opened the back door.

The sky was hard and leaden, and the brown hills that had gleamed in the sun the day before looked dark and bare. The east wind, like a razor, stripped the trees, and the leaves, crackling and dry, shivered and scattered with the wind's blast. Nat stubbed the earth with his boot. It was frozen hard. He had never known a change so swift and sudden. Black winter had descended in a single night.

The children were awake now. Jill was chattering upstairs and young Johnny crying once again. Nat heard his wife's voice, soothing, comforting. Presently they came down. He had breakfast ready for them, and the routine of the day began.

"Did you drive away the birds?" asked Jill, restored to calm because of the kitchen fire, because of day, because of breakfast.

"Yes, they've all gone now," said Nat. "It was the east wind brought them in. They were frightened and lost, they wanted shelter."

"They tried to peck us," said Jill. "They went for Johnny's eyes."

"Fright made them do that," said Nat. "They didn't know where they were in the dark bedroom."

"I hope they won't come again," said Jill. "Perhaps if we put bread for them outside the window they will eat that and fly away."

She finished her breakfast and then went for her coat and hood, her schoolbooks and her satchel. Nat said nothing, but his wife looked at him across the table. A silent message passed between them.

"I'll walk with her to the bus," he said. "I don't go to the farm today."

And while the child was washing in the scullery he said to his wife, "Keep all the windows closed, and the doors too. Just to be on the safe side. I'll go to the farm. Find out if they heard anything in the night." Then he walked with his small daughter up the lane. She seemed to have forgotten her experience of the night before. She danced ahead of him, chasing the leaves, her face whipped with the cold and rosy under the pixie hood.

"Is it going to snow, Dad?" she said. "It's cold enough."

He glanced up at the bleak sky, felt the wind tear at his shoulders.

---

2. **scullery** (skul′ ər ē) n. a room next to the kitchen where pots and pans are washed and stored.

Literary Analysis
Foreshadowing
Overnight, "black winter" has taken hold of the countryside. What might the suddenness of this change foreshadow?

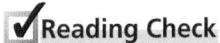**Reading Check**

What does Nat ask his wife to do before he leaves the house?

"No," he said, "it's not going to snow. This is a black winter, not a white one."

All the while he searched the hedgerows for the birds, glanced over the top of them to the fields beyond, looked to the small wood above the farm where the rooks and jackdaws gathered. He saw none.

The other children waited by the bus stop, muffled, hooded like Jill, the faces white and pinched with cold.

Jill ran to them, waving. "My dad says it won't snow," she called, "it's going to be a black winter."

She said nothing of the birds. She began to push and struggle with another little girl. The bus came ambling up the hill. Nat saw her on to it, then turned and walked back towards the farm. It was not his day for work, but he wanted to satisfy himself that all was well. Jim, the cowman, was clattering in the yard.

"Boss around?" asked Nat.

"Gone to market," said Jim. "It's Tuesday, isn't it?"

He clumped off round the corner of a shed. He had no time for Nat. Nat was said to be superior. Read books, and the like. Nat had forgotten it was Tuesday. This showed how the events of the preceding night had shaken him. He went to the back door of the farmhouse and heard Mrs. Trigg singing in the kitchen, the wireless[3] making a background to her song.

"Are you there, missus?" called out Nat.

She came to the door, beaming, broad, a good-tempered woman.

"Hullo, Mr. Hocken," she said. "Can you tell me where this cold is coming from? Is it Russia? I've never seen such a change. And it's going on, the wireless says. Something to do with the Arctic Circle."

"We didn't turn on the wireless this morning," said Nat. "Fact is, we had trouble in the night."

"Kiddies poorly?"

"No . . ." He hardly knew how to explain it. Now, in daylight, the battle of the birds would sound absurd.

He tried to tell Mrs. Trigg what had happened, but he could see from her eyes that she thought his story was the result of a nightmare.

"Sure they were real birds," she said, smiling, "with proper feathers and all? Not the funny-shaped kind that the men see after closing hours on a Saturday night?"

"Mrs. Trigg," he said, "there are fifty dead birds, robins, wrens, and such, lying low on the floor of the children's bedroom. They went for me; they tried to go for young Johnny's eyes."

▲ **Critical Viewing**
Compare and contrast the mood of the painting with the mood of the story so far. **[Compare and Contrast]**

---

3. wireless (wīr′ lis) *n.* radio.

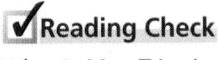

Landscape From a Dream, 1936–38, Paul Nash, Tate Gallery, London

Mrs. Trigg stared at him doubtfully.

"Well there, now," she answered, "I suppose the weather brought them. Once in the bedroom, they wouldn't know where they were to. Foreign birds maybe, from that Arctic Circle."

"No," said Nat, "they were the birds you see about here every day."

"Funny thing," said Mrs. Trigg, "no explaining it, really. You ought to write up and ask the *Guardian.* They'd have some answer for it. Well, I must be getting on."

She nodded, smiled, and went back into the kitchen.

✔ **Reading Check**

What is Mrs. Trigg's response to Nat's story?

Nat, dissatisfied, turned to the farm gate. Had it not been for those corpses on the bedroom floor, which he must now collect and bury somewhere, he would have considered the tale exaggeration too.

Jim was standing by the gate.

"Had any trouble with the birds?" asked Nat.

"Birds? What birds?"

"We got them up our place last night. Scores of them, came in the children's bedroom. Quite savage they were."

"Oh?" It took time for anything to penetrate Jim's head. "Never heard of birds acting savage," he said at length. "They get tame, like, sometimes. I've seen them come to the windows for crumbs."

"These birds last night weren't tame."

"No? Cold, maybe. Hungry. You put out some crumbs."

Jim was no more interested than Mrs. Trigg had been. It was, Nat thought, like air raids in the war. ♦ No one down this end of the country knew what the Plymouth folk had seen and suffered. You had to endure something yourself before it touched you. He walked back along the lane and crossed the stile to his cottage. He found his wife in the kitchen with young Johnny.

"See anyone?" she asked.

"Mrs. Trigg and Jim," he answered. "I don't think they believed me. Anyway, nothing wrong up there."

"You might take the birds away," she said. "I daren't go into the room to make the beds until you do. I'm scared."

"Nothing to scare you now," said Nat. "They're dead, aren't they?"

He went up with a sack and dropped the stiff bodies into it, one by one. Yes, there were fifty of them, all told. Just the ordinary, common birds of the hedgerow, nothing as large even as a thrush. It must have been fright that made them act the way they did. Blue tits, wrens—it was incredible to think of the power of their small beaks jabbing at his face and hands the night before. He took the sack out into the garden and was faced now with a fresh problem. The ground was too hard to dig. It was frozen solid, yet no snow had fallen, nothing had happened in the past hours but the coming of the east wind. It was unnatural, queer. The weather prophets must be right. The change was something connected with the Arctic Circle.

The wind seemed to cut him to the bone as he stood there uncertainly, holding the sack. He could see the white-capped seas breaking down under in the bay. He decided to take the birds to the shore and bury them.

♦ *Preparing for the Blitz*

As he prepares for the birds' attack, Nat again draws a parallel between this situation and World War II. After striking British Royal Air Force (RAF) bases in August and September of 1940, German forces believed that they had destroyed the RAF. They then began to bomb civilian targets in what was called the *Blitz* (the German word for "lightning"). The Blitz continued until May of 1941, with raids almost every night. Blackout boards and shelters became a familiar part of British life during that difficult time.

A World War II Bomb Shelter

Literary Analysis
Foreshadowing What might the "unnatural" weather foreshadow?

When he reached the beach below the headland he could scarcely stand, the force of the east wind was so strong. It hurt to draw breath, and his bare hands were blue. Never had he known such cold, not in all the bad winters he could remember. It was low tide. He crunched his way over the shingle[4] to the softer sand and then, his back to the wind, ground a pit in the sand with his heel. He meant to drop the birds into it, but as he opened up the sack the force of the wind carried them, lifted them, as though in flight again, and they were blown away from him along the beach, tossed like feathers, spread and scattered, the bodies of the fifty frozen birds. There was something ugly in the sight. He did not like it. The dead birds were swept away from him by the wind.

"The tide will take them when it turns," he said to himself.

He looked out to sea and watched the crested breakers, combing green. They rose stiffly, curled, and broke again, and because it was ebb tide the roar was distant, more remote, lacking the sound and thunder of the flood.

Then he saw them. The gulls. Out there, riding the seas.

What he had thought at first to be the whitecaps of the waves were gulls. Hundreds, thousands, tens of thousands . . . They rose and fell in the trough of the seas, heads to the wind, like a mighty fleet at anchor, waiting on the tide. To eastward, and to the west, the gulls were there. They stretched as far as his eye could reach, in close formation, line upon line. Had the sea been still they would have covered the bay like a white cloud, head to head, body packed to body. Only the east wind, whipping the sea to breakers, hid them from the shore.

Nat turned and, leaving the beach, climbed the steep path home. Someone should know of this. Someone should be told. Something was happening, because of the east wind and the weather, that he did not understand. He wondered if he should go to the call box by the bus stop and ring up the police. Yet what could they do? What could anyone do? Tens of thousands of gulls riding the sea there in the bay because of storm, because of hunger. The police would think him mad, or drunk, or take the statement from him with great calm. "Thank you. Yes, the matter has already been reported. The hard weather is driving the birds inland in great numbers." Nat looked about him. Still no sign of any other bird. Perhaps the cold had sent them all from upcountry? As he drew near to the cottage his wife came to meet him at the door. She called to him, excited. "Nat," she said, "it's on the wireless. They've just read out a special news bulletin. I've written it down."

"What's on the wireless?" he said.

"About the birds," she said. "It's not only here, it's everywhere. In London, all over the country. Something has happened to the birds."

Together they went into the kitchen. He read the piece of paper lying on the table.

"Statement from the Home Office at 11 A.M. today. Reports from all over the country are coming in hourly about the vast quantity of birds

Reading Strategy
Predicting Do you think Nat will call the police? Why?

 **Reading Check**

What does Nat see riding the seas?

---

4. **shingle** *n.* area of beach covered with waterworn gravel.

The Birds ◆ 59

flocking above towns, villages, and outlying districts, causing obstruction and damage and even attacking individuals. It is thought that the Arctic airstream, at present covering the British Isles, is causing birds to migrate south in immense numbers, and that intense hunger may drive these birds to attack human beings. Householders are warned to see to their windows, doors, and chimneys, and to take reasonable precautions for the safety of their children. A further statement will be issued later."

A kind of excitement seized Nat; he looked at his wife in triumph.

"There you are," he said. "Let's hope they'll hear that at the farm. Mrs. Trigg will know it wasn't any story. It's true. All over the country. I've been telling myself all morning there's something wrong. And just now, down on the beach, I looked out to sea and there are gulls, thousands of them, tens of thousands—you couldn't put a pin between their heads—and they're all out there, riding on the sea, waiting."

"What are they waiting for, Nat?" she asked.

He stared at her, then looked down again at the piece of paper.

"I don't know," he said slowly. "It says here the birds are hungry."

He went over to the drawer where he kept his hammer and tools.

"What are you going to do, Nat?"

"See to the windows and the chimneys too, like they tell you."

"You think they would break in, with the windows shut? Those sparrows and robins and such? Why, how could they?"

He did not answer. He was not thinking of the robins and the sparrows. He was thinking of the gulls . . .

He went upstairs and worked there the rest of the morning, boarding the windows of the bedrooms, filling up the chimney bases. Good job it was his free day and he was not working at the farm. It reminded him of the old days, at the beginning of the war. He was not married then, and he had made all the black-out boards for his mother's house in Plymouth. Made the shelter too. Not that it had been of any use when the moment came. He wondered if they would take these precautions up at the farm. He doubted it. Too easygoing, Harry Trigg and his missus. Maybe they'd laugh at the whole thing. Go off to a dance or a whist drive.[5]

"Dinner's ready." She called him, from the kitchen.

"All right. Coming down."

He was pleased with his handiwork. The frames fitted nicely over the little panes and at the bases of the chimneys.

When dinner was over and his wife was washing up, Nat switched on the one o'clock news. The same announcement was repeated, the one which she had taken down during the morning, but the news bulletin enlarged upon it. "The flocks of birds have caused dislocation in all areas," read the announcer, "and in London the sky was so dense at ten

---

5. whist drive *n.* a card game organized for a group.

o'clock this morning that it seemed as if the city was covered by a vast black cloud.

"The birds settled on rooftops, on window ledges, and on chimneys. The species included blackbird, thrush, the common house sparrow, and, as might be expected in the metropolis, a vast quantity of pigeons and starlings, and that frequenter of the London river, the black-headed gull. The sight has been so unusual that traffic came to a standstill in many thoroughfares, work was abandoned in shops and offices, and the streets and pavements were crowded with people standing about to watch the birds."

Various incidents were <u>recounted</u>, the suspected reason of cold and hunger stated again, and warnings to householders repeated. The announcer's voice was smooth and suave. Nat had the impression that this man, in particular, treated the whole business as he would an elaborate joke. There would be others like him, hundreds of them, who did not know what it was to struggle in darkness with a flock of birds. There would be parties tonight in London, like the ones they gave on election nights. People standing about, shouting and laughing . . . "Come and watch the birds!"

Nat switched off the wireless. He got up and started work on the kitchen windows. His wife watched him, young Johnny at her heels.

"What, boards for down here too?" she said. "Why, I'll have to light up before three o'clock. I see no call for boards down here."

"Better be sure than sorry," answered Nat. "I'm not going to take any chances."

"What they ought to do," she said, "is to call the Army out and shoot the birds. That would soon scare them off."

"Let them try," said Nat. "How'd they set about it?"

"They have the Army to the docks," she answered, "when the dockers strike. The soldiers go down and unload the ships."

"Yes," said Nat, "and the population of London is eight million or more. Think of all the buildings, all the flats and houses. Do you think they've enough soldiers to go around shooting birds from every roof?"

"I don't know. But something should be done. They ought to do something."

Nat thought to himself that "they" were no doubt considering the problem at that very moment, but whatever "they" decided to do in London and the big cities would not help the people here, three hundred miles away. Each householder must look after his own.

"How are we off for food?" he said.

"Now, Nat, whatever next?"

"Never mind. What have you got in the larder?"[6]

"It's shopping day tomorrow, you know that. I don't keep uncooked

---

6. **larder** (lärd´ ər) *n.* place where food is kept; pantry.

Reading Strategy
Predicting Based on the reaction to the birds, predict what you think might happen.

recounted (ri kount´ ed) *v.* told in detail; narrated

✔ **Reading Check**

What steps does Nat take to protect his family and his home?

food hanging about, it goes off. Butcher doesn't call till the day after. But I can bring back something when I go in tomorrow."

Nat did not want to scare her. He thought it possible that she might not go to town tomorrow. He looked in the larder for himself, and in the cupboard where she kept her tins. They would do for a couple of days. Bread was low.

"What about the baker?"

"He comes tomorrow too."

He saw she had flour. If the baker did not call she had enough to bake one loaf.

"We'd be better off in the old days," he said, "when the women baked twice a week, and had pilchards[7] salted, and there was food for a family to last a siege, if need be."

"I've tried the children with tinned fish, they don't like it," she said.

Nat went on hammering the boards across the kitchen windows. Candles. They were low in candles too. That must be another thing she meant to buy tomorrow. Well, it could not be helped. They must go early to bed tonight. That was, if . . .

He got up and went out of the back door and stood in the garden, looking down toward the sea. There had been no sun all day, and now, at barely three o'clock, a kind of darkness had already come, the sky <u>sullen</u>, heavy, colorless like salt. He could hear the vicious sea drumming on the rocks. He walked down the path, halfway to the beach. And then he stopped. He could see the tide had turned. The rock that had shown in midmorning was now covered, but it was not the sea that held his eyes. The gulls had risen. They were circling, hundreds of them, thousands of them, lifting their wings against the wind. It was the gulls that made the darkening of the sky. And they were silent. They made not a sound. They just went on soaring and circling, rising, falling, trying their strength against the wind.

Nat turned. He ran up the path, back to the cottage.

"I'm going for Jill," he said. "I'll wait for her at the bus stop."

"What's the matter?" asked his wife. "You've gone quite white."

"Keep Johnny inside," he said. "Keep the door shut. Light up now, and draw the curtains."

"It's only just gone three," she said.

"Never mind. Do what I tell you."

He looked inside the tool shed outside the back door. Nothing there of much use. A spade was too heavy, and a fork no good. He took the hoe. It was the only possible tool, and light enough to carry.

He started walking up the lane to the bus stop, and now and again glanced back over his shoulder.

The gulls had risen higher now, their circles were broader, wider, they were spreading out in huge formation across the sky.

He hurried on; although he knew the bus would not come to the top of the hill before four o'clock he had to hurry. He passed no one on the

sullen (sul′ ən) *adj.* gloomy

Literary Analysis
Foreshadowing What might the circling gulls foreshadow?

---

7. pilchards (pil′ chərdz) *n.* small fish similar to sardines.

way. He was glad of this. No time to stop and chatter.

At the top of the hill he waited. He was much too soon. There was half an hour still to go. The east wind came whipping across the fields from the higher ground. He stamped his feet and blew upon his hands. In the distance he could see the clay hills, white and clean, against the heavy pallor of the sky. Something black rose from behind them, like a smudge at first, then widening, becoming deeper, and the smudge became a cloud, and the cloud divided again into five other clouds, spreading north, east, south, and west, and they were not clouds at all; they were birds. He watched them travel across the sky, and as one section passed overhead, within two or three hundred feet of him, he knew, from their speed, they were bound inland, upcountry; they had no business with the people here on the peninsula. They were rooks, crows, jackdaws, magpies, jays, all birds that usually preyed upon the smaller species; but this afternoon they were bound on some other mission.

Reading Strategy
Predicting What might happen if these details about the birds were multiplied many times?

"They've been given the towns," thought Nat; "they know what they have to do. We don't matter so much here. The gulls will serve for us. The others go to the towns."

He went to the call box, stepped inside, and lifted the receiver. The exchange would do. They would pass the message on.

"I'm speaking from Highway," he said, "by the bus stop. I want to report large formations of birds traveling upcountry. The gulls are also forming in the bay."

"All right," answered the voice, laconic, weary.

"You'll be sure and pass this message on to the proper quarter?"

"Yes . . . yes . . ." Impatient now, fed-up. The buzzing note resumed.

"She's another," thought Nat, "she doesn't care. Maybe she's had to answer calls all day. She hopes to go to the pictures tonight. She'll squeeze some fellow's hand and point up at the sky and say 'Look at all them birds!' She doesn't care."

The bus came lumbering up the hill. Jill climbed out, and three or four other children. The bus went on towards the town.

"What's the hoe for, Dad?"

They crowded around him, laughing, pointing.

"I just brought it along," he said. "Come on now, let's get home. It's cold, no hanging about. Here, you. I'll watch you across the fields, see how fast you can run."

He was speaking to Jill's companions, who came from different families, living in the council houses.[8] A short cut would take them to the cottages.

"We want to play a bit in the lane," said one of them.

"No, you don't. You go off home or I'll tell your Mammy."

They whispered to one another, round-eyed, then scuttled off across the fields. Jill stared at her father, her mouth sullen.

"We always play in the lane," she said.

"Not tonight, you don't," he said. "Come on now, no dawdling."

---

8. **council houses** *n.* housing units built by the government.

**Reading Check**

What important message is Nat trying to report when he goes to the call box?

He could see the gulls now, circling the fields, coming in toward the land. Still silent. Still no sound.

"Look, Dad, look over there, look at all the gulls."

"Yes. Hurry, now."

"Where are they flying to? Where are they going?"

"Upcountry, I dare say. Where it's warmer."

He seized her hand and dragged her after him along the lane.

"Don't go so fast. I can't keep up."

The gulls were copying the rooks and crows. They were spreading out in formation across the sky. They headed, in bands of thousands, to the four compass points.

"Dad, what is it? What are the gulls doing?"

They were not intent upon their flight, as the crows, as the jackdaws had been. They still circled overhead. Nor did they fly so high. It was as though they waited upon some signal. As though some decision had yet to be given. The order was not clear.

"Do you want me to carry you, Jill? Here, come pick-a-back."

This way he might put on speed; but he was wrong. Jill was heavy. She kept slipping. And was crying too. His sense of urgency, of fear, had communicated itself to the child.

"I wish the gulls would go away. I don't like them. They're coming closer to the lane."

He put her down again. He started running, swinging Jill after him. As they went past the farm turning he saw the farmer backing his car out of the garage. Nat called to him.

"Can you give us a lift?" he said.

"What's that?"

Mr. Trigg turned in the driving seat and stared at them. Then a smile came to his cheerful, rubicund face.

"It looks as though we're in for some fun," he said. "Have you seen the gulls? Jim and I are going to take a crack at them. Everyone's gone bird-crazy, talking of nothing else. I hear you were troubled in the night. Want a gun?"

Nat shook his head.

The small car was packed. There was just room for Jill, if she crouched on top of petrol tins on the back seat.

"I don't want a gun," said Nat, "but I'd be obliged if you'd run Jill home. She's scared of the birds."

He spoke briefly. He did not want to talk in front of Jill.

"O.K.," said the farmer, "I'll take her home. Why don't you stop behind and join the shooting match? We'll make the feathers fly."

Jill climbed in, and turning the car, the driver sped up the lane. Nat followed after. Trigg must be crazy. What use was a gun against a sky of birds?

Now Nat was not responsible for Jill, he had time to look about him. The birds were circling still above the fields. Mostly herring gull, but the black-backed gull amongst them. Usually they kept apart. Now they were united. Some bond had brought them together. It was the black-

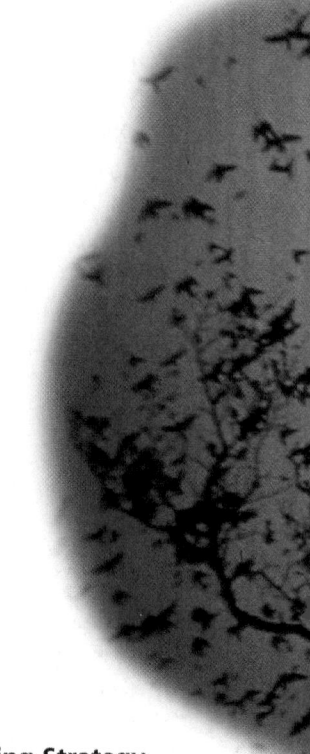

Reading Strategy
Predicting What do you predict will happen if Nat and Jill do not move along more quickly?

backed gull that attacked the smaller birds, and even newborn lambs, so he'd heard. He'd never seen it done. He remembered this now, though, looking above him in the sky. They were coming in towards the farm. They were circling lower in the sky, and the black-backed gulls were to the front, the black-backed gulls were leading. The farm, then, was their target. They were making for the farm.

Nat increased his pace toward his own cottage. He saw the farmer's car turn and come back along the lane. It drew up beside him with a jerk.

"The kid has run inside," said the farmer. "Your wife was watching for her. Well, what do you make of it? They're saying in town the Russians have done it. The Russians have poisoned the birds."

"How could they do that?" asked Nat.

"Don't ask me. You know how stories get around. Will you join my shooting match?"

"No, I'll get along home. The wife will be worried else."

▲ **Critical Viewing**
What do the scraggly tree and the scores of birds in the photograph convey about the setting of this story? **[Infer]**

✔**Reading Check**

Why does Nat ask Mr. Trigg to take Jill home?

"My missus says if you could eat gull there'd be some sense in it," said Trigg. "We'd have roast gull, baked gull, and pickle 'em into the bargain. You wait until I let off a few barrels into the brutes. That'll scare 'em."

"Have you boarded your windows?" asked Nat.

"No. Lot of nonsense. They like to scare you on the wireless. I've had more to do today than to go round boarding up my windows."

"I'd board them now, if I were you."

"Garn. You're windy. Like to come to our place to sleep?"

"No, thanks all the same."

"All right. See you in the morning. Give you a gull breakfast."

The farmer grinned and turned his car to the farm entrance.

Nat hurried on. Past the little wood, past the old barn, and then across the stile to the remaining field.

As he jumped the stile he heard the whir of wings. A black-backed gull dived down at him from the sky, missed, swerved in flight, and rose to dive again. In a moment it was joined by others, six, seven, a dozen, black-backed and herring mixed. Nat dropped his hoe. The hoe was useless. Covering his head with his arms, he ran toward the cottage. They kept coming at him from the air, silent save for the beating wings. The terrible, fluttering wings. He could feel the blood on his hands, his wrists, his neck. Each stab of a swooping beak tore his flesh. If only he could keep them from his eyes. Nothing else mattered. He must keep them from his eyes. They had not learned yet how to cling to a shoulder, how to rip clothing, how to dive in mass upon the head, upon the body. But with each dive, with each attack, they became bolder. And they had no thought for themselves. When they dived low and missed, they crashed, bruised and broken, on the ground. As Nat ran he stumbled, kicking their spent bodies in front of him.

He found the door; he hammered upon it with his bleeding hands. Because of the boarded windows no light shone. Everything was dark.

"Let me in," he shouted, "it's Nat. Let me in."

He shouted loud to make himself heard above the whir of the gulls' wings.

Then he saw the gannet, poised for the dive, above him in the sky. The gulls circled, retired, soared, one after another, against the wind. Only the gannet remained. One single gannet above him in the sky. The wings folded suddenly to its body. It dropped like a stone. Nat screamed, and the door opened. He stumbled across the threshold, and his wife threw her weight against the door.

They heard the thud of the gannet as it fell.

His wife dressed his wounds. They were not deep. The backs of his hands had suffered most, and his wrists. Had he not worn a cap they would have reached his head. As to the gannet . . . the gannet could have split his skull.

The children were crying, of course. They had seen the blood on their father's hands.

"It's all right now," he told them. "I'm not hurt. Just a few scratches.

You play with Johnny, Jill. Mammy will wash these cuts."

He half shut the door to the scullery so that they could not see. His wife was ashen. She began running water from the sink.

"I saw them overhead," she whispered. "They began collecting just as Jill ran in with Mr. Trigg. I shut the door fast, and it jammed. That's why I couldn't open it at once when you came."

"Thank God they waited for me," he said. "Jill would have fallen at once. One bird alone would have done it."

<u>Furtively</u>, so as not to alarm the children, they whispered together as she bandaged his hands and the back of his neck.

"They're flying inland," he said, "thousands of them. Rooks, crows, all the bigger birds. I saw them from the bus stop. They're making for the towns."

"But what can they do, Nat?"

"They'll attack. Go for everyone out in the streets. Then they'll try the windows, the chimneys."

"Why don't the authorities do something? Why don't they get the Army, get machine guns, anything?"

"There's been no time. Nobody's prepared. We'll hear what they have to say on the six o'clock news."

Nat went back into the kitchen, followed by his wife. Johnny was playing quietly on the floor. Only Jill looked anxious.

"I can hear the birds," she said. "Listen, Dad."

Nat listened. Muffled sounds came from the windows, from the door. Wings brushing the surface, sliding, scraping, seeking a way of entry. The sound of many bodies, pressed together, shuffling on the sills. Now and again came a thud, a crash, as some bird dived and fell. "Some of them will kill themselves that way," he thought, "but not enough. Never enough."

"All right," he said aloud. "I've got boards over the windows, Jill. The birds can't get in."

He went and examined all the windows. His work had been thorough. Every gap was closed. He would make extra certain, however. He found wedges, pieces of old tin, strips of wood and metal, and fastened them at the sides to reinforce the boards. His hammering helped to deafen the sound of the birds, the shuffling, the tapping, and more ominous—he did not want his wife or the children to hear it—the splinter of cracked glass.

"Turn on the wireless," he said, "let's have the wireless."

This would drown the sound also. He went upstairs to the bedrooms and reinforced the windows there. Now he could hear the birds on the roof, the scraping of claws, a sliding, jostling sound.

He decided they must sleep in the kitchen, keep up the fire, bring down the mattresses, and lay them out on the floor. He was afraid of the bedroom chimneys. The boards he had placed at the chimney bases might give way. In the kitchen they would be safe because of the fire. He would have to make a joke of it. Pretend to the children they were play-ing at camp. If the worst happened, and the birds forced an entry down

furtively (fur′ tiv lē) *adv.* stealthily, so as to avoid being heard

Literary Analysis
Foreshadowing Think about what Nat has done to get his house ready for this attack. What might the cracked glass foreshadow, and why?

✔**Reading Check**

What steps does Nat take to prepare his house against the birds?

the bedroom chimneys, it would be hours, days perhaps, before they could break down the doors. The birds would be imprisoned in the bedrooms. They could do no harm there. Crowded together, they would stifle and die.

He began to bring the mattresses downstairs. At sight of them his wife's eyes widened in apprehension. She thought the birds had already broken in upstairs.

"All right," he said cheerfully, "we'll all sleep together in the kitchen tonight. More cozy here by the fire. Then we shan't be worried by those silly old birds tapping at the windows."

He made the children help him rearrange the furniture, and he took the precaution of moving the dresser, with his wife's help, across the window. It fitted well. It was an added safeguard. The mattresses could now be laid, one beside the other, against the wall where the dresser had stood.

"We're safe enough now," he thought. "We're snug and tight, like an air-raid shelter. We can hold out. It's just the food that worries me. Food, and coal for the fire. We've enough for two or three days, not more. By that time . . ."

No use thinking ahead as far as that. And they'd be giving directions on the wireless. People would be told what to do. And now, in the midst of many problems, he realized that it was dance music only coming over the air. Not Children's Hour, as it should have been. He glanced at the dial. Yes, they were on the Home Service all right. Dance records. He switched to the Light program. He knew the reason. The usual programs had been abandoned. This only happened at exceptional times. Elections and such. He tried to remember if it had happened in the war, during the heavy raids on London. But of course. The B.B.C.[9] was not stationed in London during the war. The programs were broadcast from other, temporary quarters. "We're better off here," he thought; "we're better off here in the kitchen, with the windows and the doors boarded, than they are up in the towns. Thank God we're not in the towns."

At six o'clock the records ceased. The time signal was given. No matter if it scared the children, he must hear the news. There was a pause after the pips.[10] Then the announcer spoke. His voice was solemn, grave. Quite different from midday.

"This is London," he said. "A National Emergency was proclaimed at four o'clock this afternoon. Measures are being taken to safeguard the lives and property of the population, but it must be understood that these are not easy to effect immediately, owing to the unforeseen and unparalleled nature of the present crisis. Every householder must take

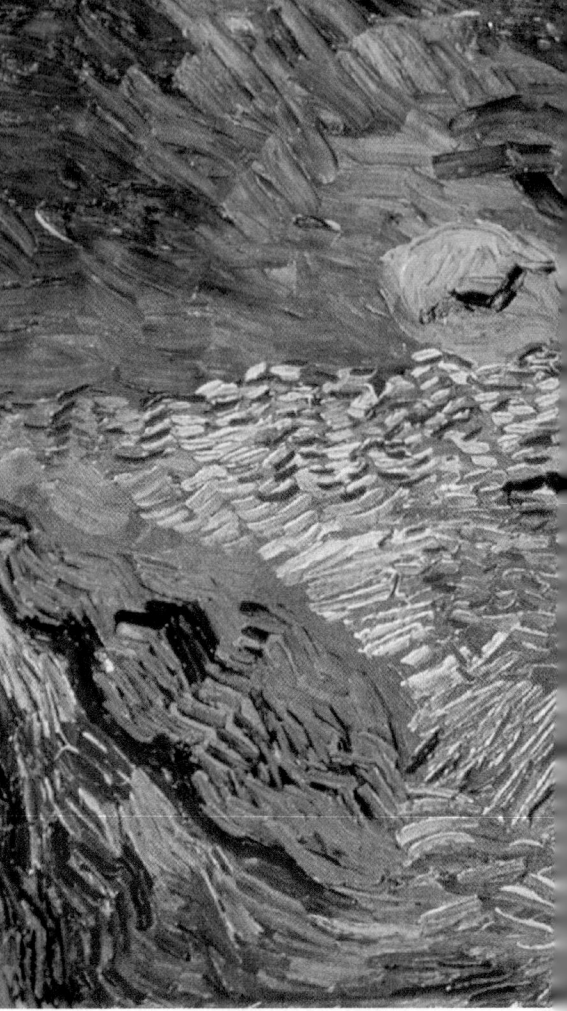

▲ **Critical Viewing**
What feelings conveyed through this painting might be similar to those conveyed through the story? **[Describe]**

---

9. B.B.C. British Broadcasting Corporation.
10. pips *n.* beeping sounds that indicate the time.

Wheatfield With Crows, Vincent van Gogh, Van Gogh Museum, Amsterdam, The Netherlands

precautions to his own building, and where several people live together, as in flats and apartments, they must unite to do the utmost they can to prevent entry. It is absolutely <u>imperative</u> that every individual stay indoors tonight and that no one at all remain on the streets, or roads, or anywhere withoutdoors.[11] The birds, in vast numbers, are attacking anyone on sight, and have already begun an assault upon buildings; but these, with due care, should be impenetrable. The population is asked to remain calm and not to panic. Owing to the exceptional nature of the emergency, there will be no further transmission from any broadcasting station until 7 A.M. tomorrow."

They played the National Anthem. Nothing more happened. Nat switched off the set. He looked at his wife. She stared back at him.

"What's it mean?" said Jill. "What did the news say?"

"There won't be any more programs tonight," said Nat. "There's been a breakdown at the B.B.C."

---

11. **withoutdoors** *adv.* old-fashioned variation of "outdoors."

imperative (im per´ ə tiv) *adj.* urgent; absolutely necessary

☑ **Reading Check**

What important news is revealed through the broadcast?

The Birds ◆ 69

"Is it the birds?" asked Jill. "Have the birds done it?"

"No," said Nat, "it's just that everyone's very busy, and then of course they have to get rid of the birds, messing everything up, in the towns. Well, we can manage without the wireless for one evening."

"I wish we had a gramophone,"[12] said Jill, "that would be better than nothing."

She had her face turned to the dresser backed against the windows. Try as they did to ignore it, they were all aware of the shuffling, the stabbing, the persistent beating and sweeping of wings.

"We'll have supper early," suggested Nat, "something for a treat. Ask Mammy. Toasted cheese, eh? Something we all like?"

He winked and nodded at his wife. He wanted the look of dread, of apprehension, to go from Jill's face.

He helped with the supper, whistling, singing, making as much clatter as he could, and it seemed to him that the shuffling and the tapping were not so intense as they had been at first. Presently he went up to the bedrooms and listened, and he no longer heard the jostling for place upon the roof.

"They've got reasoning powers," he thought; "they know it's hard to break in here. They'll try elsewhere. They won't waste their time with us."

Supper passed without incident, and then, when they were clearing away, they heard a new sound, droning, familiar, a sound they all knew and understood.

His wife looked up at him, her face alight. "It's planes," she said; "they're sending out planes after the birds. That's what I said they ought to do all along. That will get them. Isn't that gunfire? Can't you hear guns?"

It might be gunfire out at sea. Nat could not tell. Big naval guns might have an effect upon the gulls out at sea, but the gulls were inland now. The guns couldn't shell the shore because of the population.

"It's good, isn't it," said his wife, "to hear the planes?" And Jill, catching her enthusiasm, jumped up and down with Johnny. "The planes will get the birds. The planes will shoot them."

Just then they heard a crash about two miles distant, followed by a second, then a third. The droning became more distant, passed away out to sea.

"What was that?" asked his wife. "Were they dropping bombs on the birds?"

"I don't know," answered Nat. "I don't think so."

He did not want to tell her that the sound they had heard was the crashing of aircraft. It was, he had no doubt, a venture on the part of the authorities to send out <u>reconnaissance</u> forces, but they might have known the venture was suicidal. What could aircraft do against birds that flung themselves to death against propeller and fuselage, but hurtle to the ground themselves? This was being tried now, he supposed, over

Literary Analysis
Foreshadowing What might this quiet moment foreshadow?

Reading Strategy
Predicting What do you predict will happen to the planes?

reconnaissance (ri kän′ ə səns) *adj.* exploratory in nature, as when observing to seek information

---

12. gramophone (gram′ ə fōn′) *n.* phonograph; record player.

the whole country. And at a cost. Someone high up had lost his head.

"Where have the planes gone, Dad?" asked Jill.

"Back to base," he said. "Come on, now, time to tuck down for bed."

It kept his wife occupied, undressing the children before the fire, seeing to the bedding, one thing and another, while he went round the cottage again, making sure that nothing had worked loose. There was no further drone of aircraft, and the naval guns had ceased. "Waste of life and effort," Nat said to himself. "We can't destroy enough of them that way. Cost too heavy. There's always gas. Maybe they'll try spraying with gas, mustard gas. We'll be warned first, of course, if they do. There's one thing, the best brains of the country will be on to it tonight."

Somehow the thought reassured him. He had a picture of scientists, naturalists, technicians, and all those chaps they called the back-room boys, summoned to a council; they'd be working on the problem now. This was not a job for the government, for the chiefs of staff—they would merely carry out the orders of the scientists.

"They'll have to be ruthless," he thought. "Where the trouble's worst they'll have to risk more lives, if they use gas. All the livestock, too, and the soil—all contaminated. As long as everyone doesn't panic. That's the trouble. People panicking, losing their heads. The B.B.C. was right to warn us of that."

Upstairs in the bedrooms all was quiet. No further scraping and stabbing at the windows. A lull in battle. Forces regrouping. Wasn't that what they called it in the old wartime bulletins? The wind hadn't dropped, though. He could still hear it roaring in the chimneys. And the sea breaking down on the shore. Then he remembered the tide. The tide would be on the turn. Maybe the lull in battle was because of the tide. There was some law the birds obeyed, and it was all to do with the east wind and the tide.

He glanced at his watch. Nearly eight o'clock. It must have gone high water an hour ago. That explained the lull: the birds attacked with the flood tide. It might not work that way inland, upcountry, but it seemed as if it was so this way on the coast. He reckoned the time limit in his head. They had six hours to go without attack. When the tide turned again, around one-twenty in the morning, the birds would come back . . .

There were two things he could do. The first to rest, with his wife and the children, and all of them snatch what sleep they could, until the small hours. The second to go out, see how they were faring at the farm, see if the telephone was still working there, so that they might get news from the exchange.

He called softly to his wife, who had just settled the children. She came halfway up the stairs and he whispered to her.

"You're not to go," she said at once, "you're not to go and leave me alone with the children. I can't stand it."

Her voice rose hysterically. He hushed her, calmed her.

"All right," he said, "all right. I'll wait till morning. And we'll get the wireless bulletin then too, at seven. But in the morning, when the tide

Literary Analysis
Foreshadowing and Imagery In what ways does this image of experts gathering add to the tension of the story?

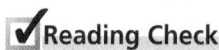

Reading Check

What does Nat think has happened to the planes?

ebbs again, I'll try for the farm, and they may let us have bread and
potatoes, and milk too."

His mind was busy again, planning against emergency. They would
not have milked, of course, this evening. The cows would be standing by
the gate, waiting in the yard, with the household inside, battened
behind boards, as they were here at the cottage. That is, if they had
time to take precautions. He thought of the farmer, Trigg, smiling at him
from the car. There would have been no shooting party, not tonight.

The children were asleep. His wife, still clothed, was sitting on her
mattress. She watched him, her eyes nervous.

"What are you going to do?" she whispered.

He shook his head for silence. Softly, stealthily, he opened the
back door and looked outside.

It was pitch dark. The wind was blowing harder than ever, coming in
steady gusts, icy, from the sea. He kicked at the step outside the door. It
was heaped with birds. There were dead birds everywhere. Under the
windows, against the walls. These were the suicides, the divers, the ones
with broken necks. Wherever he looked he saw dead birds. No trace of
the living. The living had flown seaward with the turn of the tide. The
gulls would be riding the seas now, as they had done in the forenoon.

In the far distance, on the hill where the tractor had been two days
before, something was burning. One of the aircraft that had crashed;
the fire, fanned by the wind, had set light to a stack.

He looked at the bodies of the birds, and he had a notion that if he
heaped them, one upon the other, on the windowsills they would
make added protection for the next attack. Not much, perhaps, but

▲ **Critical Viewing**
Which images found in this picture foreshadow danger? [Describe]

something. The bodies would have to be clawed at, pecked, and dragged aside before the living birds could gain purchase on the sills and attack the panes. He set to work in the darkness. It was queer; he hated touching them. The bodies were still warm and bloody. The blood matted their feathers. He felt his stomach turn, but he went on with his work. He noticed grimly that every windowpane was shattered. Only the boards had kept the birds from breaking in. He stuffed the cracked panes with the bleeding bodies of the birds.

When he had finished he went back into the cottage. He barricaded the kitchen door, made it doubly secure. He took off his bandages, sticky with the birds' blood, not with his own cuts, and put on a fresh bandage.

His wife had made him cocoa and he drank it thirstily. He was very tired.

"All right," he said, smiling, "don't worry. We'll get through."

He lay down on his mattress and closed his eyes. He slept at once. He dreamt uneasily, because through his dreams there ran a thread of something forgotten. Some piece of work, neglected, that he should have done. Some precaution that he had known well but had not taken, and he could not put a name to it in his dreams. It was connected in some way with the burning aircraft and the stack upon the hill. He went on sleeping, though; he did not awake. It was his wife shaking his shoulder that awoke him finally.

"They've begun," she sobbed, "they've started this last hour. I can't listen to it any longer alone. There's something smelling bad too, something burning."

☑ **Reading Check**

Briefly describe what Nat finds when he steps outside the cottage.

Then he remembered. He had forgotten to make up the fire. It was smoldering, nearly out. He got up swiftly and lit the lamp. The hammering had started at the windows and the doors, but it was not that he minded now. It was the smell of singed feathers. The smell filled the kitchen. He knew at once what it was. The birds were coming down the chimney, squeezing their way down to the kitchen range.

He got sticks and paper and put them on the embers, then reached for the can of paraffin.[13]

"Stand back," he shouted to his wife. "We've got to risk this."

He threw the paraffin onto the fire. The flame roared up the pipe, and down upon the fire fell the scorched, blackened bodies of the birds.

The children woke, crying. "What is it?" said Jill. "What's happened?"

Nat had no time to answer. He was raking the bodies from the chimney, clawing them out onto the floor. The flames still roared, and the danger of the chimney catching fire was one he had to take. The flames would send away the living birds from the chimney top. The lower joint was the difficulty, though. This was choked with the smoldering, helpless bodies of the birds caught by fire. He scarcely heeded the attack on the windows and the door: let them beat their wings, break their beaks, lose their lives, in the attempt to force an entry into his home. They would not break in. He thanked God he had one of the old cottages, with small windows, stout walls. Not like the new council houses. Heaven help them up the lane in the new council houses.

"Stop crying," he called to the children. "There's nothing to be afraid of, stop crying."

He went on raking at the burning, smoldering bodies as they fell into the fire.

"This'll fetch them," he said to himself, "the draft and the flames together. We're all right, as long as the chimney doesn't catch. I ought to be shot for this. It's all my fault. Last thing, I should have made up the fire. I knew there was something."

Amid the scratching and tearing at the window boards came the sudden homely striking of the kitchen clock. Three A.M. A little more than four hours yet to go. He could not be sure of the exact time of high water. He reckoned it would not turn much before half-past seven, twenty to eight.

"Light up the Primus,"[14] he said to his wife. "Make us some tea, and the kids some cocoa. No use sitting around doing nothing."

That was the line. Keep her busy, and the children too. Move about, eat, drink; always best to be on the go.

He waited by the range. The flames were dying. But no more blackened bodies fell from the chimney. He thrust his poker up as far as it could go and found nothing. It was clear. The chimney was clear. He wiped the sweat from his forehead.

"Come on now, Jill," he said, "bring me some more sticks. We'll have

---

13. **paraffin** (par´ ə fin) *n.* kerosene.
14. **Primus** (prī´ məs) *n.* small, portable stove.

Reading Strategy
Predicting What do you predict will happen next inside the house? Which details led you to this prediction?

Literary Analysis
Foreshadowing What effect does the sound of the clock have on the story? Explain.

a good fire going directly." She wouldn't come near him, though. She was staring at the heaped singed bodies of the birds.

"Never mind them," he said. "We'll put those in the passage when I've got the fire steady."

The danger of the chimney was over. It could not happen again, not if the fire was kept burning day and night.

"I'll have to get more fuel from the farm tomorrow," he thought. "This will never last. I'll manage, though. I can do all that with the ebb tide. It can be worked, fetching what we need, when the tide's turned. We've just got to adapt ourselves, that's all."

They drank tea and cocoa and ate slices of bread and Bovril.[15] Only half a loaf left, Nat noticed. Never mind though, they'd get by.

"Stop it," said young Johnny, pointing to the windows with his spoon, "stop it, you old birds."

"That's right," said Nat, smiling, "we don't want the old beggars, do we? Had enough of 'em."

They began to cheer when they heard the thud of the suicide birds.

"There's another, Dad," cried Jill, "he's done for."

"He's had it," said Nat. "There he goes, the blighter."

This was the way to face up to it. This was the spirit. If they could keep this up, hang on like this until seven, when the first news bulletin came through, they would not have done too badly.

"Give us a cigarette," he said to his wife. "A bit of a smoke will clear away the smell of the scorched feathers."

"There's only two left in the packet," she said. "I was going to buy you some from the Co-op."

"I'll have one," he said, "t'other will keep for a rainy day."

No sense trying to make the children rest. There was no rest to be got while the tapping and the scratching went on at the windows. He sat with one arm round his wife and the other round Jill, with Johnny on his mother's lap and the blankets heaped about them on the mattress.

"You can't help admiring the beggars," he said; "they've got persistence. You'd think they'd tire of the game, but not a bit of it."

Admiration was hard to sustain. The tapping went on and on and a new rasping note struck Nat's ear, as though a sharper beak than any hitherto had come to take over from its fellows. He tried to remember the names of birds; he tried to think which species would go for this particular job. It was not the tap of the woodpecker. That would be light and frequent. This was more serious, because if it continued long the wood would splinter as the glass had done. Then he remembered the hawks. Could the hawks have taken over from the gulls? Were there buzzards now upon the sills, using talons as well as beaks? Hawks, buzzards, kestrels, falcons—he had forgotten the birds of prey. He had forgotten the gripping power of the birds of prey. Three hours to go, and while they waited, the sound of the splintering wood, the talons tearing at the wood.

---

15. Bovril (bō´ vril) *n.* thick beef-flavored liquid used to make broth.

Reading Strategy
Predicting Based on the spirit Nat and his family are showing, what do you predict will happen?

✔**Reading Check**
How do the birds get into the house?

Over and Above #13, 1964, Clarence H. Carter

Nat looked about him, seeing what furniture he could destroy to fortify the door. The windows were safe because of the dresser. He was not certain of the door. He went upstairs, but when he reached the landing he paused and listened. There was a soft patter on the floor of the children's bedroom. The birds had broken through . . . He put his ear to the door. No mistake. He could hear the rustle of wings and the light patter as they searched the floor. The other bedroom was still clear. He went into it and began bringing out the furniture, to pile at the head of the stairs should the door of the children's bedroom go. It was a preparation. It might never be needed. He could not stack the furniture against the door, because it opened inward. The only possible thing was to have it at the top of the stairs.

"Come down. Nat, what are you doing?" called his wife.

"I won't be long," he shouted. "Just making everything shipshape up here."

He did not want her to come; he did not want her to hear the

▲ **Critical Viewing**
Would you expect a bird in this story to look like the bird in this picture? Explain. **[Describe]**

pattering of the feet in the children's bedroom, the brushing of those wings against the door.

At five-thirty he suggested breakfast, bacon and fried bread, if only to stop the growing look of panic in his wife's eyes and to calm the <u>fretful</u> children. She did not know about the birds upstairs. The bedroom, luckily, was not over the kitchen. Had it been so, she could not have failed to hear the sound of them up there, tapping the boards. And the silly, senseless thud of the suicide birds, the death and glory boys, who flew into the bedroom, smashing their heads against the walls. He knew them of old, the herring gulls. They had no brains. The black-backs were different; they knew what they were doing. So did the buzzards, the hawks . . .

He found himself watching the clock, gazing at the hands that went so slowly round the dial. If his theory was not correct, if the attack did not cease with the turn of the tide, he knew they were beaten. They could not continue through the long day without air, without rest, without more fuel, without . . . His mind raced. He knew there were so many things they needed to withstand siege. They were not fully prepared. They were not ready. It might be that it would be safer in the towns after all. If he could get a message through on the farm telephone to his cousin, only a short journey by train upcountry, they might be able to hire a car. That would be quicker—hire a car between tides . . .

His wife's voice, calling his name, drove away the sudden, desperate desire for sleep.

"What is it? What now?" he said sharply.

"The wireless," said his wife. "I've been watching the clock. It's nearly seven."

"Don't twist the knob," he said, impatient for the first time. "It's on the Home where it is. They'll speak from the Home."

They waited. The kitchen clock struck seven. There was no sound. No chimes, no music. They waited until a quarter past, switching to the Light. The result was the same. No news bulletin came through.

"We've heard wrong," he said. "They won't be broadcasting until eight o'clock."

They left it switched on, and Nat thought of the battery, wondered how much power was left in it. It was generally recharged when his wife went shopping in the town. If the battery failed they would not hear the instructions.

"It's getting light," whispered his wife. "I can't see it, but I can feel it. And the birds aren't hammering so loud."

She was right. The rasping, tearing sound grew fainter every moment. So did the shuffling, the jostling for place upon the step, upon the sills. The tide was on the turn. By eight there was no sound at all. Only the wind. The children, lulled at last by the stillness, fell asleep. At half-past eight Nat switched the wireless off.

"What are you doing? We'll miss the news," said his wife.

"There isn't going to be any news," said Nat. "We've got to depend upon ourselves."

fretful (fret′ fəl) *adj.* irritable and discontented

✔Reading Check

Why does Nat put the furniture at the top of the stairs?

He went to the door and slowly pulled away the barricades. He drew the bolts and, kicking the bodies from the step outside the door, breathed the cold air. He had six working hours before him, and he knew he must reserve his strength for the right things, not waste it in any way. Food, and light, and fuel; these were the necessary things. If he could get them in sufficiency, they could endure another night.

He stepped into the garden, and as he did so he saw the living birds. The gulls had gone to ride the sea, as they had done before; they sought sea food, and the buoyancy of the tide, before they returned to the attack. Not so the land birds. They waited and watched. Nat saw them, on the hedgerows, on the soil, crowded in the trees, outside in the field, line upon line of birds, all still, doing nothing.

He went to the end of his small garden. The birds did not move. They went on watching him.

"I've got to get food," said Nat to himself. "I've got to go to the farm to find food."

He went back to the cottage. He saw to the windows and the doors. He went upstairs and opened the children's bedroom. It was empty, except for the dead birds on the floor. The living were out there, in the garden, in the fields. He went downstairs.

"I'm going to the farm," he said.

His wife clung to him. She had seen the living birds from the open door.

"Take us with you," she begged. "We can't stay here alone. I'd rather die than stay here alone."

He considered the matter. He nodded.

"Come on, then," he said. "Bring baskets, and Johnny's pram.[16] We can load up the pram."

They dressed against the biting wind, wore gloves and scarves. His wife put Johnny in the pram. Nat took Jill's hand.

"The birds," she whimpered, "they're all out there in the fields."

"They won't hurt us," he said, "not in the light."

They started walking across the field towards the stile, and the birds did not move. They waited, their heads turned to the wind.

When they reached the turning to the farm, Nat stopped and told his wife to wait in the shelter of the hedge with the two children.

"But I want to see Mrs. Trigg," she protested. "There are lots of things we can borrow if they went to market yesterday; not only bread, and . . ."

"Wait here," Nat interrupted. "I'll be back in a moment."

The cows were lowing, moving restlessly in the yard, and he could see a gap in the fence where the sheep had knocked their way through, to roam unchecked in the front garden before the farmhouse. No smoke came from the chimneys. He was filled with misgiving. He did not want his wife or the children to go down to the farm.

"Don't gib[17] now," said Nat, harshly, "do what I say."

16. **pram** *n.* baby carriage.
17. **gib** (jib) *v.* hesitate.

Literary Analysis
Foreshadowing and Imagery Do you think the image of the birds waiting and watching foreshadows an end to danger?

She withdrew with the pram into the hedge, screening herself and the children from the wind.

He went down alone to the farm. He pushed his way through the herd of bellowing cows, which turned this way and that, distressed, their udders full. He saw the car standing by the gate, not put away in the garage. The windows of the farmhouse were smashed. There were many dead gulls lying in the yard and around the house. The living birds perched on the group of trees behind the farm and on the roof of the house. They were quite still. They watched him.

Jim's body lay in the yard . . . what was left of it. When the birds had finished, the cows had trampled him. His gun was beside him. The door of the house was shut and bolted, but as the windows were smashed it was easy to lift them and climb through. Trigg's body was close to the telephone. He must have been trying to get through to the exchange when the birds came for him. The receiver was hanging loose, the instrument torn from the wall. No sign of Mrs. Trigg. She would be upstairs. Was it any use going up? Sickened, Nat knew what he would find.

"Thank God," he said to himself, "there were no children."

He forced himself to climb the stairs, but halfway he turned and descended again. He could see her legs protruding from the open bedroom door. Beside her were the bodies of the black-backed gulls, and an umbrella, broken.

"It's no use," thought Nat, "doing anything. I've only got five hours, less than that. The Triggs would understand. I must load up with what I can find."

He tramped back to his wife and children.

"I'm going to fill up the car with stuff," he said. "I'll put coal in it, and paraffin for the Primus. We'll take it home and return for a fresh load."

"What about the Triggs?" asked his wife.

"They must have gone to friends," he said.

"Shall I come and help you, then?"

"No; there's a mess down there. Cows and sheep all over the place. Wait, I'll get the car. You can sit in it."

Clumsily he backed the car out of the yard and into the lane. His wife and the children could not see Jim's body from there.

"Stay here," he said, "never mind the pram. The pram can be fetched later. I'm going to load the car."

Her eyes watched his all the time. He believed she understood, otherwise she would have suggested helping him to find the bread and groceries.

They made three journeys altogether, backwards and forwards between their cottage and the farm, before he was satisfied they had everything they needed. It was surprising, once he started thinking, how many things were necessary. Almost the most important of all was planking for the windows. He had to go round searching for timber. He wanted to renew the boards on all the windows at the cottage.

Literary Analysis
Foreshadowing Do you think that the deaths of everyone at the farm foreshadow a similar fate for Nat and his family? Why or why not?

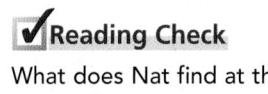

Reading Check

What does Nat find at the Triggs' farm?

Candles, paraffin, nails, tinned stuff; the list was endless. Besides all that, he milked three of the cows. The rest, poor brutes, would have to go on bellowing.

On the final journey he drove the car to the bus stop, got out, and went to the telephone box. He waited a few minutes, jangling the receiver. No good, though. The line was dead. He climbed on to a bank and looked over the countryside, but there was no sign of life at all, nothing in the fields but the waiting, watching birds. Some of them slept—he could see the beaks tucked into the feathers.

"You'd think they'd be feeding," he said to himself, "not just standing in that way."

Then he remembered. They were gorged with food. They had eaten their fill during the night. That was why they did not move this morning . . .

No smoke came from the chimneys of the council houses. He thought of the children who had run across the fields the night before.

"I should have known," he thought; "I ought to have taken them home with me."

He lifted his face to the sky. It was colorless and gray. The bare trees on the landscape looked bent and blackened by the east wind. The cold did not affect the living birds waiting out there in the fields.

"This is the time they ought to get them," said Nat; "they're a sitting target now. They must be doing this all over the country. Why don't our aircraft take off now and spray them with mustard gas? What are all our chaps doing? They must know, they must see for themselves."

He went back to the car and got into the driver's seat.

"Go quickly past that second gate," whispered his wife. "The postman's lying there. I don't want Jill to see."

He accelerated. The little Morris bumped and rattled along the lane. The children shrieked with laughter.

"Up-a-down, up-a-down," shouted young Johnny.

It was a quarter to one by the time they reached the cottage. Only an hour to go.

"Better have cold dinner," said Nat. "Hot up something for yourself and the children, some of that soup. I've no time to eat now. I've got to unload all this stuff."

He got everything inside the cottage. It could be sorted later. Give them all something to do during the long hours ahead. First he must see to the windows and the doors.

He went round the cottage methodically, testing every window, every door. He climbed on to the roof also, and fixed boards across every chimney, except the kitchen. The cold was so intense he could hardly bear it, but the job had to be done. Now and again he would look up, searching the sky for aircraft. None came. As he worked he cursed the inefficiency of the authorities.

Literary Analysis
Foreshadowing What might the dead phone line foreshadow?

"It's always the same," he muttered. "They always let us down. Muddle, muddle, from the start. No plan, no real organization. And we don't matter down here. That's what it is. The people upcountry have priority. They're using gas up there, no doubt, and all the aircraft. We've got to wait and take what comes."

He paused, his work on the bedroom chimney finished, and looked out to sea. Something was moving out there. Something gray and white amongst the breakers.

"Good old Navy," he said, "they never let us down. They're coming down-channel, they're turning in the bay."

He waited, straining his eyes, watering in the wind, towards the sea. He was wrong, though. It was not ships. The Navy was not there. The gulls were rising from the sea. The massed flocks in the fields, with ruffled feathers, rose in formation from the ground and, wing to wing, soared upwards to the sky.

The tide had turned again.

Nat climbed down the ladder and went inside the kitchen. The family were at dinner. It was a little after two. He bolted the door, put up the barricade, and lit the lamp.

"It's nighttime," said young Johnny.

His wife had switched on the wireless once again, but no sound came from it.

"I've been all round the dial," she said, "foreign stations, and that lot. I can't get anything."

"Maybe they have the same trouble," he said, "maybe it's the same right through Europe."

She poured out a plateful of the Triggs' soup, cut him a large slice of the Triggs' bread, and spread their dripping upon it.

They ate in silence. A piece of the dripping ran down young Johnny's chin and fell on to the table.

"Manners, Johnny," said Jill, "you should learn to wipe your mouth."

The tapping began at the windows, at the door. The rustling, the jostling, the pushing for position on the sills. The first thud of the suicide gulls upon the step.

"Won't America do something?" said his wife. "They've always been our allies, haven't they? Surely America will do something?"

Nat did not answer. The boards were strong against the windows, and on the chimneys too. The cottage was filled with stores, with fuel, with all they needed for the next few days. When he had finished dinner he would put the stuff away, stack it neatly, get everything shipshape, handy-like. His wife could help him, and the children too. They'd tire themselves out, between now and a quarter to nine, when the tide would ebb; then he'd tuck them down on their mattresses, see that they slept good and sound until three in the morning.

He had a new scheme for the windows, which was to fix barbed

Reading Strategy
Predicting What do you think will happen next?

✔Reading Check
What theory does Nat develop to explain why the birds do not move in the morning?

wire in front of the boards. He had brought a great roll of it from the farm. The nuisance was, he'd have to work at this in the dark, when the lull came between nine and three. Pity he had not thought of it before. Still, as long as the wife slept, and the kids, that was the main thing.

The smaller birds were at the window now. He recognized the light tap-tapping of their beaks and the soft brush of their wings. The hawks ignored the windows. They concentrated their attack upon the door. Nat listened to the tearing sound of splintering wood, and wondered how many million years of memory were stored in those little brains, behind the stabbing beaks, the piercing eyes, now giving them this instinct to destroy mankind with all the deft precision of machines.

"I'll smoke that last cigarette," he said to his wife. "Stupid of me, it was the one thing I forgot to bring back from the farm."

He reached for it, switched on the silent wireless. He threw the empty packet on the fire, and watched it burn.

Review and Assess

Thinking About the Selection

1. **Respond:** Did you find "The Birds" suspenseful? Explain.

2. **(a) Recall:** In the beginning of the story, what does the narrator say about Nat and how he spends his days?
   (b) Analyze: Do his actions suggest that Nat is sensitive to the natural world? Why or why not?

3. **(a) Recall:** According to Nat, what is different about the birds this fall? **(b) Analyze:** How might this new difference in the birds contribute to their destructive nature?

4. **(a) Recall:** When Nat cleans up after the first attack, how does he explain the birds' behavior? **(b) Evaluate:** How strongly do you think he believes his own explanation?

5. **(a) Draw Conclusions:** Why do you think the birds have begun attacking and trying to kill people? **(b) Connect:** Do you think that an animal population could suddenly turn against people? Why? **(c) Generalize:** What message do you think the story conveys about the relationship between humans and the natural world?

6. **(a) Connect:** What ending do you think most readers expect?
   (b) Evaluate: Why might this story have an inconclusive ending?

Daphne du Maurier

(1907–1989)

Du Maurier was born in London into a family of actors, artists, and writers. Her father was an actor and theater manager who specialized in playing criminals on the stage, and her grandfather was a novelist who illustrated his own writing.

The Loving Spirit (1931), du Maurier's first novel, became a bestseller, propelling her into a lifelong career as a writer. She followed with a series of romantic novels that were tinged with mystery and suspense.

Du Maurier's stories caught the attention of director Alfred Hitchcock, who specialized in suspenseful films. In addition to *The Birds*, Hitchcock made two other films based on du Maurier's tales, including *Rebecca*, which won the Academy Award for Best Picture in 1940.

Review and Assess

Literary Analysis

Foreshadowing

1. How does Nat's sighting of masses of gulls riding the sea **foreshadow** possible disaster?
2. What does the BBC announcement of a national emergency foreshadow?
3. Using a chart like this one, explain what you think the scene at Triggs' farm at the end of the story foreshadows for Nat's family.

Scene at Triggs' Farm	Possible Outcomes

Connecting Literary Elements

4. (a) Reread the description of the children's bedroom after Nat has fought off the birds in the dark of the night (p. 53). Use a chart like the one shown here to record the **imagery** in that description. (b) Explain the effect that you think each image is meant to have.

5. (a) Review the last three paragraphs of the story, and find at least two vivid details. (b) How do these details add to the suspense?

Reading Strategy

Predicting

6. What were the first hints that led you to **predict** the outcome?
7. Review the predictions you made as you read. (a) Identify one prediction that was accurate and one that you later revised. (b) For each, explain how details later in the story supported or contradicted your prediction.

Extend Understanding

8. **Science Connection:** What questions about the bird invasion might a scientist raise to help understand the events of the story?

Integrate Language Skills

Vocabulary Development Lesson

Word Analysis: Anglo-Saxon Suffix *-ful*

In "The Birds," the children are described as *fretful* about the frightening situation they face. The word *fretful* contains the Anglo-Saxon suffix *-ful*. The suffix means "having the quality of," as in *forgetful*; "having the quality that would fill," as in *handful*; or "full of," as in *fretful*. Therefore, *fretful* literally means "full of fret or worry," and it is no surprise that a fretful person is irritable or discontented.

Add the suffix *-ful* to these words. Then, using your knowledge of the suffix *-ful*, provide a definition for each of the words you generate.

1. sorrow	4. regret
2. teaspoon	5. spite
3. help	6. rest

Fluency: Clarify Word Meaning

Match each vocabulary word with its synonym.

1. placid		a.	gloomy
2. garish		b.	urgent
3. reconnaissance		c.	calm
4. sullen		d.	exploratory
5. furtively		e.	gaudy
6. imperative		f.	stealthily
7. recounted		g.	irritable
8. fretful		h.	narrated

Spelling Strategy

Most words ending in silent *e* keep the *e* before a suffix beginning with a consonant. For example, *grace* + *-ful* = *graceful*. Write the correct spelling of each word below.

1. securly   2. housful   3. discouragment

Grammar Lesson

Reflexive and Intensive Pronouns

A **reflexive pronoun** ends in *-self* or *-selves* and indicates that someone or something performs an action to, for, or upon itself. Reflexive pronouns point back to a noun or pronoun that appears earlier in the sentence. They are essential to the meaning of a sentence. In contrast, an **intensive pronoun** also ends in *-self* or *-selves* but simply adds emphasis to a noun or pronoun in the same sentence.

> **Reflexive:** "Once more he settled *himself* to sleep."
>
> **Intensive:** "You had to endure something *yourself* before it touched you."

Practice Identify whether each underlined pronoun below is reflexive or intensive.

1. Jill read <u>herself</u> a story after supper.
2. Her parents <u>themselves</u> had encouraged her.
3. They said, "If you children want to play, you will have to see to it <u>yourselves</u>."
4. Nat whispered, "I will go outside and take a look around <u>myself</u>."
5. He convinced <u>himself</u> they were safe.

Writing Application Write two sentences that include these pronouns, used as indicated.

1. himself (reflexive)
2. ourselves (intensive)

W̶G̶ Prentice Hall Writing and Grammar Connection: Chapter 16, Section 2

Writing Lesson

Bird's-Eye View of a Place

Imagine how different "The Birds" would be if it were told from the point of view of one of the birds. The action would be described from above rather than below. Write a description of a scene in the story as it would look to a bird flying overhead.

Prewriting   To see the scene from above, make a blueprint of the scene by drawing what you have chosen to describe. Label the key places.

Drafting   Refer to your sketch as you draft your bird's point of view. Include details that indicate a downward-looking perspective. For example, a bird in the sky would be able to see Nat's entire house, but it would not, for example, see the color of Nat's eyes.

Revising   Reread your description, checking for inconsistencies in viewpoint. Correct any passages that describe something from the ground up.

Model: Revising to Maintain a Consistent Viewpoint

The shingled roof of the library peeked through the ~~oak~~ trees. A

~~look through the windows showed that it was a busy place today.~~

> To keep this viewpoint consistent, details that could be seen only from ground level are eliminated.

WG *Prentice Hall Writing and Grammar Connection: Chapter 6, Section 4*

Extension Activities

Listening and Speaking In "The Birds," people try to protect themselves from birds. In real life, birds often need protection from people. In a small group, hold a **panel discussion** in which you answer the following questions:

- What dangers do humans pose to bird populations?
- What can be done to protect birds and their habitats?

Each participant should research the topic and prepare a set of concise notes for easy reference during the discussion. **[Group Activity]**

Research and Technology Prepare a research report and give a **presentation** on any four of the birds mentioned in this story. For each bird, research size, distinguishing features, natural habitats, and behaviors. Use the Internet or the CD-ROM edition of an encyclopedia to locate photographs and factual information.

 **Take It to the Net**   www.phschool.com

Go online for an additional research activity using the Internet.

from
The Perfect Storm
Sebastian Junger

"The Birds" draws its power from the transformation of a common, harmless animal into something dark and sinister.

Other authors tap the same power to transform the ordinary in nature into the extraordinary. In his 1997 book "The Perfect Storm," Sebastian Junger uses the true story of boats caught in a major storm to demonstrate the power extreme weather has on our imagination. He shows how extreme weather can transform familiar landscapes, like a gently rolling sea, into territory that is suddenly alien and hostile. In the following excerpt, people are exposed to the furious side of nature, providing insight into the different ways that people cope with danger and risk.

2:30 AM—s/v [sailing vessel] is running out of fuel, recommend we try to keep Falcon o/s [on-scene] until Tamaroa arrives.
5:29 AM—Falcon has lost comms [communication] with vessel, vessel is low on battery power and taking on water. Pumps are keeping up but are run by ele [electric].
7:07 AM—Falcon o/s, vessel has been located. Six hours fuel left. People on board are scared.

The H-3 arrives on scene around 6:30 and spends half an hour just trying to locate the *Satori.* The conditions are so bad that she's vanished from the Falcon's radar, and the H-3 pilot is almost on top of her before spotting her in the foam-streaked seas. The Falcon circles off to the southwest to prepare a life-raft drop while the H-3 takes up a hover directly over the boat. In these conditions the Falcon pilot could never line up on something as small as a sailboat, so the H-3 acts as a stand-in. The Falcon comes back at 140 knots, radar locked onto the helicopter, and at the last moment the H-3 falls away and the jet makes the drop. The pilot comes screaming over the *Satori*'s mast and the copilot pushes two life-raft packages out a hatch in the floorboards. The rafts are linked by a long nylon tether, and as they fall they cartwheel apart, splashing down well to either side of the *Satori*. The tether, released at two hundred feet into a hurricane-force wind, drops right into Bylander's hand.

The H-3 hovers overhead while the *Satori* crew haul in the packages, but both rafts have exploded on impact. There's nothing at either end of the line. The *Tamaroa* is still five hours away and the storm has retrograded[1] to within a couple of hundred miles of the coast; over the next twenty-four hours it will pass directly over the *Satori*. A daylight rescue in these conditions is difficult, and a nighttime rescue is out of the question. If the *Satori* crew is not taken off in the next few hours, there's a good chance they won't be taken off at all. Late that morning the second H-3 arrives and the pilot, Lieutenant Klosson, explains the situation to Ray Leonard. Leonard radios back that he's not leaving the boat.

It's unclear whether Leonard is serious or just trying to save face. Either way, the Coast Guard is having none of it. Two helicopters, two Falcon jets, a medium-range cutter, and a hundred air- and seamen have already been committed to the rescue; the *Satori* crew are coming off now. *"Owner refuses to leave and says he's sailed through hurricanes before,"* the Comcen[2] incident log records at 12:24 that afternoon. *"Tamaroa wants manifestly unsafe voyage so that o/o [owner-operator] can be forced off."*

A "manifestly unsafe voyage" means that the vessel has been deemed an unacceptable risk to her crew or others, and the Coast Guard has the legal authority to order everyone off. Commander Brudnicki gets on the radio with District One and requests a manifestly unsafe designation for the *Satori*, and at 12:47 it is granted. The *Tamaroa* is just a couple of miles away now, within VHF[3] range of the *Satori*, and Brudnicki raises Leonard on the radio and tells him he has no choice in the matter. Everyone is leaving the boat. At 12:57 in the afternoon, thirteen hours after weighing anchor, the *Tamaroa* plunges into view.

There's a lot of hardware circling the *Satori*. There's the Falcon, the H-3, the *Tamaroa*, and the freighter *Gold Bond Conveyor*, which has been cutting circles around the *Satori* since the first mayday call. Hardware is not the problem, though; it's time. Dark is only three hours away, and the departing H-3 pilot doesn't think the *Satori* will survive another night. She'll run out of fuel, start getting knocked down, and eventually break apart. The crew will be cast into the sea, and the helicopter pilot will refuse to drop his rescue swimmer because he can't be sure of getting him back. It would be up to the *Tamaroa* to maneuver alongside the swimmers and pull them on board, and in these seas it would be almost impossible. It's now or never.

The only way to take them off, Brudnicki decides, is to shuttle them back to the *Tamaroa* in one of the little Avons. The Avons are twenty-one-foot inflatable rafts with rigid hulls and outboard engines;

---

1. **retrograded** (re'trə grād' ed) *v.* moved backward.
2. **Comcen** (käm' sen) *abbrev.* Coast Guard abbreviation for the Command Center, which keeps track of rescue operations.
3. **VHF** *abbrev.* Very High Frequency; radio frequency used by ships for communication.

Thematic Connection
What steps do the rescue crew take to battle nature?

Reading Check
Why is it critical to save the *Satori* crew before nightfall?

one of them could make a run to the *Satori*, drop off survival suits, and then come back again to pick up the three crew. If anyone wound up in the water, at least they'd be insulated and afloat. It's not a particularly complicated maneuver, but no one has done it in conditions like this before. No one has even *seen* conditions like this before. At 1:23 PM the *Tamaroa* crew gathers at the port davits,[4] three men climb aboard the Avon, and they lower away.

It goes badly from the start. What passes for a lull between waves is in fact a crest-to-trough change of thirty to forty feet. Chief bosun[5] Thomas Amidon lowers the Avon halfway down, gets lifted up by the next wave, can't keep up with the trough and freefalls to the bottom of the cable. The lifting eye gets ripped out of its mount and Amidon almost pitches overboard. He struggles back into position, finishes lowering the boat, and makes way from the *Tamaroa*.

The seas are twice the size of the Avon raft. With <u>excruciating</u> slowness it fights its way to the *Satori*, comes up bow-to-stern,[6] and a crew member flings the three survival suits on deck. Stimpson grabs them and hands them out, but Amidon doesn't back out in time. The sailboat rides up a sea, comes down on the Avon, and punctures one of her air bladders. Things start to happen very fast now: the Avon's bow collapses, a wave swamps her to the gunwales,[7] the engine dies, and she falls away astern. Amidon tries desperately to get the engine going again and finally manages to, but they're up to their waists in water and the raft is crippled. There's no way they can even get themselves back onto the *Tamaroa*, much less save the crew of the *Satori*. Six people, not just three, now need to be rescued.

The H-3 crew watches all this <u>incredulously</u>. They're in a two o'clock hover with their jump door open, just over the tops of the waves. They can see the raft dragging heavily through the seas, and the *Tamaroa* heaving through ninety-degree rolls. Pilot Claude Hessel finally gets on the radio and tells Brudnicki and Amidon that he may have another way of doing this. He can't hoist[8] the *Satori* crew directly off their deck, he says, because the mast is <u>flailing</u> too wildly and might entangle the hoist. That would drag the H-3 right down on top of the boat. But he could drop his rescue swimmer, who would take the people off the boat one at a time and bring them up on the hoist. It's the best chance they've got, and Brudnicki knows it. He consults with District One and then gives the okay.

▲ Critical Viewing
What dangers does a rescue like the one shown here present? **[Analyze]**

excruciating (eks krōō′ shē āt′ iŋ) *adj.* agonizing

incredulously (in krej′ oo ləs lē) *adv.* unwilling or unable to believe

flailing (flāl′ iŋ) *v.* swinging freely

---

4. **port davits** (dā′ vits) *n.* cranes used to raise and lower inflatable rafts, located on the left side of a ship.
5. **Chief bosun** (bō′ sən) *n.* officer in charge of the ship's crew and equipment; also spelled boatswain.
6. **bow-to-stern** (bou tōō stɝn) *nautical term.* from the front of a ship (*bow*) to its rear (*stern*).
7. **gunwales** (gun′ əls) *n.* upper edge of the side of a boat or ship.
8. **hoist** *v.* lift by means of a special apparatus.

The rescue swimmer on Hessel's helicopter is Dave Moore, a three-year veteran who has never been on a major rescue. ("The good cases don't come along too often—usually someone beats you to them," he says. "If a sailboat gets in trouble far out we usually get a rescue, but otherwise it's just a lot of little stuff.") Moore is handsome in a baby-faced sort of way—square-jawed, blue-eyed, and a big open smile. He has a dense, compact body that is more seallike than athletic. His profession of rescue swimmer came about when a tanker went down off New York in the mid-1980s. A Coast Guard helicopter was hovering overhead, but it was winter and the tanker crew were too <u>hypothermic</u> to get into the lift basket. They all drowned. Congress decided they wanted something done, and the Coast Guard adopted the Navy rescue program. Moore is twenty-five years old, born the year Karen Stimpson graduated from high school.

Moore is already wearing a neoprene wetsuit. He puts on socks and hood, straps on swim fins, pulls a mask and snorkel down over his head, and then struggles into his neoprene gloves. He buckles on a life vest and then signals to flight engineer Vriesman that he's ready. Vriesman, who has one arm extended, gatelike, across the jump door, steps aside and allows Moore to crouch by the edge. That means that they're at "ten and ten"—a ten-foot hover at ten knots. Moore, who's no longer plugged into the intercom, signals final corrections to Vriesman with his hands, who relays them to the pilot. This is it; Moore has trained three years for this moment. An hour ago he was in the lunch line back on base. Now he's about to drop into the <u>maelstrom</u>.

Hessel holds a low hover with the boat at his two o'clock. Moore can see the crew clustered together on deck and the *Satori* making slow, plunging headway into the seas. Vriesman is seated next to Moore at the hoist controls, and avionicsman[9] Ayres is behind the copilot with the radio and search gear. Both wear flightsuits and crash helmets and are plugged into the internal communication system in the wall. The time is 2:07 PM. Moore picks a spot between waves, takes a deep breath, and jumps.

---

9. **avionicsman** (ā′ vē än′ iks man) *n.* crew member in charge of electronic equipment.

Connecting Literature Past and Present

1. How do characters in both this excerpt from *The Perfect Storm* and "The Birds" employ science and technology to deal with a natural threat?

2. (a) How are the two stories similar in their portrayal of human beings facing natural disasters? (b) Does the fact that "The Birds" is fiction affect the way you feel about the characters? Why or why not?

3. Explain the similarities and differences in the ways that characters in each selection face danger.

hypothermic (hī′ pō *thur*′ mik) *adj.* having a dangerously low body temperature

maelstrom (māl′ strəm) *n.* violent or turbulent whirl of air and water

Sebastian Junger

(b. 1962)

The widespread popularity of *The Perfect Storm* surprised even its author, Sebastian Junger. Though *The Perfect Storm* was his first book, Junger has written many articles for *Outside*, *Men's Journal*, and *The New York Times Magazine*.

Junger is drawn to the subject of ordinary people performing dangerous work. He might feel a connection to them because he has participated in dangerous work himself. His past jobs have included a freelance writing assignment in war-torn Bosnia and work as a climber for a tree removal service.

Movie Reviews

About Movie Reviews

Reviews of new films are published in most newspapers on the day they open. In addition, reviews can be found in many magazines, as well as on the Internet, radio, and TV. Writers of movie reviews usually summarize the film's plot and comment on whether they feel the film is worth seeing. Movie critics support their opinions by analyzing the plot, acting, visual appeal, and other elements of the film. Before you allow a review to influence your opinion, follow these steps:

- Distinguish between fact and opinion in the review.
- Analyze the critic's arguments.
- Evaluate the persuasive language the critic uses.

Reading Strategy

Identifying Support for Response

Reviewers know that in order to sway readers, they need to defend their views with convincing reasons. To persuade readers that their opinions are valid, film critics respond to particular elements of a film, providing examples that support their response.

For example, the author of this review of Alfred Hitchcock's *The Birds* finds the movie frightening. As you read the review, look for details he provides to support his response. Use a chart like the one below to jot down the reviewer's responses to particular elements of the film. Identify his support of those responses through his examples and explanations.

Element	Reviewer's Opinion	Support
Special Effects: Bird swooping down on townspeople in scene with gas station explosion	"... special effects in *The Birds* provide believable and extraordinary horror ..."	Special effects experts handled bird scenes so well that moviegoers exiting the theater would probably glance up at the sky fearfully.

The Birds

DeWitt Bodeen

[In his film, Hitchcock] has the cinematic advantage [over du Maurier's short story] of being able to show the birds graphically, as they gather and wait like [an evil] army and then swoop in to destroy and kill. In one scene, for example, a bird authority named Mrs. Bundy (Ethel Griffies) sits in a restaurant assuring her listeners that there are many varieties of birds, all of which stick to their own kind, making it impossible for them to unite for any form of attack. As she speaks, however, the birds outside gather and then inexplicably dive down upon the people, seemingly at random. Hitchcock has a special photographic adviser named Ub Iwerks, who, with the aid of special effects expert Laurence A. Hampton, handled the bird scenes in such an effective way that anyone coming out of a theater where *The Birds* had been screened as a matinee attraction was likely to glance up to the sky warily. *The Birds* was nominated for a special effects Academy Award in 1963, but lost to *Cleopatra* for no apparent reason, a fact that upset many critics, since the special effects in *The Birds* provide believable and extraordinary horror and are uncannily executed.

Hitchcock begins his story in San Francisco, where a bachelor attorney, Mitch Brenner (Rod Taylor), meets a wealthy, cool blonde named Melanie Daniels (Tippi Hedren). The two flirt and tease each other, and Melanie is especially taken with Mitch. She impulsively decides to visit Brenner at his home in Bodega Bay, a little north of the city, where he spends weekends with his sister Cathy (Veronica Cartwright) and mother (Jessica Tandy). Brenner's former girlfriend, Annie Hayworth (Suzanne Pleshette), also lives there, teaching at an elementary school a little apart from the main village center.

When Melanie arrives, bringing a cage with two lovebirds which she has bought for Mitch as a joke, the townspeople eye her ominously, for the birds in the area are already gathering around the town, behaving queerly and

> The reviewer provides a summary of the film's plot in paragraphs 2, 3, and 4.

> The writer identifies actors and actresses by name.

> The first part of this sentence presents a fact, while the second part offers an opinion.

The Birds

setting the people on edge. Melanie decides to rent a boat, take the birds across the bay to Mitch's house, give them to Cathy, then quietly return and wait for Mitch's reaction. When they do meet again he begins to like her more, and they fall in love, against his mother's wishes.

After these events, the birds begin more attacks. In one instance they swoop down on a service station, where an attendant is frightened and drops the gasoline line, allowing a spill to spread over the area. A driver watching the birds moving in to attack absentmindedly lights his cigarette and drops the lighted match in the path of the gasoline. There is a huge explosion, and that whole area of the town square is set afire. The camera pulls back for a full overhead shot of the disaster, while the birds sweep through the sky overhead and screech in triumph.

. . .

Hitchcock puts this dark, bizarre, frightening fairy tale before the camera with rare skill. The birds in all their terror and power were manipulated by a trainer named Ray Berwick; without him and the special effects crew, the film would not have been so believable. The picture is handsomely photographed in Technicolor by Robert Burks, and Hitchcock intensifies the spellbound, eerie atmosphere of his story by having no musical background score. Instead, he uses an electronic sound device called a Trautonium, designed by

Oskar Sala, and upon this device a toneless, monotonous, but frightening and otherworldly composition by Remi Gassman is played. The advance publicity campaign for the film was expertly handled; on billboards all over numerous cities as well as in the newspapers there appeared the warning message "The Birds Is Coming," piqueing interest in the story.

. . .

There is . . . much more to the film than merely birds. There are some seeming inconsistencies in the plot, and allusions which were criticized by contemporary reviewers are now analyzed at great length. As with all Hitchcock films there is more than a mere story; the complexities of this film are perhaps more difficult to decipher than most. It is never really clear in the film why the birds are attacking, or what, if anything, Melanie's love birds have to do with their behavior. The birds may be avenging something, but there is no evidence of what that something is. The children who are attacked are certainly innocent of any wrongdoing, and in some cases the people killed inadvertently cause their own deaths by panicking.

. . .

The true meaning of the film . . . cannot be pinpointed. This perhaps illustrates one of the greatest aspects of Hitchcock's films: so many questions are left unanswered that they can reveal new insights and nuances of meaning even after repeated viewings.

After a summary, the reviewer offers his opinion. Here, he offers praise.

The reviewer uses specific descriptive words to illustrate his opinion of film elements such as cinematography and music.

Check Your Comprehension

1. According to the reviewer, what advantage does the filmmaker have over the short story writer?
2. What did Ub Iwerks, Laurence A. Hampton, Ray Berwick, Robert Burks, Oskar Sala, and Remi Gassman contribute to the film?
3. (a) According to the reviewer, what are some of the unanswered questions raised by the film? (b) What is the reviewer's opinion of these questions?
4. How did those in charge of publicity do a good job?

Applying the Reading Strategy

Identifying Support for Response

5. Cite three examples DeWitt Bodeen gives to support his opinion that the movie is made "with rare skill."
6. Bodeen finds parts of the film "difficult to decipher," yet he does not think that this is a flaw. How does he defend this response?
7. Complete your own evaluation of the ideas in Bodeen's review. View Alfred Hitchcock's *The Birds*, and then write a brief summary comparing your response to the reviewer's.

Activity

Evaluating Movie Reviews

Choose a film currently showing in theaters. Using a chart like the one shown, record review information from a variety of sources. Then, see the film and write your own review, providing reasons for your opinion.

Compare your findings to decide which sources gave accurate, convincing, or reliable reviews and whether you agreed with the opinions stated. Then, summarize what you have learned from this exercise.

Contrasting Informational Materials

Movie Reviews and Advertisements

1. Find several movie advertisements and review them to determine the key characteristics of this form of informational material.
2. (a) What do reviews and advertisements have in common? (b) How are they different?
3. Which form do you find more reliable? Explain.

Prepare to Read

The Red-headed League

 Take It to the Net

Visit www.phschool.com for interactive activities and instruction related to "The Red-headed League," including

- background
- graphic organizers
- literary elements
- reading strategies

Preview

Connecting to the Literature

Just a quick glance at a person can give you clues to his personality. This sizing up of people is part of the unpaid detective work of everyday life. As you read "The Red-headed League," notice how the brilliant detective Sherlock Holmes uses the technique of keen observation to solve a mystery.

Background

This story is one of many tales about the exploits of the world's most famous fictional detective, Sherlock Holmes. Often shown wearing a cape and deerstalker cap, Holmes is recognized even by people who have never read a Sherlock Holmes mystery.

Literary Analysis

The Mystery

A **mystery** is a story of suspense that usually contains a crime, a crime-solver, a criminal, suspects, and key details such as clues, alibis, and characters' possible reasons for committing a crime. When you read a line like the following from "The Red-headed League," you know that you are embarking on detective work and there is a mystery to solve.

> ". . . I want to find out about them, and who they are, and what their object was in playing this prank—if it was a prank—upon me. It was a pretty expensive joke for them, for it cost them two and thirty pounds."

Read "The Red-headed League" carefully to find details the writer has provided to help you solve the mystery.

Connecting Literary Elements

In "The Red-headed League," **characterization**, the way in which characters are developed, provides vital clues to solving the mystery. Writers reveal characters through a variety of techniques, including direct statements, descriptions, and characters' words, thoughts, and actions. Notice how each character in the story is developed and which details are clues to solving the mystery.

Reading Strategy

Finding Key Details

Readers of mysteries try to solve the crime along with—or even before—the detective. This is done by noting **key details**, pieces of information that have a bearing on the crime. These key details are often clues to the mystery. For example, subtleties in a character's actions may reveal something significant. Use a chart like the one shown to record the key details that you find as you read. For each detail, note its possible importance to the case.

Vocabulary Development

singular (siŋ´ gyə lər) *adj.* rare; extraordinary (p. 97)

avail (ə vāl´) *v.* be of help (p. 103)

hoax (hōks) *n.* deceitful trick (p. 104)

introspective (in´ trə spek´ tiv) *adj.* causing one to look into one's own thoughts and feelings (p. 107)

vex (veks) *v.* annoy (p. 108)

conundrums (kə nun´ drəmz) *n.* puzzling questions or problems (p. 108)

astuteness (ə stoot´ nis) *n.* shrewdness (p. 108)

formidable (fôr´ mə də bəl) *adj.* awe-inspiring (p. 108)

CALIFORNIA STANDARDS

Instruction with this selection addresses these standards:

R 1.1*, 3.3*, 3.8*
W 2.1*
WOLC 1.2*, 1.3*
LS 1.9

* Standards tested on HS Exit Exam. For complete standards, see p. CA 4.

Key Detail

Wilson's assistant is willing to work for half wages.

Importance

It's odd that someone volunteers for less pay.

The Red-headed League

Sir Arthur Conan Doyle

I had called upon my friend, Mr. Sherlock Holmes, one day in the autumn of last year and found him in deep conversation with a very stout, florid-faced, elderly gentleman with fiery red hair. With an apology for my intrusion, I was about to withdraw when Holmes pulled me abruptly into the room and closed the door behind me.

"You could not possibly have come at a better time, my dear Watson," he said cordially.

"I was afraid that you were engaged."

"So I am. Very much so."

"Then I can wait in the next room."

"Not at all. This gentleman, Mr. Wilson, has been my partner and helper in many of my most successful cases, and I have no doubt that he will be of the utmost use to me in yours also."

The stout gentleman half rose from his chair and gave a bob of greeting, with a quick little questioning glance from his small, fat-encircled eyes.

"Try the settee,"[1] said Holmes, relapsing into his armchair and putting his finger tips together, as was his custom when in judicial moods. "I know, my dear Watson, that you share my love of all that is bizarre and outside the conventions and humdrum routine of every-day life. You have shown your relish for it by the enthusiasm which has prompted you to chronicle, and, if you will excuse my saying so, somewhat to embellish so many of my own little adventures.

"Your cases have indeed been of the greatest interest to me," I observed.

"You will remember that I remarked the other day, just before we went into the very simple problem presented by Miss Mary Sutherland, that for strange effects and extraordinary combinations we must go to life itself, which is always far more daring than any effort of the imagination."

"A proposition which I took the liberty of doubting."

"You did, Doctor, but none the less you must come round to my view, for otherwise I shall keep on piling fact upon fact on you until your reason breaks down under them and acknowledges me to be right. Now, Mr. Jabez Wilson here has been good enough to call upon me this morning, and to begin a narrative which promises to be one of the most singular which I have listened to for some time. You have heard me remark that the strangest and most unique things are very often connected not with the larger but with the smaller crimes, and occasionally, indeed, where there is room for doubt whether any positive crime has

---

1. **settee** (se tē´) *n.* small sofa.

Literary Analysis
The Mystery What does Holmes's comment about Watson indicate about the crime-solver in this mystery?

singular (siŋ´ gyə lər) *adj.* rare; extraordinary

Reading Check

Who has helped Holmes in many of his cases?

been committed. As far as I have heard it is impossible for me to say whether the present case is an instance of crime or not, but the course of events is certainly among the most singular that I have ever listened to. Perhaps, Mr. Wilson, you would have the great kindness to recommence your narrative. I ask you not merely because my friend Dr. Watson has not heard the opening part but also because the peculiar nature of the story makes me anxious to have every possible detail from your lips. As a rule, when I have heard some slight indication of the course of events, I am able to guide myself by the thousands of other similar cases which occur to my memory. In the present instance I am forced to admit that the facts are, to the best of my belief, unique."

The portly client puffed out his chest with an appearance of some little pride and pulled a dirty and wrinkled newspaper from the inside pocket of his great coat. As he glanced down the advertisement column, with his head thrust forward and the paper flattened out upon his knee, I took a good look at the man and endeavored, after the fashion of my companion, to read the indications which might be presented by his dress or appearance.

I did not gain very much, however, by my inspection. Our visitor bore every mark of being an average commonplace British tradesman, obese, pompous, and slow. He wore rather baggy gray shepherd's check trousers, a not over-clean black frock coat, unbuttoned in the front, and a drab waistcoat with a heavy brassy Albert chain, and a square pierced bit of metal dangling down as an ornament. A frayed top hat and a faded brown overcoat with a wrinkled velvet collar lay upon a chair beside him. Altogether, look as I would, there was nothing remarkable about the man save his blazing red head, and the expression of extreme chagrin and discontent upon his features.

Reading Strategy
Finding Key Details
Which details of Wilson's appearance does Watson seem to regard as most important?

Sherlock Holmes's quick eye took in my occupation, and he shook his head with a smile as he noticed my questioning glances. "Beyond the obvious facts that he has at some time done manual labor, that he takes snuff,[2] that he is a Freemason,[3] that he has been in China, and that he has done a considerable amount of writing lately, I can deduce nothing else."

Mr. Jabez Wilson started up in his chair, with his forefinger upon the paper, but his eyes upon my companion.

"How, in the name of good fortune, did you know all that, Mr. Holmes?" he asked. "How did you know, for example, that I did manual labor? It's as true as gospel, for I began as a ship's carpenter."

"Your hands, my dear sir. Your right hand is quite a size larger than your left. You have worked with it, and the muscles are more developed."

"Well, the snuff, then, and the Freemasonry?"

"I won't insult your intelligence by telling you how I read that, especially as, rather against the strict rules of your order, you use an arc-and-compass breastpin."

Literary Analysis
The Mystery Why are Holmes's observations of Wilson more meaningful than Watson's?

---

2. **snuff** powdered tobacco.
3. **Freemason** member of a secret society.

"Ah, of course, I forgot that. But the writing?"

"What else can be indicated by that right cuff so very shiny for five inches, and the left one with the smooth patch near the elbow where you rest it upon the desk?"

"Well, but China?"

"The fish that you have tattooed immediately above your right wrist could only have been done in China. I have made a small study of tattoo marks and have even contributed to the literature of the subject. That trick of staining the fishes' scales of a delicate pink is quite peculiar to China. When, in addition, I see a Chinese coin hanging from your watch-chain, the matter becomes even more simple."

Mr. Jabez Wilson laughed heavily. "Well, I never!" said he. "I thought at first that you had done something clever, but I see that there was nothing in it, after all."

"I begin to think, Watson," said Holmes, "that I make a mistake in explaining. *'Omne ignotum pro magnifico,'*[4] you know, and my poor little reputation, such as it is, will suffer shipwreck if I am so candid. Can you not find the advertisement, Mr. Wilson?"

"Yes, I have got it now," he answered with his thick red finger planted halfway down the column. "Here it is. This is what began it all. You just read it for yourself, sir."

I took the paper from him and read as follows:

To THE RED-HEADED LEAGUE:

On account of the bequest of the late Ezekiah Hopkins, of Lebanon, Pennsylvania, U. S. A., there is now another vacancy open which entitles a member of the League to a salary of £4♦ a week for purely nominal services. All red-headed men who are sound in body and mind, and above the age of twenty-one years, are eligible. Apply in person on Monday, at eleven o'clock, to Duncan Ross, at the offices of the League, 7 Pope's Court, Fleet Street.

"What on earth does this mean?" I ejaculated after I had twice read over the extraordinary announcement.

Holmes chuckled and wriggled in his chair, as was his habit when in high spirits. "It is a little off the beaten track, isn't it?" said he. "And now, Mr. Wilson, off you go at scratch and tell us all about yourself, your household, and the effect which this advertisement had upon your fortunes. You will first make a note, Doctor, of the paper and the date."

"It is *The Morning Chronicle* of April 27, 1890. Just two months ago."

"Very good. Now, Mr. Wilson?"

"Well, it is just as I have been telling you, Mr. Sherlock Holmes," said Jabez Wilson, mopping his forehead; "I have a small pawnbroker's business at Coburg Square, near the City. It's not a very large

---

4. *Omne ignotum pro magnifico* (äm´ nā ig nō´ təm prō mag nē´ fē kō) Latin for "Whatever is unknown is magnified."

Literature in context Math Connection

♦ *Pound Conversions*

The advertisement announces a League salary of four pounds a week. The pound is the monetary unit of Great Britain. Its equivalency in American dollars fluctuates, depending on current economic conditions. At the time Doyle wrote the story, one British pound equaled about $4.85, so four pounds would have equaled about $19.40. This was considered a large amount at the time in which the story is set, particularly for such simple work.

✔**Reading Check**

Who is eligible for the position posted in the advertisement?

affair, and of late years it has not done more than just give me a living. I used to be able to keep two assistants, but now I only keep one; and I would have a job to pay him but that he is willing to come for half wages so as to learn the business."

"What is the name of this obliging youth?" asked Sherlock Holmes.

"His name is Vincent Spaulding, and he's not such a youth, either. It's hard to say his age. I should not wish a smarter assistant, Mr. Holmes; and I know very well that he could better himself and earn twice what I am able to give him. But, after all, if he is satisfied, why should I put ideas in his head?"

"Why, indeed? You seem most fortunate in having an employee who comes under the full market price. It is not a common experience among employers in this age. I don't know that your assistant is not as remarkable as your advertisement."

"Oh, he has his faults, too," said Mr. Wilson. "Never was such a fellow for photography. Snapping away with a camera when he ought to be improving his mind, and then diving down into the cellar like a rabbit into its hole to develop his pictures. That is his main fault, but on the whole he's a good worker. There's no vice in him."

"He is still with you, I presume?"

"Yes, sir. He and a girl of fourteen, who does a bit of simple cooking and keeps the place clean—that's all I have in the house, for I am a widower and never had any family. We live very quietly, sir, the three of us; and we keep a roof over our heads and pay our debts, if we do nothing more.

"The first thing that put us out was that advertisement. Spaulding, he came down into the office just this day eight weeks, with this very paper in his hand, and he says:

" 'I wish to the Lord, Mr. Wilson, that I was a red-headed man.'

" 'Why that?' I asks.

" 'Why,' says he, 'here's another vacancy on the League of the Red-headed Men. It's worth quite a little fortune to any man who gets it, and I understand that there are more vacancies than there are men, so that the trustees are at their wits' end what to do with the money. If my hair would only change color, here's a nice little crib all ready for me to step into.'

" 'Why, what is it, then?' I asked. You see, Mr. Holmes, I am a very stay-at-home man,

Reading Strategy
Finding Key Details
Which details about Vincent Spaulding are unusual enough to interest Sherlock Holmes?

and as my business came to me instead of my having to go to it, I was often weeks on end without putting my foot over the doormat. In that way I didn't know much of what was going on outside, and I was always glad of a bit of news.

" 'Have you never heard of the League of the Red-headed Men?' he asked with his eyes open.

" 'Never.'

" 'Why, I wonder at that, for you are eligible yourself for one of the vacancies.'

" 'And what are they worth?' I asked.

" 'Oh, merely a couple of hundred a year, but the work is slight, and it need not interfere very much with one's other occupations.'

"Well, you can easily think that that made me prick up my ears, for the business has not been over-good for some years, and an extra couple of hundred would have been very handy.

" 'Tell me all about it,' said I.

" 'Well,' said he, showing me the advertisement, 'you can see for yourself that the League has a vacancy, and there is the address where you should apply for particulars. As far as I can make out, the League was founded by an American millionaire, Ezekiah Hopkins, who was very peculiar in his ways. He was himself red-headed, and he had a great sympathy for all red-headed men; so when he died it was found that he had left his enormous fortune in the hands of trustees, with instructions to apply the interest to the providing of easy berths to men whose hair is of that color. From all I hear it is splendid pay and very little to do.

" 'But,' said I, 'there would be millions of red-headed men who would apply.'

" 'Not so many as you might think,' he answered. 'You see it is really confined to Londoners, and to grown men. This American had started from London when he was young, and he wanted to do the old town a good turn. Then, again, I have heard it is no use your applying if your hair is light red, or dark red, or anything but real bright, blazing, fiery red. Now, if you cared to apply, Mr. Wilson, you would just walk in; but perhaps it would hardly be worth your while to put yourself out of the way for the sake of a few hundred pounds.'

"Now, it is a fact, gentlemen, as you may see for yourselves, that my hair is of a very full and rich tint, so that it seemed to me that if there was to be any competition in the matter I stood as good a chance as any man that I had ever met. Vincent Spaulding seemed to know so much about it that I thought he might prove useful so I just ordered him to put up the shutters for the day and to come right away with me. He was very willing to have a holiday,[5] so we shut the business up and started off for the address that was given us in the advertisement.

"I never hope to see such a sight as that again, Mr. Holmes. From north, south, east, and west every man who had a shade of red in his hair had tramped into the city to answer the advertisement. Fleet

Literary Analysis
The Mystery The Red-headed League seems too good to be true. What appears most suspicious about this club?

Reading Check
Why did Wilson believe he had a good chance of being chosen for the position?

---

5. **holiday** a day off from work; a vacation.

Street was choked with red-headed folk, and Pope's Court looked like a coster's orange barrow.[6] I should not have thought there were so many in the whole country as were brought together by that single advertisement. Every shade of color they were—straw, lemon, orange, brick, Irish-setter, liver, clay: but, as Spaulding said, there were not many who had the real vivid flame-colored tint. When I saw how many were waiting, I would have given it up in despair: but Spaulding would not hear of it. How he did it I could not imagine, but he pushed and pulled and butted until he got me through the crowd, and right up to the steps which led to the office. There was a double stream upon the stair, some going up in hope, and some coming back dejected: but we wedged in as well as we could and soon found ourselves in the office."

"Your experience has been a most entertaining one," remarked Holmes as his client paused and refreshed his memory with a huge pinch of snuff. "Pray continue your very interesting statement."

"There was nothing in the office but a couple of wooden chairs and a deal table, behind which sat a small man with a head that was even redder than mine. He said a few words to each candidate as he came up, and then he always managed to find some fault in them which would disqualify them. Getting a vacancy did not seem to be such a very easy matter, after all. However, when our turn came the little man was much more favorable to me than to any of the others, and he closed the door as we entered, so that he might have a private word with us.

" 'This is Mr. Jabez Wilson,' said my assistant, 'and he is willing to fill a vacancy in the League.'

" 'And he is admirably suited for it,' the other answered. 'He has every requirement. I cannot recall when I have seen anything so fine.' He took a step backward, cocked his head on one side, and gazed at my hair until I felt quite bashful. Then suddenly he plunged forward, wrung my hand, and congratulated me warmly on my success.

" 'It would be injustice to hesitate, said he. 'You will, however, I am sure, excuse me for taking an obvious precaution.' With that he seized my hair in both his hands, and tugged until I yelled with the pain. 'There is water in your eyes,' said he as he released me. 'I perceive that all is as it should be. But we have to be careful, for we have twice been deceived by wigs and once by paint. I could tell you tales of cobbler's wax which would disgust you with human nature.' He stepped over to the window and shouted through it at the top of his voice that the vacancy was filled. A groan of disappointment came up from below, and the folk all trooped away in different directions until there was not a red head to be seen except my own and that of the manager.

" 'My name,' said he, 'is Mr. Duncan Ross, and I am myself one of the pensioners upon the fund left by our noble benefactor. Are you a married man, Mr. Wilson? Have you a family?'

Reading Strategy
Finding Key Details What do you notice about how the League interviewer receives Wilson?

Literary Analysis
The Mystery What is suspicious about the way in which the vacancy was filled?

---

6. **coster's orange barrow** pushcart of a seller of oranges.

"I answered that I had not.

"His face fell immediately.

" 'Dear me!' he said gravely, 'that is very serious indeed! I am sorry to hear you say that. The fund was, of course, for the propagation and spread of the red-heads as well as for their maintenance. It is exceedingly unfortunate that you should be a bachelor.'

"My face lengthened at this, Mr. Holmes, for I thought that I was not to have the vacancy after all: but after thinking it over for a few minutes he said that it would be all right.

" 'In the case of another,' said he, 'the objection might be fatal, but we must stretch a point in favor of a man with such a head of hair as yours. When shall you be able to enter upon your new duties?

" 'Well, it is a little awkward, for I have a business already,' said I.

" 'Oh, never mind about that, Mr. Wilson!' said Vincent Spaulding. 'I should be able to look after that for you.'

" 'What would be the hours?' I asked.

" 'Ten to two.'

"Now a pawnbroker's business is mostly done of an evening, Mr. Holmes, especially Thursday and Friday evening, which is just before pay-day: so it would suit me very well to earn a little in the mornings. Besides, I knew that my assistant was a good man, and that he would see to anything that turned up.

" 'That would suit me very well,' said I. 'And the pay?'

" 'Is £4 a week.'

" 'And the work?'

" 'Is purely nominal.'

" 'What do you call purely nominal?'

" 'Well, you have to be in the office, or at least in the building, the whole time. If you leave, you forfeit your whole position forever. The will is very clear upon that point. You don't comply with the conditions if you budge from the office during that time.'

" 'It's only four hours a day, and I should not think of leaving,' said I.

" 'No excuse will <u>avail</u>,' said Mr. Duncan Ross: 'neither sickness nor business nor anything else. There you must stay, or you lose your billet.'[7]

" 'And the work?'

" 'Is to copy out the Encyclopedia Britannica. There is the first volume of it in that press. You must find your own ink, pens, and blotting-paper, but we provide this table and chair. Will you be ready tomorrow?'

" 'Certainly,' I answered.

" 'Then, good-bye, Mr. Jabez Wilson, and let me congratulate you once more on the important position which you have been fortunate enough to gain.' He bowed me out of the room, and I went home with my assistant, hardly knowing what to say or do, I was so pleased at my own good fortune.

---

7. **billet** (bil´ it) *n.* position; job.

avail (ə vāl´) *v.* be of help

Literary Analysis
The Mystery What is it about the nature of Wilson's job that sounds suspicious?

**Reading Check**
Who offered to look after Wilson's pawnbroker business while he was at his other job?

"Well, I thought over the matter all day, and by evening I was in low spirits again: for I had quite persuaded myself that the whole affair must be some great <u>hoax</u> or fraud, though what its object might be I could not imagine. It seemed altogether past belief that anyone could make such a will, or that they would pay such a sum for doing anything so simple as copying out the Encyclopedia Britannica. Vincent Spaulding did what he could to cheer me up, but by bedtime I had reasoned myself out of the whole thing. However, in the morning I determined to have a look at it anyhow, so I bought a penny bottle of ink, and with a quill-pen, and seven sheets of foolscap paper,[8] I started off for Pope's Court.

"Well, to my surprise and delight, everything was as right as possible. The table was set out ready for me, and Mr. Duncan Ross was there to see that I got fairly to work. He started me off upon the letter A, and then he left me; but he would drop in from time to time to see that all was right with me. At two o'clock he bade me good-day, complimented me upon the amount that I had written, and locked the door of the office after me.

"This went on day after day, Mr. Holmes, and on Saturday the manager came in and planked down four golden sovereigns for my week's work. It was the same next week, and the same the week after. Every morning I was there at ten, and every afternoon I left at two. By degrees Mr. Duncan Ross took to coming in only once of a morning, and then, after a time, he did not come in at all. Still, of course, I never dared to leave the room for an instant, for I was not sure when he might come, and the billet was such a good one, and suited me so well, that I would not risk the loss of it.

"Eight weeks passed away like this, and I had written about Abbots and Archery and Armor and Architecture and Attica, and hoped with diligence that I might get on to the B's before very long. It cost me something in foolscap,and I had pretty nearly filled a shelf with my writings. And then suddenly the whole business came to an end."

"To an end?"

"Yes, sir. And no later than this morning. I went to my work as usual at ten o'clock, but the door was shut and locked, with a little square of cardboard hammered on to the middle of the panel with a tack. Here it is, and you can read for yourself."

hoax (hōks) *n.* deceitful trick

---

8. foolscap paper writing paper.

He held up a piece of white cardboard about the size of a sheet of notepaper. It read in this fashion:

THE RED-HEADED LEAGUE

IS

DISSOLVED.

October 9, 1890.

Sherlock Holmes and I surveyed this curt announcement and the rueful face behind it, until the comical side of the affair so completely overtopped every other consideration that we both burst out into a roar of laughter.

"I cannot see that there is anything very funny," cried our client, flushing up to the roots of his flaming head. "If you can do nothing better than laugh at me, I can go elsewhere."

"No, no," cried Holmes, shoving him back into the chair from which he had half risen. "I really wouldn't miss your case for the world. It is most refreshingly unusual. But there is, if you will excuse my saying so, something just a little funny about it. Pray what steps did you take when you found the card upon the door?"

"I was staggered, sir. I did not know what to do. Then I called at the offices round, but none of them seemed to know anything about it. Finally, I went to the landlord, who is an accountant living on the ground floor, and I asked him if he could tell me what had become of the Red-headed League. He said that he had never heard of any such body. Then I asked him who Mr. Duncan Ross was. He answered that the name was new to him.

" 'Well,' said I, 'the gentleman at No. 4.'

" 'What, the red-headed man?'

" 'Yes.'

" 'Oh,' said he, 'his name was William Morris. He was a solicitor[9] and was using my room as a temporary convenience until his new premises were ready. He moved out yesterday.'

" 'Where could I find him?'

" 'Oh, at his new offices. He did tell me the address. Yes, 17 King Edward Street, near St. Paul's.'

"I started off, Mr. Holmes, but when I got to that address it was a manufactory of artificial kneecaps, and no one in it had ever heard of either Mr. William Morris or Mr. Duncan Ross."

"And what did you do then?" asked Holmes.

"I went home to Saxe-Coburg Square, and I took the advice of my assistant. But he could not help me in any way. He could only say that if I waited I should hear by post. But that was not quite good enough, Mr. Holmes. I did not wish to lose such a place without a struggle, so, as I had heard that you were good enough to give advice to poor folk who were in need of it, I came right away to you."

"And you did very wisely," said Holmes. "Your case is an exceedingly remarkable one, and I shall be happy to look into it. From what

---

9. **solicitor** member of the legal profession.

Literary Analysis
The Mystery At this point, another suspect enters the picture. Which clues point toward this character as a suspect?

 **Reading Check**

After eight weeks at his new job, what does Wilson find posted on the door?

you have told me I think that it is possible that graver issues hang from it than might at first sight appear."

"Grave enough!" said Mr. Jabez Wilson. "Why, I have lost four pound a week."

"As far as you are personally concerned," remarked Holmes, "I do not see that you have any grievance against this extraordinary league. On the contrary, you are, as I understand, richer by some £30, to say nothing of the minute knowledge which you have gained on every subject which comes under the letter A. You have lost nothing by them."

"No, sir. But I want to find out about them, and who they are, and what their object was in playing this prank—if it was a prank—upon me. It was a pretty expensive joke for them, for it cost them two and thirty pounds."

"We shall endeavor to clear up these points for you. And, first, one or two questions, Mr. Wilson. This assistant of yours who first called your attention to the advertisement—how long had he been with you?"

"About a month then."

"How did he come?"

"In answer to an advertisement."

"Was he the only applicant?"

"No, I had a dozen."

"Why did you pick him?"

"Because he was handy and would come cheap."

"At half-wages, in fact."

"Yes."

"What is he like, this Vincent Spaulding?"

"Small, stout-built, very quick in his ways. No hair on his face, though he's not short of thirty. Has a white splash of acid upon his forehead."

Holmes sat up in his chair in considerable excitement. "I thought as much," said he. "Have you ever observed that his ears are pierced for earrings?"

"Yes, sir. He told me that a gypsy had done it for him when he was a lad."

"Hum!" said Holmes, sinking back in deep thought. "He is still with you?"

"Oh, yes, sir; I have only just left him."

"And has your business been attended to in your absence?"

"Nothing to complain of, sir. There's never very much to do of a morning."

"That will do, Mr. Wilson. I shall be happy to give you an opinion upon the subject in the course of a day or two. Today is Saturday, and I hope that by Monday we may come to a conclusion."

"Well, Watson," said Holmes when our visitor had left us, "what do

Literary Analysis
The Mystery and Characterization Explain what is revealed in this passage about Holmes as a crime-solver.

you make of it all?"

"I make nothing of it," I answered frankly. "It is a most mysterious business."

"As a rule," said Holmes, "the more bizarre a thing is the less mysterious it proves to be. It is your commonplace, featureless crimes which are really puzzling, just as a commonplace face is the most difficult to identify. But I must be prompt over this matter."

"What are you going to do, then?" I asked.

"To smoke," he answered. "It is quite a three pipe problem, and I beg that you won't speak to me for fifty minutes." He curled himself up in his chair, with his thin knees drawn up to his hawk-like nose, and there he sat with his eyes closed and his black clay pipe thrusting out like the bill of some strange bird. I had come to the conclusion that he had dropped asleep, and indeed was nodding myself, when he suddenly sprang out of his chair with the gesture of a man who has made up his mind and put his pipe down upon the mantelpiece.

"Sarasate[10] plays at the St. James's Hall this afternoon," he remarked. "What do you think, Watson? Could your patients spare you for a few hours?"

"I have nothing to do today. My practice is never very absorbing."

"Then put on your hat and come. I am going through the City first, and we can have some lunch on the way. I observe that there is a good deal of German music on the program, which is rather more to my taste than Italian or French. It is <u>introspective</u>, and I want to introspect. Come along!"

We traveled by the Underground as far as Aldersgate; and a short walk took us to Saxe-Coburg Square, the scene of the singular story which we had listened to in the morning. It was a poky, little, shabby-genteel place, where four lines of dingy two-storied brick houses looked out into a small railed–in enclosure, where a lawn of weedy grass and a few clumps of faded laurel bushes made a hard fight against a smoke-laden and uncongenial atmosphere. Three gilt balls and a brown board with "JABEZ WILSON" in white letters, upon a corner house, announced the place where our red-headed client carried on his business. Sherlock Holmes stopped in front of it with his head on one side and looked it all over, with his eyes shining brightly between puckered lids. Then he walked slowly up the street, and then down again to the corner, still looking keenly at the houses. Finally he returned to the pawnbroker's, and, having thumped vigorously upon the pavement with his stick two or three times, he went up to the door and knocked. It was instantly opened by a bright-looking, clean-shaven young fellow, who asked him to step in.

"Thank you," said Holmes, "I only wished to ask you how you would go from here to the Strand."

"Third right, fourth left," answered the assistant promptly, closing the door.

---

10. **Sarasate** (sä rä sä′ tä) Spanish violinist and composer.

introspective (in′ trə spek′ tiv) *adj.* causing one to look into one's own thoughts and feelings

Reading Strategy
Finding Key Details
Which key details in this passage seem to be clues that help Holmes solve the crime?

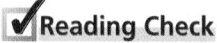**Reading Check**

What reasons does Mr. Wilson give for hiring Vincent Spaulding?

"Smart fellow, that," observed Holmes as we walked away. "He is, in my judgment, the fourth smartest man in London, and for daring I am not sure that he has not a claim to be third. I have known something of him before."

"Evidently," said I, "Mr. Wilson's assistant counts for a good deal in this mystery of the Red-headed League. I am sure that you inquired your way merely in order that you might see him."

"Not him."

"What then?"

"The knees of his trousers."

"And what did you see?"

"What I expected to see."

"Why did you beat the pavement?"

"My dear doctor, this is a time for observation, not for talk. We are spies in an enemy's country. We know something of Saxe-Coburg Square. Let us now explore the parts which lie behind it."

The road in which we found ourselves as we turned round the corner from the retired Saxe-Coburg Square presented as great a contrast to it as the front of a picture does to the back. It was one of the main arteries which conveyed the traffic of the City to the north and west. The roadway was blocked with the immense stream of commerce flowing in a double tide inward and outward, while the footpaths were black with the hurrying swarm of pedestrians. It was difficult to realize as we looked at the line of fine shops and stately business premises that they really abutted on the other side upon the faded and stagnant square which we had just quitted.

"Let me see," said Holmes, standing at the corner and glancing along the line, "I should like just to remember the order of the houses here. It is a hobby of mine to have an exact knowledge of London. There is Mortimer's, the tobacconist, the little newspaper shop, the Coburg branch of the City and Suburban Bank, the Vegetarian Restaurant, and McFarlane's carriage-building depot. That carries us right on to the other block. And now, Doctor, we've done our work, so it's time we had some play. A sandwich and a cup of coffee, and then off to violin land, where all is sweetness and delicacy and harmony, and there are no red-headed clients to <u>vex</u> us with their <u>conundrums</u>."

My friend was an enthusiastic musician, being himself not only a very capable performer but a composer of no ordinary merit. All the afternoon he sat in the stalls wrapped in the most perfect happiness, gently waving his long, thin fingers in time to the music, while his gently smiling face and his languid, dreamy eyes were as unlike those of Holmes, the sleuthhound, Holmes the relentless, keen-witted, ready-handed criminal agent, as it was possible to conceive. In his singular character the dual nature alternately asserted itself, and his extreme exactness and <u>astuteness</u> represented, as I have often thought, the reaction against the poetic and contemplative mood which occasionally predominated in him. The swing of his nature took him from extreme languor to devouring energy; and, as I knew

Literary Analysis
The Mystery What might be Holmes's motive for familiarizing himself with the order of the buildings behind Saxe-Coburg Square?

vex (veks) v. annoy

conundrums (kə nun′ drəmz) n. puzzling questions or problems

astuteness (ə stōōt′ nis) n. shrewdness

formidable (fôr′ mə də bəl) adj. awe-inspiring

well, he was never so truly <u>formidable</u> as when, for days on end, he had been lounging in his armchair amid his improvisations and his black-letter editions. Then it was that the lust of the chase would suddenly come upon him, and that his brilliant reasoning power would rise to the level of intuition, until those who were unacquainted with his methods would look askance at him as on a man whose knowledge was not that of other mortals. When I saw him that afternoon so enwrapped in the music at St. James's Hall I felt that an evil time might be coming upon those whom he had set himself to hunt down.

"You want to go home, no doubt, Doctor," he remarked as we emerged.

"Yes, it would be as well."

"And I have some business to do which will take some hours. This business at Coburg Square is serious."

"Why serious?"

"A considerable crime is in contemplation. I have every reason to believe that we shall be in time to stop it. But today being Saturday rather complicates matters. I shall want your help tonight."

"At what time?"

"Ten will be early enough."

"I shall be at Baker Street at ten."

"Very well. And, I say, Doctor, there may be some little danger, so kindly put your army revolver in your pocket." He waved his hand, turned on his heel, and disappeared in an instant among the crowd.

I trust that I am not more dense than my neighbors, but I was always oppressed with a sense of my own stupidity in my dealings with Sherlock Holmes. Here I had heard what he had heard, I had seen what he had seen, and yet from his words it was evident that he saw clearly not only what had happened but what was about to happen, while to me the whole business was still confused and grotesque. As I drove home to my house in Kensington I thought over it all, from the extraordinary story of the red-headed copier of the Encyclopedia down to the visit to Saxe-Coburg Square, and the ominous words with which he had parted from me. What was this nocturnal expedition, and why should I go armed? Where were we going, and what were we to do? I had the hint from Holmes that this smooth-faced pawnbroker's assistant was a formidable man—a man who might play a deep game. I tried to puzzle it out, but gave it up in despair and set the matter aside until night should bring an explanation.

It was a quarter past nine when I started from home and made my way across the Park, and so through Oxford Street to Baker Street. Two hansoms* were standing at the door, and as I entered the passage I heard the sound of voices from above. On entering his room I

Literature in context Cultural Connection

♦ **Hansoms**
  The hansom, also known as the hansom cab, is a two-wheeled covered carriage for two passengers, pulled by one horse. The cab was named for its inventor, Joseph Hansom (1803–1882), a London architect. By the late 1850s, the hansom was popular in New York and Boston as well as in London. Customers could enjoy a scenic and romantic ride in private with an unobstructed view, since the driver sat above and behind the passengers' cab. Today, hansom cabs are still a popular feature in New York's Central Park. However, in this story, they are a common form of transportation.

✔ **Reading Check**

Where do Holmes and Watson go after investigating at Saxe-Coburg Square?

found Holmes in animated conversation with two men, one of whom I recognized as Peter Jones, the official police agent, while the other was a long, thin, sad-faced man, with a very shiny hat and oppressively respectable frock coat.

"Ha! our party is complete," said Holmes, buttoning up his pea-jacket and taking his heavy hunting crop from the rack. "Watson, I think you know Mr. Jones, of Scotland Yard? Let me introduce you to Mr. Merryweather, who is to be our companion in tonight's adventure."

"We're hunting in couples again, Doctor, you see," said Jones in his consequential way. "Our friend here is a wonderful man for starting a chase. All he wants is an old dog to help him to do the running down."

"I hope a wild goose may not prove to be the end of our chase," observed Mr. Merryweather gloomily.

"You may place considerable confidence in Mr. Holmes, sir," said the police agent loftily. "He has his own little methods, which are, if he won't mind my saying so, just a little too theoretical and fantastic, but he has the makings of a detective in him. It is not too much to say that once or twice, as in that business of the Sholto murder and the Agra treasure, he has been more nearly correct than the official force."

"Oh, if you say so, Mr. Jones, it is all right," said the stranger with deference. "Still, I confess that I miss my rubber.[11] It is the first Saturday night for seven-and-twenty years that I have not had my rubber."

"I think you will find," said Sherlock Holmes, "that you will play for a higher stake tonight than you have ever done yet, and that the play will be more exciting. For you, Mr. Merryweather, the stake will be some £30,000: and for you, Jones, it will be the man upon whom you wish to lay your hands."

"John Clay, the murderer, thief, smasher, and forger. He's a young man, Mr. Merryweather, but he is at the head of his profession, and I would rather have my bracelets on him than on any criminal in

---

11. rubber card games.

London. He's a remarkable man, is young John Clay. His grandfather was a royal duke, and he himself has been to Eton[12] and Oxford.[13] His brain is as cunning as his fingers, and though we meet signs of him at every turn, we never know where to find the man himself. He'll crack a crib[14] in Scotland one week, and be raising money to build an orphanage in Cornwall the next. I've been on his track for years and have never set eyes on him yet."

"I hope that I may have the pleasure of introducing you tonight. I've had one or two little turns also with Mr. John Clay, and I agree with you that he is at the head of his profession. It is past ten, however, and quite time that we started. If you two will take the first hansom, Watson and I will follow in the second."

Sherlock Holmes was not very communicative during the long drive and lay back in the cab humming the tunes which he had heard in the afternoon. We rattled through an endless labyrinth of gas-lit streets until we emerged into Farrington Street.

"We are close there now," my friend remarked. "This fellow Merryweather is a bank director, and personally interested in the matter. I thought it as well to have Jones with us also. He is not a bad fellow, though an absolute imbecile in his profession. He has one positive virtue. He is as brave as a bulldog and as tenacious as a lobster if he gets his claws upon anyone. Here we are, and they are waiting for us."

We had reached the same crowded thoroughfare in which we had found ourselves in the morning. Our cabs were dismissed, and, following the guidance of Mr. Merryweather, we passed down a narrow passage and through a side door, which he opened for us. Within there was a small corridor, which ended in a very massive iron gate. This also was opened, and led down a flight of winding stone steps, which terminated at another formidable gate. Mr. Merryweather stopped to light a lantern, and then conducted us down a dark, earth-smelling passage, and so, after opening a third door, into a huge vault or cellar, which was piled all round with crates and massive boxes.

"You are not very vulnerable from above," Holmes remarked as he held up the lantern and gazed about him.

"Nor from below," said Mr. Merryweather, striking his stick upon the flags which lined the floor. "Why, dear me, it sounds quite hollow!" he remarked, looking up in surprise.

"I must really ask you to be a little more quiet!" said Holmes severely. "You have already imperiled the whole success of our expedition. Might I beg that you would have the goodness to sit down upon one of those boxes, and not to interfere?"

The solemn Mr. Merryweather perched himself upon a crate, with a very injured expression upon his face, while Holmes fell upon his knees upon the floor and, with the lantern and a magnifying lens, began to

---

12. **Eton** famous British secondary school for boys.
13. **Oxford** oldest university in Great Britain.
14. **crack a crib** break into and rob a house.

Literary Analysis
The Mystery A new suspect's name is mentioned here. What evidence suggests that John Clay might really be Vincent Spaulding?

✔ Reading Check
Who is Mr. Merryweather?

examine minutely the cracks between the stones. A few seconds sufficed to satisfy him, for he sprang to his feet again and put his glass in his pocket.

"We have at least an hour before us," he remarked, "for they can hardly take any steps until the good pawnbroker is safely in bed. Then they will not lose a minute, for the sooner they do their work the longer time they will have for their escape. We are at present, Doctor—as no doubt you have divined—in the cellar of the City branch of one of the principal London banks. Mr. Merryweather is the chairman of directors, and he will explain to you that there are reasons why the more daring criminals of London should take a considerable interest in this cellar at present."

"It is our French gold," whispered the director. "We have had several warnings that an attempt might be made upon it."

"Your French gold?"

"Yes. We had occasion some months ago to strengthen our resources and borrowed for that purpose 30,000 napoleons from the Bank of France. It has become known that we have never had occasion to unpack the money, and that it is still lying in our cellar. The crate upon which I sit contains 2,000 napoleons packed between layers of lead foil. Our reserve of bullion is much larger at present than is usually kept in a single branch office, and the directors have had misgivings upon the subject."

"Which were very well justified," observed Holmes.

"And now it is time that we arranged our little plans. I expect that within an hour matters will come to a head. In the meantime, Mr. Merryweather, we must put the screen over that dark lantern."

"And sit in the dark?"

"I am afraid so. I had brought a pack of cards in my pocket, and I thought that, as we were a *partie carrée*,[15] you might have your rubber after all. But I see that the enemy's preparations have gone so far that we cannot risk the presence of a light. And, first of all, we must choose our positions. These are daring men, and though we shall take them at a disadvantage, they may do us some harm unless we are careful. I shall stand behind this crate, and do you conceal yourselves behind those. Then, when I flash a light upon them, close in swiftly. If they fire, Watson, have no compunction about shooting them down."

I placed my revolver, cocked, upon the top of the wooden case behind which I crouched. Holmes shot the slide across the front of his lantern and left us in pitch darkness—such an absolute darkness as I have never before experienced. The smell of hot metal remained to assure us that the light was still there, ready to flash out at a moment's notice. To me, with my nerves worked up to a pitch of expectancy, there was something depressing and subduing in the sudden gloom, and in the cold dank air of the vault.

"They have but one retreat," whispered Holmes. "That is back

---

15. *partie carrée* (pär tē' cä rā') French for "group of four."

Literary Analysis
The Mystery A mystery usually includes a suspect's motive for committing a crime. What possible motive is indicated by Merryweather's revelation?

Literary Analysis
The Mystery and Characterization What do the words *they may do us some harm* reveal about the criminals?

through the house into Saxe-Coburg Square. I hope that you have done what I asked you, Jones?"

"I have an inspector and two officers waiting at the front door."

"Then we have stopped all the holes. And now we must be silent and wait."

What a time it seemed! From comparing notes afterwards it was but an hour and a quarter, yet it appeared to me that the night must have almost gone, and the dawn be breaking above us. My limbs were weary and stiff, for I feared to change my position; yet my nerves were worked up to the highest pitch of tension, and my hearing was so acute that I could not only hear the gentle breathing of my companions, but I could distinguish the deeper, heavier in-breath of the bulky Jones from the thin, sighing note of the bank director. From my position I could look over the case in the direction of the floor. Suddenly my eyes caught the glint of a light.

At first it was but a lurid spark upon the stone pavement. Then it lengthened out until it became a yellow line, and then, without any warning or sound, a gash seemed to open and a hand appeared; a white, almost womanly hand, which felt about in the center of the little area of light. For a minute or more the hand, with its writhing fingers, protruded out of the floor. Then it was withdrawn as suddenly as it appeared, and all was dark again save the single lurid spark which marked a chink between the stones.

Its disappearance, however, was but momentary. With a rending, tearing sound, one of the broad, white stones turned over upon its side and left a square, gaping hole, through which streamed the light of a lantern. Over the edge there peeped a clean-cut, boyish face, which looked keenly about it, and then, with a hand on either side of the aperture, drew itself shoulder-high and waist-high, until one knee rested upon the edge. In another instant he stood at the side of the hole and was hauling after him a companion, lithe and small like himself, with a pale face and a shock of very red hair.

"It's all clear," he whispered. "Have you the chisel and the bags? Great Scott! Jump, Archie, jump, and I'll swing for it."

Sherlock Holmes had sprung out and seized the intruder by the collar. The other dived down the hole, and I heard the sound of rending cloth as Jones clutched at his skirts. The light flashed upon the barrel of a revolver, but Holmes's hunting crop came down on the man's wrist, and the pistol clinked upon the stone floor.

"It's no use, John Clay," said Holmes blandly. "You have no chance at all."

"So I see," the other answered with the utmost coolness. "I fancy that my pal is all right, though I see you have got his coattails."

"There are three men waiting for him at the door," said Holmes.

"Oh, indeed! You seem to have done the thing very completely. I must compliment you."

"And I you," Holmes answered. "Your red-headed idea was very new and effective."

Literary Analysis
The Mystery Which details contribute to the suspense of the mystery at this point?

 **Reading Check**

How long do Holmes and his party wait for the criminals to arrive?

"You'll see your pal again presently," said Jones. "He's quicker at climbing down holes than I am. Just hold out while I fix the derbies."[16]

"I beg that you will not touch me with your filthy hands," remarked our prisoner as the handcuffs clattered upon his wrists. "You may not be aware that I have royal blood in my veins. Have the goodness, also, when you address me always to say 'sir' and 'please.' "

"All right," said Jones with a stare and a snigger. "Well, would you please, sir, march upstairs, where we can get a cab to carry your Highness to the police station?"

"That is better," said John Clay serenely. He made a sweeping bow to the three of us and walked quietly off in the custody of the detective.

"Really, Mr. Holmes," said Mr. Merryweather as we followed them from the cellar, "I do not know how the bank can thank you or repay you. There is no doubt that you have detected and defeated in the most complete manner one of the most determined attempts at bank robbery that have ever come within my experience."

"I have had one or two little scores of my own to settle with Mr. John Clay," said Holmes. "I have been at some small expense over this matter, which I shall expect the bank to refund, but beyond that I am amply repaid by having had an experience which is in many ways unique, and by hearing the very remarkable narrative of the Red-headed League."

"You see, Watson," he explained in the early hours of the morning as we sat over a glass of whisky and soda in Baker Street, "it was perfectly obvious from the first that the only possible object of this rather

---

16. **derbies** handcuffs.

fantastic business of the advertisement of the League, and the copying of the Encyclopedia, must be to get this not over-bright pawnbroker out of the way for a number of hours every day. It was a curious way of managing it, but, really, it would be difficult to suggest a better. The method was no doubt suggested to Clay's ingenious mind by the color of his accomplice's hair. The £4 a week was a lure which must draw him, and what was it to them, who were playing for thousands? They put in the advertisement, one rogue has the temporary office, the other rogue incites the man to apply for it, and together they manage to secure his absence every morning in the week. From the time that I heard of the assistant having come for half wages, it was obvious to me that he had some strong motive for securing the situation."

"But how could you guess what the motive was?"

"Had there been women in the house, I should have suspected a mere vulgar intrigue. That, however, was out of the question. The man's business was a small one, and there was nothing in his house which could account for such elaborate preparations, and such an expenditure as they were at. It must, then, be something out of the house. What could it be? I thought of the assistant's fondness for photography, and his trick of vanishing into the cellar. The cellar! There was the end of this tangled clue. Then I made inquiries as to this mysterious assistant and found that I had to deal with one of the coolest and most daring criminals in London. He was doing something in the cellar—something which took many hours a day for months on end. What could it be, once more? I could think of nothing save that he was running a tunnel to some other building.

"So far I had got when we went to visit the scene of action. I surprised you by beating upon the pavement with my stick. I was ascertaining whether the cellar stretched out in front or behind. It was not in front. Then I rang the bell, and, as I hoped, the assistant answered it. We have had some skirmishes, but we had never set eyes upon each other before. I hardly looked at his face. His knees were what I wished to see. You must yourself have remarked how worn, wrinkled, and stained they were. They spoke of those hours of burrowing. The only remaining point was what they were burrowing for. I walked round the corner, saw that the City and Suburban Bank abutted on our friend's premises, and felt that I had solved my problem. When you drove home after the concert I called upon Scotland Yard and upon the chairman of the bank directors, with the result that you have seen."

"And how could you tell that they would make their attempt tonight?" I asked.

"Well, when they closed their League offices that was a sign that they cared no longer about Mr. Jabez Wilson's presence—in other words, that they had completed their tunnel. But it was essential that they should use it soon, as it might be discovered, or the bullion might be removed. Saturday would suit them better than any other day, as it would give them two days for their escape. For all these reasons I expected them to come tonight."

Reading Strategy
Finding Key Details Even after the case is solved, Watson wonders how Holmes did it. Name the key details that explain the detective's solution.

✔**Reading Check**

As Holmes reveals his clues, what reason does he give for striking his stick against the pavement?

Integrate Language Skills

Vocabulary Development Lesson

Word Analysis: Latin Root -spec-

The Latin root -spec- means "see" or "look." The root appears in the word *introspective*, which means "looking inward." It also appears in the words *spectator, inspector,* and *spectacle.* Match each word with its definition.

1. spectator   a. a remarkable sight
2. inspector   b. one who observes
3. spectacle   c. one who looks into a matter

Spelling Strategy

When you add a prefix to a word or root, do not change the spelling of the word or root. For example, *intro-* + *spective* = *introspective*. Add a prefix such as *un-, re-, pre-,* or *mis-* to the following words to make three English words.

1. clear   2. consider   3. judge

Fluency: Context

On your paper, write the following paragraph. Using the clues you find there, fill in the blanks with words from the vocabulary list on page 95.

I'm rather shy and ___?___, but my uncle has an extremely unusual and ___?___ personality. He is both impatient and brilliant. When confronted with perplexing ___?___, he has been known to shout wildly, "Do not ___?___ me!" at no one in particular. Despite this brashness, he solves the problem. My uncle's ___?___ is regarded as ___?___ by those who respect him and as an elaborate ___?___ by those who don't. Whenever I ask for help, however, he will ___?___ himself immediately. I must say, my uncle is a very fascinating and entertaining person to know.

Grammar Lesson

Coordinate Adjectives

Adjectives are words that modify a noun or pronoun. **Coordinate adjectives** are adjectives of equal rank that separately modify the noun they precede. Use commas to separate coordinate adjectives.

To test whether adjectives are coordinate, switch their order. If the sentence still makes sense, the adjectives are coordinate.

> **Coordinate:** . . . a very *stout, florid-faced, elderly* gentleman . . .
> . . . an *elderly, florid-faced, stout* gentleman . . .
>
> **Not coordinate:** In a *few short* hours, we'll know the outcome.

Practice On your paper, write the following sentences. Supply adjectives to complete them. Separate coordinate adjectives with a comma.

1. The ___?___ ___?___ goblet was stolen.
2. The ___?___ ___?___ book contained a clue.
3. The detective outwitted the ___?___ ___?___ villain.
4. People were shocked that such a ___?___ ___?___ citizen had committed the crime.
5. The detective wore a ___?___ ___?___ coat.

Writing Application Create sentences by adding nouns to each of the following pairs of coordinate adjectives.

1. sly, perceptive   2. sneaky, greedy

W͟G Prentice Hall Writing and Grammar Connection: Chapter 29, Section 2

Writing Lesson

Detective Story

In his story, Doyle created a detective so real that readers still write to him! Write your own detective story that will appeal to today's readers.

Prewriting   Brainstorm to come up with possible crimes. Choose one of your ideas as the focus of your story. Create a diagram like the one shown, putting the crime in the center box. Elaborate with key details about the detective, the suspects, their motives, alibis, and other clues.

Detective: Sergeant Smith—intelligent, thin, quiet

Key detail: Company just changed its leadership.

Computer laptop stolen from corporate office

Suspect: Boris, janitor, works overnight

Suspect: James, office assistant, in debt

Drafting   Using your diagram as a guide, write your story. Provide readers with hints to the solution of the mystery.

Revising   Ask a classmate to read your story and use a highlighter to mark each clue he or she encounters. See if your classmate has noticed the hints you have provided. You may want to add hints or strengthen ones you have included.

 Prentice Hall Writing and Grammar Connection: Chapter 5, Section 2

Extension Activities

Listening and Speaking With a partner, **role-play an interrogation** of Spaulding by Officer Jones. When you act out the scene, focus on these kinds of body language:

- posture—the way a character stands or sits and holds his head
- gestures—how a person points or waves his hand when he talks
- eye contact—the way a person does or does not look directly at another person

After a few rehearsals, present your role play to your class. **[Group Activity]**

Research and Technology Research the science of detective work. Study fingerprinting, lie detectors, or other techniques used by detectives to arrest criminals. Refer to multiple sources, such as the Internet, journals, and criminology books, to gain more information on the subject you choose. Then, prepare a **written report.**

 **Take It to the Net**   www.phschool.com

Go online for an additional research activity using the Internet.

Prepare to Read

The Listeners ◆ Beware: Do Not Read This Poem ◆ Echo

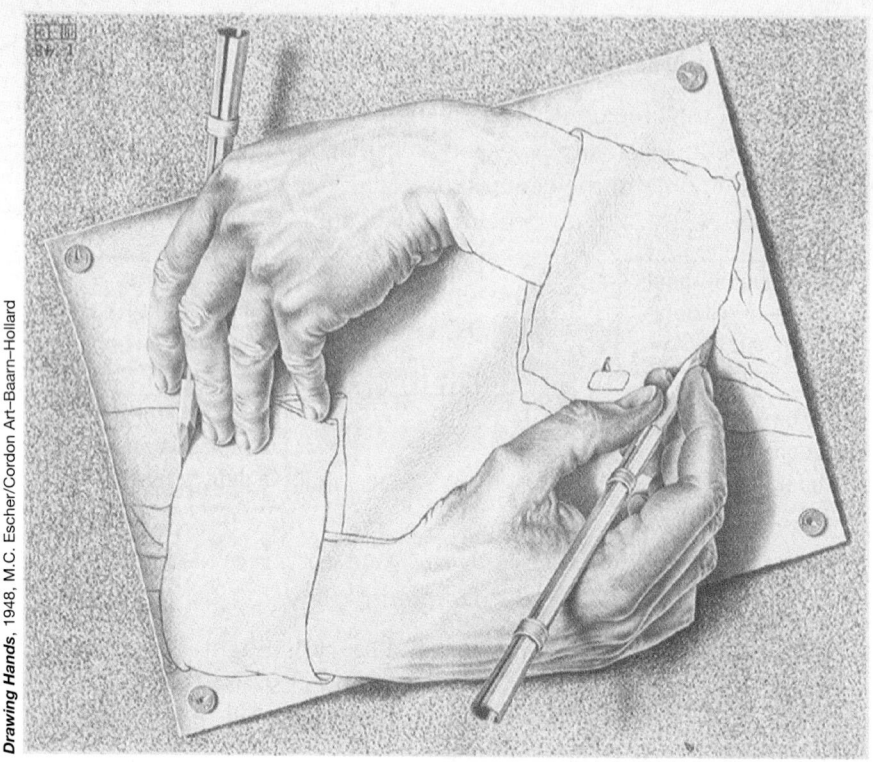

Drawing Hands, 1948, M.C. Escher/Cordon Art–Baarn–Hollard

 Take It to the Net

Visit www.phschool.com
for interactive activities
and instruction related to
the selections, including
- background
- graphic organizers
- literary elements
- reading strategies

Preview

Connecting to the Literature

A man knocks on a moonlit door. A parrot screams in a jungle. A woman disappears into a mirror. Images like these are strange, and you are not sure how they connect, yet they seem to hint at an unknown story. These poems use such images to hint at mysteries and possibilities.

Background

Just as poets create mystery in lines of poetry, artists create mysterious images with the lines they draw. Dutch artist M. C. Escher (1898–1972), for example, specialized in drawings that challenge the mind and delight the imagination. Look carefully at the Escher image above and consider why it is mysterious.

Literary Analysis

Imagery

Poets do not draw pictures with pens and brushes. However, they can use picture-painting words, called **imagery**, to help you experience their ideas with all your senses—touch, taste, smell, hearing, and sight. The poems in this section use imagery in a special way to create pictures of worlds that are haunted by mystery. Notice the vivid imagery in this passage from "Echo":

> Thousands of parrots
> screamed together
> and rock echoed.

As you read the selections, look for images that appeal strongly to your senses and paint pictures of worlds haunted by mystery.

Comparing Literary Works

Just as individual artists have their own techniques for painting a picture, individual poets have their own ways of creating imagery. Much depends on each poet's **diction**, or word choice. The poet's choice of vocabulary and vividness of language contribute to the imagery and affect its ultimate forcefulness. As you read the selections, compare the diction in the poems. Pay particular attention to the following:

- unique or interesting words that contribute to an image
- vivid or intense language that paints a clear picture

Instruction with these selections addresses these standards:

R 1.2*, 3.7*, 3.11
W 1.3*, 2.3*
WOLC 1.2*, 1.3*
LS 1.9

* Standards tested on HS Exit Exam. For complete standards, see p. CA 4.

Reading Strategy

Using Your Senses

By **using your senses** when you read a poem, you let the poem's language create a picture in your mind. As you read, experience each poem through your senses by focusing on language that tells how something looks, sounds, feels, smells, or tastes. Use a diagram like the one shown to record the sensory language in each selection. Write the words and phrases you find in their appropriate boxes.

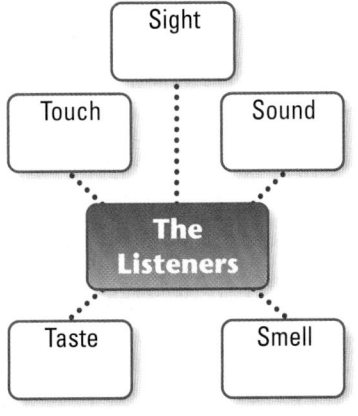

Vocabulary Development

perplexed (pər plekst') *adj.* puzzled; full of doubt (p. 122)

thronging (thrôŋ' iŋ) *adj.* crowding into (p. 122)

legendary (lej' ən der' ē) *adj.* based on legends, stories handed down from one generation to the next (p. 124)

strafing (strāf' iŋ) *adj.* attacking with machine-gun fire (p. 126)

The Listeners

Walter de la Mare

Het Blind Huis, William Degouve de Nunques, State Museum, Kroller-Muller, Otterlo, The Netherlands

▲ Critical Viewing
Does this painting convey the same feeling as "The Listeners"? Why or why not? **[Explain]**

Literary Analysis
Imagery Which words convey clear images in the first ten lines?

   'Is there anybody there?' said the Traveler,
      Knocking on the moonlit door;
   And his horse in the silence champed[1] the grasses
      Of the forest's ferny floor:
5 And a bird flew up out of the turret,
      Above the Traveler's head:
   And he smote[2] upon the door again a second time;
      'Is there anybody there?' he said.
   But no one descended to the Traveler;
10   No head from the leaf-fringed sill
   Leaned over and looked into his gray eyes,
      Where he stood <u>perplexed</u> and still.
   But only a host of phantom listeners
      That dwelt in the lone house then
15 Stood listening in the quiet of the moonlight
      To that voice from the world of men:
   Stood <u>thronging</u> the faint moonbeams on the dark stair,
      That goes down to the empty hall,
   Hearkening in an air stirred and shaken
20   By the lonely Traveler's call.
   And he felt in his heart their strangeness,

perplexed (pər plekst´) *adj.* puzzled; full of doubt

thronging (thrôn´ iŋ) *adj.* crowding into

---

1. **champed** (champt) *v.* chewed.
2. **smote** (smōt) *v.* struck hard.

Their stillness answering his cry,
While his horse moved, cropping the dark turf,
  'Neath the starred and leafy sky;
25 For he suddenly smote on the door, even
  Louder, and lifted his head:—
'Tell them I came, and no one answered,
  That I kept my word,' he said.
Never the least stir made the listeners,
30   Though every word he spake[3]
Fell echoing through the shadowiness of the still house
  From the one man left awake:
Ay, they heard his foot upon the stirrup,
  And the sound of iron on stone,
35 And how the silence surged softly backward,
  When the plunging hoofs were gone.

3. spake (spāk) *v.* spoke.

Literary Analysis
Imagery Which words paint a vivid image of a forest setting?

Review and Assess

Thinking About the Selection

1. **Respond:** Did you find this poem spooky and chilling? Why or why not?

2. **(a) Recall:** Briefly describe the time and place in which the action of the poem occurs. **(b) Analyze:** Why are the time and place important?

3. **(a) Recall:** Which words are used to describe the house? **(b) Interpret:** Which other details create the eerie, dreamlike atmosphere of the poem?

4. **(a) Recall:** What information does the poet leave out? **(b) Infer:** Why do you think there are so many unanswered questions in the poem? **(c) Speculate:** What are some possible answers to these questions?

5. **(a) Recall:** What do you learn about the traveler in the poem? **(b) Infer:** Why do you think de la Mare called the poem "The Listeners" rather than "The Traveler"?

6. **Synthesize:** Would knowing more about the Traveler's actions lessen the poem's mystery? Explain.

7. **Evaluate:** Why do you think people are compelled by mysteries like this one?

Walter de la Mare

(1873–1956)

Walter de la Mare's most famous poems, like "The Listeners," tell mysterious, incomplete stories. Perhaps de la Mare, an Englishman, used his poetry to live a more intriguing life because his daytime jobs were so unmysterious. At age seventeen, for example, he worked in the statistics department of the Anglo-American Oil Company. Poems may have been his escape from numbers!

In addition to composing poems, de la Mare wrote short stories, novels, and plays. He also edited poetry anthologies.

BEWARE:
Do Not Read This Poem
Ishmael Reed

tonite, *thriller* was
abt an ol woman, so vain she
surrounded her self w/
    many mirrors

5 It got so bad that finally she
locked herself indoors & her
whole life became the
    mirrors

one day the villagers broke
10 into her house, but she was too
swift for them. she disappeared
    into a mirror
each tenant who bought the house
after that lost a loved one to
15   the ol woman in the mirror:
      first a little girl
      then a young woman
      then the young woman/s husband

the hunger of this poem is <u>legendary</u>
20 it has taken in many victims
back off from this poem
it has drawn in yr feet
back off from this poem
it has drawn in yr legs
25 back off from this poem
it is a greedy mirror
you are into this poem. from
    the waist down
nobody can hear you can they?

Literary Analysis
Imagery What is most impressive about the image of the woman's house?

legendary (lej´ ən der´ ē) *adj.* based on legends, stories handed down from one generation to the next

30 this poem has had you up to here
        belch
    this poem aint got no manners
    you cant call out frm this poem
    relax now & go w/ this poem
35 move & roll on to this poem

        do not resist this poem
        this poem has yr eyes
        this poem has his head
        this poem has his arms
40   this poem has his fingers
        this poem has his fingertips

    this poem is the reader & the
        reader this poem

    statistic: the us bureau of missing persons reports
45   that in 1968 over 100,000 people disappeared
        leaving no solid clues
        nor trace   only
    a space   in the lives of their friends

Review and Assess

Thinking About the Selection

1. **Respond:** What feelings did Reed's poem evoke in you? Explain.

2. **(a) Recall:** What is unique about the woman's house? **(b) Analyze:** How does the description of this house add to the mystery of the poem?

3. **(a) Recall:** What does the poem say happens to those who read it? **(b) Interpret:** What does the idea of the reader's interaction suggest about the mystery of reading?

4. **(a) Recall:** Which lines in the poem refer to the poem and the reader as one? **(b) Interpret:** What message is the speaker trying to convey when he says "this poem is the reader & the/reader is this poem"? **(c) Infer:** How would you describe the speaker's tone of voice? Support your answer.

5. **(a) Analyze:** How does the sound of the poem change in the last stanza, beginning with line 44? **(b) Evaluate:** How does such an ending extend the mystery?

6. **(a) Analyze:** What details could the poet add to clarify the poem's story? **(b) Take a Position:** Considering the ways these details might alter the poem's effectiveness, would you want to include them? Explain.

Ishmael Reed

(b. 1938)

Ishmael Reed is as mysterious, many-sided, and hilarious as his poem "Beware: Do Not Read This Poem." Born in Chattanooga, Tennessee, and raised in Buffalo, New York, Reed has worked as a hospital attendant, market researcher, newspaper manager, and unemployment-office clerk.

In addition to poetry collections like *Chattanooga* (1973), Reed has written satiric novels that make fun of American westerns, as well as slave narratives, essays, plays, songs, and even operas.

Echo

Henriqueta Lisboa
Translated by
Hélcio Veiga Costa

Green parrot
let out a shrill scream.
Rock in sudden
anger, replied.

5 A great uproar
invaded the forest.
Thousands of parrots
screamed together
and rock echoed.

10 From all sides
<u>strafing</u> space
steely screams rained
and rained down.

Very piercing screams!

But no one died.

Literary Analysis
Imagery and Diction
What do you "hear" when
you read the first stanza?

strafing (strāf′ in) *adj.*
attacking with machine-
gun fire

Henriqueta Lisboa

(1903–1985)

A Brazilian poet, Lisboa uses a few well-chosen words to create powerful poems. By the age of twenty, she had already published her first book of poetry. Her early lyrics deal with traditional poetic themes, while her later poems tell about the history of her region. The themes she touched upon later in her life were not uncommon ones. Many of her contemporaries, such as Brazilian writer and poet Mário de Andrade, also spoke about the significance of Brazil in their works.

Review and Assess

Thinking About the Selection

1. **Respond:** What did you find pleasant or unpleasant about the sounds in the poem?

2. **(a) Recall:** What happens in the poem? **(b) Distinguish:** Which details in the poem could realistically occur, and which could not?

3. **(a) Recall:** What does the rock do when the green parrot first screams? **(b) Speculate:** What might the rock have been demanding of the parrot?

4. **(a) Analyze:** What effect does the poem's last line have on the meaning of the poem? **(b) Interpret:** What might be the message in this poem?

5. **(a) Evaluate:** Do you think the last line improves or weakens the poem? Explain.

Review and Assess

Literary Analysis

Imagery

1. Explain how the **imagery** in "The Listeners" helps you to hear "silence" and see invisible "listeners." Identify at least one sound-based image and one sight-based one.

2. In "Beware: Do Not Read This Poem," how does the image of "a greedy mirror" help you to experience the strangeness of reading?

3. Find two examples of imagery in "Echo" and show how they create a feeling of uncertainty.

Comparing Literary Works

4. For each example of **diction** below, explain the image created by the italicized words.

Title of Poem	Examples of Diction	Image Created
The Listeners	"*echoing* through the *shadowiness* of the *still* house"	
Beware: Do Not Read This Poem	"this poem has *yr* eyes"	
Echo	"parrot let out a *shrill* scream"	

5. How does the vividness of language in "The Listeners" compare to that in "Echo"?

6. In your opinion, which of the three poets creates the most powerful images? Justify your answer with details from the poem.

Reading Strategy

Using Your Senses

7. (a) Why is sound as important as sight in experiencing the world of "The Listeners"? (b) In which of the other two poems do you *hear* a mystery? Explain.

8. (a) Which of the poems asks you to picture yourself? (b) How are you invited to see yourself?

Extend Understanding

9. **Music Connection:** If you were setting these poems to music, what type of music would you choose for each? Explain.

Quick Review

Imagery is a picture that is painted, or created, with words.

Diction is a writer's word choice.

In reading a poem, **use your senses** to focus on language that tells how something looks, sounds, feels, smells, or tastes.

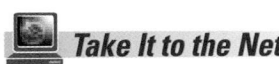 **Take It to the Net**

www.phschool.com
Take the interactive self-test online to check your understanding of the selections.

Integrate Language Skills

Vocabulary Development Lesson

Word Analysis: Poetic License and Vocabulary in Poems

Poetic license is a poet's freedom to break rules of vocabulary, grammar, or spelling in order to create a literary effect. For example, in "The Listeners," de la Mare uses *spake* for *spoke*. The word suggests an old-fashioned feeling. Answer these questions:

1. What other unusual word does de la Mare use in lines 5–7? What does it connote, or suggest to you?

2. Find an example of poetic license in line 32 of Ishmael Reed's poem. What connotation or association does the word have?

3. (a) What poetic license does Henriqueta Lisboa take in line 14 of her poem? (b) What effect does this violation of grammar have?

Fluency: Context

Copy the following paragraph. Fill in each blank with a word from the vocabulary list on page 121.

The detective entered the deserted house and stood in front of the mirror, ___?___. Deep inside the mysterious glass, he could see the ___?___ parrots, a species that had never existed. Hundreds of them were ___?___ a forest clearing, ___?___ the trees with their steely cries.

Spelling Strategy

When you add a suffix starting with a vowel to a base word ending with a consonant, do not change the spelling of the base word: *legend* + *-ary* = *legendary*. Add each suffix indicated to form a new word.

1. travel (*-er*)   2. appear (*-ance*)   3. green (*-ish*)

Grammar Lesson

Types of Adjectives

An **adjective** is a word used to describe a noun or pronoun or to give a noun or pronoun a more specific meaning. Adjectives modify nouns and pronouns by telling *what kind*, *which one*, *how many*, or *how much*. Sometimes a noun, pronoun, or verb may serve as an adjective.

> **Adjective:** the *lone* house (modifies *house*)
> **Noun as Adjective:** *phantom* listeners (modifies *listeners*)
> **Pronoun as Adjective:** felt in *his* heart (modifies *heart*)
> **Verb as Adjective:** an air *stirred* and *shaken* (modify *air*)

Practice Identify each word that serves as an adjective. Then, determine whether the word is an *adjective*, *noun*, *pronoun*, or *verb*.

1. They saw the faint moonbeams on the dark stair.
2. The silence surged backwards when the plunging hoofs disappeared.
3. Her whole life became the mirrors.
4. The forest bird let out a shrill scream.
5. Green parrots screamed piercing screams.

Writing Application Use each of the following words as an adjective in a sentence.

1. echoing   3. paper
2. strange   4. your

W͜G Prentice Hall Writing and Grammar Connection: Chapter 18, Section 1

Writing Lesson

Comparison-and-Contrast Essay

The poems in this section use imagery to create pictures. Write a comparison-and-contrast essay comparing the imagery found in two of the poems.

Prewriting   Decide which two poems generated the strongest or clearest word pictures for you. Then, complete a Venn diagram in which you jot down the similarities and differences between these two poems.

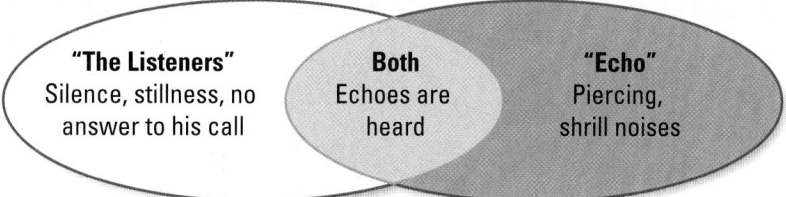

"The Listeners"
Silence, stillness, no
answer to his call

Both
Echoes are
heard

"Echo"
Piercing,
shrill noises

Drafting   Write a sentence to identify the comparison or contrast you will address. In each body paragraph of your essay, focus on one poem, citing examples of vivid language that produces an image.

Revising   Reread your essay to make sure you have used appropriate transition words. To show similarities, use words such as *all, similarly, both, in the same way,* and *equally.* To show differences, use words such as *on the other hand, in contrast,* and *however.*

W̶G̶ Prentice Hall Writing and Grammar Connection: Chapter 9, Section 2

Extension Activities

Listening and Speaking   In a small group, write a **dramatic scene** that takes place in "the lone house" of "the listeners" after the Traveler has galloped away. Assign each group member one of the following roles: actor, director, or set designer.

- Use your scene to answer some of the questions left unanswered by the poem.
- Then, act out the scene you have created.
- You may choose to videotape your drama or produce it onstage.

After acting out your scene, ask your audience to help you analyze the production. **[Group Activity]**

Research and Technology   "Echo" is set in Brazil's tropical rain forest. Give a **multimedia presentation** on this environment, taking the class on a magical mystery tour through its wonders. Use an atlas to gather information about the locations of Brazil's rain forests. Then, use the Internet to research the kinds of plants, animals, and weather found in those locations. Present your findings to the class.

 Take It to the Net   www.phschool.com

Go online for an additional research activity using the Internet.

The Listeners / Beware: Do Not Read This Poem / Echo ◆ 129

Prepare to Read

Caucasian Mummies Mystify Chinese

 Take It to the Net

Visit www.phschool.com
for interactive activities
and instruction related to
"Caucasian Mummies
Mystify Chinese," including
- background
- graphic organizers
- literary elements
- reading strategies

Preview

Connecting to the Literature

Unsolved mysteries, such as how the Egyptian pyramids were built or
why huge slabs of rock were placed in circles at Stonehenge, are popular
subjects for books, articles, and television programs. This article focuses
on the discovery of mysterious Caucasian mummies in what is now
China.

Background

While you may connect mummies with ancient Egypt, they actually
have been found all over the world, including China, Europe, Peru, and
Mexico. Because people often were buried with their clothes, tools, and
even food, mummies can teach us much about how ancient peoples lived.

Literary Analysis

News Article

The purpose of a **news article** such as "Caucasian Mummies Mystify Chinese" is to inform you—the reader—by providing facts that answer six questions: *Who? What? When? Where? Why?* and *How?* To help you answer these questions, pay close attention to the following parts of the article:

- the lead, or opening sentences
- details in the form of facts, statistics, and summaries
- opinions and quotations from experts and eyewitnesses

As you read the article, answer as many questions as you can after reading the first paragraph. Then, continue to look for additional answers in the facts and expert opinions that follow.

Connecting Literary Elements

News reporters are taught to write with **objectivity,** presenting the facts only, without opinions or judgments on the subject. By using objective language, the writer lets readers form their own opinions without influence. Pay close attention to the presentation of information in this article. Ask yourself if the writer is being objective, and notice whether certain words or details suggest an opinion or position.

Reading Strategy

Finding the Main Idea

When reading a news article, **finding the main idea** is a critical skill. The main idea in a news article is its most important point. Often, the main idea is stated in the lead paragraph. You can also determine the main idea by answering the six questions addressed in the article, and then deciding on the main point based on your answers.

As you read the article, use a chart like the one shown to record answers to the six questions: *Who? What? When? Where? Why?* and *How?*

Instruction with this selection addresses these standards:

R 1.1*, 2.1*, 2.8*
W 2.3*
WOLC 1.2*, 1.3*
LS 1.7

* Standards tested on HS Exit Exam. For complete standards, see p. CA 4.

Who?	
What?	
When?	
Where?	
Why?	
How?	

Vocabulary Development

dogmas (dôg´ məz) *n.* firmly held beliefs or doctrines (p. 133)

parched (pärcht) *adj.* dried up by heat (p. 133)

archaeologist (är´ kē äl´ ə jist) *n.* person who studies the remains of ancient ways of life (p. 133)

imperialist (im pir´ ē əl ist) *adj.* here, describing a person from a country that seeks to dominate weaker countries (p. 134)

subjugation (sub´ jə gā´ shən) *n.* enslavement (p. 136)

reconcile (rek´ ən sīl´) *v.* bring into agreement (p. 136)

Caucasian Mummies Mystify Chinese

Keay Davidson
from San Francisco **Examiner**

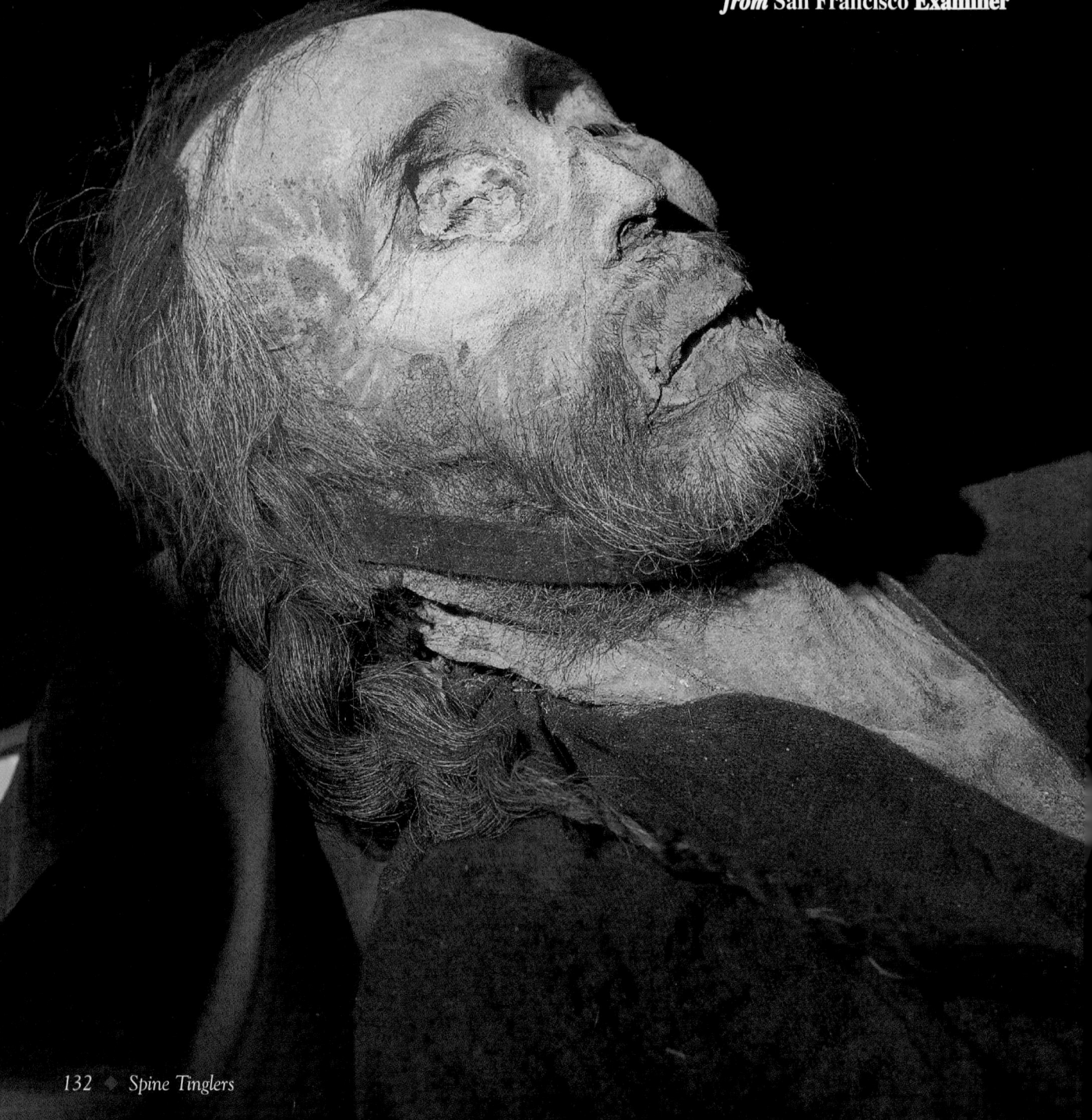

San Francisco—In dim light they appear to be sleeping, but they've been dead up to 4,000 years: more than 100 astoundingly well-preserved mummies unearthed in a Chinese desert, whose inexplicably blond hair and white skin could topple <u>dogmas</u> about early human history.

A former Stanford scientist is analyzing the mummies' DNA in hopes of answering haunting questions: Who are they? Where did they come from? And what on earth were these European-looking men, women and children doing in China's <u>parched</u> out-back 2,000 years before Jesus, when Europe was largely a dark forest? Sixteen years after the first mummies were found, the Chinese government has granted Western researchers their first close look at these faces from prehistory: a baby in colorful swaddling clothes; a 20-year-old girl with braided hair, found buried in a curled-up position with her hands by her chest, as if dozing; a man with a pigtail, scarlet-colored clothes and red, blue, and amber leg wrappings. . . .

The discovery—which could have far greater impact on our understanding of societal evolution than the lone, ancient "ice man" uncovered in the Alps in 1991—is described in an article by science writer Evan Hadingham in the April 1994 issue of *Discover* magazine. Based on the *Discover* article and *San Francisco Examiner* interviews with experts on genetics and Chinese history and culture, here's how the discoveries unfolded. In 1978 and 1979, Chinese <u>archaeologist</u> Wang Binghua found the first of what would prove to be more than 100 mummies in Xinjiang (zin jē ang´) Province. They had white skin, blond hair, long noses and skulls, and deep-set eyes—Caucasians,[1] perhaps from Northern Europe.

Little Attention in the West

Only scanty press reports have reached the West, at least partly because of the region's isolation, Chinese bureaucratic inertia and the regime's suppression of foreign contacts, particularly after the Tiananmen Square massacre[2] of 1989.

Now the cloud of mystery is lifting thanks to an investigation organized by University of Pennsylvania China scholar Victor Mair, in collaboration with researchers in China, the United States and Italy. The collaboration required delicate negotiations with Chinese officials.

It would have been "absolutely unthinkable" for Chinese authorities

---

1. **Caucasian** (kô kā´ zhən) *adj.* belonging to one of the major geographical groups of human beings, including the native peoples of Europe, who are loosely called the white race, though their skin colors may vary.
2. **Tiananmen** (tyen´ ə mən) **Square massacre** the murder of approximately 3,000 pro-democracy demonstrators by Chinese soldiers in Beijing, the capital of China, on June 3 and 4, 1989.

◀ **Critical Viewing** What features of this mummy might help scientists to deduce facts about the man and his life? [**Deduce**]

dogmas (dôg´ məz) *n.* firmly held beliefs or doctrines

parched (pärcht) *adj.* dried up by heat

Literary Analysis
News Article What questions does the writer answer in this paragraph?

archaeologist (är´ kē äl´ ə jist) *n.* person who studies the remains of ancient ways of life

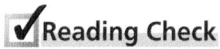✔**Reading Check**

Where were more than 100 mummies found?

hinting that the living mourned the dead: For example, a baby was buried with a sort of milk bottle fashioned from a sheep's udder.

"This is my favorite story in the seven years that I've edited *Discover* . . . because we were able to publish something monumental before anyone else," said the magazine's editor, Paul Hoffman.

Traditionally, Chinese historians insist that their society evolved on its own with little foreign input. That view has played well in modern China, which resents its past <u>subjugation</u> to foreign imperialists.

But Mair says the traditional view is hard to <u>reconcile</u> with the discovery of so many Caucasians who lived in what is now the westernmost edge of China, thousands of years before Marco Polo.[4] "The archaeological, linguistic, and textual evidence forces me to conclude that China has both significantly influenced and been influenced by other civilizations throughout history and, indeed, prehistory," Mair said. . . .

subjugation (sub′ jə gā′ shən) *n.* enslavement

reconcile (rek′ ən sīl′) *v.* bring into agreement

---

4. **Marco Polo** (1254–1324) Italian traveler and trader considered to be the first European to cross the length of Asia.

Review and Assess

Thinking About the Selection

1. **Respond:** What else would you like to know about the Caucasian mummies and the way these ancient people lived?

2. **(a) Recall:** What is remarkable about the mummies' appearance? **(b) Analyze:** Why did Chinese officials react as they did to the discovery of the mummies?

3. **(a) Recall:** Where do experts think the people found in the Chinese desert originally lived? **(b) Infer:** How has the discovery of the mummies changed historians' views of early Chinese culture?

4. **(a) Recall:** In what year were the first mummies unearthed? **(b) Interpret:** Why was there a delay between this event and the involvement of Western scholars and scientists?

5. **(a) Recall:** What tests are scientists conducting on the mummies? **(b) Speculate:** How will the tests help unlock the mystery surrounding this discovery?

6. **(a) Evaluate:** Do you think the reporter clearly communicated why the discovery of the mummies was so important? Why or why not? **(b) Assess:** What did you find most interesting about this article? Why?

7. **Extend:** Explain whether you think that real-life mysteries, like this one, are more or less interesting than those made up by storytellers.

Keay Davidson

(b. 1953)

Keay Davidson loves to write about science and technology. As a science reporter and author of books and magazine articles, he tracks the latest information on everything from NASA to tornadoes.

Davidson began as a newspaper reporter in Georgia while still in college. He moved to Florida in 1976 and later began to write about the space program. In 1981, he became a science reporter for the *Los Angeles Times* and, later, the *San Francisco Examiner*.

As a writer, Davidson coauthored *Wrinkles in Time*, a book about new scientific theories on the origins of the universe. In 1996, when the movie *Twister* swept through theaters, Davidson explained the science behind the special effects in his book *Twister: The Science of Tornadoes*.

Review and Assess

Literary Analysis

News Article

1. (a) Which details of the **news article's** lead are written to grab a reader's attention? (b) Does it make you want to read on? Why or why not?

2. (a) How do the quotations from an expert on China help you understand the news that is being reported? (b) Identify at least two quotations and explain how they extend your understanding.

3. How might this story have been different if it had been written as an encyclopedia article?

Connecting Literary Elements

4. To maintain a position of **objectivity,** the writer links positions he presents to specific authorities. Identify three opinions in the article. For each, indicate the source, or who gave the opinion.

5. How objective is Davidson's article? Support your answer.

6. How might your reaction to the article have been different if Davidson had been less objective—for example, more enthusiastic or more critical?

Reading Strategy

Finding the Main Idea

7. (a) Review the article and answer the questions in the chart shown. (b) Based on your answers to the questions, what do you think is the **main idea** of the article?

What is being tested?		**When** were the mummies found?	
Who is performing the testing?		**Why** is the discovery of these mummies important?	
Where were the mummies found?		**How** does the discovery change historians' views on early Chinese culture?	

Extend Understanding

8. **Science Connection:** In what way does the work of archaeologists have an impact on the way we live today?

Quick Review

A **news article** is written to inform you about a topic by answering six questions: *Who? What? When? Where? Why?* and *How?*

Objectivity in a news article requires the presentation of facts only, free of the writer's opinions or judgments.

The **main idea** in a news article is its most important point.

 Take It to the Net
www.phschool.com
Take the interactive self-test online to check your understanding of the selection.

Integrate Language Skills

Vocabulary Development Lesson

Word Analysis: Greek Suffix -ist

The Greek suffix -ist means "one who practices." For example, the suffix appears in the word archaeologist, which means "one who practices archaeology." Use your knowledge of -ist to define each of these words:

1. geneticist 2. linguist 3. nutritionist

Spelling Strategy

When you add an ending to a word that ends in y preceded by a consonant, change the y to i before adding the suffix. For example, when you add -ous to mystery, you form the word mysterious. For each item, write the new word formed.

1. history + -an   3. rely + -able
2. mummy + -fy   4. carry + -ed

Concept Development: Synonyms

For each item below, write the word that is the best synonym, or closest match, for the first word.

1. dogmas: (a) documents, (b) beliefs, (c) rumors
2. parched: (a) dried, (b) sophisticated, (c) curved
3. archaeologist: (a) leader, (b) caretaker, (c) scientist
4. imperialist: (a) dominating, (b) wise, (c) proud
5. subjugation: (a) enslavement, (b) freedom, (c) celebration
6. reconcile: (a) interpretation, (b) settle, (c) begin

Grammar Lesson

Proper and Compound Adjectives

A **proper adjective** is a proper noun used as an adjective or an adjective formed from a proper noun. A **compound adjective** is an adjective that is made up of more than one word. Compound adjectives are usually hyphenated. In a few cases, they are written as combined words.

Proper Adjective: *February* weather
(a proper noun used as an adjective)

Proper Adjective: *Chinese* government
(a form of a proper noun, *China*, used as an adjective)

Compound Adjective: *fur-lined* coat;
underpaid researchers

Practice Identify the proper and compound adjectives in each sentence below.

1. The mummy of a young woman in a curled-up position was found.
2. A Chinese archaeologist found the first of the mummies.
3. The mummies had deep-set eyes.
4. The Chinese government allowed Western researchers to see the findings.
5. Some of the photos of the corpses showed a woman in a fur-lined coat.

Writing Application Write four sentences, using at least two proper adjectives and at least two compound adjectives.

WG Prentice Hall Writing and Grammar Connection: Chapter 18, Section 1

Writing Lesson

News Feature

Though usually based at least indirectly on a news event, news features, like Davidson's article, provide information of general interest, explore the human-interest angle of a news story, or describe a personality. Write your own news feature about a subject of interest—perhaps a hobby, sports hero, or fashion trend.

Prewriting   Start by planning a lead that will grab the reader's attention. If none comes to mind, think of the questions you will answer in the feature. One of your answers may spark an idea.

> **Model: Grabbing the Reader's Attention**
>
> It stretches. It twists. It comes in all sizes and colors. And it never needs washing. What's the latest fad to hit high schools all across America? It's rubber-band jewelry.

> This lead gets the reader's attention by offering several details about the subject before identifying it.

Drafting   Once you have created an attention-grabbing lead, keep readers interested with details that answer *who, what, when, where, why,* and *how* about your subject. Remember to offer facts only, without your personal opinion.

Revising   Read your news feature as though you know nothing about the topic. Circle words or ideas that need more elaboration, and then add any details that will clarify the writing.

𝒲G *Prentice Hall Writing and Grammar Connection: Chapter 12, Section 2*

Extension Activities

Listening and Speaking Imagine that you were the first archaeologist to uncover the Caucasian mummies of China. Now, you have been invited by colleagues to do a **visual presentation** of your findings at an archaeology conference. Using maps and photographs, explain to your colleagues

- how you came to discover the mummies.
- what happened as a result of your discovery.
- why your discovery is so important.

Answer as many *who, what, where, when, why,* and *how* questions as possible in your presentation.

Research and Technology In a group, create a **travel brochure** promoting a tour of archaeological sites in China where mummies have been uncovered. Make sure your brochure includes maps, illustrations, and detailed explanations of the important sites. Use library resources to find photographs and information about the sites included in your brochure. **[Group Activity]**

 Take It to the Net   www.phschool.com

Go online for an additional research activity using the Internet.

Writing WORKSHOP

Narration: Autobiographical Narrative

In an **autobiographical narrative,** a writer relates an experience from his or her life. In this workshop, you will write an autobiographical narrative that tells a story from your life.

Assignment Criteria. Your autobiographical narrative should have the following characteristics:

- Yourself as the main character
- A sequence of events that suggests an insight you gained
- Action that accommodates shifts in time and mood
- Concrete details that describe sights, sounds, smells, and physical sensations
- Your personal feelings, thoughts, or views

To preview the criteria on which your autobiographical narrative may be assessed, see the Rubric on page 143.

Prewriting

Choose a topic. Write your autobiographical narrative about a topic of importance to you. Try **blueprinting** to identify an idea. First, sketch a blueprint of a place you remember well. Label each room or area. Then, jot down words or phrases you associate with these areas. Choose one of these ideas as the topic of your narrative.

Gather details. Record as many details as possible about the idea you have chosen. One idea may remind you of others. Review your notes and narrow your list to the details you will include in your narrative.

Structure the sequence. Create a detailed record of the order of events in your narrative by making a **timeline.** Write down the first event related to the subject of your narrative. Record subsequent events in the order in which they occurred.

Timeline

1 — Dad took off training wheels.

2 — Dreamed of riding bike with no training wheels.

3 — Rode two-wheeled bike and fell.

4 — Improved riding. Tried other activities.

Add personal thoughts. Look at the list of events you will include in your narrative, and note what you were thinking when each event occurred. Consider adding these thoughts to your narrative to enrich the writing.

Example

Event:	My mom suggested I play outside.
First Thought:	I thought of riding my bike without training wheels.
Second Thought:	I worried about whether I could ride a two-wheeled bike without falling.

Student Model

Before you draft your autobiographical narrative, read this student model and review the characteristics of effective autobiographical narrative.

Albert Kim
Palos Verdes, CA

Leaving Fear Behind

It all happened one day when my mom suggested that I go outside and play, not just stay inside as I usually did. At five years old, I really enjoyed staying inside my cozy house. The only outdoor activity that I ever did up to that point was ride a rusty bicycle with training wheels on it, but I often thought of what it would be like to ride it without those wheels.

> Albert is the main character in this narrative.

One night I dreamed of riding a bike with no training wheels. The bike felt large and unsteady. I couldn't keep my balance, and I fell down. I woke up right when I hit the ground. Then I was more scared than ever.

Every day I thought about riding that bike. Then I said to myself that I needed to do whatever I could to get rid of the tension. I decided that I had to do it. I had to ride a bike without those old wheels so I could feel good again.

> Words that indicate time passing suggest a sequence of events.

Late one afternoon, my dad used all kinds of tools to take off those old, rusty training wheels. My bike was ready. I got on, trying to sit still, while my dad held the back of the seat. I was still shaking because I was scared. Pedaling as fast as I could, I didn't realize that my dad had already let go. I was riding! This was unbelievable! I felt the soft, cool breeze rushing across my face.

Suddenly, something went wrong. My joy quickly faded. I couldn't stop my bike! I was barreling toward the end of the street. There was a very sharp and narrow curve ahead. To my horror, I realized I hadn't yet learned how to make a sharp turn, not even with wheels on. When I was about two feet from the curve, I turned the front wheel as hard as I could and my feet got stuck in the pedals. WHAM! I crashed and scraped my leg. The next thing I knew, I was laughing. Even though I was hurt, I was very happy and glad that I had accomplished what I had wanted to do.

> The writer describes the action using physical sensations and shifts in mood.

Since then I have tried many new things: swimming, games, and other activities. I found out that I am really good at the things I have tried. Learning to ride without training wheels was the first time I ever took a chance on trying something new. Because I was successful, I was not afraid to try other things. I crossed a threshold in my life and left fear behind.

> The writer suggests an insight he gained as a result of the experience.

Drafting

Identify your main point. As you draft your narrative, think about why the story you have chosen to tell might be meaningful to others. When you have determined what you want your audience to understand, organize your details to highlight the importance of that main point.

Organize events. The description of events adds substance to your autobiographical essay. Too much description, however, can distract a reader from your main point. Instead, choose details to accomplish these goals:

- Highlighting the central conflict that sets the events in motion.
- Creating tension that builds to a climax, or turning point.
- Offering insights related to your main point.

Elaborate. As you draft your autobiographical narrative, remember that you can make your story even more vivid by providing detailed information. The chart shown here provides some tips to help you elaborate further on an idea.

Basic Story Element	Elaboration Tip
Experience to narrate	Explain its main effect on you.
Time and place	Describe impressions using sensory details, including sights, smells, sounds, and tastes.
Suspense	Add details that raise the tension and heighten the story's problem.
Main events of story	Include thoughts or feelings that occurred to you at the time of the events.
Story outcome	Consider other possible outcomes of events.

Revising

Explode a moment. To help your readers experience the event as you did, add details that bring your thoughts and feelings to life. Read your draft and highlight moments in your narrative where you can expand your idea by telling more about what you were thinking, what it looked or felt like, or how others reacted. Then, jot down these details on a separate piece of paper and incorporate them into your revised draft.

Model: Exploding a Moment

The bike felt large and unsteady.

One night I dreamed of riding a bike with no training wheels. I couldn't keep my balance, and I fell down. I woke up right when I hit the ground. Then I was more scared than ever.

Albert adds details to describe the nervous feeling before he lost his balance.

Revise to vary your sentences. Even though your autobiographical narrative is about an event that happened to you, you should avoid beginning every sentence with *I*. Look closely at the sentences in your draft, and vary sentence beginnings to make your draft more interesting. Compare the model and the nonmodel. Why is the model more effective than the nonmodel?

Nonmodel	Model
I didn't realize that my dad had already let go. I was riding! I couldn't believe it! I felt the soft, cool breeze rushing across my face.	My dad had already let go without my realizing it. I was riding! This was unbelievable! I felt the soft, cool breeze rushing across my face.

Publishing and Presenting

Share your writing with a wider audience by presenting your story to your classmates.

Deliver an oral presentation. Practice reading your story aloud. Mark up a copy of your autobiographical narrative, underlining any dialogue, thoughts, or conversations that you believe your audience would enjoy. As you present to your classmates, emphasize those passages.

Post your essay. Create a bulletin board display of the essays written by you and your classmates. Have each writer supply a short comment about the event or idea that inspired the writing. Add photographs if they are available.

Speaking Connection
To learn more about presenting an autobiographical narrative, see the **Listening and Speaking Workshop,** p. 144.

 Prentice Hall Writing and Grammar Connection: Chapter 4

Rubric for Self-Assessment

Evaluate your autobiographical narrative using the following criteria and rating scale:

Criteria	Rating Scale				
	Not very				Very
How central are you to the action of the story?	1	2	3	4	5
How clearly organized is the sequence of events?	1	2	3	4	5
How well does the action accommodate shifts in time and mood?	1	2	3	4	5
How powerfully are concrete and sensory details used to describe events?	1	2	3	4	5
How well do you convey your insights, thoughts, and feelings?	1	2	3	4	5

Listening and Speaking WORKSHOP

Delivering a Narrative Presentation

Narrative presentations use storytelling to describe a sequence of events with meaning for an audience. You give a narrative presentation every time you tell friends what happened in a movie or sports event. Certain qualities make a narrative presentation effective—a clear story line, a description of place and time, a sense of mood, and an indication of importance to the audience or speaker.

Prepare the Presentation

Choose a compelling story. The best stories are so interesting they actually compel the audience to pay attention. For your presentation, choose a true or fictional story that lends itself easily to retelling and will have an impact on your audience.

Practice telling the story. Practice delivering your narrative to family members or friends first. After you learn which parts people like best, you can emphasize those. Your story will get better with every retelling.

Deliver the Presentation

The same aspects that you enjoy when watching an exciting performance are the ones that will make your presentation enjoyable for an audience. Incorporate these strategies into your presentation:

Use variation to hook your audience. Make your narrative more interesting by varying your voice and body language.

- Let your voice rise and fall according to the effect you want to create. Add dramatic pauses to create suspense.
- Quicken your pace to show excitement or slow it down to indicate the passage of time.
- Use gestures and facial expressions to enhance story events.

Indicate significance. When you tell a personal narrative, communicate how the event had an impact on your life. If you are giving a narrative about a larger event, such as the Civil War, explain its influence on other events of the time.

Control nervous energy. As you speak before a group, you may fidget or sway. Work to stand still, making only movements that enhance your words.

Narrative Presentation Self-Evaluation

- Do you think your audience understood the point of your presentation? If not, how could you have communicated this better?
- Which aspects of your story did others like best? Do you agree? Why?
- Which parts of your narrative were hard to describe?
- What changes would you make to improve your presentation?

 **Activity: Analyzing a Speech** Rehearse and deliver a short narrative presentation in front of a group. Use the feedback you get from others and the self-evaluation form above to help you critique your presentation.

Assessment WORKSHOP

Context Clues

The reading sections of some tests require you to read a passage and answer multiple-choice questions about word meanings. Frequently, you can determine the meanings of unfamiliar words by using context clues. The following strategies can help you answer test questions on word meanings:

- Skim the *context* of an unfamiliar word—words or phrases surrounding the word that might provide clues to its meaning.
- Search for explanations or descriptions that include details or examples.
- Consider the ideas presented in the sentences before and after an unfamiliar word or phrase. Determine a meaning consistent with the entire passage.

Test-Taking Strategies

- Use the context of an unfamiliar word to list potential substitute words.
- Reread the paragraph using the substitute words to see whether it makes sense.

Sample Test Item

Directions: Read the passage, and then answer the question that follows.

Fred was furious that Jonathan hadn't put any gas in his car after borrowing it for the day. Even though they had not discussed it, Fred was sure they had a tacit understanding that Jonathan would return the car with a full tank.

1. The word <u>tacit</u> in this passage means _____?_____

   A written
   B spoken
   C legal
   D unspoken

Answer and Explanation

D is the correct answer. There is no context that supports *A, B,* or *C.* The phrase "Even though they had not discussed it" provides a clue that *tacit* means "unspoken."

▶ Practice

Directions: Read the passage, and then answer the questions that follow.

After the entry-level position had gone unfilled for two months, Ms. Harding reviewed Carl Borden's application. He had seemed somewhat <u>reticent</u> at the start of his interview, but perhaps his silent manner was due to nervousness. After a few rounds of light <u>banter,</u> he was talking comfortably about his qualifications.

1. In this passage, the word <u>reticent</u> means _____?_____
   A untruthful
   B relaxed
   C reserved
   D argumentative

2. The word <u>banter</u> means _____?_____
   A analysis
   B debate
   C persuasion
   D small talk

UNIT 2

Challenges and Choices

Human Achievement, Tsing-Fang Chen, Lucia Gallery, NYC

Exploring the Theme

An athlete challenges herself to be the best she can be. A powerful leader makes difficult decisions that can affect an entire nation. No matter who you are, life involves facing challenges and making choices. In these stories, poems, and essays, you will see how people in many different situations confront challenges and choices in their daily lives.

Rosa Parks did not know that her refusal to give up her seat on a Birmingham bus would spark a crucial struggle in the civil rights movement. In "My Story," Parks shows us that people approach challenges in different ways and make decisions for all kinds of reasons. Some decisions are made quietly, by ordinary people with little fanfare. But they can take as much courage, and have as much impact, as the decisions of a president.

▲ **Critical Viewing** What different types of human achievement are represented in this painting? **[Analyze]**

Why Read Literature?

Whenever you read, you have a purpose, or reason. Perhaps you choose a literary work because you know little about its subject. Or maybe you pick up a selection because the subject is familiar and you enjoy reading about it. Preview some purposes you might set before reading the works in this unit.

Night Games, Ernie Barnes, The Company of Art, Los Angeles

1

Read for the Love of Literature

Interestingly, certain stories seem enhanced by their predictability. The fun is in watching the details unfold and finding out whether you guessed right in the end. Predict the winner of a showdown in ancient China in Ray Bradbury's **"The Golden Kite, the Silver Wind,"** page 178.

Most of us would come up short if asked to describe the complex give and take, graceful arcs, and physical battering of a good pickup game of basketball. If it takes a poem to capture the twists and turns, fakes, and sudden soaring movements of a beautiful game, you could do no better than Yusef Komunyakaa's **"Slam, Dunk, and Hook,"** page 228.

2

Read for Information

Even if a story is completely mythical, it can still be a rich source of information. Greek myths tell us much about the values, views, and beliefs of the ancient Greeks. Find out why a little help from the gods was not considered dishonest for a hero with fate on his side in Edith Hamilton's **"Perseus,"** page 214.

3

Read to Be Inspired

In his autobiography, Martin Luther King, Jr., reveals that he stopped looking at his notes halfway through his speech at the March on Washington. Knowing that he spoke from spontaneous heartfelt emotion could explain the power of a speech considered one of the most eloquent in human history. Join the millions who drew inspiration from King's words as you read **"I Have a Dream,"** page 164.

 Take It to the Net

Visit the Web site for online instruction and activities related to each selection in this unit.
www.phschool.com

How **to Read Literature**

Use Interactive Reading Strategies

When you read, you are not just viewing words on a page. You are also thinking about the ideas, images, and information presented in the text. With difficult or unfamiliar topics, you might find it harder to interact with the text. Use these strategies to help you get involved.

1. Establish a purpose for reading.

- Determine the reason you wish to read a work of literature. For example, you might read for entertainment or to learn information.

- Read the selection and note the facts and details that help you achieve your original purpose.

- Use a K-W-L chart, like the one at right, to help define your purpose and evaluate the selection.

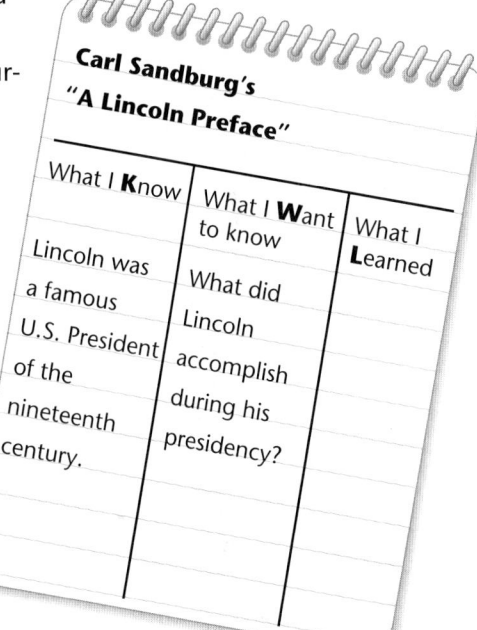

Carl Sandburg's "A Lincoln Preface"

What I **K**now	What I **W**ant to know	What I **L**earned
Lincoln was a famous U.S. President of the nineteenth century.	What did Lincoln accomplish during his presidency?	

2. Respond.

Readers bring their own set of expectations, beliefs, and experiences to the literature they read. To tap your own responses:

- Compare events in the selection with your own experiences.

- Use the author's text as a way to examine your own feelings about the subject.

- Consider the lessons of the piece and how you might use them in your own life.

3. Predict.

- Pause as you complete sections of a story to think about what might happen next.

- Base your predictions on what has already happened in the story, personal experience, or prior knowledge of the subject.

4. Generate questions.

To make sure you remain fully involved with a selection, generate questions to answer as you read.

- Use the common question words *who, what, where, when, why,* and *how* to review what you have read.

- Think about any unanswered questions you might still have as you read future passages.

- If you still have unanswered questions after finishing, discuss the work with others or do research to complete your understanding.

As you read the selections in this unit, apply these reading strategies to interact with the text.

Prepare to Read

from A Lincoln Preface

Lincoln Proclaiming Thanksgiving, Dean Cornwell, The Lincoln Museum, Fort Wayne, Indiana, a part of Lincoln National Corp.

 Take It to the Net

Visit www.phschool.com for interactive activities and instruction related to "A Lincoln Preface," including

- background
- graphic organizers
- literary elements
- reading strategies

Preview

Connecting to the Literature

Whether we admire them for their achievements, abilities, or fine qualities, we are often inspired to pay tribute to our heroes in some way. Imagine being inspired to write a six-volume biography, as Carl Sandburg did for his hero, Abraham Lincoln.

Background

Abraham Lincoln is remembered as one of our greatest presidents, yet at the time of his election in 1860, less than half the country supported him. One reason is that Lincoln was opposed to slavery—and many landowners in the south still kept slaves. After seven southern states left the Union, the Civil War broke out in April 1861. By June 1861, a total of eleven states had left the Union and joined the Confederacy.

Literary Analysis

Anecdote

An **anecdote** is a brief story about an interesting, amusing, or strange event told to illustrate a point. Carl Sandburg helps readers see Lincoln's attitude and sense of humor through anecdotes like this one:

> As [Lincoln] shook hands with the correspondent of the London *Times*, he drawled, "Well, I guess the London *Times* is about the greatest power on earth—unless perhaps it is the Mississippi River."

As you read the anecdotes in "A Lincoln Preface," jot down in a word or two what each one tells about Lincoln.

Connecting Literary Elements

Anecdotes are a type of **narration**—writing that tells a story. Sometimes, anecdotes are woven into a longer story. In this selection, for example, Sandburg weaves together anecdotes to tell the larger story of Lincoln's role in the Civil War.

Reading Strategy

Establishing a Purpose for Reading

Before you begin to read a selection, **establish a purpose**—decide *why* you are reading it. Sometimes, you read purely for enjoyment, but often you read to learn something new. For example, if you already know some information about Lincoln, you may be reading to learn more. Before reading the excerpt from "A Lincoln Preface," decide what else you would like to learn about Lincoln and start a K-W-L chart like the one shown here. Follow these steps:

- Use the title and introductory paragraphs to determine the topic of a selection, and write down what you know about that topic.
- Jot down what you hope to learn from the selection, and focus on these points as you read.

Continue to complete your chart as you read.

Instruction with this selection addresses these standards:

R 1.1*, 3.9*
W 1.8, 2.1*
WOLC 1.3*
LS 1.1

* Standards tested on HS Exit Exam. For complete standards, see p. CA 4.

What I Know

What I Want to Know

What I Learned

Vocabulary Development

despotic (des pät′ ik) *adj.* like an absolute ruler or tyrant (p. 153)

chattel (chat′ əl) *n.* a movable item of personal property (p. 153)

cipher (sī′ fər) *adj.* code (p. 155)

slouching (slouch′ iŋ) *adj.* drooping (p. 155)

censure (sen′ shər) *n.* strong disapproval (p. 156)

gaunt (gônt) *adj.* thin and bony (p. 157)

droll (drōl) *adj.* comic and amusing in an odd way (p. 158)

from A Lincoln Preface

Carl Sandburg

Lincoln Proclaiming Thanksgiving, Dean Cornwell, The Lincoln Museum, Fort Wayne, Indiana, a part of Lincoln National Corp.

▲ **Critical Viewing** What can you tell about Lincoln from this painting? **[Infer]**

In the time of the April lilacs in the year 1865, a man in the City of Washington, D.C., trusted a guard to watch at a door, and the guard was careless, left the door, and the man was shot, lingered a night, passed away, was laid in a box, and carried north and west a thousand miles; bells sobbed; cities wore crepe;[1] people stood with hats off as the railroad burial car came past at midnight, dawn or noon.

During the four years of time before he gave up the ghost, this man was clothed with <u>despotic</u> power, commanding the most powerful armies till then assembled in modern warfare, enforcing drafts of soldiers, abolishing the right of habeas corpus,[2] directing politically and spiritually the wild, massive forces loosed in civil war.

Four billion dollars' worth of property was taken from those who had been legal owners of it, confiscated, wiped out as by fire, at his instigation and executive direction; a class of <u>chattel</u> property recognized as lawful for two hundred years went to the scrap pile.

When the woman who wrote *Uncle Tom's Cabin*[3] came to see him in the White House, he greeted her, "So you're the little woman who wrote the book that made this great war," and as they seated themselves at a fireplace, "I do love an open fire: I always had one at home." As they were finishing their talk of the days of blood, he said, "I shan't last long after it's over."

An Illinois Congressman looked in on him as he had his face lathered for a shave in the White House and remarked, "If anybody had told me that in a great crisis like this the people were going out to a little one-horse town and pick out a one-horse lawyer for president, I wouldn't have believed it." The answer was, "Neither would I. But it was a time when a man with a policy would have been fatal to the country. I never had a policy. I have simply tried to do what seemed best each day, as each day came."

"I don't intend precisely to throw the Constitution overboard, but I will stick it in a

---

1. **crepe** (krāp) *n.* thin, black cloth worn to show mourning.
2. **habeas corpus** (hā bē əs kôr′ pəs) right of an imprisoned person to have a court hearing.
3. **woman . . . Cabin** Harriet Beecher Stowe (1811–1896), whose novel stirred up opinion against slavery.

despotic (des pät′ ik) *adj.* like an absolute ruler or tyrant

chattel (chat′ 'l) *n.* a movable item of personal property

Literary Analysis
Anecdote What point does this anecdote make about Lincoln's devotion to his country?

**Reading Check**

What did Lincoln do during the four years before he was killed?

hole if I can," he told a Cabinet officer. The enemy was violating the Constitution to destroy the Union, he argued, and therefore, "I will violate the Constitution, if necessary, to save the Union." He instructed a messenger to the Secretary of the Treasury, "Tell him not to bother himself about the Constitution. Say that I have that sacred instrument here at the White House, and I am guarding it with great care."

When he was renominated, it was by the device of seating delegates from Tennessee, which gave enough added votes to seat favorable delegates from Kentucky, Missouri, Louisiana, Arkansas, and from one county in Florida. Until late in that campaign of 1864, he expected to lose the November election; military victories brought the tide his way; the vote was 2,200,000 for him and 1,800,000 against him. Among those who bitterly fought him politically, and accused him of blunders or crimes, were Franklin Pierce, a former president of the United States; Horatio Seymour, the Governor of New York; Samuel F. B. Morse, inventor of the telegraph; Cyrus H. McCormick, inventor of the farm reaper; General George B. McClellan, a Democrat who had commanded the Army of the Potomac; and the *Chicago Times,* a daily newspaper. In all its essential propositions the Southern Confederacy had the moral support of powerful, respectable elements throughout the North, probably more than a million votes believing in the justice of the cause of the South as compared with the North.

While propagandas raged, and the war winds howled, he sat in the White House, the Stubborn Man of History, writing that the Mississippi was one river and could not belong to two countries, that the plans for railroad connection from coast to coast must be pushed through and the Union Pacific[4] realized.

His life, mind and heart ran in contrasts. When his white kid gloves broke into tatters while shaking hands at a White House reception, he remarked, "This looks like a general bustification." When he talked with an Ohio friend one day during the 1864 campaign, he

Peculiarsome Abe, N. C. Wyeth, The Free Library of Philadelphia

▲ **Critical Viewing**
What message does this painting convey about Lincoln? **[Describe]**

---

4. **Union Pacific** railroad chartered by Congress in 1862 to form part of a transcontinental system.

mentioned one public man, and murmured, "He's a thistle! I don't see why God lets him live." Of a devious Senator, he said, "He's too crooked to lie still!" And of a New York editor, "In early life in the West, we used to make our shoes last a great while with much mending, and sometimes, when far gone, we found the leather so rotten the stitches would not hold. Greeley is so rotten that nothing can be done with him. He is not truthful; the stitches all tear out." As he sat in the telegraph office of the War Department, reading <u>cipher</u> dispatches, and came to the words, Hosanna and Husband, he would chuckle, "Jeffy D.,"[5] and at the words, Hunter and Happy, "Bobby Lee."[6]

cipher (sī′ fər) *adj.* code

While the luck of war wavered and broke and came again, as generals failed and campaigns were lost, he held enough forces of the Union together to raise new armies and supply them, until generals were found who made war as victorious war has always been made, with terror, frightfulness, destruction, and valor and sacrifice past words of man to tell.

A <u>slouching</u>, gray-headed poet,[7] haunting the hospitals at Washington, characterized him as "the grandest figure on the crowded canvas of the drama of the nineteenth century—a Hoosier Michael Angelo."[8]

slouching (slouch′ iŋ) *adj.* drooping

His own speeches, letters, telegrams and official messages during that war form the most significant and enduring document from any one man on why the war began, why it went on, and the dangers beyond its end. He mentioned "the politicians," over and again "the politicians," with scorn and blame. As the platoons filed before him at a review of an army corps, he asked, "What is to become of these boys when the war is over?"

Reading Strategy
Establishing a Purpose for Reading What two sides of Lincoln's personality do these paragraphs reveal?

He was a chosen spokesman: yet there were times he was silent; nothing but silence could at those times have fitted a chosen spokesman; in the mixed shame and blame of the immense wrongs of two crashing civilizations, with nothing to say, he said nothing, slept not at all, and wept at those times in a way that made weeping appropriate, decent, majestic.

His hat was shot off as he rode alone one night in Washington; a son he loved died as he watched at the bed; his wife was accused of betraying information to the enemy, until denials from him were necessary; his best companion was a fine-hearted and brilliant son with a deformed palate and an impediment of speech; when a Pennsylvania Congressman told him the enemy had declared they would break into the city and hang him to a lamppost, he said he had considered "the violent preliminaries" to such a scene; on his left thumb was a scar where an ax had nearly chopped the thumb off when he was a boy; over one eye was a scar where he had been hit with a club in the hands of a man trying to steal the cargo off a

---

5. **"Jeffy D."** Jefferson Davis (1808–1889), president of the Confederacy.
6. **"Bobby Lee"** Robert E. Lee (1807–1870), commander in chief of the Confederate army.
7. **slouching . . . poet** Walt Whitman (1819–1892).
8. **Michael Angelo** Michelangelo (mik′ əl an′ jə lō′), famous Italian artist (1475–1564).

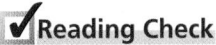**Reading Check**

Name at least three people who fought against Lincoln politically.

Mississippi River flatboat; he threw a cashiered[9] officer out of his room in the White House, crying, "I can bear <u>censure</u>, but not insult. I never wish to see your face again."

As he shook hands with the correspondent of the London *Times*, he drawled, "Well, I guess the London *Times* is about the greatest power on earth—unless perhaps it is the Mississippi River." He rebuked with anger a woman who got on her knees to thank him for a pardon that saved her son from being shot at sunrise; and when an Iowa woman said she had journeyed out of her way to Washington just for a look at him, he grinned, "Well, in the matter of looking at one another, I have altogether the advantage."

He asked his Cabinet to vote on the high military command, and after the vote, told them the appointment had already been made; one Cabinet officer, who had been governor of Ohio, came away personally baffled and frustrated from an interview, to exclaim, to a private secretary, "That man is the most cunning person I ever saw in my life"; an Illinois lawyer who had been sent on errands carrying his political secrets, said, "He is a trimmer[10] and such a trimmer as the world has never seen."

He manipulated the admission of Nevada as a state in the Union, when her votes were needed for the Emancipation Proclamation,◆ saying, "It is easier to admit Nevada than to raise another million of soldiers." At the same time he went to the office of a former New York editor, who had become Assistant Secretary of War, and said the votes of three congressmen were wanted for the required three-quarters of votes in the House of Representatives, advising, "There are three that you can deal with better than anybody else. . . . Whatever promise you make to those men, I will perform it." And in the same week, he said to a Massachusetts politician that two votes were lacking, and, "Those two votes must be procured. I leave it to you to determine how it shall be done; but remember that I am President of the United States and clothed with immense power, and I expect you to procure those votes." And while he was thus employing every last resource and device of practical politics to constitutionally abolish slavery, the abolitionist[11] Henry Ward Beecher attacked him with javelins of scorn and detestation in a series of editorials that brought from him the single comment, "Is thy servant a dog?"

When the King of Siam sent him a costly sword of exquisite

censure (sen´ shər) *n.* strong disapproval

Literature
in context History Connection

◆ **The Emancipation Proclamation**

When Lincoln signed the Emancipation Proclamation, he recognized its enormous symbolic power while understanding its limitations. Some argued it was really only a partial emancipation—freeing slaves in unconquered Confederate territory—but it was an important first step. Not only did the document give Southern blacks cause to hope, rebel, and escape, it also served as a recruitment incentive for the new black regiments of the Union Army. As the army advanced, liberating slaves along the way, it was clear that the Emancipation Proclamation had done what it was designed to do: pave the way for the total abolition of slavery.

Lincoln at the Signing of the Emancipation Proclamation

---

9. **cashiered** (ka shird´) *v.* dishonorably discharged.
10. **trimmer** (trim´ ər) *n.* person who changes his opinion to suit the circumstances.
11. **abolitionist** (ab´ ə lish´ ən ist) *n.* person in favor of doing away with slavery in the United States.

embellishment, and two elephant tusks, along with letters and a photograph of the King, he acknowledged the gifts in a manner as lavish as the Orientals. Addressing the King of Siam as "Great and Good Friend," he wrote thanks for each of the gifts, including "also two elephant's tusks of length and magnitude, such as indicate they could have belonged only to an animal which was a native of Siam." After further thanks for the tokens received, he closed the letter to the King of Siam with strange grace and humor, saying, "I appreciate most highly your Majesty's tender of good offices in forwarding to this Government a stock from which a supply of elephants might be raised on our soil. . . . our political jurisdiction, however, does not reach a latitude so low as to favor the multiplication of the elephant, and steam on land as well as water has been our best agent of transportation . . . Meantime, wishing for your Majesty a long and happy life, and, for the generous and emulous people of Siam, the highest possible prosperity, I commend both to the blessing of Almighty God."

Literary Analysis
Anecdote What does this anecdote about gifts from Siam convey about Lincoln's personality?

He sent hundreds of telegrams, "Suspend death sentence" or "Suspend execution" of So-and-So, who was to be shot at sunrise. The telegrams varied oddly at times, as in one, "If Thomas Samplogh, of the First Delaware Regiment, has been sentenced to death, and is not yet executed, suspend and report the case to me." And another, "Is it Lieut. Samuel B. Davis whose death sentence is commuted? If not done, let it be done."

While the war drums beat, he liked best of all the stories told of him, one of two Quakeresses[12] heard talking in a railway car. "I think that Jefferson will succeed." "Why does thee think so?" "Because Jefferson is a praying man." "And so is Abraham a praying man." "Yes, but the Lord will think Abraham is joking."

An Indiana man at the White House heard him say, "Voorhees, don't it seem strange to you that I, who could never so much as cut off the head of a chicken, should be elected, or selected, into the midst of all this blood?"

A party of American citizens, standing in the ruins of the Forum in Rome, Italy, heard there the news of the first assassination of the first American dictator, and took it as a sign of the growing up and the aging of the civilization on the North American continent. Far out in Coles County, Illinois, a beautiful, <u>gaunt</u> old woman in a log cabin said, "I knowed he'd never come back."

gaunt (gônt) *adj.* thin and bony

Of men taking too fat profits out of the war, he said, "Where the carcass is there will the eagles be gathered together."

An enemy general, Longstreet, after the war, declared him to have been "the one matchless man in forty millions of people," while one of his private secretaries, Hay, declared his life to have been the most perfect in its relationships and adjustments since that of Christ.

Between the days in which he crawled as a baby on the dirt floor of

**Reading Check**

What story regarding the Quakeresses did Lincoln appreciate?

---

12. **Quakeresses** (kwāk′ ər es əz) *n.* female members of the religious group known as the Society of Friends, or Quakers.

a Kentucky cabin, and the time when he gave his final breath in Washington, he packed a rich life with work, thought, laughter, tears, hate, love.

With vast reservoirs of the comic and the <u>droll</u>, and notwithstanding a mastery of mirth and nonsense, he delivered a volume of addresses and letters of terrible and serious appeal, with import beyond his own day, shot through here and there with far, thin ironics, with paragraphs having raillery[13] of the quality of the Book of Job,[14] and echoes as subtle as the whispers of wind in prairie grass.

Perhaps no human clay pot has held more laughter and tears.

The facts and myths of his life are to be an American possession, shared widely over the world, for thousands of years, as the tradition of Knute or Alfred, Lao-tse or Diogenes, Pericles or Caesar,[15] are kept. This because he was not only a genius in the science of neighborly human relationships and an artist in the personal handling of life from day to day, but a strange friend and a friendly stranger to all forms of life that he met.

He lived fifty-six years of which fifty-two were lived in the West—the prairie years.

---

13. **raillery** (rāl´ ər ē) *n.* good-natured teasing.
14. **Book of Job** (jōb) book of the Old Testament in which a man named Job is tested by God.
15. **Knute** (knōōt) **or Alfred, Lao-tse** (lou´ dzu´) **or Diogenes** (dī äj´ ə nēz), **Pericles** (per´ ə klēz) **or Caesar** (sē´ zər) well-known thinkers and leaders from different eras and places.

Review and Assess

Thinking About the Selection

1. **Respond:** Which anecdote interested you the most?
2. **(a) Recall:** To whom did Lincoln refer as "the little woman who wrote the book that made this great war"? **(b) Infer:** Why do you think Lincoln wanted to meet with this woman?
3. **(a) Recall:** How did Lincoln justify admitting Nevada to the Union? **(b) Analyze:** What other examples can you find of Lincoln's use of "practical politics"?
4. **(a) Distinguish:** How does Sandburg show that Lincoln "packed a rich life with work, thought, laughter, tears, hate, love"? **(b) Evaluate:** What do you think Sandburg thought about his subject?
5. **Evaluate:** Do you think Lincoln was justified in violating the Constitution to save the Union? Why or why not?
6. **Extend:** How does Lincoln's life, based on Sandburg's portrait, compare to the lives of other great leaders?

droll (drōl) *adj.* comic and amusing in an odd way

Carl Sandburg

(1878–1967)

At the age of thirteen, Carl Sandburg dropped out of school; for the next seven years, he worked as a porter, scene changer, truck handler, dishwasher, potter, and farm worker. Sandburg served briefly in Puerto Rico during the Spanish-American War, and that experience brought on the strong antiwar feelings that Sandburg would hold throughout his life.

After the war, Sandburg discovered literature. He read a great deal and spent eighteen years researching and writing *Abraham Lincoln: The Prairie Years* and *Abraham Lincoln: The War Years*. Sandburg received two Pulitzer Prizes—one for his Lincoln biography and one for poetry. He also gained recognition for having written what many consider the greatest historical biography of the 1900s.

Review and Assess

Literary Analysis

Anecdote

1. Use an organizer like the one shown to analyze **anecdotes** from the selection. For each, summarize the story and then identify the personality trait it reveals.

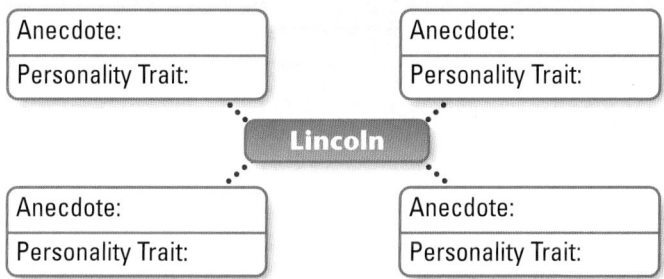

2. Why do you think Sandburg included in this work some anecdotes that portrayed Lincoln in a less-than-pleasing light?
3. Which of your previous notions about Lincoln does the narration change?

Connecting Literary Elements

4. What is the central problem that ties this **narrative** together?
5. How does Sandburg's narration paint a verbal picture of Lincoln?
6. (a) How does a biography built on anecdotes differ from other biographies you have read? (b) How do the anecdotes strengthen the narrative?

Reading Strategy

Establishing a Purpose for Reading

7. Identify two different **purposes** readers may bring to this selection.
8. Identify three pieces of information from the selection that helped you achieve the purpose of learning more about Abraham Lincoln.
9. If you were reading to learn more about the Civil War, which details in the selection would help you?

Extend Understanding

10. **Literature Connection:** Why do you think people are fascinated with political biographies that reveal the positive and negative inner workings of a politician's life?

Integrate Language Skills

Vocabulary Development Lesson

Word Analysis: Anglo-Saxon Suffix -ic

The Anglo-Saxon suffix -ic means "like" or "pertaining to." It creates the adjective form of many words, such as *despotic*, which means "like a despot, or tyrant." Define each of the following words, incorporating the definition of -ic into each answer.

    1. artistic   **2.** realistic   **3.** problematic

Spelling Strategy

To add an ending like -ic to a word that ends in a consonant, simply add the suffix. For example, *carbon* becomes *carbonic*. Create the adjective form of the following words by adding the suffix -ic to each one. Then, write a sentence using the new word.

    1. artist   **3.** class

    2. poet   **4.** patriot

Concept Development: Analogies

When you analyze vocabulary analogies, first study the relationship between a given word pair, and then complete a second word pair to show the same relationship.

Copy the following analogies. Complete each one with the appropriate word from the vocabulary list on page 151.

    1. tradition : custom :: possession : ____?____

    2. war : peace :: praise : ____?____

    3. garbled : speech :: ____?____ : message

    4. standing tall : alert :: ____?____ : tired

    5. tolerant : democratic :: repressive : ____?____

    6. well-fed : plump :: undernourished : ____?____

    7. strange : bizarre :: funny : ____?____

Grammar Lesson

Transitive and Intransitive Verbs

An action verb is **transitive** if it directs action toward someone or something named in the same sentence. An action verb is **intransitive** if it does not direct action toward something or someone named in the same sentence. To determine whether a verb is transitive or intransitive, ask *Whom?* or *What?* after the verb. If you can find the answer in the sentence, the verb is transitive. If not, the verb is intransitive.

Transitive: The president <u>read</u> the documents.

Intransitive: The president <u>read</u> every day.

Practice: Identify each underlined verb as *transitive* or *intransitive*.

    1. Several people bitterly <u>fought</u> him politically.

    2. Propagandas <u>raged</u> and the war winds <u>howled</u>.

    3. He <u>asked</u> his cabinet to vote on the issue.

    4. He <u>spoke</u> forcefully during the war.

    5. The telegrams <u>varied</u> at times.

Writing Application Write a brief paragraph about a modern-day leader. In your writing, use three transitive verbs and three intransitive verbs.

WG Prentice Hall Writing and Grammar Connection: Chapter 17, Section 1

Writing Lesson

Character Profile

Write a short profile of Lincoln, describing the traits, talents, and special skills that helped him succeed as president. Use Sandburg's narrative and your own knowledge to create your profile.

Prewriting   Use a chart like the one shown to jot down descriptions of Lincoln. Then, provide evidence for each description you list.

Model: Gathering Details About a Person

Description	Evidence
determined	He manipulated the admission of Nevada as a state into the Union to win votes for the Emancipation Proclamation.

Drafting   As you draft, use a solid organization. You might begin by explaining some of Lincoln's minor personality traits and move to addressing his most impressive traits, or do the reverse.

Revising   Reread your draft. Check to make sure that each description of Lincoln is backed up with evidence. Add any details needed to present a clear profile of Lincoln.

W/G   *Prentice Hall Writing and Grammar Connection: Chapter 5, Section 2*

Extension Activities

Listening and Speaking   In a group, conduct a **panel discussion** on Lincoln's use of "practical politics" to end slavery with the passage of the Emancipation Proclamation.

- Panel members should prepare their remarks in advance.
- Each speaker can present a brief opening statement.
- The panel can then debate the issue to reach a conclusion.

After the discussion, ask audience members to evaluate the event. **[Group Activity]**

Research and Technology   Create a **timeline** of the most significant events in Lincoln's life and presidency as Sandburg reports them. In the appropriate places, include situations in which he made famous speeches or suffered personal tragedies. Use graphics software to create your timeline, and present it to your class.

 **Take It to the Net**   www.phschool.com

Go online for an additional research activity using the Internet.

Prepare to Read

I Have a Dream ◆ *from* Rosa Parks: My Story ◆
There Is a Longing ◆ I Hear America Singing

Preview

Connecting to the Literature

Think of a time when you were inspired by a speech, a work of writing, or even a conversation. Often, as you will see in these selections, we find inspiration in the words of people who challenge us to be the best we can be.

Background

The freedom of speech guaranteed by the United States Constitution is a civil right, a freedom that people are entitled to as members of a society. Some Americans have not always enjoyed these rights and have had to struggle for equality. Their fight—marked by demonstrations and legal challenges—is known as the civil rights movement. It began in the 1950s and was led by figures such as Martin Luther King, Jr., and Rosa Parks.

Literary Analysis

Author's Purpose

An **author's purpose** is his or her reason for writing. For example, an author may want to entertain, inform, or persuade the reader. This example from "I Have a Dream" reveals the author's purpose: to urge all Americans, regardless of background, to accept one another as equals.

> With this faith, we will be able to transform the jangling discords of our nation into a beautiful symphony of brotherhood.

As you read, determine each author's purpose, and evaluate the author's techniques to decide how successfully he or she has conveyed that purpose.

Comparing Literary Works

An author's purpose helps shape his or her **tone**—the attitude toward the subject that an author conveys in a piece of writing. Identify the tone of each piece by looking for words that indicate how the author feels. Try to select adjectives that capture each tone. Then, look at the similarities and differences in the tones of the four selections.

CALIFORNIA STANDARDS

Instruction with these selections addresses these standards:

R 1.1*, 2.8*, 3.9*
W 1.3*, 2.4*
WOLC 1.2*
LS 1.4

* Standards tested on HS Exit Exam. For complete standards, see p. CA 4.

Reading Strategy

Responding

When you read something, you cannot help but **respond,** or react, to it.

- As you read, ask yourself how you are reacting.
- Note your feelings, such as anger or sympathy.
- Look for the words or ideas that have provoked your response.

Use a chart like this one to write down your responses as you read.

My Reaction

Why I React That Way

Vocabulary Development

creed (krēd) *n.* statement of belief (p. 165)

oppression (ə presh´ ən) *n.* keeping others down by the unjust use of power (p. 165)

oasis (ō ā´ sis) *n.* fertile place in the desert (p. 165)

exalted (eg zôlt´ əd) *v.* lifted up (p. 165)

prodigious (prə dij´ əs) *adj.* wonderful; of great size (p. 166)

hamlet (ham´ lit) *n.* small village (p. 166)

complied (kəm plīd´) *v.* carried out or fulfilled a request (p. 168)

manhandled (man´ han´ dəld) *v.* treated roughly (p. 169)

determination (dē tʉr´ mi nā´ shən) *n.* firm intention (p. 170)

endurance (en dʊr´ əns) *n.* ability to withstand hardship and continue on (p. 170)

"I Have a Dream"

Martin Luther King, Jr.

This speech by Martin Luther King, Jr., was part of the March on Washington, a demonstration demanding civil rights legislation and jobs. The march drew a diverse crowd of 250,000 to Washington, D.C., on August 28, 1963. In a time of unrest, King's televised speech showed the vast potential of interracial cooperation.

. . . I say to you today, my friends, that in spite of the difficulties and frustrations of the moment I still have a dream. It is a dream deeply rooted in the American dream.

I have a dream that one day this nation will rise up and live out the true meaning of its <u>creed</u>: "We hold these truths to be self-evident; that all men are created equal."

I have a dream that one day on the red hills of Georgia the sons of former slaves and the sons of former slaveowners will be able to sit down together at a table of brotherhood.

I have a dream that one day even the state of Mississippi, a desert state sweltering with the heat of injustice and <u>oppression</u>, will be transformed into an <u>oasis</u> of freedom and justice.

I have a dream that my four little children will one day live in a nation where they will not be judged by the color of their skin but by the content of their character.

I have a dream today.

I have a dream that one day the state of Alabama, whose governor's lips are presently dripping with the words of interposition and nullification,[1] will be transformed into a situation where little black boys and black girls will be able to join hands with little white boys and white girls and walk together as sisters and brothers.

I have a dream today.

I have a dream that one day every valley shall be <u>exalted</u>, every hill and mountain shall be made low, the rough places will be made plains, and the crooked places will be made straight, and the glory of the Lord shall be revealed, and all flesh shall see it together.[2]

This is our hope. This is the faith with which I return to the South. With this faith we will be able to transform the jangling discords of our nation into a beautiful symphony of brotherhood. With this faith we will be able to work together, to pray together, to

creed (krēd) *n.* statement of belief

oppression (ə presh´ ən) *n.* keeping others down by the unjust use of power

oasis (ō ā´ sis) *n.* fertile place in the desert

exalted (eg zôlt´ əd) *v.* lifted up

---

1. **interposition** (in´ tər pə zish´ ən) **and nullification** (nul´ ə fi kā´ shən) disputed doctrine that a state can reject federal laws considered to be violations of its rights.
2. **every valley . . . all flesh shall see it together** reference to a biblical passage (Isaiah 40:4–5).

◀ **Critical Viewing** What does this photograph tell you about the importance of Dr. King's message to those who heard his speech? Explain. **[Draw Conclusions]**

✔**Reading Check**

What is King's dream for his four children?

struggle together, to go to jail together, to stand up for freedom together, knowing that we will be free one day.

This will be the day when all of God's children will be able to sing with a new meaning "My country 'tis of thee, sweet land of liberty, of thee I sing. Land where my fathers died, land of the pilgrim's pride, from every mountainside, let freedom ring."

And if America is to be a great nation this must become true. So let freedom ring from the <u>prodigious</u> hilltops of New Hampshire. Let freedom ring from the mighty mountains of New York. Let freedom ring from the heightening Alleghenies of Pennsylvania!

Let freedom ring from the snowcapped Rockies of Colorado!

Let freedom ring from the curvaceous peaks of California!

But not only that: let freedom ring from Stone Mountain of Georgia!

Let freedom ring from every hill and molehill of Mississippi. From every mountainside, let freedom ring.

When we let freedom ring, when we let it ring from every village and every <u>hamlet</u>, from every state and every city, we will be able to speed up that day when all of God's children, black men and white men, Jews and Gentiles, Protestants and Catholics, will be able to join hands and sing in the words of that old Negro spiritual, "Free at last! Free at last! Thank God almighty, we are free at last!"

prodigious (prə dij´ əs) *adj.* wonderful; of great size

Reading Strategy
Responding What feelings do the words "Let freedom ring" evoke in you? Why?

hamlet (ham´ lit) *n.* small village

Review and Assess

Thinking About the Selection

1. **Respond:** What feelings does King's speech stir in you?

2. **(a) Recall:** Name at least four states King mentions in his speech. **(b) Infer:** Why do you think he refers to so many parts of the country?

3. **(a) Recall:** In your own words, briefly state King's dream. **(b) Infer:** Based on this dream, what do you think was the reality of King's life?

4. **(a) Recall:** What words does King quote from "My Country 'Tis of Thee"? **(b) Connect:** What message does he send by quoting these lines?

5. **(a) Evaluate:** How persuasive do you think King's speech is? **(b) Support:** What specific aspects of the speech make it so?

6. **(a) Make a Judgment:** Why do you think King's speech has lived on as one of the best-known speeches of all time? **(b) Evaluate:** Does it deserve this standing? Why or why not?

7. **Connect:** Do you think the dream in King's speech has been fully realized today? Support your answer.

Martin Luther King, Jr.

(1929–1968)

Born in Atlanta, Georgia, the son of a minister, Dr. Martin Luther King, Jr., was a dynamic civil rights leader of the twentieth century. During the 1950s and 1960s, King organized nonviolent protests that helped to bring about equal rights for all Americans. His tireless efforts for civil rights inspired people of all races and earned King the 1964 Nobel Peace Prize. At thirty-five, he was the youngest man and only the third black man to be awarded this prestigious honor.

CONNECTIONS
Literature and Music

Voices of Peace

People admire Martin Luther King, Jr., for his courage in preaching nonviolence during a violent era. In the lyrics to "Pride," the Irish rock group U2 pays tribute to King by celebrating his message. As a message that has survived despite King's violent death, it continues to inspire.

Pride
Bono
and
The Edge
(In The Name Of Love)

One man come in the name of love
One man come and go
One man come, he to justify
One man to overthrow
Chorus:

In the name of love
What more in the name of love
In the name of love
What more in the name of love

One man caught on a barbed wire fence
One man he resist
One man washed on an empty beach
One man betrayed with a kiss
(Chorus)

Early morning, April four
Shot rings out in the Memphis sky
Free at last
They took your life
They could not take your pride
(Chorus)

U2

U2 formed in 1978, basing its sound around the expressive vocals of lead singer Bono (Paul Hewson), the distinctive echoing style of guitarist The Edge (David Evans), and the driving rhythms of bassist Adam Clayton and drummer Larry Mullen, Jr. The band has experimented with many styles over a long career. They have used their lasting popularity to support causes ranging from famine relief to debt forgiveness for developing nations.

Connecting Literature and Music

1. What emotion does this song evoke? Explain.
2. How does the song's message relate to King's message in "I Have a Dream"?
3. (a) Why might U2 have chosen "pride" as the quality that best characterized King? (b) Which characteristic would you choose?

W hen I got off from work that evening of December 1, I went to Court Square as usual to catch the Cleveland Avenue bus home. I didn't look to see who was driving when I got on, and by the time I recognized him, I had already paid my fare. It was the same driver who had put me off the bus back in 1943, twelve years earlier. He was still tall and heavy, with red, rough-looking skin. And he was still mean-looking. I didn't know if he had been on that route before—they switched the drivers around sometimes. I do know that most of the time if I saw him on a bus, I wouldn't get on it.

I saw a vacant seat in the middle section of the bus and took it. I didn't even question why there was a vacant seat even though there were quite a few people standing in the back. If I had thought about it at all, I would probably have figured maybe someone saw me get on and did not take the seat but left it vacant for me. There was a man sitting next to the window and two women across the aisle.

The next stop was the Empire Theater, and some whites got on. They filled up the white seats, and one man was left standing. The driver looked back and noticed the man standing. Then he looked back at us. He said, "Let me have those front seats," because they were the front seats of the black section. Didn't anybody move. We just sat right where we were, the four of us. Then he spoke a second time: "Y'all better make it light on yourselves and let me have those seats."

The man in the window seat next to me stood up, and I moved to let him pass by me, and then I looked across the aisle and saw that the two women were also standing. I moved over to the window seat. I could not see how standing up was going to "make it light" for me. The more we gave in and <u>complied</u>, the worse they treated us.

I thought back to the time when I used to sit up all night and didn't

The Beginning, Artis Lane

▲ **Critical Viewing**
How does this painting reflect the ideal of equal rights for all people? **[Analyze]**

Literary Analysis
Author's Purpose Why do you think Rosa Parks included this background information in her story of the encounter on the bus?

complied (kəm plīd´) v. carried out or fulfilled a request

sleep, and my grandfather would have his gun right by the fireplace, or if he had his one-horse wagon going anywhere, he always had his gun in the back of the wagon. People always say that I didn't give up my seat because I was tired, but that isn't true. I was not tired physically, or no more tired than I usually was at the end of a working day. I was not old, although some people have an image of me as being old then.

I was forty-two. No, the only tired I was, was tired of giving in.

The driver of the bus saw me still sitting there, and he asked was I going to stand up.

I said, "No." He said, "Well, I'm going to have you arrested." Then I said, "You may do that." These were the only words we said to each other. I didn't even know his name, which was James Blake, until we were in court together. He got out of the bus and stayed outside for a few minutes, waiting for the police.

As I sat there, I tried not to think about what might happen. I knew that anything was possible. I could be <u>manhandled</u> or beaten. I could be arrested. People have asked me if it occurred to me then that I could be the test case the NAACP[1] had been looking for. I did not think about that at all. In fact if I had let myself think too deeply about what might happen to me, I might have gotten off the bus. But I chose to remain.

---

1. **NAACP** *abbr.* National Association for the Advancement of Colored People.

Rosa Parks

(b. 1913)

In 1955, Rosa Parks was arrested for breaking an unjust law—she refused to give up her seat on a public bus to a white man. This incident sparked a boycott that led to the end of segregation on the Montgomery bus system. Her courageous action marked the start of the civil rights movement. In 1999, she was granted the Congressional Gold Medal. This is the highest honor given to a civilian in the United States.

Review and Assess

Thinking About the Selection

1. **Respond:** What do you think about Rosa Parks's actions? Explain.
2. **(a) Recall:** In which section did Rosa Parks sit on the bus? **(b) Interpret:** Why did the bus driver ask the people in her row to give up their seats?
3. **(a) Recall:** Summarize her memory of her grandfather. **(b) Interpret:** How does her childhood memory affect her action that day, many years later?
4. **(a) Recall:** What reason does Rosa Parks give for staying in her seat? **(b) Interpret:** How did her refusal to stand up contribute to the civil rights movement?
5. **Compare and Contrast:** Both Rev. King and Rosa Parks helped win equality for minorities. How are their actions similar and different?
6. **Speculate:** Do you think that if Rosa Parks had given up her seat, integration would have taken place anyway? Explain.

There Is a Longing
Chief Dan George

There is a longing in the heart of my people
to reach out and grasp that which is needed
for our survival. There is a longing among
the young of my nation to secure for themselves

5   and their people the skills that will
provide them with a sense of worth and
purpose. They will be our new warriors.
Their training will be much longer and
more demanding than it was in olden days.

10 The long years of study will demand more
<u>determination</u>; separation from home and
family will demand <u>endurance</u>. But they
will emerge with their hand held forward,
not to receive welfare, but to grasp the

15 place in society that is rightly ours.

I am a chief, but my power to make war
is gone, and the only weapon left to me
is speech. It is only with tongue and speech
that I can fight my people's war.

20 Oh, Great Spirit!¹ Give me back the courage
of the olden Chiefs. Let me wrestle with
my surroundings. Let me once again,
live in harmony with my environment.
Let me humbly accept this new culture

25 and through it rise up and go on. Like
the thunderbird² of old, I shall rise again
out of the sea; I shall grab the instruments

---

1. **Great Spirit** for many Native Americans, the greatest power or god.
2. **thunderbird** a powerful supernatural creature that was thought to produce thunder
   by flapping its wings and produce lightning by opening and closing its eyes. In the
   folklore of some Native American nations, the thunderbird is in constant warfare with
   the powers beneath the waters.

determination (dē tʉr´ mi
nā´ shən) *n.* firm intention

endurance (en dʊr´ əns)
n. ability to withstand
hardship and continue on

Reading Strategy
Responding What do
you think is the most
persuasive part of the
writer's message?

We the People, Kathy Morrow, Courtesy of the artist

of the white man's success—his
education, his skills. With these new tools
30   I shall build my race into the proudest
segment of your society. I shall see our
young braves and our chiefs sitting in
the houses of law and government, ruling
and being ruled by the knowledge and
35   freedoms of *our* great land.

▲ **Critical Viewing**
Which images in this
painting reflect ideas
found in the poem?
[Interpret]

Review and Assess

Thinking About the Selection

1. **Respond:** How did you feel as you read "There Is a Longing"? Explain.

2. **(a) Recall:** What does Chief Dan George say is his community's longing? **(b) Draw Conclusions:** What is his greatest fear?

3. **(a) Recall:** What is the training the new warriors will have to endure? **(b) Analyze:** Why does Chief Dan George think this training is necessary?

4. **(a) Infer:** In what way is Chief Dan George different from his predecessors? **(b) Interpret:** What does the chief mean by fighting a war "with tongue and speech"?

5. **(a) Analyze:** In what ways does Chief Dan George believe the Great Spirit will help his people? **(b) Deduce:** What do you think the Chief himself will have to do to help them?

6. **Assess:** Do you think the Chief's goal of achieving success through education and skills is the best means for improving his people's lives? Explain.

Chief Dan George

(1899–1981)
Chief Dan George had many careers, including actor and writer. Chief of a Salish Band of Native Americans in British Columbia, Canada, he was deeply concerned about developing mutual respect between Native Americans and other North Americans. As an actor, he accepted only roles that presented Native Americans with dignity. As a writer and public speaker, he emphasized respect and understanding among people.

There Is a Longing ◆ 171

I Hear America Singing

Walt Whitman

I hear America singing, the varied carols I hear,
Those of mechanics, each one singing his as it should be
    blithe and strong,
The carpenter singing his as he measures his plank or beam,
The mason singing his as he makes ready for work, or
    leaves off work,
5 The boatman singing what belongs to him in his boat, the
    deckhand singing on the steamboat deck,
The shoemaker singing as he sits on his bench, the hatter
    singing as he stands,
The wood-cutter's song, the ploughboy's on his way in the
    morning, or at noon intermission or at sundown,
The delicious singing of the mother, or of the young wife at
    work, or of the girl sewing or washing,
Each singing what belongs to him or her and to none else,
10 The day what belongs to the day—at night the party of
    young fellows, robust, friendly,
Singing with open mouths their strong melodious songs.

Walt Whitman

(1819–1892)
Walt Whitman, one of America's greatest poets, was a lover of democracy and a champion of the common individual. Part of Whitman's mission as a poet was to inspire and vitalize the United States through the ecstatic vision of democratic life. His expansive vision and spirit are reflected in "I Hear America Singing."

Review and Assess

Thinking About the Selection

1. **Respond:** Which of the "songs" speaks to you the most? Explain.

2. **(a) Recall:** Identify three singers Whitman names.
   (b) Interpret: What does Whitman mean when he says that he hears their songs?

3. **(a) Recall:** When does the mason sing? The ploughboy?
   (b) Distinguish: Why do you think Whitman pictures the American worker in various situations and times of day?

4. **Generalize:** What kind of nation does Whitman depict?

5. **Speculate:** Do you think modern-day America is similar to the world Whitman presents? Why or why not?

Morgan Spiller

Review and Assess

Literary Analysis

Author's Purpose

1. Choose one of the selections you have just read. Using a chart like the one shown here, note details of content and style that help you determine the **author's purpose.**

Content	Style

···▶

Author's Purpose

2. How does King's use of repetition help to achieve his purpose?
3. Chief Dan George voices his appeal for his people's future. To whom is he speaking? Native Americans? Others? Explain.

Comparing Literary Works

4. (a) Analyze each writer's **tone** by completing a chart like the one shown here. For each selection, note words that reflect the writer's attitude toward the subject. Then, select a single adjective to identify the writer's tone. (b) In what ways does each writer use tone to emphasize the importance of his or her subject?

King	Word Choice	Parks
Chief Dan George		Whitman

5. Both King and Parks write about the civil rights movement in the United States. (a) How are the tones of the two pieces different? (b) What is the reason for this difference?

Reading Strategy

Responding

6. Choose one "carol" from "I Hear America Singing" and explain the **response** it generated in you.
7. Which selection provoked the strongest response in you? Explain.

Extend Understanding

8. **Social Studies Connection:** Do the ideas and issues in these selections still hold true today? Explain.

Quick Review

An **author's purpose** is his or her reason for writing.

The **tone** of a piece of writing is the author's attitude toward the subject.

When you **respond** to what you read, you acknowledge your personal reaction to the writing.

 Take It to the Net
www.phschool.com

Take the interactive self-test online to check your understanding of these selections.

Integrate Language Skills

Vocabulary Development Lesson

Word Analysis: Latin Root -cred-

Creed comes from the Latin verb *credere*, which means "to believe." Applying the meaning of *-cred-*, use each of the following words in a sentence.

a. credit   **c.** credentials

b. incredible   **d.** credibility

Spelling Strategy

Before adding a suffix beginning with a vowel to a word that ends in silent *e*, you usually drop the *e*. For example, when adding the suffix *-ance* to *endure*, the silent *e* is dropped and the word becomes *endurance*. Write the correct spelling of the following words. Then, write a sentence using each new word.

1. sense + *-ory*   **3.** like + *-able*

2. imagine + *-ary*   **4.** drive + *-ing*

Concept Development: Synonyms and Antonyms

Synonyms are words with similar meanings, such as *happy* and *cheerful*. Antonyms are words with opposite meanings, such as *light* and *dark*. Identify the relationships of the following word pairs. Use **S** for synonyms and **A** for antonyms.

1. creed, statement of doubt

2. oppression, liberty

3. oasis, desert

4. exalted, dignified

5. prodigious, remarkable

6. hamlet, city

7. complied, obeyed

8. manhandled, shoved

9. determination, weakness

10. endurance, stamina

Grammar Lesson

Action and Linking Verbs

Action verbs express physical or mental actions, like *jump* or *think*. In contrast, **linking verbs,** including forms of the verb *be*, express a state of being. They connect the subject to a word that renames or describes the subject.

Action verbs: I *saw* a seat and *took* it.

Linking verbs: I *was* tired of giving in.

Practice Copy the following sentences from the selections. Underline the action verbs and circle the linking verbs.

1. I am a chief, but my power is gone.

2. I hear America singing, the varied carols I hear.

3. I have a dream that one day every valley shall be exalted.

4. I shall build my race into the proudest segment of your society.

5. It was the same driver who had put me off the bus back in 1943, twelve years earlier.

Writing Application Write a paragraph about a person whose words or actions inspire you. Circle the verbs you have chosen, and then identify whether each is an action or a linking verb.

W͞G Prentice Hall Writing and Grammar Connection: Chapter 17, Sections 1 and 2

Writing Lesson

Proposal for a School Speaker

Consider the benefit of having a great speaker, like Martin Luther King, Jr., speak at your school. Write a proposal to your principal, presenting a persuasive argument in favor of inviting a specific speaker to a school assembly.

Prewriting   Think about problems that your classmates face daily, and consider the ways a speaker might address them. Make a list of potential speakers, and describe the benefit that each speech would provide.

Model: Gathering Evidence

Speaker	Benefit speaker will provide
Toni Morrison	Her success could inspire students to express themselves through writing.

Drafting   As you draft, explain how the speaker you have chosen could help address important issues in your school. End with an appeal that will convince the principal to act on your proposal.

Revising   Review your proposal to see that your examples are persuasive and simply stated. Check your final paragraph to be sure that you end with an appeal noting the benefits of the speaker's visit.

𝒲G *Prentice Hall Writing and Grammar Connection: Chapter 7, Section 2*

Extension Activities

Listening and Speaking Compose a **radio news report** in which you provide on-the-spot coverage of King's speech and explain his dream for America. Include the following in your report:

- background information about the civil rights movement
- excerpts from King's speech
- description of the effect it had on the crowd

Share your report with your class. Tape-record yourself while broadcasting so that you can evaluate your work later.

Research and Technology In a group, create a **multimedia presentation** on a single aspect of the American civil rights movement, such as laws, marches, or specific leaders. Assemble photographs for your presentation, as well as video or audio recordings of civil rights speeches and events. Present your findings to your class. **[Group Activity]**

 Take It to the Net   www.phschool.com

Go online for an additional research activity using the Internet.

Prepare to Read

The Golden Kite, the Silver Wind

Rectangular Box, Avery Brundage Collection, Asian Art Museum of San Francisco

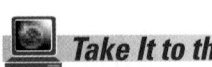
Take It to the Net

Visit www.phschool.com for interactive activities and instruction related to "The Golden Kite, The Silver Wind," including

- background
- graphic organizers
- literary elements
- reading strategies

Preview

Connecting to the Literature

Have you and a friend ever tried to outdo each other? The two of you may have become consumed by rivalry, but most likely, no one else was hurt as a result of it. In this story, a rivalry becomes so intense that it leads to widespread suffering.

Background

"The Golden Kite, the Silver Wind" was written during the Cold War, a period of intense rivalry between the United States and the former Soviet Union. During this time, each action by one country—the creation of a weapon, the launching of a satellite—was countered by a reaction from the other country. As you read, think about the parallels between the story events and the history of the Cold War.

Literary Analysis

Fable

"The Golden Kite, the Silver Wind" is a **fable,** a brief story that teaches a lesson. This lesson, or moral, may be directly stated, or it may be shown through the choices the characters make. In this fable, the actions of two rival towns teach a lesson about the value of cooperation over competition. The following example from the story highlights the unhealthy competition existing between the towns.

> "They build their wall," said the Mandarin, "in the shape of a pig! Do you see? Our own city wall is built in the shape of an orange. That pig will devour us, greedily!"

As you read, consider what lesson can be learned from this fable.

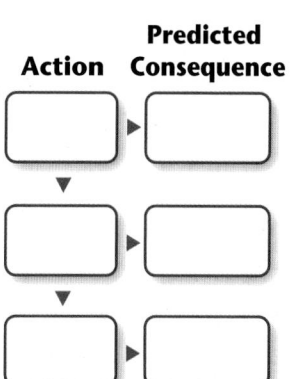

Instruction with this selection addresses these standards:

R 1.1*, 3.4*, 3.7*
W 1.3*, 2.4*
WOLC 1.3*
LS 1.9

* Standards tested on HS Exit Exam. For complete standards, see p. CA 4.

Connecting Literary Elements

A **dialogue** is a conversation between characters. As a complement to a writer's narration, dialogue is used to reveal more about a character and to advance action in a story. In this story, the dialogue quickens the action, introduces each Mandarin's tactics, and helps reveal the lesson of the fable.

Reading Strategy

Predicting Consequences of Actions

Try to **predict the consequences of each action** in a story by considering events that have already occurred. Then, read on to see whether your predictions were correct. To help you, follow these suggestions:

- Write down each event as it occurs.
- Before you read further, predict the consequences of that event.
- Look for a pattern that will lead you to the moral of the story.

Use a chart like the one shown to help you predict as you read.

Action → **Predicted Consequence**

Vocabulary Development

portents (pôr′ tentz) *n.* things that are thought to be signs of events to come; omens (p. 179)

vile (vīl) *adj.* evil; wicked (p. 179)

ravenous (rav′ ə nəs) *adj.* greedily hungry (p. 179)

acclaimed (ə klāmd′) *v.* greeted with loud applause or approval (p. 180)

pandemonium (pan′ də mōn′ nē əm) *n.* wild disorder, noise, or confusion (p. 180)

spurn (spʉrn) *v.* reject in a scornful way (p. 180)

The Golden Kite, the Silver Wind

Ray Bradbury

"In the shape of a *pig*?" cried the Mandarin.[1]

"In the shape of a pig," said the messenger, and departed.

"Oh, what an evil day in an evil year," cried the Mandarin. "The town of Kwan-Si, beyond the hill, was very small in my childhood. Now it has grown so large that at last they are building a wall."

---

1. **Mandarin** (man´ de rin) a high official of China; here, the ruling leader.

The Nymph of the Lo River, Attributed to Ku K'ai-Chih, Freer Gallery of Art, Smithsonian Institution, Washington, D.C.

"But why should a wall two miles away make my good father sad and angry all within the hour?" asked his daughter quietly.

"They build their wall," said the Mandarin, "in the shape of a pig! Do you see? Our own city wall is built in the shape of an orange. That pig will devour us, greedily!"

"Ah."

They both sat thinking.

Life was full of symbols and omens. Demons lurked everywhere, Death swam in the wetness of an eye, the turn of a gull's wing meant rain, a fan held so, the tilt of a roof, and, yes, even a city wall was of immense importance. Travelers and tourists, caravans, musicians, artists, coming upon these two towns, equally judging the <u>portents</u>, would say, "The city shaped like an orange? No! I will enter the city shaped like a pig and prosper, eating all, growing fat with good luck and prosperity!"

The Mandarin wept. "All is lost! These symbols and signs terrify. Our city will come on evil days."

"Then," said the daughter, "call in your stonemasons and temple builders. I will whisper from behind the silken screen and you will know the words."

The old man clapped his hands despairingly. "Ho, stonemasons!"

"Ho, builders of towns and palaces!"

The men who knew marble and granite and onyx and quartz came quickly. The Mandarin faced them most uneasily, himself waiting for a whisper from the silken screen behind his throne. At last the whisper came.

"I have called you here," said the whisper.

"I have called you here," said the Mandarin aloud, "because our city is shaped like an orange, and the <u>vile</u> city of Kwan-Si has this day shaped theirs like a <u>ravenous</u> pig—"

Here the stonemasons groaned and wept. Death rattled his cane in the outer courtyard. Poverty made a sound like a wet cough in the shadows of the room.

"And so," said the whisper, said the Mandarin, "you raisers of walls must go bearing trowels and rocks and change the shape of *our* city!"

The architects and masons gasped. The Mandarin himself gasped at what he had said. The whisper whispered. The Mandarin went on: "And you will change our walls into a club which may beat the pig and drive it off!"

The stonemasons rose up, shouting. Even the Mandarin, delighted at the words from his mouth, applauded, stood down from his throne. "Quick!" he cried. "To work!"

Literary Analysis

Fable Based on the Mandarin's answer to his daughter's question, what rivalry exists between the two towns?

portents (pôr´ tentz) *n.* things that are thought to be signs of events to come; omens

vile (vīl) *adj.* evil; wicked

ravenous (rav´ ə nəs) *adj.* greedily hungry

**Reading Check**

Who is whispering to the king from behind a silken screen?

When his men had gone, smiling and bustling, the Mandarin turned with great love to the silken screen. "Daughter," he whispered, "I will embrace you." There was no reply. He stepped around the screen, and she was gone.

Such modesty, he thought. She has slipped away and left me with a triumph, as if it were mine.

The news spread through the city; the Mandarin was <u>acclaimed</u>. Everyone carried stone to the walls. Fireworks were set off and the demons of death and poverty did not linger, as all worked together. At the end of the month the wall had been changed. It was now a mighty bludgeon with which to drive pigs, boars, even lions, far away. The Mandarin slept like a happy fox every night.

"I would like to see the Mandarin of Kwan-Si when the news is learned. Such <u>pandemonium</u> and hysteria; he will likely throw himself from a mountain! A little more of that wine, oh Daughter-who-thinks-like-a-son."

But the pleasure was like a winter flower; it died swiftly. That very afternoon the messenger rushed into the courtroom. "Oh, Mandarin, disease, early sorrow, avalanches, grasshopper plagues, and poisoned well water!"

The Mandarin trembled.

"The town of Kwan-Si," said the messenger, "which was built like a pig and which animal we drove away by changing our walls to a mighty stick, has now turned triumph to winter ashes. They have built their city's walls like a great bonfire to burn our stick!"

The Mandarin's heart sickened within him, like an autumn fruit upon an ancient tree. "Oh, gods! Travelers will <u>spurn</u> us. Tradesmen, reading the symbols, will turn from the stick, so easily destroyed, to the fire, which conquers all!"

"No," said a whisper like a snowflake from behind the silken screen.

"No," said the startled Mandarin.

"Tell my stonemasons," said the whisper that was a falling drop of rain, "to build our walls in the shape of a shining lake."

The Mandarin said this aloud, his heart warmed.

"And with this lake of water," said the whisper and the old man, "we will quench the fire and put it out forever!"

The city turned out in joy to learn that once again they had been saved by the magnificent Emperor of ideas. They ran to the walls and built them nearer to this new vision, singing, not as loudly as before, of course, for they were tired, and not as quickly, for since it had taken a month to rebuild the wall the first time, they had had to neglect business and crops and therefore were somewhat weaker and poorer.

There then followed a succession of horrible and wonderful days, one in another like a nest of frightened boxes.

"Oh, Emperor," cried the messenger, "Kwan-Si has rebuilt their walls to resemble a mouth with which to drink all our lake!"

acclaimed (ə klāmd´) v. greeted with loud applause or approval; hailed

pandemonium (pan´ də mōn´ nē əm) n. wild disorder, noise, or confusion

spurn (spurn) v. reject in a scornful way

Reading Strategy
Predicting Consequences of Actions What do you think will be the consequence of this latest action?

"Then," said the Emperor, standing very close to his silken screen, "build our walls like a needle to sew up that mouth!"

"Emperor!" screamed the messenger. "They make their walls like a sword to break your needle!"

The Emperor held, trembling, to the silken screen. "Then shift the stones to form a scabbard to sheathe that sword!"[2]

"Mercy," wept the messenger the following morn, "they have worked all night and shaped their walls like lightning which will explode and destroy that sheath!"

Sickness spread in the city like a pack of evil dogs. Shops closed. The population, working now steadily for endless months upon the changing of the walls, resembled Death himself, clattering his white bones like musical instruments in the wind. Funerals began to appear in the streets, though it was the middle of summer, a time when all should be tending and harvesting. The Mandarin fell so ill that he had his bed drawn up by the silken screen and there he lay, miserably giving his architectural orders. The voice behind the screen was weak now, too, and faint, like the wind in the eaves.

"Kwan-Si is an eagle. Then our walls must be a net for that eagle. They are a sun to burn our net. Then we build a moon to eclipse their sun!"

Like a rusted machine, the city ground to a halt.

At last the whisper behind the screen cried out:

"In the name of the gods, send for Kwan-Si!"

Upon the last day of summer the Mandarin Kwan-Si, very ill and withered away, was carried into our Mandarin's courtroom by four starving footmen. The two mandarins were propped up, facing each other. Their breaths fluttered like winter winds in their mouths. A voice said:

"Let us put an end to this."

The old men nodded.

"This cannot go on," said the faint voice. "Our people do nothing but rebuild our cities to a different shape every day, every hour. They have no time to hunt, to fish, to love, to be good to their ancestors and their ancestors' children."

"This I admit," said the mandarins of the towns of the Cage, the Moon, the Spear, the Fire, the Sword and this, that, and other things.

"Carry us into the sunlight," said the voice.

The old men were borne out under the sun and up a little hill. In the late summer breeze a few very thin children were flying dragon kites in all the colors of the sun, and frogs and grass, the color of the sea and the color of coins and wheat.

The first Mandarin's daughter stood by his bed.

"See," she said.

"Those are nothing but kites," said the two old men.

Literary Analysis
Fable What lesson are the mandarins beginning to learn?

**Reading Check**
What kind of wall was built to defeat Kwan-si's sun?

---

2. **scabbard** (skab´ ərd) **to sheathe** (shēth) **that sword!** case to hold the blade of the sword.

"But what is a kite on the ground?" she said. "It is nothing. What does it need to sustain it and make it beautiful and truly spiritual?"

"The wind, of course!" said the others.

"And what do the sky and the wind need to make *them* beautiful?"

"A kite, of course—many kites, to break the monotony, the sameness of the sky. Colored kites, flying!"

"So," said the Mandarin's daughter. "You, Kwan-Si, will make a last rebuilding of your town to resemble nothing more nor less than the wind. And we shall build like a golden kite. The wind will beautify the kite and carry it to wondrous heights. And the kite will break the sameness of the wind's existence and give it purpose and meaning. One without the other is nothing. Together, all will be beauty and cooperation and a long and enduring life."

Whereupon the two mandarins were so overjoyed that they took their first nourishment in days, momentarily were given strength, embraced, and lavished praise upon each other, called the Mandarin's daughter a boy, a man, a stone pillar, a warrior, and a true and unforgettable son. Almost immediately they parted and hurried to their towns, calling out and singing, weakly but happily.

And so, in time, the towns became the Town of Golden Kite and the Town of the Silver Wind. And harvestings were harvested and business tended again, and the flesh returned, and disease ran off like a frightened jackal. And on every night of the year the inhabitants in the Town of the Kite could hear the good clear wind sustaining them. And those in the Town of the Wind could hear the kite singing, whispering, rising, and beautifying them.

"So be it," said the Mandarin in front of his silken screen.

Literary Analysis
Fable and Dialogue What do you learn from the dialogue between the daughter and the two mandarins?

Review and Assess

Thinking About the Selection

1. **Respond:** Do you think the Mandarin's daughter gave her father good advice? Explain.

2. **(a) Recall:** Which event at the beginning of the story upsets and angers the Mandarin? **(b) Infer:** What does his reaction tell you about his beliefs?

3. **(a) Recall:** How does the Mandarin's daughter advise her father? **(b) Infer:** Why do you think she needs to advise him in such a way?

4. **(a) Infer:** What can you infer about the townspeople based on their response to the Mandarin's plans? **(b) Evaluate:** Should they have continued to follow his advice?

5. **Apply:** How can the lesson from this story be applied to everyday life situations?

Ray Bradbury

(b. 1920)

Born in Waukegan, Illinois, Bradbury developed a love of fantasy and suspenseful writing at an early age. In 1932, Bradbury's family moved to Tucson, Arizona, where he wrote his first stories. In 1934, they moved to Los Angeles, where he has lived ever since.

A year after he graduated from high school, Bradbury founded and edited a publication called *Futuria Fantasia*. By this time, he was already writing at least one story a week.

One of America's most celebrated science-fiction writers, Bradbury has earned the World Fantasy Award for lifetime achievement and the Grand Master Award from the Science Fiction Writers of America.

Review and Assess

Literary Analysis

Fable

1. (a) What poor choices were made by both the Mandarin and his daughter in this **fable**? (b) What happened as a result?
2. Use a chart like this one to list key responsibilities of leaders. What lesson does this fable teach us about powerful leaders and their responsibilities to the people they represent?

Responsibilities		Mandarins' Leadership Abilities
	...▶	

3. In your own words, express the moral of the fable in one sentence.

Connecting Literary Elements

4. Most of the **dialogue** in the story is provided by the daughter speaking from behind a screen. What does this dialogue reveal to us about the daughter and the Mandarin?
5. (a) Note places in the story where dialogue moves the action along more quickly. (b) Why does dialogue work better than description in the story?

Reading Strategy

Predicting Consequences of Actions

6. What were the first hints that the rivalry between the two towns would be disastrous? Support your answer.
7. At what point were you able to **predict** the outcome? Explain.
8. (a) What do you predict will be the result of the actions taken at the end of the story? (b) Which details support your answer?

Extend Understanding

9. **World History Connection:** This story was written during the Cold War. (a) Why would the story have been especially appropriate for that time? (b) Which countries or cultures from today's world could the two villages represent? Explain.

Integrate Language Skills

Vocabulary Development Lesson

Word Analysis: Latin Root -clam-

In this story, the word *acclaimed*, meaning "greeted with loud applause or approval," contains *-claim-*, a variation of the Latin root *-clam-*, meaning "call out" or "shout." Applying the meaning of *-clam-*, write a sentence for each word below.

1. exclaim **2.** proclamation **3.** clamorous

Spelling Strategy

The final consonant of a prefix sometimes changes to match the first letter of the word to which it is attached. The result is a doubled consonant. For example, the prefix *in-* changes to *ir-* in *irregular*.

Rewrite each item below by adding the given prefix. Then, write a sentence using the new word.

1. *ex-* + centric **2.** *ad-* + sign

Fluency: Context

Write each sentence below, filling in the blanks with words from the vocabulary list on page 177, or forms of those words.

The ___?___ for the kingdom were not good. The crops had failed, lightning had struck the bell tower, and a dragon was causing ___?___ across the countryside. Fierce and ___?___, the dragon terrified the peasants and devoured their livestock, leaving the people hungry and frightened. "That ___?___ dragon must be destroyed!" exclaimed the princess. ___?___ offers of assistance, she rode off to fight the dragon. On her triumphant return home, the dragon-slaying princess was ___?___ by her grateful people for her bravery and determination.

Grammar Lesson

Compound Verbs

A **compound verb** is two or more verbs that have the same subject and are joined by a conjunction such as *and* or *or*. In the following example from "The Golden Kite, the Silver Wind," the subject is underlined and the parts of the compound verb are italicized.

>   S   V   V
> **Example:** "They *ran* to the walls and *built* them nearer to this new vision. . . ."

Both *ran* and *built* have the same subject, *They*, and the verbs are connected by the conjunction *and*.

Practice Identify the compound verbs in each sentence below.

1. She spoke and directed people through the silken screen.
2. The townspeople worked all night and shaped their walls like lightning.
3. The people moaned and wept.
4. They parted and hurried back to work.
5. The wind will carry and sustain the kite.

Writing Application Use each word below as the subject in a sentence, and create compound verbs to accompany each subject.

1. Mandarin **2.** walls

W͡G Prentice Hall Writing and Grammar Connection: Chapter 20, Section 1

Writing Lesson

Persuasive Letter

Imagine you were living in one of the cities featured in "The Golden Kite, the Silver Wind." Write a letter to the Mandarin, letting him know how concerned you are about the competition between the cities and urging him to resolve the conflict.

Prewriting	Brainstorm a list of points you would like to make about the conflict. Keep your audience in mind and think about what you can say that would affect the Mandarin's thoughts about the issue.
Drafting	As you draft, make sure your arguments are supported. Whenever possible, prove your point by providing examples, facts, or details.
Revising	As you revise, underline all of your arguments and highlight the support. If a point needs more evidence, add details. If there is no stronger evidence, eliminate your point.

Model: Evaluating Support for Your Arguments

The people of the city will not survive the competition.

and people are dying

Everyone is working on the walls. Sickness has spread.

> Added information supports the argument that the people of the city will not survive.

 Prentice Hall Writing and Grammar Connection: Chapter 7, Section 4

Extension Activities

Listening and Speaking In a small group, present a **dramatic interpretation** of Bradbury's story. Make these necessary decisions to organize your interpretation properly.

- Assign the roles of the two mandarins, the daughter, and a messenger.
- Assign the role of director to one person in the group who can listen objectively and give advice on pitch and tone of voice.

Present your interpretation to the class, and ask your audience to evaluate your presentation. **[Group Activity]**

Research and Technology Bradbury's fable addresses issues raised by the Cold War. Research some aspect of the Cold War. For example, you might study the alliances each side formed or the weapons buildup that took place. Use library resources like the Internet, an atlas, and history books. Then, compare the events in Bradbury's story to produce a **historical report.**

 Take It to the Net   www.phschool.com

Go online for an additional research activity using the Internet.

Prepare to Read

The Road Not Taken ◆ To be of use ◆ New Directions

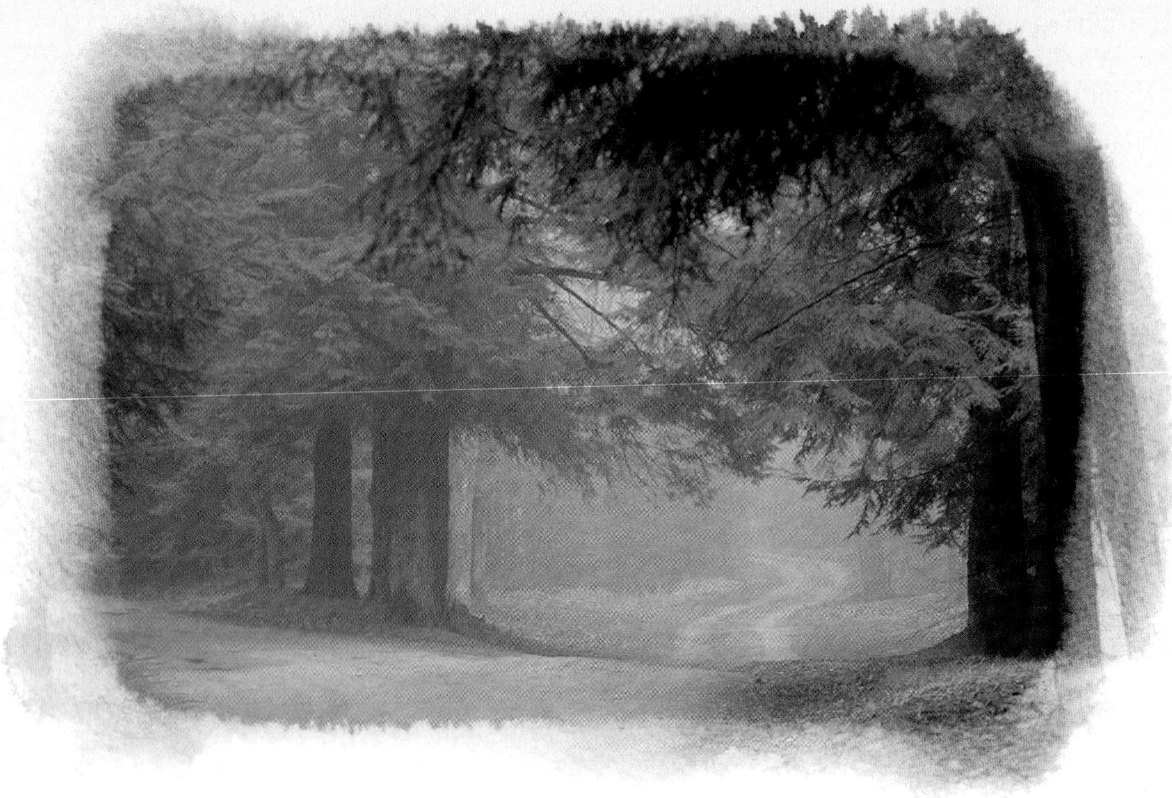

Take It to the Net

Visit www.phschool.com for interactive activities and instruction related to the selections, including

- background
- graphic organizers
- literary elements
- reading strategies

Preview

Connecting to the Literature

You face choices big and small every day. The questions of how to challenge yourself in a new way or which career path to pursue present decisions with major implications. The selections that follow explore these kinds of life choices—critical forks in the road of life.

Background

In the early 1900s, job opportunities were limited for many Americans—particularly for African Americans like Annie Johnson in Maya Angelou's "New Directions." Then, the most common jobs for African American women were cleaning, childcare, and general household labor. For women who had families, caring for someone else's household was an extra burden. No wonder Annie Johnson struck off in a "new direction."

Literary Analysis

Figurative Language

Figurative language, language that means more than it says literally, is often used to create vivid impressions by introducing comparisons between dissimilar things. Look at the following example of figurative language found in Marge Piercy's "To be of use":

> The people I love the best
> jump into work head first,
> without dallying in the shallows.

Piercy is not stating that the people she loves best are deep-sea divers. Rather, she is expressing admiration for people who take on challenges courageously. As you read the selections, take note of vivid language that implies more than its literal meaning.

Comparing Literary Works

While making difficult decisions and working toward a goal, the people you will encounter in these selections have put themselves to the test. In the words of Robert Frost, "that has made all the difference." Compare and contrast the ways each writer uses figurative language to convey larger ideas about decisions and their impact.

CALIFORNIA STANDARDS

Instruction with these selections addresses these standards:

R 1.1*, 2.3*, 3.7*
W 1.3*, 2.2*
WOLC 1.2*
LS 1.9

* Standards tested on HS Exit Exam. For complete standards, see p. CA 4.

Reading Strategy

Generating Questions

To better understand what you read, **generate questions** based on the text. Begin with the common questions words *who, what, where, when, why,* and *how.* Write questions that come to mind as you read a passage, and try to answer those questions as you progress. Use a chart like the one shown to jot down your questions and answers.

Who?	
What?	
When?	
Where?	
Why?	
How?	

Vocabulary Development

diverged (di vʉrjd´) *v.* branched out in different directions (p. 189)

dallying (dal´ ē iŋ) *v.* wasting time; loitering (p. 190)

submerged (səb mʉrjd´) *adj.* covered with something; underwater (p. 190)

harness (här´ nis) *v.* attach, as with straps for pulling or controlling (p. 190)

amicably (am´ i kə blē) *adv.* agreeably (p. 191)

meticulously (mə tik´ yoo ləs lē) *adv.* very carefully and precisely (p. 191)

specters (spek´ tərz) *n.* ghostly images; phantoms (p. 191)

ominous (äm´ ə nəs) *adj.* threatening; menacing (p. 192)

unpalatable (un pal´ it ə bəl) *adj.* distasteful; unpleasant (p. 192)

The Road Not Taken

Robert Frost

Two roads diverged in a yellow wood,
And sorry I could not travel both
And be one traveler, long I stood
And looked down one as far as I could
5   To where it bent in the undergrowth;

Then took the other, as just as fair,
And having perhaps the better claim,
Because it was grassy and wanted wear;
Though as for that, the passing there
10   Had worn them really about the same,

And both that morning equally lay
In leaves no step had trodden black.
Oh, I kept the first for another day!
Yet knowing how way leads on to way,
15   I doubted if I should ever come back.

I shall be telling this with a sigh
Somewhere ages and ages hence:
Two roads diverged in a wood, and I—
I took the one less traveled by,
20   And that has made all the difference.

diverged (di vʉrjd´) v.
branched out in different
directions

Literary Analysis
Figurative Language
What is the figurative
meaning of the two roads
diverging?

Review and Assess

Thinking About the Selection

1. **Respond:** Which of the speaker's feelings or experiences seem most relevant to your own life? Why?

2. **(a) Recall:** What two options does the speaker face?
(b) Recall: Which does he choose? **(c) Classify:** By making this choice, what sort of person does the speaker seem to be?

3. **(a) Recall:** What is the speaker sorry he could not do?
(b) Speculate: Why do you think he was sorry?

4. **(a) Interpret:** According to the fourth stanza, how does the speaker expect he will feel about the decision? **(b) Draw Conclusions:** Why do you think the speaker expects to sigh when recalling this incident in the future?

5. **Evaluate:** Robert Frost once said that a poem "begins as a lump in the throat, a sense of wrong, a homesickness, a loneliness." Would you say that description applies in any way to this poem? Explain.

6. **Apply:** Do you think it is generally a good idea to choose a less-traveled path in life? Explain.

Robert Frost

(1874–1963)
In January 1961, when John F. Kennedy took the helm as president of the United States, he called on fellow New Englander Robert Frost—at the time, America's most famous living poet—to recite two poems at the inauguration. Earlier in his career, Frost was not so well received in his native land. In 1912, unable to earn a living as a poet, he packed up his family and moved to England. After British editions of his poetry volumes *A Boy's Will* (1913) and *North of Boston* (1914) won praise on both sides of the Atlantic, Frost returned to the United States a celebrity.

To be of use

Marge Piercy

The people I love the best
jump into work head first
without <u>dallying</u> in the shallows
and swim off with sure strokes almost out of sight.
5 They seem to become natives of that element,
the black sleek heads of seals
bouncing like half-<u>submerged</u> balls.

I love people who <u>harness</u> themselves, an ox to a heavy cart,
who pull like water buffalo, with massive patience,
10 who strain in the mud and the muck to move things forward,
who do what has to be done, again and again.

I want to be with people who submerge
in the task, who go into the fields to harvest
and work in a row and pass the bags along,
15 who are not parlor generals and field deserters
but move in a common rhythm
when the food must come in or the fire be put out.

The work of the world is common as mud.
Botched, it smears the hands, crumbles to dust.
20 But the thing worth doing well done
has a shape that satisfies, clean and evident.
Greek amphoras[1] for wine or oil,
Hopi[2] vases that held corn, are put in museums
but you know they were made to be used.
25 The pitcher cries for water to carry
and a person for work that is real.

---

1. **amphoras** (am´ fər əz) *n.* tall jars that have a narrow neck and base and two handles, used by the ancient Greeks and Romans.
2. **Hopi** (hō´ pē) *n.* Pueblo tribe of Indians in northeastern Arizona.

Marge Piercy

(b. 1936)

The young Marge Piercy seemed an unlikely future writer. Born into economic hardship in Detroit, Michigan, Piercy was the first person in her family to attend college. It took her more than ten years to win recognition as a writer, during which time six of her novels were rejected for publication. Now even better known as a poet, Piercy's *To be of use* (1973) and many other highly praised verse collections have been published.

New Directions
Maya Angelou

In 1903 the late Mrs. Annie Johnson of Arkansas found herself with two toddling sons, very little money, a slight ability to read and add simple numbers. To this picture add a disastrous marriage and the burdensome fact that Mrs. Johnson was a Negro.

When she told her husband, Mr. William Johnson, of her dissatisfaction with their marriage, he conceded that he too found it to be less than he expected, and had been secretly hoping to leave and study religion. He added that he thought God was calling him not only to preach but to do so in Enid, Oklahoma. He did not tell her that he knew a minister in Enid with whom he could study and who had a friendly, unmarried daughter. They parted <u>amicably</u>, Annie keeping the one-room house and William taking most of the cash to carry himself to Oklahoma.

Annie, over six feet tall, big-boned, decided that she would not go to work as a domestic and leave her "precious babes" to anyone else's care. There was no possibility of being hired at the town's cotton gin or lumber mill, but maybe there was a way to make the two factories work for her. In her words, "I looked up the road I was going and back the way I come, and since I wasn't satisfied, I decided to step off the road and cut me a new path." She told herself that she wasn't a fancy cook but that she could "mix groceries well enough to scare hungry away and from starving a man."

She made her plans <u>meticulously</u> and in secret. One early evening to see if she was ready, she placed stones in two five-gallon pails and carried them three miles to the cotton gin. She rested a little, and then, discarding some rocks, she walked in the darkness to the saw mill five miles farther along the dirt road. On her way back to her little house and her babies, she dumped the remaining rocks along the path.

That same night she worked into the early hours boiling chicken and frying ham. She made dough and filled the rolled-out pastry with meat. At last she went to sleep.

The next morning she left her house carrying the meat pies, lard, an iron brazier,[1] and coals for a fire. Just before lunch she appeared in an empty lot behind the cotton gin. As the dinner noon bell rang, she dropped the savors into boiling fat and the aroma rose and floated over to the workers who spilled out of the gin, covered with white lint, looking like <u>specters</u>.

Most workers had brought their lunches of pinto beans and biscuits or crackers, onions and cans of sardines, but they were

---

1. **iron brazier** (brā′ zhər) pan for holding burning charcoal or coals as a heat source for cooking; a portable barbecue.

Reading Strategy
Generating Questions
What question might you ask about the character of Annie's husband?

amicably (am′ i kə blē) *adv.* agreeably

meticulously (mə tik′ yoo ləs lē) *adv.* very carefully and precisely

specters (spek′ tərz) *n.* ghostly images; phantoms

**Reading Check**

What did Annie's husband do when she told him she was dissatisfied with their marriage?

tempted by the hot meat pies which Annie ladled out of the fat. She wrapped them in newspapers, which soaked up the grease, and offered them for sale at a nickel each. Although business was slow, those first days Annie was determined. She balanced her appearances between the two hours of activity.

So, on Monday if she offered hot fresh pies at the cotton gin and sold the remaining cooled-down pies at the lumber mill for three cents, then on Tuesday she went first to the lumber mill presenting fresh, just-cooked pies as the lumbermen covered in sawdust emerged from the mill.

For the next few years, on balmy spring days, blistering summer noons, and cold, wet, and wintry middays, Annie never disappointed her customers, who could count on seeing the tall, brown-skin woman bent over her brazier, carefully turning the meat pies. When she felt certain that the workers had become dependent on her, she built a stall between the two hives of industry and let the men run to her for their lunchtime provisions.

She had indeed stepped from the road which seemed to have been chosen for her and cut herself a brand-new path. In years that stall became a store where customers could buy cheese, meal, syrup, cookies, candy, writing tablets, pickles, canned goods, fresh fruit, soft drinks, coal, oil, and leather soles for worn-out shoes.

Each of us has the right and the responsibility to assess the roads which lie ahead, and those over which we have traveled, and if the future road looms <u>ominous</u> or unpromising, and the roads back uninviting, then we need to gather our resolve and, carrying only the necessary baggage, step off that road into another direction. If the new choice is also <u>unpalatable</u>, without embarrassment, we must be ready to change that as well.

Review and Assess

Thinking About the Selections

1. **Respond:** Would you rather meet Annie Johnson or the speaker of "To be of use"? Explain.

2. **(a) Recall:** In the first stanza of "To be of use," what kind of people does the speaker say she loves best? **(b) Analyze:** What kinds of qualities or traits do these people possess?

3. **(a) Recall:** Why does Annie Johnson have to find a source of income? **(b) Infer:** Why do you think Annie Johnson chose not to pursue a factory job or a job as a domestic?

4. **(a) Recall:** How does Annie Johnson earn a living? **(b) Draw Conclusions:** What does Johnson's achievement suggest about the human spirit in general?

5. **Apply:** What are the positive consequences of feeling useful?

Maya Angelou

(b. 1928)
Three decades after Frost's appearance at the Kennedy inauguration, President-elect Bill Clinton invited fellow Arkansan Maya Angelou to read one of her poems at his inaugural ceremonies. In both her poetry and her nonfiction, Angelou draws on her own experience, frequently exploring the problems of poverty, racism, and sexism.

Review and Assess

Literary Analysis

Figurative Language

1. Why is the description of life as a road or path an effective use of **figurative language**?

2. Use a chart like this one to record four examples of figurative language from "To be of use." Explain the meaning of each example.

Figurative Language:	1. _____ _____	2. _____ _____	3. _____ _____	4. _____ _____
Meaning:				

Comparing Literary Works

3. (a) Compare Frost's "less traveled" road with the "new path" that Johnson carves for herself. (b) What similar approaches to life do these images convey?

4. (a) Contrast the way Frost's speaker approaches the roads and the way the people in Piercy's opening stanza approach the water. (b) What different approaches to life does the figurative language convey?

Reading Strategy

Generating Questions

5. Using a chart like the one shown, identify at least three of the **questions** and answers you **generated** while reading the selections.

	Who?	What?	When?	Where?	Why?	How?
Question:						
Answer:						

6. Which questions helped you understand the selections best?

Extend Understanding

7. **History Connection:** Annie Johnson's situation shows the struggle that many African American women faced in the early 1900s. How have situations changed for African Americans in the United States over the last century?

Quick Review

Figurative language is language that means more than it says literally. It is often used to create vivid impressions by setting up comparisons between dissimilar things.

To better understand what you read, **generate questions** based on the text. Begin with the common question words *who*, *what*, *where*, *when*, *why*, and *how* about a selection.

 Take It to the Net
www.phschool.com
Take the interactive self-test online to check your understanding of the selections.

Integrate Language Skills

Vocabulary Development Lesson

Word Analysis: Anglo-Saxon Suffix -ly

Words that end in -ly are often adjectives turned into adverbs of manner—adverbs that tell *how* or *in what manner*. Use the suffix -ly to turn the following adjectives into adverbs.

1. amicable (friendly)
2. meticulous (very careful or thorough)
3. ominous (menacing; threatening)

Spelling Strategy

Do not double the letters *w, h, x,* or *y* at the end of a word before adding an ending such as -ing or -ed. For example, *box + -ed = boxed*. Write the new words formed by adding the given suffixes below, and then use each word in a sentence.

1. dismay + -ed
2. catch + -ing
3. flex + -ed
4. flow + -ing

Fluency: True or False

Indicate whether each of the following statements is true or false. Explain your answer.

1. If a stream *diverged*, two parts of it probably moved in different directions.
2. If you and your friend part *amicably*, you are most likely in a bad mood.
3. If you clean your room *meticulously*, it is messy.
4. Some children dress as *specters* on Halloween.
5. A smile is usually an *ominous* expression.
6. Most chefs try to cook *unpalatable* meals.
7. Window shoppers seem to enjoy *dallying*.
8. Flowers are *submerged* in the soil.
9. In Alaska, some people *harness* dogs to a sled.

Grammar Lesson

Regular Verbs

A **verb** has four principal parts: the present, the present participle, the past, and the past participle. Most of the verbs in the English language, such as the verb *talk*, are regular, and you can form these parts following a predictable pattern. Notice that the final *e* may be dropped in forming the present participle.

Present: talk; race
Present Participle: (is) talking; (is) racing
Past: talked; raced
Past Participle: (has) talked; (has) raced

Practice Write the four principal parts of each of the following verbs.

1. look
2. diverge
3. observe
4. harvest
5. work
6. walk
7. jump
8. cook
9. expect
10. cover

Writing Application Write four sentences using each of the principal parts of the regular verb *travel*. After each sentence, identify which part you used.

W̧G Prentice Hall Writing and Grammar Connection: Chapter 23, Section 1

Writing Lesson

Evaluation of Figurative Language

By using figurative language—such as the image of a road in Frost's poem to suggest a life—writers hope to add clarity and color to their writing. Choose one of the selections and write an essay evaluating the writer's use of figurative language.

Prewriting List examples of figurative language that you find in your chosen selection. Identify the basic comparisons that are stated or implied. As you make your list, decide whether the language leaves you confused or if the choice of words is logical. Also, notice whether the comparison is an overused expression or a fresh, new idea.

Model: Evaluating Figurative Language

Figurative Language	Comments	
"[people] who pull like water buffalo, with massive patience"	This is original and makes a clear comparison to people who work diligently and patiently.	The comment evaluates the unique qualities of the poet's use of figurative language.

Drafting State your reaction to the figurative language, and then cite examples to support your reaction. Present the examples in order of importance or in the order in which they appear in the work.

Revising Make sure you have offered enough examples to support all general statements. Check to see that your sentences are logical.

 *Prentice Hall Writing and Grammar Connection: Chapter 13, Section 2*

Extension Activities

Listening and Speaking Working with another student, role-play a **job interview** that might take place between Annie Johnson and a potential employer.

- Analyze the occasion and decide what each speaker needs to say.
- Decide what the potential employer wants to hear.

During the interview, use effective, formal language to convey the character and the situation. When appropriate, use gestures and eye contact to make a point.

Research and Technology Working in a small group, **videotape an interview** with a local businessperson, a teacher, or another professional to learn about the stages of that person's career. After watching the video, compare the aspects of your subject's career to those of Annie Johnson's. **[Group Activity]**

 **Take It to the Net**   www.phschool.com

Go online for an additional research activity using the Internet.

READING INFORMATIONAL MATERIALS

Business Documents

About Business Documents

A business document is a formal piece of writing relating to the work-place. The purpose of a business document is to communicate specific information effectively by presenting facts and other pertinent details.

This chart shows the variety and function of business documents.

Types of Business Documents	
Print	Electronic
Letter: a formal, written message sent by regular mail	**Voice mail:** a spoken message recorded on an answering machine
Agenda: a schedule for a meeting	**E-mail:** a typed message sent by computer
Memo: a brief message with pertinent information for internal company use only	**Fax:** a printed copy of a handwritten or typed message transmitted via phone lines
Meeting minutes: the notes and a summary of a business meeting	
Form/application: a document filled out by an applicant	

A well-written business document meets these criteria:

- It imparts accurate information in a clear, direct, and concise way.
- It addresses specific issues and anticipates readers' questions.
- It is neatly formatted, well organized, and error-free.

Reading Strategy

Analyzing Document Structure and Format

The structure of a business document suits its purpose. Look at the structure and format of these common business documents:

A **business letter** addresses a work-related issue, such as a request for service or a clarification of company policy. The letter has six parts: the heading, inside address, salutation, body, closing, and signature. It is written in paragraph form that follows an acceptable format of indentation.

A **business agenda** outlines the schedule for a meeting. An agenda contains a title identifying the subject, a list of starting and ending times for scheduled events, and descriptions of each part of the agenda.

Letter of Welcome

In the following business letter, California senator Martha Escutia welcomes students to a college conference. Notice that the language of the letter, which uses block format, is welcoming but formal and polite.

The **heading** provides the business address of the senator.

The **salutation** identifies and greets the letter's recipients.

The **body** explains the letter writer's purpose for writing.

The **closing**, written in Spanish, means "It is possible." Typical English closings include "Sincerely" and "Yours truly."

Senator
MARTHA ESCUTIA

California State Senate 30th District

400 N. Montebello Blvd. #101
Montebello, CA 90640

Representing the communities of:

Bell

Bell Gardens

Commerce

Cudahy

East Los Angeles

Florence-Graham

Huntington Park

Maywood

Miramonte

Montebello

Norwalk

Pico Rivera

Santa Fe Springs

South El Monte

South Gate

Vernon

Walnut Park

Whittier

Dear Students:

I want to welcome you to the 8th Annual Southeast College Conference. It is my privilege to host this exciting event and to share the many educational opportunities at your disposal.

You have reached a critical time in your life, a time filled with questions. Where do you want to go in life? How will you get there? Education is definitely the vehicle to your success in any career you choose. Education will help develop you into leaders of the next generation. It will empower you intellectually and enable you to grow into valuable, contributing citizens of your community.

As a young girl I learned the importance of a college education. I armed myself with information that enabled me to pursue my dream. Believe me, my quest for higher education was not easy. I remember the financial and social obstacles my family and community had to overcome. Their sacrifices inspired me to educate myself and give back to my community.

When I was first elected to the Assembly, I was overjoyed. I finally had the opportunity to give back by passing legislation to improve the quality of life in my community. This year, as your Senator, I passed SB 1689, the Advanced Placement Challenge Grant Program. This measure allocated $16.5 million dollars to fund Advanced Placement (AP) classes in schools that lack teachers and support systems for AP students. I also passed SB 1683, which will ensure that every student at risk of not graduating will receive the extra academic help he or she needs. Its focus is to give the students the tools they need to establish a stronger educational foundation.

Please make today an opportunity of a lifetime. Ask questions, participate in the workshops, let your voice be heard and, most importantly, have fun. Today I am very proud to have the opportunity to meet the great minds of the future. I wish you the best of luck and continued success in your future educational endeavors.

SÍ, SE PUEDE

Senator Martha Escutia

Senator Martha Escutia

Conference Agenda

In addition to the business letter welcoming them to the 8th Annual Southeast College Conference, students attending also received this agenda. The agenda outlines activities from 8 A.M. to 2 P.M.

Program Agenda

> The agenda announces the exact times for each part of the program.

8:00 A.M.–9:00 A.M.
Registration/Continental Breakfast

9:00 A.M.–10:00 A.M.
Welcome
Mel Mares
Principal, Bell High School

> Descriptions in boldface letters identify what will happen during each scheduled time period.

Opening Remarks
Senator Martha Escutia

Keynote Speakers
Manny Medrano
Legal Issues Reporter, Channel 4 News

Claudio Trejos
Sports Anchor, KTLA News

10:15 A.M.–11:00 A.M.
Workshop Session I

11:15 A.M.–12:00 P.M.
Workshop Session II

12:00 P.M.–2:00 P.M.
Lunch/College Recruitment Fair

Check Your Comprehension

1. What is Senator Escutia's purpose for writing her business letter?
2. What personal information does the senator share to make her letter friendly to students?
3. According to the agenda, who is delivering the opening remarks?
4. When will Workshop Session I be held?

Applying the Reading Strategy

Analyzing Document Structure and Format

5. What is the relationship between the opening and closing paragraphs of this business letter?
6. What is the purpose of the paragraph in which the author discusses her accomplishments as senator?
7. Why do you think the senator chose to write her closing in Spanish?

Activity

Writing a Letter of Welcome to Parents

Write a business letter in which you welcome parents to a school event such as a parent-teacher conference or talent show. Assume that the letter will be distributed to parents as they enter the building. In your letter, include information that tells when and where the event takes place. Also, explain the purpose of the event. Use friendly but formal language. Keep track of the parts of your business letter by using the chart at right.

> **Outline for Letter of Welcome to Parents**
>
> **Heading:** Your Address
> **Salutation:** "Dear Parents:"
> **Body:**
> • Letter's Purpose (in opening paragraph)
> • Explanation of Event
> • Where and When
> **Polite Closing:**
> **Signature:**

Contrasting Informational Texts

Document Formats

1. For each situation below, indicate the best format to convey information. Choose voice mail, e-mail, fax, business letter, agenda, memo, meeting minutes, or application form. Explain your choice.

   (a) Formally introducing your business to a new client
   (b) Reminding a co-worker about an idea you had and asking for her input
   (c) Supplying the information needed to open a bank account
   (d) Sharing a sketch of your idea with someone in another office
   (e) Recording decisions made at a meeting
   (f) Instructing employees about a complex new policy

Old Man of the Temple

R. K. Narayan

The Talkative Man said:

It was some years ago that this happened. I don't know if you can make anything of it. If you do, I shall be glad to hear what you have to say; but personally I don't understand it at all. It has always mystified me. Perhaps the driver was drunk; perhaps he wasn't.

I had engaged a taxi for going to Kumbum, which, as you may already know, is fifty miles from Malgudi.[1] I went there one morning and it was past nine in the evening when I finished my business and started back for the town. Doss [däs], the driver, was a young fellow of about twenty-five. He had often brought his car for me and I liked him. He was a well-behaved, obedient fellow, with a capacity to sit and wait at the wheel, which is really a rare quality in a taxi driver. He drove the car smoothly, seldom swore at passers-by, and exhibited perfect judgment, good sense, and <u>sobriety</u>; and so I preferred him to any other driver whenever I had to go out on business.

It was about eleven when we passed the village

---

1. Malgudi (mäl gōō´ dē) fictional city about which Narayan often writes.

sobriety (sə brī´ə tē) *n.* moderation, especially in the use of alcoholic beverages

◀ **Critical Viewing** What mysterious events might occur in a temple like this? **[Speculate]**

Koopal [kōō päl′], which is on the way down. It was the dark half of the month and the surrounding country was swallowed up in the night. The village street was deserted. Everyone had gone to sleep; hardly any light was to be seen. The stars overhead sparkled brightly. Sitting in the back seat and listening to the continuous noise of the running wheels, I was half lulled into a drowse.

All of a sudden Doss swerved the car and shouted: "You old fool! Do you want to kill yourself?"

I was shaken out of my drowse and asked: "What is the matter?"

Doss stopped the car and said, "You see that old fellow, sir. He is trying to kill himself. I can't understand what he is up to."

I looked in the direction he pointed and asked, "Which old man?"

"There, there. He is coming towards us again. As soon as I saw him open that temple door and come out I had a feeling, somehow, that I must keep an eye on him."

I took out my torch, got down, and walked about, but could see no one. There was an old temple on the roadside. It was utterly in ruins; most portions of it were mere mounds of old brick; the walls were <u>awry</u>; the doors were shut to the main doorway, and brambles and thickets grew over and covered them. It was difficult to guess with the aid of the torch alone what temple it was and to what period it belonged.

"The doors are shut and sealed and don't look as if they had been opened for centuries now," I cried.

"No, sir," Doss said coming nearer. "I saw the old man open the doors and come out. He is standing there; shall we ask him to open them again if you want to go in and see?"

I said to Doss, "Let us be going. We are wasting our time here."

We went back to the car. Doss sat in his seat, pressed the self-starter, and asked without turning his head, "Are you permitting this fellow to come with us, sir? He says he will get down at the next milestone."

"Which fellow?" I asked.

Doss indicated the space next to him.

"What is the matter with you, Doss? Have you had a drop of drink or something?"

"I have never tasted any drink in my life, sir," he said, and added, "Get down, old boy. Master says he can't take you."

"Are you talking to yourself?"

"After all, I think we needn't care for these unknown fellows on the road," he said.

"Doss," I pleaded. "Do you feel confident you can drive? If you feel dizzy don't drive."

"Thank you, sir," said Doss. "I would rather not start the car now. I am feeling a little out of sorts." I looked at him anxiously. He closed his eyes, his breathing became heavy and noisy, and gradually his head sank.

"Doss, Doss," I cried desperately. I got down, walked to the front seat, opened the door, and shook him vigorously. He opened his eyes, assumed a hunched-up position, and rubbed his eyes with his hands, which trembled like an old man's.

"Do you feel better?" I asked.

"Better! Better! Hi! Hi!" he said in a thin, piping voice.

"What has happened to your voice? You sound like someone else," I said.

"Nothing. My voice is as good as it was. When a man is eighty he is bound to feel a few changes coming on."

"You aren't eighty, surely," I said.

"Not a day less," he said. "Is nobody going to move this vehicle? If not, there is no sense in sitting here all day. I will get down and go back to my temple."

"I don't know how to drive," I said. "And unless you do it, I don't see how it can move."

"Me!" exclaimed Doss. "These new chariots! God knows what they are drawn by, I never understand, though I could handle a pair of bullocks[2] in my time. May I ask a question?"

"Go on," I said.

"Where is everybody?"

"Who?"

"Lots of people I knew are not to be seen at all. All sorts of new fellows everywhere, and nobody seems to care. Not a soul comes near the temple. All sorts of people go about but not one who cares to stop and talk. Why doesn't the king ever come this way? He used to go this way at least once a year before."

"Which king?" I asked.

"Let me go, you idiot," said Doss, edging towards the door on which I was leaning. "You don't seem to know anything." He pushed me aside, and got down from the car. He stooped as if he had a big hump on his back, and hobbled along towards the temple. I followed him, hardly knowing what to do. He turned and snarled at me: "Go away, leave me alone. I have had enough of you."

"What has come over you, Doss?" I asked.

"Who is Doss, anyway? Doss, Doss, Doss. What an absurd name! Call me by my name or leave me alone. Don't follow me calling 'Doss, Doss.' "

"What is your name?" I asked.

"Krishna Battar [krish´ nə bə tar´], and if you mention my name people will know for a hundred miles around. I built a temple where there was only a cactus field before. I dug the earth, burnt every brick, and put them one upon another, all single-handed. And on the day the temple held up its tower over the surrounding country, what a crowd gathered! The king sent his chief minister . . ."

"Who was the king?"

"Where do you come from?" he asked.

"I belong to these parts certainly, but as far as I know there has been only a collector at the head of the district. I have never heard of any king."

---

2. **bullocks** (bŏŏl´ əks) *n.* oxen; steer.

Literature
in context Cultural Connection

Hinduism and Reincarnation

Hinduism is the religion of the majority of people in India, the setting for "Old Man of the Temple." Drawing from a set of beliefs that is thousands of years old, Hinduism teaches that death is a temporary stage in an endless cycle of reincarnations, or rebirths. The actions that someone performs in one life, good and bad, will determine the conditions of future rebirths. Therefore, it is not surprising that Narayan includes aspects of reincarnation in his story.

Reading Strategy
Distinguishing Fantasy From Reality Which clues in this paragraph sound real and which sound fantastic?

Reading Check

How old does Doss say he is when he wakes up?

"Hi! Hi! Hi!" he cackled, and his voice rang through the gloomy silent village. "Fancy never knowing the king! He will behead you if he hears it."

"What is his name?" I asked.

This tickled him so much that he sat down on the ground, <u>literally</u> unable to stand the joke any more. He laughed and coughed uncontrollably.

"I am sorry to admit," I said, "that my parents have brought me up in such utter ignorance of worldly affairs that I don't know even my king. But won't you enlighten me? What is his name?"

"Vishnu Varma [vish′ nōō vär′ mə], the emperor of emperors . . ."

I cast my mind up and down the range of my historical knowledge but there was no one by that name. Perhaps a local chief of pre-British days, I thought.

"What a king! He often visited my temple or sent his minister for the Annual Festival of the temple. But now nobody cares."

"People are becoming less godly nowadays," I said. There was silence for a moment. An idea occurred to me, I can't say why. "Listen to me," I said. "You ought not to be here any more."

"What do you mean?" he asked, drawing himself up, proudly.

"Don't feel hurt; I say you shouldn't be here any more because you are dead."

"Dead! Dead!" he said. "Don't talk nonsense. How can I be dead when you see me before you now? If I am dead how can I be saying this and that?"

"I don't know all that," I said. I argued and pointed out that according to his own story he was more than five hundred years old, and didn't he know that man's <u>longevity</u> was only a hundred? He constantly interrupted me, but considered deeply what I said.

He said: "It is like this . . . I was coming through the jungle one night after visiting my sister in the next village. I had on me some money and gold ornaments. A gang of robbers set upon me. I gave them as good a fight as any man could, but they were too many for me. They beat me down and knifed me; they took away all that I had on me and left thinking they had killed me. But soon I got up and tried to follow them. They were gone. And I returned to the temple and have been here since . . ."

I told him, "Krishna Battar, you are dead, absolutely dead. You must try and go away from here."

"What is to happen to the temple?" he asked.

"Others will look after it."

"Where am I to go? Where am I to go?"

"Have you no one who cares for you?" I asked.

"None except my wife. I loved her very much."

"You can go to her."

"Oh, no. She died four years ago . . ."

Four years! It was very puzzling. "Do you say four years back from now?" I asked.

"Yes, four years ago from now." He was clearly without any sense of time.

Reading Strategy
Distinguishing Fantasy From Reality Does the old man's story sound fantastic or realistic to you? Explain.

◀ **Critical Viewing**
How do the details of this painting compare to the details of the story's setting? **[Support]**

So I asked, "Was she alive when you were attacked by thieves?"

"Certainly not. If she had been alive she would never have allowed me to go through the jungle after nightfall. She took very good care of me."

"See here," I said. "It is <u>imperative</u> you should go away from here. If she comes and calls you, will you go?"

"How can she when I tell you that she is dead?"

I thought for a moment. Presently I found myself saying, "Think of her, and only of her, for a while and see what happens. What was her name?"

"Seetha [sē´ thə], a wonderful girl . . ."

"Come on, think of her." He remained in deep thought for a while. He suddenly screamed, "Seetha is coming! Am I dreaming or what? I will go with her . . ." He stood up, very erect; he appeared to have lost all the humps and twists he had on his body. He drew himself up, made a dash forward, and fell down in a heap.

imperative (im per´ ə tiv) *adj.* absolutely necessary; urgent

✔**Reading Check**

According to the old man, how many years ago did his wife die?

Doss lay on the rough ground. The only sign of life in him was his faint breathing. I shook him and called him. He would not open his eyes. I walked across and knocked on the door of the first cottage. I banged on the door violently.

Someone moaned inside, "Ah, it is come!"

Someone else whispered, "You just cover your ears and sleep. It will knock for a while and go away." I banged on the door and shouted who I was and where I came from.

I walked back to the car and sounded the horn. Then the door opened, and a whole family crowded out with lamps. "We thought it was the usual knocking and we wouldn't have opened if you hadn't spoken."

"When was this knocking first heard?" I asked.

"We can't say," said one. "The first time I heard it was when my grandfather was living; he used to say he had even seen it once or twice. It doesn't harm anyone, as far as I know. The only thing it does is bother the bullock carts passing the temple and knock on the doors at night . . ."

I said as a venture, "It is unlikely you will be troubled any more."

It proved correct. When I passed that way again months later I was told that the bullocks passing the temple after dusk never shied now and no knocking on the doors was heard at nights. So I felt that the old fellow had really gone away with his good wife.

venture (ven´ chər) *n.* chance

R. K. Narayan

(1906-2001)

Within a career that spanned more than sixty years, R. K. Narayan wrote more than fifteen novels, as well as numerous collections of short stories, travel books, and essays. Born in the city of Madras in southern India, he was one of nine children of a middle-class family. He attended Maharaja's College in Mysore, and after briefly working as a teacher, he became a writer.

In his novels, legends, and short stories, Narayan skillfully combines Western plots and themes with Indian subject matter. In 1958, he won the National Prize of the Indian Literary Academy, his nation's highest literary honor.

Review and Assess

Thinking About the Selection

1. **Respond:** The narrator tells you, "I don't know if you can make anything of it. If you do, I shall be glad to hear what you have to say. . . ." How would you answer him?

2. **(a) Recall:** Early in the story, what does Doss say he sees when he swerves the car? **(b) Analyze:** Why does the narrator find Doss's words unbelievable?

3. **(a) Recall:** Describe the transformation that happens to Doss. **(b) Analyze:** How does the narrator react to the change?

4. **(a) Recall:** What does the narrator say to cause the old man to think about his own situation? **(b) Infer:** Do you think the narrator is ruled more by his feelings or by reason? Why?

5. **Connect:** What purpose does the introduction of the family serve?

6. **Assess:** How might you respond if you found yourself in the narrator's situation?

Review and Assess

Literary Analysis

Fantasy

1. Why is "Old Man of the Temple" a **fantasy**?
2. How do the fantastic elements add to the story?
3. Using a chart like the one below, show how the realistic elements found in the story contribute to an atmosphere in which fantasy can develop.

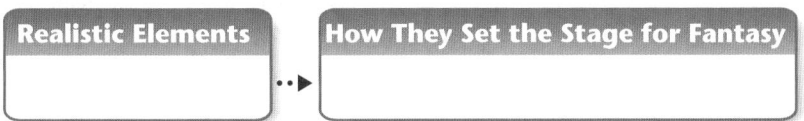

Connecting Literary Elements

4. Use a chart like the one below to help you answer the following questions. (a) How does the **setting** contribute to the fantasy in the story? (b) How does the setting contribute to the reality in the story?

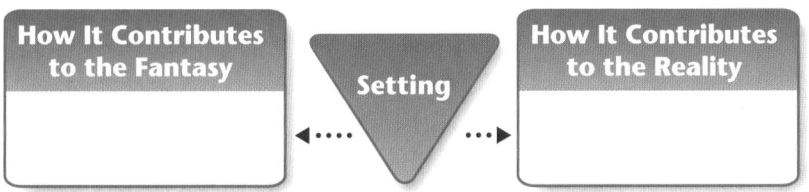

5. How might this story be different if it were set in a modern American city?

Reading Strategy

Distinguishing Fantasy From Reality

6. Name two elements of the story that are fantastic.
7. At what point in the story does the plot change from realistic to fantastic? Explain.
8. During which scenes in the story is it difficult to **distinguish fantasy from reality**? Explain.

Extend Understanding

9. **Media Connection:** Compare this story with fantasy movies. (a) Which elements are similar? (b) Which are different?

Quick Review

Fantasy is fiction that includes characters, places, and events that could not exist or happen in real life.

The **setting** of a story is the time and place in which the action occurs.

To **distinguish fantasy from reality,** determine which elements of a story could or could not happen in real life.

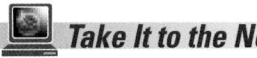 **Take It to the Net**

www.phschool.com

Take the interactive self-test online to check your understanding of the selection.

Integrate Language Skills

Vocabulary Development Lesson

Word Analysis: Latin Suffix -ity

In the word *longevity*, you find the suffix *-ity*, meaning "state of" or "condition of." One way to define *longevity* is "the condition of having a long life." Using the meaning of *-ity*, write definitions for the following words:

1. agility
2. severity
3. generosity
4. individuality

Spelling Strategy

When spelling a word that contains the *j* sound before an *e*, you usually use a *g*, as in *longevity*. There are exceptions, however, such as *subject*. For each word below, write "Correct" if the word is spelled correctly. If the spelling is incorrect, write the proper spelling.

1. suggest   2. injection   3. magesty

Concept Development: Synonyms

In each numbered item, choose the word whose meaning is closest to that of the word from the vocabulary list on page 201.

1. sobriety: (a) sadness, (b) loneliness, (c) moderation
2. awry: (a) sophisticated, (b) crooked, (c) clever
3. literally: (a) actually, (b) scholarly, (c) differently
4. longevity: (a) height, (b) endurance, (c) duration
5. imperative: (a) essential, (b) unnecessary, (c) ruler
6. venture: (a) satisfaction, (b) risk, (c) university

Grammar Lesson

Adverbs

Adverbs are words that modify verbs, adjectives, and other adverbs. They answer the questions *Where? When? In what way?* and *To what extent?* about the words they modify. You can often make descriptions more meaningful by adding an adverb to a sentence. Look at the following examples:

Modifying a Verb: Doss <u>drove</u> the car *smoothly*. (*smoothly* modifies the verb *drove*)

Modifying an Adjective: He drove an *extremely* <u>large</u> car. (*extremely* modifies the adjective *large*)

Modifying an Adverb: He drove the car *very* <u>smoothly</u>. (*very* modifies the adverb *smoothly*)

Practice Copy each sentence. Underline the word or words modified by the adverb in italics. Then, identify whether the word modified is a verb, an adjective, or an adverb.

1. He *certainly* believed that he was right.
2. His wife took *very* good care of him.
3. Doss told him that he was *absolutely* dead.
4. He laughed *uncontrollably* at the news.
5. He needed to go *away* from there.

Writing Application Use each of the following adverbs in a sentence. At the end of the sentence, write which word each one modifies.

1. completely   2. entirely   3. quietly

W͠G Prentice Hall Writing and Grammar Connection: Chapter 18, Section 2

Writing Lesson

Travel Brochure

India, where "Old Man of the Temple" takes place, is a land of ancient cultures, colorful ceremonies, and joyous celebrations—an excellent visitor destination. Using the setting of the story and additional information about India, write a travel brochure that will entice travelers to visit.

Prewriting   Decide on the features you will describe in your brochure. Review the selection and research India to gather appealing details.

Drafting   Many qualities can make the tone of your brochure persuasive. For instance, vivid descriptions will appeal to readers' imaginations and dreams, and a sense of humor will spark a receptive attitude.

Model: Using a Persuasive Tone

From mysterious and historical temple ruins to breathtaking views of snow-peaked mountains soaring to incredible heights, you can experience the splendor of a culture rich in beauty and tradition.

> Words like *breathtaking* and *soaring* convey the splendor of India and appeal to a tourist's desire for an unforgettable experience.

Revising   Reread your draft. Make sure that your readers will be persuaded to visit. Add information that can make your tone more persuasive and your travel brochure more appealing.

 Prentice Hall Writing and Grammar Connection: Chapter 7, Section 3

Extension Activities

Listening and Speaking Prepare a **dramatic monologue** in which the old man relates the story from his point of view. Follow these suggestions as you write your monologue:

- Use appropriate word choice—select words that the old man would use.
- Describe experiences found in the story.
- Enhance your performance by adding new information about the old man that you did not learn in the story.

Perform your monologue for the class.

Research and Technology Southern India, where this story takes place, is overwhelmingly Hindu. In a group, do a **research report** on Hinduism and explain how Hinduism enriches your understanding of this story. Use library resources, including the Internet, to find information to strengthen your report. **[Group Activity]**

 Take It to the Net   www.phschool.com

Go online for an additional research activity using the Internet.

Prepare to Read

Perseus

Danaë with young Perseus arriving on the island of Seripo,
Museo Archeologico, Ferrara, Italy

Take It to the Net

Visit www.phschool.com
for interactive activities
and instruction related to
"Perseus," including

- background
- graphic organizers
- literary elements
- reading strategies

Preview

Connecting to the Literature

Some people love to rise to the challenge of difficult situations, while others prefer to keep their lives on an even keel. Perseus, the main character in this selection, is the first sort of person—the type who thrives on grappling with thorny problems. Before reading, consider which type of person you relate to more.

Background

"Perseus" takes place in a mythological world populated by Greek gods and goddesses. Among them are Zeus, the chief god, who fathered a number of human children; Athena, goddess of war and wisdom; and Hermes, the messenger god. Each god plays a pivotal role in Perseus' heroic adventure.

Literary Analysis
Hero in a Myth

A **hero in a myth** is a character who performs amazing feats in a tale involving supernatural beings and fantastic events. The hero in a myth is often aided by sympathetic gods and magical elements. Nevertheless, the hero must exhibit admirable qualities such as courage, loyalty, and fairness. The following excerpt shows the loyalty and courage of Perseus, the hero in this myth.

> [Perseus] did exactly what the King had hoped he would do, declared that he would . . . go off and kill Medusa and bring back her head as his gift. . . . No one in his senses would have made such a proposal.

As you read, think about how Perseus' positive traits make him worthy of the supernatural help he gets.

Connecting Literary Elements

An **antagonist** is a character or force in conflict with the main character or hero in a story. In this story, Perseus is faced with conflicts between two antagonists, his grandfather Acrisius and the king Polydectes. As you read, take note of the actions and choices of these antagonists, which create great struggles and challenges for the hero, Perseus.

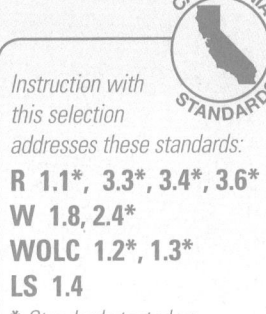

CALIFORNIA STANDARDS

Instruction with this selection addresses these standards:

R 1.1*, 3.3*, 3.4*, 3.6*
W 1.8, 2.4*
WOLC 1.2*, 1.3*
LS 1.4

* Standards tested on HS Exit Exam. For complete standards, see p. CA 4.

Reading Strategy
Predicting

When you read, you can **predict** outcomes by thinking about the world presented in the literature and about the logical consequences of the characters' actions. Use these strategies to help you predict outcomes in "Perseus":

- Look for details and facts to suggest what may occur later.
- Decide what would be the likely outcome of an event.

Use a chart like the one shown here to note your predictions.

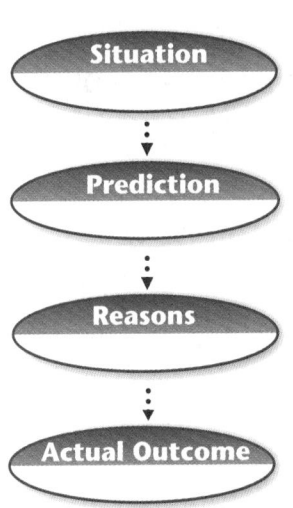

Vocabulary Development

kindred (kin´ drid) *n.* relatives (p. 215)

mortified (môrt´ ə fīd´) *adj.* embarrassed (p. 216)

despair (di sper´) *n.* hopelessness (p. 217)

wavering (wā´ vər iŋ) *adj.* flickering (p. 219)

revelry (rev´ əl rē) *n.* party (p. 219)

deity (dē´ ə tē) *n.* a god (p. 220)

reconciled (rek´ ən sīld´) *adj.* became friends again (p. 222)

Perseus

Edith Hamilton

Andromeda Liberated, Pierre Mignard. Louvre, Paris, France

▲ **Critical Viewing** The man with the sword is Perseus as an adult. Judging from this painting, how do you think others perceive him? Cite details in the art to support your answer. **[Draw Conclusions]**

King Acrisius [a kris′ ē əs] of Argos had only one child, a daughter, Danaë [dan′ ā ē]. She was beautiful above all the other women of the land, but this was small comfort to the King for not having a son. He journeyed to Delphi to ask the god if there was any hope that some day he would be the father of a boy. The priestess told him no, and added what was far worse: that his daughter would have a son who would kill him.

The only sure way to escape that fate was for the King to have Danaë instantly put to death—taking no chances, but seeing to it himself. This Acrisius would not do. His fatherly affection was not strong, as events proved, but his fear of the gods was. They visited with terrible punishment those who shed the blood of <u>kindred</u>. Acrisius did not dare slay his daughter. Instead, he had a house built all of bronze and sunk underground, but with part of the roof open to the sky so that light and air could come through. Here he shut her up and guarded her.

> So Danaë endured, the beautiful,
> To change the glad daylight for brass-bound walls,
> And in that chamber secret as the grave
> She lived a prisoner. Yet to her came
> Zeus in the golden rain.

As she sat there through the long days and hours with nothing to do, nothing to see except the clouds moving by overhead, a mysterious thing happened, a shower of gold fell from the sky and filled her chamber. How it was revealed to her that it was Zeus who had visited her in this shape we are not told, but she knew that the child she bore was his son.

For a time she kept his birth secret from her father, but it became increasingly difficult to do so in the narrow limits of that bronze house and finally one day the little boy—his name was Perseus—was discovered by his grandfather. "Your child!" Acrisius cried in great anger. "Who is his father?" But when Danaë answered proudly, "Zeus," he would not believe her. One thing only he was sure of, that the boy's life was a terrible danger to his own. He was afraid to kill him for the same reason that had kept him from killing her, fear of Zeus and the Furies who pursue such murderers. But if he could not kill them outright, he could put them in the way of tolerably certain death. He had a great chest made, and the two placed in it. Then it was taken out to sea and cast into the water.

In that strange boat Danaë sat with her little son. The daylight faded and she was alone on the sea.

> When in the carven chest the winds and waves
> Struck fear into her heart she put her arms,
> Not without tears, round Perseus tenderly
> She said, "O son, what grief is mine.
> But you sleep softly, little child,
> Sunk deep in rest within your cheerless home,
> Only a box, brass-bound. The night, this darkness visible,
> The scudding waves so near to your soft curls,
> The shrill voice of the wind, you do not heed,
> Nestled in your red cloak, fair little face."

Through the night in the tossing chest she listened to the waters that seemed always about to wash over them. The dawn came, but with no comfort to her for she could not see it. Neither could she see

Reading Strategy

Predicting What do you think will happen to Danaë and Perseus after they are sent off in the chest?

✔ **Reading Check**

What was Acrisius told would happen to him when his daughter had a son?

that around them there were islands rising high above the sea, many islands. All she knew was that presently a wave seemed to lift them and carry them swiftly on and then, retreating, leave them on something solid and motionless. They had made land; they were safe from the sea, but they were still in the chest with no way to get out.

Fate willed it—or perhaps Zeus, who up to now had done little for his love and his child—that they should be discovered by a good man, a fisherman named Dictys. He came upon the great box and broke it open and took the pitiful cargo home to his wife who was as kind as he. They had no children and they cared for Danaë and Perseus as if they were their own. The two lived there many years, Danaë content to let her son follow the fisherman's humble trade, out of harm's way. But in the end more trouble came. Polydectes [pol i dek´ tēz], the ruler of the little island, was the brother of Dictys, but he was a cruel and ruthless man. He seems to have taken no notice of the mother and son for a long time, but at last Danaë attracted his attention. She was still radiantly beautiful even though Perseus by now was full grown, and Polydectes fell in love with her. He wanted her, but he did not want her son, and he set himself to think out a way of getting rid of him.

There were some fearsome monsters called Gorgons who lived on an island and were known far and wide because of their deadly power. Polydectes evidently talked to Perseus about them; he probably told him that he would rather have the head of one of them than anything else in the world. This seems practically certain from the plan he devised for killing Perseus. He announced that he was about to be married and he called his friends together for a celebration, including Perseus in the invitation. Each guest, as was customary, brought a gift for the bride-to-be, except Perseus alone. He had nothing he could give. He was young and proud and keenly <u>mortified</u>. He stood up before them all and did exactly what the King had hoped he would do, declared that he would give him a present better than any there. He would go off and kill Medusa and bring back her head as his gift. Nothing could have suited the King better. No one in his senses would have made such a proposal. Medusa was one of the Gorgons,

> And they are three, the Gorgons, each with wings
> And snaky hair, most horrible to mortals.
> Whom no man shall behold and draw again
> The breath of life,

for the reason that whoever looked at them were turned instantly into stone. It seemed that Perseus had been led by his angry pride into making an empty boast. No man unaided could kill Medusa.

But Perseus was saved from his folly. Two great gods were watching over him. He took ship as soon as he left the King's hall, not daring to see his mother first and tell her what he intended, and he sailed to Greece to learn where the three monsters were to be found. He went to Delphi, but all the priestess would say was to bid him

216 ◆ *Challenges and Choices*

Reading Strategy
Predicting Do you think Danaë and Perseus will survive? Why?

mortified (môrt´ ə fid´) *adj.* embarrassed

Literary Analysis
Hero in a Myth What is heroic about Perseus' offer to the King?

Danaë with young Perseus arriving on the island of Seripo,
Museo Archeologico, Ferrara, Italy

▲ **Critical Viewing**
Which scene in the story
does this art illustrate?
[Assess]

seek the land where men eat not Demeter's golden grain, but only
acorns. So he went to Dodona, in the land of oak trees, where the
talking oaks were which declared Zeus's will and where the Selli lived
who made their bread from acorns. They could tell him, however, no
more than this, that he was under the protection of the gods. They
did not know where the Gorgons lived.

When and how Hermes and Athena came to his help is not told in
any story, but he must have known <u>despair</u> before they did so. At last,
however, as he wandered on, he met a strange and beautiful person.
We know what he looked like from many a poem, a young man with
the first down upon his cheek when youth is loveliest, carrying, as no
other young man ever did, a wand of gold with wings at one end,
wearing a winged hat, too, and winged sandals. At sight of him hope
must have entered Perseus' heart, for he would know that this could
be none other than Hermes, the guide and the giver of good.

This radiant personage told him that before he attacked Medusa he
must first be properly equipped, and that what he needed was in the
possession of the nymphs of the North. To find the nymphs' abode,
they must go to the Gray Women who alone could tell them the way.
These women dwelt in a land where all was dim and shrouded in twilight. No ray of sun looked ever on that country, nor the moon by

despair (di sper´) *n.*
hopelessness

✔**Reading Check**

Who is Hermes?

Perseus ◆ 217

night. In that gray place the three women lived, all gray themselves and withered as in extreme old age. They were strange creatures, indeed, most of all because they had but one eye for the three, which it was their custom to take turns with, each removing it from her forehead when she had had it for a time and handing it to another.

All this Hermes told Perseus and then he unfolded his plan. He would himself guide Perseus to them. Once there Perseus must keep hidden until he saw one of them take the eye out of her forehead to pass it on. At that moment, when none of the three could see, he must rush forward and seize the eye and refuse to give it back until they told him how to reach the nymphs of the North.

He himself, Hermes said, would give him a sword to attack Medusa with—which could not be bent or broken by the Gorgon's scales, no matter how hard they were. This was a wonderful gift, no doubt, and yet of what use was a sword when the creature to be struck by it could turn the swordsman into stone before he was within striking distance? But another great deity was at hand to help. Pallas Athena stood beside Perseus. She took off the shield of polished bronze which covered her breast and
held it out to him.
"Look into this
when you
attack the
Gorgon,"

▼ **Critical Viewing**
Who is portrayed in this art? How do you know? **[Connect]**

she said. "You will be able to see her in it as in a mirror, and so avoid her deadly power."

Now, indeed, Perseus had good reason to hope. The journey to the twilight land was long, over the stream of Ocean and on to the very border of the black country where the Cimmerians dwell, but Hermes was his guide and he could not go astray. They found the Gray Women at last, looking in the <u>wavering</u> light like gray birds, for they had the shape of swans. But their heads were human and beneath their wings they had arms and hands. Perseus did just as Hermes had said, he held back until he saw one of them take the eye out of her forehead. Then before she could give it to her sister, he snatched it out of her hand. It was a moment or two before the three realized they had lost it. Each thought one of the others had it. But Perseus spoke out and told them he had taken it and that it would be theirs again only when they showed him how to find the nymphs of the North. They gave him full directions at once; they would have done anything to get their eye back. He returned it to them and went on the way they had pointed out to him. He was bound, although he did not know it, to the blessed country of the Hyperboreans [hī per bō´ rē anz], at the back of the North Wind, of which it is said: "Neither by ship nor yet by land shall one find the wondrous road to the gathering place of the Hyperboreans." But Perseus had Hermes with him, so that the road lay open to him, and he reached that host of happy people who are always banqueting and holding joyful <u>revelry</u>. They showed him great kindness: they welcomed him to their feast, and the maidens dancing to the sound of flute and lyre paused to get for him the gifts he sought. These were three: winged sandals, a magic wallet which would always become the right size for whatever was to be carried in it, and, most important of all, a cap which made the wearer invisible. With these and Athena's shield and Hermes' sword Perseus was ready for the Gorgons. Hermes knew where they lived, and leaving the happy land the two flew back across Ocean and over the sea to the Terrible Sisters' island.

By great good fortune they were all asleep when Perseus found them. In the mirror of the bright shield he could see them clearly, creatures with great wings and bodies covered with golden scales and hair a mass of twisting snakes. Athena was beside him now as well as Hermes. They told him which one was Medusa and that was important, for she alone of the three could be killed; the other two were immortal. Perseus on his winged sandals hovered above them, looking, however, only at the shield. Then he aimed a stroke down at Medusa's throat and Athena guided his hand. With a single sweep of his sword he cut through her neck and, his eyes still fixed on the shield with never a glance at her, he swooped low enough to seize the head. He dropped it into the wallet which closed around it. He had nothing to fear from it now. But the two other Gorgons had awakened and, horrified at the sight of their sister slain, tried to pursue the slayer. Perseus was safe; he had on the cap of darkness and they could not find him.

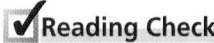

So over the sea rich-haired Danaë's son,
Perseus, on his winged sandals sped,
Flying swift as thought.
In a wallet of silver,
A wonder to behold,
He bore the head of the monster,
While Hermes, the son of Maia,
The messenger of Zeus,
Kept ever at his side.

On his way back he came to Ethiopia and alighted there. By this time Hermes had left him. Perseus found, as Hercules was later to find, that a lovely maiden had been given up to be devoured by a horrible sea serpent. Her name was Andromeda and she was the daughter of a silly vain woman,

That starred Ethiop queen who strove
To set her beauty's praise above
The sea-nymphs, and their power offended.

She had boasted that she was more beautiful than the daughters of Nereus, the Sea-god. An absolutely certain way in those days to draw down on one a wretched fate was to claim superiority in anything over any deity; nevertheless people were perpetually doing so. In this case the punishment for the arrogance the gods detested fell not on Queen Cassiopeia [kas´ ē ō pē´ ə], Andromeda's mother, but on her daughter. The Ethiopians were being devoured in numbers by the serpent; and, learning from the oracle that they could be freed from the pest only if Andromeda were offered up to it, they forced Cepheus [sē fəs], her father, to consent. When Perseus arrived the maiden was on a rocky ledge by the sea, chained there to wait for the coming of the monster. Perseus saw her and on the instant loved her. He waited beside her until the great snake came for its prey; then he cut its head off just as he had the Gorgon's. The headless body dropped back into the water; Perseus took Andromeda to her parents and asked for her hand, which they gladly gave him.

With her he sailed back to the island and his mother, but in the house where he had lived so long he found no one. The fisherman Dictys' wife was long since dead, and the two others, Danaë and the man who had been like a father to Perseus, had had to fly and hide themselves from Polydectes, who was furious at Danaë's refusal to marry him. They had taken refuge in a temple, Perseus was told. He learned also that the King was holding a banquet in the palace and all the men who favored him were gathered there. Perseus instantly saw his opportunity. He went straight to the palace and entered the hall. As he stood at the entrance, Athena's shining buckler on his breast, the silver wallet at his side, he drew the eyes of every man there. Then before any could look away he held up the Gorgon's head; and at the sight one and all, the cruel King and his servile courtiers, were turned into stone. There they sat, a row of statues,

Reading Strategy
Predicting What part do you think Andromeda will play in Perseus' journey? Why?

deity (dē´ ə tē) *n.* a god

Literary Analysis
Hero in a Myth What new challenge does Perseus face?

◀ **Critical Viewing**
Which heroic qualities
does this image illustrate?
[Support]

✔ **Reading Check**

What does Perseus learn
has happened to Dictys
and Danaë?

each, as it were, frozen stiff in the attitude he had struck when he
first saw Perseus.

When the islanders knew themselves freed from the tyrant it was easy
for Perseus to find Danaë and Dictys. He made Dictys king of the island,
but he and his mother decided that they would go back with Andromeda

to Greece and try to be <u>reconciled</u> to Acrisius, to see if the many years that had passed since he had put them in the chest had not softened him so that he would be glad to receive his daughter and grandson. When they reached Argos, however, they found that Acrisius had been driven away from the city, and where he was no one could say. It happened that soon after their arrival Perseus heard that the King of Larissa, in the North, was holding a great athletic contest, and he journeyed there to take part. In the discus-throwing when his turn came and he hurled the heavy missile, it swerved and fell among the spectators. Acrisius was there on a visit to the King, and the discus struck him. The blow was fatal and he died at once.

So Apollo's oracle was again proved true. If Perseus felt any grief, at least he knew that his grandfather had done his best to kill him and his mother. With his death their troubles came to an end. Perseus and Andromeda lived happily ever after. Their son, Electryon, was the grandfather of Hercules.

Medusa's head was given to Athena, who bore it always upon the aegis, Zeus's shield, which she carried for him.

reconciled (rek´ ən sīld´) *adj.* became friends again

Review and Assess

Thinking About the Selection

1. **Respond:** Which of Perseus' adventures would make the best action-adventure movie? Why?

2. **(a) Recall:** What prediction does the priestess make to Acrisius? **(b) Connect:** What two actions does Acrisius take to prevent the prediction from coming true? **(c) Infer:** What is revealed about Acrisius' character through the actions he takes to escape fate?

3. **(a) Recall:** Why does Perseus set out to kill Medusa? **(b) Connect:** What help does he receive from Hermes and Athena? **(c) Infer:** What detail of Perseus' background might have led Athena and Hermes to help Perseus in his quest?

4. **(a) Recall:** How does Perseus manage to kill Medusa? **(b) Hypothesize:** What might have happened to Perseus if he had not received help from the gods?

5. **Make a Judgment:** Considering the actions he takes against Danaë and Perseus, does Acrisius deserve his fate? Why or why not?

6. **Draw Conclusions:** What does this myth suggest about one's ability to escape or control fate? Explain.

7. **Extend:** This myth from ancient Greece is thousands of years old. **(a)** What lessson do you think it taught its first audiences? **(b)** In what ways is it still relevant today?

Edith Hamilton

(1867–1963)

Edith Hamilton's long journey on Earth began soon after the Civil War and ended in the Space Age. Her heart took an even longer journey—back to the worlds of ancient Greece and Rome—to find messages that modern people could apply to their lives.

Hamilton started as a groundbreaking educator who helped found the Bryn Mawr School in Baltimore, the first college preparatory school for women. She taught a generation of young women the lesson she had learned: not to limit their goals simply because they were not men.

After leaving Bryn Mawr, Hamilton began writing articles about ancient Greece, which she later turned into a book entitled *The Greek Way*, published in 1930. Her other books include *The Roman Way* (1932), *The Prophets of Israel* (1936), and *Mythology* (1942).

Review and Assess

Literary Analysis

Hero in a Myth

1. Perseus accepts the help of Hermes and Athena in his pursuit of Medusa, but which **heroic qualities** of his own does he draw upon to accomplish his goals?
2. Which heroic quality does Perseus exhibit when he decides to return to Argos to see Acrisius?
3. Which of Danaë's qualities might Perseus have inherited from her? Use the following chart to analyze the connection between mother and son. In each case, provide an example of each quality you identify.

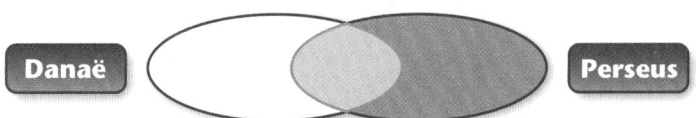

Connecting Literary Elements

4. In what ways are Acrisius and Polydectes **antagonists** of Perseus? In a chart like the following, trace their actions, the difficulties they create for Perseus, and the ways he overcomes these challenges.

Antagonist	Actions	Effect on Perseus	End Result

5. How do the actions of the two antagonists make Perseus an even stronger hero?

Reading Strategy

Predicting

6. What evidence in the story made it possible to **predict** that Perseus would be successful in killing Medusa?
7. (a) Why is Acrisius' death a logical outcome? (b) What aspects of his death could not have been predicted?

Extend Understanding

8. **Literature Connection:** (a) What situations from other works of literature, movies, or real life can you recall in which someone tried to escape or control fate? (b) What were the outcomes?

Quick Review

A **hero in a myth** is a character who performs amazing feats in a tale involving supernatural beings and fantastic events.

An **antagonist** is a character or force in conflict with the hero.

To **predict** story events, look for details and facts to suggest what may occur later.

 Take It to the Net

www.phschool.com

Take the interactive self-test online to check your understanding of the selections.

Integrate Language Skills

Vocabulary Development Lesson

Word Analysis: Latin Root -mort-

The word *mortified*, meaning "deeply humiliated," is based on the Latin root -mort-, meaning "death." Use the meaning of -mort- to help you define the following words.

1. immortality
2. mortician
3. mortally
4. immortalize

Spelling Strategy

When you add an ending that begins with a vowel to a word of more than one syllable that ends in a consonant preceded by a vowel, you normally do not double the final consonant. Thus, *cancel + -ed = canceled*. However, if the word's stress is on the final syllable, you usually double the consonant. Thus, *compel + -ing = compelling*. Add the ending shown to each of the words below.

1. wither + -ing 2. transmit + -ed 3. refer + -ed

Concept Development: Synonyms

On your paper, write the word or phrase whose meaning is closest to that of the first word. If necessary, review the vocabulary word list on page 213.

1. deity: (a) goodness, (b) god, (c) generosity
2. mortified: (a) cleansed, (b) stiff, (c) humiliated
3. revelry: (a) grand party, (b) rude awakening, (c) loud disagreement
4. despair: (a) hopelessness, (b) ruin, (c) sacrifice
5. reconciled: (a) guessed again, (b) became friends again, (c) forgot again
6. wavering: (a) greeting, (b) stumbling, (c) flickering
7. kindred: (a) relatives, (b) childhood, (c) hostility

Grammar Lesson

Active and Passive Voice

A verb in the **active voice** expresses an action done *by* its subject. A verb in the **passive voice** expresses an action done *to* its subject.

> **Active voice:** Edith Hamilton *wrote* "Perseus." [The subject, *Edith Hamilton*, performs the action of the verb *wrote*.]
>
> **Passive voice:** "Perseus" *was written* by Edith Hamilton. [The subject, "*Perseus*," receives the action of the verb *was written*.]

Sentences written in the active voice are often less wordy and more direct than those written in the passive voice. Therefore, use the active voice to create more forceful and lively writing.

Practice Copy the following sentences and underline the verb or verbs in each one. Determine whether the underlined verbs are in the active or passive voice.

1. Danaë was imprisoned by Acrisius.
2. They were placed in a chest in the sea.
3. Dictys found them on the beach.
4. In his search for Medusa, Perseus was helped by Hermes and Athena.
5. Perseus rescued Andromeda.

Writing Application Write four sentences about Perseus' heroic actions, two in the active voice and two in the passive voice.

W̸G Prentice Hall Writing and Grammar Connection: Chapter 23, Section 2

Writing Lesson

Speech of Introduction

Imagine that you have to deliver a speech introducing Perseus at a large public gathering. Your speech should tell your audience something of Perseus' background and should go on to describe and praise his deeds before finally introducing him.

Prewriting   Start by listing the important facts of Perseus' life. Then, highlight the events that will appeal to the audience in various ways—by touching people's emotions or by amusing them, for example.

Model: Listing Details That Appeal to Your Audience

1. Dictys found Perseus and his mother in a chest.
2. Perseus told Polydectes he would bring back Medusa's head.
3. He did not tell his mother, and he sailed off to Greece.
4. Perseus received help from Athena and Hermes.

> The highlighted information accents Perseus' heroic qualities—qualities audiences should find compelling.

Drafting   Organize your information in time order, or group the details into categories by focusing on each of Perseus' character traits. Then, cite details from his life that relate to each trait.

Revising   Reread your draft and make sure you have chosen the most appealing material from Perseus' story to help win over your audience.

Prentice Hall Writing and Grammar Connection: Chapter 7, Section 2

Extension Activities

Listening and Speaking Imagine that Acrisius escapes death and is brought to trial for his treatment of Danaë and Perseus. As a prosecuting attorney, present an **opening argument** to a jury of your classmates, accusing the king of intent to commit murder. Follow these tips to help you:

- Explain how Acrisius put Danaë and Perseus in a life-threatening situation.
- Point out Acrisius' motive—the reason he wanted to kill them.

Present your opening argument to the class.

Research and Technology In a group, prepare an **illustrated map** showing Perseus' travels from the time of his birth until the end of the story. Refer back to the story and list the places he goes to in his travels. Then, create your map. Illustrate the map with pictures of the various gods and monsters he meets. Use graphics software to design the map. **[Group Activity]**

 Take It to the Net   www.phschool.com

Go online for an additional research activity using the Internet.

Prepare to Read

Slam, Dunk, & Hook ◆ The Spearthrower ◆ Shoulders

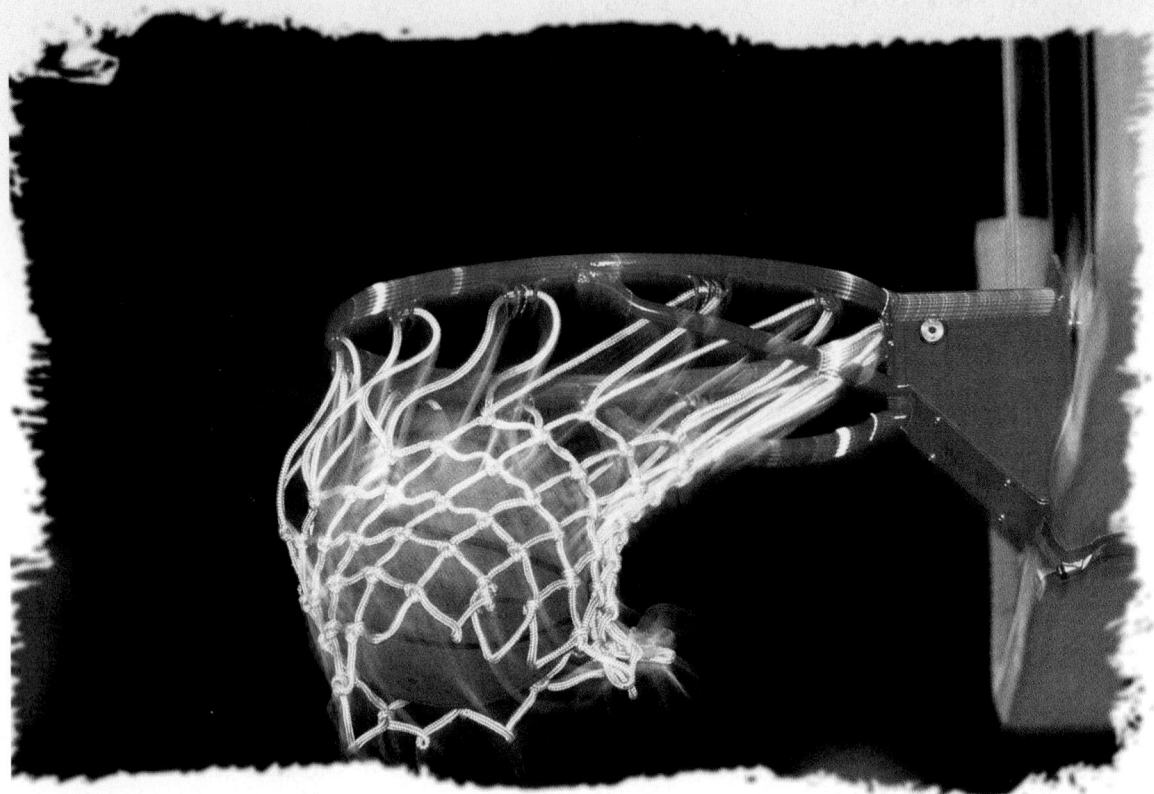

 Take It to the Net

Visit www.phschool.com
for interactive activities
and instruction related to
the selections, including

- background
- graphic organizers
- literary elements
- reading strategies

Preview

Connecting to the Literature

These poems are about the exhilaration of pure physical action that comes from a disciplined focus on an important goal. As you read, experience the sensation described and imagine what it means to spend every ounce of your strength for something you want with all your heart.

Background

The title "The Spearthrower" refers not only to a javelin thrower but also to a poet who sends her "signed song" of praise for women athletes into the "bullying dark" of athletic events once dominated by men. In associating the poet with the athlete, the poet Lillian Morrison follows a tradition from ancient Greece, where poets sang songs honoring Olympic athletics.

Literary Analysis

Theme in Poetry

On their surface, these poems vividly describe physical action, but underneath that surface is a **theme,** a central message or insight about life that sits at the center of each poem. The following lines from "The Spearthrower" address such a theme, suggesting that the athlete throws her javelin not only for herself but for other female athletes as well.

> her quick laps
> on the curving track,
> that the sprinter surge
> and the hurdler leap, . . .

As you read these poems, look for the insights or messages at their core.

Comparing Literary Works

In poetry, as in other literature, theme can be hinted at sideways or stated directly. In "The Spearthrower" and "Shoulders," the themes are stated directly. In contrast, in "Slam, Dunk, & Hook," the theme is implied; there seems to be much more than a game at stake. Compare and contrast the themes in each of the poems, paying close attention to the meaning that lies just beneath the words.

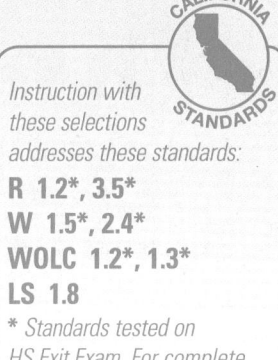

CALIFORNIA STANDARDS

Instruction with these selections addresses these standards:

R 1.2*, 3.5*
W 1.5*, 2.4*
WOLC 1.2*, 1.3*
LS 1.8

* Standards tested on HS Exit Exam. For complete standards, see p. CA 4.

Reading Strategy

Forming Mental Images

A poet writes words that let you see pictures in your mind's eye. To **form mental images** of a poem, turn the poet's words into pictures by applying your own experiences. These strategies will help you form mental images as you read poetry:

- Picture the scene that the poet sketches for you in words.
- If a picture does not come to mind easily, relate the words to events in your own life or to another poem or story you have read.

Use the chart shown at the right to help you form mental images as you read.

Words: _____
_____
_____

⋮

Image Created in Your Mind: _____
_____
_____

Vocabulary Development

metaphysical (met′ə fiz′i kəl) *adj.* spiritual; beyond the physical (p. 229)

jibed (jībd) *v.* stopped short and turned from side to side (p. 229)

feint (fānt) *v.* deliver a pretended move to catch an opponent off guard (p. 229)

surge (sʉrj) *v.* increase suddenly; speed up (p. 231)

Slam, Dunk, & Hook

Yusef Komunyakaa

Fast breaks. Lay ups. With Mercury's[1]
Insignia[2] on our sneakers,
We outmaneuvered the footwork
Of bad angels. Nothing but a hot
5 Swish of strings like silk
Ten feet out. In the roundhouse[3]
Labyrinth[4] our bodies
Created, we could almost
Last forever, poised in midair
10 Like storybook sea monsters.
A high note hung there
A long second. Off
The rim. We'd corkscrew
Up & dunk balls that exploded

---

1. **Mercury's** Mercury was the Roman god of travel, usually depicted with wings on his feet.
2. **insignia** (in sig´ nē ə) *n.* emblems or badges; logos.
3. **roundhouse** *n.* area on the court beneath the basket.
4. **labyrinth** (lab´ ə rinth) *n.* maze.

▶ **Critical Viewing** Which details in this painting relate to lines in the poem "Slam, Dunk, & Hook"? **[Connect]**

15　The skullcap of hope & good
　　　Intention. Bug-eyed, lanky,
　　　All hands & feet . . . sprung rhythm.
　　　We were <u>metaphysical</u> when girls
　　　Cheered on the sidelines.
20　Tangled up in a falling,
　　　Muscles were a bright motor
　　　Double-flashing to the metal hoop
　　　Nailed to our oak.
　　　When Sonny Boy's mama died
25　He played nonstop all day, so hard
　　　Our backboard splintered.
　　　Glistening with sweat, we <u>jibed</u>
　　　& rolled the ball off our
　　　Fingertips. Trouble
30　Was there slapping a blackjack
　　　Against an open palm.
　　　Dribble, drive to the inside, <u>feint</u>,
　　　& glide like a sparrow hawk.
　　　Lay ups. Fast breaks.
35　We had moves we didn't know
　　　We had. Our bodies spun
　　　On swivels of bone & faith,
　　　Through a lyric slipknot
　　　Of joy, & we knew we were
40　Beautiful & dangerous.

metaphysical (met´ə fiz´i kəl) *adj.* spiritual; beyond the physical

jibed (jībd) *v.* stopped short and turned from side to side

feint (fānt) *v.* deliver a pretended move to catch an opponent off guard

Review and Assess

Thinking About the Selection

1. **Respond:** Which images in this poem were clearest to you? Explain your answer.

2. **(a) Recall:** How does the speaker describe the action in lines 3–4? **(b) Infer:** Who or what do you think are the "bad angels" to which Komunyakaa refers?

3. **(a) Recall:** How does Sonny Boy play on the day his mother dies? **(b) Infer:** Why do you think he plays this way?

4. **(a) Interpret:** How does the first line of the poem convey the fast action of a game? **(b) Infer:** What might have been the purpose of starting the poem in such a way?

5. **(a) Analyze:** Why might the basketball players be both "beautiful" and "dangerous"? **(b) Infer:** What does playing basketball help the neighborhood boys to do?

6. **Apply:** Do you think sports are just for fun or do you think they help in other ways?

Yusef Komunyakaa

(b. 1947)

Komunyakaa has said that he likes "connecting the abstract to the concrete," and that is precisely what he does in "Slam, Dunk, & Hook." Komunyakaa won the Pulitzer Prize for poetry for his book *Neon Vernacular: New and Selected Poems* (1993). He grew up in Bogalusa, Louisiana, and earned the Bronze Star in Vietnam, serving as reporter and editor of the military newspaper *The Southern Cross*. He now teaches at Princeton University.

The Spearthrower

Lillian Morrison

▲ Critical Viewing
Based on the young woman's expression, what might her feelings be at this moment? **[Infer]**

She walks alone
to the edge of the park
and throws into
the bullying dark
5   her javelin
of light,
her singing sign
her signed song
that the runner may run
10 far and long
her quick laps
on the curving track,
that the sprinter surge
and the hurdler leap,
15 that the vaulter soar,
clear the highest bar,
and the discus fly
as the great crowds cry
to their heroines
20 Come on!

Reading Strategy
Forming Mental Images
Describe the picture you
see in your mind as you
read lines 1–6.

surge (sʉrj) *v.* increase
suddenly; speed up

Review and Assess

Thinking About the Selection

1. **Respond:** How did this poem make you feel when you read it? Why?

2. **(a) Recall:** What surroundings does Morrison describe at the beginning of the poem? **(b) Analyze:** Which words add mood to this description? **(c) Interpret:** Why do you think Morrison refers to the dark as "bullying"?

3. **(a) Recall:** Who "walks alone" in the poem? **(b) Evaluate:** What is the effect of starting the poem this way?

4. **(a) Recall:** Which athletes does Morrison mention in lines 9–16? **(b) Interpret:** Which details in the poem support the interpretation that the spearthrower is not an athlete, but a poet?

5. **Analyze:** What benefit does the spearthrower "pass on" to other female athletes?

6. **Speculate:** What do you think motivates great athletes the most?

7. **Extend:** Do you believe that the successes and failures a person experiences can greatly affect others? Explain.

Lillian Morrison

(b. 1917)

Lillian Morrison has worked as a librarian and has written and compiled many books. She has published several books of her own poetry, including *Whistling the Morning In* (1992). She has also edited several anthologies of poems about sports (including one focused on basketball and entitled, coincidentally, *Slam, Dunk*), along with collections of riddles, playground chants, and autograph sayings.

Shoulders

Naomi Shihab Nye

A man crosses the street in rain,
stepping gently, looking two times north and south,
because his son is asleep on his shoulder.

No car must splash him.
5 No car drive too near to his shadow.

This man carries the world's most sensitive cargo
but he's not marked.
Nowhere does his jacket say FRAGILE,
HANDLE WITH CARE.

10 His ear fills up with breathing.
He hears the hum of the boy's dream
deep inside him.

We're not going to be able
to live in the world
15 if we're not willing to do what he's doing
with one another.

The road will only be wide.
The rain will never stop falling.

Literary Analysis
Theme in Poetry Why does the poet point out that the child is not marked "fragile"?

Naomi Shihab Nye

(b. 1952)

Naomi Shihab Nye spent her teenage years in Jerusalem and has since worked as a visiting writer at several colleges and universities, including the University of Texas. Her books of poems have received such awards as the Pushcart Prize. In addition, her work has received recognition from the American Library Association. Nye says, "For me poetry has always been a way of paying attention to the world. . . ."

Review and Assess

Thinking About the Selection

1. **Respond:** Which images in the poem "spoke" to you? Why?

2. **(a) Recall:** Where are the father and child as the poem begins? **(b) Interpret:** Why might the poet have chosen this setting?

3. **(a) Recall:** Why is the father in the poem "stepping gently"? **(b) Speculate:** What does the son represent in the poem?

4. **(a) Interpret:** What warning does the poet give to the world in lines 17–18? **(b) Draw Conclusions:** What dangers does this warning seem to suggest?

5. **(a) Infer:** What does the speaker of the poem say that people must do for one another? **(b) Apply:** Do you think most people treat each other the way this man treats his son? Explain.

Review and Assess

Literary Analysis

Theme in Poetry

1. (a) What does "Slam, Dunk, & Hook" say about the role of basketball in the street life of the neighborhood kids? (b) Which details of the poem suggest that **theme**?

2. How does the "spearthrower" (that is, the poet who sings of women athletes) enable the runner to run and the discus to fly?

3. Use the chart below to analyze the insights in "Shoulders." (a) What message does the speaker convey about the role of a parent in a child's life? (b) What message is implied about the responsibility of all human beings?

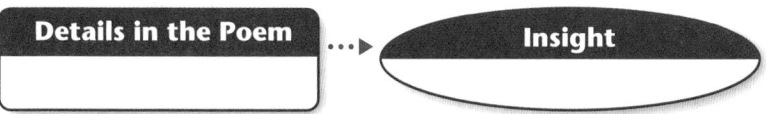

4. What idea about life is Nye expressing when she talks about the road always being wide and the rain always falling?

Comparing Literary Works

5. Using the chart below, compare the action, images, and themes of the three poems. (a) Which poem best conveys physical action? Explain. (b) Which poem best conveys emotional challenges? Explain.

Poem	Summary of Action	Images Created	Theme

Reading Strategy

Forming Mental Images

6. Which **image** in "Slam, Dunk, & Hook" creates the most vivid picture in your mind?

7. Describe what you see in the final image of "Shoulders."

Extend Understanding

8. **Sports Connection:** "The Spearthrower" shows women overcoming great obstacles in sports. Name a famous female athlete, and explain the impact she has had on sports and other athletes.

Integrate Language Skills

Vocabulary Development Lesson

Specialized Vocabulary: Jargon

Some poems use **jargon,** specialized vocabulary used in a particular occupation, sport, or other well-defined activity. For example, the term *feint* in "Slam, Dunk, & Hook" refers to a pretended move meant to take an opponent off guard. For each item, write the meaning of the jargon and the impression each word or phrase suggests.

1. dribble   3. fast breaks
2. drive to the inside   4. quick laps

Spelling Strategy

Remember the following rule: Place *i* before *e* except after *c* or when sounded like *a* as in *neighbor* and *weigh.* For each word, write "Correct" if the word is spelled correctly. If the spelling is incorrect, write the correct spelling.

1. yield   3. recieved
2. height   4. sieze

Fluency: Words in Context

Rewrite the following paragraph, filling in the blanks with words from the vocabulary list on page 227.

Emotions were high as the game entered the last quarter. The score was tied. The winning team would make it to the playoffs. We saw the center ____?____ left, then pass the ball to the right, confusing the player guarding her. The player who caught the ball then ____?____, looking for a teammate on either side of her who was closer to the basket. The moment was almost ____?____ as she found an opening among the group of girls that allowed her to ____?____ past the guard and make her shot. The home team was going to the playoffs, and the visiting team was left feeling stunned.

Grammar Lesson

Irregular Verbs

Unlike regular verbs, the past tense and past participle of **irregular verbs** are not formed by adding *-ed* to the present form. Instead, the past tense and past participle are formed in various ways. Some change vowels or consonants within the word. Others change both vowels and consonants. Some verbs use the same form for the present, past, and past participle. Look at the various forms of the verbs *run* and *catch.*

Present: run; catch

Past: ran; caught

Past Participle: (have) run; (have) caught

Practice

Test your knowledge of irregular verbs by identifying the past and past participle of each present-tense verb below. Use a dictionary if you are not sure about a particular form.

1. began   6. sing
2. hang   7. stand
3. spring   8. swing
4. fall   9. lead
5. drive   10. won

Writing Application Write three sentences using the present, past, and past participle of *spin.*

 Prentice Hall Writing and Grammar Connection: Chapter 23, Section 1

Writing Lesson

Editorial

Write an **editorial**—a brief piece of writing that presents one side of an issue—related to one of the selections. For example, using information you gathered from "Slam, Dunk, & Hook," you could write an editorial about the need for more funding for neighborhood sports because of the effect sports have on self-esteem.

Prewriting To persuade your readers, try to anticipate questions from those who might disagree with you. Imagine how opponents might question your opinions, and jot down questions and opposing viewpoints.

Model: Anticipating Readers' Questions

Topic: Our neighborhood needs more money for sports programs.

Questions: How much money will it cost our city?

Will funding come out of taxpayer money?

> Generating questions that readers might have helps you address all of the important aspects of an issue.

Drafting Write your editorial by stating the issue clearly and expressing your opinion reasonably. Address the questions you anticipated.

Revising Show your editorial to several people. Try to find at least one reader who disagrees with you. Ask that person whether your opinion sounds fair and if you have answered all objections effectively. If you hear a point you should have raised, consider adding it to your editorial.

W̷G Prentice Hall Writing and Grammar Connection: Chapter 7, Section 2

Extension Activities

Listening and Speaking A good sportscast captures the thrills of the game. Choose one of the track-and-field events in "The Spearthrower." Create a **sportscast** describing the contest from start to finish. Use these tips to guide your preparation:

- Give a play-by-play of the game.
- Focus attention on exciting or disappointing moments.
- Use vivid and lively language.

When you have written your sportscast, rehearse it and then present it to your class.

Research and Technology In a group, do a **research report** on some aspect of women's athletic competitions—for example, a biography of one outstanding athlete or an explanation of an exciting current topic. Use library resources, including the Internet and sports magazines, to help you with your research. Include photographs, recordings, and videotapes, if possible. **[Group Activity]**

 Take It to the Net   www.phschool.com

Go online for an additional research activity using the Internet.

Writing WORKSHOP

Workplace Writing: Business Letter

The form of writing commonly used by those in the workplace is a **business letter.** Business letters may take the form of job offer letters, requests for information, or letters of introduction. In this workshop, you will write a business letter to learn more about a profession.

Assignment Criteria. Your business letter should have the following characteristics:

● a heading, inside address, greeting, body, closing, and signature

● formal, polite language that outlines a clear purpose and provides relevant background information

● standard formatting with consistent spacing and indentation

To preview the criteria on which your business letter may be assessed, see the Rubric on page 239.

Prewriting

Choose a topic. To write a business letter, **list and itemize** to identify some of your strengths. In a chart like the one shown, match your strengths with "dream jobs" that require those abilities. Choose a profession from the list that you would like to learn more about. Use this career as the subject of your business letter.

Choose a Topic

Personal Strength	Dream Jobs Requiring This Strength
artistic	painter, sculptor
avid reader	teacher, writer, journalist
fast runner	professional running back
good joke teller	comedian

Make connections. Use the Internet, the classified section in the newspaper, or your local phone book to find the address, name, and title of the person to whom you will send your letter. Then, jot down any questions you might like to ask someone in that profession.

Research. Gather some background information about the dream job you have chosen. Use your school or local library or the Internet to research salary level, employment opportunities, and other pertinent information. Jot this down for use in the draft of your business letter.

Identify your purpose. Before you write your business letter, consider why you are writing. Review your notes and come up with a sentence that expresses this information clearly. You may want to incorporate this information later into the body of your draft.

> **Example:** I have taken guitar lessons for years, and I want to learn about the job of a studio musician.

Student Model

Before you begin drafting your business letter, read this model from Robin Weber, a student in St. Petersburg, Florida.

Intelligent Productions
220 Any Street, Suite 112
Any Town, NY 10000
December 13, 2001

G-2000 Computers
310 Infinite Loop
Any City, CA 94000

Dear Sirs:

My business is currently in the market for several high-end, reliable server computers. I would like to obtain more information about your line of server products.

The computers we use are operating twenty-four hours a day, seven days a week, as servers hosting a high-traffic Internet Web site. Therefore, it would be unacceptable for my company to purchase computers that require periods of inactivity in order to remain in working condition. We are also concerned about technical support issues and cost.

I would appreciate if you could send me the exact specifications on catalog items number 1444, as well as number 2314. There is no information on warranties in your product descriptions. Any information in this regard would be very helpful in making my purchasing decision. Also, would it be possible to obtain a high volume discount? How would such an order affect delivery time?

Please send me any information you have on these issues. I look forward to hearing from you.

Sincerely,

Robin Weber

Robin Weber
Intelligent Productions

> In his letter, Robin assumes the voice of a business that he created for this assignment.

> The author states his purpose clearly and concisely.

> In this paragraph, the author provides important background information.

> The author uses modified block format.

> The letter includes specific questions that Robin would like answered.

> The conclusion summarizes the request using polite language.

Drafting

Selecting a format. Select a standard format that uses traditional font and spacing. Acceptable formats for business letters include the following:

- **Block format**—each part of the letter begins at the left margin
- **Modified block format**—the heading, closing, and signature are indented to the center of the page

Adhere to standards. As you draft your business letter, be certain you have included all of the essential parts of the form. Use the checklist at right to verify that your business letter has all of the proper elements. Add any elements that are missing from your checklist.

Consider your audience. Remember that you are addressing a busy professional. Include only information that is essential; do not provide flowery elaboration that will detract from your main purpose. Make sure to provide information clearly and use formal vocabulary, style, and tone of address.

Call for action. As you draft, include information that tells your reader what you want him or her to do. For example, you may want to set up an interview, arrange a phone call, or you may want the recipient to provide you with some information. Make sure the outcome you want is clearly stated.

Business Letter Standards
☐ **Heading**—indicates the writer's address and affiliation (if any) and the date
☐ **Inside Address**—indicates where letter will be sent
☐ **Greeting**—always punctuated by a colon
☐ **Body**—states the writer's purpose
☐ **Closing**—an appropriate farewell
☐ **Signature**—a signed name

Revising

Revise to support your purpose. Your business letter must address the reasons for your writing. Verify that this reason is clearly stated early in the body of your business letter. To evaluate your letter, look over your draft to find places where you can offer detail to support your purpose.

1. Review your draft and underline your purpose for writing.

2. Highlight any other details in your business letter that reinforce your purpose for writing.

3. Cross out details that are not essential for the reader to know.

Model: Supporting Your Purpose

I would like to obtain more information about your line of server products. The computers we use are operating twenty-four hours a day, seven days a week, as servers hosting a high-traffic Internet Web site. ~~Intelligent Productions was the fastest growing privately owned company in the year 2000.~~

> This information is not essential to the writer's purpose.

Revise to make language formal. Look for words in your business letter that can be replaced to create a more formal effect. In the following example, *excels* creates a more formal effect than *is good*.

Example: He *is good* at playing chess.
He *excels* at playing chess.

Compare the model and the nonmodel. Why is the model more effective than the nonmodel?

Nonmodel	Model
I want a good, reliable server. Can you get me some information on your products?	My business is currently in the market for several high-end, reliable server computers. I would like to obtain more information about your line of server products.

Publishing and Presenting

Consider sharing your writing with a wider audience in one of the following ways.

Send your letter. If your letter is written to an existing business, mail it. When you get a response, share it with classmates.

Apply your knowledge to another situation: write a letter of complaint. Pair up with a partner. Write a letter of complaint to your partner's fictional company, using formal language and following the standard format for a business letter. Ask your partner to draft a polite business letter addressing your complaint. Afterward, discuss whether you were each satisfied with the letter you received.

 Prentice Hall Writing and Grammar Connection: Chapter 15

 Read to Write
To learn more about writing business documents, see **Reading Informational Materials**, p. 196.

Rubric for Self-Assessment

Evaluate your business letter using the following criteria and rating scale:

Criteria	Rating Scale Not very				Very
How well does the letter incorporate all the elements of a business letter?	1	2	3	4	5
How clear and formal is the language of the letter?	1	2	3	4	5
How well does the letter follow appropriate formatting?	1	2	3	4	5
How well does the letter include appropriate background information?	1	2	3	4	5
How clearly is the purpose stated?	1	2	3	4	5

Listening and Speaking WORKSHOP

Conducting Interviews

You do not need to be a talk-show host to produce a good interview. All you need is curiosity about a subject, a willingness to put in some preparation time, and a chance to connect with someone who can provide the detailed information you need.

Prepare for the Interview

Whether you are using an interview to gather data for a research paper or to find a new job, you want to start off feeling prepared. To plan:

Identify your purpose. Determine what kind of information you need to obtain from an interview. Your purpose might be to find a few personal stories for a history paper or facts for a school newspaper article.

Do research. Perform enough preliminary research so that you can ask informed questions. For a job interview, find out more about the employer. Before interviewing an expert on the psychology of twins, look at studies on twin behavior.

Draw up questions. The best questions inspire answers in which people talk about themselves and their experiences. Everyone has a conversation "combination lock." Your challenge is to find the right combination of insightful, provocative questions that lets you open that lock.

Conduct the Interview

Once your preparation is complete, consider these tips for conducting a productive interview:

Build a question staircase. Think of the answers in your interview as the steps in a staircase you are building upward. Each *question* should build on the *answer* you just received, as well as the previous question. See the chart at right for guidance.

Stick to your subject. Maintain focus by keeping your original purpose in mind. If the other person seems confused, you may have gone off-topic or asked an overly complicated question. Simplify your question, make sure it is relevant, and give examples to get back on track.

Building a Question Staircase

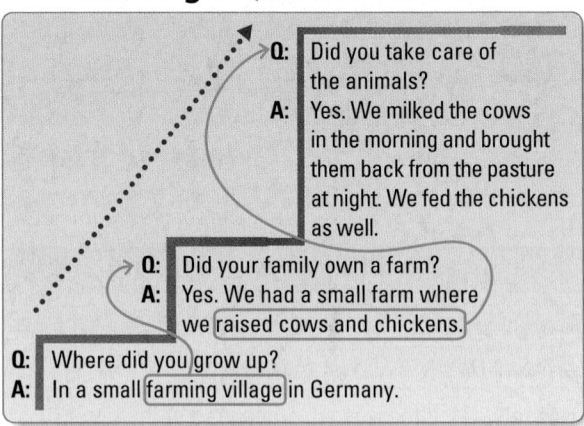

Q: Did you take care of the animals?
A: Yes. We milked the cows in the morning and brought them back from the pasture at night. We fed the chickens as well.

Q: Did your family own a farm?
A: Yes. We had a small farm where we raised cows and chickens.

Q: Where did you grow up?
A: In a small farming village in Germany.

(Activity:)
Interview and Evaluation Practice your skills by interviewing a community member with a particular expertise. Use the graphic to help you evaluate the quality of information you receive. After the interview, determine what you did well and areas you could improve.

Assessment WORKSHOP

Facts and Details

The reading sections of some tests require you to read a passage and answer multiple-choice questions about supporting ideas in a passage. The supporting ideas in a text are the facts and details that provide information about a main idea. Use the following strategies to help you answer test questions about supporting ideas:

- Think of a statement that summarizes the main idea of the passage.
- Look for facts or details that relate to the main idea.
- Check to see whether the test question is answered by the main idea or a supporting detail.
- Eliminate responses that supply details unrelated to the question.

Test-Taking Strategies

- Look at the test question before reading the passage to give yourself the appropriate focus.
- Even if you think you know the correct answer, read all the answer choices before choosing one.

Sample Test Item

Directions: Read the following passage, and then answer the question that follows.

As Yolanda read the application for summer camp counselor, she felt doubtful. She was interested in teaching art and sports, but the position required experience. Did she qualify? She made a list of what she had done: two terms of a child-development lab last year, babysitting for four years, one year as an art and soccer teacher for day camp.

1. Which of Yolanda's experiences is the closest match for the position?

  A her experience as a babysitter

  B the classes she took in child development

  C her experience as an art and soccer teacher

  D her certification in CPR

Answer and Explanation

The correct answer is *C,* which describes her art and sports experience. *A* and *B* are experiences that relate to the position, but neither is a close match. While Yolanda may be certified in CPR, this detail is not directly stated in the passage; *D* is therefore incorrect.

▶ Practice

Directions: Read the following passage, and then answer the question that follows.

Dr. Ellen Ochoa is a woman of many talents. She was born and raised in southern California, where her primary interests as a child included reading and playing flute. Graduating as the top-ranked math student in high school, she went on to earn an undergraduate degree in physics, as well as a master's and a doctorate in electrical engineering.

In 1993, she became the first Hispanic female astronaut to travel in space, where she and her team studied the sun's radiation levels. She even played the flute in space!

1. Dr. Ochoa's childhood interests included ___?___.

  A reading

  B electrical engineering

  C band

  D physics

2. What success is not included in the passage?

  A earning a doctoral degree

  B becoming an astronaut

  C graduating from high school

  D leading a university marching band

UNIT 3 *Moments of* *Discovery*

Waiting Girl, 1978, Yan Hsia, Asian American Arts Center

242 ◆ Moments of Discovery

Exploring the Theme

Any insight can be a moment of discovery—children identifying an entire animal from a fragment of jawbone or a woman suddenly recognizing a common thread that she shares with her mother and grandmother. Whether big or small, these moments of discovery teach people something about themselves, others, and the world around them.

In Amy Tan's "Rules of the Game," Waverly Jong gains sudden insights in successive waves during her childhood in San Francisco's Chinatown. Insight into the intricacies of chess allows her to succeed beyond everyone's expectations. This same success, though, alienates her from the rest of her family and a more carefree past. In just a few pages of the story, you will experience moments of discovery of every variety—exhilarating, bittersweet, and full of pain.

▲ **Critical Viewing** What emotions would you imagine this woman is experiencing? **[Analyze]**

Why Read Literature?

Perhaps we always read to gain insight or to learn more about the world around us. You might be interested in specific information or you might just enjoy the way an author puts words together. Preview these three purposes you might set before reading works in this unit.

1 Read for the Love of Literature

The early 1960s was an excruciating time for southern African American students attending formerly all-white schools. These students were pioneers, venturing into new territory where many angry voices were raised against them. Discover the meaning of personal courage in Charlayne Hunter–Gault's classic account **"In My Place,"** page 296.

Many readers enjoy stories that reveal inner truths about themselves. If you have ever regretted missing an opportunity to meet someone—for a reason too ridiculous to remember—then you may sympathize with the main character in Cynthia Rylant's **"Checkouts,"** page 282.

2 Read to Appreciate an Author's Style

When you read any of E. E. Cummings's poems, you will quickly realize that regular rules of grammar do not apply. Capital letters are reincarnated as lower case letters and parentheses appear magically out of nowhere. Although it may seem random, Cummings's style is closely tailored to the way the poem makes you feel. To gain an appreciation for Cummings's unusual choices, read **"maggie and milly and molly and may,"** page 328.

William Stafford's writing has a conversational style that can make you feel like you are listening to a friend tell a good story. See how Stafford creates this effect in **"Fifteen,"** page 286, a poem about a motorcycle and the intensity of youth.

3 Read for Information

The National Audubon Society was inspired by a group of Boston women who were horrified by the mistreatment of birds. In 1896, they banded together, boycotting products such as hats and clothing adorned with bird feathers. Their dedication, more than a century ago, has grown to include Audubon chapters nationwide. In addition to producing mailings and publications, the National Audubon Society has established a presence online to spread information and encourage action. To find out about navigating the Web to learn more about this group, see the **Audubon Society Web site,** page 257.

 Take It to the Net

Visit the Web site for online instruction and activities related to each selection in this unit.

www.phschool.com

How to Read Literature

Use Strategies for Constructing Meaning

You have to go a step beyond the literal meaning of each word on a page to fully understand what you are reading. Next steps include putting words and ideas together, forming judgments about plot and character, reading between the lines, and relating material to past experiences. This process is called constructing meaning. Use these strategies to help you construct meaning.

1. Relate generalizations and evidence.

- To find a generalization, look for a statement that is broad and strongly worded.

- Check to see whether an author backs up his or her generalization with convincing evidence. If the evidence is weak, you might decide that you disagree with the generalization.

2. Identify causes and effects.

- Find at least one reason *(cause)* for each result *(effect)* in a story.

- Use cause and effect to understand the chain of events in fiction and nonfiction. The chart at right shows the start of a cause-and-effect analysis of "The Interlopers."

3. Make inferences about character.

You can use inferences—reasonable conclusions based on details in the text—to predict how characters will react to certain situations.

- Consider the details that the author includes about characters.

- Pay close attention to physical descriptions and to actions that might shed light on character traits. Look at this example:

> I assumed he had learned from the hotel manager that I was to be in Herat for five days, and it was obvious that he felt confident that within that period he could wear me down and persuade me to buy a rug.
> —from **"The Rug Merchant"**

From this quotation, you can infer that the author is smart enough to know that he will be the target of a sales strategy. You might also infer that he is suspicious of others' motives.

4. Relate to personal experience.

Think about events in the selection and how they might resemble events in your life. Then, use your experiences to understand a story's characters and predict what might happen next.

As you read the selections in this unit, use these strategies for constructing meaning to enrich your understanding of the literature.

Cause and Effect

Question
Why does Ulrich hate Georg so deeply?

Cause
Georg repeatedly hunts without permission on land that legally belongs to Ulrich.

Effect
Ulrich is hunting down Georg so that he can settle this quarrel.

Prepare to Read

Children in the Woods

Take It to the Net

Visit www.phschool.com for interactive activities and instruction related to "Children in the Woods," including
- background
- graphic organizers
- literary elements
- reading strategies

Preview

Connecting to the Literature

Some of your ideas about how the world works may have come from observations and discoveries you made as a child. Mixing red and yellow paint to get orange, for example, might have shown you how colors are formed. In "Children in the Woods," Barry Lopez shares his thoughts on how to help children discover and understand their world.

Background

At one time, the emphasis in science was to describe the natural world in as much detail as possible. In the early nineteenth century, in fact, collecting and cataloging such objects as birds' eggs and orchids was a popular hobby. Today, although scientists need to know the names of living things, they focus more upon theories and explanations.

Literary Analysis

Reflective Essay

A **reflective essay** is a short nonfiction work that focuses on the writer's thoughts about a personal experience. Most reflective essays have a friendly tone and convey a sense of discovery. Consider the reflective nature of this statement from the selection.

> Whenever I walk with a child, I think how much I have seen disappear in my own life.

As you read, consider Lopez's "discoveries."

Connecting Literary Elements

In a reflective essay, sensory language can help readers share in the experience that the writer explores. **Sensory language** is writing or speech that appeals to one or more of the senses. Sensory language often helps you "see" what the writer is describing, but some words or phrases can also suggest sounds, textures, smells, and tastes.

Instruction with this selection addresses these standards:

R 1.1*, 2.8*, 3.4*, 3.7*
W 1.3*, 2.6
WOLC 1.3*
LS 1.3

* Standards tested on HS Exit Exam. For complete standards, see p. CA 4.

Reading Strategy

Relating Generalizations and Evidence

The key point of Lopez's reflective essay is a **generalization**—a broad principle that is supported by particulars, or **evidence**. Use these tips to relate generalizations and evidence:

- Look for broad personal opinions in the essay that might direct you toward generalizations. There may be small generalizations throughout, but somewhere there should be a large generalization that states the overall "point" of the essay.
- Find specific details to back up those generalizations.

Record your evidence and generalization on a chart like this one.

Evidence:

Generalization:

Vocabulary Development

charged (chärjd) *adj.* intense (p. 249)

acutely (ə kyōōt´ lē) *adv.* sharply (p. 249)

elucidate (ə lōō´ sə dāt´) *v.* explain (p. 249)

extrapolation (ek strap´ ə lā´ shən) *n.* conclusions drawn by speculation on the basis of facts (p. 250)

detritus (dē trīt´ əs) *n.* debris (p. 250)

effervesce (ef´ ər ves´) *v.* to be lively (p. 250)

myriad (mir´ ē əd) *adj.* countless; innumerable (p. 250)

insidious (in sid´ ē əs) *adj.* treacherous in a sly, tricky way (p. 250)

ineffable (in ef´ ə bəl) *adj.* too overwhelming to be expressed in words (p. 251)

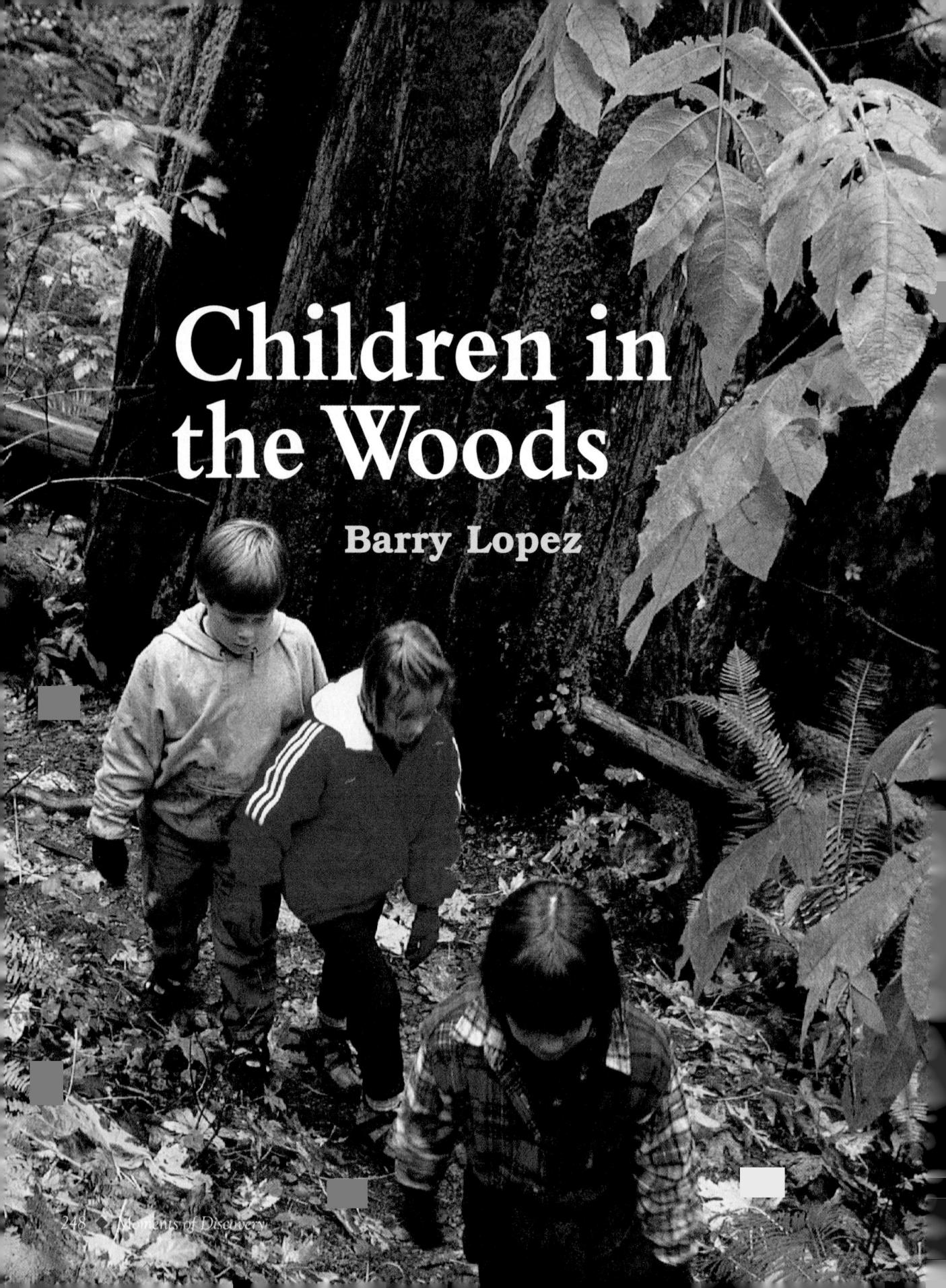

Children in the Woods

Barry Lopez

When I was a child growing up in the San Fernando Valley in California, a trip into Los Angeles was special. The sensation of movement from a rural area into an urban one was sharp. On one of these <u>charged</u> occasions, walking down a sidewalk with my mother, I stopped suddenly, caught by a pattern of sunlight trapped in a spiraling imperfection in a windowpane. A stranger, an elderly woman in a cloth coat and a dark hat, spoke out spontaneously, saying how remarkable it is that children notice these things.

I have never forgotten the texture of this incident. Whenever I recall it I am moved not so much by any sense of my young self but by a sense of responsibility toward children, knowing how <u>acutely</u> I was affected in that moment by that woman's words. The effect, for all I know, has lasted a lifetime.

Now, years later, I live in a rain forest in western Oregon, on the banks of a mountain river in relatively undisturbed country, surrounded by 150-foot-tall Douglas firs,[1] delicate deerhead orchids, and clearings where wild berries grow. White-footed mice and mule deer, mink and coyote move through here. My wife and I do not have children, but children we know, or children whose parents we are close to, are often here. They always want to go into the woods. And I wonder what to tell them.

In the beginning, years ago, I think I said too much. I spoke with an encyclopedic knowledge of the names of plants or the names of birds passing through in season. Gradually I came to say less. After a while the only words I spoke, beyond answering a question or calling attention quickly to the slight difference between a sprig of red cedar and a sprig of incense cedar,[2] were to <u>elucidate</u> single objects.

I remember once finding a fragment of a raccoon's jaw in an alder thicket. I sat down alongside the two children with me and encouraged them to find out who this was—with only the three teeth still intact in a

---

1. **Douglas firs** tall evergreen trees of the pine family.
2. **sprig of red cedar . . . incense cedar** twigs from two types of trees of the pine family.

charged (chärjd) *adj.* tensely expectant; intense

acutely (ə kyo͞ot′ lē) *adv.* sharply

Reading Strategy
Relating Generalizations and Evidence What evidence supports the generalization that Lopez loves nature and is knowledgeable about plants and animals?

elucidate (ə lo͞o′ sə dāt′) *v.* explain

✔**Reading Check**
When he first started his walks in the woods with children, how does Lopez say he spoke to them?

piece of the animal's maxilla[3] to guide them. The teeth told by their shape and placement what this animal ate. By a kind of visual extrapolation its size became clear. There were other clues, immediately present, which told, with what I could add of climate and terrain, how this animal lived, how its broken jaw came to be lying here. Raccoon, they surmised. And tiny tooth marks along the bone's broken edge told of a mouse's hunger for calcium.

We set the jaw back and went on.

If I had known more about raccoons, finer points of osteology,[4] we might have guessed more: say, whether it was male or female. But what we deduced was all we needed. Hours later, the maxilla, lost behind us in the detritus of the forest floor, continued to effervesce. It was tied faintly to all else we spoke of that afternoon.

In speaking with children who might one day take a permanent interest in natural history—as writers, as scientists, as filmmakers, as anthropologists[5]—I have sensed that an extrapolation from a single fragment of the whole is the most invigorating experience I can share with them. I think children know that nearly anyone can learn the names of things; the impression made on them at this level is fleeting. What takes a lifetime to learn, they comprehend, is the existence and substance of myriad relationships: it is these relationships, not the things themselves, that ultimately hold the human imagination.

The brightest children, it has often struck me, are fascinated by metaphor—with what is shown in the set of relationships bearing on the raccoon, for example, to lie quite beyond the raccoon. In the end, you are trying to make clear to them that everything found at the edge of one's senses—the high note of the winter wren, the thick perfume of propolis that drifts downwind from spring willows, the brightness of wood chips scattered by beaver—that all this fits together. The indestructibility of these associations conveys a sense of permanence that nurtures the heart, that cripples one of the most insidious of

> The brightest children, it has often struck me, are fascinated by metaphor . . .

---

extrapolation (ek strap′ ə lā′ shən) *n.* conclusions drawn by speculation on the basis of facts

detritus (dē trīt′ əs) *n.* debris

effervesce (ef′ ər ves′) *v.* to be lively

myriad (mir′ ē əd) *adj.* countless; innumerable

insidious (in sid′ ē əs) *adj.* treacherous in a sly, tricky way

---

3. **maxilla** (maks il′ ə) *n.* upper jaw.
4. **osteology** (äs′ tē äl′ ə jē) *n.* study of the structure and function of bones.
5. **anthropologists** (an′ *thr*ō päl′ ə jists) *n.* specialists in the study of mankind, especially the cultures of mankind.

▲ **Critical Viewing** Do you agree with the author that discoveries children make in nature can help them understand the world around them? **[Assess]**

human anxieties, the one that says, you do not belong here, you are unnecessary.

Whenever I walk with a child, I think how much I have seen disappear in my own life. What will there be for this person when he is my age? If he senses something <u>ineffable</u> in the landscape, will I know enough to encourage it?—to somehow show him that, yes, when people talk about violent death, spiritual exhilaration, compassion, futility, final causes, they are drawing on forty thousand years of human meditation on *this*—as we embrace Douglas firs, or stand by a river across whose undulating back we skip stones, or dig out a camas bulb,[6] biting down into a taste so much wilder than last night's potatoes.

The most moving look I ever saw from a child in the woods was on

---

6. **camas** (kam´ əs) **bulbs** underground buds of a sweet and edible American plant.

ineffable (in ef´ ə bəl) *adj.* too overwhelming to be expressed in words

✔**Reading Check**

What do the children learn from the raccoon jaw?

a mud bar by the footprints of a heron.[7] We were on our knees, making handprints beside the footprints. You could feel the creek vibrating in the silt and sand. The sun beat down heavily on our hair. Our shoes were soaking wet. The look said: I did not know until now that I needed someone much older to confirm this, the feeling I have of life here. I can now grow older, knowing it need never be lost.

The quickest door to open in the woods for a child is the one that leads to the smallest room, by knowing the name each thing is called. The door that leads to the cathedral is marked by a hesitancy to speak at all, rather to encourage by example a sharpness of the senses. If one speaks it should only be to say, as well as one can, how wonderfully all this fits together, to indicate what a long, fierce peace can derive from this knowledge.

---

7. **heron** (her´ ən) wading bird with a long neck, long legs, and a long, tapered bill.

Review and Assess
Thinking About the Selection

1. **Respond:** Would you like to explore the woods or parks near your home with someone like Barry Lopez? Explain.

2. **(a) Recall:** What does the elderly woman in Los Angeles say to Lopez's mother? **(b) Infer:** Why do her words affect Lopez so greatly?

3. **(a) Recall:** List three activities that take place on Lopez's walks in the woods. **(b) Infer:** Why does Lopez use the method he does to teach children about nature?

4. **(a) Interpret:** Why is the author concerned about what he tells children? **(b) Draw Conclusions:** Why does the author change his approach to teaching children about nature? **(c) Analyze:** What do children gain from an understanding of relationships in nature?

5. **(a) Infer:** How do you think Lopez himself grows and develops from the moments of discovery he shares with children? **(b) Speculate:** Do you think that a greater understanding of nature can bring more peace to a person?

6. **(a) Interpret:** Which details in the essay indicate that Lopez is concerned with the passage of time? **(b) Speculate:** Why do you think this concern is intensified by his interaction with children?

7. **Assess:** What is the greatest benefit of learning about nature?

8. **Apply:** How could you apply Barry Lopez's ideas to teaching art to children?

Barry Lopez

(b. 1945)
If you have any interest in nature, you will be moved by the poetic nonfiction of Barry Lopez. In his writing, Lopez speaks for those that cannot speak for themselves— Santa Ana winds, wolves, cottonwood trees, and more. Lopez has said, "I like to use the word *isumatug.* It's of eastern Arctic Eskimo dialect and refers to the storyteller, meaning 'the person who creates the atmosphere in which wisdom reveals itself.'"

An avid explorer, Lopez has journeyed to Alaska, the Galapagos Islands, Australia, Africa, the Antarctic, and the Arctic. In fact, he defines himself as "a writer who travels. Some writers stay at home or inside a room. I am a writer who travels."

Review and Assess

Literary Analysis

Reflective Essay

1. Which elements of "Children in the Woods" make it a good example of a **reflective essay?** Use a chart like the one below to record your answer.

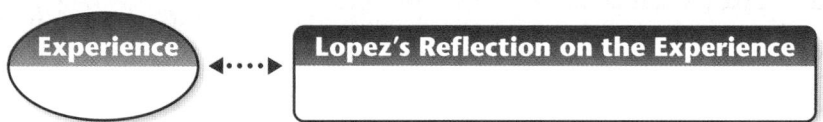

2. (a) If Lopez wrote "Children in the Woods" in the third person, telling about someone else's experiences, how would it differ from the essay he wrote? (b) Do you think it would be as effective?

Connecting Literary Elements

3. When Lopez recalls making handprints next to footprints of a heron, which **sensory language** brings that personal experience to life?

4. Using a chart like the one below, list examples of sensory language in the essay and explain why the language appeals to your senses.

Example		Sight	Sound	Taste	Touch	Smell

5. How do the images help you understand Lopez's personal thoughts?

Reading Strategy

Relating Generalizations and Evidence

6. (a) What **generalization** does the author make about speaking to children? (b) What **evidence** from his childhood in Los Angeles supports this?

7. (a) What do you think is the key point, or greatest generalization, of "Children in the Woods"? (b) Name three pieces of evidence that relate to the generalization.

Extend Understanding

8. **Career Connection:** Lopez believes that seeing relationships is better than just learning the names of things. Why might this approach help a person who is studying to be a doctor?

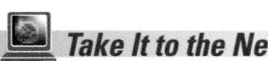

Integrate Language Skills

Vocabulary Development Lesson

Word Analysis: Latin Prefix *extra-*

Extrapolate contains the Latin prefix *extra-*, which means "outside." When you extrapolate, you put facts together to reach a conclusion that is "outside" the information you had when you started. Using the meaning of *extra-*, explain the following terms. Use a dictionary to check your answers.

1. extraordinary
2. extracurricular
3. extrasensory
4. extraterrestrial

Spelling Strategy

When adding an ending that begins with a vowel to a word that ends in a silent *e*, drop the *e* before you add the ending. For example, *make + -ing = making*. Write the word formed by adding each ending.

1. reside + *-ence*
2. invigorate + *-ing*

Fluency: Clarify Word Meaning

Identify the word from the vocabulary list on page 247 that answers each question.

1. What does soda do when you open the can?
2. What is another word for "explain"?
3. What do scientists get when they use facts to help them draw conclusions?
4. What word describes a tense game?
5. What would you find scattered around a junkyard?
6. How might someone experience a bad headache?
7. How might you describe a disease that is deadly but very hard to detect?
8. How many stars are in the sky?
9. How could you describe a feeling so strong that you could not put it into words?

Grammar Lesson

Prepositions

A **preposition** is a word that relates a noun or pronoun that appears with it to another word in the sentence. Although most prepositions, such as *at*, *by*, *in*, and *with*, are single words, some prepositions, such as *because of* and *in addition to*, are compound. In this example from "Children in the Woods," the prepositions are in italics:

> **Example:** The most moving look I ever saw *from* a child *in* the woods was *on* a mud bar *by* the footprints *of* a heron. We were *on* our knees, making handprints *beside* the footprints.

Practice Write each sentence, underlining all prepositions.

1. They saw rabbits across the stream.
2. The water flowed from the mountain and into the river.
3. The children walked along the path and looked at the roots of the tree.
4. Around the corner from the hiking trail we spotted a chipmunk.
5. The children can look at life a little differently because of the walk in the woods.

Writing Application Write a paragraph about nature using the following prepositions: *over*, *outside*, and *ahead of*.

W͟G Prentice Hall Writing and Grammar Connection: Chapter 19, Section 1

Writing Lesson

Field Guide

In "Children in the Woods," Barry Lopez vividly describes the woods around his home. A field guide provides detailed information about particular types of wildlife in a region. Write your own field guide about nature found right outside your home.

Prewriting Brainstorm for a list of animals that live near your home. For each general group, itemize by naming specific examples. From your list, select the subjects for your field guide.

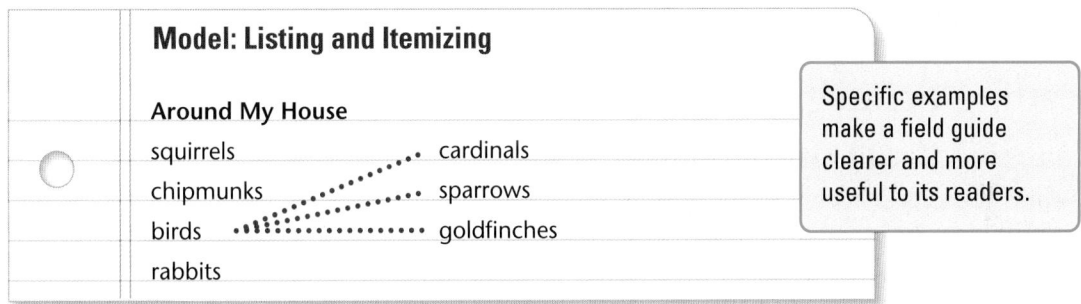

Model: Listing and Itemizing

Around My House

squirrels   cardinals
chipmunks   sparrows
birds   goldfinches
rabbits

> Specific examples make a field guide clearer and more useful to its readers.

Drafting As you draft, be specific, factual, and objective. Show what the animals look like and how they behave. For example, if you are describing the feeding habits of rabbits, tell exactly which plants they eat.

Revising Have classmates read your field guide and list their unanswered questions. Use these questions to guide your revisions.

W/G Prentice Hall Writing and Grammar Connection: Chapter 12, Section 2

Extension Activities

Listening and Speaking Keeping Barry Lopez's ideas in mind, devise a **lesson plan** to teach children about one aspect of nature. Use these suggestions as you plan:

- Select a topic that you know rather well.
- Use visuals to help inform your audience.
- Practice your lesson. If possible, videotape yourself to find room for improvement.

When you have finished preparing, teach your lesson to a child or a small group of children.

Research and Technology The woods described by Lopez are part of a temperate rain forest. In a group, prepare a **rain forest presentation.** Use resources at the library and on the Internet to find your facts. In your presentation, include a world map that shows where temperate rain forests are located. [**Group Activity**]

 **Take It to the Net**   www.phschool.com

Go online for an additional research activity using the Internet.

Web Sites

About Web Sites

A Web site is a collection of information located at a specific address on the World Wide Web, a part of the Internet accessible by computer. Software known as a browser enables an Internet user to access millions of Web sites around the world. To connect to a Web site, a user can either type a specific address or click on a word or picture that is electronically linked to the address. Often, a Web site begins with a home page, which is similar to the table of contents in a book. The user clicks on a specific home page listing, or link, to access the Web site's information on that topic.

Reading Strategy

Evaluating Credibility of Sources

When you access Web sites for information, it is important to evaluate the credibility of your sources. Use these questions to determine whether or not a source can be trusted:

- Who is the sponsor of the site?
- What are their credentials and background?
- Are both sides of issues represented?
- How current is the information?

You can trust the National Audubon Society, an established group, to give accurate Web site information on the Important Bird Area Program, a strictly factual topic. However, the Audubon Web page titled "Audubon View" sometimes presents an opinion, so you must treat that information more cautiously. Use a graphic organizer like the one shown here to rate the credibility of each link on the Audubon Web site home page.

Link	Credibility
Names of North American Birds	**Sponsor?** National Audubon Society. **Credentials?** 100-year-old organization that runs wildlife preservation programs. **Both sides shown?** Page presents factual information, not opinion. **Information current?** Yes. **Credible or not?** Credible. An organization dedicated to conservation would keep an accurate list of names of birds.

Audubon Web Site

If you are looking for information on wildlife conservation on the Internet, you are likely to come across the Web site for the National Audubon Society. The National Audubon Society is an organization that is dedicated to wildlife conservation and habitat restoration. The home page of the organization is shown below, providing a table of contents with links to the various pages of the site.

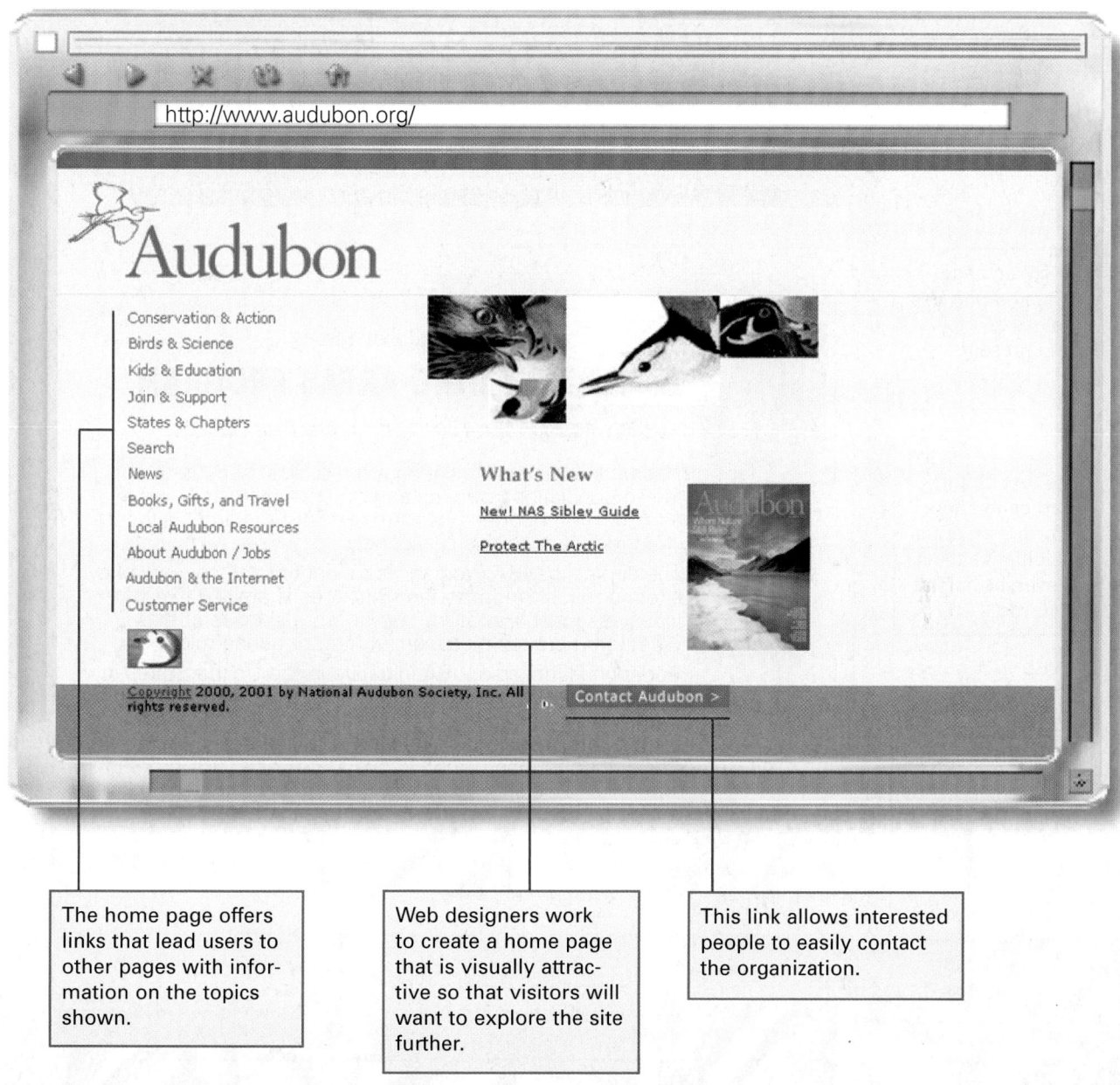

http://www.audubon.org/

Audubon

Conservation & Action
Birds & Science
Kids & Education
Join & Support
States & Chapters
Search
News
Books, Gifts, and Travel
Local Audubon Resources
About Audubon / Jobs
Audubon & the Internet
Customer Service

What's New

New! NAS Sibley Guide

Protect The Arctic

Copyright 2000, 2001 by National Audubon Society, Inc. All rights reserved.

Contact Audubon >

The home page offers links that lead users to other pages with information on the topics shown.

Web designers work to create a home page that is visually attractive so that visitors will want to explore the site further.

This link allows interested people to easily contact the organization.

Internal Pages

Since there is too much information to fit on a single page, and because the Internet is suited to the presentation of unlimited information, the Audubon site is designed with multiple levels to organize its information. Users move down a level every time they click on a link on a page. The page shown below, from the third level of the site, provides detailed information about the Important Bird Areas Program.

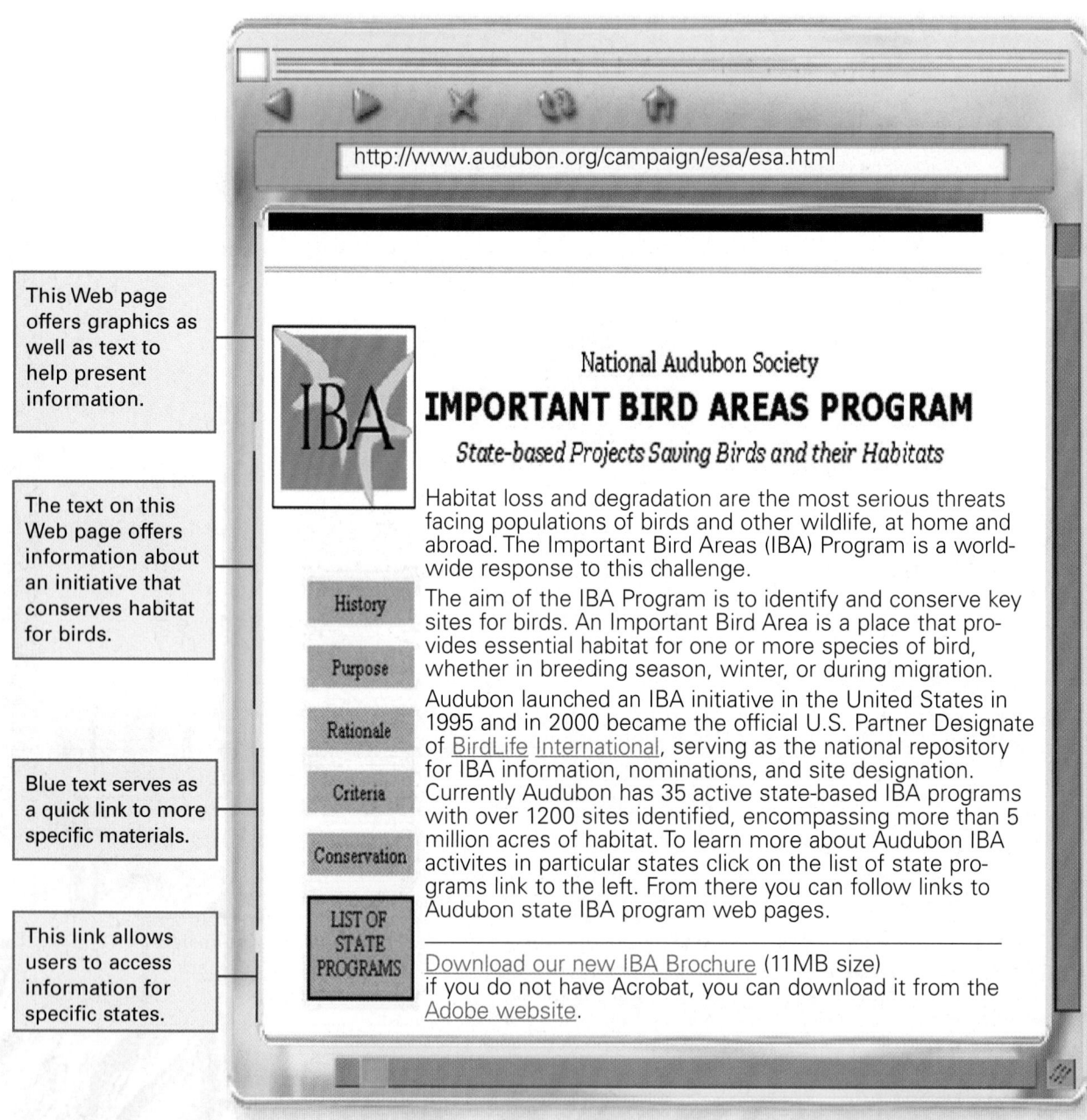

This Web page offers graphics as well as text to help present information.

The text on this Web page offers information about an initiative that conserves habitat for birds.

Blue text serves as a quick link to more specific materials.

This link allows users to access information for specific states.

http://www.audubon.org/campaign/esa/esa.html

National Audubon Society
IMPORTANT BIRD AREAS PROGRAM
State-based Projects Saving Birds and their Habitats

Habitat loss and degradation are the most serious threats facing populations of birds and other wildlife, at home and abroad. The Important Bird Areas (IBA) Program is a world-wide response to this challenge.

The aim of the IBA Program is to identify and conserve key sites for birds. An Important Bird Area is a place that provides essential habitat for one or more species of bird, whether in breeding season, winter, or during migration.

Audubon launched an IBA initiative in the United States in 1995 and in 2000 became the official U.S. Partner Designate of BirdLife International, serving as the national repository for IBA information, nominations, and site designation. Currently Audubon has 35 active state-based IBA programs with over 1200 sites identified, encompassing more than 5 million acres of habitat. To learn more about Audubon IBA activites in particular states click on the list of state programs link to the left. From there you can follow links to Audubon state IBA program web pages.

Download our new IBA Brochure (11MB size) if you do not have Acrobat, you can download it from the Adobe website.

History

Purpose

Rationale

Criteria

Conservation

LIST OF STATE PROGRAMS

Check Your Comprehension

1. Which link or links on the home page lead to information about education and resources?
2. Where would you find contact information?
3. What is the aim of the IBA program?

Applying the Reading Strategy

Evaluating Credibility of Sources

4. Cite two links on the Audubon home page that lead to information you can easily accept, along with two links you might evaluate more cautiously. Record your answers in the chart like the one below.

Credible	Explanation
Link:	
Evaluate More Cautiously	**Explanation**
Link:	

Activity

Researching a Web Site

You can find information on virtually any topic by using the World Wide Web. Choose a topic of interest to you. Then, use one or more Web sites to find information on your topic. For each site you visit, record information on an index card like the one shown here. Rank at least three sites in order of usefulness.

Conducting a Web Search

Topic:
Web address(es)
Web sponsor or author:
Credibility:
_____ Excellent _____ Good _____ Fair
_____ Poor
Date site was last updated:
Interesting facts:

Contrasting Informational Texts

Web Sites and Traditional Resources

1. Suppose that you wished to learn about the conservation of bird habitat without logging on to the Internet. (a) How could you find information on your topic in an encyclopedia? (b) Explain how this search process differs from using a Web site.
2. List resources other than the Internet and encyclopedias that you could use to find information on the conservation of bird habitat. Explain how to use each source and how using each one differs from using a Web site.

Prepare to Read

Rules of the Game

 Take It to the Net

Visit www.phschool.com for interactive activities and instruction related to "Rules of the Game," including
- background
- graphic organizers
- literary elements
- reading strategies

Preview

Connecting to the Literature

In "Rules of the Game," a generational tug of war is complicated by a conflict between Chinese and American cultures. No matter what your cultural background might be, however, the battle of wills that takes place in this selection should be familiar to you.

Background

Chess, which plays a central role in this story by Amy Tan, is believed to have evolved from a game first played in India in the sixth century. The game spread to Persia (the present Iran), and the Arab invaders who conquered Persia in the seventh century later introduced chess to other lands around the Mediterranean Sea. Today, chess is played by people of all ages and cultural backgrounds around the world.

Literary Analysis

Generational Conflict

A **generational conflict** is a struggle that exists between characters when beliefs and values change from one generation to another. The following passage from "Rules of the Game" demonstrates the generational conflict that exists in the story.

> One day, after we left a shop I said under my breath, "I wish you wouldn't do that, telling everybody I'm your daughter." My mother stopped walking. . . . "Aiii-ya. So shame be with mother?"

As you read the story, pay attention to the conflicts, or struggles, between the characters and consider why the conflicts exist.

Connecting Literary Elements

Motivation is the reason behind a character's thoughts, feelings, and actions. The motives of characters often contribute to the conflict in a story. In "Rules of the Game," young Waverly's motivation to be a successful chess player, and her mother's motivation to become involved with Waverly's success, greatly contribute to the conflict.

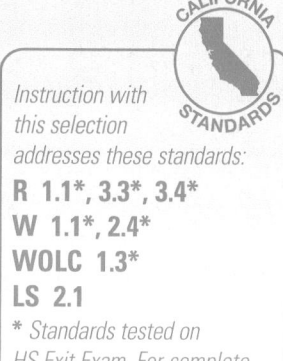

CALIFORNIA STANDARDS

Instruction with this selection addresses these standards:

R 1.1*, 3.3*, 3.4*
W 1.1*, 2.4*
WOLC 1.3*
LS 2.1

* Standards tested on HS Exit Exam. For complete standards, see p. CA 4.

Reading Strategy

Contrasting Characters

Throughout the story, you will see Waverly and her mother engaged in conflict. In order to follow the story, you need to understand how the two main characters are contrasted.

- As you read, **contrast,** or notice the differences in, the way each character expresses herself.
- Consider how each character feels about the other.

Use a chart like the one shown here to keep track of the actions, words, traits, and hopes of Waverly and her mother.

Waverly	Mrs. Jong
Born in the U.S.	Born in China
Significant Actions	
Significant Statements	
Personality Traits	
Hopes	

Vocabulary Development

pungent (pun´ jənt) *adj.* producing a sharp sensation of smell (p. 263)

benevolently (bə nev´ ə lent lē) *adv.* in a kind and well-meaning way (p. 267)

retort (ri tôrt´) *n.* sharp or clever reply (p. 267)

prodigy (präd´ ə jē) *n.* person who is amazingly talented or intelligent (p. 269)

malodorous (mal ō´ dər əs) *adj.* having a bad smell (p. 269)

concessions (kən sesh´ ənz) *n.* things given or granted as privileges (p. 270)

Rules
of the
Game

from

The Joy Luck Club

Amy Tan

I was six when my mother taught me the art of invisible strength. It was a strategy for winning arguments, respect from others, and eventually, though neither of us knew it at the time, chess games.

"Bite back your tongue," scolded my mother when I cried loudly, yanking her hand toward the store that sold bags of salted plums. At home, she said, "Wise guy, he not go against wind. In Chinese we say, Come from South, blow with wind—poom!—North will follow. Strongest wind cannot be seen."

The next week I bit back my tongue as we entered the store with the forbidden candies. When my mother finished her shopping, she quietly plucked a small bag of plums from the rack and put it on the counter with the rest of the items.

My mother imparted her daily truths so she could help my older brothers and me rise above our circumstances. We lived in San Francisco's Chinatown. Like most of the other Chinese children who played in the back alleys of restaurants and curio shops,[1] I didn't think we were poor. My bowl was always full, three five-course meals every day, beginning with a soup full of mysterious things I didn't want to know the names of.

We lived on Waverly Place, in a warm, clean, two-bedroom flat that sat above a small Chinese bakery specializing in steamed pastries and dim sum.[2] In the early morning, when the alley was still quiet, I could smell fragrant red beans as they were cooked down to a pasty sweetness. By daybreak, our flat was heavy with the odor of fried sesame balls and sweet curried chicken crescents. From my bed, I would listen as my father got ready for work, then locked the door behind him, one-two-three clicks.

At the end of our two-block alley was a small sandlot playground with swings and slides well-shined down the middle with use. The play area was bordered by wood-slat benches where old-country people sat cracking roasted watermelon seeds with their golden teeth and scattering the husks to an impatient gathering of gurgling pigeons. The best playground, however, was the dark alley itself. It was crammed with daily mysteries and adventures. My brothers and I would peer into the medicinal herb shop, watching old Li dole out onto a stiff sheet of white paper the right amount of insect shells, saffron-colored[3] seeds and <u>pungent</u> leaves for his ailing customers. It was said that he once cured a woman dying of an ancestral curse that had eluded the best of American doctors. Next to the pharmacy was a printer who specialized in gold-embossed wedding invitations and festive red banners.

Farther down the street was Ping Yuen Fish Market. The front window displayed a tank crowded with doomed fish and turtles struggling to gain footing on the slimy green-tiled sides. A hand-written sign informed tourists, "Within this store, is all for food, not for pet." Inside, the butchers with their bloodstained white smocks deftly gutted the fish while customers cried out their orders and shouted, "Give me your freshest," to which the butchers always protested, "All are freshest." On less crowded market days, we would inspect the crates of live frogs and crabs which we were warned not to poke, boxes of dried cuttlefish, and row upon row of iced prawns, squid, and slippery fish. The sanddabs made me shiver each time; their eyes lay on one flattened side and reminded me of my mother's story of a careless girl who ran into a crowded street and was crushed by a cab. "Was smash flat," reported my mother.

---

1. **curio** (kyoor′ ē ō′) **shops** shops that sell unusual or rare items.
2. **dim sum** (dim′ sum′) shells of dough filled with meat and vegetables and served as a light meal.
3. **saffron-colored** orange-yellow.

Literary Analysis
Generational Conflict
How does the mother's view of her family's situation contrast with that of the narrator?

pungent (pun′ jənt) *adj.* producing a sharp sensation of smell

✔**Reading Check**
What does the mother give to her daughter when she behaves in the candy store?

At the corner of the alley was Hong Sing's, a four-table cafe with a recessed stairwell in front that led to a door marked "Tradesmen." My brothers and I believed the bad people emerged from this door at night. Tourists never went to Hong Sing's, since the menu was printed only in Chinese. A Caucasian[4] man with a big camera once posed me and my playmates in front of the restaurant. He had us move to the side of the picture window so the photo would capture the roasted duck with its head dangling from a juice-covered rope. After he took the picture, I told him he should go into Hong Sing's and eat dinner. When he smiled and asked me what they served, I shouted, "Guts and duck's feet and octopus gizzards!" Then I ran off with my friends, shrieking with laughter as we scampered across the alley and hid in the entryway grotto[5] of the China Gem Company, my heart pounding with hope that he would chase us.

My mother named me after the street that we lived on: Waverly Place Jong, my official name for important American documents. But my family called me Meimei [mã´ mã´], "Little Sister," I was the youngest, the only daughter. Each morning before school, my mother would twist and yank on my thick black hair until she had formed two tightly wound pigtails. One day, as she struggled to weave a hard-toothed comb through my disobedient hair, I had a sly thought.

I asked her, "Ma, what is Chinese torture?" My mother shook her head. A bobby pin was wedged between her lips. She wetted her palm and smoothed the hair above my ear, then pushed the pin in so that it nicked sharply against my scalp.

"Who say this word?" she asked without a trace of knowing how wicked I was being. I shrugged my shoulders and said, "Some boy in my class said Chinese people do Chinese torture."

"Chinese people do many things," she said simply. "Chinese people do business, do medicine, do painting. Not lazy like American people. We do torture. Best torture."

M̲y older brother Vincent was the one who actually got the chess set. We had gone to the annual Christmas party held at the First Chinese Baptist Church at the end of the alley. The missionary ladies had put together a Santa bag of gifts donated by members of another church. None of the gifts had names on them. There were separate sacks for boys and girls of different ages.

One of the Chinese parishioners had donned a Santa Claus costume and a stiff paper beard with cotton balls glued to it. I think the only children who thought he was the real thing were too young to

---

4. **Caucasian** (kô kā´ zhən) *adj.* person of European ancestry.
5. **entryway grotto** (grät´ ō) *n.* entryway resembling a cave.

know that Santa Claus was not Chinese. When my turn came up, the Santa man asked me how old I was. I thought it was a trick question; I was seven according to the American formula and eight by the Chinese calendar. I said I was born on March 17, 1951. That seemed to satisfy him. He then solemnly asked if I had been a very, very good girl this year and did I believe in Jesus Christ and obey my parents. I knew the only answer to that. I nodded back with equal solemnity.

Having watched the other children opening their gifts, I already knew that the big gifts were not necessarily the nicest ones. One girl my age got a large coloring book of biblical characters, while a less greedy girl who selected a small box received a glass vial of lavender toilet water. The sound of the box was also important. A ten-year-old boy had chosen a box that jangled when he shook it. It was a tin globe of the world with a slit for inserting money. He must have thought it was full of dimes and nickels, because when he saw that it had just ten pennies, his face fell with such undisguised disappointment that his mother slapped the side of his head and led him out of the church hall, apologizing to the crowd for her son who had such bad manners he couldn't appreciate such a fine gift.

As I peered into the sack, I quickly fingered the remaining presents, testing their weight, imagining what they contained. I chose a heavy, compact one that was wrapped in shiny silver foil and a red satin ribbon. It was a twelve-pack of Life Savers and I spent the rest of the party arranging and rearranging the candy tubes in the order of my favorites. My brother Winston chose wisely as well. His present turned out to be a box of intricate plastic parts; the instructions on the box proclaimed that when they were properly assembled he would have an authentic miniature replica of a World War II submarine.

Vincent got the chess set, which would have been a very decent present to get at a church Christmas party except it was obviously used and, as we discovered later, it was missing a black pawn and a white knight. My mother graciously thanked the unknown benefactor, saying, "Too good. Cost too much." At which point, an old lady with fine white, wispy hair nodded toward our family and said with a whistling whisper, "Merry, merry Christmas."

When we got home, my mother told Vincent to throw the chess set away. "She not want it. We not want it," she said, tossing her head stiffly to the side with a tight, proud smile. My brothers had deaf ears. They were already lining up the chess pieces and reading from the dog-eared instruction book.

I watched Vincent and Winston play during Christmas week. The chess board seemed to hold elaborate secrets waiting to be untangled. The chessmen were more powerful than Old Li's magic herbs that cured ancestral curses. And my brothers wore such serious faces that I was sure something was at stake that was greater than avoiding the tradesmen's door to Hong Sing's.

Literary Analysis
Generational Conflict and Motivation What motivates Waverly to produce the right answers for Santa Claus?

Reading Strategy
Contrasting Characters What do Mrs. Jong's statement and action regarding the chess set suggest about her sense of her own worth?

✔**Reading Check**

What gift does Vincent receive at the Christmas party?

"Let me! Let me!" I begged between games when one brother or the other would sit back with a deep sigh of relief and victory, the other annoyed, unable to let go of the outcome. Vincent at first refused to let me play, but when I offered my Life Savers as replacements for the buttons that filled in for the missing pieces, he relented. He chose the flavors: wild cherry for the black pawn and peppermint for the white knight. Winner could eat both. As our mother sprinkled flour and rolled out small doughy circles for the steamed dumplings that would be our dinner that night, Vincent explained the rules, pointing to each piece. "You have sixteen pieces and so do I. One king and queen, two bishops, two knights, two castles, and eight pawns. The pawns can only move forward one step, except on the first move. Then they can move two. But they can only take men by moving crossways like this, except in the beginning, when you can move ahead and take another pawn."

"Why?" I asked as I moved my pawn. "Why can't they move more steps?"

"Because they're pawns," he said.

"But why do they go crossways to take other men. Why aren't there any women and children?"

"Why is the sky blue? Why must you always ask stupid questions?" asked Vincent. "This is a game. These are the rules. I didn't make them up. See. Here. In the book." He jabbed a page with a pawn in his hand. "Pawn. P-A-W-N. Pawn. Read it yourself."

My mother patted the flour off her hands. "Let me see book," she said quietly. She scanned the pages quickly, not reading the foreign English symbols, seeming to search deliberately for nothing in particular.

"This American rules," she concluded at last. "Every time people come out from foreign country, must know rules. You not know, judge say, Too bad, go back. They not telling you why so you can use their way go forward. They say, Don't know why, you find out yourself. But they knowing all the time. Better you take it, find out why yourself." She tossed her head back with a satisfied smile.

I found out about all the whys later. I read the rules and looked up all the big words in a dictionary. I borrowed books from the Chinatown library. I studied each chess piece, trying to absorb the power each contained.

I learned about opening moves and why it's important to control the center early on; the shortest distance between two points is straight down the middle. I learned about the middle game and why tactics between two adversaries are like clashing ideas; the one who plays better has the clearest plans for both attacking and getting out of traps. I learned why it is essential in the endgame* to have foresight, a mathematical understanding of all possible moves, and patience; all weaknesses and advantages become evident to a strong adversary and are obscured to

Literary Analysis
Generational Conflict and Motivation What motivates Waverly's desire to play? What motivates Vincent to let her play?

Literary Analysis
Generational Conflict and Motivation What motivates Mrs. Jong to tell Waverly she has to figure out the rules for herself?

a tiring opponent. I discovered that for the whole game one must gather invisible strengths and see the endgame before the game begins.

I also found out why I should never reveal "why" to others. A little knowledge withheld is a great advantage one should store for future use. That is the power of chess. It is a game of secrets in which one must show and never tell.

I loved the secrets I found within the sixty-four black and white squares. I carefully drew a handmade chessboard and pinned it to the wall next to my bed, where at night I would stare for hours at imaginary battles. Soon I no longer lost any games or Life Savers, but I lost my adversaries. Winston and Vincent decided they were more interested in roaming the streets after school in their Hopalong Cassidy[6] cowboy hats.

On a cold spring afternoon, while walking home from school, I detoured through the playground at the end of our alley. I saw a group of old men, two seated across a folding table playing a game of chess, others smoking pipes, eating peanuts, and watching. I ran home and grabbed Vincent's chess set, which was bound in a cardboard box with rubber bands. I also carefully selected two prized rolls of Life Savers. I came back to the park and approached a man who was observing the game.

"Want to play?" I asked him. His face widened with surprise and he grinned as he looked at the box under my arm.

"Little sister, been a long time since I play with dolls," he said, smiling benevolently. I quickly put the box down next to him on the bench and displayed my retort.

Lau Po, as he allowed me to call him, turned out to be a much better player than my brothers. I lost many games and many Life Savers. But over the weeks, with each diminishing roll of candies, I added new secrets. Lau Po gave me the names. The Double Attack from the East and West Shores. Throwing Stones on the Drowning Man. The Sudden Meeting of the Clan. The Surprise from the Sleeping Guard. The Humble Servant Who Kills the King. Sand in the Eyes of Advancing Forces. A Double Killing Without Blood.

There were also the fine points of chess etiquette. Keep captured men in neat rows, as well-tended prisoners. Never announce "Check" with vanity, lest someone with an unseen sword slit your throat. Never hurl pieces into the sandbox after you have lost a game, because then you must find them again, by yourself, after apologizing to all around you. By the end of the summer, Lau Po had taught me all he knew, and I had become a better chess player.

---

6. **Hopalong Cassidy** character in cowboy movies during the 1950s.

♦ **Endgame**

Endgame describes a tense period in a chess game when the end seems close at hand. With fewer pieces left, lines of attack and defense become clearer to both players. Mistakes are magnified in an endgame, when the margin between victory and defeat can be a single ill-considered move. In this story, Waverly develops a keen awareness of the strategies needed in the endgame to secure a victory.

benevolently (bə nev' ə lent lē) *adv.* in a kind and well-meaning way

retort (ri tôrt') *n.* sharp or clever reply

✓**Reading Check**

How does Waverly quench her desire to understand the rules of chess?

A small week-end crowd of Chinese people and tourists would gather as I played and defeated my opponents one by one. My mother would join the crowds during these outdoor exhibition games. She sat proudly on the bench, telling my admirers with proper Chinese humility, "Is luck."

A man who watched me play in the park suggested that my mother allow me to play in local chess tournaments. My mother smiled graciously, an answer that meant nothing. I desperately wanted to go, but I bit back my tongue. I knew she would not let me play among strangers. So as we walked home I said in a small voice that I didn't want to play in the local tournament. They would have American rules. If I lost, I would bring shame on my family.

"Is shame you fall down nobody push you," said my mother.

During my first tournament, my mother sat with me in the front row as I waited for my turn. I frequently bounced my legs to unstick them from the cold metal seat of the folding chair. When my name was called, I leapt up. My mother unwrapped something in her lap. It was her chang, a small tablet of red jade which held the sun's fire. "Is luck," she whispered, and tucked it into my dress pocket. I turned to my opponent, a fifteen-year-old boy from Oakland. He looked at me, wrinkling his nose.

As I began to play, the boy disappeared, the color ran out of the room, and I saw only my white pieces and his black ones waiting on the other side. A light wind began blowing past my ears. It whispered secrets only I could hear.

Chess Mates, 1992, Pamela Chin Lee, Courtesy of the artist

▲ **Critical Viewing**
Based on details in the painting, who do you think is winning this chess game? Why? **[Support]**

"Blow from the South," it murmured. "The wind leaves no trail." I saw a clear path, the traps to avoid. The crowd rustled. "Shhh! Shhh!" said the corners of the room. The wind blew stronger. "Throw sand from the East to distract him." The knight came forward ready for the sacrifice. The wind hissed, louder and louder. "Blow, blow, blow. He cannot see. He is blind now. Make him lean away from the wind so he is easier to knock down."

"Check," I said, as the wind roared with laughter. The wind died down to little puffs, my own breath.

My mother placed my first trophy next to a new plastic chess set that the neighborhood Tao society[7] had given to me. As she wiped each piece with a soft cloth, she said, "Next time win more, lose less."

"Ma, it's not how many pieces you lose," I said. "Sometimes you need to lose pieces to get ahead."

"Better to lose less, see if you really need."

At the next tournament, I won again, but it was my mother who wore the triumphant grin.

"Lost eight piece this time. Last time was eleven. What I tell you? Better off lose less!" I was annoyed, but I couldn't say anything.

I attended more tournaments, each one farther away from home. I won all games, in all divisions. The Chinese bakery downstairs from our flat displayed my growing collection of trophies in its window, amidst the dust-covered cakes that were never picked up. The day after I won an important regional tournament, the window encased a fresh sheet cake with whipped-cream frosting and red script saying, "Congratulations, Waverly Jong, Chinatown Chess Champion." Soon after that, a flower shop, headstone engraver, and funeral parlor offered to sponsor me in national tournaments. That's when my mother decided I no longer had to do the dishes. Winston and Vincent had to do my chores.

"Why does she get to play and we do all the work," complained Vincent.

"Is new American rules," said my mother. "Meimei play, squeeze all her brains out for win chess. You play, worth squeeze towel."

By my ninth birthday, I was a national chess champion. I was still some 429 points away from grand-master status, but I was touted as the Great American Hope, a child prodigy and a girl to boot. They ran a photo of me in *Life* magazine next to a quote in which Bobby Fischer[8] said, "There will never be a woman grand master." "Your move, Bobby," said the caption.

The day they took the magazine picture I wore neatly plaited braids clipped with plastic barrettes trimmed with rhinestones. I was playing in

---

7. **Tao** (dou) **society** group of people who believe in Taoism, a Chinese religion that stresses simplicity and unselfishness.
8. **Bobby Fischer** born in 1943, this American chess prodigy attained the high rank of grand master in 1958.

Literary Analysis
Generational Conflict and Motivation What motivates the mother to advise Waverly, instead of complimenting her daughter on her win?

prodigy (präd´ ə jē) *n.* person who is amazingly talented or intelligent

✔ **Reading Check**
Why was Waverly featured in *Life* magazine?

a large high school auditorium that echoed with phlegmy coughs and the squeaky rubber knobs of chair legs sliding across freshly waxed wooden floors. Seated across from me was an American man, about the same age as Lau Po, maybe fifty. I remember that his sweaty brow seemed to weep at my every move. He wore a dark, <u>malodorous</u> suit. One of his pockets was stuffed with a great white kerchief on which he wiped his palm before sweeping his hand over the chosen chess piece with great flourish.

In my crisp pink-and-white dress with scratchy lace at the neck, one of two my mother had sewn for these special occasions, I would clasp my hands under my chin, the delicate points of my elbows poised lightly on the table in the manner my mother had shown me for posing for the press. I would swing my patent leather shoes back and forth like an impatient child riding on a school bus. Then I would pause, suck in my lips, twirl my chosen piece in midair as if undecided, and then firmly plant it in its new threatening place, with a triumphant smile thrown back at my opponent for good measure.

I no longer played in the alley of Waverly Place. I never visited the playground where the pigeons and old men gathered. I went to school, then directly home to learn new chess secrets, cleverly concealed advantages, more escape routes.

But I found it difficult to concentrate at home. My mother had a habit of standing over me while I plotted out my games. I think she thought of herself as my protective ally. Her lips would be sealed tight, and after each move I made, a soft "Hmmmmph" would escape from her nose.

"Ma, I can't practice when you stand there like that," I said one day. She retreated to the kitchen and made loud noises with the pots and pans. When the crashing stopped, I could see out of the corner of my eye that she was standing in the doorway. "Hmmmmph!" Only this one came out of her tight throat.

My parents made many <u>concessions</u> to allow me to practice. One time I complained that the bedroom I shared was so noisy that I couldn't think. Thereafter, my brothers slept in a bed in the living room facing the street. I said I couldn't finish my rice; my head didn't work right when my stomach was too full. I left the table with half-finished bowls and nobody complained. But there was one duty I couldn't avoid. I had to accompany my mother on Saturday market days when I had no tournament to play. My mother would proudly walk with me, visiting many shops, buying very little. "This my daughter Wave-ly Jong," she said to whoever looked her way.

One day, after we left a shop I said under my breath, "I wish you wouldn't do that, telling everybody I'm your daughter." My mother stopped walking. Crowds of people with heavy bags pushed past us on the sidewalk, bumping into first one shoulder, then another.

"Aiii-ya. So shame be with mother?" She grasped my hand even tighter as she glared at me.

I looked down. "It's not that, it's just so obvious. It's just so embarrassing."

malodorous (mal ō′ dər əs) *adj.* having a bad smell

Reading Strategy
Contrasting Characters
What does this passage reveal about the way each character communicates?

concessions (kən sesh′ ənz) *n.* things given or granted as privileges

"Embarrass you be my daughter?" Her voice was cracking with anger. "That's not what I meant. That's not what I said."

"What you say?"

I knew it was a mistake to say anything more, but I heard my voice speaking. "Why do you have to use me to show off? If you want to show off, then why don't you learn to play chess." My mother's eyes turned into dangerous black slits. She had no words for me, just sharp silence.

I felt the wind rushing around my hot ears. I jerked my hand out of my mother's tight grasp and spun around, knocking into an old woman. Her bag of groceries spilled to the ground.

"Aii-ya! Stupid girl!" my mother and the woman cried. Oranges and tin cans careened down the sidewalk. As my mother stooped to help the old woman pick up the escaping food, I took off.

I raced down the street, dashing between people, not looking back as my mother screamed shrilly, "Meimei! Meimei!" I fled down an alley, past dark curtained shops and merchants washing the grime off their windows. I sped into the sunlight, into a large street crowded with tourists examining trinkets and souvenirs. I ducked into another dark alley, down another street, up another alley. I ran until it hurt and I realized I had nowhere to go, that I was not running from anything. The alleys contained no escape routes.

My breath came out like angry smoke. It was cold. I sat down on an upturned plastic pail next to a stack of empty boxes, cupping my chin with my hands, thinking hard. I imagined my mother, first walking briskly down one street or another looking for me, then giving up and returning home to await my arrival. After two hours, I stood up on creaking legs and slowly walked home.

The alley was quiet and I could see the yellow lights shining from our flat like two tiger's eyes in the night. I climbed the sixteen steps to the door, advancing quietly up each so as not to make any warning sounds. I turned the knob; the door was locked. I heard a chair moving, quick steps, the locks turning—click! click! click!—and then the door opened.

"About time you got home," said Vincent. "Boy, are you in trouble."

He slid back to the dinner table. On a platter were the remains of a large fish, its fleshy head still connected to bones swimming upstream in vain escape. Standing there waiting for my punishment, I heard my mother speak in a dry voice.

"We not concerning this girl. This girl not have concerning for us."

Nobody looked at me. Bone chopsticks[9] clinked against the insides of bowls being emptied into hungry mouths.

---

9. **chopsticks** (chäp′ stiks′) two small sticks of wood, bone, or ivory, held together in one hand and used as utensils for eating, cooking, and serving food.

Literary Analysis
Generational Conflict
What makes Waverly upset with her mother's behavior?

✔**Reading Check**

What does Waverly say to her mother when they walk through the Saturday market?

I walked into my room, closed the door, and lay down on my bed. The room was dark, the ceiling filled with shadows from the dinner-time lights of neighboring flats.

In my head, I saw a chessboard with sixty-four black and white squares. Opposite me was my opponent, two angry black slits. She wore a triumphant smile. "Strongest wind cannot be seen," she said.

Her black men advanced across the plane, slowly marching to each successive level as a single unit. My white pieces screamed as they scurried and fell off the board one by one. As her men drew closer to my edge, I felt myself growing light. I rose up into the air and flew out the window. Higher and higher, above the alley, over the tops of tiled roofs, where I was gathered up by the wind and pushed up toward the night sky until everything below me disappeared and I was alone.

I closed my eyes and pondered my next move.

Review and Assess

Thinking About the Selection

1. **Respond:** Which character did you find most realistic? Explain.

2. **(a) Recall:** Explain the salted plums incident in the beginning of the story. **(b) Analyze:** Which strategy does Waverly use with her mother even before she starts playing chess?

3. **(a) Recall:** How does Mrs. Jong teach Waverly rules of behavior? **(b) Connect:** How does Waverly use these rules to win at chess? **(c) Extend:** How does she use them in her struggle with her mother?

4. **Speculate:** The story ends without a final showdown. Who do you think will eventually "win" the game? Why?

5. **Apply:** Referring to chess, Waverly says that "for the whole game one must gather invisible strengths and see the endgame before the game begins." In which more general situations does this idea apply? Explain.

6. **Interpret:** Why do you think Amy Tan called this story "Rules of the Game"?

7. **(a) Assess:** Which elements of the struggle between Waverly and her mother are universal, relating to people from all cultures? Explain. **(b) Extend:** Which elements are uniquely Chinese American? Explain.

8. **Take a Position:** Do you think that Waverly's anger toward her mother is justified? Why or why not?

Amy Tan

(b. 1952)

Like Waverly, the nine-year-old chess champion in this story, Amy Tan was something of a child prodigy, displaying literary promise at the ripe age of eight. As a young woman, Tan supported herself as a technical writer, playing piano and writing fiction for relaxation. Through writing, she discovered her own ethnic identity. She has said in interviews that she had tried to minimize her ethnicity when she was younger. All that changed when she began to write about the painful but rich experiences of Chinese American women.

In 1985, Tan wrote "Rules of the Game," which she later included in *The Joy Luck Club*, set in Oakland, California, where she was born. The novel weaves together the stories of four Chinese mothers and their American-born daughters.

Review and Assess

Literary Analysis

Generational Conflict

1. What does Waverly resent about her mother's behavior when they are shopping together?
2. What might Mrs. Jong feel that her child does not yet understand?
3. (a) Use a chart like the one shown below to list statements made by Waverly and her mother that suggest a conflict. (b) Based on their statements, how would you rate the **generational conflict** on a scale from 1 to 10? Explain.

Speaker	Statement

Connecting Literary Elements

4. What motivates Mrs. Jong's involvement in Waverly's chess success?
5. How does Waverly's **motivation** to be a successful chess player contribute to her conflict with her mother?

Reading Strategy

Contrasting Characters

6. In what ways are Waverly and Mrs. Jong more alike than they admit? Using a chart like the one below, analyze their similarities and differences.

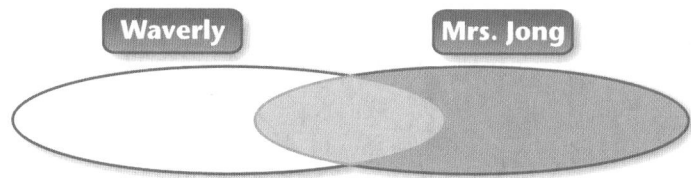

Waverly   Mrs. Jong

7. Why is Waverly in a better position than her mother to understand "American rules"?
8. What does Mrs. Jong want for her daughter that she does not have herself?

Extend Understanding

9. **Humanities Connection:** What other stories do you know in which a child uses success in some activity to outgrow a parent?

Integrate Language Skills

Vocabulary Development Lesson

Word Origins: Words From French

Several words found in "Rules of the Game" come from the French language, including *etiquette* (rules of behavior) and *souvenirs* (mementos).

In your notebook, write the English equivalent of these Old French words.

1. *rieules*   2. *circonstances*   3. *torneiement*

Spelling Strategy

Most English words ending in -gy are spelled with an *o* before the -gy. *Prodigy*, however, is one of only four words in common usage that do not follow this rule. Review the items below. If the spelling of a word is correct, write *Correct*. If the spelling is wrong, write the proper spelling.

1. strategy   2. apoligy   3. effegy

Concept Development: Synonyms

For each item below, identify the letter of the word or phrase whose meaning is closest to that of the first word.

1. concessions: (a) things granted, (b) large meetings, (c) secrets
2. retort: (a) foolish deed, (b) clever reply, (c) old wisdom
3. malodorous: (a) evil-minded, (b) bad-smelling, (c) beautiful-sounding
4. prodigy: (a) young child, (b) large amount, (c) talented person
5. pungent: (a) sweet-tasting, (b) sharp-smelling, (c) witty
6. benevolently: (a) wealthily, (b) attractively, (c) in a kind way

Grammar Lesson

Prepositional Phrases

A **prepositional phrase** is a group of words that includes a preposition and a noun or pronoun, called the *object of the preposition*. Generally, the object of the preposition is found after the preposition. In the following examples from the story, prepositional phrases are underlined, prepositions are italicized, and objects of prepositions are boldface.

> **Examples:** She won respect *from* **others**.
>
> No one knew it *at* the **time**.
>
> *During* the tense **game,** she showed great concentration.

Practice Find the prepositional phrases in the following sentences. For each, identify the object of the preposition.

1. Nobody looked at Waverly.
2. The gifts did not have names on them.
3. The tin globe had a slit for inserting money.
4. She loved the secrets she found in chess.
5. After the game, she put the pieces in the case.

Writing Application Write four sentences, using one of these prepositional phrases in each.

1. about me   3. through a strategy
2. before the game   4. after Mrs. Jong

Ꮤ᎐Ꮐ Prentice Hall Writing and Grammar Connection: Chapter 19, Section 1

Writing Lesson

Advice Column

Imagine you are a newspaper advice columnist. Write a column that provides advice to Waverly and her mother about how they can resolve their conflict.

Prewriting   Jot down all of the issues between Waverly and Mrs. Jong. Next to each issue, make a suggestion about how the conflict can be resolved.

Drafting   Your column should include suggestions for both characters. Remember to keep an objective tone—do not favor one character over another, but instead show concern for both of them.

Revising   Read your draft, paying attention to the tone. Highlight and rewrite any language that sounds biased, or overly supportive of one character. Make sure you have addressed every issue and provided reasonable solutions to their problems.

Model: Revising to Keep an Objective Tone

Biased:	Objective:
It's not surprising that Waverly was completely embarrassed when you put her on display at the market.	It's obvious that you are very proud of your daughter, but it will help both of you if you express your pride differently.

> The objective statement shows concern for both people.

W G Prentice Hall Writing and Grammar Connection: Chapter 11, Section 4

Extension Activities

Listening and Speaking With a classmate, write a **dialogue** between Waverly and her mother that takes place years after the events in this story, when Waverly is an adult.

- Consider the character traits you think Waverly will have as an adult.
- Decide whether the dialogue will reflect conflict in their relationship or a better way of communicating.

Read your dialogue aloud to the class. [**Group Activity**]

Research and Technology Imagine that you are a radio announcer. Give a **radio commentary** describing a national chess tournament in which Waverly Jong is a finalist. Start your commentary by explaining the significance of the event. Remember to use a tone of voice that captures the mood of the scene. After practicing, present the commentary to your class.

 Take It to the Net   www.phschool.com

Go online for an additional research activity using the Internet.

CONNECTIONS
Literature and Media

From Printed Page to Silver Screen

Amy Tan included "Rules of the Game" in her first novel, *The Joy Luck Club.* The book sold extremely well because readers connected emotionally with its characters. After only two weeks in print, *The Joy Luck Club* had become a best-seller. Tan was then asked to consider adapting her novel as a movie. Despite the allure of such an offer, this was not an easy decision for the young novelist to make. She feared losing creative control of her story and worried that a movie made in Hollywood might end up portraying stereotypes of Asian Americans. She also was not sure that the book, with its complex structure and notable lack of car chase scenes, could be adapted to the movie screen.

Tan managed to put her initial fears aside after meeting the director and co-writer, but during the filmmaking process she encountered a new set of worries. In the following excerpt from a newspaper article, Tan discusses how the process of making a movie from her book was more difficult—and rewarding—than she ever anticipated.

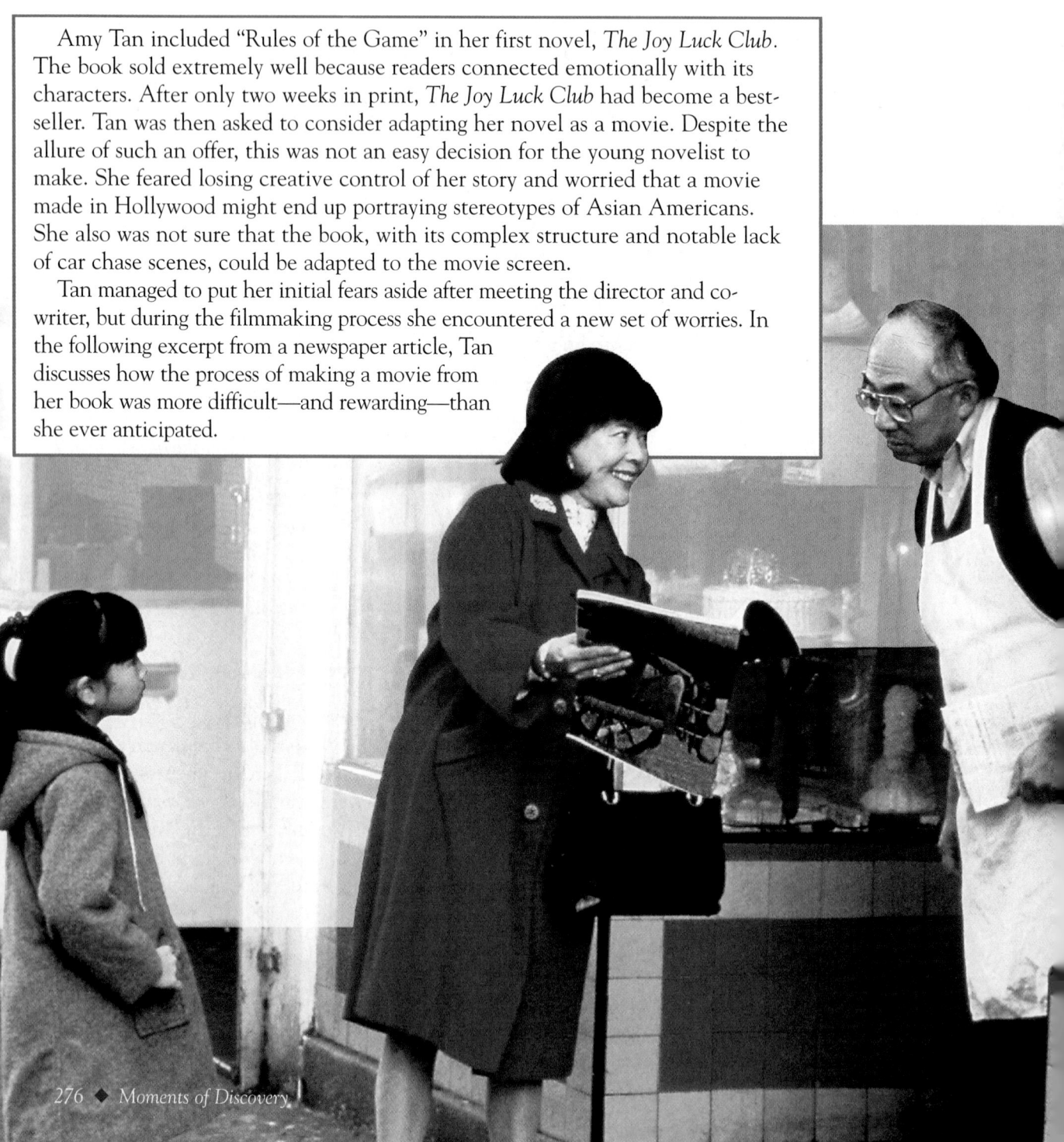

from
Joy, Luck, and Hollywood

Amy Tan

Los Angeles Times, September 5, 1993

I CRIED MY EYES OUT

I saw all the dailies,[1] most of them on video format at home. I cried throughout the making of the movie. I was very moved by what I was seeing. I was exhausted watching what the actors went through. At major stages, Ron and I worked with Wayne and the editor, Maysie Hoy, as the movie was being cut. That process was fascinating but tedious. I ended up thinking Maysie was a saint.

Around April, I got to see a first rough cut.[2] I was supposed to watch it and take notes of problem areas and such. But I was too <u>mesmerized</u> to do anything but watch it pretty much like an ordinary moviegoer. I laughed, I cried. The second time I saw it, I said to Wayne: "I want you to remember this day. We're going to get a lot of different reactions to this film later down the road. But I want us to remember that on this day, you, Ron and I were proud with what we've accomplished. We made our vision."

Ron insisted that I come to the test previews because there I'd get some of the biggest highs or lows of my life, seeing how a real audience reacted. Fortunately, it was the former. I was surprised, though, whenever people laughed during a scene I never considered funny. I suppose it was one of those <u>ironic</u> laughs, in which one recognizes the pain of some childhood humiliation.

I've now seen the movie about 25 times, and I am not ashamed to say I'm moved to tears each time.

By the time you read this, I will have seen the movie with my mother and my half sister, who just immigrated from China. So that'll be my version of life imitating art, or sitting in front of it. I'm nervous about what my mother will think. I'm afraid she'll be overwhelmed by

mesmerized (mez′mər ized′) *v.* hypnotized; fascinated

ironic (ī rän′ ik) *adj.* directly opposite to what is or what might be expected

---

1. **dailies** (dā′ lēz) *n.* movie term to describe the photographic prints made from the previous day's filming. Directors and actors use dailies to assess the progress of the film and the quality of actors' performances.
2. **rough cut** *n.* early version of an entire film. The rough cut allows the director and writers to receive reactions and suggest additional revisions for the finished film.

✔**Reading Check**

What was Amy Tan's initial reaction to seeing the first rough cut?

▲ **Critical Viewing** What impression does this portrait
convey about the author, Amy Tan? **[Respond]**

some of the scenes that are taken from her life, especially the one that depicts the suicide of her mother.

I hope those in the audience are moved by the film, that they connect with the emotions and feel changed at the end, that they feel closer to another person as a result. That's what I like to get out of a book, a connection with the world.

As to reviews, I've already imagined all the bad things that can be said. That way I'll be delighted by anything good that comes out. I'm aware that the success of this movie will depend on good reviews and word-of-mouth reactions. But there comes a point when you've done all you can. And then it's out of your control. Certainly I hope the movie's a success at the box office,[3] mostly for Wayne and Ron's sakes, as well as the cast and crew who worked on this. And certainly I hope Disney feels it was more than justified in taking a risk on this movie. By my score, however, the movie is already a success. We made the movie we wanted to make. It's not perfect, but we're happy with it. And I'll be standing in line, ready to plunk down $7 to see it.

In the meantime, I've got a whole mess of Chinese lucky charms that are absolutely guaranteed to bring the gods to the theater.

I'VE LEARNED MY LESSONS

At different points in the making of the movie, I vowed I'd never do this again. It's too time-consuming. It's <u>rife</u> with ups and downs. There's so much business. I've developed calluses and a certain sang-froid[4] attitude about some of the <u>inherent</u> difficulties of filmmaking.

Yet, against all my expectations, I like working <u>collaboratively</u> from time to time. I like fusing ideas into one vision. I like seeing that vision come to life with other people who know exactly what it took to get there.

My love of fiction is unaltered. It's my first love. But, yes, I'll make another film with Ron and Wayne. It'll probably be my second novel, "The Kitchen God's Wife." We've already started breaking the scenes out with page counts and narrative text. We started the day after we saw the first rough cut of "The Joy Luck Club."

---

3. **box office** *n.* place where movie tickets are sold.
4. **sang-froid** (sä*n* frwä') coolness under pressure. (From the French, meaning "cold blood.")

Thematic Connection
Do you think that readers react the same way to books as audiences react to movie adaptations?

rife (rīf) *adj.* abundant

inherent (in her´ənt) *adj.* existing as a natural, inborn quality

collaboratively (kə lab´ə rə tiv lē) *adv.* together as a team

> ## Connecting Literature and Media
>
> 1. Which parts of "Rules of the Game" might be difficult to adapt to the movie screen?
> 2. Which parts of the story are especially well suited to a movie adaptation?
> 3. What did Tan find most rewarding about the transformation of her work to film?

Prepare to Read

Checkouts ◆ Fifteen

Food City, 1967, Richard Estes, Collection of the Akron Art Museum, Akron, Ohio

Take It to the Net

Visit www.phschool.com
for interactive activities
and instruction related to
the selections, including

- background
- graphic organizers
- literary elements
- reading strategies

Preview

Connecting to the Literature

You get on the school bus and sit alone instead of taking a seat next to someone you do not know. You cannot go to a concert because you are battling the flu. Missed opportunities for new adventures occur just about every day. In these two selections, young people experience lost opportunities for different reasons.

Background

In "Checkouts," the main character is compared to "a Tibetan monk in solitary meditation." The Buddhist monks of Tibet live in seclusion, often meditating, or clearing the mind of all thoughts, to achieve a state of perfect calmness. In "Checkouts," the main character achieves this state by grocery shopping!

Literary Analysis

Irony

Irony is the contrast between an actual outcome and what the reader or the characters expect, or what might logically be expected. Irony can add humor to some situations; it can also invite readers to stop and think. In this example from "Checkouts," notice the discrepancy in ideas and how it creates irony.

> Then one day the bag boy dropped her jar of mayonnaise and that is how she fell in love.

You would probably expect a person to be frustrated if a bag boy dropped a jar of mayonnaise. In "Checkouts," however, the action generates an unexpected outcome.

Comparing Literary Works

The following selections share a theme of self-discovery. In "Checkouts," a girl falls in love, and in "Fifteen," a boy chances upon a riderless motorcycle. These opportunities for new experiences lead the teenagers to discoveries about themselves. As you read, compare and contrast the opportunities, losses, and discoveries each character faces.

Reading Strategy

Relating to Personal Experience

You can appreciate and understand a character's story by **relating it to your personal experience**. To do this, use the following strategies:

- Decide how the events in the story are like your own experiences.
- Consider how you or people you know would feel in the same situation.

Make a chart like the one shown here to keep track of your thoughts.

Vocabulary Development

intuition (in´ tōō ish´ ən) *n.* knowledge of something without reasoning (p. 283)

reverie (rev´ ər ē) *n.* dreamy thought of pleasant things (p. 283)

shards (shärdz) *n.* broken pieces (p. 283)

harried (har´ ēd) *adj.* worried (p. 283)

brazen (brā´ zən) *adj.* shamelessly bold (p. 283)

dishevelment (di shev´ əl ment) *n.* state of being untidy (p. 284)

perverse (pər vʉrs´) *adj.* contrary and willful (p. 284)

articulate (är tik´ yōō lāt´) *v.* express in words (p. 284)

lingered (liŋ´ gərd) *v.* stayed on, as if unwilling to leave (p. 285)

demure (di myoor´) *adj.* shy or modest (p. 286)

CALIFORNIA STANDARDS

Instruction with these selections addresses these standards:

R 1.1*, 3.8*

W 1.1*, 2.2*

WOLC 1.3*

LS 1.8

* Standards tested on HS Exit Exam. For complete standards, see p. CA 4.

Story Detail

The bag boy's job

Personal Experience the Incident Recalls

My first job as a grocery store cashier

Feelings It Evokes

Nervousness, anxiety

Checkouts

Cynthia Rylant

*H*er parents had moved her to Cincinnati, to a large house with beveled glass[1] windows and several porches and the *history* her mother liked to emphasize. You'll love the house, they said. You'll be lonely at first, they admitted, but you're so nice you'll make friends fast. And as an impulse tore at her to lie on the floor, to hold to their ankles and tell them she felt she was dying, to offer anything, anything at all, so they might allow her to finish growing up in the town of her childhood, they firmed their mouths and spoke from their chests and they said, It's decided.

▲ **Critical Viewing**
What distractions found in a supermarket might help people take their minds off their troubles? **[Analyze]**

---

1. beveled (bev´ əld) **glass** glass having angled or slanted edges.

They moved her to Cincinnati, where for a month she spent the greater part of every day in a room full of beveled glass windows, sifting through photographs of the life she'd lived and left behind. But it is difficult work, suffering, and in its own way a kind of art, and finally she didn't have the energy for it anymore, so she emerged from the beautiful house and fell in love with a bag boy at the supermarket. Of course, this didn't happen all at once, just like that, but in the sequence of things that's exactly the way it happened.

She liked to grocery shop. She loved it in the way some people love to drive long country roads, because doing it she could think and relax and wander. Her parents wrote up the list and handed it to her and off she went without complaint to perform what they regarded as a great sacrifice of her time and a sign that she was indeed a very nice girl. She had never told them how much she loved grocery shopping, only that she was "willing" to do it. She had an <u>intuition</u> which told her that her parents were not safe for sharing such strong, important facts about herself. Let them think they knew her.

Once inside the supermarket, her hands firmly around the handle of the cart, she would lapse into a kind of <u>reverie</u> and wheel toward the produce. Like a Tibetan monk in solitary meditation, she calmed to a point of deep, deep happiness; this feeling came to her, reliably, if strangely, only in the supermarket.

Then one day the bag boy dropped her jar of mayonnaise and that is how she fell in love.

He was nervous—first day on the job—and along had come this fascinating girl, standing in the checkout line with the unfocused stare one often sees in young children, her face turned enough away that he might take several full looks at her as he packed sturdy bags full of food and the goods of modern life. She interested him because her hair was red and thick, and in it she had placed a huge orange bow, nearly the size of a small hat. That was enough to distract him, and when finally it was her groceries he was packing, she looked at him and smiled and he could respond only by busting her jar of mayonnaise on the floor, <u>shards</u> of glass and oozing cream decorating the area around his feet.

She loved him at exactly that moment, and if he'd known this perhaps he wouldn't have fallen into the brown depression he fell into, which lasted the rest of his shift. He believed he must have looked the fool in her eyes, and he envied the sureness of everyone around him: the cocky cashier at the register, the grim and <u>harried</u> store manager, the bland butcher, and the <u>brazen</u> bag boys who smoked in the warehouse on their breaks. He wanted a second chance. Another chance to be confident and say witty things to her as he threw tin cans into her bags, persuading her to allow him to help her to her car so he might learn just a little about her, check out the floor of the car for signs of hobbies or fetishes and the bumpers for clues as to beliefs and loyalties.

But he busted her jar of mayonnaise and nothing else worked out for the rest of the day.

Fifteen

William Stafford

South of the bridge on Seventeenth
I found back of the willows one summer
day a motorcycle with engine running
as it lay on its side, ticking over
5 slowly in the high grass. I was fifteen.

I admired all that pulsing gleam, the
shiny flanks, the <u>demure</u> headlights
fringed where it lay; I led it gently
to the road and stood with that
10 companion, ready and friendly. I was fifteen.

We could find the end of a road, meet
the sky on out Seventeenth. I thought about
hills, and patting the handle got back a
confident opinion. On the bridge we indulged
15 a forward feeling, a tremble. I was fifteen.

Thinking, back farther in the grass I found
the owner, just coming to, where he had flipped
over the rail. He had blood on his hand, was pale—
I helped him walk to his machine. He ran his hand
20 over it, called me a good man, roared away.

I stood there, fifteen.

demure (di myoor') *adj.*
shy or modest

William Stafford

(1914–1993)

Reading a poem by William Stafford is like conversing with the poet. According to commentator Robert Bly, Stafford's poems are "spoken like a friend over coffee."

Stafford grew up in Kansas but later taught and wrote in Oregon. He did not publish his first book, *West of Your City*, until he was forty-six. From then on, he was prolific. He wrote a poem every day and published numerous collections, including *Traveling Through the Dark*, winner of the National Book Award in 1963.

Review and Assess

Thinking About the Selection

1. **Respond:** What would you have done if you had been in the speaker's place? Why?

2. **(a) Recall:** Which words in the first half of the poem make the motorcycle seem human? **(b) Infer:** On what basis is the speaker first attracted to the motorcycle?

3. **(a) Recall:** What does the boy imagine doing with the motor-cycle? **(b) Infer:** What does the motorcycle represent to him?

4. **(a) Recall:** How does the speaker help the owner of the motorcycle? **(b) Compare and Contrast:** How do the speaker's actions contrast with his fantasy? **(c) Draw Conclusions:** What does this contrast tell you about the speaker?

5. **Apply:** What message does this poem convey about the contrasts between fantasy and reality? Explain.

Review and Assess

Literary Analysis

Irony

1. Why is it **ironic** that the girl falls in love with the bag boy?
2. In "Fifteen," why is it ironic that the owner of the motorcycle calls the speaker "good man"?
3. (a) Using a chart like the one shown below, explain what is ironic about the endings of "Checkouts" and "Fifteen." (b) In each story, what point does the ironic ending make?

Action of Story	Expected Ending

···▶

Actual Ending

Comparing Literary Works

4. (a) Using a chart like the one below, compare the two characters in "Checkouts" to the boy in "Fifteen." (b) Who do you think learns the most about himself or herself? Why?

Character	Experiences	Feelings	Missed Opportunity	Self-discovery

Reading Strategy

Relating to Personal Experience

5. (a) Which **personal experiences** do the events in "Fifteen" call to mind? (b) How do your memories of these experiences help you to appreciate the speaker's feelings and actions?
6. What advice would you have given the girl in "Checkouts"?
7. Do you think that the unacknowledged romance in "Checkouts" is true to life? Why or why not?

Extend Understanding

8. **Cultural Connection:** Teenagers sometimes are said to have a culture all their own. Do you think that reading either selection would help adults understand "teen culture" better? Why or why not?

Integrate Language Skills

Vocabulary Development Lesson

Word Analysis: Latin Suffix -ment

The Latin suffix -ment means "state or condition of." It can be added to some verbs to form nouns, changing *dishevel* to *dishevelment*. Change each verb below to a noun by adding -ment, and use each new word in a sentence.

1. amuse
2. enlighten
3. disappoint
4. disillusion

Spelling Strategy

When you add an ending to words ending in y preceded by a consonant, change the y to i, unless the ending begins with an i. For example, *carry + -ed = carried*, but *carry + -ing = carrying*.

If the spelling of each word is correct, write *Correct*. If it is wrong, write the correct spelling.

1. denyed   2. denying   3. varyable

Fluency: Clarify Word Meaning

For each numbered item, choose the letter of the word that is closest in meaning to the vocabulary list word.

1. intuition
2. reverie
3. shards
4. harried
5. brazen

6. dishevelment
7. perverse
8. articulate
9. lingered
10. demure

a. daydream
b. untidiness
c. willfully contrary
d. shy
e. a feeling beyond thought
f. broken pieces
g. stayed on
h. worried
i. express in words
j. bold

Grammar Lesson

Prepositional Phrases as Modifiers

A **prepositional phrase** is made up of a preposition and a noun or pronoun, called the object of the preposition.

A prepositional phrase can function as either an adjective or an adverb, depending on the word it modifies. An adjective phrase modifies nouns and pronouns. An adverb phrase modifies verbs, adjectives, and adverbs. Look at the following examples:

Adjective phrase: The girl in the grocery store fell in love. (modifies the noun *girl*)

Adverb phrase: She smiled at the bag boy. (modifies the verb *smiled*)

Practice Identify the prepositional phrases in these sentences. Then, for each phrase, identify the word it modifies and indicate whether it is an adjective or adverb phrase.

1. He took the motorcycle to the road.
2. At the store, she looked for the boy.
3. The jar of mayonnaise fell to the floor.
4. He didn't mention the color of the bike.
5. They were at a theater with their dates.

Writing Application Use the following prepositional phrases in sentences. Explain whether the phrase is an adjective or adverb phrase.

1. after the trip
2. on the motorcycle

W̶G̶ Prentice Hall Writing and Grammar Connection: Chapter 21, Section 1

Writing Lesson

Character's Journal

In order to focus more on the feelings of the characters in "Checkouts," retell the events of the story by creating contrasting journals. For each date of an entry, prepare "he-said/she-said" entries.

Prewriting   Review the story to list three key events. For each event, note the likely response of each character.

Model: Finding Subjects for Each Journal

Girl	Event	Boy
thought the boy was very sweet	boy drops and breaks jar	mortified and wanted to hide

Drafting   Begin each paired journal entry with the date and a headline that summarizes the main idea of the entry. Then, in the voice of the character, write the ideas and emotions the event provoked.

Revising   Review your draft, looking for opportunities to tighten the connection between the entries. For example, if one character includes a specific detail, consider adding that detail—and a contrasting response—to the other character's journal.

WG Prentice Hall Writing and Grammar Connection: Chapter 13, Section 2

Extension Activities

Listening and Speaking Imagine you are the girl from "Checkouts," talking on the telephone to a friend in your old hometown. Tell the story of your infatuation with the bag boy.

- Start by telling your friend where you met the boy and why you like him.
- Use appropriate expressions to convey the emotions of the girl.

Write down the story you have created, practice reading it, and then present your **oral story** to your class.

Research and Technology In a group, develop a **script for a scene** from a teen soap opera based on the story from "Checkouts." In your script, make sure that you include stage directions to describe the action and the characters' emotions. Remember that you want your characters to speak and act in a way that will appeal to teenagers. **[Group Activity]**

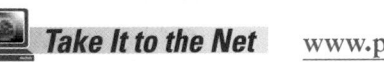 **Take It to the Net**   www.phschool.com

Go online for an additional research activity using the Internet.

Prepare to Read

Sympathy ◆ Caged Bird ◆
We never know how high we are ◆ *from* In My Place

 Take It to the Net

Visit www.phschool.com
for interactive activities
and instruction related to
the selections, including
- background
- graphic organizers
- literary elements
- reading strategies

Preview

Connecting to the Literature

The writers in this group tell about the way a dream can focus our lives. If you have ever been driven by a dream, you will be able to relate to the authors' messages—even if you have had a very different experience.

Background

Until the 1950s, Southern public schools and universities were segregated; African American students did not attend the same schools as white students. In the landmark *Brown* v. *Board of Education* decision of 1954, however, the Supreme Court overturned the doctrine of "separate but equal" schools and ruled that separate schools for different races could not offer equivalent education. In the early 1960s, various African American students like writer Charlayne Hunter-Gault enrolled at formerly all-white institutions.

Literary Analysis

Symbol

A **symbol** is an object, person, or idea that represents something beyond itself. Authors may use symbols to make a point, create a mood, or reinforce a theme. For example, in literature, springtime often represents new life and hope. Notice how the bird in the following lines from "Caged Bird" symbolizes human circumstance:

> But a bird that stalks / down his narrow cage / can seldom see through / his bars of rage. . . .

In these selections, look for details that symbolize a larger meaning.

Comparing Literary Works

As these writers suggest, dreams are part of our identity. The dream may be to acquire freedom or love or success; it may come true, or it may not. As you read these selections, compare and contrast the message each author conveys about reaching for a dream.

CALIFORNIA STANDARDS

Instruction with these selections addresses these standards:

R 1.2*, 3.7*, 3.8*
W 1.5*, 2.4*
WOLC 1.1*
LS 2.4

* Standards tested on HS Exit Exam. For complete standards, see p. CA 4.

Reading Strategy

Drawing Conclusions

Whether you are reading or just observing life, you often make sense of information by **drawing conclusions.**

- When you draw conclusions, you form an opinion about something based upon evidence that you can identify.
- Pay attention to ideas about the work that occur to you but that are not actually stated.

Each of the works in this group invites you to draw a particular conclusion about the value of aspiring to something beyond your current circumstances. Use a chart like the one shown to record your conclusions and the evidence for them.

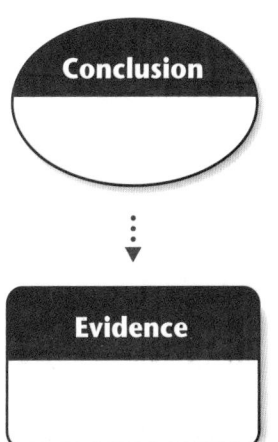

Conclusion

Evidence

Vocabulary Development

keener (kēn′ ər) *adj.* sharper (p. 292)

warp (wôrp) *v.* twist; distort (p. 295)

epithets (ep′ ə thetz) *n.* abusive words or phrases (p. 297)

effigies (ef′ i jēz) *n.* crude figures representing hated people or groups (p. 297)

disperse (di spʉrs′) *v.* drive off or scatter in different directions (p. 297)

imbued (im byo͞od′) *v.* inspired (p. 298)

perpetuated (pər pech′ o͞o āt′ id) *v.* caused to continue indefinitely (p. 298)

Sympathy

Paul Laurence Dunbar

I know what the caged bird feels, alas!
When the sun is bright on the upland slopes;
When the wind stirs, soft through the springing grass,
And the river flows like a stream of glass;
5 When the first bird sings and the first bud opes,
And the faint perfume from its chalice[1] steals—
I know what the caged bird feels!

I know why the caged bird beats his wing
Till its blood is red on the cruel bars;
10 For he must fly back to his perch and cling
When he fain[2] would be on the bough a-swing;
And a pain still throbs in the old, old scars
And they pulse again with a <u>keener</u> sting—
I know why he beats his wing!

15 I know why the caged bird sings, ah me,
When his wing is bruised and his bosom sore,—
When he beats his bars and he would be free;
It is not a carol of joy or glee,
But a prayer that he sends from his heart's deep core,
20 But a plea, that upward to Heaven he flings—
I know why the caged bird sings!

---

1. **chalice** (chalʹ is) *v.* cup or goblet; here, the cup-shaped part of a budding flower.
2. **fain** (fān) *adv.* gladly; eagerly.

keener (kēnʹ ər) *adj.* sharper

Paul Laurence Dunbar

(1872–1906)
He died before reaching his thirty-fifth birthday, but Paul Laurence Dunbar produced a tremendous outpouring of poetry and fiction during his brief lifetime. Born in Dayton, Ohio, the child of former slaves, Dunbar is widely recognized as the first African American poet of national stature.

Caged Bird

Maya Angelou

A free bird leaps
on the back of the wind
and floats downstream
till the current ends
5 and dips his wing
in the orange sun rays
and dares to claim the sky.

But a bird that stalks
down his narrow cage
10 can seldom see through
his bars of rage
his wings are clipped and
his feet are tied
so he opens his throat to sing.

15 The caged bird sings
with a fearful trill
of things unknown
but longed for still
and his tune is heard
20 on the distant hill
for the caged bird
sings of freedom.

▲ **Critical Viewing**
Which poem best captures
the spirit conveyed by this
image? Explain. **[Make a
Judgment]**

**Reading Strategy
Drawing Conclusions**
Can the bird in the
second stanza expect to
be free? Why or why not?

✔ **Reading Check**

According to "Caged
Bird," how does a free
bird interact with his
environment?

The free bird thinks of another breeze
and the trade winds soft through the sighing trees
25 and the fat worms waiting on a dawn-bright lawn
and he names the sky his own.

But a caged bird stands on the grave of dreams
his shadow shouts on a nightmare scream
his wings are clipped and his feet are tied
30 so he opens his throat to sing.

The caged bird sings
with a fearful trill
of things unknown
but longed for still
35 and his tune is heard
on the distant hill
for the caged bird
sings of freedom.

Review and Assess

Thinking About the Selections

1. **Respond:** What, if anything, has made you feel like the caged bird that Dunbar describes?

2. **(a) Recall:** What outdoor scene does the first stanza of "Sympathy" describe? **(b) Infer:** What does the caged bird feel at this time?

3. **(a) Recall:** In the second stanza of "Sympathy," what is the bird's main activity? **(b) Infer:** Why does the caged bird beat its wing against the bars of its cage?

4. **(a) Recall:** What expression appears repeatedly in "Sympathy"? **(b) Interpret:** Why do you think the speaker can sympathize so well with the caged bird?

5. **(a) Recall:** In "Caged Bird," in which stanza do readers meet the caged bird? **(b) Analyze:** Why do you think that the life of the free bird is described first?

6. **(a) Recall:** How has the caged bird been crippled?
   (b) Infer: If he still sings "with a fearful trill" despite this experience, what can you conclude about his character?

7. **(a) Recall:** How do the caged birds sing in each of the poems?
   (b) Infer: Why do they sing as they do?

8. **Speculate:** What good, if any, results from each caged bird's singing?

Maya Angelou

(b. 1928)

Born Marguerite Johnson in St. Louis, Missouri, Maya Angelou grew up in Arkansas and California. Her difficult childhood became the source for her extremely popular autobiography, *I Know Why the Caged Bird Sings* (1969), which takes its title from Paul Laurence Dunbar's "Sympathy."

In her adult life, she achieved success as a singer, an actress, a civil rights worker, and a writer of non-fiction, fiction, poetry, and plays. In her book *Wouldn't Take Nothin' for My Journey Now* (1993), she shares her reflections on life.

We never know how high we are

Emily Dickinson

We never know how high we are
Till we are asked to rise
And then if we are true to plan
Our statures touch the skies—
The Heroism we recite
Would be a normal thing
Did not ourselves the Cubits[1] warp
For fear to be a King—

Bubbles, Watercolor, 39" x 29". Courtesy of Scott Burdick

1. **Cubits** (kyoo′ bitz) ancient measure using the length of the arm from the end of the middle finger to the elbow (about 18–22 inches).

warp (wôrp) *v.* twist; distort

Review and Assess

Thinking About the Selection

1. **Respond:** What personal experiences does this poem call to mind? Explain.

2. **(a) Recall:** According to the poem, what happens when we are asked to rise to an occasion? **(b) Hypothesize:** Why might this happen?

3. **(a) Recall:** What happens "if we are true to plan"? **(b) Speculate:** How might Dickinson define heroism?

4. **(a) Recall:** According to the poem, what prevents people from acting heroically all the time? **(b) Distinguish:** Does Dickinson think people do not live to their full potential or that they are too humble to accept praise? Explain.

5. **Extend:** What advice do you think Dickinson would give someone who was just offered a challenging job opportunity?

Emily Dickinson

(1830–1886)

Emily Dickinson was born and lived most of her life in Amherst, Massachusetts. Outwardly, her life was uneventful. The range and depth of her inner life, however, are suggested by the fact that she wrote at least 1,775 poems—each one compact with emotional power. She hid these poems in a bureau drawer, where they remained until after her death.

from
In My Place
Charlayne Hunter-Gault

On January 9, 1961, I walked onto the campus at the University of Georgia to begin registering for classes. Ordinarily, there would not have been anything unusual about such a routine exercise, except, in this instance, the officials at the university had been fighting for two and a half years to keep me out. I was not socially, intellectually, or morally undesirable. I was Black. And no Black student had ever been admitted to the University of Georgia in its 176-year history. Until the landmark *Brown* v. *Board of Education* decision that in 1954 declared separate but equal schools unconstitutional, the university was protected by law in its exclusion of people like me. In applying to the university, Hamilton Holmes and I were making one of the first major tests of the court's ruling in Georgia, and no one was sure just how hard it would be to challenge nearly two hundred years of exclusive white privilege. It would take us two and a half years of fighting our way through the system and the courts, but finally, with the help of the NAACP[1] Legal Defense and Educational Fund, Inc., and with the support of our family and friends, we won the right that should have been ours all along. With the ink barely dry on the court order of three days before, Hamilton Holmes and I walked onto the campus and into history.

We would be greeted by mobs of white students, who within forty-eight hours would hurl <u>epithets</u>, burn crosses and Black <u>effigies</u>, and finally stage a riot outside my dormitory while, nearby, state patrolmen ignored the call from university officials to come and intervene. Tear gas would <u>disperse</u> the crowd, but not before I got word in my dorm room, now strewn with glass from a rock through my window, that Hamilton and I were being suspended for our own safety. It might have been the end of the story but for the fact that the University of

---

1. **NAACP** *abbr*. National Association for the Advancement of Colored People.

◀ **Critical Viewing** Which character traits does Charlayne Hunter-Gault display in this photograph? [**Analyze**]

Reading Strategy
Drawing Conclusions
What evidence supports the conclusion that Hunter-Gault faced a major struggle?

epithets (ep´ ə *the*tz) *n.* abusive words or phrases

effigies (ef´ i jēz) *n.* crude figures representing hated people or groups

disperse (di spʉrs´) *v.* drive off or scatter in different directions

✔**Reading Check**

What happened when Hunter-Gault walked onto the campus?

Georgia was now the lead case in a series of events that would become Georgia's entry into the Civil Rights Revolution. And we—like the legions of young Black students to follow in other arenas—were now <u>imbued</u> with an unshakable determination to take control of our destiny and force the South to abandon the wretched Jim Crow laws[2] it had <u>perpetuated</u> for generations to keep us in our place.

The newfound sense of mission that now motivated us evolved for me out of a natural desire to fulfill a dream I had nurtured from an early age. With a passion bordering on obsession, I wanted to be a journalist, a dream that would have been, if not unthinkable, at least undoable in the South of my early years. But no one ever told me not to dream, and when the time came to act on that dream, I would not let anything stand in the way of fulfilling it.

imbued (im byōōd′) *v.* inspired

perpetuated (pər pech′ ōō āt′ id) *v.* caused to continue indefinitely

---

2. **Jim Crow laws** upholding or practicing discrimination against African Americans. Jim Crow was a derogatory name given to African Americans from the title of a nineteenth-century minstrel song.

Review and Assess

Thinking About the Selection

1. **Respond:** If you had faced the obstacles that Hunter-Gault did, how would you have handled the situation?

2. **(a) Recall:** What had been true of the University of Georgia for 176 years? **(b) Compare and Contrast:** How was Hunter-Gault's arrival on campus different from the experiences of most other students?

3. **(a) Recall:** What specific student actions met Hunter-Gault and Hamilton Holmes at the university during their first two days? **(b) Analyze:** Why was there such a violent reaction to Hunter-Gault's attempt to attend college?

4. **(a) Recall:** How did Hunter-Gault respond when she learned that she would be suspended? **(b) Deduce:** What qualities did she need in order to succeed in her mission?

5. **(a) Recall:** With which statement does Hunter-Gault conclude her essay? **(b) Draw Conclusions:** What conclusion can you draw from this idea?

6. **(a) Connect:** How does Hunter-Gault's chosen career connect with her experiences and dreams? **(b) Generalize:** How can a sense of pursuing a larger purpose, as well as one's personal goals, give someone strength?

7. **Evaluate:** Do you think Hunter-Gault is a hero? Why or why not?

Charlayne Hunter-Gault

(b. 1942)
Born into a minister's family in South Carolina, Charlayne Hunter-Gault showed writing talent early in life and was accepted into several universities. When she was encouraged by civil rights leaders to apply to the University of Georgia, however, she made history as one of the first African American students to enter an all-white institution.

As an adult, Hunter-Gault achieved her dream of becoming a journalist, working for the "MacNeil/ Lehrer Report," the *New Yorker*, and the *New York Times*, among others. Her work in broadcast journalism has won her many awards, including two Emmys and a Peabody for excellence in broadcast journalism.

Review and Assess

Literary Analysis

Symbol

1. In Dunbar's poem, what might the cage **symbolize**?
2. In a chart like the one below, list the experiences of the birds, and then explain how their experiences symbolize those of humans.

Free ····▶ Human Experience ◀···· Caged

3. In Dickinson's poem, what might *high* and *rise* symbolize?

Comparing Literary Works

4. Use a Venn diagram to compare and contrast the spirit and behavior of the caged birds in "Sympathy" and "Caged Bird."

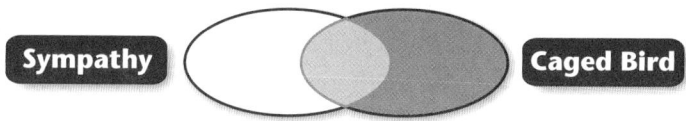

Sympathy   Caged Bird

5. Based on the message of her poem, do you think Dickinson would have seen people as caged or free? Explain.
6. Would you compare Hunter-Gault's experience to that of a caged or a free bird?

Reading Strategy

Drawing Conclusions

7. What **conclusion** can you draw from Dunbar's and Angelou's poems about freedom? Why?
8. What can you conclude from Dickinson's poem about who is responsible for a life falling short of its potential?
9. What conclusion can you draw from Hunter-Gault's circumstance about her commitment to her dream?

Extend Understanding

10. **World Events Connection:** Identify and explain a situation, past or present, in a different country from your own, in which you think one or more of these selections would apply.

Quick Review

A **symbol** is an object, person, or idea that represents something beyond itself.

To **draw conclusions**, form opinions about things based upon evidence that you can identify in your reading.

 Take It to the Net
www.phschool.com
Take the interactive self-test online to check your understanding of the selections.

Integrate Language Skills

Vocabulary Development Lesson

Levels of Diction

Diction is word choice. A writer's diction depends on his or her purpose, audience, and mood. For example, Dunbar uses elevated, or formal, diction when he refers to a song as a "carol," but Angelou uses the more down-to-earth "tune."

1. Find two more examples of old-fashioned or formal diction in "Sympathy."
2. What impression of the speaker is created?

Spelling Strategy

When adding an ending to a word that ends in more than one consonant, never double the final consonant. For example, *warp* + *-ed* = *warped*. If the spelling of each word below is correct, write *Correct*. If the spelling is incorrect, write the correct spelling.

1. protectted   2. wanting   3. deterring

Concept Development: Synonyms

For each item below, identify the letter of the word whose meaning is closest to that of the first word. If necessary, review the vocabulary words listed on page 291.

1. warp: (a) hit, (b) distort, (c) build
2. disperse: (a) scatter, (b) steal, (c) scold
3. perpetuated: (a) generated, (b) prolonged, (c) honored
4. effigies: (a) speeches, (b) insults, (c) dummies
5. keener: (a) sharper, (b) sweeter, (c) smarter
6. imbued: (a) painted, (b) placed, (c) inspired
7. epithets: (a) books, (b) slurs, (c) legends

Grammar Lesson

Preposition or Adverb?

Many words that act as prepositions can also act as adverbs, depending on their usage. A **preposition** must have an object and be part of a prepositional phrase. **Adverbs** modify verbs, adjectives, and adverbs but do not have objects.

Preposition: She had to pass *through* an angry mob. (the object is *mob*)

Adverb: She walked right *through*. (no object following *through*; modifies *walked*)

Practice Identify each underlined word as a preposition or an adverb.

1. Charlayne was not accepted <u>from</u> the moment she arrived.
2. The school had never admitted a black student <u>before</u>.
3. I'm sure she didn't even feel safe <u>inside</u>.
4. She received word that she was suspended <u>for</u> her own safety.
5. <u>After</u> the news, she decided she would continue to fight for equality.

Writing Application Use each of the following words in a sentence. Then, determine whether the word functions as a preposition or as an adverb.

1. throughout   4. around
2. outside   5. along
3. at   6. since

W͟G Prentice Hall Writing and Grammar Connection: Chapter 19, Section 1

Writing Lesson

Editorial

Write an editorial, an essay that offers an opinion on an issue, for the student newspaper at the University of Georgia at the time of Charlayne Hunter-Gault's enrollment. Try to persuade the students at the university to change their behavior toward the new African American students.

Prewriting	Jot down your point of view on the topic. Make a list of reasons to explain why students should change their behavior. Highlight the most important reasons.
Drafting	As you draft, be sure to use a solid organization. You might choose to start with your least important reasons and build toward your most important reasons, or do the reverse.
Revising	Reread your draft to make sure you have made smooth transitions between sentences. Add transition words such as *also*, *since*, and *therefore* to smooth out your writing and clarify your ideas.

Model: Adding Transitions to Smooth Writing

Although

∧They came here to seek an education, they have only dealt with

Therefore,

prejudice so far.∧It is time for us to make a change.

> Transitions like *although* and *therefore* help to connect ideas and make arguments more logical.

W̶G *Prentice Hall Writing and Grammar Connection: Chapter 11, Section 4*

Extension Activities

Listening and Speaking Plan and prepare an **oral presentation** that compares Hunter-Gault's experience with the experiences of the birds found in "Sympathy" and "Caged Bird."

- Jot down Hunter-Gault's experiences and the experiences of the free and caged birds.
- Note the similarities and differences.
- Organize your notes in a way that will clearly convey your comparison.

After you have given your presentation, ask your classmates if they agree with your views.

Research and Technology In a small group, prepare a **historical report** on the *Brown v. Board of Education* decision of 1954. In your report, explain how the Supreme Court ruling helped Charlayne Hunter-Gault attend a previously all-white school. Use library resources, including the Internet, to find information on the subject. **[Group Activity]**

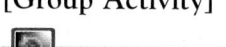 **Take It to the Net**   www.phschool.com

Go online for an additional research activity using the Internet

Prepare to Read

The Interlopers

 Take It to the Net

Visit www.phschool.com
for interactive activities
and instruction related
to "The Interlopers,"
including

- background
- graphic organizers
- literary elements
- reading strategies

Preview

Connecting to the Literature

All people get into arguments from time to time, but most disagreements do not last for a lifetime, as is the case with the characters in "The Interlopers." Think about how a long-standing dispute between two people can come to a disastrous end.

Background

A feud is a bitter, prolonged fight, typically between families or clans, that may continue for years or even generations. It may start with a single insult or injury, which provokes an act of revenge. This act in turn prompts a response, and the cycle of anger and violence is set in motion. The brutality of a feud can make for gripping drama, as it does in "The Interlopers."

Literary Analysis

Conflict

The **conflict** in a story is the struggle between opposing forces. A conflict may be internal or external. An **internal conflict** occurs within a character who experiences opposing ideas or feelings. In contrast, an **external conflict** occurs between characters or between a character and a force of nature. This passage shows a conflict between two men:

> The two enemies stood glaring at one another for a long silent moment. Each had a rifle in his hand, each had hate in his heart and murder uppermost in his mind.

As you read "The Interlopers," look for details that describe and explain the conflicts between and within the two main characters.

Connecting Literary Elements

To build the conflict of this story, the author uses **indirect characterization,** revealing only what a character does, says, and thinks. This leaves readers to draw their own conclusions about the nature of the characters and the conflict. In "The Interlopers," the writer allows the words and deeds of Ulrich and Georg to disclose what they are really like. Their actions and speech demonstrate and build the underlying conflict between them.

Reading Strategy

Identifying Causes and Effects

Understanding the causes and effects in a story can help clarify a conflict between characters.

- A **cause** is the reason for an action or event. In "The Interlopers," the cause of a long-standing feud is an old land dispute.
- An **effect** is the result of an action or event. In the story, the effect of the ancient land dispute is the personal feud between the two men.

Record the causes and effects of the story in a chart like this one.

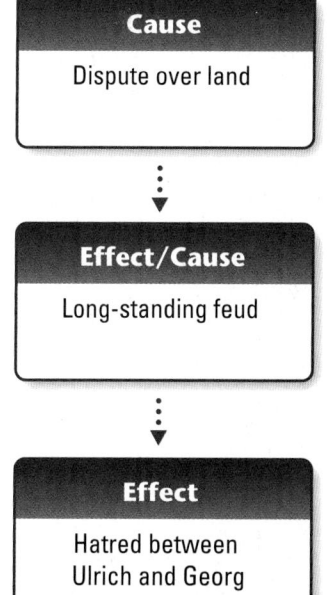

Cause
Dispute over land

Effect/Cause
Long-standing feud

Effect
Hatred between Ulrich and Georg

Vocabulary Development

precipitous (prē sip′ ə təs) *adj.* steep; sheer (p. 304)

marauders (mə rôd′ ərz) *n.* raiders; people who take goods by force (p. 305)

medley (med′ lē) *n.* mixture of things not usually found together (p. 306)

condolences (kən dō′ lən səz) *n.* expressions of sympathy with a grieving person's pain (p. 307)

languor (laŋ′ gər) *n.* lack of vigor; weakness; weariness (p. 307)

succor (suk′ ər) *n.* relief; aid; assistance (p. 309)

The Interlopers
Saki

In a forest of mixed growth somewhere on the eastern spurs of the Carpathians,[1] a man stood one winter night watching and listening, as though he waited for some beast of the woods to come within the range of his vision, and, later, of his rifle. But the game for whose presence he kept so keen an outlook was none that figured in the sportsman's calendar as lawful and proper for the chase: Ulrich von Gradwitz (ōōl´ rik fôn gräd´ vitz) patrolled the dark forest in quest of a human enemy.

The forest lands of Gradwitz were of wide extent and well stocked with game; the narrow strip of <u>precipitous</u> woodland that lay on its outskirt was not remarkable for the game it harbored or the shooting it afforded, but it was the most jealously guarded of all its owner's territorial possessions. A famous lawsuit, in the days of his grandfather, had wrested it from the illegal possession of a neighboring family of petty landowners; the dispossessed party had never acquiesced in the judgment

precipitous
(prē sip´ ə təs) *adj.*
steep; sheer

---

1. **Carpathians** (kär pā´ thē ənz) mountains in central Europe.

of the Courts, and a long series of poaching affrays[2] and similar scandals had embittered the relationships between the families for three generations. The neighbor feud had grown into a personal one since Ulrich had come to be head of his family; if there was a man in the world whom he detested and wished ill to it was Georg Znaeym (gā′ ôrg znä′ im), the inheritor of the quarrel and the tireless game-snatcher and raider of the disputed border-forest. The feud might, perhaps, have died down or been compromised if the personal ill will of the two men had not stood in the way; as boys they had thirsted for one another's blood, as men each prayed that misfortune might fall on the other, and this wind-scourged winter night Ulrich had banded together his foresters to watch the dark forest, not in quest of four-footed quarry, but to keep a lookout for the prowling thieves whom he suspected of being afoot from across the land boundary. The roebuck[3] which usually kept in the sheltered hollows during a storm wind, were running like driven things tonight, and there was movement and unrest among the creatures that were wont to sleep through the dark hours. Assuredly there was a disturbing element in the forest, and Ulrich could guess the quarter from whence it came.

He strayed away by himself from the watchers whom he had placed in ambush on the crest of the hill, and wandered far down the steep slopes amid the wild tangle of undergrowth, peering through the tree trunks and listening through the whistling and skirling of the wind and the restless beating of the branches for sight or sound of the <u>marauders</u>. If only on this wild night, in this dark, lone spot, he might come across Georg Znaeym, man to man, with none to witness—that was the wish that was uppermost in his thoughts. And as he stepped round the trunk of a huge beech he came face to face with the man he sought.

The two enemies stood glaring at one another for a long silent moment. Each had a rifle in his hand, each had hate in his heart and murder uppermost in his mind. The chance had come to give full play to the passions of a lifetime. But a man who has been brought up under the code of a restraining civilization cannot easily nerve himself to shoot down his neighbor in cold blood and without word spoken, except for an offense against his hearth and honor. And before the moment of hesitation had given way to action a deed of Nature's own violence overwhelmed them both. A fierce shriek of the storm had been answered by a splitting crash over their heads, and ere they could leap aside a mass of falling beech tree had thundered down on them. Ulrich von Gradwitz found himself stretched on the ground, one arm numb beneath him and the other held almost as helplessly in a tight tangle of forked branches, while both legs were pinned beneath the fallen mass. His heavy shooting-boots had saved his feet from being crushed to pieces, but if his fractures were not as serious

---

2. **poaching affrays** (pōch′ iŋ ə frāz′) disputes about hunting on someone else's property.
3. **roebuck** (rō′ buk′) *n.* male deer.

marauders (mə rôd′ ərz) *n.* raiders; people who take goods by force

Literary Analysis
Conflict How is the bitterness between the two landowners evident in this passage?

✔**Reading Check**
What happens to the men when they come face to face?

The Interlopers ◆ 305

as they might have been, at least it was evident that he could not move from his present position till someone came to release him. The descending twigs had slashed the skin of his face, and he had to wink away some drops of blood from his eyelashes before he could take in a general view of the disaster. At his side, so near that under ordinary circumstances he could almost have touched him, lay Georg Znaeym, alive and struggling, but obviously as helplessly pinioned down as himself. All round them lay a thick-strewn wreckage of splintered branches and broken twigs.

Relief at being alive and exasperation at his captive plight brought a strange <u>medley</u> of pious thank-offerings and sharp curses to Ulrich's lips. Georg, who was nearly blinded with the blood which trickled across his eyes, stopped his struggling for a moment to listen, and then gave a short, snarling laugh.

"So you're not killed, as you ought to be, but you're caught, anyway," he cried; "caught fast. Ho, what a jest, Ulrich von Gradwitz snared in his stolen forest. There's real justice for you!"

And he laughed again, mockingly and savagely.

"I'm caught in my own forest land," retorted Ulrich. "When my men come to release us you will wish, perhaps, that you were in a better plight than caught poaching on a neighbor's land, shame on you."

Georg was silent for a moment; then he answered quietly:

"Are you sure that your men will find much to release? I have men, too, in the forest tonight, close behind me, and *they* will be here first

medley (med′ lē) *n.* mixture of things not usually found together

▼ Critical Viewing
Why does the setting—a snowy forest like the one shown here—intensify the danger of the conflict? **[Connect]**

Untitled, Rob Wood. Illustration by Wood Ronsaville Harlin, Inc.

and do the releasing. When they drag me out from under these branches it won't need much clumsiness on their part to roll this mass of trunk right over on the top of you. Your men will find you dead under a fallen beech tree. For form's sake I shall send my <u>condolences</u> to your family."

"It is a useful hint," said Ulrich fiercely. "My men had orders to follow in ten minutes' time, seven of which must have gone by already, and when they get me out—I will remember the hint. Only as you will have met your death poaching on my lands I don't think I can decently send any message of condolence to your family."

"Good," snarled Georg, "good. We fight this quarrel out to the death, you and I and our foresters, with no cursed interlopers to come between us. Death and damnation to you, Ulrich von Gradwitz."

"The same to you, Georg Znaeym, forest-thief, game-snatcher."

Both men spoke with the bitterness of possible defeat before them, for each knew that it might be long before his men would seek him out or find him; it was a bare matter of chance which party would arrive first on the scene.

Both had now given up the useless struggle to free themselves from the mass of wood that held them down; Ulrich limited his endeavors to an effort to bring his one partially free arm near enough to his outer coat pocket to draw out his wine flask. Even when he had accomplished that operation it was long before he could manage the unscrewing of the stopper or get any of the liquid down his throat. But what a heaven-sent draft it seemed! It was an open winter, and little snow had fallen as yet, hence the captives suffered less from the cold than might have been the case at that season of the year; nevertheless, the wine was warming and reviving to the wounded man, and he looked across with something like a throb of pity to where his enemy lay, just keeping the groans of pain and weariness from crossing his lips.

"Could you reach this flask if I threw it over to you?" asked Ulrich suddenly; "there is good wine in it, and one may as well be as comfortable as one can. Let us drink, even if tonight one of us dies."

"No, I can scarcely see anything; there is so much blood caked round my eyes," said Georg, "and in any case I don't drink wine with an enemy."

Ulrich was silent for a few minutes, and lay listening to the weary screeching of the wind. An idea was slowly forming and growing in his brain, an idea that gained strength every time that he looked across at the man who was fighting so grimly against pain and exhaustion. In the pain and <u>languor</u> that Ulrich himself was feeling the old fierce hatred seemed to be dying down.

"Neighbor," he said presently, "do as you please if your men come first. It was a fair compact. But as for me, I've changed my mind. If my men are the first to come you shall be the first to be helped, as though you were my guest. We have quarreled like devils all our lives over this stupid strip of forest, where the trees can't even stand

condolences (kən dō´ lən sez) *n.* expressions of sympathy with a grieving person's pain

Literary Analysis
Conflict and Indirect Characterization What can you conclude about the men's characters from their exchange of comments here?

languor (laŋ´ gər) *n.* lack of vigor; weakness; weariness

**Reading Check**

What happens to the two men after the tree falls?

upright in a breath of wind. Lying here tonight, thinking, I've come to think we've been rather fools; there are better things in life than getting the better of a boundary dispute. Neighbor, if you will help me to bury the old quarrel I—I will ask you to be my friend."

Georg Znaeym was silent for so long that Ulrich thought, perhaps, he had fainted with the pain of his injuries. Then he spoke slowly and in jerks.

"How the whole region would stare and gabble if we rode into the market square together. No one living can remember seeing a Znaeym and a von Gradwitz talking to one another in friendship. And what peace there would be among the forester folk if we ended our feud tonight. And if we choose to make peace among our people there is none other to interfere, no interlopers from outside . . . You would come and keep the Sylvester night beneath my roof, and I would come and feast on some high day at your castle . . . I would never fire a shot on your land, save when you invited me as a guest; and you should come and shoot with me down in the marshes where the wildfowl are. In all the countryside there are none that could hinder if we willed to make peace. I never thought to have wanted to do

▲ **Critical Viewing**
What kinds of encounters or incidents might occur in this setting? **[Analyze]**

Literary Analysis
Conflict How has the nature of the conflict between the two men now changed?

other than hate you all my life, but I think I have changed my mind about things too, this last half-hour. And you offered me your wine flask . . . Ulrich von Gradwitz, I will be your friend."

For a space both men were silent, turning over in their minds the wonderful changes that this dramatic reconciliation would bring about. In the cold, gloomy forest, with the wind tearing in fitful gusts through the naked branches and whistling round the tree trunks, they lay and waited for the help that would now bring release and <u>succor</u> to both parties. And each prayed a private prayer that his men might be the first to arrive, so that he might be the first to show honorable attention to the enemy that had become a friend.

Presently, as the wind dropped for a moment, Ulrich broke silence.

"Let's shout for help," he said; "in this lull our voices may carry a little way."

"They won't carry far through the trees and undergrowth," said Georg, "but we can try. Together, then."

The two raised their voices in a prolonged hunting call.

"Together again," said Ulrich a few minutes later, after listening in vain for an answering halloo.

succor (suk´ ər) *n.* relief; aid; assistance

✓**Reading Check**

What response does Georg give when Ulrich asks him to be his friend?

"I heard something that time, I think," said Ulrich.

"I heard nothing but the pestilential wind," said Georg hoarsely.

There was silence again for some minutes, and then Ulrich gave a joyful cry.

"I can see figures coming through the wood. They are following in the way I came down the hillside."

Both men raised their voices in as loud a shout as they could muster.

"They hear us! They've stopped. Now they see us. They're running down the hill toward us," cried Ulrich.

"How many of them are there?" asked Georg.

"I can't see distinctly," said Ulrich; "nine or ten."

"Then they are yours," said Georg; "I had only seven out with me."

"They are making all the speed they can, brave lads," said Ulrich gladly.

"Are they your men?" asked Georg. "Are they your men?" he repeated impatiently as Ulrich did not answer.

"No," said Ulrich with a laugh, the idiotic chattering laugh of a man unstrung with hideous fear.

"Who are they?" asked Georg quickly, straining his eyes to see what the other would gladly not have seen.

"Wolves."

Review and Assess

Thinking About the Selection

1. **Respond:** With whom did you sympathize: Ulrich, Georg, neither, or both? Why?

2. **(a) Recall:** Whose family won possession of the disputed land in the lawsuit? **(b) Interpret:** Why does Georg not consider himself a poacher?

3. **(a) Recall:** How far back does the hatred between Ulrich and Georg go? **(b) Infer:** Which factors about the feud seem to contribute the most to Ulrich's anger at Georg?

4. **(a) Recall:** In what condition does the fallen tree leave each man? **(b) Draw Conclusions:** Why do the men end their feud?

5. **(a) Speculate:** How might the story have continued if the two men had been rescued? **(b) Support:** Why do you think so?

6. **(a) Evaluate:** Considering the cause of their predicament, do you think the two men deserved their fate? Why or why not? **(b) Extend:** What lesson can be learned from the experiences of Ulrich and Georg?

7. **(a) Apply:** What is it about human nature that leads to feuds like the one in the story? **(b) Speculate:** Will it ever be possible to end such feuds? Explain.

Saki
(1870–1916)

Saki is the pen name of the British writer H. H. Munro. Born in Burma, he was sent at age two to live in England, where he was raised in a strict household by two aunts. As a young adult, he returned to Burma to serve in the police force. Two years later, however, poor health forced him to return to England, where he began working as a jounalist. After serving as a newspaper correspondent in Russia and France, Saki settled in London.

In 1904, his first collection of short stories was published. He later wrote more short stories and two novels.

Saki was killed in France during World War I. In his honor, the king of England issued a scroll that concludes, "Let those who come after see to it that his name is not forgotten."

Review and Assess

Literary Analysis

Conflict

1. What **external conflict** pits a character against another character in "The Interlopers"?
2. Identify a conflict that pits a character against a force of nature.
3. Give an example of an **internal conflict** within Ulrich or Georg.
4. Using a chart like the one shown, analyze a conflict that changes or develops as the story continues.

Developing conflict	Reason for change

Connecting Literary Elements

5. Using a character-trait diagram like this one, list the traits you detect in each man. Cite examples from the story.

Traits   **Examples**

Character _____ ...▶ _____

_____ ...▶ _____

6. How does the use of **indirect characterization** illuminate the conflict between the two men? Give specific details.

Reading Strategy

Identifying Causes and Effects

7. (a) What **causes** the beech tree to fall over? (b) What is the **effect** of that event?
8. (a) Why do the men shout together at the end? (b) What is the effect of their shouting? (c) Is it the effect they expect?

Extend Understanding

9. **Social Studies Connection:** (a) Explain the options for resolving a bitter territorial dispute among nations in today's world.
(b) Why are such problems so complicated?

Quick Review

Conflict in a story is the struggle between opposing forces.
An **internal conflict** occurs within a character.
An **external conflict** occurs between characters or between a character and a force of nature.

When using **indirect characterization,** an author reveals only what a character does, says, and thinks, leaving readers to draw conclusions about the nature of the character.

A **cause** is the reason for an action or event.
An **effect** is what results from that action or event.

 Take It to the Net
www.phschool.com
Take the interactive self-test online to check your understanding of the selections.

Integrate Language Skills

Vocabulary Development Lesson

Word Analysis: Latin Root -dol-

The Latin root -dol- means "pain." The root appears in the word *condolence*, meaning "an expression of sympathy with a grieving person's pain." Using the meaning of -dol-, define *doleful* and *indolent* and use each in a sentence.

Spelling Strategy

For many verbs ending in y, you must change the y to i or ie when you add an ending such as -s or -ed. For those that end in y preceded by a vowel, however, the spelling remains unchanged. For example, *medley* + -s = *medleys*.

For each item, add the ending shown and write the new word created.

1. spy + -s
2. journey + -ed
3. stray + -ed
4. fly + -s

Fluency: Words in Context

Write sentences as described below, using one word from the vocabulary list on page 303 for each sentence.

1. Write the lead sentence of a news article describing a robbery.
2. Describe the site of a rock-climbing expedition.
3. Explain what a group of rescue workers provides for flood victims.
4. Begin a letter to a friend who has lost an elderly family member.
5. Describe your feelings after spending a week in bed with the flu.
6. Write a description of a program honoring the composer of many famous songs.

Grammar Lesson

Different Kinds of Conjunctions

A main clause is a group of words with a subject and a verb that makes sense even when it stands alone. In contrast, a subordinate clause makes sense only when it is linked to a main clause. **Conjunctions** connect words, word groups, or clauses.

A **subordinating conjunction** links a subordinate clause to the main clause of a sentence.

Subordinating: *Before* they moved, the tree fell on them.

A **coordinating conjunction** joins main clauses or words of equal importance.

Coordinating: They waited, *but* no one arrived.

Correlative conjunctions are pairs of conjunctions that link words of equal rank.

Correlative: Ulrich watched, *not* in quest of quarry *but* to wait for thieves.

Practice Identify the conjunctions and classify each as *subordinating*, *coordinating*, or *correlative*.

1. Ulrich and Georg were enemies.
2. A tree fell, and the two men were trapped.
3. Neither Ulrich nor Georg was brave.
4. They yelled so that help would come.
5. Interlopers arrived, but they were wolves.

Writing Application Summarize the story, making use of at least one of each type of conjunction.

*W*G *Prentice Hall Writing and Grammar Connection: Chapter 19, Section 2*

Writing Lesson

News Story

Nature's own violence spells doom for Ulrich and Georg. Imagine you are a news reporter. Write a story about the freak accident and its aftermath.

Prewriting Focus on the questions *who? what? when? where? why?* and *how?* Include facts, quotations, and details below each heading in a chart. Then, plan your lead, or opening paragraph, which should summarize the news story.

Model: Recording Details in an Organizer

Who?	What?	When?	Where?	Why?	How?
Ulrich and Georg	Hit by a tree limb	Night	Ulrich's land	A beech tree fell on them	Tree blown down by storm

Drafting As you write the body of your story, use elaboration—the development of ideas and details—to help readers understand the news event. Clarify as much of the event as you can.

Revising Read your story aloud to a classmate. Change any part of the story that is unclear or requires further elaboration.

 Prentice Hall Writing and Grammar Connection: Chapter 6, Section 2

Extension Activities

Listening and Speaking To present a **debate** about the disputed land, form groups to represent each man. Each group should

- offer reasons why its character is entitled to the land.
- use quotations and other citations from the story to support its point of view.
- present an introductory statement, a rebuttal, and a closing statement.

Allot each team the same amount of time, and then ask the audience to decide which group was more persuasive. **[Group Activity]**

Research and Technology The chilling ending of "The Interlopers" comes about because of the unexpected arrival of wolves. Create a **brochure** that presents information about wolves. Design and publish your document with software and graphics programs that make charts, maps, or other graphics. Show where wolves live and how they raise their young, form packs, and hunt.

 **Take It to the Net**   www.phschool.com

Go online for an additional research activity using the Internet.

Prepare to Read

The Rug Merchant

 Take It to the Net

Visit www.phschool.com
for interactive activities
and instruction related to
"The Rug Merchant,"
including
- background
- graphic organizers
- literary elements
- reading strategies

Preview

Connecting to the Literature

Sometimes you make up your mind and then find yourself changing it.
You think you have someone sized up and then discover that a bit more
measuring tape is needed. James Michener finds himself in this position in
"The Rug Merchant."

Background

Persian rugs—like the ones sold by Zaqir, the rug merchant in the
essay—are mostly made of wool, but the finest are made of silk. Different
designs are linked with specific regions. Most designs are abstract or geometric patterns, although some depict people, plants, and animals.

Literary Analysis

Characterization in Essays

Writers create and in essays develop their characters by means of a process called **characterization.** In an essay, a person's speech and actions, the reactions of others, and the author's comments all contribute to the person's characterization. Look at this description of Zaqir, a rug merchant in Afghanistan:

> . . . a very thin, toothy man with longish black hair and a perpetual smile entered and started throwing onto the dirt floor twenty or thirty of the most enchantingly beautiful Persian rugs I had ever seen.

Note how the author focuses on the man's appearance and behavior. While reading "The Rug Merchant," look for more details that characterize the seller.

Connecting Literary Elements

"The Rug Merchant" is a nonfiction essay that uses **first-person narration**—the author is part of the story and thus makes use of the words *I, me,* and *my.* Michener relates his own experiences with a rug merchant. In so doing, Michener ends up characterizing not only Zaqir but also himself. Authors using first-person narration inevitably tell readers as much about themselves as about other characters.

Instruction with this selection addresses these standards:

R 1.1*, 3.3*, 3.4*
W 1.3*, 2.5*
WOLC 1.3*
LS 1.7, 1.9

* *Standards tested on HS Exit Exam. For complete standards, see p. CA 4.*

Reading Strategy

Making Inferences About Characters

When you **make inferences about characters,** you draw conclusions about them by using details such as the following:

- Their appearance and actions
- What they say—including what they say about themselves—in narration and dialogue

Use a chart like the one shown to record details from "The Rug Merchant." For each detail you note, jot down the inference you draw.

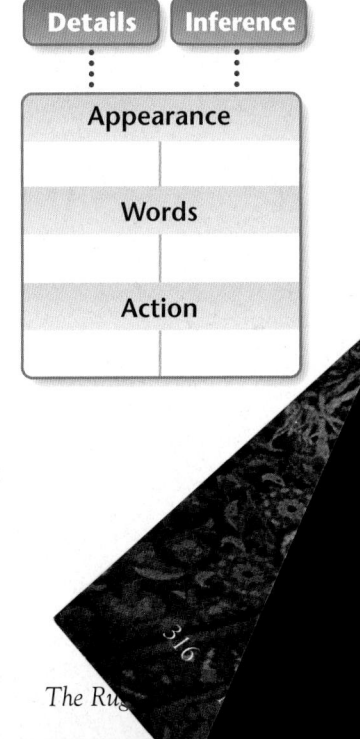

Details	Inference
Appearance	
Words	
Action	

Vocabulary Development

improvised (im′ prə vīzd) *adj.* put together spontaneously (p. 317)

laden (lād′ 'n) *adj.* burdened (p. 317)

encompassed (en kum′ pəst) *v.* surrounded (p. 317)

impose (im pōz′) *v.* put to some trouble (p. 319)

ingeniously (in jēn′ yəs lē) *adv.* very cleverly (p. 320)

316

The Rug

The Rug Merchant

James Michener

I once made a long trip over the Dasht-i-Margo, the desert in Afghanistan, to the ancient city of Herat (he rät´), where I lodged in a former mosque with earthen floors. I had been in my improvised quarters only a few minutes when a very thin, toothy man with longish black hair and a perpetual smile entered and started throwing onto the dirt floor twenty or thirty of the most enchantingly beautiful Persian rugs I had ever seen. Their designs were miraculous—intricate interweavings of Koranic symbols framed in geometric patterns that teased the eye—but their colors were also sheer delight: reds, yellows, greens and especially dark blues that were radiant.

They made my room a museum, one rug piled atop another, all peeking out at me, and when they were in place and the smiling man was satisfied with his handiwork—I supposed that this was a service of the so-called hotel—to my amazement he handed me a scrap of paper on which was written in pencil in English: "muhammad zaqir, rug merchant, herat."

Aware at last of how I had been trapped, I protested: "No! No! No rugs!" but without relaxing his smile the least bit he said in English: "No necessity to buy. I leave here. You study, you learn to like," and before I could protest further he was gone. I ran out to make him take back his rugs, for I wanted none of them, but he was already leading his laden camel away from the old mosque.

I assumed he had learned from the hotel manager that I was to be in Herat for five days, and it was obvious that he felt confident that within that period he could wear me down and persuade me to buy a rug. He started on the evening of that first day; he came back after supper to sit with me in the shadowy light cast by a flickering lamp. He said: "Have you ever seen lovelier rugs? That one from my friend in Meshed. Those two from the dealer in Bukhara. This one from a place you know, maybe? Samarkand."

When I asked him how he was able to trade with such towns in the Soviet Union[1] he shrugged: "Borders? Out here we don't bother," and with a sweep of his hand that encompassed all the rugs he said: "Not one woven in Afghanistan," and I noted the compelling pronunciation he gave that name: Ahf-han-ee-stahn.

He sat for more than an hour with me that evening, and next day he was back before noon to start his serious bargaining: "Michener-sahib,[2] name German perhaps?" I told him it was more likely English, at which he laughed: "English, Afghans, many battles, English always win but next day you march back to India, nothing change." When I corrected him: "I'm not English," he said: "I know. Pennsylvania. Three, four, maybe five of your rugs look great your place Pennsylvania."

"But I don't need rugs there. I don't really want them."

"Would they not look fine Pennsylvania?" and as if the rugs were of

---

1. **Soviet Union** The Union of Soviet Socialist Republics consisted of fifteen republics strictly controlled by the country's central government until independence movements in 1991.
2. **Michener-sahib** (sä´ ib) Mr. Michener.

The Rug Merchant ◆ 317

improvised (im´ prə vīzd) *adj.* put together spontaneously

Literary Analysis
Characterization in Essays How would you describe Michener, based on where he is lodging?

laden (lād´ ′n) *adj.* burdened

encompassed (en kum´ pəst) *v.* surrounded

Reading Check
What does the visitor bring to Michener's room?

little value, he kicked the top ones aside to reveal the glowing wonders of those below.

When he returned that second night he got down to even more serious business: "The big white and gold one you like, six hundred dollars." On and on he went, and when it was clear that I had no interest whatever in the big ones, he subtly covered them over with the smaller six- by four-foot ones already in the room; then he ran out to his camel to fetch seven or eight of the size that I had in some unconscious way disclosed I might consider, and by the end of that session he knew that I was at least a possible purchaser of four or five of the handsome rugs.

"Ah, Michener-sahib, you have fine eye. That one from China, silk and wool, look at those tiny knots." Then he gave me a lesson in rug making; he talked about the designs, the variation in knots, the wonderful compactness of the Chinese variety, the dazzling colors of the Samarkand. It was fascinating to hear him talk, and all the while he was wearing me down.

He was a persistent rascal, always watching till he saw me return to my mosque after work, then pouncing on me. On the third day, as he sat drinking tea with me while our chairs were perched on his treasury of rugs, four and five deep at some places and covering the entire floor, he knocked down one after another of my objections: "You can't take them with you? No traveler can. I send them to you, camel here, ship Karachi, train New York, truck to your home Pennsylvania." Pasted onto the pages of his notebook were addresses of buyers from all parts of the world to whom he had shipped his rugs, and I noticed that they had gone out from Meshed in Iran, Mazar-e-Sharif in Afghanistan and Bukhara (bü kär′ ə) in Russia; apparently he really moved about with his laden camel. But he also had, pasted close to the shipping address, letters from his customers proving that the rugs had finally reached their new owners. In our dealings he seemed to me an honest man.

On that third night, when it began to look as if I might escape without making a purchase even though I had shown an interest in six rugs, he hammered at me regarding payments: "Now, Michener-sahib, I can take American dollars, you know."

"I have no American dollars." Rapidly he ran through the currencies that he would accept, British, Indian, Iranian, Pakistani, Afghani, in that descending order, until I had to stop him with a truthful statement: "Muhammad, my friend, I have no money, none of any kind," and before the last word had been uttered he cried: "I take traveler's checks, American Express, Bank America in California," and then I had to tell him the sad news: "Muhammad, friend. I have no traveler's checks. Left them all locked up in the American embassy in Kabul. Because there are robbers on the road to Meshed."

"I know. I know. But you are an honest man, Michener-sahib. I take your personal check."

When I said truthfully that I had none, he asked simply: "You like those six rugs?"

"Yes, you have made me appreciate them. I do."

With a sweeping gesture he gathered the six beauties, rolled them deftly into a bundle and thrust them into my arms: "You take them. Send me a check when you get to Pennsylvania."

"You would trust me?"

"You look honest. Don't I look honest?" And he picked up one of his larger rugs, a real beauty, and showed me the fine knots: "Bukhara. I got it there, could not pay. I send the money when I sell. Man in Bukhara trusts me. I trust you."

I said I could not <u>impose</u> on him in that way. Something might happen to me or I might prove to be a crook, and the discussion ended, except that as he left me he asked: "Michener, if you had the money, what rugs would you take with you?" and I said "None, but if you could ship them, I'd take those four," and he said: "Those four you shall have. I'll find a way."

Next day he was back in the mosque right after breakfast with an astonishing proposal: "Michener-sahib, I can let you have those four rugs, special price, four hundred fifty dollars." Before I could repeat my inability to pay, he said: "Bargain like this you never see again. Tell you what to do. You write me a check."

When I said, distressed at losing such a bargain: "But I really have no blank checks," he said: "You told me yesterday. I believe you. But draw me one," and from his folder he produced a sheet of ordinary paper and a pencil. He showed me how to draw a copy of a blank check, bearing the name of the bank, address, amount, etc.—and for the first time in my life I actually drew a blank check, filled in the amount and signed it, whereupon Muhammad Zaqir placed it in his file, folded the four rugs I had bought, tied them with string and attached my name and address.

He piled the rugs onto his camel, and then mounted it to proceed on his way to Samarkand.

Back home in Pennsylvania I started to receive two different kinds of letters, perhaps fifteen of each. The following is a sample of the first category:

> I am a shipping agent in Istanbul and a freighter arrived here from Karachi bringing a large package, well wrapped, addressed to you in Pennsylvania. Upon receipt of your check for $19.50 American I will forward the package to you.

From Karachi, Istanbul, Trieste, Marseilles and heavens knows where else I received a steady flow of letters over a three-year period, and always the sum demanded was less than twenty dollars, so that I would say to myself: "Well, I've invested so much in it already, I may as well

Michener and the World

"The Rug Merchant" comes from James Michener's autobiography, *The World Is My Home: A Memoir*. In fact, Michener visited countless places around the world and wrote books about many of them. His books often relate fascinating histories and describe exotic lands. *The Bridges at Toko-Ri, Hawaii, Tales of the South Pacific, Caravans, Poland, Iberia, Chesapeake, Texas, Alaska, Caribbean,* and *Space* are some of the approximately twenty novels he wrote. The practiced eye of a lifelong traveler comes in handy for someone describing Zaqir, the merchant in this story.

impose (im pōz´) v. put to some trouble

✔ Reading Check

What kind of payment does Michener give Zaqir for the rugs?

risk a little more." And off the check would go, with the rugs never getting any closer. Moreover, I was not at all sure that if they ever did reach me they would be my property, for my unusual check had never been submitted for payment, even though I had forewarned my local bank: "If it ever does arrive, pay it immediately, because it's a debt of honor."

The second group of letters explained the long delay:

> I am serving in Kabul as the Italian ambassador and was lately in Herat where a rug merchant showed me that remarkable check you gave him for something like five hundred dollars. He asked me if I thought it would be paid if he forwarded it and I assured him that since you were a man of good reputation it would be. When I asked him why he had not submitted it sooner, he said: "Michener-sahib a good name. I show his check everybody like you, sell many rugs."

These letters came from French commercial travelers, English explorers, Indian merchants, almost anyone who might be expected to reach out-of-the-way Herat and take a room in that miserable old mosque.

In time the rugs arrived, just as Muhammad Zaqir had predicted they would, accompanied by so many shipping papers they were a museum in themselves. And after my improvised check had been used as an advertisement for nearly five years, it too came home to roost and was honored. Alas, shortly thereafter the rugs were stolen, but I remember them vividly and with longing. Especially do I remember the man who spent four days ingeniously persuading me to buy.

ingeniously (in jēn′ yəs lē) *adv.* cleverly

James Michener

(1907–1997)

James Michener was raised as a Quaker by his adoptive mother in Doylestown, Pennsylvania. After graduating from college, he worked as a book editor before joining the navy during World War II.

Michener's war experiences inspired him to write *Tales of the South Pacific* (1947), which won the Pulitzer Prize—a remarkable achievement for a first-time novelist.

Michener was a tireless portrayer of other lands and peoples. Among the many places he wrote about were the Holy Land, in *The Source* (1965), and South Africa, in *The Covenant* (1980).

Review and Assess

Thinking About the Selection

1. **Respond:** Would you have bought rugs from Zaqir? Explain.
2. **(a) Recall:** What does Zaqir do after Michener first protests that he does not want the rugs? **(b) Infer:** Why does Michener keep discussing the rugs with Zaqir?
3. **(a) Recall:** When Zaqir returns on the second night, how has he altered his sales pitch? **(b) Distinguish:** Zaqir's behavior prompts Michener to describe him as both "an honest man" and "a rascal." What provokes this reaction?
4. **(a) Recall:** What business proposal does Zaqir eventually make to Michener? **(b) Generalize:** What does the proposal suggest about the differences between Zaqir's culture and Michener's?
5. **Speculate:** What do you think Michener finally concludes about Zaqir as a result of their dealings?
6. **Extend:** What could this essay teach someone about trust and honesty?

Review and Assess

Literary Analysis

Characterization in Essays

1. As first **characterized,** does Zaqir seem believable to you? Write your response in the center of a cluster map like the one shown. Then, show which actions and words support your opinion.

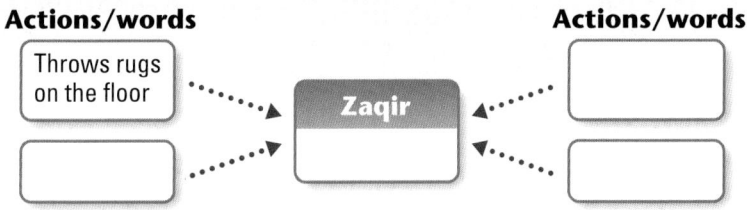

Actions/words — Throws rugs on the floor → **Zaqir** ← **Actions/words**

2. Does your overall impression of Zaqir change over the course of the story? Explain.
3. Describe Michener as a character. Base your answer on his actions, attitudes, and words.

Connecting Literary Elements

4. **First-person narration** reveals the ideas and opinions of the writer. In which specific ways is your opinion of Zaqir influenced by Michener's narration?
5. Cite specific ways in which your impression of Zaqir might be different if he had narrated the story.

Reading Strategy

Making Inferences About Characters

6. Michener pays shipping charges for three years while awaiting the rugs' arrival. What does this fact lead you to **infer** about him?
7. One detail and the responses it generates can reveal the traits of two characters. (a) What inferences can you draw about Michener based on the blank check he draws? (b) What can you infer about Zaqir based on his interaction with the check?

Extend Understanding

8. **Cultural Connection:** Which cultural differences influence the nature of the salesperson-customer relationship in this essay?

Quick Review

Characterization involves an author's use of speech, actions, reactions, and comments to create and develop characters.

In nonfiction, **first-person narration** allows the author to be part of the action and to use the words *I, me,* and *my.*

To **make inferences about characters,** draw conclusions about them from their appearance, actions, and words.

 Take It to the Net
www.phschool.com
Take the interactive self-test online to check your understanding of the selections.

Integrate Language Skills

Vocabulary Development Lesson

Word Analysis: Latin Root -vis-

The Latin root -vis- means "see." The root appears in the word *improvised,* which literally means "not seen before." It also appears in these words and phrases:

visitor	revise
supervisor	visual aid
invisible	envision

Identify the word or phrase above that matches each clue.

1. A person who oversees and directs you in your work
2. Not able to be seen
3. One who comes to see you
4. Something you see that helps explain an idea
5. To see in your mind
6. To "see again" and change

Concept Development: Synonyms

Identify the synonym, or word with nearly the same meaning, for the first word in each item.

1. laden: (a) spoon, (b) burdened, (c) hurt
2. improvised: (a) unplanned, (b) entertaining, (c) careful
3. encompassed: (a) directed, (b) watched, (c) surrounded
4. ingeniously: (a) cleverly, (b) dishonestly, (c) stupidly
5. impose: (a) arrange, (b) trouble, (c) stand

Spelling Strategy

For a word that ends in a double consonant, do not drop the final consonant before adding an ending: *encompass* + *-ed* = *encompassed.*

Identify the misspelled word or words below and correct the spelling.

1. enthraling   2. embarrasment   3. reference

Grammar Lesson

Interjections

An **interjection** is a word or phrase that expresses a feeling or an emotion and functions independently of the other words in a sentence. An interjection might express pain, joy, annoyance, or surprise.

In the following example, the interjection expresses a feeling of discovery.

> **Example:**
> *Oh,* Michener-sahib, you have a fine eye.

Punctuate mild interjections with commas and strong ones with exclamation marks.

Practice Identify the interjections below. Then, describe the emotion that each expresses.

1. No! I want no rugs!
2. Ah, Michener-sahib, I can take American dollars.
3. Well, you make me appreciate them.
4. My goodness, I've already invested so much.
5. Alas, the rugs were stolen.

Writing Application Select three sentences from "The Rug Merchant" and rewrite them, using interjections to add emotion.

WG *Prentice Hall Writing and Grammar Connection: Chapter 19, Section 2*

Writing Lesson

Letter of Recommendation

If a problem had arisen with the rugs that Michener bought from Zaqir, he might have written a letter of complaint to the merchant. Instead, he seems to have been pleased with his purchase. As Michener, write a letter encouraging others to buy from Zaqir.

Prewriting	Review the story to find examples of Zaqir's behavior and sales approach. Also, note Michener's evolving responses to Zaqir.
Drafting	Write your letter, clearly stating your feelings about the rug merchant. As a testimonial, your letter should explain Michener's experiences and draw generalizations about them.
Revising	Review your draft, underlining the main impression you want to convey to other consumers. Where necessary, add more examples to support this idea.

Model: Revising to Create a Main Impression

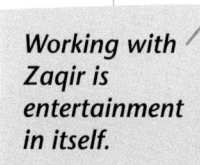

Working with Zaqir is entertainment in itself.

Personally, I received my goods years after I purchased them, but the memory of this persistent salesman—piling rug over rug—lingers.

> The added text elaborates on the writer's positive memories.

Prentice Hall Writing and Grammar Connection: Chapter 7, Section 4

Extension Activities

Listening and Speaking With a classmate, **role-play** a conversation between Michener and Zaqir. Combine dialogue from the essay with original dialogue. Follow these points:

- Analyze the situation the men are in before constructing your dialogue.
- Use nonverbal techniques—voice, gestures, and eye contact—to convey the characters' essence.

Rehearse your conversation together, using a tape recorder to check its effectiveness. Then, present the conversation to your class. **[Group Activity]**

Research and Technology Search the Internet for additional information about Persian rugs, like those described in "The Rug Merchant." Display what you learn in an **oral presentation.** Use graphics, such as pictures of vibrant rugs, to enhance the appeal and accuracy of your report, and prepare concise notes to help you in your delivery.

 **Take It to the Net**   www.phschool.com

Go online for an additional research activity using the Internet.

Prepare to Read

Combing ◆ Women ◆ maggie and milly and molly and may ◆ Astonishment

The Quiltmaker, Paul Goodnight, Color Circle Art Publishing Inc.

Take It to the Net

Visit www.phschool.com for interactive activities and instruction related to the selections, including

- background
- graphic organizers
- literary elements
- reading strategies

Preview

Connecting to the Literature

Throughout our lives, we make discoveries that show us who we are. Each of the poems that follow presents such a discovery. You may find that the discoveries of the poems' speakers lead you to discoveries of your own.

Background

In "Women," the speaker expresses admiration for African American women who fought for public school desegregation in the American South. Until the 1950s, these schools were segregated—that is, black and white students attended different schools. In 1954, the U.S. Supreme Court ruled that segregated public schooling was not permissible because it was inherently unequal. Some state governments and local school districts resisted the new ruling.

Literary Analysis

Moment of Insight

A **moment of insight** is a fresh, new thought that arises from a poet's musings or reflections. Specific details in a poem add up to a general insight into life. This excerpt from "Combing" offers one such insight:

> Bending, I bow my head
> And lay my hand upon
> Her hair, combing, and think
> How women do this for
> Each other.

The poet connects her own action with something all women have done. Look for other moments of insight as you read the four selections. Use a chart like the one shown to record the details and insights you find.

Details

She combs her daughter's hair.

Insight

She realizes that this is something all women do.

Comparing Literary Works

A moment of insight is usually closely related to a poem's **theme,** or central message about life. The poems that follow all focus on a theme, related to the issue of identity. Each poem explores a different way of thinking about identity—through family connections, nature, and an appreciation of the surrounding world. As you read, compare and contrast the messages about identity that the poems convey. With which poet's message do you most identify? Why?

Reading Strategy

Interpreting Meaning

When you **interpret the meaning** of a poem, you seek to understand the point or insight that the poet communicates. To help interpret the meaning of a poem, apply the following techniques:

- Use sensory images—things you can see, hear, taste, smell, or touch—to picture what is being described.
- Ask yourself why the poet has chosen those specific images.
- Connect what is being said to your own experience.

As you read, try to interpret the meaning of each poem.

Vocabulary Development

intent (in tent´) *adj.* firmly fixed; concentrated (p. 326)

plaiting (plāt´ iŋ) *v.* braiding (p. 326)

stout (stout) *adj.* sturdy (p. 327)

languid (laŋ´ gwid) *adj.* drooping; weak (p. 329)

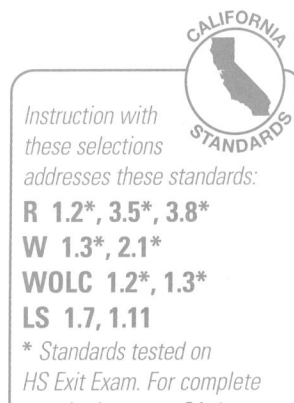

Instruction with these selections addresses these standards:
R 1.2*, 3.5*, 3.8*
W 1.3*, 2.1*
WOLC 1.2*, 1.3*
LS 1.7, 1.11
* *Standards tested on HS Exit Exam. For complete standards, see p. CA 4.*

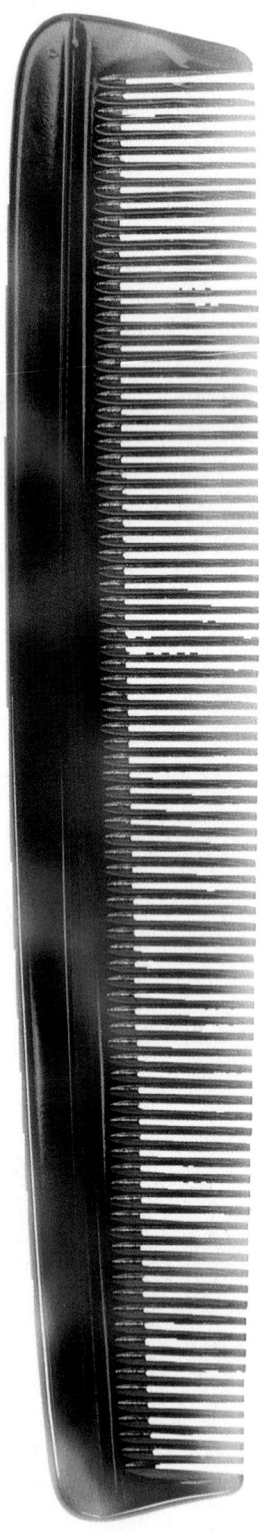

Combing

Gladys Cardiff

Bending, I bow my head
And lay my hand upon
Her hair, combing, and think
How women do this for
5 Each other. My daughter's hair
Curls against the comb,
Wet and fragrant—orange
Parings. Her face, downcast,
Is quiet for one so young.

10 I take her place. Beneath
My mother's hands I feel
The braids drawn up tight
As a piano wire and singing,
Vinegar-rinsed. Sitting
15 Before the oven I hear
The orange coils tick
The early hour before school.

She combed her grandmother
Mathilda's hair using
20 A comb made out of bone.
Mathilda rocked her oak wood
Chair, her face downcast,
Intent on tearing rags
In strips to braid a cotton
25 Rug from bits of orange
And brown. A simple act,

Preparing hair. Something
Women do for each other,
Plaiting the generations.

Reading Strategy
Interpreting Meaning
Identify the sensory language in this stanza that helps you interpret the poem's meaning.

intent (in tent´) *adj.* firmly fixed; concentrated

plaiting (plāt´ iŋ) *v.* braiding

Gladys Cardiff

(b. 1942)

Born in Montana, where her Cherokee father and Irish/Welsh mother taught school on a Blackfoot reservation, Gladys Cardiff grew up in Seattle, Washington, and received both Bachelor and Master of Arts degrees in creative writing from the University of Washington.

The Quiltmakers, Paul Goodnight, Color Circle Art Publishing, Inc.

▲ **Critical Viewing** Draw conclusions about the artist's attitude toward these women. Is it similar to the one expressed by Alice Walker? **[Draw Conclusions]**

Women
Alice Walker

They were women then
My mama's generation
Husky of voice—<u>Stout</u> of
Step
5 With fists as well as
Hands
How they battered down
Doors
And ironed
10 Starched white
Shirts
How they led
Armies
Headragged Generals
15 Across mined
Fields
Booby-trapped
Ditches
To discover books
20 Desks
A place for us
How they knew what we
Must know
Without knowing a page
25 Of it
Themselves.

stout (stout) *adj.* sturdy

Alice Walker

(b. 1944)
Alice Walker was born in Eatonton, Georgia. From the age of eight, she kept a journal and wrote poems. Many teachers encouraged her love of reading and writing.

Walker has written poetry, short stories, nonfiction, and novels, including the highly acclaimed *The Color Purple*.

maggie
and milly
and molly
and may

E. E. Cummings

maggie and milly and molly and may
went down to the beach (to play one day)

and maggie discovered a shell that sang
so sweetly she couldn't remember her troubles, and

5 milly befriended a stranded star
whose rays five <u>languid</u> fingers were;

and molly was chased by a horrible thing
which raced sideways while blowing bubbles: and

may came home with a smooth round stone
10 as small as a world and as large as alone.

For whatever we lose (like a you or a me)
it's always ourselves we find in the sea

Reading Strategy
Interpreting Meaning
What does the poet mean
by "a shell that sang"?

languid (laŋ´ gwid) *adj.*
drooping; weak

E. E. Cummings

(1894–1962)
Born in
Cambridge,
Massachusetts,
E. E. Cummings
graduated from
Harvard University. Serving in
Europe during World
War I, he was briefly
imprisoned because of his
connection to an
American who French
authorities thought was
critical of the war effort.

Both as poet and playwright, Cummings became
notorious for his unconventional style, which
reflected his individualistic
outlook. Though much of
his work is playful and lyrical, he often disregarded
rules of grammar, spelling,
and punctuation. In addition, he frequently coined
his own words and ran sentences together.

Review and Assess

Thinking About the Selections

1. **Respond:** Which of these poems did you like best? Why?
2. **(a) Recall:** How many generations of her family does the speaker in "Combing" mention? **(b) Analyze:** What do you think "plaiting the generations" means to the poet?
3. **(a) Recall:** Whom does the speaker in "Women" describe as being "husky of voice" and "stout of step"? **(b) Support:** What do these words convey about the women?
4. **(a) Interpret:** What makes women who "knew . . . without knowing" remarkable? **(b) Speculate:** How might these women have described themselves?
5. **(a) Recall:** Who are the four characters in Cummings's poem? **(b) Infer:** Do they seem different from one another? Explain.
6. **Infer:** According to Cummings, what kinds of things can you find out about yourself at sea?
7. **(a) Speculate:** Would the speaker in "Combing" or "Women" be more likely to agree with the insight in Cummings's poem? **(b) Support:** Which specific details influenced your choice?
8. **Evaluate:** Do you think a person can gain a better understanding of him- or herself by reflecting on past generations or by reflecting on individual experiences? Explain.

Astonishment

Wisława Szymborska

Translated by Grażyna Drabik, Austin Flint, and Sharon Olds

Why as one person, and one only?
Why this one, not another? And why here?
On Tuesday? At home, not in a nest?
Why in skin, not scales? With a face, not a leaf?
5   And why do I come, I myself, only once?
On this earth? Near a small star?
After many epochs[1] of absence?
Instead of always, and as all?
As all insects, and all horizons?
10 And why right now? Why bone and blood?
Myself as myself with myself? Why—
not nearby or a hundred miles away,
not yesterday or a hundred years ago—
do I sit and stare into a dark corner,
15 just as it looks up, suddenly raising its head,
this growling thing that is called a dog?

---

1. **epochs** (ep´ əks) *n.* periods or spans of time.

Reading Strategy
Interpreting Meaning To which "small star" does the speaker refer in line 6?

Wisława Szymborska

(b. 1923)

In her poem "Astonishment," Wisława Szymborska uses the word *why* eight times. "Question authority" might be the motto of this Polish poet. During World War II, when the Nazis closed Polish secondary schools and universities, Szymborska attended school illegally.

Today, Szymborska lives quietly in Poland. She prefers letting her poetry speak for her. In 1996, she was awarded the Nobel Prize for Literature.

Review and Assess

Thinking About the Selection

1. **Respond:** How do you react to the poet's style of presenting the entire poem as a series of questions? Explain.

2. **(a) Recall:** Which questioning word is used the most?
   (b) Infer: What do the questions indicate about the speaker?
   (c) Draw Conclusions: Do they all seem to point in the same direction, or not? Explain.

3. **(a) Interpret:** What does the speaker find astonishing?
   (b) Connect: How do the final lines reinforce this idea?

4. **(a) Speculate:** Would E. E. Cummings be likely to agree with the insight expressed in this poem? **(b) Support:** Draw on images and ideas in both poems to support your answer.

5. **Evaluate:** Do you think pondering the meaning of life, as the speaker does, can enrich a person's life? Why or why not?

Review and Assess

Literary Analysis

Moment of Insight

1. (a) Which details lead to the **moments of insight** in "Combing" and "Women"? (b) At what line in each poem is the insight revealed?
2. Which words express the moment of insight in "maggie and milly and molly and may"?
3. (a) What is the insight expressed in "Astonishment"? (b) What provokes it?

Comparing Literary Works

4. Exploring identity is the **theme** common to all four poems. How does each poet address this theme? In the center of a chart like this one, record the similarities you find. In the outer boxes, note the differences in the poems' ideas.

5. Of the four moments of insight, which came as the greatest surprise to you? Explain your answer.
6. Which moment of insight meant the most to you? Explain.

Reading Strategy

Interpreting Meaning

7. Which images and interpretations came to mind while you read "Combing" and "Women"?
8. In his poem, Cummings focuses on playing, while in hers, Szymborska focuses on the single question *why?* What is the effect of each poet's strategy?

Extend Understanding

9. **Career Connection:** What value might the insights in the four poems have for a teacher, a counselor, or anyone in the position of giving guidance to young people?

Quick Review

A **moment of insight** is a fresh, new thought that arises from a poet's musings.

The **theme** is the message or central insight at the heart of a work of literature.

To **interpret the meaning** of a poem, work to understand the point or insight that the poet is making.

 Take It to the Net
www.phschool.com
Take the interactive self-test online to check your understanding of the selections.

Integrate Language Skills

Vocabulary Development Lesson

Word Analysis: Words With Multiple Meanings

Some words have more than one meaning. For example, in "Women," the poet uses the word *stout* to mean "sturdy." *Stout* can also mean "courageous" or "heavyset." When a word has multiple meanings, its context determines the meaning that applies.

Write two definitions for each italicized word. Underline the definition that applies in the sentence based on the context.

1. The growling dog made its *intent* plain.
2. I was saddened to see her *downcast* expression.
3. Maggie found a *shell* on the beach that made her forget her troubles.
4. He understood the book without having read a *page* of it.

Concept Development: Antonyms

Write the word from the vocabulary list on page 325 that is an antonym for, or has the opposite meaning of, each of these words.

1. vigorous
2. unbraiding
3. distracted
4. weak

Spelling Strategy

For a word that ends in the pattern *vowel-vowel-consonant*, do not double the consonant before adding an ending.

Example: *plait + -ing = plaiting*

Think of an ending for each word shown, and use it to write a new word. Use each ending only once.

1. ghoul
2. scream
3. braid
4. appear

Grammar Lesson

Parenthetical Expressions

As you have seen in Cummings's poem, parentheses are sometimes used to set off a nonessential phrase within a sentence. Commas can also set off these **parenthetical expressions,** or nonessential words or phrases that interrupt the sentence's general flow. Look at how parenthetical expressions are used below:

Direct Address: Please help me, *Milly.*
Mild Interjection: *Well,* I never saw such a beautiful shell.
Common Expression: It is, *in my opinion,* tiny.
Transition: The ocean, *however,* is huge.
Contrast: This one, *unlike mine,* is blue.

Practice Copy each sentence, inserting any commas necessary to set off the parenthetical expression.

1. It is I think a powerful poem.
2. Oh I was amazed by what I saw.
3. Her hair was braided neatly and beautifully I might add.
4. Yes they certainly were determined and strong women.
5. Yours like mine is a smooth shell.

Writing Application Write a paragraph about one or two of the poems you liked best. Use at least two parenthetical expressions.

Prentice Hall Writing and Grammar Connection: Chapter 29, Section 2

Writing Lesson

Journal Entry on a Moment of Insight

Writing poetry is one way of exploring ideas and feelings. Journal writing is another. Write a journal entry about a moment of insight that you had in the recent past as a result of something that happened either locally or nationally.

Prewriting Start by jotting down important events that have occurred over the past several years. Then, choose one of those as your topic. Gather details by noting the sensory details of the event or experience. These will add emotional depth to your entry.

Drafting Using your notes as a starting point, recount the experience or event. Include details that will help your readers *feel* what you are describing. Reveal the moment of insight at the end of your journal entry.

Revising Read over your journal entry. Delete details that do not add to your insight. Look for places where more sensory details would add to the emotional depth of your writing.

Model: Eliminating Unnecessary Information

moving through the frenzy with silent focus

The rescue workers—dressed in blue coveralls—treated the

accident victims with great compassion.

> Words like *frenzy* and *silent focus* add to the emotional depth of the writing.

WG *Prentice Hall Writing and Grammar Connection: Chapter 1, Section 1*

Extension Activities

Listening and Speaking With three classmates, prepare an **oral reading** of "maggie and milly and molly and may."

- Plan individual speaking assignments, but read the first and last stanzas together.
- Consider your audience, and practice changing your tone of voice to improve the presentation's impact on your audience.

After you have rehearsed, perform your interpretation for your classmates and invite them to offer their reactions. **[Group Activity]**

Research and Technology Using "Combing" and "Women" as inspiration, prepare a **photo essay** about mothers and daughters. Try to include women of varying ages and backgrounds. Use the Internet to help you find photos, or take pictures of subjects you know. Then, prepare captions that reflect your response to each photo. Present a display in your classroom or school library.

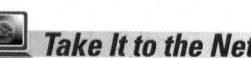 **Take It to the Net** www.phschool.com

Go online for an additional research activity using the Internet.

Writing WORKSHOP

Persuasion: Persuasive Essay

A **persuasive essay** is a work in which a writer presents a case for or against a particular position. In this workshop, you will write a persuasive essay on a topic of importance to you.

Assignment Criteria. Your persuasive essay should have the following characteristics:

- A clear thesis statement—a statement of your position on an issue
- Evidence that supports your position and anticipates your readers' counterarguments
- An effective organization
- Persuasive language that builds your argument

To preview the criteria on which your persuasive essay may be assessed, see the Rubric on page 337.

Prewriting

Choose a topic. Pair up with a classmate and brainstorm for topics that are important to each of you, noting those that cause the most disagreement. Select an issue that has compelling arguments on both sides. Then, choose a position to support.

Look at both sides. A persuasive essay is always more effective if it acknowledges and addresses counterarguments. Make a chart like the one below by jotting down facts and ideas that support or contradict your position.

Evidence for school uniforms	Evidence against school uniforms
• May reduce violence and discrimination	• Take choice away from students
• Promote school image	• Can cause resentment among students

Gather evidence. Gather evidence from a wide variety of sources. Collect quotations and facts. As you investigate, keep track of any ideas or phrases that are not your own so that you can give appropriate credit.

Write a thesis statement. Review your notes and the evidence that you have gathered from additional research. Develop a thesis statement that clearly expresses your position.

Student Model

Before you begin drafting your persuasive essay, read this student model and review the characteristics of powerful persuasion.

Braden Danbury
Cumming, GA

Dress Codes May Succeed Where School Uniforms Have Failed

School uniforms are becoming increasingly popular as a way to combat school violence and discrimination. Uniforms, while they may help somewhat, cause problems of their own. Students argue that it is their right to wear what they choose and uniforms violate that right. A less strict code is the answer to both of these problems, keeping appropriate attire in the schools while allowing individuals to choose what they wear.

> The author offers a clear thesis statement in the form of a proposal that addresses a key problem.

Uniforms require students to wear specific shirt and pant types, thus eliminating the element of choice. Dress codes, on the other hand, are less restrictive than school uniforms and cause less resentment among students. Students enjoy choosing what to wear to school each day, coordinating what they wear with how they feel. School uniforms may cause friction between students and school officials, which can have negative consequences.

While it might make sense to have students' safety as a leading justification for requiring uniforms, safety hits the bottom of the list in a press release from the National Association of Elementary School Principals. Safety ranks below such trivial things as school image. This calls into question why uniforms are touted as the answer to school safety issues. Dress codes make the difference where it counts. They keep students safe while forcing them to do nothing other than make sure their clothes meet acceptable standards. An added benefit of dress codes is that schools with uniform policies pay much more than schools with dress codes. Schools with uniforms have to design, order, sell, and distribute the uniforms they wish to have for their school. Dress codes are much less expensive to implement and follow.

> Braden finds a way to deal with counterarguments based on safety concerns.

> Braden offers evidence that supports his position.

With the rise in violence, students and their dress often come under suspicion and scrutiny. In addition, the wide variety of clothing in our high schools may lead students to make prejudicial judgments about each other. Dress codes address the problems of violence without causing resentment among students. They are less strict, giving the students more freedom in how they dress, while allowing school officials to set general guidelines. The amount of money it would take to implement a dress code is a fraction of the cost of school uniforms. Dress codes are not the only answer, but they are a step toward combating violence and discrimination in schools.

> The author restates his thesis and summarizes his evidence. He also offers an additional insight.

Drafting

Organize your arguments. It is useful to sketch out a logical structure for your essay before you write it. Decide which arguments you will present in support of your thesis statement and the order of presentation. Be sure to include a place in your outline to address counterarguments. The organization at right demonstrates one effective way to write a persuasive essay.

Provide evidence. For each point you make, provide evidence to back up your argument. Types of effective evidence include the following:

- **Statistics:** Cite numbers that show the impact of your proposal.

- **Expert opinions:** Include the advice of those who have training and experience related to your topic.

- **Personal observations:** Tell your readers about your own experiences with the topic.

- **Testimonials:** Include statements from peers that reinforce your argument.

Write with a respectful tone. Let your ideas be the strength of your essay. Avoid insulting the opposition. Instead, use a tone that shows respect.

Organizing Your Arguments

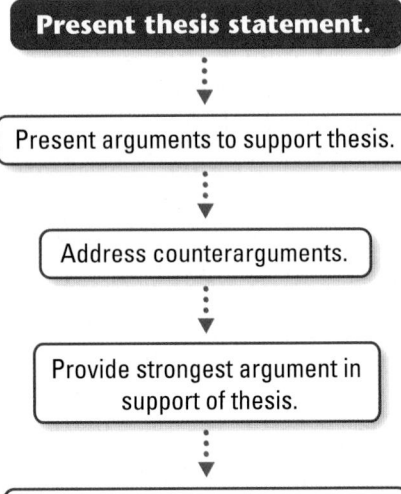

Revising

Revise to address readers' concerns. To convince those who may not agree with your position, show them that you understand their concerns.

1. Look over your draft to highlight controversial claims that a critic of your position would oppose.

2. For each of these claims, determine strong counterarguments that you can make with explanations and evidence.

3. Look for a place where you can insert this information and incorporate it into your draft.

Model: Addressing the Opposition

Dress codes make the difference where it counts. They keep students safe while forcing them to do nothing other than make sure their clothes meet acceptable standards.

Braden could provide evidence *and* address concerns by finding a statistic that shows that schools with dress codes are just as safe as, or safer than, schools with uniforms.

Revise to strengthen persuasive language. Look for words that can be replaced with more persuasive language. For example, in the following example, *refused* creates a stronger impression than *did not want*.

Example: She *did not want* to leave her home.
She *refused* to leave her home.

Compare the model and the nonmodel. Why is the model more effective than the nonmodel?

Nonmodel	Model
Students argue that it is their right to wear what they choose and that uniforms withdraw that right.	Students argue that it is their right to wear what they choose and that uniforms violate that right.

Publishing and Presenting

Present your writing to a wider audience. Sharing your persuasive essay might possibly achieve results—your ideas could inspire a positive change in behavior, open minds to a new perspective, or help change an unfair policy.

Deliver an oral presentation. Read your persuasive composition aloud in front of your classmates. After you have finished reading, take an unofficial poll to determine whether or not you convinced your audience of your position.

Publish in a newspaper. Send your essay as an opinion piece to your school or community newsletter, or condense it into a letter to the editor.

 **Speaking Connection**

To learn more about analyzing persuasive arguments, see the **Listening and Speaking Workshop**, page 338.

 Prentice Hall Writing and Grammar Connection: Chapter 7

Rubric for Self-Assessment

Evaluate your persuasive essay using the following criteria and rating scale:

Criteria	Rating Scale				
	Not very				Very
How clear is the thesis statement?	1	2	3	4	5
How well is the thesis supported by evidence?	1	2	3	4	5
How well are readers' concerns anticipated and addressed?	1	2	3	4	5
How effectively are arguments organized?	1	2	3	4	5
How powerful is the persuasive language?	1	2	3	4	5

Analyzing Types of Arguments

We normally think of an argument as a shouting match or disagreement. However, an argument, as it is used to describe speeches, essays, and debates, is a series of statements that support a particular conclusion. Learning how to analyze an argument will improve your own ability to build persuasive arguments.

Recognize Argument Structure

Just as the human body is supported by its skeleton, the body of an argument is bolstered with supporting statements, or premises. Recognizing an argument's structure will help you figure out whether it is strong—supported by many powerful premises—or weak.

Identify the conclusion. The conclusion is the main idea of an argument. It should be easy to identify because it is broadly stated, general, and supported by individual pieces of evidence.

Identify premises. Premises are the basic building blocks of an argument. The best way to find individual premises is to work backward from a conclusion to find its supporting statements or evidence.

Identify Argument Types

Persuasive speakers use a variety of argument types to convince audiences. For example, if you had to prepare a persuasive speech on why solar energy is better than energy from coal, you might use the following argument types:

- **Analogy (Making a comparison):** You could argue that not using solar energy is like paying to drive your car to school when you could take a free school bus.

- **Authority (Citing expert opinion):** You might point to specific research that links the burning of coal to air pollution.

- **Emotion (Appealing to sense of right and wrong):** You could indicate the harmful effects that pollution might have on a child with asthma.

- **Logic (Using reasoning):** You could indicate that solar energy is cleaner than coal and exists in greater supply.

- **Causation (Using cause-and-effect analysis):** You could walk your audience through the coal energy process, from the burning of coal to its effect on living organisms.

Analyzing Types of Arguments

Argument Structure

Conclusion: _____

Premise: _____   Premise: _____

Premise: _____

Argument Types

Type	Example
Analogy	
Authority	
Emotion	
Logic	
Causation	

(Activity: Observation and Analysis) Watch a video of a debate or an important speech, such as a presidential address. As you listen, complete a chart like the one shown. Note an example of each type of argument you hear in the speech. Use the flowchart to diagram one of the main arguments.

Assessment WORKSHOP

Stated and Implied Main Idea

In the reading sections of some tests, you are required to read passages and answer multiple-choice questions about stated and implied main ideas. Use the following strategies to answer such questions:

- Look for a topic sentence that is a statement of the main idea of a passage.
- If a main idea is not stated, it may be implied or suggested.
- To identify an implied main idea, read the passage and summarize the author's message in a single statement.
- To make sure that you have identified the topic sentence correctly, check that the other sentences support the idea of the sentence you have chosen.

Test-Taking Strategies

- Check implied main ideas by making sure all of the sentences support your one-sentence summary.
- Consider the title you might assign a passage. This may reinforce the main idea.

Sample Test Item

Directions: Read the passage, and then answer the question that follows.

Despite dropping temperatures and decreased daylight, finches, sparrows, and mockingbirds are birds commonly seen in winter. These species feed primarily on seeds and berries, which are plentiful even through the coldest months.

1. What is the main idea implied in this passage?

   A Birds feed on seeds and berries in winter.

   B Birds that are seen in winter are finches, sparrows, and mockingbirds.

   C During winter, birds look for food near trees and shrubs.

   D Finches, sparrows, and mockingbirds can survive the coldest winter months.

Answer and Explanation

The correct answer is **D,** because both sentences support the main idea. **A** and **B** are details, but they are not the central idea of the passage. **C** is not stated in the passage.

► Practice

Directions: Read the passage, and then answer the question that follows.

Everyone has a fever at some point. A fever is a symptom, not a disease. It is an indication that your body is fighting an infection or illness. While it causes discomfort, a fever may be a sign of recovery.

You do not need to call a doctor immediately if you develop a low-grade fever. You should drink fluids and get plenty of rest. Record your temperature every two hours, and note any change in symptoms.

1. What is the stated main idea of the first paragraph?

   A Everyone gets a fever at some point.

   B A fever is a symptom of a disease, not the disease itself.

   C A fever indicates that your body is fighting an infection or illness.

   D A fever may be a sign of your body's recovery.

Scientist's Hobby: Failure #18 of the Anti-Gravity Pack, 1992, Bruce Widdows, Courtesy of George Adams Gallery, New York

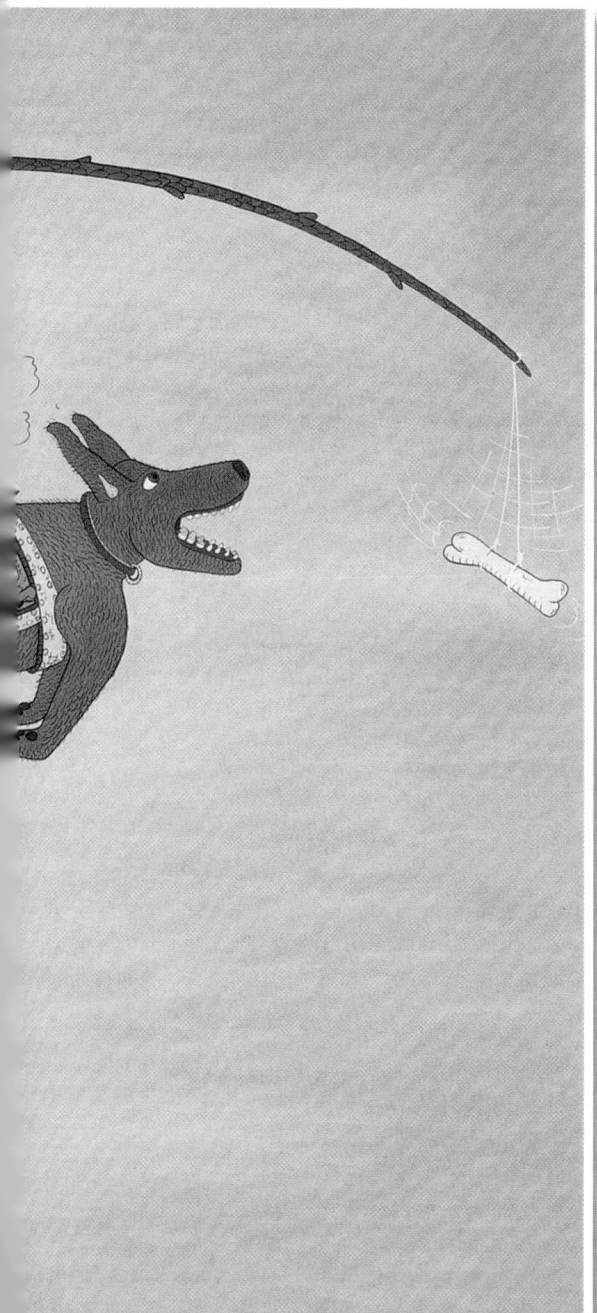

Exploring the Theme

What's so funny? It might be an animal trainer teaching 5,000 flies how to "act." It might be an overstressed husband taking a mental leave of absence, or it might be an outlandish poem told in nonsense language. Check out these stories, essays, poems, and more. You are sure to find something to make you smile.

You may never have played football on a crowded street in Philadelphia, like Bill Cosby in **"Go Deep to the Sewer."** But you will probably still laugh when you recognize yourself—and the games you improvised with your friends—in Cosby's humorous reminiscence. This is only one of the many types of laughter you will find in the pieces that follow—the laughter of recognition.

▲ **Critical Viewing** Which aspects of this drawing add to its humorous impact? **[Analyze]**

Why Read Literature?

Whenever you read, you have a purpose, or reason. You might read to find a particular type of information, to be entertained, or to further your understanding of a certain kind of literature. Preview three purposes you could set for yourself before reading works in this unit.

1 Read for the Love of Literature

In Russian literature there is a tradition of poking fun at government officials that has landed some writers in trouble. The negative reaction to Nikolai Gogol's play *The Inspector-General* caused Gogol to seek exile. See how dramatist Anton Chekhov takes Gogol's play, in which townspeople mistake a local scoundrel for a government inspector, and turns it on its head in his version of *The Inspector-General,* page 358.

You know something is not quite right when you read a poem like "Jabberwocky." Maybe it is the fact that author Lewis Carroll invents his own language as he goes along. Maybe it is the feeling that, in spite of all the bizarre phrases, you still understand what he is saying. Test your wits and chortle along with the inspired nonsense of **"Jabberwocky,"** page 400.

The Jabberwock, 1872, John Tenniel

2 Read for Information

You might be surprised at some of the trickery trainers use to get animals to do what movie directors want. Find out how one trainer coaxed five thousand winged extras to fly on cue as he takes you behind the scenes in **"Fly Away,"** page 373.

If you have ever wondered what insects eat or hungered to know the name of that bug you found crawling across your bathroom floor, you can find the answers in Patricia Volk's essay **"An Entomological Study of Apartment 4A,"** page 386.

3 Read to Be Entertained

We all have moments when we take a mental break and pretend to be somewhere or someone we are not. James Thurber attempts to answer the question "What would it be like to daydream all the time?" in his humorous story entitled **"The Secret Life of Walter Mitty,"** page 346.

 Take It to the Net

Visit the Web site for online instruction and activities related to each selection in this unit.
www.phschool.com

How to Read Literature

Use Interactive Reading Strategies

To get the most out of many things in life, you have to get involved. This rule is as true in reading as it is in playing sports or visiting new places. Use these strategies to interact with what you are reading.

1. Read back or read ahead.

Even the best readers can find themselves confused when they encounter difficult passages. If you lose focus or encounter complex sentences with unfamiliar words, follow these steps:

- Pause to think about what you have just read and to look up new words. If necessary, go back to the last portion of the text you understood and reread from that point.

- Read ahead to clear up confusion—especially when reading texts in which the action is presented before explanations are given.

2. Read between the lines.

- Notice details that might provide indications of a deeper message or future plot development.

- Keep track of suspicions you might have about characters and their motives by using a chart like the one shown.

Read Between the Lines	
Character	Driver in *The Inspector-General*
What I already know about the character	Driver knows many personal details about the new Inspector-General.
What the author might be suggesting	Driver might be able to recognize the Inspector-General if he were to meet him.

3. Recognize situational humor.

When you laugh because you relate to the set of circumstances an author is describing, you are recognizing situational humor. Keep in mind the following tips:

- Look for humor that involves familiar experiences.

- Notice techniques like contrast or exaggeration that play up the humor of a given situation.

4. Question characters' actions.

As you read, ask questions and offer explanations for why characters act the way they do. Base your answers on characters' past actions and your own experiences. For example, you might want to determine the main character's motive in this passage.

> Mr. Johnson . . . came forward and, touching his hat civilly, said, "Perhaps I can keep an eye on your little boy for you."
>
> —*from* "One Ordinary Day, With Peanuts"

Start by asking why a character might offer help. He might be acting out of kindness or expecting something in return. Use your answers to evaluate the character's behavior as you continue reading.

As you read, review these reading strategies and use the notes in the selection margin to interact with the text.

Prepare to Read

The Secret Life of Walter Mitty

Portrait XIV, Donald C. Martin, Private Collection

 Take It to the Net

Visit www.phschool.com
for interactive activities
and instruction related to
"The Secret Life of Walter
Mitty," including

- background
- graphic organizers
- literary elements
- reading strategies

Preview

Connecting to the Literature

There you are, a movie star, accepting an Academy Award. . . .
Suddenly, a dog barks, bringing you back to the real world . . . in a bus on
your way home. Perhaps you can recall daydreams that seemed sweeter
than reality. "The Secret Life of Walter Mitty" is about a man whose frequent daydreams are more real to him than his workaday existence.

Background

Psychologists say that a person's thoughts often consist of seemingly
unconnected insights, memories, and reflections, and that single incidents
can prompt an unpredictable mental response. In James Thurber's story,
random events cause Walter Mitty's thoughts to jump back and forth
between his exciting "secret" life and his humdrum everyday life.

Literary Analysis
Point of View

In stories told in the **first-person point of view,** the narrator is one of the characters. In the **third-person point of view,** the narrator does not participate in the action. The third-person point of view can be either *omniscient*, in which the narrator sees into the minds of all the characters, or *limited*, in which the narrator sees the world through one character's eyes and reveals only that character's thoughts.

This story is written from the third-person point of view. As you read, notice that the narrator lets you see Mitty's thoughts and feelings in a way you would not experience in real life.

Connecting Literary Elements

Walter Mitty, a bumbling husband but a man of action in his dreams, is an example of a **round character**—a character who exhibits many traits, including faults as well as virtues. Mrs. Mitty, a wife who does nothing but scold Walter, is an example of a **flat character**—a character who seems to have only a single surface or aspect to her personality. As you read, notice the many traits of Walter Mitty.

Instruction with this selection addresses these standards:
R 1.1*, 3.9*
W 1.5*, 2.1*
WOLC 1.2*
LS 1.9
* Standards tested on HS Exit Exam. For complete standards, see p. CA 4.

Reading Strategy
Reading Back and Reading Ahead

Walter Mitty's thoughts consistently shift from fantasy to reality. To understand the shifts in the story, read back and read ahead.

- **Read back** to see if you have overlooked any important facts.
- **Read ahead** to clarify an unclear situation.

Use a chart like this one to clarify insights you gain by reading back and reading ahead.

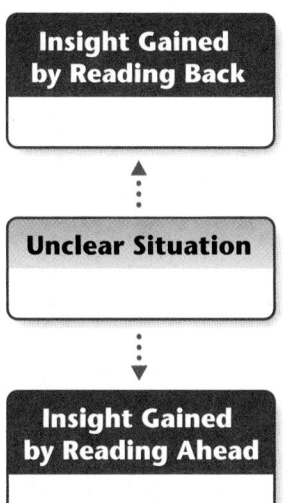

Insight Gained by Reading Back

Unclear Situation

Insight Gained by Reading Ahead

Vocabulary Development

rakishly (rāk´ ish lē) *adv.* with a trim, casual look; dashingly (p. 347)

hurtling (hʉrt´ liŋ) *adj.* moving swiftly and with great force (p. 347)

distraught (di strôt´) *adj.* extremely troubled; confused; distracted (p. 348)

haggard (hag´ ərd) *adj.* having a worn look, as from sleeplessness (p. 348)

insolent (in´ sə lənt) *adj.* boldly disrespectful (p. 349)

insinuatingly (in sin´ yoo āt´ iŋ lē) *adv.* suggesting indirectly (p. 349)

cur (kʉr) *n.* mean, contemptible person; mean, ugly dog (p. 349)

cannonading (kan´ ən ād´ iŋ) *n.* continuous firing of artillery (p. 350)

derisive (di rī´ siv) *adj.* showing contempt or ridicule (p. 352)

inscrutable (in skroot´ ə bəl) *adj.* baffling; mysterious (p. 352)

The Man With Three Masks, John Rush, Courtesy of the artist

▲ **Critical Viewing** Analyze the significance of the mask in this painting. Why might the man hold one mask up to his face and have other masks nearby? **[Analyze]**

The Secret Life of Walter Mitty

James Thurber

We're going through!" The Commander's voice was like thin ice breaking. He wore his full-dress uniform, with the heavily braided white cap pulled down rakishly over one cold gray eye. "We can't make it, sir. It's spoiling for a hurricane, if you ask me." "I'm not asking you, Lieutenant Berg," said the Commander. "Throw on the power lights! Rev her up to 8,500! We're going through!" The pounding of the cylinders increased: ta-pocketa-pocketa-pocketa-*pocketa-pocketa*. The Commander stared at the ice forming on the pilot window. He walked over and twisted a row of complicated dials. "Switch on No. 8 auxiliary!" he shouted. "Switch on No. 8 auxiliary!" repeated Lieutenant Berg. "Full strength in No. 3 turret!" shouted the Commander. "Full strength in No. 3 turret!" The crew, bending to their various tasks in the huge, hurtling eight-engined Navy hydroplane,[1] looked at each other and grinned. "The Old Man'll get us through," they said to one another. "The Old Man ain't afraid of Hell!". . .

"Not so fast! You're driving too fast!" said Mrs. Mitty. "What are you driving so fast for?"

"Hmm?" said Walter Mitty. He looked at his wife, in the seat beside him, with shocked astonishment. She seemed grossly unfamiliar, like a strange woman who had yelled at him in a crowd. "You were up to fifty-five," she said. "You know I don't like to go more than forty. You were up to fifty-five." Walter Mitty drove on toward Waterbury in silence, the roaring of the SN202 through the worst storm in twenty years of Navy flying fading in the remote, intimate airways of his mind. "You're tensed up again," said Mrs. Mitty. "It's one of your days. I wish you'd let Dr. Renshaw look you over."

Walter Mitty stopped the car in front of the building where his wife went to have her hair done. "Remember to get those overshoes while

rakishly (rāk´ ish lē) *adv.* with a trim, casual look; dashing

hurtling (hʉrt´ liη) *adj.* moving swiftly and with great force

✔**Reading Check**

Why is Mrs. Mitty upset?

---

1. **hydroplane** (hī´ drō plān´) *n.* seaplane.

I'm having my hair done," she said. "I don't need overshoes," said Mitty. She put her mirror back into her bag. "We've been all through that," she said, getting out of the car. "You're not a young man any longer." He raced the engine a little. "Why don't you wear your gloves? Have you lost your gloves?" Walter Mitty reached in a pocket and brought out the gloves. He put them on, but after she had turned and gone into the building and he had driven on to a red light, he took them off again. "Pick it up, brother!" snapped a cop as the light changed, and Mitty hastily pulled on his gloves and lurched ahead. He drove around the streets aimlessly for a time, and then he drove past the hospital on his way to the parking lot.

. . . "It's the millionaire banker, Wellington McMillan," said the pretty nurse. "Yes?" said Walter Mitty, removing his gloves slowly. "Who has the case?" "Dr. Renshaw and Dr. Benbow, but there are two specialists here, Dr. Remington from New York and Mr. Pritchard-Mitford from London. He flew over." A door opened down a long, cool corridor and Dr. Renshaw came out. He looked <u>distraught</u> and <u>haggard</u>. "Hello, Mitty," he said. "We're having the devil's own time with McMillan, the millionaire banker and close personal friend of Roosevelt. Obstreosis of the ductal tract.[2] Tertiary. Wish you'd take a look at him." "Glad to," said Mitty.

In the operating room there were whispered introductions: "Dr. Remington, Dr. Mitty. Mr. Pritchard-Mitford, Dr. Mitty." "I've read your book on streptothricosis," said Pritchard-Mitford, shaking hands. "A brilliant performance, sir." "Thank you," said Walter Mitty. "Didn't know you were in the States, Mitty," grumbled Remington. "Coals to Newcastle,[3] bringing Mitford and me up here for tertiary." "You are very kind," said Mitty. A huge, complicated machine, connected to the operating table, with many tubes and wires, began at this moment to go pocketa-pocketa-pocketa. "The new anesthetizer is giving way!" shouted an intern. "There is no one in the East who knows how to fix it!" "Quiet, man!" said Mitty, in a low, cool voice. He sprang to the machine, which was now going pocketa-pocketa-queep-pocketa-queep. He began fingering delicately a row of glistening dials. "Give me a fountain pen!" he snapped. Someone handed him a fountain pen. He pulled a faulty piston out of the machine and inserted the pen in its place. "That will hold for ten minutes," he said. "Get on with the operation." A nurse hurried over and whispered to Renshaw, and Mitty saw the man turn pale. "Coreopsis has set in," said Renshaw nervously. "If you would take over, Mitty?" Mitty looked at him and at the craven figure of Benbow, who drank, and at the grave, uncertain faces of the two great specialists. "If you wish," he said. They slipped a white gown on him; he adjusted a mask and drew on thin gloves; nurses handed him shining . . .

"Back it up, Mac! Look out for that Buick!" Walter Mitty jammed on

---

2. **obstreosis of the ductal tract** Thurber has invented this and other medical terms.
3. **coals to Newcastle** The proverb "bringing coals to Newcastle" means bringing things to a place unnecessarily—Newcastle, England, was a coal center and so did not need coal brought to it.

distraught (di strôt') *adj.* extremely troubled; confused; distracted

haggard (hag' ərd) *adj.* having a worn look, as from sleeplessness

Literary Analysis
Point of View and Round Characters How does this shift in scenes show that Walter Mitty is a round character?

the brakes. "Wrong lane, Mac," said the parking-lot attendant, looking at Mitty closely. "Gee. Yeh," muttered Mitty. He began cautiously to back out of the lane marked "Exit Only." "Leave her sit there," said the attendant. "I'll put her away." Mitty got out of the car. "Hey, better leave the key." "Oh," said Mitty, handing the man the ignition key. The attendant vaulted into the car, backed it up with <u>insolent</u> skill, and put it where it belonged.

insolent (in′ sə lənt) *adj.* boldly disrespectful

They're so cocky, thought Walter Mitty, walking along Main Street; they think they know everything. Once he had tried to take his chains off, outside New Milford, and he had got them wound around the axles. A man had had to come out in a wrecking car and unwind them, a young, grinning garageman. Since then Mrs. Mitty always made him drive to a garage to have the chains taken off. The next time, he thought, I'll wear my right arm in a sling; they won't grin at me then. I'll have my right arm in a sling and they'll see I couldn't possibly take the chains off myself. He kicked at the slush on the sidewalk. "Overshoes," he said to himself, and he began looking for a shoe store.

When he came out into the street again, with the overshoes in a box under his arm, Walter Mitty began to wonder what the other thing was his wife had told him to get. She had told him, twice, before they set out from their house for Waterbury. In a way he hated these weekly trips to town—he was always getting something wrong. Kleenex, he thought, Squibb's, razor blades? No. Toothpaste, toothbrush, bicarbonate, carborundum, initiative and referendum?[4] He gave it up. But she would remember it. "Where's the what's-its-name?" she would ask. "Don't tell me you forgot the what's-its-name." A newsboy went by shouting something about the Waterbury trial.

. . . "Perhaps this will refresh your memory." The District Attorney suddenly thrust a heavy automatic at the quiet figure on the witness stand. "Have you ever seen this before?" Walter Mitty took the gun and examined it expertly. "This is my Webley-Vickers 50.80," he said calmly. An excited buzz ran around the courtroom. The Judge rapped for order. "You are a crack shot with any sort of firearms, I believe?" said the District Attorney, <u>insinuatingly</u>. "Objection!" shouted Mitty's attorney. "We have shown that the defendant could not have fired the shot. We have shown that he wore his right arm in a sling on the night of the fourteenth of July." Walter Mitty raised his hand briefly and the bickering attorneys were stilled. "With any known make of gun," he said evenly, "I could have killed Gregory Fitzhurst at three hundred *feet with my left hand.*" Pandemonium broke loose in the courtroom. A woman's scream rose above the bedlam and suddenly a lovely, dark-haired girl was in Walter Mitty's arms. The District Attorney struck at her savagely. Without rising from his chair, Mitty let the man have it on the point of the chin. "You miserable <u>cur</u>!" . . .

insinuatingly (in sin′ yōō āt′ iŋ lē) *adv.* suggesting indirectly

cur (kʉr) *n.* mean, contemptible person; mean, ugly dog

✔**Reading Check**

Why does Mitty say that next time he will wear his arm in a sling?

---

4. **carborundum** (kär′ bə run′ dəm), **initiative** (i nish′ ē ə tiv) **and referendum** (ref ə ren′ dəm) Thurber is purposely making a nonsense list; *carborundum* is a hard substance used for scraping, *initiative* is the right of citizens to introduce ideas for laws, and *referendum* is the right of citizens to vote on laws.

"Puppy biscuit," said Walter Mitty. He stopped walking and the buildings of Waterbury rose up out of the misty courtroom and surrounded him again. A woman who was passing laughed. "He said 'Puppy biscuit,'" she said to her companion. "That man said 'Puppy biscuit' to himself." Walter Mitty hurried on. He went into an A. & P., not the first one he came to but a smaller one farther up the street. "I want some biscuit for small, young dogs," he said to the clerk. "Any special brand, sir?" The greatest pistol shot in the world thought a moment. "It says 'Puppies Bark for It' on the box," said Walter Mitty.

His wife would be through at the hairdresser's in fifteen minutes, Mitty saw in looking at his watch, unless they had trouble drying it; sometimes they had trouble drying it. She didn't like to get to the hotel first; she would want him to be there waiting for her as usual. He found a big leather chair in the lobby, facing a window, and he put the overshoes and the puppy biscuit on the floor beside it. He picked up an old copy of *Liberty* and sank down into the chair. "Can Germany Conquer the World Through the Air?" Walter Mitty looked at the pictures of bombing planes and of ruined streets.

Literary Analysis
Point of View Through whose eyes do you obtain this view of Mrs. Mitty?

. . . "The <u>cannonading</u> has got the wind up in young Raleigh,[5] sir," said the sergeant. Captain Mitty looked up at him through tousled hair. "Get him to bed," he said wearily. "With the others. I'll fly alone." "But you can't, sir," said the sergeant anxiously. "It takes two men to handle that bomber and the Archies[6] are pounding hell out of the air. Von Richtman's circus[7] is between here and Saulier." "Somebody's got to get that ammunition dump," said Mitty. "I'm going over. Spot of brandy?" He poured a drink for the sergeant and one for himself. War thundered and whined around the dugout and battered at the door. There was a rending of wood and splinters flew through the room. "A bit of a near thing," said Captain Mitty carelessly. "The box barrage is closing in," said the sergeant. "We only live once, Sergeant," said Mitty, with his faint, fleeting smile. "Or do we?" He poured another brandy and tossed it off. "I never see a man could hold his brandy like you, sir," said the sergeant. "Begging your pardon, sir." Captain Mitty stood up and strapped on his huge Webley-Vickers automatic. "It's forty kilometers through hell, sir," said the sergeant. Mitty finished one last brandy. "After all," he said softly, "what isn't?" The pounding of the cannon increased; there was the rat-tat-tatting of machine guns, and from somewhere came the menacing pocketa-pocketa-pocketa of the new flame-throwers. Walter Mitty walked to the door of the dugout humming "Auprès de Ma Blonde."[8] He turned and waved to the sergeant. "Cheerio!" he said. . . .

Something struck his shoulder. "I've been looking all over this hotel

cannonading (kan´ ən ād´ iŋ) *n.* continuous firing of artillery

Reading Strategy
Reading Back and Reading Ahead To clarify Mitty's location, would you read ahead or read back at this point? Explain.

---

5. **has got the wind up in young Raleigh** has made young Raleigh nervous.
6. **Archies** slang term for antiaircraft guns.
7. **Von Richtman's circus** German airplane squadron.
8. **"Auprès de Ma Blonde"** (ō prä´ də mä blôn´ də) "Next to My Blonde," a popular French song.

New Orleans Fantasy (detail), Max Papart, Nahan Galleries, New York

▲ **Critical Viewing** Describe a situation that might make Walter Mitty daydream about being a circus performer like the one shown. **[Hypothesize]**

for you," said Mrs. Mitty. "Why do you have to hide in this old chair? How did you expect me to find you?" "Things close in," said Walter Mitty vaguely. "What?" Mrs. Mitty said. "Did you get the what's-its-name? The puppy biscuit? What's in that box?" "Overshoes," said Mitty. "Couldn't you have put them on in the store?" "I was thinking," said Walter Mitty. "Does it ever occur to you that I am sometimes thinking?" She looked at him. "I'm going to take your temperature when I get you home," she said.

They went out through the revolving doors that made a faintly <u>derisive</u> whistling sound when you pushed them. It was two blocks to the parking lot. At the drugstore on the corner she said, "Wait here for me. I forgot something. I won't be a minute." She was more than a minute. Walter Mitty lighted a cigarette. It began to rain, rain with sleet in it. He stood up against the wall of the drugstore, smoking. . . . He put his shoulders back and his heels together. "To hell with the handkerchief," said Walter Mitty scornfully. He took one last drag on his cigarette and snapped it away. Then, with that faint, fleeting smile playing about his lips, he faced the firing squad; erect and motionless, proud and disdainful, Walter Mitty the Undefeated, <u>inscrutable</u> to the last.

derisive (di rī′ siv) *adj.* showing contempt or ridicule

inscrutable (in skro͞ot′ ə bəl) *adj.* baffling; mysterious

Review and Assess

Thinking About the Selection

1. **Respond:** Do you feel sorry for Walter Mitty? Why or why not?

2. **(a) Recall:** In the "real" world, what are Mitty and his wife actually doing? **(b) Deduce:** Does Mrs. Mitty understand the reasons for Walter's absentmindedness? Explain.

3. **(a) Recall:** What jars Mitty out of his first daydream? **(b) Compare and Contrast:** How does he behave in this daydream? In his real life?

4. **(a) Recall:** What event triggers Mitty's courtroom daydream? **(b) Draw Conclusions:** Explain the significant difference between the way people treat Mitty in his real life and the way they treat him in his daydreams.

5. **(a) Infer:** Which aspects of Mrs. Mitty's personality trigger Mitty's last daydream? **(b) Draw Conclusions:** In what way is this daydream a comment on his fate in real life?

6. **Hypothesize:** How might Mitty's life be altered if he could transfer the self-esteem he experiences in his daydreams into his conscious life?

7. **Take a Position:** Can daydreaming ever benefit a person? Explain.

James Thurber

(1894–1961)

Born in Columbus, Ohio, James Thurber began his writing career at the *Columbus Evening Dispatch*, where he was a reporter. He later achieved fame as a humorous writer and cartoonist during his many years at *The New Yorker* magazine.

Thurber's plays, stories, essays, fables, reminiscences, and verse fill more than twenty volumes. He lost his sight in the 1940s but continued to write until his death. In 1960, he won the Antoinette Perry award for his revue *A Thurber Carnival*.

Review and Assess

Literary Analysis

Point of View

1. Is there a moment when you realize that you are seeing Walter Mitty's world through his eyes? Explain.

2. How are your feelings about Mitty influenced by seeing things from his **point of view**?

3. If the **limited third-person narration** had focused on Mrs. Mitty instead of Walter, how would the story have been different? Use a Venn diagram to gather details for a response.

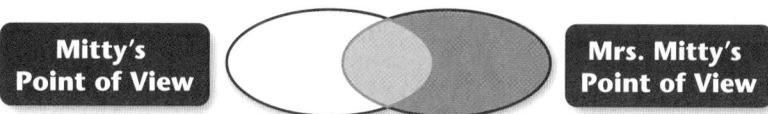

Mitty's Point of View — Mrs. Mitty's Point of View

Connecting Literary Elements

4. (a) What evidence suggests that Walter Mitty is a **round character**? (b) What evidence shows Mrs. Mitty is a **flat character**?

5. Using a chart like the one shown here, analyze the characters in Walter's daydreams.

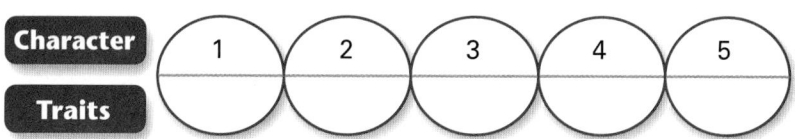

Character — 1 2 3 4 5 — Traits

6. (a) Do the characters in Mitty's daydreams seem as flat as those in his real life? (b) How does this characterization influence the story?

Reading Strategy

Reading Back and Reading Ahead

7. Cite two places where **reading back or ahead** helped you fully understand the meaning of a scene in the story.

Extend Understanding

8. **Career Connection:** (a) In reality, could Mitty perform the work he thinks about in his daydreams? Why or why not? (b) Suggest a fulfilling career for Walter. Explain your choice.

Quick Review

Point of view is the perspective from which a story is told.

A **limited third-person narrator** reveals the thoughts of only one character, through whose eyes you see the other characters.

A **round character** exhibits many traits, including both virtues and faults.

A **flat character** exhibits only a single quality or trait.

You **read back** to see if you have overlooked any important facts.

You **read ahead** to look for an explanation of a passage you do not understand.

 Take It to the Net
www.phschool.com

Take the interactive self-test online to check your understanding of the selection.

Integrate Language Skills

Vocabulary Development Lesson

Word Analysis: Latin Root -scrut-

The Latin root -scrut- means "to search carefully or examine." The word *inscrutable* literally means "not able to be searched or examined" or "not easily understood." Define each of the following words.

1. scrutiny   **2.** scrutinize   **3.** inscrutability

Spelling Strategy

When a word ends in silent *e*, you often drop the *e* before adding an ending that begins with a vowel. For example, *cannonade + -ing = cannonading*. However, there are many exceptions to this rule. For example, *manage + -able = manageable*. Write the new word that is formed when you combine these words and suffixes.

1. rake + -ing   **3.** courage + -ous
2. cure + -ative   **4.** sane + -ity

Concept Development: Synonyms

On your paper, write the letter of the word in the second column that is closest in meaning to each word in the first column. To help you, review the vocabulary list on page 345.

1. rakishly	**a.** baffling
2. hurtling	**b.** bombarding
3. distraught	**c.** implying
4. haggard	**d.** scoundrel
5. insolent	**e.** speeding
6. insinuatingly	**f.** insulting
7. cur	**g.** exhausted
8. cannonading	**h.** disrespectful
9. derisive	**i.** troubled
10. inscrutable	**j.** stylishly

Grammar Lesson

Complete Subjects and Predicates

The **complete subject** of a sentence consists of the simple subject and all the words associated with it. The **complete predicate** consists of the simple predicate, or verb, and all the words associated with it.

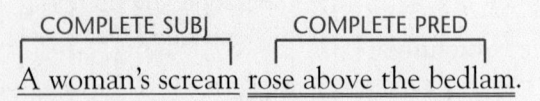

COMPLETE SUBJ   COMPLETE PRED
A woman's scream rose above the bedlam.

Practice Copy each sentence. Underline the complete subject once and the complete predicate twice.

1. The Commander spoke seriously.

2. He looked at his wife in astonishment.
3. A huge machine, connected to the operating table, was very noisy.
4. He could not remember what she asked him to buy.
5. The District Attorney spoke to the man on the witness stand.
6. War rumbled and whined at the door.

Writing Application Write two or three sentences to add more details to one of Walter Mitty's adventures in the story. Underline each complete subject once and each complete predicate twice.

Prentice Hall Writing and Grammar Connection: Chapter 20, Section 1

Writing Lesson

Character Profile

Walter Mitty sees himself as one fearless character after another. Use one of Mitty's daydreams to inspire a character profile that vividly describes a personality he becomes in his dreams.

Prewriting   Use a cluster map like the one shown to jot down details that capture the character's appearance, personality, achievements, and feelings.

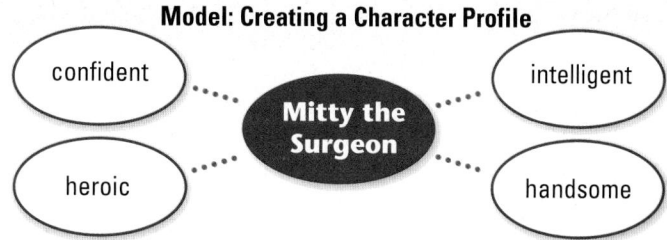

Model: Creating a Character Profile

confident — Mitty the Surgeon — intelligent

heroic — Mitty the Surgeon — handsome

Drafting   Decide on the impression you want to convey, and present details so that they all point toward it. Build toward the most important point.

Revising   Review your work to be sure you have used details from each prewriting category. Ask a classmate to identify the main impression of your character description. If the response is not what you expected, revise to clarify your focus. Provide more details that support the main impression, and eliminate those that do not.

*W*G *Prentice Hall Writing and Grammar Connection: Chapter 13, Section 2*

Extension Activities

Listening and Speaking Take these steps to adapt one of Walter Mitty's daydreams as a **dramatic skit:**

- In a group, choose the daydream you find most appealing.
- Decide who will play the various roles.

Consider incorporating the phrase *ta-pocketa-pocketa* to ensure that the scene truly captures Mitty. Perform your skit for the class. [**Group Activity**]

Research and Technology Use library resources, including the Internet, to research scientific facts and theories about daydreaming. Record the information in a **learning log,** a written record of what you discover about the topic. Compare your findings to the story. Decide whether Walter Mitty is really as different from others as he seems.

Take It to the Net   www.phschool.com

Go online for an additional research activity using the Internet.

Prepare to Read

The Inspector-General

Valmondois Sous la Neige, Maurice Vlaminck

 **Take It to the Net**

Visit www.phschool.com for interactive activities and instruction related to *The Inspector-General,* including

- background
- graphic organizers
- literary elements
- reading strategies

Preview

Connecting to the Literature

Sometimes, people hide their identities or pretend to be someone else. They may be trying to impress someone or play a practical joke. Unexpectedly, the results can be embarrassing or even funny, as the title character of this selection discovers.

Background

The Inspector-General is set in imperial Russia, before the 1917 communist revolution, when the country was ruled by an emperor, or czar. To oversee the many minor officials in Russia's vast expanse, the czars employed people called inspectors general. They observed how local schools, courts, and hospitals were functioning. Many people resented the czar's authority, however, and inspectors general were as unpopular as other officials.

Literary Analysis

Irony

When a literary work like *The Inspector-General* takes a surprising turn, it creates **irony**—a contrast between what is expected or believed and what is actual. Following are some of the types of irony used in literature:

- **Verbal irony:** A word or phrase is used to suggest the opposite of its usual meaning.
- **Dramatic irony:** There is a contradiction between what a character thinks and what the reader knows is true.
- **Situational irony:** An event directly contradicts the expectations of readers or characters.

As you will see, irony can create humor.

Connecting Literary Elements

In this play, **dialogue**—the conversation between characters—helps to convey the irony. Through dialogue, the driver's vivid descriptions paint a picture for his traveler, and the irony of the situation is revealed. Watch for the driver's descriptions of the inspector general, as revealed through his dialogue, and decide how accurate they are.

CALIFORNIA STANDARDS

Instruction with this selection addresses these standards:

R 1.1*, 3.4*, 3.8*
W 1.5*, 2.4*
WOLC 1.2*
LS 1.7, 1.9

* Standards tested on HS Exit Exam. For complete standards, see p. CA 4.

Reading Strategy

Reading Between the Lines

When you read a drama, **read between the lines,** or draw conclusions about a person or idea by using the information provided through dialogue. These tips can help you read between the lines:

- Think critically about a character based on what he or she says or does, or based on details of appearance, as revealed through dialogue.
- Pay attention to questions that one character asks another.

Use a diagram like the one shown here to record ideas that you find between the lines.

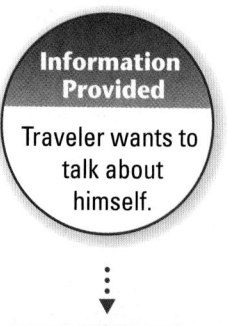

Information Provided

Traveler wants to talk about himself.

Conclusion

He thinks he is an important man.

Vocabulary Development

incognito (in käg´ ni tō´) *n*. a disguised condition (p. 359)

anonymous (ə nän´ ə məs) *adj*. without a known or acknowledged name (p. 359)

trundle (trun´ dəl) *v*. to roll along; to rotate (p. 359)

valet (val´ it) *n*. a man's personal servant who takes care of the man's clothes (p. 360)

buffet (bə´ fā´) *n*. restaurant with a counter or table where refreshments are served (p. 362)

The Inspector-General

Anton Chekhov Adapted by Michael Frayn

Valmondois Sous la Neige, Maurice de Vlaminck

▲ **Critical Viewing** What might life be like in a setting such as this one? **[Speculate]**

The curtain goes up to reveal falling snow and a cart facing away from us. Enter the STORYTELLER, *who begins to read the story. Meanwhile, the* TRAVELER *enters. He is a middle-aged man of urban appearance, wearing dark glasses and a long overcoat with its collar turned up. He is carrying a small traveling bag. He climbs into the cart and sits facing us.*

STORYTELLER. The Inspector General. In deepest <u>incognito</u>, first by express train, then along back roads, Pyotr Pavlovich Posudin[1] was hastening toward the little town of N, to which he had been summoned by an <u>anonymous</u> letter. "I'll take them by surprise," he thought to himself. "I'll come down on them like a thunderbolt out of the blue. I can just imagine their faces when they hear who I am . . ." [*Enter the* DRIVER, *a peasant, who climbs onto the cart, so that he is sitting with his back to us, and the cart begins to* <u>trundle</u> *slowly away from us.*] And when he'd thought to himself for long enough, he fell into conversation with the driver of the cart. What did he talk about? About himself, of course. [*Exit the* STORYTELLER.]

TRAVELER. I gather you've got a new Inspector-General in these parts.

DRIVER. True enough.

TRAVELER. Know anything about him? [*The driver turns and looks at the* TRAVELER, *who turns his coat collar up a little higher.*]

DRIVER. Know anything about him? Of course we do! We know everything about all of them up there! Every last little clerk—we know the color of his hair and the size of his boots! [*He turns back to the front, and the* TRAVELER *permits himself a slight smile.*]

TRAVELER. So, what do you reckon? Any good, is he? [*The* DRIVER *turns around.*]

DRIVER. Oh, yes, he's a good one, this one.

TRAVELER. Really?

DRIVER. Did one good thing straight off.

TRAVELER. What was that?

DRIVER. He got rid of the last one. Holy terror he was! Hear him coming five miles off! Say he's going to this little town. Somewhere like we're going, say. He'd let all the world know about it a month before. So now he's on his way, say, and it's like thunder and lightning coming down the road. And when he gets where he's going he has a good sleep, he has a good eat and drink—and then he starts. Stamps his feet, shouts his head off. Then he has another good sleep, and off he goes.

---

1. **Pyotr Pavlovich Posudin** (pyō´ tr pȧv lō´ vich pō syo͞o´ dən)

incognito (in käg´ ni tō´) *n.* a disguised condition

anonymous (ə nän´ ə məs) *adj.* without a known or acknowledged name

trundle (trun´ dəl) *v.* to roll along; to rotate

Literary Analysis
Irony What is ironic about the driver's words here?

**Reading Check**
What does the driver say about the last inspector general?

TRAVELER. But the new one's not like that?

DRIVER. Oh, no, the new one goes everywhere on the quiet, like. Creeps around like a cat. Don't want no one to see him, don't want no one to know who he is. Say he's going to this town down the road here. Someone there sent him a letter on the sly, let's say. "Things going on here you should know about." Something of that kind. Well, now, he creeps out of his office, so none of them up there see him go. He hops on a train just like anyone else, just like you or me. Then when he gets off he don't go jumping into a cab or nothing fancy. Oh, no. He wraps himself up from head to toe so you can't see his face, and he wheezes away like an old dog so no one can recognize his voice.

Literary Analysis
Irony Why is the description of the new inspector general ironic?

TRAVELER. Wheezes? That's not wheezing! That's the way he talks! So I gather.

DRIVER. Oh, is it? But the tales they tell about him. You'd laugh till you burst your tripes![2]

TRAVELER [*sourly*]. I'm sure I would.

DRIVER. He drinks, mind!

TRAVELER [*startled*]. Drinks?

DRIVER. Oh, like a hole in the ground. Famous for it.

TRAVELER. He's never touched a drop! I mean, from what I've heard.

DRIVER. Oh, not in public, no. Goes to some great ball—"No thank you, not for me." Oh, no, he puts it away at home! Wakes up in the morning, rubs his eyes, and the first thing he does, he shouts, "Vodka!" So in runs his <u>valet</u> with a glass. Fixed himself up a tube behind his desk, he has. Leans down, takes a pull on it, no one the wiser.

TRAVELER [*offended*]. How do you know all this, may I ask?

DRIVER. Can't hide it from the servants, can you? The valet and the coachman have got tongues in their heads. Then again, he's on the road, say, going about his business, and he keeps the bottle in his little bag. [*The* TRAVELER *discreetly pushes the traveling bag out of the* DRIVER'S *sight.*] And his housekeeper . . .

valet (val´ it) *n.* a man's personal servant who takes care of the man's clothes

TRAVELER. What about her?

DRIVER. Runs circles around him, she does, like a fox round his tail. She's the one who wears the trousers.[3] The people aren't half so frightened of him as they are of her.

TRAVELER. But at least he's good at his job, you say?

DRIVER. Oh, he's a blessing from heaven, I'll grant him that.

TRAVELER. Very cunning—you were saying.

---

2. **tripes** (trĭps) *n.* parts of the stomach, usually of an ox or a sheep.
3. **wears the trousers** has the greatest authority; is really in charge.

White Night, Edvard Munch, National Gallery, Oslo

◀ **Critical Viewing**
How well does the mood of this painting match the mood of this play? Explain. **[Connect]**

DRIVER. Oh, he creeps around all right.

TRAVELER. And then he pounces, yes? I should think some people must get the surprise of their life, mustn't they?

DRIVER. No, no—let's be fair, now. Give him his due. He don't make no trouble.

TRAVELER. No, I mean, if no one knows he's coming . . .

DRIVER. Oh, that's what *he* thinks, but *we* all know.

TRAVELER. You know?

DRIVER. Oh, some gentleman gets off the train at the station back there with his greatcoat up to his eyebrows and says, "No, I don't want a cab, thank you, just an ordinary horse and cart for me." Well, we'd put two and two together, wouldn't we! Say it was you, now, creeping along down the road here. The lads would be down there in a cab by now! By the time you got there the whole town would be as regular

Literary Analysis
Irony What makes the driver's description funny?

✔**Reading Check**
What does the driver say that the new inspector general does at night?

The Inspector-General ◆ 361

as clockwork! And you'd think to yourself, "Oh, look at that! As clean as a whistle! And they didn't know I was coming!" No, that's why he's such a blessing after the other one. This one believes it!

TRAVELER. Oh, I see.

DRIVER. What, you thought we wouldn't know him? Why, we've got the electric telegraph these days! Take today, now. I'm going past the station back there this morning, and the fellow who runs the <u>buffet</u> comes out like a bolt of lightning. Arms full of baskets and bottles. "Where are you off to?" I say. "Doing drinks and refreshments for the Inspector-General!" he says, and he jumps into a carriage and goes flying off down the road here. So there's the old Inspector-General, all muffled up like a roll of carpet, going secretly along in a cart somewhere—and when he gets there, nothing to be seen but vodka and cold salmon!

TRAVELER [*shouts*]. Right—turn around, then . . . !

DRIVER [*to the horse*]. Whoa, boy! Whoa! [*To the* TRAVELER.] Oh, so what's this, then? Don't want to go running into the Inspector-General, is that it? [*The* TRAVELER *gestures impatiently for the* DRIVER *to turn the cart around.* DRIVER *to the horse.*] Back we go, then, boy. Home we go. [*He turns the cart around, and the* TRAVELER *takes a swig from his traveling bag.*] Though if I know the old devil, he's like as not turned around and gone home again himself. [*Blackout.*]

buffet (bə fā′) *n.* restaurant with a counter or table where refreshments are served

Review and Assess

Thinking About the Selection

1. **Respond:** Did you feel any sympathy for the inspector general? Why or why not?

2. **(a) Recall:** What have townspeople learned about the inspector general's habits? **(b) Draw Conclusions:** What do these habits reveal about the official's character?

3. **(a) Recall:** What does the traveler do when the driver mentions that the inspector general keeps a flask of vodka? **(b) Infer:** What does this action tell you about the traveler?

4. **(a) Recall:** How does the driver describe the preparations for the inspector general's arrival? **(b) Interpret:** Why does this account provoke the traveler's demand to turn around?

5. **Speculate:** What kind of report might the inspector general make to the czar about his mission? Give specific details.

6. **Assess:** Based on his actions, what kind of leader do you think the inspector general will be?

7. **Evaluate:** Who do you think is the wiser man, the driver or the traveler? Explain.

Anton Chekhov

(1860–1904)

The grandson of a former serf who had purchased his freedom, Chekhov grew up in a small Russian coastal town. He later attended medical school in Moscow, where he began writing humorous sketches and short stories. Writing soon became his major focus, but he practiced medicine part-time throughout his life.

Chekhov wrote more than one thousand short stories as well as several acclaimed plays, including *The Seagull* (1896), *Uncle Vanya* (1899), and *The Three Sisters* (1901). He is considered one of the finest playwrights and short-story writers who ever lived.

Review and Assess

Literary Analysis

Irony

1. The humor in *The Inspector-General* comes from the use of **irony.** In a chart like the one shown here, note the traveler's assumptions and the driver's ironic observations.

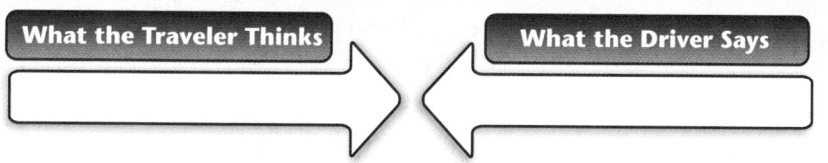

2. Explain why the traveler's attempt to hide his identity presents **situational irony.**

3. Explain why the driver's remark that the inspector general is "a good one" is an example of **verbal irony.**

Connecting Literary Elements

4. (a) What image of the inspector general is revealed through the **dialogue**? (b) Explain the irony in the driver's description of the new inspector general.

5. As the dialogue between the men continues, the situation becomes ever funnier. Use a flowchart like the one shown here to record the most important details leading to the comic reversal.

Reading Strategy

Reading Between the Lines

6. (a) When did you first realize that the traveler is the inspector general? (b) Which details led you to this conclusion?

7. As the driver goes on speaking, the traveler resorts to saying "so I gather" and "from what I've heard." **Read between the lines** to explain why he uses these expressions.

Extend Understanding

8. **Cultural Connection:** What makes a person of authority popular or unpopular in the public eye?

Integrate Language Skills

Vocabulary Development Lesson

Word Analysis: Greek Root -nym-

The Greek root -nym-, meaning "name," is used in many English words, including *anonymous*, which means "without a known name." Use a dictionary to define the following words.

1. patronymic   2. synonym   3. acronym

Spelling Strategy

When you add a suffix that begins with a vowel to a word that ends in a consonant, the spelling of the original word does not change. For example, *inspect* + *-or* = *inspector*.

Add *-ance*, *-ish*, or *-er* to each word below to form three properly spelled words.

1. child   2. travel   3. accept

Fluency: Sentence Completions

In your notebook, complete each sentence with a word from the vocabulary list on page 357.

1. The heavy trucks slowly ____?____ along the bumpy road.
2. An ____?____ donor gave ten thousand dollars to the hospital fund. We're still not sure who made the donation.
3. The ____?____ cleaned and ironed the pants of the hotel guest.
4. The ____?____ featured delicious main courses and desserts. Everyone moved along, placing their favorite foods on their plates.
5. Traveling ____?____, with sunglasses, a fake mustache, and a hat, the spy checked into the motel under a false name.

Grammar Lesson

Compound Subjects and Compound Predicates

A sentence may have two or more subjects with the same verb (a **compound subject**) or two or more verbs, or predicates, with the same subject (a **compound predicate**). It may even have both at once. The parts of a compound subject or predicate are joined by a conjunction, such as *and* or *or*.

Compound subject: <u>Glasses</u> and <u>an over-coat</u> were worn by the inspector general. <u>Glasses</u>, <u>an overcoat</u>, and <u>a traveling bag</u> were some of his belongings.

Compound predicate: They <u>traveled</u> and <u>talked</u> in the cart. The driver <u>turns</u>, <u>looks</u>, and <u>nods</u> at the traveler.

Practice Copy each sentence. Underline each compound subject once and each compound predicate twice.

1. Snow and ice make travel difficult.
2. The driver and the traveler took a ride.
3. As they ride, the traveler asks questions and hopes for the right response.
4. The driver's manner and his ideas reveal an interesting situation.
5. He makes a decision and chooses to leave.

Writing Application Write two sentences about *The Inspector-General*, using a compound subject in one and a compound predicate in the other.

Prentice Hall Writing and Grammar Connection: Chapter 20, Section 1

Writing Lesson

Ad for a New Inspector General

Imagine that you are the czar and have just fired the old inspector general. Write a newspaper ad to find a replacement. Your ad should provide information that will appeal to potential applicants and clarify whether they are qualified for the job.

Prewriting Jot down ideas in the following categories: (a) job title and responsibilities; (b) necessary experience and background; (c) salary and benefits; (d) contact information, such as the company's phone number or address.

Drafting Begin with an attention-grabbing introduction. Then, devote a short paragraph to each of the four categories.

> **Model: Grabbing Your Reader's Attention**
>
> Love to travel? Ready to take on fascinating new responsibilities? Consider becoming an inspector general!
>
> An effective ad is based on a catchy and memorable message.

Revising Compare your ad to your prewriting notes, underlining key details in your draft. If you discover information that is unclear or incomplete, revise to present a more accurate picture of the job.

WG Prentice Hall Writing and Grammar Connection: Chapter 8, Section 3

Extension Activities

Listening and Speaking With two other students, prepare to perform a **Readers Theater presentation** of *The Inspector-General*. Do not provide props or staging; instead, focus on a well-prepared reading of the play.

- Choose roles—the traveler, the driver, and a narrator who reads the introduction and any stage directions you feel should be shared.

- Experiment to find the tone of voice and style of delivery that seem to work best.

Then, perform the play in front of a small group or the entire class. **[Group Activity]**

Research and Technology Research what life was like in Russia during the rule of the czars. Explain the responsibilities of inspectors general during this time. Use two or more Internet search engines to broaden the scope of your findings. Display your findings in a **concept map** or another graphic organizer and present it to your class. Ask your class to compare inspectors general in history to the inspector general in this story.

 **Take It to the Net**   www.phschool.com

Go online for an additional research activity using the Internet.

Prepare to Read

Go Deep to the Sewer ◆ Fly Away

 Take It to the Net

Visit www.phschool.com
for interactive activities
and instruction related to
the selections, including
- background
- graphic organizers
- literary elements
- reading strategies

Preview

Connecting to the Literature

When life hands out lemons, some people make lemonade. Other people make big lemon meringue pies to toss so that others will laugh. Maybe you are one of those people who can find something funny even in difficult situations. These selections focus on the lighter side of personal experiences.

Background

For years, Ralph Helfer, an animal trainer and the author of "Fly Away," used an animal-training method based on fear. After being injured several times, Helfer developed a new system, "affection training," with which the trainer wins an animal's loyalty through understanding, patience, and love. Since using this system, neither Helfer nor any of his animals have been injured.

Literary Analysis

Humorous Remembrance

A **humorous remembrance** is a story that emphasizes what is funny in a writer's past experiences. The following excerpt from "Go Deep to the Sewer" relates a ten-year-old quarterback's instructions to his team, whose football field was an urban street in Philadelphia.

> ". . . Arnie, you go down to the corner of Locust an' fake takin' the bus. An' Cos, you do a zig out to the bakery. See if you can shake your man before you hit the rolls."

As you read the selections, notice how both writers find something to laugh about in experiences that may have had their painful moments as well.

Comparing Literary Works

Humorous remembrances are all amusing, whether or not the writers initially intended them to be. Humor is the most important ingredient in both of these stories, and laughter may be the reader's most frequent reaction. Compare the humorous and serious sides of the experiences these authors convey in each of their stories.

Reading Strategy

Recognizing Situational Humor

Situational humor, as found in these humorous remembrances, arises from conditions that mix people, actions, and settings in funny and often improbable ways:

- In "Go Deep to the Sewer," a stickball player is tagged out at third base because the car that takes the place of the base is suddenly driven away.
- In "Fly Away," the trainer amazingly gets several thousand flies to take to the air on cue.

Use a chart like this one to capture and categorize specific examples of situational humor you find as you read.

What Is Being Done?	Who Is Doing It?
Where?	**Using What?**

Vocabulary Development

lateral (lat′ ər əl) *adj.* sideways (p. 368)

yearned (yʉrnd) *v.* longed for (p. 370)

decoy (dē′ koï′) *n.* person used to lure others into a trap (p. 370)

interpretation (in tʉr′ prə tā′ shən) *n.* explanation (p. 371)

skeptical (skep′ ti kəl) *adj.* doubting; questioning (p. 375)

Go Deep to the Sewer

Bill Cosby

The essence of childhood, of course, is play, which my friends and I did endlessly on streets that we reluctantly shared with traffic. As a daring receiver in touch football, I spent many happy years running up and down those asphalt fields, hoping that a football would hit me before a Chevrolet did.

My mother was often a nervous fan who watched me from her window.

"Bill, don't get run over!" she would cry in a moving concern for me.

"Do you see me getting run over?" I would cleverly reply.

And if I ever *had* been run over, my mother had a seat for it that a scalper[1] would have prized.

Because the narrow fields of those football games allowed almost no <u>lateral</u> movement, an end run was possible only if a car pulled out and blocked for you. And so I worked on my pass-catching, for I knew I had little chance of ever living my dream: taking a handoff and sweeping to glory along the curb, dancing over the dog dung like Red Grange.

The quarterback held this position not because he was the best passer but because he knew how to drop to one knee in the huddle and diagram plays with trash.

"Okay, Shorty," Junior Barnes would say, "this is you: the orange peel."

"I don' wanna be the orange peel," Shorty replied. "The orange peel is Albert. I'm the gum."

lateral (lat´ ər əl) *adj.* sideways

Reading Strategy
Recognizing Situational Humor Why did few players get to make "end runs"? What is funny about this situation?

---

1. **scalper** (skalp´ ər) *n.* person who buys tickets and sells them later at higher than regular prices.

◀ **Critical Viewing**
How does this painting
help you picture the setting
and the characters in
Cosby's essay? **[Connect]**

Young Brothers in the Hood, Tom McKinney

"But let's make 'em *think* he's the orange peel," I said, "an' let 'em think Albert's the manhole."

"Okay, Shorty," said Junior, "you go out ten steps an' then cut left behind the black Oldsmobile."

"I'll sorta go *in* it first to shake my man," said Shorty, "an' then, when he don' know where I am, you can hit me at the fender."

"Cool. An' Arnie, you go down to the corner of Locust an' fake takin' the bus. An' Cos, you do a zig out to the bakery. See if you can shake your man before you hit the rolls."

"Suppose I start a fly pattern to the bakery an' then do a zig out to the trash can," I said.

"No, they'll be expecting that."

☑**Reading Check**

Where do Cosby and his
friends play football?

I spent most of my boyhood trying to catch passes with the easy grace of my heroes at Temple;[2] but easy grace was too hard for me. Because I was short and thin, my hands were too small to catch a football with arms extended on the run. Instead, I had to stagger backwards and smother the ball in my chest. How I <u>yearned</u> to grab the ball in my hands while striding smoothly ahead, rather than receiving it like someone who was catching a load of wet wash. Often, after a pass had bounced off my hands, I returned to the quarterback and glumly said, "Jeeze, Junior, I don' know what happened." He, of course, knew what had happened: he had thrown the ball to someone who should have been catching it with a butterfly net.

Each of these street games began with a quick review of the rules: two-hand touch, either three or four downs, always goal-to-go, forward passing from anywhere, and no touchdowns called back because of traffic in motion. If a receiver caught a ball near an oncoming car while the defender was running for his life, the receiver had guts, and possibly a long excuse from school.

I will never forget one particular play from those days when I was trying so hard to prove my manhood between the manholes. In the huddle, as Junior, our permanent quarterback, dropped to one knee to arrange the garbage offensively, I said, "Hey, Junior, make me a <u>decoy</u> on this one."

Pretending to catch the ball was what I did best.

"What's a decoy?" he said.

"Well, it's—"

"I ain't got time to learn. Okay, Eddie, you're the Dr Pepper cap an' you go deep toward New Jersey."

"An' I'll fool around short," I said.

"No, Cos, you fake goin' deep an' then buttonhook at the DeSoto. An' Harold, you do a zig out between 'em. *Somebody* get free."

Moments later, the ball was snapped to him and I started sprinting down the field with my defender, Jody, who was matching me stride for stride. Wondering if I would be able to get free for a pass sometime within the next hour, I stopped at the corner and began sprinting back to Junior, whose arm had been cocked for about fifteen seconds, as if he'd been posing for a trophy. Since Eddie and Harold also were covered, and since running from scrimmage was impossible on that narrow field, I felt that this might be touch football's first eternal play: Junior still standing there long after Eddie, Harold, and I had dropped to the ground, his arm still cocked as he tried to find some way to pass to himself.

But unlimited time was what we had and it was almost enough for us. Often we played in the street until the light began to fade and the ball became a blur in the dusk. If there is one memory of my

---

2. **Temple** Temple University in Philadelphia, Pennsylvania.

yearned (yɜrnd) *v.* longed for

decoy (dē′ koi′) *n.* person used to lure others into a trap

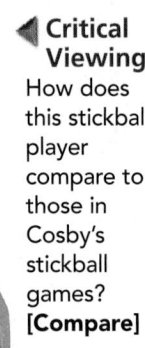

◀ **Critical Viewing** How does this stickball player compare to those in Cosby's stickball games? **[Compare]**

childhood that will never disappear, it is a bunch of boys straining to find a flying football in the growing darkness of a summer night.

There were, of course, a couple of streetlamps on our field, but they were useful only if your pattern took you right up to one of them to make your catch. The rest of the field was lost in the night; and what an adventure it was to refuse to surrender to that night, to hear the quarterback cry "Ball!" and then stagger around in a kind of grid-iron blindman's buff.

"Hey, you guys, dontcha think we should call the game?" said Harold one summer evening.

"Why do a stupid thing like that?" Junior replied.

"'Cause I can't see the ball."

"Harold, that don't make you special. Nobody can see the ball. But y' *know* it's up there."

And we continued to stagger around as night fell on Philadelphia and we kept looking for a football that could have been seen only on radar screens.

One day last year in a gym, I heard a boy say to his father, "Dad, what's a Spal*deen*?"

This shocking question left me depressed, for it is one thing not to know the location of the White House or the country that gave its name to Swiss cheese, but when a boy doesn't know what a Spal*deen* is, our educational system has failed. For those of you ignorant of basic American history, a Spal*deen* was a pink rubber ball with more bounce than can be imagined today. Baseball fans talk about the lively ball, but a lively baseball is a sinking stone compared to a Spal*deen*, which could be dropped from your eye level and bounce back there again, if you wanted to do something boring with it. And when you connected with a Spal*deen* in stickball, you put a pink rocket in orbit, perhaps even over the house at the corner and into another neighborhood, where it might gently bop somebody's mother sitting on a stoop.

I love to remember all the street games that we could play with a Spal*deen*. First, of course, was stickball, an organized version of which is also popular and known as baseball. The playing field was the same rectangle that we used for football: it was the first rectangular diamond. And for this game, we had outfield walls in which people happened to live and we had bases that lacked a certain uniformity: home and second were manhole covers, and first and third were the fenders of parked cars.

One summer morning, this offbeat infield caused a memorable <u>interpretation</u> of the official stickball rules. Junior hit a two-sewer shot and was running toward what should have been third when third suddenly drove away in first. While the bewildered Junior tried to arrive safely in what had become a twilight zone, Eddie took my throw from center field and tagged him out.

"I'm not out!" cried Junior in outrage. "I'm right here on third!"

And he did have a point, but so did Eddie, who replied, not without a certain logic of his own, "But third ain't there anymore."

Literary Analysis
Humorous Remembrance
Which details about playing at night are exaggerated?

interpretation (in tʉr′ prə tā′ shən) *n.* explanation

**Reading Check**

What is the one memory Cosby has of his childhood that he says will never disappear?

In those games, our first base was as mobile as our third; and it was a floating first that set off another lively division of opinion on the day that Fat Albert hit a drive over the spot from which first base had just driven away, leaving us without a good part of the right field foul line. The hit would have been at least a double for anyone with movable legs, but Albert's destination was first, where the play might have been close had the right fielder hit the cutoff man instead of a postman.

"Foul ball!" cried Junior, taking a guess that happened to be in his favor.

"You're out of your mind, Junior!" cried Albert, an observation that often was true, no matter what Junior was doing. "It went right over the fender!"

"What fender?"

"If that car comes back, you'll see it's got a fender," said Albert, our automotive authority.

However, no matter how many pieces of our field drove away, nothing could ever take away the sweetness of having your stick connect with a Spal*deen* in a magnificent *whoppp* and drive it so high and far that it bounced off a window with a view of New Jersey and then caromed back to the street, where Eddie would have fielded it like Carl Furillo[3] had he not backed into a coal chute.

---

3. **Carl Furillo** (kärl fər il′ ō) baseball player for the Brooklyn Dodgers in the 1950s.

Review and Assess

Thinking About the Selection

1. **Respond:** Would you enjoy playing stickball or football by the rules Bill Cosby describes? Explain.

2. **(a) Recall:** What does Cosby regret about his physical size during his boyhood? **(b) Compare and Contrast:** How was Cosby like and unlike his heroes at Temple University?

3. **(a) Recall:** Why was Junior always the quarterback for the neighborhood football games? **(b) Analyze:** Was Junior's method of calling plays successful? Explain.

4. **(a) Recall:** How does Cosby describe the experience of connecting with a Spaldeen? **(b) Interpret:** Does Cosby really mean what he says about hitting a Spaldeen? Explain.

5. **(a) Speculate:** What does Cosby mean when he says "The essence of childhood . . . is play"? **(b) Evaluate:** Do you agree with this idea? Explain.

Bill Cosby

(b. 1937)

The son of a navy cook and a domestic worker, Bill Cosby grew up in the housing projects of Philadelphia. Although he left high school to join the navy, he earned a diploma through a correspondence course. During the 1960s, he performed stand-up comedy in Philadelphia and soon became nationally famous.

Cosby has won awards for his television shows and his books, which include *Fatherhood* (1986) and *Time Flies* (1987).

Fly Away

Ralph Helfer

"I need 5,000 trained flies. Can you do it? Yes or no!" The voice at the other end of the phone was insistent.

"Well, I . . ."

"Of course you can't, Helfer. *Nobody* can. Look, I told the director I'd make a couple of calls. So, now I have. The answer is obviously NO!"

"I *can* do it," I said, fitting my sentence neatly in between my caller's constant jabber, "but I'll need a couple of days."

The voice on the phone was silent a moment. Then: "You're kidding."

"No, really. Two days, and I'll be ready. What do they have to do?"

"There's this artificial, dead-looking 'thing' lying on the ground in the forest. The director wants thousands of flies to be crawling on it without flying away."

"Okay," I said. "Consider it done."

"No, wait. Then, he wants them *all* to fly away, on command—but not before."

"Okay, no problem," I said. "Two days."

"Wait. Did you hear what I said? They can't leave until he says okay. How are you going to keep them there, let alone have them fly away when he wants them to??"

"I'll stick each of their 20,000 legs in glue! Look, don't worry. Call me later, and I'll give you the figure. 'Bye."

Sometimes affection training was not the only answer. One could not "pet" a fly or earn its respect. I knew I would have to resort to the laws of nature for the answer to this one. I'd had the opportunity to

Reading Strategy
Recognizing Situational Humor How does the caller's attitude create humor?

Reading Check

What does the director's assistant ask Helfer to do?

work with various insects in the past. But *5,000!* I hoped I hadn't bitten off more than I could chew.

I went to work, first converting an old box in which we'd been keeping crickets (we raised them to feed to the tarantulas). The box was about three feet high by two feet square. Patching up a few holes, I scrubbed it clean, fixed a crooked door, and set it inside the snake room.

The next day I visited a good friend of mine, Professor Jonathan Ziller, an entomologist and researcher. His work area consisted of twenty to thirty lab-type cages made of fine-mesh wire. Each contained a different species of insect. Over a cup of coffee, I told him of my needs. We walked over to a cage that was being heated by a special infrared lamp. Inside I could see massive swarms of maggots—fly larvae, ready to be hatched into their next stage. As I stood there, the professor calculated the exact time when they would become flies. As his watch struck the "birthing" time, thousands of flies left their maggot bodies and were suddenly airborne, buzzing about the cage.

We both agreed that these flies, an unusually large type that resembled the horsefly, would be perfect. An added plus was the fact that they were all hybrid, incapable of breeding. Hence, in releasing them I would not be running the risk of upsetting the natural balance of the environment.

The professor gave me a batch of fly larvae, which he'd calculated would hatch on the morning of the shoot, along with a vial of a special, harmless tranquilizer in a gas capsule. The gas would be released when the tip of the cigarette-sized plastic tube was broken. With the vial set inside the fly box, all the flies could be put to sleep within seconds. Once the gas had dissipated in a matter of moments, the flies would awaken. The tranquilizer was, of course, harmless to people. A handshake later, I was off, gently carrying my brood with me.

On the morning of the shoot, all the flies hatched right on schedule. I loaded up and headed for the studio location. When I arrived, I was greeted by a crew of disbelievers with tongue-in-cheek attitudes. Bets and jokes were being made in every direction, all in good-natured fun.

▲ **Critical Viewing**
What other challenges, like having flies act on cue, can you think of that might be faced by people in the film industry who work with animals? **[Speculate]**

Reading Strategy
Recognizing Situational Humor Why are the workers on the movie set making jokes? Do they expect Helfer to be successful?

The director, a big, friendly sort, came over to me with a suspicious look in his eyes. "Is it true?"

"What?"

"That you can put 5,000 flies on something and they'll crawl around, but you can guarantee they won't fly right off?"

"It's true."

"Then when I tell you to let them go, they'll all fly away immediately?"

"Give or take a few."

"A few what?"

"Flies that won't fly away."

"If you pull this off, I'll double your fee," he said in disbelief.

"Ready whenever you are," I said, and headed for my fly house.

The camera was set. The "dead thing" turned out to be a special-effects monster baby that had supposedly died a while back and was now to be swarming with flies. Somebody was to walk by, and the flies would then have to fly away.

Everything was ready.

The skeptical assistant director yelled for the "fly man." One of my trainers and I carried the fly house over and set it near the camera. The loud buzzing of an enormous number of flies was obvious. Sheets of heavy paper prevented anyone from seeing into the box.

"Now, Ralph, I'll roll the camera whenever you say—okay?" asked the director.

"Sure, but everything has to be ready. I've only got 10,042 flies—just enough for two shots."

His look told me he wasn't sure whether I was putting him on or not.

"10,042—really!" he mumbled, and walked over to the camera.

With everything set, I opened the small door of the fly house. Hiding the gas capsule in the palm of my hand and reaching inside, I broke it open, closed the door, and waited for fifteen seconds. To everybody's amazement, the buzzing stopped. Next, I opened the door and scooped out three or four handfuls of flies. I shook them out as one would when counting a pound of peanuts. Putting the little sleeping flies all over the "body," I began to dramatically count the last few: "Five-thousand twenty, five-thousand twenty-one, five-thousand twenty-one . . . that makes it half!"

I told everyone to hold still, then I gave the flies a verbal cue: "Okay guys—Jack, Bill, Mary—come on, up and at 'em!"

Slowly the flies started to awaken, then move around. In a few moments the whole mass of them was swarming all over the "thing," but they were still too drowsy to fly, as my professor friend had told me they would be.

"Okay, roll!" yelled the director. The camera rolled on the fly swarm, and I shot a look at the crew. They appeared to be in shock. Then, having gotten enough footage, the director shouted, "Okay, Ralph, *now!*"

My great moment.

"Okay, group," I said to the flies. "Get ready: on the count of three, all of you take off."

skeptical (skep´ ti kəl) *adj.* doubting; questioning

Literary Analysis

Humorous Remembrance
Helfer says he has exactly 10,042 flies. What makes this statement funny?

Reading Check

What does Helfer put in the fly house before scooping out the flies?

The crew, absolutely bug-eyed (forgive the pun), was hypnotized. "One," I counted. They looked from the flies to me.

"Two."

"Three!" I yelled, clapping my hands and stamping my foot at the same time. Five thousand twenty-one flies flew up, up, around and around. The camera hummed until the director, rousing himself from his amazed state, said, "Cut!"

The entire crew was silent for a moment, and then they burst into applause and delighted laughter.

"You did it, you really did it!" said the director, slapping me heartily on the back. "I'm not even going to ask you how. I don't even want to know. But if I ever need a trained *anything*, you're the man I'll call!"

Straight-faced, I said, "Well, actually, I've recently trained 432 flies to form a chorus line on my arm, and on cue they all kick a leg at the same time."

The director, poker-faced, looked straight at me. "Which one?" he asked.

"Which one what?"

"Which leg?"

"The left one, of course!"

We all broke up laughing and headed home.

Review and Assess

Thinking About the Selection

1. **Respond:** What did you find most interesting about Ralph Helfer's remembrance? Explain.

2. **(a) Recall:** What plan does Helfer develop to make the flies do what is needed for the movie? **(b) Draw Conclusions:** Why do you think he feels comfortable making the deal?

3. **(a) Recall:** How does Helfer know that the flies will not fly away as soon as they are released? **(b) Infer:** Why does he speak to the flies as if they understand him?

4. **(a) Recall:** What is the director's reaction to the fly stunt? **(b) Infer:** Would he want to work with Helfer again? Why?

5. **Assess:** Would it have benefited Helfer to tell the director how he did the fly trick? Explain.

6. **Speculate:** What specific skills are needed to be a good animal trainer? Explain.

7. **(a) Evaluate:** Do you think Helfer's live effects are still needed in the computer age? **(b) Support:** What would be gained or lost by using only computers for special effects?

Ralph Helfer

(b. 1937)

Ralph Helfer, one of the world's leading animal trainers, has worked in more than 5,000 movies and television programs. In his book *The Beauty of the Beasts* (1989), Helfer describes being "clawed by lions, attacked by bears, bitten by poisonous snakes, and nearly suffocated by pythons."

Since instituting affection training, however, Helfer has been bite-free. He and his trained animals have won 18 PATSY awards for the best animal performances on screen.

Review and Assess

Literary Analysis

Humorous Remembrance

1. Use a chart like the one below to record details that identify "Go Deep to the Sewer" as a **humorous remembrance.**

2. How does Cosby give readers the sense that they are part of the action as they move through the story?
3. (a) What overall impression of his work does Helfer communicate in his remembrance? (b) Which humorous details make the writing entertaining?

Comparing Literary Works

4. (a) Review each selection and compare the serious elements or ideas in each of these humorous remembrances. (b) Which selection conveyed the more serious ideas? Explain.
5. Cosby's story strings together experiences of childhood play. Helfer's memoir focuses on one memorable job. Which piece do you find more appealing? Why?

Reading Strategy

Recognizing Situational Humor

6. How does Cosby use his **situation**—being obliged to play football and stickball in the street—to humorous advantage?
7. Helfer pretends to count the sleeping flies. Why is this funny?
8. How does the audience's reaction to Helfer's achievement add to the situation's humor?

Extend Understanding

9. **Cultural Connection:** Do you think Cosby's story could only be appreciated by people who have lived in a city? Explain.

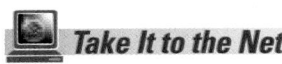

Integrate Language Skills

Vocabulary Development Lesson

Concept Development: Sports Jargon

Jargon is special language related to a particular activity, profession, sport, or art. Use a dictionary to find the meanings of the following sports terms. Then, explain how each term might be used in everyday speech.

1. slam dunk
2. punt
3. on deck
4. huddle

Spelling Strategy

When you add *-ly* to a word ending with a short vowel followed by an *l*, keep the final *l*. For example, *lateral* + *-ly* = *laterally*.

Identify the misspelled words in the following list and correct their spelling.

1. wonderfuly
2. civily
3. thoughtfully
4. politically

Concept Development: Analogies

Complete the following analogies by analyzing the word relationship in the first pair of words. Then, create the same relationship in the second pair by choosing the most suitable word.

1. forward : ahead :: lateral : ___?___
   (a) nearby (b) quickly (c) sideways (d) far
2. dislike : like :: yearn : ___?___
   (a) long for (b) realize (c) reject (d) behave
3. false : wrong :: decoy : ___?___
   (a) duck (b) bait (c) coach (d) invite
4. seasoning : spice :: interpretation : ___?___
   (a) version (b) behavior (c) satisfaction (d) play
5. prisoner : pardon :: skeptic : ___?___
   (a) remedy (b) lightly (c) convince (d) enemy

Grammar Lesson

Direct Objects

A **direct object** is the noun or pronoun that receives the action of a verb. You can determine whether a word is a direct object by asking *whom?* or *what?* after an action verb.

Examples:

Junior threw the *football* to Cosby. (threw *what?*)

He told *Albert* to pass the ball. (told *whom?*)

Junior devised elaborate *plans* for the team. (devised *what?*)

The boy asked his *father*. (asked *whom?*)

Practice In each sentence, identify the direct object and the verb whose action it completes.

1. I will never forget one particular play.
2. Suppose I start a fly pattern to the bakery.
3. "No," said Junior, "they'll be expecting that."
4. "Now, Ralph, I'll roll the camera whenever you say—okay?"
5. The professor gave me a batch of fly larvae.

Writing Application Write a short paragraph about a sports experience you have had. Try to include a direct object in every sentence. Then, underline each direct object.

Prentice Hall Writing and Grammar Connection: Chapter 20, Section 3

Writing Lesson

Humorous Personal Narrative

Choose a memorable experience and write a humorous narrative about it. Catch your readers' attention and help them anticipate the comedy in your writing. Use the essays by Cosby and Helfer as inspirations for your own brand of humor.

Prewriting   Jot down details that you know will make your readers laugh. Focus on details that can be exaggerated for comic effect.

Drafting   The best groundwork for any kind of narrative writing—especially a humorous narrative—is a strong introduction. A striking quotation is one of a number of things that will make a good start.

Model: Writing a Strong Introduction

The voice on the phone was insistent: "I need a dozen rabbits, and I need them now!"

> An interesting quotation or a surprising observation can provide a strong introduction to a narrative.

Revising   Review your draft to evaluate whether your introduction will make your readers want to read further. Then, check that your narrative maintains its humorous tone throughout.

WG Prentice Hall Writing and Grammar Connection: Chapter 4, Section 3

Extension Activities

Listening and Speaking Bill Cosby's memoir originated as part of his stand-up comedy routine. Working with a partner, use a real or imagined incident from your own life or one you have seen in a book, movie, or television show as the basis for a brief **monologue.** Your partner can help you judge whether the incident has comic potential.

- Emphasize the humor of the situation.
- End the story in a satisfying way.

Use your partner's feedback to revise your monologue before presenting it to a small group of friends or classmates. **[Group Activity]**

Research and Technology Use books, magazines, reference materials, or online resources to do research about current methods of training animals. Focus on learning about the training methods used with two or three specific kinds of animals. Organize what you learn into a **visual report** using charts, graphs, or other appropriate visual aids. Share your findings with your class.

 **Take It to the Net**   www.phschool.com

Go online for an additional research activity using the Internet.

CONNECTIONS
Literature and Childhood
Memories of Youth

In "Go Deep to the Sewer," Bill Cosby captures the sights and sounds of the Philadelphia neighborhood where he grew up. His childhood, spent playing with colorful characters with nicknames like Fat Albert and Weasel, provided him with a uniquely humorous way of looking at the world. Cosby's comedy rings true because he can summon up his childhood with such clarity, reminding us of similar experiences we otherwise might have forgotten.

The writer Gary Soto also draws upon the memories of his childhood to provide inspiration for his writing. Soto grew up in the Mexican American community of Fresno, California, and his memories of childhood are sometimes bittersweet. As you read Soto's account, you may be struck by the difference in mood that Cosby and Soto bring to their vivid memories of childhood.

The Talk
Gary Soto

My best friend and I knew that we were going to grow up to be ugly. On a backyard lawn—the summer light failing west of the mulberry tree where the house of the most beautiful girl on the street stood—we talked about what we could do: shake the second-base dirt from our hair, wash our hands of frog smells and canal water, and learn to smile without showing our crooked teeth. We had to stop spitting when girls were looking and learn not to pile food onto a fork and into a fat cheek already churning hot grub.

We were twelve, with lean bodies that were beginning to grow in weird ways. First, our heads got large, but our necks wavered, frail as crisp tulips. The eyes stayed small as well, receding into pencil dots on each side of an unshapely nose that cast remarkable shadows when we turned sideways. It seemed that Scott's legs sprouted muscle and renegade veins, but his arms, blue with ink markings, stayed short and hung just below his waist. My gangly arms nearly touched my kneecaps. In this way, I was built for picking up grounders[1] and doing cartwheels, my arms swaying just inches from the summery grass.

We sat on the lawn, with the porch light off, waiting for the beautiful girl to turn on her bedroom light and read on her stomach with one leg stirring the air. This stirred us, and our dream was a clean dream of holding hands and airing out our loneliness by walking up and down the block.

When Scott asked whom I was going to marry, I said a brown girl from the valley. He said that he was going to marry a strawberry blonde who would enjoy Millerton Lake, dirty as it was. I said mine would like cats and the sea and would think nothing of getting up at night from a warm, restless bed and sitting in the yard under the icy stars. Scott said his wife would work for the first year or so, because he would go to trade school[2] in refrigeration. Since our town was made with what was left over after God made hell, there was money in air conditioning, he reasoned.

I said that while my wife would clean the house and stir pots of nice grub, I would drive a truck to my job as a carpenter, which would allow me to use my long arms. I would need only a stepladder to hand a fellow worker on the roof a pinch of nails. I could hammer,

receding (ri sēd′ ing) *v.* withdrawing; diminishing

renegade (ren′ ə gād′) *adj.* disloyal; traitorous

gangly (gaŋ′ glē) *adj.* thin, tall, and awkward; of lanky build

Thematic Connection
How do the boys' dreams of the future compare with their present-day realities?

---

1. picking up grounders catching balls as they bounce along the ground.
2. trade school school in which students specialize in learning one set of skills for a particular profession.

saw, lift beams into place, and see the work I got done at the end of the day. Of course, she might like to work, and that would be okay, because then we could buy two cars and wave at each other if we should see the other drive by. In the evenings, we would drink Kool-Aid and throw a slipper at our <u>feisty</u> dog at least a hundred times before we went inside for a Pop-Tart and hot chocolate.

Scott said he would work hard too, but now and then he would find money on the street and the two of them could buy extra things like a second TV for the bedroom and a Doughboy swimming pool for his three kids. He planned on having three kids and a ranch house on the river, where he could dip a hand in the water, drink, and say, "Ahh, tastes good."

feisty (fīs′ tē) *adj.* full of spirit; energetic

But that would be years later. Now we had to do something about our looks. We plucked at the grass and flung it into each other's faces.

"Rotten luck," Scott said. "My arms are too short. Look at 'em."

"Maybe we can lift weights. This would make up for our looks," I said.

"I don't think so," Scott said, depressed. "People like people with nice faces."

He was probably right. I turned onto my stomach, a stalk of grass in my mouth. "Even if I'm ugly, my wife's going to be good-looking," I said. "She'll have a lot of dresses and I'll have more shirts than I have now. Do you know how much carpenters make?"

Then I saw the bedroom light come on and the beautiful girl walk into the room drying her hair with a towel. I nudged Scott's short arm and he saw what I saw. We flicked the stalks of grass, stood up, and walked over to the fence to look at her scrub her hair dry. She plopped onto the bed and began to comb it, slowly at first because it was tangled. With a rubber band, she tied it back, and picked up a book that was thick as a good-sized sandwich.

Scott and I watched her read a book, now both legs in the air and twined together, her painted toenails like red petals. She turned the pages slowly, very carefully, and now and then lowered her face into the pillow. She looked sad but beautiful, and we didn't know what to do except nudge each other in the heart and creep away to the front yard.

"I can't stand it anymore. We have to talk about this," Scott said.

"If I try, I think I can make myself better looking," I said. "I read an article about a girl whitening her teeth with water and flour."

So we walked up the street, depressed. For every step I took, Scott took two, his short arms pumping to keep up. For every time Scott said, "I think we're ugly," I said two times, "Yeah, yeah, we're in big trouble."

Connecting Literature and Childhood

1. What does the girl in the window seem to represent for the two young boys?

2. What types of character traits can you infer from the boys' choice of future careers?

3. How does the humor differ in Cosby's and Soto's recollections of their childhoods?

4. How might their stories have been written differently if Cosby and Soto had written them as children?

Gary Soto

(b. 1952)

Gary Soto was not a person who could accurately predict what he would be when he grew up. Making a living as a writer did not occur to him in a house where reading was not encouraged. In college, after a brief flirtation with geography, he discovered the allure of writing. Soto went on to write several award-winning novels, short stories, and books of poetry. Much of his writing has been inspired by his childhood in the Mexican American community of Fresno, California.

Prepare to Read

An Entomological Study of Apartment 4A

Preview

Connecting to the Literature

Often, we are fascinated by creatures that repel us. Even if you would rather not look at that many-legged thing that just scurried under the stove, you may still want to know what it is. This natural curiosity inspired writer Patricia Volk to collect the bugs she found in her apartment and take them to an expert for identification.

Background

In everyday speech, the words *insect* and *bug* are used for all sorts of pests, but no entomologist, like Louis Sorkin in this article, would use these terms loosely. An entomologist studies insects—their behavior, their eating habits, and the differences among the dozens of species that are often smaller than a human fingernail.

Literary Analysis

Feature Article

A **feature article** is a newspaper or magazine story written to entertain readers or to provide information on a subject of human interest. Such an article may be designed to evoke an emotional response to its subject's achievements or problems. One way a writer can evoke a strong response from readers is by sharing a personal experience. In this excerpt, note how Patricia Volk personalizes a common problem.

> A black crawly thing with more legs than the Rockettes had staked out the north bedroom wall . . . and a bug as shiny as patent leather had moved into the water gauge of our electric coffee maker.

Notice how Volk's subject matter entertains while informing you.

Connecting Literary Elements

A well-written article holds your attention because it never wanders far from its main idea. The **main idea** is the central or underlying point of an article. The fact that every sentence in "An Entomological Study of Apartment 4A" is related to the writer's investigation of insects and bugs shapes the article and gives it impact. By the end of the article, Volk reveals the main idea and the insights it generates.

Instruction with this selection addresses these standards:

R 1.1*, 3.8*
W 1.3*, 2.5*
WOLC 1.3*
LS 1.8

* Standards tested on HS Exit Exam. For complete standards, see p. CA 4.

Reading Strategy

Establishing a Purpose for Reading

To get the most out of what you read, **establish a purpose** for reading and then read to achieve this purpose. Your purpose may be

- to discover something new or to gather information for a report; if so, focus on obtaining useful facts.
- simply to enjoy reading; if so, look for fascinating details and descriptions.

Set a purpose for reading this selection and use a chart like this one to jot down notes that will help fulfill your purpose.

My Purpose

Notes From Selection

Vocabulary Development

microcosms (mī′ krō käz′əms) *n.* little worlds (p. 386)

metaphors (met′ə fôrz) *n.* ways of speaking of things as though they were something else (p. 386)

poignant (poin′ yənt) *adj.* drawing forth compassion; moving (p. 389)

malevolence (mə lev′ ə ləns) *n.* bad or evil feelings or intentions (p. 389)

immortalized (i môr′ tə līzd) *v.* given lasting fame (p. 390)

An Entomological Study of Apartment 4A

Patricia Volk

ouis Sorkin has a prominent forehead, gently rounded abdomen and powerful bandy legs. During the day, he can be found in the entomology department of the American Museum of Natural History. Sorkin, a senior scientific assistant, has agreed to identify the insects that have been calling my home home since we asked Fred, the building pest control operator, to stop spraying.

"God bless you," Fred used to say at the door, as if we might be seeing each other for the last time.

"What's in this stuff, anyway?" I said to him one day. Malathion, a controversial pesticide, was on the list.

Normally I admire bugs, which happens to be the scientific name for insects that have a modified beaklike mouth. As a child, I collected them in glass cigar tubes my father brought home from his restaurant. Bugs are <u>microcosms</u> and microcosms are <u>metaphors</u>. But something was eating grooves in my favorite brown hat. A black crawly thing with more legs than the Rockettes had staked out the north bedroom wall. There was a fauna in the freezer and a bug as shiny as patent leather had moved into the water gauge of our electric coffee maker. Darkest of

microcosms (mī´ krō kāz´əms) *n.* little worlds

metaphors (met´ə fôrz´) *n.* ways of speaking of things as though they were something else

all, there were definite signs of wildlife in the back-room closet a former tenant had jury-rigged into a shower. Whatever it was, it was big.

What I'm hoping Louis N. Sorkin will tell me is what eats what and whether biological warfare is an apartment possibility. California used Australian ladybugs to get rid of cottony-cushion scale. The Mormons lucked out when sea gulls saved them from the locusts. Could my pests have natural enemies on the food chain, something besides the Tokay gecko that barks at night and looks like a Tokay gecko?

Sorkin greets me in a hall stacked six feet high with drawers of Pyraustinae, a moth. We scuttle into a room crammed with journals, papers and boxes of stoppered vials. On the wall, a sign reads, "Feeling Lousy?" Sorkin's desk is littered with dental tools, mail, baby food jars and mugs with spoons—roach heaven.

I hand him my hat. He tweezes something off the brim and puts it under his microscope.

"This is a shed skin of one of the dermestid beetles in the larval stage," he says. "I think this one is the Anthrenus species. They've been grazing along it here . . . here . . . they like wool. In New York City, they live under the parquet floor.[1] Hair is a very good food source for them."

"What do they eat on hair?"

"The hair itself. It's protein."

I empty two shopping bags filled with takeout containers and hand over the freezer specimen.

It turns out that it's an immature German cockroach, which means, Sorkin says, it could have been found anywhere. Of my 21 specimens, 11 are German cockroaches. This comes as a big surprise because some look like black dots, some are pear-shaped with pale dorsal banding and some look like greasy pecan shells. Sorkin explains that roaches have a three-stage metamorphosis, going from egg to wingless nymph to adult. During the nymph stage, they molt up to seven times.

"German cockroaches are called Belgian cockroaches in Germany," Sorkin says, scratching his arm. I scratch mine too. "They're also called steam-bugs, shiners and Yankee settlers."

He studies a bug I found in my colander under the grapes.

"Oh! Otiorhynchus ovatus! A strawberry root weevil. It's an outdoor weevil that sometimes comes into homes as it migrates."

"How would it get into a fourth-floor apartment?"

"They crawl."

"Would it eat my roaches?"

"It would starve."

I show him an arachnid that has spun a web in its container. Maybe it eats strawberry root weevils.

---

1. **parquet** (pär kā´) **floor** wooden floor in which the pieces of wood fit together to form a pattern.

Reading Strategy
Establishing a Purpose for Reading What purpose have you set for reading this article?

✔**Reading Check**

What does Sorkin say is a very good food source for dermestid beetles?

"This is a jumping spider. Normally it would be outside."

Sorkin peers into the container with the north-wall stalker.

"A house centipede!" His mustache twitches. "This is a neat animal! Chilopoda have their front legs modified to inject venom. They're predators. They live on roaches and spiders and probably other centipedes."

Bingo! A natural roach enemy. "So if I introduce more Chilopods, they'll get rid of the roaches?"

"Not completely. You'd have to isolate your apartment. If you could keep them from gaining access through cracks and wall voids and holes around pipes and the door to the hallway, yeah, you could have a really insect-free zone."

The phone rings. It rings all day. Louis Sorkin is the 911 of insect emergencies. If you open your safe and bugs fly in your face or you need to know whether New Mexican centipedes produce cyanide, Sorkin's your man.

He studies two flies I found on the bathroom windowsill. There's no masking his disgust.

"These are a little moldy or fungus-y. They look like houseflies, Musca domestica."

He checks a dust ball from under our bed for dust mites, which spend their days with their mouths open, waiting for scales to drop from our skin.

"Can't see much here."

"Is it true that there are things that live on our eyelids?"

"There are two species of certain follicle mites around the nose and forehead."

"What's the reason for us to have them?"

"They're just there. Demidex folliculorum. They feed on the material in the hair follicles and usually don't cause any trouble whatsoever. Hold your skin tight like this"—Sorkin pulls his forehead to the side with four fingers—"and push it with a 3-by-5 card and look at what you pushed on a slide, you might even find them."

I try it, but even with magnification of 200, nothing shows up. Maybe moisturizer kills them.

Sorkin checks sweepings from the back-room closet shower.

"This is an American cockroach. You also have the shed skin of what looks like another Anthrenus species and an Odd beetle. The reason it has that name is because the male and female don't look alike. So you've got three different things in here."

On deck is my strangest bug. It suspends itself in liquid, like a peanut in pudding.

"Oh yeah." Sorkin recognizes it instantly. "This is a tortoise beetle. When they're alive they're sometimes gold-colored."

"How did it get in the apartment?"

"Flew."

Sorkin helps me load the containers back into the

Literary Analysis
Feature Article Which humorous lines add human interest to the article?

Reading Strategy
Establishing a Purpose for Reading What reading purpose do these odd and interesting facts support?

shopping bag. I head home thinking about the high drama that goes on behind the kitchen pegboard and wondering about the strawberry root weevil. What compelled it to climb four stories to a place where it would find nothing to eat? A strawberry root weevil entering an apartment is a suicidal gesture . . . .

The next morning, while I'm getting coffee, a juvenile roach heads for the food processor. Although I can do 3.8 m.p.h. on the treadmill and the fastest roach in the world can only go 2.9, I'm no match for it. In the sink, there's a mature female that looks like she's carrying a purse. She died with her egg case stuck in her. Before Sorkin, I never would have found this <u>poignant</u>. Sipping coffee, I gaze at the ceiling. That's when it hits me: I've neglected my prime bug habitat.

poignant (poin´ yənt) *adj.* drawing forth compassion; moving

Back at the museum, Sorkin rotates a new container with hundreds of insects and insect fragments I've retrieved from our glass ceiling fixture.

"There's . . . a hover fly . . . a spotted cucumber beetle . . . staphylinid beetles . . . a carabid stink beetle . . . ichneumon wasps . . . leaf hoppers . . . a ladybird beetle . . . a fungus beetle . . . a silverfish . . . mirid plant bugs . . . a chironomid midge . . . drugstore beetles . . . and . . . more dermestids. All these insects are attracted to light and they fly in. Then they die and the dermestids eat them."

"How do the dermestids know they're in there?"

"They smell them."

I ask Sorkin about my most surprising insect encounter:

"One night, I was making guacamole and when I put in the chili powder it started to move. How could insects live on something so hot?"

"Oh, cigarette beetles are very common in dried pepper. They do quite well. Some insects feed on insecticide."

I follow Sorkin to another room. He points to a heap of black molts from his tarantula (they would make terrific earmuffs), then lifts the lid off a plastic tray. There it is, ready to pounce, a furry ball of <u>malevolence</u>. Sorkin shows me a jar of preserved insects saved at the 100th anniversary dinner of the New York Entomological Society. There's a cerambycid larva as big as a parsnip, giant meal worms and a black thing the size of a small hamburger.

malevolence (mə lev´ ə ləns) *n.* bad or evil feelings or intentions

"This is a belostomadid, or true water bug, from Thailand. The body has a Gorgonzola cheese flavor."

Sorkin's personal favorite is grubs over easy.

"Tastes like bacon," he says.

"Are bugs kosher?"[2]

"Uh, well, yes and no. There are references in the Bible that say six species of locust are kosher, but there's some discussion that people were really referring to locust *beans*."

Sorkin is encyclopedic. Sorkin can answer anything. Talking to Sorkin is like playing "Stump the Stars": No, a roach cannot live on the glue of one postage stamp for a year. Even though we find them that

---

2. **kosher** (kō´ shər) *adj.* fit to eat according to Jewish dietary laws.

✔ Reading Check

What happens to Volk's guacamole when she adds chili powder?

way, insects don't always die on their backs. (Their legs bend in or they twitch and fall over.) There is no such thing as a *hen*-roach. It would not destroy the balance of nature if all pest species were eliminated from apartments, since that's not their natural habitat anyway. Roaches probably got into Biosphere 2 on packaging, same as we import them from the supermarket. After you've finished the bananas, fruit flies go back outside. Centipedes don't have a hundred legs. They have one pair per body segment, and 20 to 30 segments is normal. New insects are being discovered all the time. Recently Sorkin was <u>immortalized</u> by a parasitic moth mite, *Charletonia sorkini*.

"Can you look at a bite and tell what did it?"

"Sometimes," Sorkin says. "Bedbugs bite in a line. Fleas," he taps his sock, "usually bite at ground level."

I show him the back of my neck.

"None of your samples did that."

I thank Sorkin for his help. While my problem hasn't been solved, at least I know more about it. And I don't have cereal mites, black carpet beetles, termites, bedbugs, furniture carpet beetles, Trogoderma beetles, fleas and Anthrenus carpet beetles. Head lice, now that the kids are out of elementary school, are a thing of the past. If many of my insects come in with fresh air, what's the alternative? When you think about it, living close to nature, even on a tiny scale, is a privilege in a city.

When greeting, insects antennate, tapping each other with their antennae to check out who they're dealing with. Sorkin and I nod goodbye and shake hands, a Homo sapiens-specific ritual.

immortalized (i môr′ tə līzd) *v.* given lasting fame

Patricia Volk

(b. 1943)

In her youth, Volk focused on the visual arts. She worked as an art director at advertising agencies and at magazines such as *Seventeen* and *Harper's Bazaar*. A passion for writing soon emerged, and in 1988 she became a full-time writer.

Her short stories, articles, and novels—even the award-winning advertisements she has written—display her quirky sense of humor. Having spent almost all her life in New York City, she has a keen sense of the everyday humor of modern urban life.

Review and Assess

Thinking About the Selection

1. **Respond:** What was the most interesting thing you learned from this article?

2. **(a) Recall:** What reason does Patricia Volk give for visiting the entomologist? **(b) Analyze:** Does her stated reason strike you as a sensible response? Why?

3. **(a) Recall:** What do most of the bugs in the first batch turn out to be? **(b) Deduce:** Why does this surprise Volk?

4. **(a) Infer:** How is the author's attitude toward bugs changed by what she learns? **(b) Analyze:** How does she demonstrate her change in attitude? **(c) Speculate:** Do you think her new attitude will be temporary or long-term?

5. **Evaluate:** The author seems to imply that problems and annoyances are easier to cope with if you maintain a light, easygoing attitude. Do you agree or disagree? Explain.

Review and Assess

Literary Analysis

Feature Article

1. How well does "An Entomological Study of Apartment 4A" fit the criteria for a **feature article**?
2. What is one entertaining aspect of the article? Explain.
3. Using a chart like the one shown here, identify at least four facts you found in the article. For each, identify how it is useful or valuable.

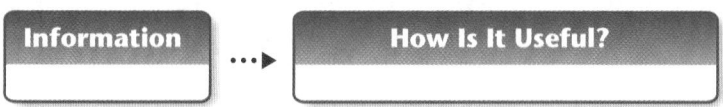

4. Do you consider Patricia Volk's article to be a genuine human-interest story? Why?

Connecting Literary Elements

5. By the end of the article, the **main idea** is revealed to the reader. (a) What is this central point? (b) Use a chart like this to explain which details from the article help to convey the main idea.

Main Idea:		
Details:	Details:	Details:

6. The author finds a dead cockroach and describes the scene as "poignant." Does a moment like this reinforce or depart from the main idea? Explain.

Reading Strategy

Establishing a Purpose for Reading

7. (a) What was your own **purpose for reading**? (b) Why did you select this particular purpose?
8. Identify at least three facts or incidents from the article that helped you achieve your purpose.

Extend Understanding

9. **Science Connection:** The use of pesticides is often a subject of debate. Do you agree with Patricia Volk's approach to pest control? Explain why or why not.

Integrate Language Skills

Vocabulary Development Lesson

Word Analysis: Greek Prefix *micro-*

The Greek prefix *micro-* means "small." Thus, the word *microcosm* means "small world." Using this information, match each of the following words with its definition.

a. microorganism **b.** microfilm **c.** microcomputer

1. an electronic device of reduced size
2. a tiny life form
3. a format for storing reduced-size images

Spelling Strategy

When you attach a prefix to a word, the spelling of the original word does not change. For example, *im-* + *mortal* = *immortal*.

Add *il-*, *mis-*, or *hemi-* to each word below to form three properly spelled words.

1. fire   2. sphere   3. legal

Fluency: Sentence Completions

On your paper, write the following sentences. Then, fill in the blanks with a form of the most appropriate word from the vocabulary list on page 389.

1. In poems and stories, a road is often a ____?____ for life.
2. The wicked villain planned to blow up the city out of sheer ____?____.
3. Philosophers have said that human beings are ____?____ of nature; by understanding people, you can understand nature.
4. The hero's adventures were ____?____ in song and story.
5. The ____?____ plot had us all sniffling by the end of the movie.

Grammar Lesson

Indirect Objects

An **indirect object** is a noun or pronoun that names the person or thing that receives the action of the verb. You can tell whether a word is the indirect object by finding the direct object and asking *to / for whom?* or *to / for what?* after the action verb. An indirect object always comes between the subject and its direct object, and it never appears in a sentence without a direct object.

	S	V	IO

Example: Patricia Volk gave <u>Louis Sorkin</u>

DO

some insects. (*gave insects to whom?*)

Practice Identify the indirect object in each sentence.

1. Fred gave Patricia Volk a promise that he would stop spraying.
2. I handed the entomologist my hat with the grooves in it.
3. Sorkin offered her some information on the bugs in her house.
4. The bugs gave them an itchy feeling.
5. Later, Sorkin showed her a jar of insects.

Writing Application Use each word below as an indirect object in a sentence.

1. cockroaches   2. apartment

WG Prentice Hall Writing and Grammar Connection: Chapter 20, Section 3

Writing Lesson

A Letter to an Expert

The entomologist Louis Sorkin played an important part in Patricia Volk's article. Write a letter asking him for information on an interesting insect you have found.

Prewriting   List insects that you frequently see around your neighborhood. Choose one that interests you. Then, jot down some questions about it.

Drafting   In the body of the letter, identify yourself, explain why you are interested in the insect, and ask your questions. Your letter should be straightforward and have the right level of formality: In this case, use the recipient's title and last name, be polite, and avoid slang.

Revising   Make sure that your letter includes a heading, an inside address, a salutation, body, closing, and signature. Then, revise to eliminate any language that may be too informal.

Model: Revising for the Right Level of Formality

several

I have noticed ~~tons of~~ gray fuzzy insects on the sidewalks

near my house. ~~Gross!~~ They appeared one day last week.

> When in doubt, use formal language. It is better to be considered too proper rather than impolite.

 Prentice Hall Writing and Grammar Connection: Chapter 15, Section 1

Extension Activities

Listening and Speaking   Patricia Volk has grown wary of pesticides. Work with a partner or a group to conduct a **print and television ad review** for pest-control products. You should

- identify the techniques used to sell these products.
- compare advertising claims for the various pesticides.

Follow up with a small-group discussion of what you have learned. **[Group Activity]**

Research and Technology   Volk's feature article is meant to entertain, yet it addresses a broad subject—the world of insects. Use the article as a springboard for your own **entomological study.** Identify the categories or criteria you will use to classify the insects you study. Then, generate a database that provides information on a variety of bugs.

 **Take It to the Net**   www.phschool.com

Go online for an additional research activity using the Internet.

READING INFORMATIONAL MATERIALS

Newspaper Articles

About Newspaper Articles

A newspaper is a form of print media. Its main purpose is to inform the public by presenting news and commentary.

- A *daily newspaper* covers international, national, state, and local news with articles on topics such as politics, economics, education, and science. Newspapers also present feature articles that showcase trends, unusual people and events, and other topics of continuing interest.

- A *weekly newspaper* usually has a smaller readership than a daily. Its articles report more personal kinds of news, such as local weddings or fires.

- A *special-interest newspaper* runs articles of interest to one particular group of people, such as teachers, parents, or immigrants.

Reading Strategy

Analyzing Text Structure

Text structure is the way a piece of writing is organized and presented. Writers use different structures for a variety of needs. In a front-page news article, for example, the first paragraph contains the basic facts of the story. In a feature article, the structure may be more relaxed.

"Cows on Parade" is a feature article written for a special-interest business newspaper, *The Business Journal* of Milwaukee. The writer adopts a casual tone and does not present any financial information until the fourth paragraph. As you read the article, use a chart like the one below to note the kinds of information—factual details, quotations, summaries—included in the text. Indicate the location of each type of information you find.

	Vivid Scene	Summary of Central Event	Details: *who, what, when, where,* or *how*	Quotation	General Background Information
Paragraph 1			*Where:* Chicago *What:* the cow		
Paragraph 2	320 painted fiberglass cows				

'Cows on parade' find sweet home in Chicago

After success in big city, cow caravan not herded for dairy state

David Schuyler

The city of Chicago has adopted one of Wisconsin's dearest symbols—the cow.

Make that 320 of them, to be exact. They're made of fiberglass, painted, prettied up by local artists and displayed about the city's streets in what may be the country's goofiest and most well-received public art project ever.

Chicago's "Cows on Parade" public art spectacle, a project of the Public Art Program of the Department of Cultural Affairs, is being credited for a boom in the tourism trade that could add an extra $100 million or more to the city's economy. Not bad for a bunch of beautified bovines that only had to hang around—literally, for some—for four months.

"We really didn't anticipate the effect they would have on people," said Dorothy Coyle, director of tourism for the city of Chicago. "The publicity was tremendous and it did result in people traveling to Chicago just to see the cows."

Given the success of the cows in the big city, what about the idea of displaying the cows in their true home state as a tourist attraction?

Members of the Milwaukee Riverwalk District

Board recently visited Chicago to view the display and consider the possibility of bringing the cows to Milwaukee, said board member Marsha Sehler.

"They were terrific, but what was more terrific was the reaction. Everybody was buying film and cameras at that Walgreens on Michigan Avenue," said Sehler.

NOT A COWTOWN

The organization, however, has since decided not to pursue the project.

Fellow Riverwalk District Board member Lisa Bailey believed that Milwaukee would not receive any benefit from hosting the cows, particularly with a number of other American cities considering a similar display.

"It didn't make sense to bring the cows here to Milwaukee," she said. "We don't want to look like a secondhand city."

If any plans to bring the cows to Wisconsin are in the works, they have yet to be made public.

The life-size cow replicas were displayed in Chicago from June 15 to Oct. 31, and received with open arms by both natives and visitors of the city with big shoulders. People crowded around cows in a variety of settings: on the sidewalks along North Michigan Avenue, outside of the Museum of Science and Industry, floating in the terminal of O'Hare International Airport, and climbing up the sides of buildings.

Cows appeared along

A quotation by someone directly involved in the event provides important information for readers.

Background information about the event helps you understand the current situation better.

continued next page

city streets adorned as ladybugs, as waiters, as Picasso paintings and, of course, as the cow that jumped over the moon. One of three representations of Mrs. O'Leary's cow, long-blamed for starting the Chicago fire of 1871, still had monkeys on its back. In one bad pun, a cow, sponsored by Harry Caray's Restaurant, had holes drilled through it to represent the late WGN sportscaster's exclamation, "Holy cow!"

This paragraph would be of particular interest to a business newspaper's readers.

Chicago adapted the idea from the Swiss. Chicago businessman Peter Hanig saw a similar display while on vacation in Zurich, Switzerland, last year and promoted the concept for the city, said Coyle.

Zurich displayed 800 cows in its "Cow Parade" project, resulting in approximately $100 million in additional tourism dollars coming into the city, Coyle said.

Chicago tourism officials won't have any figures on the project's economic impact until December, but they are confident of its success.

"We believe that we will actually surpass that amount," Coyle said.

A brief subhead signals that a new main idea will follow. You can find the main idea and its supporting details in the section that follows.

OUT-MOO-NEUVERING NYC

Chicago, however, wasn't the only city that had heard of the Zurich event. When the city discovered that New York City was also considering having a cow parade, Chicago officials moved quickly.

The city negotiated a licensing agreement with the Swiss government to exclusively feature a United States cow event for 1999.

The city received a $100,000 grant from the state of Illinois to help fund the project. An additional $100,000 was raised from Michigan Avenue businesses by the Cows on Parade Committee, co-chaired by Hanig.

The city purchased 320 fiberglass cows and charged local businesses and individuals $3,500 each to have an artist produce a cow with a design approved by the city. Businesses could also choose to have an artist draw up their own design, which still had to be approved by city officials, Coyle said.

Some more renowned artists demanded more, a cost which was picked up by the company buying the cow. One cow was reportedly sold for $11,000.

ALLEN-EDMONDS HAS A COW

Footwear businessman Hanig contacted Port Washington-based Allen-Edmonds Shoe Corp. about purchasing one of the cows, said Louis Ripple, director of sales and marketing.

The company became interested in its industry colleague's pitch and decided to buy a cow and have it displayed in front of its Michigan Avenue store.

"The customers really enjoyed it," he said. "We certainly had a lot of comments."

Ripple credits the cow—Shoe Horn—for bringing people into the store and even purchasing shoes. With the Chicago project now completed, the company plans to bring the cow to Wisconsin and have it displayed in its Port Washington headquarters, Ripple said.

The cows' combination of public art with something recognizably down-home may account for their popularity, said Curtis Carter, director of the Haggerty Museum of Art in Milwaukee.

"They are easily accessible to a wide range of the population," he said. "You don't need a degree in art history to appreciate these."

Juxtaposing a rural symbol with an urban setting also fits well with the socially provocative nature of public art and adds to the irony and wit of the sculptures, Carter said.

While Milwaukee takes a pass, at least 28 other cities are exploring their own cow parades, Coyle said. Variations on the theme are also being considered, such as pigs, lizards, lions, coffee cups and basketballs, she said.

As for Chicago, "we will come up with something completely different," said Coyle.

Check Your Comprehension

1. What effect did the cows have on tourism in Chicago?
2. Why did Milwaukee officials vote against the cows?
3. Where did the idea of the cows originate?

Applying the Reading Strategy

Analyzing Text Structure

4. How does "Cows on Parade" differ in format from an article you might see on the front page of a daily newspaper?
5. How does the paragraph about cows appearing as ladybugs, waiters, and Picasso paintings help reinforce the writer's purpose?

Activity

Developing a K-W-L Chart

Having read a newspaper article about painted fiberglass cows, you now possess a certain amount of knowledge on the subject. However, you may wish to learn even more about the topic.

Create a K-W-L chart like the one shown here. In the first column, write down important details that you already **know** about the cows. In the second column, list questions indicating what you still **want** to learn about them. Consult newspapers and magazines in a library and go to Internet Web sites to find information that can answer your questions. In the third column of the chart, record what you **learned** and how you obtained the information.

What I *Know*	What I *Want* to Know	What I *Learned* and Where
Cows were a success in Chicago.	What reaction did they generate in New York City?	
One cow was sold for $11,000.	What is the most anyone paid for a cow?	

Contrasting Informational Materials

Feature Articles, Art Reviews, and Advertisements

1. "Cows on Parade" is a feature article: The author draws in readers with humor and does not present hard facts for several paragraphs. Imagine that the cow display had been the subject of an art critic's review instead of a reporter's feature story. Explain how the information and details would have been structured differently.
2. Imagine that the cow exhibit were the subject of an advertisement or brochure meant to draw tourists to Chicago. How would the writing differ in structure from the feature article?

Prepare to Read

Jabberwocky ◆ Macavity: The Mystery Cat ◆ Problems With Hurricanes

Preview

Connecting to the Literature

You can probably remember enjoying silly nursery rhymes and songs when you were young. Not all funny poems are written for children, though. As you will see, poems like the ones you are about to read can make you laugh out loud.

Background

The farmer, or "campesino," in "Problems With Hurricanes" says, "Don't worry about the water / Don't worry about the wind—," but that is exactly what you should worry about in such a storm. As a hurricane approaches land, strong rains form huge ocean waves, called storm surges, that can cause severe flooding. Puerto Rico, the poet's homeland, is in a hurricane region where the storm season extends from August to October.

Literary Analysis

Humorous Diction

A writer's **diction**, or word choice, can help create a humorous effect. For example, writers may intentionally use the wrong word, use formal or informal English, or even invent unusual words. In the following line from "Macavity: The Mystery Cat," notice how the sophisticated words used to describe a cat contribute to the humor:

> For he's a fiend in feline shape, a monster of depravity.

As you read these three poems, think about how each writer's word choice makes you smile.

Comparing Literary Works

In each of the poems you are about to read, repetition is used to create a unique effect. **Repetition** is the use of any element of language—a sound, word, phrase, clause, or sentence—more than once. Poets use many kinds of repetition to add emphasis, drama, or musical rhythm to a poem. Compare the way lines, words, or stanzas are repeated in these poems, and consider the effect of the repetition.

CALIFORNIA STANDARDS

Instruction with these selections addresses these standards:

R 1.1*, 3.8*
W 1.2*
WOLC 1.3*
LS 2.1

* Standards tested on HS Exit Exam. For complete standards, see p. CA 4.

Reading Strategy

Contrasting the Serious and the Ridiculous

One way in which these poems achieve humor is by combining the **serious** with the **ridiculous**. Consider, for example, these lines from "Problems With Hurricanes":

> How would your family / feel if they had to tell
> The generations that you / got killed by a flying / Banana.

Death is serious indeed, but a flying banana is just plain silly, and the combination of the two details makes most readers chuckle. To help you contrast the serious and ridiculous details, use a chart like this one.

Serious Details

Ridiculous Details

Vocabulary Development

chortled (chôrt´ 'ld) *v.* made a jolly, chuckling sound (p. 401)

bafflement (baf´ əl mənt) *n.* puzzlement; bewilderment (p. 403)

levitation (lev i tā´ shən) *n.* the illusion of keeping a heavy body in the air without visible support (p. 403)

feline (fē´ līn) *adj.* catlike (p. 403)

depravity (dē prav´ ə tē) *n.* crookedness; corruption (p. 403)

larder (lärd´ ər) *n.* place where food is kept; pantry (p. 403)

suavity (swä´ və tē) *n.* quality of being socially smooth (p. 404)

projectiles (prō jek´ təlz) *n.* objects that are hurled through the air (p. 405)

Jabberwocky
Lewis Carroll

'Twas brillig, and the slithy toves
    Did gyre and gimble in the wabe;
All mimsy were the borogoves,
    And the mome raths outgrabe.

5 "Beware the Jabberwock, my son!
    The jaws that bite, the claws that catch!
Beware the Jubjub bird, and shun
    The frumious Bandersnatch!"

He took his vorpal sword in hand:
10   Long time the manxome foe he sought—
So rested he by the Tumtum tree,
    And stood awhile in thought.

The Jabberwock, 1872, John Tenniel

*L*iterature
in context   Language Connection

Alice encounters a creature called a Jabberwock in the first chapter of *Through the Looking-Glass*. She cannot understand it, so the character Humpty Dumpty explains some of its words, including these:

brillig: four o'clock in the afternoon, the time when you begin broiling things for dinner

toves: creatures that are something like badgers, something like lizards, and something like corkscrews

gyre: go round and round like a gyroscope

gimble: make holes like a gimlet (a hand tool that bores holes)

wabe: grass plot around a sundial

mome: having lost the way home

raths: something like green pigs

And as in uffish thought he stood,
    The Jabberwock, with eyes of flame,
15 Came whiffling through the tulgey wood,
    And burbled as it came!

One, two! One, two! And through and through
    The vorpal blade went snicker-snack!
He left it dead, and with its head
20   He went galumphing back.

"And hast thou slain the Jabberwock?
    Come to my arms, my beamish boy!
O frabjous day! Callooh! Callay!"
    He <u>chortled</u> in his joy.

25 'Twas brillig, and the slithy toves
    Did gyre and gimble in the wabe;
All mimsy were the borogoves,
    And the mome raths outgrabe.

chortled (chôrt′ ′ld) v. made a jolly, chuckling sound

Review and Assess

Thinking About the Selection

1. **Respond:** What images did this poem bring to mind?

2. **(a) Recall:** State in your own words the warning given in the second stanza of the poem. **(b) Analyze:** How would you describe the overall mood of "Jabberwocky"?

3. **(a) Recall:** What does the hero do after being warned about the Jabberwock? **(b) Evaluate:** One critic said that "Jabberwocky," despite its odd language, tells a story like many legends of knights and dragons. Do you agree? Why or why not? **(c) Assess:** Do you think the poem pokes fun at knighthood? Explain.

4. **(a) Interpret:** You can often tell the part of speech of a word even if you do not understand it. Identify the part of speech of three of the made-up words in this poem. Explain how you arrived at each answer. **(b) Apply:** How can a poem like "Jabberwocky" give readers a better understanding of language?

5. **Speculate:** Do you think it is easier or more challenging to write a poem with invented language? Explain.

Lewis Carroll

(1832–1898)

Charles Lutwidge Dodgson was a professor of mathematics, an ordained deacon in the Church of England, and a talented early photographer. Yet today, he is best remembered for two children's books he wrote under the pen name Lewis Carroll: *Alice's Adventures in Wonderland* (1865) and its sequel, *Through the Looking-Glass* (1871). Both feature a young girl named Alice whose curiosity leads her into amazing fantasy worlds. Huge bestsellers almost from the moment they appeared, the *Alice* books have been the basis of numerous stage plays, television adaptations, and live and animated movies.

Macavity:

T. S. Eliot

Illustration from *Old Possum's Book of Practical Cats*, Edward Gorey

◀ **Critical Viewing**
Judging from this illustration, what do you think is the spirit of the poem? **[Infer]**

The Mystery Cat

Macavity's a Mystery Cat: he's called the Hidden Paw—
For he's the master criminal who can defy the Law.
He's the <u>bafflement</u> of Scotland Yard,[1] the Flying Squad's[2]
    despair:
5 For when they reach the scene of crime—*Macavity's not*
    there!

Macavity, Macavity, there's no one like Macavity,
He's broken every human law, he breaks the law of gravity.
His powers of <u>levitation</u> would make a fakir[3] stare,
10 And when you reach the scene of crime—*Macavity's not there!*
You may seek him in the basement, you may look up in the
    air—
But I tell you once and once again, *Macavity's not there!*

Macavity's a ginger cat, he's very tall and thin;
15 You would know him if you saw him, for his eyes are sunken in.
His brow is deeply lined with thought, his head is highly
    domed;
His coat is dusty from neglect, his whiskers are uncombed.
He sways his head from side to side, with movements like a
20   snake;
And when you think he's half asleep, he's always wide awake.

Macavity, Macavity, there's no one like Macavity,
For he's a fiend in <u>feline</u> shape, a monster of <u>depravity</u>.
You may meet him in a by-street, you may see him in the
25   square—
But when a crime's discovered, then *Macavity's not there!*

He's outwardly respectable. (They say he cheats at cards.)
And his footprints are not found in any file of Scotland Yard's.
And when the <u>larder</u>'s looted, or the jewel-case is rifled,
30 Or when the milk is missing, or another Peke's[4] been stifled,
Or the greenhouse glass is broken, and the trellis past repair—
Ay, there's the wonder of the thing! *Macavity's not there!*

---

1. **Scotland Yard** London police.
2. **Flying Squad** criminal-investigation department.
3. **fakir** (fə kir′) *n.* Muslim or Hindu beggar who claims to perform miracles.
4. **Peke** short for Pekingese, a small dog with long, silky hair and a pug nose.

bafflement (baf′ əl mənt) *n.* puzzlement; bewilderment

levitation (lev i tā′ shən) *n.* the illusion of keeping a heavy body in the air without visible support

feline (fē′ līn) *adj.* catlike

depravity (dē prav′ ə tē) *n.* crookedness; corruption

larder (lärd′ ər) *n.* place where food is kept; pantry

☑Reading Check

Which unusual detail links or separates Macavity from crime scenes?

And when the Foreign Office[5] find a Treaty's gone astray,
Or the Admiralty[6] lose some plans and drawings by the way,
35 There may be a scrap of paper in the hall or on the stair—
But it's useless to investigate—*Macavity's not there!*
And when the loss has been disclosed, the Secret Service say:
'It *must* have been Macavity!'—but he's a mile away.
You'll be sure to find him resting, or a-licking of his thumbs,
40 Or engaged in doing complicated long division sums.

Macavity, Macavity, there's no one like Macavity,
There never was a Cat of such deceitfulness and <u>suavity</u>.
He always has an alibi, and one or two to spare:
At whatever time the deed took place—MACAVITY WASN'T
45   THERE!
And they say that all the Cats whose wicked deeds are widely
          known
(I might mention Mungojerrie, I might mention Griddlebone)
Are nothing more than agents for the Cat who all the time
50 Just controls their operations: the Napoleon of Crime![7]

---

5. **Foreign Office** British equivalent of the U.S. Department of State.
6. **Admiralty** British government department in charge of naval affairs.
7. **the Napoleon of Crime** a criminal mastermind; an emperor of crime—just as Napoleon Bonaparte (1769–1821) was a masterful military strategist who had himself crowned emperor.

Reading Strategy
Contrasting the Serious and the Ridiculous What is funny about lines 33–34?

suavity (swä´ və tē) *n.* quality of being socially smooth

Review and Assess

Thinking About the Selection

1. **Respond:** Did you find this poem amusing? Why or why not?
2. **(a) Recall:** Briefly describe Macavity's appearance.
   (b) Support: How does the description of his appearance contribute to the humor found in the poem?
3. **(a) Recall:** What words and phrases are repeated throughout the poem? **(b) Analyze:** Why do you think Eliot keeps repeating these words?
4. **(a) Recall:** Why are the police unable to charge Macavity?
   (b) Make a Judgment: Do you think Macavity is guilty? Explain.
5. **Speculate:** Which qualities of cats that you have known might have prompted Eliot to associate them with criminal activities?
6. **Extend:** In the collection of poems that includes "Macavity," Eliot associates a variety of human characteristics with cats. Do you think that animals possess any "human" characteristics, either good or bad? Explain.

T. S. Eliot

(1888–1965)

T. S. Eliot's collection of humorous poems, *Old Possum's Book of Practical Cats* (1939), was the inspiration for *Cats!*—one of the most popular musicals of all time. The work was something of a departure for Eliot, who was better known as a serious poet.

Although born in the United States, Eliot settled in England while still a young man, working as a teacher and bank clerk. He first won literary attention with his poetry collection *Prufrock, and Other Observations*, published in 1917. Eliot went on to become one of the world's leading poets, winning the Nobel Prize for Literature in 1948.

Problems With Hurricanes

Victor Hernández Cruz

A campesino[1] looked at the air
And told me:
With hurricanes it's not the wind
or the noise or the water.
5 I'll tell you he said:
it's the mangoes, avocados
Green plantains[2] and bananas
flying into town like <u>projectiles</u>.

How would your family
10 feel if they had to tell
The generations that you
got killed by a flying
Banana.

---

1. **campesino** (käm´ pe sē´ nō) *n.* Spanish term for a simple farmer or another person who lives in a rural area.
2. **plantains** (plan´ tins) *n.* starchy tropical fruits that resemble bananas.

projectiles (pro jek´ təlz) *n.* objects that are hurled through the air

✔ **Reading Check**

What does the campesino say is the problem with hurricanes?

Death by drowning has honor
15 If the wind picked you up
and slammed you
Against a mountain boulder
This would not carry shame
But
20 to suffer a mango smashing
Your skull
or a plantain hitting your
Temple at 70 miles per hour
is the ultimate disgrace.

25 The campesino takes off his hat—
As a sign of respect
toward the fury of the wind
And says:
Don't worry about the noise
30 Don't worry about the water
Don't worry about the wind—
If you are going out
beware of mangoes
And all such beautiful
35 sweet things.

Review and Assess

Thinking About the Selection

1. **Respond:** What amusing images does this poem create?
2. **(a) Recall:** According to the campesino, which causes of death would be worse than drowning or being slammed into a mountain by the wind? **(b) Distinguish:** What seems to be the difference for him between a noble and a shameful hurricane death?
3. **(a) Recall:** Which question does the campesino ask in the second stanza? **(b) Infer:** What is he suggesting about how one family member's death affects future generations? **(c) Assess:** Do you think the campesino is a reliable judge of human behavior?
4. **Modify:** How would the poem be affected if the last four lines were not included?
5. **(a) Analyze:** How would you describe the tone or mood of this poem? **(b) Support:** Which words or images create this tone?

Victor Hernández Cruz

(b. 1949)

A native of Puerto Rico, Victor Hernández Cruz moved to New York City with his family while still a boy. As a poet, Cruz pioneered a style called Nuyorican, a combination of English and Spanish dotted with slang that became popular among New York poets of Puerto Rican descent. He is also known for powerful oral readings that twice saw him crowned World Heavyweight Poetry Champion in Taos, New Mexico.

Review and Assess

Literary Analysis

Humorous Diction

1. Find at least three words or phrases in "Macavity" that seem typical of mystery or crime fiction. How do these words contribute to the poem's **humorous diction**?

2. (a) Rewrite three sentences from "Jabberwocky" using familiar words. (b) Is it still funny? Explain.

Comparing Literary Works

3. (a) Using a chart like the one below, compare the humorous diction found in each poem. (b) Does diction play an equally strong role in creating humor in each poem? Explain.

Poem	Serious Subject	Humorous Diction

4. (a) Compare the technique of **repetition** used in each of the poems. (b) In your opinion, which poem makes the best use of repetition?

Reading Strategy

Contrasting the Serious and the Ridiculous

5. Sum up what is most serious and most ridiculous in each of the three poems.

6. What point do you think each poet is making through this contrast?

7. Of the three, which poem do you think is the most serious? Explain your choice.

Extend Understanding

8. **Cultural Connection:** "Macavity: The Mystery Cat" refers to several qualities of cats. Cats have played an important role in human society for thousands of years. "Curiosity killed the cat" is a common saying in our society. Explain the meaning of this saying. Come up with two more sayings or legends about cats and explain their meanings.

Quick Review

Humorous diction is word choice used to create a humorous effect.

Repetition is the use of any language element—a sound, word, phrase, clause, or sentence—more than once to create an effect.

To **contrast the serious and the ridiculous,** separate details in a selection into two categories: absurd, unusual details and serious ones.

 **Take It to the Net**

www.phschool.com

Take the interactive self-test online to check your understanding of these selections.

Integrate Language Skills

Vocabulary Development Lesson

Word Origins: Portmanteau Words

"Jabberwocky" contains many invented words, including some formed by blending two words into one—like *chortled*, combining *chuckle* and *snort*, or *mimsy*, combining *miserable* and *flimsy*. Such words are now known as **portmanteau words**.

Use a dictionary, if necessary, to explain the origins of these portmanteau words:

    1. smog   **2.** brunch   **3.** motel

Spelling Strategy

The *shun/zhun* sound in a suffix is spelled *ssion* or *tion/sion*. The *shun* sound can be heard in *fission* and *levitation*; the *zhun* sound, in *invasion*.

Complete each word below with the correct form of the *shun/zhun* sound.

    1. deci___   **2.** transmi___   **3.** transla___

Fluency: Sentence Completion

Complete each sentence with a vocabulary word from the list on page 399.

1. The magician seemed to perform ___?___, for it looked as if a person floated in air.
2. Bullets and darts are types of ___?___.
3. Lions are part of the ___?___ family.
4. The poem was written in invented language, to the ___?___ of many readers.
5. Store the food in the ___?___.
6. The sinner had engaged in many forms of ___?___.
7. Jack ___?___ as he observed the outcome of his practical joke.
8. Cary Grant was an actor of great sophistication and ___?___.

Grammar Lesson

Predicate Adjectives

In sentences formed with linking verbs, the verb can be completed with a predicate adjective. A **predicate adjective** is an adjective that appears with a linking verb and describes the subject of the sentence. Linking verbs, including forms of the verb *be*, express a state of being.

                S   V PA
Example: The cat was *tall*.

A **compound predicate adjective** is two or more adjectives that appear with the linking verb and describe the subject.

                S   V   PA   PA
Example: The cat was *sneaky* and *mischievous*.

Practice Copy the following sentences. Circle the linking verb. Then, underline each predicate adjective and draw an arrow to the word it modifies.

1. His brow is deep.
2. Macavity was good at escaping.
3. He appears respectable and smart.
4. The whiskers are uncombed.
5. They have looked for him everywhere because they are thorough.

Writing Application Write two sentences using the following items as predicate adjectives.

1. deceitful
2. shocked and dismayed

W͞G Prentice Hall Writing and Grammar Connection: Chapter 20, Section 3

Writing Lesson

Fantastic Poem

The poems in this section are unusual, to say the least. Write your own unusual poem about one of the fantastic creatures or events you have just read about.

Prewriting   List precise details that you might use to describe this unusual creature or event. Choose details that you think will help you achieve an overall mood—humorous, eerie, or something else.

Drafting   Write either a free-verse poem—one without a regular rhythm or rhyme scheme—or one with a regular rhythm and rhyme scheme. Use descriptive details that contribute to your overall mood.

Revising   Read your poem aloud. Highlight weak or vague words, and replace them with more precise language.

Model: Revising to Add Precise Details

> *leaped*   *gripping*
>
> Macavity ~~came~~ out, ~~holding~~ a key in one paw,
>
> *gazed*   *admired*
>
> Curious, he ~~looked~~ around and ~~liked~~ what he saw.

Words like *leaped* and *gazed* add precise details to the poem.

WG *Prentice Hall Writing and Grammar Connection: Chapter 6, Connected Assignment*

Extension Activities

Research and Technology   The poet of "Problems With Hurricanes" is a native of Puerto Rico, a hurricane region. In a group, research and present a **television news report** on weather conditions and foods grown in Puerto Rico.

- Find maps, photographs, and other visuals.
- Look for generalizations you can draw about the climate of the region.

Rehearse and then present your broadcast to the class. **[Group Activity]**

Listening and Speaking   Write a **news article** reporting the events found in "Macavity: The Mystery Cat." Give a description of Macavity's appearance. Then, explain why he is considered a master criminal. Try to stay objective, reporting only the facts without including personal opinions. Present the news article to your class.

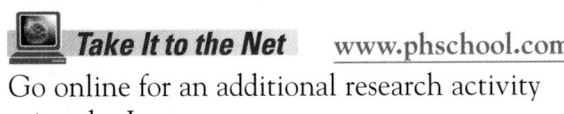 **Take It to the Net**   www.phschool.com

Go online for an additional research activity using the Internet.

Prepare to Read

Talk

 Take It to the Net

Visit www.phschool.com for interactive activities and instruction related to "Talk," including

- background
- graphic organizers
- literary elements
- reading strategies

Preview

Connecting to the Literature

Your breakfast muffin somersaults out of your hands and lands jam side down on the floor. Although the muffin may be called an "inanimate object," it seems to have a mischievous mind of its own. "Talk" is an African folk tale that whimsically nudges this idea a step further.

Background

"Talk" is set on the west coast of Africa, in the country now known as the Republic of Ghana. Many of the story's details reflect the everyday reality of life there. For example, yams, mentioned often in the story, are one of the staples of the diet of rural Ghanaians. In addition, the characters include a fisherman and a weaver, common occupations in Ghana, a country known for its beautiful hand-woven fabrics.

Literary Analysis
Humorous Folk Tale

A **folk tale** is an anonymous story passed down by word of mouth from one generation to the next. With everyday language, folk tales express the beliefs and values of the cultures that create them, and they typically present simple characters and far-fetched situations. A **humorous folk tale**, meant to entertain and to instruct, uses humor or exaggeration to appeal to its audiences. Look at the following example from "Talk":

> . . . a country man went out to his garden to dig up some yams to take to market. While he was digging, one of the yams said to him, "Well at last you're here . . ."

You will see that this fantastic idea of objects that suddenly speak is repeated throughout the story for humorous effect.

Connecting Literary Elements

Personification, often used in folk tales, occurs when a nonhuman subject is given human characteristics. In "Talk," personification contributes to the humor in the folk tale by giving objects the ability to speak. As you read, notice the nonhuman things that seem to come to life.

Reading Strategy
Recognizing Illogical Situations

When reading a folk tale, you might come across situations that could not possibly happen in real life. Illogical situations can make a work of fantasy more fantastic and entertaining. However, these situations can distract you, so it is important to **recognize illogical situations** when you read. To prevent illogical situations from distracting you, follow these strategies:

- Jot down confusing or unusual situations.
- Decide why a situation is illogical.
- Consider what the situation adds to the story.

Use a chart like the one shown here to keep track of the illogical situations you come across in "Talk."

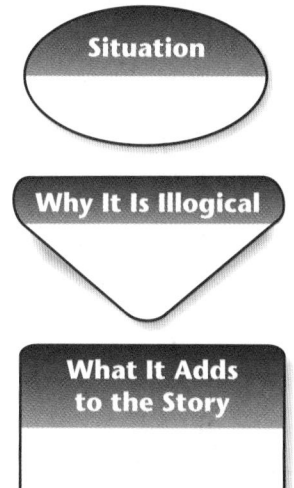

Vocabulary Development

ford (fôrd) *n.* shallow place in a river that can be crossed (p. 413)

refrain (ri frān´) *v.* hold back (p. 414)

scowling (skou´ iŋ) *v.* contracting the eyebrows and frowning to show displeasure (p. 414)

CALIFORNIA STANDARDS

Instruction with this selection addresses these standards:
R 1.1*, 3.7*, 3.8*
W 1.5*, 2.1*
WOLC 1.3*
LS 1.8, 2.3
* Standards tested on HS Exit Exam. For complete standards, see p. CA 4.

TALK

African (Ashanti) Folk Tale

Retold by Harold Courlander and George Herzog

Once, not far from the city of Accra on the Gulf of Guinea, a country man went out to his garden to dig up some yams to take to market. While he was digging, one of the yams said to him, "Well, at last you're here. You never weeded me, but now you come around with your digging stick. Go away and leave me alone!"

The farmer turned around and looked at his cow in amazement. The cow was chewing her cud and looking at him.

"Did you say something?" he asked.

The cow kept on chewing and said nothing, but the man's dog spoke up. "It wasn't the cow who spoke to you," the dog said. "It was the yam. The yam says leave him alone."

The man became angry, because his dog had never talked before, and he didn't like his tone besides. So he took his knife and cut a branch from a palm tree to whip his dog. Just then the palm tree said, "Put that branch down!"

The man was getting very upset about the way things were going, and he started to throw the palm branch away, but the palm branch said, "Man, put me down softly!"

He put the branch down gently on a stone, and the stone said, "Hey, take that thing off me!"

This was enough, and the frightened farmer started to run for his village. On the way he met a fisherman going the other way with a fish trap on his head.

"What's the hurry?" the fisherman asked.

"My yam said, 'Leave me alone!' Then the dog said, 'Listen to what the yam says!' When I went to whip the dog with a palm branch the tree said, 'Put that branch down!' Then the palm branch said, 'Do it softly!' Then the stone said, 'Take that thing off me!'"

"Is that all?" the man with the fish trap asked. "Is that so frightening?"

"Well," the man's fish trap said, "did he take it off the stone?"

"Wah!" the fisherman shouted. He threw the fish trap on the ground and began to run with the farmer, and on the trail they met a weaver with a bundle of cloth on his head.

"Where are you going in such a rush?" he asked them.

"My yam said, 'Leave me alone!'" the farmer said. "The dog said, 'Listen to what the yam says!' The tree said, 'Put that branch down!' The branch said, 'Do it softly!' And the stone said, 'Take that thing off me!'"

"And then," the fisherman continued, "the fish trap said, 'Did he take it off?'"

"That's nothing to get excited about," the weaver said. "No reason at all."

"Oh, yes it is," his bundle of cloth said. "If it happened to you you'd run too!"

"Wah!" the weaver shouted. He threw his bundle on the trail and started running with the other men.

They came panting to the <u>ford</u> in the river and found a man bathing. "Are you chasing a gazelle?" he asked them.

The first man said breathlessly, "My yam talked at me, and it said, 'Leave me alone!' And my dog said, 'Listen to your yam!' And when I cut myself a branch the tree said, 'Put that branch down!' And the branch said, 'Do it softly!' And the stone said, 'Take that thing off me!'"

The fisherman panted. "And my trap said, 'Did he?'"

The weaver wheezed. "And my bundle of cloth said, 'You'd run too!'"

"Is that why you're running?" the man in the river asked.

"Well, wouldn't you run if you were in their position?" the river said.

The man jumped out of the water and began to run with the others. They ran down the main street of the village to the house of the chief. The chief's servant brought his stool out, and he came and sat on it to listen to their complaints. The men began to recite their troubles.

Literature
in context Cultural Connection

West African Folk Tales

Every culture has its own folk tales. In West Africa, folk tales that entertain and teach lessons are an essential part of a rich oral tradition.

A common folk-tale theme, in a part of the world teeming with plant and animal life, is the relationship between nature and people. Many cultures of this region believe that all living things possess a spirit, so it is not unusual in folk tales for plants and animals to take on human qualities. For example, Anansi, the spider, is a major figure in African folklore. This spider takes on human qualities ranging from wisdom to foolishness. Even with flawed qualities, Anansi always conveys a lesson. Therefore, it is not surprising that a yam and a dog take on human characteristics in "Talk."

ford (fôrd) *n.* shallow place in a river that can be crossed

Reading Check

What happens when the country man starts digging yams?

"I went out to my garden to dig yams," the farmer said, waving his arms. "Then everything began to talk! My yam said, 'Leave me alone!' My dog said, 'Pay attention to your yam!' The tree said, 'Put that branch down!' The branch said, 'Do it softly!' And the stone said, 'Take it off me!'"

"And my fish trap said, 'Well, did he take it off?'" the fisherman said.

"And my cloth said, 'You'd run too!'" the weaver said.

"And the river said the same," the bather said hoarsely, his eyes bulging.

The chief listened to them patiently, but he couldn't <u>refrain</u> from <u>scowling</u>. "Now this is really a wild story," he said at last. "You'd better all go back to your work before I punish you for disturbing the peace."

So the men went away, and the chief shook his head and mumbled to himself, "Nonsense like that upsets the community."

"Fantastic, isn't it?" his stool said. "Imagine, a talking yam!"

refrain (ri frān´) *v.* hold back

scowling (skoul´ iŋ) *v.* contracting the eyebrows and frowning to show displeasure

Review and Assess

Thinking About the Selection

1. **Respond:** Which situation in "Talk" struck you as the funniest? Why?

2. **(a) Recall:** How does the fisherman react when the country man tells his crazy story? **(b) Analyze:** Why does he get so upset when his fish trap speaks to him?

3. **(a) Recall:** What upsets each man who joins the country man? **(b) Deduce:** What reason might the objects and animals have for speaking all of a sudden?

4. **(a) Recall:** What does the chief say to the men when they come rushing in to tell their stories? **(b) Modify:** What do you think the chief should have said to the men?

5. **(a) Hypothesize:** What might the chief say when his stool talks back to him? **(b) Evaluate:** Would the story have been funnier if it had included what the chief said or did after the stool spoke? Explain.

6. **(a) Compare and Contrast:** What aspects of the story are unique to its West African setting? What elements of the story are universal? **(b) Make a Judgment:** Would most Americans find "Talk" funny? Explain.

7. **(a) Recall:** What happens to every human character after he insults each man who is afraid? **(b) Draw Conclusions:** Which aspects of human nature does the story hold up to ridicule?

Harold Courlander

(b. 1908)

Harold Courlander has had a long, distinguished career as a builder of bridges between different cultures. The settings for his novels range from eighteenth-century Africa to rural Mississippi to the Hopi Nation before the arrival of the Europeans.

George Herzog

(1901–1983)

Born in Budapest, Hungary, George Herzog was a pioneer in the field of ethnomusicology, the study of music for its cultural values and social significance. He also taught courses in linguistics and cultural anthropology and published numerous books on folk music.

Review and Assess

Literary Analysis

Humorous Folk Tale

1. Use a chart like the one below to show how "Talk" fits the criteria of a **humorous folk tale.**

Characters	Simple Language	Far-fetched Situations	Point About Human Nature

2. What image of its culture does "Talk" seem to project? Why?

Connecting Literary Elements

3. Use a chart like the one below to show how the nonhuman characters are **personified** in the folk tale. Write the words that are spoken and the feelings that are conveyed by each character.

4. How does personification create a humorous effect in the story?

Reading Strategy

Recognizing Illogical Situations

5. What is illogical about what happens to each man in "Talk"?
6. Does the use of **illogical situations** grow funnier or less funny as the story goes on? Explain.
7. (a) Is the chief's reaction to the men logical or illogical? Explain. (b) How does his response add to the humor?

Extend Understanding

8. **Cultural Connection:** (a) If objects or animals in the United States could speak for a day, which ones might have the most to say? (b) What might they say? Explain.

Integrate Language Skills

Vocabulary Development Lesson

Word Analysis: Latin Prefix *re-*

The word *refrain* uses the Latin prefix *re-*, which means "back" or "again." Thus, the word *refrain* means "to hold oneself back." Other words that use the Latin prefix *re-* include *rewrite* (to write something *again*) and *reflect* (to think *back*).

Using the meaning of *re-*, write the word from the following list that is the best match for each definition below.

a. rethink   c. regenerate
b. refresh   d. redo

1. Produce or grow again
2. Make cooler than before
3. Start over; try again
4. Give something another thought

Concept Development: Antonyms

Write the letter of the word whose meaning is most nearly opposite to that of the first word.

1. scowling: (a) frowning, (b) smiling, (c) resting
2. ford: (a) icy canal, (b) shallow underwater spot, (c) deep underwater spot
3. refrain: (a) continue, (b) stop, (c) begin

Spelling Strategy

In words ending in two vowels plus a consonant, do not double the final consonant before adding an ending that starts with a vowel. For example, *refrain* + *-ed* = *refrained*. In your notebook, write the correct spelling of each word. Then, use each word in a sentence.

1. shout + *-ed*   2. look + *-ing*   3. weed + *-ed*

Grammar Lesson

Predicate Nominatives

A **predicate nominative** is a noun or pronoun that appears with a linking verb (commonly a form of *be*). A predicate nominative renames, identifies, or explains the subject of the sentence. The linking verb acts as an equal sign between the subject and the predicate nominative; both the subject and the predicate nominative name the same person or thing.

In the examples below, the subject is in bold-face, the linking verb is in italics, and the predicate nominative is underlined.

	S	LV	PN
Examples:	The **yam** *was* the <u>first</u> to talk.		

	S	LV		PN
Now **this** *is* really a wild <u>story</u>.				

Practice Copy the following sentences. Label the subject and verb. Then, underline the predicate nominative in each.

1. The story is a folk tale.
2. The chief was a skeptic.
3. The men were sprinters.
4. The branch and stone were talkers.
5. One object in the story was the yam.

Writing Application Use each of the following in a sentence, and then underline the predicate nominative.

1. are talking objects
2. The chief will become

WG *Prentice Hall Writing and Grammar Connection: Chapter 20, Section 3*

Writing Lesson

Humorous Folk Tale

Think of your school as a community, with its own culture, customs, and values. Write your own humorous folk tale set in your school. Use simple characters, simple language, and a far-fetched situation. To add humor, personify some of the objects in your school, just as nonhuman things were personified in "Talk."

Prewriting   Choose an event that has happened in your school. Add unusual details to the real-life event to create a far-fetched situation. Gather details about your characters, using a chart like the one shown.

Character	Actions	Description
desk	It can walk and talk.	When it "wakes up," it has a friendly and boisterous personality.

Drafting   As you draft, show, rather than tell, what is happening in the story. Use characters' actions, details of setting, and dialogue to show readers what you want them to see.

Revising   Ask a partner to read your folk tale aloud. Listen closely to the language you have included in your story. Rewrite any dialogue that sounds unnatural to make your characters sound more realistic.

W/G *Prentice Hall Writing and Grammar Connection: Chapter 5, Section 2*

Extension Activities

Listening and Speaking Imagine that a famous television interviewer or talk-show host conducts an **interview** with one of the nonhuman characters in "Talk." With another student, role-play this situation.

- Ask questions that will inform and entertain your audience.
- Use appropriate mannerisms and gestures as you talk.

Present your interview to your class. **[Group Activity]**

Research and Technology "Talk" is set in West Africa, near the Gulf of Guinea. Prepare a **cultural report** about this region. Include as many multimedia elements as you can: a map; photographs of people, land, and art; tapes of voices and music; and actual art objects and clothes, if you can find them. Consider creating a multimedia presentation to share your findings.

 **Take It to the Net**   www.phschool.com

Go online for an additional research activity using the Internet.

Prepare to Read

One Ordinary Day, With Peanuts

 **Take It to the Net**

Visit www.phschool.com for interactive activities and instruction related to "One Ordinary Day, With Peanuts," including

- background
- graphic organizers
- literary elements
- reading strategies

Preview

Connecting to the Literature

Sometimes it may seem as though there are not enough hours in the day. People often criticize the pace of modern life, complaining that they find it too hectic. As you will see, several of the characters in Shirley Jackson's story are experiencing one of life's frenzied days.

Background

Shirley Jackson's story is set in New York City. More than 8 million people live in the five boroughs that officially make up the city. On a typical workday, a few million more travel in from the suburbs—most of them to work in the island borough of Manhattan. For many people, Manhattan defines their image of New York City.

Literary Analysis

Surprise Ending

A **surprise ending** is an unexpected twist at the close of a story. The writer makes a surprise ending believable by hinting at it earlier in the story, without giving the surprise away. This example shows that the writer carefully conceals some ideas from the reader, hinting at a surprise ending:

> Finally, from half a block away, he saw what he wanted, and moved out into the center of the traffic to intercept a young man, who was hurrying . . .

Based on what you learn in the story, try to predict the ending.

Connecting Literary Elements

The **plot** is the sequence of events that drives the action. In "One Ordinary Day, With Peanuts," the story focuses on the actions of Mr. Johnson after he leaves his apartment early one morning. Events take a surprising twist when he returns home at the end of the day. Notice how the events of the plot lead you to anticipate the story's conclusion.

Reading Strategy

Questioning Characters' Actions

The title of the story suggests that Mr. Johnson's actions are ordinary, but the reader must decide if that is really the case. One way to do so is to **question a character's actions.** For each event, ask these questions:

- What reasons might the character have for this action?
- What behavior on the part of other characters may have led to this action?
- Does the action seem consistent with the character's personality or past behavior?

Use a chart like this one to record your questions and answers.

Vocabulary Development

irradiated (ir rā´ dē āt´ id) *v.* gave out; radiated (p. 421)

loitered (loit´ ərd) *v.* hung about; lingered (p. 421)

endeavoring (en dev´ ər iŋ) *v.* trying; attempting (p. 421)

ominously (äm´ ə nəs lē) *adv.* in a threatening way (p. 423)

buffeted (buf´ it ed) *v.* jostled; knocked about (p. 427)

insatiable (in sā´ shə bəl) *adj.* unable to be satisfied (p. 427)

omen (ō´ mən) *n.* sign foretelling a future event, either good or evil (p. 428)

impertinent (im pʉrt´ 'n ənt) *adj.* rude; impolite (p. 430)

Action
Mr. Johnson offers to watch the little boy.

Question
What are his motives?

Answer

"Yep," said the boy.

"Where you going?"

"Vermont."

"Nice place. Plenty of snow there. Maple sugar, too; you like maple sugar?"

"Sure."

"Plenty of maple sugar in Vermont. You going to live on a farm?"

"Going to live with Grandpa."

"Grandpa like peanuts?"

"Sure."

"Ought to take him some," said Mr. Johnson, reaching into his pocket. "Just you and Mommy going?"

"Yep."

"Tell you what," Mr. Johnson said. "You take some peanuts to eat on the train."

The boy's mother, after glancing at them frequently, had seemingly decided that Mr. Johnson was trustworthy, because she had devoted herself wholeheartedly to seeing that the movers did not—what movers rarely do, but every housewife believes they will—crack a leg from her good table, or set a kitchen chair down on a lamp. Most of the furniture was loaded by now, and she was deep in that nervous stage when she knew there was something she had forgotten to pack—hidden away in the back of a closet somewhere, or left at a neighbor's and forgotten, or on a clothesline—and was trying to remember under stress what it was.

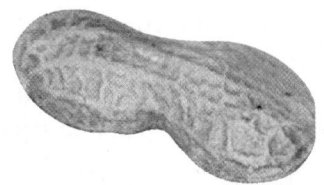

"This all, lady?" the chief mover said, completing her dismay.

Uncertainly, she nodded.

"Want to go on the truck with the furniture, sonny?" the mover asked the boy, and laughed. The boy laughed too and said to Mr. Johnson, "I guess I'll have a good time at Vermont."

"Fine time," said Mr. Johnson, and stood up. "Have one more peanut before you go," he said to the boy.

The boy's mother said to Mr. Johnson, "Thank you so much; it was a great help to me."

"Nothing at all," said Mr. Johnson gallantly. "Where in Vermont are you going?"

The mother looked at the little boy accusingly, as though he had given away a secret of some importance, and said unwillingly, "Greenwich."

"Lovely town," said Mr. Johnson. He took out a card, and wrote a name on the back. "Very good friend of mine lives in Greenwich," he said. "Call on him for anything you need. His wife makes the best doughnuts in town," he added soberly to the little boy.

"Swell," said the little boy.

"Goodbye," said Mr. Johnson.

He went on, stepping happily with his new-shod feet, feeling the warm sun on his back and on the top of his head. Halfway down the block he met a stray dog and fed him a peanut.

Reading Strategy
Questioning Characters' Actions Why do you think Mr. Johnson watched the boy?

At the corner, where another wide avenue faced him, Mr. Johnson decided to go on uptown again. Moving with comparative laziness, he was passed on either side by people hurrying and frowning, and people brushed past him going the other way, clattering along to get somewhere quickly. Mr. Johnson stopped on every corner and waited patiently for the light to change, and he stepped out of the way of anyone who seemed to be in any particular hurry, but one young lady came too fast for him, and crashed wildly into him when he stooped to pat a kitten which had run out onto the sidewalk from an apartment house and was now unable to get back through the rushing feet.

"Excuse me," said the young lady, trying frantically to pick up Mr. Johnson and hurry on at the same time, "terribly sorry."

The kitten, regardless now of danger, raced back to its home. "Perfectly all right," said Mr. Johnson, adjusting himself carefully. "You seem to be in a hurry."

"Of course I'm in a hurry," said the young lady. "I'm late."

She was extremely cross and the frown between her eyes seemed well on its way to becoming permanent. She had obviously awakened late, because she had not spent any extra time in making herself look pretty, and her dress was plain and unadorned with collar or brooch, and her lipstick was noticeably crooked. She tried to brush past Mr. Johnson, but, risking her suspicious displeasure, he took her arm and said, "Please wait."

▲ **Critical Viewing** This scene is filled with anonymous people moving about. What might Mr. Johnson think about these people? **[Speculate]**

"Look," she said <u>ominously</u>, "I ran into you and your lawyer can see my lawyer and I will gladly pay all damages and all inconveniences suffered therefrom but please this minute let me go because *I am late.*"

"Late for what?" said Mr. Johnson; he tried his winning smile on her but it did no more than keep her, he suspected, from knocking him down again.

ominously (äm´ ə nəs lē) *adv.* in a threatening way

✔Reading Check

What happens to Mr. Johnson when he stoops to pat a kitten?

"Late for work," she said between her teeth. "Late for my employment. I have a job and if I am late I lose exactly so much an hour and I cannot really afford what your pleasant conversation is costing me, be it *ever* so pleasant."

"I'll pay for it," said Mr. Johnson. Now these were magic words, not necessarily because they were true, or because she seriously expected Mr. Johnson to pay for anything, but because Mr. Johnson's flat statement, obviously innocent of irony, could not be, coming from Mr. Johnson, anything but the statement of a responsible and truthful and respectable man.

"What *do* you mean?" she asked.

"I said that since I am obviously responsible for your being late I shall certainly pay for it."

"Don't be silly," she said, and for the first time the frown disappeared. "I wouldn't expect you to pay for anything—a few minutes ago I was offering to pay *you*. Anyway," she added, almost smiling, "it *was* my fault."

"What happens if you don't go to work?"

She stared. "I don't get paid."

"Precisely," said Mr. Johnson.

"What do you mean, precisely? If I don't show up at the office exactly twenty minutes ago I lose a dollar and twenty cents an hour, or two cents a minute or . . . " She thought. ". . . Almost a dime for the time I've spent talking to you."

Mr. Johnson laughed, and finally she laughed, too. "You're late already," he pointed out. "Will you give me another four cents worth?"

"I don't understand why."

"You'll see," Mr. Johnson promised. He led her over to the side of the walk, next to the buildings, and said, "Stand here," and went out into the rush of people going both ways. Selecting and considering, as one who must make a choice involving perhaps whole years of lives, he estimated the people going by. Once he almost moved, and then at the last minute thought better of it and drew back. Finally, from half a block away, he saw what he wanted, and moved out into the center of the traffic to intercept a young man, who was hurrying, and dressed as though he had awakened late, and frowning.

"Oof," said the young man, because Mr. Johnson had thought of no better way to intercept anyone than the one the young woman had unwittingly used upon him. "Where do you think you're going?" the young man demanded from the sidewalk.

"I want to speak to you," said Mr. Johnson ominously.

The young man got up nervously, dusting himself and eyeing Mr. Johnson. "What for?" he said. "What'd *I* do?"

"That's what bothers me most about people nowadays," Mr. Johnson complained broadly to the people passing. "No matter whether they've done anything or not, they always figure someone's after them. About what you're going to do," he told the young man.

"Listen," said the young man, trying to brush past him, "I'm late,

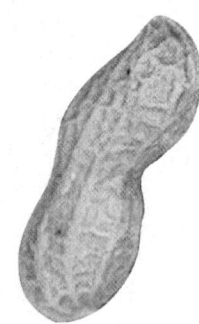

Reading Strategy
Questioning Characters' Actions What could be Mr. Johnson's motive for offering to pay for the young woman's time?

Reading Strategy
Questioning Characters' Actions What is unusual about Mr. Johnson's actions?

▲ **Critical Viewing** Based upon this photograph, what can you infer about the setting of this story? **[Infer]**

and I don't have any time to listen. Here's a dime, now get going."

"Thank you," said Mr. Johnson, pocketing the dime. "Look," he said, "what happens if you stop running?"

"I'm late," said the young man, still trying to get past Mr. Johnson, who was unexpectedly clinging.

"How much you make an hour?" Mr. Johnson demanded.

"A communist, are you?" said the young man. "Now will you please let me—"

"No," said Mr. Johnson insistently, "*how* much?"

"Dollar fifty," said the young man. "And *now* will you—"

"You like adventure?"

The young man stared, and, staring, found himself caught and held by Mr. Johnson's genial smile; he almost smiled back and then

✓ **Reading Check**

How does Mr. Johnson respond when the woman says she is late for work?

repressed it and made an effort to tear away. "I got to *hurry*," he said.

"Mystery? Like surprises? Unusual and exciting events?"

"You selling something?"

"Sure," said Mr. Johnson. "You want to take a chance?"

The young man hesitated, looking longingly up the avenue toward what might have been his destination and then, when Mr. Johnson said, "I'll pay for it," with his own peculiar convincing emphasis, turned and said, "Well, okay. But I got to see it first, what I'm buying."

Mr. Johnson, breathing hard, led the young man over to the side where the girl was standing; she had been watching with interest Mr. Johnson's capture of the young man and now, smiling timidly, she looked at Mr. Johnson as though prepared to be surprised at nothing.

Mr. Johnson reached into his pocket and took out his wallet. "Here," he said, and handed a bill to the girl. "This about equals your day's pay."

"But no," she said, surprised in spite of herself. "I mean, I *couldn't*."

"Please do not interrupt," Mr. Johnson told her. "And *here*," he said to the young man, "this will take care of *you*." The young man accepted the bill dazedly, but said, "Probably counterfeit," to the young woman out of the side of his mouth. "Now," Mr. Johnson went on, disregarding the young man, "what is your name, miss?"

"Kent," she said helplessly. "Mildred Kent."

"Fine," said Mr. Johnson. "And you, sir?"

"Arthur Adams," said the young man stiffly.

"Splendid," said Mr. Johnson. "Now, Miss Kent, I would like you to meet Mr. Adams. Mr. Adams, Miss Kent."

Miss Kent stared, wet her lips nervously, made a gesture as though she might run, and said, "How do you do?"

Mr. Adams straightened his shoulders, scowled at Mr. Johnson, made a gesture as though he might run, and said, "How do you do?"

"Now *this*," said Mr. Johnson, taking several bills from his wallet, "should be enough for the day for both of you. I would suggest, perhaps, Coney Island*—although I personally am not fond of the place—or perhaps a nice lunch somewhere, and dancing, or a matinee,[1] or even a movie, although take care to choose a really good one;

---

1. **matinee** here, an afternoon performance of an on- or off-Broadway show.

Literature in context Geography Connection

◆ Coney Island

Coney Island—the place to which Mr. Johnson suggests Miss Kent and Mr. Adams might go—is a famous beach area and amusement park in Brooklyn, one of the five boroughs of New York City. During the first half of the twentieth century, it was one of the largest amusement areas in the world. Millions of New Yorkers were drawn to its rides, games, entertainment, restaurants, and swimming each year. Although attendance was down during the early 1950s because of the polio epidemic and the resulting fear of contagion, by 1955—when this story was published—attendance was back up to 1.5 million on July 4th.

The Cyclone at Coney Island

Reading Strategy
Questioning Characters' Actions Why might Mr. Johnson have "captured" the young man?

there are so many bad movies these days. "You might," he said, struck with an inspiration, "visit the Bronx Zoo, or the Planetarium.[2] Anywhere, as a matter of fact," he concluded, "that you would like to go. Have a nice time."

As he started to move away, Arthur Adams, breaking from his dumbfounded stare, said, "But see here, mister, you *can't* do this. Why—how do you know—I mean, *we* don't even know—I mean, how do you know we won't just take the money and not do what you said?"

"You've taken the money," Mr. Johnson said. "You don't have to follow any of my suggestions. You may know something you prefer to do—perhaps a museum, or something."

"But suppose I just run away with it and leave her here?"

"I know you won't," said Mr. Johnson gently, "because you remembered to ask *me* that. Goodbye," he added, and went on.

As he stepped up the street, conscious of the sun on his head and his good shoes, he heard from somewhere behind him the young man saying, "Look, you know you don't have to if you don't want to," and the girl saying, "But unless you don't want to . . ." Mr. Johnson smiled to himself and then thought that he had better hurry along; when he wanted to he could move very quickly, and before the young woman had gotten around to saying, "Well, *I* will if *you* will," Mr. Johnson was several blocks away and had already stopped twice, once to help a lady lift several large packages into a taxi and once to hand a peanut to a seagull. By this time he was in an area of large stores and many more people and he was <u>buffeted</u> constantly from either side by people hurrying and cross and late and sullen. Once he offered a peanut to a man who asked him for a dime, and once he offered a peanut to a bus driver who had stopped his bus at an intersection and had opened the window next to his seat and put out his head as though longing for fresh air and the comparative quiet of the traffic. The man wanting a dime took the peanut because Mr. Johnson had wrapped a dollar bill around it, but the bus driver took the peanut and asked ironically, "You want a transfer, Jack?"

On a busy corner Mr. Johnson encountered two young people—for one minute he thought they might be Mildred Kent and Arthur Adams—who were eagerly scanning a newspaper, their backs pressed against a storefront to avoid the people passing, their heads bent together. Mr. Johnson, whose curiosity was <u>insatiable</u>, leaned onto the storefront next to them and peeked over the man's shoulder; they were scanning the "Apartments Vacant" columns.

Mr. Johnson remembered the street where the woman and her little boy were going to Vermont and he tapped the man on the shoulder and said amiably, "Try down on West Seventeen. About the middle of the block, people moved out this morning."

---

2. **Planetarium** the Hayden Planetarium, adjoining the American Museum of Natural History in New York City.

buffeted (buf´ it ed) *v.* jostled; knocked about

insatiable (in sā´ she bel) *adj.* unable to be satisfied

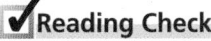Reading Check

What does Mr. Johnson offer to the man who asks him for a dime?

"Say, what do you—" said the man, and then, seeing Mr. Johnson clearly, "Well thanks. Where did you say?"

"West Seventeen," said Mr. Johnson. "About the middle of the block." He smiled again and said, "Good luck."

"Thanks," said the man.

"Thanks," said the girl, as they moved off.

"Goodbye," said Mr. Johnson.

He lunched alone in a pleasant restaurant, where the food was rich, and only Mr. Johnson's excellent digestion could encompass two of their whipped-cream-and-chocolate-and-rum-cake pastries for dessert. He had three cups of coffee, tipped the waiter largely, and went out into the street again into the wonderful sunlight, his shoes still comfortable and fresh on his feet. Outside he found a beggar staring into the windows of the restaurant he had left and, carefully looking through the money in his pocket, Mr. Johnson approached the beggar and pressed some coins and a couple of bills into his hand. "It's the price of the veal cutlet lunch plus tip," said Mr. Johnson. "Goodbye."

After his lunch he rested; he walked into the nearest park and fed peanuts to the pigeons. It was late afternoon by the time he was ready to start back downtown, and he had refereed two checker games and watched a small boy and girl whose mother had fallen asleep and awakened with surprise and fear which turned to amusement when she saw Mr. Johnson. He had given away almost all of his candy, and had fed all the rest of his peanuts to the pigeons, and it was time to go home. Although the late afternoon sun was pleasant, and his shoes were still entirely comfortable, he decided to take a taxi downtown.

He had a difficult time catching a taxi, because he gave up the first three or four empty ones to people who seemed to need them more; finally, however, he stood alone on the corner and—almost like netting a frisky fish—he hailed desperately until he succeeded in catching a cab which had been proceeding with haste uptown and seemed to draw in towards Mr. Johnson against its own will.

"Mister," the cab driver said as Mr. Johnson climbed in, "I figured you was an <u>omen</u>, like. I wasn't going to pick you up at all."

"Kind of you," said Mr. Johnson ambiguously.

"If I'd of let you go it would of cost me ten bucks," said the driver.

"Really?" said Mr. Johnson.

"Yeah," said the driver. "Guy just got out of the cab, he turned around and give me ten bucks, said take this and bet it in a hurry on a horse named Vulcan,[3] right away."

"Vulcan?" said Mr. Johnson, horrified. "A fire sign[4] on a Wednesday?"

"What?" said the driver. "Anyway, I said to myself if I got no fare between here and there I'd bet the ten, but if anyone looked like they

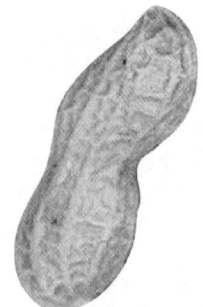

---

3. **Vulcan** also the name of the Roman god of fire.
4. **fire sign** term borrowed from astrology, referring here to Vulcan.

needed the cab I'd take it as an omen and I'd take the ten home to the wife."

"You were very right," said Mr. Johnson heartily. "This is Wednesday, you would have lost your money. Monday, yes, or even Saturday. But never never never a fire sign on a Wednesday. Sunday would have been good, now."

"Vulcan don't run on Sunday," said the driver.

"You wait till another day," said Mr. Johnson. "Down this street, please, driver. I'll get off on the next corner."

"He *told* me Vulcan, though," said the driver.

"I'll tell you," said Mr. Johnson, hesitating with the door of the cab half open. "You take that ten dollars and I'll give you another ten dollars to go with it, and you go right ahead and bet that money on any Thursday on any horse that has a name indicating . . . let me see, Thursday . . . well, grain. Or any growing food."

"Grain?" said the driver. "You mean a horse named, like, Wheat or something?"

"Certainly," said Mr. Johnson. "Or, as a matter of fact, to make it even easier, any horse whose name includes the letters C, R, L. Perfectly simple."

"Tall corn?" said the driver, a light in his eye. "You mean a horse named, like, Tall Corn?"

"Absolutely," said Mr. Johnson. "Here's your money."

"Tall Corn," said the driver. "Thank *you*, mister."

"Goodbye," said Mr. Johnson.

He was on his own corner and went straight up to his apartment. He let himself in and called "Hello?" and Mrs. Johnson answered from the kitchen, "Hello, dear, aren't you early?"

"Took a taxi home," Mr. Johnson said. "I remembered the cheesecake, too. What's for dinner?"

Mrs. Johnson came out of the kitchen and kissed him; she was a comfortable woman, and smiling as Mr. Johnson smiled. "Hard day?" she asked.

"Not very," said Mr. Johnson, hanging his coat in the closet. "How about you?"

"So-so," she said. She stood in the kitchen doorway while he settled into his easy chair and took off his good shoes and took out the paper he had bought that morning. "Here and there," she said.

"I didn't do so badly," Mr. Johnson said. "Couple young people."

"Fine," she said. "I had a little nap this afternoon, took it easy most of the day. Went into a department store this morning and accused

Reading Strategy
Questioning Characters' Actions Is Mr. Johnson's behavior in the cab consistent with the impression you have of him up to this point? Why or why not?

✔**Reading Check**

Why does Mr. Johnson have a hard time catching a cab?

the woman next to me of shoplifting, and had the store detective pick her up. Sent three dogs to the pound—you know, the usual thing. Oh, and listen," she added, remembering.

"What?" asked Mr. Johnson.

"Well," she said, "I got onto a bus and asked the driver for a transfer, and when he helped someone else first I said that he was <u>impertinent</u>, and quarreled with him. And then I said why wasn't he in the army, and I said it loud enough for everyone to hear, and I took his number and I turned in a complaint. Probably got him fired."

"Fine," said Mr. Johnson. "But you do look tired. Want to change over tomorrow?"

"I would like to," she said. "I could do with a change."

"Right," said Mr. Johnson. "What's for dinner?"

"Veal cutlet."

"Had it for lunch," said Mr. Johnson.

impertinent (im purt´ ən ənt) *adj.* rude; impolite

Review and Assess

Thinking About the Selection

1. **Respond:** How did you feel when you read the ending? Explain.

2. **(a) Recall:** Give at least three examples from the story that show how Mr. Johnson helped people. **(b) Infer:** Through his actions, what might Mr. Johnson teach people?

3. **(a) Recall:** According to what she tells her husband when he gets home, how did Mrs. Johnson spend her day? **(b) Make a Judgment:** Is this the sort of wife you would have imagined for Mr. Johnson, based on your impressions of his personality up to that point? Explain.

4. **(a) Recall:** What do the couple decide they will do on the next day? **(b) Infer:** What do you discover about the two of them? **(c) Hypothesize:** How do you suppose Mr. Johnson will treat each of the people he met today if he runs into them again tomorrow?

5. **(a) Compare:** In what ways is Mr. Johnson's day ordinary, as the title suggests? **(b) Contrast:** In what ways is his day out of the ordinary?

6. **Apply:** At which aspects of modern life does this story poke fun?

7. **(a) Extend:** How would you have responded to Mr. Johnson if you had been Miss Kent or Mr. Adams? **(b) Take a Position:** Do you think it is helpful or harmful to be suspicious of strangers doing good deeds? Explain.

Shirley Jackson

(1919–1965)

As a writer, Shirley Jackson seems to wear two hats. On one hand, she writes warm-hearted portraits of family life. On the other, she is a master of horror fiction. Jackson brings her comic eye to both forms, capturing the humor of family life and adding a touch of humor to her tales of horror by grounding strange happenings in everyday events.

Born in San Francisco, Jackson spent most of her adult life in the East. She first won attention with her short story "The Lottery," which appeared in 1948 in the literary magazine *The New Yorker*. This eerie tale of a bizarre and deadly small-town New England lottery provoked more reader reaction than other work the magazine had published. Her horror novels include *The Bird's Nest* (1954), *The Sundial* (1958), and *The Haunting of Hill House*, which became the basis of the popular 1963 film, *The Haunting*.

Review and Assess

Literary Analysis

Surprise Ending

1. Considering Mr. Johnson's behavior throughout the story, why does the ending come as a **surprise**?
2. What hints point to the unexpected ending? Explain.
3. What might the ending suggest about unexpected acts of kindness or mean behavior?

Connecting Literary Elements

4. In many stories, the climax, or high point of the **plot**, occurs toward the end, leaving the reader with more information following the climax to help tie up loose ends. Using a chart like the one shown, analyze the placement of the high point of this story.

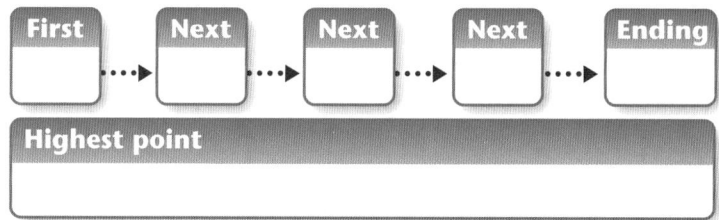

5. What is the effect of this unusual order of events?

Reading Strategy

Questioning Characters' Actions

6. What seems to motivate Mr. Johnson in his behavior toward others as he travels around New York?
7. Why do you think Mr. Johnson chose to help the particular individuals mentioned in the story?
8. What does the decision to change roles with his wife suggest about his motives?

Extend Understanding

9. **Cultural Connection:** (a) How does the setting of this story—a busy city—affect the Johnsons' work? (b) Would the story have been as successful if it had been set in a small town? Explain.

Quick Review

A **surprise ending** is an unexpected close to a story.

The **plot** is the sequence of events that drives the action.

To **question characters' actions**, look for reasons behind their words and deeds.

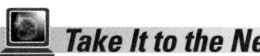 **Take It to the Net**
www.phschool.com
Take the interactive self-test online to check your understanding of the selection.

Integrate Language Skills

Vocabulary Development Lesson

Related Words: *omen*

An *omen* is "a sign or event that foretells the future." Such signs can be positive or negative, but the word *ominously* focuses only on the negative: It means "in a way that seems to foretell doom." Write the meaning of each word below, using the meaning of the related word.

1. *irradiated*—related word: *radiant*
2. *planetarium*—related word: *planet*
3. *insatiable*—related word: *satisfy*

Spelling Strategy

When you add an ending to a word that ends with two or more consonants, never double the final consonant. Thus, *impertinent* becomes *impertinently*, but *final* becomes *finally*. Write the correct spelling for each item below.

1. pass + *-ed* 2. dumb + *-ly* 3. tick + *-ing*

Grammar Lesson

Direct Object or Object of a Preposition?

A **direct object** is a noun or pronoun that receives the action of a transitive action verb. The **object of the preposition** is the noun or pronoun at the end of a prepositional phrase. Look at the following examples.

>   S   V DO
> **Direct Object:** Mr. Johnson ate *lunch.* (*lunch* receives the action of *ate*)
>
>   S   V
> **Object of a Preposition:** Mr. Johnson ate
>   PREP PHRASE
> at a pleasant *restaurant.* (*restaurant* is the object of the preposition *at*)

Concept Development: Synonyms

Choose the letter of the word that is most nearly the same in meaning as the first word.

1. irradiated: (a) darkened, (b) glowed, (c) frozen
2. loitered: (a) dirtied, (b) delivered, (c) lingered
3. endeavoring: (a) trying, (b) asking, (c) preparing
4. ominously: (a) threateningly, (b) brightly, (c) loudly
5. buffeted: (a) cooked, (b) shined, (c) shoved
6. insatiable: (a) unquenchable, (b) indefinite, (c) odd
7. omen: (a) stamp, (b) signal, (c) cause
8. impertinent: (a) impatient, (b) unrelated, (c) impolite

Practice Copy each sentence. Label the subjects and verbs. Circle each direct object. Underline each object of a preposition.

1. The woman ran into Mr. Johnson.
2. Mr. Johnson spoke to the people.
3. She watched Mr. Johnson with interest.
4. He gave peanuts to the people he met.
5. He paid her for the hours she missed.

Writing Application Write a paragraph about "One Ordinary Day, With Peanuts" that includes at least one direct object and one prepositional phrase.

Writing Lesson

Summary

A summary provides only the most important details of a story or event. Write a summary of Mrs. Johnson's day.

Prewriting   Start by imagining Mrs. Johnson's unusual day. Fill out an hour-by-hour schedule showing all her activities. Underline the most important events in your list.

Drafting   Recount the events of the day in chronological order. Use transitions like *next*, *meanwhile*, and *later* to clarify the order of events.

Revising   Reread your summary to make sure that you have included all of the important details of the day. Place boxes between sentences to help you evaluate whether you need to add transitions. Where necessary, add transition words to make your writing clearer.

Model: Revising to Add Transitions

☑She shut the door, ready to start her day. ☐ *First,* She bought

the paper, giving everyone an angry snarl. ☐ *Then,* She looked

for her first victim.

> Transition words smooth out the writing and make the sequence of events clear.

 Prentice Hall Writing and Grammar Connection: Chapter 7, Section 4

Extension Activities

Listening and Speaking Imagine meeting both Mr. Johnson and Mrs. Johnson on this not-so-ordinary day. Prepare a **monologue** describing your feelings before and after the encounter. Review the story before you write.

- Notice how people reacted to Mr. Johnson's generosity.
- Think about how Mrs. Johnson probably treated people and how her actions would compare with Mr. Johnson's.

Rehearse your monologue, and present it to your class.

Research and Technology In a small group, put together a **research report** about the setting of the story, New York City in the 1950s. Before starting your research, generate research questions about the tourist attractions in New York City and the kinds of changes that took place in the 1950s. Use library sources, including encyclopedias on CD-ROM, to help you. **[Group Activity]**

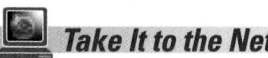 **Take It to the Net**   www.phschool.com

Go online for an additional research activity using the Internet.

Writing WORKSHOP

Writing for Assessment: Test Essay

To make sure that you are learning the information and skills you need to succeed, teachers frequently assess your knowledge. Tests, oral reports, and research papers are ways of evaluating your progress. Essay tests are the most common type of **writing for assessment**.

Assignment Criteria. Successful writing for assessment usually has the following characteristics:

- a direct response to the test question
- a thesis statement that is clearly worded and well supported
- specific information about the topic, drawn from your reading or from class discussion
- a clear organization

To preview the criteria on which your writing for assessment may be judged, see the Rubric on page 437.

Prewriting

Choose a topic. On some essay tests, a single topic is assigned. In cases in which you have the opportunity to choose a topic, use the following techniques:

- **Consider what you know.** Jot down specific details for each topic. You should choose a topic that you know well.
- **Pinpoint your strengths.** The question may ask you to *analyze*, to *predict*, or to *explain*. Choose a topic for which you can provide facts to support the type of response required.

Narrow your response. As you prepare to write your essay, circle key words in the question and take notes to help you interpret the directions. The chart on this page shows how specific verbs should direct the purpose of your writing.

Draft a single sentence. Identify in a single sentence the main idea you will develop in your essay. Once you choose your topic, jot down this sentence and refer to it to remind you of your position. Use your main idea to formulate your thesis statement when you draft.

Example

Essay Question: Discuss how someone you admire overcame an obstacle in order to succeed.

Main Idea: I will discuss how Stevie Wonder and Jackie Joyner-Kersee overcame their disabilities.

Narrow Your Response

Key Words	Essay Objectives
Analyze	Examine how various elements contribute to the whole.
Describe	Give main features and examples of each
Compare and Contrast	Stress how two wor' or other items are alike and different.
Discuss	Support a generalization with facts an examples.
Explain	Clarify by probing reasons, causes, results, and effects.
Defend	Support your positic with examples from the text.

Student Model

Before you begin drafting your writing for assessment, read this student model and review the characteristics of effective writing for assessment.

Eddie Harris
Chicago, IL

Question: In an essay, discuss how someone you admire overcame an obstacle in order to succeed.

The best way to overcome a disability is to face it head-on and not let it prevent you from achieving great things. This is the lesson I draw from the lives of two people whom I admire—the musician Stevie Wonder and the track-and-field star Jackie Joyner-Kersee. I respect them for their courage and strength in overcoming obstacles. Both are African Americans with disabilities who defied obstacles in order to be successful in their fields.

Stevie Wonder became blind after he was born prematurely and received too much oxygen. But that did not stop him from becoming one of the best musicians ever. He started out singing rock and roll songs outside a church in Detroit. Eventually, he found his way to Motown Studios at a time when Motown was one of the top recording studios in America. There his career skyrocketed. He became one of the best Motown singers even though he was only ten years old.

He has since been nominated for more Grammy awards than any other musician. His blindness is no disability for him. On the music charts, Stevie Wonder opened the gates for a new sound . . . not just for African Americans but for everyone else as well.

Another person that I admire for the way she overcame obstacles is Jackie Joyner-Kersee, a famous track-and-field star. She was born in East St. Louis, Illinois, and her family was very poor. Her parents thought that track and field were inappropriate for a girl. When she was nine, she entered her first track-and-field competition. Even though she lost, she didn't give up. Jackie entered another race. Her parents were shocked when she won.

In the late 1980s, she was diagnosed with asthma. This has not interfered with her performance as an athlete. Jackie is a world champion in both the long jump and heptathlon and has many Olympic medals to prove it.

Jackie Joyner-Kersee continues to be a role model for young people with disabilities like me. I think that Jackie Joyner-Kersee and Stevie Wonder are admirable for overcoming their disabilities. Stevie Wonder overcame blindness to bring music to the world. Joyner-Kersee stunned us with her athleticism, despite her asthma. They teach me to never give up, no matter how intimidating the obstacles I face in life.

The author uses a general statement to introduce his response to the essay question.

This author presents a thesis statement that focuses his answer to the essay question.

In the body of the essay, the author supports his general statement with specific factual information.

The author concludes by restating his thesis and reinforcing it with personal insight.

Drafting

Find a focus. Once you choose your topic, develop a focus for your essay. Consider the type of writing you are creating, and draft a statement that directly responds to the question. Use the information at right to help you focus your ideas.

Plan a structure. When you sketch an outline for your essay, divide it into three parts: introduction, body, and conclusion.

- The **introduction** should state your thesis.
- The **body** of the essay should present at least two main points that support your thesis.
- The **conclusion** should restate the answer to the essay question and sum up the main points in the body.

Fill in the details. In a test situation, you normally have limited time. List the evidence, facts, examples, and quotations you will need to prove your point. Jot down as many details as you can remember or generate. Refer to this list as you draft.

Find Your Focus

Exposition

Develop a thesis statement to address the question, gearing your response to the expectation of problem-and-solution, cause-and-effect, or comparison-and-contrast essays.

Persuasion

Choose a position to argue, and identify the support you'll use to defend it.

Response to Literature

In a single sentence, identify your focus. You may decide to evaluate a character or analyze a setting.

Revising

Revise for coherence. When you have finished writing, compare the first paragraph of your essay with the last:

1. The first paragraph should contain your focus or thesis in response to the essay question.

2. The final paragraph should restate the thesis statement and summarize your supporting evidence.

3. If the main points in the first and final paragraphs do not match, revise either paragraph to make the writing more coherent. If necessary, revise body paragraphs or add transitional sentences to make sure that the essay flows and holds together well.

Model: Revising a Conclusion

Stevie Wonder overcame blindness to bring music to the world. Joyner-Kersee stunned us with her athleticism, despite her asthma.

I think that Jackie Joyner-Kersee and Stevie Wonder are admirable for overcoming their disabilities. They teach me to never give up, no matter how intimidating the obstacles I face in my life.

Eddie could summarize his supporting arguments to give greater weight and clarity to his thesis.

Revise for formal language. Look for words in your writing that can be replaced with words that are more appropriate to your purpose. In the following example, *element* creates a more formal effect than *thing*.

Informal: The railroad was the *thing* that most contributed to the success of new businesses.

Formal: The railroad was the *element* that most contributed to the success of new businesses.

Compare the model and the nonmodel. Why is the model more effective than the nonmodel?

Nonmodel	Model
The first person I want to talk about is a great African American musician by the name of Stevie Wonder.	One person who serves as a powerful example of someone who has overcome a disability is the African American musician Stevie Wonder.

Publishing and Presenting

After you receive an essay back from your teacher with comments, keep a copy in your portfolio. Consider this suggestion to make further use of it:

Organize a study group. Compare your response with those of your classmates. Read the essays and discuss with other members of the study group the ways you could improve your essay writing. If it is helpful, list the strengths and weaknesses of each essay. Use the lists to improve your performance on your next essay test.

Rubric for Self-Assessment

Evaluate your writing for assessment using the following criteria and rating scale:

Criteria	Rating Scale Not very				Very
How directly does the essay answer the question?	1	2	3	4	5
How well is the thesis supported by evidence?	1	2	3	4	5
How specific is the supporting information?	1	2	3	4	5
How effectively is information drawn from reading or discussion incorporated?	1	2	3	4	5
How effectively are arguments organized?	1	2	3	4	5

Listening and Speaking WORKSHOP

Delivering a Descriptive Presentation

In a **descriptive presentation**, you communicate an experience by describing it in detail. The ability to deliver a memorable descriptive presentation is as important for telling a good story as it is for telling someone how to operate machinery. The following techniques will help you organize and deliver a descriptive presentation.

Prepare the Presentation

Much of the creative work that goes into putting together a descriptive presentation involves gathering details and organizing them logically.

Picture the topic that you are describing. Project yourself into the situation you are describing. Think about what you see, hear, and feel around you. Make a list of these sensory details, selecting those that would best help your audience to picture the situation. For example, you might describe the feeling of terror when the person teaching you to ride your bike let go, and you suddenly forgot how to brake.

Define your topic. Too much descriptive detail can slow you down or get you sidetracked. To avoid this problem, start off with a single generalization that sums up your presentation and suits your purpose. Then, consider whether details are essential or inessential to capturing your generalization. Adjust the balance if you feel you have too much or too little detail.

Defining Your Topic

Purpose: To entertain
Audience: Fellow students

Essential Details	Inessential Details
I received a bike for my sixth birthday.	
I felt the wheel shake when I was first gaining my balance.	My bike was a three speed.
I didn't know how to brake when my dad let go.	

Deliver the Presentation

When it comes time to deliver your presentation, use the following techniques to provide greater impact.

Be dynamic. An audience will pay closer attention to a speaker who is animated and varies his or her voice. The more interested you are in your topic, the easier it will be to give a dynamic presentation.

Gauge audience reaction. Look at the audience frequently to check how people are reacting. If you feel your audience is losing interest, leave out some details and pick up your pace. If people are actively engaged, do not be afraid to elaborate on aspects that seem to play well with your audience.

Activity:
Analyzing a Speech
Pair up with another student. Choose a topic that you know well but your partner does not. Take turns presenting to each other, using as much description as you feel necessary. When you have finished, ask your partner to recall as many details as possible. Use this feedback to evaluate your presentation.

Assessment WORKSHOP

Cause and Effect

The reading sections of some tests often require you to read a passage and answer multiple-choice questions about cause-and-effect relationships. Use these strategies to help you answer test questions on cause and effect:

- Remember that a *cause* is an event that makes something happen, and an *effect* is a result of that event.
- To recognize cause and effect, ask yourself, "What happened in this passage? Why did this event come about?"
- Do not limit your search to a single cause and effect. One cause may have several effects, and one effect may have several causes.

Test-Taking Strategies

- Look for words and phrases such as "factor," "because," and "as a result" that signal cause-and-effect statements.
- Keep track of multiple cause-and-effect relationships by circling and labeling causes and effects and drawing arrows between them.

Sample Test Item

Directions: Read the passage, and then answer the question that follows.

Marcus dressed quickly, gulped breakfast, and bolted out the door. As he hurried to school, he mentally reviewed his notes and realized that he felt confident. He had been unprepared for the last biology exam. This would be his last chance to improve his final grade. This time, he had made a serious effort to study for the exam.

1 Why did Marcus feel confident?

  A This was his last chance to pass biology.

  B He arrived at school on time.

  C He had not done well on the last exam.

  D He had studied hard for the exam.

Answer and Explanation

The correct answer is *D*. *A* and *C* might make Marcus more nervous, but not confident. *B* is not found in the paragraph.

▶ Practice

Directions: Read the passage, and then answer the question that follows.

Lauren looked at the car repair bill. She thought about the day that Shelly, her sister, had borrowed her car. Lauren had reluctantly given her the keys. Shelly had promised to be back in time for Lauren to go to work, so five hours later, Shelly returned and sheepishly explained how she had crushed the rear fender. Lauren had lost a day's pay. "Well, I've learned something," she thought.

1 Why did Lauren lose a day's pay?

  A She had to have her car repaired.

  B Shelly had an accident.

  C She couldn't go to work.

  D Shelly begged her for the car.

2 Why did Lauren give Shelly the keys to her car?

  A She needed money to pay a bill.

  B It was a rainy day.

  C They were sisters.

  D Shelly made a promise to be back on time.

UNIT 5 *Visions of the Future*

Exploring the Theme

People have always tried to imagine the future. Some have worried that today's human carelessness will produce the problems of tomorrow. Others have looked optimistically toward the future, hoping that technological progress will offer us a way to solve our current problems. Still others have predicted that each set of advancements will bring its own set of problems and solutions, in an endless cycle of human wisdom and folly.

Bryan Woolley incorporates elements of all three outlooks in his time capsule essay, "To the Residents of A.D. 2029." Addressing future citizens, Woolley acknowledges the problems of our time. Through it all, though, he manages to find perspective, humor, and a glimmer of hope.

▲ **Critical Viewing** Which elements of this picture suggest that computer technology opens infinite possibilities? **[Infer]**

Why **Read Literature?**

Whenever you read science fiction, you have a purpose, or reason. You might read to appreciate a new view of the future, or because the social issues an author raises interest you. Preview the three purposes you might set before reading works in this unit.

Read for the Love of Literature

Science fiction is particularly compelling when a writer interweaves technological progress with great moral dilemmas. If you have ever wondered—or worried—what it might be like when humans rely completely on technology, you may find a surprising answer in Isaac Asimov's **"The Machine That Won the War,"** page 456.

Many works of science fiction are tales of wayward computers destroying the world with murderous abandon. But why not try to imagine a world where technology and nature coexist peacefully? If this concept intrigues you, read Richard Brautigan's **"All Watched Over by Machines of Loving Grace,"** page 476.

Read to Be Inspired

Imprisoned for twenty-seven years for his opposition to racial segregation, Nelson Mandela served as the conscience of South Africa. After he was released and elected president, Mandela was faced with the overwhelming task of creating a just society out of poverty and inequality. See how he viewed this as an opportunity to issue a stirring call to action in **"Glory and Hope,"** page 506.

Read for Information

In 1993, when the first Internet browser was introduced, few could have predicted how important the Internet would become. How difficult is it for you to imagine the state of technology five years from now? Find out Bill Gates's vision for the future in video technology and see if it matches your own in **"The Road Ahead,"** page 446.

In 1962, pesticide use was widespread and companies dumped toxins into our streams. It took a biologist named Rachel Carson to draw the vital connection between technology and destruction of the environment. Read an excerpt from ***Silent Spring***—the book that helped spawn the environmental movement—on page 491.

 Take It to the Net

Visit the Web site for online instruction and activities related to each selection in this unit.
www.phschool.com

How to Read Literature

Use Critical Reading Strategies

When you read a work that presents an individual's perspective, it is a good idea to read critically. Reading critically involves examining and questioning the author's ideas. Use these strategies to help you read critically:

1. Recognize bias.

No matter how impartial writers seem, they inevitably bring some of their own experiences and beliefs to their writing. The bias that results influences both their writing and your reaction. To increase your awareness of bias:

- Weigh the facts that support or contradict the author's position. Then, see if your conclusion is the same as the author's.

- Consider what the author is omitting, as well as including.

- Learn about the author's background to determine which experiences may have influenced his or her writing.

2. Identify relevant details.

To help process information as you read, it is useful to screen passages for relevant detail.

- Details that have the most relevance are those that are essential to your understanding of the story's plot, characters, and setting.

- Do not expect to know what is or is not relevant from the very beginning. As you read further, the distinction will become clearer.

3. Recognize a poet's purpose.

- Look for recurring ideas and images in the poem that may provide clues to a poet's reason for writing.

- Pay close attention to the opening and closing lines of a poem. Poets will often announce their intentions in these lines.

- Remember that a poet may have multiple purposes and that every reader may bring a slightly different interpretation to a poem.

Fact vs. Opinion

Selection

"To the Residents of A.D. 2029"

Fact (Verifiable)
▶ 20th C. U.S. has the world's highest standard of living.

Opinion (Belief)
▶ We need art to feed our souls and America does not have enough art.

4. Distinguish fact from opinion.

- Facts can be verified for accuracy by checking a reference book; opinions cannot. Note the examples of the distinction between fact and opinion at right.

- Opinions, though often stated strongly, will always be an interpretation based on a writer's beliefs or values.

As you read the selections in this unit, review the critical reading strategies and apply them to interact with the text.

Prepare to Read

from The Road Ahead

 Take It to the Net

Visit www.phschool.com
for interactive activities
and instruction related to
The Road Ahead, including
- background
- graphic organizers
- literary elements
- reading strategies

Preview

Connecting to the Literature

Technology changes at an astounding pace. Computers that were marvels of technology a few years ago now lack the processing power, memory, and features to complete the new tasks people take for granted. Let this essay by computer mogul Bill Gates encourage you to speculate how future innovations will replace today's cutting-edge technology and affect your life.

Background

The Internet consists of thousands of computer networks connected via telephone lines and cable wires. The Internet provides access to vast amounts of information, including text, graphics, and sound, with links to other sites and "pages." In *The Road Ahead,* Gates envisions a new Internet service—the delivery of high-quality video programming when customers want it.

Literary Analysis

Expository Writing

Expository writing informs the reader, explaining its subject by presenting details, examples, and facts. This passage from the selection uses details to explain the concept of conventional television:

> Conventional television allows us to decide what we watch but not when we watch it. . . . Viewers have to synchronize their schedules with the time of a broadcast. . . .

Although the focus of expository writing is to present information, the writer may also express personal opinions based on experience. As you read this excerpt from *The Road Ahead*, note how the author uses facts and examples to explain his subject and support his views.

Connecting Literary Elements

In expository writing, an **author's purpose** is his or her reason for writing—to inform, to entertain, or to persuade, for example. Of course, an author may have more than one purpose: Bill Gates writes persuasively to convince you of his opinions. At the same time, he informs and entertains you. To help you organize the opinions and supporting facts in Gates's essay, use a chart like the one shown here.

Reading Strategy

Recognizing a Writer's Bias

Even within expository writing, an author may show bias—a strong feeling for or against something. To **recognize a writer's bias,** pay attention to the following:

- loaded words—words that trigger a positive or negative response
- a single viewpoint that does not address an opposing viewpoint
- an opinion or assumption that is not backed up with facts

In this selection, Gates's involvement in his software company probably influences his positive attitude toward technology.

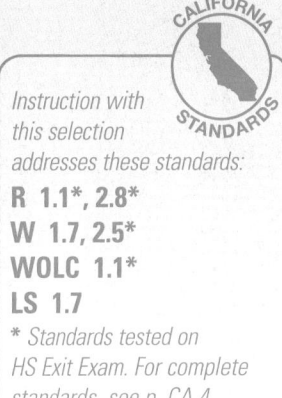

Instruction with this selection addresses these standards:
R 1.1*, 2.8*
W 1.7, 2.5*
WOLC 1.1*
LS 1.7
* Standards tested on HS Exit Exam. For complete standards, see p. CA 4.

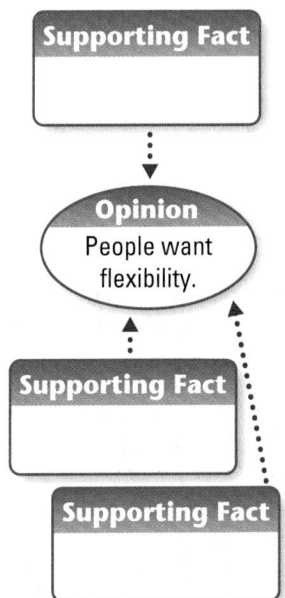

Supporting Fact

Opinion
People want flexibility.

Supporting Fact

Supporting Fact

Vocabulary Development

simultaneously (sī′ məl tā′ nē əs lē) *adv.* at the same time (p. 447)

capacious (kə pā′ shəs) *adj.* able to hold much; roomy (p. 449)

precursors (prē kur′ sərz) *n.* things that prepare the way for what will follow (p. 450)

infrared (in′ frə red′) *adj.* of light waves that lie just beyond the red end of the visible spectrum (p. 450)

parlance (pär′ ləns) *n.* style of speaking or writing; language (p. 450)

from *The Road Ahead* ◆ 445

from The Road Ahead

Bill Gates

When I was a kid, *The Ed Sullivan Show* came on at eight o'clock on Sunday nights. Most Americans with television sets tried to be at home to watch it because that might be the only time and place to see the Beatles, Elvis Presley, the Temptations, or that guy who could spin ten plates <u>simultaneously</u> on the noses of ten dogs. But if you were driving back from your grandparents' house or on a Cub Scout camping trip, too bad. Not being at home on Sunday at eight meant that you also missed out on the Monday morning talk about Sunday night's show.

Conventional television allows us to decide what we watch but not when we watch it. The technical term for this sort of broadcasting is "synchronous."[1] Viewers have to synchronize their schedules with the time of a broadcast that's sent to everybody at the same time. That's how I watched *The Ed Sullivan Show* thirty years ago, and it's how most of us will watch the news tonight.

In the early 1980's the videocassette recorder gave us more flexibility. If you cared enough about a program to fuss with timers and tapes in advance, you could watch it whenever you liked. You could claim from the broadcasters the freedom and luxury to serve as your own program scheduler—and millions of people do. When you tape a television show, or when you let your answering machine take an incoming message so that you don't have to pick up the phone, you're converting synchronous communications into a more convenient form: "asynchronous" communications.

It's human nature to find ways to convert synchronous communications into asynchronous forms. Before the invention of writing 5,000

simultaneously (sī′ məl tā′ nē əs lē) *adv.* at the same time

Literary Analysis
Expository Writing
Which details support Gates's claim that the videocassette recorder offered flexibility?

✔**Reading Check**

What does Gates say conventional television allows us to do?

---

1. **synchronous** (siṇ′ krə nəs) *adj.* happening at the same time; simultaneous.

◀ **Critical Viewing** Which details of this computer-generated art suit the double meaning of this selection's title? **[Connect]**

years ago, the only form of communication was the spoken word and the listener had to be in the presence of the speaker or miss his message. Once the message could be written, it could be stored and read later by anybody, at his or her convenience. I'm writing these words at home on a summer evening, but I have no idea where or when you'll read them. One of the benefits the communications revolution will bring to all of us is more control over our schedules.

Once a form of communication is asynchronous, you also get an increase in the variety of selection possibilities. Even people who rarely record television programs routinely rent movies from the thousands of choices available at local video rental stores for just a few dollars each. The home viewer can spend any evening with Elvis, the Beatles—or Greta Garbo.

Television has been around for fewer than sixty years, but in that time it has become a major influence in the life of almost everyone in the developed nations. In some ways, though, television was just an

▼ **Critical Viewing**
Computers and the Internet are now a part of everyday life. How do Gates's predictions about future technologies relate to your own experiences? **[Apply]**

enhancement of commercial radio, which had been bringing electronic entertainment into homes for twenty years. But no broadcast medium we have right now is comparable to the communications media we'll have once the Internet evolves to the point at which it has the broadband capacity[2] necessary to carry high-quality video.

Because consumers already understand the value of movies and are used to paying to watch them, video-on-demand is an obvious development. There won't be any intermediary VCR. You'll simply select what you want from countless available programs.

No one knows when residential broadband networks capable of supporting video-on-demand will be available in the United States and other developed countries, let alone in developing countries. Many corporate networks already have enough bandwidth,[3] but . . . even in the U.S. most homes will have to make do for some time—maybe more than a decade—with narrowband and midband access. Fortunately, these lower-capacity bandwidths work fine for many Internet-based services such as games, electronic mail, and banking. For the next few years, interactivity in homes will be limited to these kinds of services, which will be delivered to personal computers and other information appliances.

Even after broadband residential networks have become common, television shows will continue to be broadcast as they are today, for synchronous consumption. But after they air, these shows—as well as thousands of movies and virtually all other kinds of video—will also be available whenever you want to view them. If a new episode of *Seinfeld* is on at 9:00 P.M. on Thursday night, you'll also be able to see it at 9:13 P.M., 9:45 P.M., or 11:00 A.M. on Saturday. And there will be thousands of other choices. Your request for a specific movie or TV show episode will register, and the bits[4] will be routed to you across the network. It will feel as if there's no intermediary machinery between you and the object of your interest. You'll indicate what you want, and presto! you'll get it.

Movies, TV shows, and other kinds of digital information will be stored on "servers," which are computers with <u>capacious</u> disks. Servers will provide information for use anywhere on the network, just as they do for today's Internet. If you ask to see a particular movie, check a fact, or retrieve your electronic mail, your request will be routed by switches to the server or servers storing that information. You won't know whether the movie, TV show, query response, or e-mail that arrives at your house is stored on a server down the road or on the other side of the country, and it won't matter to you.

The digitized data will be retrieved from the server and routed by switches back to your television, personal computer, or telephone—your "information appliance." These digital devices will succeed for

---

2. **broadband capacity** *n.* ability to transmit a huge amount of electronic information quickly.
3. **bandwidth** *n.* amount of electronic information that can be transmitted in a given amount of time; capacity.
4. **bits** *n.* units of electronic information.

Literary Analysis
Expository Writing and Author's Purpose What is Gates's purpose in this part of his essay?

Reading Strategy
Recognizing a Writer's Bias How does Gates's bias toward technology affect his views and enthusiasm in this paragraph?

capacious (kə pā´ shəs) *adj.* able to hold much; roomy

☑ **Reading Check**

In the future, where will digital information be stored, according to the writer?

from *The Road Ahead* ◆ 449

the same reason their analog <u>precursors</u> did—they'll make some aspect of life easier. Unlike the dedicated word processors[5] that brought the first microprocessors to many offices, most of these information appliances will be general-purpose, programmable computers connected to the network.

Even if a show is being broadcast live, you'll be able to use your <u>infrared</u> remote control to start it, stop it, or go to any earlier part of the program, at any time. If somebody comes to the door, you'll be able to pause the program for as long as you like. You'll be in absolute control—except, of course, you won't be able to forward past part of a live show as it's taking place.

Most viewers can appreciate the benefits of video-on-demand and will welcome the convenience it gives them. Once the costs to build a broadband network are low enough, video-on-demand has the potential to be what in computer <u>parlance</u> is called a "killer application," or just "killer app"—a use of technology so attractive to consumers that it fuels market forces and makes the underlying invention on which it depends all but indispensable. Killer applications change technological advances from curiosities into moneymaking essentials.

5. **dedicated word processors** *n.* machines that can be used only for word processing. Unlike personal computers, dedicated machines perform only one function.

precursors (prē kur´ sərz) *n.* things that prepare the way for what will follow

infrared (in´ frə red´) *adj.* of light waves that lie just beyond the red end of the visible spectrum

parlance (pär´ ləns) *n.* style of speaking or writing; language

Review and Assess

Thinking About the Selection

1. **Respond:** What do you think about an Internet video service like the one Gates describes?

2. **(a) Recall:** Which television show does Gates cite at the start of his essay? **(b) Connect:** Why is its popularity important to the point he is trying to make?

3. **(a) Recall:** How did video delivery work when Gates wrote his essay? **(b) Compare and Contrast:** In what ways does Gates think future video delivery will be different? **(c) Infer:** Why will the Internet's broadband development be significant?

4. **(a) Recall:** How long does Gates estimate Americans will have to wait for video-on-demand to be available? **(b) Infer:** How do you think Gates feels about the length of time this development will take?

5. **Speculate:** How might the advances that Gates predicts directly affect your future?

6. **(a) Extend:** What negative impacts might video-on-demand have on our society? **(b) Assess:** Do you think the benefits outweigh the negative impacts? Explain.

Bill Gates

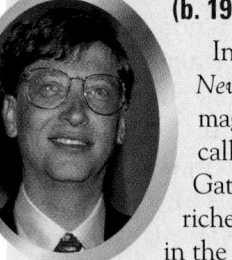

(b. 1955)
In 1997, *Newsweek* magazine called Bill Gates "the richest man in the world, and maybe the smartest." He is chief executive officer and cofounder of Microsoft Corporation, the world's largest computer software company.

In the eighth grade, Gates taught himself the computer language BASIC and began writing programs. In 1975, he and Paul Allen wrote the first version of BASIC for a microcomputer. They soon started Microsoft, which now has over 20,000 employees. In *The Road Ahead* (1996), Gates examines the future of computer technology.

Review and Assess

Literary Analysis

Expository Writing

1. Using a chart like the one shown here, identify the main idea Gates proposes. Then, identify three facts that support this idea.

2. Which details and descriptions help Gates give the essay a personal flavor?
3. Which opinions does the author introduce in his essay?

Connecting Literary Elements

4. (a) Is Gates's idea persuasive? (b) Which supporting details are most or least convincing?
5. What is the **author's** primary **purpose**? Explain.

Reading Strategy

Recognizing a Writer's Bias

6. How does Gates show a **bias** in the way he describes and explains videocassette recorders of the early 1980s?
7. (a) Use a chart like the one shown to categorize the biases in Gates's writing. Identify those details that help Gates make his case and those that do not help. (b) Do Gates's biases ultimately make his writing more or less effective for a general audience? Explain.

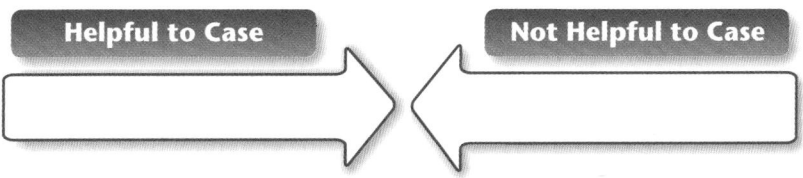

Extend Understanding

8. **Technology Connection:** In your opinion, which technological development is the most important for the present and future—the communications revolution or something else? Why?

Quick Review

Expository writing informs the reader, explaining something by presenting details, examples, and facts.

An **author's purpose** is his or her reason for writing—for example, it may be to inform, to entertain, or to persuade.

A writer's work may exhibit **bias,** a strong feeling for or against something, based on knowledge or personal experience.

 Take It to the Net
www.phschool.com

Take the interactive self-test online to check your understanding of the selection.

Integrate Language Skills

Vocabulary Development Lesson

Word Analysis: Latin Root -simul-

The Latin root -simul- means "same" or "at the same time." This fact explains the meaning of *simultaneously*—"happening at the same time." This root also appears in *simulate* and *simulcast*; identify the definition that matches each word.

1. broadcast at the same time on radio and television
2. look or act like; feign

Spelling Strategy

Do not change the spelling of a base word when you add a prefix to it. For example, *infra-* + *red* = *infrared*.

Add *un-*, *mis-*, or *pre-* to each word below to form three properly spelled words.

1. record   2. spell   3. necessary

Fluency: Word Choice

In each sentence, replace the italicized words with the appropriate one from the word list on page 445. Rephrase as necessary.

1. The expert hiker could pack an amazing amount of gear in the *large and roomy* backpack.
2. The two runners reached the finish line *at the same time*.
3. In computer *language*, restarting a computer is called "rebooting."
4. Ultraviolet radiation is more dangerous than *that of light waves beyond the red end of the spectrum*.
5. Vinyl records were the *things that came before and prepared the way for* compact discs.

Grammar Lesson

Main and Subordinate Clauses

A **clause** is a group of words with a subject and a verb. A **main,** or **independent, clause** can stand by itself as a complete sentence. In contrast, a **subordinate clause** cannot stand by itself.

In a sentence, a subordinate clause may either follow or precede a main clause.

> **Main Clause:**
>   The Internet is expanding.
> **Main Clause, Subordinate Clause:**
>   It offers more *as time passes.*
> **Subordinate Clause, Main Clause:**
>   *If we let it,* it can change our lives.

Practice Copy each sentence. Underline the main clause and circle the subordinate clause.

1. If you cared about a program, you taped it.
2. This medium will offer shows that you can watch any time.
3. The demand is growing, even as I write.
4. Before much more time passes, the revolution will succeed.
5. Viewers welcome convenience, which video-on-demand will give them.

Writing Application Rephrase each of the preceding sentences by converting main clauses to subordinate ones and subordinate clauses to main ones.

W̶G *Prentice Hall Writing and Grammar Connection: Chapter 21, Section 2*

Writing Lesson

Consumer Response

Bill Gates uses his experience as a businessman and technology specialist to offer his views about the future. In an essay that responds to his, use your experiences as a television viewer or computer user to tell technology developers which advances you would like to see.

Prewriting   Review the essay, noting key advances that Gates mentions. Evaluate the worth of each one to you. Then, brainstorm to add your own ideas for innovation. For each idea, list the benefits of your proposal.

Model: Brainstorming to Identify Benefits

Idea ⟶	Benefit
1. full-screen, real-time videophones	1. Allows people to see each other clearly, without choppiness of current technology.

> This idea comes from the writer's disappointment with existing video applications.

Drafting   Begin with an introduction that establishes your authority as a consumer. Then, devote a paragraph to each of your ideas, explaining both your innovation and its benefits.

Revising   Evaluate the body paragraphs to decide whether you have effectively argued the effects of your proposal. If necessary, add more details about current technology's shortcomings to support the need for change.

*W*G *Prentice Hall Writing and Grammar Connection: Chapter 10, Section 2*

Extension Activities

Listening and Speaking Working in a group, organize a **presentation** on important inventions of the past one hundred years.

- The group should agree on the inventions to be discussed.
- Each student should research a single invention.
- Use charts and other visuals in creating a display to support the discussion.

Conclude your presentation by inviting questions from your audience. **[Group Activity]**

Research and Technology The future is likely to see many more technological advances besides video-on-demand. Use the Internet to learn what Bill Gates and three (or more) other experts think will be the big technological breakthroughs in the coming decades. Prepare a handout with an **annotated list** of Web sites you found most helpful.

 **Take It to the Net**   www.phschool.com

Go online for an additional research activity using the Internet.

Prepare to Read

The Machine That Won the War

Take It to the Net

Visit www.phschool.com for interactive activities and instruction related to "The Machine That Won the War," including
- background
- graphic organizers
- literary elements
- reading strategies

Preview

Connecting to the Literature

The success of everyday life has come to depend on computers. Machines track store purchases, banking transactions, and school records. Sometimes, as you will see in "The Machine That Won the War," computers run important military applications.

Background

When Isaac Asimov wrote this story, computers were big, bulky machines; small, personal computers had not yet been invented. Solving problems required the setting of thousands of cables and switches by hand. The early computers had names like UNIVAC and ENIAC. Perhaps Asimov was thinking of them when he devised the name "Multivac"—the powerful computer in this story.

Literary Analysis

Science Fiction

Science fiction is a form of literature in which the writer makes free use of his or her imagination to create settings, characters, and situations not found in reality. Whatever changes the author introduces, however, are based on real science. This passage from Asimov's story describes an unreal setting and situation:

> "What do you know of the data Multivac had to use: predigested from a hundred subsidiary computers here on Earth, on the Moon, on Mars, even on Titan. . . ."

In addition to the names of actual planets and moons that Asimov cites, notice how many of the details in "The Machine That Won the War" combine imagination with scientific fact.

Connecting Literary Elements

A story's **setting** is the time and place in which the action occurs. In science fiction, the setting may be

- an alternative past.
- an altered present.
- a possible future.

Many details of Asimov's story suggest that it is set in a possible future.

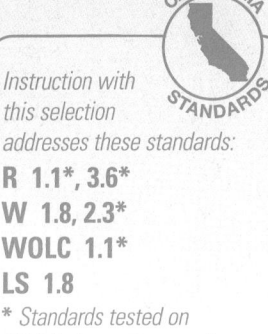

CALIFORNIA STANDARDS

Instruction with this selection addresses these standards:

R 1.1*, 3.6*
W 1.8, 2.3*
WOLC 1.1*
LS 1.8

* *Standards tested on HS Exit Exam. For complete standards, see p. CA 4.*

Reading Strategy

Identifying Relevant Details

Relevant details are those descriptions or events that are important in helping you understand the plot, characters, and setting of a story. Asimov's story mentions computers on the Moon, Mars, and Titan. These details are relevant because they make it clear that the setting is in the future.

Use a chart like the one shown to record specific details about characters, setting, technology, or the war found in the story, and explain why each is relevant.

Details	Relevance

Vocabulary Development

erratic (er rat´ ik) *adj.* irregular; random (p. 457)

grisly (griz´ lē) *adj.* horrifying; gruesome (p. 457)

imperturbable (im´ pər tur´ bə bəl) *adj.* unable to be excited or disturbed (p. 457)

oracle (ôr´ ə kəl) *n.* source of knowledge or wise counsel (p. 457)

surcease (sur sēs´) *n.* end (p. 459)

subsidiary (səb sid´ ē er´ ē) *adj.* secondary; supporting (p. 459)

circumvent (sur kəm vent´) *v.* avoid; go around (p. 460)

The Machine That Won the War

Isaac Asimov

The celebration had a long way to go and even in the silent depths of Multivac's underground chambers, it hung in the air.

If nothing else, there was the mere fact of isolation and silence. For the first time in a decade, technicians were not scurrying about the vitals of the giant computer, the soft lights did not wink out their <u>erratic</u> patterns, the flow of information in and out had halted.

It would not be halted long, of course, for the needs of peace would be pressing. Yet now, for a day, perhaps for a week, even Multivac might celebrate the great time, and rest.

Lamar Swift took off the military cap he was wearing and looked down the long and empty main corridor of the enormous computer. He sat down rather wearily in one of the technician's swing-stools, and his uniform, in which he had never been comfortable, took on a heavy and wrinkled appearance.

He said, "I'll miss it all after a <u>grisly</u> fashion. It's hard to remember when we weren't at war with Deneb, and it seems against nature now to be at peace and to look at the stars without anxiety."

The two men with the Executive Director of the Solar Federation were both younger than Swift. Neither was as gray. Neither looked quite as tired.

John Henderson, thin-lipped and finding it hard to control the relief he felt in the midst of triumph, said, "They're destroyed! They're destroyed! It's what I keep saying to myself over and over and I still can't believe it. We all talked so much, over so many years, about the menace hanging over Earth and all its worlds, over every human being, and all the time it was true, every word of it. And now we're alive and it's the Denebians who are shattered and destroyed. They'll be no menace now, ever again."

"Thanks to Multivac," said Swift, with a quiet glance at the <u>imperturbable</u> Jablonsky, who through all the war had been Chief Interpreter of science's <u>oracle</u>. "Right, Max?"

Jablonsky shrugged. He said, "Well, that's what *they* say." His broad thumb moved in the direction of his right shoulder, aiming upward.

"Jealous, Max?"

"Because they're shouting for Multivac? Because Multivac is the big hero of mankind in this war?" Jablonsky's craggy face took on an air of suitable contempt. "What's that to me? Let Multivac be the machine that won the war, if it pleases them."

Henderson looked at the other two out of the corners of his eyes. In this short interlude that the three had instinctively sought out

erratic (er rat´ ik) *adj.* irregular; random

grisly (griz´ lē) *adj.* horrifying; gruesome

imperturbable (im´ pər tʉr´ bə bəl) *adj.* unable to be excited or disturbed

oracle (ôr´ ə kəl) *n.* source of knowledge or wise counsel

✓ Reading Check

Why are the characters enjoying a brief rest as the story begins?

The Machine That Won the War ◆ 457

▲ **Critical Viewing** What attraction might the night sky, as shown here, have for science-fiction writers? **[Hypothesize]**

in the one peaceful corner of a metropolis gone mad; in this entr'acte[1] between the dangers of war and the difficulties of peace; when, for one moment, they might all find <u>surcease</u>; he was conscious only of his weight of guilt.

Suddenly, it was as though that weight were too great to be borne longer. It had to be thrown off, along with the war; now!

Henderson said, "Multivac had nothing to do with victory. It's just a machine."

"A big one," said Swift.

"Then just a big machine. No better than the data fed it." For a moment, he stopped, suddenly unnerved at what he was saying.

Jablonsky looked at him. "You should know. You supplied the data. Or is it just that you're taking the credit?"

"*No*," said Henderson angrily. "There is no credit. What do you know of the data Multivac had to use: predigested from a hundred <u>subsidiary</u> computers here on Earth, on the Moon, on Mars, even on Titan. With Titan always delayed and always feeling that its figures would introduce an unexpected bias."

"It would drive anyone mad," said Swift, with gentle sympathy.

Henderson shook his head. "It wasn't just that. I admit that eight years ago when I replaced Lepont as Chief Programmer, I was nervous. But there was an exhilaration about things in those days. The war was still long range; an adventure without real danger. We hadn't reached the point where manned vessels had had to take over and where interstellar warps could swallow up a planet clean, if aimed correctly. But then, when the real difficulties began—"

Angrily—he could finally permit anger—he said, "You know nothing about it."

"Well," said Swift. "Tell us. The war is over. We've won."

"Yes." Henderson nodded his head. He had to remember that. Earth had won, so all had been for the best. "Well, the data became meaningless."

"Meaningless? You mean that literally?" said Jablonsky.

"Literally. What would you expect? The trouble with you two was that you weren't out in the thick of it. You never left Multivac, Max, and you, Mr. Director, never left the Mansion except on state visits where you saw exactly what they wanted you to see."

"I was not as unaware of that," said Swift, "as you may have thought."

"Do you know," said Henderson, "to what extent data concerning our production capacity, our resource potential, our trained manpower—everything of importance to the war effort, in fact—had become unreliable and untrustworthy during the last half of the war? Group leaders, both civilian and military, were intent on projecting their own improved image, so to speak, so they obscured the bad and magnified the good. Whatever the machines might do, the men who programmed

_____

1. entr'acte (än trakt′) *n.* interval.

---

surcease (sʉr′ sēs′) *n.* end

subsidiary (səb sid′ ē er′ ē) *adj.* secondary; supporting

Reading Strategy
Identifying Relevant Details Which details in this paragraph are relevant to helping you understand the plot?

**Reading Check**

What does Henderson say about Multivac's role in winning the war?

The Machine That Won the War ◆ 459

them and interpreted the results had their own skins to think of and competitors to stab. There was no way of stopping that. I tried, and failed."

"Of course," said Swift, in quiet consolation. "I can see that you would."

"Yet I presume you provided Multivac with data in your programming?" Jablonsky said. "You said nothing to us about unreliability."

"How could I tell you? And if I did, how could you afford to believe me?" demanded Henderson, savagely. "Our entire war effort was geared to Multivac. It was the one great weapon on our side, for the Denebians had nothing like it. What else kept up morale in the face of doom but the assurance that Multivac would always predict and <u>circumvent</u> any Denebian move, and would always direct and prevent the circumvention of our moves? Great Space, after our Spy-warp was blasted out of hyperspace we lacked any reliable Denebian data to feed Multivac and we didn't dare make *that* public."

"True enough," said Swift.

"Well, then," said Henderson, "if I told you the data was unreliable, what could you have done but replace me and refuse to believe me? I couldn't allow that."

"What did you do?" said Jablonsky.

"Since the war is won, I'll tell you what I did. I corrected the data."

"How?" asked Swift.

"Intuition, I presume. I juggled them till they looked right. At first, I hardly dared. I changed a bit here and there to correct what were obvious impossibilities. When the sky didn't collapse about us, I got braver. Toward the end, I scarcely cared. I just wrote out the necessary data as it was needed. I even had the Multivac Annex prepare data for me according to a private programming pattern I had devised for the purpose."

"Random figures?" said Jablonsky.

"Not at all. I introduced a number of necessary biases."

Jablonsky smiled, quite unexpectedly, his dark eyes sparkling behind the crinkling of the lower lids. "Three times a report was brought to me about unauthorized uses of the Annex, and I let it go each time. If it had mattered, I would have followed it up and spotted you, John, and found out what you were doing. But, of course, nothing about Multivac mattered in those days, so you got away with it."

"What do you mean, nothing mattered?" asked Henderson, suspiciously.

"Nothing did. I suppose if I had told you this at the time, it would have spared you your agony, but then if you had told me what you were doing, it would have spared me mine. What made you think Multivac was in working order, whatever the data you supplied it?"

"Not in working order?" said Swift.

"Not really. Not reliably. After all, where were my technicians in the last years of the war? I'll tell you, they were feeding computers on a thousand different space devices. They were gone! I had to make do

circumvent (sur′ kəm vent′) v. avoid; go around

Reading Strategy
Identifying Relevant Details What are the most relevant details in this paragraph?

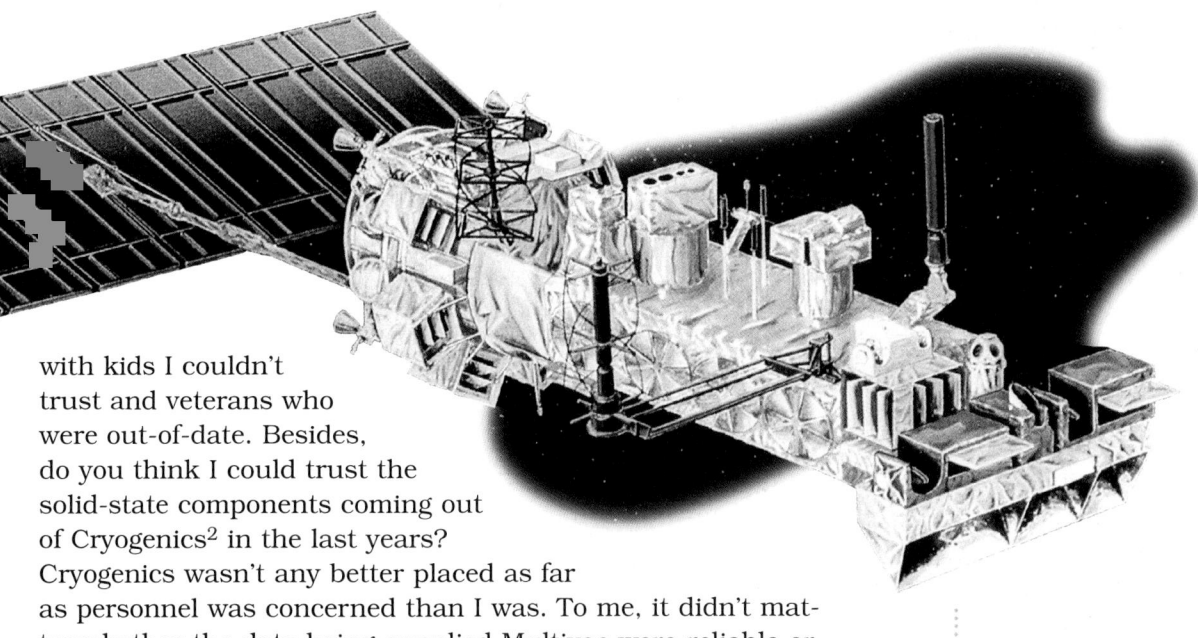

with kids I couldn't trust and veterans who were out-of-date. Besides, do you think I could trust the solid-state components coming out of Cryogenics[2] in the last years? Cryogenics wasn't any better placed as far as personnel was concerned than I was. To me, it didn't matter whether the data being supplied Multivac were reliable or not. The results weren't reliable. That much I knew."

"What did you do?" asked Henderson.

"I did what you did, John. I introduced the bugger factor. I adjusted matters in accordance with intuition—and that's how the machine won the war."

Swift leaned back in the chair and stretched his legs out before him. "Such revelations. It turns out then that the material handed me to guide me in my decision-making capacity was a man-made interpretation of man-made data. Isn't that right?"

"It looks so," said Jablonsky.

"Then I perceive I was correct in not placing too much reliance upon it," said Swift.

"You didn't?" Jablonsky, despite what he had just said, managed to look professionally insulted.

"I'm afraid I didn't. Multivac might seem to say, Strike here, not there; do this, not that; wait, don't act. But I could never be certain that what Multivac seemed to say, it really did say; or what it really said, it really meant. I could never be certain."

"But the final report was always plain enough, sir," said Jablonsky.

"To those who did not have to make the decision, perhaps. Not to me. The horror of the responsibility of such decisions was unbearable and not even Multivac was sufficient to remove the weight. But the point is I was justified in doubting and there is tremendous relief in that."

Caught up in the conspiracy of mutual confession, Jablonsky put titles aside. "What was it you did then, Lamar? After all, you did make decisions. How?"

---

2. **Cryogenics** (krī ō jen´ iks) here, a department concerned with the science of low-temperature phenomena.

✔**Reading Check**

What kind of data and interpretation of data were given to Swift during the war?

"Well, it's time to be getting back perhaps, but—I'll tell you first. Why not? I did make use of a computer, Max, but an older one than Multivac, much older."

He groped in his own pocket and brought out a scattering of small change; old-fashioned coins dating to the first years before the metal shortage had brought into being a credit system tied to a computer-complex.

Swift smiled rather sheepishly. "I still need these to make money seem substantial to me. An old man finds it hard to abandon the habits of youth." He dropped the coins, one by one, back into his pocket.

He held the last coin between his fingers, staring absently at it. "Multivac is not the first computer, friends, nor the best-known, nor the one that can most efficiently lift the load of decision from the shoulders of the executive. A machine *did* win the war, John; at least a very simple computing device did; one that I used every time I had a particularly hard decision to make."

With a faint smile of reminiscence, he flipped the coin he held. It glinted in the air as it spun and came down in Swift's outstretched palm. His hand closed over it and brought it down on the back of his left hand. His right hand remained in place, hiding the coin.

"Heads or tails, gentlemen?" said Swift.

Review and Assess

Thinking About the Selection

1. **Respond:** How did your opinion of Multivac change as you read the story?

2. **(a) Recall:** What is behind the celebration mentioned at the opening of the story? **(b) Connect:** Do the three men join in the celebratory mood? Explain.

3. **(a) Recall:** What are the job titles of the three men in the story? **(b) Compare and Contrast:** How are the men's jobs related yet different?

4. **(a) Recall:** What was Multivac's expected role in the war? **(b) Draw Conclusions:** What was its true role in the war?

5. **(a) Recall:** What did the men do to the data fed to Multivac? **(b) Deduce:** Did their actions make Multivac less reliable than Swift's "simple computing device"? Explain.

6. **Speculate:** If all three men had done their jobs properly, would the war's outcome have been different? Explain.

7. **Take a Position:** Do you think it is better to rely on information from humans or from computers? Why?

Isaac Asimov

(1920–1992)

Asimov came to the United States from Russia at the age of three. His parents spoke no English, but he taught himself to read the language before entering first grade.

Disliking the need to return library books and wanting a permanent library of his own, Asimov decided to write his own books. Overall, he wrote more than 470 books on subjects including science, history, Shakespeare, and the Bible, as well as science fiction, for which he is best known.

Some of his most famous works include *I Robot* (1950), the *Foundation* trilogy (1951–53), and *Fantastic Voyage* (1966), which was made into a movie.

Review and Assess

Literary Analysis

Science Fiction

1. In **science fiction,** some elements must be based on scientific ideas. Use a chart like this to classify key elements of the story.

Science-Based	Non-Science-Based

2. Which plot details indicate that the story is science fiction?
3. Could the characters in this story exist in real life? Why or why not?
4. Good science fiction carefully balances scientific and imaginative elements. Is this story good science fiction? Explain.

Connecting Literary Elements

5. Which details of time and place indicate that the story's **setting** is the future? Record your answers in a chart like the one below.

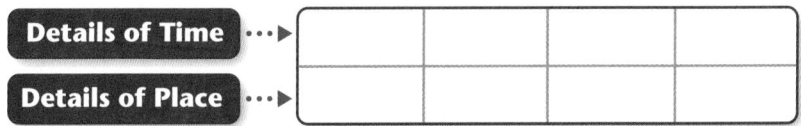

Details of Time				
Details of Place				

6. On the basis of what you know about the present and the past, does Asimov's future seem genuinely possible? Explain.
7. Could a story have the same setting as Asimov's and *not* be science fiction? Explain.

Reading Strategy

Identifying Relevant Details

8. In this story, the space program is both vast and advanced. (a) Find two details that support this statement. (b) Are these details **relevant** to the plot? Explain your answer.
9. (a) Which detail in the story shows how the monetary system in Asimov's future world differs from the present system? (b) Is the changed system relevant? Explain.

Extend Understanding

10. **Technology Connection:** Computers solve many—but not all—problems. Name areas where they are not useful now, and then speculate whether future computers might be useful in those areas.

Quick Review

Science fiction is a form of fiction in which the writer makes free use of imagination to create settings, characters, and situations not found in reality.

A story's **setting** is the time and place in which its action occurs.

To **identify relevant details,** find those that make the plot, characters, and setting understandable.

 Take It to the Net
www.phschool.com
Take the interactive self-test online to check your understanding of the selection.

Integrate Language Skills

Vocabulary Development Lesson

Word Analysis: Latin Prefix *circum-*

The Latin prefix *circum-* means "around." *Circumvent*, for instance, means "go around" or "avoid." Apply the meaning of *circum-* to define each word below. Then, use each word in a sentence.

1. circumference
2. circumscribe
3. circumstance
4. circumnavigate

Spelling Strategy

To add the suffix *-ly* to a word that ends in *-ic*, spell the suffix *-ally*. For example, *erratic* becomes *erratically*. (An exception to this rule is *publicly*.) Add *-ally* to the following adjectives to make them adverbs. Then, use each adverb in a sentence.

1. realistic
2. hectic
3. terrific

Concept Development: Synonyms

Choose the letter of the word or phrase that has the same meaning as the first word.

1. erratic: (a) slow, (b) random, (c) rapid
2. grisly: (a) private, (b) oily, (c) horrifying
3. imperturbable: (a) unexcitable, (b) increasing, (c) unhappy
4. oracle: (a) wise person, (b) loyal pet, (c) generous host
5. surcease: (a) a beginning, (b) an overabundance, (c) an end
6. subsidiary: (a) foremost, (b) subsiding, (c) secondary
7. circumvent: (a) avoid, (b) encourage, (c) reward

Grammar Lesson

Adverb Clauses and Noun Clauses

A **subordinate clause** is a group of words with a subject and verb that cannot stand alone as a sentence. An **adverb clause** is a subordinate clause that modifies a verb, an adjective, or an adverb. It tells *where, when, why, how,* or *to what extent*.

> **Adverb Clause:** Swift was surprised *when he heard the news.* (modifies the adjective *surprised* by telling *when*)

A **noun clause** is a subordinate clause that acts as a noun.

> **Noun Clause:** The decision was *whether they should trust Multivac.* (acts as predicate nominative)

Practice Identify the subordinate clause in each sentence, and tell whether it functions as an adverb clause or a noun clause.

1. The three men confessed after the war ended.
2. Each man's secret was that he had changed the rules.
3. Multivac was valuable if it was used right.
4. The computer didn't know that it was a hero.
5. Swift tossed a coin before he made a decision.

Writing Application "Since the war is won, I'll tell you what I did." Using this sentence as a model, write two original sentences that incorporate both an adverb clause and a noun clause.

 Prentice Hall Writing and Grammar Connection: Chapter 21, Section 2

Writing Lesson

Newspaper Story

Write a newspaper story about the end of the war between Earth and Deneb. Use references from "The Machine That Won the War" and your own ideas to explain what the war was about and what the victory might mean for Earthlings.

Prewriting Start by jotting down answers to the five W's—*who, what, where, when,* and *why*. Then, plan an attention-grabbing headline.

Drafting Begin your news story with a striking lead sentence that captures the effect the war has had on both Earthlings and Denebians. As you write the body of your article, make sure that each of the questions is addressed and answered.

Model: Writing an Attention-Grabbing Lead

After a ten-year struggle, Earth is at peace.
Denebians are no longer a threat, and Earthlings
must now begin to rebuild a planet shattered by war.

> Words like *struggle, peace, threat,* and *shattered* immediately grab the reader's attention.

Revising Ask a classmate to read your draft aloud to you. As you listen, consider which scenes are unclear, and then provide further elaboration.

WG Prentice Hall Writing and Grammar Connection: Chapter 13, Section 3

Extension Activities

Listening and Speaking In Asimov's story, the three main characters relied on intuition to adjust the data fed to Multivac. In a small group, conduct a **discussion** on the role of intuition in any decision. Use these questions to guide you:

- When is it proper to ignore instructions and follow your instincts?
- When may using your intuition be the wrong thing to do?

Take notes on the points group members make. Then, use your notes to share a summary of the discussion with the class. **[Group Activity]**

Research and Technology Prepare an **illustrated report** on the history of computers, including an essay accompanied by drawings, photos, and magazine ads. Incorporate Asimov's Multivac into your writing, explaining how it compares to computers throughout history. Design and publish your illustrated report by using desktop software and graphic programs.

 **Take It to the Net** www.phschool.com

Go online for an additional research activity using the Internet.

In "The Machine That Won the War," Isaac Asimov depicts a world in which humans seem to have surrendered control to powerful computers. When Asimov was writing the story in 1961, popular culture was filled with conflicting impressions about the changes that technological progress would bring. In one way, it was evident from the explosion of new products and labor-saving devices that life would become easier. In contrast, there was a deep uneasiness about depending completely on new technology and losing control to automation. The deadly spiral of nuclear warfare was the most potent symbol of this fear, hanging over this Cold War period like an ominous cloud.

Fast-forward several decades to a routine flight on a commercial jet airliner transporting author Julia Alvarez. Commercial jet technology, while new in 1961, has been around long enough for most people to take their safety for granted. Those fears about depending on technology, however, are never far from the surface. An act of nature and a mechanical failure forced the writer Alvarez to rethink her relationship with technology and her fellow humans.

AHA MOMENT

Julia Alvarez

I was in the tiny bathroom in the back of the plane when I felt the slamming jolt, then the horrible swerve that threw me against the door. Oh, Lord, I thought, this is it! Somehow I managed to unbolt the door and scramble out. The flight attendants, already strapped in, waved wildly for me to sit down. As I lunged ahead toward my seat, passengers looked up at me with the stricken expression of creatures who know they are about to die.

"I think we got hit by lightning," the girl in the seat next to mine said. She was from a small town in east Texas, and this was only her second time on an airplane. She had won a trip to England by competing in a high school geography bee and was supposed to make a connecting flight when we landed in Newark.

In the next seat, at the window, sat a young businessman who had been confidently working. Now he looked worried—something that really worries me: when confident-looking businessmen look worried. The laptop was put away. "Something's not right," he said.

The pilot's voice came over the speaker. I heard vaguely through my fear, "Engine number two. . .hit. . .emergency landing. . .New Orleans." When he was done, the voice of a flight attendant came on, reminding us of the emergency procedures she had reviewed before takeoff. Of course I never paid attention to this drill, always figuring that if we ever got to the point where we needed to use life jackets, I would have already died of terror.

Now we began a roller-coaster ride through the thunderclouds. I was ready to faint, but when I saw the face of the girl next to me I pulled myself together. I reached for her hand and reassured her that we were going to make it. "What a story you're going to tell when you get home!" I said. "After this, London's going to seem like small potatoes."

"Yes, ma'am," she mumbled.

I wondered where I was getting my strength. Then I saw that my other hand was tightly held by a ringed hand. Someone was comforting *me*—a glamorous young woman across the aisle, the female equivalent of the confident businessman. She must have seen how scared I was and reached over.

"I tell you," she confided, "the problems I brought up on this plane with me sure don't seem real big right now." I loved her southern <u>drawl</u>, her <u>indiscriminate</u> use of perfume, her soulful squeezes. I was sure that even if I survived a plane crash, I'd have a couple of broken fingers from all the T.L.C.[1] "Are you okay?" she kept asking me.

Among the many feelings going through my head during those excruciating 20 minutes was pride—pride in how well everybody was behaving. No one panicked. No one screamed. As we jolted and screeched our way downward, I could hear small pockets of soothing conversation everywhere.

I thought of something I had heard a friend say about the wonderful gift his dying father had given the family: He had died peacefully, as if not to alarm any of them about an experience they would all have to go through someday.

And then—yes!—we landed safely. Outside on the ground, attendants and officials were waiting to transfer us to alternate flights. But we passengers clung together. We chatted about the lives we now felt blessed to be living, as difficult or rocky as they might be. The young

---

1. **T.L.C.** abbreviation for "Tender Loving Care"

What do the descriptions of passengers and their varied reactions show us about dependence on technology?

drawl (drôl) *n.* a slow speech pattern, characterized by prolonged vowels

indiscriminate (in´di skrim´ i nit) *adj.* ignoring standards of good taste

businessman <u>lamented</u> that he had not had a chance to buy his two little girls a present. An older woman offered him her box of expensive Lindt chocolates, still untouched, tied with a lovely bow. "I shouldn't be eating them anyhow," she said. My glamorous aisle mate took out her cell phone and passed it around to anyone who wanted to make a call to hear the reassuring voice of a loved one.

There was someone I wanted to call. Back in Vermont, my husband, Bill, was anticipating my arrival late that night. He had been complaining that he wasn't getting to see very much of me because of my book tour. That's why I had decided to take this particular flight—oh, yes, one of those stories! I had planned to surprise him by getting in a few hours early. Now I just wanted him to know I was okay and on my way.

When my name was finally called to board my new flight, I felt almost tearful to be parting from people whose lives had so intensely, if briefly, touched mine.

Even now, back on terra firma,[2] walking down a Vermont road, I sometimes hear an airplane and look up at that small, glinting piece of metal. I remember the passengers on that fateful, lucky flight and wish I could thank them for the many acts of kindness I witnessed and received. I am indebted to my fellow passengers and wish I could pay them back.

But then, remembering my aisle mate's hand clutching mine while I clutched the hand of the high school student, I feel struck by lightning all over again: The point is not to pay back kindness but to pass it on.

---

2. **terra firma** (ter´ə fur´mə) *n.* Latin phrase meaning "solid ground."

> **lamented** (lə ment´ id) *v.* expressed sorrow; regretted

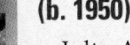

Julia Alvarez

(b. 1950)

Julia Alvarez immigrated to the United States from the Dominican Republic when she was ten years old. This sudden adjustment to an unfamiliar country with a strange language influenced her decision to write. ". . . I realized that language was going to be how I connected with these babbles. . . . Language was a portable homeland." Since this early realization, Alvarez has written several successful novels and volumes of poetry, in addition to teaching writing to college students, senior citizens, and bilingual students. Alvarez's work has been praised for its humor, sensitivity, and insight into the way people think and interact.

Connecting Literature Past and Present

1. How does Alvarez's story reflect the often hidden role technology plays in our lives?

2. Why do you think the passengers reacted the way they did when their plane was hit?

3. (a) How does the narrative reflect an "aha moment"? (b) In what ways might the experience change the writer's life? Explain.

4. (a) In what ways were the situations of the men in "The Machine That Won the War" and the passengers in the Alvarez story similar? (b) How did they differ?

5. What do both of these stories have to tell us about human faith in technology?

Prepare to Read

Fire and Ice ◆ "There Will Come Soft Rains" ◆ The Horses ◆ All Watched Over by Machines of Loving Grace

Wild Mustang, Red Desert, Wyoming

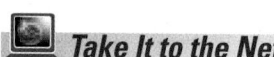 **Take It to the Net**

Visit www.phschool.com for interactive activities and instruction related to the selections, including

• background
• graphic organizers
• literary elements
• reading strategies

Preview

Connecting to the Literature

Is the world heading toward a gloomy destruction or a golden age of harmony? The poets in these four works explore their individual visions of the future. As you read the poems, consider your own ideas on the subject.

Background

Sara Teasdale's poem mentions "the war" without specifying which one. She and her husband both opposed World War I (1914–1918), even though their position was unpopular. Called at the time the Great War, it was the first one fought with machine guns, weapons that could spit out 600 to 700 bullets a minute. Soldiers on the battlefield knew that large numbers of them would be brutally cut down by machine-gun fire. The impersonality of this type of warfare horrified many.

Literary Analysis

Alliteration

Alliteration is the repetition of a consonant sound at the beginning of two or more words. Poets use this sound technique mainly to emphasize certain words but also to create musical effects and to help create a mood. In these lines from "The Horses," four words begin with *w*:

> We saw the heads
> Like a wild wave charging and were afraid.

The repetition of the sound draws attention to these words and their meaning. When read aloud, the words slow the reader's pace and suggest a sense of awe. Look for other examples of alliteration in the selections, and think about how it affects the poems' sound and meaning.

Comparing Literary Works

Each poem in this section presents a vision of the future. While one poem's vision may be more or less disturbing than another's, each poet sends a particular message or warning to people. Compare and contrast the visions presented in each poem. Decide whether a particular poem presents a hopeful, gloomy, or frightening vision of the future, and consider how effectively a message is conveyed.

Instruction with these selections addresses these standards:
R 1.1*, 3.7*, 3.8*, 3.11
W 1.2*
WOLC 1.1*
LS 1.8, 1.9
* Standards tested on HS Exit Exam. For complete standards, see p. CA 4.

Reading Strategy

Recognizing a Poet's Purpose

Each poem in this group calls attention to a troubling situation or attitude. To **recognize a poet's purpose,** or reason for writing a poem, read the work closely. Follow these suggestions:

- Look for the meaning behind the words in the poem.
- Note words that seem startling or jarring.
- Consider why the poet chose those specific words.

Use a chart like the one shown to note key details. Jot down the effects of each and determine the poet's purpose.

Key Words
perish
twice

Effects
surprising,
scary

Poet's Purpose

Vocabulary Development

perish (per´ ish) *v.* die (p. 472)

suffice (sə fīs´) *v.* be enough (p. 472)

tremulous (trem´ yōō ləs) *adj.* quivering (p. 473)

covenant (kuv´ ə nənt) *n.* agreement; pact (p. 474)

confounds (kən foundz´) *v.* bewilders; confuses (p. 474)

steeds (stēdz) *n.* horses (p. 475)

archaic (är kā´ ik) *adj.* seldom used; old-fashioned (p. 475)

Fire and Ice

Robert Frost

Some say the world will end in fire,
Some say in ice.
From what I've tasted of desire
I hold with those who favor fire.
5 But if it had to <u>perish</u> twice,
I think I know enough of hate
To say that for destruction ice
Is also great
And would <u>suffice</u>.

perish (per´ ish) *v.* die

suffice (sə fis´) *v.* be enough

Robert Frost

(1874–1963)

Like the title of his poem "Fire and Ice," Robert Frost seemed witty and warm to some, cold and bitter to others. All agreed, however, that poetry came first in his life. Frost is known for being the poet called upon to recite two poems at the inauguration of John F. Kennedy in 1961.

Frost produced a large body of work and became the most popular American poet of his time, winning four Pulitzer Prizes.

Review and Assess

Thinking About the Selection

1. **Respond:** How does the speaker's view of the future make you feel? Explain.
2. **(a) Recall:** With which opinion of the world's end does Frost first side? **(b) Interpret:** How might desire bring an end to the world?
3. **(a) Recall:** Why does Frost think the world might end in ice? **(b) Interpret:** In what way is ice a fitting metaphor for hatred?
4. **Assess:** How do the rhyming words affect the poem's mood?
5. **Speculate:** How have desire and hatred already affected the safety of people in the world?

"There Will Come Soft Rains"

(War Time)

Sara Teasdale

There will come soft rains and the smell of the ground,
And swallows circling with their shimmering sound;

And frogs in the pools singing at night,
And wild plum-trees in <u>tremulous</u> white;

5 Robins will wear their feathery fire
Whistling their whims on a low fence-wire;

And not one will know of the war, not one
Will care at last when it is done.

Not one would mind, neither bird nor tree
10 If mankind perished utterly;

And Spring herself, when she woke at dawn,
Would scarcely know that we were gone.

tremulous (trem´ yōo ləs)
adj. quivering

Review and Assess

Thinking About the Selection

1. **Respond:** Do you think that nature "has an attitude" toward humans, as this poem suggests? Explain.

2. **(a) Recall:** According to the poet, what will animals do after the war is over? **(b) Compare and Contrast:** How will the animals' fate differ from people's?

3. **Recall:** What will be Spring's reaction to human absence after the war? **(b) Generalize:** What theme about war does Spring's reaction, in combination with other details in the poem, suggest?

4. **Speculate:** Teasdale died before an even more destructive war broke out. What might her reaction have been to World War II?

Sara Teasdale

(1884–1933)

Sara Teasdale's poetry—much of it on the subject of love—was rooted in her own difficulties with personal relationships. Teasdale had a sad life and often expressed her sadness through poetry.

She once commented that "poems are written because of a state of emotional irritation" and that the poem "free[s] the poet from an emotional burden."

The Horses

Edwin Muir

Barely a twelvemonth after
The seven days war that put the world to sleep,
Late in the evening the strange horses came.
By then we had made our <u>covenant</u> with silence,
5 But in the first few days it was so still
We listened to our breathing and were afraid.
On the second day
The radios failed; we turned the knobs; no answer.
On the third day a warship passed us, heading north,
10 Dead bodies piled on the deck. On the sixth day
A plane plunged over us into the sea. Thereafter
Nothing. The radios dumb;
And still they stand in corners of our kitchens,
And stand, perhaps, turned on, in a million rooms
15 All over the world. But now if they should speak,
If on a sudden they should speak again,
If on the stroke of noon a voice should speak,
We would not listen, we would not let it bring
That old bad world that swallowed its children quick
20 At one great gulp. We would not have it again.
Sometimes we think of the nations lying asleep,
Curled blindly in impenetrable sorrow,
And then the thought <u>confounds</u> us with its strangeness.

The tractors lie about our fields; at evening
25 They look like dank sea-monsters couched and waiting.
We leave them where they are and let them rust:

covenant (kuv´ ə nənt) *n.*
agreement; pact

Literary Analysis
Alliteration What
examples of alliteration
do you see in line 20?

confounds (kən foundz´) *v.*
bewilders; confuses

▼ **Critical Viewing** In
what ways do these
horses compare to those
the poet describes?
[Connect]

'They'll moulder away and be like other loam'.[1]
We make our oxen drag our rusty ploughs,
Long laid aside. We have gone back
30 Far past our fathers' land.
                              And then, that evening
Late in the summer the strange horses came.
We heard a distant tapping on the road,
A deepening drumming; it stopped, went on again
35 And at the corner changed to hollow thunder.
We saw the heads
Like a wild wave charging and were afraid.
We had sold our horses in our fathers' time
To buy new tractors. Now they were strange to us
40 As fabulous <u>steeds</u> set on an ancient shield
Or illustrations in a book of knights.
We did not dare go near them. Yet they waited,
Stubborn and shy, as if they had been sent
By an old command to find our whereabouts
45 And that long-lost <u>archaic</u> companionship.
In the first moment we had never a thought
That they were creatures to be owned and used.
Among them were some half-a-dozen colts
Dropped in some wilderness of the broken world,
50 Yet new as if they had come from their own Eden.[2]
Since then they have pulled our ploughs and borne our loads,
But that free servitude still can pierce our hearts.
Our life is changed; their coming our beginning.

steeds (stēdz) n. horses

archaic (är kā´ ik) adj. seldom used; old-fashioned

---

1. **loam** (lōm) n. dark, rich soil.
2. **Eden** in the Bible, the garden where life began with Adam and Eve; paradise.

Review and Assess

Thinking About the Selection

1. **Respond:** How did the arrival of the horses in the poem make you feel? Explain.

2. **(a) Recall:** What has been the result of the "seven days war"? **(b) Support:** What words led you to this opinion?

3. **(a) Recall:** What did the "old bad world" do to its children? **(b) Analyze:** Is this event a sufficient explanation for the sorrow and confusion the speaker refers to?

4. **(a) Recall:** What has happened to the tractors? **(b) Interpret:** Why are the tractors and the horses placed side by side?

5. **Speculate:** Do you see any reason to believe that the note of hope the speaker associates with the horses' arrival will survive into the future? Explain your response.

Edwin Muir

(1887–1959)

A prolific writer who produced many volumes of poetry and several novels, Muir had visions of the future that were rooted in his past. He spent his first fourteen years on a farm in the Orkney Islands north of the Scottish mainland. Much of his imagery comes from this place.

Integrate Language Skills

Vocabulary Development Lesson

Word Analysis: Latin Suffix -ous

The Latin suffix -ous means "full of" or "characterized by," as in the word *tremulous*, which means "characterized by trembling." Match each word below with its definition.

1. perilous **2.** courageous **3.** clamorous

a. characterized by bravery

b. noisy; loud; marked by vehemence

c. risky; full of danger

Spelling Strategy

If a word ends in a vowel-vowel-consonant combination, do not double the consonant before adding a suffix. For example, *archaic* + *-ally* = *archaically*. Add *-ness*, *-ance*, or *-al* to each word below to form a properly spelled new word.

1. tremulous **2.** avoid **3.** stoic

Concept Development: Synonyms

Identify the word that is a synonym for, or is closest in meaning to, each word from the vocabulary list on page 471.

1. perish: (a) live, (b) die, (c) decide

2. suffice: (a) help, (b) satisfy, (c) mistake

3. steeds: (a) rewards, (b) cattle, (c) horses

4. confounds: (a) irritates, (b) surprises, (c) confuses

5. tremulous: (a) quivering, (b) huge, (c) emotional

6. archaic: (a) curved, (b) simple, (c) old-fashioned

7. covenant: (a) church, (b) argument, (c) agreement

Grammar Lesson

Adjective Clauses

A **subordinate clause** is a group of words with a subject and verb that cannot stand on its own in a sentence.

An **adjective clause** is a subordinate clause that modifies a noun or pronoun by answering the question *what kind?* or *which one?* It is usually introduced by a **relative pronoun,** such as *who, whom, whose, which,* or *that,* or by a **conjunction,** such as *where, when,* or *why.*

In this example, the adjective clause is underlined and the noun it modifies is in italics.

> **Example:** I see a *meadow* <u>where they live together.</u> (which *meadow*?)

Practice Write each sentence on your paper. Underline the adjective clauses and circle the word that each one modifies.

1. It was a seven days war that put the world to sleep.

2. There was a time when people used tractors.

3. I hold with those who favor fire.

4. We saw the horses, which could help us with our labor.

5. Listen to the plains where robins whistle.

Writing Application Write a short paragraph about the poem you liked best. Use at least three adjective clauses in your paragraph.

W͜G Prentice Hall Writing and Grammar Connection: Chapter 21, Section 2

Writing Lesson

Poem to a Future Generation

The poems in this section describe the future in order to make you think critically about the present. Write a short poem that describes the positive aspects of today's world for people of the future.

Prewriting   Decide on a positive message. Then, make a list of images drawn from the present-day world that will help convey your message. Try to use words that create alliteration and convey a particular mood.

Drafting   Use precise language and sensory details to present a clear picture of the present. Make sure that you present each image in as few words as possible.

Revising   As you discuss your poem with a classmate, highlight any words that do not create a clear picture or do not seem necessary. Consider rephrasing for clarity or eliminating the unnecessary words.

Model: Rephrasing to Clarify an Image

awash in silvery	
The sky was ~~streaming with a beautiful~~ light,	Precise adjectives like *silvery* and *somber* help build and clarify the images while keeping them forceful and brief.
the somber ravens soared	
As we sat in silence, ~~watching the birds overhead.~~	

W̶G̶ Prentice Hall Writing and Grammar Connection: Chapter 6, Section 4

Extension Activities

Listening and Speaking Prepare and present a **dramatic reading** of "Fire and Ice," "All Watched Over by Machines of Loving Grace," or "There Will Come Soft Rains."

- Concentrate on your tone of voice and use of facial expressions to express meaning.
- Practice making eye contact with your audience.

Videotape your rehearsal for later review, or practice in front of a mirror. After presenting, invite listeners to comment on the effectiveness of your reading.

Research and Technology Watch a video or TV program set in the future. As you watch, jot down some specific futuristic elements at work. As a participant in a **panel discussion,** discuss whether the program presents a positive or negative vision of the future. Then, compare this vision to the visions of the poems in this section. **[Group Activity]**

 **Take It to the Net**   www.phschool.com

Go online for an additional research activity using the Internet.

Product Information

About Product Information

Product information is printed material that comes packaged with a manufactured item. Two common types of product information are **technical directions** and **warranties.**

- Technical directions explain the safe, proper, and efficient uses of a product and may include diagrams to help convey information.
- Warranties explain the contractual obligations between a consumer and the manufacturer.

You might find these printed features after opening a new item such as a camera, computer, or calculator.

Reading Strategy

Analyzing the Purpose of Product Information

To get the most out of product information, you need to know where to locate the information you want.

Technical directions offer step-by-step instructions for using the item. They may explain procedures such as the following:

- How to assemble the item
- How to turn the item on and off
- How to operate specific features

A **warranty** explains what the manufacturer agrees to provide the consumer in terms of service and maintenance. It may tell, for example, how long the manufacturer will repair a part at no additional charge. Often, the consumer must mail in a signed warranty card to the manufacturer in order for the agreement to become effective.

As you read product information, check to see that it contains the features and purposes outlined in the chart below.

Product Information	Features	Purpose
Technical directions	• Assembling, operating, maintenance instructions • Informal language	Explains how to assemble, use, and protect the merchandise
Warranty	• Charts or graphs • Printed contract between manufacturer and user • Formal language	Details manufacturer's service obligation to user

Technical Directions

Following are technical directions for using a graphing calculator. The product manual, included with the purchase, outlines the procedures for a variety of calculating functions. The directions on this page specifically offer step-by-step instructions for displaying and tracing a graph. They assume the user has a basic knowledge of the calculator.

> The heading conveniently indicates the function being explained.

DISPLAYING AND TRACING THE GRAPH

Now that you have defined the function to be graphed and the WINDOW in which to graph it, you can display and explore the graph. You can trace along a function with TRACE.

---

1. Press **GRAPH** to graph the selected function in the viewing **WINDOW**.

   The graph of Y₁=(W–2X)(L/2–X)X is shown in the display.

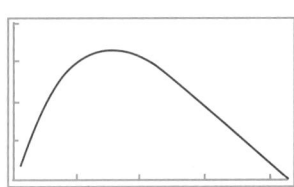

2. Press ▶ once to display the free-moving graph cursor just to the right of the center of the screen. The bottom line of the display shows the **X** and **Y** coordinate values for the position of the graph cursor.

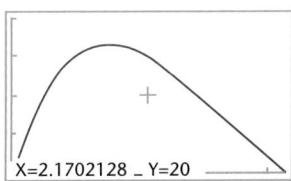

> The directions provide visual aids to accompany the instructional text.

3. Use the cursor-keys (◀, ▶, ▲ and ▼) to position the free-moving cursor at the apparent maximum of the function.

   As you move the cursor, **X** and **Y** coordinate values are updated continually with the cursor position.

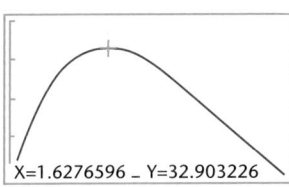

> Directions are numbered to show the user the exact order of the steps.

4. Press **TRACE**. The **TRACE** cursor appears on the Y₁ function near the middle of the screen. 1 in the upper right corner of the display shows that the cursor is on Y₁. As you press ◀ and ▶, you TRACE along Y₁, one **X** dot at a time, evaluating Y₁ at each **X**.

   Press ◀ and ▶ until you are on the maximum **Y** value. This is the maximum of Y₁(X) for the **X** pixels. (There may be a maximum "in between" pixels.)

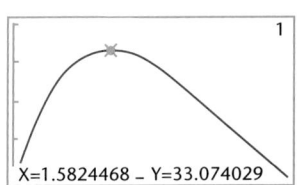

> These directions assume a certain level of knowledge, using vocabulary that is not defined in the instructions.

One-Year Limited Warranty

The warranty below is included in the product manual for the graphing calculator. Its language outlines the manufacturer's and the consumer's responsibilities. The warranty also explains the process a consumer should follow to get the product repaired.

The warranty specifies the person or persons covered by this agreement.

Subheads help the user locate specific conditions in the agreement.

The agreement states, in detail, what the manufacturer promises the consumer.

One-Year Limited Warranty

This electronic calculator warranty extends to the original consumer purchaser of the product.

Warranty Duration

This calculator is warranted to the original consumer purchaser for a period of one (1) year from the original purchase date.

Warranty Coverage

This calculator is warranted against defective materials or workmanship. This warranty is void if the product has been damaged by accident, unreasonable use, neglect, improper service, or other causes not arising out of defects in material or workmanship.

Warranty Disclaimers

Any implied warranties arising out of this sale, including but not limited to the implied warranties of merchantability and fitness for a particular purpose, are limited in duration to the above one-year period. This company shall not be liable for loss of use of the calculator or other incidental or consequential costs, expenses, or damages incurred by the consumer or any other user.

Some states do not allow the exclusion or limitations of implied warranties or consequential damages, so the above limitations or exclusions may not apply to you.

Legal Remedies

This warranty gives you specific legal rights, and you may also have other rights that vary from state to state.

Warranty Performance

During the above one-year warranty period, a defective calculator will either be repaired or replaced with a reconditioned comparable model when the product is returned, postage prepaid, to a service facility.

The repaired or replacement calculator will be in warranty for the remainder of the original warranty period or for six months, whichever is longer. Other than the postage requirement, no charge will be made for such repair or replacement.

It is strongly recommended that you insure the product for value prior to mailing.

Check Your Comprehension

1. What is the first thing you must do in order to graph the selected function in the viewing window?
2. How long does the warranty on this graphing calculator last?
3. Who must pay the postage when a damaged calculator is shipped to a service facility for repair?

Applying the Reading Strategy

Analyzing Purpose of Product Information

4. What purpose do the technical directions serve for the consumer?
5. Why do the technical directions include visuals?
6. Why would it be necessary for the manufacturer to have verification of the calculator's purchase date?
7. Why does the manufacturer recommend insuring the product prior to mailing?

Activity

Using Information From Consumer Documents

Find the product information that accompanies a product such as a VCR or a digital alarm clock. Read the manufacturer's technical directions and warranty. Use the chart below to record the three important pieces of information from each document. Explain their importance.

Product Information for _____		
	Key Information	Reasons
Technical Directions		
Warranty		

Contrasting Informational Materials

Product Information, Advertisements, and Consumer Articles

1. Technical directions and warranties are two types of product information. Advertisements are also a kind of product information since they, too, offer details about a product. However, an advertisement does not share the same purpose or language as technical directions or a warranty. Explain the differences in purpose and language between (a) technical directions and an advertisement, and (b) a warranty and an advertisement.
2. Find a product review in a magazine such as *Consumer Reports*. Explain how the purpose and language of the review differ from those found in technical directions and a warranty.

Prepare to Read

"If I Forget Thee, Oh Earth . . ." ◆ *from* Silent Spring ◆ To the Residents of A.D. 2029

 Take It to the Net

Visit www.phschool.com for interactive activities and instruction related to the selections, including
- background
- graphic organizers
- literary elements
- reading strategies

Preview

Connecting to the Literature

Perhaps you are aware of local dangers to the environment and of individuals or groups that are seeking to correct them. In these selections, the authors encourage readers to think about environmental problems and their solutions.

Background

Many environmentalists today are concerned with the ozone layer, which shields Earth from 95 to 99 percent of the sun's harmful ultraviolet rays. Since the mid-1970s, scientists have worried about a breakdown in the ozone layer caused by the use of CFCs found in aerosol sprays and refrigerants. Environmental scientists continue to monitor the situation.

Literary Analysis

Persuasive Appeal

A **persuasive appeal** is an urgent appeal or warning that aims to convince the reader to think or act in a certain way. A persuasive appeal may exist in fiction or nonfiction, and it may be stated or implied. In this excerpt from *Silent Spring*, Rachel Carson warns how the indiscriminate use of pesticides threatens our environment:

> Then a strange blight crept over the area and everything began to change . . . mysterious maladies swept the flocks of chickens; the cattle and sheep sickened and died.

As you read, find other warnings about environmental conditions.

Comparing Literary Works

The writers of these selections use **imagery**, or descriptive language, to create pictures in the reader's mind. Imagery is intended to appeal to one or more of the senses—sight, hearing, touch, taste, or smell. Compare the imagery in each selection, and decide how it strengthens the warning.

CALIFORNIA STANDARDS

Instruction with these selections addresses these standards:

R 1.1*, 3.7*, 3.8*, 3.9*
W 2.3*, 2.6
WOLC 1.3*
LS 1.5

* Standards tested on HS Exit Exam. For complete standards, see p. CA 4.

Reading Strategy

Distinguishing Between Fact and Opinion

When you read literature that makes a persuasive appeal, it is important to distinguish between fact and opinion. A **fact** is a statement that can be proved, or tested for accuracy. An **opinion** is a statement of personal preference and cannot be proved. Look at the following examples from "To the Residents of A.D. 2029."

Fact: Parts of our land are overcrowded, parts neglected, parts abused, parts destroyed.

Opinion: Our present disrespect for the natural world is our most serious stupidity to date.

Use a chart like this one to separate facts from opinions as you read.

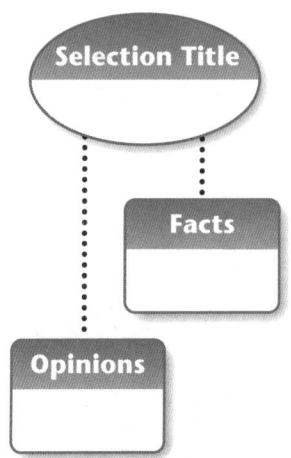

Selection Title

Facts

Opinions

Vocabulary Development

purged (purjd) *v.* cleansed (p. 487)

pyre (pīr) *n.* pile of wood on which a body is burned at a funeral (p. 489)

perennial (pər en´ ē əl) *adj.* constant (p. 489)

blight (blīt) *n.* something that destroys or prevents growth (p. 492)

moribund (môr´ i bund´) *adj.* dying (p. 493)

postulated (päs´ chə lāt´ ed) *v.* claimed (p. 497)

beleaguered (bē lē´ gərd) *adj.* worried; tormented (p. 498)

schism (siz´ əm) *n.* division (p. 498)

"If I Forget Thee, Oh Earth..."

Arthur C. Clarke

W hen Marvin was ten years old, his father took him through the long, echoing corridors that led up through Administration and Power, until at last they came to the uppermost levels of all and were among the swiftly growing vegetation of the Farmlands. Marvin liked it here: it was fun watching the great, slender plants creeping with almost visible eagerness toward the sunlight as it filtered down through the plastic domes to meet them. The smell of life was everywhere, awakening inexpressible longings in his heart: no longer was he breathing the dry, cool air of the residential levels, <u>purged</u> of all smells but the faint tang of ozone.1 He wished he could stay here for a little while, but Father would not let him. They went onward until they had reached the entrance to the Observatory, which he had never visited: but they did not stop, and Marvin knew with a sense of rising excitement that there could be only one goal left. For the first time in his life, he was going Outside.

There were a dozen of the surface vehicles, with their wide balloon tires and pressurized cabins, in the great servicing chamber. His father must have been expected, for they were led at once to the little scout car waiting by the huge circular door of the airlock. Tense with expectancy, Marvin settled himself down in the cramped cabin while his father started the motor and checked the controls. The inner door of the lock slid open and then closed behind them: he heard the roar of the great air pumps fade slowly away as the pressure dropped to zero. Then the "Vacuum" sign flashed on, the outer door parted, and before Marvin lay the land which he had never yet entered.

He had seen it in photographs, of course: he had watched it imaged on television screens a hundred times. But now it was lying all around him, burning beneath the fierce sun that crawled so slowly across the jet-black sky. He stared into the west, away from the blinding splendor of the sun—and there were the stars, as he had been told but had never quite believed. He gazed at them for a long time, marveling that anything could be so bright and yet so tiny. They were intense unscintillating points, and suddenly he remembered a rhyme he had once read in one of his father's books:

Twinkle, twinkle, little star,
How I wonder what you are.

Well, *he* knew what the stars were. Whoever asked that question must have been very stupid. And what did they mean by "twinkle"? You could see at a glance that all the stars shone with the same steady, unwavering light. He abandoned the puzzle and turned his attention to the landscape around him.

---

1. ozone (ō´ zōn) *n.* form of oxygen with a sharp odor.

purged (pʉrjd) *v.* cleansed

Reading Strategy
Distinguishing Between Fact and Opinion Is the statement "They were intense unscintillating points" a fact or an opinion? Explain.

✔**Reading Check**
Where is Marvin going for the first time in his life?

They were racing across a level plain at almost a hundred miles an hour, the great balloon tires sending up little spurts of dust behind them. There was no sign of the Colony: in the few minutes while he had been gazing at the stars, its domes and radio towers had fallen below the horizon. Yet there were other indications of man's presence, for about a mile ahead Marvin could see the curiously shaped structures clustering round the head of a mine. Now and then a puff of vapor would emerge from a squat smokestack and would instantly disperse.

They were past the mine in a moment: Father was driving with a reckless and exhilarating skill as if—it was a strange thought to come into a child's mind—he were trying to escape from something. In a few minutes they had reached the edge of the plateau on which the Colony had been built. The ground fell sharply away beneath them in a dizzying slope whose lower stretches were lost in shadow. Ahead, as far as the eye could reach, was a jumbled wasteland of craters, mountain ranges, and ravines. The crests of the mountains, catching the low sun, burned like islands of fire in a sea of darkness: and above them the stars still shone as steadfastly as ever.

There could be no way forward—yet there was. Marvin clenched his fists as the car edged over the slope and started the long descent. Then he saw the barely visible track leading down the mountainside, and relaxed a little. Other men, it seemed, had gone this way before.

Night fell with a shocking abruptness as they crossed the shadow line and the sun dropped below the crest of the plateau. The twin searchlights sprang into life, casting blue-white bands on the rocks ahead, so that there was scarcely need to check their speed. For hours they drove through valleys and past the foot of mountains whose peaks seemed to comb the stars, and sometimes they emerged for a moment into the sunlight as they climbed over higher ground.

And now on the right was a wrinkled, dusty plain, and on the left, its ramparts and terraces rising mile after mile into the sky, was a wall of mountains that marched into the distance until its peaks sank from sight below the rim of the world. There was no sign that men had ever explored this land, but once they passed the skeleton of a crashed rocket, and beside it a stone cairn[2] surmounted by a metal cross.

It seemed to Marvin that the mountains stretched on forever: but at last, many hours later, the range ended in a towering, precipitous headland[3] that rose steeply from a cluster of little hills. They drove down into a shallow valley that curved in a great arc toward the far side of the mountains: and as they did so, Marvin slowly realized that something very strange was happening in the land ahead.

The sun was now low behind the hills on the right: the valley before them should be in total darkness. Yet it was awash with a cold white

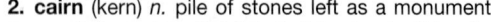

2. **cairn** (kern) *n.* pile of stones left as a monument.
3. **precipitous headland** (prē sip′ ə təs hed′ land) steep cliff.

radiance that came spilling over the crags beneath which they were driving. Then, suddenly, they were out in the open plain, and the source of the light lay before them in all its glory.

It was very quiet in the little cabin now that the motors had stopped. The only sound was the faint whisper of the oxygen feed and an occasional metallic crepitation as the outer walls of the vehicle radiated away their heat. For no warmth at all came from the great silver crescent that floated low above the far horizon and flooded all this land with pearly light. It was so brilliant that minutes passed before Marvin could accept its challenge and look steadfastly into its glare, but at last he could discern the outlines of continents, the hazy border of the atmosphere, and the white islands of cloud. And even at this distance, he could see the glitter of sunlight on the polar ice.

It was beautiful, and it called to his heart across the abyss of space. There in that shining crescent were all the wonders that he had never known—the hues of sunset skies, the moaning of the sea on pebbled shores, the patter of falling rain, the unhurried benison of snow. These and a thousand others should have been his rightful heritage, but he knew them only from the books and ancient records, and the thought filled him with the anguish of exile.

Why could they not return? It seemed so peaceful beneath those lines of marching cloud. Then Marvin, his eyes no longer blinded by the glare, saw that the portion of the disk that should have been in darkness was gleaming faintly with an evil phosphorescence:[4] and he remembered. He was looking upon the funeral <u>pyre</u> of a world—upon the radioactive aftermath of Armageddon.[5] Across a quarter of a million miles of space, the glow of dying atoms was still visible, a <u>perennial</u> reminder of the ruinous past. It would be centuries yet before that deadly glow died from the rocks and life could return again to fill that silent, empty world.

And now Father began to speak, telling Marvin the story which until this moment had meant no more to him than the fairy tales he had once been told. There were many things he could not understand: it was impossible for him to picture the glowing, multicolored pattern of life on the planet he had never seen. Nor could he comprehend the forces that had destroyed it in the end, leaving the Colony, preserved by its isolation, as the sole survivor. Yet he could share the agony of those final days, when the Colony had learned at last that never again would the supply ships come flaming down through the stars with gifts from home. One by one the radio stations had ceased to call: on the shadowed globe the lights of the cities had dimmed and died, and they were alone at last, as no men had ever been alone before, carrying in their hands the future of the race.

Then had followed the years of despair, and the long-drawn battle

---

4. **phosphorescence** (fäs′ fə res′ əns) *n.* emission of light resulting from exposure to radiation.
5. **Armageddon** (är′ mə ged′ ən) *n.* in the Bible, the place where the final battle between good and evil is to be fought.

Literary Analysis
Persuasive Appeal What warning is implied in this description of Earth?

pyre (pīr) *n.* pile of wood on which a body is burned at a funeral

perennial (pə ren′ ē əl) *adj.* constant

**Reading Check**
What does Marvin realize he is seeing?

for survival in their fierce and hostile world. That battle had been won, though barely: this little oasis of life was safe against the worst that Nature could do. But unless there was a goal, a future toward which it could work, the Colony would lose the will to live, and neither machines nor skill nor science could save it then.

So, at last, Marvin understood the purpose of this pilgrimage. He would never walk beside the rivers of that lost and legendary world, or listen to the thunder raging above its softly rounded hills. Yet one day—how far ahead?—his children's children would return to claim their heritage. The winds and the rains would scour the poisons from the burning lands and carry them to the sea, and in the depths of the sea they would waste their venom until they could harm no living things. Then the great ships that were still waiting here on the silent, dusty plains could lift once more into space, along the road that led to home.

That was the dream: and one day, Marvin knew with a sudden flash of insight, he would pass it on to his own son, here at this same spot with the mountains behind him and the silver light from the sky streaming into his face.

He did not look back as they began the homeward journey. He could not bear to see the cold glory of the crescent Earth fade from the rocks around him, as he went to rejoin his people in their long exile.

Reading Strategy
Distinguishing Between Fact and Opinion Is the statement about the Colony's need for a goal a fact or an opinion? Explain.

Arthur C. Clarke

(b. 1917)

For more than fifty years, Arthur C. Clarke has been turning out exceptional works of fiction and nonfiction. A child of Somerset, England, he wrote his first science-fiction stories during his teens.

Of more than fifty works, Clarke's most famous is his collaboration with film director Stanley Kubrick on the screenplay for *2001: A Space Odyssey*. Equally distinguished is Clarke's nonfiction. In a 1945 essay, he predicted the development of communications satellites long before they were a reality.

Review and Assess

Thinking About the Selection

1. **Respond:** Could you endure the kind of life that Marvin has with only the hope that some distant descendants could return to Earth? Explain.

2. **(a) Recall:** What rhyme does Marvin remember as he looks outside? **(b) Infer:** What evidence indicates that the story is set on the moon? **(c) Analyze:** How does the choice of setting make the story more realistic?

3. **(a) Recall:** At the end of the story, what does Marvin determine to do? **(b) Draw Conclusions:** What was the purpose of Marvin's trip with his father?

4. **(a) Infer:** How did Earth come to be destroyed? **(b) Extend:** What suggestions do you think Clark would make about how to prevent a situation like the one in the story from occurring?

from Silent Spring

Rachel Carson

There was once a town in the heart of America where all life seemed to live in harmony with its surroundings. The town lay in the midst of a checkerboard of prosperous farms, with fields of grain and hillsides of orchards where, in spring, white clouds of bloom drifted above the green fields. In autumn, oak and maple and birch set up a blaze of color that flamed and flickered across a backdrop of pines. Then foxes barked in the hills and deer silently crossed the fields, half hidden in the mists of the fall mornings.

Along the roads, laurel, viburnum and alder, great ferns and wild-flowers delighted the traveler's eye through much of the year. Even in winter the roadsides were places of beauty, where countless birds came to feed on the berries and on the seed heads of the dried weeds rising above the snow. The countryside was, in fact, famous for the abundance and variety of its bird life, and when the flood of migrants was pouring through in spring and fall people traveled from great distances to observe them. Others came to fish the streams, which flowed clear and cold out of the hills and contained shady pools where trout lay. So it had been from the days many years ago when the first settlers raised their houses, sank their wells, and built their barns.

Then a strange <u>blight</u> crept over the area and everything began to change. Some evil spell had settled on the community: mysterious maladies swept the flocks of chickens; the cattle and sheep sickened and died. Everywhere was a shadow of death. The farmers spoke of

blight (blīt) *n.* something that destroys or prevents growth

much illness among their families. In the town the doctors had become more and more puzzled by new kinds of sickness appearing among their patients. There had been several sudden and unexplained deaths, not only among adults but even among children, who would be stricken suddenly while at play and die within a few hours.

There was a strange stillness. The birds, for example—where had they gone? Many people spoke of them, puzzled and disturbed. The feeding stations in the backyards were deserted. The few birds seen anywhere were <u>moribund</u>; they trembled violently and could not fly. It was a spring without voices. On the mornings that had once throbbed with the dawn chorus of robins, catbirds, doves, jays, wrens, and scores of other bird voices there was now no sound; only silence lay over the fields and woods and marsh.

On the farms the hens brooded, but no chicks hatched. The farmers complained that they were unable to raise any pigs—the litters were small and the young survived only a few days. The apple trees

Literary Analysis
Persuasive Appeal What persuasive appeal does the author present in this paragraph?

moribund (môr´ i bund´) *adj.* dying

▼ **Critical Viewing**
What might the author think about the aerial spraying of crops to kill pests? **[Connect]**

were coming into bloom but no bees droned among the blossoms, so there was no pollination and there would be no fruit.

The roadsides, once so attractive, were now lined with browned and withered vegetation as though swept by fire. These, too, were silent, deserted by all living things. Even the streams were now lifeless. Anglers no longer visited them, for all the fish had died.

In the gutters under the eaves and between the shingles of the roofs, a white granular powder still showed a few patches; some weeks before it had fallen like snow upon the roofs and the lawns, the fields and streams.

No witchcraft, no enemy action had silenced the rebirth of new life in this stricken world. The people had done it themselves.

This town does not actually exist, but it might easily have a thousand counterparts in America or elsewhere in the world. I know of no community that has experienced all the misfortunes I describe. Yet every one of these disasters has actually happened somewhere, and many real communities have already suffered a substantial number of them. A grim specter has crept upon us almost unnoticed, and this imagined tragedy may easily become a stark reality we all shall know.

Review and Assess

Thinking About the Selection

1. **Respond:** Is Carson's technique of describing environmental problems in a fictional town effective? Explain.

2. **(a) Recall:** What is the condition of life at the beginning of Carson's story? **(b) Compare and Contrast:** How does the condition of life change as the story continues?

3. **(a) Recall:** What happens to the farm animals? **(b) Infer:** What causes this sudden change?

4. **(a) Recall:** What becomes of the vegetation in the town? **(b) Connect:** Why does the fate of the vegetation affect the fate of humans?

5. **(a) Recall:** What information about the town does Carson reveal at the end of her story? **(b) Speculate:** Would Carson's story have been more effective had the town been real? Why or why not?

6. **(a) Recall:** According to Carson, who caused the problem? **(b) Draw Conclusions:** What suggestions do you think Carson would make to humans?

7. **Apply:** Does a warning like Carson's motivate you to become more involved in environmental issues? Explain.

Rachel Carson

(1907–1964)

As a young woman, Rachel Carson studied writing at the Pennsylvania College for Women. A lifelong love of science and nature, however, caused her to change her field of study to marine biology. She was later able to pursue both fields by writing eloquently about nature.

Carson's widely praised book *The Sea Around Us* (1951) came out of her years as a biologist and editor at the United States Fish and Wildlife Service. Her most significant work was *Silent Spring* (1962), a chilling and well-documented warning about the dangers of pesticides. Before her book, few people understood the dangers of pollution or the interconnectedness of all life.

To the Residents of A.D. 2029

Bryan Woolley

Every writer's secret dream has been fulfilled for me. I know, as surely as anyone can know such things, that my works will be read fifty years from now. Well, one work, anyway.

This is because Collin County is about to dedicate a new courthouse and jail in McKinney, and somewhere in the vicinity of that structure the Collin County Historical Commission is going to bury a time capsule that will be opened in A.D. 2029, assuming that somebody's still around then, and that he can read. And I've been asked to contribute something to the capsule, probably because Mrs. Elisabeth Pink—the lady responsible for its contents—and I knew each other slightly long ago, in an era that by 2029 will be known as Prehistory.

My contribution, Mrs. Pink's letter says, "could be either on our current status or what you think the future will hold."

I wish I could report to the future that our current status is hunky-dory, that we live in the Golden Age of something or other. Until recently it was possible for Americans to believe that. There's no doubt that in the twentieth century, at least, the people of the United States have enjoyed the highest standard of living that the world has known up to this point in history. We've had so much of everything, in fact, that we've thought our supplies of the essentials of life—land, food, air, water, fuel—would last forever, and we've been wasteful. Sometimes we've even been wasteful of human life itself.

Lately, though, a sense of decline has set in. We've begun to realize that we're in trouble. We've poured so much filth into our water that much of it is undrinkable, and no life can live in it. Even the life of the ocean, the great mother of us all, is threatened. Scientists say the last wisp of pure, natural air in the continental United States was absorbed into our generally polluted atmosphere over Flagstaff, Arizona, several years ago. Parts of our land are overcrowded, parts neglected, parts abused, parts destroyed. We continue to depend on unrenewable resources—petroleum; natural gas, and coal—for most of the fuel that heats and cools our homes; runs our industry, agriculture, and business; and propels our transportation. We've suddenly discovered that those resources are disappearing forever. Without usable land, air, water, and fuel, food production would be impossible, of course. In addition, the United States and the Soviet Union are at this moment trying to make treaties that we hope will keep us from destroying all life and the possibility of life if we decide to destroy each other before the fuel runs out.

Literary Analysis
Persuasive Appeal Which words indicate that the author's persuasive appeal is beginning?

Reading Strategy
Distinguishing Between Fact and Opinion Which facts here support the writer's opinion about a sense of decline?

◀ **Critical Viewing** How can respect for wildflowers and other parts of nature improve the quality of human life? **[Speculate]**

So I would classify the current status that Mrs. Pink mentions as shaky, which makes the outlook for the future—even so near a future as A.D. 2029—uncertain.

An uncertain future is no new thing, of course. The future has always existed only in the imagination, a realm of hope and dread with which we can do little more than play games. But the games sometimes become serious. The Europeans <u>postulated</u> another land across the ocean for centuries and then came and found it. Jules Verne traveled under the sea and to the moon in his mind many years before we could make the machines to catch up with him. If, as we say, Necessity is the mother of Invention, then Desire is the father of Possibility.

Because of man's amazing record of making his dreams come true, I refuse to be pessimistic about the future, despite the frightening aspects of the present. As long as we—both as a race and as a crowd of individuals—retain our capacity for dreaming, we also keep the possibility of doing. And when doing becomes necessary, we invent a means to do so. Especially when we're in danger, as we are now.

Some of our present dangers surely will be around in 2029, for they're part of being human. We're too far from solving poverty, disease, and probably even war to be done with them in another half-century. Collin County probably will still need its courts and its jail—

▲ **Critical Viewing** How does this image relate to Woolley's vision? **[Connect]**

postulated (päs´ chə lāt´ ed) v. claimed

☑ **Reading Check**
What does Woolley say the United States and the Soviet Union are doing "at this moment"?

maybe more courts and a newer, stronger jail.

But if my generation and my sons' generation do what we must to prolong the possibility of survival and the likelihood of this being read, most of the problems about which I'm worrying may seem quaint. If so, they'll be replaced by others that will seem as serious to those who gather to open the time capsule as mine do to me. Golden Ages exist only in retrospect, never for those who are trying to cope with them.

So for the <u>beleaguered</u> residents of 2029 I wish four things:

—A deeper understanding of history, to better avoid repeating the errors of the past, for if each generation keeps on inventing its own mistakes, some of the old ones will have to be thrown out.

—A healing of the <u>schism</u> between man and the rest of nature. Our present disrespect for the natural world is our most serious stupidity to date. We must realize that man can't long outlive the other living creatures.

—A wider and more profound appreciation of beauty. Music, poetry, pictures, and stories feed the soul as surely as wheat and meat and rice feed the body, and the soul of America is malnourished.

—A sense of humor. If man ever stops laughing at himself, he can no longer endure life, nor will he have reason to.

beleaguered (bi lē′ gərd) *adj.* worried; tormented

schism (siz′ əm) *n.* division

Review and Assess

Thinking About the Selection

1. **Respond:** Based on Woolley's ideas, do you take a pessimistic or an optimistic view of the future? Why?

2. **(a) Recall:** Why is the author guaranteed an audience in the future? **(b) Infer:** What prompted the author to accept the invitation to write this essay?

3. **(a) Recall:** Name two environmental problems mentioned by the author. **(b) Analyze:** Identify at least two pessimistic signs for the future that Woolley foresees.

4. **Support:** What specific evidence does Woolley offer to support his assertion that human beings have a record of making dreams come true?

5. **(a) Analyze:** What does Woolley mean when he says "Golden Ages exist only in retrospect, never for those who are trying to cope with them"? **(b) Connect:** What does this statement reveal about the author's fears for 2029?

6. **(a) Categorize:** Review the four wishes Woolley makes at the end of his essay, and rank them in order from most important to least important. **(b) Support:** Explain the priorities you have set.

Bryan Woolley

(b. 1937)
Born in Texas, Bryan Woolley has been a teacher, a journalist, and a novelist. His novel *November 22*, about the events in Dallas on the day President John F. Kennedy was assassinated, was praised by *Texas Monthly* as an outstanding book. In 1979, the author wrote "To the Residents of A.D. 2029," addressing his concerns for the present and his hopes for the future.

Review and Assess

Literary Analysis

Persuasive Appeal

1. What details does Clarke include to make his science-fiction story believable enough to be taken seriously as **persuasive appeal**?

2. Carson creates a fictional place to show many examples of the dangers of pesticides. What effect does this have on her warning?

3. (a) What argument for an optimistic outlook does Woolley use in his writing? (b) What is the effect of his positive outlook?

Comparing Literary Works

4. (a) Using a chart like the one below, compare the **imagery** used in each selection. (b) How does each author's use of imagery strengthen the persuasive appeal?

Title of Selection	Imagery Used	How It Strengthens the Persuasive Appeal

5. In your opinion, which selection is most powerful or persuasive? Explain.

Reading Strategy

Distinguishing Between Fact and Opinion

6. Identify one **fact** and one **opinion** mentioned in Clarke's story.

7. (a) What is one opinion expressed in the chapter from *Silent Spring*? (b) Which facts support this opinion?

8. Using a chart like the one below, identify at least two facts and two opinions in Woolley's essay, and explain what makes each a fact or an opinion.

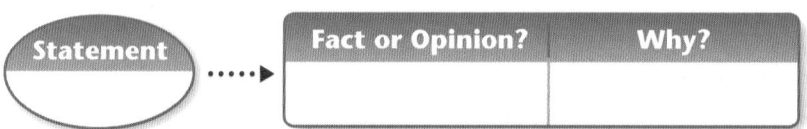

Statement	Fact or Opinion?	Why?

Extend Understanding

9. **Media Link:** Which of the three selections would be the best choice for adaptation as a science-fiction movie? Why?

Quick Review

In all forms of literature, writers may use **persuasive appeals** to warn readers and urge action. The message of such appeals may be stated or implied.

Imagery is the use of descriptive language to create pictures in the reader's mind.

A **fact** is a statement that can be proved, or tested for accuracy.

An **opinion** is a statement of personal preference and cannot be proved.

 Take It to the Net
www.phschool.com

Take the interactive self-test online to check your understanding of these selections.

Integrate Language Skills

Vocabulary Development Lesson

Word Analysis: Latin Root -ann-

The Latin root -ann- means "year." The root appears, in modified form, in the word *perennial*, meaning "through the years." Perennial flowers blossom year after year, whereas annual flowers blossom for only one season, then die. Use the meaning of -ann- to write the correct definition of each of the following words.

1. annually   **2.** biannual   **3.** semiannual

Spelling Strategy

When a word ends in two or more consonants, do not double the final consonant before adding a suffix. For example, *blight* + -ed = *blighted*. Add each suffix shown below to form a new word. Then, use each new word in a sentence.

1. quick + -ly   **3.** expect + -ation
2. catch + -ing   **4.** warn + -ing

Fluency: Sentence Completion

On your paper, rewrite the following sentences, filling in each blank with a word from the vocabulary list on page 485.

1. The ___?___ politician pleaded with his colleagues to revive the ___?___ bill he had proposed.
2. Brown spots on the shrubs warned of a ___?___ in the ___?___ garden.
3. After his death, the holy man was cremated on a ___?___.
4. The police ___?___ that the burglar would return.
5. There was a ___?___ in the group because some members of the group disagreed about an issue.
6. She wished she had ___?___ all negativity from her group.

Grammar Lesson

Compound and Complex Sentences

A **compound sentence** consists of two or more independent clauses. The clauses can be joined by a comma and a coordinating conjunction or by a semicolon. A **complex sentence** consists of one independent clause, which can stand by itself, and at least one subordinate clause, which cannot stand by itself as a sentence. In the following examples, the independent clauses are underlined and the subordinate clause is italicized.

Compound sentence: The stars shone, and he remembered an old nursery rhyme.

Complex sentence: *When the stars shone,* he remembered an old nursery rhyme.

Practice Identify each sentence below as *compound* or *complex*. For compound sentences, identify the coordinating conjunction. For complex sentences, identify the subordinate clause.

1. When he was ten, Marvin went outside.
2. He saw Earth, but no one lived there.
3. Life changed after pesticide was sprayed.
4. The animals grew ill, and vegetation died.
5. We must act now if we care about the world.

Writing Application Write a paragraph about one of these selections. Use and identify two compound sentences and two complex sentences in your writing.

𝒲𝒢 *Prentice Hall Writing and Grammar Connection: Chapter 21, Section 2*

Writing Lesson

Environmental Report

Rachel Carson's *Silent Spring* had an enormous impact on the way people viewed pest control, due partly to its well-documented facts. Using information from the selections and additional research, prepare a factual report on an environmental issue.

Prewriting   Choose an environmental issue of interest to you. Decide which facts from the selections and from your research are the most valuable. Jot these key findings on note cards. Put your cards in an order that makes sense and use your cards to make an outline.

Drafting   Write a strong introduction, body, and conclusion for your report. As you write, elaborate with facts and statistics to prove your point.

Model: Elaborating to Prove a Point

In 1995, our town had 35 ducks swimming on Birch Pond. Today, only 8 ducks remain. Why? The answer comes in a single word: pollution.

> The author provides an exact year and specific statistics to help prove the point that the waters are polluted.

Revising   Reread your draft and add any facts that would strengthen the main point you want to convey.

*W*G   *Prentice Hall Writing and Grammar Connection: Chapter 12, Section 3*

Extension Activities

Listening and Speaking   Prepare a **speech** about an environmental issue that concerns you. As you prepare and rehearse your speech, consider these tips:

- Offer strong arguments supported with facts and statistics to help you win over your audience.
- Tell listeners exactly which action you wish them to take.

After delivering the speech, invite your audience to evaluate the effectiveness of your arguments.

Research and Technology   Imagine that you are a descendant of Marvin in "If I Forget Thee, Oh Earth. . . ." You and the other members of the Colony are preparing to return to Earth. In a group, research information about the ozone layer. Write a **memo** that gives suggestions to your fellow travelers about ways they can protect Earth when they return. **[Group Activity]**

 Take It to the Net   www.phschool.com

Go online for an additional research activity using the Internet.

Prepare to Read

Gifts ◆ Glory and Hope

 Take It to the Net

Visit www.phschool.com
for interactive activities
and instruction related to
the selections, including
• background
• graphic organizers
• literary elements
• reading strategies

Preview

Connecting to the Literature

As you watch the newscast of a demonstration for freedom in a foreign land, you may not feel personally affected. Yet, as these selections show, freedom is a concern shared by people throughout the world.

Background

Apartheid, which means "apartness" in Afrikaans (one of the languages of South Africa), is the policy of segregation and discrimination that was once practiced against nonwhites by the South African government. When apartheid became law in 1948, it affected housing, education, and transportation. In order to help end apartheid, many nations reduced trade with South Africa. Apartheid was finally abolished in 1991.

Literary Analysis

Tone

Tone is the attitude a writer takes toward an audience or subject. The tone might be formal or informal, playful or serious. Recognizing the author's word choice is key to understanding the tone of a piece. Consider the formal and hopeful tone of this passage from "Glory and Hope."

> Today, all of us do, by our presence here, and by our celebrations in other parts of our country and the world, confer glory and hope to newborn liberty.

As you read, notice the tone conveyed through the author's word choice.

Comparing Literary Works

You will discover that these selections share a common theme: hope for a peaceful future and freedom for all people. Though the authors represent different lands and people, both writers show concern for peace and freedom for all. While reading, compare the ways that each author expresses his or her hopes, and pay special attention to the tone used to express the theme.

CALIFORNIA STANDARDS

Instruction with these selections addresses these standards:

R 1.1*, 3.5*, 3.11
W 1.5*, 2.4*
WOLC 1.1*, 1.3*
LS 1.8

* Standards tested on HS Exit Exam. For complete standards, see p. CA 4.

Reading Strategy

Evaluating the Writer's Message

Tone helps convey a writer's message—the idea that he or she wants to communicate. To **evaluate a writer's message,** first identify the message, and then determine whether the message meets these criteria:

- Is it logical, or clearly reasoned-out?
- Is it well-supported, or backed up with facts or personal experience?

You can evaluate a message without necessarily agreeing with it. Use a chart like the one shown to evaluate the writer's message.

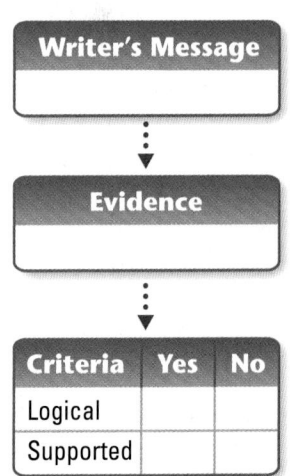

Writer's Message

↓

Evidence

↓

Criteria	Yes	No
Logical		
Supported		

Vocabulary Development

pinions (pin´ yənz) *n.* last bony sections of a bird's wings (p. 505)

hieroglyphics (hī´ ər ō´ glif´ iks) *n.* pictures that represent words or ideas (p. 505)

confer (kən fur´) *v.* to give (p. 506)

pernicious (pər nish´ əs) *adj.* destructive (p. 507)

ideology (ī´ dē äl´ ə jē) *n.* ideas on which a political, economic, or social system is based (p. 507)

chasms (kaz´ əmz) *n.* deep cracks in Earth's surface (p. 507)

covenant (kuv´ ə nənt) *n.* agreement or contract (p. 507)

inalienable (in āl´ yən ə bəl) *adj.* not able to be taken away (p. 507)

Gifts

Shu Ting

Translated by Donald Finkel

▲ **Critical Viewing** Relate this photograph to the first stanza of the poem. Which image from nature could illustrate your "dream"? **[Connect]**

My dream is the dream of a pond
Not just to mirror the sky
But to let the willows and ferns
Suck me dry.
5   I'll climb from the roots to the veins,
And when leaves wither and fade
I will refuse to mourn
Because I was dying to live.

My joy is the joy of sunlight.
10   In a moment of creation
I will leave shining words
In the pupils of children's eyes
Igniting golden flames.
Whenever seedlings sprout
15   I shall sing a song of green.
I'm so simple I'm profound!

My grief is the grief of birds.
The Spring will understand:
Flying from hardship and failure
20   To a future of warmth and light.
There my blood-stained <u>pinions</u>
Will scratch <u>hieroglyphics</u>
On every human heart
For every year to come.

25   Because all that I am
Has been a gift from earth.

pinions (pin´ yənz) *n.* last bony sections of a bird's wings

hieroglyphics (hī´ ər ō´ glif´ iks) *n.* pictures that represent words or ideas

Shu Ting

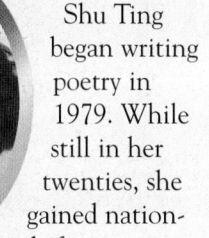

(b. 1952)

Shu Ting began writing poetry in 1979. While still in her twenties, she gained nation-wide fame as a poet.

During the 1980s, Shu Ting became known as one of the "Misty Poets of China." The term derives from a government literary critic's appraisal of an anti-communist poem by poet Gu Chen as "misty." The writings of the Misty Poets have fueled—and continue to inspire—a ceaseless struggle for democracy in China.

Shu Ting uses poetry to express her personal feelings—even though the Communist government of China has condemned such expression as anti-communist.

Review and Assess

Thinking About the Selection

1. **Respond:** Which image in the poem is most powerful? Explain.

2. **(a) Recall:** Which image does the speaker use to express her dream? **(b) Draw Conclusions:** Why does the speaker wish to be sucked dry by the willows and ferns? **(c) Interpret:** What are the seedlings that sprout from the poet's words?

3. **(a) Analyze:** How does the speaker use sunlight as a way of expressing hope? **(b) Interpret:** Why are birds an appropriate image to convey the speaker's grief? **(c) Speculate:** What kind of message do you think will be scratched by the blood-stained pinions?

4. **Apply:** How might the words in "Gifts" inspire people who are fighting for freedom?

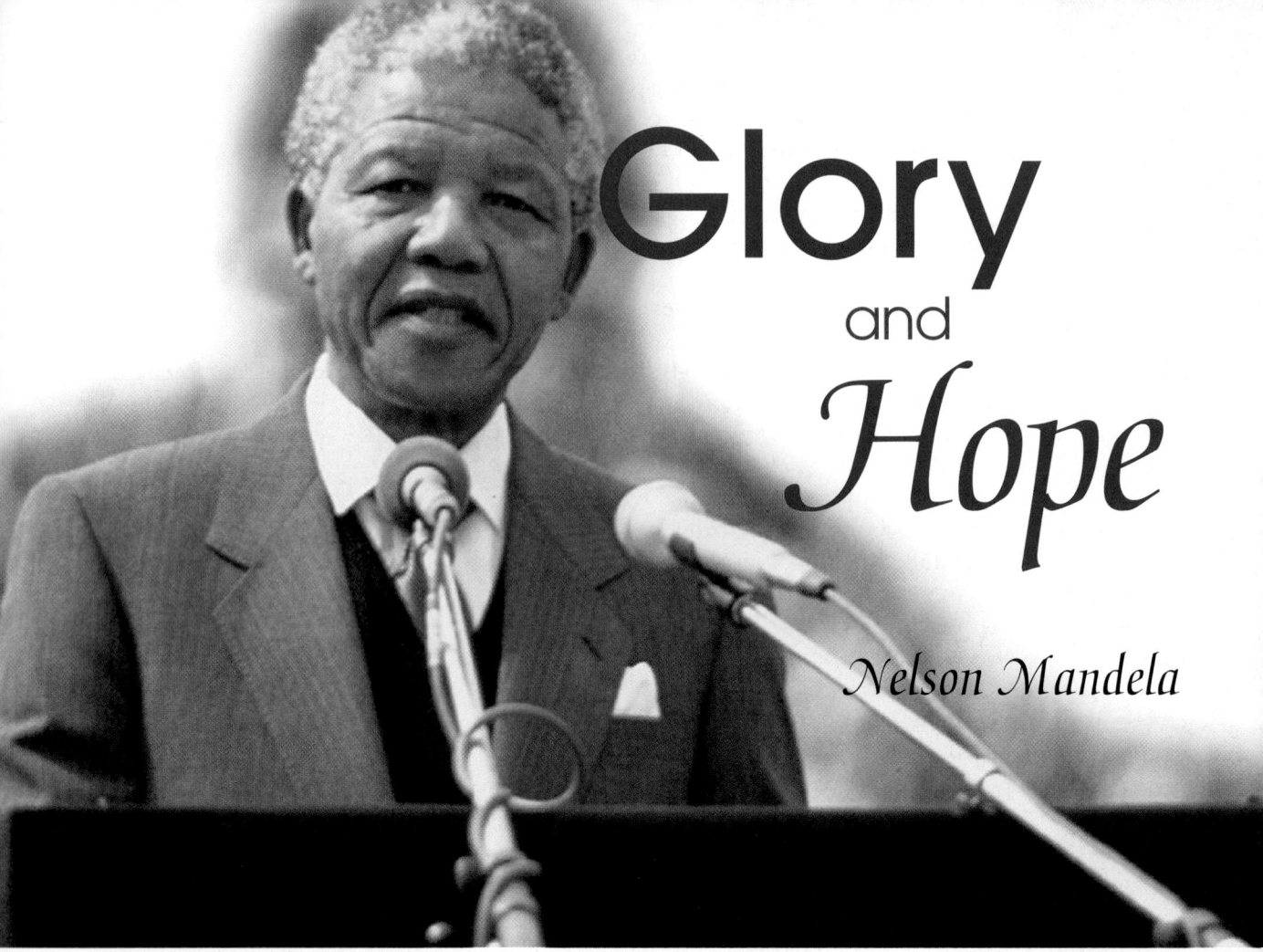

Glory and *Hope*

Nelson Mandela

Your majesties, your royal highnesses, distinguished guests, comrades and friends: Today, all of us do, by our presence here, and by our celebrations in other parts of our country and the world, <u>confer</u> glory and hope to newborn liberty.

Out of the experience of an extraordinary human disaster that lasted too long must be born a society of which all humanity will be proud.

Our daily deeds as ordinary South Africans must produce an actual South African reality that will reinforce humanity's belief in justice, strengthen its confidence in the nobility of the human soul and sustain all our hopes for a glorious life for all.

All this we owe both to ourselves and to the peoples of the world who are so well represented here today.

To my compatriots, I have no hesitation in saying that each one of us is as intimately attached to the soil of this beautiful country as are the famous jacaranda trees of Pretoria and the mimosa trees of the bushveld.[1]

---

1. **bushveld** (bŏŏsh′ velt) *n.* South African grassland with abundant shrubs and thorny vegetation.

▲ **Critical Viewing**
How do you think Mandela felt when this picture was taken as he presented this speech? **[Interpret]**

confer (kən fʉr′) *v.* to give

Literary Analysis
Tone How does the speaker establish a tone of pride in this passage?

Each time one of us touches the soil of this land, we feel a sense of personal renewal. The national mood changes as the seasons change.

We are moved by a sense of joy and exhilaration when the grass turns green and the flowers bloom.

That spiritual and physical oneness we all share with this common homeland explains the depth of the pain we all carried in our hearts as we saw our country tear itself apart in terrible conflict, and as we saw it spurned, outlawed and isolated by the peoples of the world, precisely because it has become the universal base of the <u>pernicious ideology</u> and practice of racism and racial oppression.

We, the people of South Africa, feel fulfilled that humanity has taken us back into its bosom, that we, who were outlaws not so long ago, have today been given the rare privilege to be host to the nations of the world on our own soil.

We thank all our distinguished international guests for having come to take possession with the people of our country of what is, after all, a common victory for justice, for peace, for human dignity.

We trust that you will continue to stand by us as we tackle the challenges of building peace, prosperity, nonsexism, nonracialism and democracy.

We deeply appreciate the role that the masses of our people and their democratic, religious, women, youth, business, traditional and other leaders have played to bring about this conclusion. Not least among them is my Second Deputy President, the Honorable F. W. de Klerk.

We would also like to pay tribute to our security forces, in all their ranks, for the distinguished role they have played in securing our first democratic elections and the transition to democracy, from bloodthirsty forces which still refuse to see the light.

The time for the healing of the wounds has come.

The moment to bridge the <u>chasms</u> that divide us has come.

The time to build is upon us.

We have, at last, achieved our political emancipation. We pledge ourselves to liberate all our people from the continuing bondage of poverty, deprivation, suffering, gender and other discrimination.

We succeeded to take our last steps to freedom in conditions of relative peace. We commit ourselves to the construction of a complete, just and lasting peace.

We have triumphed in the effort to implant hope in the breasts of the millions of our people. We enter into a <u>covenant</u> that we shall build the society in which all South Africans, both black and white, will be able to walk tall, without any fear in their hearts, assured of their <u>inalienable</u> right to human dignity—a rainbow nation at peace with itself and the world.

As a token of its commitment to the renewal of our country, the new Interim Government of National Unity will, as a matter of urgency, address the issue of amnesty for various categories of our people who are currently serving terms of imprisonment.

We dedicate this day to all the heroes and heroines in this country

pernicious (pər nish′ əs) *adj.* destructive

ideology (ī′ dē äl′ ə jē) *n.* ideas on which a political, economic, or social system is based

chasms (kaz′ əmz) *n.* deep cracks in Earth's surface

covenant (kuv′ ə nənt) *n.* agreement or contract

inalienable (in āl′ yən ə bəl) *adj.* not able to be taken away

✔ **Reading Check**

Which challenges does South Africa face, according to Mandela?

and the rest of the world who sacrificed in many ways and surrendered their lives so that we could be free.

Their dreams have become reality. Freedom is their reward.

We are both humbled and elevated by the honor and privilege that you, the people of South Africa, have bestowed on us, as the first President of a united, democratic, nonracial and nonsexist South Africa, to lead our country out of the valley of darkness.

We understand it still that there is no easy road to freedom.

We know it well that none of us acting alone can achieve success.

We must therefore act together as a united people, for national reconciliation, for nation building, for the birth of a new world.

Let there be justice for all.

Let there be peace for all.

Let there be work, bread, water and salt for all.

Let each know that for each the body, the mind and the soul have been freed to fulfill themselves.

Never, never and never again shall it be that this beautiful land will again experience the oppression of one by another and suffer the indignity of being the skunk of the world.

The sun shall never set on so glorious a human achievement!

Let freedom reign. God bless Africa!

Nelson Mandela

(b. 1918)
Nelson Mandela was born in South Africa, a nation whose white government maintained a strict policy of apartheid, or legal discrimination against blacks. In 1944, Mandela began protesting apartheid. Twenty years later, after several arrests, he was sentenced to life in prison for acts of sabotage.

After twenty-seven years of imprisonment, Mandela was released in 1990. He continued to fight for equal rights for all South Africans. In 1991, apartheid was finally abolished and, in 1993, Mandela and South African president F. W. de Klerk shared the Nobel Peace Prize. The next year, Mandela became the first black man to be elected president of South Africa.

Review and Assess

Thinking About the Selection

1. **Respond:** What do you admire most about the message in Mandela's speech? Why?

2. **(a) Recall:** According to Mandela, what is "newborn" in South Africa? **(b) Interpret:** Which emotion does the word "newborn" add to his remarks?

3. **(a) Recall:** Citing examples, describe what life was like in the old South Africa. **(b) Draw Conclusions:** Describe the new South Africa that Mandela envisions.

4. **(a) Recall:** What "covenant" does Mandela say the South African people are now entering? **(b) Generalize:** Which ideas in the speech are especially important for safeguarding the human rights of all people throughout today's world?

5. **(a) Connect:** How does the title of the speech connect with the ideas that Mandela conveys? **(b) Compare and Contrast:** What are the similarities and differences between "glory" and "hope"?

6. **Extend:** How do you think the people of South Africa reacted to Mandela's inaugural speech?

7. **Take a Position:** Basing your answer on Mandela's speech, what do you think was the new leader's greatest challenge? Why?

Review and Assess

Literary Analysis

Tone

1. Using a chart like the one below, analyze the **tone** of "Glory and Hope" and "Gifts."

Title	Memorable Words or Phrases	Tone	Effect of the Tone

2. Given the format of each selection, would you say the tone is appropriate in each case? Explain.

Comparing Literary Works

3. Using a chart like the one below, compare the ways that Shu Ting and Nelson Mandela express hope for a peaceful future.

4. Which selection do you feel does a better job of justifying its optimism for the future? Explain.

Reading Strategy

Evaluating the Writer's Message

5. (a) What is Nelson Mandela's **message**? (b) How does he support his message?
6. Which evidence from your own knowledge or experience would support—or challenge—the validity of Mandela's message?
7. Evaluate Shu Ting's message in "Gifts."

Extend Understanding

8. **Social Studies Connection:** What is currently being done to help oppressed people in other parts of the world attain their human rights and freedom?

Quick Review

Tone is the attitude a writer takes toward an audience or subject.

To **evaluate a writer's message,** decide whether the ideas of the writer are logical and well-supported.

 **Take It to the Net**
www.phschool.com
Take the interactive self-test online to check your understanding of these selections.

Integrate Language Skills

Vocabulary Development Lesson

Word Analysis: Greek Suffix -logy

The Greek suffix -logy means "the study, science, or theory of." The suffix appears in the word *ideology*, which means "the study of ideas" or "a set of ideas." Define each of the following words.

1. zoology   2. sociology   3. biology

Spelling Strategy

If a word ends in a single consonant preceded by a single vowel and the last syllable is accented, double the final consonant before adding most endings. For example, *confer* becomes *conferred*. However, do not double the final consonant before adding *-ence*, as in *conference*. (*Occurrence* is an exception to this rule.) For each item, add the suffix shown and write the new word. Then, use each new word in a sentence.

1. refer + -ed   2. infer + -ence   3. defer + -ing

Fluency: Sentence Completion

Identify the word from the vocabulary list on page 503 that correctly completes each sentence below.

1. The general will ____?____ a medal upon the heroic soldier.
2. In a free society, liberty and freedom are ____?____ rights for everyone.
3. A term to describe a destructive system of ideas is a ____?____ ____?____.
4. Once you enter into a ____?____, you are not supposed to back out.
5. The ____?____ on the birds' wings were red with spots of white.
6. The scientist studied the ____?____ that had been scratched into the cave wall.
7. If you should go out walking after an earthquake, do not fall into any ____?____.

Grammar Lesson

Parallelism: Clauses

Parallelism is the repetition of grammatically similar words or groups of words. The parallelism may appear in the form of related **clauses**—groups of words with subjects and verbs—if a clause is presented for the first time, and then its pattern is repeated in subsequent clauses or sentences. Parallelism gives the writing a sense of rhythm, evenness, and structure. Look at this example from "Gifts."

> **Example:** My dream is the dream of a pond.
> My joy is the joy of sunlight.
> My grief is the grief of birds.

Practice Copy each pair of sentences below. Underline the words that are repeated in order to create parallelism.

1. Let there be justice. Let there be peace.
2. To be free is a gift. To be free is a treasure.
3. The time to heal has come. The time to build has come.
4. I shall sing to life. I shall dance to love.
5. Freedom is a privilege. Life is a privilege.

Writing Application Using the parallelism you have identified, add another sentence to each practice item.

WG Prentice Hall Writing and Grammar Connection: Chapter 21, Section 2

Writing Lesson

Letter to Nelson Mandela

In his speech "Glory and Hope," Nelson Mandela presents a memorable message about the future of South Africa. Write a letter to Nelson Mandela in which you share the parts of his speech that you found most inspiring.

Prewriting   Make a list of words that describe how Mandela's speech makes you feel. Next to each word, write the section of the speech that evoked that particular emotion.

Model: Listing Words to Describe Feelings

Feeling	Example From Speech
hope	The sun shall never set on so glorious a human achievement!

> The example from the speech explains the hopeful feeling.

Drafting   As you draft, use a friendly yet respectful tone. Your opening paragraph should address your reason for writing. The body of your letter should address your feelings about his speech. In your closing paragraph, sum up the way in which the speech inspired you.

Revising   Read your letter to a classmate to make sure that you have maintained a respectful tone throughout your letter.

W̶G̶ Prentice Hall Writing and Grammar Connection: Chapter 15, Section 1

Extension Activities

Listening and Speaking   In a group, hold a **panel discussion** on the kind of world you would like to leave to future generations. Keep in mind the human rights issues that Nelson Mandela addresses in "Glory and Hope." Consider these tips:

- Make note cards to use for extemporaneous, or unrehearsed, delivery of your ideas.
- During your discussion, show respect for everyone's opinions and speak in turn.

Afterward, analyze the process to decide how you might improve future discussions. **[Group Activity]**

Research and Technology   Write a **research report** about the changes in South Africa since the end of apartheid. Use library resources, including the Internet, to gather information from at least three sources, synthesizing the details and facts you find into your writing. Then, share your report with classmates..

 **Take It to the Net**   www.phschool.com

Go online for an additional research activity using the Internet.

Writing WORKSHOP

Exposition: How-to Essays

A how-to essay or manual provides detailed step-by-step instructions that tell you how to perform a certain task. In this workshop, you will write a how-to essay on a process you know well.

Assignment Criteria. Your how-to essay should have the following characteristics:

- Specific factual information presented logically and accurately
- Rules of behavior for each particular situation
- Examples and definitions that demonstrate key concepts
- Instructions that anticipate readers' potential mistakes

To preview the criteria on which your how-to essay may be assessed, see the Rubric on page 515.

Prewriting

Choose a topic. Make a calendar of your schedule. For each day of the week, write down your activities. Then, identify an activity from your calendar to describe in a how-to manual. Or, if you prefer, describe another activity with which you are familiar.

Use a target diagram. Once you have chosen an activity to describe in a how-to manual, use the diagram on this page to narrow your topic. In the outer circle, write your general topic. Then, consider the aspect of your topic on which you will focus in your manual; write this in the inner circle. To complete the diagram, write an even narrower topic in the center of the target.

Narrowing Your Topic With a Target Diagram

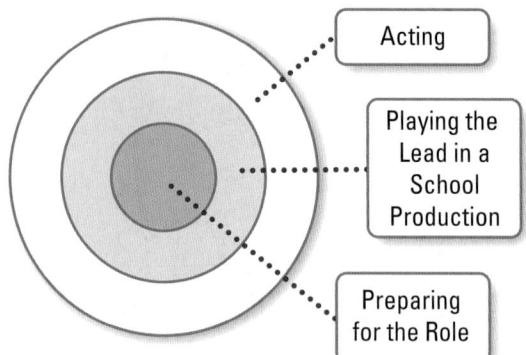

Acting

Playing the Lead in a School Production

Preparing for the Role

Gather information. As you prepare to draft your how-to manual, remember to provide your reader with all the tools needed to perform the activity you are describing:

- Make a list of materials needed
- Note all the steps involved, in the order in which they occur
- Collect any additional information or hints of use to the reader

Student Model

Before you begin drafting, read this student model and review the characteristics of effective how-to essays.

Carmen Rose Viviano-Crafts
Syracuse, NY

Preparing for a Dramatic Role

One of the first challenges of a new dramatic role is the task of memorizing lines. Use the following guidelines to memorize lines more efficiently:

1. Read the entire play at least twice to familiarize yourself with the setting and situations. When performing, it is essential to know what is going on around you in order to provide the appropriate reactions.

2. Highlight or underline all your lines to identify when your character speaks.

3. Begin to concentrate solely on your parts. Look at the script scene by scene, memorizing one or two scenes a day, depending on how much time you have. Reading the lines out loud speeds up the process by making the lines more memorable.

4. Once you feel confident enough, begin to "run" your lines (read them aloud), with another person reading the other characters' lines. This prepares you for being onstage with other actors.

5. When you begin rehearsing with fellow cast members, you will be able to try out different ways of saying things, and you'll start to develop your character. Here are the steps to use when developing a character:

   - If your role is based on a real person, research that person or observe someone in a similar situation. Try to find out as much information as you can so that you can play the part realistically.

   - If you are playing a fictional character, study the script closely. The character's words can tell you about his or her feelings, likes, and dislikes.

   - Once you have learned some aspects of your character, begin to delve into the mind and soul of the person. Make up an entire life story for your character. The more you know about the person, the easier it is to put yourself in his or her place. Think of a past experience to relate to something your character is going through. Bring the emotions you felt in that situation to your character's situation.

   - Finally, conduct general conversations with other cast members, with each of you speaking from your own character's point of view. Ask things like "How do you feel about me?" and "How do you think I feel about you?" This lets you know how you are perceived by the other actors/characters in the play, and allows you to react more realistically.

6. After each rehearsal, consider what worked well and what felt wrong to you. Use your after-rehearsal notes as feedback to improve your performance.

[sidebar] e numbering sys- n allows Carmen present informa- n logically.

[sidebar] offering time gestions, the ay anticipates ders' questions d concerns.

[sidebar] boration about earching demon- tes the writer's gestions.

[sidebar] se ideas offer s of conduct, aining the value ch strategy.

Drafting

Organize information. Now that you have gathered all the information you want to include in your draft, choose an organization that will make sense to your reader. Chronological, or step-by-step, order is usually best suited to this kind of writing. Use the chart at right to help you organize your information effectively.

Elaborate each stage in a process. Provide information to fully explain each step in the process:

- Explain why each step is important.
- Define terms.
- Include graphics where necessary.

Give thorough descriptions and explanations so your readers can complete the task you describe.

Use graphic devices. Photographs, diagrams, and drawings are a great way to help readers follow an explanation. Create or locate graphics to reinforce your instructions, and place them at the appropriate points in your essay. To work effectively, each graphic must be clear and complete. Each should illustrate a step in the process you are explaining. Finally, a graphic should include labels to make strong connections back to your essay.

Consider formatting techniques. In your how-to essay, lengthy paragraphs may not be the best way to present information. Brief paragraphs, bullets, or numbered lists will help keep your how-to essay clear and easy for readers to manage.

> **Organize Information**
> 1. State the purpose of your technical document.
> 2. List the materials and conditions necessary to complete the activity.
> 3. Provide examples to demonstrate the activity.
> 4. List steps to complete in consecutive order.
> 5. Suggest solutions to common problems when performing the activity.

Revising

Revise for clarity. Look over your draft to identify instructions, steps, or information that may be unclear to your reader. Mark these sections and go back to them, rewriting any confusing passages with language that informs in a logical manner.

Model: Revising for Clarity

—read aloud—

4. Once you feel confident enough, begin to "run" your lines with another person. ∧*This prepares you for being onstage with other actors.*

> Carmen defined a term that may be unfamiliar to readers and added information to explain the value of a strategy.

Revise for transitions. Look for sections in your draft that need transitional language to connect the steps in your activity. In the following example, adding the words *first* and *then* makes the instruction easier to understand.

> **Example:** Wash the bowl and add the eggs.
> *First,* wash the bowl, and *then* add the eggs.

Compare the model and the nonmodel. Why is the model more effective than the nonmodel?

Nonmodel	Model
Look at the script scene by scene, memorizing one or two scenes a day. Begin to "run" your lines. This prepares you for being onstage with other actors.	Begin to concentrate solely on your parts. Look at the script scene by scene, memorizing one or two scenes a day, depending on how much time you have. Once you feel confident, begin to "run" your lines. This prepares you for being onstage with other actors.

Publishing and Presenting

How-to essays or manuals are meant to be shared. Consider this option for sharing your writing with a wider audience.

Deliver an oral presentation. Prepare and distribute a handout of your draft for your classmates. Give an instructional presentation, providing elaboration if you feel something is unclear. Ask for feedback on the clarity of your how-to manual and presentation. If possible, have a classmate attempt the activity you described in order to gauge the effectiveness of your manual and presentation.

Rubric for Self-Assessment

Evaluate your how-to essay using the following criteria and rating scale:

Criteria	Rating Scale				
	Not very				Very
Is factual information expressed logically and correctly?	1	2	3	4	5
Are the rules of behavior or action for a specific situation clearly conveyed?	1	2	3	4	5
How well incorporated are examples and definitions that demonstrate concepts?	1	2	3	4	5
How well are readers' mistakes anticipated?	1	2	3	4	5

Listening and Speaking WORKSHOP

Effective Listening and Note Taking

Even when they are presenting information to an audience, some people speak very rapidly, leaving you struggling to keep up. The good news is that you can keep up with even the fastest speakers through careful listening. Once you have perfected your listening and note-taking skills, you can use them any time you need to remember something you have heard.

Listen Carefully

Listen to how something is said. Speakers often give you clues to what they consider important. If someone adds emphasis, changes his or her tone of voice, or repeats certain aspects often, then these are points you should capture in your notes.

Recognize barriers to listening. A major barrier to effective listening is the distractions all around you. Make sure to sit in a place that is as close to the speaker as possible, away from side conversations or visual distractions. Try not to let your mind wander—stay focused on what the speaker is saying.

Take Notes

Understand what the speaker is saying. Sometimes, we are too busy with the act of taking notes to think about what the speaker is saying. Focus on the speaker's ideas to decide which points are important and what form your notes should take.

Write main points and key details. You should not try to take down in your notes every word a speaker says. Instead, determine the speaker's main points and capture a few supporting details that illustrate each main point.

Rephrase and rewrite. To save time, try to rephrase the speaker's words using minimal punctuation, partial phrases, and abbreviations wherever possible. Also, the more you can rewrite the information simply, in your own words, the better you will understand it later.

Review your notes. To reinforce what you heard, review your notes as soon as possible after writing them. While your memory is still fresh, add significant details, rewrite confusing notes, and highlight important information.

Activity: Observation and Discussion With other students, watch a video of a television interview. Take notes without stopping the video. Afterward, use your notes to present a summary of the speaker's main points. Use the chart to evaluate and compare notes to see how they differ in length and emphasis.

Note-Taking Evaluation

Rating System
+ = Excellent   ✔ = Average   – = Weak

Notes:
Organization:
____ Inappropriate   ____ Sensible
Coherence:
____ Confusing   ____ Clear
Length:
____ Too Long   ____ Adequate   ____ Too Short

Summaries:
How did your note taking affect your summary?

Did you feel you missed any main points that the other students found?

Did you have any main points that you now feel should be considered supporting details (or vice versa)?

Assessment WORKSHOP

Generalizations

The reading sections of some tests require you to read a passage and answer multiple-choice questions about generalizations. Use the following strategies to help you answer these kinds of test questions:

- Remember that a generalization is a broad statement that can be applied to a variety of situations.
- Generalizations often illustrate a key theme, or lesson, of a passage.
- To make a generalization, list the main points or events in the passage. Then, devise a general principle that applies to all of the items in your list.

Test-Taking Strategies

- Generalizations can be easily recognized when they use signal words such as "in general," "most," "often," and "usually."
- Test a generalization by checking to see whether it can be applied to multiple elements of the passage.

Sample Test Item

Directions: Read the passage, and then answer the question that follows.

When you vote for class president, remember this: If you don't care about class trips or adequate funding, vote for Jessie Smith again. If you want to have more outings and more money, vote for Helen Aquino. Her plans include three fund-raising events and a class outing after each one! Make this year one to remember—vote for Helen Aquino!

1 Which of these statements is a generalization about the passage?

A Class elections are often pointless.

B Political ads try to make opponents look bad.

C A new candidate is always better.

D Most students don't vote.

Answer and Explanation

The correct answer is *B.* The advertisement characterizes her opponent as uncaring about issues that Aquino considers important. Answers *A, C,* and *D* may be applicable in other situations, but they do not reflect ideas contained in this specific passage.

Practice

Directions: Read the passage, and then answer the question that follows.

When we moved to this city a month ago, I never expected to have to make so many adjustments. I have had to consult so many transit schedules and I have gotten lost so many times that I am no longer interested in exploring my new surroundings. I also thought I would have some new friends by now.

1 Which generalization applies to the passage?

A Getting lost is part of adjusting to a new city.

B Transit schedules are often complicated.

C It takes a long time to meet people.

D Adjusting to new situations and surroundings can be difficult.

Short Stories

Reading, 1973, by Billy Morrow Jackson

Exploring the Genre

A short story is a brief visit to an imaginary world. This world could be nineteenth-century Paris, the American Southwest, or the swamp country of South Carolina. Wherever you travel, you will meet characters who deal with problems that are surprisingly real—for example, how to win someone's love or how to treat a younger brother. As you live through these problems with the characters, you may gain a deeper under- standing of the world around you.

Despite their varied content, almost all short stories have the following elements in common:

- **Plot**— the sequence of events that catches your interest and takes you through the story.

- **Characters**— the people, animals, or other beings that take part in the story's action.

- **Setting**— the time and location in which the story takes place.

- **Theme**— the message about life that the story conveys.

This unit highlights the elements of the short story while showing the power and variety of the form.

▲ **Critical Viewing** How does the mood of this painting match your notion of reading? **[Compare]**

Why Read Literature?

Whenever you read fiction, you have a purpose, or reason. You might find the topic interesting or love the characters a certain author creates. Preview three purposes you might set before reading works in this unit.

Read for the Love of Literature

We may no longer use pocket watches or sell our hair like the main characters in "The Gift of the Magi." Nevertheless, this story of a couple in love is still widely read and admired today. Find out why generations of people have treasured this simple O. Henry tale when you read **"The Gift of the Magi,"** page 524.

A powerful story may teach a lesson yet still entertain. When a woman sacrifices the financial stability of her household to appear wealthier than she is, you might appreciate the irony of her downfall in Guy de Maupassant's story, **"The Necklace,"** page 608.

Read to Appreciate an Author's Style

Some may associate lying in bed with laziness, but Mark Twain found it to be the best position to inspire good writing. Propped up with pillows, Twain would write stories with an informal, humorous style that reflected the good-natured ease of his surroundings. Fall under the spell of a master storyteller as you read Twain's **"The Invalid's Story,"** page 596.

Realism blends with fantasy in Isabel Allende's stories. Enjoy her unique style in the tale of an eccentric uncle who turns his family's town upside down in **"Uncle Marcos,"** page 577.

Read for Information

Advertisements can convey a great deal of information about a society and culture at a specific point in time. Place yourself in the shoes of a customer looking for a good automotive deal in 1913 as you scan the **"Advertisement for Automobile,"** page 536.

Stories that examine the intersection of two cultures usually end up revealing something hidden about each one. Native American ritual combines with Catholicism in unexpected ways in Leslie Marmon Silko's **"The Man to Send Rain Clouds,"** page 590.

 Take It to the Net

Visit the Web site for online instruction and activities related to each selection in this unit.
www.phschool.com

How to Read Literature

Use Strategies for Reading Fiction

Fiction is literature of the imagination. Authors of fiction invent the characters and events that populate their short stories and novels. Fiction can be closely associated with real people and events or it can be entirely fabricated. The following strategies will help you get more out of the fiction you read.

1. Ask questions.

Pause occasionally when reading to jot down two types of questions:

- Basic questions about what is happening in the story.

- Deeper-level questions about characters' motivations or the author's overall message.

2. Draw conclusions.

As soon as you find answers to your questions, you are ready to draw conclusions. Put details together to arrive at an understanding of the story, as the chart at right demonstrates.

- Carefully examine the evidence before drawing a conclusion. For example, look at characters' past actions before you attribute a general habit pattern to them.

- Make sure that your conclusions fit the general theme or tone of the story.

Drawing Conclusions

Character: Madame Loisel in Guy de Maupassant's "The Necklace"	
Details	Conclusions
Character's Action	Reason for the Action
She cries when she receives invitation to an evening party.	She is afraid she will be ridiculed if she goes to the party.

3. Identify with a character.

If you have ever sympathized with a character you might never have known in real life, you have identified with a character. Here are some tips to help you relate to the characters you encounter as you read:

- Imagine yourself in the character's situation.

- Think about how you might feel or react in that situation.

4. Use your senses.

Many stories are rich with descriptions of sensory details such as sights, sounds, and smells. As you read, make these descriptions come alive.

- Match the descriptions of sights, sounds, smells, and feelings with similar situations that you have personally experienced.

- Use your imagination and the details that the author provides to picture the action in your mind.

As you read the selections in this unit, review the reading strategies and apply them to interact with the text.

Prepare to Read

The Gift of the Magi

Wishful Thinking, Peter Szumowski, Private Collection

 Take It to the Net

Visit www.phschool.com for interactive activities and instruction related to "The Gift of the Magi," including

- background
- graphic organizers
- literary elements
- reading strategies

Preview

Connecting to the Literature

With excitement, you tear the wrapping paper off a birthday gift, only to be disappointed by the present you uncover. You hide your feelings, remembering it is the thought that counts. Gifts may be either less appropriate or more meaningful than they first appear. In "The Gift of the Magi," a husband and wife discover the problems and joys of giving gifts.

Background

In a story that was written years ago, any prices quoted may seem very low. Inflation, the steady increase in the prices of most things, is the reason: It reduces money's purchasing power. In this story, written around 1905, $32 is roughly a month's rent for Della and Jim. Today, for many people, that amount would not cover one week's rent.

Literary Analysis

Plot

Plot is the sequence of events that make up a story. Plot is divided into five stages:

- **Exposition**—the scene is set and background information is provided
- **Rising action**—the central conflict, or struggle, is introduced
- **Climax**—the high point of the conflict
- **Falling action**—the conflict lessens
- **Resolution**—the conflict concludes and loose ends get tied up

As you read "The Gift of the Magi," notice how its events apply to the stages of plot development.

Connecting Literary Elements

During the resolution, you learn how a story will end. In "The Gift of the Magi," the resolution reveals a **surprise ending,** a conclusion that differs from the reader's expectations, but in a way that is both logical and believable. As you read, look for clues to the surprise ending.

Reading Strategy

Asking Questions

To fully understand the plot of a story, **ask questions** about characters and events. Ask yourself these kinds of questions while you read:

- Why does a character act in a certain way?
- What does an event really mean?
- Why does the narrator reveal or conceal information?

Use a chart like the one shown to help you as you look for the answers to your questions in the story.

CALIFORNIA STANDARDS

Instruction with this selection addresses these standards:

R 1.1*, 3.7*, 3.9*
W 1.8, 2.2*
WOLC 1.1*
LS 1.9

* Standards tested on HS Exit Exam. For complete standards, see p. CA 4.

Question That Comes to Mind

Answer Revealed in Story

Vocabulary Development

instigates (in′ stə gāts′) v. urges on; stirs up (p. 525)

depreciate (dē prē′ shē āt′) v. reduce in value (p. 526)

cascade (kas kād′) n. waterfall (p. 526)

chaste (chāst) adj. pure or clean in style; not ornate (p. 526)

meretricious (mer′ ə trish′ əs) adj. attractive in a cheap, flashy way (p. 526)

ravages (rav′ ij iz) n. ruins (p. 527)

discreet (di skrēt′) adj. tactful; respectful (p. 529)

The Gift of the Magi

O. Henry

One dollar and eighty-seven cents. That was all. And sixty cents of it was in pennies. Pennies saved one and two at a time by bulldozing the grocer and the vegetable man and the butcher until one's cheeks burned with the silent imputation of parsimony[1] that such close dealing implied. Three times Della counted it. One dollar and eighty-seven cents. And the next day would be Christmas.

There was clearly nothing to do but flop down on the shabby little couch and howl. So Della did it. Which <u>instigates</u> the moral reflection that life is made up of sobs, sniffles, and smiles, with sniffles predominating.

While the mistress of the home is gradually subsiding from the first stage to the second, take a look at the home. A furnished flat[2] at $8 per week. It did not exactly beggar description,[3] but it certainly had that word on the lookout for the mendicancy squad.[4]

In the vestibule below was a letter-box into which no letter would go, and an electric button from which no mortal finger could coax a ring. Also appertaining thereunto was a card bearing the name "Mr. James Dillingham Young."

The "Dillingham" had been flung to the breeze during a former period of prosperity when its possessor was being paid $30 per week. Now, when the income was shrunk to $20, the letters of "Dillingham" looked blurred, as though they were thinking seriously of contracting to a modest and unassuming D. But whenever Mr. James Dillingham Young came home and reached his flat above he was called "Jim" and greatly hugged by Mrs. James Dillingham Young, already introduced to you as Della. Which is all very good.

Della finished her cry and attended to her cheeks with the powder rag. She stood by the window and looked out dully at a gray cat walking a gray fence in a gray backyard. Tomorrow would be Christmas Day, and she had only $1.87 with which to buy Jim a present. She had been saving every penny she could for months, with this result. Twenty dollars a week doesn't go far. Expenses had been greater than she had calculated. They always are. Only $1.87 to buy a present for Jim. Her Jim. Many a happy hour she had spent planning for something nice for him.

Something fine and rare and sterling—something just a little bit near to being worthy of the honor of being owned by Jim.

There was a pier glass[5] between the windows of the room. Perhaps you have seen a pier glass in an $8 flat.

---

1. **imputation** (im pyōō tā′ shən) **of parsimony** (pär′ sə mō′ nē) accusation of stinginess.
2. **flat** *n.* apartment.
3. **beggar description** resist description.
4. **it certainly . . . mendicancy** (men′ di kən′ sē) **squad** it would have been noticed by the police who arrested beggars.
5. **pier** (pir) **glass** tall mirror.

Reading Strategy
Asking Questions What question might you ask, based on this paragraph?

instigates (in′ stə gāts′) *v.* urges on; stirs up

Literary Analysis
Plot What conflict is introduced at this point?

✔**Reading Check**

How much money does Della have to buy a present for Jim?

The Gift of the Magi ◆ 525

A very thin and very agile person may, by observing his reflection in a rapid sequence of longitudinal strips, obtain a fairly accurate conception of his looks. Della, being slender, had mastered the art.

Suddenly she whirled from the window and stood before the glass. Her eyes were shining brilliantly, but her face had lost its color within twenty seconds. Rapidly she pulled down her hair and let it fall to its full length.

Now, there were two possessions of the James Dillingham Youngs in which they both took a mighty pride. One was Jim's gold watch that had been his father's and his grandfather's. The other was Della's hair. Had the Queen of Sheba[6] lived in the flat across the airshaft, Della would have let her hair hang out the window some day to dry just to <u>depreciate</u> Her Majesty's jewels and gifts. Had King Solomon been the janitor, with all his treasures piled up in the basement, Jim would have pulled out his watch every time he passed, just to see him pluck at his beard from envy.

So now Della's beautiful hair fell about her rippling and shining like a <u>cascade</u> of brown waters. It reached below her knee and made itself almost a garment for her. And then she did it up again nervously and quickly. Once she faltered for a minute and stood still while a tear or two splashed on the worn red carpet.

On went her old brown jacket; on went her old brown hat. With a whirl of skirts and with the brilliant sparkle still in her eyes, she fluttered out the door and down the stairs to the street.

Where she stopped the sign read: "Mme. Sofronie. Hair Goods of All Kinds." One flight up Della ran, and collected herself, panting. Madame, large, too white, chilly, hardly looked the "Sofronie."

"Will you buy my hair?" asked Della.

"I buy hair," said Madame. "Take yer hat off and let's have a sight at the looks of it."

Down rippled the brown cascade.

"Twenty dollars," said Madame, lifting the mass with a practiced hand.

"Give it to me quick," said Della.

Oh, and the next two hours tripped by on rosy wings. Forget the hashed metaphor. She was ransacking the stores for Jim's present.

She found it at last. It surely had been made for Jim and no one else. There was no other like it in any of the stores, and she had turned all of them inside out. It was a platinum fob chain♦ simple and <u>chaste</u> in design, properly proclaiming its value by substance alone and not by <u>meretricious</u> ornamentation—as all good things should do. It was even worthy of The Watch. As soon as she saw it she knew that

---

6. **Queen of Sheba** in the Bible, the beautiful queen who visited King Solomon to test his wisdom.

Literature in context Cultural Connection

♦ *Watch Fob Chain*

A fob chain is central to the plot of "The Gift of the Magi." The word *fob* probably entered the English language from the German dialect word *Fuppe*, meaning "pocket." During the nineteenth century, before the wristwatch became common, a man would carry a pocket watch that fit in a special vest pocket. To keep the watch from falling or becoming lost, it was fastened to the vest by means of a strap or chain (sometimes with an ornament, or fob, at the end) that was attached to a pin with a locking clasp, making it quite secure. Sometimes, as pictured at right, a chain had finely detailed metalwork, making it a work of art.

A fob chain was often handed down from father to son, as was Jim Young's in O. Henry's story. This fact alone made it very precious to its owner, despite its modest intrinsic value.

---

depreciate (dē prē′ shē āt′) *v.* reduce in value

cascade (kas kād′) *n.* waterfall

chaste (chāst) *adj.* pure or clean in style; not ornate

meretricious (mer′ ə trish′ əs) *adj.* attractive in a cheap, flashy way

it must be Jim's. It was like him. Quietness and value—the description applied to both. Twenty-one dollars they took from her for it, and she hurried home with the 87 cents. With that chain on his watch Jim might be properly anxious about the time in any company. Grand as the watch was he sometimes looked at it on the sly on account of the old leather strap that he used in place of a chain.

When Della reached home her intoxication gave way a little to prudence and reason. She got out her curling irons and lighted the gas and went to work repairing the <u>ravages</u> made by generosity added to love. Which is always a tremendous task, dear friends—a mammoth task.

Within forty minutes her head was covered with tiny, close-lying curls that made her look wonderfully like a truant schoolboy. She looked at her reflection in the mirror long, carefully, and critically.

"If Jim doesn't kill me," she said to herself, "before he takes a second look at me, he'll say I look like a Coney Island[7] chorus girl. But what could I do—oh! what could I do with a dollar and eighty-seven cents?"

At 7 o'clock the coffee was made and the frying-pan was on the back of the stove hot and ready to cook the chops.

Jim was never late. Della doubled the fob chain in her hand and sat on the corner of the table near the door that he always entered. Then she heard his step on the stair away down on the first flight, and she turned white for just a moment. She had a habit of saying little silent prayers about the simplest everyday things, and now she whispered: "Please God, make him think I am still pretty."

The door opened and Jim stepped in and closed it. He looked thin and very serious. Poor fellow, he was only twenty-two—and to be burdened with a family! He needed a new overcoat and he was without gloves.

Jim stopped inside the door, as immovable as a setter at the scent of quail. His eyes were fixed upon Della, and there was an expression in them that she could not read, and it terrified her. It was not anger, nor surprise, nor disapproval, nor horror, nor any of the sentiments that she had been prepared for. He simply stared at her fixedly with that peculiar expression on his face.

Della wriggled off the table and went for him.

"Jim, darling," she cried, "don't look at me that way. I had my hair cut off and sold it because I couldn't have lived through Christmas without giving you a present. It'll grow out again—you won't mind, will you? I just had to do it. My hair grows awfully fast. Say 'Merry Christmas!' Jim, and let's be happy. You don't know what a nice— what a beautiful, nice gift I've got for you."

---

7. **Coney Island** beach and amusement park in Brooklyn, New York.

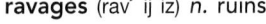

ravages (rav´ ij iz) *n.* ruins

Reading Check

What does Della sell for twenty dollars?

Hairdresser's Window, 1907, John Sloan, Wadsworth Atheneum, Hartford, Connecticut

▲ **Critical Viewing** How do you think Della felt as she approached Madame Sofronie's shop? **[Analyze]**

"You've cut off your hair?" asked Jim, laboriously, as if he had not arrived at that patent fact yet even after the hardest mental labor.

"Cut it off and sold it," said Della. "Don't you like me just as well, anyhow? I'm me without my hair, ain't I?"

Jim looked about the room curiously.

"You say your hair is gone?" he said, with an air almost of idiocy.

"You needn't look for it," said Della. "It's sold, I tell you—sold and gone, too. It's Christmas Eve, boy. Be good to me, for it went for you. Maybe the hairs of my head were numbered," she went on with a sudden serious sweetness, "but nobody could ever count my love for you. Shall I put the chops on, Jim?"

Out of his trance Jim seemed quickly to wake. He enfolded his Della. For ten seconds let us regard with <u>discreet</u> scrutiny some inconsequential object in the other direction. Eight dollars a week or a million a year—what is the difference? A mathematician or a wit would give you the wrong answer. The Magi brought valuable gifts, but that was not among them. This dark assertion will be illuminated later on.

Jim drew a package from his overcoat pocket and threw it upon the table.

"Don't make any mistake, Dell," he said, "about me. I don't think there's anything in the way of a haircut or a shave or a shampoo that could make me like my girl any less. But if you'll unwrap that package you may see why you had me going a while at first."

White fingers and nimble tore at the string and paper. And then an ecstatic scream of joy; and then, alas! a quick feminine change to hysterical tears and wails, necessitating the immediate employment of all the comforting powers of the lord of the flat.

For there lay The Combs—the set of combs, side and back, that Della had worshipped for long in a Broadway window. Beautiful combs, pure tortoise shell, with jeweled rims—just the shade to wear in the beautiful vanished hair. They were expensive combs, she knew, and her heart had simply craved and yearned over them without the least hope of possession. And now, they were hers, but the tresses that should have adorned the coveted adornments were gone.

But she hugged them to her bosom, and at length she was able to look up with dim eyes and a smile and say: "My hair grows so fast, Jim!"

And then Della leaped up like a little singed cat and cried, "Oh, oh!"

Jim had not yet seen his beautiful present. She held it out to him

discreet (di skrēt') adj. tactful; respectful

▼ Critical Viewing
How might Della have felt about an elaborate, expensive comb like this one? [Connect]

✔ Reading Check
What gift does Jim give to Della?

eagerly upon her open palm. The dull precious metal seemed to flash with a reflection of her bright and ardent spirit.

"Isn't it a dandy, Jim? I hunted all over town to find it. You'll have to look at the time a hundred times a day now. Give me your watch. I want to see how it looks on it."

Instead of obeying, Jim tumbled down on the couch and put his hands under the back of his head and smiled.

"Dell," said he, "let's put our Christmas presents away and keep 'em a while. They're too nice to use just at present. I sold the watch to get the money to buy your combs. And now suppose you put the chops on."

The Magi, as you know, were wise men—wonderfully wise men—who brought gifts to the Babe in the manger. They invented the art of giving Christmas presents. Being wise, their gifts were no doubt wise ones, possibly bearing the privilege of exchange in case of duplication. And here I have lamely related to you the uneventful chronicle of two foolish children in a flat who most unwisely sacrificed for each other the greatest treasures of their house. But in a last word to the wise of these days let it be said that of all who give gifts these two were the wisest. Of all who give and receive gifts, such as they are wisest. Everywhere they are wisest. They are the magi.

Review and Assess

Thinking About the Selection

1. **Respond:** If you were Jim or Della, how would you feel about the gift you received?

2. **(a) Recall:** How do Jim and Della feel toward each other?
   (b) Support: What evidence from the story leads you to your opinion?

3. **(a) Recall:** What does Della do to get money for Jim's present?
   (b) Infer: What does her action suggest about her character?

4. **(a) Recall:** How does Jim react when he sees that Della has cut her hair? **(b) Analyze:** Why does Della misunderstand Jim's reaction?

5. **(a) Recall:** How did Jim get the money for Della's gift?
   (b) Connect: How does he react to the watch chain?
   (c) Infer: Why does he react in such a way?

6. **Draw Conclusions:** O. Henry says of these "two foolish children" that they were "the wisest." How do you think he would define wisdom?

7. **Take a Position:** Do you believe it is wise to give up your most treasured possessions to buy something meaningful for a loved one? Why or why not?

O. Henry

(1862–1910)

William Sydney Porter, alias O. Henry, was born in Greensboro, North Carolina, and left school at sixteen to work at his uncle's drugstore. In 1882, he moved to Texas. In Austin he worked at a ranch, a general land office, and then the First National Bank. In Houston, he became a reporter, columnist, and cartoonist for the *Houston Post*.

In 1896, Porter was indicted for embezzling bank funds. He fled to Honduras but returned to Texas when he learned his wife was dying. After her death, Porter was arrested, convicted, and sent to prison in Ohio, where he began writing short stories that made him immensely popular.

Released from prison, he changed his name to O. Henry and moved to New York City. Many of his stories, including "The Gift of the Magi," draw upon his observations of the lives of everyday New Yorkers.

Review and Assess

Literary Analysis

Plot

1. What is the central conflict, or struggle, in the **plot** of "The Gift of the Magi"?
2. What occurs at the climax, or high point, of the story?
3. Which events form the resolution?
4. The exposition extends to the introduction of the central conflict. Use this graphic organizer to help you describe the remaining stages in the plot of "The Gift of the Magi."

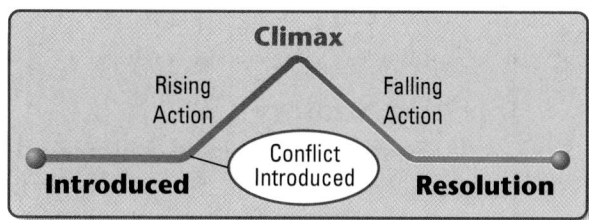

Connecting Literary Elements

5. In what ways was the ending different from what you expected?
6. Look back at the story. Which hints point to the **surprise ending**?
7. Although it was a surprise, did you find the ending logical and believable? Explain.

Reading Strategy

Asking Questions

8. Which **questions** about Della and Jim came to your mind as you read?
9. (a) List three details that the narrator reveals and three that he does not reveal. (b) What is the effect of the narrator's choice of details?

Extend Understanding

10. **History Connection:** This story takes place about a hundred years ago. How might the story—and especially Della and Jim— be different if the story took place today?

Quick Review

Plot is the sequence of events that make up a story. Plot is divided into five stages: **exposition** (the scene is set and background information is provided), **rising action** (the central conflict, or struggle, is introduced), **climax** (the high point of the conflict), **falling action** (the conflict lessens), and **resolution** (the conflict concludes and loose ends get tied up).

A **surprise ending** is a conclusion that differs from what a reader expects.

To fully understand the plot, **ask questions** about characters, events, and information the narrator reveals or conceals.

 Take It to the Net
www.phschool.com
Take the interactive self-test online to check your understanding of the selection.

Integrate Language Skills

Vocabulary Development Lesson

Word Analysis: Latin Prefix de-

In "The Gift of the Magi," you will encounter the word *depreciate*, meaning "to reduce in value." This word is derived from a Latin word meaning "price" and contains the Latin prefix *de-*, which in this case means "down." When something *depreciates*, its price goes down. The prefix *de-* can also mean "away from," as in *deviate*, or "undo," as in *defrost*.

Using what you know about the meaning of *de-*, match each phrase shown here with one of the words below.

a. demerit   **b.** derail   **c.** deform

1. run off the tracks
2. undo something's shape
3. grade for poor work

Concept Development: Synonyms

Write the word that is a synonym for, or means the same as, the vocabulary word on the left.

1. instigates		a. waterfall
2. depreciate		b. gaudy
3. cascade		c. cheapen
4. meretricious		d. pure
5. chaste		e. tactful
6. discreet		f. ruins
7. ravages		g. provokes

Spelling Strategy

If a word ends in a single consonant that is preceded by two vowels, do not double the final consonant when you add an ending. Thus, *discreet* + *-ly* = *discreetly*. Add *-ly*, *-ing*, or *-ed* to each word below to form a properly spelled new word.

1. chain   2. hour   3. kneel

Grammar Lesson

Adverb Phrases

An **adverb phrase** is a prepositional phrase that modifies a verb, an adjective, or an adverb. An adverb phrase answers the question *how? in what way? where? when?* or *to what extent?*

In this example, the adverb phrase is italicized.

Example: She let her hair fall *to its full length*. (to what extent did it fall?)

Practice Copy each of these sentences from the story. Underline the adverb phrases, and write the word or words each adverb phrase modifies.

1. Had the Queen of Sheba lived in the next flat across the airshaft, Della would have let her hair hang out the window.

2. The next two hours tripped by on rosy wings.
3. Within forty minutes her head was covered with tiny, close-lying curls.
4. He simply stared at her fixedly with that peculiar expression on his face.
5. She held it out to him eagerly upon her open palm.

Writing Application Write four sentences that contain adverb phrases. Each sentence should include a response to at least one of these questions: *How? Where? When?* Underline the phrases you have included.

W̶G Prentice Hall Writing and Grammar Connection: Chapter 21, Section 1

Writing Lesson

Story From Jim's Point of View

As you read "The Gift of the Magi," you learn about the experiences of Della and Jim through a narrator who stands outside the story. Rewrite the story, telling it from Jim's point of view.

Prewriting   Review the story and use a chart like the one shown to jot down information that is revealed about Jim. Next to each piece of information, write a sentence from Jim's perspective.

Model: Writing From a First-Person Perspective

Information From the Story	In Jim's Words
They took great pride in Jim's gold watch, which had been passed down to him.	I always cherished this watch, not for the gold, but for the memory of my father.

Drafting   Using Jim's words, draft your story. Remember that the entire narrative must be from Jim's perspective. Any information about Della that you include must be from Jim's point of view.

Revising   Reread your draft, checking for any inconsistencies in viewpoint. Decide whether Jim would truly know the information you provide. Rewrite any passage that is not written from Jim's perspective.

WG Prentice Hall Writing and Grammar Connection: Chapter 5, Section 2

Extension Activities

Listening and Speaking In a small group, prepare a **performance** of "The Gift of the Magi."

- Consider the best approach to take to show the characters and the setting.
- Work out the best way to include the information the narrator provides.
- Decide who will play each part.

If possible, tape your rehearsals for review. Perform the play for your classmates. Invite them to write a brief response. [**Group Activity**]

Research and Technology Prepare an **illustrated report** about life in New York or any other large American city around 1905, when "The Gift of the Magi" was written. Use reference books as well as an Internet search engine to find information and period illustrations. Look especially for pictures of clothing that appears very different from what people wear today.

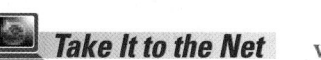 **Take It to the Net**   www.phschool.com

Go online for an additional research activity using the Internet.

CONNECTIONS
Literature and Society

Gift-Giving in the Technological World

In "The Gift of the Magi," Della spends the day before Christmas frantically searching stores for Jim's present. Had she lived in modern times, she could have saved time and trouble by shopping online via the Internet.

Search Engines

Della had no idea which store carried the platinum watch chain she sought. Today, she could use the Internet to locate the store and item. After logging on to the search engine of her choice, she would simply enter the object of her search: "watch-chain store." If her search yielded 500 watch stores in 12 different countries, she might wish to narrow her search further by doing an "AND" search. In this case, she would use the search engine's advanced search screen to add "New York

City" to her search terms. The results would list only New York City watch-chain stores, saving Della the cost of travel.

Store Web Sites

If Della already knew of stores that sold watch chains online, she could log on directly to each store's Web site. Sites sometimes include a "Search" box for typing in the name of a particular item. If the watch chain were in stock, Della might even be able to order it online and have it rush-delivered in time for Christmas. However, because online merchants are not likely to accept hair as payment, Della might have to apply for a credit card—another advance in the modern world.

Online Auctions

Della might have saved some money by bidding for her watch chain at an online auction. After logging on to an auction Web site, she would have identified the item she was seeking and found a list of available items. Della could then have bid against other buyers, with the item going to the highest bidder.

Connecting Literature and Society

1. Which method of online shopping do you think would have suited Della's needs best? Why?
2. What are the advantages of shopping online as opposed to shopping the way Della and Jim did? What are the disadvantages?

Advertisements

About Advertisements

An **advertisement** is a message intended to promote a product, a service, or an idea. People use advertisements for many purposes:

- Manufacturers advertise to persuade consumers to buy their goods.
- Companies advertise to create a positive public image of themselves.
- Politicians advertise to win votes.
- Special-interest groups advertise to promote causes they favor.
- Individuals advertise to sell homes, cars, and other property.

You can find advertisements in many places—in newspapers and magazines, on television and radio, on billboards and posters, and in your mail and e-mail.

Reading Strategy

Analyzing Persuasive Techniques: Appeal Through Expertise

Advertisers use many techniques to persuade consumers to buy products. One technique is the **appeal through expertise,** which takes advantage of the average customer's ignorance about the product.

The automobile advertisement on the next page states that the R-C-H automobile has a "semi-floating type" of rear axle. However, there is no explanation of what a semi-floating axle is or why it should be considered a unique and valuable feature. For all you know, every car is made with such an axle. Yet, the phrase sounds impressive. The ad reads as if it were written by experts, and readers might trust it, based solely on the technical language the copywriter uses.

As you read the entire ad, list each feature that it describes. Ask yourself: Is this feature likely to be familiar to customers? If the answer is no, list it in your notebook as an appeal through expertise.

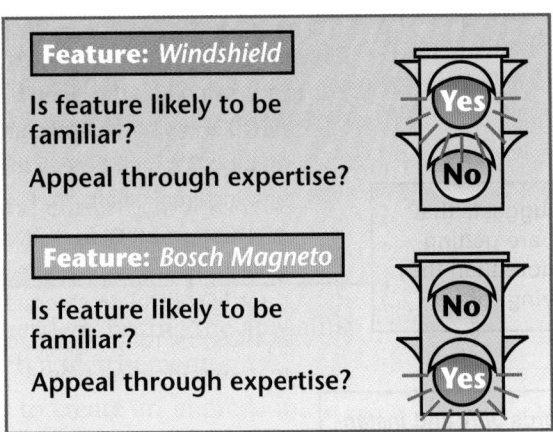

Feature: *Windshield*

Is feature likely to be familiar?

Appeal through expertise?

Feature: *Bosch Magneto*

Is feature likely to be familiar?

Appeal through expertise?

Prepare to Read

Sonata for Harp and Bicycle

 Take It to the Net

Visit www.phschool.com
for interactive activities
and instruction related to
"Sonata for Harp and
Bicycle," including

- background
- graphic organizers
- literary elements
- reading strategies

Preview

Connecting to the Literature

Mysteries are everywhere. Some people find safety in ignoring them or simply wondering about them without trying to figure them out. Certain people, however, feel compelled to solve these mysteries—even if danger is involved. In this story, a young man stumbles into a strange situation and tries to get to the bottom of it, come what may.

Background

A sonata [sə nät´ ə] is a musical composition in several movements, or parts, for one or more instruments. Sonatas are frequently written for solo piano or for piano and another instrument (such as a harp). In titling her story "Sonata for Harp and Bicycle," Joan Aiken playfully suggests a musical structure that will, like a sequence of chords, be resolved at the end.

Literary Analysis

Rising Action

The most suspenseful part of a story is the **rising action**—the part that introduces and develops the main conflict of the plot. The rising action of "Sonata for Harp and Bicycle" includes a complicated, puzzling mystery that fuels suspense as this passage from the story suggests:

> "—fire escape," he heard, as they came into the momentary hush of the carpeted entrance hall. And "—it's to do with a bicycle. A bicycle and a harp."

As you read, watch for the way in which a harp and a bicycle surprisingly converge.

Connecting Literary Elements

The rising action builds until it reaches the **climax,** or high point of interest. The climax is the emotional peak of the story—the moment toward which the plot builds. It is also the point from which the action winds down toward the resolution. As you read, use a chart like this one to record details leading to the climax and to explain the mystery.

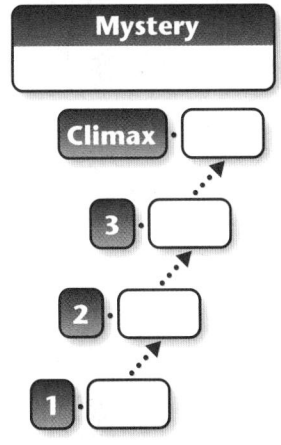

Reading Strategy

Predicting

When you **predict,** you guess what will happen on the basis of what you already know. While reading the story,

- make predictions by looking for clues about future events.
- record each clue you find, along with a prediction of where it will lead.

Revise your predictions as you read, and compare them with what actually happens at the end.

Vocabulary Development

encroaching (en krōch´ iŋ) *adj.* intruding in a sneaking way (p. 541)

tantalizingly (tan´ tə līz´ iŋ lē) *adv.* in a teasing way (p. 542)

furtive (fur´ tiv) *adj.* sneaky (p. 543)

menacing (men´ əs iŋ) *v.* threatening (p. 544)

reciprocate (ri sip´ rə kāt) *v.* return (p. 546)

ardent (ärd´ 'nt) *adj.* passionate (p. 546)

gossamer (gäs´ ə mər) *adj.* light, thin, and filmy (p. 546)

preposterous (prē päs´ tər əs) *adj.* absurd (p. 546)

engendered (en jen´ dərd) *adj.* produced (p. 547)

improbably (im präb´ ə blē) *adv.* unlikely to happen (p. 548)

Instruction with this selection addresses these standards:

R 1.3, 3.6*
W 1.1*, 1.5*
WOLC 1.1*
LS 2.3

* Standards tested on HS Exit Exam. For complete standards, see p. CA 4.

Sonata for Harp and Bicycle

Joan Aiken

"No one is allowed to remain in the building after five o'clock," Mr. Manaby told his new assistant, showing him into the little room that was like the inside of a parcel.

"Why not?"

"Directorial policy," said Mr. Manaby. But that was not the real reason.

Gaunt and sooty, Grimes Buildings lurched up the side of a hill toward Clerkenwell.[1] Every little office within its dim and crumbling exterior owned one tiny crumb of light—such was the proud boast of the architect—but toward evening the crumbs were collected as by an immense vacuum cleaner, absorbed and demolished, yielding to an uncontrollable mass of dark that came tumbling in through windows and doors to take their place. Darkness infested the building like a flight of bats returning willingly to roost.

"Wash hands, please. Wash hands, please," the intercom began to bawl in the passages at a quarter to five. Without much need of prompting, the staff hustled like lemmings along the corridors to green- and blue-tiled washrooms that mocked with an illusion of cheerfulness the <u>encroaching</u> dusk.

"All papers into cases, please," the voice warned, five minutes later. "Look at your desks, ladies and gentlemen. Any documents left lying about? Kindly put them away. Desks must be left clear and tidy. Drawers must be shut."

A multitudinous shuffling, a rustling as of innumerable bluebottle flies might have been heard by the attentive ear after this injunction, as the employees of Moreton Wold and Company thrust their papers into cases, hurried letters and invoices into drawers, clipped statistical abstracts together and slammed them into filing cabinets, dropped discarded copy into wastepaper baskets. Two minutes later, and not a desk throughout Grimes Buildings bore more than its customary coating of dust.

---

1. **Clerkenwell** district of London.

encroaching (en krōch′ iŋ) *adj.* intruding in a sneaking way

✓**Reading Check**

What is the new assistant told about being in the building after five o'clock?

"Hats and coats on, please. Hats and coats on, please. Did you bring an umbrella? Have you left any shopping on the floor?" At three minutes to five the homegoing throng was in the lifts[2] and on the stairs; a clattering, staccato-voiced flood darkened momentarily the great double doors of the building, and then as the first faint notes of St. Paul's[3] came echoing faintly on the frosty air, to be picked up near at hand by the louder chimes of St. Biddulph's-on-the-Wall, the entire premises of Moreton Wold stood empty.

"But why is it?" Jason Ashgrove, the new copywriter, asked his secretary one day. "Why are the staff herded out so fast? Not that I'm against it, mind you; I think it's an admirable idea in many ways, but there is the liberty of the individual to be considered, don't you think?"

"Hush!" Miss Golden, the secretary, gazed at him with large and terrified eyes. "You mustn't ask that sort of question. When you are taken onto the Established Staff you'll be told. Not before."

"But I want to know now," Jason said in discontent. "Do you know?"

"Yes, I do," Miss Golden answered <u>tantalizingly</u>. "Come on, or we shan't have finished the Oat Crisp layout by a quarter to." And she stared firmly down at the copy in front of her, lips folded, candyfloss hair falling over her face, lashes hiding eyes like peridots,[4] a girl with a secret.

Jason was annoyed. He rapped out a couple of rude and witty rhymes which Miss Golden let pass in a withering silence.

"What do you want for your birthday, Miss Golden? Sherry? Fudge? Bubble bath?"

"I want to go away with a clear conscience about Oat Crisps," Miss Golden retorted. It was not true; what she chiefly wanted was Mr. Jason Ashgrove, but he had not realized this yet.

"Come on, don't tease! I'm sure you haven't been on the Established Staff all that long," he coaxed her. "What happens when one is taken on, anyway? Does the Managing Director have us up for a confidential chat? Or are we given a little book called *The Awful Secret of Grimes Buildings*?"

Miss Golden wasn't telling. She opened her drawer and took out a white towel and a cake of rosy soap.

"Wash hands, please! Wash hands, please!"

Jason was frustrated. "You'll be sorry," he said. "I shall do something desperate."

"Oh no, you mustn't!" Her eyes were large with fright. She ran from the room and was back within a couple of moments, still drying her hands.

"If I took you out for a coffee, couldn't you give me just a tiny hint?"

Side by side Miss Golden and Mr. Ashgrove ran along the green-floored passages, battled down the white marble stairs among the hundred other employees from the tenth floor, the nine hundred from the floors below.

---

2. **lifts** *n.* British term for elevators.
3. **St. Paul's** famous church in London.
4. **peridots** (per′ i däts′) *n.* yellowish-green gems.

Literary Analysis
Rising Action What conflict is introduced here to begin the rising action?

tantalizingly (tan′ tə līz′ iŋ lē) *adv.* in a teasing way

Reading Strategy
Predicting Do you think the relationship between Miss Golden and Jason will develop into a romance? Which details help you decide?

He saw her lips move as she said something, but in the clatter of two thousand feet the words were lost.

"—fire escape," he heard, as they came into the momentary hush of the carpeted entrance hall. And "—it's to do with a bicycle. A bicycle and a harp."

"I don't understand."

Now they were in the street, chilly with the winter dusk smells of celery on carts, of swept-up leaves heaped in faraway parks, and cold layers of dew sinking among the withered evening primroses in the bombed areas. London lay about them wreathed in twilit mystery and fading against the barred and smoky sky. Like a ninth wave the sound of traffic overtook and swallowed them.

"Please tell me!"

But, shaking her head, she stepped onto a scarlet homebound bus and was borne away from him.

Jason stood undecided on the pavement, with the crowds dividing around him as around the pier of a bridge. He scratched his head, looked about him for guidance.

Literary Analysis
Rising Action What effect does Miss Golden's silence have on the rising action?

An ambulance clanged, a taxi hooted, a drill stuttered, a siren wailed on the river, a door slammed, a brake squealed, and close beside his ear a bicycle bell tinkled its tiny warning.

A bicycle, she had said. A bicycle and a harp.

Jason turned and stared at Grimes Buildings.

Somewhere, he knew, there was a back way in, a service entrance. He walked slowly past the main doors, with their tubs of snowy chrysanthemums, and up Glass Street. A tiny <u>furtive</u> wedge of darkness beckoned him, a snicket, a hacket, an alley carved into the thickness of the building. It was so narrow that at any moment, it seemed, the overtopping walls would come together and squeeze it out of existence.

furtive (fur′ tiv) *adj.* sneaky

Walking as softly as an Indian, Jason passed through it, slid by a file of dustbins,[5] and found the foot of the fire escape. Iron treads rose into the mist, like an illustration to a Gothic[6] fairy tale.

He began to climb.

When he had mounted to the ninth story he paused for breath. It was a lonely place. The lighting consisted of a dim bulb at the foot of every flight. A well of gloom sank beneath him. The cold fingers of the wind nagged and fluttered at the tails of his jacket, and he pulled the string of the fire door and edged inside.

Grimes Buildings were triangular, with the street forming the base of the triangle, and the fire escape the point. Jason could see two long passages coming toward him, meeting at an acute angle where he stood. He started down the left-hand one, tiptoeing in the cavelike silence. Nowhere was there any sound, except for the faraway drip of a tap.

✔**Reading Check**

Which question does Jason Ashgrove want answered by Miss Golden?

---

5. **dustbins** British term for garbage cans.
6. **Gothic** *adj.* mysterious.

and gave lessons in it. She began to <u>reciprocate</u> his love, and they used to share a picnic supper every night at eleven, and she'd stay on a while to keep him company. It was an idyll,[10] among the fire buckets and the furnace pipes.

"On Halloween he had summoned up the courage to propose to her. The day before he had told her he was going to ask her a very important question, and he came to the Buildings with a huge bunch of roses and a bottle of wine. But Miss Bell never turned up.

"The explanation was simple. Miss Bell, of course, had been losing a lot of sleep through her nocturnal romance, and so she used to take a nap in her music room between seven and ten, to save going home. In order to make sure that she would wake up, she persuaded her father, a distant relative of Graham Bell,[11] to attach an alarm-waking fixture to her telephone which called her every night at ten. She was too modest and shy to let Heron know that she spent those hours in the building, and to give him the pleasure of waking her himself.

"Alas! On this important evening the line failed, and she never woke up. The telephone was in its infancy at that time, you must remember.

"Heron waited and waited. At last, mad with grief and jealousy, having called her home and discovered that she was not there, he concluded that she had betrayed him; he ran to the fire escape, and cast himself off it, holding the roses and the bottle of wine.

"Daisy did not long survive him but pined away soon after. Since that day their ghosts have haunted Grimes Buildings, he vainly patrolling the corridors on his bicycle, she playing her harp in the room she rented. *But they never meet.* And anyone who meets the ghost of William Heron will himself, within five days, leap down from the same fatal fire escape."

She gazed at him with tragic eyes.

"In that case we must lose no time," said Jason, and he enveloped her in an embrace as prompt as it was <u>ardent</u>. Looking down at the <u>gossamer</u> hair sprayed across his pin-stripe, he added, "Just the same it is a <u>preposterous</u> situation. Firstly, I have no intention of jumping off the fire escape—" here, however, he repressed a shudder as he remembered the cold, clutching hands of the evening before— "and secondly, I find it quite nonsensical that those two inefficient ghosts have spent fifty years in this building without coming across each other. We must remedy the matter, Berenice. We must not begrudge our new-found happiness to others."

He gave her another kiss so impassioned that the electric typewriter against which they were leaning began chattering to itself in a frenzy of enthusiasm.

"This very evening," he went on, looking at his watch, "we will put matters right for that unhappy couple and then, if I really have only five more days to live, which I don't for one moment believe, we will

---

10. **idyll** (ī′ dəl) *n.* romantic scene, usually in the country.
11. **Graham Bell** Alexander Graham Bell (1847–1922), the inventor of the telephone.

---

reciprocate (ri sip′ rə kāt) *v.* return

Literary Analysis
Rising Action How does this information change the nature of the story's conflict?

ardent (ärd′ 'nt) *adj.* passionate

gossamer (gäs′ ə mər) *adj.* light, thin, and filmy

preposterous (prē päs′ tər əs) *adj.* absurd

Reading Strategy
Predicting How do you think Jason plans to "remedy the matter"?

proceed to spend them together, my bewitching Berenice, in the most advantageous manner possible."

She nodded, spellbound.

"Can you work a switchboard?" he added. She nodded again. "My love, you are perfection itself. Meet me in the switchboard room then, at ten this evening. I would say, have dinner with me, but I shall need to make one or two purchases and see an old R.A.F.[12] friend. You will be safe from Heron's curse in the switchboard room if he always keeps to the corridors."

"I would rather meet him and die with you," she murmured.

"My angel, I hope that won't be necessary. Now," he said, sighing, "I suppose we should get down to our day's work."

Strangely enough the copy they wrote that day, although <u>engendered</u> from such agitated minds, sold more packets of Oat Crisps than any other advertising matter before or since.

That evening when Jason entered Grimes Buildings he was carrying two bottles of wine, two bunches of red roses, and a large canvas-covered bundle. Miss Golden, who had concealed herself in the switchboard room before the offices closed for the night, eyed these things with surprise.

"Now," said Jason, after he had greeted her, "I want you first to ring our own extension."

"No one will reply, surely?"

"I think she will reply."

Sure enough, when Berenice rang Extension 170 a faint, sleepy voice, distant and yet clear, whispered, "Hullo?"

"Is that Miss Bell?"

"Yes."

Berenice went a little pale. Her eyes sought Jason's and, prompted by him, she said formally, "Switchboard here, Miss Bell. Your ten o'clock call."

"Thank you," the faint voice said. There was a click and the line went blank.

"Excellent," Jason remarked. He unfastened his package and slipped its straps over his shoulders. "Now plug into the intercom."

Berenice did so, and then said, loudly and clearly, "Attention. Night watchman on duty, please. Night watchman on duty. You have an urgent summons to Room 492. You have an urgent summons to Room 492." The intercom echoed and reverberated through the empty corridors, then coughed itself to silence.

"Now we must run. You take the roses, sweetheart, and I'll carry the bottles."

Together they raced up eight flights of stairs and along the passages to Room 492. As they neared the door a burst of music met them—harp music swelling out, sweet and triumphant. Jason took a bunch of roses from Berenice, opened the door a little way, and gently deposited them,

---

12. **R.A.F.** Royal Air Force.

engendered (en jen´ dərd) *adj.* produced

Literary Analysis
Rising Action and Climax
Which details in this paragraph suggest that the story is nearing its climax?

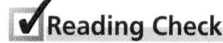**Reading Check**

According to Berenice, what happens to anyone who meets the ghost of William Heron?

with a bottle, inside the door. As he closed it again Berenice said breathlessly, "Did you see anyone?"

"No," he said. "The room was too full of music." She saw that his eyes were shining.

They stood hand in hand, reluctant to move away, waiting for they hardly knew what. Suddenly the door opened again. Neither Berenice nor Jason, afterward, would speak of what they saw but each was left with a memory, bright as the picture on a Salvador Dali[13] calendar, of a bicycle bearing on its saddle a harp, a bottle of wine, and a bouquet of red roses, sweeping <u>improbably</u> down the corridor and far, far away.

improbably (im präb´ ə blē) *adv.* unlikely to happen

"We can go now," Jason said.

He led Berenice to the fire door, tucking the bottle of Médoc in his jacket pocket. A black wind from the north whistled beneath them as they stood on the openwork platform, looking down.

"We don't want our evening to be spoiled by the thought of a curse hanging over us," he said, "so this is the practical thing to do. Hang onto the roses." And holding his love firmly, Jason pulled the rip cord of his R.A.F. friend's parachute and leaped off the fire escape.

A bridal shower of rose petals adorned the descent of Miss Golden, who was possibly the only girl to be kissed in midair in the district of Clerkenwell at ten minutes to midnight on Halloween.

---

13. **Salvador Dali** (sal´ və dôr´ dä´ lē) modern artist (1904–1989) famous for his unusual pictures.

Review and Assess

Thinking About the Selection

1. **Respond:** If you were Jason, would you try to solve the mystery of the Grimes Buildings? Explain.

2. **(a) Recall:** What three things does Miss Golden mention to Jason as they leave the Grimes Buildings at five P.M.?
   (b) Connect: How does he use this information?

3. **(a) Recall:** How has Jason changed when he sees Miss Golden the next day? **(b) Analyze Cause and Effect:** What evidence is there that his encounter in the closed building causes the change?

4. **(a) Recall:** How does Jason avoid the curse that awaits anyone who sees Heron's ghost? **(b) Speculate:** Who was more concerned about the curse—Jason or Berenice? Explain.
   (c) Infer: Why do you think Berenice agrees to assist Jason?

5. **Generalize:** What lesson do the circumstances of William Heron's death teach about the danger of making rash decisions?

Joan Aiken

(b. 1924)

Joan Aiken, the daughter of the poet Conrad Aiken, was born in England and lived with her family in an eerie old house, an experience that helped foster her fascination with mystery and the unexplained.

Aiken began writing at five and published her first story at sixteen. After working in London for a magazine, an advertising agency, and the United Nations, she decided to pursue what she has called "the family trade." Her immense output includes novels, poems, plays, and stories.

Known for her wit, Aiken called her first short-story collection *All You Ever Wanted* and her second *More Than You Bargained For.*

Like other writers, she sometimes uses personal experiences in her work. Jason Ashgrove, the main character of "Sonata for Harp and Bicycle," writes advertising copy, as Aiken once did.

Review and Assess

Literary Analysis
Rising Action

1. At what point in the story does the **rising action** begin? Explain.
2. Why do the sounds that Jason hears in the empty building increase the tension and suspense of the rising action?
3. What information keeps the action of the plot rising on the morning after Jason's escape from Heron?

Connecting Literary Elements

4. Using a chart like the one shown, identify two events in the rising action and determine which event marks the **climax** of the story.

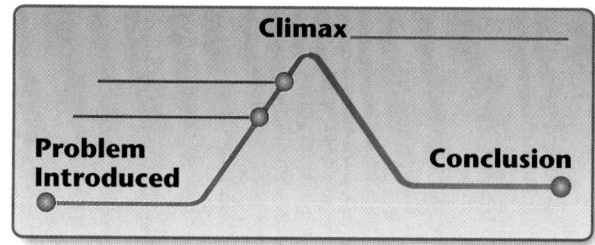

5. What makes the climax the true emotional peak?
6. Which specific events preceding the climax lead you to believe that the climax is imminent? Explain.

Reading Strategy
Predicting

7. Jason enters the Grimes Buildings after closing and hears a bicycle bell tinkling. What **predictions** did you make based on this event?
8. Using a chart like the one shown, explain which clues in the story helped you make the most accurate predictions.

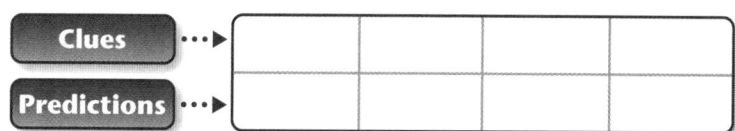

Extend Understanding

9. **Cultural Connection:** This story is set in London and refers to local landmarks. Does the effect of the story depend on its setting, or could it just as well be set in any large city? Explain.

Integrate Language Skills

Vocabulary Development Lesson

Word Analysis: Words From Myths

Many English words derive their meaning from names in Greek mythology. *Echo* is a nymph who pined away until only her voice remained. *Hercules* is a son of Zeus known for his strength. *Narcissus* is a handsome youth in love with his reflection.

Use the clues above to write a definition for each word below.

1. echo   2. herculean   3. narcissism

Spelling Strategy

If a word ends in two consonants, do not change the consonants when you add a word ending. Thus, *encroach + -ing = encroaching.* Add *-ful*, *-ive*, or *-en* to the words below to create three properly spelled new words.

1. gold   2. help   3. collect

Concept Development: Synonyms

Correctly match each word on the left with its synonym on the right. To help you, review the vocabulary list on p. 539.

1. encroaching   a. passionate
2. tantalizingly   b. threatening
3. furtive   c. created
4. menacing   d. delicate
5. reciprocate   e. teasingly
6. ardent   f. unlikely
7. gossamer   g. secretive
8. preposterous   h. intruding
9. engendered   i. nonsensical
10. improbably   j. return

Grammar Lesson

Participial Phrases

A **participle** is a verb form that acts as an adjective. A **participial phrase** is a participle with an accompanying adverb, adverb phrase, or complement. To avoid misplaced modifiers—participles or participial phrases that seem to modify the wrong words—place a participle or participial phrase as close to the word it modifies as possible.

> **Participle:** He heard a *clattering* noise. (modifies *noise*)
> **Participial Phrase:** He heard them *clattering down the stairs.* (modifies *them*)
> **Misplaced Modifier:** *Converging,* Jason saw down the corridors. (modifies *Jason*)
> **Correct:** Jason saw down the *converging* corridors. (modifies *corridors*)

Practice Identify each participle or participial phrase. Indicate the word each one modifies and correct any misplaced modifiers.

1. Frightened by what she saw, she told him the story.
2. Heron was the watchman, patrolling from dusk to dawn.
3. We will spend our time together, my bewitching Berenice.
4. He carried red roses and a covered bundle.
5. Hanging in the air, Jason felt danger.

Writing Application Rewrite three sentences from the story, using a participle or participial phrase correctly in each.

 Prentice Hall Writing and Grammar Connection: Chapter 21, Section 1

Writing Lesson

Critical Review

Joan Aiken has said, "A flat or unsatisfactory ending is the worst sin a writer can commit." Write a critical review evaluating the ending of "Sonata for Harp and Bicycle," and indicate whether Aiken has provided a satisfactory or unsatisfactory ending.

Prewriting   Make a list of the qualities that you think create satisfactory and unsatisfactory endings to stories. Then, check off the qualities that relate to Aiken's story.

Model: Evaluating a Story's Ending

Satisfactory	Unsatisfactory
☑ when problems are resolved for characters	☐ when events are predictable

Drafting   The first sentence of your review should state your opinion about the ending. Follow up by referring to examples from the story to provide support for your views.

Revising   Reread your draft. Circle any descriptive words you use to convey positive or negative criticism. If you have used vague or overused words, consider replacing them with more precise words.

W̶G̶ *Prentice Hall Writing and Grammar Connection: Chapter 13, Section 2*

Extension Activities

Listening and Speaking Develop and perform a **talk-show interview** featuring Berenice, Jason, the two ghosts, and the host of the program.

- Review the story and jot down the experiences of Berenice and Jason and the two ghosts.
- Plan the interview so that the two pairs of guests tell what happened at the Grimes Buildings from their own perspectives.
- Practice your interview, providing enough time for each character to speak.

Present your interview to your class. [**Group Activity**]

Research and Technology Research a famous real-life mystery, and create a **timeline** outlining the facts and summarizing the details. Search the Internet or the library for help in locating information about your subject. Compare the elements of the real-life mystery to those of the mystery in "Sonata for Harp and Bicycle." Present the timeline and your comparison to the class.

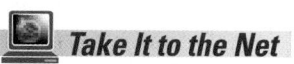 **Take It to the Net**   www.phschool.com

Go online for an additional research activity using the Internet.

Prepare to Read

The Scarlet Ibis

Take It to the Net

Visit www.phschool.com for interactive activities and instruction related to "The Scarlet Ibis," including

- background
- graphic organizers
- literary elements
- reading strategies

Preview

Connecting to the Literature

Sometimes your best pal is also the biggest pain in your neck. The narrator of "The Scarlet Ibis" has these conflicting feelings toward his younger brother. Although his brother is his closest companion, the narrator is embarrassed by him and makes tremendous demands on him.

Background

Found mostly in the South American tropics, the strikingly beautiful scarlet ibis is a wading bird with long legs, a long, slender neck, black-tipped wings, and a wingspan of more than three feet. Since it seldom appears in the United States north of Florida, the discovery of such a bird in coastal North Carolina, the setting of this story, is unexpected and dramatic.

Literary Analysis

Point of View

Point of view is the perspective from which a story is told. In **third-person point of view,** the narrator does not participate in the story. In **first-person point of view,** the narrator is a character who refers to himself or herself as "I." Look at this passage from "The Scarlet Ibis":

> . . . one afternoon as I watched him, my head poked between the iron posts of the foot of the bed, he looked straight at me and grinned. I skipped through the room, . . . shouting, "Mama, he smiled. He's all there! He's all there!" and he was.

In using this point of view, the writer enables you to experience the narrator's feelings firsthand.

Connecting Literary Elements

A first-person point of view lets you see firsthand how a character changes. A **dynamic character** is one who develops and grows during the course of a story. In contrast, a **static character** does not change. In "The Scarlet Ibis," Doodle's brother is a dynamic character whose emotions range among love, frustration, anger, and sadness over the course of the story.

Reading Strategy

Identifying With a Character

Authors who write from a first-person point of view invite you to walk through the story in the shoes of one of the characters. **Identify with the character** using these steps:

- Put yourself in his or her place.
- Consider how you would respond if you were in the same situation.

Use a chart like this one to record events from the story, the narrator's reaction to each event, and how *you* might have reacted.

Vocabulary Development

imminent (im´ ə nənt) *adj.* likely to happen soon (p. 558)

iridescent (ir ə des´ ənt) *adj.* having shifting, rainbowlike colors (p. 559)

vortex (vôr´ teks´) *n.* rushing whirl, drawing in all that surrounds it (p. 559)

infallibility (in fal´ ə bil´ ə tē) *n.* condition of being unable to fail (p. 559)

entrails (en´ trālz) *n.* internal organs, specifically intestines (p. 560)

precariously (prē ker´ ē əs lē) *adv.* insecurely (p. 561)

evanesced (ev´ ə nest´) *v.* faded away (p. 563)

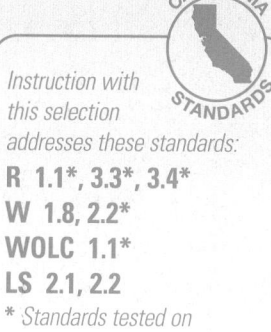

Instruction with this selection addresses these standards:

R 1.1*, 3.3*, 3.4*
W 1.8, 2.2*
WOLC 1.1*
LS 2.1, 2.2

* Standards tested on HS Exit Exam. For complete standards, see p. CA 4.

Narrator's Reaction
"He was a burden."

Event
Narrator takes Doodle everywhere

Your Reaction

The Scarlet Ibis

James Hurst

It was in the clove of seasons, summer was dead but autumn had not yet been born, that the ibis lit in the bleeding tree. The flower garden was stained with rotting brown magnolia petals and iron-weeds grew rank amid the purple phlox. The five o'clocks by the chimney still marked time, but the oriole nest in the elm was untenanted and rocked back and forth like an empty cradle. The last graveyard flowers were blooming, and their smell drifted across the cotton field and through every room of our house, speaking softly the names of our dead.

It's strange that all this is still so clear to me, now that the summer has long since fled and time has had its way. A grindstone stands where the bleeding tree stood, just outside the kitchen door, and now if an oriole sings in the elm, its song seems to die up in the leaves, a silvery dust. The flower garden is prim, the house a gleaming white, and the pale fence across the yard stands straight and spruce. But sometimes (like right now), as I sit in the cool, green-draped parlor, the grindstone begins to turn, and time with all its changes is ground away—and I remember Doodle.

Doodle was just about the craziest brother a boy ever had. Of course, he wasn't a crazy crazy like old Miss Leedie, who was in love with President Wilson and wrote him a letter every day, but was a nice crazy, like someone you meet in your dreams. He was born when I was six and was, from the outset, a disappointment. He seemed all head, with a tiny body which was red and shriveled like an old man's. Everybody thought he was going to die—everybody except Aunt Nicey, who had delivered him. She said he would live because he was born in a caul[1] and cauls were made from Jesus' nightgown. Daddy had Mr. Heath, the carpenter, build a little mahogany coffin for him. But he didn't die, and when he was three months old Mama and Daddy decided they might as well name him. They named him William Armstrong, which was like tying a big tail on a small kite. Such a name sounds good only on a tombstone.

I thought myself pretty smart at many things, like holding my breath, running, jumping, or climbing the vines in Old Woman Swamp, and I wanted more than anything else someone to race to Horsehead Landing, someone to box with, and someone to perch with in the top fork of the great pine behind the barn, where across the fields and swamps you could see the sea. I wanted a brother. But Mama, crying, told me that even if William Armstrong lived, he would never do these things with me. He might not, she sobbed, even be "all there." He might, as long as he lived, lie on the rubber sheet in the center of the bed in the front bedroom where the white marquisette curtains billowed out in the afternoon sea breeze, rustling like palmetto fronds.[2]

It was bad enough having an invalid brother, but having one who possibly was not all there was unbearable, so I began to make plans to kill him by smothering him with a pillow. However, one afternoon as I watched him, my head poked between the iron posts of the foot of the bed, he looked straight at me and grinned. I skipped through the rooms, down the echoing halls, shouting, "Mama, he smiled. He's all there! He's all there!" and he was.

When he was two, if you laid him on his stomach, he began to try to move himself, straining terribly. The doctor said that with his weak heart this strain would probably kill him, but it didn't. Trembling, he'd push himself up, turning first red, then a soft purple, and finally collapse back onto the bed like an old worn-out doll. I can still see Mama watching him, her hand pressed tight across her mouth, her eyes wide and unblinking. But he learned to crawl (it was his third winter), and we brought him out of the front bedroom, putting him on the rug before the fireplace. For the first time he became one of us.

As long as he lay all the time in bed, we called him William Armstrong, even though it was formal and sounded as if we were referring to one of our ancestors, but with his creeping around on the deerskin rug and beginning to talk, something had to be done about

---

1. caul (kôl) *n.* membrane enclosing a baby at birth.
2. palmetto fronds palm leaves.

Literary Analysis
Point of View Which details indicate the point of view from which this story is written?

**Reading Check**

How does William Armstrong respond when the narrator pokes his head through the posts of the bed to look at him?

his name. It was I who renamed him. When he crawled, he crawled backwards, as if he were in reverse and couldn't change gears. If you called him, he'd turn around as if he were going in the other direction, then he'd back right up to you to be picked up. Crawling backward made him look like a doodle-bug, so I began to call him Doodle, and in time even Mama and Daddy thought it was a better name than William Armstrong. Only Aunt Nicey disagreed. She said caul babies should be treated with special respect since they might turn out to be saints. Renaming my brother was perhaps the kindest thing I ever did for him, because nobody expects much from someone called Doodle.

Although Doodle learned to crawl, he showed no signs of walking, but he wasn't idle. He talked so much that we all quit listening to what he said. It was about this time that Daddy built him a go-cart and I had to pull him around. At first I just paraded him up and down the piazza, but then he started crying to be taken out into the yard and it ended up by my having to lug him wherever I went. If I so much as picked up my cap, he'd start crying to go with me and Mama would call from wherever she was, "Take Doodle with you."

He was a burden in many ways. The doctor had said that he mustn't get too excited, too hot, too cold, or too tired and that he must always be treated gently. A long list of don'ts went with him, all of which I ignored once we got out of the house. To discourage his coming with me, I'd run with him across the ends of the cotton rows and career him around corners on two wheels. Sometimes I accidentally turned him over, but he never told Mama. His skin was very sensitive, and he had to wear a big straw hat whenever he went out. When the going got rough and he had to cling to the sides of the go-cart, the hat slipped all the way down over his ears. He was a sight. Finally, I could see I was licked. Doodle was my brother and he was going to cling to me forever, no matter what I did, so I dragged him across the burning cotton field to share with him the only beauty I knew, Old Woman Swamp. I pulled the go-cart through the saw-tooth fern, down into the green dimness where the palmetto fronds whispered by the stream. I lifted him out and set him down in the soft rubber grass beside a tall pine. His eyes were round with wonder as he gazed about him, and his little hands began to stroke the rubber grass. Then he began to cry.

"For heaven's sake, what's the matter?" I asked, annoyed.

Two Boys in a Punt, N. C. Wyeth, Courtesy of Dr. and Mrs. William A. Morton, Jr.

▲ **Critical Viewing**
What can you tell about the brothers' relationship from this illustration and the details in the story? **[Infer]**

"It's so pretty," he said. "So pretty, pretty, pretty."

After that day Doodle and I often went down into Old Woman Swamp. I would gather wildflowers, wild violets, honeysuckle, yellow jasmine, snakeflowers, and water lilies, and with wire grass we'd weave them into necklaces and crowns. We'd bedeck ourselves with our handiwork and loll about thus beautified, beyond the touch of the everyday world. Then when the slanted rays of the sun burned orange in the tops of the pines, we'd drop our jewels into the stream and watch them float away toward the sea.

There is within me (and with sadness I have watched it in others) a knot of cruelty borne by the stream of love, much as our blood sometimes bears the seed of our destruction, and at times I was mean to Doodle. One day I took him up to the barn loft and showed him his casket, telling him how we all had believed he would die. It was covered with a film of Paris green[3] sprinkled to kill the rats, and screech owls had built a nest inside it.

Doodle studied the mahogany box for a long time, then said, "It's not mine."

"It is," I said. "And before I'll help you down from the loft, you're going to have to touch it."

"I won't touch it," he said sullenly.

"Then I'll leave you here by yourself," I threatened, and made as if I were going down.

Doodle was frightened of being left. "Don't go leave me, Brother," he cried, and he leaned toward the coffin. His hand, trembling, reached out, and when he touched the casket he screamed. A screech owl flapped out of the box into our faces, scaring us and covering us with Paris green. Doodle was paralyzed, so I put him on my shoulder and carried him down the ladder, and even when we were outside in the bright sunshine, he clung to me, crying, "Don't leave me. Don't leave me."

When Doodle was five years old, I was embarrassed at having a brother of that age who couldn't walk, so I set out to teach him. We were down in Old Woman Swamp and it was spring and the sick-sweet smell of bay flowers hung everywhere like a mournful song. "I'm going to teach you to walk, Doodle," I said.

He was sitting comfortably on the soft grass, leaning back against the pine. "Why?" he asked.

I hadn't expected such an answer. "So I won't have to haul you around all the time."

"I can't walk, Brother," he said.

---

3. **Paris green** poisonous green powder.

Literary Analysis
Point of View How would this part of the story be different if a third-person narrator told it?

**Reading Check**
What does the narrator force Doodle to touch?

"Who says so?" I demanded.

"Mama, the doctor—everybody."

"Oh, you can walk," I said, and I took him by the arms and stood him up. He collapsed onto the grass like a half-empty flour sack. It was as if he had no bones in his little legs.

"Don't hurt me, Brother," he warned.

"Shut up. I'm not going to hurt you. I'm going to teach you to walk." I heaved him up again, and again he collapsed.

This time he did not lift his face up out of the rubber grass. "I just can't do it. Let's make honeysuckle wreaths."

"Oh yes you can, Doodle," I said. "All you got to do is try. Now come on," and I hauled him up once more.

It seemed so hopeless from the beginning that it's a miracle I didn't give up. But all of us must have something or someone to be proud of, and Doodle had become mine. I did not know then that pride is a wonderful, terrible thing, a seed that bears two vines, life and death. Every day that summer we went to the pine beside the stream of Old Woman Swamp, and I put him on his feet at least a hundred times each afternoon. Occasionally I too became discouraged because it didn't seem as if he was trying, and I would say, "Doodle, don't you *want* to learn to walk?"

He'd nod his head, and I'd say, "Well, if you don't keep trying, you'll never learn." Then I'd paint for him a picture of us as old men, white-haired, him with a long white beard and me still pulling him around in the go-cart. This never failed to make him try again.

Finally one day, after many weeks of practicing, he stood alone for a few seconds. When he fell, I grabbed him in my arms and hugged him, our laughter pealing through the swamp like a ringing bell. Now we knew it could be done. Hope no longer hid in the dark palmetto thicket but perched like a cardinal in the lacy toothbrush tree, brilliantly visible. "Yes, yes," I cried, and he cried it too, and the grass beneath us was soft and the smell of the swamp was sweet.

With success so imminent, we decided not to tell anyone until he could actually walk. Each day, barring rain, we sneaked into Old Woman Swamp, and by cotton-picking time Doodle was ready to show what he could do. He still wasn't able to walk far, but we could wait no longer. Keeping a nice secret is very hard to do, like holding your breath. We chose to reveal all on October eighth, Doodle's sixth birthday, and for weeks ahead we mooned around the house, promising everybody a most spectacular surprise. Aunt Nicey said that, after so much talk, if we produced anything less tremendous than the Resurrection,[4] she was going to be disappointed.

At breakfast on our chosen day, when Mama, Daddy, and Aunt Nicey were in the dining room, I brought Doodle to the door in the go-cart just as usual and had them turn their backs, making them cross

Reading Strategy
Identifying With a Character How would you feel if you were in Doodle's situation? Why?

imminent (im′ ə nənt) *adj.* likely to happen soon

---

4. **the Resurrection** (rez′ ə rek′ shən) the rising of Jesus Christ from the dead after his death and burial.

their hearts and hope to die if they peeked. I helped Doodle up, and when he was standing alone I let them look. There wasn't a sound as Doodle walked slowly across the room and sat down at his place at the table. Then Mama began to cry and ran over to him, hugging him and kissing him. Daddy hugged him too, so I went to Aunt Nicey, who was thanks praying in the doorway, and began to waltz her around. We danced together quite well until she came down on my big toe with her brogans, hurting me so badly I thought I was crippled for life.

Doodle told them it was I who had taught him to walk, so everyone wanted to hug me, and I began to cry.

"What are you crying for?" asked Daddy, but I couldn't answer. They did not know that I did it for myself; that pride, whose slave I was, spoke to me louder than all their voices, and that Doodle walked only because I was ashamed of having a crippled brother.

Within a few months Doodle had learned to walk well and his go-cart was put up in the barn loft (it's still there) beside his little mahogany coffin. Now, when we roamed off together, resting often, we never turned back until our destination had been reached, and to help pass the time, we took up lying. From the beginning Doodle was a terrible liar and he got me in the habit. Had anyone stopped to listen to us, we would have been sent off to Dix Hill.

My lies were scary, involved, and usually pointless, but Doodle's were twice as crazy. People in his stories all had wings and flew wherever they wanted to go. His favorite lie was about a boy named Peter who had a pet peacock with a ten-foot tail. Peter wore a golden robe that glittered so brightly that when he walked through the sunflowers they turned away from the sun to face him. When Peter was ready to go to sleep, the peacock spread his magnificent tail, enfolding the boy gently like a closing go-to-sleep flower, burying him in the gloriously <u>iridescent</u>, rustling <u>vortex</u>. Yes, I must admit it. Doodle could beat me lying.

Doodle and I spent lots of time thinking about our future. We decided that when we were grown we'd live in Old Woman Swamp and pick dog-tongue for a living. Beside the stream, he planned, we'd build us a house of whispering leaves and the swamp birds would be our chickens. All day long (when we weren't gathering dog-tongue) we'd swing through the cypresses on the rope vines, and if it rained we'd huddle beneath an umbrella tree and play stickfrog. Mama and Daddy could come and live with us if they wanted to. He even came up with the idea that he could marry Mama and I could marry Daddy. Of course, I was old enough to know this wouldn't work out, but the picture he painted was so beautiful and serene that all I could do was whisper Yes, yes.

Once I had succeeded in teaching Doodle to walk, I began to believe in my own <u>infallibility</u> and I prepared a terrific development program for him, unknown to Mama and Daddy, of course. I would teach him to run, to swim, to climb trees, and to fight. He, too, now

Literary Analysis
Point of View What effect does the narrator's admission of his motive have on your perception of his development?

iridescent (ir´ ə des´ ənt) *adj.* having shifting, rainbowlike colors

vortex (vôr´ teks´) *n.* rushing whirl, drawing in all that surrounds it

infallibility (in fal´ ə bil´ ə tē) *n.* condition of being unable to fail

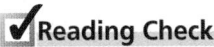 **Reading Check**

What surprise do the narrator and Doodle present to their parents?

believed in my infallibility, so we set the deadline for these accomplishments less than a year away, when, it had been decided, Doodle could start to school.

That winter we didn't make much progress, for I was in school and Doodle suffered from one bad cold after another. But when spring came, rich and warm, we raised our sights again. Success lay at the end of summer like a pot of gold, and our campaign got off to a good start. On hot days, Doodle and I went down to Horsehead Landing and I gave him swimming lessons or showed him how to row a boat. Sometimes we descended into the cool greenness of Old Woman Swamp and climbed the rope vines or boxed scientifically beneath the pine where he had learned to walk. Promise hung about us like the leaves, and wherever we looked, ferns unfurled and birds broke into song.

That summer, the summer of 1918, was blighted. In May and June there was no rain and the crops withered, curled up, then died under the thirsty sun. One morning in July a hurricane came out of the east, tipping over the oaks in the yard and splitting the limbs of the elm trees. That afternoon it roared back out of the west, blew the fallen oaks around, snapping their roots and tearing them out of the earth like a hawk at the <u>entrails</u> of a chicken. Cotton bolls were wrenched from the stalks and lay like green walnuts in the valleys between the rows, while the cornfield leaned over uniformly so that the tassels touched the ground. Doodle and I followed Daddy out into the cotton field, where he stood, shoulders sagging, surveying the ruin. When his chin sank down onto his chest, we were frightened, and Doodle slipped his hand into mine. Suddenly Daddy straightened his shoulders, raised a giant knuckly fist, and with a voice that seemed to rumble out of the earth itself began cursing heaven, hell, the weather, and the Republican Party. Doodle and I, prodding each other and giggling, went back to the house, knowing that everything would be all right.

And during that summer, strange names were heard through the house: Chateau Thierry, Amiens, Soissons, and in her blessing at the supper table, Mama once said, "And bless the Pearsons, whose boy Joe was lost at Belleau Wood."[5]

So we came to that clove of seasons. School was only a few weeks away, and Doodle was far behind schedule. He could barely clear the ground when climbing up the rope vines and his swimming was certainly not passable. We decided to double our efforts, to make that last drive and reach our pot of gold. I made him swim until he turned blue and row until he couldn't lift an oar. Wherever we went, I purposely walked fast, and although he kept up, his face turned red and his eyes became glazed. Once, he could go no further, so he collapsed on the ground and began to cry.

entrails (en´ trālz) *n.* internal organs, specifically intestines

Literary Analysis
Point of View Based on this passage, what do you learn about the narrator and his wishes for his brother?

---

5. **Château Thierry** (shá´ tō´ tē er´ ē), **Amiens** (á myan´), **Soissons** (swä sôn´), . . . **Belleau** (be lō´) **Wood** places in France where battles were fought during World War I.

"Aw, come on, Doodle," I urged. "You can do it. Do you want to be different from everybody else when you start school?"

"Does it make any difference?"

"It certainly does," I said. "Now, come on," and I helped him up.

As we slipped through dog days, Doodle began to look feverish, and Mama felt his forehead, asking him if he felt ill. At night he didn't sleep well, and sometimes he had nightmares, crying out until I touched him and said, "Wake up, Doodle. Wake up."

It was Saturday noon, just a few days before school was to start. I should have already admitted defeat, but my pride wouldn't let me. The excitement of our program had now been gone for weeks, but still we kept on with a tired doggedness. It was too late to turn back, for we had both wandered too far into a net of expectations and had left no crumbs behind.

Daddy, Mama, Doodle, and I were seated at the dining-room table having lunch. It was a hot day, with all the windows and doors open in case a breeze should come. In the kitchen Aunt Nicey was humming softly. After a long silence, Daddy spoke. "It's so calm, I wouldn't be surprised if we had a storm this afternoon."

"I haven't heard a rain frog," said Mama, who believed in signs, as she served the bread around the table.

"I did," declared Doodle. "Down in the swamp."

"He didn't," I said contrarily.

"You did, eh?" said Daddy, ignoring my denial.

"I certainly did," Doodle reiterated, scowling at me over the top of his iced-tea glass, and we were quiet again.

Suddenly, from out in the yard, came a strange croaking noise. Doodle stopped eating, with a piece of bread poised ready for his mouth, his eyes popped round like two blue buttons. "What's that?" he whispered.

I jumped up, knocking over my chair, and had reached the door when Mama called, "Pick up the chair, sit down again, and say excuse me."

By the time I had done this, Doodle had excused himself and had slipped out into the yard. He was looking up into the bleeding tree. "It's a great big red bird!" he called.

The bird croaked loudly again, and Mama and Daddy came out into the yard. We shaded our eyes with our hands against the hazy glare of the sun and peered up through the still leaves. On the topmost branch a bird the size of a chicken, with scarlet feathers and long legs, was perched <u>precariously</u>. Its wings hung down loosely, and as we watched, a feather dropped away and floated slowly down through the green leaves.

"It's not even frightened of us," Mama said.

"It looks tired," Daddy added. "Or maybe sick."

Doodle's hands were clasped at his throat, and I had never seen him stand still so long. "What is it?" he asked.

Daddy shook his head. "I don't know, maybe it's—"

Reading Strategy
Identifying With a Character How do you think Doodle feels when his brother asks him if he wants to be different from everybody else?

precariously (prē ker´ ē əs lē) *adv.* insecurely

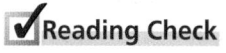Reading Check

What does Doodle find in the yard?

At that moment the bird began to flutter, but the wings were uncoordinated, and amid much flapping and a spray of flying feathers, it tumbled down, bumping through the limbs of the bleeding tree and landing at our feet with a thud. Its long, graceful neck jerked twice into an S, then straightened out, and the bird was still. A white veil came over the eyes and the long white beak unhinged. Its legs were crossed and its clawlike feet were delicately curved at rest. Even death did not mar its grace, for it lay on the earth like a broken vase of red flowers, and we stood around it, awed by its exotic beauty.

"It's dead," Mama said.

"What is it?" Doodle repeated.

"Go bring me the bird book," said Daddy.

I ran into the house and brought back the bird book. As we watched, Daddy thumbed through its pages. "It's a scarlet ibis," he said, pointing to a picture. "It lives in the tropics—South America to Florida. A storm must have brought it here."

Sadly, we all looked back at the bird. A scarlet ibis! How many miles it had traveled to die like this, in our yard, beneath the bleeding tree.

"Let's finish lunch," Mama said, nudging us back toward the dining room.

"I'm not hungry," said Doodle, and he knelt down beside the ibis.

"We've got peach cobbler for dessert," Mama tempted from the doorway.

Doodle remained kneeling. "I'm going to bury him."

"Don't you dare touch him," Mama warned. "There's no telling what disease he might have had."

"All right," said Doodle. "I won't."

Daddy, Mama, and I went back to the dining-room table, but we watched Doodle through the open door. He took out a piece of string from his pocket and, without touching the ibis, looped one end around its neck. Slowly, while singing softly "Shall We Gather at the River," he carried the bird around to the front yard and dug a hole in the flower garden, next to the petunia bed. Now we were watching him through the front window, but he didn't know it. His awkwardness at digging the hole with a shovel whose handle was twice as long as he was made us laugh, and we covered our mouths with our hands so he wouldn't hear.

When Doodle came into the dining room, he found us seriously eating our cobbler. He was pale and lingered just inside the screen door. "Did you get the scarlet ibis buried?" asked Daddy.

Doodle didn't speak but nodded his head.

"Go wash your hands, and then you can have some peach cobbler," said Mama.

"I'm not hungry," he said.

"Dead birds is bad luck," said Aunt Nicey, poking her head from the kitchen door. "Specially *red* dead birds!"

As soon as I had finished eating, Doodle and I hurried off to

▶ **Critical Viewing** How would you react if this exotic bird showed up in your back yard? **[Relate]**

Reading Strategy
Identifying With a Character With whose response toward the ibis do you identify most strongly? Why?

Scarlet Ibis, John James Audubon, New-York Historical Society

Horsehead Landing. Time was short, and Doodle still had a long way to go if he was going to keep up with the other boys when he started school. The sun, gilded with the yellow cast of autumn, still burned fiercely, but the dark green woods through which we passed were shady and cool. When we reached the landing, Doodle said he was too tired to swim, so we got into a skiff and floated down the creek with the tide. Far off in the marsh a rail was scolding, and over on the beach locusts were singing in the myrtle trees. Doodle did not speak and kept his head turned away, letting one hand trail limply in the water.

After we had drifted a long way, I put the oars in place and made Doodle row back against the tide. Black clouds began to gather in the southwest, and he kept watching them, trying to pull the oars a little faster. When we reached Horsehead Landing, lightning was playing across half the sky and thunder roared out, hiding even the sound of the sea. The sun disappeared and darkness descended, almost like night. Flocks of marsh crows flew by, heading inland to their roosting trees, and two egrets, squawking, arose from the oyster-rock shallows and careened away.

Doodle was both tired and frightened, and when he stepped from the skiff he collapsed onto the mud, sending an armada of fiddler crabs rustling off into the marsh grass. I helped him up, and as he wiped the mud off his trousers, he smiled at me ashamedly. He had failed and we both knew it, so we started back home, racing the storm. We never spoke (What are the words that can solder cracked pride?), but I knew he was watching me, watching for a sign of mercy. The lightning was near now, and from fear he walked so close behind me he kept stepping on my heels. The faster I walked, the faster he walked, so I began to run. The rain was coming, roaring through the pines, and then, like a bursting Roman candle, a gum tree ahead of us was shattered by a bolt of lightning. When the deafening peal of thunder had died, and in the moment before the rain arrived, I heard Doodle, who had fallen behind, cry out, "Brother, Brother, don't leave me! Don't leave me!"

The knowledge that Doodle's and my plans had come to naught was bitter, and that streak of cruelty within me awakened. I ran as fast as I could, leaving him far behind with a wall of rain dividing us. The drops stung my face like nettles, and the wind flared the wet glistening leaves of the bordering trees. Soon I could hear his voice no more.

I hadn't run too far before I became tired, and the flood of childish spite evanesced as well. I stopped and waited for Doodle. The sound of rain was everywhere, but the wind had died and it fell straight down in parallel paths like ropes

Literary Analysis
Point of View What might you learn about Doodle's silence here if the story were told from his point of view?

Reading Strategy
Identifying With a Character How do you think the narrator feels about his brother's failure?

evanesced (ev´ ə nest´) v. faded away

✔ **Reading Check**

What does Doodle do with the dead ibis?

hanging from the sky. As I waited, I peered through the downpour, but no one came. Finally I went back and found him huddled beneath a red nightshade bush beside the road. He was sitting on the ground, his face buried in his arms, which were resting on his drawn-up knees. "Let's go, Doodle," I said.

He didn't answer, so I placed my hand on his forehead and lifted his head. Limply, he fell backwards onto the earth. He had been bleeding from the mouth, and his neck and the front of his shirt were stained a brilliant red.

"Doodle! Doodle!" I cried, shaking him, but there was no answer but the ropy rain. He lay very awkwardly, with his head thrown far back, making his vermilion neck appear unusually long and slim. His little legs, bent sharply at the knees, had never before seemed so fragile, so thin.

I began to weep, and the tear-blurred vision in red before me looked very familiar. "Doodle!" I screamed above the pounding storm and threw my body to the earth above his. For a long long time, it seemed forever, I lay there crying, sheltering my fallen scarlet ibis from the heresy[6] of rain.

---

6. **heresy** (her´ i sē) idea opposed to the beliefs of a religion or philosophy.

Review and Assess

Thinking About the Selection

1. **Respond:** Do you blame the narrator for Doodle's death? Why or why not?

2. **(a) Recall:** How does Doodle react to Old Woman Swamp? **(b) Analyze:** What does Doodle's reaction suggest about his character?

3. **(a) Recall:** What do the brothers reveal on Doodle's sixth birthday? **(b) Deduce:** Do you think the family guessed the reason for the narrator's tears? Explain.

4. **(a) Recall:** What does the narrator want to teach Doodle to do next? **(b) Interpret:** Why do you think he sets such demanding goals for Doodle?

5. **(a) Recall:** What happens after the appearance of the scarlet ibis? **(b) Infer:** What do you think motivates Doodle to treat the ibis as he does?

6. **Compare:** How is Doodle like the scarlet ibis?

7. **Extend:** Do you think it is normal to have mixed feelings about a brother or sister? Why or why not?

James Hurst

(b. 1922)

James Hurst grew up in coastal North Carolina, a place of quiet landscapes and violent storms. Before becoming a writer, he studied both chemical engineering and opera, served in the army during World War II, and eventually took a job in a New York bank. Hurst's career at the bank lasted for thirty-four years.

While at the bank, Hurst spent his evenings writing short stories. "The Scarlet Ibis," his most popular story, was published in 1960. One of the qualities that makes it such a powerful story is Hurst's use of symbols—objects, people, or ideas that have an underlying meaning. Hurst wrote, "I wanted [the ibis] to represent [the character of Doodle]—not Doodle's physical self, but his spirit."

Review and Assess

Literary Analysis

Point of View

1. Does Hurst's use of the **first-person point of view** make you feel more involved in the story? Why or why not?
2. What is the effect of having the narrator look back at the events years after they occurred?
3. If it were told from another point of view, the story would be very different. In a chart like the one shown, record how various events might be seen from Daddy's and Mama's perspective.

Connecting Literary Elements

4. Is Doodle a **dynamic** or a **static character**? Using a chart like this one, cite story details that will help you answer the question.

5. Are the mother and father in the story **dynamic characters?** Explain.
6. (a) Do you think a first-person narrator must always be a dynamic character? (b) Would "The Scarlet Ibis" be an effective story if the narrator never changed? Why or why not?

Reading Strategy

Identifying With a Character

7. **Identify** with the narrator by describing how you might have treated Doodle if he had been your little brother.
8. What can you learn from the narrator's experiences that you can apply to your relationships?

Extend Understanding

9. **Cultural Connection:** The story refers briefly to World War I, then raging in Europe. What connections can be made between the horrors of war and the pain of ordinary life? Explain.

Quick Review

Point of view is the perspective from which a story is told.

In **third-person point of view,** the narrator does not participate in the story.

In **first-person point of view,** the narrator is a character within the story who refers to himself or herself as "I."

A **dynamic character** is one who develops and grows during the course of the story. A **static character** does not change.

To **identify with a character,** put yourself in his or her place by considering how you would act in similar circumstances.

 Take It to the Net

www.phschool.com
Take the interactive self-test online to check your understanding of the selection.

Integrate Language Skills

Vocabulary Development Lesson

Word Analysis: Latin Prefix *in-*

The Latin prefix *in-*, a variant spelling of the prefix *un-*, usually means "not." *Infallible*, then, means "not fallible" or "not able to fail." For each word below, explain how adding *in-* changes its meaning.

1. correct **2.** dependent **3.** compatible

Spelling Strategy

The plural of some words ending in *x* may be formed by changing the *x* to *ces*. Sometimes, you may need to change the vowel that precedes the *x*, too. One plural form of the word *vortex*, for example, is *vortices*.

Look up the plural form(s) of the following words, and use each plural form in a sentence.

1. index **2.** appendix **3.** apex **4.** matrix

Concept Development: Synonyms and Antonyms

Review the vocabulary word list on page 553. Then, decide whether the word pairs below are synonyms, words with similar meanings, or antonyms, words with opposite meanings. Write your answer in your notebook.

1. entrails, guts
2. infallibility, unreliability
3. precariously, securely
4. vortex, whirlpool
5. imminent, proximate
6. endured, evanesced
7. shimmering, iridescent

Grammar Lesson

Gerund Phrases

A **gerund** is a verb form ending in *-ing* that acts as a noun. In a sentence, a gerund can be the subject, object, or object of a preposition. A **gerund phrase** is a gerund with modifiers or a complement, all acting together as a noun. (Do not confuse a gerund with a **present participle,** which acts as an adjective and also ends in *-ing.*)

Look at the following examples.

Gerund: *Boating* was a challenge. (*subject*)

Gerund Phrase: *Boating with Doodle* was even harder. (*subject*)

He faced the challenge of *boating with Doodle*. (*object of preposition*)

Practice Write the gerund or gerund phrase in each sentence, and identify its function.

1. Crawling backward was a necessity.
2. Renaming my brother was my idea.
3. He learned to crawl, but he showed no signs of walking.
4. One day, after weeks of practicing, he stood alone for a few seconds.
5. Keeping a secret is hard to do, like holding your breath.

Writing Application Choose and rewrite three sentences from "The Scarlet Ibis," using gerund phrases in all of them.

WG *Prentice Hall Writing and Grammar Connection: Chapter 21, Section 1*

Writing Lesson

Journal Entry

Put yourself in the place of the narrator in "The Scarlet Ibis," and write a journal entry describing your feelings about Doodle's death.

Prewriting Start by making a list of the emotions you think the narrator might have felt after his brother's death, and the reasons for those emotions. Then, make a list of Doodle's qualities based on the story.

Model: Listing to Elaborate Emotions

Emotion	Reason
guilt	I ran away from him in the storm.

> Providing a reason for a particular emotion conveys a clear image for the journal entry.

Drafting Using the lists you have generated, write one paragraph explaining how you feel about the loss of Doodle. Then, write another paragraph explaining what you miss most about him.

Revising Read your journal entry to a classmate. Make sure that you have conveyed all of the feelings you listed. Add additional details or insights to reveal the true emotions of the narrator.

W̶G *Prentice Hall Writing and Grammar Connection: Chapter 13, Section 2*

Extension Activities

Research and Technology Coastal North Carolina—the setting of "The Scarlet Ibis"—is an area of striking natural beauty. In a group, gather information to prepare a **travel brochure** about the region.

- Use Internet resources to gather maps and photographs of the region.
- Include appealing information to make sure that the presentation is directed toward attracting tourists.

If possible, use desktop graphics software to publish your brochure. [**Group Activity**]

Listening and Speaking Research the role of the ibis in Egyptian myth and religion and deliver a **presentation** about it. Compare and contrast the Egyptian attitude toward the ibis with that of the characters in the story. After your presentation, ask your class for feedback.

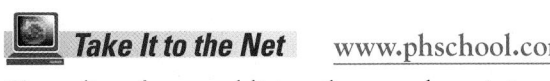 **Take It to the Net**   www.phschool.com

Go online for an additional research activity using the Internet.

Prepare to Read

Blues Ain't No Mockin Bird ◆ Uncle Marcos

 Take It to the Net

Visit www.phschool.com
for interactive activities
and instruction related to
the selections, including
- background
- graphic organizers
- literary elements
- reading strategies

Preview

Connecting to the Literature

Certain people you meet in childhood may become etched in memory forever because of their unique personality traits or the lessons they teach you. In these stories, you will meet two memorable characters who leave an indelible impression on the stories' narrators.

Background

Imagine a world in which people can float in the air and it can rain continuously for years. These fantastic details capture the way a group of writers, including Isabel Allende, use words. The authors practice a style of writing known as "magical realism," in which fantastic details blend with realistic ones to stretch the boundaries of readers' imaginations.

Literary Analysis

Characterization

Characterization refers to the way a writer reveals a character's personality traits. With **direct characterization,** writers directly state a character's personality traits. In **indirect characterization,** a writer uses a character's actions, thoughts, and feelings to suggest a character's traits. In this passage from "Uncle Marcos," the writer characterizes Marcos indirectly:

> He spent the whole night making incomprehensible movements in the drawing room; later they turned out to be exercises . . .

Notice how the authors of these selections let their characters' words and actions, along with the reactions of others, reveal what they are like.

Comparing Literary Works

A character's personality traits are often revealed through the **narrator**—the person from whose perspective a story is told.

- A **third-person narrator** is not a character in the story.
- A **first-person narrator** is a character within the story.

The narrator in "Blues Ain't No Mockin Bird" is part of the story, while the narrator of "Uncle Marcos" stands outside the story. Compare the author's choice of narrator in each selection.

Instruction with these selections addresses these standards:
R 1.1*, 3.3*, 3.4*
W 1.1*, 1.3*
WOLC 1.1*
LS 2.1
* Standards tested on HS Exit Exam. For complete standards, see p. CA 4.

Reading Strategy

Making Inferences About Characters

When you **make an inference about a character,** you draw a conclusion using details the author provides. For example, in "Uncle Marcos," you will learn that Marcos once serenaded a woman. From this, you can infer that he is romantic and unpredictable.

To make inferences, look beyond the words on the page, and ask yourself what the author implies about the characters. On a chart like this one, list details from the selections and the inferences you make from them.

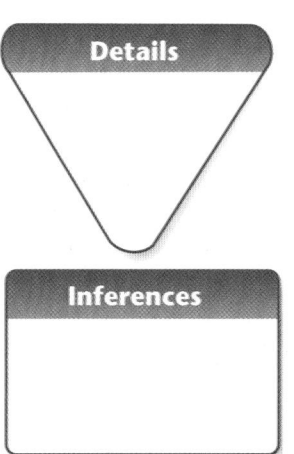

Vocabulary Development

lassoed (las´ ōd´) *adj.* wrapped around (p. 570)

formality (fôr mal´ ə tē) *n.* established rules or customs (p. 574)

pallid (pal´ id) *adj.* pale (p. 577)

vanquished (vaŋ´ kwisht) *adj.* defeated (p. 577)

fetid (fet´ id) *adj.* smelly (p. 577)

impassive (im pas´ iv) *adj.* showing no emotion (p. 578)

disconsolately (dis kän´ sə lit lē) *adv.* unhappily (p. 581)

unrequited (un ri kwīt´ id) *adj.* not reciprocated (p. 583)

BLUES AIN'T NO MOCKIN BIRD

Toni Cade Bambara

The puddle had frozen over, and me and Cathy went stompin in it. The twins from next door, Tyrone and Terry, were swingin so high out of sight we forgot we were waitin our turn on the tire. Cathy jumped up and came down hard on her heels and started tap-dancin. And the frozen patch splinterin every which way underneath kinda spooky. "Looks like a plastic spider web," she said. "A sort of weird spider, I guess, with many mental problems." But really it looked like the crystal paperweight Granny kept in the parlor. She was on the back porch, Granny was, making the cakes drunk. The old ladle dripping rum into the Christmas tins, like it used to drip maple syrup into the pails when we lived in the Judson's woods, like it poured cider into the vats when we were on the Cooper place, like it used to scoop buttermilk and soft cheese when we lived at the dairy.

"Go tell that man we ain't a bunch of trees."

"Ma'am?"

"I said to tell that man to get away from here with that camera." Me and Cathy look over toward the meadow where the men with the station wagon'd been roamin around all mornin. The tall man with a huge camera lassoed to his shoulder was buzzin our way.

"They're makin movie pictures," yelled Tyrone, stiffenin his legs and twistin so the tire'd come down slow so they could see.

"They're makin movie pictures," sang out Terry.

"That boy don't never have anything original to say," say Cathy grown-up.

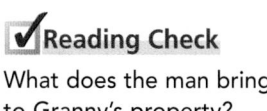

Sharecropper, Elizabeth Catlett, Courtesy Evan Tibbs Collection

▲ **Critical Viewing** As you read, compare Granny with the woman in the illustration. **[Compare and Contrast]**

By the time the man with the camera had cut across our neighbor's yard, the twins were out of the trees swingin low and Granny was onto the steps, the screen door bammin soft and scratchy against her palms. "We thought we'd get a shot or two of the house and everything and then—"

✔ **Reading Check**

What does the man bring to Granny's property?

Blues Ain't No Mockin Bird ◆ 571

"Good mornin," Granny cut him off. And smiled that smile.

"Good mornin," he said, head all down the way Bingo does when you yell at him about the bones on the kitchen floor. "Nice place you got here, aunty. We thought we'd take a—"

"Did you?" said Granny with her eyebrows. Cathy pulled up her socks and giggled.

"Nice things here," said the man, buzzin his camera over the yard. The pecan barrels, the sled, me and Cathy, the flowers, the printed stones along the driveway, the trees, the twins, the toolshed.

"I don't know about the thing, the it, and the stuff," said Granny, still talkin with her eyebrows. "Just people here is what I tend to consider."

Camera man stopped buzzin. Cathy giggled into her collar.

"Mornin, ladies," a new man said. He had come up behind us when we weren't lookin. "And gents," discoverin the twins givin him a nasty look. "We're filmin for the county," he said with a smile. "Mind if we shoot a bit around here?"

"I do indeed," said Granny with no smile. Smilin man was smiling up a storm. So was Cathy. But he didn't seem to have another word to say, so he and the camera man backed on out the yard, but you could hear the camera buzzin still. "Suppose you just shut that machine off," said Granny real low through her teeth, and took a step down off the porch and then another.

"Now, aunty," Camera said, pointin the thing straight at her.

"Your mama and I are not related."

Smilin man got his notebook out and a chewed-up pencil. "Listen," he said movin back into our yard, "we'd like to have a statement from you . . . for the film. We're filmin for the county, see. Part of the food stamp campaign. You know about the food stamps?"

Granny said nuthin.

"Maybe there's somethin you want to say for the film. I see you grow your own vegetables," he smiled real nice. "If more folks did that, see, there'd be no need—"

Granny wasn't sayin nuthin. So they backed on out, buzzin at our clothesline and the twins' bicycles, then back on down to the meadow. The twins were danglin in the tire, lookin at Granny. Me and Cathy were waitin, too, cause Granny always got somethin to say. She teaches steady with no let-up. "I was on this bridge one time," she started off. "Was a crowd cause this man was goin to jump, you understand. And a minister was there and the police and some other folks. His woman was there, too."

"What was they doin?" asked Tyrone.

"Tryin to talk him out of it was what they was doin. The minister talkin about how it was a mortal sin, suicide. His woman takin bites out of her own hand and not even knowin it, so nervous and cryin and talkin fast."

Dialect

"Blues Ain't No Mockin Bird" is written in dialect—a way of speaking that is common to people in a particular region or group. Dialect affects pronunciation, word choice, and sentence structure. You will notice, for example, that the characters in Bambara's story do not pronounce the *g* on the ends of *-ing* words—a common speech pattern in the American South. Bambara's use of dialect makes her story sound informal and intimate, as if it were being related orally.

Literary Analysis
Characterization and Narrator Who is the narrator? How do you know?

"So what happened?" asked Tyrone.

"So here comes . . . this person . . . with a camera, takin pictures of the man and the minister and the woman. Takin pictures of the man in his misery about to jump, cause life so bad and people been messin with him so bad. This person takin up the whole roll of film practically. But savin a few, of course."

"Of course," said Cathy, hatin the person. Me standin there wonderin how Cathy knew it was "of course" when I didn't and it was *my* grandmother.

After a while Tyrone say, "Did he jump?"

"Yeh, did he jump?" say Terry all eager. And Granny just stared at the twins till their faces swallow up the eager and they don't even care any more about the man jumpin. Then she goes back onto the porch and lets the screen door go for itself. I'm lookin to Cathy to finish the story cause she knows Granny's whole story before me even. Like she knew how come we move so much and Cathy ain't but a third cousin we picked up on the way last Thanksgivin visitin. But she knew it was on account of people drivin Granny crazy till she'd get up in the night and start packin. Mumblin and packin and wakin everybody up sayin, "Let's get on away from here before I kill me somebody." Like people wouldn't pay her for things like they said they would. Or Mr. Judson bringin us boxes of old clothes and raggedy magazines. Or Mrs. Cooper comin in our kitchen and touchin everything and sayin how clean it all was. Granny goin crazy, and Granddaddy Cain pullin her off the people, sayin, "Now, now, Cora." But next day loadin up the truck, with rocks all in his jaw, madder than Granny in the first place.

"I read a story once," said Cathy soundin like Granny teacher. "About this lady Goldilocks who barged into a house that wasn't even hers. And not invited, you understand. Messed over the people's groceries and broke up the people's furniture. Had the nerve to sleep in the folks' bed."

"Then what happened?" asked Tyrone. "What they do, the folks, when they come in to all this mess?"

"Did they make her pay for it?" asked Terry, makin a fist. "I'd've made her pay me."

I didn't even ask. I could see Cathy actress was very likely to just walk away and leave us in mystery about this story which I heard was about some bears.

"Did they throw her out?" asked Tyrone, like his father sounds when he's bein extra nasty-plus to the washin-machine man.

"Woulda," said Terry. "I woulda gone upside her head with my fist and—"

"You woulda done whatcha always do—go cry to Mama, you big baby," said Tyrone. So naturally Terry starts hittin on Tyrone, and next thing you know they tumblin out the tire and rollin on the ground. But Granny didn't say a thing or send the twins home or step out on the steps to tell us about how we can't afford to be fightin amongst ourselves. She didn't say nuthin. So I get into the tire to take my turn. And I could see her leanin up against the pantry table, staring at the cakes

Reading Strategy
Making Inferences About Characters What can you infer about the attitudes of the children toward Granny?

**Reading Check**

How does Granny respond when the camera crew ask her to make a statement?

she was puttin up for the Christmas sale, mumblin real low and grumpy and holdin her forehead like it wanted to fall off and mess up the rum cakes.

Behind me I hear before I can see Granddaddy Cain comin through the woods in his field boots. Then I twist around to see the shiny black oilskin cuttin through what little left there was of yellows, reds, and oranges. His great white head not quite round cause of this bloody thing high on his shoulder, like he was wearin a cap on sideways. He takes the shortcut through the pecan grove, and the sound of twigs snapping overhead and under-foot travels clear and cold all the way up to us. And here comes Smilin and Camera up behind him like they was goin to do somethin. Folks like to go for him sometimes. Cathy say it's because he's so tall and quiet and like a king. And people just can't stand it. But Smilin and Camera don't hit him in the head or nuthin. They just buzz on him as he stalks by with the chicken hawk slung over his shoulder, squawkin, drippin red down the back of the oil-skin. He passes the porch and stops a second for Granny to see he's caught the hawk at last, but she's just starin and mumblin, and not at the hawk. So he nails the bird to the toolshed door, the hammerin crackin through the eardrums. And the bird flappin himself to death and droolin down the door to paint the gravel in the driveway red, then brown, then black. And the two men movin up on tiptoe like they was invisible or we were blind, one.

"Get them persons out of my flower bed, Mister Cain," say Granny moanin real low like at a funeral.

"How come your grandmother calls her husband 'Mister Cain' all the time?" Tyrone whispers all loud and noisy and from the city and don't know no better. Like his mama, Miss Myrtle, tell us never mind the formality as if we had no better breeding than to call her Myrtle, plain. And then this awful thing—a giant hawk—come wailin up over the meadow, flyin low and tilted and screamin, zigzaggin through the pecan grove, breakin branches and hollerin, snappin past the clothes-line, flyin every which way, flyin into things reckless with crazy.

"He's come to claim his mate," say Cathy fast, and ducks down. We all fall quick and flat into the gravel driveway, stones scrapin my face. I squinch my eyes open again at the hawk on the door, tryin to fly up out of her death like it was just a sack flown into by mistake. Her body holdin her there on that nail, though. The mate beatin the air overhead and clutchin for hair, for heads, for landin space.

The camera man duckin and bendin and runnin and fallin, jigglin the

Reading Strategy
Making Inferences About Characters What inferences can you make about the camera crew from their reaction to Granddaddy Cain?

formality (fôr mal´ ə tē) *n.* established rules or customs

camera and scared. And Smilin jumpin up and down swipin at the huge bird, tryin to bring the hawk down with just his raggedy ole cap. Granddaddy Cain straight up and silent, watchin the circles of the hawk, then aimin the hammer off his wrist. The giant bird fallin, silent and slow. Then here comes Camera and Smilin all big and bad now that the awful screechin thing is on its back and broken, here they come. And Granddaddy Cain looks up at them like it was the first time noticin, but not payin them too much mind cause he's listenin, we all listenin, to that low groanin music comin from the porch. And we figure any minute, somethin in my back tells me any minute now, Granny gonna bust through that screen with somethin in her hand and murder on her mind. So Granddaddy say above the buzzin, but quiet, "Good day, gentlemen." Just like that. Like he'd invited them in to play cards and they'd stayed too long and all the sandwiches were gone and Reverend Webb was droppin by and it was time to go.

They didn't know what to do. But like Cathy say, folks can't stand Granddaddy tall and silent and like a king. They can't neither. The smile the men smilin is pullin the mouth back and showin the teeth. Lookin like the wolf man, both of them. Then Granddaddy holds his hand out— this huge hand I used to sit in when I was a baby and he'd carry me through the house to my mother like I was a gift on a tray. Like he used to on the trains. They called the other men just waiters. But they spoke of Granddaddy separate and said, The Waiter. And said he had engines in his feet and motors in his hands and couldn't no train throw him off and couldn't nobody turn him round. They were big enough for motors, his hands were. He held that one hand out all still and it gettin to be not at all a hand but a person in itself.

"He wants you to hand him the camera," Smilin whispers to Camera, tiltin his head to talk secret like they was in the jungle or somethin and come upon a native that don't speak the language. The men start untyin the straps, and they put the camera into that great hand speckled with the hawk's blood all black and crackly now. And the hand don't even drop with the weight, just the fingers move, curl up around the machine. But Granddaddy lookin straight at the men. They lookin at each other and everywhere but at Granddaddy's face.

"We filmin for the county, see," say Smilin. "We puttin together a movie for the food stamp program . . . filmin all around these parts. Uhh, filmin for the county."

"Can I have my camera back?" say the tall man with no machine on his shoulder, but still keepin it high like the camera was still there or needed to be. "Please, sir."

Then Granddaddy's other hand flies up like a sudden and gentle bird, slaps down fast on top of the camera and lifts off half like it was a calabash[1] cut for sharing.

"Hey," Camera jumps forward. He gathers up the parts into his chest and everything unrollin and fallin all over. "Whatcha tryin to do? You'll

---

1. **calabash** (kal´ ə bash) *n.* large gourdlike fruit.

Literary Analysis
Characterization and Narrator How do the narrator's memories of Granddaddy influence your reaction to him?

 **Reading Check**

What does Granddaddy do to let the camera crew know he wants their camera?

ruin the film." He looks down into his chest of metal reels and things like he's protectin a kitten from the cold.

"You standin in the misses' flower bed," say Granddaddy. "This is our own place."

The two men look at him, then at each other, then back at the mess in the camera man's chest, and they just back off. One sayin over and over all the way down to the meadow, "Watch it, Bruno. Keep ya fingers off the film." Then Granddaddy picks up the hammer and jams it into the oilskin pocket, scrapes his boots, and goes into the house. And you can hear the squish of his boots headin through the house. And you can see the funny shadow he throws from the parlor window onto the ground by the string-bean patch. The hammer draggin the pocket of the oilskin out so Granddaddy looked even wider. Granny was hummin now—high not low and grumbly. And she was doin the cakes again, you could smell the molasses from the rum.

"There's this story I'm goin to write one day," say Cathy dreamer. "About the proper use of the hammer."

"Can I be in it?" Tyrone say with his hand up like it was a matter of first come, first served.

"Perhaps," say Cathy, climbin onto the tire to pump us up. "If you there and ready."

Review and Assess

Thinking About the Selection

1. **Respond:** Which character from the story would you most like to meet? Why?

2. **(a) Recall:** How does Granny react when she notices the man with the camera? **(b) Analyze:** What does she mean when she says "we ain't a bunch of trees"?

3. **(a) Recall:** Why are the photographers filming in the area? **(b) Generalize:** What kind of message is Granny giving the men through her speech and actions?

4. **(a) Generalize:** What is the main point of Granny's story about the man who attempted suicide? **(b) Draw Conclusions:** How does the story help explain Granny's behavior?

5. **(a) Recall:** How is Granddaddy described when he first appears on the scene? **(b) Connect:** What does Granny ask Granddaddy to do when he appears? **(c) Infer:** What does the description of his actions suggest about his character?

6. **Evaluate:** Is Granddaddy's treatment of the photographers justified? Support your view with details from the story.

Toni Cade Bambara

(1939–1995)

Toni Cade Bambara's interest in her African American heritage comes through clearly in her writing. Her cultural identity is evident even in her name, Bambara—the name of an African tribe known for its textiles—which she made her own after finding it on a sketchbook belonging to her great-grandmother.

Bambara wrote two collections of short stories—*Gorilla, My Love*, where "Blues Ain't No Mockin Bird" appeared, and *The Sea Birds Are Still Alive*—as well as a novel, *The Salt Eaters*.

Uncle Marcos

from *The House of the Spirits*

Isabel Allende

. . . It had been two years since Clara had last seen her Uncle Marcos, but she remembered him very well. His was the only perfectly clear image she retained from her whole childhood, and in order to describe him she did not need to consult the daguerreotype[1] in the drawing room that showed him dressed as an explorer leaning on an old-fashioned double-barreled rifle with his right foot on the neck of a Malaysian tiger, the same triumphant position in which she had seen the Virgin standing between plaster clouds and <u>pallid</u> angels at the main altar, one foot on the <u>vanquished</u> devil. All Clara had to do to see her uncle was close her eyes and there he was, weather-beaten and thin, with a pirate's mustache through which his strange, sharklike smile peered out at her. It seemed impossible that he could be inside that long black box that was lying in the middle of the courtyard.

pallid (pal′ id) *adj.* pale

vanquished (van′ kwisht) *adj.* defeated

Each time Uncle Marcos had visited his sister Nivea's home, he had stayed for several months, to the immense joy of his nieces and nephews, particularly Clara, causing a storm in which the sharp lines of domestic order blurred. The house became a clutter of trunks, of animals in jars of formaldehyde,[2] of Indian lances and sailor's bundles. In every part of the house people kept tripping over his equipment, and all sorts of unfamiliar animals appeared that had traveled from remote lands only to meet their death beneath Nana's irate broom in the farthest corners of the house. Uncle Marcos's manners were those of a cannibal, as Severo put it. He spent the whole night making incomprehensible movements in the drawing room; later they turned out to be exercises designed to perfect the mind's control over the body and to improve digestion. He performed alchemy[3] experiments in the kitchen, filling the house with <u>fetid</u> smoke and ruining pots and pans with solid substances that stuck to their bottoms and were impossible to remove. While the rest of the household tried to sleep, he dragged his suitcases up and down the halls, practiced making strange, high-pitched sounds

fetid (fet′ id) *adj.* smelly

---

1. **daguerreotype** (də ger′ ō tīp′) *n.* early type of photograph.
2. **formaldehyde** (for mal′ də hīd′) *n.* solution used as a preservative.
3. **alchemy** (al′ kə mē) *adj.* early form of chemistry, with philosophical and magical associations.

✔**Reading Check**

How long does Uncle Marcos stay when he visits Nivea's home?

on savage instruments, and taught Spanish to a parrot whose native language was an Amazonic dialect. During the day, he slept in a hammock that he had strung between two columns in the hall, wearing only a loincloth that put Severo in a terrible mood but that Nivea forgave because Marcos had convinced her that it was the same costume in which Jesus of Nazareth had preached. Clara remembered perfectly, even though she had been only a tiny child, the first time her Uncle Marcos came to the house after one of his voyages. He settled in as if he planned to stay forever. After a short time, bored with having to appear at ladies' gatherings where the mistress of the house played the piano, with playing cards, and with dodging all his relatives' pressures to pull himself together and take a job as a clerk in Severo del Valle's law practice, he bought a barrel organ and took to the streets with the hope of seducing his Cousin Antonieta and entertaining the public in the bargain. The machine was just a rusty box with wheels, but he painted it with seafaring designs and gave it a fake ship's smokestack. It ended up looking like a coal stove. The organ played either a military march or a waltz, and in between turns of the handle the parrot, who had managed to learn Spanish although he had not lost his foreign accent, would draw a crowd with his piercing shrieks. He also plucked slips of paper from a box with his beak, by way of selling fortunes to the curious. The little pink, green, and blue papers were so clever that they always divulged the exact secret wishes of the customers. Besides fortunes there were little balls of sawdust to amuse the children. The idea of the organ was a last desperate attempt to win the hand of Cousin Antonieta after more conventional means of courting her had failed. Marcos thought no woman in her right mind could remain <u>impassive</u> before a barrel-organ serenade. He stood beneath her window one evening and played his military march and his waltz just as she was taking tea with a group of female friends. Antonieta did not realize the music was meant for her until the parrot called her by her full name, at which point she appeared in the window. Her reaction was not what her suitor had hoped for. Her friends offered to spread the news to every salon[4] in the city, and the next day people thronged the downtown streets hoping to see Severo del Valle's brother-in-law playing the organ and selling little sawdust balls with a motheaten parrot, for the sheer pleasure of proving that even in the best of families there could be good reason for embarrassment. In the face of this stain to the family reputation, Marcos was

---

4. **salon** (sə län´) *n.* regular gathering of distinguished guests that meets in a private home.

▲ **Critical Viewing** In this story, a man tries to build a flying machine. Which character traits might you find in someone who would try to do this? **[Speculate]**

impassive (im pas´ iv) *adj.* showing no emotion

forced to give up organ grinding and resort to less conspicuous ways of winning over his Cousin Antonieta, but he did not renounce his goal. In any case, he did not succeed, because from one day to the next the young lady married a diplomat who was twenty years her senior; he took her to live in a tropical country whose name no one could recall, except that it suggested negritude,[5] bananas, and palm trees, where she managed to recover from the memory of that suitor who had ruined her seventeenth year with his military march and his waltz. Marcos sank into a deep depression that lasted two or three days, at the end of which he announced that he would never marry and that he was embarking on a trip around the world. He sold his organ to a blind man and left the parrot to Clara, but Nana secretly poisoned it with an overdose of cod-liver oil, because no one could stand its lusty glance, its fleas, and its harsh, tuneless hawking of paper fortunes and sawdust balls.

That was Marcos's longest trip. He returned with a shipment of enormous boxes that were piled in the far courtyard, between the chicken coop and the woodshed, until the winter was over. At the first signs of spring he had them transferred to the parade grounds, a huge park where people would gather to watch the soldiers file by on Independence Day, with the goosestep they had learned from the Prussians. When the crates were opened, they were found to contain loose bits of wood, metal, and painted cloth. Marcos spent two weeks assembling the contents according to an instruction manual written in English, which he was able to decipher thanks to his invincible imagination and a small dictionary. When the job was finished, it turned out to be a bird of prehistoric dimensions, with the face of a furious eagle, wings that moved, and a propeller on its back. It caused an uproar. The families of the oligarchy[6] forgot all about the barrel organ, and Marcos became the star attraction of the season. People took Sunday outings to see the bird; souvenir vendors and strolling photographers made a fortune. Nonetheless, the public's interest quickly waned. But then Marcos announced that as soon as the weather cleared he planned to take off in his bird and cross the mountain range. The news spread, making this the most talked-about event of the year. The contraption lay with its stomach on terra firma,[7] heavy and sluggish and looking more like a wounded duck than like one of those newfangled airplanes they were starting to produce in the United States. There was nothing in its appearance to suggest that it could move, much less take flight across the snowy peaks. Journalists and the curious flocked to see it. Marcos smiled his immutable[8] smile before the avalanche of questions and posed for photographers without offering

---

5. **negritude** (neg′ rə to͞od′) *n.* blacks and their cultural heritage.
6. **oligarchy** (äl′ i gär′ kē) *n.* government ruled by a few.
7. **terra firma** (ter′ a fur′ ma) *n.* Latin term meaning "firm earth; solid ground."
8. **immutable** (im myo͞ot′ ə bəl) *adj.* never changing.

the least technical or scientific explanation of how he hoped to carry out his plan. People came from the provinces to see the sight. Forty years later his great-nephew Nicolás, whom Marcos did not live to see, unearthed the desire to fly that had always existed in the men of his lineage. Nicolás was interested in doing it for commercial reasons, in a gigantic hot-air sausage on which would be printed an advertisement for carbonated drinks. But when Marcos announced his plane trip, no one believed that his contraption could be put to any practical use. The appointed day dawned full of clouds, but so many people had turned out that Marcos did not want to disappoint them. He showed up punctually at the appointed spot and did not once look up at the sky, which was growing darker and darker with thick gray clouds. The astonished crowd filled all the nearby streets, perching on rooftops and the balconies of the nearest houses and squeezing into the park. No political gathering managed to attract so many people until half a century later, when the first Marxist candidate attempted, through strictly democratic channels, to become President. Clara would remember this holiday as long as she lived. People dressed in their spring best, thereby getting a step ahead of the official opening of the season, the men in white linen suits and the ladies in the Italian straw hats that were all the rage that year. Groups of elementary-school children paraded with their teachers, clutching flowers for the hero. Marcos accepted their bouquets and joked that they might as well hold on to them and wait for him to crash, so they could take them directly to his funeral. The bishop himself, accompanied by two incense bearers, appeared to bless the bird without having been asked, and the police band played happy, unpretentious music that pleased everyone. The police, on horseback and carrying lances, had trouble keeping the crowds far enough away from the center of the park, where Marcos waited dressed in mechanic's overalls, with huge racer's goggles and an explorer's helmet. He was also equipped with a compass, a telescope, and several strange maps that he had traced himself based on various theories of Leonardo da Vinci and on the polar knowledge of the Incas.[9] Against all logic, on the second try the bird lifted off without mishap and with a certain elegance, accompanied by the creaking of its skeleton and the roar of its motor. It rose flapping its wings and disappeared into the clouds, to a send-off of applause, whistlings, handkerchiefs, drumrolls, and the sprinkling of holy water. All that remained on earth were the comments of the amazed crowd below and a multitude of experts, who attempted to provide a reasonable explanation of the miracle. Clara continued to stare at the sky long after her uncle had become invisible. She thought she saw him ten minutes later, but it was only a migrating sparrow. After three days the initial euphoria that had accompanied the first airplane flight in the country died down and no one gave the episode another thought, except for Clara, who continued to peer at the horizon.

---

9. **Leonardo da Vinci** (lē´ ə när´ dō də vin´ chē) **. . . Incas** Leonardo da Vinci (1452–1519) was an Italian painter, sculptor, architect, and scientist. The Incas were Native Americans who dominated ancient Peru until the Spanish conquest.

Literary Analysis
Characterization What does the people's reaction to Marcos's plan for a plane trip tell you about him?

Reading Strategy
Making Inferences About Characters What can you infer about Uncle Marcos's motives for attempting to fly in his "bird"?

After a week with no word from the flying uncle, people began to speculate that he had gone so high that he had disappeared into outer space, and the ignorant suggested he would reach the moon. With a mixture of sadness and relief, Severo decided that his brother-in-law and his machine must have fallen into some hidden crevice of the cordillera,[10] where they would never be found. Nivea wept <u>disconsolately</u> and lit candles to San Antonio, patron of lost objects. Severo opposed the idea of having masses said, because he did not believe in them as a way of getting into heaven, much less of returning to earth, and he maintained that masses and religious vows, like the selling of indulgences, images, and scapulars,[11] were a dishonest business. Because of his attitude, Nivea and Nana had the children say the rosary,[12] behind their father's back for nine days. Meanwhile, groups of volunteer explorers and mountain climbers tirelessly searched peaks and passes, combing every accessible stretch of land until they finally returned in triumph to hand the family the mortal remains of the deceased in a sealed black coffin. The intrepid traveler was laid to rest in a grandiose funeral. His death made him a hero and his name was on the front page of all the papers for several days. The same multitude that had gathered to see him off the day he flew away in his bird paraded past his coffin. The entire family wept as befit the occasion, except for Clara, who continued to watch the sky with the patience of an astronomer. One week after he had been buried, Uncle Marcos, a bright smile playing behind his pirate's mustache, appeared in person in the doorway of Nivea and Severo del Valle's house. Thanks to the surreptitious[13] prayers of the women and children, as he himself admitted, he was alive and well and in full possession of his faculties, including his sense of humor. Despite the noble lineage of his aerial maps, the flight had been a failure. He had lost his airplane and had to return on foot, but he had not broken any bones and his adventurous spirit was intact. This confirmed the family's eternal devotion to San Antonio, but was not taken as a warning by future generations, who also tried to fly, although by different means. Legally, however, Marcos was a corpse. Severo del Valle was obliged to use all his legal ingenuity to bring his brother-in-law back to life and the full rights of citizenship. When the coffin was pried open in the presence of the appropriate authorities, it was found to contain a bag of sand. This discovery ruined the reputation, up till then untarnished, of the volunteer explorers and mountain climbers, who from that day on were considered little better than a pack of bandits.

Marcos's heroic resurrection made everyone forget about his barrel-organ phase. Once again he was a sought-after guest in all the city's salons and, at least for a while, his name was cleared. Marcos stayed in

disconsolately (dis kän´ sə lit lē) *adv.* unhappily

Reading Strategy
Making Inferences About Characters What inference can you make about Clara from her belief concerning her uncle and his fate?

**Reading Check**
What happens to Uncle Marcos after he loses his airplane?

---

10. **cordillera** (kôr´ dil yer´ə) *n.* system or chain of mountains.
11. **indulgences, images, and scapulars** (skap´ yə lərz) Indulgences are pardons for sins, images are pictures or sculptures of religious figures, and scapulars are garments worn by Roman Catholics as tokens of religious devotion.
12. **say the rosary** use a set of beads to say prayers.
13. **surreptitious** (sur´ əp tish´ əs) *adj.* secretive.

his sister's house for several months. One night he left without saying goodbye, leaving behind his trunks, his books, his weapons, his boots, and all his belongings. Severo, and even Nivea herself, breathed a sigh of relief. His visit had gone on too long. But Clara was so upset that she spent a week walking in her sleep and sucking her thumb. The little girl, who was only seven at the time, had learned to read from her uncle's storybooks and been closer to him than any other member of the family because of her prophesying powers. Marcos maintained that his niece's gift could be a source of income and a good opportunity for him to cultivate his own clairvoyance.[14] He believed that all human beings possessed this ability, particularly his own family, and that if it did not function well it was simply due to a lack of training. He bought a crystal ball in the Persian bazaar, insisting that it had magic powers and was from the East (although it was later found to be part of a buoy from a fishing boat), set it down on a background of black velvet, and announced that he could tell people's fortunes, cure the evil eye, and improve the quality of dreams, all for the modest sum of five centavos.[15] His first customers were the maids from around the neighborhood. One of them had been accused of stealing, because her employer had misplaced a valuable ring. The crystal ball revealed the exact location of the object in question: it had rolled beneath a wardrobe. The next day there was a line outside the front door of the house. There were coachmen, storekeepers, and milkmen; later a few municipal employees and distinguished ladies made a discreet appearance, slinking along the side walls of the house to keep from being recognized. The customers were received by Nana, who ushered them into the waiting room and collected their fees. This task kept her busy throughout the day and demanded so much of her time that the family began to complain that all there ever was for dinner was old string beans and jellied quince.[16] Marcos decorated the carriage house with some frayed curtains that had once belonged in the drawing room but that neglect and age had turned to dusty rags. There he and Clara received the customers. The two divines wore tunics "color of the men of light," as Marcos called the color yellow. Nana had dyed them with saffron powder, boiling them in pots usually reserved for rice and pasta. In addition to his tunic, Marcos wore a turban around his head and an Egyptian amulet around his neck. He had grown a beard and let his hair grow long and he was thinner than ever before. Marcos and Clara were utterly convincing, especially because the child had no need to look into the crystal ball to guess what her clients wanted to hear. She would whisper in her Uncle Marcos's ear, and he in turn would transmit the

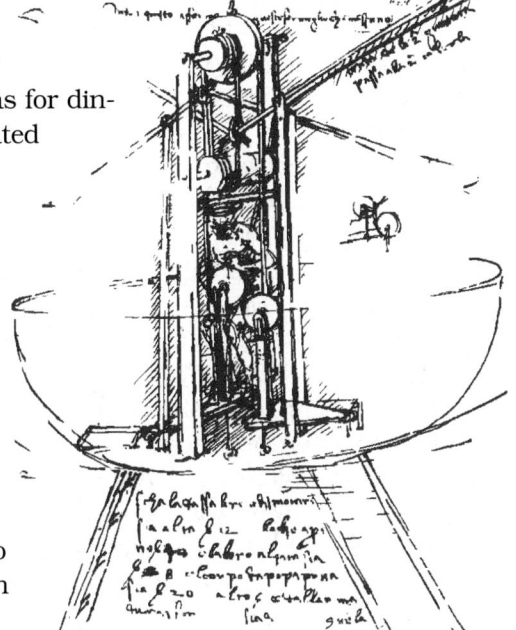

---

14. **clairvoyance** (kler voi′ əns) *n.* supposed ability to perceive unseen things.
15. **centavos** (sen tä′ vōs) *n.* coins equal to 1/100 of a cruzeiro, the basic monetary unit of Brazil.
16. **quince** (kwins) golden or greenish-yellow, hard, apple-shaped fruit.

message to the client, along with any improvisations of his own that he thought pertinent. Thus their fame spread, because all those who arrived sad and bedraggled at the consulting room left filled with hope.

<u>Unrequited</u> lovers were told how to win over indifferent hearts, and the poor left with foolproof tips on how to place their money at the dog tracks. Business grew so prosperous that the waiting room was always packed with people, and Nana began to suffer dizzy spells from being on her feet so many hours a day. This time Severo had no need to intervene to put a stop to his brother-in-law's venture, for both Marcos and Clara, realizing that their unerring guesses could alter the fate of their clients, who always followed their advice to the letter, became frightened and decided that this was a job for swindlers. They abandoned their carriage-house oracle and split the profits, even though the only one who had cared about the material side of things had been Nana.

Of all the del Valle children, Clara was the one with the greatest interest in and stamina for her uncle's stories. She could repeat each and every one of them. She knew by heart words from several dialects of the Indians, was acquainted with their customs, and could describe the exact way in which they pierced their lips and earlobes with wooden shafts, their initiation rites, the names of the most poisonous snakes, and the appropriate antidotes for each. Her uncle was so eloquent that the child could feel in her own skin the burning sting of snakebites, see reptiles slide across the carpet between the legs of the jacaranda[17] room divider, and hear the shrieks of macaws behind the drawing-room drapes. She did not hesitate as she recalled Lope de Aguirre's search for El Dorado,[18] or the unpronounceable names of the flora and fauna her extraordinary uncle had seen; she knew about the lamas who take salt tea with yak lard and she could give detailed descriptions of the opulent women of Tahiti, the rice fields of China, or the white prairies of the North, where the eternal ice kills animals and men who lose their way, turning them to stone in seconds. Marcos had various travel journals in which he recorded his excursions and impressions, as well as a collection of maps and books of stories and fairy tales that he kept in the trunks he stored in the junk room at the far end of the third courtyard. From there they were hauled out to inhabit the dreams of his descendants, until they were mistakenly burned half a century later on an infamous pyre.

Now Marcos had returned from his last journey in a coffin. He had died of a mysterious African plague that had turned him as yellow and wrinkled as a piece of parchment. When he realized he was ill, he set out for home with the hope that his sister's ministrations and Dr. Cuevas's knowledge would restore his health and youth, but he was unable to withstand the sixty days on ship and died at the latitude of

unrequited (un ri kwit´ id) *adj.* not reciprocated

---

17. **jacaranda** (jak´ ə ran´ də) type of tropical American tree.
18. **Lope de Aguirre's** (lō´ pā dā ä gēr´ rās) **. . . El Dorado** Lope de Aguirre was a Spanish adventurer (1510–1561) in colonial South America who searched for a legendary country called El Dorado, which was supposedly rich in gold.

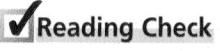**Reading Check**

What power does Marcos believe Clara holds?

Guayaquil,[19] ravaged by fever and hallucinating about musky women and hidden treasure. The captain of the ship, an Englishman by the name of Longfellow, was about to throw him overboard wrapped in a flag, but Marcos, despite his savage appearance and his delirium, had made so many friends on board and seduced so many women that the passengers prevented him from doing so, and Longfellow was obliged to store the body side by side with the vegetables of the Chinese cook, to preserve it from the heat and mosquitoes of the tropics until the ship's carpenter had time to improvise a coffin. At El Callao[20] they obtained a more appropriate container, and several days later the captain, furious at all the troubles this passenger had caused the shipping company and himself personally, unloaded him without a backward glance, surprised that not a soul was there to receive the body or cover the expenses he had incurred. Later he learned that the post office in these latitudes was not as reliable as that of far-off England, and that all his telegrams had vaporized en route. Fortunately for Longfellow, a customs lawyer who was a friend of the del Valle family appeared and offered to take charge, placing Marcos and all his paraphernalia in a freight car, which he shipped to the capital to the only known address of the deceased: his sister's house. . . .

---

19. **Guayaquil** (gwī ä kēl´) seaport in western Ecuador.
20. **El Callao** (kə yä´ ō) seaport in western Peru.

Review and Assess

Thinking About the Selection

1. **Respond:** Which of Uncle Marcos's adventures would you most like to share with him? Why?

2. **(a) Recall:** What does Uncle Marcos do to try to win the hand of Cousin Antonieta? **(b) Connect:** Is her reaction what Uncle Marcos expects? **(c) Compare and Contrast:** What subsequent actions does each take in the wake of his courtship?

3. **(a) Recall:** What does Uncle Marcos make from the materials in the "enormous boxes"? **(b) Infer:** What do you think motivates Uncle Marcos to undertake this project?

4. **(a) Recall:** How do various people in the family and community react to Uncle Marcos's disappearance? **(b) Deduce:** Do you think Marcos wanted to fool everyone about his fate? Explain.

5. **Speculate:** In the story, you see the reactions of people who knew Uncle Marcos. How do you think people who did not know him might have reacted to him? Explain.

Isabel Allende

(b. 1942)

Isabel Allende has said, "I had a very lonely life when I was a child but very interesting—only adults around me . . . a very extravagant family." She grew up in Chile, where she lived with her grandparents. Her uncle was the former Chilean president Salvador Allende.

Allende's first novel, *The House of the Spirits* (1985), from which "Uncle Marcos" is excerpted, was inspired by her family. Her other books include *Of Love and Shadows* (1987), *Eva Luna* (1988), *The Stories of Eva Luna* (1991), *The Infinite Plan* (1993), and *Paula* (1995).

Review and Assess

Literary Analysis

Characterization

1. Using a chart like this one, find examples of **indirect characterization** for two people in each story. Rewrite each example to **directly characterize** the person.

2. Which character does Isabel Allende indirectly characterize in the most detail? Support your answer.
3. Which form of characterization does each writer seem to prefer? Explain and support your answer.

Comparing Literary Works

4. Using the Venn diagram below, compare the information revealed about the characters through the **narration** in each story. Consider each character's appearance, traits, actions, and thoughts.

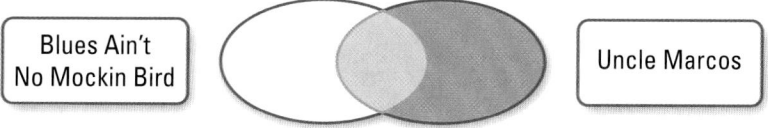

5. How would these stories be different if their narration styles were switched? Provide specific examples.

Reading Strategy

Making Inferences About Characters

6. **Make an inference** to explain how the photographer in "Blues Ain't No Mockin Bird" feels about the people he is filming.
7. In "Uncle Marcos," which details might lead you to infer that Clara is an unusual child?

Extend Understanding

8. **Media Connection:** (a) What insights might journalists gain from reading Bambara's story? (b) Are there any times when the public's right to know outweighs individual privacy? Explain.

Integrate Language Skills

Vocabulary Development Lesson

Word Analysis: Latin Prefix *dis-*

The Latin prefix *dis-* means "opposite." Thus, *disconsolate* means "the opposite of consolable," or "dejected; cheerless."

Match each word on the left with its definition on the right.

1. dishonest   **a.** take apart
2. disassemble   **b.** doubt
3. distrust   **c.** not truthful

Spelling Strategy

When you add a prefix to a word, do not change the spelling of the original word. For example, *un-* + *requited* = *unrequited*. Add *in-, im-, non-,* or *un-* to each word below to form four properly spelled new words.

1. formality   3. passive
2. cover   4. sense

Concept Development: Analogies

For each item, complete the analogy.

1. disconsolately : joyously :: rain : ___?___
   a. sunshine b. leaf c. spring d. grass
2. fetid : smelly :: pond : ___?___
   a. rain b. duck c. pool d. egg
3. formality : tuxedo :: relaxation : ___?___
   a. chair b. snow c. red d. swimsuit
4. impassive : calm :: search : ___?___
   a. find b. explore c. begin d. reason
5. lassoed : released :: day : ___?___
   a. sad b. week c. pocket d. night
6. pallid : ruddy :: bend : ___?___
   a. straighten b. swirl c. trade d. fry
7. unrequited : shared :: calm : ___?___
   a. dry b. windy c. excited d. cold
8. vanquished : beaten :: survived : ___?___
   a. persevered b. horse c. hunter d. peril

Grammar Lesson

Infinitive Phrases

An **infinitive** is a verb form preceded by the word *to* that acts as a noun, adjective, or adverb. An **infinitive phrase** is an infinitive with its modifiers or complements. Like infinitives, infinitive phrases can function as nouns, adjectives, or adverbs. Unlike a **prepositional phrase** that begins with *to* and ends with a noun, an infinitive phrase always ends with a verb.

> **Infinitive:** Granny decided *to stare.* (noun)
>
> **Infinitive Phrase:** Clara was afraid *to speak her mind.* (acts as an adverb by modifying *afraid*)
>
> **Prepositional Phrase:** Antonieta did not speak *to Marcos.*

Practice Copy the sentences below. Circle the infinitives and underline the infinitive phrases. Identify the part of speech of each phrase.

1. The men wanted to get a statement from Granny.
2. Soon there were no more hawks to chase.
3. He wanted to throw him overboard.
4. The machine was made to soar over the mountains to a new life.
5. The organ was a last attempt to win the hand of Cousin Antonieta.

Writing Application Write two sentences about each selection, using infinitives and infinitive phrases in each.

W͜G Prentice Hall Writing and Grammar Connection: Chapter 21, Section 1

Writing Lesson

Magazine Feature

These selections feature amazing characters, brought to life with vivid details. Use one of the characters in this section as the basis for a magazine feature—an article that is meant to entertain or provide information on a subject of interest.

Prewriting As you prepare, decide what makes the character truly remarkable. To help you gather relevant ideas, list specific details concerning the person's appearance, personality, and achievements.

Model: Organizing Details

Talents	Goals
adventurous	to fly
eccentric	to travel the world

These specific details, under the general ideas *Talents* and *Goals,* will support the main impression and make a feature article believable.

Drafting Use your notes to focus your writing on the main impression: the amazing qualities of your character. As you write, provide examples illustrating each characteristic you mention.

Revising Review your work to ensure that you communicate your main impression. Add more details if necessary, and discard any details that are not relevant or that detract from your focus.

Prentice Hall Writing and Grammar Connection: Chapter 13, Section 2

Extension Activities

Research and Technology Sometimes, a person like Uncle Marcos is seen as irresponsible. However, imaginative and adventurous people like him are responsible for making some of the most important discoveries in history.

- In a group, research people in history who, through their adventures, made great discoveries.
- Show how these people compare to Marcos.

Compile your notes to create a **comparison-and-contrast brochure.**

Listening and Speaking Assume that you are the cameraman in "Blues Ain't No Mockin Bird," and prepare a **monologue** explaining to your boss what happened to your camera. Do not omit anything important, and do not exaggerate. Be polite, and use language appropriate to your situation. Read or perform the monologue for a friend or a small group.

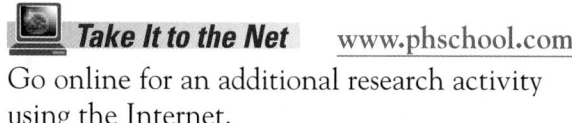 **Take It to the Net** www.phschool.com

Go online for an additional research activity using the Internet.

Prepare to Read

The Man to Send Rain Clouds ◆ The Invalid's Story

Feast Day, San Juan Pueblo, 1921, William Penhallow Henderson, National Museum of American Art, Smithsonian Institution

Take It to the Net

Visit www.phschool.com for interactive activities and instruction related to the selections, including

- background
- graphic organizers
- literary elements
- reading strategies

Preview

Connecting to the Literature

People cope with the loss of a loved one in different ways. Some try to preserve their memories of the deceased; others try to fulfill the loved one's last wishes. These stories offer two sets of circumstances surrounding death and others' responses to it.

Background

"The Man to Send Rain Clouds" explores the traditions of the Pueblo people of the southwestern United States. Over time, the Pueblo people have tried to maintain their ancient belief that if they live in harmony with the natural world, nature will give them what they need. The Pueblos' balancing of traditional and modern ways provides the central conflict in Leslie Marmon Silko's story.

Literary Analysis

Setting

In each of these stories, **setting**—the time and place in which the story unfolds—strongly influences the action. Time may include not only the historical period but also a specific year, season, or time of day. Place may involve not only the geographical place but also the social, economic, and cultural environment. The following excerpt reveals the cultural environment of "The Man to Send Rain Clouds":

> Leon stared at the new moccasins that Teofilo had made for the ceremonial dances in the summer. They were nearly hidden by the red blanket.

In some stories, the setting simply provides a backdrop for the action; in other stories, including these, setting shapes the character's actions.

Comparing Literary Works

Although both stories deal with death, the settings of the stories are very different. One is the high desert of New Mexico; the other is a train on its way to Wisconsin. While reading, compare and contrast the brief journey of the aged Pueblo with the somewhat longer one of John B. Hackett. Note the way story events seem to emerge from each distinctive setting.

Instruction with these selections addresses these standards:

R 1.1*, 3.7*
W 1.5*, 2.4*
WOLC 1.1*
LS 2.1

* Standards tested on HS Exit Exam. For complete standards, see p. CA 4.

Reading Strategy

Using Your Senses

The setting of each story, like a stifling boxcar with a smelly package, gives your **senses** a virtual workout. Draw from your own experiences to see, hear, smell, taste, or feel what each author describes. Then, try to recreate senses in your mind. Use a chart like the one shown to record key details appealing to each sense.

Sights

Sounds

Smells

Tastes

Physical Sensations

Vocabulary Development

cloister (klois´ tər) *n.* place devoted to religious seclusion (p. 594)

pagans (pā´ gənz) *n.* people who are not Christians, Muslims, or Jews (p. 594)

perverse (pər vurs´) *adj.* continuing in a stubborn way to do what is wrong or harmful (p. 594)

prodigious (pro dij´ es) *adj.* enormous (p. 597)

deleterious (del´ ə tir´ ē əs) *adj.* harmful to health or well-being (p. 598)

ominous (äm´ ə nəs) *adj.* threatening (p. 599)

judicious (jōō dish´ əs) *adj.* showing good judgment (p. 599)

placidly (plas´ id lē) *adv.* calmly; quietly (p. 599)

desultory (des´ əl tôr´ ē) *adj.* random (p. 600)

The Man To Send Rain Clouds

LESLIE MARMON SILKO

▲ **Critical Viewing**
Which physical features of
the New Mexico landscape
are revealed in this
photograph? **[Analyze]**

They found him under a big cottonwood tree. His Levi jacket and pants were faded light blue so that he had been easy to find. The big cottonwood tree stood apart from a small grove of winterbare cottonwoods which grew in the wide, sandy arroyo. He had been dead for a day or more, and the sheep had wandered and scattered up and down the arroyo. Leon and his brother-in-law, Ken, gathered the sheep and left them in the pen at the sheep camp before they returned to the cottonwood tree. Leon waited under the tree while Ken drove the truck through the deep sand to the edge of the arroyo. He squinted up at the sun and unzipped his jacket—it sure was hot for this time of year. But high and northwest the blue mountains were still in snow. Ken came sliding down the low, crumbling bank about fifty yards down, and he was bringing the red blanket.

Before they wrapped the old man, Leon took a piece of string out of his pocket and tied a small gray feather in the old man's long white hair. Ken gave him the paint. Across the brown wrinkled forehead he drew a streak of white and along the high cheekbones he drew a strip of blue paint. He paused and watched Ken throw pinches of corn meal and pollen into the wind that fluttered the small gray feather. Then Leon painted with yellow under the old man's broad nose, and finally, when he had painted green across the chin, he smiled.

"Send us rain clouds, Grandfather." They laid the bundle in the back of the pickup and covered it with a heavy tarp before they started back to the pueblo.

They turned off the highway onto the sandy pueblo road. Not long after they passed the store and post office they saw Father Paul's car coming toward them. When he recognized their faces he slowed his car and waved for them to stop. The young priest rolled down the car window.

"Did you find old Teofilo?" he asked loudly.

Leon stopped the truck. "Good morning, Father. We were just out to the sheep camp. Everything is O.K. now."

✔ **Reading Check**

How do Leon and Ken prepare the old man's body before they move it?

The Man to Send Rain Clouds ◆ 591

"Thank God for that. Teofilo is a very old man. You really shouldn't allow him to stay at the sheep camp alone."

"No, he won't do that any more now."

"Well, I'm glad you understand. I hope I'll be seeing you at Mass[1] this week—we missed you last Sunday. See if you can get old Teofilo to come with you." The priest smiled and waved at them as they drove away.

Louise and Teresa were waiting. The table was set for lunch, and the coffee was boiling on the black iron stove. Leon looked at Louise and then at Teresa.

"We found him under a cottonwood tree in the big arroyo near sheep camp. I guess he sat down to rest in the shade and never got up again." Leon walked toward the old man's bed. The red plaid shawl had been shaken and spread carefully over the bed, and a new brown flannel shirt and pair of stiff new Levi's were arranged neatly beside the pillow. Louise held the screen door open while Leon and Ken carried in the red blanket. He looked small and shriveled, and after they dressed him in the new shirt and pants he seemed more shrunken.

It was noontime now because the church bells rang the Angelus.[2] They ate the beans with hot bread, and nobody said anything until after Teresa poured the coffee.

Ken stood up and put on his jacket. "I'll see about the gravediggers. Only the top layer of soil is frozen. I think it can be ready before dark."

Leon nodded his head and finished his coffee. After Ken had been gone for a while, the neighbors and clanspeople came quietly to embrace Teofilo's family and to leave food on the table because the gravediggers would come to eat when they were finished.

The sky in the west was full of pale yellow light. Louise stood out-side with her hands in the pockets of Leon's green army jacket that was too big for her. The funeral was over, and the old men had taken their candles and medicine bags[3] and were gone. She waited until the body was laid into the pickup before she said anything to Leon. She touched his arm, and he noticed that her hands were still dusty from the corn meal that she had sprinkled around the old man. When she spoke, Leon could not hear her.

"What did you say? I didn't hear you."

"I said that I had been thinking about something."

"About what?"

"About the priest sprinkling holy water for Grandpa. So he won't be thirsty."

Leon stared at the new moccasins that Teofilo had made for the ceremonial dances in the summer. They were nearly hidden by the red blanket. It was getting colder, and the wind pushed gray dust down the

Literary Analysis
Setting Which cultural elements are represented in Louise's request to the priest?

---

1. **Mass** (mas) church service celebrated by Roman Catholics.
2. **Angelus** (an′ jə ləs) bell rung at morning, noon, and evening to announce a prayer.
3. **medicine bags** bags containing objects that were thought to have special powers.

Feast Day, San Juan Pueblo, 1921, William Penhallow Henderson, National Museum of American Art, Smithsonian Institution

narrow pueblo road. The sun was approaching the long mesa where it disappeared during the winter. Louise stood there shivering and watching his face. Then he zipped up his jacket and opened the truck door. "I'll see if he's there."

Ken stopped the pickup at the church, and Leon got out: and then Ken drove down the hill to the graveyard where people were waiting. Leon knocked at the old carved door with its symbols of the Lamb.[4] While he waited he looked up at the twin bells from the king of Spain with the last sunlight pouring around them in their tower.

The priest opened the door and smiled when he saw who it was.

---

4. **the Lamb** Jesus Christ, as the sacrificial Lamb of God.

▲ **Critical Viewing**
How do the images in this painting compare to images created by the story? **[Compare]**

☑**Reading Check**

What do the old men take with them when the funeral is over?

"Come in! What brings you here this evening?"

The priest walked toward the kitchen, and Leon stood with his cap in his hand, playing with the earflaps and examining the living room—the brown sofa, the green armchair, and the brass lamp that hung down from the ceiling by links of chain. The priest dragged a chair out of the kitchen and offered it to Leon.

"No thank you, Father. I only came to ask you if you would bring your holy water to the graveyard."

The priest turned away from Leon and looked out the window at the patio full of shadows and the dining-room windows of the nuns' <u>cloister</u> across the patio. The curtains were heavy, and the light from within faintly penetrated; it was impossible to see the nuns inside eating supper. "Why didn't you tell me he was dead? I could have brought the Last Rites[5] anyway."

Leon smiled. "It wasn't necessary, Father."

The priest stared down at his scuffed brown loafers and the worn hem of his cassock. "For a Christian burial it was necessary."

His voice was distant, and Leon thought that his blue eyes looked tired.

"It's O.K. Father, we just want him to have plenty of water."

The priest sank down into the green chair and picked up a glossy missionary magazine. He turned the colored pages full of lepers and <u>pagans</u> without looking at them.

"You know I can't do that, Leon. There should have been the Last Rites and a funeral Mass at the very least."

Leon put on his green cap and pulled the flaps down over his ears. "It's getting late, Father. I've got to go."

When Leon opened the door Father Paul stood up and said, "Wait." He left the room and came back wearing a long brown overcoat. He followed Leon out the door and across the dim churchyard to the adobe steps in front of the church. They both stooped to fit through the low adobe entrance. And when they started down the hill to the graveyard only half of the sun was visible above the mesa.

The priest approached the grave slowly, wondering how they had managed to dig into the frozen ground; and then he remembered that this was New Mexico, and saw the pile of cold loose sand beside the hole. The people stood close to each other with little clouds of steam puffing from their faces. The priest looked at them and saw a pile of jackets, gloves, and scarves in the yellow, dry tumbleweeds that grew in the graveyard. He looked at the red blanket, not sure that Teofilo was so small, wondering if it wasn't some <u>perverse</u> Indian trick—something they did in March to ensure a good harvest—wondering if maybe old Teofilo was actually at sheep camp corraling the sheep for the night. But there he was, facing into a cold dry wind and squinting at the last sunlight, ready to bury a red wool blanket while the faces of his parishioners were in shadow with the last warmth of the sun on their backs.

---

5. **the Last Rites** religious ceremony for a dying person or for someone who has just died.

cloister (klois′ tər) *n.* place devoted to religious seclusion

pagans (pā′ gənz) *n.* people who are not Christians, Muslims, or Jews

perverse (pər vurs′) *adj.* continuing in a stubborn way to do what is wrong or harmful

His fingers were stiff, and it took him a long time to twist the lid off the holy water. Drops of water fell on the red blanket and soaked into dark icy spots. He sprinkled the grave and the water disappeared almost before it touched the dim, cold sand; it reminded him of something—he tried to remember what it was, because he thought if he could remember he might understand this. He sprinkled more water; he shook the container until it was empty, and the water fell through the light from sundown like August rain that fell while the sun was still shining, almost evaporating before it touched the wilted squash flowers.

The wind pulled at the priest's brown Franciscan robe[6] and swirled away the corn meal and pollen that had been sprinkled on the blanket. They lowered the bundle into the ground, and they didn't bother to untie the stiff pieces of new rope that were tied around the ends of the blanket. The sun was gone, and over on the highway the eastbound lane was full of headlights. The priest walked away slowly. Leon watched him climb the hill, and when he had disappeared within the tall, thick walls, Leon turned to look up at the high blue mountains in the deep snow that reflected a faint red light from the west. He felt good because it was finished, and he was happy about the sprinkling of the holy water; now the old man could send them big thunderclouds for sure.

6. **Franciscan** (fran sis´ kən) **robe** robe worn by a member of the Franciscan religious order, founded in 1209 by Saint Francis of Assisi.

Literary Analysis

Setting In what ways does the setting described in the last paragraph contribute to the action in the story?

Review and Assess

Thinking About the Selection

1. **Respond:** What did you think about the way in which the tribespeople buried Teofilo's body? Why?

2. **(a) Recall:** What do Leon and Ken find at the opening of the story? **(b) Analyze:** Why doesn't Leon tell Father Paul about Teofilo's death at first?

3. **(a) Recall:** Why does Louise ask Leon to bring the priest to Teofilo's grave? **(b) Compare and Contrast:** What does this story reveal about the contrasts between Pueblo and Christian beliefs?

4. **(a) Analyze:** Why is Father Paul upset about the burial ceremony? **(b) Infer:** What insight into the Pueblo people do you think Father Paul gained during the ceremony?

5. **(a) Recall:** How are Leon's feelings described at the end of the story? **(b) Draw Conclusions:** What do Leon's thoughts after Teofilo's burial suggest about his views of death?

6. **Extend:** What lesson can be taken from this story about working out differences in cultural beliefs?

Leslie Marmon Silko

(b. 1948)

Storytelling has always been an important part of Leslie Marmon Silko's life. Raised on the Laguna Pueblo reservation in New Mexico, she grew up listening to tribal stories told by her great-grandmother and great-aunts.

In her stories, novels, and poems, Silko explores what life is like for Native Americans in today's world. Many of her works capture the contrast between traditional values and beliefs and the elements of modern-day life.

The Invalid's Story

Mark Twain

I seem sixty and married, but these effects are due to my condition and sufferings, for I am a bachelor, and only forty-one. It will be hard for you to believe that I, who am now but a shadow, was a hale, hearty man two short years ago—a man of iron, a very athlete!—yet such is the simple truth. But stranger still than this fact is the way in which I lost my health. I lost it through helping to take care of a box of guns on a two-hundred-mile railway journey one winter's night. It is the actual truth, and I will tell you about it.

I belong in Cleveland, Ohio. One winter's night, two years ago, I reached home just after dark, in a driving snowstorm, and the first thing I heard when I entered the house was that my dearest boyhood friend and schoolmate, John B. Hackett, had died the day before, and that his last utterance had been a desire that I would take his remains home to his poor old father and mother in Wisconsin. I was greatly shocked and grieved, but there was no time to waste in emotions; I must start at once. I took the card, marked "Deacon Levi Hackett, Bethlehem, Wisconsin," and hurried off through the whistling storm to the railway station. Arrived there I found the long white-pine box which had been described to me; I fastened the card to it with some tacks, saw it put safely aboard the express car, and then ran into the eating room to provide myself with a sandwich and some cigars. When I returned, presently, there was my coffin-box *back again,* apparently, and a young fellow examining around it, with a card in his hands, and some tacks and a hammer! I was astonished and puzzled. He began to nail on his card, and I rushed out to the express car, in a good deal of a state of mind, to ask for an explanation. But no—there was my box, all right, in the express car; it hadn't been disturbed. [The fact is that without my suspecting it a <u>prodigious</u> mistake had been made. I was carrying off a box of *guns* which that young fellow had come to the station to ship to a rifle company in Peoria, Illinois, and *he* had got my corpse.] Just then the conductor sang out "All aboard," and I jumped into the express car and got a comfortable seat on a bale of buckets. The expressman was there, hard at work—a plain man of fifty, with a simple, honest, good-natured face, and a breezy, practical heartiness in his general style. As the train moved off a stranger skipped into the car and set a package of peculiarly mature and capable Limburger cheese[1] on one end of my coffin-box—I mean my box of guns. That is to say, I know now that it was Limburger cheese, but at that time I never had heard of the article in my life, and of course was wholly ignorant of its character. Well, we sped through the wild night, the bitter storm raged on, a cheerless misery stole over me, my heart went down, down, down! The old expressman made a brisk remark or two about the tempest and the arctic weather, slammed his sliding doors to, and bolted them, closed his window down tight, and then went bustling around, here and there and yonder, setting things to rights, and all the time contentedly humming "Sweet By and By" in a low tone, and flatting a good deal. Presently I

---

1. **Limburger cheese** cheese with a strong odor.

◀ **Critical Viewing** How do the sensory details in this image compare to the sensory details in the story? [**Compare**]

Literary Analysis
Setting Describe the setting at the beginning of this paragraph.

prodigious (prō dij′ əs) *adj.* enormous

✔**Reading Check**

What is the first thing the narrator hears when he enters his house during a snowstorm?

began to detect a most evil and searching odor stealing about on the frozen air. This depressed my spirits still more, because of course I attributed it to my poor departed friend. There was something infinitely saddening about his calling himself to my remembrance in this dumb, pathetic way, so it was hard to keep the tears back. Moreover, it distressed me on account of the old expressman, who, I was afraid, might notice it. However, he went humming tranquilly on, and gave no sign; and for this I was grateful. Grateful, yes, but still uneasy; and soon I began to feel more and more uneasy every minute, for every minute that went by that odor thickened up the more, and got to be more and more gamy and hard to stand. Presently, having got things arranged to his satisfaction, the expressman got some wood and made up a tremendous fire in his stove. This distressed me more than I can tell, for I could not but feel that it was a mistake. I was sure that the effect would be <u>deleterious</u> upon my poor departed friend. Thompson—the expressman's name was Thompson, as I found out in the course of the night—now went poking around his car, stopping up whatever stray cracks he could find, remarking that it didn't make any difference what kind of a night it was outside, he calculated to make us comfortable, anyway. I said nothing, but I believed he was not choosing the right way. Meantime he was humming to himself just as before; and meantime, too, the stove was getting hotter and hotter, and the place closer and closer. I felt myself growing pale and qualmish,[2] but grieved

---

2. **qualmish** (kwäm´ ish) *adj.* slightly ill.

Reading Strategy
Using Your Senses Which senses can you use to experience this description? How can an "odor" be "searching"?

deleterious (del´ ə tir´ ē əs) *adj.* injurious; harmful to health or well-being

▼ **Critical Viewing**
Examine this painting of a railway station in 1874. How difficult do you think it was to get from one place to another at this time in history? Which details in the painting support your ideas?
[Support]

Sacramento Railroad Station, 1874, William Hahn, The Fine Arts Museum of San Francisco

in silence and said nothing. Soon I noticed that the "Sweet By and By" was gradually fading out; next it ceased altogether, and there was an <u>ominous</u> stillness. After a few moments Thompson said—

"Pfew! I reckon it ain't no cinnamon't I've loaded up thish-year stove with!"

He gasped once or twice, then moved toward the cof—gun-box, stood over that Limburger cheese part of a moment, then came back and sat down near me, looking a good deal impressed. After a contemplative pause, he said, indicating the box with a gesture—

"Friend of yourn?"

"Yes," I said with a sigh.

"He's pretty ripe, ain't he!"

Nothing further was said for perhaps a couple of minutes, each being busy with his own thoughts; then Thompson said, in a low awed voice—

"Sometimes it's uncertain whether they're really gone or not—*seem* gone, you know—body warm, joints limber—and so, although you *think* they're gone, you don't really know. I've had cases in my car. It's perfectly awful, becuz *you* don't know what minute they'll rise up and look at you!" Then, after a pause, and slightly lifting his elbow toward the box,—"But *he* ain't in no trance! No, sir, I go bail for *him!*"

We sat some time, in meditative silence, listening to the wind and the roar of the train; then Thompson said, with a good deal of feeling:

"Well-a-well, we've all got to go, they ain't no getting around it. Man that is born of woman is of few days and far between, as Scriptur'[3] says. Yes, you look at it any way you want to, it's awful solemn and cur'us: they ain't *nobody* can get around it; *all's* got to go—just *everybody*, as you may say. One day you're hearty and strong"—here he scrambled to his feet and broke a pane and stretched his nose out at it a moment or two, then sat down again while I struggled up and thrust my nose out at the same place, and this we kept on doing every now and then—"and next day he's cut down like the grass, and the places which knowed him then knows him no more forever, as Scriptur' says. Yes'ndeedy, it's awful solemn and cur'us; but we've all got to go, one time or another; they ain't no getting around it."

There was another long pause; then—

"What did he die of?"

I said I didn't know.

"How long has he ben dead?"

It seemed <u>judicious</u> to enlarge the facts to fit the probabilities; so I said:

"Two or three days."

But it did no good: for Thompson received it with an injured look which plainly said. "Two or three *years*, you mean." Then he went right along, <u>placidly</u> ignoring my statement, and gave his views at considerable length upon the unwisdom of putting off burials too long. Then he lounged off toward the box, stood a moment, then came back on a

---

3. **Scriptur'** scripture; the Bible.

ominous (äm´ ə nəs) *adj.* threatening

Reading Strategy
Using Your Senses How does Twain rely on sound to set the mood for the following scene?

judicious (jōō dish´ əs) *adj.* showing good judgment

placidly (plas´ id lē) *adv.* calmly; quietly

**Reading Check**

What does the narrator say depressed his spirits?

sharp trot and visited the broken pane, observing:

"'Twould 'a' ben a durn sight better, all around, if they'd started him along last summer."

Thompson sat down and buried his face in his red silk handkerchief, and began to slowly sway and rock his body like one who is doing his best to endure the almost unendurable. By this time the fragrance—if you may call it fragrance—was just about suffocating, as near as you can come at it. Thompson's face was turning gray: I knew mine hadn't any color left in it. By and by Thompson rested his forehead in his left hand, with his elbow on his knee, and sort of waved his red handkerchief toward the box with his other hand, and said:

"I've carried a many a one of 'em—some of 'em considerable overdue, too—but, lordy, he just lays over 'em all!—and does it *easy*. Cap, they was heliotrope[4] to *him*!"

This recognition of my poor friend gratified me, in spite of the sad circumstances, because it had so much the sound of a compliment.

Pretty soon it was plain that something had got to be done. I suggested cigars. Thompson thought it was a good idea. He said:

"Likely it'll modify him some."

We puffed gingerly along for a while, and tried hard to imagine that things were improved. But it wasn't any use. Before very long, and without any consultation, both cigars were quietly dropped from our nerveless fingers at the same moment. Thompson said, with a sigh:

"No, Cap, it don't modify him worth a cent. Fact is, it makes him worse, becuz it appears to stir up his ambition. What do you reckon we better do, now?"

I was not able to suggest anything: indeed, I had to be swallowing and swallowing all the time, and did not like to trust myself to speak. Thompson fell to maundering,[5] in a <u>desultory</u> and low-spirited way, about the miserable experiences of this night: and he got to referring to my poor friend by various titles—sometimes military ones, sometimes civil ones; and I noticed that as fast as my poor friend's effectiveness grew, Thompson promoted him accordingly—gave him a bigger title. Finally he said:

"I've got an idea. Suppos'n' we buckle down to it and give the Colonel a bit of a shove toward t'other end of the car?—about ten foot, say. He wouldn't have so much influence, then, don't you reckon?"

I said it was a good scheme. So we took in a good fresh breath at the broken pane, calculating to hold it till we got through: then we went there and bent over that deadly cheese and took a grip on the box. Thompson nodded "All ready," and then we threw ourselves forward with all our might: but Thompson slipped, and slumped down with his nose on the cheese, and his breath got loose. He gagged and gasped, and floundered up and made a break for the door, pawing the air and saying hoarsely, "Don't hender me!—gimme the road! I'm a-dying;

desultory (des´ əl tôr´ ē) *adj.* random

---

4. **heliotrope** (hē´ lē ə trōp´) *n.* sweet-smelling plant.
5. **maundering** (môn´ dər iŋ) *v.* talking in an unconnected way.

gimme the road!" Out on the cold platform I sat down and held his head awhile, and he revived. Presently he said:

"Do you reckon we started the Gen'rul any?"

I said no: we hadn't budged him.

"Well, then, *that* idea's up the flume. We got to think up something else. He's suited wher' he is, I reckon; and if that's the way he feels about it, and has made up his mind that he don't wish to be disturbed, you bet he's a-going to have his own way in the business. Yes, better leave him right wher' he is, long as he wants it so; becuz he holds all the trumps, don't you know, and so it stands to reason that the man that lays out to alter his plans for him is going to get left."

But we couldn't stay out there in that mad storm; we should have frozen to death. So we went in again and shut the door, and began to suffer once more and take turns at the break in the window. By and by, as we were starting away from a station where we had stopped a moment Thompson pranced in cheerily, and exclaimed:

"We're all right, now! I reckon we've got the Commodore this time. I judge I've got the stuff here that'll take the tuck out of him."

It was carbolic acid. He had a carboy[6] of it. He sprinkled it all around everywhere; in fact he drenched everything with it, rifle-box, cheese and all. Then we sat down, feeling pretty hopeful. But it wasn't for long. You see the two perfumes began to mix, and then—well, pretty soon we made a break for the door; and out there Thompson swabbed his face with his bandanna and said in a kind of disheartened way:

"It ain't no use. We can't buck agin *him*. He just utilizes everything we put up to modify him with, and gives it his own flavor and plays it back on us. Why, Cap, don't you know, it's as much as a hundred times worse in there now than it was when he first got a-going. I never *did* see one of 'em warm up to his work so, and take such a dumnation interest in it. No, sir, I never did, as long as I've ben on the road: and I've carried a many a one of 'em, as I was telling you."

We went in again after we were frozen pretty stiff; but my, we couldn't stay in, now. So we just waltzed back and forth, freezing, and thawing, and stifling, by turns. In about an hour we stopped at another station; and as we left it Thompson came in with a bag, and said—

"Cap, I'm a-going to chance him once more—just this once; and if we don't fetch him this time, the thing for us to do, is to just throw up the sponge and withdraw from the canvass.[7] That's the way I put it up."

He had brought a lot of chicken feathers, and dried apples, and leaf tobacco, and rags, and old shoes, and sulphur, and asafetida,[8]

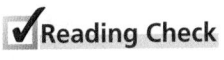

---

6. **carboy** (kär´ boï´) *n.* large glass bottle enclosed in basketwork to prevent it from breaking.
7. **withdraw from the canvass** (kan´ vəs) give up the attempt.
8. **asafetida** (as´ ə fet´ ə də) *n.* bad-smelling substance from certain plants, used as medicine.

Reading Strategy
Using Your Senses Which sense do you use when you envision the narrator and Thompson out on the platform?

▼ **Critical Viewing**
Imagine yourself on a train like the one in "The Invalid's Story." What might you see, hear, feel, and smell on such a journey? **[Connect]**

✔**Reading Check**

What does Thompson do with the carbolic acid?

and one thing or another: and he piled them on a breadth of sheet iron in the middle of the floor, and set fire to them.

When they got well started. I couldn't see, myself, how even the corpse could stand it. All that went before was just simply poetry to that smell—but mind you, the original smell stood up out of it just as sublime as ever—fact is, these other smells just seemed to give it a better hold: and my, how rich it was! I didn't make these reflections there—there wasn't time—made them on the platform. And breaking for the platform, Thompson got suffocated and fell: and before I got him dragged out, which I did by the collar, I was mighty near gone myself. When we revived, Thompson said dejectedly:

"We got to stay out here, Cap. We got to do it. They ain't no other way. The Governor wants to travel alone, and he's fixed so he can outvote us."

And presently he added:

"And don't you know, we're *pisoned*. It's our last trip, you can make up your mind to it. Typhoid fever is what's going to come of this. I feel it a-coming right now. Yes, sir, we're elected, just as sure as you're born."

We were taken from the platform an hour later, frozen and insensible, at the next station, and I went straight off into a virulent fever, and never knew anything again for three weeks. I found out, then, that I had spent that awful night with a harmless box of rifles and a lot of innocent cheese; but the news was too late to save me; imagination had done its work, and my health was permanently shattered; neither Bermuda nor any other land can ever bring it back to me. This is my last trip; I am on my way home to die.

Review and Assess

Thinking About the Selection

1. **Respond:** Did you find this story entertaining? Why or why not?

2. **(a) Recall:** What is the purpose of the narrator's journey? **(b) Speculate:** Would the story be as effective if it were not set on a train? Why or why not?

3. **(a) Recall:** What do the men believe is creating the awful smell? **(b) Recall:** What is actually creating the smell? **(c) Compare and Contrast:** How does the contrast between what they think is true and what is really true contribute to the humor?

4. **(a) Recall:** Find at least three places in the story where the narrator exaggerates details. **(b) Analyze:** How does the use of exaggeration contribute to the story's humor?

5. **Analyze:** How does Thompson's description of the corpse as deliberately trying to smell bad add to the story's humor?

6. **Extend:** Would this story make a good movie? Why or why not?

Review and Assess

Literary Analysis

Setting

1. (a) In "The Man to Send Rain Clouds," which aspects of the Native American culture affect the action, and how? (b) Why is the desert important to the action? Use a chart like the one below to analyze the story's **setting.**

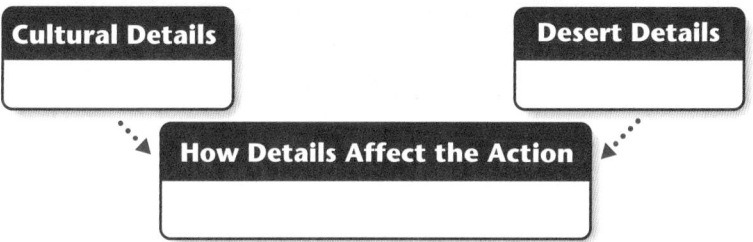

Cultural Details

Desert Details

How Details Affect the Action

2. (a) In "The Invalid's Story," describe the physical environment in which the narrator and Thompson sit. (b) Which factors in this setting drive the action of the story?

Comparing Literary Works

3. (a) Compare both stories to evaluate how the setting influences the action in each. (b) In which story is the setting more critical to the action? Explain.

4. (a) Compare the details of the winter settings found in each story. (b) How would each story be affected if it were set during a different season? Explain.

Reading Strategy

Using Your Senses

5. In "The Man to Send Rain Clouds," to which two **senses** would you say Silko appeals the most? Support your answer.

6. "The Invalid's Story" is one of the few stories to play almost exclusively to the sense of smell. Find two images in the story that most vividly capture the smell of the cheese. Explain your choice.

Extend Understanding

7. **Cultural Connection:** Silko's story illustrates conflict between cultures. (a) Describe another situation in which two cultures have clashed. (b) What can be done to resolve such conflicts?

Integrate Language Skills

Vocabulary Development Lesson

Word Analysis: Latin Suffix -ous

Several words in "The Invalid's Story" end in -ous. The Latin suffix -ous generally means "full of" or "characterized by," as in *courageous*, meaning "full of courage." Add -ous to each word to form a new word. Then, define each new word.

   1. melody   2. prestige   3. riot

Spelling Strategy

When adding a suffix to words ending in y preceded by a consonant, change the y to i unless the suffix itself starts with i. For example, *desultory* + -ly = *desultorily*. However, *try* + -ing = *trying*.

Write the new word formed by adding each suffix.

   1. lonely + -est
   2. unnecessary + -ly
   3. fly + -ing

Concept Development: Synonyms

Choose the word that is closest in meaning to the first word.

   1. deleterious: (a) delaying, (b) tasty, (c) harmful
   2. cloister: (a) retreat, (b) group, (c) injury
   3. judicious: (a) legal, (b) prudent, (c) rash
   4. desultory: (a) kind, (b) evil, (c) random
   5. placidly: (a) quietly, (b) coldly, (c) politely
   6. pagans: (a) aliens, (b) villains, (c) non-believers
   7. ominous: (a) threatening, (b) dishonest, (c) dark
   8. prodigious: (a) inventive, (b) enormous, (c) joyous
   9. perverse: (a) untidy, (b) improper, (c) clean

Grammar Lesson

Prepositional Phrase or Infinitive?

An **infinitive** is a verbal consisting of the word *to* and a verb. A **prepositional phrase**, however, consists of a preposition and a noun or pronoun, as well as any modifiers.

It is important not to confuse a prepositional phrase beginning with *to* with an infinitive. A prepositional phrase always ends with a noun or pronoun, while an infinitive always ends with a verb.

> **Examples:** **Infinitive:** He needed *to bring* the coffin on a train.
>
> **Prepositional Phrase:** Leon carried Teofilo *to the truck*.

Practice Copy each sentence in your notebook, circling each phrase beginning with *to*. Then, label each a *prepositional phrase* or an *infinitive*.

   1. Neighbors came to embrace Teofilo's family.
   2. They asked the priest to help them by sprinkling holy water.
   3. He walked to the railway station.
   4. Thompson reacted strongly to the smell.
   5. The cheese was causing them to suffer.

Writing Application Write a short paragraph about your reaction to either story, including at least two infinitives and two prepositional phrases in your writing.

*W*G *Prentice Hall Writing and Grammar Connection: Chapter 21, Section 1*

Writing Lesson

Letter From Father Paul

Imagine that you are Father Paul in "The Man to Send Rain Clouds." Write a letter to a friend addressing the cultural differences you have encountered and how you would like to deal with them.

Prewriting   Review the story. Jot down the ways Father Paul deals with the differences in the cultures. Then, note additional ways you think the two cultures can work together.

Drafting   In your opening paragraph, express the feelings of Father Paul. Next, explain the differences in the cultures from his point of view. Finally, explain the way he intends to work with the Native American culture in the future.

> ### Model: Drafting a Strong Opening Sentence
>
> I am very fortunate to be working in this community, but I feel a conflict within myself and I struggle to know the best way to handle our differences.

Words like *fortunate* and *struggle* convey the varied feelings of Father Paul.

Revising   Reread your letter. Make sure that you have addressed and explained each of the ways you think the two cultures can work together.

W *G* *Prentice Hall Writing and Grammar Connection: Chapter 11, Section 3*

Extension Activities

Listening and Speaking Prepare a **monologue** in which Thompson from "The Invalid's Story" explains the experience on the train from his perspective.

- Review the story to gain a better understanding of Thompson.
- Use the tone of voice and gestures you think Thompson would use.
- Maintain a humorous tone.

Present your monologue to the class, and ask classmates if they agree with your interpretation of Thompson.

Research and Technology In a small group, prepare a **research report** about the Pueblo people. Use library resources, including the Internet and books about Native Americans, to gather information about their traditions and beliefs. In your report, explain which elements of Silko's story reflect the Pueblo culture best. **[Group Activity]**

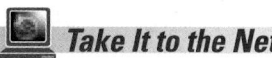 **Take It to the Net**   www.phschool.com

Go online for an additional research activity using the Internet.

Prepare to Read

The Necklace ◆ The Harvest

Campesino, 1976, Daniel DeSiga, Wright Art Gallery, University of California, Los Angeles

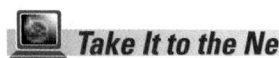
Take It to the Net

Visit www.phschool.com
for interactive activities
and instruction related to
the selections, including

- background
- graphic organizers
- literary elements
- reading strategies

Preview

Connecting to the Literature

You may remember a time when a simple or surprising discovery made a strong impression on your life. Both of these stories capture the lasting impact of a character's discovery. Watch for the moment of discovery, and think about how it changes each character's world.

Background

Moving from place to place, harvesting and processing crops for low pay, migrant workers face many obstacles in the United States, such as difficulty in obtaining unemployment compensation, disability insurance, and sufficient education for their children. A former migrant worker himself, Tomás Rivera's concern is reflected in both "The Harvest" and his work as an educator.

Literary Analysis

Theme

The **theme** of a literary work is the insight about life that it communicates. Sometimes, the theme of a work is stated directly. More often, however, the theme is expressed indirectly through the experiences of the characters, through the events and the setting of the work, or through the use of devices such as irony or symbols. The following excerpt from "The Necklace" raises questions about the importance of money and attention:

> She had no dowry, no hopes, not the slightest chance of being appreciated, understood, loved, and married by a rich and distinguished man; so she slipped into marriage with a minor civil servant at the Ministry of Education.

As you read these stories, pay attention to insights into life that are indirectly expressed.

Comparing Literary Works

Although the cultures and settings presented in the following stories are very different, both stories include a moment of discovery that greatly affects a character's life and indirectly expresses each story's theme. Compare the moments of insight the characters experience in the following stories.

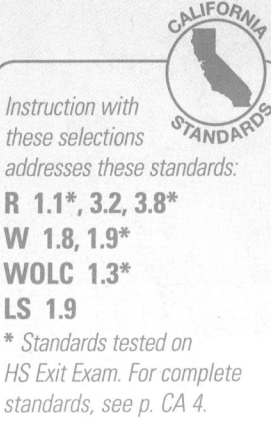

Instruction with these selections addresses these standards:

R 1.1*, 3.2, 3.8*
W 1.8, 1.9*
WOLC 1.3*
LS 1.9

* Standards tested on HS Exit Exam. For complete standards, see p. CA 4.

Reading Strategy

Drawing Conclusions

In determining a theme, you usually need to **draw conclusions** about characters and events. Follow these steps:

- Gather details about characters and events in the story.
- Make decisions about the underlying meaning of the details.

Using a chart like the one shown here, note details and draw conclusions about each character's actions. Then, decide how these actions might relate to each theme.

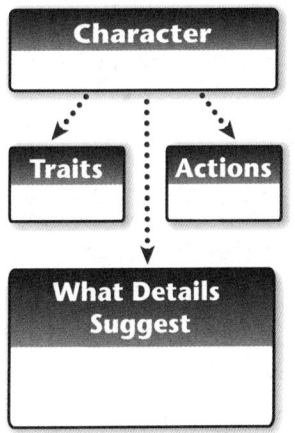

Vocabulary Development

déclassée (dā′ klä sā′) *French fem. adj.* lowered in social status (p. 609)

rueful (rōō′ fəl) *adj.* feeling sorrow or regret (p. 609)

resplendent (ri splen′ dənt) *adj.* shining brightly (p. 611)

disheveled (di shev′ əld) *adj.* disarranged and untidy (p. 614)

profoundly (prō found′ lē) *adv.* deeply and intensely (p. 615)

harrowed (har′ ōd) *v.* broken up by a harrow, a frame with spikes drawn by a horse or tractor (p. 619)

astutely (ə stōōt′ lē) *adv.* cleverly or cunningly (p. 619)

The Necklace

Guy de Maupassant

S he was one of those pretty, charming young women who are born, as if by an error of Fate, into a petty official's family. She had no dowry,[1] no hopes, not the slightest chance of being appreciated, understood, loved, and married by a rich and distinguished man; so she slipped into marriage with a minor civil servant at the Ministry of Education.

---

1. dowry (dou´ rē) *n.* property that a woman brought to her husband at marriage.

Unable to afford jewelry, she dressed simply: but she was as wretched as a _déclassée_, for women have neither caste nor breeding—in them beauty, grace, and charm replace pride of birth. Innate refinement, instinctive elegance, and suppleness of wit give them their place on the only scale that counts, and these qualities make humble girls the peers of the grandest ladies.

She suffered constantly, feeling that all the attributes of a gracious life, every luxury, should rightly have been hers. The poverty of her rooms—the shabby walls, the worn furniture, the ugly upholstery—caused her pain. All these things that another woman of her class would not even have noticed, tormented her and made her angry. The very sight of the little Breton girl who cleaned for her awoke _rueful_ thoughts and the wildest dreams in her mind. She dreamt of thick-carpeted reception rooms with Oriental hangings, lighted by tall, bronze torches, and with two huge footmen in knee breeches, made drowsy by the heat from the stove, asleep in the wide armchairs. She dreamt of great drawing rooms upholstered in old silks, with fragile little tables holding priceless knickknacks, and of enchanting little sitting rooms redolent of perfume, designed for tea-time chats with intimate friends—famous, sought-after men whose attentions all women longed for.

When she sat down to dinner at her round table with its three-day-old cloth, and watched her husband opposite her lift the lid of the soup tureen and exclaim, delighted: "Ah, a good homemade beef stew! There's nothing better . . ." she would visualize elegant dinners with gleaming silver amid tapestried walls peopled by knights and ladies and exotic birds in a fairy forest; she would think of exquisite dishes served on gorgeous china, and of gallantries whispered and received with sphinx-like smiles[2] while eating the pink flesh of trout or wings of grouse.

She had no proper wardrobe, no jewels, nothing. And those were the only things that she loved—she felt she was made for them. She would have so loved to charm, to be envied, to be admired and sought after.

She had a rich friend, a schoolmate from the convent she had attended, but she didn't like to visit her because it always made her so miserable when she got home again. She would weep for whole days at a time from sorrow, regret, despair, and distress.

Then one evening her husband arrived home looking triumphant and waving a large envelope.

"There," he said, "there's something for you."

She tore it open eagerly and took out a printed card which said:

"The Minister of Education and Madame Georges Ramponneau [ma dam′ zhôrzh ram pə nō′] request the pleasure of the company of M. and Mme. Loisel [lwa zel′] at an evening reception at the Ministry on Monday, January 18th."

Instead of being delighted, as her husband had hoped, she tossed the invitation on the table and muttered, annoyed:

---

2. **gallantries whispered and received with sphinx** (sfiŋks)**-like smiles** flirtatious compliments whispered and received with mysterious smiles.

déclassée (dā′ klä sā′) _French fem. adj._ lowered in social status

rueful (rōō′ fəl) _adj._ feeling sorrow or regret

Literary Analysis
Theme What theme might be hinted at in the description of Madame Loisel's longings?

Reading Check

Which word best describes Mme. Loisel's life?

"What do you expect me to do with that?"

"Why, I thought you'd be pleased, dear. You never go out and this would be an occasion for you, a great one! I had a lot of trouble getting it. Everyone wants an invitation; they're in great demand and there are only a few reserved for the employees. All the officials will be there."

She looked at him, irritated, and said impatiently:

"I haven't a thing to wear. How could I go?"

It had never even occurred to him. He stammered:

"But what about the dress you wear to the theater? I think it's lovely. . . ."

He fell silent, amazed and bewildered to see that his wife was crying. Two big tears escaped from the corners of her eyes and rolled slowly toward the corners of her mouth. He mumbled:

"What is it? What is it?"

But, with great effort, she had overcome her misery; and now she answered him calmly, wiping her tear-damp cheeks:

"It's nothing. It's just that I have no evening dress and so I can't go to the party. Give the invitation to one of your colleagues whose wife will be better dressed than I would be."

He was overcome. He said:

"Listen, Mathilde [ma tēld´], how much would an evening dress cost—a suitable one that you could wear again on other occasions, something very simple?"

She thought for several seconds, making her calculations and at the same time estimating how much she could ask for without eliciting an immediate refusal and an exclamation of horror from this economical government clerk.

At last, not too sure of herself, she said:

"It's hard to say exactly but I think I could manage with four hundred francs."

He went a little pale, for that was exactly the amount he had put aside to buy a rifle so that he could go hunting the following summer near Nanterre, with a few friends who went shooting larks around there on Sundays.

However, he said:

"Well, all right, then. I'll give you four hundred francs. But try to get something really nice."

As the day of the ball drew closer, Madame Loisel seemed depressed, disturbed, worried—despite the fact that her dress was ready. One evening her husband said:

"What's the matter? You've really been very strange these last few days."

And she answered:

"I hate not having a single jewel, not one stone, to wear. I shall look so dowdy.[3] I'd almost rather not go to the party."

---

3. **dowdy** (dou´dē) *adj.* shabby.

Reading Strategy
Drawing Conclusions
What conclusions can you draw about the feelings of Madame Loisel on the basis of her reaction to this invitation?

Literary Analysis
Theme Which details do you learn in these paragraphs that might suggest the story's ending and theme?

He suggested:

"You can wear some fresh flowers. It's considered very chic[4] at this time of year. For ten francs you can get two or three beautiful roses."

That didn't satisfy her at all.

"No . . . there's nothing more humiliating than to look poverty-stricken among a lot of rich women."

Then her husband exclaimed:

"Wait—you silly thing! Why don't you go and see Madame Forestier [fôr əs tyā´] and ask her to lend you some jewelry. You certainly know her well enough for that, don't you think?"

She let out a joyful cry.

"You're right. It never occurred to me."

The next day she went to see her friend and related her tale of woe.

Madame Forestier went to her mirrored wardrobe, took out a big jewel case, brought it to Madame Loisel, opened it, and said:

"Take your pick, my dear."

Her eyes wandered from some bracelets to a pearl necklace, then to a gold Venetian cross set with stones, of very fine workmanship. She tried on the jewelry before the mirror, hesitating, unable to bring herself to take them off, to give them back. And she kept asking:

"Do you have anything else, by chance?"

"Why yes. Here, look for yourself. I don't know which ones you'll like."

All at once, in a box lined with black satin, she came upon a superb diamond necklace, and her heart started beating with overwhelming desire. Her hands trembled as she picked it up. She fastened it around her neck over her high-necked dress and stood there gazing at herself ecstatically.

Hesitantly, filled with terrible anguish, she asked:

"Could you lend me this one—just this and nothing else?"

"Yes, of course."

She threw her arms around her friend's neck, kissed her ardently, and fled with her treasure.

The day of the party arrived. Madame Loisel was a great success. She was the prettiest woman there—<u>resplendent</u>, graceful, beaming, and deliriously happy. All the men looked at her, asked who she was, tried to get themselves introduced to her. All the minister's aides wanted to waltz with her. The minister himself noticed her.

She danced enraptured—carried away, intoxicated with pleasure, forgetting everything in this triumph of her beauty and the glory of her success, floating in a cloud of happiness formed by all this homage, all this admiration, all the desires she had stirred up—by this victory so complete and so sweet to the heart of a woman.

When she left the party, it was almost four in the morning. Her husband had been sleeping since midnight in a small, deserted sitting room, with three other gentlemen whose wives were having a wonderful time.

---

4. **chic** (shēk) *adj.* fashionable.

Reading Strategy
Drawing Conclusions
What conclusions can you draw about Madame Loisel's feelings toward her husband?

resplendent (ri splen´ dənt) *adj.* shining brightly

✔**Reading Check**
Why does Madame Loisel visit Madame Forestier?

The Necklace ◆ 611

He brought her wraps so that they could leave and put them around her shoulders—the plain wraps from her everyday life whose shabbiness jarred with the elegance of her evening dress. She felt this and wanted to escape quickly so that the other women, who were enveloping themselves in their rich furs, wouldn't see her.

Loisel held her back.

"Wait a minute. You'll catch cold out there. I'm going to call a cab."

But she wouldn't listen to him and went hastily downstairs. Outside in the street, there was no cab to be found; they set out to look for one, calling to the drivers they saw passing in the distance.

They walked toward the Seine,[5] shivering and miserable. Finally, on the embankment, they found one of those ancient nocturnal broughams[6] which are only to be seen in Paris at night, as if they were ashamed to show their shabbiness in daylight.

It took them to their door in the Rue des Martyrs, and they went sadly upstairs to their apartment. For her, it was all over. And he was thinking that he had to be at the Ministry by ten.

She took off her wraps before the mirror so that she could see herself in all her glory once more. Then she cried out. The necklace was gone; there was nothing around her neck.

Her husband, already half undressed, asked:

"What's the matter?"

She turned toward him in a frenzy:

"The . . . the . . . necklace—it's gone."

He got up, thunderstruck.

"What did you say? . . . What! . . . Impossible!"

And they searched the folds of her dress, the folds of her wrap, the pockets, everywhere. They didn't find it.

He asked:

"Are you sure you still had it when we left the ball?"

"Yes. I remember touching it in the hallway of the Ministry."

"But if you had lost it in the street, we would have heard it fall. It must be in the cab."

"Yes, most likely. Do you remember the number?"

"No. What about you—did you notice it?"

"No."

They looked at each other in utter dejection. Finally Loisel got dressed again.

"I'm going to retrace the whole distance we covered on foot," he said, "and see if I can't find it."

And he left the house. She remained in her evening dress, too weak to go to bed, sitting crushed on a chair, lifeless and blank.

---

5. **Seine** (sen) river flowing through Paris.
6. **broughams** (brooms) *n.* horse-drawn carriages.

▼ **Critical Viewing**
Imagine Mathilde trying on piece after piece of her wealthy friend's jewelry. What can you tell about her personality from this behavior? **[Infer]**

Her husband returned at about seven o'clock. He had found nothing.

He went to the police station, to the newspapers to offer a reward, to the offices of the cab companies—in a word, wherever there seemed to be the slightest hope of tracing it.

She spent the whole day waiting, in a state of utter hopelessness before such an appalling catastrophe.

Loisel returned in the evening, his face lined and pale; he had learned nothing.

"You must write to your friend," he said, "and tell her that you've broken the clasp of the necklace and that you're getting it mended. That'll give us time to decide what to do."

She wrote the letter at his dictation.

By the end of the week, they had lost all hope.

Loisel, who had aged five years, declared:

"We'll have to replace the necklace."

The next day they took the case in which it had been kept and went to the jeweler whose name appeared inside it. He looked through his ledgers:

"I didn't sell this necklace, madame. I only supplied the case."

Then they went from one jeweler to the next, trying to find a necklace like the other, racking their memories, both of them sick with worry and distress.

In a fashionable shop near the Palais Royal, they found a diamond necklace which they decided was exactly like the other. It was worth 40,000 francs. They could have it for 36,000 francs.

They asked the jeweler to hold it for them for three days, and they stipulated that he should take it back for 34,000 francs if the other necklace was found before the end of February.

Loisel possessed 18,000 francs left him by his father. He would borrow the rest.

He borrowed, asking a thousand francs from one man, five hundred from another, a hundred here, fifty there. He signed promissory notes,[7] borrowed at exorbitant rates, dealt with usurers and the entire race of moneylenders. He compromised his whole career, gave his signature even when he wasn't sure he would be able to honor it, and horrified by the anxieties with which his future would be filled, by the black misery about to descend upon him, by the prospect of physical privation and moral suffering, went to get the new necklace, placing on the jeweler's counter 36,000 francs.

When Madame Loisel went to return the necklace, Madame Forestier said in a faintly waspish tone:

"You could have brought it back a little sooner! I might have needed it."

She didn't open the case as her friend had feared she might. If she had noticed the substitution, what would she have thought? What would she have said? Mightn't she have taken Madame Loisel for a thief?

---

7. **promissory** (präm´ i sôr´ē) **notes** written promises to pay back borrowed money.

Reading Strategy
Drawing Conclusions
What conclusions can you draw about the personalities of M. and Mme. Loisel from their actions after the necklace is lost?

Reading Check

What do the Loisels do to replace the necklace?

The Necklace ◆ 613

Madame Loisel came to know the awful life of the poverty-stricken. However, she resigned herself to it with unexpected fortitude. The crushing debt had to be paid. She would pay it. They dismissed the maid; they moved into an attic under the roof.

She came to know all the heavy household chores, the loathsome work of the kitchen. She washed the dishes, wearing down her pink nails on greasy casseroles and the bottoms of saucepans. She did the laundry, washing shirts and dishcloths which she hung on a line to dry; she took the garbage down to the street every morning, and carried water upstairs, stopping at every floor to get her breath. Dressed like a working-class woman, she went to the fruit store, the grocer, and the butcher with her basket on her arm, bargaining, outraged, contesting each sou[8] of her pitiful funds.

Every month some notes had to be honored and more time requested on others.

Her husband worked in the evenings, putting a shopkeeper's ledgers in order, and often at night as well, doing copying at twenty-five centimes a page.

And it went on like that for ten years.

After ten years, they had made good on everything, including the usurious rates and the compound interest.

Madame Loisel looked old now. She had become the sort of strong woman, hard and coarse, that one finds in poor families. <u>Disheveled</u>, her skirts askew, with reddened hands, she spoke in a loud voice, slopping water over the floors as she washed them. But sometimes, when her husband was at the office, she would sit down by the window and muse over that party long ago when she had been so beautiful, the belle of the ball.

How would things have turned out if she hadn't lost that necklace? Who could tell? How strange and fickle life is! How little it takes to make or break you!

Then one Sunday when she was strolling along the Champs Elysées[9] to forget the week's chores for a while, she suddenly caught sight of a woman taking a child for a walk. It was Madame Forestier, still young, still beautiful, still charming.

Madame Loisel started to tremble. Should she speak to her? Yes, certainly she should. And now that she had paid everything back, why shouldn't she tell her the whole story?

She went up to her.

"Hello, Jeanne."

The other didn't recognize her and was surprised that this plainly dressed woman should speak to her so familiarly. She murmured:

"But . . . madame! . . . I'm sure . . . You must be mistaken."

"No, I'm not. I am Mathilde Loisel."

---

8. **sou** (soo) *n.* former French coin, worth very little; the centime (sän′ tēm′), mentioned later, was also of little value.
9. **Champs Elysées** (shän zā lē zā′) fashionable street in Paris.

Literary Analysis
Theme What insight into hardship does this description of Madame Loisel suggest?

disheveled (di shev′ əld) *adj.* disarranged and untidy

Her friend gave a little cry.

"Oh! Oh, my poor Mathilde, how you've changed!"

"Yes, I've been through some pretty hard times since I last saw you and I've had plenty of trouble—and all because of you!"

"Because of me? What do you mean?"

"You remember the diamond necklace you lent me to wear to the party at the Ministry?"

"Yes. What about it?"

"Well, I lost it."

"What are you talking about? You returned it to me."

"What I gave back to you was another one just like it. And it took us ten years to pay for it. You can imagine it wasn't easy for us, since we were quite poor. . . . Anyway, I'm glad it's over and done with."

Madame Forestier stopped short.

"You say you bought a diamond necklace to replace that other one?"

"Yes. You didn't even notice then? They really were exactly alike."

And she smiled, full of a proud, simple joy.

Madame Forestier, profoundly moved, took Mathilde's hands in her own.

"Oh, my poor, poor Mathilde! Mine was false. It was worth five hundred francs at the most!"

profoundly (prō found′ lē) *adv.* deeply and intensely

Guy de Maupassant

(1850–1893)

Perhaps the best-known short-story writer in the world, Guy de Maupassant is known for his realistic stories that capture the surprising twists and turns of life. Maupassant was raised in northern France. As a young man, he served in the Franco-Prussian War, gathering experiences that would later appear in some of his stories. Later, he became a government clerk and devoted his spare time to writing. Eventually, Maupassant became the literary apprentice of well-known writer Gustave Flaubert, who introduced him to other illustrious writers of the day.

Despite the wealth he accumulated, Maupassant's later years were shadowed by ill health and depression.

Review and Assess

Thinking About the Selection

1. **Respond:** Do you feel sorry for Mathilde? Why or why not?

2. **(a) Recall:** As the story begins, why is Madame Loisel so unhappy with her life? **(b) Infer:** Do you think the author wants readers to sympathize with her unhappiness at this time? Why or why not?

3. **(a) Recall:** How does Madame Loisel's husband respond to her disappointment over the invitation? **(b) Compare and Contrast:** How is Madame Loisel different from her husband?

4. **(a) Recall:** Why is Madame Loisel so happy when her husband suggests that she go to see her wealthy friend, Madame Forestier? **(b) Interpret:** What symbolic meaning does the necklace have for Madame Loisel when she wears it?

5. **(a) Recall:** How does Madame Loisel change over the ten years she works to pay off the cost of the necklace? **(b) Analyze:** What actually causes her to change?

6. **Interpret:** How is the ending of the story ironic or surprising?

7. **Speculate:** Do you think people who value material possessions too much are likely to face hardship in life? Why or why not?

Campesino, 1976, Daniel DeSiga, Wright Art Gallery, University of California, Los Angeles

The Harvest

Tomás Rivera

The end of September and the beginning of October. That was the best time of the year. First, because it was a sign that the work was coming to an end and that the return to Texas would start. Also, because there was something in the air that the folks created, an aura of peace and death. The earth also shared that feeling. The cold came more frequently, the frosts that killed by night, in the morning covered the earth in whiteness. It seemed that all was coming to an end. The folks felt that all was coming to rest. Everyone took to thinking more. And they talked more about the trip back to Texas, about the harvests, if it had gone well or bad for them, if they would return or not to the same place next year. Some began to take long walks around the grove. It seemed like in these last days of work there was a wake over the earth. It made you think.

That's why it wasn't very surprising to see Don Trine take a walk by himself through the grove and to walk along the fields every afternoon. This was at the beginning, but when some youngsters asked him if they could tag along, he even got angry. He told them he didn't want anybody sticking behind him.

"Why would he want to be all by hisself, anyway?"
"To heck with him: it's his business."
"But, you notice, it never fails. Every time, why, sometimes I don't even think he eats supper, he takes his walk. Don't you think that's a bit strange?"
"Well, I reckon. But you saw how he got real mad when we told him we'd go along with him. It wasn't anything to make a fuss over. This ain't his land. We can go wherever we take a liking to. He can't tell us what to do."
"That's why I wonder, why'd he want to walk by hisself?"

And that's how all the rumors about Don Trine's walks got started. The folks couldn't figure out why or what he got out of taking off by himself every afternoon. When he would leave, and somebody would spy on him, somehow or other he would catch on, then take a little walk, turn around and head right back to his chicken coop. The fact of the matter is that everybody began to say he was hiding the money he had earned that year or that he had found some buried treasure and every day, little by little, he was bringing it back to his coop. Then they began to say that when he was young he had run around with a gang in Mexico and that he always carried around a lot of money with him. They said, too, that even if it was real hot, he carried a belt full of money beneath his undershirt. Practically all the speculation centered on the idea that he had money.

◀ **Critical Viewing** What does this painting suggest about the lives of the migrant workers in this story? **[Infer]**

Literary Analysis
Theme What insights about life might be provided in this paragraph?

Reading Check
What does everyone see Don Trine do every afternoon?

"Let's see, who's he got to take care of? He's an old bachelor. He ain't never married or had a family. So, with him working so many years . . . Don't you think he's bound to have money? And then, what's that man spend his money on? The only thing he buys is his bit of food every Saturday. Once in a while, a beer, but that's all."

"Yeah, he's gotta have a pile of money, for sure. But, you think he's going to bury it around here?"

"Who said he's burying anything? Look, he always goes for his food on Saturday. Let's check close where he goes this week, and on Saturday, when he's on his errand, we'll see what he's hiding. Whadda you say?"

"Good'nuff. Let's hope he doesn't catch on to us."

▼ Critical Viewing
Does this image capture the setting of the story as you imagine it? Why or why not? [Evaluate]

Farmworker de Califas, Tony Ortega, Courtesy of the artist

That week the youngsters closely watched Don Trine's walks. They noticed that he would disappear into the grove, then come out on the north side, cross the road then cross the field until he got to the irrigation ditch. There he dropped from sight for a while, then he reappeared in the west field. It was there where he would disappear and linger the most. They noticed also that, so as to throw people off his track, he would take a different route, but he always spent more time around the ditch that crossed the west field. They decided to investigate the ditch and that field the following Saturday.

When that day arrived, the boys were filled with anticipation. The truck had scarcely left and they were on their way to the west field. The truck had not yet disappeared and they had already crossed the grove. What they found they almost expected. There was nothing in the ditch, but in the field that had been <u>harrowed</u> after pulling the potatoes they found a number of holes.

"You notice all the holes here? The harrow didn't make these. Look, here's some foot prints, and notice that the holes are at least a foot deep. You can stick your arm in them up to your elbow. No animal makes these kind of holes. Whadda you think?"

"Well, it's bound to be Don Trine. But, what's he hiding? Why's he making so many holes? You think the landowner knows what he's up to?"

"Naw, man. Why, look, you can't see them from the road. You gotta come in a ways to notice they're here. What's he making them for? What's he using them for? And, look, they're all about the same width. Whadda you think?"

"Well, you got me. Maybe we'll know if we hide in the ditch and see what he does when he comes here."

"Look, here's a coffee can. I bet you this is what he digs with."

"I think you're right."

The boys had to wait until late the following Monday to discover the reason for the holes. But the word had spread around so that everybody already knew that Don Trine had a bunch of holes in that field. They tried not to let on but the allusions they made to the holes while they were out in the fields during the day were very obvious. Everybody thought there had to be a big explanation. So, the youngsters spied more carefully and <u>astutely</u>.

That afternoon they managed to fool Don Trine and saw what he was doing. They saw, and as they had suspected, Don Trine used the coffee can to dig a hole. Every so often, he would measure with his arm the depth of the hole. When it went up to his elbow, he stuck in his left arm, then filled dirt in around it with his right hand, all the way up to the elbow. Then he stayed like that for some time. He seemed very satisfied and even tried to light a cigarette with one hand. Not being able to, he just let it hang from his lips. Then he dug another hole and repeated the process. The boys could not understand why

Reading Strategy
Drawing Conclusions
What conclusion would you draw about Don Trine from his mysterious behavior?

harrowed (har′ ōd) v. broken up by a harrow, a frame with spikes drawn by a horse or tractor

Reading Strategy
Drawing Conclusions
What conclusion can you draw, so far, about Don Trine based on his actions?

astutely (ə stōōt′ lē) adv. cleverly or cunningly

✔**Reading Check**

What do the youngsters witness Don Trine doing with the dirt?

he did this. That was what puzzled them the most. They had believed that, with finding out what it was he did, they would understand everything. But it didn't turn out that way at all. The boys brought the news to the rest of the folks in the grove and nobody there understood either. In reality, when they found out that the holes didn't have anything to do with money, they thought Don Trine was crazy and even lost interest in the whole matter. But not everybody.

The next day one of the boys who discovered what Don Trine had been up to went by himself to a field. There he went through the same procedure that he had witnessed the day before. What he experienced and what he never forgot was feeling the earth move, feeling the earth grasp his fingers and even caressing them. He also felt the warmth of the earth. He sensed he was inside someone. Then he understood what Don Trine was doing. He was not crazy, he simply liked to feel the earth when it was sleeping.

That's why the boy kept going to the field every afternoon, until one night a hard freeze came on so that he could no longer dig any holes in the ground. The earth was fast asleep. Then he thought of next year, in October at harvest time, when once again he could repeat what Don Trine did. It was like when someone died. You always blamed yourself for not loving him more before he died.

Review and Assess

Thinking About the Selection

1. **Respond:** What do you think of Don Trine at the end of the story? Why?

2. **(a) Recall:** At what time of year does this story take place?
   (b) Apply: How does the opening paragraph foreshadow, or hint at, the ending of the story?

3. **(a) Recall:** What do the boys think Don Trine is doing every afternoon? **(b) Infer:** What do the boys' speculations about Don Trine reveal about them?

4. **(a) Recall:** When the one boy goes into the field later, what does he learn about Don Trine? **(b) Recall:** What does he realize when he imitates Don Trine's actions? **(c) Infer:** What does this ability to understand Don Trine suggest about the boy?

5. **(a) Extend:** Don Trine finds a way to make a connection with nature. In what other ways do people connect with nature?
   (b) Speculate: Do you think most people would benefit from taking time to appreciate nature? Why or why not?

Tomás Rivera

(1935–1984)

Born in Crystal City, Texas, Tomás Rivera soon joined what he called the "migrant labor stream" that traveled throughout the farmlands of the United States. Faced with the challenge of alternating schooling with work in the fields, Rivera pursued his education tirelessly. His persistence paid off, as he eventually earned a Ph.D. in Spanish Literature.

Rivera's concern for the education of minorities led him to a career as an educator, limiting the time he could devote to his writing. Nevertheless, he has become one of the most renowned Mexican American authors in the United States. His work most often focuses on the experiences of migrant farm workers.

Review and Assess

Literary Analysis

Theme

1. Toward the end of "The Necklace," Madame Loisel thinks, "How strange and fickle life is! How little it takes to make or break you!" What does this statement suggest about the complexity of life?

2. Considering the course of events for Madame Loisel, what would you say is the **theme** of "The Necklace"? Explain.

3. Using a chart like the one below, analyze the last two paragraphs of "The Harvest" and explain the theme of the story.

Words From the Text	Insights
Theme:	

Comparing Literary Works

4. (a) Summarize the moment of insight for Madame Loisel in "The Necklace" and for the boy at the end of the "The Harvest."
(b) Using a Venn diagram like the one below, explain how their discoveries are similar and different.

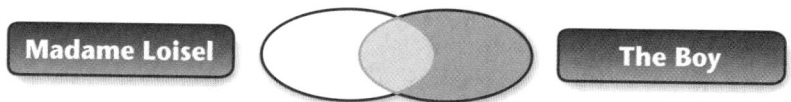

Madame Loisel — The Boy

5. Who do you think will be affected more by their insight? Explain.

Reading Strategy

Drawing Conclusions

6. Madame Loisel places a high value on material goods. On the basis of the story, what **conclusion** can you draw about such values?

7. Based on the ending of "The Harvest," what conclusion can you draw about the importance of nature to the human spirit?

Extend Understanding

8. **Cultural Connection:** (a) What does "The Necklace" show you about life in middle-class French society in the late nineteenth century? (b) Do you think there are parallels in modern American society? Explain.

Quick Review

The **theme** of a literary work is the insight about life that it communicates.

To **draw conclusions,** gather details and make decisions about the underlying meaning of these details.

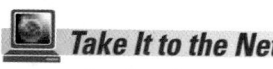 **Take It to the Net**
www.phschool.com
Take the interactive self-test online to check your understanding of the selections.

Integrate Language Skills

Vocabulary Development Lesson

Word Analysis: Latin Root -ject-

The word *dejection*, meaning "a state of sadness," is formed from the Latin word root -*ject*-, which means "to throw." Considering the meaning of -*ject*-, write a definition for each word below.

1. trajectory   2. eject   3. interject

Spelling Strategy

For words that end in silent *e*, keep the *e* before adding an ending that begins with a consonant. For example, when you add -*ful* to the word *rue*, you form the word *rueful*. Add the given suffixes to the words below. Then, write a sentence for each new word.

1. entire + -*ly*   2. hope + -*ful*   3. awe + -*some*

Concept Development: Synonyms

Choose the word or phrase that is closest in meaning to the first word.

1. astutely: (a) cleverly, (b) grandly, (c) thriftily
2. resplendent: (a) radiant, (b) wealthy, (c) sturdy
3. profoundly: (a) slowly, (b) deeply, (c) quietly
4. déclassée: (a) decorated, (b) lowered in social status, (c) tardy
5. harrowed: (a) mad, (b) frightened, (c) plowed
6. rueful: (a) angry, (b) sweet, (c) sorry
7. disheveled: (a) old, (b) messy, (c) rusty

Grammar Lesson

Appositive Phrases

An **appositive phrase** is a noun or pronoun with modifiers that is placed next to a noun or pronoun to provide more information. The modifiers added to make an appositive phrase can be adjectives, adjective phrases, or other groups of words acting as adjectives. Look at the following example from "The Necklace."

> **Example:** She had a rich <u>friend</u>, *a schoolmate from the convent she had attended,* but she didn't like to visit her because it always made her so miserable when she got home again.
>
> (The appositive phrase in italics renames *friend*.)

Practice Write the appositive phrase in each sentence and the word or words it renames.

1. Mathilde, a woman from a middle-class background, was unhappy with her life.
2. Her husband, a kind and generous man, could not provide the life she desired.
3. She spoke to Madame Forestier, a wealthy woman with an upper-class background.
4. The necklace, a strand of fake jewels, was lost.
5. She went back to her home, a meager and simple apartment, to speak to her husband.

Writing Application Write three sentences about a character in one of the stories you have just read, including an appositive phrase in each.

W͞G Prentice Hall Writing and Grammar Connection: Chapter 21, Section 1

Writing Lesson

Scene for a Television Drama

Imagine that one of the stories you have just read will be adapted for presentation as a television drama. Choose either "The Necklace" or "The Harvest" and write the final, dramatic scene for this production.

Prewriting   Make a list of the events you would like to include in the scene. Note the actions that make up the climax, or highest point of the story, and plan the events that will happen after the climax.

Drafting   As you draft your television drama, try to hear your characters speak. Create dialogue that fits each character's personality, age, and background. Use stage directions to describe each scene.

Model: Using Script Format

[Madame Loisel enters the room and looks in the mirror, reaches for her neck, and lets out a scream.]

M. Loisel: What's the matter?

Mme. Loisel: The . . . the . . . necklace—is gone.

> The stage directions in brackets and the dialogue create a dramatic interpretation.

Revising   Reread your scene to determine whether the events can be clearly understood. Rewrite any dialogue that does not sound realistic.

*W*G *Prentice Hall Writing and Grammar Connection: Chapter 5, Connected Assignment*

Extension Activities

Listening and Speaking With another student, improvise a conversation between Madame Loisel and her husband after she returns from meeting her old friend ten years later. Jot some notes before you start your **improvisation**.

- Think about how you would feel if you were Madame Loisel.
- Consider the reaction her husband would have after hearing the news.

Since you will be working without a script, work to integrate your comments and ideas with those of your partner. **[Group Activity]**

Research and Technology Farmers, like those featured in "The Harvest," make up only a small part of the population today, but just a few decades ago farmers were the bulk of the population. Research your family or community history back far enough to find farmers. Then, create a **flow chart** that shows the results of your research.

 **Take It to the Net**   www.phschool.com

Go online for an additional research activity using the Internet.

Writing WORKSHOP

Narration: Short Story

A **short story** is a work of fiction that combines plot, setting, and characters to present a brief narrative. In this workshop, you will write and revise a short story.

Assignment Criteria. Your short story should have the following characteristics:

- A main character who takes part in the action
- Details that describe a particular time and place
- A conflict, or problem, to be introduced, developed, and resolved
- A succession of events that make up the plot, incorporating changes in time and mood
- A central theme or generalization about life

To preview the criteria on which your short story may be assessed, see the Rubric on page 627.

Prewriting

Choose a topic. Use **sentence starters** to spark your creativity when brainstorming for a topic. Use one sentence starter to write freely for five minutes without worrying about grammar or sentence structure. Draw from your memories or imagination to develop interesting situations. Then, circle intriguing conflicts or themes and choose one to build into a story. Consider these sentence starters or make up your own:

- *What would happen if . . .*
- *One person I will never forget is . . .*

Based on your work, choose an idea as the basis for a story.

Summarize the plot. Briefly describe the incidents that make up the plot of your story. If you need more than a few sentences to do this, you may be trying to do too much in your writing.

Develop characters. Bring the characters and conflict of your story to life by providing enough detail for readers to imagine the world you create. Establish details about each of your characters to incorporate into your draft later.

Character	Details
Grandfather Clock	• Lonely, because everyone grows up and moves away • Wants to be loved and cared for • Is winding down from lack of human care

Student Model

Before you begin drafting your short story, read this abridged student model and its side notes. The full text of the story can be found at www.phschool.com

Katie Hartwell
Newberry, Florida

The main character in this first-person story is the grandfather clock.

Grandfather Clock

Tick, tock, tick, tock. I'm sitting here, watching the moments of my existence pass slowly away. My house has been empty for such a long time, and I'm lonely and forgotten. As I sit here, by myself, all that I can do is look back and reminisce. I could tell you stories that only walls would know. But walls can't speak.

In the opening paragraph, the author describes setting and mood.

I came to this place many years ago, tugged along behind an old man. . . . Sadly, he was with me for only three short years before he passed on. . . .

For a time, I was left alone, while people came and looked at the house. . . . Then, one day a nice couple moved in with a young son. From the beginning, their son Danny was fascinated by me, and I was completely taken with him. He always looked as if he loved the stories I told, most of which began with, "Back in my day . . ." and "When I was younger. . . ." I sometimes thought that he didn't really understand what I was saying, but it felt good to be loved. . . . When Danny went off to college, I was crushed. Soon afterward, his parents sold the house. . . .

The mood changes as time passes and new events occur.

New owners came and went. Then, one day I heard a new family was moving into the house. You can't even imagine my surprise when, out of the blue, Danny walked through the front door. He had a wife and kids now. I was so overjoyed when I saw him that I put all my energy into my daily activities. . . . I spent the next twenty years watching Danny's kids grow up, with a mixture of pride and anxiety about what would happen next.

The kids finally grew up and Danny sold the house. That was about five years ago. . . . Some of the local kids have started the rumor that the house is haunted—and, in a fashion, it is. It is haunted by the memories of all the people who have lived in it. Every second has left its mark on me. I have been counting them down and they are almost up for me. . . . I hope that someday somebody will remember me, and come to wind me again. Maybe then I'll get a new home and a chance for a whole new set of memories.

The author restates the problem and central theme in the closing lines of the story.

Drafting

Organize details. As you draft your short story, check that you have included the following story components:

- **Characters**—actors in the story with unique characteristics, attitudes, and relationships to one another
- **Setting**—the specific time and place of the action of your story
- **Conflict**—a struggle between opposing forces or characters
- **Action**—specific events in the plot that show how the conflict intensifies and how it is resolved

Elaborate. If you find yourself writing sentences that tell readers what you want them to think, challenge yourself to be a better storyteller. Provide details that will make the writing speak for itself. Follow up "telling" sentences with "showing" ones. Use the chart at right as a guide for drafting more revealing sentences.

Telling	Showing
Danny seemed to like me.	He would spend hours in front of me, staring up at my face, and raptly listening to everything I said. When I spoke, the little boy would stare up at me, smiling.

Elaborate: Show, Don't Tell

Revising

Revise to emphasize changes in mood. The power of a story depends on its ability to appeal to a reader's emotions. One dramatic technique that writers use is an abrupt shift in mood to keep the reader emotionally involved. Review your story and note instances where events occur that would fit naturally with a change in mood. Then, add descriptions to show how the characters might react emotionally to the new event.

Model: Stressing a Change in Mood

For a time I was left alone, while people came and looked at

I lost hope that the house would ever be occupied again.

the house. ∧Then, one day a nice couple moved in with a

Naturally, I was ecstatic.

young son. ∧From the beginning, their son Danny was

fascinated by me, and I was completely taken with him.

> Katie adds description and insight to show the clock's shifting emotions.

Revise to use the active voice. In sentences whose verbs take the active voice, the subject performs the action of a sentence. To create dynamic sentences in which characters are acting instead of being acted upon, choose the active voice instead of the passive voice. In the following example, the active voice makes the writing stronger.

Passive Voice: The bus was caught by Daniel.

Active Voice: Daniel caught the bus.

Compare the model and the nonmodel. Why is the model more effective than the nonmodel?

Nonmodel	Model
I hope that someday I will be remembered by somebody and that I will be wound again.	I hope that someday someone will remember me, and come to wind me again.

Publishing and Presenting

When you are satisfied with your short story, share your writing with a wider audience.

Deliver an oral presentation. Read your short story aloud to your classmates. As you read passages with dialogue, alter your voice to convey the different personalities of your characters. Ask for feedback from your classmates and consider revisions based on their comments. Then, compile your work with that of your classmates to publish an anthology or collection of your short stories in book form.

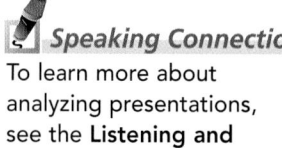

Speaking Connection
To learn more about analyzing presentations, see the **Listening and Speaking Workshop,** p. 628.

 Prentice Hall Writing and Grammar Connection: Chapter 5

Rubric for Self-Assessment

Evaluate your short story using the following criteria and rating scale:

Criteria	Rating Scale				
	Not very				Very
How well do you establish your setting?	1	2	3	4	5
Is the main character well developed?	1	2	3	4	5
How well do you develop, introduce, and resolve your central conflict?	1	2	3	4	5
How well developed is your plot?	1	2	3	4	5
How effectively does the story convey a theme or generalization about life?	1	2	3	4	5

Listening and Speaking WORKSHOP

Analyzing a Media Presentation

People enjoy watching a movie review and then agreeing—or vehemently disagreeing—with the critic's opinions. In order to explain your own reaction to a movie or television show, it is useful to know how to **analyze a media presentation.** As with any type of analysis, interpreting involves breaking different elements of a program apart and examining them.

Analyze the Media Presentation

Establish categories. Since they cannot address every aspect of a production, critics use established categories to analyze and evaluate media presentations.

- For *fiction,* including movies and television programs, critics use categories such as plot, setting, dialogue, and believability.
- For *nonfiction,* including news programs, documentaries, and infomercials, critics use categories such as clarity of presentation, credibility of sources, and appropriateness of special effects.

Note your responses. As you watch the presentation, use a chart like the one shown to record your impressions. For each category, make brief notes about aspects that struck you favorably or unfavorably. Compare the presentation to movies or shows you have seen in the past.

Rating a Media Presentation

	Category	Opinion	Evidence
FICTION	Plot		
	Setting		
	Dialogue		
	Realistic Portrayal		
NONFICTION	Clarity of Presentation		
	Credibility of Sources		
	Organization		
	Added Effects		

Evaluate the Media Presentation

When you have finished viewing, review your notes to find a central idea.

Indicate strengths and weaknesses. Describe your overall impression of the media presentation, and then assess the movie's individual aspects. You can do this by assigning numerical ratings or by choosing adjectives to convey your impressions of various aspects of the program—for example, identify a *weak* plot, *shallow* characters, *clever* dialogue, *brilliant* special effects, or *inventive* camera work.

Cite examples to support your view. Since others may not share your opinion, use your analysis as an opportunity for persuasion. Cite examples from the movie or show to justify your opinions. For example, if you criticized the dialogue as unrealistic, you might cite a ridiculous conversation between two characters to support this view.

(Activity: Analysis and Discussion**)** In a small group, watch a movie, a news report, or another type of media presentation. Using the chart shown, analyze the program. Share your reviews with the other members of the group to discuss differences in opinion.

Assessment WORKSHOP

Author's Point of View

The reading sections of some tests require you to read a passage and answer multiple-choice questions about the author's point of view. Use these strategies to help you answer test questions about the author's point of view:

- Look for language to help you understand the author's perspective or thoughts on a subject.
- Use the author's tone and choice of details as clues to his or her point of view.
- Remember that the author's point of view is often implied, not directly stated.

Test-Taking Strategies

- Look for strong language that seems calculated to sway readers' emotions. Then, infer the author's approval or disapproval.
- Examine the opening and closing statements carefully as an indication of an author's attitude.

Sample Test Item

Directions: Read the passage, and then answer the question that follows.

Jane Addams founded a settlement house in Chicago, Illinois, in 1889. Hull House offered hot lunches, child care, and tutoring in English and other subjects. Most important, Hull House developed a neighborhood spirit among recent immigrants. Addams said that she was just "a simple person," but her ideas and actions had far-reaching consequences.

1. The author views Jane Addams with ____?____.

   A suspicion

   B affection

   C admiration

   D fear

Answer and Explanation

The correct answer is *C.* The author selects facts that highlight Addams's positive qualities. The passage mentions no negative characteristics, which might justify *A* or *D.* The author does not discuss Addams in an openly personal way, so *B* is not the best answer.

▶ Practice

Directions: Read the passage, and then answer the question that follows.

Jonah Hart, a student, was in-line skating when he fell and hit his head. He was unconscious for several days. Jonah probably would have walked away with only scrapes and bruises if he had been wearing a helmet. The National Safe Kids Campaign says that wearing helmets lowers the risk of head injury by 85 percent. Kids should always wear helmets when they skate. A helmet could save your life!

1. The author's point of view is that ____?____.

   A helmets are not expensive

   B everyone should join the National Safe Kids Campaign

   C Jonah Hart could have avoided injury if he had been a better skater

   D kids risk injury if they skate without helmets

Nonfiction

Mural on PAL center depicts the diverse community in Santa Monica, CA

Exploring the Genre

If fiction takes you on imaginative flights of fancy, nonfiction grounds you in reality. This does not make nonfiction any less fascinating or diverse. When you want to encounter real people with interesting experiences, learn a new skill, or read viewpoints on a controversial issue, you can turn to nonfiction.

The nonfiction in this unit falls into several categories:

- An **autobiography** is the writer's own story, describing notable events of his or her life.

- A **biography** is the story of a life from another person's perspective.

- An **essay** is a short nonfiction work that addresses a specific subject. A **reflective essay** shares the writer's inner thoughts and feelings. A **narrative essay** tells a story about an actual event or person. An **expository essay** explains certain aspects of a subject. A **persuasive essay** attempts to convince the reader to think or act in a certain way.

- A **speech** is a talk or an address presented to an audience.

▲ **Critical Viewing** Which nonfiction subjects could this image effectively illustrate? **[Hypothesize]**

Why Read Literature?

Whenever you read nonfiction, you have a purpose, or reason. You might be curious about a topic or fascinated by an author's memory of an important event. Preview three purposes you might set before reading works in this unit.

1

Read for the Love of Literature

Even your longest-held opinions can change, if you keep an open mind. As a child, Lorraine Hansberry strongly disliked summer. Learn how her initial feelings turned into an enthusiastic embrace of the season in her eloquent essay **"On Summer,"** page 656.

Powerful literature can make unlikely heroes out of ordinary people. Some people might not think twice about an old woman walking in the snow, bent under the weight of several bags of laundry. For Isaac Bachevis Singer, though, this woman presents an opportunity to memorialize a personal hero in **"The Washwoman,"** page 650.

3

Read to Be Inspired

After you read Steve Gietschier's enthusiastic book review **"In These Girls, Hope Is a Muscle,"** page 715, you just might be tempted to pick up the book, which traces the emotional highs and lows of a women's high school basketball team.

In a sport known for emotional behavior, tennis champion Arthur Ashe never lost his cool. Yet, when others expected such a cool player to play cautiously, he attacked the ball with a fierce intensity. Learn more about this remarkable athlete in John McPhee's essay **"Arthur Ashe Remembered,"** page 682.

2

Read for Information

Lady Bird Johnson became First Lady as a result of one of the most traumatic episodes in American history: the assassination of President John F. Kennedy in 1963. Observe Johnson's impressions as momentous events swirled around her when you read **from *A White House Diary*,** page 674.

Not many people have viewed Earth from a vantage point two hundred miles away. Discover the complex answer to the question "What was it like?" when you read astronaut Sally Ride's essay **"Single Room, Earth View,"** page 636.

 Take It to the Net

Visit the Web site for online instruction and activities related to each selection in this unit.
www.phschool.com

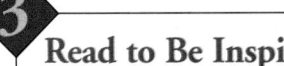

How to Read Literature

Use Strategies for Reading Nonfiction

Although works of nonfiction vary in topic, type, and purpose, they all share one common characteristic: They all claim to be true. This does not mean that you should accept everything an author writes without question. Use these strategies to help you judge the facts and form your own opinions.

1. Identify the author's attitude.

To identify an author's attitude, examine the selection of language and evidence presented in the text.

- If the text includes language with strong positive or negative connotations, this can provide you with valuable clues to the author's attitude.
- When an author uses neutral language, he or she may wish to be perceived as even-handed and objective.
- If the author highlights certain facts or details and omits others, note it as possible evidence of personal bias.

2. Find the writer's main points and support.

Taking apart a writer's argument for analysis is the first step to forming your own opinion on the subject. Use the model at right to guide you.

- To determine the main points of a selection, ask yourself what the author wants you to learn or think as a result of reading the text.
- Summarize the ideas of individual paragraphs or chapters to determine how an author is supporting the main points.

> **Finding Main Points and Support:**
>
> **"Arthur Ashe Remembered"**
>
> Ashe was a great tennis player.
> - Maintained control, even in tight spots
> - Played with energy, grace, and power
> - Willing to take risks to win games
>
> Ashe was difficult to read.
> - Didn't react emotionally, kept cool
> - Would attempt unpredictable shots

3. Vary your reading rate.

- To find specific information, skim the text quickly, looking for key words and phrases.
- To absorb a complex argument or appreciate descriptive passages, slow your reading pace.

4. Use visuals as a key to meaning.

Nonfiction authors frequently use drawings, charts, and graphs to supplement their written text. To get the most out of visuals, first summarize the main point that the visual attempts to convey. Then, determine how the illustration, chart, or graph complements the main points that the author is trying to make.

As you read the selections in this unit, review the reading strategies and apply them to interact with the text.

Prepare to Read

Single Room, Earth View

 Take It to the Net

Visit www.phschool.com for interactive activities and instruction related to "Single Room, Earth View," including

- background
- graphic organizers
- literary elements
- reading strategies

Preview

Connecting to the Literature

At street level, a city can be a confusing place. When you look at that city from a high floor of a tall building, however, its layout becomes apparent. In this essay, you will see what it is like to look down on Earth, as the astronaut Sally Ride describes her view from space.

Background

On June 18, 1983, when she soared aloft as flight engineer and mission specialist aboard the shuttle *Challenger*—the same shuttle that would explode shortly after liftoff three years later—Sally Ride became the first American woman in space. Her historic mission allowed her to experience what she recounts in "Single Room, Earth View."

Literary Analysis

Observation

An **observation** describes an event that a writer witnessed firsthand. It includes many details and uses vivid, precise words to re-create the event for readers. In this example, the vivid details are set in italics:

> We could see the Ganges River dumping *its murky, sediment-laden water* into the Indian Ocean and watch *ominous hurricane clouds expanding and rising like biscuits in the oven* . . .

As you read, notice Ride's clear, expressive observations of Earth.

Connecting Literary Elements

To enhance a written observation, writers use **description**—a portrait in words of a person, place, or object. Descriptive writing uses sensory details that appeal to sight, hearing, taste, smell, and touch. A writer may also use figurative language to draw unique and surprising comparisons that bring a subject's key qualities into focus. Notice how Sally Ride uses a variety of techniques to vividly describe her view of Earth.

Reading Strategy

Varying Your Reading Rate

When you **vary your reading rate,** you adjust your reading speed to suit your purpose.

- Read quickly if you are scanning for a particular piece of information or just want the overall idea of a nonfiction work.
- Read slowly and carefully when seeking to understand more details or more complex information.

Use a chart like this one to record changes in your reading rate.

Instruction with this selection addresses these standards:

R 1.1*, 3.7*, 3.8*
W 1.5, * 2.6
WOLC 1.2*, 1.3*
LS 1.7

* Standards tested on HS Exit Exam. For complete standards, see p. CA 4.

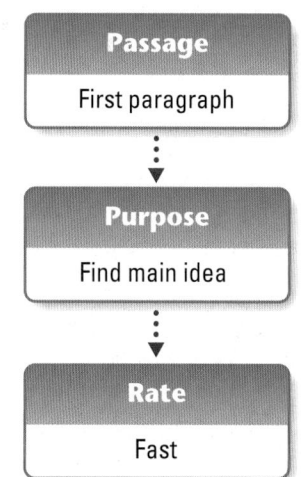

Passage
First paragraph

↓

Purpose
Find main idea

↓

Rate
Fast

Vocabulary Development

articulate (är tik′ yoo lit) *adj.* expressing oneself clearly and easily (p. 637)

surreal (sər rē′ əl) *adj.* strange (p. 637)

ominous (äm′ ə nəs) *adj.* threatening (p. 637)

novice (näv′ is) *adj.* beginner (p. 637)

muted (myoot′ əd) *adj.* weaker; less intense (p. 638)

eddies (ed′ ēz) *n.* circular currents (p. 639)

subtle (sut′ ′l) *adj.* not obvious (p. 639)

eerie (ir′ ē) *adj.* mysterious (p. 639)

diffused (di fyoozd′) *v.* spread out (p. 640)

extrapolating (ek strap′ ə lāt′ iŋ) *v.* arriving at a conclusion by making inferences based on known facts (p. 640)

Single Room, Earth View

Sally Ride

veryone I've met has a glittering, if vague, mental image of space travel. And naturally enough, people want to hear about it from an astronaut: "How did it feel . . . ?" "What did it look like . . . ?" "Were you scared?" Sometimes, the questions come from reporters, their pens poised and their tape recorders silently reeling in the words; sometimes, it's wide-eyed, ten-year-old girls who want answers. I find a way to answer all of them, but it's not easy.

Imagine trying to describe an airplane ride to someone who has never flown. An <u>articulate</u> traveler could describe the sights but would find it much harder to explain the difference in perspective provided by the new view from a greater distance, along with the feelings, impressions, and insights that go with that new perspective. And the difference is enormous: Spaceflight moves the traveler another giant step farther away. Eight and one-half thunderous minutes after launch, an astronaut is orbiting high above the Earth, suddenly able to watch typhoons form, volcanoes smolder, and meteors streak through the atmosphere below.

While flying over the Hawaiian Islands, several astronauts have marveled that the islands look just like they do on a map. When people first hear that, they wonder what should be so surprising about Hawaii looking the way it does in the atlas. Yet, to the astronauts it is an absolutely startling sensation: The islands really *do* look as if that part of the world has been carpeted with a big page torn out of Rand-McNally,[1] and all we can do is try to convey the <u>surreal</u> quality of that scene.

In orbit, racing along at five miles per second, the space shuttle circles the Earth once every 90 minutes. I found that at this speed, unless I kept my nose pressed to the window, it was almost impossible to keep track of where we were at any given moment—the world below simply changes too fast. If I turned my concentration away for too long, even just to change film in a camera, I could miss an entire land mass. It's embarrassing to float up to a window, glance outside, and then have to ask a crewmate, "What continent is this?"

We could see smoke rising from fires that dotted the entire east coast of Africa, and in the same orbit only moments later, ice floes jostling for position in the Antarctic. We could see the Ganges River dumping its murky, sediment-laden water into the Indian Ocean and watch <u>ominous</u> hurricane clouds expanding and rising like biscuits in the oven of the Caribbean.

Mountain ranges, volcanoes, and river deltas appeared in salt-and-flour relief, all leading me to assume the role of a <u>novice</u> geologist. In such moments, it was easy to imagine the dynamic upheavals that created jutting mountain ranges and the internal wrenchings that created

---

1. **Rand-McNally** publisher of atlases.

◀ **Critical Viewing** Based on this photograph, do you think you would enjoy a trip on the space shuttle? Why or why not? **[Connect]**

articulate (är tik′ yoo lit) *adj.* expressing oneself clearly and easily

surreal (sər rē′ əl) *adj.* strange

Literary Analysis
Observation Which details does Ride use to focus her observation in this paragraph?

ominous (äm′ ə nəs) *adj.* threatening

novice (näv′ is) *adj.* beginner

Reading Check

According to Ride, how have astronauts described the Hawaiian Islands?

rifts and seas. I also became an instant believer in plate tectonics;[*] India really *is* crashing into Asia, and Saudi Arabia and Egypt really *are* pulling apart, making the Red Sea wider. Even though their respective motion is really no more than mere inches a year, the view from overhead makes theory come alive.

Spectacular as the view is from 200 miles up, the Earth is not the awe-inspiring "blue marble" made famous by the photos from the moon. From space shuttle height, we can't see the entire globe at a glance, but we can look down the entire boot of Italy, or up the East Coast of the United States from Cape Hatteras to Cape Cod. The panoramic view inspires an appreciation for the scale of some of nature's phenomena. One day, as I scanned the sandy expanse of Northern Africa, I couldn't find any of the familiar landmarks—colorful outcroppings of rock in Chad, irrigated patches of the Sahara. Then I realized they were obscured by a huge dust storm, a cloud of sand that enveloped the continent from Morocco to the Sudan.

Since the space shuttle flies fairly low (at least by orbital standards; it's more than 22,000 miles lower than a typical TV satellite), we can make out both natural and manmade features in surprising detail. Familiar geographical features like San Francisco Bay, Long Island, and Lake Michigan are easy to recognize, as are many cities, bridges, and airports. The Great Wall of China is *not* the only man-made object visible from space.

The signatures of civilization are usually seen in straight lines (bridges or runways) or sharp delineations (abrupt transitions from desert to irrigated land, as in California's Imperial Valley). A modern city like New York doesn't leap from the canvas of its surroundings, but its straight piers and concrete runways catch the eye—and around them, the city materializes. I found Salina, Kansas (and pleased my in-laws, who live there) by spotting its long runway amid the wheat fields near the city. Over Florida, I could see the launch pad where we had begun our trip, and the landing strip, where we would eventually land.

Some of civilization's more unfortunate effects on the environment are also evident from orbit. Oil slicks glisten on the surface of the Persian Gulf, patches of pollution-damaged trees dot the forests of central Europe. Some cities look out of focus, and their colors <u>muted</u>, when viewed through a pollutant haze. Not surprisingly, the effects are more noticeable now than they were a decade ago. An astronaut who has flown in both Skylab and the space shuttle reported that the horizon didn't seem quite as sharp, or the colors quite as bright, in 1983 as they had in 1973.

Of course, informal observations by individual astronauts are one thing, but more precise measurements are continually being made from space: The space shuttle has carried infrared film to document

Literature in context Science Connection

◆ **Plate Tectonics**

In the 1960s, scientists proposed a theory that Earth's outer shell consists of a number of rigid segments, or "plates." The shell, called the lithosphere, is about 45 to 95 miles thick and seems to be in constant motion. The plates slowly slide on a soft, flexible layer of rock and move from 0.5 to 4 inches a year.

If one plate pushes against another, the collision can form mountains. Major earthquakes occur when two plates slide past each other. Not all scientists, however, are as convinced as Sally Ride was, circling the planet 22 miles up, that the plate tectonic theory is valid.

Reading Strategy
Varying Your Reading Rate How quickly would you read this paragraph if you wanted to learn about effects on the environment viewed from space?

muted (myo͞ot′ əd) *adj.* weaker; less intense

damage to citrus trees in Florida and in rain forests along the Amazon. It has carried even more sophisticated sensors in the payload bay. Here is one example: sensors used to measure atmospheric carbon monoxide levels, allowing scientists to study the environmental effects of city emissions and land-clearing fires.

Most of the Earth's surface is covered with water, and at first glance it all looks the same: blue. But with the right lighting conditions and a couple of orbits of practice, it's possible to make out the intricate patterns in the oceans—<u>eddies</u> and spirals become visible because of the <u>subtle</u> differences in water color or reflectivity.

eddies (ed′ ēz) *n.* circular currents

subtle (sut′ ′l) *adj.* not obvious

Observations and photographs by astronauts have contributed significantly to the understanding of ocean dynamics, and some of the more intriguing discoveries prompted the National Aeronautics and Space Administration to fly an oceanographic observer for the express purpose of studying the ocean from orbit. Scientists' understanding of the energy balance in the oceans has increased significantly as a result of the discoveries of circular and spiral eddies tens of kilometers in diameter, of standing waves hundreds of kilometers long, and of spiral eddies that sometimes trail into one another for thousands of kilometers. If a scientist wants to study features on this scale, it's much easier from an orbiting vehicle than from the vantage point of a boat.

Believe it or not, an astronaut can also see the wakes of large ships and the contrails[2] of airplanes. The sun angle has to be just right, but when the lighting conditions are perfect, you can follow otherwise invisible oil tankers on the Persian Gulf and trace major shipping lanes through the Mediterranean Sea. Similarly, when atmospheric conditions allow contrail formation, the thousand-mile-long condensation trails let astronauts trace the major air routes across the northern Pacific Ocean.

Part of every orbit takes us to the dark side of the planet. In space, night is very, very black—but that doesn't mean there's nothing to look at. The lights of cities sparkle; on nights when there was no moon, it was difficult for me to tell the Earth from the sky—the twinkling lights could be stars or they could be small cities. On one nighttime pass from Cuba to Nova Scotia, the entire East Coast of the United States appeared in twinkling outline.

When the moon is full, it casts an <u>eerie</u> light on the Earth. In its light, we see ghostly clouds and bright reflections on the water. One night, the Mississippi River flashed into view, and because of our viewing angle and orbital path, the reflected moonlight seemed to flow downstream—as if Huck Finn[3] had tied a candle to his raft.

Of all the sights from orbit, the most spectacular may be the

eerie (ir′ ē) *adj.* mysterious

**Reading Check**

What is the infrared film carried in a space shuttle used to document?

---

2. **contrails** (kän′ trāls′) *n.* white trails of condensed water vapor that sometimes form in the wake of aircraft.
3. **Huck Finn** hero of Mark Twain's novel *The Adventures of Huckleberry Finn.*

magnificent displays of lightning that ignite the clouds at night. On Earth, we see lightning from below the clouds; in orbit, we see it from above. Bolts of lightning are <u>diffused</u> by the clouds into bursting balls of light. Sometimes, when a storm extends hundreds of miles, it looks like a transcontinental brigade is tossing fireworks from cloud to cloud.

As the shuttle races the sun around the Earth, we pass from day to night and back again during a single orbit—hurtling into darkness, then bursting into daylight. The sun's appearance unleashes spectacular blue and orange bands along the horizon, a clockwork miracle that astronauts witness every 90 minutes. But I really can't describe a sunrise in orbit. The drama set against the black backdrop of space and the magic of the materializing colors can't be captured in an astronomer's equations or an astronaut's photographs.

I once heard someone (not an astronaut) suggest that it's possible to imagine what spaceflight is like by simply <u>extrapolating</u> from the sensations you experience on an airplane. All you have to do, he said, is mentally raise the airplane 200 miles, mentally eliminate the air noise and the turbulence, and you get an accurate mental picture of a trip in the space shuttle.

Not true. And while it's natural to try to liken spaceflight to familiar experiences, it can't be brought "down to Earth"—not in the final sense. The environment is different, the perspective is different. Part of the fascination with space travel is the element of the unknown—the conviction that it's different from earthbound experiences. And it is.

diffused (di fyo͞ozd´) *v.* spread out

extrapolating (ek strap´ ə lāt´ iŋ) *v.* arriving at a conclusion by making inferences based on known facts

Review and Assess

Thinking About the Selection

1. **Respond:** Would you like to be an astronaut? Why or why not?

2. **(a) Recall:** On which space shuttle did Ride travel?
   (b) Compare and Contrast: According to Ride, how is travel on the space shuttle different from travel on an airplane?

3. **(a) Recall:** Which geological features did Ride observe from orbit? **(b) Interpret:** Why did Ride find it easier to imagine geological forces from space?

4. **(a) Recall:** Which "unfortunate effects" did Ride see from orbit? **(b) Infer:** Why would these effects make colors seen in 1983 seem not as bright as those seen in 1973?

5. **(a) Draw Conclusions:** Does space travel aid in understanding conditions on Earth? **(b) Support:** Cite evidence from Ride's essay to explain your point of view.

6. **Connect:** How have Ride's descriptions of Earth changed the way you think about our planet?

Sally Ride

(b. 1951)

Although best known as an astronaut, Sally Ride was also a talented athlete in her youth. She received both undergraduate and graduate degrees from Stanford University.

In 1978, she read about NASA's search for astronauts and ultimately was chosen as one of the six women and twenty-five men accepted from among 8,000 applicants. In 1983, Sally Ride became the first American woman in space. She played a key role in the investigation of the *Challenger* tragedy in 1986.

Ride retired from NASA in 1987. She currently teaches physics at the University of California and is the author of several books on space.

Review and Assess

Literary Analysis

Observation

1. Which details in the essay show Ride's talent for **observation** in finding civilization's "signatures"?
2. How does Ride prove herself to be a careful observer of Earth's oceans?
3. Choose a particularly powerful observation of Ride's, and explain what makes it memorable. Use a chart like the following to record facts, events, and vivid details.

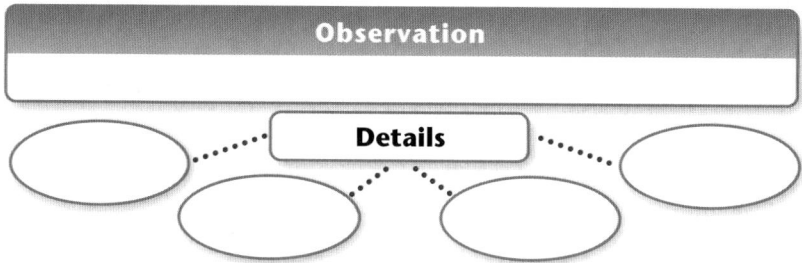

Connecting Literary Elements

4. Find an example from Ride's selection of **descriptive** language that appeals to the sense of touch.
5. How does Ride use comparisons to everyday phenomena to help readers follow her observations?
6. Does Ride's attention to descriptive details compromise her ability to be objective or strengthen her ability to convey her ideas?

Reading Strategy

Varying Your Reading Rate

7. (a) If you were reading to learn about Ride's description of cities in the United States, which paragraphs could you skim through quickly? (b) Which paragraphs would you read more carefully?
8. Why might you recommend that someone else read the entire essay slowly? Refer to the selection as you answer.

Extend Understanding

9. **Science Connection:** How has Sally Ride's essay affected what you think about the space program? Explain.

Quick Review

An **observation** describes an event that a writer saw firsthand, and it includes many details and vivid, precise words.

A **description** is a portrait in words of a person, place, or object.

To **vary your reading rate**, adjust your reading speed according to your purpose for reading.

 Take It to the Net
www.phschool.com
Take the interactive self-test online to check your understanding of the selection.

Integrate Language Skills

Vocabulary Development Lesson

Word Analysis: Latin Root -nov-

The Latin root -nov- means "new." The root appears in the word *novice*, which means "someone new to an activity; a beginner."

Use your knowledge of the root -nov- to define each of the following words, incorporating *new* into each definition.

    1. novel (*adj.*)   **2.** renovate   **3.** innovate

Spelling Strategy

If a word ends in silent *e*, drop the *e* before adding a suffix that starts with a vowel. Thus, *extrapolate* + *-ing* = *extrapolating* and *diffuse* + *-ion* = *diffusion*.

Add *-able*, *-ing*, or *-est* to each word below to form three properly spelled new words.

    1. rare   **2.** use   **3.** articulate

Fluency: Context

Fill in each blank with a word (or a form of the word) from the vocabulary list on page 635.

  1. Normally ____?____, the veteran scientist felt like a tongue-tied ____?____ speaker.

  2. The low, ____?____ murmuring of her audience was frightening and ____?____, giving her a bad feeling.

  3. She turned on the projector, and the smell of burning dust, ____?____ but unmistakable, ____?____ through the air.

  4. "This will seem weird, even ____?____," she said, putting on the strange first slide.

  5. "However, what we can ____?____ from the facts and evidence is clear."

  6. "The odd, ____?____ patterns of ____?____ and whirlpools on Planet X are mysterious signs of intelligent life."

Grammar Lesson

Subject-Verb Agreement

The **subject** is the word or group of words in a sentence that tells whom or what the sentence is about. The **verb,** or *predicate,* is the word or group of words in a sentence that expresses an action, condition, or state of being.

Subjects and verbs must agree in number. A singular subject requires a singular verb. A plural subject requires a plural verb.

	S V
Singular:	The <u>astronaut</u> *orbits* Earth.
	S V
Plural:	The <u>astronauts</u> *orbit* Earth.

Practice In each sentence, choose the form of the verb that agrees with the subject.

  1. The shuttle (circle, circles) the planet.

  2. Cameras (capture, captures) the experience.

  3. A mountain and a river (come, comes) into view.

  4. Bolts of lightning (flash, flashes) quickly.

  5. Sally Ride (describe, describes) her trip.

Writing Application Find three sentences in "Single Room, Earth View" that have a plural subject and verb, and rewrite each with a singular subject and verb.

W̶G̶ Prentice Hall Writing and Grammar Connection: Chapter 25, Section 1

Writing Lesson

Observation From Space

Imagine that you are an astronaut in space, like Sally Ride. Perhaps you are orbiting this planet in a space shuttle or planting a flag on the surface of Mars. Write an observation that describes the event for readers back home on Earth.

Prewriting   Consult actual photographs taken from space to gain a sense of what you might see as an astronaut. Make a list of the features on Earth that you want to include in your observation.

Drafting   To ensure that you get all your ideas on paper, write a first draft without stopping to change what you have written. Concentrate on getting across what you perceive through your senses.

Revising   Look for places where you can add vivid adjectives to enliven your description. Replace vague words with more exact ones.

Model: Revising to Incorporate Vivid Adjectives

gray, rocky, and desolate

I stepped onto the ⋏surface of the moon. Seeing the great

awesome

bulk of Earth overhead was an ⋏~~interesting~~ experience.

> Vivid adjectives such as *gray, rocky, desolate,* and *awesome* make the description come to life.

 Prentice Hall Writing and Grammar Connection: Chapter 6, Section 4

Extension Activities

Listening and Speaking   In a group, study detailed photographs of Earth taken from space. Design a **presentation** to share one of the images you choose.

- Conduct research to learn about the features you want to highlight.
- Let your viewers know exactly what they see in the photograph.
- Describe each important feature.

Encourage your classmates to ask questions about the information in your presentation. [Group Activity]

Research and Technology   Prepare a **report** on one aspect of space exploration, such as women astronauts or the space shuttle. Access NASA's Web site and related sites to obtain information and illustrations for your report. Where needed, identify and explain any discrepancies you find among the various Web sites.

 **Take It to the Net**   www.phschool.com

Go online for an additional research activity using the Internet.

and both must be enterprised and over-come with answerable courage.

If this capsule history of our progress teaches us anything, it is that man, in his quest for knowledge and progress, is determined and cannot be deterred. The exploration of space will go ahead, whether we join in it or not, and it is one of the great adventures of all time, and no nation which expects to be the leader of other nations can expect to stay behind in the race for space.[3]

Those who came before us made certain that this country rode the first waves of the industrial revolutions, the first waves of modern invention, and the first wave of nuclear power, and this gen-eration does not intend to founder in the backwash of the coming age of space. We mean to be a part of it—we mean to lead it. For the eyes of the world now look into space, to the moon and to the planets beyond, and we have vowed that we shall not see it governed by a hostile flag of con-quest, but by a banner of freedom and peace. We have vowed that we shall not see space filled with weapons of mass de-struction, but with instruments of knowl-edge and understanding.

Yet the vows of this Nation can only be fulfilled if we in this Nation are first, and, therefore, we intend to be first. In short, our leadership in science and in industry, our hopes for peace and security, our obliga-tions to ourselves as well as others, all require us to make this effort, to solve these mysteries, to solve them for the good of all men, and to become the world's leading space-faring nation.

We set sail on this new sea because there is new knowledge to be gained, and new rights to be won, and they must be won and used for the progress of all people. For space science, like nuclear science and all technology, has no conscience of its own. Whether it will become a force for good or ill depends on man, and only if the United States occupies a position of pre-eminence can we help decide whether this new ocean will be a sea of peace or a new terrifying theater of war. I do not say that we should or will go unprotected against the hostile misuse of space any more than we go unprotected against the hostile use of land or sea, but I do say that space can be explored and mastered without feeding the fires of war, without repeating the mistakes that man has made in extending his writ[4] around this globe of ours.

There is no strife, no prejudice, no national conflict in outer space as yet. Its hazards are hostile to us all. Its conquest deserves the best of all mankind, and its opportunity for peaceful cooperation may never come again. But why, some say, the moon? Why choose this as our goal? And they may well ask why climb the highest mountain? Why, 35 years ago, fly the Atlantic? Why does Rice play Texas?[5]

We choose to go to the moon. We choose to go to the moon in this decade and do the other things, not because they are easy, but because they are hard, because that goal will serve to organize and measure the best of our energies and skills, because that challenge is one that we are willing to accept, one we are unwilling to postpone, and one which we intend to win, and the others, too. . . .

---

3. **race for space** Starting in the 1950s, the United States and the Soviet Union competed for mastery of space. In 1961, the Soviets sent the first man into orbit.
4. **writ** (rit) *n.* here, "claims or laws."
5. **Why does Rice play Texas?** Rice, typically low-ranked in football, played games against the powerhouse Univer-sity of Texas team.

By praising the accomplishments of previous gen-erations, Kennedy appeals to the emotion of pride.

The opening sen-tence of this paragraph offers three reasons why space travel is important.

Check Your Comprehension

1. What idea does Kennedy express by quoting William Bradford?
2. What reasons does Kennedy offer for going to the moon?

Applying the Reading Strategy

Evaluating the Author's Purpose

3. How does Kennedy support his purpose by using a historical analogy about human development at the beginning of his speech?
4. Kennedy assumes that the United States will use space exploration peacefully and responsibly. (a) Explain why he makes this assumption. (b) How is it linked with the purpose of his speech?

Activity

Preparing a Bibliography

One way to evaluate the arguments in a persuasive speech is by researching the topic yourself to confirm that the speaker's facts, details, and examples are valid.

Research America's involvement in the space program during the past 30 years to determine whether Kennedy's arguments would still have merit today. Use a variety of resources to ensure accuracy, including government reports, magazine and newspaper articles, and encyclopedia articles. Then, prepare a bibliography, or a reference list of the sources you have consulted. See pages R46–R47 for bibliographical format.

Comparing Informational Materials

Persuasive Techniques in Nonfiction

1. Read or review Sally Ride's essay "Single Room, Earth View" on page 636. Compare the techniques that Ride uses to persuade readers about the virtues of the space program with the techniques that Kennedy employs. Use these questions to guide your comparison:

	Kennedy's Speech	Ride's Essay
Persuasive reasons offered		
Effectiveness of persuasion		

- How are their arguments and reasons similar or different?

- How does the format affect the writer's choice of words or details?

- Is the essay or the speech more persuasive? Why?

2. Locate and analyze NASA's Web site. (a) What techniques does the site use to persuade readers about the value of the space program? (b) How do these techniques compare to the ways Kennedy tries to persuade his audience?

Prepare to Read

The Washwoman ◆ On Summer ◆ A Celebration of Grandfathers

Don Nemesio, 1977, Esperanza Martinez

Take It to the Net

Visit www.phschool.com for interactive activities and instruction related to the selections, including

- background
- graphic organizers
- literary elements
- reading strategies

Preview

Connecting to the Literature

The authors of these selections journey deep into their past to find people who gave them gifts that were not boxed or tied with bows. Think about similar special gifts in your life, about the people who gave them to you, and about what these gifts have meant to you.

Background

In the early 1900s, Russia, Austria-Hungary, and Germany ruled the territories that make up modern Poland, the scene of "The Washwoman." In this area, few people were well off—most worked long hours merely to earn enough to survive. The area had a sizable Jewish population, most of whom spoke Yiddish and maintained their own cultural traditions. These conditions form the backdrop for Isaac Bashevis Singer's narrative essay.

Literary Analysis

Essay

An **essay** is a short piece of nonfiction in which a writer expresses a personal view on a topic. In this example, Rudolfo Anaya tells why he thinks his dying grandfather acted with uncharacteristic impatience:

> It was because he could not care for himself, because he was returning to that state of childhood, and all those wishes and desires were now wrapped in a crumbling body.

As you read, look for details that express each writer's point of view.

Comparing Literary Works

Within the broad range of essays, there are specific types, each with a different purpose.

- **Narrative essays** tell a story.
- **Persuasive essays** present an opinion in order to convince readers to accept a position or take a course of action.
- **Reflective essays** reveal a writer's feelings about a topic of personal importance.

Compare these essays by considering which category each one represents. Then, compare the specific effects each essay has on the reader.

Reading Strategy

Identifying the Author's Attitude

In an essay, the **author's attitude** toward the subject colors the presentation of information. For example, a writer describing someone he or she respects will use descriptive words and details that convey that respect.

Use a diagram like the one shown to help you identify the author's attitude. Note words or details that hint at the author's feelings. Then, indicate what these hints suggest about the author's attitude.

Instruction with these selections addresses these standards:
R 1.1*, 3.2
W 1.1*., 1.3*
WOLC 1.2*, 1.3*
LS 1.8
* Standards tested on HS Exit Exam. For complete standards, see p. CA 4.

Vocabulary Development

forebears (fôr´ bers´) *n.* ancestors (p. 650)

rancor (raŋ´ ker) *n.* deep spite or bitter hate (p. 651)

obstinacy (äb´ stə nə sē) *n.* stubbornness (p. 653)

pious (pī´ əs) *adj.* showing religious devotion (p. 654)

aloofness (ə lōōf´ nəs) *n.* state of being distant or removed (p. 656)

perplexes (pər pleks´ iz) *v.* confuses or makes hard to understand (p. 662)

permeate (pʉr´ mē āt´) *v.* spread or flow throughout (p. 663)

epiphany (ē pif´ ə nē) *n.* moment of sudden understanding (p. 664)

The Washwoman

Isaac Bashevis Singer

Our home had little contact with Gentiles.[1] The only Gentile in the building was the janitor. Fridays he would come for a tip, his "Friday money." He remained standing at the door, took off his hat, and my mother gave him six groschen.[2]

Besides the janitor there were also the Gentile washwomen who came to the house to fetch our laundry. My story is about one of these.

She was a small woman, old and wrinkled. When she started washing for us, she was already past seventy. Most Jewish women of her age were sickly, weak, broken in body. All the old women in our street had bent backs and leaned on sticks when they walked. But this washwoman, small and thin as she was, possessed a strength that came from generations of peasant forebears. Mother would count out to her a bundle of laundry that had accumulated over several weeks. She would lift the unwieldy pack, load it on her narrow shoulders, and carry it the long way home. She lived on Krochmalna Street too, but at the other end, near the

forebears (fôr´ bərs´) *n.* ancestors

---

1. **Gentiles** any persons not Jewish; here, specifically Christians.
2. **groschen** (grō´ shən) Austrian cent or penny.

Wola section. It must have been a walk of an hour and a half.

She would bring the laundry back about two weeks later. My mother had never been so pleased with any washwoman. Every piece of linen sparkled like polished silver. Every piece was neatly ironed. Yet she charged no more than the others. She was a real find. Mother always had her money ready, because it was too far for the old woman to come a second time.

Laundering was not easy in those days. The old woman had no faucet where she lived but had to bring in the water from a pump. For the linens to come out so clean, they had to be scrubbed thoroughly in a washtub, rinsed with washing soda, soaked, boiled in an enormous pot, starched, then ironed. Every piece was handled ten times or more. And the drying! It could not be done outside because thieves would steal the laundry. The wrung-out wash had to be carried up to the attic and hung on clotheslines. In the winter it would become as brittle as glass and almost break when touched. And there was always a to-do with other housewives and washwomen who wanted the attic clothesline for their own use. Only God knows all the old woman had to endure each time she did a wash!

She could have begged at the church door or entered a home for the penniless and aged. But there was in her a certain pride and love of labor with which many Gentiles have been blessed. The old woman did not want to become a burden, and so she bore her burden.

My mother spoke a little Polish, and the old woman would talk with her about many things. She was especially fond of me and used to say I looked like Jesus. She repeated this every time she came, and Mother would frown and whisper to herself, her lips barely moving, "May her words be scattered in the wilderness."

The woman had a son who was rich. I no longer remember what sort of business he had. He was ashamed of his mother, the washwoman, and never came to see her. Nor did he ever give her a groschen. The old woman told this without <u>rancor</u>. One day the son was married. It seemed that he had made a good match. The wedding took place in a church. The son had not invited the old mother to his wedding, but she went to the church and waited at the steps to see her son lead the "young lady" to the altar.

The story of the faithless son left a deep impression on my mother. She talked about it for weeks and months. It was an affront not only to the old woman but to the entire institution of motherhood. Mother would argue, "Nu, does it pay to make sacrifices for children? The mother uses up her last strength, and he does not even know the meaning of loyalty."

And she would drop dark hints to the effect that she was not certain of her own children: Who knows what they would do some day? This, however, did not prevent her from dedicating her life to us. If there was any delicacy in the house, she would put it aside for the children and invent all sorts of excuses and reasons why she herself did not want to taste it. She knew charms that went back to ancient times, and she

Literary Analysis
Essay Which type of essay do you think Singer is writing? Why?

Reading Strategy
Identifying the Author's Attitude Which words and phrases indicate the author's admiration for the washwoman?

rancor (raŋ´ kər) *n.* deep spite or bitter hate

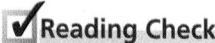**Reading Check**
Why does the washwoman's son never come to see her?

The Oldest Inhabitant, 1876, Julian Alden Weir, Butler Institute of American Art, Youngstown, Ohio

used expressions she had inherited from generations of devoted mothers and grandmothers. If one of the children complained of a pain, she would say, "May I be your ransom and may you outlive my bones!" Or she would say, "May I be the atonement for the least of your fingernails." When we ate she used to say, "Health and marrow in your bones!" The day before the new moon she gave us a kind of candy that was said to prevent parasitic worms. If one of us had something in his eye, Mother would lick the eye clean with her tongue. She also fed us rock candy against coughs, and from time to time she would take us to be blessed against the evil eye. This did not prevent her from studying *The Duties of the Heart, The Book of the Covenant,* and other serious philosophic works.

But to return to the washwoman. That winter was a harsh one. The streets were in the grip of a bitter cold. No matter how much we heated our stove, the windows were covered with frostwork and decorated with icicles. The newspapers reported that people were dying of the cold. Coal became dear. The winter had become so severe that parents stopped sending children to cheder,[3] and even the Polish schools were closed.

On one such day the washwoman, now nearly eighty years old, came to our house. A good deal of laundry had accumulated during the past weeks. Mother gave her a pot of tea to warm herself, as well as some bread. The old woman sat on a kitchen chair trembling and shaking, and warmed her hands against the teapot. Her fingers were gnarled from work, and perhaps from arthritis too. Her fingernails were strangely white. These hands spoke of the stubbornness of mankind, of the will to work not only as one's strength permits but beyond the limits of one's power. Mother counted and wrote down the list: men's undershirts, women's vests, long-legged drawers, bloomers, petticoats, shifts, featherbed covers, pillowcases, sheets, and the men's fringed garments. Yes, the Gentile woman washed these holy garments as well.

The bundle was big, bigger than usual. When the woman placed it on her shoulders, it covered her completely. At first she swayed, as though she were about to fall under the load. But an inner obstinacy seemed to call out: No, you may not fall. A donkey may permit himself to fall under his burden, but not a human being, the crown of creation.

It was fearful to watch the old woman staggering out with the enormous pack, out into the frost, where the snow was dry as salt and the air was filled with dusty white whirlwinds, like goblins dancing in the cold. Would the old woman ever reach Wola?

She disappeared, and Mother sighed and prayed for her.

Usually the woman brought back the wash after two or, at the most, three weeks. But three weeks passed, then four and five, and nothing was heard of the old woman. We remained without linens. The cold had become even more intense. The telephone wires were now as thick as ropes. The branches of the trees looked like glass. So much snow had fallen that the streets had become uneven, and sleds were able to glide

---

3. **cheder** (khā′ dər) *n.* religious school.

Reading Strategy
Identifying the Author's Attitude Based on this paragraph, what do you think the author's attitude is toward his mother?

Literary Analysis
Essay Which personal view does the author express here?

obstinacy (äb′ stə nə sē) *n.* stubbornness

Reading Check

How does the washwoman handle the unusually large bundle of laundry?

down many streets as on the slopes of a hill. Kindhearted people lit fires in the streets for vagrants[4] to warm themselves and roast potatoes in, if they had any to roast.

For us the washwoman's absence was a catastrophe. We needed the laundry. We did not even know the woman's address. It seemed certain that she had collapsed, died. Mother declared she had had a premonition, as the old woman left our house that last time, that we would never see our things again. She found some old torn shirts and washed and mended them. We mourned, both for the laundry and for the old, toil-worn woman who had grown close to us through the years she had served us so faithfully.

More than two months passed. The frost had subsided, and then a new frost had come, a new wave of cold. One evening, while Mother was sitting near the kerosene lamp mending a shirt, the door opened and a small puff of steam, followed by a gigantic bundle, entered. Under the bundle tottered the old woman, her face as white as a linen sheet. A few wisps of white hair straggled out from beneath her shawl. Mother uttered a half-choked cry. It was as though a corpse had entered the room. I ran toward the old woman and helped her unload her pack. She was even thinner now, more bent. Her face had become more gaunt, and her head shook from side to side as though she were saying no. She could not utter a clear word, but mumbled something with her sunken mouth and pale lips.

After the old woman had recovered somewhat, she told us that she had been ill, very ill. Just what her illness was, I cannot remember. She had been so sick that someone had called a doctor, and the doctor had sent for a priest. Someone had informed the son, and he had contributed money for a coffin and for the funeral. But the Almighty had not yet wanted to take this pain-racked soul to Himself. She began to feel better, she became well, and as soon as she was able to stand on her feet once more, she resumed her washing. Not just ours, but the wash of several other families too.

"I could not rest easy in my bed because of the wash," the old woman explained. "The wash would not let me die."

"With the help of God you will live to be a hundred and twenty," said my mother, as a benediction.

"God forbid! What good would such a long life be? The work becomes harder and harder . . . my strength is leaving me . . . I do not want to be a burden on anyone!" The old woman muttered and crossed herself, and raised her eyes toward heaven.

Fortunately there was some money in the house and Mother counted out what she owed. I had a strange feeling: the coins in the old woman's washed-out hands seemed to become as worn and clean and <u>pious</u> as she herself was. She blew on the coins and tied them in a kerchief. Then she left, promising to return in a few weeks for a new load of wash.

---

4. **vagrants** (vā′ grәntz) *n.* people who wander from place to place, especially those without regular jobs.

Reading Strategy
Identifying the Author's Attitude How would you describe the author's attitude toward the washwoman, based on this information about her illness?

pious (pī′ әs) *adj.* showing religious devotion

But she never came back. The wash she had returned was her last effort on this earth. She had been driven by an indomitable will to return the property to its rightful owners, to fulfill the task she had undertaken.

And now at last her body, which had long been no more than a shard[5] supported only by the force of honesty and duty, had fallen. Her soul passed into those spheres where all holy souls meet, regardless of the roles they played on this earth, in whatever tongue, of whatever creed. I cannot imagine paradise without this Gentile washwoman. I cannot even conceive of a world where there is no recompense for such effort.

---

5. **shard** (shärd) *n.* fragment or broken piece.

Reading Strategy
Identifying the Author's Attitude Which attitude toward the washwoman does Singer express here?

Review and Assess

Thinking About the Selection

1. **Respond:** Why do you think the washwoman gives so much and asks so little in return?

2. **(a) Recall:** Which job does the washwoman perform for Singer's family? **(b) Connect:** Which laborious obstacles to doing the job well does Singer describe?

3. **(a) Recall:** How does Singer's mother feel about the washwoman? **(b) Compare and Contrast:** In what ways is the washwoman like and unlike the author's mother?

4. **(a) Recall:** What prevents the washwoman from returning to the family for several months? **(b) Draw Conclusions:** What does the washwoman's eventual return tell you about her character?

5. **(a) Interpret:** What significance, beyond her work alone, does the washwoman have for Singer? **(b) Speculate:** In light of his own words, how might Singer's life have been different if he had never known her?

6. **(a) Interpret:** What difficulties does Singer imply about the washwoman? **(b) Assess:** Which details of her life are omitted from the essay? **(c) Evaluate:** What effect do these omissions have on the effectiveness of the selection?

7. **(a) Assess:** Do you think the washwoman had a fulfilling life? Explain. **(b) Apply:** What lessons can we learn from the washwoman?

8. **(a) Evaluate:** What are the benefits of a life of service? **(b) Extend:** What are the costs?

Isaac Bashevis Singer

(1904–1991)

I. B. Singer once said that he believed that "life itself is a story." This belief is reflected in his many short stories, novels, and essays that capture the lessons of everyday life.

Born in Poland, Singer moved to New York City in 1935 and later took American citizenship. Writing in Yiddish, the language of some Eastern European Jews and their descendants, Singer became a widely popular and respected writer. He won the Nobel Prize for Literature in 1978.

On Summer

Lorraine Hansberry

It has taken me a good number of years to come to any measure of respect for summer. I was, being May-born, literally an "infant of the spring" and, during the later childhood years, tended, for some reason or other, to rather worship the cold aloofness of winter. The adolescence, admittedly lingering still, brought the traditional passionate commitment to melancholy autumn—and all that. For the longest kind of time I simply thought that *summer* was a mistake.

In fact, my earliest memory of anything at all is of waking up in a darkened room where I had been put to bed for a nap on a summer's afternoon, and feeling very, very hot. I acutely disliked the feeling then and retained the bias for years. It had originally been a matter of the heat but, over the years, I came actively to associate displeasure with most of the usually celebrated natural features and social by-products of the season: the too-grainy texture of sand; the too-cold coldness of the various waters we constantly try to escape into, and the icky-perspiry feeling of bathing caps.

It also seemed to me, esthetically[1] speaking, that nature had got inexcusably carried away on the summer question and let the whole thing get to be rather much. By duration alone, for instance, a summer's day seemed maddeningly excessive; an utter overstatement. Except for those few hours at either end of it, objects always appeared in too sharp a relief against backgrounds; shadows too pronounced and light too blinding. It always gave me the feeling of walking around in a motion picture which had been too artsily-craftsily exposed. Sound also had a way of coming to the ear without that muting influence, marvelously common to winter, across patios or beaches or through the woods. I suppose I found it too stark and yet too intimate a season.

---

aloofness (ə lōōf´ nəs) *n.* state of being distant or removed

Literary Analysis
Essay What personal view does Hansberry express?

---

1. **esthetically** (es thet´ ik lē) *adv.* artistically.

My childhood Southside[2] summers were the ordinary city kind, full of the street games which other rememberers have turned into fine ballets these days and rhymes that anticipated what some people insist on calling modern poetry:

Oh, Mary Mack, Mack, Mack
With the silver buttons, buttons, buttons
All down her back, back, back
She asked her mother, mother, mother
For fifteen cents, cents, cents
To see the elephant, elephant, elephant
Jump the fence, fence, fence
Well, he jumped so high, high, high
'Til he touched the sky, sky, sky
And he didn't come back, back, back
'Til the Fourth of Ju-ly, ly, ly!

---

2. **Southside** section of Chicago, Illinois.

▲ **Critical Viewing**
How well does this photograph fit the essay? Explain. **[Evaluate]**

✓**Reading Check**

What is Hansberry's earliest memory?

Evenings were spent mainly on the back porches where screen doors slammed in the darkness with those really very special summertime sounds. And, sometimes, when Chicago nights got too steamy, the whole family got into the car and went to the park and slept out in the open on blankets. Those were, of course, the best times of all because the grownups were invariably reminded of having been children in rural parts of the country and told the best stories then. And it was also cool and sweet to be on the grass and there was usually the scent of freshly cut lemons or melons in the air. And Daddy would lie on his back, as fathers must, and explain about how men thought the stars above us came to be and how far away they were. I never did learn to believe that anything could be as far away as *that*. Especially the stars.

▼ **Critical Viewing**
How does this photograph of the Maine coast add to the descriptions in the essay?
[Connect]

My mother first took us south to visit her Tennessee birthplace one summer when I was seven or eight, I think. I woke up on the back seat of the car while we were still driving through some place called Kentucky and my mother was pointing out to the beautiful hills on both sides of the highway and telling my brothers and my sister about how her father had run away and hidden from his master in those very hills when he was a little boy. She said that his mother had wandered among the wooded slopes in the moonlight and left food for him in secret places. They were very beautiful hills and I looked out at them for miles and miles after that wondering who and what a *master* might be.

I remember being startled when I first saw my grandmother rocking away on her porch. All my life I had heard that she was a great

Literary Analysis

Essay Which details suggest that Hansberry is trying to convince you to accept her opinion about summer?

✔**Reading Check**

Whom does Hansberry visit in Tennessee?

beauty and no one had ever remarked that they meant a half century before. The woman that I met was as wrinkled as a prune and could hardly hear and barely see and always seemed to be thinking of other times. But she could still rock and talk and even make wonderful cupcakes which were like cornbread, only sweet. She was captivated by automobiles and, even though it was well into the Thirties,[3] I don't think she had ever been in one before we came down and took her driving. She was a little afraid of them and could not seem to negotiate the windows, but she loved driving. She died the next summer and that is all that I remember about her, except that she was born in slavery and had memories of it and they didn't sound anything like *Gone With the Wind.*[4]

Reading Strategy
Identifying the Author's Attitude How would you describe the author's attitude toward her grandmother?

Like everyone else, I have spent whole or bits of summers in many different kinds of places since then: camps and resorts in the Middle West and New York State; on an island; in a tiny Mexican village; Cape Cod, perched atop the Truro bluffs at Longnook Beach that Millay[5] wrote about; or simply strolling the streets of Provincetown[6] before the hours when the parties begin.

And, lastly, I do not think that I will forget days spent, a few summers ago, at a beautiful lodge built right into the rocky cliffs of a bay on the Maine coast. We met a woman there who had lived a purposeful and courageous life and who was then dying of cancer. She had, characteristically, just written a book and taken up painting. She had also been of radical viewpoint all her life; one of those people who energetically believe that the world *can* be changed for the better and spend their lives trying to do just that. And that was the way she thought of cancer; she absolutely refused to award it the stature of tragedy, a devastating instance of the brooding doom and inexplicability[7] of the absurdity of human destiny, etc., etc. The kind of characterization given, lately, as we all know, to far less formidable foes in life than cancer.

Literary Analysis
Essay Which words convey the reflective nature of Hansberry's essay?

But for this remarkable woman it was a matter of nature in imperfection, implying, as always, work for man to do. It was an *enemy*, but a palpable one with shape and effect and source; and if it existed, it could be destroyed. She saluted it accordingly, without despondency, but with a lively, beautiful and delightfully ribald anger. There was one thing, she felt, which would prove equal to its relentless ravages and that was the genius of man. Not his mysticism, but man with tubes and slides and the stubborn human notion that the stars are very much within our reach.

The last time I saw her she was sitting surrounded by her paintings with her manuscript laid out for me to read, because, she said,

3. **Thirties** the 1930s.
4. ***Gone With the Wind*** novel set in the South during the Civil War period.
5. **Millay** Edna St. Vincent Millay (1892–1950), American poet.
6. **Provincetown** resort town at the northern tip of Cape Cod, Massachusetts.
7. **inexplicability** (in eks′ pli kə bil′ ə tē) *n.* condition that cannot be explained.

she wanted to know what a *young person* would think of her thinking; one must always keep up with what *young people* thought about things because, after all, they were *change*.

Every now and then her jaw set in anger as we spoke of things people should be angry about. And then, for relief, she would look out at the lovely bay at a mellow sunset settling on the water. Her face softened with love of all that beauty and, watching her, I wished with all my power what I knew that she was wishing: that she might live to see at least one more *summer*. Through her eyes I finally gained the sense of what it might mean; more than the coming autumn with its pretentious melancholy; more than an austere and silent winter which must shut dying people in for precious months; more even than the frivolous spring, too full of too many false promises, would be the gift of another summer with its stark and intimate assertion of neither birth nor death but life at the apex; with the gentlest nights and, above all, the longest days.

I heard later that she did live to see another summer. And I have retained my respect for the noblest of the seasons.

Review and Assess

Thinking About the Selection

1. **Respond:** How do Hansberry's ideas about summer compare with your own?

2. **(a) Recall:** What are some of Hansberry's memories of childhood summers? **(b) Compare and Contrast:** Do her memories seem to support or contradict the opinion of summer she stated earlier? Explain.

3. **(a) Recall:** When does Hansberry first visit her grandmother? **(b) Infer:** Why do you think she includes the section about her grandmother in her essay?

4. **(a) Recall:** When does Hansberry's attitude toward summer change? **(b) Connect:** At the end, she calls summer "the noblest of the seasons." What do you think she means by this phrase?

5. **(a) Analyze:** What point of view does Hansberry try to persuade you to accept in her essay? **(b) Support:** What emotional appeals does she use to reach this goal?

6. **(a) Extend:** What experience have you had to cause your attitude about a season to change? **(b) Synthesize:** Is such a transformation of childhood opinions an important part of growing up? Why?

7. **Take a Position:** Which do you think affects a person's opinions more—personal experience or some other kind of learning? Explain.

Lorraine Hansberry

(1930–1965)

Lorraine Hansberry was born and raised in Chicago, Illinois. After high school, she studied art for two years before moving to New York City, where she worked for an African American newspaper called *Freedom*. While in New York, she wrote *A Raisin in the Sun*, which takes its name from a Langston Hughes poem, and in 1959 it became the first play by an African American woman to be produced on Broadway.

The essay "On Summer" comes from *To Be Young, Gifted, and Black*, a collection of Hansberry's writings that was published after her death.

A Celebration of Grandfathers

Rudolfo A. Anaya

"Buenos días le de Dios, abuelo."[1] God give you a good day, grandfather. This is how I was taught as a child to greet my grandfather, or any grown person. It was a greeting of respect, a cultural value to be passed on from generation to generation, this respect for the old ones.

The old people I remember from my childhood were strong in their beliefs, and as we lived daily with them we learned a wise path of life to follow. They had something important to share with the young, and when they spoke the young listened. These old abuelos and abuelitas[2] had worked the earth all their lives, and so they knew the value of nurturing, they knew the sensitivity of the earth. The daily struggle called for cooperation, and so every person contributed to the social fabric, and each person was respected for his contribution.

The old ones had looked deep into the web that connects all animate and inanimate forms of life, and they recognized the great design of the creation.

These *ancianos*[3] from the cultures of the Río Grande, living side by side, sharing, growing together, they knew the rhythms and cycles of time, from the preparation of the earth in the spring to the digging of the acequias[4] that brought the water to the dance of harvest in the fall. They shared good times and hard times. They helped each other through the epidemics and the personal tragedies, and they shared what little they had when the hot winds burned the land and no rain came. They learned that to survive one had to share in the process of life.

Hard workers all, they tilled the earth and farmed, ran the herds and spun wool, and carved their saints and their kachinas[5] from cottonwood late in the winter nights. All worked with a deep faith which <u>perplexes</u> the modern mind.

Their faith shone in their eyes; it was in the strength of their grip, in the creases time wove into their faces. When they spoke, they spoke plainly and with few words, and they meant what they said.

---

1. **Buenos días le de Dios, abuelo** (bwā′ nəs dē′ äs lā dā dē′ ōs ä bwä′ lō)
2. **abuelitas** (a bwä lē′ täs) grandmothers.
3. *ancianos* (än cē ä′ nōs) old people; ancestors.
4. **acequias** (ä sä kē′ əs) irrigation ditches.
5. **kachinas** (kə chē′ nəz) small wooden dolls, representing the spirit of an ancestor or a god.

Reading Strategy
Identifying the Author's Attitude Which facts about the author's past help you understand his attitude toward his subject?

perplexes (pər pleks′ iz) v. confuses or makes hard to understand

Don Nemesio, 1977, Esperanza Martinez

When they prayed, they went straight to the source of life. When there were good times, they knew how to dance in celebration and how to prepare the foods of the fiestas.[6] All this they passed on to the young, so that a new generation would know what they had known, so the string of life would not be broken.

Today we would say that the old abuelitos lived authentic lives.

Newcomers to New Mexico often say that time seems to move slowly here. I think they mean they have come in contact with the inner strength of the people, a strength so solid it causes time itself to pause. Think of it. Think of the high, northern New Mexico villages, or the lonely ranches on the open llano.[7] Think of the Indian pueblo[8] which lies as solid as rock in the face of time. Remember the old people whose eyes seem like windows that peer into a distant past that makes absurdity of our contemporary world. That is what one feels when one encounters the old ones and their land, a pausing of time.

We have all felt time stand still. We have all been in the presence of power, the knowledge of the old ones, the majestic peace of a mountain stream or an aspen grove or red buttes rising into blue sky. We have all felt the light of dusk <u>permeate</u> the earth and cause time to pause in its flow.

---

6. **fiestas** (fē es′ tez) celebrations; feasts.
7. **llano** (yä′ nō) plain.
8. **pueblo** (pweb′ lō) village or town.

▲ **Critical Viewing**
Which aspects of the man in this painting are similar to the description of the elders in the essay? **[Compare and Contrast]**

permeate (pʉr′ mē āt′) *v.* spread or flow throughout

✔**Reading Check**
Why was Anaya taught as a child to give his grandfather a proper greeting?

A Celebration of Grandfathers ◆ 663

I felt this when first touched by the spirit of Ultima, the old *curan-dera*[9] who appears in my first novel, *Bless Me, Ultima.* This is how the young Antonio describes what he feels:

> When she came the beauty of the llano unfolded before my eyes, and the gurgling waters of the river sang to the hum of the turning earth. The magical time of childhood stood still, and the pulse of the living earth pressed its mystery into my living blood. She took my hand, and the silent, magic powers she possessed made beauty from the raw, sun-baked llano, the green river valley, and the blue bowl which was the white sun's home. My bare feet felt the throbbing earth, and my body trembled with excitement. Time stood still . . .

At other times, in other places, when I have been privileged to be with the old ones, to learn, I have felt this inner reserve of strength upon which they draw. I have been held motionless and speechless by the power of curanderas. I have felt the same power when I hunted with Cruz, high on the Taos [tä´ ōs] mountain, where it was more than the incredible beauty of the mountain bathed in morning light, more than the shining of the quivering aspen, but a connection with life, as if a shining strand of light connected the particular and the cosmic. That feeling is an <u>epiphany</u> of time, a standing still of time.

But not all of our old ones are curanderos or hunters on the mountain. My grandfather was a plain man, a farmer from Puerto de Luna[10] on the Pecos River. He was probably a descendent of those people who spilled over the mountain from Taos, following the Pecos River in search of farmland. There in that river valley he settled and raised a large family.

Bearded and walrus-mustached, he stood five feet tall, but to me as a child he was a giant. I remember him most for his silence. In the summers my parents sent me to live with him on his farm, for I was to learn the ways of a farmer. My uncles also lived in that valley, the valley called Puerto de Luna, there where only the flow of the river and the whispering of the wind marked time. For me it was a magical place.

I remember once, while out hoeing the fields, I came upon an anthill, and before I knew it I was badly bitten. After he had covered my welts with the cool mud from the irrigation ditch, my grandfather calmly said: "Know where you stand." That is the way he spoke, in short phrases, to the point.

One very dry summer, the river dried to a trickle, there was no water for the fields. The young plants withered and died. In my sadness and with the impulses of youth I said, "I wish it would rain!" My grandfather touched me, looked up into the sky and whispered, "Pray for rain." In his language there was a difference. He felt connected to the cycles that brought the rain or kept it from us. His prayer was a

9. **curandera** (kōō rän dä´ rä) medicine woman.
10. **Puerto de Luna** (pwer´ tō dä lōō´ nə) Port of the Moon, the name of a town.

Literary Analysis
Essay Which of Anaya's personal experiences help him reflect on his feelings about the strength and power of the old ones?

epiphany (ē pif´ ə nē) *n.* moment of sudden understanding

Reading Strategy
Identifying the Author's Attitude What attitude toward his grandfather is the author communicating?

El Lenador, 1934, Tom Lea, Museum of Fine Arts, Museum of New Mexico

◀ Critical Viewing
How does the elderly farmer in this painting compare with the image you have of the author's grandfather? [Compare and Contrast]

meaningful action, because he was a participant with the forces that filled our world, he was not a bystander.

A young man died at the village one summer. A very tragic death. He was dragged by his horse. When he was found I cried, for the boy was my friend. I did not understand why death had come to one so young. My grandfather took me aside and said: "Think of the death of the trees and the fields in the fall. The leaves fall, and everything rests, as if dead. But they bloom again in the spring. Death is only this small transformation in life."

These are the things I remember, these fleeting images, few words.

I remember him driving his horse-drawn wagon into Santa Rosa in the fall when he brought his harvest produce to sell in the town. What a tower of strength seemed to come in that small man huddled on the seat of the giant wagon. One click of his tongue and the horses obeyed, stopped or turned as he wished. He never raised his

☑ Reading Check

What does Anaya's grandfather tell him to do when there is no water for the fields?

A Celebration of Grandfathers ◆ 665

whip. How unlike today when so much teaching is done with loud words and threatening hands.

I would run to greet the wagon, and the wagon would stop. "Buenos días le de Dios, abuelo," I would say. This was the pre-scribed greeting of esteem and respect. Only after the greeting was given could we approach these venerable old people. "Buenos días te de Dios, mi hijo,"[11] he would answer and smile, and then I could jump up on the wagon and sit at his side. Then I, too, became a king as I rode next to the old man who smelled of earth and sweat and the other deep aromas from the orchards and fields of Puerto de Luna.

We were all sons and daughters to him. But today the sons and daughters are breaking with the past, putting aside los abuelitos. The old values are threatened, and threatened most where it comes to these relationships with the old people. If we don't take the time to watch and feel the years of their final transformation, a part of our humanity will be lessened.

I grew up speaking Spanish, and oh! how difficult it was to learn English. Sometimes I would give up and cry out that I couldn't learn. Then he would say, "Ten paciencia."[12] Have patience. *Paciencia*, a word with the strength of centuries, a word that said that someday we would overcome. *Paciencia*, how soothing a word coming from this old man who could still sling hundred-pound bags over his shoulder, chop wood for hours on end, and hitch up his own horses and ride to town and back in one day.

"You have to learn the language of the Americanos,"[13] he said. "Me, I will live my last days in my valley. You will live in a new time, the time of the gringos."[14]

A new time did come, a new time is here. How will we form it so it is fruitful? We need to know where we stand. We need to speak softly and respect others, and to share what we have. We need to pray not for material gain, but for rain for the fields, for the sun to nurture growth, for nights in which we can sleep in peace, and for a harvest in which everyone can share. Simple lessons from a simple man. These lessons he learned from his past which was as deep and strong as the currents of the river of life, a life which could be stronger than death.

He was a man; he died. Not in his valley, but nevertheless cared for by his sons and daughters and flocks of grandchildren. At the end, I would enter his room which carried the smell of medications and Vicks, the faint pungent odor of urine, and cigarette smoke. Gone were the aroma of the fields, the strength of his young manhood. Gone also was his patience in the face of crippling old age. Small things bothered him; he shouted or turned sour when his expecta-tions were not met. It was because he could not care for himself, because he was returning to that state of childhood, and all those

11. **mi hijo** (mē ē′ hō) my son.
12. **Ten paciencia** (ten pä sē en′ sē ä)
13. **Americanos** (ä mer′ ē kä′ nōs) Americans.
14. **gringos** (griŋ′ gōs) foreigners; North Americans.

Reading Strategy
Identifying the Author's Attitude How would you describe the author's attitude toward the potential loss of old values?

Literary Analysis
Essay Which words in this paragraph signify that the purpose of Anaya's essay has shifted from reflection to persuasion?

wishes and desires were now wrapped in a crumbling old body.

"Ten paciencia," I once said to him, and he smiled. "I didn't know I would grow this old," he said. "Now, I can't even roll my own cigarettes." I rolled a cigarette for him, placed it in his mouth and lit it. I asked him why he smoked, the doctor had said it was bad for him. "I like to see the smoke rise," he said. He would smoke and doze, and his quilt was spotted with little burns where the cigarettes dropped. One of us had to sit and watch to make sure a fire didn't start.

I would sit and look at him and remember what was said of him when he was a young man. He could mount a wild horse and break it, and he could ride as far as any man. He could dance all night at a dance, then work the acequia the following day. He helped neighbors, they helped him. He married, raised children. Small legends, the kind that make up everyman's life.

He was 94 when he died. Family, neighbors, and friends gathered; they all agreed he had led a rich life. I remembered the last years, the years he spent in bed. And as I remember now, I am reminded that it is too easy to romanticize old age. Sometimes we forget the pain of the transformation into old age, we forget the natural breaking down of the body. Not all go gentle into the last years, some go crying and cursing, forgetting the names of those they loved the most, withdrawing into an internal anguish few of us can know. May we be granted the patience and care to deal with our ancianos.

For some time we haven't looked at these changes and needs of the old ones. The American image created by the mass media is an image of youth, not of old age. It is the beautiful and the young who are praised in this society. If analyzed carefully, we see that same damaging thought has crept into the way society views the old. In response to the old, the mass media have just created old people who act like the young. It is only the healthy, pink-cheeked, outgoing, older persons we are shown in the media. And they are always selling something, as if an entire generation of old people were salesmen in their lives. Commercials show very lively old men, who must always be in excellent health according to the new myth, selling insurance policies or real estate as they are out golfing; older women selling coffee or toilet paper to those just married. That image does not illustrate the real life of the old ones.

Real life takes into account the natural cycle of growth and change. My grandfather pointed to the leaves falling from the tree. So time brings with its transformation the often painful, wearing-down process. Vision blurs, health wanes; even the act of walking carries with it the painful reminder of the autumn of life. But this process is something to be faced, not something to be hidden away by false images. Yes, the old can be young at heart, but in their own way, with their own dignity. They do not have to copy the always-young image of the Hollywood star.

My grandfather wanted to return to his valley to die. But by then the families of the valley had left in search of a better future. It is only now that there seems to be a return to the valley, a revival. The

Literary Analysis
Essay What reflections does Anaya convey in this part of his essay?

**Reading Check**
What does Anaya's grandfather say to him as the writer struggles to learn English?

new generation seeks its roots, that value of love for the land moves us to return to the place where our ancianos formed the culture.

I returned to Puerto de Luna last summer, to join the community in a celebration of the founding of the church. I drove by my grandfather's home, my uncles' ranches, the neglected adobe[15] washing down into the earth from whence it came. And I wondered, how might the values of my grandfather's generation live in our own? What can we retain to see us through these hard times? I was to become a farmer, and I became a writer. As I plow and plant my words, do I nurture as my grandfather did in his fields and orchards? The answers are not simple.

"They don't make men like that anymore," is a phrase we hear when one does honor to a man. I am glad I knew my grandfather. I am glad there are still times when I can see him in my dreams, hear him in my reverie. Sometimes I think I catch a whiff of that earthy aroma that was his smell, just as in lonely times sometimes I catch the fragrance of Ultima's herbs. Then I smile. How strong these people were to leave such a lasting impression.

So, as I would greet my abuelo long ago, it would help us all to greet the old ones we know with this kind and respectful greeting: "Buenos días le de Dios."

---

15. adobe (ə dō′ bē) *n.* sun-dried clay brick.

Review and Assess

Thinking About the Selection

1. **Respond:** How would you describe the author's attitude toward the "old ones"?

2. **(a) Recall:** What qualities of old people does Anaya remember from his childhood? **(b) Distinguish:** How are these qualities different from the images created by American mass media?

3. **(a) Recall:** What kind of work did Anaya's grandfather do? **(b) Compare and Contrast:** How do the author's work and values differ from those of his grandfather?

4. **(a) Recall:** What is the "new time" that Anaya's grandfather mentions? **(b) Infer:** What does the author imply about this "new time"?

5. **(a) Analyze:** Why do you think the essay ends with the very same words with which it begins? **(b) Support:** Use evidence from the essay to support your view.

6. **(a) Generalize:** What perspective does Anaya offer on the way old people should be treated as they age and die? **(b) Take a Position:** Do you agree with him? Explain.

Rudolfo Anaya

(b. 1937)

Rudolfo Anaya was born in Pastura, New Mexico, and his writing reflects his Mexican American heritage.

Many of his novels, stories, and articles concern the past. His first novel, *Bless Me, Ultima* (1972), was acclaimed for its depiction of the culture and history of New Mexico. Anaya has also published *Heart of Aztlan* (1976) and *Tortuga* (1979).

His essay "A Celebration of Grandfathers" reflects on the "old ones" he remembers from his childhood.

Review and Assess

Literary Analysis

Essay

1. Using a chart like the one shown, analyze the ideas presented in each of these **essays**.

2. What personal views about life does Singer express in his essay?
3. What are some of the facts and reasons Hansberry presents to persuade you to accept her opinion about summer?
4. Rudolfo Anaya celebrates his grandfather and other "old ones." Which people or things seem, in his view, less worthy of praise?

Comparing Literary Works

5. Which essay is the most **persuasive**?
6. Which essay includes the most **reflections** by the author?
7. Which essay has the strongest emotional effect on the reader? Why?
8. How are the three authors' attitudes toward elderly people similar and different? Cite specific details.

Reading Strategy

Identifying the Author's Attitude

9. Which three adjectives might Singer use to describe his attitude toward the washwoman? Explain your answer.
10. Do you think Anaya could convince others who do not share his background to adopt his attitude? Explain.

Extend Understanding

11. **Cultural Connection:** Are today's elderly treated with what the three authors would consider appropriate respect? Explain.

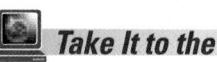

Integrate Language Skills

Vocabulary Development Lesson

Word Analysis: Anglo-Saxon Prefix *fore-*

The Anglo-Saxon prefix *fore-* means "before." The prefix appears in the word *forebears*, which means "ancestors" or "those who came before us."

Use the meaning of *fore-* to define each word below.

1. foreground   2. foresee   3. forethought

Spelling Strategy

To form the plural (or some verb forms) of words ending in *z, x, sh, ch,* or *s,* add *-es* instead of *-s.* Thus, *perplex + -es = perplexes.*

Add *-es* to each word below. Then, find four other words in the selections that would follow this rule.

1. box   2. fizz   3. clash

Fluency: Word Choice

For each item below, write the word from the vocabulary list on page 649 that best matches each clue.

1. creates confusion
2. the condition of showing disinterest, distance, or uninvolvement
3. one's relatives who lived long ago
4. the opposite of peaceful agreement and harmony
5. a sudden feeling of discovery
6. a quality of donkeys
7. deeply religious
8. what a heavy rain does when it falls on dry soil

Grammar Lesson

Consistency of Verb Tense

A **verb** is a word that expresses an action or a state of being. A verb has various **tenses,** such as past, present, and future. These forms of the verb are used to show the time of the action or condition.

To maintain a **consistency of verb tense,** analyze the verbs in your writing. If you begin a passage in the past tense, for instance, do not suddenly switch to present tense to talk about the past.

> **Unnecessary Tense Shift:** We *paid* the washwoman. She *thanks* us.
>
> **Correct:** We *paid* the washwoman. She *thanked* us.

Practice Rewrite each of the following items to maintain consistency of verb tense.

1. Yesterday I worked. Then, I will rest.
2. The woman comes early. She left late.
3. When Grandmother sings to me, I recorded her.
4. Tomorrow, we will travel and visited friends.
5. I ran to greet the wagon, and the wagon stops.

Writing Application Change the tense of the first verb in each of the practice sentences above, and then adjust the tense of the second verb to match the first.

 Prentice Hall Writing and Grammar Connection: Chapter 23, Section 1

Writing Lesson

Essay on Summer

Write an essay that summarizes the ideas Hansberry presents in her essay "On Summer." Provide your own personal connections to agree or disagree with her views.

Prewriting   List Hansberry's reflections on summer, and then list personal experiences that connect to the reflection. If you find that you do not connect with her experience, explain why.

Model: Connecting to the Author's Experience

Hansberry's Reflection	My Connection
Sleeping outside on hot summer nights	It reminds me of my camping trips to Vermont.

Drafting   As you draft, make sure to support each opinion with a specific example. In the closing paragraph of your essay, state your final views on summer.

Revising   Read your draft to a classmate. Ask your classmate if your views on summer are clear. Add any necessary details to strengthen your description of your experiences and to improve your analysis.

 Prentice Hall Writing and Grammar Connection: Chapter 13, Section 2

Extension Activities

Listening and Speaking To learn more about the authors, watch the movie version of either Lorraine Hansberry's *A Raisin in the Sun* or Isaac B. Singer's *Yentl*. Then, prepare a **movie review** for your classmates.

- Determine what you liked and disliked about the film's acting, directing, and costuming.
- Find any connection between the movie and the author's essay in this book.
- Prepare concise notes to use in an oral presentation of your review.

Later, invite your audience to evaluate the effectiveness of your review. [**Group Activity**]

Research and Technology Conduct an **interview** with an older person whom you know and admire. Find out key details about the person's life and important lessons that he or she has learned. Videotape the interview and share it with your class. After you present the video, compare the elderly person in your interview with the grandfather in "A Celebration of Grandfathers."

 **Take It to the Net**   www.phschool.com

Go online for an additional research activity using the Internet.

Prepare to Read

from A White House Diary ◆ Arthur Ashe Remembered ◆ Georgia O'Keeffe

The White Trumpet Flower, Georgia O'Keeffe, San Diego Museum of Art

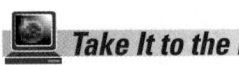

Take It to the Net

Visit www.phschool.com for interactive activities and instruction related to the selections, including

- background
- graphic organizers
- literary elements
- reading strategies

Preview

Connecting to the Literature

In the following selections, you will have a rare chance to see the private sides of three famous Americans. As you read, think about how the triumphs and tragedies in your own life have led you to discover what really matters.

Background

The assassination of President John F. Kennedy on November 22, 1963, was a stunning and unforgettable event. As the news media reported the tragedy, the United States came to a halt. People wept openly in their homes and in the streets. Kennedy had been a young, vibrant, and popular leader. A mournful nation agreed with his successor, Lyndon Johnson, who said of the assassination, "We have suffered a loss that cannot be weighed."

Literary Analysis

Biographical and Autobiographical Writing

Biographical writing is nonfiction in which a writer tells the story of another person's life. **Autobiographical writing** is nonfiction in which a writer tells the story of his or her own life. This excerpt from *A White House Diary* lets you share Lady Bird Johnson's thoughts and feelings:

> One last happy moment I had was looking up and seeing Mary Griffith leaning out of a window waving at me.

As you read, notice the emotions conveyed through each piece.

Comparing Literary Works

Biographical and autobiographical writing offer readers two distinctly different experiences. The differences in the presentation of views and experiences in each type of writing can influence the way readers interpret the events. Compare the selections and consider how each type of writing influences your attitude toward the person at the center of the work.

Reading Strategy

Finding the Writer's Main Points and Support

A key to understanding biographies and autobiographies is the ability to **find the writer's main points** and the details that **support** those points.

- Read each paragraph to determine the main idea it conveys.
- Locate the facts, events, details, or quotations that elaborate, develop, or support the main idea.
- Once you have finished reading a selection, try to determine the main points of the work as a whole.

Use a chart like the one shown here to help you as you read.

CALIFORNIA STANDARDS

Instruction with these selections addresses these standards:

R 1.1*, 3.2
W 1.1*, 1.3*
WOLC 1.2*, 1.3*
LS 1.4

* Standards tested on HS Exit Exam. For complete standards, see p. CA 4.

Writer

Main Point

Support

Vocabulary Development

tumultuous (tōō mul′ chōō əs) *adj.* greatly disturbed (p. 676)

implications (im′ pli kā′ shənz) *n.* indirect indications (p. 677)

poignant (poin′ yənt) *adj.* drawing forth pity or compassion (p. 678)

legacy (leg′ ə sē) *n.* anything handed down from an ancestor (p. 683)

enigma (i nig′ mə) *n.* puzzling or baffling matter; riddle (p. 683)

condescending (kän′ di sen′ diŋ) *adj.* characterized by looking down on someone (p. 685)

sentimental (sen′ tə ment′ 'l) *adj.* excessively emotional (p. 686)

genesis (jen′ ə sis) *n.* origin (p. 686)

rancor (raŋ′ kər) *n.* hatred (p. 689)

immutable (im myōōt′ ə bəl) *adj.* never changing (p. 689)

from

A White House Diary

Lady Bird Johnson

▲ **Critical Viewing** What does this photograph reveal about the mood in the moments leading up to the assassination? **[Infer]**

DALLAS, FRIDAY, NOVEMBER 22, 1963

It all began so beautifully. After a drizzle in the morning, the sun came out bright and clear. We were driving into Dallas. In the lead car were President and Mrs. Kennedy, John and Nellie Connally,[1] a Secret Service[2] car full of men, and then our car with Lyndon and me and Senator Ralph Yarborough.

The streets were lined with people—lots and lots of people—the children all smiling, placards, confetti, people waving from windows. One last happy moment I had was looking up and seeing Mary Griffith leaning out of a window waving at me. (Mary for many years had been in charge of altering the clothes which I purchased at Neiman-Marcus.)

Then, almost at the edge of town, on our way to the Trade Mart for the Presidential luncheon, we were rounding a curve, going down a hill, and suddenly there was a sharp, loud report. It sounded like a shot. The sound seemed to me to come from a building on the right above my shoulder. A moment passed, and then two more shots rang out in rapid succession. There had been such a gala air about the day that I thought the noise must come from firecrackers—part of the celebration. Then the Secret Service men were suddenly down in the lead car. Over the car radio system, I heard "Let's get out of here!" and our Secret Service man, Rufus Youngblood, vaulted over the front seat on top of Lyndon, threw him to the floor, and said, "Get down."

Senator Yarborough and I ducked our heads. The car accelerated terrifically—faster and faster. Then, suddenly, the brakes were put on so hard that I wondered if we were going to make it as we wheeled left and went around the corner. We pulled up to a building. I looked up and saw a sign, "HOSPITAL." Only then did I believe that this might be what it was. Senator Yarborough kept saying in an excited voice, "Have they shot the President? Have they shot the President?" I said something like, "No, it can't be."

As we ground to a halt—we were still the third car—Secret Service men began to pull, lead, guide, and hustle us out. I cast one last look over my shoulder and saw in the President's car a bundle of pink, just like a drift of blossoms, lying on the back seat. It was Mrs. Kennedy lying over the President's body.

The Secret Service men rushed us to the right, then to the left, and then onward into a quiet room in the hospital—a very small room. It was lined with white sheets, I believe.

People came and went—Kenny O'Donnell, the President's top aide, Congressman Homer Thornberry, Congressman Jack Brooks. Always there was Rufe right there and other Secret Service agents—Emory Roberts, Jerry Kivett, Lem Johns, and Woody Taylor. People spoke of how widespread this might be. There was talk about where we would go—to the plane, to our house, back to Washington.

---

1. **John and Nellie Connally** John Connally, then Governor of Texas, and his wife, Nellie.
2. **Secret Service** division of the U.S. Treasury Department, responsible for protecting the president.

Literary Analysis
Biographical and Autobiographical Writing
Which words in this passage tell you that Johnson's writing is autobiographical?

Reading Stragegy
Finding the Writer's Main Points and Support
Which details does the writer use to support her main point that she was in disbelief about the shooting?

Reading Check
Where are the Johnsons taken after a shot is heard?

from *A White House Diary* ◆ 675

Mrs. Kennedy had arrived by this time, as had the coffin. There, in the very narrow confines of the plane—with Jackie standing by Lyndon, her hair falling in her face but very composed, with me beside him, Judge Hughes in front of him, and a cluster of Secret Service people, staff, and Congressmen we had known for a long time around him—Lyndon took the oath of office.

It's odd the little things that come to your mind at times of utmost stress, the flashes of deep compassion you feel for people who are really not at the center of the tragedy. I heard a Secret Service man say in the most desolate voice—and I hurt for him: "We never lost a President in the Service." Then, Police Chief Curry of Dallas came on the plane and said, "Mrs. Kennedy, believe me, we did everything we possibly could." That must have been an agonizing moment for him.

We all sat around the plane. The casket was in the corridor. I went in the small private room to see Mrs. Kennedy, and though it was a very hard thing to do, she made it as easy as possible. She said things like, "Oh, Lady Bird, we've liked you two so much. . . . Oh, what if I had not been there. I'm so glad I was there."

I looked at her. Mrs. Kennedy's dress was stained with blood. One leg was almost entirely covered with it and her right glove was caked, it was caked with blood—her husband's blood. Somehow that was one of the most <u>poignant</u> sights—that immaculate woman exquisitely dressed, and caked in blood.

I asked her if I couldn't get someone in to help her change and she said, "Oh, no. Perhaps later I'll ask Mary Gallagher but not right now." And then with almost an element of fierceness—if a person that

▲ **Critical Viewing** This photograph shows Lyndon Johnson beginning to assume his duties as president. Based on the details in the photo, how do you think he felt at that time? Why? **[Analyze]**

poignant (poin´ yənt) *adj.* drawing forth pity or compassion

gentle, that dignified, can be said to have such a quality—she said, "I want them to see what they have done to Jack."

I tried to express how we felt. I said, "Oh, Mrs. Kennedy, you know we never even wanted to be Vice President and now, dear God, it's come to this." I would have done anything to help her, but there was nothing I could do, so rather quickly I left and went back to the main part of the airplane where everyone was seated.

The flight to Washington was silent, each sitting with his own thoughts. One of mine was a recollection of what I had said about Lyndon a long time ago—he's a good man in a tight spot. I remembered one little thing he had said in that hospital room—"Tell the children to get a Secret Service man with them."

Finally we got to Washington, with a cluster of people waiting and many bright lights. The casket went off first, then Mrs. Kennedy, and then we followed. The family had come to join her. Lyndon made a very simple, very brief, and, I think, strong statement to the people there. Only about four sentences. We got in helicopters, dropped him off at the White House, and I came home in a car with Liz Carpenter.[5]

---

5. **Liz Carpenter** Mrs. Johnson's press secretary.

Review and Assess

Thinking About the Selection

1. **Respond:** What do you admire most about Lady Bird Johnson? Why?

2. **(a) Recall:** What are the writer's thoughts about Mrs. Kennedy at the hospital? **(b) Deduce:** In what ways is Mrs. Kennedy alone?

3. **(a) Recall:** What is the most noticeable aspect of Mrs. Kennedy's appearance when Mrs. Johnson speaks with her on *Air Force One*? **(b) Interpret:** In what way is wearing the clothing a tribute to her husband?

4. **(a) Recall:** Where does Lyndon Johnson take the oath of office? **(b) Support:** Which details from the text indicate that the Johnsons are up to the tasks before them?

5. **(a) Recall:** How does Mrs. Kennedy behave after the death of her husband? **(b) Compare and Contrast:** What similarities do you find between Mrs. Kennedy and Mrs. Johnson? Explain your answer.

6. **Assess:** Why might a diary entry be an effective way for a person to grieve and cope with a tragic event?

Lady Bird Johnson

(b. 1912)
Texas-born Claudia Alta Taylor received her nickname at age two, when a nurse said she was as pretty as a lady bird. In 1934, she married Lyndon Johnson, then a congressional secretary. Throughout her husband's political career, Lady Bird was a most valued advisor and campaigner.

On November 22, 1963, after President John F. Kennedy was killed by an assassin in Dallas, Texas, Lady Bird Johnson became First Lady of the United States. Aboard *Air Force One*, the president's airplane, Vice President Johnson took the oath of office to become the thirty-sixth president of the United States. On his left stood Kennedy's widow, Jackie, her clothing still spattered with her husband's blood. On his right stood his wife, Lady Bird.

The Role of the First Lady

The excerpt from *A White House Diary* by Lady Bird Johnson offers a keen insight into the kinds of pressures and responsibilities that a president's spouse can face. Despite these pressures, first ladies often carve out their own niches by advancing special causes. Johnson went on to become a respected advocate for natural resource conservation. Throughout our nation's history, first ladies have applied their own style and personalities to the ways in which they defined and carried out their duties as the wife of the president.

Eleanor Roosevelt: Social Activist

Eleanor Roosevelt was married to Franklin D. Roosevelt, president of the United States from 1933 to 1945. During her years in the White House, Mrs. Roosevelt became the most socially active first lady in American history. Because of her husband's physical restrictions due to polio, Mrs. Roosevelt often went on fact-finding tours on his behalf. During the Depression, she spoke in cities across America to bring hope to the poor and desperate. She also traveled to Europe, Latin America, and many other parts of the

world, working for young people and minority groups. Privately, Mrs. Roosevelt urged her husband to take stronger actions on social problems like racial inequality. She raised money for humanitarian causes by writing magazine articles and a daily newspaper column. During World War II, she visited American troops overseas.

Roosevelt's Legacy

Roosevelt's activism inspired a more recent first lady, Hillary Clinton. When Mrs. Clinton worked on issues ranging from health care to children's welfare, she explicitly mentioned her debt to Mrs. Roosevelt in redefining the role of first lady. Like Mrs. Roosevelt, who went on to become a United Nations delegate, Mrs. Clinton also took on a high visibility, post-White House career—as a United States senator representing New York.

Mamie Eisenhower: Hostess and Housewife

Mamie Eisenhower was married to Dwight D. Eisenhower, president of the United States from 1953 to 1961. Mrs. Eisenhower defined her role in the White House primarily as a popular hostess. As a result of increased air travel in the 1950s, the Eisenhowers entertained more state and foreign leaders than any previous presidential couple. Beloved for her unpretentious yet dignified style, Mrs. Eisenhower personally greeted thousands of tourists at the White House. The American public regarded her as the ideal American woman of the 1950s. She described herself as "perfectly satisfied as a housewife," and served as an inspiration to homemakers across the country who felt she reflected their own values.

©White House Collection, Courtesy White House Historical Association

Eisenhower's Legacy

When emotional issues, such as school desegregation, were on people's minds, Mrs. Eisenhower largely refrained from taking public positions. On the rare occasions when she did speak out, she did so with gracious impartiality. In the 1952 election, for instance, she urged Americans to vote, even if they chose to vote for her husband's opponent, Adlai Stevenson. Her legacy can be seen in the highly visible roles that subsequent first ladies have assumed in serving as coordinators of White House social and diplomatic events.

Connecting Literature and Social Studies

1. Based on these descriptions, how did Eleanor Roosevelt and Mamie Eisenhower view their role as first lady?
2. Which first lady defined her role similarly to Lady Bird Johnson? Why?
3. What type of first lady would appeal to most Americans today? Explain your opinion.

Arthur Ashe Remembered

John McPhee

He once described his life as "a succession of fortunate circumstances." He was in his twenties then. More than half of his life was behind him. His memory of his mother was confined to a single image: in a blue corduroy bathrobe she stood in a doorway looking out on the courts and playing fields surrounding their house, which stood in the center of a Richmond playground. Weakened by illness, she was taken to a hospital that day, and died at the age of twenty-seven. He was six.

It was to be his tragedy, as the world knows, that he would leave his own child when she was six, that his life would be trapped in a medical irony as a result of early heart disease, and death would come to him prematurely, as it had to his mother.

His mother was tall, with long soft hair and a face that was gentle and thin. She read a lot. She read a lot to him. His father said of her, "She was just like Arthur Junior. She never argued. She was quiet, easygoing, kindhearted."

If by legacy her son never argued, he was also schooled, instructed, coached not to argue, and as he moved alone into alien country he fashioned not-arguing into an enigma and turned the enigma into a weapon. When things got tough (as I noted in these pages twenty-four years ago[1]), he had control. Even in very tight moments, other players thought he was toying with them. They rarely knew what he was thinking. They could not tell if he was angry. It was maddening, sometimes, to play against him. Never less than candid, he said that what he liked best about himself on a tennis court was his demeanor: "What it is is controlled cool, in a way. Always have the situation under control, even if losing. Never betray an inward sense of defeat."

---

1. **twenty-four years ago** McPhee refers to an article published in 1969.

◀ **Critical Viewing** In 1975, Arthur Ashe won the men's singles championship at Wimbledon. What do you think is going through his mind as he displays his trophy? **[Speculate]**

legacy (leg´ ə sē) *n.* anything handed down from an ancestor

enigma (i nig´ mə) *n.* puzzling or baffling matter; riddle

✔**Reading Check**

What happens to Ashe's mother at the age of twenty-seven?

And of course he never did—not in the height of his athletic power, not in the statesmanship of the years that followed, and not in the endgame of his existence. If you wished to choose a single image, you would see him standing there in his twenties, his lithe body a braid of cables, his energy without apparent limit, in a court situation indescribably bad, and all he does is put his index finger on the bridge of his glasses and push them back up the bridge of his nose. In the shadow of disaster, he hits out. Faced with a choice between a conservative, percentage return or a one-in-ten flat-out blast, he chooses the blast. In a signature manner, he extends his left arm to point upward at lobs as they fall toward him. His overheads, in fire bursts, put them away. His backhand is, if anything, stronger than his forehand, and his shots from either side for the most part are explosions. In motions graceful and decisive, though, and with reactions as fast as the imagination, he is a master of drop shots, of cat-and-mouse, of miscellaneous dinks and chips and (riskiest of all) the crosscourt half-volley. Other tennis players might be wondering who in his right mind would attempt something like that, but that is how Ashe plays the game: at the tensest moment, he goes for the all but impossible. He is predictably unpredictable. He is unreadable. His ballistic serves move in odd patterns and come off the court in unexpected ways. Behind his impassive face—behind the enigmatic glasses, the lifted chin, the first-mate-on-the-bridge look—there seems to be, even from this distance, a smile.

Reading Strategy
Finding the Writer's Main Points and Support What is the writer's main point in this paragraph?

Review and Assess

Thinking About the Selection

1. **Respond:** After reading this selection, what are your feelings about Arthur Ashe? Why?

2. **(a) Recall:** How did Ashe once describe his life?
   (b) Connect: What later proved to be tragically ironic about this statement?

3. **(a) Recall:** Which "weapon" did Ashe use against opponents on the court? **(b) Interpret:** Why did Ashe's opponents often think he was toying with them?

4. **(a) Recall:** According to his father, how was Ashe like his mother? **(b) Recall:** What does Ashe say he likes best about himself on the court? **(c) Draw Conclusions:** Based on this article, how would you describe Ashe's character?

5. **(a) Connect:** Use examples to show how the writer uses the way Arthur Ashe played tennis to illustrate how Ashe lived life. **(b) Apply:** How can one aspect of Ashe's approach to tennis—going for the difficult shot when in trouble—be applied as an approach to life?

John McPhee

(b. 1931)

After graduating from Princeton University, John McPhee worked at *Time* magazine and then at *The New Yorker*. McPhee has written many nonfiction books and essays.

McPhee has found success in writing about topics that fascinate him. One such subject is sports. In his book *Levels of the Game* (1969), an account of the 1968 U.S. Open Tennis Championship, McPhee reveals his admiration for Arthur Ashe.

The White Trumpet Flower, Georgia O'Keeffe, San Diego Museum of Art

Georgia O'Keeffe
Joan Didion

"Where I was born and where and how I have lived is unimportant," Georgia O'Keeffe told us in the book of paintings and words published in her ninetieth year on earth. She seemed to be advising us to forget the beautiful face in the Stieglitz[1] photographs. She appeared to be dismissing the rather <u>condescending</u> romance that had attached to her by then, the romance of extreme good looks and advanced age and deliberate isolation. "It is what I have done with where I have been that should be

▲ **Critical Viewing**
What can you guess about the personality of the artist from her work? **[Deduce]**

condescending (kän′ di sen′ diŋ) *adj.* characterized by looking down on someone

---

1. **Stieglitz** (stēg′ lits) Alfred Stieglitz (1864–1946); U.S. photographer and husband of Georgia O'Keeffe.

of interest." I recall an August afternoon in Chicago in 1973 when I took my daughter, then seven, to see what Georgia O'Keeffe had done with where she had been. One of the vast O'Keeffe "Sky Above Clouds" canvases floated over the back stairs in the Chicago Art Institute that day, dominating what seemed to be several stories of empty light, and my daughter looked at it once, ran to the landing, and kept on looking. "Who drew it," she whispered after a while. I told her. "I need to talk to her," she said finally.

My daughter was making, that day in Chicago, an entirely unconscious but quite basic assumption about people and the work they do. She was assuming that the glory she saw in the work reflected a glory in its maker, that the painting was the painter as the poem is the poet, that every choice one made alone—every word chosen or rejected, every brush stroke laid or not laid down—betrayed one's character. *Style is character.* It seemed to me that afternoon that I had rarely seen so instinctive an application of this familiar principle, and I recall being pleased not only that my daughter responded to style as character but that it was Georgia O'Keeffe's particular style to which she responded: this was a hard woman who had imposed her 192 square feet of clouds on Chicago.

"Hardness" has not been in our century a quality much admired in women, nor in the past twenty years has it even been in official favor for men. When hardness surfaces in the very old we tend to transform it into "crustiness" or eccentricity, some tonic pepperiness to be indulged at a distance. On the evidence of her work and what she has said about it, Georgia O'Keeffe is neither "crusty" nor eccentric. She is simply hard, a straight shooter, a woman clean of received wisdom and open to what she sees. This is a woman who could early on dismiss most of her contemporaries as "dreamy," and would later single out one she liked as "a very poor painter." (And then add, apparently by way of softening the judgment: "I guess he wasn't a painter at all. He had no courage and I believe that to create one's own world in any of the arts takes courage.") This is a woman who in 1939 could advise her admirers that they were missing her point, that their appreciation of her famous flowers was merely <u>sentimental</u>. "When I paint a red hill," she observed coolly in the catalogue for an exhibition that year, "you say it is too bad that I don't always paint flowers. A flower touches almost everyone's heart. A red hill doesn't touch everyone's heart." This is a woman who could describe the <u>genesis</u> of one of her most well-known paintings—the "Cow's Skull: Red, White and Blue" owned by the Metropolitan[2]—as an act of quite deliberate and derisive orneriness. "I thought of the city men I had been seeing in the East," she wrote. "They talked so often of writing the Great American Novel—the Great American Play—the Great American Poetry. . . . So as I was painting my cow's head on blue I thought to

---

2. **Metropolitan** Metropolitan Museum of Art in New York City.

Literary Analysis
Biographical and Autobiographical Writing
How does the author personalize her biographical writing about O'Keeffe?

Reading Strategy
Finding the Writer's Main Points and Support What is the writer's main point in this paragraph?

sentimental (sen´ tə ment´ 'l) *adj.* excessively emotional

genesis (jen´ ə sis) *n.* origin

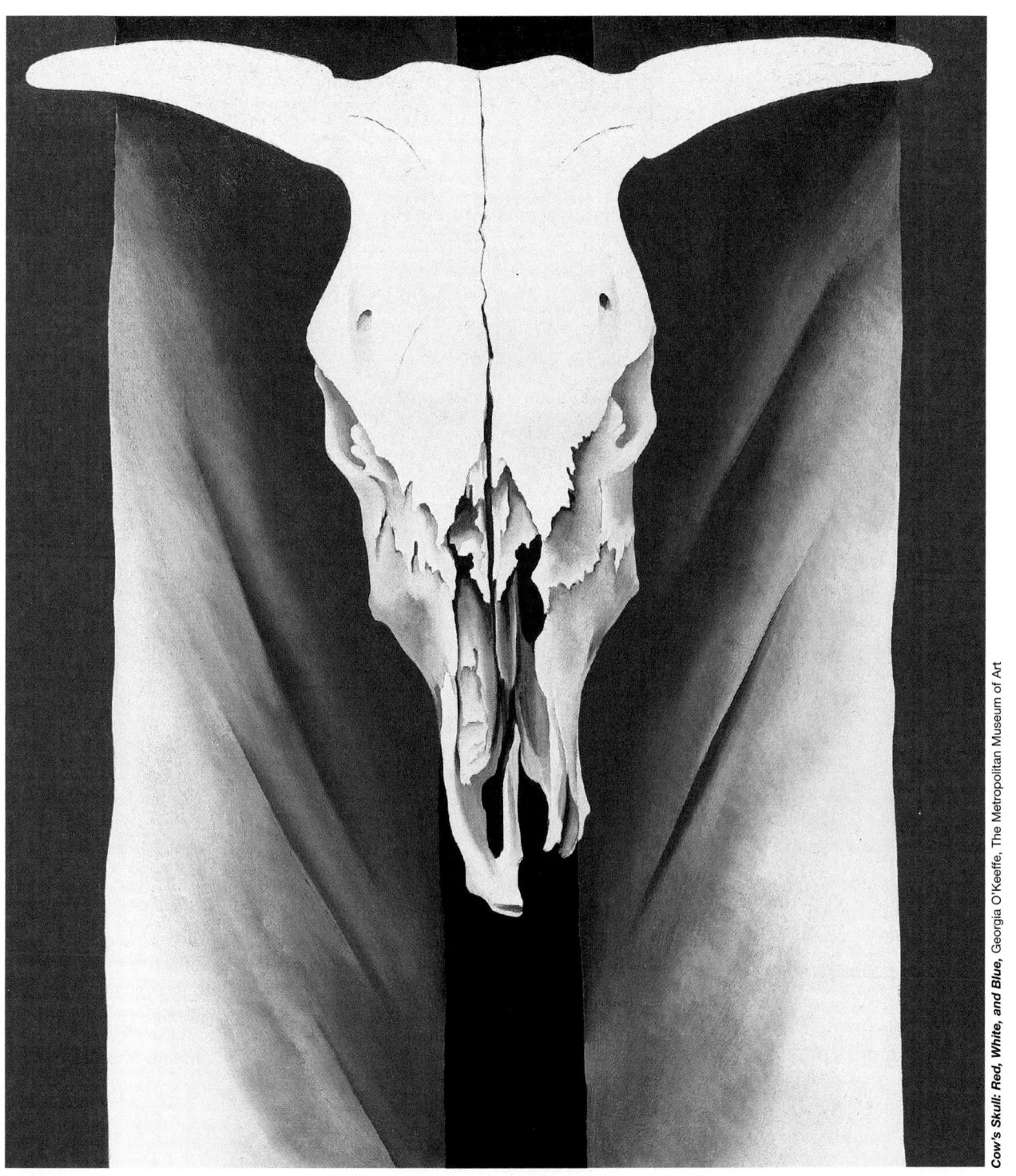

Cow's Skull: Red, White, and Blue, Georgia O'Keeffe, The Metropolitan Museum of Art

▲ **Critical Viewing** What information in the text helps you understand this painting better? **[Connect]**

The Lawrence Tree, 1929, Georgia O'Keeffe, Wadsworth Atheneum, Hartford

myself, 'I'll make it an American painting. They will not think it great with the red stripes down the sides—Red, White and Blue—but they will notice it.'"

The city men. The men. They. The words crop up again and again as this astonishingly aggressive woman tells us what was on her mind when she was making her astonishingly aggressive paintings. It was those city men who stood accused of sentimentalizing her flowers: "I made you take time to look at what I saw and when you took time to really notice my flower you hung all your associations with flowers on my flower and you write about my flower as if I

▲ **Critical Viewing**
Compare this painting with the one on page 685. What do they suggest about the artist?
[Compare and Contrast]

think and see what you think and see—and I don't." *And I don't.*
Imagine those words spoken, and the sound you hear is *don't tread
on me.*[3] "The men" believed it impossible to paint New York, so
Georgia O'Keeffe painted New York. "The men" didn't think much of
her bright color, so she made it brighter. The men yearned toward
Europe so she went to Texas, and then New Mexico. The men talked
about Cézanne,[4] "long involved remarks about the 'plastic quality' of
his form and color," and took one another's long involved remarks, in
the view of this angelic rattlesnake in their midst, altogether too seriously. "I can paint one of those dismal-colored paintings like the
men," the woman who regarded herself always as an outsider remembers thinking one day in 1922, and she did: a painting of a shed "all
low-toned and dreary with the tree beside the door." She called this
act of <u>rancor</u> "The Shanty" and hung it in her next show. "The men
seemed to approve of it," she reported fifty-four years later, her contempt undimmed. "They seemed to think that maybe I was beginning
to paint. That was my only low-toned dismal-colored painting."

Some women fight and others do not. Like so many successful
guerrillas in the war between the sexes, Georgia O'Keeffe seems to
have been equipped early with an <u>immutable</u> sense of who she was
and a fairly clear understanding that she would be required to prove
it. On the surface her upbringing was conventional. She was a child
on the Wisconsin prairie who played with china dolls and painted
watercolors with cloudy skies because sunlight was too hard to paint
and, with her brother and sisters, listened every night to her mother
read stories of the Wild West, of Texas, of Kit Carson and Billy the
Kid. She told adults that she wanted to be an artist and was embarrassed when they asked what kind of artist she wanted to be: she
had no idea "what kind." She had no idea what artists did. She had
never seen a picture that interested her, other than a pen-and-ink
Maid of Athens in one of her mother's books, some Mother Goose
illustrations printed on cloth, a tablet cover that showed a little girl
with pink roses, and the painting of Arabs on horseback that hung in
her grandmother's parlor. At thirteen, in a Dominican convent, she
was mortified when the sister corrected her drawing. At Chatham
Episcopal Institute in Virginia she painted lilacs and sneaked time
alone to walk out to where she could see the line of the Blue Ridge
Mountains on the horizon. At the Art Institute in Chicago she was
shocked by the presence of live models and wanted to abandon
anatomy lessons. At the Art Students League in New York one of her
fellow students advised her that, since he would be a great painter
and she would end up teaching painting in a girls' school, any work
of hers was less important than modeling for him. Another painted
over her work to show her how the Impressionists did trees. She had

---

3. ***Don't tread on me*** motto of the first official American flag to be flown by a naval
vessel, on December 3, 1775.
4. **Cézanne** (sā zän) Paul Cézanne (1839–1906), French Impressionist and Post-
Impressionist painter.

Literary Analysis
**Biographical and
Autobiographical Writing**
What does this paragraph
reveal about O'Keeffe?

rancor (raŋ´ kər) *n.* hatred

immutable (im my͞o͞ot´ ə bəl)
adj. never changing

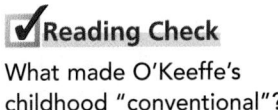
Reading Check
What made O'Keeffe's
childhood "conventional"?

not before heard how the Impressionists did trees and she did not much care.

At twenty-four she left all these opinions behind and went for the first time to live in Texas, where there were no trees to paint and no one to tell her how not to paint them. In Texas there was only the horizon she craved. In Texas she had her sister Claudia with her for a while, and in the late afternoons they would walk away from town and toward the horizon and watch the evening star come out. "That evening star fascinated me," she wrote. "It was in some way very exciting to me. My sister had a gun, and as we walked she would throw bottles into the air and shoot as many as she could before they hit the ground. I had nothing but to walk into nowhere and the wide sunset space with the star. Ten watercolors were made from that star." In a way one's interest is compelled as much by the sister Claudia with the gun as by the painter Georgia with the star, but only the painter left us this shining record. Ten watercolors were made from that star.

Review and Assess

Thinking About the Selection

1. **Respond:** Which of O'Keeffe's qualities do you admire most? Why?

2. **(a) Recall:** Which primary character trait does the writer attribute to O'Keeffe? **(b) Interpret:** What does the writer mean by "hardness"? Give examples.

3. **(a) Recall:** How does O'Keeffe respond when " 'the men' didn't think much of her bright color"? **(b) Draw Conclusions:** What does her response tell you about her character?

4. **(a) Recall:** Where does O'Keeffe move and find what she craves? **(b) Infer:** What do you think she found attractive about this place?

5. **Interpret:** What does Didion mean when she says O'Keeffe had "an immutable sense of who she was"?

6. **(a) Analyze:** What do the words "style is character" mean? **(b) Draw Conclusions:** Explain how the statement is appropriate for Georgia O'Keeffe. Cite evidence from the text to support your answer.

7. **(a) Speculate:** To what extent do you think O'Keeffe's disregard for the opinions of others contributed to her success? **(b) Assess:** Do you think an artist needs to be bold and individualistic to be successful?

Joan Didion

(b. 1934)

Joan Didion is descended from a long line of pioneers. Her great-great-grandmother went west in a covered wagon in 1846.

As a young woman, Didion won a writing contest sponsored by *Vogue* magazine. Eventually, she became an editor there. Her reputation in the literary world, however, is based on her novels and essays. Didion has said, "I write entirely to find out what I'm thinking, what I'm looking at, what I see and what it means."

The essay "Georgia O'Keeffe" pays tribute to an artist who herself displayed a strong pioneer spirit.

Review and Assess

Literary Analysis

Biographical and Autobiographical Writing

1. Using a chart like this one, provide evidence to show whether each selection is a **biography** or an **autobiography**.

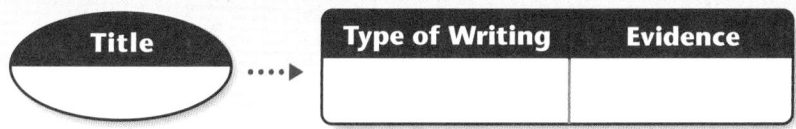

	Type of Writing	Evidence
Title		

2. What are two details from *A White House Diary* that reveal the compassion of Lady Bird Johnson?
3. What does McPhee reveal about Ashe's personal nature?
4. In what ways was Georgia O'Keeffe portrayed as a "loner"?

Comparing Literary Works

5. (a) Which of the three selections reveals the most to you about the qualities of the person portrayed? (b) Which of the three selections evokes the most emotion in you? Why?
6. (a) How would *A White House Diary* be different if it were written as a biography? (b) Use a Venn diagram like this one to compare the ways each type of writing would present Lady Bird Johnson.

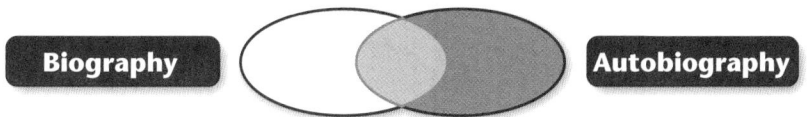

Reading Strategy

Finding the Writer's Main Points and Support

7. For each main point below, explain which details the writer provides to support the main point:
   (a) Mrs. Kennedy made Lady Bird's visit with her as easy as possible.
   (b) Remaining cool on the court was a potent weapon for Ashe.
   (c) Georgia O'Keeffe was a hard, straight shooter.

Extend Understanding

8. **Social Studies Connection:** Why are biographical and autobiographical writings valuable sources for historians and teachers?

Integrate Language Skills

Vocabulary Development Lesson

Word Analysis: Latin Root -sent-/-sens-

The Latin root *-sent-/-sens-* means "feeling." The root appears in the word *sentimental*, which means "having excessive feelings." Using the meaning of *-sent-/-sens-*, define each word below.

1. sensitize   **2.** sensitively   **3.** sentimentality

Spelling Strategy

Do not change the spelling of a base word when adding a prefix to it. For example, *im-* + *mutable* = *immutable*.

Add the prefix shown to form the new word. Then, use each word in a sentence.

1. *pre-* + eminent   **3.** *un-* + natural
2. *dis-* + service   **4.** *im-* + proper

Fluency: Definitions

Review the vocabulary list on page 673. Then, match each of the following phrases on the left with its correct definition on the right.

1. poignant genesis   **a.** emotional riddle
2. tumultuous implications   **b.** unchangeable inheritance
3. immutable legacy   **c.** patronizing hatred
4. sentimental enigma   **d.** turbulent indications
5. condescending rancor   **e.** moving beginning

Grammar Lesson

Subject-Verb Agreement: Confusing Subjects

The **subject** and **verb** in a sentence must agree in number. A singular subject takes the singular form of the verb. A plural subject takes the plural form of the verb. If a subject follows a verb in a sentence, the subject and verb must still agree.

In the following examples, the verbs are italicized and the subjects are underlined.

Singular:	There *was* a sharp, loud report.
Plural:	There *were* sharp, loud reports.

If the subject is *any* or *all*, the verb agrees with the noun to which the pronoun refers.

Singular:	All the danger *was* over.
Plural:	All the shades *were* lowered.

Practice Identify the subject in each sentence. Then, choose the correct verb to complete each sentence.

1. There (was, were) Secret Service men all over.
2. His entire life (was, were) a series of victories.
3. Some of his opponents (was, were) baffled.
4. There on the wall (was, were) her paintings.
5. Each painting in the group (was, were) a masterpiece.

Writing Application Use each item as the subject in a sentence. Make sure you use a verb that agrees in number with the subject.

1. tennis players   2. painter

 Prentice Hall Writing and Grammar Connection: Chapter 25, Section 1

Writing Lesson

Awards Speech

Imagine that you are an official at an awards ceremony for Lady Bird Johnson, Arthur Ashe, or Georgia O'Keeffe. Using the selections you have just read, write a speech that introduces the award winner.

Prewriting Select the person from these selections whom you admire most. Jot down the points you would like to make about that person.

Drafting Begin your speech with an attention-grabbing opening. In the body of your speech, present your main points in a logical order.

Revising Read your speech and ask a classmate to suggest places where you can add details to make your ideas more coherent. Add transition words, such as *then* and *as a result,* to clarify your speech.

Model: Adding Smooth Transitions

Tonight we are honoring an admirable woman.

But even more importantly,

∧We are honoring a great American. She has worked tirelessly

As a result,

for our country.∧ $he has brought all of us closer together.

> The inserted words create smoother transitions between sentences.

---

*W*G *Prentice Hall Writing and Grammar Connection: Chapter 7, Section 4*

Extension Activities

Listening and Speaking In a small group, develop and present a **radio news report** on the assassination of President Kennedy.

- Use library resources to find relevant information on the subject.
- Use details such as quotations and anecdotes in your report.
- Organize the information in the best possible order, using transition words where helpful.

Present your radio news report to the class. **[Group Activity]**

Research and Technology Prepare a **visual presentation** on the paintings of Georgia O'Keeffe. Find reproductions of her paintings and use them as your primary source of information. Then, use the Internet to find more information about her and her paintings. Write informational captions for each painting. Present your findings to your class.

 **Take It to the Net**   www.phschool.com

Go online for an additional research activity using the Internet.

Prepare to Read

excerpt from Understanding Comics

Preview

Connecting to the Literature

Most people associate comics with superheroes, humorous animals, and amusing people with exaggerated facial features. As you read this excerpt from *Understanding Comics,* consider how much the writer/illustrator changes your impressions and ideas about a typical comic strip.

Background

Comics first appeared in American newspapers in the late 1800s. One early strip featuring a character called the Yellow Kid was so popular that it boosted sales for its newspaper. Soon, other newspapers were running their own comics, too. Comic books first appeared in the 1930s. The *Superman* comic began in 1938 and is still popular today. In recent years, the popularity of comic books has increased dramatically among adults.

Literary Analysis

Visual Essay

A **visual essay** is an exploration of a topic that conveys its ideas through visual elements as well as language. Like a standard essay, a visual essay presents an author's views of a topic. Unlike other essays, however, much of the meaning in a visual essay is conveyed through illustrations or photographs. For example, the following excerpt from *Understanding Comics* will take on new meaning when you read it along with a visual element in the comic:

> The artform—the *medium*—known as comics is a *vessel* which can hold any *number* of *ideas* and *images*.

Note how the visual elements of *Understanding Comics* heighten your understanding and appreciation of the text.

Connecting Literary Elements

The **tone** of a visual essay is the writer's attitude toward his or her audience and subject, and it can be conveyed through both words and images. Often, the tone can be described in a single adjective, such as *formal* or *informal*, *serious* or *playful*, *bitter* or *ironic*. As you read a comic, consider how the pictures and the letters—for example, the size of the letters and the repetition of words—contribute to the author's overall tone.

Reading Strategy

Using Visuals as a Key to Meaning

You can **use visuals as a key to meaning** by looking carefully at each illustration or photograph and deciding how it adds to the ideas presented in the written text. Pictures can reinforce and extend words in the following ways:

- They add humor to apparently straightforward statements.
- They add details, without having to use additional words.
- They signal flashbacks in time or the element of fantasy.

Use a chart like the one shown to record details about the text and the illustrations. Then, explain how the visual extends meaning.

Vocabulary Development

obsessed (əb sest´) *adj.* greatly occupied with

aesthetic (es thet´ ik) *adj.* relating to the appreciation of beauty

arbitrary (är´ bə trer´ē) *adj.* not fixed by rules, but left to one's judgment

Instruction with this selection addresses these standards:

R 1.1*, 3.9*
W 1.8, 2.2*
WOLC 1.3*
LS 1.7

* *Standards tested on HS Exit Exam. For complete standards, see p. CA 4.*

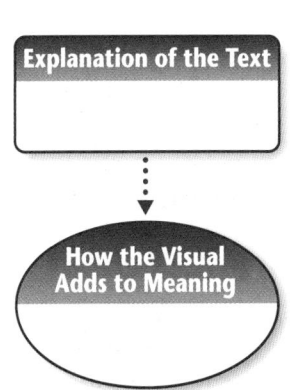

Explanation of the Text

How the Visual Adds to Meaning

excerpt from

UNDERSTANDING COMICS

Scott McCloud

HI, I'M *SCOTT McCLOUD.*

WHEN I WAS A *LITTLE KID* I KNEW *EXACTLY* WHAT COMICS WERE.

COMICS WERE THOSE *BRIGHT, COLORFUL MAGAZINES* FILLED WITH *BAD ART, STUPID STORIES* AND *GUYS IN TIGHTS.*

I READ *REAL* BOOKS, NATURALLY. I WAS MUCH TOO *OLD* FOR COMICS!

BUT WHEN I WAS IN *8th GRADE,* A FRIEND OF MINE (WHO WAS A LOT *SMARTER* THAN I WAS) CONVINCED ME TO GIVE COMICS ANOTHER LOOK AND LENT ME HIS COLLECTION.

SOON, I WAS HOOKED!

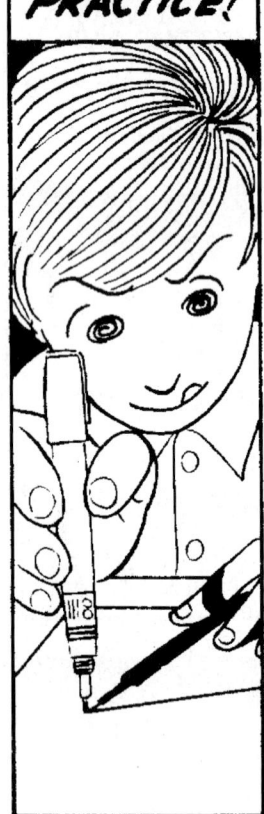

--WHILE NOT BEING **SO** BROAD AS TO INCLUDE ANYTHING WHICH IS CLEARLY **NOT** COMICS.

"COMICS" IS THE WORD WORTH DEFINING, AS IT REFERS TO THE MEDIUM *ITSELF,* NOT A SPECIFIC *OBJECT* AS *"COMIC BOOK"* OR *"COMIC STRIP"* DO.

WE CAN ALL VISUALIZE **A** COMIC.

THE WORLD OF COMICS IS A *HUGE* AND *VARIED* ONE. OUR DEFINITION MUST ENCOMPASS ALL THESE TYPES--

BUT WHAT--

--IS--

--COMICS?

excerpt from *Understanding Comics* ◆ 699

THE ARTFORM--THE *MEDIUM*--KNOWN AS COMICS IS A *VESSEL* WHICH CAN HOLD ANY *NUMBER* OF *IDEAS* AND *IMAGES*.

COMICS

Writers
ARTISTS
Trends
GENRES
STYLES
Subject matter
THEMES

THE *"CONTENT"* OF THOSE IMAGES AND IDEAS IS, OF COURSE, UP TO *CREATORS*, AND WE ALL HAVE DIFFERENT *TASTES*.

GLUG
GLUG

PTUI!!!

GAAK
WHEEEEZ
KAF! KAF!
GLUGH· GGH...

ahem

THE *TRICK* IS TO NEVER MISTAKE THE *MESSAGE*--

--FOR THE *MESSENGER*.

COMICS

AT ONE TIME OR ANOTHER VIRTUALLY *ALL* THE GREAT MEDIA HAVE RECEIVED *CRITICAL EXAMINATION,* IN AND OF *THEMSELVES.*

WRITTEN WORD

MUSIC

VIDEO

THEATRE

VISUAL ART

FILM

BUT FOR *COMICS,* THIS ATTENTION HAS BEEN *RARE.* *

LET'S SEE IF WE CAN HELP *RECTIFY* THE SITUATION.

excerpt from *Understanding Comics* ◆ 701

© and ™ 1994 Scott McCloud

excerpt from *Understanding Comics* ◆ 703

The complete *Understanding Comics* is 215 pages in 9 chapters and examines all aspects of comics. The above excerpt is from Chapter One.

© and ™ 1994 Scott McCloud

Review and Assess

Thinking About the Selection

1. **Respond:** Did you enjoy this selection? Why or why not?

2. **(a) Recall:** How does McCloud's view of comics change from his early childhood view to his present view? **(b) Make a Judgment:** Do you accept McCloud's final definition of comics, which says nothing about their entertainment value? Explain.

3. **Evaluate:** Do you think McCloud is justified in comparing comics to art forms such as film, music, and theater? Explain.

Scott McCloud

(b. 1960)

Scott McCloud started drawing comics at the age of twelve. After graduating from Syracuse University in 1982, he began his career as a cartoonist. He has since published an award-winning comic book series called *Zot!* as well as *Destroy!*, a parody of superhero comics.

Review and Assess

Literary Analysis

Visual Essay

1. Using a chart like this one, identify the main idea of this selection. Show how both the visuals and the text convey this idea.

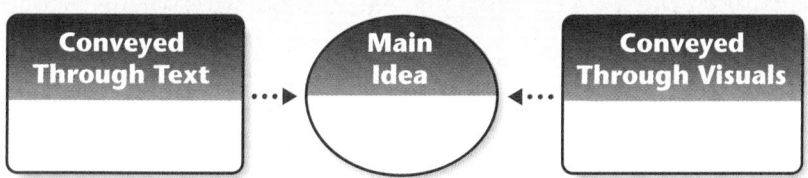

2. Would the selection lose its impact if either the words or the visuals were eliminated? Explain.

3. How does McCloud's selection fit Will Eisner's description of comics as "sequential art"?

Connecting Literary Elements

4. Using a chart like this, analyze the varying **tone** of the selection.

Text	Visuals		Tone
		···▶	

5. Which word best describes the overall tone of the essay? Explain.

Reading Strategy

Using Visuals as a Key to Meaning

6. Find three places in which visuals add humor to text that is straightforward and serious. Explain each example.

7. Identify two illustrations that add meaning to McCloud's definition of a comic. Explain.

8. Find two illustrations that help explain the meaning of the term "sequential art." Explain how the visuals illustrate the meaning.

Extend Understanding

9. **Media Connection:** McCloud briefly addresses the difference between comics and animation. (a) What are some additional differences between comics and animation? (b) Which medium do you think is more effective in conveying a message? Why?

Quick Review

A **visual essay** is a piece of nonfiction that conveys its ideas through visual elements as well as language.

The **tone** in a literary work is the writer's attitude toward his or her audience and subject.

To **use visuals as a key to meaning,** rely on illustrations or photographs to help you understand and appreciate the meaning of accompanying text.

 Take It to the Net
www.phschool.com
Take the interactive self-test online to check your understanding of the selection.

Integrate Language Skills

Vocabulary Development Lesson

Word Analysis: Latin Root -stat-

The Latin root -stat- means "to stand." The root appears in the word *static*, which describes something that stands unchanging. Write a definition of each word below, incorporating the meaning of -stat- in your definition.

1. statue   2. stationary   3. statistics

Spelling Strategy

If a base word ends in two consonants, retain both consonants when adding a suffix. For example, *obsess* + *-ed* = *obsessed*.

Add the suffix shown and write each new word. Then, use each new word in a sentence.

1. lurk + *-ing*   3. content + *-ment*
2. harsh + *-ly*   4. vast + *-ness*

Concept Development: Analogies

On your paper, write the word that best completes each analogy. Then, write a sentence or two that explains the relationship between the words in each pair.

1. ecstatic : happy :: obsessed : ____?____
   a. overwhelmed
   b. unconcerned
   c. interested
2. stationary : fixed :: arbitrary : ____?____
   a. random
   b. specific
   c. cruel
3. physical : sports :: aesthetic : ____?____
   a. people
   b. art
   c. running

Grammar Lesson

Varieties of English: Standard and Nonstandard

Standard English can be either formal or informal. Formal English is used to address subjects in a serious way. Informal English is used when you want to achieve a conversational tone for casual writing. **Nonstandard English** is language that does not follow the rules of proper English usage.

Formal: Each successive frame of a movie is projected on exactly the same space.

Informal: Hi, I'm Scott McCloud. When I was a little kid I knew . . .

Nonstandard: Don't gimme that comic book talk!

Practice Identify each sentence as *formal, informal,* or *Nonstandard* English.

1. Comics are a visual and sequential art.
2. They're kinda like cartoons on paper.
3. Reading comics is really lots of fun.
4. To define comics, one must separate form from content.
5. I usta think comics were sorta uncool.

Writing Application Write a five-sentence paragraph about your reaction to McCloud's comics. Include both Standard and Nonstandard English, and then label each sentence *formal, informal,* or *Nonstandard.*

W̶G *Prentice Hall Writing and Grammar Connection: Chapter 3, Section 3*

Writing Lesson

Essay on Humor

Write a short essay about McCloud's use of humor in this excerpt from *Understanding Comics*. Discuss his use of visuals and other techniques, and explain how he uses humor both to entertain and to inform.

Prewriting   Review the selection to determine the ways McCloud uses humor. On separate note cards, write each main point and the details that support the main point.

Model: Gathering Relevant Details

Main point I want to prove:

    McCloud's humor is original.

Examples of original humor:

    The image of the globe to convey the world of comics

    The images he uses to explain sequential art

> Specific details provide support for one main point.

Drafting   Use your note cards to include references from the text that support your points. Include quotations or descriptions of images.

Revising   Reread your draft, making sure you have used modifiers that clearly convey your thoughts and feelings. For example, the word *brilliant* conveys high praise, while *adequate* conveys mild praise.

WG   *Prentice Hall Writing and Grammar Connection: Chapter 13, Section 2*

Extension Activities

Listening and Speaking In a group, research the subject of comics in all their variety and prepare a **visual presentation.** Follow these steps:

- Divide comics into five or fewer categories, such as superhero comic books, newspaper comic strips, and comic book adaptations of classic novels.

- Show an example of each type of comic.

- Discuss how each category began and how it has developed over the years.

Share your presentation with your class. [**Group Activity**]

Research and Technology Choose an activity that interests you and create a **comic strip** of your own based on the activity. Locate comics from the newspaper and consider using them as models. Use publishing software and graphic programs to publish your strip. Your tone can be serious or humorous, depending on your message.

 **Take It to the Net**   www.phschool.com

Go online for an additional research activity using the Internet.

Prepare to Read

Earhart Redux ◆ In These Girls, Hope Is a Muscle

 **Take It to the Net**

Visit www.phschool.com for interactive activities and instruction related to the selections, including
- background
- graphic organizers
- literary elements
- reading strategies

Preview

Connecting to the Literature

Sometimes a failure can be the most powerful incentive for a new victory. If you have ever wanted something, lost it, and then wanted it even more, you will know the truth at the heart of these true stories.

Background

In 1932, at age thirty-five, Amelia Earhart became the first woman to fly solo across the Atlantic Ocean. Five years later, she attempted to fly around the world, accompanied only by a navigator. After circling three quarters of the globe, the pair disappeared on July 1, 1937, near New Guinea. Earhart's final message reported empty fuel tanks. Her plane was never found. In 1997, Linda Finch successfully re-created and completed Earhart's flight around the world in a similar aircraft.

Literary Analysis

Career Writing

Writing is an important part of a wide range of occupations—for example, television reporting, advertising, even police work. **Career writing** is any writing that is done as part of a person's job responsibilities. In this example, writer Tracy Kidder presents his review of a fellow reporter's work:

> This book is the product of a perfect marriage. The subject is timely and fascinating, and Madeleine Blais is a first-rate reporter and writer.

As you read the selections, note the type of career writing that each represents. Then, consider the qualities that the pieces share.

Comparing Literary Works

Each of the following selections tells about real women who are defined by the challenges they take on. As you read, compare the different experiences and challenges of the women in each piece, as well as the ways these writers address their subjects' struggles.

CALIFORNIA STANDARDS

Instruction with these selections addresses these standards:

R 1.1*
W 1.2*, 1.4*
WOLC 1.3*
LS 1.8

* Standards tested on HS Exit Exam. For complete standards, see p. CA 4.

Reading Strategy

Determining the Author's Purpose

Career writing is shaped most of all by its purpose—the goal the writer sets out to achieve. When you **determine the author's purpose,** you seek to understand the writer's goal, which may be to inform, to entertain, or to persuade. You can determine the writer's purpose by paying close attention to details in the writing. Use a chart like the one shown to record details and identify each writer's purpose.

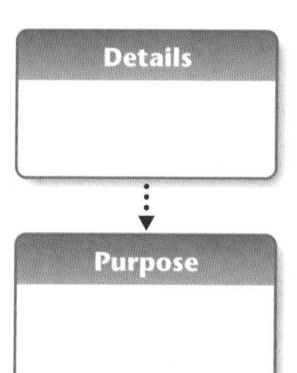

Details

↓

Purpose

Vocabulary Development

aerodynamics (er´ ō dī nam´ iks) *n.* branch of mechanics dealing with the forces exerted by air or other gases in motion (p. 711)

hydraulic (hī drô´ lik) *adj.* operated by the movement and pressure of liquid (p. 713)

pursue (pər sōō´) *v.* seek (p. 715)

improbable (im präb´ ə bəl) *adj.* unlikely to happen (p. 715)

derides (di rīdz´) *v.* ridicules (p. 715)

legacy (leg´ ə sē) *n.* anything handed down from an ancestor (p. 715)

riveting (riv´ it iŋ) *adj.* firmly holding attention (p. 717)

ruminative (rōō´ mə nə təv) *adj.* meditative (p. 717)

adept (ə dept´) *adj.* highly skilled; expert (p. 717)

compelling (kəm pel´ iŋ) *adj.* forceful (p. 718)

Earhart Redux

Alex Chadwick

On March 17, 1997, national interest was piqued as Linda Finch set off to complete the flight that Amelia Earhart had attempted sixty years earlier. Alex Chadwick, a radio reporter for National Public Radio, conducted a radio interview with Linda Finch before her flight. The following is the script of Chadwick's interview.

BOB EDWARDS, HOST: This is *Morning Edition.* I'm Bob Edwards.

In Oakland, California, this morning, pilot Linda Finch takes off on an adventure that actually started 60 years ago. On this day in 1937, Amelia Earhart began her attempt to become the first person to fly around the world at the equator. She failed.

Her plane disappeared over the Pacific Ocean, but in that, she achieved a measure of immortality.

In the latest National Geographic Radio Expedition, NPR's[1] Alex Chadwick reports Linda Finch hopes to finish what Amelia Earhart began.

SOUNDS OF MACHINERY

ALEX CHADWICK, NPR REPORTER: The door to the hangar is bigger than any big theater movie screen. And it's opening slowly and improbably, folding outward on a horizontal midline and upward from the bottom. And there is Linda Finch's amazing airplane: 1930s aerodynamics, like an artifact from an old movie, or a dream.

LINDA FINCH, PILOT: The aircraft is very rare. There were only fifteen manufactured initially in the twenties and thirties, and there are only two left in the world.

CHADWICK: Ms. Finch is pretty rare herself. A 46-year-old grandmother who owns several nursing homes in Texas, and a pilot who restores and flies vintage fighters. Even so, replicating Amelia Earhart's flight is difficult. And though she doesn't like to say so, a little risky.

SOUNDS OF DOORS OPENING AND CLOSING

FINCH: We'll be flying in an aircraft that is the exact same model Amelia flew. And we'll be following the same route that she flew around the world.

CHADWICK: Well, I'm sure some people hearing about this flight would say, what is the point of setting off in an aircraft that's already failed in this once? I mean, it's dangerous. Maybe recklessly dangerous.

FINCH: Well, I have a lot of advantages that Amelia didn't have. We will have modern navigation, communication, and flight instruments that she just didn't have available at the time. The flight, I believe, needs to be done in the right airplane, to be historically correct, to generate the excitement in order to communicate our message.

I started learning about Amelia and really feel like I came to know her. And although I think that flying was definitely a part of her being,

---

1. **NPR's** National Public Radio's.

aerodynamics (er´ ō dī nam´ iks) *n.* branch of mechanics dealing with the forces exerted by air or other gases in motion

Reading Strategy
Determining the Author's Purpose
What is the author's goal in this passage?

✔**Reading Check**
What does Linda Finch hope to accomplish?

that she really flew to get the recognition to convince people that they could do what they wanted. Especially women in the 1930s. That people weren't limited to small lives. That they could have their dreams.

CHADWICK: Amelia Earhart was an aviation pioneer, daring and determined. The second flyer after Lindbergh[2] to solo across the Atlantic. Fourteen others had died trying to repeat his flight, and Amelia nearly did when a crucial instrument failed in bad weather.

Here's that earlier flyer after her Atlantic flight, when President Hoover presented her with a gold medal from the National Geographic Society.

AMELIA EARHART, PILOT: I came down until I could see the flight path blinking in the darkness. If it had been a smooth sea, I might have come too far. Whether I was 50 feet off the water or 150, I do not know, without my altimeter. I was too close, however.

CHADWICK: The plane that Amelia used on her round-the-world attempt, the Lockheed Electra 10-E, is 38.5 feet long, with a 55-foot wingspan. The tail angles back on a small, solid rubber rear wheel. The nose tilts upwards toward the sky. She glows like a polished aluminum athlete, broad-shouldered. Beautiful as a swan dive.

SOUND OF AIRPLANE ENGINE

She carries two nine-cylinder radial Pratt and Whitney Wasp engines. These are the first air-cooled engines developed. At 650 pounds, they produced more than 400 horsepower when they were introduced in 1926, and that was an extraordinary weight-power ratio for the time.

Linda Finch's plane has later, more powerful versions of that engine, as did Amelia Earhart's. Except for new navigation and communication gear, their planes are identical.

FINCH: The aircraft was in boxes and pieces and parts. And one of the things that I discovered was that prior to World War II, there were no parts manuals. You get just a big box of pieces, and it's like a jigsaw puzzle, you have to figure out how to put it together.

CHADWICK: She describes the Electra as graceful and slow in flight. Almost peaceful. Amelia did all her flying, but carried a navigator co-pilot. And so will Linda. The cockpit is a narrow, confined space, barely enough room for twin controls. And the enormous, banquet-sized steering wheels.

SOUND OF WHEELS TURNING

What do these wheels feel like? They look like they came out of

Literary Analysis
Career Writing
What information did Chadwick need to research in order to prepare this writing assignment?

---

2. **Lindbergh** Charles Lindbergh (1902–1974) made the first solo nonstop flight across the Atlantic Ocean on May 20–21, 1927.

1940s British sports cars or something.

FINCH: Exactly, and the wood is so worn. We actually had some new ones we could have put in. But I like these because they're worn and they've been in the airplane, obviously, since it was new.

CHADWICK: So, this is all human-powered controls for turning things and making the airplane fly?

FINCH: Absolutely. People are very surprised that there is just a thin cable and actually you move the cable. Everyone always says, does it have <u>hydraulic</u> controls? Absolutely not.

CHADWICK: These things here, these switches and hand controls. Those are original on the plane. This is what Amelia Earhart flew.

FINCH: Exactly. There are many things, the controls, throttle, and the propeller and mixture controls, the fuel selector gauges, the magneto switches, the gear indicator. All of the things that have to do with the airplane mechanically are in fact the same as Amelia's.

CHADWICK: The plane was in the airport in Memphis, en route for tests elsewhere. Linda, and navigator Bob Fodge, had refilled the main battery the evening before, and something had gone wrong. Overnight it leaked acid, eating away at a small panel of the undercarriage. They had to remove it.

The technology is 60 and 70 years old. Linda Finch knows how it works. Why it works. Why it's reliable. But she is attempting to fly around the world in an airplane where the rivets all show. And the cockpit windows slide open, and little accidents cause the flawless aluminum skin to weaken and decay.

The navigation electronics are as good as you could get. She has an on-board satellite link to the Internet. Schools can check her progress hourly. But the actual airplane is decades older than Linda Finch herself. And on many portions of this flight, she's going to have to overload that plane with fuel in order to cross open water.

What does your daughter think? What does your family think, when you are setting off to re-create a flight that Amelia Earhart did not survive?

FINCH: Well, my daughter is very supportive and excited and pleased. And is real involved in the project. On the other hand, she's a worrier. So, she always worries.

And she's most happy that we'll actually be sending the airplane's position back on the Internet every hour. So, I think she'll be watching that quite closely to see where we are.

CHADWICK: Oakland; across the country to Miami; then San Juan, Puerto Rico; Cumana, Venezuela; Paramari, Vos Serena; down to Natale in Brazil, and across to Africa. Dakkar, Injamana, Khartoum. It'll be hot over the desert. Karachi, Calcutta, Rangoon. In a couple of

hydraulic (hī drô´ lik) *adj.* operated by the movement and pressure of liquid

✔️ Reading Check

How does Finch say her family has responded to her adventure?

months, she'll get to Lahe, New Guinea, the last place that Amelia Earhart was ever seen.

Here's Amelia, after flying the Atlantic.

EARHART: I hope that the flight has meant something to women in aviation. If it has, I shall feel it justified. But I can't claim anything else.

CHADWICK: And here is Linda Finch. In a tan wool gabardine flight suit, strains showing in her face a little from the work and the stress, but mostly looking eager to go finish that great adventure.

FINCH: Well, I don't know what happened to Amelia Earhart, and neither does anyone else, certainly. When I'm reading a book about Amelia and I get to the last communications that they heard from her, that's really where I stop reading. Because I just think it doesn't matter. What does matter is what Amelia did with her life, and that's really the focus of our project.

SOUND OF AN AIRPLANE PROPELLER

CHADWICK: Pilot Linda Finch, who sets out today to fly around the world in a Lockheed Electra 10-E, the plane Amelia Earhart flew.

For Radio Expeditions, this is Alex Chadwick reporting.

Review and Assess

Thinking About the Selection

1. **Respond:** Do you admire Linda Finch for undertaking her adventure? Explain.

2. **(a) Recall:** As the interview begins, what words does Alex Chadwick use to describe Finch? **(b) Analyze:** How does Chadwick seem to feel about Finch and her mission?

3. **(a) Recall:** What happened to Amelia Earhart when she attempted to fly around the world at the equator?
   (b) Evaluate: What details of the report add to the suspense about the outcome of Finch's endeavor?

4. **(a) Recall:** How often is Amelia Earhart's voice heard in the interview? **(b) Speculate:** What effect does Chadwick create by including the voice of Earhart?

5. **(a) Recall:** What sound effects does Chadwick use in his interview? **(b) Draw a Conclusion:** Why does Chadwick use the sound effects in his work?

6. **Evaluate:** In the interview, Earhart says, "I hope that the flight has meant something to women in aviation." What do you think Finch's flight might mean to these women?

7. **Assess:** How might Finch inspire the general public?

Alex Chadwick

(b. 1947)

As you read "Earhart Redux," you may have noticed the references to sound effects. Alex Chadwick's work as a correspondent for National Public Radio for more than twenty years has been marked by his use of such sounds to anchor his stories in reality.

Before becoming a radio correspondent, Chadwick earned a degree in communications from American University in Washington, D.C., and worked in Maine as both a radio reporter and a commercial fisherman.

Chadwick's accomplishments in radio include his essays and features on the critically acclaimed radio programs *Morning Edition* and *All Things Considered*. He also co-hosted the Public Broadcasting Service television series *Childhood* in 1991.

In These Girls, Hope Is a Muscle

Book Review by *Steve Gietschier*

If you have not yet had the opportunity to give your heart to a women's high school basketball team or to feel the passion of women's athletics in general, reading this book may be the start of something big. Although its poetic title alone could win an award, the text is even better: beautifully written, heartfelt, gently humorous but most important, forthright in its insistence that women as well as men should be able to <u>pursue</u> genuine excellence through sports.

Blais explains how <u>improbable</u> it is to find a championship basketball team of either gender, John Calipari's Massachusetts' squad[1] excluded, in Amherst, Mass., a town she <u>derides</u> as "probably the only place in the United States where men can wear berets and not get beaten up." Amherst, she says, "is, for the most part, smoke free, nuclear free and eager to free Tibet."[2] It is the proud home of Bread & Circus, the self-proclaimed world's largest health food store. More significantly, Amherst is, in Blais' view, "an achingly democratic sort of place in which tryouts for Little League, with their inevitable rejections, have caused people to suggest that more teams should be created so that no one is left out."

Far from an athlete herself, Blais nevertheless was still able to find unfolding within Amherst's "self-absorbed loftiness" the glistening struggle of superb competitors, the Lady Hurricanes of Amherst Regional High School. Picking up their story with the final game of the 1991–92 season, Blais followed their efforts throughout 1992–93, an epic campaign dedicated to overcoming a long <u>legacy</u> of being good, but just not good enough.

On the surface, then, this book is a simple tale of a singular basketball season. . . . Readers looking for no more than a good story

pursue (pər sōō′) *v.* seek

improbable (im präb′ ə bəl) *adj.* unlikely to happen

derides (di rīdz′) *v.* ridicules

Reading Strategy
Determining the Author's Purpose Why does Gietschier include Blais's quote about the qualities of Amherst?

legacy (leg′ ə sē) *n.* anything handed down from an ancestor

---

1. **John Calipari's Massachusetts' squad** coach of an excellent basketball team at University of Massachusetts.
2. **to free Tibet** Once a semi-independent state, Tibet has been part of China since the 1950s.

can chart the season game by game and turn one page after another in anticipation of the next victory.

But there is so much more here to savor and absorb. The young women who give themselves so completely to their team's quest are extraordinary each in her own way. Burdened with the pains of adolescence, the duties that high school imposes and, in some cases, the tough circumstances of families rent asunder,[3] they learn from one another how to dig deep to find the resources they need to reach their goal.

In the process, they journey in so many ways to places Amherst women have never gone before, proving to themselves, their families, their town and all who will look with open eyes that women's sports can be an astoundingly fulfilling and moving experience.

---

3. **rent asunder** (ə sun′ dər) torn apart.

▶ **Critical Viewing**
How might this player's facial expression reflect the experiences of the Lady Hurricanes? **[Infer]**

As part of the marketing of a book, many publishers include brief reviews by well-known writers or public figures. Following are some of the comments that appeared on the book jacket of Madeleine Blais's book.

Book Jacket Copy for
In These Girls, Hope Is a Muscle   Madeleine Blais

Advance praise for *In These Girls, Hope Is a Muscle*:

This book is the product of a perfect marriage. The subject is timely and fascinating, and Madeleine Blais is a first-rate reporter and writer.
                                                                                —*Tracy Kidder*

Blais's narrative gift has produced a touching, exciting book about a subject largely ignored until now, namely women athletes. Her story of a year in the life of a high school basketball team and its hometown goes far beyond the obvious to illuminate how people really feel, how things really work.
                                                                                —*Anne Bernays*

Begun as an article that appeared in the *New York Times Magazine*, *In These Girls, Hope Is a Muscle* offers a <u>riveting</u> close-up of the girls on a high school basketball team whose passion for the sport is rivaled only by their loyalty to one another. Reminiscent of John McPhee's *A Sense of Where You Are* and H. G. Bissinger's *Friday Night Lights*, Pulitzer Prize–winning journalist Madeleine Blais's book takes the reader through a singular season in the history of the Lady Hurricanes of Amherst, Massachusetts.

For years they had been known as a finesse team, talented and hard-working players who in the end lacked that final hardscrabble ingredient that would take them over the top to the state championship. They seemed doomed to mirror the college town they represented: kindly, <u>ruminative</u>, at times ineffectual; more <u>adept</u> at quoting Emily Dickinson[1] and singing nature songs than going to the basket.

One season, all that changed. Madeleine Blais takes us from try-outs to practices during the regular season, up through the final championship game against the mighty Hillies from Haverhill. The result is an astoundingly moving narrative that captures the complexities of girls' experiences in high school, in sports, and in our society.

---

1. **Emily Dickinson** (1830–1886), poet who was born and lived most of her life in Amherst, Massachusetts.

riveting (riv´ it iŋ) *adj.* firmly holding attention

ruminative (ro͞o´ mə nə təv) *adj.* meditative

adept (ə dept´) *adj.* highly skilled; expert

Reading Strategy
Determining the Author's Purpose What are two goals the writer exhibits in this passage?

As their coach says, unlike training boys—whose arrogance and confidence often have to be eroded before a team can pull together—working with girls is all constructive. The way to build a girls' team is to build each player's self-confidence. During the course of this season we see the Amherst Lady Hurricanes in their fierce, funny, sisterhood-is-powerful quest for excellence.

As Blais reports, "This is just one team in one season. It alone cannot change the discrimination against girls and their bodies throughout history." But it is a <u>compelling</u>, funny, and touching literary exploration of one group of girls' fight for success and, perhaps most of all, respect. *In These Girls, Hope Is a Muscle* is both a dramatization of the success of the women's movement and a testimony to all the changes that have yet to come.

Madeleine Blais worked at the *Miami Herald* for eight years. A collection of her work, *The Heart Is an Instrument: Portraits in Journalism,* was published by the University of Massachusetts Press in 1992. Now a resident of Amherst, she has been on the faculty at the University of Massachusetts for six years.

compelling (kəm pel′ iŋ)
adj. forceful

Review and Assess

Thinking About the Selection

1. **Respond:** Does reading the review and the book-jacket blurb of *In These Girls, Hope Is a Muscle* make you want to read the book itself? Explain.

2. **(a) Recall:** In the opening of his review, which words does Gietschier use to describe Blais's book? **(b) Analyze:** Why do you think Gietschier likes Blais's book?

3. **(a) Recall:** What is the subject of the book *In These Girls, Hope Is a Muscle?* **(b) Infer:** Based on Gietschier's review, why do you think Blais chose to write the book?

4. **(a) Recall:** According to the book review, what do the girls prove about women's sports? **(b) Speculate:** Who do you think would be most persuaded to buy this book after reading the review?

5. **(a) Recall:** What two people are quoted in the book-jacket copy? **(b) Compare:** What do their comments have in common? **(c) Summarize:** Since the information following the quotes closely echoes the author's writing in the book, what would you say is Blais's main idea and attitude toward the subject?

6. **Compare and Contrast:** How is the format of the book-jacket blurb different from that of Gietschier's review?

Steve Gietschier

(b. 1948)
Steve Gietschier holds the game of basketball dear to his heart: His experiences coaching his daughter's team led him to seek out the assignment of reviewing *In These Girls, Hope Is a Muscle,* Madeleine Blais's gripping account of a high-school girls' basketball team's championship season.

Born in New York City, Gietschier earned his bachelor's degree from Georgetown University in Washington, D.C., and his doctorate from Ohio State University.

Since 1986, Gietschier has been the Director of Historical Records at *The Sporting News* in St. Louis, Missouri, the newspaper that originally published his review of Blais's book.

Review and Assess

Literary Analysis

Career Writing

1. Why is it important for a radio journalist to be a good writer?
2. Using a chart like the one below, list the characteristics of good radio journalism, as well as the characteristics of a well-written book review and book-jacket blurb.

Radio Journalism	Book Review	Book-Jacket Blurb

3. Based on your chart, how effective is each selection that you read?

Comparing Literary Works

4. Using a chart like the one below, compare the challenges faced by Linda Finch and the Lady Hurricanes.

Person/Group		Challenges	Strengths
	····▶		

5. How is a challenge to a team different from a challenge to an individual?
6. In your opinion, which selection is more successful at conveying the challenge its subject faces?

Reading Strategy

Determining the Author's Purpose

7. What do you think is Chadwick's **purpose** in conducting his interview with Linda Finch?
8. (a) Explain the different purposes of the book-jacket copy and the review. (b) Do you think the book review or the book-jacket copy is more effective in persuading people to read the book? Why?

Extend Understanding

9. **Career Link:** What other occupations can you think of in which writing is particularly important?

Quick Review

Career writing is writing that is done as part of a person's job.

To **determine the author's purpose,** seek to understand the writer's goal—to inform, to entertain, or to persuade, for example.

 Take It to the Net
www.phschool.com
Take the interactive self-test online to check your understanding of these selections.

Integrate Language Skills

Vocabulary Development Lesson

Word Analysis: Greek Root *-dyna-*

The Greek root *-dyna-* means "power" or "strength." The root appears in the word *aerodynamics*, which means "the branch of mechanics dealing with the power exerted by air or other gases in motion." Write the definition for each word below. Use a dictionary if you need help.

    1. dynasty   2. hydrodynamic

Spelling Strategy

To create the adverbial form of an adjective of more than one syllable that ends in *-le,* change the *e* to *y.* Do not double the *l.* For example, *improbable* becomes *improbably.* In one-syllable words ending in *-le,* the final consonant may double, as in *whole* and *wholly.* Write the adverbial form of each word below.

    1. noble   2. capable   3. legible

Concept Development: Synonyms

Write the word or phrase that means the same as the first word in each item. To help you, review the list of vocabulary words on page 709.

1. hydraulic: (a) strong, (b) liquid-powered
2. pursue: (a) chase, (b) quarrel
3. aerodynamics: (a) air movement, (b) flight
4. riveting: (a) pretty, (b) gripping
5. improbable: (a) unlikely, (b) impossible
6. compelling: (a) noisy, (b) fascinating
7. adept: (a) clumsy, (b) skillful
8. ruminative: (a) meditative, (b) wealthy
9. legacy: (a) victory, (b) heritage
10. derides: (a) ridicules, (b) ignores

Grammar Lesson

Usage: *there, their, they're*

Because the words *there, their,* and *they're* sound alike, they are often misused in sentences. **There** can be used either as an adverb meaning "at that place" or as an expletive at the start of a sentence. **Their,** a possessive pronoun, always modifies a noun. **They're** is a contraction for *they are.* Look at the following examples:

There:	Linda's airplane is over *there.* (used to mean "at that place")
There:	*There* were only fifteen manufactured. (used as an expletive)
Their:	Some players got *their* rejections. (used to modify *players*)

They're:	*They're* brave to fly in that plane. (used as a contraction)

Practice For each item below, indicate how the underlined word is used.

1. They're playing in a championship game.
2. Their coach is very nervous.
3. The flight manual is over there.
4. There are few differences between them.
5. Have you heard news of their arrival?

Writing Application Use *there, their,* and *they're* in a paragraph about these two selections.

WG Prentice Hall Writing and Grammar Connection: Chapter 27, Section 2

Writing Lesson

Letter to Linda Finch

Write a letter to Linda Finch explaining how you feel about her adventure. Whether you admire her or think she is taking too much of a risk, let her know in a respectful and friendly manner.

Prewriting Make a list of your feelings about Finch's endeavor. Then, provide a reason for each feeling.

Drafting In your introductory paragraph, explain why you are writing to her. In the next two paragraphs, explain how you feel about her adventure. Your final paragraph should explain what you have learned.

Revising Review your draft, underlining each point you have made. Then, highlight the support you have provided. Add any details needed to support your feelings on the subject.

Model: Highlighting to Find Support

I am impressed with your devotion and determination. You understand the risk involved, but your desire to live out a dream is stronger than your fear.

> The highlighted information shows that the point has been effectively supported.

 Prentice Hall Writing and Grammar Connection: Chapter 13, Section 2

Extension Activities

Listening and Speaking In a group, stage a **book chat** in which you review a book that the entire group has recently read. Ask each group member to prepare note cards about the following aspects of the book:

- Characters
- The writer's style
- The theme, or message, of the book

During the discussion, express what you liked or disliked about each aspect of the book, using your note cards. Give examples from the book.

Research and Technology In a small group, do a **research project** about one aspect of the role of women in aviation—for example, women who have flown in space or who have piloted planes in wartime. Develop your main idea through descriptions of the women and their experiences. Present your information as an oral report with visual displays. **[Group Activity]**

 Take It to the Net www.phschool.com

Go online for an additional research activity using the Internet.

Writing WORKSHOP

Exposition: Problem-and-Solution Essay

A **problem-and-solution essay** identifies and explains a problem and then proposes a practical solution. In this workshop, you will write a problem-and-solution essay.

Assignment Criteria. Your problem-and-solution essay should have the following characteristics:

● A statement of the problem and a suggested solution

● Facts, statistics, and details that show the problem's scope and indicate how it can be solved

● Language appropriate to the level of knowledge of your audience

● A logical organization

To preview the criteria on which your problem-and-solution essay may be assessed, see the Rubric on page 725.

Prewriting

Choose a topic. Write your problem-and-solution essay about an issue of interest to you. One strategy is to conduct a **media scan,** reviewing local newspapers and television news programs for items about community issues and problems. List problems for which you can imagine practical solutions. Choose one as your essay topic.

Create a problem profile. Once you have chosen a topic, create a profile to help you determine which aspect of the problem you will address in your essay. Answer the following questions about the problem:

● Who or what is affected by the problem?

● What causes the problem to occur?

● What are some possible solutions to the problem?

Gather information. Collect the information you will need to start your draft. Assess all the possible solutions and weed out the less practical ones to narrow your list.

Identify your audience. Keep a specific audience in mind while you write: readers who have the ability to implement your suggestions. As you narrow your list of solutions, identify the aspects of each idea that will most likely appeal to your target audience.

Problem Profile

Problem: Litter is creating an unsafe environment.

Who is affected? *Everyone on Earth.*

What causes the problem?

Lack of:

• *responsibility*

• *environmental education*

• *sense of ownership*

What are possible solutions? *Stiffer fines, more policing, more environmental education, volunteer trash pickup*

Student Model

Before you begin drafting your problem-and-solution essay, read this student model and review the characteristics of effective problem-and-solution essays.

Naomi Barrowclough
Maplewood, NJ

Environmental Un-Consciousness

During a recent Earth Day cleanup, I became disgusted by the amount of trash I picked up within a two-hour period. People had thrown little papers, bits of plastic, and candy wrappers until the mess formed a multicolored carpet over the green grass. What people who litter may not realize is that litter creates serious environmental problems, in addition to prompting concerns over appearance.

> In the opening paragraph, the author provides a general statement of the problem.

We've all been told not to litter, but it does not seem to sink in. One person may think his or her contribution is only a microscopic addition when viewed against the whole. But if every person shared this sense of irresponsibility, Earth would soon be overwhelmed by pollution.

Litter is harmful for many reasons. For one, roadside litter is eventually washed into our waterways and oceans—water we use for drinking and recreation. Also, animals might entangle themselves or mistake trash for food and swallow it. In our public spaces, children spend a great deal of time in areas where they could be physically harmed by the pollution caused by litter.

> Here, the author provides greater detail to explain the problem more fully.

There is no simple solution to the problem of litter, only an array of possible solutions with one strategy in common: Create a feeling of ownership over public spaces. Some of the most popular sites for litter are beaches and parks because people feel no sense of ownership over these places. These same people might think twice about littering in their own homes.

> The author introduces a general solution here.

To create a feeling of ownership, it is necessary to educate children early about the environmental consequences of littering. Schools could lead field trips to local beaches or parks where students pick up trash and test water quality. If kids have to fish two shopping carts from the side of a stream, as I did, they might think twice about throwing something else on the ground. If they see that contaminated water is harmful to humans and wildlife, they might stop someone they see littering.

> In this paragraph, specific strategies for achieving the solution are introduced.

There is no easy way to stop littering. Fines and policing alone will not do the trick because people will just look before they litter. Until people understand that littering is irresponsible and has devastating environmental consequences, there will continue to be litterbugs. The solution lies in education and creating a sense of ownership about our public spaces.

> In the final paragraph, the author addresses a potential concern and then restates her solution.

Drafting

Organize your ideas. An effective organization for your essay breaks your ideas into clear categories. After an introduction that raises your audience's interest, develop the problem with detailed examples. Next, offer a solution. Use your conclusion to drive home the soundness of your ideas.

Elaborate. In order to persuade your readers, consider these types of evidence:

- **Statistics:** Provide numbers to show how many people would be affected by your solution.
- **Expert opinions:** Include the advice of those who have training and experience related to your topic.
- **Personal anecdotes:** Tell your readers about your own experiences with the problem or solution.
- **Testimonials:** Include comments from others on the effectiveness of your proposed solution.

Address readers' concerns. To convince those who may not approve of your solution, show them that you understand their concerns. Address their objections with explanations and evidence that suggest your solution is the best course of action.

Elaborate to Provide Evidence

Subject: Problem-and-solution essay on litter

Statistics to include:

    Number of tons of litter deposited in local park/year

    Water quality studies related to pollution from litter

Experts to cite:

    Environmental organizations

    Park and beach sanitation officials

    Local police

Anecdote to include:

    Earth Day trash pickup experience

Testimonials to provide:

    Educators involved with environmental issues

    Park officials

Revising

Revise to support generalizations. Look at each paragraph to be sure that the details support or explain the main idea of its topic sentence. Use the following strategies:

1. Highlight your topic sentence, the general statement from which the rest of the paragraph flows.

2. Underline the supporting sentences that develop this main idea.

3. Eliminate any sentences that do not support the main idea and cut those that simply restate it.

Model: Supporting Generalizations

Litter is harmful for many reasons. For one, roadside litter is eventually washed into our waterways and oceans— water we use for drinking and recreation. It is also unpleasant to see trash floating in the water. Also, animals might entangle themselves or mistake trash for food and swallow it.

> Naomi chose to eliminate the third sentence since it did not relate directly to her topic sentence.

Revise to evaluate and refine word choice. Review your draft as if you were a member of your target audience. Find terms that need to be defined, or vocabulary that seems too difficult or easy for your readers. Then, make changes accordingly.

General Audience: Another way to fight fatigue is to exercise regularly.

Target Audience of Experts: Another way to raise low levels of blood sugar is to get more exercise.

Compare the two sentences below. Why would the model be more appropriate than the nonmodel if you were presenting an essay to third graders?

Nonmodel	Model
But if every person shared this sense of irresponsibility, Earth would soon be overwhelmed by pollution.	If no one cared about how much pollution he or she caused, Earth would be completely polluted.

Publishing and Presenting

To make the best use of your problem-and-solution essay, share it with the people who can help you make a difference.

Send a letter. Send your essay to the appropriate government official, agency, or group. Share any responses you receive with classmates.

Read to Write

To see another example of problem-and-solution writing, see "To the Residents of A.D. 2029" on page 495.

 Prentice Hall Writing and Grammar Connection: Chapter 11

Rubric for Self-Assessment

Evaluate your problem-and-solution essay using the following criteria and rating scale:

Criteria	Rating Scale				
	Not very				Very
Is the problem explored adequately in the essay?	1	2	3	4	5
How effective is the suggested solution?	1	2	3	4	5
Do facts, statistics, and details effectively illustrate the problem and solution?	1	2	3	4	5
How appropriate is the language for the audience's knowledge level?	1	2	3	4	5
Was the information logically organized and presented?	1	2	3	4	5

Listening and Speaking WORKSHOP

Evaluating a Speech

Public speaking can be daunting for someone who is not used to presenting ideas in front of an audience. It may be easier to be evaluating the speech as an audience member. The two skills are closely related. In this workshop, you will learn how to **evaluate a speech**, which will give you a solid basis for preparing your own oral presentation.

Evaluate Content

Assess arguments for quality. A convincing speech should present arguments that are easily understood. While evaluating speeches, you may catch flaws or "holes" in poorly presented arguments. To find errors in arguments, use the following tips:

- Determine the type of argument the speaker uses.
- Decide whether you can identify a potential flaw, or consider whether you know of specific information that contradicts the argument.

Use the chart at right to anticipate common weaknesses in these types of arguments.

Type of Argument	Potential Flaw
Analogy: Compares one situation to another	Are the two situations really alike?
Authority: Cites the opinion of an expert	Is the expert knowledgeable and unbiased?
Emotion: Appeals to audience's feelings	Is the full argument balanced between logic and emotion?
Logic: Appeals to sense of rationalism	
Causation: Shows cause-and-effect relationship	Does the argument oversimplify?

Evaluate development of arguments. A good speech has a logical development and organization. Main points are introduced and developed with supporting evidence in the form of facts, statistics, anecdotes, charts, or graphs. In a conclusion, the speaker summarizes the main argument. The speaker might vary this organization slightly, but the structure should always be apparent to the audience.

Evaluate Delivery

Observe the speaker's choice of language. Speakers often include powerful language to make their speech more memorable and persuasive. As you listen, note instances where the speaker uses words or phrases with strong positive or negative *connotations,* or associations. Think about how the use of this language influences your own attitude toward the topic. Be alert to the fact that some speakers may rely on powerful or emotional language instead of reasoned arguments to advance their ideas.

Listen to the speaker's voice. Determine whether the speaker's voice is varied enough to hold an audience's attention and whether key points are emphasized. Also, think about whether the speaker's delivery creates a mood and tone that are appropriate to the subject.

Activity:
Analyzing a Speech Evaluate a famous speech, such as Martin Luther King's "I Have a Dream" speech, with your classmates. As a group, assess the argument for quality and generate a list of positive and negative qualities of that speech.

Assessment WORKSHOP

Connotation and Denotation

The reading sections of some tests require you to read a passage and answer multiple-choice questions about the meaning of a word or phrase. Use these strategies to help you distinguish between two different types of meaning:

- *Denotation* refers to the literal, or exact, meaning of a word. Denotations are characterized by a neutral, objective tone. For example, *thin* and *skinny* have similar denotations. They each describe a quality of depth or size.

- *Connotation* is the implied, or suggested, meaning of a word or phrase. A connotation can be positive or negative, depending on its context and each reader's past experience. For example, many people would say *thin* has a positive connotation but *skinny* has a negative one.

Test-Taking Strategies

- To determine a word's connotation, notice the reaction a word or phrase elicits from you.
- When searching for a denotation, look for a synonym that defines the word exactly, without placing it in a positive or negative light.

Sample Test Item

Directions: Read the passage, and then answer the question that follows.

Arlene Johnson's 1956 Cadillac convertible was a <u>battleship</u>. With its long silver body and huge chrome tail fins, this well-cared-for antique cruised through the streets of Coberton every morning with Arlene sitting proudly at the wheel. She was a petite woman, and even with the top down, the car swallowed her up.

1. What is the connotation of <u>battleship</u> in this passage?
   A large warship with guns and armor
   B large, powerful vehicle
   C compact, new vehicle
   D dilapidated, unsafe vehicle

Answer and Explanation

The correct answer is **B,** the implied meaning of *battleship*. **A** is a literal definition of battleship and is therefore a denotation that does not make sense in the context of the passage. **C** and **D** are incorrect because the passage indicates an older, larger vehicle that is well maintained.

▶ Practice

Directions: Read the passage, and then answer the questions that follow.

The Elmont High School Blazers struggled through their <u>worst</u> football season ever. Each week, they walked onto Elmont Field with the hope of victory and walked off with another loss. After four losses, with the stands nearly empty, the team still <u>strode</u> onto the field with pride.

1. What is the denotation of <u>worst</u> in this passage?
   A most embarrassing
   B most stunning
   C most difficult
   D most bad

2. What is the connotation of <u>strode</u> in this passage?
   A walked slowly and dejectedly
   B walked purposefully
   C raced at a quick pace
   D moved hesitantly

The Sheridan Theatre, 1937, Edward Hopper, Collection of the Newark Museum

Exploring the Genre

When you read a play, *you* are the director; *you* breathe life into the characters. As you read the works in this unit, notice the following elements, which can help bring the dramas to life in your mind:

- **Dialogue** In drama, much of what you learn about the characters, setting, and events is revealed through dialogue—conversations among the characters.

- **Stage Directions** These notes convey information to the cast, crew, and readers of the drama about sound effects, actions, sets, and line readings.

- **Characters** Dramatic characters are brought to life by their dialogue and actions onstage.

- **Plot** Most dramas contain a plot in which events unfold, develop to a climax, and are resolved.

- **Theme** A theme is the central message the playwright conveys to the audience.

▲ **Critical Viewing** Why do you think the painter chose to show a portion of this theater without showing the stage or actors? **[Infer]**

Why **Read Literature?**

A dramatic work can have multiple dimensions. You might explore one dimension while reading and then find something completely new after learning more about its history. Preview these examples that show how you can explore many sides of a single work of literature.

Read for the Love of Literature

No other author has been as widely read and admired as William Shakespeare. Discover Shakespeare for yourself as you read *Romeo and Juliet,* page 770.

Read for Information

It is one thing to imagine the action as you read *Romeo and Juliet,* but quite another to picture a performance in Shakespeare's time. Find out why the role of Juliet was always played by a young boy—along with other interesting facts—when you travel back to the stage of seventeenth-century England in **"The Shakespearean Theater,"** page 764.

One reason Shakespeare's plays have gained worldwide popularity is that they touch on so many aspects of the human experience. You may be amazed at just how adaptable his plays are when you read this unit's *Connections* feature, **"Shakespeare in Today's World,"** page 878.

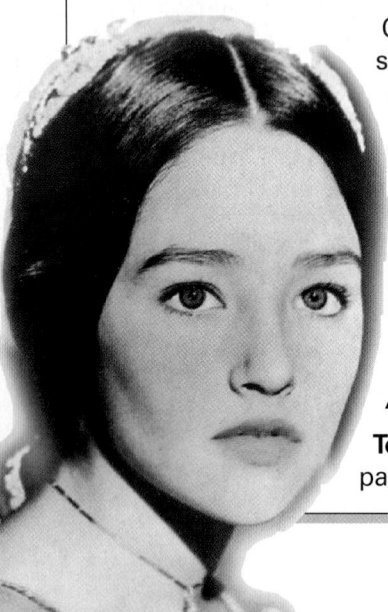

Read to Be Inspired

Shakespeare's story of two young lovers kept apart by a senseless feud still retains its power today. In 1993, when a young Serb man and his Muslim lover died in each other's arms during bitter ethnic warfare in Bosnia, they were instantly dubbed "Romeo and Juliet." As you read *Romeo and Juliet,* you will understand why this story continues to inspire comparison today.

 Take It to the Net

Visit the Web site for online instruction and activities related to each selection in this unit.
www.phschool.com

How to Read Literature

Use Strategies for Reading Drama

While drama shares many elements with prose, fiction, and poetry, the greatest difference is that dramas are designed to be performed on a stage before an audience. Since you will not have the benefit of a performance to help you interpret the text, use the following strategies when reading drama.

1. Picture the action.

- Use stage directions to form a mental image of the way characters move around on stage and interact with one another.

- Pay close attention to stage directions related to setting. For example, if the action takes place in a 1950s drugstore, it will have a much different feel than if it is set in a character's living room.

2. Use text aids.

Text aids are notes outside the main text that clarify the meaning of a word or phrase or add detailed information.

- Try not to let text aids interrupt the flow of your reading. If you come to an unfamiliar phrase, first try to figure it out from context.

- If you need to use a text aid, substitute the footnoted language directly into the original sentence, and then reread the new sentence with the surrounding text.

3. Read blank verse.

Blank verse is a poetic form that uses a regular meter to create a certain mood and rhythm. The author often uses blank verse to create a more formal atmosphere. To get used to the feel of blank verse, read passages aloud, stressing every second syllable. Read at a steady pace, and pause only when you see punctuation, as the model at right suggests.

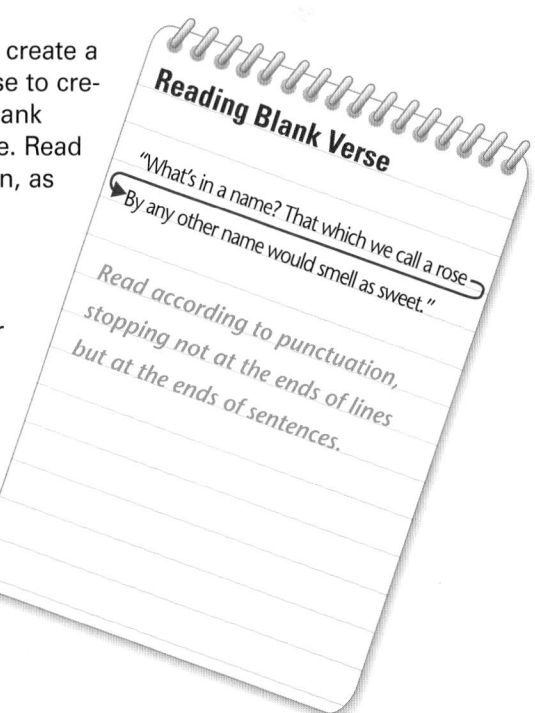

Reading Blank Verse

"What's in a name? That which we call a rose
By any other name would smell as sweet."

Read according to punctuation, stopping not at the ends of lines but at the ends of sentences.

4. Paraphrase.

Paraphrase, or summarize, a key idea or passage in your own words to ensure that you understand what you have read.

- Replace formal language with words that are more commonly used.

- When summarizing, eliminate ideas that are not essential to the meaning of the passage.

As you read the selections in this unit, review the reading strategies and apply them to strengthen your understanding of the text.

Prepare to Read

The Dancers

 **Take It to the Net**

Visit www.phschool.com for interactive activities and instruction related to "The Dancers," including

- background
- graphic organizers
- literary elements
- reading strategies

Preview

Connecting to the Literature

Like most people, you probably experience times when your social life does not go smoothly. You might go to a party and find that you do not know anyone, or mistakenly make plans with two different people for the same evening. As you read this play, notice how the characters respond to such awkward situations.

Background

In the 1950s, the setting for "The Dancers," people danced differently from the way they do now. Partners held each other, and their movements were synchronized and determined by the type of dance they were doing. It was not uncommon for children to take dance lessons in which they learned ballroom dances such as the waltz, the fox trot, and the cha-cha.

Literary Analysis

Staging

Staging is one of the ways in which a script is brought to life. It includes the sets, lighting, sound effects, costumes, and the way the actors move and deliver their lines. Staging is based on the stage directions, which are often bracketed and italicized. The staging excerpt below provides a brief description of the appearance and actions of one character, Emily, as she arrives on stage. In addition, it gives the time of day in which the scene takes place:

> [ELIZABETH CREWS *and her daughter* EMILY *come into the drugstore.* EMILY *is about seventeen and very pretty. This afternoon, however, it is evident that she is unhappy.*]

As you read the play, use the dialogue, stage directions, and your imagination to stage the play in your mind's eye.

Instruction with this selection addresses these standards:

R 1.2*, 3.4*, 3.10*
W 1.8
WOLC 1.2*, 1.3*
LS 1.7

* *Standards tested on HS Exit Exam. For complete standards, see p. CA 4.*

Connecting Literary Elements

A drama relies completely on staging and dialogue to tell a story. **Dialogue** is a conversation between characters. It is used to reveal the qualities and situations of the characters and to advance the action of the play. As you read, notice how the staging and dialogue work together to reveal the events of the play.

Reading Strategy

Picturing the Action

Plays are meant to be performed, so it is important to **picture the action** as you read. To picture the action, you should use these strategies:

- Read stage directions carefully and draw from your own experience to connect to the scene being set.
- Notice subtleties about characters' emotions, insecurities, or hopes.

Using a chart like the one on the right, note descriptions of characters and details of setting to help you picture the action.

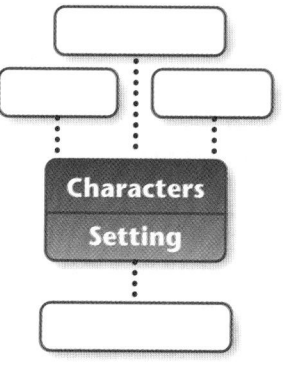

Vocabulary Development

genteel (jen tēl´) *adj.* polite (p. 741)

mortified (môrt´ ə fīd´) *v.* humiliated (p. 742)

defiance (dē fī´ əns) *n.* open resistance (p. 743)

console (kən sōl´) *v.* comfort (p. 751)

The

CHARACTERS

A **WAITRESS** in the local drugstore

INEZ STANLEY, Horace's older sister

ELIZABETH CREWS, Emily's mother

EMILY CREWS, a popular seventeen
    year old

HERMAN STANLEY, Inez's husband

HORACE, a sensitive eighteen year old

MARY CATHERINE DAVIS, a
    plainer girl of Emily's
    age

VELMA MORRISON, another
    young girl

TOM DAVIS, Mary Catherine's
    father

MRS. DAVIS, Mary Catherine's mother

SETTING

Harrison, Texas

Dancers

Horton Foote

[*Scene: The stage is divided into four acting areas: downstage left is the living room of* INEZ *and* HERMAN STANLEY. *Downstage right is part of a small-town drugstore. Upstage right is the living room of* ELIZABETH CREWS. *Upstage left, the yard and living room of* MARY CATHERINE DAVIS. *Since the action should flow continuously from one area to the other, only the barest amount of furnishings should be used to suggest what each area represents. The lights are brought up on the drugstore, downstage right.* WAITRESS *is there.* INEZ STANLEY *comes into the drugstore. She stands for a moment thinking. The* WAITRESS *goes over to her.*]

WAITRESS. Can I help you?

INEZ. Yes, you can if I can think of what I came in here for. Just gone completely out of my mind. I've been running around all day. You see, I'm expecting some company tonight. My brother Horace. He's coming on a visit.

[ELIZABETH CREWS *and her daughter* EMILY *come into the drugstore.* EMILY *is about seventeen and very pretty. This afternoon, however, it is evident that she is unhappy.*]

Hey . . .

ELIZABETH. We've just been by your house.

INEZ. You have? Hello, Emily.

EMILY. Hello.

ELIZABETH. We made some divinity[1] and took it over for Horace.

INEZ. Well, that's so sweet of you.

ELIZABETH. What time is he coming in?

INEZ. Six-thirty.

ELIZABETH. Are you meeting him?

INEZ. No—Herman. I've got to cook supper. Can I buy you all a drink?

ELIZABETH. No, we have to get Emily over to the beauty parlor.

INEZ. What are you wearing tonight, Emily?

ELIZABETH. She's wearing that sweet little net[2] I got her the end of last summer. She's never worn it to a dance here.

INEZ. I don't think I've ever seen it. I'll bet it looks beautiful on her. I'm gonna make Horace bring you by the house so I can see you before the dance.

WAITRESS. Excuse me. . . .

INEZ. Yes?

WAITRESS. Have you thought of what you wanted yet? I thought I could be getting it for you.

INEZ. That's sweet, honey . . . but I haven't thought of what I wanted yet. [*To* ELIZABETH *and* EMILY.] I feel so foolish, I came in here for something, and I can't remember what.

WAITRESS. Cosmetics?

INEZ. No . . . you go on. I'll think and call you.

WAITRESS. All right. [*She goes.*]

INEZ. Emily, I think it's so sweet of you to go to the dance with Horace. I know he's going to be thrilled when I tell him.

ELIZABETH. Well, you're thrilled too, aren't you, Emily?

EMILY. Yes, ma'm.

ELIZABETH. I told Emily she'd thank me some day for not permitting her to sit home and miss all the fun.

EMILY. Mama, it's five to four. My appointment is at four o'clock.

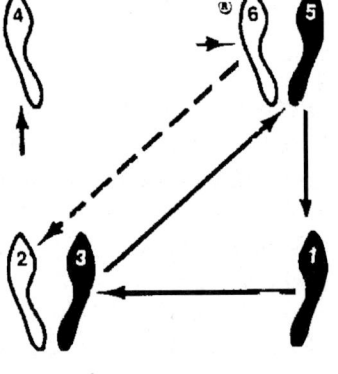

Reading Strategy
Picturing the Action
What kind of expression do you think Emily has on her face when she responds to her mother? Why?

---

1. **divinity** soft, creamy candy made of sugar, egg whites, corn syrup, flavoring, and nuts.
2. **sweet little net** dress made of delicate, lacy fabric.

ELIZABETH. Well, you go on in the car.

EMILY. How are you gonna get home?

ELIZABETH. I'll get home. Don't worry about me.

EMILY. OK. [*She starts out.*]

INEZ. 'Bye, Emily.

EMILY. 'Bye. [*She goes on out.*]

ELIZABETH. Does Horace have a car for tonight?

INEZ. Oh, yes. He's taking Herman's.

ELIZABETH. I just wondered. I wanted to offer ours if he didn't have one.

INEZ. That's very sweet—but we're giving him our car every night for the two weeks of his visit. Oh—I know what I'm after. Flowers. I have to order Emily's corsage for Horace. I came in here to use the telephone to call you to find out what color Emily's dress was going to be.

ELIZABETH. Blue.

INEZ. My favorite color. Walk me over to the florist.

ELIZABETH. All right.

[*They go out as the lights fade. The lights are brought up downstage left on the living room of* INEZ STANLEY. HERMAN STANLEY *and his brother-in-law,* HORACE, *come in.* HERMAN *is carrying* HORACE'S *suitcase.* HERMAN *is in his middle thirties.* HORACE *is eighteen, thin, sensitive, but a likable boy.*]

HERMAN. Inez. Inez. We're here.

[*He puts the bag down in the living room.* INEZ *comes running in from stage right.*]

INEZ. You're early.

HERMAN. The bus was five minutes ahead of time.

INEZ. Is that so? Why, I never heard of that. [*She kisses her brother.*] Hello, honey.

HORACE. Hello, sis.

INEZ. You look fine.

HORACE. Thank you.

INEZ. You haven't put on a bit of weight though.

HORACE. Haven't I?

INEZ. Not a bit. I'm just going to stuff food down you and put some weight on you while you're here. How's your appetite?

HORACE. Oh, it's real good. I eat all the time.

Reading Strategy
Picturing the Action
Picture in your mind how Emily looks as she starts to leave the drugstore. Is she in a hurry?

Literary Analysis
Staging What kind of staging do you think could be added to this dialogue between Horace and Inez?

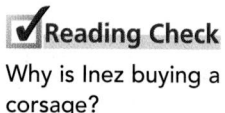**Reading Check**
Why is Inez buying a corsage?

The Dancers ◆ 737

INEZ. Then why don't you put on some weight?

HORACE. I don't know. I guess I'm just the skinny type.

INEZ. How are the folks?

HORACE. Fine.

INEZ. Mother over her cold?

HORACE. Yes, she is.

INEZ. Dad's fine?

HORACE. Just fine.

INEZ. Oh, Herman, did you ask him?

HERMAN. Ask him what?

INEZ. Ask him what? About his tux.

HERMAN. No, I didn't. . . .

INEZ. Honestly, Herman. Here we have him a date with the prettiest and most popular girl in Harrison and Herman says ask him what. You did bring it, didn't you, Bubber?

HORACE. Bring what?

INEZ. Your tux.

HORACE. Oh, sure.

INEZ. Well, guess who I've got you a date with. Aren't you curious?

HORACE. Uh. Huh.

INEZ. Well, guess. . . .

[*A pause. He thinks.*]

HORACE. I don't know.

INEZ. Well, just try guessing. . . .

HORACE. Well . . . uh . . . [*He is a little embarrassed. He stands trying to think. No names come to him.*] I don't know.

INEZ. Emily Crews. Now isn't she a pretty girl?

HORACE. Yes. She is.

INEZ. And the most popular girl in this town. You know her mother is a very close friend of mine and she called me day before yesterday and she said I hear Horace is coming to town and I said yes you were and she said that the boy Emily is going with is in summer school and couldn't get

away this week-end and Emily said she wouldn't go to the dance at all but her mother said that she had insisted and wondered if you'd take her. . . .

HORACE. Her mother said. Does Emily want me to take her?

INEZ. That isn't the point, Bubber. The point is that her mother doesn't approve of the boy Emily is in love with and she likes you . . .

HORACE. Who likes me?

INEZ. Emily's mother. And she thinks you would make a very nice couple.

HORACE. Oh. [*A pause.*] But what does Emily think?

INEZ. Emily doesn't know what to think, honey. I'm trying to explain that to you. She's in love.

HORACE. Where am I supposed to take her to?

INEZ. The dance.

HORACE. But, Inez, I don't dance well enough. . . . I don't like to go to dances . . . yet . . .

INEZ. Oh, Horace. Mother wrote me you were learning.

HORACE. Well . . . I am learning. But I don't dance well enough yet.

INEZ. Horace, you just make me sick. The trouble with you is that you have no confidence in yourself. I bet you can dance.

HORACE. No, I can't. . . .

INEZ. Now let's see. [INEZ *goes to the radio and turns it on. She comes back to him.*] Now, come on. Show me what you've learned. . . .

HORACE. Aw, Sis . . .

HERMAN. Inez. Why don't you let the boy alone?

INEZ. Now you keep out of this, Herman Stanley. He's my brother and he's a stick. He's missing all the fun in life and I'm not going to have him a stick. I've sat up nights thinking of social engagements to keep him busy every minute of these next two weeks—I've got three dances scheduled for him. So he cannot dance. Now come on, dance with me. . . . [*He takes her by the arm awkwardly. He begins to lead her around the room.*] Now, that's fine. That's just fine. Isn't that fine, Herman?

HERMAN. Uh. Huh.

INEZ. You see all you need is confidence. And I want you to promise me you'll talk plenty when you're with the girl, not just sit there in silence and only answer when you're asked a question. . . . Now promise me.

HORACE. I promise.

Reading Strategy
Picturing the Action How do you picture Horace's reaction to the news about Emily?

**Reading Check**

Why does Horace say he does not like to go to dances?

INEZ. Fine. Why, I think he dances real well. Don't you, Herman?

HERMAN. Yes, I do. Just fine, Inez.

INEZ. Just a lovely dancer, all he needs is confidence. He is very light on his feet. And he has a fine sense of rhythm—why, brother, you're a born dancer—

[HORACE *is smiling over the compliments, half wanting to believe what they say, but then not so sure. He is dancing with her around the room as the lights fade. They are brought up on the area upstage right.* EMILY CREWS *is in her living room. She has on her dressing gown.*[3] *She is crying.* ELIZABETH, *her mother, comes in from upstage right.*]

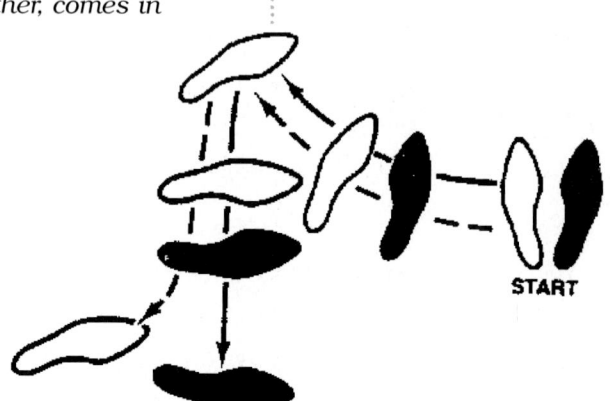

ELIZABETH. Emily.

EMILY. Yes, ma'm.

ELIZABETH. Do you know what time it is?

EMILY. Yes, ma'm.

ELIZABETH. Then why in the world aren't you dressed?

EMILY. Because I don't feel good.

ELIZABETH. Emily . . .

EMILY. I don't feel good . . . [*She begins to cry.*] Oh, Mother. I don't want to go to the dance tonight. Please, ma'm, don't make me. I'll do anything in this world for you if you promise me . . .

ELIZABETH. Emily. This is all settled. You are going to that dance. Do you understand me. You are going to that dance. That sweet, nice brother of Inez Stanley's will be here any minute. . . .

EMILY. Sweet, nice brother. He's a goon. That's what he is. A regular goon. A bore and a goon. . . .

ELIZABETH. Emily . . .

EMILY. That's all he is. Just sits and doesn't talk. Can't dance. I'm not going to any dance or any place else with him and that's final.

[*She runs out stage right.*]

ELIZABETH. Emily . . . Emily . . . You get ready this minute . . . [*The doorbell rings. Yelling.*] Emily . . . Emily . . . Horace is here. I want you down those stairs in five minutes . . . dressed.

[*She goes out stage left and comes back in followed by* HORACE, *all dressed up. He has a corsage box in his hand.*]

Hello, Horace.

---

3. **dressing gown** loose robe.

HORACE. Good evening.

ELIZABETH. Sit down, won't you, Horace? Emily is a little late getting dressed. You know how girls are.

HORACE. Yes, ma'm.

[*He sits down. He seems a little awkward and shy.*]

ELIZABETH. Can I get you something to drink, Horace?

HORACE. No, ma'm.

[*A pause.* ELIZABETH *is obviously very nervous about whether* EMILY *will behave or not.*]

ELIZABETH. Are you sure I can't get you a coca-cola or something?

HORACE. No. Thank you.

ELIZABETH. How's your family?

HORACE. Just fine, thank you.

ELIZABETH. I bet your sister was glad to see you.

HORACE. Yes, she was.

ELIZABETH. How's your family? Oh, I guess I asked you that, didn't I?

HORACE. Yes, you did.

[ELIZABETH *keeps glancing off stage right, praying that* EMILY *will put in an appearance.*]

ELIZABETH. I understand you've become quite an accomplished dancer. . . .

HORACE. Oh . . . well . . . I . . .

ELIZABETH. Inez tells me you do all the new steps.

HORACE. Well—I . . .

ELIZABETH. Excuse me. Let me see what is keeping that girl.

[*She goes running off stage right.* HORACE *gets up. He seems very nervous. He begins to practice his dancing. He seems more unsure of himself and awkward. . . . We can hear* ELIZABETH *offstage knocking on* EMILY'S *door. At first* HORACE *isn't conscious of the knocking or the ensuing conversation and goes on practicing his dancing. When he first becomes conscious of what's to follow he tries to pay no attention. Then gradually he moves over to the far left side of the stage. The first thing we hear is* ELIZABETH'S <u>genteel</u> *tapping at* EMILY'S *door. Then she begins to call, softly at first, then louder and louder.*]

Emily. Emily. Emily Crews. Emily Carter Crews. . . . [*The pounding offstage is getting louder and louder.*] Emily. I can hear you in there. Now open that door.

Literary Analysis
Staging and Dialogue
Does the dialogue effectively convey Elizabeth's nervousness mentioned in the stage directions? Explain.

Reading Strategy
Picturing the Action
Describe how you picture Horace's body language as he overhears the conversation going on offstage.

genteel (jen tēl') *adj.* polite

Reading Check

Why is Emily still in her dressing gown and crying when Horace arrives?

EMILY. [*Screaming back.*] I won't. I told you I won't.

ELIZABETH. Emily Carter Crews. You open that door immediately.

EMILY. I won't.

ELIZABETH. I'm calling your father from downtown if you don't open that door right this very minute.

EMILY. I don't care. I won't come out.

ELIZABETH. Then I'll call him. [*She comes running in from stage right.* HORACE *quickly gets back to his chair and sits.*] Excuse me, Horace.

> [*She crosses through the room and goes out upstage right.* HORACE *seems very ill at ease. He looks at the box of flowers. He is very warm. He begins to fan himself.* ELIZABETH *comes back in the room from upstage right. She is very nervous. But she tries to hide her nervousness in an overly social manner.* ELIZABETH *has decided to tell a fib.*]

Horace, I am so sorry to have to ruin your evening, but my little girl isn't feeling well. She has a headache and a slight temperature and I've just called the doctor and he says he thinks it's very advisable that she stay in this evening. She's upstairs insisting she go, but I do feel under the circumstances I had just better keep her in. I hope you understand.

HORACE. Oh, yes ma'm. I do understand.

ELIZABETH. How long do you plan to visit us, Horace?

HORACE. Two weeks.

ELIZABETH. That's nice. [*They start walking offstage left.*] Please call Emily tomorrow and ask her out again. She'll just be heartbroken if you don't.

HORACE. Yes, ma'm. Good night.

ELIZABETH. Good night, Horace. [HORACE *goes out.* ELIZABETH *calls out after him.*] Can you see, Horace? [*In the distance we hear* HORACE *answer.*]

HORACE. Yes, ma'm.

ELIZABETH. Now you be sure and call us tomorrow. You hear? [*She stands waiting for a moment. Then she walks back across stage to upstage right, screaming at the top of her voice.*] Emily Carter Crews. You have <u>mortified</u> me. You have mortified me to death. I have, for your information, called your father and he is interrupting his work and is coming home this very minute and he says to tell you that you are not to be allowed to leave this house again for two solid weeks. Is that perfectly clear?

> [*She is screaming as she goes out upstage right. The lights are brought down. They are brought up immediately downstage right on*

Reading Strategy
Picturing the Action
How do you picture the facial expressions of Horace and Elizabeth as she apologizes to him?

mortified (môrt′ ə fīd) *v.* humiliated

the drugstore. It is half an hour later. HORACE *comes in. He seats himself at the counter. He still has the box of flowers. The drugstore is deserted. A* WAITRESS *is up near the front with her arms on the counter. She keeps glancing at a clock.* HORACE *is examining a menu . . .]*

HORACE. Can I have a chicken salad sandwich?

WAITRESS. We're all out of that.

HORACE. Oh.

[*He goes back to reading the menu.*]

WAITRESS. If it's all the same to you, I'd rather not make a sandwich. I'm closing my doors in ten minutes.

HORACE. Oh. Well, what would you like to make?

WAITRESS. Any kind of ice cream or soft drinks. [*She looks up at the ice cream menu.*] Coffee is all gone.

HORACE. How about a chocolate ice cream soda?

WAITRESS. O.K. Coming up. [*She starts to mix the soda. She talks as she works.*] Going to the dance?

HORACE. No.

WAITRESS. The way you're all dressed up I thought for sure you were going.

HORACE. No. I was, but I changed my mind.

[MARY CATHERINE DAVIS *comes in the drugstore from downstage right. Somehow in her young head she has gotten the idea that she is a plain girl and in* <u>defiance</u> *for the pain of that fact she does everything she can to make herself look plainer.*]

WAITRESS. Hello, Mary Catherine. Been to the movies?

MARY CATHERINE. Yes, I have.

[*The* WAITRESS *puts the drink down in front of* HORACE. *He begins to drink.*]

WAITRESS. What'll you have, Mary Catherine?

MARY CATHERINE. Vanilla ice cream.

▲ **Critical Viewing**
What does this photograph reveal about life in the 1950s, the setting for "The Dancers"? **[Infer]**

defiance (dē fī´ əns) *n.* open resistance

✔**Reading Check**

What excuse does Elizabeth give for Emily's refusal to go to the dance?

The Dancers ◆ 743

WAITRESS. O.K. [*She gets the ice cream. She talks as she does so.*] There weren't many at the picture show tonight, I bet. I can always tell by whether we have a crowd in here or not after the first show. I guess everybody is at the dance.

MARY CATHERINE. I could have gone, but I didn't want to. I didn't want to miss the picture show. Emily Crews didn't go. Leo couldn't get home from summer school and she said she was refusing to go. Her mother made a date for her with some bore from out of town without consulting her and she was furious about it. I talked to her this afternoon. She said she didn't know yet how she would get out of it, but she would. She said she had some rights. Her mother doesn't approve of Leo and that's a shame because they are practically engaged.

WAITRESS. I think Emily is a very cute girl, don't you?

MARY CATHERINE. Oh, yes. I think she's darling.

[HORACE *has finished his drink and is embarrassed by their talk. He is trying to get the* WAITRESS's *attention but doesn't quite know how. He finally calls to the* WAITRESS.]

HORACE. Miss . . .

WAITRESS. Yes?

HORACE. How much do I owe you?

WAITRESS. Twenty cents.

HORACE. Thank you.

[*He reaches in his pocket for the money.*]

WAITRESS. Emily has beautiful clothes, doesn't she?

MARY CATHERINE. Oh, yes. She does.

WAITRESS. Her folks are rich?

MARY CATHERINE. She has the prettiest things. But she's not a bit stuck up. . . .

[*He holds the money out to the* WAITRESS.]

HORACE. Here you are.

WAITRESS. Thank you. [*She takes the money and rings it up in the cash register.* HORACE *goes on out.* WAITRESS *shakes her head as he goes.*] There's a goofy nut if I ever saw one. He's got flowers under his arm. He's wearing a tux and yet he's not going to the dance. Who is he?

MARY CATHERINE. I don't know. I never saw him before.

[*The* WAITRESS *walks to the edge of the area and looks out. She comes back shaking her head. She sits on the stool beside* MARY CATHERINE.]

Literary Analysis
Staging What do you think Horace is doing in this scene to get the waitress's attention?

Reading Strategy
Picturing the Action How do you picture Horace, based on the waitress's description?

WAITRESS. [*While laughing and shaking her head.*] I ought to call the Sheriff and have him locked up. Do you know what he's doing?

MARY CATHERINE. No. What?

WAITRESS. Standing on the corner. Dancing back and forth. He's holding his arm up like he's got a girl and everything. Wouldn't it kill you? [*Goes to the front and looks out.*] See him?

MARY CATHERINE. No. He's stopped.

WAITRESS. What's he doing?

MARY CATHERINE. Just standing there. Looking kind of lost.

[MARY CATHERINE *comes back to the counter. She starts eating her ice cream again.*]

WAITRESS. Well—it takes all kinds.

MARY CATHERINE. I guess so.

[*She goes back to eating her ice cream. The lights are brought down. The lights are brought up on the area downstage left. The living room of the* STANLEYS. INEZ *is there reading a book.* HERMAN *comes in.*]

HERMAN. Hi, hon.

INEZ. Hello. . . .

HERMAN. What's the matter with you? You look down in the dumps.

INEZ. No, I'm just disgusted.

HERMAN. What are you disgusted about?

INEZ. Horace. I had everything planned so beautifully for him and then that silly Emily has to go and hurt his feelings.

HERMAN. Well, honey, that was pretty raw, the trick she pulled.

INEZ. I know. But he's a fool to let that get him down. He should have just gone to the dance by himself and proved her wrong. . . . Why like I told him. Show her up. Rush a different girl every night. Be charming. Make yourself popular. But it's like trying to talk to a stone wall. He refused to go out any more. He says he's going home tomorrow.

HERMAN. Where is he now?

INEZ. Gone to the movies.

HERMAN. Well, honey. I hate to say it, but in a way it serves you right. I've told you a thousand times if I've told you once. Leave the boy alone. He'll be all right. Only don't push him. You and your mother have pushed the boy and pushed him and pushed him.

INEZ. And I'm going to keep on pushing him. I let him off tonight

Literary Analysis

Staging Would additional stage directions convey a clearer image of Horace, or is the dialogue sufficient? Explain.

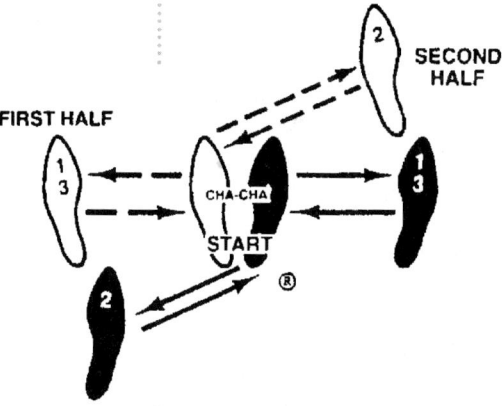

✔**Reading Check**

Why is Inez disgusted?

The Dancers ◆ 745

because his feelings were hurt, but tomorrow I'm going to have a long talk with him.

HERMAN. Inez. Leave the boy alone.

INEZ. I won't leave him alone. He is my brother and I'm going to see that he learns to have a good time.

HERMAN. Inez . . .

INEZ. Now you just let me handle this, Herman. He's starting to college next year and it's a most important time in his life. He had no fun in high school . . .

HERMAN. Now. He must have had some fun. . . .

INEZ. Not like other people. And he's not going through four years of college like a hermit with his nose stuck in some old book . . . [*She jumps up.*] I'll never forgive Elizabeth for letting Emily behave this way. And I told her so. I said Elizabeth Crews. I am very upset . . .

[*She is angrily walking up and down as the lights fade. They are brought up downstage right on the drugstore area. The* WAITRESS *is there alone.* MARY CATHERINE *comes in from downstage right.*]

WAITRESS. Did you go to the movies again tonight?

MARY CATHERINE. Uh-huh. Lila, do you remember when I was telling you about Emily's date and how she wouldn't go out with him because he was such a bore?

WAITRESS. Uh . . .

MARY CATHERINE. Oh, I just feel awful. That was the boy sitting in here . . .

WAITRESS. Last night . . . ?

MARY CATHERINE. Yes. I went riding with Emily and some of the girls this afternoon and we passed by his sister's house and there sat the boy.

WAITRESS. Sh . . . sh . . . [*She has seen* HORACE *come in to the area from downstage right. He comes to the counter. He seems very silent. He picks up a menu.*] Back again tonight?

HORACE. Uh-huh.

WAITRESS. What'll you have?

HORACE. A cup of coffee. . . .

WAITRESS. All out. We don't serve coffee after eight unless we happen to have some left over from supper time. . . .

HORACE. Thanks. [*He gets up.*]

WAITRESS. Nothing else?

Literary Analysis
Staging and Dialogue
Which traits of Inez are revealed through the dialogue?

Reading Strategy
Picturing the Action How do you picture Mary Catherine as she explains the situation with Emily's date to the waitress?

◀ **Critical Viewing**
Why do you think several scenes in "The Dancers" take place in the drugstore? **[Hypothesize]**

HORACE. No, thanks.

[*He goes over to the magazine rack. He picks up a magazine and starts looking through it.* EMILY CREWS *comes in from downstage right. She doesn't see* HORACE. *She goes right over to* MARY CATHERINE.]

EMILY. Leora and I were riding around the square and we saw you sitting here . . .

[MARY CATHERINE *points to* HORACE. *She turns around and sees him.* EMILY *looks a little embarrassed. He happens to glance up and sees her.*]

HORACE. Hello, Emily.

✓ **Reading Check**

What does Mary Catherine realize about Horace?

The Dancers ◆ 747

EMILY. Hello, Horace. . . . Do you know Mary Catherine Davis?

HORACE. No. How do you do.

MARY CATHERINE. How do you do.

EMILY. I feel awfully bad about last night, Horace. My mother says that you know I wasn't really sick. I just wanted to tell you that it had nothing to do with you, Horace. It was a battle between me and my mother. Mary Catherine can tell you. I promised the boy I go with not to go with any other boys . . .

HORACE. Oh, that's all right, I understand.

EMILY. You see, we've gone steady for two years. All the other boys in town understand it and their feelings are not a bit hurt if I turn them down. Are they, Mary Catherine?

MARY CATHERINE. No.

EMILY. Mary Catherine is my best friend and she can tell you I'm not stuck up. And I would have gone, anyway, except I was so mad at my mother . . .

MARY CATHERINE. Emily is not stuck up a bit. Emily used to date all the boys before she began going with Leo steadily. . . . Didn't you, Emily?

EMILY. Uh-huh. How long are you going to be here, Horace?

HORACE. Well, I haven't decided, Emily.

EMILY. Well, I hope you're not still hurt with me.

HORACE. No, I'm not, Emily.

EMILY. Well, I'm glad for that. Mary Catherine, can you come with us?

MARY CATHERINE. No, I can't, Emily. Velma came in after the first show started and I promised to wait here for her and we'd walk home together.

EMILY. Come on. We can ride around and watch for her.

MARY CATHERINE. No. I don't dare. You know how sensitive Velma is. If she looked in here and saw I wasn't sitting at this counter she'd go right home and not speak to me again for two or three months.

EMILY. Velma's too sensitive. You shouldn't indulge her in it.

MARY CATHERINE. I'm willing to grant you that. But you all are going off to college next year and Velma and I are the only ones that are going to be left here and I can't afford to get her mad at me.

EMILY. O.K. I'll watch out for you and if we're still riding around when Velma gets out, we'll pick you up.

MARY CATHERINE. Fine. . . .

EMILY. 'Bye. . . .

Literary Analysis
Staging and Dialogue
Would staging enhance the dialogue in this scene? Explain.

Reading Strategy
Picturing the Action How do you picture Horace as Emily apologizes to him?

MARY CATHERINE. 'Bye. . . .

EMILY. 'Bye, Horace.

HORACE. Good-bye, Emily.

[*She goes out downstage right.*]

MARY CATHERINE. She's a lovely girl. She was my closest friend until this year. Now we're still good friends, but we're not as close as we were. We had a long talk about it last week. I told her I understood. She and Eloise Dayton just naturally have a little more in common now. They're both going steady and they're going to the same college. [*A pause.*] They're going to Sophie Newcomb.[4] Are you going to college?

HORACE. Uh-huh.

MARY CATHERINE. You are? What college?

HORACE. The University. . . .

MARY CATHERINE. Oh. I know lots of people there. [*A pause.*] I had a long talk with Emily about my not getting to go. She said she thought it was wonderful that I wasn't showing any bitterness about it. [*A pause.*] I'm getting a job next week so I can save up enough money to go into Houston to Business School. I'll probably work in Houston some day. If I don't get too lonely. Velma Morrison's oldest sister went into Houston and got herself a job but she almost died from loneliness. She's back here now working at the Court House. Oh, well . . . I don't think I'll get lonely. I think a change of scenery would be good for me.

[VELMA MORRISON *comes in downstage right. She is about the same age as* MARY CATHERINE. *She is filled with excitement.*]

VELMA. Mary Catherine, you're going to be furious with me. But Stanley Sewell came in right after you left and he said he'd never forgive me if I didn't go riding with him. . . . I said I had to ask you first. As I had asked you to wait particularly for me and that I knew you were very sensitive.

MARY CATHERINE. I'm very sensitive. You're very sensitive. . . . I have never in my life stopped speaking to you over anything.

---

4. **Sophie Newcomb** H. Sophie Newcomb College for Women in New Orleans, Louisiana.

Literature in context Cultural Connection

The 1950s Drugstore

Many of the scenes in "The Dancers" are set in a drugstore. In addition to selling medicine, soap, and other necessities, the drugstore of the 1950s offered people a place to hear local gossip and get something to eat at the soda fountain. Few drugstores today have soda fountains that sell ice cream cones and sundaes.

Back in the 1950s, you could sit at the counter and have a small sandwich and a soda while you listened to the jukebox. Many owners expanded their stores by adding booths and tables and by extending the menu to include hot dogs, hamburgers, and French fries. Many booths had their own "private" jukeboxes, on which couples could play their favorite songs. Horton Foote's play captures just this type of shop.

Reading Check

Why does Mary Catherine want to wait for Velma?

[*A car horn is heard off stage.*]

VELMA. Will you forgive me if I go?

MARY CATHERINE. Oh, sure.

[VELMA *goes running out.*]

VELMA. Thank you.

[*She disappears out the door.*]

MARY CATHERINE. I'm not nearly as close to Velma as I am to Emily. I think Emily's beautiful, don't you?

HORACE. Yes. She's very pretty.

MARY CATHERINE. Well, Lila's going to kill us if we don't stop holding her up. Which way do you go?

HORACE. Home.

MARY CATHERINE. I go that way, too. We can walk together.

HORACE. O.K. [*They go out of the area.*]

MARY CATHERINE. Good night, Lila.

WAITRESS. Good night.

[*They continue walking out downstage left as the lights fade. The lights are brought up on the living room of the* CREWS' *house.* ELIZABETH CREWS *is there, crying.* EMILY *comes in.*]

EMILY. Mother, what is it? Has something happened to Daddy?

ELIZABETH. No. He's in bed asleep.

EMILY. Then what is it?

ELIZABETH. Inez blessed me out and stopped speaking to me over last night. She says we've ruined the boy's whole vacation. You've broken his heart, given him all kinds of complexes and he's going home tomorrow. . . .

▼ **Critical Viewing** The characters in "The Dancers" probably danced to music played on a record player like the one in this picture. How does this equipment compare to modern-day music players? [**Compare and Contrast**]

EMILY. But I saw him at the drugstore tonight and I had a long talk with him and he said he understood . . .

ELIZABETH. But Inez doesn't understand. She says she'll never forgive either of us again.

[*She starts to cry.*]

EMILY. Oh, Mother. I'm sorry . . .

ELIZABETH. Emily, if you'll do me one favor. I promise you I'll never ask another thing of you again as long as I live. And I will never nag you about going out with Leo again as long as I live. . . .

EMILY. What is the favor, Mother?

ELIZABETH. Let that boy take you to the dance day after tomorrow. . . .

EMILY. Now, Mother . . .

ELIZABETH. Emily. I get down on my knees to you. Do me this one favor . . . [*A pause.*] Emily . . . Emily . . . [*She is crying again.*]

EMILY. Now, Mother, please. Don't cry. I'll think about it. I'll call Leo and see what he says. But please don't cry like this. . . . Mother . . . Mother.

[*She is trying to <u>console</u> her as the lights fade. The lights are brought up on upstage left. It is* MARY CATHERINE'*s yard and living room. Music can be heard in the distance.* HORACE *and* MARY CATHERINE *come walking in downstage left, go up the center of the stage until they reach the upstage area.*]

MARY CATHERINE. Well, this is where I live.

HORACE. In that house there?

MARY CATHERINE. Uh-huh. [*A pause.*]

HORACE. Where is that music coming from?

MARY CATHERINE. The Flats. . . .

HORACE. What's the Flats?

MARY CATHERINE. I don't know what it is. That's just what they call it. It's nothing but a bunch of barbecue restaurants and beer joints down there and they call it the Flats. There used to be a creek running down there that they called Willow Creek but it's all dry now. My father says when he was a boy, every time the river flooded, Willow Creek would fill up. The river doesn't overflow any more since they took the raft[5] out of it. I like to come out here at night and listen to the music. Do you like to dance . . . ?

HORACE. Well . . . I . . .

---

5. **raft** natural dam formed by debris, leaves, and trees.

Literary Analysis
Staging What role do sound effects play in these staging directions?

console (kən sōl') *v.* comfort

**Reading Check**

What favor does Elizabeth ask of Emily?

MARY CATHERINE. I love to dance.

HORACE. Well . . . I don't dance too well.

MARY CATHERINE. There's nothing to it but confidence.

HORACE. That's what my sister says . . .

MARY CATHERINE. I didn't learn for the longest kind of time for lack of confidence and then Emily gave me a long lecture about it and I got confidence and went ahead and learned. Would you like to come in for a while?

HORACE. Well . . . if it's all right with you. . . .

MARY CATHERINE. I'd be glad to have you.

HORACE. Thank you.

[*They go into the area.* MARY CATHERINE's *father,* TOM DAVIS, *is seated there in his undershirt. He works in a garage.*]

MARY CATHERINE. Hello, Daddy.

TOM. Hello, baby.

MARY CATHERINE. Daddy, this is Horace.

TOM. Hello, son.

HORACE. Howdy do, sir.

[*They shake hands.*]

MARY CATHERINE. Horace is Mrs. Inez Stanley's brother. He's here on a visit.

TOM. That's nice. Where's your home, son?

HORACE. Flatonia.

TOM. Oh, I see. Well, are you young people going to visit for a while?

MARY CATHERINE. Yes, sir.

TOM. Well, I'll leave you then. Good night.

MARY CATHERINE. Good night, Daddy.

HORACE. Good night, sir. [*He goes out upstage left.*] What does your father do?

MARY CATHERINE. He works in a garage. He's a mechanic. What does your father do?

HORACE. He's a judge.

MARY CATHERINE. My father worries so because he can't afford to send me to college. My mother told him that was all foolishness. That I'd rather go to business school anyway.

HORACE. Had you rather go to business school?

Reading Strategy
Picturing the Action Do the staging directions or the dialogue provide a clearer image of Mary Catherine's dad? Explain.

Literary Analysis
Staging If you could add a description of the set at this point, what would it be?

MARY CATHERINE. I don't know. [*A pause.*] Not really. But I'd never tell him that. When I was in the seventh grade I thought I would die if I couldn't get there, but then when I was in the ninth, Mother talked to me one day and told me Daddy wasn't sleeping at nights for fear I'd be disappointed if he couldn't send me, so I told him the next night I decided I'd rather go to business school. He seemed relieved. [*A pause.*]

HORACE. Mary Catherine. I . . . uh . . . heard you say a while ago that you didn't dance because you lacked confidence and uh . . . then I heard you say you talked it over with Emily and she told you what was wrong and you got the confidence and you went ahead . . .

MARY CATHERINE. That's right. . . .

HORACE. Well . . . It may sound silly and all to you . . . seeing I'm about to start my first year at college . . . but I'd like to ask you a question. . . .

MARY CATHERINE. What is it, Horace?

HORACE. How do you get confidence?

MARY CATHERINE. Well, you just get it. Someone points it out to you that you lack it and then you get it. . . .

HORACE. Oh, is that how it's done?

MARY CATHERINE. That's how I did it.

HORACE. You see I lack confidence. And I . . . sure would like to get it. . . .

MARY CATHERINE. In what way do you lack confidence, Horace? . . .

HORACE. Oh, in all kinds of ways. [*A pause.*] I'm not much of a mixer[6]. . . .

MARY CATHERINE. I think you're just mixing fine tonight.

HORACE. I know. That's what's giving me a little encouragement. You're the first girl I've ever really been able to talk to. I mean this way. . . .

MARY CATHERINE. Am I, Horace . . . ?

HORACE. Yes.

MARY CATHERINE. Well, I feel in some ways that's quite a compliment.

HORACE. Well, you should feel that way. [*A pause.*] Mary Catherine . . .

MARY CATHERINE. Yes, Horace?

HORACE. I had about decided to go back home tomorrow or the next day, but I understand there's another dance at the end of the week . . .

MARY CATHERINE. Uh-huh. Day after tomorrow.

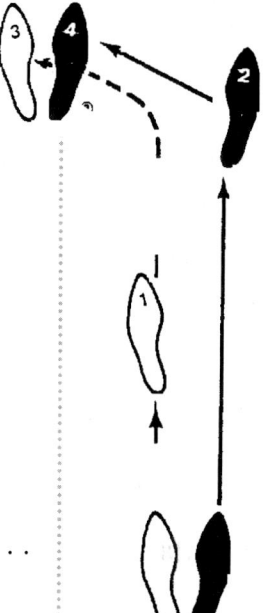

START

6. **a mixer** someone who socializes easily.

Reading Check

What does Horace say he lacks?

HORACE. Well . . . I . . . don't know if you have a date or not . . . but if you don't have . . . I feel if I could take you . . . I would gain the confidence to go . . . I mean . . .

MARY CATHERINE. Well, Horace . . . You see . . .

HORACE. I know I'd gain the confidence. My sister is a swell dancer and she'll let me practice with her every living minute until it's time for the dance. Of course I don't know if I could learn to jitterbug by then or rumba or do anything fancy, you understand, but I know I could learn the fox trot and I can waltz a little now . . .

MARY CATHERINE. I'm sure you could.

HORACE. Well, will you go with me?

MARY CATHERINE. Yes, Horace. I'd love to. . . .

HORACE. Oh, thank you, Mary Catherine. I'll just practice night and day. I can't tell you how grateful Inez is going to be to you. . . . Mary Catherine, if we played the radio softly could we dance now?

MARY CATHERINE. Why certainly, Horace.

HORACE. You understand I'll make mistakes. . . .

MARY CATHERINE. I understand. . . .

[*She turns the radio on very softly.*]

HORACE. All right.

MARY CATHERINE. Yes. . . .

[*He approaches her very cautiously and takes her in his arms. He begins awkwardly to dance.* MARY CATHERINE *is very pleased and happy.*]

Why, you're doing fine, Horace. Just fine.

HORACE. Thank you, Mary Catherine. Thank you.

[*They continue dancing.* HORACE *is very pleased with himself although he is still dancing quite awkwardly. The lights fade. The lights are brought up on the area downstage left. It is early next morning.* INEZ *is there reading.* HORACE *comes in whistling. He seems brimming over with happiness.*]

INEZ. What are you so happy about?

HORACE. I'm just happy.

INEZ. Wait until you hear my news and you'll be happier.

HORACE. Is that so?

INEZ. Miss Emily has seen the light.

HORACE. What?

INEZ. She has succumbed.

► **Critical Viewing** Do you think Horace would have a better time at a dance like the one shown here if he were with Mary Catherine or with Emily? Why? **[Speculate]**

**Literary Analysis
Staging** What role does lighting play in these stage directions?

HORACE. What do you mean?

INEZ. She has crawled on her knees.

HORACE. She's crawled on her knees? I don't get it. . . .

INEZ. She has eaten dirt.

HORACE. Sister, what's this all about?

INEZ. Last night around ten o'clock she called in the meekest kind of voice possible and said, Inez, I've called up to apologize to you. I have apologized to Horace in the drugstore. Did she?

HORACE. Uh. Huh.

INEZ. And now I want to apologize to you and to tell you how sorry I am I behaved so badly. . . .

HORACE. Well. Isn't that nice of her, Inez?

INEZ. Wait a minute. You haven't heard the whole thing. And then her highness added, tell Horace if he would like to invite me to the dance to call me and I'd be glad to accept. And furthermore, Elizabeth called this morning and said they were leaving for Houston to buy her the most expensive evening dress in sight. Just to impress you with.

HORACE. Oh . . . [*He sits down on a chair.*]

INEZ. Brother. What is the matter with you? Now are you gonna start worrying about this dancin' business all over again? You are the biggest fool sometimes. We've got today and tomorrow to practice.

HORACE. Inez . . .

INEZ. Yes?

HORACE. I already have a date with someone tomorrow. . . .

INEZ. You do?

HORACE. Yes. I met a girl last night at the drugstore and I asked her.

INEZ. What girl did you ask?

HORACE. Mary Catherine Davis. . . .

INEZ. Well, you've got to get right out of it. You've got to call her up and explain just what happened.

HORACE. But, Inez . . .

INEZ. You've got to do it, Horace. They told me they are spending all kinds of money for that dress. I practically had to threaten Elizabeth with never speaking to her again to bring this all about. Why, she will never forgive me now if I turn around and tell her you can't go. . . . Horace. Don't look that way. I can't help it. For my sake, for your sister's sake you've got to get out of this date with Mary Catherine Davis . . . tell her . . . tell her . . . anything . . .

HORACE. O.K. [*A pause. He starts out.*] What can I say?

INEZ. I don't know, Horace. [*A pause.*] Say . . . well just tell her the truth. That's the best thing. Tell her that Emily's mother is your sister's best friend and that Emily's mother has taken her into Houston to buy her a very expensive dress . . .

HORACE. What if Mary Catherine has bought a dress . . .

INEZ. Well, she can't have bought an expensive dress. . . .

HORACE. Why not?

INEZ. Because her people can't afford it. Honey, you'll be the envy of every young man in Harrison, bringing Emily Crews to the dance. . . . Why, everybody will wonder just what it is you have . . .

HORACE. I'm not going to do it.

INEZ. Horace . . .

HORACE. I don't want to take Emily, I want to take Mary Catherine and that's just what I'm going to do.

INEZ. Horace . . .

HORACE. My mind is made up. Once and for all. . . .

INEZ. Then what am I gonna do? [*She starts to cry.*] Who's gonna speak to Elizabeth? She'll bless me out putting her to all this trouble. Making her spend all this money and time . . . [*She is crying loudly now.*] Horace. You just can't do this to me. You just simply can't. . . .

HORACE. I can't help it. I'm not taking Emily Crews—

INEZ. Horace . . .

HORACE. I am not taking Emily Crews.

> [*He is firm. She is crying as the lights fade. The lights are brought up on the upstage left area.* MARY CATHERINE'*s father is seated there. He is in his undershirt. In the distance dance music can be heard.* MRS. DAVIS *comes in from stage left.*]

MRS. DAVIS. Don't you think you'd better put your shirt on, Tom? Mary Catherine's date will be here any minute.

TOM. What time is it?

MRS. DAVIS. Nine o'clock.

TOM. The dance has already started. I can hear the music from here.

MRS. DAVIS. I know. But you know young people, they'd die before they'd be the first to a dance. Put your shirt on, Tom.

TOM. O.K.

Literary Analysis
Staging What does "a pause" convey about Horace's feelings?

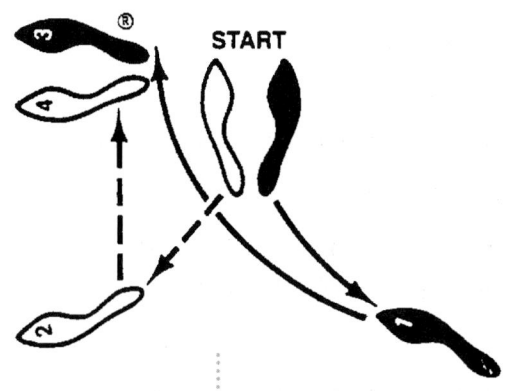

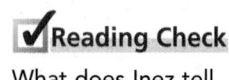**Reading Check**

What does Inez tell Horace about Emily?

MRS. DAVIS. As soon as her date arrives we'll go.

TOM. O.K.

[MARY CATHERINE *comes in from stage left. She has on an evening dress and she looks very pretty.*]

MRS. DAVIS. Why, Mary Catherine. You look lovely. Doesn't she look lovely, Tom?

TOM. Yes, she does.

MRS. DAVIS. Turn around, honey, and let me see you from the back. [*She does so.*] Just as pretty as you can be, Mary Catherine.

MARY CATHERINE. Thank you.

[HORACE *comes in downstage left in his tux with a corsage box. He walks up the center of the stage to the upstage left area.*]

That's Horace. [*She goes to the corner of the area.*] Hello, Horace.

HORACE. Hello, Mary Catherine.

MARY CATHERINE. You've met my mother and father.

HORACE. Yes. I have. I met your father the other night and your mother yesterday afternoon.

MRS. DAVIS. Hello, Horace.

TOM. Hello, son.

MRS. DAVIS. Well, we were just going. You all have a good time tonight.

HORACE. Thank you.

MRS. DAVIS. Come on, Tom.

TOM. All right. Good night and have a nice time.

MARY CATHERINE. Thank you, Daddy. [*They go out stage left.* HORACE *hands her the corsage box. She takes it and opens it.*] Oh, thank you, Horace. Thank you so much. [*She takes the flowers out.*] They're just lovely. Will you pin them on for me?

HORACE. I'll try. [*He takes the corsage and the pin. He begins to pin it on.*] Will about here be all right?

MARY CATHERINE. Just fine. [*He pins the corsage on.*] Emily told me about the mix-up between your sister and her mother. I appreciate your going ahead and taking me anyway. If you had wanted to get out of it I would have understood. Emily and I are very good friends . . . and . . .

Reading Strategy
Picturing the Action
How do you picture the expressions on both characters' faces at this point? Why?

HORACE. I didn't want to get out of it, Mary Catherine. I wanted to take you.

MARY CATHERINE. I'm glad you didn't want to get out of it. Emily offered to let me wear her new dress. But I had already bought one of my own.

HORACE. It's very pretty, Mary Catherine.

MARY CATHERINE. Thank you. [*A pause.*] Well, the dance has started. I can hear the music. Can't you?

HORACE. Yes.

MARY CATHERINE. Well, we'd better get going. . . .

HORACE. All right. [*They start out.*] Mary Catherine. I hope you don't think this is silly, but could we practice just once more . . .

MARY CATHERINE. Certainly we could. . . .

[*They start to dance.* HORACE *has improved although he is no Fred Astaire. They are dancing around and suddenly* HORACE *breaks away.*]

HORACE. Mary Catherine. I'm not good enough yet. I can't go. I'm sorry. Please let's just stay here.

MARY CATHERINE. No, Horace. We have to go.

HORACE. Please, Mary Catherine . . .

MARY CATHERINE. I know just how you feel, Horace, but we have to go. [*A pause.*] I haven't told you the whole truth, Horace. This is my first dance, too. . . .

HORACE. It is?

MARY CATHERINE. Yes. I've been afraid to go. Afraid I wouldn't be popular. The last two dances I was asked to go and I said no.

HORACE. Then why did you accept when I asked you?

MARY CATHERINE. I don't know. I asked myself that afterwards. I guess

✓**Reading Check**

What does Horace want to do once more before the dance?

The Dancers ◆ 759

because you gave me a kind of confidence. [*A pause. They dance again.*] You gave me confidence and I gave you confidence. What's the sense of getting confidence, Horace, if you're not going to use it?

[*A pause. They continue dancing.*]

HORACE. That's a pretty piece.

MARY CATHERINE. Yes, it is.

[*A pause. They dance again.* HORACE *stops.*]

HORACE. I'm ready to go if you are, Mary Catherine.

MARY CATHERINE. I'm ready. [*They start out.*] Scared?

HORACE. A little.

MARY CATHERINE. So am I. But let's go.

HORACE. O.K.

[*They continue out the area down the center of the stage and off downstage right as the music from the dance is heard.*]

Horton Foote

(b. 1916)

Born in Wharton, Texas, Horton Foote left his hometown after high school to attend acting school. While studying in New York, he formed friendships with several fellow actors; together, they formed an off-Broadway theater company. He began writing plays, and since then, writing has been the focus of his career.

During the 1950s and early 1960s, television's "golden age," Foote wrote scripts for live television. One of his first teleplays, *The Trip to Bountiful,* was later made into an award-winning film. Many of Foote's plays are set in the fictional town of Harrison, Texas, based on his hometown and the people he has known.

He says that his plays are often concerned "with defining what home is and where home is and how we get to home." Recurring themes include human shortcomings, family issues, and relationships between generations.

Review and Assess

Thinking About the Selection

1. **Respond:** Do you admire Horace? Why or why not?

2. **(a) Recall:** Why is Inez determined to set up Horace with Emily? **(b) Recall:** Why is Elizabeth determined to set up Emily with Horace? **(c) Compare and Contrast:** Which qualities do Elizabeth and Inez seem to have in common?

3. **(a) Recall:** Why does Emily refuse to go to the dance with Horace? **(b) Make a Judgment:** Do you think Emily's behavior is justified? Explain.

4. **(a) Recall:** What does Emily tell Horace the next day about why she did not go to the dance? **(b) Analyze:** What does this action tell you about Emily's character?

5. **(a) Recall:** How does Horace meet Mary Catherine? **(b) Infer:** In what ways are Horace and Mary Catherine well suited to be friends? **(c) Analyze:** After asking Mary Catherine to the dance, how does Horace demonstrate that he is a sensitive and considerate person?

6. **Speculate:** Do you think the adults or the teenagers acted more maturely in this play?

7. **(a) Extend:** Identify one insight about human relationships that you gained from this play. **(b) Apply:** How can this insight be applied to your own life?

Review and Assess

Literary Analysis

Staging

1. (a) Using a chart like the one below, select two examples of stage directions in "The Dancers" that leave most of the specifics up to the imagination. (b) How might you add to the **staging** you have listed to better explain the place, action, or event described in your examples? (c) Why might the author have left staging vague?

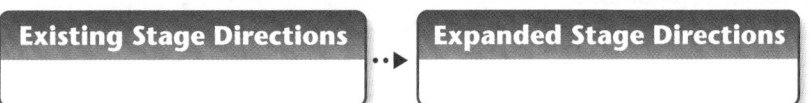

2. (a) What kind of lighting would be most effective in the drugstore scenes? (b) What kind of lighting would be most effective when Horace is dancing with Mary Catherine? Why?

Connecting Literary Elements

3. Using a chart like the one below, explain which **dialogue** in the play reveals the most about each character.

Character	Dialogue		Reveals

4. Give two examples of staging directions that enhance the dialogue and provide a clearer image of a character or situation. Explain your answer.

Reading Strategy

Picturing the Action

5. In the opening scene, you learn that Emily is unhappy. How might Emily's face, posture, and actions show this?

6. **Picture** the scene in which Mary Catherine tells the waitress about the date Emily Crews wanted to break. (a) How do you think Horace might act as he sits at the counter? (b) What do you think the waitress might do as she listens?

Extend Understanding

7. **Drama Connection:** The characters spend most of their time in a drugstore. If you were to update this play, where might you set it to reflect today's trends? Why?

Quick Review

Staging is one of the ways a script is brought to life. It includes descriptions of the sets, lighting, sound effects, costumes, and directions about the way the actors should move and deliver their lines.

Dialogue is a conversation between characters that reveals the qualities and situations of the characters and advances the action of the play.

To **picture the action** in a play, read descriptions carefully, and draw from your own experience to see characters and actions in your mind's eye.

 Take It to the Net
www.phschool.com

Take the interactive self-test online to check your understanding of the selection.

Integrate Language Skills

Vocabulary Development Lesson

Concept Development: Homographs

In "The Dancers," Emily tries to console her mother, who has been crying. *Console* is a homograph—a word that has two or more meanings but is always spelled the same. *Console* can be a verb meaning "to comfort"; it is also a noun meaning "a television cabinet that is made to stand on the floor." The only way to determine the proper meaning and pronunciation of a homograph is to look at the context in which it appears. Choose the letter of the correct homograph for each use of *contract*.

   a. **contract** (kən trakt′) to get, as a disease
   b. **contract** (kän′ trakt) a binding agreement

   1. The partners signed a *contract*.
   2. Did Paul *contract* pneumonia?

Concept Development: Antonyms

Write the letter of the word that means the opposite of the first word.

   1. genteel: (a) gentle, (b) refined, (c) impolite
   2. mortified: (a) honored, (b) humiliated, (c) loved
   3. defiance: (a) resistance, (b) anger, (c) cooperation
   4. console: (a) cause grief, (b) ease grief, (c) table

Spelling Strategy

When you add a suffix to a word that ends in *y* preceded by a consonant, change the *y* to *i* and then add the suffix: *mortify* + *-ed* = *mortified*. Write the word formed by adding the ending to each word below. Then, use the new word in a sentence.

   1. try + *-ed* 2. empty + *-ness* 3. cleanly + *-ness*

Grammar Lesson

Pronoun Case

Case is the form of a noun or a pronoun that indicates its use in a sentence. The three **pronoun cases** are the **nominative,** in which a pronoun is used as a subject or predicate nominative; the **possessive,** in which a pronoun is used to show ownership; and the **objective,** in which a pronoun is used as a direct object, an indirect object, the object of a preposition, or the object of a verb.

Nominative:	*He* danced very well with Mary Catherine.
Possessive:	*His* sister was responsible for the disappointing outcome.
Objective:	She gave *him* dancing lessons.

Practice Identify the case of each underlined pronoun.

   1. Horace thought <u>they</u> were going to the dance together.
   2. <u>She</u> was tired of <u>her</u> mother's intrusive behavior.
   3. Horace understood the explanation <u>she</u> gave <u>him.</u>
   4. <u>He</u> ignored Inez and <u>her</u> demands.
   5. <u>Their</u> conversation helped <u>him</u> gain more confidence.

Writing Application Use three pronouns in a sentence about "The Dancers." Then, identify the case of each pronoun.

W̶G̶ *Prentice Hall Writing and Grammar Connection: Chapter 24, Section 1*

Writing Lesson

Diary Entry

Write a diary entry that Horace might have written after Emily refused to go with him to the dance.

Prewriting   Review the play to make a list of the emotions you think Horace might have felt. Think about how he felt when Inez first told him about her plans for him and Emily, and think about his confidence level at the beginning of the play.

Drafting   As you draft, use a tone you think Horace would use. Show the range of emotions he felt from first hearing about his date to being rejected by Emily. Then, express Horace's feelings about Inez and Elizabeth.

Revising   Reread your draft, circling any vague words and replacing them with more precise language.

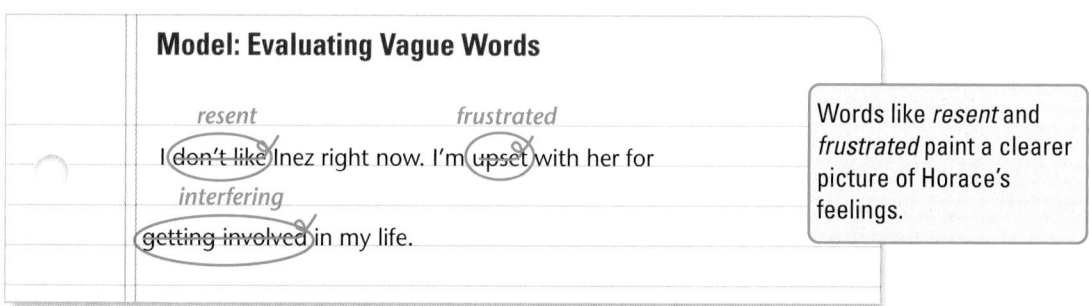

Model: Evaluating Vague Words

resent   *frustrated*

I ~~don't like~~ Inez right now. I'm ~~upset~~ with her for

interfering

~~getting involved~~ in my life.

> Words like *resent* and *frustrated* paint a clearer picture of Horace's feelings.

 Prentice Hall Writing and Grammar Connection: Chapter 6, Section 4

Extension Activities

Listening and Speaking In a small group, compile a **soundtrack** for a film version of "The Dancers." Consider the following points as you plan your music:

- Since the play is set in the 1950s, select some popular music from that era.
- Include music that relates to the particular mood of a scene.

When you present your soundtrack to your class, explain why you chose each piece and how it connects to the play. [**Group Activity**]

Research and Technology Write a **movie proposal** in which you explain how you would turn "The Dancers" into a movie. Start by researching clothing from the 1950s, and create a costume design catalog with the designs you think are best. Then, decide which actor you would cast in the role of each character. Share your proposal with your class.

 **Take It to the Net**   www.phschool.com

Go online for an additional research activity using the Internet.

The Shakespearean Theater

ROMEO AND JULIET

Of all the love stories ever written, that of Romeo and Juliet is the most famous. To many people, Shakespeare's tragic lovers represent the essence of romantic love. When Shakespeare wrote *The Tragedy of Romeo and Juliet,* he was a young man, and the play is a young man's play about young love.

The Theater in Shakespeare's Day

Romeo and Juliet, like most of Shakespeare's plays, was produced in a public theater. Public theaters were built around roofless courtyards without artificial light. Performances, therefore, were given only during daylight hours. Surrounding the courtyard were three levels of galleries with benches on which wealthier playgoers sat. Less wealthy spectators, called groundlings, stood and watched a play from the courtyard, which was called the pit.

Most of Shakespeare's plays were performed in the Globe theater. No one is certain exactly what the Globe looked like, though Shakespeare tells us it was round or octagonal. We know that it was open to the sky and held between 2,500 and 3,000 people. Scholars disagree about its actual dimensions and size. The discovery of its foundation in 1990 was exciting because the eventual excavation will reveal clues about the plays, the actors, and the audience. The tiny

▼ Critical Viewing
Which attribute of the Globe theater is emphasized in this painting? **[Analyze]**

The Globe Theatre, London

part of the foundation initially uncovered yielded a great number of hazelnut shells. Hazelnuts were Elizabethan popcorn; people munched on them all during the performance.

The stage was a platform that extended into the pit. Actors entered and left the stage from doors located behind the platform. The portion of the galleries behind and above the stage was used primarily as dressing and storage rooms. The second-level gallery right above the stage, however, was used as an upper stage. It would have been here that the famous balcony scene in *Romeo and Juliet* was enacted.

There was no scenery in the theaters of Shakespeare's day. Settings were indicated by references in the dialogue. As a result, one scene could follow another in rapid succession. The actors wore elaborate clothing. It was, in fact, typical Elizabethan clothing, not costuming. Thus, the plays produced in Shakespeare's day were fast-paced, colorful productions. Usually, a play lasted two hours.

One other difference between Shakespeare's theater and today's is that acting companies in the sixteenth century were made up only of men and boys. Women did not perform on the stage. This was not considered proper for a woman. As a general rule, boys of eleven, twelve, or thirteen—before their voices changed—performed the female roles.

▲ **Critical Viewing**
Which part of the replica of the Globe theater do you think is being built in this picture? **[Speculate]**

The Globe Today

Building a replica of Shakespeare's Globe was the dream of American actor Sam Wanamaker. After long years of fund-raising and construction, the theater opened in London to its first full season on June 8, 1997, with a production of *Henry V*. Like the earlier Globe, this one is made of wood, with a thatched roof and lime plaster covering the walls. The stage and the galleries are covered, but the "bear pit," where the modern-day groundlings stand, is open to the skies, exposing the spectators to the weather.

Prepare to Read

The Tragedy of Romeo and Juliet

William Shakespeare (1564–1616)

Almost 400 years after Shakespeare's death, his 37 plays continue to be read widely and produced frequently throughout the world. They have as powerful an impact on audiences today as when they were first staged.

Starting in Stratford Not much is known about Shakespeare's early life. One reason for this lack of information is that playwrights during Shakespeare's time were not considered very important people socially. Therefore, no biographies were written about him until many years after his death. Church and town records in his hometown of Stratford-on-Avon—a busy market town about seventy-five miles northwest of London—provide some clues about Shakespeare's beginnings, however. His mother, whose maiden name was Mary Arden, was the daughter of his father's landlord. His father, John, was a prosperous merchant in Stratford and even served a term as the town's mayor. John Shakespeare's social standing made it possible for William to attend Stratford Grammar School free of charge until the age of fourteen. There, he studied Latin and Greek, as well as British and world history. Shakespeare would later put all of these lessons to use in his plays about historic figures such as Julius Caesar, Pericles, Macbeth, Richard III, and Henry IV.

Building a Love of Theater Because Stratford was a commercial center, traveling companies of professional actors visited several times a year. Young William probably attended many of these performances, inspiring his interest in the stage. In 1582, at the age of eighteen, Shakespeare married and was soon the father of three children. It is uncertain how Shakespeare spent the next few years, but he did not settle down in Stratford. His heart was set on London and the theater, so he followed his heart there sometime before 1592, leaving his patient

Elizabethan Language

As you read *Romeo and Juliet*, most of the unfamiliar words from Elizabethan English that you encounter will be explained in footnotes. The following, however, appear so frequently that learning them now will make your reading of the play easier.

against for; in preparation for
alack alas (an exclamation of sorrow)
an, and if
anon soon
aye yes
but only; except
e'en even
e'er ever
haply perhaps

happy fortunate
hence away; from here
hie hurry
hither here
marry indeed
whence where
wilt will
withal in addition; notwithstanding
would wish

family behind. Stratford nevertheless remained an important part of Shakespeare's life, and he visited often. Once he had achieved success in London, Shakespeare purchased one of Stratford's nicest homes for his family, and he retired there after his playwriting career ended.

Stage Celebrity By 1594, William Shakespeare, now a Londoner, had developed a reputation as an actor, had written several plays, and had become the principal playwright of the Lord Chamberlain's Men, a successful London theater company. He was also a part owner of the company, which meant that he earned money in three ways—from fees for his plays, from his acting salary, and from his share of the profits of the company. In 1599, the company built the famous Globe theater, where most of Shakespeare's plays were performed. When James I became king in 1603, Shakespeare and his partners renamed the company The King's Men. Shakespeare stayed with the company until 1610, when he retired to Stratford-on-Avon.

When Were They Written? Because Shakespeare wrote his plays to be performed, not published, no one knows exactly when each play was written. However, scholars have charted several distinct periods in Shakespeare's development as a playwright. During his early years, he wrote a number of comedies, several histories, and two tragedies. *Romeo and Juliet*—inspiration for the musical *West Side Story* as well as ballets, songs, stories, and movies—was written around 1595. Between that date and the turn of the seventeenth century, Shakespeare wrote several of his finest romantic comedies (*As You Like It*, *Twelfth Night*, and *Much Ado About Nothing*). During the first decade of the seventeenth century, Shakespeare created his greatest tragedies (*Hamlet*, *Othello*, *King Lear*, *Macbeth*, *Antony and Cleopatra*, and *Coriolanus*). Finally, toward the end of his career, Shakespeare wrote sev-

eral plays referred to as romances or tragicomedies. Shakespeare's plays were finally published in a one-volume edition in 1623, seven years after his death. More than 1,000 copies of the first printing were sold for the considerable sum of one pound each—equivalent to more than $50 in today's currency.

Shakespeare's Impact on English

No other individual has played a more significant role in shaping the English language than William Shakespeare. In addition to introducing many new words into the language, Shakespeare penned hundreds of memorable lines that are familiar to millions of people throughout the world—even people who have never read one of Shakespeare's plays. Following are just a few of his most famous lines. See how many you recognize.

From *Hamlet:*
> To be, or not to be: that is the question:
> Whether 'tis nobler in the mind to suffer
> The slings and arrows of outrageous fortune,
> Or take arms against a sea of troubles, . . .

From *Romeo and Juliet:*
> What's in a name? That which we call a rose
> By any other name would smell as sweet.
>
> . . . parting is such sweet sorrow, . . .

From *Macbeth:*
> Fair is foul, and foul is fair.

From *Julius Caesar:*
> Friends, Romans, countrymen, lend me your ears;
> I come to bury Caesar, not to praise him.

From *As You Like It:*
> All the world's a stage,
> And all the men and women merely players . . .

From *Richard the Third:*
> A horse, a horse! My kingdom for a horse!

From *Twelfth Night:*
> If music be the food of love, play on . . .

Prepare to Read

The Tragedy of Romeo and Juliet, Act I

 Take It to the Net

Visit www.phschool.com
for interactive activities
and instruction related to
*The Tragedy of Romeo and
Juliet,* including
- background
- graphic organizers
- literary elements
- reading strategies

Preview

Connecting to the Literature

The world is filled with rivalries—among countries, families, schools, even groups of friends. Occasionally, rivalries become so fierce that the members of one group refuse to associate with their rivals. In extreme cases, as you will see in this play, rivalries can even erupt into violence.

Background

Shakespeare based his play about star-crossed lovers from feuding Italian families on a poem published in 1562 by Arthur Brooke. Brooke's 3,000-line poem has a highly moral tone: Disobedience, as well as fate, leads to the deaths of the two lovers. Brooke's poem, in turn, was based on a French version of the story, written in 1559.

Literary Analysis

Character

Characters are the people or animals who take part in a literary work. Some characters are fully developed, while others are not as complex.

- A **round character** has many personality traits, like a real person.
- A **flat character** is one-dimensional, embodying only a single trait. Shakespeare's plays often include flat characters who provide comic relief.

As you read the play, use a chart like the one shown to note round and flat characters and their personality traits.

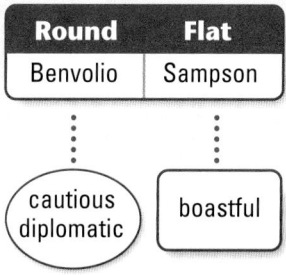

Round	Flat
Benvolio	Sampson

cautious diplomatic | boastful

Connecting Literary Elements

A **dramatic foil** is a character who highlights the traits of another character through contrast. For example, in Act I, Benvolio, who tries to quiet a group of brawling servants, is a foil to Tybalt, who has a fiery hot temper. As you read, look for foils by identifying characters who possess contrasting personality traits. This will help you determine key differences among characters.

Reading Strategy

Using Text Aids

The way the characters speak in Shakespeare's play, which was written over 400 years ago, will probably be unfamiliar to you. To make sure that you understand the dialogue, it is crucial that you use the **text aids**—the numbered explanations of Shakespeare's language that appear alongside the text.

- If you are confused by a passage, check to see if there is a footnote and read the corresponding explanation.
- Reread the passage, using your new knowledge from the footnote, to be sure that you grasp the meaning of the passage.

The footnotes should add to your enjoyment of the play by clarifying confusing language.

Vocabulary Development

pernicious (pər nish′ əs) *adj.* causing great injury or ruin (p. 774)

augmenting (ôg ment′ iŋ) *v.* increasing; enlarging (p. 775)

grievance (grēv′ əns) *n.* injustice; complaint (p. 776)

transgression (trans gresh′ ən) *n.* wrongdoing; sin (p. 777)

heretics (her′ ə tiks) *n.* those who hold to a belief opposed to the established teachings of a church (p. 780)

Instruction with this selection addresses these standards:
R 1.1*, 3.4*, 3.10*
W 2.4*, 2.5*
WOLC 1.3*
LS 1.11
* *Standards tested on HS Exit Exam. For complete standards, see p. CA 4.*

GREGORY. But thou art not quickly moved to strike.

SAMPSON. A dog of the house of Montague moves me.

GREGORY. To move is to stir, and to be valiant is to stand. Therefore, if thou art moved, thou run'st away.

10 **SAMPSON.** A dog of that house shall move me to stand. I will take the wall[6] of any man or maid of Montague's.

GREGORY. That shows thee a weak slave; for the weakest goes to the wall.

SAMPSON. 'Tis true; and therefore women, being the weaker
15 vessels, are ever thrust to the wall. Therefore I will push Montague's men from the wall and thrust his maids to the wall.

GREGORY. The quarrel is between our masters and us their men.

SAMPSON. Tis all one. I will show myself a tyrant. When I have fought with the men, I will be civil with the maids—I will cut
20 off their heads.

GREGORY. The heads of the maids?

SAMPSON. Ay, the heads of the maids or their maidenheads. Take it in what sense thou wilt.

GREGORY. They must take it in sense that feel it.

25 **SAMPSON.** Me they shall feel while I am able to stand; and 'tis known I am a pretty piece of flesh.

GREGORY. Tis well thou art not fish; if thou hadst, thou hadst been Poor John. Draw thy tool![7] Here comes two of the house of Montagues.

[*Enter two other Servingmen,* ABRAM *and* BALTHASAR.]

30 **SAMPSON.** My naked weapon is out. Quarrel! I will back thee.

GREGORY. How? Turn thy back and run?

SAMPSON. Fear me not.

GREGORY. No, marry. I fear thee!

SAMPSON. Let us take the law of our sides;[8] let them begin.

35 **GREGORY.** I will frown as I pass by, and let them take it as they list.[9]

SAMPSON. Nay, as they dare. I will bite my thumb[10] at them, which is disgrace to them if they bear it.

ABRAM. Do you bite your thumb at us, sir?

SAMPSON. I do bite my thumb, sir.

40 **ABRAM.** Do you bite your thumb at us, sir?

SAMPSON. [*Aside to* GREGORY] Is the law of our side if I say ay?

6. take the wall assert superiority by walking nearer the houses and therefore farther from the gutter

Literary Analysis
Character What does this conversation reveal about the Capulets and the Montagues?

7. tool weapon.

8. take . . . sides make sure the law is on our side.
9. list please.
10. bite . . . thumb make an insulting gesture.

Reading Strategy
Using Text Aids How does footnote 8 help you understand Sampson's logic in line 34?

GREGORY. [*Aside to* SAMPSON] No.

SAMPSON. No, sir, I do not bite my thumb at you, sir; but I bite my thumb, sir.

45   **GREGORY.** Do you quarrel, sir?

ABRAM. Quarrel, sir? No, sir.

SAMPSON. But if you do, sir, I am for you. I serve as good a man as you.

ABRAM. No better.

SAMPSON. Well, sir.

[*Enter* BENVOLIO.]

50   **GREGORY.** Say "better." Here comes one of my master's kinsmen.

SAMPSON. Yes, better, sir.

ABRAM. You lie.

SAMPSON. Draw, if you be men. Gregory, remember thy swashing[11] blow.   [*They fight.*]

55   **BENVOLIO.** Part, fools!
Put up your swords. You know not what you do.

[*Enter* TYBALT.]

TYBALT. What art thou drawn among these heartless hinds?[12]
Turn thee, Benvolio; look upon thy death.

BENVOLIO. I do but keep the peace. Put up thy sword,
60   Or manage it to part these men with me.

TYBALT. What, drawn, and talk of peace? I hate the word
As I hate hell, all Montagues, and thee.
Have at thee, coward!   [*They fight.*]

[*Enter an* OFFICER, *and three or four* CITIZENS *with clubs or partisans.*[13]]

OFFICER. Clubs, bills,[14] and partisans! Strike! Beat them down!
65   Down with the Capulets! Down with the Montagues!

[*Enter old* CAPULET *in his gown, and his* WIFE.]

CAPULET. What noise is this? Give me my long sword, ho!

LADY CAPULET. A crutch, a crutch! Why call you for a sword?

CAPULET. My sword, I say! Old Montague is come
And flourishes his blade in spite[15] of me.

[*Enter old* MONTAGUE *and his* WIFE.]

70   **MONTAGUE.** Thou villain Capulet!—Hold me not; let me go.

LADY MONTAGUE. Thou shalt not stir one foot to seek a foe.

Literary Analysis
Character How would you describe Gregory and Sampson in this scene?

11. swashing hard downward swordstroke.

12. heartless hinds cowardly servants. *Hind* also meant "a female deer."

Literary Analysis
Character and Dramatic Foil Which contrasting personality traits do Benvolio and Tybalt reveal in their brief conversation?

13. partisans spearlike weapons with broad blades.

14. bills weapons consisting of hook-shaped blades with long handles.

15. spite defiance.

✔**Reading Check**
Whom does Tybalt fight?

[*Enter* PRINCE ESCALUS, *with his Train.*[16]]

PRINCE. Rebellious subjects, enemies to peace,
          Profaners[17] of this neighbor-stainèd steel—
          Will they not hear? What, ho! You men, you beasts,
75   That quench the fire of your <u>pernicious</u> rage
          With purple fountains issuing from your veins!
          On pain of torture, from those bloody hands
          Throw your mistempered[18] weapons to the ground
          And hear the sentence of your moved prince.
80   Three civil brawls, bred of an airy word
          By thee, old Capulet, and Montague,
          Have thrice disturbed the quiet of our streets
          And made Verona's ancient citizens
          Cast by their grave beseeming ornaments[19]
85   To wield old partisans, in hands as old,
          Cank'red with peace, to part your cank'red hate.[20]
          If ever you disturb our streets again,
          Your lives shall pay the forfeit of the peace.
          For this time all the rest depart away.
90   You, Capulet, shall go along with me;
          And, Montague, come you this afternoon,
          To know our farther pleasure in this case,
          To old Freetown, our common judgment place.
          Once more, on pain of death, all men depart.

[*Exit all but* MONTAGUE, *his* WIFE, *and* BENVOLIO.]

95 MONTAGUE. Who set this ancient quarrel new abroach?[21]
              Speak, nephew, were you by when it began?

    BENVOLIO. Here were the servants of your adversary
              And yours, close fighting ere I did approach.
              I drew to part them. In the instant came
100   The fiery Tybalt, with his sword prepared;
              Which, as he breathed defiance to my ears,
              He swung about his head and cut the winds,
              Who, nothing hurt withal, hissed him in scorn.
              While we were interchanging thrusts and blows,
105   Came more and more, and fought on part and part,[22]
              Till the Prince came, who parted either part.

    LADY MONTAGUE. O, where is Romeo? Saw you him today?
                   Right glad I am he was not at this fray.

    BENVOLIO. Madam, an hour before the worshiped sun
110   Peered forth the golden window of the East,
              A troubled mind drave me to walk abroad:
              Where, underneath the grove of sycamore
              That westward rooteth from this city side,
              So early walking did I see your son.

Literary Analysis
Character What can you infer about Benvolio based on his interaction with Romeo's parents?

115   Towards him I made, but he was ware[23] of me
    And stole into the covert[24] of the wood.
    I, measuring his affections[25] by my own,
    Which then most sought where most might not be found,[26]
    Being one too many by my weary self,
120   Pursued my humor not pursuing his,[27]
    And gladly shunned who gladly fled from me.

MONTAGUE. Many a morning hath he there been seen,
    With tears <u>augmenting</u> the fresh morning's dew,
    Adding to clouds more clouds with his deep sighs;
125   But all so soon as the all-cheering sun
    Should in the farthest East begin to draw
    The shady curtains from Aurora's♦ bed,
    Away from light steals home my heavy[28] son
    And private in his chamber pens himself,
130   Shuts up his windows, locks fair daylight out,
    And makes himself an artificial night.
    Black and portentous[29] must this humor prove
    Unless good counsel may the cause remove.

BENVOLIO. My noble uncle, do you know the cause?

135 **MONTAGUE.** I neither know it nor can learn of him.

BENVOLIO. Have you importuned[30] him by any means?

MONTAGUE. Both by myself and many other friends;
    But he, his own affections' counselor,
    Is to himself—I will not say how true—
140   But to himself so secret and so close,
    So far from sounding[31] and discovery,
    As is the bud bit with an envious worm
    Ere he can spread his sweet leaves to the air
    Or dedicate his beauty to the sun.
145   Could we but learn from whence his sorrows grow,
    We would as willingly give cure as know.

23. ware aware; wary.

24. covert hidden place.

25. measuring . . . affections judging his feelings.

26. Which . . . found which wanted to be where there was no one else.

27. Pursued . . . his followed my own mind by not following after Romeo.

augmenting (ôg ment′ iŋ) v. increasing; enlarging

28. heavy sad, moody.

29. portentous promising bad fortune.

30. importuned questioned deeply.

31. sounding understanding.

✓ **Reading Check**

How does the Prince respond to the fight between Benvolio and Tybalt?

*L*iterature
in context Humanities Connection

♦ *Aurora*

Aurora was the Latin goddess of the dawn who began each day riding a chariot from the River Oceanus to heaven to announce the coming of the sun. She was said to dip her rosy fingers into a cup filled with dew and sprinkle drops on flowers and trees. Aurora had special feelings for young people like Romeo, whose lives were just dawning. Unlike Aurora, the moody Romeo roams at night and shuts himself in his room at dawn (I, i, 127).

[*Enter* ROMEO.]

BENVOLIO. See, where he comes. So please you step aside;
I'll know his <u>grievance</u>, or be much denied.

MONTAGUE. I would thou wert so happy by thy stay
150 To hear true shrift.³² Come, madam, let's away.

[*Exit* MONTAGUE *and* WIFE.]

BENVOLIO. Good morrow, cousin.

ROMEO.   Is the day so young?

BENVOLIO. But new struck nine.

ROMEO.   Ay me! Sad hours seem long.
Was that my father that went hence so fast?

BENVOLIO. It was. What sadness lengthens Romeo's hours?

155 **ROMEO.** Not having that which having makes them short.

BENVOLIO. In love?

ROMEO. Out—

BENVOLIO. Of love?

ROMEO. Out of her favor where I am in love.

160 **BENVOLIO.** Alas that love, so gentle in his view,³³
Should be so tyrannous and rough in proof!³⁴

ROMEO. Alas that love, whose view is muffled still,³⁵
Should without eyes see pathways to his will!
Where shall we dine? O me! What fray was here?
165 Yet tell me not, for I have heard it all.
Here's much to do with hate, but more with love.³⁶
Why then, O brawling love, O loving hate,
O anything, of nothing first created!
O heavy lightness, serious vanity,
170 Misshapen chaos of well-seeming forms,

---

grievance (grēvʹ əns) *n.*
injustice; complaint

32. I . . . shrift I hope you
are lucky enough to hear
him confess the truth.

Literary Analysis
Character Which
personality traits are
revealed by Benvolio's
concern for Romeo?

33. view appearance.
34. in proof when experienced.

35. whose . . . still Cupid is
traditionally represented as
blindfolded.

36. but . . . love loyalty to
family and love of fighting. In
the following lines, Romeo
speaks of love as a series of
contradictions—a union of
opposites.

▶ **Critical Viewing**
How would you describe
the feelings of each
character, based on this
photograph? **[Analyze]**

776 ◆ *Drama*

Feather of lead, bright smoke, cold fire, sick health,
Still-waking sleep, that is not what it is!
This love feel I, that feel no love in this.
Dost thou not laugh?

BENVOLIO.   No, coz,[37] I rather weep.

ROMEO. Good heart, at what?

175 **BENVOLIO.**   At thy good heart's oppression.

ROMEO. Why, such is love's <u>transgression</u>.
Griefs of mine own lie heavy in my breast,
Which thou wilt propagate, to have it prest
With more of thine.[38] This love that thou hast shown
180 Doth add more grief to too much of mine own.
Love is a smoke made with the fume of sighs;
Being purged, a fire sparkling in lovers' eyes;
Being vexed, a sea nourished with loving tears.
What is it else? A madness most discreet,[39]
185 A choking gall,[40] and a preserving sweet.
Farewell, my coz.

BENVOLIO.   Soft![41] I will go along.
And if you leave me so, you do me wrong.

ROMEO. Tut! I have lost myself; I am not here;
This is not Romeo, he's some other where.

190 **BENVOLIO.** Tell me in sadness,[42] who is that you love?

ROMEO. What, shall I groan and tell thee?

BENVOLIO.   Groan? Why, no;
But sadly tell me who.

ROMEO. Bid a sick man in sadness make his will.
Ah, word ill urged to one that is so ill!
195 In sadness, cousin, I do love a woman.

BENVOLIO. I aimed so near when I supposed you loved.

ROMEO. A right good markman. And she's fair I love.

BENVOLIO. A right fair mark, fair coz, is soonest hit.

ROMEO. Well, in that hit you miss. She'll not be hit
200 With Cupid's arrow. She hath Dian's wit,[43]
And, in strong proof[44] of chastity well armed,
From Love's weak childish bow she lives uncharmed.
She will not stay[45] the siege of loving terms,
Nor bide th' encounter of assailing eyes,
205 Nor ope her lap to saint-seducing gold.
O, she is rich in beauty; only poor
That, when she dies, with beauty dies her store.[46]

BENVOLIO. Then she hath sworn that she will still live chaste?

Literary Analysis
Character What do Romeo's words in lines 171–174 reveal about his personality?

37. **coz** cousin.

transgression (trans gresh´ ən) *n.* wrongdoing; sin

38. **Which . . . thine** Which griefs you will increase by adding your own sorrow to them.

39. **discreet** intelligently sensitive.

40. **gall** a bitter liquid.

41. **Soft!** Hold on a minute.

Reading Strategy
Using Text Aids Why is footnote 41 helpful here?

42. **in sadness** seriously.

Literary Analysis
Character Which details in line 195 indicate that Romeo is a round character?

43. **Dian's wit** the mind of Diana, goddess of chastity.
44. **proof** armor.
45. **stay** endure; put up with.
46. **That . . . store** In that her beauty will die with her if she does not marry and have children.

✔**Reading Check**
What reason for his sadness does Romeo give to Benvolio?

ROMEO. She hath, and in that sparing make huge waste;
210   For beauty, starved with her severity,
    Cuts beauty off from all posterity.[47]
    She is too fair, too wise, wisely too fair
    To merit bliss by making me despair.[48]
    She hath forsworn to[49] love, and in that vow
215   Do I live dead that live to tell it now.

BENVOLIO. Be ruled by me; forget to think of her.

ROMEO. O, teach me how I should forget to think!

BENVOLIO. By giving liberty unto thine eyes.
    Examine other beauties.

ROMEO.   'Tis the way
220   To call hers, exquisite, in question more.[50]
    These happy masks that kiss fair ladies' brows,
    Being black puts us in mind they hide the fair.
    He that is strucken blind cannot forget
    The precious treasure of his eyesight lost.
225   Show me a mistress that is passing fair:
    What doth her beauty serve but as a note
    Where I may read who passed that passing fair?[51]
    Farewell. Thou canst not teach me to forget.

BENVOLIO. I'll pay that doctrine, or else die in debt.[52]   *[Exit all.]*

Scene ii. *A street.*

[Enter CAPULET, COUNTY PARIS, *and the* CLOWN, *his servant.]*

CAPULET. But Montague is bound as well as I,
    In penalty alike; and 'tis not hard, I think,
    For men so old as we to keep the peace.

PARIS. Of honorable reckoning[1] are you both,
5   And pity 'tis you lived at odds so long.
    But now, my lord, what say you to my suit?

CAPULET. But saying o'er what I have said before:
    My child is yet a stranger in the world,
    She hath not seen the change of fourteen years;
10   Let two more summers wither in their pride
    Ere we may think her ripe to be a bride.

PARIS. Younger than she are happy mothers made.

CAPULET. And too soon marred are those so early made.
    Earth hath swallowed all my hopes[2] but she;
15   She is the hopeful lady of my earth.[3]
    But woo her, gentle Paris, get her heart;
    My will to her consent is but a part.

47. in . . . posterity By denying herself love and marriage, she wastes her beauty, which will not live on in future generations.

48. She . . . despair She is being too good—she'll earn happiness in heaven by dooming me to live without her love.

49. forsworn to sworn not to.

50. 'Tis . . . more That way will only make her beauty more strongly present in my mind.

Literary Analysis

Character and Dramatic Foil What contrasting attitudes are revealed in this exchange between Romeo and Benvolio?

51. who . . . fair who surpassed in beauty that very beautiful woman.

52. I'll . . . debt I'll teach you to forget, or else die trying.

1. reckoning reputation.

Literary Analysis

Character What can you tell about Lord Capulet's character traits based on his talk with Paris?

2. hopes children.

3. She . . . earth My hopes for the future rest in her; she will inherit all that is mine.

An she agree, within her scope of choice
Lies my consent and fair according voice,[4]
20 This night I hold an old accustomed feast,
Whereto I have invited many a guest,
Such as I love; and you among the store,
One more, most welcome, makes my number more.
At my poor house look to behold this night
25 Earth-treading stars[5] that make dark heaven light.
Such comfort as do lusty young men feel
When well-appareled April on the heel
Of limping Winter treads, even such delight
Among fresh fennel buds shall you this night
30 Inherit at my house. Hear all, all see,
And like her most whose merit most shall be;
Which, on more view of many, mine, being one,
May stand in number, though in reck'ning none.[6]
Come, go with me. [*To* SERVANT, *giving him a paper*]
      Go, sirrah, trudge about
35 Through fair Verona; find those persons out
Whose names are written there, and to them say
My house and welcome on their pleasure stay.[7] [*Exit with* PARIS.]

SERVANT. Find them out whose names are written here? It is written
    that the shoemaker should meddle with his yard and the tailor
40 with his last, the fisher with his pencil and the painter with his
    nets;[8] but I am sent to find those persons whose names are
    here writ, and can never find what names the writing person
    hath here writ. I must to the learned. In good time![9]

[*Enter* BENVOLIO *and* ROMEO.]

BENVOLIO. Tut, man, one fire burns out another's burning;
45   One pain is less'ned by another's anguish;
    Turn giddy, and be holp by backward turning;[10]
        One desperate grief cures with another's languish.
    Take thou some new infection to thy eye,
    And the rank poison of the old will die.

50 **ROMEO.** Your plantain leaf[11] is excellent for that.

BENVOLIO. For what, I pray thee?

ROMEO.   For your broken shin.

BENVOLIO. Why, Romeo, art thou mad?

ROMEO. Not mad, but bound more than a madman is;
    Shut up in prison, kept without my food,
55 Whipped and tormented and—God-den,[12] good fellow.

SERVANT. God gi' go-den. I pray, sir, can you read?

ROMEO. Ay, mine own fortune in my misery.

4. and . . . voice If she
agrees, I will consent to and
agree with her choice.

5. Earth-treading stars
young ladies.

6. Which . . . none If you
look at all the young girls,
you may see her as merely
one among many, and not
worth special admiration.

Reading Strategy
Using Text Aids Using
footnote 6, explain the
main idea of Capulet's
proposal to Paris.

7. stay await.

8. shoemaker . . . nets The
servant is confusing workers
and their tools. He intends
to say that people should
stick with what they know.

9. In good time! Just in
time! The servant has seen
Benvolio and Romeo, who
can read.

10. Turn . . . turning If you
are dizzy from turning one
way, turn the other way.

11. plantain leaf leaf used
to stop bleeding.

12. God-den good after-
noon; good evening.

✓Reading Check

What does Capulet tell
Paris he wishes for his
daughter?

SERVANT. Perhaps you have learned it without book.
But, I pray, can you read anything you see?

60 **ROMEO.** Ay, if I know the letters and the language.

SERVANT. Ye say honestly. Rest you merry.[13]

ROMEO. Stay, fellow; I can read. [*He reads the letter.*]
"Signior Martino and his wife and daughters;
County Anselm and his beauteous sisters;
65 The lady widow of Vitruvio;
Signior Placentio and his lovely nieces;
Mercutio and his brother Valentine;
Mine uncle Capulet, his wife and daughters;
My fair niece Rosaline; Livia;
70 Signior Valentio and his cousin Tybalt;
Lucio and the lively Helena."
A fair assembly. Whither should they come?

SERVANT. Up.

ROMEO. Whither? To supper?

75 **SERVANT.** To our house.

ROMEO. Whose house?

SERVANT. My master's.

ROMEO. Indeed I should have asked you that before.

SERVANT. Now I'll tell you without asking. My master is the great
80 rich Capulet; and if you be not of the house of Montagues, I pray
come and crush a cup of wine. Rest you merry. [*Exit.*]

BENVOLIO. At this same ancient[14] feast of Capulet's
Sups the fair Rosaline whom thou so loves;
With all the admirèd beauties of Verona.
85 Go thither, and with unattainted[15] eye
Compare her face with some that I shall show,
And I will make thee think thy swan a crow.

ROMEO. When the devout religion of mine eye
Maintains such falsehood, then turn tears to fires:
90 And these, who, often drowned, could never die,
Transparent <u>heretics</u>, be burnt for liars![16]
One fairer than my love? The all-seeing sun
Ne'er saw her match since first the world begun.

BENVOLIO. Tut! you saw her fair, none else being by,
95 Herself poised with herself in either eye;[17]
But in that crystal scales[18] let there be weighed
Your lady's love against some other maid
That I will show you shining at this feast,
And she shall scant show well that now seems best.

13. **Rest you merry** May God keep you happy—a way of saying farewell.

Literary Analysis
Character Is the servant a round or flat character? Why?

14. **ancient** long-established; traditional.

15. **unattainted** unprejudiced.

heretics (her´ ə tiks) *n.* those who hold to a belief opposed to the established teachings of a church

16. **When . . . liars!** When I see Rosaline as just a plain-looking girl, may my tears turn to fire and burn my eyes out!

Reading Strategy
Using Text Aids How does footnote 16 convey Romeo's feelings for Rosaline?

17. **Herself . . . eye** Rosaline compared with no one else.

18. **crystal scales** your eyes.

100 **ROMEO.** I'll go along, no such sight to be shown,
　　　But to rejoice in splendor of mine own.[19]

[*Exit all.*]

19. mine own my own love, Rosaline.

Scene iii. *A room in* CAPULET'*s house.*

[*Enter* CAPULET'S WIFE, *and* NURSE.]

　　LADY CAPULET. Nurse, where's my daughter? Call her forth to me.

　　NURSE. Now, by my maidenhead at twelve year old,
　　　　I bade her come. What, lamb! What, ladybird!
　　　　God forbid, where's this girl? What, Juliet!

[*Enter* JULIET.]

　5 **JULIET.** How now? Who calls?

　　NURSE.　　　　　　　　　　Your mother.

　　JULIET.　　　　　　　　　　　　　Madam, I am here
　　　　What is your will?

　　LADY CAPULET. This is the matter—Nurse, give leave[1] awhile;
　　　　We must talk in secret. Nurse, come back again.
　　　　I have rememb'red me; thou's hear our counsel.[2]
　10　　Thou knowest my daughter's of a pretty age.

　　NURSE. Faith, I can tell her age unto an hour.

　　LADY CAPULET. She's not fourteen.

　　NURSE.　　　　　　　　　　I'll lay fourteen of my teeth—
　　　　And yet, to my teen[3] be it spoken, I have but four—
　　　　She's not fourteen. How long is it now
　　　　To Lammastide?[4]

　15 **LADY CAPULET.**　　　A fortnight and odd days.[5]

　　NURSE. Even or odd, of all days in the year,
　　　　Come Lammas Eve at night shall she be fourteen.
　　　　Susan and she (God rest all Christian souls!)

1. give leave Leave us alone.

2. thou's . . . counsel You shall hear our conference.

Reading Strategy
Using Text Aids Based on footnotes 1 and 2, what facial expression might the Nurse have during Lady Capulet's speech?

3. teen sorrow.

4. Lammastide August 1, a holiday celebrating the summer harvest.

5. A fortnight and odd days two weeks plus a few days.

◀ **Critical Viewing**
What do this picture and the conversation among Juliet, Lady Capulet, and the Nurse tell you about their relationship? **[Infer]**

✔**Reading Check**
What does Romeo agree to do with Benvolio?

Were of an age.[6] Well, Susan is with God;
20   She was too good for me. But, as I said,
    On Lammas Eve at night shall she be fourteen;
    That shall she, marry; I remember it well.
    'Tis since the earthquake now eleven years.
    And she was weaned (I never shall forget it),
25   Of all the days of the year, upon that day;
    For I had then laid wormwood to my dug,
    Sitting in the sun under the dove house wall.
    My lord and you were then at Mantua.
    Nay, I do bear a brain. But, as I said,
30   When it did taste the wormwood on the nipple
    Of my dug and felt it bitter, pretty fool,
    To see it tetchy and fall out with the dug!
    Shake, quoth the dovehouse! 'Twas no need, I trow,
    To bid me trudge.
35   And since that time it is eleven years,
    For then she could stand high-lone; nay, by th' rood,
    She could have run and waddled all about;
    For even the day before, she broke her brow;
    And then my husband (God be with his soul!
40   'A was a merry man) took up the child.
    "Yea," quoth he, "dost thou fall upon thy face?
    Thou wilt fall backward when thou hast more wit;
    Wilt thou not, Jule?" and, by my holidam,
    The pretty wretch left crying and said, "Ay."
45   To see now how a jest shall come about!
    I warrant, and I should live a thousand years,
    I never should forget it. "Wilt thou not, Jule?" quoth he,
    And, pretty fool, it stinted and said, "Ay."

    LADY CAPULET. Enough of this. I pray thee hold thy peace.

50 **NURSE.** Yes, madam. Yet I cannot choose but laugh
    To think it should leave crying and say, "Ay."
    And yet, I warrant, it had upon it brow
    A bump as big as a young cock'rel's stone;
    A perilous knock; and it cried bitterly.
55   "Yea," quoth my husband, "fall'st upon thy face?
    Thou wilt fall backward when thou comest to age,
    Wilt thou not, Jule?" It stinted and said, "Ay."

    JULIET. And stint thou too, I pray thee, nurse, say I.

    NURSE. Peace, I have done. God mark thee to His grace!
60   Thou wast the prettiest babe that e'er I nursed.
    And I might live to see thee married once,
    I have my wish.

    LADY CAPULET. Marry, that "marry" is the very theme
    I came to talk of. Tell me, daughter Juliet,

6. Susan . . . age Susan, the Nurse's child, and Juliet were the same age.

Reading Strategy
Using Text Aids How does the information in footnote 6 help you understand the Nurse's devotion to Juliet?

Literary Analysis
Character Which character traits does the Nurse reveal in her speech?

Literary Analysis
Character and Dramatic Foil In what ways does the Nurse's character contrast with those of Lady Capulet and Juliet?

65   How stands your dispositions to be married?

JULIET. It is an honor that I dream not of.

NURSE. An honor? Were not I thine only nurse,
    I would say thou hadst sucked wisdom from thy teat.

LADY CAPULET. Well, think of marriage now. Younger than you,
70   Here in Verona, ladies of esteem,
    Are made already mothers. By my count,
    I was your mother much upon these years
    That you are now a maid.[7] Thus then in brief;
    The valiant Paris seeks you for his love.

75 **NURSE.** A man, young lady! Lady, such a man
    As all the world— Why, he's a man of wax.[8]

LADY CAPULET. Verona's summer hath not such a flower.

NURSE. Nay, he's a flower, in faith—a very flower.

LADY CAPULET. What say you? Can you love the gentleman?
80   This night you shall behold him at our feast.
    Read o'er the volume of young Paris' face,
    And find delight writ there with beauty's pen;
    Examine every married lineament,
    And see how one another lends content;[9]
85   And what obscured in this fair volume lies
    Find written in the margent[10] of his eyes.
    This precious book of love, this unbound lover,
    To beautify him only lacks a cover.[11]
    The fish lives in the sea, and 'tis much pride
90   For fair without the fair within to hide.
    That book in many's eyes doth share the glory,
    That in gold clasps locks in the golden story;
    So shall you share all that he doth possess,
    By having him making yourself no less.

95 **NURSE.** No less? Nay, bigger! Women grow by men.

LADY CAPULET. Speak briefly, can you like of Paris' love?

JULIET. I'll look to like, if looking liking move;[12]
    But no more deep will I endart mine eye
    Than your consent gives strength to make it fly.[13]

[*Enter* SERVINGMAN.]

100 **SERVINGMAN.** Madam, the guests are come, supper served up, you
    called, my young lady asked for, the nurse cursed in the pantry,
    and everything in extremity. I must hence to wait. I beseech
    you follow straight.   [*Exit.*]

LADY CAPULET. We follow thee. Juliet, the County stays.[14]

105 **NURSE.** Go, girl, seek happy nights to happy days.   [*Exit all.*]

7. I . . . maid I was your mother when I was as old as you are now.

8. he's . . . wax He's a model of a man.

Reading Strategy

Using Text Aids Why is footnote 8 essential for your understanding?

9. Examine . . . content: Examine every harmonious feature of his face, and see how each one enhances every other. Throughout this speech, Lady Capulet compares Paris to a book.

10. margent margin. Paris's eyes are compared to the margin of a book, where whatever is not clear in the text (the rest of his face) can be explained by notes.

11. cover metaphor for *wife.*

12. I'll . . . move If looking favorably at someone leads to liking him, I'll look at Paris in a way that will lead to liking him.

13. But . . . fly But I won't look harder than you want me to.

14. the County stays The Count, Paris, is waiting.

✔Reading Check

Why has Lady Capulet come to talk to Juliet?

Scene iv. *A street*

[*Enter* ROMEO, MERCUTIO, BENVOLIO, *with five or six other* MASKERS; TORCHBEARERS.]

 ROMEO. What, shall this speech¹ be spoke for our excuse?
  Or shall we on without apology?

 BENVOLIO. The date is out of such prolixity.²
  We'll have no Cupid hoodwinked with a scarf,
5 Bearing a Tartar's painted bow of lath,
  Scaring the ladies like a crowkeeper,
  Nor no without-book prologue, faintly spoke
  After the prompter, for our entrance;
  But, let them measure us by what they will,
10 We'll measure them a measure and be gone.

 ROMEO. Give me a torch. I am not for this ambling.
  Being but heavy,³ I will bear the light.

 MERCUTIO. Nay, gentle Romeo, we must have you dance.

 ROMEO. Not I, believe me. You have dancing shoes
15 With nimble soles; I have a soul of lead
  So stakes me to the ground I cannot move.

 MERCUTIO. You are a lover. Borrow Cupid's wings
  And soar with them above a common bound

 ROMEO. I am too sore enpiercèd with his shaft
20 To soar with his light feathers; and so bound

Reading Strategy
Using Text Aids How would you restate Romeo's questions in lines 1–2 in contemporary English?

1. this speech Romeo asks whether he and his companions, being uninvited guests, should follow custom by announcing their arrival in a speech.

2. The . . . prolixity Such wordiness is outdated. In the following lines, Benvolio says, in sum: "Let's forget about announcing our entrance with a show. The other guests can look over as they see fit. We'll dance a while, then leave."

3. heavy weighed down with sadness.

▼ **Critical Viewing**
Which details in this photograph show how Romeo and his friends prepare to attend the feast? **[Infer]**

I cannot bound a pitch above dull woe.
Under love's heavy burden do I sink.

MERCUTIO. And, to sink in it, should you burden love—
Too great oppression for a tender thing.

25 **ROMEO.** Is love a tender thing? It is too rough,
Too rude, too boist'rous, and it pricks like thorn.

MERCUTIO. If love be rough with you, be rough with love.
Prick love for pricking, and you beat love down.
Give me a case to put my visage[4] in.
30 A visor for a visor![5] What care I
What curious eye doth quote deformities?[6]
Here are the beetle brows shall blush for me.

BENVOLIO. Come, knock and enter; and no sooner in
But every man betake him to his legs.[7]

35 **ROMEO.** A torch for me! Let wantons light of heart
Tickle the senseless rushes[8] with their heels;
For I am proverbed with a grandsire phrase,[9]
I'll be a candleholder and look on;
The game was ne'er so fair, and I am done.[10]

40 **MERCUTIO.** Tut! Dun's the mouse, the constable's own word![11]
If thou art Dun,[12] we'll draw thee from the mire
Of this sir-reverence love, wherein thou stickest
Up to the ears. Come, we burn daylight, ho!

ROMEO. Nay, that's not so.

MERCUTIO.   I mean, sir, in delay
45 We waste our lights in vain, like lights by day.
Take our good meaning, for our judgment sits
Five times in that ere once in our five wits.[13]

ROMEO. And we mean well in going to this masque,
But 'tis no wit to go.

MERCUTIO.   Why, may one ask?

ROMEO. I dreamt a dream tonight.

50 **MERCUTIO.**   And so did I.

ROMEO. Well, what was yours?

MERCUTIO.   That dreamers often lie.

ROMEO. In bed asleep, while they do dream things true.

MERCUTIO. O, then I see Queen Mab[14] hath been with you.
She is the fairies' midwife, and she comes
55 In shape no bigger than an agate stone
On the forefinger of an alderman,
Drawn with a team of little atomies[15]

4. visage mask.

5. A visor . . . visor! A mask for a mask—which is what my real face is like!

6. quote deformities notice my ugly features.

7. betake . . . legs start dancing.

8. Let . . . rushes Let fun-loving people dance on the floor coverings.

9. proverbed . . . phrase directed by an old saying.

10. The game . . . done No matter how much enjoyment may be had, I won't have any.

11. Dun's . . . word!: Lie low like a mouse—that's what a constable waiting to make an arrest might say.

12. Dun proverbial name for a horse.

13. Take . . . wits Understand my intended meaning. That shows more intelligence than merely following what your senses perceive.

14. Queen Mab the queen of fairyland.

15. atomies creatures.

Literary Analysis
Character and Dramatic Foil In what way is Mercutio a foil for the sulky Romeo?

✔**Reading Check**

What advice about love does Mercutio give Romeo?

Over men's noses as they lie asleep;
Her wagon spokes made of long spinners'[16] legs,
60   The cover, of the wings of grasshoppers;
Her traces, of the smallest spider web;
Her collars, of the moonshine's wat'ry beams;
Her whip, of cricket's bone; the lash, of film;[17]
Her wagoner, a small gray-coated gnat,
65   Not half so big as a round little worm
Pricked from the lazy finger of a maid;
Her chariot is an empty hazelnut,
Made by the joiner squirrel or old grub,[18]
Time out o' mind the fairies' coachmakers.
70   And in this state she gallops night by night
Through lovers' brains, and then they dream of love;
On courtiers' knees, that dream on curtsies straight;
O'er lawyers' fingers, who straight dream on fees;
O'er ladies' lips, who straight on kisses dream,
75   Which oft the angry Mab with blisters plagues,
Because their breath with sweetmeats[19] tainted are.
Sometimes she gallops o'er a courtier's nose,
And then dreams he of smelling out a suit;[20]
And sometime comes she with a tithe pig's[21] tail
80   Tickling a parson's nose as 'a lies asleep,
Then he dreams of another benefice.[22]
Sometime she driveth o'er a soldier's neck,
And then dream he of cutting foreign throats,
Of breaches, ambuscadoes,[23] Spanish blades,
85   Of healths[24] five fathom deep; and then anon
Drums in his ear, at which he starts and wakes,
And being thus frighted, swears a prayer or two
And sleeps again. This is that very Mab
That plats[25] the manes of horses in the night
90   And bakes the elflocks[26] in foul sluttish hairs,
Which once untangled much misfortune bodes.
This is the hag, when maids lie on their backs,
That presses them and learns them first to bear,
Making them women of good carriage.[27]
This is she—

95   **ROMEO.**   Peace, peace, Mercutio, peace!
Thou talk'st of nothing.

MERCUTIO.   True, I talk of dreams;
Which are the children of an idle brain,
Begot of nothing but vain fantasy;
Which is as thin of substance as the air,
100   And more inconstant than the wind, who woos
Even now the frozen bosom of the North
And, being angered, puffs away from thence,
Turning his side to the dew-dropping South.

16. **spinners** spiders.

17. **film** spider's thread.

18. **old grub** an insect that bores holes in nuts.

Literary Analysis
Character Which character traits does Mercutio reveal in his Queen Mab speech?

19. **sweetmeats** candy.

20. **smelling . . . suit** finding someone who has a petition (suit) for the king and who will pay the courtier to gain the king's favor for the petition.

21. **tithe pig** a pig donated to a parson.

22. **benefice** a church appointment that included a guaranteed income.

23. **ambuscadoes** ambushes.

24. **healths** toasts ("To your health!").

25. **plats** tangles.

26. **elflocks** tangled hair.

27. **carriage** posture.

Literary Analysis
Character and Dramatic Foil How do lines 95–96 emphasize the contrast between Romeo and Mercutio?

BENVOLIO. This wind you talk of blows us from ourselves.
105   Supper is done, and we shall come too late.

    ROMEO. I fear, too early; for my mind misgives
    Some consequence yet hanging in the stars
    Shall bitterly begin his fearful date
    With this night's revels and expire the term
110   Of a despisèd life, closed in my breast,
    By some vile forfeit of untimely death.[28]
    But he that hath the steerage of my course
    Direct my sail! On, lusty gentlemen!

    BENVOLIO. Strike, drum.

             [*They march about the stage, and retire to one side.*]

Scene v. *A hall in* CAPULET'S *house.*

[SERVINGMEN *come forth with napkins.*]

    FIRST SERVINGMAN. Where's Potpan, that he helps not to
    take away? He shift a trencher![1] He scrape a trencher!

    SECOND SERVINGMAN. When good manners shall lie all in one or two
    men's hands, and they unwashed too, 'tis a foul thing.

5 **FIRST SERVINGMAN.** Away with the join-stools, remove the
    court cupboard, look to the plate. Good thou, save me a
    piece of marchpane,[2] and, as thou loves me, let the porter
    let in Susan Grindstone and Nell. Anthony, and Potpan!

    SECOND SERVINGMAN. Ay, boy, ready.

10 **FIRST SERVINGMAN.** You are looked for and called for,
    asked for and sought for, in the great chamber.

    THIRD SERVINGMAN. We cannot be here and there too.
    Cheerly, boys! Be brisk awhile, and the longer liver
    take all.   [*Exit.*]

[*Enter* CAPULET, *his* WIFE, JULIET, TYBALT, NURSE, *and all the* GUESTS *and*
GENTLEWOMEN *to the* MASKERS.]

15 **CAPULET.** Welcome, gentlemen! Ladies that have their toes
    Unplagued with corns will walk a bout[3] with you.
    Ah, my mistresses, which of you all
    Will now deny to dance? She that makes dainty,[4]
    She I'll swear hath corns. Am I come near ye now?
20   Welcome, gentlemen! I have seen the day
    That I have worn a visor and could tell
    A whispering tale in a fair lady's ear,
    Such as would please. 'Tis gone, 'tis gone, 'tis gone.
    You are welcome, gentlemen! Come, musicians, play.
                   [*Music plays, and they dance.*]
25   A hall,[5] a hall! Give room! And foot it, girls.

---

28. my mind . . . death My mind is fearful that some future event, fated by the stars, shall start to run its course tonight and cut my life short.

Reading Strategy
Using Text Aids Using note 28 as a text aid, restate Romeo's words in lines 109–111 in modern English.

1. trencher wooden platter.

2. marchpane marzipan, a confection made of sugar and almonds.

Literary Analysis
Character How do flat characters like the servingmen add to the play?

3. walk a bout dance a turn.

4. makes dainty hesitates, acts shy.

5. A hall clear the floor, make room for dancing.

✔Reading Check
What does Romeo fear might happen in the near future?

More light, you knaves, and turn the tables up,
And quench the fire; the room is grown too hot.
Ah, sirrah, this unlooked-for sport comes well.
Nay, sit; nay, sit, good cousin Capulet;
30　For you and I are past our dancing days.
How long is't now since last yourself and I
Were in a mask?

SECOND CAPULET.　　　By'r Lady, thirty years.

CAPULET. What, man? 'Tis not so much, 'tis not so much;
35　'Tis since the nuptial of Lucentio,
Come Pentecost as quickly as it will,
Some five-and-twenty years, and then we masked.

SECOND CAPULET. 'Tis more, 'tis more. His son is elder, sir;
His son is thirty.

CAPULET.　　　　　Will you tell me that?
40　His son was but a ward[6] two years ago.

ROMEO. [*To a* SERVINGMAN] What lady's that which doth
enrich the hand
Of yonder knight?

SERVINGMAN. I know not, sir.

ROMEO. O, she doth teach the torches to burn bright!
It seems she hangs upon the cheek of night
45　As a rich jewel in an Ethiop's ear—
Beauty too rich for use, for earth too dear!
So shows a snowy dove trooping with crows
As yonder lady o'er her fellows shows.
The measure done, I'll watch her place of stand
50　And, touching hers, make blessèd my rude hand.
Did my heart love till now? Forswear[7] it, sight!
For I ne'er saw true beauty till this night.

TYBALT. This, by his voice, should be a Montague.
Fetch me my rapier, boy. What! Dares the slave
55　Come hither, covered with an antic face,[8]
To fleer[9] and scorn at our solemnity?
Now, by the stock and honor of my kin,
To strike him dead I hold it not a sin.

CAPULET. Why, how now, kinsman? Wherefore storm you so?

60　**TYBALT.** Uncle, this is a Montague, our foe,
A villain, that is hither come in spite
To scorn at our solemnity this night.

CAPULET. Young Romeo is it?

TYBALT.　　　　　　'Tis he, that villain Romeo.

▲ Critical Viewing
What can you tell about
Romeo's personality from
the fact that he has taken
off his mask? **[Draw
Conclusions]**

6. **ward** minor.

7. **Forswear** deny.

8. **antic face** strange, fantastic mask.

9. **fleer** mock.

Reading Strategy
Using Text Aids What
does Tybalt mean by
saying that Romeo has
come to the party with an
"antic face, / To fleer and
scorn at our solemnity"?

CAPULET. Content thee, gentle coz,[10] let him alone.

65 'A bears him like a portly gentleman,[11]
And, to say truth, Verona brags of him
To be a virtuous and well-governed youth.
I would not for the wealth of all this town
Here in my house do him disparagement.[12]

70 Therefore be patient; take no note of him.
It is my will, the which if thou respect,
Show a fair presence and put off these frowns,
An ill-beseeming semblance[13] for a feast.

TYBALT. It fits when such a villain is a guest.
I'll not endure him.

75 **CAPULET.** He shall be endured.
What, goodman[14] boy! I say he shall. Go to![15]
Am I the master here, or you? Go to!
You'll not endure him, God shall mend my soul![16]
You'll make a mutiny among my guests!

80 You will set cock-a-hoop.[17] You'll be the man!

TYBALT. Why, uncle, 'tis a shame.

CAPULET. Go to, go to!
You are a saucy boy. Is't so, indeed?
This trick may chance to scathe you.[18] I know what.
You must contrary me! Marry, 'tis time–

85 Well said, my hearts!—You are a princox[19]—go!
Be quiet, or—more light, more light!—For shame!
I'll make you quiet. What!—Cheerly, my hearts!

TYBALT. Patience perforce with willful choler meeting[20]
Makes my flesh tremble in their different greeting.

90 I will withdraw; but this intrusion shall,
Now seeming sweet, convert to bitt'rest gall.   [*Exit.*]

ROMEO. If I profane with my unworthiest hand
    This holy shrine,[21] the gentle sin is this:
My lips, two blushing pilgrims, ready stand

95   To smooth that rough touch with a tender kiss.

JULIET. Good pilgrim, you do wrong your hand too much,
    Which mannerly devotion shows in this;
For saints have hands that pilgrims' hands do touch
    And palm to palm is holy palmers'[22] kiss.

100 **ROMEO.** Have not saints lips, and holy palmers too?

JULIET. Ay, pilgrim, lips that they must use in prayer.

ROMEO. O, then, dear saint, let lips do what hands do!
    They pray; grant thou, lest faith turn to despair.

JULIET. Saints do not move,[23] though grant for prayers' sake.

10. **coz** Here coz is used as a term of address for a relative.

11. **'A . . . gentleman** He behaves like a dignified gentleman.

12. **disparagement** insult.

13. **ill-beseeming semblance** inappropriate appearance.

14. **goodman** term of address for someone below the rank of gentleman.

15. **Go to!** expression of angry impatience.

16. **God . . . soul!** expression of impatience, equivalent to, "God save me!"

17. **You will set cock-a-hoop** You want to swagger like a barnyard rooster.

18. **This . . . you** This trait of yours may turn to hurt you.

19. **princox** rude youngster; wise guy.

20. **Patience . . . meeting** enforced self-control mixing with strong anger.

Literary Analysis
Character Which character traits do Romeo and Juliet reveal in their words to each other?

21. **shrine** Juliet's hand.

22. **palmers** pilgrims who at one time carried palm branches from the Holy Land.

23. **move** initiate involvement in earthly affairs.

✔**Reading Check**

How does Capulet respond when Tybalt says he will not tolerate Romeo's presence at the party?

105   **ROMEO.** Then move not while my prayer's effect I take.
     Thus from my lips, by thine my sin is purged.   *[Kisses her.]*

  JULIET. Then have my lips the sin that they have took.

  ROMEO. Sin from my lips? O trespass sweetly urged!²⁴
     Give me my sin again.   *[Kisses her.]*

  JULIET.   You kiss by th' book.²⁵

110   **NURSE.** Madam, your mother craves a word with you.

  ROMEO. What is her mother?

  NURSE.   Marry, bachelor,
     Her mother is the lady of the house,
     And a good lady, and a wise and virtuous.
     I nursed her daughter that you talked withal.
115   I tell you, he that can lay hold of her
     Shall have the chinks.²⁶

  ROMEO.   Is she a Capulet?
     O dear account! My life is my foe's debt.²⁷

  BENVOLIO. Away, be gone; the sport is at the best.

  ROMEO. Ay, so I fear; the more is my unrest.

120   **CAPULET.** Nay, gentlemen, prepare not to be gone;
     We have a trifling foolish banquet towards.²⁸
     Is it e'en so?²⁹ Why then, I thank you all.
     I thank you, honest gentlemen. Good night.
     More torches here! Come on then; let's to bed.
125   Ah, sirrah, by my fay,³⁰ it waxes late;
     I'll to my rest.   *[Exit all but* JULIET *and* NURSE.]

▲ **Critical Viewing**
What does this picture suggest about Romeo and Juliet's feelings for each other? **[Infer]**

24. **O . . . urged!** Romeo is saying, in substance, that he is happy. Juliet calls his kiss a sin, for now he can take it back—by another kiss.

25. **by th' book** as if you were following a manual of courtly love.

26. **chinks** cash.

27. **My life . . . debt** Since Juliet is a Capulet, Romeo's life is at the mercy of the enemies of his family.

Reading Strategy
Using Text Aids What do you learn from the text aid that helps you understand Romeo's conflict?

28. **towards** being prepared.

29. **Is . . . so?** Is it the case that you really must leave?

30. **fay** faith.

JULIET. Come hither, nurse. What is yond gentleman?

NURSE. The son and heir of old Tiberio.

JULIET. What's he that now is going out of door?

130 **NURSE.** Marry, that, I think, be young Petruchio.

JULIET. What's he that follows here, that would not dance?

NURSE. I know not.

JULIET. Go ask his name—If he is married,
    My grave is like to be my wedding bed.

135 **NURSE.** His name is Romeo, and a Montague,
    The only son of your great enemy.

JULIET. My only love, sprung from my only hate!
    Too early seen unknown, and known too late!
    Prodigious[31] birth of love it is to me
140   That I must love a loathèd enemy.

NURSE. What's this? What's this?

JULIET.   A rhyme I learnt even now.
    Of one I danced withal.   [*One calls within,* "Juliet."]

NURSE.   Anon, anon!
    Come, let's away; the strangers all are gone.   [*Exit all.*]

31. Prodigious monstrous; foretelling misfortune.

Review and Assess

Thinking About Act I

1. **Respond:** If you were Romeo or Juliet, would you pursue a relationship? Explain.

2. **(a) Recall:** Based on Act I, what facts do you know about Romeo's and Juliet's lives? **(b) Compare and Contrast:** How are these characters' personalities alike and different?

3. **(a) Recall:** What information about the two households is presented in the Prologue? **(b) Connect:** How does Juliet's comment in Act I, Scene v, lines 137–138, echo the Prologue?

4. **Analyze:** How do the comments of Montague and Benvolio in Act I help you understand the character of Romeo?

5. **(a) Analyze:** What threats to Romeo and Juliet's love already exist in Act I? **(b) Support:** How does Shakespeare use these threats to generate suspense in the first act?

6. **Evaluate:** Based on Romeo's behavior in Act I, do you think Shakespeare accurately portrays a teenager in love? Explain.

Review and Assess

Literary Analysis

Character

1. Which single personality trait makes Gregory and Sampson **flat characters**?
2. Which personality traits make Mercutio and Benvolio **round characters**? Use a chart like the one shown to list their character traits.

Character	Personality Traits	Character Type

3. Is Romeo a round or flat character? Explain.

Connecting Literary Elements

4. How is Benvolio a **dramatic foil** for Romeo? Using a chart like the one shown, record their contrasting personality traits.

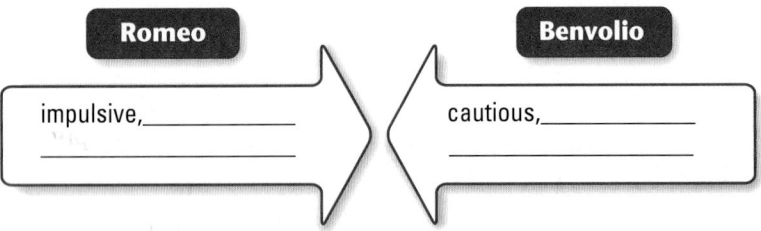

Romeo — impulsive, _____ _____

Benvolio — cautious, _____ _____

5. How is Mercutio a dramatic foil for Romeo?
6. Does Juliet have a foil? Explain.

Reading Strategy

Using Text Aids

7. (a) Use the **text aids** to restate Capulet's scolding of Tybalt in Act I, Scene v, lines 77–87. (b) Express his meaning in your own words.
8. Using text aids, explain the play on words in Juliet's speech in Act I, Scene v, lines 96–99.

Extend Understanding

9. **Social Studies Connection:** Identify a city or region in the world today where a couple from rival groups might have great difficulty establishing a relationship. Explain your choices.

Integrate Language Skills

Vocabulary Development Lesson

Word Analysis: Latin Prefix *trans-*

The Latin prefix *trans-* means "through" or "across," as in *transgression*, "the act of going across the boundary of appropriate behavior." Using the meaning of *trans-*, write a definition for each word below.

1. transport   **2.** translate   **3.** transform

Spelling Strategy

If a word ends in two consonants, do not double the final consonant when adding a suffix: *augment* + *-ing* = *augmenting*. Add *-ful*, *-al*, or *-or* to each word below to form three correct words.

1. respect   **2.** ornament   **3.** instruct

Concept Development: Analogies

In your notebook, write the word that best completes each analogy, or comparison.

1. thoughtful : kind :: pernicious : ____?____
   (a) useful, (b) helpful, (c) harmful
2. decreasing : less :: augmenting : ____?____
   (a) fewer, (b) more, (c) several
3. problem : solution :: grievance : ____?____
   (a) satisfaction, (b) complaint, (c) sadness
4. habitation : home :: transgression : ____?____
   (a) blessing, (b) crime, (c) illness
5. believers : agree :: heretics : ____?____
   (a) heresy, (b) dissent, (c) outcasts

Grammar Lesson

Pronoun Case in Elliptical Clauses

In an **elliptical clause,** one or more words are unstated because they are understood. To determine the correct case of a pronoun in an elliptical clause, determine the placement of the unstated words. If the unstated words come after the pronoun, use a **nominative case pronoun.** If the unstated words come before the pronoun, use an **objective case pronoun.** In these examples, the unstated word or words are shown in brackets.

Nominative:	Juliet is younger than *he* [is].
Objective:	They gave Juliet the same warning as [they gave] *him.*

Practice Choose the correct pronoun to complete each item. State the word or phrase missing from the elliptical clause.

1. Romeo was as love-struck as (she, her).
2. He listens to him more than to (she, her).
3. No one else felt as upset as (he, him).
4. Capulet was friendlier than (he, him).
5. Nurse felt closer to Juliet than to (he, him).

Writing Application Write two sentences about Act I, using elliptical clauses in each.

WG *Prentice Hall Writing and Grammar Connection: Chapter 24, Section 2*

Extension Activities

Writing As Romeo or Juliet, write a letter requesting help with the problem of falling in love with the wrong person. In a **letter to an advice columnist,** explain your dilemma. Then, write the columnist's response.

Listening and Speaking Select a scene from Act I to perform with classmates. Practice reading your lines aloud and perform your **oral reading** for the class. Then, discuss how delivery of the lines affects the mood of the scene. **[Group Activity]**

Prepare to Read

The Tragedy of Romeo and Juliet, Act II

CALIFORNIA STANDARDS

Instruction with this selection addresses these standards:

R 1.1*, 3.1*, 3.3*, 3.4*, 3.7*

W 1.1*, 2.4*

WOLC 1.2*

LS 1.11

* Standards tested on HS Exit Exam. For complete standards, see p. CA 4.

Literary Analysis

Blank Verse

Blank verse is unrhymed poetry written in iambic pentameter, or lines of five stressed beats in which every second syllable is stressed. For example, when Romeo sees Juliet appear at her window, he exclaims,

> But soft! What light through yonder window breaks?
> It is the east, and Juliet is the sun!

Much of *Romeo and Juliet* is written in blank verse. This formal meter is well suited to serious subjects. As you read, say some of the lines aloud and note the effect of the stressed syllables and words spoken in blank verse.

Connecting Literary Elements

In a play, you generally learn about characters from the things they say and do and the way they speak. In Shakespeare's plays, blank verse helps reinforce **character rank:** Important or aristocratic characters typically speak in blank verse. Minor or comic characters often do not speak in verse. Use a chart like the one shown to identify a character's rank in this play.

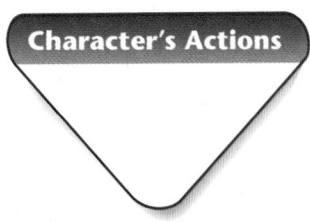

Character's Speech
- Formal
- Informal

Character's Actions

Reading Strategy

Reading Blank Verse

When **reading blank verse,** remember that thoughts or phrases often run past the end of a line. To determine its full meaning, read blank verse in sentences, pausing according to the punctuation and not necessarily at the end of each line.

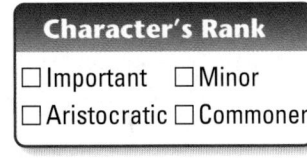

Character's Rank
- ☐ Important ☐ Minor
- ☐ Aristocratic ☐ Commoner

Vocabulary Development

cunning (kun′ iŋ) *n.* cleverness; slyness (p. 799)

procure (prō kyoor′) *v.* get (p. 801)

vile (vīl) *adj.* worthless (p. 803)

predominant (prē däm′ ə nənt) *adj.* having dominating influence over others (p. 803)

intercession (in′ tər sesh′ ən) *n.* the act of pleading on behalf of another (p. 804)

sallow (sal′ ō) *adj.* of a sickly, pale-yellowish complexion (p. 804)

waverer (wā′ vər ər) *n.* one who changes or is unsteady (p. 805)

lamentable (lə men′ tə bəl) *adj.* distressing; sad (p. 806)

unwieldy (un wēl′ dē) *adj.* awkward; clumsy (p. 811)

Review and Anticipate

Act I reveals a bitter, long-standing feud between the Montagues and the Capulets. It also introduces the play's title characters, who meet at a feast and immediately fall in love, only to discover that they come from opposing sides of the feud.

Based on what you have learned about the personalities of Romeo and Juliet, how do you expect them to respond to their love for each other and to the problems it poses? How do you think their families will react?

[*Enter* CHORUS.]

CHORUS. Now old desire[1] doth in his deathbed lie,
    And young affection gapes to be his heir;[2]
That fair[3] for which love groaned for and would die,
    With tender Juliet matched, is now not fair.
5 Now Romeo is beloved and loves again,
    Alike bewitchèd[4] by the charm of looks;
But to his foe supposed he must complain,[5]
    And she steal love's sweet bait from fearful hooks.
Being held a foe, he may not have access
10   To breathe such vows as lovers use to swear,

1. old desire Romeo's love for Rosaline.

2. young . . . heir Romeo's new love for Juliet is eager to replace his love for Rosaline.

3. fair beautiful woman (Rosaline).

4. Alike bewitched Both Romeo and Juliet are enchanted.

5. complain address his words of love.

And she as much in love, her means much less
    To meet her new belovèd anywhere;
But passion lends them power, time means to meet,
Temp'ring extremities with extreme sweet.[6]   [*Exit.*]

6. **Temp'ring . . . sweet**
easing their difficulties
with great delights.

Scene i. *Near* CAPULET's *orchard.*

[*Enter* ROMEO *alone.*]

ROMEO. Can I go forward when my heart is here?
    Turn back, dull earth,[1] and find thy center[2] out.

[*Enter* BENVOLIO *with* MERCUTIO. ROMEO *retires.*]

BENVOLIO. Romeo! My cousin Romeo! Romeo!

MERCUTIO.   He is wise.
    And, on my life, hath stol'n him home to bed.

5 **BENVOLIO.** He ran this way and leapt this orchard wall.
    Call, good Mercutio.

MERCUTIO.   Nay, I'll conjure[3] too.
    Romeo! Humors! Madman! Passion! Lover!
    Appear thou in the likeness of a sigh;
    Speak but one rhyme, and I am satisfied!
10   Cry but "Ay me!" pronounce but "love" and "dove";
    Speak to my gossip[4] Venus one fair word,
    One nickname for her purblind son and heir,
    Young Abraham Cupid, he that shot so true
    When King Cophetua loved the beggar maid!
15   He heareth not, he stirreth not, he moveth not;
    The ape is dead,[5] and I must conjure him.
    I conjure thee by Rosaline's bright eyes,
    By her high forehead and her scarlet lip,
    By her fine foot, straight leg, and quivering thigh,
20   And the demesnes that there adjacent lie,
    That in thy likeness thou appear to us!

BENVOLIO. And if he hear thee, thou wilt anger him.

MERCUTIO. This cannot anger him. 'Twould anger him
    To raise a spirit in his mistress' circle
25   Of some strange nature, letting it there stand
    Till she had laid it and conjured it down.
    That were some spite; my invocation
    Is fair and honest; in his mistress' name,
    I conjure only but to raise up him.

30 **BENVOLIO.** Come, he hath hid himself among these trees
    To be consorted[6] with the humorous[7] night.
    Blind is his love and best befits the dark.

MERCUTIO. If love be blind, love cannot hit the mark.

1. **dull earth** lifeless
body.
2. **center** heart, or
possibly soul (Juliet).

Literary Analysis
Blank Verse Line 3
breaks the pattern of
blank verse. Why is this
break suited to the emo-
tion of the line?

3. **conjure** recite a spell
to make Romeo appear.

4. **gossip** merry old lady.

Reading Strategy
Reading Blank Verse
When reading Mercutio's
speech (lines 6–21),
where should you pause
and where should you
come to a complete
stop?

5. **The ape is dead**
Romeo, like a trained
monkey, seems to be
playing.

6. **consorted** associated.
7. **humorous** humid;
moody, like a lover.

Now will he sit under a medlar tree

35 And wish his mistress were that kind of fruit
As maids call medlars[8] when they laugh alone.
O, Romeo, that she were, O that she were
An open *et cetera*, thou a pop'rin pear!
Romeo, good night. I'll to my truckle bed;[9]

40 This field bed is too cold for me to sleep.
Come, shall we go?

BENVOLIO.   Go then, for 'tis in vain
To seek him here that means not to be found.

[*Exit with others.*]

8. **medlars** applelike fruits.

9. **truckle bed** trundlebed, placed under a larger bed when not in use.

S**cene ii.** CAPULET'*s orchard.*

ROMEO. [*Coming forward*] He jests at scars that never felt a wound.

[*Enters* JULIET *at a window.*]

But soft! What light through yonder window breaks?
It is the East, and Juliet is the sun!
Arise, fair sun, and kill the envious moon,

5 Who is already sick and pale with grief
That thou her maid art far more fair than she.
Be not her maid, since she is envious.
Her vestal livery[1] is but sick and green,
And none but fools do wear it. Cast it off.

10 It is my lady! O, it is my love!
O, that she knew she were!
She speaks, yet she says nothing. What of that?
Her eye discourses; I will answer it.
I am too bold; 'tis not to me she speaks.

15 Two of the fairest stars in all the heaven,
Having some business, do entreat her eyes
To twinkle in their spheres[2] till they return.
What if her eyes were there, they in her head?
The brightness of her cheek would shame those stars

20 As daylight doth a lamp; her eyes in heaven
Would through the airy region stream so bright
That birds would sing and think it were not night.
See how she leans her cheek upon that hand,
O, that I were a glove upon that hand,
That I might touch that cheek!

JULIET.   Ay me!

25 **ROMEO.**   She speaks.
O, speak again, bright angel, for thou art
As glorious to this night, being o'er my head,
As is a wingèd messenger of heaven
Unto the white-upturnèd wond'ring eyes

Literary Analysis
Blank Verse What effect does Shakespeare achieve by breaking up a rhymed couplet—a pair of rhyming lines—into two separate scenes?

1. **livery** clothing or costume worn by a servant.

2. **spheres** orbits.

Reading Strategy
Reading Blank Verse Why does reading Romeo's speech in complete sentences instead of line by line help you grasp its meaning?

✔**Reading Check**
Whom does Romeo see at the window?

30 Of mortals that fall back to gaze on him
When he bestrides the lazy puffing clouds
And sails upon the bosom of the air.

JULIET. O Romeo, Romeo! Wherefore art thou Romeo?[3]
Deny thy father and refuse thy name;
35 Or, if thou wilt not, be but sworn my love,
And I'll no longer be a Capulet.

ROMEO. [*Aside*] Shall I hear more, or shall I speak at this?

JULIET. Tis but thy name that is my enemy.
Thou art thyself, though not[4] a Montague.
40 What's Montague? It is nor hand, nor foot,
Nor arm, nor face, nor any other part
Belonging to a man. O, be some other name!
What's in a name? That which we call a rose
By any other name would smell as sweet.
45 So Romeo would, were he not Romeo called,
Retain that dear perfection which he owes[5]
Without that title. Romeo, doff[6] thy name;
And for thy name, which is no part of thee,
Take all myself.

ROMEO.   I take thee at thy word.
50 Call me but love, and I'll be new baptized;
Henceforth I never will be Romeo.

JULIET. What man art thou, thus bescreened in night,
So stumblest on my counsel?[7]

ROMEO.   By a name
I know not how to tell thee who I am.
55 My name, dear saint, is hateful to myself
Because it is an enemy to thee.
Had I it written, I would tear the word.

JULIET. My ears have yet not drunk a hundred words
Of thy tongue's uttering, yet I know the sound.
60 Art thou not Romeo, and a Montague?

ROMEO. Neither, fair maid, if either thee dislike.

JULIET. How camest thou hither, tell me, and wherefore?
The orchard walls are high and hard to climb,
And the place death, considering who thou art,
65 If any of my kinsmen find thee here.

ROMEO. With love's light wings did I o'erperch[8] these walls;
For stony limits cannot hold love out,
And what love can do, that dares love attempt.
Therefore thy kinsmen are no stop to me.

70 JULIET. If they do see thee, they will murder thee.

3. Wherefore . . . Romeo? Why are you Romeo—a Montague?

4. though not even if you were not.

5. owes owns; possesses.

6. doff remove.

7. counsel secret thoughts.

Literary Analysis
Blank Verse As in some other lines in this scene, the five beats of line 53 are split between two speakers. How is this suited to the fact that the two speakers are in love?

8. o'erperch fly over.

ROMEO. Alack, there lies more peril in thine eye
  Than twenty of their swords! Look thou but sweet,
  And I am proof[9] against their enmity.

JULIET. I would not for the world they saw thee here.

75 **ROMEO.** I have night's cloak to hide me from their eyes;
  And but[10] thou love me, let them find me here.
  My life were better ended by their hate
  Than death proroguèd,[11] wanting of thy love.

JULIET. By whose direction found'st thou out this place?

80 **ROMEO.** By love, that first did prompt me to inquire.
  He lent me counsel, and I lent him eyes.
  I am no pilot; yet, wert thou as far
  As that vast shore washed with the farthest sea,
  I should adventure[12] for such merchandise.

85 **JULIET.** Thou knowest the mask of night is on my face;
  Else would a maiden blush bepaint my cheek
  For that which thou hast heard me speak tonight.
  Fain would I dwell on form[13]—fain, fain deny
  What I have spoke; but farewell compliment![14]
90 Dost thou love me? I know thou wilt say "Ay";
  And I will take thy word. Yet, if thou swear'st,
  Thou mayst prove false. At lovers' perjuries,
  They say Jove laughs. O gentle Romeo,
  If thou dost love, pronounce it faithfully.
95 Or if thou thinkest I am too quickly won,
  I'll frown and be perverse[15] and say thee nay,
  So thou wilt woo; but else, not for the world.
  In truth, fair Montague, I am too fond,[16]
  And therefore thou mayst think my havior light;[17]
100 But trust me, gentleman, I'll prove more true
  Than those that have more cunning to be strange.[18]
  I should have been more strange, I must confess,
  But that thou overheard'st, ere I was ware,
  My truelove passion. Therefore pardon me,
105 And not impute this yielding to light love,
  Which the dark night hath so discoverèd.[19]

ROMEO. Lady, by yonder blessèd moon I vow,
  That tips with silver all these fruit-tree tops—

JULIET. O, swear not by the moon, th' inconstant moon,
110 That monthly changes in her circle orb,
  Lest that thy love prove likewise variable.

ROMEO. What shall I swear by?

JULIET.   Do not swear at all;
  Or if thou wilt, swear by thy gracious self,

Literary Analysis
Blank Verse In line 72, what is the effect of the stressed syllable *swords*? Explain.

9. **proof** protected, as by armor.

10. **And but** unless.

11. **proroguèd** postponed.

12. **adventure** risk a long journey, like a sea adventurer.

13. **Fain . . . form** eagerly would I follow convention (by acting reserved).

14. **compliment** conventional behavior.

15. **be perverse** act contrary to my true feelings.

16. **fond** affectionate.

17. **my havior light** my behavior immodest or unserious.

cunning (kun´ iŋ) *n.* cleverness; slyness

18. **strange** distant and cold.

19. **discoverèd** revealed.

Reading Check

Why does Romeo say his name is hateful to him?

Which is the god of my idolatry,
And I'll believe thee.

115 **ROMEO.**   If my heart's dear love—

JULIET. Well, do not swear. Although I joy in thee,
I have no joy of this contract[20] tonight.
It is too rash, too unadvised, too sudden;
Too like the lightning, which doth cease to be
120 Ere one can say it lightens. Sweet, good night!
This bud of love, by summer's ripening breath,
May prove a beauteous flow'r when next we meet.
Good night, good night! As sweet repose and rest
Come to thy heart as that within my breast!

125 **ROMEO.** O, wilt thou leave me so unsatisfied?

JULIET. What satisfaction canst thou have tonight?

ROMEO. Th' exchange of thy love's faithful vow for mine.

JULIET. I gave thee mine before thou didst request it;
And yet I would it were to give again.

130 **ROMEO.** Wouldst thou withdraw it? For what purpose, love?

JULIET. But to be frank[21] and give it thee again.
And yet I wish but for the thing I have.
My bounty[22] is as boundless as the sea,
My love as deep; the more I give to thee,

20. **contract** betrothal.

Reading Strategy
Reading Blank Verse
How would you rephrase in Standard English what Romeo and Juliet are saying to each other?

21. **frank** generous.

22. **bounty** what I have to give.

◄ **Critical Viewing**
How does Juliet's expression in this picture match the feelings she has conveyed in the play so far? **[Connect]**

135 The more I have, for both are infinite,
I hear some noise within. Dear love, adieu!

[NURSE *calls within.*]

Anon, good nurse! Sweet Montague, be true.
Stay but a little, I will come again.   [*Exit.*]

ROMEO. O blessèd, blessèd night! I am afeard,
140 Being in night, all this is but a dream,
Too flattering-sweet to be substantial.[23]

[*Enter* JULIET *again.*]

JULIET. Three words, dear Romeo, and good night indeed.
If that thy bent[24] of love be honorable,
Thy purpose marriage, send me word tomorrow,
145 By one that I'll procure to come to thee,
Where and what time thou wilt perform the rite;
And all my fortunes at thy foot I'll lay
And follow thee my lord throughout the world.

NURSE. [*Within*] Madam!

150 **JULIET.** I come anon.—But if thou meanest not well,
I do beseech thee—

NURSE.   [*Within*] Madam!

JULIET.   By and by[25] I come.—
To cease thy strife[26] and leave me to my grief.
Tomorrow will I send.

ROMEO.   So thrive my soul—

JULIET. A thousand times good night!   [*Exit.*]

155 **ROMEO.** A thousand times the worse, to want thy light!
Love goes toward love as schoolboys from their books;
But love from love, toward school with heavy looks.

[*Enter* JULIET *again.*]

JULIET. Hist! Romeo, hist! O for a falc'ner's voice
To lure this tassel gentle[27] back again!
160 Bondage is hoarse[28] and may not speak aloud,
Else would I tear the cave where Echo[29] lies
And make her airy tongue more hoarse than mine
With repetition of "My Romeo!"

ROMEO. It is my soul that calls upon my name.
165 How silver-sweet sound lovers' tongues by night,
Like softest music to attending ears!

JULIET. Romeo!

ROMEO.   My sweet?

Literary Analysis
Blank Verse Analyze lines 135–136. Do they meet the criteria of blank verse? Explain.

23. **substantial** real.

24. **bent** purpose; intention.

procure (prō kyoor′) *v.* get

Literary Analysis
Blank Verse Two speakers share the rhythm of line 151. Does the Nurse's interruption complete or break the blank verse?

25. **By and by** at once.

26. **strife** efforts.

27. **tassel gentle** male falcon.

28. **Bondage is hoarse** Being bound in by my family restricts my speech.

29. **Echo** In classical mythology, the nymph Echo, unable to win the love of Narcissus, wasted away in a cave until nothing was left of her but her voice.

✔**Reading Check**

What plan do Romeo and Juliet make for the following day?

JULIET. What o'clock tomorrow
Shall I send to thee?

ROMEO. By the hour of nine.

JULIET. I will not fail. 'Tis twenty year till then.
170   I have forgot why I did call thee back.

ROMEO. Let me stand here till thou remember it.

JULIET. I shall forget, to have thee still stand there,
    Rememb'ring how I love thy company.

ROMEO. And I'll stay, to have thee still forget,
175   Forgetting any other home but this.

JULIET. 'Tis almost morning. I would have thee gone—
    And yet no farther than a wanton's[30] bird,
    That lets it hop a little from his hand,
    Like a poor prisoner in his twisted gyves,[31]
180   And with a silken thread plucks it back again,
    So loving-jealous of his liberty.

ROMEO. I would I were thy bird.

JULIET. Sweet, so would I.
    Yet I should kill thee with much cherishing.
    Good night, good night! Parting is such sweet sorrow
185   That I shall say good night till it be morrow.   [*Exit.*]

ROMEO. Sleep dwell upon thine eyes, peace in thy breast!
    Would I were sleep and peace, so sweet to rest!
    Hence will I to my ghostly friar's[32] close cell,[33]
    His help to crave and my dear hap[34] to tell.   [*Exit.*]

*S*cene iii. FRIAR LAWRENCE's *cell.*

[*Enter* FRIAR LAWRENCE *alone, with a basket.*]

FRIAR. The gray-eyed morn smiles on the frowning night,

*L*iterature
in context Literature Connection

Hyperbole
Hyperbole is deliberate exaggeration in writing or speech. For example, in lines 71–72, when Romeo says the look in Juliet's eyes is more dangerous than twenty of her kinsmen's swords, he uses hyperbole to express the power in the beauty of her eyes. Several times in this scene, as in line 169, both young lovers use hyperbole to emphasize their love.

Check'ring the eastern clouds with streaks of light;
And fleckèd[1] darkness like a drunkard reels
From forth day's path and Titan's burning wheels.[2]
5   Now, ere the sun advance his burning eye
The day to cheer and night's dank dew to dry,
I must upfill this osier cage[3] of ours
With baleful[4] weeds and precious-juicèd flowers.
The earth that's nature's mother is her tomb.
10   What is her burying grave, that is her womb;
And from her womb children of divers kind[5]
We sucking on her natural bosom find,
Many for many virtues excellent,
None but for some, and yet all different.
15   O, mickle[6] is the powerful grace[7] that lies
In plants, herbs, stones, and their true qualities;
For naught so vile that on the earth doth live
But to the earth some special good doth give;
Nor aught so good but, strained[8] from that fair use,
20   Revolts from true birth,[9] stumbling on abuse.
Virtue itself turns vice, being misapplied,
And vice sometime by action dignified.

[*Enter* ROMEO.]

Within the infant rind[10] of this weak flower
Poison hath residence and medicine power;[11]
25   For this, being smelt, with that part cheers each part;[12]
Being tasted, stays all senses with the heart.[13]
Two such opposèd kings encamp them still[14]
In man as well as herbs—grace and rude will;
And where the worser is predominant,
30   Full soon the canker[15] death eats up that plant.

ROMEO. Good morrow, father.

FRIAR.   *Benedicite!*[16]
What early tongue so sweet saluteth me?
Young son, it argues a distemperèd head[17]
So soon to bid good morrow to thy bed.
35   Care keeps his watch in every old man's eye,
And where care lodges, sleep will never lie;
But where unbruisèd youth with unstuffed[18] brain
Doth couch his limbs, there golden sleep doth reign,
Therefore thy earliness doth me assure
40   Thou art uproused with some distemp'rature;[19]
Or if not so, then here I hit it right—
Our Romeo hath not been in bed tonight.

ROMEO. That last is true. The sweeter rest was mine.

FRIAR. God pardon sin! Wast thou with Rosaline?

1. **fleckèd** spotted.
2. **Titan's burning wheels** wheels of the sun god's chariot.
3. **osier cage** willow basket.
4. **baleful** poisonous.
5. **divers kind** different kinds.
6. **mickle** great.
7. **grace** divine power.
8. **strained** turned away.

vile (vīl) *adj.* worthless

9. **Revolts . . . birth** conflicts with its real purpose.
10. **infant rind** tender skin.
11. **and medicine power** and medicinal quality has power.
12. **with . . . part** with that quality—odor—revives each part of the body.
13. **stays . . . heart** kills (stops the working of the five senses along with the heart).

predominant (prē däm′ ə nənt) *adj.* having dominating influence over others

14. **still** always.
15. **canker** a destructive caterpillar.
16. *Benedicite!* God bless you!
17. **distemperèd head** troubled mind.
18. **unstuffed** not filled with cares.
19. **distemp'rature** illness.

✔**Reading Check**

When Romeo leaves Juliet, what reason does he give for visiting the Friar?

45 **ROMEO.** With Rosaline, my ghostly father? No.
       I have forgot that name and that name's woe.

FRIAR. That's my good son! But where hast thou been then?

   ROMEO. I'll tell thee ere thou ask it me again.
       I have been feasting with mine enemy,
50   Where on a sudden one hath wounded me
       That's by me wounded. Both our remedies
       Within thy help and holy physic[20] lies.
       I bear no hatred, blessèd man, for, lo,
       My <u>intercession</u> likewise steads my foe.[21]

55 **FRIAR.** Be plain, good son, and homely in thy drift.[22]
       Riddling confession finds but riddling shrift.[23]

   ROMEO. Then plainly know my heart's dear love is set
       On the fair daughter of rich Capulet;
       As mine on hers, so hers is set on mine,
60   And all combined, save[24] what thou must combine
       By holy marriage. When and where and how
       We met, we wooed, and made exchange of vow,
       I'll tell thee as we pass; but this I pray,
       That thou consent to marry us today.

65 **FRIAR.** Holy Saint Francis! What a change is here!
       Is Rosaline, that thou didst love so dear,
       So soon forsaken? Young men's love then lies
       Not truly in their hearts, but in their eyes.
       Jesu Maria! What a deal of brine[25]
70   Hath washed thy <u>sallow</u> cheeks for Rosaline!
       How much salt water thrown away in waste
       To season love, that of it doth not taste!
       The sun not yet thy sighs from heaven clears,
       Thy old groans ring yet in mine ancient ears.
75   Lo, here upon thy cheek the stain doth sit
       Of an old tear that is not washed off yet.
       If e'er thou wast thyself, and these woes thine,
       Thou and these woes were all for Rosaline.
       And art thou changed? Pronounce this sentence then:
80   Women may fall[26] when there's no strength[27] in men.

   ROMEO. Thou chidst me oft for loving Rosaline.

   FRIAR. For doting,[28] not for loving, pupil mine.

   ROMEO. And badst[29] me bury love.

   FRIAR.   Not in a grave
       To lay one in, another out to have.

85 **ROMEO.** I pray thee chide me not. Her I love now
       Doth grace[30] for grace and love for love allow.[31]
       The other did not so.

---

20. physic (fiz´ ik) medicine.

21. My . . . foe my plea also helps my enemy (Juliet, a Capulet).

intercession (in´ tər sesh´ ən) *n.* the act of pleading on behalf of another

22. and . . . drift and simple in your speech.

23. Riddling . . . shrift A confusing confession will get you uncertain forgiveness. The Friar means that unless Romeo speaks clearly, he will not get clear and direct advice.

24. And . . . save and we are united in every way, except for (save).

25. brine salt water (tears).

sallow (sal´ ō) *adj.* of a sickly, pale-yellowish complexion

26. fall be weak or inconstant.

Literary Analysis
Blank Verse Which important words are stressed in the last six lines of the Friar's speech?

27. strength constancy; stability.

28. doting being infatuated.

29. badst urged.

30. grace favor.
31. allow give.

FRIAR.   O, she knew well
         Thy love did read by rote, that could not spell.[32]
         But come, young <u>waverer</u>, come go with me.
90   In one respect I'll thy assistant be;
         For this alliance may so happy prove
         To turn your households' rancor[33] to pure love.

ROMEO. O, let us hence! I stand on[34] sudden haste.

FRIAR. Wisely and slow. They stumble that run fast.   [*Exit all.*]

Scene iv. *A street.*

[*Enter* BENVOLIO *and* MERCUTIO.]

MERCUTIO. Where the devil should this Romeo be?
         Came he not home tonight?

BENVOLIO. Not to his father's. I spoke with his man.

MERCUTIO. Why, that same pale hardhearted wench, that Rosaline,
5   Torments him so that he will sure run mad.

BENVOLIO. Tybalt, the kinsman to old Capulet,
         Hath sent a letter to his father's house.

MERCUTIO. A challenge, on my life.

BENVOLIO. Romeo will answer it.

10 **MERCUTIO.** Any man that can write may answer a letter.

BENVOLIO. Nay, he will answer the letter's master, how he dares,
         being dared.

MERCUTIO. Alas, poor Romeo, he is already dead: stabbed
         with a white wench's black eye; run through the ear
15   with a love song; the very pin of his heart cleft with the
         blind bow-boy's butt-shaft;[1] and is he a man to encounter Tybalt?

BENVOLIO. Why, what is Tybalt?

MERCUTIO. More than Prince of Cats.[2] O, he's the coura-
         geous captain of compliments.[3] He fights as you sing
20   pricksong[4]—keeps time, distance, and proportion; he
         rests his minim rests,[5] one, two, and the third in your
         bosom! The very butcher of a silk button,[6] a duelist, a
         duelist! A gentleman of the very first house,[7] of the first
         and second cause.[8] Ah, the immortal *passado!* The
25   *punto reverso!* The hay![9]

BENVOLIO. The what?

MERCUTIO. The pox of such antic, lisping, affecting fantas-
         ticoes—these new tuners of accent![10] "By Jesu, a very
         good blade! A very tall man! A very good whore!" Why,

32. Thy . . . spell your love recited words from memory with no understanding of them.

waverer (wā′ vər ər) *n.* one who changes or is unsteady

33. rancor hatred.

34. stand on insist on.

1. blind bow-boy's butt-shaft Cupid's blunt arrow.

2. Prince of Cats Tybalt, or a variation of it, is the name of the cat in medieval stories of Reynard the Fox.

3. captain of compliments master of formal behavior.

4. as you sing prick-song with attention to precision.

5. rests . . . rests observes all formalities.

6. button an exact spot on his opponent's shirt.

7. first house finest school of fencing.

8. the first and second cause reasons that would cause a gentleman to challenge another to a duel.

9. *passado! . . . punto reverso! . . . hay!* lunge . . . backhanded stroke . . . home thrust.

10. The pox . . . accent May the plague strike these absurd characters with their phony manners—these men who speak in weird, newfangled ways!

✔ **Reading Check**

What does the Friar think Romeo and Juliet's love will do for the Capulets and Montagues?

30   is not this a <u>lamentable</u> thing, grandsir, that we
should be thus afflicted with these strange flies, these
fashionmongers, these pardon-me's,[11] who stand so
much on the new form that they cannot sit at ease on
the old bench? O, their bones, their bones!

[*Enter* ROMEO.]

35   **BENVOLIO.** Here comes Romeo! Here comes Romeo!

  MERCUTIO. Without his roe, like a dried herring.[12] O flesh,
flesh, how art thou fishified! Now is he for the numbers[13] that Petrarch flowed in. Laura,[14] to his lady, was
a kitchen wench (marry, she had a better love to be-
40   rhyme her), Dido a dowdy, Cleopatra a gypsy, Helen
and Hero hildings and harlots, Thisbe a gray eye or so,
but not to the purpose. Signior Romeo, *bon jour!*
There's a French salutation to your French slop. You
gave us the counterfeit fairly last night.

45   **ROMEO.** Good morrow to you both. What counterfeit did I
give you?

  MERCUTIO. The slip,[15] sir, the slip. Can you not conceive?

  ROMEO. Pardon, good Mercutio. My business was great,
and in such a case as mine a man may strain courtesy.

lamentable (lə men´ tə bəl)
adj. distressing; sad

11. these pardon-me's
these men who are
always saying "Pardon
me" (adopting ridiculous
manners).

**12. Without . . . her-
ring** worn out.

13. numbers verses of
love poems.

14. Laura Laura and the
other ladies mentioned
are all notable figures of
European love literature.
Mercutio is saying that
Romeo thinks that none
of them compare with
Rosaline.

15. slip escape. *Slip* is
also a term for counter-
feit coin.

Literary Analysis
Blank Verse Why do you
think the conversation
between Romeo and his
friends is not in blank
verse?

◀ **Critical Viewing**
How is the rowdy
behavior of the young
Montagues, as shown in
this picture, typical of a
group of teenage friends?
[Generalize]

◀ **Critical Viewing**
How do the men in this picture compare with your image of the three men in this scene? [Generalize]

50 **MERCUTIO.** That's as much as to say, such a case as yours constrains a man to bow in the hams.[16]

ROMEO. Meaning, to curtsy.

MERCUTIO. Thou hast most kindly hit it.

ROMEO. A most courteous exposition.

55 **MERCUTIO.** Nay, I am the very pink of courtesy.

ROMEO. Pink for flower.

MERCUTIO. Right.

ROMEO. Why, then is my pump[17] well-flowered.

MERCUTIO. Sure wit, follow me this jest now till thou hast
60 worn out thy pump, that, when the single sole of it is worn, the jest may remain, after the wearing, solely singular.[18]

ROMEO. O single-soled jest, solely singular for the single-ness![19]

65 **MERCUTIO.** Come between us, good Benvolio! My wits faints.

ROMEO. Swits and spurs, swits and spurs; or I'll cry a match.[20]

MERCUTIO. Nay, if our wits run the wild-goose chase, I am done; for thou hast more of the wild goose in one of

16. **hams** hips.

17. **pump** shoe.

18. **when . . . singular**
the jest will outwear the shoe and will then be all alone.

19. **O . . . singleness!** O thin joke, unique for only one thing—weakness!

20. **Swits . . . match**
Drive your wit harder to beat me or else I'll claim victory in this match of word play.

✔ **Reading Check**
How does Romeo respond when Mercutio says Romeo gave them "the slip" the night before?

70 thy wits than, I am sure, I have in my whole five. Was I
with you there for the goose?

ROMEO. Thou wast never with me for anything when thou
wast not there for the goose.

MERCUTIO. I will bite thee by the ear for that jest.

75 **ROMEO.** Nay, good goose, bite not!

MERCUTIO. Thy wit is a very bitter sweeting;[21] it is a most sharp
sauce.

ROMEO. And is it not, then, well served in to a sweet goose?

MERCUTIO. O, here's a wit of cheveril,[22] that stretches from an inch
80   narrow to an ell broad!

ROMEO. I stretch it out for that word "broad," which added
to the goose, proves thee far and wide a broad goose.

MERCUTIO. Why, is not this better now than groaning for
love? Now art thou sociable, now art thou Romeo; now
85   art thou what thou art, by art as well as by nature. For
this driveling love is like a great natural[23] that runs
lolling[24] up and down to hide his bauble[25] in a hole.

BENVOLIO. Stop there, stop there!

MERCUTIO. Thou desirest me to stop in my tale against the hair.[26]

90 **BENVOLIO.** Thou wouldst else have made thy tale large.

MERCUTIO. O, thou art deceived! I would have made it
short; for I was come to the whole depth of my tale,
and meant indeed to occupy the argument[27] no longer.

ROMEO. Here's goodly gear![28]

[*Enter* NURSE *and her Man,* PETER.]

95   A sail, a sail!

MERCUTIO. Two, two! A shirt and a smock.[29]

NURSE. Peter!

PETER. Anon.

NURSE. My fan, Peter.

100 **MERCUTIO.** Good Peter, to hide her face; for her fan's the
fairer face.

NURSE. God ye good morrow, gentlemen.

MERCUTIO. God ye good-den, fair gentlewoman.

NURSE. Is it good-den?

105 **MERCUTIO.** 'Tis no less, I tell ye; for the bawdy hand of the

21. **sweeting** a kind of apple.

22. **cheveril** easily stretched kid leather.

23. **natural** idiot.

24. **lolling** with tongue hanging out.

25. **bauble** toy.

Literary Analysis
Blank Verse and Character Rank How does Shakespeare reveal Mercutio's intelligence despite the fact that the character does not speak in blank verse?

26. **the hair** natural inclination.

27. **occupy the argument** talk about the matter.

28. **goodly gear** good stuff for joking (Romeo sees Nurse approaching).

29. **A shirt and a smock** a man and a woman.

dial is now upon the prick of noon.

NURSE. Out upon you! What a man are you!

ROMEO. One, gentlewoman, that God hath made, himself to mar.

NURSE. By my troth, it is well said. "For himself to mar,"
110   quoth 'a? Gentlemen, can any of you tell me where I
may find the young Romeo?

ROMEO. I can tell you; but young Romeo will be older
when you have found him than he was when you sought
him. I am the youngest of that name, for fault³⁰ of a
115   worse.

NURSE. You say well.

MERCUTIO. Yea, is the worst well? Very well took,³¹ i' faith! Wisely,
wisely.

NURSE. If you be he, sir, I desire some confidence³² with you.

120 **BENVOLIO.** She will endite him to some supper.

MERCUTIO. A bawd, a bawd, a bawd! So ho!

ROMEO. What hast thou found?

MERCUTIO. No hare, sir; unless a hare, sir, in a lenten pie,
that is something stale and hoar ere it be spent.

> [*He walks by them and sings.*]

125   An old hare hoar,
                And an old hare hoar,
                Is very good meat in Lent;
                But a hare that is hoar
                Is too much for a score
130   When it hoars ere it be spent.

Romeo, will you come to your father's? We'll to dinner thither.

ROMEO. I will follow you.

MERCUTIO. Farewell, ancient lady. Farewell, [*singing*] "Lady, lady,
lady."³³
                    [*Exit* MERCUTIO, BENVOLIO.]

135 **NURSE.** I pray you, sir, what saucy merchant was this that
was so full of his ropery?³⁴

ROMEO. A gentleman, nurse, that loves to hear himself talk
and will speak more in a minute than he will stand to
in a month.

140 **NURSE.** And 'a³⁵ speak anything against me, I'll take him
down, and 'a were lustier than he is, and twenty such
Jacks; and if I cannot, I'll find those that shall. Scurvy
knave! I am none of his flirt-gills;³⁶ I am none of his

30. **fault** lack.

31. **took** understood.

32. **confidence** Nurse
means *conference*.

33. **"Lady . . . lady"**
line from an old ballad,
"Chaste Susanna."

34. **ropery** Nurse
means *roguery*, the talk
and conduct of a rascal.

35. **'a** he.

36. **flirt-gills** common
girls.

✔**Reading Check**

Who interrupts Romeo
and his friends to ask
about Romeo?

skainsmates.[37] And thou must stand by too, and suffer
145   every knave to use me at his pleasure!

PETER. I saw no man use you at his pleasure. If I had, my
   weapon should quickly have been out, I warrant you. I
   dare draw as soon as another man, if I see occasion in
   a good quarrel, and the law on my side.

150 **NURSE.** Now, afore God, I am so vexed that every part about
   me quivers. Scurvy knave! Pray you, sir, a word; and,
   as I told you, my young lady bid me inquire you out.
   What she bid me say, I will keep to myself; but first let
   me tell ye, if ye should lead her in a fool's paradise, as
155   they say, it were a very gross kind of behavior, as they
   say; for the gentlewoman is young; and therefore, if
   you should deal double with her, truly it were an ill
   thing to be off'red to any gentlewoman, and very
   weak[38] dealing.

160 **ROMEO.** Nurse, commend[39] me to thy lady and mistress.
   I protest unto thee—

NURSE. Good heart, and i' faith I will tell her as much.
   Lord, Lord, she will be a joyful woman.

ROMEO. What wilt thou tell her, nurse? Thou dost not
165   mark me.

NURSE. I will tell her, sir, that you do protest, which, as I
   take it, is a gentlemanlike offer.

ROMEO. Bid her devise
   Some means to come to shrift[40] this afternoon;
170   And there she shall at Friar Lawrence' cell
   Be shrived and married. Here is for thy pains.

NURSE. No, truly, sir; not a penny.

ROMEO. Go to! I say you shall.

NURSE. This afternoon, sir? Well, she shall be there.

175 **ROMEO.** And stay, good nurse, behind the abbey wall.
   Within this hour my man shall be with thee
   And bring thee cords made like a tackled stair.[41]
   Which to the high topgallant[42] of my joy
   Must be my convoy[43] in the secret night.
180   Farewell. Be trusty, and I'll quit[44] thy pains.
   Farewell. Commend me to thy mistress.

NURSE. Now God in heaven bless thee! Hark you, sir.

ROMEO. What say'st thou, my dear nurse?

NURSE. Is your man secret? Did you ne'er hear say,
185   Two may keep counsel, putting one away?[45]

---

37. **skainsmates** criminals; cutthroats.

Literary Analysis
Blank Verse and Character Rank Why do you think Shakespeare chose to write the Nurse's lines without attention to blank verse?

38. **weak** unmanly.

39. **commend** convey my respect and best wishes.

40. **shrift** confession.

Reading Strategy
Reading Blank Verse How would you rephrase Romeo's words in lines 170–171?

41. **tackled stair** rope ladder.

42. **topgallant** summit.

43. **convoy** conveyance.

44. **quit** reward; pay you back for.

45. **Two . . . away** Two can keep a secret if one is ignorant, or out of the way.

ROMEO. Warrant thee my man's as true as steel.

NURSE. Well, sir, my mistress is the sweetest lady. Lord,
   Lord! When 'twas a little prating⁴⁶ thing— O, there is a
   nobleman in town, one Paris, that would fain lay knife
190   aboard;⁴⁷ but she, good soul, had as lieve⁴⁸ see a toad,
   a very toad, as see him. I anger her sometimes, and tell
   her that Paris is the properer man; but I'll warrant
   you, when I say so, she looks as pale as any clout⁴⁹
   in the versal world.⁵⁰ Doth not rosemary and Romeo
195   begin both with a letter?

ROMEO. Ay, nurse; what of that? Both with an *R*.

NURSE. Ah, mocker! That's the dog's name.⁵¹ *R* is for the—
   No; I know it begins with some other letter; and she
   hath the prettiest sententious⁵² of it, of you and rosemary,
200   that it would do you good to hear it.

ROMEO. Commend me to thy lady.

NURSE. Ay, a thousand times. [*Exit* ROMEO.] Peter!

PETER. Anon.

NURSE. Before, and apace.⁵³   [*Exit, after* PETER.]

Scene *v.* CAPULET's *orchard.*

[*Enter* JULIET.]

JULIET. The clock struck nine when I did send the nurse;
   In half an hour she promised to return.
   Perchance she cannot meet him. That's not so.
   O, she is lame! Love's heralds should be thoughts,
5   Which ten times faster glides than the sun's beams
   Driving back shadows over low'ring¹ hills.
   Therefore do nimble-pinioned doves draw Love,²
   And therefore hath the wind-swift Cupid wings.
   Now is the sun upon the highmost hill
10   Of this day's journey, and from nine till twelve
   Is three long hours; yet she is not come.
   Had she affections and warm youthful blood,
   She would be as swift in motion as a ball;
   My words would bandy her³ to my sweet love,
15   And his to me.
   But old folks, many feign⁴ as they were dead—
   Unwieldy, slow, heavy and pale as lead.

[*Enter* NURSE *and* PETER.]

   O God, she comes! O honey nurse, what news?
   Hast thou met with him? Send thy man away.

46. **prating** babbling.

47. **fain . . . aboard**
eagerly seize Juliet for
himself.

48. **had as lieve** would as
willingly.

49. **clout** cloth.

50. **versal world** universe.

51. **dog's name** *R* sounds
like a growl.

52. **sententious** Nurse
means *sentences*—clever,
wise sayings.

53. **Before, and apace** Go
ahead of me, and quickly.

1. **low'ring** darkening.
2. **Therefore . . . Love**
therefore, doves with
quick wings pull the
chariot of Venus, god-
dess of love.

Literary Analysis
Blank Verse What is the
effect of hearing Juliet's
blank verse right after the
Nurse's prose speeches?

3. **bandy her** send her
rapidly.

4. **feign** act.

unwieldy (un wēl′ dē) *adj.*
awkward; clumsy

✔ **Reading Check**

What does Romeo ask the
Nurse to tell Juliet?

NURSE.   O God's Lady dear!
Are you so hot?[11] Marry come up, I trow.[12]
Is this the poultice[13] for my aching bones?
Henceforward do your messages yourself.

65 **JULIET.** Here's such a coil![14] Come, what says Romeo?

NURSE. Have you got leave to go to shrift today?

JULIET. I have.

NURSE. Then hie you hence to Friar Lawrence' cell;
There stays a husband to make you a wife.
70 Now comes the wanton[15] blood up in your cheeks:
They'll be in scarlet straight at any news.
Hie you to church: I must another way,
To fetch a ladder, by the which your love
Must climb a bird's nest soon when it is dark.
75 I am the drudge, and toil in your delight:
But you shall bear the burden soon at night.
Go; I'll to dinner; hie you to the cell.

JULIET. Hie to high fortune! Honest nurse, farewell.   [*Exit all.*]

Scene vi. FRIAR LAWRENCE's *cell.*

[*Enter* FRIAR LAWRENCE *and* ROMEO.]

FRIAR. So smile the heavens upon this holy act
That afterhours with sorrow chide us not![1]

ROMEO. Amen, amen! But come what sorrow can,
It cannot countervail[2] the exchange of joy
5 That one short minute gives me in her sight.
Do thou but close our hands with holy words,
Then love-devouring death do what he dare—
It is enough I may but call her mine.

FRIAR. These violent delights have violent ends
10 And in their triumph die, like fire and powder,[3]
Which, as they kiss, consume. The sweetest honey
Is loathsome in his own deliciousness
And in the taste confounds[4] the appetite.
Therefore love moderately: long love doth so;
15 Too swift arrives as tardy as too slow.

[*Enter* JULIET.]

Here comes the lady. O, so light a foot
Will ne'er wear out the everlasting flint.[5]
A lover may bestride the gossamers[6]
That idles in the wanton summer air,
20 And yet not fall; so light is vanity.[7]

11. hot impatient; hot-tempered.

12. Marry . . . trow Indeed, cool down, I say.
13. poultice remedy.
14. coil disturbance.

Literary Analysis
Blank Verse Why do you think Shakespeare broke the pattern of blank verse in line 67?

15. wanton excited.

Literary Analysis
Blank Verse What effect is created by making Juliet's last line rhyme with the Nurse's last line?

1. That . . . not! that the future does not punish us with sorrow.
2. countervail equal.

3. powder gunpowder.

4. confounds destroys.

5. flint stone.
6. gossamers spider webs.

7. vanity foolish things that cannot last.

JULIET. Good even to my ghostly confessor.

FRIAR. Romeo shall thank thee, daughter, for us both.

JULIET. As much to him,[8] else is his thanks too much.

ROMEO. Ah, Juliet, if the measure of thy joy
25 Be heaped like mine, and that thy skill be more
To blazon it,[9] then sweeten with thy breath
This neighbor air, and let rich music's tongue
Unfold the imagined happiness that both
Receive in either by this dear encounter.

30 **JULIET.** Conceit, more rich in matter than in words,
Brags of his substance, not of ornament.[10]
They are but beggars that can count their worth;
But my true love is grown to such excess
I cannot sum up sum of half my wealth.

35 **FRIAR.** Come, come with me, and we will make short work;
For, by your leaves, you shall not stay alone
Till Holy Church incorporate two in one.   *[Exit all.]*

8. **As . . . him** the same greeting to him.

Reading Strategy
Reading Blank Verse
How can you read Romeo's lines most effectively to grasp their meaning as well as their poetry?

9. **and . . . it** and if you are better able to proclaim it.

10. **Conceit . . . ornament** Understanding does not need to be dressed up in words.

Review and Assess

Thinking About Act II

1. **Respond:** Do you think Friar Lawrence is wise to agree to marry Romeo and Juliet? Explain.

2. **(a) Recall:** Where do Romeo and Juliet first mutually declare their love for each other? **(b) Interpret:** What role does darkness play in the scene?

3. **(a) Recall:** What doubts and fears does Juliet express even as she realizes that Romeo loves her? **(b) Make a Judgment:** Do you think the couple will be able to overcome these problems? Explain.

4. **(a) Recall:** What weakness in Romeo does the Friar point out before agreeing to help? **(b) Compare and Contrast:** How do the Friar's motives differ from the couple's own motives?

5. **(a) Recall:** For whom does Juliet wait in Act II, Scene v? **(b) Interpret:** What are Juliet's feelings as she waits to hear the message Romeo has sent?

6. **Analyze:** What tragic events to come are foreshadowed in Act II?

7. **Evaluate:** Why do you think the love scene in Capulet's garden is one of the most famous in all of literature?

Prepare to Read

The Tragedy of Romeo and Juliet, Act III

CALIFORNIA STANDARDS

Instruction with
this selection
addresses these standards:

R 1.2*, 1.3, 3.1*, 3.7*
W 2.3*, 2.4*
WOLC 1.3*
LS 1.8

* Standards tested on
HS Exit Exam. For complete
standards, see p. CA 4.

Literary Analysis

Soliloquy, Aside, and Monologue

Shakespeare's characters often deliver these types of dramatic speeches:

- A **soliloquy** is a lengthy speech in which a character—usually alone on stage—expresses his or her thoughts to the audience.
- An **aside** is a brief remark by a character revealing thoughts or feelings to the audience, unheard by other characters.
- A **monologue,** like a soliloquy, is a lengthy speech. However, a monologue is addressed to other characters on stage, not to the audience.

As you read, notice the effect created by each type of speech.

Connecting Literary Elements

Within their dramatic speeches, characters often make **allusions**—references to well-known people, places, or events from myths or literature. Shakespeare's characters often allude to figures in myths or popular stories to add meaning to their speeches. In Act II, Mercutio insultingly calls Tybalt "Prince of Cats," alluding to a cat named Tybalt in French fables. As you read Act III, record allusions you find in a chart like the one shown.

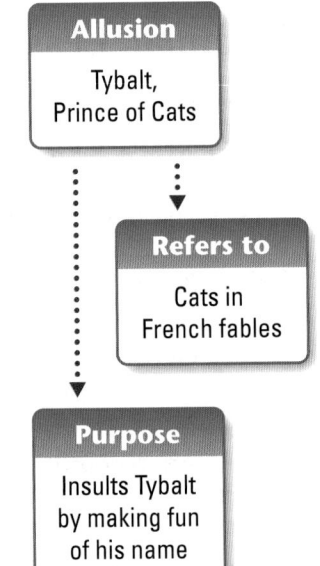

Allusion

Tybalt, Prince of Cats

Refers to

Cats in French fables

Purpose

Insults Tybalt by making fun of his name

Reading Strategy

Paraphrasing

Shakespearean language and style can be difficult to understand today. One way to make sense of difficult passages is to paraphrase them. To **paraphrase,** restate text in your own words.

> **Shakespeare's version:** This gentleman, the prince's near ally / My very friend hath got his mortal hurt / In my behalf. . . .

> **Paraphrase:** My good friend, a close relative of the prince, has been fatally wounded defending me.

As you read Act III, paraphrase passages to help you clarify meaning.

Vocabulary Development

gallant (gal´ ənt) adj. brave and noble (p. 822)

fray (frā) n. noisy fight (p. 823)

martial (mär´ shəl) adj. military (p. 824)

exile (eks´ īl´) v. banish (p. 824)

eloquence (el´ ə kwəns) n. speech that is vivid, forceful, graceful, and persuasive (p. 825)

fickle (fik´ əl) adj. changeable (p. 836)

Review and Anticipate

In Act II, Romeo and Juliet express their mutual love and enlist the aid of Juliet's nurse and Friar Lawrence to arrange a secret marriage ceremony. As the act closes, the young couple are about to be married. Before performing the ceremony, the Friar warns, "These violent delights have violent ends. . . ." How might this statement hint at events that will occur in Act III or later in the play?

Scene i. A public place.

[*Enter* MERCUTIO, BENVOLIO, *and* MEN.]

BENVOLIO. I pray thee, good Mercutio, let's retire.
The day is hot, the Capels are abroad,
And, if we meet, we shall not 'scape a brawl,
For now, these hot days, is the mad blood stirring.

5   **MERCUTIO.** Thou art like one of these fellows that, when he enters the confines of a tavern, claps me his sword upon the table and says, "God send me no need of thee!" and by the operation of the second cup draws him on the drawer,[1] when indeed there is no need.

10   **BENVOLIO.** Am I like such a fellow?

1. **and . . . drawer** and by the effect of the second drink, draws his sword against the waiter.

✔**Reading Check**

Why does Benvolio want to get off the street?

MERCUTIO. Come, come, thou art as hot a Jack in thy mood as any in Italy; and as soon moved to be moody, and as soon moody to be moved.[2]

BENVOLIO. And what to?

15 **MERCUTIO.** Nay, and there were two such, we should have none shortly, for one would kill the other. Thou! Why, thou wilt quarrel with a man that hath a hair more or a hair less in his beard than thou hast. Thou wilt quarrel with a man for cracking nuts, having no other reason but because thou hast hazel eyes. What eye but
20 such an eye would spy out such a quarrel? Thy head is as full of quarrels as an egg is full of meat; and yet thy head hath been beaten as addle[3] as an egg for quarreling. Thou hast quarreled with a man for coughing in the street, because he hath wakened thy dog that hath lain asleep in the sun. Didst thou not fall out
25 with a tailor for wearing his new doublet[4] before Easter? With another for tying his new shoes with old riband?[5] And yet thou wilt tutor me from quarreling![6]

BENVOLIO. And I were so apt to quarrel as thou art, any man should buy the fee simple[7] of my life for an hour and a quarter.[8]

30 **MERCUTIO.** The fee simple? O simple![9]

[*Enter* TYBALT, PETRUCHIO, *and* OTHERS.]

BENVOLIO. By my head, here comes the Capulets.

MERCUTIO. By my heel, I care not.

TYBALT. Follow me close, for I will speak to them.
35   Gentlemen, good-den. A word with one of you.

MERCUTIO. And but one word with one of us? Couple it with something; make it a word and a blow.

TYBALT. You shall find me apt enough to that, sir, and you will give me occasion.[10]

40 **MERCUTIO.** Could you not take some occasion without giving?

TYBALT. Mercutio, thou consortest[11] with Romeo.

MERCUTIO. Consort?[12] What, dost thou make us minstrels? And thou make minstrels of us, look to hear nothing but discords.[13] Here's my fiddlestick; here's that shall make you dance.
45   Zounds,[14] consort!

BENVOLIO. We talk here in the public haunt of men.
    Either withdraw unto some private place,
    Or reason coldly of your grievances,
    Or else depart. Here all eyes gaze on us.

50 **MERCUTIO.** Men's eyes were made to look, and let them gaze.
    I will not budge for no man's pleasure, I.

2. **and . . . moved** and as quickly stirred to anger as you are eager to be so stirred.

Literary Analysis
Soliloquy, Aside, and Monologue Which details of Mercutio's speech indicate that it is a monologue and not a soliloquy?

3. **addle** scrambled; crazy.

4. **doublet** jacket.
5. **riband** ribbon.
6. **tutor . . . quarreling** instruct me not to quarrel.

7. **fee simple** complete possession.

8. **an hour and a quarter** length of time that a man with Mercutio's fondness for quarreling may be expected to live.

9. **O simple!** O stupid!

Reading Strategy
Paraphrasing How would you paraphrase the exchange between Tybalt and Mercutio to make its tone and meaning understandable to a reader today?

10. **occasion** cause; reason.
11. **consortest** associate with.

12. **Consort** associate with; *consort* also meant a group of musicians.

13. **discords** harsh sounds.
14. **Zounds** exclamation of surprise or anger ("By God's wounds").

[*Enter* ROMEO.]

TYBALT. Well, peace be with you, sir. Here comes my man.[15]

MERCUTIO. But I'll be hanged, sir, if he wear your livery.[16]
    Marry, go before to field,[17] he'll be your follower!
55   Your worship in that sense may call him man.

TYBALT. Romeo, the love I bear thee can afford
    No better term than this: thou art a villain.[18]

ROMEO. Tybalt, the reason that I have to love thee
    Doth much excuse the appertaining[19] rage
60   To such a greeting. Villain am I none.
    Therefore farewell. I see thou knowest me not.

TYBALT. Boy, this shall not excuse the injuries
    That thou hast done me; therefore turn and draw.

ROMEO. I do protest I never injured thee,
65   But love thee better than thou canst devise[20]
    Till thou shalt know the reason of my love;
    And so, good Capulet, which name I tender[21]
    As dearly as mine own, be satisfied.

MERCUTIO. O calm, dishonorable, vile submission!
70   *Alla stoccata*[22] carries it away.   [*Draws.*]
    Tybalt, you ratcatcher, will you walk?

TYBALT. What wouldst thou have with me?

MERCUTIO. Good King of Cats, nothing but one of your nine lives.
    That I mean to make bold withal,[23] and, as you shall use me
75   here-after, dry-beat[24] the rest of the eight. Will you pluck your
    sword out of his pilcher[25] by the ears? Make haste, lest mine be
    about your ears ere it be out.

TYBALT. I am for you.   [*Draws.*]

ROMEO. Gentle Mercutio, put thy rapier up.

80 **MERCUTIO.** Come, sir, your *passado!*   [*They fight.*]

ROMEO. Draw, Benvolio; beat down their weapons.
    Gentlemen, for shame! Forbear this outrage!
    Tybalt, Mercutio, the Prince expressly hath
    Forbid this bandying in Verona streets.
85   Hold, Tybalt! Good Mercutio!

        [TYBALT *under* ROMEO's *arm thrusts* MERCUTIO *in, and flies.*]

MERCUTIO.   I am hurt.
    A plague a[26] both houses! I am sped.[27]
    Is he gone and hath nothing?

BENVOLIO.   What, art thou hurt?

---

15. **man** the man I'm looking for; "man" also meant "manservant."

16. **livery** servant's uniform.

17. **field** dueling place.

18. **villain** low, vulgar person.

19. **appertaining** appropriate.

20. **devise** understand; imagine.

21. **tender** value.

22. *Alla stoccata* at the thrust—an Italian fencing term that Mercutio uses as a nickname for Tybalt.

23. **make bold withal** make bold with; take.

24. **dry-beat** thrash.

25. **pilcher** scabbard.

26. **a** on.

27. **sped** wounded; done for.

Reading Check

What is the outcome of the duel between Tybalt and Mercutio?

Romeo and Juliet, Act III, Scene i ◆ *821*

For blood of ours shed blood of Montague.
O cousin, cousin!

145 **PRINCE.** Benvolio, who began this bloody fray?

BENVOLIO. Tybalt, here slain, whom Romeo's hand did slay.
Romeo, that spoke him fair, bid him bethink
How nice[40] the quarrel was, and urged withal
Your high displeasure. All this—utterèd
150 With gentle breath, calm look, knees humbly bowed—
Could not take truce with the unruly spleen[41]
Of Tybalt deaf to peace, but that he tilts[42]
With piercing steel at bold Mercutio's breast;
Who, all as hot, turns deadly point to point,
155 And, with a <u>martial</u> scorn, with one hand beats
Cold death aside and with the other sends
It back to Tybalt, whose dexterity
Retorts it. Romeo he cries aloud,
"Hold, friends! Friends, part!" and swifter than his tongue,
160 His agile arm beats down their fatal points,
And 'twixt them rushes; underneath whose arm
An envious[43] thrust from Tybalt hit the life
Of stout Mercutio, and then Tybalt fled;
But by and by comes back to Romeo,
165 Who had but newly entertained[44] revenge,
And to't they go like lightning; for, ere I
Could draw to part them, was stout Tybalt slain;
And, as he fell, did Romeo turn and fly.
This is the truth, or let Benvolio die.

170 **LADY CAPULET.** He is a kinsman to the Montague;
Affection makes him false, he speaks not true.
Some twenty of them fought in this black strife,
And all those twenty could but kill one life.
I beg for justice, which thou, Prince, must give.
175 Romeo slew Tybalt; Romeo must not live.

PRINCE. Romeo slew him; he slew Mercutio.
Who now the price of his dear blood doth owe?

MONTAGUE. Not Romeo, Prince; he was Mercutio's friend;
His fault concludes but what the law should end,
The life of Tybalt.[45]
180 **PRINCE.** And for that offense
Immediately we do <u>exile</u> him hence.
I have an interest in your hate's proceeding.
My blood[46] for your rude brawls doth lie a-bleeding;
But I'll amerce[47] you with so strong a fine
185 That you shall all repent the loss of mine.
I will be deaf to pleading and excuses;

Nor tears nor prayers shall purchase out abuses.
Therefore use none. Let Romeo hence in haste,
Else, when he is found, that hour is his last.
190 Bear hence this body and attend our will.[48]
Mercy but murders, pardoning those that kill.

[*Exit with others.*]

Scene ii. CAPULET'S *orchard.*

[*Enter* JULIET *alone.*]

JULIET. Gallop apace, you fiery-footed steeds,[1]
Towards Phoebus' lodging![2] Such a wagoner
As Phaëton[3] would whip you to the west
And bring in cloudy night immediately.
5 Spread thy close curtain, love-performing night,
That runaways' eyes may wink,[4] and Romeo
Leap to these arms untalked of and unseen.
Lovers can see to do their amorous rites,
And by their own beauties; or, if love be blind,
10 It best agrees with night. Come, civil night,
Thou sober-suited matron all in black,
And learn me how to lose a winning match,
Played for a pair of stainless maidenhoods.
Hood my unmanned blood, bating in my cheeks,[5]
15 With thy black mantle till strange[6] love grow bold,
Think true love acted simple modesty,
Come, night; come, Romeo; come, thou day in night;
For thou wilt lie upon the wings of night
Whiter than new snow upon a raven's back.
20 Come, gentle night; come, loving, black-browed night;
Give me my Romeo; and when I shall die,
Take him and cut him out in little stars,
And he will make the face of heaven so fine
That all the world will be in love with night
25 And pay no worship to the garish sun
O, I have bought the mansion of a love,
But not possessed it; and though I am sold,
Not yet enjoyed. So tedious is this day
As is the night before some festival
30 To an impatient child that hath new robes
And may not wear them. O, here comes my nurse,

[*Enter* NURSE, *with cords.*]

And she brings news; and every tongue that speaks
But Romeo's name speaks heavenly <u>eloquence</u>.
Now, nurse, what news? What hast thou there, the cords
That Romeo bid thee fetch?

35 NURSE.   Ay, ay, the cords.

48. attend our will
await my decision.

1. fiery-footed steeds
horses of the sun god,
Phoebus.

2. Phoebus' lodging
below the horizon.

3. Phaëton Phoebus' son,
who tried to drive his
father's horses but was
unable to control them.

**4. That runaways' eyes
may wink** so that the eyes
of busybodies may not see.

5. Hood . . . cheeks hide
the untamed blood that
makes me blush.

6. strange unfamiliar.

**Literary Analysis
Soliloquy, Aside, and
Monologue** Should
Juliet's speech be
classified as a monologue,
a soliloquy, or an aside?
Why?

eloquence (el′ ə kwəns) *n.*
speech that is vivid,
forceful, graceful, and
persuasive

**Reading Check**

What punishment does the
Prince order for Romeo?

JULIET. Ay me! What news? Why dost thou wring thy hands?

NURSE. Ah, weraday![7] He's dead, he's dead, he's dead!
    We are undone, lady, we are undone!
    Alack the day! He's gone, he's killed, he's dead!

JULIET. Can heaven be so envious?

40 **NURSE.**   Romeo can,
    Though heaven cannot. O Romeo, Romeo!
    Who ever would have thought it? Romeo!

JULIET. What devil art thou that dost torment me thus?
    This torture should be roared in dismal hell.
45   Hath Romeo slain himself? Say thou but "Ay,"
    And that bare vowel "I" shall poison more
    Than the death-darting eye of cockatrice.◆
    I am not I, if there be such an "Ay,"[8]
    Or those eyes' shot[9] that makes thee answer "Ay."
50   If he be slain, say "Ay"; or if not, "No."
    Brief sounds determine of my weal or woe.

NURSE. I saw the wound, I saw it with mine eyes,
    (God save the mark![10]) here on his manly breast.
    A piteous corse,[11] a bloody piteous corse;
55   Pale, pale as ashes, all bedaubed in blood,
    All in gore-blood. I sounded[12] at the sight.

JULIET. O, break, my heart! Poor bankrout,[13] break at once!
    To prison, eyes; ne'er look on liberty!
    Vile earth, to earth resign;[14] end motion here,
60   And thou and Romeo press one heavy bier![15]

NURSE. O Tybalt, Tybalt, the best friend I had!
    O courteous Tybalt! Honest gentleman!
    That ever I should live to see thee dead!

---

7. **Ah, weraday!** alas!

Literary Analysis
Allusions What is the effect of Juliet's allusions to hell in lines 43–44? Explain.

8. **"Ay"** yes.
9. **eyes' shot** the Nurse's glance.

10. **God save the mark!** may God save us from evil!

11. **corse** corpse.

12. **sounded** swooned; fainted.

13. **bankrout** bankrupt.

14. **Vile . . . resign** let my body return to the earth.

15. **bier** platform on which a corpse is displayed before burial.

---

*L*iterature
in context Humanities Connection

◆ *Cockatrice*

    In a play on words, Juliet links "Ay" with the dangerous "eye" of a cockatrice (III, ii, 47). The cockatrice is a serpent that, according to myth, could kill with a look or transform people into stone. The creature resembled a snake with the head and yellow feathers of a rooster. It feared the song of the rooster as well as its own reflection in the mirror. Juliet alludes to a cockatrice to reinforce the tormenting nature of her conversation with the Nurse.

JULIET. What storm is this that blows so contrary?[16]
65   Is Romeo slaught'red, and is Tybalt dead?
        My dearest cousin, and my dearer lord?
        Then, dreadful trumpet, sound the general doom![17]
        For who is living, if those two are gone?

NURSE. Tybalt is gone, and Romeo banishèd;
70   Romeo that killed him, he is banishèd.

JULIET. O God! Did Romeo's hand shed Tybalt's blood?

NURSE. It did, it did! Alas the day, it did!

JULIET. O serpent heart, hid with a flow'ring face!
        Did ever dragon keep so fair a cave?
75   Beautiful tyrant! Fiend angelical!
        Dove-feathered raven! Wolvish-ravening lamb!
        Despisèd substance of divinest show!
        Just opposite to what thou justly seem'st—
        A damnèd saint, an honorable villain!
80   O nature, what hadst thou to do in hell
        When thou didst bower the spirit of a fiend
        In mortal paradise of such sweet flesh?
        Was ever book containing such vile matter
        So fairly bound? O, that deceit should dwell
        In such a gorgeous palace!

85 **NURSE.**   There's no trust,
        No faith, no honesty in men; all perjured,
        All forsworn,[18] all naught, all dissemblers.[19]
        Ah, where's my man? Give me some *aqua vitae*.[20]
        These griefs, these woes, these sorrows make me old.
        Shame come to Romeo!

90 **JULIET.**   Blistered be thy tongue
        For such a wish! He was not born to shame.
        Upon his brow shame is ashamed to sit;
        For 'tis a throne where honor may be crowned
        Sole monarch of the universal earth.
95   O, what a beast was I to chide at him!

NURSE. Will you speak well of him that killed your cousin?

JULIET. Shall I speak ill of him that is my husband?
        Ah, poor my lord, what tongue shall smooth thy name
        When I, thy three-hours wife, have mangled it?
100   But wherefore, villain, didst thou kill my cousin?
        That villain cousin would have killed my husband.
        Back, foolish tears, back to your native spring!
        Your tributary[21] drops belong to woe,
        Which you, mistaking, offer up to joy.
105   My husband lives, that Tybalt would have slain;

16. contrary in opposite directions.

17. dreadful . . . doom let the trumpet that announces doomsday be sounded.

Reading Strategy
Paraphrasing Restate lines 78–79 in your own words.

18. forsworn are liars.
19. dissemblers hypocrites.
20. *aqua vitae* brandy.

21. tributary in tribute.

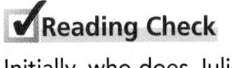**Reading Check**

Initially, who does Juliet think is dead?

And Tybalt's dead, that would have slain my husband.
All this is comfort; wherefore weep I then?
Some word there was, worser than Tybalt's death,
That murd'red me. I would forget it fain;
110 But O, it presses to my memory
Like damnèd guilty deeds to sinners' minds!
"Tybalt is dead, and Romeo—banishèd."
That "banishèd," that one word "banishèd,"
Hath slain ten thousand Tybalts. Tybalt's death
115 Was woe enough, if it had ended there;
Or, if sour woe delights in fellowship
And needly will be ranked with²² other griefs,
Why followed not, when she said "Tybalt's dead,"
Thy father, or thy mother, nay, or both,
120 Which modern²³ lamentation might have moved?
But with a rearward²⁴ following Tybalt's death,
"Romeo is banishèd"—to speak that word
Is father, mother, Tybalt, Romeo, Juliet,
All slain, all dead. "Romeo is banishèd"—
125 There is no end, no limit, measure, bound,
In that word's death; no words can that woe sound.
Where is my father and my mother, nurse?

NURSE. Weeping and wailing over Tybalt's corse.
Will you go to them? I will bring you thither.

130 JULIET. Wash they his wounds with tears? Mine shall be spent,
When theirs are dry, for Romeo's banishment.
Take up those cords. Poor ropes, you are beguiled,
Both you and I, for Romeo is exiled.
He made you for a highway to my bed;
135 But I, a maid, die maiden-widowèd.
Come, cords; come, nurse. I'll to my wedding bed;
And death, not Romeo, take my maidenhead!

NURSE. Hie to your chamber. I'll find Romeo
To comfort you. I wot²⁵ well where he is.
140 Hark ye, your Romeo will be here at night.
I'll to him; he is hid at Lawrence' cell.

JULIET. O, find him! Give this ring to my true knight
And bid him come to take his last farewell.   [*Exit* with NURSE]

S*cene iii.* FRIAR LAWRENCE'S *cell.*

[*Enter* FRIAR LAWRENCE.]

FRIAR. Romeo, come forth; come forth, thou fearful man.
Affliction is enamored of thy parts,¹
And thou art wedded to calamity.

Literary Analysis
Soliloquy, Aside, and Monologue Is Juliet's lengthy speech a soliloquy? Why or why not?

22. needly . . . with must be accompanied by.

23. modern ordinary.
24. rearward follow up; literally, a rear guard.

Reading Strategy
Paraphrasing How would you paraphrase the Nurse's reply to Juliet?

25. wot know.

Reading Strategy
Paraphrasing Paraphrase in modern English the Friar's opening lines to Romeo.

1. Affliction . . . parts misery is in love with your attractive qualities.

[*Enter* ROMEO.]

ROMEO. Father, what news? What is the Prince's doom?[2]
5   What sorrow craves acquaintance at my hand
    That I yet know not?

FRIAR.   Too familiar
    Is my dear son with such sour company.
    I bring thee tidings of the Prince's doom.

ROMEO. What less than doomsday[3] is the Prince's doom?

10 **FRIAR.** A gentler judgment vanished[4] from his lips—
    Not body's death, but body's banishment.

ROMEO. Ha, banishment? Be merciful, say "death";
    For exile hath more terror in his look,
    Much more than death. Do not say "banishment."

15 **FRIAR.** Here from Verona art thou banishèd.
    Be patient, for the world is broad and wide.

ROMEO. There is no world without[5] Verona walls,
    But purgatory, torture, hell itself.
    Hence banishèd is banished from the world,
20   And world's exile is death. Then "banishèd"
    Is death mistermed. Calling death "banishèd,"
    Thou cut'st my head off with a golden ax
    And smilest upon the stroke that murders me.

FRIAR. O deadly sin! O rude unthankfulness!
25   Thy fault our law calls death;[6] but the kind Prince,
    Taking thy part, hath rushed[7] aside the law,
    And turned that black word "death" to "banishment."
    This is dear mercy, and thou seest it not.

ROMEO. 'Tis torture, and not mercy. Heaven is here,
30   Where Juliet lives; and every cat and dog
    And little mouse, every unworthy thing,
    Live here in heaven and may look on her;
    But Romeo may not. More validity,[8]
    More honorable state, more courtship lives
35   In carrion flies than Romeo. They may seize
    On the white wonder of dear Juliet's hand
    And steal immortal blessing from her lips,
    Who, even in pure and vestal modesty,
    Still blush, as thinking their own kisses sin;
40   But Romeo may not, he is banishèd.
    Flies may do this but I from this must fly;
    They are freemen, but I am banishèd.
    And sayest thou yet that exile is not death?
    Hadst thou no poison mixed, no sharp-ground knife,

2. **doom** final decision.

3. **doomsday** my death.

4. **vanished** escaped; came forth.

5. **without** outside.

6. **Thy fault . . . death** for what you did our law demands the death penalty.

7. **rushed** pushed.

Reading Strategy
Paraphrasing Restate Romeo's complaint in lines 29–33.

8. **validity** value.

✔**Reading Check**
What punishment does the Friar say Romeo could have received for his crime?

45 No sudden mean⁹ of death, though ne'er so mean,¹⁰
    But "banishèd" to kill me—"banishèd"?
    O friar, the damnèd use that word in hell;
    Howling attends it! How hast thou the heart,
    Being a divine, a ghostly confessor,
50 A sin-absolver, and my friend professed,
    To mangle me with that word "banishèd"?

    FRIAR. Thou fond mad man, hear me a little speak.

    ROMEO. O, thou wilt speak again of banishment.

    FRIAR. I'll give thee armor to keep off that word;
55 Adversity's sweet milk, philosophy,
    To comfort thee, though thou art banishèd.

    ROMEO. Yet "banishèd"? Hang up philosophy!
    Unless philosophy can make a Juliet,
    Displant a town, reverse a prince's doom,
60 It helps not, it prevails not. Talk no more.

    FRIAR. O, then I see that madmen have no ears.

Literary Analysis
Soliloquy, Aside, and Monologue Which characteristics of a monologue are present in Romeo's lament?

9. **mean** method.

10. **mean** humiliating.

Reading Strategy
Paraphrasing Summarize Romeo's ideas in lines 57–60. What do they suggest about his state of mind?

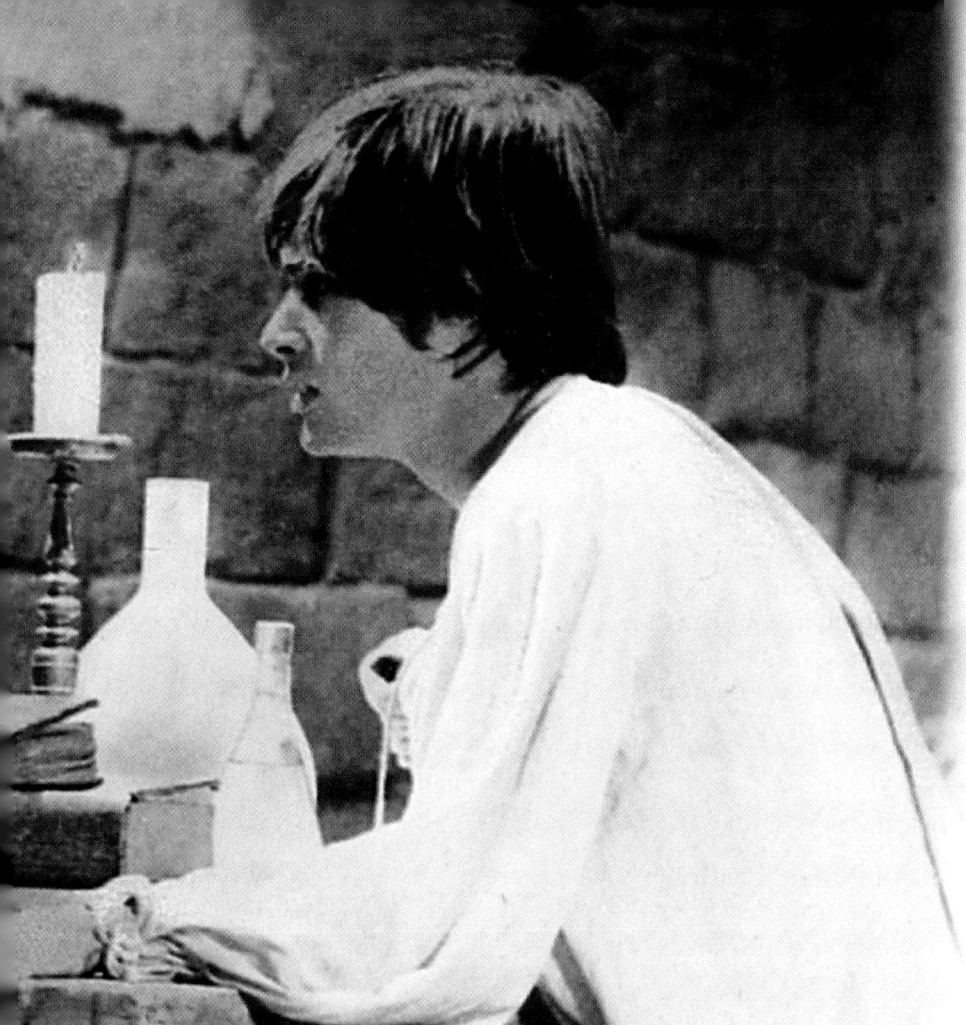

◀ **Critical Viewing**
How does Romeo's
expression in this picture
compare to your impres-
sion of him as you read?
[Analyze]

ROMEO. How should they, when that wise men have no eyes?

FRIAR. Let me dispute[11] with thee of thy estate.[12]

ROMEO. Thou canst not speak of that thou dost not feel.
65   Wert thou as young as I, Juliet thy love,
    An hour but married, Tybalt murderèd,
    Doting like me, and like me banishèd,
    Then mightst thou speak, then mightst thou tear thy hair,
    And fall upon the ground, as I do now,
70   Taking the measure of an unmade grave.

[*Enter* NURSE *and knock.*]

    FRIAR. Arise, one knocks. Good Romeo, hide thyself.

    ROMEO. Not I; unless the breath of heartsick groans
    Mistlike infold me from the search of eyes. [*Knock.*]

    FRIAR. Hark, how they knock! Who's there? Romeo, arise;
75   Thou wilt be taken.—Stay awhile!—Stand up; [*Knock.*]
    Run to my study.—By and by![13]—God's will,

11. dispute discuss.

12. estate condition;
situation.

Reading Strategy
Paraphrasing How would
you paraphrase Friar
Lawrence's words in lines
74–78?

13. By and by! In a minute!
(said to the person knocking).

✔**Reading Check**

What word does Romeo
use repeatedly while
speaking to the Friar?

Romeo and Juliet, Act III, Scene iii ◆ 831

What simpleness[14] is this.—I come, I come! [*Knock.*]
Who knocks so hard? Whence come you? What's your will?

[*Enter* NURSE.]

NURSE. Let me come in, and you shall know my errand.
I come from Lady Juliet.

80 **FRIAR.**   Welcome then.

NURSE. O holy friar, O, tell me, holy friar,
Where is my lady's lord, where's Romeo?

FRIAR. There on the ground, with his own tears made drunk.

NURSE. O, he is even in my mistress' case,
85   Just in her case! O woeful sympathy!
Piteous predicament! Even so lies she,
Blubb'ring and weeping, weeping and blubb'ring.
Stand up, stand up! Stand, and you be a man.
For Juliet's sake, for her sake, rise and stand!
90   Why should you fall into so deep an O?[15]

ROMEO. [*Rises.*] Nurse—

NURSE. Ah sir, ah sir! Death's the end of all.

ROMEO. Spakest thou of Juliet? How is it with her?
Doth not she think me an old murderer,
95   Now I have stained the childhood of our joy
With blood removed but little from her own?
Where is she? And how doth she? And what says
My concealed lady[16] to our canceled love?

NURSE. O, she says nothing, sir, but weeps and weeps;
100   And now falls on her bed, and then starts up,
And Tybalt calls; and then on Romeo cries,
And then down falls again.

ROMEO.   As if that name,
Shot from the deadly level[17] of a gun,
Did murder her; as that name's cursèd hand
105   Murdered her kinsman. O, tell me, friar, tell me,
In what vile part of this anatomy
Doth my name lodge? Tell me, that I may sack[18]
The hateful mansion.

[*He offers to stab himself, and* NURSE *snatches the dagger away.*]

FRIAR.   Hold thy desperate hand.
Art thou a man? Thy form cries out thou art;
110   Thy tears are womanish, thy wild acts denote
The unreasonable fury of a beast.
Unseemly[19] woman in a seeming man!
And ill-beseeming beast in seeming both![20]

14. simpleness silly behavior (Romeo does not move).

15. O cry of grief.

16. concealed lady secret bride.

17. level aim.

18. sack plunder.

19. Unseemly inappropriate (because unnatural).

20. And . . . both! Romeo has inappropriately lost his human nature because he seems like a man and woman combined.

Thou hast amazed me. By my holy order,
115 I thought thy disposition better tempered.
Hast thou slain Tybalt? Wilt thou slay thyself?
And slay thy lady that in thy life lives,
By doing damnèd hate upon thyself?
Why railest thou on thy birth, the heaven, and earth?
120 Since birth and heaven and earth, all three do meet
In thee at once; which thou at once wouldst lose.
Fie, fie, thou shamest thy shape, thy love, thy wit,[21]
Which, like a usurer,[22] abound'st in all,
And usest none in that true use indeed
125 Which should bedeck[23] thy shape, thy love, thy wit.
Thy noble shape is but a form of wax,
Digressing from the valor of a man;
Thy dear love sworn but hollow prejury,
Killing that love which thou hast vowed to cherish;
130 Thy wit, that ornament to shape and love,
Misshapen in the conduct[24] of them both,
Like powder in a skilless soldier's flask,[25]
Is set afire by thine own ignorance,
And thou dismemb'red with thine own defense.[26]
135 What, rouse thee, man! Thy Juliet is alive,
For whose dear sake thou wast but lately dead.[27]
There art thou happy.[28] Tybalt would kill thee,
But thou slewest Tybalt. There art thou happy.
The law, that threat'ned death, becomes thy friend
140 And turns it to exile. There art thou happy.
A pack of blessings light upon thy back;
Happiness courts thee in her best array;
But, like a misbehaved and sullen wench,[29]
Thou puts up[30] thy fortune and thy love.
145 Take heed, take heed, for such die miserable.
Go get thee to thy love, as was decreed,
Ascend her chamber, hence and comfort her.
But look thou stay not till the watch be set,[31]
For then thou canst not pass to Mantua,
150 Where thou shalt live till we can find a time
To blaze[32] your marriage, reconcile your friends,
Beg pardon of the Prince, and call thee back
With twenty hundred thousand times more joy
Than thou went'st forth in lamentation.
155 Go before, nurse. Commend me to thy lady,
And bid her hasten all the house to bed,
Which heavy sorrow makes them apt unto.[33]
Romeo is coming.

NURSE. O Lord, I could have stayed here all the night
160 To hear good counsel. O, what learning is!
My lord, I'll tell my lady you will come.

---

21. **wit** mind; intellect.
22. **Which, like a usurer** who, like a rich money-lender.

23. **bedeck** do honor to.

Literary Analysis
Soliloquy, Aside, and Monologue Is the Friar's long speech addressed to another character? Is it a monologue or a soliloquy?

24. **conduct** management.
25. **flask** powder flask.
26. **And thou . . . defense** the friar is saying that Romeo's mind, which is now irrational, is destroying rather than aiding him.

27. **but lately dead** only recently declaring yourself dead.

28. **happy** fortunate.
29. **wench** low, common girl.

30. **puts up** pouts over.

31. **watch be set** watchmen go on duty.

32. **blaze** announce publicly.

33. **apt unto** likely to do.

 **Reading Check**
What three reasons does the Friar give to persuade Romeo to change his attitude?

ROMEO. Do so, and bid my sweet prepare to chide.[34]

[NURSE *offers to go in and turns again.*]

NURSE. Here, sir, a ring she bid me give you, sir.
Hie you, make haste, for it grows very late.   [*Exit.*]

165 **ROMEO.** How well my comfort is revived by this!

FRIAR. Go hence; good night; and here stands all your state:[35]
Either be gone before the watch be set,
Or by the break of day disguised from hence.
Sojourn[36] in Mantua. I'll find out your man,
170 And he shall signify[37] from time to time
Every good hap to you that chances here.
Give me thy hand. 'Tis late. Farewell; good night.

ROMEO. But that a joy past joy calls out on me,
It were a grief so brief to part with thee.
175 Farewell.   [*Exit all.*]

Scene iv. *A room in* CAPULET'S *house.*

[*Enter old* CAPULET, *his* WIFE, *and* PARIS.]

CAPULET. Things have fall'n out, sir, so unluckily
That we have had no time to move[1] our daughter.
Look you, she loved her kinsman Tybalt dearly,
And so did I. Well, we were born to die.
5 'Tis very late; she'll not come down tonight.
I promise you, but for your company,
I would have been abed an hour ago.

PARIS. These times of woe afford no times to woo.
Madam, good night. Commend me to your daughter.

10 **LADY.** I will, and know her mind early tomorrow;
Tonight she's mewed up to her heaviness.[2]

CAPULET. Sir, Paris, I will make a desperate tender[3]
Of my child's love. I think she will be ruled
In all respects by me; nay more, I doubt it not.
15 Wife, go you to her ere you go to bed;
Acquaint her here of my son[4] Paris' love
And bid her (mark you me?) on Wednesday next—
But soft! What day is this?

PARIS.   Monday, my lord.

CAPULET. Monday! Ha, ha! Well, Wednesday is too soon.
20 A[5] Thursday let it be—a Thursday, tell her,
She shall be married to this noble earl.
Will you be ready? Do you like this haste?
We'll keep no great ado[6]—a friend or two;
For hark you, Tybalt being slain so late,

---

34. chide rebuke me (for slaying Tybalt).

Reading Strategy
Paraphrasing What does Romeo mean when he says, "Bid my sweet prepare to chide"?

35. here . . . state this is your situation.

36. Sojourn remain.

37. signify let you know.

Reading Strategy
Paraphrasing Is Romeo's parting with the Friar angry, sad, or something else? Explain.

1. move discuss your proposal with.

Literary Analysis
Soliloquy, Aside, and Monologue Is Lady Capulet's brief remark in lines 10–11 an aside? Why or why not?

2. mewed . . . heaviness locked up with her sorrow.

3. desperate tender risky offer.

4. son son-in-law.

5. A on.

6. We'll . . . ado We won't make a great fuss.

25   It may be thought we held him carelessly,[7]
     Being our kinsman, if we revel much.
     Therefore we'll have some half a dozen friends,
     And there an end. But what say you to Thursday?

     PARIS. My lord, I would that Thursday were tomorrow.

30   **CAPULET.** Well, get you gone. A Thursday be it then.
     Go you to Juliet ere you go to bed;
     Prepare her, wife, against[8] this wedding day.
     Farewell, my lord.—Light to my chamber, ho!
     Afore me,[9] it is so very late
35   That we may call it early by and by.
     Good night.   [*Exit all.*]

Scene v. CAPULET'S *orchard.*

[*Enter* ROMEO *and* JULIET *aloft.*]

     JULIET. Wilt thou be gone? It is not yet near day.
     It was the nightingale, and not the lark,[1]
     That pierced the fearful hollow of thine ear.
     Nightly she sings on yond pomegranate tree.
5   Believe me, love, it was the nightingale.

     ROMEO. It was the lark, the herald of the morn;
     No nightingale. Look, love, what envious streaks
     Do lace the severing[2] clouds in yonder East.
     Night's candles[3] are burnt out, and jocund day
10   Stands tiptoe on the misty mountaintops.
     I must be gone and live, or stay and die.

     JULIET. Yond light is not daylight; I know it, I.
     It is some meteor that the sun exhales[4]
     To be to thee this night a torchbearer
15   And light thee on thy way to Mantua.
     Therefore stay yet; thou need'st not to be gone.

     ROMEO. Let me be ta'en, let me be put to death.
     I am content, so thou wilt have it so.
     I'll say yon gray is not the morning's eye,
20   'Tis but the pale reflex of Cynthia's brow;[5]
     Nor that is not the lark whose notes do beat
     The vaulty heaven so high above our heads.
     I have more care to stay than will to go.
     Come, death, and welcome! Juliet wills it so.
25   How is't, my soul? Let's talk; it is not day.

     JULIET. It is, it is! Hie hence, be gone, away!
     It is the lark that sings so out of tune,
     Straining harsh discords and unpleasing sharps.[6]
     Some say the lark makes sweet division;[7]

30 This doth not so, for she divideth us.
    Some say the lark and loathèd toad change eyes;[8]
    O, now I would they had changed voices too,
    Since arm from arm that voice doth us affray,[9]
    Hunting thee hence with hunt's-up[10] to the day.
35 O, now be gone! More light and light it grows.

ROMEO. More light and light—more dark and dark our woes.

[*Enter* NURSE.]

NURSE. Madam!

JULIET. Nurse?

NURSE. Your lady mother is coming to your chamber.
40 The day is broke; be wary, look about.   [*Exit.*]

JULIET. Then, window, let day in, and let life out.

ROMEO. Farewell, farewell! One kiss, and I'll descend.
                                                    [*He goeth down.*]

JULIET. Art thou gone so, love-lord, ay husband-friend?
    I must hear from thee every day in the hour,
45 For in a minute there are many days.
    O, by this count I shall be much in years[11]
    Ere I again behold my Romeo!

ROMEO. Farewell!
    I will omit no opportunity
50 That may convey my greetings, love, to thee.

JULIET. O, think'st thou we shall ever meet again?

ROMEO. I doubt it not; and all these woes shall serve
    For sweet discourses[12] in our times to come.

JULIET. O God, I have an ill-divining[13] soul!
55 Methinks I see thee, now thou art so low,
    As one dead in the bottom of a tomb.
    Either my eyesight fails, or thou lookest pale.

ROMEO. And trust me, love, in my eye so do you.
    Dry sorrow drinks our blood.[14] Adieu, adieu!   [*Exit.*]

60 **JULIET.** O Fortune, Fortune! All men call thee <u>fickle</u>.
    If thou art fickle, what dost thou[15] with him
    That is renowned for faith? Be fickle, Fortune,
    For then I hope thou wilt not keep him long
    But send him back.

[*Enter* MOTHER.]

65 **LADY CAPULET.** Ho, daughter! Are you up?

    JULIET. Who is't that calls? It is my lady mother.

---

8. change eyes exchange eyes (because the lark has a beautiful body with ugly eyes and the toad has an ugly body with beautiful eyes).

9. affray frighten.

10. hunt's-up morning song for hunters.

Reading Strategy
Paraphrasing Restate Romeo's complaint in line 36 to explain the contrast he makes between light and dark.

11. much in years much older.

Reading Strategy
Paraphrasing Translate Romeo and Juliet's conversation in lines 48–53 into modern English.

12. discourses conversations.

13. ill-divining predicting evil.

14. Dry sorrow . . . blood it was once believed that sorrow drained away the blood.

fickle (fik´əl) *adj.* changeable

15. dost thou do you have to do.

Literary Analysis
Allusion To which quality of Fortune, the Greek goddess of chance, does Juliet allude?

Is she not down so late,[16] or up so early?
What unaccustomed cause procures her hither?[17]

LADY CAPULET. Why, how now, Juliet?

JULIET.   Madam, I am not well.

70 **LADY CAPULET.** Evermore weeping for your cousin's death?
What, wilt thou wash him from his grave with tears?
And if thou couldst, thou couldst not make him live.
Therefore have done. Some grief shows much of love;
But much of grief shows still some want of wit.

75 **JULIET.** Yet let me weep for such a feeling[18] loss.

LADY CAPULET. So shall you feel the loss, but not the friend
Which you weep for.

JULIET.   Feeling so the loss,
I cannot choose but ever weep the friend.

LADY CAPULET. Well, girl, thou weep'st not so much for his death
80 As that the villain lives which slaughtered him.

JULIET. What villain, madam?

LADY CAPULET.   That same villain Romeo.

JULIET. [*Aside*] Villain and he be many miles asunder.[19]—
God pardon him! I do, with all my heart;
And yet no man like he doth grieve my heart.

85 **LADY CAPULET.** That is because the traitor murderer lives.

JULIET. Ay, madam, from the reach of these my hands.
Would none but I might venge my cousin's death!

LADY CAPULET. We will have vengeance for it, fear thou not.
Then weep no more. I'll send to one in Mantua,
90 Where that same banished runagate[20] doth live,
Shall give him such an unaccustomed dram[21]
That he shall soon keep Tybalt company;
And then I hope thou wilt be satisfied.

JULIET. Indeed I never shall be satisfied
95 With Romeo till I behold him—dead[22]—
Is my poor heart so for a kinsman vexed.
Madam, if you could find out but a man
To bear a poison, I would temper[23] it;
That Romeo should, upon receipt thereof,
100 Soon sleep in quiet. O, how my heart abhors
To hear him named and cannot come to him,
To wreak[24] the love I bore my cousin
Upon his body that hath slaughtered him!

LADY CAPULET. Find thou the means, and I'll find such a man.

---

16. Is she . . . late Has she stayed up so late?

17. What . . . hither? What unusual reason brings her here?

18. feeling deeply felt.

Literary Analysis
Soliloquy, Aside, and Monologue Which characteristics of an aside do you find in Juliet's words in lines 82–84?

19. asunder apart.

20. runagate renegade; runaway.

21. unaccustomed dram unexpected dose of poison.

22. dead Juliet is deliberately ambiguous here. Her mother thinks *dead* refers to Romeo. But Juliet is using the word with the following line, in reference to her heart.

23. temper mix; weaken.

24. wreak (reek) avenge; express.

**Reading Check**

Who leaves Juliet's chambers just before Lady Capulet arrives?

Stuffed, as they say, with honorable parts,[47]
Proportioned as one's thought would wish a man—
185 And then to have a wretched puling[48] fool,
A whining mammet,[49] in her fortune's tender,[50]
To answer "I'll not wed, I cannot love;
I am too young, I pray you pardon me"!
But, and you will not wed, I'll pardon you!
190 Graze where you will, you shall not house with me.
Look to't, think on't; I do not use to jest.
Thursday is near; lay hand on heart, advise:[51]
And you be mine, I'll give you to my friend;
And you be not, hang, beg, starve, die in the streets,
195 For, by my soul, I'll ne'er acknowledge thee,
Nor what is mine shall never do thee good.
Trust to't. Bethink you. I'll not be forsworn.[52]   [*Exit.*]

JULIET. Is there no pity sitting in the clouds
That sees into the bottom of my grief?
200 O sweet my mother, cast me not away!
Delay this marriage for a month, a week;
Or if you do not, make the bridal bed
In that dim monument where Tybalt lies.

LADY CAPULET. Talk not to me, for I'll not speak a word.
205 Do as thou wilt, for I have done with thee.   [*Exit.*]

JULIET. O God!—O nurse, how shall this be prevented?
My husband is on earth, my faith in heaven.[53]
How shall that faith return again to earth
Unless that husband send it me from heaven
210 By leaving earth?[54] Comfort me, counsel me.
Alack, alack, that heaven should practice stratagems[55]
Upon so soft a subject as myself!
What say'st thou? Hast thou not a word of joy?
Some comfort, nurse.

NURSE.   Faith, here it is.
Romeo is banished; and all the world to nothing[56]
That he dares ne'er come back to challenge[57] you;
Or if he do, it needs must be by stealth.
Then, since the case so stands as now it doth,
I think it best you married with the County.
220 O, he's a lovely gentleman!
Romeo's a dishclout to him.[58] An eagle, madam,
Hath not so green, so quick, so fair an eye
As Paris hath. Beshrew my very heart,
I think you are happy in this second match,
225 For it excels your first; or if it did not,
Your first is dead—or 'twere as good he were
As living here and you no use of him.

47. **parts** qualities.

48. **puling** whining.
49. **mammet** doll.
50. **in . . . tender** when good fortune is offered her.

51. **advise** consider.

52. **forsworn** made to violate my promise.

Reading Strategy
Paraphrasing In lines 200–204, what options does Juliet offer her mother?

53. **my faith in heaven** my marriage vow is recorded in heaven.

54. **leaving earth** dying.
55. **stratagems** tricks; plots.

56. **all . . . nothing** the odds are overwhelming.

57. **challenge** claim.

58. **a dishclout to him** a dishcloth compared with him.

JULIET. Speak'st thou from thy heart?

NURSE. And from my soul too; else beshrew them both.

230 **JULIET.** Amen!

NURSE. What?

JULIET. Well, thou hast comforted me marvelous much.
Go in; and tell my lady I am gone,
Having displeased my father, to Lawrence' cell,
235 To make confession and to be absolved.[59]

NURSE. Marry, I will; and this is wisely done.   [*Exit.*]

JULIET. Ancient damnation![60] O most wicked fiend!
Is it more sin to wish me thus forsworn,
Or to dispraise my lord with that same tongue
240 Which she hath praised him with above compare
So many thousand times? Go, counselor!
Thou and my bosom henceforth shall be twain.[61]
I'll to the friar to know his remedy.
If all else fail, myself have power to die.   [*Exit.*]

59. absolved receive forgiveness for my sins.

60. Ancient damnation! Old devil!

61. Thou . . . twain You will from now on be separated from my trust.

Review and Assess

Thinking About Act III

1. **Respond:** What would you do if you were in Romeo or Juliet's situation?

2. **(a) Recall:** Why do Mercutio and Tybalt fight in Act III, Scene i? **(b) Interpret:** What does Mercutio mean by his dying exclamation, "A plague on both your houses!"? **(c) Connect:** How do these lines echo the ideas set forth in the play's prologue?

3. **(a) Recall:** How and why does Romeo kill Tybalt? **(b) Interpret:** What does Romeo mean when he says, after killing Tybalt, "I am fortune's fool!"?

4. **(a) Recall:** What punishment does the prince order for Romeo? **(b) Draw Conclusions:** Why does the Prince decide not to sentence Romeo to death, despite his threat in Act I?

5. **(a) Recall:** Describe the clashing emotions Juliet feels when Nurse reports Tybalt's death and Romeo's punishment. **(b) Compare and Contrast:** What reactions—both similar and different—do Juliet and Romeo have to Romeo's punishment?

6. **Speculate:** Do you think Romeo's punishment is fair? Support your answer.

Review and Assess

Literary Analysis

Soliloquy, Aside, and Monologue

1. Analyze the thoughts and feelings Juliet reveals in the **soliloquy** that opens Scene ii of Act III.

2. Which criticisms of Romeo does the Friar address in his Scene iii **monologue** beginning "Hold thy desperate hand"?

3. (a) In Act III, Scene v, when her mother refers to Romeo as a villain, Juliet utters the **aside**, "Villain and he be many miles asunder." What does Juliet mean? (b) Why is it important that the audience, but not Lady Capulet, hear this remark?

Connecting Literary Elements

4. How does Mercutio use an **allusion** to incite Tybalt to fight him in Act III, Scene i?

5. When Juliet alludes to Phoebus and Phaëton in her soliloquy opening Act III, Scene ii, what is she hoping will happen soon?

6. What do Juliet's allusions to mythology in her speeches reveal about her character?

7. Do you need to understand an allusion to understand a character's ideas? Why or why not?

Reading Strategy

Paraphrasing

8. Using a chart like the one shown, paraphrase lines 29–51 in Act III, Scene iii.

Shakespeare's Words	My Words

9. Paraphrase lines 215–227 in Act III, Scene v.

10. To reverse the process, write two sentences about Romeo and Juliet. Then, restate them in Shakespearean language.

Extend Understanding

11. **Cultural Connection:** For Romeo, being exiled from his homeland is a very harsh punishment. What important role does a person's homeland play in modern life?

Quick Review

A **soliloquy** is a lengthy speech in which a character, alone on stage, expresses his or her thoughts to the audience.

An **aside** is a character's brief remark made to the audience, unheard by other characters on stage.

A **monologue** is a lengthy speech addressed to other characters on stage.

Within their dramatic speeches, characters often make **allusions**—references to well-known people, places, or events from myths or literature.

Paraphrasing is restating text in your own words.

 Take It to the Net

www.phschool.com
Take the interactive self-test online to check your understanding of Act III.

Integrate Language Skills

Vocabulary Development Lesson

Word Analysis: Words From Myths

Nemesis is the Greek goddess of vengeance. *Mercury* is the swift Roman messenger to the gods. *Odysseus* is the Greek hero who wanders for years. Using these mythological clues, write a definition for each word below.

1. nemesis   2. mercurial   3. odyssey

Spelling Strategy

To make a present-tense verb agree with a third-person singular subject, add *-s* to the verb. (*He visits her.*) If the verb ends in *ss*, *sh*, or *ch*, add *-es*. (*She touches his hand.*) Choose the correctly spelled word in each item below.

1. tauntes, taunts   2. reaches, reachs

Concept Development: Synonyms

Write the word that is the best synonym for the first word in each item. To help you, review vocabulary words on page 818.

1. gallant: (a) enchanting, (b) courageous, (c) cowardly
2. fray: (a) brawl, (b) condition, (c) truce
3. martial: (a) financial, (b) deputy, (c) warlike
4. exile: (a) expel, (b) discourage, (c) arrive
5. eloquence: (a) beauty, (b) expressiveness, (c) value
6. fickle: (a) fruitful, (b) constant, (c) erratic

Grammar Lesson

Pronoun Case: *who* and *whom*

Use the pronoun **who** when it is the subject of the verb or is a predicate nominative. Use the pronoun **whom** when it receives the action of the verb or is the object of a preposition.

| Subject: | Who knocks so hard? |
| Direct Object: | It shall be Romeo, whom you know I hate? |

Practice In your notebook, complete each sentence with *who* or *whom*.

1. ___?___ began the tragic argument?
2. Romeo, ___?___ wanted peace, intervened.
3. He is someone to ___?___ bad things happen.
4. Romeo is the man ___?___ Juliet loves.
5. Tybalt was the man ___?___ Romeo killed.

Writing Application Write two additional sentences about Act III, using *who* in one sentence and *whom* in the other.

*W*G *Prentice Hall Writing and Grammar Connection: Chapter 24, Section 2*

Extension Activities

Writing Imagine that you are the editor of the Verona newspaper. Write an **editorial** addressing the Prince's response to Tybalt's death. Decide whether the ruling was appropriate, and support your arguments with details from Acts I through III.

Listening and Speaking View a film of the ballet *Romeo and Juliet*. Take notes on how the dance communicates the play's ideas. Then, use your notes to present a **film review** for your classmates. **[Group Activity]**

Prepare to Read

The Tragedy of Romeo and Juliet, Act IV

CALIFORNIA STANDARDS

Instruction with this selection addresses these standards:

R 1.1*, 3.6*, 3.8*
W 1.2*, 2.4*
WOLC 1.3*
LS 1.7

* *Standards tested on HS Exit Exam. For complete standards, see p. CA 4.*

Literary Analysis

Dramatic Irony

Dramatic irony is a contradiction between what a character thinks or says and what the audience or reader knows to be true. For example, in Act III, Lord Capulet decides that the way to ensure Juliet's future happiness is to have her wed Paris. He does not know what you know—that Juliet is already married. Dramatic irony involves you emotionally in the story. You may even feel the urge to step into the play to help the characters see a situation correctly.

Connecting Literary Elements

Suspense is a feeling of curiosity or uncertainty about the outcome of events in a literary work. Suspense often results from the use of dramatic irony, as the audience anxiously wonders whether characters will discover the truth before it is too late. As you read the events of Act IV, notice how Shakespeare builds suspense through Juliet's words and actions.

Reading Strategy

Predicting

When you **predict,** you make educated guesses about what may happen next in a literary work. To predict, consider each character's personality and what information he or she knows. Also, look for places where the author hints at future events. In this passage, Juliet's remark hints at deadly consequences:

> If in thy wisdom thou canst give no help,
> Do thou but call my resolution wise
> And with this knife I'll help it presently.

Use a chart like this one to make and assess predictions as you read.

What I Predict

Juliet will not marry Paris.

Why?

She says she will kill herself instead.

Actual Outcome

Vocabulary Development

pensive (pen´ siv) *adj.* thinking deeply or seriously (p. 846)

vial (vī´ əl) *n.* small bottle containing medicine or other liquids (p. 848)

enjoined (en joind´) *v.* ordered (p. 849)

wayward (wā´ wərd) *adj.* headstrong; willful (p. 850)

dismal (diz´ məl) *adj.* causing gloom or misery (p. 850)

loathsome (lōth´ səm) *adj.* disgusting (p. 851)

pilgrimage (pil´ grim ij) *n.* long journey, often for religious purposes (p. 855)

Review and Anticipate

Romeo and Juliet are married for only a few hours when disaster strikes. In Act III, Juliet's cousin Tybalt kills Mercutio, and then Romeo kills Tybalt. This leads to Romeo's banishment from Verona. To make matters worse, Juliet's parents are determined to marry her to Paris. Will Romeo and Juliet ever be able to live together as husband and wife? What, if anything, can the lovers now do to preserve their relationship?

Scene i. FRIAR LAWRENCE's cell.

[*Enter* FRIAR LAWRENCE *and* COUNTY PARIS.]

FRIAR. On Thursday, sir? The time is very short.

PARIS. My father[1] Capulet will have it so,
And I am nothing slow to slack his haste.[2]

FRIAR. You say you do not know the lady's mind.
5   Uneven is the course;[3] I like it not.

PARIS. Immoderately she weeps for Tybalt's death,
And therefore have I little talked of love;
For Venus smiles not in a house of tears.
Now, sir, her father counts it dangerous

1. **father** future
father-in-law.

2. **I . . . haste** I won't
slow him down by
being slow myself.
3. **Uneven . . . course**
irregular is the plan.

✔Reading Check

What is the Friar's complaint to Paris about the impending wedding?

10   That she do give her sorrow so much sway,
     And in his wisdom hastes our marriage
     To stop the inundation⁴ of her tears,
     Which, too much minded⁵ by herself alone,
     May be put from her by society.
15   Now do you know the reason of this haste.

     FRIAR. [*Aside*] I would I knew not why it should be slowed.—
     Look, sir, here comes the lady toward my cell.

[*Enter* JULIET.]

     PARIS. Happily met, my lady and my wife!

     JULIET. That may be, sir, when I may be a wife.

20   **PARIS.** That "may be" must be, love, on Thursday next.

     JULIET. What must be shall be.

     FRIAR.   That's a certain text.⁶

     PARIS. Come you to make confession to this father?

     JULIET. To answer that, I should confess to you.

     PARIS. Do not deny to him that you love me.

25   **JULIET.** I will confess to you that I love him.

     PARIS. So will ye, I am sure, that you love me.

     JULIET. If I do so, it will be of more price,⁷
     Being spoke behind your back, than to your face.

     PARIS. Poor soul, thy face is much abused with tears.

30   **JULIET.** The tears have got small victory by that,
     For it was bad enough before their spite.⁸

     PARIS. Thou wrong'st it more than tears with that report.

     JULIET. That is no slander, sir, which is a truth;
     And what I spake, I spake it to my face.

35   **PARIS.** Thy face is mine, and thou hast sland'red it.

     JULIET. It may be so, for it is not mine own.
     Are you at leisure, holy father, now,
     Or shall I come to you at evening mass?

     FRIAR. My leisure serves me, <u>pensive</u> daughter, now.
40   My lord, we must entreat the time alone.⁹

     PARIS. God shield¹⁰ I should disturb devotion!
     Juliet, on Thursday early will I rouse ye.
     Till then, adieu, and keep this holy kiss.   [*Exit.*]

     JULIET. O, shut the door, and when thou hast done so,
45   Come weep with me—past hope, past care, past help!

---

4. inundation flood.
5. minded thought about.

Literary Analysis
Dramatic Irony In what way does Paris' comment show that he does not understand the real reason that Juliet is crying?

6. That's . . . text
That's a certain truth.

7. price value.

8. before their spite
before the harm that the tears did.

Reading Strategy
Predicting Based on this dialogue, do you think Juliet will consider Paris an ally? Why or why not?

pensive (pen´ siv) *adj.* thinking deeply or seriously

9. entreat . . . alone
ask to have this time to ourselves.
10. shield forbid.

FRIAR. O Juliet, I already know thy grief;
It strains me past the compass of my wits.[11]
I hear thou must, and nothing may prorogue[12] it,
On Thursday next be married to this County.

50 **JULIET.** Tell me not, friar, that thou hearest of this,
Unless thou tell me how I may prevent it.
If in thy wisdom thou canst give no help,
Do thou but call my resolution wise
And with this knife I'll help it presently.[13]
55 God joined my heart and Romeo's, thou our hands;
And ere this hand, by thee to Romeo's sealed,
Shall be the label to another deed,[14]
Or my true heart with treacherous revolt
Turn to another, this shall slay them both.
60 Therefore, out of thy long-experienced time,
Give me some present counsel; or, behold,
'Twixt my extremes and me[15] this bloody knife
Shall play the umpire, arbitrating[16] that
Which the commission of thy years and art
65 Could to no issue of true honor bring.[17]
Be not so long to speak. I long to die
If what thou speak'st speak not of remedy.

FRIAR. Hold, daughter. I do spy a kind of hope,
Which craves[18] as desperate an execution
70 As that is desperate which we would prevent.
If, rather than to marry County Paris,
Thou hast the strength of will to slay thyself,
Then is it likely thou wilt undertake
A thing like death to chide away this shame,
75 That cop'st with death himself to scape from it;[19]
And, if thou darest, I'll give thee remedy.

JULIET. O, bid me leap, rather than marry Paris,
From off the battlements of any tower,
Or walk in thievish ways,[20] or bid me lurk
80 Where serpents are; chain me with roaring bears,
Or hide me nightly in a charnel house,[21]
O'ercovered quite with dead men's rattling bones,
With reeky[22] shanks and yellow chapless[23] skulls;
Or bid me go into a new-made grave
85 And hide me with a dead man in his shroud—
Things that, to hear them told, have made me tremble—
And I will do it without fear or doubt,
To live an unstained wife to my sweet love.

FRIAR. Hold, then. Go home, be merry, give consent
90 To marry Paris. Wednesday is tomorrow.
Tomorrow night look that thou lie alone;

11. **past . . . wits** beyond the ability of my mind to find a remedy.

12. **prorogue** delay.

Reading Strategy
Predicting What do you predict Juliet will do if there is no way to prevent her marriage to Paris?

13. **presently** at once.
14. **Shall . . . deed** shall give the seal of approval to another marriage contract.

15. **'Twixt . . . me** between my misfortunes and me.

16. **arbitrating** deciding.
17. **Which . . . bring** which the authority that derives from your age and ability could not solve honorably.

18. **craves** requires.

19. **That cop'st . . . it** that bargains with death itself to escape from it.

20. **thievish ways** roads where criminals lurk.

21. **charnel house** vault for bones removed from graves to be reused.

22. **reeky** foul-smelling.
23. **chapless** jawless.

✔Reading Check

What does the Friar tell Juliet she should do when she goes home?

Let not the nurse lie with thee in thy chamber.
Take thou this <u>vial</u>, being then in bed,
And this distilling liquor drink thou off;
95 When presently through all thy veins shall run
A cold and drowsy humor;[24] for no pulse
Shall keep his native[25] progress, but surcease;[26]
No warmth, no breath, shall testify thou livest;
The roses in thy lips and cheeks shall fade
100 To wanny ashes,[27] thy eyes' windows[28] fall
Like death when he shuts up the day of life;
Each part, deprived of supple government,[29]
Shall, stiff and stark and cold, appear like death;
And in this borrowed likeness of shrunk death
105 Thou shalt continue two-and-forty hours,
And then awake as from a pleasant sleep.
Now, when the bridegroom in the morning comes
To rouse thee from thy bed, there art thou dead.
Then, as the manner of our country is,
110 In thy best robes uncovered on the bier[30]
Thou shalt be borne to that same ancient vault
Where all the kindred of the Capulets lie.
In the meantime, against[31] thou shalt awake,
Shall Romeo by my letters know our drift;[32]
115 And hither shall he come; and he and I
Will watch thy waking, and that very night
Shall Romeo bear thee hence to Mantua.
And this shall free thee from this present shame,
If no inconstant toy[33] nor womanish fear
120 Abate thy valor[34] in the acting it.

JULIET. Give me, give me! O, tell not me of fear!

vial (vī′ əl) *n.* small bottle containing medicine or other liquids

24. humor fluid; liquid.

25. native natural.

26. surcease stop.

27. wanny ashes to the color of pale ashes.

28. eyes' windows eyelids.

29. supple government ability for maintaining motion.

30. uncovered on the bier displayed on the funeral platform.

31. against before.

32. drift purpose; plan.

33. inconstant toy passing whim.

34. Abate thy valor lessen your courage.

◀ **Critical Viewing**
According to the play, what power does the vial hold? **[Connect]**

FRIAR. Hold! Get you gone, be strong and prosperous
In this resolve. I'll send a friar with speed
To Mantua, with my letters to thy lord.

125 **JULIET.** Love give me strength, and strength shall help afford.
Farewell, dear father.   *[Exit with* FRIAR.]

Scene ii. *Hall in* CAPULET'*s house.*

[*Enter* FATHER CAPULET, MOTHER, NURSE, *and* SERVINGMEN, *two or three.*]

CAPULET. So many guests invite as here are writ.   [*Exit a* SERVINGMAN.]
Sirrah, go hire me twenty cunning¹ cooks.

SERVINGMAN. You shall have none ill, sir; for I'll try² if they can lick
their fingers.

5 **CAPULET.** How canst thou try them so?

SERVINGMAN. Marry, sir, 'tis an ill cook that cannot lick his own fin-
gers.³ Therefore he that cannot lick his fingers goes not with me.

CAPULET. Go, begone.   *[Exit* SERVINGMAN.]
We shall be much unfurnished⁴ for this time.
10 What, is my daughter gone to Friar Lawrence?

NURSE. Ay, forsooth.⁵

CAPULET. Well, he may chance to do some good on her.
A peevish self-willed harlotry it is.⁶

[*Enter* JULIET.]

NURSE. See where she comes from shrift with merry look.

15 **CAPULET.** How now, my headstrong? Where have you been gadding?

JULIET. Where I have learnt me to repent the sin
Of disobedient opposition
To you and your behests,⁷ and am <u>enjoined</u>
By holy Lawrence to fall prostrate⁸ here
20 To beg your pardon. Pardon, I beseech you!
Henceforward I am ever ruled by you.

CAPULET. Send for the County. Go tell him of this.
I'll have this knot knit up tomorrow morning.

JULIET. I met the youthful lord at Lawrence' cell
25 And gave him what becomèd⁹ love I might,
Not stepping o'er the bounds of modesty.

CAPULET. Why, I am glad on't. This is well. Stand up.
This is as't should be. Let me see the County.
Ay, marry, go, I say, and fetch him hither.
30 Now, afore God, this reverend holy friar,
All our whole city is much bound¹⁰ to him.

Literary Analysis
Dramatic Irony What information does Juliet now know that Romeo does not?

1. **cunning** skillful.

2. **try** test.

3. **'tis . . . fingers** It's a bad cook that won't taste his own cooking.
4. **unfurnished** unprepared.

5. **forsooth** in truth.

6. **A peevish . . . it is** It is the ill-tempered, self-ish behavior of a woman without good breeding.

7. **behests** requests.
enjoined (en joind´) *v.* ordered

8. **fall prostrate** lie face down in humble submission.

9. **becomèd** suitable; proper.

10. **bound** indebted.

✔ **Reading Check**

What does the Friar say will happen when Juliet drinks the contents of the vial?

JULIET. Nurse, will you go with me into my closet[11]
To help me sort such needful ornaments[12]
As you think fit to furnish me tomorrow?

35 **LADY CAPULET.** No, not till Thursday. There is time enough.

CAPULET. Go, nurse, go with her. We'll to church tomorrow.

[*Exit* JULIET *and* NURSE.]

LADY CAPULET. We shall be short in our provision.[13]
'Tis now near night.

CAPULET.   Tush, I will stir about,
And all things shall be well, I warrant thee, wife.
40 Go thou to Juliet, help to deck up her.[14]
I'll not to bed tonight; let me alone.
I'll play the housewife for this once. What, ho![15]
They are all forth; well, I will walk myself
To County Paris, to prepare up him
45 Against tomorrow. My heart is wondrous light,
Since this same <u>wayward</u> girl is so reclaimed.   [*Exit with* MOTHER.]

Scene iii. JULIET'*s chamber.*

[*Enter* JULIET *and* NURSE.]

JULIET. Ay, those attires are best; but, gentle nurse,
I pray thee leave me to myself tonight;
For I have need of many orisons[1]
To move the heavens to smile upon my state,[2]
5 Which, well thou knowest, is cross[3] and full of sin.

[*Enter* MOTHER.]

LADY CAPULET. What, are you busy, ho? Need you my help?

JULIET. No, madam; we have culled[4] such necessaries
As are behoveful[5] for our state tomorrow.
So please you, let me now be left alone,
10 And let the nurse this night sit up with you:
For I am sure you have your hands full all
In this so sudden business.

LADY CAPULET.   Good night.
Get thee to bed, and rest: for thou hast need.

[*Exit* MOTHER *and* NURSE.]

JULIET. Farewell! God knows when we shall meet again.
15 I have a faint cold fear thrills through my veins
That almost freezes up the heat of life.
I'll call them back again to comfort me.
Nurse!—What should she do here?
My <u>dismal</u> scene I needs must act alone.

---

11. **closet** private room.
12. **ornaments** clothes.

13. **short . . . provision** lacking time for preparation.

14. **deck up her** dress her; get her ready.

15. **What, ho!** Capulet is calling for his servants.

wayward (wā′ wərd) *adj.* headstrong; willful

Literary Analysis
Dramatic Irony What is ironic about Lord Capulet's relief and joy?

1. **orisons** prayers.
2. **state** condition.
3. **cross** selfish; disobedient.

4. **culled** chosen.
5. **behoveful** desirable; appropriate.

Literary Analysis
Dramatic Irony and Suspense In what ways does Juliet's statement— "I have a faint cold fear thrills through my veins"—add suspense to the drama?

dismal (diz′ məl) *adj.* causing gloom or misery

20   Come, vial.
What if this mixture do not work at all?
Shall I be married then tomorrow morning?
No, no! This shall forbid it. Lie thou there. [*Lays down a dagger.*]
What if it be a poison which the friar
25   Subtly hath minist'red[6] to have me dead,
Lest in this marriage he should be dishonored
Because he married me before to Romeo?
I fear it is; and yet methinks it should not,
For he hath still been tried[7] a holy man.
30   How if, when I am laid into the tomb,
I wake before the time that Romeo
Come to redeem me? There's a fearful point!
Shall I not then be stifled in the vault,
To whose foul mouth no healthsome air breathes in,
35   And there die strangled ere my Romeo comes?
Or, if I live, is it not very like
The horrible conceit[8] of death and night,
Together with the terror of the place—
As in a vault, an ancient receptacle
40   Where for this many hundred years the bones
Of all my buried ancestors are packed;
Where bloody Tybalt, yet but green in earth,[9]
Lies fest'ring in his shroud; where, as they say,
At some hours in the night spirits resort—
45   Alack, alack, is it not like[10] that I,
So early waking—what with loathsome smells,
And shrieks like mandrakes[11] torn out of the earth,
That living mortals, hearing them, run mad—
O, if I wake, shall I not be distraught,[12]
50   Environèd[13] with all these hideous fears,
And madly play with my forefathers' joints,
And pluck the mangled Tybalt from his shroud,
And, in this rage, with some great kinsman's bone
As with a club dash out my desp'rate brains?
55   O, look! Methinks I see my cousin's ghost
Seeking out Romeo, that did spit his body
Upon a rapier's point. Stay, Tybalt, stay!
Romeo, Romeo, Romeo, I drink to thee.
              [*She falls upon her bed within the curtains.*]

Scene iv. *Hall in* CAPULET's *house.*

[*Enter* LADY OF THE HOUSE *and* NURSE.]

    LADY CAPULET. Hold, take these keys and fetch more spices, nurse.

    NURSE. They call for dates and quinces[1] in the pastry.[2]

6. minist'red given me.

7. tried proved.

Literary Analysis
Dramatic Irony and Suspense How do Juliet's anxieties add to the suspense for readers or audiences?

8. conceit idea; thought.

9. green in earth newly entombed.

10. like likely.

loathsome (lōtħ´ səm) *adj.* disgusting

11. mandrakes plants with forked roots that resemble human legs. The mandrake was believed to shriek when uprooted and cause the hearer to go mad.

12. distraught insane.
13. Environèd surrounded.

Reading Strategy
Predicting What do you think will happen when Juliet's "lifeless" body is found on her bed?

1. quinces golden apple-shaped fruit.
2. pastry baking room.

✔ **Reading Check**

What does Juliet do after her mother and the Nurse leave her chambers?

The County Paris hath set up his rest
That you shall rest but little. God forgive me!
Marry, and amen. How sound is she asleep!
I needs must wake her. Madam, madam, madam!
10   Ay, let the County take you in your bed;
He'll fright you up, i' faith. Will it not be?

                                    [*Draws aside the curtains.*]

What, dressed, and in your clothes, and down again?[3]
I must needs wake you. Lady! Lady! Lady!
Alas, alas! Help, help! My lady's dead!
15   O weraday that ever I was born!
Some *aqua vitae*, ho! My lord! My lady!

[*Enter* MOTHER.]

LADY CAPULET. What noise is here?

NURSE.   O lamentable day!

LADY CAPULET. What is the matter?

NURSE.   Look, look! O heavy day!

LADY CAPULET. O me, O me! My child, my only life!
20   Revive, look up, or I will die with thee!
Help, help! Call help.

[*Enter* FATHER.]

CAPULET. For shame, bring Juliet forth; her lord is come.

NURSE. She's dead, deceased; she's dead, alack the day!

LADY CAPULET. Alack the day, she's dead, she's dead, she's dead!

25   **CAPULET.** Ha! Let me see her. Out alas! She's cold,
Her blood is settled, and her joints are stiff;
Life and these lips have long been separated.
Death lies on her like an untimely frost
Upon the sweetest flower of all the field.

NURSE. O lamentable day!

30 **LADY CAPULET.**   O woeful time!

CAPULET. Death, that hath ta'en her hence to make me wail,
Ties up my tongue and will not let me speak.

[*Enter* FRIAR LAWRENCE *and the* COUNTY PARIS, *with* MUSICIANS.]

FRIAR. Come, is the bride ready to go to church?

CAPULET. Ready to go, but never to return.
35   O son, the night before thy wedding day
Hath Death lain with thy wife. There she lies,
Flower as she was, deflowerèd by him.
Death is my son-in-law, Death is my heir;

My daughter he hath wedded. I will die

40   And leave him all. Life, living, all is Death's.

PARIS. Have I thought, love, to see this morning's face,
And doth it give me such a sight as this?

LADY CAPULET. Accursed, unhappy, wretched, hateful day!
Most miserable hour that e'er time saw

45   In lasting labor of his <u>pilgrimage</u>!
But one, poor one, one poor and loving child,
But one thing to rejoice and solace[4] in,
And cruel Death hath catched it from my sight.

NURSE. O woe! O woeful, woeful, woeful day!

50   Most lamentable day, most woeful day
That ever ever I did yet behold!
O day, O day, O day! O hateful day!
Never was seen so black a day as this.
O woeful day! O woeful day!

55   **PARIS.** Beguiled,[5] divorcèd, wrongèd, spited, slain!
Most detestable Death, by thee beguiled,
By cruel, cruel thee quite overthrown.
O love! O life!—not life, but love in death!

CAPULET. Despised, distressèd, hated, martyred, killed!

60   Uncomfortable[6] time, why cam'st thou now
To murder, murder our solemnity?[7]
O child, O child! My soul, and not my child!
Dead art thou—alack, my child is dead,
And with my child my joys are burièd!

65   **FRIAR.** Peace, ho, for shame! Confusion's cure lives not
In these confusions.[8] Heaven and yourself
Had part in this fair maid—now heaven hath all,
And all the better is it for the maid.
Your part in her you could not keep from death,

70   But heaven keeps his part in eternal life.
The most you sought was her promotion,
For 'twas your heaven she should be advanced;
And weep ye now, seeing she is advanced
Above the clouds, as high as heaven itself?

75   O, in this love, you love your child so ill
That you run mad, seeing that she is well.[9]
She's not well married that lives married long,
But she's best married that dies married young.
Dry up your tears and stick your rosemary[10]

80   On this fair corse, and, as the custom is,
And in her best array bear her to church:
For though fond nature[11] bids us all lament,
Yet nature's tears are reason's merriment.[12]

Romeo and Juliet, Act IV, Scene v ◆ 855

Literary Analysis

Dramatic Irony How do Paris' words contribute to the dramatic irony?

pilgrimage (pil′ grim ij) *n.* long journey, often for religious purposes

4. **solace** find comfort.

5. **Beguiled** cheated.

6. **Uncomfortable** painful, upsetting.

7. **solemnity** solemn rites.

Reading Strategy

Predicting What might Capulet's remarks in lines 63–64 foreshadow about the future?

8. **Confusion's . . . confusions** The remedy for this calamity is not to be found in these outcries.

9. **well** blessed in heaven.

10. **rosemary** an evergreen herb signifying love and remembrance.

11. **fond nature** mistake-prone human nature.

12. **Yet . . . merriment** while human nature causes us to weep for Juliet, reason should cause us to be happy (since she is in heaven).

✔**Reading Check**

What does the Nurse find when she draws aside the curtains in Juliet's chamber?

Review and Assess

Literary Analysis

Dramatic Irony

1. What **dramatic irony** results when Juliet encounters Paris in Friar Lawrence's cell?
2. What makes Act IV, Scene iv, in which Capulet prepares for Juliet's wedding, an example of dramatic irony?
3. Find at least one other example of dramatic irony in the first four acts. Use a diagram like the one shown to indicate how a character's thoughts or actions contradict what the audience knows is true.

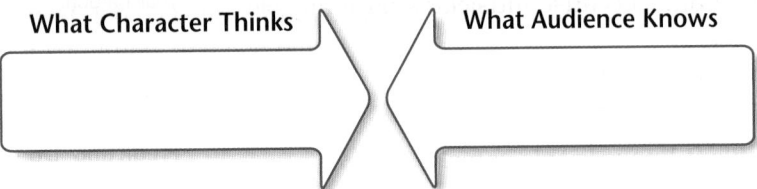

What Character Thinks   **What Audience Knows**

Connecting Literary Elements

4. What possible outcomes generate the feeling of **suspense** in Act IV, Scene i, when the Friar proposes his secret plan to Juliet?
5. Why does suspense build when Juliet holds the dagger and the potion in Act IV, Scene iii?
6. Why does the audience feel suspense in Act IV, Scene iv, as the Nurse prepares to waken Juliet?

Reading Strategy

Predicting

7. How do Juliet's comments to Paris in Act IV, Scene i, lead you to **predict** that she will never marry him?
8. What parts of the Friar's plan do you predict could lead to potential problems? Explain.
9. (a) In what ways is death a main focus throughout Act IV?
   (b) How might this focus foreshadow real tragedy in Act V?

Extend Understanding

10. **Cultural Connection:** How are the customs related to marriage and death in the play similar to or different from those generally followed in the United States today?

Quick Review

Dramatic irony is a contradiction between what a character thinks or says and what the audience or reader knows to be true.

Suspense is a feeling of curiosity or uncertainty about the outcome of events in a literary work.

To **predict,** make educated guesses about what may happen next in a literary work.

 Take It to the Net
www.phschool.com
Take the interactive self-test online to check your understanding of Act IV.

Integrate Language Skills

Vocabulary Development Lesson

Word Analysis: Anglo-Saxon suffix *-ward*

The Anglo-Saxon suffix *-ward* means "in a direction." The suffix appears in the word *wayward,* meaning "insistent upon going in one's own direction." Using the meaning of *-ward,* define each word below.

   1. forward   **2.** skyward   **3.** outward

Spelling Strategy

The *ij* sound at the end of a word is usually spelled *age,* as in *pilgrimage.* Write each of these words, filling in the missing ending.

   1. wreck__?__   **2.** post__?__   **3.** voy__?__

Concept Development: Analogies

Complete each analogy, or comparison, with a word from the vocabulary list on page 844.

   1. *Bright* is to *glistening* as *gloomy* is to __?__.
   2. *Requested* is to *asked* as *commanded* is to __?__.
   3. *Exhausted* is to *rested* as *pleasant* is to __?__.
   4. *Wet* is to *rain* as *long* is to __?__.
   5. *Car* is to *sedan* as *container* is to __?__.
   6. *Dark* is to *light* as *obedient* is to __?__.
   7. *Nervous* is to *edgy* as *thoughtful* is to __?__.

Grammar Lesson

Degrees of Comparison

Use the **comparative** degree of an adjective to compare two things. Use *-er* or *more* to form the comparative degree of most adjectives.

Use the **superlative** form of an adjective to compare three or more things. Generally use *-est* or *most* to form the superlative degree.

Comparative:	Juliet has *greater* love for Romeo than for Paris.
Superlative:	Romeo considers Juliet the *sweetest* and *most* beautiful woman he has known.

Practice Complete each sentence with the correct degree of the adjective.

   1. Romeo is (older, oldest) than Juliet.
   2. Juliet is the (kinder, kindest) Capulet.
   3. Act IV is the (shorter, shortest) act.
   4. Romeo is the (more, most) impulsive of the two lovers.
   5. Act II is the (more, most) memorable act.

Writing Application Use both degrees of comparison in two sentences comparing characters in the play.

*W*G *Prentice Hall Writing and Grammar Connection: Chapter 26, Section 1*

Extension Activities

Writing Use your prediction skills to write your own **ending** for the play. Create a narrative of events that will occur in your version of Act V. Make sure that your ending develops naturally out of the events in Acts I through IV.

Listening and Speaking With a partner, prepare an informal **presentation** on Renaissance music. Collect examples of music that would have been played by musicians in Act IV, Scene v. Present your findings to your class. **[Group Activity]**

Prepare to Read

The Tragedy of Romeo and Juliet, Act V

Literary Analysis

Tragedy

A **tragedy** is a drama in which the central character, who is usually of
noble stature, meets with disaster or great misfortune. The tragic hero's
downfall is usually the result of fate, a serious character flaw, or a combination of both. A great tragedy is not necessarily depressing, however. It
uplifts the audience by showing the greatness of spirit of which people are
capable. This spirit is reflected in these lines near the end of the play:

> For I will raise her statue in pure gold,
> That whiles Verona by that name is known,
> There shall no figure at such rate be set
> As that of true and faithful Juliet.

As you read Act V of *Romeo and Juliet*, consider the reasons for the tragic
events and analyze how the events make you feel about the human spirit.

Connecting Literary Elements

A **character's motive** is the reason behind an individual's thoughts or
actions. In Shakespeare's tragedies, the hero's motives are basically good,
although sometimes misguided. The character's fate, therefore, often
seems worse than what he or she deserves.

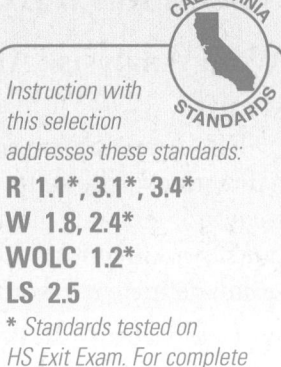

*Instruction with
this selection
addresses these standards:*
R 1.1*, 3.1*, 3.4*
W 1.8, 2.4*
WOLC 1.2*
LS 2.5
* *Standards tested on
HS Exit Exam. For complete
standards, see p. CA 4.*

Reading Strategy

Identifying Causes and Effects

Tragedies often involve a chain of causes and effects that advances the
plot and leads to the final tragic outcome.

- A **cause** is an action, an event, or a situation that produces a
  result.
- An **effect** is the result produced by a cause.

Use a chart like this one to record the causes and effects in Act V.

Vocabulary Development

remnants (rem´ nənts) *n.* remaining
persons or things (p. 862)

penury (pen´ yo͞o rē) *n.* extreme
poverty (p. 862)

haughty (hôt´ ē) *adj.* arrogant (p. 866)

sepulcher (sep´ əl kər) *n.* tomb
(p. 869)

ambiguities (am´ bə gyo͞o´ ə tēz) *n.*
statements or events whose meanings are unclear (p. 872)

scourge (skʉrj) *n.* whip or other
instrument for inflicting punishment
(p. 873)

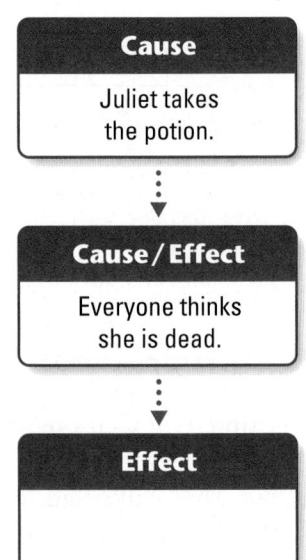

Cause

Juliet takes
the potion.

Cause/Effect

Everyone thinks
she is dead.

Effect

Review and Anticipate

To prevent her marriage to Paris, Juliet has taken the Friar's potion and, as Act V begins, is in a temporary deathlike sleep. Her unsuspecting family plans her funeral. Meanwhile, the Friar has sent a messenger to Mantua to tell Romeo of the ruse, so that he may return and rescue Juliet from her family tomb. What do you think might go wrong with the Friar's plan?

cene i. *Mantua. A street.*

[*Enter* ROMEO.]

    ROMEO. If I may trust the flattering truth of sleep,[1]
    My dreams presage[2] some joyful news at hand.
    My bosom's lord[3] sits lightly in his throne,
    And all this day an unaccustomed spirit
5   Lifts me above the ground with cheerful thoughts.
    I dreamt my lady came and found me dead
    (Strange dream that gives a dead man leave to think!)
    And breathed such life with kisses in my lips
    That I revived and was an emperor.
10   Ah me! How sweet is love itself possessed,
    When but love's shadows[4] are so rich in joy!

---

1. flattering . . . sleep pleasing illusions of dreams.

2. presage foretell.

3. bosom's lord heart.

4. shadows dreams; unreal images.

✔**Reading Check**

Why is Romeo in a good mood?

Romeo and Juliet, Act V, Scene i ◆ 861

[*Enter* ROMEO'S MAN, BALTHASAR, *booted.*]

    News from Verona! How now, Balthasar?
    Dost thou not bring me letters from the friar?
    How doth my lady? Is my father well?
15   How fares my Juliet? That I ask again,
    For nothing can be ill if she be well.

MAN. Then she is well, and nothing can be ill.
    Her body sleeps in Capels' monument,[5]
    And her immortal part with angels lives.
20   I saw her laid low in her kindred's vault
    And presently took post[6] to tell it you.
    O, pardon me for bringing these ill news,
    Since you did leave it for my office,[7] sir.

ROMEO. Is it e'en so? Then I defy you, stars!
25   Thou knowest my lodging. Get me ink and paper
    And hire post horses. I will hence tonight.

MAN. I do beseech you, sir, have patience.
    Your looks are pale and wild and do import
    Some misadventure.[8]

ROMEO.   Tush, thou art deceived.
30   Leave me and do the thing I bid thee do.
    Hast thou no letters to me from the friar?

MAN. No, my good lord.

ROMEO.   No matter. Get thee gone.
    And hire those horses. I'll be with thee straight.   [*Exit* BALTHASAR.]
    Well, Juliet, I will lie with thee tonight.
35   Let's see for means. O mischief, thou art swift
    To enter in the thoughts of desperate men!
    I do remember an apothecary,[9]
    And hereabouts 'a dwells, which late I noted
    In tatt'red weeds, with overwhelming brows,
40   Culling of simples.[10] Meager were his looks,
    Sharp misery had worn him to the bones;
    And in his needy shop a tortoise hung,
    An alligator stuffed, and other skins
    Of ill-shaped fishes; and about his shelves
45   A beggarly account[11] of empty boxes,
    Green earthen pots, bladders, and musty seeds,
    <u>Remnants</u> of packthread, and old cakes of roses[12]
    Were thinly scatterèd, to make up a show.
    Noting this <u>penury</u>, to myself I said,
50   "And if a man did need a poison now
    Whose sale is present death in Mantua,
    Here lives a caitiff[13] wretch would sell it him."
    O, this same thought did but forerun my need,

Literary Analysis
Tragedy and Character's Motive What motivates Romeo's questions?

5. **Capels' monument** the Capulets' burial vault.

6. **presently took post** immediately set out on horseback.

7. **office** duty.

Literary Analysis
Tragedy Which words in the exchange between Romeo and the man suggest that fate plays a role in the tragedy?

8. **import / Some misadventure** suggest some misfortune.

9. **apothecary** one who prepares and sells drugs and medicines.

10. **In tatt'red . . . simples** in torn clothing, with overhanging eyebrows, sorting out herbs.

11. **beggarly account** small number.

12. **cakes of roses** pressed rose petals (used for perfume).

remnants (rem´ nənts) *n.* remaining persons or things

penury (pen´ yoo rē) *n.* extreme poverty

13. **caitiff** miserable.

And this same needy man must sell it me.
55 As I remember, this should be the house.
Being holiday, the beggar's shop is shut.
What, ho! Apothecary!

[*Enter* APOTHECARY.]

APOTHECARY.   Who calls so loud?

ROMEO. Come hither, man. I see that thou art poor.
Hold, there is forty ducats.[14] Let me have
60 A dram of poison, such soon-speeding gear[15]
As will disperse itself through all the veins
That the life-weary taker may fall dead,
And that the trunk[16] may be discharged of breath
As violently as hasty powder fired
65 Doth hurry from the fatal cannon's womb.

APOTHECARY. Such mortal drugs I have; but Mantua's law
Is death to any he that utters[17] them.

ROMEO. Art thou so bare and full of wretchedness
And fearest to die? Famine is in thy cheeks,
70 Need and oppression starveth in thy eyes,
Contempt and beggary hangs upon thy back:
The world is not thy friend, nor the world's law;
The world affords no law to make thee rich;
Then be not poor, but break it and take this.

75 APOTHECARY. My poverty but not my will consents.

ROMEO. I pay thy poverty and not thy will.

APOTHECARY. Put this in any liquid thing you will
And drink it off, and if you had the strength
Of twenty men, it would dispatch you straight.

80 ROMEO. There is thy gold—worse poison to men's souls,
Doing more murder in this loathsome world,
Than these poor compounds[18] that thou mayst not sell.
I sell thee poison; thou hast sold me none.
Farewell. Buy food and get thyself in flesh.
85 Come, cordial[19] and not poison, go with me
To Juliet's grave; for there must I use thee.   [*Exit all.*]

Scene ii. FRIAR LAWRENCE'S *cell.*

[*Enter* FRIAR JOHN *to* FRIAR LAWRENCE.]

JOHN. Holy Franciscan friar, brother, ho!

[*Enter* FRIAR LAWRENCE.]

LAWRENCE. This same should be the voice of Friar John.

Reading Strategy
Identifying Causes and Effects What causes Romeo to buy poison from the apothecary?

14. ducats (duk´ əts) gold coins.

15. soon-speeding gear fast-working stuff.

16. trunk body.

17. utters sells.

Literary Analysis
Tragedy and Character's Motive What motivates the apothecary to sell Romeo poison?

18. compounds mixtures.

19. cordial health-giving drink.

✔**Reading Check**
What does Romeo learn from Balthasar?

PRINCE. Come, Montague; for thou art early up
To see thy son and heir more early down.

210 **MONTAGUE.** Alas, my liege,[46] my wife is dead tonight!
Grief of my son's exile hath stopped her breath.
What further woe conspires against mine age?

PRINCE. Look, and thou shalt see.

MONTAGUE. O thou untaught! What manners is in this,
215 To press before thy father to a grave?

PRINCE. Seal up the mouth of outrage[47] for a while,
Till we can clear these <u>ambiguities</u>
And know their spring, their head, their true descent;
And then will I be general of your woes[48]
220 And lead you even to death. Meantime forbear,
And let mischance be slave to patience.[49]
Bring forth the parties of suspicion.

FRIAR. I am the greatest, able to do least,
Yet most suspected, as the time and place
225 Doth make against me, of this direful[50] murder;
And here I stand, both to impeach and purge[51]
Myself condemnèd and myself excused.

PRINCE. Then say at once what thou dost know in this.

FRIAR. I will be brief, for my short date of breath[52]
230 Is not so long as is a tedious tale.
Romeo, there dead, was husband to that Juliet;
And she, there dead, that's Romeo's faithful wife.
I married them; and their stol'n marriage day
Was Tybalt's doomsday, whose untimely death
235 Banished the new-made bridegroom from this city;
For whom, and not for Tybalt, Juliet pined.
You, to remove that siege of grief from her,
Betrothed and would have married her perforce
To County Paris. Then comes she to me
240 And with wild looks bid me devise some mean
To rid her from this second marriage,
Or in my cell there would she kill herself.
Then gave I her (so tutored by my art)
A sleeping potion; which so took effect
245 As I intended, for it wrought on her
The form of death. Meantime I writ to Romeo
That he should hither come as[53] this dire night
To help to take her from her borrowed grave,
Being the time the potion's force should cease,
250 But he which bore my letter, Friar John,
Was stayed by accident, and yesternight
Returned my letter back. Then all alone

46. liege (lēj) Lord.

Reading Strategy
Identifying Causes and Effects How did Romeo's exile affect his mother?

47. mouth of outrage violent cries.

ambiguities (am´ bə gyoo´ ə tēz) *n.* statements or events whose meanings are unclear

48. general . . . woes leader in your sorrow.

49. let . . . patience be patient in the face of misfortune.

50. direful terrible.
51. impeach and purge accuse and declare blameless.

52. date of breath term of life.

Literary Analysis
Tragedy What examples of fate or character flaws contribute to the tragedy the Friar recounts?

53. as on.

At the prefixèd hour of her waking
Came I to take her from her kindred's vault;
255 Meaning to keep her closely[54] at my cell
Till I conveniently could send to Romeo.
But when I came, some minute ere the time
Of her awakening, here untimely lay
The noble Paris and true Romeo dead.
260 She wakes; and I entreated her come forth
And bear this work of heaven with patience;
But then a noise did scare me from the tomb,
And she, too desperate, would not go with me,
But, as it seems, did violence on herself.
265 All this I know, and to the marriage
Her nurse is privy;[55] and if aught in this
Miscarried by my fault, let my old life
Be sacrificed some hour before his time
Unto the rigor[56] of severest law.

270 **PRINCE.** We still have known thee for a holy man.
Where's Romeo's man? What can he say to this?

BALTHASAR. I brought my master news of Juliet's death;
And then in post he came from Mantua
To this same place, to this same monument.
275 This letter he early bid me give his father,
And threat'ned me with death, going in the vault,
If I departed not and left him there.

PRINCE. Give me the letter. I will look on it.
Where is the County's page that raised the watch?
280 Sirrah, what made your master[57] in this place?

BOY. He came with flowers to strew his lady's grave;
And bid me stand aloof, and so I did.
Anon comes one with light to ope the tomb;
And by and by my master drew on him;
285 And then I ran away to call the watch.

PRINCE. This letter doth make good the friar's words,
Their course of love, the tidings of her death;
And here he writes that he did buy a poison
Of a poor pothecary and therewithal
290 Came to this vault to die and lie with Juliet.
Where be these enemies? Capulet, Montague,
See what a <u>scourge</u> is laid upon your hate,
That heaven finds means to kill your joys with love.
And I, for winking at[58] your discords too,
295 Have lost a brace[59] of kinsmen. All are punished.

CAPULET. O brother Montague, give me thy hand.
This is my daughter's jointure,[60] for no more

54. **closely** hidden; secretly.

55. **privy** secretly informed about.

56. **rigor** strictness.

Reading Strategy
Identifying Causes and Effects What could the Friar have done differently that might have prevented the tragedy from happening?

57. **made your master** was your master doing.

Literary Analysis
Tragedy Explain the tragedy of Paris' circumstances.

58. **winking at** closing my eyes to.

59. **brace** pair (Mercutio and Paris).

60. **jointure** wedding gift; marriage settlement.

scourge (skʉrj) *n.* whip or other instrument for inflicting punishment

✔**Reading Check**

How do the details of the letter compare with the Friar's story?

Can I demand.

MONTAGUE. But I can give thee more;
For I will raise her statue in pure gold,
300   That whiles Verona by that name is known,
There shall no figure at such rate[61] be set
As that of true and faithful Juliet.

CAPULET. As rich shall Romeo's by his lady's lie—
Poor sacrifices of our enmity![62]

305 **PRINCE.** A glooming[63] peace this morning with it brings.
The sun for sorrow will not show his head.
Go hence, to have more talk of these sad things;
Some shall be pardoned, and some punishèd;
For never was a story of more woe
310   Than this of Juliet and her Romeo.   [*Exit all.*]

61. **rate** value.

62. **enmity** hostility.

63. **glooming** cloudy; gloomy.

Review and Assess

Thinking About Act V

1. **Respond:** Were you in any way surprised by the way in which this play ends? Why or why not?

2. **(a) Recall:** In Act V, Scene i, what news causes Romeo to exclaim, "Then I defy you, stars"? **(b) Connect:** How are Romeo's words consistent with what you know of his character?

3. **(a) Recall:** Identify at least three events that cause the Friar's scheme to fail. **(b) Analyze:** Why is it not surprising that the scheme fails?

4. **(a) Recall:** How do Romeo and Juliet die? **(b) Make a Judgment:** Which is most to blame for the lovers' deaths— chance, the lovers themselves, or their families? Explain.

5. **(a) Speculate:** How do you think events would have turned out if the apothecary had refused to sell poison to Romeo? **(b) Hypothesize:** What other unique actions in the chain of events, if avoided, could have changed the play's outcome?

6. **(a) Recall:** How does the relationship of the feuding families change at the end of the play? **(b) Draw Conclusions:** Were Romeo and Juliet's deaths necessary for the feud to end? Explain. **(c) Assess:** Do you think tragedies always lead to peace?

7. **Evaluate:** In what ways does Shakespeare's play provide a valuable lesson about the destructive effects of hatred?

Review and Assess

Literary Analysis

Tragedy

1. Use a chart like the one shown to list the elements that contribute to the **tragedy.**

Romeo's and Juliet's Personalities	Fate or Chance	Other Causes

2. What theme or message does Shakespeare attempt to convey through the tragic events in the play? Explain.
3. What positive message about the human spirit does Shakespeare convey through the play? Explain.

Connecting Literary Elements

4. (a) What is the Friar's **motive** for helping Romeo and Juliet? (b) Why does his plan ultimately fail?
5. What is the Nurse's motive for defying the wishes of the Capulets?
6. What are the fathers' motives for building monuments to their children at the end of the play?
7. Who is most guilty for the tragedy? Explain your choice.

Reading Strategy

Identifying Causes and Effects

8. Use a chart like this one to summarize the chain of **causes and effects** outlined by the Friar in his monologue in Act V, Scene iii.

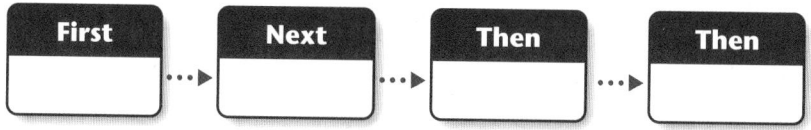

9. What chain of events leads to the death of Paris?

Extend Understanding

10. **World Events Connection:** How might the lesson that the play teaches be applied to a specific situation in today's world?

Quick Review

A **tragedy** is a drama in which a central character of noble rank meets with disaster or overwhelming misfortune.

A **character's motive** is the reason an individual thinks and acts in a certain way.

A **cause** is an action, an event, or a situation that produces a result.

An **effect** is the result produced by a cause.

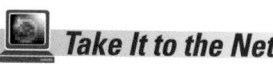 **Take It to the Net**
www.phschool.com
Take the interactive self-test online to check your understanding of Act V.

Integrate Language Skills

Vocabulary Development Lesson

Word Analysis: Latin Prefix *ambi-*

The Latin prefix *ambi-* means "both." It appears in *ambiguities*, which means "statements or events having two or more possible meanings." In your notebook, complete each sentence below with one of the following words.

   a. ambidextrous   **b.** ambilateral

1. The __?__ man used both hands with equal skill.
2. The __?__ pain hurt both sides of my body.

Spelling Strategy

If a noun ends in *y* preceded by a consonant, change the *y* to *i* and add *-es* to form the plural. For example, *ambiguities* is the plural of *ambiguity*. Write the plural of each of these nouns.

   1. tragedy   **2.** fury   **3.** enmity

Concept Development: Synonyms

In your notebook, write the word that is the best synonym for the first word. To help you, review the vocabulary list on page 860.

1. remnants: (a) cloths, (b) remains, (c) factors
2. penury: (a) poverty, (b) currency, (c) disease
3. haughty: (a) timid, (b) friendly, (c) arrogant
4. sepulcher: (a) monument, (b) tomb, (c) cemetery
5. ambiguities: (a) vows, (b) details, (c) uncertainties
6. scourge: (a) sorrow, (b) punishment, (c) hatred

Grammar Lesson

Agreement With Indefinite Pronouns

Indefinite pronouns refer to people, places, or things, often without specifying which ones. Indefinite pronouns may be singular (such as *each*, *neither*, or *one*) or plural (such as *both* or *many*).

When you write a sentence with a personal pronoun that has an indefinite pronoun as its antecedent, you must make sure the pronouns agree in number. In the examples below, the indefinite pronoun is underlined and the personal pronoun is in italics.

Singular:	<u>One</u> of the friars stayed in *his* quarters.
Plural:	<u>Both</u> of the friars were quarantined in *their* house.

Practice Write each sentence, circling the indefinite pronoun and choosing the personal pronoun that completes the sentence correctly.

1. Both of the lovers lost (his, their) lives.
2. Each of the fathers mourned (his, their) child.
3. Many were shocked by (its, their) discovery.
4. One of the lovers poisoned (his, their) lips.
5. Neither of the families was happy with (its, their) loss.

Writing Application Write two sentences about Act V, using a singular indefinite pronoun and personal pronoun in one and a plural indefinite pronoun and personal pronoun in the other.

WG Prentice Hall Writing and Grammar Connection: Chapter 25, Section 2

Writing Lesson

Persuasive Letter

A letter from Friar Lawrence to both families, urging them to end their feud, might have saved Romeo and Juliet's lives. As the Friar, develop a persuasive letter to send to both families right after you have married their children.

Prewriting   Your letter should appeal both to reason and to emotion. Make a list of factual evidence and emotional pleas that might convince the families to end their feud.

Drafting   Begin your draft by announcing the marriage ceremony you have just performed. Then, arrange your persuasive appeals in a logical order.

Revising   Read your draft as if you were Montague or Capulet. Determine whether the letter appeals equally to both your mind and heart. If not, revise it so that the appeals are both strong and balanced.

Model: Revising to Balance Persuasive Appeals

They each live behind gated walls and have to sneak into each other's homes to be together.

The hatred between your families is forcing your children to be apart and is threatening their happiness. They are even afraid that something bad might happen if they attempt to tell their families of their marriage. Do you want your children to be miserable?

Adding factual information makes the letter more persuasive by balancing appeals to reason and emotion.

Prentice Hall Writing and Grammar Connection: Chapter 7, Section 4

Extension Activities

Listening and Speaking Hold a **mock trial** to investigate the causes of the tragedy. Follow these steps:

- Assign roles—the main characters, the lawyer, the judge, and the jury.
- Take depositions in which each character tells the story from his or her perspective.

When the court is in session, lawyers should question and cross-examine witnesses before the jury reaches a verdict. **[Group Activity]**

Research and Technology Imagine that you and a group of classmates have been hired to create a **set design** for a modern-day version of *Romeo and Juliet*. Decide on an appropriate setting for the adaptation, such as in a large modern city. Then, use computer software or posterboard to create diagrams for your set design.

 Take It to the Net   www.phschool.com

Go online for an additional research activity using the Internet.

After reading *Romeo and Juliet*, you may be inspired to view a production of the play. You have plenty of options. Shakespeare's plays, though 400 years old, are still performed on stages throughout the world. In addition, his works have been adapted successfully as movies, television dramas, musicals, operas, and ballets.

Adaptations of *Romeo and Juliet*

If you care to watch a video of *Romeo and Juliet*, one choice is the 1968 film directed by Franco Zeffirelli. Another is the 1996 movie starring Leonardo DiCaprio. Both films remain faithful to Shakespeare's language and plot. In the 1996 version, however, the actors wear modern clothing and even drive around in cars!

To see *Romeo and Juliet* as a ballet, you could watch the 1966 film starring Rudolph Nureyev and Margot Fonteyn. This adaptation tells the story entirely through dance and contains no words.

In 1957, *Romeo and Juliet* served as the basis for a successful Broadway musical, *West Side Story*. The show's creators borrowed the basic Shakespearean plot but modernized the characters and events. The feuding Montagues and Capulets were replaced by rival New York City street gangs, the Jets and Sharks. The famous balcony scene with Juliet and Romeo became a fire-escape scene with Maria and Tony. The musical was made into a popular movie in 1961.

In 1998, the Academy Award for Best Movie went to *Shakespeare in Love*. Its story surmises the circumstances under which Shakespeare wrote *Romeo and Juliet*. You will find parallels between the characters in the story and the characters in Shakespeare's play, and knowledge of the play will enhance your understanding of the film starring Gwyneth Paltrow.

More Shakespeare at the Movies

Most of Shakespeare's plays have been adapted as movies. The first Shakespearean movie ever made was *King John*, in 1899. It was directed by Sir Herbert Beerbohm Tree, who also played the title role.

Today, popular film adaptations of Shakespeare's plays include the following:

- *Love's Labour's Lost* (2000), with Nathan Lane and Alicia Silverstone
- *Othello* (1995), with Lawrence Fishburne and Kenneth Branagh
- *Hamlet* (1990), with Mel Gibson and Glenn Close
- *Julius Caesar* (1970), with Jason Robards, Charlton Heston, and Diana Rigg; there is also a 1953 version, with Marlon Brando and John Gielgud
- *10 Things I Hate About You* (1999), a modern-day teenage comedy based on *The Taming of the Shrew*

Shakespeare on Stage

Stage directors all over the world have experimented with unusual techniques and interpretations of Shakespeare's works. For example, in 1970, Peter Brook staged *A Midsummer Night's Dream* using a large white box for the set, while two of the main characters swung on trapezes above the other actors.

Titus Andronicus is one of Shakespeare's most violent plays. In 1955, when Peter Brook staged it quite vividly at Stratford, England, with Laurence Olivier and Vivien Leigh, audience members had to be carried away in ambulances every night!

Many playwrights have created original plays based on Shakespeare's works. One noted example is Tom Stoppard's comedy *Rosencrantz and Guildenstern Are Dead*, which highlights two minor characters from *Hamlet*.

Shakespeare in Musicals

West Side Story is not the only popular Broadway musical based on a Shakespearean play. Another famous example is Cole Porter's *Kiss Me, Kate*, which presents backstage bickering among actors during their out-of-town tryout of *The Taming of the Shrew*. As the musical unfolds, the lives of the actors parallel the lives of the Shakespearean characters they portray.

Television Productions

All of Shakespeare's plays have been adapted as television dramas. Notable productions include the following:

- *Othello* (BBC, 1983), with Anthony Hopkins
- *Love's Labour's Lost* (BBC, 1984), set in the 1700s

Connecting Literature and Media

1. Why do you think Shakespeare's plays have such popular appeal as modern movies and musicals?
2. Some people object to any modernization of Shakespeare's plays, claiming that such productions cheapen the original. What is your opinion?

READING INFORMATIONAL MATERIALS

Atlas Entries

About Atlas Entries

An atlas is a book of maps showing physical features of the world, such as cities, mountains, rivers, and roads. Some atlases include facts and statistics about the places depicted. Many modern atlases, like the Dorling Kindersley atlas (whose pages are shown here), provide brief articles on topics such as these:

- Population
- Climate
- Government
- Transportation
- Tourism

The maps in an atlas usually are accompanied by a *legend*, a key that explains the symbols and colors used in the map. For example, symbols might represent features such as national or state capitals. Color codes might be used to indicate land height or density of population. The legend also indicates to what mileage the map is scaled.

Reading Strategy

Skimming and Scanning

Atlases and other reference materials provide a broad range of information. To find what you need, adjust your reading rate by skimming or scanning.

- By **skimming,** you can get an idea of the organization and scope of a work before reading it. To skim, read quickly, taking in words in groups. Stop for headings and other text that is set off, such as bold text.

- By **scanning,** you can locate specific information fast. Move your eyes quickly over the page. Look for words related to the information you are seeking. Stop and read the paragraphs that contain the words you are seeking.

Skim the atlas entry on the following pages. Use a graphic organizer like the one at right to record each kind of information you can find on the page.

Subjects Covered	How I Know
Climate of Italy	Listed as a heading on the page
Transportation in Italy	Listed as a heading on the page, shown with icons of a ship and a plane

ITALY

Adapted from *Dorling Kindersley World Reference Atlas*

ITALY
Total Land Area : 294 060 sq. km
(301 270 sq. miles)

POPULATION

over 1 000 000	▢
over 500 000	◉
over 100 000	◎
over 50 000	○
over 10 000	●

LAND HEIGHT

3000m/9843ft
2000m/6562ft
1000m/3281ft
500m/1640ft
200m/656ft
Sea Level

The legend explains the meaning of the symbols found on the map.

The map shows the cities and towns of Italy.

N

0 — 100 km
0 — 100 miles

ITALY

Official Name: *Italian Republic*
Capital: *Rome*
Population: *57.2 million*
Currency: *Italian lira*
Official Language: *Italian*

Lying in southern Europe, Italy comprises the famous boot-shaped peninsula stretching 500 miles into the Mediterranean and a number of islands—Sicily and Sardinia being the largest. The Alps form a natural boundary to the north, while the Apennine Mountains run the length of the peninsula. The south is an area of seismic activity, epitomized by the volcanoes of Mounts Etna and Vesuvius. United under ancient Roman rule, Italy subsequently developed into a series of competing kingdoms and states, not fully reunited until 1870. Italian politics was dominated by the Christian Democrats (CD) from 1945 to 1992 under a system of political patronage and a succession of short-lived governments. Investigations into corruption from 1992 on led to the demise of this system in the elections of 1994.

CLIMATE

Southern Italy has a Mediterranean climate; the north is more temperate. Summers are hot and dry, especially in the south. Temperatures range from 75°F to over 81°F in Sardinia and Sicily. Southern winters are mild; northern ones are cooler and wetter. The mountains usually experience heavy snow. The Adriatic coast suffers from cold winds such as the bora.

TRANSPORTATION

 Leonardo da Vinci (Fiumicino), Rome 15.55m passengers
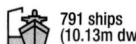 791 ships (10.13m dwt)

Many of Italy's key routes are congested. The trans-Apennine *autostrada* (expressway) from Bologna to Florence is being doubled in size. A high-speed train program (*treno ad alta velocità—TAV*) is planned to link Turin, Milan, Venice, Bologna, Florence and Naples to Rome. Most of Italy's exports travel by road, via Switzerland and Austria. Only 16% goes by sea.

TOURISM

 27.5m visitors
 Up 4% in 1994

Italy has been a tourist destination since the 16th century and probably invented the concept. Roman Popes consciously aimed to make their city the most beautiful in the world to attract travelers. In the 18th century, Italy was the focus of any Grand Tour. Today, its many unspoilt centers of Renaissance culture continue to make Italy one of the world's major tourism destinations. The industry accounts for 3% of Italy's GDP, and hotels and restaurants employ one million out of a working population of 21 million.

Most visitors travel to the northern half of the country, to cities such as Rome, Florence, Venice and Padova. Many are increasingly traveling to the northern lakes. Beach resorts such as Rimini attract a large, youthful crowd in summer. Italy is also growing in popularity as a skiing destination.

PEOPLE

 Italian, German, French, Rhaeto-Romanic, Sardinian
 505 people per sq. mile

Italy is a remarkably homogenous society. Most Italians are Roman Catholics, and Italy has far fewer ethnic minorities than its EU neighbors. Most are fairly recent immigrants from Ethiopia, the Philippines and Egypt. A sharp rise in illegal immigration in the 1980's and 1990's, from North and West Africa, Turkey and Albania, generated a right-wing backlash and tighter controls. It became a major election issue in 1993 and a factor in the rise of the federalist Northern League.

Check Your Comprehension

1. Which four seas border Italy?
2. What is the approximate population of Napoli?
3. What percentage of Italy's exports travel by sea?

Applying the Reading Strategy

Skimming and Scanning

4. (a) By skimming and scanning, find and list the languages of Italy.
   (b) Where did you find the information?
5. Why is *Rome* printed in bold, capital letters on the map?
6. Which symbol indicates a city with more than 50,000 people?

Activity

Asking Questions About an Atlas Entry

An atlas entry presents a large amount of information. Some details are found in the map itself, and other details are found in the accompanying text.

Help your classmates assess how well they understand the atlas entry about Italy. Write several questions based on information located in the map and in the accompanying articles. Challenge your classmates to supply the answers, using the atlas entry.

Contrasting Informational Texts

Atlases and Guidebooks

1. The atlas entry you read is one place to find information about Italy. However, if you were touring Italy, you would probably use a guidebook instead of an atlas to learn about the country. Find a tourist guidebook for Italy or any other country. Skim and scan it to determine the kinds of information it offers. Completing a chart like the one shown, note key differences between the sources.

Contrasting Sources		
	Tourist Guidebook	Atlas Entry
Maps		
Articles		

2. Using the information in your chart, explain how the purpose of informational materials determines their content.

3. Read several sections in your tourist guidebook. Choose one section that you find particularly interesting and helpful. Offer a brief summary of the information to classmates.

Writing WORKSHOP

Response to Literature

When you write a **response to literature,** you explore *how, what,* and *why* a piece of writing communicates to you. In this workshop, you will write a response to a piece of literature that engages you as a reader.

Assignment Criteria. Your response to literature should have the following characteristics:

- An analysis of the work's content, its related ideas, or its effect on the reader
- A thesis statement that characterizes your response
- A focus on a single aspect or an overall view of the work
- Evidence from the literary work or other texts to support the opinions you present

To preview the criteria on which your response to literature may be assessed, see the Rubric on page 887.

Prewriting

Choose a topic. Think of novels, poems, and other works of literature that you consider memorable. Create a top-ten list by writing down the titles and authors of these works. Next to each, note any ideas you would like to share about the literature. Review your list and choose a topic.

Gather details. Return to the piece of literature you have selected to find examples, excerpts, and direct quotations that relate directly to your topic. You will use this evidence to help frame your main idea and supporting ideas.

Gathering Details

What I want to prove:
General Zaroff's civilized exterior conceals a ruthless, cunning, heartless murderer.

How I can prove it:
- Describe the wealth of his castle
- Include quote: "The weak were created to please the strong."

Clarify your purpose. Whether you are sharing your enthusiasm for a new writer, interpreting a well-known poem, or responding to a short story, include details that support your writing goal. Consider these tips:

- **To praise,** include concrete details about what you liked.
- **To analyze,** back up your ideas with evidence from the text.
- **To explain a personal response,** show how the work connects to your own experience or ideas.

Student Model

Before you begin drafting your response to literature, read this student model and review the characteristics of effective responses to literature.

Jeff Rutherford
Broken Arrow, OK

Characterization of General Zaroff

What lies at the heart of a refined man? In Richard Connell's short story "The Most Dangerous Game," the deranged, yet cunning and elegant, General Zaroff shares his taste for hunting with an unsuspecting visitor. Although he is civilized in his choice of lifestyle, Zaroff's beliefs reveal the murderous mind behind the illusion of a charming, charismatic man.

> The title indicates that the essay is limited to a single character.

> Jeff uses strong language to clearly state his thesis.

When we first encounter General Zaroff, our initial reaction is one of delight and admiration for his wealth and charm. Zaroff lives in a massive castle, feasts on the finest delicacies, and wears expensive clothes. His luxurious surroundings and lifestyle reflect a highly civilized, eloquent, and proper gentleman. As readers soon learn, however, there is more to Zaroff than food and elegance.

Beneath Zaroff's fine qualities, though, lies an overwhelming attitude of arrogance. This attitude comes from his firm belief that his way of thinking is superior to that of the average person. Zaroff also fancies himself a phenomenal hunter: "My hand was made for the trigger," he claims. It is this deadly mixture of arrogance, superior hunting skills, and belief that it is natural for the strong to prevail over the weak that makes him disregard the value of human life.

Zaroff's extreme beliefs lead him to conclude that only the intelligent mind of a human being can provide him with the dangerous game he desires. Rationalizing that "the weak were created to please the strong," he chooses to hunt humans instead of animals. Unfortunately, Rainsford steps into this situation. The major conflicts in "The Most Dangerous Game" demonstrate what happens during such an inhumane hunt.

> Direct quotations provide evidence for this characterization of Zaroff.

However, the general's arrogance and disregard for human life blind him to the fear and desperation of his prey. His attitude leads to his own demise at the hands of Rainsford, his prey. The characterization of Zaroff as a murderer hiding behind a mask of civility shows that beneath even the most beautiful rose can lie a sharp and deadly thorn.

> Jeff concludes his response with an analogy that neatly summarizes his analysis.

Drafting

Identify your thesis. Your draft should have a clear thesis statement that you will develop throughout the essay. Review your notes to draft a single statement that brings together the ideas and evidence you have accumulated. Use this sentence, your thesis statement, to direct your essay writing.

Organize your ideas. Use the organizational chart at right to help you present your ideas in a logical way as you draft your essay.

Elaborate to prove your interpretation. Include citations from the literary work to support the points you are making. Consider these specific suggestions:

- **Quotations** can illustrate a character's attitude, a writer's word choice, or an essay's argument.

- **Examples** of a character's actions or of a specific literary element can enhance your analysis of literature.

- **Paraphrases** can help you interpret a writer's theme, discuss the conflict, analyze the character, or restate key ideas from the literature.

Organize Your Ideas

Introduction
- Grab attention with opening
- Identify author and title
- Offer brief summary of the work
- Present thesis

Details
- Present supporting ideas
- Introduce each new idea in a new paragraph
- Use details to support each idea

Conclusion
- Restate thesis
- Make a final point or present a final question or insight

Revising

Revise to eliminate unnecessary information.
Read your draft to identify instances in which the information you provide may distract from your main idea.

1. Highlight sentences that do not support your thesis.
2. Consider revising details to make a tighter connection to your main idea.
3. Eliminate any paragraphs or details that do not clearly contribute to your analysis.

Model: Cutting Unnecessary Details

When we first encounter General Zaroff, our initial reaction is one of delight and admiration for his wealth and charm. Zaroff lives in a massive castle, feasts on the finest delicacies, and wears expensive clothes. He had previously been in the army, and his strong personality has a frightening quality.

Jeff eliminates this sentence because it does not support his main point effectively.

Revise to indicate precise evaluation. In order to clarify your position, the words you use to convey praise or criticism in your response must be precise. In the following example, note how the word *honest* is more precise than *factual*.

> **Vague:** Her *factual* portrayal of her family's experiences captured the audience's attention.

> **Precise:** Her *honest* portrayal of her family's experiences captured the audience's attention.

Compare the model and the nonmodel. Why is the model more effective than the nonmodel?

Nonmodel	Model
However, the general's harsh attitude blinds him to the fear and desperation of his prey.	However, the general's arrogance and disregard for human life blind him to the fear and desperation of his prey.

Publishing and Presenting

Share your writing with a wider audience by presenting your views to your classmates.

Deliver an oral presentation. Read your response to literature aloud. You may want to have a copy of the literary work to which you are responding on hand in the event that your classmates want to review it.

Publish a collection of reviews. Gather the essays of several of your classmates. Organize them in a binder and make your ideas available in the school library.

 Prentice Hall Writing and Grammar Connection: Chapter 13

Speaking Connection
To learn more about presenting an oral response to literature, see the **Listening and Speaking Workshop**, p. 888.

Rubric for Self-Assessment

Evaluate your response to literature using the following criteria and rating scale:

Criteria	Rating Scale Not very				Very
How well does the the response analyze the work's content, its related ideas, or its effect on the reader?	1	2	3	4	5
How well does the thesis statement communicate the nature of the response?	1	2	3	4	5
Is the response well focused?	1	2	3	4	5
How effectively does the work use evidence to support the writer's opinion?	1	2	3	4	5

Listening and Speaking WORKSHOP

Presenting an Oral Response to Literature

Certain works of literature provoke a strong emotional response. Capturing those feelings in words can be a challenging task. When you present an **oral response to literature,** you articulate your response and support it with evidence from the text.

Define Your Response

Before you present a response to others, you must first determine how you feel about a selection. Review the Writing Workshop on pages 884–887. Use these steps to help you focus and define your feelings:

Summarize the main ideas. Finding the main idea gives you a basic skeleton around which to organize your response. In nonfiction, the main idea is generally found in the introduction or conclusion. For a fictional work, limit yourself to the most important ideas. Then, gather details from the work that are especially important or memorable to you.

Characterize your response. Decide whether you agree or disagree with the main ideas you have selected and determine why. Turn these reactions into a single thesis statement that captures the way you feel, and jot down at least three reasons for your reaction. These reasons will be your supporting arguments.

Find evidence to support your response. Use examples from the literature as evidence to support your arguments. Direct quotations or paraphrases give greater depth and power to the arguments you develop in your oral response.

Offer Your Response

Organize your thoughts. If possible, keep your organization clear and simple, and include these elements:

- A brief introduction outlining your thesis
- A body presenting supporting arguments along with key evidence
- A summary of your main argument

Use evocative language. To make your presentation more memorable, choose words and phrases that will have powerful associations for your audience and generate a reaction.

(Activity:) Book Club Forming a book club can enhance your enjoyment of reading by exchanging views with others. Discuss a work of literature in a small group. Take turns presenting and evaluating all of the group's presentations, using the chart shown. Discuss interesting variations in interpretation or response.

**Feedback Form for
Oral Response to Literature**

Rating System
+ = Excellent   ✔ = Average   – = Weak

Content
_____ Clarity of thesis
_____ Support of ideas with evidence
_____ Validity of interpretation

Delivery
_____ Presentation clearly organized and presented
_____ Use of appropriate language to describe response

Answer the following questions:

Do you agree with the interpretation of the work?

What would have made the presentation more effective?

Assessment WORKSHOP

Responses and Interpretations

The reading sections of some tests require you to read a passage and write short, essay-type answers that respond to and interpret the written text. Use the following strategies to help you defend your responses and interpretations:

- To determine your reaction, think about how the text makes you feel and how it might influence your opinions.
- When you interpret a text, give your own ideas about what the text means.
- Base your response and interpretation on information contained in the text, supporting your opinions with references.

Test-Taking Strategies

- To defend your ideas about a fictional work, use the language, plot details, and character descriptions as support.
- Search for facts, quotations, and statistics to support your interpretation of nonfiction.

Sample Test Item

Directions: Read the passage, and then answer the question that follows.

Geographers use globes and maps to represent Earth. A globe is more accurate than a map. Shaped like Earth, a globe gives a true picture of the size and shape of landmasses and of distance across oceans. Globes are awkward to carry around, however, so most people use maps instead. Even so, maps have a major drawback. Because Earth's surface is curved and maps are flat, all maps distort Earth's image in some way.

1. For what reason would you use a map? For what reason would you use a globe? Support your answers.

Answers and Explanations

Possible Answers:

You might use a map to find out how to drive to a new place. You might use a globe to see how far the United States is from China.

A successful answer should incorporate the different attributes of globes and maps.

Practice

Directions: Read the passage, and then answer the questions that follow.

Hoover Dam was built in the 1930s during the Great Depression to control the Colorado River and irrigate the farmlands of the southwestern United States. It has also provided electric power and formed a giant reservoir, Lake Mead, for drinking water, swimming, boating, and fishing. However, Hoover Dam has also changed the river's ecology, hurting some native fish and other species and flooding some parts of the Grand Canyon.

1. In what ways have technology and human intervention served the needs of the United States?

2. Do you think the advantages outweighed the disadvantages in the construction of Hoover Dam? Support your answer with evidence from the text.

Garden of Delights, watercolor, 11" x17", Sandy Novak, Omni-Photo Communications, Inc.

Exploring the Genre

The poet T. S. Eliot said that poetry can be enjoyed before it is understood. A powerful poem uses language to draw you in, invite you to reread, and inspire you to find a new layer of meaning each time. A poet carefully chooses words to capture a unique and personal vision. Poetry combines meaning with sound to add music and rhythm to ideas. Each reader brings a different set of associations to a poem based on the people, places, and experiences that he or she has known.

These terms will help you discuss the variety of poems in this unit:

- **Lyric poetry** expresses vivid thoughts and feelings.

- **Narrative poetry** tells a story.

- **Dramatic poetry** uses techniques of drama, such as speaker and conflict, to tell a story.

- **Musical devices** such as alliteration, onomatopoeia, assonance, consonance, meter, repetition, and rhyme give poems a melodious quality.

- **Figurative language** uses simile, lyrical metaphor, and personification in creative, unexpected comparisons and descriptions.

▲ **Critical Viewing** Which details of this picture suggest poetry to you? **[Connect]**

Read Literature?

There are many different reasons to read a poem. You might read poetry because you like the way certain poets put words together or because you find their perspectives unique and intriguing. Preview three purposes you might set before reading the poems in this unit.

1

Read for the Love of Literature

A poem can provide a window into the writing process. Find out how choosing the right words for a poem is a little like eating overripe blackberries in Galway Kinnell's **"Blackberry Eating,"** page 914.

Good literature makes connections and illustrates universal themes. If you ever have been forced to stay inside and clean while others played, you can appreciate the way Julia Alvarez transforms household drudgery into personal discovery in **"Woman's Work,"** page 920.

2

Read for Information

With the rapid advances in science and technology in the last century, you might wonder how doctors, scientists, and librarians keep up with recent developments in their fields. Explore the world of professional journals in this unit's **Reading Informational Materials,** page 964.

3

Read to Appreciate an Author's Style

The eagle, subject of Alfred, Lord Tennyson's poem, has long been one of the most recognizable symbols of grace, power, and authority. See how Tennyson adds majesty to the list when you read **"The Eagle,"** page 906.

When the playwright Lorraine Hansberry read one of Langston Hughes's poems, she was so moved by his insights that she used a line from one of his works to name her play *A Raisin in the Sun.* Read Hughes's powerful poem **"Dream Deferred,"** page 904.

 Take It to the Net

Visit the Web site for online instruction and activities related to each selection in this unit.
www.phschool.com

How to Read Literature

Use Strategies for Reading Poetry

If you are used to reading prose, getting accustomed to poetry may take a slight adjustment. The payoff comes when you suddenly gain insight into a poet's ideas. Here are some strategies to help make the shift from prose to poetry:

1. Use your senses.

One way to appreciate a poem more fully is to use all of your senses to place yourself in the situation the poet describes.

- Determine the poem's setting before you try to imagine individual sensations.

- Look for descriptive words that convey a specific physical sensation.

- Be aware of words that appeal to sight, sound, taste, touch, and smell.

2. Paraphrase.

Since the language of a poem can be abstract, it is helpful to rephrase lines to make sure that you understand their meaning.

- Choose words you commonly use when rephrasing what the author is saying.

- Use simple sentences and change the word order if it helps you understand the meaning better.

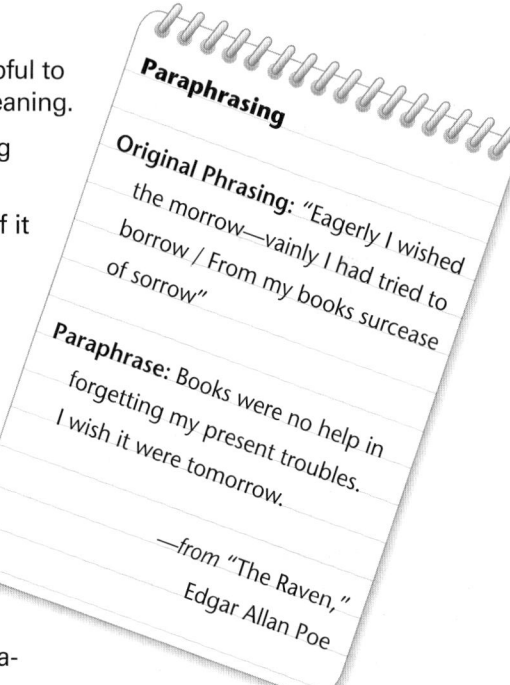

Paraphrasing

Original Phrasing: "Eagerly I wished the morrow—vainly I had tried to borrow / From my books surcease of sorrow"

Paraphrase: Books were no help in forgetting my present troubles. I wish it were tomorrow.

—from "The Raven," Edgar Allan Poe

3. Draw inferences about the speaker.

When you read a poem, you hear the voice of the poem's speaker, or the imaginary voice assumed by the poet. As you read, think about how you might describe the person voicing those particular lines of poetry. Use this knowledge to achieve a deeper understanding of the poem's meaning.

4. Read in sentences.

- Use punctuation, not the ends of lines, as the indication of where to pause when reading a poem.

- Periods, commas, colons, semicolons, and dashes signal where to pause or to stop reading.

As you read the selections in this unit, review the reading strategies and look at the notes in the side columns. Use the suggestions to apply the strategies and interact with the text.

Prepare to Read

I Wandered Lonely as a Cloud

 Take It to the Net

Visit www.phschool.com for interactive activities and instruction related to "I Wandered Lonely as a Cloud," including
- background
- graphic organizers
- literary elements
- reading strategies

Preview

Connecting to the Literature

You probably have moments in your life that you replay in your memory—images to which photographs or videos cannot do justice because they cannot capture your feelings. In this poem, William Wordsworth captures both the images and the feelings connected to a special moment in his life.

Background

Dorothy Wordsworth was William's friend as well as his sister. She kept a journal of their activities, including what they saw as they took walks through England's Lake District. On April 15, 1802, she recorded her impressions after they suddenly saw a field crowded with daffodils. Wordsworth used his sister's comments as inspiration for this poem.

Literary Analysis

Rhyme Scheme

A **rhyme scheme** is a regular pattern of rhyming words that appear at the ends of lines in a poem. You indicate the pattern of a poem's rhymes by using letters of the alphabet, assigning a new letter to each rhyme. The first stanza of "I Wandered Lonely as a Cloud" follows a rhyme scheme of *ababcc*. Look at the first three lines of the stanza:

> I wandered lonely as a cloud (a)
> That floats on high o'er vales and hills, (b)
> When all at once I saw a crowd, (a)

Since *cloud* and *crowd* are rhyming words, lines 1 and 3 are assigned the letter *a. Hills* does not rhyme with *cloud*, so line 2 is assigned the letter *b*. As you read the other stanzas, determine whether Wordsworth keeps to his rhyme scheme or if he breaks the pattern he has established.

Connecting Literary Elements

A **simile** is a figure of speech in which *like* or *as* is used to make a comparison between ideas that are basically dissimilar. The title of Wordsworth's poem contains a simile in which the speaker compares himself to a cloud. As with the rhyme scheme in a poem, similes require writers to carefully consider their use of language—assessing both the words that they choose and the impressions that those words make.

Reading Strategy

Using Your Senses

Once you have a basic idea of what is happening in a poem, **using your senses** can give you a greater appreciation of the ideas the poem conveys.

- Pay attention to images that appeal to your senses of sight, smell, sound, taste, and touch.
- Consider the impression each image conveys.

As you read, use a chart like the one shown to note the images that appeal to your senses, and then record how they make you feel.

Vocabulary Development

host (hōst) *n.* great number (p. 897)

glee (glē) *n.* joy (p. 898)

pensive (pen´ siv) *adj.* thinking deeply (p. 898)

bliss (blis) *n.* great joy or happiness (p. 898)

CALIFORNIA STANDARDS

Instruction with this selection addresses these standards:

R 1.1*, 1.2*, 3.7*, 3.8*
W 1.2*, 1.3*
WOLC 1.1*
LS 1.7

* Standards tested on HS Exit Exam. For complete standards, see p. CA 4.

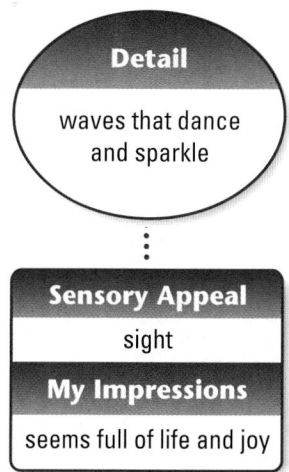

Detail

waves that dance and sparkle

⋮

Sensory Appeal

sight

My Impressions

seems full of life and joy

I Wandered Lonely

as a Cloud

William Wordsworth

I wandered lonely as a cloud
That floats on high o'er vales[1] and hills,
When all at once I saw a crowd,
A <u>host</u>, of golden daffodils;
5   Beside the lake, beneath the trees,
Fluttering and dancing in the breeze.

Continuous as the stars that shine
And twinkle on the milky way,
They stretched in never-ending line
10 Along the margin of a bay:
Ten thousand saw I at a glance,
Tossing their heads in sprightly dance.

host (hōst) *n.* great number

✔ **Reading Check**

What was most remarkable about the flowers that the speaker saw?

---

1. o'er vales over valleys.

The waves beside them danced; but they
Outdid the sparkling waves in <u>glee</u>;
15 A poet could not but be gay,
In such a jocund² company;
I gazed—and gazed—but little thought
What wealth the show to me had brought:

For oft, when on my couch I lie
20 In vacant or in <u>pensive</u> mood,
They flash upon that inward eye
Which is the <u>bliss</u> of solitude;
And then my heart with pleasure fills,
And dances with the daffodils.

---

2. jocund (jäk´ ənd) *adj.* cheerful.

glee (glē) *n.* joy

pensive (pen´ siv) *adj.*
thinking deeply

bliss (blis) *n.* great joy or
happiness

William Wordsworth

(1770–1850)

Wordsworth was born in England's rural Lake District. As a young man, he spent time in France and became a supporter of the French Revolution's ideals of freedom, equality, and brotherhood. Although Wordsworth abandoned his desire for political change as the French Revolution turned bloody, he was able to bring about revolutionary changes in British literature.

In 1798, Wordsworth and fellow poet Samuel Taylor Coleridge published a book of poetry entitled *Lyrical Ballads*. Unlike the formal, highly intellectual poems that were popular at the time, the poems in the book used simple language to exalt the remarkable moments of everyday life.

Review and Assess
Thinking About the Selection

1. **Respond:** Why do you think this experience created such a strong impression in Wordsworth's memory?

2. **(a) Recall:** Where are the daffodils, and what are they doing? **(b) Analyze:** To what are the daffodils compared in stanza 2? **(c) Interpret:** What does the comparison suggest about the daffodils?

3. **(a) Recall:** In stanza 3, which words does the speaker use to describe the daffodils? **(b) Interpret:** How does the sight of the daffodils affect the speaker?

4. **(a) Recall:** What does the speaker say happens when he is alone in a "pensive mood"? **(b) Connect:** What "wealth" do memories of the scene give him?

5. **Assess:** How are natural scenes like the one presented in this poem valuable?

6. **Apply:** Have you ever made an observation that caused you to feel the type of connection to nature that the speaker feels? Explain.

Review and Assess

Literary Analysis

Rhyme Scheme

1. Complete the following chart to show the **rhyme scheme** of "I Wandered Lonely as a Cloud."

Stanza #		Rhyme Scheme
	....▶	

2. What happens in the rhyme scheme to set off the final two lines of each stanza?

3. How does setting off the final two lines of each stanza reinforce the meaning?

Connecting Literary Elements

4. (a) In the first stanza, what words does the speaker use to describe the clouds? (b) When the speaker compares himself to a cloud, what is he saying about himself?

5. (a) What mood or "feeling" is set by the title? (b) Is the **simile** found in the title of the poem an effective one? Explain.

6. Find and analyze another simile in the poem. Explain which two objects are being compared and what the comparison suggests.

Reading Strategy

Using Your Senses

7. (a) Which details help express the great numbers of daffodils? (b) Which of these details appeal to you most? Explain.

8. Using a chart like the one shown, explain which **senses** you engaged in reading this poem.

Detail	Sight	Sound	Smell	Touch	Taste

Extend Understanding

9. **Art Connection:** Wordsworth's poem paints a vivid portrait of the daffodils. (a) Compare and contrast his poem with a photograph or painting of the same type of scene. (b) What could not be conveyed in a photograph or painting?

Quick Review

A **rhyme scheme** is a regular pattern of rhyming words that appear at the ends of lines in a poem.

A **simile** is a figure of speech in which *like* or *as* is used to make a comparison between two ideas that are basically dissimilar.

To use your **senses** while reading poetry, pay attention to images that appeal to your senses of sight, smell, sound, taste, and touch.

 Take It to the Net
www.phschool.com
Take the interactive self-test online to check your understanding of the selection.

Integrate Language Skills

Vocabulary Development Lesson

Specialized Vocabulary: Poetic Contractions

Poets sometimes use **poetic contractions**—words in which one or more letters are left out—to sustain a rhythm or rhyme scheme. For example, Wordsworth uses the contraction *o'er*—short for *over*—to maintain the rhythm of line 2.

Identify the meanings of these contractions.

1. 'twill   **2.** 'twasn't   **3.** fore'er

Spelling Strategy

When adding a suffix that begins with a consonant to a word that ends in silent *e*, do not drop the *e*. For example, *pensive* + *-ly* = *pensively*. Add the suffix to each word below.

1. grace + *-ful*   **2.** love + *-ly*   **3.** place + *-ment*

Concept Development: Antonyms

Review the vocabulary list on page 895 and notice Wordsworth's use of the words in the poem. Then, in your notebook, write the word that is the antonym, or the opposite in meaning, of the first word.

1. glee: (a) intelligence, (b) happiness, (c) sorrow

2. pensive: (a) careless, (b) cheerful, (c) thoughtful

3. host: (a) army, (b) small number, (c) innkeeper

4. bliss: (a) intelligence, (b) happiness, (c) misery

Grammar Lesson

Semicolons and Colons

A **semicolon** is used to join independent clauses that are closely related. It is also used to separate independent clauses or items in a series that already contain a number of commas.

A **colon** is used mainly to list items following an independent clause. Look at how the semicolon and the colon are used in the following sentences:

Semicolon:	The field of daffodils appeared unexpectedly; the sight greatly impressed Wordsworth.
Colon:	The flowers moved in ways that seemed almost human: fluttering, nodding, and dancing.

Practice Write these sentences on your paper, adding semicolons or colons wherever necessary.

1. Dorothy Wordsworth was many things a sister, a friend, and an inspiration.

2. She wrote often in her journal her comments are fascinating.

3. She described the field of daffodils vividly many of her details appear in this poem.

4. According to her journal, the daffodils did the following things tossed, reeled, danced, and laughed.

5. He used her journal entries to create his poem it was written just as beautifully.

Writing Application Write two sentences about Wordsworth's poem. Use a semicolon in one sentence and a colon in the other.

W͟G Prentice Hall Writing and Grammar Connection: Chapter 29, Section 3

Writing Lesson

Description of a Natural Scene

Wordsworth uses words to create a vivid portrait of a natural scene. Create your own descriptive word picture in the form of either a few paragraphs or a brief poem. Describe a beautiful natural scene that you have witnessed or seen in photographs.

Prewriting   Jot down details that are related to the scene you have chosen. Next, decide on the purpose for your description. Eliminate details that do not fit your purpose and replace them with more precise details.

Drafting   Decide whether your description will be a poem or a set of paragraphs. Use your notes to write your first draft.

Revising   As you evaluate your writing, circle vague words and replace them with words that are more appealing to the senses. Also, eliminate details that confuse the purpose.

Model: Avoiding Unnecessary Details

Breathless,

I stood on the side of the crater. ~~I wondered what time it was.~~
∧

                                                    massive
The sun threw shadows across the crater's ~~large~~ bowl.

> Taking out unnecessary details and adding more precise words adds to the appeal of the word picture.

 Prentice Hall Writing and Grammar Connection: Chapter 6, Section 4

Extension Activities

Listening and Speaking Prepare a **visual presentation** about England's Lake District, where Wordsworth grew up. Follow this plan:

- Look for pictures of the region.
- Find connections between the landscape and the imagery that Wordsworth used.
- Practice giving the presentation so that you will feel comfortable speaking and displaying the visuals.

In your presentation, read Wordsworth's poem aloud to the class, and then explain your findings.

Research and Technology Wordsworth is one of the most famous British Romantic poets. With a few classmates, find out about the other Romantic poets, such as John Keats or Samuel Taylor Coleridge. Collect examples of their poetry. Using word-processing software, create an **anthology** of the poems and include an explanation of each choice. [**Group Activity**]

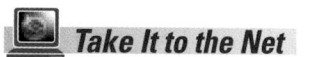 **Take It to the Net**   www.phschool.com

Go online for an additional research activity using the Internet.

Prepare to Read

Dream Deferred ◆ Dreams ◆ The Eagle ◆ "Hope" is the thing with feathers—

Bernard's Daddy, Raymond Lark, Edward Smith and Company

Take It to the Net

Visit www.phschool.com for interactive activities and instruction related to the selections, including
- background
- graphic organizers
- literary elements
- reading strategies

Preview

Connecting to the Literature

In your dreams, you can accomplish anything. Your hopes and dreams can provide you with the motivation you need to keep reaching for a goal. These poems explore the significance of hopes—and some of them look at what happens when dreams are shattered.

Background

Harlem is a center for New York City's African American population. During the 1920s, Harlem blossomed with hope; writers and artists living there took part in a literary and cultural movement know as the Harlem Renaissance. When Langston Hughes wrote "Dream Deferred" in 1951, much of Harlem was marked by extreme poverty. As a result, many of those who lived in Harlem at the time felt a sense of hopelessness.

Literary Analysis

Figurative Language

Figurative language is writing or speech that is not meant to be taken literally. Instead, it is used to create vivid impressions by setting up comparisons between dissimilar things. Three common uses of figurative language are simile, metaphor, and personification.

- A **simile** compares one thing to another using *like* or *as*. Hughes uses a simile when he asks whether a dream deferred "stinks like rotten meat."
- A **metaphor** compares one thing to another without using *like* or *as*. Hughes uses a metaphor when he writes, "Life is a barren field."
- **Personification** gives human characteristics to an animal, object, or idea. Tennyson personifies an eagle by giving it "hands."

As you read, take note of language that creates an impression through unusual comparisons.

Comparing Literary Works

The power of figurative language is in the connotations of the words poets choose to compare. The **connotation** of a word is the idea, subtle meaning, or feeling associated with it. Hughes compares a dream deferred to a festering sore. Because the connotations of these words are powerfully negative, he conveys a feeling of sickness and despair. Compare the connotations conveyed through figurative language in these four selections.

CALIFORNIA STANDARDS

Instruction with these selections addresses these standards:

R 1.2*, 3.7*, 3.8*
W 1.6*, 2.2*
WOLC 1.1*
LS 1.3

* Standards tested on HS Exit Exam. For complete standards, see p. CA 4.

Reading Strategy

Paraphrasing

When you **paraphrase,** you use your own words to express what someone else has written. For example, Hughes's line "Hold fast to dreams" can be paraphrased as "Do not let go of dreams."

- Work through the poem one line at a time.
- Find a simpler way of expressing confusing lines.

Record your paraphrases in a chart like the one shown.

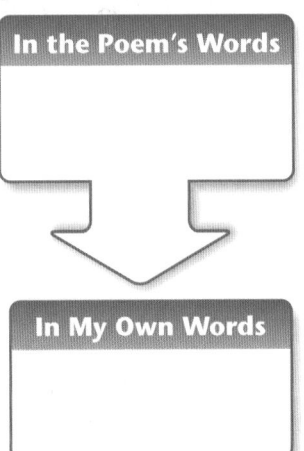

In the Poem's Words

In My Own Words

Vocabulary Development

deferred (di furd´) *adj.* put off until a future time (p. 904)

fester (fes´ tər) *v.* form pus (p. 904)

barren (bar´ ən) *adj.* empty (p. 905)

azure (azh´ ər) *adj.* blue (p. 906)

sore (sôr) *adj.* fierce; cruel (p. 908)

abash (ə bash´) *v.* embarrass (p. 908)

Bernard's Daddy, Raymond Lark, Edward Smith and Company

▲ **Critical Viewing** Explain why you do or do not think this piece of art is an effective illustration for the two poems. **[Evaluate]**

Dream Deferred

Langston Hughes

Harlem

What happens to a dream <u>deferred</u>?

    Does it dry up
    like a raisin in the sun?
5 Or <u>fester</u> like a sore——
    And then run?
    Does it stink like rotten meat?
    Or crust and sugar over——
    like a syrupy sweet?

10 Maybe it just sags
    like a heavy load.

    Or does it explode?

deferred (di furd´) *adj.* put off until a future time

fester (fes´ tər) *v.* form pus

Dreams

Langston Hughes

Hold fast to dreams
For if dreams die
Life is a broken-winged bird
That cannot fly.

5   Hold fast to dreams
For when dreams go
Life is a <u>barren</u> field
Frozen with snow.

barren (bar´ən) *adj.* empty

Review and Assess

Thinking About the Selections

1. **Respond:** Which poem affected you more? Why?
2. **(a) Recall:** What is the first question asked in "Dream Deferred"? **(b) Infer:** How is the question answered? **(c) Speculate:** Why does Hughes use six questions and only one statement in the poem?
3. **(a) Compare and Contrast:** How does the last line of "Dream Deferred" contrast with the rest of the poem? **(b) Draw Conclusions:** What is the effect of this contrast?
4. **(a) Recall:** To what two things does the speaker in "Dreams" compare life? **(b) Interpret:** Restate in your own words the advice that "Dreams" offers.
5. **Apply:** How might you apply the advice Hughes gives in "Dreams" to your own life?
6. **(a) Assess:** What might your life be like if you were prevented from pursuing your dreams or goals? **(b) Extend:** Which personal qualities are needed to hold on to dreams in adversity?

Langston Hughes

(1902–1967)
Langston Hughes, born in Joplin, Missouri, was the first African American to have a strictly literary career. As a young man, he held a variety of jobs—teacher, ranch hand, farmer, seaman, and night-club cook, among others. He drew on all of these experiences, but even more so on his experience as an African American man, to create his great body of work. "Dream Deferred" and "Dreams" illustrate his ability to express the spirit of black America.

The Eagle

Alfred, Lord Tennyson

He clasps the crag[1] with crooked hands;
Close to the sun in lonely lands,
Ring'd with the <u>azure</u> world, he stands.

> azure (azh´ ər) *adj.* blue

The wrinkled sea beneath him crawls;
5   He watches from his mountain walls,
And like a thunderbolt he falls.

---

1. **crag** (krag) *n.* steep, rugged rock that juts out from a rock mass.

Review and Assess

Thinking About the Selection

1. **Respond:** How did you feel as you read "The Eagle"? Why?

2. **(a) Recall:** When the poem opens, where is the eagle?
   (b) Interpret: Why does Tennyson place the eagle in that setting?

3. **(a) Interpret:** What is meant by the words "close to the sun"?
   (b) Assess: What effect does this phrase have on your response to the eagle?

4. **(a) Recall:** What is the eagle doing? **(b) Make a Judgment:** Is "falls" the right word for the action of the eagle in line 6? Explain.

5. **(a) Compare and Contrast:** How is the first stanza different from the second? **(b) Evaluate:** Why do you think Tennyson breaks such a short poem into two stanzas?

6. **(a) Assess:** Which words would you use to describe an eagle?
   (b) Extend: Why do you think an eagle is the national emblem of the United States?

Alfred, Lord Tennyson

(1809–1892)
The most popular of British poets during his lifetime, Alfred, Lord Tennyson rose from the quiet of humble beginnings to the glory of the position of poet laureate of England. Although he was enthralled by the technological advances of the Victorian era, Tennyson remained a poet of nature, bringing both imagination and feeling to the landscape and its inhabitants.

"Hope"
is the thing with
feathers—

Emily Dickinson

"Hope" is the thing with feathers—
That perches in the soul—
And sings the tune without the words—
And never stops—at all—

5 And sweetest—in the Gale[1]—is heard—
And <u>sore</u> must be the storm—
That could <u>abash</u> the little Bird
That kept so many warm—

I've heard it in the chillest land—
10 And on the strangest Sea—
Yet, never, in Extremity,
It asked a crumb—of Me.

---

1. **gale** (gāl) *n.* strong wind.

sore (sôr) *adj.* fierce; cruel

abash (ə bash´) *v.* embarrass

Emily Dickinson

(1830–1886)

Shy, solitary, and brilliant, Emily Dickinson led a life filled with loneliness in Amherst, Massachusetts. Yet, despite her quiet exterior, an inner life continually raged, enabling her to produce at least 1,775 poems.

Dickinson is known for her deceptively simple subjects from nature—flies buzzing at the moment of human death, birds coming down a walk. She wrote most frequently about death, love, and some of her religious beliefs. Whatever her subject, however, Dickinson's treatment was imaginative, complex, and thought-provoking.

Review and Assess

Thinking About the Selection

1. **Respond:** How do your views about hope compare with those expressed in Dickinson's poem?

2. **(a) Recall:** What is hope compared to in the poem?
   (b) Analyze: What do the two items have in common?

3. **(a) Recall:** According to the speaker, what does hope do?
   (b) Interpret: Why is it significant that hope sings a tune without words?

4. **(a) Infer:** When does hope sing the "sweetest" tune?
   (b) Interpret: Why would it sing so well at this time?

5. **Extend:** In what kinds of situations might hope keep people "warm"?

Review and Assess

Literary Analysis

Figurative Language

1. List the similes found in "Dream Deferred." Which similes are the most effective? Why?

2. (a) Change the two metaphors in "Dreams" into similes by adding *like*. (b) Does this alter the effect or meaning of the poem? Explain.

3. Using a chart like the one shown, list the **figurative language** in "'Hope' is the thing with feathers—" and "The Eagle." Then, write the comparison being made for each.

Poem	Simile	Metaphor	Personification

Comparing Literary Works

4. Using a chart like the one shown, compare the **connotations** of the figurative language found in each of the poems.

Poem	Figurative Language		Connotation

5. (a) Which poem connotes, or suggests, a feeling of despair? How? (b) Which poem connotes optimism and perseverance? How?

Reading Strategy

Paraphrasing

6. (a) **Paraphrase** the last stanza of "Dreams." (b) According to the poem, how would your life feel if it were empty of dreams?

7. Paraphrase the last stanza of "'Hope' is the thing with feathers—". Be sure to supply a noun to take the place of the pronoun *it*.

Extend Understanding

8. **Social Studies Connection:** How might civil rights leaders have used any of these poems in support of their cause?

Integrate Language Skills

Vocabulary Development Lesson

Specialized Vocabulary: Color Words

Azure, a shade of blue, is just one of the many words that poets use to convey meaning with more exactness and feeling.

Use a dictionary to find the meanings of these color words: *vermilion*, *emerald*, *ivory*, and *ebony*.

Spelling Strategy

If a word of more than one syllable ends in a single consonant following a single vowel, and the accent falls on the last syllable, the final consonant is usually doubled when a suffix starting with a vowel is added. For example, *defer + -ed = deferred*. Write the word formed by adding each ending. Use a dictionary to check your spelling.

1. plan + *-ed* **2.** control + *-er* **3.** regret + *-ed*

Concept Development: Context

Review the vocabulary list on page 903. Then, substitute a vocabulary word for the word or phrase in italics below.

1. The donation helped greatly after the *fierce* hurricane struck the family's home.
2. Changes in the work calendar resulted in *delayed* vacations, which upset the students.
3. The clouds were bright white against the *blue* sky, creating an unforgettable view.
4. Kim was feeling so confident that nothing could *embarrass* her.
5. Matt's cut began to *run with pus*.
6. The field behind the farmhouse seemed curiously *empty of life*.

Grammar Lesson

Dashes

Dashes are part of Emily Dickinson's poetic style. In everyday use, the **dash** functions in three basic ways: to dramatically set off an interrupting idea, to set off a summary statement, or to indicate an abrupt change of thought.

> **Interrupting Idea:** Dickinson—one of the greatest American poets—did not achieve fame during her lifetime.
>
> **Summary Statement:** Thomas Higginson and Helen Jackson—these are two of the few friends who recognized her talent.
>
> **Abrupt Change:** Let me read you this example of—now, where did I put that book of poems?

Practice Copy these sentences, adding dashes where appropriate.

1. She is an amazing writer to think that she was never acknowledged in her lifetime.
2. Her poem so beautifully crafted is just one of thousands she wrote.
3. Only a handful of poems seven, in fact appeared in print before Dickinson's death.
4. Intensely personal, simple in language rather free in form Dickinson's poetry ran contrary to literary tastes of that time.
5. Perhaps if she had published more but I suppose we will never know.

Writing Application Write a paragraph about hope that uses each function of the dash.

W͜G Prentice Hall Writing and Grammar Connection: Chapter 29, Section 5

Writing Lesson

Analytical Essay

Review the poems in this section, and write an essay in which you interpret the message that the poet conveys in one of the poems.

Prewriting Decide which poem you would like to interpret. Consider the message you think it conveys, and then make a list of words or lines from the poem that support your interpretation.

Drafting In the first paragraph, make sure you identify the title and author of the poem and provide a brief overview of your interpretation. In the body of your essay, develop your ideas and provide examples from the poem. Your last paragraph should restate your main point.

Revising Review your draft to determine whether you have conveyed your ideas clearly. Replace any vague language with more precise words.

Model: Replacing Vague Language

It conveys the power of hope, for even in ~~bad~~ *desperate*

provide comfort and strength
times, hope can ~~help.~~

> The inserted words provide more precise language and clarify the interpretation.

WG Prentice Hall Writing and Grammar Connection: Chapter 13, Section 3

Extension Activities

Listening and Speaking Use the poems of Dickinson and Hughes as the basis for an **inspirational speech** about the importance of hopes and dreams.

- Make sure that your speech includes a main idea that conveys hope.
- Prepare a conclusion that restates your main idea in a powerful way.
- Practice your speech in front of a friend.

As you present your speech, use body language and eye contact to convey your sincerity. Ask your audience to give you feedback about your performance.

Research and Technology In a small group, prepare a **biographical report** about Tennyson, Dickinson, or Hughes. In your writing, provide information about the writer's life, and use quotations from his or her work to show the writer's character. Use library resources, including the Internet, to gather information, and be sure to include citations of your materials where appropriate. [**Group Activity**]

 **Take It to the Net** www.phschool.com

Go online for an additional research activity using the Internet.

Prepare to Read

Blackberry Eating ◆ **Memory** ◆ **Eulogy for a Hermit Crab** ◆
Meciendo ◆ **Woman's Work**

Take It to the Net

Visit www.phschool.com
for interactive activities
and instruction related to
the selections, including
- background
- graphic organizers
- literary elements
- reading strategies

Preview

Connecting to the Literature
With a little thought, you can often find deeper meaning in routine
events and observations. For example, gazing upon the ocean might make
you think of the immensity and timelessness of nature. As these poems
illustrate, one of the great qualities of poetry is that it can lead you toward
such insights.

Background
One of the poems in this group is about a hermit crab, an animal that
carries around an abandoned shell to cover its soft, unprotected abdomen.
As a hermit crab grows, it must continually find larger shells—a dilemma
that causes much competition among hermit crabs.

Literary Analysis

Imagery

Imagery is the descriptive language that paints pictures in readers' minds. An image may appeal to any of the five senses: sight, sound, taste, smell, or touch. The following example from Margaret Walker's "Memory" uses imagery that appeals to the senses of touch and sight:

> I can remember wind-swept streets of cities
> on cold and blustery nights, on rainy days;

As you read, use a chart like this one to note memorable images and to analyze the senses to which each image appeals.

Image: fat, overripe, icy, black blackberries	
Sight	✓
Sound	
Taste	✓
Smell	
Touch	✓

Comparing Literary Works

Two poets can use the same word to create different images, or they can describe similar images in different ways. For example, one poet uses *icy* to describe juicy blackberries, but another uses *icy* to describe the painful, sharp wind. Similarly, one poet describes the movement of the sea as *spinning*, whereas another describes it as *rocking*. Compare the imagery in each of the following poems and determine the effect each has on you as a reader.

Reading Strategy

Picturing the Imagery

To appreciate the ideas that are being presented in a poem, form a mental **picture** of **each image.**

- Pay attention to descriptive words in the poem, and consider each word's descriptive meaning.
- Using your imagination, try to place yourself in the poem and experience what the speaker experiences at that moment.
- If possible, relate the image in the poem to something that you yourself have experienced.

As you relate to each image, remember to not only *see* but also *hear*, *feel*, *taste*, and *smell* what the poet describes.

Vocabulary Development

unbidden (un bid′ ′n) *adj.* without being asked; uninvited (p. 914)

sinister (sin′ is tər) *adj.* threatening harm; ominous (p. 915)

meticulously (mə tik′ yoo ləs lē) *adv.* very carefully; scrupulously (p. 916)

divine (də vīn′) *adj.* holy; sacred (p. 919)

primed (prīmd) *v.* prepared (p. 920)

CALIFORNIA STANDARDS

Instruction with these selections addresses these standards:

R 1.1*, 3.7*
W 1.3*, 2.1*
WOLC 1.1*
LS 1.7

* *Standards tested on HS Exit Exam. For complete standards, see p. CA 4.*

BLACKBERRY EATING

Galway Kinnell

I love to go out in late September
among the fat, overripe, icy, black blackberries
to eat blackberries for breakfast,
the stalks very prickly, a penalty
5   they earn for knowing the black art
of blackberry-making; and as I stand among them
lifting the stalks to my mouth, the ripest berries
fall almost <u>unbidden</u> to my tongue,
as words sometimes do, certain peculiar words
10 like *strengths* or *squinched*,
many-lettered, one-syllabled lumps,
which I squeeze, squinch open, and splurge well
in the silent, startled, icy, black language
of blackberry-eating in late September.

unbidden (un bid´ ′n) *adj.*
without being asked;
uninvited

Review and Assess

Thinking About the Selection

1. **Respond:** Which description in this poem is most appealing?
2. **(a) Recall:** Identify two words that the speaker compares to blackberries. **(b) Compare and Contrast:** What do these words have in common with blackberries?
   c) **Analyze:** What special meaning does eating blackberries have for the speaker?
3. **Make a Judgment:** Which aspect of writing does "Blackberry Eating" capture in lines 9–13? Explain.
4. **Speculate:** Do you think the speaker of this poem enjoys writing poetry? Why or why not?

Galway Kinnell

(b. 1927)

Galway Kinnell is an American poet whose writing addresses the themes of the inevitability of death, selfhood, and the power of nature. He has taught at various universities and has been active in the civil rights movement.

Memory

Margaret Walker

I can remember wind-swept streets of cities
on cold and blustery nights, on rainy days;
heads under shabby felts¹ and parasols
and shoulders hunched against a sharp concern;
5   seeing hurt bewilderment on poor faces,
smelling a deep and <u>sinister</u> unrest
these brooding people cautiously caress;
hearing ghostly marching on pavement stones
and closing fast around their squares of hate.
10 I can remember seeing them alone,
at work, and in their tenements at home.
I can remember hearing all they said:
their muttering protests, their whispered oaths,
and all that spells their living in distress.

sinister (sin′ is tər) *adj.*
threatening harm; ominous

---

1. **felts** felt hats.

Review and Assess

Thinking About the Selection

1. **Respond:** What thoughts and feelings did "Memory" evoke in you? Explain.

2. **(a) Recall:** Describe the setting and weather in Walker's poem. **(b) Interpret:** What effect does the weather have on your understanding of the lives of the people in "Memory"?

3. **Interpret:** Explain how "Memory" can be seen as a criticism of an injustice in society.

4. **Speculate:** What do you think is a possible result of a life lived in distress? Explain.

Margaret Walker

(1915–1998)

A poet and novelist, Margaret Walker is considered one of the legends of African American literature. She is best known for *Jubilee* (1966), her narrative on the life of the daughter of a slave and a slave owner. As a writer, Walker focused on the experiences and hardships of African Americans.

Eulogy for a Hermit Crab

Pattiann Rogers

You were consistently brave
On these surf-drenched rocks, in and out of their salty
Slough holes around which the entire expanse
Of the glinting grey sea and the single spotlight
5 Of the sun went spinning and spinning and spinning
In a tangle of blinding spume and spray
And pistol-shot collisions your whole life long.
You stayed. Even with the wet icy wind of the moon
Circling your silver case night after night after night
10 You were here.

And by the gritty orange curve of your claws,
By the soft, wormlike grip
Of your hinter body, by the unrelieved wonder
Of your black-pea eyes, by the mystified swing
15 And swing and swing of your touching antennae,
You maintained your name <u>meticulously</u>, you kept
Your name intact exactly, day after day after day.
No one could say you were less than perfect
In the hermitage of your crabness.

20 Now, beside the racing, incomprehensible racket
Of the sea stretching its great girth forever
Back and forth between this direction and another,
Please let the words of this proper praise I speak
Become the identical and proper sound
25 Of my mourning.

Reading Strategy
Picturing the Imagery
Which words in this description help you imagine being at the seashore?

meticulously (mə tik′ yoo ləs lē) *adj.* very carefully; scrupulously

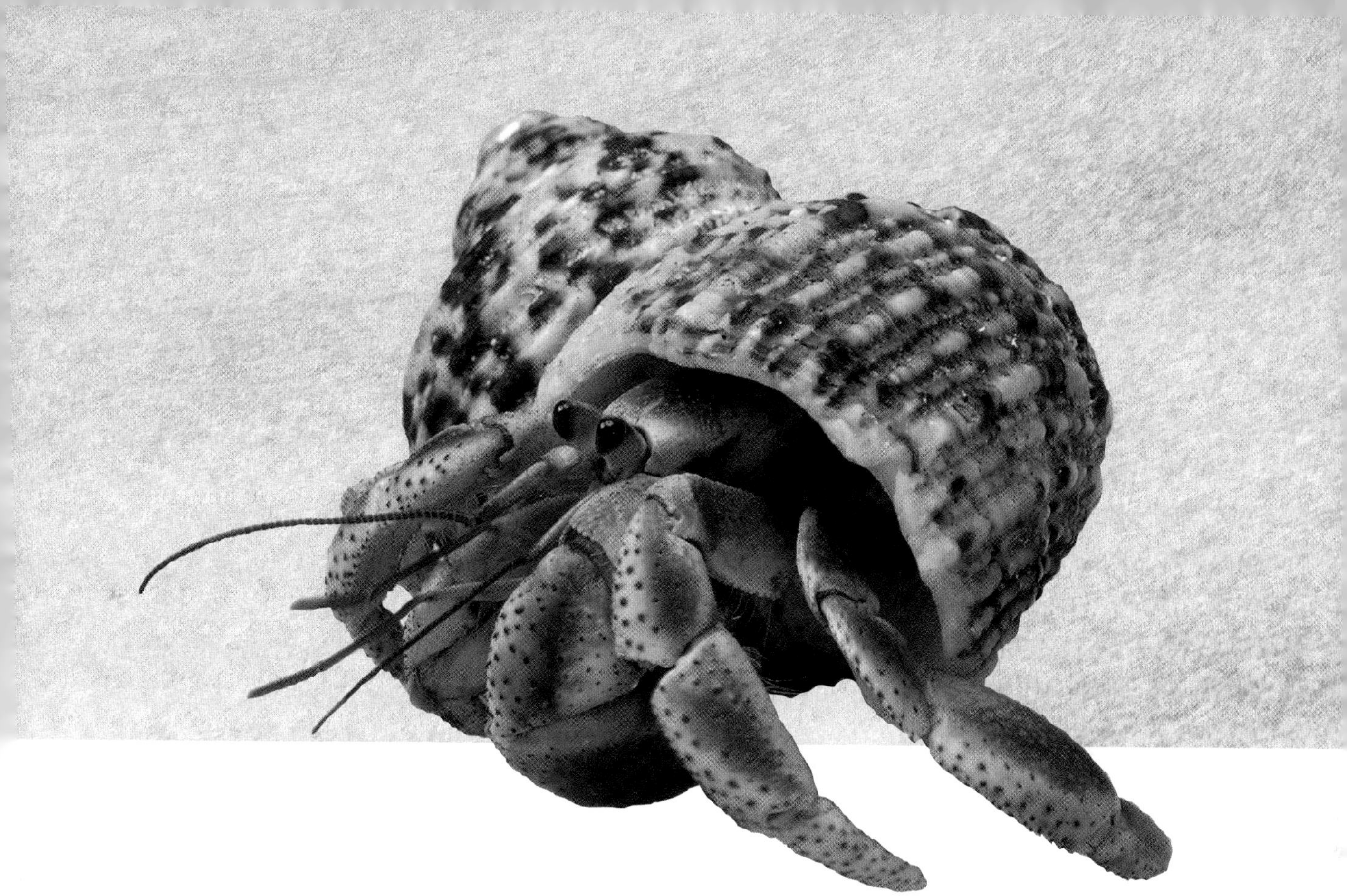

▲ **Critical Viewing**
What can you learn about hermit crabs from this photograph? **[Infer]**

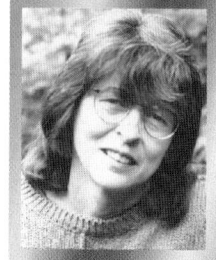

Review and Assess

Thinking About the Selection

1. **Respond:** Which image in this poem do you like best? Why?
2. **(a) Recall:** Identify two details from the first stanza that describe the hermit crab's environment. **(b) Infer:** How was that environment a constant challenge? **(c) Interpret:** What evidence proves that the crab was "consistently brave"?
3. **(a) Recall:** What does the speaker say about the crab in lines 18–19? **(b) Infer:** Why might the speaker feel the need to speak on the crab's behalf?
4. **(a) Recall:** In the final line of the poem, what is the speaker's main thought about the dead hermit crab? **(b) Connect:** What do lines 23–24 suggest about the speaker's feelings of helplessness?
5. **(a) Extend:** Did your view of hermit crabs change after reading this poem? Why or why not? **(b) Apply:** Based on this poem, what lesson can people learn from hermit crabs?
6. **Take a Position:** Are funerals or memorials for pets important? Why or why not?

Pattiann Rogers

(b. 1940)

Known for the scientifically exact language of her writing, Pattiann Rogers says that the natural world has always provided a way for her to consider the important questions of why we are here.

Meciendo

Gabriela Mistral

El mar sus millares de olas
mece, divino.
Oyendo a los mares amantes,
mezo a mi niño.

5 El viento errabundo en la noche
mece a los trigos.
Oyendo a los vientos amantes,
mezo a mi niño.

Dios Padre sus miles de mundos
10 mece sin ruido.
Sintiendo su mano en la sombra,
mezo a mi niño.

Rocking

(Meciendo)

Gabriela Mistral Translated by Doris Dana

The sea rocks her thousands of waves.
The sea is <u>divine</u>.
Hearing the loving sea,
I rock my son.

5 The wind wandering by night
rocks the wheat.
Hearing the loving wind,
I rock my son.

God, the Father, soundlessly rocks
10 His thousands of worlds.
Feeling His hand in the shadow,
I rock my son.

Review and Assess

Thinking About the Selection

1. **Respond:** What emotion does the poem evoke in you? Explain.

2. **(a) Recall:** Which forces of nature does the speaker name in the first two stanzas? **(b) Compare and Contrast:** What do these forces have in common with what the speaker is doing?

3. **(a) Recall:** Describe the scene in the third stanza.
   (b) Interpret: Why do you think that the speaker concludes the poem with a reference to God? **(c) Infer:** What do references to nature and God reveal about the speaker's feelings about motherhood?

4. **Generalize:** Does the sea always convey a sense of peace? Explain.

Gabriela Mistral

(1889–1957)
Born in Chile and given the name Lucila Godoy y Alcayaga, this writer formed her pen name from the names of two of her favorite writers, Gabriele D'Annunzio and Frederic Mistral. The 1945 recipient of the Nobel Prize for Literature, Mistral wrote many poems about children and motherhood.

Woman's Work

Julia Alvarez

Who says a woman's work isn't high art?
She'd challenge as she scrubbed the bathroom tiles.
Keep house as if the address were your heart.

We'd clean the whole upstairs before we'd start
5   downstairs. I'd sigh, hearing my friends outside.
Doing her woman's work was a hard art

to practice when the summer sun would bar
the floor I swept till she was satisfied.
She kept me prisoner in her housebound heart.

10   She'd shine the tines of forks, the wheels of carts,
cut lacy lattices[1] for all her pies.
Her woman's work was nothing less than art.

And, I, her masterpiece since I was smart,
was primed, praised, polished, scolded and advised
15   to keep a house much better than my heart.

I did not want to be her counterpart!
I struck out . . . but became my mother's child:
a woman working at home on her art,
housekeeping paper as if it were her heart.

---

1. lattices (lat′ is əz) narrow strips of pastry laid on the pie in a crisscross pattern.

Literary Analysis
Imagery Compare the image of the way the mother treats her daughter to the image of the way she treats her house.

primed (prīmd) v. prepared

Review and Assess

Thinking About the Selection

1. **Respond:** How do you feel about the mother in this poem? Why?

2. **(a) Recall:** What ambition does the mother have for her daughter? **(b) Analyze:** Why does the speaker reject that ambition? **(c) Infer:** How can you tell that the daughter both admires and resents her mother?

3. **Compare and Contrast:** How does the final stanza suggest that the daughter is similar to her mother, after all?

4. **Assess:** Do you think housekeeping can be considered an art? Explain.

Julia Alvarez

(b. 1950)

Julia Alvarez moved from the Dominican Republic to New York City with her family when she was ten years old. She says that the complexity of the many cultures in the United States is "part of what makes us rich and makes us strong."

Review and Assess

Literary Analysis

Imagery

1. Which **images** in "Memory" appeal to your sense of hearing?
2. Which images in "Eulogy for a Hermit Crab" reveal the most about the crab's world?
3. An image that appeals to the sense of touch or movement runs throughout "Meciendo." Name that image and explain its appeal.

Comparing Literary Works

4. (a) Use a chart like the one shown to identify words in "Blackberry Eating" and "Memory" that convey emotion. (b) Which poem conveys a feeling of contentment?

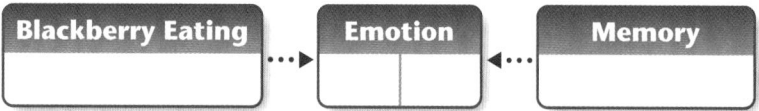

5. How do the images of the ocean in "Meciendo" and "Eulogy for a Hermit Crab" differ?

Reading Strategy

Picturing the Imagery

6. "Blackberry Eating" contains the adjectives *icy* and *prickly*, which seem unpleasant. Why, then, is picturing the images in this poem a pleasant experience?
7. Using a chart like the one below, name three images from the poems in this section that appeal to your senses, and explain how you picture the imagery.

Image	Sense Used	How I Picture It

Extend Understanding

8. **Science Connection:** (a) What can you learn about marine biology by reading "Eulogy for a Hermit Crab"? (b) What does the poem achieve that a biology book could not?

Quick Review

Imagery is the descriptive language used to create mental pictures by appealing to sight, sound, taste, touch, or smell.

To **picture the imagery,** imagine experiencing what the speaker experiences at that moment, or relate the image in the poem to something that you yourself have experienced.

 Take It to the Net
www.phschool.com
Take the interactive self-test online to check your understanding of the selections.

Integrate Language Skills

Vocabulary Development Lesson

Word Analysis: Latin Root -prim-

The word *prime* comes from the Latin root -*prim*-, which means "first in time or in importance." In "Woman's Work," *primed* means "coached beforehand." Using your knowledge of -*prim*-, define each of these words or phrases:

1. prime witness   3. primary election
2. primitive   4. primary color

Spelling Strategy

Before adding an ending that begins with a vowel to a word that ends in silent *e*, drop the *e*: *prime* + -*ed* = *primed*. Write the new word formed by adding the suffix to each word below. Then, use each new word in a sentence.

1. dive + -*ing*   2. revise + -*ing*   3. confide + -*ence*

Concept Development: Synonyms

In your notebook, write the letter of the word that means about the same as the first word. To help you, review the vocabulary list on page 913.

1. unbidden: (a) uninvited, (b) unusual, (c) ordered
2. sinister: (a) innocent, (b) evil, (c) sisterly
3. primed: (a) allowed, (b) coached, (c) followed
4. meticulously: (a) carefully, (b) quickly, (c) sloppily
5. divine: (a) godlike, (b) congested, (c) divided

Grammar Lesson

Ellipsis Points

Ellipsis points (. . .) are punctuation marks that are used to show that something has not been expressed. Usually, ellipsis points indicate one of the following situations:

- Words have been left out of a quotation
- A series continues beyond the items mentioned
- Time passes or action occurs in a narrative

This example, from the final stanza of "Woman's Work," indicates the passage of time or action:

> **Example:**   I struck out . . . but became my mother's child.

Practice Choose the blank that marks the most reasonable place to insert ellipsis points.

1. Her memories of the city ___ are clear, vivid ___ and poignant.
2. Walker refers to ___ "wind-swept streets of cities ___ on rainy days."
3. The people ___ who live in "Memory" face ___ conditions that are windy, cold, ___ and generally unpleasant.
4. The speaker remembers ___ seeing them "alone, at work, and ___ at home."
5. They keep their discontent to ___ themselves ___ but will they ___ do so forever?

Writing Application Write about one of the poems in this group, and illustrate at least two of the ellipsis rules in your sentences.

WG Prentice Hall Writing and Grammar Connection: Chapter 29

Writing Lesson

Letter About a Memorable Moment

These five poems use imagery to describe memorable moments. Choose a moment that was memorable for you, whether it occurred in real life or in a picture or a movie. Write a letter about that remarkable time and place, using imagery to capture your experience.

Prewriting   Once you have chosen an important moment, list sensory details that convey the main impression, such as joy, fear, pride, or awe. Gather details to show how the place or event appealed to your senses of sight, sound, taste, touch, and smell.

Drafting   Use your prewriting notes to draft your letter, focusing on the main impression you want to convey. Organize your details in order of time, space, or importance.

Revising   As you reread your letter, ask yourself whether each sensory detail contributes to the main impression. Add or change details to strengthen the main impression.

Model: Revising to Strengthen the Main Impression

teemed with life

Every inch of the rain forest ~~was alive.~~ Trees, brushes, and

jostled for position

vines ~~were everywhere.~~

> These revisions build the image of a vibrant and living landscape.

WG *Prentice Hall Writing and Grammar Connection: Chapter 6, Section 4*

Extension Activities

Listening and Speaking In her poem, Rogers offers a description of the hermit crab that is both beautiful and highly accurate. Plan a visual **presentation of artwork** that combines the same qualities.

- Look for art that you consider to be both beautiful and true to life.
- Make brief notes about each picture.
- Practice making your presentation while displaying your pictures.

Present your findings to your class and ask them for feedback on your art choices.

Research and Technology In a small group, prepare a **research report** about how women's roles have changed over the past several decades. You might use "Woman's Work" to help you generate questions for research. Use library resources, including the Internet, and personal interviews to help you gather facts and information. [**Group Activity**]

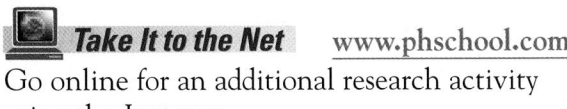 **Take It to the Net**   www.phschool.com
Go online for an additional research activity using the Internet.

Prepare to Read

Uphill ◆ Summer ◆ Ecclesiastes 3:1–8 ◆ The Bells

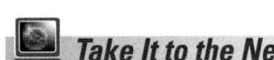 **Take It to the Net**

Visit www.phschool.com
for interactive activities
and instruction related to
the selections, including

- background
- graphic organizers
- literary elements
- reading strategies

Preview

Connecting to the Literature

Sweating through an August afternoon, you realize that the summer heat will soon change to the chill of autumn. You see parents and children enjoying the outdoors and realize that toddlers grow to adulthood. Nature and life have predictable cycles and stages. The following poems explore these cycles.

Background

Throughout the ages, poets have explored the stages and patterns of life. Scientists, too, describe life as comprising cycles and seasons, stages and patterns. Advances in medicine may extend life expectancy, but medicine has not been able to alter the basic cycle of life in which we are born, grow, and inevitably die.

Literary Analysis

Lyric Poetry and Sound Devices

These poems are examples of **lyric poetry**—verse that expresses the observations and feelings of a single speaker through a highly musical style. That style comes from various **sound devices,** including the following:

- **Rhythm:** the pattern of beats or stresses in language
- **Alliteration:** the repetition of initial consonant sounds
- **Rhyme:** the repetition of sounds at the ends of words
- **Onomatopoeia:** the use of words, like *buzz* and *whirr*, that imitate the sounds that they name

As you read, notice the musical sounds in each poem.

Comparing Literary Works

As these poems suggest, life is filled with cycles and stages. Whether addressing life milestones, the journey from birth to death, or the natural progression of seasons, each poem reveals patterns that apply to life. As you move from one poem to the next, compare and contrast the patterns and cycles presented in each to determine whether each presents a hopeful or a despairing message.

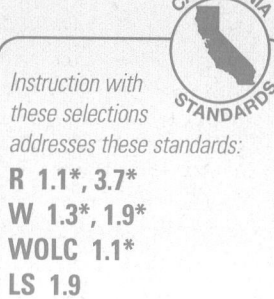

Instruction with these selections addresses these standards:

R 1.1*, 3.7*
W 1.3*, 1.9*
WOLC 1.1*
LS 1.9

* Standards tested on HS Exit Exam. For complete standards, see p. CA 4.

Reading Strategy

Listening to Poetic Sounds

To appreciate the musical quality of lyric poems, read them aloud and **listen to the sound** of the lines. Follow these points to help you:

- Read the poem aloud to yourself or to a partner. If you wish, record your reading.
- Listen for the musical sounds created by the words.
- Consider the mood or feeling created by the sounds.

Use a chart like the one shown to help you analyze how the sound reinforces the poem's meaning.

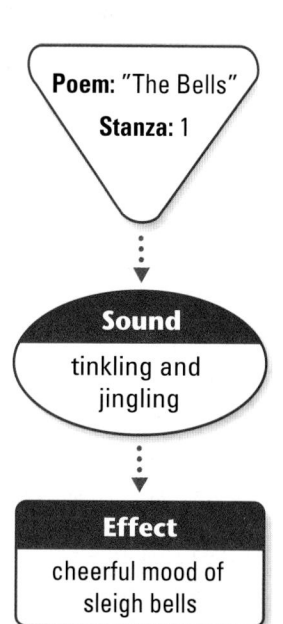

Poem: "The Bells"

Stanza: 1

Sound
tinkling and jingling

Effect
cheerful mood of sleigh bells

Vocabulary Development

wayfarers (wā′ fer′ ərz) *n.* travelers (p. 926)

voluminously (və lōōm′ ə nəs lē) *adv.* fully; in great volume (p. 932)

palpitating (pal′ pə tāt′ iŋ) *adj.* beating rapidly; throbbing (p. 933)

monotone (män′ ə tōn′) *n.* uninterrupted repetition of the same tone (p. 933)

pæan (pē′ ən) *n.* song of joy or triumph (p. 933)

Uphill

Christina Rossetti

Does the road wind uphill all the way?
    Yes, to the very end.
Will the day's journey take the whole long day?
    From morn to night, my friend.

5 But is there for the night a resting place?
    A roof for when the slow dark hours begin.
May not the darkness hide it from my face?
    You cannot miss that inn.

Shall I meet other <u>wayfarers</u> at night?
10   Those who have gone before.
Then must I knock, or call when just in sight?
    They will not keep you standing at that door.

Shall I find comfort, travel-sore and weak?
    Of labor you shall find the sum.
15 Will there be beds for me and all who seek?
    Yea,[1] beds for all who come.

---

1. **yea** (yā) indeed; truly.

wayfarers (wā′ fer′ ərz) *n.* travelers

Christina Rossetti

(1830–1894)

Christina Rossetti is considered by some critics to be the best female poet in English literature. Her father had come from Italy to live in England, and the famous poet and painter Dante Gabriel Rossetti was her brother. Her best-known work is the long poem "Goblin Market," a kind of supernatural fairy tale.

Summer

Walter Dean Myers

I like hot days, hot days
Sweat is what you got days
Bugs buzzin from cousin to cousin
Juices dripping
5 Running and ripping
Catch the one you love days

Birds peeping
Old men sleeping
Lazy days, daisies lay
10 Beaming and dreaming
Of hot days, hot days,
Sweat is what you got days

Review and Assess

Thinking About the Selections

1. **Respond:** How do you feel about the journey described in "Uphill"? Why?

2. **(a) Recall:** According to the final stanza of "Uphill," how will the traveler feel at journey's end? **(b) Interpret:** What might the uphill winding of the road represent? Explain.

3. **(a) Recall:** According to the final stanza, what is waiting for all travelers at the end of the journey? **(b) Interpret:** What is the final destination of the journey?

4. **(a) Recall:** In lines 1–2 of "Summer," how does Myers describe summer? **(b) Infer:** What kinds of juices might be dripping?

5. **(a) Recall:** What do birds do in summer? **(b) Contrast:** How does their activity contrast with that of old men?

6. **Take a Position:** Which poet more effectively conveys a particular feeling to you? Explain.

Walter Dean Myers

(b. 1937)
As a child, acclaimed author Walter Dean Myers never imagined himself becoming a writer. He was born into poverty in West Virginia and was writing poems and stories by his early teens, but he believed that his dream of being a writer would never be realized. Myers's dream was fulfilled, however, when he won a writing contest sponsored by the Council on Interracial Books for Children for his book *Where Does a Day Go?*

ECCLESIASTES 3:1-8

(King James Version)

To every thing there is a season, and a time to
    every purpose under the heaven:
A time to be born, and a time to die; a time to
    plant, and a time to pluck up that which is planted;
A time to kill, and a time to heal; a time to break
    down, and a time to build up;
A time to weep, and a time to laugh; a time to
    mourn, and a time to dance;
5   A time to cast away stones, and a time to gather
    stones together; a time to embrace, and a time to
    refrain from embracing;
A time to get, and a time to lose; a time to keep,
    and a time to cast away;
A time to rend,[1] and a time to sew; a time to keep
    silence, and a time to speak;
A time to love, and a time to hate; a time of war,
    and a time of peace.

---

1. **rend** (rend) v. tear.

Reading Strategy
Listening to Poetic Sounds How does the rhythm of these lines illustrate the main idea of the passage?

◀ **Critical Viewing** How do the contrasts in these pictures reflect the poem? **[Connect]**

Review and Assess

Thinking About the Selection

1. **Respond:** Do you find this passage comforting? Explain why or why not.

2. **(a) Recall:** Which verse begins differently from the other verses? **(b) Analyze:** What is the relationship between that verse and the rest of the passage?

3. **(a) Recall:** Which words are repeated throughout the poem? **(b) Analyze:** Why do you think these words are repeated?

4. **(a) Recall:** Identify four pairs of actions mentioned in the passage. **(b) Infer:** What activity is suggested by the words "A time to cast away stones, and a time to gather stones together"? **(c) Analyze:** How does the pairing of opposite ideas help to communicate the message of the passage?

5. **Apply:** What comfort or guidance can a person of today find in these verses written thousands of years ago?

The King James Bible

The King James Version of the Bible was published in 1611. It was the work of a committee of English churchmen led by Lancelot Andrews. The language of the King James Version is considered by many to be so beautiful that the Bible is often ranked in English literature with the works of William Shakespeare.

According to tradition, Ecclesiastes, the section from which this selection is taken, was written by Solomon, the wise Hebrew king, who died around 932 B.C.

▲ **Critical Viewing** How would you describe the mood of this painting? What do you predict the mood of the poem might be? **[Interpret]**

The Bells

Edgar Allan Poe

I

Hear the sledges[1] with the bells—
Silver bells!
What a world of merriment their melody foretells!
How they tinkle, tinkle, tinkle,
5   In the icy air of night!
While the stars, that oversprinkle
All the heavens, seem to twinkle
With a crystalline delight;
Keeping time, time, time,
10   In a sort of Runic[2] rhyme,
To the tintinnabulation[3] that so musically wells
From the bells, bells, bells, bells,
Bells, bells, bells—
From the jingling and the tinkling of the bells.

---

1. **sledges** (slej´ əz) *n.* sleighs.
2. **Runic** (roo´ nik) *adj.* songlike; poetical.
3. **tintinnabulation** (tin´ ti nab´ yoo la´ shən) *n.* ringing of bells.

II

15   Hear the mellow wedding bells,
Golden bells!
What a world of happiness their harmony foretells!
Through the balmy air of night
How they ring out their delight!
20   From the molten golden-notes,
And all in tune,
What a liquid ditty[4] floats
To the turtle-dove[5] that listens, while she gloats
On the moon!
25   Oh, from out the sounding cells,
What a gush of euphony[6] <u>voluminously</u> wells!
How it swells!
How it dwells
On the future! how it tells
30   Of the rapture that impels
To the swinging and the ringing
Of the bells, bells, bells,
Of the bells, bells, bells, bells
Bells, bells, bells—
35   To the rhyming and the chiming of the bells!

III

Hear the loud alarum[7] bells!
Brazen[8] bells!
What a tale of terror now their turbulency tells!
In the startled ear of night
40   How they scream out their affright!
Too much horrified to speak,
They can only shriek, shriek,
Out of tune,
In a clamorous appealing to the mercy of the fire,
45   In a mad expostulation[9] with the deaf and frantic fire
Leaping higher, higher, higher,
With a desperate desire,
And a resolute endeavor
Now—now to sit or never,
50   By the side of the pale-faced moon.
Oh, the bells, bells, bells!
What a tale their terror tells

voluminously (və lōōm′ ə nəs lē) *adv.* fully; in great volume

Reading Strategy
Listening to Poetic Sounds What do the sounds in these lines suggest? Explain.

---

4. **ditty** (dit′ ē) *n.* song.
5. **turtle-dove** The turtle-dove is traditionally associated with love.
6. **euphony** (yōō′ fə nē) *n.* pleasing sound.
7. **alarum** (ə ler′ əm) *adj.* sudden call to arms; alarm.
8. **brazen** (brā′ zən) *adj.* made of brass; having the sound of brass.
9. **expostulation** (eks päs′ chə lā′ shən) *n.* objection; complaint.

Of Despair!
How they clang, and clash, and roar!
55   What a horror they outpour
On the bosom of the <u>palpitating</u> air!
Yet the ear it fully knows,
By the twanging
And the clanging,
60   How the danger ebbs and flows;
Yet the ear distinctly tells,
In the jangling,
And the wrangling,
How the danger sinks and swells,
65 By the sinking or the swelling in the anger of the bells—
Of the bells—
Of the bells, bells, bells, bells,
Bells, bells, bells—
In the clamor and the clangor of the bells!

IV

70   Hear the tolling of the bells—
Iron bells!
What a world of solemn thought their monody[10] compels!
In the silence of the night,
How we shiver with affright
75   At the melancholy menace of their tone!
For every sound that floats
From the rust within their throats
Is a groan.
And the people—ah, the people—
80   They that dwell up in the steeple,
All alone,
And who tolling, tolling, tolling,
In that muffled <u>monotone</u>,
Feel a glory in so rolling
85   On the human heart a stone—
They are neither man nor woman—
They are neither brute nor human—
They are Ghouls:[11]
And their king it is who tolls;
90   And he rolls, rolls, rolls,
Rolls
A <u>pæan</u> from the bells!
And his merry bosom swells
With the pæan of the bells!

Literary Analysis
Lyric Poetry and Sound Devices What effect is created by the sound devices in lines 73–78?

monotone (män´ ə tōn´) n. uninterrupted repetition of the same tone

pæan (pē´ ən) n. song of joy or triumph

☑ **Reading Check**

What kind of story do the wedding bells tell?

---

10. monody (män´ ə dē) n. poem of mourning; a steady sound; music in which one instrument or voice is dominant.
11. Ghouls (goolz) n. evil spirits that rob graves.

95   And he dances and he yells;
         Keeping time, time, time,
         In a sort of Runic rhyme,
         To the pæan of the bells—
             Of the bells:
100   Keeping time, time, time,
         In a sort of Runic rhyme,
         To the throbbing of the bells—
         Of the bells, bells, bells—
         To the sobbing of the bells;
105   Keeping time, time, time,
         As he knells, knells, knells,
         In a happy Runic rhyme,
         To the rolling of the bells—
         Of the bells, bells, bells—
110   To the tolling of the bells,
     Of the bells, bells, bells, bells,
         Bells, bells, bells—
To the moaning and the groaning of the bells.

Review and Assess

Thinking About the Selection

1. **Respond:** What feelings did each section of "The Bells" evoke in you?

2. **(a) Recall:** What kinds of bells are described in each of the four sections of "The Bells"? **(b) Infer:** What scenes or situations does each of the sections suggest?

3. **(a) Recall:** Identify five words in the poem that refer to the sounds that bells make. **(b) Evaluate:** How successful is Poe in capturing the sounds of bells in words? Explain.

4. **(a) Recall:** Are the lines in "The Bells" of a consistent length? Explain. **(b) Speculate:** Why do you think Poe chose to present the lines in this way?

5. **(a) Analyze:** What similarities among the four sections do you see? **(b) Compare and Contrast:** Does the mood or spirit of the poem vary from one section to another, or is it basically the same throughout? Explain.

6. **Assess:** The poet T. S. Eliot once said that poetry can be enjoyed before it is understood. Could "The Bells" be used as evidence in support of this idea? Explain.

7. **Apply:** Do you associate various feelings with different bell sounds in your own life? Explain.

Edgar Allan Poe

(1809–1849)

Edgar Allan Poe may be best known for chilling tales like "The Cask of Amontillado," but he was also a talented poet. As poems like "The Bells" illustrate, Poe was a master at using rhythm and sound effects to emphasize meaning and create a powerful musical effect.

Many scholars believe that the idea for "The Bells" was suggested to Poe by Marie Louise Shew, a woman with medical training who treated Poe when his health began to fail during his final years.

Review and Assess

Literary Analysis

Lyric Poetry and Sound Devices

1. (a) Using a chart like the one shown, check off the **sound devices** used in each poem. (b) Based on your chart, which poem has the strongest musical qualities? Explain.

Poem	Line #	Rhythm	Alliteration	Rhyme	Onomatopoeia
"Summer"	3	✓	✓ b and c sound	✓ buzzin/ cousin	✓ buzzin

2. (a) List at least four examples of onomatopoeia in "The Bells." (b) How does the use of onomatopoeia add to the poem?

3. In the **lyric poem** "Uphill," how does the speaker feel about life's journey and its ultimate destination? Support your answer.

4. (a) What emotion does "Summer" convey? (b) If you were to retitle the poem, what would you call it? Why?

Comparing Literary Works

5. (a) Compare the views of the nature of human life that are expressed in these poems. (b) Which poem most strongly conveys the theme of life's cycles? Explain.

6. (a) Which three poems deal with death? (b) How do the poems' perspectives on death differ?

Reading Strategy

Listening to Poetic Sounds

7. (a) How does reading the poems aloud help you appreciate the use of rhyme in the poems? (b) Which other sound devices are revealed by reading aloud?

8. Which poem's meaning became clearer to you when you read it aloud? Explain.

Extend Understanding

9. **Cultural Connection:** Which poem, "Uphill" or Ecclesiastes 3:1–8, might be more comforting to people who are mourning a loss? Explain your answer.

Quick Review

Lyric poetry is verse that expresses the observations and feelings of a single speaker through a highly musical style. That style comes from **sound devices** such as these:

Rhythm: the pattern of beats or stresses in language

Alliteration: the repetition of initial consonant sounds

Rhyme: the repetition of sounds at the ends of words

Onomatopoeia: the use of words that imitate the sounds that they name

To **listen to poetic sounds,** read the poem aloud, listen to the musical sound created, and consider the mood or feeling the sound suggests.

 Take It to the Net

www.phschool.com

Take the interactive self-test online to check your understanding of the selections.

Integrate Language Skills

Vocabulary Development Lesson

Word Analysis: Greek Prefix *mono-*

The word *monotone* contains the Greek prefix *mono-*, which means "one." You might guess, therefore, that *monotone* means "one tone," which is close to the actual meaning, "uninterrupted repetition of the same tone."

Match each word containing the prefix *mono-* with its definition on the right.

1. monorail
2. monopoly
3. monochromatic
4. monolith

  a. exclusive control of the selling of something
  b. single large block of stone
  c. railway with a single rail as a track
  d. having or being of one color

Fluency: Clarify Word Meaning

Copy the paragraph below, completing it with words from the vocabulary list on page 925.

Commuters, ___?___ heading home from work, ___?___ packed the railroad platform. With their hearts ___?___, they listened to an announcement delivered in a ___?___. When the voice proclaimed that their train was about to arrive, they sang a ___?___ as one!

Spelling Strategy

A prefix attached to a word does not affect the spelling of the original word. For example, *mono-* + *tone* = *monotone*. Rewrite each word below by adding the given prefix. Then, use each new word in a sentence.

1. *un-* + necessary
2. *dis-* + satisfied
3. *re-* + construct
4. *pre* + determine

Grammar Lesson

End Punctuation

End punctuation is the period, question mark, or exclamation mark at the end of a sentence. A **period** indicates the end of a sentence or an abbreviation. A **question mark** follows a word, phrase, or sentence that asks a question. An **exclamation mark** indicates strong feeling or emotion, including surprise. In the following examples, notice how the end punctuation affects the meaning of these sentences:

Statement:	The road winds uphill.
Question:	The road winds uphill?
Exclamation:	The road winds uphill!

Practice Write each item below, using the appropriate end punctuation for the emotion indicated in parentheses.

1. I will meet other wayfarers at night (anxiety)
2. You like hot days (disbelief)
3. Please, listen to the bells (anger)
4. The time has come to dig up what we have planted (informative)
5. I hear the sound of the bells (excitement)

Writing Application Write five sentences that reflect on one of the poems you have just read. Use each type of end punctuation at least once.

W̶G̶ Prentice Hall Writing and Grammar Connection: Chapter 29, Section 1

Writing Lesson

Rap Song

Like lyric poems, rap songs are musical expressions of a speaker's thoughts and feelings. Write a rap song that conveys your feelings about a season, a stage of life, or another topic that interests you.

Prewriting   Choose your topic and make preliminary notes about it. Decide on your message and your key ideas. Then, think about which words or lines you could repeat to help drive home your points.

Drafting   As you draft your rap song, focus on establishing a strong rhythm. Use rhymes at the ends of lines to create a musical effect. Also, consider including a refrain, a line or group of lines that is repeated throughout the song.

Revising   Read your rap song aloud to check its rhythm. Make sure that your use of repetition highlights your main ideas. Make any revisions needed to improve the sound of the song.

Model: Analyzing Word Choice for Use of Repetition

abound

Fall—everywhere I look I find leaves ~~all over~~!

falling

Yellow, red, orange, brown are ~~going~~ to the ground.

> The rhyming words *abound* and *ground* and the repeated use of *fall* improve the sound of the song.

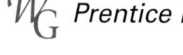 *Prentice Hall Writing and Grammar Connection: Chapter 6, Connected Assignment*

Extension Activities

Listening and Speaking Prepare and present a **dramatic reading** of "The Bells" to capture the poem's musical quality.

- Read the poem aloud to yourself.
- Make notes about which words to emphasize and when to change your reading pace.
- Practice your reading, recording yourself, if possible, so that you can hear and fix problem spots.

After you present your dramatic reading, ask your listeners what they liked best about it.

Research and Technology In a group, create an **illustrated version** of the poem "Summer." Look on the Internet for images, or use photographs and original artwork that you prepare. As you conduct your visual research, try to capture the mood of the poem. Combine the poem with the art and share it with classmates. **[Group Activity]**

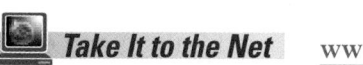 **Take It to the Net**   www.phschool.com

Go online for an additional research activity using the Internet.

Prepare to Read

The Raven ◆ The Seven Ages of Man

Take It to the Net

Visit www.phschool.com
for interactive activities
and instruction related to
the selections, including

- background
- graphic organizers
- literary elements
- reading strategies

Preview

Connecting to the Literature

Why do people act the way they do? Adults often explain the behavior
of young people by saying, "It's just a phase. . . ." Do you think people go
through "phases" all their lives, or do specific events in an individual's life
shape his or her behavior? These two selections present different answers
to the question.

Background

"The Seven Ages of Man" is a speech from William Shakespeare's
comedy *As You Like It*. The play is about a duke who has been deprived
of his rights and exiled to the forest by his own brother. The duke's
attendant, Jacques, delivers the speech to his master and reveals a cold
and bitter outlook on life.

Literary Analysis

Narrative and Dramatic Poetry

"The Raven" is a poem that has characters, a setting, and a plot. These elements make it **narrative poetry**—poetry that tells a story. The first line of "The Raven" opens in storytelling style:

> Once upon a midnight dreary, while I pondered, weak and weary,

"The Seven Ages of Man," in contrast, is a **dramatic poem**—a poem in which the lines are spoken by one or more characters to express their thoughts and feelings. The poem is spoken by a character named Jacques:

> All the world's a stage,
> And all the men and women merely players:

Comparing Literary Works

These two poems present different perspectives on human life. As you read, compare the speakers' views on love, hope, aging, loss, and suffering. Also, consider how the style and language of each speaker help express his feelings about life. For example, you may notice that the narrative speaker is sad and intense as he presents his story, while the dramatic speaker is direct and sarcastic in his monologue.

Reading Strategy

Drawing Inferences About the Speaker

Readers sometimes mistakenly assume that a poem's speaker is always the poet. Actually, the speaker is often an imaginary voice assumed by the poet. To understand a poem, it is helpful to identify who the speaker is and then to **draw inferences**—educated guesses based on evidence—about the speaker's situation, attitudes, and personality traits. Use a chart like the one shown to record words and details that reveal information about each speaker.

Vocabulary Development

quaint (kwānt) *adj.* strange; unusual (p. 940)

beguiling (bi gīl´ iŋ) *adj.* tricking; charming (p. 942)

respite (res´ pit) *n.* rest; relief (p. 942)

desolate (des´ ə lit) *adj.* deserted (p. 942)

pallid (pal´ id) *adj.* pale (p. 943)

woeful (wō´ fəl) *adj.* full of sorrow (p. 945)

treble (treb´ əl) *n.* high-pitched voice (p. 946)

Speaker's Words

Weak
Weary

Inferences

Speaker is in a gloomy mood.

Speaker's Actions

Worries about opening door
Whispers first; then shrieks

The Raven

Edgar Allan Poe

Once upon a midnight dreary, while I pondered, weak and weary,
Over many a <u>quaint</u> and curious volume of forgotten lore,[1]
While I nodded, nearly napping, suddenly there came a tapping,
As of someone gently rapping, rapping at my chamber door.
5 "'Tis some visitor," I muttered, "tapping at my chamber door—
　　Only this, and nothing more."

Ah, distinctly I remember it was in the bleak December,
And each separate dying ember wrought its ghost upon the floor.
Eagerly I wished the morrow—vainly I had tried to borrow
10 From my books surcease[2] of sorrow—sorrow for the lost Lenore—
For the rare and radiant maiden whom the angels name Lenore—
　　Nameless here for evermore.

And the silken, sad, uncertain rustling of each purple curtain
Thrilled me—filled me with fantastic terrors never felt before;
15 So that now, to still the beating of my heart, I stood repeating
"'Tis some visitor entreating entrance at my chamber door—
Some late visitor entreating entrance at my chamber door—
　　This it is and nothing more."

Presently my soul grew stronger; hesitating then no longer,
20 "Sir," said I, "or Madam, truly your forgiveness I implore;
But the fact is I was napping, and so gently you came rapping,
And so faintly you came tapping, tapping at my chamber door,
That I scarce was sure I heard you"—here I opened wide the door—
　　Darkness there, and nothing more.

25 Deep into that darkness peering, long I stood there wondering,
　　fearing,
Doubting, dreaming dreams no mortal ever dared to dream before;
But the silence was unbroken, and the darkness gave no token,[3]
And the only word there spoken was the whispered word, "Lenore!"
This *I* whispered, and an echo murmured back the word, "Lenore!"
30 　　Merely this, and nothing more.

---

1. **quaint . . . lore** strange book of ancient learning.
2. **surcease** (sʉr sēs´) *n.* end.
3. **token** (tō´ kən) *n.* sign.

Literary Analysis
Narrative and Dramatic Poetry Which background details does the speaker provide in the first two stanzas to set the scene for the story?

Reading Strategy
Drawing Inferences About the Speaker Which words or actions by the speaker show that he is getting more and more nervous?

Then into the chamber turning, all my soul within me burning,
Soon I heard again a tapping somewhat louder than before.
"Surely," said I, "surely that is something at my window lattice;⁴
Let me see, then, what thereat⁵ is, and this mystery explore—
35 Let my heart be still a moment and this mystery explore—
          'Tis the wind, and nothing more!"

Open here I flung the shutter, when, with many a flirt⁶ and flutter,
In there stepped a stately raven of the saintly days of yore;
Not the least obeisance⁷ made he; not an instant stopped or
          stayed he;
40 But, with mien⁸ of lord or lady, perched above my chamber door—
Perched upon a bust of Pallas⁹ just above my chamber door—
          Perched, and sat, and nothing more.

Then this ebony bird beguiling my sad fancy¹⁰ into smiling,
By the grave and stern decorum of the countenance¹¹ it wore,
45 "Though thy crest be shorn and shaven, thou," I said, "art sure
          no craven,¹²
Ghastly grim and ancient raven wandering from the Nightly shore—
Tell me what thy lordly name is on the Night's Plutonian¹³ shore!"
          Quoth¹⁴ the raven, "Nevermore."

Much I marveled this ungainly fowl to hear discourse so plainly,
50 Though its answer little meaning—little relevancy bore;
For we cannot help agreeing that no sublunary¹⁵ being
Ever yet was blessed with seeing bird above his chamber door—
Bird or beast upon the sculptured bust above his chamber door,
          With such name as "Nevermore."

55 But the raven, sitting lonely on the placid bust, spoke only
That one word, as if his soul in that one word he did outpour.
Nothing farther then he uttered—not a feather then he fluttered—
Till I scarcely more than muttered, "Other friends have flown before—
On the morrow *he* will leave me, as my hopes have flown before."
60   Quoth the raven, "Nevermore."

Literary Analysis
Narrative and Dramatic Poetry Which elements of a story plot are evident in the first eight stanzas of the poem?

---

4. **lattice** (lat´ is) *n.* framework of wood or metal.
5. **thereat** (*th*er at´) *adv.* there.
6. **flirt** (flʉrt) *n.* quick, uneven movement.
7. **obeisance** (ō bā´ səns) *n.* bow or another sign of respect.
8. **mien** (mēn) *n.* manner.
9. **bust of Pallas** (pal´ əs) sculpture of the head and shoulders of Pallas Athena (ə thē´ nə), the ancient Greek goddess of wisdom.
10. **fancy** (fan´ sē) *n.* imagination.
11. **countenance** (koun´ tə nəns) *n.* facial appearance.
12. **craven** (krā´ vən) *n.* coward (usually an adjective).
13. **Plutonian** (ploo tō´ nē ən) *adj.* like the underworld, ruled over by the ancient Roman god Pluto.
14. **quoth** (kwōth) *v.* said.
15. **sublunary** (sub loon´ ər ē) *adj.* earthly.

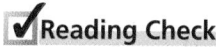
Reading Check
What is tapping at the speaker's chamber door?

Wondering at the stillness broken by reply so aptly spoken,
"Doubtless," said I, "what it utters is its only stock and store,
Caught from some unhappy master whom unmerciful Disaster
Followed fast and followed faster—so, when Hope he would adjure,[16]
65 Stern Despair returned, instead of the sweet Hope he dared adjure—
    That sad answer, 'Nevermore.'"

But the raven still <u>beguiling</u> all my sad soul into smiling,
Straight I wheeled a cushioned seat in front of bird, and bust, and
    door;
Then upon the velvet sinking, I betook myself to linking
70 Fancy unto fancy, thinking what this ominous bird of yore—
What this grim, ungainly, ghastly, gaunt, and ominous bird of yore
    Meant in croaking "Nevermore."

Reading Strategy
**Drawing Inferences
About the Speaker** What
does the speaker's action
in line 68 suggest about
his state of mind?

beguiling (bi gīl' iŋ) *adj.*
tricking; charming

This I sat engaged in guessing, but no syllable expressing
To the fowl whose fiery eyes now burned into my bosom's core;
75 This and more I sat divining,[17] with my head at ease reclining
On the cushion's velvet lining that the lamplight gloated o'er,
But whose velvet violet lining with the lamplight gloating o'er,
    She shall press, ah, nevermore!

Then, methought, the air grew denser, perfumed from an unseen
    censer[18]
80 Swung by angels whose faint footfalls tinkled on the tufted floor.
"Wretch," I cried, "thy God hath lent thee—by these angels he hath
    sent thee
<u>Respite</u>—respite and Nepenthe[19] from thy memories of Lenore!
Let me quaff[20] this kind Nepenthe and forget this lost Lenore!"
    Quoth the raven, "Nevermore."

respite (res' pit) *n.* rest;
relief

85 "Prophet!" said I, "thing of evil!—prophet still, if bird or devil!—
Whether Tempter[21] sent, or whether tempest tossed thee here
    ashore,
<u>Desolate</u>, yet all undaunted, on this desert land enchanted—
On this home by Horror haunted—tell me truly, I implore—
Is there—is there balm in Gilead?[22]—tell me—tell me, I implore!"
90   Quoth the raven, "Nevermore."

"Prophet!" said I, "thing of evil!—prophet still, if bird or devil!
By that Heaven that bends above us—by that God we both adore—

desolate (des' ə lit) *adj.*
deserted

---

16. **adjure** (ə joor') *v.* appeal to.
17. **divining** (də vīn' iŋ) *v.* guessing.
18. **censer** (sen' sər) *n.* container for burning incense.
19. **Nepenthe** (ni pen' thē) *n.* drug used in ancient times to cause forgetfulness of sorrow.
20. **quaff** (kwäf) *v.* drink.
21. **Tempter** devil.
22. **balm** (bäm) **in Gilead** (gil' ē əd) cure for suffering; the Bible refers to a medicinal
    ointment, or balm, made in a region called Gilead.

Tell this soul with sorrow laden if, within the distant Aidenn,[23]
It shall clasp a sainted maiden whom the angels name Lenore—
95 Clasp a rare and radiant maiden whom the angels name Lenore."
     Quoth the raven, "Nevermore."

"Be that word our sign of parting, bird or fiend!" I shrieked,
    upstarting—
"Get thee back into the tempest and the Night's Plutonian shore!
Leave no black plume as a token of that lie thy soul hath spoken!
100 Leave my loneliness unbroken!—quit the bust above my door!
Take thy beak from out my heart, and take thy form from off
    my door!"
     Quoth the raven, "Nevermore."

And the raven, never flitting, still is sitting, still is sitting
On the pallid bust of Pallas just above my chamber door;
105 And his eyes have all the seeming of a demon that is dreaming,
And the lamplight o'er him streaming throws his shadow on
    the floor;
And my soul from out that shadow that lies floating on the floor
    Shall be lifted—nevermore!

pallid (pal′ id) *adj.* pale

23. **Aidenn** name meant to suggest Eden or paradise.

Review and Assess
Thinking About the Selection
1. **Respond:** How do you feel about the poem's speaker? Why?
2. **(a) Recall:** Who is Lenore and what has happened to her?
   (b) Infer: What can you infer about the speaker's relationship with Lenore? Explain.
3. **(a) Recall:** Which two adjectives does the speaker use to describe his mood at the beginning of the poem? **(b) Draw Conclusions:** Which adjectives would you use to describe the speaker's mood at the end of the poem? Explain. **(c) Analyze Cause and Effect:** What has caused the speaker's mood to change?
4. **(a) Recall:** What one word does the Raven speak? **(b) Draw Conclusions:** Do you think the raven is merely repeating a sound, or is it responding to each of the narrator's questions?
5. **(a) Connect:** Describe how your impression of the raven changes as the poem progresses. **(b) Analyzing Cause and Effect:** What causes your impression to change?
6. **Evaluate:** Poe considered having a parrot repeat the word "Nevermore." Would the poem have been as effective if Poe had used a parrot instead of a raven? Explain.

Edgar Allan Poe

(1809–1849)
Although he is re-membered mostly for his eerie short stories, Edgar Allan Poe was also a gifted poet. The haunting mood of "The Raven," his best-known poem, reflects the impact of the many misfortunes that Poe experienced during his brief, tragic life. As a young boy, Poe lost both of his parents and was taken in by a wealthy Virginia mer-chant, John Allan, but their relationship was often stormy.

During his literary career, Poe published numerous short stories and poems but never achieved financial success as a writer. Despite his financial struggles, Poe experienced a period of hap-piness following his mar-riage to Virginia Clemm in 1835. This happiness was shattered, however, by his wife's death in 1847. (For more on Edgar Allan Poe, see pp. 12 and 934.)

The Seven Ages of Man, Folger Shakespeare Library, Washington, D.C.

▲ **Critical Viewing** How do the images in this stained glass window add to your understanding of the poem? **[Relate]**

The Seven Ages of Man

William Shakespeare

All the world's a stage,
And all the men and women merely players:[1]
They have their exits and their entrances;
And one man in his time plays many parts,
5   His acts being seven ages.[2] At first the infant,
Mewling[3] and puking in the nurse's arms.
And then the whining schoolboy, with his satchel,
And shining morning face, creeping like snail
Unwillingly to school. And then the lover,
10   Sighing like furnace, with a <u>woeful</u> ballad
Made to his mistress' eyebrow. Then a soldier,
Full of strange oaths, and bearded like the pard,[4]
Jealous in honor,[5] sudden and quick in quarrel,
Seeking the bubble reputation
15   Even in the cannon's mouth. And then the justice,[6]
In fair round belly with good capon[7] lined,
With eyes severe and beard of formal cut,

---

1. **players** actors.
2. **ages** periods of life.
3. **mewling** (myoo͞l´ in) *adj.* whimpering; crying weakly.
4. **pard** (pärd) *n.* leopard or panther.
5. **Jealous in honor** very concerned about his honor.
6. **justice** judge.
7. **capon** (kā´ pän) *n.* roasted chicken.

Literary Analysis
Narrative and Dramatic Poetry Which qualities of both poetry and drama does the selection embody?

woeful (wō´ fəl) *adj.* full of sorrow

Full of wise saws and modern instances;[8]
And so he plays his part. The sixth age shifts
20 Into the lean and slippered pantaloon,[9]
With spectacles on nose and pouch on side,
His youthful hose[10] well saved, a world too wide
For his shrunk shank;[11] and his big manly voice,
Turning again toward childish <u>treble</u>, pipes
25 And whistles in his sound. Last scene of all,
That ends this strange eventful history,
Is second childishness, and mere oblivion,
Sans[12] teeth, sans eyes, sans taste, sans everything.

treble (treb´ əl) *n.* high-pitched voice

---

8. **wise saws and modern instances** wise sayings and modern examples that show the truth of the sayings.
9. **pantaloon** (pan´ təl o͞on´) *n.* thin, foolish old man—originally a character in old comedies.
10. **hose** (hōz) *n.* stockings.
11. **shank** (shank) *n.* leg.
12. **sans** (sanz) *prep.* without; lacking.

William Shakespeare

(1564–1616)

Theatergoers of Shakespeare's time expected to see action, humor, and passion played out on the stage, and to hear impressive dramatic speeches like those in classical drama. Shakespeare was able to forge a perfect blend of high drama and exalted language that met his audience's twin expectations.

Altogether, Shakespeare wrote more than three dozen plays, most of which continue to be read and performed today. Because of the beauty of his language and the timelessness of his themes, speeches in his plays are quoted more often than those of any other writer. "The Seven Ages of Man" is considered one of his best speeches. (For more on William Shakespeare, see p. 766.)

Review and Assess

Thinking About the Selection

1. **Respond:** Do you agree with the speaker's view of the seven stages of life? Explain.

2. **(a) Recall:** List the seven different people mentioned by the speaker. **(b) Interpret:** Which stage of life does each of these people represent?

3. **(a) Recall:** How does the speaker describe the soldier and the judge? **(b) Infer:** Are they characterized in a positive or negative way? Explain.

4. **(a) Recall:** According to the speaker, which items do the people in the final stage lack? **(b) Interpret:** How does the last age bring people back full circle to the start?

5. **(a) Draw Conclusions:** What attitude toward life does the speaker seem to be expressing?
   (b) Compare and Contrast: Do you think the speaker of "The Raven" would express the same attitude? Explain.

6. **Take a Position:** Which speaker better represents your opinion? Explain.

7. **Assess:** Does this poem in any way change your perspective about the stages of life? Why or why not?

8. **Extend:** If you could meet the speaker, which of his insights about life would you like to discuss?

Review and Assess

Literary Analysis

Narrative and Dramatic Poetry

1. Summarize the story told in the **narrative poem** "The Raven."
2. How do the rhythm and rhyme scheme of "The Raven" enhance its story?
3. "The Seven Ages of Man" is from Shakespeare's play *As You Like It*. Do you think the **dramatic poem** is clear and complete by itself? Why or why not?

Comparing Literary Works

4. Briefly compare and contrast the two speakers' attitudes toward life and death, using a chart like the one shown.

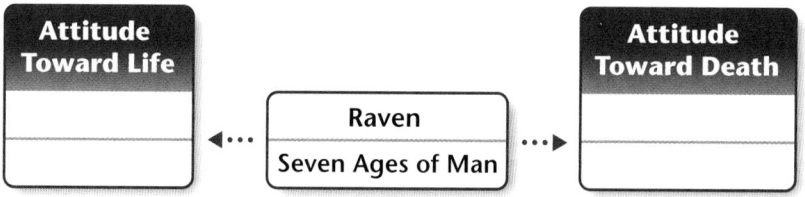

5. (a) How does the tone or attitude of Poe's narrative poem differ from that of Shakespeare's dramatic poem? (b) Which words or techniques used by the poets help to create the tone of each poem?
6. If the speakers of each poem were to meet, what advice would Shakespeare's speaker give Poe's speaker?

Reading Strategy

Drawing Inferences About the Speaker

7. In "The Raven," what can you infer about the speaker's level of education and social class from his style of speaking? Provide examples to support your answer.
8. What else can you infer about the speaker of "The Raven" from other details in the poem? Explain.
9. In lines 9–15 of "The Seven Ages of Man," what do the speaker's words reveal about his attitude toward lovers and soldiers?

Extend Understanding

10. **Cultural Connection:** Would you describe the final two stages of modern life differently from the way Jacques does? Explain.

Quick Review

Narrative poetry tells a story.

The lines of **dramatic poetry** are spoken by one or more characters to express their thoughts and feelings.

You can **draw inferences** (make educated guesses) about the speaker of a poem by noting the speaker's words, actions, and emotions.

 Take It to the Net
www.phschool.com

Take the interactive self-test online to check your understanding of these selections.

Integrate Language Skills

Vocabulary Development Lesson

Word Analysis: Latin Root -sol-

The Latin root -sol- means "alone." This root contributes to the definition of *desolate*, meaning "deserted" or "abandoned." Use the meaning of -sol- to write a definition of each italicized word.

1. A *solitary* tree remains where a forest once stood.
2. Maria enjoyed the *solitude* of the morning.
3. The *isolated* cottage is surrounded by fields.

Spelling Strategy

When a word ends in silent *e*, drop the *e* when adding a suffix that begins with a vowel. For example, *beguile* + *-ing* = *beguiling*.

Add the suffix in italics to each item below, and write the new word in your notebook.

1. rustle (*-ing*) 2. forgive (*-able*) 3. donate (*-tion*)

Concept Development: Analogies

For each sentence below, write the word from the vocabulary list on page 939 that best completes each comparison. Then, explain your reasoning.

1. *Tired* is to *energetic* as ____?____ is to *crowded*.
2. *Baritone* is to *man* as ____?____ is to *child*.
3. *Amusing* is to *entertaining* as ____?____ is to *strange*.
4. *Faded* is to *fabric* as ____?____ is to *skin*.
5. *Tiny* is to *enormous* as ____?____ is to *joyful*.
6. *Teasing* is to *tormenting* as ____?____ is to *tricking*.
7. *Work* is to *exert* as ____?____ is to *relax*.

Grammar Lesson

Punctuation With Quotation Marks

In direct quotations, quotation marks enclose the exact words a person speaks. Interrupting expressions, such as *he said* or *she asked*, are set off with commas. A comma or period is placed inside the final quotation mark, but a question mark or exclamation mark is set inside the final quotation mark only if the end mark is part of the quotation.

> **Example:**
>
> "There is a visitor," he remarked, "knocking on my door." (interrupter set off with commas)
>
> I yelled, "There's someone at my door!" (exclamation mark is part of quote)

Practice Copy the following sentences, adding the proper punctuation.

1. The only word spoken was the word *Lenore!*
2. Surely said I, something's at my window
3. That's the last word I'll hear from you! I shrieked.
4. The lover declares She is lovely!
5. The soldier, he said, is quick to exclaim Let's fight!

Writing Application Expand each sentence to include a direct quotation. Punctuate correctly.

1. The school boy whined.
2. I remember said the old man.

WG *Prentice Hall Writing and Grammar Connection: Chapter 29, Section 4*

Writing Lesson

Scene for a Movie

Imagine that you have been hired by a film studio to create a movie based on "The Raven." Write a detailed description of the scene that a scriptwriter could use to develop a script. In your description, provide detailed instructions about the mood, setting, characters, and events of the scene.

Prewriting   Start by thinking about how the poem could be expanded into a movie. Review the poem to jot down details about people, events, and setting that might appear in the opening scene.

Drafting   Using the ideas you have gathered, draft your description. Start with a paragraph describing the mood you want to establish. Then, follow with paragraphs about the plot, characters, and setting.

Revising   Look for places where you can add precise details to set a gloomy mood. Have one of your classmates assume the role of a scriptwriter to read your description and tell you if you have conveyed the feeling of the poem. Add further details if they are needed.

Model: Revising to Add Descriptive Details

lit by a single lamp that casts soft, eerie shadows on the wall,

In a darkened room ∧ a man sits reading a heavy book.

> Words such as *single lamp* and *eerie* help develop the scene.

 Prentice Hall Writing and Grammar Connection: Chapter 6, Section 4

Extension Activities

Listening and Speaking   Stage a **debate** based on "The Seven Ages of Man."

- Form two teams of two to four speakers.
- One team should support the views expressed in "The Seven Ages of Man," while the second team should support a more optimistic view.
- Speakers for each group should present their side to the class, backing up points with examples from real life.

Afterward, have the class decide which side presented the stronger argument. **[Group Activity]**

Research and Technology   Gather information for a **fact sheet** on ravens. Include details on what the birds look like, where they are found, what they eat, and other key facts. If possible, include information from Internet or encyclopedia sources that provide photos or film footage of ravens. Compare the details in your fact sheet to details about the raven found in Poe's poem.

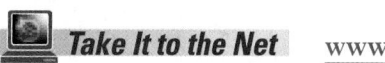 **Take It to the Net**   www.phschool.com

Go online for an additional research activity using the Internet.

Although aging and dying are natural parts of the life cycle, we often try to put thoughts about such subjects out of our minds. Shakespeare's poem "The Seven Ages of Man" makes it clear why most people prefer not to think about their own mortality. The poem traces a gloomy pathway through life. Growing old gracefully does not seem to enter into the equation. With such a hopeless view of the end of the road, who would want to be reminded of aging and death?

Sometimes, certain events—a birthday we do not wish to acknowledge or the death of a friend or relative—make aging and dying harder to ignore. When Detroit sportswriter Mitch Albom read an interview that revealed a favorite college professor was dying, Albom made the difficult decision to visit his former teacher, Morrie. Teacher and student quickly rekindled their friendship, despite years of separation. In the remaining weeks of his life, Morrie again assumed the role of teacher. The subject was savoring life and old age, even in the face of death.

from
Tuesdays with Morrie
Mitch Albom

Later that day, we talked about aging. Or maybe I should say the fear of aging—another of the issues on my what's-bugging-my-generation list. On my ride from the Boston airport, I had counted the billboards that featured young and beautiful people. There was a handsome young man in a cowboy hat, . . . two beautiful young women smiling over a shampoo bottle, a sultry-looking teenager . . . and a sexy woman in a black velvet dress, next to a man in a tuxedo. . . .

Not once did I see anyone who would pass for over thirty-five. I told Morrie I was already feeling over the hill, much as I tried desperately to stay on top of it. I worked out constantly. Watched what I ate. Checked my hairline in the mirror. I had gone from being proud to say my age—because of all I had done so young—to not bringing it up, for fear I was getting too close to forty and, therefore, professional oblivion.

Morrie had aging in better perspective.

"All this emphasis on youth—I don't buy it," he said. "Listen, I know what a misery being young can be, so don't tell me it's so great. All these kids who came to me with their struggles, their strife, their feelings of inadequacy, their sense that life was miserable. . . .

"And, in addition to all the miseries, the young are not wise. They have very little understanding about life. Who wants to live every day when you don't know what's going on? When people are manipulating you, telling you to buy this perfume and you'll be beautiful, or this pair of jeans and you'll be sexy—and you believe them! It's such nonsense."

Weren't you *ever* afraid to grow old, I asked?

"Mitch, I *embrace* aging."

Embrace it?

"It's very simple. As you grow, you learn more. If you stayed at twenty-two, you'd always be as ignorant as you were at twenty-two. Aging is not just decay, you know. It's growth. It's more than the negative that you're going to die, it's also the positive that you *understand* you're going to die, and that you live a better life because of it."

Yes, I said, but if aging were so valuable, why do people always say, "Oh, if I were young again." You never hear people say, "I wish I were sixty-five."

He smiled. "You know what that reflects? Unsatisfied lives. Unfulfilled lives. Lives that haven't found meaning. Because if you've found meaning in your life, you don't want to go back. You want to go forward. You want to see more, do more. You can't wait until sixty-five.

"Listen. You should know something. All younger people should know something. If you're always battling against getting older, you're always going to be unhappy, because it will happen anyhow.

"And Mitch?"

He lowered his voice.

"The fact is, *you* are going to die eventually."

I nodded.

"It won't matter what you tell yourself."

I know.

"But hopefully," he said, "not for a long, long time."

He closed his eyes with a peaceful look, then asked me to adjust the pillows behind his head. His body needed constant adjustment to stay comfortable. It was propped up in the chair with white pillows, yellow foam, and blue towels. At a quick glance, it seemed as if Morrie were being packed for shipping.

"Thank you," he whispered as I moved the pillows.

oblivion (ə blivˊ ē ən) *n.* condition of being forgotten

Thematic Connection
How does Morrie's view of aging contrast with that of Jacques, the speaker of "The Seven Ages of Man"?

No problem, I said.

"Mitch. What are you thinking?"

I paused before answering. Okay, I said, I'm wondering how you don't envy younger, healthy people.

"Oh, I guess I do." He closed his eyes. "I envy them being able to go to the health club, or go for a swim. Or dance. Mostly for dancing. But envy comes to me, I feel it, and then I let it go. Remember what I said about detachment? Let it go. Tell yourself, 'That's envy, I'm going to separate from it now.' And walk away."

He coughed—a long, scratchy cough—and he pushed a tissue to his mouth and spit weakly into it. Sitting there, I felt so much stronger than he, ridiculously so, as if I could lift him and toss him over my shoulder like a sack of flour. I was embarrassed by this superiority, because I did not feel superior to him in any other way.

How do you keep from envying . . .

"What?"

Me?

He smiled.

"Mitch, it is impossible for the old not to envy the young. But the issue is to accept who you are and <u>revel</u> in that. This is your time to be in your thirties. I had my time to be in my thirties, and now is my time to be seventy-eight.

"You have to find what's good and true and beautiful in your life as it is now. Looking back makes you competitive. And, age is not a competitive issue."

He exhaled and lowered his eyes, as if to watch his breath scatter into the air.

"The truth is, part of me is every age. I'm a three-year-old, I'm a five-year-old, I'm a thirty-seven-year-old, I'm a fifty-year-old. I've been through all of them, and I know what it's like. I delight in being a child when it's appropriate to be a child. I delight in being a wise old man when it's appropriate to be a wise old man. Think of all I can be! I am every age, up to my own. Do you understand?"

I nodded.

"How can I be envious of where you are—when I've been there myself?"

revel (revˊəl) *v.* take delight or pleasure

Mitch Albom

(b. 1958)

Building a career in newspaper journalism, nonfiction writing, and television commentary, Mitch Albom accomplished a great deal at an early age. He has been voted America's best sports-writer thirteen times by the Associated Press Sports Editors for his columns in the *Detroit Free Press*. He appears regularly on television and has his own radio show. Still, the impending death of his former professor made him take a step back to reevaluate his own life. *Tuesdays with Morrie* (1997) was the result of this soul-searching. More than 5 million copies of the book have been sold, securing its place on bestseller lists since its publication.

Connecting Literature Past and Present

1. How might you apply Morrie's advice on growing older to your own life?

2. How might the author's perspective have changed after hearing Morrie's views on aging and death?

3. Assess the different views on aging presented by "The Seven Ages of Man" and by Morrie. With which do you agree more?

Prepare to Read

Three Haiku ◆ Hokku Poems ◆
On the Grasshopper and the Cricket ◆ Sonnet 30

 Take It to the Net

Visit www.phschool.com
for interactive activities
and instruction related to
the selections, including
- background
- graphic organizers
- literary elements
- reading strategies

Preview

Connecting to the Literature

Almost everyone has regrets—memories of losses, disappointments, and mistakes—that can ruin the enjoyment of the present. In Sonnet 30, Shakespeare offers a way to put aside regrets about the past. The other poems in this section present a way to keep focused on the present through careful observation of nature.

Background

It is not surprising that the poet Keats chose the cricket and the grasshopper when he wanted to write about the poetry of nature. These two "musical" insects produce sounds by rubbing one part of the body against another. Male crickets rub the rough surfaces of their wing covers together. Male grasshoppers usually rub a leg against a wing with a sawing motion.

Literary Analysis

Haiku and Sonnets

The poems in this section represent two poetic forms with strict rules. The first seven poems in this section are **haiku,** a form of poetry developed in Japan that consists of three unrhymed lines of verse. The first and third lines have five syllables each. The second line has seven syllables. With very few words, haiku presents one or two striking images.

The other two poems are **sonnets**—lyric poems of fourteen lines, usually written in rhymed iambic pentameter (ten-syllable lines in which every second syllable is accented). Symbols for stressed syllables (´) and unstressed syllables (˘) show the meter in the first line of Keats's poem:

> Thĕ póetrў ŏf eárth ĭs néveř deád . . .

Comparing Literary Works

These poems present contrasting observations of the natural world. As you read, compare the natural images in each poem. Decide which element of nature each poet addresses. Consider these typical points of emphasis:

- Nature's beauty
- Nature's power
- The freedom nature embodies

Record your analysis in a diagram like the one shown. Then, consider the way each poet's thoughts of nature reflect his or her thoughts about how people live.

Reading Strategy

Reading in Sentences

In a poem, a sentence may extend for several lines and end in the middle of a line so that the poet can keep to a rhythm and rhyme scheme. To understand the literal meaning of a poem, **read in sentences,** letting the punctuation tell you when to pause or when to come to a complete stop. Notice that the comma in this haiku indicates the poem's single internal pause:

> Dragonfly catcher,
> How far have you gone today
> In your wandering?

Vocabulary Development

ceasing (sēs´ iŋ) *v.* stopping (p. 959)

wrought (rôt) *v.* formed; fashioned (p. 959)

drowsiness (drou´ zē nes) *n.* sleepiness (p. 959)

woes (wōz) *n.* great sorrows (p. 960)

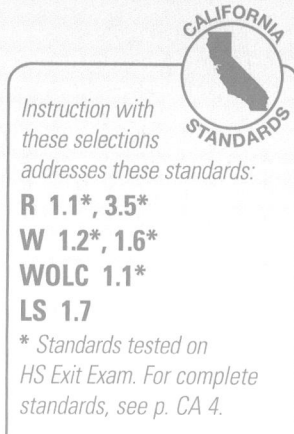

Instruction with these selections addresses these standards:

R 1.1*, 3.5*
W 1.2*, 1.6*
WOLC 1.1*
LS 1.7

* Standards tested on HS Exit Exam. For complete standards, see p. CA 4.

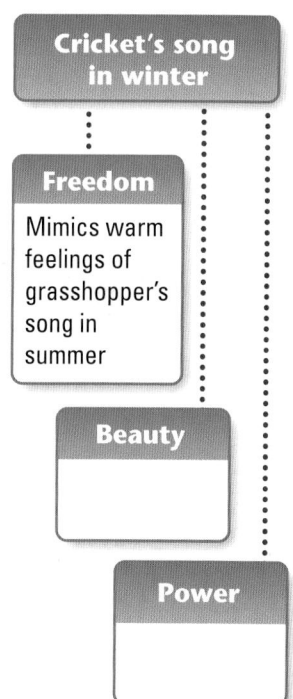

Cricket's song in winter

Freedom — Mimics warm feelings of grasshopper's song in summer

Beauty

Power

Three Haiku

Temple bells die out.
The fragrant blossoms remain.
A perfect evening!
—BASHŌ

Dragonfly catcher,
How far have you gone today
In your wandering?
—CHIYOJO

Bearing no flowers,
I am free to toss madly
Like the willow tree.
—CHIYOJO

Haiku Poets

Bashō (1644–1694)

Bashō [bash´ ō] is regarded as one of the greatest Japanese poets. In his youth, he lived in luxury as the companion to the son of a lord. Later, however, he lived apart and devoted himself to writing haiku.

Chiyojo (1887–1959)

Chiyojo [chē yō jō] was the wife of a samurai's servant. When her husband died, she became a nun and began studying poetry with a well-known teacher of haiku. Scholars celebrate the lightness of spirit in her poems.

Hokku Poems

Richard Wright

Make up your mind snail!
You are half inside your house
And halfway out!

In the falling snow
A laughing boy holds out his palms
Until they are white

Keep straight down this block
Then turn right where you will find
A peach tree blooming

Whose town did you leave
O wild and drowning spring rain
And where do you go?

Review and Assess

Thinking About the Selections

1. **Respond:** Which of the seven haiku do you like best? Why?

2. **(a) Recall:** To which senses does Bashō's haiku appeal?
   (b) Analyze Cause and Effect: In what ways do the two things that are sensed help to make the evening perfect?

3. **(a) Recall:** In what two ways does Chiyojo say she is like a willow tree? **(b) Interpret:** What impression is she trying to convey by the comparison?

4. **(a) Recall:** Which two weather events does Richard Wright describe in his haiku? **(b) Interpret:** What different feelings does he convey about these two weather events? **(c) Analyze:** Which words in each poem help to convey the feelings?

5. **(a) Distinguish:** Which of the haiku convey humor, and which seem serious? **(b) Make a Judgment:** Do you think that the haiku form works better with a more solemn or a more humorous content? Explain.

Richard Wright

(1908–1960)

Richard Wright is best known for his acclaimed novel *Native Son* (1940), which chronicles the life of an African American boy raised in poverty in Chicago. However, Wright also produced a wide range of other types of works, including essays and poems. As a poet, Wright experimented with different forms, including the traditional Japanese haiku.

On the Grasshopper and the Cricket

John Keats

The poetry of earth is never dead:
When all the birds are faint with the hot sun,
And hide in cooling trees, a voice will run
From hedge to hedge about the new-mown mead;[1]
5   That is the Grasshopper's—he takes the lead
In summer luxury,—he has never done
With his delights; for when tired out with fun
He rests at ease beneath some pleasant weed.
The poetry of earth is <u>ceasing</u> never:
10 On a lone winter evening, when the frost
Has <u>wrought</u> a silence, from the stove there shrills
The Cricket's song, in warmth increasing ever,
And seems to one in <u>drowsiness</u> half lost,
The Grasshopper's among some grassy hills.

ceasing (sēs´ iŋ) *v.* stopping

wrought (rôt) *v.* formed; fashioned

drowsiness (drou´ zē nes) *n.* sleepiness

---

1. **mead** (mēd) *n.* meadow.

Review and Assess

Thinking About the Selection

1. **Respond:** Which scene painted by the poet appeals more to you? Why?

2. **(a) Compare and Contrast:** In what ways are the two insects alike and different? **(b) Associate:** How are the two insects connected in the speaker's mind?

3. **(a) Interpret:** What does the speaker mean by saying "The poetry of earth is never dead"? **(b) Analyze:** In which other line of the poem do you find this line closely echoed? **(c) Interpret:** Do you think there is a difference in meaning between these related lines? Explain.

4. **Generalize:** What one word would you use to describe this poem? Explain your choices.

5. **Make a Judgment:** Does the sonnet form help or hinder Keats in getting across his meaning? Explain.

6. **Apply:** In your environment, what "poetry of nature" do you experience at different times of the year? Explain, citing examples from at least two seasons.

John Keats

(1795–1821)
The poems of John Keats are among the most admired in the English language. Remarkably, Keats accomplished this distinction in spite of his premature death at the age of twenty-five.

Keats is considered one of the main poets of the Romantic Movement, a group of writers who stressed the importance of individual experience and the spiritual connection between people and nature.

SONNET 30

William Shakespeare

When to the sessions of sweet silent thought
I summon up remembrance of things past,
I sigh the lack of many a thing I sought,
And with old <u>woes</u>' new wail my dear times waste:[1]
5   Then can I drown an eye, unused to flow,
For precious friends hid in death's dateless[2] night,
And weep afresh love's long since cancelled woe,
And moan the expense[3] of many a vanished sight:
Then can I grieve at grievances foregone,[4]
10   And heavily from woe to woe tell o'er[5]
The sad account of fore-bemoanèd moan,[6]
Which I new pay as if not paid before.
But if the while I think on thee, dear friend,
All losses are restored and sorrows end.

woes (wōz) *n.* great sorrows

---

1. **And . . . waste** and by grieving anew for past sorrows, ruin the precious present.
2. **dateless** endless.
3. **expense** loss.
4. **foregone** past and done with.
5. **tell o'er** count up.
6. **fore-bemoanèd moan** sorrows suffered in the past.

Review and Assess

Thinking About the Selection

1. **Respond:** Would you want the speaker of the poem as a friend? Explain?

2. **(a) Recall:** In the opening lines of Sonnet 30, how does the speaker refer to his memories? **(b) Infer:** In general, how does the speaker feel when he remembers the past? Explain.

3. **(a) Infer:** In line 5, what does "drown an eye" mean? **(b) Analyze Cause and Effect:** Which thoughts cause the speaker to "drown an eye"? Why?

4. **Clarify:** What is the speaker describing in lines 10–12?

5. **Hypothesize:** How would the effect of this poem be different without the final two lines?

6. **Evaluate:** Do you agree with the assessment of the value of friendship? Why or why not?

William Shakespeare

(1564–1616)
William Shakespeare was as much a poet as a playwright. He not only wrote his 37 plays in verse, but also composed 154 sonnets. Taken together, the sonnets seem to tell a story. The "plot" is not always clear, but it seems obvious that the main characters are a young nobleman, a lady, a poet (probably Shakespeare himself), and a rival poet. Some of the best sonnets, like Sonnet 30, are addressed to the nobleman. (For more on William Shakespeare, see p. 766.)

Review and Assess

Literary Analysis

Haiku and Sonnets

1. (a) What are the two main images in Wright's second **haiku**?
   (b) What is the connection between these images?

2. A Shakespearean **sonnet** usually presents an idea or question in the first quatrain (four lines), explores the idea in the next two quatrains, and reaches a conclusion in the couplet (two lines) at the end. Use a chart like this to analyze the content of Sonnet 30.

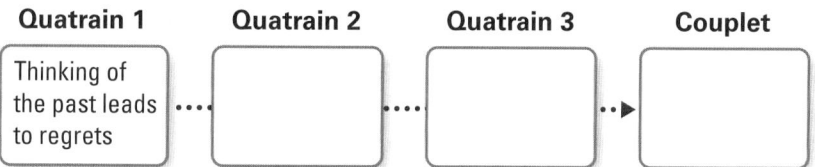

Quatrain 1 | Quatrain 2 | Quatrain 3 | Couplet

Thinking of the past leads to regrets

3. Keats's **sonnet** is Petrarchan, a form consisting of an octave (eight lines) and a sestet (six lines). In his poem, how is the content of the octave and the sestet related?

Comparing Literary Works

4. (a) Which of these poets use images from the natural world to explain something about human nature? (b) Which of these poets seem to focus primarily on the natural world rather than on people?

5. Do you think the haiku writers would agree with Keats that "the poetry of earth is never dead"? Explain your answer.

Reading Strategy

Reading in Sentences

6. In Sonnet 30, why do lines 1 and 10 lack punctuation marks?

7. In "On the Grasshopper and the Cricket," why do lines 1 and 9 end in colons rather than in periods?

8. How do the haiku writers use or omit punctuation to convey a dominant impression in their poems?

Extend Understanding

9. **Science Connection:** In what ways can scientists develop a different understanding of nature by reading poems that focus on natural images?

Quick Review

A **haiku** is a poem in three unrhymed lines (of five, seven, and five syllables each) that conveys a single, dominant impression by means of images from nature.

A **sonnet** is a lyric poem of fourteen lines, usually written in rhymed iambic pentameter.

To understand the literal meaning of a poem, **read in sentences** rather than lines, using punctuation to determine when to pause or stop.

 Take It to the Net
www.phschool.com
Take the interactive self-test online to check your understanding of these selections.

Integrate Language Skills

Vocabulary Development Lesson

Word Analysis: Anglo-Saxon Suffix -ness

In his sonnet "On the Grasshopper and the Cricket," Keats describes a person half lost in drowsiness. *Drowsiness* ends in the Anglo-Saxon suffix *-ness*, meaning "in the state or condition of." When added to the adjective *drowsy*, the suffix *-ness* forms the noun *drowsiness*, meaning "in the state of being drowsy or sleepy."

For each definition below, add *-ness* to the adjective in italics to create a noun.

1. state of being *happy*
2. state of acting *friendly*
3. state of being *thoughtful*
4. state of being *shrill* in tone
5. state of being *weary*

Concept Development: Antonyms

In your notebook, write the lettered word that is most nearly opposite to the first word.

1. wrought: (a) created, (b) seen, (c) destroyed
2. ceasing: (a) escaping, (b) rewarding, (c) beginning
3. drowsiness: (a) frankness, (b) alertness, (c) quietness
4. woe: (a) terror, (b) ease, (c) joy

Spelling Strategy

When adding a suffix to a word ending in *y* preceded by a consonant, change the *y* to *i* and then add the suffix: *drowsy* + *-ness* = *drowsiness*

Add the suffix in italics to each word below, and then use the new word in a sentence.

1. grassy + *-er*   2. heavy + *-ly*   3. marry + *-ed*

Grammar Lesson

Hyphens

A **hyphen** (-) is often used to connect two or more modifiers that are used together. You should use a hyphen to connect a compound modifier that comes *before* a noun. If the compound modifier comes *after* the noun, however, the hyphen is dropped.

In these examples, the compound modifier is in italics and the noun is underlined.

> **Before noun:** The grasshopper jumped from hedge to hedge in the *new-mown* <u>meadow</u>.

> **After noun:** The grasshopper's <u>song</u> was *well rehearsed*.

Practice Copy the following sentences in your notebook. Insert hyphens where they are needed.

1. We revel in the never ending poetry of earth.
2. The pleasure seeking grasshopper rests under a plant.
3. The weed ridden meadow is full of insects.
4. The hills are frost covered and silent.
5. The cricket's song has an ever increasing tempo.

Writing Application Write sentences that contain these hyphenated compound modifiers.

1. long-lost   2. tear-stained

 Prentice Hall Writing and Grammar Connection: Chapter 29, Section 5

Writing Lesson

Haiku Series

Write three related haiku, either about the same subject or on the same theme. Remember that a haiku captures a feeling with one or two concrete images and follows a strict format: three unrhymed lines of five, seven, and five syllables each.

Prewriting List several possible topics for the three haiku. Then, jot down several concrete images that each topic suggests.

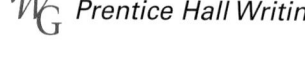

Model: Listing and Itemizing Haiku Images

Topics	Images
Birds	Flying freely
Basketball	Singing brightly
Autumn	Fleeing winter

> The images for the chosen topic are concise, yet descriptive.

Drafting As you draft, do not worry about getting exactly the right number of syllables—you can perfect the form as you revise.

Revising Count the syllables in each line. If you do not have the correct number, decide which words you can change, leave out, or add to achieve the desired number of syllables. In addition, make sure that each of your haiku conveys the impression you intended.

Prentice Hall Writing and Grammar Connection: Chapter 6, Section 2

Extension Activities

Listening and Speaking Images from the natural world are fundamental to most haiku, particularly those created by Japanese poets. Prepare a brief **oral presentation** connecting the Japanese landscape and haiku.

- Research the geography and art of Japan.
- Print out or copy several pieces of Japanese art to accompany your presentation.

After your presentation, explain how the Japanese haiku you have read relate to the country's landscape and art.

Research and Technology Shakespeare penned 154 sonnets. Write a **research paper** about the information that is known about his sonnets. Explain the stories they tell, as well as their characters. In addition to Sonnet 30, read at least three more of his sonnets. In your report, incorporate quotations from the sonnets to support your ideas.

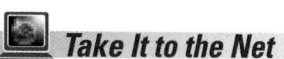 **Take It to the Net** www.phschool.com

Go online for an additional research activity using the Internet.

Professional Journals

About Professional Journals

A professional journal is a magazine or newspaper published for people who work in a specific field or industry, such as computer technology, agriculture, or finance. The articles in a professional journal inform readers about new products, techniques, and trends. "Passing Time in Times Past," excerpted here, is from *Book Links*, a professional journal for teachers and librarians.

Professional journals often present a complex, in-depth view of a subject that can be understood only by specialists in that field. For instance, different medical journals might present research on cell biology or cardiology or pediatric medicine. The editors of each journal assume that readers already possess basic knowledge of their subject, so the article can focus on presenting specific research results and analysis.

Reading Strategy

Identifying a Target Audience's Purpose

When authors write a magazine article, they do so with a specific purpose in mind, such as to entertain, to inform, or to persuade. Likewise, when you read a magazine article, you also have a specific purpose in mind. You may be reading purely for amusement, to learn about a subject, or to help you make a decision.

Readers of a professional journal like *Book Links* also have specific purposes for reading. They may read to achieve goals such as the following:

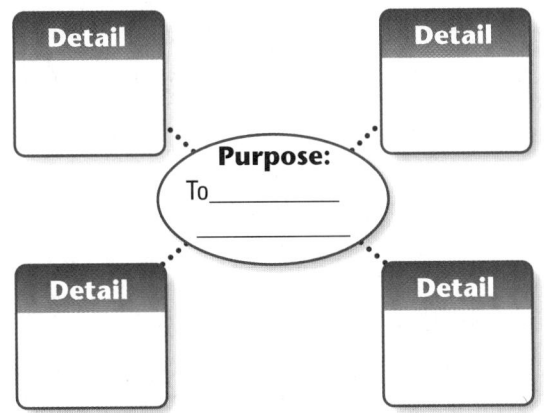

- To recommend new books to students
- To order books for the library
- To keep up with the latest trends and issues

As you read this excerpt from "Passing Time in Times Past," put yourself in the place of a teacher or librarian. Identify your purpose for reading, and then write down details you find that help you achieve that purpose.

Books and Bytes: Digital Connections
Passing Time in Times Past
Virginia A. Walter

Both pundits and parents like to complain about the lack of historical knowledge displayed by today's young people. Test scores and anecdotes alike document the failure of teenagers to recognize the names of historical figures such as Lenin (frequently mistaken for a dead rock star) or Joan of Arc (some times confused with a biblical character who was swallowed by a whale).

> This article starts with humorous examples that capture readers' interest in the topic.

On the other hand, we observe the popularity of the historical series Dear America . . . and note how enthusiastically middle-school girls read the historical novels of Karen Cushman. Certainly, some children have found reading and learning about past times to be a favorite pastime, not just a dull chunk of the social studies curriculum; and there are many skilled, creative teachers who know how to make history come alive for children whose preoccupation with the present and fascination with the future sometimes seem to leave little time for the past.

> This article provides readers with an annotated list of resources.

CD-ROMs and the Internet have proven to be excellent vehicles for putting some of the raw materials of history, the primary sources used by scholars to re-create the past, in the hands of young

> Each entry includes the author, title, and price of a recommended item, as well as a brief description.

historians. The interactive nature of CD-ROMs has also made them natural vehicles for edutainment ventures, creating game-like environments and simulations in which children can explore historical themes and events and learn while they play. The best of these CD-ROMs can support classroom learning, provide information for school reports, or provide independent, informal learning opportunities at home and in the library.

Here are some CD-ROMs and a few tantalizing books, grouped under broad topics that lend themselves to further exploration, to help more children find the delights of traveling into the past.

Castles

CD-ROMs

Castle Explorer. 1996. $29.95.

Ages 9–12. Children act as spies to the king, playing the role of maid or page boy, learning a great deal about daily life in a medieval castle while they search for answers to four questions and pieces of a map. Six books in a chained library and pop-up text provide explanatory text in this cleverly designed history game, based on Steven Biesty's book *Castle*.

Books

Macaulay, David. *Castle.* 1977. 74p. $16 (0-395-25784-0); paper, $7.95 (0-395-32920-5).

Ages 9–12. This Caldecott Honor Book for 1978 tells the story of the construction of a thirteenth-century castle with a refreshing combination of humor and authority.

Winthrop, Elizabeth. *The Castle in the Attic.* 1985. 179p. $15.95 (0-8234-0579-6); paper, $4.99 (0-440-40941-1)

Ages 9–12. The adventures begin when William shrinks to fit into the realistic toy castle in the attic.

Journalism

CD-ROMs

Chronicle of the 20th Century. 1996. $39.95.

Ages 9–up. A charmingly anachronistic newspaper editor's office, complete with a manual typewriter and a ticker tape machine, is the starting point for this exploration of twentieth-century history up to the early days of 1996. There are multiple access points for young people searching for specific events, dates, or names, as well as some intriguing opportunities for browsing and for more in-depth research on eight major focus areas, such as the Russian Revolution, the two world wars, space exploration, and the fall of Communism. All entries contain visual materials as well as text, and many also include sound or video clips, such as Orson Welles' famous "War of the Worlds" broadcast and Yasir Arafat addressing the United Nations in Arabic. With newspapers and headlines making up the framework for this CD-ROM, it also makes a good springboard to books about journalism.

Books

Fleischman, Paul. *Dateline: Troy.* 1996. 79p. $15.99 (1-56402-469-5).

Ages 11–up. The author juxtaposes the history of the Trojan War with newspaper clippings of contemporary events, making the parallels between Homer's world and our own unmistakably clear.

Granfield, Linda. *Extra! Extra! The Who, What, Where, When, and Why of Newspapers.* Illus. by Bill Slavin. 1994. 72p. $16.99 (0-531-98683-6); paper, $7.95 (0-531-07049-2).

Ages 9–12. This book contains everything kids ever wanted to know about how a newspaper is published—including information on how to publish their own.

The Gold Rush

CD-ROMs

Klondike Gold. 1996. $39.95.

Ages 11–up. American children more familiar with the California gold rush will find some interesting differences and similarities in the Klondike gold rush that took place in the far north of Canada in 1896. A pan of gold nuggets serves as the main menu on this CD-ROM, leading to information about this rip-roaring episode in Yukon history, an interactive exploration of the placer mining process, and a rich segment on "The Cremation of Sam McGee" by Robert Service, the bard of the Yukon. Historical photographs form the foundation for multiple hypertext links to related topics, and honky-tonk music sets the tone.

Books

Fleischman, Sid. *Bandit's Moon.* Illus. by Jos. A. Smith. 1998. 136p. $15 (0-688-15830-7).

Ages 9–12. Twelve-year-old orphan Annyrose tells what happened when she was taken in by Joaquin Murieta and his band of outlaws during the California gold rush.

Service, Robert W. *The Cremation of Sam McGee.* Illus. by Ted Harrison. 1987. 32p. $18 (0-688-06903-7).

Ages 9–up. An illustrated edition of the poetic tall tale about a frozen gold miner that is featured in the *Klondike Gold* CD-ROM.

Yee, Paul. *Tales from Gold Mountain.* Illus. by Simon Ng. 1999. 64p. $18.95 (0-88899-098-7).

Ages 9–12. Yee blends folklore, fact, and fiction in these eight haunting stories about Chinese immigrants in North America.

Information is presented in three categories: *Castles, Journalism,* and *The Gold Rush.*

Teachers and librarians may find the inclusion of books and CD-ROMS especially useful.

Formatting, such as the use of titles and subheads, helps readers locate the content they wish to find.

Check Your Comprehension

1. What is the advantage to children in learning from a CD-ROM, according to Virginia A. Walter?
2. What is the subject of Paul Fleischman's book *Dateline: Troy*?
3. How does Walter organize the materials that she recommends?

Applying the Reading Strategy

Identifying a Target Audience's Purpose

4. Use a chart like the one shown to identify three purposes that either a librarian or a teacher might have for reading the article in *Book Links*. For each, indicate which details in the article meet that purpose.

Purposes of Specific Audiences

A. Librarian Purpose
 1.
 2. Details
 3.

B. Teacher Purpose
 1.
 2. Details
 3.

Activity

Writing an Annotated Discography

The article presented here offers reviews of books and CD-ROMs devoted to certain subjects. When the subject of a review is music, it often takes the form of an annotated discography. An annotated discography lists songs or CDs by a particular artist or in a specific genre and offers opinions about their quality. Using the chart below as a guide, write an annotated discography reviewing a category of music. Include your evaluation of each item and provide details to support our opinions.

Music Title	Your Reaction	Supporting Detail

Contrasting Informational Materials

Professional Journals and General Newspapers

1. Imagine that the books presented by Walter were reviewed in a daily newspaper with a general adult readership. (a) What book information does the professional journal article contain that a newspaper might omit? (b) What details might be expanded in a newspaper review? (c) What other information might a newspaper include that was omitted in this article?
2. Suppose that the same books in this article were reviewed in a magazine or newspaper written for young people. (a) How would the content of such a review differ from the content in the article presented here? (b) How would the style of the two kinds of reviews be different?

Writing WORKSHOP

Exposition: Comparison-and-Contrast Essay

A **comparison-and-contrast essay** addresses two or more subjects to show their similarities and differences. It may describe or explain, reveal strengths and weaknesses, or persuade readers to value one subject over another. In this workshop, you will write a comparison-and-contrast essay on subjects that are suitable to this type of exposition.

Assignment Criteria. Your comparison-and-contrast essay should have the following characteristics:

● Analysis and discussion of similarities and differences between two or more things, people, places, or ideas

● Factual details about each subject

● A purpose for comparison and contrast

● Equal presentation of each subject using one of two organizations: subject-by-subject or point-by-point

To preview the criteria on which your comparison-and-contrast essay may be assessed, see the Rubric on page 971.

Prewriting

Choose a topic. Explore topics in terms of clear opposites (winter/summer), clear similarities (baseball/cricket), or close relationships (book/movie). **Brainstorm** for topics by starting with names of people, places, objects, or ideas. Then, note related subjects that come to mind. Notice relationships that interest you, and then choose one to develop.

Identify your audience. Your intended audience will direct the type of information you include—from the level of vocabulary you use to the level of analysis you pursue. Consider your audience as you gather information.

Specify your purpose. To identify a purpose for your essay, consider the following possibilities:

● *To persuade*—You want readers to accept your opinion that one subject is preferable to another.

● *To explain*—You want readers to understand something special about the subjects.

● *To describe*—You want readers to understand the basic similarities and differences between your subjects.

Gather details. As you generate the details to use in your comparison-and-contrast essay, look at the ideas you have collected and consider the main elements you will discuss.

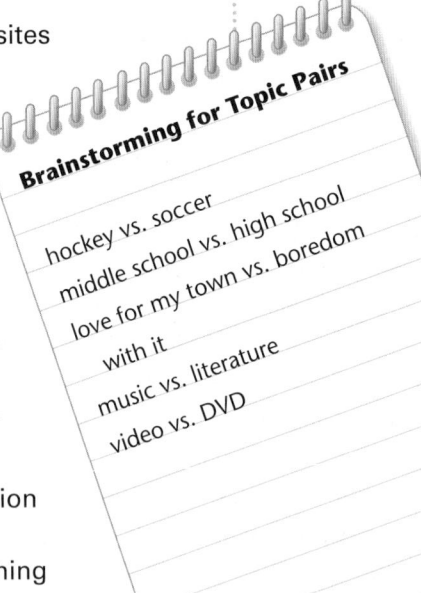

Brainstorming for Topic Pairs

hockey vs. soccer

middle school vs. high school

love for my town vs. boredom with it

music vs. literature

video vs. DVD

Student Model

Before you begin drafting your comparison-and-contrast essay, read this student model and review the characteristics of an effective comparison-and-contrast essay.

Lauren DeLoach
Bernice, Louisiana

Ambivalence

When I consider my conflicting feelings about my hometown, I see that there are things that I love and hate about living in Bernice, Louisiana, a nineties version of Mayberry. I love the security of a small town, and I hate it. I love the way that my town is not clouded by the smog of a city, and I hate it too. I love it and I hate that I love it.

> Lauren's essay will compare two feelings: what she loves and what she hates about her hometown.

I love and hate the security in my town for a number of reasons. I love it because I know that it is my dogs scratching at my door at 5:30 in the morning and not some dangerous stranger. In my town, a fifteen-car traffic jam is front-page news. On the other hand, I hate that it gets a little boring sometimes. I don't want criminals at my door, but a little excitement would be nice.

> Using a point-by-point organization, Lauren addresses the first contrast in her attitudes about her town: She feels ambivalence about its security.

I am fond of the size of Bernice and I detest it, too. I'm glad that only fifteen cars is a major traffic jam. But I hate that I have to drive sixteen miles to the nearest major store. I love and hate that my town is so small that I know everybody's first, middle, and last names. I like it because I have a "tab" at the grocery story and the drug store, so that eliminates the necessity of money. I hate that everybody knows me because that means that everybody finds out about whom I'm dating, whom I once dated, my height, weight, and age. I also hate that we all know each other so well that the most entertaining news we can come up with to put in the Bernice Banner is that Peggy Jane and her brother JC visited their Aunt Goosey Lou in the nursing home. But by knowing everyone so well, I've made friends who are trustworthy because we know all of each other's deepest secrets.

> These facts support the writer's ideas and opinions.

Even though I say that I detest some things, home wouldn't be home without these silly quirks. I love that my parents and their friends are known as the "elite group" because they have traveled beyond Texas, Arkansas, and Mississippi. I love saying that I have read the *Iliad* to people who think I would not read such a book. I know that it sounds like I love the provincialism that small towns can impose, but the smells of fresh-cut grass and the gardenia bush outside my door are what make my home my home.

This is what I love and what I say I hate, but I don't really. The overall feeling I get from living in Bernice is ambivalence. I love it and I hate that I love such goofy things. But the parts of home that seem so trivial are the ones that make you who you are. That makes a place your home.

> Lauren's comparison allows her to be funny, but also helps her reflect on her ideas.

Drafting

Choose an organization. Choose an organization that suits your topic. Point-by-point and subject-by-subject plans are the most common types of comparison-and-contrast writing:

- **Point-by-point organization:** This organization allows you to move between your subjects, sharpening your points of comparison and contrast and addressing each feature for both subjects.

- **Subject-by-subject organization:** This organization allows you to compare your subjects as complete units. First, address all aspects of one subject, and then devote full attention to the other. Be careful to address the same features and devote equal time to each subject.

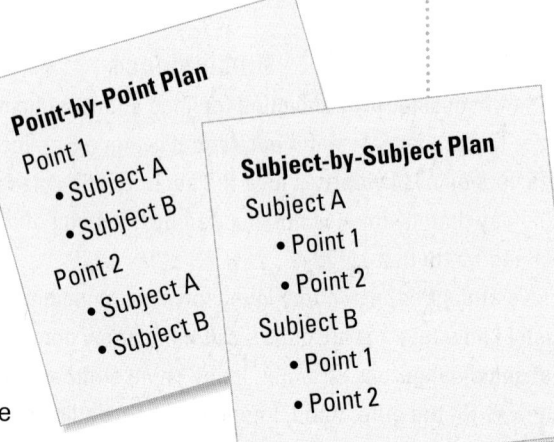

Point-by-Point Plan

Point 1
- Subject A
- Subject B

Point 2
- Subject A
- Subject B

Subject-by-Subject Plan

Subject A
- Point 1
- Point 2

Subject B
- Point 1
- Point 2

Support generalizations with specifics. As you point out similarities and differences, include facts or information to back up your assertions. For example, if you compare and contrast the climates of Antarctica and Australia, you should provide statistics of their annual temperatures, rainfall records, and other specific evidence to demonstrate your points.

Revising

Revise to make comparisons and contrasts clear. Review each paragraph to be sure that you lead the reader to see the comparisons and contrasts you draw. Using two different colors, mark your draft to distinguish between the two subjects you discuss. Then, evaluate the places where the two subjects meet. Add transitional words or phrases to make the shift clear.

Model: Revising for Clarity

I love and hate the security in my town for a number of reasons.

I love it because I know that it is my dogs scratching at my door at 5:30 in the morning and not some dangerous stranger. In my town, a fifteen-car traffic jam is front-page news.

On the other hand,

I hate that it gets a little boring sometimes. I don't want criminals at my door, but a little excitement would be nice.

A topic sentence helps call out the point of comparison. The transition *on the other hand* shows readers the shift between subjects.

Revise to add detail. To help your readers understand the comparison you make, add enough detail to explain the differences and similarities you see. Review your draft to find vague language. Wherever you can, add information that strengthens your description or analysis.

Vague: In contrast to literature, popular music forms a soundtrack in our lives.

Specific: In contrast to literature that we must read to enjoy, popular music, like the top 40 tunes we hear on the radio, forms a soundtrack for our lives. We can hear it as we drive, shop, or even fall asleep at night.

Compare the model and the nonmodel. Why is the model more effective than the nonmodel?

Nonmodel	Model
I know that it sounds like I love the things that small towns include, but the smells outside my door are what make my home a home.	I know that it sounds like I love the provincialism that small towns can impose, but the smells of fresh-cut grass and the gardenia bush outside my door are what make my home a home.

Publishing and Presenting

When you are satisfied with your draft, share your ideas and your writing with a wider audience.

Deliver an oral presentation. Read your comparison-and-contrast essay aloud to an audience of your classmates. If you attempted in your essay to persuade your audience to see the benefits of one subject over another, consider asking classmates whether or not they agree with your position after hearing your evidence.

 Prentice Hall Writing and Grammar Connection: Chapter 9

Rubric for Self-Assessment

Evaluate your comparison-and-contrast essay using the following criteria and rating scale:

Criteria	Rating Scale				
	Not very				Very
How well does the essay identify similarities and differences?	1	2	3	4	5
How well does the essay provide factual details about each subject?	1	2	3	4	5
How well defined is the purpose of the essay?	1	2	3	4	5
How effective is the organization of the essay?	1	2	3	4	5

Listening and Speaking WORKSHOP

Comparing Media Coverage

Whether information comes from the Internet or a 24-hour cable network, it is useful to know how to analyze and compare media coverage.

Prepare to View

Every news format and news source has strengths and weaknesses. As you follow news stories, consider the way they are filtered and presented to you.

Consider your sources. Certain types of news media are designed to cover specific types of news events. Consider these sources and the variety and quality of reporting they represent:

● nightly network news or local television news

● Internet Web pages of news organizations

● public radio

● national magazines or daily newspapers

● cable news channels

Recognize differences. Before you compare media coverage, think about the differences you are likely to find among sources. A good general news source might present news coverage of a variety of topics— science, politics, and entertainment. However, if you are looking for coverage of one issue, you might be concerned with the depth of coverage rather than variety.

Identify bias. Bias occurs when an organization has a special interest in reporting the news in a particular way. If you anticipate bias, you will have a heightened awareness when you view the news source. Find out which organization sponsors the coverage, and think about how that might influence reporting of a particular issue or group of issues.

Using Criteria to Compare Coverage

Accuracy
• Are there any mistakes in the facts presented?
• Are the news reports misleading viewers by leaving out essential information?

Comprehensiveness
• Do the news reports support their assertions with evidence?
• Do the reports present an adequate level of detail and complexity?

Credibility
• How close were the reporters to the events they are reporting?
• Do the reports cite well-known authorities or published studies?

Objectivity
• Do news sources present more than one side of an issue?
• Does any source have a vested interest in presenting facts in a particular way?

View and Compare

Use consistent criteria. When you watch or listen to coverage of a news story reported by several sources, you are likely to notice differences. Consider the questions in the chart shown on this page.

Make comparisons. Once you have evaluated each news source, a side-by-side comparison, using the same criteria, should be straightforward. Notice the similarities and differences among the reports you find to determine the news sources you can trust.

(Activity:)
Research and Discussion
Choose a current issue to research as a group. Find three sources from television, radio, or the Internet. Compare coverage of that issue and discuss your findings.

Assessment WORKSHOP

Analogies

The reading sections of some tests often require you to answer multiple-choice questions to complete analogies. Use the following strategies to help you:

- An *analogy* establishes a relationship between one pair of words so that a similar relationship can be established between a second pair.

- To complete an analogy, identify the relationship between the initial pair of words, and then look for a second pair with a similar relationship.

- Common relationships to look for are synonyms, antonyms, cause and effect, part and whole, example and group, and product and function.

Test-Taking Strategies

- Say the relationship of the first word pair aloud to yourself in a test sentence. For example, "joy/smile" would be "When you feel joy, you smile."

- Use the same relationship when putting the second pair of words into a sentence. Discard pairs that do not make sense in your test sentence.

Sample Test Item

Directions: Read the word pair, and then choose the letter of the word pair that is most similar to the example.

1. MINT : HERB ::
   A garage : car
   B score : game
   C snow : precipitation
   D sow : harvest

Answer and Explanation

C is the correct answer. To arrive at the correct answer, identify the relationship first: "Mint is a type of herb." Then, look for a word pair that has a similar relationship. Since garage is *not* a type of car, score is *not* a type of game, and sow is *not* a type of harvest, the answer cannot be *A, B,* or *D.* Snow is a type of precipitation, therefore *C* is the correct choice.

▶ Practice

Directions: Read each word pair, and then choose the letter of the word pair that is most similar to the example.

1. SUNSCREEN : PROTECT ::
   A shampoo : rinse
   B sand : bucket
   C curtains : drapes
   D label : inform

2. STATEMENT : CONFIDENCE ::
   A excitement : happiness
   B proposal : intuition
   C question : confusion
   D interruption : disappointment

3. CONDUCTOR : SYMPHONY ::
   A orchestra : violin
   B driver : bus
   C tour guide : argument
   D official : relaxation

UNIT 10 The Epic

Ulysses Deriding Polyphemus, 1819, J.M.W. Turner, The National Gallery, London

Exploring the Genre

Turn the page to enter a world of heroes, gods, and sweeping adventures. Tradition tells us that the blind poet Homer wrote the *Odyssey* after it had been passed down by generations of Greek singers. If it had not been for this ancient scribe, many generations of readers would never have learned about the heroic exploits of Odysseus and his companions.

An **epic** is a long narrative poem about the deeds of gods or heroes. Early in the *Odyssey*, Homer presents an epic question. Odysseus asks:

> "Where shall a man find sweetness
> to surpass his own home and his
> parents? In far lands he shall not,
> though he find a house of gold. What
> of my sailing, then, from Troy?"

The *Odyssey* itself is the answer.

▲ **Critical Viewing** In this painting, inspired by the *Odyssey*, which dangers seem to present themselves? **[Interpret]**

Why **Read Literature?**

As you read an ancient work of literature, it is interesting to think about its influence on subsequent generations of authors and readers. The *Odyssey* is a powerful tale that has been read for many different reasons since it was first written down. Here is a sampling of reasons to read this epic and the works that follow:

1

Read for the Love of Literature

The singers who spread the tale of the *Odyssey* before it was written down were highly skilled poets. Each would change the tale slightly, embellishing certain parts to create his own dramatic effects and style. Enjoy the final product of many skillful poets as you read an excerpt from the ***Odyssey***, page 980.

A powerful story can take on new life when it is read by authors who are inspired to create works of their own. See which lesson Constantine Cavafy took from Odysseus' long absence from home when you read his poem **"Ithaca,"** page 1058.

2

Read to Be Entertained

Great adventures are not limited to the pages of ancient epics. Find the connection between ancient Greek adventure and a heart-pounding modern-day odyssey through space as you read the excerpt from ***Lost Moon***, page 1064.

3

Read for Information

In 1962, John Glenn was the first American to orbit Earth. Thirty-six years later, at the age of 77, he joined the crew of the space shuttle to go into orbit again, eliciting both admiration and controversy. Read both sides of the debate over Glenn's 1998 space flight in **Reading Informational Materials: Newspaper Editorials,** page 1066.

 Take It to the Net

Visit the Web site for online instruction and activities related to each selection in this unit.
www.phschool.com

How to Read Literature

Use Strategies for Reading an Epic

In ancient societies, wandering storytellers told stories of gods and heroes that would sometimes take days to complete. To help the storytellers remember such lengthy pieces, epic tales were composed in poetry and recited to musical accompaniment. Their language and sentence structure may present some difficulty for you as you read. Apply the following strategies to help you.

1. Summarize.

You can be certain that you have understood a passage when you are able to offer a clear, concise summary of the action. Stop to summarize what has happened at each pause in the action. Eliminate any aspects or events that are not directly related to the basic plot.

2. Read in sentences.

You may become confused if you stop at the end of every line of verse in an epic because sentences frequently flow to the next line.

- Be guided by the punctuation, not simply the ends of lines, in determining where to pause.

- Use periods and the ends of paragraphs to maintain the natural flow of words.

3. Compare and contrast.

Finding similarities and recognizing differences can help you understand your reactions to different texts.

- Choose basic categories such as style, subject, and viewpoint to compare and contrast.

- Compare specific passages that are similar enough to enable you to draw effective comparisons and contrasts.

> The lovely voices in ardor appealing over the water
> made me crave to listen, . . .
>
> —from the *Odyssey*

> I don't enjoy singing
> this trio, fatal and valuable.
>
> —from "Siren Song"

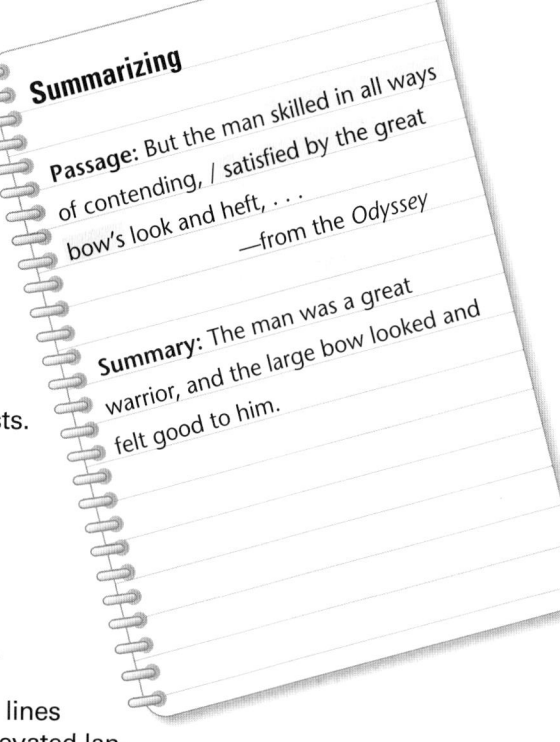

Summarizing

Passage: But the man skilled in all ways of contending, / satisfied by the great bow's look and heft, . . .
        —from the *Odyssey*

Summary: The man was a great warrior, and the large bow looked and felt good to him.

The subject of these two passages is the same, but the lines express different viewpoints. The *Odyssey* uses formal, elevated language, whereas "Siren Song" uses informal language. The *Odyssey* passage simply tells the story, but "Siren Song" hints at a deeper meaning.

As you read the selections in this unit, review the reading strategies and look at the notes in the side column. Use the suggestions to apply the strategies and interact with the text.

Prepare to Read

from the Odyssey, Part 1

"Circe Meanwhile had gone her Ways . . . ," 1924, William Russell Flint, New York Public Library

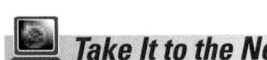
Preview

Connecting to the Literature

Whether you are journeying across town or to another country, it sometimes seems to take forever to reach your destination. Just getting there can be quite an adventure! In the *Odyssey*, you will follow a journey that took far longer than expected and experience the amazing adventures that took place along the way.

Background

The *Odyssey* describes what happened to the Greek hero Odysseus on his way home after the Trojan War. According to legend, the Trojan War was sparked when Paris, son of the king of Troy, ran off with Helen, the most beautiful woman in the world and the wife of Menelaus of Sparta. A Greek force attacked Troy (in modern-day Turkey) to recapture her and was finally victorious after ten years of fighting.

Literary Analysis
The Epic Hero

An epic is a long poem about the adventures of gods or heroes. The epic's central character, its **epic hero,** is a larger-than-life figure from history or legend. The hero undertakes a dangerous voyage, demonstrating traits—such as courage, loyalty, and honor—that are valued by the society in which the epic originates. In this passage, Odysseus shows his bravery and leadership:

> Now, by the gods, I drove my big hand spike
> deep in the embers, charring it again,
> and cheered my men along with battle talk
> to keep their courage up; no quitting now.

As you read, use a chart like the one shown to record traits or actions that prove Odysseus to be an epic hero.

Connecting Literary Elements

At the center of every epic is a **conflict**—a struggle between opposing forces. Conflicts may occur between characters, between a character and nature, or within a character's mind. In an epic, conflicts often put the traits of the epic hero on display. In the *Odyssey*, notice that conflicts arise as the hero confronts his enemies and as he wrestles with his own thoughts.

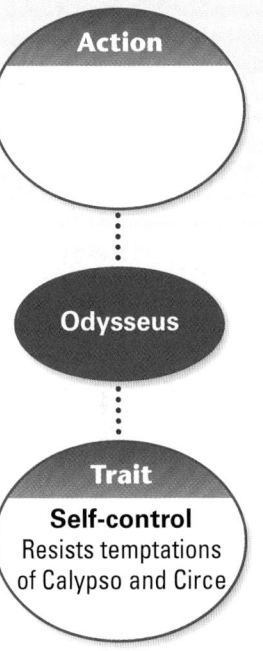

Reading Strategy
Reading in Sentences

To get the most out of a story told in verse, ignore the line breaks and **read in sentences.** Although the line breaks reveal the structure of the verse, they may make it harder for you to follow the meaning. Read the *Odyssey* the same way you might read a magazine article or a novel: Let the words flow to you in complete sentences. In some cases, you may need to rephrase the sentences in your own words to make the meaning clearer.

Vocabulary Development

plundered (plun´ dərd) *v.* took goods by force; looted (p. 981)

squall (skwôl) *n.* brief, violent storm (p. 984)

dispatched (di spacht´) *v.* finished quickly (p. 990)

mammoth (mam´ əth) *adj.* enormous (p. 993)

titanic (tī tan´ ik) *adj.* of great size or strength (p. 997)

assuage (ə swāj´) *v.* calm; pacify (p. 1000)

bereft (bi reft´) *adj.* deprived (p. 1003)

ardor (är´ dər) *n.* passion; enthusiasm (p. 1007)

insidious (in sid´ ē əs) *adj.* characterized by craftiness and betrayal (p. 1011)

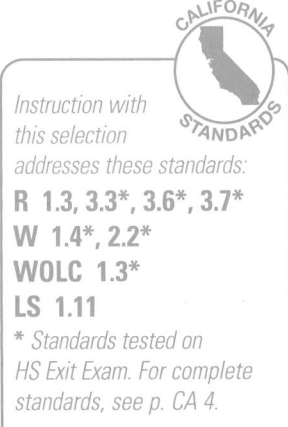

Instruction with this selection addresses these standards:
R 1.3, 3.3*, 3.6*, 3.7*
W 1.4*, 2.2*
WOLC 1.3*
LS 1.11
* *Standards tested on HS Exit Exam. For complete standards, see p. CA 4.*

Ulysses Deriding Polyphemus, 1819, J.M.W. Turner, The National Gallery, London

▲ **Critical Viewing** Do the images in this painting evoke feelings of hope or doom? [Analyze]

from the

Odyssey

Homer Translated by Robert Fitzgerald

PART 1
The Adventures of Odysseus

In the opening verses, Homer addresses the muse of epic poetry. He asks her help in telling the tale of Odysseus.

Sing in me, Muse,[1] and through me tell the story
of that man skilled in all ways of contending,
the wanderer, harried for years on end,
after he <u>plundered</u> the stronghold
5   on the proud height of Troy.[2]
                                  He saw the townlands
and learned the minds of many distant men,
and weathered many bitter nights and days
in his deep heart at sea, while he fought only
to save his life, to bring his shipmates home.
10 But not by will nor valor could he save them,
for their own recklessness destroyed them all—
children and fools, they killed and feasted on
the cattle of Lord Helios,[3] the Sun,
and he who moves all day through heaven
15 took from their eyes the dawn of their return.
Of these adventures, Muse, daughter of Zeus,[4]
tell us in our time, lift the great song again.

Note: In translating the *Odyssey*, Fitzgerald spelled Greek names to suggest the sound of the original Greek. In these excerpts, more familiar spellings have been used. For example, Fitzgerald's "Kirkê," "Kyklops," and "Seirênês" are spelled here as "Circe," "Cyclops," and "Sirens."

---

1. Muse (myooz) any one of the nine goddesses of the arts, literature, and the sciences; the spirit that is thought to inspire a poet or other artist.

plundered (plun´ dərd) v. took goods by force; looted

2. Troy (troi) city in northwest Asia Minor; site of the Trojan War.

3. Helios (hē´ lē äs´) sun god.

4. Zeus (zoos) king of the gods.

✔**Reading Check**

Which act led to an epic journey?

CHARACTERS

Alcinous (al sin′ ō əs)—king of the Phaeacians, to whom Odysseus tells his story

Odysseus (ō dis′ ē əs)—king of Ithaca

Calypso (kə lip′ sō)—sea goddess who loved Odysseus

Circe (sur′ sē)—enchantress who helped Odysseus

Zeus (zoos)—king of the gods

Apollo (ə päl′ ō)—god of music, poetry, prophecy, and medicine

Agamemnon (ag′ ə mem′ nän′)—king and leader of Greek forces

Poseidon (pō sī′ dən)—god of sea, earthquakes, horses, and storms at sea

Athena (ə thē′ nə)—goddess of wisdom, skills, and warfare

Polyphemus (päl′ i fē′ məs)—the Cyclops who imprisoned Odysseus

Laertes (lā ur′ tēz′)—Odysseus' father

Cronus (krō′ nəs)—Titan ruler of the universe; father of Zeus

Perimedes (per′ ə mē′ dēz)—member of Odysseus' crew

Eurylochus (yoo ril′ ə kəs)—another member of the crew

Tiresias (tī rē′ sē əs)—blind prophet who advised Odysseus

Persephone (pər sef′ ə nē)—wife of Hades

Telemachus (tə lem′ ə kəs)—Odysseus and Penelope's son

Sirens (sī′ rənz)—creatures whose songs lure sailors to their deaths

Scylla (sil′ ə)—sea monster of gray rock

Charybdis (kə rib′ dis)—enormous and dangerous whirlpool

Lampetia (lam pē′ shə)—nymph

Hermes (hur′ mēz′)—herald and messenger of the gods

Eumaeus (yoo mē′ əs)—old swineherd and friend of Odysseus

Antinous (an tin′ ō əs)—leader among the suitors

Eurynome (yoo rin′ ə mē)—housekeeper for Penelope

Penelope (pə nel′ ə pē)—Odysseus' wife

Eurymachus (yoo ri′ mə kəs)—suitor

Amphinomus (am fin′ ə məs)—suitor

Sailing from Troy

Ten years after the Trojan War, Odysseus departs from the goddess Calypso's island. He arrives in Phaeacia, ruled by Alcinous. Alcinous offers a ship to Odysseus and asks him to tell of his adventures.

"I am Laertes'[5] son, Odysseus.

                      Men hold me
formidable for guile[6] in peace and war:
20 this fame has gone abroad to the sky's rim.

My home is on the peaked sea-mark of Ithaca[7]
under Mount Neion's wind-blown robe of leaves,
in sight of other islands—Dulichium,
Same, wooded Zacynthus—Ithaca
25 being most lofty in that coastal sea,
and northwest, while the rest lie east and south.
A rocky isle, but good for a boy's training;
I shall not see on earth a place more dear,
though I have been detained long by Calypso,[8]
30 loveliest among goddesses, who held me
in her smooth caves, to be her heart's delight,
as Circe of Aeaea,[9] the enchantress,
desired me, and detained me in her hall.
But in my heart I never gave consent.
35 Where shall a man find sweetness to surpass
his own home and his parents? In far lands
he shall not, though he find a house of gold.

What of my sailing, then, from Troy?

                      What of those years
of rough adventure, weathered under Zeus?
40 The wind that carried west from Ilium[10]
brought me to Ismarus, on the far shore,
a strongpoint on the coast of Cicones.[11]
I stormed that place and killed the men who fought.
Plunder we took, and we enslaved the women,
45 to make division, equal shares to all—
but on the spot I told them: 'Back, and quickly!
Out to sea again!' My men were mutinous,[12]
fools, on stores of wine. Sheep after sheep
they butchered by the surf, and shambling cattle,

---

5. Laertes (lā ʉr´ tēz´)

6. guile (gīl) *n.* craftiness; cunning.

7. Ithaca (ith´ ə kə) island off the west coast of Greece.

Reading Strategy
Reading in Sentences
Why do these opening lines sound more natural when you ignore the line breaks?

8. Calypso (kə lip´ sō)

9. Circe (sʉr´ sē) **of Aeaea** (ē´ ē ə)

10. Ilium (il ē əm) Troy.

11. Cicones (si kō´ nēz)

12. mutinous (my<u>oo</u>t´ ən əs) *adj.* rebellious.

✔**Reading Check**
Who has asked Odysseus to tell his tale?

Odyssey, Part 1, The Adventures of Odysseus ◆ 983

50 feasting,—while fugitives went inland, running
    to call to arms the main force of Cicones.
    This was an army, trained to fight on horseback
    or, where the ground required, on foot. They came
    with dawn over that terrain like the leaves
55 and blades of spring. So doom appeared to us,
    dark word of Zeus for us, our evil days.
    My men stood up and made a fight of it—
    backed on the ships, with lances kept in play,
    from bright morning through the blaze of noon
60 holding our beach, although so far outnumbered;
    but when the sun passed toward unyoking time,
    then the Achaeans,[13] one by one, gave way.
    Six benches were left empty in every ship
    that evening when we pulled away from death.
65 And this new grief we bore with us to sea:
    our precious lives we had, but not our friends.
    No ship made sail next day until some shipmate
    had raised a cry, three times, for each poor ghost
    unfleshed by the Cicones on that field.

13. Achaeans (ə kē´ ənz) Greeks; here, Odysseus' men.

The Lotus-Eaters

70 Now Zeus the lord of cloud roused in the north
    a storm against the ships, and driving veils
    of <u>squall</u> moved down like night on land and sea.
    The bows went plunging at the gust; sails
    cracked and lashed out strips in the big wind.
75 We saw death in that fury, dropped the yards,
    unshipped the oars, and pulled for the nearest lee:[14]
    then two long days and nights we lay offshore
    worn out and sick at heart, tasting our grief,
    until a third Dawn came with ringlets shining.
80 Then we put up our masts, hauled sail, and rested,
    letting the steersmen and the breeze take over.

    I might have made it safely home, that time,
    but as I came round Malea the current
    took me out to sea, and from the north
85 a fresh gale drove me on, past Cythera.
    Nine days I drifted on the teeming sea
    before dangerous high winds. Upon the tenth
    we came to the coastline of the Lotus-Eaters,
    who live upon that flower. We landed there

squall (skwôl) *n.* brief, violent storm

14. lee (lē) *n.* area sheltered from the wind.

90   to take on water. All ships' companies
    mustered alongside for the mid-day meal.
    Then I sent out two picked men and a runner
    to learn what race of men that land sustained.
    They fell in, soon enough, with Lotus-Eaters,
95   who showed no will to do us harm, only
    offering the sweet Lotus to our friends—
    but those who ate this honeyed plant, the Lotus,
    never cared to report, nor to return:
    they longed to stay forever, browsing on
100   that native bloom, forgetful of their homeland.
    I drove them, all three wailing, to the ships,
    tied them down under their rowing benches,
    and called the rest: 'All hands aboard;
    come, clear the beach and no one taste
105   the Lotus, or you lose your hope of home.'
    Filing in to their places by the rowlocks
    my oarsmen dipped their long oars in the surf,
    and we moved out again on our sea faring.

Reading Strategy
Reading in Sentences
Read lines 94–98 as a complete sentence. How does doing so help your understanding of the passage?

Literary Analysis
The Epic Hero Which characteristics of a hero and leader does Odysseus show in the episode with the Lotus-Eaters?

Review and Assess

Thinking About the Selection

1. **Respond:** What is your first impression of Odysseus? Which of his qualities do you admire?

2. **(a) Recall:** Describe the events on Ismarus.
   (b) Interpret: What lessons can be learned from the defeat of Odysseus and his men at Ismarus?

3. **(a) Recall:** Where is Odysseus' home? **(b) Interpret:** What significant role does his home play in Odysseus' epic journey?

4. **(a) Recall:** How do Calypso and Circe keep Odysseus from reaching home? **(b) Interpret:** What were Odysseus' feelings when he was with Calypso and Circe?

5. **(a) Recall:** What happens to the men who eat the Lotus?
   (b) Infer: What does this episode suggest about the main problem that Odysseus has with his men? **(c) Speculate:** What do you think about the way Odysseus responds to the three men who long to stay with the Lotus-Eaters?

6. **Compare and Contrast:** In what ways is the world of the *Odyssey* similar to today's world? In what ways is it different?

7. **Take a Position:** Do you admire Odysseus? Why or why not?

The Cyclops

In the next land we found were Cyclopes,[15]
110 giants, louts, without a law to bless them.
In ignorance leaving the fruitage of the earth in mystery
to the immortal gods, they neither plow
nor sow by hand, nor till the ground, though grain—
wild wheat and barley—grows untended, and
115 wine-grapes, in clusters, ripen in heaven's rains.
Cyclopes have no muster and no meeting,
no consultation or old tribal ways,
but each one dwells in his own mountain cave
dealing out rough justice to wife and child,
120 indifferent to what the others do. . . .

As we rowed on, and nearer to the mainland,
at one end of the bay, we saw a cavern
yawning above the water, screened with laurel,
and many rams and goats about the place
125 inside a sheepfold—made from slabs of stone
earthfast between tall trunks of pine and rugged
towering oak trees.

                        A prodigious[16] man
slept in this cave alone, and took his flocks
to graze afield—remote from all companions,
130 knowing none but savage ways, a brute
so huge, he seemed no man at all of those
who eat good wheaten bread; but he seemed rather
a shaggy mountain reared in solitude.
We beached there, and I told the crew
135 to stand by and keep watch over the ship:
as for myself I took my twelve best fighters
and went ahead. I had a goatskin full
of that sweet liquor that Euanthes' son,
Maron, had given me. He kept Apollo's[17]
140 holy grove at Ismarus; for kindness
we showed him there, and showed his wife and child,
he gave me seven shining golden talents[18]
perfectly formed, a solid silver winebowl,
and then this liquor—twelve two-handled jars
145 of brandy, pure and fiery. Not a slave
in Maron's household knew this drink; only
he, his wife and the storeroom mistress knew;
and they would put one cupful—ruby-colored,
honey-smooth—in twenty more of water,

---

15. Cyclopes (sī klō′ pēz′)
n. plural form of **Cyclops**
(sī′ kläps′), a race of giants
with one eye in the middle
of the forehead.

Literary Analysis
**The Epic Hero and
Conflict** Based on
Odysseus' description of
Cyclopes, what conflicts
might arise for Odysseus
and his men?

16. prodigious (prō dij′ əs)
adj. enormous.

Reading Strategy
Reading in Sentences
Rephrase the description
of the Cyclops in lines
130–133, using your own
words.

17. Apollo (ə päl′ ō) god of
music, poetry, prophecy, and
medicine.

18. talents units of money
in ancient Greece.

150 but still the sweet scent hovered like a fume
over the winebowl. No man turned away
when cups of this came round.

                                        A wineskin full

I brought along, and victuals[19] in a bag,
for in my bones I knew some towering brute
155 would be upon us soon—all outward power,
a wild man, ignorant of civility.

We climbed, then, briskly to the cave. But Cyclops
had gone afield, to pasture his fat sheep,
so we looked round at everything inside:
160 a drying rack that sagged with cheeses, pens
crowded with lambs and kids,[20] each in its class:
firstlings apart from middlings, and the 'dewdrops,'

19. victuals (vit′ əls) *n.*
food or other provisions.

20. kids *n.* young goats.

☑**Reading Check**

What does Odysseus
bring along when he goes
to inspect the Cyclops'
cave?

◀ **Critical Viewing** How
does this image of Apollo
compare with your
impressions of the other gods
Odysseus has encountered?
[Compare and Contrast]

or newborn lambkins, penned apart from both.
And vessels full of whey[21] were brimming there—
165 bowls of earthenware and pails for milking.
My men came pressing round me, pleading:

'Why not
take these cheeses, get them stowed, come back,
throw open all the pens, and make a run for it?
We'll drive the kids and lambs aboard. We say
170 put out again on good salt water!'

Ah,
how sound that was! Yet I refused. I wished
to see the cave man, what he had to offer—
no pretty sight, it turned out, for my friends.
We lit a fire, burnt an offering,
175 and took some cheese to eat; then sat in silence
around the embers, waiting. When he came
he had a load of dry boughs[22] on his shoulder
to stoke his fire at suppertime. He dumped it
with a great crash into that hollow cave,
180 and we all scattered fast to the far wall.
Then over the broad cavern floor he ushered
the ewes he meant to milk. He left his rams
and he-goats in the yard outside, and swung
high overhead a slab of solid rock
185 to close the cave. Two dozen four-wheeled wagons,
with heaving wagon teams, could not have stirred
the tonnage of that rock from where he wedged it
over the doorsill. Next he took his seat
and milked his bleating ewes. A practiced job
190 he made of it, giving each ewe her suckling;
thickened his milk, then, into curds and whey,
sieved out the curds to drip in withy[23] baskets,
and poured the whey to stand in bowls
cooling until he drank it for his supper.
195 When all these chores were done, he poked the fire,
heaping on brushwood. In the glare he saw us.

'Strangers,' he said, 'who are you? And where from?
What brings you here by seaways—a fair traffic?
Or are you wandering rogues, who cast your lives
200 like dice, and ravage other folk by sea?'

21. whey (hwā) *n.* thin, watery part of milk separated from the thicker curds.

22. boughs (bouz) *n.* tree branches.

23. withy (with´ ē) *adj.* made from tough, flexible twigs.

We felt a pressure on our hearts, in dread
of that deep rumble and that mighty man.
But all the same I spoke up in reply:

'We are from Troy, Achaeans, blown off course
205 by shifting gales on the Great South Sea;
homeward bound, but taking routes and ways
uncommon; so the will of Zeus would have it.
We served under Agamemnon,[24] son of Atreus—
the whole world knows what city
210 he laid waste, what armies he destroyed.
It was our luck to come here; here we stand,
beholden for your help, or any gifts
you give—as custom is to honor strangers.
We would entreat you, great Sir, have a care
215 for the gods' courtesy; Zeus will avenge
the unoffending guest.'

                                    He answered this
from his brute chest, unmoved:

                                    'You are a ninny,
or else you come from the other end of nowhere,
telling me, mind the gods! We Cyclopes
220 care not a whistle for your thundering Zeus
or all the gods in bliss; we have more force by far.
I would not let you go for fear of Zeus—
you or your friends—unless I had a whim[25] to.
Tell me, where was it, now, you left your ship—
225 around the point, or down the shore, I wonder?'

He thought he'd find out, but I saw through this,
and answered with a ready lie:

                                    'My ship?
Poseidon[26] Lord, who sets the earth a-tremble,
broke it up on the rocks at your land's end.
230 A wind from seaward served him, drove us there.
We are survivors, these good men and I.'

Neither reply nor pity came from him,
but in one stride he clutched at my companions
and caught two in his hands like squirming puppies
235 to beat their brains out, spattering the floor.
Then he dismembered them and made his meal,
gaping and crunching like a mountain lion—
everything: innards, flesh, and marrow bones.

Literary Analysis
The Epic Hero Which quality of an epic hero does Odysseus demonstrate by addressing the mighty man?

24. Agamemnon (ag´ ə mem´ nän´) king who led the Greek army during the Trojan War.

Literary Analysis
The Epic Hero and Conflict What conflict is revealed in lines 217–223?

25. whim (hwim) *n.* sudden thought or wish to do something.

26. Poseidon (pō sī´ dən) god of the sea, earthquakes, horses, and storms at sea.

Reading Check

What does Odysseus tell Cyclops happened to their ship?

We cried aloud, lifting our hands to Zeus,
240 powerless, looking on at this, appalled;
but Cyclops went on filling up his belly
with manflesh and great gulps of whey,
then lay down like a mast among his sheep.
My heart beat high now at the chance of action,
245 and drawing the sharp sword from my hip I went
along his flank to stab him where the midriff
holds the liver. I had touched the spot
when sudden fear stayed me: if I killed him
we perished there as well, for we could never
250 move his ponderous doorway slab aside.
So we were left to groan and wait for morning.

When the young Dawn with fingertips of rose
lit up the world, the Cyclops built a fire
and milked his handsome ewes, all in due order,
255 putting the sucklings to the mothers. Then,
his chores being all <u>dispatched</u>, he caught
another brace²⁷ of men to make his breakfast,
and whisked away his great door slab
to let his sheep go through—but he, behind,
260 reset the stone as one would cap a quiver.²⁸
There was a din²⁹ of whistling as the Cyclops
rounded his flock to higher ground, then stillness.
And now I pondered how to hurt him worst,
if but Athena³⁰ granted what I prayed for.
265 Here are the means I thought would serve my turn:

a club, or staff, lay there along the fold—
an olive tree, felled green and left to season³¹
for Cyclops' hand. And it was like a mast
a lugger³² of twenty oars, broad in the beam—
270 a deep-sea-going craft—might carry:
so long, so big around, it seemed. Now I
chopped out a six foot section of this pole
and set it down before my men, who scraped it;
and when they had it smooth, I hewed again
275 to make a stake with pointed end. I held this
in the fire's heart and turned it, toughening it,
then hid it, well back in the cavern, under
one of the dung piles in profusion there.
Now came the time to toss for it: who ventured
280 along with me? whose hand could bear to thrust
and grind that spike in Cyclops' eye, when mild

Reading Strategy
Reading in Sentences
Reread lines 244–250 in complete sentences, ignoring the line breaks, to help you understand the passage.

dispatched (di spacht´) *v.* finished quickly

27. **brace** (brās) *n.* pair.

28. **cap a quiver** (kwiv´ ər) close a case holding arrows.

29. **din** *n.* loud, continuous noise; uproar.

30. **Athena** (ə thē´ nə) goddess of wisdom, skills, and warfare.

31. **felled green and left to season** chopped down and exposed to the weather to age the wood.

32. **lugger** (lug´ ər) *n.* small sailing vessel.

Literary Analysis
The Epic Hero Which heroic qualities does Odysseus reveal as he plots against Cyclops?

sleep had mastered him? As luck would have it,
the men I would have chosen won the toss—
four strong men, and I made five as captain.

285 At evening came the shepherd with his flock,
his woolly flock. The rams as well, this time,
entered the cave: by some sheepherding whim—
or a god's bidding—none were left outside.
He hefted his great boulder into place
290 and sat him down to milk the bleating ewes
in proper order, put the lambs to suck,
and swiftly ran through all his evening chores.
Then he caught two more men and feasted on them.
My moment was at hand, and I went forward
295 holding an ivy bowl of my dark drink,
looking up, saying:

                                'Cyclops, try some wine.
Here's liquor to wash down your scraps of men.
Taste it, and see the kind of drink we carried
under our planks. I meant it for an offering
300 if you would help us home. But you are mad,
unbearable, a bloody monster! After this,
will any other traveler come to see you?'

He seized and drained the bowl, and it went down
so fiery and smooth he called for more:

305 'Give me another, thank you kindly. Tell me,
how are you called? I'll make a gift will please you.
Even Cyclopes know the wine grapes grow
out of grassland and loam in heaven's rain,
but here's a bit of nectar and ambrosia!'[33]

310 Three bowls I brought him, and he poured them down.
I saw the fuddle and flush come over him,
then I sang out in cordial tones:

                                'Cyclops,
you ask my honorable name? Remember
the gift you promised me, and I shall tell you.
315 My name is Nohbdy: mother, father, and friends,
everyone calls me Nohbdy.'

                            And he said:

Literary Analysis
The Epic Hero What plan
do you think Odysseus
has in mind by offering the
drink?

33. nectar (nek´ tər)
and ambrosia (am brō´
zhə) drink and food of
the gods.

Reading Strategy
Reading in Sentences
How would you write
Odysseus' sly lie in
ordinary prose?

✔**Reading Check**

What does Odysseus give
to Cyclops to drink?

'Nohbdy's my meat, then, after I eat his friends.
Others come first. There's a noble gift, now.'

Even as he spoke, he reeled and tumbled backward,
320 his great head lolling to one side; and sleep
took him like any creature. Drunk, hiccuping,
he dribbled streams of liquor and bits of men.

Now, by the gods, I drove my big hand spike
deep in the embers, charring it again,
325 and cheered my men along with battle talk
to keep their courage up: no quitting now.
The pike of olive, green though it had been,
reddened and glowed as if about to catch.
I drew it from the coals and my four fellows
330 gave me a hand, lugging it near the Cyclops
as more than natural force nerved them; straight
forward they sprinted, lifted it, and rammed it
deep in his crater eye, and leaned on it
turning it as a shipwright turns a drill
335 in planking, having men below to swing
the two-handled strap that spins it in the groove.
So with our brand we bored[34] that great eye socket
while blood ran out around the red-hot bar.
Eyelid and lash were seared; the pierced ball
340 hissed broiling, and the roots popped.

                              In a smithy
one sees a white-hot axehead or an adze
plunged and wrung in a cold tub, screeching steam—
the way they make soft iron hale and hard—:
just so that eyeball hissed around the spike.
345 The Cyclops bellowed and the rock roared round him,
and we fell back in fear. Clawing his face
he tugged the bloody spike out of his eye,
threw it away, and his wild hands went groping;
then he set up a howl for Cyclopes
350 who lived in caves on windy peaks nearby.
Some heard him; and they came by divers[35] ways
to clump around outside and call:
                              'What ails you,
Polyphemus?[36] Why do you cry so sore
in the starry night? You will not let us sleep.
355 Sure no man's driving off your flock? No man
has tricked you, ruined you?'

Reading Strategy
Reading in Sentences
What is the main idea of
lines 323–326?

34. bored (bôrd) *v.*
made a hole in.

35. divers (dī´ vərz) *adj.*
several; various.

36. Polyphemus (päl´ i
fē´ məs)

992 ◆ *The Epic*

Out of the cave
the <u>mammoth</u> Polyphemus roared in answer:

'Nohbdy, Nohbdy's tricked me, Nohbdy's ruined me!'

To this rough shout they made a sage[37] reply:

360 'Ah well, if nobody has played you foul
there in your lonely bed, we are no use in pain
given by great Zeus. Let it be your father,
Poseidon Lord, to whom you pray.'

So saying
they trailed away. And I was filled with laughter
365 to see how like a charm the name deceived them.
Now Cyclops, wheezing as the pain came on him,
fumbled to wrench away the great doorstone
and squatted in the breach with arms thrown wide
for any silly beast or man who bolted—
370 hoping somehow I might be such a fool.
But I kept thinking how to win the game:
death sat there huge; how could we slip away?
I drew on all my wits, and ran through tactics,
reasoning as a man will for dear life,
375 until a trick came—and it pleased me well.
The Cyclops' rams were handsome, fat, with heavy
fleeces, a dark violet.

Three abreast
I tied them silently together, twining
cords of willow from the ogre's bed;
380 then slung a man under each middle one
to ride there safely, shielded left and right.
So three sheep could convey each man. I took
the woolliest ram, the choicest of the flock,
and hung myself under his kinky belly,
385 pulled up tight, with fingers twisted deep
in sheepskin ringlets for an iron grip.
So, breathing hard, we waited until morning.

When Dawn spread out her fingertips of rose
the rams began to stir, moving for pasture,
390 and peals of bleating echoed round the pens
where dams with udders full called for a milking.
Blinded, and sick with pain from his head wound,
the master stroked each ram, then let it pass,

mammoth (mam´ əth) *adj.*
enormous

37. sage (sāj) *adj.* wise.

Reading Strategy
Reading in Sentences
How many questions do
the other Cyclopes ask
Polyphemus? What two
basic things do they want
to know?

Literary Analysis
The Epic Hero Which
heroic quality does
Odysseus demonstrate in
lines 371–375?

**Reading Check**

What do the other
Cyclopes think
Polyphemus is saying
when he says, "Nohbdy's
tricked me"?

but my men riding on the pectoral[38] fleece
395 the giant's blind hands blundering never found.
Last of them all my ram, the leader, came,
weighted by wool and me with my meditations.
The Cyclops patted him, and then he said:

'Sweet cousin ram, why lag behind the rest
400 in the night cave? You never linger so,
but graze before them all, and go afar
to crop sweet grass, and take your stately way
leading along the streams, until at evening
you run to be the first one in the fold.
405 Why, now, so far behind? Can you be grieving
over your Master's eye? That carrion rogue[39]
and his accurst companions burnt it out
when he had conquered all my wits with wine.
Nohbdy will not get out alive, I swear.
410 Oh, had you brain and voice to tell
where he may be now, dodging all my fury!
Bashed by this hand and bashed on this rock wall
his brains would strew the floor, and I should have
rest from the outrage Nohbdy worked upon me.'

415 He sent us into the open, then. Close by,
I dropped and rolled clear of the ram's belly,
going this way and that to untie the men.
With many glances back, we rounded up
his fat, stiff-legged sheep to take aboard,
420 and drove them down to where the good ship lay.
We saw, as we came near, our fellows' faces
shining; then we saw them turn to grief
tallying those who had not fled from death.
I hushed them, jerking head and eyebrows up,
425 and in a low voice told them: 'Load this herd;
move fast, and put the ship's head toward the breakers.'
They all pitched in at loading, then embarked
and struck their oars into the sea. Far out,
as far off shore as shouted words would carry,
430 I sent a few back to the adversary:

'O Cyclops! Would you feast on my companions?
Puny, am I, in a cave man's hands?
How do you like the beating that we gave you,

38. pectoral (pek´ tə rəl)
adj. located in or on the chest.

39. carrion (kar´ ē ən) **rogue**
(rōg) repulsive scoundrel.

**Reading Check**

How do the men escape from the Cyclops' cave?

Polyphemus, The Cyclops, N. C. Wyeth, Delaware Art Museum

▲ **Critical Viewing** Odysseus and his surviving men escape in their ship as the blinded Cyclops hurls boulders and curses. How does this illustration compare to your mental image of the scene? **[Analyze]**

you damned cannibal? Eater of guests
435 under your roof! Zeus and the gods have paid you!'

The blind thing in his doubled fury broke
a hilltop in his hands and heaved it after us.
Ahead of our black prow it struck and sank
whelmed in a spuming geyser, a giant wave
440 that washed the ship stern foremost back to shore.
I got the longest boathook out and stood
fending us off, with furious nods to all
to put their backs into a racing stroke—
row, row, or perish. So the long oars bent
445 kicking the foam sternward, making head
until we drew away, and twice as far.
Now when I cupped my hands I heard the crew
in low voices protesting:

                         'Godsake, Captain!
Why bait the beast again? Let him alone!'

450 'That tidal wave he made on the first throw
all but beached us.'

                              'All but stove us in!'
'Give him our bearing with your trumpeting,
he'll get the range and lob a boulder.'

                                      'Aye
He'll smash our timbers and our heads together!'
455 I would not heed them in my glorying spirit,
but let my anger flare and yelled:

                              'Cyclops,
if ever mortal man inquire
how you were put to shame and blinded, tell him
Odysseus, raider of cities, took your eye:
460 Laertes' son, whose home's on Ithaca!'

At this he gave a mighty sob and rumbled:
'Now comes the weird[40] upon me, spoken of old.
A wizard, grand and wondrous, lived here—Telemus,[41]
a son of Eurymus;[42] great length of days
465 he had in wizardry among the Cyclopes,
and these things he foretold for time to come:
my great eye lost, and at Odysseus' hands.

Literary Analysis
The Epic Hero Despite his heroism, which human weaknesses does Odysseus reveal as he sails away?

Reading Strategy
Reading in Sentences Rephrase the sentence in lines 450–451.

40. **weird** n. fate or destiny.
41. **Telemus** (tel e´ məs)
42. **Eurymus** (yoo rim´ əs)

Always I had in mind some giant, armed
in giant force, would come against me here.
470 But this, but you—small, pitiful and twiggy—
you put me down with wine, you blinded me.
Come back, Odysseus, and I'll treat you well,
praying the god of earthquake[43] to befriend you—
his son I am, for he by his avowal
475 fathered me, and, if he will, he may
heal me of this black wound—he and no other
of all the happy gods or mortal men.'

Few words I shouted in reply to him:

'If I could take your life I would and take
480 your time away, and hurl you down to hell!
The god of earthquake could not heal you there!'

At this he stretched his hands out in his darkness
toward the sky of stars, and prayed Poseidon:

'O hear me, lord, blue girdler of the islands,
485 if I am thine indeed, and thou art father:
grant that Odysseus, raider of cities, never
see his home: Laertes' son, I mean,
who kept his hall on Ithaca. Should destiny
intend that he shall see his roof again
490 among his family in his father land,
far be that day, and dark the years between.
Let him lose all companions, and return
under strange sail to bitter days at home.'

In these words he prayed, and the god heard him.
495 Now he laid hands upon a bigger stone
and wheeled around, <u>titanic</u> for the cast,
to let it fly in the black-prowed vessel's track.
But it fell short, just aft the steering oar,
and whelming seas rose giant above the stone
500 to bear us onward toward the island.
                                    There
as we ran in we saw the squadron waiting,
the trim ships drawn up side by side, and all
our troubled friends who waited, looking seaward.
We beached her, grinding keel in the soft sand,
505 and waded in, ourselves, on the sandy beach.
Then we unloaded all the Cyclops' flock

43. god of earthquake
Poseidon.

Reading Strategy
Reading in Sentences
Rephrase the second
sentence of Cyclops'
prayer to Poseidon.

titanic (tī tan´ ik) *adj.* of
great size or strength

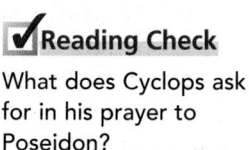
Reading Check

What does Cyclops ask
for in his prayer to
Poseidon?

Odysseus in the Land of the Dead, N. C. Wyeth, Delaware Art Museum

▲ **Critical Viewing** What can you infer about ancient Greek beliefs concerning death and the afterlife from the text and this illustration? **[Infer]**

to make division, share and share alike,
only my fighters voted that my ram,
the prize of all, should go to me. I slew him
510 by the seaside and burnt his long thighbones
to Zeus beyond the stormcloud, Cronus'[44] son,
who rules the world. But Zeus disdained my offering:
destruction for my ships he had in store
and death for those who sailed them, my companions.
515 Now all day long until the sun went down
we made our feast on mutton and sweet wine,
till after sunset in the gathering dark
we went to sleep above the wash of ripples.

When the young Dawn with fingertips of rose
520 touched the world, I roused the men, gave orders
to man the ships, cast off the mooring lines;
and filing in to sit beside the rowlocks
oarsmen in line dipped oars in the gray sea.
So we moved out, sad in the vast offing,[45]
525 having our precious lives, but not our friends.

The Land of the Dead

*Odysseus and his men sail to Aeolia,[46] where Aeolus, king of the
winds, sends Odysseus on his way with a gift: a sack containing
all the winds except the favorable west wind. When they are near
home, Odysseus' men open the sack, letting loose a storm that
drives them back to Aeolia. Aeolus casts them out, having decided
that they are detested by the gods. They sail for seven days and
arrive in the land of the Laestrygonians,[47] a race of cannibals.
These creatures destroy all of Odysseus' ships except the one he is
sailing in. Odysseus and his reduced crew escape and reach
Aeaea, the island ruled by the sorceress-goddess Circe. She transforms half of the men into swine. Protected by a magic herb,
Odysseus demands that Circe change his men back into human
form. Before Odysseus departs from the island a year later, Circe
informs him that in order to reach home he must journey to the
land of the dead, Hades, and consult the blind prophet Tiresias.*

Literary Analysis
The Epic Hero Which admirable quality does Odysseus show in his actions with the stolen sheep?

44. Cronus (krō' nəs) Titan who was ruler of the universe until he was over-thrown by his son Zeus.

45. offing *n.* distant part of the sea visible from the shore.

46. Aeolia (ē ō' lē ə)

47. Laestrygonians (les tri gō' ni anz)

✔**Reading Check**

What does Circe say Odysseus must do in order to reach home?

We bore down on the ship at the sea's edge
and launched her on the salt immortal sea,
stepping our mast and spar in the black ship;
embarked the ram and ewe and went aboard
530 in tears, with bitter and sore dread upon us.
But now a breeze came up for us astern—
a canvas-bellying landbreeze, hale shipmate
sent by the singing nymph with sunbright hair;[48]
so we made fast the braces, took our thwarts,
535 and let the wind and steersman work the ship
with full sail spread all day above our coursing,
till the sun dipped, and all the ways grew dark
upon the fathomless unresting sea.

By night
our ship ran onward toward the Ocean's bourne,
540 the realm and region of the Men of Winter,
hidden in mist and cloud. Never the flaming
eye of Helios lights on those men
at morning, when he climbs the sky of stars,
nor in descending earthward out of heaven;
545 ruinous night being rove over those wretches.
We made the land, put ram and ewe ashore,
and took our way along the Ocean stream
to find the place foretold for us by Circe.
There Perimedes and Eulylochus[49]
550 pinioned[50] the sacred beasts. With my drawn blade
I spaded up the votive[51] pit, and poured
libations[52] round it to the unnumbered dead:
sweet milk and honey, then sweet wine, and last
clear water; and I scattered barley down.
555 Then I addressed the blurred and breathless dead,
vowing to slaughter my best heifer for them
before she calved, at home in Ithaca,
and burn the choice bits on the altar fire;
as for Tiresias, I swore to sacrifice
560 a black lamb, handsomest of all our flock.
Thus to <u>assuage</u> the nations of the dead
I pledged these rites, then slashed the lamb and ewe,
letting their black blood stream into the wellpit.
Now the souls gathered, stirring out of Erebus,[53]
565 brides and young men, and men grown old in pain,
and tender girls whose hearts were new to grief;
many were there, too, torn by brazen lanceheads,
battle-slain, bearing still their bloody gear.

48. singing nymph . . . hair Circe.

Reading Strategy
Reading in Sentences
Reread the sentences in lines 539–541 to explain what happens to their ship by night.

49. Perimedes (per´ ə mē´ dēz) **and Eurylochus** (yōō ril´ ə kəs)

50. pinioned (pin´ yənd) *v.* confined or shackled.

51. votive (vōt´ iv) *adj.* done in fulfillment of a vow or pledge.

52. libations (lī bā´ shənz) *n.* wine or other liquids poured upon the ground as a sacrifice to a god.

assuage (ə swāj´) *v.* calm; pacify

53. Erebus (er´ ə bəs) dark region under the earth through which the dead pass before entering the realm of Hades.

From every side they came and sought the pit
570 with rustling cries; and I grew sick with fear.
But presently I gave command to my officers
to flay those sheep the bronze cut down, and make
burnt offerings of flesh to the gods below—
to sovereign Death, to pale Persephone.[54]
575 Meanwhile I crouched with my drawn sword to keep
the surging phantoms from the bloody pit
till I should know the presence of Tiresias.[55]

One shade came first—Elpenor, of our company,
who lay unburied still on the wide earth
580 as we had left him—dead in Circe's hall,
untouched, unmourned, when other cares compelled us.
Now when I saw him there I wept for pity
and called out to him:

       'How is this, Elpenor,
how could you journey to the western gloom
585 swifter afoot than I in the black lugger?'
He sighed, and answered:

       'Son of great Laertes,
Odysseus, master mariner and soldier,
bad luck shadowed me, and no kindly power;
ignoble death I drank with so much wine.
590 I slept on Circe's roof, then could not see
the long steep backward ladder, coming down,
and fell that height. My neckbone, buckled under,
snapped, and my spirit found this well of dark.
Now hear the grace I pray for, in the name
595 of those back in the world, not here—your wife
and father, he who gave you bread in childhood,
and your own child, your only son, Telemachus,[56]
long ago left at home.

       When you make sail
and put these lodgings of dim Death behind,
600 you will moor ship, I know, upon Aeaea Island;
there, O my lord, remember me, I pray,
do not abandon me unwept, unburied,
to tempt the gods' wrath, while you sail for home;
but fire my corpse, and all the gear I had,
605 and build a cairn[57] for me above the breakers—
an unknown sailor's mark for men to come.

Literary Analysis
The Epic Hero and
Conflict Which outside
forces and inner feelings
does Odysseus confront
as he faces the spirits of
the dead?

54. Persephone (pər
sef′ ə nē) wife of Hades.

55. Tiresias (tī rē′ sē əs)

Reading Strategy
Reading in Sentences As
you read Elpenor's words,
where do you pause if you
read in sentences?

56. Telemachus
(tə lem′ ə kəs)

57. cairn (kern) n. conical
heap of stones built as a
monument.

✔Reading Check
What does Elpenor say
happened to him on
Circe's roof?

Heap up the mound there, and implant upon it
the oar I pulled in life with my companions.'

He ceased, and I replied:

          'Unhappy spirit,
610 I promise you the barrow and the burial.'

So we conversed, and grimly, at a distance,
with my long sword between, guarding the blood,
while the faint image of the lad spoke on.
Now came the soul of Anticlea, dead,
615 my mother, daughter of Autolycus,[58]
dead now, though living still when I took ship
for holy Troy. Seeing this ghost I grieved,
but held her off, through pang on pang of tears,
till I should know the presence of Tiresias.
620 Soon from the dark that prince of Thebes[59] came forward
bearing a golden staff; and he addressed me:

'Son of Laertes and the gods of old,
Odysseus, master of landways and seaways,
why leave the blazing sun, O man of woe,
625 to see the cold dead and the joyless region?
Stand clear, put up your sword;
let me but taste of blood, I shall speak true.'

At this I stepped aside, and in the scabbard
let my long sword ring home to the pommel silver,
630 as he bent down to the somber blood. Then spoke
the prince of those with gift of speech:

         'Great captain,
a fair wind and the honey lights of home
are all you seek. But anguish lies ahead;
the god who thunders on the land prepares it,
635 not to be shaken from your track, implacable,
in rancor for the son whose eye you blinded.
One narrow strait may take you through his blows:
denial of yourself, restraint of shipmates.
When you make landfall on Thrinacia first
640 and quit the violet sea, dark on the land
you'll find the grazing herds of Helios
by whom all things are seen, all speech is known.

58. Autolycus (ô täl´ i kəs)

59. Thebes (thēbz)

Reading Strategy
Reading in Sentences
In ordinary language, rephrase the lines in which Odysseus puts away his sword.

Avoid those kine,[60] hold fast to your intent,
and hard seafaring brings you all to Ithaca.
645　But if you raid the beeves, I see destruction
for ship and crew. Though you survive alone,
<u>bereft</u> of all companions, lost for years,
under strange sail shall you come home, to find
your own house filled with trouble: insolent men
650　eating your livestock as they court your lady.
Aye, you shall make those men atone in blood!
But after you have dealt out death—in open
combat or by stealth—to all the suitors,
go overland on foot, and take an oar,
655　until one day you come where men have lived
with meat unsalted, never known the sea,
nor seen seagoing ships, with crimson bows

60. kine (kīn) *n.* cattle.

bereft (bi reft´) *adj.*
deprived

✔**Reading Check**

What does Odysseus
learn has happened to his
mother?

▲ **Critical Viewing** How does the description of the characters in this art compare
to your image of the characters in the *Odyssey*? **[Compare and Contrast]**

and oars that fledge light hulls for dipping flight.
The spot will soon be plain to you, and I
660 can tell you how: some passerby will say,
"What winnowing fan is that upon your shoulder?"
Halt, and implant your smooth oar in the turf
and make fair sacrifice to Lord Poseidon:
a ram, a bull, a great buck boar; turn back,
665 and carry out pure hecatombs[61] at home
to all wide heaven's lords, the undying gods,
to each in order. Then a seaborne death
soft as this hand of mist will come upon you
when you are wearied out with rich old age,
670 your country folk in blessed peace around you.
And all this shall be just as I foretell.'

61. hecatombs (hek´ ə tōmz´) *n.* large-scale sacrifices in ancient Greece; often, the slaughter of 100 cattle at one time.

Review and Assess

Thinking About the Selection

1. **Respond:** What do you think of Odysseus' plan for escaping from Polyphemus?

2. **(a) Recall:** Before the meeting with the Cyclops, what had Odysseus received from Maron at Ismarus?
   (b) Generalize: What does the encounter with Maron reveal about ancient Greek attitudes regarding hospitality?

3. **(a) Recall:** How do Odysseus and his companions expect to be treated by the Cyclops? **(b) Infer:** What "laws" of behavior and attitude does Polyphemus violate in his treatment of the Greeks?

4. **(a) Recall:** How do Odysseus and his crew ultimately escape from the Cyclops? **(b) Evaluate:** Which positive and negative character traits does Odysseus demonstrate in his adventure with the Cyclops?

5. **(a) Recall:** Whom does Odysseus encounter in the Land of the Dead? **(b) Interpret:** Which character trait does Odysseus display in the Land of the Dead that he did not reveal earlier?

6. **(a) Recall:** What difficulties does Tiresias predict for the journey to come? **(b) Speculate:** Why would Odysseus continue, despite the grim prophecies?

7. **(a) Assess:** Based on Tiresias' prediction, which heroic qualities will Odysseus need to rely upon as he continues his journey? Explain.

The Sirens

*Odysseus returns to Circe's island. The goddess reveals his course
to him and gives advice on how to avoid the dangers he will face:
the Sirens, who lure sailors to their destruction; the Wandering
Rocks, sea rocks that destroy even birds in flight; the perils of the
sea monster Scylla and, nearby, the whirlpool Charybdis;*[62] *and
the cattle of the sun god, which Tiresias has warned Odysseus not
to harm.*

62. Charybdis (kə rib´ dis)

As Circe spoke, Dawn mounted her golden throne,
and on the first rays Circe left me, taking
her way like a great goddess up the island.
675 I made straight for the ship, roused up the men
to get aboard and cast off at the stern.
They scrambled to their places by the rowlocks
and all in line dipped oars in the gray sea.
But soon an offshore breeze blew to our liking—
680 a canvas-bellying breeze, a lusty shipmate
sent by the singing nymph with sunbright hair.
So we made fast the braces, and we rested,
letting the wind and steersman work the ship.
The crew being now silent before me, I
685 addressed them, sore at heart:

        'Dear friends,
more than one man, or two, should know those things
Circe foresaw for us and shared with me,
so let me tell her forecast: then we die
with our eyes open, if we are going to die,
690 or know what death we baffle if we can. Sirens
weaving a haunting song over the sea
we are to shun, she said, and their green shore
all sweet with clover; yet she urged that I
alone should listen to their song. Therefore
695 you are to tie me up, tight as a splint,
erect along the mast, lashed to the mast,
and if I shout and beg to be untied,
take more turns of the rope to muffle me.'

I rather dwelt on this part of the forecast,
700 while our good ship made time, bound outward down
the wind for the strange island of Sirens.

Literary Analysis

The Epic Hero What does
Odysseus reveal about his
character by sharing
information with his men?

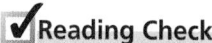**Reading Check**

What has Odysseus asked
his shipmates to do in
order to deal with the
Sirens?

Then all at once the wind fell, and a calm
came over all the sea, as though some power
lulled the swell.

                        The crew were on their feet

705 briskly, to furl the sail, and stow it; then,
each in place, they poised the smooth oar blades
and sent the white foam scudding by. I carved
a massive cake of beeswax into bits
and rolled them in my hands until they softened—
710 no long task, for a burning heat came down
from Helios, lord of high noon. Going forward
I carried wax along the line, and laid it
thick on their ears. They tied me up, then, plumb
amidships, back to the mast, lashed to the mast,
715 and took themselves again to rowing. Soon,
as we came smartly within hailing distance,
the two Sirens, noting our fast ship
off their point, made ready, and they sang:

> This way, oh turn your bows,
> 720   Achaea's glory,
> As all the world allows—
>   Moor and be merry.
>
> Sweet coupled airs we sing.
>   No lonely seafarer
> 725 Holds clear of entering
>   Our green mirror.
>
> Pleased by each purling note
>   Like honey twining
> From her throat and my throat,
> 730   Who lies a-pining?
>
> Sea rovers here take joy
>   Voyaging onward,
> As from our song of Troy
> Graybeard and rower-boy
> 735   Goeth more learnèd.
>
> All feats on that great field
>   In the long warfare,
> Dark days the bright gods willed,
>   Wounds you bore there,

Reading Strategy
Reading in Sentences
Reread lines 704–715 as
sentences, ignoring the
line breaks. What happens
in each of the four
sentences?

Literary Analysis
**The Epic Hero and
Conflict** Which details in
the Sirens' song are
calculated to tempt a hero
and bring him down?

740 *Argos' old soldiery*[63]
     On Troy beach teeming,
     Charmed out of time we see.
     No life on earth can be
     Hid from our dreaming.

63. Argos' old soldiery soldiers from Argos, a city in ancient Greece.

745 The lovely voices in <u>ardor</u> appealing over the water
     made me crave to listen, and I tried to say
     'Untie me!' to the crew, jerking my brows;
     but they bent steady to the oars. Then Perimedes
     got to his feet, he and Eurylochus,
750 and passed more line about, to hold me still.
     So all rowed on, until the Sirens
     dropped under the sea rim, and their singing
     dwindled away.

                         My faithful company
     rested on their oars now, peeling off
755 the wax that I had laid thick on their ears;
     then set me free.

ardor (är′ dər) *n.* passion; enthusiasm

Reading Strategy
Reading in Sentences
Explain what happens in the sentence in lines 753–756.

Scylla and Charybdis

                         But scarcely had that island
     faded in blue air than I saw smoke
     and white water, with sound of waves in tumult—
     a sound the men heard, and it terrified them.
760 Oars flew from their hands; the blades went knocking
     wild alongside till the ship lost way,
     with no oar blades to drive her through the water.

     Well, I walked up and down from bow to stern,
     trying to put heart into them, standing over
765 every oarsman, saying gently,

                                        'Friends,
     have we never been in danger before this?
     More fearsome, is it now, than when the Cyclops
     penned us in his cave? What power he had!
     Did I not keep my nerve, and use my wits
770 to find a way out for us?

                              Now I say

     by hook or crook this peril too shall be
     something that we remember.

☑ Reading Check

What does Odysseus put in his shipmates' ears before they hear the Sirens sing?

▲ **Critical Viewing** The beautiful sorceress Circe both helps and hinders Odysseus on his journey home. What can you tell about Circe from this illustration? **[Deduce]**

Heads up, lads!

We must obey the orders as I give them.
Get the oar shafts in your hands, and lay back
775 hard on your benches; hit these breaking seas.
Zeus help us pull away before we founder.
You at the tiller, listen, and take in
all that I say—the rudders are your duty;
keep her out of the combers and the smoke;[64]
780 steer for that headland; watch the drift, or we
fetch up in the smother, and you drown us.'

That was all, and it brought them round to action.
But as I sent them on toward Scylla,[65] I
told them nothing, as they could do nothing.
785 They would have dropped their oars again, in panic,
to roll for cover under the decking. Circe's
bidding against arms had slipped my mind,
so I tied on my cuirass[66] and took up
two heavy spears, then made my way along
790 to the foredeck—thinking to see her first from there,
the monster of the gray rock, harboring
torment for my friends. I strained my eyes
upon the cliffside veiled in cloud, but nowhere
could I catch sight of her.

And all this time,

795 in travail,[67] sobbing, gaining on the current,
we rowed into the strait—Scylla to port
and on our starboard beam Charybdis,[68] dire
gorge[69] of the salt seatide. By heaven! when she
vomited, all the sea was like a cauldron
800 seething over intense fire, when the mixture
suddenly heaves and rises.

The shot spume

soared to the landside heights, and fell like rain.
But when she swallowed the sea water down
we saw the funnel of the maelstrom,[70] heard
805 the rock bellowing all around, and dark
sand raged on the bottom far below.
My men all blanched against the gloom, our eyes

Reading Strategy
Reading in Sentences
How would you rewrite Odysseus' pep talk in paragraph form without poetic line breaks?

64. the combers (kōmʹ ərs) **and the smoke** the large waves that break on the beach and the ocean spray.

65. Scylla (silʹ ə)

66. cuirass (kwi rasʹ) *n.* armor for the upper body.

67. travail (trə vālʹ) *n.* very hard work.

68. Charybdis (kə ribʹ dis)
69. gorge (gôrj) *n.* hungry, consuming mouth.

70. maelstrom (mālʹ strəm) *n.* large, violent whirlpool.

✔**Reading Check**
What orders does Odysseus give his shipmates?

were fixed upon that yawning mouth in fear
of being devoured.

                              Then Scylla made her strike,
810 whisking six of my best men from the ship.
I happened to glance aft at ship and oarsmen
and caught sight of their arms and legs, dangling
high overhead. Voices came down to me
in anguish, calling my name for the last time.

815 A man surfcasting on a point of rock
for bass or mackerel, whipping his long rod
to drop the sinker and the bait far out,
will hook a fish and rip it from the surface
to dangle wriggling through the air:

                                             so these
820 were borne aloft in spasms toward the cliff.

She ate them as they shrieked there, in her den,
in the dire grapple, reaching still for me—
and deathly pity ran me through
at that sight—far the worst I ever suffered,
825 questing the passes of the strange sea.

                              We rowed on.
The Rocks were now behind; Charybdis, too,
and Scylla dropped astern.

The Cattle of the Sun God

In the small hours of the third watch, when stars
that shone out in the first dusk of evening
830 had gone down to their setting, a giant wind
blew from heaven, and clouds driven by Zeus
shrouded land and sea in a night of storm;
so, just as Dawn with fingertips of rose
touched the windy world, we dragged our ship
835 to cover in a grotto, a sea cave
where nymphs had chairs of rock and sanded floors.
I mustered all the crew and said:

Reading Strategy
Reading in Sentences By
reading in sentences
rather than line breaks,
explain what happens in
lines 810–814.

Literary Analyis
The Epic Hero How does
Odysseus show the heroic
quality of loyalty in lines
823–825?

'Old shipmates,
our stores are in the ship's hold, food and drink;
the cattle here are not for our provision,
840 or we pay dearly for it.

Fierce the god is
who cherishes these heifers and these sheep:
Helios; and no man avoids his eye.'

To this my fighters nodded. Yes. But now
we had a month of onshore gales, blowing
845 day in, day out—south winds, or south by east.
As long as bread and good red wine remained
to keep the men up, and appease their craving,
they would not touch the cattle. But in the end,
when all the barley in the ship was gone,
850 hunger drove them to scour the wild shore
with angling hooks, for fishes and seafowl,
whatever fell into their hands; and lean days
wore their bellies thin.

The storms continued.
So one day I withdrew to the interior
855 to pray the gods in solitude, for hope
that one might show me some way of salvation.
Slipping away, I struck across the island
to a sheltered spot, out of the driving gale.
I washed my hands there, and made supplication
860 to the gods who own Olympus,[71] all the gods—
but they, for answer, only closed my eyes
under slow drops of sleep.

Now on the shore Eurylochus
made his <u>insidious</u> plea:

'Comrades,' he said,
'You've gone through everything; listen to what I say.
865 All deaths are hateful to us, mortal wretches,
but famine is the most pitiful, the worst
end that a man can come to.

Will you fight it?
Come, we'll cut out the noblest of these cattle
for sacrifice to the gods who own the sky;
870 and once at home, in the old country of Ithaca,

Reading Strategy
Reading in Sentences
Explain the instructions
that Odysseus gives his
crew in lines 838–840.

Literary Analysis
**The Epic Hero and
Conflict** What conflict is
likely to arise from the
crew's hunger?

71. Olympus (ō lim´
pəs) Mount Olympus,
home of the gods.

insidious (in sid´ ē əs) *adj.*
characterized by crafti-
ness and betrayal

**Reading Check**

What does Scylla do to
the six men she takes
from the ship?

if ever that day comes—
we'll build a costly temple and adorn it
with every beauty for the Lord of Noon.[72]
But if he flares up over his heifers lost,
875 wishing our ship destroyed, and if the gods
make cause with him, why, then I say: Better
open your lungs to a big sea once for all
than waste to skin and bones on a lonely island!'

Thus Eurylochus; and they murmered 'Aye!'
880 trooping away at once to round up heifers.
Now, that day tranquil cattle with broad brows
were gazing near, and soon the men drew up
around their chosen beasts in ceremony.
They plucked the leaves that shone on a tall oak—
885 having no barley meal—to strew the victims,
performed the prayers and ritual, knifed the kine
and flayed each carcass, cutting thighbones free
to wrap in double folds of fat. These offerings,
with strips of meat, were laid upon the fire.
890 Then, as they had no wine, they made libation
with clear spring water, broiling the entrails first;
and when the bones were burnt and tripes shared,
they spitted the carved meat.
                                        Just then my slumber
left me in a rush, my eyes opened,
895 and I went down the seaward path. No sooner
had I caught sight of our black hull, than savory
odors of burnt fat eddied around me;
grief took hold of me, and I cried aloud:

'O Father Zeus and gods in bliss forever,
900 you made me sleep away this day of mischief!
O cruel drowsing, in the evil hour!
Here they sat, and a great work they contrived.'[73]

Lampetia[74] in her long gown meanwhile
had borne swift word to the Overlord of Noon:

905 'They have killed your kine.'
                                        And the Lord Helios
burst into angry speech amid the immortals:

'O Father Zeus and gods in bliss forever,

---

72. Lord of Noon
Helios.

Literary Analysis
The Epic Hero and Conflict Do you think Eurylochus' beliefs are in conflict with Odysseus' beliefs?

Reading Strategy
Reading in Sentences Read in complete sentences to rephrase lines 894–900.

73. contrived (kən trīvd´) v. thought up; devised.

74. Lampetia (lam pē´ shə) a nymph.

Literary Analysis
The Epic Hero Which important ancient Greek value does Odysseus reveal through his actions concerning the sacrifice?

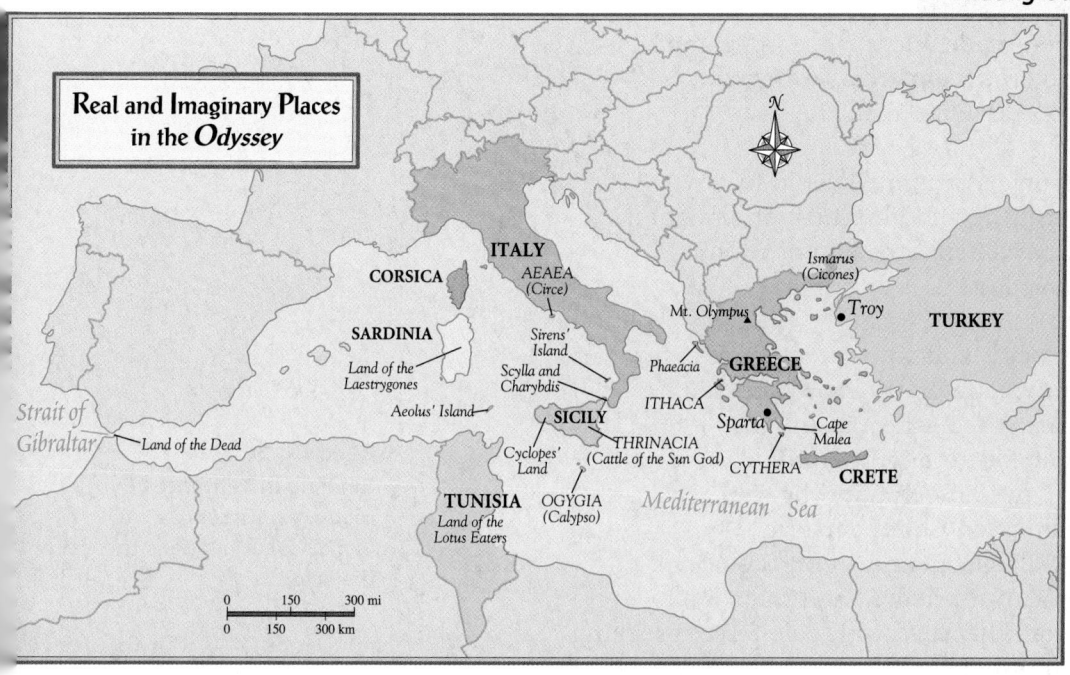

Real and Imaginary Places in the *Odyssey*

Tracing Odysseus' Route

Odysseus' journey carries him to real places, like Troy and Sparta, and fictitious places, like Aeolia and Aeaea. Modern historians have tried to determine Odysseus' actual route. Here is one theory:

• From Troy (in present-day Turkey), Odysseus proceeded across the Aegean Sea, passing between Sparta and Crete.

• He then sailed westward on the Mediterranean Sea to Sicily, where he confronted the Cyclops. Nearby islands were home to the Lotus-Eaters, the Sirens, and Aeolus.

• After circling Sicily, Odysseus sailed north-eastward until he finally reached the island of Ithaca, his home.

▲ **Critical Viewing** The entrance to the Land of the Dead is believed to have been the Strait of Gibraltar. Why might the ancient Greeks have considered this location frightening? **[Analyze]**

punish Odysseus' men! So overweening,
now they have killed my peaceful kine, my joy
910 at morning when I climbed the sky of stars,
and evening, when I bore westward from heaven.
Restitution or penalty they shall pay—
and pay in full—or I go down forever
to light the dead men in the underworld.'

915 Then Zeus who drives the stormcloud made reply:

'Peace, Helios: shine on among the gods,
shine over mortals in the fields of grain.
Let me throw down one white-hot bolt, and make
splinters of their ship in the winedark sea.'

✔**Reading Check**

What do the shipmates do while Odysseus is sleeping?

Odyssey, Part 1, The Adventures of Odysseus ◆ 1013

920 —Calypso later told me of this exchange,
     as she declared that Hermes[75] had told her.
     Well, when I reached the sea cave and the ship,
     I faced each man, and had it out; but where
     could any remedy be found? There was none.
925 The silken beeves[76] of Helios were dead.
     The gods, moreover, made queer signs appear:
     cowhides began to crawl, and beef, both raw
     and roasted, lowed like kine upon the spits.

     Now six full days my gallant crew could feast
930 upon the prime beef they had marked for slaughter
     from Helios' herd; and Zeus, the son of Cronus,
     added one fine morning.

                              All the gales
     had ceased, blown out, and with an offshore breeze
     we launched again, stepping the mast and sail,
935 to make for the open sea. Astern of us
     the island coastline faded, and no land
     showed anywhere, but only sea and heaven,
     when Zeus Cronion piled a thunderhead
     above the ship, while gloom spread on the ocean.
940 We held our course, but briefly. Then the squall
     struck whining from the west, with gale force, breaking
     both forestays, and the mast came toppling aft
     along the ship's length, so the running rigging
     showered into the bilge.

                              On the afterdeck
945 the mast had hit the steersman a slant blow
     bashing the skull in, knocking him overside,
     as the brave soul fled the body, like a diver.
     With crack on crack of thunder, Zeus let fly
     a bolt against the ship, a direct hit,
950 so that she bucked, in reeking fumes of sulphur,
     and all the men were flung into the sea.
     They came up 'round the wreck, bobbing awhile
     like petrels[77] on the waves.

                              No more seafaring
     homeward for these, no sweet day of return;
955 the god had turned his face from them.

                              I clambered

75. **Hermes** (hur´ mēz)
herald and messenger
of the gods.

76. **beeves** (bēvz) *n.*
plural of *beef.*

Reading Strategy
Reading in Sentences By
reading in sentences,
explain what happens to
the ship.

77. **petrels** (pe´ trəlz)
small, dark sea birds.

fore and aft my hulk until a comber
split her, keel from ribs, and the big timber
floated free; the mast, too, broke away.
A backstay floated dangling from it, stout
960 rawhide rope, and I used this for lashing
mast and keel together. These I straddled,
riding the frightful storm.

                                                    Nor had I yet

seen the worst of it: for now the west wind
dropped, and a southeast gale came on—one more
965 twist of the knife—taking me north again,
straight for Charybdis. All that night I drifted,
and in the sunrise, sure enough, I lay
off Scylla mountain and Charybdis deep.
There, as the whirlpool drank the tide, a billow
970 tossed me, and I sprang for the great fig tree,
catching on like a bat under a bough.
Nowhere had I to stand, no way of climbing,
the root and bole[78] being far below, and far
above my head the branches and their leaves,
975 massed, overshadowing Charybdis pool.
But I clung grimly, thinking my mast and keel
would come back to the surface when she spouted.
And ah! how long, with what desire, I waited!
till, at the twilight hour, when one who hears
980 and judges pleas in the marketplace all day
between contentious men, goes home to supper,
the long poles at last reared from the sea.

Now I let go with hands and feet, plunging
straight into the foam beside the timbers,
985 pulled astride, and rowed hard with my hands
to pass by Scylla. Never could I have passed her
had not the Father of gods and men,[79] this time,
kept me from her eyes. Once through the strait,
nine days I drifted in the open sea
990 before I made shore, buoyed up by the gods,
upon Ogygia[80] Isle. The dangerous nymph
Calypso lives and sings there, in her beauty,
and she received me, loved me.

Literary Analysis
The Epic Hero Which of Odysseus' heroic qualities are revealed in lines 959–962?

78. bole (bōl) *n.* tree trunk.

79. Father . . . men Zeus.

80. Ogygia (o jij´ ĭ a).

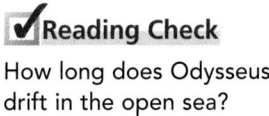**Reading Check**

How long does Odysseus drift in the open sea?

▲ **Critical Viewing** In the *Odyssey*, Telemachus searches for his father in a ship like this one. From what you observe in the painting, how does this ship compare with modern ships? [**Compare and Contrast**]

But why tell
the same tale that I told last night in hall
995   to you and to your lady? Those adventures
made a long evening, and I do not hold
with tiresome repetition of a story."

Review and Assess

Thinking About the Selection

1. **Respond:** In which adventure in this section does Odysseus act most heroically? Explain.

2. **(a) Recall:** How do the Sirens lure travelers to their destruction? **(b) Compare and Contrast:** How does the danger posed by the Sirens compare to that posed by the Lotus-Eaters?

3. **(a) Recall:** What are Scylla and Charybdis, and why do they pose dangers for travelers? **(b) Analyze:** Why does Odysseus choose to sail toward Scylla rather than Charybdis?

4. **(a) Make a Judgment:** Was Odysseus right not to tell his men about his decision to sail toward Scylla? **(b) Hypothesize:** What would have happened if Odysseus had told them everything?

5. **(a) Recall:** What does Eurylochus say to persuade Odysseus' men to slaughter and eat the cattle of Helios, the sun god? **(b) Analyze:** Why is Odysseus unable to keep his men from killing the cattle? **(c) Apply:** If you had been in their situation, do you think you would have eaten the cattle? Why or why not?

6. **Make a Judgment:** Do the members of the crew deserve the punishment they receive for killing the cattle?

Review and Assess

Literary Analysis

The Epic Hero

1. As an **epic hero,** Odysseus has both heroic and mortal qualities. Identify some of his qualities in both categories.
2. When Odysseus introduces himself in lines 18–37, which heroic traits does he reveal?
3. Based on Odysseus' actions in these episodes, which values did the ancient Greeks admire?

Connecting Literary Elements

4. Some of Odysseus' **conflicts** involve battles with enemies, and some involve clashes with thoughts and feelings within himself. On a chart like the one shown, list Odysseus' external and internal conflicts.

External Conflicts   **External Conflicts**

5. In which of the adventures does Odysseus come into conflict with forces of nature?
6. Which character traits help Odysseus to be victorious in most of his conflicts?

Reading Strategy

Reading in Sentences

7. (a) How many complete stops should you make in reading lines 398–408? (b) Where are they?
8. Rewrite lines 704–715 as a paragraph, using your own words.

Extend Understanding

9. **History Connection:** Which political or military leader whom you have read or heard about seems similar to Odysseus? Explain.

Quick Review

The **epic hero**—the central character in a long poetic tale of adventure—undertakes a dangerous voyage, demonstrating traits that are valued by the society in which the epic originates.

A **conflict** is a struggle between opposing forces. It may occur between characters, between a character and nature, or within a character's mind.

To get the most out of a story told in verse, **read in sentences**, using punctuation and ignoring the line breaks.

 Take It to the Net

www.phschool.com

Take the interactive self-test online to check your understanding of the selection.

Integrate Language Skills

Vocabulary Development Lesson

Word Origins: Words From Myths

Titanic, meaning "huge or powerful," comes from *Titans*, giant Greek gods who once ruled the world. Define each word and explain its link to mythology.

1. helium 2. odyssey 3. museum 4. siren

Spelling Strategy

If a word of more than one syllable has a vowel-consonant ending and the accent is not on the last syllable, do not double the final consonant before adding a suffix beginning with a vowel: *plunder* + *-ed* = *plundered*. Correct any misspellings below.

1. mentorring 2. flowerred 3. travelers

Concept Development: Antonyms

After reviewing the vocabulary on page 979, match each word below with its opposite.

1. dispatched   a. restored to its owner
2. bereft   b. begun
3. plundered   c. joyfully acquired
4. squall   d. tiny
5. mammoth   e. small and weak
6. assuage   f. calm, sunny weather
7. insidious   g. honest
8. titanic   h. aggravate
9. ardor   i. indifference

Grammar Lesson

Usage: *like, as,* and *as if*

The words *like, as,* and *as if* all suggest comparisons, but they are often used incorrectly. **Like** is a preposition and should not be used instead of the conjunctions **as** or **as if** to introduce a clause.

Incorrect: *Like* he had boasted, he was mighty.
Correct: *As* he had boasted, he was mighty.

Incorrect: He held the men *like* they were squirming puppies.
Correct: He held the men *as if* they were squirming puppies.
Correct: He held the men *like* squirming puppies.

Practice Write these sentences on your paper, using the correct word(s) in parentheses.

1. He ate (as if, like) he had been starving.
2. The men wept (as if, like) children.
3. (Like, As) a dead man, he slept unmoving.
4. The men felt (like, as if) they were doomed.
5. Odysseus' bragging sounded (like, as) a donkey's bray to the Cyclops.

Writing Application Write three sentences about Odysseus, using *like, as,* or *as if* in one sentence each.

W͞G Prentice Hall Writing and Grammar Connection: Chapter 27, Section 2

Extension Activities

Listening and Speaking Pick one episode from Part 1 of the *Odyssey*, and describe the action as a **play-by-play broadcast**. Reread the episode and jot down the key actions. Draft a script. Practice your broadcast and record it to play for the class.

Writing In a **comparison-and-contrast essay**, explore the concept of the hero. In your essay, show similarities and differences between Odysseus and other heroes, real or imaginary. Include several different points of comparison.

Prepare to Read

from the Odyssey, Part 2

Literary Analysis

Epic Simile

An **epic simile**, sometimes called a Homeric simile, is an elaborate comparison that may extend for several lines. Epic similes may use the words *like, as, just as,* or *so* to make the comparison. In Part 1, lines 268–271, Odysseus uses an epic simile to describe the fallen tree from which he creates the weapon used to blind the Cyclops.

> And it was like a mast / a lugger of twenty oars, broad in the beam— / a deep-sea-going craft—might carry: / so long, so big around, it seemed.

As you read, notice Homer's use of epic similes to bring descriptions to life.

Connecting Literary Elements

Similes are one example of **imagery**—descriptive language that creates word pictures. These pictures, or images, are created with details of sight, sound, taste, touch, smell, or movement. An epic simile contains imagery that shows how something looks or acts by comparing it to something else. For example, comparing a fallen tree to a broad mast stresses the size of the tree.

Reading Strategy

Summarizing

You can better understand the events in an epic like the *Odyssey*—or in any other work of literature with a complicated plot—by **summarizing** the events as you read. Retell the plot briefly in your own words, jotting down details about what events occurred and why.

Use a chart like the one shown to summarize episodes in the *Odyssey*.

Vocabulary Development

dissemble (di sem′ bəl) *v.* conceal under a false appearance; disguise (p. 1022)

lithe (līth) *adj.* supple; limber (p. 1024)

incredulity (in′ krə dōō′ lə tē) *n.* inability to believe (p. 1024)

bemusing (bi myōōz′ iŋ) *adj.* stupefying or muddling (p. 1027)

glowering (glou′ ər iŋ) *adj.* staring with sullen anger; scowling (p. 1029)

equity (ek′ wit ē) *n.* fairness; impartiality; justice (p. 1032)

maudlin (môd′ lin) *adj.* tearfully or foolishly sentimental (p. 1032)

contempt (kən tempt′) *n.* disdain or scorn; scornful feelings or actions (p. 1040)

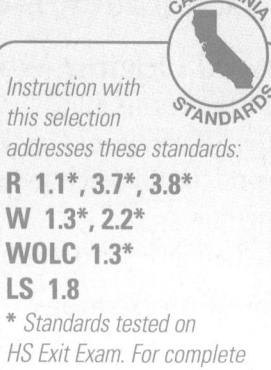

Instruction with this selection addresses these standards:

R 1.1*, 3.7*, 3.8*
W 1.3*, 2.2*
WOLC 1.3*
LS 1.8

* *Standards tested on HS Exit Exam. For complete standards, see p. CA 4.*

What Happens

As a beggar, Odysseus meets Telemachus. He is changed by Athena. He reveals his identity.

Why?

His disguise helps him find out what has changed in Ithaca. He needs his son's help.

Summary

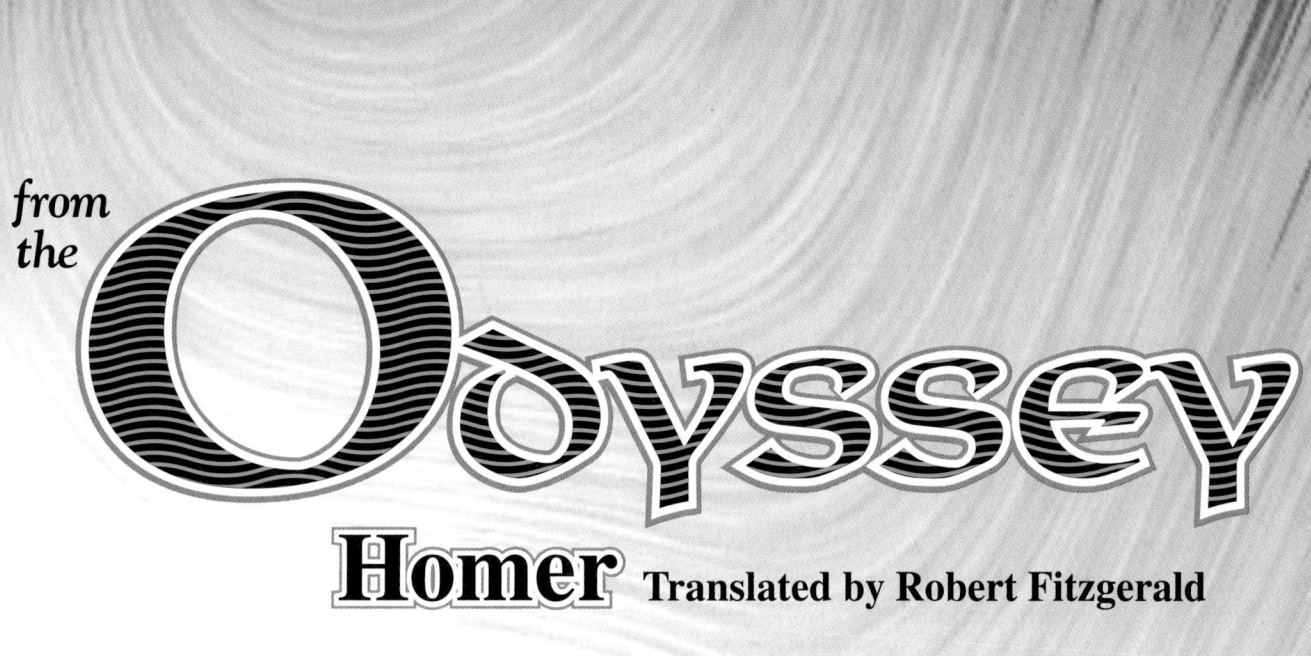

from the

Odyssey

Homer Translated by Robert Fitzgerald

PART 2
The Return of Odysseus

Review and Anticipate

In Part 1 of the *Odyssey*, Odysseus and his companions face many perils on their voyage from Troy to Ithaca. At some moments, they are tempted by others to forsake their voyage; at others, their lives are endangered by powerful enemies. Ultimately, Odysseus' men bring about their own destruction at the hand of Zeus when they kill the cattle belonging to Helios.

As Part 2 begins, Odysseus is alone when he reaches Ithaca after a twenty-year absence. What do you predict will happen when Odysseus arrives home?

"Twenty years gone, and I am back again . . ."

Odysseus has finished telling his story to the Phaeacians. The next day, young Phaeacian noblemen conduct him home by ship. He arrives in Ithaca after an absence of twenty years. The goddess Athena appears and informs him of the situation at home. Numerous suitors, believing Odysseus to be dead, have been continually seeking the hand of his wife, Penelope, in marriage, while overrunning Odysseus' palace and enjoying themselves at Penelope's expense. Moreover, they are plotting to murder Odysseus' son, Telemachus, before he can inherit his father's lands. Telemachus, who, like Penelope, still hopes for his father's return, has journeyed to Pylos and Sparta to learn what he can about his father's fate. Athena disguises Odysseus as a beggar and directs him to the hut of Eumaeus,[1] his old and faithful swineherd. While Odysseus and Eumaeus are eating breakfast, Telemachus arrives. Athena then appears to Odysseus.

1. **Eumaeus** (yōō mē´ əs)

. . . From the air

    she walked, taking the form of a tall woman,
    handsome and clever at her craft, and stood
1000 beyond the gate in plain sight of Odysseus,
    unseen, though, by Telemachus, unguessed,
    for not to everyone will gods appear.
    Odysseus noticed her; so did the dogs,
    who cowered whimpering away from her. She only
1005 nodded, signing to him with her brows,
    a sign he recognized. Crossing the yard,
    he passed out through the gate in the stockade
    to face the goddess. There she said to him:

    "Son of Laertes and the gods of old,
1010 Odysseus, master of landways and seaways,
    <u>dissemble</u> to your son no longer now.
    The time has come: tell him how you together
    will bring doom on the suitors in the town.
    I shall not be far distant then, for I
1015 myself desire battle."

Literary Analysis
Epic Simile and Imagery
Is the description of the goddess in lines 997–1007 written as an epic simile? Why or why not?

dissemble (di sem´ bəl) v. conceal under a false appearance; disguise

☑**Reading Check**

What does Athena reveal to Odysseus about his situation at home?

Eumaeus, the Swineherd, N. C. Wyeth, Delaware Art Museum

▲ **Critical Viewing** What can you tell about Eumaeus from this illustration? **[Infer]**

Saying no more,
she tipped her golden wand upon the man,
making his cloak pure white, and the knit tunic
fresh around him. Lithe and young she made him,
ruddy with sun, his jawline clean, the beard
1020 no longer gray upon his chin. And she
withdrew when she had done.

               Then Lord Odysseus
reappeared—and his son was thunderstruck.
Fear in his eyes, he looked down and away
as though it were a god, and whispered:

                       "Stranger,
1025 you are no longer what you were just now!
Your cloak is new; even your skin! You are
one of the gods who rule the sweep of heaven!
Be kind to us, we'll make you fair oblation[2]
and gifts of hammered gold. Have mercy on us!"

1030 The noble and enduring man replied:

"No god. Why take me for a god? No, no.
I am that father whom your boyhood lacked
and suffered pain for lack of. I am he."

Held back too long, the tears ran down his cheeks
1035 as he embraced his son.

                 Only Telemachus,
uncomprehending, wild
with incredulity, cried out:

                      "You cannot
be my father Odysseus! Meddling spirits
conceived this trick to twist the knife in me!
1040 No man of woman born could work these wonders
by his own craft, unless a god came into it
with ease to turn him young or old at will.
I swear you were in rags and old,
and here you stand like one of the immortals!"

1045 Odysseus brought his ranging mind to bear
and said:

                 "This is not princely, to be swept
away by wonder at your father's presence.
No other Odysseus will ever come,
for he and I are one, the same; his bitter
1050 fortune and his wanderings are mine.

lithe (līth) adj. supple;
limber

2. oblation (äb lā´ shən)
n. offering to a god.

incredulity (in´ krə dōō´ lə
tē) n. inability to believe

Twenty years gone, and I am back again
on my own island.

As for my change of skin,
that is a charm Athena, Hope of Soldiers,
uses as she will; she has the knack

1055   to make me seem a beggar man sometimes
and sometimes young, with finer clothes about me.
It is no hard thing for the gods of heaven
to glorify a man or bring him low."

When he had spoken, down he sat.

Then, throwing

1060   his arms around this marvel of a father
Telemachus began to weep. Salt tears
rose from the wells of longing in both men,
and cries burst from both as keen and fluttering
as those of the great taloned hawk,

1065   whose nestlings farmers take before they fly.
So helplessly they cried, pouring out tears,
and might have gone on weeping so till sundown,
had not Telemachus said:

"Dear father! Tell me
what kind of vessel put you here ashore

1070   on Ithaca? Your sailors, who were they?
I doubt you made it, walking on the sea!"

Then said Odysseus, who had borne the barren sea:

"Only plain truth shall I tell you, child.
Great seafarers, the Phaeacians, gave me passage

1075   as they give other wanderers. By night
over the open ocean, while I slept,
they brought me in their cutter,[3] set me down
on Ithaca, with gifts of bronze and gold
and stores of woven things. By the gods' will

1080   these lie all hidden in a cave. I came
to this wild place, directed by Athena,
so that we might lay plans to kill our enemies.
Count up the suitors for me, let me know
what men at arms are there, how many men.

1085   I must put all my mind to it, to see
if we two by ourselves can take them on
or if we should look round for help."

Telemachus

replied:

Reading Strategy
Summarizing How does Odysseus explain the change in his appearance?

Literary Analysis
Epic Simile In this epic simile, what is being compared?

3. **cutter** (kutʹər) *n.* small, swift ship or boat carried aboard a large ship to transport personnel or supplies.

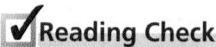
Reading Check

Why is Telemachus initially doubtful of Odysseus' words?

"O Father, all my life your fame
as a fighting man has echoed in my ears—
1090   your skill with weapons and the tricks of war—
but what you speak of is a staggering thing,
beyond imagining, for me. How can two men
do battle with a houseful in their prime?[4]
For I must tell you this is no affair
1095   of ten or even twice ten men, but scores,
throngs of them. You shall see, here and now.
The number from Dulichium alone
is fifty-two picked men, with armorers,
a half dozen; twenty-four came from Same,
1100   twenty from Zacynthus; our own island
accounts for twelve, high-ranked, and their retainers,
Medon the crier, and the Master Harper,
besides a pair of handymen at feasts.
If we go in against all these
1105   I fear we pay in salt blood for your vengeance.
You must think hard if you would conjure up
the fighting strength to take us through."

                                        Odysseus

who had endured the long war and the sea
answered:

                              "I'll tell you now.
1110   Suppose Athena's arm is over us, and Zeus
her father's, must I rack my brains for more?"

Clearheaded Telemachus looked hard and said:

"Those two are great defenders, no one doubts it,
but throned in the serene clouds overhead;
1115   other affairs of men and gods they have
to rule over."

                              And the hero answered:

"Before long they will stand to right and left of us
in combat, in the shouting, when the test comes—
our nerve against the suitors' in my hall.
1120   Here is your part: at break of day tomorrow
home with you, go mingle with our princes.
The swineherd later on will take me down
the port-side trail—a beggar, by my looks,
hangdog and old. If they make fun of me
1125   in my own courtyard, let your ribs cage up

Reading Strategy
Summarizing Summarize
Telemachus' response to
his father in lines
1089–1092. What is his
concern?

4. in their prime in the
best or most vigorous
stage of their lives.

▼ **Critical Viewing**
Why do you think scenes
such as this were depicted
on Greek pottery?
[Speculate]

your springing heart, no matter what I suffer,
no matter if they pull me by the heels
or practice shots at me, to drive me out.
Look on, hold down your anger. You may even
1130 plead with them, by heaven! in gentle terms
to quit their horseplay—not that they will heed you,
rash as they are, facing their day of wrath.
Now fix the next step in your mind.

                                    Athena,

counseling me, will give me word, and I
1135 shall signal to you, nodding: at that point
round up all armor, lances, gear of war
left in our hall, and stow the lot away
back in the vaulted storeroom. When the suitors
miss those arms and question you, be soft
1140 in what you say: answer:

                           'I thought I'd move them
out of the smoke. They seemed no longer those
bright arms Odysseus left us years ago
when he went off to Troy. Here where the fire's
hot breath came, they had grown black and drear.
1145 One better reason, too, I had from Zeus:
suppose a brawl starts up when you are drunk,
you might be crazed and bloody one another,
and that would stain your feast, your courtship. Tempered
iron can magnetize a man.'

                                 Say that.

1150 But put aside two broadswords and two spears
for our own use, two oxhide shields nearby
when we go into action. Pallas Athena
and Zeus All-Provident will see you through,
bemusing our young friends.

                          Now one thing more.

1155 If son of mine you are and blood of mine,
let no one hear Odysseus is about.
Neither Laertes, nor the swineherd here,
nor any slave, nor even Penelope.
But you and I alone must learn how far
1160 the women are corrupted; we should know
how to locate good men among our hands,
the loyal and respectful, and the shirkers⁵
who take you lightly, as alone and young."

Reading Strategy
Summarizing Summarize Athena's role in Odysseus' plan.

Reading Strategy
Summarizing Summarize the events of Odysseus' reunion with Telemachus.

bemusing (bi myōōz´ iŋ) *adj.* stupefying or muddling

5. shirkers (shʉrk´ ərz) *n.* people who get out of doing (or leave undone) something that needs to be done.

✔**Reading Check**
How does Odysseus tell his son to respond if the suitors "practice shots" on Odysseus?

Argus

*Odysseus heads for town with Eumaeus. Outside the palace,
Odysseus' old dog, Argus, is lying at rest as his long-absent
master approaches.*

While he spoke

an old hound, lying near, pricked up his ears

1165 and lifted up his muzzle. This was Argus,
trained as a puppy by Odysseus,
but never taken on a hunt before
his master sailed for Troy. The young men, afterward,
hunted wild goats with him, and hare, and deer,

1170 but he had grown old in his master's absence.
Treated as rubbish now, he lay at last
upon a mass of dung before the gates—
manure of mules and cows, piled there until
fieldhands could spread it on the king's estate.

1175 Abandoned there, and half destroyed with flies,
old Argus lay.

But when he knew he heard

Odysseus' voice nearby, he did his best
to wag his tail, nose down, with flattened ears,
having no strength to move nearer his master.

1180 And the man looked away,
wiping a salt tear from his cheek; but he
hid this from Eumaeus. Then he said:

"I marvel that they leave this hound to lie
here on the dung pile;

1185 he would have been a fine dog, from the look of him,
though I can't say as to his power and speed
when he was young. You find the same good build
in house dogs, table dogs landowners keep
all for style."

And you replied, Eumaeus:

1190 "A hunter owned him—but the man is dead
in some far place. If this old hound could show
the form he had when Lord Odysseus left him,
going to Troy, you'd see him swift and strong.
He never shrank from any savage thing

1195 he'd brought to bay in the deep woods; on the scent
no other dog kept up with him. Now misery

has him in leash. His owner died abroad,
and here the women slaves will take no care of him.
You know how servants are: without a master
1200   they have no will to labor, or excel.
For Zeus who views the wide world takes away
half the manhood of a man, that day
he goes into captivity and slavery."

Eumaeus crossed the court and went straight forward
1205   into the megaron[6] among the suitors:
but death and darkness in that instant closed
the eyes of Argus, who had seen his master,
Odysseus, after twenty years.

The Suitors

*Still disguised as a beggar, Odysseus enters his home.
He is confronted by the haughty[7] suitor Antinous.[8]*

But here Antinous broke in, shouting:

                                                        "God!

1210   What evil wind blew in this pest?

                                          Get over,

stand in the passage! Nudge my table, will you?
Egyptian whips are sweet
to what you'll come to here, you nosing rat,
making your pitch to everyone!
1215   These men have bread to throw away on you
because it is not theirs. Who cares? Who spares
another's food, when he has more than plenty?"

With guile Odysseus drew away, then said:

"A pity that you have more looks than heart.
1220   You'd grudge a pinch of salt from your own larder
to your own handyman. You sit here, fat
on others' meat, and cannot bring yourself
to rummage out a crust of bread for me!"

Then anger made Antinous' heart beat hard,
1225   and, <u>glowering</u> under his brows, he answered:

                                             "Now!
You think you'll shuffle off and get away
after that impudence?[9] Oh, no you don't!"

The stool he let fly hit the man's right shoulder
on the packed muscle under the shoulder blade—
1230   like solid rock, for all the effect one saw.
Odysseus only shook his head, containing
thoughts of bloody work, as he walked on,
then sat, and dropped his loaded bag again
upon the door sill. Facing the whole crowd
1235   he said, and eyed them all:

                                    "One word only,
my lords, and suitors of the famous queen.
One thing I have to say.
There is no pain, no burden for the heart
when blows come to a man, and he defending
1240   his own cattle—his own cows and lambs.
Here it was otherwise. Antinous
hit me for being driven on by hunger—
how many bitter seas men cross for hunger!
If beggars interest the gods, if there are Furies[10]
1245   pent in the dark to avenge a poor man's wrong, then may
Antinous meet his death before his wedding day!"

Then said Eupeithes' son, Antinous:

                                    "Enough.
Eat and be quiet where you are, or shamble elsewhere,
unless you want these lads to stop your mouth
1250   pulling you by the heels, or hands and feet,
over the whole floor, till your back is peeled!"

But now the rest were mortified, and someone
spoke from the crowd of young bucks to rebuke him:

"A poor show, that—hitting this famished tramp—
1255   bad business, if he happened to be a god.
You know they go in foreign guise, the gods do,
looking like strangers, turning up
in towns and settlements to keep an eye
on manners, good or bad."

                                    But at this notion
1260   Antinous only shrugged.

9. impudence (im′ pyo͞o dəns) *n.* quality of being shamelessly bold; disrespectful.

10. Furies (fyoor′ ōz) three terrible spirits who punish those whose crimes have not been avenged.

after the blow his father bore, sat still
without a tear, though his heart felt the blow.
Slowly he shook his head from side to side,
containing murderous thoughts.

Penelope
1265 on the higher level of her room had heard
the blow, and knew who gave it. Now she murmured:

"Would god you could be hit yourself, Antinous—
hit by Apollo's bowshot!"

And Eurynome[11]
her housekeeper, put in:

"He and no other?
1270 If all we pray for came to pass, not one
would live till dawn!"

Her gentle mistress said:

"Oh, Nan, they are a bad lot; they intend
ruin for all of us; but Antinous
appears a blacker-hearted hound than any.
1275 Here is a poor man come, a wanderer,
driven by want to beg his bread, and everyone
in hall gave bits, to cram his bag—only
Antinous threw a stool, and banged his shoulder!"

So she described it, sitting in her chamber
1280 among her maids—while her true lord was eating.
Then she called in the forester and said:

"Go to that man on my behalf, Eumaeus,
and send him here, so I can greet and question him.
Abroad in the great world, he may have heard
1285 rumors about Odysseus—may have known him!"

Penelope

In the evening, Penelope interrogates the old beggar.

"Friend, let me ask you first of all:
who are you, where do you come from, of what nation
and parents were you born?"

Reading Strategy
Summarizing Summarize lines 1261–1264. How is Telemachus feeling?

11. Eurynome (yo͞o rin´ əm ē)

Literary Analysis
Epic Simile Is the comparison made between Antinous and a hound in line 1274 an epic simile? How do you know?

**Reading Check**

How does Antinous respond to Odysseus, who is disguised as a beggar?

And he replied:

"My lady, never a man in the wide world
1290   should have a fault to find with you. Your name
has gone out under heaven like the sweet
honor of some god-fearing king, who rules
in <u>equity</u> over the strong: his black lands bear
both wheat and barley, fruit trees laden bright,
1295   new lambs at lambing time—and the deep sea
gives great hauls of fish by his good strategy,
so that his folk fare well.

O my dear lady,
this being so, let it suffice to ask me
of other matters—not my blood, my homeland.
1300   Do not enforce me to recall my pain.
My heart is sore; but I must not be found
sitting in tears here, in another's house:
it is not well forever to be grieving.
One of the maids might say—or you might think—
1305   I had got <u>maudlin</u> over cups of wine."

And Penelope replied:

"Stranger, my looks,
my face, my carriage,[12] were soon lost or faded
when the Achaeans crossed the sea to Troy,
Odysseus my lord among the rest.
1310   If he returned, if he were here to care for me,
I might be happily renowned!
But grief instead heaven sent me—years of pain.
Sons of the noblest families on the islands,
Dulichium, Same, wooded Zacynthus,[13]
1315   with native Ithacans, are here to court me,
against my wish; and they consume this house.
Can I give proper heed to guest or suppliant
or herald on the realm's affairs?

How could I?
wasted with longing for Odysseus, while here
1320   they press for marriage.

Ruses[14] served my turn
to draw the time out—first a close-grained web
I had the happy thought to set up weaving
on my big loom in hall. I said, that day:
'Young men—my suitors, now my lord is dead,
1325   let me finish my weaving before I marry,

equity (ek´ wit ē) *n.* fairness; impartiality; justice

Literary Analysis
Epic Simile To what does Odysseus compare his wife in the epic simile in lines 1290–1297?

maudlin (môd´ lin) *adj.* tearfully or foolishly sentimental

12. carriage (kar´ ij) *n.* posture.

13. Zacynthus (za sin´ thus)

14. ruses (rōōz´ əz) *n.* tricks.

or else my thread will have been spun in vain.
It is a shroud I weave for Lord Laertes
when cold Death comes to lay him on his bier.
The country wives would hold me in dishonor
1330   if he, with all his fortune, lay unshrouded.'
I reached their hearts that way, and they agreed.
So every day I wove on the great loom,
but every night by torchlight I unwove it;
and so for three years I deceived the Achaeans.
1335   But when the seasons brought a fourth year on,
as long months waned, and the long days were spent,
through impudent folly in the slinking maids
they caught me—clamored up to me at night;
I had no choice then but to finish it.
1340   And now, as matters stand at last,
I have no strength left to evade a marriage,
cannot find any further way; my parents
urge it upon me, and my son
will not stand by while they eat up his property.
1345   He comprehends it, being a man full-grown,
able to oversee the kind of house
Zeus would endow with honor.

                           But you too

confide in me, tell me your ancestry.
You were not born of mythic oak or stone."

---

*Penelope again asks the beggar to tell about himself. He makes
up a tale in which Odysseus is mentioned and declares that
Penelope's husband will soon be home.*

1350   "You see, then, he is alive and well, and headed
homeward now, no more to be abroad
far from his island, his dear wife and son.
Here is my sworn word for it. Witness this,
god of the zenith, noblest of the gods,[15]
1355   and Lord Odysseus' hearthfire, now before me:
I swear these things shall turn out as I say.
Between this present dark and one day's ebb,
after the wane, before the crescent moon,
Odysseus will come."

15. god of the zenith, noblest of the gods Zeus.

☑**Reading Check**

How does Odysseus initially respond to Penelope's questions about his past?

▲ **Critical Viewing** The winner of the archery contest will win Penelope's hand in marriage. How does the artist capture the tension in this scene? **[Interpret]**

The Challenge

Pressed by the suitors to choose a husband from among them, Penelope says she will marry the man who can string Odysseus' bow and shoot an arrow through twelve axhandle sockets. The suitors try and fail. Still in disguise, Odysseus asks for a turn and gets it.

And Odysseus took his time,

1360 turning the bow, tapping it, every inch,
for borings that termites might have made
while the master of the weapon was abroad.
The suitors were now watching him, and some
jested among themselves:

"A bow lover!"

1365 "Dealer in old bows!"

"Maybe he has one like it

at home!"

"Or has an itch to make one for himself."

"See how he handles it, the sly old buzzard!"

And one disdainful suitor added this:

"May his fortune grow an inch for every inch he bends it!"

1370 But the man skilled in all ways of contending,
satisfied by the great bow's look and heft,
like a musician, like a harper, when
with quiet hand upon his instrument
he draws between his thumb and forefinger
1375 a sweet new string upon a peg: so effortlessly
Odysseus in one motion strung the bow.
Then slid his right hand down the cord and plucked it,
so the taut gut vibrating hummed and sang
a swallow's note.

Reading Check

How does Penelope decide she will choose a suitor?

In the hushed hall it smote the suitors
1380 and all their faces changed. Then Zeus thundered
overhead, one loud crack for a sign.
And Odysseus laughed within him that the son
of crooked-minded Cronus had flung that omen down.
He picked one ready arrow from his table
1385 where it lay bare: the rest were waiting still
in the quiver for the young men's turn to come.
He nocked[16] it, let it rest across the handgrip,
and drew the string and grooved butt of the arrow,
aiming from where he sat upon the stool.

                                           Now flashed
1390 arrow from twanging bow clean as a whistle
through every socket ring, and grazed not one,
to thud with heavy brazen head beyond.

                                          Then quietly

Odysseus said:

                              "Telemachus, the stranger
you welcomed in your hall has not disgraced you.

▲ Critical Viewing
Compare Odysseus'
grace, described in line
1375, with the grace of
the hunter pictured here.
[Compare and Contrast]

16. nocked set an
arrow against the bow-
string.

1395   I did not miss, neither did I take all day
         stringing the bow. My hand and eye are sound,
         not so contemptible as the young men say.
         The hour has come to cook their lordships' mutton—
         supper by daylight. Other amusements later,
1400   with song and harping that adorn a feast."

         He dropped his eyes and nodded, and the prince
         Telemachus, true son of King Odysseus,
         belted his sword on, clapped hand to his spear,
         and with a clink and glitter of keen bronze
1405   stood by his chair, in the forefront near his father.

Review and Assess

Thinking About the Selection

1. **Respond:** If you were Telemachus or Penelope, how would you react to the stranger's arrival?

2. **(a) Recall:** Who does Telemachus think Odysseus is when they first reunite? **(b) Compare and Contrast:** Compare Odysseus' emotions with those of Telemachus at their reunion.

3. **(a) Recall:** Who is Argus? **(b) Recall:** How does Argus react to Odysseus' return? **(c) Analyze:** Is it a coincidence that Argus dies just when Odysseus returns? Explain.

4. **(a) Recall:** Describe Antinous' treatment of Odysseus. **(b) Analyze Causes and Effects:** Why do you think Antinous treats Odysseus so badly?

5. **(a) Analyze:** How does Penelope feel about the suitors in her house? **(b) Compare and Contrast:** How might Odysseus' feelings about the suitors differ from Penelope's?

6. **(a) Recall:** What does Odysseus tell Penelope about himself? **(b) Infer:** Why do you think Odysseus chooses not to reveal his identity to his wife?

7. **Take a Position:** Is it wrong for Odysseus to deceive his wife? Explain.

▲ **Critical Viewing** Do you think Odysseus' desire to fight the suitors is justified? Explain. **[Make a Judgment]**

Odysseus' Revenge

Now shrugging off his rags the wiliest[17] fighter of the islands
leapt and stood on the broad doorsill, his own bow in his hand.
He poured out at his feet a rain of arrows from the quiver
and spoke to the crowd:

> "So much for that. Your clean-cut game is over.
1410 Now watch me hit a target that no man has hit before,
> if I can make this shot. Help me, Apollo."

He drew to his fist the cruel head of an arrow for Antinous
just as the young man leaned to lift his beautiful drinking cup,
embossed, two-handled, golden: the cup was in his fingers:
1415 the wine was even at his lips: and did he dream of death?
How could he? In that revelry[18] amid his throng of friends
who would imagine a single foe—though a strong foe indeed—
could dare to bring death's pain on him and darkness on his eyes?
Odysseus' arrow hit him under the chin
1420 and punched up to the feathers through his throat.

Backward and down he went, letting the winecup fall
from his shocked hand. Like pipes his nostrils jetted
crimson runnels, a river of mortal red,
and one last kick upset his table
1425 knocking the bread and meat to soak in dusty blood.
Now as they craned to see their champion where he lay
the suitors jostled in uproar down the hall,
everyone on his feet. Wildly they turned and scanned
the walls in the long room for arms; but not a shield,
1430 not a good ashen spear was there for a man to take and throw.
All they could do was yell in outrage at Odysseus:

"Foul! to shoot at a man! That was your last shot!"

"Your own throat will be slit for this!"

> "Our finest lad is down!
You killed the best on Ithaca."

> "Buzzards will tear your eyes out!"

1435 For they imagined as they wished—that it was a wild shot,
an unintended killing—fools, not to comprehend
they were already in the grip of death.
But glaring under his brows Odysseus answered:

"You yellow dogs, you thought I'd never make it
1440 home from the land of Troy. You took my house to plunder. . . .
You dared bid for my wife while I was still alive.

---

17. wiliest (wīl′ ē əst)
adj. craftiest; slyest.

18. revelry (rev′ əl rē)
n. boisterous festivity.

Literary Analysis
Epic Simile and Imagery
What color images appear
in the epic simile about
Antinous' wounds?

Reading Strategy
Summarizing Summarize
Odysseus' interactions
with Antinous and the
other suitors to this point.
What do you think will
happen next?

✓Reading Check
What happens to
Antinous?

Contempt was all you had for the gods who rule wide heaven,
contempt for what men say of you hereafter.
Your last hour has come. You die in blood."

contempt (kən tempt´) *n.*
disdain or scorn; scornful
feelings or actions

1445 As they all took this in, sickly green fear
pulled at their entrails, and their eyes flickered
looking for some hatch or hideaway from death.
Eurymachus[19] alone could speak. He said:

19. Eurymachus (yoo
ri´ mə kəs)

"If you are Odysseus of Ithaca come back,
1450 all that you say these men have done is true.
Rash actions, many here, more in the countryside.
But here he lies, the man who caused them all.
Antinous was the ringleader, he whipped us on
to do these things. He cared less for a marriage
1455 than for the power Cronion has denied him
as king of Ithaca. For that
he tried to trap your son and would have killed him.
He is dead now and has his portion. Spare
your own people. As for ourselves, we'll make
1460 restitution of wine and meat consumed,
and add, each one, a tithe of twenty oxen
with gifts of bronze and gold to warm your heart.
Meanwhile we cannot blame you for your anger."

Reading Strategy
Summarizing Summarize
the plea made by
Eurymachus to Odysseus.

Odysseus glowered under his black brows
1465 and said:
                    "Not for the whole treasure of your fathers,
all you enjoy, lands, flocks, or any gold
put up by others, would I hold my hand.
There will be killing till the score is paid.
You forced yourselves upon this house. Fight your way out,
1470 or run for it, if you think you'll escape death.
I doubt one man of you skins by."

They felt their knees fail, and their hearts—but heard
Eurymachus for the last time rallying them.

"Friends," he said, "the man is implacable.
1475 Now that he's got his hands on bow and quiver
he'll shoot from the big doorstone there
until he kills us to the last man.
                    Fight, I say,
let's remember the joy of it. Swords out!
Hold up your tables to deflect his arrows.
1480 After me, everyone: rush him where he stands.

If we can budge him from the door, if we can pass
into the town, we'll call out men to chase him.
This fellow with his bow will shoot no more."

He drew his own sword as he spoke, a broadsword of fine
    bronze,
1485   honed like a razor on either edge. Then crying hoarse and loud
he hurled himself at Odysseus. But the kingly man let fly
an arrow at that instant, and the quivering feathered butt
sprang to the nipple of his breast as the barb stuck in his liver.
The bright broadsword clanged down. He lurched and fell aside,
1490   pitching across his table. His cup, his bread and meat,
were spilt and scattered far and wide, and his head slammed
        on the ground.
Revulsion, anguish in his heart, with both feet kicking out,
he downed his chair, while the shrouding wave of mist closed on
        his eyes.

Amphinomus now came running at Odysseus,
1495   broadsword naked in his hand. He thought to make
the great soldier give way at the door.
But with a spear throw from behind Telemachus hit him
between the shoulders, and the lancehead drove
clear through his chest. He left his feet and fell
1500   forward, thudding, forehead against the ground.
Telemachus swerved around him, leaving the long dark spear
planted in Amphinomus. If he paused to yank it out
someone might jump him from behind or cut him down with a
        sword
at the moment he bent over. So he ran—ran from the tables
1505   to his father's side and halted, panting, saying:

"Father let me bring you a shield and spear,
a pair of spears, a helmet.
I can arm on the run myself; I'll give
outfits to Eumaeus and this cowherd.
1510   Better to have equipment."

                                        Said Odysseus:

"Run then, while I hold them off with arrows
as long as the arrows last. When all are gone
if I'm alone they can dislodge me."

                                                Quick

upon his father's word Telemachus

Literary Analysis
Epic Simile Why is the comparison of Eurymachus' sharp sword to a razor a simile but not an epic simile?

Reading Strategy
Summarizing In your own words, briefly describe the events of the battle of Odysseus and Telemachus with the suitors thus far.

✔**Reading Check**
What does Telemachus want to bring to his father to help him fight the suitors?

1515 ran to the room where spears and armor lay.
He caught up four light shields, four pairs of spears,
four helms of war high-plumed with flowing manes,
and ran back, loaded down, to his father's side.
He was the first to pull a helmet on
1520 and slide his bare arm in a buckler strap.
The servants armed themselves, and all three took their stand
beside the master of battle.

                      While he had arrows
he aimed and shot, and every shot brought down
one of his huddling enemies.
1525 But when all barbs had flown from the bowman's fist,
he leaned his bow in the bright entryway
beside the door, and armed: a four-ply shield
hard on his shoulder, and a crested helm,
horsetailed, nodding stormy upon his head,
1530 then took his tough and bronze-shod spears. . . .

---

*Aided by Athena, Odysseus, Telemachus, Eumaeus, and other
faithful herdsmen kill all the suitors.*

And Odysseus looked around him, narrow-eyed,
for any others who had lain hidden
while death's black fury passed.

                    In blood and dust
he saw that crowd all fallen, many and many slain.

1535 Think of a catch that fishermen haul in to a half-moon bay
in a fine-meshed net from the whitecaps of the sea:
how all are poured out on the sand, in throes for the salt sea,
twitching their cold lives away in Helios' fiery air:
so lay the suitors heaped on one another.

Penelope's Test

Penelope tests Odysseus to prove he really is her husband.

1540 Greathearted Odysseus, home at last,
was being bathed now by Eurynome
and rubbed with golden oil, and clothed again
in a fresh tunic and a cloak. Athena
lent him beauty, head to foot. She made him
1545 taller, and massive, too, with crisping hair

**Literary Analysis
Imagery and Epic Simile**
In reading the epic simile
in lines 1535–1539, what
do you picture?

**Literary Analysis
Epic Simile** To what is
Odysseus' hair compared?
Is this comparison an epic
simile?

in curls like petals of wild hyacinth
but all red-golden. Think of gold infused
on silver by a craftsman, whose fine art
Hephaestus♦ taught him, or Athena: one
1550　whose work moves to delight: just so she lavished
beauty over Odysseus' head and shoulders.
He sat then in the same chair by the pillar,
facing his silent wife, and said:

　　　　　　　　　　　　　　"Strange woman,
the immortals of Olympus made you hard,
1555　harder than any. Who else in the world
would keep aloof as you do from her husband
if he returned to her from years of trouble,
cast on his own land in the twentieth year?

Nurse, make up a bed for me to sleep on.
1560　Her heart is iron in her breast."

　　　　　　　　　　　　　　　Penelope
spoke to Odysseus now. She said:

　　　　　　　　　　　　　　"Strange man,
if man you are . . . This is no pride on my part
nor scorn for you—not even wonder, merely.
I know so well how you—how he—appeared
1565　boarding the ship for Troy. But all the same . . .

Make up his bed for him, Eurycleia.
Place it outside the bedchamber my lord
built with his own hands. Pile the big bed
with fleeces, rugs, and sheets of purest linen."

1570　With this she tried him to the breaking point,
and he turned on her in a flash raging:

"Woman, by heaven you've stung me now!
Who dared to move my bed?
No builder had the skill for that—unless
1575　a god came down to turn the trick. No mortal
in his best days could budge it with a crowbar.
There is our pact and pledge, our secret sign,
built into that bed—my handiwork
and no one else's!

　　　　　　　　　　　　An old trunk of olive
1580　grew like a pillar on the building plot,

ℒiterature
in context　Mythology Connection

♦ Hephaestus

Any craftsman taught by Hephaestus, the Greek god of fire and metalworking, would be worth his weight in gold. His counterpart in Roman mythology was the mighty fire god Vulcan. Hephaestus was renowned for his work at the forge, crafting such items as Athena's spear, Achilles' shield, and Zeus' thunderbolts. Hephaestus was the only god with a physical deformity, caused when his father Zeus hurled him from Olympus. During his recovery, he learned how to craft beautiful objects from underwater coral and metals.

Statue of Vulcan, Hephaestus' Roman counterpart

✓Reading Check

How does Odysseus describe Penelope's attitude toward him?

▲ **Critical Viewing** How does your image of the events in the *Odyssey* compare to this artist's interpretation of the events? **[Compare]**

and I laid out our bedroom round that tree,
lined up the stone walls, built the walls and roof,
gave it a doorway and smooth-fitting doors.
Then I lopped off the silvery leaves and branches,
1585   hewed and shaped that stump from the roots up
into a bedpost, drilled it, let it serve
as model for the rest. I planed them all,
inlaid them all with silver, gold and ivory,
and stretched a bed between—a pliant web
1590   of oxhide thongs dyed crimson.

                                   There's our sign!
I know no more. Could someone else's hand
have sawn that trunk and dragged the frame away?"

Their secret! as she heard it told, her knees
grew tremulous and weak, her heart failed her.
1595   With eyes brimming tears she ran to him,
throwing her arms around his neck, and kissed him,
murmuring:

                      "Do not rage at me, Odysseus!
No one ever matched your caution! Think
what difficulty the gods gave: they denied us
1600   life together in our prime and flowering years,
kept us from crossing into age together.
Forgive me, don't be angry. I could not
welcome you with love on sight! I armed myself
long ago against the frauds of men,
1605   impostors who might come—and all those many
whose underhanded ways bring evil on! . . .
But here and now, what sign could be so clear
as this of our own bed?
No other man has ever laid eyes on it—
1610   only my own slave, Actoris, that my father
sent with me as a gift—she kept our door.
You make my stiff heart know that I am yours."

Now from his breast into his eyes the ache
of longing mounted, and he wept at last,
1615   his dear wife, clear and faithful, in his arms,

Reading Strategy
Summarizing How would
you describe Penelope's
feelings in lines
1593–1596?

✔**Reading Check**
What difficulty does
Penelope say the gods
gave to her and
Odysseus?

longed for as the sunwarmed earth is longed for by a swimmer
spent in rough water where his ship went down
under Poseidon's blows, gale winds and tons of sea.
Few men can keep alive through a big surf
1620   to crawl, clotted with brine, on kindly beaches
in joy, in joy, knowing the abyss[20] behind:
and so she too rejoiced, her gaze upon her husband,
her white arms round him pressed as though forever.

20. abyss (ə bis') *n.*
ocean depths.

The Ending

*Odysseus is reunited with his father. Athena commands that
peace prevail between Odysseus and the relatives of the slain
suitors. Odysseus has regained his family and his kingdom.*

Review and Assess

Thinking About the Selection

1. **Respond:** Do you think that Odysseus' revenge is justified?
   Why or why not?
2. **(a) Recall:** Which act begins Odysseus' revenge on the
   suitors? **(b) Analyze:** Why does this act catch the suitors by
   surprise?
3. **(a) Recall:** What planning does Odysseus do before battling
   the suitors? **(b) Analyze:** How does his planning help him
   defeat his opponents?
4. **(a) Recall:** How does the fight turn out? **(b) Analyze:** Even
   though some suitors have been crueler than others, why does
   Odysseus take equal revenge on all of them?
5. **(a) Recall:** What is Penelope's test, and how does Odysseus
   pass it? **(b) Infer:** Why does Penelope feel the need to test
   Odysseus, even though he has abandoned his disguise?
   (c) Interpret: Is the mood after the test altogether happy?
   Explain.
6. **(a) Connect:** Are Odysseus' actions in dealing with the
   suitors consistent with his actions in earlier episodes of the
   epic? Explain. **(b) Assess:** Do you consider him heroic?
7. **Evaluate:** How do you think the problem of the suitors should
   have been handled? Why?

Homer

(circa 800 B.C.)

A legendary
poet and his-
torian, Homer
is credited
with two of
the most
famous and
enduring epics of
all time: the *Iliad* and the
Odyssey. Their impressive
length and scope have
resulted in the coining of
an adjective from the
author's name: *homeric,*
meaning "large-scale, massive, or enormous."

Facts about Homer's life
have been lost over time.
Scholars even disagree
about whether the *Iliad* and
the *Odyssey* were written
by the same person—and
whether Homer existed at
all! According to tradition,
however, Homer was born
in western Asia Minor, and
he was blind.

In later centuries, the
Iliad and the *Odyssey* were
the basis of Greek and
Roman education.

Review and Assess

Literary Analysis

Epic Simile

1. Identify at least three **epic similes** in Part 2 of the *Odyssey*.
2. Using a chart like the one shown, note what is being compared in each of the epic similes you identified and the purpose of the comparison.

Lines	Comparison	Purpose

Connecting Literary Elements

3. What **imagery** involving sight, sound, and movement does Homer include in the epic simile in lines 1061–1065?
4. In lines 1412–1425, to which senses do the images used in describing Antinous' death appeal?
5. (a) What is the epic simile in lines 1613–1624? (b) Why is this simile a powerful image for the conclusion of the epic?

Reading Strategy

Summarizing

6. To **summarize** Part 2, use a timeline like this to list, in order, the main events.

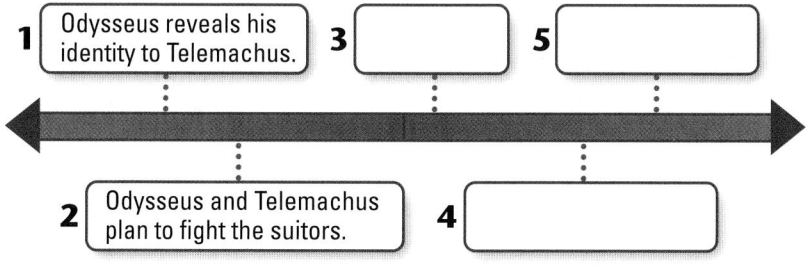

7. Explain the cause and effect of each event that you listed.

Extend Understanding

8. **Cultural Connection:** Why do you think contemporary readers still relate to the characters and the events in the *Odyssey*?

Integrate Language Skills

Vocabulary Development Lesson

Word Analysis: Latin Root -equi-

The Latin root -equi-, meaning "same" or "equal," appears in the word equity, which means "fairness" or "justice." Complete each sentence below with one of the following -equi- words.

a. equinox   **b.** equivalent   **c.** equidistant

1. Two nickels are ___?___ to a dime.
2. Since the two restaurants are ___?___, we could reach either one in the same time.
3. At the vernal ___?___, day and night are of the same duration.

Spelling Strategy

When adding a suffix beginning with a vowel to a word that ends in silent e, drop the e and add the suffix: bemuse + -ing = bemusing.

Add the suffix in italics to each word below, and write the new word in your notebook.

1. believe + -able   2. sense + -ible   3. secure + -ity

Grammar Lesson

Usage: among and between

The prepositions among and between are sometimes used incorrectly. **Among** always implies a relationship involving three or more items, while **between** generally is used with only two.

Among: Eumaeus went into the megaron among the suitors. (many suitors)

Between: Odysseus will come between this present dark and one day's ebb. (two times)

Practice Copy these sentences, using among or between to complete each one.

1. Suddenly a beggar stood ___?___ all of the suitors.

Concept Development: Synonyms

Review the words in the vocabulary list on page 1020. Then, choose the word or phrase whose meaning is closest to that of the first word.

1. dissemble: (a) resemble, (b) take apart, (c) disguise
2. lithe: (a) alert, (b) young, (c) limber
3. incredulity: (a) disbelief, (b) anger, (c) naiveté
4. bemusing: (a) allowing, (b) muddling, (c) entertaining
5. glowering: (a) shining, (b) scowling, (c) laughing
6. equity: (a) fairness, (b) horses, (c) calmness
7. maudlin: (a) boring, (b) tired, (c) sentimental
8. contempt: (a) scorn, (b) pity, (c) doubt

2. A clash ___?___ him and Antinous quickly developed.
3. Sounds of protest spread ___?___ the onlookers, but Antinous paid them no heed.
4. Odysseus' deadly arrow struck ___?___ Antinous' neck and shoulder.
5. Odysseus' skill as an archer is well known ___?___ the Greeks.

Writing Application Write four sentences about events in the Odyssey. Use among correctly in two of the sentences and between correctly in the other two.

𝒲𝒢 *Prentice Hall Writing and Grammar Connection: Chapter 27, Section 2*

Writing Lesson

Character Study

Odysseus is an epic hero, but he may not be a good role model. In a character study, evaluate Odysseus' status as a hero by analyzing his actions and motives. Support your analysis with examples and quotations from the epic.

Prewriting   Decide what you want to prove about Odysseus. To get started, write several different completions to this statement: *What I want to prove is . . .* Then, for each statement, list lines from the poem that can help you prove your point.

Drafting   Develop a thesis statement that expresses your main idea. Then, organize your points in a logical order. As you draft, be sure to include quotations from the text to illustrate your ideas.

> ### Model: Using Quotations to Illustrate Points
>
> When the men are escaping from the Cyclops, Odysseus taunts Polyphemus against his crew's wishes. He notes, "I would not heed them in my glorying spirit, but let my anger flare and yelled" (lines 455–456).

> Quotations from the text and line citations help readers see a strong connection between an argument and the text.

Revising   Review your draft to determine whether your ideas come across clearly and are well supported with quotations.

*W*G *Prentice Hall Writing and Grammar Connection: Chapter 13, Section 3*

Extension Activities

Listening and Speaking With several classmates, prepare a **debate** to determine whether Odysseus should be prosecuted for murder in the slaying of Penelope's suitors.

- Divide into two opposing teams.
- Prepare an argument expressing your team's position, and support it with details from the *Odyssey* or from actual legal cases found in library or Internet sources.
- Present arguments before the class.

Ask class members to decide which side presented its argument most successfully. **[Group Activity]**

Research and Technology Create an **Odyssey map** that traces Odysseus' voyage. Conduct library and Internet research to help you determine locations and distances between them. You might also refer to the map on page 1013. When you have completed your map, calculate the actual straight-line distance from Troy to Ithaca. Then, based on your map, approximate how far Odysseus traveled.

 Take It to the Net   www.phschool.com

Go online for an additional research activity using the Internet.

Prepare to Read

An Ancient Gesture ◆ Siren Song ◆
Prologue and Epilogue *from the* Odyssey ◆ Ithaca

Penelope and the Suitors, 1912, J.M. Waterhouse, Aberdeen Art Gallery and Museum, Scotland

Take It to the Net

Visit www.phschool.com
for interactive activities
and instruction related to
the selections, including

- background
- graphic organizers
- literary elements
- reading strategies

Preview

Connecting to the Literature

Two or more people looking at the same event are likely to describe it in distinctly different ways. In these selections, four writers bring their own perspectives to the events in the *Odyssey*.

Background

The authors of these four poems are twentieth-century men and women. Thus, their views of society and of men's and women's roles in society are very different from Homer's. For much of history in most cultures, women have had fewer legal rights and fewer opportunities than men. In fact, women in the United States did not even have the right to vote until 1920. Further progress for women was slow; they did not gain career and educational opportunities until the last few decades of the twentieth century.

Literary Analysis

Contemporary Interpretations

The characters and events of the *Odyssey* are timeless and universal in their interest and significance. They are so rich in meaning that every generation sees in them ideas and values that ring true. **Contemporary interpretations** of the epic—present-day conceptions or understandings—have produced poems, plays, novels, and essays by countless writers. For instance, in "Ithaca," Constantine Cavafy transforms Ithaca from a physical place to a spiritual ideal:

> Ithaca has given you the beautiful voyage.
> Without her you would never have taken the road.

Notice how the poets use ideas from Homer's work to convey contemporary thoughts, values, beliefs, and feelings.

Comparing Literary Works

Contemporary interpretations of an epic like the *Odyssey* can differ widely in purpose, theme, and artistic method. Consider the impact the backgrounds, ideas, and feelings of these writers may have had on their interpretations of the *Odyssey*. Then, compare the ways each poet reflects and adapts ideas from Homer's epic.

CALIFORNIA STANDARDS

Instruction with these selections addresses these standards:

R 1.1*, 3.2
W 1.8, 2.3*
WOLC 1.3*
LS 1.1

* Standards tested on HS Exit Exam. For complete standards, see p. CA 4.

Reading Strategy

Comparing and Contrasting

In reading a piece of literature based on an earlier work, look for the similarities and differences between the original and the updated work.

- **Compare** an updated work with its original to discover how elements in the works are alike.
- **Contrast** an updated work with its original to decide how elements in the works are different.

As you read, use a Venn diagram like the one shown to identify similarities and differences between each poem and Homer's *Odyssey*.

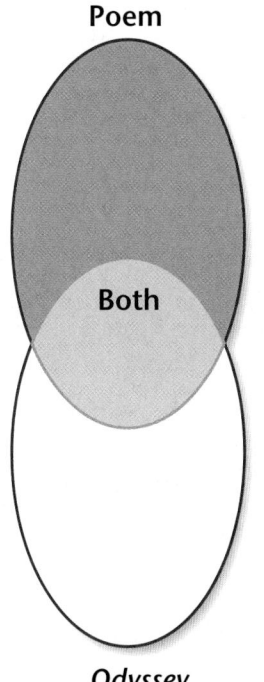

Poem

Both

Odyssey

Vocabulary Development

beached (bēcht) *adj.* washed up and lying on a beach (p. 1054)

picturesque (pik´ chər esk´) *adj.* like or suggesting a picture (p. 1055)

tempests (tem´ pists) *n.* violent storms with strong winds (p. 1056)

amber (am´ bər) *n.* yellowish resin used in jewelry (p. 1059)

ebony (eb´ ə nē) *n.* hard, dark wood used for furniture (p. 1059)

defrauded (dē frôd´ id) *v.* cheated (p. 1060)

AN ANCIENT GESTURE

Edna St. Vincent Millay

▲ **Critical Viewing** What is Penelope's attitude toward the suitors? How can you tell? **[Infer; Support]**

I thought, as I wiped my eyes on the corner of my apron:
Penelope did this too.
And more than once: you can't keep weaving all day
And undoing it all through the night;
5   Your arms get tired, and the back of your neck gets tight;
And along towards morning, when you think it will never be light,
And your husband has been gone, and you don't know where,
     for years,
Suddenly you burst into tears;
There is simply nothing else to do.

10   And I thought, as I wiped my eyes on the corner of my apron:
This is an ancient gesture, authentic, antique,
In the very best tradition, classic, Greek;
Ulysses did this too.
But only as a gesture,—a gesture which implied
15   To the assembled throng that he was much too moved to speak.
He learned it from Penelope . . .
Penelope, who really cried.

Reading Strategy
Comparing and Contrasting How are the reasons for the speaker's tears similar to the reasons for Penelope's tears?

Review and Assess

Thinking About the Selection

1. **Respond:** Does this poem make you feel more or less sympathetic to Penelope than the *Odyssey* did? Explain.

2. **(a) Recall:** What similarity does the speaker of "An Ancient Gesture" see between herself and Penelope?
   (b) Analyze: What has caused the speaker to employ this "ancient gesture"?

3. **(a) Recall:** Which characters from the *Odyssey* does Millay incorporate in her poem? **(b) Distinguish:** What differences between these characters does the speaker point out?

4. **(a) Assess:** What questions about the speaker and her husband are left unanswered? **(b) Extend:** What effect is created by these unanswered questions?

5. **Speculate:** What advice do you think Penelope would give to the speaker of this poem? Explain.

Edna St. Vincent Millay

(1892–1950)

Like many other American writers of her time, Edna St. Vincent Millay is remembered for her artistic experimentation and her rebelliousness. She published several successful poetry collections, including *The Harp Weaver and Other Poems* (1923), which earned her a Pulitzer Prize.

SIREN SONG

Margaret Atwood

This is the one song everyone
would like to learn: the song
that is irresistible:

the song that forces men
5   to leap overboard in squadrons
even though they see the <u>beached</u> skulls

the song nobody knows
because anyone who has heard it
is dead, and the others can't remember.

10   Shall I tell you the secret
and if I do, will you get me
out of this bird suit?[1]

beached (bēcht) *adj.*
washed up and lying on
a beach

---

1. bird suit Sirens are usually represented as half bird
and half woman.

I don't enjoy it here
squatting on this island
15 looking <u>picturesque</u> and mythical

with these two feathery maniacs,
I don't enjoy singing
this trio, fatal and valuable.

I will tell the secret to you,
20 to you, only to you.
Come closer. This song

is a cry for help: Help me!
Only you, only you can,
you are unique

25 at last. Alas
it is a boring song
but it works every time.

picturesque (pik′ chər esk′) *adj.* like or suggesting a picture

Review and Assess

Thinking About the Selection

1. **Respond:** How do you feel about the experience of the speaker of the poem?
2. **(a) Recall:** What does the Siren reveal about the song? **(b) Analyze:** The Siren describes the song as "fatal and valuable." Why might it be valuable?
3. **(a) Recall:** How does the speaker of "Siren Song" say she feels about being a Siren? **(b) Infer:** To whom might the Siren be speaking as she describes her feelings?
4. **Assess:** How much of "Siren Song" is based on Homer's *Odyssey* and how much is Atwood's original creation?
5. **Speculate:** What relationship between men and women does she portray in this poem?
6. **Extend:** Do you think most women would appreciate or dislike this poem?

Margaret Atwood

(b. 1939)

Since the 1960s, this Canadian author has been writing about what it means to be a woman in a period of social change. For example, her novel *The Handmaid's Tale* (1985) explores a futuristic society in which women's roles are strictly defined.

Another of Atwood's central themes is the role of mythology in people's lives. These two concerns come together in "Siren Song," an ironic look at Homer's Sirens.

Prologue and Epilogue from the Odyssey

Derek Walcott

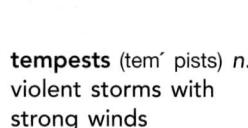

PROLOGUE

Sound of surf.

BILLY BLUE (*Sings*)
Gone sing 'bout that man because his stories please us,
Who saw trials and <u>tempests</u> for ten years after Troy.

I'm Blind Billy Blue, my main man's sea-smart Odysseus,
Who the God of the Sea drove crazy and tried to destroy.

5   Andra moi ennepe mousa polutropon hos mala polla . . .
The shuttle of the sea moves back and forth on this line,

All night, like the surf, she shuttles and doesn't fall
Asleep, then her rosy fingers at dawn unstitch the design.

When you hear this chord
(Chord)
               Look for a swallow's wings,
10 A swallow arrowing seaward like a messenger

Passing smoke-blue islands, happy that the kings
Of Troy are going home and its ten years' siege is over.

So my blues drifts like smoke from the fire of that war,
Cause once Achilles was ashes, things sure fell apart.

15 Slow-striding Achilles, who put the hex on Hector
A swallow twitters in Troy. That's where we start.
(Exit.)

tempests (tem´ pists) *n.*
violent storms with
strong winds

Literary Analysis
**Contemporary
Interpretations** Which
details in the prologue
give a modern twist to
the *Odyssey*?

EPILOGUE

BILLY BLUE (*Sings*)

I sang of that man against whom the sea still rages,
Who escaped its terrors, that despair could not destroy,

Since that first blind singer, others will sing down the ages
20 Of the heart in its harbour, then long years after Troy, after Troy.

And a house, happy for good, from a swallow's omen,
Let the trees clap their hands, and the surf whisper amen.

For a rock, a rock, a rock, a rock-steady woman
Let the waves clap their hands and the surf whisper amen.

25 For that peace which, in their mercy, the gods allow men.
(*Fade. Sound of surf.*)

Review and Assess

Thinking About the Selection

1. **Respond:** Do you think the narrator is someone you would like to know? Explain.
2. **(a) Recall:** Who is the narrator? **(b) Interpret:** Which qualities of the narrator's character do the words in these passages convey?
3. **(a) Recall:** Which characters from the *Odyssey* does the narrator mention by name in the Prologue? **(b) Recall:** How does he describe Penelope in the Epilogue? **(c) Infer:** What seems to be his attitude toward her? Explain your answer.
4. **(a) Recall:** Who is the "first blind singer" referred to in the Epilogue? **(b) Analyze:** Does this reference explain why Billy Blue *sings* the Epilogue? Explain.
5. **(a) Generalize:** Overall, which elements from the *Odyssey* seem most interesting to Walcott? **(b) Assess:** How faithful is this interpretation of Homer's *Odyssey*?
6. **Evaluate:** Do you think the poet treats the original text with respect? Explain.

Derek Walcott

(b. 1930)

Born on the Caribbean island of St. Lucia, Walcott writes poems that reflect the influence of his background. His work has won worldwide acclaim, and in 1992 he won the Nobel Prize for Literature for his book *Omeros* (1990), which draws on Homer's epic. While granting the award, the Swedish Academy said, "West Indian culture has found its great poet."

In addition to being a poet, Walcott is a successful playwright and director. "Prologue" and "Epilogue" are from his stage version of the *Odyssey*.

▲ **Critical Viewing** The poet uses classical images from the *Odyssey*, like those pictured here, to make a connection to modern life. Which experiences in your life could correspond to some of the classical images mentioned in the poem? **[Connect]**

ITHACA

Constantine Cavafy

When you start on your journey to Ithaca,
then pray that the road is long,
full of adventure, full of knowledge.
Do not fear the Lestrygonians[1]
5   and the Cyclopes and the angry Poseidon.
You will never meet such as these on your path,
if your thoughts remain lofty, if a fine
emotion touches your body and your spirit.
You will never meet the Lestrygonians,
10 the Cyclopes and the fierce Poseidon,
if you do not carry them within your soul,
if your soul does not raise them up before you.

Then pray that the road is long.
That the summer mornings are many,
15 that you will enter ports seen for the first time
with such pleasure, with such joy!
Stop at Phoenician markets,
and purchase fine merchandise,
mother-of-pearl and corals, <u>amber</u> and <u>ebony</u>,

---

1. **Lestrygonians** (les tri gō´ nē ənz) cannibals who destroy all of Odysseus'
ships except his own and kill the crews.

amber (am´ bər) *n.* yellow-ish resin used in jewelry

ebony (eb´ ə nē) *n.* hard, dark wood used for furniture

✔**Reading Check**

What advice does the speaker give listeners or readers about meeting the Lestrygonians?

Integrate Language Skills

Vocabulary Development Lesson

Word Analysis: French Suffix -esque

The French suffix -esque means "like" or "having the quality of." In "Siren Song," one of the Sirens complains of having to look too *picturesque*, which means "like or suggesting a picture." The suffix also appears in *statuesque* and *arabesque*.

Complete each sentence with one of the -esque words below:

a. picturesque **b.** statuesque **c.** arabesque

1. The ___?___ mountain view lingered in my mind for several days.
2. The carpet was covered with ___?___ designs resembling Moorish calligraphy.
3. The ___?___ actress commanded the attention of the audience with her regal bearing and stunning diamonds.

Concept Development: Analogies

Complete each analogy below with a word from the vocabulary list on page 1051.

1. *Melodious* is to *voice* as __?__ is to *appearance*.
2. *Marble* is to *statue* as __?__ is to *necklace*.
3. *Fallen* is to *leaves* as __?__ is to *shells*.
4. *Floods* are to *water* as __?__ are to *wind*.
5. *Aluminum* is to *can* as __?__ is to *table*.
6. *Spoke* is to *conversed* as __?__ is to *cheated*.

Spelling Strategy

If a word ends in a vowel-vowel-consonant combination, do not double the final consonant before adding a suffix. Thus, *defraud* + -ed = *defrauded*. Add the suffix to each word below and then use the new word in a sentence.

1. sweet + -est **2.** break + -age **3.** veil + -ed

Grammar Lesson

Varying Sentence Length

When you **vary sentence length,** you alternate between long and short sentences in order to make your sentences more interesting and readable. The varied rhythm of the passage below helps emphasize its meaning.

> **Example:** Cavafy uses the journey to Ithaca as a metaphor for one's own life journey. Enjoy life, says the poet. (*Long sentence followed by short sentence*)

If you write many long sentences, it will help the flow of your writing if you break some into shorter sentences.

Practice Rewrite each sentence as two shorter sentences. Simplify where possible.

1. Penelope cries for Odysseus, who is her husband, who has been away for years.
2. Sailors cannot resist the call of the Sirens' song, which lures men to their deaths.
3. Walcott introduces Billy Blue, who substitutes for Homer, narrator of the *Odyssey*.
4. Ithaca, which may symbolize the end of life, is the goal to focus on.
5. Each poet offers an interpretation of the *Odyssey*, the epic by Homer, who lived long ago.

Writing Application Write a paragraph describing your reaction to one of the poems. Work to vary your sentence lengths.

W/*G* *Prentice Hall Writing and Grammar Connection: Chapter 22, Section 3*

Writing Lesson

Comparison-and-Contrast Essay

All four of the poems in this section draw their inspiration from Homer's *Odyssey*. Write an essay in which you compare and contrast one of the selections with the appropriate portion of Homer's original work.

Prewriting   After choosing the selection you wish to compare and contrast, list the ways that the poem and the *Odyssey* are similar and different. Prepare a comparison chart to organize the information.

Model: Finding Points of Comparison

Cavafy's "Ithaca"	Homer's *Odyssey*
1. Hopes the journey is long.	1. Hopes the journey will end.
2.	2.
3.	3.

> A comparison chart is a useful tool for organizing the information to be used in an essay.

Drafting   Use the notes in your chart as the starting point from which to write your draft. Use words such as *like*, *unlike*, *similarly*, and *in contrast* to show points of difference and resemblance.

Revising   When you revise your essay, make sure that it is clearly organized by points of comparison and contrast. In addition to checking for accuracy, be sure you have clarified the meaning of the passages to which you draw your readers' attention.

W̶G Prentice Hall Writing and Grammar Connection: Chapter 9, Section 2

Extension Activities

Listening and Speaking Watch a film version of the *Odyssey*. Then, prepare a **movie review** for your classmates. In writing your review, consider these key elements of the task:

- Focus on the movie's themes and imagery.
- Formulate your own judgments about the film.
- Support those judgments with evidence.

Read your review aloud to your classmates and invite them to ask questions. **[Group Activity]**

Research and Technology Organize a **collection of literary works** inspired by the *Odyssey*. Use the Internet to help you search. Find enough information so that you can include a summary of each work you choose. If possible, use software to design your collection.

 **Take It to the Net**   www.phschool.com

Go online for an additional research activity using the Internet.

The *Odyssey* recounts the trials and adventures of Odysseus. Two decades is a long time to be away from home, dependent on the whims of the gods and facing dangers in battle with men and monsters. Still, risk has its rewards, and ultimately the story has a happy ending.

In April 1970, the three-man crew of the *Apollo 13* spacecraft embarked on a modern-day odyssey to the moon. Like Odysseus, they set out with a spirit of anticipation and adventure. But the exploration of space has its own perils. On the third day of their mission, just as they were getting ready to sleep in the command module nicknamed Odyssey, an onboard oxygen tank ruptured. After several nerve-wracking days, the crew finally managed to return safely to Earth. In this case, survival was the ultimate reward. The following excerpt from one astronaut's narrative describes the moment when the gas leak was first discovered.

Lost Moon
The Perilous Voyage
of
Apollo 13

Jim Lovell
and
Jeffrey Kluger

"It looks to me," Lovell told the ground uninflectedly, "that we are venting something." Then, for impact, and perhaps to persuade himself, he repeated: "We are venting something into space."

"Roger," Lousma responded in the mandatory matter-of-factness of the Capcom, "we copy your venting."

"It's a gas of some sort," Lovell said.

"Can you tell us anything about it? Where is it coming from?"

"It's coming out of window one right now, Jack," Lovell answered, offering only as much detail as his limited vantage point provided.

The understated report from the spacecraft tore through the control room like a bullet.

"Crew thinks they're venting something," Lousma said to the loop at large.

"I heard that," Kranz said.

"Copy that, Flight?" Lousma asked, just to be sure.

"Rog," Kranz assured him. "O.K. everybody, let's think of the kinds of things we'd be venting. GNC, you got anything that looks abnormal on your system?"

"Negative, Flight."

"How about you, EECOM? You see anything with the instrumentation you've got that could be venting?"

"That's affirmed, Flight," Liebergot said, thinking, of course, of oxygen tank two. If a tank of gas is suddenly reading empty and a cloud of gas is surrounding the spacecraft, it's a good bet the two are connected, especially if the whole mess had been preceded by a suspicious, ship-shaking bang. "Let me look at the system as far as venting is concerned," Liebergot said to Flight.

"O.K., let's start scanning," Kranz agreed. "I assume you've called in your backup EECOM to see if we can get some more brain power on this thing."

"We got one here."

"Rog."

The change on the loop and in the room was palpable. No one said anything out loud, no one declared anything officially, but the controllers began to recognize that Apollo 13, which had been launched in triumph just over two days earlier, might have just metamorphosed from a brilliant mission of exploration to one of simple survival.

Jim Lovell

(b. 1928)

Jim Lovell was a test pilot for U.S. Navy fighter aircraft before joining the space program as an astronaut. Lovell was the first man to rendezvous two spacecraft and to journey twice to the moon. He coauthored this account of the harrowing journey of *Apollo 13*'s three-man crew.

Jeffrey Kluger

(b. 1954)

Jeffrey Kluger, a senior writer for *Time* magazine, frequently writes on science and space issues. With *Apollo 13* astronaut Jim Lovell, he coauthored the book *Lost Moon*, which served as the basis for the Ron Howard film about the mission.

Connecting Literature Past and Present

1. How would you have reacted to the discovery of the oxygen leak?
2. Did the astronauts deal with adversity in a manner similar to Odysseus'? If not, how did they differ?
3. Do the roles played by the gods have any type of counterpart in the account of the flight of *Apollo 13*? Explain

READING INFORMATIONAL MATERIALS

Newspaper Editorials

About Newspaper Editorials

A newspaper editorial is an article in which the newspaper's publisher or editor expresses his or her opinion on a current event or issue, such as criticizing or praising the actions of a public official or group. In some cases, an editorial might also attempt to persuade readers to take a particular action. For example, an editorial may promote certain political candidates and urge readers to vote for them in an upcoming election. Like a persuasive essay, an editorial can be effective only if strong arguments support the writer's opinion.

Reading Strategy

Analyzing Bias

Bias is a writer's tendency to favor one side of an issue. Writers show bias when they present unfavorable facts, use language intended to provoke an emotional response, or do not examine opposing points of view.

Both editorials that follow use loaded language—words intended to trigger a positive or negative response without reasoned support.

- The *Minneapolis Star and Tribune* refers to Senator John Glenn's decision to go into space as "volunteering." The word is meant to elicit a positive response from readers.

- *The Kansas City Star* calls Glenn's flight a "junket," a word suggesting that it is a pleasure trip. The word is intended to elicit a negative response.

As you read both editorials, use a chart like the one shown to record each instance of bias you find.

	"Veteran"	"Wrong Orbit"
Main idea		
Support		
Loaded words		
Opposing point not considered		There is symbolic value to Glenn's flight.
Facts not considered		

Veteran Returns, Becomes Symbol

**Editorial in the
Minneapolis Star and Tribune,
January 19, 1998**

John Glenn went into orbit in 1962 and took America's hearts soaring with him. Who better to fire the nation's imagination again about the promise of space exploration?

NASA has done itself and its cause great good by announcing that Glenn, the astronaut-turned-U.S. senator, will fly into space once more. Though Glenn has represented Ohio in the Senate for five terms and run for president once, many Americans still consider his name synonymous with the nation's manned space program.

At a time when all astronauts were esteemed as America's best and brightest, Glenn stood out. Though not the first American in space, nor the one to seize the space-race prize—a moon landing—Glenn possessed an appeal that surpassed that of his peers.

Just as Glenn's orbital heroics inspired America when he was a young man, by joining the shuttle crew in October at age 77, he can inspire the nation again. He can reignite curiosity about the benefits and challenges for humankind that lie beyond Earth. He can let a watchful public share vicariously his delight at leaving Earth's bounds once more.

And he can again be an exemplar for his generation—a generation already setting new standards for vigor and productivity past age 70. Glenn's flight should dramatically demonstrate that age is no limit to derring-do, nor to service to one's country.

Volunteering for a space ride isn't an option for most septuagenarians. But many of Glenn's contemporaries are also volunteering, lending a hand to the young, old, sick and needy in their own communities. As America honors Glenn's past and future career in space, let the nation also take grateful note of the good works senior citizens are doing here on the ground.

The Wrong Orbit

Senator Has No Legitimate Business Blasting Into Space

Editorial in *The Kansas City Star*, January 20, 1998

Most Americans think of political lobbying as something done by special interest groups trying to curry favor with lawmakers to affect some legislation. Not so in the case of Sen. John Glenn and his former employer, the National Aeronautics and Space Administration.

Glenn, a Democratic senator from Ohio, has lobbied NASA for some time in hope of returning to space. Glenn, who will turn 77 in July, was the first American to orbit the Earth.

He plans to retire from the Senate, but for his next engagement he wants to strap on a space suit under the pretense of scientific merit. Glenn says his space jaunt would help the space program understand the effects of weightlessness on the aging human form. (C'mon, Senator, it's doubtful even you believe that, so don't expect anyone else to.)

There are much better uses for the taxpayers' money than Glenn's planned junket in space via the Discovery mission in October. Besides, as the senator ought to know, workers in the space program are being laid off around the country due to downsizing at NASA. And there's something questionable, if not downright indecent, about a U.S. senator who has been a NASA ally in Congress, calling on the space agency for a favor. Whether on this planet or another, a quid pro quo is the same.

. . .

John Glenn became a hero after his pioneering space flight, and he parlayed that status into what was said to be a successful political career. His political career was jeopardized by his involvement in the Keating Five scandal, and he became excessively shrill this year during committee hearings as the Senate defender of the Democratic presidential fund-raising debacle.

Certainly, there are times when good science and good politics mix, as happened with the launch of the U.S. space program as part of the space race with former Soviet Union.

But Glenn's proposed junket in space is neither good science nor good politics.

> The writer uses the loaded word "pretense" in this paragraph.

> Here, the writer acknowledges an opposing point of view. Later, the writer will argue that the position is wrong.

> The editorial concludes with a restatement of the writer's opinion.

Check Your Comprehension

1. What were John Glenn's two careers?
2. What is unusual about Glenn's proposed ride in space?
3. Which editorial opposes Glenn's planned space ride?

Applying the Reading Strategy

Analyzing Bias

4. Cite two uses of loaded words in each editorial.
5. Identify two issues raised by the Kansas City editorial that are ignored by the Minneapolis editorial.

Activity

Writing an Editorial Analysis

These two editorials offer opposing points of view about John Glenn's proposed space trip. Create an outline like the one shown, listing the arguments in each editorial. Then, explain which editorial you find more convincing and why.

Contrasting Informational Texts

Editorials and News Reports

Editorials serve a different purpose from news reports. You read an editorial to discover a different perspective, or opinion, of an event. You watch a news report to collect information that is largely free of opinion.

1. Consider the differences between the two types of writing and answer the following questions:
   (a) How would a news article presenting John Glenn's proposed space voyage differ in tone and content from an editorial on the subject?
   (b) What is the benefit of each kind of writing?
2. In a current newspaper, find two letters to the editor that present opposing views on the same topic. Summarize the arguments that each writer presents.

I. ***Minneapolis Star and Tribune***

   A. Main idea _____

   _____

   B. Supporting arguments
     1. _____
     2. _____
     3. _____

   C. My conclusion _____

   _____

II. ***The Kansas City Star***

   A. Main idea _____

   _____

   B. Supporting arguments
     1. _____
     2. _____
     3. _____

   C. My conclusion _____

   _____

Writing WORKSHOP

Research Writing: Research Report

A **research report** interprets and presents information gathered through the extensive study of a subject. In this workshop, you will write a research report that presents your findings on a subject.

Assignment Criteria. Your research report should have the following characteristics of research writing:

- A thesis statement that is clearly expressed
- Factual support from a variety of credited sources
- A clear organization that includes an introduction, body, and conclusion
- A bibliography or works-cited list that provides a complete listing of research sources

To preview the criteria on which your research report may be assessed, see the Rubric on page 1075.

Prewriting

Choose a topic. Identify an area of general interest, and **brainstorm** for a list of more specific categories. For example, from the general area of art, you might choose the following categories: sculpture, Impressionism, and Pop Art. Using these categories, find a topic you would like to research.

Identify your purpose. Before you begin your report, consider a question that you would like to answer through your research. Review your notes and jot down a question that expresses this idea clearly. You may want to incorporate this information in a slightly different form into your draft when you start writing.

Question: How did the school of painting called Impressionism begin?

Gather and organize information. As you locate information, take notes to aid you in drafting your paper and creating a reference list.

- **Source cards:** Create a separate card to note the author, title, publisher, city, date of publication, and page number of each source you consult.
- **Note cards:** For each item of information, create a separate note card to record facts accurately, as in the chart shown.

If you choose to keep an electronic log of information, be sure to include all source details. Electronic logs offer you the advantage of using key word searches to locate source details.

Organize Information with Note Cards

Marsh, Peter, M.D. *Eye to Eye: How People Interact.* Topsfield, MA: Salem House Publishers, 1988. (p. 54)

Gestures vary from culture to culture. The American "OK" symbol (thumb and forefinger) is considered insulting in Greece and Turkey.

Student Model

Before you begin your research report, read this student model and review the characteristics of an effective research report.

Lyndsey Regan
Canyon Country, CA

Body Language

When we speak to other people, they are not only listening to our actual words, but sensing our facial expression, tone of voice, gestures, level of eye contact, posture, and movements as well. Nonverbal communication, or body language, makes up approximately 65 percent of human communication (Aylesworth 3). Body language has a major impact on how others perceive what we say. It can also be a tool for miscommunication when the speaker and listener are from different cultures or are communicating through technology that deprives them of visual cues. In fact, we often realize the importance of body language only when we cannot interpret someone else's body language correctly.

> The opening line is meant to capture the reader's attention by presenting a surprising perspective.

> The author expresses her thesis statement clearly and concisely.

In *Eye to Eye: How People Interact*, Dr. Peter Marsh explains that before we speak, our gestures, posture and facial expressions are already broadcasting messages to those around us. While we are speaking, these gestures continue to communicate messages—usually clarifying what we are saying, but sometimes contradicting us in telltale ways (Marsh 116–119).

Often, body language is an unconscious act that triggers the most developed senses in other people—hearing and sight (Aylesworth 18). That is why body language is such a great way to emphasize words and ideas. Many people take advantage of this. Advertisers, for example, hire actors in their commercials who use body language that appeals to viewers.

Studies have shown that people's body language changes when they are not telling the truth (Vrij, Edward, Roberts, and Bull 239–263). If someone's body language is inconsistent with what he or she is saying, people tend to believe what the body is telling them. A good way for people to convey a positive message is to avoid certain movements, like fidgeting or letting your eyes wander. Instead, good communicators maintain steady eye contact, nod in agreement, and smile. You may notice that people on television, like hosts of infomercials and talk-show hosts, generally display this positive body language when speaking.

Writing WORKSHOP *continued*

Drafting

Propose a thesis statement. An effective thesis statement expresses an idea that can be supported by research. Review your notes and take a focused position that can be supported by most of the data you have gathered. Incorporate this position into your draft in the form of a statement.

Sample Thesis Statement
Claude Monet's handling of light in his water lily paintings is typical of Impressionist techniques.

Create an outline. To expand your ideas before writing the draft, use an outline. Organize your outline by using headings, as modeled in the chart shown. To construct a sentence outline, identify a topic sentence in each section. You can use these sentences to develop your draft.

Prepare to credit sources. When you include a direct quotation, present an original idea that is not your own, or report a fact that is available in only one source, you must include documentation. As you draft, circle ideas or words that are not your own. Use parentheses to note the author's last name and the page numbers of the material used. Later, you can use this record to create formal citation.

Outline Using Headings

Thesis Statement: Body language has a major impact on how others perceive what we say.
I. Introduction—Body language definition and thesis
II. Importance of body language
A. To emphasize key points
B. To recognize falsehoods
III. Poorly understood body language
A. Cultural differences
B. Text or voice technology
IV. Summary and conclusion

Revising

Revise to consider your sources. When presenting material as *fact*—information that is true and can be proven—you must confirm that the source of your information is reliable.

Underline any fact in your draft that may not have a trustworthy source. For example, you may have found an idea on another student's Web site or in a newspaper known for exaggerating ideas or events. Check to see if the fact you have marked is repeated in another, more reliable source, such as an established encyclopedia, a scholarly Web site, or a more trustworthy newspaper or magazine. If the fact is essential to your argument, you *must* find the fact in another source. If this fact is not essential to your argument, consider removing it from your draft.

Model: Evaluating Sources

A good way to convey a positive message is to avoid certain movements. ~~When people cross their arms it is always a sign of defensiveness.~~

> Lyndsey found that this was a controversial claim that was supported by only one source. Since it was inessential to her basic argument, she chose to eliminate it.

Revise to examine word choice. Except for the specific terminology associated with your topic, avoid using the same word over and over. Identify words that are key to your topic, and review your writing to find words that you have repeated. Circle them as you read. Using a thesaurus, generate a list of possible synonyms, and substitute them as appropriate. Look at these examples:

Example Synonym Banks

> *technology*: innovation, invention, product, brainchild
>
> *theory*: belief, policy, system, position, idea
>
> *Ronald Reagan*: president, government official, leader

Finalize your research report. Before you publish your research report, you should document your sources of information. A works-cited page provides readers with complete information on each source you cite in your paper. A bibliography lists every work you used when researching, even if you did not cite it in the body of the report.

Standards for documentation are set by several organizations. Identify the format your teacher prefers. Following that format, check that each entry is complete and properly punctuated. (For more information, see Writing Criticism and Citing Sources, pages R30 and R31.)

Publishing and Presenting

Share your writing with a wider audience.

Deliver an oral presentation. Read your research report aloud in front of your classmates. You may want to provide classmates with a copy of your bibliography or works-cited page if they care to learn more about your topic.

 Prentice Hall Writing and Grammar Connection: Chapter 12

Rubric for Self-Assessment

Evaluate your research report using the following criteria and rating scale:

Criteria	Rating Scale				
	Not very				Very
How clearly is the thesis statement expressed?	1	2	3	4	5
How sufficient is factual support from a variety of sources?	1	2	3	4	5
Is the research report well organized?	1	2	3	4	5
How comprehensive is the bibliography or works-cited list?	1	2	3	4	5

Delivering an Expository Presentation

In an **expository presentation,** a speaker explains a topic for an audience. Expository presentations are common in the business, scientific, and academic worlds. As with any public speech, the success of an expository presentation depends on thoughtful preparation and enthusiastic delivery.

Prepare the Presentation

Chose a topic. Decide what information you will present. You may decide to introduce your audience to your favorite hobby, to explain an interesting development in current events, or to discuss a musician whose work you admire. Narrow your topic so that you can address it in a brief presentation.

Consider your audience. The content of your presentation depends on the level of knowledge your audience already possesses. If they know little to nothing about your topic, do not present high-level material with complex detail. Conversely, do not expect an audience that is already familiar with a topic to be interested in basic-level description.

Prepare visuals. Plan to incorporate visuals to add interest to your presentation. These enhancements may include charts, graphs, bulleted outlines, illustrations, and fine art. Visuals should meet these criteria:

- They should be concise but clear.
- They should support your main thesis.
- They should present material in a new and interesting way.

Deliver the Presentation

Choose an appropriate tone. Develop a tone appropriate to the subject. If you are delivering a presentation on a serious subject, such as a bloody battle of the Civil War, adopt a serious tone. Use dramatic language and graphic visuals. Consider adding humor only when you want to put your audience at ease and inject some appropriate variety into your presentation.

Make use of source material. Direct references and quotations from source material can bring a presentation to life. Whenever appropriate, cite your sources or quote experts.

Offer varying interpretations. If a topic is controversial, address the varying interpretations of the subject. Stay on the subject when doing this, and offer your own conclusions to clarify ideas for your audience. Visual aids can help to eliminate confusion when you discuss complex topics.

(Activity:)
Presentation and Feedback Choose a historical topic to present. Research your topic, and then deliver an expository presentation that incorporates visual aids as well as material culled from a variety of sources. Critique your presentation with the feedback form at right, and ask other students to offer their feedback.

Feedback Form for Expository Presentation

Rating System
+ = excellent   ✔ = average   – = weak

Preparation
Scope of Topic _____
Level of Detail _____
Use of Visuals _____

Delivery
Tone _____
Reference to Source Materials _____
Introduction of Varying Interpretations _____

Answer the following questions:
What did you learn that you did not know before?

What questions do you have about the content?

What improvements to the presentation would you recommend? Why?

Assessment WORKSHOP

Grammar, Usage, and Mechanics

The reading portions of some standardized tests require you to read a sentence or passage and answer multiple-choice questions about grammar, usage, and mechanics. Use the following information to help you:

- Grammar and usage questions test your knowledge of the parts of speech and the rules of sentence structure.

- To answer grammar and usage questions, check to see if all the parts of the sentence agree in number (singular or plural) and gender (masculine or feminine). Then, look to see whether every sentence expresses a complete thought.

- *Mechanics* refers to correct punctuation and capitalization. As you read each passage, determine whether the text makes correct use of these elements of writing.

Test-Taking Strategies

- Try to "hear" each sentence. If it sounds incorrect, check to see if all the parts of the sentence agree. If it is so long that you run out of breath, check for missing punctuation.

- If a word looks wrong, examine its spelling and capitalization.

Sample Test Item

Directions: Read the sentence and choose the best correction for the underlined word or words. If no correction is required, choose "Correct as is."

1. The use of sundials for telling time <u>span</u> many centuries.

   A are spanning

   B is spanning

   C spans

   D Correct as is

Answer and Explanation

The correct answer is *C*. *Use* is the subject and is singular. Therefore, the verb with which it agrees should be in its singular form, *spans*. *A* is plural and is therefore incorrect. *B* is incorrect because it describes an action in the present progressive tense, which does not make sense in the context of this sentence. *D* is incorrect because the verb does not agree in number with the subject.

▶ Practice

Directions: Read each sentence and choose the best correction for the underlined word or words. If no correction is required, choose "Correct as is."

1. Harold went to the barber <u>shop he</u> also went to the store.

   A shop. He

   B shop, he

   C shop—he

   D Correct as is

2. Although we want more <u>information. We</u> don't know where to look.

   A information: we

   B information, we

   C information—we

   D Correct as is

3. The pile of books on the table <u>are</u> heavy.

   A is

   B were

   C are not

   D Correct as is

RESOURCES

Following are some suggestions for longer works that will give you the opportunity to experience the fun of sustained reading. Each of the suggestions further explores one of the themes in this book. Many of the titles are included in the **Prentice Hall Literature Library**.

Unit One

A Tale of Two Cities
Charles Dickens

This historical novel, set in London and Paris during the French Revolution, is filled with suspenseful plot twists such as false accusations, look-alike characters, and bitter people thirsting for revenge. At the center of it all is beautiful Lucy Manette—whose father wavers between sanity and madness after spending eighteen years in a French prison, and whose husband is later unjustly imprisoned and sentenced to die by the guillotine.

To Kill a Mockingbird
Harper Lee

This novel, set in the South in the early 1930s, is narrated by a strong-willed girl named Scout. Through Scout's narration, readers meet her older brother, Jem, and her beloved father, Atticus, a respected lawyer who defends an African American accused of attacking a white woman. Scout also recounts the chilling legend of Boo Radley, a neighborhood recluse, feared by all the children, who seems to be following Scout and her brother.

The Strange Case of Dr. Jekyll and Mr. Hyde
Robert Louis Stevenson

This is the story of a mild-mannered doctor who explores his dark side—with terrifying results. Fascinated with the idea of evil, the story's main character, Dr. Jekyll, develops a potion that changes him into the violent Mr. Hyde. Before long, however, Jekyll finds himself transforming into Hyde without the aid of the potion, leaving him, along with terrified readers, to wonder which personality will finally win out.

Unit Two

The Old Man and the Sea
Ernest Hemingway

This novel tells of a man's heroic struggle with nature. The battle begins when the old fisherman Santiago hooks a giant marlin after months without a catch. The old man puts up a fierce effort to conquer the huge and powerful fish, fighting exhaustion, hunger, injury, and even a pack of sharks. This story, told in Hemingway's lean, straightforward style, is a timeless tale of courage and adventure.

The Miracle Worker
William Gibson

This moving play is based on the true story of Helen Keller, who was left blind, deaf, and unable to speak following an illness when she was an infant. The title refers to Helen's teacher, Annie Sullivan, a young woman determined to meet the challenge of helping Helen to communicate. This play, Gibson's most famous, inspired an Academy Award-winning movie.

Rosa Parks: My Story
Rosa Parks with Jim Haskins

One of the pivotal moments of the American civil rights movement occurred on December 1, 1955, when Rosa Parks, an African American, chose not to give up her seat to a white rider on a bus in Montgomery, Alabama. Through this memoir, readers get a firsthand account of that dramatic event and its aftermath, as well as biographical information about one of the leaders of the civil rights movement.

Unit Three

Great Expectations
Charles Dickens

Set in nineteenth-century England, this classic novel traces the passage of a boy called Pip into adulthood. Along the way, he encounters many memorable characters, including a pair of escaped convicts, a wealthy old woman who hasn't left her house since being jilted on her wedding day, and a beautiful young girl who captures his heart. Through a series of adventures, Pip makes many discoveries about himself, the people close to him, and the society in which he lives.

When the Legends Die
Hal Borland

This is the story of a young man who discovers his identity and cultural heritage as he struggles with the challenges of nature. After his father kills another brave, Thomas Black Bull and his parents flee the Ute reservation in southwestern Colorado to live in the wilderness. There, they follow the old ways of Native Americans—hunting, fishing, and fighting for survival. Life is good until Thomas's parents die and he is left on his own.

The House on Mango Street
Sandra Cisneros

This book, a mixture of poetry and prose, tells the story of Esperanza Cordero, a young girl living in Chicago. Through her neighbors on Mango Street, Esperanza makes many discoveries about life as she explores questions such as these: Should a girl get married or pursue her education? How does writing help people express their ideas and solve their problems? Why is growing up so confusing?

Unit Four

The Prince and the Pauper
Mark Twain

In this social satire, set in sixteenth-century England, a young prince and a London street beggar exchange identities. Twain uses both understatement and exaggeration to describe the confusing events that follow. The amusing twists and turns of the plot ultimately reveal a deeper message—that it is wrong to judge people by their outward appearances and that anyone can be a king.

Alice's Adventures in Wonderland
Lewis Carroll

In this fanciful story, a young girl falls down a rabbit hole and finds herself in a strange country where nothing seems to make sense. At times, she grows huge as a giant; at other times, she shrinks to the size of a mouse. Along the way, Alice meets an assortment of extraordinary characters, including a talking rabbit, a sleepy dormouse, and a grinning Cheshire cat. More than just a children's story, this book uses satire and symbolism to poke fun at society.

Childhood
Bill Cosby

In this entertaining book, funnyman Bill Cosby shares humorous reminiscences of his childhood. He recalls getting scolded for his bad manners, acting up in school, suffering through crushes on girls, and playing sports on the streets of Philadelphia. Each tale is told in the sidesplitting style that has secured for Cosby his place as one of the country's best-loved comedians.

Unit Five

Fahrenheit 451
Ray Bradbury

This book is set in a time when firemen start fires—fires that burn books. Guy Montag is a fireman who enjoys his job and never thinks of questioning the system. Then, he meets a teenage girl who tells him of a time when people were not afraid to think for themselves. Suddenly Montag realizes that he can no longer blindly accept the laws of his society.

The Time Machine
H. G. Wells

In this classic science-fiction tale, written more than one hundred years ago, H. G. Wells provides a grim view of the future. The story focuses on an inventor who travels into the future in a time machine he has built. During his travels, he views the progressive destruction of society and even life itself, eventually witnessing a time when giant crabs are the only surviving life form and the sun and Earth are dying.

Dragonsong
Anne McCaffrey

Set in the imaginary world of Pern, *Dragonsong* tells the story of Menolly, a young musician. When the laws of her society prevent Menolly from developing her musical talents, she wanders away from her home and discovers a group of rare and enchanting fire lizards. Menolly's relationship with the fire lizards and her unshakeable love for her music are the basis of this fantasy story.

abash (ə bash´) v.: Embarrass

acclaimed (ə klāmd´) v.: Greeted with loud applause or approval; hailed

acutely (ə kyoot´ lē) adv.: Sharply

adept (ə dept´) adj.: Highly skilled; expert

aerodynamics (er´ ō dī nam´ iks) n.: Branch of mechanics dealing with the forces exerted by air or other gases in motion

aloofness (ə loof´ nəs) n.: State of being distant, removed, or uninvolved

amber (am´ bər) n.: Yellowish resin used in jewelry

ambiguities (am´ bə gyoo´ ə tēz) n.: Statements or events whose meanings are unclear

amicably (am´ i kə blē) adv.: Agreeably

anonymous (ə nän´ ə məs) adj.: Without a known or acknowledged name

archaeologist (är´ kē äl´ ə jist) n.: Person who practices the scientific study of the remains of ancient ways of life

archaic (är kā´ ik) adj.: Seldom used; old-fashioned

ardent (ärd´ 'nt) adj.: Passionate

ardor (är´ dər) n.: Passion; enthusiasm

articulate (är tik´ yoo lāt) v.: Express in words

articulate (är tik´ yoo lit) adj.: Expressing oneself clearly and easily

assuage (ə swāj´) v.: Calm; pacify

astutely (ə stoot´ lē) adv.: Cleverly or cunningly

astuteness (ə stoot´ nis) n.: Shrewdness

augmenting (ôg ment´ iŋ) v.: Increasing; enlarging

avail (ə vāl´) v.: Be of help

awry (ə rī´) adj.: Not straight

azure (azh´ ər) n.: Blue

bafflement (baf´ əl mənt) n.: Puzzlement; bewilderment

barren (bar´ ən) adj.: Empty

beached (bēcht) adj.: Washed up and lying on a beach

beguiling (bi gīl´ iŋ) adj.: Tricking; charming

beleaguered (bi lē´ gərd) adj.: Worried; tormented

bemusing (bi myooz´ iŋ) adj.: Stupefying or muddling

benevolently (bə nev´ ə lənt lē) adv.: In a kind and well-meaning way

bereft (bi reft´) adj.: Deprived

bizarre (bi zär´) adj.: Odd in appearance

blandly (bland´ lē) adv.: In a mild and soothing way

blight (blīt) n.: Something that destroys or prevents growth

bliss (blis) n.: Great joy or happiness

brazen (brā´ zən) adj.: Shamelessly bold

buffet (bə fā´) n.: Counter or table where refreshments are served

buffeted (buf´ it ed) v.: Jostled; knocked about

cannonading (kan´ ən ād´ iŋ) n.: Continuous firing of artillery

capacious (kə pā´ shəs) adj.: Able to hold much; roomy

ceasing (sēs´ iŋ) v.: Stopping

censure (sen´ shər) n.: Strong disapproval

charged (chärjd) adj.: Tensely expectant; intense

chasms (kaz´ əmz) n.: Deep cracks in Earth's surface; narrow gorges

chaste (chāst) adj.: Pure or clean in style; not ornate

chattel (chat´ əl) n.: Movable item of personal property

chortled (chôrt´ əld) v.: Made a jolly, chuckling sound

cipher (sī´ fər) adj.: Code

circumvent (sur´ kəm vent´) v.: Avoid; go around

cloister (klois´ tər) n.: Place devoted to religious seclusion

compelling (kəm pel´ iŋ) adj.: Forceful

complied (kəm plīd´) v.: Carried out or fulfilled a request

concessions (kən sesh´ ənz) n.: Things given or granted as privileges

condescending (kän´ di sen´ diŋ) adj.: Characterized by looking down on someone

condolence (kən dō´ ləns) n.: Expression of sympathy for a grieving person

confer (kən fur´) v.: To give

confounds (kən foundz´) v.: Bewilders; confuses

console (kən sōl´) v.: Comfort

contempt (kən tempt´) n.: Actions or attitude of a person toward someone or something he or she considers low or worthless

conundrums (kə nun´ drəmz) n.: Puzzling questions or problems

covenant (kuv´ ə nənt) n.: Agreement; pact

creed (krēd) n.: Statement of belief

cunning (kun´ iŋ) n.: Clever; sly

cur (kur) n.: Mean, contemptible person; mean, ugly dog

dallying (dal´ ē iŋ) v.: Wasting time; loitering

déclassée (dā´ klä sā´) French fem. adj.: Lowered in social status

decoy (dē´ koi) n.: Person or thing used to lure others into a trap

deferred (di furd´) adj.: Put off until a future time

defiance (di fī´ əns) n.: Open resistance

defrauded (di frôd´ əd) v.: Cheated

deity (dē´ ə tē) n.: A god

deleterious (del´ ə tir´ ē əs) adj.: Injurious; harmful to health or well-being

demure (di myoor´) adj.: Shy or modest

depravity (dē prav´ ə tē) n.: Wickedness; corruption

derides (di rīdz´) v.: Ridicules

derisive (di rī´ siv) adj.: Showing contempt or ridicule

desolate (des´ ə lit) adj.: Deserted; abandoned

despair (di sper´) n.: Hopelessness

despotic (des pät´ ik) adj.: Like or in the manner of an absolute ruler or tyrant

desultory (des´ əl tôr´ ē) adj.: Random

determination (dē tur´ mi nā´ shən) n.: Firm intention

detritus (di trīt´ əs) n.: Debris

diffused (di fyoozd´) v.: Spread out

discreet (dis krēt´) adj.: Tactful; respectful

disheveled (di shev´ əld) adj.: Disarranged and untidy

dishevelment (di shev´ əl mənt) n.: A state of being untidy

dismal (diz´ məl) adj.: Causing gloom or misery

dispatched (dis pacht´) v.: Finished quickly

disperse (di spurs´) v.: Drive off or scatter in different directions

dissemble (di sem´ bəl) v.: Conceal with false appearances; disguise

distraught (di strôt´) adj.: Extremely troubled; confused; distracted

diverged (dī vurjd´) v.: Branched out in different directions

divine (də vīn´) adj.: Holy; sacred

dogmas (dôg´ məz) n.: Firmly held beliefs or doctrines

droll (drōl) adj.: Comic and amusing in an odd way

drowsiness (drou´ zē nes) n.: Sleepiness

ebony (eb´ ə nē) n.: Hard, dark wood used for furniture

eddies (ed´ ēz) n.: Circular currents

eerie (ir´ ē) adj.: Mysterious

effervesce (ef´ ər ves´) v.: To be lively

effigies (ef´ i jēz) n.: Crude figures or dummies representing hated people or a group

eloquence (el´ ə kwəns) n.: Speech that is vivid, forceful, graceful, and persuasive

elucidate (i loo´ sə dāt´) v.: Explain

encompassed (en kum´ pəst) v.: Surrounded

encroaching (en krōch´ iŋ) adj.: Intruding in a gradual or sneaking way

endeavoring (en dev´ ər iŋ) n.: Trying; attempting

endurance (en door´ əns) n.: Ability to withstand hardship and stress and to carry on

engendered (en jen´ dərd) v.: Produced

enigma (i nig´ mə) n.: Puzzling or baffling matter; riddle

enjoined (en joind´) v.: Ordered

entrails (en´ trālz) n.: Internal organs, specifically intestines

epiphany (ē pif´ ə nē) n.: Moment of sudden understanding

epithets (ep´ ə thetz) n.: Abusive words or phrases; slurs

equity (ek´ wit ē) n.: Fairness; impartiality; justice

erratic (er rat´ ik) adj.: Irregular; random

evanesced (ev ə nest´) v.: Faded away

exalted (eg zôlt´ əd) v.: Lifted up

exile (eks´ īl´) v.: Banish

extrapolating (ek strap´ ə lāt´ iŋ) v.: Arriving at a conclusion by making inferences based on known facts

extrapolation (ek strap′ ə lā′ shən) *n.*: Conclusions drawn by speculation on the basis of facts

feint (fānt) *v.*: Pretended move to catch an opponent off guard

feline (fē′ līn) *adj.*: Catlike

fester (fes′ tər) *v.*: Form pus

fickle (fik′əl) *adj.*: Changeable

ford (fôrd) *n.*: Shallow place in a river that can be crossed

forebears (fôr′ bɛrs′) *n.*: Ancestors

formality (fôr mal′ ə tē) *n.*: Established rules or customs

formidable (fôr′ mə də bəl) *adj.*: Awe-inspiring

fray (frā) *n.*: Noisy fight

fretful (fret′ fəl) *adj.*: Irritable and discontented

furtive (fur′ tiv) *adj.*: Preventing observation; sneaky

furtively (fur′ tiv lē) *adv.*: Stealthily, so as to avoid being heard

futile (fyōōt′ əl) *adj.*: Useless; hopeless

gallant (gal′ ənt) *adj.*: Brave and noble

garish (gar′ ish) *adj.*: Too bright or gaudy

gaunt (gônt) *adj.*: Thin and bony

genesis (jen′ ə sis) *n.*: Birth; origin; beginning

genteel (jen tēl′) *adj.*: Refined; polite

glee (glē) *n.*: Joy

glowering (glou′ ər iŋ) *adj.*: Staring with sullen anger; scowling

gossamer (gäs′ ə mər) *adj.*: Light, thin, and filmy

grievance (grēv′ əns) *n.*: Injustice; complaint

grisly (griz′ lē) *adj.*: Horrifying; gruesome

grotesque (grō tesk′) *adj.*: Having a strange, bizarre design

haggard (hag′ ərd) *adj.*: Having a wild, worn look, as from sleeplessness

hamlet (ham′ lit) *n.*: Very small village

harness (här′ nis) *v.*: Attach, as with straps for pulling or controlling

harried (har′ ēd) *adj.*: Worried

harrowed (har′ ōd) *v.*: Broken up and leveled by a harrow, a frame with spikes or disks, drawn by a horse or tractor

haughty (hôt′ ē) *adj.*: Arrogant

heretics (her′ ə tiks) *n.*: Those who hold to a belief opposed to the established teachings of a church

hieroglyphics (hī′ ər ō′ glif iks) *n.*: Pictures or symbols that represent words or ideas

hoax (hōks) *n.*: Deceitful trick

host (hōst) *n.*: A great number

hurtling (hurt′ liŋ) *adj.*: Moving swiftly and with great force

hydraulic (hī drô′ lik) *adj.*: Operated by the movement and pressure of liquid

ideology (ī′ dē äl′ ə jē) *n.*: Ideas on which a political, economic, or social system is based

imbued (im byōōd′) *v.*: Inspired

imminent (im′ ə nənt) *adj.*: Likely to happen soon

immortalized (im môrt′ 'l īzd) *v.*: Given lasting fame

immutable (im′ myōōt′ ə bəl) *adj.*: Never changing

imperative (im per′ ə tiv) *adj.*: Absolutely necessary; urgent

imperialist (im pir′ ē əl ist) *adj.*: Here, describing a person from a country that seeks to dominate weaker countries

impertinent (im purt′ ən ənt) *adj.*: Rude; impolite

imperturbable (im′ pər tur′ bə bəl) *adj.*: Unable to be excited or disturbed

implications (im′ pli kā′ shənz) *n.*: Suggestions or indirect indications

impose (im pōz′) *v.*: Put to some trouble

improbable (im präb′ ə bəl) *adj.*: Unlikely to happen

improvised (im′ prə vīzd) *adj.*: Put together on the spur of the moment

inalienable (in āl′ yən ə bəl) *adj.*: Not able to be taken away or transferred

incognito (in käg′ ni tō′) *n.*: A disguised condition

incredulity (in′ krə dōō′ lə tē) *n.*: Inability to believe

indolently (in′ də lənt lē) *adv.*: Lazily; idly

ineffable (in ef′ ə bəl) *adj.*: Too overwhelming to be expressed in words

infallibility (in fal′ ə bil′ ə tē) *n.*: Condition of being unable to fail

infrared (in′ frə red′) *adj.*: Of light waves that lie just beyond the red end of the visible spectrum

ingeniously (in jēn′ yəs lē) *adv.*: Cleverly

insatiable (in sā′ shə bəl) *adj.*: Unable to be satisfied

inscrutable (in skrōōt′ ə bəl) *adj.*: That which cannot be easily understood; baffling; mysterious

insidious (in sid′ ē əs) *adj.*: Treacherous in a sly, tricky way

insinuatingly (in sin′ yoo āt′ iŋ lē) *adv.*: Hinting or suggesting indirectly; implying

insolent (in′ sə lənt) *adj.*: Boldly disrespectful in speech or behavior

instigates (in′ stə gāts′) *v.*: Urges on; stirs up

intent (in tent′) *adj.*: Firmly fixed; concentrated

intercession (in′ tər sesh′ ən) *n.*: The act of pleading on behalf of another

interpretation (in tur′ prə tā′ shən) *n.*: Explanation

introspective (in′ trō spek′ tiv) *adj.*: Causing one to look into one's own thoughts and feelings

intuition (in′ tōō ish′ ən) *n.*: Knowledge of something without reasoning

iridescent (ir′ i des′ ənt) *adj.*: Having shifting, rainbowlike colors

irradiated (ir rā′ dē āt′ id) *v.*: Gave out; radiated

jibed (jībd) *v.*: Stopped short and turned from side to side

judicious (jōō dish′ əs) *adj.*: Showing good judgment

keener (kēn′ ər) *adj.*: More clear; sharper

kindred (kin′ drid) *n.*: Relatives

laden (lād′ ən) *adj.*: Burdened

lamentable (lam′ ən tə bəl) *adj.*: Distressing; sad

languid (laŋ′ gwid) *adj.*: Drooping; weak

languor (laŋ′ gər) *n.*: Lack of vigor; weakness

larder (lärd′ ər) *n.*: Place where food is kept; pantry

lassoed (las′ ōd) *v.*: Wrapped around

lateral (lat′ ər əl) *adj.*: Sideways

legacy (leg′ ə sē) *n.*: Anything handed down from an ancestor

legendary (lej′ ən der′ ē) *adj.*: Based on legends, or stories handed down for generations

levitation (lev ə tā′ shən) *n.*: The illusion of keeping a heavy body in the air without visible support

lingered (liŋ′ gərd) *v.*: Stayed on, as if unwilling to leave

literally (lit′ ər əl ē) *adv.*: Actually; in fact

lithe (līth) *adj.*: Supple; limber

loathsome (lōth′ səm) *adj.*: Disgusting

loitered (loit′ ərd) *v.*: Hung about; lingered

longevity (län jev′ ə tē) *n.*: The length or duration of a life

malevolence (mə lev′ ə ləns) *n.*: Bad or evil feelings or intentions

malodorous (mal ō′ dər əs) *adj.*: Having a bad smell

mammoth (mam′ əth) *adj.*: Enormous

manhandled (man′ han′ dəld) *v.*: Treated roughly

marauders (mə rôd′ ərz) *n.*: Raiders; people who take goods by force

martial (mär′ shəl) *adj.*: Military

maudlin (môd′ lin) *adj.*: Tearfully or foolishly sentimental

medley (med′ lē) *n.*: Mixture of things not usually found together

menacing (men′ əs iŋ) *v.*: Threatening

meretricious (mer′ ə trish′ əs) *adj.*: Attractive in a cheap, flashy way

metaphors (met′ ə fôrz′) *n.*: Figures of speech in which things are spoken of as if they were something else

metaphysical (met′ ə fiz′ i kəl) *adj.*: Spiritual; beyond the physical

meticulously (mə tik′ yōō ləs lē) *adv.*: Very carefully; scrupulously

microcosms (mī′ krō kä′ zəmz) *n.*: Little worlds

monotone (män′ ə tōn′) *n.*: Uninterrupted repetition of the same tone

moribund (môr′ i bund′) *adj.*: Dying

mortified (môrt′ ə fīd′) *v.*: Embarrassed

muted (myōōt′ əd) *adj.*: Weaker; less intense

myriad (mir′ ē əd) *adj.*: Countless; innumerable

naive (nä ēv′) *adj.*: Unsophisticated

novice (näv′ is) *adj.*: Beginner

oasis (ō ā′ sis) *n.*: Fertile place in the desert

obstinacy (äb′ stə nə sē) *n.*: Stubbornness

omen (ō′ mən) *n.*: Sign foretelling a future event, either good or evil

ominous (äm′ ə nəs) *adj.*: Threatening; menacing

ominously (äm′ ə nəs lē) *adv.*: In a threatening way

oppression (ə presh′ ən) *n.*: Keeping others down by the unjust use of power

oracle (ō′ rə kəl) *n.*: Source of knowledge or wise counsel

paean (pē′ ən) *n.*: Song of joy or triumph

pagans (pā′ gənz) *n.*: People who are not Christians, Muslims, or Jews

pallid (pal′ id) *adj.*: Pale

pallor (pal´ ər) n.: Paleness

palpable (pal´ pə bəl) adj.: Able to be touched or felt

palpitating (pal´ pə tāt´ iŋ) adj.: Beating rapidly; throbbing

pandemonium (pan´ də mō´ nē əm) n.: Wild disorder, noise, or confusion

parched (pärcht) adj.: Dried up by heat

parlance (pär´ ləns) n.: Style of speaking or writing; language

pensive (pen´ siv) adj. Thinking deeply or seriously

penury (pen´ yōō rē) n.: Extreme poverty

perennial (pə ren´ ē əl) adj.: Lasting through the year or for a long time

perish (per´ ish) v.: Die

permeate (pur´ mē āt) v.: Spread or flow throughout

pernicious (pər nish´ əs) adj.: Causing great injury or ruin; destructive

perpetuated (pər pech´ ōō āt id) v.: Caused to continue indefinitely; prolonged

perplexed (pər plekst´) adj.: Puzzled; full of doubt

perplexes (pər´ pleks´ iz) v.: Confuses or makes hard to understand

perverse (pər vurs´) adj.: Continuing in a stubborn way to do what is wrong or harmful; improper; willful

picturesque (pik´ chər esk´) adj.: Like or suggesting a picture

pilgrimage (pil´ grim ij) n.: Long journey

pinions (pin´ yənz) n.: The last bony sections of a bird's wings

pious (pī´ əs) adj.: Showing religious devotion

placid (plas´ id) adj.: Tranquil; calm

placidly (plas´ id lē) adv.: Calmly; quietly

plaiting (plāt´ iŋ) v.: Braiding

plundered (plun´ dərd) v.: Took goods by force; looted

poignant (poin´ yənt) adj.: Drawing forth pity or compassion; moving

portents (pôr´ tentz) n.: Things that are thought to be signs of events to come; omens

postulated (päs´ chə lāt´ ed) v.: Claimed

precariously (prē ker´ ē əs lē) adv.: Insecurely

precipitous (prē sip´ ə təs) adj.: Steep; sheer

precluded (prē klōōd´ id) v.: Prevented; made impossible in advance

precursors (prē kur´ sərz) n.: Things that prepare the way for what will follow

predominant (prē däm´ ə nənt) adj.: Having dominating influence over others

preposterous (pri päs´ tər əs) adj.: Absurd

primed (prīmd) v.: Made ready; prepared

procure (prō kyōōr´) v.: Get; obtain

prodigious (prō dij´ əs) adj.: Wonderful; of great size

prodigy (präd´ ə jē) n.: Person who is amazingly talented or intelligent

profoundly (prō found´ lē) adj.: Deeply and intensely

projectiles (prō jek´ təlz) n.: Objects that are hurled through the air

pungent (pun´ jənt) adj.: Producing a sharp sensation of smell

purged (purjd) v.: Cleansed; emptied

pursue (pər sōō´) v.: Seek

pyre (pīr) n.: Pile of wood on which a body is burned at a funeral

quaint (kwānt) adj.: Strange; unusual

rakishly (rāk´ ish lē) adv.: With a careless, casual look; dashing

rancor (raŋ´ kər) n.: Deep spite or bitter hate

ravages (rav´ ij iz) n.: Ruins; devastating damages

ravenous (rav´ ə nəs) adj.: Greedily hungry

reciprocate (ri sip´ rə kāt) v.: Return

reconcile (rek´ ən sīl´) v.: Bring into agreement

reconciled (rek´ ən sīld) adj.: Became friends again

reconnaissance (ri kän´ ə səns) adj.: Exploratory in nature, as when examining or observing to seek information

recounted (ri kount´ ed) v.: Told in detail; narrated

refrain (ri frān´) v.: To hold back

remnants (rem´ nənts) n.: Remaining persons or things

respite (res´ pit) n.: Rest; relief

resplendent (ri splen´ dənt) adj.: Shining brightly

retort (ri tôrt´) n.: Sharp or clever reply

retribution (re trə byōō´ shən) n.: Payback; punishment for a misdeed or reward for a good deed

revelry (rev´ əl rē) n.: Party

reverie (rev´ ər ē) n.: Dreamy thought of pleasant things

riveting (riv´ it iŋ) adj.: Firmly holding attention

rueful (rōō´ fəl) adj.: Feeling sorrow or regret

ruminative (rōō´ mə nə təv) adj.: Meditative

sallow (sal´ ō) adj.: Of a sickly, pale-yellowish complexion

schism (siz´ əm) n.: Split or division

scourge (skurj) n.: Whip or other instrument for inflicting punishment

scowling (skoul´ iŋ) v.: Contracting the eyebrows and frowning to show displeasure

scruples (skrōō´ pəlz) n.: Misgivings about something one feels is wrong

sentimental (sen´ tə ment´ əl) adj.: Excessively or foolishly emotional

sepulcher (sep´ əl kər) n.: Tomb

shards (shärdz) n.: Broken pieces

simultaneously (sī´ məl tā´ nē əs lē) adv.: At the same time

singular (siŋ´ gyə lər) adj.: Extraordinary; rare

sinister (sin´ is tər) adj.: Threatening harm; ominous

skeptical (skep´ ti kəl) adj.: Doubting; questioning

slouching (slouch´ iŋ) adj.: Drooping

sobriety (sə brī´ ə tē) n.: Moderation, especially in the use of alcoholic beverages

sore (sôr) adj.: Fierce; cruel

specters (spek´ tərz) n.: Ghostly images; phantoms

spurn (spurn) v.: Reject in a scornful way

squall (skwôl) n.: Brief, violent storm

steeds (stēdz) n.: Horses

stout (stout) adj.: Sturdy; forceful

strafing (strāf´ iŋ) adj.: Attacking with machine-gun fire

suavity (swäv´ ə tē) n.: Quality of being socially smooth

subjugation (sub´ jə gā´ shən) n.: Enslavement

submerged (səb murjd´) adj.: Covered with something; underwater

subsidiary (səb sid´ ē er´ ē) adj.: Secondary; supporting

subtle (sut´ 'l) adj.: Not obvious

succor (suk´ ər) n.: Aid; help; relief

suffice (sə fīs´) v.: To be enough

sullen (sul´ ən) adj.: Gloomy; dismal

surcease (sur sēs´) n.: An end

surge (surj) v.: Increase suddenly; speed up

surreal (sə rē´ əl) adj.: Strange

tantalizingly (tan´ tə liz´ iŋ glē) adv.: In a teasing or tormenting way

tempests (tem´ pists) n.: Violent storms with strong winds

thronging (throŋ´ iŋ) adj.: Crowding into

titanic (ti tan´ ik) adj.: Of great size or strength

transgression (trans gresh´ ən) n.: Wrongdoing; sin

treble (treb´ əl) n.: High-pitched voice

tremulous (trem´ yōō ləs) adj.: Quivering

trundle (trun´ dəl) v.: To roll along; to rotate

tumult (tōō´ məlt) n.: Noisy commotion

tumultuous (tōō mul´ chōō əs) adj.: Greatly disturbed

unbidden (un bid´ ən) adj.: Without being asked; uninvited

unpalatable (un pal´ ət ə bəl) adj.: Distasteful; unpleasant

unwieldy (un wēl´ dē) adj.: Awkward; clumsy

valet (val´ it) n.: A man's personal servant who takes care of the man's clothes

vanquished (vaŋ´ kwisht) adj.: Defeated

venture (ven´ chər) n.: Chance

vex (veks) v.: Annoy

vial (vī´ əl) n.: Small bottle containing medicine or other liquids

vile (vīl) adj.: Evil; wicked; worthless; cheap; low

voluminously (və lōōm´ ə nəs lē) adv.: Fully; in great volume

vortex (vôr´ teks) n.: Center of a situation, which draws in all that surrounds it

warp (wôrp) v.: Bend or twist out of shape; distort

waverer (wā´ vər ər) n.: One who changes or is unsteady

wavering (wā´ vər iŋ) adj.: Flickering

wayfarers (wā´ fer ərz) n.: Travelers

wayward (wā´ wərd) adj.: Insistent upon having one's own way; headstrong

woeful (wō´ fəl) adj.: Full of sorrow

woes (wōz) n.: Great sorrows

wreathed (rēthd) v.: Curled around

writhing (rīth´iŋ) v.: Twisting; turning

wrought (rôt) v.: Formed; fashioned

yearned (yurnd) v.: Longed for; desired

ACT *See* Drama.

ALLEGORY An *allegory* is a story or tale with two or more levels of meaning—a literal level and one or more symbolic levels. The events, setting, and characters in an allegory are symbols for ideas and qualities.

ALLITERATION *Alliteration* is the repetition of initial consonant sounds. Writers use alliteration to give emphasis to words, to imitate sounds, and to create musical effects. In the following lines from Walter de la Mare's "The Listeners," notice how the *s* sound imitates a whisper:

Ay, they heard his foot upon the stirrup,
    And the sound of iron on stone,
And how the silence surged softly backward. . .

ALLUSION An *allusion* is a reference to a well-known person, place, event, literary work, or work of art. In "The Gift of the Magi" (p. 524), O. Henry writes about a young couple and the Christmas gifts they give to each other. At the end of the story, the narrator explains the biblical allusion in the title: "The Magi, as you know, were wise men—wonderfully wise men—who brought gifts to the Babe in the manger. They invented the art of giving Christmas presents. Being wise, their gifts were no doubt wise ones. . . ."

ANALOGY An *analogy* makes a comparison between two or more things that are similar in some ways but otherwise unalike.

ANECDOTE An *anecdote* is a brief story about an interesting, amusing, or strange event told to entertain or to make a point. In "A Lincoln Preface" (p. 152), Carl Sandburg tells anecdotes about Abraham Lincoln.
See also Narrative.

ANTAGONIST An *antagonist* is a character or force in conflict with a main character, or protagonist.

ANTICLIMAX Like a climax, an *anticlimax* is the turning point in a story. However, an anticlimax is always a letdown. It's the point at which you learn that the story will not turn out the way you had expected. In Thayer's "Casey at the Bat," the anticlimax occurs when Casey strikes out instead of hitting a game-winning run as everyone had expected.

ASIDE An *aside* is a short speech delivered by an actor in a play. Traditionally, the aside is directed to the audience and is presumed to be inaudible to the other actors.

ASSONANCE *Assonance* is the repetition of vowel sounds followed by different consonants in two or more stressed syllables. Assonance is found in the phrase "weak and weary" in Edgar Allan Poe's "The Raven" (p. 940).

ATMOSPHERE *See* Mood.

AUTOBIOGRAPHY An *autobiography* is a form of nonfiction in which a writer tells his or her own life story. An autobiography may tell about the person's whole life or only a part of it.
See also Biography *and* Nonfiction.

BALLAD A *ballad* is a songlike poem that tells a story, often one dealing with adventure and romance. Most ballads are written in four- to six-line stanzas and have regular rhythms and rhyme schemes. A ballad often features a refrain—a regularly repeated line or group of lines.
See also Oral Tradition.

BIOGRAPHY A *biography* is a form of nonfiction in which a writer tells the life story of another person. Biographies have been written about many famous people, historical and contemporary, but they can also be written about "ordinary" people.
See also Autobiography *and* Nonfiction.

BLANK VERSE *Blank verse* is poetry written in unrhymed iambic pentameter lines. This verse form was widely used by William Shakespeare.
See also Meter.

CHARACTER A *character* is a person or an animal who takes part in the action of a literary work. The main character, or protagonist, is the most important character in a story. This character often changes in some important way as a result of the story's events. In Richard Connell's "The Most Dangerous Game" (p. 18), Rainsford is the main character and General Zaroff is the antagonist, or character who opposes the main character.

Characters are sometimes classified as round or flat, dynamic or static. A *round character* shows many different traits—faults as well as virtues. A *flat character* shows only one trait. A *dynamic character* develops and grows during the course of the story; a *static character* does not change.
See also Characterization and Motivation.

CHARACTERIZATION *Characterization* is the act of creating and developing a character. In *direct characterization*, the author directly states a character's traits. In

"Uncle Marcos," for example, a character states that "Uncle Marcos's manners were those of a cannibal."

In *indirect characterization*, an author tells what a character looks like, does, and says, as well as how other characters react to him or her. It is up to the reader to draw conclusions about the character based on this indirect information.

The most effective indirect characterizations usually result from showing characters acting or speaking.
See also Character.

CLIMAX The *climax* of a story, novel, or play is the high point of interest or suspense. The events that make up the rising action lead up to the climax. The events that make up the falling action follow the climax.
See also Conflict, Plot, *and* Anticlimax.

COMEDY A *comedy* is a literary work, especially a play, that has a happy ending. Comedies often show ordinary characters in conflict with society. These conflicts are resolved through misunderstandings, deceptions, and concealed identities, which result in the correction of moral faults or social wrongs. Types of comedy include *romantic comedy*, which involves problems among lovers, and the *comedy of manners*, which satirically challenges the social customs of a sophisticated society. Comedy is often contrasted with tragedy, in which the protagonist meets an unfortunate end.

COMIC RELIEF *Comic relief* is a technique that is used to interrupt a serious part of a literary work by introducing a humorous character or situation.

CONFLICT A *conflict* is a struggle between opposing forces. Characters in conflict form the basis of stories, novels, and plays.

There are two kinds of conflict: external and internal. In an external conflict, the main character struggles against an outside force. This force may be another character, as in Richard Connell's "The Most Dangerous Game" (p. 18), in which Rainsford struggles with General Zaroff. The outside force could also be the standards or expectations of a group, such as the family prejudices that Romeo and Juliet struggle against. Their story (p. 770) shows them in conflict with society. The outside force may be nature itself, a person-against-nature conflict. The two men who are trapped by a fallen tree in Saki's "The Interlopers" (p. 304) face such a conflict.

An *internal conflict* involves a character in conflict with himself or herself. In "Checkouts" (p. 282), two young people who meet by chance in a supermarket agonize over whether they should speak to each other.
See also Plot.

CONNOTATION The *connotation* of a word is the set of ideas associated with it in addition to its explicit meaning. In his poem "Sympathy" (p. 292), Paul Laurence Dunbar speaks of a "caged bird," which connotes a sad, trapped creature.
See also Denotation.

COUPLET A *couplet* is a pair of rhyming lines, usually of the same length and meter. In the following couplet from a poem by William Shakespeare, the speaker comforts himself with the thought of his love:

For thy sweet love remember'd such wealth brings
That then I scorn to change my state with kings.
See also Stanza.

DENOTATION The *denotation* of a word is its dictionary meaning, independent of other associations that the word may have. The denotation of the word *lake*, for example, is an inland body of water. "Vacation spot" and "place where the fishing is good" are connotations of the word *lake*.
See also Connotation.

DENOUEMENT *See* Plot.

DESCRIPTION A *description* is a portrait in words of a person, place, or object. Descriptive writing uses sensory details, those that appeal to the senses: sight, hearing, taste, smell, and touch. Description can be found in all types of writing. Rudolfo Anaya's essay "A Celebration of Grandfathers" (p. 662) contains descriptive passages.

DEVELOPMENT *See* Plot.

DIALECT *Dialect* is the form of language spoken by people in a particular region or group. Pronunciation, vocabulary, and sentence structure are affected by dialect. In "The Invalid's Story" (p. 596), Mark Twain uses dialect:

"Friends of *yourn*?"
"Yes," I said with a sigh.
"He's pretty ripe, *ain't* he!"

DIALOGUE A *dialogue* is a conversation between characters. It is used to reveal character and to advance action. In a story or novel, quotation marks are generally used to indicate a speaker's exact words. A new paragraph usually indicates a change of speaker. Look at an example from "The Scarlet Ibis" (p. 554). The narrator is a boy who is urging his frail younger brother, Doodle, to stand up and walk fast:

> "Aw, come on Doodle," I urged. "You can do it. Do you want to be different from everybody else when you start school?"
>
> "Does it make any difference?"
>
> "It certainly does," I said. "Now come on," and I helped him up.

A drama depends entirely on dialogue and actions. Quotation marks are not used in the *script*, which is the printed version of a play. Instead, the dialogue follows the name of the speaker. Here is an example from *The Dancers* (p. 734):

> HORACE. Miss . . .
>
> WAITRESS. Yes?
>
> HORACE. How much do I owe you?

DICTION *Diction* is word choice, including the vocabulary used, the appropriateness of the words, and the vividness of the language. Diction can be formal, as in this excerpt from O. Henry's "The Gift of the Magi" (p. 524):

> In the vestibule below was a letter-box into which no letter would go, and an electric button from which no mortal finger could coax a ring.

Diction can also be informal and conversational, as in these lines from Ernest Lawrence Thayer's "Casey at the Bat" (p. 42):

> It looked extremely rocky for the Mudville nine
>   that day;
> The score stood two to four; with but an inning
>   left to play.
> So, when Cooney died at second, and Burrows
>   did the same,
> A pallor wreathed the features of the patrons of
>   the game.

See also Connotation *and* Denotation.

DIRECT CHARACTERIZATION *See* Characterization.

DRAMA A *drama* is a story written to be performed by actors. The script of a drama is made up of *dialogue*—the words the actors say—and *stage directions*, which are comments on how and where action happens.

The drama's *setting* is the time and place in which the action occurs. It is indicated by one or more sets that suggest interior or exterior scenes. *Props* are objects,

such as a sword or a cup of tea, that are used onstage.

At the beginning of most plays, a brief exposition gives the audience some background information about the characters and the situation. Just as in a story or novel, the plot of a drama is built around characters in conflict.

Dramas are divided into large units called *acts,* which are divided into smaller units called *scenes*. A long play may include many sets that change with the scenes, or it may indicate a change of scene with lighting.

See also Dialogue, Genre, Stage Directions, *and* Tragedy.

DRAMATIC IRONY *See* Irony.

DRAMATIC MONOLOGUE A *dramatic monologue* is a poem or speech in which a fictional character addresses the listener.

DRAMATIC POETRY *Dramatic poetry* is poetry that utilizes the techniques of drama. The dialogue used in Edgar Allan Poe's "The Raven" (p. 940) makes it dramatic dialogue. A *dramatic monologue* is a poem spoken by one person, addressing a silent listener.

END RHYME *See* Rhyme.

EPIC An *epic* is a long narrative poem about the deeds of gods or heroes. Homer's *Odyssey* (p. 980) is an example of epic poetry. It tells the story of the Greek hero Odysseus, the king of Ithaca.

An epic is elevated in style and usually follows certain patterns. The poet begins by announcing the subject and asking a Muse—one of the nine goddesses of the arts, literature, and sciences—to help.

See also Epic Simile *and* Narrative Poem.

EPIC SIMILE An *epic simile*, also called *Homeric simile*, is an elaborate comparison of unlike subjects. In this example from the *Odyssey* (p. 980), Homer compares the bodies of men killed by Odysseus to a fisherman's catch heaped up on the shore:

> Think of a catch that fishermen haul in to a
>   half-moon bay
> in a fine-meshed net from the whitecaps of the sea:
> how all are poured out on the sand, in throes
>   for the salt sea,
> twitching their cold lives away in Helios' fiery air:
>   so lay the suitors heaped on one another.

See also Figurative Language *and* Simile.

ESSAY An *essay* is a short nonfiction work about a particular subject. While classification is difficult, five types of essays are sometimes identified.

A *descriptive essay* seeks to convey an impression about a person, place, or object. In "A Celebration of Grandfathers" (p. 662), Rudolfo Anaya describes the cultural values that his grandfather and other "old ones" from his childhood passed down.

A *narrative essay* tells a true story. In "The Washwoman," Isaac Bashevis Singer tells of his childhood in Poland.

An *expository essay* gives information, discusses ideas, or explains a process. In "Single Room, Earth View" (p. 636), Sally Ride describes what it is like to be in outer space.

A *persuasive essay* tries to convince readers to do something or to accept the writer's point of view. In the essay, "To the Residents of A.D. 2029" (p. 495), Bryan Woolley advises future generations how to avoid calamities.

A *visual essay* is an exploration of a topic that conveys its ideas through visual elements as well as language. Like a standard essay, a visual essay presents an author's views of a single topic. Unlike other essays, however, much of the meaning in a visual essay is conveyed through illustrations or photographs.
See also Description, Exposition, Genre, Narration, Nonfiction, *and* Persuasion.

EXPOSITION *Exposition* is writing or speech that explains a process or presents information. In the plot of a story or drama, the exposition is the part of the work that introduces the characters, the setting, and the basic situation.

EXTENDED METAPHOR In an *extended metaphor*, as in regular metaphor, a writer speaks or writes of a subject as though it were something else. An extended metaphor sustains the comparison for several lines or for an entire poem. The "caged bird" of Paul Laurence Dunbar's "Sympathy" (p. 292) is an extended metaphor for a person who is not free.
See also Figurative Language *and* Metaphor.

FALLING ACTION *See* Plot.

FANTASY A *fantasy* is highly imaginative writing that contains elements not found in real life. Examples of fantasy include stories that involve supernatural elements, stories that resemble fairy tales, and stories that deal with imaginary places and creatures.
See also Science Fiction.

FICTION *Fiction* is prose writing that tells about imaginary characters and events. The term is usually used for

novels and short stories, but it also applies to dramas and narrative poetry. Some writers rely on their imaginations alone to create their works of fiction. Others base their fiction on actual events and people, to which they add invented characters, dialogue, and plot situations.
See also Genre, Narrative, *and* Nonfiction.

FIGURATIVE LANGUAGE *Figurative language* is writing or speech not meant to be interpreted literally. It is often used to create vivid impressions by setting up comparisons between dissimilar things.

Some frequently used figures of speech are *metaphors, similes*, and *personifications*.
See also Literal Language.

FOIL A *foil* is a character who provides a contrast to another character. In *Romeo and Juliet* (p. 770), the fiery temper of Tybalt serves as a foil to the good nature of Benvolio.

FOOT *See* Meter.

FORESHADOWING *Foreshadowing* is the use in a literary work of clues that suggest events that have yet to occur. This technique helps to create suspense, keeping readers wondering about what will happen next.
See also Suspense.

FREE VERSE *Free verse* is poetry not written in a regular rhythmical pattern, or meter. Free verse seeks to capture the rhythms of speech.
See also Meter.

GENRE A *genre* is a category or type of literature. Literature is commonly divided into three major genres: poetry, prose, and drama. Each major genre is in turn divided into smaller genres, as follows:
1. Poetry: Lyric Poetry, Concrete Poetry, Dramatic Poetry, Narrative Poetry, and Epic Poetry
2. Prose: Fiction (Novels and Short Stories) and Nonfiction (Biography, Autobiography, Letters, Essays, and Reports)
3. Drama: Serious Drama and Tragedy, Comic Drama, Melodrama, and Farce
See also Drama, Poetry, *and* Prose.

HAIKU The *haiku* is a three-line verse form. The first and third lines of a haiku each have five syllables. The second line has seven syllables. A haiku seeks to convey a single vivid emotion by means of images from nature.

HOMERIC SIMILE *See* Epic Simile.

HYPERBOLE A *hyperbole* is a deliberate exaggeration or overstatement. In Mark Twain's "The Notorious Jumping Frog of Calaveras County," the claim that Jim Smiley would follow a bug as far as Mexico to win a bet is a hyperbole. As this example shows, hyperboles are often used for comic effect.

IAMB *See* Meter.

IMAGE An *image* is a word or phrase that appeals to one or more of the five senses—sight, hearing, touch, taste, or smell. Writers use images to re-create sensory experiences in words.
See also Description.

IMAGERY *Imagery* is the descriptive or figurative language used in literature to create word pictures for the reader. These pictures, or images, are created by details of sight, sound, taste, touch, smell, or movement.

INDIRECT CHARACTERIZATION *See* Characterization.

INTERNAL RHYME *See* Rhyme.

IRONY *Irony* is the general term for literary techniques that portray differences between appearance and reality, or expectation and result. In *verbal irony*, words are used to suggest the opposite of what is meant. In *dramatic irony*, there is a contradiction between what a character thinks and what the reader or audience knows to be true. In *irony of situation*, an event occurs that directly contradicts the expectations of the characters, the reader, or the audience.

LITERAL LANGUAGE *Literal language* uses words in their ordinary senses. It is the opposite of *figurative language*. If you tell someone standing on a diving board to jump in, you speak literally. If you tell someone on the street to jump in a lake, you are speaking figuratively.
See also Figurative Language.

LYRIC POEM A *lyric poem* is a highly musical verse that expresses the observations and feelings of a single speaker. In ancient times, lyric poems were sung to the accompaniment of the lyre, a type of stringed instrument. Modern lyric poems are not usually sung. However, they still have a musical quality that is achieved through rhythm and other devices such as alliteration and rhyme.

MAIN CHARACTER *See* Character.

METAPHOR A *metaphor* is a figure of speech in which one thing is spoken of as though it were something else. Unlike a simile, which compares two things using *like* or *as*, a metaphor implies a comparison between them. In "Dreams" (p. 905), Langston Hughes uses a metaphor to show what happens to a life without dreams:

> . . . if dreams die
> Life is a broken-winged bird
> That cannot fly.

See also Extended Metaphor *and* Figurative Language.

METER The *meter* of a poem is its rhythmical pattern. This pattern is determined by the number and types of stresses, or beats, in each line. To describe the meter of a poem, you must scan its lines. Scanning involves marking the stressed and unstressed syllables, as shown with the following two lines from "I Wandered Lonely as a Cloud" by William Wordsworth (p. 896):

> Ĭ wán|dered lone|lý as| ă cloud
> That floats |on high| o'er vales| and hills.

As you can see, each strong stress is marked with a slanted line (ˊ) and each unstressed syllable with a horseshoe symbol (˘). The stressed and unstressed syllables are then divided by vertical lines (|) into groups called *feet*. The following types of feet are common in English poetry:

1. *Iamb:* a foot with one unstressed syllable followed by a stressed syllable, as in the word "again"
2. *Trochee:* a foot with one stressed syllable followed by an unstressed syllable, as in the word "wonder"
3. *Anapest:* a foot with two unstressed syllables followed by one strong stress, as in the phrase "on the beach"
4. *Dactyl:* a foot with one strong stress followed by two unstressed syllables, as in the word "wonderful"
5. *Spondee:* a foot with two strong stresses, as in the word "spacewalk"

Depending on the type of foot that is most common in them, lines of poetry are described as *iambic, trochaic, anapestic*, and so forth.

Lines are also described in terms of the number of feet that occur in them, as follows:

1. *Monometer:* verse written in one-foot lines
   All things
   Must pass
   Away.

2. *Dimeter:* verse written in two-foot lines
   Thomas | Jefferson
   What do | you say
   Under the | gravestone
   Hidden | away?
   —Rosemary and Stephen Vincent Benét,
   "Thomas Jefferson, 1743–1826"

3. *Trimeter:* verse written in three-foot lines
   I know | not whom | I meet
   I know | not where | I go.

4. *Tetrameter:* verse written in four-foot lines

5. *Pentameter:* verse written in five-foot lines

6. *Hexameter:* verse written in six-foot lines

7. *Heptameter:* verse written in seven-foot lines

Blank verse is poetry written in unrhymed iambic pentameter. Poetry that does not have a regular meter is called *free verse.*

MONOLOGUE A *monologue* is a speech by one character in a play, story, or poem. An example from Shakespeare's *Romeo and Juliet* (p. 770) is the speech in which the Prince of Verona commands the Capulets and Montagues to cease feuding (Act 1, Scene i, lines 62–84).
See also Dramatic Poetry *and* Soliloquy.

MONOMETER *See* Meter.

MOOD *Mood,* or *atmosphere,* is the feeling created in the reader by a literary work or passage. The mood is often suggested by descriptive details. Often the mood can be described in a single word, such as lighthearted, frightening, or despairing. Notice how this passage from Edgar Allan Poe's "The Cask of Amontillado" (p. 6) contributes to an eerie, fearful mood:

> "The niter!" I said; "see, it increases. It hangs like moss upon the vaults. We are below the river's bed. The drops of moisture trickle among the bones. Come, we will go back ere it is too late."

See also Tone.

MORAL A *moral* is a lesson taught by a literary work. A fable usually ends with a moral that is directly stated.

MOTIVATION *Motivation* is a reason that explains or partially explains why a character thinks, feels, acts, or behaves in a certain way. Motivation results from a combination of the character's personality and the situation he or she must deal with. Nat Hocken in "The Birds" (p. 50) is motivated by his fear of being killed by birds to board up windows and stay inside.
See also Character *and* Characterization.

MYTH A *myth* is a fictional tale that explains the actions of gods or the causes of natural phenomena. Unlike legends, myths have little historical truth and involve supernatural elements. Every culture has its collections of myths. Among the most familiar are the myths of the ancient Greeks and Romans. The *Odyssey* (p. 980) is a mythical story attributed to the ancient poet Homer.
See also Oral Tradition.

NARRATION *Narration* is writing that tells a story. The act of telling a story in speech is also called narration. Novels and short stories are fictional narratives. Nonfiction works—such as news stories, biographies, and autobiographies—are also narratives. A narrative poem tells a story in verse.
See also Anecdote, Essay, Narrative Poem, Nonfiction, Novel, *and* Short Story.

NARRATIVE A *narrative* is a story told in fiction, nonfiction, poetry, or drama.
See also Narration.

NARRATIVE POEM A *narrative poem* is one that tells a story. "Casey at the Bat" (p. 42) is a humorous narrative poem about the last inning of a baseball game. Edgar Allan Poe's "The Raven" (p. 940) is a serious narrative poem about a man's grief over the loss of a loved one.
See also Dramatic Poetry, Epic, *and* Narration.

NARRATOR A *narrator* is a speaker or character who tells a story. The writer's choice of narrator determines the story's *point of view,* which directs the type and amount of information the writer reveals.

When a character in the story tells the story, that character is a *first-person narrator.* This narrator may be a major character, a minor character, or just a witness. Readers see only what this character sees, hear only what he or she hears, and so on. The first-person narrator may or may not be reliable. We have reason, for example, to be suspicious of the first-person narrator of Edgar Allan Poe's "The Cask of Amontillado" (p. 6).

When a voice outside the story narrates, the story has a *third-person narrator.* An omniscient, or all-knowing, third-person narrator can tell readers what any character thinks and feels. For example, in Guy de Maupassant's "The Necklace" (p. 608), we know the feelings of both Monsieur and Madame Loisel. A limited third-person narrator sees the world through one character's eyes and reveals only that character's thoughts. In James Thurber's "The Secret Life of Walter Mitty" (p. 346), the narrator reveals only Mitty's experiences and feelings.
See also Speaker.

NONFICTION *Nonfiction* is prose writing that presents and explains ideas or that tells about real people, places, ideas, or events. To be classified as nonfiction, a work must be true. "Single Room, Earth View" (p. 636) is a nonfictional account of the view of Earth from space.

See also Autobiography, Biography, *and* Essay.

NOVEL A *novel* is a long work of fiction. It has a plot that explores characters in conflict. A novel may also have one or more subplots, or minor stories, and several themes.

OCTAVE *See* Stanza.

ONOMATOPOEIA *Onomatopoeia* is the use of words that imitate sounds. *Whirr, thud, sizzle,* and *hiss* are typical examples. Writers can deliberately choose words that contribute to a desired sound effect.

ORAL TRADITION The *oral tradition* is the passing of songs, stories, and poems from generation to generation by word of mouth. Many folk songs, ballads, fairy tales, legends, and myths originated in the oral tradition.

See also Myth.

PARADOX A *paradox* is a statement that seems contradictory but that actually may be true. Because a paradox is surprising, it catches the reader's attention.

PENTAMETER *See* Meter.

PERSONIFICATION *Personification* is a type of figurative language in which a nonhuman subject is given human characteristics. William Wordsworth personifies daffodils when he describes them as "Tossing their heads in sprightly dance" (p. 896).

See also Figurative Language.

PERSUASION *Persuasion* is writing or speech that attempts to convince the reader to adopt a particular opinion or course of action.

PLOT *Plot* is the sequence of events in a literary work. In most novels, dramas, short stories, and narrative poems, the plot involves both characters and a central conflict. The plot usually begins with an *exposition* that introduces the setting, the characters, and the basic situation. This is followed by the *inciting incident*, which introduces the central conflict. The conflict then increases during the *development* until it reaches a high point of interest or suspense, the *climax*. All the events leading up to the climax make up the *rising action*. The climax is followed by the *falling action*, which leads to the *denouement,* or *resolution,* in which a general insight or change is conveyed.

POETRY *Poetry* is one of the three major types of literature, the others being prose and drama. Most poems make use of highly concise, musical, and emotionally charged language. Many also make use of imagery, figurative language, and special devices of sound such as rhyme. Poems are often divided into lines and stanzas and often employ regular rhythmical patterns, or meters. However, some poems are written out just like prose, while others are written in free verse.

See also Genre.

POINT OF VIEW *See* Narrator.

PROSE *Prose* is the ordinary form of written language. Most writing that is not poetry, drama, or song is considered prose. Prose is one of the major genres of literature and occurs in two forms: fiction and nonfiction.

See also Fiction, Genre, *and* Nonfiction.

PROTAGONIST The *protagonist* is the main character in a literary work.

See also Antagonist *and* Character.

QUATRAIN A *quatrain* is a stanza or poem made up of four lines, usually with a definite rhythm and rhyme scheme.

REPETITION *Repetition* is the use of any element of language—a sound, a word, a phrase, a clause, or a sentence—more than once.

Poets use many kinds of repetition. Alliteration, assonance, rhyme, and rhythm are repetitions of certain sounds and sound patterns. A refrain is a repeated line or group of lines. In both prose and poetry, repetition is used for musical effects and for emphasis.

See also Alliteration, Assonance, Rhyme, *and* Rhythm.

RESOLUTION *See* Plot.

RHYME *Rhyme* is the repetition of sounds at the ends of words. *End rhyme* occurs when the rhyming words come at the ends of lines, as in "The Desired Swan Song" by Samuel Taylor Coleridge:

Swans sing before they die—'twere no bad *thing*
Should certain persons die before they *sing*.

Internal rhyme occurs when the rhyming words appear in the same line, as in the first line of Edgar Allan Poe's "The Raven" (p. 940):

Once upon a midnight *dreary*, while I pondered, weak and *weary*,

See also Repetition *and* Rhyme Scheme.

RHYME SCHEME A *rhyme scheme* is a regular pattern of rhyming words in a poem. The rhyme scheme of a poem is indicated by using different letters of the alphabet for each new rhyme. In an *aabb* stanza, for example, line 1 rhymes with line 2 and line 3 rhymes with line 4. William Wordsworth's poem "I Wandered Lonely as a Cloud" (p. 896) uses an *ababcc* rhyme pattern:

I wandered lonely as a cloud	a
That floats on high o'er vales and hills,	b
When all at once I saw a crowd,	a
A host, of golden daffodils;	b
Beside the lake, beneath the trees,	c
Fluttering and dancing in the breeze.	c

Many poems use the same pattern of rhymes, though not the same rhymes, in each stanza.
See also Rhyme.

RHYTHM *Rhythm* is the pattern of *beats*, or *stresses*, in spoken or written language. Some poems have a very specific pattern, or meter, whereas prose and free verse use the natural rhythms of everyday speech.
See also Meter.

RISING ACTION *See* Plot.

ROUND CHARACTER *See* Character.

SCENE *See* Drama.

SCIENCE FICTION *Science fiction* is writing that tells about imaginary events involving science or technology. Many science-fiction stories are set in the future. Arthur C. Clarke's "If I Forget Thee, Oh Earth . . ." (p. 486) is set on the moon after a nuclear disaster on Earth.
See also Fantasy.

SENSORY LANGUAGE *Sensory language* is writing or speech that appeals to one or more of the senses.
See also Image.

SESTET *See* Stanza.

SETTING The *setting* of a literary work is the time and place of the action. Time can include not only the historical period—past, present, or future—but also a specific year, season, or time of day. Place may involve not only the geographical place—a region, country, state, or town—but also the social, economic, or cultural environment.

In some stories, setting serves merely as a backdrop for action, a context in which the characters move and speak. In others, however, setting is a crucial element.
See also Mood.

SHORT STORY A *short story* is a brief work of fiction. In most short stories, one main character faces a conflict that is resolved in the plot of the story. Great craftsmanship must go into the writing of a good story, for it has to accomplish its purpose in relatively few words.
See also Fiction *and* Genre.

SIMILE A *simile* is a figure of speech in which *like* or *as* is used to make a comparison between two basically unlike ideas. "Claire is as flighty as Roger" is a comparison, not a simile. "Claire is as flighty as a sparrow" is a simile.
See also Figurative Language.

SOLILOQUY A *soliloquy* is a long speech expressing the thoughts of a character alone on stage. In William Shakespeare's *Romeo and Juliet* (p. 861), Romeo gives a soliloquy after the servant has fled and Paris has died (Act V, Scene iii, lines 74–120).
See also Monologue.

SONNET A *sonnet* is a fourteen-line lyric poem, usually written in rhymed iambic pentameter. The *English*, or *Shakespearean*, sonnet consists of three quatrains (four-line stanzas) and a couplet (two lines), usually rhyming *abab cdcd efef gg*. The couplet usually comments on the ideas contained in the preceding twelve lines. The sonnet is usually not printed with the stanzas divided, but a reader can see distinct ideas in each. See the English sonnet by William Shakespeare on page 960.

The *Italian*, or *Petrarchan*, sonnet consists of an octave (eight-line stanza) and a sestet (six-line stanza). Often, the octave rhymes *abbaabba* and the sestet rhymes *cdecde*. The octave states a theme or asks a question. The sestet comments on or answers the question.
See also Lyric Poem, Meter, *and* Stanza.

SPEAKER The *speaker* is the imaginary voice assumed by the writer of a poem. In many poems, the speaker is not identified by name. When reading a poem, remember that the speaker within the poem may be a person, an animal, a thing, or an abstraction. The speaker in the following stanza by Emily Dickinson is a person who has died:

Because I could not stop for Death—
He kindly stopped for me—
The Carriage held but just Ourselves—
And Immortality.

STAGE DIRECTIONS *Stage directions* are notes included in a drama to describe how the work is to be performed or staged. These instructions are printed in italics and are not spoken aloud. They are used to

describe sets, lighting, sound effects, and the appearance, personalities, and movements of characters.
See also Drama.

STANZA A *stanza* is a formal division of lines in a poem, considered as a unit. Often, the stanzas in a poem are separated by spaces.

Stanzas are sometimes named according to the number of lines found in them. A *couplet*, for example, is a two-line stanza. A *tercet* is a stanza with three lines. Other types of stanzas include the following:
1. *Quatrain:* a four-line stanza
2. *Cinquain:* a five-line stanza
3. *Sestet:* a six-line stanza
4. *Heptastich:* a seven-line stanza
5. *Octave:* an eight-line stanza

See also Haiku *and* Sonnet.

STATIC CHARACTER *See* Character.

SURPRISE ENDING A *surprise ending* is a conclusion that violates the expectations of the reader but in a way that is both logical and believable.

O. Henry's "The Gift of the Magi" (p. 524) and Guy de Maupassant's "The Necklace" (p. 608) have surprise endings. Both authors were masters of this form.

SUSPENSE *Suspense* is a feeling of uncertainty about the outcome of events in a literary work. Writers create suspense by raising questions in the minds of their readers.

SYMBOL A *symbol* is anything that stands for or represents something else. An object that serves as a symbol has its own meaning, but it also represents abstract ideas. Marks on paper can symbolize spoken words. A flag symbolizes a country. A flashy car may symbolize wealth. Writers sometimes use such conventional symbols in their work, but they may also create symbols of their own through emphasis or repetition.

In James Hurst's "The Scarlet Ibis" (p. 554), the ibis symbolizes the character named Doodle. Doodle and the ibis have many traits in common. Both are beautiful and otherworldly. Both struggle against great odds. Both meet an unfortunate fate. Since a story says something about life or people in general, the ibis, in a larger sense, becomes a symbol for those who struggle.

TETRAMETER *See* Meter.

THEME A *theme* is a central message or insight into life revealed through a literary work.

The theme of a literary work may be stated directly or implied. When the theme of a work is implied, readers think about what the work suggests about people or life.

TONE The *tone* of a literary work is the writer's attitude toward his or her audience and subject. The tone can often be described by a single adjective, such as *formal* or *informal, serious* or *playful, bitter* or *ironic.* When O. Henry discusses the young couple in "The Gift of the Magi" (p. 524), he uses a sympathetic tone. By contrast, Margaret Walker uses a grieving tone in her poem "Memory" (p. 915).
See also Mood.

TRAGEDY A *tragedy* is a work of literature, especially a play, that results in a catastrophe for the main character. In ancient Greek drama, the main character was always a significant person—a king or a hero—and the cause of the tragedy was a tragic flaw, or weakness, in his or her character. In modern drama, the main character can be an ordinary person, and the cause of the tragedy can be some evil in society itself. Tragedy not only arouses fear and pity in the audience, but also, in some cases, conveys a sense of the grandeur and nobility of the human spirit.

Shakespeare's *Romeo and Juliet* (p. 770) is a tragedy. Romeo and Juliet both suffer from the tragic flaw of impulsiveness. This flaw ultimately leads to their deaths.
See also Drama.

TRIMETER *See* Meter.

UNIVERSAL THEME A *universal theme* is a message about life that can be understood by most cultures. Many folk tales and examples of classic literature address universal themes such as the importance of courage, the effects of honesty, or the danger of greed.

VERBAL IRONY *See* Irony.

VILLANELLE A *villanelle* is a lyric poem written in three-line stanzas, ending with a four-line stanza. It has two refrain lines that appear initially in the first and third lines of the first stanza; they then appear alternately as the third line of subsequent stanzas and finally as the last two lines of the poem.

VISUAL ESSAY A *visual essay* is an exploration of a topic that conveys its ideas through visual elements as well as language. Like a standard essay, a visual essay presents an author's views of a single topic. Unlike other essays, however, much of the meaning in a visual essay is conveyed through illustrations or photographs.

THE WRITING PROCESS

A polished piece of writing can seem to have been effortlessly created, but most good writing is the result of a process of writing, rethinking, and rewriting. The process can roughly be divided into stages: prewriting, drafting, revising, editing, proofreading, and publishing.

It is important to remember that the writing process is one that moves backward as well as forward. Even while you are moving forward in the creation of your composition, you may still return to a previous stage—to rethink or rewrite.

Following are stages of the writing process, with key points to address during each stage.

Prewriting

In this stage, you plan out the work to be done. You prepare to write by exploring ideas, gathering information, and working out an organization plan. Following are the key steps to take at this stage.

Step 1: Analyze the writing situation. Start by clarifying your assignment, so that you know exactly what you are supposed to do.

- *Focus your topic.* If necessary, narrow the topic—the subject you are writing about—so that you can write about it fully in the space you have.
- *Know your purpose.* What is your goal for this paper? What do you want to accomplish? Your purpose will determine what you include in the paper.
- *Know your audience.* Who will read your paper influences what you say and how you say it.

Step 2: Gather ideas and information. You can do this in a number of ways:

- *Brainstorm.* When you brainstorm, either alone or with others, you come up with possible ideas to use in your paper. Not all of your ideas will be useful or suitable. You will need to evaluate them later.
- *Consult other people about your subject.* Speaking informally with others may suggest an idea or an approach you did not see at first.
- *Make a list of questions about your topic.* When your list is complete, find the answers to your questions.
- *Do research.* Your topic may require information that you do not have, so you will need to go to other sources to find information. There are numerous ways to find information on a topic.

The ideas and information you gather will become the content of your paper. Not all of the information you gather will be needed. As you develop and revise your paper, you will make further decisions about what to include and what to leave out.

Drafting

When you draft, you put down your ideas on paper in rough form. Working from your prewriting notes and your outline or plan, you develop and present your ideas in sentences and paragraphs.

Organize. First, make a rough plan for the way you want to present your information. Sort your ideas and notes. Decide what goes with what and which points are the most important. You can make an outline to show the order of ideas, or you can use some other organizing plan that works for you.

There are many ways in which you can organize and develop your material. Use a method that works for your topic. Following are common methods of organizing information in the development of a paper:

- *Chronological Order* In this method, events are presented in the order in which they occurred. This organization works best for presenting narrative material or explaining in a "how-to" format.
- *Spatial Order* In spatial order, details are presented as seen in space; for example, from left to right, top to bottom, or from foreground to background. This order is good for descriptive writing.
- *Order of Importance* This order helps readers see the relative importance of ideas. You present ideas from the most to least important or from the least to most important.
- *Main Idea and Details* This logical organization works well to support an idea or opinion. Present each main idea, and back it up with appropriate support.

Once you have chosen an organization, begin writing your draft. Do not worry about getting everything perfect at the drafting stage. Concentrate on getting your ideas down.

Write your draft in a way that works for you. Some writers work best by writing a quick draft—putting down all their ideas without stopping to evaluate them. Other writers prefer to develop each paragraph carefully and thoughtfully, making sure that each main idea is supported by details.

As you are developing your draft, keep in mind your purpose and your audience. These determine what you say and how you say it.

Do not be afraid to change your original plans during drafting. Some of the best ideas are those that were not planned at the beginning. Write as many drafts as you like, until you are happy with the results.

Develop an Essay Most papers, regardless of the topic, are developed with an introduction, a body, and a conclusion. Here are tips for developing these parts:

Introduction In the introduction to a paper, you want to engage your readers' attention and let them know the purpose of your paper. You may use the following strategies in your introduction:

- Startle your readers.
- Use an anecdote.
- Take a stand.
- Quote someone.

Body of the Paper In the body of your paper, you present your information and make your points. Your organization is an important factor in leading readers through your ideas. Elaborating on your main ideas is also important. Elaboration is the development of ideas to make your written work precise and complete. You can use the following kinds of details to elaborate your main ideas:

- Facts and statistics
- Sensory details
- Explanations and definitions
- Anecdotes
- Examples
- Quotations

Conclusion The ending of your paper is the final impression you leave with your readers. Your conclusion should give readers the sense that you have pulled everything together. Following are some effective ways to end your paper:

- Summarize and restate.
- State an opinion.
- Call for action.
- Ask a question.
- Tell an anecdote.
- Provide an insight.

Revising

Once you have a draft, you can look at it critically or have others review it. This is the time to make changes—on many levels. Revising is the process of reworking what you have written to make it as good as it can be.

Revising Your Overall Structure Start by examining the soundness of your structure, or overall organization. Your ideas should flow logically from beginning to end. You may strengthen the structure by reordering paragraphs or by adding information to fill in gaps.

Revising Your Paragraphs Next, examine each paragraph in your writing. Consider the way each sentence contributes to the point of the paragraph. As you evaluate

your draft, rewrite or eliminate any sentences that are not effective.

Revising Your Sentences When you study the sentences in your draft, check to see that they flow smoothly from one to the next. Look to see that you have avoided the pattern of beginning most of your sentences in the same way, and vary your sentence length.

Revising Your Word Choice The final step in the process of revising your work is to analyze your choice of words. Consider the connotations, or associations each word suggests, and make sure that each word conveys the exact meaning you intended. Also, look for the repetition of words, and make revisions to polish your writing.

Peer Review After you have finished revising your draft, work with one or more classmates to get a fresh perspective on your writing. First, have your reviewer look at one element of your writing, and ask your reviewer a specific question to get the most focused feedback possible. Weigh the responses you receive, and determine which suggestions you want to incorporate in your draft.

Editing

When you edit, you look more closely at the language you have used to ensure that the way you expressed your ideas is the most effective.

- Replace dull language with vivid, precise words.
- Cut or change unnecessary repetition.
- Cut empty words and phrases—those that do not add anything to the writing.
- Check passive voice. Usually, active voice is more effective.
- Replace wordy expressions with shorter, more precise ones.

Proofreading

After you finish your final draft, proofread it, either on your own or with the help of a partner.

It is useful to have both a dictionary and a usage handbook available to help you check that your work is correct. Here are the tasks in proofreading:

- Correct errors in grammar and usage.
- Correct errors in punctuation and capitalization.
- Correct errors in spelling.

Publishing

Now your paper is ready to be shared with others. Consider sharing your writing with classmates, family, or a wider audience.

THE MODES OF WRITING

Writing is a process that begins with the exploration of ideas and ends with the presentation of a final draft. Often, the types of writing are grouped into modes according to form and purpose.

The modes addressed in this handbook are

- Narration
- Description
- Persuasion
- Exposition
- Research Writing
- Response to Literature
- Writing for Assessment
- Workplace Writing

NARRATION

Whenever writers tell any type of story, they are using **narration.** Although there are many kinds of narration, most narratives share certain elements, such as characters, a setting, a sequence of events, and, often, a theme. Following are some types of narration:

Autobiographical Writing Autobiographical writing tells a true story about an important period, experience, or relationship in the writer's life. An autobiographical narrative can be as simple as a description of a recent car trip or as complex as the entire story of a person's life. Effective autobiographical writing includes

- A series of events that involve the writer as the main character
- Details, thoughts, feelings, and insights from the writer's perspective
- A conflict or an event that affects the writer
- A logical organization that tells the story clearly
- Insights that the writer gained from the experience

A few types of autobiographical writing are autobiographical incidents, personal narratives, autobiographical narratives or sketches, reflective essays, eyewitness accounts, anecdotes, and memoirs.

Short Story A short story is a brief, creative narrative—a retelling of events arranged to hold a reader's attention. Most short stories include

- Details that establish the setting in time and place
- A main character who undergoes a change or learns something during the course of the story
- A conflict or a problem to be introduced, developed, and resolved
- A plot, the series of events that make up the action of the story
- A theme or generalization about life

A few types of short stories are realistic stories, fantasies, historical narratives, mysteries, thrillers, science-fiction stories, and adventure stories.

DESCRIPTION

Descriptive writing is writing that creates a vivid picture of a person, place, thing, or event. Descriptive writing can stand on its own or be part of a longer work, such as a short story. Most descriptive writing includes

- Sensory details—sights, sounds, smells, tastes, and physical sensations
- Vivid, precise language
- Figurative language or comparisons
- Adjectives and adverbs that paint a word picture
- An organization suited to the subject

Some examples of descriptive writing include description of ideas, observations, travel brochures, physical descriptions, functional descriptions, remembrances, and character sketches.

PERSUASION

Persuasion is writing or speaking that attempts to convince people to accept a position or take a desired action. When used effectively, persuasive writing has the power to change people's lives. As a reader and a writer, you will find yourself engaged in many forms of persuasion. Here are a few of them:

Persuasive Essay A persuasive essay presents your position on an issue, urges your readers to accept that position, and may encourage them to take an action. An effective persuasive essay

- Explores an issue of importance to the writer
- Addresses an issue that is arguable
- Uses facts, examples, statistics, or personal experiences to support a position
- Tries to influence the audience through appeals to the readers' knowledge, experiences, or emotions
- Uses clear organization to present a logical argument

Persuasion can take many forms. A few forms of persuasion include editorials, position papers, persuasive speeches, grant proposals, advertisements, and debates.

Advertisements An advertisement is a planned communication meant to be seen, heard, or read. It attempts to persuade an audience to buy a product or service, accept an idea, or support a cause. Advertisements may appear in printed form—in newspapers and magazines, on billboards, or as posters or flyers. They may appear on radio or television, as commercials or public-service announcements. An effective advertisement includes

- A memorable slogan to grab the audience's attention
- A call to action, which tries to rally the audience to do something
- Persuasive and/or informative text
- Striking visual or aural images
- Details that provide such information as price, location, date, and time

Several common types of advertisements are public-service announcements, billboards, merchandise ads, service ads, online ads, product packaging, and political campaign literature.

EXPOSITION

Exposition is writing that informs or explains. The information you include in expository writing is factual or based on fact. Effective expository writing reflects a well-thought-out organization—one that includes a clear introduction, body, and conclusion. The organization should be appropriate for the type of exposition you are writing. Here are some types of exposition:

Comparison-and-Contrast Essay A comparison-and-contrast essay analyzes the similarities and differences between two or more things. You may organize your essay either point by point or subject by subject. An effective comparison-and-contrast essay

- Identifies a purpose for comparison and contrast
- Identifies similarities and differences between two or more things, people, places, or ideas
- Gives factual details about the subjects being compared
- Uses an organizational plan suited to its topic and purpose

Types of comparison-and-contrast essays are product comparisons, essays on economic or historical developments, comparison and contrast of literary works, and plan evaluations.

Cause-and-Effect Essay A cause-and-effect essay examines the relationship between events, explaining how one event or situation causes another. A successful cause-and-effect essay includes

- A discussion of a cause, event, or condition that produces a specific result
- An explanation of an effect, outcome, or result

- Evidence and examples to support the relationship between cause and effect
- A logical organization that makes the explanation clear

Some appropriate subjects for cause-and-effect essays are science reports, current-events articles, health studies, historical accounts, and cause-and-effect investigations.

Problem-and-Solution Essay A problem-and-solution essay describes a problem and offers one or more solutions to it. It describes a clear set of steps to achieve a result. An effective problem-and-solution essay includes

- A clear statement of the problem, with its causes and effects summarized for the reader
- The most important aspects of the problem
- A proposal of at least one realistic solution
- Facts, statistics, data, or expert testimony to support the solution
- Language appropriate to the audience's knowledge and ability levels
- A clear organization that makes the relationship between problem and solution obvious

Some types of issues that might be addressed in a problem-and-solution essay include consumer issues, business issues, time-management issues, and local issues.

RESEARCH WRITING

Research writing is based on information gathered from outside sources, and it gives a writer the power to become an expert on any subject. A research paper—a focused study of a topic—helps writers explore and connect ideas, make discoveries, and share their findings with an audience. Effective research writing

- Focuses on a specific, narrow topic, which is usually summarized in a thesis statement
- Presents relevant information from a wide variety of sources
- Structures the information logically and effectively
- Identifies the sources from which the information was drawn

Besides the formal research report, there are many other specialized types of writing that depend on accurate and insightful research, including multimedia presentations, statistical reports, annotated bibliographies, and experiment journals.

Documented Essay A documented essay uses research gathered from outside sources to support an idea. What distinguishes this essay from other categories of research is the level and intensity of the research. In a documented essay, the writer consults a limited number of sources to elaborate an idea. In contrast, a formal research paper may include many more research sources. An effective documented essay includes

- A well-defined thesis that can be fully discussed in a brief essay
- Facts and details to support each main point
- Expert or informed ideas gathered from interviews and other sources
- A clear, coherent method of organization
- Full internal documentation to show sources of information

Subjects especially suited to the documented essay format include health issues, current events, and cultural trends.

Research Paper A research paper presents and interprets information gathered through an extensive study of a subject. An effective research paper has

- A clearly stated thesis statement
- Convincing factual support from a variety of outside sources, including direct quotations whose sources are credited
- A clear organization that includes an introduction, body, and conclusion
- A bibliography, or works-cited list, that provides a complete listing of research sources

Some research formats you may encounter include lab reports, annotated bibliographies, and multigenre research papers.

RESPONSE TO LITERATURE

When you write a **response-to-literature essay,** you give yourself the opportunity to discover *what, how,* and *why* a piece of writing communicated to you. An effective response

- Contains a reaction to a poem, story, essay, or other work of literature
- Analyzes the content of a literary work, its related ideas, or the work's effect on the reader
- Presents a thesis statement to identify the nature of the response
- Focuses on a single aspect of the work or gives a general overview

- Supports opinion with evidence from the work addressed

The following are just a few of the ways you might respond in writing to a literary work: reader's response journals, character analyses, literary letters, and literary analyses.

WRITING FOR ASSESSMENT

One of the most common types of school **assessment** is the written test. Most often, a written test is announced in advance, allowing you time to study and prepare. When a test includes an essay, you are expected to write a response that includes

- A clearly stated and well-supported thesis or main idea
- Specific information about the topic derived from your reading or from class discussion
- A clear organization

In your school career, you will probably encounter questions that ask you to address each of the following types of writing: explain a process; defend a position; compare, contrast, or categorize; and show cause and effect.

WORKPLACE WRITING

Workplace writing is probably the format you will use most after you finish school. It is used in offices, factories, and by workers on the road. Workplace writing includes a variety of formats that share common features. In general, workplace writing is fact-based writing that communicates specific information to readers in a structured format. Effective workplace writing

- Communicates information concisely to make the best use of both the writer's and the reader's time
- Includes a level of detail that provides necessary information and anticipates potential questions
- Reflects the writer's care if it is error-free and neatly presented

Some common types of workplace writing include business letters, memorandums, résumés, forms, and applications.

Clauses A **clause** is a group of words with a subject and a verb.

An **independent clause** has a subject and a verb and can stand by itself as a complete sentence.

A **subordinate clause** has a subject and a verb but cannot stand by itself as a complete sentence; it can only be part of a sentence.

An **adjective clause** is a subordinate clause that modifies a noun or a pronoun by telling *what kind* or *which one*.

> Walter Mitty stopped the car in front of the building *where his wife went to have her hair done.*
>
> —"The Secret Life of Walter Mitty," p. 346

An **adverb clause** modifies a verb, an adjective, an adverb, or a verbal by telling *where, when, in what way, to what extent, under what condition,* or *why.*

> The hunter shook his head several times, *as if he was puzzled.*
>
> —"The Most Dangerous Game," p. 18

A **noun clause** is a subordinate clause that acts as a noun.

> . . . I discovered *that the intoxication had worn off* . . .
>
> —"The Cask of Amontillado," p. 6

SUMMARY OF CAPITALIZATION AND PUNCTUATION

Capitalization

Capitalize the first word of a sentence and also the first word in a quotation if the quotation is a complete sentence.

> I said to him, "My dear Fortunato, you are luckily met."
> —"The Cask of Amontillado," p. 6

Capitalize all proper nouns and adjectives.

> O. Henry   Ganges River   Great Wall of China

Capitalize a person's title when it is followed by the person's name or when it is used in direct address.

> Madame   Dr. Mitty   General Zaroff

Capitalize titles showing family relationships when they refer to a specific person, unless they are preceded by a possessive noun or pronoun.

> Uncle Marcos   Granddaddy Cain

Capitalize the first word and all other key words in the titles of books, periodicals, poems, stories, plays, paintings, and other works of art.

> *Odyssey*   "I Wandered Lonely as a Cloud"

Punctuation

End Marks Use a **period** to end a declarative sentence, an imperative sentence, an indirect question, and most abbreviations.

> Mr. Jabez Wilson laughed heavily.
>
> —"The Red-headed League," p. 96

Use a **question mark** to end a direct question, an incomplete question, or a statement that is intended as a question.

> Shall I meet other wayfarers at night?
>
> —"Uphill," p. 926

Use an **exclamation mark** after a statement showing strong emotion, an urgent imperative sentence, or an interjection expressing strong emotion.

> Free at last! Free at last!
> Thank God almighty, we are Free at last!
>
> —"I Have a Dream," p. 164

Commas Use a **comma** before the coordinating conjunction to separate two independent clauses in a compound sentence.

> All at once . . . she came upon a superb diamond necklace, and her heart started beating with overwhelming desire.   —"The Necklace," p. 608

Use commas to separate three or more words, phrases, or clauses in a series.

> My brothers and I would peer into the medicinal herb shop, watching old Li dole out onto a stiff sheet of white paper the right amount of insect shells, saffron-colored seeds, and pungent leaves for his ailing customers.
>
> —"Rules of the Game," p. 262

Use commas to separate adjectives of equal rank. Do not use commas to separate adjectives that must stay in a specific order.

> The big cottonwood tree stood apart from a small group of winterbare cottonwoods which grew in the wide, sandy arroyo.
>
> —"The Man to Send Rain Clouds," p. 590

> In autumn those that had not migrated overseas . . . were caught up in the same driving urge . . .
>
> —"The Birds," p. 50

Use a comma after an introductory word, phrase, or clause.

> When Marvin was ten years old, his father took him through the long, echoing corridors . . .
>
> > —"If I Forget Thee, Oh Earth . . . ," p. 486

Use commas to set off parenthetical and nonessential expressions.

> An evil place can, so to speak, broadcast vibrations of evil.
>
> > —"The Most Dangerous Game," p. 18

Use commas with places, dates, and titles.

> Poe was raised in Richmond, Virginia.
>
> On September 1, 1939, World War II began.
>
> Dr. Martin Luther King, Jr., was born in 1929.

Use a comma to set off a direct quotation, to prevent a sentence from being misunderstood, and to indicate the omission of a common verb in a sentence with two or more clauses.

> Michele said, "I'm going to the game tonight."
>
> *Faulty:* She stifled the sob that rose to her lips and lay motionless.
>
> *Revised:* She stifled the sob that rose to her lips, and lay motionless.
>
> In the *Odyssey,* the Cyclops may symbolize brutishness; the Sirens, knowledge.

Semicolons
Use a **semicolon** to join independent clauses that are not already joined by a conjunction.

> The lights of cities sparkle; on nights when there was no moon, it was difficult for me to tell the Earth from the sky. . . .
>
> > —"Single Room, Earth View," p. 636

Use a semicolon to join independent clauses separated by either a conjunctive adverb or a transitional expression.

> Edward Way Teale wrote nearly thirty books; moreover, he was also an artist and a naturalist.

Use semicolons to avoid confusion when independent clauses or items in a series already contain commas.

> Unable to afford jewelry, she dressed simply; but she was as wretched as a *déclassée,* for women have neither caste nor breeding—in them beauty, grace, and charm replace pride of birth.
>
> > —"The Necklace," p. 608

Colons
Use a **colon** in order to introduce a list of items following an independent clause.

> The authors we are reading include a number of poets: Robert Frost, Lewis Carroll, and Emily Dickinson.

Use a colon to introduce a formal quotation.

> I have a dream that one day this nation will rise up and live out the true meaning of its creed: "We hold these truths to be self-evident; . . ."
>
> > —"I Have a Dream," p. 164

Quotation Marks
A **direct quotation** represents a person's exact speech or thoughts and is enclosed in quotation marks.

> "Where I was born and where and how I have lived is unimportant," Georgia O'Keeffe told us in the book of paintings and words published in her ninetieth year on earth.
>
> > —"Georgia O'Keeffe," p. 685

An **indirect quotation** reports only the general meaning of what a person said or thought and does not require quotation marks.

> The driver of the bus saw me still sitting there, and he asked was I going to stand up . . .
>
> > —from *Rosa Parks: My Story,* p. 168

Always place a comma or a period inside the final quotation mark.

> "I don't know," he said slowly. "It says here the birds are hungry."   —"The Birds," p. 50

Place a question mark or an exclamation mark inside the final quotation mark if the end mark is part of the quotation; if it is not part of the quotation, place it outside the final quotation mark.

> "That pig will devour us, greedily!"
>
> > —"The Golden Kite, the Silver Wind," p. 178
>
> Have you ever read the poem "Dreams"?

Use single quotation marks for a quotation within a quotation.

> "'But,' said I, 'there would be millions of red-headed men who would apply.'"
>
> > —"The Red-headed League," p. 96

Use quotation marks around the titles of short written works, episodes in a series, songs, and titles of works mentioned as parts of a collection.

> "I Hear America Singing"   "Both Sides Now"

Dashes Use **dashes** to indicate an abrupt change of thought, a dramatic interrupting idea, or a summary statement.

> The streets were lined with people—lots and lots of people—the children all smiling, placards, confetti, people waving from windows.
>
> —from *A White House Diary*, p. 674

Parentheses Use **parentheses** to set off asides and explanations only when the material is not essential or when it consists of one or more sentences.

> One last happy moment I had was looking up and seeing Mary Griffith . . . (Mary for many years had been in charge of altering the clothes which I purchased) . . .
>
> —from *A White House Diary*, p. 674

Hyphens Use a **hyphen** with certain numbers, after certain prefixes, with two or more words used as one word, and with a compound modifier coming before a noun.

> seventy-six   Post-Modernist

Apostrophes Add an **apostrophe** and -*s* to show the possessive case of most singular nouns.

> Thurmond's wife   the playwright's craft

Add an apostrophe to show the possessive case of plural nouns ending in -*s* and -*es*.

> the sailors' ships   the Wattses' daughter

Add an apostrophe and -*s* to show the possessive case of plural nouns that do not end in -*s* or -*es*.

> the children's games   the people's friend

Use an apostrophe in a contraction to indicate the position of the missing letter or letters.

> You'll be lonely at first, they admitted, but you're so nice you'll make friends fast.
>
> —"Checkouts," p. 282

GLOSSARY OF COMMON USAGE

among, between
Among is usually used with three or more items. *Between* is generally used with only two items.

> *Among* the poems we read this year, Margaret Walker's "Memory" was my favorite.

> Mark Twain's "The Invalid's Story" includes a humorous encounter *between* the narrator and a character named Thompson.

amount, number
Amount refers to a mass or a unit, whereas *number* refers to individual items that can be counted. Therefore, *amount* generally appears with a singular noun, and *number* appears with a plural noun.

> Annie Sullivan's work with Helen Keller must have required a huge *amount* of patience.

> In her poem, "Uphill," Christina Rossetti uses a *number* of intriguing symbols.

any, all
Any should not be used in place of *any other* or *all*.

> Rajika liked Amy Tan's "Rules of the Game" better than *any other* short story.

> Of *all* O. Henry's short stories, "The Gift of the Magi" is one of the most famous.

around
In formal writing, *around* should not be used to mean *approximately* or *about*. These usages are allowable, however, in informal writing or in colloquial dialogue.

> Shakespeare's *Romeo and Juliet* had its first performance in *approximately* 1595.

> Shakespeare was *about* thirty when he wrote this play.

as, because, like, as to
The word *as* has several meanings and can function as several parts of speech. To avoid confusion, use *because* rather than *as* when you want to indicate cause and effect.

> *Because* Cyril was interested in the history of African American poetry, he decided to write his report on Paul Laurence Dunbar.

Do not use the preposition *like* to introduce a clause that requires the conjunction *as*.

> Dorothy Parker conversed *as* she wrote—wittily.

The use of *as to* for *about* is awkward and should be avoided.

> Rosa has an interesting theory *about* E. E. Cummings's unusual typography in his poems.

bad, badly

Use the predicate adjective *bad* after linking verbs such as *feel, look*, and *seem*. Use *badly* whenever an adverb is required.

> Sara Teasdale's poem "There Will Come Soft Rains" shows clearly that the author felt *bad* about the destruction of war.

> In O. Henry's "The Gift of the Magi," Della *badly* wants to buy a wonderful Christmas present for her husband, Jim.

because of, due to

Use *due to* if it can logically replace the phrase *caused by*. In introductory phrases, however, *because of* is better usage than *due to*.

> The popularity of Frank Stockton's "The Lady or the Tiger?" is largely *due to* the story's open ending.

> *Because of* her feeling that Bennie's mother had enough to worry about already, Bennie's grandmother keeps the doctor's conclusions to herself.

being as, being that

Avoid these expressions. Use *because* or *since* instead.

> *Because* the protagonist of James Hurst's "The Scarlet Ibis" is a dynamic character, he changes significantly in the course of the story.

> *Since* Romeo and Juliet were from feuding families, their relationship involved secrecy and risk.

beside, besides

Beside is a preposition meaning "at the side of" or "close to." Do not confuse *beside* with *besides,* which means "in addition to." *Besides* can be a preposition or an adverb.

> When our group discussed William Least Heat Moon's "Nameless, Tennessee," Luis sat *beside* Eileen.

> *Besides* "The Bells," can you think of any other poems by Edgar Allan Poe?

can, may

The verb *can* generally refers to the ability to act. The verb *may* generally refers to permission to act.

> The mysterious listeners in Walter de la Mare's poem *can* hear the words of the lonely traveler.

> *May* I tell you why I admire Edgar Lee Masters's "George Gray"?

compare, contrast

The verb *compare* can involve both similarities and differences. The verb *contrast* always involves differences. Use *to* or *with* after *compare*. Use *with* after *contrast*.

> Theo's paper *compared* James Weldon Johnson's style in "The Creation" *with* the style of African American sermons of the same period.

> In the opening lines of the famous speech in Shakespeare's *As You Like It*, the world is *compared to* a stage and men and women to actors or players.

> The speaker's tone of hysteria in the closing stanzas of Poe's "The Raven" *contrasts with* the quiet opening of the poem.

different from, different than

The preferred usage is *different from*.

> The structure of "The Meadow Mouse" is quite *different from* that of "I Wandered Lonely as a Cloud."

farther, further

Use *farther* when you refer to distance. Use *further* when you mean "to a greater degree" or "additional."

> The *farther* Rainsford traveled in the jungle in "The Most Dangerous Game," the nearer the baying of the hounds sounded.

> Despite his men's advice, Odysseus *further* insults the Cyclops and provokes the monster's curse.

fewer, less

Use *fewer* for things that can be counted. Use *less* for amounts or quantities that cannot be counted.

> Poetry often uses *fewer* words than prose to convey ideas and images.

> T. S. Eliot's humorous poems have received *less* critical attention than his serious verse has.

good, well

Use the adjective *good* after linking verbs such as *feel, look, smell, taste*, and *seem*. Use *well* whenever you need an adverb.

> In Walt Whitman's "I Hear America Singing," the "varied carols" sound *good* to the speaker.

> Dickens wrote especially *well* when he described eccentric characters.

hopefully

You should not loosely attach this adverb to a sentence, as in "*Hopefully*, the rain will stop by noon." Rewrite the sentence so that *hopefully* modifies a specific verb. Other possible ways of revising such sentences include using the adjective *hopeful* or a phrase such as "everyone *hopes* that."

> Dr. Martin Luther King, Jr., wrote and spoke *hopefully* about his dream of racial harmony.

> Akko was *hopeful* that he could find some of the unusual words from Lewis Carroll's "Jabberwocky" in an unabridged dictionary.

> Everyone *hopes* that the class production of *Romeo and Juliet* will be a big success.

its, it's

Do not confuse the possessive pronoun *its* with the contraction *it's*, used in place of "it is" or "it has."

> Ancient Greek society must have recognized many of *its* ideal values in the *Odyssey*.

> In Walter de la Mare's "The Listeners," the traveler thinks *it's* strange that no one replies to his call.

just, only

When you use *just* as an adverb meaning "no more than," be sure you place it directly before the word it logically modifies. Likewise, be sure you place *only* before the word it logically modifies.

> Shakespeare's Sonnet 30 offers *just* one remedy for the speaker's grief and depression: the thought of a dear friend.

> A stereotyped character exhibits *only* those traits or behavior patterns that are assumed to be typical.

kind of, sort of

In formal writing, you should not use these colloquial expressions. Instead, use a word such as *rather* or *somewhat*.

> Alfred is *rather* irresponsible in Morley Callaghan's story "All the Years of Her Life."

> In "The Secret Life of Walter Mitty," James Thurber characterizes Mitty as *somewhat* absentminded.

lay, lie

Do not confuse these verbs. *Lay* is a transitive verb meaning "to set or put something down." Its principal parts are *lay, laying, laid, laid*. *Lie* is an intransitive verb meaning "to recline." Its principal parts are *lie, lying, lay, lain*.

> In Heyerdahl's *Kon-Tiki,* the narrator says that after the ship hit the reef, Herman *lay* pressed flat across the ridge of the cabin roof.

> Homer describes the slaughtered suitors *lying* dead in a heap on the floor of Odysseus' hall.

leave, let

Be careful not to confuse these verbs. *Leave* means "to go away" or "to allow to remain." *Let* means "to permit."

> In Tennyson's "The Eagle," the bird *leaves* the crag and plunges like a thunderbolt toward the sea.

> The lovesick Romeo asks his friends to *leave* him alone while they go to Capulet's party.

> "*Let* wantons light of heart / Tickle the senseless rushes with their heels," he says.

literally, figuratively

Literally means "word for word" or "in fact." The opposite of *literally* is *figuratively*, meaning "metaphorically." Be careful not to use *literally* as a synonym for *nearly*, as in informal expressions like this: "He was *literally* beside himself with rage."

> Certain specific details in "I Hear an Army" show that James Joyce does not intend us to interpret the army *literally*. Instead, the army and the speaker's nightmare are meant *figuratively* to suggest his despair at his abandonment by his love.

of, have

Do not use *of* in place of *have* after auxiliary verbs like *would, could, should, may*, or *might*.

> Sir Arthur Conan Doyle might *have* continued to practice medicine, but soon after the publication *of* his first Sherlock Holmes stories, he decided to write full time.

raise, rise

Raise is a transitive verb that usually takes a direct object. *Rise* is an intransitive verb and never takes a direct object.

> In "Casey at the Bat," Ernest Lawrence Thayer suspensefully *raises* the reader's expectations throughout the poem, only to end the narrative with a mighty anticlimax.

> Jorge *rose* to the challenge of interpreting Gabriel García Márquez's story "A Very Old Man With Enormous Wings."

set, sit

Do not confuse these verbs. *Set* is a transitive verb meaning "to put (something) in a certain place." Its principal parts are *set, setting, set, set*. *Sit* is an intransitive verb meaning "to be seated." Its principal parts are *sit, sitting, sat, sat*.

> The opening sentence of Saki's "The Interlopers" *sets* a tone of tension and conflict for the story.

> While Walter Mitty *sat* in a big leather chair in the hotel lobby, he picked up a copy of a magazine.

so, so that

Be careful not to use the coordinating conjunction *so* when your context requires *so that*. *So* means "accordingly" or "therefore" and expresses a cause-and-effect relationship. *So that* expresses purpose.

> He wanted to check the clues, *so* he read "The Red-headed League" again.

> The priest wanted to locate Teofilo's body *so that* he could give him the Last Rites.

than, then

The conjunction *than* is used to connect the two parts of a comparison. Do not confuse *than* with the adverb *then*, which usually refers to time.

> I enjoyed reading "Jacob Lawrence: American Painter" more *than* "Autumn Gardening."

> Sally Ride earned a doctorate in physics and *then* became the first American woman in space.

that, which, who

Use the relative pronoun *that* to refer to things or people. Use *which* only for things and *who* only for people.

> The phrase *that* James Thurber dislikes is "you know."

> Donald Justice wrote "Incident in a Rose Garden," *which* is a dramatic poem.

> The sea goddess *who* loved Odysseus was Calypso.

unique

Because *unique* means "one of a kind," you should not use it carelessly to mean "interesting" or "unusual." Avoid such illogical expressions as "most unique," "very unique," and "extremely unique."

> Homer occupies a *unique* position in the history of Western literature.

when, where

Do not directly follow a linking verb with *when* or *where*. Also, be careful not to use *where* when your context requires *that*.

> *Faulty:* Foreshadowing is *when* an author uses clues to suggest future events.

> *Revised:* In foreshadowing, an author uses clues to suggest future events.

> *Faulty:* Ithaca was *where* Penelope awaited Odysseus.

> *Revised:* Penelope awaited Odysseus on Ithaca.

who, whom

In formal writing, remember to use *who* only as a subject in clauses and sentences and *whom* only as an object.

> Richard Wright, *who* is widely admired for his novel *Native Son,* also wrote haiku verse.

> Leslie Marmon Silko, *whom* Mark quoted in his oral report, was raised on the Laguna Pueblo reservation in New Mexico.

Introduction to the Internet

The Internet is a series of networks that are interconnected all over the world. The Internet allows users to have almost unlimited access to information stored on the networks. Dr. Berners-Lee, a physicist, created the Internet in the 1980s by writing a small computer program that allowed pages to be linked together using key words. The Internet was mostly text-based until 1992, when a computer program called the NCSA Mosaic (National Center for Supercomputing Applications) was created at the University of Illinois. This program was the first Web browser. The development of Web browsers greatly eased the ability of the user to navigate through all the pages stored on the Web. Very soon, the appearance of the Web was altered as well. More appealing visuals were added, and sound, too, was implemented. This change made the Web more user-friendly and more appealing to the general public.

Using the Internet for Research

Key Word Search

Before you begin a search, you should identify your specific topic. To make searching easier, narrow your subject to a key word or a group of key words. These are your search terms, and they should be as specific as possible. For example, if you are looking for the latest concert dates for your favorite musical group, you might use the band's name as a key word. However, if you were to enter the name of the group in the query box of the search engine, you might be presented with thousands of links to information about the group that is unrelated to what you want to know. You might locate such information as band member biographies, the group's history, fan reviews of concerts, and hundreds of sites with related names containing information that is irrelevant to your search. Because you used such a broad key word, you might need to navigate through all that information before you could find a link or subheading for concert dates. In contrast, if you were to type in "Duplex Arena and [band name]," you would have a better chance of locating pages that contain this information.

How to Narrow Your Search

If you have a large group of key words and still do not know which ones to use, write out a list of all the words you are considering. Once you have completed the list, scrutinize it. Then, delete the words that are least important to your search, and highlight those that are most important.

These **key search connectors** can help you fine-tune your search:

AND: Narrows a search by retrieving documents that include both terms. For example: *baseball* AND *playoffs*

OR: Broadens a search by retrieving documents including any of the terms. For example: *playoffs* OR *championships*

NOT: Narrows a search by excluding documents containing certain words. For example: *baseball* NOT *history of*

Tips for an Effective Search

1. Remember that search engines can be case-sensitive. If your first attempt at searching fails, check your search terms for misspellings and try again.

2. If you are entering a group of key words, present them in order from the most important to the least important key word.

3. Avoid opening the link to every single page in your results list. Search engines present pages in descending order of relevancy. The most useful pages will be located at the top of the list. However, read the description of each link before you open the page.

4. Some search engines provide helpful tips for specializing your search. Take the opportunity to learn more about effective searching.

Other Ways to Search

Using Online Reference Sites How you search should be tailored to what you are hoping to find. If you are looking for data and facts, use reference sites before you jump onto a simple search engine. For example, you can find reference sites to provide definitions of words, statistics about almost any subject, biographies, maps, and concise information on many topics. Here are some useful online reference sites:

Online libraries

Online periodicals

Almanacs

Encyclopedias

You can find these sources using subject searches.

Conducting Subject Searches As you prepare to go online, consider your subject and the best way to find information to suit your needs. If you are looking for general information on a topic and you want your search results to be extensive, consider the subject search indexes on most search engines. These indexes, in the form of category and subject lists, often appear on the first page of a search engine. When you click on a specific highlighted word, you will be presented with a new screen containing subcategories of the topic you chose.

Evaluating the Reliability of Internet Resources

Just as you would evaluate the quality, bias, and validity of any other research material you locate, check the source of information you find online. Compare these two sites containing information about the poet and writer Langston Hughes:

Site A is a personal Web site constructed by a college student. It contains no bibliographic information or links to sites that he used. Included on the site are several poems by Langston Hughes and a student essay about the poet's use of symbolism. It has not been updated in more than six months.

Site B is a Web site constructed and maintained by the English Department of a major university. Information on Hughes is presented in a scholarly format, with a bibliography and credits for the writer. The site includes links to other sites and indicates new features that are added weekly.

For your own research, consider the information you find on Site B to be more reliable and accurate than that on Site A. Because it is maintained by experts in their field who are held accountable for their work, the university site will be a better research tool than the student-generated one.

Tips for Evaluating Internet Sources

1. Consider who constructed and who now maintains the Web page. Determine whether this author is a reputable source. Often, the URL endings indicate a source.
   - Sites ending in *.edu* are maintained by educational institutions.
   - Sites ending in *.gov* are maintained by government agencies (federal, state, or local).
   - Sites ending in *.org* are normally maintained by non-profit organizations and agencies.
   - Sites ending in *.com* are commercially or personally maintained.

2. Skim the official and trademarked Web pages first. It is safe to assume that the information you draw from Web pages of reputable institutions, online encyclopedias, online versions of major daily newspapers, or government-owned sites produce information as reliable as the material you would find in print. In contrast, unbranded sites or those generated by individuals tend to borrow information from other sources without providing documentation. As information travels from one source to another, it could have been muddled, misinterpreted, edited, or revised.

3. You can still find valuable information in the less "official" sites. Check for the writer's credentials, and then consider these factors:
   - Do not be misled by official-looking graphics or presentations.
   - Make sure that the information is updated enough to suit your needs. Many Web pages will indicate how recently they have been updated.
   - If the information is borrowed, notice whether you can trace it back to its original source.

Respecting Copyrighted Material

Because the Internet is a relatively new and quickly growing medium, issues of copyright and ownership arise almost daily. As laws begin to govern the use and reuse of material posted online, they may change the way that people can access or reprint material.

Text, photographs, music, and fine art printed online may not be reproduced without acknowledged permission of the copyright owner.

Writing Criticism

Literary criticism involves studying, analyzing, inter-preting, and evaluating works of literature. It can be as brief as an answer to a question or as lengthy as an essay or a book. Following are examples of three types of criticism.

Analysis

You are frequently asked to analyze, or break down into parts and examine, a passage or a work. Often you must support your analysis with specific references to the text. In this brief analysis, the writer uses words from the question to write a topic sentence and embeds quotations from the text as support.

Question In "Heat" by H.D., how does the speaker create the impression that heat is almost a solid substance?

Answer The speaker in "Heat" uses repetition and imagery to convey the impression that heat is almost a solid substance. By repeating the word *heat* in each of the three stanzas, the speaker emphasizes its physical presence. Further, the speaker uses images that appeal to the sense of touch in describing heat as if it were a sub-stance. In the first stanza, the speaker asks the wind to "cut apart the heat," and in the third stanza, to "plow through it."

Biographical Criticism Critics who take a biographical approach use information about a writer's life to explain his or her work. In this passage of biographical criticism, Kenneth Silverman explains Edgar Allan Poe's preoccupa-tion with death as Poe's response to the early death of his mother, Eliza.

"Much of his later writing, despite its variety of forms and styles, places and characters, is driven by the ques-tion of whether the dead remain dead. . . . The most per-suasive and coherent explanation, . . . comes from the modern understanding of childhood bereavement. . . . [C]hildren who lose a parent at an early age, as Edgar lost Eliza Poe, . . . invest more feeling in and magnify the par-ent's image. . . . The young child . . . cannot comprehend the finality of death. . . . "

Historical Criticism Using this approach, a critic explains how an author's work responds to the events, circum-stances, or ideas of the author's historical era. In the fol-lowing passage of historical criticism, Jean H. Hagstrum shows how William Blake's character Urizen symbolizes the Enlightenment ideas of Newton, Locke, and Bacon that Blake detested.

"Urizen is also an active force. Dividing, partitioning, dropping the plummet line, applying Newton's compasses to the world, he creates abstract mathematical forms. Like Locke, he shrinks the senses, narrows the percep-tions, binds man to natural fact. Like Bacon, he creates the laws of prudence and crucifies passion."

Using Ideas From Research

Below are three common methods of incorporating the ideas of other writers into your work. Choose the most appropriate style by analyzing your needs in each case. In all cases, you must credit your source.

- **Direct Quotation:** Use quotation marks to indicate the exact words.
- **Paraphrase:** To share ideas without a direct quotation, state the ideas in your own words.
- **Summary:** To provide information about a large body of work, identify the writer's main idea.

Avoiding Plagiarism

Whether you are presenting a formal research paper or an opinion paper on a current event, be careful to give credit for any ideas or opinions that are not your own. Presenting someone else's ideas, research, or opinion as your own—even if you have rephrased it in different words—is plagiarism, the equivalent of academic steal-ing, or fraud.

You can avoid plagiarism by synthesizing what you learn: Read from several sources, and let the ideas of experts help you draw your own conclusions and form your own opinions. When you choose to use someone else's ideas or work to support your view, credit the source of the material.

Preparing a Manuscript

The presentation of your written work is important. Your work should be neat, clean, and easy to read. Follow your teacher's directions for placing your name and class, along with the title and date of your work, on the paper.

Research Papers

Most formal research papers have these features:

- Title Page
- Table of Contents or Outline
- Works-Cited List or Bibliography

Citing Sources

In research writing, cite your sources. In the body of your paper, provide a footnote, an endnote, or an internal citation, identifying the sources of facts, opinions, or quotations. At the end of your paper, provide a bibliography or a works-cited list, a list of all the sources you cite. Follow an established format, such as Modern Library Association (MLA) Style.

Works-Cited List (MLA Style)

A works-cited list must contain accurate information sufficient to enable a reader to locate each source you cite. The basic components of an entry are as follows:

- Name of the author, editor, translator, or group responsible for the work
- Title
- Place and date of publication
- Publisher

For print materials, the information required for a citation generally appears on the copyright and title pages of a work. For the format of works-cited list entries, consult the examples at right and in the chart on page R32.

Internal Citations (MLA Style)

An internal citation briefly identifies the source from which you have taken a specific quotation, factual claim, or opinion. It refers the reader to one of the entries on your works-cited list. An internal citation has the following features:

- It appears in parentheses.
- It identifies the source by the last name of the author, editor, or translator.
- It gives a page reference, identifying the page of the source on which the information cited can be found.

Punctuation An internal citation generally falls outside a closing quotation mark but within the final punctuation of a clause or sentence. For a long quotation set off from the rest of your text, place the citation at the end of the excerpt without any punctuation following.

Special Cases

- If the author is an organization, use the organization's name, in a shortened version if necessary.
- If you cite more than one work by the same author, add the title or a shortened version of the title.

Sample Works-Cited Lists

Carwardine, Mark, Erich Hoyt, R. Ewan Fordyce, and Peter Gill. *The Nature Company Guides: Whales, Dolphins, and Porpoises.* New York: Time-Life Books, 1998.
Whales in Danger. "Discovering Whales." 18 Oct. 1999. <http://whales.magna.com.au/DISCOVER>

Neruda, Pablo. "Ode to Spring." *Odes to Opposites.* Trans. Ken Krabbenhoft. Ed. and illus. Ferris Cook. Boston: Little, Brown and Company, 1995.
The Saga of the Volsungs. Trans. Jesse L. Byock. London: Penguin Books, 1990.

An anonymous work is listed by title.

Both the title of the work and of the collection in which it is found are listed.

Sample Internal Citations

It makes sense that baleen whales such as the blue whale, the bowhead whale, the humpback whale, and the sei whale (to name just a few) grow to immense sizes (Carwardine, Hoyt, and Fordyce 19–21). The blue whale has grooves running from under its chin to partway along the length of its underbelly. As in some other whales, these grooves expand and allow even more food and water to be taken in (Ellis 18–21).

Author's last name

Page numbers where information can be found

MLA Style for Listing Sources

Book with one author	Pyles, Thomas. *The Origins and Development of the English Language*. 2nd ed. New York: Harcourt Brace Jovanovich, Inc., 1971.
Book with two or three authors	McCrum, Robert, William Cran, and Robert MacNeil. *The Story of English*. New York: Penguin Books, 1987.
Book with an editor	Truth, Sojourner. *Narrative of Sojourner Truth*. Ed. Margaret Washington. New York: Vintage Books, 1993.
Book with more than three authors or editors	Donald, Robert B., et al. *Writing Clear Essays*. Upper Saddle River, NJ: Prentice-Hall, Inc., 1996.
Single work from an anthology	Hawthorne, Nathaniel. "Young Goodman Brown." *Literature: An Introduction to Reading and Writing*. Ed. Edgar V. Roberts and Henry E. Jacobs. Upper Saddle River, NJ: Prentice-Hall, Inc., 1998. 376–385. [Indicate pages for the entire selection.]
Introduction in a published edition	Washington, Margaret. Introduction. *Narrative of Sojourner Truth*. By Sojourner Truth. Ed. Washington. New York: Vintage Books, 1993. v–xi.
Signed article in a weekly magazine	Wallace, Charles. "A Vodacious Deal." *Time*, 14 Feb. 2000: 63.
Signed article in a monthly magazine	Gustaitis, Joseph. "The Sticky History of Chewing Gum." *American History*, Oct. 1998: 30–38.
Unsigned editorial or story	"Selective Silence." Editorial. *Wall Street Journal*, 11 Feb. 2000: A14. [If the editorial or story is signed, begin with the author's name.]
Signed pamphlet	[Treat the pamphlet as though it were a book.]
Pamphlet with no author, publisher, or date	*Are You at Risk of Heart Attack?* n.p. n.d. [n.p. n.d. indicates that there is no known publisher or date]
Filmstrips, slide programs, videocassettes, DVDs, and other audiovisual media	*The Diary of Anne Frank*. Dir. George Stevens. Perf. Millie Perkins, Shelley Winters, Joseph Schildkraut, Lou Jacobi, and Richard Beymer. 1959. DVD. Twentieth Century Fox, 2004.
Radio or television program transcript	"Washington's Crossing of the Delaware" Host Liane Hansen. Guest David Hackett Fischer. *Weekend Edition Sunday*. Nat'l Public Radio. WNYC, New York City. 23 Dec. 2003. Transcript.
Internet	"*Fun Facts About Gum.*" NACGM site. National Association of Chewing Gum Manufacturers. 19 Dec. 1999 <http://www.nacgm.org/consumer/funfacts.html> [Indicate the date you accessed the information. Content and addresses at Web sites change frequently.]
Newspaper	Thurow, Roger. "South Africans Who Fought for Sanctions Now Scrap for Investors." *Wall Street Journal*, 11 Feb. 2000: A1+ [For a multipage article that does not appear on consecutive pages, write only the first page number on which it appears, followed by a plus sign.]
Personal interview	Smith, Jane. Personal interview. 10 Feb. 2000.
CD (with multiple publishers)	Simms, James, ed. *Romeo and Juliet*. By William Shakespeare. CD-ROM. Oxford: Attica Cybernetics Ltd.; London: BBC Education; London: HarperCollins Publishers, 1995.
Signed article from an encyclopedia	Askeland, Donald R. "Welding." *World Book Encyclopedia*. 1991 ed.

Index of Authors and Titles

Page numbers in *italics* refer to biographical information.

Index of Skills

Humor, recognizing situational, 367, 368, 372, 373, 374, 377
Identifying a target audience's purpose, 964, 967
Identifying causes and effects, 245, 303, 305, 311, 860, 863, 864, 867, 868, 869, 871, 872, 873, 875
Identifying relevant details, 443, 455, 459, 460, 463
Identifying support for response, 90, 93
Identifying the author's attitude, 633, 649, 651, 653, 654, 655, 660, 662, 664, 666, 669
Identifying with a character, 521, 553, 554, 558, 562, 563, 565
Images, forming mental, 227, 231, 233
Interactive reading, 149, 343
Interpreting meaning, 325, 326, 329, 330, 331
Key details, finding, 95, 98, 100, 102, 107, 115, 117
Listening to poetic sounds, 925, 929, 932, 935
Literal comprehension strategies, 3
Main idea:
    finding the, 131, 134, 135, 137
    implied, 339
    stated, 339
Making inferences about characters, 245, 315, 318, 321, 569, 573, 574, 580, 581, 585
Movie reviews, 90
Paraphrasing, 731, 818, 820, 822, 823, 824, 827, 828, 829, 830, 831, 834, 835, 836, 838, 840, 842, 893, 903, 909
Personal experience, relating to, 245, 281, 284, 287
Photo essay, 333
Picturing the action, 731, 733, 736, 737, 739, 741, 742, 744, 746, 748, 752, 756, 758, 761
Picturing the imagery, 913, 916, 919, 921
Predicting, 3, 49, 51, 53, 59, 61, 63, 64, 66, 70, 74, 75, 81, 83, 149, 213, 215, 216, 219, 220, 223, 539, 542, 546, 549, 844, 846, 847, 851, 854, 855, 857, 858
Predicting consequences of actions, 177, 180, 183
Purpose, establishing a, 151
Purpose for reading, establishing a, 155, 159
Questioning characters' actions, 343, 419, 422, 424, 426, 429, 431
Questions, generating, 187, 191, 192, 193
Read for information, 2, 148, 244, 342, 442, 520, 632, 730, 892, 976
Read for the love of literature, 2, 148, 244, 342, 442, 520, 632, 730, 892, 976
Reading ahead, 345, 350, 353
Reading back, 345, 350, 353
Reading back or reading ahead, 343
Reading between the lines, 343, 357, 363

Reading blank verse, 731, 794, 796, 797, 800, 802, 810, 812, 815, 816
Reading drama, 731
Reading fiction, 521
Reading in sentences, 893, 955, 961, 977, 979, 983, 985, 986, 990, 991, 992, 993, 996, 997, 1000, 1001, 1002, 1006, 1007, 1009, 1010, 1011, 1012, 1014, 1018
Reading nonfiction, 633
Read to appreciate an author's style, 244, 520, 892
Read to be entertained, 2, 342, 976
Read to be inspired, 148, 442, 632, 730
Recognizing a poet's purpose, 443, 471, 477
Recognizing author's point of view, 629
Recognizing a writer's bias, 445, 449, 451
Recognizing bias, 443
Recognizing facts and details, 241
Recognizing illogical situations, 411, 415
Recognizing situational humor, 343, 367, 368, 372, 373, 374, 377
Relating generalizations and evidence, 245, 247, 249, 253
Relating to personal experience, 245, 281, 284, 287
Relevant details, identifying, 455, 459, 460, 463
Responding, 149, 163, 166, 169, 170, 173
Scanning, 880, 883
Senses, 521, 589, 598, 599, 601, 603
    using your, 121, 127, 899
Sentences, breaking down confusing, 5, 10, 13
Skimming, 880, 883
Stated and implied main idea, 339
Strategies for reading an epic, 977
Strategies for reading poetry, 893
Summarizing, 3, 41, 44, 45, 977, 1020, 1025, 1026, 1027, 1028, 1029, 1031, 1033, 1039, 1040, 1041, 1045, 1047
Text aids, 731, 769, 772, 779, 780, 781, 782, 783, 784, 787, 788, 790, 792
Using context clues, 3, 17, 23, 24, 31, 37
Using interactive reading strategies, 343
Using literal comprehension strategies, 3
Using strategies for reading an epic, 977
Using text aids, 731, 769, 772, 779, 780, 781, 782, 783, 784, 787, 788, 790, 792
Using visuals as a key to meaning, 695, 705
Using your senses, 121, 127, 521, 589, 598, 599, 601, 603, 893, 895
Varying your reading rate, 635, 638, 641
Visuals as a key to meaning, 695, 705

GRAMMAR, USAGE, MECHANICS

Action verbs, 174, R20
Active voice, 224
Adjective clauses, 478, R22
Adjective phrases, 288, R21
Adjectives, 128, R20
    compound, 138
    coordinate, 118
    modifying, 210
    predicate, 408
    proper, 138
Adverb clauses, 464, R22
Adverb phrases, 288, 532, R21
Adverbs, 210, 300, R21
    modifying, 210
Agreement with indefinite pronouns, 876
Antecedents, 38
Apostrophes, R24
Appositive phrase, 622, R21
Capitalization, R22
Case, 762
Clauses, 510, R22
    adjective, 478, R22
    adverb, 464, R22
    independent, 452, R22
    main, 452
    noun, 464, R22
    subordinate, 452, 464, 478, R22
Colons, 900, R23
Commas, R22–R23
Common expression, 332
Commonly confused words:
    among and *between*, 1048, R24
    amount and *number*, R24
    any and *all*, R24
    around, R25
    as, because, like, and *as to*, R24
    bad and *badly*, R25
    because of and *due to*, R25
    being as and *being that*, R25
    beside and *besides*, R25
    can and *may*, R25
    compare and *contrast*, R25
    different from and *different than*, R25
    farther and *further*, R25
    fewer and *less*, R25
    good and *well*, R25
    of and *have*, R26
    hopefully, R26
    its and *it's*, R26
    just and *only*, R26
    kind of and *sort of*, R26
    lay and *lie*, R26
    leave and *let*, R26
    like, as, and *as if*, 1019
    literally and *figuratively*, R26
    raise and *rise*, R27
    set and *sit*, R27
    so and *so that*, R27
    than and *then*, R27
    that, which, and *who*, R27
    there, their, and *they're*, 720
    unique, R27

CRITICAL THINKING AND VIEWING

WRITING

Writing Applications

Writing Strategies

Index of Features

The Business Journal Serving Greater Milwaukee "'Cows on parade' find sweet home in Chicago" by David Schuyler. "This article appeared in Volume 17, No. 7 of *The Business Journal* Serving Greater Milwaukee on November 12, 1999. It has been reprinted by *The Business Journal* serving Greater Milwaukee and further reproduction by any other party is prohibited. Copyright © 1999 by *The Business Journal* serving greater Milwaukee, 600 W Virginia Street, Suite 500, Milwaukee, WI 53204, 414-278-7788." Used by permission.

Richard Curtis Associates, Inc. "Fly Away" from *The Beauty of the Beasts: Tales of Hollywood's Wild Animal Stars* by Ralph Helfer. Copyright © 1990 by Ralph Helfer. Reprinted by permission of Richard Curtis Associates, Inc.

Abigail de Oliveira Carvalho "Echo" by Henriqueta Lisboa, from *Poems Escolbidos: Chosen Poems,* translated by Helcio Veiga Costa, copyright © 1987 by Ed. Editora e Distribuidora, Ltda. Reprinted by permission of Abigail de Oliveira Carvalho, Henriqueta Lisboa's niece.

Curtis Brown, Ltd., London "The Birds" from *Kiss Me Again Stranger* by Daphne du Maurier. Reproduced by permission of Curtis Brown, Ltd., London, on behalf of the Chichester Partnership, copyright 1952 by Daphne du Maurier.

Jonathan Clowes Ltd., on behalf of Andrea Plunket "The Red-headed League" from *The Adventures of Sherlock Holmes* by Sir Arthur Conan Doyle. Copyright © 1996 Sir Arthur Conan Doyle Copyright Holders. Reprinted by kind permission of Jonathan Clowes Ltd., London, on behalf of Andrea Plunket, the Administrator of the Sir Arthur Conan Doyle Copyrights.

Coffee House Press "Problems With Hurricanes" by Victor Hernandez Cruz, from *Red Beans.* Copyright © 1991 by Victor Hernandez Cruz. Reprinted by permission of Coffee House Press.

Don Congdon Associates, Inc. "The Golden Kite, the Silver Wind" by Ray Bradbury. Copyright © 1953 by Epoch Associates; renewed 1981 by Ray Bradbury. Reprinted by permission of Don Congdon Associates, Inc.

Joan Daves Agency for the Estate of Gabriela Mistral "Meciendo" by Gabriela Mistral ("Rocking"), translated by Doris Dana from *Selected Poems of Gabriela Mistral,* translated and edited by Doris Dana. Copyright © 1961, 1964, 1970, 1971 by Doris Dana. Reprinted by permission of the Joan Daves Agency on behalf of the estate of the author.

Dial Books for Young Readers, a division of Penguin Putnam, Inc. From *Rosa Parks: My Story* by Rosa Parks with Jim Haskins. Copyright © 1992 by Rosa Parks. Used by permission of Dial Books for Young Readers, an imprint of Penguin Putnam Books for Young Readers, a division of Penguin Putnam, Inc.

Sandra Dijkstra Literary Agency for Amy Tan From "Joy, Luck, and Hollywood" by Amy Tan. Copyright © 1993 by Amy Tan. First appeared in the *Los Angeles Times,* Sunday, September 5, 1993. Reprinted with permission of the author and the Sandra Dijkstra Literary Agency.

Doubleday, a division of Random House, Inc. "The Machine That Won the War," copyright © 1961 by Mercury Press, Inc., from *Isaac Asimov: The Complete Stories, Vol. I* by Isaac Asimov. "The Birds," copyright 1952 by Daphne du Maurier, from *Kiss Me Again Stranger* by Daphne du Maurier. From *Tuesdays with Morrie* by Mitch Albom, copyright © 1997 by Mitch Albom. Used by permission of Doubleday, a division of Random House, Inc. "The Gift of the Magi" from *The Complete Works of O. Henry* by O. Henry. Published by Press Publications Company.

Martha Escutia "Business Letter and Agenda for the 8th Annual Southeast College Conference" by Martha Escutia. Used by permission of the author.

Faber and Faber Limited and Oxford University Press, Inc. "The Horses" from *Collected Poems* by Edwin Muir, copyright © 1960 by Willa Muir. Used by permission of Faber and Faber Limited and Oxford University Press, Inc.

Farrar, Straus & Giroux, Inc. "Georgia O'Keeffe" from *The White Album* by Joan Didion. Copyright © 1979 by Joan Didion. "The Washwoman" from *A Day of Pleasure* by Isaac Bashevis Singer. Copyright © 1969 by Isaac Bashevis Singer. Excerpts from *The Odyssey: A Stage Version* by Derek Walcott. Copyright © 1993 by Derek Walcott. From *In My Place* by Charlayne Hunter-Gault. Copyright © 1992 by Charlayne Hunter-Gault. Excerpts from the *Odyssey* by Homer, translated by R. Fitzgerald. Copyright © 1961, 1963 by Robert Fitzgerald and renewed 1989 by Benedict R. C. Fitzgerald.

Gale Group Excerpts from "The Birds" by DeWitt Bodeen from pp. 249–252 of *Magill's Survey of Cinema* edited by Frank N. Magill. Copyright © 1981 by Frank N. Magill. Reprinted by permission.

Graywolf Press and The Estate of William Stafford "Fifteen," copyright 1966, 1998 by the Estate of William Stafford. Reprinted from *The Way It Is: New & Selected Poems* with the permission of Graywolf Press, Saint Paul, Minnesota, and Kim Stafford for the Estate of William Stafford.

Alice R. Abbott "Perseus" by Edith Hamilton from *Mythology.* Copyright © 1940, 1942, by Edith Hamilton, renewed 1969. Used by permission.

Harcourt, Inc. "Women" from *Revolutionary Petunias & Other Poems,* copyright © 1972, 2000 by Alice Walker. "Macavity: The Mystery Cat" from *Old Possum's Book of Practical Cats,* copyright 1939 by T. S. Eliot and renewed 1967 by Esme Valerie Eliot. "A Lincoln Preface," copyright 1953 by Carl Sandburg and renewed 1981 by Margaret Sandburg, Janet Sandburg, and Helga Sandburg Crile. "Ithaca" from *The Complete Poems of Cavafy,* copyright © 1961 and renewed 1989 by Rae Dalven. Reprinted by permission of Harcourt, Inc.

HarperCollins Publishers "Summer" from *Brown Angels: An Album of Pictures and Verse* by Walter Dean Myers. Copyright © 1993 by Walter Dean Myers. Used by permission of HarperCollins Publishers.

Helmut Hirnschall "There is a Longing..." from *My Heart Soars* by Chief Dan George and Helmut Hirnschall. Copyright © 1974 by Clarke Irwin. Used by permission of the author.

Henry Holt and Company, Inc. "Talk" from *The Cow-Tail Switch and Other West African Stories* by Harold Courlander and George Herzog, © 1947, 1974 by Harold Courlander. "Fire and Ice" from *The Poetry of Robert Frost,* edited by Edward Connery Lathem. Copyright © 1951 by Robert Frost, Copyright © 1923, 1969 by Henry Holt and Company, Inc. Reprinted by permission of Henry Holt and Company, LLC. "The Road Not Taken" from *The Poetry of Robert Frost,* edited by Edward Connery Lathem. Published by Henry Holt and Company, Inc.

Horton Foote and The Barbara Hogenson Agency, Inc. *The Dancers* by Horton Foote. Copyright © 1955, 1983 by Horton Foote. Reprinted by arrangement with Horton Foote and the Barbara Hogenson Agency, Inc.

Rosemary Thurber and The Barbara Hogenson Agency, Inc.
"The Secret Life of Walter Mitty" from *My World—And Welcome To It* copyright © 1942 by James Thurber; copyright renewed © 1971 by James Thurber. Reprinted by arrangement with Rosemary Thurber and the Barbara Hogenson Agency. All rights reserved.

Houghton Mifflin Company "Blackberry Eating" from *Mortal Acts, Mortal Words* by Galway Kinnell. Copyright © 1980 by Galway Kinnell. Excerpt from *Lost Moon: The Perilous Voyage of Apollo 13.* Copyright © 1994 by Jim Lovell and Jeffrey Kluger. "All Watched Over by Machines of Loving Grace" by Richard Brautigan, from *Trout Fishing in America, The Pill versus the Springhill Mine Disaster,* and *In Watermelon Sugar.* Copyright © 1968, by Richard Brautigan. Reprinted by permission of Houghton Mifflin Co. All rights reserved. "Siren Song" from *You Are Happy* by Margaret Atwood. Copyright © 1974 by Margaret Atwood. Reprinted by permission of Houghton Mifflin Company.

Houghton Mifflin Company and Frances Collin, Literary Agent Excerpt from *Silent Spring* (pp. 1–3) by Rachel Carson. Copyright © 1962 by Rachel L. Carson, renewed 1990 by Roger Christie. Reprinted by permission of Houghton Mifflin Co. and Frances Collin, Literary Agent. All rights reserved.

James R. Hurst "The Scarlet Ibis" by James Hurst, published in *The Atlantic Monthly,* July 1960. Copyright © 1988 by James Hurst. Reprinted by permission of the author.

International Creative Management, Inc. "Single Room, Earth View" by Sally Ride, published in the April/May 1986 issue of *Air & Space/Smithsonian Magazine,* published by The Smithsonian Institution. Reprinted by permission of International Creative Management, Inc.

Japan Publications "Three Haiku" (originally titled "Temple bells die out" by Bashō; and "Dragonfly catcher" and "Bearing no flowers" by Chiyojo) from *One Hundred Famous Haiku* by Daniel C. Buchanan, Copyright © 1973 by Japan Publications. Used by permission.

The Kansas City Star "The wrong orbit. Senator has no legitimate business blasting into space," an editorial from *The Kansas City Star, 1/20/98.* Reprinted by permission of The Kansas City Star.

Lyndon B. Johnson Library From *A White House Diary* by Lady Bird Johnson. Reprinted by permission of the L.B.J. Library c/o Betty Tilson, assistant to Mrs. Lyndon B. Johnson.

Junior League of Seattle "Combing" by Gladys Cardiff from *Puget Soundings,* March 1971. Reprinted by permission of the Junior League of Seattle.

The Estate of Martin Luther King, Jr., c/o Writer's House "I Have a Dream" from *The Words of Martin Luther King, Jr.* Copyright 1963 by Martin Luther King, Jr., copyright renewed 1991 by Coretta Scott King. Reprinted by arrangement with the Estate of Martin Luther King, Jr., c/o Writer's House as agent for the proprietor.

Alfred A. Knopf, a division of Random House, Inc. "Uncle Marcos" from *The House of the Spirits* by Isabel Allende, translated by Magda Bogin, copyright © 1985 by Alfred A. Knopf, A Division of Random House, Inc. "Dream Deferred" and "Dreams" from *The Collected Poems of Langston Hughes* by Langston Hughes. Copyright © 1994 by The Estate of Langston Hughes. "To be of use" from *Circles on the Water* by Marge Piercy, copyright © 1982 by Marge Piercy. Used by permission of Alfred A. Knopf, a division of Random House, Inc.

Little, Brown and Company, Inc. "Perseus" from *Mythology* by Edith Hamilton. Copyright © 1942 by Edith Hamilton; Copyright © renewed 1969 by Dorian Fielding Reid and Doris Fielding Reid. #254, "'Hope' is the thing with feathers—" and #1176, "We never know how high we are" from *The Complete Poems of Emily Dickinson,* edited by Thomas H. Johnson. Copyright 1929, 1935 by Martha Dickson Bianchi; Copyright © renewed 1957, 1963 by Mary L. Hampson. By permission of Little, Brown and Company, Inc.

Liveright Publishing Corporation, an imprint of W. W. Norton & Company "maggie and milly and molly and may," copyright © 1956, 1984, 1991 by The Trustees for the E. E. Cummings Trust, from *Complete Poems: 1904–1962* by E. E. Cummings. Edited by George J. Firmage. Used by permission of Liveright Publishing Corporation.

Marie-Christine MacAndrew "The Necklace" from *Boule de Suif and Selected Stories* by Guy de Maupassant, translated by Andrew MacAndrew. Translation copyright © 1964 by Andrew MacAndrew. Reprinted by permission of Marie-Christine MacAndrew.

Macmillan, a division of Simon & Schuster, Inc. "Jabberwocky" from *The Collected Verse of Lewis Carroll* (New York: Macmillan, 1933). "There Will Come Soft Rains" by Sara Teasdale. Reprinted from *The Collected Poems of Sara Teasdale.* Published by Macmillan, a division of Simon & Schuster, Inc.

John McPhee "Arthur Ashe Remembered" by John McPhee, first published in *The New Yorker,* March 1, 1993. Reprinted by permission of the author.

Methuen Publishing, Limited "The Inspector-General" from *The Sneeze: Plays and Stories* by Anton Chekhov, translated and adapted by Michael Frayn, published by Methuen Drama. Originally from *An Awl in a Sack* by Anton Chekhov, 1885. Random House, UK, Ltd. Used by permission of Methuen Publishing, Limited.

Milkweed Editions "Eulogy for a Hermit Crab" by Pattiann Rogers from *Song of the World Becoming: New and Collected Poems 1981–2001* (Minneapolis: Milkweed Editions, 2001). Copyright © 1994, 2001 by Pattiann Rogers. Reprinted with permission from Milkweed Editions.

Edna St. Vincent Millay Society "An Ancient Gesture" by Edna St. Vincent Millay. From *Collected Poems,* HarperCollins. Copyright © 1954, 1982 by Norma Millay Ellis. All rights reserved. Reprinted by permission of Elizabeth Barnett, literary executor.

National Audubon Society "Audubon Web Site" from www.audubon.org. Used by permission of the National Audubon Society.

National Public Radio "Earhart Redux" by Alex Chadwick. Copyright © National Public Radio 1997. The news report by NPR's Alex Chadwick was originally broadcast on National Public Radio's and National Geographic Society's "Radio Expeditions" on March 17, 1997, and is used with the permission of National Public Radio, Inc. and the National Geographic Society. Any unauthorized duplication is strictly prohibited.

Charles Neider "The Invalid's Story" from *The Comic Mark Twain Reader,* edited by Charles Neider. Copyright © 1977 by Charles Neider. Reprinted by permission of the author.

New American Library, a division of Penguin Putnam, Inc. From *The Tragedy of Romeo and Juliet* by William Shakespeare, edited by J. A. Bryant, Jr. Published by New American Library, a division of Penguin Putnam, Inc.

North Point Press, a division of Farrar, Straus & Giroux, Inc. "Gifts" by Shu Ting from *A Splintered Mirror: Chinese Poetry from the Democracy Movement*, translated by Donald Finkel. Translation copyright © 1991 by Donald Finkel.

Naomi Shihab Nye "Shoulders" from *Red Suitcase* by Naomi Shihab Nye. Copyright © 1994 Naomi Shihab Nye. All rights reserved. Reprinted by permission of the author.

W. W. Norton and Company, Inc. From *The Perfect Storm* by Sebastian Junger. Copyright © 1997 by Sebastian Junger. Used by permission of W. W. Norton and Company, Inc.

Orchard Books, an imprint of Scholastic, Inc. "Checkouts" from *A Couple of Kooks and Other Stories About Love* by Cynthia Rylant. Copyright © 1990 by Cynthia Rylant. Reprinted by permission.

Oxford University Press, Canada "Siren Song" by Margaret Atwood from *Selected Poems 1966–1984*. Copyright © Margaret Atwood 1990. Reprinted by permission of Oxford University Press, Canada.

Playbill Magazine "On Summer" by Lorraine Hansberry, reprinted from *Playbill Magazine*, June, 1960. Copyright © Playbill, Inc. Playbill ® is a registered trademark of Playbill Incorporated, NYC. All rights reserved. Used by permission.

Polygram International Music Publishing "Pride (In the Name of Love)," lyrics by Bono and The Edge, music by U2. Copyright © 1984 by Polygram International Music Publishing. Reprinted by permission of Polygram International Music Publishing.

G.P. Putnam's Sons, a division of Penguin Putnam, Inc. "Rules of the Game" from *The Joy Luck Club* by Amy Tan, copyright © 1989 by Amy Tan. Used by permission of G.P. Putnam's Sons, a division of Penguin Putnam, Inc.

Quarterly Review of Literature "Astonishment" by Wisława Szymborska, translated by Grazyna Drabik, Austin Flint, and Sharon Olds. Copyright *Quarterly Review of Literature Poetry Series*, Volume XXIII, edited by T. and R. Weiss. Used by permission.

Random House, Inc. "Caged Bird," copyright © 1983 by Maya Angelou, from *Shaker, Why Don't You Sing?* by Maya Angelou. "New Directions" from *Wouldn't Take Nothin for My Journey Now* by Maya Angelou, copyright © 1993 by Maya Angelou. "Blues Ain't No Mockin Bird" by Toni Cade Bambara, copyright © 1971 by Toni Cade Bambara, from *Gorilla, My Love* by Toni Cade Bambara. "The Rug Merchant" from *The World Is My Home: A Memoir* by James Michener, copyright © 1992 by James Michener. Used by permission of Random House, Inc.

Marian Reiner, Literary Agent for Lillian Morrison "The Spearthrower" from *The Sidewalk Racer and Other Poems of Sports and Motion* by Lillian Morrison. Copyright 1965, 1967, 1968, 1977 by Lillian Morrison. © Renewed Lillian Morrison. Reprinted by permission of Marian Reiner for the author.

Scovil Chichak Galen Literary Agency "If I Forget Thee, Oh Earth . . ." from *Expedition to Earth* by Arthur C. Clarke. Copyright © 1951 by Columbia Publications, Inc. Reprinted by permission of the author and the author's agent, Scovil Chichak Galen Literary Agency, Inc.

The Literary Trustees of Walter de la Mare and The Society of Authors "The Listeners" from *The Complete Poems of Walter de la Mare* by Walter de la Mare. Used by permission of the Literary Trustees of Walter de la Mare and the Society of Authors as their representative.

San Francisco Examiner and Keay Davidson "Caucasian Mummies Mystify Chinese" by Keay Davidson, published March 13, 1994. Copyright © San Francisco Examiner. Reprinted by permission of the author.

The Sporting News Book review by Steve Gietschier of *In These Girls, Hope Is a Muscle* by Madeleine Bais, originally published in *The Sporting News, Mary 15, 1995*. Reprinted by permission of The Sporting News.

Sterling Lord Literistic, Inc. "Children in the Woods" from *Crossing Open Grounds* by Barry Lopez. Copyright © 1988 by Barry Holstun Lopez. Reprinted by permission of Sterling Lord Literistic, Inc.

Texas Instruments From *TI-82 Graphing Calculator Guidebook*. "Graphing Calculator and Warranty" by Texas Instruments. Copyright © 1993 by Texas Instruments, Incorporated. Used by kind permission of Texas Instruments.

Thacher Proffitt & Wood, as attorney-in-fact for Ishmael Reed "Beware: Do Not Read This Poem" from *New and Collected Poems* by Ishmael Reed. Copyright © 1966, 1971, 1972, 1973, 1978, 1988 by Ishmael Reed. Reprinted by permission of the author.

University Press of New England Gary Soto, "The Talk" from *A Summer Life*. © 1990 by University Press of New England. Used by permission.

Viking Penguin, A division of Penguin Putnam, Inc. "Go Deep to the Sewer" from *Childhood* by Bill Cosby. Copyright © 1991 by William H. Cosby, Jr. Used by permission of Viking Penguin, a division of Penguin Putnam, Inc. From *The Road Ahead* by Bill Gates. Copyright © 1995 by William H. Gates III. "Old Man of the Temple" from *Under the Banyan Tree* by R. K. Narayan, copyright © 1985 by R. K. Narayan. Used by permission of Viking Penguin, a division of Penguin Putnam, Inc. "The Interlopers" from *The Complete Short Stories of Saki* by Saki (H.H. Munro). Published by The Viking Press.

Vital Speeches of the Day "Glory and Hope," by Nelson Mandela, from *Vital Speeches of the Day*, June 1, 1994. Reprinted by permission of Vital Speeches of the Day.

Watkins/Loomis Agency for Patricia Volk "An Entomological Study of Apartment 4A" by Patricia Volk, from *The New York Times Magazine*, March 5, 1995. Reprinted by permission of Patricia Volk and the Watkins/Loomis Agency.

Wesleyan University Press with the University Press of New England "Slam, Dunk, & Hook," from *Magic City* by Yusef Komunyakaa. Copyright © 1992 by Yusef Komunyakaa, Wesleyan University Press with the University Press of New England. Reprinted by permission of Wesleyan University Press of New England.

Bryan Woolley "To the Residents of A.D. 2029" from *The Time of My Life* by Bryan Woolley. Copyright © Bryan Woolley, 1984. Reprinted by permission of the author.

The Wylie Agency, Inc. "The Man to Send Rain Clouds" from *Storyteller* by Leslie Marmon Silko. Copyright © 1981 by Leslie Marmon Silko, reprinted by permission of The Wylie Agency, Inc.

Note: Every effort has been made to locate the copyright owner of material reprinted in this book. Omissions brought to our attention will be corrected in subsequent printings.

Art Credits

Cover and Title Page *The Fog Warning*, 1885, oil on canvas, 30 1/4 x 48 1/2", Winslow Homer, Courtesy, Museum of Fine Arts, Boston. Reproduced with permission. ©2000 Museum of Fine Arts, Boston. All Rights Reserved. Otis Norcross Fund, 94.72; **xxv** ©The Stock Market/John Henley; **vii** Corel Professional Photos CD-ROM™; **viii** *Peculiarsome Abe*, N.C. Wyeth, Children's Special Collections, The Free Library of Philadelphia; **ix** Corel Professional Photos CD-ROM™; **x** Murray Wilson/Omni-Photo Communications, Inc.; **xi** Corel Professional Photos CD-ROM™; **xii** ©Alon Reininger/Contact Press/The Stock Market; **xiii** *The Oldest Inhabitant*, 1876, Julian Alden Weir, oil on canvas, 65 1/2 x 32" Signed, upper left. Butler Institute of American Art, Youngstown, Ohio; **xiv** Culver Pictures, Inc.; **xv** White/Pite/International Stock Photography, Ltd.; **xvi** ©Wolfgang Kaehler/CORBIS; **xvii** ©Araldo de Luca/CORBIS; **xviii** *Keying Up—The Court Jester* (detail), 1875, William Merritt Chase, Courtesy of the Pennsylvania Academy of the Fine Arts, Philadelphia, Gift of the Chapellier Galleries; **xx** ©The Stock Market/Pete Saloutos; **xxi** *The Quiltmakers*, Paul Goodnight, 22 11/16" x 24", Color Circle Art Publishing Inc.; **xi** Corel Professional Photos CD-ROM™; **xvi-xvii** Hulton Getty/Liaison Agency; **1** *The Storm*, 1893, Edvard Munch, Oil on canvas, 36 1/8 x 51 1/2" (91.8 x 130.8cm). The Museum of Modern Art, New York, Gift of Mr. and Mrs. H. Irgens Larsen and acquired through the Lillie P. Bliss and Abby Aldrich Rockefeller Funds. ©1997 The Museum of Modern Art, New York; **2** (t) *Baseball Players Practicing*, 1875, Thomas Eakins, Museum of Art, Rhode Island School of Design, Jesse Metcalf Fund and Walter H. Kimball Fund, (b) CORBIS; **4** ©Photo Researchers, Inc.; **6** *Keying Up—The Court Jester* (detail), 1875, William Merritt Chase, Courtesy of the Pennsylvania Academy of the Fine Arts, Philadelphia, Gift of the Chapellier Galleries; **9** ©Photo Researchers, Inc.; **11** SuperStock; **12** CORBIS-Bettmann; **16** Dr. E.R. Degginger; **18–19** *Peering Through the Jungle*, Larry Noble, Sal Barracca & Associates; **21** *Hat, Knife, and Gun in Woods*, David Mann, Sal Barracca & Associates; **22** Corel Professional Photos CD-ROM™; **26** Sovfoto/Eastfoto; **28** Grace Davies/Omni-Photo Communications, Inc.; **30** CORBIS; **31** Ann Shamel/Graphicstock; **33** CORBIS; **34** ©The Stock Market/John Dominis; **36** NYT Pictures; **40** *Baseball Players Practicing*, 1875, Thomas Eakins, Museum of Art, Rhode Island School of Design, Jesse Metcalf Fund and Walter H. Kimball Fund; **42** *Baseball Players Practicing*,1875, Thomas Eakins, Museum of Art, Rhode Island School of Design, Jesse Metcalf Fund and Walter H. Kimball Fund; **48** ©The Stock Market/Zefa Germany; **50** *Attack of the Birds*, 1994, Lev Tabenkin, Oil on canvas, 59" x 78", Maya Polsky Gallery; **52–53** Corel Professional Photos CD-ROM™; **56–57** *Landscape from a Dream*, 1936–38, Paul Nash, Tate Gallery, London/Art Resource, NY; **58** Art Hudson/American Red Cross; **60–61** Corel Professional Photos CD-ROM™; **65** ©The Stock Market/Zefa Germany; **68–69** *Wheatfield with Crows*, 1890, Vincent van Gogh, Van Gogh Museum, Amsterdam, The Netherlands, Art Resource, NY; **72–73** Corel Professional Photos CD-ROM™; **76** *Over and Above #13*, 1964, Clarence Holbrook Carter, oil on canvas, Courtesy of the Artist; **80–81** Corel Professional Photos CD-ROM™; **82** AP/Wide World Photos; **86** © Stone; **88** © John Darling/Stone; **89** Sonia Moskowitz/Globe Photos, Inc.; **91** Photofest; **94** Tony Cordoza/Liaison Agency; **96** The Granger Collection, New York; **99** © Simon Jauncey/Stone; **100–106** The Granger Collection, New York; **109** Historical Picture Archive/CORBIS; **110, 114** The Granger Collection, New York; **116** *Sir Arthur Conan Doyle* (detail), H. L. Gates, The National Portrait Gallery, London; **120** *Drawing Hands*, 1948, 1995 M.C. Escher/Cordon Art - Baarn - Holland. All rights reserved.; **122** *Het Blinde Huis*, William Degouve

de Nunques, State Museum, Kröller-Müller, Otterlo, The Netherlands; **123** ©Faber & Faber Ltd; **132** Jeffery Newbury/Discover Magazine; **136** Courtesy of the author; **140** ©Tony Freeman/PhotoEdit; **146–147** *Human Achievement*, Tsing-Fang Chen, Lucia Gallery, New York City/SuperStock; **148** (b.l.) CORBIS; **148** (t) *Night Games*, Ernie Barnes, Oil on canvas, 48 x 24, Courtesy of The Company of Art, Los Angeles; **148** (b.r.) *Perseus and Andromeda* (detail), ca.1580, Paolo Veronese, Musee des Beaux-Arts, Rennes, France, Erich Lessing/Art Resource, NY; **150, 152–153** *Lincoln Proclaiming Thanksgiving*, Dean Cornwell, The Lincoln Museum, Fort Wayne, Indiana, (#1153); **154** *Peculiarsome Abe*, N.C. Wyeth, Children's Special Collections, The Free Library of Philadelphia; **156** Courtesy of the Library of Congress; **158** *Carl Sandburg*, Miriam Svet, The National Portrait Gallery, Smithsonian Institution, Washington, D.C./Art Resource, New York; **162** AP/Wide World Photos; **164** CORBIS; **166** AP/Wide World Photos; **167** Neal Preston/CORBIS; **168** *The Beginning*, Artis Lane, Courtesy of the artist; **169** AP/Wide World Photos; **170–171** *We the People*, Kathy Morrow, Original scratchboard painting with hand-loomed beadwork, Courtesy of the artist; **171** Alan Markfield/Globe Photos, New York; **172** The Granger Collection, New York; **176** Rectangular box, detail, Woven bamboo and painted lacquer, Late Ming Dynasty, early 17th century, H. 12.1 cm x W. 34.3 cm x L. 48.3 cm, H. 4 3/4" x W. 13 1/2" x L. 19", China, Avery Brundage Collection, #B60 M427, Asian Art Museum of San Francisco; **178** *The Nymph of the Lo River*, section of a handscroll. (H.9 1/2") Attributed to Ku K'ai-chih, Courtesy of the Freer Gallery of Art, Smithsonian Institution, Washington, D.C. #14.53; **182** Thomas Victor; **186** ©The Stock Market/Alan Goldsmith; **188** ©The Stock Market/Alan Goldsmith; **189** Dimitri Kessel/Life Magazine; **190** AP/Wide World Photos; **192** Henry McGee/Globe Photos; **200** Charles Weckler/The Image Bank; **202–203** Charles Weckler/The Image Bank; **205** Historical Picture Archive/CORBIS; **207** Indian, Mughal, Leaf from a royal manuscript of the Shah-Jehan Nameh: A procession in a palace courtyard, gouache on paper, mid 17th century, 28.9 x19.7 cm. Kate S. Buckingham Endowment Fund, 1975.555. Photograph © 1996, The Art Institute of Chicago. All Rights Reserved.; **208** AP/Wide World Photos; **212** *Danae with young Perseus arriving on the island of Seripo*, Museo Archeologico, Ferrara, Italy. Scala/Art Resource, NY; **214** *Andromeda Liberated*, Pierre Mignard, Louvre, Paris, France, Erich Lessing/Art Resource, NY; **217** *Danae with young Perseus arriving on the island of Seripo*, Museo Archeologico, Ferrara, Italy. Scala/Art Resource, NY; **218** Terre del Greco Ascione Collections/Superstock; **221** *Perseus and Andromeda* (detail), ca.1580, Paolo Veronese, Musée des Beaux-Arts, Rennes, France, Erich Lessing/Art Resource, NY; **222** UPI/CORBIS–Bettmann; **226** © David Madison/Stone; **228** *Night Games*, Ernie Barnes, Oil on canvas, 48 x 24, Courtesy of The Company of Art, Los Angeles; **229** Photo by Mandy Sayer; **230** ©Allsport/Tony Duffy; **231** Photo by Isidro Rodriquez; **232** Photo by Michael Nye; **236** Corel Professional Photos CD-ROM™; **242–243** *Waiting Girl*, 1978, Yan Hsia, Asian American Arts Center; **244** (b) Corel Professional Photos CD-ROM™; **246** ©Jack Hollingsworth/Index Stock Imagery/PictureQuest; **248** ©The Stock Market/Mark Gamba; **249** Corel Professional Photos CD-ROM™; **251** ©The Stock Market/Mark Gamba; **252** Thomas Victor; **260** CORBIS; **262–267** Digital Imagery ©Copyright 2001 PhotoDisc, Inc.; **268** *Chess Mates*, 1992, Pamela Chin Lee, Courtesy of the artist, Photo by John Lei/Omni-Photo Communications, Inc.; **269, 271** Digital Imagery ©Copyright 2001 Photo-Disc, Inc.; **272** Robert Foothorap; **276** Photofest; **278** ©Robert Foothorap/Black Star Publishing/PictureQuest; **280, 282**

Food City, 1967, Richard Estes, Oil acrylic and graphite on fiberboard, 48" x 68", Collection of the Akron Art Museum, Akron, Ohio, Museum Acquisition Fund, Photo by Richman Haire, ©Richard Estes/Licensed by VAGA, New York, NY/Courtesy Marlborough Gallery, NY; **286** Kit Stafford; **290** Horrillo Iriola/A.G.E. FotoStock; **292** The Granger Collection, New York; **293** Horrillo Iriola/A.G.E. FotoStock; **294** Henry McGee/Globe Photos; **295** (t) *Bubbles*, watercolor, 39" x 29", Courtesy of Scott Burdick, (b) The Granger Collection, New York; **296** UPI/CORBIS-Bettmann; **298** AP/Wide World Photos; **302** David De Lossy/The Image Bank; **304** R. Ashenbrenner/Stock Boston; **306** David De Lossy/The Image Bank; **308–309** Kenneth Redding/The Image Bank; **310** The Granger Collection, New York; **314** Tina Buckman/Index Stock Photography, Inc.; **316** Patrick Ward/Stock Boston; **318** Tina Buckman/Index Stock Photography, Inc.; **319** Digital Imagery ©Copyright 2001 PhotoDisc, Inc.; **320** Adam Scull/Globe Photos; **324** *The Quiltmakers*, Paul Goodnight, 22 11/16" x 24", Color Circle Art Publishing Inc.; **326** Digital Imagery ©Copyright 2001 PhotoDisc, Inc.; **327** (t) *The Quiltmakers*, Paul Goodnight, 22 11/16" x 24" Color Circle Art Publishing Inc., (b) Thomas Victor; **328** (t), (m), (b) Corel Professional Photos CD-ROM™; **329** E. E. Cummings (detail), 1958, Self-Portrait, The National Portrait Gallery, Smithsonian Institution, Washington, D.C./Art Resource, New York; **330** AP/Wide World Photos; **334** Laima Druskis/Pearson Education; **340–341** *Scientist's Hobby: Failure #18 of the Anti-Gravity Pack*, 1992, Bruce Widdows, acrylic on canvas, 84 x 132 inches, Courtesy of George Adams Gallery, New York; **342** (t) *The Jabberwock*, 1873, John Tenniel, The Granger Collection, New York, (b), ©Danny Brass/Photo Researchers, Inc.; **344** *Portrait XIV*, Private Collection/Donald C. Martin/SuperStock; **346** *The Man With Three Masks*, John Rush, Courtesy of the artist; **351** *New Orleans Fantasy* (detail), 1985, Max Papart, Lithograph, Courtesy of Nahan Galleries, New York; **352** CORBIS-Bettmann; **356, 358** *Valmondois Sous La Neige*, Maurice de Vlaminck, Superstock; **361** *White Night*, 1901, Edvard Munch, oil on canvas, 45 1/2 x 43 1/2 in. (115.5 x 111 cm) Photo: J. Lathion ©Nasjonalgalleriet 1997; **362** CORBIS-Bettmann; **366** Chromosohm/Sohm/Stock Boston; **369** *Young Brothers in the Hood*, 17x22, Tom McKinney, Courtesy of the artist; **370** Henry Horenstein/StockBoston; **372** Globe Photos; **374** Chromosohm/Sohm/Stock Boston; **376** Courtesy of the author; **380** Michael Newman/PhotoEdit; **382** ©David Muench/CORBIS; **383** Dianne Trejo; **384** © Anthony Banniste; Gallo Images/CORBIS; **386** (t) ©Stephen Dalton/Photo Researchers, Inc., (b) ©Sturgis McKeever/Photo Researchers, Inc.; **387** ©Pat Lynch/Photo Researchers, Inc.; **388** ©R.J. Erwin/Photo Researchers, Inc.; **389** ©Louis Quitt/Photo Researchers, Inc.; **390** (t) ©John M. Burnley/Photo Researchers, Inc., (b) Photo by Larry Sillen; **395** "Hey Diddle, Diddle" by William McBride and Michael Stack, Courtesy of McBride & Kelley Architects; **398** © Churchill Kheler/Stone; **400** *The Jabberwock*, 1873, John Tenniel, The Granger Collection, New York; **401** Gernsheim Collection, Harry Ransom Humanities Research Center, The University of Texas at Austin; **402** From *Old Possum's Book of Practical Cats*, Copyright 1939 by T. S. Eliot: renewed 1967 by Esme Valerie Eliot, Reproduced by permission of Harcourt Brace Jovanovich, Inc., Illustration by Edward Gorey; **404** T. S. Eliot (detail), 1888–1965, Sir Gerald Kelly, National Portrait Gallery, Smithsonian Institution, Art Resource, New York; **405** (l) Corel Professional Photos CD-ROM™, (r) Corel Professional Photos CD-ROM™; **406** (t.l.), (t.r) Corel Professional Photos CD-ROM™, (b) Photo by William Lewis; **414** © 1966 by Michael Courlander; **418** ©R. Gates/Archive Photos; **420** Murray Wilson/Omni-Photo Communications, Inc.; **423** UPI/CORBIS-Bettmann; **425** ©R. Gates/Archive Photos; **426** Eugene Gordon/Pearson Education/PH College; **429** Murray Wilson/Omni-Photo Communications, Inc.; **430** AP/Wide World Photos; **434**

Tony Freeman/PhotoEdit; **440** Michael Agliolo/International Stock Photography, Ltd.; **442** (r) Index Stock Photography, Inc., (l) Gideon Mendel/Magnum Photos, Inc.; **444** Digital Imagery ©Copyright 2001 PhotoDisc, Inc.; **446** Sanford/Agliolo/International Stock Photography, Ltd.; **448** Index Stock Photography, Inc.; **450** Andrea Renault/Globe Photos; **454** NASA; **456–457** Corel Professional Photos CD-ROM™; **458** Corel Professional Photos CD-ROM™; **461** NASA; **462** Thomas Victor; **466** Digital Imagery ©Copyright 2001 PhotoDisc, Inc.; **466** (inset) Corel Professional Photos CD-ROM™; **469** Prentice Hall; **470** © Eastcott/Momatiuk/Stone; **472** Dimitri Kessel/Life Magazine, (l) (r) Corel Professional Photos CD-ROM™; **473** (t) Corel Professional Photos CD-ROM™, (b) CORBIS-Bettmann; **474** Corel Professional Photos CD-ROM™; **475** Mark Gerson Photography; **476** © Vernon Merritt/Time Inc.; **484** ©Alan L. Detrick/Photo Researchers, Inc.; **486–487** NASA; **490** UPI/CORBIS-Bettmann; **491** Corel Professional Photos CD-ROM™; **492–493** Frank Whitney/The Image Bank; **494** UPI/CORBIS-Bettmann; **495** ML Sinibaldi/©The Stock Market; **496** Digital Imagery ©Copyright 2001 PhotoDisc, Inc.; **497** Ryan Williams/International Stock Photography, Ltd.; **498** Photo by Judy Walgreen; **502** Gideon Mendel/Magnum Photos, Inc.; **504** Corel Professional Photos CD-ROM™; **505** Dorothy Alexander; **506** Gideon Mendel/Magnum Photos, Inc.; **508** AP/Wide World Photos; **512** © Myrleen Cate/Stone; **518–519** *Reading*, 1973, oil on masonite, Billy Morrow Jackson, Wichita Art Museum, purchased with funds donated by Mr. and Mrs. Donald C. Slawson; **520** ©Hulton Getty/Archive Photos; **522** *Wishful Thinking*, Peter Szumowski, Private Collection/Bridgeman Art Library, London/New York; **524** Jeff Spielman/The Image Bank; **527** Corel Professional Photos CD-ROM™; **528** *Hairdresser's Window*, 1907, John Sloan, oil on canvas, 1947.240, Wadsworth Atheneum, Hartford. The Ella Gallup Sumner and Mary Catlin Sumner Collection Fund; **529** Carved Tortoiseshell Comb, mid 19th century, England or France, Cooper-Hewitt National Design Museum, Smithsonian Institution/Art Resource, NY, Bequest of Mrs. John Innes Kane, 1926-22-545, photo by Richard Goodbody; **530** CORBIS-Bettmann; **534** Amazon.Com Books, Inc.; **536** CORBIS; **538** Carl Purcell/Photo Researchers, Inc.; **540–541** ©The Stock Market/ZEFA; **544–545** ©Alon Reininger/Contact Press/The Stock Market; **552** John Kaprielian/Photo Researchers, Inc.; **556** *Two Boys in a Punt*, N. C. Wyeth, Courtesy of Dr. and Mrs. William A. Morton, Jr., Photograph from Brandywine River Museum; **562–563** *Scarlet Ibis*, John James Audubon, ©Collection of The New-York Historical Society; **568** CORBIS-Bettmann; **571** *Sharecropper*, Elizabeth Catlett, Courtesy The Estate of Thurlow E. Tibbs, Jr., ©Elizabeth Catlett/Licensed by VAGA, New York, NY; **574** Digital Imagery ©Copyright 2001 PhotoDisc, Inc.; **576** Nikky Finney; **578, 582** CORBIS-Bettmann; **584** Inge Morath/Magnum Photos; **588** *Feast Day*, San Juan Pueblo, 1921, William Penhallow Henderson, National Museum of American Art, Smithsonian Institution; Given in Memory of Joshua C. Taylor/Art Resource, New York; **590–591** Corel Professional Photos CD-ROM™; **593** *Feast Day*, San Juan Pueblo, 1921, William Penhallow Henderson, National Museum of American Art, Smithsonian Institution; Given in Memory of Joshua C. Taylor/Art Resource, New York; **595** Thomas Victor; **596** ©Hulton Getty/Archive Photos; **598** *Sacramento Railroad Station*, 1874, William Hahn, Fine Arts Museum of San Francisco; **601** The Granger Collection, New York; **602** *Samuel Langhorne Clemens (Mark Twain)* (detail), 1935, Frank Edwin Larson, National Portrait Gallery, Smithsonian Institution, Washington, D.C./Art Resource, New York; **606** *Campesino*, 1976, Oil on canvas, 50 1/2 x 59 1/2 inches, Daniel DeSiga, Wight Art Gallery, University of California, Los Angeles, Collection of Alfredo Aragon, Photo by Grey Crawford; **608** Christie's Images; **612** *The New Necklace*, 1910, William McGregor Paxton, Courtesy, Museum of Fine Arts, Boston. Repro-

Staff Credits

The people who made up the *Prentice Hall Literature: Timeless Voices, Timeless Themes* team—representing design services, editorial, editorial services, market research, marketing services, media resources, online services & multimedia development, production services, project office, and publishing processes—are listed below. Bold type denotes the core team members.

Susan Andariese, Rosalyn Arcilla, Laura Jane Bird, Betsy Bostwick, **Anne M. Bray,** Evonne Burgess, **Louise B. Capuano, Pam Cardiff,** Megan Chill, Ed Cordero, Laura Dershewitz, Philip Fried, **Elaine Goldman,** Barbara Goodchild, Barbara Grant, **Rebecca Z. Graziano, Doreen Graizzaro,** Dennis Higbee, **Leanne Korszoloski,** Ellen Lees, David Liston, **Mary Luthi, George Lychock,** Gregory Lynch, Sue Lyons, **William McAllister,** Frances Medico, Gail Meyer, Jessica S. Paladini, Wendy Perri, Carolyn Carty Sapontzis, **Melissa Shustyk, Annette Simmons, Alicia Solis,** Robin Sullivan, Cynthia Sosland Summers, Lois Teesdale, **Elizabeth Torjussen, Doug Utigard,** Bernadette Walsh, Helen Young

The following persons provided invaluable assistance and support during the production of this program.

Gregory Abrom, Robert Aleman, Diane Alimena, Michele Angelucci, Gabriella Apolito, Penny Baker, Sharyn Banks, Anthony Barone, Barbara Blecher, Helen Byers, Rui Camarinha, Lorelee J. Campbell, John Carle, Cynthia Clampitt, Jaime L. Cohen, Martha Conway, Dina Curro, Nancy Dredge, Johanna Ehrmann, Josie K. Fixler, Steve Frankel, Kathy Gavilanes, Allen Gold, Michael E. Goodman, Diana Hahn, Kerry L. Harrigan, Jacki Hasko, Evan Holstrom, Beth Hyslip, Helen Issackedes, Cathy Johnson, Susan Karpin, Raegan Keida, Stephanie Kota, Mary Sue Langan, Elizabeth Letizia, Christine Mann, Vickie Menanteaux, Kathleen Mercandetti, Art Mkrtchyan, Karyl Murray, Kenneth Myett, Stefano Nese, Kim Ortell, Lissette Quinones, Erin Rehill-Seker, Patricia Rodriguez, Mildred Schulte, Adam Sherman, Mary Siener, Jan K. Singh, Diane Smith, Barbara Stufflebeem, Louis Suffredini, Lois Tatarian, Tom Thompkins, Lisa Valente, Ryan Vaarsi, Linda Westerhoff, Jeff Zoda

Prentice Hall gratefully acknowledges the following teachers who provided student models for consideration in the program.

Kate Anders, Suzanne Arkfeld, Elizabeth Bailey, Bill Brown, Diane Cappillo, Mary Chapman, Deedee Chumley, Terry Day, Cheryl Devoe, Dan Diercks, Ellen Eberly, Nancy Fahner, Terri Fields, Patty Foster, Joanne Giardino, Julie Gold, Christopher Guarraia, Dianne Hammond, Jo Higgins, Pauline Hodges, Gaye Ingram, Charlotte Jefferies, Bill Jones, Ken Kaiser, Linda Kramer, Karen Lopez, Catherine Lynn, Ashley MacDonald, Kathleen Marshall, LouAnn McCarty, Peggy Moore, Ann Okamura, Will Parker, Maureen Rippee, Tucky Roger, Terrie Saunders, Marilyn Shaw, Ken Spurlock, Mary Stevens, Sandra Sullivan, Wanda Thomas, Jennifer Watson, Amanda Wolf